Major Companies
of the
Arab World 1991/92

Edited by
Giselle C Bricault

Graham & Trotman
A member of Wolters Kluwer Academic Publishers

Sterling House, 66 Wilton Road, London SW1V 1DE, United Kingdom

Telephone: 071-821 1123   Telex: 298878 Gramco G   Facsimile: 071-630 5229

Fifteenth edition published in 1991 by
Graham & Trotman Limited,
Sterling House, 66 Wilton Road,
London SW1V 1DE, United Kingdom

DIRECTORY PUBLISHERS
A S S O C I A T I O N

British Library Cataloguing in Publication Data

Major Companies of the Arab World — 1991-92
1. Corporations — Arab countries Directories
338.740974927.
ISSN 0144-1594
ISBN 978-94-011-7482-4   ISBN 978-94-011-7480-0 (eBook)
DOI 10.1007/978-94-011-7480-0
Library of Congress CIP data is available from the publisher

© 1991 Graham & Trotman Limited
Softcover reprint of the hardcover 1st edition 1991

Contents

Introduction

Usage of the indexes

Abbreviations

Graham & Trotman Ltd is one of Europe's leading publishers of business books and reports on the Arab world.

For full details of our comprehensive range of titles contact:

Sales Department
Graham & Trotman Ltd
Sterling House
66 Wilton Road
London SW1V 1DE

Telephone: 071-821 1123
Telex: 298878 Gramco G
Cable: Infobooks London
Fax: 071-630 5229

Graham & Trotman
A member of Wolters Kluwer Academic Publishers

THE RECONSTRUCTION AND RE-EQUIPMENT OF KUWAIT:

NEW BUSINESS OPPORTUNITIES

WRITTEN AND RESEARCHED BY ROBERT BAILEY AND JOHN WHELAN

In response to the urgent need for detailed information on the current situation, Graham & Trotman is delighted to announce the publication of **The Reconstruction and Re-Equipment of Kuwait: New Business Opportunities.** This is a major new series of quarterly Reports, which will identify the essential requirements and priorities as Kuwait seeks to reactivate its infrastructure, industry and commerce.

Each Report provides a detailed and systematic overview on a sectoral basis, advising subscribers on where to focus attention and conduct business and identifying the right channels through which to direct prequalification particulars, secure tender documents and enter contract negotiations. It also includes commentaries on legal and contractual matters affecting all aspects of the reconstruction of Kuwait.

This publication is produced on a quarterly basis to ensure that it remains completely up-to-date and flexible enough to adapt to the developing political, economic and commercial situation in Kuwait. Each quarterly Report is a self-contained working document - together the Reports will build into a complete overview of Kuwait's changing requirements as the reconstruction process develops, and will be an invaluable source of information and advice for all companies seeking to capitalise on the new business opportunities available.

Make sure your Company is not left behind in the race for business - enter your subscription without delay.

Contents

Introduction; After the Storm; Decision Makers; Tendering; Private Sector; Manpower; Trading Partners; GCC States; Financing Recovery; Government; Legal, Regulatory and Contractual Requirements; Appendices; Cumulative and Classified Index.

1991 Subscription (3 issues) -- £297.00/US$645.00
Issue No. 1 due: June 1991.

For further details please contact:
The Marketing Department, Graham & Trotman, Sterling House, 66 Wilton Road, London SW1V 1DE
Telephone 071-821 1123   Fax 071-630 5229

Introduction

This book represents the fifteenth edition of the leading reference work MAJOR COMPANIES OF THE ARAB WORLD.

This volume has been completely updated compared to last year's edition (with the exception of Iraq due to the circumstances of war). Many new companies have also been included this year.

This year, the Kuwaiti section contains an appendix giving addresses for relocated Kuwaiti companies (with telephone/telefax numbers where possible). This appendix allows the reader to cross-refer the Kuwaiti company to its relocation entry in the relevant Arab country or to contact them direct if they have relocated to a non-Arab country.

The publishers remain confident that MAJOR COMPANIES OF THE ARAB WORLD contains more information on the major industrial and commercial companies than any other work. The information in the book was submitted mostly by the companies themselves, completely free of charge. To all those companies, which assisted us in our research operation, we express grateful thanks. To all those individuals who gave us help as well, we are similarly very grateful.

Definition of a major company

The criteria we have applied for the selection of companies of major status for inclusion in this book are a mixture of the following:

1 The company must have a significant sales turnover and/or issued capital, relative to other Arab companies.
2 The company must have a strong position in its national or international markets.
3 The company must have shareholders and/or directors who are persons of prominence in the business life of their company.
4 The company should be making a notable contribution to the economic growth of its country or region.
5 The company may be a significant branch of a major international corporation. Foreign bank branches and representatives offices have also been included.
6 The company may be recently established but nonetheless have sufficient capital, sufficiently prominent shareholders, and be aiming to serve a sufficiently growth-oriented market, to have significant expansion prospects.
7 Certain companies have been included which, although they may not be very large, are nonetheless important firms wishing to import and export. Shipping agents are an example.

IMPORTANT

All company entries have been entered in MAJOR COMPANIES OF THE ARAB WORLD absolutely free of charge, thus ensuring a totally objective approach to the information given.

Whilst the publishers have made every effort to ensure that the information in this book was correct at the time of press, no responsibility or liability can be accepted for any errors or omissions, or for the consequences thereof.

ABOUT GRAHAM & TROTMAN LTD

Graham & Trotman Ltd, a member of the Kluwer Academic Publishers Group, is a publishing organisation specialising in the research and publication of business and technical information for industry and commerce in many parts of the world.

Whilst maintaining and regularly updating a considerable volume of information on companies business conditions and markets in the Arab World, Graham & Trotman Ltd also publish books on energy resources, fuel technology, pollution control, finance, business law, business management techniques, and several other subject areas.

Graham & Trotman Ltd have over 450 publications in print which variously are sold throughout the world. Readers are welcome to write, phone or telex for a free copy of our illustrated complete catalogue of publications.

The Major Companies Series

A long established and reliable source of business information, providing you with essential data on today's leading Corporations from around the world.

POWERFUL INFORMATION – Each company listed has a full profile giving the following key information:

- Company Name, Address, Telephone, Fax and Telex.
- Names of Chairman/President, Senior Executives with Titles.
- Principal Activities, Parent Company, Principal Subsidiaries, Principal Banks, Number of Employees.

In addition, the following financial information is given to enable you to assess a company's status and prospects (where available);

- Sales Turnover, Profit before Tax, Profit after Tax, Retained Profits, Dividends, Dividends per Share, Earnings per Share, Share Capital, and Shareholders' Funds.

RESEARCHED AND INDEXED – For ease of use, each directory in the series has three indexes: Alphabetically; Alphabetically by Country; Alphabetically by Business and Activity by Country. The information presented is the result of an extensive and careful research programme carried out by experienced editors. The information is obtained directly from the companies concerned and thoroughly checked.

Major Companies of Europe 1991/92

With over 8,000 of Europe's leading Companies in three volumes:

Volume 1 Continental EEC: Belgium, Denmark, France, Germany, Greece, Ireland, Italy, Luxembourg, Netherlands, Portugal and Spain

Volume 2 UK

Volume 3 Non EEC: Austria, Finland, Liechtenstein, Norway, Sweden and Switzerland

Major Companies of the Arab World 1991/92

There are over 7,000 of the most important companies in the following countries:

Algeria, Bahrain, Egypt, Iraq, Jordan, Kuwait, Lebanon, Libya, Mauritania, Morocco, Oman, Qatar, Saudi Arabia, Somalia, Sudan, Syria, Tunisia, United Arab Emirates, North and South Yemen (Yemeni Republic)

Major Companies of the Far East and Australasia 1991/92

In three volumes and covering over 8,000 companies

Volume 1 Brunei, Indonesia, Malaysia, Philippines, Singapore and Thailand

Volume 2 China, Hong Kong, Japan, Korea and Taiwan

Volume 3 Australia and New Zealand

Medium Companies of Europe 1991/92

This is the companion set to the **Major Companies of Europe 1991/92**, published for the first time. It provides you with over 7,000 Companies with the data presented in the same way as its companion, in three volumes - Volume 1 EEC, Volume 2 UK, Volume 3 Non-EEC.

Major Business Organisations of Eastern Europe and the Soviet Union

Provides information on over 3,000 organisations in a similar way to the Major Companies (but no financial details) in three principal areas:

1. **Business Organisations** - includes Manufacturers, Service organisations, Banks, Joint ventures, Foreign Trade organisations

2. **Ministries** - may often be a valuable first stop for Businessmen visiting the region.

3. **Chambers of Commerce** - They provide information and advice on trade, promotion and law for the region or country concerned.

Covers the following countries:
Albania, Bulgaria, Czechoslovakia, Hungary, Poland, Romania, USSR, Yugoslavia.

For more information contact:
Directories Marketing, Graham & Trotman Ltd.
Sterling House, 66 Wilton Road
London SW1V 1DE
Tel: 071-821 1123, Fax: 071-630 5229

Published by Graham & Trotman Ltd
A Member of the Kluwer Academic Publishers Group

BANKING BOOKS

Graham & Trotman Ltd

Global Electronic Wholesale Banking

by Dr A S Mookerjee & Professor J I Cash Jr

Global Electronic Wholesale Banking is the first to address this subject, part of the broader category collectively known as Global Information Systems, and will help eliminate confusion and add to the limited collection of literature. This important new book gives a detailed account of the services provided, their strategic importance and the new product development of global information systems.

Topics include the four global electronic wholesale banking(GEWB) services

    Global Balance Reporting
    Global Funds Transfer
    Global Custody
    Global Letter of Credit

and also it addresses the inherent problems in managing the privately owned processing delivery systems through which the wholesale banks deliver these services.

The work presented is based on a survey of delivery system structures and operational performance of GEWB services provided by a selected group of banks and an extensive review of literature.

ISBN 1 85333 415 4   Pages 176
Size 216mm x 138mm   Hardback

The European Bank for Reconstruction and Development

A Comparative Analysis of the Constituent Agreements
by Ibrahim F I Shihata
- *General Counsel, World Bank*
- *Secretary General, ICSID.*

In May 1990, forty countries, together with the EEC and the European Investment Bank, signed the agreement establishing the European Bank for Reconstruction and Development.

This authoritative critical analysis of the Agreement concentrates on the three main areas relevant to the activities of the EBRD: its financing, its operations, and its organization and management.

The discussion is not limited to the provisions of the EBRD Agreement and and its other basic documents, but includes a thorough comparison of such provisions with those of other

international financial institutions. It also includes the full text of the EBRD basic documents, published for the first time in the Appendices.

ISBN 1 85333 482 0   Pages 240
Size 234mm x 156mm   Hardback

International Banking and Financial Systems: A Comparison

by Andrew Mullineux

This title presents an extensive comparative survey of banking and financial procedures of selected countries. These include the United States, France, Japan, Germany, Switzerland and the United Kingdom. It also includes Socialist and Islamic banking, banking in a developing country and off-shore banking.

"Concise in style and fluency, the book dispenses with unnecessary jargon and will be a pleasure to read for those who seek analytical information coupled with a well structured presentation."

Arab Banker 1988

ISBN 0 86010 916 X   Pages 256
Size 234mm x 156mm   Hardback

Effective Management in Financial Services

by Gerald Cohen

This book is on the recommended reading list for the Institute of Banker's Management syllabus

Effective Management in Financial Services is the third edition of the highly successful textbook (formerly entitled The Nature of Management). It has been fully revised and up-dated to conform to the new developments and amendments to the syllabus for the Institute of Banking examinations.

It reflects the most important recent changes in the management of the banking and finance community - the increaslingly blurred distinction between banks and building societies, the greater integration of marketing into management activities, and it includes a long-term view of developments affecting management in the financial sector.

Contents

Introduction - The Financial Environment - Theories of Management - Organisation of Structure - Management Techniques - Planning and Control - The Nature of People - Motivation theories - Communication - The Manager/ Subordinate Relationships - Leadership - Staffing - Training - Rewards and Benefits - Industrial Relations

ISBN: 1 85333 456 1   Pages 362
Size 246mm x 189mm   Paperback

Abbreviations

AD	ALGERIAN DINARS
BD	BAHRAIN DINARS
£E	EGYPTIAN POUNDS
ID	IRAQI DINARS
JD	JORDANIAN DINARS
KD	KUWAITI DINARS
LL	LEBANESE POUNDS
LD	LIBYAN DINARS
UM	MAURITANIAN OUGUIYA
MDh	MOROCCAN DIRHAMS
OR	OMANI RIALS
QR	QATAR RIYALS
SR	SAUDI RIYALS
SO SHs	SOMALI SHILLINGS
£S	SUDANESE POUNDS
SP	SYRIAN POUNDS
DT	TUNISIAN DINARS
DH	UAE DIRHAMS
YR	YEMENI RIYALS
US$	USA DOLLARS
£	POUND STERLING

Usage of the Index

This book has been arranged to allow the reader to locate the company entries in three ways.

Firstly the Contents page at the front of the book lists the countries which are covered in the book and the pages on which they can be found.

Secondly the companies are listed alphabetically within each country, allowing any particular company to be located quickly. As for many readers English may be a second or third language the alphabetic ordering used is a strict one and arranged as though the name including initials is one word.

For example:

ADE Engineering appears before Aden Engineering but after ACE Engineering

Thirdly three cross-referenced indexes are situated at the end of the book.

a) An alphabetical listing of all companies included in *Major Companies of the Arab World*
b) An alphabetical listing of the companies included in each country section
c) A business activity index of all companies in *Major Companies of the Arab World* subdivided into the categories listed below.

BUSINESS ACTIVITIES INDEX

AGRICULTURE
0005 ☐ Agriculture & horticulture
0010 ☐ Agricultural & horticultural equipment & services
0015 ☐ Fishing
0018 ☐ Forestry
0020 ☐ Irrigation equipment
0030 ☐ Livestock, animal feeds & pet foods
0040 ☐ Timber industries

CHEMICALS AND ALLIED INDUSTRIES
0050 ☐ Fertilisers & agricultural chemicals
0051 ☐ Biotechnology
0055 ☐ Explosives
0060 ☐ General chemicals
0065 ☐ Industrial gases
0070 ☐ Paints, inks & dyestuffs
0080 ☐ Petrochemicals
0090 ☐ Pharmaceuticals
0100 ☐ Plastics & plastic products
0110 ☐ Soaps, detergents & other cleaning products
0120 ☐ Specialty chemicals

CONSTRUCTION, BUILDING MATERIALS, PROPERTY
0130 ☐ Building materials & fittings
0140 ☐ Cement & bricks
0145 ☐ Ready mixed concrete
0150 ☐ Civil engineering & construction
0160 ☐ Civil engineering consultants
0170 ☐ Construction equipment & plant hire
0180 ☐ Glass
0190 ☐ Property, real estate

CONSUMER GOODS
0200 ☐ Domestic ceramics
0210 ☐ Furniture & components
0220 ☐ Hardware
0230 ☐ Jewellery
0240 ☐ Leisure goods & giftware
0250 ☐ Medical supplies
0260 ☐ Toiletries & cosmetics

DISTRIBUTIVE TRADES
0270 ☐ Non-food retailing
0280 ☐ Food & drink retailing
0290 ☐ Wholesalers
0300 ☐ Mail order services

ELECTRICAL AND ELECTRONIC ENGINEERING
0310 ☐ Data processing equipment
0311 ☐ Computer software & services
0320 ☐ Domestic electrical appliances
0330 ☐ Electrical & electronic equipment
0335 ☐ Electrical engineering
0340 ☐ Electrical engineering consultants
0350 ☐ Electrical machinery & components
0355 ☐ Welding equipment & services
0360 ☐ Power equipment
0370 ☐ Telecommunications
0375 ☐ Defence electronics

ENERGY
0380 ☐ Coal mining
0385 ☐ Coal products
0390 ☐ Fuel distribution
0400 ☐ Natural gas supply
0405 ☐ Electricity supply
0410 ☐ Oil & gas exploration & production
0420 ☐ Oil & gas services & equipment
0430 ☐ Oil refining
0440 ☐ Nuclear engineering

FINANCIAL SERVICES AND TRADING
0450 ☐ Banks, finance & investment
0460 ☐ Insurance
0465 ☐ Leasing & rental services
0470 ☐ General trading companies & agents
0480 ☐ Commodity trading

FOOD, DRINK AND TOBACCO
0490 ☐ Baking & flour milling
0500 ☐ Brewing, wines & spirits
0510 ☐ Cereal products
0520 ☐ Non-alcoholic beverages
0525 ☐ Coffee
0528 ☐ Tea
0530 ☐ Confectionery
0533 ☐ Snack products
0536 ☐ Soups, sauces & other relishes
0538 ☐ Infant & dietetic foods
0540 ☐ Dairy products
0550 ☐ Fish & fish processing
0560 ☐ Fruit products
0565 ☐ Vegetable products
0570 ☐ Meat & meat processing
0575 ☐ Frozen & ready prepared food products
0580 ☐ Oils & fats
0590 ☐ Sugar
0600 ☐ Tobacco

INDUSTRIAL PLANT AND EQUIPMENT
0610 ☐ Chemical plant
0620 ☐ Food & beverage plant
0625 ☐ Industrial fasteners
0630 ☐ Industrial equipment
0640 ☐ Generators
0650 ☐ Elevators, lifting equipment & conveyors
0660 ☐ Machine tools
0670 ☐ Pollution control equipment
0680 ☐ Process engineering

INSTRUMENT ENGINEERING
0685 ☐ Control & measuring equipment
0690 ☐ Medical instruments
0700 ☐ Optical equipment
0710 ☐ Photographic & copying equipment & services
0720 ☐ Scientific instruments
0730 ☐ Watches & clocks

OTHER MANUFACTURING INDUSTRIES
0735 ☐ Abrasives
0740 ☐ Cables & wires
0750 ☐ Defence & armaments
0760 ☐ Educational equipment
0770 ☐ Heating, ventilation & refrigeration
0780 ☐ Industrial ceramics
0785 ☐ Insulation products
0790 ☐ Office equipment
0793 ☐ Writing equipment
0795 ☐ Medical & surgical equipment
0800 ☐ Rubber & rubber goods
0805 ☐ Safety equipment
0810 ☐ Security equipment
0820 ☐ Toys & games

MECHANICAL ENGINEERING
0830 ☐ General mechanical engineering
0840 ☐ Hand tools
0850 ☐ Industrial engines
0860 ☐ Mechanical engineering consultants
0870 ☐ Mechanical engineering plant
0880 ☐ Mechanical handling equipment
0890 ☐ Pumps, valves & compressors
0900 ☐ Textile machinery

METALS AND METAL FABRICATION
0910 ☐ Aluminium
0920 ☐ Metal forgings, castings & stampings
0930 ☐ Copper & copper alloys
0940 ☐ Iron & steel
0950 ☐ Metal fabrication
0955 ☐ Metal treatment & related services
0960 ☐ Non-ferrous metals
0970 ☐ Precious metals

MINING AND QUARRYING
0980 ☐ Mining & quarrying
0990 ☐ Mining equipment

PAPER, PRINTING AND PUBLISHING
1000 ☐ Packaging
1005 ☐ Paper & packaging machinery
1010 ☐ Paper & board
1020 ☐ Printing & binding
1025 ☐ Printing machinery & equipment
1030 ☐ Publishing & information services

SERVICES
1032 ☐ Accountants & lawyers
1034 ☐ Architecture & town planning
1035 ☐ Educational & training services
1040 ☐ Advertising, public relations & market research
1041 ☐ Manpower services
1045 ☐ Management services & consultants
1050 ☐ Betting & gambling
1060 ☐ Broadcasting, films, theatre
1063 ☐ Commercial & industrial institutes & associations
1064 ☐ Government bodies
1065 ☐ Health care
1070 ☐ Hotels, restaurants & catering
1073 ☐ Industrial design
1075 ☐ Recreational services
1080 ☐ Laundries & dry cleaning
1081 ☐ Cleaning & waste disposal services
1083 ☐ Building maintenance & refurbishment
1085 ☐ Security services
1090 ☐ Travel & tourism
1095 ☐ Telecommunications services
1098 ☐ Postal services
1100 ☐ Public services
1102 ☐ Funeral services & related products
1105 ☐ Water supply & treatment services

TEXTILES, CLOTHING, FOOTWEAR, LEATHER
1110 ☐ Carpets
1120 ☐ Clothing
1130 ☐ Footwear
1140 ☐ Furs
1150 ☐ Knitted goods
1160 ☐ Leather goods, accessories & luggage
1170 ☐ Man-made fibres
1180 ☐ Other textiles
1190 ☐ Spinning & weaving
1200 ☐ Textile finishing
1210 ☐ Woollen goods

TRANSPORT EQUIPMENT AND COMPONENTS
1220 ☐ Aerospace equipment & components
1230 ☐ Motor vehicles
1235 ☐ Motor vehicle components
1240 ☐ Motorcycles & bicycles
1245 ☐ Mobile homes, caravans & campers
1250 ☐ Railroad vehicles & equipment
1260 ☐ Ship & boat building & marine engineering

TRANSPORT SERVICES
1270 ☐ Air transport & airport services
1280 ☐ Freight forwarding
1285 ☐ Storage & warehousing
1290 ☐ Railway vehicles & equipment
1300 ☐ Road haulage
1310 ☐ Shipping and port services

BUSINESS ACTIVITIES INDEX – FRENCH

AGRICULTURE
0005 ☐ Agriculture et horticulture
0010 ☐ Matériel et services agricoles et horticoles
0015 ☐ Pêche
0018 ☐ Sylviculture
0020 ☐ Matériel d'irrigation
0030 ☐ Aliments pour bétail et animaux
0040 ☐ Industries du bois

INDUSTRIES CHIMIQUES ET CONNEXES
0050 ☐ Engrais et produits agrochimiques
0051 ☐ Biotechnologie
0055 ☐ Explosifs
0060 ☐ Produits chimiques généraux
0065 ☐ Gaz industriels
0070 ☐ Peintures et vernis, encres et matières colorantes
0080 ☐ Produits pétrochimiques
0090 ☐ Produits pharmaceutiques
0100 ☐ Plastiques et produits plastiques
0110 ☐ Savons, détersifs et autres produits de nettoyage
0120 ☐ Produits chimiques spécialisés

CONSTRUCTION, MATERIAUX DE CONSTRUCTION, IMMOBILIER
0130 ☐ Matériaux et accessoires de construction
0140 ☐ Ciment et briques
0145 ☐ Béton prémélangé
0150 ☐ Travaux publics et construction
0160 ☐ Conseils en travaux publics
0170 ☐ Location de matériel et d'engins de construction
0180 ☐ Verre
0190 ☐ Biens, immobilier

BIENS DE CONSOMMATION
0200 ☐ Céramique domestique
0210 ☐ Meubles et composants
0220 ☐ Quincaillerie
0230 ☐ Bijouterie
0240 ☐ Articles loisir et cadeaux
0250 ☐ Fournitures médicales
0260 ☐ Produits de toilette et de beauté

DISTRIBUTION
0270 ☐ Commerce non alimentaire de détail
0280 ☐ Commerce de détail des aliments et des boissons
0290 ☐ Grossistes
0300 ☐ Ventes par correspondance

ELECTRICITE ET ELECTRONIQUE
0310 ☐ Matériel informatique
0311 ☐ Logiciel et services d'informatique
0320 ☐ Appareils électro-ménagers
0330 ☐ Matériel électrique et électronique
0335 ☐ Electrotechnique
0340 ☐ Conseils en électricité
0350 ☐ Machines et composants électriques
0355 ☐ Matériel et services de soudure
0360 ☐ Matériel fonctionnant à l'électricité
0370 ☐ Télécommunications
0375 ☐ Electronique défense

ENERGIE
0380 ☐ Exploitation de la houille
0385 ☐ Produits houilliers
0390 ☐ Commerce de combustibles
0400 ☐ Alimentation en gaz
0405 ☐ Alimentation en électricité
0410 ☐ Exploration et production de pétrole et de gaz
0420 ☐ Services et matériel de pétrole et de gaz
0430 ☐ Raffinage du pétrole
0440 ☐ Génie nucléaire

SERVICES FINANCIERS ET COMMERCE
0450 ☐ Banques, financements et investissements
0460 ☐ Assurances
0465 ☐ Services de location et leasing
0470 ☐ Commerce général sociétés et agences
0480 ☐ Commerce des denrées

ALIMENTATION, BOISSONS ET TABAC
0490 ☐ Boulangerie et meunerie
0500 ☐ Bières, vins et spiritueux
0510 ☐ Produits céréaliers
0520 ☐ Boissons non alcoolisées
0525 ☐ Café
0528 ☐ Thé
0530 ☐ Confiserie
0533 ☐ Snacks
0536 ☐ Potages, sauces et condiments
0538 ☐ Aliments nourrissons et diététiques
0540 ☐ Produits laitiers
0550 ☐ Poisson et transformation des produits de la pêche
0560 ☐ Produits à base de fruits
0565 ☐ Produits à base de légumes
0570 ☐ Viande et transformation de la viande
0575 ☐ Aliments prêts; congelés et surgelés
0580 ☐ Huiles et graisses
0590 ☐ Sucre
0600 ☐ Tabac

INSTALLATION ET EQUIPEMENT INDUSTRIELLES
0610 ☐ Usines chimiques
0620 ☐ Usines alimentaires et de boissons
0625 ☐ Fermetures industrielles
0630 ☐ Matériel industriel
0640 ☐ Générateurs
0650 ☐ Elévateurs, matériel de levage et transporteurs
0660 ☐ Machine-outils
0670 ☐ Matériel de contrôle de la pollution
0680 ☐ Techniques de transformation

INSTRUMENTS
0685 ☐ Equipement de contrôle et de mesure
0690 ☐ Instruments médicaux
0700 ☐ Matériel optique
0710 ☐ Photographie et photocopie — matériel et services
0720 ☐ Instruments scientifiques
0730 ☐ Montres et horloges

AUTRES INDUSTRIES DE FABRICATION
0735 ☐ Abrasifs
0740 ☐ Câbles et fils
0750 ☐ Défense et armement
0760 ☐ Matériel d'enseignement
0770 ☐ Chauffage, ventilation et réfrigération
0780 ☐ Céramique industrielle
0785 ☐ Produits isolants
0790 ☐ Matériel de bureau
0793 ☐ Articles papeterie
0795 ☐ Equipements médicaux et chirurgicaux
0800 ☐ Caoutchouc et produits en caoutchouc
0805 ☐ Dispositifs de sécurité
0810 ☐ Matériel de sécurité
0820 ☐ Jouets et jeux

MECANIQUE
0830 ☐ Mécanique générale
0840 ☐ Outils manuels
0850 ☐ Moteurs industriels
0860 ☐ Conseils en mécanique
0870 ☐ Engins mécaniques
0880 ☐ Matériel de manutention mécanique
0890 ☐ Pompes, soupapes et compresseurs
0900 ☐ Machines textiles

METAUX ET FABRICATION DES METAUX
0910 ☐ Aluminium
0920 ☐ Moulages, pièces forgées et bocardages métalliques
0930 ☐ Cuivre et alliages de cuivre
0940 ☐ Fer et acier
0950 ☐ Fabrication des métaux
0955 ☐ Traitement des métaux et services connexes
0960 ☐ Métaux non ferreux
0970 ☐ Métaux précieux

EXPLOITATION DES MINES ET DES CARRIERES
0980 ☐ Exploitations des mines et des carrières
0990 ☐ Matériel d'exploitation minière

PAPETERIE, IMPRIMERIE ET EDITION
1000 ☐ Emballage
1005 ☐ Machines papier et emballage
1010 ☐ Papier et carton
1020 ☐ Impression et reliure
1025 ☐ Machines et équipements d'imprimerie
1030 ☐ Edition et services d'informations

SERVICES
1032 ☐ Comptables et hommes de loi
1034 ☐ Architecture et urbanisme
1035 ☐ Education et formation professionnelle
1040 ☐ Publicité, relations publiques et étude de marché
1041 ☐ Services d'emploi
1045 ☐ Services gestion et conseils
1050 ☐ Paris et jeux de hasard
1060 ☐ Radiodiffusion, cinéma, théâtre
1063 ☐ Associations et instituts commerciaux et industriels
1064 ☐ Organisations gouvernementales
1065 ☐ Articles et services santé
1070 ☐ Hôtels, bars et restaurants
1073 ☐ Conception industrielle
1075 ☐ Services de loisirs
1080 ☐ Blanchisseries et nettoyage à sec
1081 ☐ Services de nettoyage et d'enlèvement de déchets
1083 ☐ Entretien et rénovation des bâtiments
1085 ☐ Services de sécurité
1090 ☐ Voyages et tourisme
1095 ☐ Services de télécommunications
1098 ☐ Services postaux
1100 ☐ Services publics
1102 ☐ Pompes funèbres et articles associés
1105 ☐ Distribution et traitement des eaux

TEXTILES, VETEMENTS, CHAUSSURES, CUIR
1110 ☐ Tapis
1120 ☐ Vêtements
1130 ☐ Chaussures
1140 ☐ Fourrures
1150 ☐ Articles tricotés
1160 ☐ Articles en cuir, accessoires et bagages
1170 ☐ Fibres synthétiques
1180 ☐ Autres textiles
1190 ☐ Filature et tissage
1200 ☐ Finition textile
1210 ☐ Articles en laine

MATERIEL DE TRANSPORT ET COMPOSANTS
1220 ☐ Matériel et composant aérospatiaux
1230 ☐ Automobiles
1235 ☐ Pièces de véhicules automobiles
1240 ☐ Motocyclettes et bicyclettes
1245 ☐ Caravanes et autocaravanes
1250 ☐ Véhicules et matériel de chemin de fer
1260 ☐ Construction et mécanique navale

SERVICES DE TRANSPORT
1270 ☐ Transport aérien et services d'aéroport
1280 ☐ Frêteurs — expéditeurs
1285 ☐ Entreposage/stockage
1290 ☐ Transport en commun (train et autobus)
1300 ☐ Transport de marchandises
1310 ☐ Messageries maritimes et services portuaires

Major Companies of
ALGERIA

AFRIC MAILLE
4 rue Murat, Oran
Tel: 36464, 36562
Cable: Afima oran
Telex: 22929

PRINCIPAL ACTIVITIES: Production of knitted goods and clothing
Principal Bankers: Banque Exterieure d'Algerie

AGENOR
Agence Nationale pour la Transformation et la Distribution de l'Or et Autres Metaux Precieux
50 rue Larbi Ben M'Hidi, Algiers
Tel: 638013/16, 638059
Cable: Agenor Alger
Telex: 67138

Directors: Abdellah Lansari (Director General)
Senior Executives: Younsi Brouri (Commercial Director), Mohamed Hamrat (Financial Director)

PRINCIPAL ACTIVITIES: Processing and distribution of gold and other precious metals
Branch Offices: Algiers, Oran, Constantine
Principal Bankers: Banque Exterieure d'Algerie
Financial Information: Responsible to the Ministry of Finance

Principal Shareholders: State-owned

ANEP
Agence Nationale d'Edition et de Publicite
1 Avenue Pasteur, Algiers
Tel: 791114, 791115, 790852/3
Cable: Anep Alger
Telex: 61344
Telefax: 795180

Chairman: Mohammed Raouraoua
Directors: Badreddine Mili (Marketing & Information Director), Ali Nassakh (Regie-Presse Director)

PRINCIPAL ACTIVITIES: Publishing and distribution of commercial publicity under state monopoly
Branch Offices: Agence Oran, 12 rue des Freres Assane, Tel 345829, Telex 22559; Agence Constantine, 7e Km Route d'Alger, Tel 938781, Telex 92422; Agence Centre (Bab El Oued), Tel 620306, Telex 61440; Imprimerie Rouiba, Zone Industrielle, Tel 807320, Telex 68117
Principal Bankers: Credit Populaire d'Algerie
Financial Information: Responsible to the Ministry of Information and Culture

Principal Shareholders: State-owned

BANQUE ALGERIENNE DE DEVELOPPEMENT
B.A.D.
12 Bld Colonel Amirouche, Algiers
Tel: 02-738950, 745254
Cable: Badev Alger
Telex: 67221, 67222 Bad Alger

Directors: Sassa Aziza (Director General), Idri Rafik (Finance Director), Bachtarzi Med Araslane (Administration Director)

PRINCIPAL ACTIVITIES: Financing of investments in public companies in the inudstrial, touristic, commercial and transport sectors by means of long-term domestic credits and setting of foreign credits; control and administration of private investment
Branch Offices: BAD, Direction Regionale de Constantine, 1 Place Mohamed Khemisti, Constantine; BAD, Direction Regionale d'Oran, 18 Rue Guillaume Apollinaire, Oran; BAD, Direction Regionale de Annaba, Imm Ensid, Chaiba, Annaba;

Banque Algerienne de Commerce Exterieur SA, Zurich, Switzerland
Financial Information:

	1990 AD'000
Profits	350.000
Authorised capital	100.000
Paid-up capital	83.000
Total assets	200.701.000

Principal Shareholders: State-owned
Date of Establishment: 1963
No of Employees: 470

BANQUE ALGERIENNE DE DEVELOPPEMENT RURAL
B.A.D.R.
17 Blvd Colonel Amirouche, Algiers
Tel: 647264
Telex: 52487 BADR Alger

PRINCIPAL ACTIVITIES: Medium and long term loans for agricultural development projects

Date of Establishment: 1982

BANQUE CENTRALE D'ALGERIE
B.C.A.
8 Boulevard Zirout Youcef, Algiers
Tel: 647500, 647400
Cable: Algeban Alger
Telex: 67499, 67180, 67310, 67379, 67377

Governor: Bader Eddine Nouioua
Vice Governor: Ahmed Hanifi
Senior Executives: Salah Mouhoubi (Director of Studies & Banking Regulations), Mohamed Kirat (Director Foreign Banking Services), Hacen Messai (General Inspector), Mansour Benabid (Admin Director), Slimane Zalene (Director Data Processing), Bachir Sail (Director Foreign Exchange), Mustapha Guerdoud (General Cashier)

PRINCIPAL ACTIVITIES: Central banking

Date of Establishment: January 1963

BANQUE EXTERIEURE D'ALGERIE
B.E.A.
11 Boulevard Colonel Amirouche, Algiers
Tel: 611252, 621811, 620845
Telex: 67448, 67317, 67082, 67389, 67390/1/2, 66099

President: Mourad Khellef (Director General)
Directors: Houcine Hannachi (Deputy General Manager), Boualem Benaissa (Deputy General Manager), Abdelaziz Kara Mostefa (Director General Inspection), Faycal Lamande (Director Public Sector Financing), Abderrahim Moussaoui (Director Network), Mohamed Amine Abed (Director Legal Dept), Mohamed Salah Boulahbal (Director Private Commitments), Youcef Belabdelouahab (Director Staff & Training), Mohamed OUis (Director Logistics), Kamel Bouabbas (Director International Activities), Mohamed Reda Smahi (Director Organisation & Budget), Omar Hamli (Director Treasury & Accounting)

PRINCIPAL ACTIVITIES: General banking, principally concerned with foreign trade transactions and the financing of industrial development in Algeria
Branch Offices: 62 branches in Algeria
Associated Companies: Arab Bank for Investment and Foreign Trade, Abu Dhadi, UAE; Banque Intercontinentale Arabe, Paris, France
Financial Information:

	AD'million
Authorised capital	1,000
Paid-up capital	1,000

Principal Shareholders: State-owned
Date of Establishment: October 1967
No of Employees: 2,669

BANQUE NATIONALE D'ALGERIE
B.N.A.
8 Blvd Che Guevara, Algiers
Tel: 620530/4, 626080
Cable: Watani
Telex: 52788

Chairman: Abdel Malek Temam
Directors: Mahfoud Zerouta, Selim Belattar, Abdelkader Iles, Jean Claude Melki, Ali Guerrak, Rachid Aous, Brahim Yahia Cherif, Mohamed Ifticene, Mohamed Guermouche, Ferhat Mecibah

PRINCIPAL ACTIVITIES: Commercial banking, control over the financial activities of the State enterprises. Finance to foreign trade operations and to agriculture
Branch Offices: Representative offices in Paris, France; and Beirut, Lebanon
Associated Companies: European Arab Holding; Banque Europeenne Arabe (Bruxelles); Union Mediterraneenne de Banques

Principal Shareholders: State-owned

BATA ALGERIE SA
Consul d'Attile Beo St, Algiers
Tel: 656105
Telex: 52719

PRINCIPAL ACTIVITIES: Manufacture of leather and plastic shoes, sandals and sports shoes
Principal Bankers: Banque Exterieure d'Algerie

BRICKI ET FRERES SNC
Faubourg Sidi Said, Tlemcen
Tel: 3657
Cable: Tapi Said

PRINCIPAL ACTIVITIES: Manufacture of hand-made carpets
Principal Bankers: Banque Nationale d'Algerie

BUREAU CENTRAL D'ETUDES DES TRAVAUX PUBLICS D'ARCHITECTURE ET D'URBANISME
E.T.A.U.
70 Chemin Larbi Alik, Hydra, Algiers
Tel: 602105, 602922

PRINCIPAL ACTIVITIES: Design and engineering consultants, architecture and town planning
Financial Information: Responsible to the Ministry of Public Works

Principal Shareholders: State-owned

C ITOH & CO LTD
See ITOH, C, & CO LTD

CAISSE ALGERIENNE D'AMENAGEMENT DU TERRITOIRE
C.A.D.A.T.
49 Blvd Mohamed V, Algiers
Tel: 631340/5

PRINCIPAL ACTIVITIES: Housing bank for the development and improvement of Algeria
Parent Company: Responsible to the Ministry of Housing & Construction, Telex 52680

Principal Shareholders: State-owned

CAISSE ALGERIENNE D'ASSURANCE ET DE REASSURANCE
C.A.A.R.
48 rue Didouche-Mourad, Algiers
Tel: 631195, 645432
Cable: Recar Alger
Telex: 52894

PRINCIPAL ACTIVITIES: Insurance and reinsurance
Financial Information: Responsible to the Ministry of Finance, Telex 52062

Principal Shareholders: State-owned

CAISSE CENTRALE DE COOPERATION ECONOMIQUE
C.C.C.E.
22 Larbi Alih St, Hydra, BP 35 Birmandreis, Alger

PRINCIPAL ACTIVITIES: Bank specialising in development loans

Principal Shareholders: State-owned

CAISSE NATIONALE DE MUTUALITE AGRICOLE
C.N.M.A.
24 Boulevard Victor Hugo, Algiers
Tel: 637682/86
Cable: Grelal
Telex: 52815

Chairman: Brahim Yahia-Cherif
Directors: A Asselah, S Bachtarzy, M Brakchi, A Belhadj

PRINCIPAL ACTIVITIES: Agricultural insurance
Branch Offices: (40) Alger, Oran, Constantine, Annaba, Boufarik, Tiaret, Belabbes
Principal Bankers: Banque Exterieure d'Algerie, Banque Nationale d'Algerie
Financial Information: Responsible to the Ministry of Agriculture, Algiers, Tel 638950

Date of Establishment: 1972
No of Employees: 1,500

CAISSE NATIONALE D'EPARGNE ET DE PREVOYANCE
C.N.E.P.
40-42 rue Larbi Ben M'Hidi, Algiers
Tel: 632510, 633475
Telex: 52037 CNEP Alger

PRINCIPAL ACTIVITIES: Savings bank
Financial Information: Responsible to the Ministry of Finance, Algiers, Telex 52062

Principal Shareholders: State-owned

CIE DES SERVICES DOWELL SCHLUMBERGER
PO Box 214, Alger-Gare, Algiers
Tel: 646996/98
Cable: Bigrorange Alger
Telex: 52424 Bigor

PRINCIPAL ACTIVITIES: Oil industry service company
Branch Offices: PO Box 16, Hassi Messaoud, Oasis, Algeria, Tel Hassi Messaoud 19
Parent Company: Compagnie des Services Dowell-Schlumberger, France

Date of Establishment: 1961
No of Employees: 130

CIE GENERALE DE GEOPHYSIQUE
C.G.G.
PO Box 23, Algiers El Mouradia
Tel: 9208408
Telex: 27713 Cggec

PRINCIPAL ACTIVITIES: Airborne; land and marine exploration, using all geophysical methods applied to mining and oil industry; civil engineering. Oceanological, meteorological and geodetic surveys; environment studies; data processing geophysical technique research
Subsidiary/Associated Companies: Sercel, AMG, AMPG, Argas, Geoterrex, Georex

COMMISSARIAT NATIONAL A L'INFORMATIQUE
C.N.I.
Cinq Maisons, El Harrach, Algiers
Tel: 637781/83, 637520/24

PRINCIPAL ACTIVITIES: Advising and procuring computers to all Algerian state organisations and ministries and training Algerians in the use of computers, data processing

Principal Shareholders: State-owned

COMPAGNIE CENTRALE DE REASSURANCE
C.C.R.
21 Blvd Zirout Youcef, Algiers
Tel: 640271/2, 637288/9
Telex: 67091, 67092 ALRE DZ

Chairman: Chouaib Djamel Eddine Chouiter (General Manager)
Senior Executives: Ahmed El Azhar Nechachby (Deputy General Manager Technical Affairs), Abdelhadi Meraoubi (Deputy General Manager Administration), Aoumeur Hadj Said (Marine Manager), Mourad Brouri (Non Marine Manager), Boualem Oubaiche (International Business Manager)

PRINCIPAL ACTIVITIES: Reinsurance
Subsidiary Companies: Mediterranean Insurance & Reinsurance Co, London, UK
Principal Bankers: BEA Banque Exterieure d'Algerie
Financial Information:

	AD'000
Authorised capital	80,000
Paid-up capital	80,000

Principal Shareholders: State-owned
Date of Establishment: October 1973
No of Employees: 110

CREDIT POPULAIRE D'ALGERIE
C.P.A.
2 Bvd Colonel Amirouche, Algiers 16000
Tel: 611334, 632855, 638410
Cable: Crepopal Alger
Telex: 67170 Crepopal, 67147 CPA DG

President: Mahfoud Zerouta (also Director General)
Directors: Mourad Damardji (Deputy Manager), Cherif Idjakirene (Deputy Manager)
Senior Executives: Tahar Hadj Saddok (Director Private Financing), Abdenour Kashi (Director Public Financing), Mohamed Baba Ameur (Personnel Director), Boumediene Abderrahmane (Director Legal Dept), Ahmed Bouzidi (Director Data Processing & Accounting)

PRINCIPAL ACTIVITIES: Banking, finance for the development of light industries, building and public works, tourism, transport
Branch Offices: 90 throughout Algeria
Subsidiary Companies: Banco Arabe Espanol, Spain

Financial Information:

	AD'000
Authorised capital	800,000
Paid-up capital	800,000

Principal Shareholders: State-owned
Date of Establishment: December 1966
No of Employees: 2,829

DAHOUN, TAYEB, PLOUGH MANUFACTURING CO
3 rue Amirouche, RN5 Rouiba
Telex: 217218 Rouiba

Senior Executives: A Dahoun (General and Technical Manager)

PRINCIPAL ACTIVITIES: Construction, repair and sale of farming implements and agricultural equipment

DIESEL ALGERIE
D.I.A.L.
47 Bd Kouchai Boualem, Algiers
Tel: 662055, 662057
Cable: Dial
Telex: 52356

PRINCIPAL ACTIVITIES: Distributor of industrial and public works equipment and machinery; after sales service
Principal Agencies: Perkins; Lucas; JCB; Dale
Principal Bankers: Banque Nationale d'Algerie

DNC/ANP
Direction Nationale des Cooperatives de l'Armee Nationale Populaire
Qued Smar, Algiers
Tel: 763760
Cable: Coopanp
Telex: 52039

PRINCIPAL ACTIVITIES: A wide range of engineering services for the army and for a number of state-owned companies (building projects in the education fields etc)
Financial Information: Responsible to the Ministry of Defence

ECOTEC
Bureau National d'Etudes Economiques et Techniques
6 bld Bougara, BP 33 Birmandreis, Algiers
Tel: 606044, 606044, 608622
Cable: Ecotec Alger
Telex: 52737

PRINCIPAL ACTIVITIES: ECOTEC is responsible for carrying out economic and technical studies for government projects in the field of housing and construction
Branch Offices: Algiers; Constantina; Tizi Ouzou; Batna; Annaba; Oran
Subsidiary Companies: Ecosult; Entreprise Etamcheite Extecto; Entreprise Electricite Batiments
Principal Bankers: Credit Populaire d'Algerie, Banque Algerienne de Developpement
Financial Information: Responsible to the Ministry of Housing and Construction

Principal Shareholders: State-owned
No of Employees: 8,500

ECOTEX (COMPLEXE TCB)
PO Box 110, Bejaia
Tel: 920813/5
Telex: 83052

PRINCIPAL ACTIVITIES: Cotton spinning and weaving, manufacture and processing of textiles, production of underwear clothing and sportswear
Parent Company: ECOTEX: Box 324, Route Des Avres, Bejaia
Principal Bankers: Banque Nationale d'Algerie, Bejaia

ENT NATIONALE DE TRANSPORT MARITIME DE MARCHANDISES

E.N.T.M.M./C.N.A.N.

BP 299, Alger Gare
Tel: 579999, 579567, 579021, 579734, 579489
Cable: Cnalnan Alger
Telex: 61349, 61348, 61544, 61537, 61208

Chairman: Abdessalam Touati (General Manager)

PRINCIPAL ACTIVITIES: Transportation of oil, gas, wine and other goods. The company has a monopoly of handling facilities in all Algerian ports. It operates a shipping fleet for freight and passenger services
Branch Offices: Algiers Maritime; Oran; Annaba; Bedjaia
Parent Company: Responsible to the Ministry of Transport, Algiers
Associated Companies: Societe Nationale de Manutention (SONAMA)
Principal Bankers: Banque Exterieure d'Algerie

Principal Shareholders: State-owned
Date of Establishment: 1963

ENTREPRISE NATIONALE D'AMEUBLEMENT ET DE TRANSFORMATION DU BOIS

E.N.A.T.B.

PO Box 18 Bouinan, Wilaya de Blida
Tel: 483582
Telex: 52726

PRINCIPAL ACTIVITIES: Timber industry, manufacture of furniture

Principal Shareholders: State-owned

ENTREPRISE NATIONALE DE CANALISATION

E.N.A.C

Terminal Sidi Arcine, BP 54 El Harrach, Algiers
Tel: 763866/69
Telex: 54097

PRINCIPAL ACTIVITIES: Pipelines for the transport of hydrocarbons

Principal Shareholders: State-owned

ENTREPRISE NATIONALE DE COMMERCE

E.N.C.

6/9 rue Belhaffaf Ghazali, Haussein Dey, Algiers
Tel: 774320/2, 774503/4, 774503
Cable: Encom Alger
Telex: 52063

PRINCIPAL ACTIVITIES: Monopoly of import, distribution and export of all types of hardware including office, household equipment, electrical appliances, hand tools
Financial Information: Responsible to the Ministry of Commerce, Algiers

Principal Shareholders: State-owned

ENTREPRISE NATIONALE DE FORAGE

E.N.A.F.O.R.

1 Bir Hakeim Sq, El Biar, Algiers
Tel: 784623/25
Cable: Enafor-Algiers
Telex: 52712, 53677 ENAFO DZ

PRINCIPAL ACTIVITIES: Drilling contractors
Branch Offices: Hassi Messaoud, Telex 52827
Parent Company: SONATRACH
Principal Bankers: BEA (Banque Exterieure d'Algerie)

Principal Shareholders: State owned
Date of Establishment: 1-1-82
No of Employees: 2,800

ENTREPRISE NATIONALE DE RAFFINAGE ET DE DISTRIBUTION DES PRODUITS PETROLIERS

N.A.F.T.A.L.

Route des Dunes, Cheraga, Tipaza
Tel: 810969
Telex: 53079

PRINCIPAL ACTIVITIES: Refining and distribution of petroleum products

Principal Shareholders: State-owned

ENTREPRISE NATIONALE DE TRAVAUX D'ELECTRIFICATION

K.A.H.R.I.F.

Villa Malwall, Ain D'heb, Medea
Tel: 506127, 505242, 505293
Telex: 74061

PRINCIPAL ACTIVITIES: Research and contracting for electrical works and infrastructure (low and medium tensions)

Principal Shareholders: State-owned

ENTREPRISE NATIONALE DE TRAVAUX ET MONTAGES ELECTRIQUES

K.A.H.R.A.K.I.B.

127 Bld Salah Bouakouir, Algiers
Tel: 645885, 645891
Telex: 52899

PRINCIPAL ACTIVITIES: Research and contracting for electrical works and infrastructure (High tension)

Principal Shareholders: State-owned

ENTREPRISE NATIONALE D'ENGINEERING ET DE DEVELOPPEMENT DES INDUSTRIES LEGERES

E.D.I.L.

50 rue Khelifa Boukhalfa, Algiers
Tel: 663390
Cable: Edil Alger
Telex: 65153 DZ

Chairman: Hamid Haddadj (Director General)

PRINCIPAL ACTIVITIES: Consultants to a number of state organisations on industrial projects from the feasibility and design stage through to completion. Also for a number of larger projects it has entered into joint ventures with foreign consulting/contracting groups
Branch Offices: Alger - Boumerdes
Financial Information: Responsible to the Ministry of Light Industries

Principal Shareholders: State-owned
Date of Establishment: April 1982
No of Employees: 450

ENTREPRISE NATIONALE DES GRANDS TRAVAUX PETROLIERS

E.N.G.T.P.

Zone Industrielle BP 9 Reghaia, Boumerdes
Tel: 800680/94
Telex: 54845, 54361

PRINCIPAL ACTIVITIES: Consultancy and research for
industrial installations for the oil and gas industry

Principal Shareholders: State-owned

ENTREPRISE NATIONALE DES INDUSTRIES PETROCHIMIQUES

E.N.I.P.

Zone Industrielle BP 115, Skikda
Tel: 956336
Telex: 87098

PRINCIPAL ACTIVITIES: Production and distribution of
petrochemical products (benzene, methanol, ethylene,
xylenes)

Principal Shareholders: State-owned

ENTREPRISE NATIONALE DES PECHES

E.N.A.P.E.C.H.E.

Quai d'Aigues Mortes, Algiers
Tel: 620100
Telex: 61346 ENAP DZ

Chairman: El Okbi Benouaar

PRINCIPAL ACTIVITIES: Fishing industry. Trawling and canned
sea food organisation storage and processing plants
Branch Offices: Export Office: 1 Place de la Pecherie, Algiers,
Tel 627290/1, 627119; Units in Ghazaouet, Mostaganem,
Oran, Beni Saf, Jijel, Collo, El Kala, Tenes, Kaemisti, El Bahri
Principal Bankers: Credit Populaire d'Algerie

Principal Shareholders: State-owned
Date of Establishment: November 1969
No of Employees: 400

ENTREPRISE NATIONALE D'EXPLOITATION ET DE SECURITE AERONAUTIQUES

E.N.E.S.A.

1 Avenue de l'Independence, BP 829, Algiers
Tel: (213) 2 663303
Cable: Direnesa Alger
Telex: 65070

Chairman: M Harrati (Director General)
Directors: F Kellil (Deputy Director General)

PRINCIPAL ACTIVITIES: Air traffic control, and operation and
maintenance of all aerodromes
Financial Information: Responsible to the Ministry of Transport

Principal Shareholders: State-owned
Date of Establishment: May 1983
No of Employees: 1,470

ENTREPRISE NATIONALE DU SUCRE

E.N.A. SUCRE

PO Box 63 Khemis Miliana, Chlef
Tel: 455748

PRINCIPAL ACTIVITIES: Sugar production

Principal Shareholders: State-owned

ENTREPRISE SOCIALISTE DE DEVELOPPEMENT NATIONAL DE LA CONSTRUCTION

E.S.D.N.C.

27 rue Negrier, Hussein Dey, Algiers
Tel: 772882, 771935, 771881
Telex: 52039

PRINCIPAL ACTIVITIES: Engineering and construction
Financial Information: Responsible to the Ministry of Housing &
Construction

Principal Shareholders: State-owned

FOTEX SARL

Route Nationale Fouka Marine, Algiers
Tel: 064 Alger

Senior Executives: Chaib Hamou (Manager)

PRINCIPAL ACTIVITIES: Weaving mill; polyester fabrics

GAOUAR, MOUNIR, ET CIE

18 rue Mohamed Sebagh, Tlemcen
Tel: 203678
Cable: Manubet-Tlemcen
Telex: 22040

Directors: Mounir Gaouar (Managing Director)

PRINCIPAL ACTIVITIES: Manufacture of hand-made carpets,
rugs, tapestries, fabrics and yarns
Principal Bankers: Banque Nationale d'Algerie

HENRI MASCHAT ETS

See MASCHAT, HENRI, ETS

HOTEL EL AURASSI

Les Tagarius, Ave Frantz Fanon, Algiers
Tel: 648262
Telex: 52475

PRINCIPAL ACTIVITIES: Hotel
Parent Company: Sonatour

INDUSTRIELLE DES PLASTIQUES ET METAUX

9 rue Puvis de Chavannes, Oran
Tel: 54790, 54532

PRINCIPAL ACTIVITIES: Manufacture of kitchenware,
aluminium cookers, electrical household appliances
Principal Bankers: Banque Nationale d'Algerie

INSTITUT ALGERIEN DE NORMALISATION ET DE PROPRIETE INDUSTRIELLE

I.N.A.P.I.

5 rue Abou Hamou Moussa, Algiers
Tel: 635180, 639638

PRINCIPAL ACTIVITIES: INAPI is responsible for the
registration of designs (patents) and establishing norms in
Algeria
Associated Companies: Institut National Algerien du Commerce
Exterieur (COMEX)

Principal Shareholders: State-owned

INSTITUT NATIONAL DE LA PRODUCTIVITE ET DU DEVELOPPEMENT INDUSTRIEL

I.N.P.E.D.

BP 99, 126 bis rue Didouche Mourad, Algiers
Tel: 644100
Telex: 52488

PRINCIPAL ACTIVITIES: Management training and industrial
development

Financial Information: Responsible to the Ministry of Light Industry

Principal Shareholders: State-owned

INSTITUT NATIONAL DES HYDROCARBURES ET DE LA CHIMIE
I.N.H.C.
Boumerdes
Tel: 414507
Telex: 53604

PRINCIPAL ACTIVITIES: Management training in the fields of hydrocarbons and chemical industry

Principal Shareholders: State-owned

INSTITUT PASTEUR D'ALGERIE
rue du Docteur Laveran, Algiers
Tel: 668860/62
Telex: 53715

Chairman: Pr M Benhassine (Director General)
Directors: Mrs Boulahbal
Senior Executives: Mr Harrat (Secretary-General)

PRINCIPAL ACTIVITIES: Production of vaccines, sera, culture, media, reagents for medical diagnostic use; research and training in microbiology, parasitology, immunology
Principal Bankers: Banque Nationale d'Algerie

Principal Shareholders: State-owned
Date of Establishment: 1910

ITOH, C, & CO LTD
23 Boulevard Zirout Youcef, Algiers
Tel: 649372/74
Telex: 52826 Itohchu-Alger; 52323

PRINCIPAL ACTIVITIES: Miscellaneous trades, particularly textiles, machinery, metal products, chemicals, foodstuffs, etc (From/to Japan and third world countries)
Branch Offices: Offices in the Middle East: Egypt; Libya; Lebanon; Iraq; Kuwait; Bahrain; Saudi Arabia; Iran

Principal Shareholders: A member of the C Itoh & Co Ltd Group of Japan

MANUFACTURE DE BONNETERIE ET CONFECTION
M.B.C.
13 rue Mohamed Mada, Algiers
Tel: 662751

Chairman: B K Slimane
Directors: Y Bennacer

PRINCIPAL ACTIVITIES: Weaving and spinning, woollen and worsted, hosiery and other knitted goods
Branch Offices: Zone Industrielle Guerrara (Dep Laghouat)

MANUFACTURE DE TISSUS MAILLE
2 rue de la Gare, Rouiva, Algiers
Tel: 763480
Cable: Tismail

Senior Executives: Sellaoui Djemai (Manager)

PRINCIPAL ACTIVITIES: Weaving mill, fabric finishing
Principal Bankers: Banque Exterieure d'Algerie

MAPA INTERNATIONAL GROUP
C/o Creal, 10 rue Khalaf Mustapha Ben Aknoun, Algiers
Tel: 781540/4
Telex: 52595 Sida Dz

PRINCIPAL ACTIVITIES: General contractors, mechanical, electrical, chemical, exploration, drilling, petroleum, construction, project management, engineering, pipelines construction, inspection and surveying, instrumentation, power plants, process plants, training of local staff
Branch Offices: Kuwait; Saudi Arabia; Libya; Pakistan; India; Indonesia; and Far East
Parent Company: Head office in UK
Subsidiary/Associated Companies: Mapa-Creal International Group; ZFS-Enterprises; Mapa-Tis Iran Ltd; Tis Iran Ltd; Mas International; Syd Bros

Principal Shareholders: Private company

MASCHAT, HENRI, ETS
Place Abdellah Chadi, Constantine
Tel: 5901/5
Cable: Maschat Constantine

President: Henri Maschat (Director General)

PRINCIPAL ACTIVITIES: Manufacture of metallic office furniture, general household goods, residential, hospital, school furniture
Principal Bankers: Banque Exterieure d'Algerie

MOUNIR GAOUAR ET CIE
See GAOUAR, MOUNIR, ET CIE

OAIC
Office Algerien Interprofessionnel de Cereales
5 rue Ferhat Bousaad, Algiers
Tel: 662832/5
Cable: Oaic Alger
Telex: 52798; 52121

PRINCIPAL ACTIVITIES: Storage and distribution of cereals; monopoly of trade in wheat, rice, maize, barley and their products
Principal Bankers: Banque Nationale d'Algerie
Financial Information: Responsible to the Ministry of Agriculture and Agrarian Reform

Principal Shareholders: State-owned

OFLA
Office des Fruits et Legumes d'Algerie
12 rue des 3 Freres Bouadou, PO Box 42, Bimandreis, Algiers
Tel: 603694, 600951, 600299, 609009
Cable: Ofla Algiers
Telex: 52823; 52703; 52884

PRINCIPAL ACTIVITIES: Growing, marketing and export of fruit and vegetables
Financial Information: Responsible to the Ministry of Agriculture and Agrarian Reform

Principal Shareholders: State-owned

ONACO
Office National de Commercialisation
29 Rue Larbi Ben M'Hidi, Algiers
Tel: 640275/77, 631095, 614457, 640275/77
Telex: 52992, 52882

Chairman: Sabri Laid (Managing Director)
Directors: Hamrit Abd El Kader (Assistant Managing Director), Annaui Kamel Eddine (Director of Purchasing)

PRINCIPAL ACTIVITIES: Monopoly of import and distribution of foodstuffs and groceries throughout Algeria
Branch Offices: 31 Commercial Offices, 4 Port Offices, 4 Cold Storage
Principal Bankers: Banque Nationale d'Algerie (BNA)
Financial Information: Responsible to the Ministry of Commerce

Principal Shareholders: State-owned
Date of Establishment: 1962
No of Employees: 11,459

ONAFEX
Office National des Foires et Expositions

Palais des Expositions, Pins Maritimes, PO Box 656, Algiers

Tel: 763100/04

Cable: Onafex Alger

Telex: 52828

PRINCIPAL ACTIVITIES: Trade expansion and promotion, holding of the annual Algiers International Trade Fair, national fairs, commercial representation of Algeria abroad

Subsidiary Companies: Several delegations abroad

Financial Information: Responsible to the Ministry of Commerce

Principal Shareholders: State-owned

ONALAIT
Office National du Lait et des Produits Laitiers

1 Place Carnot, Hussein Dey, Algiers

Tel: 770952, 770167, 773995

Cable: Onal Alger

Telex: 52550

PRINCIPAL ACTIVITIES: Development and operation of the milk processing industry. It holds the monopoly for the import and distribution of fresh milk and cream, powder milk and butter, oil and dairy cattle (ONACO holds the monopoly for the import and distribution of butter, cheese, and condensed and evaporated milk)

Financial Information: Responsible to the Ministry of Agriculture and Agrarian Reform

Principal Shareholders: State-owned

ONALFA
Office National de l'Alfa

Immmeuble des Forets, Bois de Boulogne, Le Golf, Algiers

Tel: 604300/4

Cable: Onalfa Alger

Telex: 52854

PRINCIPAL ACTIVITIES: Production and marketing of vegetable hair and alfa grass

Principal Bankers: Banque Nationale d'Algerie

Financial Information: Responsible to the Ministry of Agricultural and Agrarian Reform

Principal Shareholders: State-owned

ONAMA
Office National de Materiel Agricole

15 Rue Arab Si Ahmed, Birkadem, Algiers

Tel: 602392, 666543, 666862

Cable: Onama Alger

Telex: 52948

PRINCIPAL ACTIVITIES: Distribution and repair facilities for agricultural machinery and equipment which ONAMA sells or hires to agricultural producers in both the public and private sectors. It either purchases its requirements direct from the manufacturer or, if required to do so under monopoly legislation, through the SONACOME. It also has set up several small factories manufacturing agricultural equipment

Financial Information: Responsible to the Ministry of Agriculture and Agrarian Reform

Principal Shareholders: State-owned

ONAT
Office National Algerien de la Promotion et de l'Information Touristique

25-27 Rue Khelifa Boukhalfa, Algiers

Tel: 612655, 612986

Cable: Offtour Alger

Telex: 52947

Telefax: 66383, 66339

PRINCIPAL ACTIVITIES: Development and promotion of the tourist industry

Principal Bankers: Credit Populaire d'Algerie

Financial Information: Responsible to the Ministry of Tourism

	AD'000
Authorised capital	6,700
Paid-up capital	3,000

Principal Shareholders: State-owned
No of Employees: 80

ONCIC
Office National pour la Commercialisation des Industries Cinematographiques

Les Asphodeles, Ben Aknoun, Algiers

Tel: 786452, 781302, 782255

Telex: 52506

PRINCIPAL ACTIVITIES: Import, distribution and production of cinema films

Financial Information: Responsible to the Ministry of Information

Principal Shareholders: State-owned

ONCN
Office National de Constructions Navales

Chantier Naval, Mers El Kebir, Oran

PRINCIPAL ACTIVITIES: Shipbuilding and marine construction

Financial Information: Responsible to the Ministry of Defence

Principal Shareholders: State-owned

ONCV
Office National de Commercialisation des Produits Viti-Vinicoles

112 Quai Sud, Algiers

Tel: 630940/44, 633730/34

Cable: Oncv Alger

Telex: 67074, 67363

Directors: E Menia (Director General)

PRINCIPAL ACTIVITIES: Monopoly of import for wine and alcoholic beverages; marketing and distribution of ethyl alcohol, grapes, wines, barrels and bottles

Branch Offices: Oran, Ain Temouchent, Mostaganem, Alger, Annaba

Principal Bankers: Banque Nationale d'Algerie; Banque Exterieure d'Algerie; Banque Algerienne de Developpement Rural

Financial Information: Responsible to the Ministry of Agriculture and Agricultural Reform

Principal Shareholders: State-owned
Date of Establishment: 1968
No of Employees: 1,600

ONEX
Office National de Substances Explosives

5 Bld Mustapha Ben Boulaid, PO Box 509, Algiers

Tel: 618606

Telex: 52678

PRINCIPAL ACTIVITIES: Import, production and distribution of all explosives

Financial Information: Responsible to the Ministry of National Defence

Principal Shareholders: State-owned

ONP
Office National des Ports
Quai d'Arcachon, Port d'Alger, PO Box 830, Algiers
Tel: 626221, 625748/51, 626611, 625255
Telex: 52738

PRINCIPAL ACTIVITIES: Operation and development of all ports in Algeria
Financial Information: Responsible to the Ministry of Transport

Principal Shareholders: State-owned

ONTF
Office National des Travaux Forestiers
Imm des Forets et des Sols, Petit Atlas, Le Golf, Algiers
Tel: 604097, 604804
Telex: 52984

PRINCIPAL ACTIVITIES: Production of timber and the care and maintenance of forests
Financial Information: Responsible to the Ministry of Agriculture and Agrarian Reform

Principal Shareholders: State-owned

ORGANISME DE CONTROLE TECHNIQUE DE LA CONSTRUCTION
O.C.T.E.C.
Rue Kaddour Rahim, Hussein Dey, Algiers
Tel: 772345/48
Telex: OCTEC 52425 DZ

Chairman: Ahcen Tadrist
Directors: Amarouche Bachir, Abdelhamid Abbes
Senior Executives: Omar Terki, Abdelkrim Bentama, Bouhouche Said, Yassini Tahar, Mustapha Salhi

PRINCIPAL ACTIVITIES: Establishment of technical and safety standards for the construction and building industry; technical control of buildings
Branch Offices: Alger; Blida; Bouira; Boumerdes; Medea; Tipaza; Tizi-Ouzou
Parent Company: Responsible to the Ministry of Housing, Town Planning & Construction
Principal Bankers: CPA
Financial Information:

	1990 DA'000
Sales turnover	174,000
Paid-up capital	40,000

Principal Shareholders: State-owned
Date of Establishment: December 1971
No of Employees: 300

PAPETERIE CARTONNERIE MODERNE
Quartier Sainte Corine, Maison Carree, District of Algiers
Tel: 766680

PRINCIPAL ACTIVITIES: Paper industry (Output: 10,000 tons per year)

PHARMACIE CENTRALE ALGERIENNE (PCA)
2 rue Bichat, Algiers
Tel: 660936, 662827/9, 669210
Cable: Algephar Alger
Telex: 52993

PRINCIPAL ACTIVITIES: Production and primary distribution and monopoly on pharmaceutical goods, medical supplies and equipment. It is responsible for the import and

distribution of these products to the public sector and to the private retail chemists
Financial Information: Responsible to the Ministry of Public Health

Principal Shareholders: State-owned

PYRAF
Route d'Oran, Ain Defla, El-Asnam
Tel: 1252

PRINCIPAL ACTIVITIES: Production of mining, blasting and safety fuses, electric detonators, etc
Principal Bankers: Banque Nationale d'Algerie

RADIODIFFUSION TELEVISION ALGERIENNE
R.T.A.
21 Boulevard des Martyrs, Algiers
Tel: 602300/04, 780310/13
Cable: Rta Alger
Telex: 52042

PRINCIPAL ACTIVITIES: Monopoly for radio and television broadcasting
Financial Information: Responsible to the Ministry of Information and Culture

Principal Shareholders: State-owned

SAIPEM SPA SUCCURSALE D'ALGERIE
24 Bougainville St, PO Box 60, El Mouradia, Algiers
Tel: 606370/1/2

PRINCIPAL ACTIVITIES: Engineers, constructors, pipeline contractors, drilling contractors
Branch Offices: Italy; Libya; Algeria; Tunisia; Iraq; Abu Dhabi (UAE); Iran; Tanzania; etc

SAP
Ste Agricole de Prevoyance
19 rue Khodjet El Djeld, Birmandreis, Algiers
Tel: 603720, 603999
Cable: Dgsap Alger
Telex: 52296

PRINCIPAL ACTIVITIES: Import and distribution of seeds and agricultural materials

Principal Shareholders: State-owned

SNAMPROGETTI
16 rue Payen-Hydra, PO Box 496, Algiers
Tel: 600812/4
Cable: Snamproge Elger
Telex: 91751

PRINCIPAL ACTIVITIES: Consultant engineering contractors for refineries, petrochemical and power plants
Branch Offices: Italy; Algeria; Libya; Iraq; Iran

SNB TRAPAL
Ste Nationale du Batiment et de Travaux Publics d'Alger
PO Box 7, Route de Blida, El Achour, Algiers
Tel: 811543, 811525
Telex: 53854

PRINCIPAL ACTIVITIES: Civil engineering, building and public works in Algiers
Associated Companies: SNB TRAPCO (Societe Nationale du Batiment et des Travaux Publics de Constantine)
Financial Information: Responsible to the Ministry of Housing and Construction

Principal Shareholders: State-owned

SNB TRAPCO
Ste Nationale du Batiment et des Travaux Publics de Constantine
28 rue Kaddour Boumedouir, Constantine
Tel: 939829

PRINCIPAL ACTIVITIES: Civil engineering, building and public
   works in Constantine
Financial Information: Responsible to the Ministry of Housing
   and Construction

Principal Shareholders: State-owned

SNCOTEC
Ste Nationale de Commercialisation des Textiles et des Cuirs
3 Boulevard Anatole France, PO Box 94, Algiers
Tel: 625763/66
Cable: Sncotec Alger
Telex: 52072

PRINCIPAL ACTIVITIES: Import and distribution of textiles,
   ready-made clothing and leather clothing, footwear, skins and
   leather. SNCOTEC holds the monopoly for the import and
   distribution of the above products
Associated Companies: SONITEX and SONIPEC
Principal Bankers: Banque Exterieure d'Algerie
Financial Information: Responsible to the Ministry of Commerce

Principal Shareholders: State-owned

SNED
Ste Nationale d'Edition et de Diffusion
3 Boulevard Zirout Youcef, Algiers
Tel: 639643, 639712/13, 639670
Cable: Sneda Alger

President: Sid Ahmed Baghli (also Director General)

PRINCIPAL ACTIVITIES: Monopoly for the import and export of
   newspapers and magazines, and the import of school and
   office supplies and all types of stationery. Also development
   and operation of factories in the public sector manufacturing
   school and office supplies
Financial Information: Responsible to the Ministry of Information
   and Culture

Principal Shareholders: State-owned

SNEMA
Ste Nationale des Eaux Minerales
21 Rue Bellouchat Mouloud, Hussein Dey, Algiers
Tel: 771791/93, 771022
Telex: 52310

PRINCIPAL ACTIVITIES: Development and management of the
   mineral waters industry
Financial Information: Responsible to the Ministry of Light
   Industries

Principal Shareholders: State-owned

SNIC
Ste Nationale des Industries Chimiques
Route des 5 Maisons, El Harrach, Algiers
Tel: 763782/5
Cable: Snicent Alger
Telex: 52840

PRINCIPAL ACTIVITIES: Production and distribution of paint
   and varnish, cosmetics, chlorine, insecticides, glass,
   hydrochloric acid, ammonia, detergents, shampoos, talcum
   and razor blades. It holds the monopoly of chemical products
Branch Offices: Administrative Office: 24 Blvd Zirout Youcef,
   Algiers, Tel 632910. Financial Office: 15 rue Victor Hugo,
   Hussein Dey, Algiers. Commercial Office: Route des 5
Maisons, El Harrach, Algiers, Tel 763782/5, Telex 52840.
   Engineering Office: 29 rue Didouche Mourad, Algiers, Tel
   630421/5, Telex 52521
Subsidiary Companies: Unite Verre (SNIC), Oran, Tel 40911,
   Telex 22056
Financial Information: Responsible to the Ministry of Light
   Industry

Principal Shareholders: State-owned

SNIV
Ste Nationale des Industries du Verre
Avenue des Martyrs, Es-Senia-Oran
Tel: (3)40911, (3)41317/18
Telex: 22056

PRINCIPAL ACTIVITIES: Development and management of
   glass and chinaware factories in the public sector

Principal Shareholders: State-owned

SNLB
Ste Nationale des Industries des Lieges et du Bois
1 Rue Kaddour Rahim, PO Box 61, Hussein-Dey, Algiers
Tel: 775000, 775834, 775220
Telex: 52726 Dz Liebois

PRINCIPAL ACTIVITIES: Manufacture of furniture, office
   equipment, building materials, doors and windows, cork
   products, plywood, hardboard and general timber products
Subsidiary Companies: Mischler Afrique, 28 Av des Martyrs,
   Oran
Financial Information: Responsible to the Ministry of Light
   Industry

Principal Shareholders: State-owned

SNMC
Ste Nationale des Materiaux de Construction
Route de L'Arbea, El Harrach, Algiers
Tel: 763199
Telex: 52811

PRINCIPAL ACTIVITIES: Manufacture and sale of building
   materials (bricks, cement, lime, plaster, zinc). Holds the
   monopoly for the import of all building materials and ceramic
   sanitary ware
Branch Offices: Commercial Office: Route de l'Arbea, El
   Harrach, Algiers. Production Office: PO Box 712, 88 rue
   Didouche Mourad, Algiers, Tel 664672. Technical Office: Gue
   de Constantine, Kouba, Algiers, Tel 766933/4, 766890/1,
   Telex 52861
Financial Information: Responsible to the Ministry of Light
   Industry

Principal Shareholders: State-owned

SN-METAL
Ste Nationale de Constructions Metalliques
110 rue de Tripoli, Hussein Dey, Algiers
Tel: 772810
Cable: DP Metal Alger
Telex: 52594

PRINCIPAL ACTIVITIES: Structural steel builders to draw up
   complexes and sub-complexes for the iron and steel industry,
   the chemical industry, the building materials industry.
   Responsible for the management and the operation of public
   sector plants for general mechanics, metal working and boiler
   making. SN METAL absorbs a large portion of the iron and
   steel production of SNS and transforms it into equipment for
   use in Algeria's industrial projects
Branch Offices: Plastic Unit: Avenue de l'ALN, Hussein-Dey,
   Algiers. Engineering Unit; Rue du Sergeant Addoun,
   Caroubier, Hussein Dey, Algiers, Tel 779110, 779211, 779524.

Development Office: Route de Meftah, Oued Smar, PO Box 25, El Harrach, Algiers, Tel 766411/2

Financial Information: Responsible to the Ministry of Heavy Industry

SNNGA

Ste Nationale "Les Nouvelles Galeries Algeriennes"

67 Rue Larbi Tebessi, PO Box 150, Algiers

Tel: 662963, 662971,662988

Cable: Snga Alger

Telex: 52776

PRINCIPAL ACTIVITIES: Operation of many department stores; also distribution to private wholesalers and retailers of a wide range of consumer goods for which it holds the import monopoly

Financial Information: Responsible to the Ministry of Commerce

Principal Shareholders: State-owned

SN-REPAL

Ste Nationale Repal

Chemin du Reservoir, PO Box 105, Hydra

Tel: 602090/97

Cable: Repal Alger

Telex: 91917

PRINCIPAL ACTIVITIES: Integrated petroleum activity, petroleum prospecting

Parent Company: SONATRACH

Financial Information: A subsidiary of SONATRACH

Principal Shareholders: State-owned

Date of Establishment: 1926

SNS

Ste Nationale de la Siderugie

5 rue Abu-Moussa, PO Box 296, Algiers

Tel: 647560/4

Cable: Algersider

Telex: 52887 Sidejar Algiers; 52309

Chairman: Lakhdar Bentebbal

Directors: Reski Hocine (Director General)

PRINCIPAL ACTIVITIES: Production and distribution of iron and steel products, conversion of steel, production and conversion of non-ferrous metals, importation of metals on a monopoly basis. Responsible for the duty, design, construction and operation of iron and steel plants

Branch Offices: Commercial Office: Hydra, Algiers, Tel 601544, 600158, 608000, Telex 52819, 52950. Engineering Office: 116 Route Neuve, La Bruyere, Bouzareah, Algiers, Tel 781465/7, 781958. Financial Office: 2 rue de Chenoua, La Paradou, Hydra, Algiers, Tel 603711, 603384, 608084. Aluminium Office: Gue de Constantine, Kouba, Algiers, Tel 765993/4. Industrial Gas Office: 2 Blvd Aissat Idir, Algiers, Tel 669863/6, 664718. Tubes Offices: Reghaia, Algiers, Tel 800441/2. El Hadjar Office: Annaba, Telex 92718, 92727

Subsidiary Companies: Genisider (SNS 51%; Razel 49%); Sidal (SNS 51%; Air Liquide 49%)

Principal Bankers: Banque Algerienne de Developpement; Banque Exterieure d'Algerie

Principal Shareholders: State-owned

No of Employees: 35,000

SN-SEMPAC

Ste Nationale de Semouleries, Meuneries, Fabriques de Pates Alimentaires et Couscous

6bd Zirout Youcef, PO Box 17, Algiers

Tel: 630490/92, 639297

Cable: Snsempac

Telex: 52923; 52912; 52507

PRINCIPAL ACTIVITIES: Production and distribution of cereal foods, couscous, pasta, flour, bran, biscuits, sweets. SEMPAC holds the monopoly for the import and export of these products

Branch Offices: Financial Office: 8 rue Rene Tilley, Algiers, Tel 614535/7. Technical Office: 5 rue Aristide Briand, El Harrach, Algiers, Tel 765225. Commercial Office: 28 Blvd Colonel Bougara, Algiers, Tel 764184, 764973, 765517, Telex 52912

Principal Bankers: Banque Nationale d'Algerie

Financial Information: Responsible to the Ministry of Light Industries

Principal Shareholders: State-owned

SNTA

Ste Nationale des Tabacs et Allumettes

40 rue Hocine Nourredine, Belcourt, Algiers

Tel: 656943/44, 661868

Cable: Sntabac

Telex: 52780

Chairman: Mourad Medeci

PRINCIPAL ACTIVITIES: Monopoly of manufacture of trade in tobacco and matches, cigarettes, cigars, pipe tobacco; manufacture of several foreing cigarette brands under licence

Branch Offices: Commercial Office: 5 rue Marquis de Montcalm, Bab El Qued, Algiers

Principal Bankers: Banque Nationale d'Algerie

Principal Shareholders: State-owned

No of Employees: 4,400

SNTF

Ste Nationale des Transports Ferroviaires

21/23 Blvd Mohamed V, Algiers

Tel: 611510

Telex: 52455

PRINCIPAL ACTIVITIES: Rail transport, freight and passenger

Associated Companies: Societe Nationale d'Etudes et de Realisations de l'Infrastructure Ferroviaire

Financial Information: Responsible to the Ministry of Transport

Principal Shareholders: State-owned

Date of Establishment: 1959

SNTR

Ste Nationale des Transports Routiers

27 rue des 3 Freres Bouaddou, Birmandreis, Algiers

Tel: 602477, 604392

Cable: Sntr

Telex: 52962

PRINCIPAL ACTIVITIES: The company has a monopoly of commercial road transport on long distances

Financial Information: Responsible to the Ministry of Transport

Principal Shareholders: State-owned

SNTV

Ste Nationale de Transport des Voyageurs

19 rue Raban Midat, Algiers

Tel: 663341

Telex: 52903

PRINCIPAL ACTIVITIES: All long-distance road passenger transport

Subsidiary Companies: Agence de Voyage Algerienne (AVA), 9 Bld Zirout Youssef, Algiers, Tel 639041/4, Telex 52903

Financial Information: Responsible to the Ministry of Transport

Principal Shareholders: State-owned

SOGEDIA

Ste de Gestion et de Developpement des Industries Alimentaires

13 Av Claude Debussy, Algiers
Tel: 643801, 643833
Telex: 52837; 52539; 52316

PRINCIPAL ACTIVITIES: Formerly known as the Societe Nationale de Gestion et de Developpement des Industries du Sucre (SOGEDIS). Since its formation it has absorbed the Societe Nationale des Conserveries Algeriennes (SOALCO), and the Societe Nationale des Corps Gras (SNGC). SOGEDIA is responsible for the operation and development of sugar plants and processing plants for food and fruit juices in public sector

Principal Bankers: Banque Nationale d'Algerie

Financial Information: Responsible to the Ministry of Light Industries

Principal Shareholders: State-owned

SONACOB

Ste Nationale de Commercialisation des Bois et Derives

2 Boulevard Mohamed V, Algiers
Tel: 638532/26
Telex: 52508 Cobalger

President: Abdelmadjid Bentchikou (also Director General)

PRINCIPAL ACTIVITIES: Monopoly for the import and distribution of wood and wood by-products such as plywood and particle board

Associated Companies: Societe Nationale de Lieges et du Bois (SNLB)

Financial Information: Responsible to the Ministry of Commerce

Principal Shareholders: State-owned

SONACOME

Ste Nationale de Constructions Mecaniques

18 avenue Mustapha Ouali, Algiers
Tel: 567084, 568790
Cable: Sonacome Alger
Telex: 52800; 52367

Directors: Abdallah Daba

PRINCIPAL ACTIVITIES: SONACOME has the exclusive monopoly on imports of mechanical products. Sole manufacturer and importer of motor vehicles, industrial and agricultural equipment, public works equipment, cars, motorcycles, pumps and allied products. Promotion of mechanical equipment, marketing of such products and control of their imports. Responsible for the management of factories producing mechanical equipment

Branch Offices: Engineering & Public Works Dept, Route de Dely Brahim, Cheraga; Home Market Dept, 18 Avenue Mustapha Ouali, Algiers; Import Sales, Avenue de l'Aln, Algiers

Principal Shareholders: State-owned
Date of Establishment: August 1967
No of Employees: 30,000

SONADE

Ste Nationale de Distribution d'Eau Potable et Industrielle

8 Rue Sergent Addoun, Algiers
Tel: 634334, 638577
Cable: Sonade Alger
Telex: 52879

PRINCIPAL ACTIVITIES: Monopoly for the distribution of water to domestic and industrial users; maintenance and renewal of production and distribution installations

Principal Shareholders: State-owned

SONAGTHER

Ste Nationale des Grands Travaux Hydrauliques et d'Equipement Rural

22 Chemin de la Madeleine, El Bair, Algiers
Tel: 782361/63
Cable: Sonagther Alger
Telex: 52519

Directors: Abdelaziz Kellout

PRINCIPAL ACTIVITIES: SONAGTHER is responsible for hydraulic works (dams, bore holes, irrigation schemes, etc) and rural equipment. (It has replaced the previous hydraulics company, SONATHYD, which was dissolved)

Principal Shareholders: State-owned

SONAMA

Ste Nationale de Manutention

6 rue de Beziers, Algiers
Tel: 646561, 649201, 630317
Cable: Sonama
Telex: 52339; 52330

PRINCIPAL ACTIVITIES: Monopoly of all lighterage and associated activities in Algerian ports, previously the responsibility of the Compagnie Nationale Algerienne de Navigation (Transport)

Financial Information: Responsible for the Ministry of Transport

Principal Shareholders: State-owned

SONAREM

Ste Nationale de Recherches et d'Exploitations Minieres

127 Boulevard Salah Bouakir, PO Box 860, Algiers
Tel: 63155/62
Telex: 52910 Minebar

PRINCIPAL ACTIVITIES: Mining prospecting excluding hydrocarbons; exploration and valorization of the national mineral wealth (iron and zinc ore, lead and phosphate); marketing of mineral products. SONAREM holds the import monopoly of all mineral products

Principal Bankers: Banque Nationale d'Algerie

Financial Information: Responsible to the Ministry of Heavy Industry

Principal Shareholders: State-owned

SONATIBA

Ste Nationale de Travaux d'Infrastructure et de Batiment

Route Nationale No 1, PO Box 53, Birmandreis, Algiers
Tel: 605266
Telex: 52060

Chairman: Belkacem Benbatouche (Director General)

PRINCIPAL ACTIVITIES: Building and civil engineering contract work in the construction of buildings, factories, roads, ports, airports, dams, etc

Branch Offices: Algiers; Oran; Constantina; Skikda; Annaba
Principal Bankers: CPA; CCP
Financial Information: Responsible to the Ministry of Housing and Construction

Principal Shareholders: State-owned
No of Employees: 18,000

SONATITE

Ste Nationale des Travaux d'Infrastructure des Telecommunications

Quai d'Angkor, PO Box 816, Algiers
Tel: 628352/4, 628855, 629407
Telex: 52568

PRINCIPAL ACTIVITIES: General civil engineering and construction work in the telecommunications field

Principal Shareholders: State-owned

SONATMAG

Ste Nationale de Transit et des Magasins Generaux

8 Rue Said Babel, Algiers
Tel: 648636/38, 649060/61
Cable: Sonatmag
Telex: 52071

PRINCIPAL ACTIVITIES: Dealing with the transit, transport, handling, cold storage, and warehousing of goods. It does not have a monopoly, and a number of private firms are still operating in this field
Financial Information: Responsible to the Ministry of Commerce

Principal Shareholders: State-owned

SONATOUR

Ste Nationale Algerienne de Tourisme et d'Hotellerie

Grand Hotel de Chenoua Plage, BP G Tipaza, Wilaya de Blida , Algiers
Tel: 461450
Telex: 53600

PRINCIPAL ACTIVITIES: Tourism and hotels; operation of public sector hotels and tourist complexes
Branch Offices: Commercial Office: 51 Blvd Ben Boulaid, Algiers, Tel 641550/1, 641286
Subsidiary Companies: Organisme National de Congres et Conferences; Societe Nationale Algerienne de l'Hotellerie Urbaine; Entreprise Nationale des Etudes Touristiques
Financial Information: Responsible to the Ministry of Tourism, 42 rue Khelifa Boukhalfa, Algiers, Tel 663353

Principal Shareholders: State-owned

SONATRACH

Ste Nationale pour la Recherche, la Production, le Transport, la Transformation, et la Commercialisation des Hydrocarbures

80 Avenue Ahmed Ghermoul, Algiers
Tel: 663300, 662707, 662890
Cable: Sonatrach
Telex: 52916; 52790

President: Ahmed Ghozali (Director General)
Directors: Nourredine Ait Laoucine (Distribution Vice-President), Othmane Khouani (Engineering and Development Vice-President), Mohamed Mazouni (Petrochemicals LNG and Refinery Vice-President), Hassen Mefti (Hydrocarbons Vice-President), Hacene Kahlouche (Organisation and Planning Vice-President)

PRINCIPAL ACTIVITIES: Monopoly of exploration, production, transport, processing, marketing and distribution of oil products, derivatives of liquid and natural gas (hydrocarbons, fertilisers, plastics and petrochemicals)
Branch Offices: Distribution Dept: Imm Mauretania, Algiers, Tel 638800. Engineering and Development Dept: 10 rue du Sahara, Hydra, Algiers, Tel 600600. Petrochemicals, GNI and Refinery Dept; Zone Industrielle, Arzew, Tel 376381. Hydrocarbons Dept: Imm Mauretania, Algiers, Tel 611366. Financial Dept: 76 Ave Ahmed Ghermoul, Tel 669892. Production Dept: 8 Chemin du Reservoir, Hydra, Algiers, Tel 609200, 602629. LNG Dept: 17 Bld Khemisti, Algiers, Tel 606044. Transport Dept: 9 rue Abou Nouas, Hydra, Algiers, Tel 609000. Central Engineering Dept: 10 rue du Sahara, Hydra, Algiers, Tel 606633. Commercialisation Dept: 46 Bld Mohamed V, Algiers, Tel 638800
Subsidiary/Associated Companies: ASCOOP, CREPS, SOTHRA, SOELGAZ, COMES, ALTRA, SN REPAL, SOPEG, SONEMS, ALFOR, ALGEO, Ste de la Raffinerie d'Alger
Principal Bankers: Banque Exterieure d'Algerie
Financial Information: SONATRACH holds the import monopoly for many hydrocarbon chemical and petrochemical products including fertilisers. It owns all oil and gas pipelines in Algeria and controls 80% of Algeria's oil production

Principal Shareholders: State-owned

SONATRACH (USINE GL4Z)

HQ and Plant, PO Box 11, Arzew
Tel: 376233
Telex: 22076

PRINCIPAL ACTIVITIES: Natural gas liquefaction
Branch Offices: 17 bld Mohamed Khemisti, Algiers, Tel 646844/81, Telex 52704

Principal Shareholders: State-owned
Date of Establishment: 1963, nationalised in 1978
No of Employees: 400

SONATRAM

Ste Nationale de Travaux Maritimes

1 rue de Dole, Port d'Alger, Algiers
Tel: 657073/4, 657053/6, 653620
Telex: 52074

PRINCIPAL ACTIVITIES: Port construction, civil, electro-mechanical engineering, power construction
Financial Information: Responsible to the Ministry of Public Works

Principal Shareholders: State-owned

SONATRO

Ste Nationale de Travaux Routiers

1 Boulevard Anatole France, Algiers
Tel: 620881/82
Cable: Sonatro
Telex: 52759

PRINCIPAL ACTIVITIES: Road and earthmoving contractors; construction and maintenance of roads and related works
Financial Information: Responsible to the Ministry of Public Works, 135 rue Didouche Mourad, Algiers

Principal Shareholders: State-owned

SONELEC

Ste Nationale de Fabrication et de Montage du Materiel Electrique et Electronique

Rue de Constantine, Kouba, Algiers
Tel: 765680
Telex: 52219

PRINCIPAL ACTIVITIES: Production of electric and telephonic cables, wet and dry batteries, electrical equipment and electro-mechanical appliances, public lighting equipment, motors and transformers. Holds the import monopoly of electrical and electronic equipment

Financial Information: Responsible to the Ministry of Heavy Industry

Principal Shareholders: State-owned

SONELGAZ
Ste Nationale de l'Electricite et du Gaz

2 Blvd Salah Bouakouir, Algiers
Tel: 648260
Telex: 91898

Chairman: Mostefa Harrati

PRINCIPAL ACTIVITIES: The monopoly of production, distribution and transport of electric power to domestic and industrial consumers in the country; exportation of electric power. Transport and distribution of gaz to domestic and industrial consumers

Branch Offices: Algiers; Blida; Oran; Chlef; Constantine; Annaba; Setif; Bechar; Ouargla

Financial Information: Responsible to the Ministry of Energy and Petrochemical Industries

	AD'million
Sales turnover	3.390

Principal Shareholders: State-owned
Date of Establishment: 1969
No of Employees: 18,000

SONIC
Ste Nationale des Industries de la Cellulose

64 rue Ali Haddad, El Mouradia, Algiers
Tel: 663800/1
Telex: 52933

Chairman: Chaib Cherif Bralium
Directors: Bourouina Sadek

PRINCIPAL ACTIVITIES: Production of cellulose, pulp, paper and cardboard, papier mache, writing and printing paper, tissue paper. SONIC holds the monopoly of import and export of material and goods required for the manufacture of paper and associated products

Principal Bankers: Banque Exterieure d'Algerie

Financial Information: Responsible to the Ministry of Light Industry

Principal Shareholders: State-owned
Date of Establishment: 1968
No of Employees: 7,778

SONIC UNITE BABA ALI

PO Box 32, Elmouradia, Algiers
Cable: Baba Ali (Alger)
Telex: 91789

PRINCIPAL ACTIVITIES: Paper industry (Output: 23,000 tons per year)

Parent Company: Societe Nationale des Industries de la Cellulose (SONIC)

Principal Shareholders: State-owned

SONIPEC
Ste Nationale des Industries des Peaux et Cuirs

100 rue de Tripoli, Hussein-Dey, Algiers
Tel: 772604, 772042
Telex: 52832; 52068

PRINCIPAL ACTIVITIES: Development and production of leather, leather clothing and leather shoes

Associated Companies: SNCOTEC

Financial Information: Absorbed in 1972 the two state companies: Societe Nationale de Tanneries Algeriennes (TAL) and Societe Nationale des Industries de la Chaussure (SIAC)

Principal Shareholders: State-owned; responsible to the Ministry of Light Industry

SONITEX
Ste Nationale des Industries Textiles

22 rue des Fusilles, Les Annassers, Algiers
Tel: 659314/8
Telex: 52871

PRINCIPAL ACTIVITIES: Production of textile and clothing. Responsible for the marketing, planning and construction of new textile plants

Associated Companies: SNCOTEC (Societe Nationale de Commercialisation de Textiles de Cuirs) (see separate entry)

Financial Information: Responsible to the Ministry of Light Industry

Principal Shareholders: State-owned
Date of Establishment: 1966
No of Employees: 33,000

STE ALGERIENNE D'ASSURANCES
S.A.A.

5 Boulevard Che Guevara, Algiers
Tel: 622944
Telex: 52716

President: Farid Benbouzid (Director General)

PRINCIPAL ACTIVITIES: All types of Insurance
Financial Information: Responsible to the Ministry of Finance

Principal Shareholders: State-owned

STE ALGERIENNE D'EMAILLAGE ET DE GALVANISATION
S.A.E.G.

12 rue Ali Boumendjel, Algiers
Telex: 52040 Alger

President: Abdel Majid Kerrar

PRINCIPAL ACTIVITIES: Manufacture of household articles made of enamel, lead, galvanised or printed sheets
Branch Offices: Place du Marche, Isser, Grand Kabylie
Principal Bankers: Banque Nationale d'Algerie

STE ALGERIENNE DES ETS BROSSETTE
Ets Brossette

3 rue de Tripoli, Hussein-Dey, Algiers
Tel: 772790
Cable: Brosetmeto
Telex: 91830 Brosset

PRINCIPAL ACTIVITIES: Oil service company; representative for Byron Jackson Inc, also wholesale metals, iron, plumbing supplies, hardware

STE ALGERIENNE DES ETS MORY & CO
Ets Mory & Co

8 Bd Colonel Amirouche, PO Box 234, Algiers
Tel: 631962/5
Cable: Mory, Algiers
Telex: 52906

PRINCIPAL ACTIVITIES: Shipping agent

STE ALGERIENNE D'OUVRAGES EN PLASTIQUE
S.A.C.O.P.

35 Av de Martyrs, PO Box 1012, Lamur, Oran
Tel: 43885

PRINCIPAL ACTIVITIES: Production polyethylene bags, covers and films
Principal Bankers: Banque Exterieure d'Algerie

STE ALGERIENNE SIMMONS

SIMMONS

1 route de Meftah, PO Box 65, Algiers
Tel: 765965
Cable: Cosimmons Alger

PRINCIPAL ACTIVITIES: Production of mattresses and spring mattresses
Principal Bankers: Banque Exterieure d'Algerie

STE DE LA RAFFINERIE D'ALGERIE

Raffinerie de Sidi Arcine, PO Box 71, El Harrach
Tel: 764865
Telex: 52842 Rafinal

President: A Khodja (Director General)

PRINCIPAL ACTIVITIES: Oil refining. Production: 2,000,000 tons per year
Branch Offices: 5 rue Michel-Ange, Paris 16e, France, Tel 5255151

Principal Shareholders: Sonatrach (80%), Compagnie Francaise des Petroles (20%)

STE DE PEINTURES DE L'OUEST ALGERIEN

S.P.O.A.

22 Avenue Khiali Ben Salein, Oran
Tel: 354143
Telex: 22090 Tamesol

Directors: Mohamed Soltane, Habib Soltane
Senior Executives: Mustapha Soltane (Commercial Director), Tayeb Boumedjout (Financial Director)

PRINCIPAL ACTIVITIES: Production of paints for industrial, marine and construction usage
Principal Bankers: Banque Exterieure d'Algerie; Banque Nationale Algerienne

STE D'ECONOMIE MIXTE BRASSERIES ET GLACIERES D'ALGERIE

Brasseries et Glacieres d'Alger

PO Box 22, El-Harrach, Algiers
Tel: 765840/43

PRINCIPAL ACTIVITIES: Brewery and soft drinks manufacture
Branch Offices: 3 branches in Algeria

STE DES APPLICATIONS TECHNIQUES INDUSTRIELLES

S.A.T.I.

rue Badjarah Hussein-Dey, PO Box 72, Algiers
Tel: 770834/6
Cable: Michelinaf
Telex: 52747

PRINCIPAL ACTIVITIES: Tyre industry, rubber contractors
Principal Agencies: Michelin

STE NATIONALE DES TRANSPORTS AERIENS

Air Algerie

1 Place Maurice Audin, Algiers
Tel: 742428, 631282/89
Telex: 54436 Algah
Telefax: 610553

Chairman: Mohamed Salah Ouaari (Director General)

Directors: Chakib Belleili (Deputy General Manager for Finance & Commerce), Benouis M'hamed (Deputy General Manager for Technical and Operation)
Senior Executives: Mahfoud Benkhelil (General Secretary), M Bekhaled (Personnel Manager), Mustapha Benaissa (Commercial Manager), Saddek Ouldabedlkader (Finance Manager), Omar Hamchaoui (Technical Manager), Faycal Hanafi (Operations Manager), Omar Mesbah (Purchasing Manager), M Belkheir (Legal Manager)

PRINCIPAL ACTIVITIES: Air transport, passengers and freight
Principal Agencies: All major international foreign airlines
Branch Offices: Paris: 19 Avenue de l'Opera, Paris 1 er; Frankfurt: 9 Munchenerstrasse; Moscow: Koutouzovski Prospect Dom 7/4 Bat 6 Apt 20; London: 10 Baker St, W1; Rome: Via 4 Fontane 177; Madrid: Torre de Madrid Piso II Officina 2
Principal Bankers: Banque Nationale d'Algerie; Banque Exterieure d'Algerie
Financial Information:

	1989/90 DA'000
Sales turnover	2.982.000
Profits	231.000
Authorised capital	28.672
Paid-up capital	28.672
Total assets	4.778.000

Principal Shareholders: State-owned
Date of Establishment: 1947; nationalised in 1972
No of Employees: 8,807

STE NORD AFRICAINE DE CONSTRUCTION ET DE REPRESENTATIONS AGRICOLES ET MECANIQUES

S.N.A.C.R.A.M.

PO Box 12, 207 bis rue Hassiba, Ben-Bouali, Hussein Dey, Algiers
Tel: 663788/9
Cable: Sacrafnor

PRINCIPAL ACTIVITIES: Production of heavy machinery, agricultural and mechanical equipment
Principal Bankers: Banque Nationale d'Algerie; Banque Exterieure d'Algerie

TAYEB DAHOUN PLOUGH MANUFACTURING CO

See DAHOUN, TAYEB, PLOUGH MANUFACTURING CO

UNITE VERRE

Ave des Martyrs, El-Senia, Oran
Tel: 40911
Telex: 22056

PRINCIPAL ACTIVITIES: Ceramics, glass works
Parent Company: Ste Nationale des Industries Chimiques (SNIC)

Major Companies of BAHRAIN

A A ZAYANI & SONS (MERCANTILE DIVISION)
See ZAYANI, A A, & SONS (MERCANTILE DIVISION)

A J M KOOHEJI & SONS
See KOOHEJI, A J M, & SONS

A M YATEEM BROS
See YATEEM, A M, BROS

A R BOKHAMMAS
See BOKHAMMAS, A R,

ABBAS ALI REZA HAMEDE
PO Box 5182, Manama
Tel: 259199, 230043
Cable: Jahromy
Telex: 8924 Abasco BN

Proprietor: Abbas Ali Reza Hamede (Managing Director)
Senior Executives: S M Kamal (General Manager), S B Soman (Projects Manager), S V Shirodkar (Contracts Manager), N S Chudda (Planning Manager), P K Mukundan (Administration Manager)

PRINCIPAL ACTIVITIES: Civil, electrical and mechanical engineering contractors, plant hire, supply of all types of building materials and construction equipment
Principal Agencies: Peabody International, USA; Mannesmann Demag, W Germany; Losenhausen Maschinen Bau, W Germany; Intradym AG, Switzerland; Wagner GmbH, W Germany; Osaki Ltd, Japan
Principal Bankers: National Bank of Abu Dhabi; Banque Paribas; Al Ahli Commercial Bank

Date of Establishment: 1975
No of Employees: 515

ABBAS BILJEEK & SONS
See BILJEEK, ABBAS, & SONS

ABDUL AAL CONSTRUCTION SERVICES
Diplomatic Area, PO Box 20418, Manama
Tel: 533999
Telex: 8454 Walid BN
Telefax: 0973-533236

Chairman: Ebrahim Abdul Aal
Directors: Ebrahim Abdul Aal (Managing Director)
Senior Executives: Y P Madan (General Manager), V D Dandanayak (Deputy General Manager)

PRINCIPAL ACTIVITIES: Electro mechanical contracting, building and civil construction and trading in: oil and water storage tanks, gas scrubbing plants, oil and gas pile lines, water proofing and surface treatment, thermal insulation and refractory works, pumping station and distribution networks, domestic/industrial electrical installation, industrial maintenance and turnkey projects, furnishing of hospitals, school and commercial establishments, fire protection and safety and security equipment; supply of electronic items, garments; livestock
Principal Agencies: Suedrohrbau; U.P. State Bridge Corp; Aturia, Italy; Astaldi Estero, Italy; Klockner Ina, W Germany; Best & Crompton, India
Branch Offices: Oman; Qatar; Abu Dhabi; Dubai; Saudi Arabia
Associated Companies: Petroleum Development Services; Abdul Aal Safety & Security Services; Abdul Aal Commercial Services; Waleed Electronics; Fyfield Commercial Corp; Transworld Enterprises; Gulf Somali Export Corp
Principal Bankers: Algemene Bank Nederland, Bahrain

Principal Shareholders: Ebrahim Abdul Aal
Date of Establishment: 1976
No of Employees: 450

ABDUL AZIZ SULAIMAN AL BASSAM
See AL BASSAM, ABDUL AZIZ SULAIMAN,

ABDUL HADI ALAFOO
See ALAFOO, ABDUL HADI,

ABDUL RAHMAN & JALAL ALMEER
See ALMEER, ABDUL RAHMAN & JALAL,

ABDULKAREM DARWISH TATTAN
See TATTAN, ABDULKAREM DARWISH,

ABDULLA AHMED NASS
See NASS, ABDULLA AHMED,

ABDULLA YUSUF FAKHRO CO
See FAKHRO, ABDULLA YUSUF, CO

ABDULRAHMAN & OSMAN KHONJI
See KHONJI, ABDULRAHMAN & OSMAN,

ABDULRAHMAN EBRAHIM AL MOOSA EST
See AL MOOSA, ABDULRAHMAN EBRAHIM, EST

ABDULRAHMAN KHALIL ALMOAYED
See ALMOAYED, ABDULRAHMAN KHALIL,

ABDULREHMAN AHMED ZUBARI & SONS
See ZUBARI, ABDULREHMAN AHMED, & SONS

ABEDALI ESSA AL NOOH & SONS CO WLL
See AL NOOH, ABEDALI ESSA, & SONS CO WLL

ADEL AHMADI CONSULTING ENGINEERS (FORMERLY MODULE 2 BAHRAIN LTD)
PO Box 20285, Sheikh Daij Bldg, 4th Floor, Manama
Tel: 252908, 245371
Cable: Module 2 Bah
Telex: 9053 Modbah BN
Telefax: 275198

Chairman: Adel Mohd Ahmadi (Managing Director)
Directors: Omman Koshy (Finance & Administration Director)
Senior Executives: E W Lant, Nader Boutrus, R Mundany, Pia Abdulla

PRINCIPAL ACTIVITIES: Planners, architects and engineering consultants
Principal Bankers: National Bank of Bahrain; Al Ahli Commercial Bank

Principal Shareholders: Sole proprietorship
Date of Establishment: 1978

AERADIO TECHNICAL SERVICES WLL (ATS WLL)
PO Box 26803, Manama
Tel: 727790
Cable: Aertech
Telex: 8226 Ats BN
Telefax: 727811

Chairman: Mubarrak Jassim Kanoo
Directors: A Dawes (Managing Director), Fawzi Ahmed Kanoo, Ali Abdulaziz Kanoo, J Baker, C Sansom

PRINCIPAL ACTIVITIES: Land, marine, electronic and avionic sales installations; repair and maintenance services; system planning; process control instrumentation; fire safety and security; liferaft survey/repair
Principal Agencies: Decca; SP Radio; Kelvin Hughes; Chubb; Falcon International; Sperry; Raytheon; Marconi; Simrad; Dunlop; Kent; Gould Instruments; RFD; General Electric; Multitone; Wilcox; Pharos Marine; Bull Groupe Computers; Exicom; British Telecom
Branch Offices: Saudi Arabia (Jeddah, Dammam)

Parent Company: Yusuf bin Ahmed Kanoo, PO Box 45, Bahrain
Associated Companies: International Aeradio plc, Southall UK
Principal Bankers: National Bank of Bahrain
Financial Information:

	1990
	BD'000
Sales turnover	1,700
Profits	58
Authorised capital	40
Paid-up capital	40
Total assets	1,000

Principal Shareholders: Y B A Kanoo; International Aeradio plc
Date of Establishment: 1961
No of Employees: 71

AFRICAN & EASTERN (NEAR EAST) LTD & ASSOCIATED COMPANIES

PO Box 49, Manama
Tel: 254745/6/7
Cable: Ethiop
Telex: 8223 BN

PRINCIPAL ACTIVITIES: Marketing, wholesaling and distribution
of general merchandise, including provisions, drinks, building
materials, refrigeration design, installation and servicing,
office equipment and business systems, and insurance
agents
Principal Agencies: Unilever, Liptons, Rootes, Tempair and
Keeprite (air conditioners), Hygena, Austinsuite, G Plan

Principal Shareholders: UAC International Ltd (Unilever),
Bahrain Tourism Company, National Hotels Company,
Investment & Trading (Gulf) Enterprises

AHMADI INDUSTRIES WLL

PO Box 34, Manama
Tel: 271333
Cable: Beverages
Telex: 8336 Ahmadi
Telefax: (973) 262593

Chairman: Abdulla Hussain Ahmadi
Directors: Ali A Ahmadi (Managing Director), Khalid Abdulla
Ahmadi

PRINCIPAL ACTIVITIES: Bottling of soft drinks, Pepsi and
Mirinda, juices, milk and ice cream
Principal Agencies: Pepsicola International
Principal Bankers: National Bank of Bahrain; Standard
Chartered Bank; Al Ahli Commercial Bank

Date of Establishment: 1953
No of Employees: 325

AHMED & ESSA AL JALAHEMA

See AL JALAHEMA, AHMED & ESSA,

AHMED MANSOOR AL A'ALI

See AL A'ALI, AHMED MANSOOR,

AHMED OMER TRADING & CONTRACTING EST

PO Box 5098, Gudaibiya Avenue, Gudaibiya
Tel: 258529, 258545
Cable: AOTEST
Telex: 8904 Aotest BN
Telefax: 233882

Chairman: A O Saleh
Directors: Hisham A O Saleh, Raed A O Saleh

PRINCIPAL ACTIVITIES: Building contractors and engineering
consultants; construction plant
Principal Agencies: Duraflex, UK
Subsidiary Companies: Oasis Travel & Tourism; Modern
Architect

Principal Bankers: Standard Chartered Bank; Bank of Bahrain &
Kuwait; National Bank of Bahrain; Arab Bank; Al Ahli
Commercial Bank

Principal Shareholders: Ahmed Omer Saleh
Date of Establishment: 1972
No of Employees: 80

AHMED S H AL GHARABALLY

See AL GHARABALLY, AHMED S H,

AIRMECH EASTERN ENGINEERING WLL

PO Box 20137, Manama
Tel: 593013, 593022
Cable: Elect Bahrain
Telex: 8382 Elect BN
Telefax: 593113

Chairman: Mohammed Y Jalal
Directors: Jalal M Jalal, J C M Thomas, S H Matlub (Managing
Director)
Senior Executives: R C Bean (Engineering Manager), W S
McCorkindale (Financial Controller), P Smith (Commercial
Manager), D J Kemp (Contracts Manager)

PRINCIPAL ACTIVITIES: Electrical and mechanical engineering,
contracting, steel fabrication engineers
Principal Agencies: BICC-Pyrotenax
Branch Offices: Bahrain; Oman
Parent Company: Mohammed Jalal & Sons
Subsidiary Companies: Bahrain Trading Agencies (A/C Division)
Principal Bankers: Banque Paribas, Standard Chartered Bank,
Al Ahli Bank

Principal Shareholders: Moh'Jalal & Sons
Date of Establishment: 1969
No of Employees: 650

AL A'ALI, AHMED MANSOOR,

PO Box 778, Shaikh Sulman Highway, Manama
Tel: 250521
Cable: Tawfic
Telex: 8285 Tawfic BN
Telefax: (973) 262323

President: Ahmed Mansoor Al-A'Ali
Directors: Jalal Al-A'Ali (Vice-President), Hassan Abdul Aziz Al-
A'Ali (Managing Director)
Senior Executives: Anthony Brady (Chief Executive)

PRINCIPAL ACTIVITIES: Traders, civil and mechanical
engineers, contractors, landlords, agents and sponsors,
suppliers of construction materials, plant and equipment,
vehicles, and labour, shipping and forwarding agents,
manufacturers of oxygen, nitrogen argon and acetylene
gases, drinking water, concrete blocks, tiles, aggregates and
other building materials, agents for land, sea, and air cargo
services
Subsidiary/Associated Companies: Ahmed Mansoor Al-Aali
(Heavy Construction Division); AMA (Civil Engineering
Division); Middle East Transport; Middle East Block & Tiles
Factory; Middle East Crusher Plant; Bahrain Medical &
Industrial Gas Plant; Eastern Asphalt & Readymix Concrete
Co; Comsip Al A'Ali; Overseas Cargo Services (Bahrain)
Principal Bankers: National Bank of Bahrain; Bank of Bahrain &
Kuwait; Standard Chartered Bank; Bahraini Saudi Bank
Financial Information:

	1990
	BD'000
Sales turnover	29,500
Total assets	50,000

Principal Shareholders: Proprietorship
Date of Establishment: 1954
No of Employees: over 3,500

AL AALI ENTERPRISES

Sh Hamad Rd, PO Box 979, Manama
Tel: 258198, 275346
Cable: Ahmabros-Bahrain
Telex: 8792 Ahma BN

Owner: Ali Moosa Al-Aali
Directors: Adel Al Aali

PRINCIPAL ACTIVITIES: Importers and dealers in all types of
furniture for houses and offices, airconditioners, refrigerators,
cookers, water coolers, carpets, curtains, wallpapers
Principal Agencies: Tappan, USA; EBCO Mfg Co, USA;
Georgian Carpets Ltd, UK; Templeton Carpets Ltd, UK; World
Carpets Ltd, USA; Abbot Bros, UK; Sekisei Co, Japan;
Sankey Sheldon Ltd, UK; Mobilest SpA, Italy, Alco, Japan;
Nerelle, Italy; Boro, Belgium; Hill Int., Italy; Dico, Holland;
Good Furniture, Italy; Gen. Export, Italy, Vaghi, Italy
Principal Bankers: Standard Chartered Bank; Bank of Bahrain &
Kuwait; National Bank of Bahrain

Principal Shareholders: Family Company
Date of Establishment: 1960
No of Employees: 75

ALAFOO, ABDUL HADI,

PO Box 611, Manama
Tel: 250807, 254469, 254503
Cable: Contractor
Telex: 8287 Alafoo BN

Chairman: Abdul Hadi Alafoo

PRINCIPAL ACTIVITIES: General contracting and labour
suppliers; building and civil engineering contractors; plant
hire; import and distribution of heavy machinery and
earthmoving equipment, and spare parts; electrical and
mechanical engineering
Principal Agencies: Millars Wellpoint Int, UK; Boiraud Cie,
France
Principal Bankers: British Bank of the Middle East

No of Employees: 1,325

AL AHLI COMMERCIAL BANK BSC

Government Road, PO Box 5941, Manama
Tel: 244333
Cable: Ahlico BN
Telex: 9130/1/2 BN

Chairman: Mohammad Yousuf Jalal
Directors: Abdul Rahman Hassan Taqi, Qasim Ahmed Fakhro,
Jasim Mohamed Al Saffar, Ali Bin Ebrahim Abdul A'Al, Abdul
Rahman Gholum Mohadded Amin, Taqi Mohamed Al
Baharna, Abdulla Ahmed Bin Hindi, Mohammed Abdul Gaffar
Al Alawi, Mohammed Abdulla Al Mannai
Senior Executives: Qasim Mohamed Qasim (General Manager),
Abdul Rahman Fakhro (Deputy General Manager)

PRINCIPAL ACTIVITIES: Commercial banking
Branch Offices: Municipality Branch: Shaikh Mubarak Building;
Gudabiya Branch: Lloyds Building; Diplomatic Branch:
Diplomatic Area
Principal Bankers: London: Bank of America NT&SA; Barclays
Bank; Lloyds Bank; National Westminster Bank; New York:
Bankamerica International; Irving Trust Co; Marine Midland
Bank
Financial Information:

	1989
	BD'000
Profits	1,916
Authorised capital	50,000
Paid-up capital	8,000
Total assets	168,243

Principal Shareholders: Bahraini public shareholding company
(8,200 shareholders)
Date of Establishment: September, 15, 1978
No of Employees: 201

AL AHLIA INSURANCE COMPANY

Chamber of Commerce Bldg, King Faisal Rd, PO Box 5282,
Manama
Tel: 258860, 244363
Cable: Ahlinsure
Telex: 8761 Aico BN

Chairman: Qasim Ahmed Fakhro
Directors: Ali Saleh Al-Saleh (Deputy Chairman), Taqi M Al-
Baharna (Managing Director), Abdul Rahman H Taqi, Dr
Essam Abdulla Fakhro, Abdul Ali Hassan Al Modaifa, Ebrahim
Eshaq A Rahman

PRINCIPAL ACTIVITIES: Insurance and reinsurance (all classes)
Branch Offices: In Saudi Arabia: PO Box 9, Alkhobar, Telex
870132; PO Box 12651, Jeddah, Telex 604757 Zamil SJ
Principal Bankers: National Bank of Bahrain; Bank of Bahrain &
Kuwait; Al Ahli Commercial Bank

Principal Shareholders: Public Shareholding Company
Date of Establishment: 22nd February, 1976
No of Employees: 45

AL ALAWI FACTORIES

Shaikh Salman Rd, PO Box 704, Manama
Tel: 252663
Cable: Yakaza
Telex: 8384 Yakaza BN

Chairman: Alawi Sayed Moosa Al-Alawi
Directors: Jalal Alawi, Phidias G Koursoumbas, Hadi Al Alawi,
Hussain S K Alawi, John Strongylos

PRINCIPAL ACTIVITIES: Manufacture and supply of concrete
blocks, washed aggregate and sand and neon signs;
servicing of air conditioners, refrigerators and household
appliances. Manufacturer's representation
Principal Agencies: Singer, Atlas Copco, JCB, Burgmann,
Huggler, Hatz Diesel, General Electric; International Harvester
Subsidiary/Associated Companies: Alko Construction Co Ltd,
(PO Box 5545, Bahrain); Alko Mechanical & Electrical, (PO
Box 5813, Bahrain); Bahrain Neon (PO Box 704, Bahrain); Al
Yakaza Trading Stores (PO Box 190, Bahrain); United Motors
(PO Box 5405, Bahrain); BRAMCO (PO Box 20260, Bahrain)
Principal Bankers: National Bank of Bahrain; Bank of Bahrain &
Kuwait; Continental Bank Ltd

Date of Establishment: 1961
No of Employees: 600; 1350 in group total

AL ALAWI, HASHIM, CONTRACTING

PO Box 5043, Manama
Tel: 252257
Cable: Aboalawi
Telex: 8375 BN

Chairman: Sayed Hashim Al Alawi

PRINCIPAL ACTIVITIES: General trading and contracting,
import and distribution of building materials and sanitary ware
Principal Agencies: SK Iron Foundry & Engineering, India; SAER
Elettroneccanica, Italy; Intercommerciale Italia, Italy; Ceramica
Venus, Italy
Principal Bankers: Bank of Bahrain and Kuwait; National Bank
of Bahrain; Banque de Paris

AL BAHAR, MOHAMED ABDULRAHMAN,

PO Box 5357, Mina Sulman, Manama
Tel: 243466
Cable: Moatasim Bahrain
Telex: 8299 Bahar BN

Chairman: Mohamed Abdulrahman Al Bahar

PRINCIPAL ACTIVITIES: Importers and distributors of heavy construction machinery and trucks; electrical equipment; car dealers

Principal Agencies: Caterpillar; Koehring (Bantam & Lorain); Barber Greene; Munster; Raugo; Volvo Cars & Trucks; Ingram; Crane Fruehauf; Oshkosh; Telsmith

Branch Offices: Abu Dhabi; Dubai; Sharjah; Qatar; Oman

Parent Company: Head Office in Kuwait

ALBAHARNA, SADIQ & TAQI,

PO Box 179, Manama

Tel: 253816, 262815

Cable: Sadiq

Telex: 9042 Bahrna BN

Telefax: 246013

Chairman: Sadiq Albaharna

Directors: Taqi Albaharna (Managing Director)

Senior Executives: N K Nair (General Manager)

PRINCIPAL ACTIVITIES: Import and distribution of electrical, refrigeration equipment and office equipment

Principal Agencies: Amana Refrigeration Int'l Inc, USA; Mitsubishi Electric Corpn, Japan; Letraset, UK; Kardex Systems, UK; Danza Zuthen & Aagaard, Denmark; Toshiba Corp, Japan; Bell & Howell, UK; OEM(S)P Ltd, Singapore; Scanida Randers, Denmark; Nikko, Japan; International Prestige, Italy; Typewriter Continental, Switzerland

Associated Companies: Continental Office Equipment Services, Bahrain

Principal Bankers: Bank of Bahrain and Kuwait; National Bank of Bahrain; Al Ahli Commercial Bank

Principal Shareholders: Partnership

Date of Establishment: 1946

No of Employees: 42

ALBARAKA ISLAMIC INVESTMENT BANK BSC (EC)

PO Box 1882, Al Hedaya Bldg No1, 7th & 8th Floor, Govt Road, Manama

Tel: 259641, 254269

Telex: 8220 BARAKA BN

Telefax: 252093, 274364

Chairman: Mahmoud J Hassoubah

Directors: Dr Mohammed A Yamani (Deputy Chairman), Haj Saeed Ahmed Lootah, Abdul Latif Janahi, Abdulla Saleh Abdulla Kamel, Abdul Elah A Rahim Sabahi, Mohammad Ismaeel Habes

Senior Executives: Abdulla Abolfatih (General Manager), Mohammed Abdul Rahim Mohammed (Asst General Manager)

PRINCIPAL ACTIVITIES: Investment banking, projects development, trade finance and other banking activities in conformity with Islamic principles. Special preference in investment will be given to Arab and Islamic countries in Asia

Parent Company: Albaraka Investment & Development Co, Jeddah

Associated Companies: Albaraka Investment & Development Co, Saudi Arabia; Beit Ettamweel Alsaudi Altunisi, Tunisia; Albaraka Investment Co, UK; Albaraka International Ltd, UK; Albaraka Bank, Sudan; Arab Thai Investment Co, Thailand; Albaraka Turkish Finance House, Turkey; Albaraka Mauritania Islamic Investment Bank, Mauritania; Albaraka Bank Bangladesh Ltd, Bangladesh; Subsidiary company: Altawfeek Co for Investment Funds, Bahrain

Principal Bankers: Gulf International Bank, New York; Deutsche Bank, Frankfurt; Saudi International Bank, London; Saudi British Bank, Riyadh

Financial Information:

	1988 US$'000	1989 US$'000
Total income	4,579	7,653
Profits	2,735	4,328
Authorised capital	200,000	200,000
Paid-up capital	50,000	50,000
Total assets	282,311	333,907

Principal Shareholders: Sh Saleh A Kamel (Saudi Arabia); Sh Hussein M AlHarthy (Saudi Arabia); Albaraka Investment and Development Co (Saudi Arabia); Jordan Islamic Bank for Finance & Investment (Jordan); Bahrain Islamic Bank (Bahrain); Bahrain Islamic Investment Co (Bahrain); Dubai Islamic Bank (Dubai); Dr Nasser Ibrahim Al Rasheed (Saudi Arabia); Haj Saeed Ahmed Lootah (Dubai); Dr Hassan Abdulla Kamel (Saudi Arabia); Abdul Aziz Abdulla Kamel (Saudi Arabia); Dr Mohamed Abdou Yamani (Saudi Arabia); Abdul Latif Abdul Rahim Janahi (Bahrain); Mahmoud Jameel Hassoubah (Saudi Arabia); Shaikh Saleh Abdul Aziz Al Rajhi (Saudi Arabia)

Date of Establishment: 21 February, 1984

No of Employees: 25

AL BASSAM, ABDUL AZIZ SULAIMAN,

PO Box 26699, Manama

Tel: 250228, 727049

Cable: Albassam

Chairman: Abdul Aziz Sulaiman Al Bassam

PRINCIPAL ACTIVITIES: Manufacture of aluminium products and supply, glass, property and investment, estate agents

Parent Company: Bassam Aluminium

Principal Bankers: Al Ahli Commercial Bank; Bahrain Saudi Bank

Date of Establishment: 1965

No of Employees: 35

AL BOURSHAID TRADING & CONTRACTING

Bourmed Industries Company

PO Box 22451, Manama

Tel: 731677, 731685

Telex: 9501 BORMED BN

President: Salman I Al-Bourshaid

Directors: Dawood S Al-Bourshaid (Vice President), Issa Al-Jalahema (Director Medical Division)

PRINCIPAL ACTIVITIES: Manufacture of plastic and rubber medical disposables, contract supplies and trading for educational and medical equipment, civil construction, workshop and manpower services

Principal Agencies: Bigla, Switzerland; ASS School Furniture, Germany; Cosmark Co, UK; J W Plant, UK; Fullers, UK; Denford Machines, UK; Swish Products, UK; John Norris, UK; Luna Int'l, UK; B Braun, W Germany

Branch Offices: NTH Sitra Industrial Estate, Bahrain

Subsidiary Companies: Al-Bourshaid Contracting; Al-Bourshaid Trading

Principal Bankers: British Bank of the Middle East; National Bank of Bahrain; Arab Bank; Bank of Bahrain & Kuwait; AlBaraka Islamic Bank

Financial Information:

	BD'000
Sales turnover	9,500
Authorised capital	1,200
Paid-up capital	1,050

Principal Shareholders: Salman I Al-Bourshaid; Dawood S Al-Bourshaid, Issa Al-Jalahema

No of Employees: 135

ALGEMENE BANK NEDERLAND NV
ABN Bank
Government Ave, PO Box 350, Manama
Tel: 255420 general, 273311 Dealing, 250123 Inv. Banking
Cable: Bancolanda
Telex: 8356 ABN BAH BN (General), 8433 ABN EXC BN
(Dealing), 8614 ABN REG BN (Regional Management &
Invest. Banking)
Telefax: 973 - 262241 (General), 257424 (Regional Management
& Invest. Banking), 274593 (Dealing & Treasury)

Senior Executives: P V Callenfels (Regional Manager Middle
East & Africa), Yusuf A Abdulrahman (Manager Bahrain
Branch), V H van der Kwast (Investment Banking & OBU
Manager), P J Scholten (Deputy Manager), J Fernandes
(Principal Dealer), K S Fakhruddin (Marketing Officer), T
Hussain (Dealer)

PRINCIPAL ACTIVITIES: International commercial banking,
investment offshore banking
Parent Company: Head office: Amsterdam, Netherlands

Date of Establishment: in Bahrain: 1974

AL GHARABALLY, AHMED S H,
PO Box 191, Manama
Tel: 254823, 256172, 256178
Cable: Al Gharabally
Telex: 8355 Grably BN

Chairman: Ahmed Sayed Hashim Gharabally
Senior Executives: E J Ghattas (General Manager & Executive
Representative)

PRINCIPAL ACTIVITIES: General trading and contracting,
import and distribution of electrical appliances, office
equipment, shoes, automobiles and auto spare parts,
insurance agents
Principal Agencies: Fiat, Royal Insurance Co, Lotus Shoes,
Heavenhill, Shoes, Bally Shoe Switzerland, Pierre Cardin
France
Branch Offices: Throughout the Gulf states
Parent Company: Head office in Kuwait
Principal Bankers: British Bank of the Middle East; Arab Bank
Ltd

Date of Establishment: 1950 in Bahrain

AL GHAZAL CONSTRUCTION & DEVELOPMENT CO
PO Box 822, Manama
Tel: 245123
Telex: 9284 GIC BN

Chairman: Salah Mohammed Amin Al Rayes

PRINCIPAL ACTIVITIES: Construction, industrial maintenance,
construction management, equipment programs, oil refineries,
gas processing, chemicals/fertilisers, power generation,
supporting facilities
Parent Company: Head office in Kuwait

Principal Shareholders: Kuwait public company

ALGOSAIBI DIVING & MARINE SERVICES
PO Box 5526, Mina Sulman
Tel: 243435
Telex: 8516 Adams BN

Directors: Khalifa A Algosaibi

PRINCIPAL ACTIVITIES: Import and distribution of equipment
for civil engineering and offshore construction; SBM
installations and maintenance services; contractors plant hire;
civil engineering and pipeline inspection
Parent Company: Head office in Saudi Arabia

ALI AMIRI ESTABLISHMENT
PO Box 5233, Bank Saderat Bldg, Government Rd, Manama
Tel: 253002
Cable: Civilcon
Telex: 8456 Civil BN

PRINCIPAL ACTIVITIES: Civil construction, contracting and
supply of building materials and heavy equipment

ALI BIN EBRAHIM ABDUL AAL EST
PO Box 507, Manama
Tel: 274577, 252577
Cable: Nader-Bahrain
Telex: 8757 Anwar BN

Chairman: Ali Bin Ebrahim Abdul Aal
Directors: Jemil Ali Ebrahim (Managing Director), Jalal Ali
Ebrahim (Assistant Managing Director)
Senior Executives: Saleh Ali Ebrahim (General Manager, Nader
Gas)

PRINCIPAL ACTIVITIES: General merchants and contractors;
distribution of petroleum products, protective coatings,
transformers and switchgear, LP Gas and cookers,
manufacture and laying of asphalt; importers, wholesalers
and retailers of foodstuffs, safety and security equipment,
communications equipment, medical, educational and
scientific equipment
Principal Agencies: L & C Arnold, W Germany; Leybold
Herraeus, W Germany; John Prutscher, Australia;
Tecquipment Int'l, UK; Stierlen Macquet, W Germany; W & J
Leigh & Co, UK; Joy Compressors, USA, Brush
Transformers, UK; Beasley Industries Ltd, Australia; Remploy,
UK; Delmahro, France; Ariston, Italy; Ferranti OSL, UK; Mitel,
UK; Palmer Bioscience, UK; Racal Safety, UK; General Data
Comm, UK; Hyssna, Denmark; Ayala, UK; Denco, UK;
Emerson, USA; Electrolux Foodservices, Sweden, American
Pipe, USA
Associated Companies: Nader Gas; Nader Trading &
Refrigerating Co Ltd; Marhaba Super Market; United Gulf
Asphalt Co WLL; Nader Safety; Nader Retreads, Interlink,
Interspares, Intec
Principal Bankers: National Bank of Bahrain; Chartered Bank;
Al-Ahli Commercial Bank; Banque Paribas; British Bank of the
Middle East

Date of Establishment: 1954
No of Employees: 850

ALIREZA & SONS
PO Box 79, Manama
Tel: 253654, 258320, 250235, 250535, 255018
Telex: 8396 Alreza

Chairman: Alireza Abbas Alireza
Directors: S Alireza, N Alireza

PRINCIPAL ACTIVITIES: General trading, property owners and
real estate agents, import and distribution of carpets, cigars
and cigarettes, canned foodstuffs, and juice, textiles and
clothing, furniture, electronic equipment and appliances
Principal Agencies: King Edward Cigars, USA, etc
Subsidiary Companies: Global Travel & Tour
Principal Bankers: National Bank of Bahrain; Bank of Bahrain &
Kuwait

Date of Establishment: 1940
No of Employees: 25

ALIREZA, YOUSUF AKBAR, & SONS
PO Box 77, Manama
Tel: 253429
Cable: Akbar
Telex: 8343 Akbar BN

Chairman: Mohamed Yousuf Akbar Alireza
Directors: Abdulla Akbar Alireza, Ebrahim Akbar Alireza,
Mohamed Akbar Alireza

BAHRAIN

Senior Executives: Ahmed Mohamed Al-Asseeri (General Manager)

PRINCIPAL ACTIVITIES: General trading, import and distribution of foodstuffs, building materials, insulation products, chemicals, ceramics, furniture and timber products and investments

Principal Agencies: General Electric Co; Newalls Insulation Co Ltd; Petrolite Ltd; Porter Bros Ltd; Knoll International; Sansho Corp; William Moore & Sons; Swiss Insulation Works Ltd; Cape Insulation

Branch Offices: Ebrahim Yousuf Akbar Alireza, PO Box 243, Jeddah, Saudi Arabia; Yousuf Akbar Alireza & Sons, PO Box 543, Dubai, UAE

Subsidiary Companies: Middle East Engineering Ltd, Bahrain; International Trading Co Ltd, Bahrain

Principal Bankers: National Bank of Bahrain; Standard Chartered Bank; Citibank; British Bank of the Middle East; Bank Melli Iran; Al-Ahli Commercial Bank; Arab Bank Ltd; Banque Paribas

Principal Shareholders: Mohamed Akbar Alireza & Bros
Date of Establishment: 1910
No of Employees: 120

AL JALAHEMA, AHMED & ESSA,

PO Box 619 and 5357, Manama
Tel: 713607, 254832
Cable: Al Jalahema
Telex: 8299 BN

Directors: Ahmed Al-Jalahema, Essa Al-Jalahema

PRINCIPAL ACTIVITIES: Import and distribution of earth moving equipment, heavy machinery, marine diesel engines
Principal Agencies: Caterpillar, Coleman, USA; Motorfabriken Bukh, Denmark; Center Company, Germany; Stetter
Branch Offices: Bahrain; Saudi Arabia (Alkhobar branch)

AL JAZIRA COLD STORE CO WLL

PO Box 26087, Manama
Tel: 714914 (15 lines)
Cable: Coldzira
Telex: 8312 Jazira BN
Telefax: 712923, 713185

Chairman: Abdul Hussain Khalil Dawani (Managing Director)
Directors: Mohd Sadiq Khalil Dawani (Deputy Chairman & General Manager), Ali Reza Murteza Dawani, Abdul Hameed Mohd Hassan Dawani
Senior Executives: Ebrahim H Ismail (Supermarket Manager), Ali Abbas Jalal (Sales Manager), Savio Noronha (Accounts Manager), Joaquim Fernandes (Purchasing Manager), Abdul Hodi Abbas (Sales Manager), Tommy D'Souza (Personnel Manager)

PRINCIPAL ACTIVITIES: Wholesalers, retailers, supermaket operators and shipchandlers for frozen and dry foodstuffs, household goods and cosmetics and perfumes
Principal Agencies: UK: HJ Heinz Co; Spillers Foods; John West Foods; Spillers Milling; Unilever Export; Robertsons Foods; United Biscuits; Deeko; Kimberly-Clark; USA: General Mills; Rockingham Poultry Mktg; Green Giant; The RT French Co; CPC Int'l; Uncle Ben's; Denmark: CO-RO Food; Plumrose; MD Foods; France: Volvic; L'Oreal; Zone 2 Oceans; Australia: Kitchens of Sara Lee; W Germany: H Bahlsens Keksfabrik; Dalli-Weke Maurer + Wirtz, etc
Principal Bankers: Standard Chartered Bank, Bahrain
Financial Information:

	1990 BD'000
Authorised capital	4,000
Paid-up capital	4,000

Principal Shareholders: Abdul Hussain Khalil Dawani, Sadiq Khalil Dawani, Ali Reza Murtaza Dawani, Abdul Hameed Mohd Hassan Dawani
Date of Establishment: 1965
No of Employees: 140

AL JAZIRA CONTRACTING & INVESTMENT CO EC

PO Box 20456, Manama
Tel: 233287, 233558
Telex: 9294 Aljaco BN

Chairman: H R H Mohammad Bin Fahd Bin Abdul Aziz
Directors: Fawzi Musaad Al Saleh (Vice Chairman), Jasem Mohammad Nase Al Issa (Managing Director Technical Affairs), Dawood Buhaimed (Managing Director Investment Affairs), Jawad A Bukhamsin, Fahd Al Athel, Musaad Bader Al Sayer, Mohammad Yousef Mohammad, Sheikh Hamad Bin Ibrahim Al Khalifa, Fawzi Ahmad Kanoo

PRINCIPAL ACTIVITIES: Contractors for all types of civil engineering works, investments in securities, real estate and industrial ventures
Branch Offices: Baghdad Office: PO Box 2229 Alawiyeh, Tel 5552775, Telex 213295 Jaira IK, Baghdad, Iraq; Kuwait Office: PO Box 25960 Safat, Tel 846440, 848104, Telex 44101 Jazira KT
Financial Information:

	US$'000
Share capital	79,500
Paid-up capital	72,300

AL-JISHI CORPORATION

PO Box 617, Al-Khalifa Road, Manama
Tel: 233544
Cable: Jishi Bahrain
Telex: 8371 Jishi BN
Telefax: 255602

Chairman: Rasul Al-Jishi
Directors: Fouad Al-Jishi
Senior Executives: Ghassan Al Jishi, Maysa Al Jishi

PRINCIPAL ACTIVITIES: Dealers in pharmaceuticals, baby products, hospital and lab furniture, chemicals, veterinary products, surgical and lab equipment, agricultural products, perfumes and cosmetics
Principal Agencies: Merck Sharp & Dhome, Medishield Corporation, Smith Kline & French Laboratories, 3M (Medical), G D Searle, Richardson-Vicks Ltd, Beecham Research International, Ethicon, Scholl, Cappucci, Blendax, etc
Branch Offices: Outlets: Gulf Hotel Gift Shop; Al Farabi Pharmacy; Al Jishi Pharmacy; East Pharmacy
Subsidiary Companies: Abu Dhabi, UAE; Dubai, UAE
Principal Bankers: National Bank of Bahrain; Bank of Bahrain & Kuwait

Date of Establishment: 1959
No of Employees: 50

AL KHAJAH GROUP OF COMPANIES

PO Box 5042, Manama
Tel: 730811
Cable: Stabalka Bahrain
Telex: 8619 Ake BN

Chairman: Ahmed Al Khajah
Directors: Jassim Al Khajah (Managing Director), Fareed Al Khajah (Director), Abdul Rahman Al Khajah (Director)

PRINCIPAL ACTIVITIES: Electrical, mechanical and civil engineering, contractors, manufacture of AC units, switchboards, lighting fittings, agents, stockists and distributors of electrical equipment & materials
Principal Agencies: Dorman Smith, UK; Daikin Kogyo Co, Japan; Associated Lighting Ind, Australia; Mobil Oil Inc, USA;

Electronic Space Systems Corp, USA; KSU Kapp Schnellmann, Switzerland; Krupp Ind, Germany
Subsidiary Companies: Al Khajah Factories WLL, North Sitra Industrial Area, Bahrain; Refrigeration & General Airconditioning, Bahrain; Ahmed Al Khajah Est, PO Box 7265, Dubai, UAE; Al Mehar Trading & Contracting Est, PO Box 2978, Doha, Qatar; Saudi Arabian Industrial & Trading Est, PO Box 37, Dammam, Saudi Arabia; Almahar Appliances, PO Box 22672, Bahrain; Deera Exhibition, PO Box 26065, Bahrain
Principal Bankers: National Bank of Bahrain; Algemene Bank; Bank of Bahrain & Kuwait; Grindlays Bank; Al Ahli Bank

Principal Shareholders: Ahmed Alkhajah; Jassim Alkhajah; Fareed Al Khajah; Abdul Rahman Al Khajah
Date of Establishment: 1972
No of Employees: 750

ALKO CONSTRUCTION CO LTD

PO Box 5545, Manama
Tel: 252663
Cable: Yakaza
Telex: 8384 Yakaza BN

Chairman: Alawi S M Al-Alawi
Directors: Phidias G Koursoumbas (Managing Director), Jalal S M Al-Alawi

PRINCIPAL ACTIVITIES: Building, civil, electrical and mechanical engineering contractors; plant hire
Branch Offices: Alkomed; PO Box 5813, Manama, Bahrain
Associated Companies: Phidias G Koursoumbas Limited (Cyprus); Al-Alawi Factories
Principal Bankers: Bank of Bahrain and Kuwait

Principal Shareholders: Alawi S M Al-Alawi, Phidias G Koursoumbas, Jalal S M Al-Alawi

ALKOMED ENGINEERING SERVICES CO WLL

PO Box 5813, Manama
Tel: 691011 (4 lines)
Telex: 9271 Almed BN
Telefax: (0973) 692025

Chairman: Alawi S Moosa Al Alawi
Directors: John Chr Strongylos (Managing Director), George N Mavrikios (Executive Director), Jalal S Moosa Al Alawi (Director)
Senior Executives: John Chr Strongylos, George N Mavrikios, K Yiacoumi (Contracts Manager), E G Zambas (Manager Administration)

PRINCIPAL ACTIVITIES: Electrical and mechanical engineers and general contractors. Installation and maintenance - A/C; electrical, plumbing, refrigeration water sewage (distribution and treatment). Distributors for: electrical and air conditioning equipment, industrial equipment, cables, lifts, cold stores, welding equipment, water and sewage treatment plants
Branch Offices: Ma-Stro Ltd, PO Box 2071, Nicosia, Cyprus, Telex 2595 Strong Cy, Tel 0357-2-452021, Fax (0357) 2456072
Parent Company: Al Alawi Factories, Bahrain
Principal Bankers: National Bank of Bahrain; British Bank of the Middle East

Principal Shareholders: Al Alawi Factories, Bahrain
Date of Establishment: 1976
No of Employees: 250

ALLIED BANKING CORPORATION - BAHRAIN

PO Box 20493, Manama
Tel: 246616, 261461
Telex: 9349 Allied BN

PRINCIPAL ACTIVITIES: Offshore banking
Branch Offices: Guam, London; representative office: Singapore

Parent Company: Allied Banking Corporation, Manila, Philippines
Subsidiary Associated Companies: Allied Capital Resources, HK Ltd; Oceanic Bank, San Francisco, USA

Date of Establishment: In Bahrain: 18th August, 1980

ALMEER, ABDUL RAHMAN & JALAL,

PO Box 512, Manama
Tel: 255107
Cable: Almeer
Telex: 8771 Almeer BN

Chairman: Jalal Almeer
Directors: Abdul Rahman Almeer
Senior Executives: Jalal Almeer (General Manager), Sadiq M Jaffer (Asst General Manager), Abdulla Almeer (Cargo Clearing Superintendent)

PRINCIPAL ACTIVITIES: Distribution and sale of sanitary ware, tiles and water heaters
Principal Agencies: Ceramiche Girardi, Italy; Cisa, Italy; Saime, Italy; Cesame, Italy; Belco, England; Carron, Scotland
Principal Bankers: National Bank of Bahrain

ALMOAYED, ABDULRAHMAN KHALIL,

PO Box 363, Almoayed Bldg, Al Khalifa Road, Manama
Tel: 251212
Cable: Akatrade
Telex: 8267 Aka BN
Telefax: (973) 273372

Chairman: Abdulrahman Khalil Almoayed
Directors: Khalid Abdulrahman Almoayed (Managing Director), Emad Almoayed
Senior Executives: Capt Hakon Vik (Shipping Manager), Alan Rooke (Commercial Manager), Jos Thomas (Chief Accountant)

PRINCIPAL ACTIVITIES: Building materials stockists, production, import and distribution of timber and steel products and all building materials
Principal Agencies: Stephens & Carter, UK; Bolton Gate, UK; CCL Systems, UK; British Steel Tubes, UK; Darlington Fencing, UK; Expanded Metal, UK; Master Builders, USA; Ruberoid Building Products, UK; H H Robertson, UK, France, USA; Nidermeyer Martin, USA; Jotun, Norway; Hauserman, USA; Lippi Est, France; Buchtal, Germany; Marconi, UK; Schlegel, UK, USA; Wilh Wilhelmsen, Norway; Barber Blue Sea, USA; Willine, Norway; Scancarriers, Norway; Weiser, UK; Toyo Scaffolding, Japan; Dainichi Nippon Cables, Japan; Macchi, Italy; Kurvers, UK; Honeywell, USA; Prodeco, Italy; Genpack, Italy; Chavonnet, France; Weber & Broutin, France; Alcatel, Belgium
Associated Companies: BRC Weldmesh (Gulf) Ltd; Almoayed-Barwil Ltd; International Supplies & Services; United Building Materials; Electra Centre
Principal Bankers: Grindlays Bahrain Bank, AlAhli Commercial Bank, British Bank of the Middle East

Date of Establishment: 1935
No of Employees: 120

ALMOAYED BARWIL LTD

2nd Floor, A K Almoayed Bldg, Al Khalifa Road, PO Box 5535, Manama
Tel: 211177
Cable: BARWIL
Telex: 8708 BARWIL BN
Telefax: 210899

Directors: Abdulrahman Khalil Almoayed, Khalid Almoayed, Wilhelm Wilhelmsen, Arne O Haugmo
Senior Executives: Khalid Almoayed, Arne O Haugmo, Jan Fr Maeland (General Manager)

PRINCIPAL ACTIVITIES: Shipping agency, stevedoring, tally contractors clearing and forwarding agents, P & I Hull insurance agents

Principal Agencies: Barber Blue Sea; Willine; Scancarriers; Qatar National Navigation & Transport Co; Vega; Unitas; A K Jebson

Associated Companies: Dubai; Dammam; Kuwait; Iran; Riyadh; Jeddah and Worldwide

Principal Bankers: Al Ahli Commercial Bank

Principal Shareholders: A K Almoayed, Bahrain; Wilhelm Wilhelmsen, Norway

Date of Establishment: 1st June 1976

No of Employees: 2632

ALMOAYED STATIONERY EST WLL

73 Alkhalifa Avenue, PO Box 5745, Manama 304

Tel: 253434

Cable: Stationery

Telex: 8854 Equipt BN

Directors: Omar Almoayed, Hisham Almoayed, Fatima Almoayed

PRINCIPAL ACTIVITIES: Import and sale of stationery business equipment and systems, office furniture, computers, contract furnishings and interior designers, sponsorships, real estate, financial investments

Principal Agencies: Facit, Twinlock, Righini, Develop, Triumph Alder, Leabank, F C Brown, DRG Stationery, Westinghouse ASD, Dymo, Myers, Ideal, Mutoh, Solvit, Stielow, Sokkisha, Francotyp, Casio, Efficienta, Meto, Satas, Dictaphone, Mikuni, Artin, Wilson & Garden, Rexel, Helix, H A Coombs, Fisco, Pelikan, Winsor & Newton, Linex, Leitz, Staedtler, Faber Castell, Fireking Int, Cincinnati Time, Aarque, British Thornton, Moresecure, Chartsign, Systema and Checker, Com, Cazzaro, Interface, Planhold, A B Dick, Bertello Int'l, Skema, Giaiotti, Virco, Burroughs

Parent Company: M A Almoayed Family

Associate Companies: Almoayed Data Group; Homes

Principal Bankers: National Bank of Bahrain; Bank of Bahrain and Kuwait; Alahli Commercial Bank

Financial Information:

	US$'000
Authorised capital	1,380
Paid-up capital	1,380

Principal Shareholders: Nabeel Almoayed, Omar Almoayed, Afeef Almoayed, Fatima Almoayed, Hisham Almoayed, Ebrahim Almoayed, Fayza Almoayed, Hayat Almoayed

Date of Establishment: 1946

No of Employees: 171

ALMOAYYED INTERNATIONAL GROUP

PO Box 26259, Manama

Tel: 700777

Cable: AISIT

Telex: 9297 AISIT BN

Telefax: 701211

Chairman: Farouk Y Almoayyed (Chief Executive Officer)

Senior Executives: C V Ramana Murthy (General Manager)

PRINCIPAL ACTIVITIES: Computer distribution and agency, software development, computer maintenance, turnkey contracting for the construction of computer room, fire alarm system, access control system, etc

Principal Agencies: Wang Computers, Redstone IBM Compatible PCs, IBS Radix Hand Held Computers, Apple Computers, ICL DTS Datachecker, Case Communications, Wright Air Conditioning, Cardkey System, Exide Electronics, Minolta, Ricoh, Taxan, etc

Member Companies: Almoayyed Computers; Almoayyed Commercial Services; Almoayyed Trading & Contracting; Apple Centre

Principal Bankers: National Bank of Bahrain; Bank of Bahrain & Kuwait; Al Ahlia Commercial Bank

Financial Information:

	1990
	US$'000
Sales turnover	5,900
Profits	1,200
Total assets	1,800

Principal Shareholders: Farouk Almoayyed (Sole Proprietor)

Date of Establishment: 1979

No of Employees: 110

ALMOAYYED, YOUSUF KHALIL, & SONS WLL

PO Box 143, Almoayyed Bldg, Manama

Tel: 271271

Cable: Almoayyed

Telex: 8270 Moayed BN

Telefax: (0973) 254130

Chairman: Yousuf Almoayyed

Directors: Farouk Almoayyed, Fareed Almoayyed

Senior Executives: Farouk Almoayyed (Managing Director), S M Joseph (Financial Controller), S J Mustafa (Technical Manager), Fareed Y Almoayyed (Executive Director), Abdul Aziz Abdulla Jassim (Executive Director)

PRINCIPAL ACTIVITIES: Import, retail, property, distribution of automobiles, heavy machinery and spare parts, home appliances, electronic items, air conditioners, office furniture and equipment, tools, building materials

Principal Agencies: Nissan Motor Co; Toshiba Corp; Blue Circle Ind; Ford New Holland; Ford Motor Co; Ignis Spa; Thorn Domestic Appliances; Potain; GEC; York Int; Crane Ltd; Wolf Electric Tools; Express Lift Co; Sykes Pumps; ACE Machinery; Komatsu; Hepworth; Pirelli; Kohler & Co; H & R Johnson; Nissan Diesel Motor Co; GEC Group; Simon Group UK

Subsidiary Companies: Almoayyed Airconditioning Contracting; Almoayyed Express Lift Company Ltd; Almoayyed Motors WLL

Principal Bankers: National Bank of Bahrain; Standard Chartered Bank; Al Ahli Commercial Bank; Banque Paribas

Financial Information:

	1989	1990
	BD'000	BD'000
Sales turnover	19,000	20,000
Authorised capital	3,000	3,000
Paid-up capital	3,000	3,000

Principal Shareholders: Y K Almoayyed family

Date of Establishment: 1938

No of Employees: 450

AL MOOSA, ABDULRAHMAN EBRAHIM, EST

PO Box 1058, Manama

Tel: 254650, 714989

Telex: 8387 Amoosa BN

President: Abdulrahman Ebrahim Al Moosa

PRINCIPAL ACTIVITIES: Importers and commission agents of building materials and construction equipment (refineries, bulk plants, wells, dams, off-shore platforms, pipelines, roads, piers). Building and civil engineering contractors

Principal Agencies: John & Joseph Goodare Ltd; Quentsplass Ltd; Sentrymatic Ltd; Buildscaff; Mingori SA, Paris; Zaidan House Beirut; Fimet, Italy; Petroleum Products Co, USA

Principal Bankers: Bank of Bahrain & Kuwait

ALMULLA ENGINEERING & CONTRACTING

PO Box 5355, Manama

Tel: 258988

Telex: 8782 Ameco BN

Directors: Majid Al Mulla

PRINCIPAL ACTIVITIES: Electrical and mechanical engineering contractors

AL NOOH, ABEDALI ESSA, & SONS CO WLL

PO Box 320, Manama
Tel: 253994, 252427
Cable: Alnooh
Telex: 8330 Alnooh BN, 8404 Agency BN

Directors: Abedali Essa Al-Nooh

PRINCIPAL ACTIVITIES: Import and distribution of building
materials, sanitary ware, tools and hardware, iron and steel,
timber and plywood
Principal Agencies: Dowidat Tools, Lamontite, McKechine

AL SHAKAR, EBRAHIM, & SONS (ESSCO)

PO Box 5344, Manama
Tel: 255472
Cable: Lumitron
Telex: 8588 Essco BN

Chairman: Khalil Al-Shakar
Directors: Salman Al-Shakar (Chief Accountant), Faisel Al-
Shakar (Stores Officer), Fouad Al-Shakar (Sales Officer)

PRINCIPAL ACTIVITIES: Electrical engineers, contractors and
distributors, manufacturers' representatives and agents
Principal Agencies: ITE World Trade Corporation, USA; Millers
Falls, Ingersoll-Rand USA; Hawker Siddeley Electric Export
Ltd, UK; Linolite Ltd, UK; Superswitch Electric Appliances Ltd,
UK; Calor SA, France; Felten & Guilleume AG, Austria; Hioki
Electric Works Ltd, Japan; Telemecanique, France
Principal Bankers: National Bank of Bahrain; British Bank of the
Middle East; Rafidain Bank

ALSHARIF SHIPPING AGENCY

PO Box 40, Manama
Tel: 255005, 256177, 255542
Cable: Alsharif
Telex: 8341 Shipco BN

Directors: Mohamed Taher Alsharif, Abdul Hussain Alsharif,
Abdul Rasool Alsharif

PRINCIPAL ACTIVITIES: Shipping and forwarding agents,
labour contractors and ship chandlers

ALUBAF ARAB INTERNATIONAL BANK EC

PO Box 11529, UGB Tower, Diplomatic Area, Manama
Tel: 531212 (General), 532929 (Forex)
Telex: 9671 Alubaf BN (General), 9458 Alubaf BN (Forex)
Telefax: 523100

Chairman: Rashid Al Zayani
Directors: Mohamed Abduljawad (Vice-Chairman), Ahmed
Bennani, Tarek Al Tukmachi, Hamdi El Menabawi, Masoud
Hayat, Mrs Awattif Al Hakman, Mokhazni Mohamed, Hadi
Coobar, Dr Michel Marto, Hussein Hag Ahmed, Essam Al
Usaimi
Senior Executives: Patrick J Mason (General Manager),
Christopher C Briars (Asst General Manager Credit &
Marketing), Mutassim K Mahmassani (Asst General Manager
Administration & Financial Operations), Paul Lind (Senior Vice
President & Treasurer), Ahmed El Bashary (Vice President
Investment Banking)

PRINCIPAL ACTIVITIES: Offshore banking unit
Subsidiary Companies: ALUBAF International Bank-Tunis,
Tunisia
Financial Information:

	1988/89 US$'000
Deposits	715,982
Loans & advances	269,036
Reserves	14,070
Authorised capital	200,000
Paid-up capital	52,000
Total assets	845,644

Principal Shareholders: UBAC Curacao NV (60%), Bank of
Bahrain & Kuwait BSC (5.85%), Alahli Bank of Kuwait KSC
(5.83%), Al Bahrain Arab African Bank EC (5.83%), Banque
Exterieure d'Algerie (4.15%), Central Bank of Egypt (4.15%),
Libyan Arab Foreign Bank (4.15%), Bank of Jordan Ltd
(1.63%), Ministry of Finance & Economy (Oman) (1.63%),
Yemen Bank for Reconstruction & Development (1.63%),
National Bank of Yemen (1.00%)
Date of Establishment: November 1982
No of Employees: 69

ALUMINIUM BAHRAIN BSC (C)
ALBA

PO Box 570, Manama
Tel: 661751
Cable: Alba
Telex: 8253 Alba BN
Telefax: (973) 830083

Chairman: H E Yousif A Shirawi
Directors: HE Yousif A Shirawi, HE Habib Kassim, Shk. Isa Bin
Abdulla Bin Hamad Al Khalifa, HE Abdul Aziz Al Zamil, G
Rohrseitz, Ibrahim A Salamah, Ibrahim A Al Hamar
Senior Executives: Gudvin K Tofte (Chief Executive), A S Al
Noaimi (General Manager Finance), A J de Vries (General
Manager Power & Project), A K Salimi (Deputy Chief
Executive), M H Ghaith (General Manager Metal Production),
J Amiri (General Manager Carbon and Metal Services), J Kerr
(General Manager Engineering & Maintenance), M M Daylami
(General Manager Administration), I W Reid (General Manager
Smelter Expansion)

PRINCIPAL ACTIVITIES: Aluminium smelting including
manufacture of carbon anodes for this process and casting of
aluminium in various forms; capacity: 210,000 mt.
Principal Bankers: Bahrain: National Bank of Bahrain; Bank of
Bahrain & Kuwait; Alahli Commercial Bank; London: United
Bank of Kuwait; New York: Chase Manhattan Bank
Financial Information:

	1990 BD'000
Authorised capital	100,000
Paid-up capital	25,000

Principal Shareholders: Bahrain Government (74.9%); Breton
Investments Ltd (5.1%); Saudi Public Investments Fund (20%)
Date of Establishment: 9.8.1968
No of Employees: 1,600

ALWARDI TRANSPORT & CONSTRUCTION

PO Box 26378, Manama
Tel: 730626/7/8, 730141, 730959
Telex: 8709 Alward BN
Telefax: 731565

Chairman: Abdulla Ali Alwardi
Directors: Ali Abdulla Alwardi, Tariq Abdulla Alwardi
Senior Executives: Ebrahim Ali Al Ghaisi (General Manager),
Mohammed Ali Ishmael (Operations Manager), G D Rao
(Financial Controller)

PRINCIPAL ACTIVITIES: Transport contractors and labour
suppliers; supply of light and heavy auto equipment (cars,
trucks, trailers, cranes, compressors, fork lifts, earthmoving
equipment etc); civil engineers; suppliers of machinery and
equipment to the construction and allied industries
Principal Agencies: Kobelco, P&H Cranes, Norton Clipper,
Arcomet, Powerscreen, Peddinghaus
Principal Bankers: British Bank of the Middle East; Grindlays
Bahrain Bank

Principal Shareholders: Abdulla Alwardi
Date of Establishment: 1974
No of Employees: 380

BAHRAIN

AL-ZAMIL GROUP OF COMPANIES

PO Box 285, Manama
Tel: 253445
Cable: Al Zamil
Telex: 8381 Zamil BN

Chairman: Mohamed A Alzamil
Directors: Fahad A Alzamil, Ahmed A Alzamil, Adib A Alzamil, Sulaiman A Alzamil, Khalid A Alzamil, Hamed A Alzamil, Zamil A Alzamil, Waleed A Alzamil

PRINCIPAL ACTIVITIES: Property leasing and development; manufacture of air conditioning equipment and steel buildings, aluminium doors, window and screens, marble products, nails and screws, also agents and manufacturers' representatives
Principal Agencies: Freudenberg Floors, Needlefelt Carpets, Emerson Electric Co, Allis Chalmers, Siemens Allis, Al Ahlia Insurance, Teledyne, Texas International, Societa Anonima Electrificazione, Intergulf Steel, Arenco, Heitmann Bruun, Harrier Marine Ltd (UK); Teroson, Daihatsu, Phipher International
Branch Offices: A H Alzamil & Sons, Al Khobar, Riyadh, Jubail, Jeddah, Dammam, Saudi Arabia
Subsidiary Companies: Al-Zamil Aluminium Factory, Bahrain; Al-Zamil Nails & Screws Factory, Bahrain; Al-Zamil Marble Factory, Bahrain; Zamil Aluminium Factory, Damman; Al Zamil Refrigeration Industries, Damman; Zamil Steel Bldg Co Ltd, Damman; Zamil Food Industries Co Ltd., Jubail, Saudi Arabia; Arabian Gulf Construction Co, Dammam; Zamil Operation & Marine Co, Alkhobar; Zamil Travel Bureau, Alkhobar; Zamil Plastic Ware Factory, Dammam; Zamil-Corelab, Alkhobar; Overseas Offices: Al-Zamil Co, Inc., 2640 Fountainview, Suite 200, Houston, Texas 77057 (USA); A H Al-Zamil & Sons (UK) Ltd, 25 Chesham St, London SW1, UK; Zamil Coatings, Bahrain; Zamil Furniture, Alkhobar, Saudi Arabia
Principal Bankers: National Bank of Bahrain; Bank of Bahrain & Kuwait; Grindlays Bank; Saudi French Bank; Chase Manhattan Bank; Al-Ahli Commercial Bank

Principal Shareholders: Alzamil Family
No of Employees: 7,000

AL ZAYANI COMMERCIAL SERVICES

PO Box 5553, Manama
Tel: 243186, 231177
Telex: 8624 KHMZ BN

Chairman: Khalid Al Zayani
Directors: Hamid Al Zayani

PRINCIPAL ACTIVITIES: International trading in all fields, including chemicals, building materials, marine industry and silicones
Principal Agencies: Rochem Chemicals, Sigma Coating, Kalmar LMV, Valmet, Sisu, Burgess Ceilings, Denco Flooring, DLW Flooring & Carpeting
Principal Bankers: Bank of Bahrain and Kuwait

Principal Shareholders: Al Zayani Investments

AL ZAYANI INVESTMENTS WLL

PO Box 5553, Diplomatic Area, Manama
Tel: 531177
Telex: 8624 KHMZ BN
Telefax: 530659

Chairman: Khalid R Al Zayani
Directors: Hamid R Al Zayani (Managing Director), Dr Yousif Al Memar
Senior Executives: Ali Fadel, Ali Ewais

PRINCIPAL ACTIVITIES: Investment company specialising in computers (Almakateb), electronic office equipment, furniture (Aldar), services industry (Hotels Delmon & Habara), car hire (Avis rent-a-car), travel agency (Al Zayani Travel & Tours), drycleaning (Martinizing), joint ventures in aluminium cables, manufacture (Midal Cables), tendering in bulk materials,

agency for Kone lift & escalators, and other businesses in Saudi Arabia
Branch Offices: Alkhobar, Saudi Arabia
Subsidiary Companies: Aldar, Al Makateb, Avis Rent-a-Car, Delmon Hotel, Habara Hotel, Martinizing Laundry, Al Zayani Travels & Tours, Tree of Life, Al Zayani Properties, Al Zayani Trading & Tendering

Date of Establishment: 1980

AMERICAN EXPRESS BANK LTD

PO Box 93, Manama
Tel: 231383, 253660
Cable: Amexbank
Telex: 8536 BN

PRINCIPAL ACTIVITIES: Offshore banking
Branch Offices: Dubai, UAE; Cairo, Egypt
Parent Company: Head office in New York, USA

AMERICAN EXPRESS INTERNATIONAL INC

PO Box 5990, Manama
Tel: 232373
Telex: 8851 AMEXCD BN, 9327 AMEXCD BN Authorisations
Telefax: 256385

Directors: George Efthyvoulidis (VP & General Manager)
Senior Executives: P Dean (Finance Controller), Magdi Hanna (Director of Operations), John Pickles (Manager Marketing), Baqer Hassan (Manager Personnel)

PRINCIPAL ACTIVITIES: Travel related and financial services, delivered through American Express travellers cheques and cards
Branch Offices: Bahrain Car Park & Commercial Centre, Manama; Amman; Beirut; Jeddah; Riyadh; Alkhobar; Dammam; Damascus; Muscat; Doha; Abu Dhabi; Dubai; Kuwait; Cairo; Alexandria; Luxor; Sana'a
Parent Company: American Express Company

Date of Establishment: 1980
No of Employees: 150

AMIRI CONSTRUCTION & MAINTENANCE EST

PO Box 564, Manama
Tel: 243622
Cable: Amiri Bahrain
Telex: 8316 Amiri BN

Directors: Mahmood Amiri (Managing Director), Jassim Amiri

PRINCIPAL ACTIVITIES: Civil, mechanical, electrical & maintenance contractors; manufacturers' agents
Principal Agencies: Isocrete Group Sales, UK; Magna Allys & Research Pty Ltd, Australia; Hertalan Roofing BV, Netherlands; Kirlosker, India; Demag, Germany; Hino Motors, Japan; General Motors (Oldsmobile), USA; Opel, Germany; Worthington Meccanica, Italy; Aston Martin, GB; Isucu (Holden), Japan
Subsidiary Companies: Amiri Motors, PO Box 564, Manama, Bahrain
Principal Bankers: Algemene Bank; Nederland
Financial Information:

	US$'000
Authorised capital	3,500
Paid-up capital	3,500

Date of Establishment: 1957
No of Employees: 205

ANAZA

PO Box 231, Manama
Tel: 277888
Telex: 8280 Conserv BN

PRINCIPAL ACTIVITIES: Manufacturers' representatives, supply of foodstuffs, general trading

ARAB ASIAN BANK (EC)

Diplomat Tower, Diplomatic Area, PO Box 5619 Manama
Tel: 532129
Telex: 8583 Abmal BN
Telefax: 530976

Chairman: Mohammed Al Batati
Directors: Abdulla Bahamdan, Harry A Cockrell, Tony Khoury,
Saeed I Chaudhry
Senior Executives: Saeed I Chaudhry (Managing Director),
Saleh H A Hussain (Vice President Operations)

PRINCIPAL ACTIVITIES: Offshore commercial and merchant
and investment banking
Parent Company: Middle East Financial Group SA, Luxembourg
Principal Bankers: Barclays International, London; Fidelity Intl.
Bank New York; National Commercial Bank, Saudi Arabia
Financial Information:

	1990
	US$'000
Authorised capital	100,000
Paid-up capital	37,000

Principal Shareholders: Middle East Financial Group SA, Sheikh
Khalid Bin Salim Bin Mahfouz
Date of Establishment: 21.1.1981
No of Employees: 22

ARAB BANK PLC

Regional Management & OBU, PO Box 813, Manama
Tel: 272040 (Regional), 256398 (OBU), 275303 (OBU)
Cable: Bankarabi
Telex: 8657 (Regional), 8647 (OBU), 8658 OP, 9559 CR, 9333
FX
Telefax: 231640

PRINCIPAL ACTIVITIES: Regional Management, commercial
banking and offshore banking
Branch Offices: In Bahrain: Commercial banking, PO Box 395,
Manama, Tel 255988; Jordan (Head Office); PO Box 950544,
Shmeisani, Amman; Cyprus; Egypt; France; Greece; Lebanon;
Qatar; Singapore; United Arab Emirates (Abu Dhabi, Dubai,
AlMaktoum); United Kingdom; USA; Yemen Republic; China;
Japan
Parent Company: Arab Bank Plc, Jordan
Subsidiary/Associated Companies: Arab Bank (Switzerland) Ltd;
Arab Tunisian Bank, Tunis; Arab Bank Investment Co Ltd,
UK; UBAF, France; UBAE Arab German Bank, W Germany;
Arab Bank Maroc, Morocco; Oman Arab Bank, Oman; Arab
National Bank, Saudi Arabia; Nigeria Arab Bank, Nigeria;
UBAF (Hong Kong) Ltd; UBAF Arab American Bank, USA;
UBAE Arab German Bank, Luxembourg; UBIC; Arab Bank
(Austria) AG

ARAB BANKING CORPORATION (BSC)

ABC Tower, Diplomatic Area, PO Box 5698, Manama
Tel: 532235
Cable: ABCBANK
Telex: 9432 ABC BAH BN, 9433 ABC BAH BN
Telefax: 533163, 533062

Chairman: Abdulmohsen Y Al-Hunaif
Directors: Abdulla A Saudi (Deputy Chairman, President & Chief
Executive), Mohammed E Al-Meraikhi (Deputy Chairman),
Khalifa Mohamed Al Muhairy (Director), Ali Gassem Tantush
(Director), Salem Masoud Jueily (Director), Saleh Mohamed Al
Yousef (Director), Nasser Ahmed Al Suwaidi (Director),
Abdulwahad Ali Al Tammar (Director), Dr Abdulaziz Mohamed
Al Dukheil (Director), Farouk Almoayyed (Director), Giuma K
Said (Secretary to the Board)
Senior Executives: Abdulla A Saudi (President & Chief
Executive), Hikmat Nashashibi (Senior Advisor Investment
Banking), Morven C Hay (SVP Commercial Banking),
Mohamed S Khleif (SVP & General Manager Bahrain Main
Branch), Joe Hili (First VP Information Technology & Support
Division and Chief Accountant), Giuma K Said (First VP

Branches, Subsidiaries & Affiliates Division), Adnan A Yousif
(First VP Global Marketing & Institutional Relations Division),
Roger Lawson (First VP Global Treasury), Farid F Araman
(First VP & Financial Controller), Jan Peter Faberij de Jonge
(First VP Portfolio Management)

PRINCIPAL ACTIVITIES: Commercial, merchant and investment
banking
Branch Offices: Bahrain; New York; London; Singapore; Milan;
Grand Cayman; Paris; Representative Offices in Hongkong;
Houston, Los Angeles, Rome, Tokyo, Tripoli, Tunis
Associated/Subsidiary Companies: Subsidiaries: ABC Banque
Internationale de Monaco, Monaco; ABC Finanziaria Spa,
Italy; ABC Group (UK) Properties Ltd, UK; ABC International
Bank Plc, UK; ABC Investment & Services Co (EC), Bahrain;
ABC (London) Services Co Ltd, UK; Arab Banking
Corporation- Daus & Co GmbH, W Germany; Arab Banking
Corporation, Jordan; Banco Atlantico SA, Spain; International
Bank of Asia Ltd, Hong Kong; Affiliates: Arab Financial
Services Co EC, Bahrain; Arlabank International EC, Bahrain;
Banco ABC-Roma SA, Brazil
Principal Bankers: New York: Manufacturers Hanover Trust;
London: Midland Bank
Financial Information:

	1989	1990
	US$'million	US$'million
Total Assets	21,730	20,549
Deposits	18,088	16,618
Loans & Marketable		
Securities	11,018	12,088
Total Shareholders Equity	1,150	1,386
Profits (loss)	-	(91)
Authorised capital	1,500	1,500
Paid-up capital	750	1,000

Principal Shareholders: A publicly quoted company (Bahrain and
Paris Stock Exchanges) whose principal shareholders are the
Ministry of Finance (Kuwait), Central Bank of Libya and the
Abu Dhabi Investment Authority
Date of Establishment: January 1980
No of Employees: 5,129 (ABC Group)

ARAB COMMERCIAL ENTERPRISES WLL

Suite 205, 230 Government Ave, Manama 315, PO Box 781
Tel: 251656
Cable: Comment Bahrain
Telex: 8608 Ace BN
Telefax: 250806

Chairman: HRH Prince Fahd Bin Khalid Bin Abdulla Al Saud
Directors: Prince Salman Bin Khalid Al Saud, George S
Medawar, Richard Titley, Dr Ibrahim A Al Moneef, Adrian
Platt, Abdulaziz A Abussuud
Senior Executives: A A Abussuud (President & Chief Executive
Officer)

PRINCIPAL ACTIVITIES: Insurance and reinsurance agents and
brokers, surveyors and travel agents
Principal Agencies: Al Nisr Insurance Co SAL; Saudi Arabian
Insurance Co Ltd EC; Mitsui Marine & Fire Ins Co Ltd; Legal
& General; Arab Japanese Insurance Co Ltd EC
Branch Offices: approx 40 offices in the Middle East and one
office in New York
Parent Company: Arab Commercial Enterprises Ltd, Saudi
Arabia
Subsidiary/Associated Companies: Reinsurance & Insurance
Management Services; Al Nisr Ins Co SAL; Saudi Arabian Ins
Co Ltd; Arab Japanese Insurance Co
Principal Bankers: Citibank
Financial Information:

	1989
	US$'000
Sales turnover	126,000
Total assets	72,000

Principal Shareholders: The Almawarid Group and the Sedgwick Group, London
Date of Establishment: 1952 in Al Khobar (Saudi Arabia)
No of Employees: 300 (Worldwide)

ARAB CONSTRUCTION CO EC

PO Box 5755, Chamber of Commerce Bldg, King Faisal Road, Manama
Tel: 255665
Cable: Manza Bahrain
Telex: 9179 Arabcc BN

PRINCIPAL ACTIVITIES: General contractors, and engineering consultants

ARAB ENGINEERING & CONTRACTING CO WLL (ARENCO)

PO Box 823, Manama
Tel: 243244
Cable: Arenco
Telex: 8379 Arenco BN

Chairman: Mohammed Jalal
Directors: Emile F El-Khazen (Managing Director)

PRINCIPAL ACTIVITIES: General contracting, ground improvement, piling, waterproofing, sprayed fire protection, separation layer, thermal insulation, structural repairs, structural steel, pumps, terraline well casings
Principal Agencies: Mandoval; Braas; ICI Fibres; Cementation Piling & Foundations Ltd; Cleveland Bridge & Engineering Co Ltd; Wanner Isofi; Weir & Mono Pumps, Demco
Parent Company: Mohammed Jalal Corporation
Subsidiary/Associate Companies: Arenco/Cementation Ground Engineering Ltd, Cementation/Frankipile Overseas Ltd, Cementation Chemicals Ltd; Associate Companies: Arenco Fairclough WLL
Principal Bankers: Standard Chartered Bank; Banque Paribas

Principal Shareholders: Mohammed Jalal, Emile F El-Khazen
Date of Establishment: 1964
No of Employees: 500

ARAB FINANCIAL SERVICES CO

PO Box 2152, Manama
Tel: 532525
Cable: Arabfin
Telex: 7212 AFS BN
Telefax: 530943, 530499

Chairman: Abdulla A Saudi
Directors: Ebrahim Al Ebrahim (Deputy Chairman), Mustafa Saleh Gibril, Hadi Giteli, Mohamed Abdul Jawad, Hassan Juma, Abdul Rahman Ahmed Mahdi, Khalid Salim Bin Mahfouz, Hikmat Nashashibi, Abdul Rahman Al Rajhi, Ayoub Farid M Saab, Mohamed Akil Tawfiqi, Abdel Rahman S Touqan, Tarik Talib Al Tukmachi
Senior Executives: Dr Medhat Sadek (General Manager), Derek J Pearmund (Deputy General Manager), Bryn J Rees (Head of Finance), Ken H Dubbins (Head of Operations), J Mark Johnson (Head of Sales & Marketing)

PRINCIPAL ACTIVITIES: Financial services specialising in travel related finances; travellers cheques, visa card, business consultancy in field of data processing & communications
Associated Companies: Arab Banking Corporation
Principal Bankers: Arab Banking Corporation
Financial Information:

	1990 US$'000
Authorised capital	50,000
Paid-up capital	30,000

Principal Shareholders: Arab banks and financial institutions
Date of Establishment: April 1984
No of Employees: 77

ARAB HOTELS & CATERING CO

PO Box 5546, Manama
Tel: 233331
Cable: Orient Bahrain
Telex: 9392 Arabtl BN
Telefax: 240149

Directors: Majeed Al Zeera (Managing Director), Mohamed Akram Al Zeera
Senior Executives: Mohsin Rajaei

PRINCIPAL ACTIVITIES: Hotel management and catering
Subsidiary Companies: Oriental Palace Hotel; Bristol Hotel
Principal Bankers: Al Ahli Commercial Bank

Principal Shareholders: Directors as described
Date of Establishment: 1979
No of Employees: 50

ARAB INSURANCE GROUP (ARIG)

Arig House, Diplomatic Area, PO Box 26992, Manama
Tel: 531110
Telex: 9395, 9396 ARIG BN
Telefax: (0973) 531155, 530289

Chairman: Abdul Wahab A Al Tammar
Directors: Nasser M Al Nowais (Vice-Chairman), Kassem M Sherlala (Vice Chairman), Anis A Al Jallaf, Taher Dau H Benlaba, Hisham A Razzuqi
Senior Executives: Gunnar Maltegard (Executive Manager Facultative Div), G Rangarajan (Executive Manager Treaty Div), P V Unnikrishnan (Invesment Dept Manager), Ismail Mudhaffar Ali (Administration & Personnel Manager), Loay M Al Naqib (CEO UK Subsidiary)

PRINCIPAL ACTIVITIES: Insurance and reinsurance
Branch Offices: Hong Kong Branch Office, Fax 0852 8660821; Tunis Branch Office, Fax 0216 1 785397
Subsidiary Companies: Ang Insurance Co Ltd, London, Fax 071-286 1923
Principal Bankers: United Bank of Kuwait; Bank of Bahrain and Kuwait; Arab Banking Corporation
Financial Information:

	1988/89 US$'000	1989/90 US$'000
Gross premium	153,644	143,039
Net profit	29,490	30,915
Authorised capital	3,000,000	3,000,000
Paid-up capital	150,000	150,000
Total assets	514,918	537,681

Principal Shareholders: Kuwait; United Arab Emirates; Libya
Date of Establishment: 1980
No of Employees: 203

ARAB INTERNATIONAL BANK

PO Box 1114, Diplomat Tower, Manama
Tel: 531611
Cable: AIBBAH
Telex: 9489 AIBBAH BN, 9538 AIBEX BN

Chairman: Dr Mostafa Khalil
Directors: Abdalla Ammar Saudi, Dr Hassan Abbas Zaki, Ali Mohamed Nigm, Ghanim Fares Al-Mazrui, Hadi Mohamed Giteli, Hikmat Sayed Ahmed Rizk, Abdel Latif El Kib, Mohamed Ali El Barbary, Mohamed Fouad Osman, Mohamed Hussein Layas, Mohamed Al-Fazzani, Khalifa Mohamed Al-Mouheiry, Khalifa Al-Gaith Khalifa Al-Qubeisi, Khalifa Mohamed Seif Al-Shamsi, Isa Mohamed Al-Suwaidi, Dr Omar Al-Zawawy, Sakr Zaher Al-Merikhi
Senior Executives: Abdel Latif El Kib (Managing Director), Hadi M El Fighi (General Manager)

PRINCIPAL ACTIVITIES: Money market operation, loans and syndications, marketable securities, acceptances, guarantees and letters of credit
Parent Company: Head Office: Arab International Bank, 35 Abdul Khalek Sarwat Street, Cairo, Egypt

Principal Bankers: Mellon Bank Int'l, New York; Banque
Nationale de Paris, Paris; Dresdner Bank, Frankfurt; Lloyds
Bank, London; Sumitomo Bank, Tokyo; National Commercial
Bank, Jeddah
Financial Information:

	1990
	US$'000
Authorised capital	150,000
Paid-up capital	150,000

Principal Shareholders: The Arab Republic of Eygpt; Socialist
People's Libyan Arab Jamahiriya; The United Arab Emirates;
The Sultanate of Oman; The State of Qatar; Private Arab
Participants
Date of Establishment: 1st March 1984
No of Employees: 25

ARAB INTERNATIONAL DEVELOPMENT CO EC

PO Box 26626, Manama
Tel: 242391, 242392
Telex: 9226 Aidco BN

Directors: Essa Bahman, Salah Ahmed Al-Ayoub, Abdulla Al-
Wazzan, Khalid Nasser Al-Saleh, Faisal Al Dabboos, Faisal
Al-Dawood, Ghazi Al-Mutawwa
Senior Executives: Essa Bahman (Managing Director), Mussa M
Barakat (General Manager)

PRINCIPAL ACTIVITIES: Investment, real estate, property,
precious metals, joint venture etc.
Branch Offices: Kuwait Office: PO Box 26315 Safat, Kuwait
Associated Companies: Arab Development Co for Contracting
(KSCC) Kuwait
Principal Bankers: Burgan Bank (KSC), Kuwait; Bank of Bahrain
& Kuwait, Bahrain
Financial Information:

	US$'000
Authorised capital	53,000
Paid-up capital	30,213
Issued capital	39,750

Principal Shareholders: Public
Date of Establishment: May 1979

ARAB SAUDI BANK (FORMERLY ARAB SOLIDARITY BANK)

PO Box 10100, 8th & 9th Floors, BKIC House, Diplomatic Area,
Manama
Tel: 530011 (General)
Cable: Tadhamon
Telex: 9373 Bahasb BN (Forex), 7218 Bahash BN (General)
Telefax: 530788

Chairman: HH Prince Fahad Bin Abdullah Bin Abdul Rahman Al
Saud
Directors: Sheikh Amin Jamil Dahlawi (Vice Chairman), HH
Prince Saud Bin Abdullah Bin Abdul Rahman Al Saud
(Executive Committee Member), Sheikh Hassan Jamil Al
Dahlawi (Executive Committee Member), Sheikh Othman
Jamil Al Dahlawi, Sheikh Abdul Aziz Mohamed Bin Nafisah
(Executive Committee Member), Sheikh Abdulla Mohamed
Amin Al Dahlawi, HH Prince Khalid Bin Saud Bin Abdulla Bin
Abdul Rahman Al Saud, Tarek A Mowafi (Director & General
Manager), Hatim Sharif Zubi (Secretary to the Board & Legal
Advisor)
Senior Executives: Tarek A Mowafi (Director & General
Manager), Abdulla M Yateem (VP Credit & Marketing), Leslie
J Rice (VP Financial Control), Canute A D'Sa (VP Operations
& Administration), Ebrahim Al Yahya (Money Markets
Manager), Valerian Crasto (Back-Office Settlements Manager)

PRINCIPAL ACTIVITIES: Bank registered in Cayman Islands,
British West Indies in 1978. Has an OBU in Bahrain and
handles foreign exchange, money market operations and
project finance/commercial loans, letters of credit and
guarantees

Principal Bankers: Frankfurt: Arab Banking Corp, Daus & Co;
Hong Kong: International Bank of Asia; London: Barclays
Bank; Milan: Arab Banking Corp; New York: American
Express Bank, Security Pacific International Bank, Fidelity
International Bank; Paris: Barclays Bank; Tokyo: Sumitomo
Bank Ltd; Zurich: Credit Suisse

Principal Shareholders: Private sector
Date of Establishment: Bahrain OBU commenced operations in
1980
No of Employees: 26

ARAB SHIPBUILDING & REPAIR YARD CO (ASRY)

PO Box 50110, Hidd
Tel: 671111
Cable: Asry
Telex: 8455 Asry BN
Telefax: 670236

Chairman: HE Shaikh Daij Bin Khalifa Al Khalifa (Bahrain),
(Alternate Ebrahim Hassan Salman)
Directors: Issa Abdul Rahman Al Mannai (Qatar), Alternate
Sultan Nasser Al Sowaidi, Ebrahim Al Ghanim (Kuwait),
Alternate Wael Al Madaf, HE Nasser Al Sharhan (UAE),
Alternate Ahmed Mohamed Saeed Majid, Abdul Rahim Al
Saban (Saudi Arabia), Alternate Hassan Ishaq Azzouz,
Mohamed Otaiwi Mohamed (Iraq), Alternate Sabah Jumma,
Ageli Abdul Salam Breni (Libya), Alternate Abu Zaid Ramadan
Al Omrani, Mohamed M Al Khatib (Secretary to the Board of
Directors and Asrymar Managing Director and Legal Advisor)
Senior Executives: Hans G Frisk (General Manager), A Redha
Faraj (Deputy General Manager), Fawzi Al-Qusaibi
(Commercial Manager), Dr A C Antoniou (Production
Manager)

PRINCIPAL ACTIVITIES: Ship repairs; steel fabrication and land
work; mechanical and electrical engineering
Branch Offices: Agents in Australia, Brazil, France, Germany,
Greece, Hong Kong, India, Italy, Japan, Norway, Spain,
Sweden, UK, USA, Singapore, South Korea, Portugal
Associated Companies: Arab Shipbuilding and Repair Yard
Marketing Services (Asrymar) Limited, 39 Pall Mall, London
SW1Y5JG, UK; ASRYWELD, Bahrain; ASRYPROPEL, Bahrain
Principal Bankers: National Bank of Bahrain
Financial Information:

	1990
	US$'000
Sales turnover	44,000
Profits	7,600
Paid-up capital	340,000

Principal Shareholders: 7 OAPEC State of Saudi Arabia,
Bahrain, Kuwait, Qatar, United Arab Emirates, Libya and Iraq
Date of Establishment: 30th November 1974
No of Employees: 738

ARAB WINGS

PO Box 1044, Manama
Tel: 258616
Telex: 8918 Alia BN

Chairman: Ali Ghandour

PRINCIPAL ACTIVITIES: Air taxi service
Associated Companies: ALIA The Royal Jordanian Air Line

Date of Establishment: April 1975

ARABCONSULT

Almoayyed Bldg, North Side, 6th Floor, PO Box 551, Manama
Tel: 251006
Cable: Arabconsult Bahrain
Telex: 8263 FAKHRI BN

Chairman: Ahmed A Fakhri
Directors: Leonara Consunji

PRINCIPAL ACTIVITIES: Government relations, public relations, marketing, advertising and publishing

Principal Agencies: Ministry of Information, State of Bahrain; YBA Kanoo, Ministry of Development & Industry, Bahrain Petroleum Co, Bahrain Telecommunications Co, Directorate of Tourism & Archeology, Ford of Europe Inc, Gulf Petrochemical Industries Co

Branch Offices: Arabconsult, Saudi Arabia

Subsidiary Companies: ArabCommunicators; ArabVision; ArabAd

Principal Bankers: Grindlays Bank; Bank of Bahrain & Kuwait

Principal Shareholders: Private company
Date of Establishment: 1969
No of Employees: 12

ARABIAN AVIATION CORPORATION EC

PO Box 10476, Manama
Tel: 532308, 530972
Telex: 9289 HELI BN
Telefax: 530032

Chairman: C M Ryland
Deputy Chairman: I J Blackie
Senior Executives: I T Dallimore (General Manager), Mrs Linda A H Smythe (Company Secretary & Finance Manager), W N Robertson (Marketing Manager)

PRINCIPAL ACTIVITIES: Aircraft and helicopter sales
Principal Agencies: Bell Helicopter Textron; Pilatus Britten-Norman; Avco Lycoming
Parent Company: Hawker Pacific Pty Ltd
Principal Bankers: Standard Chartered Bank

Date of Establishment: 1979

ARABIAN EXHIBITION MANAGEMENT WLL

PO Box 20200, Manama
Tel: 250033
Telex: 9103 Exhib BN
Telefax: 242381

Chairman: Shaikh Mohamed Bin Abdulla Al Khalifa
Directors: H B G Montgomery, L P Kelly, H R W Johnson
Senior Executives: Stephen C Key (Chief Executive)

PRINCIPAL ACTIVITIES: Exhibition organisers
Associated Companies: Overseas Exhibition Services, London, UK
Principal Bankers: Grindlays Bahrain Bank

Date of Establishment: 1977

ARLABANK INTERNATIONAL EC

PO Box 5070, Manama Center, (part IV), Manama
Tel: GEN 232124, DEALING 232118
Telex: GEN 9345 ARLABK BN, DEALING 9393 ARLAFX BN
Telefax: 246239

Chairman: Abdulla A Saudi
Directors: Abdulrasool Y Abulhasan (First Vice Chairman), Cesar Rodriguez Batlle (Vice Chairman), Nooruddin A Nooruddin (Executive Director), Ahmad M A Bastaki, Mohamed H Layas, Salem Zenaty, Ahmed Saeed Al Badi, Arab Banking Corporation (Rep Giuma K Said), Banco do Brasil (Rep Narciso Da Fonseca Carvalho), Banco Nacional de Desarrollo (Rep Roberto Luis Arano), Banco Arabe Espanol (Rep Rafael Gomez Perezagua), Banco de la Nacion (rep Manuel Chavez), Arab International Bank (Rep Abdulatif A Elkib), Corporacion de Fomento de la Produccion (Rep Ismael Ibarra)
Senior Executives: Christian Rodriguez Camilloni (General Manager), M Farouk Qadir (Deputy General Manager), Qutub Yousafali (Senior Manager Controllership/Secretariat), Adil A Al Mannai (Manager Business Development), Akbar N Mohammed (Manager & Chief Dealer)

PRINCIPAL ACTIVITIES: Merchant, commercial and investment banking

Branch Offices: Aralabank International EC, Edificio Vallarino, Elvira Mendez y Calle, 52 Panama, PO BOx 6-8082 El Dorado, Panama. Arlabank International EC, PO Box 707, Grand Cayman, British West Indies

Subsidiary Companies: Arab Latin American Bank, Lima, Peru; Alpha Lambda Investment & Securities Corp, Tortola, British Virgin Islands

Principal Bankers: Manufacturers Hanover Trust Co; ABN; Credit Suisse; BNP; Bank of Tokyo; Lloyds Bank Plc; Banco Arabe Espanol; National Westminster Bank; Saudi British Bank; Osterreichische Landerbank

Financial Information:

	1989 US$'million
Total finance income	20.6
Net profit	5.2
Capital & reserves	56
Share capital	184
Deposits	916
Total assets	1,315

Principal Shareholders: Abu Dhabi Authority; Arab Banking Corporation; Banco Arabe Espanol; Banco do Brasil; Banco Nacional de Desarrollo; Kuwait Foreign Trading & Contracting Co; Libyan Arab Foreign Bank
Date of Establishment: 22 February 1983
No of Employees: 80

ASHRAF BROTHERS WLL

PO Box 62, Manama
Tel: 534439, 534441
Cable: Ashraf
Telex: 8477 Ashraf BN
Telefax: 534406

Chairman: Mrs Ingeborg Ashraf
Directors: Mrs Romana Ashraf (Deputy Chairman), Miss Reshma Ashraf (Executive Director)
Senior Executives: Virendra Gulati (General Manager), N R C Nair (Group Financial Controller), Antony Thomas, N Premkumar, Ali Rahma, A R Chandran, Munawar Akhtar, Nanda Kumar

PRINCIPAL ACTIVITIES: Import, export, retailing, wholesaling of electrical and electronic appliances and equipment, household goods, photographic goods, business equipment, watches and lighters, cosmetics and perfumes, clothing and food; confectionery; rasors; batteries; etc
Principal Agencies: Kodak, Sony, Nikon, Trio-Kenwood, Gillette, U-Bix, Durst, Hasselblad, NCL, Casio, Data Card, Brother, Yves Saint Laurent, Christian Dior, Lancome, Elizabeth Arden, Shulton, Maruman, Mondi, Jaeger, Chanel, Noritake, Royal Doulton, WMF, Hutschenreuther, Nivada, Milus, Swatch, Everready, Perrier, Orangina, Replay, Melitta, Red Tulip, etc
Branch Offices: Dubai
Associated Companies: Ashraf Bros, Dubai; Ashraf Distributors WLL, Bahrain; Gulf Colour Laboratories, Bahrain; Ashraf Supermarkets, Bahrain
Principal Bankers: British Bank of the Middle East
Financial Information:

	1989/90 BD'000
Sales turnover	11,000
Profits	480
Authorised capital	720
Paid-up capital	720
Total assets	7,890

Date of Establishment: 1st April 1913
No of Employees: 350

ASSOCIATED CONSULTING ENGINEERS (ACE)

PO Box 844, Manama
Tel: 250947, 252314
Telex: 8731 ACEBAH BN

PRINCIPAL ACTIVITIES: Civil engineering consultants
Branch Offices: Abu Dhabi, Kuwait

AWAL CONTRACTING & TRADING CO (AWALCO) WLL

PO Box 741, Manama
Tel: 725100
Cable: Shaheen
Telex: 8277 Awalco BN
Telefax: 728997

Chairman: Shaheen S Shaheen
Directors: Mohamed A Mattar (Vice Chairman), Khalid M Mattar (Managing Director), Adel M Mattar (Director Airconditioning Dept)

PRINCIPAL ACTIVITIES: Contractors/charterers of tug boats, utility boats and barges, contractors/suppliers/manufacturers/importers/exporter of airconditioning, refrigeration and watercooling equipment; contractors/suppliers and installation of electrical equipment and fire alarm systems
Principal Agencies: Friedrich Airconditioning & Refrigeration Co, USA; Uawithiya Industries Co, Thailand; S C Engineering, Thailand; McQuay Inc, USA; M K Refrigeration, UK; Frimont Spa, Italy
Branch Offices: Awalco, PO Box 3735, Dubai, Tel 228536; Awalco, 353 Monticello Park, Conroe, Texas 77302, USA
Subsidiary Companies: Awal Products Co WLL; Gulf Services Co WLL
Principal Bankers: British Bank of the Middle East; Al Ahli Commercial Bank BSC

Principal Shareholders: Shaheen S Shaheen, Mohammed A Mattar
Date of Establishment: 1957
No of Employees: 400

AWAL PLASTICS WLL

PO Box 693, Manama
Tel: 254728
Cable: Plastico
Telex: 9237 Signs BN
Telefax: (973) 259956

Directors: M A Ali (Managing Director), Abdulla A Rahim (Technical Director), Adel M Ali (Executive Director)

PRINCIPAL ACTIVITIES: Producing taylor-made plastic illuminated and non-illuminated sign boards, reflective traffic signs, screen printing, electroplating, rubber stamps and stereos, engraving, PVC welding, advertising & promotional items, etc
Principal Agencies: 3M Co, Chimei, Fasson, Thomas Fattorini, X-Film
Principal Bankers: Bank of Bahrain & Kuwait; National Bank of Bahrain
Financial Information:

	1989 BD'000
Sales turnover	3,134
Authorised capital	2,000
Paid-up capital	2,000
Total assets	3,718

Principal Shareholders: Mohammed Ali (50%), Abdulla A Rahim (50%)
Date of Establishment: 1969
No of Employees: 165

AWAL REFRIGERATION & AIRCONDITIONING WORKSHOP

PO Box 955, Manama
Tel: 294502, 293388, 293377
Cable: Refrigeration-Bahrain
Telex: 8534 Otoobi BN
Telefax: 294524

Proprietor: Ahmed Abdulla Khalid (also Managing Director)
Senior Executives: Yousif A A Alkhaja (General Manager)

PRINCIPAL ACTIVITIES: Mechanical contractors specialising in airconditioning and refrigeration, also all types of electrical appliances, interior decoration, sanitary ware, and household appliances, electronic components, local manufacturers of Gulf Star brand water cooler, refrigerators, and stainless steel food service equipment
Principal Agencies: Fedders, USA; Airtemp, USA; ESTA, Denmark; Brandt, France; Croydon, Brazil; Alax, Switzerland, DWM Copeland, W Germany; Vulcan, USA; Aspera, Italy; Agut, Spain; Winner, Spain
Branch Offices: Head office & Showroom at Hoora, Tel 293388; Factory at Mina Sulman Industrial Area, Tel 727040; Muharraq showroom
Subsidiary Companies: Ahmed Abdulla Khalid Contracting Est (Civil Contractors)
Principal Bankers: National Bank of Bahrain, Manama

Date of Establishment: 1963
No of Employees: 145

BADER BROS

PO Box 5157, Manama
Tel: 252694
Cable: Buildcentre
Telex: 8803 BN

Directors: Reza Bader (Managing Director), Jawad Bader, Bahram Bader

PRINCIPAL ACTIVITIES: Contractors, engineering consultants, and interior designers suppliers of building materials and equipment

BAHRAIN AIRPORT SERVICES BSC (C)

PO Box 22285, Muharraq
Tel: 321777
Cable: Airserve Bahrain
Telex: 8971 Basba BN
Telefax: 335304

Directors: Mubarak Jassem Kanoo (Vice Chairman)
Senior Executives: Khalil Zaman (General Manager), Alan Brough (Manager Cargo), N Warringer (Manager Traffic Services), Pactrick Beasley (Manager Engineering Services), Abdul Latif Al Goud (Manager Personnel & Training), Joao Luis Aguiar (Manager Aircraft Catering Services)

PRINCIPAL ACTIVITIES: Airport handling agents for aircraft and airline operators, providing full range of traffic, catering, engineering and cargo services for all aircraft types
Principal Bankers: Bank of Bahrain and Kuwait; National Bank of Bahrain; Al Alhi Commercial Bank

Principal Shareholders: Gulf Air (30%); Y B A Kanoo (30%); various travel agents in Bahrain (40%)
Date of Establishment: 1st August 1977
No of Employees: 1,681

BAHRAIN ARAB INTERNATIONAL BANK EC (BAIB)

PO Box 20488, Manama
Tel: 230491, 230492
Cable: BAIB Bahrain
Telex: 9380 Baib BN; 9382 Baib BN
Telefax: 243798

Chairman: Mohamed Ali E Al Qadhi

Directors: Issam Abdul Aziz Al Usaimi (Vice Chairman), Walid Mohamad S A Al Qattan (Executive Director), Abdullah Saad Al Munaifi (Director), Ahmed Nasser Al Hamlan (Director)
Senior Executives: Ezzat El Kilany (General Manager), Omar Mourad (Assistant General Manager), Ibrahim Al Jallabi (Credit Follow Up), Nabil Hamdan (Marketing & Correspondent Banking), Ali Harun (Operations), Nora Baluchi (Treasury)

PRINCIPAL ACTIVITIES: Offshore commercial and merchant banking
Parent Company: Arab African International Bank, Cairo
Principal Bankers: Bank of New York, New York; ABC-New York, New York; National Westminster Bank, London; Credit Suisse, Zurich; Dresdner Bank, Frankfurt; Banque Nationale de Paris, Paris
Financial Information:

	1990 US$'000
Authorised capital	200,000
Paid-up capital	100,000

Principal Shareholders: Kuwait Foreign Trading Contracting & Investment Co, Kuwait (47.88%); Kuwait & Middle East Financial Investment Co, Kuwait (47.88%); Kuwait Investment Authority, Kuwait (3.15%); Bank Al Jazira, Saudi Arabia (1.09%)
Date of Establishment: October 1979
No of Employees: 40

BAHRAIN ATOMISERS INTERNATIONAL BSC (C)

PO Box 5328, Manama
Tel: 261158
Cable: Bahratom
Telex: 8253 ALBA BN
Telefax: 273279

Chairman: Ahmed J Hubail
Directors: Yousif Alkhaja, Gert Roherseitz, Abdulla Al Thawadi, Gens Kallmeyer
Senior Executives: Hameed Ali (General Manager), Joseph Castelino (Accountant)

PRINCIPAL ACTIVITIES: Production of atomised aluminium powder
Principal Bankers: National Bank of Bahrain
Financial Information: Bahrain (51%) Breton Investments (49%)

	1989 BD'000
Sales turnover	15,000
Authorised capital	1,000
Paid-up capital	400

Principal Shareholders: Bahrain Government (51%), Breton Investments Ltd (49%)
Date of Establishment: 1972
No of Employees: 44

BAHRAIN BEDDING FACTORY (AL ANSARI)

PO Box 5648, Manama
Tel: 727407, 727073
Telex: 9493 BMF BN
Telefax: 729796

Chairman: Abdul Jaleel Al Ansari
Directors: Ahmed Al-Ansari, Abdullah Al Ansari
Senior Executives: Ali Abdulla Muttawah (Sales Manager), M G Joy (Office Manager)

PRINCIPAL ACTIVITIES: Mattress and bed manufacturing
Principal Bankers: Banque du Caire
Financial Information: Bahraini owned (100%)

Principal Shareholders: Al Ansari Group of Companies
Date of Establishment: 1974
No of Employees: 55

BAHRAIN CAR PARKS COMPANY BSC

PO Box 5298, Manama
Tel: 244130, 244283, 230514
Telex: 9321 BHCP BN

Chairman: Mahmoud Mahmoud Husain
Directors: Jasim Mohammed Murad (Managing Director), Yacoub Yousef (Vice Chairman), Mubarak Al Hassawi (Director), Yaseen Al Hassawi (Director), Ahmed Aqueel Janahi (Director), Abdulwahid M Noor (Director), Ebrahim Eshaq (Director), Ali Saleh Al Saleh (Director), Ahmed Yusuf Mahmood Husain (Director)
Senior Executives: Mohammed Al Kooheji (Manager Operations), S Suthakar (Financial Controller)

PRINCIPAL ACTIVITIES: Car park building and managing
Principal Bankers: National Bank of Bahrain, Al Ahli Commercial Bank, Bank of Bahrain & Kuwait
Financial Information:

	1989 BD'000	1990 BD'000
Total income	1,195	1,200
Profits	728	729
Authorised capital	10,000	10,000
Paid-up capital	7,032	7,032
Total assets	9,397	9,500

BAHRAIN CINEMA COMPANY

PO Box 26573, Manama
Tel: 258900
Telex: 8300 Cinema BN
Telefax: 273680

Chairman: Ali Yousuf Fakhro
Directors: Farooq Al Moayyad, Mohammed Kanoo, Esam Fakhro, Ali Ubaidly, Jalal Jalal, Farooq Al Alawi, Jamil Ebrahim
Senior Executives: Esam Fakhro (Managing Director), Ahmed Rashed (General Manager)

PRINCIPAL ACTIVITIES: Motion picture exhibitors, film distributors, video wholesalers, video shop owners
Subsidiary Companies: The Bahrain Cinema Co, PO Box 521, Dubai
Principal Bankers: Bank of Bahrain & Kuwait; National Bank of Bahrain; Al Ahli Commercial Bank
Financial Information:

	1989 BD'000
Sales turnover	917
Profits	364
Authorised capital	1,500
Paid-up capital	1,500
Total assets	2,673

Principal Shareholders: Public shareholding company
Date of Establishment: 1968
No of Employees: 85

BAHRAIN COMMERCIAL FACILITIES COMPANY BSC (C)

PO Box 1175, Tariq Building, Government Road, Manama
Tel: 250099
Telex: 9168 BN
Telefax: 276056

Chairman: Isa Borshaid
Directors: Fuad Kanoo, Mohammed Khalaifat, Abdul Razak Hassan, Hassan Al Jalahma, Jalal M Jalal, Ebrahim Buhindi, Khalid Al Zayani, Abdul Rahman Y Fakhro, Yusuf Khalaf
Senior Executives: Paul E Birch (General Manager), Mohamad Ahmed Al Jaber (Finance Manager), Jalil Zaber (New Business Manager)

PRINCIPAL ACTIVITIES: Instalment credit & leasing
Subsidiary Companies: National Motor Company WLL

Principal Bankers: Banque Paribas; Bank of Bahrain & Kuwait; National Bank of Bahrain

Financial Information:

	1990 US$'000
Sales turnover	19,000
Profit	2,000
Authorised capital	26,500
Paid-up capital	17,250
Total assets	37,000

Principal Shareholders: Bank of Bahrain & Kuwait; National Bank of Bahrain; General Organisation for Social Insurance

Date of Establishment: 1983

BAHRAIN CONSTRUCTION CO

PO Box 5009, Manama
Tel: 250297, 250325
Cable: Baconco
Telex: 8415 Makk BN

PRINCIPAL ACTIVITIES: Industrial and public works contractors

Branch Offices: Works at Issa Town (Tel 68071)

Associated Companies: KB Reinforcements Gulf Ltd, Tel 681037; Industrial Automation; Multiblok Concrete; Inaco Structural Eng, Tel 681071; Sitra Blocks and Tiles Co, Tel 661796

BAHRAIN ESTATE CO

PO Box 805, Al-Khalifa Rd, Manama
Tel: 255413, 250379, 256430
Cable: Bestco Bahrain
Telex: 8728 Bestco BN

Directors: Hassan Saleh A R Al-Baluchi, (Partner) Khalifa Saleh Ali (Partner)

PRINCIPAL ACTIVITIES: Distribution and sale of household furniture and household articles, carpet and furnishing

Principal Agencies: Silentnight (Export Ltd), UK; Avalon Furniture Ltd, UK; Lancaster Carpets Ltd, UK; Annmed (Importers & Exporters) Ltd, UK

Principal Bankers: British Bank of the Middle East

BAHRAIN FLOUR MILLS CO

PO Box 26787, Mina Sulman
Tel: 729984
Cable: Almatahin
Telex: 8585 Bfmill BN
Telefax: 729312

Chairman: Ali Bin Yusuf Fakhroo

Directors: Jassim Mohamed Al-Saffar, Khalid Abdulla Al-Saqur, Sadiq Mohamed Al-Baharna, Rashid Abdulrahman Al-Zayani, Khalil Mutawa, Abdulla Rashid Al Madany, Abdulla Ahmed Mansour

Senior Executives: Shamsan Al Waswasi (General Manager)

PRINCIPAL ACTIVITIES: Flour milling

Principal Bankers: National Bank of Bahrain; Bank of Bahrain and Kuwait; Al Ahlia Commercial Bank; Arab Bank

Financial Information:

	1990 BD'000
Sales turnover	3,621
Profits	279
Authorised capital	10,000
Paid-up capital	2,150
Total assets	6,171

Principal Shareholders: Government of Bahrain; Kuwait Flour Mills Co; Individuals

Date of Establishment: May 1972

No of Employees: 165

BAHRAIN GAS

PO Box 254, Manama
Tel: 255319
Cable: Bahrain Gas
Telex: 8988 Bahgas BN
Telefax: (973) 242261

Directors: Mohammed Bin Ali Al-Hasan, Bashar Mohammed Al-Hasan (Deputy Director)

Senior Executives: Mohammed Noor Pathan (Administration Manager)

PRINCIPAL ACTIVITIES: Production and distribution of LP gas and petroleum products and kitchen appliances

Principal Agencies: Dresser Wayne, USA; TI Creda int, UK; Magic Chef, USA; Hoechst AG, W Germany; Primus Sievert, Sweden; Kosan AS, Denmark; Zanussi, Italy; Leon Guilbert, France; FAC Metal, Taiwan; W Warne, USA; Selin Group, Taiwan; W Clasmann, USA; Bosch, W Germany; Dalworth Tank, USA; Nova Comet, Italy; Viking Pump, USA; Koetser, USA; Dover Int, Holland; Raywall, USA

Branch Offices: Alhasan Bldg, Diplomatic Area, Manama

Subsidiary Companies: M A Alhasan General Trading & Airport Service Station

Principal Bankers: British Bank of the Middle East; Standard Chartered Bank

Principal Shareholders: Mohammed Bin Ali Al Hasan

Date of Establishment: 1962

No of Employees: 120

BAHRAIN HOTELS COMPANY BSC

PO Box 580, Manama
Tel: 713000
Telex: 8241 Gulftl BN
Telefax: 713040

Chairman: Ahmed Ali Kanoo

Directors: Salim Bin Ali Nasser Assiyabi (Vice Chairman), Farouk Yousuf Almoayyed (Managing Director), Ali Mohammed Al Jassim, Mohamed Husain Yateem, Fowzie Ahmed Ali Kanoo, Mubarak Jassim Kanoo, Mohamed Noor Sultan

Senior Executives: Mohamed J Buzizi (General Manager), Aqeel G M Raees (General Manager Gulf Hotel), Philip Stephen (Financial Controller/Company Secretary), Michael Fuhrmann (Food & Beverage Manager), Moosa A Ali (Personnel & Training Manager), Alan Pendleton (Director of Sales), Abdul Nabi Amini (Rooms Division Manager)

PRINCIPAL ACTIVITIES: Hotel business

Subsidiary Companies: Gulf Cellar

Principal Bankers: National Bank of Bahrain

Financial Information:

	1990 BD'000
Sales turnover	9,022
Profits	2,119
Authorised capital	8,484
Paid-up capital	8,484
Total assets	15,527

Principal Shareholders: Gulf Air

Date of Establishment: 1969

No of Employees: 407

BAHRAIN HOUSING BANK

PO Box 5370, Manama
Tel: 233321
Telex: 8599

Chairman: Shaikh Khaled bin Abdulla Al Khalifa

Directors: Dr Abdul Latif Kanoo (Deputy Chairman), Ibrahim Abdulla Al Hamer, Shaikh Isa bin Ibrahim Al Khalifa, Ahmed Hubail, Abdul Rahman Zayani, Abdul Karim Al Aliwat

Senior Executives: Isa Sultan Al-Thawadi (General Manager)

BAHRAIN

PRINCIPAL ACTIVITIES: Housing finance, long term housing loans; finance to the contruction industry
Principal Bankers: National Bank of Bahrain

Date of Establishment: 1979
No of Employees: 55

BAHRAIN INSURANCE COMPANY BSC

PO Box 843, Manama
Tel: 255641, 259291, 257011, 251244
Cable: Tameen BN
Telex: 8463 BN
Telefax: 973-242389

Chairman: Sadiq Mohammed Al Baharna
Directors: Yousuf Ahmed AL Saie (Vice Chairman), Ali H Yateem, Hameed A E Al-Nooh
Senior Executives: Ali H Yateem (Managing Director), Mun'em Al Khafaji (General Manager), Mohammad Ali A Rehman (Deputy General Manager), Mohamd Kadem (Motor Dept Manager), Mahdi Al Aradi (Marine & Reinsurance Manager), A Balakrishnan (Fire & General Accident Manager)

PRINCIPAL ACTIVITIES: Insurance; general insurance of all kinds of risks and life assurance
Branch Offices: In Bahrain: Muharraq, Tel 331740; Riffa, Tel 664655; Sitra, Tel 732270; Hamad Town, Tel 421277
Principal Bankers: National Bank of Bahrain, Bank of Bahrain & Kuwait, Al Ahli Commercial Bank, Rafidain Bank
Financial Information:

	1988/89 BD'000	1989/90 BD'000
Gross premium	3,320	3,322
Net profit	1,032	427
Authorised capital	5,000	5,000
Paid-up capital	1,200	1,200
Total assets	4,277	4,349

Principal Shareholders: Bahrain public (66.66%), Insurance Companies of Iraq (33.34%)
Date of Establishment: Operation commenced 7 January 1971
No of Employees: 77

BAHRAIN INTERNATIONAL AIRPORT

PO Box 586, International Airport, Muharraq
Tel: 321332
Telex: 9186 Airciv BN

Senior Executives: Mohammad Al Khan (Director of Admin & Finance), Yousif Ahmed (Superintendent Operations)

PRINCIPAL ACTIVITIES: Civil aviation operations, passengers and cargo handling

Principal Shareholders: Responsible to the Ministry of Industry & Development

BAHRAIN INTERNATIONAL BANK EC

PO Box 5016, Bahrain Commercial Complex, 10th & 11th Floors, Manama
Tel: 534545
Telex: 9832 BIB BN
Telefax: 535141

Chairman: Dr Salim Jaber Al Ahmad Al-Sabah
Directors: Sami Salman Kaiksow (Vice Chairman), Sheikh Mubarak Jaber Al Ahmed Al Sabah (Chairman Executive Committee), Adel Abdulla Fakhro (Vice Chairman Executive Committee), Prince Faisal bin Abdul Aziz bin Faisal Al Saud (Director), Abdul Aziz Khalid Al Abdul Razzak (Director), Faisal Yousif Al-Marzouk (Director), Abdul Aziz Faisal Al-Zabin (Director), Abdul Wahab Yousef Al Nafisi (Director)
Senior Executives: Donald J Selinger (General Manager & Chief Executive Officer), M C George (Senior Vice President - Controller), Arnold J Haake (Vice President), Sameer Al Aradi (Vice President), William H Casey (Vice President), Osama T Al Ghoussein (Vice President), Mohamed A R Hussain (Vice President), Pradeep K Verma (Asst Vice President),

Mohammed Yusuf Chaknam (Operations Officer), Basem Al Shater (Operations Officer)

PRINCIPAL ACTIVITIES: Offshore banking
Subsidiary Companies: BIB Real Estate Co NV; BIB Holdings (Bermuda) Ltd; BIB Holdings (Nederland) BV; BIB Holdings (USA) Inc; Dilmun Investments Inc; BIB Holdings (USA) II Inc; BIB Holdings (USA) III Inc; BIB (USA) Inc
Principal Bankers: Lloyds Bank, London; Credit Suisse, Zurich; Security Pacific, Frankfurt; Societe Generale, Paris; Algemene Bank, Amsterdam; Al Ahli Commercial Bank, Bahrain; Albank Alsaudi Alhollandi, Jeddah/Riyadh/Alkhobar; Commercial Bank of Kuwait, Kuwait; National Bank of Abu Dhabi, UAE; Qatar National Bank, Doha; Bank of Tokyo, Tokyo; Mellon Bank Int'l, New York; Westpac Banking Corp, Sydney; etc
Financial Information:

	1989 US$'000
Net income	15,461
Retained earnings	11,943
Authorised capital	300,000
Paid-up capital	179,901
Deposits	189,220
Total assets	425,830

Principal Shareholders: GCC Public Shareholding Company
Date of Establishment: May 1982
No of Employees: 31

BAHRAIN INTERNATIONAL CARGO SERVICES WLL

PO Box 45, Manama
Tel: 727881 (10 lines)
Cable: Bics Bahrain
Telex: 8676 Kanofs BN
Telefax: 727024

Directors: Fawzi Ahmed Kanoo
Senior Executives: Tawfiq Taki (Manager)

PRINCIPAL ACTIVITIES: Freight clearing and forwarding, warehousing and jetty activities and air cargo services (both import and export)
Branch Offices: Branches in the Bahrain International Airport and Minasulman Port; also air cargo offices in Manama, Airport and Mahooz
Parent Company: Y B A Kanoo WLL, PO Box 45, Manama, Bahrain

Principal Shareholders: Yusuf Bin Ahmed Kanoo, Bahrain, Saudi Arabia and United Arab Emirates
No of Employees: 50

BAHRAIN INTERNATIONAL TRAVEL (BIT)

PO Box 1044, Chamber of Commerce Bldg, King Faisal Road, Manama
Tel: 253315/6, Airport 321289, 321290
Cable: Bahtravel
Telex: 9242 BitBah BN
Telefax: 210175

Directors: E Eshaq (Joint Managing Director), A L Eshaq (Joint Managing Director)
Senior Executives: Paul Clabburn (General Manager)

PRINCIPAL ACTIVITIES: Full service travel agency, tour operator and freight forwarder, car rental
Principal Agencies: Alia, Air Lanka, Ethiopian Airlines, Air Nevada, Kenya Airlines, Iran Air, Japan Airlines, Singapore Airlines, TWA, Woods Car Rental, Muller Airfreight, South County Self Drive Car Hire
Branch Offices: Hilton Hotel
Associates Companies: Middle East Traders; Hilton Hotel Bahrain
Principal Bankers: Bank of Bahrain & Kuwait

Date of Establishment: 1972
No of Employees: 30

BAHRAIN INVESTMENT BANK BSC

PO Box 5808, Manama
Tel: 530042, 530424
Cable: ISTITHMAR
Telex: 8937 Invest BN
Telefax: 530848

Chairman: Shaikh Isa Bin Ibrahim Al Khalifa
Senior Executives: Jaffar Al Salman (Manager)

PRINCIPAL ACTIVITIES: Development and corporate finance, real estate, portfolio management, equity participation, trading
Parent Company: General Organisation for Social Insurance
Principal Bankers: Bank of Bahrain & Kuwait; National Bank of Bahrain; Al Ahli Commercial Bank
Financial Information:

	1990
	BD'000
Authorised capital	50,000
Paid-up capital	16,000

Principal Shareholders: General Organisation for Social Insurance
Date of Establishment: July 1977

BAHRAIN ISLAMIC BANK BSC

PO Box 5240, Government Rd, Manama
Tel: 231402 (6 lines)
Cable: Islamic Bank
Telex: 9388 Besmeh BN

Chairman: Sheikh Abdul Rahman Bin Mohamed Bin Rashid Al Khalifa
Directors: Khalid Rashid Al Zayani (Deputy Chairman), Mohamed Yousuf Al Roumi (Deputy Chairman), Abdul Latif Abdul Rahim Janahi (Managing Director), Ibrahim Mohamed Zainal (Deputy Managing Director), Mohamed Abdulla Al Hamed Al Zamil, Mubarak Jassim Kanoo, Ahmad Mansour Al Aly, Mohamed Bardan Mohamed, Yousuf Mohamed Saleh Al Awadi, Yousif Hussain Mado, Sh Said Ahmed Lotah, Ibrahim Ahmed Yalli

PRINCIPAL ACTIVITIES: Banking in accordance with Islamic principles
Branch Offices: Muharraq; Gudaibiya
Associated Companies: Bahrain Islamic Investment Co, Bahrain; Albaraka Islamic Investment Bank, Bahrain; Islamic Insurance & Reinsurance Co, Bahrain; Arabian Agri-Business Consultants Int'l, Bahrain; Altadaman Islamic bank, Sudan; Islamic Bank of West Sudan, Sudan; Bangladesh Islamic Bank, Dhaka; Islamic Int'l Paints & Chemical Industry Co, Cairo; Al Baraka Turkish Finance House, Turkey
Financial Information:

	BD'000
Authorised capital	23,000
Subscribed capital	11,500
Paid-up capital	5,750

Date of Establishment: 1979 (1400 H)

BAHRAIN ISLAMIC INVESTMENT CO BSC (C)

PO Box 5571, 23 Sheikh Daij Bin Hamad Bldg, Government Rd, Manama
Tel: 271296
Cable: ISLMIN
Telex: 9720 ISLMIN BN
Telefax: 277741

Chairman: HE Sh Isa Bin Mohamed Al Khalifa
Directors: A Latif Janahi (Vice Chairman), Ebrahim M Zainal, Hassan E Kamal, Mohd Y Al Roomi, Sh Saeed A Lootah, Sh Essa E Al Khalifa, Khalid R Zayani, Mohamed A Al Khudhairy, Khalid A Al Zeer, Ahmed A Harmas
Senior Executives: Ebrahim M Zainal (Managing Director), Abdulla A Abdul Rahim (Manager), Mohamed Saeed Turki (Secretary to the Board)

PRINCIPAL ACTIVITIES: Investment according to Islamic law
Principal Bankers: Bahrain Islamic Bank; Kuwait Finance House
Financial Information:

	1988	1989
	BD'000	BD'000
Investments	4,373	4,451
Net profit	377	153
Authorised capital	5,000	5,000
Paid-up capital	5,000	5,000
Total assets	8,793	9,594

Principal Shareholders: Bahrain Islamic Bank; General Organization for Social Insurance; Kuwait Finance House; Dubai Islamic Bank; Others
Date of Establishment: August 1981

BAHRAIN KUWAIT INSURANCE CO BSC

PO Box 10166, Manama
Tel: 532323 (PABX), 531555 (Management)
Cable: Bahramin
Telex: 8672 BKIC BN
Telefax: (0973) 530799

Chairman: Ali Bin Yusif Fakhroo
Directors: Sulaiman Al Dalali (Vice Chairman), Abdul Rahman Yusif Fakhroo (Managing Director), Yacoob Yousif Al Saqar, Faisal Saood Al Fozan, Osama Mohd Yousif Al Nisf, Khalifa Abdulla Al Mannai, Hassan Mohamed Zainal-Abedin, Khalid Rashid Al Zayani, Issa Ahmed Al Khalaf
Senior Executives: Peter L Atkinson (General Manager), Mian Mohd Rafique (Deputy General Manager), Waleed Mohd Al Mudhaf (Dy GM / General Manager Kuwait Branch), A Hameed Al Nasser (Asst General Manager), John Rodrigues (Manager Underwriting Div), Ali Hassan Follad (Manager Finance & Admin Div), Ahmed Yusif Abbas (Manager Motor Div), Yahya Nooruddin (Manager Marketing)

PRINCIPAL ACTIVITIES: All classes of insurance (except-life)
Branch Offices: Kuwait: PO Box 26728 Safat, Tel 2468544, Telex 46020 BKIC KT, Fax 2468545
Principal Bankers: Bank of Bahrain & Kuwait; National Bank of Bahrain; Al Ahli Commercial Bank
Financial Information:

	1988/89	1989/90
	BD'000	BD'000
Gross premiums	5,732	5,252
Profits	193	226
Authorised capital	1,200	1,200
Paid-up capital	1,200	1,200
Total assets	10,634	8,634

Principal Shareholders: 50% Bahraini Nationals; 50% Five Kuwaiti National Insurance & Reinsurance Companies
Date of Establishment: 1975
No of Employees: 101 (Bahrain and Kuwait)

BAHRAIN LIGHT INDUSTRIES CO

PO Box 26700, Manama
Tel: 830222
Cable: Blico
Telex: 8538 BN
Telefax: 830399

Chairman: Hamid R Al Zayani
Directors: Mohamed E Al Wazzan (Managing Director)
Senior Executives: Hamed Faleh (General Manager), Hussein Al Leathy (Technical Manager), Seena R Jaberi (Sales Manager), Abdulaziz Al Majid (Administration Manager), R S Rajan (Finance Executive)

PRINCIPAL ACTIVITIES: Development of light industrial projects; manufacture of wooden furniture
Branch Offices: Tylos Furniture Showroom, Manama
Principal Bankers: Al Ahli Commercial Bank; National Bank of Bahrain

BAHRAIN

Financial Information:

	1989/90 BD'000
Sales turnover	1,100
Authorised capital	10,000
Paid-up capital	2,500
Total assets	4,650

Principal Shareholders: Gulf Investment, Bahrain (48%); National Bank of Bahrain (10%); General Organization of Social Insurance (15%); Bahraini Interests (27%)
Date of Establishment: 1980
No of Employees: 150

BAHRAIN MARBLE FACTORY
PO Box 285, Mina Sulman
Tel: 713085, 243375
Telex: 8381 Zamil BN

Directors: Fahad Al Zamil (Managing Director)

PRINCIPAL ACTIVITIES: Production of marble products, stairways and flooring materials
Associated Companies: Gulf Aluminium Factory

BAHRAIN MARINE CONTRACTING
PO Box 716, Manama
Tel: 731325
Cable: Caterpillar
Telex: 8235 Frutan BN
Telefax: 731324

Chairman: Mohamed Jaffar Froutan
Directors: Masood M J Froutan (Managing Director), Abdul Rasool M J Froutan (Finance Director)

PRINCIPAL ACTIVITIES: Marine and offshore chartering, supply of vessels and barges
Branch Offices: Bahrain Marine Contracting, PO Box 5275, Sharjah, UAE
Principal Bankers: The British Bank of the Middle East

Date of Establishment: 1926
No of Employees: 65

BAHRAIN MARITIME & MERCANTILE INTERNATIONAL BSC (C)
PO Box 828, 125 Al Khalifa Road, Government Avenue, Manama 304
Tel: 211535
Cable: Marint Bahrain
Telex: 8212 BMMI BN
Telefax: 210925

Chairman: Khalid Abdulrahman Almoayed
Directors: D G John, Sami Salman Kaiksow, Abdul Rahman Fakhro, Faisal Hassan Jawad, Ali Saleh Al Saleh, A G Davies, M Smith, N J E H Monk

PRINCIPAL ACTIVITIES: Shipping, travel, insurance, general trading, freight forwarding
Principal Agencies: Hapag Lloyd, P & O, Cunard Ellerman, Beecham, Yardley, Lucas, Glynwed, Poulain Chocolat, etc
Associated Companies: An Associate of the Gray Mackenzie group of Companies
Principal Bankers: British Bank of the Middle East, National Bank of Bahrain, Ali Ahli Commercial Bank, Standard Chartered Bank, Bank of Bahrain & Kuwait
Financial Information:

	1990/91 BD'000
Authorised capital	9,000
Paid-up capital	5,400

Principal Shareholders: Gray Mackenzie & Co Ltd (48%); Bahraini interests (52%)
Date of Establishment: October 1980
No of Employees: 200

BAHRAIN MIDDLE EAST BANK (EC)
PO Box 797, BMB Centre, Diplomatic Area, Manama
Tel: 532345 (General), 530123 (Dealers)
Cable: BMB
Telex: 9706/9446 BMB BN (General), 9418 BMB FX (Dealers)
Telefax: 530526

Chairman: H E Abdul Rahman Salem Al-Ateeqi
Directors: Sheikh Ebrahim Bin Hamad Bin Abdulla Al Khalifa (Vice Chairman), Sheikh Ali Jarrah Al Sabah (Chairman of the Executive Committee), Sheikh Ahmed Al Abdulla Al Ahmed Al Sabah, Mohammad Yousuf Abdulla Al Roomi, Mohammed Aqiel Tawfiqi, Adwan Mohamad Al Adwani

Senior Executives: K J A Katchadurian (Chief Executive), Mathews Kuruvilla (North American Group Head & SVP, General Manager BMB New York Agency), Omar Ali (European Group Head & SVP and Senior Representative and General Manager, UMH Finance BV), David L Dale (UK Group Head & SVP and Senior Representative and General Manager BMB International Ltd), R Anthony Samms (VP Credit Administration), Amar Saksena (General Counsel), Stewart Hay (Group Financial Controller), Maher Helal (VP Administration), Khalifa Al Dossery (AVP Senior Dealer), A Ali Al Anzoor (AVP Senior Dealer), G A Dass (AVP Head of General Banking), Fadeela Ali Khan (AVP General Banking), Abdulali Shams (AVP General Banking), Hugh Farias (AVP Internal Control Unit), B R Bhat (AVP & Manager Operations), Mirza Najmuddin (Chief Accountant)

PRINCIPAL ACTIVITIES: Merchant, commercial & private banking
Branch Offices: New York: 18th Flr, Tower 49, 12 East 49th Street, New York NY 10017; London Representative Office: 1 College Hill, London EC4R 2RA; Amsterdam Representative Office: Paleistraat, PO Box 11465, 1001 GL Amsterdam; Grand Cayman Branch: PO Box 694, Grand Cayman, Cayman Islands

Subsidiary/Associated Companies: BMB Property Services (EC) Manama, Bahrain (100%); Universal Investment Co SAK, Kuwait (49%); BMB Int'l Ltd, London, UK (100%); BMB-H Investment Co Ltd, Jersey, Channel Islands (75%), BMB-H Ltd, London, UK (75%), BMB-H Investment Trading Ltd, Georgetown, Grand Cayman (75%); BMB New York Agency, USA (100%); Grand Cayman Branch, Georgetown, Grand Cayman (100%); BMB Finance Ltd, Grand Cayman (100%), Netherlands Ant (100%); Universal Merchant Holdings NV, Amsterdam (100%); UMH Finance BV, Amsterdam (100%); BMB Curacao Netherlands NV, Netherlands Antilles (100%); Universal Finance Holding NV, Amsterdam (100%); European Universal Bank NV, Amsterdam NV, Amsterdam (100%); London Amsterdam Merchant Bank, Amsterdam (15%), etc

Financial Information:

	1988/89 US$'000	1989/90 US$'000
Authorised capital	500,000	500,000
Issued capital	200,000	200,000
Paid up capital	139,944	139,944
Reserves	2,105	4,091
Deposits	358,050	476,658
Cash & banks	115,964	110,658
Investments	126,743	139,315
Loans	242,374	367,593
Total assets	514,200	642,457

Principal Shareholders: 72% owned by Gulf Co-Operation Council (GCC) country nationals; 28% owned by Burgan Bank SAK, Kuwait

Date of Establishment: March 1982
No of Employees: 554

BAHRAIN MONETARY AGENCY

PO Box 27, Manama
Tel: 535535
Cable: Nakdelbahr
Telex: 8295 Bahmon BN
Telefax: 259273

Chairman: Sheikh Khalifah Bin Sulman Al Khalifah
Directors: HE Ibrahim Abdul Karim (Deputy Chairman), Abdulla Saif (Governor), Abdul Rahman Taqi (Member), Abdul Rahman Al Moayyed (Member), Mohamed Jawad Al Modaifa'a (Member), Sheikh Ebrahim Al Khalifa (Deputy Governor)
Advisers & Officers: Nazir Ahmad Chaudhary (Organisation & Methods Adviser), Al Rashied Abdul Wahab (Adviser to Economic Research Directorate), K L Deshpande (IMF Adviser to Economic Research Directorate), Nabeel Hussain Mattar (Director of Accounts), Abbas Mahmood Radhi (Director of Economic Research), A Rahman Al Wazzan (Executive Director for Banking Control), Abdulla Khalifa Al Khalifa (Director of Bank Supervision), Anwar Khalifa Al Sadah (Director of Financial Institutions Supervision), Ahmed Saqer Al Khalifa (Executive Director for Banking Operations), Salman Khalifa Al Khalifa (Director of Banking Services), Faisal Jafer Al Alawi (Director of Currency Issue)

PRINCIPAL ACTIVITIES: To organize the issue and circulation of the currency of the State of Bahrain; to maintain the value of Bahrain Dinar; to organize the banking business and control the banking system; to control and direct bank credit so as to realise the objectives of the economic policy of the State of Bahrain
Financial Information:

	1988/89 BD'000	1989/90 BD'000
Profits	17,749	24,816
Authorised capital	20,000	20,000
Paid-up capital	20,000	100,000
Reserve fund	124,628	60,574
Total assets	311,850	320,705

Principal Shareholders: Owned by Government
Date of Establishment: December 5th 1973
No of Employees: 120

BAHRAIN NATIONAL COLD STORAGE & WAREHOUSING CO (BANZ)

PO Box 2244, Manama
Tel: 727874
Telex: 8874 A/B: Storag BN
Telefax: 725435

Chairman: Abdulla Buhindi
Directors: Ali Amin, Jassim Fakhroo, Abdul Rahman Jamsheer, Jalal Mohd Jalal, Fahad Al Zamil, Mohd Buhindi
Senior Executives: Taefeeq Khalaf (General Manager), Khalil Ghreeb (Operations Manager), Douglas Godsman (Board's Advisor for Transhipment)

PRINCIPAL ACTIVITIES: Cold Storage, warehousing, distribution and inventory management services, specialising in container handling
Principal Agencies: Kuwait United Poultry, Kuwait Livestock Co, Tilly Chichen (France), Kuwait Food Co
Principal Bankers: Grindlays Bank; Al Ahli Commercial Bank
Financial Information:

	1988/89 BD'000
Sales turnover	1,300
Authorised capital	2,700
Paid-up capital	2,700
Total assets	2,700

Principal Shareholders: Abdulla Buhindi (30%); National Investment Co (20%); Trafco (17%)
Date of Establishment: October 1979
No of Employees: 70

BAHRAIN NATIONAL GAS CO BSC

PO Box 29099, Manama
Tel: 756222
Cable: BANAGAS JEBEL
Telex: 9317 BANGAS BN
Telefax: 756991

Chairman: Sheikh Hamad Bin Ibrahim Al Khalifa
Directors: A Nabi A Mansour (Vice Chairman), Ali Al Jalahema, Ibrahim Laham, Majid A Shafea, Sheikh Mohamed Bin Khalifa Al Khalifa (Company Secretary)
Senior Executives: Ali A Gindy (General Manager - Production), Sheikh Mohamed Bin Khalifa Al Khalifa (General Manager Administration & Finance), A Hashim (Operations Manager), Mohsin Al Mahoozi (Maintenance Manager), A Aziz Mohamed Al Beloshy (Manager Administration), S A A Rahman (Finance Manager), M A Burashid (Technical Services / Projects Manager)

PRINCIPAL ACTIVITIES: Liquefaction of associated hydrocarbon gases
Principal Bankers: National Bank of Bahrain; Bank of Bahrain & Kuwait; Bahrain Monetary Agency
Financial Information:

	1990/91 BD'000
Sales turnover	19,231
Profits	1,200
Authorised capital	8,900
Paid-up capital	8,000
Total assets	26,321

Principal Shareholders: The Government of Bahrain (75%); Caltex (Bahrain) Limited (12.5%); Arab Petroleum Investments Corporation (12.5%)
Date of Establishment: March 22nd, 1979
No of Employees: 321

BAHRAIN NATIONAL OIL CO (BANOCO) (THE)

PO Box 25504, Awali, Bahrain
Tel: 754666
Cable: Banoco
Telex: 8670 Banoco BN, 9524 Taswik BN
Telefax: 753230

Chairman: HE Yousif Ahmed Al-Shirawi (Minister of Development & Industry)
Directors: Shaikh Isa Bin Abdulla Al-Khalifa (Vice-Chairman), Hamad Al-Rumaihi, Shaikh Mohamed Attiyatullah Al-Khalifa, Abdulla Rashid Al-Absi, Abdul Hameed Al-Aradi, Yacoub Yousif Al-Majid, Kadhim Al-Hashimi
Senior Executives: Mohamed Saleh Shaikh Ali (Chief Executive), Rashid M Fakhro (General Manager Finance & Administration), Mohamed Fathalla (General Manager Producing & Technical), Adel K Al-Moayyed (General Manager Marketing), Abdul Rahman Abdulla (General Manager Management Services), Ebrahim M Abdulla (Manager Financial Accounting), Yousif Zainalabedin (Manager Local Marketing), Khalil H Ahmed (Manager International Sales), Hashim A Hashim (Manager Supply & Marine Operations), Abdul Rahman A Rahim (Manager Production), Faisal M Kaladari (Manager Administration), Gary Gollobin (Senior Coordinator Management & Information Systems), Adel H Al Maskati (Manager Projects), Abdul Jalil Al Samahiji (Manager Exploration & Development), Faisal Al Mahroos (Manager Petroleum Engineering), D J Chamberlain (Manager Management Accounting), Mohamed Reza Al Khaja (Senior Superintendent Drilling), Roger Willis (Head of Training)

PRINCIPAL ACTIVITIES: Representation of the interests of the State of Bahrain in all aspects of petroleum exploration, production, processing and marketing (Local and International)
Principal Bankers: National Bank of Bahrain

Financial Information:

	1988/89 BD'000
Sales turnover	639,319
Authorised capital	100,000
Paid-up capital	5,000
Total assets	143,965

Principal Shareholders: The Government of the State of Bahrain
Date of Establishment: July 1976
No of Employees: 706

BAHRAIN NORWICH WINTERTHUR INSURANCE CO BSC (C)

PO Box 45, Manama
Tel: 213515
Telex: 8215 Kanoo BN
Telefax: 213308

Chairman: Mubarak Jassim Kanoo
Directors: H R Strickler, G W H Jones, Abdulrehman Jassim Kanoo, Fawzi Ahmed Kanoo, J A Gilmour, Akbar Mahmood Sa'ati
Senior Executives: I L Reid (General Manager), Ashraf Hussein (Non-Marine Underwriter), F D Evans (Marine Underwriter), Mohamed Makee (Chief Accountant & Manager)

PRINCIPAL ACTIVITIES: All classes of insurance and reinsurance (except life)
Principal Bankers: British Bank of the Middle East

Principal Shareholders: Yusuf Bin Ahmed Kanoo (51%); Winterthur Insurance (Gulf) Ltd (49%)
Date of Establishment: 1990
No of Employees: 26

BAHRAIN PETROLEUM CO BSC (C)

Awali, Bahrain
Tel: 750005
Cable: Bapco Bahrain
Telex: 8214 BN

Chairman: HE Yusuf Ahmed Shirawi
Directors: Shaikh Isa bin Abdulla Al Khalifa, Ali Ibrahim Al Mahrous, Shaikh Ebrahim bin Khalifa bin Ali Al Khalifa, Ibrahim Abdulla Al-Hamer, Abdulla Mansoor, R F Johnson, P J Ward, R G Fernie, G W Trumbull

PRINCIPAL ACTIVITIES: Refining of oil, manufacture of petroleum products and fuels

Principal Shareholders: Government of Bahrain (60%); Caltex petroleum Corp (40%)
Date of Establishment: 1981
No of Employees: 3,460

BAHRAIN PRECAST CONCRETE CO WLL

PO Box 20095, Manama
Tel: 682974
Telex: 9105 BPC BN
Telefax: 687328

Chairman: Haji Hassan Bin Ali Al A'Ali
Directors: Chris Hviid, Ahmed Ali Al A'Ali, Adel Hassan Al A'Ali, Peter Hansen
Senior Executives: Tom Gyllenborg (General Manager), Peter Spoer (Chief Engineer/Sales Manager), Hans Jorgen Jensen (Production Manager), Preben Jensen (Manager Repair & Maintenance)

PRINCIPAL ACTIVITIES: Production and erection of all kinds of large size precast industrial and building components, including prestressed hollowcore slabs, modular building and housing systems, GRC (glass reinforced concrete) and maintenance and repair of concrete structures
Principal Bankers: Standard Chartered Bank, Manama

Principal Shareholders: Haji Hassan Trading & Contracting Co WLL, Bahrain; Rasmussen & Schiotz A/S, Denmark
Date of Establishment: 1977
No of Employees: 200

BAHRAIN SAINRAPT CONTRACTING CO WLL

PO Box 20210, Manama
Tel: 742318, 742319
Telex: 9069 BRISA BN

PRINCIPAL ACTIVITIES: Dredging and reclamation works, civil engineering works
Parent Company: Sainrapt & Brice (SOGEA France)

BAHRAIN SHERATON HOTEL

PO Box 30, 5 Palace Avenue, Manama
Tel: 233233
Cable: Sherhotel
Telex: 9440 Sherat BN

President: Gerry Morin (also Director of Operations)
Directors: Sami Zoghbi (Exec. V.P/Regional Director of Operations -Middle East)

PRINCIPAL ACTIVITIES: Hotel business
Principal Bankers: British Bank of the Middle East

Date of Establishment: 1981
No of Employees: 350

BAHRAIN SHIP REPAIRING & ENGINEERING CO
B.A.S.R.E.C.

PO Box 568, Manama
Tel: 725300
Cable: Basrec Bahrain
Telex: 8297 Basrec BN
Telefax: 729891

Chairman: Ahmed Ali Kanoo
Directors: Abdullah Yousuf Akbar Ali Reza, Abdul Rehman Kanoo, Mubarak Jasim Kanoo, Khalid Mohamed Kanoo, Eng Khalid Yousuf Abdul Rehman
Senior Executives: Eric Cockerill (General Manager)

PRINCIPAL ACTIVITIES: Ship repairing and maintenance of mobile rigs and offshore vessels, mechanical and electrical engineering (including all hull repairs, diesel engines overhauls)
Principal Agencies: Howaldswerft Deutsche Werft, Philadelphia Resins, Nicol and Andrew, MWM, AEG, Baldor, Allis Chalmers, ABS Pumpen
Associated Companies: TEAMS (Bahrain) Technical, Engineering & Marine Services, PO Box 568, Bahrain
Principal Bankers: National Bank of Bahrain; British Bank of the Middle East

Principal Shareholders: Public shareholding company
Date of Establishment: 1963
No of Employees: 300

BAHRAIN TECHNICAL & TRADING CO WLL

PO Box 49, Manama
Tel: 253252
Cable: Finniya Bahrain
Telex: 8223 Ethiop BN
Telefax: 274095

Chairman: Abdulrahman Ghuloom Mohd Amin
Directors: Abdul Rahman Ali Al Wazzan, Mohd Yousuf Jalal, P R Gartrell, P G Evans, W N Beddall
Senior Executives: P R Gartrell (Managing Director), P J Punnen (Chief Accountant), W N Beddall, M S Chappell

PRINCIPAL ACTIVITIES: Marketing, wholesaling, importing and distribution of general merchandise, including provisions, furniture, specialising in air conditioning, refrigeration design, installation and servicing, desalination plants, office equipment and business systems and insurance agents

Principal Agencies: Keeprite, qualitair, GEC, Heatrae Sadia, Belling, Danfoss, Caravell, Houseman, Searle, Rowntree Mackintosh, Pearce Duff, Slazenger, Swedish Match, Kimberly Clark, Roneo, Monroe, 3M Middle East, Unilever Export Ltd

Branch Offices: Bahrain; UAE (Dubai and Abu Dhabi); Oman

Parent Company: African & Eastern (Near East) Limited

Associated Companies: Technical & Trading Co, Dubai, UAE; Thani Murshid & African & Eastern (Near East) Ltd, Abu Dhabi, UAE; Sharikat Fanniya Omaniya (Muscat) Muscat, Oman; African & Eastern (Near East) Ltd, 2 Blackfrairs Rd, London SE1

Principal Bankers: Standard Chartered Bank, BBME, Grindlays Bahrain Bank

Principal Shareholders: Abdulrahman Ghuloom Mohd Amin, Abdulla Ghuloom Mohd Amin, International Agencies Co Ltd, Mohd Yousuf Jalal, African & Eastern (Near East) Ltd

No of Employees: 122

BAHRAIN TELECOMMUNICATIONS CO (BSC)

PO Box 14, Manama
Tel: 270270
Cable: Batelco Bahrain
Telex: 8201 BTCADM BN
Telefax: 248451

Chairman: HE Ebrahim M Humaidan

Directors: Sh Isa Bin Ebrahim Al Khalifa (First Deputy Chairman), J D Munday (Second Deputy Chairman), Abdulla Hassan Buhindi, Dr Rasheed J Ashoor, Rasheed M Al Maraj, Abdulla Mohammed Juma, Hassan Ali Juma, Murad Ali Murad, Brian R Divett

Senior Executives: Brian Wood (General Manager), R Loweth (Divisional Manager Finance), D Bamford (Divisional Manager Commercial & Operations), Jasim Al Binali (Divisional Manager Administration), Henry Buesnel (Divisional Managaer Engineering)

PRINCIPAL ACTIVITIES: Provision of national and international telecommunications

Principal Bankers: National Bank of Bahrain

Financial Information:

	1989/90
	BD'000
Turnover	46,709
Net profit	17,752
Authorised capital	80,000
Issued capital	60,000
Total assets	105,585

Principal Shareholders: Bahrain (Government, institutions and individuals) (80%); Cable & Wireless (20%)

Date of Establishment: July 1981

No of Employees: 2,000

BAHRAIN TOURISM CO (BSC)

PO Box 5831, Manama
Tel: 530530
Telex: 8929 Toursm BN
Telefax: 530154

Chairman: Mohamed Yousuf Jalal

Directors: Shaikh Isa Bin Ibrahim Al-Khalifa (Vice Chairman), Qassim Mohamed Fakhroo (Managing Director), Shaikh Rashid Bin Khalifa Al-Khalifa, Mahmood Mahmood Hussain, Mohamed Abdulla Zamil, Hassan Khalifa Jalahma, Ahmed Sayed Abdul Rahman

Senior Executives: A Nabi Daylami (General Manager)

PRINCIPAL ACTIVITIES: General financing, travel and tourism, hotel and catering, property and real estate

Principal Bankers: National Bank of Bahrain, Bank of Bahrain & Kuwait, Al-Ahli Commercial Bank

Financial Information:

	1988/89	1989/90
	BD'000	BD'000
Sales turnover	2,644	2,768
Profits	624	676
Authorised capital	15,000	15,000
Paid-up capital	7,200	7,200
Total assets	12,994	13,149

Principal Shareholders: Government of State of Bahrain, General Organisation of Social Insurance

Date of Establishment: 1974

No of Employees: 261

BAHRAIN WORKSHOP COMPANY WLL

PO Box 404, Manama
Tel: 251730, 253289
Cable: Bahworks
Telex: 8460 BN

PRINCIPAL ACTIVITIES: General engineering, manufacturers representation, supply of heavy machinery and equipment, construction plant, safety equipment, oilfield supplies and generating equipment

Principal Agencies: BOC, Worthington Pumps, Petter Engines, Protector Safety Equipment, Hobart Welding Equipment, Bristol Compressors

BAHRAINI SAUDI BANK BSC

PO Box 1159, Manama
Tel: 263111
Telex: 7232 BSB BN (General), 7380 BSB BN (Forex)
Telefax: 263048

Chairman: Sh Ibrahim Bin Hamad Al Khalifa

Directors: Fahad M Al Athel (Vice Chairman), Sami S Kaiksow, Farouk Y Almoayyed (Deputy Chairman), Jassim A Al Zayani, Mohammed A Alhasan, Abdul Kareem Z Al Quraishi, Khalid M El Seif, Ebrahim J Al Ahmedi, Sadiq M Al Baharna, Abedlelah M S Kaki (Chairman Executive Committee), Hamad A Al Zamil

Senior Executives: Mansoor Al Sayed (General Manager), Pankaj Mehra (Manager Operations & Financial Controls), A J Jaganathan (Manager Corporate Banking), Ali Qahtan (Manager Treasury)

PRINCIPAL ACTIVITIES: Commercial banking

Financial Information:

	1988/89
	BD'000
Net income	2,083
Profits (loss)	(2,801)
Authorised capital	50,000
Paid-up capital	20,000
Total assets	85,764

Principal Shareholders: 1,600 Saudi and Bahraini Nationals

Date of Establishment: December 1983

No of Employees: 47

BALCO

Bahrain Saudi Aluminium Marketing Co BSC (C)

PO Box 20079, Manama
Tel: 973-532626
Cable: BALCO
Telex: 9110 BALCO BN
Telefax: 973-532727

Chairman: Shaikh Isa Bin Abdulla Al-Khalifa (Under Secretary, Ministry of Development & Industry)

Directors: Zamil Al Jowesir (Vice Chairman), Ahmed Hubail, Ahmed Al Sayed Abdulrahman, Mohammed Al Hindi, Yousif Hassan

Senior Executives: Mahmoud Al Soufi (General Manager), Ebrahim A R Esbai (Manager Metal Purchase Control &

Shipping), Hussain Al Ali (Sales Manager), Ebrahim Tadayyon (Finance & Administration Manager)

PRINCIPAL ACTIVITIES: BALCO markets Bahrain and Saudi Arabia's 94.9% offtake of primary aluminium (in standard, rolling and extrusion ingot forms) from the ALBA smelter; BALCO also markets Bahrain's 51% offtake of aluminium powder from Bahrain Atomisers

Associated Companies: Alba (Aluminium Bahrain); BAI (Bahrain Atomisers International); Balexco (Bahrain Aluminium Extrusion Co), Garmco (Gulf Aluminium Rolling Mill Co)

Principal Bankers: National Bank of Bahrain, Gulf International Bank

Financial Information:

	1989 US$'000	1990 US$'000
Sales revenue	408,000	341,800

Principal Shareholders: State of Bahrain (74.33%); Sabic Marketing Limited (25.67%)

Date of Establishment: 1 May 1978

BALEXCO
Bahrain Aluminium Extrusion Co BSC

PO Box 1053, Manama
Tel: 730221
Cable: Balexco
Telex: 8634 Balexc BN
Telefax: 731678

Chairman: Salah Ali Al Madani
Directors: Ahmed Hubail, Hassan Falah, Abdulla Juma, Saager Shaheen, Abdul Latif Zaayani, Isa Thawadi, Saud Kanoo, Sulaiman Al Zamil
Senior Executives: Mahmood Al Soufi (General Manager), Ali Al Abbasi (Technical Manager), Abdulla Al Swaidi (Production Manager), Fareed Ahmed (Sales Manager), Abdul Wahab Naqi (Finance & Administration Manager), Hussain Ramadhan (Head of Personnel & Training), Basim Al Saie (Act Marketing & Technical Support Manager)

PRINCIPAL ACTIVITIES: Aluminium sections and profiles anodised in colinal bronze, gold, black, plain matt or brushed finishes, or powder coated for architectural purposes; licencee to produce and market the Technal French System, licencee to produce the Alussuisse range of AS-200 curtian walling system, and Alsec 2000 thermally broken systems, agents for alucobond Facia decoration panels and Alucopan Insulation Panels, producers of telephone booths, lamp posts, bus shelters, flag poles, and goal posts

Principal Bankers: National Bank of Bahrain; Bank of Bahrain & Kuwait; Al Ahli Commercial Bank; Grindlays Bahrain Bank; British Bank of the Middle East

Date of Establishment: Production started: 15 March 1977
No of Employees: 257

BALUCH ASHBY & HORNER

PO Box 64, Manama
Tel: 259034
Telex: 8499 Baluch BN

Chairman: I U Baluch
Directors: K Rafiuddin

PRINCIPAL ACTIVITIES: Construction, interior design, shopfitting, joinery
Principal Agencies: Henga Carpet Tiles, Bobrick Washroom Equipment, Alifabs, Treetex Ceilings
Branch Offices: Associates in Sri Lanka and Singapore
Principal Bankers: Bank of Bahrain & Kuwait

Principal Shareholders: U C Baluch
Date of Establishment: 1977
No of Employees: 100

BALUCH, USMAN C,

PO Box 64, Manama
Tel: 253201
Cable: Baluch Bahrain
Telex: 8499 Baluch BN
Telefax: 257572

Chairman: Ismail U Baluch
Directors: Jalal Baluch, Miss Emma Baluch
Senior Executives: Ramesh Rao (Financial Controller)

PRINCIPAL ACTIVITIES: General merchants, import and distribution of curtains, furniture, carpets, household accessories, perfumes and cosmetics, real estate
Principal Agencies: Estee Lauder, Jovan, Clarins, Sopadima, Reminiscence
Subsidiary Companies: Baluch Ashby & Horner, Baluch Habitat
Principal Bankers: Bank of Bahrain & Kuwait

Principal Shareholders: U C Baluch

BANK MELLI IRAN

PO Box 785, Manama
Tel: 259910
Cable: Bank Melli
Telex: 8266 Bkmeli BN

PRINCIPAL ACTIVITIES: Commercial banking
Parent Company: Head office in Tehran, Iran

BANK OF AMERICA NT & SA

PO Box 5280, Manama
Tel: 530500, 532400 FX
Cable: BOABOB BN
Telex: 8616, 8768 FX
Telefax: 531236

Senior Executives: R Zakir Mahmood (Vice President & Manager), Faisal Al Meshqab (Asst Vice President Operations), K Fareed Khan (Vice President & Treasurer)

PRINCIPAL ACTIVITIES: Offshore banking unit
Parent Company: Bank of America, San Francisco, USA

BANK OF BAHRAIN & KUWAIT BSC

PO Box 597, 43 Government Avenue, Manama
Tel: 253388
Cable: Bahkubank
Telex: 8919 Bakubk Bn
Telefax: 275785

Chairman: Rashid Abdul Rahman Al-Zayani
Directors: Saleh Mubarak Al Falah, Ebrahim Eshaq A Rahman, Hilal Mushari Al Mutairi, Hassan Haider Darwish, Yousif Abdulla Al Awadi, Ebrahim Abdulla Al Yahya, Seraj Saleh Al Baker, Ali Saleh Al Saleh
Senior Executives: Murad Ali Murad (General Manager & CEO), Amjad Karim (Asst General Manager Operation), A Wahed Noor (Asst General Manager Domestic Branches), Peter F Stevenson (Asst General Manager International), Ahmed Al Banna (Asst General Manager Human Resources & Services), Antony Butler (Asst General Manager Credit)

PRINCIPAL ACTIVITIES: Commercial banking, and offshore banking unit
Branch Offices: Bank of Bahrain and Kuwait, PO Box 24396, Safat, Kuwait; also in Istanbul, Turkey and in Bombay, India
Associated Companies: Bank of Oman, Bahrain and Kuwait; Union de Banques Arabes et Francaises (UBAF); Kuwait Asia Bank
Financial Information:

	1990 BD'000
Authorised capital	100,000
Paid-up capital	55,000

Principal Shareholders: (24.76%) Citizens of the State of Bahrain; (11.96%) Pension Fund Commission; (10.61%)

General Organisation for Social Insurance; (2.67%) Military Pension Fund; (6.75%) National Bank of Kuwait SAK; (6.75% Al Ahli Bank of Kuwait KSC; (6.75%) Gulf Bank KSC; (6.75%) Bank of Kuwait & the Middle East KSC; (6.75%) Burgan Bank SAK; (3.75% Kuwait Foreign Trading Contracting & Invesmtnet Co SAK; (3.75%) Kuwait Investment Co SAK; (2.00%) Kuwait International Investment Co SAK
Date of Establishment: 16 March 1971
No of Employees: 550

BANK OF BARODA

PO Box 1915, Manama
Tel: 262537, 262538
Cable: Barodabank Bahrain
Telex: 9449 Baroda BN

Senior Executives: K L Majumdar (Manager Operations)

PRINCIPAL ACTIVITIES: Offshore banking
Parent Company: Head office in Baroda, India
Subsidiary Companies: IBU International Finance Ltd, HongKong; Bank of Baroda (Uganda), Kampala

BANK OF CREDIT & COMMERCE INTERNATIONAL SA

Bab Al Bahrain Bldg, Government Road, PO Box 569, Manama
Tel: 245520 (General), 256501 (dealers)
Cable: Bancrecom
Telex: 8346 BCCI BH
Telefax: 274702

Senior Executives: Ali Abbas (Branch Manager)

PRINCIPAL ACTIVITIES: Offshore banking

BANK OF OMAN LTD

PO Box 20654, Manama
Tel: 232882, 257858, 252176, 252167
Cable: BANOMAN
Telex: 9566 BOL BK BN, 9565 BOL FX BN
Telefax: 231096

PRINCIPAL ACTIVITIES: Offshore banking
Branch Offices: Head Office: Dubai, UAE
Principal Bankers: Bank of America, New York; Bankers Trust Co, New York; Dresdner Bank, Hamburg; Tokai Bank, Tokyo

Date of Establishment: 1981 in Bahrain

BANK OF TOKYO LTD (THE)

PO Box 5850, Manama
Tel: 246518, 246519 (forex), 256011 (Rep Office)
Cable: Tohbank
Telex: 9066 TOHBK BN (OBU), 9096 (FOREX), 8922 (Rep)

PRINCIPAL ACTIVITIES: Offshore banking and representative office
Branch Offices: 33 branch offices in Japan and overseas network of over 250 offices

Date of Establishment: January 1980 (O.B.U.)
No of Employees: 29 (OBU), 3 (Rep)

BANK SADERAT IRAN

PO Box 825, Manama
Tel: 250809, 256487, 255977, 255318
Telex: 8363, 8688 BN

PRINCIPAL ACTIVITIES: Banking (also offshore banking)

BANKERS TRUST COMPANY

PO Box 5905, Manama
Tel: 259841
Cable: Bantrusbah
Telex: 9020, 9064, 8955 BN

PRINCIPAL ACTIVITIES: Offshore banking unit
Parent Company: Head Office: 280 Park Ave, New York, USA

Date of Establishment: 1978
No of Employees: 21

BANQUE ARABE ET INTERNATIONALE D'INVESTISSEMENT

PO Box 5333, Manama
Tel: 531373
Telex: 8542 BAII BN
Telefax: 531224

Senior Executives: Mounir Lyan (Senior Representative), B Phillips (Representative)

PRINCIPAL ACTIVITIES: Representative office
Parent Company: Banque Arabe et Internationale d'Investissement, Paris
Principal Bankers: Manufacturers Hanover Trust, New York; BNP PLC, London; National Commercial Bank, Jeddah

Date of Establishment: 1976

BANQUE DU CAIRE

PO Box 815, Awal Bldg, Government Road, Manama
Tel: 254454, 275672
Cable: Banquecaire
Telex: 8298 Bcaire BN

PRINCIPAL ACTIVITIES: Commercial banking (also offshore banking)
Parent Company: Head office: 22 Adly Street, PO Box 1495, Cairo, Egypt

Date of Establishment: 1972

BANQUE FRANCAISE DE L'ORIENT (GROUPE BANK INDOSUEZ)

PO Box 5820, Kanoo Tower, Manama
Tel: 257319
Telex: 8969 BFOBAH BN
Telefax: 261685

Chairman: Bernard Vernhes (CEO)
Senior Executives: Herman Dom (Regional Manager)

PRINCIPAL ACTIVITIES: Offshore banking unit
Parent Company: Head Office: 33 rue de Monceau, Paris 8, France

Principal Shareholders: Banque Indosuez (35%); Al Bank Al Saudi Al Fransi (30%); Holding de la Mediterranee BV (30%); Banque Libano-Francaise SAL (2.9%); Societe de Banque Thomson (2.1%)
Date of Establishment: July 1989

BANQUE INDOSUEZ (OBU)

PO Box 5410, Manama
Tel: 531345
Cable: Indosuez Manama
Telex: 8976 BN
Telefax: 531476

Senior Executives: Philippe Favre (General Manager), William Roberts (Operations Manager), Stephen Austen (Senior Manager Investment Banking), Tim Mattar (Manager Investment Banking), Jawad Nasser (Manager Treasury), Simon Bedle (Manager Forex)

PRINCIPAL ACTIVITIES: Offshore banking unit
Parent Company: Banque Indosuez, 96 Boulevard Haussmann, 75008 Paris, France

Date of Establishment: 1976
No of Employees: 40

BAHRAIN

BANQUE NATIONALE DE PARIS

PO Box 5253, Manama
Tel: 531152 (General), 531116 (Dealing)
Cable: Natiopar Bahrain
Telex: 8595 BNP BN
Telefax: 531237

Senior Executives: Maurice Blanchet (General Manager), M C
   Tomchek (Deputy Genera Manager), J M Bonnici (Treasury
   Manager), J P Leclere (Administration Manager), Paul Firino-
   Martell (Portfolio Manager)

PRINCIPAL ACTIVITIES: Offshore banking unit
Parent Company: Head office: 16 Blvd des Italiens, Paris 9,
   France

Date of Establishment: March 1976
No of Employees: 37

BANQUE PARIBAS

PO Box 5241, Manama
Tel: 253119
Cable: Pariba Bahrain
Telex: 8458 BN

PRINCIPAL ACTIVITIES: Commercial banking (also offshore
   banking unit)
Branch Offices: Gulf Branches: Abu Dhabi; Dubai; Qatar; Oman;
   Bahrain
Parent Company: Head Office: 3 rue d'Antin, 75002 Paris,
   France

BAQER FURNISHINGS WLL

PO Box 88, Manama
Tel: 400800, 400900
Cable: Baqer Bahrain
Telex: 8446 Baqer BN
Telefax: 400020

Directors: Hussain M Baqer (Managing Director), Jassim M
   Baqer
Senior Executives: T K Thomas (Overseas Purchase Manager)

PRINCIPAL ACTIVITIES: Importers of furniture, carpets,
   curtains, furnishing fabrics, interior decoration materials, and
   light fittings, household linen items
Principal Agencies: Rufflette (Export), UK; Renz & Sohn,
   Germany; Slumberland, UK; Meubelfabriek Van Pelt, Belgium;
   Velda, Belgium; Commercial Plastics, UK, Tintawn Carpets,
   Ireland; Vidal Grau, Spain; Mico Estelles, Spain; Gautier,
   France; Lawn Comfort, Belgium; Dreammakers
   Manufacturing, Singapore
Parent Company: Mohammed Hussain Haji Baqer WLL
Subsidiary Companies: Diana Furnishings, PO Box 640, Doha,
   Qatar; White Corner, PO Box 88, Manama, Bahrain
Principal Bankers: Al-Ahli Commercial Bank

Date of Establishment: 1946
No of Employees: 75

BARCLAYS BANK PLC

PO Box 5120, Manama
Tel: 242024
Telex: 8747 Barint BN
Telefax: 254221

PRINCIPAL ACTIVITIES: Offshore banking unit/representative
   office

BATA SHOE CO BAHRAIN WLL

Fariq Kanoo, Abu-Huraira Road, Manama
Tel: 253076
Cable: Batasale
Telex: 8630 Bata BN

Chairman: Mumtaz Ahmed

PRINCIPAL ACTIVITIES: Indenting business: booking orders for
   wholesale and retail in Arabian Gulf and Saudi Arabia
Principal Bankers: British Bank of the Middle East

Principal Shareholders: Mumtaz Ahmed, Northern Investment
   Co of Bermuda
Date of Establishment: 1952

BEHBEHANI BROS LTD

PO Box 168, Manama
Tel: 253872, 255297, 252488

Directors: Mohamed Saleh Behbehani, Reza Yousuf Behbehani,
   Morad Yousuf Behbehani
Senior Executives: A Rezak, A Majeed (Manager)

PRINCIPAL ACTIVITIES: Import and distribution of automobiles
   and spare parts and consumer goods (watches)
Principal Agencies: Volkswagen, Omega, Piaget
Branch Offices: United Arab Emirates
Parent Company: Head office in Kuwait

BERGER PAINTS BAHRAIN WLL

PO Box 26688, Manama
Tel: 730700, 730771
Telex: 9660 Berger BN
Telefax: 730689

Chairman: Vijay Mallya
Directors: Amitav Sur (Managing Director)
Senior Executives: D Mahapatra (Sales Manager), Dr J C Dalal
   (Technical Manager)

PRINCIPAL ACTIVITIES: Manufacture of paints and protective
   coatings
Parent Company: Jenson & Nicholson Ltd, PO Box 2,
   Dagenham, Essex RM18 1RU, UK
Associated Companies: Nigeria, Kenya, Mozambique,
   Zimbabwe, Uganda, Malawi, Tanzania, Angola, Pakistan,
   Bangladesh, India, Jamaica, Trinidad, Barbados, Singapore,
   Hongkong, Malta, United Arab Emirates
Principal Bankers: British Bank of the Middle East, Bahrain
Financial Information:

	1990/91 BD'000
Authorised capital	418
Paid-up capital	418
Total assets	460

Principal Shareholders: 100% subsidiary of J & N, UK
Date of Establishment: 1981

BHATIA & CO (BAHRAIN) WLL

PO Box 95, Manama
Tel: 730449, 730781
Cable: Bhatia
Telex: 8361 BN
Telefax: (973) 730746

Directors: J M Bhatia (Managing Director)
Senior Executives: V Mathew (General Sales Manager), K
   Aravindakshan (Finance Manager), P L Asarpota
   (Administration Manager)

PRINCIPAL ACTIVITIES: Import and distribution of general
   motor vehicles, spare auto parts, batteries, pumps, tyres and
   tubes, bearings, cables, marine equipment, hoses, wire ropes,
   lubrication systems, asbestos, safety equipment, welding
   equipment
Principal Agencies: Lincoln, USA; Detroit Diesel Corp; Kiddle;
   Farr; Redwing International; FAG; National; General Motors
Principal Bankers: Banque Paribas

Date of Establishment: 1948
No of Employees: 60

BILJEEK, ABBAS, & SONS

PO Box 308, Manama
Tel: 253131, 254317
Cable: BILJEEK-BAHRAIN
Telex: 8420 BILJEK BN
Telefax: 276252

Chairman: Abbas Biljeek (Managing Director)
Directors: Dawood Biljeek, Mohamed Biljeek, Ali Biljeek
Senior Executives: K K Kutty (Office Manager), A Nadim (Sales Engineer)

PRINCIPAL ACTIVITIES: Import of construction machinery, wood working machinery, generators, engines, pumps, compressors, welding equipment, portable electrical tools, building materials, etc
Principal Agencies: Kohler, USA; Norton, USA; SCM, Italy; Abet Print, Italy; P C Henderson, UK; Croda, UK; Spit, France; Joseph Scheppach, W Germany; Kress, W Germany; MWM, W Germany; Dorma, W Germany; Deutz-MWM, W Germany; AEG Power Tools, W Germany; Leitz, Austria
Subsidiary Companies: Arabia Glass & Mirrors Co; Awal Aluminium Factory
Principal Bankers: British Bank of the Middle East; Al Ahli Commercial Bank

Principal Shareholders: Family concern
Date of Establishment: 1950
No of Employees: 35

BIN ABDULLATIF, MOSTAFA,

PO Box 18, Manama
Tel: 253417, 253510
Cable: Mostafa

Directors: Shaikh Eshaq Abdulrahman, Shaikh Mohamed Y Najihi

PRINCIPAL ACTIVITIES: General trading; import and distribution of electrical household appliances, refrigerators, freezers, air conditioners, cookers, washing machines, sanitary ware; pearl and diamond business
Branch Offices: Dubai, also in Pakistan and India
Principal Bankers: All banks in Bahrain

BOKHAMMAS, A R,

PO Box 151, Manama
Tel: (Head Office) 261457, (Manama Off) 253756, (Muharraq Br) 320056, 320249
Cable: Bokhammas Bahrain
Telex: 8810 Khammas BN

Directors: Abdulerehman Bokhammas (Managing Director)
Senior Executives: Ahmed A R Bokhammas (Sales & Marketing), Rashid A R Bokhammas (Technical), Essa A R Bokhammas (Purchasing)

PRINCIPAL ACTIVITIES: Suppliers and stockists of hardware, tools, paints, varnishes, paint brushes, fishing accessories, building materials and ironmongery
Principal Agencies: Federated paints, Scotland; Bostik Ltd, UK; Nobel Brushes, Scotland; Impex, Germany; Union Locks & Hardware, UK; Peugeot, France; Kango-Electric Drills & Hammers; James Neill Group; Britool; M & W; Eclipse; Tioa Paints; Royal Paints, Italy; Rawlplug Fastners, UK; Yale Locks, UK/Italy/USA; Flag Stone Paints; GKN Fastners
Branch Offices: Manama and Muhurraq
Principal Bankers: National Bank of Bahrain; Bank of Bahrain and Kuwait; Al Ahli Commercial Bank

Date of Establishment: over 100 years
No of Employees: 25

BOKHAMMAS ESTABLISHMENT

PO Box 5262, Manama
Tel: (Head Office) 742040, 714174
Cable: AWladead
Telex: 8770 Bokms BN
Telefax: (0973) 712612

Chairman: Eid Bokhammas
Directors: Mohammed Eid Bokhammas (Managing Director)
Senior Executives: Yousuf Eid Bokhammas (General Manager), Ali Eid Bokhammas (Sales Manager), Aziz Eid Bokhammas (Branch Manager), Hassan Eid Bokhammas (Accounts Manager), Adnan Eid Bokhammas (Branch Manager), Jasim Mohammed Bokhammas (Branch Manager)

PRINCIPAL ACTIVITIES: General trading and contracting
Principal Agencies: British Screws Co Ltd UK; Stanley group of companies; Neill Tools Ltd UK; Leyland Paints & Wall Paper Ltd UK; Evode (Evostick) Ltd UK; Rawl Plug Co Ltd UK; Yale Group of Companies; Union Locks, Josiah Parks & Sons Ltd UK; Hilti Corporation Switzerland; Rustoleum Paints Holland; Kontrad Germany; Thomas Hardson Stocks UK; Cuprinol UK; Metabo Drills Germany; Dyrup paint Denmark; Hammerite Paint, UK; Hycraft Insulation, Eire; Diplomat Steel Furniture, Korea
Branch Offices: Manama, Central Market, Muharraq, Isa Town (HO), Hoora
Parent Company: Bokhammas Center, Isa Town
Principal Bankers: National Bank of Bahrain, Bank of Bahrain & Kuwait, British Bank of the Middle East, Al-Ahli Commercial Bank, Chartered Bank, National Westminster Bank UK, American Express Bank,
Financial Information:

	1990 BD'000
Sales turnover	2,500
Profits	750
Authorised capital	8,200
Paid-up capital	2,500
Total assets	8,500

Principal Shareholders: Bokhammas Family
Date of Establishment: 1875
No of Employees: 96

BP ARABIAN AGENCIES LIMITED

PO Box 299, Manama
Tel: 254741/4
Cable: Beepee Bahrain
Telex: 8259 Bahrain Beepee BN

PRINCIPAL ACTIVITIES: Marketing, distribution and sale of BP products
Branch Offices: Bahrain; United Arab Emirates; Oman; Kuwait; Saudi Arabia; Qatar

BRAMCO WLL

PO Box 20260, Manama
Tel: 250954, 250981
Cable: Bramco Bahrain
Telex: 9261 Bramco BN
Telefax: 272725

Chairman: Jamil A Wafa
Directors: Mohamed Zubari (Vice Chairman), Vinay Kumar Dewan (President)
Senior Executives: V K Dewan, J K Jain

PRINCIPAL ACTIVITIES: Blasting and quarrying contractors, building and civil contractors, drilling contractors, etc
Parent Company: Unitag WLL
Subsidiary Companies: UBF Industries WLL
Principal Bankers: Banque Paribas

BAHRAIN

Financial Information:

	1990 BD'000
Sales turnover	3,056
Profits	58
Authorised capital	200
Paid-up capital	200
Total assets	1,079

Principal Shareholders: Unitag, V K Dewan
Date of Establishment: 1978
No of Employees: 300

BRC WELDMESH (GULF) WLL

PO Box 5341, Manama
Tel: 728222
Cable: Brenforce Bahrain
Telex: 8503 BRCBAH BN
Telefax: (973) 725562

Chairman: A K Almoayed
Directors: K A Almoayed, R N C Hall, J Hall, E Almoayed
Senior Executives: Emad Almoayed (Managing Director &
Company Secretary)

PRINCIPAL ACTIVITIES: Manufacture and supply of electrically
cross-welded steel wire mesh in sheets and rolls
Parent Company: A K Almoayed; Hall Engineering (Holdings) Plc
Principal Bankers: Al Ahli Commercial Bank, British Bank of the
Middle East

Principal Shareholders: A K Almoayed
Date of Establishment: 1973
No of Employees: 48

BRITISH BANK OF THE MIDDLE EAST (THE)

PO Box 57, Manama
Tel: 255933
Cable: Bactria Bahrain
Telex: 8230 BN
Telefax: 256822

Chairman: W Purves CBE DSO
Directors: J R H Bond, F J French, J M Gray, A P Hill CBE, S
Robertson, P J Wrangham
Senior Executives: A D Whyte (Area Manager), N Dinan
(Manager Corporate Banking), R S Webber (Manager Retail
Banking), J H K Crichton (Manager Credit), I J Carruthers
(Credit Control Manager), Saleh Salman Al Kowary
(Management Accountant), N P Stickland (Manager OBU), S
G D Walker (Asst Manager OBU)

PRINCIPAL ACTIVITIES: Commercial banking (also offshore
banking unit)
Branch Offices: Throughout the Middle East; Bahrain; India;
Jordan; Lebanon; Oman; Qatar; United Arab Emirates; and
United Kingdom
Parent Company: The Hongkong and Shanghai Banking Corp
Ltd
Subsidiary Companies: Saudi British Bank; Middle East Finance
Co Ltd

Principal Shareholders: The Hong Kong and Shanghai Banking
Corp Ltd
Date of Establishment: Incorporated by Royal Charter in 1889
No of Employees: approx 300 in Bahrain

BROWN AND ROOT (GULF) EC

PO Box 780, Manama
Tel: 243243
Telex: 8274 BN
Telefax: 727697

Directors: Jerry D Slaughter (Managing Director)
Senior Executives: Barry Kihneman (Finance & Admin Manager),
Dean Campbell (Marketing & Business Development
Manager)

PRINCIPAL ACTIVITIES: Offshore engineering contractors,
offshore works, structural and mechanical installations,
submarine pipelay contrators
Branch Offices: PO Box 90, Alkhobar, Saudi Arabia, Tel
8954016/8954036, Telex 670589 SJ
Parent Company: Brown & Root Int'l Inc
Principal Bankers: Citibank; British Bank of the Middle East

BUCHEERY CONSTRUCTION SERVICES

PO Box 561, Manama
Tel: 664700
Telex: 8315 Argus BN

Chairman: Ali Mohammed Haji Bucheery

PRINCIPAL ACTIVITIES: General contractors engaged in civil
works (comprising major sewerage and drainage projects,
land reclamation, and industrial construction), electrical,
mechanical and instrumentation installations, plant, equipment
and transport hire
Associated Companies: Bucheery -A.C.T. Joint Venture;
Bucheery Technical & Trading Establishment

C ITOH MIDDLE EAST EC

See ITOH, C, MIDDLE EAST EC

CALTEX BAHRAIN

PO Box 25125, Awali
Tel: 753131
Cable: Caltex Bahrain
Telex: 7039 Caltex BN
Telefax: 753122

Senior Executives: J D M Weir (Managing Director), M A Shafea
(General Manager Logistics & Marketing), W B Umberfield
(Manager Finance & Administration), R A Maxwell (Manager
Marketing)

PRINCIPAL ACTIVITIES: Oil trading, refining and marketing
Associated Companies: Bahrain Petroleum Co BSC; Bahrain
National Gas Co BSC; Bahrain Aviation Fuelling Co BSC

Date of Establishment: 1981

CELMEC

PO Box 26252, Manama
Tel: 730096, 731249
Cable: CELMEC
Telex: 8594 Celmec BN
Telefax: (973) 730860

Chairman: Atiyatullah Omardin

PRINCIPAL ACTIVITIES: Civil, electrical & mechanical
engineering and contracting, manufacturers' representatives

Date of Establishment: 1978
No of Employees: 50

CHASE MANHATTAN BANK NA

PO Box 368, Manama
Tel: 251401
Cable: Chamanbank Bahrain
Telex: 8286 Cmbbah BN
Telefax: 259670

Senior Executives: Steven Fullenkamp (VP General Manager),
Mufeed Rajab (Manager Operations, Systems &
Administration)

PRINCIPAL ACTIVITIES: Commercial banking; and offshore
banking unit
Parent Company: Head office: 1 Chase Manhattan Plaza, New
York NY 10015, USA

Date of Establishment: 1971
No of Employees: 60

CHEMICAL BANK

PO Box 5492, Manama
Tel: 252619
Cable: Chemical
Telex: 8562 CHEMBK BN

PRINCIPAL ACTIVITIES: Offshore banking unit
Parent Company: Chemical New York Corporation

Date of Establishment: 1976 (in Bahrain)
No of Employees: 35 (in Bahrain)

CITIBANK NA

PO Box 548, Manama
Tel: 257124
Telex: 8225 Citibk BN
Telefax: 243027

Senior Executives: Flavian Pinto (Senior Country Operations
   Officer), Mohammed Al Shroogi (Country Corporate Officer),
   Richard Berry (Head of Financial Institutions)

PRINCIPAL ACTIVITIES: Commercial and offshore banking
Branch Offices: In the Middle East: United Arab Emirates,
   Bahrain, Jordan, Lebanon, Egypt, Oman
Parent Company: Head office: 399 Park Ave, New York NY
   10043, USA

Date of Establishment: January 1970
No of Employees: 130

CITICORP INVESTMENT BANK

PO Box 2465, Manama
Tel: 247670, 274117
Telex: 8225 CITIBK BN
Telefax: 243027

Senior Executives: Mohammed Al Shroogi (Investment Bank
   Head)

PRINCIPAL ACTIVITIES: Investment banking
Branch Offices: Dubai
Parent Company: Head office in New York, 399 Park Ave,
   NY10043, USA

Date of Establishment: 1980
No of Employees: 88

COMMERZBANK AG

UGB Tower, 4th Floor, Diplomatic Area, PO Box 11800,
   Manama
Tel: 531431, 531432
Cable: Commerzrep
Telex: 8567 CBKBAH BN
Telefax: 531435

Senior Executives: Eberhard Brodhage (Chief Representative),
   Hans-Peter Amrein (Representative)

PRINCIPAL ACTIVITIES: Representative office
Parent Company: Head office in Frankfurt, West Germany

Date of Establishment: 1976

CREDIT SUISSE

PO Box 5100, Manama
Tel: 232123
Telex: 8418 CREDGN
Telefax: 261987

Senior Executives: Ruedi Schmid (Branch Manager), J C Doge
   (Senior Representative), Ebrahim Al Yamani (Operations
   Manager)

PRINCIPAL ACTIVITIES: Offshore banking unit and commercial
   banking branch

DAIWA BANK LTD

PO Box 26937, 4th Floor Part 1, Manama Centre, Manama
Tel: 255845
Cable: Daiwabk
Telex: 8584 Daibnk BN
Telefax: (973) 256023

Senior Executives: H Nakazawa (Chief Representative), Y Saiki
   (Representative)

PRINCIPAL ACTIVITIES: Representative office
Parent Company: Head Office in Osaka, Japan

Date of Establishment: January 1981

DANISH BAHRAIN DAIRY CO LTD

PO Box 601, Manama
Tel: 258500
Cable: Dabadco
Telex: 8590

PRINCIPAL ACTIVITIES: Production and supply of dairy
   products

DAR AL TASMEEM ATKINS

PO Box 11267, Manama
Tel: 251548
Telex: 8803 HHPART BN
Telefax: 252694

PRINCIPAL ACTIVITIES: Planning, engineering, management
   and agricultural consultants and architects
Branch Offices: In the Middle East: Kuwait, Oman, Dubai, Abu
   Dhabi
Parent Company: W S Atkins Ltd, UK

DARWISH, HASSAN HAIDER,

PO Box 272, Manama
Tel: 253178
Cable: ALDARWISH
Telex: 8653 HASSAN BN
Telefax: 240088

Chairman: Hassan Haider Darwish (Chairman)
Directors: Harith Hassan Darwish, Dr Mohamed Hassan
   Darwish, Adel Hassan Darwish
Senior Executives: Rakesh Grover (Chief Executive)

PRINCIPAL ACTIVITIES: General merchants, commission
   agents, contractors and manufacturers'representatives,
   importers, wholesale dealers, distributors of foodstuffs,
   cigarettes, electrical home appliances and bathroom furniture
Principal Agencies: R J Reynolds Tobacco, USA; Domo
   Melkprodukten Bedrijven Beilen, Holland; Tanko, Holland;
   Spontex, France; Areilos, Italy; Sanwa Industries, Japan;
   Godrej & Boyce, India; ROV, USA; Cricket, France; Daiden,
   Japan; Osteo, Switzerland; Acalor, UK; Chr Fabers Fabriker,
   Denmark; Simu, France; Huppe, Germany; Dickson Constant,
   France; Somfy, France; Allibert, France; George Payne, Sri
   Lanka
Branch Offices: PO Box 424, Muscat, Sultanate of Oman
Subsidiary Companies: Al-Darwish Trading & Electrical
   Contractors; Al-Darwish Awnings & Blinds Factory; Al-
   Darwish Cooker Factory; Al-Darwish Travel Agency; Al-
   Darwish Trading & Construction; Bahrain & Kuwait Co for
   Light Industries & Commerce; Al Darwish Dairy & Agroserve
Principal Bankers: Alahli Commercial Bank; Bank Melli Iran;
   Algemene Bank

Date of Establishment: 1953
No of Employees: 150

DEBENHAM TEWSON INTERNATIONAL

PO Box 5084, Manama
Tel: 252237
Telefax: 233249

Chairman: Richard Lay

BAHRAIN

Directors: David C Watt, Keith M Stockdale
Senior Executives: Cliff Langford (Resident Manager), Naser Al Arrayedh (International Investment Manager)

PRINCIPAL ACTIVITIES: Independent property advice including valuation, leasing, development advice, feasability studies, property/project management and investment, funding advice
Branch Offices: Australia, Belgium, France, W Germany, Netherlands, Singapore, USA
Parent Company: Head office: 44 Brook Street, London W1, UK
Principal Bankers: Standard Chartered Bank, Bahrain; National Westminster Bank, UK

Date of Establishment: 1974 in Bahrain

DELMON GULF CONSTRUCTION
PO Box 5786, Manama
Tel: 258842, 258209, 257884
Cable: Gulcon
Telex: 9055 Delcon BN

Chairman: Sheikh Abdulrahman Bin Mohammed Al Khalifa
Directors: Sh Rashid Abdulrahman Al Khalifa, Ahmed Mahfooth Al Aali

PRINCIPAL ACTIVITIES: Building contractors and other civil works
Principal Bankers: Bank of Bahrain & Kuwait; National Bank of Bahrain

Principal Shareholders: Chairman and directors as described
Date of Establishment: 1977
No of Employees: 300

DELMON POULTRY CO BSC
PO Box 20535, Manama
Tel: 631993
Telex: 9669 DEPCO BN
Telefax: 632426

Chairman: Mohamed Al-Mannai
Directors: Yousuf Al-Saleh (Managing Director), Dr Jalil Halwachi (General Manager)
Senior Executives: Abdulla Mohamed Ali (Asst General Manager), Hani Ahmed (Feed Mill Manager), Mohsin Durazi (Processing Plant Manager)

PRINCIPAL ACTIVITIES: Animal and poultry feed, production of broiler processing plant, by-product renderring plant, broiler farms and hatchery under construction
Principal Bankers: National Bank of Bahrain; Bank of Bahrain & Kuwait; Al-Ahli Commercial Bank
Financial Information:

	1989 BD'000
Sales turnover	5,300
Profits	370
Authorised capital	10,000
Paid-up capital	3,000
Total assets	5,890

Principal Shareholders: Government (15%); Public (85%)
Date of Establishment: March 1980
No of Employees: 145

DELOITTE HASKINS & SELLS
PO Box 5475, Manama
Tel: 271400
Telex: 9644 DHS BN
Telefax: 256973

Managing Partner: Pen Wilson
Partner in Charge: Doug W Watts
Senior Executives: Edward R Crater (Partner), Salman Ahmed (Senior Manager)

PRINCIPAL ACTIVITIES: Chartered accountants, management consulting, auditing and tax services (incl US expatriate taxation)

Branch Offices: Offices in the Middle East: Abu Dhabi; Bahrain; Cyprus; Dubai; Greece; Kuwait; Oman; Sharjah; Saudi Arabia; Turkey; and other offices worldwide
Parent Company: Head Offices in London and New York

Date of Establishment: 1/10/81

DEUTSCHE BANK AG
PO Box 20619, Manama Centre 1, 6th Floor, Government Ave, Manama
Tel: 276630
Telex: 8493 Deutbank BN
Telefax: 274136

Senior Executives: Dr Hans Juergen Koch (Chief Representative), Michael Fritz (Representative)

PRINCIPAL ACTIVITIES: Banking (representative office)
Parent Company: Head office in Frankfurt, Germany

Date of Establishment: 1982

DHL INTERNATIONAL EC
Regional Office, Awazi Bldg, Old Palace Road, PO Box 5741, Manama
Tel: 534800
Telex: 9503 DHL RO BN
Telefax: 535722

Senior Executives: G Davey (Regional Manager), K Allen (Regional Finance Manager), M Wood (Regional Sales & Marketing Manager), M Stone (Operations Manager)

PRINCIPAL ACTIVITIES: Worldwide courier service, documents and small parcels
Branch Offices: Bahrain office: DHL International (Bahrain) WLL, Ammar Bldg, Diplomatic Area, PO Box 5741, Manama, Tel 534141, Telex 8876 DHL BAH BN; and offices in the Middle East: Kuwait, Oman, Qatar, Saudi Arabia, Yemen, Abu Dhabi, Dubai, Sharjah, Jordan, Egypt, Lebanon, Cyprus

DIPLOMAT HOTEL
PO Box 5243, Manama
Tel: 531666
Telex: 9555 Dipotl BN
Telefax: 530843

PRINCIPAL ACTIVITIES: Hotel operation

DRESDNER BANK AG
Yateem Centre, 6th Floor, PO Box 5567, Manama
Tel: 256526
Telex: 8744 Dresag BN
Telefax: 276529

Senior Executives: Klaus H F Muller (Middle East Representative)

PRINCIPAL ACTIVITIES: Banking (representative office)
Parent Company: Head Office in Frankfurt, West Germany

Date of Establishment: 1976

EBRAHIM AL SHAKAR & SONS (ESSCO)
See AL SHAKAR, EBRAHIM, & SONS (ESSCO)

ELDERS AUSTRALIA MIDDLE EAST EC
PO Box 5812, 2nd Floor, DMB Centre, Diplomatic Area, Manama
Tel: 531163
Telex: 9472 Elders BN
Telefax: 530465

PRINCIPAL ACTIVITIES: Representative office of Elders IXL Ltd
Parent Company: Elders IXL Ltd, Garden Street, South Yarra, Victoria 3141, Australia

ERNST & YOUNG

PO Box 140, 14th Floor, The Tower, Sheraton Commercial
  Complex, Manama
Tel: 535455
Cable: Ernstaudit Bahrain
Telex: 8453 ERNST BN
Telefax: 535405

Chairman: Ismail M Amin (Chief Executive)
Resident Partners: I D Williams (Managing Partner), N R Abid,
  M T Sadiq
Senior Executives: P J Griffiths, T D Trafford, P W Gillam

PRINCIPAL ACTIVITIES: Accountants and management
  consultants
Branch Offices: Worldwide and as follows in Middle East:
  Bahrain; Egypt; Jordan; Kuwait; Lebanon; Libya; Morocco;
  Oman; Qatar; Saudi Arabia; United Arab Emirates

Date of Establishment: 1928 (in Bahrain)
No of Employees: 40 (in Bahrain)

ESSO MIDDLE EAST MARKETING INC

PO Box 5170, Manama
Tel: 253421
Cable: Essoma
Telex: 8438 Essoma BN

PRINCIPAL ACTIVITIES: Marketing of lubricants
Parent Company: Exxon Corp

Principal Shareholders: Exxon Corp

FAKHRO, ABDULLA YUSUF, CO

PO Box 39, Manama
Tel: 275000, 253531, 259843, 274500
Cable: Fakhrabad
Telex: 8867 FAKHRO BN
Telefax: 273947

Proprietor: Abdulla Yusuf Fakhro
Directors: Dr Esam Fakhro (Director), Adel Fakhro (Managing
  Director)
Senior Executives: R F Paes (Company Secretary)

PRINCIPAL ACTIVITIES: Import and distribution of marine
  diesel engines and spare parts, automobile and road
  transport vehicles and spares, tyres, tubes, hoses, rubber
  footwear and other general rubber goods, building materials,
  electrical goods and machinery, sponsorship services, car
  rental, fuel supply, courier services, insurance agents,
  shipping agents, garage & tyre shop equipment, cathodic
  protection, car batteries, electronic products, marine supplies
Principal Agencies: L Gardner & Sons Ltd, UK; Dunlop Ltd, UK
  and subsidiaries & associates companies in other countries;
  General Accident Fire & Life Assurance Corp, UK; American
  Life Insurance Co, USA; Budget Rent a Car; Bergsoe Anti
  Corrosion, Denmark; Canada Wire & Cable, Canada
Subsidiary Companies: Al Sabah & Abdulla Fakhro WLL,
  Kuwait; Ahmad & Abdulla Fakhro, Bahrain; Gulf Agency Co
  (Bahrain) WLL, Bahrain; Budget Rent A Car; TNT Skypak
  Bahrain WLL; Fakhro Electronics WLL
Principal Bankers: National Bank of Bahrain; Standard
  Chartered Bank; Arab Bank Ltd

Principal Shareholders: Sole Proprietorship
Date of Establishment: 1888

FAKHRO COMMERCIAL SERVICES

PO Box 2200, Manama, Bahrain
Tel: 263344
Telex: 7152 FCS BN
Telefax: 259723, 263100

President: Adel Abdulla Fakhro
Senior Executives: Mathew Daniel (Marine Services & Food
  Division Sales Manager), Dinesh Pillay (Electrical Sales
  Manager), Prabhu Samson (Sales Manager Kitchen Magic)

PRINCIPAL ACTIVITIES: Distribution of electrical goods,
  marketing of electrical machinery and cables; distribution and
  installation of fitted kitchens and other kitchen furniture;
  marine supplies and shipchandling services; industrial
  supplies; import & distribution of food and drink products
Principal Agencies: MK Electric Ltd; Barton Conduits; Canada
  Wire & Cable Co; Stromberg Transformers; Unitor Ship
  Services; Unitor Rochem Marine Chemicals; Bobbe
  Associates; Inter Floridana Fruit Juices; Hochland Cheese;
  Hak Bottles Vegetables
Subsidiary Companies: Middle East Marine Services; Kitchen
  Magic; Adel Fakhro Enterprises
Principal Bankers: Al-Ahli Commercial Bank; ABN Bank;
  Standard Chartered Bank

Principal Shareholders: President
Date of Establishment: 1984

FAKHRO ELECTRONICS

PO Box 39, Manama
Tel: 263344
Telex: 7152 FCS BN
Telefax: 263100

Chairman: Abdulla Yusuf Fakhro
Directors: Yousif A Fakhro (Managing Director)
Senior Executives: Malcolm Kemp (General Manager), Alfredo
  D'souza (Manager Business Equipment Sales)

PRINCIPAL ACTIVITIES: Marketing and distribution of business
  and telecommunication equipment, facsimiles, modems,
  PABXs, radios, printers, computer networks
Principal Agencies: NEC; Bosch; OKI; Proteon; GPT; Ericsson;
  V Band; Riso; Dell; Copam
Branch Offices: The Phone Shop
Parent Company: Abdulla Yusuf Fakhro
Principal Bankers: Standard Chartered Bank; Al Ahli
  Commercial Bank; Arab Bank

Date of Establishment: 1985
No of Employees: 30

FAKHRO SHIPPING AGENCY LTD

PO Box 5826, Awal Building, Government Road, Manama
Tel: 262125
Cable: Dhows
Telex: 8693 BN

Chairman: Abdullah Yusuf Fakhro
Directors: Adel Abdullah Fakhro, Skjalm Bang
Senior Executives: S Bang (Managing Director)

PRINCIPAL ACTIVITIES: Shipping; freight clearing and
  forwarding; transport

Date of Establishment: 1976
No of Employees: 30

FAKHROO, MOHAMED, & BROS

PO Box 439, Manama
Tel: 253529, 253329
Cable: Al Fakhroo
Telex: 8679 BN

Directors: Mohamed Yousuf Fakhroo, Ali Yousuf Fakhrro,
  Ebrahim Yousuf Fakhroo

PRINCIPAL ACTIVITIES: General trading and contracting,
  import and distribution of building materials (asbestos pipes
  and sheets, pipes and fittings, timber, plywood, hard and soft
  boards, formica), electrical household appliances, tyres, air
  conditioners and refrigerators, heavy machinery
Principal Agencies: N V Phillips, Holland; Turner Asbestos
  Cement Ltd; Newman Hattersley Int Ltd; J D Marshall Int Inc;
  Stanton & Staveley Ltd

BAHRAIN

FAKHROO, QASIM AHMAD,

PO Box 633, Manama
Tel: 255225, 712336, 257199
Cable: Tagheezat Bahrain
Telex: 8829 GETRAD BN

Chairman: Qasim Ahmad Fakhroo
Senior Executives: K N Gupta, D N Saigal

PRINCIPAL ACTIVITIES: General trading, distributing, and
contracting all kinds of building materials, pipes, insulation
materials, partitions
Principal Agencies: Johns-Manville International Corp, Expandite
Ltd, Omark International, Alveolite Light Foam Concrete,
Grace Italiana, Plastica Italiana
Associated Companies: Qasim Fakhroo Gulf Eternit WLL, PO
Box 633, Manama
Principal Bankers: Bahrain; United Arab Emirates (Abu Dhabi
and Dubai)

FAKHROO, YUSUF BIN YUSUF,

PO Box 214, Bahrain
Tel: 253532
Cable: Alyusuf
Telex: 8545 BN

Chairman: Yusuf Bin Yusuf Fakhroo

PRINCIPAL ACTIVITIES: Electrical engineering, import and
distribution and of air-conditioning equipment, radio and TV
receivers, electronic items, and all electrical household
appliances
Principal Agencies: Airtemp Chyrsler, Siera, Theio Denko

FAYSAL ISLAMIC BANK OF BAHRAIN EC

Massraf Faysal Al Islami Al Bahrain EC

PO Box 20492, Chamber of Commerce Bldg, King Faisal Road,
Manama
Tel: 275040
Cable: Masfaslam
Telex: 9270 Faisbk BN
Telefax: 277305

Chairman: Abdullah Ahmed Zainal Alireza
Directors: HRH Prince Saud Alabdallah Al Faisal (Deputy
Chairman), Sheikh Mohamed Abdullah El Khereiji, Omar Abdi
Ali, Zafar Ahmed Khan, Moustapha Mohamed Sakkaf,
Khedher Mohsin Alibrahim, Nabil Nassief (Managing Director)
Senior Executives: Imtiaz Pervez (General Manager), Saeed
Ahmad (Asst General Manager), Abdulaziz Aba Al Khail
(Senior Manager), Salim Abdul Sattar (Actg Senior Manager),
Abdulrahman Shehab Ahmed (Operations Manager), Luis
Ballesteros (EDP Manager), Mousa A Husain (Deputy
Manager Credit & Marketing), Abdulaziz Al Mutlaq (Deputy
Manager Credit & Marketing), Juma Abull (Deputy Manager
Control & Coordination)

PRINCIPAL ACTIVITIES: Offshore banking, all functions of the
bank are performed in conformity with the principles of
Islamic Sharia'a
Branch Offices: Pakistan: Karachi, Faisalabad

Principal Shareholders: Dar Al Maal Al Islami Trust (89%),
Islamic Takafol Company of Bahrain (10%), HRH Prince
Mohamed Al Faisal Al Saud (1%)
Date of Establishment: 1982

FORTUNE PROMOSEVEN WLL

Promosen Holdings EC

PO Box 5989, Sheikh Murabak Bldg, Government Ave, Manama
Tel: 250148, 245233
Telex: 8980 Promo BN
Telefax: 271451,211457

Chairman: Jamil Al Wafa
Directors: Akram Miknas (President - Network), Ahmed Abu
Reesh (Vice President - Network), Mohd Zubari

Senior Executives: Akram Miknas (President & CEO), Steven
Samuel (Production & Marketing Director), J I Desai (Financial
Controller), Issa Juma A Wahab (Senior Account Director),
Fares Abou Hamad (Clients Servicing Manager), Mrs Kamilia
Ahmed Long (Public Relations Officer)

PRINCIPAL ACTIVITIES: Advertising and public relations
services, marketing, newspaper, radio and television
commercials, etc
Principal Agencies: BMW, Ceylon Tea, Cathay Pacific, Coca
Cola, AMLC, Austrade, Gulf Danish Dairy, DDB, National
Organisation of Greece, The British Bank of the Middle East,
Beiersdorf AG
Branch Offices: UAE: PO Box 6834, Deira, Dubai; Lebanon: PO
Box 11-6777, Hamra, Pavillion Centre, Beirut; Egypt: Aboul
Fotouh Promoseven, 17 Dr El Mahrouki St, Midan Aswan,
Agouza, Giza, Cairo, London: 27 Curzon Street, London
SW1V 7AE; Saudi Arabia: PO Box 20675, Jeddah 21465; PO
Box 53038, Riyadh 11583; Sultanate of Oman: Muscat
Advertising Agency, PO Boc 5316, Ruwi
Subsidiary Companies: PROMOVISION (Still Commercials,
Audio Visuals, and Film); Arab Animation (Animated Films and
Cartoon)
Principal Bankers: Standard Chartered Bank, Bahrain; British
Bank of the Middle East, Bahrain & London, Chase
Manhattan Bank

Principal Shareholders: Unitag; Promoseven; A Miknas
Date of Establishment: 1968, reorganised in 1989
No of Employees: 260

FRAB BANK (MIDDLE EAST) EC

PO Box 5290, Manama
Tel: 259921, 259862
Cable: Frabahrain
Telex: 9024; 9025; 9251 Frabah BN

Chairman: Mohamed Abdul Muhsin Al Kharafi
Directors: Abdul Aziz Al Sulaiman (Vice Chairman), Ibrahim
Dabdoub, Tony Jadoune, Neville Mills

PRINCIPAL ACTIVITIES: Offshore banking unit
Parent Company: Frab Holding
Principal Bankers: Philadelphia Intl Bank-NY; Frab Bank Intl-
Paris; Bayerische Landesbank-Munich; Societe General-
London
Financial Information:

	US$'000
Authorised capital	12,000
Paid-up capital	12,000

Principal Shareholders: Frab Holding
Date of Establishment: May 1978

FUJI BANK LTD (THE)

PO Box 26899, Manama Centre, Government Road, Manama
Tel: 231158
Telex: 9415 Fujibk BN
Telefax: 263125

Senior Executives: Kiminori Nagano (Chief Representative)

PRINCIPAL ACTIVITIES: Representative office

Date of Establishment: November 1980

GENERAL POULTRY COMPANY

PO Box 5472, Manama
Tel: 631004
Telex: 8344 Tanmya BN, 8678

Chairman: Siddiq Al Alawi
Directors: Nasser Abdulla Abbas (General Manager)

PRINCIPAL ACTIVITIES: Production of poultry feed and eggs
Principal Bankers: National Bank of Bahrain

GENERAL TRADING & FOOD PROCESSING CO BSC

PO Box 20202, Manama
Tel: 729731, 729766, 241019
Cable: Trafco Bahrain
Telex: 9165 BN
Telefax: (973) 727380

Chairman: Ali Rashid Al Amin
Directors: Mohammed Baqer Al Tajir (Vice Chairman), Mohsin Mohamed Ali Al Arjaani, Hassan Ebrahim Hassan Kamal, Yousuf Saleh Al Saleh, Ebrahim Mohamed Ali Zainal, Hassan Isa Al Khayat, Mohamed Abdulla Al Zamil, Khalid Abdulrahman Almoayed, Abdul Reda Mohamed Al Daylami
Senior Executives: Ram Narain (Manager), Aziz Al Mulla (Assistant Manager), K V Madhan Rao (Chief Accountant), Ali Ramadan Nasser (Cold Store Manager), Mohamed Abdulla (Catering & Branches Manager)

PRINCIPAL ACTIVITIES: Import and distribution of foodstuffs, frozen, canned and fresh, cold storage, catering
Principal Agencies: Arnotts Biscuits; Vegetable Oil Pty Ltd; SPC Ltd, Australia; Honig; United Dairymen, Holland; Juice Bowl, USA; American Marketing Corp USA; Anglia Canners UK; Inga's Butter Cookies; Nowaco Denmark
Branch Offices: Main Office, Mina Salman, Tel 245206, 727208; Central Market, Manama, Tel 241019; Muharraq Branch, Tel 320278; East Riffa Branch, Tel 662417
Subsidiary Companies: BMMI; Danish-Bahrain Dairy Co; Food Supply Co Ltd; Delmon Poultry Co
Principal Bankers: National Bank of Bahrain, Bank of Bahrain & Kuwait, Al Ahli Commercial Bank; Grindlays Bahrain Bank BSC; Bahrain Islamic Bank BSC

Principal Shareholders: Government (20%) and Public (Bahrainis only)
Date of Establishment: March 1978
No of Employees: 100

GKN KELLER GMBH

Gulf Branch, PO Box 5452, Manama
Tel: 256905, 258641
Telex: 8625 GKNKG BN

Chairman: Dr J M West
Directors: K Kirsch, K Esters, W T Kueblbeck

PRINCIPAL ACTIVITIES: Ground engineering contractors, vibro compaction, piling, drilling and grouting
Parent Company: GKN Keller GmbH, 6050 Offenbach, Germany
Principal Bankers: Al Ahli Commercial Bank

Date of Establishment: 1973 (In Bahrain)
No of Employees: 40 (In Bahrain)

GRAY MACKENZIE & CO LTD

PO Box 210, Manama
Tel: 712750
Cable: Gray
Telex: 7068 BN
Telefax: 712749

Chairman: D G John
Directors: Alan G Davies (Chief Executive), Martyn Smith (Director Finance)
Senior Executives: N J E H Monk (General Manager Shipping Services & Admin), A P Schofield (Group Personnel Manager), T Stokes (Group Consumer Manager), R A C Rice (Group Planning & Development Manager), P McElwaine (Group Wines & Spirits Manager), T Casey (Group Travel Manager), B Molland (Group Industrial Manager)

PRINCIPAL ACTIVITIES: Industrial services, marketing and distribution of fast consumer goods, Lloyds Agents, P&I club agencies and surveying, travel agents, marine craft operators, dry cargo ship and tanker agents, freight forwarders, general merchants, port operators, services and products to the oil, gas and water industry, engineering workshop activities
Principal Agencies: P&O Containers, Ellerman, Hapag-Lloyd, Maersk, Lauritzen, Jugolinija, Showa, NCHP, CMB, Texaco, Shell Int'l, EP, Exxon, Japan Line, Sanka, Olympic; Beecham Products, Yardleys, Ferrero, CPC, Henkel, United Biscuits, Berec, Unicharm, Heineken, Amstel, United Distillers, Lanson, Calvet, Adet Seward, Signode, SSI Fix, Saunders, Daniel Ind, Brickhouse Broads (GBBI), Lotus, Shaw Wallace, Jagajit, Cameron Iron Works, Rochester Instruments, Moore Products, Nalco Italiana, Budenberg, Tomoe, Camco, TK Valves, Angus Fire Armour; British Airways, KLM, Air India, Qantas, American Airlines, Cunard
Parent Company: Inchcape Plc, St James's House, 23 King Street, London SW1Y 6QY, UK
Associated Companies: Bahrain Maritime & Mercantile Int'l BSC, PO Box 828, Bahrain; Kuwait Maritime & Mercantile Co KSC, PO Box 78 Safat, 13001 Kuwait; Oman United Agencies LLC, PO Box 3985, Ruwi; Oman United Agencies (Dhofar) LLC, PO Box 18179, Salalah; United Engineering Services LLC, PO Box 5638, Ruwi; Abu Dhabi Maritime & Mercantile Int'l, PO Box 247, Abu Dhabi; Maritime & Mercantile Int'l (Pvt) Ltd, PO Box 70, Dubai; Fujairah Maritime & Mercantile Int'l (Pvt) Ltd, PO Box 259, Fujairah; Ras Al Khaimah Maritime & Mercantile Int'l Ltd, PO Box 4888, Ras-al-Khaimah; Port Rashid Authority, PO Box 2149, Dubai; Gray Mackenzie & Co Ltd, PO Box 11365-1953, Tehran, Iran
Principal Bankers: Standard Chartered Bank; British Bank of the Middle East; National Bank of Bahrain; Bank of Bahrain & Kuwait; ABN
Financial Information:

	1990 St£'000
Authorised capital	7,500
Paid-up capital	7,500

Principal Shareholders: Inchcape Plc, UK
No of Employees: 1,100

GRINDLAYS BAHRAIN BANK BSC (C)

PO Box 793, Manama Centre, Manama
Tel: 250805, 257687
Cable: Grindlay
Telex: 8335 Grndly BN

Chairman: Mohamed Abdulla Al-Zamil
Directors: M A Al-Zamil, A Anderson, A R Al Wazzan, M E Kanoo, J G Davenport

PRINCIPAL ACTIVITIES: Full commercial banking
Branch Offices: Grindlays Group
Financial Information:
Paid-up capital   BD3,000,000

Principal Shareholders: Bahraini Shareholders (60%); Grindlays (40%)

GULF ADVERTISING & MARKETING

PO Box 726, Manama
Tel: 250014
Cable: Alaqat
Telex: 8494 BN
Telefax: 230025

Chairman: Abdulnabi Al Sho'ala
Directors: Khamis Al Muqla (Managing Director), Hasan Al Jishi, Robert M Hughes
Senior Executives: Robert M Hughes (Director)

PRINCIPAL ACTIVITIES: Advertising consultants
Branch Offices: Jeddah, Riyadh, Saudi Arabia; Cairo, Egypt; Muscat, Oman; Dubai, UAE; Kuwait
Parent Company: Gulf Public Relations, PO Box 726, Manama, Bahrain
Subsidiary Companies: Gulf Media Services, PO Box 726, Manama, Bahrain
Principal Bankers: Bank of Bahrain & Kuwait, Bahrain

BAHRAIN

Principal Shareholders: Abdulnabi Al Sho'ala, Khamis Al Muqla, Hasan Al Jishi
Date of Establishment: 1974
No of Employees: 33

GULF AGENCY CO (BAHRAIN) WLL

Awal Bdlg, Government Rd, PO Box 412, Manama
Tel: 254228, 243381
Cable: Confidence Bahrain
Telex: 8211 Gac BN

Directors: Abdulla Yousuf Fakhro, S Bang (Managing Director)

PRINCIPAL ACTIVITIES: Shipping agents; stevedores, clearing and forwarding agents, packers and marine contractors
Principal Agencies: NYK, Yamashita Shinnihon Steamship Co Ltd, Hinode Kisen Co Ltd, Exxon Tankers, Effoa
Subsidiary/Associated Companies: Associated companies in Iran, Kuwait Saudi Arabia, Abu Dhabi, Dubai, Sharjah, Ras-Al-Khaimah, Oman, Lebanon, Syria, Cyprus, Turkey, UK, Italy, Norway, Hong Kong, Greece, Sweden, USA, Nigeria
Principal Bankers: Standard Chartered Bank; National Bank of Bahrain; Arab Bank

Principal Shareholders: Abdulla & Ahmed Fakhro
Date of Establishment: 1957
No of Employees: 90

GULF AIR
Gulf Aviation Co Ltd

PO Box 138, Manama
Tel: 322200, 531166
Cable: Gulfav Bahrain
Telex: 8255 GULFHQ BN
Telefax: 530385, 531035

Chairman: HE Abdulla Bin Saleh Al Mana (Chairman of the Board & Executive Committee)
Directors: HE Ali Bin Khalfan Al Dhahry (Deputy Chairman of the Board), HE Yousuf Ahmed Shirawi, HE Sh Hamoud Bin Abdulla Al Harthy, HE Nasser Mohamed Ali Al Nuweis, HE Ahmed M Obaidly, HE Sh Hamdan Bin Mubarak Al Nahyan (Member of Exec Committee), HE Sh Isa Bin Abdulla Al Khalifa, HE Abdulla Hassan Saif (Member of Exec Committee), HE Sh Hamad Bin Abdulla Al Khalifa, HE Salim Bin Ali Nasser Assiyabi, HE Sulaiman Bin Muhanna Bin Said Al Adawy (Member of Exec Committee), HE Tariq Mohamed Amin Al Manthery, HE Abdulla Hussain Salatt (Member of Exec Committee), HE Abdulla Bin Hamad Al Attiyah, HE Abdulaziz Mohamed Al Noaimi, HE Ali Ibrahim Al Malki
Senior Executives: Ali Ibrahim Al Malki (President & Chief Executive)

PRINCIPAL ACTIVITIES: Airline transportation of passenger, cargo and mail, hotel management, handling services, engineering and maintenance services
Branch Offices: USA; Jordan; Bahrain; Lebanon; India; Saudi Arabia; Qatar; Pakistan; England; Oman; UAE; Colombo; Manila; Frankfurt; Paris; Amsterdam; Hong Kong; Athens; Bangkok; Cairo; Kuwait; Seoul; Nicosia; Tunis; Dacca; Sudan; Sanaa; Taipei; Frankfurt
Subsidiary Companies: Gulf Helicopters Ltd; Gulf Hotel, Bahrain and Muscat
Principal Bankers: National Bank of Bahrain; Bank of Bahrain & Kuwait
Financial Information:

	1989/90 BD'000
Sales turnover	192,877
Profits	27,294
Share capital	64,000
Reserves	49,970
Total assets	246,890

Principal Shareholders: Jointly owned by the governments of Bahrain, Qatar, Abu Dhabi and Oman
Date of Establishment: March 1950
No of Employees: 4,600

GULF ALUMINIUM FACTORY

Mina Sulman Industrial Estate, PO Box 285, Manama
Tel: 243377, 713085
Cable: Alzamil
Telex: 8381 BN

Directors: Fahad A Al Zamil (Managing Director)

PRINCIPAL ACTIVITIES: Manufacture of aluminium doors, windows, building and shop fronts, office partitionings, etc
Associated Companies: Bahrain Marble Factory

Principal Shareholders: Part of the A H Al Zamil Group of Companies, Saudi Arabia

GULF ALUMINIUM ROLLING MILL CO (GARMCO)

PO Box 20725, Manama
Tel: 731000
Telex: 9786 GARMCO BN

Chairman: Ahmed A R Al-Manna
Directors: Khalid Ashoor (Managing Director)

PRINCIPAL ACTIVITIES: Aluminium rolling mill
Principal Bankers: National Bank of Bahrain; Bank of Bahrain and Kuwait; Al-Ahli Commercial Bank
Financial Information:

	BD'000
Authorised capital	24,000
Paid-up capital	24,000

Principal Shareholders: Saudi Arabia (20%); Iraq (20%); Bahrain (20%); Kuwait (20%); Qatar (10%); Oman (10%)
Date of Establishment: Production started in 1985
No of Employees: 260

GULF COMPUTER LEASE CO WLL

PO Box 2057, Manama
Tel: 262515/16/25
Telex: 7181 Gulflc BN
Telefax: 274023

Directors: Afeef Almoayed, Christopher Power
Senior Executives: Christopher Power (Chief Executive)

PRINCIPAL ACTIVITIES: Lease and sale of IBM computer equipment
Principal Bankers: National Bank of Bahrain; Al Ahli Commercial Bank; Standard Chartered Bank; Wardleys (Middle East) Ltd

Date of Establishment: December 1983

GULF CONSTRUCTION (ME) CO WLL

PO Box 370, Manama
Tel: 252373
Cable: Genco
Telex: 8424 Genco BN

Chairman: A R Sa'ai
Directors: Ghazi Al-Faris (Managing Director)

PRINCIPAL ACTIVITIES: Civil engineers and contractors; building and maintenance
Principal Agencies: Evode (Export) Ltd, UK; Pillar Naco, Malaysia; American Building Co, USA; Davy Plants Management, UK; Dresser Clarke, USA
Principal Bankers: British Bank of the Middle East; National Bank of Bahrain

Principal Shareholders: A R Sa'ai (51%); Ghazi Al Faris (49%)
Date of Establishment: 1954
No of Employees: 150

GULF EST MAINTENANCE PETROL EQUIPMENT (GEMPE)
PO Box 5342, Manama
Tel: 664858
Cable: RINCO

Directors: Saleh Mohd Saleh, Hassan Asad Ali
Senior Executives: M D Shah (Engineer), K K Sreedharan (Accountant)

PRINCIPAL ACTIVITIES: Building contracting, erection, prefabricated houses civil engineering, welding and construction
Principal Bankers: Bank Melli Iran, Manama

Date of Establishment: 1967
No of Employees: 40

GULF HOTEL
Qudaibiya Bay, PO Box 580, Bahrain
Tel: 233000
Cable: Gulfotel
Telex: 8241 Gulftl BN
Telefax: 713040

Chairman: Ahmed Kanoo
Directors: Ali Al Malki, Farouk Almoayyed, Mubarak Kanoo, Abdulla Al Madani, Sayed Al Marzooq, Ali Al Jassim, Khalil Ebrahim Al Thawadi
Senior Executives: Mohamed J Buzizi (General Manager), Aqeel G M Raees (Resident Manager), K Vivekanandan (Financial Controller), Abdul Nabi Amini (Rooms Division Manager), Michael Fuhrmann (Food & Beverage Manager), Moosa A Ali (Personnel & Training Manager)

PRINCIPAL ACTIVITIES: Hotel business
Parent Company: Bahrain Hotels Company BSC
Principal Bankers: National Bank of Bahrain
Financial Information:

	1988/89 BD'000
Sales turnover	8,643
Profits	2,004
Authorised capital	8,484
Paid-up capital	8,484
Total assets	17,341

Principal Shareholders: Gulf Air, Government of Bahrain
Date of Establishment: 1969
No of Employees: 450

GULF INDUSTRIAL INVESTMENT CO EC
PO Box 50177, Hidd
Tel: 673311
Cable: GULFIC Bahrain
Telex: 9993 GIIC BN
Telefax: 675258

Chairman: Awwad B Al Khaldi (Managing Director)
Directors: Abdullatif Hamad Al Tourah (Vice Chairman), Ahmed Mohamed Al Awadi, Nasser Bader Al Tukhaim, Mohamed Ali Jazzaf, Essa Mohamed Al Oun, Kamel A Harami
Senior Executives: Mohamad Yousuf Obaydli (Services & Public Relations Manager), Joseph T Rahal (Finance Manager & Personnel Manager), Khodair Al Majid (Quality Control Manager/Technical Coordinator to Commercial Dept), Khalid Al Qadeeri (Commercial Manager), Dr Ali Basdag (Production Manager), J Frost (Technical Manager)

PRINCIPAL ACTIVITIES: Production of iron oxide pellets
Branch Offices: Gulf Industrial Investment Co EC Kuwait, PO Box 26565 Safat 13126, Telex 22446 GCBC KT, Fax 2405732
Principal Bankers: National Bank of Bahrain, Bank of Bahrain & Kuwait, Grindlays Bank, Bahrain

Financial Information:

	1990 US$'000
Authorised capital	160,000
Paid-up capital	150,000

Principal Shareholders: Santa Fe International Corporation, Abdulateef Hamad Al Tourah, Ahmed Mohamed Al Awadi, Abdulla Abdul Noor Jamal
Date of Establishment: 17 February 1988
No of Employees: 300

GULF INTERNATIONAL BANK BSC
Al-Dowali Building, 3 Palace Avenue, PO Box 1017, Manama
Tel: 534000
Swift: GULFBHBM
Telex: 8802 Dowali BN
Telefax: 522633

Chairman: Abdulla Hassan Saif
Directors: Bader Al Rushaid, Rasheed Al Marag, Hisham A Razzuqi, Ahmed Abdullatif, Dr Abdulla El Kuwaiz, Mustafa Bin Ali Bin Sulaiman Mohamed, Hussain Bin Mohamed Hassan Al Saleh, Hareb M Al Darmaki, Majed M M Al Saad, Sakr Al Merikhi, Abdul Majeed Al Ani, Tariq Hashim Al Khatib
Senior Executives: Ghazi M Abdul-Jawad (General Manager), Mohammad A Aziz Al Moammar (Asst General Manager Marketing), Chehlaoui (EVP Special Projects), George Morton (EVP Banking Group Head), Jurgen Klimm (EVP Operations & Admin Group Head), Bashir Barbir (EVP Assets & Liabilities Group Head), Hussain Al Ansari (SVP Human Resources), Clive Temple-Court (SVP Risk Management Group Head), Michael Barnes (SVP Head of Asset Management), Mahmoud Difrawy (VP Corporate Banking Div Head), Antony Maw (SVP Operations & Administration Group Head), Abdulla Mubarak (SVP Administrative Services Division Head), Ahmed Al Moataz (VP Chief Representative), Abdul Elah Al Amer (VP Board Secretary & Public Relations), Anthony James (SVP Financial Controller), Masood Zafar (SVP Chief Auditor)Issa Baconi (SVP New York Branch Manager), Hayder Al Uzri (SVP Latin America & Corporate Finance Head), Mohannad Farouky (SVP London Branch Manager), Atef Sakr (SVP Chief Credit Officer, ME & Asia), Peter F Smith (VP Singapore Chief Representative)

PRINCIPAL ACTIVITIES: International wholesale bank offering a range of commercial and merchant banking services
Branch Offices: London Branch: 2-6 Cannon Street, London EC4M 6XP, UK; New York Branch: 380 Madison Avenue, NY 10017, USA; Cayman Branch: New York Office; Singapore Representative Office: Unit 1101-1106, Shell Tower, 50 Raffles Place, Singapore 0104; Abu Dhabi Representative Office: PO Box 27051, Abu Dhabi, UAE
Subsidiary Companies: Gibcorp Oman LLC
Principal Bankers: Westpac Banking Corp, Sydney; Swiss Bank Corp, Zurich; Deutsche Bank, Frankfurt; Gulf International Bank, London/New York/Singapore; Citibank, New York; Hongkong & Shanghai Banking Corp, Honkong; Saudi British Bank, Jeddah
Financial Information:

	1988/89 US$'000	1989/90 US$'000
Cash & Bank	52,509	50,585
Loans & discounts	5,081,725	5,110,188
Placements	2,912,052	3,006,364
Other assets	248,475	616,400
Deposits	7,724,378	8,766,599
Issued share capital	641,910	1,001,114
Shareholders' equity	725,826	392,537
Total assets	9,203,544	9,892,973

Principal Shareholders: The governments of Bahrain, Iraq, Kuwait, Oman, Qatar, Saudi Arabia and Abu Dhabi Investment Authority and Gulf Investment Corporation
Date of Establishment: 13th November, 1975
No of Employees: 206

BAHRAIN

GULF INVESTMENTS

PO Box 822, Manama
Tel: 245123
Telex: 9284 GIC BN

Chairman: Sabah Mohammed Al-Rayes

PRINCIPAL ACTIVITIES: Investments in real estate, financial
  services, energy
Branch Offices: Kuwait Office: PO Box 25667 Safat, Kuwait, Tel
  2416033/4, Telex 46616 Ginvco Kt
Financial Information:

	US$'000
Authorised capital	500,000
Paid-up capital	289,932

Principal Shareholders: A Bahraini Shareholding Public Co
  (offshore)
Date of Establishment: 1979

GULF MARKETS INTERNATIONAL

PO Box 5854, Manama
Tel: 230654, 233228
Cable: Gulfmarket
Telex: 9344 Shoala BN
Telefax: 243625

Chairman: Abdulnabi Al Shoala
Directors: Mrs Rabab Al Mahroos, S A M Jaffari
Senior Executives: S A M Jaffari (Managing Director), S V
  Chellappa (Finance Manager), Fahad Al Hamad (Manager), Ali
  Yawar (Sales Manager), Mohd Abdul Haque (Sales Manager)

PRINCIPAL ACTIVITIES: General trading, business consultants
  and promoters, sponsorships, joint ventures
Principal Agencies: Harper, Rholac, Swantex, Linpac, Polarpak,
  Pokka, Etc
Branch Offices: Pearl Enterprises International, PO Box 7745,
  Doha, Qatar
Subsidiary Companies: Falcon Publishing, Bahrain; Gulf Public
  Relations, Bahrain
Principal Bankers: Bahrain Islamic Bank
Financial Information:

	1989/90 US$'000
Sales turnover	5,000
Authorised capital	265
Paid-up capital	265

Principal Shareholders: Abdulnabi Al Sho'ala; Mrs Rabab Al
  Mahroos
Date of Establishment: 1976
No of Employees: 50

GULF MOTOR AGENCY CO WLL

PO Box 1973, Salmabad
Tel: 686791
Telex: 9991 BAA BN
Telefax: 973 687049

Chairman: Makki Mohd Tammam
Senior Executives: C Rajan (Deputy Manager), Ghuloom
  Hussain (Supervisor Garage & Workshop), Jaffar Juma
  Fardan (Supervisor Spare Parts), Genevieve Q Manlanpaz
  (Executive Secretary)

PRINCIPAL ACTIVITIES: Sales and service of cars, sale of
  motor oil and auto spare parts
Principal Agencies: Hyundai Motor Co, Coma Oils Ltd, Hankook
  Tire Mnfg Co
Subsidiary Companies: Salmabad Car Exhibition, PO Box 5009,
  Salmabad, Bahrain
Principal Bankers: Bank of Bahrain & Kuwait

Principal Shareholders: Makki Mohd Tammam, Ahmed Buallay
Date of Establishment: 1983
No of Employees: 53

GULF OIL MIDDLE EAST TRADING CO

PO Box 113, Manama
Tel: 254356
Cable: Gometco
Telex: 8512 Gomet BN

Senior Executives: Regional Manager - International Lubricant
  Sales & Business Development

PRINCIPAL ACTIVITIES: Production and distribution of oil
  products
Branch Offices: Tokyo, Singapore, London
Parent Company: Gotco NV
Principal Bankers: Bank of America

Date of Establishment: November 1984
No of Employees: 150

GULF PACKING COMPANY

PO Box 5035, Umm-Al-Hassam Avenue, Umm-Al-Hassam,
  Bahrain
Tel: 722412 (Office), 730722 (Warehouse) 722408, 722409 (Head
  Office)
Cable: Gulfpack
Telex: 8857 GPC BN
Telefax: 721709

Chairman: Hussain Abdullah Mohammed Khalfan (Managing
  Director)
Directors: Idris Jowhar, Ismail Jowhar
Senior Executives: Mohamed Hasan Al-Bakali (Administrative
  Manager), A M Khalfe (Regional Manager), Joaquim F Nunes
  (Sales Representative), Mahmood Abbas Ghougle (Export
  Sales Manager)

PRINCIPAL ACTIVITIES: Packing; air and sea freight
  forwarders; removals service; customs clearance;
  warehousing
Principal Agencies: Delcher Intercontinental, USA; Allied Van
  Lines International Corp, USA; Ocean Air, USA; Marsh Stenail
  Machine Co, UK; Livingston Internation Freight, UK
Branch Offices: Gulf Packing Services; Shaikh Abdulla Road,
  Manama; and Gulf Packing Co, 1703, Sitra Road, Sitra,
  Bahrain
Principal Bankers: Citibank; Standard Chartered Bank
Financial Information:

	1990 BD'000
Sales turnover	9,500

Date of Establishment: 1958
No of Employees: 55

GULF PETROCHEMICAL INDUSTRIES CO BSC

PO Box 26730, Manama
Tel: 731777
Cable: PETROKEMIA
Telex: 9897 GPIC BN
Telefax: 731047

Chairman: Dr Tawfeeq Abdulrahman Almoayed
Directors: Abdullatif Al Haddad (Vice Chairman), Hassan Ali
  Falah, Awad Alkhaldi, Nassir Ahmed Al Sayyari (Managing
  Director), Nasser Bader Al Tukhaim, Hamed Abdul Rahman Al
  Mufada, Khalid Ashoor, Zalool Al Rabih
Senior Executives: Mustafa Al Sayed (General Manager), Khalil
  Ebrahim Al Obaidat (General Manager Technical Division),
  Ugo Fiorentino (Plant Manager), Abdulrahman Jawahery
  (Operations Manager), Yousif Abdulla Yousif (Maintenance
  Manager), Luigi Mazzasra (Technical Services Manager),
  Mohamed A Taqi (Administration Manager), Alexander P
  Klemen (Finance Manager), Yousif Fakhroo (Marketing
  Manager), Fawzi Ahmed Al Jaber (Public Relations Manager)

PRINCIPAL ACTIVITIES: Methanol and ammonia production
Principal Bankers: National Bank of Bahrain, Bahrain; Al-Ahli
  Commercial Bank, Bahrain; Gulf International Bank, Bahrain

Financial Information:

	1989
	BD'000
Sales turnover	45,000
Profits	4,000
Authorised capital	60,000
Paid-up capital	60,000
Total assets	160,000

Principal Shareholders: State of Bahrain, Petrochemical Industries Co. (Kuwait); Saudi Basic Industries Corporation (Saudi Arabia)
Date of Establishment: 1979
No of Employees: 350

GULF PLASTIC INDUSTRIES

PO Box 894, Manama
Tel: 243366,727877
Cable: Gulfplas
Telex: 8405 Gpi BN
Telefax: 728987

Chairman: Ahmad Abdulrahman Zayani (Proprietor)
Directors: Riyadh Zayani (General Manager)

PRINCIPAL ACTIVITIES: Manufacturers of UPVC and polyethylene pipes (pressure, irrigation, soil, waste, sewer, telephone, cable duct and conduits)
Principal Agencies: Key Terrain Systems, Durapipe PVC, Redi Spa
Branch Offices: Plastic Products Est, PO Box 3148, Alkhobar 31952, Saudi Arabia, Tel 8985097, 8980244, Telex 872125 PPE SJ
Subsidiary Companies: Plastic Products Est, PO Box 3148, Alkhobar, Saudi Arabia
Principal Bankers: Banque Paribas; British Bank of the Middle East

Date of Establishment: 1970
No of Employees: 200

GULF RIYAD BANK EC

Manama Centre, PO Box 20220, Manama
Tel: 232030
Telex: 9088 Creryd BN
Telefax: 250102

Chairman: Ibrahim Shams
Directors: Jean Deflassieux (Deputy Chairman), Talal Al Qudaibi, Abdul Rehman Al Amoudi, Bernard Thiolon, Bernard Jaquet (Alternate Director)
Senior Executives: Jean-Yves Le Paulmier (General Manager)

PRINCIPAL ACTIVITIES: Offshore banking unit engaged in interbank transactions, syndications, short and medium term financing, foreign exchange, marketable securities and letters of credit
Parent Company: Riyad Bank, Riyadh (60%); Credit Lyonnais, Paris (40%)
Principal Bankers: Riyad Bank, Riyadh; Credit Lyonnais, New York
Financial Information:

	1989	1990
	US$'000	US$'000
Sales turnover	57,831	44,068
Profits	-	592
Authorised capital	50,000	50,000
Paid-up capital	50,000	50,000
Total assets	743,190	432,940

Principal Shareholders: Riyad Bank, Riyadh, Saudi Arabia (60%); Credit Lyonnais, 75002 Paris, France (40%)
Date of Establishment: 8 March 1978
No of Employees: 21

GULF SERVICES COMPANY WLL

PO Box 405, Manama
Tel: 729739, 729811
Cable: Radar Bahrain
Telex: 8277 Awalco BN
Telefax: 243854

Owners: Shaheen S Shaheen, Mohammed Mattar
Directors: Khalid Mattar (Managing Director)

PRINCIPAL ACTIVITIES: Sale installation and maintenance of electrical distribution, fire protection, commercial catering and laundry equipment
Principal Agencies: Lucy, Dale, Brush Fusegear, Tann-synchronome, Wandsworth
Principal Bankers: British Bank of the Middle East

Date of Establishment: 1954
No of Employees: 24

GULF TRADERS

PO Box 941, 32 Sh Hamad Road, 303 Manama
Tel: 254594, 245577, 263963
Cable: Baseltrade
Telex: 8700 Aryan BN
Telefax: 242445

Chairman: H M Aryan (Proprietor)
Senior Executives: Basel H Aryan (Executive Manager), K Salim Pillay (Manager), Hanif Rowther (Sales Manager)

PRINCIPAL ACTIVITIES: General trading, import-export, manufacturers' representation; trade consultants, organisers, stage, TV theatre equipment, seatings and lighting, real estate dealing in property, house, lease rent, sales and purchases, and sponsorship
Principal Agencies: ASEA, Sweden; ASEA KABEL, Sweden; Jarankonst, Sweden; Electro-Invest, Sweden; Slingsby, UK; Henry Mason, UK; Lepper-Dominit, W Germany; Peglers, UK; Chemische Fabrik Grunau, W Germany, Parker Hannifen (UK) Ltd, UK, Basco, UK; CPC, Italy; Stuart Edgar Ltd, UK; Boet, UK
Branch Offices: Rentacolour, tel 713843; Handy Hardwares, tel 254594, Arya Contractors, tel 253017; Intergulf Media Services, tel 254594
Subsidiary Companies: Universal Electro Engineering Co, Tel 693726; Technical Protection Engineering, Tel 693725
Principal Bankers: British Bank of the Middle East; Bank of Bahrain & Kuwait

Date of Establishment: 1973

GULF TRADING & EXPORT AGENCY

PO Box 1063, Manama
Tel: 250023, 253025
Telex: 8233 BN

PRINCIPAL ACTIVITIES: Supply of building materials and construction equipment, glass products, steel and aluminium products, furniture, fire extinguishers, plywood, tiles, lifts etc
Principal Agencies: Hitachi; Twyfords; Emco; Shell; Eternit; Emerald; Ostara Fliesen; Eraflex; Grohe; Wash Perle, etc

HABIB BANK LIMITED

PO Box 566, Regional Office Manama Centre, Manama
Tel: 271402, 273083, 271811
Cable: HABIBANK
Telex: 9448 HBLREG BN
Telefax: 276685

President: Maqbool A Soomro
Directors: Masood Akhtar, Fasihiddin Khan, Himayat ALi Khan, Fazal Karim Khilji, Nizam A Shah, Tahir Ai Tayebi
Senior Executives: Sh Muhammed Ahmed (EVP & General Manager)

PRINCIPAL ACTIVITIES: Commercial and offshore banking

Branch Offices: Bahrain; Abu Dhabi; Dubai; Sharjah; Ras Al
Khaimah; Al Ain; Ajman; Umm Al Qaiwan; Oman; Lebanon

Parent Company: Habib Bank Limited, Head Office, Habib Bank
Plaza, Karachi (Pakistan)

Subsidiary Companies: Habib Finance International Ltd, Hong
Kong; Habib Finance (Australia) Ltd, Sydney

HAJI HASSAN GROUP WLL

PO Box 530, Manama
Tel: 232260
Cable: Abuali
Telex: 8366 Asphlt BN
Telefax: 254813

Chairman: Haji Hassan Bin Ali Al-Aali

Directors: Ebrahim Ali Al-Aali, Ahmed Ali Al-Aali, Adel Hassan
Al-Aali, Khalid Hassan Al-Aali

PRINCIPAL ACTIVITIES: Crushing plants, asphalt plants,
calcium silicate bricks and block factory, all types and size of
concrete blocks, lintel blocks and interlocking tiles, housing
projects, road contracts, ready mixed concrete, washed
aggregate and sand suppliers, building materials, and building
chemicals, hire of plant, machinery and equipment, real estate
development, dredging and reclamation, reinforcing bar and
welded mesh stock holders, manufacturers of precast
concrete components, developing and renting of offices,
show rooms and residential accommodation

Principal Agencies: Ricambi Trattori, Italy; Action One, Italy;
Technoil, Italy; Metraco, Italy; CGR Ghanassi, Italy;
Technocar, Italy; ASBO seals, Italy; Fichtel & Sachs,
Germany; Tip Top Int, Germany; Meyle Products, Germany;
Fina Chemicals, UK; China National Import & Export Corp,
China; RHP Bearings, Japan; NTN Bearings, Japan; Dai Kin
CLutch, Japan, Izumi Int, Japan

Parent Company: Haji Hassan Al-Aali Trading and Contracting
Co WLL

Subsidiary Companies: Bahrain Asphalt Est; Bahrain Blocks;
Bahrain Calcium Silicate Bricks and Block Factory; Haji Hasan
Ready Mix Div; Haji Hasan Construction Div; Haji Hasan
Reinforcements; Bahrain Precast Concrete Co (JV); Gulf
Concrete Services (JV); Isola Building Chemicals

Principal Bankers: Standard Chartered Bank; British Bank of
the Middle East; National Bank of Bahrain; Bank of Bahrain &
Kuwait; Al-Ahli Commercial Bank

Financial Information:

	1989
	BD'000
Authorised capital	4,350
Paid-up capital	4,350

Principal Shareholders: Private Limited Company
Date of Establishment: 1954
No of Employees: About 1,000

HALLIBURTON LTD BAHRAIN

Regional Office, PO Box 515, Manama
Tel: 258866
Cable: Halliburt Bahrain
Telex: 8231 Halmeb BN

PRINCIPAL ACTIVITIES: Oil services, marine services, supply of
equipment to the oil industry, warehousing, oil well servicing

Branch Offices: In the Middle East; Abu Dhabi; Bahrain; Dubai;
Qatar; Saudi Arabia; Kuwait; Oman; India; Pakistan

Associated Companies: Brown & Root; Jackson Marine; Otis;
Imco Services, Taylor Diving Service

Principal Bankers: Citibank

Principal Shareholders: Wholly owned subsidiary of Halliburton
Services, Oklahoma, USA

HANIL BANK (BAHRAIN BRANCH)

PO Box 1151, Manama
Tel: 243503, 256624 FX
Cable: Bankhanil Bahrain
Telex: 7048 Hanil BN
Telefax: 271812

Senior Executives: Doo Hong Lee (Senior General Manager for
the Middle East), Yeo Won Yoon (Deputy General Manager)

PRINCIPAL ACTIVITIES: Offshore banking unit
Parent Company: Head office in Seoul, Korea

Date of Establishment: October 1983
No of Employees: 9

HASAN & HABIB S/O MAHMOOD

See MAHMOOD, HASAN & HABIB S/O,

HASAN MANSOURI

See MANSOURI, HASAN,

HASHIM AL ALAWI CONTRACTING

See AL ALAWI, HASHIM, CONTRACTING

HASSAN HAIDER DARWISH

See DARWISH, HASSAN HAIDER,

HEMPEL'S MARINE PAINTS (BAHRAIN) WLL

PO Box 997, Mina Sulman Industrial Area, Bahrain
Tel: 728668
Cable: Hempaturi
Telex: 8258 Hempel BN

Chairman: Sheikh Khalid Ahmed Al-Khalifa

Directors: Sheikh Ali bin Khalifa Alkhalifa, Sadiq Mohammed Al
Baharna, Abdul Rahman Ali Alwazzan, Sheikh Nasser Sabah
Al-Ahmed Al-Sabah, Saud Abdulaziz Al-Rashed, Borge
Hansen, Jorn Lillelund

PRINCIPAL ACTIVITIES: Manufacture of paints for marine,
industrial and domestic use

Principal Agencies: Elcometer Instruments Ltd, UK; GRACO
France SA, France; Airblast, Holland; Alentec, UK

Principal Bankers: Algemene Bank Nederland; Bank of Bahrain
and Kuwait; British Bank of the Middle East

Principal Shareholders: Chairman and Directors as described
Date of Establishment: 1979
No of Employees: 35

HEPWORTH BUILDING PRODUCTS INTERNATIONAL

Almoayyed Bldg (North), 3rd Floor, PO Box 143, Manama
Tel: 250518
Telex: 8403 Hepbah BN
Telefax: 254130

Senior Executives: A D McKeown (Area Manager)

PRINCIPAL ACTIVITIES: Sales and service
Parent Company: Hepworth Iron Company Limited, UK
Principal Bankers: Grindlays Bank Limited

Date of Establishment: 1977

HILTON INTERNATIONAL BAHRAIN

PO Box 1090, Manama
Tel: 535000
Cable: Hiltels Bahrain
Telex: 8288 Hilton BN
Telefax: 533097

Senior Executives: Emmanuel Matsakis (General Manager)

PRINCIPAL ACTIVITIES: Hotel management and operation
Parent Company: Hilton International

Principal Bankers: Bank of Bahrain and Kuwait

Principal Shareholders: Ladbroke
No of Employees: 240

HOLIDAY INN BAHRAIN
PO Box 5831, Diplomatic Area, Manama
Tel: 531122
Telex: 9000 Holinn Bn

PRINCIPAL ACTIVITIES: Hotel business

HOTEL DELMON
PO Box 2226, Government Road, Manama
Tel: 234000/8
Cable: Delmonotel
Telex: 8224 Delhtl BN
Telefax: 246236

Chairman: Khalid R Zayani
Directors: Hamid R Zayani (Managing Director)
Senior Executives: Ali Ewais (General Manager)

PRINCIPAL ACTIVITIES: Hotel business
Parent Company: Al Zayani Investments Group
Principal Bankers: British Bank of the Middle East

Principal Shareholders: Chairman and director as described
Date of Establishment: 1968
No of Employees: 170

HYUNDAI ENGINEERING & CONSTRUCTION CO LTD
PO Box 22266, Muharraq
Tel: 671011/5
Cable: Hyundaico
Telex: 8551; 8753; 8618 Hydbah BN

PRINCIPAL ACTIVITIES: Engineering and construction for industrial plants, harbour and dredging, civil, electrical, mechanical, marine and offshore and architectural works
Branch Offices: Middle East Branches: Al Khobar, Riyadh, Jeddah, Abu Dhabi, Kuwait, Sana'a, Bahrain, Doha, Baghdad, Jordan, Benghazi, Tripoli
Parent Company: Hyundai Engineering & Construction Co Ltd (Head Office: 140-2, Kye-Dong, Chongro-Ku, Seoul, Korea)
Principal Bankers: National Bank of Bahrain; Grindlays Bank, Bahrain; Bank of America, Bahrain; Continental Bank, Bahrain; Gulf International Bank, Bahrain; Bank of Tokyo, Bahrain

Principal Shareholders: Asan Foundation; Ju Yung Chung, Mong Hun Chung, Mong Ke Chung

INDUSTRIAL BANK OF JAPAN LTD
PO Box 5759, Manama
Tel: 273740, 273749
Telex: 9775 IBJBAH BN
Telefax: 276128

Senior Executives: Hiroo Harada (Chief Representative), Osamu Takiguchi (Representative)

PRINCIPAL ACTIVITIES: Representative office

Date of Establishment: March 1982

INTERMARKETS BAHRAIN
PO Box 5047, Manama
Tel: 250760
Cable: Intmarkets Bahrain
Telex: 8400 Market BN
Telefax: 263295

Chairman: Erwin Guerrovich
Directors: Raymond Hanna, Ramzi Raad, Khalil Bitar

PRINCIPAL ACTIVITIES: Advertising and public relations
Principal Agencies: Clients: Procter & Gamble, British Airways, White Westinghouse, Reckitt & Coleman, Citizen, Braun,

Kraft, Nissan, RJ Reynolds, Borden, Lanvin, Ellen Betrix, Indian Tea Board, IBM
Branch Offices: Kuwait: PO Box 20604; UAE: PO Box 156/7434; Egypt: 42 Abdel Moniem Riad St, Dokki, Cairo; Saudi Arabia: PO Box 4635, Jeddah; Jordan: PO Box 926976, Amman; Lebanon: PO Box 55434, Sin el Fil, Beirut; Yemen AR: PO Box 1372, Sana'a; UK: The Kiln House, 210 New Kings Road, London SW6
Parent Company: Intermarkets SAL, PO Box 110963, Beirut, Lebanon, Tel 482812/4, Telex 40477 Market LE
Subsidiary Companies: Burson Marsteller/Intermarkets
Principal Bankers: National Bank of Bahrain; Banque Nationale de Paris Intercontinentale; Banque Audi SAL

Principal Shareholders: Intermarkets SAL (all shareholding held by executives of the organisation)
Date of Establishment: 1971
No of Employees: 184

INTERNATIONAL AGENCIES CO LTD
PO Box 584, Manama
Tel: 254275
Cable: Intercol
Telex: 8273 Intcol BN; 8661; 8517; Intcol BN

Directors: Sadiq M Albaharna, Abdulrahman Ali Alwazzan

PRINCIPAL ACTIVITIES: Shipping, travel, insurance, trading, catering, marine operations, construction, manufacturers & distributors, clearing and forwarding, advertising, management & sponsorship consultants
Principal Agencies: Representatives from Australia, United Kingdom, New Zealand, Switzerland, France, Holland, Denmark, USA, Singapore, Japan, Taiwan
Subsidiary/Associated Companies: Bahrain Marine Supply Co; Bahrain Catering & Supply Co; International Marine Services Ltd; International Travel Bureau; New India Assurance Co Ltd; Hempel's Marine Paints (Bahrain) WLL; Bahrain Technical & Trading Co; New Zealand Meat & Food Corp; Consolidated Contractors Co (Bahrain) WLL
Principal Bankers: The Arab Bank Ltd; Bank of Bahrain and Kuwait; National Bank of Bahrain

Date of Establishment: 1957

INTERNATIONAL MARINE SERVICES LTD
PO Box 584, Mina Sulman Industrial Area, Manama
Tel: 254275, 727089, 727096
Cable: Intercol
Telex: 8273; 8517 BN

Directors: Sadiq M Albaharna, Abdulrahman Ali Alwazzan, Dr Nazar Albaharna, Capt T Kose, Capt Y Tamaka, Guy Baldwin, Capt S Ayoama

PRINCIPAL ACTIVITIES: Chartering, marine services, mechanical engineering and marine works

INTERNATIONAL TURNKEY SYSTEMS
PO Box 1344, Manama
Tel: 273280
Telex: 9752 ITS BN
Telefax: 273281

Chairman: Abdul Jalil Al Gharabally
Directors: Abdul Jalil Al Gharabally, Faisal Al Khatrash, Samir Al Nafisi, Mohammed Al Khudairy
Senior Executives: Saad Al Barrak (General Manager), Khalifa Al Soulah (Asst General Manager), Ebrahim Ali (Country Manager Bahrain), Mustafa Shehata (Country Manager UAE)

PRINCIPAL ACTIVITIES: Engaged in marketing, support, installation and maintenance of turnkey computer solutions (hardware and software), computer consultancy services, etc
Principal Agencies: Tandem Computers Inc, USA; Sequent Computer Systems Inc, USA
Parent Company: Head office in Kuwait
Principal Bankers: Bahrain Islamic Bank, Bahrain

INVESTCORP BANK EC

Investcorp House, PO Box 5340, Manama
Tel: 532000 (General), 531011 (Dealing Room)
Telex: 9664 INCORP BN, 8573 INCORP BN (Dealing Room)
Telefax: 530816

Chairman: H E Abdul Rahman Salem Al-Ateeqi
Directors: Ahmed Ali Kanoo (Vice Chairman), Nemir A Kirdar
(President and Chief Executive Officer), Omar Aggad,
Abdullah Taha Bakhsh, Mustafa Jassim Boodai, Hussain I Al-
Fardan, Faraj Ali Bin Hamoodah, Mohammed Y Jalal, Abdul
Aziz J Kanoo, Juma Al Majid, Ahmed Abdullah Al Mannai, Dr
Nasser Al Rashid, Abdul Rahman Ali Al-Turki, Mohammed
Abdullah Al-Zamil, Khalid Rashid Al Zayani
Management Committee: Nemir A Kirdar, Salman A Abbasi,
Yusef Abu Khadra, Cem N Cesmig, William Flanz, Robert V
Glaser, Elias N Hallack, Abdul Khalik Jallad, Michael L Merritt,
Oliver E Richardson, Paul W Soldatos, John A Thompson,
Savio W Tung, Philip Buscombe, Lee R Thomas, Linda A
Cates

PRINCIPAL ACTIVITIES: Investment banking; undertaking
international and regional investments on behalf of clients and
the firm in real estate, corporate investment, and portfolio
investment; providing traditional investment banking services
to regional clients and international clients in the region;
undertaking traditional treasury activities including FX, deposit
and securities trading
Subsidiary/Associated Companies: Representative Office:
Investcorp Bank EC, 65 Brook Street, London W1, UK;
Investcorp International Ltd, 65 Brook Street, London W1,
UK; Investcorp International Inc, 280 Park Ave, 37th Floor,
New York NY10017
Principal Bankers: Bankers Trust Co, Manufacturers Hanover
Trust Co, Deutsche Bank AG, Bank of Tokyo, Credit Suisse,
Midland Bank, Algemene Bank Nederland, Credit Lyonnais,
Banco Bilbao Vizcaya, National Bank of Bahrain, Westpac
Banking Corporation, National Commercial Bank
Financial Information:

	1989 US$'000	1990 US$'000
Operating income	77,763	99,250
Profits	51,782	66,308
Issued capital	100,000	100,000
Paid-up capital	100,000	100,000
Total net worth	194,597	243,217
Total assets	813,938	943,945

Principal Shareholders: Approximately 10,000 public
shareholders from Saudi Arabia, Kuwait, Bahrain, Qatar, the
United Arab Emirates and Oman
Date of Establishment: July 1982
No of Employees: 158

INVESTMENT & TRADING (GULF) ENTERPRISES

PO Box 773, Manama
Tel: 255734, 251194
Telex: 8313 BN

Chairman: Abdul Latif Eshag
Directors: Ebrahim Eshag (Managing Director)

PRINCIPAL ACTIVITIES: General trading and import; investment
finance, property developers and participation in joint
ventures
Subsidiary Companies: Joint-venture bank: Continental Bank
Ltd of Bahrain (together with the Continental Illinois National
Bank and Trust Company of Chicago), (17% stake in African
& Eastern (Near East) of Bahrain

ITOH, C, MIDDLE EAST EC

PO Box 992, Manama
Tel: 262270
Cable: Citoh Bahrain
Telex: 8275 CITOH BN

PRINCIPAL ACTIVITIES: Off-shore trading and related financing
(import and export of textiles, machinery, metals, foodstuff,
general merchandise, petroleum, gas, chemicals and mineral
ores and constructional engineering)
Principal Bankers: National Bank of Bahrain; Bank of Tokyo Ltd
(Bahrain)

Principal Shareholders: C Itoh & Co Ltd, Japan
Date of Establishment: Oct 25 1980

JACKSON MARINE SA

PO Box 26788, Manama
Tel: 730011
Cable: Jacmac
Telex: 8261 Jacmac BN

PRINCIPAL ACTIVITIES: Supply and tug boat operators
Branch Offices: Jackson Marine SA, PO Box 2537, Deira, Dubai

Date of Establishment: 1967

JALAL COSTAIN WLL

PO Box 5985, Manama
Tel: 712650
Cable: JACO
Telex: 9742 MJCONT BN
Telefax: 714181

Chairman: Mohammed Yousuf Jalal (Bahrain)
Directors: Jalal M Jalal (Managing Director/Bahrain), M Lee
(Bahrain), A J D Franklin (UK), J W H Lawson (UK), C C
Preece (Bahrain)
Senior Executives: C C Preece (General Manager), A C Hoslin
(Chief Quantity Surveyor), M R Youngs (Accountant/Company
Secretary)

PRINCIPAL ACTIVITIES: Civil engineering and construction
Principal Bankers: Standard Chartered Bank, Manama

Principal Shareholders: Mohammed Jalal & Sons Company Ltd
(Bahrain) (51%); Costain (Overseas) Ltd (49%)
Date of Establishment: May 1979
No of Employees: 180

JALAL, MOHAMMED, & SONS CO LTD
Jalal, Mohammed, Contracting

PO Box 113, Manama
Tel: 255544, 252606
Cable: Jalal Bahrain
Telex: 8791 Jalal BN; 8233 Majal BN
Telefax: 256246

Chairman: Mohammed Y Jalal
Directors: Jalal Mohd Jalal (Managing Director), Ahmed Mohd
Jalal, Sami Mohd Jalal, Fuad Mohd Jalal, P M F Melhuish
(Secretary to the Board)
Senior Executives: C C Preece (General Manager), A C Hoslin
(Commercial Manager), M R Youngs (Chief Accountant)

PRINCIPAL ACTIVITIES: Trading. Civil, mechanical and
electrical contracting. Distribution of motor cars, tyres and
tubes, auto spare parts, heavy machinery and equipment for
construction and for the oil industry. Building materials, office
and domestic furniture, office equipment, stationery,
sanitaryware and interior furnishings and fittings. Industrial
catering, travel agency, computers
Principal Agencies: Chrysler, UK; Jaguar Cars Ltd, UK; Citroen,
France; Alfa Romeo, Italy; Peugeot, France; Suzuki, Japan;
Tideland Signal Corp; Ingersoll Rand International; Subaru,
Japan; IBM; Schindler; Rothmans of Pall Mall
Branch Offices: Bahrain, UAE, Kuwait, Jordan, USA, Australia,
UK
Principal Bankers: Standard Chartered Bank, Bahrain; National
Bank of Bahrain; Al-Ahli Commercial Bank, Bahrain

Principal Shareholders: Privately Owned Family Business
Date of Establishment: 1947
No of Employees: Approx. 1,500

JASHANMAL & SONS WLL

PO Box 16, Manama
Tel: 251431
Cable: Jashanmal
Telex: 8216 Jashan BN
Telefax: (0973) 234392

Chairman: Atma Jashanmal
Directors: Bharat Jashanmal, Hiro Jashanmal, Mohan Jashanmal, Tony Jashanmal
Senior Executives: Gangu Batra (Group Managing Director), T B K Menon (Bahrain General Manager)

PRINCIPAL ACTIVITIES: Retailers, wholesalers and agents, general merchants for household goods, electrical equipment, leisure goods, clothing, shoes and leather goods, toiletries, and photographical equipment and general consumer goods
Principal Agencies: Hoover Ltd, England; Yashica Co Ltd, Japan and Hong Kong; Jaeger Sales Ltd, England; A T Cross, USA; Clarks Overseas Shoes Ltd, England; Max Factor & Co, England; Christofle, France; Alladdin, UK and USA
Branch Offices: Associates: Kuwait: PO Box 5138; Dubai: PO Box 1545; Abu Dhabi: PO Box 316
Associated Companies: Jashanmal National Co (UAE), PO Box 1545, Dubai; Emirates Markets & Stores (Pvt) Ltd, PO Box 8060, Dubai; Jashanmal National Co (UAE), PO Box 316, Abu Dhabi; Jashanmal & Partners Ltd, Kuwait; Overseas Courier Service (BAH) WLL, PO Box 16, Bahrain; Fragrances & Beauty Inc, PO Box 16, Bahrain
Principal Bankers: National Bank of Bahrain

JASSIM TRADING & AGROSERVE

PO Box 1059, Manama
Tel: 730710, 731969
Cable: Seyagha
Telex: 9526 SEYAGH BN
Telefax: 730236

Chairman: Jassim Mohamed Al Sayegh
Directors: Nabeel Jassim Al Sayegh
Senior Executives: K Kumar (Sales Manager), H Jassim Saigh (Garden Centre Manager)

PRINCIPAL ACTIVITIES: Trading and irrigation work; sale and distribution agricultural equipment, sale of household and industrial chemicals, fire extinguishers, safety items, landscaping contractors
Principal Agencies: Gebruder Holder, West Germany; L & K Co, UK; Zinge, Denmark; Wintrich, Germany; Amoa, UK; Kaaz, Japan; Fisons, UK; Hardie Irrigation
Branch Offices: Jassim Garden Centre; Delmon Chemicals
Subsidiary Companies: Jassim Fire & Safety Systems WLL, PO Box 1059, Manama
Principal Bankers: Grindlays Bank Ltd; Bank of Bahrain & Kuwait
Financial Information:

	1989 US$'000
Sales turnover	1,000
Profits	250
Authorised capital	1,000
Paid-up capital	500
Total assets	2,000

Date of Establishment: 1974
No of Employees: 50

JAWAD COLD STORE

PO Box 430, Manama
Tel: 253032
Cable: Jawad
Telex: 8347 Jawad BN
Telefax: 273866

Chairman: Ali Hassan Jawad
Directors: Faisal Hassan Jawad (Managing Director), Fatima Hassan Jawad, Sabah Hassan Jawad

Senior Executives: Abbas Abdulla Dehdari (General Manager), Shailendra Malhotra (Financial Controller)
PRINCIPAL ACTIVITIES: Cold storage, import and distribution of foodstuffs, warehousing, operation of supermarkets and bakeries
Principal Agencies: General Foods, Borden, New Zealand Dairy Board, Whitworths, Nestle (Libby's), Findus, American Poultry Int'l
Parent Company: Hassan Mohamed Jawad & Sons Co WLL
Associated Companies: Dairy Queen; Jawad Bakery; Al Safina Restaurant; British Home Stores (BhS) Franchise Bahrain
Principal Bankers: National Bank of Bahrain
Financial Information:

	1989/90 US$'000
Sales turnover	20,000
Authorised capital	5,000
Paid-up capital	5,000
Total assets	10,000

No of Employees: 250

JOTUN MARINE & INDUSTRIAL PAINTS

PO Box 363, Manama
Tel: 210882, 211155
Cable: Aka Trade
Telex: 8267 BN
Telefax: 210894

Chairman: Abdul Gaffar
Directors: Knut Hanssen (Managing Director)
Senior Executives: Anand Karmandi (Area Manager), P Richardson (Sales Manager), P Richardson (Sales Manager), Tuan Cheng Ewe (Marketing Manager), J Shaw (Export Manager), U Mistry (Production Manager), R Sundaram (Financial Controller), A Skjonberg (Technical Manager), Z Hegazi (Personnel Manager)

PRINCIPAL ACTIVITIES: Production and supply of marine, industrial paints and decorative paints
Principal Agencies: A K Almoayyed, Bahrain
Branch Offices: Regional Office: United Arab Emirates (PO Box 3671, Dubai)
Parent Company: Jotun Norway
Subsidiary Companies: Jotun Bahrain, Jotun Saudi, Jotun Oman, Jotun Doha, Jotun Kuwait
Principal Bankers: Grindlays Bank Bahrain

Principal Shareholders: Jotun Protective Coatings (Norway)
No of Employees: 140

JUMA ABD MOHAMED & SONS

PO Box 727, Manama
Tel: 252151
Cable: Welder
Telex: 8413 BN

Directors: Juma Abd Mohamed

PRINCIPAL ACTIVITIES: Construction and maintenance contractors, import, distributors, sale and hire of heavy machinery, construction and earth-moving equipment; manufacturers' representatives and agents for industrial machinery, earth-moving plants, and welding accessories, transport contractors

KAIKSOW, SALMAN AHMED, & SONS

PO Box 20733, Government Avenue, Manama
Tel: 252227, 253735, 258384
Cable: Kaiksow Bahrain
Telex: 8553 Sakco BN

Chairman: Abdulla S Kaiksow (Managing Director)
Directors: Ahmed S Kaiksow, Sami S Kaiksow, Nabeel S Kaiksow, Najeeb S Kaiksow, Ali S Kaiksow

PRINCIPAL ACTIVITIES: General trade; civil and electromechanical contractors; hoteliers; distributors of air conditioning equipment electrical machinery, and building materials; travel agents and marketing of computers

Principal Agencies: Ames Crosta Babcock, UK; China National Light Industries Imp & Exp, China; Cosmos India Rubber Works, India; Foster Refrigerator UK; Hepworth Plastics, UK; Hawker Siddeley Electric Export UK; Kwikset Sales & Service, USA; Pye Industries Sales, Australia; Singer, USA; Staff KG, W Germany; Sitapur, India; Thyssen, W Germany; Teledyne Wisconsin Motor, USA; A O Smith Corp, Netherlands; Ward Brothers, UK; Kia Co, South Korea; Goulds Pumps, USA; Alno Moebelwerke, W Germany; Trilux Lenze, W Germany; Commodore Electronics, USA; Gromenco, USA; Mitsubishi Central Airconditioning

Subsidiary/Associated Companies: Tylos Hotel, PO Box 1086, Manama; Taram Travel; International Business Enterprises

Principal Bankers: British Bank of the Middle East; Grindlays Bank; Al Ahli Commercial Bank

Date of Establishment: 1938
No of Employees: 215

KANOO, YUSUF BIN AHMED, WLL

PO BOX 45, Manama
Tel: 254081
Cable: Kanoo Bahrain
Telex: 8215 Kanoo BN
Telefax: 246093

Chairman: Ahmed Ali Kanoo

Directors: Mohamed Jassim Kanoo (Deputy Chairman), Abdulla Ali Kanoo (Chief Executive Officer & Chairman Y B A Kanoo Saudi Arabia), Mubarak Jassim Kanoo (Deputy Chief Executive Officer & Chairman Y B A Kanoo Bahrain), Abdul Rehman Jassim Kanoo (Deputy Chairman Y B A Kanoo Bahrain), Abdul Aziz Jassim Kanoo (Deputy Chief Executive Officer & Deputy Chairman Y B A Kanoo Saudi Arabia), Hamed Ali Kanoo (Chairman The Kanoo Group UAE & Oman)

Senior Executives: Khalid Mohamed Kanoo (Managing Director Saudi Arabia), Yusuf Ahmed Kanoo (Managing Director UAE & Oman), Fawzi Ahmed Kanoo (Managing Director Bahrain), Ali Abdul Aziz Kanoo (Deputy Managing Director Saudi Arabia), Saud Abdul Aziz Kanoo (Managing Director Property & Deputy Managing Director Bahrain)

PRINCIPAL ACTIVITIES: Manufacturer's representatives in construction and mechanical equipment, shipping agents, travel agents and insurance agents, wholesale holidays, property developers, computer bureau operators, local sponsorship, joint venture operators, aircraft handling, chemical products suppliers, oilfied supplies & services and agriculture consultants and services

Principal Agencies: Shipping: United Arab Shipping Co, A P Moller, Nedlloyd, Hoegh-Ugland, Concordia Line, Mitsui Osk Line, Blue Star Line; Air Travel: British Airways, Qantas, MEA, AirIndia, KLM, Swiss Air, Singapore Airlines, PIA; General Trading: BASF, ESSO, Serck, Baroid, Associated Octel, British American Tobacco; Machinery: Grove, Hyster, Massey-Ferguson, Elequip, Benford, GEC, Perkins Engines, Cummins Engines, Sumitomo Metal Industries, Consolidated Pneumatic, Thyseen; Insurance: Norwich Winterthur

Branch Offices: The Kanoo Group: Dubai: PO Box 290; Abu Dhabi: PO Box 245; Ras Al Khaimah: PO Box 151; Jebel Dhanna: PO Box 245; Al Ain: PO Box 1779; Oman: PO Box 1310 Muscat; Saudi Arabia: Yusuf Bin Ahmed Kanoo, PO Box 37, Dammam; Kanoo Centre, Alkhobar; PO Box 711, Ras Tanura; PO Box 753, Riyadh; PO Box 812, Jeddah; PO Box 88, Yanbu

Joint Ventures: Bahrain Airport Services; Foster Wheeler Saudi Arabia Co Ltd; Greyhound Services (Saudi Arabia) Ltd; Saudi Enterprise and Port Services Co; International Paint Saudi Arabia Ltd; Otis Saudi Ltd; Dar Al Bahrain WLL; Charilaos Apostolides (Bahrain) WLL; Bahrain Ship Repair and Engineering Co BSC; Aeradio Technical Services WLL; Kanoo

Serck Services WLL; International Paint (Gulf) Ltd; Dubai Express; Baroid Saudi Arabia Ltd; Kanoo Terminal Services Ltd; King Wilkingson Saudi Arabia Ltd; Norwich Winterthur Insurance (SA) EC; Shipping and Marine Services Co Ltd; Watson Gray (Saudi Arabia) Ltd; Saudi Computer Information and Maintenance Co; Decca Survey Saudi Arabia Ltd; Saudi Arabian Lube Additives Co Ltd; Elbar Turbine Saudi Arabia Ltd; Saudi United Arab Shipping Agencies Co; Johnson Controls Saudi Arabia Ltd; Watson Gray (UAE); Smit Tak (UAE)

Principal Shareholders: Family company
Date of Establishment: 1890

KAZEROONI CONTRACTING & DESIGN CENTRE

PO Box 5385, Manama
Tel: 254334, 259111
Cable: Kazcontrac
Telex: 9295 Kazcon BN

Directors: Abdul Rahman Kazerooni, Mahmood Kazerooni

PRINCIPAL ACTIVITIES: Building contractors, architects, interior designers; civil engineering consultants
Subsidiary Companies: Ramsis Cont Maintenance Service Co (Mechanical engineering and safety equipment)
Principal Bankers: Standard Chartered Bank; National Bank of Bahrain

No of Employees: 400

KHALAIFAT ESTABLISHMENT

PO Box 5111, Manama
Tel: 250529
Cable: Leena
Telex: 8359 BN
Telefax: 730261

Chairman: Mohamed A S Khalaifat

PRINCIPAL ACTIVITIES: Distributors of electrical appliances, building materials, flooring and ceiling products, air-conditioning equipment, furnishing and design
Principal Agencies: Saporiti, Italy; De Sede, Switzerland; Artifort, Holland; Hotpoint, USA; Flintkote, USA; Dunlop Semtex Ltd, UK; Siemens, W Germany; Bradford White Corp, USA; Robert Bosch, W Germany; Vestfrost, Denmark; Caloric Corp, USA; Uniflow Manufacturing, USA; Central Airconditioning Co, Bangkok; Jim Walter Sales, USA; Westpoint, Singapore
Subsidiary Companies: Touchwood, Bahrain
Principal Bankers: Bank of Bahrain and Kuwait; Al Ahli Commercial Bank; Standard Chartered Bank

Date of Establishment: 1967
No of Employees: 50

KHATIB & ALAMI
Consolidated Engineering Co

PO Box 5083, Manama
Tel: 742131
Telex: 8783
Telefax: 973-742120

President: Prof Mounir El Khatib
Directors: Dr Zuheir Y Alami (Senior Partner)
Senior Executives: Othman Ayaso (Resident Manager Bahrain)

PRINCIPAL ACTIVITIES: Consulting engineers, architects, planners, and designers
Branch Offices: Saudi Arabia (Jeddah, Riyadh, Alkhobar), UAE (Abu Dhabi, Dubai, Sharjah), Oman (Ruwi)
Parent Company: Head office in Beirut
Principal Bankers: Arab Bank Ltd

KHONJI, ABDULRAHMAN & OSMAN,

PO Box 101, Manama
Tel: 253826, 253571

Directors: Abdulrahman Khonji, Osman Khonji

PRINCIPAL ACTIVITIES: Dealers representing household and office furniture, furnishing fabrics, ceramic tiles, television sets, refrigerators, air conditioners, cookers, washing-machines, freezers, dish-washers, lighting fixtures, carpets
Principal Agencies: Frigidaire, Admiral, Tyler (Prestcold), Schreiber

KOBELCO MIDDLE EAST EC

PO Box 2309, Manama
Tel: 531717, 530661, 530660, 530662
Fax: 530629
Telex: 7303 Kobelc BN

Chairman: Y Tanno (Managing Director)
Directors: T Okugawa, T Negami, T Watanabe
Senior Executives: Takafumi Okugawa (General Manager), Yukio Doi (Deputy General Manager)

PRINCIPAL ACTIVITIES: Sales, engineering, construction, trading, management and financing
Parent Company: Kobe Steel Ltd, Tokyo, Japan
Principal Bankers: Citibank, Bahrain

Principal Shareholders: Kobe Steel Ltd, Tokyo, Japan
Date of Establishment: 1984

KONTRA

PO Box 1618, Government Avenue, Manama
Tel: 255729
Cable: Kontra
Telex: 8317 Kontra BN
Telefax: 210074

Chairman: Mohammad Y Jalal
Directors: Sami M Jalal
Senior Executives: David Murthick (General Manager)

PRINCIPAL ACTIVITIES: Supply of household goods and furnishings, carpets, interior designers and partitions contractors, joinery works, GRG tiles
Principal Agencies: Armstrong, Intalite, 3M
Parent Company: Mohammad Jalal & Sons
Financial Information:

	1990
	BD'000
Sales turnover	4,000

No of Employees: 230

KOOHEJI, A J M, & SONS

PO Box 74, Manama
Tel: 403304
Cable: KOOHEJYAN
Telex: 8386 BN KOHEJI
Telefax: 403800

President: Abdul Hameed Kooheji
Directors: Abdulla Kooheji (Vice President), Mahmood Kooheji (Vice President), Jamal Kooheji (Director), Mohammed Kooheji (Director)
Senior Executives: N J Bhatia (General Manager), N O Rajan (Finance Manager)

PRINCIPAL ACTIVITIES: Distributors and general merchants of: home appliances, tyres, fork lifts, boats and out board motors, diesel engines, dealers in furniture, carpets and curtains
Principal Agencies: Admiral International, USA; Goldstar Co, Korea; Bridgestone, Japan; Yamaha Motor, Japan; Yanmar Diesel Engine; Fairline Boats, UK; Cougar Boats, USA/UK; Mitsubishi Heavy Industries, Japan
Subsidiary Companies: Kooheji Marine Centre, PO Box 74, Bahrain, Tel 330303; Al Ahliya Chemical Co, PO Box 74, Bahrain, Tel 270027; Delmon Furniture Factory, PO Box 74, Bahrain, Tel 700999; Abdullah Trading, PO Box 26470,

Bahrain, Tel 40377; Al Ahlia Investment Co, PO Box 26470, Bahrain
Principal Bankers: The British Bank of the Middle East; Bahrain Islamic Bank; Al Ahli Commercial Bank

Date of Establishment: 1900
No of Employees: 100

KOREA DEVELOPMENT BANK (THE)

PO Box 5970, Manama
Tel: 273256/7
Telex: 9751 KDB BN
Telefax: 273257

PRINCIPAL ACTIVITIES: Representative office

Date of Establishment: September 1981

KOREA EXCHANGE BANK

PO Box 5767, Manama
Tel: 258282, 259333, 255418
Cable: KOEXBANK, BAHRAIN
Telex: 8846 BN

PRINCIPAL ACTIVITIES: Offshore banking unit
Parent Company: Korea Exchange Bank, IPO Box 2924, Seoul, Korea

Date of Establishment: 30th April, 1977
No of Employees: 24

KPMG FAKHRO

PO Box 710, Manama
Tel: 254807, 233440
Telex: 9100 Fest BN
Telefax: 273443, 233449

Managing Partner: Jamal Fakhro

PRINCIPAL ACTIVITIES: Accountants and management consultants
Branch Offices: Worldwide (650 offices)
Parent Company: Klynveld Peat Marwick Goerdeler
Principal Bankers: Bank of Bahrain & Kuwait, Alahli Commercial Bank, National Bank of Bahrain

Date of Establishment: 1968
No of Employees: 95

KUWAIT ASIA BANK EC

PO Box 10401, Manama
Tel: 532111
Swift: KABKBH
Telex: 9611 KAB BN
Telefax: 530831

Chairman: Hamad Mishari Ahmed Al Humaidhi
Directors: Ebrahim Eshaq Abdul-Rahman (Deputy Chairman), Ahmed Fahad Suleiman Al-Fahad, Abdul Rahman A Al Mughni, Rasheed Yacoob Al Nafeesi, Faisal Fahad Al-Shayaa, Hassan Ali Juma, Abdul Aziz Ebrahim Al Nabhan, Mustafa Ebrahim Al Saleh, Habib Hassan Jowhar Hayat, Ali Abdul Nabi Khaja, Suliman Al Ghunaim
Senior Executives: Omar Hadeed (General Manager), Alphonso D'Costa (SVP Administration & Operations), V Sawhney (SVP International Division), John Bonnici (SVP Treasury), Younis Zubhchevich (VP International Division), Abdulla Al Fuwaires (VP Investment Division), A Rahman Al Ansary (VP Treasury)

PRINCIPAL ACTIVITIES: To identify, promote, serve and participate in all kinds of banking, financial, and investment activities to develop industrial, commercial, financial, and investment relations relevant to the economies of the Middle East, Far East, and Australasia
Branch Offices: Singapore
Associated Companies: Kuwair Asia (New Zealand) Ltd, Auckland, New Zealand; Korea Investment & Finance Corp, Seoul, Korea; Panin Holdings Ltd, Hongkong; Kuwait Asia (Australia) Ltd, Melbourne, Australia

Principal Bankers: Manufacturers Hanover Trust Co, New York; National Westminster Bank, London; Commercial Bank of Kuwait, Kuwait; Al Bank Al Saudi Al Fransi, Saudi Arabia, etc

Financial Information:

	1988 US$'000	1989 US$'000
Net income	6,587	6,618
Deposits	99,801	57,670
Loans & advances	64,230	67,574
Other liabilities	221,259	178,947
Authorised capital	150,000	150,000
Paid-up capital	100,000	100,000
Total shareholders'equity	88,243	93,963
Total assets	309,502	272,916

Principal Shareholders: Kuwait: Public Institution for Social Security (32%); Kuwait International Investment Co (9%); Al-Ahli Bank of Kuwait (5%); Commercial Bank of Kuwait (5%); The Industrial Bank of Kuwait (5%); Kuwait Projects Co (5%); Kuwait Real Estate Bank (5%); Kuwait Real Estate Investment Consortium (5%); Pearl Holding (Luxembourg) SA (5%); Gulf Insurance Co (4%); Kuwait Insurance Co (4%); Al-Ahleia Insurance Co (2%); Warba Insurance Co (2%); Bahrain: Bank of Bahrain & Kuwait (5%); National Bank of Bahrain (5%); Al Ahli Commercial Bank, Bahrain (2%)
Date of Establishment: March 1981
No of Employees: 53

LAW OFFICES OF AHMED ZAKI YAMANI

Suite 071, National Bank of Bahrain Tower, PO Box 342, Manama
Tel: 231277, 252882
Telex: 8991 Yamani BN
Telefax: 231278

Directors: Dr Zaki Mustafa (Senior Resident Partner), Omer O El Mardi (Resident Partner)

PRINCIPAL ACTIVITIES: Legal Consultancy
Branch Offices: Head Office in Saudi Arabia; Jeddah: PO Box 1351; Jeddah, Tel 6429550/1, Telex 6605853; Fax 6437511; and Branch Office in Riyadh: PO Box 7159, Tel 4646921; Telex 203609; Fax 4648718
Principal Bankers: Grindlays Bank

Date of Establishment: In Jeddah: 1952, In Bahrain: 1980

LONG-TERM CREDIT BANK OF JAPAN LTD (THE)

PO Box 26908, Manama
Tel: 262900
Cable: Bankchogin
Telex: 9463 LTCB BN

PRINCIPAL ACTIVITIES: Representative office
Branch Offices: Head Office: 2-4 Ohtemachi I-Chome, Chiyoda-ku, Tokyo, Japan

Date of Establishment: November 1980

M A MALABARI SONS & CO WLL

See MALABARI, M A, SONS & CO WLL

M D MINASIAN

See MINASIAN, M D,

MAERSK LINE BAHRAIN APS

PO Box 45, Manama
Tel: 727896
Cable: Maersktop
Telex: 8676 Kanofs BN

PRINCIPAL ACTIVITIES: Shipping line
Branch Offices: Rep offices in Kuwait, Dubai, Dammam, Riyadh, Jeddah
Parent Company: Head office in Denmark

MAHMOOD, HASAN & HABIB S/O,

PO Box 302, Manama
Tel: 254303, 254159
Cable: Mahmoodco
Telex: 8329 Hashab BN
Telefax: 230024

Directors: Habib Mahmood, Ali Hasan Mahmood (Managing Director)
Senior Executives: Fareed Hasan Mahmood (General Manager)

PRINCIPAL ACTIVITIES: Civil engineering, building and labour contractors, importers of foodstuffs; general merchants; manufacturers; general commission agents; property developers; shipowners; bakery and supermarket owners; soft drink bottlers
Branch Offices: Branches in Dubai, Sharjah (UAE)
Subsidiary Companies: Eastern Bakery; Interiors; Fine Food Supermarket; Gulf Cold Store & Ice Plant Co; Canada Dry International
Principal Bankers: National Bank of Bahrain; Standard Chartered Bank

Principal Shareholders: Directors as described
Date of Establishment: 1942
No of Employees: 750

MAKIYA ASSOCIATES

PO Box 667, Manama
Tel: 252650
Cable: Architect

Chairman: Dr M S Makiya
Directors: Dr Nazar Makiya, Kanan Makiya, Mrs M Makiya
Senior Executives: Ahmed Mahdi (Manager)

PRINCIPAL ACTIVITIES: Consultant architects, planners and engineers
Branch Offices: Dubai (PO Box 4234); Qatar (PO Box 5074, Doha); Kuwait (PO Box 2873); London
Parent Company: Makiya Associates, Baghdad, Iraq
Principal Bankers: Citibank; National Bank of Abu Dhabi; National Bank of Kuwait

Principal Shareholders: Dr M S Makiya
Date of Establishment: 1971 in Bahrain
No of Employees: 160

MALABARI, M A, SONS & CO WLL

PO Box 61, Manama
Tel: 253710, 251429
Cable: Malabari

Chairman: Mustafa Malabari
Directors: Abdul Latif Malabari, Ali Bin Ahmed Al-Qaseer

PRINCIPAL ACTIVITIES: Importers, exporters, manufacturers' representatives, commission agents and general merchants
Principal Agencies: Beecham Products Overseas, UK; O Kauli A/S, Norway; Honig Foods B V, Holland; Government Soap Factory, India; 20th Century Foods, Singapore; Barker Dobson Confectionery, UK, etc
Branch Offices: M A Malabari & Sons, PO Box 959, Abu Dhabi
Principal Bankers: British Bank of the Middle East, National Bank of Bahrain, Habib Bank, Bahrain Islamic Bank

Principal Shareholders: Chairman and directors as described
Date of Establishment: 1910

MANNAI ENGINEERING CO LTD

PO Box 849, Government Rd, Manama
Tel: 251329, 259470
Cable: Mannai
Telex: 8419 Mannai BN
Telefax: 259605

Chairman: Dr Salem Abdulla Almannai
Directors: Isa Abdulla Almannai (Managing Director)

Senior Executives: S V Raghuram (Financial & Administrative Manager)

PRINCIPAL ACTIVITIES: Structural and civil contracting and engineering, sanitary works and building materials supplies
Principal Agencies: Kirby Building System, Kuwait; Industrial Technology (ME) Ltd, Dubai; Montan Engineering, W Germany
Principal Bankers: Bank of Bahrain & Kuwait
Financial Information:

	1990 US$'000
Sales turnover	12,000

Principal Shareholders: Chairman as described
Date of Establishment: 1972
No of Employees: 200

MANNAI TRADING & CONTRACTING EST

PO Box 5664, Manama
Tel: 290383
Cable: Manestab
Telex: 8785 Mantra BN
Telefax: 292372

Chairman: Salim Ahmed Mannai (Proprietor)
Senior Executives: Anil Krishnan Nair (Marketing Manager)

PRINCIPAL ACTIVITIES: Trading and contracting
Principal Agencies: Rockwool, Denmark; UBM Overseas, UK; Dennis & Robinson, UK; Lancing, UK; Fujairah Marble & Tiles Factory, Fujairah; Long Products, UK; etc
Subsidiary Companies: Panorama Contracting & Engineering Services Ltd, PO Box 5602, Manama
Principal Bankers: Bank of Bahrain and Kuwait
Financial Information:

	1989 BD'000
Sales turnover	304
Profits	50
Authorised capital	100
Paid-up capital	100
Total assets	300

Principal Shareholders: Proprietorship
Date of Establishment: 1976
No of Employees: 100

MANNAI TRADING & INVESTMENT CO LTD

PO Box 968, Manama
Tel: 251557
Cable: Matric
Telex: 9118 Matric BN
Telefax: 275758

Chairman: Mohammed A Mannai
Directors: Darwish A Mannai (General Director)
Senior Executives: A H Magra (Financial Controller), P Richardos (Factory Manager)

PRINCIPAL ACTIVITIES: Trading, agencies and sponsorship, business ventures, aluminium fabrication, insulating glass manufacturing; real estate
Principal Agencies: Gulf Oil Corpn, USA/UK; Bernard Sunley, UK; Pye Telecommunication, UK; Sargent Welch, USA; AEI Cables, UK; Permanite, UK; Redifusion Simulation, UK; Wicksteed Leisure, UK; Goddard & Gibbs, UK; Crown House Eng, UK; W S Atkins & Partners, UK; Hardall Intl, UK; Nor Control, Norway; Purafil, UK; D D Lamson, UK; Koolshade, UK; HAM, Holland; Fijitsu, Japan; Fairey Engineering, UK; Rush & Tompkins, UK; Cogelex, France; Hawker Siddley Power Engineering UK; Unilock Group, UK; Tripower, UK; Interspiro, UK; Defence Equipment & Systems, UK; General Electric Plastics, France; Crow Industries, Australia; Laidlaw Thomson Group, UK; Pearce Signs, UK; Pearce Security Systems, UK; Neuro Co, Germany; Alico Impalloy, Sharjah;

Bruder Eckelt & Co, Austria; Biwater Shelabear, UK; La Nuova Dibiten, Italy; Fairy Marine, UK; Form & Test Seidner, Germany
Subsidiary Companies: Kirkland Whittaker (Bahrain) WLL (same address); Mannai Aluminium & Glass (Architectural Aluminium & Glass Divn)
Principal Bankers: Bank of Bahrain & Kuwait

Principal Shareholders: Mohammed A Mannai, Darwish A Mannai
Date of Establishment: 1976
No of Employees: 80

MANSOURI, HASAN,

PO Box 5185, Manama
Tel: 728144
Cable: Crane
Telex: 8948 Hasman BN
Telefax: 729976

Chairman: Hasan Mansouri
Directors: Karim Mansouri (Managing Director)
Senior Executives: Ken Malone (General Manager), Jim Green (Works Manager)

PRINCIPAL ACTIVITIES: General contracting and construction; architects and planning consultants; plant hire; portable buildings, hoteliers, steel fabrication and erection; property letting; shipping, cargo haulage and forwarding; import of chemicals
Principal Agencies: ERF Commercial Vehicles; Thomas McInerney & Sons Building Materials; Mineralite; Protective Materials Ltd
Associated Companies: Mansouri McInerney WLL, Bahrain; Near East Structures Co (NESCO) WLL, Bahrain; Spacemaker
Principal Bankers: Banque Paribas; National Bank of Bahrain

Principal Shareholders: Private company
Date of Establishment: 1960
No of Employees: 450

MANSOURI MCINERNEY WLL

PO Box 5697, Manama
Tel: 663627
Telex: 8767 MCBAH BN
Telefax: 661837

Chairman: Hasan Mansouri
Directors: Karim Mansouri, Bob Allen, Lawrence Leavy
Senior Executives: Denis E Davis (General Manager)

PRINCIPAL ACTIVITIES: General construction by conventional and prefabricated methods, temporary accommodation, workcamps, offices and timber houses
Parent Company: McInerney Properties Plc, Ireland
Principal Bankers: British Bank of Middle East; Grindlays Bahrain Bank

Principal Shareholders: Hasan Mansouri, Inerney Anstalt (wholly owned subsidiary of McInerney Properties Plc)
Date of Establishment: 1976
No of Employees: 200

MANUFACTURERS HANOVER TRUST CO

PO Box 5471, Manama
Tel: 254353, 254375, 242030
Cable: Mantrust
Telex: 8556 BN (General), 8600 MHTBFX (Foreign Exchange)
Telefax: 251568

Senior Executives: A I Kittaneh (Managing Director), Abdul Aziz Abdul Malik (Vice President & Deputy Manager), George Karam (Vice President/Marketing), Riad J Kallas (Vice President/Marketing), Michael Hayhurst (Chief Dealer)

PRINCIPAL ACTIVITIES: Offshore banking unit

Parent Company: Head Office: 270 Park Ave, New York NY 10017, USA

Date of Establishment: 1976
No of Employees: 50

MASKATI BROS & CO

PO Box 24, Manama
Tel: 729911 PABX
Cable: Maskati Bahrain
Telex: 8621 Paper BN
Telefax: (973) 725454

Chairman: Hussain Maskati (Managing Director)
Directors: Khalid H Maskati (General Manager)
Senior Executives: P Kumar (Purchasing Manager), T K Antony (Production Manager), A Ali Jassim (Personnel Manager), P Joseph (Admin Manager)

PRINCIPAL ACTIVITIES: Paper converting factory, manufacture and distribution of paper and polyethelene products, airline catering disposables, products include facial & toilet tissue, kitchen rolls, handtowels, garbage bags, grocery bags, cutlery items, cups, dishes and hospital disposables
Branch Offices: Bahrain and other Arabian Gulf States
Subsidiary Companies: Maskati Commercial Services; Gulf Trading & Development Co; Tylos Paper Factory
Principal Bankers: British Bank of the Middle East; National Bank of Bahrain; Bank of Bahrain & Kuwait
Financial Information:

	1990 US$'000
Sales turnover	10,000
Authorised capital	4,000
Paid-up capital	4,000
Total assets	8,000

Principal Shareholders: Maskati Bros
Date of Establishment: 1958
No of Employees: 300

MECHANICAL CONTRACTING & SERVICES CO WLL (MCSC)

PO Box 5238, Manama
Tel: 255544, 623723, 623002
Cable: Majal
Telex: 9275 MCSC BN
Telefax: 624082

Partners: Moh'd Jalal, Jalal Moh'd Jalal, William Abu Hamad
Senior Executives: William Abu Hamad (Chief Executive)

PRINCIPAL ACTIVITIES: Mechanical and civil engineers
Branch Offices: Mechanical Contracting & Services Co WLL, Issa Town, PO Box 5238, Tel 623723
Subsidiary/Associated Companies: Mohammed Jalal & Sons
Principal Bankers: Chartered Bank

Date of Establishment: 1972

METRAS WLL

PO Box 575, Manama
Tel: 252862
Telefax: 272675

Chairman: Jasim Mohd Al-Saffar
Directors: Wael Jasim Al-Saffar
Senior Executives: Martin Johnson (Sales Manager)

PRINCIPAL ACTIVITIES: Marketing of steel frame buildings and allied services
Principal Agencies: Varco Pruden; Martin Roberts; Butterley; Systems Floors (UK) Ltd; Tarkett, Altro; Sound Acoustics
Branch Offices: PO Box 21853 Safat, Kuwait
Principal Bankers: British Bank of Middle East, Bahrain

Principal Shareholders: Jasim & Wael Al-Saffar
Date of Establishment: 1969

MIDAL CABLES LTD

PO Box 5939, Manama
Tel: 662050
Cable: Midal Cable
Telex: 9127 Midal BN

Chairman: Khalid R Zayani
Directors: Hamid R Zayani, Omar H Khalifati

PRINCIPAL ACTIVITIES: Manufacture of aluminium power transmission and distribution cables and EC grade re - draw rod
Principal Bankers: Bank of Bahrain & Kuwait, Chartered Bank, Chase Manhattan Bank, British Bank of the Middle East

Principal Shareholders: Intersteel of Bahrain, Saudi Cable Company, Jeddah and Olex Cables Ltd of Australia
Date of Establishment: 1977
No of Employees: 120

MIDDLE EAST CONSULTANCY CENTER WLL

PO Box 1013, 2nd Floor, Jashanmal Bldg, Al Khalifa Avenue, Manama
Tel: 213223
Cable: Mideast
Telex: 9246 Mecon BN
Telefax: 244670

Chairman: Dr Adnan N Bseisu (Managing Director)
Directors: Dr Adnan N Bseisu, Mrs Alima A Bseisu, Amjad A Bseisu, Ashraf A Bseisu, Dina A Bseisu
Senior Executives: Amjad A Bseisu (Director), Ashraf A Bseisu (Executive Director), Savio Rodrigues (Senior Manager Marketing & Research), Sree Kant (Manager Marketing & Sales)

PRINCIPAL ACTIVITIES: Management, financial, banking, business & aviation consultants, sponsorship & representation services and publishers' representatives, advertising, public relations, and executive recruitment
Principal Agencies: Graham & Trotman Ltd; Kluwer Academic Publishers; MEED; Euromoney Publications Ltd; Lloyd's of London Press; Europa Publications; Financial Times Business Information; Longman Group; Woodhead-Faulkner; The Economic Intelligence Unit-UK; IFR; Simon & Schuster International Group; Prentice Hall International; McGrawill Book Co (UK) Ltd; etc
Branch Offices: Subsidiary Co: Near East Contracting Co WLL, PO Box 1013, Manama, Bahrain; Manama Publishing WLL, PO Box 1013, Manama, Bahrain
Associated Companies: Andrew Ronaldson Associates, UK; Davis International Banking Consultants, UK; Charles Barker Management Selection International Ltd, UK; Aviation Systems International, USA; MEIRC SA, Greece; Overseas Companies Registration Agencies Ltd, Isle of Man; Middle East Marketing & Consultants, Bahrain
Principal Bankers: Bank of Bahrain & Kuwait, Main Office Bahrain; Arab Bank Ltd, Manama/New York/Geneva; Midland Bank Ltd, London; Union Bank of Switzerland, Zurich

Principal Shareholders: Fully owned by the Directors
Date of Establishment: February 1978

MIDDLE EAST EQUIPMENT CO

PO Box 5156, Mina Sulman
Tel: 8737/9
Cable: Meeco
Telex: 8327 BN

PRINCIPAL ACTIVITIES: Distribution and hiring of heavy machinery and earth-moving equipment (cranes, excavators, shovels, pipe-drivers) for the offshore oil and gas industries and heavy industries and petrochemical industries
Principal Agencies: Manitomac, Unit Crane and Shovel Corp, Hydrojet, Vulcan
Parent Company: A Long & Co Ltd, Wembley, UK

MIDDLE EAST TRADERS

PO Box 311, Manama
Tel: 255350, 253311
Telex: 8712 ESHAQ BN

Directors: Ebrahim Eshaq, Abdullatif Eshaq
Senior Executives: P H Scrine (Manager Building Supplies Div),
M Mustafa (Manager Furniture Div)

PRINCIPAL ACTIVITIES: Sanitaryware, boards and panels,
storage, lamination, ceiling and floors, partitions, castors and
wheels, spiral staircases etc
Principal Agencies: Armitage Shanks, Cape Boards & Panels,
Dexion, Formica, Hunter Douglas, Marley Vinyl, Flexello
Castors, Floating Floors, Lewes Design, etc
Principal Bankers: Bank of Bahrain & Kuwait, National Bank of
Bahrain, Standard Chartered Bank, Al Ahlia Commercial Bank

Date of Establishment: 1954
No of Employees: 120

MIDLAND BANK PLC

PO Box 5675, Manama
Tel: 530108
Telex: 9099 BN
Telefax: 530801

PRINCIPAL ACTIVITIES: Group representative office

MINASIAN, M D,

PO Box 198, Manama
Tel: 253577
Cable: Minasian

Chairman: M D Minasian

PRINCIPAL ACTIVITIES: Import, export; general trading;
contracting; mechancal engineering. Distribution of
mechanical equipment; air-conditioning equipment; heavy
machinery and spare parts; diesel engines; earth-moving
equipment
Principal Agencies: Parker concrete mixers, Johnson dumpers

MITSUBISHI BANK LTD

PO Box 26977, Manama
Tel: 232829
Cable: BishBank Bahrain
Telex: 9498 Bishba BN
Telefax: 258724

Senior Executives: Y Kawaguchi (Chief Representative for the
Middle East), T Hiraishi (Representative), S Kanai
(Representative)

PRINCIPAL ACTIVITIES: Representative office
Parent Company: Head office: 7-1 Marunouchi, 2-Chome,
Chiyoda Ku, Tokyo 100, Japan

Date of Establishment: February 1981

MITSUBISHI CORP (MIDDLE EAST) EC

PO Box 26864, Manama
Tel: 250669
Telex: 9423 MCMID BN
Telefax: 251985

Chairman: M Inoue (Chairman & Managing Director)
Directors: K Takahashi (Deputy Chairman)
Senior Executives: K Nakagawa (Director Manager
Coordination)

PRINCIPAL ACTIVITIES: Offshore trading

MITSUI & CO (MIDDLE EAST) EC

PO Box 20262, Manama Centre, Ent 2 Room 101, Government
Rd, Manama
Tel: 254824, 258599
Cable: Mitsui Bahrain
Telex: 9220 Mitsui BN
Telefax: 276612

Chairman: Yasuhiko Uryu (Managing Director)
Senior Executives: Osamu Takahashi (Deputy Managing
Director)

PRINCIPAL ACTIVITIES: Trading, offshore, finance and related
import/export of all types of commodities
Parent Company: Mitsui & Co Ltd, Japan
Principal Bankers: Bank of Tokyo, Bahrain; Grindlays Bahrain
Bank; Gulf International Bank

Date of Establishment: June 1983
No of Employees: 20

MITSUI BANK LTD

PO Box 26859, Manama Centre, Room 303 Part II, Government
Road, Manama
Tel: 253805
Telex: 9427

PRINCIPAL ACTIVITIES: Representative office
Parent Company: Head Office: 1-2 Yurakuchoo 1-Chome,
Chiyoda-Ku, Tokyo 100, Tokyo, Japan

Date of Establishment: November 1980

MOHAMED ABDULRAHMAN AL BAHAR

See AL BAHAR, MOHAMED ABDULRAHMAN,

MOHAMED ALI ZAINAL ABDULLA

See ZAINAL, MOHAMED ALI, ABDULLA

MOHAMED FAKHROO & BROS

See FAKHROO, MOHAMED, & BROS

MOHAMED JASIM AL HAIKI & AHMED MANSOOR NAIM

Shaikh Hamed Rd, PO Box 5020, Manama
Tel: 256771, 261145, 276089
Cable: Khyber Bahrain
Telex: 8868 Khyber BN
Telefax: (973) 234067

Directors: Mohamed Jasim Al Haiki, Ahmed Mansoor Naim
Senior Executives: Hussain M J Al Haiki (Personnel Manager), V
A Mammen (Construction Manager)

PRINCIPAL ACTIVITIES: Civil engineering and construction
Principal Agencies: Tarkett, Sweden
Principal Bankers: Bank of Bahrain and Kuwait; Al Ahli
Commercial Bank, National Bank of Bahrain

Principal Shareholders: Directors as described
Date of Establishment: 1962
No of Employees: 500

MOHAMED SALAHUDDIN CONSULTING ENGINEERING BUREAU

See SALAHUDDIN, MOHAMED, CONSULTING ENGINEERING
BUREAU

MOHAMED SHARIF MOHAMED & SONS

Sharif Garment Factory

Bab Al Bahrain Road, PO Box 739, Manama
Tel: 254910, 244449, 230997
Cable: Mosharm
Telex: 8202 Bahtag BN RE: 118
Telefax: 231515

Chairman: Mohamed Sharif Mohamed

Directors: Othman Mohamed Sharif (General Manager)
Senior Executives: Abdul Rahman Mohd Sharif (Manager Branch), Waleed Mohd Sharif (Manager Branch)

PRINCIPAL ACTIVITIES: Dealing in electronic and electrical items, watches & wall clocks, tailoring department, textiles
Principal Agencies: Garuda, Singapore; Libra, India; Jerger, Germany; Dugena, Switzerland
Subsidiary Companies: Mohd Sharif Mohd & Sons Tailoring
Principal Bankers: British Bank of the Middle East, Bahrain Islamic Bank

Date of Establishment: 1956
No of Employees: 39

MOHAMMED JALAL & SONS CO LTD
See JALAL, MOHAMMED, & SONS CO LTD

MOHAMMED JALAL CONTRACTING
See JALAL, MOHAMMED, CONTRACTING

MOON ORGANISATION
PO Box 247, Manama
Tel: 728631, 729381
Cable: Moonstores
Telex: 8308 Plaza BN, 9063 Duty BN

Directors: Sharokh Akhtarzadeh, Ali Akhtarzadah, Goli Akhtarzadeh

PRINCIPAL ACTIVITIES: Importers, exporters, distributors, manufacturers' representatives and agents, hoteliers, and owners of cold stores, supermarkets, musical instrument shops, flower shops, boutiques, perfumery shops and furniture shops
Principal Agencies: Carnation Int, Holland; Smedley-HP Foods, UK; Campbells, UK; Triumph, Austria; Sanyei Electronics, Japan; S & W Fine Foods, USA; Wrigley, USA; Purex, USA; Suchard, Switzerland; Bourjois, France; Marbert, Germany; Avon USA; Femia, W Germany; Fribad, Germany; Chemco, Italy; Eikosha Musical Inst, Japan; Elgam Electronica, Italy; H Mukai, Japan; Giaccaglia, Italy; Henry Selmer; Jen Electronica, Italy; Ludwig Int, USA; Shinto Sangyo, Japan
Subsidiary Companies: Akhtarzadeh Superstores; Moon Flower Shop; Moon Musical Shop; Shehab Cold Stores; Moon Plaza Hotel
Principal Bankers: Bank of Bahrain & Kuwait; National Bank of Bahrain; Al Ahli Commercial Bank

Date of Establishment: 1946
No of Employees: 150

MOSTAFA BIN ABDULLATIF
See BIN ABDULLATIF, MOSTAFA,

MUHARRAQ ENGINEERING WORKS
PO Box 5476, Manama
Tel: 727301, 729101, 729698
Cable: Drilco Bahrain
Telex: 8293 Drilco BN

Directors: Ahmed Ebrahim (Managing Director)
Senior Executives: Farooq Ahmed Ebrahim (Transport Manager), Samir Ahmed Ebrahim (Director)

PRINCIPAL ACTIVITIES: Import and distribution of machinery and equipment for the oil industry, marine and other works, also stud bolts, nuts, wires, ropes, steel products, etc. Steel fabrication works, material sales and service
Principal Agencies: Verlinde, France; MTE Ltd, UK; Robey of Lincoln Ltd, UK; Eur Contolitalia, Italy; Copes Vulcan, UK; LSJ Int, UK; Neptune Glenfield, UK; Taprogge GmbH, W Germany; Rockwell Int, USA; Plicaflex Inc, USA; Kemwell, UK; Band-it, USA; PPD, UK; Mac Michael Gaskets, UK; Velan, Canada; Bruntons, UK; FEMA, Italy; Smitweld, Holland; Euro Drill Equipment, UK; Hockman Lewis, USA; British Ropes, UK

Branch Offices: Sales Dept: Muharraq Engg Works (Mercantile Div), PO Box 798, Manama, Tel 729609, Telex 8589
Principal Bankers: Bank of Bahrain & Kuwait; National Bank of Bahrain; British Bank of the Middle East; Al Ahlia Commercial Bank

Date of Establishment: 1964

NADER TRADING & REFRIGERATING CO LTD
PO Box 409, Manama
Tel: 590002/3
Cable: Reefer Bahrain
Telex: 8410 Nader BN
Telefax: 590103

PRINCIPAL ACTIVITIES: Catering services and contractors, cold store operations (300,000 cubic-foot cold storage), agencies, wholesale, retail and supermarkets
Principal Agencies: Mars, Kraft, RHM, Hero, Anchor Foods, SPC, Borthwicks, Lyons, Ross, Coroli, Hills
Parent Company: Ali Bin Ebrahim Abdul Aal
Principal Bankers: Standard Chartered Bank

Principal Shareholders: Ali Bin Ebrahim Abdul Aal
Date of Establishment: 1977 (Previously J H Raynor Est 1955)
No of Employees: 84

NASS, ABDULLA AHMED,
PO Box 669, Manama
Tel: 243425
Cable: Nascon
Telex: 8243 Nascon BN
Telefax: 728184

Chairman: Abdulla Ahmed Nass (also Managing Director)
Directors: Samir Abdulla Nass, Sami Abdulla Nass

PRINCIPAL ACTIVITIES: Civil, electrical and mechanical engineering and plumbing contractors, import and distribution of heavy machinery and spare parts, building materials, buses, electrical cables, cement, aggregates, furniture, carpets, curtains, foodstuffs, motor vehicles, cargo handling, chartering of marine vessels and ship chandlering, sand dredging, sand washing, bakery, laundry, supply of manpower, plant and equipment, real estate
Principal Agencies: Poclain, France; Premier Automobile India Ltd; Retesa, Spain; Moda, Texas, USA; Fracasso, Italy; Neylor, UK
Branch Offices: Bahrain; Qatar; UAE (branch in Abu Dhabi, PO Box 2416, Tel 22373)
Subsidiary Companies: Delmon Ready Mix Concrete & Product Co Ltd, United Building Factories Industries WLL
Principal Bankers: British Bank of the Middle East; Bank of Bahrain and Kuwait; National Bank of Bahrain; Al Ahli Commercial Bank; National Bank of Abu Dhabi

Principal Shareholders: Abdulla Ahmed Nass
No of Employees: 1,500

NASSER ABD MOHAMMED EST
PO Box 984, Manama
Tel: 700888
Cable: Nasco
Telex: 8828 Nasco BN

Founder: Nasser Abd Mohammed
Directors: Mohammed Nasser, Ali Nasser

PRINCIPAL ACTIVITIES: Mechanical and civil engineering, metal fabrication and erection, tank building, repairs and maintenance, plant hire, cranes, trailers, welding machines, air compressors, dump trucks and other construction equipment
Principal Bankers: Al Ahli Commercial Bank

Date of Establishment: 1952
No of Employees: 250

NATIONAL BANK OF ABU DHABI

PO Box 5247, Manama
Tel: 250824, 251398, 251689
Cable: Masraf
Telex: 8483 BN

PRINCIPAL ACTIVITIES: Commercial banking
Branch Offices: Abu Dhabi; Dubai; Sharjah; Fujairah; Ras Al
   Khaimah; Bahrain; Egypt; Sudan; Oman; Qatar; UK (London)
Parent Company: Head office in Abu Dhabi, PO Box 4, UAE

NATIONAL BANK OF BAHRAIN BSC

PO Box 106, Manama
Tel: 258800
Cable: Natbank
Telex: 8242 Natbnk BN
Telefax: 263876 (General Hedaya), 272406 (NBB Tower),
   754194 (Awali Br)

Chairman: Ahmed Ali Kanoo
Directors: Essa Abdulla Burshaid (First Deputy Chairman),
   Hussain Ali Yateem (Second Deputy Chairman), Yousuf Khalil
   Al-Moayyed (Third Deputy Chairman), Khalil Ebrahim Kanoo
   (Director), Hassan Al-Nusuf (Director), Ali Mohamed Al-Noor
   (Director), Fahad Ebrahim Al-Wazzan (Director), Nooruddin
   Abdulla Nooruddin (Director), Abdulla Yousuf Akbar Alireza
   (Director)
Senior Executives: Hassan Ali Juma (Chief General Manager),
   Yacoob Y Mohammed (Acting General Manager), A Razak A
   Hassan (AGM Credit Administration & Marketing), Mohamed
   Hassan Ali (Manager Personnel & Training), B
   Balasubramanian (Manager Property Management), A
   Rahman Hussain (Senior Manager Systems), Mrs Sabah Al
   Moayyed (Senior Manager Corporate Banking), Hussain S Ali
   Al Hussaini (Manager Treasury), Yousif A Karim (Manager
   Retail Services), A Rahman Khalil (Asst Manager Treasury
   Operations)

PRINCIPAL ACTIVITIES: Commercial banking and offshore
   banking unit
Branch Offices: Bahrain (19 branches)
Principal Bankers: Bank of New York; Chase Manhattan;
   Barclays Bank
Financial Information:

	1990
	BD'000
Sales turnover	517,340
Profits	9,000
Authorised capital	100,000
Paid-up capital	28,000
Total assets	605,800

Principal Shareholders: Government of Bahrain (49%), Bahraini
   interests (51%)
Date of Establishment: 1957
No of Employees: 464

NATIONAL BANK OF PAKISTAN

PO Box 775, Manama
Tel: 244191, 244183, 244186, 244185
Cable: MILLATBANK, BAHRAIN
Telex: 9221, 9222, 9405 NatPak BN
Telefax: 274411

Directors: Abdur Rashid (Vice President)
Senior Executives: Khalid Pervaiz (General Manager OBU &
   Middle East Area)

PRINCIPAL ACTIVITIES: Offshore banking unit
Parent Company: NBP Head Office: Karachi
Subsidiary Companies: Bank Al Jazira (Saudia Arabia)

Date of Establishment: 1949; OBU in Bahrain, February 1979

NATIONAL COMPUTER SERVICES LTD

PO Box 26766, Manama
Tel: 261220
Telex: 8391 NCS BH
Telefax: 274390

Senior Executives: Omar Taha (Digital Operations Manager),
   Arun L Jain (Business Manager)

PRINCIPAL ACTIVITIES: Installation and maintenance of
   computer systems
Principal Agencies: Digital, Alis, Oracle, Infotron, Paradyne,
   Liebert
Parent Company: NCS Ltd, PO Box 766, Safat, Kuwait, Tel
   742275, Telex 22272
Principal Bankers: ABN Bank

Date of Establishment: 1980

NATIONAL HOTELS COMPANY

PO Box 5243, Manama
Tel: 530838, 530839
Telex: 8729 Hotels BN
Telefax: 530991

Chairman: Ahmed A Rahman Al Zayani
Directors: Abdulla Ahmed Al Qabandi (Vice Chairman), Hassan
   Ali Al Khaja, Ali M Murad, Yousef A Al Jassim, Abdulla Al
   Mansour, Faisal A Al Zayani
Senior Executives: Abdul Rahman Ali Morshed (General
   Manager), P J Kuruvilla (Chief Accountant)

PRINCIPAL ACTIVITIES: Hoteliers
Branch Offices: Diplomat Hotel, PO Box 5243, Manama, Tel
   531666
Principal Bankers: National Bank of Bahrain
Financial Information:

	1990
	BD'000
Sales turnover	4,000
Profits	32%
Authorised capital	14,442
Paid-up capital	14,442

Principal Shareholders: Bahrain Pension Fund, KFTCIC
Date of Establishment: August 1973
No of Employees: 322

NATIONAL IMPORT & EXPORT CO

PO Box 1080, Manama
Tel: 535005
Cable: Estrad
Telex: 8257 Estrad BN
Telefax: 533436

Chairman: Abdul Rahman Taki
Directors: Mohammed Baqer Al Tager (Vice Chairman), Abdul
   Rahman Jamsheer (Managing Director), Mohd A Ghaffar Al
   Alawi, Khalil E Al Motawa, Mohamed Y Jalal, Ebrahim H
   Kamal, Ali E Abdul Aal, Sadiq M Al Baharna, Mohammed H
   Diwani
Senior Executives: Abdulbari Abdulghaffar (General Manager), A
   Ameer M Redi (Asst General Manager Admin & Financial
   Affairs)

PRINCIPAL ACTIVITIES: Import of cement and basic building
   materials, rice, white sugar, vegetable ghee
Principal Bankers: National Bank of Bahrain; Bank of Bahrain
   and Kuwait; Al Ahi Commercial Bank, Bahrain Islamic Bank,
   Grindlays Bank Bahrain
Financial Information:

	1990
	BD'000
Sales turnover	12,658
Profits	1,036
Authorised capital	6,000
Paid-up capital	6,000
Total assets	15,461

BAHRAIN

Principal Shareholders: Public Company, 10% State owned
Date of Establishment: 1973
No of Employees: 23

NATIONAL INSURANCE CO BSC (C)

Unitag House, Government Av, PO Box 1818, Manama
Tel: 244181
Cable: Secure BN
Telex: 8908 Secure BN
Telefax: 230228

Chairman: Jamil A Wafa (also Chief Executive)
Deputy Chairman: M J Zubari
Senior Executives: Sameer Al Wazzan (General Manager), K
   Gopi Rao (Deputy General Manager), Adli Al Aseeri (Asst
   General Manager), Jassim Seyadee (Asst General Manager)

PRINCIPAL ACTIVITIES: All classes of insurance
Principal Bankers: Standard Chartered Bank
Financial Information:

	1990 BD'000
Gross premiums	4,322
Profits	481
Authorised capital	805
Paid-up capital	805
Total assets	4,578

Principal Shareholders: Unitag; Bahrain Financing Co; A A
   Nass; Haji Hassan, Ali Rashid Al Amin
Date of Establishment: May 1982 (previously National Insurance
   Services)
No of Employees: 49

NATIONAL SHIPPING AGENCY

PO Box 762, Manama
Tel: 255542, 255005, 256117
Cable: Nashipco
Telex: 8341 Shipco BN

PRINCIPAL ACTIVITIES: Shipping and forwarding agents

NCR CORPORATION GULF

Sheikh Mubarak Bldg, Government Rd, PO Box 265, Manama
Tel: 244233, 253711
Cable: Nacareco
Telex: 8306 Ncrco BN

PRINCIPAL ACTIVITIES: Sale and distribution of business
   equipment, computers and terminals, electronic data,
   processing equipment
Branch Offices: PO Box 2952, Kuwait; PO Box 1185, Dubai,
   UAE; PO Box 350, Abu Dhabi, UAE; PO Box 867, Doha,
   Qatar; PO Box 4728, Ruwi, Muscat, Oman; PO Box 6293,
   Sharjah, UAE; PO Box 5345, Karachi, Pakistan; PO Box 520,
   Dhaka, Bangladesh

Date of Establishment: 1956
No of Employees: 276

NEDERLANDSCHE MIDDENSTANDSBANK NV

NMB Bank

PO Box 788, Manama
Tel: 254010
Telex: 8448 NMB BAH
Telefax: 273116

PRINCIPAL ACTIVITIES: Commercial and investment banking
   (representative office)
Parent Company: NMB Bank NV: PO Box 1800, Amsterdam
Principal Bankers: NMB Bank, Amsterdam

Date of Establishment: 1927 (Head Office)
No of Employees: 3 (Bahrain)

NEDLLOYD AREA MANAGEMENT MIDDLE EAST

PO Box 603, Y.B.A. Kanoo Building F/2, Manama
Tel: 728849, 255327
Cable: Nedship
Telex: 8256 Nedlld BN

PRINCIPAL ACTIVITIES: Shipping liner services, regional
   management; RoRo services East Coast USA to Middle East;
   Container/conventional services NW
   Europe/UK/Mediterranean to M E ports; Indian Sub Continent
Branch Offices: Representatives in Riyadh, Jeddah, Dammam,
   Dubai, Kuwait
Parent Company: Royal Nedlloyd Group NV, Rotterdam, Holland

NEW INDIA ASSURANCE CO LTD

PO Box 584, Bahrain
Tel: 254275, 256058
Cable: 'NIASURANCE'
Telex: 8273 INTCOL BN
Telefax: 727509

Chairman: S K Seth
Directors: S Kannan, H B Desai, Prenjit Singh, D N Desai, F K
   Daruwalla, A S Mitra, S C Gaur

PRINCIPAL ACTIVITIES: Insurance (general)
Parent Company: The New India Assurance Co Ltd, Bombay,
   India
Principal Bankers: State Bank of India; The British Bank of the
   Middle East

Principal Shareholders: General Insurance Corporation of India
   (Government Holding) 99.6%

NIKKO INVESTMENT BANKING (MIDDLE EAST) EC

PO Box 830, Bahrain
Tel: 271750
Telex: 9619 NIKOSE BN
Telefax: 275760

Chairman: Masao Inagaki
Directors: Yasuo Kanzaki, Jun Okano
Senior Executives: Keigo Otani (Manager Admin & Accounting),
   Hisashi Onuma (Deputy General Manager), Hayato Kodama
   (Manager)

PRINCIPAL ACTIVITIES: Exempt company
Principal Bankers: National Bank of Bahrain
Financial Information:

	1990 US$'000
Authorised capital	15,000

Date of Establishment: 2 July 1988
No of Employees: 13

NOMURA INVESTMENT BANKING (MIDDLE EAST) EC

10th & 11th Floors, BMB Centre, Diplomatic Area, PO Box
   26893, Manama
Tel: 530531
Cable: Nomura (Bahrain)
Telex: 9070 Nomura BN (General), 9010 Nomura BN (Banking),
   9506 Nomura BN (Investment), 9058 Nomura BN (Investment)
Telefax: 530365

Chairman: Akira Ogino (Japan)
Directors: Tetsu Hirano (Deputy Chairman), Yoshihiko Tahara
   (Director Investment), Hiroaki Yokomachi (Director
   Administration & Accounting)

PRINCIPAL ACTIVITIES: Offshore investment banking
Parent Company: The Nomura Securities Company Ltd, Tokyo
Principal Bankers: National Bank of Bahrain, Bahrain; Mitsui
   Bank, Japan; Bankers Trust Co, New York

Financial Information:

	1988/89 US$'000
Profits	13,700
Authorised capital	50,000
Paid-up capital	25,000
Total assets	568,890

Principal Shareholders: The Nomura Securities Co Ltd, Japan
Date of Establishment: 1982
No of Employees: 54

NORWICH WINTERTHUR INSURANCE (GULF) LTD

PO Box 45, Manama
Tel: 2210778
Cable: Kanoo Bahrain
Telex: 8215 Kanoo BN
Telefax: 274192

Chairman: Yusuf Ahmed Kanoo
Directors: G W H Jones, E J Sainsbury, J D Campbell, Yusuf Ahmed Kanoo, I L Reid, H R Strickler, J A Gilmour
Senior Executives: I L Reid (General Manager), Ashraf Hussein (Non-Marine Underwriter & Manager), F D Evans (Marine Underwriter), Mohamed Makee (Chief Accountant)

PRINCIPAL ACTIVITIES: All classes of insurance and reinsurance (except life)
Branch Offices: Bahrain PO Box 45 Manama Bahrain; Dubai PO Box 290, Dubai; Abu Dhabi; PO Box 245, Abu Dhabi; Sharjah PO Box 153, Sharjah; Oman PO Box 3833, Ruwi, Oman
Parent Company: Norwich Winterthur Holdings Ltd
Associated Companies: Norwich Winterthur Insurance (Saudi Arabia) EC, Jeddah, Riyadh, Alkhobar; Bahrain Norwich Winterthur Insurance Co BSC(C), Manama, Bahrain
Principal Bankers: British Bank of the Middle East

Principal Shareholders: Norwich Union Fire Insurance Society Ltd (46.5%); Winterthur Swiss Insurance Group of Switzerland (46.5%), Chiyoda Fire and Marine Insurance Company of Japan (7%)
Date of Establishment: 1979
No of Employees: 60

OCEANAIR WLL

Adliya, PO Box 113, Manama
Tel: 714237, 714216
Cable: Coexpress Bahrain
Telex: 8974 BEXB BN
Telefax: 712545

Chairman: Mohammed Jalal
Directors: Jalal Jalal
Senior Executives: Patricia Ekins (General Manager)

PRINCIPAL ACTIVITIES: Packing, international removals, forwarding, storage, and customs clearing
Principal Agencies: Schenker Int'l
Branch Offices: Selwa, Bahrain
Parent Company: Mohammed Jalal Group, Bahrain
Principal Bankers: Grindlays Bank, Standard Chartered Bank

Principal Shareholders: Mohammed Jalal
Date of Establishment: 1973 in Bahrain

ORIENTAL PRESS

PO Box 161, Manama
Tel: 233323 (10 lines)
Cable: Orient
Telex: 8806 Orient BN
Telefax: (0973) 240149

Directors: Majeed Al-Zeera, Mohamed Akram Al-Zeera

PRINCIPAL ACTIVITIES: General commercial printing, security printing, books & magazines, computer stationery, packaging and paper merchants

Branch Offices: Security Printing Division
Subsidiary Companies: Delmon Press, Oriental Palace Hotel, Issa Zeera Real Estate Co, Issa Zeera Corporation Dubai
Principal Bankers: National Bank of Bahrain; Al Ahli Commercial Bank
Financial Information:

	1990 BD'000
Paid-up capital	1,000

Principal Shareholders: Majeed Al Zeera, Mohamed Al Zeera
Date of Establishment: 1952
No of Employees: 300

OVERSEAS FINANCIAL SERVICES

PO Box 5499, Manama Centre, Manama
Tel: 210616
Telex: 7214 Muna BN
Telefax: 210402

Chairman: Kevin Mudd
Directors: Joe Silk
Senior Executives: Marcus Osborne (Country Manager), Tony Mustafa (Associate Director), Ken Paul

PRINCIPAL ACTIVITIES: Independent financial advisors, marketing investment products, international tax consultants, real estate finance, international pension consultants
Branch Offices: Oman, Kuwait, Indonesia, Malaysia, Thailand, Botswana, Netherlands
Principal Bankers: Barclays Bank

Date of Establishment: 1982

PAN ARAB CONSULTING ENGINEERS WLL P.A.C.E.

PO Box 10207, Manama
Tel: 533073
Telex: 8612 Pace BN
Telefax: 973-533069

Partners: Sabah Al Rayes, Hamid A Shuaib (Managing Partner)
Senior Executives: Hakam Jarrar (Technical Manager), Geoff Pollitt (General Manager, Bahrain Office), Shawkat Odeh (Financial & Administration Manager), Kais Dakkak (Head of Supervision), Raad Al Shedidi (Manager for International Projects), Michael Gebhart (Chief Architect), Gretchen Addi (Chief Interior Designer), Michael Nason (Chief Landscape Architect), Richard Hattersley (Chief Quantity Surveyor), Mohammed Sabbagh (Chief Public Health Engineer), Wid Al Amer (Act Chief Mechanical Engineer), Hoda El Sayyad (Chief Electrical Engineer), Sunil Manchanda (Act Chief Structural Engineer), Essam Al Khawam (Head Computer Dept), Ali Al Saleh (Personnel & Purchasing Manager), Hilda Jubran (Office Executive Manager)

PRINCIPAL ACTIVITIES: Architects, engineers and planners
Branch Offices: Abu Dhabi: PO Box 315, Tel 213013, Telex 23157
Parent Company: Head office in Kuwait
Subsidiary Companies: Pace UK Ltd, Grosvenor Gardens House, 35/37 Grosvenor Gardens, London SW1W 0BS, UK

Principal Shareholders: Partners as described
Date of Establishment: 1968

PEARL INVESTMENT CO EC

PO Box 5809, Government Road, Unitag House, Manama
Tel: 246570, 232578
Telefax: 210606

Chairman: Khaled Al Marzooq
Directors: Mubarak Jaber Al Ahmad Al Sabah (Vice Chairman), Saad Al Nahad (Managing Director), Yousif E Al-Ghanim, Hussein M Juma, Hamad A Al-Saqar, Abdul Salam Al-Awadi, A Razaq S Aman, Hamad A Al-Hamad, Ahmad A Al-Nakeeb

Senior Executives: Abdulaziz Al Meshaal (General Manager), Khalid Al Bassam (Bahrain Office Manager), Adnan Zakhout (Investment Manager)

PRINCIPAL ACTIVITIES: Investment company
Branch Offices: Kuwait: PO Box 23859 Safat, Telex 44461 JORI
Subsidiary/Associated Companies: Pearl Holding, Luxembourg; Pearl Real Estate, Kuwait; Pearl Properties Co NV, Grand Cayman; Pearl Cayman Co NV, Grand Cayman, Kuwait & French Bank, Swiss-Kuwaiti Bank
Principal Bankers: Kuwait Real Estate Bank; Bank of Bahrain & Kuwait
Financial Information:

	1990 US$'000
Profits	7,291
Authorised capital	200,000
Paid-up capital	100,000
Total assets	193,533

Principal Shareholders: Kuwait Pearl Investment Co and others
Date of Establishment: 1979
No of Employees: 30

PRICE WATERHOUSE
PO Box 26403, Unitag House, Government Rd, Manama
Tel: 233266
Telex: 8964 PWBAH BN
Telefax: 271459

Senior Executives: T V Hopcroft (Partner), J M Keane (Manager), K Y Abdulla (Manager), D J McIntyre (Manager), D L Maunder (Manager Management Consultancy)

PRINCIPAL ACTIVITIES: Public accountants and consultants

PROCESS ENGINEERING CO WLL (PENCO)
PO Box 5258, Manama
Tel: 293222
Cable: PENCO BN
Telex: 9630 PENCO BN
Telefax: 294411

Directors: Sami Al Alawi (Managing Director), Saeed Al Alawi

PRINCIPAL ACTIVITIES: Agents and general trading, chemical services suppliers, domestic and industrial pump, filteration technique, industrial process engineering, instrumentation, irrigation, meetering dosing pumps, swimming pools, water treatment and desalination
Principal Agencies: Ciba Geigy Additives, UK/Switzerland; American Cynamid Chemical, USA; Rohm & Hass, Italy; Kronos Titon, Germany; Brunswick, USA; Cuno, USA; Ametik, USA; Kane May, UK; Gestra, Germany; EFLO, UK; Great Lakes Instruments, USA; Prominent Doseritechnik, Germany; Taprogge, Germany; Adams, Germany; Jung Pumpen, Germany; WSA Engg System, USA; Scem, Italy; Emco, USA; Alkawther Ind, Saudi Arabia; Ecodyne Lindsay, Belgiuim, Finish Thomson, USA; Tintometer, UK; Reugger,Switzerland
Branch Offices: S K Al Alawi & Sons Group of Companies, PO Box 3000, Manama, Bahrain
Principal Bankers: National Bank of Bahrain; Bahraini Saudi Bank; Banque Paribas
Financial Information:

	1989/90 US$'000
Authorised capital	265
Paid-up capital	265

Principal Shareholders: Sami Al Alawi
Date of Establishment: 1979

PROJECTS & PROPERTIES
PO Box 801, Manama
Tel: 271184
Telex: 7077 PRO-HLD BN
Telefax: 272324

Chairman: Sheikh Ebrahim Bin Hamad Al Khalifa
Directors: Sheikh Abdullah Bin Hamad Al Khalifa, C Kennett, H P G Turner

PRINCIPAL ACTIVITIES: Estate agents
Principal Agencies: Callander Wright, Uk; Kennett Turner, UK
Branch Offices: Kennett Turner, 59 Cadogan St, London SW3
Principal Bankers: Al Ahli Commercial Bank

Principal Shareholders: Sheikh Ebrahim Bin Hamad Al Khalifa
Date of Establishment: April 1977

PROJECTS UBM
PO Box 801, Sitra
Tel: 731087, 251217
Telex: 8819 Pro Ag BN
Telefax: 732189

PRINCIPAL ACTIVITIES: Building contractors and developers
Associated Companies: Projects (Properties Ltd); Project Systems Ltd; Project-PMA; Pan Gulf Posters Ltd; Projects-Modric Allgood

PROSPERITY TRADING & CONTRACTING EST
PO Box 998, Tariq Bldg, Government Rd, Manama
Tel: 255884, 254704, 251833
Cable: Prosperity Bahrain
Telex: 8506 Kholud BN

Chairman: Essa Abdulla Moosa (also Sole Proprietor)

PRINCIPAL ACTIVITIES: Sales and distribution of chemicals, refrigerant gases, spare parts, automobile batteries, paints, tapes and abrasives, welding materials, sandblasting sand, chamois leather, perspex clear sheet; also labour suppliers
Principal Agencies: Galex, France; S Dyrup & Co AS, Denmark; 3M Middle East Inc, Dubai; Korea Iron & Steel, South Korea; Chinhae Battery Co Ltd, South Korea; Kenmore AS, Norway; Danokan, Denmark; G W Russell & Sons, UK; A S E Europe, NV Belgium; Clamyer International Corp, New York; Welfare Development Co Ltd, Taiwan; Chemproha Chemical Export BV, Holland
Principal Bankers: Bank of Bahrain and Kuwait; Grindlays Bank; British Bank of the Middle East; Banque Paribas

QASIM AHMAD FAKHROO
See FAKHROO, QASIM AHMAD,

RAFIDAIN BANK
PO Box 607, Government Road, Manama
Tel: 255456, 275796
Cable: Rafidbank
Telex: 8332 Rafdbk BN

PRINCIPAL ACTIVITIES: Commercial banking
Parent Company: Head office in Baghdad, Iraq

Date of Establishment: 1979

RAMADA HOTEL
PO Box 5750, Manama
Tel: 714921
Cable: Ramada
Telex: 8855 Ramada BN
Telefax: 742809

PRINCIPAL ACTIVITIES: Hotel operation
Principal Agencies: Ramada Hotels International
Parent Company: Ramada Hotel Group; Phoenix, Arizona
Principal Bankers: Bank of Bahrain & Kuwait

Principal Shareholders: Tourism Investment Company, Manama
Date of Establishment: July 1977
No of Employees: 130

REDMACK INDUSTRIAL SERVICES (BAHRAIN) WLL

PO Box 29040, Riffa
Tel: 700375, 700370
Telex: 8675 Redmac BN
Telefax: 275758

Chairman: Mohamed Abdullah Al Mannai
Directors: Mohamed Ali Al Hassan, Darwish A Mannai
Senior Executives: R J Fox (General Manager), A H Magra (Financial Controller)

PRINCIPAL ACTIVITIES: Industrial and marine maintenance and cleaning; high pressure water jetting; chemical cleaning; waste management; hydraulic hose repair and supply services; domestic and industrial drain cleaning services; high pressure on-line leak sealing services
Principal Agencies: Dynorod drain cleaning; Sibex on line leak sealing; Catalyst handling services

Principal Shareholders: Mohamed Abdullah Al Mannai; Mohamed Ali Al Hasan; Darwish A Mannai
Date of Establishment: April 1975

REFRESHMENT TRADING CO (BAHRAIN)

PO Box 713, Bahrain
Tel: 252588, 250201
Cable: Eshrab
Telex: 8631 Eshrab BN

Directors: Ahmed Al-Jalahema, Essa Al-Jalahema
Senior Executives: Mustafa Radwan (Plant Manager)

PRINCIPAL ACTIVITIES: Soft drinks bottling
Principal Agencies: Seven-Up, USA; Crush, USA; Dixi, Dubai; Sohat, Lebanon
Principal Bankers: Arab Bank Ltd; Bank of Bahrain and Kuwait; British Bank of the Middle East

Date of Establishment: 1967
No of Employees: 203

REFRIGERATION & ELECTRICAL SERVICES

PO Box 75, Manama
Tel: 254819
Cable: Refelec Bahrain
Telex: 8390 Reflec BN

Directors: Naji Murad

PRINCIPAL ACTIVITIES: Electrical engineering contractors; refrigeration and air conditioning engineers; distributors and retailers of electrical appliances and equipment
Principal Agencies: White-Westinghouse Int Co, USA; Thorn Lighting Ltd, UK; MK Electric, UK; KEC, Kuwait; Schlumberger, Sangamo, UK; IMI Paxman, UK; Hemcol Ltd, UK; Ricardo Soriano, Spain
Principal Bankers: Standard Chartered Bank, Bahrain

Date of Establishment: 1962

REGENCY INTER-CONTINENTAL BAHRAIN (THE)

PO Box 777, Manama
Tel: 231777
Cable: Regent Bahrain
Telex: 9400 Regent BN
Telefax: 240028

Directors: Jamil A Wafa (Managing Director United Hotels Company)
Senior Executives: Phillipe Leroy (General Manager)

PRINCIPAL ACTIVITIES: Hotel business
Parent Company: United Hotels Company
Associated Companies: Seibu Saisan, Tokyo, Japan

Principal Bankers: Standard Chartered Bank

Date of Establishment: November 1980
No of Employees: 400

RUMAIHI HOUSING & CONSTRUCTION EST

PO Box 1028, Manama
Tel: 251497
Cable: Rumaihi
Telex: 8289 Gulmar BN

Chairman: Amer Mohd Rumaihi (Managing Director)

PRINCIPAL ACTIVITIES: Import and erection of Pre-fab houses, trading in building materials, household appliances etc; kitchen furniture assembly factory; hotel operations and management
Principal Agencies: Chain Link Fencing, UK; Walwin Pumps, UK; Salvarani SpA, Italy

No of Employees: 200

SABA & CO

PO Box 421, Manama
Tel: 254302
Cable: Sabaco Bahrain
Telex: 8769 Saba BN

PRINCIPAL ACTIVITIES: Public accountants, management and industrial property consultants
Branch Offices: Lebanon; Cyprus; Algeria; Bahrain; Egypt; Iraq; Jordan; Kuwait; Libya; Morocco; Oman; Qatar; Saudi Arabia; Syria; United Arab Emirates; Yemen

SADIQ & TAQI ALBAHARNA

See ALBAHARNA, SADIQ & TAQI,

SALAHUDDIN, MOHAMED, CONSULTING ENGINEERING BUREAU

123 Salahuddin Bldg, Road 402, Manama 304
Tel: 253663
Telefax: 240199

Chairman: Mohamed Salahuddin (Managing Director)
Directors: Ahmed Salahuddin
Senior Executives: Ebrahim Salahuddin (Administration Manager), K U Bangera (Projects Director)

PRINCIPAL ACTIVITIES: Consulting architects and engineers for all types of building projects
Associated Companies: Salahuddin - Travers Morgan (Consulting Engineers & Planners)
Principal Bankers: Standard Chartered Bank; Bank of Bahrain and Kuwait; Ahli Commercial Bank

Date of Establishment: 1970
No of Employees: 35

SALMAN AHMED KAIKSOW & SONS

See KAIKSOW, SALMAN AHMED, & SONS

SANTA FE INTERNATIONAL SERVICES INC

Middle East Regional Office, Alhasan Building, PO Box 5425, Manama
Tel: 252288
Telex: 8354 Sanafe BN

PRINCIPAL ACTIVITIES: On- and offshore oilwell drilling contractors and related services
Branch Offices: Santa Fe International (Egypt) Inc, PO Box 341, Cairo, Egypt; Kuwait Drilling Company, PO Box 9066, Ahmadi, Kuwait; Santa Fe International Services Inc, PO Box 219, Abqaiq, Saudi Arabia; Santa Fe International Services Inc, PO Box 4396, Doha, Qatar
Principal Bankers: Chase Manhattan Bank

SANWA BANK LTD (THE)

PO Box 20530, 3rd Floor, Yateem Centre, Manama
Tel: 256140
Telex: 9479 Snwbah BN
Telefax: 263423

Chairman: Kenji Kawakatsu (Japan)

PRINCIPAL ACTIVITIES: Representative office
Parent Company: Head office in Osaka, Japan

Date of Establishment: 1981

SARDAR & SONS

PO Box 691, Manama
Tel: 253938
Cable: Oldcar
Telex: 8714 BN

Directors: Abdul Nabi Sardar (Managing Director)
Senior Executives: A Karim Sardar (Plant Manager), A Khaliq Sardar (Yard Manager)

PRINCIPAL ACTIVITIES: Hiring of heavy plant and equipment, also distribution of drinking water
Principal Bankers: Bank of Bahrain & Kuwait; Bank Melli Iran

Date of Establishment: 1950
No of Employees: 30

SAUDI NATIONAL COMMERCIAL BANK

Zayani Bldg, PO Box 20363, Manama
Tel: 231182
Telex: 9298

PRINCIPAL ACTIVITIES: Offshore banking
Parent Company: Head office in Jeddah, Saudi Arabia

Date of Establishment: Licensed in 1979

SHEHABI TRADING & CONTRACTING

PO Box 5136, Manama
Tel: 276836
Cable: Shehabi Bahrain
Telefax: 274811

Chairman: Dr Ali Saleh Shehabi (Managing Director)
Senior Executives: Yahya Zaki (Construction Manager), K R Babu (Tourism Manager)

PRINCIPAL ACTIVITIES: Building, civil, electrical and mechanical contracting, manufacture of concrete blocks, import and wholesale of building materials
Principal Agencies: Emanex de Briare, France; Benfra SPA, Italy; Officine Meccaniche Fiori, Italy; BDC, UK; Jori Spa, Italy
Subsidiary Companies: Shehabi Travels
Principal Bankers: Banque du Caire, Bahrain
Financial Information:

	1990 BD'000
Annual turnover	1,000
Profits	100
Paid-up capital	1,500

Date of Establishment: 1968
No of Employees: 300 + Subcontractors

SHUTDOWN MAINTENANCE SERVICES WLL

PO Box 5871, Manama
Tel: 742961, 742962
Cable: Contesco
Telex: 8724 Sms BN
Telefax: 713691

Directors: Shawki Ali Fakhroo, John A Witter (Managing Director)
Senior Executives: Talal Reda, John A Witter Jr

PRINCIPAL ACTIVITIES: Refinery maintenance, gritblasting coatings, anti corrosion treatments, industrial painting, fibreglass applications, commercial cleaning and maintenance, security
Principal Bankers: Bank of Bahrain and Kuwait

Principal Shareholders: Shawki A Fakhroo, John A Witter
Date of Establishment: 1972
No of Employees: 220

SMIT INTERNATIONAL MIDDLE EAST

PO Box 5510, Manama
Tel: 727201, 727206/7
Cable: Smitbahr
Telex: 8659 Sime BN

PRINCIPAL ACTIVITIES: Marine services, salvage, antipollution, heavy lift, towage, chartering, diving services
Branch Offices: Smit Tak Offshore Services, PO Box 5687, Sharjah, UAE
Parent Company: Head Office: Smit International Group, 1 Zalmstraat, PO Box 1042, 3000 BA Rotterdam
Principal Bankers: AMRO Bank; ABN Bank

Date of Establishment: Bahrain: January 1976

SOLAR ENERGY CENTRE EC

PO Box 32225, Manama
Tel: 272425
Telex: 9648 ARCO ME

PRINCIPAL ACTIVITIES: Marketing, sales, installation and maintenance of solar powered systems and ''absolyte batteries''
Principal Agencies: Arco Solar Products; GNB Batteries Inc
Principal Bankers: Citibank, Bahrain

Principal Shareholders: ARCO Solar Inc; B M Harper; M H Harper
Date of Establishment: June 1981

STANDARD CHARTERED BANK

PO Box 29, Government Rd, Manama
Tel: 255946
Cable: STANCHART
Telex: 8229 SCBAH BN
Telefax: 230503

Senior Executives: A R Holden (Manager), P J Preston (Senior Manager Corporate Banking), Y A R Buchiri (Business Adviser), A F King (Manager Operations)

PRINCIPAL ACTIVITIES: Commercial banking
Branch Offices: In Bahrain: Manama (Main Office), Al Hoora, Muharraq, East Rifa'a, Diplomatic Area; Consumer Finance Division
Parent Company: Head Office in London, UK

Date of Establishment: 1920 in Bahrain
No of Employees: 275

STATE BANK OF INDIA

PO Box 5466, Manama
Tel: 245256, 253640, 253832
Cable: State Bank
Telex: 8636; 8804 BN
Telefax: 263045

Chairman: M N Goiporia
Senior Executives: T K Sinha (Managing Director), Bharat Bhattacharya (Dy Managing Director), M P Radhakhrishnan (Chief Manager Bahrain & Representative for Middle East)

PRINCIPAL ACTIVITIES: Offshore banking unit

Principal Shareholders: Reserve Bank of India
Date of Establishment: January 1977
No of Employees: 3740

SUMITOMO BANK LTD (THE)
Manama Centre, Part III 4th Floor, PO Box 20483, Manama
Tel: 231211
Telex: 9301 Sumtbk BN

Senior Executives: Tsunesaburo Suyama (General Manager & Chief Representative), Bunichi Yokoi (Representative)

PRINCIPAL ACTIVITIES: Banking (representative office)
Parent Company: Head Office in Osaka, Japan
Subsidiary Companies: In the Middle East: Sumitomo Finance (Middle East) EC

Date of Establishment: October 1979
No of Employees: 7

SUMITOMO FINANCE (MIDDLE EAST) EC
PO Box 20483, Manama
Tel: 270 710
Telex: 9938, 9939 SFME BN
Telefax: 271452

Senior Executives: Tsunesaburo Suyama (Managing Director & General Manager)

PRINCIPAL ACTIVITIES: Investment banking
Parent Company: The Sumitomo Bank Ltd

Principal Shareholders: The Sumitomo Bank Limited (100%)
Date of Establishment: April 1983
No of Employees: 9

SWISS BANK CORPORATION
PO Box 5560, Manama
Tel: 257221
Cable: Swissbank Bahrain
Telex: 8814 Swibah BN
Telefax: 274315

Senior Executives: Philip J White (Senior Vice President & Branch Manager)

PRINCIPAL ACTIVITIES: Offshore banking unit
Branch Offices: Head Office: Basel, Switzerland

Date of Establishment: In Bahrain: 1976

SYSCON TRADING & MECHANICAL SERVICES CO WLL
PO Box 5278, Manama
Tel: 254571, 263247
Cable: SYSCON - BAHRAIN
Telex: 8775 SYSCON BN
Telefax: 272912

Chairman: Hassan M Zainalabedin
Directors: Abdul Aziz Eshaq, Yousuf M Najibi

PRINCIPAL ACTIVITIES: Installation of Mitsubishi lift & escalator, industrial chemicals, packing and gaskets, pumps, valves, conveyor belts, mechanical seal, construction equipment and window cleaning equipment
Principal Agencies: Mitsubishi, Japan; Unispec Int'l; IMP, UK; Zep Mnfg Co, USA; Sealol, Kuwait; Allweiler, W Germany
Branch Offices: Khamis
Associated Companies: Abul Aziz Eshaq Est
Principal Bankers: Bank of Bahrain & Kuwait; British Bank of the Middle East, Manama

Principal Shareholders: Hassan M Zainalabedin, Yousuf M Najibi, Abdul Aziz Eshaq
Date of Establishment: 1976
No of Employees: 42

TALAL ABU GHAZALEH & CO
Talal Abu Ghazaleh Associates Ltd
PO Box 990, Manama
Tel: 251950
Cable: Auditors
Telex: 8350 BN

PRINCIPAL ACTIVITIES: Public accountants, management and industrial consultants
Branch Offices: Damman, Riyadh, Jeddah, Manama, Abu Dhabi, Dubai, Sharjah, Ras Al Khaimah, Ajman, Sulalah, Muscat, Doha, Amman, Damascus, Cairo, Beirut, Hudeidah, Sanaa, Aden, Baghdad
Parent Company: Head office in Kuwait

TATTAN, ABDULKAREM DARWISH,
PO Box 523, Manama
Tel: 253172, 230653
Cable: Foodco
Telex: 9178 Foodco BN

Chairman: A K D Tattan
Senior Executives: S Tattan (Marketing Manager)

PRINCIPAL ACTIVITIES: General merchants and commission agents (foodstuffs, household products, cosmetics and tobacco)
Principal Agencies: Reckitt & Colman (Overseas) Ltd, England; Alcan Aluminium, UK; Drackett Products Co, USA; Douwe Egberts, Holland
Principal Bankers: British Bank of the Middle East, National Bank of Bahrain

Date of Establishment: 1950

TECHNICAL, ENGINEERING & MARKETING SERVICES
T.E.A.M.S. Bahrain
PO Box 568, Manama
Tel: 243302, 243303
Cable: Teams Bahrain
Telex: 8297 Basrec BN
Telefax: 725584

Chairman: Ahmed Ali Kanoo
Directors: Mubarek Jasim Kanoo, Mohamed Yousuf Akbar Ali Reza, Abdul Rahman Kanoo, Khalid Mohamed Kanoo, Eng Khalid Abdul Rehman

PRINCIPAL ACTIVITIES: Marketing and installation of numerous products and equipment, mainly associated with the construction industry
Principal Agencies: Allenwest-Simplex GE, ICI, Willy Meyer & Sohn GmbH & Co, ABS Pumpen GmbH Ltd, Westag Getalit
Associated Companies: The Bahrain Ship Repairing and Engineering Company, PO Box 568, Bahrain
Principal Bankers: National Bank of Bahrain; British Bank of the Middle East

Principal Shareholders: Public shareholding company

THOMAS COOK TRAVELLERS CHEQUES LTD
Regional Headquarters, PO Box 5805, Manama
Tel: 530108
Cable: Cookbanker
Telex: 9099 Thcook
Telefax: 530801

PRINCIPAL ACTIVITIES: Sales marketing and distribution centre for travellers cheques within Gulf & Saudi Arabia
Parent Company: Midland Bank PLC

Principal Shareholders: Midland Bank Group
Date of Establishment: 1977

TNT SKYPAK INTERNATIONAL (BAHRAIN) EC

PO Box 20504, Al Matrook Bldg, Diplomatic Area, Manama
Tel: 533113
Telex: 9584 SKYPAK BN
Telefax: 533080

Chairman: John Robertson (Managing Director)
Directors: J Sancheti (Regional Financial Controller)
Senior Executives: Sean Bradley (UAE), Anton Barneveld
   (Regional Operations Manager), David Stasey (Regional Sales
   Manager), Paul Holmes (Bahrain)

PRINCIPAL ACTIVITIES: Worldwide courier service, collection,
   clearance and delivery of documents and commercial value
   items
Branch Offices: 400 Worldwide
Parent Company: TNT Thomas Nationwide Transport Ltd
Subsidiary/Associated Companies: TNT Overnite; TNT Comet
Principal Bankers: Grindlays Bank

TRADING & SERVICES CO (TASCO)

PO Box 20053, Al Khalifa Avenue, Manama
Tel: 256360, 256542
Cable: TASCO
Telex: 8233 Majal BN

PRINCIPAL ACTIVITIES: Manufacturers' representation, general
   trading and contracting

TRANS ARABIAN DEVELOPMENT CO EC

PO Box 20222, Manama
Tel: 533179
Telex: 9106 Trarab BN

Chairman: Iqbal G Mamdani
Directors: Mrs Shelby M Mamdani, A Baroom

PRINCIPAL ACTIVITIES: Financial, investment consultancy, and
   real estate services
Associated Companies: Transar Investment Co, Florida, USA;
   Transar Realty of Florida, USA; Transar Management Co,
   West Palm Beach, Florida; Trans Arabian Investment Bank
   EC, Bahrain
Principal Bankers: Paribas, Bahrain; Royal Trust Bank, Isle of
   Man

Date of Establishment: April 1978

TRANS ARABIAN INVESTMENT BANK EC (TAIB)

PO Box 20485, Sehl Centre, Diplomatic Area, Manama
Tel: 533334
Cable: TAIB Bahrain
Telex: 8598 Taib Bn, 9634 Taib FXBN
Telefax: 533174

Honorary Chairman: HRH Prince Saud Bin Naif Bin Abdulaziz
Directors: Sheikh Abdulrahman Al Jeraisy (Chairman), Iqbal G
   Mamdani (Vice Chairman & Chief Executive), Sheikh
   Abdulaziz Al-Rashid, Sheikh Ahmed M Baroom, Sheikh
   Mahfooz Bin Mahfooz, David D Carpita, Mohammed Al Attas,
   Nigel Astbury
Senior Executives: Iqbal G Mamdani (Chief Executive Officer),
   Nagaraj N Rao (Senior Vice President & General Manager),
   Ibrahim Sharif (Vice President & Asst General Manager), Jai N
   Gupta (Vice President), Fakhruddin Goga (VP & Group
   Financial Controller), Walter J Rathod (VP & Group Internal
   Auditor), Dayanand Shetty (Vice President)

PRINCIPAL ACTIVITIES: Merchant and investment banking
Branch Offices: Overseas Offices: New York; Hong Kong;
   Istanbul; Cairo
Parent Company: TAIB Holdings SA, Luxembourg
Subsidiary/Associated Companies: Subsidiaries: TAIB
   Investment Management Co EC, Bahrain; Yatirim Bank AS,
   Istanbul, Turkey. Associates: Creditcorp Ltd, London, UK;

Creditcorp SA, Geneva, Switzerland; Creditcorp International
   Inc, New York, USA; Creditcorp Asia Ltd, Hong Kong
Principal Bankers: Manufacturers Hanover Trust Co; American
   Express Bank, Lloyds Bank; Bank of Tokyo; Swiss Bank
   Corp
Financial Information:

	1988/89 US$'000	1989/90 US$'000
Authorised capital	100,000	100,000
Paid-up capital	75,000	75,000
Deposits	89,776	73,549
Loans & advances	80,358	118,628
Total assets	266,437	279,267
Net income	10,722	11,672

Principal Shareholders: Prominent Saudi Arabian businessmen
Date of Establishment: November 1979 (Exempt Company)
No of Employees: 74 Group

TRANSGULF TRADING INTERNATIONAL SA

PO Box 20400, Manama
Tel: 712303
Telex: 8704 TGT INT BN
Telefax: 712450

Directors: J M Fakhroo, A P Hedges, John Morgan

PRINCIPAL ACTIVITIES: Market research for general trading,
   real estate, mergers and acquisitions, financial services
Principal Agencies: Heston Middle East Ltd; Continental Land
   Investments Ltd; Jet Supply Ltd, Strom International;South
   Australian Breweries Ltd; John Holland Holdings Ltd;
   McWilliams Wines Ltd; Croucher Reoch and Partners Ltd;
   King Robert II Whisky Co; Pennant Holdings Ltd
Principal Bankers: Standard Chartered Bank, Lloyds Bank

Principal Shareholders: J M Fakhroo, A P Hedges
Date of Establishment: 1978

TRANSITEC GULF

PO Box 830, Unitag House, Manama
Tel: 252123
Cable: Transitec
Telex: 8622 Unitag BN
Telefax: 250838

Chairman: Jamil A Wafa
Directors: Shaikh Ali Bin Khalifa Al-Khalifa, Jamil A Wafa
Senior Executives: George Lyons (Executive Vice President)

PRINCIPAL ACTIVITIES: Electrical, mechanical, consulting
   engineers
Principal Agencies: Siemens AG, Germany; Ferranti Engineering
   Ltd, UK; Woma, Germany; Scharmann, Germany; Wilson
   Walton, UK; Wemco, UK
Associated Companies: UNITAG; Bahrain Weighing Equipment
Principal Bankers: Standard Chartered Bank

Date of Establishment: 1976

UCO MARINE CONTRACTING

PO Box 1074, Manama
Tel: 730816/8, 730206/8, 730851, 730006
Cable: Ucomarine Bahrain
Telex: 8260 UCO BN
Telefax: (0973) 732131

Directors: Ali Al Mussalam, Hassan Al Sabah, Bader A Kaiksow
Senior Executives: Akeel Ahmed Essa, A Hakim Bukamal

PRINCIPAL ACTIVITIES: Supply and rentals of tugs, barges,
   cargo vessels, utility boats; supply of Ras Al Khaimah
   aggregate; cranes/wheel loader/fork-lift/dump trucks hire;
   sales of dredged marine sand; sales and services of radio
   and radar equipment
Principal Agencies: Furuno; Standard, Japan
Branch Offices: PO Box 2137, Sharjah, UAE; Tel 351582, Telex
   68370 Uco EM, Fax (09716) 526508

Parent Company: UCO Marine Contracting WLL
Subsidiary Companies: Armcon, Bahrain; UCO Engineering; UCO Cold Store; Bahrain Bulk Handling
Principal Bankers: National Bank of Bahrain; Bank of Bahrain & Kuwait

Principal Shareholders: Directors as above
Date of Establishment: 1973
No of Employees: 250

UNION BANK OF SWITZERLAND

PO Box 795, Manama
Tel: 250811
Cable: Bankunion
Telex: 8222 Ubsbah BN

PRINCIPAL ACTIVITIES: Representative office

UNION DE BANQUES ARABES ET FRANCAISES
U.B.A.F.

PO Box 5595, Manama
Tel: 257393, 250985, 259539
Telex: 8840 BN

PRINCIPAL ACTIVITIES: Offshore banking unit

UNITAG GROUP

Unitag House, Government Avenue, PO Box 830, Manama
Tel: 246246
Cable: Unitag Bahrain
Telex: 8622 Unitag BN
Telefax: 250838

Chairman: Jamil A Wafa (Also Chief Executive)
Directors: Koshy Zachariah (Executive Vice President Finance), Faiz Rabeyeh (Vice President Personnel), Khalid Jamsheer (Vice President Administration & Special Projects)
Senior Executives: Mohamed J Zubari (Chairman Unitraco WLL), Farid K Junblatt (Executive Vice President), Koshy Zachariah (Executive Vice President), George Lyons (Executive Vice President)

PRINCIPAL ACTIVITIES: Company representation, contracting and trading, airlines representation and general travel services, general catering services, construction and civil engineering, specialist electrical engineering, quarry and mining services, general insurance and special engineering equipment supplies, money broking, hotel management
Principal Agencies: UTA French Airlines; Pan Am; Cathay Pacific; Ansett of Australia; Rolls Royce Ltd, UK; Air Inter, Air Afrique; Philippine Airlines, Canadian International Airways, Northwest Airlines, Iceland-Air, Siemens, Germany; Kraftwerk Union, Germany; B & B Italia, Italy; ICM Airport Technics, Germany; Scanrisk EC; Clearwater Systems, UK; Mareno Industries, Italy; Liquid Engineering, UK; Allied Medical Group, UK; Hanaoka Sharyo Co, Japan ; Thomson CSF, France; Hidada, Saudi Arabia; Whipp & Bourne, UK; Compagnie Generale de Geophysique, France; Airport Ground Equipment, France; Voko, Germany
Subsidiary/Associated Companies: World Travel Service, Transitec Gulf, Building Raw Materials Company, (Bramco), National Insurance Co, United Caterers & Contractors, Charles Fulton (Gulf) WLL, Bahrain Sainrapt Contracting Co, Bahrain Weighing & Equipment Est, UBFI, Regency Intercontinental Hotel, Sunshine Tours, Unitag WLL, Unitraco, Anaza, Bahrain Markets, Sedgwick Bahrain
Principal Bankers: Standard Chartered Bank

Principal Shareholders: Ali Bin Khalifa Al Khalifa, Salman Bin Khalifa Al Khalifa, Jamil Wafa and Mohammed Zubari
Date of Establishment: 1974

UNITED ARAB BROKING CO

PO Box 5488, Government Road, Manama
Tel: 251231/251375 (General)
Telex: 8604/5/6/7 UNABCO

Chairman: Sheikh Mohammed Bin Abdulla Al-Khalifa
Directors: David V Gladman, Charles Gregson

PRINCIPAL ACTIVITIES: Foreign exchange and deposit money brokers
Branch Offices: Head Office: Harlow Meyer Sawage Ltd, London Bridge, Adelaide House, London, UK
Subsidiary/Associated Companies: Mills & Allen International PLC (Parent Company) London
Principal Bankers: National Bank of Bahrain; Grindlays Bank Ltd

Principal Shareholders: Sheikh Mohammed Bin Abdulla Al-Khalifa (51%); Mills & Allen International PLC (49%)
Date of Establishment: February 1976
No of Employees: 18

UNITED ARAB SHIPPING CO SAG

PO Box 5367, Manama
Tel: 291291, 291726
Cable: UASCO
Telex: 9049 UASCO BN
Telefax: 291737

Chairman: Abdulaziz H Salatt
Directors: Eid Abdulla Yousuf (Director Bahrain)
Senior Executives: Farouk Nafawa (UASC Acting Chief Executive), Yousuf Zuwayed (Bahrain Branch Manager), Hajaj Bu Khadour (Regional Marketing Manager - Gulf)

PRINCIPAL ACTIVITIES: Shipping company, container service and cargo handling, line services
Principal Agencies: Yousuf Bin Ahmed Kanoo
Branch Offices: Abu Dhabi; Dubai; Saudi Arabia; Iraq; Qatar; Jordan; UK; Japan; USA
Parent Company: Head Office in Kuwait
Subsidiary Companies: Kuwait Shipping Agencies Co SAK, Arab Transport Co SAK ARATRANS
Financial Information:

	1989 KD'000
Authorised capital	500,000
Paid-up capital	280,000

Principal Shareholders: Government of Kuwait, Saudi Arabia, Bahrain, Qatar, United Arab Emirates, Iraq
Date of Establishment: 1976
No of Employees: 700

UNITED BANK LTD

PO Box 546, Manama
Tel: 254032/4
Telex: 8247 BN

PRINCIPAL ACTIVITIES: Commercial banking
Branch Offices: In the Middle East; Abu Dhabi; Dubai; Sharjah; Ras Al Khaimah; Umm Al Qaiwan; Ajman; Qatar; Bahrain; Saudi Arabia; Yemen
Parent Company: Head office in Karachi, Pakistan

UNITED BANK OF KUWAIT

PO Box 5494, Manama
Tel: 256774
Cable: Kuwfex Bn
Telex: 8651 BN
Telefax: (973) 259804

Chairman: Fahad Mazad Al Rajaan
Executive Committee: Ghanem Hamad Al Dabbous, Abdullah A Al Gabandi, Saad Ali A Nahedh, Hamad Abdulaziz Al Sagar, Najeeb Hamad Musaed Al Saleh

PRINCIPAL ACTIVITIES: Representative Office
Branch Offices: London (2 Branches); New York (1 Branch)

Parent Company: Head Office: The United Bank of Kuwait Ltd, 3 Lombard Street, London EC3V 9DT, UK

Subsidiary Companies: UBK Customer Services, PO Box 2616 Safat, Kuwait 13027, Tel 2527988, Fax 2520644, Telex 30296 UBKCS; UBK Asset Management (Guernsey); UBK Leasing Finance Ltd, UK; UBK Export Finance Ltd, UK; Venture Factors Plc, UK

Principal Shareholders: National Bank of Kuwait; Kuwait Investment Company; Commercial Bank of Kuwait; Gulf Bank; Kuwait Foreign Trading Contracting and Investment Co; Alahli Bank; Bank of Kuwait and the Middle East; Burgan Bank; Kuwait International Investment Co; Kuwait Real Estate Investment Consortium; Industrial Bank of Kuwait; Kuwait Real Estate Bank

Date of Establishment: Head Office 1966 - Bahrain 1976

UNITED BUILDING FACTORIES

PO Box 5761, Manama
Tel: 270439, 270445, 270499, 270636
Cable: Unibild
Telex: 8527 Ubfind BN
Telefax: 230614

Chairman: Abdulla Ahmed Nass
Directors: Mohammed Zubari (Vice-Chairman), V K Dewan (Managing Director), Sami A Nass, G Thomas, K Zachariah

PRINCIPAL ACTIVITIES: Precast concrete manufacturers, building contractors
Branch Offices: Factory, Tel 270636, 270445
Principal Bankers: Standard Chartered Bank
Financial Information:

	1989 BD'000
Sales turnover	2,000
Authorised capital	400
Paid-up capital	400

Principal Shareholders: A A Nass; Bramco WLL
Date of Establishment: 1976
No of Employees: 200

UNITED CATERERS & CONTRACTORS LTD

Unitag House, Government Avenue, PO Box 830, Manama
Tel: 250839
Cable: Unitag-Bahrain
Telex: 8622 Unitag BN
Telefax: 250838

Directors: Jamil A Wafa (Managing Director), Albert Abela (Chairman & Chief Executive, Albert Abela Corp)

PRINCIPAL ACTIVITIES: Industrial catering and camp services, foodstuffs and general supplies
Parent Company: Albert Abela Corporation, Monaco & London, UK
Associated Companies: Unitag Group of Companies, Bahrain; Albert Abela Group of Companies, London, UK
Principal Bankers: Chartered Bank; Bahrain; British Bank of the Middle East, Bahrain

Principal Shareholders: Unitag Group (51%); Albert Abela Group (49%)
Date of Establishment: August 1974
No of Employees: 180

UNITED COMMERCIAL AGENCIES

PO Box 166, Manama
Tel: 245250
Cable: UNITED
Telex: 8394 UNITED BN

Chairman: Mohanlal F Bhatia
Senior Executives: Latesh Gajria (Sales Manager), Chandu Bhatia (Manager)

PRINCIPAL ACTIVITIES: Agents and distributors

Principal Agencies: Honda Motor, Japan; Yuasa Batteries, Japan; Kuraray Hoses, Japan
Principal Bankers: British Bank of the Middle East
Financial Information:

	US$'000
Sales turnover	25,000

Date of Establishment: 1954

UNITED GULF ASPHALT CO WLL

PO Box 32129, Manama
Tel: 700116
Telex: 9830 UGA BN
Telefax: 700368

PRINCIPAL ACTIVITIES: Suppliers of asphalt and surfacings, bitumen, and emulsions; road surfacing contractors

UNITED GULF BANK BSC EC

UGB Tower, Diplomatic Area, PO Box 5964, Manama
Tel: 533233 General, 530532 Marketing
Cable: Unitedgulf
Telex: 9556 UGBADM
Telefax: 533137

Chairman: Mohammad Abdullah Boodai
Directors: Faisal Hamad Al Ayar, Ebrahim Abdulla Shehab, Tareq Khalid AL Sabeeh, Adel Yousif Al Muzaini, Abdul Aziz Abdul Razaq Al Jassar, Mubarak Mohammad Al Maskati, Masood Jowher Hayat, Najeeb Mohammad Hamadan, Amer Theyab Al Tameemi, Abdul Mohsen Jawher Hayat, Abdul Aziz Ebrahim Al Nabhan
Senior Executives: Abdul Mohsen J Hayat (Managing Director), Mohammad Haroon (Vice President Credit & Marketing), Ali Al Laith (Manager Operations & Admin), Sawsan Siddiqui (Manager Data Processing & Accounts)

PRINCIPAL ACTIVITIES: Investment banking
Parent Company: Kuwait Investment Projects Co, Kuwait
Subsidiary Companies: United Gulf Services Ltd, New York, USA; United Gulf Limited, London, UK
Financial Information:

	1989/90 US$'000
Net profit	10,568
Authorised capital	250,000
Paid-up capital	200,000
Total shareholders'equity	212,233
Total assets	230,713

Principal Shareholders: Kuwait Investment Projects Company, Kuwait
Date of Establishment: June 1980

UNITED GULF COMPANY

PO Box 988, Manama
Tel: 781002
Cable: Transarab Bahrain
Telex: 8340 Transa BN
Telefax: 686023

Chairman: Hussain Ali Bin Janahi
Directors: Ahmed Hussain Ali Janahi
Senior Executives: Mahmoud Mohd Mahmoud (Operations Manager)

PRINCIPAL ACTIVITIES: Importers, distributors and stockists of industrial/mechanical handling products and spare parts, chemicals
Principal Agencies: Lansing Ltd (UK), Esab (Sweden), Steelfab Ltd, Watts Tyres (Overseas) Ltd, Jones Cranes Ltd, Stothert & Pitt Ltd (Crane and Deck M Div), Storeline, Planmarine
Principal Bankers: Bank of Bahrain & Kuwait; United Bank Ltd

Principal Shareholders: Hussain Ali Bin Janahi, Ahmed Hussain Janahi
Date of Establishment: 1971

UNITED PARCEL SERVICE (UPS)

PO Box 113, Manama
Tel: 273123
Telex: 8540
Telefax: 263866

Senior Executives: Brent Edwards (Regional Manager)

PRINCIPAL ACTIVITIES: International courier service

UNIVERSAL ENTERPRISES

PO Box 1062, Manama
Tel: 290303 (6 lines), 292452
Cable: Gulfprize
Telex: 8318 Gprize BN
Telefax: 277567 Att Universal Ent

President: Mohammad Al Mannai (also Managing Director)
Directors: Talal M Al Mannai (Vice President)
Senior Executives: Nasir Raoof (Manager)

PRINCIPAL ACTIVITIES: Business promotion and sponsorship;
import of fresh and frozen meat; food and dairy products;
office equipment; computers; prefabricated houses;
home/office furniture and carpets, supermarkets, shelving and
warehousing
Principal Agencies: Portakabin, UK; Nashua Corp, USA;
Postalia, W Germany; Casio Computer, Japan; Fichet Bauche,
France; New Zealand Dairy Board; BSI Typewriters; Amanc,
Japan; GBC, Italy; Flakt Air Handling, UK; McCain Foods,
Canada; Meatcut, Denmark; United Foods Ltd, UAE; National
Foods, Pakistan; Tenani Furnitures, Italy; Baskin-Robbins,
USA; Galadari (Galaxy) Ice Cream, UAE
Branch Offices: Universal Enterprises (Overseas) Pvt Ltd, PO
Box 5886, Sharjah, UAE
Parent Company: Mannai Trading Co, PO Box 76, Doha, Qatar;
Telex: 47816, Tel: 593796/594329
Principal Bankers: National Bank of Bahrain; Al Ahli Commercial
Bank; Bank of Bahrain & Kuwait

Principal Shareholders: Proprietorship
Date of Establishment: 1972
No of Employees: 180

UNIVERSAL SHIPPING & TECHNOLOGY WLL

PO Box 5249, Manama
Tel: 253830, 253401, 240099
Cable: Uniship Bahrain
Telex: 8476 Unisip BN

Chairman: Mahmood Adeeb (Managing Director)
Directors: Nabeel Al Mahroos
Senior Executives: F F d'Souza (General Manager), C H
d'Almeida (Manager), Raffie Adeeb (Administrative Manager)

PRINCIPAL ACTIVITIES: Ship agents, clearing, forwarding,
transporting and forwarding agents, mechanical handling
equipment and transport contractors, traders, importers,
exporter, manufacturers of foodstuffs
Principal Agencies: Norasia Line, Orient Overseas Container
Line, Lauritzen Reefers
Subsidiary Companies: Delmon Heavy Transport Co; Universal
Chemical WLL; Universal Palace; Universal Food Factory
Principal Bankers: British Bank of the Middle East; Bank of
Bahrain & Kuwait

Date of Establishment: 1975
No of Employees: 54

USMAN C BALUCH

See BALUCH, USMAN C,

VENTURE GULF GROUP

PO Box 5553, Diplomatic Area, Manama
Tel: 232421
Telex: 8624 KHMZ BN

PRINCIPAL ACTIVITIES: Metal recycling plant; transport and
commercial vehicles hiring service, car hire, manufacturers'
representation, supply of industrial and construction
equipment, fibreglass products and chemicals, tanks, and
swimming pools contracting, plant hire
Branch Offices: Dubai, Qatar

WATSON HAWKSLEY

PO Box 5150, Manama
Tel: 712542, 712543
Telex: 8423 Culvrt BN

PRINCIPAL ACTIVITIES: Consultants for sewerage, sewage
disposal and water supply
Branch Offices: Dubai, Oman
Parent Company: Watson Hawksley, Terriers House, Amersham
Road, High Wycombe, Bucks, UK

YAMAICHI INTERNATIONAL (MIDDLE EAST) EC

PO Box 26894, Manama
Tel: 533422
Telex: 9468, 9469 Yamabh BN
Telefax: 533384

Directors: Yoshiyuki Atarashi (Managing Director)
Senior Executives: Katsuhiko Abe (Deputy General Manager)

PRINCIPAL ACTIVITIES: Investment banking
Branch Offices: Head Office: 4-1 Yaesu 2-Chome, Chuo-ku,
Tokyo 104, Japan
Parent Company: Yamaichi Securities Co Ltd
Principal Bankers: The Fuji Bank, Limited

Principal Shareholders: Yamaichi Securities Co Ltd
Date of Establishment: May 27, 1983
No of Employees: 21

YATEEM, A M, BROS

PO Box 60, Manama
Tel: 253177, 253450, 272601, 256675
Cable: Yateem
Telex: 8314, 9195, 8901 BN
Telefax: 274705

Chairman: Hussain Ali Yateem
Directors: Ali Yateem, Mohammed Yateem

PRINCIPAL ACTIVITIES: Real estate agents, general trading,
import and distribution of air-conditioning equipment, and
service; manufacture and supply of medical and industrial
oxygen, engineering equipment and service
Principal Agencies: Carrier; BKW; Brown Boveri; Nalco Italiana;
Cutler Hammer; Condair; Beckman; Wavin; Landir & Gyr;
Brooks etc
Principal Bankers: National Bank of Bahrain

Date of Establishment: 1910
No of Employees: 250

YATEEM INFORMATION SYSTEMS

PO Box 60, Manama
Tel: 274721
Telex: 8314 Yateem BN

Chairman: Husain Yateem
Directors: Ali Husain Yateem, Mohamed Husain Yateem
Senior Executives: Pradipta Guha (Manager), Amitabha Neil Ray
(Systems Incharge), Sarbajit Deb (Hadrware Engineer), Murali
Srinivasan (Sales Executive)

PRINCIPAL ACTIVITIES: Marketing and servicing of Mini and
Micro computers, supply of application software packages.
Marketing of computer media, access control system and
third party maintenance; marketing of voltage stabilisers
Principal Agencies: Management Assistence Inc, USA; Sord
Computer Corp, Japan; Arab Latin Information Systems,
Canada; VERBATIM - Datalife Diskettes; Cordata - IBM

Compatible Personal Computers; Lydiastar; Ling LDS Power Conditioner; Citizen Printers, UK; CMS Enhancements, USA; SBT Corp, USA
Branch Offices: Key Information Technology, PO Box 6856, Dubai, UAE
Parent Company: A M Yateem Bros
Principal Bankers: National Bank of Bahrain

Date of Establishment: 1981

YOUSUF AKBAR ALIREZA & SONS

See ALIREZA, YOUSUF AKBAR, & SONS

YOUSUF KHALIL ALMOAYYED & SONS WLL

See ALMOAYYED, YOUSUF KHALIL, & SONS WLL

YOUSUF MAHMOOD HUSAIN

Tijjar Rd, PO Box 23, Manama
Tel: 253547 (3 lines)
Cable: Husain
Telex: 8462 Husain BN
Telefax: 251607

Chairman: Ahmad Yousuf Mahmood
Directors: Aziz Yousuf Mahmood (Managing Director)
Senior Executives: Mukutar G Baqer (Sales & Admin Executive), Abbas Mohd Abbas (Sales Director), Kishor Tirathdas (Finance Director)

PRINCIPAL ACTIVITIES: General trading, import and distribution of pharmaceuticals, chemicals, detergents, vocational training aids and educational equipment, laboratory, veterinary and hospital equipment and furniture
Principal Agencies: Glaxo Group; A Wander; Baird & Tatlock; Boehringer; Colgate Palmolive, UK and USA; Eli Lilly; Imperial Chemical Industries; Johnson & Johnson International, UK and USA; Ciba-Geigy; May & Baker; Nicholas Laboratories; Parke Davis, UK and USA; Pfizer; Roussel Laboratories; S C Johnson & Son
Principal Bankers: Standard Chartered Bank; National Bank of Bahrain

Principal Shareholders: Ahmad Yousuf Mahmood and Abdul-Aziz Yousuf Mahmood
Date of Establishment: 1930
No of Employees: 50

YUSUF BIN AHMED KANOO WLL

See KANOO, YUSUF BIN AHMED, WLL

YUSUF BIN YUSUF FAKHROO

See FAKHROO, YUSUF BIN YUSUF,

ZAINAL, MOHAMED ALI, ABDULLA

PO Box 593, Manama
Tel: 254138, 250941
Cable: Zainaleyan
Telex: 8425 Zainal BN
Telefax: (973) 276746

Chairman: Ebrahim Zainal
Directors: Mohamed Sharif Zainal
Senior Executives: Mohamed Hussain Hassan, Yaseen Zainal

PRINCIPAL ACTIVITIES: Wholesale importers and distributors of all foodstuffs
Principal Agencies: Various food agencies and owners of private registered 'MAZA' label for food and general grocery
Principal Bankers: National Bank of Bahrain; The British Bank of the Middle East; Bank of Bahrain & Kuwait; Algemene Bank; Alahli Commercial Bank; Bahrain Islamic Bank

Principal Shareholders: Private family company
Date of Establishment: 1930

ZAYANI, A A, & SONS (MERCANTILE DIVISION)

PO Box 932, Manama
Tel: 251411, 255921
Cable: Zayani
Telex: 8367 Ahlan BN

Directors: Rashid Zayani, Ahmed Zayani, Jassim Zayani
Senior Executives: Faisal Zayani (Manager)

PRINCIPAL ACTIVITIES: General trading, manufacturer's representation
Principal Agencies: Imperial Chemical Industries Ltd; Otis International; Sanyo, Japan; Winget, UK; Serviced, UK; Eaton Corporation; Wickham Engineering Co, UK; Wacker, W Germany; Kelvinator International Inc; Godrej, India; Tecalemit, UK; SGB Export Ltd, UK
Branch Offices: A A Zayani & Sons, PO box 281, Abu Dhabi, A A Zayani & Sons, PO Box 167, Dubai; A A Zayani & Sons, PO Box 102, Alkhobar, Saudi Arabia
Subsidiary Companies: Kuwait Automobile & Trading, PO Box 41, Kuwait; Middle East Traders, PO Box 273, Doha, Qatar
Principal Bankers: Standard Chartered Bank; British Bank of the Middle East; Bank of Bahrain & Kuwait

ZAYANI COMPUTER SYSTEMS

PO Box 5918, Manama
Tel: 276278
Cable: PLANS BAHRAIN
Telex: 9015 PLANS BN
Telefax: 271761

Chairman: Faisal A Zayani
Senior Executives: Vivek Jaitpal (Manager), A Kanak (Hardware Engineer)

PRINCIPAL ACTIVITIES: Marketing various computers ranging from home computers to mini computers, providing total hardware and software support marketing facsimile machines, and various computer accessories such as floppy disks, mag tapes, etc
Principal Agencies: OKI Electric Industry Co, Japan; Hewlett-Packard, USA; BBC-Acorn, UK
Principal Bankers: British Bank of the Middle East

Date of Establishment: January 1983
No of Employees: 20

ZUBARI, ABDULREHMAN AHMED, & SONS

PO Box 82, Manama
Tel: 253375

Chairman: Mohammed Zubari

PRINCIPAL ACTIVITIES: Importers and distributors of mechanical and electrical appliances (ropes, steel pipes and fittings, oil-well equipment, paints, varnishes, safety equipment, etc)
Principal Agencies: James Walker & Co Ltd; Wilson Pipe Fittings; Namila Cordage Co; G B Kent; Excelsior Ropes Ltd; Van Leeuwen Buizer; Solten Export Trading; Joseph Nason & Co Ltd

Major Companies of EGYPT

ABOUKIR ENGINEERING INDUSTRIES CO

Aboukir, Alexandria
Tel: 560140, 560538
Cable: Fakir-Aboukir Alex
Telex: 54179 AEI UN

Chairman: Eng Mousa Fargly Hassan
Senior Executives: Eng Raouf Ragib (Production Manager),
Hamed Ebrahim Rizk (Financial Manager), Ali Hafez Ali
(Commercial Manager)

PRINCIPAL ACTIVITIES: Production of cans, aerosols
containers, sporting cartridges, plastic caps, aluminium
bottles and cans, tin plate cans, ovens, water desalination
units, transportation and moving line for stores and factories

Principal Shareholders: Public sector company

ABU SIMBEL SHIPPING AGENCY

71 El Horriya Street, Alexandria
Tel: 4937110, 4937111
Telex: 54129, 54491 Simbel UN

PRINCIPAL ACTIVITIES: Shipping agency

Principal Shareholders: Part of the Alexandria Co for Shipping
Agencies

ABU ZAABAL CO FOR SPECIALITY CHEMICALS

Abu Zaabal, Cairo
Tel: 875856/7, 692489
Cable: Ardob
Telex: 92283 NITRO

Chairman: Eng El Sayed Younis Darwish

PRINCIPAL ACTIVITIES: Production of nitro-cellulose, gun
powder, stearic acid, ether, dynamite, margarine
Branch Offices: 23 Talaat Harb St, Cairo
Subsidiary Companies: Wasaabal Co for Projects - Johnson
Wax
Principal Bankers: National Bank of Egypt

Principal Shareholders: Public sector company

ABU ZAABAL FERTILIZER & CHEMICAL CO

17 Sh Kasr El Nil, Cairo
Tel: 978330, 977177, 977155, 924324

PRINCIPAL ACTIVITIES: Production of calcium superphosphate,
sulphuric acid, oleum
Branch Offices: Factory: Abu Zaabal, Tel 869682, 877132 and
phosphoric plant in the Al-Sibaiyah West
Parent Company: Responsible to the Ministry of Industry

Principal Shareholders: Public sector company

AFRO ASIAN ORGANISATION FOR ECONOMIC CO-OPERATION

AFRASEC

Chamber of Commerce Bldg, 4 Midan Al Falaki, Cairo
Tel: 32941, 32983
Cable: Afrasec

President: Zakaria Tewfik Abdel Fattah

PRINCIPAL ACTIVITIES: Industrialisation and economic
relations between the Central Chambers of Commerce of 45
countries

AGREXPORT

PO Box 153, Alexandria
Tel: 4820654
Cable: Agrexport Alexandria
Telex: 54053 Comlx UN, 54304 Manx UN

Chairman: Adib Elias Hamaty

PRINCIPAL ACTIVITIES: Export of agricultural products, fruit
and vegetables, fresh and frozen, spices, seeds, herbs,
aromatic plants
Principal Bankers: Bank of Alexandria

Principal Shareholders: Private company
Date of Establishment: 1968

AL AHRAM ORGANISATION

Sharia El Galaa, Cairo
Tel: 758333, 745666, 755500
Cable: Al-Ahram-Cairo
Telex: 92544, 92001 Ahram UN

Chairman: Abdalla Abdel Bari
Directors: Ibrahim Nafei, Dr Gamal El Oteifi, Salah Montasser,
Salah Galal, Sayed El Gabri, Aly Abdel Naby, Aly Ghoneim

PRINCIPAL ACTIVITIES: Printing, publishing and advertising
Branch Offices: In major towns in Egypt, and representatives
worldwide
Subsidiary Companies: Al Ahram Investment Co; Al Ahram
Commercial Printing Co; Pyramid Advertising Agency; Al
Ahram Distributing Agency; Microfilm & Organisation Centre;
AMAC Al Ahram Management & Computer Centre; Al Ahram
Centre for Scientific Translation; SICEP Societe industrielle
des Crayons et Plastiques SAE
Principal Bankers: National Bank of Egypt; Suez Canal Bank

Date of Establishment: 1875
No of Employees: 5,000

AL-AKARIA CO

2 Abdelhamid Said St, Talaat Harb, Cairo
Tel: 48235, 54033
Cable: Makakom
Telex: 92412 UN

Chairman: Eng Abdel Wahab M Selim
Directors: Eng M Sani Eldin (General Manager)

PRINCIPAL ACTIVITIES: Land reclamation, civil contracting and
commercial agency
Principal Agencies: Komatsu, Japan; CIFA, Italy; Astra, Italy;
Longinotti, Italy; Marini, Italy; Bulgari, Italy; Baioni, Italy;
Ruggeri, Italy
Branch Offices: Saudi Arabia: Ehsaa
Subsidiary/Associated Companies: Joint venture with Arab
Organization for Engineering and Contracting, Saudi Arabia
Principal Bankers: Bank Misr, Cairo; Banque du Caire, Cairo;
International Arab Bank, Cairo

Principal Shareholders: Public sector

AL CHARK INSURANCE CO SAE

15 Kasr El-Nil St, Cairo
Tel: 753238, 740660
Cable: Viechark
Telex: 92276 Chark UN

Chairman: Ezzat Abdel Bary
Directors: Ahmed Fouad Abou Haggar (Vice-Chairman),
Mahmoud El-Khodary, Gamal Shata, Hassan Atteya, Aly
Selait
Senior Executives: Dr Korayem El Daif (Life), Nabil Morsy (Life),
Mohamed El Gamal (Fire), Reda Hussein (Marine & Motor),
Aly Badawi (Accident), Mohamed Abdullah (Energy &
Engineering), Galal Madkour (Reinsurance), Anwar Bismark
(Reinsurance)

PRINCIPAL ACTIVITIES: Life, fire, marine & motor, accident,
energy & engineering, reinsurance
Branch Offices: 152 branches
Principal Bankers: Banque du Caire, Delta Bank, Egypt;
National Westminster Bank, UK; UBAF, France

Principal Shareholders: Public Sector company responsible to the Ministry of Economy & Foreign Trade, and supervised by Egyptian Insurance Supervisory Authority
Date of Establishment: 1931
No of Employees: 4720

ALCOTAN COTTON TRADING & EXPORT CO

16 Sharia Sesostris, Alexandria
Tel: 4824667
Cable: Alfacot-Alex
Telex: 54026 ALFAC UN
Telefax: 4839601

Chairman: Dr Shamel Abaza
Directors: Said Sourour (Commercial Director), Abdel Fattah Gomaa (Financial Director), Badr El Dln Saleh (Sales Director), Maria Messina Salib (Marketing Director), Ahmed Bassouni (Purchasing Director), Ibrahim Gad (Personnel Director), Hussein Salama (Technical Director)

PRINCIPAL ACTIVITIES: Export of cotton
Branch Offices: 41 Sherif Street, Cairo, Tel 44644; Damanhour; Kafr Zayat; Benha; Zagazig; Zifta; Mehalla Kobra; Mansourah (Lower Egypt); Samallout; Assiout; Sohag; Girga (Upper Egypt)
Parent Company: Responsible to the Ministry of Trade
Principal Bankers: Banque du Caire, Alexandria

Principal Shareholders: Public sector company
No of Employees: 1,000

ALEXANDRIA BRASS FOUNDRY

Leon Froundjian & Co

76 Al Gomhouria St, Cairo
Tel: 915264
Cable: Phosbronze

Chairman: Leon Froundjian (also General Manager)
Directors: Joseph Froundjian (Technical Manager), Rafik Froundjian (Accounting Manager)

PRINCIPAL ACTIVITIES: Production and sale of phosphor bronze bars (sold and hollow) and anti-friction white metal
Branch Offices: Factory: 41 Port Said St (Industrial Zone), Cairo PO Box 72, Faggala, Cairo, Tel 876632
Principal Bankers: Banque de Caire; Chase Manhattan Bank

Principal Shareholders: Private company
Date of Establishment: 1940
No of Employees: 50

ALEXANDRIA CO FOR METAL PRODUCTS

72 ElShahid Galal ElFessouki Sh, PO Box 386, Alexandria
Tel: 4927069

PRINCIPAL ACTIVITIES: Manufacture of enamelled sheet iron, domestic ware, gas cookers, razor blades, metal barrels
Branch Offices: Iron Sheets & Razor Blades Factory; Metal Products Factory
Parent Company: Responsible to the Ministry of Industry

Principal Shareholders: Public sector company

ALEXANDRIA CO FOR SHIPPING AGENCIES

71 El Horreya Street, PO Box 405, Alexandria
Tel: 4916624, 4916753
Cable: Margent
Telex: 54086, 54487 Alag UN

PRINCIPAL ACTIVITIES: Shipping agents, clearing & forwarding agents, touristic agents, IATA members
Parent Company: Responsible to the Ministry of Maritime Transport
Subsidiary Companies: Abu Simbel Shipping Agency; Amoun Shipping Agency; Memphis Shipping Agency; Thebes Shipping Agency; Thebes Tourism (IATA member)

Principal Bankers: Banque du Caire; National Bank of Egypt; Alexandria Commercial & Maritime Bank

Principal Shareholders: Public sector company

ALEXANDRIA COMMERCIAL & MARITIME BANK

PO Box 2376, 85 Avenue El Horreya, Alexandria
Tel: 4921556, 4921237, 4929203
Cable: Comarit
Telex: 54553 ACMB UN
Telefax: 4913706

Chairman: Adel Ghaleb Mahmoud
Directors: Dr Naim Abou Taleb, Fouad Bayoumi Hashem, Mohamed Ibrahim Hassan, Abdel Aziz El Tayeb Kouratem, Bakr Abdel Ghani El Badri, Moustafa Gaber Mahmoud, Ahmed Zaki Mansour, Hussein Hussein El Hawari, Ahmed Dia Eldin Mohamed Fahmy, Sayed Mohamed Saleh, Eng Mohamed Mahmoud Abdel Nabi, Mohamed Fahmy Abdel Aal, Omar Mohamed Tamoum, Mohamed Adel Mohamed El Gammal, Moustafa Mohamed Nour Eldin
Senior Executives: Mohamed M Fahmy (Managing Director)

PRINCIPAL ACTIVITIES: Full range of banking services with emphasis on maritime business
Branch Offices: Cairo: PO Box 2216, 10 Talaat Harb St, Tel 767233, 771244, Telex 20387
Financial Information:

	US$'000
Authorised capital	30,000
Paid-up capital	30,000

Principal Shareholders: National Investment Bank, Bank of Alexandria, National Bank of Egypt, Misr Insurance Co, Egyptian Co for Maritime Transport, Alexandria Maritime Agencies Co, Canal Maritime Agencies Co, Arab Stevedoring Co, Egyptian Shipbuilding & Repair Co, Famco Insurance & Pension Fund
Date of Establishment: 1981
No of Employees: 158

ALEXANDRIA COMMERCIAL CO SAE

1 Sharia Ahmed Abdulsalem, PO Box 623, Alexandria
Tel: 4927360, 4927368, 4927369, 4930005
Cable: Commodate-Alex
Telex: 54067 Comod UN, 54411 Comod UN

PRINCIPAL ACTIVITIES: Export of cotton
Branch Offices: Delta & Upper Egypt
Parent Company: Responsible to the Ministry of Trade
Principal Bankers: Public Sector Banks

Principal Shareholders: Public Sector company
Date of Establishment: September 1923
No of Employees: 900

ALEXANDRIA GENERAL CONTRACTING CO

16 Sharia Adly, Cairo
Tel: 916788

PRINCIPAL ACTIVITIES: Civil engineering and construction
Branch Offices: 2 Sharia Mahmoud Azmi, Alexandria, Tel 30303
Parent Company: Responsible to the Ministry of Housing

Principal Shareholders: Public sector company

ALEXANDRIA HARBOUR AUTHORITY

66 Tarik Gamal Abdel Nasser, Alexandria
Tel: 4934321/4

PRINCIPAL ACTIVITIES: Supervision and management of the Port of Alexandria
Parent Company: Responsible to the Ministry of Maritime Transport

Principal Shareholders: Public sector company

ALEXANDRIA KUWAIT INTERNATIONAL BANK

Head Office, 10 Talaat Harb Street, Evergreen Bldg/4th Floor, Cairo
Tel: 779766, 764644, 762733
Cable: AKIBANK
Telex: 21394 AKIHO UN, 20398 AKIEX UN
Telefax: 764844

Chairman: Elsayed El Habashy (Managing Director)
Directors: Kamal Eldin A Zayed, Salah El Din Hassan Basyony, Abdullah A A Alshrahan, Mubarak M Elotaibi, Abdul Azeem A Azzam, Mufeed M Elaradi
Senior Executives: Mahmoud A W Shehata (Senior Deputy General Manager), Ahmed Fawzi El Shahed (Senior Deputy General Manager), Mohamed A Naguib (Deputy General Manager), Hassan M A Hassanein (Deputy General Manager), Mohamed A R Gohar (Deputy General Manager), Moustafa Abdel Wahab Khallaf (Asst General Manager), Moustafa Shoukry Ahmed (Asst General Manager), Farouk El Ghazawi (Asst General Manager), Abd El Aziz Mohamed Ali (Asst General Manager), Reda Askar (Asst General Manager), Nabil El Dardiry (Asst General Manager)

PRINCIPAL ACTIVITIES: Commercial banking
Branch Offices: Cairo Branch: 110 Kasr El Eini St, Tahrir Square, PO Box 10004, Cairo; Alexandria Branch; 29 El Naby Danial St, PO Box 3014, Alexandria; Al-Azhar branch: 106 Al Azhar Street, Cairo, Heliopolis Branch: 80 Khalifa Al-Mamouen St, Roxy; Mohandeseen Branch: 4 Syria Street, Mohandeseen
Subsidiary Companies: Suez Cement Co, Nile Shoes Manufacturing Co, Middle East Investment Co, Al Timsah Co for Touristic Projects

Principal Shareholders: Egypt: Bank of Alexandria (25%), Bank for Development and Agriculture Credit (4.46%), Egyptian Individuals (18.13%), Egyptian Companies (8.8%), Emirates Interests (13.41%), Kuwaiti Individuals (28.23%), Arab Individuals (2%)
Date of Establishment: 1978
No of Employees: 366

ALEXANDRIA OIL & SOAP CO

Soc D'Alexandrie des Huileries et Savonneries

76 Sharia Canal El Mahmoudieh, PO Box 402, Alexandria
Tel: 4927234, 4925671

PRINCIPAL ACTIVITIES: Production of cotton seed, oil and margarine, animal fodder, glycerine, caustic soda, chlore, industrial detergents, chemicals, hydrogen
Branch Offices: Cairo Office: 11 Midan El Tahrir, Tel 974379, Cable Emadoil
Parent Company: Responsible to the Ministry of Industry

Principal Shareholders: Public sector company

ALEXANDRIA PASSENGERS TRANSPORT AUTHORITY

PO Box 466, 3 Aflatone Street, Chatby, Alexandria
Tel: 5961810, 5975223
Cable: Ramelec/PO Box 466
Telex: 54637 APTA/UN

Chairman: Eng Mohamed Salah Eldin Abd Elmoneim
Senior Executives: Mustafa Hossen (GM Financial Affairs), Aly Abd El Hameed Saad (GM Purchasing & Stores), Mohamed Fathy Abd El Moneim (GM Admin Affairs)

PRINCIPAL ACTIVITIES: Public transport around Alexandria city by buses and tramcars
Principal Bankers: National Bank of Egypt, Alexandria

Date of Establishment: 1860
No of Employees: 8,988

ALEXANDRIA PETROLEUM COMPANY

PO Box 3, Mex, Alexandria
Tel: 4922833, 4923600
Cable: Petmex, Alex
Telex: 54369 Petax UN

PRINCIPAL ACTIVITIES: Oil refining
Parent Company: Affiliated to the Egyptian General Petroleum Corp
Principal Bankers: National Bank of Egypt, Alexandria
Financial Information: Responsible to the Ministry of Petroleum

Principal Shareholders: EGPC
Date of Establishment: June 1957
No of Employees: 1,700

ALEXANDRIA PHARMACEUTICALS & CHEMICAL INDUSTRIES CO

10 Sharia Sidi Metwalli, Alexandria
Tel: 4924146, 4937273, 4937434

PRINCIPAL ACTIVITIES: Distribution of chemicals and pharmaceuticals
Branch Offices: Cairo Office: 6 Sharia Abdel Hamid Said, Tel 973744, 83722
Parent Company: Responsible to the Ministry of Health

Principal Shareholders: Public sector company

ALEXANDRIA PORTLAND CEMENT CO

Mex, Alexandria
Tel: 4923605, 4924974
Cable: CEMALEX
Telex: 54243 ALEX UN

Chairman: Moustafa Mohamed Abou Zeid
Senior Executives: Eng Hassan Foula (General Manager), Kamel Mahmoud Abd Allah (Finance Manager), Abd El Kader Mokhtar (Production Manager), Eng Mohamed Nagy (Technical Manager)

PRINCIPAL ACTIVITIES: Production of ordinary Portland cement, rapid hardening cement, Portland blast furnace cement, sea water cement
Branch Offices: Cairo Office: 5 Sharia 26 July, Cairo
Parent Company: Responsible to the Organisation of Building Materials & Housing
Principal Bankers: Bank of Alexandria, National Bank of Egypt, Bank Misr, Suez Canal Bank, Bank of Cairo
Financial Information:

	1990/91 E£'000
Sales turnover	46,009
Profits	11,629
Authorised capital	34,919
Paid-up capital	34,919
Total assets	159,708

Principal Shareholders: Public sector company
Date of Establishment: 1948
No of Employees: 1,500

ALEXANDRIA SHIPYARD

Gate 36, Kabbary, Alexandria 21553
Tel: 4453090, 4455090, 4454420
Cable: Alexyard
Telex: 54069 Alxard UN, 55486 Alxard UN
Telefax: 4454672

Chairman: Eng T A El-Magraby
Directors: M Reda Eldieb (Technical Director), E Bayomi (Financial Director), Eng M Farag (Ship Repair Director)
Senior Executives: H Abdel Maboud (Production Director), Hassan A Abouraya (Information Systems General Manager)

PRINCIPAL ACTIVITIES: Ship building and repairing, offshore units building and repairing, manufacturing of heavy steel structures and heavy lifting equipment and cranes,

manufacturing of containers, ship scrapping, spare parts
manufacturing
Parent Company: Responsible to the Ministry of Industry
Principal Bankers: National Bank of Egypt
Financial Information:

| | 1990 |
	E£'000
Sales turnover	92,000
Authorised capital	56,000

Principal Shareholders: Government owned
Date of Establishment: 1970
No of Employees: 5,600

ALEXANDRIA WATER GENERAL AUTHORITY

61 Tareek El Horreya, Alexandria
Tel: 4923047, 4932847
Cable: Waterworks Alex
Telex: 54307 Awga UN

Chairman: Eng Mohamed Ahmed Marzouk

PRINCIPAL ACTIVITIES: Water supply
Branch Offices: 9 branch offices
Parent Company: Responsible to the Governorate of Alexandria
Principal Bankers: Banque du Caire
Financial Information:

	E£'000
Authorised capital	32,000

Principal Shareholders: Public sector company

AL HANA CO

Sohair Nawar & Partners

PO Box 82 Aurman, 66 Abu-Maaty St, Aguza, Geiza
Tel: 808358, 805965
Telex: 94004 UN

Chairman: Dr Ahmed El Shafei
Directors: Mrs Sohair Abu Mandoor Nawar

PRINCIPAL ACTIVITIES: Export, import, contracting, market
consulting, building materials, paints, sanitaryware, irrigation
services, mechanical engineering, plastic and metal products,
real estate, agencies
Principal Agencies: Dynamic Industries, Cardinal Scale Co,
Nissan Kizai Co, Natelco Co, Nufins Co
Branch Offices: Bilbis, Alexandria
Associated Companies: El Murra Lakes Investment Co; Plastic
Pipes & Products Manufacturing Co; El Shafei Food Co;
Green Fields Co
Principal Bankers: Cairo Bank; El-Nile Bank

Principal Shareholders: Dr El-Shafei Family
Date of Establishment: 1978
No of Employees: 30

AL-KAHIRA COTTON TRADING CO

12 Talaat Nooman St, Alexandria
Tel: 808477, 808536
Cable: Kaircot-Alex
Telex: 54144 Kaircot

PRINCIPAL ACTIVITIES: Export of cotton
Parent Company: Responsible to the Ministry of Trade

Principal Shareholders: Public sector company

AL KAHIRA PHARMACEUTICAL & CHEMICAL INDUSTRIES CO

46A Sharia Kasr El Eini, Cairo
Tel: 25094/7
Cable: Dosenal

PRINCIPAL ACTIVITIES: Production of pharmaceuticals and
chemicals
Parent Company: Responsible to the Ministry of Health

Principal Shareholders: Public sector company

AL KAMAR FACTORY FOR OILS PAINTS & CHEMICALS

32 Zaher Bayoumi St, Hadara, PO Box 75, Alexandria
Tel: 70559

PRINCIPAL ACTIVITIES: Production of synthetic paints,
lacquers, marine, plastic, thermal and anti-acid paints and
varnishes for ground and paintings

Principal Shareholders: Private Company

AL TAHRIR PRINTING & PUBLISHING HOUSE

24 Zakaria Ahmed Street, Cairo
Tel: 751511, 744166, 741611
Cable: Annonce Cairo
Telex: 92475 Tahrir UN
Telefax: 776399

Chairman: Samir Ragab
Directors: Mahmoud Rasheed (General Manager)
Senior Executives: Edward Attia (Deputy General Manager)

PRINCIPAL ACTIVITIES: Printing, publishing and advertising
Principal Agencies: SEP; SOP; Al Gomhouria for Press; United
Distribution
Branch Offices: Alexandria and all provinces
Parent Company: Al Tahrir, holding company
Associated Companies: United Distribution Co; Societe
Egyptienne de Publicite (see separate entry); Al Gomhouria
Press; Societe Orientale de Publicite
Principal Bankers: National Bank of Egypt, Banque de Caire,
Citibank, Bank of Greece
Financial Information:

| | 1990 |
	E£'000
Sales turnover	15,000
Total assets	40,000

Principal Shareholders: Shoura consultative Council; Supreme
Council For Press
Date of Establishment: 1953
No of Employees: 7,400

ALUMINIUM COMPANY OF EGYPT

5 Abd Elkhalek Sarwat Street, Cairo
Tel: 924710, 924787, 922284
Cable: Egyptalum
Telex: 92119 EGTAL UN, 94131 EGTAL UN

Chairman: Eng Soliman Reda
Directors: Eng Ismail Mahmod (Chief of Projects), Ramzi
Shaaban (Chief of Industrial Relation), Mohamed Zaki (Chief
of Financial Sectors), Galal Lotfi (Chief of Commercial Sector)

PRINCIPAL ACTIVITIES: Production of primary aluminium
Branch Offices: Alexandria, (2 Horreya Road); Safaga
Parent Company: Responsible to the Ministry of Industry
Principal Bankers: Bank of Alexandria, Cairo

Principal Shareholders: Public sector company
Date of Establishment: 1975
No of Employees: 8,000

ALWATANY BANK OF EGYPT

PO Box 750, 1113 Corniche El Nil, Cairo
Tel: 760070, 753479, 740728, 740762
Cable: Alwatany Cairo
Telex: 93268, 21168 Watan UN, 21108
Telefax: 772959

Chairman: Fathalla R Mohamed
Directors: Adel Hussein Ezzi, Tawfik J Yassin, Abdul M Seoudi,
Galal S Madkour, Ahmed F Hussein, Ali A Al Agroudi, Subeah
A Dief, Hassan G Sheba
Senior Executives: Tawfik J Yassin (Managing Director &
General Manager)

PRINCIPAL ACTIVITIES: Commercial banking

Branch Offices: Alexandria, Cornish El Nil, Sarwat, Heliopolis, Dokki branch for Islamic Operations

Financial Information:

	1990
	E£'000
Authorised capital	28,000
Paid-up capital	17,500

Principal Shareholders: Private and public sectors
Date of Establishment: 1980
No of Employees: 326

ALY, MAHMOUD & ABDEL RAZEK, & CO

47 Ramses St, PO Box 1600, Cairo
Tel: 743982, 743993
Cable: Alarazek Cairo Egypt
Telex: 92709 Omda UN

Chairman: Abdel Razek UN
Directors: Emad Abdel Razek (General Manager)

PRINCIPAL ACTIVITIES: Import of automotive and spare parts and earthmoving equipment; agents and general traders
Principal Agencies: A W Chesterton, Boston, USA; Federal Mogul, Jacksonville; Protexa Contractors, Mexico; Wheatherby Engineering, USA
Branch Offices: 2 Abdel Hamid Loufty St, Cairo Tel 704052; 46 Mohamed Farid St, Cairo, Tel 976982
Principal Bankers: National Societe Generale; National Bank of Egypt

Date of Establishment: 1952

AMERICAN EXPRESS BANK LTD

PO Box 1824, 4A Ibn Zanki Street, Zamalek, Cairo
Tel: 412287, 410236, 404253
Telex: 93610 AMBNK UN

Senior Executives: N A Chowdhury (General Manager), A Dabbous (Marketing Manager), A Hamdy (Operations Manager)

PRINCIPAL ACTIVITIES: Banking

AMOCO EGYPT OIL COMPANY

14 Road 252, Digla, Maadi
Tel: 3530703
Cable: Amocoegypt
Telex: 92027 Amocoegypt UN
Telefax: 3530703 ext 143

President: D F Work (Chairman & General Manager)
Senior Executives: E R McHaffie (General Manager Administrative & Financial Affairs), T G Russel (Exploration Manager), Y H Serry (Financial Manager), A El Aguizy (Administrative Manager), D Hutchinson (Human Resources Manager)

PRINCIPAL ACTIVITIES: Oil exploration and production
Parent Company: Standard Oil Company (Indiana)

Principal Shareholders: Wholly owned subsidiary of Amoco Production Company. Amoco Egypt Oil Co owns petroleum rights in the Gulf of Suez and Western Desert jointly with the state owned Egyptian General Petroleum Corporation (EGPC)
No of Employees: 79

AMOUN SHIPPING AGENCY

17 El Horriya Street, Alexandria
Tel: 4937115, 4931470
Telex: 54127, 54507

PRINCIPAL ACTIVITIES: Shipping Agency

Principal Shareholders: Part of Alexandria Co for Shipping Agencies

ANTIBIOTIC & VACCINES AUTHORITY

51 Sharia Wizaret El Ziraha, Agouza, Cairo
Tel: 807180, 81776

PRINCIPAL ACTIVITIES: Production of antibiotics and vaccines
Parent Company: Responsible to the Ministry of Health
Financial Information: 19?

Principal Shareholders: Public sector company

ARAB AFRICAN INTERNATIONAL BANK

PO Box 60 (Magles El Chaab), 11516 Cairo
Tel: 3545094/5/6
Cable: Arabafro HO
Telex: 93531 AAIB UN, 21266 AAIB UN, 21566 AAIB UN, 22306 AABEX UN
Telefax: (202) 3558493

Chairman: Ali Abdul Rahman R Albader
Directors: Mohamed Ibrahim Farid (Vice Chairman & Managing Director), Abdel Aziz Abdel Razzak Al Jassar, Mahmoud A Al Nouri, Badr Salman Al Rashoud, El Sayed Maghrabi Singer, Mohamed Taher El Ashry, Mohamed Al Hadi Mohamed Al Anwar Salem, Saadoun Abdel Razzak Kubba, Dr Abdul Meguid Qasem Nasser, Mansour M Lotaief (General Secretary to the Board)
Senior Executives: Sami El Halawany (General Manager), Mohsen Khaled (General Manager London), Hussein Gamgoum (General Manager Admin & Visa), Mansour Lotaief (General Secretary & Legal Counsellor), Mostafa Yassin (Deputy General Manager EDP), Aly El Labban (Deputy General Manager Correspondent Banking), Zohair Fahmy (Deputy General Manager Credit & Int'l Finance), Ahmed Gad (Manager Portfolio Control), Mohamed Abdel Fatah (Manager Operations), Ahmed Gad (Manager Portfolio Control), Abdel Kerim Kotb (Manager Budgets & Accounts)

PRINCIPAL ACTIVITIES: Commercial and investment banking
Branch Offices: Branches in Egypt (Cairo: PO Box 1143, Tel 3916710, 3911309, Telex 22363, 92071, Branch Manager Amin Al Aroussy; Alexandria: 73 Eng Ahmed Mohamed Ismail St, Tel 4221120, Telex 54789, Manager Aly Saleh; Heliopolis: PO Box 5842, Heliopolis West, Cairo, Tel 667413, Telex 23313, Manager Bahaa Farwiz); also in UAE (Dubai, Abu Dhabi); Lebanon (Beirut); UK (London); USA (New York)
Subsidiary Companies: Egypt Arab African Bank; Tunis Arab African Bank
Financial Information:

	1989/90
	US$'000
Shareholders funds	504,559
Loans & advances	1,094,579
Deposits	1,565,461
Reserves	4,290
Total assets	2,398,628

Principal Shareholders: Capital held by the Governments of Kuwait (43.66%), Egypt (43.66), Iraq (10%), Jordan (1%), Algeria (0.62%), Bank Al Jazira, Saudi Arabia (0.50%), Qatar (0.25%), Individuals and Arab Institutions (0.31%)
Date of Establishment: 1964 as Arab African Bank, in 1978 as AAIB

ARAB ALUMINIUM CO SAE

3 Ahmed El Dardeery St, Heliopolis, Cairo
Tel: 665149, 2915196, 667206
Cable: Arabalum Cairo
Telex: 92539 Arbal UN

Chairman: Eng Fikry Abdel Wahab Fahmy
Directors: Eng Ali Taha El Husseini (Managing Director)
Senior Executives: Wagdy G Elias (Finance Manager), Nashed El Khatab (Marketing Manager), Eng Wagdy El Kollali (Purchasing Manager), Eng Adel El Sissy (Production Manager), Eng Ossama Gharib (Technical Manager)

PRINCIPAL ACTIVITIES: Aluminium manufacturers; continuous casting, extrusion, heat treatment, surface treatment and dye manufacturing
Principal Bankers: EAB; Credit Suisse; Arab Investment Bank; National Bank of Egypt
Financial Information:

	1990
	E£'000
Sales turnover	50,000
Profits	5,000
Authorised capital	6,354
Paid-up capital	12,000

Principal Shareholders: M A Kharafi, Kuwait; Egyptian Co for General Investments; University Education Endowment Fund
Date of Establishment: 1976
No of Employees: 423

ARAB AMERICAN VEHICLE CORP

Kilo 4.5 Cairo, Suez Road, Heliopolis, Cairo
Tel: 603427, 914583
Telex: 93791 AAV UN

PRINCIPAL ACTIVITIES: Vehicle manufacturing
Financial Information:

	US$'000
Authorised capital	6,000

Principal Shareholders: Motor Corp (Jeep), USA (49%)
Date of Establishment: 1979
No of Employees: 650

ARAB BANK PLC

PO Box 2006, 28 Tala't Harb St, Cairo
Tel: 746026, 746165, 746218
Cable: Bankarabi
Telex: 21401 Arbnk UN, 92716

Senior Executives: Hatem Sadek (Senior Manager Egypt)

PRINCIPAL ACTIVITIES: Commercial and investment banking
Branch Offices: Throughout the Arab World and also in London and major European cities
Parent Company: Head office: PO Box 69, Amman, Jordan

ARAB BUREAU FOR DESIGN & TECHNICAL CONSULTATIONS

Nasr City, Abbassia, Cairo
Tel: 2833099, 2833232
Cable: Ddesignarc Cairo
Telex: 93040 ABDEC UN
Telefax: 202-2833669

Chairman: Eng Salah El Din Mohamed Nassar
Directors: Arch Mohamed El Sherbiny (Vice Chairman for Technical Affairs), Taher Abdel Wahab Mashhour (Vice Chairman for Financial Affairs)
Senior Executives: Arch Ahmed Fahmy Zaky (Head of Construction Supervision Sector), Arch Morad R Bebawy (Head of Research & Information Sector), Eng George Halim (Head of Structural Engineering Sector), Arch Yousef Abdel Hamid (Head of Architectural Design Sector), Arch Moustafa Kamel (Head of Planning Sector)

PRINCIPAL ACTIVITIES: Engineering consultants, designing and architecture, urban planning, construction supervision, research
Parent Company: Responsible to the Ministry of Housing & Reconstruction
Principal Bankers: Banque du Caire
Financial Information:

	1990
	E£'000
Profits	2,714
Authorised capital	3,000
Paid-up capital	3,000

Principal Shareholders: Public sector company
Date of Establishment: 1965
No of Employees: 832

ARAB CO FOR LAND RECLAMATION

Mogamma Islah El Aradi, Dokki, Cairo
Tel: 705737
Cable: Araklam

Chairman: Eng Ismail Ibrahim Badawi
Directors: Eng Ibrahim Shahin, Eng Mohamed Mogazy, Mohamed Gazally, Falhat El Shahid, Foad El Alfi, Nagiba Mokhtar, Abdelfatah Bahakim

PRINCIPAL ACTIVITIES: Land reclamation, drainage, fish plant
Parent Company: Responsible to the Ministry of Land Reclamation
Principal Bankers: Banque du Caire

Principal Shareholders: Public sector
Date of Establishment: 1964
No of Employees: 1,119

ARAB CONTRACTORS
Osman Ahmed Osman & Co

34 Adly St, Cairo
Tel: 3935006, 3935455, 3935011
Cable: Osmason Cairo
Telex: 92239 Osman UN, 92367 Osman UN
Telefax: 3925728

Chairman: M S Hassaballah
Directors: M A F Refaat (Senior Vice President), Hassan Nassef (Vice President Executive Sector), Abdelrahim Elhoushy (Vice President Executive Sector), Bahig Ragab (Director Technical Affairs), Hassan Madkour (Director), Ismail Osman (Director Finance), M Said Azmi (Director), Rizk Elshenawy (Director), Adel Ayoub (Director)

PRINCIPAL ACTIVITIES: Building and civil engineering contractors for heavy construction and erection works; land reclamation; agriculture; engineering services; also food production; medical care and transportation
Branch Offices: Egypt; Cairo, Alexandria, Aswan, Ismailia, Tanta, Helwan, Nasr City, Shubra Abroad: Libya; Kuwait; Sudan; Iraq; Abu Dhabi; Saudi Arabia
Subsidiary Companies: The Saudi Contractors; The Libyan Company for Contracting; Misr Consulting; Kuwait Engineering Company; Osman Ahmed Osman (Abu Dhabi); ICON; ARAAB; ALUMISR; ACROMISR; Woody; A C Medical Centre; A C Investments
Principal Bankers: National Bank of Egypt; Banque du Caire; Banque Misr; Arab International Bank
Financial Information:

	1990
	E£'000
Sales turnover	1,060,000
Profits	34,000
Authorised capital	200,000
Paid-up capital	138,000
Total assets	1,800,000

Principal Shareholders: State owned
Date of Establishment: 1954
No of Employees: 45,000

ARAB DRUG COMPANY

5 El Masanei St, Cairo
Tel: 862806

Chairman: Dr Ahmed Loutfi Ebrahim
Directors: Dr Saad Helmy (Production Manager), Dr Foad Kotb Daha (Research Manager), Dr Sami Aguib (Planning Manager), Ismail Oways (Financial Manager)

PRINCIPAL ACTIVITIES: Production of pharmaceuticals and chemicals
Principal Agencies: Pharmakon, Switzerland; Gilagchemie, France; Seigfrieud, Switzerland; Knoll, West Germany
Branch Offices: Branch in Mansheya Sq, Alexandria

ARAB ELEVATORS CO
Schindler Egypt SAE
23 Talaat Harb St, Cairo
Tel: 741632, 74533, 752127, 754274
Cable: Swislift
Telex: 92371 UN

Chairman: Eng Yehia Zakaria Yehia
Directors: Eng Raouf Abou Osbaa (General Director)
Senior Executives: Eng Samir Mohsen (Project Manager), Eng Mohsen Salem (Production Manager), Eng Magdi Shafik (Executive Manager), Eng Mounir El Komos (Executive Manager), Eng Khairy Fawaz (Executive Manager)

PRINCIPAL ACTIVITIES: Production, erection and maintenance of lifts
Principal Agencies: Schindler & Co, Switzerland
Branch Offices: Factory: Airport Rd, Helicopolis, Cairo Erection and Maintenance Division; 1 Seket El Fadl, Cairo Alexandria Branch; 66 El Horreya St
Principal Bankers: Banque de Caire; Lloyds Bank; Nisr International Bank

Principal Shareholders: Egypt, Saudi Arabia, Kuwait, Libya, Switzerland
Date of Establishment: January 1976, production started in 1978
No of Employees: 533

ARAB ENGINEERING & DISTRIBUTION CO
2 El Saray El Kobra St, PO Box 901, Garden City, Cairo
Tel: 3545432, 3547313, 3545174
Telex: 92477 AEDCO UN

Senior Executives: Amin Marei (Deputy General Manager)

PRINCIPAL ACTIVITIES: Agents and representatives of foreign companies in the field of telecommunications, transportation, industry, chemicals, electricity and electrical products

ARAB FOREIGN TRADE COMPANY
12 Sharia Youssef El Guindi, Cairo
Tel: 28562, 28565, 23595
Cable: Arabimex

Chairman: Samir Mahmoud Sami
Senior Executives: Ahmed Zaki Abdel Rahman (Import Manager), Mohamed Talaat Anous (Export Manager)

PRINCIPAL ACTIVITIES: Import/export, general trade. Import of chemicals, metals, tools, machines, electrical appliances, iron, insulating materials, spare parts; export of wool, linen and milk products, yarn and fabrics
Branch Offices: 6 Tarik Gamal Abdel Nasser, Alexandria, Tel 39065
Parent Company: Responsible to the Ministry of Trade

Principal Shareholders: Public sector company

ARAB FOUNDATIONS CO (VIBRO)
6 Sharia Champollion, Cairo
Tel: 753951
Cable: Foundation
Telex: 94203 Vibro UN
Telefax: 761531

Chairman: Eng M El Tokhy

Directors: M Maatook (Managing Director), Taher Salim (General Manager), Eng Magda Shawky (Technical Director), Eng Faisal Abd El Hamed (Technical Director), Abd El Halim Mohamed (Financial Director)

PRINCIPAL ACTIVITIES: Contracting, foundation contracting, civil engineering and construction
Branch Offices: 5 Kasr El Nil St, Cairo; 16 Fawzy Fahmy Guindi St, Alexandria
Principal Bankers: Banque du Caire, National Bank of Egypt

Principal Shareholders: State-owned
Date of Establishment: March 1929
No of Employees: 2,500

ARAB GENERAL CONTRACTING CO
26A Sharia Sherif, PO Box 105, Cairo
Tel: 48039, 974754

PRINCIPAL ACTIVITIES: Contracting, civil engineering and construction
Branch Offices: 10 Ibn el-Sayegh Street, Alexandria, Tel 268884
Parent Company: Responsible to the Ministry of Housing and Reconstruction

Principal Shareholders: Public sector company

ARAB INTERNATIONAL BANK
35 Abdel Khalek Sarwat St, Cairo
Tel: 916120, 917893
Cable: Arabinbank
Telex: 92079 Aib UN

Chairman: Dr Mostafa Khalil
Directors: Abdalla Ammar Saudi (Deputy Chairman), Dr Hassan Abbas Zaki (Deputy Chairman), Ali Mohamed Nigm (Deputy Chairman), Ghanim Fares Al Mazroui (Deputy Chairman), Hadi Mohamed Giteli (Managing Director), Hikmat Sayed Rizk (Managing Director), Abdel Latif El Kib (Managing Director)

PRINCIPAL ACTIVITIES: Offshore and investment banking
Branch Offices: Branch in Cairo, Alexandria, Port Said, Egypt
Principal Bankers: European Arab Bank; Societe Arabe Internationale de Banque
Financial Information:

	US$'000
Issued capital	150,000

Principal Shareholders: Arab Republic of Egypt, Libyan Arab People Socialist Jamahireya, United Arab Emirates, Sultanate of Oman, State of Qatar, and private Arab participations

ARAB INTERNATIONAL CO FOR HOTELS & TOURISM
4 Ahmed Pasha Street, Garden City, Cairo
Tel: 3540509, 3542559
Telex: 92558 AICHT UN

Senior Executives: M Maged Abaza (General Manager)

PRINCIPAL ACTIVITIES: Promotion of hotels and tourism

ARAB INTERNATIONAL INSURANCE CO
PO Box 2704, 28 Sharia Talaat Harb, Cairo
Tel: 746322, 777939, 776320
Cable: Rabins Cairo
Telex: 92599 Rabins UN
Telefax: 02-760053

Chairman: Hassan M Hafez (Managing Director)
Directors: M G El Husseiny, W A H Abu El Ela, Fahad Al Ibrahim, Issa A Al Khalaf, W Hazelden, Alternate Don Lyal, Detleu Bremkamp, Dr Remo Vergna, Takashi Kagawa
Senior Executives: Hassan M Hafez (Managing Director), Hussein Sirry Koraiem (Deputy General Manager & Financial Manager), Miss Afifa Mikhail (Deputy General Manager & Underwriting Manager), Mrs Safinaz I El Gawish (General Secretary)

PRINCIPAL ACTIVITIES: Marine, general and international insurance and reinsurance business generated by the free zones in Egypt, under legislation on foreign investment, these are established in the Suez Canal Area, Alexandria, Port Said, Ismailia, Cairo, etc

Branch Offices: Alexandria; PO Box 479, 65 Horreia Rd, Tel 4926078; Port Said: Corner Abdel Salam Aref St and Al Sultan Mahmoud St, Tel 21716

Principal Bankers: Misr Iran Development Bank, Cairo; Arab International Bank, Cairo; National Bank of Abu Dhabi, Cairo; Bank of Credit and Commerce, Cairo

Financial Information:

| | 1989/90 |
	US$'000
Net income	1,210
Net profit	764
Authorised capital	4,000
Paid-up capital	4,000
Shareholders'funds	6,011
Total assets	18,401

Principal Shareholders: Misr Insurance Company, The Arab Investment Co, Al Ahleia Insurance Co, Kuwait Insurance Co, Gulf Insurance Co, AFIA Finance Corporation, Commercial Union Assurance Co Plc, Willis Faber & Dumas Ltd, UAP International, Allianze AG Holding, Assicurazioni Generali, Tokio Marine & Fire Insurance Co, Zurich Insurance Co

Date of Establishment: March 1976

No of Employees: 45

ARAB INVESTMENT BANK

PO Box 826, 8 Abdul Khalek Tharwat Street, Cairo Sky Center Bldg, Cairo

Tel: 360031, 770376

Cable: INVESBANK CAIRO

Telex: 20191 INVBK UN

Telefax: 707329

Chairman: Prof Dr Fouad Hashem Awad

Directors: Kamal Soliman Youness, Ahmed Shawky Mahmoud, Hussein Ahmed Hussein, Mahmoud Hassan Helal, Hassab El Nabi Ahmed Assal, Abdel Moneim Abu El Saad

Senior Executives: Dr Nawal Abd El Moneim El Tatawy (General Manager Loans & Supervisor Head Office Depts), Mourad Selim Fahmy (General Manager Branches), Abdel Halim Amin Ibrahim (General Manager & Supervisor Central Depts), Abd El Hamid Ahmed El Gohary (Asst General Manager & Azhar Branch Manager), Mohamed Abd El Hamid Mahmoud (General Manager & Cairo Branch Manager), Mahmoud Hamed Soliman (Asst General Manager Credit Dept), Dr Beshir Selim Saleh (Asst General Manager Holdings & Investments), Ashraf Mohamed El Salamony (Asst General Manager Islamic Branches)

PRINCIPAL ACTIVITIES: Commercial and investment banking

Branch Offices: Croniche El Nil Branch: 1113 Corniche El Nil Cairo; Alexandria Branch: 68 El Horreya Road-Alexandria; El Azhar Branch: 24 A Beibars St, El Hamzawy El Azhar; Zamalek Branch for Islamic Transactions: 8 El Mansour Mohamed, Zamalek, Cairo; Nasr City Branch: Nasr Centre Bldg, Abbas El Akkad St, Nasr City, Cairo; Giza Branch: Sky Center Bldg, 28 Mourad St; Port Said Branch: Freeport Bldg, El Nahda St; Maadi Branch: 206 St (Salah Salem) Degla Maadi; Alexandria Branch for Islamic Transactions: 68 El Horeya Road; Heliopolis Branch: 21 Ramsis St, El Korba, Heliopolis, Cairo

Financial Information:

| | 1989/90 |
	E£'000
Total income	73,986
Net profit	314
Deposits	556,093
Loans & advances	521,765
Authorised capital	US$40,000,000
Paid-up capital	18,500
Shareholders'funds	50,322
Total assets	809,293

Date of Establishment: 1978

No of Employees: 450

ARAB LAND BANK

33 Abdul Khalek Sarwat St, Cairo

Tel: 748506, 758786

Cable: Arakari Cairo

Telex: 92208 UN

PRINCIPAL ACTIVITIES: Banking

Branch Offices: Jordan, Egypt

ARAB MULTINATIONAL FINANCE CO (AMFCO)

PO Box 312, Cairo

Tel: 982205

Cable: AMFCO

Telex: 93124 AMFCO UN

Chairman: Ebrahim Al Ebrahim (and Managing Director)

Directors: Abdul Kader El Seessi (Vice-Chairman), Dr Hassan Helmi Zahed (Vice-Chairman), Hamed Al ShaKankiri, Dr Nezpat El Tayeb (Managing Director), Hussein El Baz, Adnan El Tayyar, Ahmad Al Duaij

PRINCIPAL ACTIVITIES: Investment in projects, financing, participating in international loans, underwriting, buying, and selling securities and shares, issuing guarantees, trading in precious metals

Branch Offices: Registered office: 10 Aldringen St, Luxembourg; Regional Representative office: 3 Abdel Kader Hamza, Cairo; Kuwait Advisory office: PO Box 4743, Safat

Associated Companies: In Egypt; Inland Transport and Tourism (Intratour); Al El Tehad Al Arabi for Metal Industries (Omico); Egyptian Granite and Marble Co; El Shams Hotels & TourismCo; Golden Farm; Misr Iran Air Conditioning Co (Miraco); Arab Multinational Trading Co (AMTCO); Suez Cement Co; Egyptian Gulf Bank; Artoc Suez Ltd; National Beverage Co; Jordan Lime and Brick Silicate (Jordan); Artoc Diamond Ltd (Morocco); Twin Holdings, Wembley Trust (UK); Artoc America (Lee National Corporation), USA; Artoc Bank and Trust Ltd (Cayman Islands); Arab Capital Corp (Cayman Islands); Beaverton Properties (Singapore); Prism Resources Ltd (Canada); Kumiss Co (USA)

Principal Bankers: Arab African International Bank; Al Ahli Bank of Kuwait; Banque de Caire; Artoc Bank & Trust Ltd (Bahamas); UBAF (Paris); European Banking Co (London); Arab Bank Ltd (Jordan); Arab Japanese Finance Ltd; Saudi National Commercial Bank; Banque Arabe et Internationale d'Investissement; Alexandria Kuwait International Bank (Cairo)

Principal Shareholders: Arab African International Bank; Blue Sea Co (Kuwait); Ahmad Gosaibi & Bros; Artoc (Kuwait); Salem Bin Laden; Musaid Al Saleh Real Estate Co; Ghanem Al Thani (UK); W J Towell; Kamal Ahmad Achour; Kuwait Real Estate Investment Consortium; Esaaf Abdel Rahman El Azm; Tawfik Abdul Kerim El Nassar; Dr Gad Noueish; HE Dr Omar Zawawi; Abdul Aziz Al Ali Al Wazan & Sons & Partners; Yussef Abdul Aziz Al Muzainy

ARAB ORGANIZATION FOR INDUSTRIALIZATION

2D Abbasseya Sq, PO Box 770, Cairo
Tel: 823377, 932822, 603015, 745190
Cable: Sonarab
Telex: 92090; 92014 Aoi UN

Chairman: Ahmed Zandou
Directors: HH Prince Bandar Bin Fahad Bin Khaled (First Deputy Chairman), Lieutenant General Mohamed Mahmoud (Second Deputy Chairman), HE Sheikh Faisal Sultan El-Kassimy (Third Deputy Chairman), HE Dr Mohamed El-Mulhim, Ahmed Zendo, Eng Yousif Moustafa, Lieutenant General Awad El-Khalidy, Dr Ahmed El-Malek, Colonel General Mohamed Said El-Bady, Captain Faleh Fahad El-Shahwany, Captain Ahmed Saleh El-Manaay
Senior Executives: Abdel Khalek Akl (General Manager)

PRINCIPAL ACTIVITIES: Defence and armaments
Branch Offices: Paris Office; 53 Rue Montaigne, Paris, France
Subsidiary Companies: Sakr Factory for Developing Industries; Kader Factory for Developing Industries; Aircraft Factory; Engines Factory; Electronics Factory. Joint venture companies: Arab British Co for Dynamics; Arab American Vehicles Co; Arab British Co for Helicopters; Arab British Co for Engines
Principal Bankers: Credit Lyonnais (Paris); Bank of America (London); Arab African Bank (Cairo); Deutsche Bank (Frankfurt); Barclays Bank (London); Societe Generale (Paris); Midland Bank (London); International Saudi Bank (London)

Principal Shareholders: United Arab Emirates, State of Qatar, Kingdom of Saudi Arabia, Arab Republic of Egypt
Date of Establishment: 1975
No of Employees: 17,000

ARAB PETROLEUM PIPELINES CO SUMED

431 El Geish Avenue, PO Box 2056, Alexandria
Tel: 5862613, 5864139, 5861579
Telex: 54108, 54295, 54033 Sumed UN

Chairman: Eng Hafez Mohamed El Sherbini (Managing Director)
Directors: Eng Bakr Abdul Samad Khoja (Deputy Chairman and Managing Director for Marketing & Operations), Eng Rafik Nosseir Mahmoud (General Operations Manager), Ahmed Hafez Amin (General Administrative Manager), Saleh Abdullah Al Shalfan (Deputy Chairman and Managing Director for Engineering & Planning Affairs)

PRINCIPAL ACTIVITIES: Construction of pipelines for petroleum transportation from the Suez Gulf to the Mediterranean, operation thereof and associated industrial and commercial work
Branch Offices: 10 Shehab St, Mohandsin, Dokki, Cairo, Tel 3480966, Telex 92747; Suez Terminal, Sukhna Suez, Tel 791128, 778146; Sidi Krir Terminal, KI 27 Highway Alexandria, Matrouh, Tel 491714
Parent Company: Affiliated to the Egyptian General Petroleum Authority
Principal Bankers: Arab & African International Bank; Chase National Bank
Financial Information:

	1990 US$'000
Authorised capital	400,000
Paid-up capital	400,000

Principal Shareholders: Egypt, Saudi Arabia, Kuwait, Abu Dhabi, Qatar
Date of Establishment: January 1974
No of Employees: 328

ARAB RESEARCH & ADMINISTRATION CENTRE (ARAC)

1119 Corniche El Nil, PO Box 782, Cairo
Tel: 603762, 777077
Cable: Aracairo
Telex: 92799 Maaref UN

Chairman: Gamal El Din Zaki

PRINCIPAL ACTIVITIES: Advertising, training, research, studies
Parent Company: Responsible to the United Arab Press Authority, Cairo

Principal Shareholders: Public sector company

ARAB STEVEDORING CO

13 Ahmed Orabi St, Alexandria
Tel: 38550, 38558/9

PRINCIPAL ACTIVITIES: Loading, unloading and stevedoring
Branch Offices: Port Said Office: 20 Palestine St, Tel 2688, 23376; Suez Office: PO Box 94
Parent Company: Responsible to the Ministry of Maritime Transport

Principal Shareholders: Public sector company

ARABIAN INK FACTORY (REINZ)

455 Ramses Ave, Abbassia, Cairo
Tel: 820927, 906028
Telex: 20391 Elbat UN

Chairman: Hany Dikran Boghossian
Directors: Dikram O Boghossian
Senior Executives: Gamil Radouan (Chemist), Kamal Mechreky (Chemist)

PRINCIPAL ACTIVITIES: Production of writing ink, stamp pad ink, marking ink, numbering ink, glue and plastic school articles, staples
Branch Offices: 437 Port Said St, Cairo
Subsidiary Companies: Arabian Office Articles Co
Principal Bankers: Banque du Caire

Principal Shareholders: Private company
Date of Establishment: 1960
No of Employees: 35

ARABIAN OFFICE EQUIPMENT CO

Head Office, 54 Abbas El Akkad Street, Nasr City, Cairo
Tel: 2608441, 2608250, 2606004, 2606005
Cable: Royimp Cairo
Telex: 22317 Andco UN
Telefax: 2608440

Directors: Samir Antoun Guirguis (General Director)
Senior Executives: Eikry Earid, Naim Silvanos

PRINCIPAL ACTIVITIES: Import and distribution of all office equipment and machines
Principal Agencies: Taichi Co ltd, Japan; Eba Maschinenfabrik, W Germany; Meito Shokai, Japan; Ricoh Co Ltd, Japan; Rotaprint, W Germany; ATF Davidson, USA; Itomanco, Japan
Branch Offices: 8 Talaat Harb Street, Alexandria, Tel 4824573; Port Said, Tel 224860; Mansoura, Tel 353712
Subsidiary Companies: National Development Co, Cairo
Principal Bankers: Mohandes Bank, Cairo; Pyramids Bank, Cairo; El Watany Bank of Egypt, Cairo

Principal Shareholders: Samir Antoun Guirguis; Heirs of Fouad Shukri; Naim Silwanos; Fikri Farid Milad; Mrs Wafaa Farid milad; Mrs May Youssif Boulos
Date of Establishment: 1971

ARDAMAN-ACE

7 Soliman Abaza Street, Dokki, Cairo
Tel: 710955, 702683
Telex: 21274 Vipco UN
Telefax: 3444429

EGYPT

Chairman: Dr Ahmed Moharram

Directors: Dr Mohamed Sheta (General Manager), Eng Reda El Rahed

Senior Executives: Abdel Monem Soliman (Finance Manager), Eng Nadia Haggag (Company Secretary)

PRINCIPAL ACTIVITIES: Soil investigations, geotechnical engineering, concrete testing

Principal Bankers: Bank of Alexandria

Financial Information:

	1990 US$'000
Authorised capital	600

Principal Shareholders: Ardaman and Associates, Orlando, Fl, USA; Arab Consulting Engineers ACE, Egypt

Date of Establishment: 1974

No of Employees: 59

ARTHUR ANDERSEN SHAWKI & CO

PO Box 2095, 153 Mohamed Farid Street, Cairo

Tel: 3917299, 3926000

Cable: Mostafaki

Telex: 92195 AASCO UN, 93649 AAS UN

Telefax: 3939430

Chairman: Mostafa Shawki

Senior Executives: Dr Ahmed Shawki (Managing Director)

PRINCIPAL ACTIVITIES: Accounting, auditing and management consultancy

Branch Offices: Alexandria

Parent Company: Arthur Andersen & Co

Principal Bankers: Misr International Bank; Misr America International Bank

Principal Shareholders: Arthur Andersen & Co, USA; Shawki & Co, Egypt

Date of Establishment: 1980

No of Employees: 350

ARTHUR YOUNG & CO

PO Box 2808, Cairo

Tel: 757512, 748661

Telex: 94245 ZAROX UN

PRINCIPAL ACTIVITIES: Accounting and management consulting

Branch Offices: 90 Avenue El Horreya, Alexandria, Tel 802777, 4936341, 4920039

ARTOC SUEZ GROUP

15 Giza Street, PO Box 1666, Cairo 11511

Tel: 727827, 727386

Telex: 23573 ARTOC UN, 93298 EICC UN

Telefax: 726654

Chairman: S A El Haddad

Directors: M Shafik Gabr (Managing Director)

Senior Executives: A Abdel Azim (Deputy General Manager)

PRINCIPAL ACTIVITIES: The company has three divisions: project investment, engineering & consultancy, utility equipment

Branch Offices: Cairo, Alexandria, Tenth of Ramadan, Athens, and Washington DC

Subsidiary/Associated Companies: American Engineering Technology, Adel Gabr Consultant Co, Alphametal, Egyptian Equipment Co, Tobex Ltd, Egyptian Investment & Consulting Co

Principal Bankers: Egypt Arab African Bank

Financial Information:

	1989 US$'000
Sales turnover	22,000
Authorised capital	2,000
Paid-up capital	1,300

Date of Establishment: 1978

No of Employees: 52

ASSIUT SHIPPING AGENCY

9 Mostafa Kamel St, PO Box 128, Port Said

Tel: 2722, 5205

Cable: Assiuship

Telex: 4262 Assiut UN

PRINCIPAL ACTIVITIES: Shipping agents, clearing and forwarding agents

Branch Offices: Suez Branch: 1 Abdel Khalek St, Abou Ghabban Bldg, Suez, Tel 2790, 3025, Cable Assiuship, Telex 4187 Suezag

Principal Bankers: Banque du Caire

Principal Shareholders: Part of the Canal Shipping Agencies

ASSOCIATED CHEMICAL INDUSTRIES

Madinet Hassan Mohamed, 363 Pyramids Rd, Giza

Tel: 852930, 854253

PRINCIPAL ACTIVITIES: Production of scientific and medical equipment, laboratory steel furniture, shakers, mills, water stills, colorimeters, safety equipment, flame photometers, cooling and heating apparatus; assembly of microscopes under licence of Komax

Principal Agencies: Komax, Japan

Principal Shareholders: Private company

ASSWAN SHIPPING AGENCY

8 El Goumhouria St, Port Said

Tel: 3194/6, 3521/3

Cable: Swana

Telex: 63261 Swan UN

PRINCIPAL ACTIVITIES: Shipping agency, clearing and forwarding agency

Branch Offices: Suez Branch: 1 El Gueish St, PO Box 4, Port Tewfik, Suez, Tel 2074, 2149, 3216, Cable Swana, Telex 54187 Agency UN

Principal Bankers: Suez Canal Bank, Port Said

Principal Shareholders: Part of the Canal Shipping Agencies Co

AT & T INTERNATIONAL

El Nasr Building, Nile Street, 22nd Floor, Giza

Tel: 728872, 726998

Telex: 92444 ATTI UN

Senior Executives: I N Shalaby (General Manager), J L Bloom (Project Manager), G K Guirguis (Finance Manager), R E Hippchen (Engineering Manager)

PRINCIPAL ACTIVITIES: Telecommunications, computer systems

Principal Agencies: Arab Engineering & Distribution Co (Agents); Egyptian Automated Equipment (Computer distributor)

Parent Company: AT & T International, Basking Ridge, NJ 07920

Principal Bankers: Chase National, European Arab Bank

No of Employees: 65 in branch

ATLANTIC INDUSTRIES LTD

PO Box 7052, Nasr City Free Zone, 6th District, Nasr City

Tel: 609841, 607535

Telex: 20561 COKAT UN

Senior Executives: Rafik J Cressaty (Resident Manager)

PRINCIPAL ACTIVITIES: Manufacture and supply of Coca Cola concentrate to approved bottlers in the Middle East
Principal Agencies: Coca Cola
Parent Company: Coca Cola Export Corp

ATLAS GENERAL CONTRACTING

23 Sharia Kasr El Nil, PO Box 910, Cairo
Tel: 741378
Telex: 93247 Atlas UN

PRINCIPAL ACTIVITIES: Contracting, civil engineering and construction
Branch Offices: El Horria Rd, Alexandria, Tel 39471
Parent Company: Responsible to the Ministry of Housing & Reconstruction

Principal Shareholders: Public sector company

AZZA PLASTICS FACTORY

9 Istamboul St, Alexandria
Tel: 21926 Alexandria
Cable: Plastaz

Chairman: Abdel Aziz Mohammed Osman
Directors: Nabeel A Osman, Said A Osman

PRINCIPAL ACTIVITIES: Production of polyethylene sacks, and all kinds of plastic works and products; manufacture of extruder machines, moulding machines, blowing machines, pressing machines, electric-tubes machines, electric baking machines and many other kinds of machines

Principal Shareholders: Private company

BALSAM ENGINEERING LTD

12 Gezira Street, Zamalek, Cairo
Tel: 807125
Telex: 93920

PRINCIPAL ACTIVITIES: Electrical engineering, telecommunication, power equipment and systems
Principal Agencies: Mitel

BANCA COMMERCIALE ITALIANA

3 Ahmad Nessim Street, PO Box 2663, Cairo
Tel: 980427
Cable: COMITBANCA
Telex: 92669 BCICAI UN

PRINCIPAL ACTIVITIES: Commercial banking
Parent Company: Head Office in Milan, Italy

BANK MELLI IRAN

15 Kasr el-Nil St, Cairo
Tel: 750971, 753197, 747505
Telex: 92633 Cameli

PRINCIPAL ACTIVITIES: Commercial banking
Parent Company: Head Office in Tehran, Iran

BANK OF ALEXANDRIA

Head office, 49 Kasr El Nil Street, Cairo
Tel: 3916079, 3926822, 3900940
Telex: 22286 BNALX UN, 21732 GMALX UN
Telefax: 3910481

Chairman: Abdel Ghani Hamed Gameh
Directors: Mohamed Gamal El Din El Shazly (Vice Chairman), Mohamed Said Abou Seoud (Vice Chairman), Hassen Ali El Leissy (Senior Executive General Manager), Mohamed Moharem Soliman El Asfar (Senior Executive General Manager), Dr Mohamed M El Sayed El Gazzar, Dr Abdel Moneim Ali Rady

PRINCIPAL ACTIVITIES: Commercial banking
Branch Offices: Alexandria Main Branch: 6 Salah Salem St, Alexandria, Tel 4836073, 4824056, 48344980, Telex 54600 Balsz UN, Fax 4839968; and over 130 branches & agencies

throughout Egypt: Greater Cairo Region; Alexandria Region; Lower Egypt; Upper Egypt; Canal Zone; Sinai Region
Subsidiary Companies: Joint venture banks: The Egyptian American Bank; Suez Canal Bank; Alexandria Kuwait International Bank; Delta International Bank; Misr Iran Development Bank; Housing & Development Bank; Alexandria Commercial & Maritime Bank; National Development Bank; Joint Arab Investment Corporation; Misr Arab African Bank; Export Development Bank of Egypt; Pyramids Bank; Egypt Investment Finance Corporation; Egyptians Abroad for Investment & Development Inc. Also joint ventures in the Industrial, Foodstuffs, Construction & Housing, Tourism & Hotels, Publishing and Technology sectors
Financial Information:

	1988/89 E£'000	1989/90 E£'000
Net profit	13,905	15,069
Deposits	4,569,078	5,231,528
Loans & advances	2,579,268	2,932,108
Shareholders' equity	100,093	103,878
Total assets	5,756,672	6,700,668

Principal Shareholders: State-owned
Date of Establishment: 1957; formerly Barclays Bank DCO (Est 1925)
No of Employees: 5,387

BANK OF AMERICA NT & SA

106 Kasr El Aini St, Cairo
Tel: 773133, 3547508, 3547509
Telex: 92425, 93804 BOFA UN
Telefax: (202) 3555023

Senior Executives: Omar A Sakr (Vice President & Regional Manager), M Atef Abdallah (Vice President & Operations Officer)

PRINCIPAL ACTIVITIES: Banking
Branch Offices: 10 Patrice Lumumba St, Alexandria

BANK OF COMMERCE & DEVELOPMENT (AL EGARYOON)

13 26 July St, Sphinx Square, Mohandisseen, PO Box 1373, Cairo
Tel: 3472056, 3472063, 3475584
Cable: Tegaryoon
Telex: 21607 BCD UN, 93508 BCD UN

Chairman: Dr Abd El Aziz Mohamed Hegazi
Directors: Samir M Fouad ElKasry (Vice Chairman & General Manager)
Senior Executives: Ahmed Sabie (Deputy General Manager), Ahmed Koura (Deputy General Manager), Dr Ahmed El Gowainy (Deputy General Manager)

PRINCIPAL ACTIVITIES: Banking
Branch Offices: Ramses Branch, Garden City Branch, Alexandria Branch, Islamic Dealing Bank, El Azhar, Islamic Dealing Unit, Mohandiseen
Subsidiary Companies: Egyptian Match Co, Fast Food Co, El Ektissadia Co for Food Development, Misr International Hospital, Egyptian Car Service & Maintenance Co, Economic Islamic Trade & Distribution Co, Economic Co for Development of Tourist Services, Misr International Towers, Egyptian Sanitary Ware Co, Economic Printing & Publishing Co, Egyptian Co for Medical Products

Principal Shareholders: Commercial Syndicate, Education Occupations Syndicate, Practitioners Syndicate, Lawyers Syndicate, National Bank of Egypt, National Investment Bank, East Insurance Co, Egyptian Reinsurance Co, General Authority for Social Security
Date of Establishment: 1980
No of Employees: 402

EGYPT

BANK OF CREDIT & COMMERCE (MISR) SAE

Cairo Centre Bldg, 106 Kasr-El-Aini Street, Garden City, Cairo
Tel: 762415
Cable: Ainicrecom
Telex: 94130 BCCMS UN

PRINCIPAL ACTIVITIES: Commercial banking
Branch Offices: In Egypt: Ahmed Orabi Street, Roushdy, Safia
Zaghloul Street, Assuit, Giza, Heliopolis, Moski el Azhar Nile
Hilton, Orabi Square, Sarwat, Sherif Street, Shubra, Talaat
Harb, 26 July Street, Zamalek, Port Said, Tanta

BANK OF NOVA SCOTIA

PO Box 656, 3 Ahmed Nessim St, Giza, Cairo
Tel: 977605, 973723
Cable: Scotiacare
Telex: 92336 BNSC UN

PRINCIPAL ACTIVITIES: Commercial banking

BANK OF TOKYO

26 July Street, PO Box 942, Cairo
Tel: 53860
Cable: TOHBANK
Telex: 92392

PRINCIPAL ACTIVITIES: Banking (representative office)
Parent Company: Head office in Tokyo, Japan

BANK SADERAT IRAN

4 Bahler Bldg, Kasr Al Nile Street, PO Box 462, Cairo
Tel: 58742
Telex: 92611

PRINCIPAL ACTIVITIES: Banking
Parent Company: Head office in Tehran, Iran

BANKERS TRUST CO

17 Kasr El Nil Street, 3rd Floor, Mohd Farid Station, PO Box
308, Cairo
Tel: 743427, 762628, 778522
Telex: 93826 BTKRO UN, 93514 BTCAI UN

PRINCIPAL ACTIVITIES: Banking (representative office)

BANQUE DU CAIRE BARCLAYS INTERNATIONAL SAE

12 Midan El Sheikh Youssef, Garden City, PO Box 2335, Cairo
Tel: 3549415, 3542195, 3552746, 3549422
Cable: Caibarint
Telex: 92343, 93734 Cabar UN

Chairman: Mahmoud Hassan Abdallah
Directors: J H Whicher (Deputy Chairman), Mohamed Abo El
Fath Abdel Aziz (Joint Managing Director), D L James, Maitre
Ragaie Selim Shenouda, Edigio Cutayar (Joint Managing
Director), R C Whittet, Mrs Fawzia Ibrahim Youssef,
Mamdouh Said El Nadoury
Senior Executives: Fuad Mohamed Zaki (General Managers'
Assistant Head Office), Youssef E Esmat (General Manager
Cairo Branch), Raafat Bassyoni (Chief Manager Alexandria
Branch)

PRINCIPAL ACTIVITIES: Investment and merchant banking in
Egyptian and foreign currencies in both Egypt and abroad
Branch Offices: Cairo Branch: 12 Midan El Sheikh Youssef,
Garden City, PO Box 2335, Cairo; Alexandria Branch: 10 El
Fawatem St, PO Box 1097, Alexandria, Tel 4821307,
4821308, 4820660, Telex 54337, 54680

Principal Shareholders: Banque du Caire, Egypt (51%), Barclays
Bank Plc, UK (49%)
Date of Establishment: September 1975
No of Employees: 208

BANQUE DU CAIRE ET DE PARIS SAE

3 Latin America St, Garden City, PO Box 2441, Cairo
Tel: 3548323
Telex: 93722, 21819 BACAP UN
Telefax: 3540619

Chairman: Mohamed Abdo El Sabbagh
Directors: Jean Claude Clarac (Vice Chairman), de Gayardon de
Fenoyl, Marcel Guichard, Mohd Abdel Wekil Gaber, Dr Prof El
Sayed Aly Abdel Mawla, Zakareya Abdel Hamid Ibrahim,
Mohd Adel El Fazzari
Senior Executives: Mohamed Adel El Fazzari (Managing
Director), Jean Thibault (Deputy Managing Director)

PRINCIPAL ACTIVITIES: Banking
Branch Offices: Alexandria: 11 Dr Ibrahim Abdel Sayed St, Po
Box 2417, Alexandria, Tel 4938959, Telex 54651 BACAX UN;
Heliopolis: 79 El Merghani, Heliopolis, PO Box 2917 Al
Horeya, Tel 678711, Telex 20315 BACAH UN
Financial Information:

	1989/90
	E£'000
Net profit	2,870
Authorised capital	10,326
Paid-up capital	10,326
Total assets	243,205

Principal Shareholders: Banque du Caire (51%), Banque
Nationale de Paris (49%)
Date of Establishment: 1977
No of Employees: 210

BANQUE DU CAIRE (SAE)

Banque du Caire Tower, 30 Roushdy St, PO Box 1495,
Abdin/Cairo
Tel: 3904554
Cable: Bankaher
Telex: 92022, 92838, 23438 Bnkhr UN, 20701 Bdcac UN
Telefax: 3908992

Chairman: Mahmoud Hassan Abdalla
Directors: Mahmoud Mohamed Youssef (Deputy Chairman),
Mamdouhh Said El Nadoury (Deputy Chairman), Mohamed
Adel El Fazzary (Member), Mrs Doria Osman El Degwey
(Member), Mohamed Hassan El Sabbagh (Member), Dr El
Sayed Ali Abdel Mawla (Specialised Member), Dr Hassan
Mahmoud Ebrahim (Specialised Member)

PRINCIPAL ACTIVITIES: Commercial banking
Branch Offices: Egypt: Cairo (46), Alexandria (15), Delta (34),
Suez Canal (7), Upper Egypt (36); Bahrain; United Arab
Emirates (Abu Dhabi, Dubai, Sharjah, Ras Al Khaimah)
Subsidiary/Associated Companies: Joint ventures: Cairo Amman
Bank, Jordan; Banque du Caire Barclays Int'l SAE, Egypt;
Banque du Caire et de Paris SAE, Egypt; Cairo Far East
Bank, Egypt; Saudi Cairo Bank, Saudi Arabia. Participations
in: Suez Canal Bank; Housing & Development Bank; National
Bank for Development; Egyptian Gulf Bank; Egypt Arab
African Bank; Pyramids Bank; Export Development Bank of
Egypt; Kalyoubia National Bank for Development; Misr
America International Bank
Financial Information:

	1988/89
	E£'000
Total income	534,000
Net profits	40,000
Authorised capital	100,000
Capital & reserves	689,000
Total assets	2,427,000

Principal Shareholders: Public sector
Date of Establishment: 5 May 1952
No of Employees: 6,870

BANQUE MISR

151 Mohamed Farid St, Cairo
Tel: 912711
Cable: Banisr Cairo
Telex: 92242, 92325, 21783, 21730 BANISR UN

Chairman: Mahmoud Mohamed Mahmoud
Directors: Mohamed Aly Hafez (Deputy Chairman), Ahmed
Raafat Abdou (Deputy Chairman)

PRINCIPAL ACTIVITIES: All banking transactions
Branch Offices: 311 Branches throughout Egypt, and branch in
Paris, France
Subsidiary Companies: 50 affiliated companies (Banque Misr
Group)

Principal Shareholders: Wholly State owned
Date of Establishment: 1920
No of Employees: 13,000

BANQUE NATIONALE DE PARIS

4 Latin America Street, Garden City, PO Box 2441, Cairo
Tel: 31913, 33854
Cable: Natiopar
Telex: 92419 NATPAR UN

PRINCIPAL ACTIVITIES: Representative office
Parent Company: Head office in Paris, France

Date of Establishment: 1975

BANQUE PARIBAS

Arab African Int'l Building, 5 El Birgas Street, Garden City, Cairo
Tel: 540391, 547323
Telex: 20747 UN, 22332 UN

PRINCIPAL ACTIVITIES: Commercial banking
Parent Company: Head office in Paris, France

BARAKA INTERNATIONAL

Mahmoud Fathi Mahmoud

18 Abou Bakr El Sedik Street, PO Box 156 Orman, Dokki, Cairo
Tel: 702152, 701219
Telex: 22212 BARAKA UN

President: Mahmoud Fathi Mahmoud

PRINCIPAL ACTIVITIES: Import export of foodstuffs and animal
feeds, also production of poultry

BECHTEL COMPANIES IN EGYPT

Cairo Center Bldg/5th Floor, 2 Abdel Kader Hamza St, Garden
City, Cairo
Tel: 3554611 (6lines)
Telex: 22324 WATEX UN, 94251

Senior Executives: Said M Ahmed (VP & Project Manager
Overseas Bechtel Inc), Arun K Nayar (Project Procurement
Manager Overseas Bechtel Inc)

PRINCIPAL ACTIVITIES: Engineering, construction,
management and related services

BELAYIM PETROLEUM COMPANY

PETROBEL

155 Sharia Mohamed Farid, Cairo
Tel: 913233, 913351, 913710
Cable: Petrobel Cairo
Telex: 92449 UN

PRINCIPAL ACTIVITIES: Oil exploration, drilling and production
Parent Company: Affiliated to the Egyptian General Petroleum
Corporation

BLACK & VEATCH ACE

2 Champolion St, Cairo
Tel: 744876, 753610
Telex: 92578 MOBA UN

Senior Executives: Dr Ahmed Moharam (General Manager)
PRINCIPAL ACTIVITIES: Consulting engineers
Branch Offices: PO Box 543, Alexandria

Principal Shareholders: Black & Veach International, USA (50%)
Date of Establishment: 1974
No of Employees: 323

CAIRO CLOTHING & HOSIERY CO

6 El Madares St, Kobba Gardens, Cairo
Tel: 821156, 823044, 829203, 833267
Cable: Tricona Cairo
Telex: 93589 Trcon UN
Telefax: 02-836755

Chairman: Eng Abd El Khalek Yassin
Senior Executives: Ahmed Hassan El Masrey (Commercial
Manager), Mounir Ghali (Export Manager), Atef Afifi (Import
Manager), Ahmed Selim (Finance Manager), Abdalla El
Helbaway (Purchasing Manager), Ezzat Istafanous (Personnel
Manager), Eng Adel Abd El Fatah (Technical Manager)

PRINCIPAL ACTIVITIES: Production of knitted clothing, socks
and ribbons, underwear, outerwear garments, sport garments
etc
Parent Company: Responsible to the Ministry of Industry
Principal Bankers: Bank Misr Overseas, Cairo

Principal Shareholders: Public sector company

CAIRO FAR EAST BANK

PO Box 757, 104 Corniche El Nil, Dokki, Cairo
Tel: 710280, 713064, 713554
Telex: 93977 Casol UN

Chairman: Ahmad Abou Ismail
Directors: Jong I Kim (Deputy Chairman)
Senior Executives: Kamal Saleh Radi (Managing Director), Joon
Jeong Woon (Managing Director)

PRINCIPAL ACTIVITIES: Commercial banking
Branch Offices: Alexandria Branch; Cairo Islamic Branch

Principal Shareholders: Korea Exchange Bank; Banque du
Caire; Al Chark Insurance Co; Commercial Bank of Korea;
Hanil Bank; Cho Heung Bank Ltd; Korea First Bank; Bank of
Seoul & Trust Co; Ahmed Abou Ismail and others
Date of Establishment: 1978

CAIRO GENERAL CONTRACTING CO

El Thawra Bldg, 5 Al-Alfi St, Cairo
Tel: 905389, 903830, 908792, 923877
Cable: CAICONTRA
Telex: 92826 CAGEC, UN

Chairman: Eng Mohamed Mostafa Ali
Directors: Hassanein Ali Hassanein (Vice Chairman)
Senior Executives: Taher A Bary, Eng Mahmoud Soliman, Eng
Ahmed Sadek, Eng Ibrahim El Massry

PRINCIPAL ACTIVITIES: Contracting, civil engineering and
construction
Branch Offices: Alexandria, Luxor, Egypt; Saudi Arabia; Libya
Parent Company: Responsible to the Ministry of Housing &
Reconstruction
Subsidiary Companies: Saudi - Egyptian Co, Saudi Arabia
Principal Bankers: Cairo Bank; Arab International Bank
Financial Information:

	E£'000
Authorised capital	10,000
Paid-up capital	7,000

Principal Shareholders: State-owned

CAIRO MARRIOTT HOTEL

PO Box 33, Zamalek, Cairo
Tel: 3408888
Telex: 93464, 93465 MAR UN
Telefax: 3406667

Senior Executives: Harry Bosschaart (Area Vice President & General Manager), Andrew Houghton (Director of Sales & Marketing)

PRINCIPAL ACTIVITIES: Hotel business
Parent Company: Marriott Corporation (Washington DC - USA)

Principal Shareholders: EGOTH (Egyptian government)
Date of Establishment: 1982
No of Employees: 1,600

CAIRO METAL PRODUCTS CO

Sharia El Madaress, Embabah, Cairo
Tel: 800260, 801922, 801487

PRINCIPAL ACTIVITIES: Manufacture of cast iron household utensils and sanitary ware, enamelled sheet, tin containers and other metal products
Branch Offices: Cairo Office: 18 Emad El-Din St, Tel 44723
Parent Company: Responsible to the Ministry of Industry

Principal Shareholders: Public sector company

CAIRO PLASTICS

41 Naguib El Rehany St, PO Box 2696, Cairo
Tel: 908191, 920508
Telex: 93971 Nesco UN att Semir Cairo Plastic

Chairman: Ahmed Mohamed Ahmed
Directors: Medhat Ahmed Mohamed

PRINCIPAL ACTIVITIES: Injection moulding and blow moulding of plastics for electrical components, household utensils, toys, cosmetics appliances and packages

Principal Shareholders: Private company

CAIRO PUBLIC TRANSPORT AUTHORITY

El Gabal El Ahmar, Nasr City, Cairo
Tel: 825633

Senior Executives: Hassam Abdoun (Manager of Purchases)

PRINCIPAL ACTIVITIES: Public transport
Parent Company: Responsible to the Ministry of Transport and Communications

Principal Shareholders: Public sector company

CAIRO REFRIGERATION & ICE MAKING CO

22 Sharia Galaa, Cairo
Tel: 975671, 54460
Telex: 975671, 54460

PRINCIPAL ACTIVITIES: Refrigeration and cold storage
Parent Company: Responsible to the Ministry of Supply

Principal Shareholders: Public sector company

CAIRO SAND BRICKS CO

33 Sharia Seka El Baida, Abbassia, Cairo
Tel: 822511, 605446
Cable: Sand Bricks Cairo

Chairman: Hussein Siam (also Managing Director)
Directors: Eng A Alaasar, Eng Khamis Bannassy, M Ghoneim, Bahi El Din Taha

PRINCIPAL ACTIVITIES: Manufacture of building materials
Branch Offices: Factories in Cairo and Menoufia, Alexandria and Minia
Parent Company: Responsible to the Ministry of Housing and Reconstruction
Principal Bankers: Bank of Alexandria, Sherif Branch

Principal Shareholders: Public sector company
Date of Establishment: 1910
No of Employees: 2,500

CAIRO SHERATON HOTEL & CASINO

PO Box 11, Galaa Square, Giza, Cairo
Tel: 3488600, 3488700
Cable: Sheraco Cairo
Telex: 92041; 22382 Shera UN
Telefax: 3489051/91

Senior Executives: Adel O Cherif (General Manager), Ola Leheta (Public Realtions Director), Mrs Claudette Nassif (Director of Sales & Promotion), Amr Basmi (Resident Manager), Hisham El Enna (Financial Controller), Derek Barnard (Casino Director)

PRINCIPAL ACTIVITIES: Hotel business
Branch Offices: Heliopolis Sheraton Hotel, Oruba Street, PO Box 2466, Horreya, Heliopolis, Cairo, Tel 665500, Telex 93300; El Gezirah Sheraton Hotel & Tower, El Gezirah Island, PO Box 264, Orman, Giza, Cairo, Tel 3411333, Telex 22812
Parent Company: Part of the ITT Sheraton Corporation
Principal Bankers: Commercial International Bank, Giza; Misr Bank, Cairo
Financial Information:

	1990 US$'000
Sales turnover	21,000
Profits	35%
Total assets	57,000

Date of Establishment: 1970
No of Employees: 1025

CAIRO SILK TEXTILES CO

3 Sharia El Moutasser, Subra El Kheima, Cairo
Tel: 943524, 943822, 940226
Cable: Kaheratex Cairo

Directors: Hassan Morsy (Commercial Director)

PRINCIPAL ACTIVITIES: Cotton yarn, cotton and silk fabrics, mixed fabrics, printing and dyeing
Parent Company: Responsible to the Ministry of Industry
Principal Bankers: Misr Bank

Principal Shareholders: Public sector company
No of Employees: 7,000

CALTEX EGYPT SAE

Isis Bldg, 7 Lazoughly St, Garden City, PO Box 1608, Cairo
Tel: 3548428/9, 3557790
Telex: 92383, 22335 CLTX UN
Telefax: 3557790

Chairman: S M F El Kilany (General Manager)
Directors: M W Saunders, H Hagin (Asst General Manager), M Gouda, M Hermina
Senior Executives: Samir El Kilany (Chairman & General Manager)

PRINCIPAL ACTIVITIES: Storage & marketing of petroleum products, lubricant sales, marine fuel oil sales, retail sales to service stations and deliveries of jet fuel at Cairo International Airport blendings, bunkering in Egyptian ports and deliveries of jet fuel at Cairo International Airport
Branch Offices: Suez Terminal, Airport Aviation Service Station, Alexandria Warehouse
Parent Company: Caltex Petroleum Corporation jointly owned by Texaco and Chevron
Principal Bankers: National Bank of Egypt, Misr America International Bank
Financial Information:

	1990 US$'000
Authorised capital	1,000

Principal Shareholders: Caltex Petroleum Corporation, USA
Date of Establishment: 1937
No of Employees: 51

CANAL SHIPPING AGENCIES CO

26 Palestine Street, PO Box 262, Port Said
Tel: 20662, 20666
Cable: Canaship
Telex: 63075 Agen UN Port Said

PRINCIPAL ACTIVITIES: Sole shipping agents at the ports of
area, handling import, export, transit and transhipment cargo,
transit stores, containers' yard, clearing and forwarding
agents, tourist agents and IATA members, Lloyd's agents,
marine surveyors and underwriters' settling agents, agents
for approx 2000 shipping lines
Branch Offices: Cairo; Suez; Port Said; Safaga; Kosseir; Ras
Gharib; Hamrawein; Wadifiran; Ras Shukeir; Ain El Sukhna; El
Sadat; Abou Rudeis
Parent Company: Responsible to the Ministry of Maritime
Transport
Subsidiary/Associated Companies: (see separate entries):
Assiut Shipping Agency; Asswan Shipping Agency;
Damanhour Shipping Agency; El Menia Shipping Agency;
Cairo Shipping Agency

Principal Shareholders: Public sector company
No of Employees: 2,000

CANALTEX VINYL FLOORING CO

7 Sharia Abdel Khalek Sarwat, Cairo
Tel: 974500

PRINCIPAL ACTIVITIES: Manufacture of vinyl tiles and
sanitaryware
Parent Company: Responsible to the Ministry of Housing and
Reconstruction

Principal Shareholders: Public sector company

CARLIN MIDDLE EAST

2A Beni Amer Street, Giza, Cairo
Tel: 737550, 723164
Telex: 93636, 22334 CME UN

President: Eng M Hady Tarrab
Directors: Hoda Tarrab

PRINCIPAL ACTIVITIES: Sales and service distributors to
foreign manufacturers
Principal Agencies: Carrier International, USA; GM Detroit
Diesel Allison, USA; Barber Greene Overseas, USA; Eaton
Corp, USA; Paccar International Inc, USA; Kenworth Trucks,
USA; Harnischfeger Corp, USA

CATTLE INSURANCE FUND

18 Shareh Boursa, Tewfikieh, Ramses Post Office, Cairo
Tel: 72750, 56028

Chairman: Dr Amin Zaher
Directors: Dr Ismail Kadry (Director-General)
Senior Executives: Dr M Zein-El-Dine (Technical Counsellor), Dr
Shoukry El-Maraghy (Technical Counsellor), Edward Michael
(Financial Director)

PRINCIPAL ACTIVITIES: Insurance of cattle and buffaloes
against death or forced slaughter
Subsidiary Companies: Branches in all Governorates of Egypt

CENTRAL BANK OF EGYPT

31 Kasr El Nil St, Cairo
Tel: 3926108
Cable: Markazi Cairo
Telex: 92237, 22386 CBECR UN
Telefax: 3926361

Governor: Dr Salah Hamed
Deputy Governor: Mohamed Aly El Barbary

Sub-Governors: Fouad Osman (Banking Affairs), Hamdy El
Menebawy (Legal Advisor), El Sayed Singer (Foreign
Relations), Abdel Moneim Aboul Saad (Economic Research),
Hassan Abdel Tawab (Banknote Printing Plant)

PRINCIPAL ACTIVITIES: Central banking
Branch Offices: Branches in Alexandria (3 Tosson St, Telex
54729 CBEFX UN) and Port Said (Gomhoreya St, Telex 63266
CBEPS UN)

CENTRAL DESERT MINING CO

2 Mohamed Sabry Abu Alam St, PO Box 2548, Cairo
Tel: 3933545, 3920151
Cable: Motakholy/Cairo
Telex: 92867 NID UN

Chairman: Helal Abdalla Helal (Accountant)
Directors: Samir H Motawea (Accountant)
Senior Executives: Hassanein H El Kholy (Commercial
Manager), Shoukry El Masry (Mines Manager)

PRINCIPAL ACTIVITIES: Mining of fluorspar, graphite,
magnesite, asbestos, feldespar, chrome, talc, barite,
corundum; quarrying of granite, marble
Subsidiary Companies: IDFU East, Upper Egypt
Principal Bankers: Arab International Bank; Bank Misr

Date of Establishment: 1974
No of Employees: 40

CHAKERT, RUDOLPH, CO FOR PUMPS

95 El Gumhuria St, Cairo
Tel: 908988, 908186

Chairman: Anwar Kaddis

PRINCIPAL ACTIVITIES: Supply and installation of pumps

Principal Shareholders: Private company

CHEMICAL BANK

14 Talaat Harb Street, PO Box 2171, Ataba, Cairo
Tel: 740707, 762357, 740652, 750727
Cable: Chembank Cairo
Telex: 92066 Chembk, 23423

Senior Executives: Shakil A Riaz (VP & Regional Manager)

PRINCIPAL ACTIVITIES: Banking (representative office)
Parent Company: Head office in New York, USA

CIC UNION EUROPEENNE INTERNATIONALE ET CIE

3 Ahmad Nessim Street, Giza, Cairo
Tel: 3610586, 3610591
Cable: Norbankrep
Telex: 92450 Amin UN
Telefax: 3610586

Chairman: Amin Fakhry Abdelnour (General Delegate)

PRINCIPAL ACTIVITIES: Representative office
Parent Company: CIC-Union Europeenne International et Cie,
Paris, France

CITIBANK NA

PO Box 188, 4 Ahmed Pasha St, Garden City, Cairo
Tel: 3551877, 3549523, 3547246
Cable: Citibank
Telex: 92162 Citare UN

PRINCIPAL ACTIVITIES: Banking
Branch Offices: In Egypt: PO Box 638, Port Said, Tel 21773,
24675, Telex 63254; and PO Box 1445, Alexandria, Tel
4916376, 4925183, Telex 54296; Heliopolis, Tel 664337
Parent Company: Citibank, New York

Date of Establishment: 1812 in the USA, 1975 in Egypt
No of Employees: 124

EGYPT

COLGATE-PALMOLIVE (EGYPT) SAE

PO Box 43, Alexandria
Tel: 4300638, 4301408, 4301409, 4300638, 4301408, 4301409
Cable: Cogal Alexandria
Telex: 54576 COPAL UN
Telefax: 03-4302261

Directors: Sayed M Fayed (Managing Director)
Senior Executives: Marc P Bernard (Financial Controller), Adel F
    Saleh (Plant Manager), Tamer K Eisa (Sales Manager), Yehia
    Lutfy (Export & Purchasing Manager), Mohamed Mustafa
    (Information Resources Manager)

PRINCIPAL ACTIVITIES: Manufacture of toiletries, household
    and personal care products
Parent Company: Colgate Palmolive Co, USA
Principal Bankers: Bank of Credit & Commerce, Bank of
    America, Cairo
Financial Information:

	1990 US$'000
Sales turnover	5,000
Authorised capital	2,000
Paid-up capital	2,000

Principal Shareholders: Colgate Palmolive Co, USA (90%)
Date of Establishment: 1979
No of Employees: 200

COMMERCIAL INTERNATIONAL BANK (EGYPT) SAE (JOINT VENTURE BANK)

21-23 Giza Street, Nile Tower Bldg, Giza, Cairo
Tel: 726132/215/221, 726376/423/564
Cable: Chasnat Egypt
Telex: 20201, 92394 CNBCA UN

Chairman: Ahmed Ismail (Managing Director)
Directors: Mahmoud M Helal (Asst Managing Director)
Senior Executives: Adel Youssry (Senior General Manager
    Credit & Marketing), Mohamed El Turky (General Manager
    Operations, Treasury, Institutional & Trade Finance),
    Mohamed El Khouly (General Manager Audit Dept)

PRINCIPAL ACTIVITIES: Commercial banking
Branch Offices: Cairo (7), Alexandria (3), Port Said (1), Tanta (1)
Financial Information:

	E£'000
Authorised capital	70,000
Paid-up capital	50,000

Principal Shareholders: National Bank of Egypt and its entities
    (100%)
Date of Establishment: September 1975
No of Employees: 710

COMMERCIAL SERVICES CORP

10 El Mansour Mohamed St, Zamalek, Cairo
Tel: 3407568, 3407729, 3407618, 3407668, 3400951
Cable: Mimalak
Telex: 92486 Malak UN, 22240 CSC UN
Telefax: (202) 3402342

Chairman: M G Malak
Senior Executives: W Khodier (Manager Electrical &
    Telecommunication Division), N S Kamel (Deputy General
    Manager)

PRINCIPAL ACTIVITIES: General trading and representation of
    foreign international companies in Egypt
Principal Bankers: Hongkong Egyptian Bank, Zamalek, Cairo;
    Export Development Bank of Egypt

COMMERZBANK AG

2 Ali Labib Gabr Street, PO Box 1944, Cairo
Tel: 744203
Telex: 92194 CBK UN

PRINCIPAL ACTIVITIES: Banking (representative office)
Parent Company: Head office in Frankfurt, West Germany

COMPUTER CONSULTING & SUPPLIES CO (CCS)

33B Mohamed Mazhar Street, Zamalek, Cairo
Tel: 3402557, 3415424, 3418529, 3402558
Telex: 21006 CCS UN
Telefax: 3413624

Chairman: Kamal Zaghloul (General Manager)
Directors: Hassan Hegazi (Asst Manager), Ali El Rafei (Finance
    & Admin Manager), Said Boseila (Sales Manager)
Senior Executives: Kamal A Zaghloul (General Manager)

PRINCIPAL ACTIVITIES: Computer supplies and consulting,
    hardware and software
Principal Agencies: IBM, CDC, Xidex Corp
Principal Bankers: National Societe Generale Bank, Lloyds
    Bank, Hongkong Bank, Credit International Bank

Principal Shareholders: Kamal Zaghloul (50%), Amr Soliman
    (25%), Khaled Soliman (25%)
Date of Establishment: 1977

CONOCO EGYPT

58 Road 105, PO BOx 16, Maadi, Cairo
Tel: 3502026, 3503726, 3504053
Telex: 92345, 20749 CONCO UN

PRINCIPAL ACTIVITIES: Petroleum exploration

CONSUMERS COOPERATIVE SOCIETY

Omar Effendi

25 Sharia Adly, Cairo
Tel: 745011, 745332, 745253, 769470
Cable: Omar Effendi

Chairman: Sayed Ahmed Mohamad Giresha
Directors: Mohamad Abrahim Ahmed (Commercial Manager)
Senior Executives: Abdel Moniem Abd El Mouity

PRINCIPAL ACTIVITIES: General trade
Branch Offices: 60 branches
Parent Company: Responsible to the Ministry of Supply
Principal Bankers: Misr Bank

Principal Shareholders: Public sector company
Date of Establishment: 1856
No of Employees: 6,000

CORE LABORATORIES INTERNATIONAL LTD

PO Box 45, Maadi, Cairo
Tel: 637970
Cable: Corelabor
Telex: 94302 Core UN

PRINCIPAL ACTIVITIES: Worldwide petroleum reservoir
    engineering and field services
Parent Company: Core Laboratories Inc
Principal Bankers: Chase National Bank

Date of Establishment: 1975
No of Employees: 73

CREDIT FONCIER EGYPTIEN

11 El Mashadi Street, Off Kasr El-Nil, PO Box 141, Cairo
Tel: 910197
Cable: Foncier
Telex: 93863 CFEBK UN

Directors: Aly Salem Gommah (General Manager), Ibrahim Kheir
    El Din (General Manager), Eng. Mohamad S El Dine El

Bendari (Specialized Director), Dr Ahmad R Moussa (Specialized Director)

Senior Executives: Mostafa Hamam (General Manager, Legal Department), Yussef Adel Mansour (General Manager, Engineer & Survey Department), Mohamad El Far (General Manager, Accounts Department)

PRINCIPAL ACTIVITIES: Mortgage and real estate banking
Branch Offices: 17 Talaat Harb Street, Alexandria, Tel 29731, Port Said, Mansoura, Zakazeek, Tanta, Minia, Helwan
Subsidiary Companies: Al Shams Company for Housing and Reconstruction (Cairo); Egyptian Real Estate Investment Co
Principal Bankers: Central Bank of Egypt
Financial Information:

	£E'000
Authorised capital	25,000
Paid-up capital	25,000

Principal Shareholders: 100% Government owned
Date of Establishment: January 1880
No of Employees: 595

CREDIT INTERNATIONAL D'EGYPTE SAE

PO Box 831, 2 Talaat Harb Street, Cairo
Tel: 759738
Cable: Credegypt
Telex: 93680 CIE UN

Chairman: Abd El Ghani Hamed Gameh
Directors: Ahmad I A Ismail, Gamil B H B Balbaa, Moumir H Y Hemaya, Mohamed Sami El Halawani, Ahmed Wagdy, Hans A Denfield, Francois Jorda, Noel Bazoche
Senior Executives: Anis Rezkalla, Marc Demeulenaere

PRINCIPAL ACTIVITIES: Banking
Financial Information:

	US$'000
Authorised capital	10,000
Paid-up capital	10,000

Principal Shareholders: National Bank of Egypt (51%), Credit Commercial de France (39%), Berliner Handels und Frankfurter Bank (10%)
Date of Establishment: 1977
No of Employees: 55

CREDIT LYONNAIS

3 rue Manchaet, Al Kataba, PO Box 2652, Cairo
Tel: 741910, 746141, 779158
Telex: 92577 CRELYO UN; 94077 CRELY UN

PRINCIPAL ACTIVITIES: Commercial banking (full branch)
Parent Company: Head office in Paris, France

Date of Establishment: 1975

CREDIT SUISSE

6 Oqba Street, PO Box 224, Dokki, Cairo
Tel: 3484333, 3484777
Cable: Credswiss
Telex: 94128 CSCA UN
Telefax: 3485237

Directors: Magdi N Hanna (First Vice President & Branch Manager)
Senior Executives: Mrs N Hoda Abu Basha (Vice President & Deputy Branch Manager), Thomas Schuppius (Asst Vice President & Operation Manager)

PRINCIPAL ACTIVITIES: Commercial banking
Parent Company: Head office in Zurich, Switzerland

DAMANHOUR SHIPPING AGENCY

1 Safia Zaghloul St, PO Box 126, Port Said
Tel: 220351/6
Cable: Damanship
Telex: 63264, 63146 Daman UN
Telefax: (20 66) 35978

Directors: Abdel Rahman Mahmoud
Senior Executives: Abdel Rahman Mahmoud (General Manager), Aboul Ela Aly (Commercial Manager), Shawky El Gayyar (Financial Manager)

PRINCIPAL ACTIVITIES: Shipping agency, clearing and forwarding
Principal Agencies: A P Moller; P & O; Shipping Corp of India; Evergreen; United Arab Shipping; Duch Oost Africa; Hapag Lloyd, Ato Shioggia
Branch Offices: Suez Branch: Canal Shipping Agencies Co Bldg, PO Box 4, Suez, Tel 29661, 29676, Cable Damanship, Telex 66022 AGENCY UN
Principal Bankers: National Bank of Egypt

Principal Shareholders: Part of the Canal Shipping Agencies Company
Date of Establishment: 1965

DAR EL MAAREF PRINTING & PUBLISHING HOUSE

1119 Corniche El Nil, Cairo
Tel: 777077, 775877
Cable: Damaref
Telex: 92199 UN

Chairman: Salah Montasar
Directors: El Mahdi Hamza (Managing Director)
Senior Executives: Azza Harouni (Import Manager), Kamel Okasha (Export Manager)

PRINCIPAL ACTIVITIES: Publishing, printing, distribution import-export of Arabic and foreign books
Branch Offices: 18 branches from Aswan to Alexandria
Parent Company: Responsible to the United Arab Press Authority, Cairo
Principal Bankers: Bank Misr, Cairo

Principal Shareholders: State-owned
Date of Establishment: 1897
No of Employees: 1,600

DELTA COTTON GINNING CO

19 Sharia El Gumhuriya, Cairo
Tel: 910821, 919034, 916350

PRINCIPAL ACTIVITIES: Cotton ginning
Branch Offices: 17 Salah Salem St, Alexandria, Tel 25161
Parent Company: Responsible to the Ministry of Trade

Principal Shareholders: Public sector company

DELTA GENERAL CONTRACTING CO

19 Sharia Kasr El Nil, Cairo
Tel: 970230, 972149
Telex: 93278 Delta UN

PRINCIPAL ACTIVITIES: Contracting, civil engineering and construction
Parent Company: Responsible to the Ministry of Housing and Reconstruction

Principal Shareholders: Public sector company

DELTA INDUSTRIAL CO (IDEAL)

Ramses Street Extension, Nasr City, Cairo
Tel: 2846081/2/3
Cable: Rabsteel Cairo
Telex: 92218 DTC UN, 20583 DTC UN
Telefax: 2846075

Chairman: Eng Mohamed Moheib Eldin Abou Alam
Senior Executives: Abdel Rahman Fahmy (Managing Director), Mrs Roshdia Abdel Sayed (Finance Director), Eid Abdel Gelil (Sales Director), Mrs Nabila H Mattar (Export Director), Anwar I El Ghoneimy (Marketing Director), Ibrahim El Naggar (Purchasing Director), Eng Badr Attia (Production Director), Fouad Abdallah (Personnel Director), Mrs Souhir Moussa (Admin Director)

PRINCIPAL ACTIVITIES: Manufacture of steel furniture; electrical appliances; washing machines; kitchen equipment; refrigerators; slotted angles
Branch Offices: Alexandria, Tanta, Mansouro, Port Said, Sohag, Bany Sweef, Luxor, Aswan, Marsa Matrouh
Principal Bankers: Alexandria Bank; Cairo Bank; Misr Bank
Financial Information: Responsible to the Ministry of Industry

	1989/90 E£'000
Sales turnover	211,000
Profits	1,946
Authorised capital	25,000
Paid-up capital	25,000

Principal Shareholders: Public sector company
Date of Establishment: 1920
No of Employees: 8,103

DELTA INTERNATIONAL BANK
1113 Corniche El Nil, PO Box 1159, Cairo
Tel: 743456, 753484, 750989, 753492
Cable: Bankdelta Cairo
Telex: 93833 Delta UN, 22674 Delta UN, 93319 Dib UN

Chairman: Mahmoud Sidky Mourad (also Managing Director)
Directors: Ibrahim Shehata Moustafa, Ahmed Abdel Aziz El Aley El Metawaa, El Syaed El Syaed El Gohary, Gamal El Din Mohamed Shata, Eng Hussein Sultan, Ragaa Hamed El Mekawy, Abdel Elah Mohamed Saleh Kaaki, Eng Aly Nour El Din Nassar, Fouad El Kommos Sidrak, Eng Mohamed El Mahdy Hegazi, Eng Mohamed Farid Akl, Moustafa Mohamed El Beledi, Eng Niazi Ibrahim Moustafa, Sheikh Hani Al Emam
Senior Executives: Ibrahim Shehata Moustafa (General Manager), Hamed Badr El Din (Senior Deputy GM Financing Investment & Foreign Relations), Mohy Hassan Badr (Senior Deputy GM Credit Facilities), Mohamed Refaat Sakr (Deputy GM Financial Affairs), Ahmed Mahmoud El Baga (Deputy GM Financing & Investment), Adel Kamel Seddik (Deputy GM Public Affairs & Branches), Mrs Elham Shoukry (Deputy GM Planning & Marketing), Guirguis Abdel Sayed (Asst GM Foreign Relations), Moussa Mohamed Khalifa (Asst GM Credit Facilities), Aboul Ezz Ahmed Abdallah (asst GM Follow Up of Credit Facilities), Ahmed El Mourshidy (Manager pf Inspection), Mahmoud El Kelany (Asst GM Electronic Data Processing), Wagih Sayed Hassanein (Asst GM Financial Affairs)

PRINCIPAL ACTIVITIES: Commercial banking
Branch Offices: Head Office Cairo; Dokki (Cairo); Heliopolis (Cairo); Cairo Airport (Cairo); Tahrir (Cairo); Maadi (Cairo); Mohandessin (Cairo); Merghany (Cairo); Shubra (Cairo); Shallalat (Alexandria); Selsela (Alexandria); Tanta; Suez; Minia; Port Said

Principal Shareholders: Bank of Alexandria; El Shark Insurance Co; Eastern Cotton Co; Cairo Investments and Development Co; Ahmed and Mohamed Saleh El Kaki Co; Sheikh Kamal J Adham; Financial & Investment Services for Asia Ltd (Hong Kong)
Date of Establishment: 1978
No of Employees: 675

DELTA STEEL MILL CO
18 Sh Emad El Din, Cairo
Tel: 754955
Telex: 94220 UN
Telefax: (202) 2205648

Chairman: Dr Aly Helmy
Directors: Eng Adel El Miniawi (Head of Works Sector), Eng Amin Zanati (Head of Technical Sector), Essam El Karrar (Head of Financial Sector), Eng M El Serafy (Head of Commercial Sector)

PRINCIPAL ACTIVITIES: Production and marketing of hot rolling steel products, cold drawing products, wire mesh, steel castings, cast irons, etc

Branch Offices: Works: Mostorod-Bahtim, Tel 2205831, 2205837
Principal Bankers: Bank of Alexandria, Misr Bank, National Bank

Date of Establishment: 1947
No of Employees: 4,321

DEN NORSKE CREDITBANK
3 Ahmad Nessim Street, Giza, Cairo
Tel: 727825, 729499
Telex: 93750 USSI UN

PRINCIPAL ACTIVITIES: Representative office
Parent Company: Head office in Oslo, Norway

DEUTSCHE BANK AG
23 Kasr El Nile Street, PO Box 2306, Cairo
Tel: 762341, 741373
Cable: Deutbank
Telex: 92306 Deucai UN

PRINCIPAL ACTIVITIES: Banking (representative office)
Parent Company: Head office in Frankfurt, West Germany

DEVELOPMENT & POPULAR HOUSING CO
4 Latin America Street, Garden City, Cairo
Tel: 28353/5

PRINCIPAL ACTIVITIES: Designing of housing, public buildings, hotels, hospitals and industrial buildings, also urban planning

Principal Shareholders: Public sector company

DEVELOPMENT INDUSTRIAL BANK
Head Office, 110 El-Galaa St, Cairo
Tel: 779188, 779247, 779087
Cable: Devbank
Telex: 92643 DIBAK UN

Directors: Hussein Mahmoud El Sennary (Acting Chairman), Mrs Zeinal Amin El Feky (General Manager), Mohamed Abdel Moneim Turk (General Manager), Samir Mahmoud Hamdy (General Manager), Dr Mohamed Abdel Aziz Agamia, Dr Atef El Sayed Ahmed

PRINCIPAL ACTIVITIES: Short, medium and long-term loans to industrial projects
Branch Offices: Cairo (2); Alexandria (2); Tanta
Associated Companies: Misr America International Bank, Cairo, Egypt
Principal Bankers: Bank of Alexandria, Bank of America; Banque du Caire

Principal Shareholders: Central Bank of Egypt
Date of Establishment: 1975
No of Employees: 507

DHL EGYPT WLL
20 Gamal Edin Abul Mahassin St, Garden City, Cairo
Tel: 3557301, 3557118, 3546710
Telex: 94045 DHLEG UN

Senior Executives: Tony Sloan (General Manager), Mona Kabel (Sales Manager), Mostafa Tawfik (Financial Manager)

PRINCIPAL ACTIVITIES: Worldwide courier service
Branch Offices: In the Middle East: Bahrain, Cyprus, Egypt (Cairo, Port Said: tel 34335/7, telex 63210; Alexandria: tel 5970953, 5968830, telex 54253), Iran, Iraq, Jordan, Kuwait, Lebanon, Oman, Qatar, Saudi Arabia (AlKhobar, Jeddah, Riyadh, Jubail, Tabuk, Taif), Sudan, UAE (Abu Dhabi, Dubai, Sharjah)

DOWELL SCHLUMBERGER (WESTERN) SA (CEG)
PO Box 89, Maadi, Cairo
Tel: 631476, 771372, 766911
Telex: 94064 Orang UN

PRINCIPAL ACTIVITIES: Oil service company
Branch Offices: Abu Dhabi; Sharjah; Saudi Arabia; Kuwait;
Oman; Syria; Jordan; Yemen; India; Pakistan; Turkey

Principal Shareholders: Dow Chemical Co; Schlumberger Ltd

DRESDNER BANK AG
Representative Office, Nile Tower Bld, 21/23 Giza Street, Cairo
Tel: 7234511
Cable: Dresagent
Telex: 92603 Dresag UN
Telefax: 7237826

Senior Executives: Fritz W Fahlbusch (Representative)

PRINCIPAL ACTIVITIES: Banking (representative office)
Parent Company: Head office in Frankfurt, Germany

DREXEL OILFIELD EQUIPMENT (EGYPT)
47 Road 250, Digla, New Maadi, Cairo
Tel: 3527041, 3528960, 3524329
Telex: 22973 Drexl UN

PRINCIPAL ACTIVITIES: Oilfield service

DYESTUFFS & CHEMICALS CO
Kafr El-Dawar
Tel: 902734, 902745
Cable: Ismadye Egypt
Telex: 54083 Dych UN
Telefax: 4838975 (Alexandria)

Chairman: Lotfi Khatab
Directors: Ali Tawfik (Head of Production Sector), D Hamdi Abd
El Dayem (Head of Technical Sector), Sayed Kassem (Head
of Engineering Sector), Salah El Toukhi (Head of Financial &
Admin Sector), Abd El Fatah Risk (Head of Commercial
Sector)

PRINCIPAL ACTIVITIES: Manufacture, sale and export of
dyestuffs and chemicals; pesticides, auxilliaries, detergents,
organic chemicals, pharmaceuticals, industrial services
Branch Offices: Alexandria Office: 48 El Houria Ave, Tel
4822952, 4838975; Cairo Office: 8 Shampolion St, Tel 753860,
741356, 746147
Parent Company: Responsible to the Ministry of Industry
Subsidiary Companies: Egyptian German Co for Dyes & Resins
(Joint Venture with Hoescht)
Principal Bankers: Bank of Alexandria, Alexandria; Bank Misr,
Kafr El-Dawar
Financial Information:

	1990
	E£'000
Sales turnover	42,000
Profits	3,600
Paid-up capital	28,361
Total assets	25,671

Principal Shareholders: State owned
Date of Establishment: 1964
No of Employees: 1,755

E & D INDUSTRIAL CALIFORNIA OVERSEAS CO
10 Shawarbi St, Cairo
Tel: 757218, 757499, 772526
Telex: 318 ADELCO

Senior Executives: Adel T Agha (General Manager)

PRINCIPAL ACTIVITIES: Textile manfacturing
Financial Information:

	US$'000
Authorised capital	3,500

Date of Establishment: 1974
No of Employees: 300

EASTERN COTTON EXPORT CO
8 Tarik El Horriya, Alexandria
Tel: 37120/24
Cable: Marba-Alex
Telex: 54150 Marboc UN

PRINCIPAL ACTIVITIES: Export of cotton
Branch Offices: Cairo Office: 37 Kasr El Nil St, Tel 979051
Parent Company: Responsible to the Ministry of Trade

Principal Shareholders: Public sector company

EASTERN PLASTICS PRODUCTS
46 Nehmat Moukhtar-Hadra St, Alexandria
Tel: 72518, 70277

Chairman: Mohamed Abdel Rahman Hamouda
Directors: Amin Mohamed Abdel Rahman

PRINCIPAL ACTIVITIES: Thermosetting; thermoplastics
Principal Bankers: National Bank of Egypt; Banque du Caire

EASTERN TOBACCO CO SAE
450 El Ahram St, Giza, PO Box 1543, Cairo
Tel: 724711
Cable: Comtern-Giza
Telex: 92596 Comtr UN

PRINCIPAL ACTIVITIES: Manufacture and distribution of
tobacco and cigarettes
Branch Offices: Alexandria Branch
Parent Company: Responsible to the Ministry of Industry

Principal Shareholders: Public sector company
Date of Establishment: 1920
No of Employees: 9,450

EBASCO SERVICES INTERNATIONAL INC
5 Mahmoud Azmy Street, Zamalek, Cairo
Tel: 3402138, 3409582, 3407125, 3414934
Telex: 93920 BALSM UN

Directors: Ahmed Seif El Din Khorshid

PRINCIPAL ACTIVITIES: Engineering and construction services
in the field of power generating plants, heavy industrial plants

EDFINA CO FOR FOOD PROCESSING & CANNING
Ras Soda, Montaza, PO Box 937, Alexandria
Tel: 67054, 69447

PRINCIPAL ACTIVITIES: Production of canned vegetables,
juices and fruits, frozen shrimps and fish, pilchards,
anchovies, fish powder, smoked fish and sardines
Branch Offices: Cairo Commercial Office: 9/11 Orabi St, Tel
827816, 55984
Parent Company: Responsible to the Ministry of Industry

Principal Shareholders: Public sector company

EGYPT ARAB AFRICAN BANK
BP 61, Magless El Shaab, 5 Midan Al Saray Al Koubra, Garden
City, Cairo
Tel: 3551513, 3550948, 3551698
Cable: EGYRABAF
Telex: 23569, 20965, 20597 EAAB UN
Telefax: 3556239

Chairman: Mohamed Ibrahim Farid (Managing Director)
Directors: Mohamed Samy El Halawany (Deputy Chairman),
Samir Helmy Awad, Dr Adel Gazareen, Hussein Gamal Eldin
Gamgoum, Mohsen Mohamed Khaled, Mohamed Moharram
Alasfer, Ibrahim Dousouki Sabe, Kamal Zaki Abou Eleid, Dr
Mohamed Ahmed Lotfi Hassouna, Mansour Lotief, Dr Ahmed
Abdel Wahab El Ghandour, Mohamed M El Mouafi
Senior Executives: Bahieddin Moustafa El Sadek (General
Manager), Mohamed Moustafa Allam (Deputy General
Manager)

EGYPT

PRINCIPAL ACTIVITIES: Investment banking
Branch Offices: Cairo (Fax 3556239), Alexandria (Fax 3-4839675), Sarwat, Tenth of Ramadan (15-364074), Mohandessin (Fax 702481)
Principal Bankers: Correspondent banks in Amsterdam, Brussels, Frankfurt, Hongkong, London, Milan, New York, Paris, Tokyo, Zurich
Financial Information:

	1989 E£'000	1990 E£'000
Total income	37,197	48,481
Reserves & profit	44,962	49,484
Loans & advances	320,754	403,911
Deposits	330,512	430,436
Authorised capital	20,000	20,000
Paid-up capital	20,000	20,000
Total assets	508,203	841,140

Principal Shareholders: Arab African International Bank (49%); Bank of Alexandria (7%); Development Industrial Bank (7%); Egyptian Reinsurance Co (7%); Banque du Caire (7%); Arab African International Pension Funds (7%); Egyptian businessmen (16%)
Date of Establishment: 1982
No of Employees: 298

EGYPT FREE SHOP CO

106 Gamat EL Dewal El Arabia, Mohandseen
Tel: 3497094
Cable: 12411
Telex: 92479
Telefax: 3486948

Chairman: Mohamed Abd El Fattah Ebaid
Directors: Mohamed Khalil Hussen

PRINCIPAL ACTIVITIES: General trade; import and export of consumer goods
Parent Company: Responsible to the Ministry of Trade

EGYPTAIR

Cairo International Airport, Cairo
Tel: 968866, 2459316, 2454400, 2450260
Cable: Egyoair
Telex: 92221 Egair UN, 92116 Egy Opr UN
Telefax: 245931

Chairman: M F Rayan
Directors: Wafik Abd El Hamid (Vice President Avation Division), Ismail El Sherif (Vice President Corporate Planning & Finance), Mamdouh Abd El Kader (Vice President Commercial Division), Mohamed Abou Setta (Vice President Engineering, Ground & Technical Divisions)

PRINCIPAL ACTIVITIES: Air transport
Branch Offices: Karnak Office: 12 Kasr El Nil, Tel 750600; Adly Office: 6 Adly Street, Cairo, Tel 3900999, 3902444
Principal Bankers: Bank Misr
Financial Information:

	1990 E£'000
Authorised capital	8,500

Date of Establishment: 1932
No of Employees: 13,000

EGYPTEX

Mahmoud Al Tallawi

18 El Mansour Mohamed Street, Zamalek, Cairo
Tel: 3412578
Telex: 23713 MT UN
Telefax: 200154

President: Mahmoud Tallawi

PRINCIPAL ACTIVITIES: Non woven products manufacturing, carpets, floor covering and industrial felts; sea water desalination plants
Branch Offices: Tarsana Center, Mohandisseen, Cairo, Tel 3464018; Factory: El Badrashin, Giza, Cairo, Tel 200017
Principal Bankers: National Bank for Development

Date of Establishment: 1973
No of Employees: 300

EGYPTIAN ADVANCED TECHNOLOGIES SAE (BALSAM)

3 Osman Ibn Affan Street, Mohandessin
Tel: 3443001, 3447703/5
Telex: 22516, 93920 BALSM UN
Telefax: 3447704

Chairman: Dr Ahmed S Foda
Directors: Yehia Labib (Managing Director), Mahmoud S Foda (Managing Director), Mohamed Hamed Abdel Aziz (Finance Director)
Senior Executives: Salem El Badawi (General Manager), Adel Sioufi (Sales Manager Microcomputers), Salama Yousef (Sales Manager Communications), Hossam El Alfi (Systems Manager), Mounir El Karamani (Maintenance Manager), Soher Amer (Education Centre Manager)

PRINCIPAL ACTIVITIES: Computers sales service, software and education
Principal Agencies: Telecommunications (Wire & Wireless); Mitel, Wang, Northern Telecom, Sola, DTS, Canadian Marconi
Branch Offices: Alexandria
Subsidiary Companies: Egyptian Telecommunications Project Balsam
Principal Bankers: Egyptian American Bank, Chase National Bank

Date of Establishment: 1978
No of Employees: 250

EGYPTIAN AMERICAN AGRICULTURAL CO

220 Avenue el Horreya, Alexandria
Tel: 73524, 77472
Telex: 54756 LMTC UN

PRINCIPAL ACTIVITIES: Vegetable farming for export
Financial Information:

	US$'000
Authorised capital	1,500

Principal Shareholders: World Farms, USA (55%)
Date of Establishment: 1981
No of Employees: 100 full time + 500 labourers

EGYPTIAN AMERICAN BANK

4 Hassan Sabri Street, Zamalek, Cairo
Tel: 3416150/7/8/9
Cable: Egypambank
Telex: 92683 EGAMB UN

Chairman: Abdel Ghani Gameh
Directors: Dr Farid W Saad (Vice Chairman), Elie J Baroudi (Managing Director)
Senior Executives: Elie J Baroudi (Managing Director), Imran R Khan (General Manager), Peter Schofield (General Manager Operations), Adel Senoussi (General Manager & Counsel)

PRINCIPAL ACTIVITIES: Commercial banking
Branch Offices: Cairo: Kasr El Nil Branch; Garden City Branch; Abdel Khalek Sarwat Branch; Mohamdessine Branch; Pyramids Branch; Alexandria: Main Branch, 14 Salah Salem Street, Tel 801288, Telex 54387
Parent Company: American Express Bank; Bank of Alexandria
Principal Bankers: American Express Bank

Financial Information:

	1988/89 E£'000
Profits	27,354
Deposits	1,132,601
Loans & advances	484,257
Authorised capital	22,000
Paid-up capital	22,000
Total assets	1,487,732

Principal Shareholders: Joint venture between American Express Banking Corp (49%) and Bank of Alexandria (51%)
Date of Establishment: June 1976
No of Employees: 650

EGYPTIAN AMERICAN INSURANCE CO

9 Talaat Harb St, PO Box 2012, Cairo
Tel: 3932808, 3822955
Cable: Egaminco
Telex: 92845 EGAM UN, 20446 Egam UN
Telefax: 3913384

Chairman: Koraim El Daif
Senior Executives: Mohamed Ihab Hilal (Managing Director), Mohamed Samir Ibrahim (Asst General Manager Finance), Kamel Ragai Ali (Asst General Manager Underwriting)

PRINCIPAL ACTIVITIES: Reinsurance transactions in Egypt & Worldwide and insurance in Free Zone
Branch Offices: Alexandria, Port Said
Principal Bankers: Commercial International Bank (Egypt) SAE; Egyptian American Bank
Financial Information:

	1989/90 US$'000
Profits	321
Authorised capital	3,000
Paid-up capital	3,000
Total assets	20,648

Principal Shareholders: Al Chark Insurance Company (50%), American International Underwriters Overseas (AIUO) (50%)
Date of Establishment: 1977
No of Employees: 44

EGYPTIAN AMERICAN SANITARY WARES CO

117, El Thawra Street, Heliopolis, Cairo
Tel: 2900394, 2909872
Telex: 20404 ESANX UN
Telefax: 2901108

Chairman: Mohamed Selim Zaki
Directors: R David Chapman (Managing Director)
Senior Executives: A G Gono (Finance Manager), Abdel Hamid Hamdy (Personnel Manager)

PRINCIPAL ACTIVITIES: Manufacture of sanitary ware
Parent Company: American Standard Inc Licensee
Financial Information:

	1989/90 E£'000
Authorised capital	20,000
Paid-up capital	7,500

Principal Shareholders: American Standard Inc, USA (59%)
Date of Establishment: 1983
No of Employees: 200

EGYPTIAN AVIATION & TRAVEL SERVICES

20 Talaat Harb Street, Cairo
Tel: 762660, 782660
Telex: 93999 EATS UN

President: Mohamed Beltagui

PRINCIPAL ACTIVITIES: Air transport and travel services

Date of Establishment: 1953

EGYPTIAN CATERING & CONTRACTING CO LTD

10 Abdul Rahman Fahmi St, Garden City, Cairo
Tel: 29433, 22362
Cable: Catcon-Cairo
Telex: 92067 Mefco UN

PRINCIPAL ACTIVITIES: Industrial catering and camp services, construction, hotel management
Associated Companies: Gulf Catering & Contracting Ltd

EGYPTIAN CEMENT OFFICE

21 26th July Street, Cairo
Tel: 740938, 740817, 740797, 740776, 740655
Cable: Portland
Telex: 21989 E C O UN

Chairman: Mohamed Abdel Hamid Metwalli
Directors: Mohamed Anwar Abdel Latif (Deputy for Commercial Affairs), Gamal Eldin Abbass Mohamed (Deputy for Financial Affairs)

PRINCIPAL ACTIVITIES: Marketing and distribution of cement
Parent Company: Responsible to the Ministry of Housing and Reconstruction
Principal Bankers: Banque du Caire; Bank of Alexandria

Principal Shareholders: Public sector company
Date of Establishment: 1932

EGYPTIAN CHEMICAL INDUSTRIES (KIMA)

12 Sh Talaat Harb, Cairo
Tel: 970605/6, 971544/5
Cable: Kimanile Aswan

PRINCIPAL ACTIVITIES: Production of calcium ammonium nitrate 26, heavy water, calcium carbide, ferrosilicon
Branch Offices: Head Office and factory in Aswan
Parent Company: Responsible to the Ministry of Industry

Principal Shareholders: Public sector company

EGYPTIAN CO FOR CHEMICAL TRADING

10 Champollion St, Cairo
Tel: 50761, 50862

Senior Executives: Eng M Hamouda (General Purchasing Director)

PRINCIPAL ACTIVITIES: Import, export and marketing of chemicals
Parent Company: Responsible to the Ministry of Trade

Principal Shareholders: Public sector company

EGYPTIAN CO FOR ELECTRICAL APPLIANCES (SHAHER)

27 Sharia Talaat, Harb, Cairo
Tel: 49991/2, 87578, 56122

PRINCIPAL ACTIVITIES: Production and distribution of electrical equipment and electrical household appliances
Parent Company: Responsible to the Ministry of Supply

Principal Shareholders: Public sector company

EGYPTIAN CO FOR FISH MARKETING

42 Sharia El Thawra, Heliopolis, PO Box 917, Cairo
Tel: 963049
Cable: Asmak, Cairo

PRINCIPAL ACTIVITIES: Production and distribution of fish and fish products
Parent Company: Responsible to the Ministry of Supply

Principal Shareholders: Public sector company

EGYPT

EGYPTIAN CO FOR FOOD 'BISCOMISR'

Soc Egyptienne pour l'Aliment 'Biscomisr'

Sharia El Sawah, Amiria, Koubbeh, PO Box 1470, Cairo
Tel: 866906
Cable: Biscomsir
Telex: 92649 Bisco Un

Directors: Saleh Mostafa Ammar (Commercial Director), William
Aziz, Mohamed Atef Abdel Kader

PRINCIPAL ACTIVITIES: Production of bread, biscuits, wafer
biscuits, boiled sweets, halawa, chocolates, chewing gum
Parent Company: Responsible to the Ministry of Industry
Principal Bankers: Bank of Alexandria; National Bank of Egypt

Principal Shareholders: Public sector company
Date of Establishment: 1957
No of Employees: 3,500

EGYPTIAN CO FOR LEATHER MANUFACTURE

Model Tanneries Co

Bassatin, Maadi, Cairo
Tel: 636366, 636437
Cable: Medabaghine
Telex: 23026 ELCO UN

Chairman: Chem Emam Hassanien
Directors: Chem Abdel Kader Abdel Hameed Abbas (Factories
Director), Saad Atalla (Commercial Director), Farouk Sayed
Ahmed Ghoraba (Administrative Director)

PRINCIPAL ACTIVITIES: Leather tanning
Branch Offices: 37 Sharia Kasr El Nil, Cairo, Tel 744378
Parent Company: Responsible to the Ministry of Industry

Principal Shareholders: Public sector
Date of Establishment: 1964
No of Employees: 2,000

EGYPTIAN CO FOR MANUFACTURE OF LIGHT TRANSPORT EQUIPMENT (AL TRAMCO)

Wadi Hof, Helwan
Tel: 30154, 38109
Cable: Al Tramco

PRINCIPAL ACTIVITIES: Manufacture of bicycles; mopeds;
vans; microbuses
Branch Offices: 70 El Goumhouriya St, Cairo, Tel 913341
Parent Company: Responsible to the Ministry of Industry

Principal Shareholders: Public sector company

EGYPTIAN CO FOR MARITIME TRANSPORT (MARTRANS)

7 Abdel Khalek Sarwat St, PO Box 2196, Cairo
Tel: 970317/9, 41283
Telex: 92243 Martrans

PRINCIPAL ACTIVITIES: Shipping and transport

EGYPTIAN CO FOR MEAT & DAIRY PRODUCTION

14 Midan El Goumhouria, Cairo
Tel: 919221, 919448

PRINCIPAL ACTIVITIES: Production and distribution of meat
and dairy products
Parent Company: Responsible to the Ministry of Supply

Principal Shareholders: Public sector company

EGYPTIAN CO FOR MEAT, POULTRY & FOODSTUFFS SUPPLIES

7A Sharia Youssef Naguib, Ataba, Cairo
Tel: 901066, 904059

PRINCIPAL ACTIVITIES: Distribution of foodstuffs, meat and
poultry
Parent Company: Responsible to the Ministry of Supply

Principal Shareholders: Public sector company

EGYPTIAN CO FOR METAL CONSTRUCTION METALCO

5A Sharia 26 July, Cairo
Tel: 910092, 910377, 910420, 910484
Telex: 93094 Mtlco UN

PRINCIPAL ACTIVITIES: Production of heavy metal structures,
fluvial and marine units erection and repairs, storage tanks,
production of steel pipes for waterworks and drainage
Branch Offices: Shoubrah El Mozzalat Factory; Damanhour
Factory
Parent Company: Responsible to the Ministry of Industry
Subsidiary Companies: Ferrometal Co (Joint venture between
Metalco, Egypt and Ferrosstaal, Germany)

Principal Shareholders: Public sector company
Date of Establishment: 30-6-1968

EGYPTIAN CO FOR METAL TRADE (SIGAL)

17 Gomhouria Street, PO BOx 691, Cairo
Tel: 3924763, 3912012
Cable: Sigalcair
Telex: 20430
Telefax: 3910566

Senior Executives: Mohamed El Sayed (Commercial Director)

PRINCIPAL ACTIVITIES: Distribution of metals, and metal
products
Parent Company: Responsible to the Ministry of Supply

Principal Shareholders: Public sector company

EGYPTIAN CO FOR PACKING & DISTRIBUTION OF FOODSTUFFS

16B 26 July Street, Cairo
Tel: 756838
Cable: SHEMTO, Cairo

Chairman: Eng A M Elasfouri

PRINCIPAL ACTIVITIES: Packaging and distribution of
foodstuffs
Parent Company: Responsible to the Ministry of Supply

Principal Shareholders: Public sector company
No of Employees: 1,200

EGYPTIAN CO FOR PAPER & STATIONERY

30 Sherief Street, Cairo
Tel: 3925643, 3936477, 3936538
Telex: 20786 Romney UN

Chairman: Reffat Dissouki
Directors: Alfy Bishara, Samir Abd El Monem

PRINCIPAL ACTIVITIES: Trading in paper, stationery, office
supplies and office equipment
Principal Agencies: Roneo Alcatel
Branch Offices: Alexandria
Parent Company: Responsible to the Ministry of Supply & Home
Trade
Principal Bankers: Bank Misr, National Bank of Egypt

Principal Shareholders: Public sector company

EGYPTIAN CO FOR PORTLAND CEMENT, TOURAH

Soc Egyptienne de Ciment Portland, Tourah

17 Sharia Kasr El Nil, Cairo
Tel: 47855

PRINCIPAL ACTIVITIES: Production of portland cement, rapid hardening cement, sulphate resisting cement and low-heat cement
Branch Offices: Factory in Tourah, near Cairo, tel 34116
Parent Company: Responsible to the Ministry of Housing and Reconstruction

Principal Shareholders: Public sector company

EGYPTIAN CO FOR RADIOS & TRANSISTORS

3 Fatma Roushdi St, Guiza, Cairo
Tel: 850336, 850379
Cable: Transegypt

PRINCIPAL ACTIVITIES: Manufacture of radios and transistors
Branch Offices: 33 Kasr El-Nil St, Cairo, Tel 49506, 44757
Parent Company: Responsible to the Ministry of Industry

Principal Shareholders: Public sector company

EGYPTIAN CO FOR TRADE OF CHEMICALS

10 Sharia Champollion, Cairo
Tel: 42185, 50761

PRINCIPAL ACTIVITIES: Distribution of chemicals and chemicals products
Parent Company: Responsible to the Ministry of Supply

Principal Shareholders: Public sector company

EGYPTIAN CO FOR WHOLESALE TRADE OF FOODSTUFFS

7A Sharia Youssef Naguib, Ataba, Cairo
Tel: 900288, 900689

PRINCIPAL ACTIVITIES: Wholesale and distribution of foodstuffs
Parent Company: Responsible to the Ministry of Supply

Principal Shareholders: Public sector company

EGYPTIAN CO FOR WOOL SPINNING & WEAVING (WOOLTEX)

PO Box 1938, Shoubra El Kheima, Cairo
Tel: 2201866, 2201080
Cable: Siftilia Cairo
Telex: 93420 Woltex UN
Telefax: 2201089

Chairman: Eng Abd El Khalek El Awad
Directors: Mahmoud Ebd El Hamid Hassan (Managing Director), Ahmed El Mahdy (Finance Director), Abd El Monem El Bashbishi (Commercial Director)

PRINCIPAL ACTIVITIES: Production of wool yarn and fabrics, knitted wool, blankets dyeing and finishing, ready made garments
Branch Offices: Factory at Shoubra El Kheima, Cairo, Tel 941866, 941197
Parent Company: Responsible to the Ministry of Industry

Principal Shareholders: Public sector company
Date of Establishment: 1938
No of Employees: 6,000

EGYPTIAN COMPUTER SYSTEMS

56 Gamet El Dowal Al Arabiya St, Mohandesseen, PO Box 1913, Cairo
Tel: 3608801/02/03/04
Telex: 92096 EKA UN, 93644 ALKAN UN
Telefax: 3608805

Chairman: Eng Mohamed Mahmoud Nosseir
Directors: Akil Beshir, Magdi Rasekh (Marketing Director), Shawki Moghazy
Senior Executives: Mohamed Magdi Rasekh (General Manager & Managing Director)

PRINCIPAL ACTIVITIES: Sales and services of personal computers
Principal Agencies: IBM authorised dealers
Branch Offices: 3A El Moaskar El Romany Street, Roshdy, Alexandria, Tel 852660
Principal Bankers: Commercial International Bank; Arab African International Bank; Egyptian Gulf Bank
Financial Information:

	1990
	E£'000
Authorised capital	5,000
Paid-up capital	2,000

Principal Shareholders: M Nosseir, Akil Beshir, Shawki Moghazy, Magdi Rasekh
Date of Establishment: 1983
No of Employees: 70

EGYPTIAN CONTRACTING CO (EL ABD)

8 Talaat Harb Str, Cairo
Tel: 747484, 757252
Cable: Nasr Contra
Telex: 92833 EL ABD UN

Chairman: Eng Samy Taha Khalifa
Directors: Eng Kamal Amin (Vice Chairman), Eng Mahmoud Sobh (Head sector of Abu Qir Zone & Member of Board), Eng Ahmed El-sayed (Head Sector of Cairo Zone & Member of Board), Hagrass Ahmed Hagrass (Head of Administration Sector), Sobhy Nageeb (Head of Financial Sector)
Senior Executives: Eng Nashaat Nageeb (Head Sector of Alexandria Zone), Eng Abd El-Moneim El-Sharkawi (Head Sector of El-Mansoura Zone), Eng Abd El-Gafaar (Head Sector of Delta Zone), Eng Samir Gergess (General Manager of Upper Egypt Zone), Eng Aly El-Din (Head of Projects Sector)

PRINCIPAL ACTIVITIES: Industrial, building, power plants, irrigation drainage, pumping station, marine works, hospital
Branch Offices: Cairo, Alexandria, Abu Qir, El Mansoura, Delta, Canal, Upper Egypt
Subsidiary Companies: Misr Austrian Plastic
Principal Bankers: National Bank of Egypt; Arab International Bank; Banque du Caire
Financial Information:

	E£'000
Authorised capital	8,000
Paid-up capital	5,110

Date of Establishment: 1951
No of Employees: 3,153

EGYPTIAN COPPER WORKS CO

Head Office and Works, Hagar El Nawatieh, Alexandria
Tel: 5864434/5
Cable: Copperworks Alexandria
Telex: 54293 Copr UN

Chairman: Eng Mohamed Tawfik Ahmed
Directors: Eng Ahmed Marghany (Technical Director), Mohamed Mohmod Abu Ouf (Commercial Director), Awad Mohamed Awad (Financial Director)

PRINCIPAL ACTIVITIES: Production of steel rolls, steel casting, steel wire ropes, brass and aluminium discs, aluminium foil, non-ferrous tubes and wire, agricultural spraying equipment and other copper products
Branch Offices: Cairo Office: 66 Sharia El Goumhouria, Tel 906231; and 90 Al Azhar St, Tel 901436; Alexandria Office: 79 Abu Al Dordar St, Tel 4926141
Parent Company: Responsible to the Ministry of Industry
Principal Bankers: Bank of Alexandria

Principal Shareholders: Public sector company

EGYPT

EGYPTIAN ELECTRO-CABLE CO

40 Talaat Harb St, Cairo

Tel: 876000

Cable: Lectrocab

PRINCIPAL ACTIVITIES: Manufacture and sale for cable wires, telephone and power cables, armoured cables

Branch Offices: Ismailia Canal Rd, Mostorod, Km4

Parent Company: Responsible to the Ministry of Industry

Principal Bankers: National Bank of Egypt; Bank of Alexandria

Principal Shareholders: Public sector company

EGYPTIAN ENGINEERING & INDUSTRIAL OFFICE

Eng Fayez Guindi & Co

Head office, 18 Hoda Shaarawi St, PO Box 1631, Cairo

Tel: 752776, 742588, 742609

Cable: Egyptdustry

Telex: 92963 Egeio UN

Chairman: Fayez Guindi (also Managing Director)

Directors: Mrs F Guindi (Deputy Managing Director), Eng Adel Guindi (Director of Technical Section)

PRINCIPAL ACTIVITIES: Agents and general traders, contractors and Government suppliers of hospital, scientific and educational equipment; hotel and equipment furniture, sanitary ware, electrical and electronic equipment, material handling

Principal Agencies: Hotel section: Ets Bonnet, Carpigiani Bruto, Frimont Spa, BRAS, GICO, Silber Herthel, Officine Giuseppe Cimbali, Blodgett, ISA; Medical Section: Vickers Medical, Asmund Laerdal, Shimadzu Corp, Cape Engineering, Becton Dickinson, Bio-Medical Research; Educational & Laboratory Section: Armfield Technical Education Co, Broadhead Garrett Co, Terco AB, ISI Impianti, Technolab SA de Lorenzo, August Sauter, Boeckel & Co; Miscellaneous Section: Rapistan Lande, Stanley Magic Doors, NKI

Branch Offices: Workshop and Technical Services: 16 Sh El Nabawi El Mohandess, Embaba, Cairo

Principal Bankers: Chase National Bank; Bank of Alexandria; National Bank of Egypt

Date of Establishment: 1956

No of Employees: 120

EGYPTIAN EQUIPMENT CO

10 Ahmed Nessim Street, Giza, Cairo

Tel: 753485, 776505

Telex: 23097 Prompt UN

President: Hassan Marei

PRINCIPAL ACTIVITIES: Manufacturers' representatives, supply of engineered and industrial equipment and heavy machinery

EGYPTIAN FINANCE COMPANY

4 Hassan Sabri Street, PO BOx 1824, Zamalek, Cairo

Tel: 3401116, 3404385, 3407510, 3410056

Telex: 92672 EFC UN

Chairman: Farid W Saad

Directors: Mounir F Abdelnour (Managing Director), Jamil W Saad (Managing Director), Gilbert N Gargour, Akram Hijazi, Elie Baroudi, Farid El Azem

PRINCIPAL ACTIVITIES: Merchant banking, investments

Principal Shareholders: American Express International Banking Corp; Olayan Investment Co; Middle East Associates, Azemco Holdings

Date of Establishment: 1976

EGYPTIAN FINANCIAL & INDUSTRIAL CO

Soc Financiere et Industrielle Egyptienne d'Egypte

43 Ahmed Maher Street, Kafr El Zayat, Egypt

Tel: 002-040-329355, 2100

Cable: Super Chaux - Kafr El Zayat

Telex: 24057 SFIE UN

Chairman: Eng Azab Soliman

Directors: Chem Abdul Monem Darwesh (Assiut Factory Director), Chem Zakria El Manfi (Kafr El Zayat Factory Director)

PRINCIPAL ACTIVITIES: Production of calcium superphosphate, sulphuric acid

Branch Offices: Works: Kafr El Zayat Factory; Assuit Factory: Mankbad, Assuit

Parent Company: Responsible to the Ministry of Industry

Principal Shareholders: Public sector company

EGYPTIAN FISHERIES CO FOR FISHING & FISH GEARS

53 Hourriah Avenue, Alexandria

Tel: 4911464, 4933285, 4921538

Cable: SAFINA ALEXANDRIA

Telex: 54148 SAFINA UN, 54649 MODAT UN

Telefax: 4911464

Chairman: Prof Dr Farouk El Gayar

Directors: Bashir Hassan Bashir (General Manager), Omar Hafez (Head of Financial Sector), Abou El Azzayem Shalaby (General Manager Marketing)

PRINCIPAL ACTIVITIES: Production and distribution of fish, fish products and fishing equipment and supplies

Branch Offices: Mahmoud Azmy St, Alexandria, Tel 806023, 805322; 61 El Nabi Danyal St, Alexandria, Tel 4917276; 19 El Gish and Abdel Moneim St, Port Said, Tel 28633, 26998; El Sweis, Tel 2884; Kafr El Sheikh, Tel 2881; Aswan, Tel 24232

Principal Bankers: Bank Misr, Alexandria; Bank Alexandria, Alexandria; Bank of Cairo, Alexandria

Financial Information:

| | 1989/90 |
	E£'000
Sales turnover	9,395
Profits	421
Authorised capital	20,000
Paid-up capital	13,921
Total assets	17,801

Principal Shareholders: Public sector company

Date of Establishment: 1985

No of Employees: 275

EGYPTIAN GENERAL CO FOR TOURISM & HOTELS

4 Latin America St, Garden City, Cairo

Tel: 32158, 27408

Cable: Egoth

Telex: 92363 Egoth UN

PRINCIPAL ACTIVITIES: Owners of public sectors, hotels and internationally operated hotels; development of tourism and hotels in Egypt

Principal Bankers: National Bank of Egypt

Principal Shareholders: State-owned

Date of Establishment: 1961

No of Employees: 373

EGYPTIAN GENERAL PETROLEUM AUTHORITY

20 Sharia Osman Abdel Hafiz, Nasr City, PO Box 2130, Cairo
Tel: 837388, 836105, 837514, 837126
Cable: Petmist
Telex: 92061 Petmisr; 92049

PRINCIPAL ACTIVITIES: Responsible for the control and coordination of the petroleum industry
Parent Company: Responsible to the Ministry of Petroleum
Subsidiary Companies: General Petroleum Co, Alexandria Petroleum Co, Arab Petroleum Pipelines Co, Compagnie Orientale de Petroles, El Nasr Petroleum Co, Misr Petroleum Co, Petroleum Cooperative Society, Petroleum Pipelines Co, Suez Oil Processing Co, Petroleum Gases Co

Principal Shareholders: Public sector company

EGYPTIAN GULF BANK

El Orman Plaza Bldg, 8/10 Ahmed Nessim St, PO Box 56, El Orman
Tel: 3606640, 3606457, 3606580
Cable: Engulfbank Giza
Telex: 20214, 20517 EGUB UN
Telefax: 3606512

Chairman: Kamal Hassan Aly
Senior Executives: Naabil El Sahar (General Manager), Mrs Sanaa Mahmoud Hanafy (Deputy General Manager), Elsayed Wafa Ragab (Deputy General Manager)

PRINCIPAL ACTIVITIES: Commercial and investment banking
Branch Offices: Cairo: PO Box 50 Maglis Al Shaab; Al Azhar Islamic Br: 24A Beibars St, Al Hamzawy, PO Bag Al Ghoreyah, Al Azhar; Heliopolis Br: 15 Al Khalifa Al Maamoun St, PO Box 277, Heliopolis, Cairo; Alexandria Br: 81 Al Sultan Hussein St, Bab Sharki, PO Bag Al Mesallah, Mansoura
Financial Information:

	1989/90 E£'million
Shareholders equity	30
Deposits	441
Loans & investments	290
Profits	4
Authorised capital	18
Paid-up capital	18
Total assets	613
Contra a/c	89

Principal Shareholders: Banque du Caire (10%); Misr Insurance Co (9.5%); Kuwait Real Estate Investment Consortium (9.9%); Tunis International Bank (9%); Red Sea Insurance Co, Jeddah (5%); Arab Investment Co, Kuwait (5%); Jawad & Hayder Abul Hassan Co, Kuwait (4.5%); Egyptian and Arab Businessmen (47.1%)
Date of Establishment: 1981, started operations in January 1983
No of Employees: 361

EGYPTIAN GYPSUM MARBLE & QUARRIES CO

4 Sh Mohamed Hamed Fahmy, Dokki, PO Box 329, Cairo
Tel: 700705, 700122
Telex: 92500 GYMCO UN

PRINCIPAL ACTIVITIES: Production of gypsum, marble and granite (block & slabs)
Parent Company: Responsible to the Ministry of Housing and Reconstruction

Principal Shareholders: Public sector company

EGYPTIAN HOTELS COMPANY

c/o Continental Hotel, 10 Opera Square, Cairo
Tel: 3919261, 3911030
Cable: Egotels
Telex: 92726 EGYPTL UN
Telefax: 3911322

Chairman: Mohamed Kamal Kandil
Senior Executives: Hamdy El Sheikh (DG Administration Dept), Hamed Zaki (DG Financial Dept), Abd El Aziz Abed (DG Marketing Dept), Salah Sharaf (DG Public Relations Dept)

PRINCIPAL ACTIVITIES: Hotel management (incorporating Shepheard, Upper Egypt and Tour Hotel companies), owner of 18 hotels throughout Egypt, most of them being run by national and international hotel managements
Parent Company: Responsible to the Ministry of Tourism

Principal Shareholders: EGOTH (Egyptian Co for Tourism and Hotels)

EGYPTIAN INSURANCE SUPERVISORY AUTHORITY

28 Talaat Harb Street, PO Box 2545, Cairo
Tel: 2-758423, 758807
Cable: Insurcontr
Telex: 92276 Chark UN
Telefax: 758645

Chairman: Abdel Hamid El Sarrag
Directors: Khairy Selim (Deputy Chairman), Dr Mohamed Salah El Din Sedky, Mohamed Fouad Osman, Gaser Fahmy Ewaiss, Ibrahim Lamiy Ibrahim, Dr Hosni Hafez Abdel Rahman, Farahat Mansour, Ghonaimy Ahmed Selim, Salah A Fattah Salama
Senior Executives: Nahed F Ismael (General Manager), Kamal A Abu Saif (General Manager), Adel M Rateb (General Manager), Ahmed M Anwar (General Manager)

PRINCIPAL ACTIVITIES: Supervision and control of the insurance business in Egypt

Principal Shareholders: State-owned
Date of Establishment: 270

EGYPTIAN INTERNATIONAL TRADING & ENGINEERING CO LTD (EITECO)

18 Maamal El Sukkar Street, 6th Floor, Garden City, Cairo
Tel: 3551175, 3545370
Telex: 20367 MKEN UN

Directors: Kamal Nabih (Managing Director)

PRINCIPAL ACTIVITIES: Manufacturers' representatives and engineering consultants

EGYPTIAN IRON & STEEL CO

54 Sh Abdel Khalek Sarwat, Cairo
Tel: 3916220, 3900622, 3900686, 3900684, 3913040
Cable: Hadisolb Cairo
Telex: 92007 UN
Telefax: 3913526

Chairman: Dr Ali Helmy
Senior Executives: Eng Hassan Abu El Dahab (Production Director), Eng Ziad El Sherbiny (Production Director), Eng Mohamed Ezezza (Production Director), Maher Saad (Production Director), Mohamed El Husseiny Younes (Utilities & Services Director)

PRINCIPAL ACTIVITIES: Manufacture iron and steel products
Branch Offices: Works: El-Tebin-Helwan, Tel 790311, 709242, 790513, 790615, 790442, 790498, Fax 791546; Alexandria Office: 5 Salah Salem Street, Tel 4822776, Fax 3-4822776
Parent Company: Responsible to the Ministry of Industry
Financial Information:

	1990 E£'000
Sales turnover	625,000
Profits	30,000
Authorised capital	540,000
Paid-up capital	540,000
Total assets	1,342,000

Principal Shareholders: Public sector company

EGYPTIAN LAND BANK

11 Mashhadi St, Kasr El Nil, Cairo
Tel: 910197, 919977

Chairman: Dr Aly Sabri Yason
Directors: Ahmad Zaki Aboul Nasr (Deputy Chairman)
Senior Executives: Aly Salem Gomaa (General Manager), Raouf
    Chalaby (General Manager), Ibrahim Abdel Halim Kheir El-
    Dine (General Manager)

PRINCIPAL ACTIVITIES: Banking

EGYPTIAN MARINE SUPPLY & CONTRACTING CO (CONSUP)

2 El-Horrya Avenue, PO Box 2025, Alexandria
Tel: 4820958, 4830550
Cable: Consup
Telex: 54183 Consup

Chairman: Nabil El Boluk
Directors: Abdel Aziz Abdel Halim, Hussein Gabr, Said Sahim
Senior Executives: Wadia Tadros (Financial Director)

PRINCIPAL ACTIVITIES: Ship chandlers and marine
    contracting; maintenance works; stockists and distributors
Principal Agencies: International Red Hand Marine Coating,
    Perolin Co Ltd, British Admiralty Charts
Branch Offices: Port Said: Al Goumhouria & Gabarti St, Tel
    227588, Telex 63030; Alexandria: PO Box 923, Mahmoudia
    Customs House, Gate No 27, Tel 805234, 802564, Telex
    54183; Suez: Huzaien Bldg, Port Tawfic, Tel 220132, Telex
    66132; Damietta: Al Araiess City, Ras El Bar, Tel 227955,
    Telex 63030; Safaga: Port Safaga; Noubaa: El Sultan Qabous
    Port
Parent Company: Public Sector Organisation for Maritime
    Transport
Principal Bankers: National Bank of Egypt; Bank Misr
Financial Information:

	1990 E£'000
Sales turnover	25,759
Profits	6,421
Authorised capital	3,320
Paid-up capital	3,20
Total assets	32,497

Principal Shareholders: State-owned company
Date of Establishment: 1962
No of Employees: 1,279

EGYPTIAN MARITIME NAVIGATION CO

2 Tarik El Nasr, Alexandria
Tel: 803608, 803536, 800503

PRINCIPAL ACTIVITIES: Owners and operators of Egypt's
    mercantile marine
Branch Offices: Cairo Office: 20 Sharia Talaat Harb, Tel 941166,
    976278, 979258; Port Said: Plaestine St, Tel 4041; Suez:
    Khedivial Bldg, Tel 3987
Parent Company: Responsible to the Ministry of Maritime
    Transport

Principal Shareholders: Public sector company

EGYPTIAN MARITIME TRANSPORT CO

7 Sh Abdel Khalek Sarwat, PO Box 2196, Cairo
Tel: 755633
Cable: Martrans
Telex: 92909 Martrans UN

Chairman: Mohamed Shawki Younes

PRINCIPAL ACTIVITIES: Operators of the shipping agency in
    Egypt
Principal Agencies: Schenker; Worms services Maritimes
Branch Offices: Alexandria; Port Said
Parent Company: Responsible to the Ministry of Maritime
    Transport

Principal Bankers: National Bank; Misr Bank; Suez Canal Bank

Principal Shareholders: Public sector company
Date of Establishment: 1962

EGYPTIAN MECHANICAL PRECISION INDUSTRIES CO (SABI)

41 Kasr El Nil St, PO Box 2457, Cairo
Tel: 907697, 915719, 755528
Cable: SABI Gypt Cairo
Telex: 92848 Sabget UN

Chairman: Eng Talaat Samak
Directors: Eng Omar Abdel Hamid (Factories Director), Saad
    Galal (Commercial Director), Reda Fayez (Financial Director),
    Mahmoud El Manshiliny (Administration Director), Mohd
    Rashad Mostafa (Sales & Marketing Directors)

PRINCIPAL ACTIVITIES: Manufacture of locks and padlocks,
    hinges, steel builders hardware, taps and valves, grinding
    wheels and other mechanical precision equipment
Branch Offices: Factory: Moahda Bridge Mostorod, Ismailia
    Route, Tel 864727, 690204, 873274, Telex 92848
Parent Company: Responsible to the Ministry of Industry

Principal Shareholders: Public sector company
Date of Establishment: 1958
No of Employees: 2,500

EGYPTIAN PHARMACEUTICAL TRADING CO

18 Adly Street, Cairo
Tel: 746522, 746613
Cable: Egydrug
Telex: 93677 Egbrg Un

PRINCIPAL ACTIVITIES: Import and distribution of
    pharmaceuticals
Branch Offices: Cairo Office: 23 Sharia Abdel Khalek Sarwat,
    Tel 56641, 56480
Parent Company: Responsible to the Ministry of Health
Principal Bankers: Bank Misr

Principal Shareholders: Public sector company
Date of Establishment: 1965
No of Employees: 4,000

EGYPTIAN PIPES & CEMENT PRODUCTS CO (SIEGWART)

15 Sharia Sherif, Cairo
Tel: 756402, 756711, 763504
Cable: Siegwart
Telex: 93244 SGWRT UN

Chairman: Eng Hassan Abdel Kader Zaki (also Managing
    Director)
Directors: Gamal Sadek (Commercial Director)

PRINCIPAL ACTIVITIES: Production of asbestos pipes,
    asbestos sheets and accessories, concrete pipes and fittings,
    concrete poles and accessories, products, clay and
    refractories, etc
Branch Offices: Factories: Maassarah, Shubra, Maadi Area
Parent Company: URAMISR (Responsible to the Ministry of
    Housing and Reconstruction)
Principal Bankers: National Bank, Alexandria Bank, Misr Bank

Principal Shareholders: Public sector company
Date of Establishment: 1927
No of Employees: 5,500

EGYPTIAN PLASTICS & ELECTRICAL INDUSTRIES CO

5 Ibn Okeil St, Victoria, Alexandria
Tel: 64664/3
Cable: Egyplastic
Telex: 54223

Chairman: Farouk Hussein Garrana

Directors: Hamed El Sharkawy, Saad Morsi, Gamal Abdel Salam, Mohamed Mostafa

PRINCIPAL ACTIVITIES: Manufacture of batteries, plastic products, artificial leather, floor covering, wallpaper and buttons

Branch Offices: Cairo Branch: 7 A Midan El Ataba St; Alexandria Branch: 5 Midan Ahmed Orabi

Parent Company: Responsible to the Ministry of Industry

Principal Shareholders: Public sector company
No of Employees: 2,600

EGYPTIAN RAILWAYS

Midan Ramses, Cairo
Tel: 47600

Chairman: Eng Abdel Moneim Heshmat Gadr

PRINCIPAL ACTIVITIES: Railways services
Parent Company: Responsible to the Ministry of Transport and Communications

Principal Shareholders: Public sector company

EGYPTIAN REAL PROPERTY CO

Soc Fonciere d'Egypte

2 Sharia Dr Abdel Hamid Saeed, Cairo
Tel: 57753, 58626

Chairman: Eng Abdel Wahab Selim

PRINCIPAL ACTIVITIES: Land reclamation
Parent Company: Responsible to the Ministry of Agriculture and Irrigation

Principal Shareholders: Public sector company

EGYPTIAN REFRACTORIES CO

23 Sh Talaat Harb, Cairo
Tel: 975512, 975301

Chairman: Eng Mohamed El Secoufi
Directors: Chem Fouad Abdel Rahim Hussein (Alexandria Factory), Dr Mohamed Abdel Rageh Abdel Salam (El Tebbin Factory)

PRINCIPAL ACTIVITIES: Production of ceramics, refractories, blue bricks, tiles, and all kinds of building materials. Also construction and consultancy work
Branch Offices: Cairo Factory: El Tebbin, Helwan, Tel 39062, 38488; Alexandria Factory: El Nouzha, Tel 970826
Parent Company: Responsible to the Ministry of Industry

Principal Shareholders: Public sector company

EGYPTIAN REINSURANCE CO (THE)

7 Dar El Shifa St, Garden City, PO Box 950, Cairo
Tel: 3543354, 3541603
Cable: Egyptre
Telex: 92245, 23047 EDTRE UN
Telefax: 20-2-355473

Chairman: Essam El Dine Omar
Directors: Ahmed M Salem (Director & General Manager Finance), M Hosny Mecky (Director & General Manager Administration), Ahmed Taher Bassiouni (Director & General Manager Marine & Aviation), Rashad Mohamed Kamaly (Director & General Manager Non Marine), Dr Hassan Hosni (Director), Mrs Elham A Shaheen (General Manager Marketing), M Helmy Abdel Salam (General Manager Information Systems)

PRINCIPAL ACTIVITIES: All classes of reinsurance
Branch Offices: London Contact Office: 90 Fenchurch St, London EC3N 3DA, UK, Fax 44-1-4882038
Principal Bankers: Midland Bank; Dresdner Bank AG; National Bank of Kuwait SAK

Financial Information:

	1990
	E£'000
Gross premium income	212,960
Net premium income	148,059
Authorised capital	100,000
Paid-up capital	43,000
Total assets	443,944

EGYPTIAN SALT & SODA CO

Sharia Canal El-Mahmoudieh, Moharrem Bey, Alexandria
Tel: 4925875/8
Telex: 54015 Salt UN

Chairman: Eng Aly Abdel Rahman Amin
Directors: Zaghloul Reda El Bahay (General Commercial Manager)

PRINCIPAL ACTIVITIES: Production of cottonseed oil, maize oil, margarine, animal fodder, soap, sodium silicate, floor polish, pharmaceuticals and industrial glycerine, fatty acids, candles
Parent Company: Responsible to the Ministry of Industry and Mining

Principal Shareholders: Public sector company

EGYPTIAN SAUDI FINANCE BANK

Head office, 8 Ibrahim Naguib Street, El Sabbah Tower, Garden City, Cairo
Tel: 3546208, 3546489
Cable: Tamwilsodi
Telex: 20623, 22926 Esfbk UN
Telefax: 3542911

Chairman: Sheikh Saleh A Kamel
Directors: Hazem B Mansour (Managing Director)
Senior Executives: Moustafa Khalil Ibrahim (General Manager)

PRINCIPAL ACTIVITIES: Commercial banking according to the Islamic Sharia
Branch Offices: Cairo, Heliopolis, Alfy
Principal Bankers: Bank of New York, New York; Al Baraka Bank, London; Banque Nationale de Paris, France; Arab Banking Corporation, Frankfurt; Swiss Bank Corp, Basle; Unibank, Copenhagen; Credito Italiano, Milano; Ubaf Bank, Tokyo; Amsterdam Rotterdam Bank, Amsterdam; Saudi Cairo Bank, Jeddah
Financial Information:

	1989/90
	E£'000
Authorised capital	60,200
Paid-up capital	60,200
Total assets	183,551

Principal Shareholders: National Bank of Egypt; Bank Misr; Banque du Caire; Bank of Alexandria; Misr Insurance Co; Al Baraka Investment & Developmemt Co, Dallah International Holding Co (Egyptian Joint Stock Co) and others
Date of Establishment: 1980
No of Employees: 215

EGYPTIAN SHIPBUILDING & REPAIRS CO

Customs Area, Alexandria
Tel: 803588, 803859
Cable: SHIPREPCO
Telex: 54717 REPCO UN
Telefax: 802808

Chairman: Eng Mohamed H Abdelwahab
Directors: Eng Ahmed Shawky (Technical Director), Eng Yehia Rageb (Production Director)

PRINCIPAL ACTIVITIES: Ship repairs, builders of tugs, barges, launches, floating cranes, ferries and fishing boats
Branch Offices: Work: Bab El Karasta
Parent Company: Responsible to the Ministry of Maritime Transport

Financial Information:

	1990
	E£'000
Sales turnover	16,857
Profits	141
Authorised capital	7,159
Paid-up capital	7,159
Total assets	48,705

Principal Shareholders: Public sector company
Date of Establishment: 1880
No of Employees: 3000

EGYPTIAN SHOE CO (BATA)

61 Sharia El Akhshid, Alexandria
Tel: 4935790, 4924640
Cable: Batashoe Alexandria
Telex: 54473 Bata UN

Chairman: Mohamed Adel El Habashy
Directors: Ali Ahmed Badawi (Commercial Director), Fawzi Chafik (Financial Director), Naguib Iskandar (Technical Director), Said Abdou (Administrative Director)

PRINCIPAL ACTIVITIES: Production, marketing and distribution of leather and plastic footwear and sport shoes
Branch Offices: 5, 26th July St, Cairo, Tel 912804
Parent Company: Responsible to the Ministry of Supply & Home Trade
Principal Bankers: National Bank; Misr Bank

Principal Shareholders: Public sector
Date of Establishment: 1927
No of Employees: 5,800

EGYPTIAN STARCH YEAST & DETERGENT CO

30 Salah Salem St, Alexandria
Tel: 805851, 805437, 808462

Chairman: Eng Mohamed Ahmed Abdel Gelil

PRINCIPAL ACTIVITIES: Production of rice starch, glucose, fresh and dried yeast, fatty alcohols, wetting agents for use in spinning and weaving, leather and paper industries
Branch Offices: Cairo Office: 28 Talaat Harb St
Parent Company: Responsible to the Ministry of Industry
Principal Bankers: Bank of Alexandria; Bank Misr

Principal Shareholders: Public sector company

EGYPTIAN SUPPLIES COMPANY

7 Abdel Hamid Said St, PO Box 1723, Cairo
Tel: 40487
Cable: Egysupco
Telex: 92336 Alfcai (063/Ato)

Chairman: Samir Antoun Guirguis (also General Manager)
Directors: Fikri Farid Milad (Deputy General Manager)

PRINCIPAL ACTIVITIES: Import and distribution of office equipment
Principal Agencies: Ricoh Nederland BV, Hasler Cash Registers Ltd, Switzerland; Tokyo Electric, Japan
Principal Bankers: Arab Investment Bank, Cairo

Date of Establishment: 1974

EGYPTIAN TRADING & INDUSTRIAL CO (RAGAB)

18 El Horrya Avenue, PO Box 736, Alexandria
Tel: 4834210, 4827051
Cable: MARAGAB Alexandria
Telex: 54024 Ragab UN, 54728 Ragab UN
Telefax: (03) 4826831

President: Mohamed Abdel Fattah Ragab (Executive Partner)
Directors: Eng Abdel Fattah M Ragab (Vice President), Eng Alaa El Din M Ragab (Managing Director)

Senior Executives: Yehia Sheta (General Manager Cairo Branch), Abdel Razek Morsi (General Manager Alexandria Marketing), Hassan Khalil (General Manager Finance & Administration), Adly Abdoun (General Manager Cairo Marketing), Mahmoud Elgkondokly (General Manager Alexandria Sales), Fathy Ibrahim (Manager Spare Parts), Eng Moustafa Abul Enien (Manager Construction Machinery), Abdel Moneim Hossein (Manager Export), Mohamed Bakry (Manager Foodstuff)

PRINCIPAL ACTIVITIES: Import and export of agricultural equipment, construction and industrial machinery and equipment, vehicles, steel products, chemicals, electrical equipment, raw materials, cereals, foodstuffs and cotton, textile machinery, commodities, general contracting and manufacturers' representation
Principal Agencies: IMT Tractors, Yugolavia; Hino Motor, Japan; Yanmar, Japan; Vicon, Holland; Daihatsu Motor, Japan; Komatsu Forklift, Japan; Tadano, Japan; Kawasaki Heavy Industries, Japan; Mitsui Engineering & Shipbuilding, Japan; Hitachi Construction Machinery, Japan; Rieter, Switzerland; Officine Savio, Italy; Durkopp, W Germany; British Northrop, UK; Bond Textile Machinery, USA; Nuovo Pignone, Italy; Teikoku Kanaosa Kogyosho, Japan; Alvi, Italy; J Schwarzer, W Germany; Magitex, Italy; Bethlehem Steel, USA; Ferranti, UK; Capitol Pipes, USA; Braibanti, Italy; Sequipag, France; Zegward, Holland; Brown & Sites, USA; Interpack, USA; Sherne, USA; Aqua Assistance, Belgium; Schering, W Germany; Ciba Geigy, Switzerland; Gaf, Holland; Guyomarch 11, France; Rexolin Chemicals, Sweden; Simelhag, Denmark; Leroy Somer, France; Labour Pumps, UK Westico, UK
Branch Offices: Cairo: 1 Talaat Harb Square, Suite 41/42, 6th Floor; Tel 3930496, 3933565, 3921175, Telex 93106 Ragco UN, Fax (02) 3937191
Subsidiary Companies: The International Contracting & Engineering Co, Alexandria and Cairo
Principal Bankers: National Bank of Egypt, National Bank of Abu Dhabi, Citibank NA, Bank of America, Egyptian American Bank, Misr America International Bank, Misr International Bank, Islamic International Bank

Date of Establishment: 1949

EGYPTIAN VINEYARD & DISTILLING CO

122 El Shahid Galal Dessouki, Alexandria
Tel: 4221728, 4220056, 4221980
Cable: Rumdy Alexandria
Telex: 54047
Telefax: 4221980

Chairman: Eng Raouf Abdalla Atta
Directors: Sobhy Khalifa (Director Agriculture), Raouf Abukela (Industrial Production Director), Abdel Monem Elsayed (Finance Director), Nabil Abdelhamid (Marketing Director)

PRINCIPAL ACTIVITIES: Production of brandy, rum, arak, fenet, vermouth, ouzo, syrups and liqueurs
Branch Offices: Cairo Office: 4 Sharia Shawarbi, Tel 44137
Parent Company: Responsible to the Ministry of Agriculture
Principal Bankers: Bank of Alexandria, Banque du Caire, National Bank of Egypt

Principal Shareholders: Public sector company
Date of Establishment: 1968
No of Employees: 1,786

EGYPTIAN WOODWORKING CO (WOODCO)

5 Talaat Harb St, Kasr El Nil, Cairo
Tel: 750175
Cable: Egywood
Telex: 93753 Wdco

Directors: Abdel Khalek Al Badry (Production Director), Ahmed Fouad (Technical Director), Mohamed Al-Minsheliny (Commercial Director), Mohamed Hashem (Financial Director)

PRINCIPAL ACTIVITIES: Production of plywood, blockboard, veneer, steam bent chairs and furniture
Branch Offices: Imbaba; Shoubra; Helwan; Alexandria
Parent Company: Responsible to the Ministry of Industry
Principal Bankers: Bank of Alexandria

Principal Shareholders: Public sector
Date of Establishment: 1961
No of Employees: 1,800

EL BASSATIN FACTORY FOR METAL PRODUCTS

2 Maroof St, Cairo
Tel: 759055, 749169
Cable: Saftide Cairo
Telex: 93787 Saft UN

Chairman: M A El-Saftawi

PRINCIPAL ACTIVITIES: Production of barbed wires, electric insulators and screws, metal furniture, wire products, plastic coating, printing by silk-screen and advertising
Branch Offices: Factory: Industrial Zone, Bassatin, Cairo, Tel 930721
Principal Bankers: National Bank of Egypt; National Bank of Abu Dhabi

Principal Shareholders: Private company
Date of Establishment: 1960
No of Employees: 250

EL KAHIRA OIL & SOAP CO

Soc du Caire des Huileries et Savonneries

6 Midan El Falaki, Cairo
Tel: 22825/7, 25046
Cable: El Mizan Cairo

Directors: Eng Fathi Gouda Santawi (Factories Director), Fayez Darwish (Commercial Director)

PRINCIPAL ACTIVITIES: Production of soap, industrial glycerine, margarine, animal fodder, oil and stearine
Branch Offices: Alexandria Office: 12 Sharia Talaat harb
Parent Company: Responsible to the Ministry of Industry

EL MASRI SHOES FACTORY

15 El Kawa St, El Guesh St, Cairo
Tel: 917002

Chairman: Kamal Hafez Ramadan

PRINCIPAL ACTIVITIES: Production of ladies' and men's shoes

Principal Shareholders: Private company

EL MENIA SHIPPING AGENCY

31 El Goumhouria St, PO Box 328 & 130, Port Said
Tel: 8672/4
Cable: Minship
Telex: 4263 Menia Un

Senior Executives: Abdel Rahman Mahmoud (General Manager)

PRINCIPAL ACTIVITIES: Shipping agency, clearing and forwarding
Branch Offices: Suez Branch: 66 Adly Yakan St, PO Box 4, Suez, Tel 2639, 3085, Cable Minship, Telex 4187 Suezag
Principal Bankers: National Bank of Egypt

Principal Shareholders: Part of Canal Shipping Agencies Company

EL MOTTAHIDA

United Co for Housing and Development

13 Salah Salem St, Alexandria
Tel: 29585

Directors: Eng Mohamed Ali Mahmoud (Technical Director)

PRINCIPAL ACTIVITIES: Contracting, building construction

Parent Company: Responsible to the Ministry of Housing and Reconstruction

Principal Shareholders: Public sector company

EL NASR AUTOMOTIVE MANUFACTURING CO (NASCO)

Wadi Hof, Helwan, Cairo
Tel: 3741901
Cable: Automotive Helwan
Telex: 92063 Autoc UN; 92064 Autohel UN
Telefax: 202-3742612

Chairman: Eng Ezzeddin Haikal
Directors: Yehia Zaki Eddin (Head of Financial Sector), Eng Said El Naggar (Head of Planning & Technical Sectors), Eng Salah El Hadary (Head of Sales & Service Sectors)

PRINCIPAL ACTIVITIES: Manufacture of truck, buses, tractors, cars, mini-buses and engines and spare parts
Principal Agencies: Iveco Magirus, Deutz, Fiat, Zastava (Yugoslavia), Pol-Mot (Poland), IMR (Yugoslavia)
Branch Offices: Sales & Service: 1081 Corniche El Nil, Garden City, Cairo; Service Stations: 4 Meniawy Street, Ghamra, Cairo and 12 Sedi El Khayashy Street, Kom El Kekka, Alexandria
Parent Company: Responsible to the Ministry of Industry
Subsidiary Companies: Wood Manufacturing J.V. Co; Egyptian Co for Car Service & Maintenance
Principal Bankers: Bank of Alexandria; National Bank of Egypt
Financial Information:

	1989/90 E£'000
Sales turnover	471,037
Profits	6,525
Authorised capital	60,000
Paid-up capital	45,570
Total assets	952,547

Principal Shareholders: Public sector company
Date of Establishment: 1959
No of Employees: 11,234

EL NASR BOILERS & PRESSURE VESSELS MANUFACTURING CO

Manial Shiha, Guiza
Tel: 35031, 36135, 36138, 816309

Directors: Eng Ahmed Fouad El Sayed (Director of Construction), Eng Ahmad Fouad Abdel Meguid (Director of Factories), Eng Ibrahim Ahmed Fahmy (Technical Director), Ahmed Rateb (Commercial Director)

PRINCIPAL ACTIVITIES: Manufacture of boilers, pressure vessels, chemical plant
Parent Company: Responsible to the Ministry of Industry

Principal Shareholders: Public sector company

EL NASR BOTTLING CO (SICO)

1 Sharia El Tahrir, Dokki, Cairo
Tel: 983912, 980619
Cable: Sico Cairo

Directors: Alaa Al-Hadidi (Factories Director)

PRINCIPAL ACTIVITIES: Production of carbonated soft drinks
Branch Offices: Alexandria Office: 118 Sharia El Shahid Galal El Dessouki, Tel 4925943
Parent Company: Responsible to the Ministry of Industry

Principal Shareholders: Public sector company

EL NASR CASTING & ALUMINIUM CO

5 Sh Emad El Din, Cairo
Tel: 915785, 914151
Cable: Castings

Directors: Eng El Dai Mohamed El Hamamy (Technical Director), Eng Abdel Razek Hussein Radwan (Cairo Factory Director), Eng Mohamed Rafie El Serrafy (Alexandria Factory Director)

PRINCIPAL ACTIVITIES: Production of cast iron, high pressure water pipes, pumps, valves
Branch Offices: Works: Tanash, Embabeh, Cairo; Moharrem Bey, Alexandria
Parent Company: Responsible to the Ministry of Industry

Principal Shareholders: Public sector company

EL NASR CIVIL ENGINEERING CO
26 Sharia Sherif, Immobilia Bldg, PO Box 987, Cairo
Tel: 47426, 54396, 40567, 44050

PRINCIPAL ACTIVITIES: Contracting, civil engineering and construction
Parent Company: Responsible to the Ministry of Housing and Reconstruction

Principal Shareholders: Public sector company

EL NASR CLOTHING & TEXTILE CO
407 Canal El Mahmoudieh St, Hadra, Alexandria
Tel: 4216585, 4216586
Cable: Mogakabo
Telex: 54204 Kabo Un
Telefax: 4210923

Chairman: Hassan Abdel Kader (Also Managing Director)
Senior Executives: Soliman El Sheikh (Financial Manager), Hussein Mohamed (Commercial Manager), Fayek Abdel Kader (Export Manager), El Sayed Abdel Aziz (Marketing Manager), Mohamed Metwally (Purchasing Manager), Samir Shalouh (Production Manager), Sami Mosaad (Personnel Manager), Nagui Gobrial (Technical Manager)

PRINCIPAL ACTIVITIES: Production of knitted fabrics, underwear, ribbons, ready made garments, scarfs; dyeing and printing
Principal Bankers: Bank of Alexandria; Banque Misr; Banque du Caire; National Bank of Egypt

Principal Shareholders: Public Sector (76.3%), Private Sector (23.7%)
Date of Establishment: 1940
No of Employees: 5,920

EL NASR CO FOR BUILDING & CONSTRUCTION (EGYCO)
106 Sharia Mohamed Farid, Cairo
Tel: 751861, 759695
Cable: Egyconasr
Telex: 92903 Egyco Un

Chairman: Eng Abdel Rahman El Kashef
Directors: Eng Shawki Mossad (Vice Chairman), Eng Hussen Abdel Ali (Head of Project), Eng Louis George (Head of Equipment)

PRINCIPAL ACTIVITIES: Contracting, civil engineering and construction (marine works, prefabricated and traditional housing construction, earthmoving and levelling works, industrial construction)
Branch Offices: 33 Saffia Zaghloul St, Alexandria, Tel 4928151
Parent Company: Responsible to the Ministry of Housing and Reconstruction
Principal Bankers: Banque du Caire, Misr International Bank

Principal Shareholders: Public sector company
Date of Establishment: 1936
No of Employees: 2,286

EL NASR CO FOR COKE & CHEMICALS
16 Sharia Sherif, Cairo
Tel: 744189, 741731
Cable: Chemicoke Helwan
Telex: 93926 COKE UN

Chairman: Eng Adel El Mouzy

PRINCIPAL ACTIVITIES: Production of metallurgical coke, pure ammonium nitrate, fertilisers, coal tar, distillates
Branch Offices: Factory: El Tabin, Helwan, Cairo, Tel 790695, 790259
Principal Bankers: Bank of Alexandria

Principal Shareholders: Public sector company

EL NASR CO FOR DEHYDRATING AGRICULTURAL PRODUCTS (SOHAG)
4 Sharia Maarouf, PO Box 1991, Cairo
Tel: 758755, 756270, 746377
Telex: 92965

Directors: Emam Abbas Ahmed (Purchasing Director), Eng Shalabi Yussouf Shalabi (Commercial Director)

PRINCIPAL ACTIVITIES: Production and export of dehydrated onions and other vegetables
Parent Company: Responsible to the Ministry of Trade

Principal Shareholders: Public sector company

EL NASR CO FOR ELECTRICAL & ELECTRONIC APPARATUS (PHILIPS)
26 Sharia Adly, Cairo
Tel: 49748, 59928, 74983
Cable: Philor Cairo

Directors: Eng Zoheir Abdel Hamid (Technical Director and Philips Representative), Eng Nasr El Din Shehta (Director of Factories), Eng Mahmoud Taha Wali (Financial & Commercial Director)

PRINCIPAL ACTIVITIES: Production of electrical and electronic equipment
Principal Agencies: Philips, Pye
Parent Company: Responsible to the Ministry of Industry

Principal Shareholders: Public sector company

EL NASR CO FOR HOUSING, DEVELOPMENT & MAINTENANCE OF BUILDINGS
26A Sharia Sherif, Cairo
Tel: 970113/5, 974923, 974826

Directors: Eng Eli Saweris (Technical Director), Eng Elsayed Abo El-Nour (Technical Director)

PRINCIPAL ACTIVITIES: Contracting, civil engineering, construction and maintenance
Parent Company: Responsible to the Ministry of Housing and Reconstruction

Principal Shareholders: Public sector company

EL NASR CO FOR PENCIL MANUFACTURE & GRAPHITE PRODUCTS
Ramses St Extension, Nasr City, Cairo
Tel: 832434, 835176
Cable: NASRAFIT CAIRO
Telex: 20082, 20382, 20682, 20982, 21282 PBGIA UN Att. Pencil Co

PRINCIPAL ACTIVITIES: Manufacture of pencils, graphite products, carbon electrodes, writing inks, carbon paper, typewriter ribbons
Parent Company: Responsible to the Ministry of Industry

Principal Shareholders: Public sector company

EL NASR CO FOR PRODUCTION OF REFRACTORIES & CERAMICS (SORNAGNA)
22 Sharia Kasr El Nil, Cairo
Tel: 751566, 751695
Cable: Hayaryat
Telex: 92006 SRNAG UN

Chairman: Dr Nawal Shalaby
Directors: Eng Mohamed Kamal Aldin Naguib (Head of
  Technical Engineering Sector), Mohamed Azmy Al-Mandouh
  (Head of Commercial Sector), Mohamed Abd Allah Fahmy
  (Head of Industrial Sector), Abd Al Ghaffar Al-Abd (Head of
  Financial Sector), Monir Hanna (Head of Administrative
  Sector)

PRINCIPAL ACTIVITIES: Production of ceramics tiles, sanitary
  ware, blue bricks, refractories, magnesite and chrome
  magnesite, sewer clay pipes, art ware
Branch Offices: Factory: El Wadi, Guiza; Factory: Mostorod,
  Kaluobia Tel 448966, 438885; Factory: Canal El Mahmoudia,
  Alexandria, Tel 38531
Parent Company: Responsible to the Ministry of Industry
Principal Bankers: Bank of Alexandria

Principal Shareholders: Public sector company
Date of Establishment: 1956
No of Employees: 1,700

EL NASR CO FOR PUBLIC UTILITIES & INSTALLATIONS

49 Abd ElKhalek Tharwat St, PO Box 1042, Cairo
Tel: 912329, 918947
Telex: 21204 Erect

Chairman: Eng Mohd Khaled Mostafa
Directors: Eng Mohd Elmenebawi (Projects Dept), Eng Dolar
  Shoukry (Execution Dept), Farouk Mahdy (Financial Dept),

PRINCIPAL ACTIVITIES: Utility services and installations, water,
  waterwaste, irrigation
Branch Offices: Alexandria: 14 Fawzi Fahmi St, Tel 37283
Parent Company: Responsible to the Ministry of Housing and
  Utilities
Principal Bankers: Banque du Caire, Egyptian Gulf Bank

Principal Shareholders: Public sector company
Date of Establishment: 1961
No of Employees: 1,000

EL NASR CO FOR RUBBER PRODUCTS (NAROBIN)

22 Sharia Soliman El Halaby, PO Box 1586, Cairo
Tel: 911722, 910800, 90356, 935186
Cable: Narubin
Telex: 93834 Narub UN

Chairman: Mahmoud Khalid Ateiba
Directors: Eng Ahmed Fouad El Sayed (Managing Director)
Senior Executives: Ahmed Abd El Hafiz Diab (Finance Director),
  Mohamed Ali Gabr (Commercial Director), Ahmed Rashid El
  Difrawi (Production Director)

PRINCIPAL ACTIVITIES: Manufacture of rubber transmission
  and conveyor belts, rubber tiles, sheets, mouldings, hoses,
  rubber domestic goods, sponges, foam, rubber boots, and
  rubber accessories for textile industry
Parent Company: Responsible to the Ministry of Industry
Subsidiary Companies: SEFCA
Principal Bankers: Bank of Alexandria; Suez Canal Bank; Misr
  Bank

Principal Shareholders: Public sector company
No of Employees: 2,100

EL NASR CO FOR TRANSFORMERS & ELECTRICAL PRODUCTS (EL-MAKO)

17 El Sheikh El Shabrawi St, Rod El Farag, PO Box 1916, Cairo
Tel: 943476, 943644
Cable: ELMACO
Telex: 93415 ELMCO UH

Chairman: Eng M Nasr
Directors: Eng Ismail Attia, Eng I F Issa
Senior Executives: J Hassan (Sales Manager)

PRINCIPAL ACTIVITIES: Manufacture of electrical and
  electronic equipment and transformers
Parent Company: Responsible to the Ministry of Electricity
Principal Bankers: Alexandria Bank

EL NASR DYEING & FINISHING CO MEHALLA EL KOBRA

Tarik El-Mahsoura, Mehalla El Kobra
Tel: 3864, 3758. 4980

Chairman: Dr Omar Hussein El Hamamsy

PRINCIPAL ACTIVITIES: Bleaching, dyeing, printing and
  finishing
Branch Offices: Cairo Office: 6 Sharia Moudiret El Tahrir,
  Garden City, Tel 32401
Parent Company: Responsible to the Ministry of Industry

Principal Shareholders: Public sector company

EL NASR ENGINEERING & REFRIGERATION CO (KOLDAIR)

Sakiet Mekki, Guiza, PO Box 1148, Cairo
Tel: 896780, 898397/8
Cable: Koldair Cairo

Chairman: Eng Mohamed Aly El Habashi

PRINCIPAL ACTIVITIES: Manufacture and installation of
  refrigeration equipment
Parent Company: Responsible to the Ministry of Industry

Principal Shareholders: Public sector company

EL NASR EXPORT & IMPORT CO

28A Talaat Harb St, Cairo
Tel: 748500
Cable: Shintam
Telex: 92232

Chiefs of Sectors: Mohamed Abdul Karim (Administrative
  Sector), Imam Abdul Rahman (Export Sector), Hassan Sadek
  (Import Sector), Mohey Fathi (Overseas Branches Sector),
  Abdulla Etman (Financial Sector)
Executives: Ibrahim Abbas (Import General Manager for Animal
  & Industrial Goods), Nabil Mostafa (Import General Manager
  for Foodstuffs), Abdel Hay Ahmed (Import General Manager
  for Metal & Engineering goods), Mohamed Abdel Latif (Import
  General Manager for Minerals & Refrectories), Ahmed Zaki
  (General Manager for Import Services), Salah Hemdan (Import
  General Manager Chemicals & Textiles), Ahmed El Biadi
  (Import General Manager for Special Operations), Abdel
  Menem Etabi (Export General Manager for Industrial Goods),
  Esam Amer (General Manager for Export Services), Amin El
  Sayed (General Manager for Maritime Transport), Hussien
  Ebrahim (General Manager for Agricultural Goods &
  Foodstuffs), Ahmed Kamoon (Export General Manager for
  Textiles)

PRINCIPAL ACTIVITIES: Import of foodstuffs, tobacco, dairy
  products, canned food, livestock, frozen fish and meat,
  chemicals, fertilizers and insecticides, metals, textiles, paper
  and timber, synthetic leather, toys, blankets, raw hides and
  rubber; export of industrial and metal product, textiles,
  agricultural products, foodstuffs, carpets, pharmaceutical
  products, cosmetics, books etc
Branch Offices: Cameroon; Congo Brazzaville; Zaire; Ivory
  Coast; Ghana; Guinea; Kenya; Liberia; Mali; Mauritania; Niger;
  Nigeria; Central African Republic; Senegal; Sierra Leone;
  Chad; Togo; Uganda; Benin; Kuwait; Jordan; Syria; Lebanon;
  France; Upper Volta
Principal Bankers: National Bank of Egypt; Misr Bank

Principal Shareholders: Public sector
Date of Establishment: 1958
No of Employees: 1,500

EGYPT

EL NASR FINE SPINNING & WEAVING CO (DAMIETTA)

50 Sharia El Gomhouriya, Cairo
Tel: 916029, 911765, 41428

PRINCIPAL ACTIVITIES: Production of cotton yarn and fabrics, embroidered
Branch Offices: Factory: 3 Saad Zaghloul St, Damietta, Tel 3066/7
Parent Company: Responsible to the Ministry of Industry

Principal Shareholders: Public sector company

EL NASR FOR PRESERVED FOOD (KAHA)

43 Abdel Khalek Sarwat St, PO Box 319, Cairo
Tel: 921480, 921487, 939662
Cable: Fabkaha Cairo

Chairman: Abdel Hameed Said
Senior Executives: Eng Hassan Abbas Khalil, Aly Abdel Rashid Nasr, Eng Taher Mehasseb Ebrahim

PRINCIPAL ACTIVITIES: Production of canned and frozen foods
Branch Offices: Kaha Factory, Qualyobia; Abu Kebir Factory, Sharkia; Korin Factory, Sharkia; Tabia Factory, Alexandria; Tahir Factory, Mouderiet El Tahrir; Badrashin Factory, Giza; Rashid Factory, Behira
Parent Company: Responsible to the Ministry of Industry
Principal Bankers: Bank of Alexandria

Principal Shareholders: Public sector
Date of Establishment: 1940
No of Employees: 4,000

EL NASR FORGING COMPANY

18 Emad El-Din St, Cairo
Tel: 757984, 790798, 790813, 790112
Cable: Matrokat
Telex: 92007 Solb Un Att Matrokat
Telefax: (202) 790798

Chairman: Eng Talaat Hoballah El Deeb
Directors: Dr Eng Nabil Akl (Commercial Director), Eng Adel Balaba (Factories Director), Eng Ahmed Ezzeldin (Technical Director), Abel Badr Eldin (Financial Director)

PRINCIPAL ACTIVITIES: Steel forging and stampings for vehicles and tractors and for engines, railways, wagons; production of hand tools and machine tools, etc. Production capacity 14,000 tons p.a.
Branch Offices: Works: El Tebbin, Helwan, PO Box 15, Tel 790798, 790813, 790112 Cable Matrokatt
Parent Company: Responsible to the Ministry of Industry
Principal Bankers: Bank of Alexandria

Principal Shareholders: Public sector company
Date of Establishment: 1965
No of Employees: 2,000

EL NASR GLASS & CRYSTAL CO

11 Sh El Sherifein, Cairo
Tel: 977495, 945322

Directors: Eng Mounir Moh Ramadan (Alexandria Factory Director), Eng Saad Moh El Sakhawi (Shoubra Factory Director), Omar Moh Salem Tamoum (Commercial Director)

PRINCIPAL ACTIVITIES: Production of glass, household glassware, safety glass, glass wool, lamp glass, pharmaceutical glassware, polyester
Branch Offices: Cairo Factory; Shoubra El Kheima, Dokki, Tel 57907, 803049; Alexandria Factory: El Hadara, Tel 71609
Parent Company: Responsible to the Ministry of Industry

Principal Shareholders: Public sector company

EL NASR HARDBOARD CO (FARASKOUR)

Sharia Saray El Azbakia, Cairo
Tel: 910559, 905136

Chairman: Chem Ibrahim Taha Hendam

PRINCIPAL ACTIVITIES: Manufacture of hardboard and wood products
Branch Offices: Head Office: Kafr Abu Admah, Faraskour
Parent Company: Responsible to the Ministry of Housing and Reconstruction

Principal Shareholders: Public sector company

EL NASR PETROLEUM COMPANY

6 Sharia Orabi, PO Box 1634, Cairo
Tel: 46260, 49700
Cable: Nasr Oil
Telex: 4080

Senior Executives: Eng Said Saadallah Kandil (General Manager for Technical Affairs)

PRINCIPAL ACTIVITIES: Oil refining
Branch Offices: 32 Ahmed Orabi Street, PO Box 99, Alexandria, Tel 34200, 30124, 30129
Parent Company: Egyptian General Petroleum Authority (Responsible to the Ministry of Petroleum)

Principal Shareholders: Public sector company

EL NASR PHOSPHATE CO

23 Talaat Harb St, Cairo
Tel: 50765/66, 50793, 47791
Cable: Phonaer Cairo

Chairman: Ibrahim Kamel Ahmed
Directors: Hassan Ismail Hamdy (Commercial Director)

PRINCIPAL ACTIVITIES: Production of phosphates, talc, feldspar, fluorspar, asbestos, calcium carbonate, barite
Parent Company: Responsible to the Ministry of Industry

Principal Shareholders: Public sector company

EL NASR SALINE CO

2 Av Gamal Abd El Nasser, PO Box 490, Alexandria
Tel: 906955, 806584
Cable: Soegysel
Telex: 54290 Sali UN Alex

Chairman: Dr Mohamed Kamaleldin El Kuramani
Directors: Salah Daoud (Director of Mex Salines), Eng Mohamed Shatia (Technical Director), Kadry Arafat (Financial Director), Anwar Abou Sir (Commercial Director)

PRINCIPAL ACTIVITIES: Salt mining, production and marketing of salt
Branch Offices: Cairo Office: 1 Sharia 26th July, Cairo, Tel 917144, 917639; Port Said Salines, Tel 3320, 5750; Mex Salines, Tel 28602
Parent Company: Responsible to the Ministry of Industry
Principal Bankers: Bank of Alexandria

Principal Shareholders: Public sector company
Date of Establishment: 1952
No of Employees: 1,816

EL NASR SPINNING & WEAVING CO (PORT SAID & ZAGAZIG)

El Kabouty, Port Said
Tel: 4801, 2187, 3405, 2985

Chairman: Mahmoud Khalil
Directors: Farouk Hemdan (Commercial Director)

PRINCIPAL ACTIVITIES: Production of wool yarn, wool and mixed fabrics, knitted woollen fabrics, fishing nets, heavy cotton and linen

Branch Offices: Cairo Office: 83 Sharia El Azhar, Tel 41421
Parent Company: Responsible to the Ministry of Industry

Principal Shareholders: Public sector company

EL NASR SPINNING, WEAVING & KNITTING CO (CHOURBAGUI)

PO Box 1890, Sharia el Sudan, Embabeh, Cairo
Tel: 3471249, 3443860, 3471159, 3475836
Cable: Al Subuh Cairo
Telex: 21683 NSWKC UN
Telefax: 3471160

Chairman: Acc El Sayed Mohamed El Passyoni
Senior Executives: Mohamed Passyoni (Head of Commercial Sector), Samir Hamed (Head of Administrative Sector), Khaled Marei (Head of Financial Sector), Khaled El Nozahi (Head of Spinning & Weaving Sector)

PRINCIPAL ACTIVITIES: Production of cotton yarn and fabrics, knitted underwear, hosiery, printing, bleaching, dyeing and finishing
Parent Company: Responsible to the Ministry of Industry

Principal Shareholders: Public sector company
Date of Establishment: April 1947
No of Employees: 4,460

EL NASR STEEL PIPES & FITTINGS CO

PO Box 6, Helwan, Cairo
Tel: 38966
Cable: Tubenasr
Telex: 92590 Tubnsr Un

Chairman: Eng Tarek Hassanein
Directors: Mousa Mansour, Eng A Koraiem (Technical Director), Eng Mohamed Metwaly, Adel Shams

PRINCIPAL ACTIVITIES: Production of steel tubes (black and galvanized), welded pipes, pipe fittings, spare parts, street lights and steel scaffoldings

EL NASR TANNING CO ALEXANDRIA

6 Sharia El Horreya, Tarik Gamal Abdel Nasser, Alexandria
Tel: 805877
Telex: 54088 NTC UN

Chairman: Yehia Mohamed El-Saead El-Mokadem
Directors: Mahmoud Ahmed Shabara (Commercial Director), Eng Ibrahim Lotfy El Sayed (Factories Director), Mohamed Ibraheam Al-Khawanky (Administrative Director)

PRINCIPAL ACTIVITIES: Leather tanning
Branch Offices: Cairo Office: 34 Abdel Meguid El-Laban St, Sayeda, Zeinab, Tel 843569
Parent Company: Responible to the Ministry of Industry

Principal Shareholders: Public sector company

EL NASR TELEVISION & ELECTRONICS CO

Dar El Salam, Maadi, Cairo
Tel: 843466, 840826
Cable: Telenasrco
Telex: 92662

Chairman: Eng Ali Ismail Fahmi
Directors: Eng Abdel Zaki Darwish (Technical Director), Eng Abdel Hafeez El Oteify (Factories Director), Esmat Abaza (Commercial Director)

PRINCIPAL ACTIVITIES: Production of television sets, and electronic equipment
Branch Offices: Town Offices: 35a Sharia Mansour, Bab El Louk, Tel 27466
Parent Company: Responsible to the Ministry of Industry
Principal Bankers: Bank of Alexandria, Cairo

Principal Shareholders: Public sector company

EL NASR TOBACCO & CIGARETTES CO

5 Sharia Ghafar, Talbia, Giza, Cairo
Tel: 851411/7
Cable: Tabacnasr
Telex: 2734 Tabnas

Chairman: Mostafa Kamal Salem
Directors: Eng Yehia Ahmed El Sharkawi, Eid Grandet Iskandar, M Eid, M Fakahany

PRINCIPAL ACTIVITIES: Production of tobacco, cigarettes, cigars, snuff
Branch Offices: Alexandria Factories; Menouf Factory; Abou Tig Factory
Parent Company: Responsible to the Ministry of Industry
Principal Bankers: National Bank of Egypt; Bank of Alexandria

Principal Shareholders: Public sector
Date of Establishment: 1962
No of Employees: 6,500

EL NASR WOOLLEN & SELECTED TEXTILES CO (STIA)

Prince Ibrahim St, Nouzha, Alexandria
Tel: 4213070
Cable: Setworks
Telex: 54712 STIA UN
Telefax: 4212939

Chairman: Eng Ahmed Aboul Wafa (also Managing Director)

PRINCIPAL ACTIVITIES: Production of cotton yarns, grey and finished cotton fabrics, cotton T shirts, sets of bed sheets, wool fabrics, blended fabrics, blankets, etc
Branch Offices: Cairo Office: 49 Abdel Khalek Sarwat St, Tel 3905323, 3907074
Parent Company: Responsible to the Ministry of Industry
Financial Information:

	1990 E£'000
Sales turnover	117,000
Net profit	17,000
Authorised capital	10,000
Paid-up capital	5,500
Total assets	226,000

Principal Shareholders: Public sector company
Date of Establishment: 1948
No of Employees: 6,128

EL SALAM HOTEL CAIRO

PO Box 5614, Abdel Hamid Badawi Street, Heliopolis, Cairo
Tel: 2455155, 2452155
Telex: 92184 Elhyat UN
Telefax: 2455755

Directors: Ali W El Masri (General Manager)
Senior Executives: Mohamed El Sawi (Director of Training & Personnel), A Abdelkader (Director of Sales)

PRINCIPAL ACTIVITIES: Hotel business

Date of Establishment: 1978
No of Employees: 420

EL SAWAF, FOUAD AHMED, & CO

PO Box 405, 33 Abdel Khaleh Sarwat St, Cairo
Tel: 756144

Directors: F A E Sawaf (Partner), R I Farag (Partner), S G Soliman (Partner)

PRINCIPAL ACTIVITIES: Accountants and management consultants (correspondence with Ernst & Whinney)

EL SHAMS CO FOR HOUSING & DEVELOPMENT

Immobilia Bldg, 26A Sherif St, Cairo
Tel: 976070

Chairman: Waguih Hamdi
Directors: Eng Youssef Hassan Fouad (Technical Director)

PRINCIPAL ACTIVITIES: Housing and construction architectural services, contracting and civil engineering
Parent Company: Responsible to the Ministry of Housing and Reconstruction

Principal Shareholders: Public sector company

EL SHARIF GROUP OF COMPANIES
El Hegaz Street, Heliopolis, Cairo

Chairman: Abdul Latif Sharif

PRINCIPAL ACTIVITIES: Investments; land reclamation; housing and construction; department stores; manufacture of electrical appliances and foodstuffs; production of chemicals and plastic raw materials
Principal Agencies: Sulzer, Switzerland
Branch Offices: London; Bahrain; Dubai
Subsidiary Companies: El Sharif Co for Economic Development; El Sharif Co for Investments; El Sharif Plastics Co; El Sharif Co for Plastic Raw Materials
Financial Information:

	US$'000
Authorised capital	12,000

Principal Shareholders: Private company
No of Employees: 5,000

EL WADI EXPORT CO FOR AGRICULTURAL PRODUCTS
17 Sharia Abd El Salam Ariff, Cairo
Tel: 740070, 740077
Cable: El Wadi
Telex: 92253 Cairo; 54070 Alex

Chairman: Moustafa Roushdi Sayed

PRINCIPAL ACTIVITIES: Export of agricultural produce (crops and fruits)
Branch Offices: Alexandria
Parent Company: Responsible to the Ministry of Trade

Principal Shareholders: Public sector company

ELEKTESSADIA
2 Mohamed Farid Wagdi Street, Manial, Cairo
Tel: 980521, 842215, 846702
Telex: 92679 Zidan UN

Directors: Henry M Zaidan (Managing Director)

PRINCIPAL ACTIVITIES: Manufacture and distribution of automotive and construction equipment
Branch Offices: Cairo, Alexandria, Port Said

Date of Establishment: 1945

ENGINEERING CONSTRUCTION OFFICE (ENCO)
2 Abdel Moniem El Hosseiny St, Nasr City, Cairo
Tel: 607585, 605255, 2600393
Cable: Zakaminco
Telex: 92841 ENCO UN

Chairman: Eng Kamal Guirguis Ibrahim (Managing Director)
Senior Executives: Mahmoud Samy (Engineer), Farouk Abdel Hamid (Accountant)

PRINCIPAL ACTIVITIES: Electrical and mechanical engineering and contracting, industrial turnkey projects
Principal Bankers: Misr International Bank, Heliopolis; Chase National Bank, Heliopolis; National Bank of Egypt

Financial Information:

	1989/90 EE'000
Sales turnover	1,900
Authorised capital	50
Total assets	250

Date of Establishment: 1965
No of Employees: 52

ENGINEERING CONSULTANTS GROUP (ECG)
PO Box 1167, Cairo 11511
Tel: 2614711
Cable: Handiskawi Cairo
Telex: 93873 Ecgee Un
Telefax: 02-2622546

Chairman: M Sami Abdelkawi
Directors: Ashraf Allouba (President), M Tewfik Abdelaziz (Senior Vice President Environmental Division), Mostafa Saad (Projects Manager), Emad Rasmi (Vice President Systems Division), Fouad El Taher (Senior Vice President Business Development Division), Edmund J McDonald (Vice President Process/Industrial Division)
Senior Executives: Mahmoud Suliman (Manager Finance Dept), Ashraf Khalil (Deputy Head Business Development), Geny Christo (Personnel Manager), Hani Elkhoraibie (Manager Technical Administration Dept), Wahid Michel (Regional Manager Business Development)

PRINCIPAL ACTIVITIES: Consultancy engineering, economics, planning, operations research, construction management
Branch Offices: Alexandria; Kafr El Sheikh; Abu Sultan; Talkha; Suez; Kanater; Fayoum; Basateen (South Cairo)
Associated Companies: MEAG Middle East Advisory Group; TEA Computers; Horema Ltd
Principal Bankers: Suez Canal Bank

Principal Shareholders: M Sami Abdelkawi, Ashraf H Allouba
Date of Establishment: 1955 (renamed ECG in 1969)
No of Employees: 500

ENGINEERING ENTERPRISES FOR STEEL WORK CO
STEELCO
39 Sharia Kasr El Nil, Cairo
Tel: 3934458, 3934337
Cable: Egysteelco
Telex: 93130 Stlco UN

Chairman: Eng Ahmed Fouad Soliman
Directors: Abd El Fatah Ibrahim (Commercial Director), Mohamed El Agamy (Financial Director), Eng Adel Mohamed Thabet (Technical Director), Eng Salah Talat El Abd (Marketing Director), Eng Samy Hamed Ibrahim (Director of Research & Development)

PRINCIPAL ACTIVITIES: Manufacture of metal and wooden products for constructional works; storage tanks; cast iron and copper valves; pipes and fittings; pumps; steel structures; overhead cranes; furnaces; river barges; selling of cars, lorries, agricultural tractors, spare parts, domestic appliances, refrigerators, washing machines, gas ovens etc
Principal Bankers: Alexandria Bank; Misr Bank; Chase National Bank
Financial Information: Responsible to the Ministry of Industry

	1989/90 EE'000
Authorised capital	10,000
Paid-up capital	6,000

Principal Shareholders: State owned
Date of Establishment: 1940

ENGINEERING GENERAL CO

9-11 Sharia Orabi, Cairo
Tel: 751300, 751181
Cable: EGICI CAIRO
Telex: 92269, 92249

Chairman: Zakaria Abdel Mohsen Aly
Directors: Abdel Kader Kheidr (Projects Manager), Ihab Abaza (Commercial Manager), M Abdel Fattah Ebeid (General Manager)

PRINCIPAL ACTIVITIES: General engineering, import and export of mechanical machinery and equipment, electrical and petroleum equipment, drilling and railway equipment
Branch Offices: 25 Talaat Harb St, Alexandria, Tel 34756, 25024, Cable EGC
Parent Company: Responsible to the Ministry of Economy and Foreign Trade
Financial Information:

	E£'000
Authorised capital	500,000

Principal Shareholders: Public sector
Date of Establishment: 1962
No of Employees: 3,500

ENPPI

Engineering for the Petroleum & Process Industries

PO Box 2521, El Horreya, Heliopolis, Cairo
Tel: 667635, 2900367, 2901797, 2901163
Telex: 93258 ENPPI UN
Telefax: 2901804

Chairman: Dr M El Rifai (Chief Executive)
Senior Executives: Hassan Madkour (Finance Manager), Reda Morsi (Procurement Manager), Hassan Hamdan (Admin Manager)

PRINCIPAL ACTIVITIES: Basic and detailed engineering, procurement, inspection, construction supervision and turnkey projects for petroleum, oil production, refining, chemicals and petrochemicals industry processing for the petroleum industry, turnkey projects, etc
Branch Offices: Technical Office: 24 El Shaheed Abdel Moneim Hafiz St, Almaza, Heliopolis, Cairo; Procurement Office: 104 El Thawra St, Almaza, Heliopolis, Cairo; and in Alexandria, also in Milan, Houston
Parent Company: Egyptian General Petroleum Corporation
Financial Information:

	1989
	E£'000
Total income	106,000
Authorised capital	1,400
Paid-up capital	,400
Total assets	137,500

Principal Shareholders: Egyptian General Petroleum Corporation
Date of Establishment: 1978
No of Employees: 550

ERECTION & INDUSTRIAL SERVICES CO

26 Sharia Adly, PO Box 297, Cairo
Tel: 48600, 49506, 974315

Chairman: Eng Khaled Awad Tamer
Directors: Eng Ahmed Rashad El Koly (Technical Director), Eng Samir Fahmy Tadross (Industrial Production Director), Eng Moustafa Abdel Hadi Al Kadi (Operations Director)

PRINCIPAL ACTIVITIES: Civil engineering, construction and foundations
Parent Company: Responsible to the Ministry of Industry

Principal Shareholders: Public sector company

ESSAM INTERNATIONAL AGENCIES

5 Amin El Shamsy Street, 11361 Heliopolis, Cairo
Tel: 2452267, 2449107
Cable: ESSAMCO CAIRO
Telex: 94115 Arts UN, 20083 PBMGC UN att Fahim, 20815 PBESC UN att Essam
Telefax: 3461258

Chairman: Fahim Abdel Razek
Directors: Essam Mohamed Fahim, Mohamed Labib, Dr Nabil Abdel Kader
Senior Executives: Dr Eng Alla El Hifny, Dr R Soubhy

PRINCIPAL ACTIVITIES: Import, export, agents, consultants, engineers, import of chemicals, machinery, electronics, abrasives, raw materials, refractories, furnaces, petroleum equipment supplies, construction and installation, export of medicinal plants, essentials oils, readymade garments, vegetables, cotton yarn etc
Branch Offices: 1 Ahmed Fouad Darwish St, Bulkely, Alexandria, and 6 Stanly Bay St, Bulkely, Alexandria, Tel 847638; Farms at Tah Shoubra, Quesna, Monofia
Subsidiary Companies: Safari Co; El-Salam Co; Ranyamedco; Rami Petroleum Supplies; Hefni Petroleum Services
Principal Bankers: Alexandria Bank, Suez Canal Bank; Misr International Bank

Principal Shareholders: Private company
Date of Establishment: HISACO Co in 1971, changed name to Essam in 1979
No of Employees: 135

ESSO EGYPT EXPLORATION PRODUCTION SA

Esso Egypt Inc

Esso Suez Inc

3 Abu Elfeda Street, Zamalek, Cairo
Tel: 3404631, 3404642, 3403150
Telex: 21148 ESOSZ UN, 92378 ESOEG UN

Senior Executives: Harvey D Attra (General Manager)

PRINCIPAL ACTIVITIES: Petroleum exploration, production, refining, transportation and marketing
Branch Offices: Abu Dhabi; Egypt; Qatar; Saudi Arabia; Yemen AR
Parent Company: Exxon Corporation, New York, USA

ESSO STANDARD (NE) INC

2 Midan Kasr El Doubara, Garden City, PO Box 313, Cairo
Tel: 3548330
Cable: Essosales Cairo
Telex: 22369 Esneeg Un

Chairman: Loutfi A Mazhar (General Manager)
Senior Executives: A K Rizk, E Elzoheary, N Sobhi, I Harty

PRINCIPAL ACTIVITIES: Marketing of petroleum products
Branch Offices: Work units at Cairo Airport, Mostorod, Mex, Port Said and Suez
Parent Company: Exxon Corporation, USA

Date of Establishment: 1950
No of Employees: 200

ETS NASSIB-TORCOM & FILS

See NASSIB-TORCOM, ETS, & FILS

EXPORT DEVELOPMENT BANK OF EGYPT

PO Box 2096 Ataba, 10 Talaat Harb Street, Cairo
Tel: 68109, 769964, 777003
Telex: 20850, 20872 EDBE UN

Chairman: Hazem Abdel Aziz El Beblawi (Chief Executive)
Directors: Mahmoud Samir El Sharkawy, Baher Mohamed Alam, Mohamed A M Hilal Sheta, El Sayed Sabri Ghaith, Aly El

Leithy, Ahmed Fawzi Attia, Mahmoud Abdel Salam Omar, Farouk Osman

PRINCIPAL ACTIVITIES: Providing financial and non financial services for the development of Egyptian exports
Financial Information:

	E£'000
Authorised capital	50,000

Principal Shareholders: National Invesment Bank; National Bank of Egypt; Bank of Alexandria; Banque du Caire; Banque Misr
Date of Establishment: 1983

EXTRACTED OIL & DERIVATIVES CO

25 Tarik Canal El Suez, Moharem Bey, Alexandria
Tel: 4926199, 4927215
Cable: Exoil
Telex: 54548 Exoil UN

Chairman: Eng Gamal Moursi El Kazak

PRINCIPAL ACTIVITIES: Production of oils, animal fodder and toilet soap, laundry soap, margarine, glycerine, cottonseed cakes
Branch Offices: Cairo Office: 3 Midan Mustafa Kamel, Tel 903777
Parent Company: Responsible to the Ministry of Industry
Principal Bankers: Bank of Alexandria

Principal Shareholders: Public sector company
No of Employees: 1962

EXXON CHEMICAL NEAR EAST EGYPT

Abu El Feda Bldg, 3 Abu El Feda Street, Zamalek, PO Box 989, Cairo
Tel: 3404642, 3404631
Telex: 92378 ESOEG UN, 21148 ESOSZ UN

Senior Executives: Moheb Kassabgui (Manager)

PRINCIPAL ACTIVITIES: Marketing of petrochemicals
Parent Company: Exxon Chemical Company

Date of Establishment: 1981

FADALI, FATHI, ORGANISATION FOR TRADING & INVESTMENT

9 Emad El Din Street, Cairo
Tel: 906500, 909176
Cable: Fadimex
Telex: 93973 Fadco UN
Telefax: 924342

Chairman: Eng Fathi Fadali
Directors: Gen Fouad Nassar (Managing Director)
Senior Executives: Sherif Fadali (General Manager)

PRINCIPAL ACTIVITIES: Export, import, agent, technical and financial
Principal Agencies: British Steel Corp; Victaulic; Dorman Long Oveseas; Trafalgar Group; Thos Storey Eng Ltd; Abbey Etna Machine
Branch Offices: 10 Kanist Debana, Alexandria
Principal Bankers: Banque du Caire
Financial Information:

	1990 US$'000	1990 E£'000
Sales turnover	1,328	-
Profits	358	-
Authorised capital	-	363
Paid-up capital	-	363

Principal Shareholders: Private company
Date of Establishment: 1957
No of Employees: 40

FAISAL ISLAMIC BANK OF EGYPT

1113 Corniche El Nil, PO Box 2446, Cairo
Tel: 753109, 753165, 742113, 743364
Cable: Faisal Bank Cairo
Telex: 93877 Fbank UN, 93878
Telefax: 777301

Chairman: HRH Prince Mohamed Al Faisal Al Saud
Directors: El Sayed Ahmed Zandou, Dr Ahmed Thabet Ewaida, Dr Ibrahim Gamil Badran, Eng Ahmed Helmy Abdel Maggid, Mohamed Gamal Ek Shinawy, Khedr Mohsen Al Ebrahim, Eng Hasan Anwar Abdel Wahab, Sheikh Haider Ben Laden, Dr Sultan Abou Ali, Dr Abdel Aziz Abd Allah Al Fada, Ali Ahmed Hamdi, Dr Omar Abdi Ali, Mohamed Kamal Abdel Aziz Hashem, Dr Youssef Abd Allah El Karadawy
Senior Executives: El Sayed Ahmed Zandou (Governor), Counsellor Ahmed Amin EHassan (Deputy Governor & Trustee General), Abdel Hamid Abou Mousa (Deputy Governor for Operations), Mohamed Mustafa Kamel (Deputy Governor for Services), Dr Shawky Ismail Shehata (Financial Advisor & Supervisor of the Zakat Fund)

PRINCIPAL ACTIVITIES: Banking and investments in accordance with the Islamic Sharia Law
Branch Offices: Cairo, El Azhar, Ghamra, Heliopolis, Alexandria, Damenhour, Tanta, Banha, Assiut, Suez, Mansoura, Souhag
Subsidiary Companies: Islamic Co to Animal Wealthfare; Islamic Co for Electric Refrigerators; Islamic Foreign Trade Co; Islamic Co for Acrylic Products; Islamic Co for Packing and Printing Materials; Islamic Co for Pharmaceuticals, Chemicals & Medical Requisites; Islamic Co for Manufacturing, Packing & Distribution of Food Commodities; Islamic Clay Bricks Co, Souhag; Islamic Clay Bricks Co, Assiut; Islamic Clay Bricks Co, Suez; Damazeen Co for Agricultural & Livestock Production; Electronin Industries Co; Cairo Medical Centre; Misr International Hospital; General Investment Co; Islamic Co for Investment & Development; Islamic Development Co Ltd; El Salam Investment Co; Ismailia National Co for Foodstuff Industries; Islamic Co for Engineering Industries; Industrial Detergents Co; PVC Floor Tiles Co; Mansoura Medical Centre; Faisal Islamic Bank of Sudan; Dar El Maal El Islami; Sudanese Islamic Bank; Islamic Bank of West Sudan; Faisal Finance Institute; Arab Co for Purification Works; Pan Islamic Consulting Group; etc
Financial Information:

	1990 US$'000
Deposits	1,451,569
Reserves	39,180
Authorised capital	500,000
Issued capital	100,000
Paid-up capital	70,000
Total assets	1,831,270

Principal Shareholders: (51%) Egyptian Interests; (49%) Saudi and other Moslems Interests
Date of Establishment: 1977
No of Employees: 1111

FATHI FADALI ORGANISATION FOR TRADING & INVESTMENT

See FADALI, FATHI, ORGANISATION FOR TRADING & INVESTMENT

FAYOUM PETROLEUM CO
FAPCO

1097 Corniche El-Nil St, PO Box 2400, Cairo
Tel: 31883, 31884

PRINCIPAL ACTIVITIES: Exploration and production of oil; operation of Abu Gharadig gas project and pipelines
Parent Company: Egyptian General Petroleum Authority (Responsible to the Ministry of Petroleum)

Principal Shareholders: Public sector company

FEDERATION OF EGYPTIAN INDUSTRIES

26 A Sherif St, Immobilia Bldg, PO Box 251, Cairo
Tel: 49488, 49489
Cable: Pertinax

Chairman: Hamed Al Maamoon Habib
Directors: Ahmed Tawfik (General Director)
Senior Executives: Moustapha Hamed (Financial and Admin Manager), Bahey El-Din Saleh (Alexandria Manager), Galal Ezzat (Public Relations), Wafik El Guindy (Planning Dept)

PRINCIPAL ACTIVITIES: Representation of Egyptian industrial community
Branch Offices: Alexandria Office: 65 Gamal Abdel Nasser, Alexandria, Tel 28622
Parent Company: Responsible to the Ministry of Industry

Principal Shareholders: Public sector company

FINE TEXTILE FACTORY (DIOVEERA)

327 Shoubra St, PO Box 1180, Cairo
Tel: 947530, 944167
Cable: Dioveera Cairo

Chairman: Eng Mohamed Ghannam
Directors: Adnan Ghannam
Senior Executives: M Mowafak (Director of Machinery)

PRINCIPAL ACTIVITIES: Production of textiles and ready-made clothes for women and children
Principal Bankers: Bank Misr; Bank of Alexandria

FLOPETROL TECHNICAL SERVICES INC

Near East District Office, PO Box 35, Maadi, Cairo
Tel: 504510
Telex: 21064 FLNED UN

Senior Executives: R Attal (District Manager)

PRINCIPAL ACTIVITIES: Oil and gas services

FORCE BATTERY COMPANY

9 St 47, Industrial Zone, Abbassia, Cairo
Tel: 820014, 751549, 840929

Chairman: Kamel Ibrahim Arafa
Directors: Salah Eldin Kamel Arafa, Moustafa Kamel Ibrahim Arafa

PRINCIPAL ACTIVITIES: Production of acid batteries for scooters, cars and practical and industrial purposes all kinds of batteries box, battery, supporters, and dry batteries
Branch Offices: Service Centre: 49 St Manyal Al Roda, Cairo, Tel 820014, 840929
Principal Bankers: Bank Misr

Principal Shareholders: Private company
Date of Establishment: 1958
No of Employees: 40

FORD AEROSPACE & COMMUNICATIONS INTERNATIONAL INC

13 Ramez Street, Mohandesseen, Cairo
Tel: 715016, 715947
Telex: 21280 FACI UN

PRINCIPAL ACTIVITIES: Engineering design and turnkey projects of telecommunications systems
Parent Company: Ford Motor Co, USA

FOUAD AHMED EL SAWAF & CO

See EL SAWAF, FOUAD AHMED, & CO

FOUR WINDS INTERNATIONAL

11A Corniche El Nil, PO Box 213, Maadi, Cairo
Tel: 3500113, 3501046
Telex: 94333 AMIC UN

PRINCIPAL ACTIVITIES: Customs clearance and international freight forwarding
Branch Offices: Cairo, Alexandria, Port Said
Parent Company: Four Winds International, San Diego, California, USA

FUTAINASR TRADING CO SAE

5 Zaki Street, Tawfikia, PO Box 59, Cairo
Tel: 748488, 748936, 748587
Telex: 92581 Futnsr UN

Directors: Mostafa Abdel Halim (General Manager)

PRINCIPAL ACTIVITIES: Manufacturers' representatives, assembly of equipment and distribution of cars, motorcycles, spare parts, tyres, engines, trucks and buses, electronics and home appliances, telecommunications
Principal Agencies: Honda; Toyo; Yanmar; NGK; Hino; Fisher; Indesit; NEC

GENERAL AUTHORITY FOR CAIRO AIRPORT

Cairo Airport, Cairo
Tel: 963277, 966270, 963310, 960607

PRINCIPAL ACTIVITIES: Management and control authority for Cairo International Airport
Parent Company: Responsible to the Ministry of Tourism and Civil Aviation

Principal Shareholders: Public sector company

GENERAL AUTHORITY FOR CINEMA, THEATRE & MUSIC

Cinema City, Pyramids Rd, Cairo
Tel: 850346

Chairman: Eng Mohamed El Desoki Ibrahim
Senior Executives: Mohamed Lamie Abdel Rahman (General Manager)

PRINCIPAL ACTIVITIES: General responsibility for the entertainment industry
Branch Offices: 27 Abdel Khalek Sarwat St, Cairo, Tel 970283
Parent Company: Responsible to the Ministry of Information and Culture

Principal Shareholders: Public sector company

GENERAL AUTHORITY FOR COOPERATIVE BUILDING & HOUSING

Nasr City, Abbassia, Cairo
Tel: 838494, 835202

Chairman: Eng Abdel Rahman Labib Abu Shanab
Senior Executives: Eng Ramzi Nazim Shenouda (General Manager for Technical Affairs)

PRINCIPAL ACTIVITIES: Contracting, building construction
Parent Company: Responsible to the Ministry of Housing and Reconstruction

Principal Shareholders: Public sector company

GENERAL CO FOR BATTERIES

17 El Gomhouria St, Cairo
Tel: 933851
Cable: Genbatt

Chairman: Mohamed El Yassaki
Directors: Nabieh Abdel Messieh Mikhail (Financial & Commercial Director)

PRINCIPAL ACTIVITIES: Manufacture of lead acid and dry cells batteries
Parent Company: Responsible to the Ministry of Industry
Principal Bankers: Bank of Alexandria

Principal Shareholders: Public sector company

GENERAL CO FOR CERAMICS & PORCELAIN PRODUCTS

PO Bag Ramsis, Cairo
Tel: 2441907, 2441908
Telex: 92467 Chini UN

Chairman: Eng Gamal Mostafa Rashwan
Directors: Ahmed Hamdy El Aasar (Financial & Commercial Director), Eng Mahmoud F Goneima (Production Director), Mohamed Talaat Abul Fadl (Commercial Director)
Senior Executives: Mostafa K A Said (Technical Manager), Eng Mabrouk Farghal (Production Manager Sanitaryware), Eng Foad El Lakkany (Production Manager Porcelain)

PRINCIPAL ACTIVITIES: Manufacture and marketing of glazed tiles, sanitary ware, and other household, hard porcelain dinnerware and hotel chinaware, earthenware etc
Parent Company: Responsible to the Ministry of Industry
Subsidiary Companies: Arab Ceramics Co SAE, Egypt (33%)
Principal Bankers: Bank of Alexandria
Financial Information:

	1988/89
	E£'000
Sales turnover	33,000
Profits	3,500
Authorised capital	2,421
Paid-up capital	2,421
Total assets	34,849

Principal Shareholders: State (74.7%); Individuals (25.3%)
Date of Establishment: May 1955
No of Employees: 2,960

GENERAL CO FOR ELECTRICAL PROJECTS (ILLIGAT)

12 Sh Youssef El Guindi, Bab-El-Louk, PO Box 1921, Cairo
Tel: 20100, 23344, 33508

PRINCIPAL ACTIVITIES: Electrical engineering
Parent Company: Responsible to the Ministry of Electric Power

Principal Shareholders: Public sector company

GENERAL CO FOR FOUNDATIONS

1 Sharia El Makhazen, Giza, Cairo
Tel: 981121

Chairman: Mustafa Kamal El Masri

PRINCIPAL ACTIVITIES: Contracting, civil engineering and construction, foundations
Branch Offices: 3 El Horria Rd, Alexandria, Tel 4927701
Parent Company: Responsible to the Ministry of Housing and Reconstruction

Principal Shareholders: Public sector company

GENERAL CO FOR PAPER INDUSTRY (RAKTA)

El-Tabia Rashid Line, Alexandria
Tel: 5601760/1/2/3
Cable: RAKTACO
Telex: 54090 RAKTA UN
Telefax: 5601300

Chairman: Dr Hassan Ibrahim
Directors: Ezz El-Deen Fayed (Financial Director), Eng Nader El-Baroudy (Production Director), Wagdy Abu Nazel (Commercial), Eng Aly Soliman (Engineering Director)

PRINCIPAL ACTIVITIES: Manufacture of cardboard, printing and writing paper, pulp
Branch Offices: 3 Behlar Street, Cairo; 6 Gamal Abd El-Nasser Street, Alexandria
Principal Bankers: Bank Misr, Attareen Alexandria; Bank Alexandria, Alexandria; National Bank Alexandria

Financial Information:

	1988
	E£'000
Sales turnover	89,000
Profits	6,800
Authorised capital	12,000
Paid-up capital	11,600
Total assets	130,100

Principal Shareholders: Government (81.3%); Public Sector (10.6%); Private Sector (8.1%)
Date of Establishment: 1958
No of Employees: 2,360

GENERAL CO FOR RESEARCH & GROUND WATER (REGWA)

19 Sharia Emad El Din, Cairo
Tel: 934644, 934535, 904151
Cable: Regwa

Directors: Eng Mohamed Moussa Sadik

PRINCIPAL ACTIVITIES: Irrigation
Parent Company: Responsible to the Ministry of Agriculture and Irrigation

Principal Shareholders: Public sector company

GENERAL CO FOR SILOS

1 Swwah Square, Cairo
Tel: 2594967, 259426
Cable: Cairo Silos
Telex: 23154 Silos UN
Telefax: 2594664

Chairman: Eng Ahmed Shams El Din Abdel Hafez
Senior Executives: Refaat Abu Zeina (Head Financial Sector), Gen Salah Moustafa (Head Foreign Purchasing Committee), Sayed Badawi (Head Internal Purchase Sector), Salah Ragab El Khadrawi (Head Administration Sector), Salah Zein El Abedih (Head Technical Sector), Magdy Aby Zeid (Head Legal Sector)

PRINCIPAL ACTIVITIES: Silos and storage, transport, clearance, import
Branch Offices: Alexandria Silos, 25 Salah Salem St; Port Said Silos, Sultan Hussain St; Suez Silos, PO Box 125; Safaga Silos
Parent Company: General Authority for Milling, Silos & Bakeries, responsible to the Ministry of Supply

Date of Establishment: 1890
No of Employees: 6,000

GENERAL CO FOR TRADING & CHEMICALS

26 Sharia Sherif, Cairo
Tel: 976800
Cable: Chemtrade

Chairman: Abdel Aziz Abdel Kader Salam

PRINCIPAL ACTIVITIES: Import, export and marketing of chemicals, paints, dyes, scientific and photographic equipment, watches and razor blades
Parent Company: Responsible to the Ministry of Trade

Principal Shareholders: Public sector company

GENERAL CONSTRUCTION CO ROLLIN
Soc Generale d'Entreprise

5 Sharia 26th July, Cairo
Tel: 915684, 915755
Telex: 93803 ROLIN UN

Chairman: Eng Ahmed Lotfi Mansour
Directors: Eng Mahmoud Khater (Member of the Board), Eng Fahmy Bassily (Technical Director), Eng Kamal Sedik (Technical Director), Eng Wiliam Sourial (Technical Director),

Eng Fathi Farag (Technical Director), Eng Abdalla Rached (Technical Director), Eng Adel Hakim (Technical Director)

PRINCIPAL ACTIVITIES: Contracting, civil engineering and construction
Branch Offices: Alexandria; Aswan; Assuit; Ismailia
Principal Bankers: El-Kahira Bank; Arab International Bank
Financial Information:

	1988
	E£'000
Sales turnover	32,898
Profits	2,216
Authorised capital	4,000
Paid-up capital	3,388
Total assets	12,901

Principal Shareholders: Public sector company
Date of Establishment: 1902
No of Employees: 793

GENERAL CONTRACTING CO FOR SANITARY INSTALLATION

8 Shawarby St, PO Box 92, Cairo
Tel: 976927 (6 lines), 974073
Cable: Eniotna Cairo

Chairman: Shawky Zaitoun
Senior Executives: Norbert Mounir Fouad (Manager, Commercial Dept)

PRINCIPAL ACTIVITIES: Installation of sanitary equipment and general trading
Principal Agencies: Fraisa, Switzerland; Riello, Italy; Enka, Turkey; Kolben, Seeger, Germany
Branch Offices: Alexandria Branch: 15 Gare du Caire
Principal Bankers: Banque du Caire; Bank Misr

Principal Shareholders: State owned

GENERAL DYNAMICS CORPORATION

39 Beirut Street, PO Box 2872, El Horreya, Heliopolis, Cairo
Tel: 663731, 667677
Telex: 93408 GDARE UN

PRINCIPAL ACTIVITIES: Marine electronics, aerospace, material services

GENERAL EGYPTIAN AUTHORITY FOR CIVIL AVIATION

31 Sharia 26 July, Cairo
Tel: 970086, 974594, 971510

PRINCIPAL ACTIVITIES: Authority and control of civil aviation
Branch Offices: Cairo Airport Office: Tel 963277
Parent Company: Responsible to the Ministry of Tourism and Civil Aviation

Principal Shareholders: Public sector company

GENERAL EGYPTIAN AUTHORITY FOR GEOLOGICAL SURVEY & MINING PROJECTS

3 Tarik Salah Salem, Abbassia, Cairo
Tel: 831377, 831242, 831625
Cable: Geosurvey

PRINCIPAL ACTIVITIES: Preparing the conditions and rules for venture agreement with foreign investors for exploration and exploitation of deposits
Principal Agencies: Egyptian Black Sands Co, 2 Tarik El Horreya, Alexandria and Ballah Gypsum Co, Sharikat El Petrol St, Ghamra, Cairo
Parent Company: Responsible to the Ministry of Industry
Principal Bankers: Central Bank of Egypt

GENERAL EGYPTIAN BOOK ORGANISATION

Corniche El Nil, Boulac, Cairo
Tel: 972649, 973436,
Cable: GEBO Cairo
Telex: 93932 BOOK UN

PRINCIPAL ACTIVITIES: Import and distribution of books, printing, organisation of the Cairo International Book Fair
Parent Company: Responsible to the High Council for Culture

Principal Shareholders: Public sector company

GENERAL EGYPTIAN CO FOR RAILWAY EQUIPMENT (SEMAF)

El Hamamat, Ein Helwan, Cairo
Tel: 38715, 38306
Cable: Semaf Helwan

Chairman: Eng Fouad Abou Zaghla
Directors: Eng Hussein Ahmed El Borsiki (Factories Director), Eng Hussein Fathi Bayoumi (Technical Director)

PRINCIPAL ACTIVITIES: Manufacture of railway wagons and rolling stock. Production and marketing of light and heavy metals
Parent Company: Responsible to the Ministry of Industry

Principal Shareholders: Public sector company

GENERAL ELECTRIC COMPANY

1085 Corniche El Nil, Garden City, Cairo
Tel: 3550561, 3544869, 3552809
Telex: 92410 GETSC UN

Senior Executives: Fawzy El Katsha (Regional Manager Egypt & Sudan)

PRINCIPAL ACTIVITIES: Manufacture of power generating equipment, aircraft engines and electrical equipment

GENERAL ENGINEERING & REFRIGERATION CO (GERCO)

15 Sharia Emad El Din, Cairo
Tel: 44399, 59746, 976639

Chairman: Eng Moh Kamal El Eryan
Directors: Mohamed Said Abdel Karim (Commercial Director)

PRINCIPAL ACTIVITIES: Refrigeration, cold storage and general engineering
Parent Company: Responsible to the Ministry of Supply

Principal Shareholders: Public sector company

GENERAL METALS COMPANY

5 Sh 26 July, Cairo
Tel: 910233
Cable: Plataurum

Chairman: Eng Mohamed Adel Ahmed El Danaf
Directors: Eng Mostafa Kamal Farahat (Technical Director), Hassan Nesseim Hilal (Commercial Director), Salah El Deen Mowafi (Financial Director)

PRINCIPAL ACTIVITIES: Production of electrolytic copper, non-ferrous alloys, copper, brass, zinc, lead and aluminium sheets, etc; precious metals; production of gray and red lead oxides, pressure and gravity casting for aluminium and zinc alloys, hot rolling continuous casting aluminium and zinc
Branch Offices: Works: Abbassiah, Cairo; Khan Abou, Taqia, Camalia, Cairo, Tebbin, Helwan
Parent Company: Responsible to the Ministry of Industry
Principal Bankers: Bank of Alexandria

Principal Shareholders: Public sector company
Date of Establishment: November 1937
No of Employees: 1,800

GENERAL MOTORS EGYPT SAE

3 Abu El Feda St, Zamalek, Po Box 108, Gezira, Cairo
Tel: 3412116, 3404004
Telex: 20407, 22670 GME UN
Telefax: 200818

Chairman: Ronald G Nardi (also Managing Director)
Directors: M J Willocq, Y Yamanouchi, A S Zeidy, A Kaki, D C Hunter
Senior Executives: Michel J Willocq (Director of Finance), Pal Singh (Sales Manager), Dale C Hunter (Factory Manager), Sherif Magdi (Government & PR Manager), Yuichi Yamanouchi (Planning & Product Engg Manager), Harry Gnacke (Director Materials Management)

PRINCIPAL ACTIVITIES: Joint venture company for the manufacturing of commercial vehicles (trucks and buses)
Principal Agencies: Dealers: Mansour Chevrolet; Magar Bros; Ghabbour Bros; Modern Motors; Mounir Magar; El Seoudi Cars; National Motors
Branch Offices: Factory at 6th October City
Parent Company: General Motors Corporation
Principal Bankers: Commercial International Bank; Misr International Bank; Egyptian American Bank
Financial Information:

	1988/89	1989/90
	E£'000	E£'000
Sales turnover	132,527	174,227
Profit	5,443	13,109
Authorised capital	25,200	25,200
Paid-up capital	25,200	25,200
Total assets	99,964	111,034

Principal Shareholders: General Motors Corporation, USA (31%); Isuzu Motors Ltd (20%)
Date of Establishment: 1983
No of Employees: 521

GENERAL NILE CO FOR CONSTRUCTION & PAVING

32 Sharia El Falaki, Cairo
Tel: 25661, 24625, 30419, 982399
Cable: RASFROAD
Telex: 22032 GNCP UN

Chairman: Eng Fawzy El Ashmawy
Directors: Eng Abd El Azim Mahrous, Eng Ibrahim El Azab, Eng Hamdi Moubarek, Gamil Aziz

PRINCIPAL ACTIVITIES: Contracting, civil engineering and construction
Branch Offices: 22 Ghorfa El Tougaria St, Ramli Station, Alexandria, Tel: 807115
Parent Company: Responsible to Road & Bridges Authority
Principal Bankers: Banque du Caire

Principal Shareholders: State-owned
Date of Establishment: 1950
No of Employees: 1,300

GENERAL NILE CC FOR DESERT ROADS

10 Sharia Youssef Sherif, Manial El Roda, Cairo
Tel: 983464, 847933

PRINCIPAL ACTIVITIES: Contracting, civil engineering and construction; desert roads

Principal Shareholders: Public sector company

GENERAL NILE CO FOR ROAD CONSTRUCTION

4 Sh Mahmoud Talaat, Nasr City, Cairo
Tel: 836784, 835653, 835765

PRINCIPAL ACTIVITIES: Contracting, civil engineering and construction; roads

Parent Company: Responsible to the Ministry of Housing and Reconstruction

Principal Shareholders: Public sector company

GENERAL NILE CO FOR ROADS & BRIDGES

7 El Sharikat St, Ard El Fawala, Abdien, Cairo
Tel: 3905501, 3905502, 3905503
Cable: Workom Cairo
Telex: 93235 RBUN

Chairman: Fawzi Messiha Abd El Malek
Directors: Adel M Abd El Gawad (Responsible for Administrative Sector), Kamal F Bedwany (Responsible for Mechanical & Transportation Sectors), Hamed Sabry Aly (Chief for the Paving & Bridges Executive Sector), Farouk M Faragallah (Chief for the Paving Executive Sector), Mohamed Yousef Sharaf El Din (Chief of Financial & Economic Sector)
Senior Executives: Magdi Fouad Abd El Saied (Chief of Transportation Sector), Adel Alfonse Guirguis (Chief of Marine Sector), Abd El Rahman Sami Abbadi (Chief of Contruction & Bridges), Mohamed Shebl Ahmad Mahmoud (Chief of Local Paving Sector), Mohamed Yahya Ahmad Mousa (General Manager of Productive Workshops), Mohamed Mahmoud Abdel Rahman (General Manager of Equipment Engineering), Hamdy Abd El Khalek El Serri (General Manager of Transportation Equipment), Abdalla Badr El Dine (General Manager of General Accounts)

PRINCIPAL ACTIVITIES: Contracting, civil engineering and construction roads, bridges, railway works and construction, offshore work, ports, harbours, airports runways, dams
Principal Bankers: Banque du Caire
Financial Information:

	1989
	E£'000
Authorised capital	64,961

Date of Establishment: 1963
No of Employees: 4,400

GENERAL ORGANISATION FOR INDUSTRIAL & MINING COMPLEXES

El Thowra Bldg, El Alfi St, PO Box 754, Cairo
Tel: 917071, 923640
Cable: STLCOMPLEX
Telex: 92364 Ori Un

Chairman: Eng Abdel Aziz Kamal
Deputy Chairman: Abdel Salam Meazawi

PRINCIPAL ACTIVITIES: Execution of industrial and mining complexes
Parent Company: Responsible to the Ministry of Industry

Principal Shareholders: Public sector company
Date of Establishment: 1979
No of Employees: 1,500

GENERAL ORGANISATION FOR INDUSTRIALISATION

G.O.F.I.

6 Khalil Agha St, Garden City, Cairo
Tel: 3540677, 3540678
Cable: TANFIZ Cairo
Telex: 23389 Tanfiz UN
Telefax: 3548738

Chairman: Minister of Industry
Directors: Dr Eng Mohammed Abdel Fattah Mongi (Deputy Chairman and General Manager)

PRINCIPAL ACTIVITIES: All General Organisations were abolished in 1976 with the exception of this General Organisation for Industrialisation which concludes most contracts for goods exceeding E£50,000 in value in all the industrial sectors. Trade however is conducted directly with all the Egyptian State Companies for all other contracts

Branch Offices: Alexandria; Damietta; El Sadat; Al Aresh; Sixth
October; Zagazig; Tenth Ramadan; Assiut; Aswan
Parent Company: Responsible to the Ministry of Industry

Principal Shareholders: State owned organisation
Date of Establishment: 1958
No of Employees: 1,300

GENERAL ORGANIZATION FOR INTERNATIONAL EXHIBITIONS & FAIRS

Exhibition Ground, Nasr City, Cairo
Tel: 2607810/19
Cable: Nefertiti Cairo
Telex: 92600 Fair UN
Telefax: 2607845

Chairman: Hamed Atwa
Directors: Ragaa Rady (Deputy Chairman of GOIEF), Helmy El
Basha (Director General of Cairo International Fair), Mohamed
Sharaf (Director General of Security), Mrs Bousayna El
Maghraby (Director General of Engineering & Technical
Affairs), Mrs Afaf Habib (Director General of Contracts
Financial & Administrative Affairs), Mrs Hanaa Shaker
(Director of Publicity), Mrs Bahiga El-Sayed (Director of
Commercial Affairs), Mrs Sania Bahnasy (Director of
Information Center), Gamal Abdel Latif (Director of Exhibitors
Services)

PRINCIPAL ACTIVITIES: Supervision and management of trade
fairs and exhibitions in Egypt (especially Cairo International
Fair) and promotion of Egyptian goods abroad and exhibitions
Parent Company: Responsible to the Ministry of Economy &
Foreign Trade

Date of Establishment: 1956
No of Employees: 600

GENERAL PETROLEUM COMPANY

8 Sh Dr Moustafa Abu Zahr, Nasr City, PO Box 743, Cairo
Tel: 835433, 837573
Cable: Petrogen Cairo
Telex: 92049; 92345

PRINCIPAL ACTIVITIES: Oil exploration, drilling and production
Parent Company: Egyptian General Petroleum Authority
(Responsible to the Ministry of Petroleum)

Principal Shareholders: Public sector company

GENERAL SPRING & TRANSPORT EQUIPMENT MANUFACTURING CO (YAYAT)

8 Sharia El Massaneh, El Amiria, Cairo
Tel: 869635, 862790, 872968
Cable: Yayatmisr

Directors: Eng Ahmad Badawi Sakr (Technical Director), Eng
Hafez Ahmed Amin (Brakes Factory Director), Eng Amin Zaki
Fakh El Din (Springs Factory Director)

PRINCIPAL ACTIVITIES: Manufacture of springs for railway and
road vehicles; brake and clutch parts
Parent Company: Responsible to the Ministry of Industry

Principal Shareholders: Public sector company

GEOPHYSICAL SERVICE INC

61 Orouea St, Heliopolis, Cairo
Tel: 966229, 961496
Cable: Geesinc
Telex: 92327 Geesy

Senior Executives: S T Zaynoun (General Manager)

PRINCIPAL ACTIVITIES: Geophysical data processing
Associated Companies: Geophysical Service International

GEORGE WIMPEY (EGYPT) SAE

See WIMPEY, GEORGE, (EGYPT) SAE

GEORGE ZAIDAN & CO

See ZAIDAN, GEORGE, & CO

GIZA GENERAL CONTRACTING CO

46 Sharia El Falaki, Bab El-Louk, Cairo
Tel: 23728, 20706

Chairman: Eng Sharif Zaki El Maghraby
Directors: Eng Mandouh Hafeez (Technical Director)

PRINCIPAL ACTIVITIES: Contracting, civil engineering and
construction
Parent Company: Responsible to the Ministry of Housing and
Reconstruction

Principal Shareholders: Public sector company

GRAND HOTELS OF EGYPT COMPANY

18a Sharia El Borsa El Tewfikia, Cairo
Tel: 973775/8

PRINCIPAL ACTIVITIES: Hotel management
Parent Company: Responsible to the Ministry of Tourism and
Civil Aviation

GULF AGENCY CO LTD

PO Box 304, Port Said
Tel: 21909, 21910
Cable: Gacship Portsaid
Telex: via Athens 216344 a/b GAC GR

PRINCIPAL ACTIVITIES: Shipping, forwarding, packing and
warehousing, tugs and barges, marine contracting
Branch Offices: PO Box 78, Suez, Tel 26318, 25059; PO Box
174, Alexandria, Tel 802010, 808941

GULF OF SUEZ PETROLEUM CO GUPCO

Palestine Street, 4th Sector, New Maadi, Cairo
Tel: 3520060
Cable: Gupcooil Cairo
Telex: 92248 Gupco Un

Chairman: Hamdi El Bahbi (Managing Director)

PRINCIPAL ACTIVITIES: Petroleum exploration; GUPCO
developed the El Morgan oilfield in the Gulf of Suez, and also
holds other exploration concessions in the Gulf of Suez and
the Red Sea
Subsidiary Companies: Fayoum Petroleum Company (FAPCO);
Nile Petroleum Company

Principal Shareholders: Partnership between the General
Egyptian Petroleum Authority and Amoco Oil (a subsidiary of
Standard Oil of Indiana)

HALLIBURTON LTD

14 Abdel Kamy Osman St, Guiza, PO Box 1227, Cairo
Tel: 853856, 853001
Cable: Halliburton Cairo
Telex: 92320 Halco Un

PRINCIPAL ACTIVITIES: Oil service company

HELWAN DIESEL ENGINES CO

Ein Helwan
Tel: 782731, 781467
Cable: Diewan Helwan
Telex: 93448 Diewan UN, 92167 Lotfi UN, 92737 HMTCO
UN/Diewan

Chairman: Acc Soliman Kandil
Directors: Eng Farouk Shalash (Helwan Factory General
Manager), Eng Loutfy El Hennawy (Shoubra Factory General
Director), Wagdy Hassib (Financial & Economical Director)

PRINCIPAL ACTIVITIES: Production of water-cooled diesel
engines, air cooled diesel engines (under licence DEUTZ),

generating and welding sets, water pumps, air compressors and bearings

Branch Offices: Sales Dept: 18 Emad El Din St, Cairo, Tel 755919, 755993

Parent Company: Responsible to the Ministry of Military Production

Subsidiary Companies: Incorporating: Egyptian Co for Manufacturing Diesel Engines & Accessories

Principal Bankers: National Bank of Egypt

Principal Shareholders: General sector

Date of Establishment: 1960

No of Employees: 2,600

HELWAN NON-FERROUS METALS INDUSTRIES

Helwan, Cairo
Tel: 738360, 781950
Cable: Cobral, Helwan
Telex: 92461 Coprl UN

Chairman: Eng Mohamed Mokhtar Noor Edin

Directors: Eng Mohammad Okasha (Technical Director), Eng Mohammad Magid Zohdy (Commercial Director), Dr Eng Abdel Baset El Sebai (Planning Director)

Senior Executives: Eng Hassan El Shami (Production Manager), Mrs Mahasen Hilal (Marketing Manager)

PRINCIPAL ACTIVITIES: Production of aluminium cables, copper and aluminium plates, rods, sheets, tubes; aluminium foil, irrigation sprinkler and tubing

Parent Company: Responsible to the Ministry of Military

Financial Information: Production

	£E'000
Sales turnover	50,000
Profits	3,000
Authorised capital	12,000
Paid-up capital	12,000

Date of Establishment: 1954

No of Employees: 4,000

HELWAN PORTLAND CEMENT CO

Head Office & Factory, PO Box 16 Helwan 11421
Tel: 790550, 790177, 790059, 790268
Cable: Cemhelwan, PO BOx 16 Helwan
Telex: 92773
Telefax: 790059

Chairman: M S Dessouki

Senior Executives: Mahmoud Ibrahim (Finance Director), Hassan Kamel (Technical Director), Fikry A Fishara (Commercial Director), Mohamed Nour (Administration Director)

PRINCIPAL ACTIVITIES: Production of Portland grey cement, white Portland cement and building materials

Branch Offices: Cairo Office: PO Box 75, Cairo 11599

Parent Company: Responsible to the Ministry of Housing

Financial Information:

	1990
	£E'000
Sales turnover	214,354
Profits	23,950
Authorised capital	250,000
Paid-up capital	130,552
Total assets	1,104,481

Principal Shareholders: Public sector company

Date of Establishment: 1929

No of Employees: 3,553

HONGKONG EGYPTIAN BANK SAE

Abu El Feda Bldg, 3 Abu El Feda Street, Zamalek, Cairo
Tel: 3404849
Cable: Honegbank
Telex: 20471 HKEB UN, 22505 HKEB UN
Telefax: 3414010

Chairman: Hamed Abdel Latif El Sayeh

Directors: Keith Holt (Chief Executive)

Senior Executives: Mohd A L Nour (General Manager), T W Haddon (Senior Manager), Assaad M Assaad (Cairo Branch Manager), Hesham Guemeih (Heliopolis Branch Manager)

PRINCIPAL ACTIVITIES: Commercial banking

Branch Offices: Heliopolis Branch: 1 Roxy Square, Heliopolis, Cairo, Tel 2583152, 2582585, 2583184, 2583123, Telex 20614

Parent Company: The Hongkong Bank

Principal Bankers: The Hongkong & Shanghai Banking Corp, Chemical Bank, Midland Bank

Financial Information:

	1988/89
	£E'000
Total income	31,831
Profits	2,057
Loans & Advances	161,809
Deposits	240,677
Authorised capital	16,800
Paid-up capital	16,800
Total assets	336,746

Principal Shareholders: HongKong & Shanghai Banking Corp; Egyptian Reinsurance Company; Prominent Egyptian Individuals; other Arab Interests

Date of Establishment: 1982

No of Employees: 142

HUGHES AIRCRAFT INTERNATIONAL

2 Messaha Square, Dokki, PO Box 1913, Cairo
Tel: 3484635
Telex: 20008 HACMN UN

PRINCIPAL ACTIVITIES: Communications and military electronics

IBM WORLD TRADE CORPORATION

Aboul Fottouh Bldg, 56 Gamat El Dowal El Arabia St, Mohandisseen, Giza
Tel: 3492533
Telex: 22016 INBUS UN

Senior Executives: Mohamed Aly El Hamamsy (General Manager)

PRINCIPAL ACTIVITIES: Data processing products and services, and typewriters

Branch Offices: IBM Egypt Branch Cairo

Parent Company: IBM World Trade Corporation, Paris, France (Headquarters)

Date of Establishment: 1954 (Egypt Branch)

No of Employees: 130

IEOC COMPANY INC

PO Box 311, 2 Wadi El Nil St, Mohandessin, Cairo
Tel: 461194/7, 460861/4
Cable: PETRODELTA CAIRO
Telex: 21351, 93573, 93739 IEOC UN

Senior Executives: Primo Maioli (General Manager, Egyptian Branch)

PRINCIPAL ACTIVITIES: Oil exploration activities in various concession areas by virtue of agreements with EGPC. An operating co Petrobel, undertakes production duties

Subsidiary Companies: IEOC has participation in joint ventures in Egypt with the following companies: Amoco; Phillips; Total; British Petroleum; Elf Aquitaine; Marathon

INDUSTRIAL & TECHNICAL ADVISERS CO (ITACO)

15 Sherif St, Flat 3, Cairo
Tel: 53253, 54191

PRINCIPAL ACTIVITIES: Business and engineering consultants
Branch Offices: Greece (PO box 1435, Athens)
Parent Company: Head office in Lebanon (PO Box 4639, Beirut)

INDUSTRIAL DEVELOPMENT CENTRE FOR ARAB STATES

I.D.C.A.S.

PO Box 1297, Cairo
Tel: 3619/2/3/4
Cable: Idcasal-Cairo

Directors: Ayad El Azzabi (Director General), Dr Eng Abdul Kerim Hilmi (Director of the Technology & Design Dept), Dr Thabet El Gader (Director of the Industrial Institution & Services Dept), Dr Saleh Rouak (Director of Industrial Cooperation Dept), Eng Mrs Faria Zahawi (Director of the Documentation & Industrial Computation Dept), Hicham Habbab (Director of Financial & Administration Dept), Mohamed Hilal (Director of the Industrial Policies & Plans Dept), Eng Hyder Tarabishi (Field Activities Supervisor)

PRINCIPAL ACTIVITIES: Non-profit organisation with the aim of co-ordinating work among Arab States to promote industrialisation.

INDUSTRIAL ESTABLISHMENT FOR SILK & COTTON (ESCO)

Ets Industriel pour la Soie et le Coton

15 Sharia Gawad Hosni, Cairo
Tel: 45280, 50963, 43071

PRINCIPAL ACTIVITIES: Production of cotton yarn and fabrics, wool yarn and fabrics, artificial silk, silk fabrics, knitting wool
Branch Offices: Factories: Mostorod, Tel 866073; Bahtim, Tel 867195
Parent Company: Responsible to the Ministry of Industry

Principal Shareholders: Public sector company

INDUSTRIAL GASES CO

74 Sh El Gomhouria, Cairo
Tel: 913014, 913042, 913163

PRINCIPAL ACTIVITIES: Production of compressed gases, oxygen, acetylene, hydrogen, medical gases and welding electrodes. Carbon-dioxide and dry ice, assembly of fire extinguishing equipment
Branch Offices: Factories: Mostorod, Cairo, Tel 861899; Moharram Bey, Alexandria
Parent Company: Responsible to the Ministry of Industry

Principal Shareholders: Public sector company

INGERSOLL RAND COMPANY

23A Ismail Mohamed Street, Zamalek, PO Box 820, Cairo
Tel: 3415190, 3418927, 3411560, 3415710
Telex: 92711, 23471 IRNEA UN
Telefax: 3403648

Senior Executives: Eng M Medhat Soliman (General Manager), Mohamed Zein (Sales Manager), Hassan El Emary (Admin Manager)

PRINCIPAL ACTIVITIES: Manufacture of air compressors, drilling equipment, water well rigs, building equipment, pumps, etc
Principal Agencies: Mantrac, Pico, Combi Egypt, Shehab Co

INTER NILE MANUFACTURING CO SAE

47 Demashk Street, PO Box 117, Mohandessin, Cairo
Tel: 3490055, 3490375
Telex: 23290 INILE UN

Chairman: I K Sid Ahmed
Directors: J N Nahas (Managing Director), B R G Thomas, A Pons de Vier, Z El Far, P Khoury (Alternate), A Kheir (Alternate)
Senior Executives: S Atwia (Factory Manager), K Seif El Nasr (Marketing Manager), P Khoury (Financial Controller), S Riad (Personnel Officer), R El Abbar (Sales Manager)

PRINCIPAL ACTIVITIES: Manufacture of razor blades and toiletries
Parent Company: The Gillette Company, Boston
Principal Bankers: Chase National Bank, Cairo; Egyptian American Bank, Cairo

Principal Shareholders: Gillette, USA (80%)
Date of Establishment: 1980
No of Employees: 150

INTERNATIONAL AGENCY GROUP (IAG)

8 Abdel Rahman Fahmy St, Garden City, PO Box 315 Mohd Farid, Cairo
Tel: 3553010
Telex: 93127 SEIF UN

Directors: Mohamed Abdel Latif (Managing Director)

PRINCIPAL ACTIVITIES: General representation, procurement agents, business consultancy, general contracting, supply of office and household furniture, interior decoration, etc

INTERNATIONAL CO FOR GUM & CONFECTIONERY

7 Roshdi Pasha St, Apt 3, Roshdi, Raml Alex PO Box 2247, Alexandria
Tel: 840559

Senior Executives: Elie Anid (General Manager)

PRINCIPAL ACTIVITIES: Chewing gum and food manufacturing
Financial Information:

	US$'000
Authorised capital	2,500

Principal Shareholders: Warner Lambert Co, USA (57%)
Date of Establishment: 1980
No of Employees: 100

INTERNATIONAL COMPUTERS LTD

ICL

1 Abu El Mahasin St, El Shazli, Dokki, Cairo
Tel: 3470016
Telex: 22374
Telefax: 3447332

Directors: Eng Walid Gad (General Manager), Eng Samir Ibrahim (Deputy General Manager & Marketing Manager)
Senior Executives: K Merrith (Controller), M Refaai (Account Systems Manager), Eng Mohamed Rotaba (National Sales Manager), M Abdallah (Purchasing Manager), Nasmy Nasralla (Personnel Manager), Mohamed Salama (Business Centre Manager)

PRINCIPAL ACTIVITIES: Computer industry
Branch Offices: Cairo (Head Office) & Alexandria
Parent Company: ICL - UK
Principal Bankers: Egyptian American Bank

Principal Shareholders: International Computers Ltd, London, UK
Date of Establishment: 1938
No of Employees: Egypt Branch: 200

INTERNATIONAL CONTRACTING & TRADING SERVICES CORP

2 El Salsoul St, Garden City, Cairo
Tel: 26826, 222020
Telex: 92486 Malak Un

President: M G Malak

PRINCIPAL ACTIVITIES: General trading and contracting

INTERNATIONAL FINANCE CORP

3 Elbergas Street, Garden City, Cairo
Tel: 25045
Cable: IFCAI
Telex: 93110

PRINCIPAL ACTIVITIES: Banking (representative office)
Parent Company: Head office in Washington, USA

INTERNATIONAL GENERAL SUPPLY CO (GESCO)

47 Ramses St, Cairo
Tel: 78308, 865005

PRINCIPAL ACTIVITIES: Production of concrete mixers, electrical and mechanical installations
Branch Offices: Factories: 67 Horrya Ave, Alexandria, Tel 31160; Midan Ibn el Hakam-Helmieh-el-Zaitous, 1 Solaiman el Halaby St, Cairo

Principal Shareholders: Private company

INTERNATIONAL GROUP

International Co for Commercial Exchanges

8 Kasr El Nil St, PO Box 2210, Cairo
Tel: 750997
Cable: Income
Telex: 92350 Income UN

President: Eng Mohamed Sheta
Directors: Hesham Sheta, Khaled Sheta

PRINCIPAL ACTIVITIES: Holding company for the subsidiary companies listed below
Principal Agencies: Welco Oil, UK; Ruby, India; Doraghwa, Korea; Oberim, Spain; Procercia, Spain; Soprodec, Italy; Lithos, Holland; 3M, USA; Monroe Int, USA; A Debs, Japan; Bulkoil, UK; Triocean, UK; Chimo, Canada; TBS, Canada; MECL, USA; Toyomenka, Japan; Unilever Export, UK; Christian Dior, France; Bristol Myers, USA
Branch Offices: Alexandria, Port Said
Subsidiary Companies: International Co for Commercial Exchanges (Income), (Import of chemicals, foodstuffs, building materials); International Co for Manufacturing & Trading of Perfumery & Cosmetics (Parfico), (Production & trade of perfumery & cosmetics); International Co for Building Investments & Construction (Conetrin), (Investment in housing projects); International Co for Data & Computers (Datacomp), (Import & supply of computers, electronic equipment, visual & microfilm products); International Co for Petroleum Services (Petroserve), (Import & export of crude oil & petrochemicals)
Principal Bankers: Egyptian American Bank, Suez Canal Bank, National Bank of Egypt

Principal Shareholders: Eng Mohamed Sheta
Date of Establishment: 1974
No of Employees: 500

INVESTMENT & FREE ZONES AUTHORITY

8 Adly St, PO Box 1007, Cairo
Tel: 906796, 906804
Cable: Investazon
Telex: 92235 INVST UN

Chairman: Dr Sultan Abu Ali
Senior Executives: Abd El Nasser El Kadeem (Industrial Sector), Ahmed Shawky (Financial & Services Sector), Hassan Affify (Agricultural & Construction), Tawfik Donia (Free Zones Sector), Dr Wahby G Wahba (Research, Information and Promotion), Mahmoud El Sherbini (Legal Affairs), Nour Saiid (General Administration)

PRINCIPAL ACTIVITIES: Development and investment in industrial projects, and promotion of foreign investment in joint ventures

No of Employees: 1,000

ISLAMIC INTERNATIONAL BANK FOR INVESTMENT & DEVELOPMENT

PO Box 180, 4 Adly Street, Massah Square, Dokki, Cairo
Tel: 843936, 843278
Telex: 94248, 94190

Chairman: Ahmad Amin Fouad (Managing Director)
Directors: Saad M Shams El Din, Samir A Oraby, Hussein H Hassan, Ibrahim Wali, Hussein Morsy, Samir H Gaafar, Abdel A A Lokmah, Abdel Hamid El Hagazaly, Mustafa M Moemen, Mohamed Gamea, Mohamed S Eliesh, Said M Emara, Omar A Marie, Mohamed F Hewaidy

PRINCIPAL ACTIVITIES: Islamic banking for investment and development

Date of Establishment: 1981

ITT AFRICA & THE MIDDLE EAST

3 Abu El Feda Street, 13th Floor, Zamalek, PO Box 2034, Cairo
Tel: 3414611
Telex: 93991 ITTEG UN

PRINCIPAL ACTIVITIES: Telecommunications, radar equipment, electro optical products, military communications, electronics, engineered products, civil engineering contracting

JOHNSON WAX EGYPT

20 Wadi El Neal Street, Mohandssine, Cairo
Tel: 3474701, 3474702, 3476883
Telex: 21267 JOWAX UN

Chairman: Mazen Abdel Motaal
Senior Executives: Mostafa El-Halwagy (Managing Director)

PRINCIPAL ACTIVITIES: Manufacture and marketing of household products and industrial cleaners
Parent Company: S C Johnson & Son Inc, USA
Principal Bankers: Misr International Bank
Financial Information:

	1989 US$'000
Authorised capital	4,100
Paid-up capital	4,100
Total assets	15,000

Principal Shareholders: S C Johnson & Son Inc, USA
Date of Establishment: 1979
No of Employees: 100

JOINT ARAB INVESTMENT CORPORATION SAE (JAICORP)

PO Box 121 Orman, 32 Gameat El Doual El Arabia, Giza, Cairo
Tel: 3471361, 3471495, 3471476, 3460477
Cable: Jaicorp Egypt
Telex: 92840, 93567 Jaico UN
Telefax: 3461265

Chairman: H E Mohamed Khalifa Al Youssef (Director Dept of Economic Affairs/Ministry of Foreign Affairs UAE)
Directors: H E Juan Salem (Under Secretary of State/Dept of Finance Abu Dhabi), Khalifa Mohamed El Shamsy (Abu Dhabi Investment Authority), Obaid El Dhahiry (Abu Dhabi Investment Authority), Issa Al Suwaidi (Abu Dhabi Investment Authority), Fouad Gad Khamis (Banque du Caire), Dr Ibrahim Fawzy (Egyptian National Insurance Co), Dr Moheiddin El Ghareeb (Al Shark Insurance Co), Mohamed Said Abu El

Seaoud (Bank of Alexandria), Mrs Afaf Maged (National Bank of Egypt)
Senior Executives: Gamal Mohamed Shata (General Manager), Moustafa Kamel Mourad (Projects Manager), Samir Whdan (Financial Manager), Mohamed Salah Salem (Manager Merchant Banking), Mohamed Moustafa El Behairy (Manager Administration)

PRINCIPAL ACTIVITIES: Investment and merchant banking
Branch Offices: Abu Dhabi
Subsidiary/Associated Companies: Arab Sunley Construction Co; Gypsum Blocks Co (GYPCO); Nile Shoes Co; Joint Arab Co for Hotels & Tourism; Egypt Financial Investment Co
Principal Bankers: National Bank of Egypt, Bank of Alexandria, Banque du Caire, Banque Misr
Financial Information:

	1988/89 US$'000
Loans & advances	41,534
Reserves	556
Deposits	18,078
Authorised capital	50,000
Paid-up capital	50,000
Total assets	80,114

Principal Shareholders: Abu Dhabi Investment Authority (50%), Banque du Caire (8.7%), National Bank of Egypt (8.5%), Egyptian National Insurance Co (11.45%), Al Sharq Insurance Co (3.65%), Bank of Alexandria (6.95%), Banque Misr (6.25%), Egyptian Reinsurance Co (4.5%)
Date of Establishment: 1978
No of Employees: 37

KAFR EL ZAYAT PESTICIDES & CHEMICALS CO

Head Office & Factory, Kafr El Zayat
Tel: 582444, 582761 (Kafr El Zayat), 700435 (Cairo Office)
Cable: Mobidat Kafr Zayat
Telex: 23982 KZ UN

Chairman: Eng Abd El Fatah Abou Zaid
Directors: Salah El Din Namoury (Head of Financial Sector), Kamal El Damaty (Head of Commercial Sector), Younis Abd El Halim (Head of Production Sector), Abd El Salam El Madbouly (Head of Technical Sector)

PRINCIPAL ACTIVITIES: Manufacture of pesticides and chemicals
Parent Company: Responsible to the Ministry of Industry

Date of Establishment: 1957
No of Employees: 800

KHODEIR GROUP

6 Adly Street, PO Box 1057, Cairo 11511
Tel: 910650, 919789

Directors: Mohamed Abdel Halim Khodeir (Managing Director)

PRINCIPAL ACTIVITIES: Import and distribution of office equipment and supplies, paper; also oilfield services, testing equipment and materials, consultancy and design services

KODAK (EGYPT) SA

20 Adly St, Cairo
Tel: 3929399, 3929037
Cable: Kodak Cairo
Telex: 93138 Kodak UN
Telefax: 3931199

Chairman: Farag Mansour
Directors: John R McDermott (Managing Director)
Senior Executives: John D Diffenderfer (Marketing Manager), Michael Simonian (Operations Manager), W T Galal (Finance & Planning Manager)

PRINCIPAL ACTIVITIES: Marketing Kodak photographic products

Parent Company: Eastman Kodak Company
Principal Bankers: National Bank of Egypt, Egyptian American Bank
Financial Information:

	1989/90 E£'000
Sales turnover	25,000
Authorised capital	200
Paid-up capital	200
Total assets	12,300

Principal Shareholders: Eastman Kodak Company
Date of Establishment: 1912
No of Employees: 120

KUWAIT AIRWAYS CORPORATION

4 Talat Harb Street, Cairo
Tel: 747944
Telefax: 747288

Chairman: Ahmad Hamad Al Mishari

PRINCIPAL ACTIVITIES: Air transport

KUWAITI EGYPTIAN INVESTMENT CO SAE

34 Kasr Elnil St, Cairo
Tel: 744572, 754543
Cable: Dasman Cairo
Telex: 22341 REMCO

President: Ezat Abdel Bary
Directors: Mohamed Abdel Halim (Vice President and Managing Director), Ahmed Salem, Youssef El Hassawy, Saleh El Shalfan, Dr Abo Soud El Soda
Senior Executives: Eng Adel Sultan (Assistant Managing Director)

PRINCIPAL ACTIVITIES: Investment company; business consultancy; promotion and development of joint-ventures and companies involved in industry and commerce; real estate investment
Subsidiary/Associated Companies: Kuwaiti Egyptian Co for Shoes and Leather Products SAE; Kuwaiti Egyptian Co for Plastic Pipe 'Eslon Egypt' SAE; Kuwaiti Egyptian Co for Building Materials SAE
Principal Bankers: Arab African International Bank, Cairo
Financial Information:

	US$'000
Authorised capital	25,000
Paid-up capital	23,375

Principal Shareholders: Kuwait Foreign Trade, Contracting & Investment Co, National Investment Bank, Egypt; Misr Insurance Co, Egypt; Alshark Insurance Co, Egypt
Date of Establishment: 1974
No of Employees: 40

LASHEEN PLASTICS INDUSTRIES

22 Nehru St, PO Box 251, Heliopolis, Cairo
Tel: 2587451, 2587452
Cable: Laplinco
Telex: 92623 Lashen Un
Telefax: (202) 2582986

President: Mohamed Lasheen
Directors: Ahmed Lasheen (Managing Director), Sameh Mohsen

PRINCIPAL ACTIVITIES: Manufacture of polypropylene woven sacks, polythene heavy duty sacks and polythene refuse sacks
Associated Companies: Cairo Contracting Co, Abu Dhabi; Crushers Limited, Muscat, Oman, Lasheen Trading & Contracting (Crushers); Cleopatra Hospital, Heliopolis Egypt, Lasheen Plast, Tenth Ramadan City
Principal Bankers: Banque du Caire

EGYPT

Financial Information:

	US$'000
Authorised capital	6,000
Paid-up capital	6,000

Principal Shareholders: Eng Mohamed Lasheen, Eng Ahmed Lasheen, Eng Sameh Mohsen
Date of Establishment: 1975
No of Employees: 450

LLOYDS BANK PLC
PO Box 97, Zamalek, 44 Mohamed Mazhar St, Cairo 11211
Tel: 3415929, 3406437, 3406508, 3418366
Cable: Interloyd, Cairo
Telex: 92344 Lloyd Un, 22400

PRINCIPAL ACTIVITIES: Commercial banking
Branch Offices: City Centre Branch: 48/50 Abdel Khalek Tharwat St, PO Box 218, Cairo; Tel 933384, 911699, Telex 94104 Lloyd Un; Alexandria Branch: 48 Safia Zaghloul St, PO Box 1214, Alexandria, Telex 54435 Lloyd Un

LOTUS CO
PO Box 429, Horia, Heliopolis, Cairo
Tel: 876180
Cable: Lotus
Telex: 93832 Lotus Un

Directors: Adel Kamel Siddiq (General Manager)
Senior Executives: Tariq Omar (Sales Manager)

PRINCIPAL ACTIVITIES: Wholesale and retail, representation agents
Principal Agencies: Brandt, Tecnogas, Calor, Seiko, Sharp
Principal Bankers: Banque du Caire

Principal Shareholders: Private company

MAHMOUD & ABDEL RAZEK ALY & CO
See ALY, MAHMOUD & ABDEL RAZEK, & CO

MANTRAC
10 El Kamel Mohamed Street, Zamalek, Cairo
Tel: 3409429, 3410112, 3410480
Telex: 93280 MTRC UN

Chairman: Youssef Loutfy Mansour (also Managing Director)
Senior Executives: Salem Raafat (Marketing Manager), Amr Azim (VP Marketing), Onsi Nagui (VP Finance), Alastair Petrie (VP Product Support)

PRINCIPAL ACTIVITIES: Import and distribution of heavy machinery and equipment, tyres, construction plant, and water well drilling products
Principal Agencies: Caterpillar; Ingersoll Rand; Michelin

Principal Shareholders: The Mansour Family
Date of Establishment: 1977
No of Employees: 480

MANUFACTURERS HANOVER TRUST CO
El Nasr Bldg/1st Floor, El Nil Street, Giza, PO Box 1962, Cairo
Tel: 727830, 728972
Telex: 21635 Mhtro UN

PRINCIPAL ACTIVITIES: Banking (representative office)

MARATHON PETROLEUM EGYPT
16 Road 253, PO Box 52 Digla, Maadi, Cairo
Tel: 3523102, 3523019, 3523065
Telex: 93695, 22619 MAROL UN
Telefax: 3523174 ext 273

PRINCIPAL ACTIVITIES: Petroleum exploration
Parent Company: US Steel Corp, USA

MCDERMOTT INTERNATIONAL INC (A R E BRANCH)
3 Abu El Feda Street, PO Box 1786, Zamalek, Cairo
Tel: 3402622
Telex: 92082 Jaramac UN

PRINCIPAL ACTIVITIES: Construction of offshore oil production platforms and marine pipelines
Parent Company: McDermott International Inc

MEMPHIS CHEMICAL COMPANY
8 Elsawaah, Amiria, Cairo
Tel: 2593523, 2572107, 2572106
Cable: Memphis Cairo
Telex: 94164 MEMCO
Telefax: 2593523

Chairman: Dr Galal Gorab
Directors: Dr Ragai El Nagar (Production Manager), Dr Salah Abdel Baki (Planning Manager), Dr Mohamed El Rais (Research & Control Manager)
Senior Executives: Dr Hasan Kamel, Dr Ismail Youssef

PRINCIPAL ACTIVITIES: Production of pharmaceuticals and chemicals (methoxsalem, khellin etc)
Branch Offices: Alexandria
Subsidiary Companies: Arab Co for Medicinal Plants; Ibeco International for Pharmaceuticals
Principal Bankers: Banque du Caire
Financial Information:

	1989/90 E£'000
Sales turnover	70,000
Authorised capital	7,000
Total assets	4,600

Date of Establishment: 1940
No of Employees: 1,800

MEMPHIS SHIPPING AGENCY
17 Sharia Sessostris, Alexandria
Tel: 808951, 808400
Telex: 54162, 54502 MEMS UN

PRINCIPAL ACTIVITIES: Shipping agency

Principal Shareholders: Part of the Alexandria Co for Shipping Agencies

MERIDIEN HOTEL
Corniche El Nile St, PO Box 2288, Cairo
Tel: 845444
Cable: Homer Cairo
Telex: 92325 Homer Un
Telefax: (202) 3621927

President: Edouard Speck
Directors: Sherif Hosny (Asst General Manager), Hicham Aidarous (Director of Marketing & Sales)
Senior Executives: Mokhtar Tantawi (Finance Director), Mrs Tamara Barakat (Purchasing Director), Abdel Aziz Shehata (Personnel Director), Mohamed El Naggar (Technical Manager), Mrs Yvette Abdallah (Admin Director)

PRINCIPAL ACTIVITIES: Hotel business
Parent Company: Le Meridien
Subsidiary Companies: Part of Soc des Hotels Meridien (Air France)

Principal Shareholders: Egoth
Date of Establishment: June 1974
No of Employees: 540

MIDDLE EAST PAPER CO (SIMO)
Soc du Papier du Moyen-Orient
37 Kasr el Nil Street, Cairo
Tel: 754596, 752153
Cable: Warkim
Telex: 93816 Simo-UN

Chairman: Chem Y M Youssef
Directors: Sayed Nassar (Technical Manager), Talaat El Zawy (Commercial Manager), Mahmond El Nemr (Financial Manager)

PRINCIPAL ACTIVITIES: Manufacture of cardboard, wrapping paper
Branch Offices: Factory: 4 Bahtim Road, Mostorod, Kalubia
Parent Company: Responsible to the Ministry of Industry
Principal Bankers: Bank of Alexandria, Egypt

No of Employees: 1,500

MISR AIR CONDITIONING MNFG CO SAE
Miraco York
48 El Batal Ahmed Abdel Aziz St, Mohandisseen, Cairo
Tel: 3483369 (5 lines)
Cable: Miraco
Telex: 93100 MIRCO UN
Telefax: (02) 3498124

Chairman: Eng A Barakat (Managing Director)
Directors: Eng H Barakat (General Manager Sales & Contracting), Eng M Labib, Eng S Shalaby (Production Director)
Senior Executives: Eng T Danish (Marketing Director)

PRINCIPAL ACTIVITIES: Manufacture, sales and service of air conditioning equipment
Principal Agencies: Under licence from York, USA
Branch Offices: Heliopolis, Alexandria, Luxor
Principal Bankers: Misr Iran Development Bank
Financial Information:

	1989/90 US$'000
Sales turnover	30,000
Authorised capital	2,785

Principal Shareholders: Misr Iran Bank, Misr Insurance Co, York International
Date of Establishment: 1977
No of Employees: 700

MISR AMERICA INTERNATIONAL BANK SAE
PO Box 1003, 5 El Saraya El Kobra St, Garden City, Cairo
Tel: 3554359, 3554360/3
Cable: MAIBEHLAIR
Telex: 23505 MAIB UN, 23050

Chairman: Dr Mohammad Dakrouri
Directors: Fred Pascher (Managing Director), F Serour (Asst Managing Director)

PRINCIPAL ACTIVITIES: Commercial banking
Branch Offices: 5 branches in Egypt: 68 El Horreya St, Alexandria; 6 Boutros Basha Ghali St, Heliopolis; 81 El Gueish St, Tanta

Principal Shareholders: Bank of American NT & SA, Misr Insurance Co, Development Industrial Bank, Kuwait Real Estate Bank, First Arabian Corporation
Date of Establishment: 1977
No of Employees: 197

MISR CAR TRADING CO
12 Abdel Khalek Sarwat St, Cairo
Tel: 758055, 758116, 745800 (Head Office), 746007 (Import Department)
Cable: Automisr
Telex: 92362 Miscar Un

Chairman: Eng Adel El Serafy
Directors: Youssef El Hayatmy (Commercial Director), Eng Maurice Fouad (Technical Director), Tewfik Ismail (Financial Director)

PRINCIPAL ACTIVITIES: Import, export and marketing of cars, fire fighting vehicles, trucks, trailers, loaders, generators sets, cranes, lorries, motorcycles, bicycles, tyres, technical and electrical spare parts
Principal Agencies: Mercedes-Benz, W Germany; Motokov, Czechoslovakia; Moguer, Hungary; Baribbi, Italy; Spencer, UK; Volvo Loaders, Sweden; Lucas, Hartridge, UK; Blumhardt, Ackerman; Schmitz, W Germany
Parent Company: Responsible to the Ministry of Trade
Principal Bankers: National Bank of Egypt; Banque du Caire

Principal Shareholders: Public sector
Date of Establishment: 1961

MISR CHEMICAL INDUSTRIES CO
1 Sharia Boustan, Cairo
Tel: 43128, 979961, 979867
Cable: Misr Chemico
Telex: 54119 KMISR UN

Chairman: Chem Abdel Moez Okeil
Directors: Eng Abdel Moneim Bibars, Chem Mahmoud Borham, Eng Ahmed Amin Wahba, Eng Fayez El Bouriny, Eng Ibrahim Youssef

PRINCIPAL ACTIVITIES: Production of caustic soda, chlorine and its by-products, soda ash, sodium bicarbonate, hydrogen peroxide, bleaching powder
Branch Offices: Head Office and Factory: El Mex, Alexandria, Tel 38420, 38426/7/8
Parent Company: Responsible to the Ministry of Industry
Principal Bankers: Central Bank; Bank of Alexandria

Principal Shareholders: Public sector company

MISR CO FOR MECHANICAL & ELECTRICAL PROJECTS (KAHROMIKA)
3 Sharia El Seluly, Dokki, Cairo
Tel: 3486488, 3485154
Cable: KAHROMIKA
Telex: 92653 KAHRO UN

Chairman: Eng M S Souidan
Directors: Eng M H Masoud (Vice Chairman), Eng F A Rifaie (Technical Director), Eng A M Zeftawi (Vice Chairman)

PRINCIPAL ACTIVITIES: Execution of mechanical, electrical and industrial projects
Parent Company: National Sector Authority For Construction and Electric Industries (Responsible to the Ministry of Electric Power)
Principal Bankers: Alexandria Bank

Date of Establishment: 1972
No of Employees: 3,700

MISR CO FOR PHARMACEUTICAL INDUSTRIES
92 Mataria St, Mataria, Cairo
Tel: 2572093, 2573865
Cable: Dawamisr
Telex: 21343 MPCI UN

Chairman: Dr Farghaly Farid Hassan
Directors: Dr Kadry Ismail (Research Director), Dr Mervet El Ahawani (Production Director), Dr Hussam Darwish (Commercial Director), Hussein Khafaby (Financial Director), Dr Omar Shawer (Sales Manager), Dr Salah El Gandour (Export Manager), Mahmoud Rostom (Purchasing Manager), Ahmed Fikry (Personnel Manager

PRINCIPAL ACTIVITIES: Production of pharmaceuticals; research and development of new drugs

Principal Agencies: Solco Laboratories, Switzerland; Mycofarm Delft, Holland; Chemie Linz, Austria; Syntex, UK
Branch Offices: Head Office and Labs: 92 Mataria St, Mataria, Cairo Scientific Dept: 34A Kasr El-Nil St, Tel 742101, 754555; Alexandria Branch: 47 Nabi Danial St, Tel 4937370, 4933826
Parent Company: Responsible to the Ministry of Health
Principal Bankers: Banque du Caire

Principal Shareholders: Public sector company
Date of Establishment: 1939
No of Employees: 2,600

MISR CONCRETE DEVELOPMENT CO

21 July St, Cairo
Tel: 750711, 750762
Cable: Misrkrasan
Telex: 92682 Micode Un

Chairman: Eng Salah Hassan
Directors: Ibrahim El Said Ibrahim (Vice President for Financial & Administrative Affairs), Eng Elwy Abdel Razik El Habashi (Vice Chairman for Technical Affairs), Eng Ahmed Samir Abou Arab (Vice Chairman for Technical Affairs), Eng Mohsein Kaddah (Vice Chairman for Technical Affairs), Eng Mostafa Amer (Construction Director)

PRINCIPAL ACTIVITIES: Civil engineers, contractors and consultants
Branch Offices: Sudan Branch: Banque Misr Bldg, Khartoum, PO Box 290, Tel 72027, Telex 517 Micode Iraq Branch: Mahmoud El-Sarraf Bldg, Mafrak El-Karada, PO Box 2161, Alweya Baghdad, Tel 95126, 95127, Telex 2324 Misr Libya Branch: Abu-Zeid Bldg, El-Isteklal St, Benghazi, PO Box 1198, Tel 94956
Parent Company: Responsible to the Ministry of Reconstruction and New Communities
Principal Bankers: Banque du Caire, Cairo; The Arab International Bank, Cairo
Financial Information:

	E£'000
Authorised capital	25,000
Paid-up capital	21,000

Principal Shareholders: State-owned
Date of Establishment: 1938
No of Employees: 9,000

MISR ENGINEERING & TOOLS CO

El Amiriya, Soubrah, Cairo
Tel: 882070, 875471

Directors: Eng Mohamed Rafie Al Serafi (Technical Director), Mahmoud Mounih Mohamed (Commercial Director)

PRINCIPAL ACTIVITIES: Manufacture of dye-cast products and reconditioned tyres
Branch Offices: 33 Kasr El-Nil St, Cairo
Parent Company: Responsible to the Ministry of Industry

Principal Shareholders: Public sector company

MISR EXTERIOR BANK SAE

PO Box 272, Cairo Plaza Building, Corniche El Nil, Cairo
Tel: 778464, 778380
Telex: 94061 UN

Chairman: Mohamed Nabil Ibrahim
Directors: Jose Fabrega Tome (Vice Chairman), Abdulla Abdel Fatah Tayel (Managing Director), Juan Jose Puyol (Managing Director)

PRINCIPAL ACTIVITIES: Commercial banking
Branch Offices: Cairo, Heliopolis, Alexandria
Financial Information:

	E£'000
Authorised capital	14,000
Paid-up capital	14,000

Principal Shareholders: Banque Misr (40%); Banco Exterior de Espana (40%); private shareholders (20%)
Date of Establishment: 1981

MISR FOOD & DAIRY PRODUCTS CO
Soc Misr pour les Produits Laitiers et Alimentaires

26 Sharia El Sawah, Amiria, Cairo
Tel: 869450, 861417

Chairman: Eng Mostafa Sobhi
Directors: Mohamed Ahmed Nooh (Financial & Commercial Director)

PRINCIPAL ACTIVITIES: Production of pasteurized milk, butter, cheese, yoghourt, dried milk, ice cream and cream
Branch Offices: Commercial Dept: 37 Sh Talaat Harb, Cairo, Cable Somlait
Parent Company: Responsible to the Ministry of Industry

Principal Shareholders: Public sector company

MISR FOREIGN TRADE COMPANY

1 Sharia Kasr El Nil, Cairo
Tel: 759966, 759837
Cable: Misr Comex
Telex: 92233; 92782; 92370;

Chairman: Mamdouh M El-Masry
Senior Executives: Mostafa El Ghazzawi (General Manager Planning & Research)

PRINCIPAL ACTIVITIES: Import/export, general trade. Mineral raw materials, coal, paper, paper pulp, sugar, tobacco, etc. Export of clothing, yarn and fabrics, carpets, leather products etc
Branch Offices: Alexandria Office: El Falaki Street
Parent Company: Responsible to the Ministry of Economy & Foreign Trade
Principal Bankers: National Bank of Egypt; Banque du Caire
Financial Information:

	E£'000
Paid-up capital	9,000

Date of Establishment: December 3rd, 1955
No of Employees: 829

MISR HOTELS COMPANY

1 Talaat Harb Square, Cairo
Tel: 3931418, 3936776
Telex: 94074 MISTL UN
Telefax: 3920821

Chairman: Abd El Hamid Fargly Dahis
Directors: Mahmoud Abd El Wahab
Senior Executives: Mrs Yousria Salama

PRINCIPAL ACTIVITIES: Hotel management and establishment of tourist villages centres
Parent Company: Misr Hotels Company
Subsidiary Companies: Egyptrav, Misr Touristic Villages
Principal Bankers: Misr International Bank; Egyptian American Bank; Exterior Bank; Delta International Bank; Banque du Caire; Arab Investment Bank
Financial Information:

	1990
	E£'000
Authorised capital	5,000
Paid-up capital	18,000

Principal Shareholders: Misr Insurance Co; Banque Misr; EGOTH; Misr Hotels Co
Date of Establishment: 1955
No of Employees: 200

MISR IMPORT & EXPORT CO

6 Sharia Adly, Cairo
Tel: 911733, 911217, 911524
Cable: Impexmisr cairo, Toirmique Cairo
Telex: 92251, 92385 impexmisr Cairo

Chairman: Mahmoud Abdel Kader Sabour

PRINCIPAL ACTIVITIES: Import/export, general trade mainly
foodstuffs, also paper, books, pharmaceuticals, furniture and
chemicals, cold storage for meat, fish and poultry
Branch Offices: 5 Salah Salem St, Alexandria, Tel 31400; Port
Said; Suez; also in India; Bangladesh; Sri Lanka; Ethiopria;
Somalia; UAE; Qatar; Bahrain; Oman; Indonesia
Parent Company: Responsible to the Ministry of Trade
Principal Bankers: National Bank of Egypt

Principal Shareholders: Public sector
No of Employees: 1,200

MISR INSURANCE COMPANY

44 A Dokki Street, Giza
Tel: 700158, 700425, 700693
Cable: Tamin
Telex: 93320 MSRIN UN
Telefax: 700428

Chairman: Fathi Mohamed Ibrahim
Directors: Ahmed Zaki Abd El Hadi (Deputy Chairman), Abd El
Khalek Sarwat (Director & General Manager), Dr Abou El
Saoud El Soda (Director & General Manager), Yousry El
Fedawi (Director & General Manager), Dr Mohamed Tolba
Oweeda (Director), Dr Sarwat Badawy (Director)

PRINCIPAL ACTIVITIES: Direct insurance and reinsurance
business
Branch Offices: Cairo Office: 7 Talaat harb St, Cairo, Tel
752600, Telex 92281; Alexandria Office: 66 El Horreya St,
Alexandria, Tel 4827250, Telex 54475; Lower Egypt Office: 26
El Gaish St, Tanta, Tel 333888; Upper Egypt Office: Al
Gomhuria St, Sohag, Tel 323875; Suez Canal Office: Orabi
Square, Ismalia, Tel 20914
Parent Company: Responsible to the Ministry of Trade
Subsidiary Companies: Arab International Insurance Co
Principal Bankers: Banque du Caire, Cairo; Arab International
Bank, Cairo; Midland Bank, London; Chase Manhattan Bank,
New York; Swiss Bank, Zurich; Deutsche Bank, Munich;
Banque Misr, Paris
Financial Information:

	1988/89
	E£'000
Gross premium income	223,844
Paid up capital	17,000
Total reserves	584,055
Total investments	887,921
Total assets	998,804

Date of Establishment: 1934

MISR INTERNATIONAL BANK SAE
MIBANK

14 Alfy St, PO Box 631, Cairo
Tel: 932747, 922053, 922676, 904927, 918907, 931002
Cable: Mibankcai
Telex: 92165 Mib Cai, 92688 Mib Cai, 93384 Mib Cai

Chairman: Sarwat Abdel Ghaffar
Directors: William G Curran (Deputy Chairman), Mahmoud
Mohamed Mahmoud (Vice Chairman, Managing Director), Dr
Abdel Ahad Gamal Eddine, Martin J White, Hussein Mohamed
Amer, Samir Mahmoud Dessouki, Mahmoud Ahmed Roubi

PRINCIPAL ACTIVITIES: All banking activities, foreign exchange
Branch Offices: Alexandria; Cairo: Heliopolis, Kasr El Nil; Maadi,
Glym, Mohandeseen, Guiza, Corniche El Nil, Zamalek
Parent Company: Banque Misr Group, ARE

Principal Shareholders: Banque Misr; First National Bank of
Chicago; Banco di Roma, Luxembourg; UBAF Bank, London;
Europartners (Holding) SA, Luxembourg; Misr Insurance Co;
Mitsui Bank
No of Employees: 456

MISR IRAN DEVELOPMENT BANK

Nile Tower Bldg, 21-23 Giza Street, Giza, PO Box 219 Orman,
Cairo
Tel: 727311
Cable: MIRBANK
Telex: 20474, 22407 MIDB UN
Telefax: 721168

Chairman: Fathi M Ibrahim
Directors: Mohamed El Asfar (Vice Chairman), Dr Al Motaz
Mansour (Managing Director), Hassan Abu Halawa, Abdel
Kader Salem, Dr Ibrahim Mokhtar, Sayed Sherif Razavi,
Siavash Naghshineh
Senior Executives: Dr Al Motaz Mansour (Managing Director),
Dr Ibrahim Moukhtar (General Manager), Mohamed M Aly
(GM & Legal Adviser), Ahmed Abdel Moneim (DGM Head of
Investment Sector), Adel Abou El Magd (AGM Financial
Affairs)

PRINCIPAL ACTIVITIES: Merchant banking, development bank
engaged in the finance and management of Egyptian
development projects in all sectors & providing a full
spectrum of investment & commercial banking services
Branch Offices: Cairo Branch, 8 Adly St, PO Box 666, Cairo, Tel
3911806; and branches in Port Said; Gezira Sheraton Hotel;
Ramada Hotel; Joli Ville Hotel
Associated Companies: Egyptian Aluminium Products Co; Misr
American Consultants Co; Misr Financing Co for Construction
& Building Materials; Misr Iran Air Conditioning Co; Misr Iran
Furniture Co; Misr Iran Hotels Co; Misr Real Estate &
Touristic Investment Co; Egyptian Granite & Marble Co; Misr
Iran Co for Building Materials; Egyptian International
Development & Management Group; Pyramids Paper Mills
Co; Misr Iran Touristic & Office Building Co (Nile Tower); Misr
American Agricultural System Co; International Co for
Blankets & Textiles; Misr Investment Finance Co; Modern
Packaging Products Co; Ariculture & Food Industrial
Investment Co; Ismalia Poultry Co; Bechtel Egypt Co; Misr
American Co for Greenhouses; Misr Compressors
Manufacturing Co; etc
Financial Information:

	1989/90
	E£'000
Profits	7,655
Paid-up capital	77,011

Principal Shareholders: Bank of Alexandria (37.5%); Misr
Insurance Company (37.5%); Bank Melli Iran (12.5%); Bank of
Industry & Mine (12.5%)
Date of Establishment: 27 May 1975
No of Employees: 318

MISR PETROLEUM COMPANY

PO Box 228, 6 Sharia Orabi, Cairo
Tel: 755000, 755023
Cable: Misrpetrol, Cairo

PRINCIPAL ACTIVITIES: Petroleum products, marketing and
distribution (including LPG)
Parent Company: Egyptian General Petroleum Authority
(Responsible to the Ministry of Petroleum)

Principal Shareholders: Public sector company

MISR PHOSPHATE CO

5A El Goheini St, Dokki, Cairo
Tel: 982849, 982826

Chairman: Mahmoud Aly Abou-Elenein
Directors: Mahmoud El Sherif (Financial & Commercial Director)

PRINCIPAL ACTIVITIES: Production of phosphates, mining and exploration

Parent Company: Responsible to the Ministry of Industry

Principal Shareholders: Public sector company

MISR RAYMOND FOUNDATION SAE

20 Haroun St, Dokki, Giza
Tel: 849628, 983718
Telex: 94019 SPECC UN

PRINCIPAL ACTIVITIES: Foundation contractors soils investigation, soils and concrete labs, land and hydrographic surveys, hydrographic surveys

Principal Shareholders: Raymond Int of Delaware, Houston, Texas, USA (49%)

Date of Establishment: 1979
No of Employees: 250

MISR ROMAMIAN BANK SAE

PO Box 35, Zamalek, Cairo
Tel: 3418045, 3414081, 3402795, 3403292
Cable: ROMISBANK
Telex: 93653 MRB, 93854 MRB

Chairman: Essam Eddin Mohamed Al Ahmady

Directors: Samir Mohamoud Dessouky (Deputy Chairman & General Manager), Cristescu Gabriel (Deputy Chairman & General Manager)

Senior Executives: Horia Demian (Deputy General Manager), Imam Hussein Hassan (Manager Cairo Branch)

PRINCIPAL ACTIVITIES: Commercial banking

Branch Offices: Cairo Branch: 15 Abu El Fida Street, Zamalek, Cairo; Heliopolis Branch: 31 Hegaz St, Heliopolis, Tel 2583120, 2592030, Telex 23245; Alexandria Branch: 17 Port Said Street, El Chatby, Alexandria, Tel 5977103, 5964095, Telex 54415; Bucharest Branch: PO Box 1-850, Bucharest, Romania, Fax 40-0-153682

Financial Information:

	1989 E£'000
Total balance sheet	440,027
Total deposits	242,681
Capital & reserves	95,167
Net income	4,855

Principal Shareholders: Banque Misr (51%), Romanian Bank for Foreign Trade (19%), Bank for Agriculture & Food Industry (15%), Investment Bank (15%)

Date of Establishment: 22 February 1977
No of Employees: 97

MISR SHEBIN EL KOM SPINNING & WEAVING CO

Shebin El Kom
Tel: 22514, 22433, 22635
Cable: SHEBINTEX
Telex: 23908 SHEB UN, 54163 SHEB UN

Chairman: Eng Salah Mohamed Abd El Salam

PRINCIPAL ACTIVITIES: Production of cotton yarn
Principal Agencies: Shebin El Kom, Egypt
Parent Company: Responsible to the Ministry of Industry
Financial Information:

	E£'000
Authorised capital	25,000
Paid-up capital	15,716

Principal Shareholders: Public sector company
Date of Establishment: 1959
No of Employees: 10,739

MISR SPINNING & WEAVING CO

Mehalla El Kubra
Tel: 3000, 3564, 3762, 3881
Cable: GHAZL
Telex: 92040, 54009 Ghazl UN

PRINCIPAL ACTIVITIES: Production of cotton yarn and fabrics, wool yarn, and fabrics, medical cotton, ready made garments
Branch Offices: Cairo: 1097 Cornish El Nil Ave, Garden City, Tel 29134, 29084; Alexandria: 37 Sidi El Mitwalli Street, Tel 28028, 25538
Parent Company: Responsible to the Ministry of Industry
Principal Bankers: Banque Misr

Principal Shareholders: Public sector company
Date of Establishment: 1927
No of Employees: 33,000

MISR TRAVEL & SHIPPING CO

1 Sharia Talaat Harb, PO Box 1000, Cairo
Tel: 3930077, 3930032, 3928215
Telex: 22666, 20771 MRSHIP UN
Telefax: 3924440

Chairman: Mohamed Samir Halawa

PRINCIPAL ACTIVITIES: Travel and shipping agency
Branch Offices: 45 in Egypt
Parent Company: Responsible to the Ministry of Tourism
Financial Information:

	1990 E£'000
Authorised capital	13,104

Principal Shareholders: Public sector company
Date of Establishment: 1934
No of Employees: 2,711

MISR-HELWAN SPINNING & WEAVING CO

Kafr El Elou, Helwan
Tel: 38030, 39180
Cable: Somso Helwan

Directors: Eng Ahmed El Baz (Works Director), Farouk Hamama (Commercial Director)

PRINCIPAL ACTIVITIES: Textile manufacturing (spinning, weaving, finishing, embroidery, ready-made garments)
Parent Company: Responsible to the Ministry of Industry
Principal Bankers: Alexandria Bank; Misr Bank

Principal Shareholders: Public sector company

MOBIL OIL EGYPT SA

1097 Corniche El Nil Street, Garden City, Cairo
Tel: 3554850, 3554860
Telex: 92091 Mobil UN

Senior Executives: Samir Moufid Mohamed (Marketing Manager), Andre Kemula (Planning & External Areas Manager), Hassan Abul Nafa (Relations Manager), Adel Hashish (Accounting & Finance Manager), Louis William (Legal Affairs Manager)

PRINCIPAL ACTIVITIES: Marketing and distribution of petroleum products

MODERN BUILDING SYSTEMS

23 El Montazah Street, Heliopolis, Cairo
Tel: 2444128, 2428048, 2442456
Telex: 21842 MBS UN
Telefax: 2466452

Chairman: Bahaa Makkawi
Senior Executives: Eng Mohsen Matareed (Technical Director), Eng Alaa Tawfik (Mnfg & Purchasing Director), Eng Adel Samaha (Construction Director), Mrs Hoda El Kadi (Chief Accountant & Admin Manager), Tarek Fahmy (Sales Director)

PRINCIPAL ACTIVITIES: Design and construction of pre-engineered steel buildings; general contracting; industrial and commercial projects
Principal Bankers: Mohandes Bank; Export Development Bank; Arab African Bank
Financial Information:

	1990 E£'000
Sales turnover	6,000
Authorised capital	200
Paid-up capital	200
Total assets	1,748

Principal Shareholders: Bahaa Makkawi
Date of Establishment: 1979
No of Employees: 65

MOHANDES BANK
30 Ramses Street, PO Box 2778, Cairo
Tel: 748659, 751973, 751708
Telex: 93950, 93391 MB UN

Chairman: Ahmad Ali Kamal
Directors: Mohamed Abdel Salam Badr El Din (Managing Director), Ahmad Zaki Helmi, Abdel Aziz Ahmad Lokma, Mohamed Ezzat Adel, Ahmad Aly Mazen, Abdel Aziz Ahmad El Said

PRINCIPAL ACTIVITIES: Commercial banking

Date of Establishment: 1979

MORGAN GRENFELL & CO LTD
1 Latin America St, Garden City, Cairo
Tel: 548018, 557479
Cable: Morganile
Telex: 92390 Morgn Un

Senior Executives: Dr Khalil Nougaim (Middle East Representative)

PRINCIPAL ACTIVITIES: Bank representative office
Parent Company: Morgan Grenfell & Co Limited, London

Date of Establishment: 1974

NASR CITY CO FOR HOUSING & REHABILITATION
Youssef Abbas St, Nasr City, Abbassia, Cairo
Tel: 835544

Senior Executives: Essam El Din Abd El Hady (Managing Director), Bakr El Essawi (Construction Director), Mohamed Nour El Din Hassanen (Accounting Director), Mohamed El Galad (Technical Director), Abd El Razik El Barachy (Technical Director), Amwar Amin Kamali (Law Director), Nashwa Yehya Twefik (Public Relations Director)

PRINCIPAL ACTIVITIES: Housing and construction
Parent Company: Responsible to the Ministry of Housing and Reconstruction

Principal Shareholders: Public sector company
No of Employees: 300

NASR GENERAL CONTRACTING CO
Hassan M Allam
7 Sh Abdel Khalek Tharwat, PO Box 43, Cairo
Tel: 758327, 758214, 758316
Cable: CONTRALAM
Telex: 92292 COLAM UN
Telefax: 755811

Chairman: Samir Hassan Allam
Directors: Eng Youssef El-Taher (Vice Chairman), Eng Salama Salem (Vice Chairman), Eng Hosny E Hanafy (Head of Construction Building Sector & Member), Mamdouh Hassan (Head of Administrative Sector & Member), Said Farid (Head of Financial Sector & Member), Eng Mostafa Ramadan (Head of Construction Building Sector & General Manager Alexandria), Eng Magdy Ibrahim (Head of Projects Sector)
Senior Executives: Eng Kamal Faheem (Head of External Activities Sector), Eng Tamim Naguib (Head of Bridges Sector), Eng Mohamed Misry (General Manager Buildings), Eng Samir Mattar (General Manager Utilities)

PRINCIPAL ACTIVITIES: Contracting, civil engineering and construction
Branch Offices: Alexandria: Hassan Allam St, Smouha, Alexandria
Parent Company: Responsible to the Ministry of Housing
Principal Bankers: Banque du Caire, Cairo; Egyptian National Bank, Cairo
Financial Information:

	1988 E£'000	1989 E£'000
Sales turnover	207,070	223,329
Profits	1,000	1,000
Authorised capital	28,000	28,000
Paid-up capital	28,000	28,000
Total assets	108,945	128,650

Principal Shareholders: Public sector company
Date of Establishment: 1936
No of Employees: 10,300

NASSER SOCIAL BANK
35 Kasr El Nil St, Cairo
Tel: 979030, 41836, 414191
Cable: Nasrban Cairo
Telex: 92754

PRINCIPAL ACTIVITIES: Interest-free savings and investment bank for social and economic development, pension and social security business
Branch Offices: Branches throughout Egypt
Parent Company: Responsible to the Ministry of Trade

No of Employees: 1,000

NASSIB-TORCOM, ETS, & FILS
PO Box 582, 15 Emad El-Din Street, Cairo
Tel: 911800, 911102
Cable: Nascom Cairo

PRINCIPAL ACTIVITIES: Import and distribution of lighting equipment, building materials, electrical appliances, and printers' requirements
Principal Agencies: Mazda, Pirelli Mattresses, Faber Venetian Blinds, Kaymet Anodised Ware, Fidenza Vetraria Glass Blocks

Principal Shareholders: Private company

NATIONAL BANK FOR DEVELOPMENT (NBD)
5 El Borsa El Gedida St, PO Box 647, Cairo
Tel: 3923528
Cable: Bandevelop
Telex: 20878 NBD UN
Telefax: 2936719

Chairman: Mohamed Zaki El Orabi
Directors: Hassan Morsy Salama, Adel Abdel Kader, Mohamed Aly A Hegab, Abdel Rahman Sayed Abdel Nabi, Adel Hussein Ezzy, Nabil Hussein Mohamed, Mohamed Said Kamel, Salah El Din A Hamid, Dr Ahmed Mahmoud Omar, Maher Mohamed Aly, Fathalla Amin Zayed, Abdel Rahman Abdel Tawab
Senior Executives: Sarwat Hassan Aly (GM Regional Banks), Said Barakat (Legal Advisor), Abdel Aziz M Salem (GM Foreign Affairs), Wadie Labib (GM Investment), Mansour Mohamed Mansour (GM Main Office), Helmy Nadiem (GM Regional Banks), Saleh El Desouky (GM Credit)

PRINCIPAL ACTIVITIES: Commercial and investment banking, participation in development projects

Branch Offices: Sarwat Br; Bab El Louk Br; Helwan Br;
Zamalek Br; El Azhar Br; Kasr El Nil Br; Heliopolis Br; El
Borsa Br; Alexandria Br; Sawah Br; and Islamic Br

Subsidiary Companies: 16 National Banks for Development: El
Gharbia NBD; El Giza NBD; El Kalioubia NBD; Port Said NBD;
Assiut NBD; El Sharkeya NBD; El Beheira NBD; El Minia
NBD; El Fayoum NBD; Kafr El Sheikh NBD; Sohag NBD;
Sinai NBD; Damietta NBD; Ismailia NBD; El Menoufia NBD;
Qena NBD

Financial Information:

	1988	1989
	E£'000	E£'000
Total income	5,278	6,140
Profits	4,421	5,140
Authorised capital	50,000	50,000
Paid-up capital	37,500	37,500
Total assets	1,117,175	1,203,041

Principal Shareholders: National Bank for Investment; National
Bank of Egypt; Banque Misr; Bank of Alexandria; Banque du
Caire; Misr Insurance Co; El Shark Insurance Co; National
Insurance Co; Arab Contractors Co; Suez Canal Authority;
Egyptian General Petroleum Corp; Nasser Social Bank; Credit
Foncier Egyptien; Arab Land Bank; Suez Canal Bank;
Mohandes Bank; Industrial Development Bank; General
Authority for Social Insurance; Principal Bank for
Development & Agricultural Credit; Canal Co for Shipping
Agencies; Egyptian Reinsurance Co; Alexandria Co for
Shipping Agencies; Al Ahram Investment Co; Chamber of
Commerce Association; and other privately owned companies
and individuals

Date of Establishment: 1980

No of Employees: 1,005

NATIONAL BANK OF ABU DHABI

Nile Tower Bldg, 21 Giza Street, Giza, Cairo
Tel: 722768, 724640, 722989
Cable: Banzabi
Telex: 22734 Bnzab UN

Senior Executives: Abdul Aziz Al A'Assar (Regional Manager
Egypt Branches)

PRINCIPAL ACTIVITIES: Investment banking
Branch Offices: Alexandria, Cairo, Port Said
Parent Company: Head office: PO Box 4, Abu Dhabi, United
Arab Emirates

Principal Shareholders: Government of the Emirate of Abu
Dhabi
Date of Establishment: 1975 in Egypt
No of Employees: 190 in Regional Management & Egypt
branches

NATIONAL BANK OF EGYPT

24 Sherif St, Cairo
Tel: 3924175, 3924143, 3924184
Cable: National
Telex: 92238, 92832, NBE UN
Telefax: 3931778, 3923531, 3923550, 3936481

Chairman: Mohamed Nabil Ibrahim
Directors: Mahmoud Abdel Aziz (Deputy Chairman), Abdel
Kerim M Abdel Hamid (Deputy Chairman), Aly Chahine (Senior
Executive General Manager), Gamil Balbaa (Senior Executive
General Manager), Mohamed Madbouly (Senior Executive
General Manager), Saad M Azzam (Specialist Member)
Senior Executives: Essam El Tohami (General Manager
Research), Mrs Afaf Maged (General Manager International),
Ahmed Deiae El Din (General Manager Finance), Salma
Mahrous Saber (General Manager Marketing), Abdel Salam
Abdel Hakam (General Manager Main Branch), Baher El
Kerdani (General Manager Investment Certificates), Mostafa
Kewan (General Manager Credit), Farook Mehanna (General
Manager Legal), Nagy Youssef (General Manager Data
Processing)

PRINCIPAL ACTIVITIES: Commercial banking
Branch Offices: 278 throughout Egypt (Cairo 91, Alexandria 32,
Canal Zone & Sinai 43, Lower Egypt 52, Upper Egypt 58) and
2 branches in London, UK
Subsidiaries/Associates Companies: Commercial Internationl
Bank (Egypt); Credit International d'Egypte; National Societe
Generale Bank; Suez Canal Bank; Societe Arabe
Internationale de Banque; Development and Housing Bank;
Bank of Commerce & Development (Al Tegareyoon);
Alexandria Commercial & Maritime Bank; National Bank for
Development; Export Development Bank of Egypt; Egyptian
Saudi Finance Bank; Multitrade Holding SA, Luxembourg

Financial Information:

	June 1990
	E£'million
Deposits	15,004
Loans & advances	8,619
Reserves	193
Surplus for distribution	48
Authorised capital	100
Paid-up capital	100
Total assets	23,191

Principal Shareholders: State owned (100%)
Date of Establishment: 1898
No of Employees: 8,165

NATIONAL BANK OF GREECE

PO Box 127 Zamalek, 11211 Cairo
Tel: 3406610, 3411772
Cable: Ethnobank
Telex: 92825 NATCA UN
Telefax: 3418530

Senior Executives: George Caracostas (Branch Manager)

PRINCIPAL ACTIVITIES: All banking operations in foreign
currencies
Parent Company: Head office in Athens, Greece

Date of Establishment: 1978

NATIONAL BANK OF PAKISTAN

7 Arab Socialist Union Bldg, Corniche El Nile, PO Box 168,
Cairo
Tel: 750795
Telex: 92527 Millat UN

PRINCIPAL ACTIVITIES: Commercial banking
Parent Company: Head office in Pakistan

NATIONAL CO FOR CEMENT PRODUCTION

Head Office and Factory El Tabbin, Helwan
Tel: 39020, 39027

Chairman: Dr Ahmed Hassanein Sheraf El Din (also Managing
Director)

PRINCIPAL ACTIVITIES: Production of sulphate resisting
cement and portland cement
Parent Company: Responsible to the Ministry of Housing and
Reconstruction

Principal Shareholders: Public sector company

NATIONAL INSURANCE CO OF EGYPT

PO Box 446, 33 El-Nabi Denial Street, Alexandria
Tel: 4920712
Cable: INSURANCE
Telex: 54212 Nice UN

Chairman: Ahmed Fouad El Ansary
Directors: Ezat Abdel Azeem, Abd El Halim Moussa, Ahmed
Talaat Sherif

PRINCIPAL ACTIVITIES: All classes of insurance and
reinsurance
Branch Offices: 41 Kasr El-Nil St, Cairo, Tel 914644, Telex
92372 and Branches in Qatar, Kuwait, Abu Dhabi and France

Principal Bankers: Banque du Caire, Cairo; Bank of Alexandria; National Bank of Egypt; Misr Bank; Chase National Bank; Suez Canal Bank; Egyptian American Bank

Principal Shareholders: State owned
Date of Establishment: 1900
No of Employees: 2,560

NATIONAL METAL INDUSTRIES CO

18 Sh Emad El Din, PO Box 1673, Cairo 11001
Tel: 748721, 753940, Works 698085
Cable: Namtin Cairo
Telex: 21624 SFNMT UN
Telefax: Cairo 765937, Works 698192

Chairman: Chem Said A Elhadidy
Directors: Mohammad El Khalaifa Ahmad (Commercial Director), Eng A Shatilla (Technical Director), Rizkalla Shokralla (Factories Director)

PRINCIPAL ACTIVITIES: Production of steel, reinforcing bars, wire, metal casting
Branch Offices: Works: Abu Zaabal, Kalyoubiyah, Tel 698428, 698718
Parent Company: Metallurgical Industries Corporation (Responsible to the Ministry of Industry)
Principal Bankers: Bank of Alexandria, Cairo
Financial Information:

	1989/90 E£'000
Authorised capital	30,000
Paid-up capital	11,000

Principal Shareholders: Public sector
Date of Establishment: 1949
No of Employees: 2,800

NATIONAL PAPER CO

El Tabia Alexandria
Tel: 5601810, 5601811, 5601813, 5601712
Cable: Quertass
Telex: 54458 Un Tabia

Chairman: Mahmoud Borham El Malky
Directors: Galal Gamaa (Engineering Manager), Moustafa Mahdy (Commercial Manager), Mechael Shenouda (Technical Manager), Osman Abdel Manem (Finance Manager), Al Hosseiny Salama (Production Manager)

PRINCIPAL ACTIVITIES: Manufacture of wrapping paper, printing and writing paper, kraft paper, board
Branch Offices: Cairo Office: 19 Adly St, Tel 3939624; Alexandria Office: 44 Saad Zaghloul St, Tel 4832210
Parent Company: Responsible to the Ministry of Industry
Subsidiary Companies: Meharren Bey Mill, Tel 4221303, 4221004
Principal Bankers: Bank Misr

Principal Shareholders: Public sector company
Date of Establishment: 1934
No of Employees: 2,500

NATIONAL PLASTICS CO

15 Sharia Emad El Din, Cairo
Tel: 914315, 914500

Directors: Eng Moh Moh Ibrahim Barghous (Factories Director), Eng Moh Moh Lasheen (Giza Factory Director), Eng Hussein Abdel Hassan (Financial & Commercial Director)

PRINCIPAL ACTIVITIES: Production of domestic plastic goods, toys and games, bottles and jars, laminates, artifical leathers, automobile batteries
Branch Offices: Factories: Subra El Kheima, Cairo; El Giza, Cairo; Gabbary, Alexandria
Parent Company: Responsible to the Ministry of Industry

Principal Shareholders: Public sector company

NATIONAL SOCIETE GENERALE BANK SAE

10 Talaat Harb Street, PO Box 2664, Cairo
Tel: 770291, 747396, 747498, 774940, 770529
Cable: Nasgebca Cairo
Telex: 22307, 93893 Nasog
Telefax: 776249

Chairman: Mahmoud Abdel Aziz
Directors: Martial Lesay (Deputy Chairman), Mohamed Madbouly, AHmed Wagdy Ibrahim, Mostafa Fouad Kiwan, Jean Marie Beaux, Jacques Chevaillot
Senior Executives: Ahmed Nabil El Menoufy (General Manager), Francois Saintigny (General Manager), Mohamed E Alam El Din (Deputy General Manager)

PRINCIPAL ACTIVITIES: Investment and merchant bank
Branch Offices: Semiramis Branch; Mohandessin Branch; Heliopolis Branch
Financial Information:

	1989 E£'000
Total income	44,839
Net profit	2,265
Authorised capital	50,000
Paid-up capital	15,000
Total assets	454,785

Principal Shareholders: National Bank of Egypt (51%), Societe Generale (49%)
Date of Establishment: 1978

NCR EGYPT LTD

Nile Tower Bldg, 21-23 Giza Street, Giza, Cairo
Tel: 729784, 729794, 729866, 729664, 729778
Telex: 23211 NCEL UN

Directors: A A Hedayat (Area Managing Director - Egypt, Sudan & Jordan)

PRINCIPAL ACTIVITIES: Marketing of NCR electronic data processing equipment, electronic cash registers, accounting machines, office printing, supplies and maintenance
Principal Agencies: Mohawk Data Science Corp, Addressograph-Multigraph Ltd
Branch Offices: Field Engineering & Systemedia Div: 21 Talaat Harb St, Cairo, Tel 754055, 758846; Telex 92092 NCR UN; Alexandria Branch: Saad Zaghloul Square, Tel 4929265, 4914711
Parent Company: NCR Corporation, Dayton, Ohio
Principal Bankers: Chase National Bank; Banque du Caire

Principal Shareholders: NCR Corporation, Maryland
Date of Establishment: 1936
No of Employees: 200

NEFERTITI TRADE & EXPORT CO

32 Sharia Mrowa, Dokki, Cairo
Tel: 56558

PRINCIPAL ACTIVITIES: Distributors of automobiles
Principal Agencies: Honda

NILE BANK SAE (THE)

35 Ramses Street, Cairo
Tel: 756296, 743674, 741417, 751105, 764435
Cable: Nilbangypt Cairo
Telex: 22344, 20785, 20825 BANIL UN
Telefax: 756296

Chairman: Issa Ismail El Ayouty
Directors: Eng Hamed Abdel Moneim El Zoghby, Anton Saidhom Ibrahim, El Sayed Ibrahim El Ayouty, Anton Ibrahim Saidhoum, Drr Eng Ahmed Moustafa Abdel Warith, Eng Fowzi Rizk El Fata, Mrs Aleya Issa El Ayouty, Mohamed Fouad Abdel Moein, Dr Ashraf Abdel Latif Ghorbal, Eng Ismail Baligh Sabri, Eng Hanna Fahim Bakhoum, Counsellor Ahmed Mohamed El Hefny, Saad Mohamed El Sherbiny, Moufid Kamal El Deeb, Eng Amer Aref Ahmed Kamel

EGYPT

Senior Executives: Mrs Aleya Issa El Ayouty (Managing Director), Hamed Moustafa El Ghammaz (General Manager), Mrs Iffat Saleh Badawy (Finance Director), Dr Mohamed Aboud (Marketing Director)

PRINCIPAL ACTIVITIES: Commercial banking
Branch Offices: 15 branches in Egypt
Subsidiary Companies: Nile Co for Agricultural Industries; Nile Co for Printing & Packaging; Nile Co for Reconstruction; Nile Co for Agriculture & Food Industries; Nile Co for Manufacturing Building Materials; Nile Co for Metal Industries; Nile Co for Fodders & Chickens; Nile Co for Projects & Trade; Nile Co for Tourism; Modern Arab Co for Timber Industries; Cairo Investment & Development Co; Mansoura Poultry Co; Cairo Radiology Center; Nile Co for Chemical Industries & Packaging; Nile Co for Investment & Economic Development
Principal Bankers: Chemical Bank, New York; Hambros Bank, London; Swiss Bank Corporation, Zurich; UBAF, Commerzbank, Frankfurt
Financial Information:

	1989
	E£'000
Total income	69,208
Net profit	17,389
Authorised capital	US$40 million
Paid-up capital	US$40 milion

Principal Shareholders: 100% Egyptian Nationals
Date of Establishment: 1978
No of Employees: 655

NILE CO FOR THE EXPORT OF AGRICULTURAL CROPS

19 Sharia El Goumhouria, Cairo
Tel: 919544, 919546, 919541, 919237, 919798
Cable: NILEXPORT CAIRO
Telex: 22241, 23426 NILEX

Chairman: Fawzi Abd El Shahid Barsoom
Directors: Mohamed Nassar (Marketing General Manager), Abd El Aaty Ahmed Aly (Administrative General Manager), Ibrahim Lufy Yasseen (General Financial Manager), Farouk El Aassar (General Export Manager)

PRINCIPAL ACTIVITIES: Export of agricultural crops and products (rice, potatoes, groundnuts, fruits and vegetables, medical plants, onions, flowers)
Branch Offices: Alexandria; Port Said
Parent Company: Responsible to the Ministry of Economy & Foreign Trade

No of Employees: 1,000

NILE GENERAL CO FOR REINFORCED CONCRETE (SPICO)

5 Sharia 26 July, PO Box 719, Cairo
Tel: 915322, 914089

Chairman: Eng Adly Ayoub Ghattas
Directors: Eng Fathy Ayoub Ghattas (Vice-Chairman), Eng Mansour Hassan Mansour (Technical Director)

PRINCIPAL ACTIVITIES: Manufacture of reinforced concrete
Parent Company: Responsible to the Ministry of Housing and Reconstruction

NILE HILTON HOTEL (HILTON INTERNATIONAL CO)

Tahrir Sq, Cairo
Tel: 740777, 750666
Cable: Hiltels Cairo
Telex: 92222 Hiltls UN

Directors: Roman O Rickenbacher (General Manager)

PRINCIPAL ACTIVITIES: Hotel business
Parent Company: Hilton International Company

Principal Shareholders: Wholly-owned subsidiary of TWC

NILE MATCH COMPANY

19 Sharia El Sahafa, PO Box 1508, Manshia, Alexandria
Tel: 800588, 800367
Cable: Sonit-Alexandria

PRINCIPAL ACTIVITIES: Production of safety matches
Branch Offices: Cairo Office: 49 Sharia Abdel Khalek Sarwat, Tel 901905, Cable Matchnil Cairo; Factory: Mahmoudia Canal St, Moharram Bey, Alexandria, Tel 32886
Parent Company: Responsible to the Ministry of Industry

Principal Shareholders: Public sector company

NILE OIL & DETERGENTS CO SAE

33 Sh Orabi, PO Box 2221, Cairo
Tel: 751574, 978836/37
Cable: Sunlight Cairo

Chairman: Dr Abed El Aziz Azab
Directors: Abd El Fattah El Adely (Managing Director), Mories El Gaiar (Finance Sector Director), Mahmoud Mohammed Saleh (Marketing Sector Director), Abd El Rehim Youssef (Technical Director)

PRINCIPAL ACTIVITIES: Production of detergents, soaps, edible oils, hydrogenated vegetable margarine, cosmetics, toothpaste, sodium silicade, sulphoric acid
Parent Company: Responsible to the Ministry of Industry

Principal Shareholders: Public sector company
Date of Establishment: 1946

NILE PLASTICS & INDUSTRIAL CO

6 Aly Eltorgoman Boulac St, Cairo
Tel: 971012
Cable: Saladinari

Chairman: Eng Salah D Azhari
Senior Executives: M Magdy (Sales Manager)

PRINCIPAL ACTIVITIES: Plastic products; custom moulders; mould fabricators
Principal Bankers: Banque du Caire

Principal Shareholders: S D Azhari; M Azhari; E Azhari; Mrs N M Moharram
Date of Establishment: 1959

NILE STORES OF EGYPT

44 Sherif Pacha St, PO Box 123, Cairo
Tel: 979387, 974331, 973509, 43421
Cable: Etcalex Cairo
Telex: 385 Etcal Un; 93994 Lacte Un

Directors: Mrs Nimet Alexane (Managing Director), Robert Canaan (General Manager)

PRINCIPAL ACTIVITIES: Importers, agents and manufacturers' representatives; also manufacturers under licence or in joint ventures
Principal Agencies: Nestle Corp, Lab Delagrange, Richardson-Merrell, Swiss Serum & Vaccine Institute, Lab Egic, SEITA, R Twining & Co, Gillette, Nordisk Insulin Lab, Leo Pharmaceutical Products, Beiersdorf AG, BV Chemische Industrie 'Katwijk', Pharmacie Centrale de France, Ets Givaudan Lavirotte et Cie, Nicholas Lab Ltd, Byron Chemical Co, C H Boehringer, Saint-Gobain Industries, Industrias Quimicas Y Tartaricas, Zimmer Orthopaedic Ltd, A/S Syntetic, Fisons Ltd, Richards & Appleby Ltd, Cogecot SA, Colgate Palmolive, Wiggins Teape
Branch Offices: Alexandria: 3 Aly Amin Maher St, PO Box 1183 Alexandria Port Said: 5A Ramses and El Tor St, Port Said Assiut: 4 Nefertiti St Mansoura: 9A Aly Pacha Mubarak St, Touril Area

Principal Bankers: Bank of America; Lloyds Bank International; Suez Canal Bank

Principal Shareholders: Cherif E Alexane

NILE VALLEY AVIATION
14 Damascus St, Heliopolis, Cairo
Tel: 2580161, 2575703 (Head Office), 2914255/66/77/88 (Airport Office)
Telex: 92792 NIVA UN
Telefax: 2565966

President: Tarek El Tambouly
Senior Executives: Hosam Awaddlla

PRINCIPAL ACTIVITIES: Handling, aviation services
Branch Offices: Cairo International Airport Office: Tel 2914255, Fax 2907681; Luxor International Airport Office: Tel 384875, Fax 382370; Paris Office: Tel 47890323, Fax 47890674
Subsidiary Companies: Niva Aviation Services
Principal Bankers: Misr America International Bank

Principal Shareholders: Tarek El Tambouly, Mrs Fatma El Tambouly, Mrs Amina El Tambouly
Date of Establishment: April 15th, 1976
No of Employees: 75

NIMOS ENGINEERING COMPANY
1282 Immobilia Bldg, 26 Sherif Street, Cairo
Tel: 74822, 745714, 745573
Telex: 22366 Nimos UN

Senior Executives: Hatem N Mostafa (Managing Director)

PRINCIPAL ACTIVITIES: Manufacturers' representatives, supply of engineered equipment, electrical and agricultural equipment, transportation, building materials; also agricultural services and supplies

NORTHROP INTERNATIONAL
46 Bahgat Ali Street, Apt 20, Zamalek, Cairo
Tel: 3411226, 3410053
Telex: 20506 NORCA UN, 21973 AERCO UN

Senior Executives: William J Oakes (Corporate Regional Manager)

PRINCIPAL ACTIVITIES: Design, development, manufacture and support of aerospace and defense aviation equipment

NOVELTY STORES CO
Benzion Rivoli and Ades
25 Sharia Sherif, Cairo
Tel: 46118, 46110

Chairman: Mohamed Abu Hamila
Directors: Abdel Fattah Mahmoud Hamed (Commercial Director), Salahedin Abdel Moti Gafar (General Director)

PRINCIPAL ACTIVITIES: Production and distribution of consumer goods
Parent Company: Responsible to the Ministry of Supply

Principal Shareholders: Public sector company

NUCLEAR POWER PLANTS AUTHORITY
PO Box 8191, Masaken, Nasr City
Tel: 836877, 837236
Telex: 93580 HQNPP UN, 92157 ENPPA UN

Chairman: Dr A F El Saiedy

Directors: Dr H R Heggy, Dr E M Hassan, M Eldeeb, Eng M M Ashour
Senior Executives: A Sheha (Finance Manager), F Yousef (Marketing Manager), A El Rafei (Personnel Manager), S B Abdel Hamid (Research Manager)

PRINCIPAL ACTIVITIES: Nuclear power station

Date of Establishment: 1976
No of Employees: 400

OFFSHORE INTERNATIONAL SA
PO Box 1997, Cairo
Tel: 853500, 854081, 854178
Cable: Offdrill Cairo
Telex: 92322 Offduil UN

PRINCIPAL ACTIVITIES: Offshore drilling contractor

ORIENT LINEN & COTTON CO
111 Tarik Mustafa Kamel, Ras El Soda, Alexandria
Tel: 866404, 866950, 867519
Cable: Linorient
Telex: 54074 Orlin UN
Telefax: 203-869936

Chairman: Ahmed Rashad Abdou
Directors: Eng Nashat Helmy (Plant Director)

PRINCIPAL ACTIVITIES: Production of linen yarn, cotton yarn, cotton, silk and nylon fabrics, bed linen and households products, terry towels
Parent Company: Responsible to the Ministry of Industry
Principal Bankers: Bank Misr, Alexandria; Bank of Alexandria
Financial Information:

	1990
	E£'000
Sales turnover	50,000
Profits	5,000
Authorised capital	7,000
Paid-up capital	2,000
Total assets	35,000

Principal Shareholders: Public sector company
Date of Establishment: 1962
No of Employees: 4,500

OTIS ELEVATOR CO (EGYPT) SAE
11 Dr Mohamed Mandour Street, Nasr City, Cairo
Tel: 3465220, 3467507
Cable: Lyndentree Cairo
Telex: 92970 OTIS UN

Chairman: Evelio E Gil (also Managing Director)
Directors: Imam Abbas (Finance Director), Jacques Lalo, Hassan Kamel
Senior Executives: Samir Hendawy (Zone Operations Manager), Salah A'Hakeim (Adminsitration Manager), Sami Asaad (Technical & Quality Manager)

PRINCIPAL ACTIVITIES: Elevator manufacturing, installing and servicing
Branch Offices: Alexandria; Port Said; Assiut; Tanta; Mansourah
Parent Company: United Technologies, USA
Principal Bankers: Egyptian American Bank; Banque du Caire et de Paris
Financial Information:

	1989
	US$'000
Sales turnover	7,600
Authorised capital	500
Paid-up capital	500

Principal Shareholders: Otis Elevator Company, USA
Date of Establishment: 1955
No of Employees: 360

PAINTS & CHEMICAL INDUSTRIES CO

1 Sh El Masaneh, El Kubba, Mataria, Cairo
Tel: 871468, 868980
Cable: Bakim

Chairman: Chem Ibrahim Adel Mahmoud Zein El Din
Directors: Eng Chafik Samy Tadross (Factories Director), Eng Abdel Fatah Taha El Tanbouby (Commercial Director), Eng Sayed Abou El-Eneen Askalany (Planning & Production Research Director)

PRINCIPAL ACTIVITIES: Production of paints, varnishes and lacquers, animal charcoal, rice, oil, printing inks
Branch Offices: Cairo Office: 165 Sh Mohamed Farid, Tel 914144
Parent Company: Responsible to the Ministry of Industry

Principal Shareholders: Public sector company

PAPER CONVERTING CO (VERTA)

42 Sharia Mehatet El Souk, Bacous, Alexandria
Tel: 5700939, 5701938, 5708325, 5703717, 5701327
Cable: Verta Alexandria
Telex: 54392 Verta UN
Telefax: 5700429

Chairman: Chem Abdel Aal Atwan
Directors: Eng Adel El Shinawy (Engineering Director), Mohamed Shaheen (Commercial Manager), Rafaat Mekawy (Financial Manager), Nagib Sadaka (Administration Manager), Chem Mohamed Nafady (Planning & Project Director)
Senior Executives: Eng Abdel Halim Rehab (Corrugated Box Plant Manager), Ahmed Sabry (Sales Manager), Shafik Barakat (Purchasing Manager)

PRINCIPAL ACTIVITIES: Paper converting for all types of corrugated boxes, stationery, tabulating machines forms, cardboard, waxed paper, cellophane, laminated and aluminium foil, polyethylene, clay coated and flint paper, polythene containers, and tubes for the textile industry
Branch Offices: Corrugated Box Plant, Kafr El Zayat Ghorbiya District
Parent Company: Responsible to the Ministry of Industry
Principal Bankers: Bank of Alexandria; Bank Misr; Banque du Caire
Financial Information:

	1990
	E£'000
Sales turnover	107,737
Profits	6,012
Authorised capital	10,276
Total assets	22,112

Principal Shareholders: State-owned
Date of Establishment: 1935
No of Employees: 2,505

PARSONS BRINCKERHOFF/SABBOUR

35 Abdel Moheim Riad St, Mohandessin
Tel: 710232
Telex: 21161 SAPBI
Telefax: 3615039

Chairman: Mohamed Salah El Din Hegab
President: Mohamed Maher El Sadek
Senior Executives: Tawfik H Nawar (Manager Admin & Finance)

PRINCIPAL ACTIVITIES: Consulting engineers
Parent Company: Sabour Associates; Parsons Brinckerhoff International
Principal Bankers: Commercial International Bank, Cairo

Principal Shareholders: Parsons Brinckerhoff Int, New York, USA (50%); Sabour Associates; Cairo, Egypt (50%)
Date of Establishment: 1979
No of Employees: 120

PEAT MARWICK HASSAN & CO JOINT MANAGEMENT CONSULTANTS SAE

72 Mohd El Din Abou El Ezz St, Mohandisseen, Cairo
Tel: 3495127, 3495128, 708058, 709718
Telex: 93796 HHCO UN

PRINCIPAL ACTIVITIES: Management consultancy services, audit and taxation
Associated Companies: Hazem Hassan & Co (Public Accountants)

PEPSI COLA INTERNATIONAL

20A Road 10, PO Box 51, Maadi, Cairo
Tel: 3505607, 3505156, 3516034, 3516057
Telex: 92691 PEPSI UN

PRINCIPAL ACTIVITIES: Soft drinks, Pepsi Cola products

PETROLEUM CO-OPERATIVE SOCIETY

Soc Co-Operative des Petroles

94 Sharia El Eini, Cairo
Tel: 551800, 551900
Cable: Copetrole Cairo
Telex: 92230

Chairman: Mahmoud Rizk Eguez
Directors: Eng Mohamed Abdo Saad (Operations Manager)

PRINCIPAL ACTIVITIES: Petroleum products distribution service and filling station operators, marine service and Lube oil
Branch Offices: 23 Tahir Sq, Alexandria, Tel 4935720/8/9
Parent Company: Egyptian General Petroleum Corporation (Responsible to the Ministry of Petroleum)
Principal Bankers: Misr Intl Bank, Cairo

Principal Shareholders: Public sector company

PETROLEUM DEVELOPMENT SERVICES CORPORATION

36 Kambees St, Dokki, Guiza, PO Box 1955, Cairo
Tel: 700077/79
Cable: Pidias
Telex: 22355 Pds Um

President: Fadl El Dandarawy
Directors: Abdallah El Dandarawy, Galal Fakhr El Din

PRINCIPAL ACTIVITIES: Refining; marketing crude oil and petroleum products; technical services and consultancy
Subsidiary Companies: International Petroleum Consultants Company; Petroleum Development Services for Refining Co
Principal Bankers: Chase National Bank, Egypt; Chase Manhattan Bank, Switzerland

Principal Shareholders: Fadl El Dandarawi & Associates
Date of Establishment: 1969

PETROLEUM PIPELINES COMPANY

Mostorod, PO Box 1104, Cairo
Tel: 869019, 861366
Cable: Petlines, Olive Gardens
Telex: 92068

PRINCIPAL ACTIVITIES: Transport of petroleum products, pipelines Suez-Mostorod (Cairo) Helwan, Alexandria Kafr El Dawar
Parent Company: Egyptian General Petroleum Authority (Responsible to the Ministry of Petroleum)

Principal Shareholders: Public sector company

PFIZER EGYPT SAE

47 Ramses St, PO Box 2357, Cairo 11511
Tel: 741022, 741103, 741474, 766486
Cable: Pfizer Cairo
Telex: 92403 Pfzer UN
Telefax: (202) 767305

Chairman: Dr M M Attia

Directors: T D Granger (Managing Director & Deputy Chairman)

Senior Executives: M El Shamy (Finance Manager), Dr A R Shaheen (Pharmaceutical Div Manager), S Sharara (Animal Health Div Manager), M S Roushdy (Marketing Manager), A Amin (Materials Manager), Dr M Khatab (Production Manager), T Salem (Manpower Development Manager), J H Orphanides (Technical Manager), Dr A Gaber (Medical Director), A H Dawood (Corporate Affairs Director)

PRINCIPAL ACTIVITIES: Manufacture, distribution and sale of Pfizer pharmaceutical and animal health products, sales of Pfizer chemical products

Principal Agencies: Egyptian Co for Trading Drugs (ECTD); Middle East Chemicals Ltd (MEC)

Branch Offices: Alexandria: 3 Zancarole Street

Parent Company: Pfizer Corporation, New York, USA

Principal Bankers: National Bank of Egypt

Financial Information:

	1989 E£'000
Sales turnover	52,092
Profits	1,838
Authorised capital	10,000
Paid-up capital	5,270
Total assets	40,995

Principal Shareholders: Pfizer Corporation (60%), Local shareholders (40%)

Date of Establishment: 1961

No of Employees: 500

PHARMACEUTICAL PACKING & OPTICAL CO

47 Sharia Madkour, Industrial District, Abbassia, Cairo

Tel: 836144, 821669, 826453

Cable: Planet

Telex: 92931 Haby UN

Chairman: I A Wafa

Directors: Sobhi El Afany (Planning Manager), M Naeim (Production Manager), Said Mohsen (Financial Manager)

PRINCIPAL ACTIVITIES: Production of all sorts of packings; plastic crates, plastic film, paper, board, tin, aluminium, etc; optical lenses and frames; hospital and house appliances; moulds for plastic processing

Parent Company: Responsible to the Ministry of Health

No of Employees: 2,000

PHILLIPS PETROLEUM COMPANY (EGYPT BRANCH)

PO Box 63, 32 rue Lumumba, Bab Sharki, Alexandria

Tel: 4938554, 4938558, 4938562

Cable: Philalexia

Telex: 54066 PPCO UN

Telefax: 4938559

Senior Executives: Gerald W Berk (Manager), Said El Salmy (Deputy General Manager), T G Hilten (Engineering Manager), Fred Ineh (Geological Manager), K R Kass (Geophysical Manager)

PRINCIPAL ACTIVITIES: Exploration and production of oil

Branch Offices: 29 Abul Feda Street, Zamalek, Cairo, Tel 3410678, 3400420, Telex 92748 PPRS UN, Fax 3410678

Parent Company: Head office: Bartlesville, Oklahoma, USA, Telex 492455

Principal Shareholders: Phillips Petroleum Co, USA

Date of Establishment: 1963

PORT SAID METAL WORKS CO (MOG)

95 El Gomhoreya St, PO BOx 1899, Cairo

Tel: 930515, 838734

President: Mohamed Kamel

Partners: Ahmed Mohamed Kamel (Manager), Amr Mohamed Kamel (Manager), Khaled Mohamed Kamel (Manager)

PRINCIPAL ACTIVITIES: Manufacture of washing machines, sheet metal works, steel furniture & stainless steel catering equipment, display refrigerating cabinets, industrial refrigerators, turnkey tenders for hotels, hospitals and supermarkets

Branch Offices: 2 Factories: 10th Ramadan City; and Cairo Nasr City Industrial Estate

Principal Bankers: Banque du Caire, El Mohandiseen Bank, Cairo

Principal Shareholders: Private company

Date of Establishment: 1961

PRICE WATERHOUSE

Suite 19, 3 Bahgat Aly St, Zamalek, Cairo

Tel: 3400052, 3405122, 3400586

Telex: 23432 PW UN

PRINCIPAL ACTIVITIES: Management, financial, tax and audit consultancy

Principal Shareholders: Price Waterhouse, New York (25.5%)

Date of Establishment: 1983

No of Employees: 25

PROJECTS & INVESTMENTS CONSULTING CO (PICO)

3 Shagaret El Dor Street, Zamalek, Cairo

Tel: 3415915, 3411207, 3418743

Telex: 92735 TAG UN, 22116 DIAB UN

President: Dr Kamel Tawfik Diab

PRINCIPAL ACTIVITIES: Manufacturers' representatives, supply of heavy machinery and industrial equipment, power equipment, chemicals

Principal Agencies: FMC; Ingersoll Rank; Dresser Swaco; Vetco; Amoco; Portakamp; Meco; BJ Hughes; Rockwell; Gearhart Geodata

RAFIDAIN BANK

PO Box 239 Orman, 114 Tahrir Street, Dokki, Cairo

Tel: 715608, 715628

Cable: Rafdbank

Telex: 22502 Rafdbank UN

PRINCIPAL ACTIVITIES: Commercial banking

Parent Company: Head office in Baghdad, Iraq

RAMSES HILTON HOTEL

1115 Corniche El Nil, Cairo

Tel: 744400, 758000, 777444

Telex: 94260 Hiram UN

PRINCIPAL ACTIVITIES: Hotel business

Branch Offices: Nile Hilton, Corniche El Nil, Cairo, Tel 750666, 740777, telex 92222 Hiltls Un; Hilton International Luxor, Tel 758075

RAYCHEM MIDDLE EAST INTERNATIONAL INC

8 Midan Haiet El Tadris St, PO Box 330, Dokki, Cairo

Tel: 710250, 702723

Telex: 94308 Rakem UN

Senior Executives: Dr Mohd El Sayed Nofal (Manager Egypt)

PRINCIPAL ACTIVITIES: Supply of products to the petroleum industry, electrical, engineering, telecommunications and military sectors

RED SEA PHOSPHATE CO

PO Box 1421, 4 Mohamed Hamed St, Dokki, Cairo

Tel: 700212, 700193

Cable: Saphosco Cairo

Telex: 93850 Safos UN

Chairman: Eng M Talal El Din Abd El Telil

PRINCIPAL ACTIVITIES: Production of phosphates, mining and
exploration
Branch Offices: Cairo and Quena
Parent Company: Mining & Refractory Industries Corporation
(Responsible to the Ministry of Industry)

Principal Shareholders: Public sector company
Date of Establishment: 1908
No of Employees: 2,700

ROYAL BANK OF CANADA
3 Abou El Feda Street, Zamalek, Cairo
Tel: 405972, 408115
Telex: 92725 Rocar UM

PRINCIPAL ACTIVITIES: Banking (representative office)
Parent Company: Head office in Montreal, Canada

RUDOLPH CHAKERT CO FOR PUMPS
See CHAKERT, RUDOLPH, CO FOR PUMPS

SABA & CO
Isis Bldg, 7 Lazghli St, Garden City, PO Box 380, Cairo
Tel: 32294, 27257
Cable: Profession Cairo

PRINCIPAL ACTIVITIES: Chartered accountants and
management consultants, industrial property
Branch Offices: Lebanon; Cyprus; Bahrain; Egypt; Iraq; Jordan;
Kuwait; Libya; Morocco; Oman; Qatar; Saudi Arabia; Syria;
United Arab Emirates; Yemen

SANTA FE INTERNATIONAL (EGYPT) INC
2 Saray El Gezira St, Zamalek, PO Box 341, Cairo
Tel: 3411599, 3410771, 3411025, 3404099
Cable: Santafe Cairo
Telex: 92266, 22049 SNTF UN

Senior Executives: Ali Awad (Vice President & General
Manager)

PRINCIPAL ACTIVITIES: Drilling contractors, supply of heavy
equipment and transportation, rigs and personnel to oil
companies

Principal Shareholders: A subsidiary of Santa Fe International
(USA)

SAUDI EGYPTIAN CONSTRUCTION CO
PO Box 145, Cairo
Tel: 749779, 757477
Telex: 92526 UN
Telefax: 772944

Chairman: Mohamed Abdallah Al Sharief
Directors: Eng Mohamed Abdel Hamed Al Toody (Vice
Chairman)
Senior Executives: Abdel Moneim Attia (General Manager)

PRINCIPAL ACTIVITIES: Construction and real estate, general
contracting
Branch Offices: Alexandria and Assiout
Subsidiary Companies: Saudi Egyptian Building Co, 17 Ismail
Mohamed St, Zamalek, Cairo
Principal Bankers: National Bank of Egypt, Suez Canal Bank,
Arab African International Bank
Financial Information:

| | 1988 |
	E£'000
Sales turnover	25,600
Net profit	5,000
Authorised capital	50,000
Paid-up capital	50,000
Total assets	162,000

Principal Shareholders: Government of Egypt (50%),
Government of Saudi Arabia (50%)
Date of Establishment: 1975

SAUDI EGYPTIAN INVESTMENT & FINANCE SAE
9 Talaat Harb St, Cairo, Egypt
Tel: 740533, 769533
Cable: Secfinance
Telex: 92566 Secfi UN

Chairman: Mohamed Mahmoud Nosseir
Senior Executives: Sh Abdul Latif M A Al Khaznadar (Managing
Director)

PRINCIPAL ACTIVITIES: Finance for joint Saudi Egyptian
industrial projects; syndication and undertaking
Principal Bankers: Banque du Caire; Bank of Credit &
Commerce Misr; National Societe Generale; Egyptian
American Bank; Mohandes Bank

Principal Shareholders: Saudi Development & Commercial Co
WLL (Saudi Arabia); Al Chark Insurance Co (Egypt); National
Insurance Co (Egypt)
Date of Establishment: May 1976

SCHLUMBERGER LOGELCO SA
13 Syria Street, Mohandesin, Cairo
Tel: Cairo 651474, 802943
Telex: 92046 Logel UN

PRINCIPAL ACTIVITIES: Oil service comany

SCIENTIFIC SERVICES
145 Mohamed Farid Street, PO Box 1902, Cairo
Tel: 908414, 715450, 481424
Cable: Consulserv
Telex: 93039 SAADY UN

Chairman: Mohamed El Saady (also General Manager)
Directors: Mrs Farida El Saady
Senior Executives: Al Hussain Maklad

PRINCIPAL ACTIVITIES: Commercial representation and
technical agency for manufacturers of scientific and
laboratory equipment, sales, installation and maintenance
Principal Agencies: Pye Unicam, MSE Scientific Instruments,
Corning Medical, Griffin & George, J J Lloyds Ltd, Feedback
Instruments Ltd, ABMTM (package dealer), Fosselectic Co,
Transfer Technology (package dealer)
Branch Offices: 2 Ebn Sobiah Street, Alexandria; Sales &
Service Dept in Cairo; 20 Shihab Street, Medinat Mohandesin,
Cairo
Principal Bankers: Lloyds International; Misr Bank; National
Bank of Egypt

Date of Establishment: 1974
No of Employees: 30

SHELL WINNING NV
19 Aziz El Masry Street, Boktor Square, Heliopolis, Cairo
Tel: 694421, 693467, 692090, 692113
Cable: Shell Helio
Telex: 93431 SHELW UN

Senior Executives: T A Heggy, P R Anderson, D R Scoffham

PRINCIPAL ACTIVITIES: Oil exploration
Principal Agencies: BADR Petroleum Company
Parent Company: Shell International Petroleum (The
Netherlands)
Principal Bankers: Egyptian American Bank

Principal Shareholders: Shell International Petroleum
Date of Establishment: 1/5/1979
No of Employees: 150

SHEPHEARDS HOTEL

Corniche El-Nil St, Garden City, Cairo
Tel: 3553800, 3553900
Cable: Shepheards Cairo
Telex: 21379 SHEPOT UN

Chairman: Enan Galaly
Directors: Soren Grasto

PRINCIPAL ACTIVITIES: Hotel business
Principal Agencies: Scandinavia Management Co
Branch Offices: Palestine Management Co
Principal Bankers: Bank of Credit & Commerce, Cairo

Principal Shareholders: Enan Galaly
No of Employees: 1,000

SIDLEY, AUSTIN & NAGUIB

12 Midan El Sheikh Youssef, Garden City, Cairo
Tel: 3540608
Telex: 21014 SAN UN

Chairman: Gamal M Naguib
Senior Executives: Frederick W Taylor (Managing Director), Dr
Ashraf A Ghorbar (Senior Consultant)

PRINCIPAL ACTIVITIES: Legal consultants

Principal Shareholders: Sidley, Austin Co, Chicago, Illinois, USA
(50%)
Date of Establishment: 1982
No of Employees: 40

SINAI MANGANESE CO

1 Sharia Abdel Salaam Aref, Cairo
Tel: 970395, 970397

Chairman: Hussein Abdel Abu Youssef
Directors: Eng Foued Hussein Shalaby (Technical Director),
Ahmed Mahmoud Al-Kanawaty (Commercial Director)

PRINCIPAL ACTIVITIES: Manganese mining and exploration;
production of metals and alloys
Parent Company: Responsible to the Ministry of Industry

Principal Shareholders: Public sector company

SOC ARABE INTERNATIONALE DE BANQUE SAE

PO Box 124, 56 Gamet El Dowal El Arabia St, Mohandesseen,
Giza
Tel: 3499460, 3499464, 3499463
Cable: SOARINBANK Mohandesseen
Telex: 22087 SBANK UN, 92693 SOBANK UN
Telefax: 3603487

Chairman: Dr Hasan A Zaki
Directors: Aly Dabbous Ahmed Yehia, El Sayed Tageldin, Dr
Abul Seoud El Soda, Mansour Ibrahim Mansour, Abdel Laatif
Al Kib, Dr Omar Al Zawawi, Mohammad S Al Din Nour, Fathi
A Hassan, Kamel M Raouf, Hassaballah M Kassem,
Mohamed El Teir
Senior Executives: Hisham El Shiaty (General Manager), Omar
Abdel Halin (Deputy General Manager), M I Ragab (Assistant
General Manager)

PRINCIPAL ACTIVITIES: Commercial and investment banking
Branch Offices: Cairo Branch: 10 Abdel Salam Aref St, PO BOx
2673, Cairo; Al Azhar Branch, Cairo; Alexandria Branch
Financial Information:

	1988/89 US$'000
Total deposits	87,875
Profits	2,320
Authorised capital	16,000
Paid-up capital	16,000
Total assets	191,365

Principal Shareholders: Compagnie Arabe de Financement
International (49%); National Bank of Egypt (5.2%); Misr

Insurance (20.3%); Arab Contractors Investment Company
(17.3%); Individuals (8.2%)
Date of Establishment: 1976
No of Employees: 143

SOC DE BIERE PYRAMIDES

2 Sharia El Sarwat, PO box 88, Giza, Cairo
Tel: 982722, 982673, 982914
Cable: Tabira

PRINCIPAL ACTIVITIES: Production of malt and beer
Parent Company: Responsible to the Ministry of Industry

Principal Shareholders: Public sector company

SOC DES SUCRERIES ET DISTILLERIES D'EGYPTE

12 Sharia Gawad Hosny, PO Box 763, Cairo
Tel: 749077, 749158
Cable: El Sukka Misr

PRINCIPAL ACTIVITIES: Production of sugar, molasses,
alcohol, carbon dioxide, perfumery, cosmetics, paper pulp
Branch Offices: Alexandria Office: 11 Tarik Gamal Abdel
Nasser, Tel 4920258
Parent Company: Responsible to the Ministry of Industry

Principal Shareholders: Public sector company

SOC EGYPTIENNE D'ENTREPRISES

Moukhtar Ibrahim

199 26 July Street, Agouza, Giza, PO Box 2263, Cairo
Tel: 3471507/9, 3417119, 3471529, 3448712/6
Cable: Moukhtarim Cairo
Telex: 22971, 92013 Mktrm UN

President: Eng Attef Zeid
Directors: Eng Sobhi Labib (VP for Sites Technical Affairs),
Hussein Ghoniem (VP for Administrative Affairs), Eng Fawzi
Khattab (VP for Technical Affairs), Eng Farouk Gobran
(Member of Board for Technical Affairs)

PRINCIPAL ACTIVITIES: Civil contrators for waste water
disposal, potable water, industry, public buildings, roads,
bridges, land reclamation, electric power and housing projects
Branch Offices: In Egypt: Alexandria, Tanta, Damietta, Suez,
Ismailia, El Menia, Assiut, Sohag, Kena, Aswan; In Algeria:
Algiers, Ennabba, Wahran
Parent Company: Under the supervision of the Ministry of
Development, New Communities, Housing & Utilities
Principal Bankers: Banque du Caire, Banque Misr, National
Bank of Egypt, Misr International Bank, Arab International
Bank
Financial Information:

	E£'000
Authorised capital	35,000
Paid-up capital	20,170

Principal Shareholders: State owned
Date of Establishment: 1936
No of Employees: 8,300

SOC EGYTIENNE DE PUBLICITE (SEP)

24 Zakaria Ahmed St, Cairo
Tel: 744166
Cable: Annonce
Telex: 92475 Tahrir
Telefax: 776399

Chairman: Samir Ragab
Directors: Khadr Abdel Salam (General Manager Al Tahrir
Printing & Publishing House), Mahmoud Rasheed (General
Manager Societe Egyptienne de Publicite), Edward Attia (Asst
General Manager), Samira Khalil (Foreign Dept Manager)

PRINCIPAL ACTIVITIES: All kinds of advertising; television,
radio, press, posters, cinema, etc. Market research, public
relations

Principal Agencies: Strategies Int, France; Overseas, UK
Branch Offices: Alexandria Office: 1 Dr Ahmed Abd El Salam St,
Tel 4927366; Ismailia; Port Said
Parent Company: Al Tahrir Printing & Publishing House
Subsidiary Companies: SOP-NEON-United Distribution
Principal Bankers: First National City Bank; Bank of Greece;
Banque du Caire; Misr Bank
Financial Information:

	1989 £E'000
Sales turnover	15,000
Paid-up capital	26
Total assets	10,200

Principal Shareholders: Al Tahrir (The Holding Company)
Date of Establishment: 1949
No of Employees: 760

SOC EL NASR D'ENGRAIS ET D'INDUSTRIES CHIMIQUES SAE

El Nasr Fertilizers & Chemical Industries Co SAE

PO Box 1179, Immobilia Bldg, 26 Sharia Sherif Pasha, Cairo
Tel: 3932033, 3938186, 3938264, 3938145
Cable: Semadco-Cairo
Telex: SMADO 92609 UN
Telefax: 02-3935790

Chairman: Eng Sedky Ghoneim
Senior Executives: Acc Hamdy Mohamed Meshref (Head
Commercial Affairs Sectors)

PRINCIPAL ACTIVITIES: Production of calcium nitrate,
ammonium sulphate, heavy chemicals, urea fertilizers, and
ammonium nitrate
Branch Offices: Factories: Attaka, Suez, Tel 328881/3, Telex
66002; Talkha, Tel 327505, Telex 23682; Alexandria office, 23
Tahrir Square, Tel 4823490, Fax 4835121
Parent Company: Responsible to the Ministry of Industry
Principal Bankers: Bank of Alexandria, Cairo

Principal Shareholders: Public sector company
Date of Establishment: 1946
No of Employees: 13,000

SOC GENERALE EGYPTIENNE DE MATERIEL DE CHEMINS DE FER (SEMAF)

Ein Helwan, Cairo
Tel: 782177, 782358, 782623, 782625
Telex: 92364 ORI UN

Chairman: Eng Twakol El Maghraby
Directors: Dr Eng Lotfy Melek (Technical Manager), El Sayed
Amin (Financial Manager)

PRINCIPAL ACTIVITIES: Manufacture of railway equipment and
materials
Branch Offices: Ein Helwan, Cairo
Principal Bankers: Bank of Alexandria, Bank Misr, National
Bank of Egypt

Principal Shareholders: Public sector company
Date of Establishment: 1955
No of Employees: 3,960

SOC INDUSTRIELLE MOHARREM PRESS SAE

Canal Mahmoudieh (Rive Sud), Alexandria
Tel: 76682/5
Cable: Mohapress
Telex: 54386 Moha UN

Chairman: Taher Bishr Moustafa
Directors: Omar Hindi

PRINCIPAL ACTIVITIES: Packaging and offset printing,
manufacture of carton boxes (for packaging industrial and

consumer goods); gummed paper; waterproof paper; heat
sealing paper; playing cards; micro flute; corrugated boxes
Parent Company: Responsible to the Ministry of Industry
Subsidiary Companies: Printing Center, Cairo
Principal Bankers: Bank of Alexandria

Date of Establishment: 1885
No of Employees: 3,000

SOCIETE GENERALE

9 Talaat Harb Street, PO Box 2590, Cairo
Tel: 3937957, 3932346
Telex: 92512 SGCAI
Telefax: 3932888

Senior Executives: Regional Delegate Egypt/Yemen/Saudi
Arabia

PRINCIPAL ACTIVITIES: Banking (representative office)
Parent Company: Head office in Paris, France

SONAT OFFSHORE SA

143 Road 270, Part 4, PO Box 352, New Maadi, Cairo
Tel: 3520269, 3521543, 3520783
Telex: 22322 Sonat UN

PRINCIPAL ACTIVITIES: Offshore drilling constractors

SPECIALISED CONTRACTING & INDUSTRIES CO

20 Haroun Street, Dokki, Cairo
Tel: 983500
Telex: 94019 SPECC UN

Directors: Eng Mahmoud Osman Ahmad Osman

PRINCIPAL ACTIVITIES: Contracting, precast concrete works,
soil research and land reclamation

SQUIBB EGYPT

17 Studio Misr St, PO Box 4, Pyramids, Giza, Cairo
Tel: 856384, 853716
Telex: 92522 SQUIBB UN

PRINCIPAL ACTIVITIES: Pharmaceutical manufacturing
Financial Information:

	US$'000
Authorised capital	4,600

Principal Shareholders: E R Squibb & Sons Inc, USA (100%)
Date of Establishment: 1976
No of Employees: 220

STANDARD BUSINESS SUPPLIES

PO Box 2529, Cairo
Tel: 901253, 855433
Cable: Business-Cairo
Telex: 92437 Tagaud UN; 93980 Group UN

Chairman: Abdul Ghani El Ajou
Directors: Dr Sami Sibaie (Managing Director)

PRINCIPAL ACTIVITIES: Manufacture of office and business
machine supplies; paper conversion
Principal Bankers: Bank of Credit and Commerce Int; Chase
National Bank (Egypt) SAE

STATE BANK OF INDIA

15 Kamel Al Shinawy Street, Garden City, Cairo
Tel: 3543504, 3542522
Telex: 93068 SBICA UN

Senior Executives: R Ram Mohan (Representative)

PRINCIPAL ACTIVITIES: Banking (representative office)
Parent Company: Head office in Bombay, India

SUEZ CANAL BANK

11 Sabry Abou Alam Street, PO Box 2620, Cairo
Tel: 751033, 751066, 751215
Cable: BANCANAL
Telex: 22391, 93852 SCB UN

Chairman: Ahmed Fouad (Managing Director)
Directors: Hekmat Sayed Ahmed Rizk, Ahmed Zaki Abdel Hady, Tag Abdel Rehim Mahmoud, El Sayed Sabri Hassan Ghaith, Hassan Ibrahim Abu Halawa, Ahmed Kamal Shawki, Eng Mohamed Ezzat Adel, Elsayed Ahmed Enaba, Eng Abdel Aziz Ahmed Lokma
Senior Executives: Mohamed Abdulla El Sherif (Managing Director), Moustafa Fayez Hablas (General Manager)

PRINCIPAL ACTIVITIES: Commercial banking
Branch Offices: Alexandria, Suez, Port Said, Ismailia, Maadi, Heliopolis, Dokki, Mohandessin, Giza, Tanta

Principal Shareholders: Arab International Bank, Banque Misr, Bank of Alexandria, National Bank of Egypt, Banque du Caire, Suez Canal Authority, Misr Insurance Co, Arab Contractors Co, others
Date of Establishment: 1978

SUEZ CEMENT COMPANY

Nile Bank Bldg, 35 Ramses Street, PO Box 2691, Cairo
Tel: 741608, 740084
Telex: 93630 SUCEM UN

Chairman: Ahmed A Shaker (Managing Director)

PRINCIPAL ACTIVITIES: Manufacture of cement and building materials
Branch Offices: Plants in Suez and Qattamia

SUEZ GULF PETROLEUM CO (GAPCO)

1097 Corniche El Nil St, Garden City, PO Box 2400, Cairo
Tel: 31883, 26097
Cable: Pamentoil Cairo
Telex: 92053 Gapco; 92248

PRINCIPAL ACTIVITIES: Exploration and production of oil
Parent Company: General Egyptian Petroleum Authority (Responsible to the Ministry of Petroleum)

Principal Shareholders: General Egyptian Petroleum Authority; Amoco (USA)

SUEZ OIL PROCESSING COMPANY

15 Sharia Nabil El Wakkad, Dokki, Cairo
Tel: 814544, 809516
Cable: Petro Suez Cairo
Telex: 92058

PRINCIPAL ACTIVITIES: Oil refining and production of petrochemicals
Branch Offices: Suez, Tel 3903, 3555
Parent Company: Egyptian General Petroleum Authority (Responsible to the Ministry of Petroleum)

Principal Shareholders: Public sector company

SUMITOMO BANK LTD

Immobilia Bldg, 26 Sherif Street, Cairo
Tel: 755765, 772609
Cable: Banksumit Cairo
Telex: 92470 Sumbk

PRINCIPAL ACTIVITIES: Banking (representative office)
Parent Company: Head office in Osaka, Japan

Date of Establishment: October 1975

SWISS BANK CORPORATION

PO Box 142 Orman, 3 Ahmad Nessim Street, Giza, Cairo
Tel: 727005, 729384
Cable: SUIBANK CAIRO
Telex: 92469 SBCET UN
Telefax: 726603

Senior Executives: Haig Croubalian (Resident Representative)

PRINCIPAL ACTIVITIES: Banking (representative office)
Parent Company: Head office in Basle, Switzerland

Date of Establishment: 1975

TANTA FLAX & OIL CO

Head Office, Mit Hebeish El Baharia, Tanta
Tel: 24455, 22484, 24871
Cable: Teflaco-Tanta
Telex: 93226 TAFCO UN

Chairman: Dr Hosny Mohamed Moawad
Directors: Abd El Salam Raslan (Commercial Director)

PRINCIPAL ACTIVITIES: Production of flax, flax-seed oil, ropes, twine, particle board
Branch Offices: Cairo Office: 40 Talaat Harb Street, Cairo, Tel 745613, 745622; Alexandria Office: 22 El Horria Ave, Tel 34838
Parent Company: Responsible to the Ministry of Industry
Principal Bankers: Bank of Alexandria, Alexandria

Principal Shareholders: Public sector company

TANTA OIL & SOAP CO
Soc Tanta des Huileries et Savonneries

23 Sharia Kasr El Nil, Cairo
Tel: 970410

Chairman: Mohamed Reda El Wataty

PRINCIPAL ACTIVITIES: Production of cottonseed oil and cake, margarine, soap, pure glycerine, stearine, hydrogenation of oil, animal fodder
Branch Offices: PO Box 15, Tanta, Tel 3300, 3046, Cable Amoud Tanta; Fodder factory at Tela and oil factory at Benha
Parent Company: Responsible to the Ministry of Industry

Principal Shareholders: Public sector company

TEA COMPUTERS SA

7 Horreya St, PO Box 2439, Heliopolis, Cairo
Tel: 660865
Cable: Teamincomp
Telex: 92478 Teacom Un

Directors: Amr H Allouba (Managing Director)

PRINCIPAL ACTIVITIES: Marketing of computers; software & word processing systems
Principal Agencies: Data General; Centronics; Data Products; Applied Digital Data Systems; Pyral; CPT
Principal Bankers: Arab International Bank; National Bank of Egypt; Suez Canal Bank

TELEVISION & BROADCASTING UNION

TV Bldg, Corniche El Nil, Cairo
Tel: 759616
Telex: 92147

Chairman: Hussein Enan
Directors: Mohamed Said Sabry (Secretary General), Safia El Mohander (Broadcasting), Hemat Mostafa (TV), Farouk Ibrahim (Broadcasting Engineering), Mohamed Abdel Fatah (Financial & Economic Affairs)

PRINCIPAL ACTIVITIES: Television and broadcasting

Date of Establishment: 1970

EGYPT

TEXACO INTERNATIONAL
50 Road 105, Maadi, Cairo
Tel: 3515136, 3515267
Telex: 23323 TXACO UN

PRINCIPAL ACTIVITIES: Oil exploration

TEXTILE INDUSTRIES CORPORATION
PO Box 190 (Moh Farid), Taher Street, Cairo
Tel: 3905153
Cable: Egotextile - Cairo
Telex: 92026 UN EGOTEX
Telefax: 3905235

Chairman: Dr S Dahmoush
Directors: M Ibrahim, M Malek, H Abd El Kader, M Abd El Maksood, S Abdelsalam
Senior Executives: M El Zeiny (Sales Manager), I El Beltagi (Personnel Manager), A Aly (Finance Manager), S Zaki (Technical Manager)

PRINCIPAL ACTIVITIES: Textile industries corporation is the holding Co
Parent Company: Responsible to the Ministry of Industry
Subsidiary Companies: Misr Spinning & Weaving Co, Mehalla Kobra; Misr Fine Spinning & Weaving Co, Kafr El-Dawar; Misr Helwan Spinning & Weaving Co; Etablissement Industries Pour la Soie et le Coton Esco; Nasr Spinning & Weaving & Dyeing Co, Mehalla Kubra; Unirab Spinning & Weaving Co; Misr Shebin El-Kom Spinning & Weaving Co; Nasr Wool & Selected Textiles Co STIA; National Spinning & Weaving Co; Misr Beida Dyers Co; The Egyptian Spinning & Weaving Co for Wool Wooltex; Nasr Spinning & Weaving & Knitting Co, Shourbagi; Misr Rayon Co, Kafr El-Dawar; Upper Egypt Spinning & Weaving Co; Middle Egypt Spinning & Weaving Co; Orient Linnen & Cotton Co; Damietta Spinning & Weaving Co; Port-Said Spinning & Weaving Co; Arab Carpet & Upholstery Co, Damanhour; Siouf Spinning & Weaving Co; Alexandria Spinning & Weaving Co; Dakahlia Spinning & Weaving Co; Delta Spinning & Weaving Co; Nasr Clothing & Textiles Co, Kabo; Cairo Dyeing & Finishing Co; Cairo Silk Textile Co; Modern Textiles Co; General Jute Products Co; Misr Textile Equipment; Sharkia Spinning & Weaving Co, Zagazig Manufacturing Co; Cairo Clothing & Hosiery Co, Tricona
Principal Bankers: National Bank of Egypt, Misr Bank, Cairo Bank, Alexandria Bank
Financial Information:

	1989/90 E£'000
Sales turnover	3,435,000
Net profit	301,000

No of Employees: 232,594

THEBES SHIPPING AGENCY
71 El Horriya Street, Alexandria
Tel: 4937113, 4937114
Telex: 54128, 54513 Thebes UN

PRINCIPAL ACTIVITIES: Shipping agency

Principal Shareholders: Part of the Alexandria Co for Shipping Agencies

TRACTOR & ENGINEERING CO
18 Sharia Emed El Din, PO Box 366, Cairo
Tel: 46336, 46339, 45317
Telex: 92247

Directors: Emile Aziz El Masry (Financial Director), Abdel Aleem Abu Yousef (Project Director), El Sayed El Badawi Attia (Branch Director), Ahmed Mohamed Shalaby (Commercial Manager)

PRINCIPAL ACTIVITIES: Import and production of tractors and heavy machinery, lifting equipment and cranes, and general mechanical engineering; distributors and dealers. Export of clothing, leather products, and furniture
Principal Agencies: Caterpillar
Branch Offices: Import & Export Dept: 23 Sharia El Bustan, Cairo, Tel 30490, 30462, 32723, 32724, and PO Box 668, Alexandria
Parent Company: Responsible to the Ministry of Trade

Principal Shareholders: Public sector company

TRANS-ARABIAN INVESTMENT BANK EC
5 Talaat Harb Street, Cairo
Tel: 3920002
Telex: 23474 TAIBC UN
Telefax: 3920002

PRINCIPAL ACTIVITIES: Investment banking, representative office
Parent Company: Head office in Bahrain: PO Box 20485, Manama

TRANSPORT & ENGINEERING CO (TRENCO)
Head Office & Factory, 389 Smouha, Alexandria
Tel: 44277, 37821
Cable: Tranconiser

PRINCIPAL ACTIVITIES: Manufacture of rubber tyres and tubes for trucks, motor-cycles, motor-cars and bicycles
Branch Offices: Cairo: 8 Sharia Champollion, Tel 59240
Parent Company: Responsible to the Ministry of Industry

Principal Shareholders: Public sector company

UNION CARBIDE EGYPT SAE
6 Dokki Street, PO Box 340, Dokki, Cairo
Tel: 719747, 719763, 711547, 711586
Cable: Unicarbide
Telex: 22273 Ucare Un

Directors: Subir R Dasgupta (Managing Director Egypt)

PRINCIPAL ACTIVITIES: Manufacture and distribution of dry cell batteries;chemicals, plastics, carbon products and gases; technical services
Principal Agencies: Union Carbide Corporation and affiliates
Principal Bankers: Chase National Bank Egypt

UNION DE BANQUES ARABES ET FRANCAISES
UBAF
4 Baehler Street, Kasr El Nile, Cairo
Tel: 744654
Telex: 93277 UBAFC UN

PRINCIPAL ACTIVITIES: Banking (representative office)
Parent Company: Head office in Paris, France

UPPER EGYPT GENERAL CONTRACTING CO
5 Sharia 26 July, Cairo
Tel: 916296, 912617

Chairman: Eng Bahieldin Mohamed Ahmed

PRINCIPAL ACTIVITIES: Contracting, civil engineering and construction
Parent Company: Responsible to the Ministry of Housing and Reconstruction

Principal Shareholders: Public sector company

WADI KOMOMBO DAR EL-SALAM
Soc Anonyme de Wade Komombo
Dar Elsalam, Misr Elkadima, Cairo
Tel: 845066, 988150
Cable: Komombo, Cairo

PRINCIPAL ACTIVITIES: Land reclamation
Branch Offices: Kom-Omb, Aswan, Upper Egypt

Parent Company: Responsible to the Ministry of Rehabilitation, Development and Land Reclamation
Principal Bankers: Banque du Caire, Giza

Principal Shareholders: Public sector company

WESTERN ARABIAN GEOPHYSICAL CO
12 Tolombat St, Garden City, PO Box 443, Cairo
Tel: 3550281, 3549656
Cable: Wesarbco
Telex: 23346 WGCAI UN

Senior Executives: B M King, V W Vagt (Supervisor)

PRINCIPAL ACTIVITIES: Geophysical and services to the oil industry
Parent Company: Western Geophysical Co of America

WIMPEY, GEORGE, (EGYPT) SAE
5th Floor, 4(D) Gezira Street, Zamalek, Cairo
Tel: 3401751, 3401651
Telex: 93761 Zetco UN

PRINCIPAL ACTIVITIES: Building and civil engineering and contractors, mechanical, electrical and chemical engineering
Parent Company: Head office: Hammersmith Grove, London W6, UK

XEROX-EGYPT SAE
2 Lebanon St, Mohandessin, PO Box 30, Cairo
Tel: 3461221, 3461059
Telex: 93055 XEGPT UN

PRINCIPAL ACTIVITIES: Manufacturing and servicing photocopying machines and supplies; regional training, centre for technical and management development
Branch Offices: 177, 26th July Rd, Sidi Gaber, Alexandria, Tel: 851085, 840523, 840786
Financial Information:
Authorised capital   US$4,000,000

Principal Shareholders: Xerox Corp, USA (50%)
Date of Establishment: 1978
No of Employees: 325

ZAIDAN, GEORGE, & CO
26 Chereif Pasha St, Immobilia Bldg, Cairo
Tel: 3928244 (Office), 846425, 849585 (Factory)
Cable: Chemegypt Cairo
Telex: 92624 Pertix Un

Chairman: George J Zaidan (also Proprietor)
Directors: Jean Zaidan

PRINCIPAL ACTIVITIES: Factory producing paints, detergents, and auxiliary chemicals for industry
Branch Offices: Cairo: Naguib El Rihani St; Factory: El Kharta El Guidida St, Amam Madraset El Zahraa, Old Cairo
Principal Bankers: Bank Misr; Banque du Caire
Financial Information:

	1990 E£'000
Sales turnover	1,000

Principal Shareholders: Family concern
Date of Establishment: 1934
No of Employees: 50

EGYPT

Major Companies of IRAQ

Due to the circumstances of war, the publishers were unable to update the Iraqi section in this year's edition of MAJOR COMPANIES OF THE ARAB WORLD. The companies have nevertheless been listed for reference.

ADNAN ROUMANI & CO

See ROUMANI, ADNAN, & CO

AGRICULTURAL COOPERATIVE BANK OF IRAQ

PO Box 5112, Rashid Street, Baghdad
Tel: 8884191, 8889081
Cable: Almasraf Baghdad

PRINCIPAL ACTIVITIES: Finance for agriculture and cooperative societies

Principal Shareholders: 100% State-owned
Date of Establishment: 1936

AL AHLIA CARTON INDUSTRY CO SA

Zaafaraniya, PO Box 10010, Baghdad
Tel: 7731151/2
Cable: CartcoBaghdad

PRINCIPAL ACTIVITIES: Production of corrugated boxes for packing

Principal Shareholders: Mixed sector company

AL BUNNIA, H MAHMOOD J, & SONS CO

Al-Bunnia Bldg, Al-Khulafaa Street, Baghdad
Tel: 4168231/5, 4160852, 4165559
Cable: Albunnia-Baghdad
Telex: 212310 Bunnia IK, 213048 Jasmin IK

Chairman: Abdul Wahab Mahmood J Al-Bunnia
Directors: Saadoon Mohamood J Al-Bunnia, Abdul Latif Mahmood J Al-Bunnia

PRINCIPAL ACTIVITIES: Foodstuff production; general trading and contracting for roads and bridges
Subsidiary Companies: National Confectionery Products Co; Iraqi Sweets & Biscuits Industry Co; Eastern Frozen Foods Co; Iraqi Flour Mill Factory; National Agricultural Products Industry Co; Al-Bunnia & Sons Contractors; National Food Products Development Co; Iraqi Chocolate Production Co; Eastern Flour Mill; Protein Manufacturing Factory; Rafidain Paper Bags Manufacturing Co; Um Qara Co; Al-Alamain Flour Mill Factory; National Marketing Co Ltd; Al Nasr Building Materials Co Ltd; Chewing Gum Co Ltd; Iraqi Transport Services Co Ltd; Meat Processing Int'l Co Ltd; Al Nasr Station for Cows; Al Rafidain Co for Health Water Ltd; Al Mansour Co for the Production of Salts Ltd; Al Nour Real Estate Co Ltd; Al Tayseer Co for the Manufacture of Sweets & Foodstuffs Ltd; Al Andaleeb Bakery Co for the Production of Bread Ltd

Date of Establishment: 1910

AL-DIEAH CO FOR ELECTRONIC INDUSTRIES LTD

PO Box 20213, 102/41/8, Al Sa'adoun Street, Baghdad
Tel: 7182849
Telex: 212449 Artecs IK

PRINCIPAL ACTIVITIES: Production of light fittings

Principal Shareholders: Private sector company

AL FAYHA PERLON CO WLL

Bahbahani Bldg, Shorja, Baghdad
Tel: 8882371

PRINCIPAL ACTIVITIES: Production of synthetic textiles
Branch Offices: Factory: Jamilah Industrial Estate, Baghdad, Tel 8882314

AL FURAT CO FOR ELECTRICAL INDUSTRIES

Khykafa Street, behind State Ent for Baghdad Electricity, Baghdad
Tel: 8871062

Senior Executives: Husham Al Darzy (Manager)

PRINCIPAL ACTIVITIES: Production of electricity distribution control panels and light fittings

Principal Shareholders: Private sector company

AL HILAL INDUSTRIAL COMPANY

PO Box 2147, Za'afaraniya Industrial District, Baghdad
Tel: 7733600, 7733611
Telex: 212414, 214185 Hilalnco IK

PRINCIPAL ACTIVITIES: Manufacturing company

Principal Shareholders: Mixed sector company

AL HURIYA PRINTING HOUSE

Karantina, Sarrafiya, Baghdad
Tel: 69721
Cable: Houseprint Baghdad
Telex: 212228 Ilam IK

PRINCIPAL ACTIVITIES: Printing, import and distribution of paper, paper board, photographic paper, materials and machinery for printing

Principal Shareholders: State-owned

AL KHAYAM TRICOT CO WLL

Mustansir St, PO Box 11212, Baghdad
Tel: 8884065

Directors: E Moses, S M Salman

PRINCIPAL ACTIVITIES: Production of knitted wear
Branch Offices: Factory: Sarah Khatoon Camp, Baghdad, Tel 96674

AL KHAZEN CONSULTING ENGINEERS

33 Mirjan Bldg, South Gate, Baghdad
Tel: 8889978, 8889979
Cable: Istishary
Telex: 212448 Khazen IK

President: Dr Abdul-Karim A Ali
Directors: Dr Khalid Shakir Mahmood

PRINCIPAL ACTIVITIES: Consulting engineers for industrial works, bridges, highways and railway projects; water and sewerage schemes; institution buildings, etc
Principal Bankers: Rafidain Bank

Principal Shareholders: Dr Abdul-Karim A Ali, Dr Khalid Shakir Mahmood

AL MAHARA CO PRODUCTIVE INDUSTRIES LTD

123/53/ Bldg Mohamed Asker, Al Sheikh Omar Street, Baghdad
Tel: 8861417, 8874016

PRINCIPAL ACTIVITIES: Production of auto spare parts, cutting machines, moulds, presses, rollers, dyes

Principal Shareholders: Private sector company

AL MAHMOOD, HAMMOOD, SONS & NAIF KHALIL SONS CONSTRUCTION CO LTD

Muasker Rashid Rd, PO Box 772, Alwiyah, Baghdad
Tel: 7194340, 719682, 7196710
Telex: 212384 Hammood IK

Chairman: Jassim H Al-Mahmood
Directors: Hashim H Al-Mahmood, Rashid Haji Neyif
Senior Executives: Sami Naif Khalil

PRINCIPAL ACTIVITIES: Civil engineering and construction
Subsidiary Companies: Eastern Welded Mesh Factory
Principal Bankers: Rafidain Bank

Date of Establishment: 1952
No of Employees: 500

AL MANSOUR MELIA

PO Box 6153, Baghdad
Tel: 5370041
Telex: 212768

PRINCIPAL ACTIVITIES: Hotel business

AL MEETHAQ CO FOR AUTO PARTS MANUFACTURING

514/6/14 Jamila Industrial Estate, Hay Al Qaudes, Baghdad
Tel: 8820006
Telex: 214252 HZN IK

Senior Executives: Subhi Sa'aid

PRINCIPAL ACTIVITIES: Production of auto spares and accessories

Principal Shareholders: Private sector company

AL NAHREN FACTORY

PO Box 6003, Baghdad
Tel: 7182927

Senior Executives: Ahmad Musa Yousef (Manager)

PRINCIPAL ACTIVITIES: Production of water coolers

Principal Shareholders: Private sector company

AL RAHMANI CO FOR PLASTIC INDUSTRIES LTD

PO Box 215, Baghdad
Tel: 5425742, 5419362
Telex: 212929 Raid IK

PRINCIPAL ACTIVITIES: Production of plastic ballpens

Principal Shareholders: Private sector company

AL RAWI, FAROUK MAHDI,

Hay Al Saadoun, Mahalat 101, Street 18 No-59, PO Box 24049, Baghdad
Tel: 7186469, 7182026, 8874103
Cable: Alkawn
Telex: 212417 Alkawn IK, 213028 Saif IK
Telefax: (01) 7183852

Chairman: Farouk Mahdi Al Rawi
Directors: Salah M Al Rawi, Saad M Al Rawi, Adil M Al Rawi, Zuhair M Al Rawi

PRINCIPAL ACTIVITIES: General trading and contracting; import-export; manufacture of various household products, and confectionery goods
Subsidiary/Associated Companies: Zuhair Confectionery Factory; Iraqi Threads Manufacturing Co WLL; Al Murshid Manufacturing Co WLL; Middle East Plastic Factory; Associated Industries WLL; Al Rawi Press; Venus Industrial Co WLL; Al Manar Iron Manufacturing Co Ltd; Al Wafa Tissue Paper Manufacturing Co Ltd; Al Sayef Gum & Candies Manufacturing Co Ltd; Rafidain Soap Co Ltd
Principal Bankers: Rafidain Bank, Al Rashid Bank

AL RAZI CHEMICAL INDUSTRIES CO WLL

Al-Wathik St, PO Box 2099, Baghdad
Tel: 7198202, 7192640
Cable: Chemist Baghdad
Telex: 213745 Razico IK

Chairman: A J A Sabri
Directors: Anmar A J A Sabri (General Manager)

PRINCIPAL ACTIVITIES: Production of cosmetics and pharmaceutical products
Principal Agencies: Yardley, Beecham, BDF (Beiresdorf), Hans Schwarzkopf, Tokalon
Principal Bankers: Al Rasheed Bank, Al Rafidain Bank

Financial Information:

	1988/89 US$'000
Sales turnover	2,60
Profits	1,210
Authorised capital	850
Paid-up capital	350

Principal Shareholders: Family owned company
Date of Establishment: 1962
No of Employees: 35

AL SAMAN TEXTILE & SEWING CO WLL

Mustansir St, Baghdad
Tel: 8887656
Cable: Sammanco Baghdad

Chairman: E M Al-Saman (also Managing Director)

PRINCIPAL ACTIVITIES: Production of synthetic textiles
Branch Offices: Factory: 1 Wadi Hajur, Mosul, Ninevah Governorate, Tel 70780

AL TAYSEER COMMERCIAL AGENCIES BUREAU

PO Box 11369, Masarif, Usama Ben Zayed St, Al-Samual, Baghdad
Tel: 8880944
Cable: CHRICO Baghdad
Telex: 213081 Taysir IK

Chairman: Fadhil Salmam

PRINCIPAL ACTIVITIES: General commission agents, textiles and yarns, general raw materials, construction and machinery, leather products, rubber products, wood products, paper, cardboard, stationary, lime, cement, ceramic and coloured tiles, iron, steel products, silver, platinum and precious metals, other metal products
Principal Bankers: Rafidain Bank, Khullani Branch, Baghdad

Date of Establishment: 1982

AL WATAN AL ARABI CO

Al Said Co for Developed Industries

PO Box 5878, Sheikh Dhari Street, Jordan Square, Baghdad
Tel: 5412574, 8870519
Cable: WATANCO
Telex: 213637

Directors: Abdul Salam Mohamed Saeed (Manager)

PRINCIPAL ACTIVITIES: Production of ceramic tiles, sanitaryware, paints, fibreglass, synthetic marble

Principal Shareholders: Private sector company

AMANAT AL-ASIMA (BAGHDAD MUNICIPALITY)

Khulafa Street, Khullani Square, Baghdad
Tel: 8889011/9
Cable: Amanat Al Asima Baghdad
Telex: 212638 Asima

PRINCIPAL ACTIVITIES: Municipal and public services
Subsidiary Companies: Baghdad Water Supply Administration, Baghdad Sewerage Board

Principal Shareholders: State-owned institution

ARAB CO FOR DETERGENT CHEMICALS

PO Box 27064, Baghdad
Tel: 5413830, 5419893, 5418805, 5415213
Telex: 213312 Aradet IK

PRINCIPAL ACTIVITIES: Production of cleaning materials, detergents, chemicals

Principal Shareholders: Private sector company

ARAB ENGINEERING PROFILES CO LTD

101/75/7, Hay Al Sa'adoun, Baghdad
Tel: 8887705, 8880605
Telex: 213066 Profl IK

Senior Executives: Salem Majeed Sulaiman (Manager)

PRINCIPAL ACTIVITIES: Production of perforated, galvanised
steel angles and accessories

Principal Shareholders: Private sector company

ARAB FEDERATION FOR ENGINEERING INDUSTRIES

PO Box 509, Saadoun St, Alwiyah, Baghdad
Tel: 7186204, 7186213
Cable: Afei Baghdad
Telex: 212724 Afei IK

Chairman: Eng Abdulaziz Essassi
Senior Executives: Mustafa Salih (Secretary General), Minchawi
Al Sanee (Finance Manager)

PRINCIPAL ACTIVITIES: Coordination and cooperation among
the Member Arab Companies in the field of engineering
industries, preparation of marketing research, feasibility
studies and organisation of conferences and seminars
Branch Offices: Tunisia: PO Box 67, Tunis Carthage
Principal Bankers: Rafidain Bank, Baghdad; Alexandria Bank,
Cairo; Banque Internationale Arabe de Tunisie

Principal Shareholders: Member Countries: Algeria, Bahrain,
Egypt, Iraq, Jordan, Kuwait, Lebanon, Morocco, Saudi Arabia,
Syria, Tunisia, Yemen
Date of Establishment: 29 December 1975
No of Employees: 175

ARAB INDUSTRIAL INVESTMENT CO (AIIC)

PO Box 2154 Jadriya, Baghdad
Tel: 7189215, 7198632
Cable: ARABINVEST
Telex: 212628 Aiic IK

Chairman: Adnan Abdul Majid Jasim (Iraq)
Directors: Jamaz Abdullah Al Suhaimi (Saudi Arabia), Mubarak
Abdullah Al Khafra (Saudi Arabia), Tariq Ismail Ahmed (Iraq),
Faisal Zaied Ben Zaied (Libya), Nouri Al Nouri (Kuwait)
Senior Executives: Eng Zuhair Ismail Kadouri (Director General),
Mohamed El Attar (General Secretary to Board of Directors),
Dr Hassan Abdel Fadiel (Director of Studies & Projects)

PRINCIPAL ACTIVITIES: Studying, sponsoring, establishing and
investing in engineering industries in the Arab World
Principal Bankers: Rafidain Bank, Iraq; Jordan Gulf Bank,
Jordan
Financial Information:

	1989
	ID'000
Authorised capital	150,000
Paid-up capital	16,800

Principal Shareholders: Governments of Iraq, Saudi Arabia,
Kuwait, Libya, Jordan, Qatar, Tunisia, Yemen, Morocco
Date of Establishment: 22 Nov 1978
No of Employees: 35

ARAB PLASTIC INDUSTRIES CO LTD

Plastic Bldg, Khilani St, Sinak, Baghdad
Tel: 8887532, 8884242
Cable: Amjan Baghdad

Chairman: A M Jan
Directors: S A Jan

PRINCIPAL ACTIVITIES: Manufacture of PVC resins and plastic
products
Branch Offices: Kamillia, Baghdad, Tel 7711168
Principal Bankers: Rafidain Bank

Principal Shareholders: A M Jan & Sons
Date of Establishment: 1962
No of Employees: 120

ARAB TIMBER CO SA (THE)

PO Box 293, Mosul Nineveah
Tel: 060-810060
Cable: Alakhshad Mosul Iraq

PRINCIPAL ACTIVITIES: Manufacture and compressed wood,
wood products and furniture

Principal Shareholders: Mixed sector company

ARABIAN AERATED WATER CO (SA)

PO Box 2138 Alwiya, Baghdad
Tel: 7190028, 7190029, 7192842
Cable: Sinalco Baghdad
Telex: 213858 SINAL IK

Chairman: Mohamed Ahmed Al Ghanim (Kuwait)
Directors: Mohammed Amin Al Rahmani (Managing Director)
Senior Executives: Muayad M Kassab (Consulting Engineer)

PRINCIPAL ACTIVITIES: Production of soft drinks and soda
Principal Agencies: Sinalco, West Germany; Canada Dry, Beirut
Branch Offices: Basrah Factory
Principal Bankers: Rafidain Bank
Financial Information:

	US$'000
Authorised capital	3,200
Paid-up capital	3,200

Principal Shareholders: Mohammed Ahmed Al Ghanim and
others
Date of Establishment: 1956
No of Employees: 450

ATH-THAWRA HOUSE FOR PRESS & PUBLISHING

PO Box 2009, Uqba Bin Nafia Sq, Baghdad
Tel: 7196161
Cable: Ath-Thawra-Baghdad
Telex: 212215 Thawra IK

PRINCIPAL ACTIVITIES: Newspaper printing and publishing
Principal Bankers: Rafidain Bank

AUTOMOBILE STATE ENTERPRISE

Near Andulus Sq, Off Nidhal St, PO Box 3270, Baghdad
Tel: 7195071
Cable: Automobile Baghdad
Telex: 212342 Auto IK

PRINCIPAL ACTIVITIES: Import and distribution of vehicles and
spare parts, motorcycles and spare parts, ball bearings,
garage tools
Parent Company: State Trade Organisation for Capital Goods

Principal Shareholders: State-owned

BAGHDAD ALUMINIUM & IRON WORKS CO WLL

PO Box 238, Baghdad
Tel: 62550

PRINCIPAL ACTIVITIES: Manufacture of aluminium doors,
windows and building materials
Branch Offices: Factory: Waziriya Industrial Estate, Waziriya,
Baghdad

BAGHDAD HOTEL

Saadoun St, Baghdad
Tel: 8889031/50
Cable: Bagotel
Telex: 212200

PRINCIPAL ACTIVITIES: Hotel business

BAGHDAD PACKAGING INDUSTRIES CO SA

Zafaranyeh, PO Box 29012, Baghdad
Tel: 7731151, 7731152, 7739210, 7739835
Cable: Cartco
Telex: 213477 Cartco IK

Chairman: Khadouri Khadouri
Directors: M Abbas, A Khalid, J B Friej (Managing Director)
Senior Executives: S A Aita (Purchase and Import Manager)

PRINCIPAL ACTIVITIES: Manufacture of corrugated cardboard
boxes for packaging purposes
Principal Bankers: Rafidain Bank
Financial Information:

	1989 ID'000
Paid-up capital	600
Total assets	3,000

Principal Shareholders: Major shareholders are members of the
board
Date of Establishment: Formerly National Carton Industries
No of Employees: 290

CENTRAL BANK OF IRAQ

Rasheed Street, PO Box 64, Baghdad
Tel: 7765171
Cable: Markazi Baghdad
Telex: 212203, 212558, 212296

Governor: Subhi N Frankool
Directors & Original Members: T Al Tukmachi (Deputy
Governor), Abdul Wahab Al Kassab (Advisor), Ibrahim Abdul
Karim Al Mushahidi, Abdul Qhader Abdul Latif ALi, Dr Faiq
Abdul Rasool, Majeed Abid Jaafer, Tariq Al Khateeb, Dr Basil
Al Bustany, Abdul Majeed Abdul Hameed Al Jubury, Falih Ali
Al Saleh (Alternate Member), Dr Khaleel Al Shama (Alternate
Member), Dr Qubais Saeed Abdul Fattah (Alternate Member)
Senior Executives: Abdul Majeed Abdul Hameed Al Jubury (DG
Administration & Buildings), Sadik H Taha (DG Loans &
Agreements), Assim M Saleh (DG Foreign Exchange Control),
Dr A M Rasheed (DG Investments), Osama Al Chalabi (DG
Credit & Foreign Payments), Sami Atto (DG Research &
Statistics), Adeeb Saleem (DG Accounts), Nooh H Saeed (DG
Vaults & Issue)

PRINCIPAL ACTIVITIES: Central Banking
Branch Offices: Basra, Mosul

Principal Shareholders: State-owned
Date of Establishment: 1947
No of Employees: 1,998

CONCRETE WORKS COMPANY

Bataween, PO Box 3143, Baghdad
Tel: 8883568

PRINCIPAL ACTIVITIES: Manufacture of concrete products and
building materials
Branch Offices: Factory: Kadhamiya, Baghdad, Tel 4413441

CONSOLIDATED CONTRACTORS CO SAL

PO Box 3199, Baghdad
Tel: 7199730
Cable: Consolid Baghdad

PRINCIPAL ACTIVITIES: General construction and engineering
contractors, pipeline contractors, marine, civil and mechanical
works
Parent Company: Managing Office: Consolidated Contractors Int
Co Ltd, PO Box 61092, Amaroussion, Athens

CONSOLIDATED MODERN ENTERPRISES CO LTD

903/33/6, Fatih Sq, PO Box 2058 Alwiyah, Baghdad
Tel: 7192386, 7199160
Cable: Cosmodent
Telex: 213419 COSMO IK

Directors: Mohammad H Hadid (Managing Director)
Senior Executives: Khaddouri Khaddouri (Finance Manager),
Salam Khaddouri (Marketing Manager), Asim Sliwa (Sales
Managaer), Masoud Adel Assad (Technical Manager)

PRINCIPAL ACTIVITIES: Production of insecticides, household
products, cosmetic products, particularly in aerosol form
Principal Bankers: Rafidain Bank, Baghdad
Financial Information:

	1988/89 ID'000
Sales turnover	1,135
Profits	517
Authorised capital	500
Paid-up capital	500
Total assets	1,490

Principal Shareholders: Mohammad Hadid, Zaha Hadid,
Forester & Sabbagh Co, Khaddouri Khaddouri, Naseer
Chadirchi, Salam Khaddouri
Date of Establishment: 1968
No of Employees: 35

CONTRACTING & TRADING CO WLL

Contracting & Trading Co (Iraq) WLL

Jamhouriya St, Alhikma Bldg, PO Box 2049, Baghdad
Tel: 64665
Cable: Cat

PRINCIPAL ACTIVITIES: Structural and civil engineering and
contracting, construction of pipelines, erection of plants and
machinery
Principal Agencies: Mothercat Ltd, Lebanon
Branch Offices: Lebanon; UAE; Saudi Arabia; Sudan; Iraq;
Nigeria

DAR AL-IMARAH

56 Maghrib St, Waziriya, Baghdad
Tel: 25021, 25022
Cable: Darimarah

Chairman: Kahtan Al-Madfai
Directors: Husham Al-Madfai

PRINCIPAL ACTIVITIES: Consultants on planning, architecture
and engineering and industrial design and agro industry.
Principal Bankers: Rafidain Bank

Principal Shareholders: Partners only
Date of Establishment: 1954

DAR BAGHDAD CONSULTING ENGINEERS

PO Box 3250, Saadoun St, Baghdad
Tel: 7199575
Cable: Derseriah

Chairman: Dr Ahmed M El-Dujaili

PRINCIPAL ACTIVITIES: Consulting engineering, planning,
studies, designs, specifications and tender documents and
supervision of construction
Parent Company: Dar Baghdad
Principal Bankers: Rafidain Bank

Principal Shareholders: Dr Dujaili and sons
Date of Establishment: 1967

DIJLA PAINTS CO

Sadoon St, Near Baghdad Hotel, PO Box 3218, Baghdad
Tel: 8881709
Cable: Diginco Baghdad

PRINCIPAL ACTIVITIES: Manufacture of paints
Branch Offices: Factory: Obaidi City, Baghdad

DIRECTORATE GENERAL OF CONTRACTS & PURCHASING
PO Box 552, Baghdad
Tel: 5375171
Cable: Contdef - Baghdad
Telex: 212202 Mindef IK

PRINCIPAL ACTIVITIES: Purchasing for the Ministry of Defence
Parent Company: Part of the Ministry of Defence

Principal Shareholders: State-owned

DIRECTORATE GENERAL OF GENERATION & TRANSMISSION OF ELECTRICITY
4/356 Al Masbah Bldg, PO Box 1098, Baghdad
Tel: 7199007, 7190929
Cable: Genelect
Telex: 212590 Majelect IK

PRINCIPAL ACTIVITIES: Generation, transmission of electrical energy
Parent Company: Responsible to the State Organisation of Electricity

Principal Shareholders: State-owned organisation

DIRECTORATE GENERAL OF GEOLOGICAL SURVEY & MINERAL INVESTIGATION
PO Box 986, Alwiya, Al Sadoon Park Area, Baghdad
Tel: 7195123
Cable: Geosurv Baghdad
Telex: 212292 Som IK

PRINCIPAL ACTIVITIES: Investigations for various minerals

Principal Shareholders: State-owned

DIRECTORATE GENERAL OF MEDICAL SUPPLIES
PO Box 17041, Baghdad
Tel: 5212092
Cable: Civmedstores Baghdad
Telex: 212375 Civmedst

PRINCIPAL ACTIVITIES: Import of surgical, laboratory x-ray materials and hospital equipment & furniture
Parent Company: Part of the Ministry of Health
Principal Bankers: Central Bank of Iraq

Principal Shareholders: State-owned

DIWANIYA STATE COTTON TEXTILE CO
PO Box 79, Diwaniya, Qadisiya
Tel: (0336) 23503
Cable: Cottentex Diwaniya
Telex: 216508 DSET IK

PRINCIPAL ACTIVITIES: Manufacture of cotton and polyester yarn and textiles
Parent Company: Part of the State Organisation for Textile Industries
Principal Bankers: Rafidain Bank

Principal Shareholders: State-owned
No of Employees: 2,850

EASTERN BREWERY CO SA
Mirjan Bldg, South Gate, Baghdad
Tel: 8885104/5, 8882084
Cable: Brewhouse Baghdad

PRINCIPAL ACTIVITIES: Brewery and ice-cream manufacturing
Branch Offices: Factory: Zafaraniya, Baghdad

EASTERN PLASTIC CO
Khan Al Jibin Bldg, Mamoon Street, Baghdad
Tel: 8884081
Cable: Pelican Baghdad

PRINCIPAL ACTIVITIES: Manufacture of PVC resins
Branch Offices: Faluja, Al-Anbar, Tel 2358

EASTERN RUBBER INDUSTRIES CO
Akd Al-Jam, Bab-Agha, Rashid St, Baghdad
Tel: 8884259

PRINCIPAL ACTIVITIES: Manufacture of rubber products
Branch Offices: Jamilah Industrial Estate, Baghdad, Tel 61733

ELECTRONIC INDUSTRIAL COMPANY
PO Box 29042, Baghdad
Tel: 7733551, 7733030
Telex: 212442 Logic IK

PRINCIPAL ACTIVITIES: Production of electrical and electronics equipment and appliances

Principal Shareholders: Mixed sector company

ENGINEERING ENTERPRISES BUREAU
42 Kerradat-out, Baghdad
Tel: 7197810, 7197410
Cable: Endazyar

Chairman: B Dilair
Directors: B A Jamil, J M Amin

PRINCIPAL ACTIVITIES: General engineering consultants, construction, contracting and trading
Principal Agencies: Polytechna; Pacific, Japan; Swiss-Consult, Switzerland
Principal Bankers: Rafidain Bank

FAROUK MAHDI AL RAWI
See AL RAWI, FAROUK MAHDI,

FINE TEXTILE STATE CO
PO Box 2, Hilla, Babylon
Tel: (030) 223200/2
Cable: Hiltex Hilla
Telex: 216207 FTSC IK

PRINCIPAL ACTIVITIES: Manufacture of fine textiles
Branch Offices: Baghdad: Sadoon St, Opposite to Iraqi Airways, Tel 8888922
Parent Company: Part of the State Organisation of Textile Industries

Principal Shareholders: State-owned

GENERAL EST FOR BAKERIES & OVENS
Al Nidhal Street, Near Saddoun Park, PO Box 109, Baghdad
Tel: 8887161

PRINCIPAL ACTIVITIES: Government bakeries and control of private sector bakeries
Branch Offices: Baghdad, Milla, Basrah, Kerbala, Diwaniya, Najaf, Mosul, Arbil, Kirkuk, Nasiriya, Samawa, Baquba, Amara, Sulaimaniya, and Dohuk
Parent Company: Part of the State Organisation for Grains

Principal Shareholders: State-owned

GENERAL EST FOR DRUGS & MEDICAL SUPPLIES
Mansour City, PO Box 6138, Baghdad
Tel: 5379171
Telex: 212504 Kimadia IK; 212672

PRINCIPAL ACTIVITIES: Control and supervision for the trade of pharmaceutical products
Parent Company: Responsible to the Ministry of Health

Principal Shareholders: State-owned organisation

GENERAL EST FOR FLOUR MILLS

Entrance to Hurriyah City, PO Box 170, Baghdad
Tel: 4414001/8
Cable: Rafmill Baghdad
Telex: 212453 Mills IK

PRINCIPAL ACTIVITIES: Flour milling and distribution of flour
Branch Offices: Flour Mills in Baghdad, Mosul, Basrah
Parent Company: Part of the State Organisation for Grains

Principal Shareholders: State-owned

GENERAL EST FOR GRAIN TRADING

Bab al-Muadam, PO Box 329, Baghdad
Tel: 68121
Cable: Silowat baghdad
Telex: 212225 Silowat IK

PRINCIPAL ACTIVITIES: Import and export, storage and
distribution of wheat, barleyand rice
Parent Company: Part of the State Organisation for Grains

Principal Shareholders: State-owned

GENERAL EST FOR IRAQI RAILWAYS

Damascus Sq, Karkh, Baghdad
Tel: 5370011
Cable: Transrail Baghdad
Telex: 212272 Railway IK
Telefax: 5370450

Chairman: Mohammed Younis Al Ahmed (Director General)
Directors: Elyas Gebrail Elyas (Director of Civil Engineering)

PRINCIPAL ACTIVITIES: Passenger and freight railway
services; responsible for the planning, supervision, control of
the following Departments listed below
Parent Company: Responsible to the Ministry of Transport &
Communications
Subsidiary Companies: Department of Traffic and Operation;
Department of Civil Engineering; Department of Electrical
Mechanical Engineering

Principal Shareholders: State-owned

GENERAL EST FOR LAND TRANSPORT SERVICES

PO Box 1006, off Shaikh Omar St, Al Nahda Garage, Baghdad
Tel: 69491, 64280
Cable: Khadber Baghdad
Telex: 212718

PRINCIPAL ACTIVITIES: Repair and maintenance of transport
vehicles; import and storage of specific requirements for the
State Organisation for Land Transport
Parent Company: Part of the State Organisation for Land
Transport

Principal Shareholders: State-owned

GENERAL EST FOR PASSENGER TRANSPORT

Garage Al Nahda, Off Shaikh Omar St, Baghdad
Tel: 69771, 69715, 63608

PRINCIPAL ACTIVITIES: Control of inter-city passenger
transport (buses and taxis)
Parent Company: Part of the State Organisation for Land
Transport

GENERAL EST FOR PASSENGER TRANSPORT IN BAGHDAD

Near Garage Maslaha No 5, Opp Mustansiriya University,
Waziriya, Baghdad
Tel: 8822000
Cable: Maslaha Baghdad

PRINCIPAL ACTIVITIES: Passenger transport inside Baghdad
Governorate

Parent Company: Part of the State Organisation for Land
Transport

Principal Shareholders: State-owned

GENERAL EST FOR SPECIALISED TRANSPORT

Abdul Aziz Al Baghdadi Bldg, Near Kullani Sq, PO Box 5745,
Baghdad
Tel: 8876491
Cable: Getco
Telex: 212264 Getco IK

PRINCIPAL ACTIVITIES: Transportation of specialised goods in
bulk
Parent Company: Part of the State Organisation for Land
Transport

GENERAL EST FOR TRANSPORT OF GENERAL CARGO

A H Al-Baghdadi Bldg, Jumhouriya St, Near Kullani Sq, PO Box
5745, Baghdad
Tel: 8876491
Cable: Getco Baghdad
Telex: 212264 Getco IK

PRINCIPAL ACTIVITIES: Freight transport throughout Iraq and
abroad
Parent Company: Part of the State Organisation for Land
Transport

Principal Shareholders: State-owned

GENERAL EST FOR WOOLLEN TEXTILE

PO Box 9114, Khadhumiya, Baghdad
Tel: 4226060
Cable: Mansujat Baghdad
Telex: 212639

PRINCIPAL ACTIVITIES: Manufacture of woollen blankets,
socks and stockings, textiles and yarns
Parent Company: Part of the State Organisation for Textile
Industries

Principal Shareholders: State-owned

H MAHMOOD J AL BUNNIA & SONS CO

See AL BUNNIA, H MAHMOOD J, & SONS CO

HAJ YOUNIS WEAVING CO SA

Mosul, Ninevah Governate
Tel: 2122
Cable: Nassij

Chairman: Ali Haj Younis
Directors: Tayyeb Haj Younis

PRINCIPAL ACTIVITIES: Production of various types of cotton
and synthetic textiles, import of various types of yarns,
dyestuffs and auxiliary products
Principal Bankers: Rafidain Bank

HAMMOOD AL MAHMOOD SONS & NAIF KHALIL SONS CONSTRUCTION CO LTD

See AL MAHMOOD, HAMMOOD, SONS & NAIF KHALIL SONS
CONSTRUCTION CO LTD

HILAL INDUSTRIAL CO SA

PO Box 2147, Alwiyah, Baghdad
Tel: 7733600
Cable: Hilalinco
Telex: 212559 Hilalinco IK

Chairman: Hussein Hamza
Directors: Jasim M Al-Saidi (Managing Director)

PRINCIPAL ACTIVITIES: Manufacture of air conditioners, air coolers, stainless steel sinks, electrodes and auto spring sheets
Principal Bankers: Industrial Bank; Rafidain Bank

Principal Shareholders: Industrial Bank (75%), private interests (25%)

IDRISI CENTRE FOR ENGINEERING CONSULTANCY (ICEC)
Museum Square, Karkh, PO Box 14077, Baghdad
Tel: 5376101
Cable: Idrisi Baghdad
Telex: 213192 IK

Chairman: Saad Al Zubaidi (Director General)
Senior Executives: Fakhira Dogmachi

PRINCIPAL ACTIVITIES: Consulting engineering services for the building sector, architecture and town planning, structural and engineering services covering electrical, mechanical and public health, roads and bridges, also quantity surveying
Parent Company: Responsible to the Ministry of Housing and Construction
Financial Information:

	1989 ID'000
Authorised capital	2,000

Principal Shareholders: State-owned organisation
Date of Establishment: 1987
No of Employees: 240

INDUSTRIAL BANK
Industrial Bank Bldg, Al-Khallani Sq, PO Box 5825, Baghdad
Tel: 8872181/9
Cable: Sinaibank Baghdad
Telex: 212224 Sinai Bk IK

PRINCIPAL ACTIVITIES: Financing and promoting investment in national industry, and and general bank operations
Branch Offices: Mosul; Kirkuk; Hilla; Kerbala; Basrah; Arbil; Najaf; Sulaymania
Principal Bankers: Central Bank of Iraq; Rafidain Bank

Principal Shareholders: The capital of the bank is provided by the Iraqi Government
Date of Establishment: 1940
No of Employees: 200

INDUSTRIAL COMPLEX IN BAQUBA
Khan Al-Pasha Bldg, Samawal St, PO Box 5819, Baghdad
Cable: Dialco
Telex: 216006 dialieco IK

PRINCIPAL ACTIVITIES: Manufacture of electrical appliances and equipment for domestic and industrial use; electric motors and transformers and sanitary fittings
Branch Offices: PO Box 7, Baquba Tel (0255) 22364
Parent Company: Part of the State Organisation for Engineering Industries

Principal Shareholders: State-owned

INTERMEDIATE MATERIALS FOR PLASTIC INDUSTRIES CO SA
Zafaraniya Industrial Area, PO Box 2378, Alwiya, Baghdad
Tel: 8880897, 97616
Cable: Dopanol
Telex: 212224 Sinai Bk

PRINCIPAL ACTIVITIES: Production of plastics
Principal Bankers: Industrial Bank

Principal Shareholders: Industrial Bank and other governmental companies

IRAQI AIRWAYS
Baghdad International Airport
Tel: 5519999, 5513642
Cable: Airways
Telex: 212589 Iactmacc IK

PRINCIPAL ACTIVITIES: Airline transport
Parent Company: Responsible to the Ministry of Transport & Communications
Principal Bankers: Central Bank of Iraq; Rafidain Bank

Principal Shareholders: State-owned organisation

IRAQI BEVERAGES CO
Sadoon St, Alwiya, PO Box 2339, Baghdad
Tel: 99057
Cable: Sevenup Baghdad

PRINCIPAL ACTIVITIES: Production of soft drinks
Branch Offices: Factory: Zafaraniya, Baghdad, Tel 90096, 99958

IRAQI BICYCLES & METAL TUBES MANUFACTURING CO SA
PO Box 1176, Mahmoudiya, Babylon Governorate, Baghdad
Tel: 0202 62910
Cable: BYCIRAK Baghdad
Telex: 212953 IBMT IK

PRINCIPAL ACTIVITIES: Manufacture of bicycles and metal tubes

Principal Shareholders: Mixed sector company

IRAQI BOTTLING & CANNING CO SA
PO Box 5779, Baghdad
Tel: 7190037, 7190038
Cable: Bottling Baghdad
Telex: 212339 Tayeb IK

Chairman: Nadhim Mohamed Tayeb
Directors: Younis Kamala (Managing Director), Ramzi Al Umari (Head of Legal Dept)

PRINCIPAL ACTIVITIES: Production and bottling of soft drinks
Branch Offices: Factory: Radshid Camp St, Baghdad
Principal Bankers: Rafidain Bank
Financial Information:

	1988/89 ID'000
Sales turnover	1,400
Profits	150
Authorised capital	500
Paid-up capital	500
Total assets	1,500

Date of Establishment: 1962
No of Employees: 107

IRAQI BROADCASTING & TELEVISION EST
Broadcasting & TV Bldg, Karkh, Baghdad
Tel: 5371121, 5371151
Cable: IDAAH Baghdad
Telex: 212246 IK

Chairman: Dr Majid Ahmed Al Samarraie

PRINCIPAL ACTIVITIES: Radio broadcasting and television network; import and export of films and TV programmes
Parent Company: Responsible to the Ministry of Information
Principal Bankers: Rafidain Bank

Principal Shareholders: State-owned organisation
Date of Establishment: 1936 (Radio); 1956 (TV); 1976 (Colour TV)
No of Employees: 2,000

IRAQI BRUSHES MANUFACTURING CO LTD

PO Box 14064, Baghdad
Tel: 4250727
Cable: Safina Baghdad
Telex: 213647 Safin IK

Directors: Abdul Amir Ali Abed (Managing Director)

PRINCIPAL ACTIVITIES: Manufacture of all kinds of brushes

Principal Shareholders: Private sector company

IRAQI CEMENT STATE ENTERPRISE

Muaskar Al Rashid St, PO Box 2050, Alwiyah, Baghdad
Tel: 7736071
Cable: Iraq Cement
Telex: 212413 Cement IK

PRINCIPAL ACTIVITIES: Production and marketing of Portland
Cement, moderate and sulphate resisting Portland Cement
Branch Offices: Works at Hindiyah; Fallujah; Kufa; Baghdad
Parent Company: Part of the State Organisation for
Construction Industries
Principal Bankers: Rafidain Bank, Baghdad

Principal Shareholders: State-owned

IRAQI CO FOR CARTON MANUFACTURING

Zaafaraniya Industrial Complex, PO Box 29029, Baghdad
Tel: 7730541, 7730561, 7730530, 7730517
Cable: ICCM Baghdad
Telex: 214217 ACCM IK

Chairman: R Al-Uraiby
Directors: M Al-Khayat, S N Jassim
Senior Executives: Miss R Al-Bayatie (Managing Director)

PRINCIPAL ACTIVITIES: Production of carton boxes and
products
Principal Bankers: Industrial Bank, Baghdad; Rafidian Bank,
Zaafara'niya
Financial Information:

	ID'000
Authorised capital	2,500
Paid-up capital	2,500

Principal Shareholders: Mixed sector company
Date of Establishment: 1979
No of Employees: 230

IRAQI CO FOR DOMESTIC APPLIANCES INDUSTRY

Za'afaraniya Industrial District, PO Box 29026, Baghdad
Tel: 7733305, 7735301
Telex: 213413 Muktalt IK

PRINCIPAL ACTIVITIES: Production of domestic appliances

Principal Shareholders: Mixed sector company

IRAQI CO FOR VENTILATION FANS

Industrial Estate, Baquba Road, Bob Al Sham, Baghdad
Tel: 7768333

Senior Executives: Yousef Jabry (Manager)

PRINCIPAL ACTIVITIES: Production of ventilation fans and
electricity distribution panels

Principal Shareholders: Private sector company

IRAQI ENGINEERING INDUSTRIAL CO

PO Box 35049, Baghdad
Tel: 7181475
Telex: 212224 BK IK

PRINCIPAL ACTIVITIES: Engineering contracting

Principal Shareholders: Mixed sector company

IRAQI FAIRS ADMINISTRATION

Baghdad International Fair, Al-Mansour, PO Box 6188, Baghdad
Tel: 5519336
Cable: Almaaridh Baghdad
Telex: 212231 Tamra IK

PRINCIPAL ACTIVITIES: Fairs and exhibitions affairs locally and
abroad, fairs licence; responsible for the annual Baghdad
International Fair
Parent Company: Responsible to the State Organisation for
Export

Principal Shareholders: State-owned

IRAQI FILTERS CO

PO Box 5974, Al Sinak, Near Industrial Bank, Baghdad
Tel: 8888976, 8877204
Cable: Clayson

PRINCIPAL ACTIVITIES: Production of air, oil, fuel and gas
filters

Principal Shareholders: Private sector company

IRAQI INSURANCE COMPANY

Aqaba Bin Nafie Square, PO Box 989, Baghdad
Tel: 7192184 (5 lines)
Cable: Hayat
Telex: 213818

Chairman: Abdul Khaliq Raouf Khalil

PRINCIPAL ACTIVITIES: All classes of insurance and
reinsurance
Principal Bankers: Al Rasheed Bank, Baghdad
Financial Information:

	1989 ID'000
Sales turnover	28,867
Profits	2,650
Authorised capital	5,000
Total assets	73,043

Principal Shareholders: State-owned company
Date of Establishment: 1959
No of Employees: 430

IRAQI METAL WEAVING CO WLL

Saad Bldg, South Gate, PO Box 7, Baghdad
Tel: 8880934
Cable: Newtraco Baghdad

PRINCIPAL ACTIVITIES: Manufacture of wire netting and wire
mesh
Branch Offices: Factory: Al-Ubaidi City, Baghdad, Tel 715336

IRAQI NAILS MANUFACTURING CO WLL

Faris Bldg, Tahir Square, Baghdad
Tel: 8880565
Cable: Hudjan Baghdad

PRINCIPAL ACTIVITIES: Manufacture of nails
Branch Offices: Factory: Al-Ubaidi City, Baghdad

IRAQI NATIONAL OIL CO
INOC

Dhaman Al-Gtimaie Bldg, Khullani Sq, PO Box 476, Baghdad
Tel: 8871115, 8889061
Cable: Petrolna Baghdad
Telex: 212204 Inoc IK

PRINCIPAL ACTIVITIES: Direction and control of the oil
industry, oil field prospecting and drilling
Branch Offices: PO Box 1, Kirkuk, Tel (050) 215050; Telex
218611 Kirkuk; and PO Box 240, Basrah, Tel (043) 210016,
Telex 207003

Subsidiary Companies: Incorporating the State Organisation for Oil & Gas Production

Principal Shareholders: State-owned

IRAQI NEWS AGENCY

28 Nissan Complex, Al Salihiya, Baghdad
Tel: 5383161
Cable: INA Baghdad
Telex: 212267 Ina IK, 212513

Chairman: Taha Yassin Hassan Al Basri (also Director General)

PRINCIPAL ACTIVITIES: News agency
Branch Offices: Offices in London; New Delhi; Paris; Tunis; Moscow; Amman; Rabat; Vienna; Cairo; Correspondents in Ankara; Sana'a; Belgrad; Abu Dhabi; New York; Bonn; Sydney; Dhaka; Srilanka; Madrid; Islamabad; Nicosia; Kenya
Principal Bankers: Rafidain Bank
Financial Information:

	US$'000
Authorised capital	6,000
Paid-up capital	6,000

Date of Establishment: 1959
No of Employees: 600

IRAQI OIL TANKERS CO

PO Box 37, Basrah
Tel: 219990/7, 5188
Cable: Tankpetro Basrah
Telex: 212007 IK

PRINCIPAL ACTIVITIES: Transportation of crude oil, international trading
Parent Company: Responsible to the Ministry of Oil
Principal Bankers: Rafidain Bank, Basrah; Central Bank of Iraq, Baghdad

Principal Shareholders: State-owned

IRAQI PHARMACEUTICAL INDUSTRY CO WLL

PO Box 722, New Baghdad, Baghdad
Tel: 7711381
Cable: Ipico Baghdad

PRINCIPAL ACTIVITIES: Manufacture of pharmaceutical products and cosmetics

IRAQI REFRESHMENTS CO (SEVEN UP)

PO Box 2339, Zaafaraniya Industrial Area, Baghdad
Tel: 7731141
Cable: Seven Up Baghdad
Telex: 212224 Sinai MK IK Att Seven Up

PRINCIPAL ACTIVITIES: Production of non alcoholic beverages

IRAQI REINSURANCE CO

Khalid Bin Al Waleed St, Uqba Bin Nafee Sq, PO Box 297, Baghdad
Tel: 7195131, 7195132, 7187381, 7187356
Cable: Iraqre
Telex: 212233 Iraqre IK

Chairman: Kays M Al-Mudaries
Members: Mowaffaq H Ridha, Abdul Khaliq R Khalil, Asim M Saleh, Jassim M Al Khalaf, Mohammed Z Abdul Rahman
Senior Executives: Ghazi H Al Siaidi (Senior Accounts Managerg), Samir J Shamaan, Nabil A Kazanchi, Samir S Qattan (Acting Planning Manager), Antranik Kevorkyan, Suhail K Aslan (Investment Manager)

PRINCIPAL ACTIVITIES: Reinsurance business
Branch Offices: London Contact Office, 31-35 Fenchurch St, London, EC3, Telex 887901
Principal Bankers: Rafidain Bank, Baghdad

Financial Information:

	ID'000
Authorised capital	5,000

Principal Shareholders: State-owned
Date of Establishment: 1960
No of Employees: 320

IRAQI SPARE PARTS MANUFACTURING CO SA

PO Box 5415, Baghdad
Tel: 7186213, 5555451
Telex: 212724

Senior Executives: Yassin A J Al Samarraie (Manager)

PRINCIPAL ACTIVITIES: Production of brake discs, brakes and clutches

Principal Shareholders: Private sector company

IRAQI STATE ENTERPRISE FOR MARITIME TRANSPORT

PO Box 766, Basrah
Tel: (040) 310206, 319390
Cable: Bawakhir Basrah
Telex: 207052 Irakline; 207069 IK

PRINCIPAL ACTIVITIES: Passenger and freight sea transportation
Branch Offices: Baghdad, PO Box 13038, Al Jadriyah, Al Huriya, Telex 212565, Tel 7763201
Parent Company: Part of the State Organisation for Iraqi Water Transport
Principal Bankers: Rafidain Bank

Principal Shareholders: State-owned
Date of Establishment: 1952
No of Employees: 800

IRAQI STATE IMPORT ORGANISATION

Masbah Area, PO Box 5642, Baghdad
Tel: 7195030, 7155937
Cable: IRAIMPORTS BAGHDAD
Telex: 212524

PRINCIPAL ACTIVITIES: Import of heavy machinery, motor vehicles, tyres, batteries, spare parts, building materials (steel, iron, timber, cement, sanitaryware, hardware, furniture, glass) and chemicals (aerosols, insecticides, paints)
Parent Company: Responsible to the Ministry of Trade

Principal Shareholders: State-owned

IRAQI STEEL CONSTRUCTION CO LTD

PO Box 2160, Baghdad
Tel: 7180138/9
Telex: 212110 Haddad IK

PRINCIPAL ACTIVITIES: Production of ventilators, prefabricated houses and cold stores and complete metal cladding systems

Principal Shareholders: Private sector company

IRAQI TEXTILE STATE EST

Al Nawab St, Khadhumiya, PO Box 9106, Baghdad
Tel: 4412091/9
Cable: Nasij Baghdad
Telex: 212787 Nasij IK

PRINCIPAL ACTIVITIES: Manufacture of textiles, cotton yarns, cloth and bandages
Parent Company: Part of the State Organisation for Textile Industries

Principal Shareholders: State-owned

IRAQI TOBACCO STATE EST
Karrada Al-Sharkiya, Nadhimiya, PO Box 10026, Baghdad
Tel: 7762012
Cable: Cigarettes Baghdad
Telex: 212261 Cigarettes IK

PRINCIPAL ACTIVITIES: Manufacture and distribution of
cigarettes and matches
Parent Company: Part of the State Organisation for Food
Industries

Principal Shareholders: State-owned

IRAQI TRADING STATE CO
Masbah, PO Box 17, Baghdad
Tel: 7196218
Cable: Unifresco Baghdad
Telex: 212291 Unifresco IK

PRINCIPAL ACTIVITIES: Import, distribution, wholesale and
retail of domestic electrical appliances, industrial electrical
equipment, and general consumer accessories and equipment
air conditioning, tyres, tubes, batteries, electronic goods
Parent Company: Part of the State Trade Organisation for
Consumer Goods

Principal Shareholders: State-owned

IRAQI-JORDANIAN CO FOR DETERGENTS MANUFACTURING
PO Box 2182, Alwiyah, Baghdad
Tel: 7197896, 7186503
Telex: 212159 IJIC IK

PRINCIPAL ACTIVITIES: Production of detergents and cleaning
materials

Principal Shareholders: Private sector company

ISHTAR SHERATON HOTEL
Unknown Soldier Square, Sadoun Street, Baghdad
Tel: 8889500/9
Telex: (21) 3146/7/8/9/50

PRINCIPAL ACTIVITIES: Hotel business
Branch Offices: Basra Sheraton Hotel, PO Box 760, Basra Tel
219310, Telex 207078
Parent Company: The Sheraton Corporation

No of Employees: 430

JUMA ELECTRICAL INDUSTRIES CO
PO Box 5464, Baghdad
Tel: 8888067, 8876108, 4442507 (Factory)
Cable: VLAT
Telex: 213653

PRINCIPAL ACTIVITIES: Manufacture of electricity distribution
control panels for high and low tension

Principal Shareholders: Private sector company

KAMAL MIQDADI
See MIQDADI, KAMAL,

KUT COTTON TEXTILE STATE CO
PO Box 25, Kut
Tel: 23967, 22962
Cable: Nasijkut
Telex: 217906 Nasij IK

PRINCIPAL ACTIVITIES: Manufacture of cotton textiles, yarns,
socks, underwear and woollen knitted clothing
Principal Agencies: State Establishment for Iraqi Stores
Parent Company: Part of the State Organisation for Textile
Industries
Principal Bankers: Rafidain Bank, Kut

Principal Shareholders: State-owned
Date of Establishment: 1971
No of Employees: 2,000

LIGHT INDUSTRIES CO SA
Zaafaraniya, PO Box 164, Baghdad
Tel: 7733100/4
Telex: 212414 Litbagd IK

PRINCIPAL ACTIVITIES: Manufacture and assembly of gas and
kerosene heaters, cookers, and refrigerators

Principal Shareholders: Mixed sector company

MAEEN CO FOR PLASTIC INDUSTRY
Bahbahani Bldg, Shorja, PO Box 301, Baghdad
Tel: 8882746, 8882551

PRINCIPAL ACTIVITIES: Manufacture of plastic products
Branch Offices: Factory: Kamalliya, Baghdad, Tel 61788

MIQDADI, KAMAL,
Moosa Al Kadhim St, Attaifiyah, PO Box 6049, Baghdad
Tel: 32611, 35420, Res 5510332
Cable: Miqdadi

Chairman: Kamal Miqdadi

PRINCIPAL ACTIVITIES: Construction of industrial buildings;
general civil engineering contracting
Principal Bankers: Rafidain Bank

MISAN SUGAR STATE ENTERPRISE
PO Box 9, Amara, Misan
Tel: 321660
Cable: Kasab
Telex: 212372 Kajab IK

PRINCIPAL ACTIVITIES: Plantation of sugar cane, production of
cane sugar, yeast and molasses
Branch Offices: Baghdad: PO Box 3028, Tel 8885968
Parent Company: Part of the State Organisation for Food
Industries

Principal Shareholders: State-owned

MISHRAQ SULPHUR STATE ENTERPRISE
PO Box 54 (Mosul), Al-Mishraq, Mosul
Tel: 815333, 819145
Cable: Mishraq Mosul
Telex: 8028, 8073
Telefax: 810555

Chairman: Alsafi

PRINCIPAL ACTIVITIES: Production and marketing of sulphur
Branch Offices: Mishraq Coordinate Office, Baghdad, Tel
8867600
Principal Bankers: Central Bank of Iraq; Rafidain Bank

Principal Shareholders: State-owned
Date of Establishment: 1969
No of Employees: 1,500

MODERN BUILDING CONTRACTING CO
Ja'far Allawi's Office, Mifjan Bldg, Baghdad
Tel: 83193

Senior Executives: Tawfiq Allawi, Ja'far Allawi, Kereem Allawi

PRINCIPAL ACTIVITIES: Contractors for multi-storey buildings
and various types of building

MODERN CHEMICAL INDUSTRIES CO
Abu Nawas St, PO Box 5654, Baghdad
Tel: 94559, 94438, 93585
Cable: Alcohol Baghdad
Telex: 212648, Alcohol IK

PRINCIPAL ACTIVITIES: Production of alcoholic beverages
Branch Offices: Factory: Albo-Shajah, Karada, Baghdad, Tel 94192, 92040

MODERN CONSTRUCTION MATERIALS INDUSTRY CO SA

PO Box 5603, Baghdad
Tel: 8880897
Telex: 212224 SINAI BK IK att Const Nat Co

PRINCIPAL ACTIVITIES: Manufacture of bricks, tiles, concrete and gypsum blocks

Principal Shareholders: Mixed sector company

MODERN PAINTS INDUSTRIES CO SA

PO Box 2436, Alwiya
Tel: 7734041/5
Cable: Paintmix Baghdad
Telex: 213911, 214080 Paint IK

PRINCIPAL ACTIVITIES: Production of paints
Branch Offices: Factory: Zaafaraniya Industrial Complex, Baghdad

Principal Shareholders: Mixed sector company

MOSUL BUILDING MATERIALS STATE CO

PO Box 13, Mosul
Tel: (0607) 71031
Cable: Mosul Cement
Telex: 298014

PRINCIPAL ACTIVITIES: Manufacture of Portland cement, concrete blocks, lime and lime bricks
Parent Company: Part of the State Organisation for Construction Industries

Principal Shareholders: State-owned

MOSUL SUGAR STATE CO

PO Box 42, Gizlany St, Mosul
Tel: (0607) 85251
Cable: Benjer-Mosul
Telex: 298012 Bangar IK

PRINCIPAL ACTIVITIES: Production of beet sugar and yeast
Parent Company: Part of the State Organisation for Food Industries

Principal Shareholders: State-owned

NABIL CO FOR FOOD PRODUCTS

Sarah Khatoon Camp, PO Box 11065, Baghdad
Tel: 7616748, 7618732
Cable: Indusdeal Baghdad
Telex: 2815 IK Ideal

Chairman: Nabil Rassam

PRINCIPAL ACTIVITIES: Manufacture of food products
Principal Bankers: Rafidain Bank

Principal Shareholders: Raouf Yousif Rassam, Nabil Rassam, Salma Hana Baraz
Date of Establishment: 1966
No of Employees: 120

NADIR FOOD PRODUCTS CO LTD

PO Box 3200, Baghdad
Tel: 7191120, 7182514, 7185134, 7185185
Cable: Kamanjati Baghdad
Telex: 212435 Nadrfood IK

Chairman: Subhi Al Khudairi
Directors: Munim Hamid (Managing Director)

PRINCIPAL ACTIVITIES: Production of foodstuffs
Branch Offices: Factory: Zafaraniya, Baghdad, Tel 7737116, 7737366

Principal Bankers: Rafidain Bank
Financial Information:

	ID'000
Paid-up capital	1,000

Date of Establishment: 1966
No of Employees: 100

NASIR WATCH CO WLL

Mustansir St, PO Box 11387, Baghdad
Tel: 8886725
Cable: Steelmesh Baghdad
Telex: 212749 Bauer IK

Senior Executives: H Al Banna (Managing Director)

PRINCIPAL ACTIVITIES: Production of watches and clocks

NATIONAL CENTRE FOR ENGINEERING & ARCHITECTURAL CONSULTANCY

Rashid St, PO Box 3290, Baghdad
Tel: 88876761
Cable: Tasamin
Telex: 212260 Tasamim IK

PRINCIPAL ACTIVITIES: Engineering and architectural consultancy of diversified nature, but mainly in public works projects, services include preparation of feasibility studies, technical and legal documentation and supervision of execution
Parent Company: Part of the Ministry of Housing & Construction
Principal Bankers: Central Bank of Iraq

Principal Shareholders: State-owned
Date of Establishment: 1972
No of Employees: 202

NATIONAL CHEMICAL & PLASTIC INDUSTRIES CO SA

PO Box 2302 Alwiyah, Zaafaraniya Industrial Area, Baghdad
Tel: 7730001, 8884211, 8885558
Cable: Sponge
Telex: 212627, 213950 NCPI
Telefax: 7730531

PRINCIPAL ACTIVITIES: Producer of flexible, latex type and rigid foam, artificial leather, PVC compounding, PVC pipes, PS sheets and foils foam leather, plastic crates for bottles
Principal Bankers: Industrial Bank; Rafidain Bank

NATIONAL COMPUTER CENTRE

PO Box 3267, Saadoon and Nafoora Sq, Baghdad
Tel: 8868151/2/3, 8886151
Telex: 212218 PI IK

Chairman: Minister of Planning

PRINCIPAL ACTIVITIES: Control and coordination of the Iraqi computer industry
Parent Company: Responsible to the Ministry of Planning

Principal Shareholders: State-owned

NATIONAL ELECTRICAL INDUSTRIES CO LTD

Sadoon St, PO Box 3053, Baghdad
Tel: 7186092, 7186095
Cable: Ras Baghdad
Telex: 213381 HAS IK

Chairman: Hickmet Shaban
Directors: Hickmet Shaban (Managing Director)

PRINCIPAL ACTIVITIES: Manufacture of plastic-coated electric wires and cables, switchboards, industrial light fittings
Branch Offices: Factory: Aweereg, Baghdad
Principal Bankers: Rafidain Bank (Saadoun Branch)

Financial Information:

	1988/89 US$'000
Sales turnover	6,500
Authorised capital	1,450

Principal Shareholders: Hickmet Shaban; Widad Abdul Hussein
Date of Establishment: 1968
No of Employees: 68

NATIONAL FOOD INDUSTRIES CO SA

Zaafaraniya, PO Box 3210, Baghdad
Tel: 7730311
Cable: Hospmalt Baghdad
Telex: 212224 Sinai BK IK Att NFI

PRINCIPAL ACTIVITIES: Food processing and canning, also
beer and fruit juices production

Principal Shareholders: Mixed sector company

NATIONAL HOUSE FOR PUBLISHING, DISTRIBUTING & ADVERTISING

Al Jamhuria St, Baghdad
Tel: 8868391
Cable: Donta
Telex: 212392 Donta IK

PRINCIPAL ACTIVITIES: Sole importers of books and
periodicals as well as exporters of Iraqi books; also
monopoly of advertising in Iraq
Parent Company: Responsible to the Ministry of Information
Principal Bankers: Rafidain Bank

Principal Shareholders: State-owned

NATIONAL INSURANCE CO

Khullani St, PO Box 248, Baghdad
Tel: 8860730
Cable: Natamin
Telex: 212397 Natamin IK

Chairman: Mowafaq Hassan Ridha
Directors: Dr Khalil Alshamaa, Talal F Al-Faisal, Aziz J Hassan,
Kais M Al Mudaris, Abdul Khaliq R Khalil, Izzi Deen H Shawqi

PRINCIPAL ACTIVITIES: All classes of direct insurance and life
assurance
Principal Bankers: Rafidain Bank, Baghdad
Financial Information:

	1989 ID'000
Authorised capital	20,000
Paid-up capital	20,000

Principal Shareholders: State-owned
Date of Establishment: 1950
No of Employees: 1,629

NATIONAL PLASTIC FACTORY

Wathba St, PO Box 1015, Baghdad
Tel: 62255
Cable: Piombaba Baghdad

PRINCIPAL ACTIVITIES: Manufacture of plastic pipes, bags and
other products
Branch Offices: Jamilah Industrial Estate, Baghdad, Tel 61142

NATIONAL TOBACCO STATE CO

PO Box 6, Arbil
Tel: (0665) 21505
Cable: Arcig, Arbil
Telex: 218506 TB Arbil IK

PRINCIPAL ACTIVITIES: Manufacture and distribution of
cigarettes

Parent Company: Part of the State Organisation for Food
Industries

Principal Shareholders: State-owned

NORTHERN CEMENT PUBLIC ENTERPRISE

PO Box 1, Sulaimaniya
Tel: (0532) 27426
Telex: 218906 CHNAR IK

PRINCIPAL ACTIVITIES: Manufacture of portland and sulphate
resisting cement
Parent Company: Responsible to the State Organisation of
Construction Industries

Principal Shareholders: State-owned

ORIENT FACTORY FOR MODERN WAREHOUSING EQUIPMENT

Naji Khudairi Bldg, Rashid St, Baghdad
Tel: 8882309
Cable: Lifting Baghdad

PRINCIPAL ACTIVITIES: Manufacture and installation of racking
and related warehousing equipments and prefabricated
warehouses; design of storage systems
Principal Bankers: Rafidain Bank; Industrial Bank

Principal Shareholders: Sole Proprietor Abdul Ghani Nassief

PALESTINE MERIDIEN HOTEL

PO Box 3100, between Sadoun & Abu Nawas Strs, Mahalat
102, Baghdad
Tel: 8875641/8
Cable: HOMER-BAGHDAD
Telex: 213151/5

PRINCIPAL ACTIVITIES: Hotel business
Parent Company: Air France

Date of Establishment: May 1982
No of Employees: 370

PETRA NAVIGATION & INTERNATIONAL TRADING CO LTD

Hai Al Wahda Mahalat 906, 906 Zukak 50, House No 14,
Baghdad
Tel: 7190252
Telex: 212503 Trans IK

Chairman: Ahmad Armoush
Directors: Ali Armoush

PRINCIPAL ACTIVITIES: Vessel operation, chartering, lines
agents, related services
Parent Company: Head office in Amman, Jordan

RAFID SHOE MANUFACTURING CO LTD

PO Box 489, Baghdad
Tel: 7191502, 7197401
Cable: Shorafid
Telex: 212115 Rafid IK

Chairman: A A Al-Shakiry
Directors: Ali Mohd Ali

PRINCIPAL ACTIVITIES: Shoe and rubber products
manufacturing
Subsidiary Companies: Abid Polymers Products Manufacturing
Co WLL
Principal Bankers: Rafidain Bank
Financial Information:

	ID'000
Authorised capital	1,000
Paid-up capital	1,000

Principal Shareholders: Private company
Date of Establishment: 1966
No of Employees: 400

RAFIDAIN BANK
New Banks' St, PO Box 11360, Massarif, Baghdad
Tel: 4158001, 8870548
Cable: Rafdbank
Telex: 212211 Rafd Bk IK

Chairman: Tariq Al-Tuckmachi
Directors: Abdul Majid Hameed (General Manager), Falih A Al
Salih, Abdul Khalik Rao'of, Yaqoob Y Shonia, Dr Abdul
Munim S Ali, Abdul Husein Sahib, Asim M Salih

PRINCIPAL ACTIVITIES: All commercial banking transactions
Branch Offices: 218 branches in Iraq
Financial Information:

	ID'000
Authorised capital	100,000
Paid-up capital	100,000

Principal Shareholders: State-owned
Date of Establishment: 1941
No of Employees: 12,557

RAFIDAIN EQUIPMENT CO
Shaheen Bldg, Mafrak Karada, PO Box 3115, Baghdad
Tel: 95659
Cable: Rafcool Baghdad

PRINCIPAL ACTIVITIES: Manufacture of air coolers, gas stoves
and household goods
Branch Offices: Factory: Obaidi City, Shama'ia, Baghdad, Tel
93715

RAYON STATE ESTABLISHMENT
Hindiya, Babylon
Tel: 2911
Cable: Rayon Baghdad
Telex: 216206 Rayon IK

PRINCIPAL ACTIVITIES: Manufacture of rayon fibres, cotton
and woollen threads, sulphuric acid and caustic soda
Branch Offices: Baghdad: PO Box 11230, Tel 8897725
Parent Company: Part of the State Organisation for Textile
Industries

Principal Shareholders: State-owned

READY MADE CLOTHES INDUSTRIES CO SA
PO Box 5769, Mahmoudia, Baghdad
Tel: (0220) 22526
Cable: Pyjama Baghdad

PRINCIPAL ACTIVITIES: Manufacture of ready made clothing

Principal Shareholders: Mixed sector company

REAL ESTATE BANK
Karradat Mariam, PO Box 14185, Baghdad
Tel: 5375165
Telex: 212635 IK

PRINCIPAL ACTIVITIES: Banking, loans to the building industry

Principal Shareholders: State-owned
Date of Establishment: 1948

ROUMANI, ADNAN, & CO
PO Box 3144, Sadoon St, Baghdad
Tel: 96761, 90959
Cable: Tradany
Telex: 212151 IK

Directors: Adnan Roumani
Senior Executives: R S Issa

PRINCIPAL ACTIVITIES: General trade, transportation clearing
and forwarding and customs clearance, commission agents

SABA & CO
Shahin Bldg, Mafrag Karada Al-Sharqiya, PO Box 2319,
Alawiya, Baghdad
Tel: 99080/9
Cable: Sabaco Baghdad
Telex: 212154 IK

PRINCIPAL ACTIVITIES: Public accountants and management
consultants
Branch Offices: Lebanon; Cyprus; Egypt; Iraq (Basra and
Mosul); Jordan; Kuwait; Libya; Morocco; Oman; Qatar; Saudi
Arabia; Syria; United Arab Emirates; Yemen

SABA'PILE LTD
PO Box 2074, Aiwiyah, Baghdad
Tel: 7199065, 7199066
Telex: 212330 Sapile IK

Chairman: Saad M H Saba' (Civil Engineering)

PRINCIPAL ACTIVITIES: Piling and foundation contractors
Principal Bankers: Rafidain Bank

No of Employees: 80

SARCHINAR STATE CEMENT ENTERPRISE
PO Box 1, Sarchina, Sulaimaniya
Tel: 20311
Cable: Sarchinar Cement

PRINCIPAL ACTIVITIES: Manufacture of Portland and sulphate
resisting cement
Parent Company: Part of the State Organisation for
Construction Industries

Principal Shareholders: State-owned

SINAAT ALADDIN (IRAQ) WLL
Rashid St, Baghdad
Tel: 8885126/7/8
Cable: Sinalir
Telex: 212311 IK Sinalir

Chairman: M Hassoun
Directors: S N Sabbagh, H Al Umari, N Chaderji, Z Abbosh, K
Sabbagh, Y Allos

PRINCIPAL ACTIVITIES: Manufacture of heating and cooking
appliances (oil and gas)
Subsidiary/Associated Companies: Aladdin Industries Ltd, UK
Principal Bankers: Rafidain Bank

SOUTHERN CEMENT ENTERPRISE
PO Box 5, Samawah
Tel: (0377) 22961/2, 22844
Cable: Cemunit
Telex: 6607 Cemunit IK

Chairman: A H Kudair (Director General)
Directors: M Kamel

PRINCIPAL ACTIVITIES: Manufacture of Portland cement, lime
bricks and thermostone
Branch Offices: Cement Marketing Office in Muthena; Factories
at Muthena, Samawa, Um Kussir
Parent Company: Part of the State Organisation for
Construction Industries
Principal Bankers: Rafidain Bank, Samawah

Principal Shareholders: State-owned

SPECIALISED INSTITUTE FOR ENGINEERING INDUSTRIES (SIEI)
PO Box 5798, Baghdad
Tel: 7750880
Cable: Mahad
Telex: 2226 SIEI IK

PRINCIPAL ACTIVITIES: Production design and development; production technology; quality control; industrial information; training; techno economic studies

Parent Company: Part of the State Organisation for Engineering Industries

Principal Shareholders: State-owned
Date of Establishment: 1973
No of Employees: 200

STATE BATTERY MANUFACTURING EST

PO Box 190, Waziriya, Baghdad
Tel: 8825100
Cable: Batren
Telex: 212712 Batren IK

PRINCIPAL ACTIVITIES: Manufacture of dry and wet batteries
Parent Company: Part of the State Organisation for Engineering Industries
Principal Bankers: Rafidain Bank

Principal Shareholders: State-owned

STATE CO FOR FAIRS & COMMERCIAL SERVICES

Baghdad Al Nidhal Street, PO Box 5642 - 5760, Baghdad
Tel: 7196649, 7190354
Telex: 212524 ISOI IK

Directors: Falah Mirza Mahmood (Director General)

PRINCIPAL ACTIVITIES: Responsible for developing Iraqi exports (except oil and oil products), responsible for internal and foreign fairs and provision of export-import services for both the public and the private sectors; control and supervision of the four following committees: Fairs Committee, Export Committee, Import Committee, Commercial Services Division
Principal Bankers: Rafidain Bank, Khullani Branch

Principal Shareholders: State-owned organisation
Date of Establishment: Formerly the Iraqi State Export Organisation
No of Employees: 1,464

STATE CO FOR OIL PROJECTS (SCOP)

Ministry of Oil Complex, Port Said St, PO Box 198, Baghdad
Tel: 8869622, 7741310
Cable: Inshaat
Telex: 212806 SCOP IK
Telefax: 8763744

Chairman: A H Ijam (Director General)
Directors: Dr T Hattab (Project Director), A Al Ani (Design Director), H A Mahmoud (Construction Director)

PRINCIPAL ACTIVITIES: Design, construction and supervision of oil and gas projects
Principal Agencies: North Oil Co (NOC); South Oil Co (SOC); Oil Ref Est
Parent Company: Responsible to the Ministry of Oil
Principal Bankers: Rafidain Bank; Central Bank of Iraq; Al Rashid Bank
Financial Information:

	1989
	ID'000
Authorised capital	25,000

Principal Shareholders: State-owned
Date of Establishment: 1964
No of Employees: 3,000

STATE CO FOR SALTS

PO Box 2330, Alwiya, Saadoun Street, Baghdad
Tel: 7192361
Telex: 212292 SOMIK

PRINCIPAL ACTIVITIES: Salt mining

Principal Shareholders: State-owned

STATE CONTRACTING BUILDINGS CO

PO Box 19036, Al Nahda Area, Baghdad
Tel: 8889761, 8889735
Telex: 212577

PRINCIPAL ACTIVITIES: Building and construction
Financial Information: Succeeding the State Constructional Contracts Company which was dissolved in 1980

Principal Shareholders: State-owned
Date of Establishment: 1981

STATE CONTRACTING INDUSTRIAL PROJECTS CO

PO Box 5784, Baghdad
Tel: 8872006, 8884161
Telex: 212301 El Cont IK

PRINCIPAL ACTIVITIES: Civil engineering contracting
Financial Information: Succeeding the State Constructional Contracts Company which was dissolved in 1980

Principal Shareholders: State-owned
Date of Establishment: 1981

STATE CONTRACTING PILING & FOUNDATIONS CO

PO Box 22072, Baghdad
Tel: 8871211, 8889948
Cable: RAKAIZ
Telex: 212234 Contract IK

PRINCIPAL ACTIVITIES: Piling and foundations
Branch Offices: Basrah, Tel 410830
Principal Bankers: Rafidain Bank
Financial Information: Succeeding the State Constructional Contracts Company which was dissolved in 1980

Principal Shareholders: State-owned
Date of Establishment: 1981
No of Employees: 1,000

STATE CONTRACTING WATER & SEWAGE PROJECTS CO

Street No 52, Alwiya, PO Box 5738, Baghdad
Tel: 7192355
Cable: Projects Baghdad
Telex: 212534 WASP IK

PRINCIPAL ACTIVITIES: Main contractors for water and sewage projects
Parent Company: Responsible to the Ministry of Local Affairs

Principal Shareholders: State-owned

STATE ELECTRICAL INDUSTRIES CO

PO Box 1118, Waziria, Baghdad
Tel: 8826051
Cable: Ajheza Baghdad
Telex: 212620 Ajhiza IK

PRINCIPAL ACTIVITIES: Manufacture of electric motors, pumps, oil transformers, light fittings, sockets and electrical fans
Parent Company: Part of the State Organisation for Engineering Industries

Principal Shareholders: State-owned

STATE ENGINEERING CO FOR INDUSTRIAL DESIGN & CONSTRUCTION

Nidhal St, PO Box 5614, Baghdad
Tel: 8872006, 8867616
Cable: Tasmisinai
Telex: 213078 Sn IK

PRINCIPAL ACTIVITIES: Feasibility studies, design, construction, supervision of construction projects and sites, civil design, inspection
Principal Bankers: Rafidain Bank

Principal Shareholders: State-owned company financed by central government and self supply

STATE ENT. FOR ALUMINIUM SEMI PRODUCTS

PO Box 38, Nasiriyah
Tel: (042) 230412
Cable: Nascap Nasiriyah
Telex: 217806 Nascap IK

PRINCIPAL ACTIVITIES: Manufacture of aluminium semi products, sheets and wires, circles, profiles, foils
Parent Company: Part of the State Organisation for Engineering Industries
Principal Bankers: Central Bank of Iraq, Baghdad; Rafidain Bank, Main branch - Baghdad

Principal Shareholders: State-owned
Date of Establishment: 1975
No of Employees: 1,000

STATE ENT. FOR ASBESTOS & PLASTIC INDUSTRIES

Zaafarania, PO Box 2418, Baghdad
Tel: 7730393
Cable: Asbestos
Telex: 212358 Asbestos IK

PRINCIPAL ACTIVITIES: Manufacture of asbestos cement pipes, flat and corrugated sheets; Rekajoints; PVC pipes and HDPE pipes, and thermostone blocks
Branch Offices: Basrah Asbestos Factory: Basrah; Kirkuk Asbestos Factory: Kirkuk; Misan Plastic Pipes Factory: Misan
Parent Company: Part of the State Organisation for Construction Industries
Principal Bankers: Rafidain Bank

Principal Shareholders: State-owned

STATE ENT. FOR AUTOMOTIVE INDUSTRY

Iskandariya
Tel: (030) 222718
Cable: Scandeen Iskandariya
Telex: 216211 SEAI IK

PRINCIPAL ACTIVITIES: Assembly of trucks, buses, trailers and heavy vehicles
Parent Company: Part of the State Organisation for Engineering Industries
Principal Bankers: Rafidain Bank, Iskandariya

Principal Shareholders: State-owned

STATE ENT. FOR BRICKS INDUSTRIES

Khalid Bin Walid Street, Baghdad
Tel: 7195833
Cable: Tabouk, Baghdad
Telex: 212418 Tabouk

PRINCIPAL ACTIVITIES: Manufacture of clay bricks
Parent Company: Part of the State Organisation for Construction Industries

Principal Shareholders: State-owned

STATE ENT. FOR CABLES & WIRES

PO Box 44, Nassiriyah
Tel: (042) 230232
Cable: Cabwire Nassiriyah
Telex: 217807 Scwe IK

PRINCIPAL ACTIVITIES: Manufacture of cables and wires
Branch Offices: Factory: Nassiriya
Parent Company: Part of the State Organisation for Engineering Industries

Principal Shareholders: State-owned

STATE ENT. FOR CANNING IN KERBALA

Kerbala
Tel: (0323) 23232
Cable: Taleeb, Kerbala
Telex: 216406 Taaleeb K

PRINCIPAL ACTIVITIES: Canning of fruit, vegetables, date syrup, jams, and pickles
Branch Offices: Baghdad: Tel 5518347
Parent Company: Part of the State Organisation for Food Industries

Principal Shareholders: State-owned

STATE ENT. FOR CONCRETE INDUSTRIES

Abu-Ghraib, PO Box 6188, Baghdad
Tel: (0203) 42370
Cable: Concrete, Baghdad
Telex: 213138 Concret IK

PRINCIPAL ACTIVITIES: Manufacture of concrete pipes and blocks
Parent Company: Part of the State Organisation for Construction Industries

Principal Shareholders: State-owned

STATE ENT. FOR DAIRY PRODUCTS

PO Box 11183, Abu Ghraib, Baghdad
Tel: 5554287
Cable: Alban Baghdad
Telex: 212210 Alban IK

PRINCIPAL ACTIVITIES: Production of dairy products
Parent Company: Part of the State Organisation for Food Industries

Principal Shareholders: State-owned

STATE ENT. FOR DRUG INDUSTRIES

PO Box 271, Samarra
Tel: 2940/9
Cable: Drugs Indust Samarra
Telex: 216707

PRINCIPAL ACTIVITIES: Production and marketing of pharmaceutical products, import of chemicals, capsules and pharmaceutical preparations
Branch Offices: Baghdad, Tel 8888142
Parent Company: Responsible to the Ministry of Health

Principal Shareholders: State-owned

STATE ENT. FOR FERTILIZERS

PO Box 74, Basrah
Tel: (040) 215720/1/2
Cable: Asmida Basrah
Telex: 207001 Asmida Basrah IK

PRINCIPAL ACTIVITIES: Production of urea and ammonium sulphate fertilisers, ammonia gas and sulphuric acid
Branch Offices: PO Box 1000, Khor Az Zubair, Tel 213790, Telex 207054

Parent Company: Part of the State Organisation for Chemical Industries
Principal Bankers: Rafidain Bank, Basrah

Principal Shareholders: State-owned company

STATE ENT. FOR FOODSTUFFS TRADING

Midan Square, PO Box 548, Baghdad
Tel: 4155807
Cable: Mubayaat Baghdad
Telex: 212232 IK

PRINCIPAL ACTIVITIES: Import in bulk and distribution to local agents of foodstuffs (tea, milk powder, sugar); and wood charcoal
Parent Company: Part of the State Trade Organisation for Consumer Goods
Principal Bankers: Rafidain Bank

Principal Shareholders: State-owned

STATE ENT. FOR GLASS & CERAMIC INDUSTRIES

Ramadi, Al Anbar
Tel: (0244) 22942
Cable: Zoujaj, Ramadi
Telex: 216106 Zoujaj IK

PRINCIPAL ACTIVITIES: Manufacture of glass sheets, glass bottles and jars and household glassware
Parent Company: Part of the State Organisation for Construction Industries

Principal Shareholders: State-owned

STATE ENT. FOR GYPSUM INDUSTRIES

Nidhal Street, PO Box 3176, Baghdad
Tel: 8872971, 8877051
Cable: GYPSUM
Telex: 212968 Gypsum IK

PRINCIPAL ACTIVITIES: Manufacture of gypsum products
Parent Company: Part of the State Organisation for Construction Industries

Principal Shareholders: State-owned

STATE ENT. FOR HAND WOVEN CARPETS

Al Nasir Sq, Arbil
Tel: (0665) 22983/4
Cable: Hand Woven Carpets Arbil

PRINCIPAL ACTIVITIES: Production of hand-made carpets
Parent Company: Part of the State Organisation for Textile Industries

Principal Shareholders: State-owned

STATE ENT. FOR IRON & STEEL INDUSTRIES (SCICI)

Khor Al Zubair, PO Box 348, Basrah
Tel: (040) 216527
Cable: Statisco Basrah
Telex: 207046 Scisi IK

PRINCIPAL ACTIVITIES: Manufacture and marketing of iron and steel products
Branch Offices: Baghdad Sales Office: Tel 5520959
Parent Company: Part of the State Organisation for Engineering Industries
Principal Bankers: Rafidain Bank

Principal Shareholders: State-owned

STATE ENT. FOR MARITIME AGENCIES

Basrah
Tel: (040) 213805

PRINCIPAL ACTIVITIES: Shipping agents for all freight steamers and oil tanker ships

Parent Company: Part of the State Organisation for Iraqi Water Transport

Principal Shareholders: State-owned

STATE ENT. FOR MARKETING EQUIPMENT & MAINTENANCE

Daura, PO Box 12014, Baghdad
Tel: 5545771
Cable: Nemco
Telex: 212394 Nemco IK

PRINCIPAL ACTIVITIES: Marketing and maintenance of motor vehicles tractors manufactured by State organization for engineering industries
Branch Offices: Mosul; Basrah; Babylon; Diala; Kut; Qadesiya; Kirkuk
Parent Company: Part of the State Organisation for Engineering Industries
Principal Bankers: Rafidain Bank

Principal Shareholders: State-owned
Date of Establishment: 1976

STATE ENT. FOR MECHANICAL INDUSTRIES

PO Box 5763, Iskandariya
Tel: (030) 222722
Cable: Statengco Iskamdariya
Telex: 216208 SEMI IK

PRINCIPAL ACTIVITIES: Manufacture of nuts and bolts, agricultural equipment and tools, also assembly of cars, buses and tractors and operation of foundry
Branch Offices: Factory: Iskandariya
Parent Company: Part of the State Organisation for Engineering Industries
Principal Bankers: Rafidain Bank

Principal Shareholders: State-owned

STATE ENT. FOR PETROCHEMICAL INDUSTRIES

Khor Al Zubair, PO Box 933, Basrah
Tel: (040) 216581, 218610
Cable: Petchem Basrah
Telex: 207042
Telefax: (01) 8872557

Chairman: Gassan A Ali (Director General)

PRINCIPAL ACTIVITIES: Production of petrochemical materials for the plastic industry
Parent Company: Part of the Ministry of Industry
Principal Bankers: Rafidain Bank

Principal Shareholders: State-owned
Date of Establishment: 1978
No of Employees: 1,800

STATE ENT. FOR PHOSPHATES

PO Box 5954, East Gate, Sadoon St, Baghdad
Tel: 8873027, 8889708, 8889709, 8889700
Cable: Phosphate Baghdad
Telex: 216117 Phosphate IK

Directors: F K Al-Amir (Director General)

PRINCIPAL ACTIVITIES: Exploration and production of phosphate and production of phosphatic fertilisers (MAP, TSP, NPK) and other by-products
Branch Offices: Al Anbar, Al Qaim
Principal Bankers: Central Bank of Iraq

Principal Shareholders: State-owned
Date of Establishment: 1976
No of Employees: 2,171

STATE ENT. FOR PULP & PAPER INDUSTRIES

PO Box 248, Hartha District, Basrah
Tel: (040) 213142
Cable: Warak Basrah
Telex: 207030

PRINCIPAL ACTIVITIES: Manufacture of pulp, paper and cardboard
Branch Offices: PO Box 108, Misan, Tel (043) 320578, Telex 217708 Sulzmi IK
Parent Company: Part of the State Organisation for Chemical Industries
Principal Bankers: Rafidain Bank, Basrah

Principal Shareholders: State-owned company

STATE ENT. FOR RAW BUILDING MATERIALS

PO Box 5890 Alwiya, Near Unknown Soldier, Saadoun Street, Baghdad
Tel: 7192361
Cable: Managim
Telex: 212292 Som IK

PRINCIPAL ACTIVITIES: Production of gravel, sand, stone and marble

Principal Shareholders: State-owned

STATE ENT. FOR RIVER TRANSPORT

Kerrada Dakhil, Zewiya, Baghdad
Tel: 7763201

PRINCIPAL ACTIVITIES: Loading and offloading of river boats and steamers
Parent Company: Part of the State Organisation for Iraqi Water Transport

Principal Shareholders: State-owned

STATE ENT. FOR RUBBER INDUSTRIES

PO Box 71, Diwaniya
Tel: (0366) 20756
Cable: Tyco
Telex: 216506 Tyre IK

PRINCIPAL ACTIVITIES: Manufacture of tyres and tubes and other rubber products
Parent Company: Part of the State Organisation for Chemical Industries
Principal Bankers: Rafidain Bank

Principal Shareholders: State-owned
Date of Establishment: 1977
No of Employees: 800

STATE ENT. FOR SHOPPING CENTRES

PO Box 3095, Al Wahda District, Khalid Bin Al Waleed St, Baghdad
Tel: 7193353
Cable: SHOPEC Baghdad
Telex: 212196 Freeshop IK

PRINCIPAL ACTIVITIES: Import and distribution of consumer goods, household appliances, electrical and electronic goods, toiletries, tobacco, leisure goods, shoes and clothing, beverages, food, etc
Parent Company: Responsible to the Ministry of Trade

Principal Shareholders: State-owned

STATE ENT. FOR SOFT & ALCOHOLIC DRINKS

PO Box 5689, Sara Khatoon Camp, Baghdad
Tel: 95021/9
Cable: Entaesh
Telex: 212235 IK

PRINCIPAL ACTIVITIES: Production and bottling of soft drinks (crush cola, pepsi cola, crush orange) and manufacture of plastic crates
Parent Company: Part of the State Organisation for Food Industries

Principal Shareholders: State-owned

STATE ENT. FOR TEXTILE & SPINNING PRODUCTS IMPORTING & DISTRIBUTION

Al-Zawria Bldg, Al-Hindiya, PO Box 5856, Baghdad
Tel: 92719, 93454
Cable: Textile Baghdad

PRINCIPAL ACTIVITIES: Import, distribution, wholesale and retail of textiles and carpets
Parent Company: Part of the State Trade Organisation for Consumer Goods

Principal Shareholders: State-owned

STATE ENT. FOR VEGETABLE OILS

PO Box 2379, Muaskar Al Rashid Rd, Baghdad
Tel: 95171, 92306/8, 90041
Cable: Zuyout Baghdad
Telex: 212221 Zuyout IK

PRINCIPAL ACTIVITIES: Production of vegetable cooking oils and fats, soaps, cosmetics, toothpaste, detergents
Parent Company: Part of the State Organisation for Food Industries

Principal Shareholders: State-owned

STATE ENT. FOR WOOD INDUSTRIES

Abu Sukhair, PO Box 20, Najaf
Tel: 69061/8
Telex: 212205 Mi Ind IK

PRINCIPAL ACTIVITIES: Manufacture of wooden sheets for the furniture industry
Branch Offices: Baghdad Office: c/o State Organisation for Chemical Industries, Khullani Sq, Baghdad
Parent Company: Part of the State Organisation for Chemical Industries

Principal Shareholders: State-owned

STATE EST. FOR CIVIL AIRPORTS

Baghdad International Airport, Baghdad
Tel: 8874331, 8885161
Telex: 212500 YIA IK

PRINCIPAL ACTIVITIES: Land and air services and airport maintenance
Parent Company: Responsible to the Ministry of Transport & Communications

Principal Shareholders: State-owned

STATE EST. FOR IRAQI STORES

PO Box 26 & PO Box 5856, Baghdad
Tel: 7182752
Cable: Orosdi Baghdad
Telex: 212365 Orosdi IK, 212601 Textile IK

PRINCIPAL ACTIVITIES: Import, distribution wholesale and retail of domestic consumer goods, household goods, glassware, cutlery, cosmetics and toiletries, sport goods, ready made clothing, tobacco, beverages, haberdashery goods etc
Parent Company: Part of the State Trade Organisation for Consumer Goods

Principal Shareholders: State-owned

STATE EST. FOR IRRIGATION PROJECTS

Karantina, Near Sarafiya Bridge, Baghdad
Tel: 8889194
Cable: Rifdel Baghdad

PRINCIPAL ACTIVITIES: Responsible for irrigation services, and drainage projects
Parent Company: Part of the State Organisation for Irrigation Projects

Principal Shareholders: State-owned organisation

STATE EST. FOR LEATHER INDUSTRIES

Karrada Al-Sharkiya, Hurriya Sq, PO Box 3079, Baghdad
Tel: 7765081
Cable: Jilood
Telex: 212237 Jilood IK

PRINCIPAL ACTIVITIES: Tanning of skins, manufacture of suitcases, handbags, briefcases, belts, shoes and other leather products
Parent Company: Part of the State Organisation for Textile Industries

Principal Shareholders: State-owned

STATE MACHINERY CO

Sara Camp, PO Box 2218, Baghdad
Tel: 7196601, 7196649, 7196645
Cable: Smic Baghdad
Telex: 212193

PRINCIPAL ACTIVITIES: Production and distribution of agricultural, industrial and construction machinery and earthmoving equipment
Parent Company: Part of the State Trade Organisation for Capital Goods

Principal Shareholders: State-owned

STATE ORG. FOR AGRICULTURAL MECHANISATION & AGRICULTURAL SUPPLIES

PO Box 26028, Waziriya, opp Al Bakr University, Baghdad
Tel: 8826417
Telex: 212222 Zerra IK

PRINCIPAL ACTIVITIES: Agricultural services and equipment
Parent Company: Responsible to the Ministry of Agriculture & Agrarian Reform
Subsidiary Companies: General Establishment for Operation & Maintenance; State Establishment for Agricultural Mechanisation, General Establishment for Agricultural Supplies

Principal Shareholders: State-owned

STATE ORG. FOR ANIMAL PRODUCTION

Zafaraniya Area, Near Post Office, Baghdad
Tel: 7762613, 7732246
Telex: 212223 Yakteen IK

PRINCIPAL ACTIVITIES: Control for the production of commercial livestock and poultry
Parent Company: Responsible to the Ministry of Agriculture & Agrarian Reform
Subsidiary Companies: State Enterprise for Poultry for Central Area, Baghdad; State Enterprise for Poultry for Northern Area, Arbil; State Enterprise for Poultry for Southern Area, Basrah; State Enterprise for Animal Feed, Baghdad; State Enterprise for Livestock Projects, Baghdad

STATE ORG. FOR BUILDINGS

Museum Square, Karkh, Baghdad
Tel: 5376101
Telex: 212282 Mabanam IK

PRINCIPAL ACTIVITIES: Construction of governmental buildings
Parent Company: Responsible to the Ministry of Housing & Construction
Subsidiary Companies: State Establishment for Buildings, Northern Area, Mosul; State Establishment for Buildings, Central Area, Karkh, Baghdad; State Establishment for Buildings, Southern Area, Amara, Midan

Principal Shareholders: State-owned

STATE ORG. FOR CHEMICAL INDUSTRIES

Jumhuriya St, Khullani Sq, PO Box 5424, Baghdad
Tel: 8889121, 8870891
Cable: Indust Baghdad
Telex: 212205 Mi Ind IK

PRINCIPAL ACTIVITIES: Responsible for the planning, supervision and control of the following establishments in the chemical industry
Parent Company: Responsible to the Ministry of Industry & Minerals
Subsidiary Companies: State Enterprise for Fertilisers; State Enterprise for Paper and Pulp Industries; State Enterprise for Rubber Industries; State Enterprise for Wood Industries; State Enterprise for Petrochemical Industries

Principal Shareholders: State-owned organisation

STATE ORG. FOR CONSTRUCTION INDUSTRIES

PO Box 2101, Baghdad
Tel: 8872006
Cable: Stoki Baghdad
Telex: 212236 Stoki IK

PRINCIPAL ACTIVITIES: Responsible for the planning, supervision and control of the following establishments in the building and construction industries
Parent Company: Responsible to the Ministry of Light Industries
Subsidiary Companies: Iraqi Cement State Enterprise; Mosul State Enterprise for Cement; Southern Cement Enterprise; Sarchinar State Enterprise for Cement; State Enterprise for Asbestos & Plastic Industries; State Enterprise for Bricks Industries; State Enterprise for Concrete Industries; State Enterprise for Glass & Ceramics Industries; State Enterprise for Gypsum Industries

Principal Shareholders: State-owned organisation

STATE ORG. FOR DAMS

Saadoun Street, Baghdad
Tel: 7182236
Telex: 212107 DAMS IK

PRINCIPAL ACTIVITIES: Design and construction for dams
Parent Company: Responsible to the Ministry of Irrigation
Subsidiary Companies: Mosul Dam; Haditha Dam; Hemreen Dam

Principal Shareholders: State-owned

STATE ORG. FOR ELECTRICITY

Off Al Jumhuriya St, Bldg 166, Nafoora Square, PO Box 5796, Baghdad
Tel: 8880051
Cable: Statelect
Telex: 212220 Electric IK

PRINCIPAL ACTIVITIES: Generation, transmission and distribution of electricity throughout Iraq
Parent Company: Responsible to the Ministry of Industry & Minerals

Principal Shareholders: State-owned

STATE ORG. FOR ENGINEERING INDUSTRIES

Ministry of Industry Bldg, Al Nidal Street, PO Box 5614, Baghdad
Tel: 8872006
Cable: Industator Baghdad
Telex: 212226 Soei IK

PRINCIPAL ACTIVITIES: Responsible for the planning, supervision, control of the following establishments in the metallurgical and light industries
Parent Company: Responsible to the Ministry of Industry & Minerals
Subsidiary/Associated Companies: Industrial Complex in Baquba; State Enterprise for Marketing and Maintenance of Engineering Equipment; Specialised Institute for Engineering Industries; State Battery Manufacturing Enterprise; State Enterprise for Aluminium Semi Products; State Enterprise for Automotive Industry; State Enterprise for Cables and Wires; State Enterprise for Iron and Steel Industries; State Enterprise for Mechanical Industries; State Electrical Industries Establishment; Vocational Training Centre for Engineering Industries in Iskandariya; Directorate Transformer Plant Project, Diala; Taji Industrial Complex, Taji

Principal Shareholders: State-owned organisation

STATE ORG. FOR FISHERIES

PO Box 3296, Baghdad
Tel: 8828151
Cable: Statefish
Telex: 212643 State Fish IK

PRINCIPAL ACTIVITIES: Production and distribution of fish and fish products; establishment of fish breeding farms
Parent Company: Responsible to the Ministry of Agriculture & Agrarian Reform
Subsidiary/Associated Companies: State Enterprise for Sea Fishing, Basrah; State Enterprise for Inland Water Fishing, Aqaba Bin Nafea Square, Muaskar Al Rashid Rd, Baghdad; Fish Research Centre, Zaafaraniya, Baghdad

Principal Shareholders: State-owned

STATE ORG. FOR INDUSTRIAL DEVELOPMENT

Khullani Square, Khulafa Street, Baghdad
Tel: 8875401
Telex: 212224 Sinaibk IK

PRINCIPAL ACTIVITIES: Promotion and development and industrial projects in the public and private sectors
Parent Company: Responsible to the Ministry of Light Industries

Principal Shareholders: State-owned organisation

STATE ORG. FOR IRAQI CIVIL AVIATION

Al Mansour, Baghdad
Tel: 5519443
Telex: 212662 Civil IK

PRINCIPAL ACTIVITIES: Supervision of airports and airways
Parent Company: Part of the Ministry of Transport & Communications
Subsidiary/Associated Companies: State Establishment for Iraqi Airways; State Enterprise for Civil Airport; Civil Aviation Institute

Principal Shareholders: State-owned

STATE ORG. FOR IRAQI PORTS

Iraqi Ports Est

Maqal, Basrah
Tel: 7711
Cable: Mawani Basrah
Telex: 207008 Port IK

PRINCIPAL ACTIVITIES: Administration of Iraqi ports, import of port and dockside equipment, including dredgers, compressors, steel ropes, welding materials, tractors, hand tools, etc
Parent Company: Responsible to the Ministry of Transport & Communications
Subsidiary Companies: State Establishment for Ma'aqal Port; State Establishment for Um Qasr Port; State Establishment for Khor Al-Zubair Port; State Establishment for River Wharves; State Establishment for Port Services

Principal Shareholders: State-owned

STATE ORG. FOR IRRIGATION PROJECTS

Northgate, Karanteena, PO Box 148, Baghdad
Tel: 8889194, 8889199
Telex: 212290 Irrigat IK

PRINCIPAL ACTIVITIES: Design and execution of irrigation projects
Parent Company: Responsible to the Ministry of Irrigation
Subsidiary Companies: General Est of Studies & Designs, PO Box 10011, Baghdad; State Enterprise for Irrigation Projects, Baghdad; Higher Council for the Euphrates Basin Projects, Baghdad

Principal Shareholders: State-owned

STATE ORG. FOR LAND RECLAMATION

Amiriya, Abu Ghraib, PO Box 6161, Baghdad
Tel: 5550400
Cable: Soslr Baghdad
Telex: 212117 Soslr IK

PRINCIPAL ACTIVITIES: Responsible for soil and land reclamation
Parent Company: Responsible to the Ministry of Irrigation

Principal Shareholders: State-owned organisation

STATE ORG. FOR LAND TRANSPORT

Safey Al Deen Al Helly St, Waziriya, PO Box 14155, Baghdad
Tel: 8822000
Cable: Nakelber Baghdad
Telex: 212594 IK

PRINCIPAL ACTIVITIES: Responsible for the planning, supervision and control of the following establishments in the transport sector, also import of trucks, lorries, trailers and auto-spare parts
Parent Company: Responsible to the Ministry of Transport & Communications
Subsidiary Companies: General Establishment for Land Transport Services; General Establishment for Passenger Transport in the City of Baghdad; General Establishment for Passenger Transport, General Establishment for Specialised Transport; General Establishment for Transport of General cargo
Principal Bankers: Central Bank of Iraq; Rafidain Bank

Date of Establishment: 1977
No of Employees: 11,263

STATE ORG. FOR OIL PRODUCTS & GAS DISTRIBUTION

Khayam Cinema St, Southgate, PO Box 302, Baghdad
Tel: 8889911
Cable: Tawzee Baghdad
Telex: 212247 Adop Bgd IK

PRINCIPAL ACTIVITIES: Distribution of oil products and gas in Iraq; responsible for the planning, supervision and control of the following establishments
Parent Company: Responsible to the Ministry of Oil
Subsidiary/Associated Companies: State Enterprise for Distribution of Oil Products and Gas for Central Area, Baghdad; State Enterprise for Distribution of Oil Products and Gas for Northern Area, Mosul, Nineveh; State Enterprise for

Distribution of Oil Products and Gas for Southern Area, Basrah; State Enterprise for Distribution of Oil Products and Gas for Central Euphrates Area, Hilla, Babil

Principal Shareholders: State-owned organisation

STATE ORG. FOR POST TELEGRAPH & TELEPHONE

Karada Dakhil, Baghdad
Tel: 7760080, 7180400
Cable: Postgen, Baghdad
Telex: 212002; 212212 Postgen IK

PRINCIPAL ACTIVITIES: National and international postal, telegraph, telex and telephone services
Parent Company: Responsible to the Ministry of Transport & Communications
Subsidiary Companies: State Establishment for Telegraph and Telephone; Postal Authority; State Establishment for Telecommunication
Principal Bankers: Rafidain Bank

Principal Shareholders: State-owned

STATE ORG. FOR ROADS & BRIDGES

Karradat Mariam, Karkh, PO Box 917, Baghdad
Tel: 5372141
Cable: Turuqjesoor
Telex: 212673 Roads IK

PRINCIPAL ACTIVITIES: Responsible for roads and bridges construction projects; building and civil engineering
Parent Company: Responsible to the Ministry of Housing
Subsidiary Companies: General Establishment for the Execution of Roads, Northern Area, Kirkuk, Tel 216291; General Establishment for the Execution of Roads, Central Area, Karkh, Baghdad, Tel 33161; General Establishment for the Execution of Roads, Southern Area, Nasiriyah, Tel 230002; General Establishment for the Execution of Bridges, Karkh, Baghdad, Tel 36146

Principal Shareholders: State-owned organisation

STATE ORG. FOR TECHNICAL INDUSTRIES

Khullani St, Baghdad
Tel: 8887141

PRINCIPAL ACTIVITIES: Supervision of industrial establishments
Parent Company: Part of the Ministry of Industry & Minerals

Principal Shareholders: State-owned

STATE ORG. FOR TOURISM

PO Box 2387 Alwiyah, Saadoon St, Karrada Al-Basra, Baghdad
Tel: 8871611, 8889101, 7188017
Cable: Tourism
Telex: 212265 Tourism IK

PRINCIPAL ACTIVITIES: Planning of state tourist policies, building and managing of state tourist establishments, information activities
Branch Offices: Basrah; Mosul
Parent Company: Responsible to the Ministry of Information
Subsidiary Companies: National Company for Tourist Investment, PO Box 1220, Baghdad; State Enterprise for Management of Tourist Utilities, Baghdad
Principal Bankers: Rafidain Bank; Iraqi Industrial Bank

Principal Shareholders: State-owned organisation

STATE SEWING CO

PO Box 14007, Waziriya, Baghdad
Tel: 8829391
Cable: Wingdust Baghdad
Telex: 212249

PRINCIPAL ACTIVITIES: Manufacture of ready made garments, also uniforms for the Armed Forces

Parent Company: Part of the State Organisation for Textile Industries
Principal Bankers: Rafidain Bank

Principal Shareholders: State-owned

STATE STEEL PIPES CO

PO Box 352, Um Qasr, Basrah
Tel: 19
Telex: 207031 Sspc IK

PRINCIPAL ACTIVITIES: Manufacture of spiral steel pipes
Parent Company: Part of the State Organisation for Engineering Industries

Principal Shareholders: State-owned

STATE TRADE ORG. FOR CAPITAL GOODS

D Al-Ijtimai Bldg, Jumhuriya St, Al Khullani Sq, PO Box 5948, Baghdad
Tel: 8889703, 7196065
Cable: Tresto Baghdad
Telex: 212227 Tresto IK

PRINCIPAL ACTIVITIES: Responsible for the planning, supervision and control of the following establishments dealing in foreign trade of capital goods
Parent Company: Responsible to the Ministry of Trade
Subsidiary/Associated Companies: Automobile State Enterprise; State Enterprise for Distribution of Construction Materials; State Trading Enterprise for Equipment and Hand-tools; State Machinery Company; Steel and Timber State Enterprise; Iraqi State Import Organisation

Principal Shareholders: State-owned organisation

STATE TRADE ORG. FOR CONSUMER GOODS

Al-Masbah Area, Aqaba Ibn Nafaa Sq, Baghdad
Tel: 7196076, 7198239
Cable: Consumers Baghdad
Telex: 212378 Consumer IK

PRINCIPAL ACTIVITIES: Responsible for the planning, supervision and control of the following establishments dealing in foreign and internal trade of consumer goods
Parent Company: Responsible to the Ministry of Trade
Subsidiary/Associated Companies: State Establishment for Iraqi Stores; Iraqi Trading State Enterprise; State Enterprise for Foodstuffs Trading; State Trading Enterprise for Precision Instruments; State Enterprise for Shopping Centres

Principal Shareholders: State-owned organisation

STATE TRADING CO FOR CONSTRUCTION MATERIALS

PO Box 602 - 5720, Baghdad
Tel: 7195071/2/3/4/5/
Cable: Gecimco baghdad
Telex: 212257 Gecimco IK, 212227 Tresto IK

PRINCIPAL ACTIVITIES: Import and distribution, of sanitaryware and building materials
Parent Company: Part of the State Trade Organisation for Capital Goods

Principal Shareholders: State-owned

STATE TRADING ENT. FOR EQUIPMENT & HANDTOOLS

Khalid Bin Al-Waleed St, PO Box 414, Baghdad
Tel: 7197700, 7197754, 7197833
Cable: Adanat Baghdad
Telex: 212192 Shet IK

PRINCIPAL ACTIVITIES: Import, distribution and wholesale and retail of handtools and electrical equipment

Parent Company: Part of the State Trade Organisation for Capital Goods

Principal Shareholders: State-owned

STATE TRADING ENT. FOR PRECISION INSTRUMENTS

Saadoun St, PO Box 3164, Baghdad
Tel: 7188280
Cable: Ajdak Baghdad
Telex: 212294 Ajdac IK

PRINCIPAL ACTIVITIES: Import and distribution of office equipment, stationery, paper, optical and photographic equipment, films, watches and clocks, surveying instruments
Parent Company: Part of the State Trade Organisation for Consumer Goods

Principal Shareholders: State-owned

STEEL & TIMBER STATE ENTERPRISE

Arasat Al Hindya St, S Daoud Al Haydar Bldg, PO Box 602, Baghdad
Tel: 7195091/3, 7191113
Cable: Gecist Baghdad
Telex: 212289 Gecist IK

PRINCIPAL ACTIVITIES: Production, distribution, wholesale and retail of iron and steel; timber and formica
Parent Company: Part of the State Trade Organisation for Capital Goods

Principal Shareholders: State-owned

SULAIMANIYAH SUGAR STATE CO

PO Box 5, Sulaimaniyah
Tel: 053220212
Cable: Sheren
Telex: 218911 IK

PRINCIPAL ACTIVITIES: Production of white sugar
Parent Company: Part of the State Organisation for Food Industries
Principal Bankers: Rafidain Bank

Principal Shareholders: State-owned
No of Employees: 1,250

SYPIS CO FOR PAINTS & PASTES WLL

Al-Sijad Bldg, Sadoon St, PO Box 3113, Baghdad
Tel: 8883359
Cable: Pluto Baghdad

PRINCIPAL ACTIVITIES: Manufacture of paints, varnishes and pastes
Branch Offices: Factory: Industrial Estate, Waziriya, Baghdad, Tel 69548

TIN BOX MANUFACTURING CO WLL

PO Box 2157, Baghdad
Tel: 7194493
Cable: Boxtin Baghdad

PRINCIPAL ACTIVITIES: Manufacture of tin cans and crates
Branch Offices: Factory: Husam Al-Deen St, Near 52nd St, Baghdad

UNITED DYEING & PRINTING CO WLL

Khan Al-Zeroor, Shorja, PO Box 11373, Baghdad
Tel: 8886886
Cable: Udyprint Baghdad

PRINCIPAL ACTIVITIES: Dyeing and printing of textiles
Branch Offices: Factory: Thaalibah, Rashdiya Rd, Baghdad

VOCATIONAL TRAINING CENTRE FOR ENGINEERING & METALLIC INDUSTRIES

Iskandariya, Babil Governorate
Tel: 221077
Cable: TADRIEB
Telex: 212226 Soei IK

PRINCIPAL ACTIVITIES: Training of technicians and engineering staff
Parent Company: Responsible to the State Organisation for Engineering Industries

Principal Shareholders: State-owned

WOOLLEN INDUSTRIES FACTORY OF ARBIL

PO Box 101, Arbil
Tel: (0665) 23696, 23867, 20282
Cable: Sufarbil Iraq
Telex: 218507 Sufarbil IK

PRINCIPAL ACTIVITIES: Manufacture of woollen yarns, textiles (worsted fabrics 45% wool - 55% polyester)
Parent Company: State Establishment for Woollen Industries
Subsidiary Companies: Duhouk Textiles Factory; Arbil Hand-Woven Carpets Factory
Principal Bankers: Rafidain Bank, Arbil

Principal Shareholders: State-owned
Date of Establishment: 1976
No of Employees: 900

WOOLLEN TEXTILE STATE EST IN NASSIRIYAH

PO Box 108, Nassiriyah
Tel: (0422) 30243
Cable: Nasij Sofi Nasiriya

PRINCIPAL ACTIVITIES: Spinning and weaving, manufacture of woollen and mixed yarns and textiles
Parent Company: Part of the State Organisation for Textile Industries

Principal Shareholders: State-owned

IRAQ

Major Companies of JORDAN

A H HAMMUDEH

See HAMMUDEH, A H,

ABDALY TRADING CO LTD

PO Box 2651, Amman
Tel: 625961, 655594
Cable: Walid Amman
Telex: 21533 Alayan

Chairman: W A Alayan

PRINCIPAL ACTIVITIES: Import of agricultural equipment and irrigation systems
Principal Agencies: Lombardini Motori, Italy

ABDUL-HADI, WAEL R, & CO

PO Box 925292, Amman
Tel: 669561, 669631
Cable: Mekano
Telex: 21266 Mekano Jo
Telefax: 605251

Chairman: Wael Radi Abdul-Hadi (Director General)
Directors: Radi Wael Abdul-Hadi (Manager)
Senior Executives: Amal Fayyad (Finance Manager), Radi Mahmoud (Sales Manager), Osama Abdulhadi (Marketing Manager), Dr Ahmad Abdulhadi (Purchasing Manager), Sameh Attari (Technical Manager)

PRINCIPAL ACTIVITIES: Telecommunications and electrical contracting works, manufacturers' representatives, import of electrical, electronic, mechanical, telecommunications equipment and medical equipment
Principal Agencies: Agents for number of companies and firms in Europe and USA
Principal Bankers: Jordan Investment Bank; Arab Land Bank

Date of Establishment: 1970
No of Employees: 25

ABU KHADER, NICOLA, & SONS CO LTD

PO Box 739, Amman
Tel: 722141
Cable: Abukader
Telex: 21342 Nicola
Telefax: 722147

President: George Abu Khader
Directors: Salim Abu Khader, Isabelle Abu Khader
Senior Executives: Joseph Abu Khader (Vice President - Operations Manager), Manuel Azzam (Finance Manager), Nabil Abu Khader (Marketing Manager)

PRINCIPAL ACTIVITIES: Import and wholesale of automotive spares, garage tools, lubricants, additives batteries and tyres
Principal Agencies: Japan Storage Battery Co, Tokyo; NGK Spark Plug Co, Hoppecke Brilon
Branch Offices: 2 branches in Amman
Associated Companies: Auto Trade; Ghattas & Abu Khader Co, 5 Marouf Street, Cairo, Egypt
Principal Bankers: Jordan National Bank; British Bank of the Middle East
Financial Information:

	1990 US$'000
Sales turnover	14,000
Authorised capital	1,250
Paid-up capital	1,250

Principal Shareholders: George Abu Khader, Salim Abu-Khader, Isabelle Abu Khader
Date of Establishment: 1952
No of Employees: 54

ABU ROZA TRADING CO

POB 5280, Amman
Tel: 661415
Telex: 21754 ABUROZ JO, 23774 ABUROZ JO
Telefax: (962-6) 661415

Chairman: Mohammad Abu Roza
Directors: Mrs Salma Abu Roza
Senior Executives: Tareq Abu Roza (Managing Director), Mustafa Abu Roza (Marketing Director), Miss Fida Abu Roza (Personnel Director), Mrs Nadia Odeh (Company Secretary)

PRINCIPAL ACTIVITIES: Agents and distributors
Principal Agencies: Villeroy & Boch, Germany and France; Paul Keune & Co, Keuco, Germany; Hansa Mettallwerke, Germany; Bosch Hausegerate, Germany; Duker Karlstadt, Germany; Villeroy & Boch, Germany and Luxembourg; Ardex, Germany; Jacuzzi, Italy and USA; Uponor (12 factories); Kohler Co, USA; Ultra Seal, USA; Gail Architectural Ceramics, W Germany; Ifo Sanitar AB, Sweden; Gustavsberg, Sweden
Subsidiary Companies: Abu Roza Trading Agencies
Principal Bankers: Arab Bank, Amman, Jordan

Principal Shareholders: Mohammad Abu Roza; Mrs Salma Abu Roza
Date of Establishment: 1975

ABU ZEID & NAZZAL CO

PO Box 194, Amman
Tel: 624104/7
Cable: Nakel
Telex: 21229 Nakelmar Jo, 21604 Telstar Jo

PRINCIPAL ACTIVITIES: Shipping agency, stevedores and chartering, travel and tourism, lighterage contractors and general contractors (port works, transport by land, sea, air)
Principal Agencies: Waterman Steamship Corp, USA; Nippon Yusen Kaisha, Japan; Maldevian Nat Trading Corp, Colombo
Branch Offices: Aqaba, PO Box 8
Associated Companies: Maritime Agencies (Jordan) Co, PO Box 1619, Tel 23006

ABUJABER, SA'D, & SONS

Abujaber Bldg, Prince Mohamed St, PO Box 312, Amman
Tel: 625161/3
Cable: Sabujaber
Telex: 21323 Jo Abujbr

Chairman: Farhan Sa'd Abujaber
Directors: Raouf Abujaber, Fouad Abujaber, Fayek Abujaber, Farouk Abujaber
Senior Executives: Elias Kattan

PRINCIPAL ACTIVITIES: Import, production and distribution of alcoholic drinks, shipping agents, insurance, advertising
Principal Agencies: James Buchanan & Co Ltd, UK; Courvoisier Ltd, France; Martini & Rossi, Italy; Hiram Walker & Sons, Canada
Subsidiary Companies: Central Groceries, Amman
Principal Bankers: Grindlays Bank plc

Date of Establishment: 1946
No of Employees: 300

ADNAN SHA'LAN & CO

King Hussein St, PO Box 1428, Amman
Tel: 621121/2, 894441/2
Cable: Shalan
Telex: 21613 Shalan Jo
Telefax: 626946

Chairman: Adnan Sha'lan
Directors: Ghaleb Sha'lan, Fawaz Sha'lan
Senior Executives: Ghaleb A Sha'lan (Managing Director), Fawaz A Sha'lan (General Manger of Paints, Cosmetics, Industries), Mahmoud Adwan (Plant Manager), Rateb Abu-Awad (Manager of Commercial Trade Operations), Khalil Flaifel (Senior Accountant), Khalil Asfour (Financial Manager)

PRINCIPAL ACTIVITIES: Importers and stockists of household appliances, manufacturers of paints, glues, refrigerators, gas cookers, dairy products and cosmetics, real estate, land, buildings

Principal Agencies: Zanussi household appliances; Bompani, MacGraw Edison, Electrolux

Branch Offices: Cairo, Egypt

Subsidiary Companies: Jordan Trading & Contracting Co, Amman, Jordan; Raghadan Trading Est, Riyadh, Saudi Arabia; Alsharqiah Metal Industries, Egypt

Principal Bankers: Arab Bank Ltd; Bank Al Mashrek; Bank of Credit & Commerce; Cairo Bank Amman; Arab-African Bank, Cairo

Financial Information:

	1988/89 US$'000
Sales turnover	10,000
Profits	1,500
Authorised capital	3,000

Principal Shareholders: Adnan Shalan; Ghaleb A Shalan; Fawaz A Shalan

Date of Establishment: 1953

No of Employees: 400

AGRICULTURAL CREDIT COOPERATION

PO Box 77, Amman
Tel: 661105/8
Cable: ACC Amman
Telex: 24194 CRDCOR JO

Chairman: Yousef Al Jaber (Minister of Agriculture)

Directors: Dr Sami Sunna'a (Director General), Ziad Freez, Abd Al Majid Al Qasem, Raja'e Al Mu'asher, Sa'ed Al Ghazawi, Hammad Al Ma'itah, Sa'ad Hael Al-Soroor, Abd Al Hadi Hammoudeh

Senior Executives: Burhan Sharabi (Deputy Director General), Abdallah Abu Hammad (Deputy Director General/Loans), Nimer Nabulsi (Deputy Director General/Finance)

PRINCIPAL ACTIVITIES: Government organisation exclusively engaged in extending supervised credit to farmers

Branch Offices: 14 branches in East Bank of Jordan, 4 branches in West Bank

Financial Information:

	JD'000
Authorised capital	12,000
Paid-up capital	9,707

Principal Shareholders: Government of Jordan

Date of Establishment: 1960

No of Employees: 208

AGRICULTURAL MATERIALS CO LTD

PO Box 431, Amman
Tel: 669873, 668973
Cable: Agrimatco Amman
Telex: 21425 AGMAT
Telefax: 678973

Chairman: Khaled Miqdadi
Directors: Mustafa Miqdadi
Senior Executives: Issam Miqdadi

PRINCIPAL ACTIVITIES: Import and dealing in fertilisers, vegetable and flower seeds, agricultural materials and farming equipment

Principal Agencies: ICI, Sandoz, etc

Branch Offices: Irbid, Zarqa, Wehdat

Subsidiary Companies: A.M.C., Riyadh, Saudi Arabia

Principal Bankers: Arab Bank

Principal Shareholders: Miqdadi Family, AMC Employees

Date of Establishment: 1936

No of Employees: 200

AL ARAB CONSTRUCTION CO LTD

PO Box 9318, Amman
Tel: 675300
Cable: SHECO/AMMAN
Telex: 22296 SHECO JO
Telefax: 605300

Founder: Shukri Hamzeh (Managing Director)

Senior Executives: Julio Abed Rabbo (Project Manager), Ziad Sakkal (Project Engineer), Munzer Malak (Production Engineer), Samih Nimri (Project Manager), Ziad Shboul (Site Engineer), Bashar Saifi (Site Engineer)

PRINCIPAL ACTIVITIES: Civil engineering and buildings construction

Principal Bankers: Petra Bank, Shmeisani, Amman; Arab Bank, Mahata Br

Financial Information:

	JD'000
Sales turnover	1,200
Authorised capital	400
Paid-up capital	400

Principal Shareholders: Shukri Hamzeh; Hanan Hamzeh

Date of Establishment: 1980

No of Employees: 100

ALBERT ABELA

PO Box 2620, Zomot Bldg, Khatib St, 2nd Circle, Amman
Tel: 644419, 641830
Cable: Alabela Amman
Telex: 22335 Abela Jo

Chairman: Albert Abela

PRINCIPAL ACTIVITIES: Industrial catering and camp services, construction, hotel management

Associated Companies: Representing the Albert Abela Group of Companies

Principal Bankers: Jordan National Bank

Date of Establishment: 1973

AL CHARK INSURANCE CO

PO Box 312, Amman
Tel: 625161
Cable: Al-Chark
Telex: 21323 Abujaber

Chairman: Raouf Sa'd Abujaber
Directors: Mrs Mireille Raouf Abujaber
Senior Executives: Charly Seikaly, Miss Bassima Abujaber, Suleiman Dajjani, Moh'd Odeh

PRINCIPAL ACTIVITIES: All types of insurance in Jordan

Parent Company: Al Chark Insurance Co, Cairo

Associated Companies: United Insurance Co Ltd

Principal Bankers: Grindlays Bank; Arab Land Bank

Principal Shareholders: Egyptian Government

Date of Establishment: In Cairo: 1931; In Jordan: 1946

No of Employees: 22

AL HUSSAM PLASTICS INDUSTRIES CO

PO Box 7518, Amman
Tel: 953611/2
Cable: Kolaghassi
Telex: 41425 Kofam JO
Telefax: 962-9-954382

Chairman: Ali R Kolaghassi
Directors: Eng Hussein Ali R Kolaghassi, Walid H Kolaghassi, Eng Hani A K Kalha

PRINCIPAL ACTIVITIES: Manufacture of plastic products, packaging materials, etc

Branch Offices: Factory in Marca Amman

Principal Bankers: Bank of Credit & Commerce International

Financial Information:

	1990 US$'000
Authorised capital	5,000

Principal Shareholders: Ali Kolaghassi and family
Date of Establishment: 1988
No of Employees: 200

ALIA
Royal Jordanian Airline

Housing Bank Bldg, PO Box 302, Amman
Tel: 672872
Telex: 21501 Alia Jo
Telefax: 679243

Chairman: Ali Ghandour (Chief Executive Officer)

PRINCIPAL ACTIVITIES: Airline passenger and cargo services
Branch Offices: Worldwide
Subsidiary Companies: Arab Wings, Royal Tours, Arab Air
  Services, Arab Air Cargo, Far East Tourism & Travel Co,
  Jordan Express Travel (JET), Simulator Project, Royal
  Falcons, Alia Boutique & Duty Free Shop, Arab International
  Hotels, Jordan Holiday Inn Co
Principal Bankers: Arab Bank
Financial Information:

	US$'000
Authorised capital	60,900
Paid-up capital	60,900

Principal Shareholders: Government of Jordan
Date of Establishment: 15-12-1963
No of Employees: 4,627

ALLIED CHEMICAL MANUFACTURING & TRADING CO

PO Box 926797, Amman
Tel: 817119, 630764
Telex: 21292 Grand JO

Directors: W S Hammad, I A Taziz

PRINCIPAL ACTIVITIES: Production of aerosols, cosmetics,
  detergents and cleaning materials; trading in all types of raw
  materials, chemicals, machines, foodstuff and furniture
Principal Agencies: ACMA SpA; Cloister Labels; Durham
  Chemicals; Zimmermann Hobbs; Gariboldi & C; CMB SpA;
  Barnett & Foster Ltd; Newmans Labeling Machines; BP
  detergents; Hansa Chemie
Subsidiary Companies: Arab Aerosol Manufacturing Co
Principal Bankers: Arab Bank, Shmaisani
Financial Information:

	JD'000
Authorised capital	180
Paid-up capital	150

Principal Shareholders: Private owned company
Date of Establishment: 1979
No of Employees: 42

AL MAZARE'S NATIONAL FEED MANUFACTURING CO LTD

PO Box 1318, Amman
Tel: 644133

Directors: Nadim Salim Dajani (Managing Director)

PRINCIPAL ACTIVITIES: Manufacture of animal feeds

AL NASR TRADE & COMMISSION AGENCIES & CO

PO Box 1049, Jabal Weibdeh, Amman
Tel: 624560
Cable: Victor Amman
Telex: 21569 Victor Jo

PRINCIPAL ACTIVITIES: Import and distribution of drilling
  equipment and supplies, building materials, manufacturers'
  representatives; export of phosphates

AL OMARI IMPORT & TRADING CO

PO Box 922254, Amman
Tel: 674255, 605736
Telex: 21418 Shell JO

PRINCIPAL ACTIVITIES: Supply of petroleum products
Principal Agencies: Shell Lubricants
Principal Bankers: British Bank of the Middle East
Financial Information:

	JD'000
Sales turnover	1,200

Date of Establishment: 1982

AL TEWFIK AUTOMOBILE & EQUIPMENT CO

PO Box 253, Station Street, Amman
Tel: 656273, 656274, 651591
Cable: Interfire
Telex: 21296 Tabbaa Jo
Telefax: (09626) 647814

Chairman: Haj Tewfik Tabbaa
Directors: Hamdi Tabbaa (Managing Director), Bandar Tabbaa,
  Abdul Ilah Tabbaa
Senior Executives: Awni Issa (Finance Manager), Bahjat Majali
  (Sales Manager), Hassan Tabbaa (Marketing Manager), Nader
  Abu Ragheb (Purchasing Manager), Emile Bajjali (Personnel
  Manager), Ismat Shabsough (Technical Manager), Adel Bajes
  (Administration Manager)

PRINCIPAL ACTIVITIES: Import and distribution of electro-
  mechanical equipment, diesel generators, trucks, construction
  equipment, cars and spare parts, pumps and air compressors
Principal Agencies: Renault; Rolls Royce; Jaguar; Hawker
  Siddeley Power Plant; Lister; CompAir; Kawasaki; Wild;
  Benford; Bucyrus-Erie
Subsidiary Companies: Trans-Orient Co; United Trading Group
Principal Bankers: Cairo Amman Bank; Jordan Islamic Bank

Principal Shareholders: Chairman and directors
Date of Establishment: 1942
No of Employees: 85

AMBASSADOR HOTEL

PO Box 925390, Shmeisani, Amman
Tel: 665161, 665384
Cable: Ambas
Telex: 21628 Ambas Jo

Chairman: Isam Dakkak
Directors: Hisham Dakkak (General Manager), Said Abu El Niel,
  Yousef Izzidin Dakkak
Senior Executives: Miss Khadijeh Dakkak (Rooms Division
  Manager), Walid Abu El Niel (Finance Manager)

PRINCIPAL ACTIVITIES: Hotel business
Parent Company: Union of Tourism Hotels Company
Principal Bankers: Jordan National Bank, Arab Bank, Petra
  Bank
Financial Information:

	JD'000
Paid-up capital	750

Principal Shareholders: Dakkak Family and Abu El Niel Family
Date of Establishment: 1977
No of Employees: 70

AMIANTIT JORDAN CO LTD

PO Box 102, Amman
Tel: 636180, 636188
Cable: Tours Amman
Telex: 21839 Amiant Jo

President: George S Tannous

Directors: Khalil A Chehab (Manager)

PRINCIPAL ACTIVITIES: Manufacture of asbestos cement pipes
Associated Companies: Amiantit Plastics Jordan Co Ltd
  (Manufacture of PVC and PE (pipes)
Principal Bankers: Arab Banb

Date of Establishment: 20/2/1977
No of Employees: 200

AMIN KAWAR & SONS CO WLL

See KAWAR, AMIN, & SONS CO WLL

AMMAN FINANCIAL MARKET

PO Box 8802, Amman
Tel: 663170/3
Telex: 21711 Sukmal JO
Telefax: 686830

Chairman: Hashem Sabbagh (General Manager)
Directors: Munther Al Fahoum, Saeed Heyasat, Mansour
  Haddadeen, Adeeb Haddad, Mohammad Balbeisi, Abdel Ilah
  tabaa, Abdel Hadi Jaradeh, Mohammad Asfour
Senior Executives: Munther Al Fahoum (Acting Chairman),
  Ibrahim Balbeisi (Acting General Manager)

PRINCIPAL ACTIVITIES: Stock exchange

Date of Establishment: 1978
No of Employees: 64

ANZ GRINDLAYS BANK PLC

PO Box 3, King Hussein St, Amman
Tel: 630104/8
Cable: Grindlay Amman
Telex: 21209 Jo

PRINCIPAL ACTIVITIES: Commercial banking
Branch Offices: General Manager's Office, Shmeissani, Amman,
  PO Box 9997, Tel: 660201/7, 660301, Telex 21980; 8
  branches in Amman, and branches in Zerka; Irbid; Akaba;
  Kerak

Date of Establishment: In Jordan 1927
No of Employees: 300

AQABA SHIPPING CO (PVT) LTD

PO Box 5350, 18 Elia Abu Madi St, Shmeisani, Amman
Tel: 962-6-679892/3, 690491
Cable: AQABMAR
Telex: 21807 Aqbmar JO, 23969 Aqbmer JO
Telefax: (962 6) 679891

Chairman: Kamel Amin Kawar
Directors: Walid Faddoul Kawar (General Manager)
Senior Executives: Ghassoub Faddoul Kawar (Asst General
  Manager), Amin K Kawar (Manager), Rimon Atallah
  (Marketing Manager), Hani ra'fat (Personnel Manager), Shafiq
  Abu Ghazaleh (Accountant)

PRINCIPAL ACTIVITIES: Liner and charter agents (on
  forwarding to Iraq)
Principal Agencies: Mediterranean Shipping Co, Geneva,
  Maersk Line Copenhagen; Maritrade Bangkok; Redcliffe, UK
Branch Offices: Aqaba: PO Box 246, Tel 314218, Telex 62264,
  Fax (962 3) 313618
Parent Company: Kawar Group of Companies
Principal Bankers: Arab Bank plc

Principal Shareholders: Kamel Kawar; Walid Kawar; Issam
  Kawar; Ghassoub Kawar
Date of Establishment: 1978
No of Employees: 40

ARAB AFRICAN INTERNATIONAL BANK

PO Box 926180, Amman
Tel: 65221
Telex: 21919 Arafro JO

PRINCIPAL ACTIVITIES: Representative office
Parent Company: Head office in Cairo, Egypt

Date of Establishment: 1980

ARAB ALUMINIUM INDUSTRY CO LTD

PO Box 35042, Amman
Tel: 843965, 847145, 847146
Cable: ARAL - JORDAN
Telex: 21483 Aral JO
Telefax: 962-6-847145

Chairman: Rajab Al-Sa'ad
Directors: Fuad Ayoub, Salah Rimawi, Hisham Ezzideen, Nabil
  Asaad, Mohammed El Daoud, Mufleh Aqel, Mohamed
  Jerdaneh, Adel Hujurat
Senior Executives: Eng Fouad Ayoub (General Manager), Ghazi
  Barqawi (Marketing Manager), Eng K Sawalha (Plant
  Manager), Mohammad Ibrahim (Head of Financial Dept),
  Youssef Miqdadi (Head of Purchasing Dept), Eng Khalil Refai
  (Manager Remelting Plant), Mohammed Debie (Head of
  Personnel Dept), Firyal Rida Akar (Executive Secretary)

PRINCIPAL ACTIVITIES: Extruding and anodizing aluminium
  profiles for architectural purposes, electrostatic painting for
  aluminium profiles, remelting and casting of aluminium scrap
Principal Bankers: Jordan Kuwait Bank, Arab Bank Ltd, Jordan
  Investment & Finance Bank
Financial Information:

	1988/89	1989/90
	JD'000	JD'000
Sales turnover	7,684	9,637
Profits	904	1,360
Authorised capital	4,000	4,000
Paid-up capital	4,000	4,000
Total assets	7,873	8,079

Principal Shareholders: Jordanian citizens
Date of Establishment: 1976
No of Employees: 250

ARAB BANK PLC

PO Box 950544 & 950545, Amman
Tel: 660131, 660115
Cable: Bankarabi
Telex: 23091 Arabnk Jo
Telefax: 962-6-606793, 606830

Chairman: Abdulmajeed A H Shoman
Directors: Khalid A H Shoman (Deputy Chairman), Abdel Hamid
  A M Shoman (Asst General Manager), Hasib J Sabbagh,
  Mahmoud M Beydoun, George S Tannous, Farouk K Jabre,
  Munib R Masri, Abdul Aziz Nasrallah, Rafic B Al Hariri, Saad
  A Alnahedh, Ishaq Quttaineh (Secretary)

PRINCIPAL ACTIVITIES: Commercial banking
Branch Offices: Jordan (Head Office) (50), Bahrain (4), Qatar (2),
  UAE (8), Egypt (4), Lebanon (11), Yemen (3), United Kingdom
  (3), France (2), Greece (1), USA (2), Singapore (1), Cyprus (5),
  Korea (1), Italy (1). Representative offices in China and Japan
Associated Companies: Arab Bank Maroc, Morocco; Nigeria
  Arab Bank Ltd, Nigeria; Arab Bank (Switzerland) Ltd, Geneva,
  Zurich; Arab National Bank, Saudi Arabia; UBAE Arab
  German Bank, Frankfurt, Luxembourg; Arab Tunisian Bank,
  Tunis; Finance Accountancy & Mohassaba SA, Geneva; Oman
  Arab Bank, Ruwi; Arab Australia Ltd, Sydney; Arab Bank
  (Austria) AG, Vienna
Principal Bankers: Arab Bank Ltd, London; Arab Bank Ltd, New
  York; Bank of New York, New York

Financial Information:

	1988/89	1989/90
	US$'000	US$'000
Total shareholders'equity	765,150	792,491
Profits	80,857	98,110
Authorised capital	90,123	86,930
Paid-up capital	90,123	86,930
Deposits	12,525,780	12,978,692
Loans	3,291,952	3,778,096
Total assets	13,505,803	13,402,551

Date of Establishment: 1930
No of Employees: 3,500

ARAB BANKING CORPORATION/JORDAN

PO Box 926691, Amman
Tel: 664183/5, 674184/5
Cable: ABC JO
Telex: 23022 ABCFX JO, 22258 ABC JO
Telefax: 686291

Chairman: Mohammed E Al Meraikhi
Directors: Jawad Hadid (Deputy Chairman), Saleh M Al Yousef, Mohamed S Khleif, Farid F Araman, Abdel Kader Dweik, Na'el Zu'bi
Senior Executives: Jawad Hadid (General Manager), Amer Salti (Deputy General Manager), Mohammad Sallam (Asst General Manager)

PRINCIPAL ACTIVITIES: Commercial banking
Branch Offices: 4 local branches
Parent Company: Arab Banking Corporation, Bahrain (Holder of 60% of equity)
Principal Bankers: Arab Banking Corp, Bahrain, Milan, Tokyo, Frankfurt, London, Paris, New York; Jordan International Bank, London; UBAF Bank, Paris, Tokyo; Arab National Bank, Riyadh
Financial Information:

	1990
	JD'000
Cash at banks	25,214
Investments	2,788
Loans & discounts	27,721
Other assets	2,000
Total assets	57,723
Deposits	27,759
Other liabilities	14,851
Capital/Equity	15,113
Total liabilities	57,723

Principal Shareholders: Arab Banking Corporation, Bahrain (60%); Housing Bank (25.46%); others (15.54%)
Date of Establishment: 21 January 1990
No of Employees: 108

ARAB BREWERIES CO LTD

PO Box 312, Amman
Tel: 625161, 657679
Cable: Arab Breweries
Telex: 21323 Abujbr JO
Telefax: 962 6 628167

Chairman: Khalil Lahleh
Directors: Sa'd Abujaber
Senior Executives: Mohammad Abdul Fattah (Brewmaster)

PRINCIPAL ACTIVITIES: Brewing
Principal Agencies: Henninger Beer under licence of Henninger International in Frankfurt/Germany
Principal Bankers: Grindlays Bank, Amman

Financial Information:

	1990
	JD'000
Sales turnover	1,100
Profits	200
Authorised capital	220
Paid-up capital	220
Total assets	600

Principal Shareholders: General Investment Co Ltd
Date of Establishment: 1970
No of Employees: 57

ARAB CONSTRUCTION & CONTRACTING CO LTD

PO Box 2277, Jebel Amman, Amman
Tel: 638733, 623367
Cable: Coden Amman
Telex: 22231 Cordon Jo

PRINCIPAL ACTIVITIES: Civil engineering and construction
Branch Offices: Saudi Arabia; Kuwait; Lebanon

ARAB DEVELOPMENT CO

PO Box 6147, Amman
Tel: 637314, 625261
Cable: Drilcoamn
Telex: 21227 Drilco Jo

Directors: Munib R Masri, Tarif W Ayoubi

PRINCIPAL ACTIVITIES: Site investigations, land reclamation and development, civil and mechanical engineering, water well drilling
Branch Offices: Offices in Lebanon; Syria; Saudi Arabia; Oman; Abu Dhabi; Ras Al Khaimah; London and the Liechtenstein
Principal Bankers: Arab Bank Ltd

Date of Establishment: 1971

ARAB DEVELOPMENT ENGINEERING CO (ADECO)

PO Box 653, Amman
Tel: 624110, 623550
Cable: Adeco
Telex: 23332 ADECO JO
Telefax: 640526

President: S F Ghawi
Directors: Abdallah Shafakoj (Personnel Manager), H S Ghawi (General Manager)
Senior Executives: Suheil Abu Hanna (Marketing Manager), Shafik Freihat (Financial Manager)

PRINCIPAL ACTIVITIES: Manufacturers' representatives, electrical, mechanical and telecommunications contracting engineers
Principal Agencies: Darwish Telecom Intl, Garrett GmbH
Subsidiary Companies: ADECO International Ltd, UK; ADECO (Jersey) Ltd
Principal Bankers: Arab Bank, Amman

Principal Shareholders: S F Ghawi; J S Ghawi
Date of Establishment: 1954

ARAB FEED MANUFACTURING CO LTD

PO Box 470, King Hussein St, Amman
Tel: 637763
Cable: Feedina
Telex: 21238 Parole Jo
Telefax: 625701

Chairman: Jack G Khayyat
Directors: J G Khayyat, Y Mouasher, A Tash, J Mouasher, Dr R Mousher
Senior Executives: George Khayyat

PRINCIPAL ACTIVITIES: Manufacture of feed for poultry
Principal Bankers: Grindlays Bank

JORDAN

Financial Information: National General Investment Co

	1989/90 JD'000
Sales turnover	2,000
Authorised capital	250
Paid-up capital	250
Total assets	1,079

Principal Shareholders: J Khayyat, Y Mouasher, A Tasn, J Mouasher, Dr R Mousher
Date of Establishment: 1964
No of Employees: 35

ARAB FINANCE CORPORATION (JORDAN)

PO Box 35104, Chamber of Commerce Bldg, Shmeisane, Amman
Tel: 666148/9
Telex: 21875 AFC JO

Chairman: Khalil Salim (General Manager)
Directors: Khaled Khan, Chafic Akhras, Adnan Khayal, Abdel Wahab Majali, Marwan Hamoud, Abdel Hadi Hammoudeh

PRINCIPAL ACTIVITIES: Merchant banking
Financial Information:

	JD'000
Authorised capital	2,125
Paid-up capital	2,125

Principal Shareholders: Al Saudi Bank Group; private Jordanian interests
Date of Establishment: 1979

ARAB INVESTMENT & INTERNATIONAL TRADE CO LTD

PO Box 94, Al Raqueem
Tel: 731191, 731504
Cable: INTREX
Telex: 23216 INTREX
Telefax: 731504

Chairman: Rajab Al Sa'id
Directors: Abdul Malik Sa'id, Farouq Al Arif, Sulaiman Al Hafiz, Loa'i Jardaneh, Ghassan Arafat, Samir Jaradat, Talal Kokash, Adnan El Husseini
Senior Executives: Adnan El Husseini (General Manager)

PRINCIPAL ACTIVITIES: Manufacturing baby diaper, toilet rolls, kitchen towels, tissues, sanitary napkins and toilet soap
Principal Bankers: Jordan Kuwait Bank, Petra Bank, Arab Bank
Financial Information:

	1990 JD'000
Sales turnover	808
Authorised capital	3,488
Paid-up capital	3,423
Total assets	2,550

Principal Shareholders: Jordan Trade Facilities Co Ltd, National Industrial Co Ltd, Petra Bank, Jordan Kuwait Bank, Jordan Industrial Development Bank, Jordan Gulf Insurance Co Ltd, Jerusalem Insurance Co Ltd
Date of Establishment: 1976
No of Employees: 60

ARAB JORDAN INVESTMENT BANK

Comm Complex of Housing Bank, Shmeisani, PO Box 8797, Amman
Tel: 664126/7, 668626/7
Cable: AJIBANK
Telex: 21719 Ajib Jo, 22087 Ajib Jo

Chairman: Abdul Kader Qadi (General Manager)
Directors: Abdul Hadi Shayef, Khalifa Muhairi, Dr Jamil Jishi, Abdullah El Attiya, Bassam Atari, Mohammed Allagi, Jawdat Sha'sha'a, Jawad Hadid, Dr Kamal Sha'er, Dawud Qutub

PRINCIPAL ACTIVITIES: Merchant and wholesale commercial bank with emphasis on provision of medium and long-term financing for development projects, soliciting savings accounts, fixed-term deposits and carrying out money market operations
Branch Offices: Jabal Al Hussein Br: Near Firas Circle, PO Box 925233, Tel 672111/3

Principal Shareholders: Qatar National Bank, Qatar; Abu Dhabi Investment Authority, Abu Dhabi/UAE; The Arab Investment Co, Riyadh/Saudi Arabia; Libyan Arab Foreign Bank, Libya; National Commercial Bank, Jeddah/Saudi Arabia; The Housing Bank, Jordan; Arab Bank Ltd, Jordan; Jordan Insurance Co, Jordan; Jordan National Bank, Jordan; Bank of Jordan, Jordan; The Cairo Amman Bank, Jordan; Government Pension Fund, Jordan
Date of Establishment: 1978
No of Employees: 105

ARAB LAND BANK

Jordan Regional Head Office, PO Box 6729, Amman
Tel: 628357/8, 646157/8
Cable: ARAKARI
Telex: 21208 Arakari Amm
Telefax: 646274

Chairman: Hassouneh Hasib
Senior Executives: Fayiz Qutob (Acting General Manager), Elia Atalla (Manager Foreign Dept)

PRINCIPAL ACTIVITIES: Commercial and mortgage bank
Branch Offices: 9 branches in Jordan (Amman, Zarka, Irbid, Almafrak, Marka, Russaifa, Jabel Amman, Aqaba, Shmisani)
Parent Company: Head Office: 33 Abdul Khalek Sarwat Street, Cairo, Egypt

ARAB MINING COMPANY

PO Box 20198 Amman
Tel: 642637
Cable: Armico
Telex: 21489 Armico Jo, 21169

Chairman: Dr Abdul Razzak Al-Hashimi
Directors: Akram Karmoul, Suliaman Al-Mandeel, Abdullah Al-Angari, Faisal Salman Al-Tamimi, Saleh Al-Mahmoudi, Ateeq Abdul Rahman Ateeq, Hussein Ibrahim Al Jasem, Ibrahim Amer Al Mughrabi, Bader Bazee Al Yaseen

PRINCIPAL ACTIVITIES: Involved in all technical, industrial and commercial activities connected with mining
Subsidiary Companies: Equity shareholding in the following companies: Arab Potash Co (25%); Jordan Fertiliser Co (10%); Somali Arab Mining Co (33.33%); National Construction & Industrial Materials Co, North Yemen (35%); Lead Central Smelter, Morocco (25%); SNIM, Mauritania (6.75%); Societe des Chimiques du Fluor, Tunisia (26.6%); Sidi Lahcen Lead and Zinc Project, Morocco (40%); Zgounder Silver Project, Morocco (40%); Iron Pelletizing Plant, Bahrain (10%); Akjoujt Copper Project, Mauritania (20%)
Principal Bankers: Jordan & Kuwait Bank; Central Bank of Jordan; Gulf International Bank; Petra Bank

Principal Shareholders: The Hashemite Kingdom of Jordan, The United Arab Emirates, The Kingdom of Saudi Arabia, The Democratic Republic of Sudan, The Syrian Arab Republic, The Democratic Republic of Somalia, The Republic of Iraq, The Kuwait Foreign Trading & Contracting Investment Co SAK on behalf of the State of Kuwait, The Arab Republic of Egypt, The Arab Republic of Libya, The Yemen Arab Republic, The People's Democratic Republic of Yemen, The Arab Investment Co in the Kingdom of Saudi Arabia, The Kingdom of Morocco, The Republic of Tunisia, Mauritania
Date of Establishment: 1975

ARAB PHARMACEUTICAL MANUFACTURING CO LTD

Head Office, PO Box 42, Sult
Tel: Sult: 554961, 554962, 554963
Cable: Aladwiyeh
Telex: 21315 APMC JO, 43403 APMC JO
Telefax: 06-685131 Amman, 05-551897 Sult

Chairman: Amin Shocair
Directors: A Mua'sher, Dr K A Shae'r, T Homsi, H Saket, Dr M Khalaf, Dr M Shuqair, Dr Sh Shakhshir, N Nasrawi
Senior Executives: Dr Ma'an Shuqair (President), Dr Shukri Shakhshir (Vice President Production), Naser Nasrawi (Vice President Finance), Samih Qaryouti (Vice President Manpower), Dr Mohamed Shubair (Vice President R & D), Ibrahim Kharouf (Vice President Marketing), Nidal Husari (Vice President Quality), Bassam Haddad (Public Relations Manager)

PRINCIPAL ACTIVITIES: Manufacture of pharmaceutical products
Branch Offices: PO Box 1695 Amman, Tel 673121, 685121; Scientific Office for the Arab Pharm Manfg Co Ltd: PO Box 2418, Damascus, Syria
Principal Bankers: Arab Bank Ltd; Bank of Credit & Commerce International
Financial Information:

	1989	1990
	JD'000	JD'000
Sales turnover	16,546	18,525
Profits	4,131	4,622
Authorised capital	7,000	7,000
Paid-up capital	5,000	5,000
Total assets	36,939	37,696

Principal Shareholders: A total of 17,490 shareholders
Date of Establishment: 1964
No of Employees: 905

ARAB PLAST CO LTD
Nassar, Zaki M, & Brother

PO Box 340481, Amman
Tel: 894689
Cable: Nassar Amman
Telex: 21731 Nassar Jo

Chairman: Zaki M Nassar
Directors: Nicola M Nassar
Senior Executives: John M Nassar (Executive Manager)

PRINCIPAL ACTIVITIES: Refrigeration, airconditioning, microphones, electrical equipment, central heating spare parts, manufacture of plastic products by extrusion, injection and by blow moulding
Principal Agencies: Danfoss, Denmark; AKG Acoustics, Austria
Parent Company: Zaki M Nassar & Brother
Principal Bankers: Jordan Kuwait Bank; Petra Bank; Bank of Credit & Commerce
Financial Information:

	1988/89
	US$'000
Sales turnover	1,500
Profits	15%
Authorised capital	750
Paid-up capital	750

Principal Shareholders: Zaki M Nassar, Nicola M Nassar, John M Nassar
Date of Establishment: 1964
No of Employees: 40

ARAB POTASH COMPANY LTD

PO Box 1470, Amman
Tel: 666165, 666166, 663811, 687281
Cable: Potash Amman
Telex: 21683, 22152, 23910, 23832 Potash Jo
Telefax: 674416 Amman, 03-314441 Aqaba, 377125 Site

Chairman: Omar A Dokhgan
Directors: Ali Ensour (Managing Director)
Senior Executives: S Hawari (Deputy Managing Director & Finance Manager), Nasser Al Sadoun (Deputy Managing Director for Technical Affairs & Plant Manager)

PRINCIPAL ACTIVITIES: Production of potash, and future exploitation of other dead sea minerals
Principal Agencies: Mitsubishi, Tokyo; Woodward and Dickinson; Philadelphia; EMC, Paris
Principal Bankers: Arab Bank Ltd
Financial Information:

	JD'000
Authorised capital	72,450
Paid-up capital	70,517

Principal Shareholders: Jordan Government, Arab Mining Company, Islamic Development Bank, Governments of Iraq, Libya, Kuwait, Saudi Arabia, Jordan Post Office Saving Services, other shareholders
Date of Establishment: 1956
No of Employees: 1,335

ARAB PROJECTS CO SA LTD

PO Box 1318, Amman
Tel: 771256, 778468, 778181/183
Cable: Nasajani
Telex: 21530 Apco Jo, 22269 Crownjo

Chairman: Nadim S Al-Dajani (also Managing Director)
Directors: Sa'ad Al-Dajani, Yousuf Zahran, Aktham Tall
Senior Executives: Jum'a Abdul Fattah (Manager Automotive Division), Yousuf Zahran (Manager Accounting), Rasem Ahmad (Manager Central Stores)

PRINCIPAL ACTIVITIES: Hospitals, communications systems, electronics, general contracting, hoteliers, finance
Branch Offices: PO Box 7973, Beirut, Lebanon; PO Box 1972, Riyadh, Saudi Arabia
Subsidiary Companies: The Anglo-Arab Engineering Co; Bureau of Travel Tourism & Transport; The Turf Hotel & Club; Prex Coop for the Export of Prefabricated Building GmbH & Co
Principal Bankers: Bank of Credit and Commerce International; Citibank; Cairo Amman Bank

Principal Shareholders: Nadim S Al Dajani, Leila N S Al-Dajani
Date of Establishment: 1952
No of Employees: 178

ARAB SHIPPING COMPANY

King Hussein St, PO Box 757, Amman
Tel: 623135/7
Cable: Arabship
Telex: 21225 Arabship Jo; 21435
Telefax: 962/6 638137

Chairman: Hamad El-Farhan (also Managing Director)
Directors: Rifad El Farhan
Senior Executives: D Sweidan (General Manager), Taha Tilfah (Manager Operations), A Rjoub (Manager Marketing)

PRINCIPAL ACTIVITIES: Shipping agents and shipping charterers
Principal Agencies: Nedlloyd Line Rotterdam; Scan Dutch, Copenhagen; Shipping Corp, India; Egyptian Navigation Co, Alexandria; Barber Lines, Oslo; Jinyang, Seoul; ScanCarriers, Oslo; Epirotiki Lines, Piraeus; Naftomar, Athens
Branch Offices: Arab Shipping Co, PO Box 46, Aqaba
Subsidiary Companies: Jordan Resources Co Ltd, PO Box 6401, Amman; Petra Clearing & Transport Co, PO Box 183464, Amman

JORDAN

Principal Bankers: Bank of Jordan
Financial Information:

	1990
	JD'000
Sales turnover	200
Profits	10%
Authorised capital	60
Paid-up capital	60
Total assets	170

Principal Shareholders: Hamad El Farhan, Rifad El Farhan
Date of Establishment: 1958
No of Employees: 70

ARAB TRADING & DEVELOPMENT CO LTD

PO Box 6141, Amman
Telex: 21300 Tec Amman

Chairman: Tewfic Kattan
Directors: Fuad Kattan (Managing Director), Yussif Khoury

PRINCIPAL ACTIVITIES: Agents, representatives, import and distribution of agricultural machinery and equipment, automobiles, pipeline contractors
Branch Offices: PHB, W Germany; Sublin, W Germany; Klockner Humholdt Deutz, W Germany; Borgward

ARAB TRADING & MARKETING CO LTD

PO Box 925395, Amman
Tel: 669785 (2 lines)
Telex: 22458 ATM JO
Telefax: 962-6-660598

Chairman: Hisham Mufti
Directors: Hisham Mufti (Director General), Samir Farah (Technical Director)
Senior Executives: Mahmoud Odeh (Sales Director)

PRINCIPAL ACTIVITIES: Trading
Principal Agencies: Donn; Alphacoustic; Texas Instruments; S.K.W.; Panel; Meynadier; Dynamit Nobel; Gyproc; Profil Vertrieb
Principal Bankers: Arab Bank Ltd, Jordan National Bank

Date of Establishment: May 1981

ARAB UNION INTERNATIONAL INSURANCE CO LTD

PO Box 7241/7289, Amman
Tel: 684459, 685048, 686820, 684085
Telex: 21763 Abonin JO

Chairman: Nazieh Abed El Hussein (General Manager)
Directors: Haitham M Safadi (Deputy General Manager)

PRINCIPAL ACTIVITIES: General insurance

Principal Shareholders: Nazieh Abed El Hussein, Syrian General Insurance Co, Syria; Overseas Insurance & Reinsurance Co, Lebanon
Date of Establishment: 1985
No of Employees: 26

ARAB WINGS CO LTD

PO Box 341018, Amman
Tel: 891994, 894484 (Operation), 893901/4 (Administration), 893486 (Maintenance)
Cable: Sita Ammcdrj
Telex: 21608 Wings Jo
Telefax: 893158

Chairman: Khaldoon Abu Hassan
Directors: Khaled Shouman, Mahmoud Jamal Balqaz, Eng Moh'd Rajab Al-Baomor, Brig Ihsan Shourdum, Hussam Abu Ghazaleh
Senior Executives: Sharif Ghazi Rakan Nasser (Managing Director), Faisal Haddadin (A M D Engineering &

Maintenance), Capt Nazir Latif (A M D Operation & Chief Pilot), Mrs Aysar Akrawi (A M D Administration & Tax Services), Wael Khatib (Dir Finance), Asad Nammari (Dir Ground Operations), Samir Bazbaz (Dir Marketing & Sales)

PRINCIPAL ACTIVITIES: Business jet charter service, aircraft handling, air ambulance, package cargo, maintenance centre
Branch Offices: General Sales Agents: Alia/The Royal Jordanian Airline
Parent Company: Alia
Principal Bankers: Arab Bank Ltd

Principal Shareholders: Alia/The Royal Jordanian Airline (64%), Sultanate of Oman (36%)
Date of Establishment: May 1975
No of Employees: 48

ARABIA INSURANCE CO LTD SAL

PO Box 543, Amman
Tel: 644334/5
Cable: Arabiaco
Telex: 22370 Arabia Jo

PRINCIPAL ACTIVITIES: All classes of insurance and reinsurance
Principal Agencies: Arab Properties Co Ltd SAL; Middle East Insurance Co, Amman; Arabia Insurance Co (Morocco) SA; Groupe des Assurances de Tunisie
Branch Offices: Jordan; Bahrain (PO Box 745); Kuwait (PO Box 868); Dubai (PO Box 1050); Abu Dhabi (PO Box 867); Tunis (PO Box 540); Jeddah (PO Box 2114); Riyadh (PO Box 1075); Dammam (PO Box 847); Oman (PO Box 4); Qatar (PO Box 771); Morocco; and Lebanon (Head Office: PO Box 11-2172)
Principal Bankers: Arab Bank; Jordan National Bank

Principal Shareholders: Arab Bank Ltd, Al-Mashrek Financial Investment Co, Badr Sa'id Fahoum, Faud M Es-Said, Suleiman Tannous & Sons Ltd, His Excellency Nasser Bin Khalid Al-Thani (Qatar), Mohamed Abdul Rahman Bahr (Kuwait), Sheikh Abdul Aziz Suleiman (Saudi Arabia), Sheikh Youssef Zahed (Saudi Arabia), Moussa Abdul Rahman Hassan (Muscat), Jumaa Al-Majid (Dubai), Mohamed Jalal (Bahrain)
Date of Establishment: 1944

ARATRANS JORDAN SAG
Arabian Transport Co
PO Box 8454, Amman
Tel: 661527, 661284
Cable: Aratrans Jordan
Telex: 21353 Jtrans

PRINCIPAL ACTIVITIES: International freight forwarding by land, sea and air
Branch Offices: Jordan, PO Box 233 Aqaba; Kuwait (Head Office), Saudi Arabia, Dubai and Abu Dhabi
Parent Company: Aratrans is a subsidiary of the United Arab Shipping Corp
Principal Bankers: Arab Land Bank; Jordan Kuwait Bank

AS SALAM FORWARDING & CLEARING CO

PO Box 6894, Amman
Tel: 638351, 624261, 645125
Cable: Salamcom
Telex: 21241 Provim Jo
Telefax: 962-6-659061

Chairman: Hisham Zabian
Directors: Yousef Ahmed Abdul Hadi (General Manager), Emile S Sakkab (Deputy General Manager)

PRINCIPAL ACTIVITIES: Clearing and customs agents, forwarders, transport contractors
Branch Offices: Branches at Aqaba port; Ramtha; Amman Airport

Principal Bankers: Cairo Amman Bank; Bank of Jordan; Petra Bank

Date of Establishment: 1969
No of Employees: 27

BAKI, NAJEEB, & SONS (JORDAN) LTD

PO Box 572, Amman
Tel: 636121
Cable: Najeeb Baki

Chairman: Najeeb Baki

PRINCIPAL ACTIVITIES: Import and distribution of agricultural, industrial and electrical equipment and materials (water pumps)

BANK AL MASHREK SAL

PO Box 1226, Amman
Tel: 636750
Cable: Mashrek Bank
Telex: 21318 Jo

PRINCIPAL ACTIVITIES: Commercial banking
Parent Company: Head office in Lebanon

BANK OF CREDIT & COMMERCE INTERNATIONAL SA

PO Box 2958, Jabal Amman, Amman
Tel: 644391
Cable: Bancrecom
Telex: 21990 Bcci Jo
Telefax: 649564

Senior Executives: Fakhri Bilbeisi (General Manager), Abrar Zaidi (Manager)

PRINCIPAL ACTIVITIES: Commercial banking
Branch Offices: King Hussain Street Branch; Jabel Amman Branch; Station Road Branch
Parent Company: BCCI Holdings (Luxembourg) SA

Date of Establishment: 1975 in Jordan
No of Employees: 92

BANK OF JORDAN LTD

Head Office, Jabal Amman, 3rd Circle, PO Box 2140, Amman
Tel: 644327/8
Cable: Bank Jordan
Telex: 21479 Banjor, 21946 Banjor, 22033 Banjor
Telefax: 656642

Chairman: Tawfiq Fakhoury
Directors: Mawloud Abdel Qader (Deputy Chairman), Dr Sami Halabi, George Khnouf, Jalal Husni El Kurdi, Nabil Jamil Safadi, Yousef Marto, Mrs Hind Husni El Kurdi, Mamdouh Abu Hassan, Dr Ashraf El Kurdi
Senior Executives: Mohamed Ali Ibrahim (Secretary of Board)

PRINCIPAL ACTIVITIES: All banking activities
Branch Offices: 26 Branches
Principal Bankers: Midland, Chase Manhattan, Mantrust, UBAF, Union Bank of Switzerland, Bankamerica
Financial Information:

	JD'000
Authorised capital	5,250
Paid-up capital	5,250

Principal Shareholders: Public Shareholders
Date of Establishment: 1960
No of Employees: 568

BANQUE NATIONALE DE PARIS

PO Box 35207, Amman
Tel: 641932, 624461
Telex: 22104
Telefax: 624461

Senior Executives: H Hutter (Representative)

PRINCIPAL ACTIVITIES: Representative office
Parent Company: Head office in Paris, France

Date of Establishment: 1980

BILBEISI, ISMAIL, & CO

PO Box 213, King Hussein Street, Amman
Tel: 638103/4, 622815, 624934
Cable: Bilbeisi Amman
Telex: 21513 Bilco Jo
Telefax: 658542

Chairman: Emile Haddad (and Director)
Directors: Najib Bilbeisi
Senior Executives: George Haddad, Nihad Haddad

PRINCIPAL ACTIVITIES: Agents, importers and distributors of electrical equipment, office equipment, mechanical engineering components and air conditioning systems
Principal Agencies: Toyota Motor Sales Co Ltd, Japan; Matsushita Electric Trading Co, Ltd, Japan; National, Japan
Branch Offices: Irbid, Jordan
Principal Bankers: Arab Bank Ltd, Amman; Cairo-Amman Bank, Amman; Grindlays Bank, Amman; Bank of Credit & Commerce, Amman
Financial Information:

	1989/90 US$'000
Sales turnover	62,000
Profits	14,000
Authorised capital	12,000
Paid-up capital	12,000

Principal Shareholders: Emile Haddad; Najib Bilbeisi; Munther Bilbeisi; Ziad Bilbeisi; Mutasim Bilbeisi
Date of Establishment: 1945
No of Employees: 220

BISHARAT, GHALEB SHAKER, & CO

PO Box 305, Amman
Tel: 638890
Cable: Bisharat
Telex: 21596 Shaker Jo

Chairman: Ghaleb Shaker Bisharat
Directors: Shaker Ghaleb Bisharat, Charlie Ghaleb Bisharat
Senior Executives: Jamal Daoud

PRINCIPAL ACTIVITIES: Supply of agricultural machinery and chemicals; local government machinery and supplies; civil defence supplies
Principal Agencies: Agria; Hudson; Uniroyal; Sharpstow; Celamerck; Tennant; Same; Tifone; Comet; As Motor, Kuka; Otto; O & K; Ruthmann; CRS; Modern Environmental Services; Baribbi
Branch Offices: Sales Department: King Hussein St, PO Box 305, Amman; Industrial Zone, Irbid
Principal Bankers: Jordan-Kuwait Bank

Date of Establishment: 1963

BRITISH BANK OF THE MIDDLE EAST (THE)

PO Box 444, King Hussein St, Amman
Tel: 636175/7, 638175/6, 637247
Cable: Bactria
Telex: 21253 Jo BBME

Chairman: W Purves CBE DSO
Directors: J R H Bond, F J French, J M Gray, J A P Hill CBE, S Robertson, P J Wrangham

PRINCIPAL ACTIVITIES: Commercial banking
Branch Offices: Area Management Office: PO Box 925286, Shmeisani, Near Haya Centre, Amman; Tel 669121/2/3, Cable Bactria, Telex 22338 BBME JM; Jebel Hussein Office: PO Box 922376, Firas Circle, Jebel Hussein, Amman, Tel 660471/2/3, 667651/2, 673601; Abdalli Office: PO Box

925259, Abdalli, Amman, Tel 662239; Al Wendat Office: PO Box 520301, Al Wehdat, Amman, Tel 770810
Parent Company: The Hongkong and Shanghai Banking Corp Ltd

Principal Shareholders: The Hongkong and Shanghai Banking Corporation
Date of Establishment: 1949 (Jordan)
No of Employees: 160 (Jordan)

BUKHARI TRADING & INDUSTRIAL CO

PO Box 364, Amman
Tel: 637709, 628209
Cable: BUKHARI
Telex: 21605 Bukhari Jo
Telefax: 648713

President: Mamoun Bukhari
Directors: Imad Bukhari (Vice President)
Senior Executives: Jalil Imseeh, Tarek Bukhari

PRINCIPAL ACTIVITIES: Trading, manufacturing, contractors to military and governmental bodies
Subsidiary Companies: Abdul Hamid Trdg Corp, Jeddah, Saudi Arabia; United National Trading Co, Riyadh, Saudi Arabia; Bukhari Trading Establishment, Jeddah, Saudi Arabia
Principal Bankers: Cairo Amman Bank; Jordan & Gulf Bank
Financial Information:

| | 1990 |
	JD'000
Sales turnover	1,500
Authorised capital	300
Paid-up capital	300
Total assets	800

Principal Shareholders: Mamoun Bukhari; Imad Bukhari
Date of Establishment: 1979
No of Employees: 25

BUSINESS BANK (THE)

PO Box 3103, 11th August Street, Shmeisane, Amman
Tel: 672543, 672495
Cable: Ahlena Amman
Telex: 23455, 21345
Telefax: 672459

Chairman: Dr Rajai Muasher
Directors: Nabil Mouasher, Nazir Sati, Mahmoud El Kayed, Petra Bank, Housing Bank, General Insurance Co, Jordan Worsted Mills, Dr Ramzi Muasher, Samir Zabiri
Senior Executives: Rajai Muasher (Chairman & General Manager), George Dallal (Deputy General Manager)

PRINCIPAL ACTIVITIES: Investment banking
Branch Offices: City Branch
Subsidiary Companies: National Securities Co
Principal Bankers: Manufacturers Hanover Trust Co, National Westminster Bank
Financial Information:

| | 1989 |
	JD'000
Profits	943
Authorised capital	3,200
Paid-up capital	3,200
Total assets	48,419

Date of Establishment: 1981
No of Employees: 42

CAIRO AMMAN BANK

PO Box 715, Shabsough St, Amman
Tel: 639321/7
Cable: Cairam
Telex: 21240, 21794, 23215
Telefax: 639328

Chairman: J Shasha'a (and General Manager)

Directors: Izzedine Mahmoud Ali (Vice Chairman), Usama Salfiti, Issam Salfiti, Talal Chalabi, Yahya Kassab (Rep Jordan Civil Pension Fund), Sabih Masri, Usama Asfour, Abdel Karim Kabariti (Rep INMA Co)
Senior Executives: Ishak Abu Khadra (Deputy General Manager), Usama Asfour (Deputy General Manager)

PRINCIPAL ACTIVITIES: Commercial banking
Branch Offices: Amman Main Branch; Station Rd; Jebel Amman; Jordan University; Jebel Weibdeh; Jebel Hussein; Queismeh; Wadi Seer; Wehdat; Zerka; Russaifa; Ma'addi; Irbed; Fuhais; Al Waha; Nablus (occupied West Bank)
Associated Companies: Banque du Caire, Egypt
Principal Bankers: Amsterdam: Amsterdam Rotterdam Bank; Brussels: Societe Generale de Banque; Frankfurt: Deutsche Bank; Hong Kong: BankAmerica Int'l; London: American Express Int'l Banking Corp; Bank of America NT & SA; Barclays Bank; Manufacturers Hanover Trust; Midland Bank; National Westminster Bank; Societe Generale; Milan: Banca d'America e d'Italia; New York: American Express Int'l Banking Corp; BankAmerica Int'l; Chase Manhattan Bank; Irving Trust; Manufacturers Hanover Trust; Paris: Societe Generale; San Francisco & Singapore: BankAmerica Int'l; Tokyo: Bank of Tokyo; Zurich: Union Bank of Switzerland

Principal Shareholders: Jordan Civil Pension Fund; Banque du Caire; Halim Salfiti & Sons
Date of Establishment: 1960
No of Employees: 503

CENTRAL BANK OF JORDAN

PO Box 37, Amman
Tel: 630301/9
Cable: Markazi
Telex: 21250 Bankzi JO; 21476 Bakazi JO
Telefax: 638889

Governor: Husayn S Kasim
Directors: Dr Michel Marto (Deputy Governor), Zuhair Asfour, Khaled Shoman, Ziad Annab, Tawfiq Kawar

PRINCIPAL ACTIVITIES: Central banking
Branch Offices: Aqaba and Irbid (Jordan)

Principal Shareholders: 100% state owned

CITIBANK NA

PO Box 5055, Amman
Tel: 644065
Cable: Citibank
Telex: 21314 JO, 23235 JO, 23772 JO
Telefax: 658693

Senior Executives: Miss Ghada Debbas (Vice President & Managing Director), Khaled Dajani (Manager)

PRINCIPAL ACTIVITIES: Commercial banking
Parent Company: Head Office: 399 Park Ave, New York, NY 10022, USA

Date of Establishment: 1974
No of Employees: 43

CIVIL CONSTRUCTION CO (CILCON) LTD

PO Box 5011, Shmeisani, Amman
Tel: 661293, 685967
Telex: 21505 Cilcon Jo
Telefax: 679304

Chairman: Raja F Halazon (Managing Director)
Directors: Siham Halazon
Senior Executives: Hassan Al Adwan (Projects Manager), Ayoub Neiroukh (Financial Manager)

PRINCIPAL ACTIVITIES: General contractors, ornamental stone buildings, counsellors for expatriate firms and management advisors in construction contracting, real estate development projects

Principal Bankers: Petra Bank, Shmeisani; National Finance
Corporation
Financial Information:

	1990
	JD'000
Authorised capital	450
Paid-up capital	450

Principal Shareholders: Raja F Halazon; Siham R Halazon
Date of Establishment: 1967
No of Employees: 40

COMEDAT - JORDAN ECONOMIC DEVELOPMENT & TRADING CO

Po Box 2146, Amman
Tel: 642096, 644096
Cable: Comedat
Telex: 21288 Khalid Jo
Telefax: 642319

Chairman: Eng Khalid Al Rifa'i
Directors: Mokbel K Shukri (General Manager)

PRINCIPAL ACTIVITIES: Earthmoving and mining contractors
Principal Bankers: Arab Bank Ltd, Amman
Financial Information:

	1989
	US$'000
Sales turnover	11,000
Authorised capital	1,500
Paid-up capital	1,500
Total assets	9,000

Principal Shareholders: Eng Khalid Al-Rifa'i; Samer Judeh;
Mokbel Shukri
Date of Establishment: 1973
No of Employees: 300

COMMERCIAL & INDUSTRIAL CO LTD

PO Box 379, Amman
Tel: 624396, 651397
Cable: Nawal
Telex: 21311 Jo

Chairman: Shehadeh Twal

PRINCIPAL ACTIVITIES: Import and distribution of diesel
engines and equipment, automobiles, electrical and electronic
appliances and equipment (radios and TV sets), office
equipment
Principal Agencies: Campbell; Ford; Mullard; Leabank; Rolls-
Royce; ITT; David Brown; Nissam Diesel

CONSOLIDATED CONTRACTORS CO

Roundabout Muntazah Al Almaneh, Jabal Al-Loueibdeh, Amman
Tel: 625827, 630827
Telex: 21745 Cicici Jo

PRINCIPAL ACTIVITIES: Building and civil engineering
contractors, marine and mechanical works, pipeline
contractors
Branch Offices: Managing Office in Greece: PO Box 61092,
Athens

CONSOLIDATED ENGINEERING CO

Alami & Abdulhadi

PO Box 35256, Amman
Tel: 822136
Cable: HADICO
Telex: 23012 Cec JO
Telefax: 822137

Chairman: Dr Zuheir Alami
Directors: Samir Abdulhadi
Senior Executives: Dr Saleh Rusheidat (Resident Manager)

PRINCIPAL ACTIVITIES: Consulting engineers, architects,
planners and designers

Parent Company: Khatib and Alami, Beirut
Principal Bankers: Jordan Gulf Bank, Arab bank

Principal Shareholders: Dr Z Alami; Samir Abdulhadi
Date of Establishment: 1980

CONSTRUCTION EQUIPMENT & MACHINERY CO LTD

3rd Circle, (Tala Centre), PO Box 435, Amman
Tel: 641228, 642668, 661714
Cable: Cemaco
Telex: 21641 Cemaco Jo

Chairman: Omar M Abou Zeid
Directors: M Maher M Abou Zeid

PRINCIPAL ACTIVITIES: Stockists of construction equipment,
machinery, and building materials; manufacturers'
representatives
Principal Agencies: Stetter GmbH; Linde AG; Theis & Co,
Germany; Wysepower Ltd, UK; CCL Plant Ltd, UK; Oyh Wilh
Schauman, Finland; Linden Alimak, Sweden; Salzgitter Stahl,
Germany; Zaidan House, Lebanon
Subsidiary Companies: General Trade Building Materials Ltd,
Amman
Principal Bankers: Cairo-Amman Bank, Amman; Al-Mashrek
Bank, Amman

Principal Shareholders: Omar M Abou Zeid
Date of Establishment: 1974

CREDIT LYONNAIS

PO Box 1047, Amman
Tel: 642065
Cable: Credit Jo
Telex: 22095 Credly JO
Telefax: 634277

Senior Executives: Jean Louis Laguens (Regional
Representative), Mrs Adele Habache Khalaf (Resident
Representative)

PRINCIPAL ACTIVITIES: Representative office
Parent Company: Head office: 19 Bld des Italiens, 75002 Paris,
France

Date of Establishment: 1981 in Jordan

DAMIR INDUSTRIAL ENGINEERING TRADING & CONTRACTING CO (DIETCO)

PO Box 15245 Marka, Amman
Tel: 894866-894907
Cable: DIETCO
Telex: 21514 Damir JO

President: Mohamed Hassan Damir (General Manager)

PRINCIPAL ACTIVITIES: Mechanical contracting, sheet metal
fabricator, steel structure, boilers, concrete mixer, tanks,
chassis, silos & pipeline
Principal Bankers: Jordan Kuwait Bank

Principal Shareholders: Khalil M H Damir; Nabil M H Damir;
Hussam M H Damir; Awad M H Damir; Amjad M H Damir;
Alah M H Damir
Date of Establishment: February 7 1976
No of Employees: 80

DEEB, SHUKRI, & SONS LTD

King Hussein St, PO Box 523, Amman

PRINCIPAL ACTIVITIES: Import and distribution of motor cars
and spare parts, paints and varnish, tyres and tubes,
refrigerators, hardware, ironmongery and tools
Principal Agencies: Zenith Carburettors; GMC Trucks; Pontiac;
Opel; Goodrich; Frigidaire

DHL OPERATIONS (JORDAN)

PO Box 927111, Amman
Tel: 818351-3
Telex: 22292 DHL Jo

PRINCIPAL ACTIVITIES: Worldwide courier service and cargo, airfreight service
Branch Offices: In the Middle East: Bahrain, Cyprus, Jibouti, Egypt (Cairo, Alexandria), Iraq, Iran, Jordan, Kuwait, Lebanon, Oman, Qatar, Saudi Arabia (AlKhobar, Jeddah, Riyadh, Jubail, Tabuk, Taif), Sudan, Turkey, UAE (Abu Dhabi, Dubai, Sharjah), UK, USA, Europe, Far East

Date of Establishment: 1980
No of Employees: 20

EASTERN COMPANY

King Hussein St, PO Box 131, Amman
Tel: 622727
Cable: Eastern
Telex: 21521 Marto Jo

Chairman: Yousef M Marto

PRINCIPAL ACTIVITIES: Agricultural requirements, seed, pesticides, fertilizers, industrial machinery, importers
Principal Agencies: Shell International Chemical Co Ltd; Hoechst AG; Hurst Gunson Cooper Taber Ltd
Associated Companies: Marzo & Hazou (dealing in automotive requirements)
Principal Bankers: British Bank of the Middle East; Jordan National Bank

EL KURDI, HAJ ALI, SONS & CO

Sa'ada St, PO Box 1177, Amman

PRINCIPAL ACTIVITIES: Engineering contractors, import and distribution of heating and air conditioning equipment, heavy machinery, pharmaceuticals, toiletries, paper and board, and printing equipment
Subsidiary Companies: Modern Print Company Division (PO Box 612); Kurdi Drugstore Division (PO Box 981)

ELBA HOUSE CO LTD

PO Box 3449, Amman
Tel: 842600/1, 844013
Cable: Elba Khoury, Amman
Telex: 22060 EH JO
Telefax: 842603

Chairman: Usama Musa Khoury
Directors: Nadim Khoury, Zuhair Khoury
Senior Executives: Eng Sami Khoury (Project & Sales Manager), Eng Ma'an Husseini (Technical Advisor), Rawhi Massis (Financial Advisor), Eng Kamal Saber (Planning Manager), Salim Khoury (Supply & Marketing Manager), Eng Husni Albarghothi (Production Manager), Issam Shourbaji (Personnel Manager)

PRINCIPAL ACTIVITIES: Supply of prefab houses, mobile caravans, cabins on skids, sandwich panels, steel hangars, steel buildings, structural steel works for all purposes, wooden doors and PVC accordian doors
Branch Offices: Baghdad, Iraq, Tel 7185920; Tripoli, Libya, Tel 831131, 832982; Abu Dhabi, UAE, Tel 325884
Principal Bankers: Arab Bank Ltd; Jordan Gulf Bank; Jordan Kuwait Bank
Financial Information:

	1989/90 US$'000
Sales turnover	15,000
Authorised capital	1,500
Paid-up capital	1,500
Total assets	6,000

Principal Shareholders: Usama Musa Khoury; Zuhair Musa Khoury; Nadim Musa Khoury
Date of Establishment: 1976
No of Employees: 250

ELECTRICAL LIGHTING CO LTD

PO Box 9163, Jabal Hussain, Amman
Tel: 663431, 662347, 606342
Cable: ANWAR CO
Telex: 21792 Elco JO

Directors: T M Abu Zayyad (Managing Director), Issam A Huda, A Moury
Senior Executives: Arshad A Zubairi (Assistant General Manager)

PRINCIPAL ACTIVITIES: Electrical traders and contractors
Principal Agencies: Zumtobel AG, Austria; Square'D'Ltd, UK/USA; EGA Ltd, UK; Bergers Elastomers, UK; Bega GmbH, Germany; B G Light, Austria; Futurit Werk, Austria; Willy Meyer & Shon, Germany; Staff KG, Germany; Carters, UK; Petitjean & Cie, France; Contactum, UK; Duraplug, UK
Branch Offices: ELC, PO Box 4109, Abu Dhabi, UAE; ELC, PO Box 5700, Sharjah, UAE; ELC, PO Box 11178, Dubai, UAE
Parent Company: Electrical Lighting Co, Abu Dhabi, UAE
Subsidiary Companies: General Electric Co, PO Box 4109, Abu Dhabi, UAE
Principal Bankers: Jordan Kuwait Bank, Cairo Amman Bank

Principal Shareholders: The directors
Date of Establishment: 1960
No of Employees: 500

EL KAMAL ENTERPRISES EST

PO Box 621, Amman
Tel: 678855
Cable: Hammad
Telex: 23800 Elkam
Telefax: 678855

Directors: Khaled Kamal

PRINCIPAL ACTIVITIES: Import and distribution of telecommunication and electronic equipment, power cables, fire extinguishers and construction equipment
Principal Bankers: BCCI, Amman

EL KOUR TRADING AGENCY

PO Box 1675, Amman
Tel: 624759
Cable: El-Kour

PRINCIPAL ACTIVITIES: Import and distribution of motor cars and spare parts, tyres and tubes, ironmongery, hand tools, machine tools, stationery, clothing, underwear and toiletries

EL NASR EXPORT & IMPORT CO

PO Box 7146, Amman
Tel: 625019, 625159
Cable: Shintam Amman
Telex: 21242

PRINCIPAL ACTIVITIES: Import and export of cereals, foodstuffs, fodders, fertilizers, canned food (vegetables and meat), household utensils, building materials, leather (raw and tanned), phosphates, oils, batteries, paper, pipes, refrigerators, rice, ropes, nylon bags, leather bags, sanitary equipment, sesame seeds, sugar, textiles, threads, timber, tyres, underwear, detergents, cigarettes, cement

EL SHAMMAA, MAHMOUD, & SONS CO LTD

PO Box 29, Amman
Tel: 23830, 55058, 33038
Cable: El-Shammaa

Chairman: Zuhair Mahmoud El-Shammaa
Directors: Walid Mahmoud El-Shammaa, Khalid Mahmoud El-Shammaa

Senior Executives: Mahmoud Z El-Shammaa (Technical Manager), A G Nassar (Administration Manager), S A El-Awwad (Sales Manager)

PRINCIPAL ACTIVITIES: Manufacture of steel furniture; import/export and commission agents
Branch Offices: Al-Nassr Stores: PO Box 29, Amman; Al-Nassr Steel Furniture Factory: PO Box 29, Amman; Mahmoud El-Shammaa & Sons Co Ltd (Commission & General Agents): PO Box 29, 6143, 9881, Amman
Principal Bankers: Rafidain Bank; Bank of Jordan

ENEX CONTRACTING CORPORATION

Shmeisani, Barakat Bldg, PO Box 926982, Amman
Tel: 667424
Telex: 22460 Enexco JO

Chairman: Abdel Majid Afanah (Managing Director)
Directors: Marwan A Dajani
Senior Executives: Hani Awartani, Samir Ghuneim, Khalil Ellaham

PRINCIPAL ACTIVITIES: General construction
Principal Bankers: Arab Bank Ltd, Shmeisani branch
Financial Information:

	JD'000
Sales turnover	2,000
Authorised capital	400
Paid-up capital	400

Principal Shareholders: A M Afanah; M A Dajani
Date of Establishment: January 1979

ESSCO
Equipment Sales & Service Corporation

PO Box 6, Amman
Tel: 641410, 641910, 778148
Telex: 21992 Essco JO

Chairman: Mohammad Abu-Kurah (Managing Director)

PRINCIPAL ACTIVITIES: Import, sales and service of heavy machinery, trucks, buses and parts
Principal Agencies: John Deere; Mitsubishi Motors; Hyster; Montabert; Bofors
Principal Bankers: Arab Bank; Jordan Gulf Bank; Petra Bank

Principal Shareholders: Mohammad Abu-Kurah; Leonard Land BV/Holland
Date of Establishment: 10/10/1977
No of Employees: 55

ETCO
Engineering Trading Contracting

PO Box 3391, Amman
Tel: 642260
Telex: 21401 Audi JO

Chairman: Adib F Audi
Directors: Nabil F Audi
Senior Executives: Fadi A Audi (Sales & Administration Manager), Wajih Dababneh (Accounts Head Office), Khalil Barajakly (Service Manager)

PRINCIPAL ACTIVITIES: Sales and service of heavy construction equipment, and spare parts for all equipment
Principal Agencies: Grove Cranes; Liebherr Batching Plants; Excavators; Bulldozers; Industrial Plants; Furukawa Wheel Loaders; Champion Graders; Bomag Rollers
Branch Offices: ETCO - Lebanon: PO Box 114986, Beirut, Tel 353670/1, Telex 22441 ADIB B LE; ETCO - Syria: PO Box 5610, Damascus, Tel 453125, Telex 411165 AUDI SY
Subsidiary Companies: Letec, Lebanon; Diab Medical, Lebanon
Principal Bankers: Cairo Amman Bank; Jordan Islamic Bank

Principal Shareholders: Adib F Audi; Mrs Najat I Zeine
Date of Establishment: 1976
No of Employees: 25

EUROPCAR
National Car Rental

Khatab St, PO Box 2020, Jabal Amman, Amman
Tel: 639197, 642401
Cable: SHEPHERD Amman
Telex: 21410 SHEPRD JO

Chairman: George Shalhoub
Directors: Nader Shalhoub (General Manager)
Senior Executives: Bassem Haddadeen

PRINCIPAL ACTIVITIES: Car hire
Principal Agencies: National Car Rental, USA; Natcar, Australia; Tilden, Canada
Branch Offices: Marriott Hotel Amman; Regency Palace Hotel Amman; Amra Forum Hotel Amman; Queen Alia International Airport
Subsidiary Companies: Amra Rent A Car
Principal Bankers: Grindlays Bank; Industrial Development Bank; Citibank; Jordan Leasing Corporation

Date of Establishment: 1976

F A KETTANEH & CO LTD

See KETTANEH, F A, & CO LTD

FARHAT TRADING ORGANISATION

PO Box 2500, Amman
Tel: 661716, 663724
Cable: Faisal Tabbah
Telex: 21265 Faisal Jordan

Chairman: Faisal Tabbah
Directors: Farhat Tabbah (International Marketing and Contracting), Tareef Tabbah (Home Industries and Middle East Marketing)

PRINCIPAL ACTIVITIES: Trading in fields of transportation, engineering, textile industries, military equipment, chemicals and fertilizers, and credit and financing
Principal Agencies: Daniel Illingworth; Sunkyong Ltd; Hyundai Shipbuilding; Manta NV; Sisma; Silk Italia; Top Management SPA
Branch Offices: Kuwait; Saudi Arabia; Egypt; Syria; Iraq; United Arab Emirates; Libya; South Korea; UK
Subsidiary/Associated Companies: Farhat Industrial Co, Amman; Farhat Trading Co, Amman; United Tailoring & Contracting Co, Amman; Overseas Trade Enterprises, Amman; Decora Gallery, Amman
Principal Bankers: Cairo Amman Bank; Barclays Bank; Grindlays Bank
Financial Information:

	JD'000
Sales turnover	18,000
Paid-up capital	1,000

Principal Shareholders: Farhat Tabbah; Tareef Tabbah
Date of Establishment: 1955
No of Employees: 300

FARRADJ & CO
Fuad Abujaber & Sons

PO Box 974, Amman
Tel: 621662, 625616, 893020, 885980, 885981, 781844
Cable: Farradj
Telex: 21317 Farraj Jo, 21323 Farraj Jo.
Telefax: 891205

Chairman: Fuad S Abujaber
Directors: Kim F Abujaber (Managing Director)
Senior Executives: M Abu Othman (Marketing/Finance Manager), Khalid Kiwan (Sales & Service Manager), Saliba Khasho (Purchasing/Spare Parts Manager), Sa'd Aghabi (Service Manager)

PRINCIPAL ACTIVITIES: Import and distribution of heavy machinery, earthmoving equipment, cranes, forklift trucks, diesel engines, generating sets, automatic transmissions, road building equipment, mining equipment, concrete pumps, mixers, plants and ancillary equipment, industrial plants, ductile pipe, concrete pipe & brick making plant, spare parts, railroad & railway equipment and accessories, contractors'representatives

Principal Agencies: Detroit Diesel Corp, Allison Transmission Div of General Motors, FMC Link Belt, Krupp Industrietechnik, Thyssen GmbH, Aveling Barford Intl, Schwing GmbH, Stetter GmbH, Yale Materials Handling, Forsheda AG, Pedersaab Maskinfabrik, Donaldson Filter Components, American Hoist, Kent Moore, Gregg Co, Pool Co, Simmons Machine Tool, Pachal, Potain, Goodwin Barsby, Interroll

Branch Offices: Zerka Free Zone, Zarka, Jordan; Al Wahdat Street, Amman, Jordan, Tel 781844

Principal Bankers: Arab Bank Ltd, Cairo Amman Bank; Arab Jordan Investment Bank

Principal Shareholders: Chairman & directors as described
Date of Establishment: 1956
No of Employees: 40

FINANCE & CREDIT CORPORATION

PO Box 815352, Jabal Amman, 3rd Circle, Amman
Tel: 642701, 642667, 642383
Cable: Mali
Telex: 23281, 23128 Mali JO
Telefax: 645270

Chairman: Dr Ahmad Al Chalabi
Directors: Suhail Khoury, Ebraheem Al Ebraheem, Ebrahemm Abu Jabal, Dr Shahib Ammari, Abdel Hamid Abdel Aziz, Munjed Al Sukhtian, Samir Al Masri, Radwan Hajjar
Senior Executives: Hani Aqaish (Deputy General Manager), Samir Haddad (Branches Manager & Asst General Manager)

PRINCIPAL ACTIVITIES: Merchant banking
Financial Information:

	JD'000
Authorised capital	6,000
Paid-up capital	4,684
Total assets	46,727

Principal Shareholders: Petra Bank; Cairo Amman Bank; Housing Bank; Jordan Insurance Co; Public interests
Date of Establishment: 1982
No of Employees: 50

FOXBORO INTERCONTINENTAL LTD

PO Box 3361, Amman
Tel: 962-6664417, 6664517
Cable: Foxmeco
Telex: 21725 Foxme Jo
Telefax: 962-6601382

Chairman: F Joe Merten (General Manager Amman)
Senior Executives: Suhail Hanania (Sales Manager), E Khabaz (Manager Business Operations)

PRINCIPAL ACTIVITIES: Sales and service of process instrumentation, analyzers, controls, and computer system products of Foxboro Co
Branch Offices: Kuwait; Abu Dhabi
Parent Company: The Foxboro Company, Foxboro USA
Principal Bankers: British Bank of the Middle East, Amman

Principal Shareholders: Foxboro Intercontinental Ltd is a subsidiary of Foxboro Company, USA
Date of Establishment: January 1977 in Amman

G M KHOURY

See KHOURY, G M,

GARGOUR, T, & FILS

PO Box 419, Amman
Tel: 622307/8, 633587, 638896
Cable: Trust
Telex: 21213 Trust Jo; 23042 Trust Jo; 21072 Trust Jo; 21378 Trust Jo

Chairman: John Gargour
Directors: Nadim Gargour (Managing Director), Nicolas Gargour, Habib Gargour, Allenby Gargour

PRINCIPAL ACTIVITIES: Shipping agents and owners; importers and exporters specialising in motor vehicles and parts; general traders, hoteliers, industrialists, manufacturers; investment and finance
Principal Agencies: Hapag Lloyd; Mitsui OSK Lines; American Export Lines; United States Lines; Lloyd Braziliero; Daimler Benz; Sudan Shipping Line; Red Sea Line; Lloyd Triestino; Usinor; Alfa Laval; Akzo Chemie; Carnaud; Cofran; Elf Aquitaine; Clarke; TCM
Branch Offices: Lebanon: PO Box 110371, Lebanon, Telex 230886; UK: 5 Cromwell Place, London SW7 2JP, Telex 299238, Tel: 581 5717; France: 30 Rue de Gramont, 75002, Paris; Aqaba: Telex 62231; London: Telex 887692; Paris: Telex 230886; Cairo: Telex 54034; Limassol: Telex 2031; Kuwait: Telex 2094; Lattakia: Telex 51025; Tunis: Telex 12384; Hamburg: Telex 214577
Parent Company: T Gargour et Fils, Luxembourg
Associated Companies: Lebanese Ceramic Factory (LECICO), Associated Levant Lines (ALL), Uniceramic, Middle East Associates, International Trust Insurance, Lecico (Egypt), Egyptian Finance Co
Principal Bankers: British Bank of the Middle East; Grindlays Bank Ltd; Jordan National Bank SA; Arab Bank Ltd

Principal Shareholders: Private company
Date of Establishment: 1928
No of Employees: 2,400

GENERAL INVESTMENT CO LTD

Prince Mohammed St, PO Box 312, Amman
Tel: 625161/2
Cable: Bira
Telex: 21323 Abujaber Jo
Telefax: 628167

Chairman: Farhan Abujaber
Directors: Raouf Abujaber (General Manager)
Senior Executives: Khalil Lahleh (Manager), Mohammad Saleh (Production Manager), Suhail Kharoufeh (Technical Manager)

PRINCIPAL ACTIVITIES: Production of beer and soft drinks; financial investments and real estate
Associated Companies: Amstel International BV, Holland
Principal Bankers: Grindlays Bank, Arab Bank plc, Jordan Finance & Investment Bank
Financial Information:

	1988/89 US$'000	1989/90 US$'000
Sales turnover	6,228	4,373
Profits	1,819	1,000
Authorised capital	10,000	5,152
Paid-up capital	10,000	5,152
Total assets	13,070	8,750

Principal Shareholders: Sa'd Abujaber & Sons
Date of Establishment: 1955
No of Employees: 70

GHADIR ENGINEERING & CONTRACTING CO LTD

Jalil Street, Firas Square, Jabal Al-Hussain, PO Box 7354, Amman
Tel: 660503, 673544
Cable: Ghadir/Amman
Telex: 21724 Ace JO

Chairman: Mousa Moh'd Ramadan Himmo
Directors: Ahmed Moh'd Saed Al-Aloul, Ali Mansour Al-Hindawi, Nuhad Moh'd Haikal, Mufid Abdul Rahman Kanaan
Senior Executives: Izziddin Abdo Fahd (Chief Engineer), Abdul Majid Kanaan (Administrative Assistant), Nabil A Himmo (Chief Accountant)

PRINCIPAL ACTIVITIES: Civil engineering and construction
Subsidiary Companies: Ghadir Agricultural Co Ltd, PO Box 7354, Amman, Jordan
Principal Bankers: Arab Bank; Islamic Bank; Jordan Kuwaiti Bank
Financial Information:

	JD'000
Sales turnover	1,000
Authorised capital	500
Paid-up capital	500

Principal Shareholders: Private stock Co
Date of Establishment: 1978
No of Employees: 125

GHALEB SHAKER BISHARAT & CO
See BISHARAT, GHALEB SHAKER, & CO

GHUL, ZAKI A,
PO Box 2375, Amman
Tel: 678944 Shmeisany
Cable: Zamzam
Telex: 21788 Zamzam Jo
Telefax: 682944

President: Zaki A Ghul
Senior Executives: A/Nasser Z Ghul

PRINCIPAL ACTIVITIES: Import of electronic, electrical and medical equipment
Principal Agencies: Sony Corporation, Japan; 'Bouyer' Montauban, France
Branch Offices: Jabal Amman, Tel 621770
Principal Bankers: Grindlays Bank

Date of Establishment: 1950

GRAND FLOUR MILL CO (AMMAN)
PO Box 355, Amman
Tel: 655980

Directors: Abdullah Wahdeh Tomasi

PRINCIPAL ACTIVITIES: Flour milling

HADDAD INVESTMENT CO (HICTIC)
PO Box 9161, Amman
Tel: 661636, 663669, 661526, 664034
Cable: Hictic
Telex: 21628 Amb Haddad

Chairman: Mohd A Haddad
Directors: N M Haddad (General Director), Faris M Haddad (Contracting Director), Anas M Haddad (Trading Director), Ammar M Haddad (Industry Director)

PRINCIPAL ACTIVITIES: Export and import; building contractors; precasting houses and buildings, furnished appartments
Branch Offices: Huwara Branch
Parent Company: Al-Khibra Engineering office
Principal Bankers: Arab Land Bank (Al-Akari)

Date of Establishment: Sept 1975

HAJ ALI EL KURDI SONS & CO
See EL KURDI, HAJ ALI, SONS & CO

HAJ TAHER HUDHUD & SONS CO
See HUDHUD, HAJ TAHER, & SONS CO

HALABY & BROS CO
PO Box 488, King Hussein St, Amman
Tel: 636565, 622795
Cable: Halabros

Chairman: A Halaby

PRINCIPAL ACTIVITIES: Import and distribution of pharmaceuticals, toiletries, chemicals, surgical and medical appliances and equipment, and hospital supplies

HAMDI & IBRAHIM MANGO LTD
See MANGO, HAMDI & IBRAHIM, LTD

HAMMUDEH, A H,
PO Box 499, Amman
Tel: 625617, 636243, 638243
Cable: Hammudeh
Telex: 21241 Provimi Jo
Telefax: 659061

Chairman: A H Hammudeh
Directors: N Hammudeh
Senior Executives: S Hammudeh

PRINCIPAL ACTIVITIES: Import and distribution of chemical products, animal feeds, industrial raw materials, arms and sporting ammunition, paper, leather, and electrical accessories and spare parts
Parent Company: Jordan Chemical Co
Subsidiary Companies: Jordan Feed Company
Principal Bankers: Grindlays Bank, Arab Bank
Financial Information:

	US$'000
Sales turnover	25,000
Authorised capital	3,000
Paid-up capital	3,000

Principal Shareholders: A H Hammoudeh and Sons
Date of Establishment: 1964
No of Employees: 250

HEDJAZ JORDAN RAILWAY
PO Box 582, Amman
Tel: 655028, 655413, 655414
Cable: Jordan Railway
Telex: 21541 MOT (ATT HJR)

Chairman: Eng Ali Assheimat (Minister of Transport)
Directors: Eng. Hashem Taher, M R Qoseini, Dr Abdel Salam Abbadi, Ali Gharaibeh, Marwan Irsheidat, Ahmed Agaileh
Senior Executives: M R Qoseini (Director General)

PRINCIPAL ACTIVITIES: Passenger and freight transportation
Principal Bankers: Cairo Amman Bank, Amman
Financial Information:

	JD'000
Authorised capital	5,989
Paid-up capital	5,989

Principal Shareholders: Jordan Government
Date of Establishment: May 1948
No of Employees: 300

HOTEL INTERCONTINENTAL
PO Box 1827, Jebel Amman, Amman
Tel: 641361
Cable: Inhotelcor/Amman
Telex: 21207

PRINCIPAL ACTIVITIES: Hotel business
Parent Company: Intercontinental Hotels

HOUSING BANK

Police College St, PO Box 7693, Amman
Tel: 667126
Cable: Iskan
Telex: 21693, 22061, 23460 Iskan Jo
Telefax: 678121

Chairman: Zuhair Khouri (and General Manager)
Directors: Badr Al Rasheed (Vice Chairman), Mansour Haddadin, Mohammad Jaser, Yosef Hiyasat, Abdullah Al Qawari, Ibrahim Al Ibrahim, Ahmad Abdel Khaliq, Abdul Mohsin Kattan, Munther Fahoum, Tharwat Al Barghouthi
Senior Executives: Zuhair Khouri (General Manager), Abdul Kader Dwaik (Deputy General Manager), Ghasan Shahatit (Asst Deputy General Manager/Operations), Mahmoud Abuelteen (Asst Deputy General Manager/Administration), Owdeh Khalil (Manager of Audit Dept), Muhie Dein Ali (Manager of Personnel Dept), Nader Khanfer (Manager of Central Accounting Dept), Abdulaziz Haikal (Manager of Research & Investment Dept), Awad Fadayel (Manager of Foreign Dept), Saleem Jarar (Manager of Legal Dept), Omran Abu Ghoush (Manager of Deposits Dept), Nabeeh Halawah (Manager of Real Estate Investment Dept), Mohd Abu Zeid (Manager of PR Dept), Salah Rimawi (Manager Computer Dept), Ibrahim Al Thaher (Manager Low Cost Housing Dept), Ali Hamada (Manager of Loan Dept)

PRINCIPAL ACTIVITIES: Granting mortgage loans, accepting deposits, real-estate and financial investments
Branch Offices: 99 branches in Jordan
Subsidiary Companies: Jordan Securities Corp (45%), Jordan Real Estate Co (24.2%), Jordan Bricks & Tiles Manufacturing Co (95.7%), Jordan Holiday Inn Hotel Co (30%), Industrial Development Bank (27.9%), Darco for Investment & Housing Co (62%), minority interests in 40 other companies
Financial Information:

	1988/89 JD'000	1989/90 JD'000
Total deposits	378,500	434,000
Loans & advances	322,800	334,100
Profits	3,160	3,420
Authorised capital	18,000	18,000
Paid-up capital	12,000	12,000
Total assets	518,200	573,800

Principal Shareholders: The Government of Jordan; Kuwait Investment Authority, Kuwait; Ministry of Finance and Petroleum, Qatar; Ministry of Economic Affairs & Finance, Iran; Directorate General of Finance, Sultanate of Oman; Private Shareholders (Jordanian & Arab Citizens)
Date of Establishment: 1973
No of Employees: 1,517

HUDHUD, HAJ TAHER, & SONS CO

PO Box 446, Amman
Tel: 636354/5/6, 644420
Cable: Hudhud
Telex: 21345 HUDHUD
Telefax: 962-641928

Chairman: Mohamed T Hudhud
Directors: Suleiman T Hudhud (Managing Director)
Senior Executives: Najib S Hudhud (Marketing Manager)

PRINCIPAL ACTIVITIES: Contractors, import and distribution of building materials, timber, ironmongery and chemical products, general trade, cosmetics, perfumes, soap industry
Principal Agencies: Errut Products Ltd, UK; Potratz Dumpers, West Germany; YSL France; DMP Electronics, Italy
Branch Offices: Saudi Arabia, Kuwait, Bahrain, Dubai
Subsidiary Companies: Hudhudshand Ltd (Contractors), Avon Center (cosmetics)
Principal Bankers: Arab Bank Ltd, Jordan National Bank, Jordan Bank

Principal Shareholders: Mohamad T Hudhud, Nadim T Hudhud, Salim T Hudhud, Suleiman T Hudhud & Husam T Hudhud
Date of Establishment: 1936
No of Employees: 45

I TILLAWI & SONS LTD

See TILLAWI, I, & SONS LTD

INDUSTRIAL COMMERCIAL & AGRICULTURAL CO LTD (ICA)

PO Box 6066, Amman
Tel: 09/951945/7, 951197
Cable: ICA AMMAN-JORDAN
Telex: 41434 ICA JO
Telefax: 962-9-951198

Chairman: Mohammad Abu Hassan
Directors: Qasem Abu El Sheikh, Nabil Hamoudeh, Dr Fayez Al Tarawneh, Saadeddine Jum'a, Zahed Assaifi, Osama Asfour, Wael Brakat, Omar Bdeir
Senior Executives: Eng Yahya R Alami (General Manager), Hani Omar El Qasem (Deputy General Manager)

PRINCIPAL ACTIVITIES: Industrial, commercial and agricultural investment, operation of various factories and production of soap, detergents, toiletries, paints, biscuits, ice-cream and plastic containers, cleaners, desinfectants
Principal Agencies: Working under licence with Imperial Chemical Industries, Dulux, Pentalite Unilever, Surf, Signal, Pepsodent, Sunsilk, Lux Soap, Henkel, Persil, Dixan, Fa Soap, etc
Associated Companies: Jordan Converting & Printing Co
Principal Bankers: Arab Bank plc
Financial Information:

	1988/89 JD'000	1989/90 JD'000
Sales turnover	7,540	9,290
Profits	273	541
Authorised capital	5,000	5,000
Paid-up capital	3,466	3,466
Total assets	8,828	9,196

Date of Establishment: 1961

INDUSTRIAL DEVELOPMENT BANK

PO Box 1982, Jabal Amman, Amman
Tel: 642216/9
Cable: Banksinai
Telex: 21349 IDB JO
Telefax: 962-6-647821

Chairman: Rouhi El-Khatib
Directors: Munzer Fahoum, Sa'ad Tell, Zuhair El Khori, Mohammad Saleh Hourani, Yazeed Mufti, Edward S Far, Hassan Saoudi, Dr Safwan Toukan, Khaldoun Abu Hassan
Senior Executives: Dr Taher Kanaan (General Manager), Rajab Assaad (Deputy General Manager)

PRINCIPAL ACTIVITIES: Banking; finance for industry and tourism (long and medium-term loans); finance for small industry, portfolio management, underwriting operations of shares and bonds, syndication of loans, project identification, training of managerial personnel
Financial Information:

	1988/89 JD'000	1989/90 JD'000
Profits before provisions	1,240	1,536
Authorised capital	6,000	6,000
Paid-up capital	5,691	6,000
Current assets	32,814	42,286
Total assets	60,306	74,612

Principal Shareholders: Government of Jordan (18.5%); others (81.5%)
Date of Establishment: 1965
No of Employees: 122

INDUSTRIAL SUPPLIES BUREAU

PO Box 108, Amman
Tel: 624139, 625917
Cable: Cat Insbau
Telex: 22069 Insbau Jo

PRINCIPAL ACTIVITIES: Import and distribution of electrical
appliances and equipment, refrigerators, compressors, drilling
equipment, air conditioning and heating equipment, pumps,
fire extinguishers, contractors for general supplies

INTERNATIONAL CO FOR ELECTRIC LIFTS & ESCALATORS

PO Box 925458, Amman
Tel: 601420
Telex: 24239 Zurgat JO

Chairman: Mohammad Zuregat (Managing Director)
Directors: E Zuregat

PRINCIPAL ACTIVITIES: Manufacture of electric passenger lifts
and escalators
Principal Agencies: CEAM, Italy
Principal Bankers: Arab Bank; Petra Bank

Principal Shareholders: Chairman and director as mentioned
Date of Establishment: 1981

INTERNATIONAL CONTAINERS SERVICES CO

PO Box 9708, King Hussein Street, Amman
Tel: 639449, 635162
Telex: 21174 Sadaram JO

Chairman: Ahmad Armoush
Directors: Nabil Karam
Senior Executives: Samir El Sa'eh (Financial Manager), Fouad
Miqdad (Commercial Manager)

PRINCIPAL ACTIVITIES: Shipping agents, land transport
Principal Agencies: Compagnie Maritime d'Affretement, France
Branch Offices: PO Box 485, Aqaba, Jordan
Principal Bankers: Jordan Gulf Bank, Amman; Bank of Credit &
Commerce International, Amman
Financial Information:

	US$'000
Sales turnover	2,000
Authorised capital	155
Paid-up capital	155

Principal Shareholders: Ahmad Armoush; Piere Haddad
Date of Establishment: 1981

INTERNATIONAL CONTRACTING & INVESTMENT CO

PO Box 19170, Amman
Tel: 813781/2/3
Cable: Intervest
Telex: 21977 Icico Jo

Chairman: Sahel Hamzeh (Managing Director)
Directors: Dr Mohammad Mahdi Al Farhan (Vice Chairman),
Basel Jardaneh, Bassam Attari, Eng Mohammad Al Bataineh,
Eng A/Muniem Atteya, Dr Issam Al Taher, Khalil Sarraf,
Anwar Ajlouni, Ali Jafar, Sameeh Mikawi
Senior Executives: Eng Hamid Hashisho (Deputy Managing
Director), Assem Khair (Chief of Administrative Section),
Adnan Abu Obeid (Chief of Finance Section)

PRINCIPAL ACTIVITIES: Building, civil construction, heavy
works, etc
Branch Offices: Aqaba, Jordan; Baghdad, Iraq
Principal Bankers: Housing Bank; Jordan Investment Bank;
Jordan-Kuwait Bank; Islamic Bank; Grindlays Bank; Al Ahli
Bank; Jordan Gulf Bank; Petra Bank

Principal Shareholders: The Housing Bank; The Pension Fund;
Ministry of Finance: and a group of more than 80 highly
specialized engineers
Date of Establishment: 2/5/1977
No of Employees: 122

INTERNATIONAL FOODSTUFFS CO

PO Box 1746, Amman
Tel: 661413, 661778, 664419
Cable: Alwalid
Telex: 21614 Ifco; 21252 Deeb

Chairman: Mohammad Haj Deeb

PRINCIPAL ACTIVITIES: Import of canned foods, frozen meats,
frozen fish, dairy products, livestock and animal feeds, all
items relating to hotels, catering and civil airlines, glass, juice
and soft drinks, and agricultural produce
Principal Agencies: NCZ, Amsterdam, Holland; Fromageries Bel,
Paris, France; Scangoods Ltd, Denmark; Ribno Stopanstvo,
Sofia, Bulgaria; Oemolk, Wieun, Austria
Subsidiary/Associated Companies: National Foodstuffs Co, PO
Box 1331, Damascus, Syria
Principal Bankers: British Bank of the Middle East, Amman;
Jordan Gulf Bank SA, Amman; Bank of Jordan, Amman;
Cairo Amman Bank; Petra Bank, Amman

Principal Shareholders: Mohammad Haj Deeb (50%); Ribhi Haj
Deeb (25%); Jawad Sukarieh (25%)

INTERNATIONAL TECHNICAL CONSTRUCTION CO

PO Box 950279, Amman
Tel: 677069
Cable: ITCC Amman
Telex: 24099 Ghadi JO
Telefax: 962 6 677069

Chairman: George Salman
Directors: Saadat Hammoudeh
Senior Executives: George Salman (General Manager), Saadat
Hammoudeh (Projects Manager)

PRINCIPAL ACTIVITIES: Mechanical, tankage, pipelines, water
and sewerage schemes, structural engineers, electrical,
instrumentation, plant maintenance shutdown, industrial
coating, NDT services, associated civil works, suppliers of
specialist materials
Branch Offices: Black Cat Construction, Doha, Qatar
Principal Bankers: Grindlays Bank, Shmeisani, Amman
Financial Information:

	1988/89 JD'000
Profits	20
Authorised capital	400
Paid-up capital	135
Total assets	200

Principal Shareholders: George Salman, Sylvia Salman, Saadat
Hammoudeh, Rasmeyeh Hammoudeh
Date of Establishment: 1985
No of Employees: 50

ISMAIL BILBEISI & CO

See BILBEISI, ISMAIL, & CO

JAMCO GROUP OF COMPANIES

Na'our Roud, PO Box 5003-5186-5063, Amman
Tel: 791191/2/3
Cable: Jamco-Amman
Telex: 21773 JAMCO JO
Telefax: 791194

Directors: H Tarawneh, V Karmandarian, G Haffar

PRINCIPAL ACTIVITIES: Aluminium works, steel furniture,
partitions, kitchen cabinets, PVC products, heavy steel works,
steel structure

Principal Agencies: Signode (Strapping Systems); Adshead Ratcliffe (Arbo Sealants); Sodem (Profiles)
Subsidiary/Associated Companies: Jordan Metal Works Co; Modern Decoration Co; International Plastic Co; Jordan Aluminium Mfg Co
Principal Bankers: Arab Bank; Grindlays Bank; Jordan Bank; Jordan Gulf Bank

Principal Shareholders: G Haffar, V Karmandarian, H Tarawneh
Date of Establishment: 1965
No of Employees: 200

JORDAN AUTO PARTS CO LTD

PO Box 281, Amman
Tel: 630112, 630113/4, 621350
Cable: Zoka
Telex: 21373 Khorma Jo

Chairman: Ahmad E Khorma
Senior Executives: Shahid A Mustafa (Manager)

PRINCIPAL ACTIVITIES: General traders, contractors, manufacturers' representatives, importers and commission agents (motorcycles, electronic audio/video/TV Equipment)
Principal Agencies: Akai Electric Co Ltd, Japan; Pioneer Electronic Co Ltd, Japan; Kawasaki Heavy Industries Ltd, Japan; Shimwa Bussan Kaisha, Japan; Namco Corp, Japan; Roadstar Corp, Japan
Branch Offices: Zerqa City, King Abdulla Street; Kawasaki Showroom -Wadi Saqra St, Amman
Subsidiary Companies: International Services Co, PO Box 281, Amman
Principal Bankers: Petra Bank, Shemaisani Branch

Principal Shareholders: A Khorma & Sons
Date of Establishment: 1964

JORDAN BATA SHOE CO LTD

Marka, PO Box 486, Amman
Tel: 892136, 892203
Telex: 21099

PRINCIPAL ACTIVITIES: Footwear manufacture
Branch Offices: Jordan and throughout the Arab world

JORDAN CARPET MNFG CO

PO Box 7414, Amman
Tel: 731711
Cable: JOCARPET
Telex: 21615 Asfour JO
Telefax: 731078

Chairman: Kamal Asfour
Directors: Hassan Safadi, Siad Malas, Mohamed El Shash, Soliman Hudhud
Senior Executives: Hassan Safadi (Managing Director)

PRINCIPAL ACTIVITIES: Production of Persian design carpets kashan and tabriz, decoration handing wall carpets, praying carpets
Branch Offices: Amman, Tel 640197; Zarka, Tel 996656
Principal Bankers: Arab Bank; Jordan Gulf Bank; Jordan Syrian Bank
Financial Information:

	1989/90 JD'000
Sales turnover	4,000
Paid-up capital	1,400

Date of Establishment: 1973
No of Employees: 53

JORDAN CEMENT FACTORIES CO LTD

PO Box 610, Jabal Amman, 1st Circle, Amman
Tel: 729901
Cable: Cement Factories
Telex: 21239, 23098 Cement Jo
Telefax: 729921

Chairman: Ziad Ennab
Directors: Dr Khaldon Al Dhahir (Managing Director), Eng Hatem Halawani (Deputy Managing Director)
Senior Executives: Wadie Al Sayegh (Asst Managing Director Admin Affairs), Eng Hani Khammash (Asst Managing Director Technical Affairs), Fathi Al Shami (Financial Manager)
PRINCIPAL ACTIVITIES: Cement manufacture; sole suppliers for Jordanian market and export of type I & V cement to other countries
Branch Offices: Amman Office: Abdaly Commercial Centre Bldg, Tel 674186, 665109; Cement Plants at Fuhais and Rashadiya
Principal Bankers: Arab Bank, Jordan Bank, Housing Bank, Cairo Amman Bank, Grindlays Bank, Credit & Commercial Bank, Jordan National Bank
Financial Information:

	JD'000
Authorised capital	50,000
Paid-up capital	50,000

Principal Shareholders: State; Social Security Corp; Pension Fund; Arab Bank; Housing Bank; others
Date of Establishment: 1951
No of Employees: 1,617

JORDAN CERAMIC INDUSTRIES CO LTD

PO Box 910253, Amman
Tel: 621170
Cable: CERAMCO
Telex: 21610 CERAMCO-JO
Telefax: 962-9 996721

Chairman: Mamduh Abu Hassan
Directors: Fathi Mizyed Hiasat (General Director)

PRINCIPAL ACTIVITIES: Production of sanitary ware and wall tiles
Principal Bankers: Grindlays Bank, Shmissani, Amman; Jordan Gulf Bank, Jabal Amman
Financial Information:

	1990 JD'000
Authorised capital	2,000
Paid-up capital	2,000

Date of Establishment: 1974
No of Employees: 380

JORDAN CLOTHING COMPANY

PO Box 457, Amman
Tel: 793151, 793152, 795814
Telefax: 793153

Chairman: Mrs Suhaila K Maqdah
Directors: Samir K Maqdah, Jad K Maqdah
Senior Executives: Samir D Faraj (Finance & Accounting), Samir K Maqdah (Local Sales & Marketing), Jad K Maqdah (General Trading Section)

PRINCIPAL ACTIVITIES: Manufacturers of men's wear light clothings, retailers and wholesalers of all types of garments for men. Distributors of paper and stationery
Principal Agencies: Jockey, USA
Branch Offices: King Hussein Street, Amman, Tel 630931; Jabal Amman, Tower Building, Amman, Tel 645832; Prince Shaker Street, Zarka, Tel 982022; Housing Bank Bldg, Amman, Tel 698728
Subsidiary Companies: Jordan National Trading Co; Jordan National Paper Converting Co; Al Fayrouz Ready Wear Co, Cairo, Egypt
Principal Bankers: The British Bank of the Middle East; Arab Bank Ltd; Jordan National Bank

Financial Information:

	1988/89	1989/90
	JD'000	JD'000
Sales turnover	1,200	1,900
Authorised capital	400	400
Paid-up capital	400	400

Principal Shareholders: Mrs Suhaila K Maqdah and Sons
Date of Establishment: 1949
No of Employees: 145

JORDAN COMPUTER TRADING CO

Prince Mohd Street, Jabal Amman, PO Box 5320, Amman
Tel: 645581, 643896
Telex: 24254 JCTC JO
Telefax: 686790

Chairman: Hani Daniel
Directors: F Darwazeh
Senior Executives: N Nijim (Sales Manager), A Nimer (Technical Supervisor)

PRINCIPAL ACTIVITIES: Sales and after sales service of computers and associated peripheral, cash registers and software services
Principal Agencies: ADDS (Applied Digital Data Systems), USA; Epson, Japan; Casio, Japan; Dysan
Principal Bankers: Arab Bank Ltd; British Bank for the Middle East

Principal Shareholders: H Daniel; F Darwazeh
Date of Establishment: 1977

JORDAN CONSTRUCTION MATERIALS CO LTD

PO Box 6125, Amman
Tel: 779171/4
Cable: Omran
Telex: 23033 Omran Jo
Telefax: 779175

Chairman: Mohammad Ali Bdeir
Directors: Abdulhadi Idelbi (Managing Director), Nadim Hudhud (Sales & Marketing Director)

PRINCIPAL ACTIVITIES: Import of wood and steel for construction
Branch Offices: Dubai; Abu Dhabi; Oman; Kuwait; Qatar; Bahrain
Principal Bankers: Arab Bank Ltd, Bank of Jordan, National Bank of Jordan
Financial Information:

	1990
	US$'000
Sales turnover	17,900
Authorised capital	11,800
Paid-up capital	11,800
Total assets	22,200

Principal Shareholders: Transjordan Building Materials Co; Hamdi & Ibrahim Mango Co; Haj Taher Hudhud Co; Hamzeh Malas & Sons Co; Sabella Co
Date of Establishment: 1967
No of Employees: 125

JORDAN COOPERATIVE ORGANISATION

PO Box 1343, King Hussein Street, Amman
Tel: 65171/6
Telex: 21835 Aloun JO

President: Hassan S Nabulsi (Director General)
Directors: Khaled Al Radhadi, Hassan Al Gharaybeh, Walid Kharallah, Salem Ghazi, Wasef Azar, Abdel Wahhab Tarawneh, Khalaf Abu Nuwayer, Said Al Gharaybeh, Abdel Jawad Al Azeh

PRINCIPAL ACTIVITIES: Specialised credit banking
Branch Offices: Amman, Zerka, Irbid, Ajloun, Kerak, Tafileh, Madaba, Salt, Jerash, Mafreq, Ma'an, Shouna, Jordan Valley
Principal Shareholders: Ministry of Finance of Jordan; Cooperative Societies
Date of Establishment: 1968

JORDAN ELECTRICITY AUTHORITY

PO Box 2310, Amman
Tel: 815615-620, 817615-619
Cable: Saka Amman
Telex: 21259 Jeasak Jo, 23270 Jea Jo
Telefax: 818336

Chairman: T Taher (Minister of Energy & Mineral Resources)
Directors: M S Arafah (Director General)

PRINCIPAL ACTIVITIES: Generation, transmission and distribution of electric power in Jordan
Branch Offices: Zarka, Jordan Valley, Aqaba, Karak, Tafeelah, Ma'an
Subsidiary Companies: Pole Cement Factory
Principal Bankers: Cairo Amman Bank
Financial Information:

	JD'000
Authorised capital	97,761
Paid-up capital	97,761

Principal Shareholders: Governmental Department
Date of Establishment: 22/2/1967
No of Employees: 1,846

JORDAN ENGINEERING DRILLING & CONTRACTING ASSOCIATION (JEDCA)

6 Mohd Shureiqi Street, Jabal Weibdeh, PO Box 1111, Amman
Tel: 636442
Cable: Jedca Amman
Telex: 21793 Jedca Jo
Telefax: 633442

Directors: O A Sabri Abaza (Director General)
Senior Executives: Adham Abaza (Executive Engineer), Majed A Husseini (Finance Director)

PRINCIPAL ACTIVITIES: Contractors in electrical power (generation and distribution) and water works (domestic and irrigation), manufacturers representatives, suppliers of machines and plants and spare parts, electro-mechanical contractors; water treatment
Principal Agencies: Mannesmann-Sumerbank; A Friedr Flender GmbH & Co AG, W Germany; VAG-Armaturen GmbH, W Germany; MABEX, W Germany; Rain Soft Water Conditioning Co, USA; Lakos Separators, USA; Osmonics, USA; Modern Trade Agency, USA
Branch Offices: Amman: Hashimi Branch
Subsidiary Companies: Adamant Metalock Engineering Repairs Ltd (AMER); Eng Osman Abaza & Partners Co
Principal Bankers: Arab Land Bank Ltd, Rafidain Bank
Financial Information:

	1988/89
	JD'000
Sales turnover	400
Profits (loss)	(98)
Authorised capital	50
Paid-up capital	120
Total assets	92

Principal Shareholders: Osman Ahmad Sabri Abaza, Adham Osman Abaza, Janset Osman Abaza
Date of Establishment: 1st February, 1959

JORDAN EXPRESS CO

Police Academy St, PO Box 2143, Amman
Tel: 662722, 662723, 601498, 601489, 601481
Cable: Jordex
Telex: 21635 Jordex Jo

Chairman: Isa J Majaj

JORDAN

Senior Executives: Ahmad Zeidan, V Venkata Rao

PRINCIPAL ACTIVITIES: Export/import agents; transport contractors; packing courier, clearing agents

Principal Agencies: Macmillan Ring-Free Oil Co, Inc, USA; Pennzoil Co, USA

Branch Offices: Aqaba, Ramtha, Queen Alia Intl. Airport

Subsidiary Companies: Reem International, Beirut, Lebanon

Principal Bankers: Grindlays Bank Ltd; Almashrek Bank

Principal Shareholders: Isa J Majaj (95%); Abla Majaj (5%)

Date of Establishment: 15 April, 1962

No of Employees: 41

JORDAN FERTILIZER INDUSTRY CO LTD

PO Box 5142, Amman

Tel: 812281/812282

Cable: JFI-Amman

Telex: 21549 Jfi Jo, 22333 Jfi Jo

Chairman: H E Walid Asfour

Directors: Abdul Raoof Rawabda, Adel Al-Qdah, Dr Hashem Sabag, Thabet El-Taher, Wasef Azar, Dr Mahmud Mardi, Saleh Haddad, Dr Ezzat El-Azizi

Senior Executives: Dr Mahmoud Mardi (General Manager)

PRINCIPAL ACTIVITIES: Production of phosphatic fertilizers and aluminium fluoride

Principal Bankers: Arab Bank Ltd

Principal Shareholders: Government of Jordan; Jordan Phosphate Mines Co; Arab Mining Co; Arab petroleum Investments Corporation; International Finance Corporation; Islamic Development Bank and public

Date of Establishment: 27.3.1975

No of Employees: 848

JORDAN FINANCE HOUSE

PO Box 925993, Amman

Tel: 663141-5, 670022 FX Dealing

Cable: TAMWEEL JO

Telex: 22487 TAMWEL JO

Telefax: 683247

Chairman: Isa M Kazmi

Directors: Ali M Al Qirim (Deputy Chairman), Afif El Hasan (General Manager), Asa'd Ali Asa'd, Abdulrazak Al Nsour, Nizar F Al Alami, Riyad M Atalla, Naser A Al Lawzi

Senior Executives: Abdulrahman Dweik (Manager - Foreign Relations), Ibtesam Baghdadi (Manager -Accounting), Dawood Jaafar (Manager Operations)

PRINCIPAL ACTIVITIES: Saving and time deposits in all currencies, all project finance operations, participating in equities and financial syndicates, investment and portfolio management, foreign exchange, gold and silver trading, brokerage in Amman stock exchange

Branch Offices: Shmeisani Branch - Main; City Branch; Amman Financial Market, PO Box 925993, Amman; City Branch Office

Principal Bankers: Citibank, NY; National Westminster, London; Credit Swiss, Zurich; Central Bank of Jordan

Financial Information:

	JD'000
Authorised capital	6,000
Paid-up capital	6,000

Principal Shareholders: Major pension funds and institutions in Jordan and a number of leading businessmen and investors from Jordan and the Gulf States

Date of Establishment: 1981

No of Employees: 50

JORDAN FRENCH INSURANCE CO LTD
JOFICO

PO Box 3272, Amman

Tel: 642210, 642230, 642418

Cable: JOFICO

Telex: 21656 Jofico JO

Telefax: (9626) 644086

Chairman: HRH Sharif Jamil Bin Nasser

Directors: Wael Ayoub Zurub (Vice Chairman - President)

Senior Executives: Theodore Shomaly (Vice President Production), Amin Momani (Vice President Claims/Recoveries), Jamal Sous (Finance)

PRINCIPAL ACTIVITIES: Insurance of all classes

Principal Agencies: Lloyds Brokers; NY Insurance Syndicates

Branch Offices: Irbed, Jordan; Akaba, Jordan; Zerka, Jordan

Subsidiary Companies: Dubai: PO Box 1846, Deira, Tel 246001, Telex 47378 JOFIC EM; Abu Dhabi: PO Box 6406, Tel 338020, Telex 23491 JOFIC EM; Lebanon: PO Box 11-4861, Beirut, Tel 340910, 345386, Telex 21603, 21077 AFIA LE

Principal Bankers: Jordan Kuwait Bank; Bank of Credit & Commerce Int'l

Financial Information:

	1990 JD'000
Authorised capital	2,200
Paid-up capital	2,200

Principal Shareholders: Compagnie Financiere du Groupe Victoire, Paris, France; HRH Sharif Jamil Bin Nasser; Wael Ayoub Zurub

Date of Establishment: 1st June 1976

No of Employees: 41

JORDAN GLASS INDUSTRIES CO LTD

PO Box 3079, Jabal Al Hussein, Karim Centre, 2nd Floor, Amman

Tel: 641882, 625892

Cable: ZUZACO

Telex: 21412 Zuzaco JO

Chairman: Farhi A Obeid (General Manager)

Directors: Eng M Saudi (Vice Chairman)

Senior Executives: Rida Kharraz (Deputy General Manager)

PRINCIPAL ACTIVITIES: Production of white, clear & coloured bronze sheet glass using Pittsburg process and under technical supervision of Glaverbel SA Belgium

Principal Bankers: Bank of Jordan

Financial Information:

	1989 JD'000
Authorised capital	9,000
Paid-up capital	8,010

Principal Shareholders: Jordan Treasury; Jordan Pension Fund; Jordan Social Security; Arab Investment Co (Riyadh); Housing Bank

Date of Establishment: 23/7/1974

No of Employees: 235

JORDAN GULF BANK SA

Shmeisani, Jordan Gulf Bank Bldg, PO Box 9989, Amman

Tel: 603931

Cable: Arijbk

Telex: 21959 Jgbank Jo

Telefax: 664110

Chairman: HE Walid Asfour

Members: Jawad Al Anani (Deputy Chairman), Walid A Khairallah, Ahmad Abdel Fattah, Hisham Safadi

Senior Executives: Walid A Khairallah (General Manager), Faiz A Wazani (Senior Asst General Manager), Mohammad Ali Maree (Asst General Manager Facilities), Yousef Said (Asst General Manager Administration)

PRINCIPAL ACTIVITIES: Commercial banking
Branch Offices: Main Branch: PO Box 7736, Amman; Jabal
Amman Branch; Al-Wahdat Branch; Zerka Branch; Madaba
Branch; Commercial Area Branch; Jabal Al-Hussein Branch;
Nazzal Branch; Shmeisani Branch; Quweismeh Branch;
Sahab Br; Abu Alanda; Camp Hitteen Br; Traffic Dept Br;
Fheis Br; As-Salt Br; Mu'addi Br; Ramtha Br; Aqaba Branch;
Bayader Wadi Al Seer Br; Mecca St Br; Irbid Br
Principal Bankers: London Correspondents: Midland Bank;
Barclays Bank; New York Correspondents: Manufacturers
Hanover Trust Co
Financial Information:

	1990 JD'000
Deposits	54,951
Paid up capital	6,000
Reserves	4,452
Total assets	119,741
Contra a/c	14,825

Principal Shareholders: Jordanian Interest (73%); Kuwait (25%)
and other Arab Countries (2%)
Date of Establishment: May 3, 1977
No of Employees: 491

JORDAN GULF INSURANCE CO LTD

King Hussein Street, PO Box 1911, Amman
Tel: 636015, 637790
Cable: JOTAMIN
Telex: 22099 Jotam
Telefax: 646810

Chairman: Ibrahim A Al Ayed (Managing Director)
Directors: Rajab Barghouthi (Deputy Chairman)

PRINCIPAL ACTIVITIES: All classes of insurance
Branch Offices: Saudi Arabia: PO Box 5469, Riyadh 11422,
Telex 404388 MAMDOUH SJ
Principal Bankers: National Bank of Jordan, Housing Bank,
Arab Bank, Business Investment Bank
Financial Information:

	1988/89 JD'000	1989/90 JD'000
Total gross premium	3,148	4,283
Profits	464	473
Authorised capital	1,125	1,125
Paid-up capital	1,125	1,125
Total assets	4,148	4,227

Principal Shareholders: Main shareholders are Jordanians (in
Jordan and abroad) and Kuwaiti shareholders
Date of Establishment: June 1981
No of Employees: 46

JORDAN HOLIDAY HOTELS CO

PO Box 6399, Al Hussein Ben Ali, Amman
Tel: 663100
Cable: Phil Ho JO
Telex: 21859 Phil Ho JO
Telefax: 962-6-665160

Chairman: Zuhair Khoury
Directors: T & N Nazzal, Aql Biltaji, Zuhair Khalifeh
Senior Executives: Micheal Nazzal, Tony Nazzal

PRINCIPAL ACTIVITIES: Hotel business
Branch Offices: Aqaba: Kings Blvd, Tel 2426, Telex 263
Principal Bankers: Housing Bank
Financial Information:

	1989 JD'000
Sales turnover	3,500
Profits	1,000
Authorised capital	2,400
Paid-up capital	2,400
Total assets	12,000

Principal Shareholders: T & N Nazzal, Housing Bank,
Government, Royal Jordanian
Date of Establishment: 1972
No of Employees: 350

JORDAN INDUSTRIAL INVESTMENTS CORPORATION

PO Box 927021, Amman
Tel: 625775
Telex: 23228 JMC JO

Chairman: Zeid Shasha
Directors: Said Hammami, Dr Shabib Ammari, Farouk Ghaniem

PRINCIPAL ACTIVITIES: Holding company undertaking
industrial development projects in Jordan (household
appliances, metal furniture, sanitary fittings)
Branch Offices: Jojepco, Djbouti; Al Sharqia Metal Industries
Co, Cairo Eygpt
Subsidiary Companies: National Casting Co; Arab Metal
Industries Co; Jordan Electroplating Co; Jordan Metal
Furniture Manufacturing Co; Jordan Solar Heating Co; Overall
Jordan Co
Principal Bankers: Petra Bank; Amman Cairo Bank; Credit &
Finance Corp
Financial Information:

	JD'000
Authorised capital	11,000
Paid-up capital	2,000

Principal Shareholders: Arab International Investments Co;
Imwas Trading Investments Co; Social Security Corp; Zeid
Sha'sha'a Bros; Zeid Shasha; Munir Sukhtian Co
Date of Establishment: December 1980
No of Employees: 770

JORDAN INSULATIONS MATERIALS CO

PO Box 7518, Amman
Tel: 09-953611
Cable: Kolaghassi
Telex: 41425 Kofam JO
Telefax: 962-9-954382

Chairman: Ali R Kolaghassi
Directors: Walid H Kolaghassi, Rasheed H Kolaghassi, Hussein
Ali R Kolaghassi

PRINCIPAL ACTIVITIES: Manufacture of expandable
polystyrene, insulations boards, boxes, tiles, etc
Branch Offices: Factory in Russaufa
Subsidiary Companies: Kolaghassi Foam & Mattress Co,
Amman
Principal Bankers: Bank of Credit & Commerce International
Financial Information:

	1990 US$'000
Authorised capital	2,000

Principal Shareholders: Kolaghassi family
Date of Establishment: 1975
No of Employees: 60

JORDAN INSURANCE CO LTD

PO Box 279, Amman
Tel: 634161 (5 lines), 649194, 639850, 638446
Cable: Jordico
Telex: 21486 Jic Jo
Telefax: 637905

Chairman: Jawdat ShaSha'a
Directors: Khaldun Abu Hassan, Othman Bdeir, Ahmed Abdul
Khalig, Sabeeh Al Masri, Mohammad Abu Hassan, Tannous
Faghali, Hani Al Fayyad
Senior Executives: Khaldun Abuhassan (Vice Chairman), Ahmed
Abdul Khaliq (General Manager), Mustafa Dahbour (Asst
General Manager Finance), Shukri Costantine (Motor Accident
Manager), Salim Nukho (Life Insurance Manager), Samir

JORDAN

Farah (Asst General Manager Technical), Simon Khamis (Reinsurance Accounts Supervisor), Wajdi Abdelhadi (Marine Production & Claims Supervisor), Ahmed Bitar (Policy Supervisor)

PRINCIPAL ACTIVITIES: All classes of insurance and reinsurance

Branch Offices: Lebanon; Kuwait; United Arab Emirates (Dubai; Abu Dhabi; Al Ain); Saudi Arabia (Riyadh; Jeddah; Al Khobar)

Principal Bankers: British Bank of the Middle East; Grindlays Bank plc, Cairo Amman Bank, Arab Bank Ltd

Financial Information:

	1988/89 JD'000	1989/90 JD'000
Sales turnover	4,958	6,741
Profits	689	697
Authorised capital	5,000	5,000
Paid-up capital	5,000	5,000
Total assets	12,453	13,709

Date of Establishment: 1951
No of Employees: 70 in Jordan only

JORDAN INVESTMENT & FINANCE CORPORATION

Matalka Bldg, 3rd Floor, Bani Hani Street, Shmeisane, Amman
Tel: 665145, 665164
Telex: 23181/2 JFCORP JO

Chairman: Nizar Jardaneh
Directors: Khalid Abu Saud, Jaffar Shami, Khalil Talhouni, Michael Marto, Nabil Kaddoumi, Bassam Attari, Amin Hassan, Raoul Abu Jaber, Issam Salfiti, Basil Jardaneh

PRINCIPAL ACTIVITIES: Investment and merchant banking
Financial Information:

	JD'000
Authorised capital	6,000
Paid-up capital	3,000

Principal Shareholders: Jordanian banks, insurance companies, pension funds, and businessmen
Date of Establishment: 1982

JORDAN IRON & STEEL INDUSTRY CO LTD

PO Box 1972, Jebel Amman, Al-Tamine Bldg, Amman
Tel: 638117, 638118
Cable: Had Eco
Telex: 21279 Amman

Chairman: Riad Al-Mufleh
Directors: Mohamed Y El Taher, Othman Nassief, Farah Tamari, Hassan Haj Hassan

PRINCIPAL ACTIVITIES: Production of concrete reinforcement rods and steel bars
Branch Offices: Jordan (factories in Awajan and Al-Zerka)

Principal Shareholders: State-owned company

JORDAN ISLAMIC BANK FOR FINANCE & INVESTMENT

Head Office, Shmeisani, PO Box 926225, Amman
Tel: 677377
Cable: Islambank
Telex: 21125, 23993 Islami Jo
Telefax: 666326

Chairman: Shaikh Saleh Abdullah Kamel
Directors: Bader M Sa'eed Hirsh (Vice Chairman), Haj Salem Hussein Abu Assaf, Al-Baraka Investment & Development Co, Kamal Sami Asfour, Dallah Group Co, Haj Hamdi Tabbaa
Senior Executives: Musa A Shihadeh (General Manager), Faisal M Rasheed (Deputy General Manager), Saleh El Shanteer (Asst General Manager), Ali Elayan (Banking Relations Manager)

PRINCIPAL ACTIVITIES: All banking and financing operations in accordance with islamic principles

Branch Offices: 16 branches
Financial Information:

	1990 JD'000
Total assets	244,831
Total deposits	190,382
Total finance & investment	148,878
Capital & reserves	11,947
Net income	3,065

Principal Shareholders: Private sector (98%); Government (2%)
Date of Establishment: 1978
No of Employees: 682

JORDAN KUWAIT BANK

PO Box 9776, Amman
Tel: 688814
Cable: Arkubank
Telex: 21994 Arkubk Jo, 22234 Arkubk Jo
Telefax: 687452

Chairman: Sheikh Hamad Sabah Al-Ahmed Al Sabah
Directors: Sufian I Yasin Sartawi (Vice Chairman), Amin M Hassan (Member), Farouq Al-Aref (Member), Abdulaziz Al Jassar (Member), Faisal A Al-Mutawwaa (Member), Dawood Al Kurd (Member)
Senior Executives: Mohammad M Jamjoum (General Manager), Farouq Aref Al Aref (Deputy General Manager), Juma'a Sharif (Asst General Manager), M Yasser Al Asmar (Asst General Manager), Ibrahim Awad (Asst General Manager), Lutfi Zein (Manager, Foreign Relations)

PRINCIPAL ACTIVITIES: Commercial banking activities
Branch Offices: 15 branches in Jordan
Principal Bankers: Manufacturers Hanover, New York; Midland Bank, National Westminster, London; Commerzbank, Deutsche Bank, Frankfurt
Financial Information:

	1989/90 JD'000
Profits	937
Loans & advances	94,782
Deposits	132,478
Authorised capital	5,000
Paid-up capital	5,000
Total assets	156,900

Principal Shareholders: Sheikh Naser S A Al Sabah; Sufian I Y Sartawi; and a large number of shareholders
Date of Establishment: 25 October 1976
No of Employees: 526

JORDAN LIFT & CRANE MNFG CO

PO Box 6367, Amman
Tel: 630671
Cable: Jolift Amman
Telex: 21582

Directors: Moris L Sawalha (Managing Director)

PRINCIPAL ACTIVITIES: Fabrication, installation and servicing of lifts, electric overhead travelling cranes and escalators and pathways
Principal Agencies: Thyssen Aufzuge GmbH, West Germany
Branch Offices: Factory: PO Box 44, Madaba, Jordan, Tel 394/5/6
Subsidiary/Associated Companies: Syria: Eng Zaki Mannaa, PO Box 4170, Damascus; Dubai: Arab Technical Construction Co, PO Box 3399, Dubai; Qatar: Brothers Trading of Qatar, PO Box 2525, Doha; Saudi Arabia: Al Ajou Trading Agencies, PO Box 343, Alkhobar; Abu Dhabi: Saidoun Contracting Co, PO Box 871, Abu Dhabi
Principal Bankers: Citibank, Amman Al Mashrek Bank, Amman; Grindlays Bank

JORDAN MANAGEMENT & CONSULTANCY CORP

PO Box 927021, Amman
Tel: 625775
Telex: 23228 JMC JO

Chairman: Munjid Sukhtian
Directors: Said Hammami, Shabib Ammari
Senior Executives: Dr Shabib Ammari (General Manager), Dr
  Muin Kakish (Research Director), Hani Hunaidi (Administration
  & Finance Manager)

PRINCIPAL ACTIVITIES: Providing management consulting
  services, conducting research and investing on long term
  basis in development projects by private sector
Subsidiary Companies: Jordan Department Stores Co; Mas
  Industries Co; Jordan Spinning & Weaving Co
Principal Bankers: Housing Bank; Jordan Security Corp; Credit
  & Finance Corp; Cairo Amman Bank; Petra Bank
Financial Information:

	JD'000
Authorised capital	4,000
Paid-up capital	2,642

Principal Shareholders: Pension Fund, The Housing Bank, Cairo
  Amman Bank, Petra Bank, Finance & Credit Corp, Jordan
  Securities Corp, National General Investment Co, Jordan
  Industrial Investments Co
Date of Establishment: August 1982

JORDAN MARKETING CORP

PO Box 927234, Amman
Tel: 669291/2
Telex: 21312

Chairman: Jawdat Shashaa
Directors: Musa Shehadeh, Osama Asfour, George Dallal, Zied
  Shashaa, Akel Beltagi, Kamal Qaqish, F A Hijleh, Ezz Al-Deen
  Jwihan, Said Hamami, Dr Ahmed Al Chalabi
Senior Executives: Fouad Abu Hijleh (Managing Director)

PRINCIPAL ACTIVITIES: Export of Jordanian products, import
  and supply of industrial raw materials, trading in and supply
  of commodities and foodstuff, trading in department stores
  and grocery items
Branch Offices: Dijibouti, Cairo, Italy
Principal Bankers: Cairo Amman Bank; Petra Bank; Jordan
  National Bank; National Inv Financial Corp; Credit & Finance
  Corp

Principal Shareholders: Cairo Amman Bank; Petra Bank;
  National Inv Financial Corp; Credit & Finance Corp; Arab
  Multinational Finance Co (Luxembourg); Albaraka Inv &
  Development Corp (Saudi Arabia); Blue Seas Co (Kuwait);
  Housing Bank; Jordan Securities Corp; Jordan National Bank;
  GT Tawel (Kuwait); Jordan Management & Consultancy Corp
Date of Establishment: 1984
No of Employees: 27

JORDAN NATIONAL BANK SA

PO Box 1578, Amman
Tel: 642391/93
Cable: AhliBank
Telex: 21820 Head office Alahli Jo, 21206 Ahlibk Jo Amman
  Main Branch
Telefax: 634126, 628809

Chairman: HE Abdulkader Tash (also General Manager)
Directors: Yousif Mouasher (Deputy Chairman), Dr Abder
  Rahman S Touqan (Deputy General Manager), Arabia
  Insurance Co, Spiro Haddad, Kuwait Investment Co, Rajaee
  Mouasher & Bros Co, Michel Saliba, Abdullah M A Sha'ban,
  Wafa Abou Al Wafa Dajani, Rajaee Sukkar
Senior Executives: Dr Khalid Amin Abdullah (Asst General
  Manager), Samih Shahin (Asst General Manager)

PRINCIPAL ACTIVITIES: Commercial banking
Branch Offices: Jordan; Lebanon; Cyprus
Financial Information:

	1988/89 JD'000
Operating income	14,980
Profits	2,219
Authorised capital	9,127
Paid-up capital	9,127
Total assets	174,797

Date of Establishment: 1956
No of Employees: 830

JORDAN OVERALL COMPANY

PO Box 927021, Amman
Tel: 625775
Telex: 23228

Chairman: Zeid Sha'sha'a
Directors: Dr Shabib Ammari

PRINCIPAL ACTIVITIES: Production of gas stoves, washing
  machines, electrical water heaters, ovens for domestic use
Branch Offices: Plant at Russeifah, Zerqa
Principal Bankers: Cairo Amman Bank, Finance & Credit
  Corporation
Financial Information:

	JD'000
Sales turnover	1,000
Authorised capital	500
Paid-up capital	500

Principal Shareholders: Jordan Industrial Investments
  Corporation
Date of Establishment: 1972
No of Employees: 134

JORDAN PAPER & CARDBOARD FACTORIES CO LTD

PO Box 1051, Zerka, Jordan
Tel: 981411/2 Zerka
Cable: Warak
Telex: 41458 Warak Jo
Telefax: 9-993481

Chairman: Zuhair Asfour
Directors: Dr Abdelnour Habaybeh (Managing Director)
Senior Executives: Mamdouh Al Hassan (Finance Director), Hani
  Sa'adeh (Sales Director), Lutfi Amin (Export Sales Director),
  Fayez Attawneh (Purchasing Director), Eng Khalil Al Far
  (Production Director), Eng Mikhaeil AL Far (Technical
  Director)

PRINCIPAL ACTIVITIES: Manufacture of paper, board and
  corrugated boxes
Branch Offices: Amman: PO Box 1717, Tel 622158/9
Principal Bankers: Cairo Amman Bank, Amman; Arab Bank,
  Zerka
Financial Information:

	1990 JD'000
Sales turnover	8,490
Profits	2,149
Authorised capital	3,000
Paid-up capital	3,000
Total fixed assets	2,815

Principal Shareholders: Jordan Government (7.4%); Industrial
  Development Bank (9.6%); Cairo/Amman Bank (5.3%);
  Retirement Fund (20%); Housing Bank (6.6%); Arab
  Investment Company (26.7%)
Date of Establishment: March 1973
No of Employees: 315

JORDAN

JORDAN PETROLEUM REFINERY CO

PO Box 1079, Amman
Tel: 630151/59, 657811, 657911
Cable: Jopetrol
Telex: 21246, 21688 Petrol Jo
Telefax: 657934

Chairman: Abdul Majeed Shoman

Directors: Farid El Saad, Mohammad Yousef El Taher, Ali
Hendawi, Hassan Sa'udi, Dr Jamal Salah, Sa'ad Tell, Ramez
Malhis, Ibrahim Baker, K Abu Hassan, Jameel Barakat, M
Samour, Ahmad Hamad Nuaimi

Senior Executives: Sa'ad Tell (General Manager), Brhan Abdul
Hadi (Refinery Manager)

PRINCIPAL ACTIVITIES: Petroleum refining; loading, transport
and distribution of refined products; manufacture of drums
and cans for lube oil products; manufacture of LPG cylinders,
and manufacture of asphalt drums, and underground tank,
storage, blending and marketing lubeoil

Branch Offices: Zarka Refinery: PO Box 176, Zarka, Jordan, Tel
911211/15

Principal Bankers: Arab Bank, Amman

Financial Information:

	1988/89	1989/90
	JD'000	JD'000
Sales turnover	245,202	274,461
Profits	5,987	7,264
Authorised capital	32,000	32,000
Paid-up capital	32,000	32,000
Total assets	151,263	145,797

Principal Shareholders: Arab Investment Co; Islamic Bank;
Jordan Government Employees Pension Funds; Arab Bank
Ltd; and approximately 32,798 other shareholders
Date of Establishment: 1956
No of Employees: 3,332

JORDAN PHOSPHATE MINES CO LTD (JPMC)

PO Box 30, Amman
Tel: 660141, 660147
Cable: Phosphate-Amman
Telex: 21223, 22435 Phosphate
Telefax: 926-06-682290

Chairman: Husain Al Kasim

Directors: M Alsaqqaf, M Qatameen, M Horani, K Abu Hassan,
W Azar, W Kurdi, M Al-Farhan, Z Khalifeh, F Assaosi, A Al
Hamad

Senior Executives: Wasef Azar (Managing Director), Dr I Jallad
(Deputy Managing Director for Technical Research &
Projects), Dr A Abu Hassan (Deputy Managing Director for
Production & Handling), M Rishaydat (Financial Manager), S
Oqlah (Supply Manager), K Sunna (Projects Manager), F Khub
(Administrative Manager), M Zoraikat (Marketing & Sales
Manager), J Wraikat (Transport Manager), Anwar Sunna
(Maintenance Manager), Mohamed Bederkhan (Eshidiya
Project Manager), Omar Abu Murry (Exploration Manager), A
Shaare (Aqaba Branch Manager), M Mubaydeen (Alhassa
Mine Manager), M Tanash (Abiad Mine Manager), O Abadi
(Ruseifa Mine Manager)

PRINCIPAL ACTIVITIES: Exploration, production and export of
phosphates; import of mining machinery and trucks
Principal Agencies: E I D Parry; Soconomar; Yugo Ageant;
Mitsubishi Corp Citis; Wang Shou; Jesslo
Branch Offices: Aqaba office
Principal Bankers: Arab Bank; Housing Bank; Jordan National
Bank; Bank of Jordan; Bank of Credit & Commerce

Financial Information:

	1988/89
	JD'000
Sales turnover	140,900
Profits	22,405
Authorised capital	34,200
Paid-up capital	34,200
Total assets	226,378

Principal Shareholders: The government holds a controlling
interest
Date of Establishment: 1953
No of Employees: 4,428

JORDAN PIPES MANUFACTURING CO LTD

PO Box 6899, Amman
Tel: 651468, 651451, 651452
Cable: Anabeeb
Telex: 21517 Anabeb Jo
Telefax: 651451

Chairman: Moh'd Ali Budeir
Directors: Moh'd Ali Budeir, Ali H Mango, Moh'd T Hudhud,
Emile Shaker, Burhan Kamal, Zakariya Stetieh, Mahmoud El-
Khawaja, Khaled Kanaan, Houda Twal, Said Malas, Nasouh
Malas
Senior Executives: Khalid Kanaan (General Manager), Suleiman
Halassa (Administrative Manager), Abu Safieh (Technical
Manager)

PRINCIPAL ACTIVITIES: Manufacturing of steel water and gas
pipes
Principal Bankers: Arab Bank
Financial Information:

	1990
	JD'000
Authorised capital	2,500
Paid-up capital	2,500

Principal Shareholders: Shehadeh S Twal; Housing Bank; Mohd
Ali Bedir; Ali H Mango; Mohd T Hudhud; Yacoub Sabella &
Son Co; Saeb Nahhas
Date of Establishment: 1968 as Private Limited Co then 1974 as
Public Co
No of Employees: 165

JORDAN PLASTICS COMPANY

PO Box 2394, Amman
Tel: 773144
Cable: Abuatah
Telex: 21712 JPC JO

Chairman: Tawfiq G Abueita
Directors: Isam E Abueita

PRINCIPAL ACTIVITIES: Production of plastics, housewares,
film sheets, hoses and other items on order; form mattresses
and sheets; neoprene adhesives; spring mattresses 'Comfort'
Associated Companies: Jordan Plastics Co (Beit Sahur)
Principal Bankers: Jordan National Bank; Bank of Credit and
Commerce International

JORDAN READY-TO-WEAR MANUFACTURING CO LTD

Salt Industrial Area, PO Box 660, Salt
Tel: 655657
Cable: JORAM
Telex: 43404 Joram JO

Chairman: Abdullah Hawamdeh
Senior Executives: Fawwaz H Abboushi (General Manager),
Talal H Khoffash (Finance & Administration Manager)

PRINCIPAL ACTIVITIES: Manufacturing and marketing of Lee
Cooper jeans, ordinary trousers, safari suits, and various
work clothes
Principal Agencies: Licensee of Lee Cooper Group (Jeans), UK

Principal Bankers: Jordan Securities Corporation, PO Box 926691 Amman

Principal Shareholders: Jordanian Pension Fund; Jordanian Postal Saving; Jordan Industrial Development Bank; National Invest Group/Kuwait; Jordan Social Security Est
Date of Establishment: January 1st 1982
No of Employees: 100

JORDAN RESOURCES CO LTD

King Hussein St, PO Box 6401, Amman
Tel: 636772, 623135/6
Cable: Jordan Resource
Telex: 21225 Arabship Jo
Telefax: 638137

Chairman: H El-Farhan
Directors: Eng R El Farhan
Senior Executives: Ali Telfah (Manager)

PRINCIPAL ACTIVITIES: Representation of manufacturers; import and sales of chemicals, building materials, production of industrial projects; tenders; contracting; industrial consultations; travel and tours
Principal Agencies: Associated Octel Co, UK; Cremer & Warner Consulting Engineers, UK; Jacobs Engineering International, Pasadena, USA; Air India and several other transport and manufacturing industrial firms
Subsidiary Companies: Jordan Resources Co, Irbid, North Jordan; Arab Shipping Co Ltd, Amman
Principal Bankers: Bank of Jordan

Principal Shareholders: Hamad El Farhan; Mohammad Toukan; Rifad El Farhan
Date of Establishment: 1957

JORDAN SALES COMPANY

Ras-Elain St, PO Box 23111, Amman
Tel: 773152
Cable: Rimalinco
Telex: 21366 Husari

Directors: Kamel Taleb Amer (Partner), Abdulhadi Jaradeh (Partner)

PRINCIPAL ACTIVITIES: Import and distribution of sanitary-ware, fixtures, pipes, ceramic tiles and central heating equipment
Principal Agencies: Carrara-Matta Plastics, Italy; Eurokalor Radiators, Italy; AKMI Ceramic Tiles, Greece; Kerafina, Greece; Perla, Greece
Subsidiary Companies: The Financial Investment House
Principal Bankers: Chase Manhattan Bank

Principal Shareholders: Partners as described
Date of Establishment: 1.5.1976

JORDAN SPINNING & WEAVING CO LTD

Arab Bank Bldg, Mahatta Road, PO Box 12099, Amman
Tel: 651423
Cable: SAWCO/Amman
Telex: 21562 Spin JO

Chairman: Dr Maher Shukri
Senior Executives: Baha Nabulsi (General Manager)

PRINCIPAL ACTIVITIES: Spinning
Principal Bankers: Arab Bank; Amman/Cairo Bank; Rafidain Bank; Finance & Credit Corp
Financial Information:

	JD'000
Authorised capital	4,000
Paid-up capital	4,000

Principal Shareholders: Government of Jordan; Cairo/Amman Bank; Arab Bank; City Bank; Housing Bank; Pension Fund; Social Security Corp; Industrial Bank; Jordan Management &

Consultancy Corp; Jordan Securities Corp; Al Barka Company
Date of Establishment: 1974
No of Employees: 230

JORDAN STEEL INDUSTRIES CO LTD

PO Box 19190, Amman
Tel: 826795
Cable: JSICO Amman
Telex: 22493

Chairman: Rajai H Aweidah
Directors: Fathi A Barakat (Asst General Manager), Rashed Dajani (Finance Director)
Senior Executives: Mohd Naser Aweidah (Production Manager), Abdul Rahman S Alomari (Administration Manager)

PRINCIPAL ACTIVITIES: Manufacture of steel radiators, boilers, cylinders, basins
Principal Bankers: British Bank of the Middle East, Amman
Financial Information:

	1989/90 JD'000
Authorised capital	1,000
Paid-up capital	500
Total assets	1,250

Principal Shareholders: Rajai Aweidah; Fathi Barakat, Rashad Dajani, Dr R F Nashashibi, Dr Rajai I Sbaih, Dr M Abu Lafi
Date of Establishment: April 1977
No of Employees: 50

JORDAN TANNING CO LTD

PO Box 776, Amman
Tel: 651774, 651337, Zerka 981403
Cable: Jortan Amman
Telex: 41423 Jortan Jo

Chairman: Hassan Khateeb
Directors: Talal Ghezawi (General Manager)
Senior Executives: Rushdi Khateeb (Deputy General Manager)

PRINCIPAL ACTIVITIES: Manufacture of shoe uppers, sole leather, and other products, tannery
Subsidiary Companies: International Leather Products Ltd, Amman
Principal Bankers: Arab Bank, Amman
Financial Information:

	JD'000
Authorised capital	1,000
Paid-up capital	1,000

Date of Establishment: 1957
No of Employees: 85

JORDAN TOBACCO & CIGARETTE CO LTD

Ras El Ain St, PO Box 59, Amman
Tel: 777112 (4 lines)
Cable: Radar
Telex: 21204 Radar, 22427 Expo
Telefax: 743308

Chairman: HE Farid Sa'd
Directors: Bandar Tabba, Mohamad Ali Farid Sa'd, Antoine Soussa, Sami Habibi, Joseph Ghanem, HE Burhan Kamal, Nabil Ghanem

PRINCIPAL ACTIVITIES: Manufacture and trade in cigarettes; tobacco
Principal Bankers: Arab Bank Ltd; Grindlays Bank

Date of Establishment: 1931
No of Employees: 700

JORDAN TRACTOR & EQUIPMENT CO LTD

PO Box 313, Amman
Tel: 661141/3, 638363
Telex: 21226

Chairman: Jafa'r Shami (also General Manager)

PRINCIPAL ACTIVITIES: Distribution of earth-moving machines, agricultural machines, industrial machines, diesel engines
Principal Agencies: Caterpillar; John Deere; FMC (Peerless Pumps); Kohring; Coles Cranes; Hawker Siddeley; Hyster; CPT; Marion; British Leyland Richier; Marini; Berliet; Marshall; Eversman & Sheepbridge
Branch Offices: Jordan; Syria; Lebanon
Parent Company: M Ezzat Jallad et Fils, Beirut, Lebanon

JORDAN WOOD INDUSTRIES CO LTD

PO Box 5272, Amman
Tel: 798171, 798172
Cable: Jorwood
Telex: 21404 Wood Jo
Telefax: 794672

Chairman: Najib A Qubain (also General Manager)
Directors: Makram A Qubain, Tawfiq Kawar, Hani Anani, Anis Mouasher, Fouad Farraj, Ziad Innab
Senior Executives: Makram Qubain (Asst General Manager), Akef Najjar (Technical Manager), Munther Hadidi (Production Manager), Jawdat Thalji (Personnel & Admin Manager), Munir Rihani (Finance Manager)

PRINCIPAL ACTIVITIES: Production of interior and exterior wooden doors, kitchen cabinets, bedroom furniture and office furniture
Principal Agencies: Aqaba, Irbid, Zerka, Amman
Branch Offices: Iraq, Baghdad
Principal Bankers: Arab Bank; Jordan National Bank Bank; British Bank of the Middle East; Arab Finance Corp; Industrial Development Bank
Financial Information:

	1989/90 US$'000
Sales turnover	7,400
Profits	700
Authorised capital	4,286
Paid-up capital	4,286
Total assets	9,530

Principal Shareholders: Publicly-owned
Date of Establishment: November 1975
No of Employees: 175

JORDAN WORSTED MILLS CO LTD

PO Box 6060, Amman
Tel: 981428 Zerka
Cable: Worsted Amman
Telex: 21313 Jo

Directors: Yousef Mouasher

PRINCIPAL ACTIVITIES: Woollen, terylene and worsted piece goods
Principal Bankers: Arab Bank; Grindlays Bank

JORDANIAN PHARMACEUTICAL & MEDICAL EQUIPMENT CO LTD

PO Box 94, Naor
Tel: 661911, 727207, 727641
Telex: 21290 JPM JO

Chairman: Z Abbas
Directors: R Sh Ali, Musa Dajani, Adel Al Kenah, H Khatib
Senior Executives: Dr A A Badwan (General Manager), A Abumalooh (Research and Development Manager), Mrs L Oais (Quality Control Manager), Dr M Takeiddin (Production Manager)

PRINCIPAL ACTIVITIES: Manufacturing of pharmaceuticals and parapharmaceuticals
Principal Agencies: Al Karmel Drugstore
Principal Bankers: Jordan Islamic Bank; Cairo Amman Bank; Jordan Kuwait Bank, Petra Bank

Financial Information:

	1990 JD'000
Authorised capital	1,000
Paid-up capital	760

Date of Establishment: 1978
No of Employees: 70

JORDANIAN SYRIAN LAND TRANSPORT CO

Jebbel El Hussein, PO Box 20686, Amman
Tel: 661134, 661820, 661135
Cable: Josyco
Telex: 21384 Josyco Jo
Telefax: 669645

Chairman: Hisham Asfour (Director General)
Directors: Fares Saraireh, Rajeh Ramadan, Esa Abdullah, Ahmad Bashir Shahin, Gassan Qaddur
Senior Executives: Adnan E Abedalla (Deputy Director General), Hasan Quteish (Commercial Manager), Walid H Samman (Financial Manager), Hisham Moussalli (Fleet Manager), Mamdouh El Tall (Stores Manager), Abdul Rahman Abu Meizer (Workshop Manager)

PRINCIPAL ACTIVITIES: Land transportation
Branch Offices: Branches in Aqaba, Jordan; Lattakia, Syria; Tartus, Syria
Subsidiary Companies: The United Co for Land Transport Organisation
Principal Bankers: Syrian Jordanian Bank, Amman; Commercial Bank of Syria, Lattakia, Tartus
Financial Information:

	1989 JD'000
Authorised capital	8,000
Paid-up capital	5,000
Total assets	15,000

Principal Shareholders: Government of Jordan (50%); Government of Syria (50%)
Date of Establishment: 1975
No of Employees: 708

KAKISH, MUNTHER, & CO

PO Box 6200, Amman
Tel: 642624
Cable: Petcol Amman
Telex: 21676 Kakish Jo

Chairman: Munther Kakish
Directors: Eng Munther Kakish (Managing Director)
Senior Executives: Costa Khalil (Trading Dept), Nabil Aghabi (Tender & Commission Dept), Yacub Azam (Chief Accountant), Fares Kakish (Export Manager)

PRINCIPAL ACTIVITIES: General contracting and tenders' participation, manufacturers' representation, import of safety equipment, building materials, and consumer goods
Principal Agencies: Werner and Pfleiderer, W Germany; Cavanna Wrapping Machine, Italy; Zeelandia, Holland; Macron Fire, UK; Tekfire, UK; Remploy Textile, UK; Friedrich Pink, W Germany; manfred Vetter, W Germany; Sports Comp, USA
Subsidiary Companies: Ghantous & Bandack Trading Co, PO Box 476, Amman; Eastraco, PO Box 5142, Damascus, Syria; Arcon, PO Box 6675, Jeddah, Saudi Arabia; Shaker Hamoud Est, PO Box 6108, Sharjah; PO Box 1063, Dubai; PO Box 2870, Abu Dhabi, UAE; Turkish-Jordanian Trade Centre, PO Box 6200, Amman, Jordan
Principal Bankers: Housing Bank, Amman; Arab Land Bank, Amman

Principal Shareholders: Munther Kakish, Humam Kakish, Fares Kakish
Date of Establishment: 1985

KAWAR, AMIN, & SONS CO WLL

24 Sharif Abdulhamid Sharaf St, Shemisani, PO Box 222,
Amman
Tel: 603703 (13 lines)
Cable: Kawarship
Telex: 21212 Kawar, 23111 Kawar
Telefax: (962-6) 672170

Chairman: Tawfiq Amin Kawar (also Managing Director)
Directors: Kamel Amin Kawar (Vice Chairman)
Senior Executives: Ghassoub F Kawar (General Manager),
Walid Kawar (General Manager Aqaba Branch), Abdul Aziz
Kasaji (Shipping Manager), Jamil Said (Liner Manager),
Yousef Abdulla (Manager Aqaba Branch), Isam F Kawar (Asst
Manager Aqaba Branch)

PRINCIPAL ACTIVITIES: Chartering & liner agents, P & I Club
correspondents, clearing and forwarding, travel and tourist
agents, airfreight, industry, import-export commission
Principal Agencies: DSR, Rostock; Germanscher Llyods,
Hamburg; Mitsubishi, Tokyo; NKK, Tokyo; Hinode Line,
Tokyo; Showa Line, Tokyo; Hual, Oslo; PIL, Singapore; China
Ocean Shipping, Bejing; Kawar Egypt, Port Said; Navrom,
Constanza; POL, Gdansk; Thennamaris, Athens;
Transammonia, Zurich; Great Eastern, Bombay; Chowgule
Steamship, Bombay; Atlanska Plovidba, Dubrovnik;
Judoinspekt, Belgrade; Lloyd Register, London, etc
Branch Offices: Aqaba: PO Box 22, Tel 314217, Telex 62220
Kawar, Fax 313618
Associated Companies: Amin Kawar & Sons (Lebanon); Aqaba
Shipping Co Ltd, Amman; Red Sea Shipping Agency, Amman
Principal Bankers: Arab Bank Ltd, Jordan; Petra Bank, Amman;
Grindlays Bank, Amman

Principal Shareholders: Tawfiq Amin Kawar; Kamel Amin Kawar;
Mrs Mary (Widow Amin Kawar); Nadim R Kawar; Mrs Ghadah
Hourani Kawar
Date of Establishment: 1946 (Trading), 1955 (Shipping & other
activities)
No of Employees: 215

KAWAR INSURANCE AGENCY

PO Box 222, Amman
Tel: 672122, 672201, 603703
Cable: Kawarship
Telex: 21212 Kawar JO
Telefax: (962-6) 672170

Chairman: Samir E Kawar
Directors: R T Kawar, K T Kawar
Senior Executives: Samir E Kawar (General Manager)

PRINCIPAL ACTIVITIES: Insurance brokers (marine, fire,
accident)
Parent Company: United Insurance Co Ltd, Amman Jordan
Principal Bankers: Arab Bank Ltd

Date of Establishment: 1988

KETTANEH, F A, & CO LTD

PO Box 485, Amman
Tel: 636144, 636145, 636 246
Cable: Tanis Amman
Telex: 21234, 21173 Tanis JO

Chairman: Desire Kettaneh
Directors: Charles Kettaneh Jr (Managing Director)

PRINCIPAL ACTIVITIES: General trading and contracting,
appliances department, electrical electronics equipment and
telecommunication department, mechanical department,
medical, pharmaceuticals and cosmetics department,
chemical department, industrial and packaging department,
maintenance and general stores department
Principal Agencies: General Electric, USA; Siemens, West
Germany; Atlas Copco, Sweden; Lepetit, Italy; Minnesota 3M
laboratories, UK; Ransomes & Rapier, UK; Fuchs, West

Germany; Dynapac, Sweden; Dow Chemicals, USA; American
Steriliser Co; Rapid Metal Development Co; Kohler Co, USA
Branch Offices: Zerqa, Aqaba
Parent Company: ETS F A Kettaneh, Beirut, Lebanon
Principal Bankers: British Bank of the Middle East, Jordan
National Bank, Almashrek Bank, Grindlays Bank

Date of Establishment: 1948
No of Employees: 95

KHALAF STORES

PO Box 586, Amman
Tel: 636720, 625149, 627397
Cable: Fareedka
Telex: 21231 Khalaf Jo
Telefax: (962-6)634349

Directors: Maurice F Khalaf

PRINCIPAL ACTIVITIES: General trading and distribution of
foodstuffs, general groceries, alcoholic drinks, confectionery,
frozen foods, detergents and toiletries
Principal Agencies: General Foods International; General Mills
Inc; Khorr; CPC International; Nabisco Inc
Principal Bankers: Cairo Amman Bank; Bank Al Mashrek

Principal Shareholders: Private Proprietorship
Date of Establishment: 1950
No of Employees: 48

KHALIFEH INDUSTRIAL CO

PO Box 340920, Amman
Tel: 891890
Telex: 21030 IC JO
Telefax: 884212

Chairman: Eng Abdalla Farid Khalifeh (Owner and Managing
Director)
Senior Executives: Rami A Khalifeh (Deputy Managing Director)

PRINCIPAL ACTIVITIES: Manufacturers and distributors of
brass gate, valves, ball valves, brass bibcock
Branch Offices: Riyadh, Saudi Arabia; Alexandria, Egypt
Subsidiary Companies: Industrial Co for Casting; Middle East
Co for Industry
Principal Bankers: Arab Bank, Cairo Amman Bank

Principal Shareholders: A F Khalifeh, F A Khalifeh, R A Khalifeh
Date of Establishment: 1983
No of Employees: 50

KHOURY, G M,

PO Box 306, Amman
Tel: 827920 (4 lines)
Cable: Pharma
Telex: 21603 Jo
Telefax: 962 6 827923

Chairman: George M Khoury (also Managing Director)
Directors: Ramzi G Khoury (Director Hotel & Hospital
Supplies/Food & Beverage), Rajai G Khoury (Director
Pharmaceuticals & Dental Supplies), Rafiq G Khoury (Director
Medical Supplies)

PRINCIPAL ACTIVITIES: Import and distribution of
pharmaceutical, surgical and medical supplies, dental
equipment, hotel and hospital supplies and services,
cosmetics, wines and spirits, general foods
Principal Agencies: Bayer; Upjohn; Astra; May & Baker; Marcel
Rochas; Faberge; Nina Ricci; Maurer & Wirtz; Camus; Booth;
William Whitely; Philip Morris; CO-RO Foods; Merieux;
Stafford-Miller; Kabivitrum; Nybgaard; Torres; Olympus;
Terumo; Portex
Subsidiary Companies: Orion Trading Co
Principal Bankers: Grindlays Bank plc; British Bank of the
Middle East

JORDAN

Financial Information:

	1989
	US$'000
Sales turnover	4,000
Authorised capital	625
Paid-up capital	625

Date of Establishment: 1952
No of Employees: 45

KHOURY INTERNATIONAL TRADING CO

PO Box 459, Amman
Tel: 623458
Cable: Fatkhoury

PRINCIPAL ACTIVITIES: Import and distribution of training aids, electrical equipment, recording and telecommunications equipment, defence electronic equipment

KIMA CO

PO Box 2225, Amman
Tel: 642919, 725096
Cable: Amman Kima
Telex: 21966 Serin JO
Telefax: 644590

Chairman: Saleh Azzouni
Directors: Sabri Azzouni
Senior Executives: Khaldoun Azzouni (Commercial Manager)

PRINCIPAL ACTIVITIES: Production of powder detergents, toiletries and medicated soaps, scouring and bleaching powders, skin care products, desinfectants, etc
Principal Bankers: Arab Bank
Financial Information:

	1988/89
	US$'000
Sales turnover	9,120
Profits	487
Authorised capital	5,100
Paid-up capital	3,500
Total assets	4,400

Principal Shareholders: Azzouni family
Date of Establishment: 1977
No of Employees: 108

LUSWI CENTRE

PO Box 7117, Amman
Tel: 624986, 657192
Cable: LUSWI AMMAN

Chairman: Yousef A Luswi
Senior Executives: Sleiman A Luswi (A/Manager), Moussa A Luswi (Finance Officer)

PRINCIPAL ACTIVITIES: Supermarket, import of household appliances, cutlery, carpets, shoes, silverware, crafts and gifts, stainless steel appliances, cosmetics, etc
Branch Offices: Yousef Luswi Stores (wholesale), PO Box 7117, Amman, Tel 624986; Yousef Luswi (Retail), PO Box 266, Amman, Tel 637192
Principal Bankers: Finance and Credit Corporation; Petra Bank

Date of Establishment: 1959
No of Employees: 30

M Z SHADID ENGINEERING BUREAU

See SHADID, M Z, ENGINEERING BUREAU

MAHMOUD EL SHAMMAA & SONS CO LTD

See EL SHAMMAA, MAHMOUD, & SONS CO LTD

MANGO, HAMDI & IBRAHIM, LTD

PO Box 14, Faisal St, Amman
Tel: 636164/5
Cable: Mango
Telex: 23428 Himcon Jo

Chairman: Ali Mango
Directors: Dr Ahmed Mango, Adnan Mango, Omar Mango

PRINCIPAL ACTIVITIES: General contracting and supply of of motor cars, auto accessories and spare parts, tyres, generating parts, earthmoving equipment, telecommunication products, agricultural machinery and equipment, diesel engines, foodstuffs (rice and frozen meat)
Principal Agencies: J I Case; Chrysler; Fiat; Scania-Vabis; W H Dorman & Co; Westinghouse; English Electric; Royal Rubber International
Principal Bankers: Arab Bank
Financial Information:

	US$'000
Authorised capital	3,000
Paid-up capital	3,000

Date of Establishment: 1931
No of Employees: 150

MANUFACTURERS HANOVER TRUST CO

PO Box 5196, Amman
Tel: 36151, 44424
Telex: 22343

PRINCIPAL ACTIVITIES: Representative office
Parent Company: Head office in New York, USA

Date of Establishment: 1981

MARAR, TOUFIC, ETS

PO Box 1569, Amman
Tel: 625461
Cable: Mararco
Telex: 21808 Mebcom
Telefax: 962 6 827113

Chairman: Tawfiq Marar
Directors: Suheil Marar (Managing Director)
Senior Executives: Jyriess Sawalha (Sales & Purchasing Manager), Amjad Marar (Marketing & Technical Manager)

PRINCIPAL ACTIVITIES: Import and distribution of building materials, sanitary ware, nuts and bolts, pipe fittings, surveying instruments, storage systems, hardware and hand tools
Principal Agencies: Link 51 Ltd, Rawlplug, Kern
Subsidiary Companies: Middle East Building Materials Co; Olympia Hotel
Principal Bankers: Arab Bank, Cairo Amman Bank, Jordan National Bank
Financial Information:

	1989/90
	US$'000
Sales turnover	1,500
Authorised capital	500
Paid-up capital	500
Total assets	1,250

Principal Shareholders: Private Ownership
Date of Establishment: 1958

MARRIOTT AMMAN HOTEL

Queen Alia Street, Shmeisani, PO Box 926333, Amman
Tel: 660100
Telex: 21145 Marriott Jo
Telefax: 670100

Chairman: Francis Keenan (General Manager)
Senior Executives: Ghassan Ismail, Milos Cveticanin (Food & Beverage Director), Khalil Zaboura (Controller), Asma Ma'ani (Personnel Manager), Yousef Batshon (Chief Engineer), Jan Heesbeen (Director of Sales & Marketing)

PRINCIPAL ACTIVITIES: Hotel business
Parent Company: Marriott Corporation
Principal Bankers: Cairo Amman Bank

Financial Information:

	1989/90 JD'000
Sales turnover	5,600
Profits	1,500
Authorised capital1	1,500
Paid-up capital	7,100
Total assets	16,000

Principal Shareholders: Jordan Investment Company
Date of Establishment: 1974
No of Employees: 300

MATALKA & MUSA INTERNATIONAL FREIGHT FORWARDERS

PO Box 538, Al Sayegh Commercial Center, 6th Floor Al Abdali, Amman
Tel: 649052, 649053
Telex: 24241 Musa JO
Telefax: 633052

Chairman: Michael Matalka
Directors: Awad Musa (President), Issa Matalka (Joint Managing Director), Mohammad Musa (Joint Managing Director)
Senior Executives: Ahmad Musa (Marketing Manager), Ahmad Tawalbeh (Amman Manager), Ahmad Abu Rabeh (Aqaba Manager), Badri Shawagfeh (Zarka Free Zone Manager)

PRINCIPAL ACTIVITIES: International freight forwarding, clearing agents, national & international road transport, containers, storage, chartering
Branch Offices: Aqaba: PO Box 240, Tel 312381, 314512, Telex 62268 Musa; Ramtha: PO Box 64, Tel 283063, 283078, Telex 55505 Mtalka; Zarka Free Zone: PO Box 14, Tel 916126/8
Principal Bankers: Arab Bank, Alahli Bank

Principal Shareholders: Michael Matalka, Awad Musa
Date of Establishment: 1942
No of Employees: 60

MAZZAWI TRADING COMPANY

PO Box 9151, Amman
Tel: 667731, 621910
Cable: Mazzawi Amman
Telex: 21067 Mazawi Jo

Directors: Eng Adel Mazzawi (Partner)

PRINCIPAL ACTIVITIES: Heating, ventilation, air-conditioning, trading and import and stockist
Principal Agencies: Sealed Motor Construction Co Ltd, UK; F.lli Perani, Italy; Allen Ygnis Boilers Ltd, UK; Trox Bros, UK; Vema SpA, Italy; Nu-way Ltd, UK; Myson Int Ltd, UK; Armaflex, UK
Principal Bankers: British Bank of the Middle East; Jordan Kuwaiti Bank

Date of Establishment: 1973

MECHANICAL ENGINEERING CO LTD

PO Box 1, Amman
Tel: 624198, 624199, 623354
Cable: Tec Amman
Telex: 21300

PRINCIPAL ACTIVITIES: Import and distribution of heavy machinery and earth-moving equipment, mechanical engineering and contracting
Principal Agencies: JCB Sales Ltd

MEDICO TRADING & GENERAL CONTRACTING CO

Jabal Amman, First Circle, PO Box 3096, Amman
Tel: 623314, 639222
Cable: Medico
Telex: 21177 Medico Jo

President: Tawfik Abu Khajil

PRINCIPAL ACTIVITIES: Importers; contractors; agents, chemicals, fertilisers, animal feeds, cosmetics, computer hardware
Associated Companies: Nears East Contracting Co, Amman, Jordan
Principal Bankers: Petra Bank; Jordan & Kuwait Bank

MEDITERRANEAN ENGINEERING CO

PO Box 5110 (Zahran), Amman
Tel: 642787
Cable: Wasat
Telex: 21461 Wasat Jo

Directors: Bader Hirsh, M S Barakat

PRINCIPAL ACTIVITIES: Mechanical erection, electrical installations, heavy civil works
Principal Agencies: MWM, DEMAG (Baumaschinen)
Subsidiary Companies: Barakat Trading & Electrical Contracting, Kuwait; Al Fao Trading & Contracting Co, Kuwait; Jofi Plastic, Jordan
Principal Bankers: Bank of Credit and Commerce International, Amman and Frankfurt; National Bank of Kuwait, Kuwait; Jordan Kuwait Bank, Arab Bank

Principal Shareholders: Bader Hirsh, M S Barakat

METAL INDUSTRIES CO LTD

PO Box 4051, Amman
Tel: 894586, 894686
Telex: 21437 Handsa Jo
Telefax: 962 6 888049

Chairman: M Jardaneh
Directors: M Y Gharaibeh (Managing Director), N Omran, L Jardaneh, S Omran
Senior Executives: N Jarrar (Financial Manager)

PRINCIPAL ACTIVITIES: Manufacture of steel panel radiators, boilers, props, telescopic beams and scaffolding, hot water cylinders and heat exchangers, steam boilers
Principal Agencies: Runtalrad, Ireland; Pilosio SPA, Italy; Kunzel, West Germany
Principal Bankers: Arab Bank; Industrial Development Bank; Jordan Investment Bank
Financial Information:

	1990 US$'000
Sales turnover	1,600
Profits	225
Authorised capital	448
Paid-up capital	448
Total assets	2,000

Principal Shareholders: E Susa, M Gharaibeh, M Jardaneh, N Omran
Date of Establishment: 1976
No of Employees: 90

MIDDLE EAST AGRICULTURAL & TRADING CO LTD

PO Box 470, King Hussein Street, Amman
Tel: 624290, 637763, 627309
Cable: Parole
Telex: 21238 Parole Jo
Telefax: 625701

Chairman: Jack G Khayyat
Directors: George Khayyat
Senior Executives: Muna Khayyat (Sales Director), Tony Faran (Finance Director), Boulos Khoury (Administration Director)

PRINCIPAL ACTIVITIES: Sales of agricultural equipment, feed, day-old chicks, hatching eggs, veterinary products, and general trade activities
Principal Bankers: Grindlays Bank, Jordan Bank

JORDAN

Financial Information:

	1990
	JD'000
Sales turnover	3,000
Authorised capital	400
Paid-up capital	400
Total assets	2,000

Principal Shareholders: Jack Khayyat, George Khayyat, Josephine Khayyat
Date of Establishment: 1966
No of Employees: 125

MIDDLE EAST DEVELOPMENT CO

PO Box 781, Amman
Tel: 641323
Cable: Philtay
Telex: 21297 Medco

Chairman: Samir F Kawar
Directors: Fakhry F Kawar, Ibrahim Nursi (Director, Middle East Refrigeration Co), George Kawar (Director, Insustrong, Insulation Material Manufacturing Co)

PRINCIPAL ACTIVITIES: General agents, industries, telecommunication and electronics, refrigeration and food processing, earth-moving and construction equipment
Principal Agencies: Gram; Lindholst; Ranie; Pash & Silkaborg, Denmark; Italtel (Seimens) Breda, Italy; Rohde & Schwartz; Bomag; Gardner Denver
Associated Companies: Middle East Refrigeration Co
Principal Bankers: Cairo Amman Bank; Grindlays Bank; IBCC, Amman

MIDDLE EAST INSURANCE CO PLC

PO Box 1802, Amman
Tel: 605144
Cable: Insurance
Telex: 21420 Insure Jo
Telefax: 605950

Chairman: Samir F Kawar
Directors: Sami I Gammoh (Vice-Chairman), Abdel Hadi Hammoudeh, Dr Osama Al Talhouni, Wasef Azar, Mikdad Innab, Suleiman Al Hafez, Antoine Cazard, Roland Baldensperger
Senior Executives: Riyad Batchon (Deputy General Manager/Life Manager), Adel Shatara (Finance Manager), Jamal Madbak (Fire & General Accident/Reinsurance Manager), Issa Haddad (Motor Claims Manager), Awni Jawdat (Motor Dept Manager)

PRINCIPAL ACTIVITIES: Insurance and reinsurance
Branch Offices: Jordan: Jabal Hussein, City, Irbid, Zerka, Wihdat, and Saudi Arabia (Jeddah)
Principal Bankers: ANZ Grindlays Bank, Amman; Ahli Bank, Amman; Arab Bank, Amman; British Bank of the Middle East, Amman
Financial Information:

	1990
	JD'000
Sales turnover	3,483
Profits	594
Authorised capital	2,200
Paid-up capital	2,200
Total assets	5,888

Principal Shareholders: Samir Kawar; Union des Assurances de Paris (UAP); Astra Investment Co
Date of Establishment: 1962
No of Employees: 65

MIDDLE EAST TELECOM & ELECTRONICS CO LTD

PO Box 3089, Amman
Tel: 828424, 828425
Telex: 21867 Mete Jo
Telefax: 828426

Chairman: Hesham Khalaf (Managing Director)
Senior Executives: A Laham (Technical Dept), Miss Maha Hanayneh (Administration Dept)

PRINCIPAL ACTIVITIES: Telecommunications, electrical, electronic and power equipment, general engineering contractors
Principal Agencies: Fuji Electric, Japan; WUI, USA; Harmer & Simmons, UK; Magnus, USA; Tungstone, UK; C Itoh, Japan; ADB, Belgium; Comele, France; Wartburg Cars, East Germany; Allen Bradley, USA; Toshiba CB, Japan
Branch Offices: Intaf Services SA, 5 route de Chene, CH-1207 Geneva, Switzerland
Subsidiary Companies: METE Car Division, INTAF, Geneva
Principal Bankers: Cairo Amman Bank, Mahatta; Arab Bank, Shmeisani
Financial Information:

	1989/90
	US$'000
Sales turnover	1,000
Authorised capital	300
Paid-up capital	300

Principal Shareholders: Hesham Khalaf (90%), Liala Khalaf (10%)
Date of Establishment: 1975

MOUASHER BROTHERS CO LTD

PO Box 168, Amman
Tel: 622349
Cable: Mouasher

Chairman: Faris Elias Mouadher
Directors: Faris Elias Mouasher, Said I Mouasher

PRINCIPAL ACTIVITIES: Civil engineering contractors, manufacturers' representatives, import and distribution of tractors, motor cars, diesel engines, tyres and tubes, electrical household appliances; agricultural machinery and equipment, concrete mixers
Principal Agencies: Winget Concrete Mixers, Kelvinator; Kelly Italiana SpA, NKF Kabel BV
Subsidiary Companies: United Engineering & Mechanical Co, PO Box 1400, Amman, Jordan
Principal Bankers: British Bank of the Middle East; Arab Bank

MUNIR SUKHTIAN GROUP
See SUKHTIAN, MUNIR, GROUP

MUNTHER KAKISH & CO
See KAKISH, MUNTHER, & CO

NABER & CO INTERNATIONAL FORWARDERS

Queen Alia Intl Airport Rd, Madaba Exit, PO Box 6233, Amman
Tel: 784097, 778537, 07-51102, 07-51109
Cable: Nabco
Telex: 21606 Jo, 21157 Naber Co Jo
Telefax: 736426

Chairman: Salim Odeh Naber
Directors: Hilmi Armoush
Senior Executives: George Y Najjar (General Manager), Samir O Naber (Technical Manager)

PRINCIPAL ACTIVITIES: Transport, shipping, packing, air freight, transit, forwarding, warehousing, insurance and customs clearance

Branch Offices: Aqaba, PO Box 122, Tel 312367, Telex 62265;
Ramtha, Tel 283942, PO Box 374, Telex 55506; H4, Tel 89,
Amman Customs, Queen Alia International Airport
Associated Companies: Odeh Naber & Sons Transport
Principal Bankers: Arab Bank, Jordan National Bank, Amman

Principal Shareholders: Salim Odeh Naber, Hilmi Armoush,
Samir Odeh Naber, George Y Najjar
Date of Establishment: 1937
No of Employees: 85

NAJEEB BAKI & SONS (JORDAN) LTD

See BAKI, NAJEEB, & SONS (JORDAN) LTD

NASSAR, YOUSEF, & CO

Prince Mohammed St, PO Box 1019, Amman
Tel: 624219
Cable: Charlie
Telex: 24188 Cynas
Telefax: 625072

Chairman: Y M Nassar
Senior Executives: C Y Nassar (General Manager), W G
Jawharieh (Asst General Manager)

PRINCIPAL ACTIVITIES: Import and distribution of insecticides
and equipment for their application, veterinary preparations
and materials, canned and frozen foods, biscuits,
confectionery, disinfectants, detergents, air-fresheners,
polishes and cleaning material
Principal Agencies: Vestindisk Handelskompagni A/S, Wellcome
Foundation Ltd (except medical products), Motan GmbH,
Racasan Ltd, B V Chem Parm Ind, Luxan, H Walli GmbH;
Coopers Animal Health; Vettex AB; Raak
Principal Bankers: Bank of Jordan, Al-Mashrek Bank

Date of Establishment: 1960

NASSAR, ZAKI M, & BROTHER

PO Box 808, Amman
Tel: 624513, 627032
Cable: Nassar Amman
Telex: 21731 Nassar JO
Telefax: 962-6-624513

President: Nicola M Nassar
Directors: Zaki M Nassar (President of Subsidiary Arab Plast
Co)
Senior Executives: Miss Muna Nassar (Electrical Engineer)

PRINCIPAL ACTIVITIES: Wholesalers and retailers of electrical
and electronic apparatus and equipment, refrigeration
compressors and parts, airconditioning and
telecommunication equipment; manufacture of plastic pipes
and accessories
Principal Agencies: Danfoss, Denmark; AKG, Austria; Skywood,
Canada; Jetty Ent, Taiwan; Oertli, Switzerland; Lawson Fuses,
UK
Branch Offices: Salt Road, Tel 627032; Mekka Road, Tel
821687
Parent Company: Zaki M Nassar & Brother
Subsidiary Companies: Arab Plast Co Ltd, PO Box 340481,
Amman, Tel 894689
Principal Bankers: Jordan Kuwait Bank; Bank of Credit and
Commerce
Financial Information:

	1989	1990
	US$'000	US$'000
Sales turnover	1,000	600
Profits	25%	25%
Authorised capital	750	450
Paid-up capital	750	450
Total assets	750	450

Principal Shareholders: Nicola M Nasser & Sons
Date of Establishment: 1952
No of Employees: 30

NATIONAL AHLIA INSURANCE CO LTD

Said Kutob St, Shmeisani, PO Box 6156 & 2938, Amman
Tel: 681979, 688369, 677689, 671169
Cable: Natinsure
Telex: 21309 Natsur Jo, 23503 Ahlan Jo
Telefax: 684900

Chairman: Mustafa Abu-Goura
Directors: G Dakessian, R Barajekly, G Abu-Goura, K Abu-
Ragheb, A Majali, A Taba'a, N Majali, M A Al Hussein,
National Insurance Co of Egypt
Senior Executives: Ghaleb Abu-Goura (General Manager),
George K Ballan (Deputy General Manager), Khaled M Abu-
Goura (Asst Manager), Maher Majali (Asst Manager)

PRINCIPAL ACTIVITIES: All classes of insurance (except life)
Branch Offices: General agents throughout Jordan and branch
in Zarka and Aqaba
Principal Bankers: Jordan National Bank; Arab Bank Ltd;
Grindlays Bank plc; Housing Bank; Bank of Jordan; Cairo-
Amman Bank; Jordan Gulf Bank; Jordan Kuwait Bank; Jordan
Islamic Bank; Petra Bank; Bank of Credit & Commerce Int'l
Financial Information: The company was established in 1986
through the merging of the National Insurance Co and the
Ahlia Insurance Co

	1989
	JD'000
Sales turnover	1,444
Net profits	342
Authorised capital	1,250
Paid-up capital	1,250
Total assets	2,765

Principal Shareholders: George Dakassian, Nour Alden Ibrahim,
Mustafa Abu Goura, Mohammad Abu Goura, Ahmad Abu
Goura, Rashad Barajikli, Abdul Rahman Abu Ragheb, Bandar
Taba'a, Tawfiq Taba'a, Abdul Hai Majali, National Insurance
Co of Egypt, United Trading Co, National Portfolio Securities
Co
Date of Establishment: 1986 (see above)
No of Employees: 50

NATIONAL CONSTRUCTION & HOUSING CO LTD

PO Box 3324, Amman
Tel: 642230
Cable: Nachco
Telex: 21685 Genpex Jo

Chairman: HH Sharif Jamil Binn Nasser
Directors: Muhammed Amin Madi (Vice-Chairman), Elie Banayan
(General Manager)

PRINCIPAL ACTIVITIES: Construction
Principal Bankers: Grindlays Bank; Cairo Amman Bank

Principal Shareholders: HRH Prince Ali Ben Naif; General Import
& Export Co; HH Sharif Jamil Bin Nasser; Eng Muhammed
Amin Madi; Eng Elie Banayan
Date of Establishment: 1976

NATIONAL DEVELOPMENT & SUPPLY CO

PO Box 109, Amman
Tel: 630778, 630052
Cable: Talhouni
Telex: 21245 Granflo

PRINCIPAL ACTIVITIES: General trading, import and distribution
of foodstuffs, household appliances, office equipment and
machinery

NATIONAL TRADING CORPORATION

Zuhair Khoury Bldg, PO Box 2369, Amman
Tel: 625082, 625032
Cable: Tradingcorp
Telex: 21189 NTC JO

Chairman: R Abdini

Directors: John L Tannous (General Manager)
Senior Executives: Simon A Najm (Design & Projects Engineer)

PRINCIPAL ACTIVITIES: Import sale and installation of A/C
  equipment
Principal Agencies: Carrier International Corp; Cleaver Brooks
  Boilers
Branch Offices: Aqaba, Irbid, Zerka
Parent Company: National Trading Corp, Beirut
Principal Bankers: Jordan National Bank

Date of Establishment: 1966
No of Employees: 20

NEAR EAST ENGINEERING CO

PO Box 1838, Amman
Tel: 672013
Cable: Engineering
Telex: 21211 Enginr Jo

President: Munir H Atalla
Directors: Nicola A Nijmeh
Senior Executives: George Ammari, Bader Mustafa, Kamel
  Masarweh

PRINCIPAL ACTIVITIES: Agents and representatives for the
  aviation, electronics and engineering sectors
Branch Offices: Riyadh; Saudi Arabia
Subsidiary/Associated Companies: Near East Equipment Co;
  Communication Development Co
Principal Bankers: Arab Bank

Principal Shareholders: Munir H Atalla; Nicola A Nijmeh
Date of Establishment: 1963
No of Employees: 93

NICOLA ABU KHADER & SONS CO LTD

See ABU KHADER, NICOLA, & SONS CO LTD

NUQUL BROTHERS CONTRACTING CO

PO Box 154, Second Circle, Jebel Amman, Amman
Tel: 625109, 624719, 841571
Cable: Nubros
Telex: 21216 Nuqul Jo

PRINCIPAL ACTIVITIES: Building and civil engineering
  contractors, production of paper products, (facial tissues,
  toilet paper etc); import and distribution and agricultural
  machinery and equipment; foodstuffs, paper converting
  factory
Branch Offices: Jordan; Lebanon

ODEH NABER & SONS TRANSPORT CO

PO Box 866, Amman
Tel: 771523, 778537, 773121, 736621, 736426
Cable: Nabresco
Telex: 22196 Nbrsco Jo, 21606 Naber Jo, 21157 Nabrco Jo

Chairman: Salim Odeh Naber
Senior Executives: Samir O Naber (Mechanical Engineer)

PRINCIPAL ACTIVITIES: Transport, steel erection, crane hire,
  import of spare parts & management, operation of truck fleets
Principal Agencies: Aeroquip (UK) Ltd, Goodyear Industrial,
  Hella Electrical Parts, Steyr-Daimler-Puch AG, Eaton Ltd
Branch Offices: Iraq
Subsidiary Companies: Naber Trading Co; The Yarmouk Co Ltd;
  Naber & Co International Forwarders; Odeh Naber & Sons
  Transport Hella Branch
Principal Bankers: Arab Bank Ltd; Jordan Gulf Bank; Petra
  Bank
Financial Information:

	JD'000
Authorised capital	17,200
Paid-up capital	17,200

Principal Shareholders: Salim Odeh Naber; Samir Odeh Naber
Date of Establishment: 1949
No of Employees: 1,500

OESTERREICHISCHE LANDERBANK AG

PO Box 35297, Amman
Tel: 666361
Telex: 24319 OELBAN JO
Telefax: 677464

PRINCIPAL ACTIVITIES: Representative office
Parent Company: Head office in Vienna, Austria

Date of Establishment: 1978

PETRA BANK

PO Box 6854, Amman
Tel: 630396, 638361
Cable: PETRABANK
Telex: 21868 Petrab

Chairman: Dr Ahmad Shalabi (General Manager)
Directors: Ibrahim Alil, Rushdi Shalabi, Samir Kawar, Imad
  Baydoun, Faisal Al Marzouq, Mohammad Haj Dib, Said
  Mouasher, Abdel Mutalib Al Kathimi, Farouk Touqan

PRINCIPAL ACTIVITIES: Commercial banking

Principal Shareholders: Jordanian nationals (60%), Middle East
  Banking Co (20%), and other Arab interests (20%)
Date of Establishment: 1977

PETRA NAVIGATION & INTERNATIONAL TRADING CO LTD

White Star Bldg, PO Box 8362, Amman
Tel: 662421
Cable: Petra JO
Telex: 21755 Petra JO
Telefax: 601362

Chairman: Ahmad Armoush
Directors: Ali Armoush
Senior Executives: Farouq Al Khatib (Aqaba Office Manager),
  Anwer Subeh (Financial Manager), Tony Feghali (Asst General
  Manager), Marwan Bittar (Forwarding Manager), Hussam
  Qattan (Shipping Manager)

PRINCIPAL ACTIVITIES: Vessel operation, chartering, lines
  agents, P&I clubs representative, and related services
Branch Offices: Aqaba Br: Armoush Bldg, PO Box 485, Aqaba;
  Cairo Br: 18 Huda Sharawi St, Cairo, Tel 767136; Baghdad
  Office: Hai Al Wahda Mahalat 906, 906 Zukak 50, House 14,
  Baghdad, Tel 7190252, Telex 212503 Trans IK
Financial Information:

	1989 US$'000
Sales turnover	5,000
Authorised capital	500
Paid-up capital	500

Date of Establishment: 1978
No of Employees: 100

PHILADELPHIA INTERNATIONAL HOTEL

PO Box 6399, Amman
Tel: 663100
Cable: Philadelphia Hotel
Telex: 2189 Phil Ho Jo
Telefax: 665160

Chairman: Zuhair Khoury
Directors: Tawfiq Nazzal (Managing Director), Nabih Nazzal
  (Finance Director)
Senior Executives: Faisal Abu Nuwar (General Manager),
  Antoun Nazzal (Vice-President, Operations & Marketing),
  Michel Nazzal (Vice-President, Administration & Finance)

PRINCIPAL ACTIVITIES: Hotel management and operation
Principal Agencies: International Hotel Management Group

Branch Offices: T & N Nazzal, Altajir Bldg, Beirut, Lebanon
Principal Bankers: Arab Bank; Citibank; Chase Manhattan Bank; Bank Al Mashrek
Financial Information:

	1989 JD'000
Sales turnover	3,500
Profits	1,200
Total assets	15,000

Principal Shareholders: Housing Bank, Jordan Investment Est, T & N Nazzal Co, Royal Jordanian Airlines
Date of Establishment: 1979
No of Employees: 200

PREFABRICATED BUILDING CO

PO Box 5186, Amman
Tel: 771191/4
Cable: Prefab
Telex: 21773 Jamco Jo

Directors: Omar Maani (General Manager), Ali Maani

PRINCIPAL ACTIVITIES: Manufacture and import of prefabricated buildings and elements, insulation materials, floor and ceiling materials, etc
Associated Companies: Jordan Aluminium Mfg Co; Jordan Metal Works Co Ltd; International Plastic Co Ltd; Modern Decoration Co

Principal Shareholders: Directors as mentioned
No of Employees: 75

PREFABRICATED STRUCTURES MANUFACTURING CO

PO Box 1387, Amman
Tel: 624907, 639907
Cable: Sabcont
Telex: 21456 Sabco Jo

Chairman: Anis Mouasher
Directors: Samir Mouasher
Senior Executives: Kamil Zakka (Director, Aluminium Unit), Issa Nazek (Sales Manager), Zahi Al-As (Financial Advisor), R J Chuter (Purchasing Manager)

PRINCIPAL ACTIVITIES: Production of aluminium products and prefabricated buildings and erection
Principal Agencies: Distributors of Tildenet Shade Netting and Tilden Kee Klamp Fittings
Associated Companies: Mouasher Cousins Company
Principal Bankers: Arab Bank Ltd; Grindlays Bank; Jordan National Bank

Principal Shareholders: Chairman and director as described
Date of Establishment: 1972

PUBLIC MINING CO LTD

PO Box 922075, Amman
Tel: 667163, 667164
Cable: Minco Jo
Telex: 21578 Jo

Chairman: Eng Yousif Nimri
Directors: Eng Yousif Nimri (Director General)
Senior Executives: M Wazani (Finance & Admin Manager), A Sasa (Technical Manager), F Banna (Production Manager), G Ghassib (Personnel Manager)

PRINCIPAL ACTIVITIES: Mining and marketing of industrial rocks and non-metallic minerals such as clay, marble, kaolin, glass sand, feldspar, tripoli, gypsum, travartine and limestone
Principal Bankers: Arab Bank Ltd

Financial Information:

	1990 JD'000
Profits	272
Authorised capital	1,000
Paid-up capital	1,000
Total assets	1,745

Principal Shareholders: Jordanian Government (51%), private shareholders (49%)
Date of Establishment: 1973
No of Employees: 42

QADDOUMI TRADING EST

King Hussein Str, PO Box 3373, Amman
Tel: 639538, 622812
Cable: Qaddoumi
Telex: 21029 Qte

Directors: M Awni Qaddoumi (Director and General Manager), Fathi Shaker (Sales Manager), Muen Qaddoumi (Commercial Manager)
Senior Executives: Mohamed Hassan (Mechanical Engineer), Mohamed Ali Sakran (Electrical Engineer)

PRINCIPAL ACTIVITIES: Generators, water pumps and construction equipment, swimming pools, fountains
Principal Agencies: RTD Swan, UK; Huntley & Sparks, UK
Subsidiary/Associated Companies: Qaddoumi Agricultural Company
Principal Bankers: Jordan Kuwait Bank

Principal Shareholders: M Awni Qaddoumi
Date of Establishment: Jan 1977

RAFIDAIN BANK

PO Box 1194, Amman
Tel: 624365/66/67, 624076
Cable: Rafdbank
Telex: 21334 Jo Rafdbk

PRINCIPAL ACTIVITIES: Commercial banking
Parent Company: Head Office: Rashid Street, Baghdad, Iraq

RAZAN TRADING & CONTRACTING CORP

PO Box 927173, Amman
Tel: 605634
Telefax: (962 6) 605634

President: M Walid Sinnokrot

PRINCIPAL ACTIVITIES: Office and home furniture, contracting, electronics, tenders
Principal Agencies: Interface Carpet Tiles
Principal Bankers: British Bank of the Middle East

Date of Establishment: 2/8/1980

RED SEA SHIPPING CO WLL

24 Sharif Abdulhamid Sharaf St, Shemisani, PO Box 1248, Amman
Tel: 603771, 603776
Cable: Redship
Telex: 21912 Redship Jo
Telefax: 672170

Chairman: Tawfiq A Kawar
Directors: Walid F Kawar (Vice Chairman)
Senior Executives: Ghassoub Kawar (General Manager - Amman), Abdul Aziz Kasaji (Chartering Manager), Jamil Said (Liner Manager)

PRINCIPAL ACTIVITIES: Shipping and chartering agents, P&I Club correspondents, forwarding
Branch Offices: Aqaba: PO Box 22, Tel 314217/9, Telex 62220 Kawar Jo, Fax 313618
Parent Company: Amin Kawar & Sons Co (Pvt) Ltd
Subsidiary Companies: Aqaba Shipping Co

Principal Bankers: Arab Bank Ltd, Jordan; Petra Bank, Jordan; Grindlays Bank, Jordan

Principal Shareholders: Tawfiq A Kawar, Walid F Kawar, Nadim R Kawar, Mary widow of Amin Kawar
Date of Establishment: 1955
No of Employees: 30

REGENCY PALACE HOTEL
PO Box 927000, Queen Alia Street, Sport City Road, Amman
Tel: 926-6-660000/15
Telex: 22244/5 Regpal JO
Telefax: 660013

Chairman: Sami H Sawalha
Directors: Said H Sawalha, Ghaleb Sawalha
Senior Executives: Said Sawalha (Rooms Division Manager), Ghaleb Sawalha (Director of Sales and Marketing), Hassan Kabariti (Food & Beverage Director)

PRINCIPAL ACTIVITIES: Hotel
Parent Company: Grand Palace Hotels Co
Principal Bankers: Citibank NA, Amman

Principal Shareholders: Grand Palace Hotels Co; Sawalha Family
Date of Establishment: 1980
No of Employees: 250

SABA & CO
Jordan Insurance Co Bldg, Jabal Amman, PO Box 248, Amman
Tel: 644967, 622563, 622163
Cable: Sabaco Amman
Telex: 21665 Sabaco Jo
Telefax: 654197

Senior Executives: Mazen K Dajani (Partner)

PRINCIPAL ACTIVITIES: Public accountants and management consultants; industrial property
Branch Offices: Lebanon (Head Office); Cyprus; Algeria; Bahrain; Egypt; Iraq; Jordan; Kuwait; Libya; Morocco; Oman; Qatar; Saudi Arabia; Syria; United Arab Emirates; Yemen

Date of Establishment: 1926
No of Employees: 44

SA'D ABUJABER & SONS
See ABUJABER, SA'D, & SONS

SAKKAB TRADING EST
PO Box 9295, Amman
Tel: 624261, 616786, 647053
Cable: Sakkab
Telex: 21241 Provim Jo
Telefax: (962-6) 659061

Chairman: Emile S Sakkab
Directors: Mrs Henriette E Sakkab (Manager), Eng Simon Sakkab (Purchasing Manager), Eng Ibrahim Sakkab (Marketing Manager)
Senior Executives: Eng Sam'an Emile Sakkab

PRINCIPAL ACTIVITIES: Manufacturers' representation, commission agents, general trade, import and export, stationery and office requirements
Principal Bankers: Bank of Jordan; Bank Al Mashrek

Date of Establishment: 1976

SAMCO TRADING CO
PO Box 7531, Amman
Tel: 824800, 824801
Cable: LOTUS-AMMAN
Telex: 22303 Samco JO
Telefax: 817507

Directors: Sami R Abu-Ajweh (Managing Director)
Senior Executives: Mrs K Ghole, Miss D Shareef

PRINCIPAL ACTIVITIES: Import and distribution of perfumes and cosmetics plus gift items
Principal Agencies: Estee Lauder, USA; Trussardi, Italy; COFCI, France; Parfums Illustree, France; Salvador Dali, France; Sayidaty Products Ltd, UK
Principal Bankers: Grindlays Bank Ltd; British Bank of the Middle East

Principal Shareholders: Sami R Abu-Ajweh; Ahmad A Sacca
Date of Establishment: 1972

SCIENTIFIC & MEDICAL SUPPLIES CO
PO Box 1387, Amman
Tel: 624907, 639907, 638883
Cable: Mouasherco
Telex: 21456 Sabco Jo
Telefax: 628258

President: Anis Mouasher
Vice President: Samir Mouasher (Managing Director)
Senior Executives: Mohammad Shammout (Commercial Director), Zahi Al Assi (Financial Director)

PRINCIPAL ACTIVITIES: Import and distribution of laboratory, hospital, scientific, teaching equipment, mini computers, personal computers & peripherals, test instruments, X-ray and diagnostic equipment, open heart equipment and supplies
Principal Agencies: Hewlett Packard; IBM Office Equipment; Seward Surgical; Biomet Orthopaedic; General Electric, Boehringer Mannheim; Pfizer Hospital Products; Oticon
Branch Offices: Mouasher Showroom
Parent Company: Mouasher Cousins Company
Subsidiary/Associated Companies: Prefabricated Structures Manufacturing Co; Science and Educational Supplies; Sabco Engineering Co Ltd; ADATCO (Amman Drug & Trading Co)
Principal Bankers: Arab Bank, Grindlays Bank
Financial Information:

	1989/90 US$'000
Sales turnover	6,000
Authorised capital	600
Paid-up capital	600
Total assets	2,000

Principal Shareholders: Anis Mouasher, Samir Mouasher, Mohammad Shammout, Zahi Al Asi
Date of Establishment: 1953
No of Employees: 48

SENDAN EQUIPMENT & STEEL STRUCTURE WORKS
PO Box 2570, Amman
Tel: 794700/1
Cable: Technologia Amman
Telex: 21881 Sendan Jo
Telefax: 796158

Chairman: Hani El Sayegh (Director General)
Directors: Nazem E Sayegh (Finance Director)
Senior Executives: Saad F Jabaji (Executive Manager)

PRINCIPAL ACTIVITIES: Manufacture of all kinds of equipment and steel structures
Parent Company: Sendan Middle East Ltd, Limassol, Cyprus
Principal Bankers: Arab Bank, Amman; Bank of Credit & Commerce, Limassol, Cyprus
Financial Information:

	1989/90 JD'000
Authorised capital	500
Paid-up capital	500
Total assets	4,200

Principal Shareholders: Hani El Sayegh (sole owner)
Date of Establishment: 1976
No of Employees: 62

SETI JORDAN LTD
King Hussein St, PO Box 8053, Amman
Tel: 621867
Cable: Kellimp Amman
Telex: 21395 Kelimp Jo
Telefax: 647415

Chairman: Salim H Hakim
Directors: Hanna S Hakim, Basem S Hakim
Senior Executives: Raymond Sawalha (Sales and Parts Manager)

PRINCIPAL ACTIVITIES: General trading, import and distribution of heavy machinery, construction equipment and earth-moving equipment; maintenance; woodworking industry, hardware, building materials, vertical pumps
Principal Agencies: Blaw Knox Construction Eq Inc; Onan; Wirtgen; Fleetguard Filters, Johnston Pump Co; Cummins Engine Co; Acmetrack
Principal Bankers: British Bank of the Middle East

Principal Shareholders: Salim H Hakim, Hanna S Hakim, Basem S Hakim
Date of Establishment: 1966

SHADID, M Z, ENGINEERING BUREAU
PO Box 922072, Amman
Tel: 810709, 810694
Telex: 24062 Shadid JO

Chairman: Mohammed Zuhair Shadid
Senior Executives: Hussein Hassanain (Senior Engineering Geologist), Abdel Fattah Shami (Senior Engineering Geologist), Jack Said (Senior Civil Engineer), Anwar Tumaizi (Geological Engineer)

PRINCIPAL ACTIVITIES: Geotechnical engineering, quality control, geology, hydrogeology, geophysics and mining
Subsidiary Companies: Geopol, Poland; Geoconsult, Austria; Data Sondaj, Turkey
Principal Bankers: Arab Bank (Abdali Branch), Housing Bank (Tila Ali Branch), Bank of Trade & Commerce International (Station Rd Branch)

Principal Shareholders: M Z Shadid
Date of Establishment: 1985
No of Employees: 25

SHAMI TRADING CO
PO Box 1083, Amman
Tel: 625558, 635441
Cable: Nestra
Telex: 23212 Carbo JO
Telefax: 962-6-643720

Chairman: Hanna Shami
Directors: Hani Shami (Managing Director)
Senior Executives: Mahfouz Khouri (Marketing Manager)

PRINCIPAL ACTIVITIES: Commission agents, chemicals, industrial raw materials, textiles, etc
Principal Bankers: British Bank of the Middle East

Date of Establishment: 1960

SHEPHERD HOTEL AMMAN
Khatab St, PO Box 2020, Jabal Amman, Amman
Tel: 639197, 639198
Cable: Shepherd Amman
Telex: 21410 Sheprd Jo

Chairman: George Shalhoub
Directors: Nader Shalhoub (General Manager)

PRINCIPAL ACTIVITIES: Hoteliers and caterers
Principal Bankers: Jordan National Bank; Chase Manhattan Bank; Grindlays Bank; Industrial Development Bank

SHUKRI DEEB & SONS LTD
See DEEB, SHUKRI, & SONS LTD

SIGMA CONSULTING ENGINEERS
PO Box 20076, Amman
Tel: 661031, 662612, 670235
Cable: Sigma
Telex: 21888 Sigma Jo
Telefax: 678320

Chairman: Hani Hakki
Directors: Malak Hakki

PRINCIPAL ACTIVITIES: Engineering and architectural consulting service, construction management
Principal Bankers: Bank of Credit and Commerce International
Financial Information:

	1988/89 US$'000
Sales turnover	1,246
Profits	15
Authorised capital	40
Paid-up capital	40
Total assets	1,750

Principal Shareholders: Directors as described
Date of Establishment: 1975
No of Employees: 82

SOCIETE GENERALE
PO Box 35192, Amman
Tel: 660016
Telex: 23191
Telefax: 675870

Senior Executives: Roland de Lattre (Senior Representative)

PRINCIPAL ACTIVITIES: Representative office
Branch Offices: Bahrain, Iraq, Jordan, Kuwait, Lebanon, Oman, Qatar, Syria, UAE
Parent Company: Head office: 29 Boulevard Haussmann, 75009 Paris, France

Date of Establishment: 1982

SOUFAN BROS CO
PO Box 1340, Amman
Tel: 665354, 668578
Cable: Soufan
Telex: 21723 Soufan Jo
Telefax: 678875

Chairmen: Issam Soufan
Directors: Wafa I Soufan, Abdulla I Soufan

PRINCIPAL ACTIVITIES: Import and distribution of electrical household appliances and accessories, wires and fittings, air conditioning units
Principal Agencies: Daiken, Mazda, Matsushita
Parent Company: International Electric Supplies
Principal Bankers: Arab Bank

Date of Establishment: 1940
No of Employees: 30

SPINNEYS 1948 LTD
PO Box 40, Amman
Tel: 779141
Cable: Spinneys Amman
Telex: 21814 Spinex, Jo
Telefax: 779782

Senior Executives: George Jarjura (Acting Manager), Anton Hazboun (Finance Manager)

PRINCIPAL ACTIVITIES: Importers, wholesale food distribution, agency representations and Lloyds agents

Principal Agencies: Kraft, Heinz, Kellogs, Wrigleys, Fox's Biscuits, Tulip, H P Foods, Unilever, Haig, Gordons, Ion, Maltagliati
Parent Company: Spinneys 1948 Ltd
Principal Bankers: British Bank of the Middle East; ANZ Grindlays

Principal Shareholders: Branch of Spinneys (1948) Ltd
Date of Establishment: 1936
No of Employees: 40

SUKHTIAN, MUNIR, GROUP

PO Box 1027, Amman
Tel: 663216/7/8/9
Cable: Sukhdrug Amman
Telex: 21316 Jo
Telefax: 601568

Chairman: Nidal Munir Sukhtian (Group President)
Directors: Ghiath Munir Sukhtian (Group Senior Vice President), Munjed Munir Sukhtian (Group Vice President)
Senior Executives: Dr Taher Assaf (Asst General Manager), Abdel Raheem Obeidi (Commercial Manager), Bassam Shreideh (Manager Veterinary Div), Rima Haddad (Manager Pharmaceutical Div), Rajab Abu Elhalawa (Manager Chemical Div), Ali Sayyed (Manager Finance Dept), Mohammad Amireh (Manager Agricultural Division), Iqab Attiyeh (Manager Electronics Div)

PRINCIPAL ACTIVITIES: Import and distribution of pharmaceuticals, medical and surgical equipment, toiletries, animal feed, lubricating oil, consumer electronics, chemicals, laboratory accessories and equipment, communications systems etc, manufature of household goods and toiletries, also soft drinks plant and greenhouse manufacturing, farming
Principal Agencies: Sterling Drug Intl, The Boots Co, Cyanamid Intl, Xerox, Sterling Winthrop, Medimpex, Farmos, Biolab, Protex, Delmar Avionics, Schwarzkopf, Warner Communication, G.E., Marconi, Harris, 3M, Dow Corning, Arco Chemicals, Occidental, Dupont, etc
Subsidiary Companies: Munir Sukhtian Co Ltd; Jaffa Juice & Beverages Co; Jordan Greenhouse Manufacturing; Household & Toiletries Manufacturing Co; Sukhtian & Yahya Electronics Co Ltd; Safa Foodstuffs Manufacturing Co Ltd; Jordan Chemical Labs, Beit Jala; Lotus Paper Conversion, Nablus; Mineral Oil Co, Nablus; Takamul National Agricultural Est, Riyadh, Saudi Arabia; Hashemiah Ariculture Co, Cairo, Egypt; Rayyan Intl BV, Aalsmeer, Holland; GE Mor Inc, Taylorville, Ill, USA; United Pharmaceuticals Manufacturing Co, Jordan; Sukhtian Trading Co, Sana'a Yemen; Munir Sukhtian Co, Baghdad, Iraq; Flower Club, Amman
Principal Bankers: Arab Bank Ltd; Jordan National Bank; Cairo Amman Bank; Jordan Kuwait Bank; Credit & Finance Corp; Jordan Bank
Financial Information:

	1988/89 US$'000
Sales turnover	80,000
Paid-up capital	20,000
Total assets	50,000

Principal Shareholders: Nidal, Ghiath and Munjed Sukhtian
Date of Establishment: 1933
No of Employees: 627

SULEIMAN TANNOUS & SONS CO

See TANNOUS, SULEIMAN, & SONS CO

SUPPLIES AND CONTRACTS CO

PO Box 748, Amman
Tel: 622881
Cable: Sac Amman
Telex: 21451 Sacjor Jo

PRINCIPAL ACTIVITIES: Design and execution of electro-mechanicl and civil works including industrial projects
Principal Bankers: Arab Bank Ltd

SUPPLY AGENCIES FOR TECHNICAL & INDUSTRIAL EQUIPMENT CO LTD
S.A.T.I.C.O.

King Hussein St, PO Box 7701, Amman
Tel: 638580
Cable: Satico
Telex: 21335 Comcnt Jo

Chairman: Iklil Sati
Directors: Ahmed Y Asali (General Manager)

PRINCIPAL ACTIVITIES: Import and heavy equipment and roads and house construction, agricultural machines and equipment, after sales services and spare parts
Principal Agencies: Motor Iberica SA, Spain; Empresa Nacional de Autocamiones SA, Spain; Dale Electric Ltd, UK; The Liner Concrete Machinery Co Ltd, UK; F E Weatherill Ltd, UK; Lansing Henley Ltd, UK; Burnett Atalanta Int'l Ltd, UK; Prestcold Searle Int'l Ltd, UK; ACE Machinery Ltd, UK; Irrigation & Industrial Development Corp, USA; Hayward Tyler & Co Ltd, UK; Sumo Pumps Ltd, UK; Komatsu Forklift, Japan
Associated Companies: Irrigation and Agricultural Projects Development Co
Principal Bankers: Grindlays Bank plc; Bank of Credit and Commerce International SA

SYNCO
Jordan Services & Representations Co Ltd

PO Box 1168, Amman
Tel: 962-6-698135/6
Cable: Synco
Telex: 21268 Synco Jo
Telefax: 962060698137

Chairman: Miss Rania Sabella
Directors: Ali Al Hayari (Managing Director), Emile Srouji (Managing Director)
Senior Executives: Victor Suleiman

PRINCIPAL ACTIVITIES: General commission agents, manufacturers' representatives, contractors, insurance, shipping and forwarding agents, import and building materials, foodstuffs, etc
Principal Bankers: Jordan National Bank, Amman
Financial Information:

	1990 US$'000
Sales turnover	10,000

Principal Shareholders: Family owned
Date of Establishment: 1960

SYRIAN JORDANIAN BANK

PO Box 926636, King Hussain Street, Amman
Tel: 661138, 661139
Cable: SYJOBANK
Telex: 22102 Syjobk
Telefax: 661484

Chairman: Mohammed S Horani
Directors: Dr Saleh Khasawneh, Dr Abdul Majid Qasem, Dr Zuhair A Khalifeh
Senior Executives: Hisham J Safadi (General Manager), Ahmed A Eideh (Manager Amman Main Branch)

PRINCIPAL ACTIVITIES: Commercial banking
Branch Offices: Amman Main Branch: PO Box 926940
Principal Bankers: London: Jordan International Bank Plc; New York: American Express Bank; Paris: UBAF; Amsterdam: Amro Bank; Rome: UBAE; Banca Nazionale del Lavoro; Frankfurt: Dresdner Bank AG; Zurich: Union Bank of Switzerland; Tokyo: UBAF

Financial Information:

	1988/89 JD'000
Profits	14
Authorised capital	1,000
Paid-up capital	1,000
Total assets	12,432

Principal Shareholders: Social Security Corporation; Jordan Investment Corporation
Date of Establishment: 1979
No of Employees: 34

SYRIAN JORDANIAN CO FOR INDUSTRY

PO Box 925411, Amman
Tel: 667411, 669173
Telex: 21009 INSYJO
Telefax: 662292

Chairman: Muneer Al Humosh
Directors: Mustafa Zahran, Mohammed Shalalfa, Eid Abu-Karaki, Dr Mustafa Jamoos, Dr Ghayath Zein Al A'bideen, Fuad Ryzig, Mohammed Tawalbeh
Senior Executives: Hisham El-Taher (General Manager)

PRINCIPAL ACTIVITIES: Joint venture between Jordan and Syria aiming at the establishment of joint industries (cement, carpets, pesticides)
Branch Offices: Damascus
Subsidiary Companies: Arab Company for White Cement Industry
Principal Bankers: Syrian Jordanian Bank; Arab Bank; Jordan Bank
Financial Information:

	1989 JD'000
Authorised capital	20,000
Paid-up capital	13,978
Total assets	14,893

Principal Shareholders: Jordanian & Syrian Governments
Date of Establishment: 1976

T GARGOUR & FILS

See GARGOUR, T, & FILS

TANNOUS, SULEIMAN, & SONS CO

PO Box 102, Prince Mohammed St, Amman
Tel: 636188, 624768
Cable: Tours

Senior Executives: George Suleiman Tannous (Managing Director), Fouad S Tannous

PRINCIPAL ACTIVITIES: Import and distribution of cars and parts, tyres, tractors and agricultural machinery, pharmaceuticals, electrical household appliances and surgical supplies

TECHNICAL SERVICES BUREAU CO

PO Box 6970, Amman
Tel: 622183, 622037
Cable: TEKSERVICE
Telex: 21407 TSB JO
Telefax: 646074

Partners: Louis F Batshone (Managing Partner), Michael F Moussa
Senior Executives: Bassam F Batshone (Chief Engineer)

PRINCIPAL ACTIVITIES: Contracting for water and power projects
Principal Agencies: NEI - WH Allen; Weir Pumps; Pleuger Pumps; Sparling Watermeters; HS Brackette Screens; Viking Johnson Couplings, Guest Chrimes Valves
Branch Offices: Electrical Switchgear assembly plant, Amman, Tel 736638; Showrooms, Amman, Tel 777450

Principal Bankers: British Bank of Middle East; Jordan Kuwaiti Bank; Al-Mashrek Bank
Financial Information:

	1990 JD'000
Sales turnover	2,200
Authorised capital	250
Paid-up capital	250

Principal Shareholders: As partners described
Date of Establishment: 1977
No of Employees: 20

TELECOMMUNICATIONS CORPORATION

PO Box 1689, Amman
Tel: 638301/5, 642301/5
Cable: Jortel Amman
Telex: 21221 A/B Jortel Amman

Chairman: Minister of Communications
Directors: Mohd Shahid Ismail
Senior Executives: Saleh Atiyat (Development Asst), Mohd Al Ekoor (Asst for Finance and Administration Affairs), Walid D Waek (Governates Assistant)

PRINCIPAL ACTIVITIES: Public services for telecommunications
Branch Offices: 10 Governates and district directorate and telecommunication centre for training
Parent Company: Responsible to the Ministry of Communications
Principal Bankers: Central Bank of Jordan

Principal Shareholders: Government owned
Date of Establishment: 1971
No of Employees: 3,300

TILLAWI, I, & SONS LTD

Mahatta Street, PO Box 593, Amman
Tel: 654301, 654302
Cable: Ismailtillawi
Telex: 21010 Booth Jo Att: I Tillawi&Sons
Telefax: 640180

Chairman: Shafiq I Tillawi
Directors: Mohamed Sh Tillawi (Managing Director)
Senior Executives: Ibrahim Sh Tillawi (Manager), Mohamed Tillawi

PRINCIPAL ACTIVITIES: Manufacturers' representatives and contractors for consumer goods, household appliances, machinery tools, electrical and industrial equipment, garage equipment and fairs and shows representatives
Principal Agencies: C & E Fein, W Germany; Gedore, W Germany; BMI, W Germany; Record Marples, UK; Bahco Verktyk, Sweden; Conjoint, UK; Wirminghaus & Funcke, W Germany
Parent Company: Jordan Est for Industrial Engineering Equipment, PO Box 593, Amman, Jordan, Tel 654301/2
Principal Bankers: Arab Bank Ltd, Petra Bank,

Principal Shareholders: Chairman and directors as described
Date of Establishment: 1920

TOUFIC MARAR ETS

See MARAR, TOUFIC, ETS

TRANSJORDAN BUILDING MATERIALS CO LTD

PO Box 276, Hashimi St, Amman
Tel: 624192
Cable: Binardon
Telex: 21876 TBMCO Jo
Telefax: 794620

Chairman: M A Bdeir
Directors: Isam Bdeir, Seif Eddin Bdeir, Abdul Hadi Edliby, Othman Bdeir

PRINCIPAL ACTIVITIES: Import and distribution of building materials, sanitary ware, timber, paints, decorative materials and general contracting
Principal Bankers: Arab Bank; Jordan National Bank

Date of Establishment: 1947
No of Employees: 28

TRANSJORDAN ENGINEERING CO

PO Box 1, Amman
Tel: 639181/4
Cable: Tec
Telex: 21300

Chairman: Fuad Kattan
Directors: Tony Kattan
Senior Executives: Samir Khalil, Noman Shequem, Michael Serouji, Isam Shoush, Farouk El-Amad

PRINCIPAL ACTIVITIES: Engineering equipment (mechanical, electrical, agricultural construction), TV and household, foodstuffs, contracting, electro mechanical and medical maintenance, cosmetics
Principal Agencies: Perkins Engines, Wolf Electric, BOC, James F Low, Philips, Nestle, Haden, BBC, Hospitalia International, L'Oreal
Branch Offices: West Bank; Irbid, Aqaba
Principal Bankers: Arab Bank

Principal Shareholders: Fuad Kattan, Tony Kattan
Date of Establishment: 1940
No of Employees: 200

TRANSJORDAN TRADING CO LTD

PO Box 129, Amman
Tel: 651331/2
Telex: 22190 Titco Jo

PRINCIPAL ACTIVITIES: Import and distribution of diesel engines and equipment, automobiles, auto spare parts, tyres and tubes, motorcycles, household goods
Principal Agencies: Perkins, Kelly Tyres, Triumph Dodge, Austin

TROCON - TRANS-ORIENT ENGINEERING & CONTRACTING CO LTD

PO Box 2079, Amman
Tel: 640141/2/3
Cable: Trocon
Telex: 21893 Trocon JO
Telefax: 649745

President: Radwan A Hajjar (Managing Director)
Directors: Eng M Mansour Tabbaa, Eng Raouf Kharouba
Senior Executives: Eng Iyad Sati

PRINCIPAL ACTIVITIES: Civil and building contractors
Branch Offices: Trocon (Iraq), Baghdad, Iraq; Trocon (Malaysia), Kuala Lumpur, Malaysia
Subsidiary Companies: Technical Engineering Services (UK)
Principal Bankers: Cairo Amman Bank; Bank of Credit & Commerce International; Petra Bank
Financial Information:

	1989
	JD'000
Sales turnover	20,000
Authorised capital	2,500
Paid-up capital	2,500

Principal Shareholders: United Trading Company; Eng R Hajjar; Eng M Tabbaa; Eng B Olabi
Date of Establishment: 1972
No of Employees: 945

UNION BUILDING MATERIALS CO

PO Box 404, Amman
Tel: (Office) 622359, 625053, 638671, (Sales) 893411, 894411
Cable: Union Amman
Telex: 21094 Union Jo
Telefax: 650279

Chairman: Mahmoud Kamal Kattan
Directors: Kamal M Kattan, Imad M Kattan

PRINCIPAL ACTIVITIES: Manufacturers' representatives, general merchants and contractors, suppliers of building materials, hardware and tools
Principal Agencies: Assa-Stenman AB, Sweden, Teka Decor AB, Sweden
Principal Bankers: British Bank of the Middle East; Arab Bank Ltd; Cairo Amman Bank

Date of Establishment: 1950
No of Employees: 20

UNITED ENGINEERING & MECHANICAL CO (MODACO)

PO Box 1400, Amman
Tel: 622349
Cable: Modaco
Telex: 21590 Muabco

Chairman: Faris E Muasher

PRINCIPAL ACTIVITIES: Distributors and agents
Principal Agencies: Petters Ltd, UK; Petter Power Generation Ltd, UK; Stewart-Warner Ltd, UK; Bristol Pneumatic Ltd, UK
Principal Bankers: Grindlays Bank

UNITED INSURANCE CO LTD

PO Box 7521, Amman
Tel: 625828, 635778, 648501, 648503
Cable: Safety
Telex: 21323 Abujbr Jo
Telefax: 629417

Chairman: Dr Raouf Sa'd Abujaber
Directors: Tawfiq Kawar, Nizar Darwazeh, Michael Seikaly, Abdulla Sha'aban, Kamal Asfour, Nizar Jardaneh, Fouad Abujaber, Samir Seikaly, New India Assurance Co of Bombay, Al Chark Insurance Co of Egypt
Senior Executives: Michael Susu (General Manager), Nazeh Azar (Asst General Manager)

PRINCIPAL ACTIVITIES: Transacting all classes of insurance: fire and allied risks, marine cargo and general accident insurance
Principal Bankers: Grindlays Bank; Industrial Development Bank
Financial Information:

	1989
	JD'000
Sales turnover	1,552
Profits	315
Authorised capital	1,500
Paid-up capital	1,500
Total assets	3,010

Principal Shareholders: Chairman and directors as described, also New India Assurance Co; Amin Kawar & Sons Co; Yacoub Sabella & Son Co; Sa'd Abujaber & Sons Co; Albert N Muzber; Isaq H Halaby; General Investment Co; Al Chark Insurance Co
Date of Establishment: 1972
No of Employees: 23

UNITED TRADING CO LTD

PO Box 1408, Amman
Tel: 672188, 672086, 672146, 672137
Cable: Al-Tawfic
Telex: 21203; 21440 UTC JOR JO

Chairman: Tawfic Sabri Tabbaa

Directors: Taj Hajjar (President)
Senior Executives: Abdul Hai Majali, Bandar Tabbaa

PRINCIPAL ACTIVITIES: General merchants and traders, insurance agents, government contractors; suppliers of various commodities (wheat, flour, sugar), and engineering machinery and industrial raw materials (cement, steel); also engineering contractors, tourism and travel agents
Principal Agencies: AM General, World Flour (Holland), White Engines, Teledyne, Fujitsu, TOA Electric, Furukawa Electric Co, Nissho Iwai, Northern, Telecom, SANSUI
Associated Companies: Al-Ahlia Insurance Co (Jordan) Ltd; Jordan Flour Mills Co Ltd; TROCON-Trans-Orient Engineering & Contracting Co; Bestours-United Tourism & Transport Co Ltd; Murray Clayton Ltd, UK; United Trading Corp (USA) Inc, Virginia, USA; UTC Energy Resources Inc, Texas, USA; UTC (Japan) Ltd, Tokyo; UTC (Singapore) Pte Ltd; United General Agencies Est, Abu Dhabi; also associated companies in Cairo, Egypt; Damascus, Syria; Riyadh and Jeddah, Saudi Arabia; Kuwait; Baghdad, Iraq; Dubai, UAE; Switzerland; Gibraltar; Jersey; West Germany; Spain; Italy; Thailand; Malaysia; Canada
Principal Bankers: Allied Arab Bank Ltd, London; Arab Bank Ltd, Amman and London; UBAF, Paris; Banque de Credit et Commerce, Amman; Petra Bank, Amman

Date of Establishment: 1969
No of Employees: 700

VACU-LUG TRACTION TYRE CO

Station Rd, PO Box 768, Amman
Tel: 655296, 894772
Cable: Vacu-Lug
Telex: 21442 Bemih Jo

Directors: Nicola Kawar (Managing Director)
Senior Executives: Rami Kawar

PRINCIPAL ACTIVITIES: Retreading all sizes of earth-mover tyres
Branch Offices: Amman, Marka
Principal Bankers: Jordan National Bank

Date of Establishment: 1967

WAEL R ABDUL-HADI & CO

See ABDUL-HADI, WAEL R, & CO

WAFA DAJANI & SONS CO

Wafa Dajani Bldg, Jabal Lweibdeh, near Saadi Mosque, PO Box 33 Amman
Tel: 624179, 624170, 624111/2
Cable: Wafadajani
Telex: 21336 Dajani Jo
Telefax: 630618

Chairman: Wafa Dajani
Directors: Wafa A W Dajani, Wael A W Dajani, Mohammad A W Dajani
Senior Executives: A N Dajani (Pharmaceutical), F Koro (Lubeoil), W Ramdan (Petroleum)

PRINCIPAL ACTIVITIES: Service and gas stations; supply of electro-mechanical equipment; power engineering; telecommunications; trading and contracting; supply of pharmaceuticals, lubricants, domestic electrical appliances, office equipment
Principal Agencies: Mobil Oil Corp; GEC General Electric Co, UK; NCR; ITT; Schaub Lorenz; Pont-A-Mousson; Pitney Bowes; Pirelli General Cable; Halberg; Stork; Denco Miller; Gillette; Aspro; W Warner; Admiral Corp; Avery; Socam; McGraw Edison; Flexibox; Multi-Amp; Thomson-LGT; Eclatec; ISC Cardion; AMF Bowling
Branch Offices: Several branches in Amman, showrooms and service & gas stations

Subsidiary/Associated Companies: Wafa Dajani (Drugs) Co; Near East Tourist Center (GSA Swissair); Najjarr Bros & Co; Abul Wafa Dajani & Sons (NCR); Kwik Print Centre
Principal Bankers: Cairo-Amman Bank; Arab Bank; Bank of Jordan; Jordan National Bank

Principal Shareholders: Chairman and directors as described above
Date of Establishment: 1924
No of Employees: 140

WOOLLEN INDUSTRIES CO LTD

PO Box 1728, Amman
Tel: 892723
Cable: Soofyah
Telex: 21834 MARCO JO
Telefax: 885732

President: Dr Jamil S Maraqa
Directors: Hani S Maraqa
Senior Executives: Hani S Maraqa (General Manager), Marwan Arafeh (Senior Accountant), Abdul Mutaleb Abu Ali (Marketing Manager), Eng Mrs Kornelia Najar (Production Manager), Eng Fathi Idrisi (Technical Manager), Mazen Abdeen (Personnel Manager)

PRINCIPAL ACTIVITIES: Manufacture of blankets and textiles
Branch Offices: Jordan; Iraq
Principal Bankers: Arab Bank Ltd
Financial Information:

	1989 JD'000	1990 JD'000
Sales turnover	621	675
Authorised capital	500	500
Paid-up capital	500	500
Total assets	1,000	1,000

Principal Shareholders: Orphanage Institute and Social Security Corporation
Date of Establishment: 1961
No of Employees: 50

YEAST INDUSTRIES CO LTD

PO Box 9310, King Hussein St, Amman
Tel: 639053, 885114
Cable: Astrico
Telex: 21753 Yeast Jo
Telefax: 885325

Chairman: Ibrahim M Zeine
Directors: Rashad Barajakly, Hamdi Tabbaa, Universal Foods Corporation
Senior Executives: Eng Remon Halteh (General Manager)

PRINCIPAL ACTIVITIES: Manufacture of fresh and active dry yeast
Principal Bankers: Arab Bank Ltd
Financial Information:

	1989 JD'000	1990 JD'000
Sales turnover	1,110	1,838
Profits	350	457
Authorised capital	480	480
Paid-up capital	480	480
Total assets	1,600	1,661

Principal Shareholders: R Barajakly, I Zeine, S Ghannam, H Tabbaa, R Halteh, M Barajakly, I Barajakly, K Barajakly, Y Barajakly, I Barajakly, Mrs M Barajakly, Universal Foods Corporation
Date of Establishment: 1974
No of Employees: 50

YOUSEF NASSAR & CO

See NASSAR, YOUSEF, & CO

JORDAN

ZAKI A GHUL
See GHUL, ZAKI A,

ZAKI M NASSAR & BROTHER
See NASSAR, ZAKI M, & BROTHER

ZAKI M NASSAR & BROTHER
See NASSAR, ZAKI M, & BROTHER

ZEINE & COMPANY
PO Box 101, Amman
Tel: 622121
Cable: Zeine

PRINCIPAL ACTIVITIES: Manufacturers' representatives, import
of electrical and electronic equipment, air conditioning and
heating equipment, office equipment and safety equipment
Principal Agencies: Hoover, Philco, Coleman, Roneo, Imperial,
Chubb, Necchi

ZEYAD SALAH CONTRACTING
PO Box 7245, Amman
Tel: 661947, 661948, 666055
Telex: 21757 Zeyad Jo

Chairman: Zeyad Salah
Directors: Gen Sadeq Al-Share, Abdul Fattah Hanbali
Senior Executives: Gen Sadeq Al-Share (Managing Director),
Abdul Fattah Hanbali (Technical Manager)

PRINCIPAL ACTIVITIES: Contracting
Principal Bankers: Petra Bank, Amman; Jordan Kuwaiti Bank

Principal Shareholders: Private
Date of Establishment: 6/6/1978
No of Employees: 500

Major Companies of
KUWAIT

The Kuwaiti section is followed this year by an appendix of relocation addresses (with telephone/ telefax numbers where possible). This appendix allows the reader to cross-refer the Kuwaiti company to its relocation entry in the relevant Arab country or to contact them direct if they have relocated to a non-Arab country.

A H AL SAGAR & BROS
See AL SAGAR, A H, & BROS

ABBAS AHMAD AL SHAWAF & BROS CO WLL
See AL SHAWAF, ABBAS AHMAD, & BROS CO WLL

ABBAS ALI HAZEEM & SONS CO
See HAZEEM, ABBAS ALI, & SONS CO

ABDALLA CONTRACTING & TRADING
PO Box 714 Safat, 13008 Kuwait
Tel: 2438452, 2437400
Cable: Absam Kuwait
Telex: 22128 Absam Kwt

President: Abdalla Saleh Bassam
Senior Executives: I A Bassam (Senior Executive), B A Bassam (Senior Executive), V Ribeiro (Manager)

PRINCIPAL ACTIVITIES: Trading in commodities, import of iron and steel, cement and other building materials; civil, mechanical and electrical contracting, fabrication of oil and chemical tanks, fire-fighting systems; suppliers of industrial and protective footwear, telephone/power cables
Principal Agencies: Dunlop
Branch Offices: In Kuwait: PO Box 42472, Shuwaikh, Tel: 810381, 810732; Saudi Arabia: Abdul Aziz Saleh Al-Bassam, King Abdul Aziz St, Crossing 21, Al-Khobar, Saudi Arabia
Subsidiary Companies: General Electric & Refrigeration Co, Bahjat Jewellers WLL, PO Box 5681, Safat, Kuwait
Principal Bankers: National Bank of Kuwait

Principal Shareholders: Sole-proprietor Abdalla Saleh Al-Bassam
Date of Establishment: 1962

ABDEL AZEEZ AL WAZZAN & SONS
See AL WAZZAN, ABDEL AZEEZ, & SONS

ABDUL AZIZ A ALARFAJ GENERAL TRADING
See ALARFAJ, ABDUL AZIZ A, GENERAL TRADING

ABDUL AZIZ S AL BABTAIN
See AL BABTAIN, ABDUL AZIZ S,

ABDUL AZIZ YOUSUF AL ESSA & CO WLL
See AL ESSA, ABDUL AZIZ YOUSUF, & CO WLL

ABDUL RAHMAN ALBISHER & ZAID ALKAZEMI CO
See ALBISHER, ABDUL RAHMAN, & ZAID ALKAZEMI CO

ABDULAZIZ & ALI YOUSUF AL MUZAINI
See AL MUZAINI, ABDULAZIZ & ALI YOUSUF,

ABDULAZIZ ABDULMOHSIN AL RASHED SONS CO WLL
See AL RASHED, ABDULAZIZ ABDULMOHSIN, SONS CO WLL

ABDULAZIZ ALI AL MUTAWA
See AL MUTAWA, ABDULAZIZ ALI,

ABDULAZIZ MUHALHIL AL KHALED EST
See AL KHALED, ABDULAZIZ MUHALHIL, EST

ABDULHAMID MANSOOR MAZIDI
See MAZIDI, ABDULHAMID MANSOOR,

ABDULHAMID YOUSUF AL ESSA
See AL ESSA, ABDULHAMID YOUSUF,

ABDULLA ALOMAR AL YAGOUT
See AL YAGOUT, ABDULLA ALOMAR,

ABDULLA SAYID HASHIM AL GHARABALLY CO
See AL GHARABALLY, ABDULLA SAYID HASHIM, CO

ABDULMOHSEN ABDULAZIZ AL-BABTAIN CO
See AL-BABTAIN, ABDULMOHSEN ABDULAZIZ, CO

ABDULRAZAK, SAUD & IBRAHIM, TRADING & CONTRACTING CO
PO Box 1511 Safat, 13016 Kuwait
Tel: 2432945, 2449606
Cable: Razak
Telex: 22541 Razak KT

PRINCIPAL ACTIVITIES: Building, civil and general contracting

ABOUD TRANSPORTATION
PO Box 13045, Kaifan, 71951 Kuwait
Tel: 812453, 816149, 819626, 819650
Cable: Najafi
Telex: 22340 Abound Kt

Proprietor: Abdul Razak Mohamed Aboud
Senior Executives: Naim S Khuffash (General Manager), R S Bhasin (Marketing Manager)

PRINCIPAL ACTIVITIES: Road transportation, warehousing, clearing, forwarding and general agency
Principal Agencies: Beverol Works Ltd, Holland; Lipe Rollway Ltd, UK; MGM Brakes Ltd, USA; Le-Lis, Belgium; Weatherhead, USA; Dreyco Inc, USA; Propellerhaus Schaferbarthold, Germany; Suddetusche Kuhlerfabrik, Germany
Principal Bankers: Commercial Bank of Kuwait; National Bank of Kuwait; Gulf Bank Ltd

Date of Establishment: 1959
No of Employees: 175

ABUD ALRAZZAQ ALQADDUMI & SONS CO
See ALQADDUMI, ABUD ALRAZZAQ, & SONS CO

ADEL BEHBEHANI GENERAL TRADING CO WLL
See BEHBEHANI, ADEL, GENERAL TRADING CO WLL

ADWANI CO WLL
PO Box 538 Safat, 13006 Kuwait
Tel: 2429714, 2423818
Cable: DYANA
Telex: 23485 DYANA

Directors: A M Adwani
Senior Executives: M N Karkesh (General Manager)

PRINCIPAL ACTIVITIES: Contracting and aggregate suppliers
Principal Bankers: Alahli Bank; Commercial Bank of Kuwait

Principal Shareholders: M N Karkesh; A M Adwani
Date of Establishment: 1970
No of Employees: 75

AFRO ARAB CO FOR INVESTMENT & INTERNATIONAL TRADE
A.F.A.R.C.O.
PO Box 5024 Safat, 13051 Kuwait
Tel: 2423380/1/2/3
Cable: Afarco
Telex: 22081 Afarco; 22496 Afarco

Chairman: Yousuf Abdulaziz Al-Muzaini (and Managing Director)

Senior Executives: Anwar Amin (General Manager), Ali Al Refai (Deputy General Manager)

PRINCIPAL ACTIVITIES: International trade and investment in the Arab and African countries (economic, agricultural, industrial, mining and housing fields)
Branch Offices: Nairobi (PO Box 30444); Damascus (PO Box 5169); and Cairo (PO Box 1929); Mauritania; Singapore; Baghdad, Iraq; Geneva, Switzerland; Morocco; Turkey; Paris, France; USA
Principal Bankers: National Bank of Kuwait, Kuwait; Burgan Bank, Kuwait; United Bank of Kuwait, London; Alahli Bank of Kuwait, Kuwait; Commercial Bank of Kuwait, Kuwait; Commercial Bank of Africa, Nairobi; Arab African Bank, Cairo; United Overseas Bank, Geneva
Financial Information:

	US$'000
Authorised capital	70,000
Paid-up capital	35,000

Principal Shareholders: Kuwait Foreign Trading Contracting & Investment Co (KFTCIC), SAK (51%); Gulf Financial Center (49%)
Date of Establishment: 1972
No of Employees: 200

AGRICULTURAL FOOD PRODUCTS CO KSC

PO Box 24090 Safat, 13101 Kuwait
Tel: 4849007, 4848870, 4846088
Cable: Zariyah
Telex: 23269 AFPC KT, 46130 AFPC KT
Telefax: 4842723

Chairman: Fahad Mohammed Al Othman
Directors: Faisal Al Shathi (Deputy Chairman), Khalid A Al Othman (Managing Director), Jasim Habib, Adel Al Sarawy, Dr Salem Al Muhanna
Senior Executives: Mohammed Al Othebi (Finance Manager), Khalid A Al Haddad (Marketing Manager), Fahd Abdul Latief Al Adwani (Purchasing Manager), Hassan Al Najjar (Personnel Manager), Yousef M Al Bedah (Local Marketing Manager), Magdi Abdul Aziz (Production Manager)

PRINCIPAL ACTIVITIES: Import of agricultural foodstuffs, specially fresh, dried, canned fruits and vegetables, also import of sugar, grains such as rice, barley and maize
Branch Offices: 40 branches in Kuwait
Associated Companies: Kuwait Supply Co; Kuwait United Fisheries Co
Principal Bankers: Bank of Kuwait & The Middle East; Gulf Bank; Commercial Bank of Kuwait; National Bank of Kuwait; Burgan Bank; Kuwait Finance House
Financial Information:

	1988/89 KD'000
Sales turnover	7,108
Authorised capital	4,557
Paid-up capital	4,557
Total assets	3,376

Principal Shareholders: Kuwaiti Companies, Kuwaiti Citizens and Government of Kuwait
Date of Establishment: 1976
No of Employees: 700

AHMADIAH CONTRACTING & TRADING CO WLL

PO Box 446 Safat, 13005 Kuwait
Tel: 4814477, 4814848
Cable: Ahmadiah
Telex: 23314 Ahmadia Kt
Telefax: 4831367

Chairman: Abdul Mohsen Faisal Al Thuwainy
Directors: Ahmad Faisal Al Thuwainy, Tony Najib Najjar
Senior Executives: Magdi K Magdallah, Ahmed F Chahbaz

PRINCIPAL ACTIVITIES: Civil engineering and contracting, supply of building materials; supply, installation and maintenance of elevators and escalators
Principal Agencies: Hitachi, Japan
Branch Offices: Shuwaikh Industrial Area
Subsidiary Companies: International Contracting Co, Kuwait; Sister Company: Thuwaini Trading Co
Principal Bankers: National Bank of Kuwait; Commercial Bank of Kuwait
Financial Information:

	1988 KD'000	1989 KD'0000
Sales turnover	5,848	10,762
Profits	1,882	1,592
Authorised capital	3,000	3,000
Paid-up capital	3,000	3,000

Principal Shareholders: Thuwainy; Najjar
Date of Establishment: 1954
No of Employees: 1,180

AHMED AL AIBAN & PARTNERS
See AL AIBAN, AHMED, & PARTNERS

AHMED HAMID AL NAKIB EST
See AL NAKIB, AHMED HAMID, EST

AHMED SAYID HASHIM AL GHARABALLY
See AL GHARABALLY, AHMED SAYID HASHIM,

AHMED YOUSIF ABDULHADI ALMAILEM & BROS CO (GROUP OF COMPANIES)
See ALMAILEM, AHMED YOUSIF ABDULHADI, & BROS CO (GROUP OF COMPANIES)

AL BAHAR & BARDAWIL SPECIALITIES CO WLL

PO Box 20376 Safat, 13064 Kuwait
Tel: 4812144 (10 lines)
Telex: 30405 BNB KT
Telefax: 4836193

Chairman: Adnan A Al Bahar
Directors: Philip F Bardawil, Jassim M A Al Bahar, Issam M A A Bahar
Senior Executives: Kamal Moulayes (General Manager)

PRINCIPAL ACTIVITIES: Suppliers and stockists of building materials, concrete admixtures, jointing materials, underground waterproofing and fire protection systems; sub-contractors for roof protection systems; representatives and consultants for aviation suppliers
Branch Offices: PO Box 3880, Dubai, UAE and PO Box 936, Abu Dhabi, UAE
Associated Companies: Bardawil & Co, PO Box 110967, Beirut, Lebanon; Bahareth Organisation (Specialities Div), PO Box 3934, Jeddah, Saudi Arabia; Bahareth Organisation (Specialities Div), PO Box 593, Dammam, Saudi Arabia; Syria Equipment Co SA, PO Box 241, Damascus, Syria
Principal Bankers: Kuwait Finance House

Principal Shareholders: Philip F Bardawil, Adnan A Al Bahar, Talal I M A Al Bahar, Marzouk I M A Al Bahar
Date of Establishment: 1989
No of Employees: 65

AL YAGOUT, ABDULLA ALOMAR,

PO Box 206 Safat, 13003 Kuwait
Tel: 2432716, 2436492, 2466330/1
Cable: Alyagout
Telex: 22423 A/B Alyagout
Telefax: (965) 2433712

Chairman: Abdulla Alomar Al Yagout
Directors: Omar Abdulla Al Yagout (Managing Director)
Senior Executives: Francis B Pereira (General Manager)

PRINCIPAL ACTIVITIES: Import, wholesale and retail of readymade garments, household goods and furnishing, foodstuffs, furniture

Principal Agencies: Confecciones Elvira Gosalbez, Spain; Egeria (Towels), West Germany; Hudson Int, West Germany; Freyval Products, Switzerland, etc

Branch Offices: Supermarkets and departmental stores in shopping centre, foodstuff division, furniture showrooms

Subsidiary/Associated Companies: Tayseer Tdg Co (Sanitary ware); Mediator Tdg Co (Plastics); Alyagout Company, Los Angeles, USA; Supplying Stores Co WLL; Al-Sedrah Company (Furniture); Agents & Sole Distributors for Sony and Sanyo products; Agents for Maxell

Principal Bankers: Alahli Bank of Kuwait; Gulf Bank; National Bank of Kuwait; Commercial Bank of Kuwait; Bank of Kuwait and Middle East

Principal Shareholders: Proprietory concern
Date of Establishment: 1952
No of Employees: 34

AL ABRAQ TRADING CO WLL

PO Box 1858 Safat, 13019 Kuwait
Tel: 2419666, 2419777
Telex: 22444 Alabraq KT

PRINCIPAL ACTIVITIES: Manufacturers' representatives, distribution of electrical and electronic equipment, household appliances, office equipment

AL ADASANI, YOUSIF KHALID, ENT
Plastic Pipes & Fittings Factory

PO Box 1653 Safat, 13017 Kuwait
Tel: 4743800/1, 4714901
Cable: Youkadsan
Telex: 23807 PVC PIPE

Chairman: Yousif Khalid Al-Adasani (also General Manager)
Senior Executives: Ahmed Yousif (Production Manager), Yasin Jad (Financial Manager), Mrs Samia Amarneh (Quality Control & Follow-up Manager), Abdul Aziz Sibakhi (Administrative Manager)

PRINCIPAL ACTIVITIES: Production of PVC pipes and their fittings
Branch Offices: Sabhan Industrial Area
Principal Bankers: National Bank of Kuwait
Financial Information:

	1989 KD'000
Authorised capital	2,500

Principal Shareholders: Owned by Yousif Khalid Al-Adasani
Date of Establishment: 1974
No of Employees: 105

ALAHLI BANK OF KUWAIT KSC

PO Box 1387 Safat, 13014 Kuwait
Tel: 2400900, 2411100
Cable: Ahilbank
Telex: General: 22067, 22705, 23256, 23257, 22174; Money Market & Foreign Exchange: 44428, 44429, 44430, 44432, 46857; Securities: 44431, 44434
Telefax: General: 2424557, General Manager: 2433184, Dealing Room: 2428731

Chairman: Morad Yousuf Behbehani
Directors: Abdul Salam Abdalla Al Awadi (Deputy Chairman & Managing Director), Mohamed Saleh Yousuf Behbehani (Member), Habib Hasan Jowhar Hayat (Member), Salah Ahmad Al Sarhan (Member), Sheikh Talal Khalid Al Ahmad Al Sabah (Member), Abdul Wahab Ahmad Al Munayes (Member), Dr Abdullah Muhana Salem Ghanem (Member)
Senior Executives: Hendrik J Kwant (General Manager), Masaud Jowhar Hayat (Deputy General Manager Domestic

Credit), Seraj Saleh Al Baker (Deputy General Manager Treasury, Investment & International)

PRINCIPAL ACTIVITIES: Banking
Financial Information:

	1988/89 KD'000
Profits	4,275
Authorised capital	45,693
Paid-up capital	45,693
Total assets	1,752,733

Principal Shareholders: Kuwaiti individuals
Date of Establishment: 23 May 1967
No of Employees: 792

AL AHLIA INSURANCE CO SAK

Al Sour Street, PO Box 1602 Safat, 13017 Kuwait
Tel: 2435011, 2435028/29, 2435036
Cable: Al Ahleia
Telex: 22213 Kwt; 23585 Kwt
Telefax: (965) 2430308

Chairman: Yousef Ibrahim Al-Ghanim
Directors: Yacoub Yousef Al-Humaidi (Vice Chairman), Issa Ahmad Al-Khalaf, Hamad Abdullah Al-Saqr, Fawzi Mohammed Al-Kharafi, Isam Mohammed Al-Bahar, Osamah Mohammed Al-Nisf (Managing Director), Abdul Aziz Abdul Razzaq Al Jassar
Senior Executives: Dr Raouf H Makar (General Manager), Rajai Sweis (Deputy General Manager), Abdel Raouf Kotb (Asst General Manager Reinsurance), Nasser Al Gharibeh (Manager Production & Branches), Omar Abdul Hadi (Finance Manager), Talal Al Qattami (Marine Manager), Jamal Al Holi (Motor Manager), Issa Al Rashid (General Accident Manager)

PRINCIPAL ACTIVITIES: Insurance and reinsurance (life, fire, general accident, marine and aviation)
Branch Offices: Correspondents throughout the world
Subsidiary Companies: The Hawk Insurance Co Ltd, London
Principal Bankers: National Bank of Kuwait; Kuwait Real Estate Bank; Al-Ahli Bank of Kuwait; Gulf Bank; Bank of Kuwait and the Middle East; Commercial Bank of Kuwait; Burgan Bank, Kuwait; United Bank of Kuwait (London); National Bank of Dubai Ltd (Dubai and Abu Dhabi); National Commercial Bank (Saudi Arabia); Al-Ahli Bank Ltd, Dubai
Financial Information:

	1988 KD'000	1989 KD'000
Premium income	12,834	12,507
Profits	2,118	2,532
Authorised capital	9,200	9,660
Paid-up capital	9,200	9,660
Total assets	35,960	39,057

Principal Shareholders: Kuwaiti Shareholding Company
Date of Establishment: 1962
No of Employees: 237 Head office

AL AHLIA INVESTMENT CO KSC

PO Box 22816 Safat, 13089 Kuwait
Tel: 2445744, 2445844, 2443369, 2452581, 2452582, 410346, 410318
Cable: Investco
Telex: 22504 Ahlvest

Chairman: Badr Ahmed Al-Sharhan (also Managing Director)
Directors: Tarek Bader Al Salem (Vice Chairman), Jamil Sultan Al-Issa, Sulaiman Abdul Razzaq Al Muttawa, Bader Mohammed Al Saad, Hamed Abdul Razzaq Al-Khalid
Senior Executives: Nabeel Wafa Dajani (Consultant to the Board), Wafa H Al-Shihabi (Operations Manager), Aref Al-Junaidi (General Secretary), Ibrahim Dbies (Chief Accountant)

PRINCIPAL ACTIVITIES: Financial, industrial, real estate investment, industrial activities, etc

Subsidiary Companies: Shuaiba Paper Products Co; Kuwait
Food Processing Co; Al Assriya Printing Press & Libraries Co
Ltd; Systems Technology Arabia (Star); Al Ahlia Contracting
Company; Al Ahlia Chemicals & Concrete Additives Co
Principal Bankers: Gulf Bank KSC; Bank of Kuwait and the
Middle East; National Bank of Kuwait; Burgan Bank

Principal Shareholders: 100% Kuwaitis
Date of Establishment: 1974
No of Employees: 100

ALAJEEL, ESSA A, EST

PO Box 1676 Safat, 13017 Kuwait
Tel: 2434172, 2420284
Cable: Nabbel

Chairman: Essa A Alajeel
Directors: Majed E Alajeel (Managing Director), Malek E Alajeel
(Finance Director), Ahmad Alajeel (Marketing Director)

PRINCIPAL ACTIVITIES: General trading and commission
agencies, building contracting, import of building materials,
prefabricated houses, electrical and mechanical equipment,
medical supplies, chemicals, foodstuffs, furniture, timber and
paper
Principal Bankers: National Bank of Kuwait

Principal Shareholders: Essa Alajeel
Date of Establishment: 1959
No of Employees: 149

ALAM STEEL INDUSTRIES

PO Box 1011 Safat, 13011 Kuwait
Tel: 831522
Cable: Alamsteel
Telex: 22519 Alam Kt, 44793 Astrad Kt
Telefax: 4831868

Senior Executives: Ali Alamuddin (General Manager), Adel
Barbir (Financial Manager), Samir Abu Hamzeh (Asst General
Manager Trading Division)

PRINCIPAL ACTIVITIES: Manufacture of steel tipping bodies,
cargo bodies, water, sewage, bitumen and fuel tankers,
vacuum tanks, garbage collectors and compactors waste
disposal products, storage tanks and containers, silos, trailers
and semi-trailers, and other steel products; general trading
Principal Bankers: Commercial Bank of Kuwait; Al Ahli Bank of
Kuwait; Bank of Kuwait & the Middle East

Principal Shareholders: Sheikh Salem Sabah Al Nasser Al
Sabah; Abdul Aziz Al Fulaij; Hani Alameddine; Adel
Alameddine
Date of Establishment: 1962
No of Employees: 150

AL ARABI PLASTIC FACTORY

PO Box 231 Safat, 13003 Kuwait
Tel: 4743385, 4711866
Cable: Khudairi
Telex: 22306 Hamed
Telefax: 4738685

Chairman: Hamed Al Khudairi (General Manager)

PRINCIPAL ACTIVITIES: Manufacture of plastic products
Parent Company: Munief & Ali Abdulaziz Al Khudairi Co
Principal Bankers: Kuwait Finance House, Gulf Bank

No of Employees: 45

ALARFAJ, ABDUL AZIZ A, GENERAL
TRADING

PO Box 2410 Safat, 13025 Kuwait
Tel: 5712492/3
Cable: Alarfaj
Telex: 22914 Alarfaj
Telefax: 5753529

Chairman: Saud Abdul Aziz A Alarfaj
Directors: Miss Shaikha A Alarfaj (Managing Director)
Senior Executives: Ehsan Asslan (Manager International Trading
Div), Mazen Al Khatheeb (Manager Waste Treatment Div), U
K Nambiar (Manager Inter Cleaning Div), E K Vijayan (Finance
Manager)

PRINCIPAL ACTIVITIES: Industrial & commercial refuse
collection; industrial maintenance, water jet cleaning, plant
repairs & maintenance; waste recycling; cleaning &
maintenance of offices, factories and commercial
establishments; civil construction & building finishing;
international trading
Principal Agencies: Varta Batteries, Germany; Wallace &
Tiernan, Germany; Sitel, France; Industria, Holland; Agema
Infra Red Systems, UK; Preformed Line Products, UK; Bush
Compressors, USA
Principal Bankers: Industrial Bank of Kuwait
Financial Information:

	1989
	KD'000
Sales turnover	3,300
Profits	660
Authorised capital	2,200
Paid-up capital	2,200
Total assets	4,400

Principal Shareholders: Family owned
Date of Establishment: 1960
No of Employees: 600

AL-ASSFOOR INTERNATIONAL

PO Box 5504 Safat, 13056 Kuwait
Tel: 2446644, 2466060, 2467766
Cable: Assfoortrade
Telex: 22323 Asfoorco Kt
Telefax: (965) 2466777

Chairman: Abdullah Mahmood Al-Assfoor (also Proprietor)
Senior Executives: C J Mathews (Manager)

PRINCIPAL ACTIVITIES: Import, export, commission agents;
supply of electronic and telecommunications equipment, also
commission agency for electrical items, oilfield supplies and
oil pollution control equipment and materials, etc
Principal Agencies: La Triveneta Cavi, Italy; BPT, Italy; Fuji
Electric Co, Japan; Iwasaki Electric Co, Japan; Dialfone, Hong
Kong; Tri State Oil Tools, UK; Messina Int, UK; Dasic Int, UK;
Flanval Int, Spain; Icom Inc, Japan; Klippon Electricals, UK;
Vynckier NV, Belgium; Linder Licht, W Germany; Miyakawa
Corp, Japan; Norpol Environmental Services, Norway;
Simmons Drilling, Canada; Darron Oil Tools, UK; OMI, UK
Principal Bankers: The Gulf Bank KSC, Kuwait; Bank of Kuwait
& the Middle East, Kuwait

Date of Establishment: 1964
No of Employees: 25

AL BABTAIN, ABDUL AZIZ S,

PO Box 599 Safat, 13006 Kuwait
Tel: 2412368, 2422848, 2412730/6/8
Cable: Shurook
Telex: 22632 Shurook Kt

Chairman: Abdul Aziz S Al-Babtain
Directors: Abdul Latef S Al-Babtain (Riyadh Office), Abdul
Wahab S Al-Babtain (Al Khobar Office), Abdul Karim S Al-
Babtain (Managing Director)

PRINCIPAL ACTIVITIES: General trading company; cigarettes,
lighters, perfumes, general merchandise, government and oil
companies tenders, refrigerators, colour TVs, washing
machines, cleaners, radios, videos, tape recorders, household
appliances; banking & real estate investment overseas.
Manufacturing plastic drums in sizes
Principal Agencies: Philip Morris International, New York;
Eastern Co, Cairo; Kortnig Radio Werke GmbH, West

Germany; Sencor, Japan; Indesit, Italy; Unisef, Singapore; Suly, Taiwan
Subsidiary Companies: Abdul Lateef Al Babtain, PO Box 2711, Riyadh PO Box 494, Alkhobar, Saudi Arabia
Principal Bankers: National Bank of Kuwait SAK; Commercial Bank of Kuwait SAK; Bank of Bahrain & Kuwait

Principal Shareholders: Private
Date of Establishment: 1956
No of Employees: 7,000

AL-BABTAIN, ABDULMOHSEN ABDULAZIZ, CO

PO Box 2198 Safat, 13022 Kuwait
Tel: 4719581, 2448230
Telex: 22272 Kt Babtain

PRINCIPAL ACTIVITIES: General trading, import and distribution of cars, accessories and spare parts, garage equipment
Principal Agencies: Datsun Cars; GS Batteries; NGK Plugs; National Tyres; AGIP Oil
Parent Company: Part of the Al Babtain Group of Companies

AL BABTAIN GROUP OF COMPANIES

PO Box 766 Safat, 13008 Kuwait
Tel: 2443583, 2443598, 2443592
Cable: Babtain Kuwait
Telex: 22272 Babtain Kt; 22641 Asko Kt; 23055 Babtnco Kt

PRINCIPAL ACTIVITIES: General trading and contracting, distribution of cars, heavy duty vehicles and construction equipment, manufacture of construction plant, plastic products, office furniture, shipping agency, manufacturers representation
Principal Agencies: Nissan; Datsun; International Harvester; Rexnord Concrete Equipment, USA; Tadano Cranes, Japan; Thomas Built Buses Co, USA; Heil Co, USA; Plan Transportfahrzeuge, West Germany, etc
Branch Offices: Office in Kuwait: Souk Al Kabir Bldg, Fahed Al Salem Street
Subsidiary/Associated Companies: Abdulmahsin Abdulaziz Al Babtain Co; Al Babtain Trading & Contracting Co; Al Babtain Body Manufacturing Co; Al Ahlia Plastic Co; Al Nawal Trading & Contracting Co; Al Babtain Shipping Co; Al Babtain Furniture Co; Al Jeel Trading Co; Datsun Ltd Ireland; United Gulf Construction Co; Interasco

AL BABTAIN SHIPPING CO

PO Box 2198 Safat, 13022 Kuwait
Tel: 2428821, 2428947
Cable: Asko
Telex: 22641 Asko Kt

PRINCIPAL ACTIVITIES: Shipping agency, freight forwarding and customs agency
Parent Company: Part of the Al Babtain Group of Companies

AL BABTAIN TRADING & CONTRACTING CO

PO Box 766 Safat, 13008 Kuwait
Tel: 4745233, 4745949
Cable: Babtain
Telex: 30166

Chairman: Barrak A Al-Babtain
Directors: Abdul-Aziz A Al-Babtain, Khalid A Al-Babtain, Saleh A Al-Babtain
Senior Executives: Saad I Baddar (General Manager)

PRINCIPAL ACTIVITIES: Distribution of cars and commercial vehicles, trucks and fork-lifts; construction equipment, cranes, mixers, rollers
Principal Agencies: International Harvestor, USA; Rexnord, USA; Conveyencer Climax, UK; Tadano Crane Co, Japan; Potain Tower Cranes, France; Arrow Dumpers, UK; ATO/Huber, Smith & Scott Constn. equipment, USA; The Heil Co, USA; J D Marshal International, USA; G S Batteries, Japan; NGK Plugs, Japan; Dunlop Tyres, UK; Citroen, France

Parent Company: Part of the Al Babtain Group of Companies
Principal Bankers: Commercial Bank of Kuwait; National Bank of Kuwait; First National Bank of Wisconsin, USA

Date of Establishment: 1965
No of Employees: 177

AL BAHAR, JASSIM M, & PARTNERS WLL

PO Box 1990 Safat, 13020 Safat, Kuwait
Tel: 4717010, 4717040
Cable: Hexa Kuwait
Telex: 31065 JBPHEXA KT
Telefax: 4745478

Chairman: Jassim M Al-Bahar
Directors: Issam M Al-Bahar
Senior Executives: Ibrahim A Subhi (General Manager)

PRINCIPAL ACTIVITIES: Trading and contracting, manufacturers of shampoo/detergent, adhesives, blending of automobile paints for all cars under "Dupont" trade name, suppliers of raw materials for paint, plastic and sponge industries; suppliers of industrial chemicals, chemicals for oil and fertilizers; building chemicals and materials
Principal Agencies: Du Pont de Nemours (Belgium) SA/USA: Unilever Export Ltd; Plus Products Ltd; Fibreglass Ltd; Don Construction Chemicals, UK; A Wilson Ltd; BB Allen Ltd; Urachem International; General Electric Silicone, USA; Ipisystem, SPA; Chemetall, Germany
Principal Bankers: Bank of Kuwait & the Middle East; National Bank of Kuwait SAK; Commercial Bank of Kuwait SAK; Gulf Bank KSC
Financial Information:

	1988/89 KD'000
Sales turnover	850
Authorised capital	138
Paid-up capital	138
Total assets	800

Principal Shareholders: Directors as described above
Date of Establishment: 1972
No of Employees: 42

AL-BAHAR, MOHAMED ABDULRAHMAN,

PO Box 148 Safat, 13002 Kuwait
Tel: 810855, 2433881 (6 lines)
Cable: Moatasim
Telex: 22302 Moatasim Kt, 22068 Moayasim Kt

Chairman: Mohamed Abdulrahman Al Bahar
Senior Executives: Jassim M Al Bahar (President), Issam M Al Bahar (Executive Vice President & Group General Manager), Mohamed Numan (Deputy Group General Manager), Anton Hayek (General Parts & Service Manager), Walid Shtayyeh (Central Personnel Manager)

PRINCIPAL ACTIVITIES: Import and distribution of heavy machinery, electrical domestic appliances, consumer products; foodstuffs; office equipment and computers; and furniture; building products; shipping and general trading and contracting
Principal Agencies: General Electric Co, USA; Fay Int Ltd, UK; Lipton Ltd, UK; Burroughs Corp, USA; Koehring Overseas Corp; Caterpillar Overseas; British Ropes; 3M Co, USA; Raygo Int Inc, USA; Barber Greene Ltd, UK & USA; SKF, Sweden; etc
Branch Offices: Abu Dhabi: PO Box 441, Tel 554200, Telex 22988 BAHAR EM; Al-Ain: PO Box 15354, Tel 825060, Telex 33556 BAHAR EM; Bahrain: PO Box 5357, Manama, Tel 243466, Telex 8299 BAHAR BN; Dubai: PO Box 1170, Deira, Tel 660255, Telex 45445 BAHAR EM; Kuwait: PO Box 148, Safat, Tel 810855, Telex 22302 MOATASIM KT; Qatar: PO Box 2171, Doha, Tel 810222, Telex 4255 BAHAR DH; Sharjah: PO Box 6038, Tel 352271, Telex 68680 BAHAR EM; Oasis Trading & Equipment Co: Muscat: PO Box 7002,

Mutrah, Tel 592549, Telex 5074 Moatasim ON; Salalah: PO Box 19010 Tel 460837, Telex: 7700 MOATASIM ON
Parent Company: Mohamed Abdulrahman Al-Bahar
Associated Companies: Mohamed Abdulrahman Al-Bahar & Partners, PO Box 609 Safat, 13007 Kuwait; Oasis Trading Co Ltd, PO Box 409 Safat, 13005 Kuwait; Al-Bahar Travel Agency, PO Box 381 Safat, 13004 Kuwait; Oasis Advertising Agency, PO Box 148 Safat, 13002 Kuwait; Oasis Trading & Equipment Co, Muscat PO 7002 Mutrah
Principal Bankers: National Bank of Kuwait SAK, Kuwait; Bank of Kuwait and the Middle East KSC, Kuwait; Alahli Bank of Kuwait KSC, Kuwait; Commercial Bank of Kuwait SAK, Gulf Bank of Kuwait KSC, Kuwait

No of Employees: 1,470

AL BAIDAA TRADING & CONTRACTING CO

PO Box 24890 Safat, 13109 Kuwait
Tel: 4716274, 4716248, 2446543
Cable: Al-Qumsieh
Telex: 23736 KT QUMSIEH
Telefax: 4762181, 2409680

Managing Partner: Makram Jamil Qumsieh
Senior Executives: Said Jumah Obeid (Chief Engineer), Firas Ghunaim (Technical Manager), Mohammed Barghouthi (Finance Manager), Khalid Musleh (Administrative Manager), Samir Banayot (Electronic Systems Division Manager), Walid Qumsieh (Office Manager), Kamal Yunis (Medical Division Manager), Elias Qumsieh (Ready Made Clothes Division Manager), Ziad Abu Ziadah (Readymix Concrete Division Manager)

PRINCIPAL ACTIVITIES: Building construction contractors (industrial, public, commercial and housing); manufacturers of ready made garments; design and installation of electronic systems (computers, telecommunication, optical readers); suppliers of laboratory/scientific and medical equipment and consumables; suppliers of health/beauty care products; general trading; production of readymix concrete
Principal Agencies: USA: Amtec Inc, Diamedix, Eppendorf Inc, 5-Prime 3-Prime, Genetic Design, Genex, Gull Laboratories Inc, Medex Products, Micron Separations Inc, New England Biolabs, Polysciences Inc, SA Scientific, Scantron, Syntellect, Vector Laboratories, UK: Apollo Enterprises, Immunodiagnostic Systems, Lab M Ltd, Savan & Co, Cambridge Bioscience, Winlab Ltd, W Germany: Berthold Hermle, Eppendorf Geratebau, Heinrich AD Berkemann, GFL, Slee Technik, Witeg, Switzerland: Datascan, Hamilton Bonaduz, Ebnat Swiss Brush, France: Diagnostica Stago, Belgium: Janssen Life Sciences, Austria: EDE Electronic, Czecholovakia: Pragoexport, Italy: Bio Otica
Subsidiary Companies: International Group for Equipment & Contracting WLL, PO Box 25790 Safat, Kuwait
Principal Bankers: Burgan Bank of Kuwait; The Gulf Bank; The Commercial Bank of Kuwait; National Bank of Kuwait
Financial Information:

	1988/89 KD'000
Sales turnover	15,000
Profits	5%
Authorised capital	1,000
Paid-up capital	1,000
Total assets	8,000

Principal Shareholders: Saleh Abdul Rahman Al Ghunaim, Ibrahim Yousuf Al Ragum, Makram Jamil Qumsieh
Date of Establishment: 1976
No of Employees: 500 approx

AL BELAD CONTRACTING BUILDING MATERIALS TRADING CO

PO Box 5144 Safat, 13052 Kuwait
Tel: 2464560
Cable: BELAD HOME
Telex: 46187 BELADGE

Chairman: Fahd Mohamd Said
Directors: Eng Gamal Ali Said

PRINCIPAL ACTIVITIES: Civil contracting, building materials trading
Subsidiary Companies: Al Metrass Contracting Co
Principal Bankers: Al Ahli Bank of Kuwait

Date of Establishment: 1979
No of Employees: 35

ALBISHER, ABDUL RAHMAN, & ZAID ALKAZEMI CO

PO Box 47 Safat, 13001 Kuwait
Tel: 2410120/5
Cable: Albisher Kuwait
Telex: 22026 Albisher Kuwait
Telefax: 2420676

Chairmen: Abdul Rahman Albisher (Owner)
Directors: Dr Nouri Zaid Alkazemi, Bisher A R Albisher, Usamah Z Alkazemi, Mohammed A R Albisher
Senior Executives: Udo W Danzer (General Manager), Sakher Al Khatib (Marketing Manager), George Nunu (Accounts Manager)

PRINCIPAL ACTIVITIES: General distribution of Daimler-Benz AG for Kuwait; Mercedes-Benz passenger cars, cross-country vehicles, trucks, buses, Unimogs, MB tracs and industrial engines; general distribution of Motoren-Und-Turbinen Friedrichshafen GmbH for Kuwait
Principal Agencies: Rosenbauer; Guardian Royal Exchange Assurance; Imperial Chemical Industries (ICI); Fuchs Oil
Branch Offices: Service Station & Spare Parts (Shuwaikh), Tel 810277, Telex 23247, Fax 841763
Subsidiary Companies: Etemadco Exchange Co Ltd; Kuwait Plastic Mfg Co; Albisher & Alkazemi Travels; Watches & Gifts Division; Pharmaceutical & Trading Division
Principal Bankers: National Bank of Kuwait; Bank of Kuwait and the Middle East; Alahli Bank; Gulf Bank; Commercial Bank of Kuwait; Burgan Bank
Financial Information:

	KD'000
Authorised capital	10,000
Paid-up capital	10,000

Date of Establishment: 1935
No of Employees: 700

AL BUNYAN ENGINEERING & CONTRACTING CO

PO Box 1899 Safat, 13019 Kuwait
Tel: 4842566, 4842337
Telex: 46962 Bunyan KT

Chairman: Khalid A Al Sagar
Directors: Mishari A R Al Bahar, Hamad A Al Sagar, Nabil N Atiyeh, Khaldoun M Atiyah
Senior Executives: Nabil N Atiyeh (Managing Director), Khaldoun M Atiyah (Construction Manager)

PRINCIPAL ACTIVITIES: Construction, general contractors, medical equipment supply and services
Principal Agencies: CGR Compagnia General Di Radiloia, Italy; CGR Mev Thomson Group, France; Sopha Medical SNI, France; Astralux, Austria; Cawo Photo Chemische Fabrik, W Germany; Roche Laboratory Equipment, Switzerland
Branch Offices: Al Bunyan Medical Supplies & Services, PO Box 1899 Safat, 13019 Kuwait, Tel 5627091, 5635741, Telex 44414 Bunyan
Principal Bankers: Bank of Kuwait & the Middle East, Kuwait

Principal Shareholders: Directors as described
Date of Establishment: 1975
No of Employees: 100

AL DABBOOS, NAIF H, & SONS

PO BOx 464 Safat, Shuwaikh Industrial Area, 13005 Kuwait
Tel: 815899
Cable: Dabboosine
Telex: 22227 Area KT

PRINCIPAL ACTIVITIES: Building, civil and general contracting

AL DAR CONSULTING CO (ADCO)

PO Box 4729 Safat, 13048 Kuwait
Tel: 2449934, 2440925
Cable: Dafecon
Telex: 30849 Tagco KT
Telefax: 2440111

President: Dr Nabil S Faour
Senior Executives: Eng Raji Al Kaliouby (Partner in Charge Kuwait), Dr Ali Anani (Partner in Charge Sana'a/Yemen), Dr Mohammed S Kaddo (Partner in Charge Riyadh/Saudi Arabia), Ibrahim Al Afghani (Partner in Charge Alkhobar/Saudi Arabia)

PRINCIPAL ACTIVITIES: Project study and preparation; systems and organisation; financial analysis; technical and engineering studies; personnel; business consultancy services; special services
Principal Agencies: Professional cooperation agreements with: DGB Systems Integrators Inc, Montreal, Canada; British Teleconsult, Southall, UK; American Management Systems, Arlington, USA; STERIA, Paris, France
Branch Offices: Jordan (Amman, Irbid), Saudi Arabia (Riyadh, Jeddah, Alkhobar, Jubail, Al Ahsa), Qatar, Bahrain, Lebanon, UAE (Abu Dhabi, Dubai, Sharjah, Ajman, Ras Al Khaimah), Oman (Muscat, Salalah), Egypt (Cairo), Yemen (Sana'a, Hodeidah, Taiz, Aden)
Parent Company: Talal Abu Ghazaleh International
Associated Companies: Saudi Arab Projects Co (SAPCO), Abu Ghazaleh & Co Consulting (AGCOC)
Principal Bankers: Commercial Bank of Kuwait; National Bank of Kuwait

Principal Shareholders: Abdullah Rakiyam Al Ajmi, Bassam Sulaiman Al Otaibi, Dr Nabil S Faour
Date of Establishment: 1982
No of Employees: 57

AL-DUAIJ, Y Y, TRADING & CONTRACTING

PO Box 2364 Safat, 13024 Kuwait
Tel: 2436075, 2418540, 2418545
Cable: SDREK
Telex: 2788 Sdrek KT

Chairman: Yacoub Y Al-Duaij
Directors: Ibrahim Sulaiman Al-Duaij
Senior Executives: Abdulla Yousef Al-Duaij (Manager)

PRINCIPAL ACTIVITIES: Construction
Principal Agencies: Homa, Avon, Raclet
Subsidiary Companies: Touristic Towers Co. WLL; Garden & Leisure Centre Co WLL; Nazaka Cleaning; Kuwait Military Bureau
Principal Bankers: Gulf Bank, Kuwait

Date of Establishment: 1965
No of Employees: 40

AL ESSA, ABDUL AZIZ YOUSUF, & CO WLL

PO Box 3562 Safat, 13036 Kuwait
Tel: 4833051, 4832229, 4833064, 4833075
Cable: Labnhosp
Telex: 23576 SAUIDKT
Telefax: (965) 4840629

Chairman: Abdul Aziz Yousuf Al Essa
Directors: K T Mathew (Managing Director), John Mathew
Senior Executives: Dr Issa M Alzard (Sales Manager Lab Supplies Division), George Koshy (Sales Manager Hospital Supplies Division), K K Cherian (Sales Manager Welding Equipment Division), Nasser Sefien, G M Nair (Technical Manager)

PRINCIPAL ACTIVITIES: Supplies of chemical products, welding equipment and generators, hospital and medical supplies, laboratory equipment, piped medical gases system pharmaceutical products
Principal Agencies: Duckhams, Eschmann, Ohmeda, Imed, Varian, Kendall, Howmedica
Associated Companies: Arab Equipment Group Co
Principal Bankers: Gulf Bank, Kuwait
Financial Information:

	1989 US$'000
Sales turnover	10,000

Date of Establishment: 1978
No of Employees: 200

AL ESSA, ABDULHAMID YOUSUF,

PO Box 1350 Safat, 13019 Kuwait
Tel: 2423166
Cable: Yousco
Telex: 22558 Imad

Chairman: Abdul Hamid Yousuf Al Essa

PRINCIPAL ACTIVITIES: Civil and building contractors, airconditioning, sanitaryware, building materials, hardware, carpentry workshop, doors, electric fittings and lighting
Principal Agencies: Trane Airconditioning
Principal Bankers: National Bank of Kuwait; Gulf Bank Kuwait

Date of Establishment: 1956

AL ESSA, TAREQ, TRADING & CONTRACTING CO WLL

PO Box 25904 Safat, 13120 Kuwait
Tel: 2413973, 2425769, 2468300, 2426167
Cable: SAMI SULTAN
Telex: 30256 TALSUTA KT

Directors: Tareq Sami Sultan Al-Essa (General Manager)
Senior Executives: Kazi Mohammed Shareef (Construction Manager - Steel Department), Moosa Essa Ameera (Project Manager - Civil Const)

PRINCIPAL ACTIVITIES: Civil construction (residential complexes, villas etc), erection of steel structures (pre-engineered), also, fabrication works related to steel structures, erection of steel tanks, including maintenance of existing steel structures (additions/alterations)
Subsidiary Companies: Sami Sultan & Sons Co
Principal Bankers: Kuwait Finance House

Date of Establishment: 1979
No of Employees: 140

AL FAHED TRADING & CONTRACTING CO WLL

PO Box 5757 Safat, 13058 Kuwait
Tel: 2421046/47/48
Cable: Fahedco Kuwait
Telex: 22183 Fahedco Kt

Chairman: Saleh Khaleel Ibrahim Al Tamimi (General Manager)

PRINCIPAL ACTIVITIES: Trading and contracting in air-conditioning equipment; heavy machinery and power equipment
Principal Agencies: Collins Machinery; USA; Elgen Manufacturing Corpn, USA; Filtrine Corpn, USA; International Marketing Group, USA; Powers Regulators, USA
Branch Offices: PO Box 2819, Dubai, and PO Box 824, Abu Dhabi
Principal Bankers: Alahli Bank of Kuwait; Commercial Bank of Kuwait; International Bank of Kuwait

KUWAIT

ALFARSI, SHAIKHAN AHMAD,

PO Box 121 Safat, 13002 Kuwait
Tel: 471466, 471468
Cable: Shaikhan Kuwait
Telex: 46915 Shaikhan, 23006 Shaikan KT

Chairman: Shaikhan Ahmad Alfarsi
Senior Executives: W C Spikins (Admin Manager)

PRINCIPAL ACTIVITIES: Supply of valves, flanges, fittings, pipelines and carpets; engineering and fabrication works; repair and maintenance contractors (DRILCO licensed workshop for recutting rotary shouldered connections for drill string equipment)
Principal Agencies: DRILCO Division of Smith International, USA
Branch Offices: Workshop and Warehouse: PO Box 9132, East Ahmadi, Kuwait, Tel 3981026, 3980646
Principal Bankers: Bank of Kuwait and the Middle East

Principal Shareholders: Private Establishment
Date of Establishment: 1947

AL-FAYHA REAL ESTATE ENTERPRISE CO SAK

PO Box 42235 Shuwaikh, 70653 Kuwait
Tel: 818995, 831713, 831736
Cable: ORASH
Telex: 23489 KT Orash

Directors: Osama Kabbara (General Manager)

PRINCIPAL ACTIVITIES: Real estate, building construction, etc

AL GHANIM & AL QUTUB SHIPPING AGENCIES CO WLL

PO Box 25267 Safat, 13113 Kuwait
Tel: 4747815/8, 4747819, 4737000
Cable: Maltrans Kt
Telex: 23057, 23447, 23448, 23836
Telefax: 4749742

Chairman: Captain Faisal Al Ghanim
Directors: Dawood Y Al Qutub (Managing Director)
Senior Executives: R Clarke (General Manager), Falah A Falah (Deputy General Manager), Moiz Al Imam (Projects Director), Abdel Hak Sami Abdel Hak (Marketing Director), A R Humaid (Shipping Director), I Nakhalah (Financial & Admin Director)

PRINCIPAL ACTIVITIES: Shipping agencies; cargo transportation, international freight promoters by land, sea and air; custom's house brokers, removal experts
Principal Agencies: Wallenius Lines; Hyundai Merchant Marine; Messina Line
Branch Offices: 21 Branches and Associates in Abu Dhabi; Dubai; Egypt; Greece; Japan; Jordan; Yemen; Saudi Arabia (Jeddah, Riyadh, Damman), UK; Lebanon; Roumania
Principal Bankers: National Bank of Kuwait
Financial Information:

	US$'000
Sales turnover	300,000
Paid-up capital	10,000

Principal Shareholders: Capt Faisal Al Ghanim, D Y Al Qutub
Date of Establishment: March 1978
No of Employees: 135

ALGHANIM, ALI & FOUAD, EST

PO Box 1083 Safat, 13011 Kuwait
Tel: 2439264/7
Cable: Marata
Telex: 22142 Kt

Directors: Ali M T Alghanim, Fouad M T Alghanim
Senior Executives: Rifat Hanano (General Manager Mechanical), Sami Farhan (Commercial Manager), Eisa A Khalaf (General Manager Administration)

PRINCIPAL ACTIVITIES: Manufacturers' representatives; civil, mechanical and electrical contractors; import and distribution of electrical equipment, building materials, heavy machinery and earth-moving equipment; transportation
Principal Agencies: AEG-Telefunken, Germany; Klein, Schanzlin & Becker AG, Germany; Deutsche Babcock AB, Germany; Passavant Werke, Germany; Salzgitter Stahl, Germany; Lurgi, Germany; Mogurt, Hungary; Plessey, UK; Johnsons Machinery, UK; Stoner Communications, USA; Storno A/S, Denmark; Ring Master A/S, Norway; Northern Offshore, Germany; Poclain, France; Rockwell, USA; Fruin Colnon, USA; Renoil, Belgium; Beckman Instrumentation, Switzerland; Doka, Austria
Branch Offices: Steel Factory & Carpentry; Mechanical Engineering Div; Electrical Engineering Div; Civil Engineering Div; Transportation (internal & International); General Trading; Electronic Engineering; Medical Equipment & Chemicals Div; Investment Dept. (National & International); Marine Department (Shipowners and Charterers)
Subsidiary/Associated Companies: Ali Alghanim Est; Fouad M T Alghanim; Riham Trading & Contracting Co; Kuwait Refinery Engineering & Maintenance Co; Kuwait Paper Industries Co; Kuwait Aluminium Industries; Burgan Trading & Contracting Co; Kuwait Press House; Gulf Marine & Transport Co; Arab Real Estate Group; Kuwait Projects Co; Kuwait Sanitary Industries Co; Middle East International Contracting Co
Principal Bankers: Commercial Bank of Kuwait; Kuwait Real Estate Bank; Ali Ahli Bank of Kuwait; Bank of Kuwait and the Middle East

Principal Shareholders: Directors as described
Date of Establishment: 1960

ALGHANIM INDUSTRIES CORPORATE DEVELOPMENT

PO Box 24172 Safat, 13102 Kuwait
Tel: 842988, 843988
Cable: GHANIMINDS
Telex: 22069 YAAS Kt

PRINCIPAL ACTIVITIES: Commercial representations, manufacturing, shipping, wholesale and retail, construction

ALGHANIM, K & M, CO

PO Box 20755 Safat, 13068 Kuwait
Tel: 616156, 639281, 632299
Cable: Deconim
Telex: 23344 Sohab

Directors: Mahmoud Alghanim (Managing Director)
Senior Executives: Abdel Kader Al Azm (General Manager)

PRINCIPAL ACTIVITIES: Design and interior decoration, retail of domestic and office furniture, furnishing tenderers, contracts
Principal Agencies: Saporiti Italia; B & B; Molteni; Unifor; Jean Charles; J M Cardel; Jacques Charpentier; Mico Y Esteles
Principal Bankers: Commercial Bank of Kuwait; Bank of Kuwait and the Middle East; Al Ahli Bank of Kuwait; Gulf Bank

Principal Shareholders: Kutayba Alghanim; Mahmoud M Alghanim
Date of Establishment: 1970
No of Employees: 40

ALGHANIM, YUSUF AHMAD, & SONS WLL

PO Box 223 Safat, 13003 Kuwait
Tel: 4842988, 4843988
Cable: Autoarabi
Telex: 44900 GANIM, 22069 YAAS - Kt
Telefax: 4847244, 4842614

Chairman: Kutayba Yusuf Alghanim
Directors: Bassam Yusuf Alghanim (President)

PRINCIPAL ACTIVITIES: Contracting, electronics and electrical engineering, general trading, import and distribution of cars and spare parts, domestic electrical appliances, industrial lubricants, communications equipment, mechanical and industrial equipment; also shipping and forwarding, car hire and travel agents; toys retailing division, cameras, insulation materials

Principal Agencies: Opel, Pontiac, Chevrolet, Cadillac, Bedford, Philips, Frigidaire, Yale & Towne, BP, Terex, Foster, British Airways, Gulf Air, Air India, Hitachi, Galion, Toys'r'Us, Minolta

Branch Offices: Representations in New York; London; Beirut; Cairo

Subsidiary/Associated Companies: Alghanim Travel Agencies; Alghanim Express Packing; Alghanim Rent-a-car; Impact & Echo advertising; Alghanim Insurance; Radiator Repair Co WLL; Gulf Trading & Refrigeration Co; Alghanim Barber Shipping; Kirby Building Systems; Kuwait Insulation Materials Manufacturing Co KIMMCO

Principal Bankers: All Kuwaiti Banks; Chase Manhattan Bank; Citibank; ABN; Lloyds Bank; Algemene Bank; Gulf Intl Bank; Credit Suisse and All Saudi Bank

No of Employees: 3,035

ALGHANIM, YUSUF IBRAHIM, & CO

PO Box 435 Safat, 13005 Kuwait
Tel: 4832600
Cable: Clyde Kuwait
Telex: 23607 Yiaco Kt
Telefax: 4844954

Chairman: Abdullah Y Alghanim

Directors: Yusuf Ibrahim Alghanim, Jassim Al Qatami, Diraar Y Alghanim

Senior Executives: Ibrahim Y Alghanim (General Manager), Dr Mohamed Afifi (Commercial Manager)

PRINCIPAL ACTIVITIES: Import and distribution of pharmaceuticals, hospital equipment and supplies, dental materials and equipment, scientific equipment and supplies

Principal Agencies: Hoechst, Bayer, Schering, Smith Kline, Beecham, Squibb, Rorer International, Dupont, Kavo, Bego, Detrey/Dentsply

Principal Bankers: National Bank of Kuwait

Financial Information:

	1988/89 US$'000
Sales turnover	35,000
Authorised capital	3,500
Paid-up capital	3,500

Principal Shareholders: Yusuf Ibrahim Alghanim, Jassim Al Qatami, Diraar Y Alghanim
Date of Establishment: 1953
No of Employees: 160

AL GHARABALLY, ABDULLA SAYID HASHIM, CO

PO Box 426 Safat, 13005 Kuwait
Tel: 4814744, 4832005
Cable: Alnajat
Telex: 22186 Gbly Kt, 44801 Gbly Kt
Telefax: 4830739

Chairman: Mezher A Al Gharabally
Directors: Dr K T B Menon (Managing Director)
Senior Executives: P P Nair (General Manager)

PRINCIPAL ACTIVITIES: Engineering contractors, manufacturers' representatives, commission agents, plant hire and motor rewinding

Principal Agencies: Ishikawajima-Harima Heavy Industries Co Ltd, Japan; Taisei Corporation, Japan; Curtiss-Wright Corporation, USA; Fibreglass Pilkington, India; Mitsubishi Heavy Industries, Japan; Hindustan Machine Tools, India; Kirloskar Electric Co, India; Pirelli, Italy

Subsidiary Companies: Gharabally International Company

Principal Bankers: National Bank of Kuwait; Commercial Bank of Kuwait

No of Employees: 150

AL GHARABALLY, AHMED SAYID HASHIM,

PO Box 98 and 136, Ali Salem St, Kuwait
Tel: 2438150 (8 lines)
Cable: Gharabally, Kuwait
Telex: GARBALY 22369 KT

Chairman: Ahmed Sayid Hashim Al-Gharabally
Directors: Hashim Al-Gharabally, Zaid Al-Gharabally
Senior Executives: George Oommen, Sami Ramadan, Samuel Mathen

PRINCIPAL ACTIVITIES: General merchants, manufacturers' representatives, engineering contractors, insurance agents, importers and distributors of building materials, motor cars, spare parts, electrical stockists and distributors

Principal Agencies: Royal Insurance Co, Fiat, Nestle World Trade Corp, Fiat Autos, Royal Insurance co, Bata Shoes

Branch Offices: Kuwait; United Arab Emirates; Bahrain

Subsidiary Companies: Gulf Electrical Eng Co WLL; Gharabally Ltd, PO Box 136, Kuwait (electrical, engineering and contracting); and also branches in Dubai (PO Box 1004); Abu Dhabi (PO Box 646); Bahrain (PO Box 191)

Principal Bankers: Bank of Kuwait & The Middle East; National Bank of Kuwait

Principal Shareholders: Owned by the family
Date of Establishment: 1910
No of Employees: 450

AL GHARABALLY, BADER AL SAYID HASHIM,

PO Box 158 Safat, 13002 Kuwait
Tel: 2432913, 2437636, 2425632
Cable: Anteopolis
Telex: 22738 BASHAG KT
Telefax: 2425631

Proprietor: Bader Al Gharabally
Directors: Basil B Al Gharabally (Managing Director)
Senior Executives: N G Abraham (Commercial Manager)

PRINCIPAL ACTIVITIES: Manufacturers' representatives, commission agents, general merchants and contractors (tenderers and suppliers to government of Kuwait and all oil companies operating in Kuwait), importer/retailers footwear, leather goods, garments etc

Principal Bankers: Gulf Bank KSC

Principal Shareholders: Bader Al Gharabally
Date of Establishment: 1952
No of Employees: 50

AL GHAZAL CONSTRUCTION & DEVELOPMENT CO KSCC

PO Box 24260 Safat, 13103 Kuwait
Tel: 2439410-9
Telex: 30631 GAZELLE KT

Chairman: Salah Mohammed Amin Al Rayes
Directors: Najeeb Al-Humaidhi (Vice-Chairman), Ahmed Al-Sabti (Member), Adnan Al-Rayes (Member), Rashed Al-Khaldi (Member)
Senior Executives: F E Barth (General Manager), R R Hufford (Manager-Business Development), R Lee (Manager-Equipment Division)

PRINCIPAL ACTIVITIES: Full construction, construction management, equipment programs, industrial maintenance, oil refineries, gas processing, chemicals/fertilizers, power generation, supporting facilities

Branch Offices: Al Ghazal Construction & Development Co, PO Box 822, Manama, Bahrain

Associated Companies: Engineering Equipment, Inc. Manila, Philippines; affiliated offices in London, Paris, Geneva, New York, Marbella, Houston, Tokyo

Principal Bankers: Commercial Bank of Kuwait; Alahli Bank of Kuwait; The Gulf Bank; Burgan Bank; National Bank of Kuwait

Financial Information:

	KD'000
Authorised capital	30,000
Paid-up capital	30,000

Principal Shareholders: Over 3000 Kuwait Shareholders
Date of Establishment: 1983
No of Employees: 383

ALHABIB METAL FURNITURE FACTORY WLL

PO Box 24001 Safat, 13101 Kuwait
Tel: 4675335, 4675336
Cable: ALHABIB KUWAIT
Telex: ALHABIB 23086 KT
Telefax: 4675350

Owners: Abdul Samad Habib, Abdul Aziz Habib
Senior Executives: Amin Sultan Amin (Factory Manager)

PRINCIPAL ACTIVITIES: Manufacture of metal furniture, desks, cabinets, tables, chairs, cupboards, angles and shelves, lockers, files etc

Principal Bankers: Bank of Kuwait & the Middle East
Financial Information:

	1988/89 KD'000
Sales turnover	800
Authorised capital	1,250
Paid-up capital	1,250

Date of Establishment: 1976
No of Employees: 131

ALHADI ALUMINIUM

Mohd H A AL-Awadi

PO Box 5817 Safat, 13059 Kuwait
Tel: 713056, 713061
Cable: Igaby
Telex: 30170 Hadi Kt
Telefax: (965) 4735810

Chairman: Abdulsalam A Al-Awadi
Senior Executives: Ziad Omar Sheibani (General Manager), Nabil Ismail (Production Engineer)

PRINCIPAL ACTIVITIES: Manufacture of aluminium doors and windows; and various building materials

Principal Bankers: National Bank of Kuwait; Bank of Kuwait & the Middle East; Commercial Bank of Kuwait; Burgan Bank; Alahli Bank of Kuwait

Date of Establishment: 1974
No of Employees: 120

ALHAJERY COMMERCIAL BUREAU

PO Box 4771 Safat, 13048 Kuwait
Tel: 2425926/7
Cable: Acob Kuwait
Telex: 22640 Hajery Kt
Telefax: 2401156

Chairman: Yacoub Ibrahim Alhajery (Owner)
Senior Executives: K P Peethambaran (Office Manager)

PRINCIPAL ACTIVITIES: Supply of scientific and medical equipment; educational equipment; electrical and electronic appliances and scientific instruments

Principal Agencies: Nuclear Data, USA; Dosimeter, USA; Petrotest, W Germany; Hellige, USA; Medrad, USA; Oriel Corp, USA; Andersen Samplers, USA; Jouan France; Toni Technik, West Germany

Branch Offices: PO Box 15749, Riyadh, Saudi Arabia

Associated Companies: Alshaea Trading Est, PO Box 846, Riyadh, Saudi Arabia; Mohamed Alhajeri & Sons Ltd, PO Box 152, Safat, Kuwait

Principal Bankers: Bank of Kuwait and the Middle East

Date of Establishment: 1963

AL HAMRA GROUP OF COMPANIES

Hameng Holdings Ltd

PO Box 2048 Safat, 13021 Kuwait
Tel: 833744 (10 lines)
Cable: Al Hamra
Telex: 22355 Hamra; 23926

Partners: Yacoub Y Al Hamad (Chairman), Hanna N Ayoub (President), Zakhem International SA
Senior Executives: E Shalhoub (Managing Director, Kuwait), M Shalhoub (General Manager, Sharjah), H Shalhoub (General Manager, Riyadh), E Talbot (General Manager, London), M Shalhoub (General Manager, Beirut), A Nassif (General Manager, Amman), E Shalhoub (Legal Advisor Al Hamra Group)

PRINCIPAL ACTIVITIES: Import, distribution and supply of building materials including roofing, waterproofing, insulation, electrical and mechanical fire fighting, plumbing equipment, also civil, electrical, mechanical engineering contractors

Principal Agencies: Swimquip, USA; Vandex, Denmark; Ruberoid, UK; Mundo Rubber, Italy; Grace, Italy; Marius Dufour, France; Noxcrete Chemicals, USA; Rehau GmbH; Mapei, Italy; Siplast, France; Oy Nokia, Finland; Cementone, UK; Washperle, France; PVI, USA; Froling, Germany; Hoff, Denmark; Woltra, Denmark; Carlise, USA; Cape Contracts, UK; Boston, Italy

Associated Companies: Al Hamra Beirut, PO Box 116040 Beirut, Lebanon; Al Hamra Kuwait, PO Box 2048 Safat, Kuwait; Al Hamra Sharjah, PO Box 769 Sharjah, UAE; Al Hamra London, UK; Al Hamra Amman, PO Box 926475 Amman, Jordan; Al Hamra Saudia, PO Box 10223 Riyadh, S.Arabia

Principal Bankers: National Bank of Kuwait
Financial Information:

	US$'000
Authorised capital	4,800

Principal Shareholders: Partners as described
Date of Establishment: 1966
No of Employees: 1,000

AL HANI CONSTRUCTION & TRADING BUREAU

PO 3062 Safat, 13031 Kuwait
Tel: 2439471/2
Cable: Tradbur
Telex: 22109 Tradbur
Telefax: 2411804

Chairman: Khalid Yousuf Al-Mutawa
Directors: Abdul Muhsen Hasan Al-Kattan (Managing Director), Hisham Ahmed Shibl (General Manager), Rashid Fawzi Kassim (Deputy General Manager, Chief Engineer)

PRINCIPAL ACTIVITIES: Building construction and electro-mechanical contracting and trading in building and electrical materials

Principal Agencies: Armstrong Cork International, USA; Gallenkamp Laboratory Equip, UK; Danacoustic A/S, Denmark; Mazda Lighting, Paris, France; Lechler Industrial Paints, West Germany; Sealocrete Group, UK; Eternit SAL, Lebanon

Branch Offices: United Arab Emirates; Saudi Arabia; Jordan
Affiliated Companies: Solico Lebanese Construction & Contracting Co, Lebanon & Saudi Arabia; The Modern Air Conditioning & Refrigeration Co, Kuwait

Principal Bankers: National Bank of Kuwait, Alahli Bank of Kuwait, Gulf Bank of Kuwait

Financial Information:

	1989
	KD'000
Authorised capital	2,400
Paid-up capital	2,400
Total assets	15,200

Principal Shareholders: Khalid Y Mutawa; A M Kattan
Date of Establishment: 1964

ALI & FOUAD ALGHANIM EST
See ALGHANIM, ALI & FOUAD, EST

ALI AL QURAISH TRADING CO WLL
See AL QURAISH, ALI, TRADING CO WLL

ALI SAYEGH CONTRACTING CO WLL
PO Box 9014 Ahmadi, East Ahmadi, 61001 Kuwait
Tel: 3982020, 3984098, 3984099, 3983638, 3981980, 3980189
Cable: Aliscoltd
Telex: 44216 Vigo KT
Telefax: (965) 3985888

Partners: Dr Jasem M Al Sayegh (General Manager), Eng Hisham F Khammash (General Manager)
Senior Executives: Dr Samir Yousif Banoub (Financial & Administrative Manager), Eng Michael Issa Tannous (Chief Engineer Rods Dept), Eng Usama Ahmad Zidan (Chief Engineer Construction Dept)

PRINCIPAL ACTIVITIES: Building, civil and general contracting, asphalt & bitumen
Branch Offices: Fahed Al Salem Street, PO Box 21853 Safat, Kuwait 13079, Tel 2414679, 2410874
Principal Bankers: Kuwait Real Estate Bank
Financial Information:

	1989
	KD'000
Sales turnover	334
Authorised capital	500
Paid-up capital	500
Total assets	3,000

Principal Shareholders: Partners as described
Date of Establishment: 1970
No of Employees: 650

ALINJAZ CONTRACTING CO SAK
PO Box 25215 Safat, 13113 Kuwait
Tel: 4832615, 4832616
Telex: 22395 ALINJAZ KT
Telefax: 4848052 c/o MH AlShaya Co

Chairman: Abdul Wahab Al Shaya
Directors: Khalid Al Shaya, Abd. Al Aziz Al Shaya, Hamad Al Shaya, Abd. Rehman Al Shaya
Senior Executives: Mohammad Yousef Al Abdullah (General Manager), M Al Sabbagh (Technical Manager), S R Sarma (Construction Manager), Abdulrahman Sabri (Financial & Admn Manager)

PRINCIPAL ACTIVITIES: Electrical and mechanical engineering and contracting
Principal Agencies: Walter Kidde UK; Pipex, UK; International Gas Detection System, UK
Branch Offices: Abha Contracting Co, PO Box 4509, Al Medinah Al Munawwara, Saudi Arabia
Associated Companies: Merrol Fire Protection Engineering Ltd, UK; Crown House Engineering Ltd, UK
Principal Bankers: National Bank of Kuwait, SAK; Commercial Bank of Kuwait SAK

Principal Shareholders: M H Al Shaya Company
Date of Establishment: 1976
No of Employees: Office 50, Construction Sites 150

ALJASSAR, DAKHEEL, EST
PO Box 145 Safat, 13002 Kuwait
Tel: 4811722, 4813582, 4849484
Cable: ALJASSAR
Telex: 22288 KT ALJASSAR
Telefax: 4810067, 4843260

Chairman: Dakheel Aljassar
Directors: Abdullah Dakheel Aljassar (Managing Director)
Senior Executives: M H Dalle (Electrical Industries Division Director), Mohammed Afzal (Tenders Division Manager), Jassar D Al Jassar (Administration & Financial Account Manager)

PRINCIPAL ACTIVITIES: Manufacture of low, medium and high voltage switchgear, wholesale and retail trade of electrical products and domestic appliances, tenders for electrical, mechanical and chemical products and equipment; also trading in all kinds of paper and paper products
Principal Agencies: Felten & Guilleaume, Germany; GEC Distribution Equipment, UK; CMC Carl Maier, Switzerland; JA Crabtree, UK; Haani Cables, UK; Westinghouse Electric, USA; NK Electric, Japan; ABB Stromberg Control, Finland; Omas, Italy; Philco, USA & Italy; Schreiber, UK; Gower, UK; Takara Standard, Japan, La Germania, Italy; Linde, Germany; Canficorp, Canada; Everest Ind, UAE; TMT Trading, Hongkong; Oripyo, Korea; Fakir Werk, Germany; Kasuga, Japan; General Cable, Spain; Teba, Turkey; Derby, Denmark; Indo Asian Fusegear, India; Fulgor, Greece; Kabelmetal Electro, Germany; National Ind, Norway; Toktas, Turkey; Ottermill Switchtgear, UK; Stella, Italy; Harrison Access, UK; VRG Papier, Holland; Bunzl Pulp & Paper, UK; Wipco, Austria; TPS Technitube, Germany; Toshiba Electric, Japan; Sa Des Construccions Industriales, Spain
Branch Offices: Electrical Industries Division; Trading Division; Domestic Appliances Division; Tenders Division
Principal Bankers: Kuwait Finance House; National Bank of Kuwait; Gulf Bank; Burgan Bank; Al Ahli Bank of Kuwait; Bank of Kuwait & the Middle East

Principal Shareholders: Dakheel Aljassar
Date of Establishment: 28/4/1959
No of Employees: Approx 175

AL JASSAR, FAHAD, SONS FOR GENERAL TRADING & CONTRACTING CO
PO Box 2607 Safat, 13027 Kuwait
Tel: 4815105, 4816107, 4816514
Cable: Akhshab
Telex: 23566 Wood Kt
Telefax: 4837864

Directors: Abdul Mohsen Al-Jassar (Managing Director), Musaed Fahad Al Jassar
Senior Executives: Mohamed Awad (Marketing Manager), Mohammed Amir Uddin (Company Secretary)

PRINCIPAL ACTIVITIES: Trading, commission agents and sale of all construction and building materials, hardware, timber, blockboard, all kinds of plywood, formica and doors
Principal Agencies: Hermanns & Co, Germany; UTC, Switzerland; Lamex ronnys int, Italy; Nichimen Co, Japan
Principal Bankers: National Bank of Kuwait, Kuwait Finance House, Burgan Bank

No of Employees: 40/50

ALJASSIM, MAHMOOD, & BROS
PO Box 168 Safat, 13002 Kuwait
Tel: 2440472, 2434859
Cable: ALJASSIM-Kuwait
Telex: 3213 Aljasim

Chairman: Mishari M AlJassim
Directors: Mishari M Aljassim, Sa'dun M Aljassim

PRINCIPAL ACTIVITIES: Real estate, trading, government tenders and general contracting; telecommunications, electrical engineering, cables, electrical equipment, etc

Principal Bankers: National Bank of Kuwait SAK; Commercial Bank of Kuwait SAK; Alahli Bank of Kuwait KSC; Bank of Kuwait and the Middle East

Date of Establishment: 1945

AL JAZERA CONSULTANTS

PO Box 25328 Safat, 13114 Kuwait
Tel: 5312400 (5 lines)
Telex: 23935 Jihayem KT
Telefax: 5319533

Directors: Ahmad A Al Jihayem (Managing Director)
Senior Executives: Sameer Higazi (Technical Manager)

PRINCIPAL ACTIVITIES: Planners, architects, engineering consultants

Principal Bankers: Bank of Kuwait & the Middle East

Date of Establishment: 1978
No of Employees: 77

ALJUMA, HUSAIN MAKKI,

Ali Salem St, PO Box 153 Safat, 13002 Kuwait
Tel: 2418896, 2418897, 2418898
Cable: Aljuma
Telex: 22065

President: Husain Makki Aljuma
Senior Executives: Mahmoud Sharawi (General Manager)

PRINCIPAL ACTIVITIES: Import and distribution of building materials, steel products, textile piece goods, ready-made garments, carpets, blankets and general merchandise, government supplies

Principal Agencies: C Itoh & Co Ltd, Osaka, Japan; China National Textiles Imp & Exp Corpn, Samsung Co Ltd, Seoul, Korea; Salts (Saltaire) Ltd, UK; Pepper Lee & Co Ltd, UK; Hagihara Trading Co Ltd, Japan; Santista, Brazil

Principal Bankers: Alahli Bank of Kuwait

Date of Establishment: 1958

AL KAZEMI INTERNATIONAL COMMERCIAL GROUP

PO Box 403 Safat, 13005 Kuwait
Tel: 2463150
Cable: United
Telex: 22105 United; 22722 United

Chairman: Abdul Latif Alkazemi
Directors: Dhiya Alkazemi, Hani Alkazemi, Moh Alaam Al Kazemi

PRINCIPAL ACTIVITIES: Shipping, forwarding, trading, contracting, engineering consultancy, hotel owners, food-chain and catering, international exchange, financial and investment advisory services, import and export, ticketing and travel agent business, real estate, cleaning, skypak courier services

Subsidiary Companies: United Shipping Trading & Contracting Services WLL; Al Kazemi Real Estate Co; Al Kazemi Travel Agencies; Al Kazemi Import & Export Co; Al Kazemi International Exchange Co; Pullman Hotel; Sief Engineering Consultants; Gulf Trading & Maritime Est

Principal Bankers: National Bank of Kuwait; Commercial Bank of Kuwait; Bank of Bahrain & Kuwait; Bank of Kuwait & the Middle East

Date of Establishment: 1957

AL KAZEMI, ZAID, SONS TRADING CO

PO Box 30 Safat, 13001 Kuwait
Tel: 2437200, 2437217
Cable: Al Kazemi Kuwait
Telex: 22339 Kazemi Kt
Telefax: 2437287

Partners: Usamah Z Al Kazemi, Dr Nouri Z Al Kazemi, Malek Z Al Kazemi, Adnan Z Al Kazemi
Directors: Nouri Z Al Kazemi, Usamah Z Al Kazemi, Malek Z Al Kazemi
Senior Executives: George B Karam (Deputy Managing Director, Marketing & Dev), George Haik (Financial Manager)

PRINCIPAL ACTIVITIES: General trading and contracting (agents, distributors, tenderers), marine vessels & equipment, envrironmental engineering, material handling machinery & services, industrial cleaning equipment, chemicals and catalysts for oil drilling, refinery and petrochemical industries, hoses, protective clothing, civil defence systems and vehicles, logistic command, control and communication systems, agricultural equipment

Principal Agencies: Bourg, Belgium; Eskofot, Denmark; GBC, USA; Repromaster, Italy; Katsuragawi Electric, Japan; Meteor Siegen, Germany; Norfin, Germany; Rotaprint, Germany; Rotaprint Industries, UK; Twinlock, UK; Citizen Europe, UK; Centech, USA; CMS, USA; DSC Nestar Systems, UK; Facit, Sweden; GVC, Taiwan, ICS, UK; Inform, Germany; Mitac, Taiwan; Microteck, Taiwan; Sampo, Taiwan; Sekonic, Japan; TVM, Taiwan; Dulevo, Italy; Azimut Benetti, Italy; Singapore Shipyard, Singapore; IVG, Italy; Library Bureau, USA; Sabre Safety, UK; Ferranti Int Engineering, UK
Branch Offices: Industrial Machines, Shuwaikh Industrial Area
Associated Companies: Nouri & Usamah Zaid Al Kazemi Trading Co WLL, Kuwait
Principal Bankers: Bank of Kuwait & the Middle East; Commercial Bank of Kuwait
Financial Information:

	1989 KD'000
Authorised capital	3,000
Paid-up capital	3,000

Date of Establishment: 1974
No of Employees: 75

AL KHALED, ABDULAZIZ MUHALHIL, EST

PO Box 23887 Safat, 13099 Kuwait
Tel: 2417711

Chairman: Abdulaziz M Al Khaled
Directors: A Nabil Abdul-Fattah
Senior Executives: Eng Sabry Al Fattah (Technical Manager)

PRINCIPAL ACTIVITIES: General trading and contracting; supply of building materials and general consumer goods

AL KHALED, HAMAD, & BROS CO

PO Box 22402 Safat, 13085 Kuwait
Tel: 2424540, 2424538, 2413987, 2443713
Cable: Nazdad Kuwait
Telex: 22433 Nazdad Kt

Chairman: Hamad Abdul Razaq Al Khaled (Managing Director)
Directors: Abdul Aziz Al Khaled, Sultan Al Khaled

PRINCIPAL ACTIVITIES: Participation in tenders issued by various government and private authorities; commission agents; wholesale and retail of ready made garments & textiles, pharmaceuticals, auto spare parts; general consumer goods; transport and car rental services, automobile garages

Principal Agencies: Athletik GMBH, Austria; Asahi Yuki Hanbai Co, Japan; Elko Organization, Italy; Perma Pipe Midwesco, USA; Piccardo Carta, Italy; Switship Inc, USA; Tecfinance Group, Italy
Principal Bankers: Bank of Kuwait & the Middle East; Burgan Bank; Kuwait Finance House

Principal Shareholders: Abdul Azeez Alkhaled; Faisal Alkhaled; Hamad Alkhaled
Date of Establishment: 1971
No of Employees: 1,200

ALKHALID, HOMOUD AL-ZAID, CO

PO Box Safat 212, 13003 Kuwait
Tel: 2440010, 2440514, 2434050
Cable: Homoudzaid
Telex: 22999 Homozad Kt

Chairman: Faisal Homoud Alkahlid
Directors: Zeid Homoud Alkhalid

PRINCIPAL ACTIVITIES: General trading, commission agency, manufacturers' representatives for construction materials, cement; wholesalers and retailers
Principal Bankers: National Bank of Kuwait SAK

Principal Shareholders: Faisal Homoud Alkhalid & Bros

AL KHARAFI, KHALID ALI, & BROS CO WLL (KHARAFI STEEL)

PO Box 2886 Safat, 13029 Kuwait
Tel: 4817289, 4813127
Telex: KAL 22549 KT
Telefax: 4835501

Chairman: Khalid Ali Al Kharafi
Partners: Hamad Ali Al Kharafi, Hussain Ali Al Kharafi (General Manager)
Senior Executives: N K Shah (Senior Engineer)

PRINCIPAL ACTIVITIES: Builidng contractors, specialised in sandwich panels and the fabrication/erection of structural steel and cladding works, tanks, platforms, towers, etc
Branch Offices: Factory at Doha, Kuwait, Tel 4873400, 4873500, Fax 4873014
Principal Bankers: Commercial Bank of Kuwait; Bank of Kuwait & the Middle East; Gulf Bank

Date of Establishment: 1975
No of Employees: 175

AL KHORAFI, BADER AHMAD,
Petro-Chemie & Energy

PO Box 1100 Safat, 13011 Kuwait
Tel: 835565
Cable: MUHALLAB
Telex: 23183 BAKH KT

President: Abdulla B Al Khorafi
Directors: Tareq Al Zaidan
Senior Executives: Dastagir Anwar (Manager - Petro-Chemie and Energy)

PRINCIPAL ACTIVITIES: Engineers, contractors, general traders and manufacturers
Principal Agencies: Kawasaki Heavy Industries, Japan; A O Smith -Inland, USA; Solarex, USA; Chemap, Switzerland
Subsidiary Companies: Bader Khorafi Plastic Industries, Kuwait; Bader Khorafi Paints, Kuwait
Principal Bankers: Bank of Kuwait & Middle East; Commercial Bank of Kuwait

Date of Establishment: 1950
No of Employees: 600

AL-MAATOUK GENERAL TRADING & CONTRACTING EST

PO Box 3422 Safat, 13035 Kuwait
Tel: 2439760, 2439788, 2416611
Cable: Al-Maatouk
Telex: 22365 MAATOUK

Directors: M K Al-Maatouk (Managing Director)

PRINCIPAL ACTIVITIES: General trading and contracting

Principal Agencies: Regency Electronics Inc, USA; Regency Communications Inc, USA

Principal Shareholders: M K Al-Maatouk
Date of Establishment: 1965

ALMAILEM, AHMED YOUSIF ABDULHADI, & BROS CO (GROUP OF COMPANIES)

PO Box 4692 Safat, 13047 Kuwait
Tel: 832611, 832860, 818774
Cable: Abdulhadi
Telex: 22511 Sasco Kt, 44297 Sasco Kt

Chairman: Ahmed Yousif Abdulhadi Almailem
Directors: Ibrahim Yousif Abdulhadi Almailem, Fahad Yousif Abdulhadi Almailem, Musaed Yousif Abdulhadi Almailem, Yousif A Y Abdulhadi Almailem
Senior Executives: Kuldeep Singh (Managing Director)

PRINCIPAL ACTIVITIES: Import and distribution of tyres, tubes, batteries, and auto spare parts
Principal Agencies: Ceat, Italy; Semperit, Austria; Vredestein, Holland; Hankook, S Korea; BF Goodrich, USA; Kelly Springfield, USA; Continental, Germany
Subsidiary Companies: Abdulhadi Almailem Trading Co WLL; Al Sudasiyah Auto Spare Parts Co WLL (SASCO); Sasco Hotel, Hospital & Scientific Equipt Division; Sasco Oilfield & Industrial Equipt Division; Al Jabariya Auto Spare Parts Co WLL
Principal Bankers: Bank of Kuwait & The Middle East; Commercial Bank of Kuwait

No of Employees: 220 (Total Group)

AL MAJID SHIPPING AGENCIES

PO Box 1712 Safat, 13018 Kuwait
Tel: 2421439, 2429399
Cable: Alzayed
Telex: 22275 Kt Alzayed
Telefax: 2402184

Chairman: Bader Yousuf Al-Majid
Directors: Talal Al-Majid (Managing Director)
Senior Executives: Ahmed Hussain (General Manager, Shipping)

PRINCIPAL ACTIVITIES: Shipping and trading
Principal Agencies: Pakistan Shipping; Bangladesh Shipping; Panislamic Shipping; Paninslamic Steamship Co
Branch Offices: Shuwaikh Port, Warehouse 26
Subsidiary Companies: Al Kawthar Aluminium Co, Industrial Area, Al Raye, Tel 4745080; Silver Marble Industry, Tel 2642914; Almajid Auto Centre
Principal Bankers: National Bank of Kuwait; Bank of Bahrain and Kuwait; Gulf Bank

Principal Shareholders: Bader Yousuf Al Majid
Date of Establishment: 1962

AL MALIK'S, SALEM, SONS CO

PO Box 4481 Safat, 13045 Kuwait
Tel: 2429379, 811051
Cable: Maleksons
Telex: 23133 Kt Dakika, KT 44360 Mathew

Chairman: Sheikh Salem Al-Malik M Salem Al Sabah (Managing Director)
Directors: Abdullah Al Malik
Senior Executives: Jaya Prakash (Contracts Manager), Khalid Al-Malik (Manager), Samsudeen (Sales Manager)

PRINCIPAL ACTIVITIES: Trading and contracting, import, export and commission agents dealing in air conditioning, building materials, carpets, hardware, timber and plywood, watches, electronic goods and computers, ready made garments
Principal Agencies: IEMSA, Italy
Principal Bankers: Commercial Bank of Kuwait; Gulf Bank

Principal Shareholders: Sheikh Salem Mohammad Sulman Al Sabah
Date of Establishment: 1975
No of Employees: 108

AL MANSOUR & AL ABDALY TRADING & CONTRACTING CO WLL

PO Box 1207 Safat, 13013 Kuwait
Tel: 844300
Cable: Alzamil
Telex: MAC 22199 KT

Directors: Abdulrahman M Alzamil (Partner), Saleh A Abdaly (Partner), Abdulaziz A Alzamil (General Manager)
Senior Executives: Munir Al-Sarraj (Chief Engineer), Fateh Alla Abbass (E.D.P. Manager), Irfan S Touqan (Financial Manager)

PRINCIPAL ACTIVITIES: General trading, general and civil engineering contracting; import and distribution of general merchandise
Branch Offices: PO Box 21, Riyadh 11411, Saudi Arabia
Principal Bankers: Commercial Bank of Kuwait; Alahli Bank of Kuwait; Bank of Kuwait and Middle East; Bank of Bahrain and Kuwait
Financial Information:

	KD'000
Authorised capital	1,750
Paid-up capital	1,750

Date of Establishment: 1960
No of Employees: 1,200

AL-MARWAH TRADING & CONTRACTING CO

PO Box 3656 Safat, 13037 Kuwait
Tel: 4738285, 4741200
Cable: THARWAT
Telex: 23047 KT THARWAT
Telefax: 4733478

Chairman: Adnan M A Al Wazzan
Directors: Jamal A R Marouf (Managing Director)
Senior Executives: Mahmoud A Al-Khalidi (Chief Engineer), Omar M Salha (Chief Engineer), Samir R Marouf (Chief Engineer), Nabil A R Marouf (Engineer)

PRINCIPAL ACTIVITIES: Contracting dealing in the construction of various types of buildings, roads and water reservoirs
Principal Agencies: Bermaho, France; Gines Navarro Constructiones, Spain; EXEKTE, Greece; Space Engineering, France; BV Nemaho, Netherlands
Associated Companies: Al-Mawrid Trading & Contracting Co, Kuwait; Burhan Kuwaiti Trading & Contracting Co, Kuwait; Aswan Trading & Contracting Est, Kuwait; Safco, Kuwait; Al Diyar Trading & Contracting Co, Kuwait
Principal Bankers: Al-Ahli Bank of Kuwait; Bank of Kuwait & Middle East; National Bank of Kuwait; Commercial Bank of Kuwait; Gulf Bank
Financial Information:

	US$'000
Annual turnover	45,000
Authorised capital	3,500
Paid-up capital	3,500

Principal Shareholders: Adnan M Al Wazzan, Jamal A R Marouf; Mahmoud Al-Khalidi; Omar Salha; Samir Marouf; Nabil Marouf
Date of Establishment: February, 1973
No of Employees: 900

AL-MARZOUK, SALEM, & SABAH ABI-HANNA WLL

PO Box 1913 Safat, 13020 Kuwait
Tel: 5312830 (10 lines)
Cable: Abihanna-Kuwait
Telex: 30533/4 Abihana Kt
Telefax: 5330634

Directors: Salem Al-Marzouk, Sabah Abi-Hanna, Charles Bosel, Abdul Ridha Al Sukhni, John Abi Hanna
Associates: Mohammad Hussein Ali, John Kinloch, Steven Abi Hanna, Brian Hogg

PRINCIPAL ACTIVITIES: Architects, engineers and planners
Associated Companies: Sabah Abi-Hanna & Associates, Lebanon, SSC Consultants Ltd, UK
Principal Bankers: National Bank of Kuwait; Bank of Kuwait & the Middle East; Hill Samuel & Co Ltd, UK and Jersey
Financial Information:

	1989 US$'000
Sales turnover	8,500
Authorised capital	340
Paid-up capital	340

Principal Shareholders: Salem Al Marzouk, Sabah Abi Hanna, Charles Bosel
Date of Establishment: 1961
No of Employees: 269

AL MUHALAB CONTRACTING & TRADING CO

PO Box 3245 Safat, 13033 Kuwait
Tel: 2438955, 2438933
Cable: Namashi
Telex: 22567 Namashi Kt
Telefax: 2402000

Directors: Abdul Ghani Al-Ghani
Senior Executives: Khalid Abdul Ghani Al-Ghani (Managing Director)

PRINCIPAL ACTIVITIES: Exporters, importers and manufacturers of water coolers; electrical contractors, suppliers of cement and bricks
Associated Companies: Sabaa Construction & Contracting Establishment, Kuwait; Concrete Chemical Materials Co WLL
Principal Bankers: Commercial Bank of Kuwait

Date of Establishment: 1968

AL MUKABBER TRADING & CONTRACTING CO WLL

PO Box 23263 Safat, 13093 Kuwait
Tel: 2401571/2, 2401508
Cable: Al Mukabber
Telex: 23207 NANCY KT

Chairman: Abdullah Mubarak Al Banwan
Directors: Abdullah Abdul Mughni, Mohamed Barakat (Manager)
Senior Executives: Ziad Ammous (Area Manager Iraq), Anwar Al Omar (Area Manager Kuwait), Nasif Dawood (Chief Engineer Kuwait)

PRINCIPAL ACTIVITIES: Trading and contracting, construction, building materials, chemicals, tools, construction equipment
Principal Agencies: Mc-Bauchemie Muller, Germany; Pfeifer Seil & Hebetechnik, Germany; Pilosio, Italy; Texsa, Spain; Upat, Germany; Vatta, Italy; Crescent of Cambridge, UK; Surban, UK
Branch Offices: Al Mukabber Trading Industrial & Contracting Co, PO Box 3456 Amman, Jordan
Subsidiary Companies: International Group for Equipments & Contracting Co
Principal Bankers: Gulf Bank; Commercial Bank of Kuwait; Bank of Kuwait & the Middle East

Principal Shareholders: Abdullah Mubarak Al Banwan, Abdullah Abdul Mughni, Riad Hijawi, Khalid Sadik, Jamal Anabtawi, Mohamed Joudeh
Date of Establishment: 1974
No of Employees: 220

AL MULLA, BADER, & BROS CO WLL

PO Box 177 Safat, 13002 Kuwait
Tel: 2445040 (60 lines)
Cable: AlMulla Kuwait
Telex: 22012, 23150 AlMulla KT
Telefax: 2437285

Chairman: Najeeb A Al Mulla
Directors: Najeeb Abdulla Al Mulla, Anwar Abdulla Al Mulla,
Nabil A Al Mulla, Lutfi A Al Mulla, Apkar Hovaguimian, D R
Mirchandani, Vaiz Karamat, R K Sethi, H N Elowe, Ivan
Pacheco, A S Narenthiran, Minoo Patel
Senior Executives: Anwar A Al Mulla (Deputy Chairman), Apkar
Hovaguimian (Managing Director), D R Mirchandani (Deputy
Managing Director), Vaiz Karamat (Financial Director), A S
Narenthiran (Commercial Director), H N Elowe (Director &
Divisional General Manager), Ivan Pacheco (Director &
Divisional Manager), Minoo Patel (Deputy Financial Director)

PRINCIPAL ACTIVITIES: Dealing in passenger and commercial
vehicles, oil products, spare parts and accessories, service
garages and workshop, cleaning, maintenance and repair
services, heating, ventilation, air-conditioning, mechanical and
electrical services, project engineering, consumer products,
domestic appliances, construction equipment, boats, and
marine equipment, food, fast food restaurants, computers,
security services, travel freight, fire fighting equipment,
Government tenders, insurance, etc
Principal Agencies: White Westinghouse, Chrysler, Mister
Donut, Minolta, Gulf Oil, Mercury Engines & Boats, John Deer
Int, International Marine, Kohler, Oki Electric, Shin Meiwa,
Swensen Middle East, Mitsubishi Heavy Ind, Integrated
Automation, KLM Royal Dutch Airlines, A & W Restaurants,
Laserdata, Toshiba Battery, Express Lift Co, Bull, Robert
Krups Stifting & Co
Parent Company: Al Mulla Group
Associated Companies: Saleh Jamal & Co WLL, Maseelah
Trading Co WLL, Al Mulla Rental & Leasing of Vehicles &
Equipment Co WLL, Al Mulla Security Services Co WLL, Al
Mulla Environmental Systems Co WLL, Al Mulla International
Trading & Contracting Co WLL, Al Mulla Travel Bureau, Al
Mulla Cleaning & Maintenance Services Co WLL, Hiba
Advertising Co WLL, Al Mulla Real Estate Co WLL, Al Mulla
Consultancy Co WLL, Gulf Trading Group WLL, Al Mulla
Aviation Agencies
Principal Bankers: Bank of Kuwait & the Middle East, Kuwait;
National Bank of Kuwait, Kuwait; Commercial Bank of Kuwait,
Kuwait; Chemical Bank, Bahrain; Chase Manhattan Bank,
Bahrain
Financial Information:

	1988/89 US$'000
Sales turnover	51,680
Authorised capital	9,564
Paid-up capital	9,564
Total assets	46,900
Total reserves	8,730

Principal Shareholders: Najeeb Al Mulla, Anwar Al Mulla, Nabeel
Al Mulla, Lutfi Al Mulla, Abdullah Bader Al Mulla, Mrs Badria
Khalid Al Ghunaim
Date of Establishment: 1947
No of Employees: 2,000

AL MULLA GROUP OF COMPANIES

PO Box 177 Safat, 13002 Kuwait
Tel: 2445040 (10 lines)
Cable: Almulla
Telex: 22012 Almulla Kt

Chairman: Najeeb Abdulla Al Mulla
Directors: Anwar Abdulla Al Mulla (Deputy Chairman), Nabil
Abdulla Al Mulla (Vice-Chairman Project Engineering), Lufti
Abdulla Al Mulla (Vice-Chairman Automotive)
Senior Executives: A Hovaguimian (Managing Director), P G M
Barnes (Financial Director), D R Mirchandani (Commercial

Director), V Karamat (Deputy Financial Director), E Hammond
(Director Corporate Planning & Development), Raj Sethi
(Director - Project Engineering), Ivan Pacheco (Director &
Divisional General Manager), Hussam Elowe (Director &
Divisional General Manager), A Narenthiran (Director -
Management Accounts)

PRINCIPAL ACTIVITIES: Merchants and contractors,
distributors of passenger cars, parts and accessories,
commercial vehicles, heavy equipment, domestic appliances,
Hifi & TV equipment, office equipment, electrical equipment
and equipment for the oil industry, tools and machinery,
garage equipment, consumer goods, boats and marine
engines, plant-hire, travel agents and real estate,
environmental systems, security equipment and services,
cleaning & maintenance services, airconditioning & project
engineering; computer services, wholesale food suppliers,
fast food restaurants, marketing and advertising services,
aerial survey and mapping, financial consultants, inspection
etc
Principal Agencies: Chrysler, Airtemp, White Westinghouse, Gulf
oil, KLM Airlines; Pirelli Cables; Mitsubishi Motors; Mercury
Marine; General Electric Co; Securicor; Cluttons; Nippo; BSI
(Holland); Inter rent; Teac; A & W - Great Food Restaurant;
Mr Donut - (Multi Foods Intl USA); Swensens; Carrier &
Norfrig Transport Refrigerated Systems; Okifax; Minolta;
Zanussi; Nordmende; Mitsubishi-Daiya Airconditioners;
Glastron; Hammond; Silverline; Keith Blackman (UK); BIX Gulf
(Dubai); Civil Protection (UK); Electric Machinery Industrial
Controls (USA); GKN Sankey (UK); Liebert Intl Sales (USA);
Technipol Intl (USA); Integrated Automation (USA); Carters of
Burnley (UK); Roell & Korthaus (W Germany); Roell &
Korthaus Amsler Prufmaschinen (Switzerland); SA Equipment
(UK); SGN (UK); K & T Intl (Japan); Glyndova (UK); Pritchard
Services Group; Typewriters; Fuji Kinden (Office Equipment);
Nakajima; Glory (Japan); Kohler Generators; Kato Cranes;
Shinmeiwa Cranes & Loaders; Mitsubishi Forklifts; BFI (USA);
Kansai (Japan); Satchwell (UK); Andrex (Denmark); Saval
Kronenburg (Holland); Woods of Colchester; California Farms
& Canners Inc (USA); Richter & Co (Germany); Weinrich & Co
(Germany); MEA; Garuda Intl Airways; Intl Brokerage &
Leasing; Longdin & Browning (Surveys); Clyde Surveys;
Lamont & Partners
Associated Companies: Maseelah Trading Co WLL; Al Mulla
Rental & Leasing of Vehicles & Equipment Co WLL; Bader Al
Mulla & Bros Co WLL; Saleh Jamal & Co WLL; Al Mulla
Travel Bureau; Al Mulla International Trading & Contracting
Co WLL; Al Mulla Environmental Systems WLL; Al Mulla
Cleaning & Maintenance Services Co WLL; Al Mulla Security
Services Co WLL; Hiba Advertising Co WLL

Date of Establishment: 1938
No of Employees: 3,000

ALMUNAYES TRADING & CONTRACTING EST

PO Box 4405 Safat, 13045 Kuwait
Tel: 2461395, 2461396, 2462868, 416327
Cable: Emerald
Telex: 22278 Sami Kt

Chairman: Abdullatif Abdulkarim Almunayes (also proprietor)

PRINCIPAL ACTIVITIES: Import and distribution of foodstuffs
(sugar, rice, tea, edible oil, milk and of canned foodstuffs,
vegetables, juices, soft drinks, confectionery, tomato paste)
Principal Agencies: La Doria SAS, Italy; Hopewell International
Corp, Taiwan; Crown Yeast Co, UK; IVAN Chocolates, UK
Associated Companies: Abdullatif Abdulkarim Almunayes, PO
Box 2446, Kuwait
Principal Bankers: Commercial Bank of Kuwait; Gulf Bank; Bank
of Kuwait & the Middle East

Date of Establishment: 1967

KUWAIT

AL MUTAWA, ABDULAZIZ ALI,

PO Box 164 Safat, 13002 Kuwait
Tel: 2433108, 2432081, 2418720
Cable: Salam
Telex: 22317 Salam Kt

Chairman: Abdulaziz Ali Mutawa
Directors: Mohamed A A Mutawa
Senior Executives: Omar Mutawa (Managing Director)

PRINCIPAL ACTIVITIES: Import and distribution of automotive
products (cars, trucks, and components), construction
materials, sanitary ware, general trading and tendering
Principal Agencies: AB Volvo, Sweden; Bosch, Germany; Mintex
Ltd, UK
Associated Companies: Abdulaziz Ali Mutawa, PO Box 1123,
Riyadh, Saudi Arabia; Kuwait & Arab States Company
(KASCO), Cairo
Principal Bankers: Gulf Bank, Bank of Kuwait and the Middle
East; Commercial Bank of Kuwait

Principal Shareholders: Chairman as described

AL MUZAINI, ABDULAZIZ & ALI YOUSUF,

PO Box 2156 Safat, 13022 Kuwait
Tel: 440626, 2435147, 2435161/4
Cable: Almuzaini
Telex: 22129 Kt; 22002 Kt; 22432 Kt

Directors: Abdulaziz Al Muzaini, Ali Yousuf Al Muzaini

PRINCIPAL ACTIVITIES: Money changers and stock brokers,
international foreign exchange dealers, real estate and local
shares dealers
Associated Companies: Arab Trust Co, Kuwait; Yousuf Al
Muzaini Trading Company

AL NAKIB, AHMED HAMID, EST

PO Box 3770 Safat, 13038 Kuwait
Tel: 2415544
Cable: Dair
Telex: 22373 Dair

Chairman: Ahmed Hamid Al Nakib
Directors: Salim H Alameddine (Partner and Manager)

PRINCIPAL ACTIVITIES: Trading and contracting
Principal Bankers: Commercial Bank of Kuwait; Burgan Bank of
Kuwait; Gulf Bank of Kuwait

AL NASR MIDDLE EAST

PO Box 23730 Safat, 13098 Kuwait
Tel: 4818902
Cable: Welding
Telex: 23574 NME
Telefax: 4818902

Chairman: Salim Said Huneidi
Directors: Said Salim Huneidi (Managing Director)
Senior Executives: Amer Salim Huneidi (General Manager)

PRINCIPAL ACTIVITIES: Distributors of welding equipment
Principal Agencies: Uniweld, USA
Principal Bankers: National Bank of Kuwait; Bank of Kuwait &
the Middle East

Principal Shareholders: Salim Said Huneidi
Date of Establishment: 1974

ALNOURI & ADLOUNI TRADING & CONTRACTING CO WLL

PO Box 23676 Safat, 13097 Kuwait
Tel: 2419482, 2412914
Cable: Adlotec, Kuwait
Telex: 23238 Adlotec Kt
Telefax: 2419087

Chairman: Nouri Abdul Khaliq Al Nouri
Directors: A K Adlouni (Director General)

Senior Executives: Dr Mithqal Sartawi (Technical Manager)

PRINCIPAL ACTIVITIES: Trading and contracting, electrical and
civil contractors, supplies, machinery and tools, chemical and
petrochemical products, ready made garments, clothing,
paper and stationery, scientific and research instruments
Parent Company: Nouri Industrial Est; Kuwait & Adlouni Trading
& Contracting Co, Lebanon
Principal Bankers: National Bank of Kuwait
Financial Information:

	1988/89
Sales turnover	US$7,000,000
Authorised capital	KD100,000
Paid-up capital	KD50,000

Principal Shareholders: Al Nouri (51%), Adlouni (49%)
Date of Establishment: 1981

AL-NUSIF, WAEL, TRADING CO WLL

PO Box 25384 Safat, 13114 Kuwait
Tel: 4845772
Cable: Awaseer
Telex: 30404 WNC KT
Telefax: (965) 4840553

Chairman: Wael Al Nusif
Directors: Saleh Al Towaim, Raymond Elias Matta
Senior Executives: Raymond Elias Matta (General Manager),
George Mokdassi (Marketing Manager), Mohd Zook (Projects
Manager), Vram Nalbandian (Technical Manager), Rafeq Jamil
Abu Abbas (Administration & Finance Manager), Mohamed
Abdul Hamid (Purchasing Manager), Usman Sulaiman Abdul
Hadi (Personnel Manager)

PRINCIPAL ACTIVITIES: Dealing in cleaning chemicals,
materials & equipment and foostuffs
Principal Agencies: Economics Laboratory, Soteco, Cimex, St
Nicolas, Nejem
Principal Bankers: National Bank of Kuwait; Bank of Kuwait &
the Middle East
Financial Information:

	1988/89
	KD'000
Sales turnover/tenders	3,233
Authorised capital	210
Paid-up capital	210
Total assets	1,839

Principal Shareholders: Chairman and directors as described
Date of Establishment: 1978
No of Employees: 3,000

AL OMAR MECHANICAL ENGINEERING CO WLL

PO Box 392 Safat, 13004 Kuwait
Tel: 847849, 849555, 846311
Cable: Omarco
Telex: 22152 Omarco Kt

Directors: M A Al Omar, A M Al Kulaib

PRINCIPAL ACTIVITIES: Mechanical engineering, marine
engineering dealing in all types of hand and precision tools,
road construction machinery, workshop and garage
equipment, welding machines, electrodes fuel injection
equipment and spare parts, safety equipment and materials,
industrial goods etc
Principal Agencies: Lucas Group of Companies, UK; Mitutoyo,
Japan

AL OMRANIAH CO LTD

PO Box 23368 Safat, Kuwait 13094
Tel: 4835547 (6 lines)
Telex: 23250 Meba KT
Telefax: 4835548

Chairman: Abdul Hussain Bahaman (Managing Director)
Senior Executives: Issam Mohd Malas (General Manager)

PRINCIPAL ACTIVITIES: Import of all kinds of building materials, steel, plywood, timber, sanitary fittings, tiles, ceramics and construction chemicals

Principal Agencies: FEB, UK & UAE; Brastimber, Cyprus; Brasteel, Brazil, Hadeed, Saudi Arabia

Principal Bankers: Gulf Bank, Commercial Bank of Kuwait, Kuwait Real Estate Bank

Financial Information:

	1989 US$'000
Paid-up capital	10,000

Principal Shareholders: HE Sheikh Ahmad Al Jaber Al Sabah, Abdul Hussain Bahaman

Date of Establishment: 1976

AL OTHMAN TRADING & CONTRACTING CO WLL

PO Box 1539 Safat, 13016 Kuwait
Tel: 4815846
Cable: Othmanco
Telex: Douma 23581 KT
Telefax: 4845052

Chairman: Suleiman Ghanim Al Othman

Directors: Abdullah G Al Othman, Bader S Al Othman (Managing Director), Turki S Al Othman (Asst Managing Director)

Senior Executives: Ghanim A Al Othman (Manager), Basil S Al Othman (Manager)

PRINCIPAL ACTIVITIES: General trading, construction, and agents

Principal Agencies: Rupp, Austria; Intermont, France; Strabag, Germany; Toppan Moore Paragon, Malaysia, etc

Subsidiary Companies: Al Hidhab Trading & Contracting Co (for Computer Supplies and General Trading); Adel Al Othman Est; Al Hilal Advertising Co

Principal Bankers: Al Ahli Bank of Kuwait

Financial Information:

	1989 KD'000
Sales turnover	6,500
Authorised capital	300
Paid-up capital	300
Total assets	1,500

Principal Shareholders: Suleiman G Al Othman, Abdullah G Al Othman

Date of Establishment: 1959

No of Employees: 1,000 approx

AL QABAS NEWSPAPER

PO Box 21800 Safat, 13078 Kuwait
Tel: 4812822
Cable: Qabas Kuwait
Telex: 23370 Qabas Kt
Telefax: 4834251, 4835367

Chairman: Abdulaziz Mohammed Al Shaya

Directors: Mohammed J Al-Sager (Chief Editor), Wafa H Shihabi (General Manager)

Senior Executives: Omar T Audeh (Financial Manager), Saber Amin (Advertising Manager), Fadi Husseini (Asst Managing Editor), K V Rajagopal (Press Manager)

PRINCIPAL ACTIVITIES: Press, printing and publishing The Arabic daily newspaper 'Al Qabas' (115,972 copies daily as per ABC London) and the international edition printed and published from London/Paris/Marseille

Branch Offices: Al Qabas (England) Int'l, Unit 4, Bramber Court, 2 Bramber Road, London W14 9PB, Telex 24980 Qabas G; Al Qabas (France) Int'l, 34 Av George V, 75008 Paris, Telex 648475 Qabas F

Principal Bankers: Al Ahli Bank, Shuwaikh; Gulf Bank, Shuwaikh

Principal Shareholders: Five
Date of Establishment: February 1972
No of Employees: 400

ALQADDUMI, ABUD ALRAZZAQ, & SONS CO

PO Box 22370 Safat, 13084 Kuwait
Tel: 2413667

Chairman: Abud Alrazzaq Alqaddumi

Directors: Salah Eddin Subhi (Managing Director)

Senior Executives: Fuad Abdu Al Razzaq Al Qaddumi (Finance Manager), Muhammad Faiz Khalil Al Mardini (Sales Manager), Wael Salah Eddin (Marketing Manager), Eng Walid Mustafa Alakhrass (Production Manager), Salah Muhammad Hadad (Admin Manager)

PRINCIPAL ACTIVITIES: Construction contracting and building materials trading

Principal Agencies: Laston, Italy; Panfilli Special Isoledil Trieste

Principal Bankers: Burgan Bank

Date of Establishment: 1973
No of Employees: 50

AL QATAMI INTERNATIONAL TRADING & CONTRACTING CO WLL

PO Box 619 Safat, 13007 Kuwait
Tel: 4832370/71
Telex: 46158 AITC KT

Chairman: Naser Abdul Wahab Al Qatami

Directors: B T Gidwani (Finance Director), S M Bilgrami (Sales Director)

Senior Executives: Harish Asrani, K Rao

PRINCIPAL ACTIVITIES: General traders and stockists, building materials, fire fighting systems, sanitaryware, pipes and fittings

Principal Agencies: Acrow Automation, UK; Mecalux, Spain; Sumitomo Cement Co, Japan; Nittetsu Cement Co, Japan; Tokuyama, Japan; Fire Fighter, UK

Parent Company: Naser Abdul Wahab Al Qatami & Sons

Associated Companies: Naser Abdulwahab Al Qatami & Co; Al Qatami Shipping and Trading Co WLL

Principal Bankers: Gulf Bank; Commercial Bank of Kuwait; National Bank of Kuwait

Principal Shareholders: B T Gidwani, S M Bilgrami
No of Employees: 30

AL QURAISH, ALI, TRADING CO WLL

PO Box 2505 Safat, 13026 Kuwait
Tel: 2454232, 2434076
Cable: Kreshan
Telex: KRESHAN 30498 KT
Telefax: (965) 2403984

Chairman: Ali Zaid Al-Quraishi

Senior Executives: Ahmed H Al Mohaisin (Managing Director)

PRINCIPAL ACTIVITIES: Import and distribution of tobacco and cigarettes and general consumer goods

Principal Agencies: Philip Morris International, USA

Parent Company: Ali Zaid Al Quraishi & Bros, Dammam, Saudi Arabia

Principal Bankers: Alahli Bank of Kuwait KSC; National Bank of Kuwait

Date of Establishment: 1961

AL RABIAH CONSTRUCTION CO WLL (ARABCO)

PO Box 3592 Safat, 13036 Kuwait
Tel: 844241, 842947, 818846
Cable: Arabco
Telex: 22181 Arabco Kt

Chairman: Saleh Rashid Burislee

Directors: Horst Hubert Weniger (Managing Partner), Rashed S Burislee

PRINCIPAL ACTIVITIES: Construction and trading; fabrication and erection of prefab prestressed concrete elements
Principal Agencies: Comsip Enterprises, France; Big Lift, Holland
Subsidiary Companies: Geccis, Bander Seri Begawan, Brunei
Principal Bankers: Commercial Bank of Kuwait; Al Ahli Bank of Kuwait
Financial Information:

	US$'000
Sales turnover	40,000
Paid-up capital	2,500

Principal Shareholders: Saleh Rashid Burislee, Horst Hubert Weniger, Rashed S Burislee
No of Employees: 350

AL RASHED, ABDULAZIZ ABDULMOHSIN, SONS CO WLL

Al Rashed Group

PO Box 242 Safat, 13003 Kuwait
Tel: 2401400, 2421833, 2421856, 2421886
Cable: Ghoson
Telex: 31106 AB Ghoson KT
Telefax: 2421774

Chairman: Saud Abdulaziz A Al Rashed
Directors: Saad Abdulaziz A Al Rashed (Vice Chairman & President), Abdulmohsin A Al Rashed (Managing Director), Abdulaziz Rashed A Al Rashed (Director), Khaled Saud Al Rashed (Director), Esam Saud Al Rashed (Director), Basem Saud Al Rashed (Director),Khalid Abdulmohsin Al Rashed (Director)
Senior Executives: Yousef J Milhim (Technical Manager)

PRINCIPAL ACTIVITIES: General merchants, importers, exporters and contractors to government and oil companies. Dealers in building materials, office furniture, machines and supplies, domestic electrical and gas appliances, valves, pipe fittings and oilfield equipment, automation and control equipment/systems for process industry, electronic and telecommunication equipment, commercial laundry equipment, kitchen and catering equipment, hospital equipment and supplies, storage/racking system equipment/supplies, scooters and threewheelers, arms and ammunition. Suppliers to government and oil companies.
Principal Agencies: General Electric Co, Foxboro Co, Alcatel Business Systems, Vickers Furniture, CGE-Alsthom Int, Expanded Metal Co, Miele & Cie, Piaggio & Co, Magic Chef Inc, Cooperheat, Volund Laundry Machines, Ericsson Info Systems AB (Facit), Wertheim Werke Ag, Krautkramer GmbH, Junkers Division, Robert Bosch GmbH, Masoneilan Div, Dresser Industries Inc, M W Kellogg Co, Korea Heavy Industries & Construction Co, Atlantic, Gulf & Pacific Co of Manila Inc, Automatic Switch Co, Ceilcote Co, Fluidic Techniques Inc, Autodynamics Inc, Technomatic Spa, Dual Drilling Co, Joseph Gleave & Son, Xerox Corp, Scott Aviation Int Operations, Talco SA, Memorex Telex Corp, etc
Subsidiary/Associated Companies: Al Rashed Trading, Industrial & Contracting Co, PO Box Safat 3320, 13034 Kuwait (General trading, import and export. Manufacturers of cement and steel products, distributors of building materials. Civil engineering contractors); Al Rashed Shipping Agencies, PO Box Safat 3320 (Shipping agents, charterers, clearing and forwarding agents, tug and lighterage contractors); Al Rashed Travel Company, PO Box Safat 241, 13003 Kuwait (Airline and travel agency); Saud Abdulaziz Alrashed & Bros, PO Box 242, 13003 Kuwait (General merchants, importers, exporters and dealers of communication equipment, hospital equipment, oilfield equipment); Steamco Shipping Agencies, PO Box Safat 484 (Shipping agents, charterers, clearing and forwarding agents); Taima'a Trading & Contracting Co WLL, PO Box 3320, 13034 Safat, Kuwait (General merchants &

contractors, dealers in automobile spares, tyres, batteries, garage equipment); Gulf Travel Agency, PO Box 4600, 13046 Safat, Kuwait (Travel Agency); AFFILIATED COMPANIES: Hempel's Marine Paints (Kuwait) WLL, PO Box Safat 3400, 13034 Safat, Kuwait (Manufacturers of paints); Kuwait Metal Furniture Manufacturing Co KSC, PO Box 42301, 70654 Shuwaikh, Kuwait (Manufacturers of steel furniture)
Principal Bankers: Gulf Bank, Kuwait; National Bank of Kuwait; Bank of Kuwait and the Middle East; Commercial Bank of Kuwait; Al Ahli Bank of Kuwait

Principal Shareholders: Saud Abdulaziz Al Rashed, Saad Abdulaziz Al Rashed, Abdulmohsin Abdulaziz Al Rashed, Abdulaziz Rashed Al Rashed
Date of Establishment: In 1911 by Abdulaziz Abdulmohsin Al Rashed

AL RASHED INDUSTRIAL & CONTRACTING CO

PO Box 3320 Safat, 13034 Kuwait
Tel: 833011, 833168
Telex: 23296 ARICC Kt

PRINCIPAL ACTIVITIES: General trading, import and export. Manufacturers of cement and steel products, distributors of building materials, fire fighting equipment. Civil engineering contractors
Principal Agencies: Walter Kiddle & Co Ltd, UK
Parent Company: Part of the Al Rashed Group of Companies

AL RIFAI, SAYID RAJAB,

PO Box Safat 161, 13002 Kuwait
Tel: 2423444, 2424222
Cable: Sayidrajab Kuwait
Telex: 22073

President: Sayid Rajab Al-Rifai
Senior Executives: N K Menon (Sales Manager), A Qayum Shaikh (Administration Manager)

PRINCIPAL ACTIVITIES: Manufacturers' representatives and general suppliers, distributors of foodstuffs, chemicals, urethane foam equipment; steam generators, pipework and water treatment systems etc
Principal Agencies: Rolls-Royce Ltd, Hawker Siddeley Dynamics Ltd, Imperial Chemical Industries Ltd, BTP Tioxide Ltd, Vicking Eng Co Ltd, Steinmuller Int, R Twining & Co Ltd, Skanska Cementgjuteriet
Branch Offices: PO Box 2000, Dubai (UAE), Tel 660755/8, Telex 45439 and 6 Curzon Place, London W1 (UK), Tel 071-629 7843/5
Principal Bankers: National Bank of Kuwait; Commercial Bank of Kuwait; Gulf Bank

Principal Shareholders: Solely owned by the President
Date of Establishment: 1948

AL ROUMI, YOUSEF ABDUL RAHMAN,

PO Box 21876 Safat, 13079 Kuwait
Tel: 2419424, 4746469, 4744352
Cable: ALFODARKO
Telex: 23073 LULWANI

President: Mohammed Yousef Abdul Rahman Al Roumi

PRINCIPAL ACTIVITIES: General trading, agricultural, machinery, material and products, laboratory instruments
Principal Bankers: Kuwait Finance House; Gulf Bank

Date of Establishment: 1972

AL SAGAR, A H, & BROS

PO Box 244 Safat, 13003 Kuwait
Tel: 4810655, 4810656, 4810708
Cable: Alsagar KT
Telex: 46354 Sgrland KT; 22085 Alsagar KT; 22420 Alsagar KT
Telefax: 4811155

Chairman: Jasim Hamad Al Sagar

Directors: Hamad Abdulla Al Sagar, Hamad Abdulaziz Al Sagar, Khalid Abdulla Al Sagar, Wael Jasim Al Sagar

Senior Executives: Walid El Aker (Elect/Mech Div Technical Manager), Saad Jeiroudi (Project Div Manager), N K Mehra (HVAC Div Sales Manager), Hashim Kayyali (General Manager Shipping), Ahmad Mustafa (Manager Cable Laying), Ahmed Dick (Asst Sales Manager Oil & Gas Equipment Dept)

PRINCIPAL ACTIVITIES: Import and distribution of electrical and air conditioning equipment, electrical submersible pumps, well heads, downhole equipment, valves and oilfield chemicals, electrical and mechanical contractors, shipping agents and transportation contractors; also representatives of international contractors

Principal Agencies: York International - Borg Warner Corp, USA; York Shipley, USA; Furnas Elect Co, USA; Singer Co - Link Miles, USA; Hawker Siddeley, UK; Degremont, France; Petitjean, France; Italstrade, Italy; Ansaldo Impianti, Italy; Asea, Sweden; Jarnkonst, Sweden; Castolin, Switzerland; Union Carbide, USA; Showa Electric Wire & Cable, Japan, Oil Dynamics, USA; Manifold Systems, USA; PetroTech Tools, USA; Albright & Wilson, UK

Branch Offices: A H Alsagar & Bros, Engineering Projects Co, PO Box 697, Abu Dhabi, UAE

Subsidiary/Associated Companies: Al Sagar Line WLL; Al Sagar Transport; Affiliated companies: Al Bunyan Eng & Contg Co; Kuwait National Bottling Co (Pepsi Cola); Kuwait Automotive Imports Co (Dealers of Mazda & Peugeot cars & Michelin tyres)

Principal Bankers: National Bank of Kuwait

Principal Shareholders: Family partnership
Date of Establishment: 1895
No of Employees: approx 600

AL SAHL TRADING CO

PO Box 4196 Safat, 13042 Kuwait
Tel: 2415408, 2415437
Cable: Sahltrad
Telex: 22959 Sahltrad Kwt

Directors: Mohammed Al-Rifai
Senior Executives: K Pillai (Commercial Manager)

PRINCIPAL ACTIVITIES: Importers and exporters, stockists and distributors, commission agents

Principal Agencies: Consolidated Contracting Co, USA; Volkar Brothers (India); D A Abesinghe & Co, Ceylon; C Abdulkader & Sons, Ceylon; Pearl Special Int-Taiwan; T S Hsin Kao & Co

Branch Offices: PO Box 15261, Al-Ain, Abu Dhabi
Principal Bankers: Al-Ahli Bank of Kuwait

AL SALEH, MUSAAD, & SONS LTD

PO Box 1092 Safat, 13011 Kuwait
Tel: 845261, 841834
Cable: Fawzi
Telex: 23368 Mssltdc KT
Telefax: 4832657

Chairman: Dawood Musaad Al Saleh

Directors: Hamad M Al Saleh, Nouri M Al Saleh, Mohammed M Al Saleh, Fawzi M Al Saleh, Najeeb H M Al Saleh, Moayed H M Al Saleh, Fouad M Al Saleh

PRINCIPAL ACTIVITIES: Building and civil engineering contractors, importers and distributors of building materials, construction and earth-moving equipment, heavy machinery and contractors' plant

Principal Agencies: Clark Equipment, USA; Clark Int Marketing, W Germany; Delmag, W Germany; Acrow Wolf, W Germany; Bureau Veritas, France; Dale Electric, UK; AG (LMF), Austria; Acrow Eng, UK; A Air Filter Co, USA; Schlieren Elevators, Switzerland; Sika Compounds; Culligan; USA; De Jongs Maschinefabriek, Holland

Branch Offices: PO Box 4093, Abu Dhabi, UAE; 2 rue Annaba, Rabat, Morocco; London, UK; Manama, Bahrain; Cairo, Egypt; and USA

Parent Company: Musaad Al Saleh & Sons Investment Group

Associated Companies: Mass Equipment & Trading; Musaad Al Saleh & Sons Travel Co (Shipping Dept); Kuwait Building Industries; Kuwait Co for Process Plant Construction & Contracting; Kuwait Computer Services Co; Uniceramic, Lebanon; Union Bank of Oman, Oman

Principal Bankers: Gulf Bank; Burgan Bank; Al Ahli Bank of Kuwait

Financial Information:

	1989 KD'000
Authorised capital	4,000
Paid-up capital	4,000

Principal Shareholders: Hamad M Al Saleh; Dawood M Al Saleh; Mohammed M Al Saleh; Foad M Al Saleh; Nouri M Al Saleh; Fawzi M Al Saleh

Date of Establishment: 1937
No of Employees: 1,200

AL SALEM, IBRAHIM A, & CO

PO Box 1532 Safat, 13016 Kuwait
Tel: 2431658
Cable: JAMES
Telex: 22133, 22307 James-Kuwait

Chairman: Ibrahim A Al Salem
Directors: Ibrahim A Al Salem, Sulaiman Haddad

PRINCIPAL ACTIVITIES: Import, export and commision agency, building materials, furniture, hardware and carpets

Principal Agencies: 'Comag' Carpet Industries, Brussels; Rural Coir Industries

Principal Bankers: National Bank of Kuwait SAK, Commercial Bank of Kuwait SAK

Date of Establishment: 22nd April 1960

AL SANE CONSTRUCTION

PO Box 25901 Safat, 13120 Kuwait
Tel: 2444721, 2444731
Telex: 44080 Saneium Kt

Chairman: Mustafa Abdul Hamid Al Sane (Proprietor)

PRINCIPAL ACTIVITIES: General trading, contracting and construction, building materials, plant and equipment

Principal Agencies: Volvo Penta Marine & Industrial Engines; Storebro Leisure Boats & Workboards; CSL Silicone Products

ALSAWAN CO WLL

PO Box 576 Safat, 13006 Kuwait
Tel: 4746019, 4740886
Cable: SAWAN
Telex: 30035 Kt

Chairman: Mohamed Alsawan
Directors: A W Al-Sawan

PRINCIPAL ACTIVITIES: Shipping, forwarding, travel agents and general agents

Principal Agencies: Saudia, Sabena, Alia Jordanian Airlines, Czechoslovakian Airlines, Johnson Line, Everett Steamship Corp, San Rocco Line, Arcepey Shipping Co, Czechoslovak Shipping

Branch Offices: Ahmadi, Fahaheel (Kuwait), Syria, Lebanon, Czechoslovakia

Date of Establishment: 1963
No of Employees: 141

KUWAIT

AL SAYER, MOHD NASER, & SONS EST

PO Box 485 Safat, 13005 Kuwait

Tel: 4713622 (10 lines)

Cable: Shahnan Kuwait

Telex: 30187 Shahnan Kt, 40987 Toyota Kt

Telefax: 4718692

President: Naser Mohamed Al-Sayer

Directors: Faisal Bader Al-Sayer (Vice Chairman), Musaed
  Bader Al-Sayer, Sayer Bader Al-Sayer, Mubarak N Al Sayer,
  Mohamed N Al-Sayer

Senior Executives: Dennis A Stickley (Managing Director &
  Chief Executive)

PRINCIPAL ACTIVITIES: Distribution of automobiles; auto spare
  parts, forklifts, engineering goods; transportation;
  manufacture and marketing of cattle and poultry feeds, soft
  drinks; car rental; manufacturers' representation; electrical
  contractors; printing; stationery; travel & tourism

Principal Agencies: Toyota Motor Corp, Japan; Yokohama
  Rubber Co, Japan; Furukawa Batteries, Japan; Beecham, UK;
  RC Cola, USA; Parle, India; Kawasaki, Japan; Hitachi
  Excavators, Japan; Lotus Cars, UK; Nippon Shario, Japan

Branch Offices: PO Box 8765, Dubai, UAE

Subsidiary Companies: Bahra Trading Co, Green Belt Transport
  Co, United Marketing Co (Kuwait), Al Sayer Soft Drinks
  Factory, Kuwait Animal Feed Factory; Musaed Bader Al Sayer
  printing Press; Musaed Bader Al Sayer Est; Al Sayer Travel &
  Tourism

Principal Bankers: National Bank of Kuwait; Commercial Bank
  of Kuwait; Gulf Bank

Principal Shareholders: Family concern

Date of Establishment: 1955

No of Employees: 1,000

AL SHARHAN AEROSOL EST

PO Box 424 Safat, 13005 Kuwait

Tel: 813801/1/2/3

Cable: Alsharhan

Telex: 22239 Aerosol Kt

Telefax: 4830585

Chairman: Ahmed A Al Sharhan

Directors: Walid A Al Sharhan (Managing Director), Laurence J
  Bennett (Technical Director)

Senior Executives: Munzer Saddiq (Sales Manager), Jasser
  Kaddoumi (Production Manager), Khalid A Al Sharhan
  (Personnel Manager), Issac Fernandes (Technical Supervisor),
  Ms Munira Makawi (Company Secretary)

PRINCIPAL ACTIVITIES: Manufacture and marketing of
  aerosols, detergents, and toiletry items; packaging
  contractors

Branch Offices: Office and Factory: Canada Dry St, Industrial
  Area, Shuwaikh, Kuwait

Parent Company: Al Sharhan Est

Subsidiary Companies: Al Sharhan Envelopes Est; United Food
  Centre Co; Kuwait Paper Products Mnfg Co

Principal Bankers: Al Ahli Bank of Kuwait; Gulf Bank; National
  Bank of Kuwait

Financial Information:

	1989
	KD'000
Sales turnover	1,000
Authorised capital	300
Paid-up capital	300

Date of Establishment: 1968

No of Employees: 200

AL SHAWAF, ABBAS AHMAD, & BROS CO WLL

PO Box 1902 Safat, 13020 Kuwait

Tel: 4719530, 4716477 (5 lines)

Cable: Alshawafco

Telex: 23035, 23071 SWF

Telefax: 4749580

Chairman: Abbas Ahmad Al-Shawaf

Directors: Saleh Al Shawaf (Managing Director)

Senior Executives: Zaid Saleh Al Shawaf (Deputy Managing
  Director and Service Manager), Ahmad Saleh Al Shawaf
  (Deputy Managing Director and Spare Parts Manager)

PRINCIPAL ACTIVITIES: Automobile agents, autoparts,
  batteries and tyres, central air conditioning and electronic
  appliances

Principal Agencies: Nissan Vehicles & Accessories, Copam
  Computers, Calegro Products (Medical)

Branch Offices: Fahaheel, Kuwait

Subsidiary Companies: Gulf Quadripartite Trading Co; Ali
  Ahmad Al Shawaf & Bros

Principal Bankers: National Bank of Kuwait; Commercial Bank
  of Kuwait; Alahli Bank of Kuwait; Burgan Bank; Gulf Bank

Financial Information:

	1989
	US$'000
Sales turnover	25,000
Authorised capital	12,000
Paid-up capital	6,000

Principal Shareholders: Al-Shawaf Family

Date of Establishment: 1951

No of Employees: 200

ALSHAYA, MOHAMMED HOMOOD, CO

PO Box 181 Safat, 13002 Kuwait

Tel: 4843025, 4843825, 4841964

Cable: Alshaya

Telex: 22322 Alshaya KT

Telefax: 4848051

Owners: Saleh Ali Homood Alshaya, Abdullatif Ali Homood
  Alshaya, Abdulaziz Mohammad Homood Alshaya (Chairman)

Directors: Hamad Abdul Aziz Alshaya (Managing Director),
  Muhammad Abdul Aziz Alshaya (Executive Director), Ayman
  Abdul Latif Alshaya Alshaya (Executive Director), Saoud Abdul
  Aziz Alshaya (Personnel Director)

PRINCIPAL ACTIVITIES: Real estate, importers, wholesalers &
  retailers, agencies, sanitaryware and building materials,
  consumer goods and accessories, electrical appliances and
  catering equipment, earthmoving equipment, industrial
  equipment and tools and industrial supplies, household
  accessories, maternity & childrens wear, bedlinen, department
  store operations, foodstuffs

Principal Agencies: Clairol; Buchtal; Bobrick; Delorme; Sottini;
  Mothercare; Elefaten; Primigi; Lanvin; Oshkosh; BhS; Frette;
  Swaroski; Favols; Stefnbok; Match 1; Ceramica Imola; Ferrari;
  Move Werk; Vincenzo Zucci; Industries Bures; Calida; Gedy;
  Luis Calle; Nicobond; Ospag Laufen; Doberg; Marrie pierre;
  Anne de Solene; Inda; Lysdrap; Dieweitte Laeter; Jasminie St
  Onge; New Holland Ford; Amman Duommat; Alvan Blanch;
  Burnett; Pracht; Dari; Warwick; Concrete Vibration; Asada;
  Pedrollo; MEP; Ullrich; Karl M Rich; MCM; Kubota; Weda
  Okuda; Witco; Reed; China North Ind; Stephen & Carter;
  Hospital Equipment Komatsu; Electrolux; Cefla; Foemm;
  Frimont Scotman; Carpigiani; BMIL; Caddie; Clarke; American
  Lincoln; Gorenje; David & Booder; Zeiss; Ikon; etc

Branch Offices: Affiliates:PO Box 543, Riyadh, Saudi Arabia and
  PO Box 1277, Deira, Dubai, UAE

Subsidiary Companies: Intermarkets; Redsea Import & Export
  Co; Alinjaz Contracting Co; Oriental Hotels Co; Pan Arab
  Computer Centre (PACC); Kuwait Automotive Import Co;
  Medinah Oberoi Hotel

Principal Bankers: Commercial Bank of Kuwait; National Bank of Kuwait; Bank of Kuwait and the Middle East

Financial Information:

	1989 US$'000
Paid-up capital	30,000

Principal Shareholders: Saleh, Abdul Latif and Abdul Aziz Alshaya

Date of Establishment: 1890

No of Employees: Approx 200 (excluding subsidiaries and affiliates)

AL-TOWAIJRI TRADING & CONTRACTING CO WLL

PO Box 4450 Safat, 13045 Kuwait

Tel: 4716554, 4716880

Cable: ALTOWAIJRI

Telex: 23084 TOWIJRI

Chairman: Khalid Ibrahim Al-Towaijri

Directors: Hamad Al-Towaijri (Deputy General Manager), Fahed Al-Towaijri (Asst General Manager)

PRINCIPAL ACTIVITIES: Contractors (construction - aluminium works), interior designing and decorating; supply of furniture and tiles, import, wholesale and retail of mercedes truck spare parts, manufacturers' representatives and tenders

Principal Agencies: Clyde Industries, Australia; Alco Power Inc, Auburn New York; Control and Applications, Spain; Cubiertas, Spain

Subsidiary Companies: Maps-Kuwait

Principal Bankers: Burgan Bank SAK

No of Employees: 150

AL WAZZAN, ABDEL AZEEZ, & SONS

PO Box 1251, Kuwait

Tel: 910555

Telex: 22410 Wazaniah Kt

Chairman: Mohamed Abdel-Azeez Al-Wazzan

Directors: Yousef Abdel-Azeez Al-Wazzan, Homoud Abdel-Azeez Al-Wazzan

PRINCIPAL ACTIVITIES: Construction, sewerage, asphalt, real estate, money exchange, hospitals, carpentries, building materials, crushers, pharmaceuticals

Principal Agencies: Sony, Sanyo, Hitachi, Afel'er (German Asphalt Plants)

Branch Offices: Kuwait; UK; Syria

Subsidiary:/Associated Companies: Mohamed Abdel Azeez Al-Wazzan & Partners, PO Box 2678, Kuwait

Principal Bankers: Al-Ahli Bank, Kuwait

AL WAZZAN, MOHAMMED, STORE CO WLL

PO Box 2678, Kuwait

Tel: 4816232, 4833692

Cable: Mazen

Telex: 23151 Sahni Kt

Telefax: 4833693

Chairman: Mohd Abdul Aziz Al-Wazzan

Directors: K S Sahni (Managing Director)

Senior Executives: J S Sahni

PRINCIPAL ACTIVITIES: Import and distribution of auto parts and accessories and commission agents, computer dealers

Principal Agencies: United Incandescent Lamp & Elec Co, Hungary; Dayco, USA; Simoniz, UK; Stenor, UK; GMN Georg Muller Kugellarfabric, W Germany; Holt Chemicals; Turtle Wax Polishes

Branch Offices: Faheel Industrial Area, Faheel, Kuwait

Principal Bankers: Al-Ahli Bank of Kuwait; Gulf Bank KSC

Principal Shareholders: Mohd A Al Wazzan; K S Sahni; Mutlak Saleh Mustafa

Date of Establishment: July 1960

No of Employees: 35

ALYAN TRADING CORPORATION

PO Box 935 Safat, 13010 Kuwait

Tel: 433292, 2413795, 2413798

Cable: Alyan

Telex: 22970 ALTEST

Chairman: Yousuf Alyan

Senior Executives: Basim Nimer (Manager), Islam Darwish (Manager)

PRINCIPAL ACTIVITIES: Importers, exporters and manufacturers' goods; soaps, detergents and stationery

Associated Companies: Kuwait Times; ALTCO (Import and Export)

Principal Bankers: Gulf Bank

Principal Shareholders: Proprietorship

Date of Establishment: 1961

AL ZAYANI TRADING CO

Thunayan Al Ghanim Bldg, PO Box 41 Safat, 13001 Kuwait

Tel: 4833514, 4833478, 2437426, 4718944, 4741887, 4735220, 4739155

Cable: Automobile

Telex: 23005 Mobile KT, 44403 Zayani KT

Telefax: 4744631

Chairman: Jassim Al Zayani

Directors: Mohammed Al Zayani

Senior Executives: Nail Zayani (General Manager), Varughese Easaw (General Sales Manager), Mohammed Reedy (Financial Manager), Talat Othman (Legal Adviser), Michel Ayat (Commercial Vehicles Division Manager)

PRINCIPAL ACTIVITIES: Import and distribution of cars and spare parts, trucks and buses, consumer goods, office furniture, lubricants, tyres, batteries, garage equipment, vehicles, service & repairs, tools, industrial machinery, jewellery and boats & accessories

Principal Agencies: Daihatsu Motor, Japan; Tata Export, India; Esso Middle East Marketing, Bahrain; Godrej & Boyce, India; Houtoku Co, Japan; Itoki, Japan; Tecalemit Garage Equip, UK; Crypton Triangle, UK; Hockman Lewis, USA; Devilbiss, USA, UK and Canada; OEM Singapore; Diethelm, Singapore; Estel, Italy; Calus, Italy; Rotary Lift Exports, USA; Muller, France; Chloride, UK; T I Bradbury, UK; M A Nas, Turkey; Bayliner Marine Corp, USA

Sister Companies: Kuwait Automobile & Trading Co

Principal Bankers: Bank of Bahrain & Kuwait; Bank of Kuwait & Middle East; Commercial Bank of Kuwait; Gulf Bank; National Bank of Kuwait

Financial Information:

	1989 KD'000
Sales turnover	5,000
Profits	350
Authorised capital	1,000
Paid-up capital	1,000

Principal Shareholders: Jassim Al Zayani; Mohammed Al Zayani; Nail Al Zayani

Date of Establishment: 1952

No of Employees: 250

AMIRY CONTRACTING & TRADING CO

PO Box 110 Safat, 13002 Kuwait

Tel: 847258, 845346, 845972

Cable: Abubakre

Telex: 30408 AMTRAC KT

Telefax: 4841208

Chairman: Ahmad Saad Al-Amiry

KUWAIT

Directors: Musaed Al-Amiry (Director General)
Senior Executives: Ghassan Rajeh (Finance Manager), Ali Kauser (Sales Manager), Gul Advani (Sales Manager), Ali Al Harbi (Personnel & Admin Manager)

PRINCIPAL ACTIVITIES: Construction and trading; electronic industries; yachts; food products
Principal Agencies: Bertram Yacht, Division of Whittaker
Subsidiary Companies: Printed Circuits and Electronic Industries; Amiry International Food WLL; Amiry International Marine WLL
Principal Bankers: Al Ahli Bank; Commercial Bank of Kuwait; Burgan Bank
Financial Information:

	1989
	KD'000
Sales turnover	4,000
Profits	250
Authorised capital	750
Paid-up capital	750
Total assets	3,500

Principal Shareholders: Ahmad Al-Amiry, Musaed Al-Amiry, Hamed Al-Amiry
Date of Establishment: 1960
No of Employees: 1,500

ARAB ADVERTISING AGENCY

PO Box 2221 Safat, 13023 Kuwait
Tel: 2435921, 2435950
Cable: Offarabe
Telex: 22348 Kt Offarabe
Telefax: 2419692

President: Hassan A K Haikal (also Managing Director)
Directors: Souad Haikal (General Manager)
Senior Executives: Hisham Jaafari (Executive Managing Director), Ghassan Haikal, Walid Haikal, Hadi Al Alawi

PRINCIPAL ACTIVITIES: Advertising, marketing research and public relations
Branch Offices: Bahrain, UAE, Lebanon
Associated Companies: Arab Advertising Agency, Beirut, Lebanon
Principal Bankers: Alahli Bank of Kuwait; National Bank of Kuwait; Commercial Bank of Kuwait

Principal Shareholders: Hassan Haikal
Date of Establishment: 1936
No of Employees: 60

ARAB AGRICULTURAL CO KSC

PO Box 25310 Safat, 13114 Kuwait
Tel: 2442060, 2442061, 2413587
Cable: IETEEMAN
Telex: 22628 ATC KT

Chairman: Fawaz Ibrahim Al Qattan
Directors: Abdullah Rashed Bu Qammaze

PRINCIPAL ACTIVITIES: Landscaping, design, irrigation and maintenance works for private gardens and public areas
Parent Company: Arab Trust Company KSC
Principal Bankers: Commercial Bank of Kuwait; Midland Bank

Principal Shareholders: Arab Trust Company; Nassar Al Nassar
Date of Establishment: September 1978
No of Employees: 100

ARAB BUILDERS MERCANTILE CO WLL

PO Box 22779 Safat, 13088 Kuwait
Tel: 2460725, 2460727, 2460726, 2460728
Cable: ARBIDM
Telex: 46019 ARBILD KT
Telefax: 2460727

Chairman: Abdulredha A Khorsheed
Directors: Waleed A Khorsheed (Managing Partner)

Senior Executives: Eng Jawdat Atiya (Commercial Division Manager), Rasheed Abu Jaber (Transport Manager)

PRINCIPAL ACTIVITIES: Construction, representing construction companies; joint ventures, trade in construction materials and equipment
Principal Agencies: Clay Cross (Iron & Foundries), UK; Electroimpex, Bulgary; West-East Trading Co, Canada; 4Seasons Log Homes, Canada; Sonoco Tubes Co, Canada; Zeongan Industrial Co, South Korea; Enpoco Ltd, Canada; Pelagonija, Yugoslavia; Institute of Earthquake Engineering and Engineering Seismology, Yugoslavia; Anglo-Deutsche Engineering Services, UK
Subsidiary Companies: Al-Maha Transport & Clearing Est, PO Box 22779 Safat, Kuwait; Future Est for Food Trading, Kuwait
Principal Bankers: Bank of Kuwait & The Middle East; Al-Ahli Bank of Kuwait
Financial Information:

	1989
	KD'000
Sales turnover	2,000
Profits	150
Authorised capital	200
Paid-up capital	200
Total assets	500

Principal Shareholders: Abdulredha A Khorsheed; Waleed A Khorsheed
Date of Establishment: 1981
No of Employees: 85

ARAB BUILDING MATERIALS CO

PO Box 697 Safat, 13007 Kuwait
Tel: 4817971/2, 4810240
Cable: Shiral
Telex: 23117 Arma
Telefax: 481755

Chairman: Mohamad Ali Boudair
Directors: Abdul Hussain Haji Mohd Bahman, Ali Mango, Mohd T Hudhud, Said H Malas, Mohd A Malas
Senior Executives: Mohammed Walid Malas

PRINCIPAL ACTIVITIES: Import, stocking, wholesale, and retail of building materials, timber, steel bars, and plywood, terrazzo tiles, white cement, marble chips, teak squares
Associated Companies: Jordan Construction Materials Co Ltd, Amman, Jordan; Arab Building Materials Co, Dubai; Arab Building Materials Co, Abu Dhabi; Arab Building Materials & Co, Qatar; Delmon Building Materials Est, Bahrain; Saudi Building Materials Est, Riyadh, Dammam and Jeddah; Arab Building Materials Co, Muscat, Oman
Principal Bankers: National Bank of Kuwait; Alahli Bank; Gulf Bank; Kuwait Real Estate Bank; Commercial Bank of Kuwait
Financial Information:

	1988/89
	US$'000
Sales turnover	31,442
Profits net	2,437
Authorised capital	6,250
Paid-up capital	6,250
Current & fixed assets	22,569
Total assets less depreciation	14,030

Date of Establishment: 1959
No of Employees: 45

ARAB COMMERCIAL ENTERPRISES (KUWAIT)

PO Box 2474 Safat, 13025 Kuwait
Tel: 2430718, 2431498
Cable: Comment Kuwait
Telex: 22076 Ace Kt

Senior Executives: Aziz Abussoud (Vice President), Sami Bikhazi (Manager Kuwait)

PRINCIPAL ACTIVITIES: Insurance agents and brokers, surveyors and settling agents, travel agents
Branch Offices: Saudi Arabia; Lebanon; Kuwait; Bahrain; Qatar; Oman; United Arab Emirates; Yemen; Jordan; USA
Parent Company: Head Office in Riyadh, Saudi Arabia
Principal Bankers: First National Bank of Chicago, Geneva

Principal Shareholders: Abdullah Al Ajel, Suleiman S Olayan
Date of Establishment: 1959

ARAB CONTRACTOR CO KSC

PO Box 26664 Safat, 13127 Kuwait
Tel: 4730088, 4730818
Cable: Developco
Telex: BIULDUP 23058 KT

Chairman: Mustafa Al Sani
Directors: Saleh Salem Abdul Haid (Managing Director)
Senior Executives: Basim Al Boutie (General Manager)

PRINCIPAL ACTIVITIES: Contractors for civil engineering and construction works; also dealing with building materials and construction equipment
Associated Companies: Kuwait Development Co (Investment and Real Estate Co); Arab Trust Co (Financial Investment Co)
Principal Bankers: Commercial Bank of Kuwait

Principal Shareholders: Kuwait Development Co, Arab Trust Co

ARAB EUROPEAN FINANCIAL MANAGEMENT CO SAK

A.R.E.F.

PO Box 24100 Safat, 13101 Kuwait
Tel: 2410180 (5 lines)
Cable: Coaref
Telex: 22631, 22810, 23912 Coaref KT
Telefax: 2413749

Chairman: Abdul Muhsen Al Thuwainy
Directors: Leon D'Halloy (Vice Chairman), Ahmad Saleh Al-Shaya, Raed Abdulatif Al Thuwainy, Marcel Guichard, Khaled Yousef Al Modaf, Abdullah Al Qassar, Muthana Al Hamad, Ali Al Bahar
Senior Executive: Guy Jumelle (General Manager), Joel Letouze (Secretary General), Akram Dabbagh (Gulf Marketing), Ghalis Omar (Business Development), Roy J Boustani (Portfolio Department), Abdelhalim Kadi (Legal Department), C N Hariharan (Dealing Room), Ahmed Al Bahar (Consumer Loans Department)

PRINCIPAL ACTIVITIES: Investment consultants, portfolio management, real estate investment, foreign exchange, acquisitions in Europe
Branch Offices: London, Madrid, Paris
Principal Bankers: Banque Nationale de Paris; National Bank of Kuwait SAK; Commercial Bank of Kuwait SAK

Principal Shareholders: Avecles Investment Ltd, Bermuda (27%); Banque Nationale de Paris (22%), Al Thuwainy Trading Co (15%), Hamad A Al Hamad (14%)
Date of Establishment: January 1976
No of Employees: 59

ARAB EUROPEAN INTERNATIONAL TRADING CO

A.R.T.O.C.

PO Box 23074 Safat, 13091 Kuwait
Tel: 2421390/4
Cable: Falcon
Telex: 22366 Acsa; 22945 Acsa

Chairman: Abdullah Omar Al-Yagout
Directors: Suleiman Ahmed Al-Haddad (Deputy Chairman & Managing Director), Mahmoud Khaled Aladasani (Advisor to the Board), Peter John de Savary (Managing Director), Abdul

Baki El-Nouri, Hussain Mohammed Elbaz (General Manager), John C Walker, Albert V Styrum

PRINCIPAL ACTIVITIES: Agents and representatives involved in various commercial operations, including settlement of international accounts, multilateral and trade exchange operations; purchasing and selling, property, brokerage, and participation in investment projects
Principal Agencies: Willco Oil Inc, UK; Holland Bergen Op Zoom; Independent Oil Corp, France; International Harvester, USA
Associated Companies: Tate & Lyle, UK; Astley & Pearce, UK; Wyld Leytens Diamond, Belgium; Paktank BV, Netherlands
Principal Bankers: Alahli Bank of Kuwait; Commercial Bank of Kuwait; Bank of Kuwait and the Middle East; Banque De Paris; Artoc Bank and Trust

Principal Shareholders: Hussain Mohammed El-Baz, Suleiman Ahmed Al-Haddad, Abdulla Alomar Alyagout, Mohammed Abdl Aziz El-Wazzan, Abdul Baki El-Nouri, Mahdi and Abdulsamed Habib Al-Zahr, Abdul Aziz Soliman Aldousri, Mahmoud Khaled El-Adasani, Husain Makki Aljuma, Abdul Aziz Ahmed Al-Essa, Ibrahim Al-Ibrahim, Abdul Taha El-Ali, Peter J de Savary, Paul J de Savary, Tate & Lyle, Pak Tank

ARAB FINANCIAL CONSULTANTS CO SAK

PO Box 23767, 13098 Kuwait
Tel: 2441742, 2441747, 2419498
Cable: Kaptsmali
Telex: 22421 Afcc, 22346 Arficon
Telefax: 2416274

Chairman: Abdullah Ahmed Al Sumait (also Managing Director)
Directors: Suleiman Abdul Aziz Al Dossari (Vice Chairman)
Senior Executives: Bader Abdullah Al Sumait (General Manager)

PRINCIPAL ACTIVITIES: Management and placement of public debt issues, management of funds, arrangement of corporate finance, short-term money market operations, indentification and evaluation of new projects and arrangement of real estate transactions
Principal Bankers: Philadephia International Bank; The Taiyo Kobe Bank; Commerzbank AG; Euroclear, Brussels
Financial Information:

	1989
	KD'000
Authorised capital	2,000
Paid-up capital	1,325

Date of Establishment: January 12th, 1975

ARAB FOOD SERVICES CO

PO Box 25414 Safat, 13115 Kuwait
Tel: 5721684, 5724177, 5716156
Cable: Foodserv
Telex: 22800 KT Dhow
Telefax: 5732299

Chairman: Mahmoud Alghanim

PRINCIPAL ACTIVITIES: Bakeries, fast food (20 outlets)
Principal Bankers: Commercial Bank of Kuwait; Bank of Kuwait & Middle East
Financial Information:

	1989
	KD'000
Sales turnover	2,000
Profits	170
Authorised capital	500
Paid-up capital	500
Total assets	1,115

Principal Shareholders: Mahmoud Alghanim
Date of Establishment: 1978
No of Employees: 193

KUWAIT

ARAB FUND FOR ECONOMIC & SOCIAL DEVELOPMENT

PO Box 21923 Safat, 13080 Kuwait
Tel: 2451580, 2453120
Cable: Inmarabi Kuwait
Telex: 22143 Kt Inmarabi, 22153, 23265 Inmarabi KT
Telefax: 2416758

Chairman: Abdlatif Y Al Hamad (Director General)
Members of Board: Ibrahim Fayez (Director), Badr Al Humaidi (Director), Hamoud Ibrahim Soomar (Director), Saleh Al Humaidan (Director), Othman Saadi (Director), Kais Al Badri (Director), Mabrouk Al Ajeil (Director), Mostafa Sahel (Director), Zein Mestiri (Deputy Director), Eissa Bourshaid (Deputy Director), Bashar Kabbarah (Deputy Director), Ismail Sidky Hafez (Deputy Director), Sayyid Ali Ahmed Zaki (Deputy Director), Ziyad Fareez (Deputy Director), Fathi Salem (Deputy Director)
Senior Executives: Omar El Nass (Director of Legal Dept), Ismail El Zabri (Director of Research & Studies), Mohammed M Azzuz (Internal Auditor), Mohammed Al Qatami (Acting Administration Director), Shibly Jadaa (Acting Finance Director), Idris Mahmoud (Acting Operations Director)

PRINCIPAL ACTIVITIES: Participates in financing economic and social development and inter-Arab projects in Arab countries
Principal Bankers: Most of the leading international Banks
Financial Information:

	KD'000
Authorised capital	800,000
Paid-up capital	644,221

Principal Shareholders: Governments of the Arab countries
Date of Establishment: 1968 (started operations in 1974)
No of Employees: 164

ARAB GROUP FOR EQUIPMENT & CONSTRUCTION

PO Box 23112 Safat, 13092 Kuwait
Tel: 4835320, 4835321
Cable: AGECOMPA
Telex: 23237 AGECO
Telefax: 4834337

Chairman: Ali A Al-Ghanem
Directors: Elias N Hauranieh (Managing & Sales Director)
Senior Executives: Horst Rosenauer (Technical Manager)

PRINCIPAL ACTIVITIES: Agents for tower cranes, batching plants, transit mixers, excavators, bulldozers, concrete pumps, trailer type and truck mounted, plastering machines, wheel loader, road and airport sweepers, rubber airsprings, hoist lifts, spare parts and after sales services
Principal Agencies: Liebherr-Export AG, Switzerland; Putzmeister-Werk, W Germany; Johnston Engineering, UK; Taurus Hungarian Rubber Works, Hungary; Kubota, Japan; Tumac, Sweden
Principal Bankers: Bank of Kuwait & the Middle East (HO); Gulf Bank (HO)
Financial Information:

	1989 KD'000
Sales turnover	1,000
Profits	200
Authorised capital	405
Paid-up capital	405

Date of Establishment: 1976

ARAB MARITIME PETROLEUM CO

Arab Maritime Petroleum Transport Co

PO Box 22525 Safat, 13086 Kuwait
Tel: 2411815/20/30, 2448260/4
Cable: Arabtanco
Telex: 22360 Tankers; 22180 Amptc; 23175 Arabmar

Chairman: Sheikh Rashed Owaidha Al Thani (Qatar)
Directors: Sheikh Rashid Owaidha Al Thani (Chairman, Qatar), Abdul Rahman Ahmed Al Sultan (Vice-Chairman & Managing Director, Kuwait), Ibrahim Al Tahir Abu Rakhis (Vice-Chairman, Libya), Abdul Aziz Al-Abdulla Al Turki (Saudi Arabia), Sheeba Said Al Hamily (UAE), Peljuedj Mourad (Algeria), Eid Abdullah Yousef (Bahrain), Moujed Abed Al-Zahra Hamza Al-Obeidi (Iraq)

PRINCIPAL ACTIVITIES: Maritime transport of hydrocarbon substances (crude oil, petroleum products, liquified gases and petrochemicals)
Branch Offices: Saudi Arabia; Libya; Qatar; United Arab Emirates; Algeria; Iraq; Bahrain; Egypt
Principal Bankers: United Bank of Kuwait, London; National Bank of Kuwait; Gulf Bank of Kuwait
Financial Information:

	US$'000
Authorised capital	500,000
Paid-up capital	459,354

Principal Shareholders: AMPTC is owned and financed by the Governments of United Arab Emirates, Algeria, Bahrain, Egypt, Iraq, Kuwait, Libya, Qatar, Saudi Arabia
Date of Establishment: 1973
No of Employees: 46

ARAB PETROLEUM CONSULTANTS

PO Box 22699 Safat, 13087 Kuwait
Tel: 2415860, 2412561, 2415890
Cable: Abtaruju Kuwait
Telex: 22598 Zilfi

Chairman: Sheikh Abdullah Hamoud Tariki
Directors: Sheikh Abdullah H Tariki, Dr Hamed Kamal El Din, Dr Aziz S Audeh, George A Zeito

PRINCIPAL ACTIVITIES: Petroleum consultants
Branch Offices: APC Services Inc, Dallas, Texas, USA
Principal Bankers: National Bank of Kuwait, Kuwait; Republic National Bank of Dallas

ARAB TRANSPORT CO/ARATRANS KUWAIT SAK

PO Box 20599 Safat, 13066 Kuwait
Tel: 4842160, 4848190, 4849618
Cable: Forwarder
Telex: 22659 Ktrans Kt, 30407 Ktrans Kt
Telefax: 4845388

Chairman: Saud Abdulaziz Al Zamel
Senior Executives: Kahtan Al Sheraidah (Manager), Amer Mubarek Al Ajmi (Deputy Manager), Nouri Al Saad (Marketing & Operations Manager)

PRINCIPAL ACTIVITIES: International fowarders by land, sea and air
Principal Agencies: Various Freight Forwarders throughout the world
Parent Company: United Arab Shipping Company SAG
Subsidiary Companies: Sister Companies: Dubai, Abu Dhabi
Principal Bankers: Gulf Bank KSC, Commercial Bank of Kuwait
Financial Information:

	1988/89 KD'000
Sales turnover	2,000
Profits	400
Authorised capital	500
Paid-up capital	500

Principal Shareholders: United Arab Shipping Co SAG
Date of Establishment: 1969
No of Employees: 24

ARAB TRUST COMPANY KSC

PO Box 5365 Safat, 13054 Kuwait
Tel: 2442060/1
Cable: Ieteeman
Telex: 22628 Atc Kt, 46693 ATC KT, 22716 FORATC KT
Telefax: 2418957

Chairman: Jassim Marzouk Boodai
Directors: Fawaz Ibrahim Al Qattan (Deputy Chairman), Ahmed
   Nasser Abdulla Al Hamlan, Saleh Yacoub Al Homaidi, Tarik
   Abdul Karim
Senior Executives: Riad O Assad (Adviser to the Board),
   Abdullah Bou Qammaz (General Manager), Yacoub Al
   Sharhan (Banking & Trust Manager), M B Madhusudan (
   Financial Manager), Nawal Taji (Administration Manager)

PRINCIPAL ACTIVITIES: Merchant banking activities with
   emphasis upon consultancy in all fields of industry and
   commerce
Subsidiary Companies: Arab Agricultural Co KSC; Basmah Real
   Estate Co KSC; Electrical Projects Co KSC
Principal Bankers: Commercial Bank of Kuwait; Chase
   Manhattan Bank; United Bank of Kuwait; Deutsche Bank,
   Sumitomo Bank, Bank Leu
Financial Information:

	1988/89
	KD'000
Profits	18
Authorised capital	5,000
Paid-up capital	5,000
Total shareholders funds	7,260
Total assets	38,075

Principal Shareholders: Commercial Bank of Kuwait; Kuwait
   Insurance Company; plus 31 other Kuwaiti Shareholders
Date of Establishment: October 1975
No of Employees: 19

ARABI COMPANY WLL

PO Box 4090 Safat, 13041 Kuwait
Tel: 737316, 743086
Cable: Hamsef
Telex: 23012 Hamsef KT

Chairman: Abdulla Ahmed Al-Eissa
Directors: Abdul Aziz Yousuf Al-Essa (Managing Director)
Senior Executives: Nabil Shtayyeh (General Manager)

PRINCIPAL ACTIVITIES: Import and distribution of hand tools,
   power equipment, heavy machinery, garage equipment, and
   electrical equipment, air conditioning equipment and spare
   parts
Principal Agencies: Hunter Engineering Co, USA; Rainbird
   International, USA; ABS Pumps, Germany; Grundfos,
   Denmark; Dow Corning, Belgium; TRW Williams, USA; Hoke
   Int, USA; Nishinion Generator Manufacturing Co, Japan;
   SFEME, France; Emil Steidle, Germany; Skyclimber Europe,
   Belgium
Branch Offices: Canada Dry Branch, Kuwait (Tel 835343)
Associated Companies: Industrial Services & Supplies Co, PO
   Box 5581, Fahaheel, Kuwait; Gulf Services & Industrial
   Supplies Co, Ruwi, Muscat; Formost Irrigation Co, Kuwait;
Principal Bankers: Gulf Bank KSC: Burgan Bank SAK

Principal Shareholders: Chairman and directors as described
Date of Establishment: 1964
No of Employees: 110

ARABIAN CO FOR INSULATIONS CHEMICALS & CONSTRUCTION MATERIALS WLL

PO Box 4658 Safat, 13047 Kuwait
Tel: 4848376, 4847584, 4842194
Cable: LEAKPROOF
Telex: 23495 LIKPRUF
Telefax: 4841754

Chairman: Abbas J H Al Dashti
Directors: Khalid A Youssef, Mohd Khalid Katmeh
Senior Executives: Majd M K Al Katmeh (Managing Director),
   Ahmed Shaker (Finance Manager), Sali Fahmi (Sales
   Manager), Jamal Shehadeh (Export Sales Manager), Samer
   Meselmani (Marketing Manager), Fouad Ayash (Technical
   Manager), Iman Hussein (Admin Manager)

PRINCIPAL ACTIVITIES: Waterproofing, insulations, flooring,
   maintenance
Principal Agencies: Zedcor, Meynadier, Interplastic, Villas, L B
   Chemicals
Branch Offices: Egypt, Lebanon
Parent Company: ARABICON
Subsidiary Companies: Jasim & Sediq Cashcount
Principal Bankers: National Bank of Kuwait; Burgan Bank
Financial Information:

	1989
	KD'000
Sales turnover	1,500
Profits	27%
Authorised capital	700
Paid-up capital	700
Total assets	1,100

Date of Establishment: 1977
No of Employees: 50

ARABIAN GULF MECHANICAL SERVICES & CONTRACTING CO LTD

PO Box 1348 Safat, 13014 Kuwait
Tel: 2410100/4
Cable: Fraih Kuwait
Telex: 22312 Fraih KT
Telefax: 2435868

President: Abdul Rahman Farhan Al Fraih
Directors: Emad Abdul Rahman Al Fraih (Managing Director
   Finance), Choei Mutoh (Managing Director Operation, Projects
   and Technical)
Senior Executives: Kuniyasu Nakagami (Manager Marine &
   Technical Affairs)

PRINCIPAL ACTIVITIES: Offshore oilfield marine services and
   offshore oil production facilities maintenance services; supply
   of tug, crew, mooring, utility, service boats and barges
Branch Offices: Kuwait and Saudi Arabia
Subsidiary Companies: Food Supply Co WLL
Principal Bankers: National Bank of Kuwait; Gulf Bank of
   Kuwait; Bank of Kuwait and Middle East

Principal Shareholders: Abdul Rahman Farhan Al Fraih, Emad Al
   Fraih
Date of Establishment: 1960
No of Employees: About 300

ARABIAN LIGHT METALS KSC

PO Box 2230 Safat, 13023 Kuwait
Tel: 3985206/7/8/9/10
Cable: Kualex-Kuwait
Telex: 44243 ALM KT
Telefax: (965) 3984925

Chairman: Mohammed Naki (Managing Director)
Directors: Nasser Naki, Abdul Aziz Naki
Senior Executives: Adeeb Al Naimi, George Thaliath, Leslie
   Braganza

PRINCIPAL ACTIVITIES: Aluminium profile extrusion,
   anodization, powder coating of aluminium profiles, paint line,
   remelting and casting aluminium billets, die design and
   manufacture; Sandalor process, thermal barrier profiles
Subsidiary Companies: Kuwait Aluminium Co KSC; United Glass
   Co WLL; Kuwaiti Sudanese Aluminium Co Ltd (Al-Khartoum)
Principal Bankers: Burgan Bank; National Bank of Kuwait; Gulf
   Bank

Financial Information:

	1989
	KD'000
Sales turnover	4,566
Profits	144
Authorised capital	6,500
Paid-up capital	5,000
Total assets	5,038

Principal Shareholders: Kuwait Aluminium Company, Mohammed Naki
Date of Establishment: 1976
No of Employees: 250

ARABIAN TRANSPORTATION VEHICLES INDUSTRIAL CO (ATVICO)

PO Box 5106 Safat, 13052 Kuwait
Tel: 4675966, 4675381, 4675410, 4675895, 4675614
Cable: ATVICO
Telex: 23042 ATVICO
Telefax: 4675381

Chairman: Bassam Sulaiman Al Otaibi
Directors: Sameer Al-Omani, Samer Khanachet, Robert Lohr, Ali Ghadhanfari, Mohammad Al Majed
Senior Executives: Sameer Al Omani (Vice Chairman), Abdul Latif Al-Onaizi (General Manager), Jawad Abul (Planning & Sales Manager)

PRINCIPAL ACTIVITIES: Manufacture of industrial vehicles (trailers, semitrailers, tankers, tippers, car-carriers, lowbeds, tank transporters, garbage collecting systems, etc)
Principal Agencies: Liquid, Australia; FX Meiller, West Germany
Parent Company: National Automative Manufacturing & Trading Co, PO Box 4555 Safat, Kuwait
Principal Bankers: Commercial Bank of Kuwait (HO)
Financial Information:

	1989
	KD'000
Sales turnover	495
Profits	128
Authorised capital	1,600
Paid-up capital	1,480
Total assets	563

Principal Shareholders: National Automotive Manufacturing & Trading Co, Kuwait; Industrial Bank of Kuwait; Lohr SA, France
Date of Establishment: 25th June 1977
No of Employees: 72

ARTOC BANK & TRUST LTD

PO Box 23074 Safat, 13098 Kuwait
Tel: 2421390/4
Telex: 22366 Acsa Kt; 22945 Acsa Kt

PRINCIPAL ACTIVITIES: Provides all international banking facilities and specialises in investment in Western Countries

Principal Shareholders: Member of the ARTOC SAK group of companies

ASWAN ENGINEERING EST

PO Box 2390 Safat, 13024 Kuwait
Tel: 2447326, 2426729
Telex: 23421 Aswanco KT

Chairman: Yacoub S Mosleh
Directors: Hanna Y Qaqundha

PRINCIPAL ACTIVITIES: Contracting and trading
Principal Agencies: Townson & Coxson, UK; Delhi Iron & Steel Co
Branch Offices: Electrical Department Section; Zaid Al Khalid Bldg, Rasem Al Ghadban, Tel 2419050

Principal Shareholders: Chairman and Director as described

ATEEQY TRADING & ENGINEERING ENTERPRISES

PO Box 699 Safat, 13007 Kuwait
Tel: 4717945/6/7, 4717941, 4713059
Cable: Ateeq Kuwait
Telex: 23007 Ateeq Kt

President: Abdullah Salem Al-Ateeqy
Directors: Hamad Al-Ateeqy (Senior Vice President), Nayef Al-Ateeqy (Vice President)
Senior Executives: Shah Mohammed Siyal (Sales Manager), Riyadh Al Naji (Contracts Manager)

PRINCIPAL ACTIVITIES: Trading in diesel engines, generating sets, building materials and equipment, construction machines; copper tubing, electrical equipment, engineering items, construction work and specialised finishes and services
Principal Agencies: Klockner-Humboldt-Deutz AG, Germany; Zettelmeyer Maschinenfabrik GmbH, Germany; Schildknecht Innenausban, Germany; Irmer & Elze, Germany; Mogurt, Hungarian Trading Co for Motor Vehicles; Auto Panels Electrical Systems Ltd, UK; JM Engineering Services, UK; Meprocon AG, Holland; Lucky Engineering Co Ltd, Korea; Hartl PGC Engg Ltd, Austria; Litwin Engineers & Constructors, USA
Branch Offices: Washington, USA
Principal Bankers: National Bank of Kuwait; Al Ahli Bank of Kuwait; Bank of Kuwait & Middle East

Date of Establishment: 1961
No of Employees: 500

ATKINS, W S, OVERSEAS LIMITED

PO Box 25356 Safat, 13114 Kuwait
Tel: 5652436, 5650759
Telex: 23611 Kinskwt KT
Telefax: 5652136

PRINCIPAL ACTIVITIES: Architecture, engineering, planning, management and landscaping consultants
Branch Offices: In the Middle East: Abu Dhabi, Dubai, Bahrain, Oman, Saudi Arabia
Parent Company: W S Atkins Ltd, Epsom, Surrey, UK

ATLAS COMMERCIAL (KUWAIT) LTD

PO Box 5609 Safat, 13057 Kuwait
Tel: 813633, 813141, 813357
Cable: Atlasco
Telex: 22003 Atlasco Kwt; 23466 Ackl Kt

Chairman: Mustafa Jassim Boodai
Directors: Mozes Jacobs (Managing Director)
Senior Executives: Samuel Jacobs (Executive Director)

PRINCIPAL ACTIVITIES: Commission agents; import and stocking of building materials, cement, steel, timber and plywood
Principal Bankers: Commercial Bank of Kuwait (Shuwaikh Branch); Bank of Kuwait and the Middle East (Head Office); Burgan Bank (Shuwaikh Branch)

Principal Shareholders: Chairman and directors as described
Date of Establishment: December 1962
No of Employees: 28

AUJAN, SAUD, & BROS CO WLL

PO Box 29 Safat, 13001 Kuwait
Tel: 4336131
Cable: Aujan/Kuwait
Telex: 30029 Aujan
Telefax: (965) 2560451

Senior Executives: Faried Aujan (General Manager), Faisal Aujan (Sales Manager Beverages), Sh Ibrahim Shamsuddin (Finance & Administration Manager), Kamal K Al Ashi (Sales Manager Tobacco Div), Nizar Ersheid (Marketing & Sales Manager Foodstuffs)

PRINCIPAL ACTIVITIES: Importers and distributors of cigarettes, tobacco and smokers' requisites, soft drinks, foodstuffs and confectionery

Principal Agencies: Gallaher Int'l, UK; SEITA, France; Royal Theodorous Niemeyer, Holland; J N Nichols (Vimto), UK; Chupa Chups, Spain; China National Cereals & Foodstuffs, China; Pastificio Maltagliati, Italy; United States Playing Card Co, USA

Parent Company: A W Aujan & Bros Co, Saudi Arabia

Subsidiary Companies: Aujan Soft Drink Industries, Saudi Arabia; Aujan Industrial Supplies Co, Saudi Arabia; Aujan Crestwood Co, Saudi Arabia; A R Aujan & Sons, Bahrain

Principal Bankers: Commercial Bank of Kuwait

Financial Information:

	1990 KD'000
Authorised capital	300
Paid-up capital	300

Principal Shareholders: Aujan family

Date of Establishment: 1905 as a group, 1947 in Kuwait

No of Employees: 55

AWAZ, SAYED ALI SAYED,

PO Box 2591 Safat, 13026 Kuwait
Tel: 2422360
Cable: Najeeb
Telex: 22052 Alawi Kt
Telefax: 2433061

Directors: Ali Awaz Alawi (Owner)
Senior Executives: Moiz Kapasi (Electrical Division)

PRINCIPAL ACTIVITIES: Commission agents, import and distribution of electrical equipment and fittings (wire, cables, conduit); auto spare parts and ready made garments

Branch Offices: Alawi Novelty Exhibition; Alawi Readymade Garments Exhibition

Subsidiary Companies: Kuwait Electronics Co WLL; Alawi & Al-Kahla Textiles Co

Principal Bankers: National Bank of Kuwait; Gulf Bank of Kuwait

Date of Establishment: 1952

AYYAD TRADING CO WLL

PO Box 23601 Safat, 13097 Kuwait
Tel: 4840500, 4840986, 4840961
Cable: Ayyadpart
Telex: 22502 Ayyad Kt
Telefax: 4836874

Directors: Zuhair M Abdulla (Managing Director), Faraj W Matar (Partner/Director), Mrs Mariam Al Essa (Partner/Director)

PRINCIPAL ACTIVITIES: Agents and distributors of foodstuffs and beverages

Principal Agencies: Manley, UK; Kellogg's; H J Heinz; Lindt, Switzerland; S&W, USA; Juice Bowl, USA; Hillsdown, UK; HP Foods, UK; Tuborg, Denmark; Yurita, Spain; T W Beach, UK; Cross Paperware, UK; Jacobs Coffee, Germany; Trappys, USA; Jones Dairy Products, USA; Lea & Perrins, UK; Fox's Biscuits, UK; Dibona, Germany; Hero, Switzerland; HP Bulmers, UK

Subsidiary Companies: Louthan Foodstuff Co, Kuwait

Principal Bankers: Gulf Bank of Kuwait

Financial Information:

	US$'000
Sales turnover	10,000
Authorised capital	1,200
Paid-up capital	1,200

Principal Shareholders: Directors as described

Date of Establishment: 1972

No of Employees: 65

BADER AHMAD AL KHORAFI

See AL KHORAFI, BADER AHMAD,

BADER AL SAYID HASHIM AL GHARABALLY

See AL GHARABALLY, BADER AL SAYID HASHIM,

BADER AL MULLA & BROS CO WLL

See AL MULLA, BADER, & BROS CO WLL

BAHAR & FALAH GENERAL TRADING & CONTRACTING CO

PO Box 25781 Safat, 13118 Kuwait
Tel: 2430237, 2427406
Cable: Fahouse
Telex: 44686 Bafaco

Chairman: Adnan A Al Bahar

Directors: Adnan Abdulaziz Al-Bahar, Bader Nasir Al Falah

Senior Executives: Salah A Khalaf (Transport), Mahadi Abdul Razik (Vending & Catering), O A Ghaffar (Tender & General Trading)

PRINCIPAL ACTIVITIES: General trading and contracting; import, agents and representatives, electrical and catering equipment and leisure goods; vending machines and transportation, electrical and mechanical contractors

Principal Agencies: Brook Bond Vending System; Drinkmaster; Instra Bru; J K N Sankey

Principal Bankers: Commercial Bank of Kuwait; Burgan Bank; Kuwait Finance House

Principal Shareholders: Adnan Abdulaziz Al-Bahar; Bader Nasir Al Falah

Date of Establishment: 1979

BAHMAN, ESSA & ABEDALI, CO

PO Box 339 Safat, 13004 Kuwait
Tel: 2442040, 2435984
Cable: Essabahman Kuwait
Telex: 22448 Essa

Chairman: Essa Bahman

Directors: Abedali Bahman

PRINCIPAL ACTIVITIES: Supply of tyres and tubes, timber, cement, steel, construction materials, telecommunication & electrical equipment, insurance agency

Branch Offices: Dubai

Principal Bankers: Commercial Bank of Kuwait; National Bank of Kuwait

BANK OF BAHRAIN & KUWAIT

PO Box 24396 Safat, 13104 Kuwait
Tel: 2417140
Cable: Bahkubank
Telex: 23220 Kuwbbk
Telefax: 2440937

Chairman: Rashid Abdul Rahman Al Zayani (Head Office Bahrain)

Directors: Saleh Mubarak Al Falah, Ebrahim Abdullah Al Hamar, Faisal Mohammed Al Radwan, Mohammed Abdul Rahman Al Yahya, Ali Saleh Al Saleh, Ebrahim Eshaq Abdul Rahman, Hassan Haider Darwish, Hilal Mushari Al Mutairi, Hassan Khalifa Al Jalahma, Yousif Abdulla Al Awadi, Masoud Mahmood Jawher Hayat

Senior Executives: V T Tudball (General Manager), Hamad Al Sagar (Deputy General Manager), Abdul Latif Al Abdul Razzaq (Senior Operations Manager), Thunayan Al Ghanim (Treasurer), Abdul Aziz Al Rashed (Manager Customer Services), Assad Fleifel (Manager General Services), Mohamad Al Duraie (Senior Marketing Manager)

PRINCIPAL ACTIVITIES: Commercial banking

Parent Company: Head office in Bahrain

Associated Companies: Bank of Oman, Bahrain & Kuwait (49%)

KUWAIT

Principal Shareholders: Bahraini Individuals (50%); Kuwaiti Banks and Financial Institutions (50%)

Date of Establishment: Kuwait branch opened for business in April 1978

No of Employees: 135 (Kuwait branch)

BANK OF KUWAIT AND THE MIDDLE EAST KSC

PO Box 71 Safat, 13001 Kuwait

Tel: 2459771 (50 lines)

Cable: Bankuwait

Telex: 22045 Kwt

Telefax: 2461430

Chairman: Fahad Abdulrahman Al-Bahar

Directors: Ali Mohammed Al-Otaibi (Deputy Chairman), Fawzi Hamad Al-Sultan, Usama Zaid Al Kazemi, Barrak Abdul Mohsen Al Tukhaim, Shaker Abdul Majeed Al Kazemi, Abdul Wahab Ahmed Al Fahad, Suleiman Hamad Al Dalali, Hamed Saleh Al Saif

Senior Executives: Saleh M Al-Falah (General Manager), Saud A Al Gharabally (Deputy General Manager, Corporate Banking & Foreign Div), Issam A Al Usaimi (Deputy General Manager, Retail & Branches), Ali M Bedah (Deputy General Manager, Administration), Johnston L Evans (Advisor to the Board), Mohammed S Al Rasheed (Asst General Manager, Personal Banking Div)

PRINCIPAL ACTIVITIES: Commercial banking

Branch Offices: 19 branches in Kuwait

Associated Companies: Banque Arabe et Internationale d'Investissement, Paris; Bank of Bahrain and Kuwait, Bahrain; Arab International Bank of Tunisia, Tunisia; Industrial Bank of Kuwait KSC, Kuwait; Moroccan-Kuwait Development Group, Casablanca; Kuwait Reinsurance Co KSC, Kuwait; Compagnie Arabe et Internationale d'Investissement, Luxembourg; United Bank of Kuwait, London; Kuwait Clearing Co SAK, Kuwait; Kuwait & M E Finance Investment Co, Kuwait; Securities Group SAK, Kuwait

Date of Establishment: 1971

No of Employees: 703

BEHBEHANI, ADEL, GENERAL TRADING CO WLL

Behbehani Commercial Complex, Sharq, PO Box 24555 Safat, Kuwait 13106

Tel: 2457831/3

Cable: Reza Kuwait

Telex: 30237 Almidco KT

Telefax: (0965) 2457832

Chairman: Ahmed Yousuf Behbehani

Directors: Mohd Reza Yousuf Behbehani, Adel M R Behbehani

Senior Executives: C George John (General Manager)

PRINCIPAL ACTIVITIES: Projects, general and industrial trading, investments, agents and distributors

Principal Agencies: Water Engineering, UK; Costain Int'l, UK; Land & Marine, UK; Foundation Engineering, Dubai; Von Poll, Switzerland; Rexnord, USA; Durametallic Corp, USA; Epic Inc, USA; Linde AG, Germany; Krupp Atlas, Germany; Krupp Industrietechnik, Germany; National Building Contruction, India; Sintel, Spain; Telefonica, Spain

Associated Companies: Ahmed Yousuf Behbehani Est, Kuwait & Geneva; Mohd Saleh & Reza Yousuf Behbehani, Kuwait; Morad Yousuf Behbehani Group of Cos

Principal Shareholders: Ahmed Yousuf Behbehani, Adel M R Behbehani

Date of Establishment: 1982

BEHBEHANI, MOHAMED SALEH & REZA YOUSUF,

PO Box 341 Safat, 13004 Kuwait

Tel: 4719888, 4719023

Cable: Shereen Kuwait

Telex: 30180 Shereen KT

Telefax: 4760070

President: Mohammad Saleh Behbehani

Directors: Mohammad Reza Behbehani (Vice President), Jasem M S Behbehani, Abdulaziz M S Behbehani, Adel M R Behbehani, Abdul Wahab M S Behbehani, Abdul Ghani M S Behbehani

Senior Executives: Osmond M Louis

PRINCIPAL ACTIVITIES: Import of electrical appliances, watches, printing machinery, laboratory test equipment, communication equipment, STP products, cars, tyres and auto spare parts

Principal Agencies: Morris Ashby Ltd, STP Corporation, Jeep International, General Motors, Communications Co, Collins Radio, Polar Mohr; Heidelberger Druckmaschinen AKT; Abscania Vabis; Skyway Luggage, Isuzu Motors

Branch Offices: Bahrain: Behbehani Bros Ltd, PO Box 168, Tel 253872 UAE: Mirage General Trading Est, PO Box 3551, Dubai, Tel 60276

Associated Companies: Mohamed Saleh Y Behbehani, PO Box 370 (Insurance and shipping Agents); Seven-Up Bottling Co Ltd, PO Box 4076, Safat, Kuwait

Principal Bankers: Alahli Bank of Kuwait; Commercial Bank of Kuwait

Principal Shareholders: Mohammad Saleh Behbehani; Mohammad Reza Behbehani

Date of Establishment: 1947

No of Employees: 225

BEHBEHANI, MORAD YOUSUF,

PO Box 146 Safat, 13002 Safat, Kuwait

Tel: 4844000 (10 Lines)

Cable: Barakat Kuwait

Telex: 22048 Behbehani Kt, 23496 Motors Kt

Telefax: (00965) 4844053

President: Morad Yousuf Behbehani

Senior Executives: Ali Morad Behbehani (Vice President), K H Watt (Adviser), W R Sukkari (Sales Manager Engineering Div), G Dzierzon (General Manager Motors Division)

PRINCIPAL ACTIVITIES: Distributors for Volkswagen, Audi and Porsche cars and garage operators. Airconditioning engineering and engineering services, including diesel and gas generators, electric boilers. Retailers and wholesalers of consumer goods, TV, audio, video, watches, luggage. Electronic engineering and scientific equipment, general sales and travel agents, investment and real estate

Principal Agencies: Akai Electric Co, Japan; Carrier Int Corp, USA; Ericsson, Sweden; John Brown Engineering, UK; Nestle Corp, Switzerland; Omega, Switzerland; Petbow Ltd, UK; Piaget, Switzerland; Samsonite Corp, USA; Sansui Electric Co, Japan; Volkswagenwerk, Audi Group; Baume & Mercier, Switzerland; Wild Heerblugg, Switzerland; Tissot, Switzerland; Novado, Switzerland; Barco NV, Belgium; Toa Electric Co, Japan; Alpine Electronics, Japan

Subsidiary/Associated Company: Behbehani Motors Co, Shuwaikh, PO Box 4222, Safat, Kuwait; Behbehani Travel Bureau, Fahad Al Salem St, PO Box 3488, Safat Kuwait; Behbehani Airconditioning Co; Ali Morad Behbehani Est; General Trading & Contracting; Behbehani Bros Ltd, Bahrain; Mirage General Trading Est, UAE; Behbehani Investments Co, Kuwait; Behbehani Real Estate Co, Kuwait

Principal Bankers: Alahli Bank of Kuwait; Commercial Bank of Kuwait; National Bank of Kuwait; Gulf Bank

Principal Shareholders: Morad Yousuf Behbehani (owner)

Date of Establishment: 1936

No of Employees: 650

BEHBEHANI MOTORS COMPANY

PO Box 4222 Safat, 13043 Kuwait
Tel: 4844000 (10 lines)
Cable: Motors Kuwait
Telex: 23496 Motor Kt
Telefax: 4844053

President: Morad Yousuf Behbehani
Directors: Ahmed Yousuf Behbehani
Senior Executives: George Dzierzon (General Manager), K H
Watt (Financial Controller)

PRINCIPAL ACTIVITIES: Importers, distributors, spare parts
and repair service for Volkswagen, Audi, Porsche
Principal Agencies: Volkswagen; Audi; Porsche; Mariner;
Rustoleum Corp; Becker Auto Radio
Branch Offices: Kuwait and Ahmadi
Parent Company: The Morad Yousuf Behbehani Establishment
Associated Companies: Behbehani Airconditioning Co, PO Box
22750 Safat, 13088 Kuwait; Behbehani Travel Bureau, PO
Box 3488 Safat, 13035 Kuwait
Principal Bankers: Alahli Bank; Commercial Bank of Kuwait;
Gulf Bank, National Bank of Kuwait

Date of Establishment: 1954
No of Employees: 150

BOODAI TRADING CO LTD

PO Box 1287 Safat, 13013 Kuwait
Tel: 2427158, 2427159, 2427120-127
Cable: Columbus Kuwait
Telex: 22050 KT, 22210 KT
Telefax: 4848368

Chairman: Mustafa J Boodai
Directors: Jassim Marzook Boodai (Deputy Chairman), Marwan
Marzook Boodai (Managing Director), Jassim Mustafa Boodai
(Regional Director)
Senior Executives: Fawaz Ibrahm Al Qattan (Corporate
Manager), Walid F Kaassamani (Corporate Treasurer), Aziz H
Siddiqui (Corporate Financial Controller)

PRINCIPAL ACTIVITIES: Import and distribution of all types of
construction machinery and engineering goods, oilfield
equipment, garage equipment, machine tools, building
materials
Principal Agencies: Harnischfeger, USA; Lincoln Electric, USA;
Bros Road Machinery, USA; HAP Krane, W Germany;
Pedershaab Maskinfabrik, Denmark; Blaw Knox, UK;
Westinghouse Air Brake, USA; Kobe Steel, Japan; J I Case,
USA; James F Low Engineers, UK; Zenith Maschinenfabrik,
W Germany; Manitou, France; Elba Werk Maschinen, W
Germany; Leonhard Schmid, W Germany; Dynapac Maskin,
Sweden; Nissan Diesel Motor, Japan; Mitsubishi Heavy
Industries, Japan; Furukawa, Japan; Flygt, Sweden; Hudig, W
Germany; British Labour Pumps, UK; F G Wilson
(Engineering), UK; Saude Getriebe, W Germany; SEAM, Italy;
Mannesmann Demag, W Germany; Toyo Umpanki, Japan;
Hokuetsu Industries, Japan; Machinoexport, Bulgaria; Black &
Decker, UK; Ridge Tool, USA; Secalt, Luxembourg; Enerpac,
Switzerland; Crosby, USA; James & Stone, UK; CRC Crose,
USA; Clemco, West G Bruntons, UK; Jenkins Bros, Canada;
Gauges-Bourdon, UK; Est Bourdon, France; Spirax Sarco,
UK; BKL Alloys, UK; Dancord, Denmark; Flexitallic, UK; E H
Wach, USA; Widder, USA; Victor Equipment, USA; Thermal
Dynamics; USA; Usha Martin Black, India; Crane, USA;
Osborn Int, W Germany; Kango Wolf Power Tools, UK; Elora
Werkzeugfabrik, W Germany; Elektron Battery Chargers, W
Germany; James Neill Tools, UK
Branch Offices: PO Box 5108, Dubai, UAE, Tel 660080, Telex
45597; PO Box 6027, Abu Dhabi, UAE, Tel 320581, Telex
22983; PO Box 4569, Doha, Qatar, Tel 322982, Telex 44074;
PO Box 5215, Ruwi, Oman, Tel 701163, Telex 3154
Subsidiary Companies: Arab Equipment Est, PO Box 1660,
Dammam, Saudi Arabia

Principal Bankers: The National Bank of Kuwait, SAK - Kuwait;
The Commercial Bank of Kuwait, SAK - Kuwait

Principal Shareholders: Mustafa Jassim Boodai; Jassim
Marzook Boodai; Marwan Marzook Boodai
Date of Establishment: January, 1958
No of Employees: 400

BP MIDDLE EAST LTD

PO Box 36566, Raas Al Salmiya, 24756 Kuwait
Tel: 4835218, 4842988 ext 2814
Cable: Britpet Kuwait
Telex: 22069 Yaas Kt, 44901 Ganim Kt
Telefax: 4835218

PRINCIPAL ACTIVITIES: Supply and marketing of oil products,
lubricants and marine oil
Principal Agencies: Agents for BP (AA) Kuwait: Yusuf A
Alghanim & Sons

BRIAN COLQUHOUN & PARTNERS

See COLQUHOUN, BRIAN, & PARTNERS

BRITISH AEROSPACE

PO Box 26199 Safat, 13122 Kuwait
Tel: 4875208
Telex: 44306 SASHOTL KT

PRINCIPAL ACTIVITIES: Military aircraft
Parent Company: British Aerospace, UK

BUILDING & ROADS CO (BARCO) WLL

PO Box 1666 Safat, 13017 Kuwait
Tel: 2415957/58
Telex: 44147 KT
Telefax: 2415995

Senior Executives: Elias Zurub (Resident Engineer)

PRINCIPAL ACTIVITIES: Building contractors, roads and
flyovers
Parent Company: Contracting & Trading Co (CAT), PO Box 11-
1-36, Beirut, Lebanon

BURGAN BANK SAK

PO Box 5389 Safat, 13054 Kuwait
Tel: 2439000 (20 lines)
Cable: Burganbank
Telex: 23309, 22730, 22767 (General), 23152 (Dealing)
Telefax: 2461148

Chairman: Sheikh Ahmed Abdullah Al Ahmed Al Sabah (also
Managing Director)
Members: Ghanem Hamad Al Dabbous (Deputy Chairman),
Edwan Mohamad Abdulaziz Al Edwani, Hisham Abdulrazzak
Razzuqi, Dr Safaq Abdulla Al Rukaibi, Barrak Khalid Al
Dawood Al Marzouq, Jassim Ahmed Yousef Al Nusif, Jassim
Bader Al Majed, Salem Abdullatif Al Musallam
Senior Executives: Mohamed A Tawfiqi (General Manager),
Ahmed A Al-Hilal (Executive Manager, Administration), Abdulla
D Al Dakhil (Executive Manager, International Banking), Dr
Zouhair Kronfol (Senior Legal Advisor International Affairs),
Richard Stutely (Chief Economist), Aubyn Hill (Deputy Exec
Manager Marketing Dept), Terrance Dupuis (Deputy Exec
Manager Operations), Khodr Temsah (Deputy Exec Manager
Syndications), Vijay Caleb (Chief Credit Officer), Menon P A
Jayachandran (Loan Examiner), Syed Hasib (Chief Internal
Auditor), Christopher Wood (Manager Money Market -
Treasury)

PRINCIPAL ACTIVITIES: All activities relating to commercial
banking and investment
Associated Companies: Bank of Bahrain & Kuwait BSC,
Bahrain; Kuwait Reinsurance Co KSC, Kuwait; Industrial Bank
of Kuwait KSC, Kuwait; United Bank of Kuwait Ltd, London;
Arab Hellenic Bank SA, Athens; Kuwait Clearing Co SAK,

KUWAIT

Kuwait; Bahrain Middle East Bank EC, Bahrain; Arab Financial Service Co EC, Bahrain

Financial Information:

	1988/89 US$'000
Authorised capital	215,882
Issued & paid up capital	215,882
Total shareholders equity	571,269
Total assets	4,478,325

Principal Shareholders: Government of Kuwait represented by Ministry of Finance and public Kuwaiti investors

Date of Establishment: December 1975, operations commenced April 1977

No of Employees: 526

BURHAN KUWAIT INDUSTRIAL & CONSTRUCTION CO WLL

PO Box 20593 Safat, 13066 Kuwait

Tel: 818910

Telex: 44324 Buranco KT

PRINCIPAL ACTIVITIES: Building contractors, general contractors, turnkey services, manufacture of aluminium, glass products and building materials

BUSINESS MACHINES CO WLL

PO Box 21399 Safat, 13074 Kuwait

Tel: 2433960 (10 lines), 2416444, 2417555, 2429768

Cable: Cooperation

Telex: 23921 Makateb Kt

Chairman: Abdulla Omar Al Yaqout

Senior Executives: Mohammad Mubarak Al Rufaidi (General Manager), Omar Sabbah (Financial & Administrative Controller)

PRINCIPAL ACTIVITIES: Import and distribution of business machines, office equipment and supplies; steel case system furniture, word processor, computer accessories, micrographic equipment, bank security systems, engineering systems

Principal Agencies: Steelcase, USA; Diebold, USA; Mitsubishi, Japan; Technology Int'l, USA; Interface Int'l, USA; Microbox, Germany

Principal Bankers: Commercial Bank of Kuwait; Alahli Bank of Kuwait; Gulf Bank; National Bank of Kuwait

Principal Shareholders: Abdulla Omar Al Yaqout, Mohammad Mubarak Al Rufaidi, Sami Jasim Naqi

Date of Establishment: 1971

No of Employees: 105

CANAR TRADING & CONTRACTING CO

PO Box 1322 Safat, 13014 Kuwait

Tel: 2421802, 2411469, 2451480

Cable: Canarco

Telex: 22175 Canar Kt

Telefax: 2451481

Directors: Abdulkarim K Shawwa (Managing Partner)

Senior Executives: Omar Shawwa (Manager), Yusuf Khatib

PRINCIPAL ACTIVITIES: Supply of machinery and equipment and contracting for the oil, gas, petro-chemicals, water and power generation and related industries

Principal Agencies: Fluor, USA; Technipetrol, Italy; Union Pump, USA

Associated Companies: Mass Consultants & Services Co, Kuwait; Instruments Installation & Maintenance Co, Kuwait

Principal Bankers: Alahli Bank of Kuwait; Bank of Kuwait & The Middle East

Date of Establishment: 1970

No of Employees: 50

CARTON INDUSTRIES CO KSC

PO Box 24551 Safat, 13106 Kuwait

Tel: 4736516

Telex: 23811 Flexo Kt

PRINCIPAL ACTIVITIES: Manufacture of corrugated carton sheets and boxes

CENTRAL BANK OF KUWAIT

PO Box 526 Safat, 13006 Kuwait

Tel: 2449200, 2449219

Telex: 22101; 22173; 22118

Governor: Abdelwahab Ali Al Tammar

Directors: K A Al-Attiqi (Deputy Governor), I A Yelli, A H Al Hamad, Y I Al Ghanem, Y M Al Nisf, Y A Al Shalfan, H M Al Ali

Senior Executives: M Al Kadhi (Manager Research Department), Saleh Baqir (Manager Banking Supervision), Mubarak Al Noot (Manager Foreign Operations), Yassim Al Rushoud (Manager Administration)

PRINCIPAL ACTIVITIES: Banking; administration of State currency and credit policies

CHEMICAL & INDUSTRIAL SUPPLIES CO

PO Box 4040 Safat, 13041 Kuwait

Tel: 816739, 832017

Cable: Chemistry

Telex: 22112 Kt Cisco

President: Hani Jamil Qaddumi

Partner: William Abou Kalil

Senior Executives: Dr Nabil Qaddumi (Vice President), Muzaffar Hasan (Manager)

PRINCIPAL ACTIVITIES: Manufacturers' representatives and commission agents

Principal Agencies: Bayer AG, Germany; Eckart-Werke, Germany; Bignier Schmid Laurent, France; Ethyl SA, Belgium; Chemische Werk Huels, Germany; Cray Valley Products, UK; Capital Control, USA; Maschinenfabrik Hennecke, Germany; Katalysatorenwerke Houndry Huls, Germnay; Pluess Stauffer, Switzerland; Pleuger, Germany; Shamban International, USA; Schlegel Lining Technology, Germany and UK; Lurgi GMBH, Germany

Associated Companies: William Abou Kalil, Rabiya, Lebanon; William Abou Kalil, PO Box 1005, Damascus, Syria; William Abou Kalil, PO Box 919, Amman, Jordan; Industrial Chemicals Co, PO Box 6349, Sharjah (UAE); Safwan Trading & Contracting Enterprises, PO Box 20704 Safat, Kuwait

Principal Bankers: Commercial Bank of Kuwait; Bank of Kuwait and the Middle East; Chase Manhattan Bank, Bahrain

Principal Shareholders: Hani Jamil Qaddumi, William Abou Khalil

Date of Establishment: 1966

CHINA HARBOURS ENGINEERING CO (MIDDLE EAST)

PO Box 5449 Safat, 13055 Kuwait

Tel: 2540457, 2540474, 2540459

Telex: 23545 CHEC KT

Telefax: 2540763

PRINCIPAL ACTIVITIES: Marine construction, building and general contractors

Branch Offices: Abu Dhabi, Khartoum, Beirut, Cairo; also in Kuwait: PO BOx 44093 Hawally, 32055 Kuwait

Parent Company: China Harbours Engineering Company

Principal Bankers: Bank of China; Al Ahli Bank of Kuwait

COAST INVESTMENT & DEVELOPMENT CO KSC

PO Box 26755 Safat, 13128 Kuwait

Tel: 2468388

Cable: Sahelco

Telex: 46056, 46807

Telefax: 2415364

Chairman: Sheikh Saud Bin Sagar Al Qassimi

Directors: Waleed A Al Nusf, Mohammad J Al Sagar, Ahmed M Al Nagdi, Khalid A Al Shaya, Salem J Al Baker, Saleh M Al Falah, Abdullatif S Al Luhaib, Ahmad R Al Haroun, Abdullah S Al Mazroui, Yousef A A Al Bader

Senior Executives: Mohammad J Al Sager (Managing Director), Faisal Ben Khadra (General Manager), Dr Farouq A Zuaiter (Deputy General Manager)

PRINCIPAL ACTIVITIES: Investment company

Branch Offices: Ras Al Khaimah (UAE): PO Box 5413

Subsidiary/Associated Companies: Coast Holdings Int'l SA, Luxembourg; Coast Holdings Ltd, UK; Coast Securities Ltd, UK; Coast Management Ltd, UK; Dana Real Estate Co WLL, Kuwait; Thebes Agricultural Co WLL, Kuwait; Arab Investment & Development Group SAE, Egypt

Principal Bankers: National Bank of Kuwait, Kuwait; United Bank of Kuwait, London

Principal Shareholders: Kuwaiti businessmen (89%), UAE businessmen (10%), others (1%)

Date of Establishment: 1980

No of Employees: 63

COLQUHOUN, BRIAN, & PARTNERS

PO Box 36048, Al Raas, 24751 Kuwait

Tel: 5735307, 5744540, 5744708

Telex: 44306 SASHOTL KT

PRINCIPAL ACTIVITIES: Consulting engineering services covering highways and bridges, airports, marine works, defence installations, transportation planning, hotels and hospitals, industrial, residential, commercial and institutional buildings, electric power generation and distribution, water supply, sewerage and sewage disposal

Parent Company: Head Office: 42 Upper Grosvenor Street, London WI, UK

COMBINED BUILDING MATERIALS CO (COMBICO)

PO Box 1443 Safat, 13015 Kuwait

Tel: 4817848, 4817618, 4833291, 4833408, 4835204

Telex: 23313, 44354 Combico KT

Telefax: 4832124

PRINCIPAL ACTIVITIES: Supply of building materials, concrete admixtures, and industrial flooring

Parent Company: Fosroc Construction Chemicals, UK

COMMERCE & TECHNOLOGY CO COTECO

PO Box 25975 Safat, 13120 Kuwait

Tel: 2424525/6, 2426805

Telex: 44164 Coteco Kt

Senior Executives: Nabeel Al Fadhel (General Manager), Ghazi K Al Bader (General Manager)

PRINCIPAL ACTIVITIES: Consultancy, security and control systems

COMMERCIAL BANK OF KUWAIT SAK

PO Box 2861 Safat, 13029 Kuwait

Tel: 2411001 (50 lines)

Cable: Banktijari

Telex: 22004 CBK KT; 22470 CBK KT; 23307 CBK KT; 23739 CBK KT; 46758 CBK KT; 22167 CBK FX KT; 22300 CBK FX FT; 22458 CBK FX KT; 23768 VISA CBK KT

Telefax: 2450150

Chairman: Hamad A A Al Hamad

Directors: Faisal Yousuf Al Marzook (Deputy Chairman), Naser Al Athby Al Sabah (Member), Jasem Mishary Al Bader (Member), Talal Marzook Al Ghanim (Member), Rasheed Yacoub Al Nafisi (Member), Mohammad Ibrahim Al Fraih (Member), Sulaiman Khalil Al Yasin (Member), Fawaz Ibrahim Al Qattan (Member), Anwar Abdul Aziz Al Usaimi (Member), Hamad Al Yahya (Secretary to the Board), Hassan A E Dahabiyeh (Financial Adviser)

Senior Executives: Mohamed Abdulrahman Al Yahya (Chief General Manager), Richard K O Carey (General Manager), Terence L Hewett (General Manager), Mahmoud I Barhoum (Asst General Manager), Dalal A Al Ghanim (Asst General Manager), Jirar J Orfali (Asst General Manager), Hamad S M Al Sager (Asst General Manager), Norbert M Tiedemann (Asst General Manager), Michael S Baldwin (Asst General Manager), Ahmed N Al Hamlan (Asst General Manager)

PRINCIPAL ACTIVITIES: Commercial banking

Branch Offices: 1 in New York: 350 Park Avenue NY 10022, 1 European Representative Office: St Alphage House, 2 Fore Street, London EC2Y 5DA

Associated Banks & Affiliations: Kuwait Reinsurance Co, Kuwait; Kuwait Prefabricated Building Co, Kuwait; Arab Trust Co, Kuwait; Bank of Bahrain & Kuwait, Bahrain; Industrial Bank of Kuwait, Kuwait; Kuwait Pearl Investment Co, Kuwait; Investment Industrial Co, Kuwait; Kuwait Asia Bank, Bahrain; Kuwait Clearing Co, Kuwait; Pearl Holding Co, Luxembourg; Rif Bank, Lebanon; United Bank of Kuwait; UK

Principal Correspondents: Credit Lyonnais, New York, Citibank, New York; Continental Illinois National Bank, Chicago, United Bank of Kuwait, Kuwait; Deutsche Bank, Dusseldorf; Kuwait French Bank, Kuwait; Generale Bank, Bruxelles; Kredietbank, Bruxelles; Canadian Imperial Bank of Commerce, Toronto; Westpac Banking Corporation, Sydney; Sanwa Bank, Tokyo; Sumitomo Bank, Tokyo; Amsterdan Rotterdam Bank, Amsterdam

Financial Information:

	1988/89 US$'000
Profits	18,337
Authorised capital	174,249
Paid-up capital	174,249
Loans & advances	4,041,818
Deposits	5,759,353
Total assets	6,317089
Total balance sheet	7,269,938

Date of Establishment: June 1960

No of Employees: 1,126

COMMERCIAL FACILITIES CO SAK

PO Box 24284 Safat, 13103 Safat Kuwait

Tel: 2417050/7

Cable: TASSHILAT

Telex: 22812 KT TASSHIL

Telefax: 2455275

Chairman: Mishari Khalid Zaid Al-Khalid

Directors: Nasser Saad Abdulaziz Al-Saad (Vice Chairman), Abdallah Saud Al-Humaidhi (Managing Director), Musaed Bader Al-Sayer, Reda Yousef Al-Behbehani, Saleh Abdulmohsen Abdulaziz Al-Babtain, Adel Ahmad Al Woqoyan

Senior Executives: Kenneth Smith (General Manager), Fouad Al Zamer (Asst General Manager), Mustafa Al Redi (Customer Accounts Manager), Mohammed Bader (Accounts Manager), Mohammed Jaafar Ibrahim (Customer Services Manager),

Azmi Tawfiq (Computer Manager), Jaafar Hassouneh (Marketing Manager), Fahad Al Hajri (Branches Manager)

PRINCIPAL ACTIVITIES: Instalment credit, consumer and commercial; investment dealing

Branch Offices: Fahaheel, Kuwait; Jahra, Kuwait; Hawalli, Kuwait; Riqqai, Kuwait

Associated Companies: Financial & General Bank Plc, 13 Lowndes Street, London SW1X 9EX, UK

Principal Bankers: National Bank of Kuwait, The Gulf Bank, Commercial Bank of Kuwait, Alahli Bank, Burgan Bank, Bank of Kuwait & the Middle East, Bank of Bahrain & Kuwiat

Financial Information:

	1988/89 KD'000
Total income	4,691
Net income	3,374
Authorised capital	10,519
Paid-up capital	10,519
Shareholders'equity	18,556
Total assets	75,136

Principal Shareholders: 140 Kuwaiti Shareholders: Government (57%); Companies and private citizens

Date of Establishment: January 1977

No of Employees: 150

CONCORD INTERNATIONAL

PO Box 3862 Safat, 13039 Kuwait

Tel: 813009, 831463, 834950

Cable: Sparking

Telex: 22561 Tiger Kt

Directors: Ismail A Sayed (Managing Director)

PRINCIPAL ACTIVITIES: Electro-mechanical engineers, contractors, importers, stockist, representatives, diesel steam and gas power plants, underground networks, telephone exchange and communication systems; oil, water and gas pipe lines, pumping stations, fire fighting systems, air conditioning and ventilation

Principal Bankers: Gulf Bank of Kuwait, National Bank of Kuwait SAK

CONSOLIDATED CONTRACTORS CO (CONCO)

PO Box 509 Safat, 13006 Kuwait

Tel: 3980355, 3980250

Cable: Conco

Telex: 44215 Kt

Chairman: Hasib J Sabbagh

Directors: Said T Khoury (President), Fawzi Kawash (Group VP -Operations), Nabil Shawwa (Group VP - Finance & Corporate Development), Kevork Toroyan (Group VP - Construction Support & Administration)

Senior Executives: Yousef E Hayek (General Manager, Kuwait & Bahrain)

PRINCIPAL ACTIVITIES: General construction and engineering contractors, pipeline contractors, marine, civil and mechanical works

Branch Offices: Throughout the Middle East; Managing Office: Consolidated Contractors International Company Limited, Atrina Center, 32A Kifissias Ave, PO Box 61092, Amaroussion, Athens, Greece; Tel 219551, 219734; Telex 6829200

Parent Company: Consolidated Contractors Group (Limited)

Subsidiary Companies: Middle East Construction and Services Ltd, Liberia; Consolidated Contractors Co (Underwater Engineering) Ltd, Liberia; Consolidated Contractors Co WLL, Saudi Arabia; Consolidated Contractors Co SAL, Lebanon; Consolidated Contractors Co (Bahrain) WLL; Consolidated Contractors Co (Netherlands Antilles) NV, Curacao; and its wholly owned subsidiary Consolidated Contractors Co Europe BV, Holland; Jordanian Consolidated Contractors Co Ltd

Principal Bankers: Al Ahli Bank of Kuwait; National Bank of Kuwait; Kuwait Real Estate Bank

Financial Information:

	US$'000
Authorised capital	10,000
Paid-up capital	10,000

Principal Shareholders: Hassib Sabbagh and Said Khoury

Date of Establishment: 1952

No of Employees: 2,500 (Only in Kuwait)

CONSULTATIVE CENTRE FOR SCIENCE & TECHNOLOGY

PO Box 2607 Safat, 13027 Kuwait

Tel: 2424584

Telex: 23566 Wood KT

Telefax: 4837864

Directors: Abdulmohsen Al Jassar

Senior Executives: Maqsood Ali (Manager)

PRINCIPAL ACTIVITIES: Sales of video films relating to the development of science and technology

Date of Establishment: 1981

CONTRACTING & MARINE SERVICES SAK

PO Box 22853 Safat, 13089 Kuwait

Tel: 2410270/4

Cable: Mariserve

Telex: 22324 Marine Kt

Chairman: Mohammed A A Al Hamad

Directors: Abdullah A Jamal (Vice Chairman), Hisham S Al Otaibi (Managing Director), Saud A Al Rashed, Sulaiman N Al Omani, Anwar A Al Mullah, Yousef A Al Omani, Adnan A Al Bahar

PRINCIPAL ACTIVITIES: Marine construction works and services, construction of petroleum related projects offshore drilling

Subsidiary Companies: International Marine Construction Co SAK; Gulf Dredging Co SAK and Kuwait Drilling Company

Principal Bankers: Commercial Bank of Kuwait

Principal Shareholders: Major Participation by the Kuwaiti Ministry of Oil

Date of Establishment: 1973

CONTRACTING & TRADING CO (CAT)

PO Box 19 Safat, 13001 Kuwait

Tel: 2415957/58

Telex: 44147 KT

PRINCIPAL ACTIVITIES: Construction services for the oil industry; also civil, mechanical, and electrical engineering work

Principal Agencies: Mothercat

Branch Offices: Alkhobar, Riyadh, Jeddah, Abu Dhabi, Sharjah, Oman (Seeb)

Parent Company: Head office: PO Box 11-1-36, Beirut, Lebanon

COPRI CONSTRUCTION ENTERPRISES WLL

PO Box 4720 Safat, 13048 Kuwait

Tel: 818071, 818951

Cable: Coprico

Telex: 22718 Copri Kt

PRINCIPAL ACTIVITIES: Civil and building contractors, turnkey services

Branch Offices: Abu Dhabi

DAKHEEL ALJASSAR EST

See ALJASSAR, DAKHEEL, EST

DAMA TRADING CO WLL

PO Box 4726 Safat, 13048 Kuwait
Tel: 2414555
Cable: Bonwe
Telex: 22239 Aerosol Kt

Directors: Bader Al Sharhan

PRINCIPAL ACTIVITIES: General trading and contracting
specialising in building materials, prefabricated houses,
earthmoving equipment, safety equipment, trailers and
transportation equipment
Principal Bankers: Gulf Bank

DAR AL WATAN KSC

PO Box 1142 Safat, 13012 Kuwait
Tel: 4840950
Cable: Al Watan
Telex: 22565 Al Watan
Telefax: 4818481

Chairman: Mohamed Musaed Al Saleh
Directors: Musaid Al Jarallah, Jassim Al Mutawa, Othman
Yacoub Al Nasralah, Ghazi Bader Al Salem, Abdel Razaq Al
Muzaini
Senior Executives: Abdullah Ali Hindi (General Manager)

PRINCIPAL ACTIVITIES: Journalism, printing and publishing,
distributing 90,000 copies
Branch Offices: London, Morocco, Egypt, Bahrain, Lebanon,
Syria, Oman, Jordan, and USA
Parent Company: Gulf Distributing Co; Kuwait Paper Trading &
Industry; Commercial Guide Agencies
Principal Bankers: The Gulf Bank; Bank of Kuwait & the Middle
East; National Bank of Kuwait; Burgan Bank
Financial Information:

| | 1989 |
	KD'000
Authorised capital	5,000
Paid-up capital	5,000
Total assets	8,400

Date of Establishment: 1973
No of Employees: 450

DHLA INTERNATIONAL TRANSPORTATION CO

PO Box 26523 Safat, 13126 Kuwait
Tel: 2442375
Telex: 44881 DHLA KWI KT
Telefax: 2443995

Chairman: Dr Faisal Al Kazemi

PRINCIPAL ACTIVITIES: Worldwide courier service; worldwide
parcel express service
Branch Offices: In the Middle East; Bahrain, Cyprus, Egypt
(Cairo, Alexandria), Jordan, Kuwait, Lebanon, Oman, Qatar,
Saudi Arabia (AlKhobar, Jeddah, Riyadh, Jubail, Tabuk, Taif),
UAE (Abu Dhabi, Dubai, Sharjah), Iraq
Parent Company: DHL International Ltd

DIJLA TRADING & CONTRACTING CO WLL

PO Box 26723 Safat, 13128 Kuwait
Tel: 2450320, 2450338
Telex: 46029 Luther KT

Chairman: Imad Abdul Hameed Al-Khudairy
Directors: Muhammad Imad Kamal Mahdy
Senior Executives: Ali A Hasan (Architect), Sabri A Husain
(Technical Engineer), Sabah Situ (Technical Engineer)

PRINCIPAL ACTIVITIES: General trading, civil, plumbing, fire
fighting contracting
Principal Bankers: Alahli Bank of Kuwait; Kuwait Finance House

Principal Shareholders: Soroor Al-Samaree
Date of Establishment: 1975
No of Employees: 350

DIRECTORATE GENERAL OF CIVIL AVIATION

PO Box 17 Safat, 13001 Kuwait
Tel: 4710222
Telex: 23038 Kt
Telefax: 4744649

PRINCIPAL ACTIVITIES: Civil aviation authority
Principal Agencies: CAA, UK

DOWELL SCHLUMBERGER CORPORATION

North Gulf District, PO Box 9574, Ahmadi, 61006 Kuwait
Tel: 3981208, 3985709, 3980674
Cable: ORANGE KUWAIT
Telex: 30103 ORANGE K

PRINCIPAL ACTIVITIES: Oil service company, cementing,
testing, stimulation
Branch Offices: Dubai; Abu Dhabi; Saudi Arabia; Oman; Egypt;
Jordan

No of Employees: 40

DRESSER (KUWAIT) SAK

PO Box 4544 Safat, 13046 Kuwait
Tel: 3262455/6/7
Cable: Dresserind Kuwait
Telex: 44911
Telefax: 3262434

Chairman: Abdulaziz Alaradi
Directors: Mohammed Darwish Alaradi, Khalid Al-Fassam

PRINCIPAL ACTIVITIES: Supply and sale of oilwell drilling mud
products, drilling bits; production of chemicals and equipment
Principal Agencies: Magcobar/Imco; Security; Swaco; Guiberson
Branch Offices: Territories covered: Kuwait; Iraq; Syria; Jordan;
Qatar; Bahrain; Cyprus
Parent Company: M I Drilling Fluids Co, Houston
Associated Companies: Dresser Industries Inc
Principal Bankers: Bank of Kuwait & Middle East

Date of Establishment: 1966
No of Employees: 65

EL HOSS ENGINEERING & TRANSPORT CO

PO Box 9304 Ahmadi, 61004 Kuwait
Tel: 3981388/9
Cable: Hoss Kuwait
Telex: 44213 Hoss
Telefax: 3981585

Chairman: Jaber El Hoss
Partners: Jaber El Hoss (Managing Director), Tarif El Hoss
(Managing Director)
Senior Executives: Ronald Jiggens (Marketing Manager),
George Kassis (Finance Manager)

PRINCIPAL ACTIVITIES: Contractors, fabrication, erection,
maintenance and transportation
Principal Agencies: Cooper-Industries SA (Gas & Oil); Paccar
USA
Parent Company: El-Hoss Engineering & Trading Co, Beirut,
Lebanon, PO Box 113-5130
Subsidiary Companies: Mechanical Equipment & Maintenance
Co Ltd
Principal Bankers: National Bank of Kuwait
Financial Information:

| | 1988/89 |
	US$'000
Sales turnover	10,000
Profits	750
Authorised capital	1,400
Paid-up capital	1,400
Total assets	12,000

Principal Shareholders: Faisal Al Ghanim, Makki Al Jumma, Jaber El Hoss, Tarif El Hoss
Date of Establishment: 1947
No of Employees: 450

ELECTRICAL BOARDS MANUFACTURING CO KSC

PO Box 25428 Safat, 13115 Kuwait
Tel: 4735418, 4745948
Telex: 30008 Ebomac KT
Telefax: 4713054

Chairman: Mahdi Q Al Shammary

PRINCIPAL ACTIVITIES: Manufacture of electrical boards
Principal Agencies: Merlin Gerin, France; Asea Brown Boveri, Germany

Date of Establishment: 1979
No of Employees: 150

ELECTRICAL PROJECTS CO KSC

PO Box 24668 Safat, 13107 Kuwait
Tel: 4732225, 4743340/2
Cable: ELECPROJ
Telex: 30164 EPCO FAC KT

Chairman: Abdulla Booquamaz
Directors: Hashim B Al-Gharabally (Vice Chairman & Managing Director), Naser A Babteen (Member)
Senior Executives: Mohd Salah Al Sayeed (Financial & Admin Manager)

PRINCIPAL ACTIVITIES: Erection of indoor and outdoor electrical installations, trading in electrical, mechanical and allied products, manufacture of L.V. switchgear and motor control centres
Principal Agencies: Telemecanique Electrique, France; Sider Export, Italy; Claude Lyons Ltd, UK; Aga Infrared Systems Ltd, UK; Dalmine Spa, Italy; R & A G Crossland Ltd, UK
Principal Bankers: Commercial Bank of Kuwait; Burgan Bank; National Bank of Kuwait; Bank of Kuwait & Bahrain

Principal Shareholders: Kuwait Development Company, Arab Trust Company, A A Al-Sanea, M I Al-Mufarrij, A M Al-Sabij, F A M Al-Mutair, A H Dosari, Khalid Al-Babteen, Naser Al-Babteen
Date of Establishment: 1977
No of Employees: 65

ELECTRONIC APPLIANCES CORPORATION

PO Box 2449 Safat, 13025 Kuwait
Tel: 2448040
Cable: Transistor Kuwait
Telex: 22019 Eack, 46557 Eacorp
Telefax: 2442688

Chairman: Adel F Risheq (also Managing Director)
Senior Executives: Abdulaziz S Al-Fulaij (Deputy Managing Director), Khalid Risheq (General Manager)

PRINCIPAL ACTIVITIES: Import of air-conditioners, electrical and electronic equipment and appliances, watches, office equipment, consumer goods, lighters and other household appliances and department stores merchandise
Principal Agencies: Fedders, USA; Admiral Intl, USA; K Hattori, Japan; Toshiba, Japan; Shin-Shirasuna Electric, Japan; Siera Electronics, Netherlands; Girmi Subalpina, Italy; Uchida Yoko, Japan; A Debs, Japan; Yoshinaga Prince, Japan; Elba, Italy; W Greer, Sussex; Burlington, USA; Rubbermaid, USA; Goldstar Co, Korea
Branch Offices: 26 Retail outlets
Subsidiary/Associated Companies: Araco (Arab Refrigeration & Airconditioning Company); Pan Arab (Pan Arab Advertising Company); The Grand Stores; Arabian Business Machines Company; Arab Arts Productions

Principal Bankers: Commercial Bank of Kuwait; National Bank of Kuwait; Alahli Bank of Kuwait; Bank of Kuwait and the Middle East; Gulf Bank
Financial Information:

	1988/89 KD'000
Sales turnover	11,353
Profits	447
Authorised capital	3,000
Paid-up capital	3,000
Total assets	10,631

Principal Shareholders: Mohamed Ahmed Al Rashed, Adel Falah Risheq, Abdulrahman Al Hadlaq, Abdulla Al Hadlaq, Abdulaziz Saud Fulaij
Date of Establishment: 1961
No of Employees: 310

ELMALA, GHANEM, & CO

PO Box 32073, Rumathiyah, 25551 Kuwait
Tel: 2443610
Cable: Ghanemcar
Telex: 22457

Directors: Ghanem Elmala

PRINCIPAL ACTIVITIES: General trading and contracting, import and distribution of cars and spare parts
Principal Bankers: Al Ahlia Bank

ENERGY SAVING SYSTEMS CO WLL (ESSCO)

PO Box 23801 Safat, 13099 Kuwait
Tel: 2436970
Telex: 44715 ESSCO KT

PRINCIPAL ACTIVITIES: Manufacture and supply of insulated panels, partitions and light weight construction systems

ERNST & YOUNG

Al Aiban, Ahmed, & Partners

PO Box 74 Safat, 13001 Kuwait
Tel: 2452880/7
Cable: Ernstaudit, Kuwait
Telex: 23125 Ernst KT
Telefax: 2456419

Partners: D A Dahman (Managing Partner), A M Al-Aiban, P J Duke, M L Hunter, R S Feddah, N R Abid, W Al Osaimi, L J Willard
Senior Executives: T C Sole, P Moir, P W Gillam, F Mohammad, R A Arnouq, P Harris, I A Sharif, E B Smith, A H Issa, M M Masoud, S S Khawani

PRINCIPAL ACTIVITIES: Accountants, tax advisers and management consultants
Branch Offices: In the Middle East: Bahrain; Egypt; Jordan; Kuwait; Lebanon; Oman; Qatar; Saudi Arabia; United Arab Emirates; Yemen

Date of Establishment: 1952
No of Employees: 95

ESSA & ABEDALI BAHMAN CO

See BAHMAN, ESSA & ABEDALI, CO

ESSA A ALAJEEL EST

See ALAJEEL, ESSA A, EST

EURO-KUWAITI INVESTMENT CO KSC

PO Box 43 Safat, 13001 Kuwait
Tel: 2449561, 2449571 (15 lines)
Cable: Cooperation - Kuwait
Telex: 44645; 44649 EKIC KT

Chairman: Abdul-Hamid Mansour Mazidi

Directors: Mishari Mohammed Al-Jassim, Manaf Mohammad Al-Hamad, Abdul-Rahman Mansour Al-Zamel, Ismail Ali Dashti, Ali Murad Behbehani, Mohammad Ibrahim Ma'Arafi, Turkey Suleiman Al-Othman

Senior Executives: Abdul Hamid Mansour Al-Mazidi (Chairman), Mishari Mohammad Al-Jassim (Deputy Chairman), Manaf Mohammad Al-Hamad (Managing Director), Mahmoud Ahmed Abu Ghaida (Company Secretary)

PRINCIPAL ACTIVITIES: Investment & Portfolio Management, local & international stockbroking, corporate finance & services, special projects

Subsidiary Companies: Euro Kuwaiti Investment Management NV; Arles Finance Co SA

Principal Bankers: Al Ahli Bank of Kuwait; Gulf Bank; National Bank of Kuwait; Bank of Bahrain & Kuwait; Commercial Bank of Kuwait; Chase Manhattan Bank; Burgan Bank; Merrill Lynch International Bank, United Bank of Kuwait

Date of Establishment: September, 1976
No of Employees: 75

FADDAN GENERAL TRADING & CONTRACTING CO WLL

PO Box 5874 Safat, 13059 Kuwait
Tel: 4749854, 4749864
Cable: ARROW
Telex: 22485 ARROW KT
Telefax: 4710973

Directors: Barges Hamoud Al Barges, Mohd. Samih Barakat
Senior Executives: Mounir Freij (Asst General Manager), Husam Zayed (Special Systems Manager), Haitham Barakat (Deputy General Manager)

PRINCIPAL ACTIVITIES: Trading, civil, electrical and mechanical contracting, electrical manufacturing, auto filter manufacturing (Gulf Filters), supply and maintenance of elevators, street lighting poles

Principal Agencies: Federal Electric, UK; Simplex GE, UK; John Rusling, UK; Edison Halo Ltd, UK; FED Ltd, UK; GTC Gas Turbine, UK; Regiolux, Germany; Schwabe, Germany; Disano, Italy; Fael Luce, Italy; Siemens, Germany

Principal Bankers: National Bank of Kuwait; Commercial Bank of Kuwait

Financial Information:

	1989
	US$'000
Sales turnover	5,000
Authorised capital	900
Total assets	1,000

Principal Shareholders: Partnership Company
Date of Establishment: 1965
No of Employees: Above 250

FAHAD AL JASSAR SONS FOR GENERAL TRADING & CONTRACTING CO

See AL JASSAR, FAHAD, SONS FOR GENERAL TRADING & CONTRACTING CO

FAHAD SULTAN SONS & CO WLL

PO Box 208 Safat, 13003 Kuwait
Tel: 2459361/2/3
Cable: Fasulco
Telex: 22427 Fasulco
Telefax: 2459363

Chairman: Salah Fahad Sultan (also Managing Director)
Directors: Basil Fahad Sultan (Director for Kuwaiti Investments), Ghassan Fahad Sultan (Director for International Investments & Commercial), Mazin Fahad Sultan (Director for Marine)

PRINCIPAL ACTIVITIES: Direct investments in Kuwaiti companies, real estate development, international investments

Principal Agencies: Hatteras Boats, Cobia Boats, Netherland Kable Fa (NKF), Sellotape
Principal Bankers: Gulf Bank, Kuwait; Burgan Bank, Kuwait
Financial Information:

	1989
	KD'000
Authorised capital	23,040
Paid-up capital	23,040
Total assets	44,376

Date of Establishment: 1974
No of Employees: 50

FAWAZ REFRIGERATION & AIR CONDITIONING CO WLL

Fawaz Group International

PO Box 20423 Safat, 13065 Kuwait
Tel: 5749306 (8 lines), 5749323/4, 5751044, 5752344, 5754744
Cable: Fawazhawa
Telex: 22351 Dalia Kt, 44786 Coolair Kt, 23464 SKM Kt
Telefax: 5714150, 5715297

Directors: Osama Mohammad Hussain Ali (Managing Director)
Senior Executives: Eng Azzam Saffarini (Executive Manager), Eng Naseer A Saeed (Technical & Marketing Manager), Eng Fahed Al Hajeri (Personnel & Admin Manager), Inder K Sharma (Finance Manager), A A Allan (Export Manager), Hussam Arrafa (Sales Executive)

PRINCIPAL ACTIVITIES: General contractors, air conditioning, refrigeration equipment, electrical and mechanical engineering

Principal Agencies: USA: Dunham Bush, Miracle Adhesives, Cambridge Filter, Reliable Auto Sprinkler, W W Grainger, Philips, Drew Chemical; Japan: Ebara Corp, Daikin Industries, Shinwa Sangyo, Yazaki Corp, Chino, Fuji Koki, Asada, Japan Fire Cont, Sinko Kogyo; UK: Eltron, Myson, Sound Atenuators; Nittan, Rossell Fluid, Airflow Dev; Italy: Ciodue; Switzerland: Sauter; W Germany: DWM Copeland, Zierhut Electronic, GDR Nazema Kitchen, Rothenberger Tools; Korea: Unison Vibration Control; Thailand: Aeroflex Insulations; Holland: J V Stork Ventilators

Branch Offices: UAE: Sharjah, Dubai, Abu Dhabi; Saudi Arabia: Jeddah, Alkhobar, Riyadh; Qatar: Doha; Iraq; Jordan: Amman; Aden

Subsidiary Companies: Sharjah & Kuwait Manufacturing Co; Kuwait Industrial Centre; Kuwaiti Japanese Airconditioning Co

Principal Bankers: Gulf Bank; Burgan Bank; Commercial Bank of Kuwait, National Bank of Kuwait

Principal Shareholders: Mubarak Abdul Aziz Al Hassawi, Osama Mohammad Hussain Ali, Abdul Jalil Mahmood Al Baker
Date of Establishment: May 1973
No of Employees: 500

FINANCIAL GROUP OF KUWAIT KSCC

PO Box 23986 Safat, 13100 Kuwait
Tel: 2444087/91
Cable: Fingroup
Telex: 22653 Malia Kt; 22723 FGK Kt
Telefax: 2436874

Chairman: Ahmed A Al-Marzouk (Managing Director)
Directors: Ahmed A Al Marzouk (Chairman), Mrs Wafaa A Al Qatami (Vice Chairman), Ali Rashid Al Bader, Abdulaziz A Al Nahed (Deputy Managing Director Local Investments), Abdulaziz A Al Meshal, Talal Fahad Al Mishan, Fahad Al Mubaraki, Sameer Al Gharaballi

Senior Executives: Sameer Al Gharaballi (Deputy General Manager), Othman Sharaf (Forex Branch Manager), Salman Rashid (Investment Officer)

PRINCIPAL ACTIVITIES: Investment and finance, foreign exchange and financial consultants

Financial Information:

	1989
	KD'000
Profits	150
Authorised capital	5,000
Paid-up capital	5,000
Total assets	9,454

Principal Shareholders: Kuwait Real Estate Bank (33.8%), Pearl of Kuwait Real Estate Co (61.2%), Ahmed A Al Marzouk (5%)

Date of Establishment: June 1976

No of Employees: 30

FINANCIAL SECURITY HOUSE

PO Box 26061 Safat, 13121 Kuwait
Tel: 2424957, 2414368
Telex: 44713 TADKIK DT

Chairman: Jassem Mohammed Al-Mousa (also Managing Director)

Directors: Ussama Zerid Al-Kazemi (Vice Chairman), Wael Jassem Al-Saqr, Ibraham Yousuf Al-Raqm, Suleiman Khaled Al-Shali, Farouq Hamad Al-Sultan, Mammoud Abdulrazzaq Razzouqi

PRINCIPAL ACTIVITIES: Finance company

FIRST NATIONAL INVESTMENT GROUP

PO Box 25062 Safat, 13111 Kuwait
Tel: 447774/5, 2421627
Telex: 44864 GADCO KT

Chairman: Fouad Mohammed Thunayan Al-Ghanim

Directors: Abdulwahab Ali Abdulwahab Al-Mutawa (Managing Director), Faisal Abdulaziz Al-Zahem (Vice Chairman), Hamad Mohammed Abdulaziz Al-Wazzan, Najeeb Hamad Musaad Al-Saleh, Adel Yaqoub Shaheen

PRINCIPAL ACTIVITIES: Investment company

Principal Shareholders: Kuwait Foreign Trading & Contracting & Investment Co, Kuwait Real Estate Investment Consortium, Securities Group SAK, Investment Co, other interests

Date of Establishment: 1982

GAZAL DRILLING COMPANY

PO Box 9366 Ahmadi, 61004 Kuwait
Tel: 3981045, 3980184, 3980898
Cable: Comagency Kuwait
Telex: Strolk 44217 Kt

Chairman: Najib Al-Mulla
Directors: Anwar Al-Mulla
Senior Executives: Mustafa S Husseini

PRINCIPAL ACTIVITIES: Drilling and contracting
Branch Offices: Head Office: PO Box 9366, Ahmadi, Tel 3986079
Parent Company: Al Mulla & Husseini Co WLL (Drilling & Maintenance)
Subsidiary Companies: Kuwait Commercial Agency Co WLL
Principal Bankers: Bank of Kuwait & Middle East

Date of Establishment: 1958
No of Employees: 25

GENERAL SYNDICATE TRADING LTD

PO Box 635 Safat, 13007 Kuwait
Tel: 2402650/1, 2402653/4
Cable: Akhawan
Telex: 22742 Akhawan, 44197 Syndica
Telefax: 2432870

Directors: Eng Najati H Al Khakhshir (Deputy General Manager)
Senior Executives: Eng Khairi Al Johary (Manager), Eng Mohamed Shaheen (Manager), Eng Moosa W Damerchie (Manager)

PRINCIPAL ACTIVITIES: Engineering, highways, motorways, roads construction, infrastructure, water pipe laying works, sanitary engineering, landscaping and plant building, building industry, trading & contracting, import and export

Principal Agencies: EAB Industries, Germany; Aquatech, USA; Rib-Loc, Australia

Associated Companies: Al Shurafa Construction & Contracting Co; Golden Falcon Contracting & Building Materials Co, Gulf Horizons Trading & General Contracting Co, N M Qabazard Electrical Est, M H Qabazard Construction Materials Co; Qabazard & Al Basha Building Materials Co, Arab Tourism & Travel Agency; Sons of Mansour Qabazard & Real Estate & Shares; M Qabazard & N Marashly Co for Maintenance

Principal Bankers: Al Ahli Bank of Kuwait; Gulf Bank; Burgan Bank

Financial Information:

	1989
	KD'000
Sales turnover	15,000
Authorised capital	1,000

Principal Shareholders: Mansour Hussain Qabazard, Nader Mansour Qabazard, Nasser Mansour Qabazard, Hussain Mansour Qabazard

Date of Establishment: 1956

No of Employees: 900

GENERAL TRADING CO LTD

PO Box 1079 Safat, 13011 Kuwait
Tel: 2425101/5
Cable: Muftakhar
Telex: 22277 Getco Kt
Telefax: 2421027

Directors: Sheikh Duaij Jaber Al Ali Al Sabah, Abdulaziz Shakhashir, Aref Wasfi Bsisu
Senior Executives: Aref Wasfi Bsisu (General Manager)

PRINCIPAL ACTIVITIES: General trading, civil contractors, heavy industrial kitchen equipment, manufacturers of marine decorative paints, adhesive factory, representatives of brand name crystal and silverware; supply and application of insulation and waterproofing system and expansion joints; supply of power and communications cables, switchgears, power transformers, cable joints, supply and installation of ring main substation, pumps, valves etc, catering services, road marking and traffic signaling

Principal Agencies: Kingson Int, USA; ZSE Power Engineering Industries, Czechoslovakia; Overseas Medical Supplies, UK; Aluminium Wire & Cable, UK; Goulds Pumps, USA; Firey Insulator, UK; Canterbury Eng Co, New Zealand; Elektrim Poland; KOVO Foreing Trade, Czechoslovakia; Mostostal, Poland; Ivan Milutinovic PIM, Yugoslovia; Pumpenfabrik Ernst Vogel, Austria, Hidada, Saudi Arabia; Saudi Cable Co, Saudi Arabia; Potters Ballatoni, UK; Walter Hofmann, W Germany; Ray-o-Lite, Ferro Corp, USA; Atab, Belgium; Instrument Transformers, UK

Branch Offices: Office in Kuwait: Issa Al Saleh Bldg, Fahed Al Salem Street; Mahamy Trading (UK) Ltd, 45 Cumberland Mansion, Seymour Place, London, W1, UK

Principal Bankers: National Bank of Kuwait, Al Ahli Bank of Kuwait

Financial Information:

	KD'000
Sales turnover	5,500
Authorised capital	250
Paid-up capital	250

Principal Shareholders: Abdulaziz Shakhashir, Sheikh Duaij Jaber Al Ali Al Sabah, Aref Wasfi Bsisu

Date of Establishment: 1959

No of Employees: 300

GENERAL TRANSPORTATION & EQUIPMENT CO

PO Box 1096 Safat, 13011 Kuwait
Tel: 833380/1/2
Cable: Khairallah
Telex: 22279 Gte Kt

Chairman: Khaled S Olayan
Directors: Abdulla S Olayan
Senior Executives: Mohammed Refai (Regional Manager)

PRINCIPAL ACTIVITIES: Factories and manufacturers' representatives, transportation of rigs
Principal Agencies: Cummins Engine Company, USA; Etnyre Equipment, USA; Fleetguard Filters, USA Atlas Copco, Sweden; Dale Electric, UK; Warner & Swasey, Switzerland; Koehring Skid Steer Loader, USA
Parent Company: Olayan Saudi Holding Co
Subsidiary Companies: General Contracting Company, Saudi Arabia; General Trading Company, Saudi Arabia; Saudi General Transportation Company, Saudi Arabia
Principal Bankers: Bank of Kuwait and the Middle East, Kuwait; National Bank of Kuwait

No of Employees: 25

GHANEM ELMALA & CO

See ELMALA, GHANEM, & CO

GOLDEN TULIP MESSILAH BEACH

PO Box 3522 Safat, 13036 Kuwait
Tel: 5624111
Cable: Beachotel
Telex: 22215 Memotel Kuwait
Telefax: 5629402

Chairman: Ali Ahmed Al Ghanem Al Jabr
Senior Executives: T A Barlow (General Manager), Souheil El Assad (Executive Manager)

PRINCIPAL ACTIVITIES: Hotel business
Associated Companies: Management: Kuwait Hotels Co SAK
Principal Bankers: Burgan Bank, Commercial Bank of Kuwait

Date of Establishment: 1974
No of Employees: 250

GULF BANK KSC (THE)

PO Box 3200 Safat, 13032 Kuwait
Tel: 2449501 (20 lines)
Cable: Gulfbank
Telex: 22001 Gulfbank; 22783 Gulfbank
Telefax: 2445212

Chairman: Dr Abdul Aziz Sultan Al Essa
Members: Ali Mishari Al Hilal Al Mutairi (Vice Chairman), Abdul Wahab Rashed Al Haroon, Ali Ahmed Al Ghanim Al Jabr, Maher Abdul Latif Ben Naji, Mohammed Ibrahim Ma'rafi, Mohammed Khalid Saleh Al Roomi, Mohammed Yousef Al Nafisi, Najeeb Hamad Musaed Al Saleh, Omara Abdulaziz Al Ali Al Mutawa, Sheikh Ali Abdullah Al Sabah, Tariq Ahmed Al Ayyoub
Senior Executives: Ziad Sarawan (General Manager Treasury & Investment Banking Group), Alan Beauregard (General Manager International Banking Group), Hisham Issa Al Sultan (Deputy General Manager Technology & General Services Group), Ted Fenner (Asst General Manager Credit Policy & Review & Acting Head Domestic Banking Group), Ahmed Meri (Corporate Secretary), Adrian V McKay (General Auditor), Sunder Vaswani (Senior Manager Public Affairs), Surour Al Samerai (Senior Manager Human Resources Development), Ibrahim Ibrahim (Senior Manager Middle East Africa Div), John Carlough (Senior Manager Branches Supervision Div), Dr Abdul Wahab Al Ameen (Economic Advisor)

PRINCIPAL ACTIVITIES: Commercial banking
Branch Offices: Location of Head Office in Kuwait: Mubarak Alkabeer Street; and 28 other branches in Kuwait; also representative office in UK: 1 College Hill, London EC4 2RA, Tel 071-248 2843, Fax 071-489 0407, Telex 887688; and branch in Singapore and Cayman Islands
Associated Companies: Industrial Bank of Kuwait (Kuwait); United Bank of Kuwait (London); Bank of Bahrain and Kuwait (Bahrain); Compagnie Arabe et Internationale d'Investissement (Luxembourg); Banque Arabe et Internationale d'Investissement (Paris); Yemen Kuwait Bank for Trade & Investment (Sanaa); Kuwait Reinsurance Co (Kuwait); Kuwait Clearing Co (Kuwait)
Principal Bankers: Amsterdam Rotterdam Bank, Amsterdam; Societe Generale de Banque, Brussels; Barclays Bank Plc, London; United Bank of Kuwait, London; Banca Nationale del Lavoro, Rome; Banca Commerciale Italiana, Milan; Citibank, New York; Bankers Trust Co, New York; Credit Lyonnais, Paris; Union Bank of Switzerland, Zurich; Den Danske Bank, Copenhagen; Banco de Vizcaya, Madrid; Den Norske Credit Bank, Oslo; Scandinaviska Enschilda Banken, Stockholm; Creditsanstalt Bankverein, Vienna
Financial Information:

	1989
	KD'000
Profits	8,631
Authorised capital	61,501
Paid-up capital	61,501
Total assets	2,258,614

Principal Shareholders: 100% Kuwaiti public
Date of Establishment: 1960
No of Employees: 968

GULF CABLE & ELECTRICAL INDUSTRIES CO

PO Box 1196 Safat, 13012 Kuwait
Tel: 4675244
Cable: Wiregulf
Telex: 23063 Guceico KT
Telefax: 4675305

Chairman: A E Al-Fares
Senior Executives: Naif Mahmoud (Chief Accountant), Mohd Al Kandari (Sales Incharge), Diab Fench (Asst Purchase Manager), Mohd Ali Imam (Operation Manager), Emad Masud (Personnel Manager)

PRINCIPAL ACTIVITIES: Manufacture of power cables, telephone cables and joints
Principal Bankers: National Bank of Kuwait

Principal Shareholders: Kuwaiti Shareholders (67%) and (33%) Government of Kuwait
Date of Establishment: 1975
No of Employees: 252

GULF CEMENT COMPANY

PO Box 25001 Safat, 13111 Kuwait
Tel: 2467935/6/7
Telex: 44562 GCC KT
Telefax: 2464975

Chairman: Saleh A Al Shalfan
Directors: Abdul Wahab Al Qallaf (Managing Director)

PRINCIPAL ACTIVITIES: Cement manufacturers and products suppliers
Principal Bankers: Al Ahli Bank of Kuwait
Financial Information:

	1989
	US$'000
Sales turnover	33,500

Principal Shareholders: Kuwait Real Estate Investment (19.5%), Government of Ras Al Khaimah (16/5%), Consortium KSC Kuwaiti Governmental Company
Date of Establishment: 1977
No of Employees: 414

KUWAIT

GULF CONSULT

PO Box 22412 Safat, 13085 Kuwait
Tel: 843565, 846175, 842037
Telex: 22638 Tainc Kuwait

Directors: Hamad Thunayan Alghanim, Mohamed Tawil

PRINCIPAL ACTIVITIES: Architectural design, housing, roads, sewerage; multi-storey car parks; touristic projects, industrial, precast concrete
Principal Bankers: Gulf Bank; Commercial Bank of Kuwait

Principal Shareholders: Hamad Thunayan Alghanim; Mohamed Tawil
Date of Establishment: 1967

GULF DEVELOPMENT TRADING CO

PO Box 3150 Safat, 13032 Kuwait
Tel: 2440642, 2436872
Telex: 30373 LMR Kt

President: Dr T Al Amar
Directors: A S Akram Ali, K S Mubarak

PRINCIPAL ACTIVITIES: Trade, project, investments, money brokerage, agro-industry
Principal Bankers: Commercial Bank of Kuwait
Financial Information:

	US$'000
Authorised capital	10,000

Date of Establishment: 1977
No of Employees: 30

GULF DREDGING CO SAK

PO Box 24054 Safat, 13101 Kuwait
Tel: 2447041, 2447052, 2447164, 2423081/6
Cable: Dredging
Telex: 22708; 44087 Gdc Kt
Telefax: 2447164

Chairman: Maher Marafie
Directors: Abdullah Abdul Noor Jamal (Vice Chairman)
Senior Executives: Fadel Abu-Abbas (General Manager), Abdullah Hammad (Finance Manager), Abdul Ridha Jumaih (Personnel & Admin Manager)

PRINCIPAL ACTIVITIES: Dredging, deepening and cleaning of ports and waterchannels, pile driving and marine construction works
Principal Bankers: Commercial Bank of Kuwait, Gulf Bank
Financial Information:

	1988 KD'000	1989 KD'000
Revenue	1,000	3,020
Profits	200	919
Authorised capital	1,500	1,500
Paid-up capital	1,500	1,500
Total assets	5,000	5,000

Principal Shareholders: Contracting and Marine Services, Kuwait; Kuwait Ship Building and Repair Yard, Kuwait
Date of Establishment: December 1975
No of Employees: 225

GULF ELECTRICAL ENGINEERING SAK

PO Box 9051, Ahmadi, 61001 Kuwait
Tel: 982010, 982011
Cable: Gulf Electric Kuwait
Telex: 44280 Gelect
Telefax: 3987907

Chairman: Zaid Sayid Ahmed Al-Gharabally
Directors: Zaid Sayid Ahmed Al-Gharabally, Musa'ad Sayid Ahmed Al-Gharabally, Hashim Sayid Ahmed Al-Gharabally, Abdul-Hamid Sayid Ahmed Al-Gharabally

PRINCIPAL ACTIVITIES: Electrical engineering and instrumentation contractors and motor & generator rewind specialists
Principal Bankers: Bank of Kuwait and the Middle East, Kuwait

Principal Shareholders: Zaid Sayid Ahmed Al-Gharabally
Date of Establishment: 1st January, 1964
No of Employees: 95

GULF FISHERIES CO WLL

PO Box 3389, 13034 Kuwait
Tel: 2423017, 518100, 532172
Cable: Hamoor Kuwait
Telex: 222041; 2089 Hamoor

Chairman: Sheikh Naser Sabah Al-Hamad Sabah
Senior Executives: Abdul Kareem Marzooq, George Varghese, Mohamed Al Ma'moom

PRINCIPAL ACTIVITIES: Fishing and fish processing

GULF GLASS MANUFACTURING CO KSC

PO Box 26996 Safat, 13130 Kuwait
Tel: 3260455/6
Cable: Glasman
Telex: 31904 Glasman KT

Chairman: So'od A Al Saleh
Directors: Sulaiman S Al Zaid (Vice Chairman)
Senior Executives: Ahmad A Al Najdi (Deputy General Manager)

PRINCIPAL ACTIVITIES: Manufacture of glass containers
Branch Offices: Factory: Tel 3260456, 3260455, 3262257, 3262252
Principal Bankers: Gulf Bank; National Bank of Kuwait
Financial Information:

	1988/89 KD'000
Sales turnover	3,000
Authorised capital	5,250
Paid-up capital	5,250
Total assets	9,500

No of Employees: 230

GULF INDUSTRIAL INVESTMENT CO EC

PO Box 26565 Safat, 13126 Kuwait
Telex: 224466 GCBC KT
Telefax: 2405732

Chairman: Awwad B Al Khaldi (Managing Director)
Senior Executives: Khalid Al Qadeeri (Commercial Manager)

PRINCIPAL ACTIVITIES: Production of iron oxide pellets
Parent Company: Head office in Bahrain
Financial Information:

	1989 US$'000
Authorised capital	160,000
Paid-up capital	150,000

Principal Shareholders: Santa Fe International Corporation, Abdulateef Hamad Al Tourah, Ahmed Mohamed Al Awadi, Abdulla Abdul Noor Jamal

GULF INSURANCE CO KSC

PO Box 1040 Safat, 13011 Kuwait
Tel: 2423384 (7 lines)
Cable: Khalijmin
Telex: 22203 Kwt, 44143 KT
Telefax: 2422320

Chairman: Sulaiman Hamad Al Dalali (also Managing Director)
Directors: Abdul Aziz Saoud Al Fulaij (Vice Chairman), Khaled Jassim Al Wazzan, Abdullah Fahad Al Rushaid, Abdullah Mohammad Al Mansour, Abdullatif Ahmad Al Bahar, Ahmed Fahed Sulaiman Al Fahed, Dr Khaled Mohammad Al Sa'ad
Senior Executives: Saleh Mohammad Al Omar (Deputy General Manager, Finance), Sargon Dawood Lazar (Deputy General

Manager), Khaled Saoud Al Hassan (Deputy General Manager), Mohammad Abdul Hamid Hassan (Secretary General), Elias N Bedewi (Technical Consultant)

PRINCIPAL ACTIVITIES: Insurance and investment
Principal Bankers: National Bank of Kuwait, Gulf Bank
Financial Information:

	1988 KD'000	1989 KD'000
Sales turnover	11,607	10,374
Profits	2,566	2,501
Authorised capital	11,310	11,310
Paid-up capital	11,310	11,310
Total assets	40,640	39,235

Principal Shareholders: Ministry of Finance
Date of Establishment: 1962
No of Employees: 199

GULF INTERNATIONAL GROUP (KUWAIT)

PO Box 3389 Safat, 13034 Kuwait
Tel: 2448310/6
Telex: 22041 Hamoor Kwt; 2089 Kamoor Kwt; 2698 Gig Kwt

PRINCIPAL ACTIVITIES: Holding company, dealing in chemicals, textiles, building materials, packaging materials, agricultural services, hotels and catering, publicity etc
Branch Offices: Sudan, Egypt; Saudi Arabia; Lebanon; Nigeria; Senegal; UK; France; Austria
Subsidiary/Associated Companies: The Group comprises the following companies: Kuwait; Gulf Fisheries Co WLL; Arabian Textile Co WLL; Sudan: Sudan Textile Industry Ltd, Sudanese Glass Co Ltd, Modern Match Producing & Distributing Co Ltd; National Agriculture Organisation Ltd; Sudanese Chemical Industries; Medical & Sanitary Products Ltd; Sudan All Wear Industries, Khartoum Publicity Ltd; Gulf Services Co Ltd; Sudanese Kuwait Packaging Co Ltd; Chipboard & Particle Boards Ltd; Egypt: Gulf-Egypt Hotels Co; Lebanon: Gulf International for Hotels and Tourism SARL; Saudi Arabia: Saudi Arabian Hotels Corp; Saudi Danish Dairy Co

GULF INVESTMENT CORPORATION

PO Box 3402 Safat, 13035 Kuwait
Tel: 2431911
Cable: GICORP
Telex: 44002, 23146 GICORP KT
Telefax: 2448894

Chairman: HE Shaikh Mohammed Ali Abalkail
Directors: HE Qais Bin Abdul Munim Al Zawawi (Deputy Chairman), HE Ibrahim Abdul Karim Mohammed, HE Ahmed Humaid Al Tayer, HE Shaikh Abdulaziz Bin Khalifa Al Thani, HE Jassim Mohammed Al Khorafi, Mohammed Khalfan Khirbash, Rashid Esmail Al Meer, HE Shaikh Hamad Saud Al Sayari, HE Mohammed Bin Mousa Al Yousef, Naser Mohammed Al Hajri, HE Abdulmohsen Yousef Al Hunaif
Senior Executives: Dr Khaled Al Fayez (Chief Executive Officer), Hisham Razzuqi (Executive VP Finance Group), Dr Jassim Al Mannai (Executive VP Projects Group), Uwe Janke (SVP Corporate Finance), Tawfiq Al Fraih (VP Deputy Treasurer), Jeremy Brewin VP Portfolio Management), Roger Webster (SVP Business Development/Project Management), John Leckie (SVP Investment Evaluation/Project Appraisal), Sulaiman Al Ali (SVP Administration), Dr Munir Bushara (VP Economics & Research)

PRINCIPAL ACTIVITIES: Investment banking, project finance and development, funds management, capital market makers
Principal Bankers: National Bank of Abu Dhabi; Amsterdam Rotterdam Bank; Euroclear; Deutsche Bank; Commerz Bank; National Commercial Bank of Jeddah; Central Bank of Kuwait; National Bank of Kuwait; Barclays Bank; Gulf International Bank; National Bank of Bahrain; Sociate Generale; Citibank; Brown Bros; Harriman & Co; Bank of Tokyo; Royal Bank of Canada; Credit Suisse

Financial Information:

	1988/89 US$'000
Profits	38,366
Paid-up capital	540,000
Shareholders'equity	729,705
Total assets	1,717,039

Principal Shareholders: Member States of the GCC (100%)
Date of Establishment: November 1982
No of Employees: 162

GULF MARINE TRANSPORT CO KSC

PO Box 25344 Safat, 13114 Kuwait
Tel: 2449978
Cable: Gumatrco
Telex: 23481 GMTC

Chairman: Fouad Mohammad Thunayan Al Ghanim
Directors: Nasser Mohammad Al Sayer (Deputy Chairman), Khalid Abdul Mohsin Al Motair (Managing Director), Mufarrej Ibrahim Al Mufarrej (Executive Committee)

PRINCIPAL ACTIVITIES: Shipowners and shipping services
Associated Companies: Associated with Gray MacKenzie & Co Ltd
Principal Bankers: The Gulf Bank

Principal Shareholders: 146 Private shareholders throughout Arabian Gulf
Date of Establishment: 1977

GULF PALACE FURNISHINGS CO
H H Abdullah & M R Daneshyar & Co

PO Box 25004 Safat, 13111 Kuwait
Tel: 2637450, 2612182, 2653120, 2665628
Telex: 23337 Khlood
Telefax: 2649183

President: Mohamad Riaz Daneshyar
Directors: Habib Hamzeh Abdullah, Ibrahim M Daneshyar (Vice President & Geneal Manager)

PRINCIPAL ACTIVITIES: Manufacture of carpets and wholesales distribution of carpets and furniture in Kuwait and the GCC Countries, also major government contractors for turnkey furnishing projects in Kuwait
Principal Agencies: Gulf Textile Inc, USA; Dantex Carpet, USA; Balta, Belgium; Fenaux, Belgium
Associated Companies: Gulf Textile Inc, USA
Principal Bankers: Al Ahli Bank of Kuwait
Financial Information:

	1989
Sales turnover	US$2,500,000
Profits	20%
Authorised capital	KD100,000
Paid-up capital	KD100,000

Principal Shareholders: Habib Hamzeh Abdullah, Abed Al Wahab Al Tammar, Mohammad R Daneshyar, Ibrahim M Daneshyar
Date of Establishment: 1987
No of Employees: 28

GULF PAPER MANUFACTURING CO KSC

PO Box 7506 Fahaheel, 64006 Kuwait
Tel: 3262067, 3262072
Cable: GPMC Kuwait
Telex: 44209 GPMC KT
Telefax: 3260393

President: Abdulla Al Hunaidi
Directors: Saqer Ahmed Al Moasherji (Managing Director & General Manager)
Senior Executives: Tareq Mohd Al Moasherji (Deputy General Manager, Faisal Sayed Ahmed Al Eidan (Sales & Marketing

Manager), Sami Hafez Al Meligi (Finance & Admin Manager), Jim Peace (Mill Engineer)

PRINCIPAL ACTIVITIES: Manufacture of paper (packaging material and facial tissue) of various grammage
Parent Company: Al Moasherji & Al Rashed Group
Principal Bankers: Industrial Bank of Kuwait
Financial Information:

	1988/89 KD'000
Sales turnover	4,910
Authorised capital	3,000
Paid-up capital	3,000
Total assets	8,286

Principal Shareholders: Industrial Bank of Kuwait, Kuwait Development Co, Abdulla Al Sharhan, Paper Tradine & Industry, Othman Al Ayar, A/Aziz Al Otaibi, Khaled Al Babtain
Date of Establishment: 1977
No of Employees: 255

GULF PETROLEUM EQUIPMENT & CONTRACTING CO LTD

PO Box 2742 Safat, 13028 Kuwait
Tel: 2410272, 2410292
Cable: Oilserv
Telex: 22751 Oilserv KT
Telefax: (965) 2456349

Chairman: Saad Mohd Al Saad
Directors: Saad El Din Hammad (General Manager), Walid Bibi (Director)
Senior Executives: Ali Jafarawi (Financial Manager)

PRINCIPAL ACTIVITIES: Sales and services for oil industry, supply for oilfield/refinery/petrochemicals equipment, electrical equipment, industrial equipment and parts, industrial chemicals, oil and water drilling contractors, mechanical and electrical maintenance contractors
Principal Agencies: Norton Chemical Process Products, UK; Sonpetrol, Spain; AG Flender, Germany; R Stahl, Germany; LMF, Austria; Cooper Tools, USA; Voerst Alpine AG, Austria; Bulgargeomin, Bulgaria; Phoceenne Gulf, UAE; DSI, Germany; Born Heaters, UK; Brembana, Italy; Abex World Trade, USA; Aqua Hydraulic, UK; Polservice, Poland; Hobbs International, USA
Subsidiary Companies: Kuwait European Industrial Inspection Co
Principal Bankers: Burgan Bank; Gulf Bank
Financial Information:

	1989/90
Sales turnover	US$12,000,000
Authorised capital	KD700,000
Paid-up capital	KD700,000

Principal Shareholders: Saad Mohd Al Saad, Saad Hammad, Walid Bibi, Ali Jafarawi
Date of Establishment: 1976
No of Employees: 150

GULF STAR SYSTEMS

PO Box 27050 Safat, 13131 Kuwait
Tel: 2402550
Telex: 30361 GSS KT
Telefax: 2402557

Chairman: Abdullah Al Romaizon
Directors: Wafa H Shihabi
Senior Executives: Charles Allen (General Manager)

PRINCIPAL ACTIVITIES: Supply of computer systems and software
Principal Agencies: Novell, Computer Associates, AST Research
Branch Offices: Riyadh, Jeddah, Alkhobar
Principal Bankers: Bank of Bahrain & Kuwait

Financial Information:

	1989 KD'000
Authorised capital	250
Paid-up capital	250

Date of Establishment: 1977

GULF TRADING & REFRIGERATING CO WLL

PO Box 72 Safat, 13001 Kuwait
Tel: 4842988, 4843988
Cable: REEFER KUWAIT
Telex: 22216 REEFER KT
Telefax: 4847244

Chairman: Kutayba Y Alghanim
Directors: Kutayba Alghanim, Bassam Alghanim, Brian P Skinner
Senior Executives: Geoffrey I Walker (Managing Director), Fouad Al Masri (General Manager), Sari Dajani (Sales Manager), Ian Anderson (General Sales Manager), Gamal Yousef (Financial Controller)

PRINCIPAL ACTIVITIES: Importers and distributors of foodstuffs and cold store operation
Principal Agencies: Kraft; Mars confectionery; Pedigree petfoods; Rowntree; Ross Foods; Rank Hovis MacDougal; Weddel; Hills Biscuits; Sunshine Biscuits; Hanover Brands Inc - Maryland Chief; Royal Foods; Kodak Batteries; Buitoni; Colgate Palmolive
Principal Bankers: Bank of Kuwait and the Middle East

Principal Shareholders: Yusuf Ahmed Alghanim & Sons and Partners
Date of Establishment: 1951
No of Employees: 99

HALLIBURTON LTD KUWAIT

PO Box 9022, Ahmadi, 61001 Kuwait
Tel: 981177/8
Cable: Hallkuwait
Telex: 44214 Kalkurt

PRINCIPAL ACTIVITIES: Oil service company; marine services; cementing; special tools, formation testing stimulation services, and industrial cleaning services
Branch Offices: Bahrain: PO Box 515, Manama

HAMAD AL KHALED & BROS CO

See AL KHALED, HAMAD, & BROS CO

HAMOUDI TRADING ESTABLISHMENT

PO Box 22284 Safat, 13083 Kuwait
Tel: 2439143
Cable: Dynamic
Telex: 22140 Hamoudi Kt

Chairman: Jassim M A Hogel

PRINCIPAL ACTIVITIES: Supply of processing equipments, chemicals etc; contracting and consultancy in civil, mechanical and chemical engineering fields; marketing of building materials, foodstuffs, etc
Principal Bankers: Gulf Bank

HASSAWI EQUIPMENT CO LTD WLL

PO Box 705 Safat, 13008 Kuwait
Tel: 2432962, 833492
Cable: Hassawico
Telex: 22294 Gajaria Kt; 22871 Asswaf Kt

Chairman: Mohammad Abdulla Hassawi
Directors: H R Gajaria, K V Varghese

PRINCIPAL ACTIVITIES: Import/export of machinery, equipment, hand tools, mechanical and electrical tools, precision tools, hardware, chemicals, automobile accessories and spare parts

Subsidiary/Associated Companies: Hassawi & Gajaria Co Ltd
(WLL); Hassawi Construction Co (WLL); Hassawi Contracting
Co (WLL); Hassawi Trading Est; Nina Trading Est
Principal Bankers: National Bank of Kuwait

Date of Establishment: 1975

HAYAT TRADING & CONTRACTING CORP

PO Box 1668 Safat, 13017 Kuwait
Tel: 835080, 819448, 819435, 831087
Cable: Corp & Habib
Telex: 22916 Habib

Chairman: Habib Hassan Jowhar Hayat
Directors: Ali J Hayat, Alaa H J Hayat

PRINCIPAL ACTIVITIES: Trading and contracting
Principal Agencies: Taprogge, West Germany; Vereinigte
Deutsche Metallwerke, West Germany; Cheverton Workboat,
UK; Bouygues, France; Buss Ltd, Switzerland; Lloyds
(Burton), UK; Kuang Cheng Industrial, Taiwan; etc
Subsidiary Companies: Al Hayat Trading Co, WLL, Kuwait
(Food, Paper & Office Equipment); Hassan Jowhar Hayat &
Sons, Kuwait (Construction Materials); Hayat Marble Co,
Kuwait
Principal Bankers: Alahli Bank of Kuwait

Date of Establishment: 1967
No of Employees: 50

HAZEEM, ABBAS ALI, & SONS CO

PO Box 273 Safat, 13003 Kuwait
Tel: 4745200
Cable: RADAR
Telex: 30085 RADAR KT

Chairman: Abbas Ali Hazeem
Directors: Shaker Al Hazeem (General Manager), Fadhil Al
Hazeem (Deputy General Manager)

PRINCIPAL ACTIVITIES: General trading, contracting, interior
decorators and manufacturers (carpet and furniture)
Principal Agencies: Brintons, UK; Heuge Overseas, Holland;
Textilcommerz, E Berlin, GDR; Louis De Poortere, Belgium;
Comag Carpet Industries, Belgium; Centrotex,
Czechoslavakia; Sib Import & Export, Yugoslavia
Branch Offices: Location in Kuwait: Hazeem Showroom
Complex, Airport Road, Farwaniya; also in Dubai; Abu-Dhabi;
Sultanate of Oman; Egypt and the USA
Subsidiary Companies: Hazeem Mattress Factory, Kuwait;
Chrome Furniture Factory, Kuwait
Principal Bankers: Bank of Kuwait & Middle East, Kuwait; Gulf
Bank of Kuwait; Commercial Bank of Kuwait

Date of Establishment: 1930
No of Employees: 500

HEMPELS MARINE PAINTS (KUWAIT) WLL

PO Box 3400 Safat, 13034 Kuwait
Tel: 4813366, 4813471, 4834126
Cable: Hempaturi
Telex: 22191 Hemp Kwt
Telefax: 4843307

Chairman: Saud Abdulaziz Al Rashed
Directors: HE Sheikh Nasser Sabah Al-Ahmed Al-Sabah, Saad
Abdulaziz Al Rashed, John Schwartzbach, Consul Borge
Hansen
Senior Executives: Jorn H Lillelund (General Manager)

PRINCIPAL ACTIVITIES: Manufacturers of paints and coatings
for marine, industrial, offshore, container yacht and building
sector uses, materials and tools for surface preparation and
application of such coatings, including provision of advisory
services
Principal Agencies: ANZA paint brushes and rollers, BERGSOE
zinc anodes, ELCOMETER testing and measuring equipments

for surface coatings, and GRACO airless spraying
equipments
Branch Offices: Ahmadi: PO Box 3400 Safat, 13034 Kuwait, Tel
3981268, 3988253
Associated Companies: Saudi Arabian Packaging Industry WLL,
PO Box 1966, Dammam 31441, Saudi Arabia; Kuwait
Chemical Manufacturing Co KSC, PO Box 26011, Safat,
13121 Kuwait
Principal Bankers: National Bank of Kuwait

Principal Shareholders: Chairman and directors as described;
and J C Hempel Holding A/S, Denmark
Date of Establishment: 1966

HOLIDAY INN HOTEL

PO Box 18544, Farwaniya, 81006 Kuwait
Tel: 4742000, 4732100
Telex: 46460, 46448 Holinn Kt
Telefax: 4732020

Directors: Fethi Abdennadher (General Manager)
Senior Executives: Z E Zia (Financial Controller), Ghassan Jaber
(Director of Sales & Marketing), Shafic Haddad (Executive
Asst Manager), Kousay Sammaraie (Front Office Manager)

PRINCIPAL ACTIVITIES: Hotel business

Date of Establishment: 1982
No of Employees: 350

HOMOUD AL-ZAID ALKHALID CO

See ALKHALID, HOMOUD AL-ZAID, CO

HONEYWELL KUWAIT KSC

PO Box 20825 Safat, 13069 Kuwait
Tel: 2421327/8/9
Cable: Honeywell Kwt
Telex: 22218 Honeywell Kwt

Chairman: Wael Al Sagar

PRINCIPAL ACTIVITIES: Building automation, industrial process
controls instrumentation, computers, engineering, sales,
commissioning, service, maintenance
Principal Agencies: McDonnell & Miller, ITT, USA; Rochester
Instrument Systems, USA
Principal Bankers: Bank of Kuwait and the Middle East

Date of Establishment: 1970

HOTEL MERIDIEN KUWAIT

PO Box 26302 Safat, 13124 Kuwait
Tel: 2455550
Cable: MERIHOTEL
Telex: MERIHTL 44458 KT
Telefax: 2438391, 2455550 ext 2315

Chairman: Ghazi Alnafisi
Senior Executives: Keaton S Woods (General Manager), Fahd
Abushar (Resident Manager), Miss Nadia Ayad (Director of
Sales), Fareed Tello (Front Office Manager)

PRINCIPAL ACTIVITIES: Hotel business
Principal Agencies: Air France, Meridien hotels and sales offices
worldwide
Parent Company: Air France
Principal Bankers: Commercial Bank of Kuwait

Principal Shareholders: Salhia Real Estate
Date of Establishment: 1980
No of Employees: 322

HOUSE OF TRADE & CONTRACTING CO

PO Box 2518 Safat, 13026 Kuwait
Tel: 3986197, 3986198
Cable: Hometrade
Telex: 30138, 30014 Homet KT

KUWAIT

PRINCIPAL ACTIVITIES: Electrical and mechanical engineering, general trading
Branch Offices: Location in Kuwait: East Ahmadi

HUNGARO-KUWAIT TRADING CO LTD

PO Box 21834 Safat, 13079 Kuwait
Tel: 2436219
Cable: Hunkutex
Telex: HUKU 23649 KT

Chairman: Musead Al Sayer
Directors: Abdulla Ahmed Abu Taqa (Managing Director), Drs V Jankovits (Marketing Director)
Senior Executives: Abdulla Ahmed Abu Taqa (Deputy Managing Director)

PRINCIPAL ACTIVITIES: Marketing and trading in all types of textiles, ready-made garments, carpets, footwear and furniture
Principal Agencies: Hungarotex; Hungarocoop; Artex; Konsumex; Budaflax; Modex; Tricotex; Sancilla; Electroimpex of Hungary
Parent Company: Hungarotex, PO Box 100, H 1804 Budapest, Hungary
Associated Companies: Al Sayer & Abu Taqa General Trading Co, PO Box 23068 Safat, 13091 Kuwait
Principal Bankers: National Bank of Kuwait; Commercial Bank of Kuwait; Bank of Kuwait and the Middle East

Principal Shareholders: Hungarotex, Al Sayer & Abu Taqa General Trading Co
Date of Establishment: 1971
No of Employees: 40

HUSAIN MAKKI ALJUMA

See ALJUMA, HUSAIN MAKKI,

HUSSAIN & MALIK TRADING & CONTRACTING CO LTD

PO Box 2991 Safat, 13030 Kuwait
Tel: 2439974, 2447115
Cable: Maliktrade
Telex: 22859 Malik Kt

Directors: Malik H R Awan, Hussain Ali Hajih Shamsa

PRINCIPAL ACTIVITIES: Trading in textiles, readymade garments, footwear, furnishings, blankets, paints, building materials
Principal Agencies: Rasilan, Spain; Samarah, Spain; Gilmas, Spain; Andrisons, UK; Copertificio Agostini, Italy; Copertifico G Melani, Italy; Starlite, Pakistan; Shaheen, Pakistan; Altus, Japan; Eskimo, Switzerland; Deritex Ardura, Belgium; Besana, Italy; Linth Textile, Switzerland
Principal Bankers: National Bank of Kuwait SAK, Commercial Bank of Kuwait

Principal Shareholders: Directors as described
Date of Establishment: 1969

I H I KUWAIT COMPANY KSC

PO Box 9267, Ahmadi, 61003 Kuwait
Tel: 984482 (3 lines)
Fax: 830739
Telex: 30513 KT

Chairman: Muzher Al Gharabally
Directors: Dr K T B Menon, Montasser Al Gharabally, Sabah Al Gharabally
Senior Executives: Shawkat Barghouthi (General Manager)

PRINCIPAL ACTIVITIES: Rental of construction and heavy equipment, steel fabrication, transportation, repair and maintenance, civil and mechanical contractors and commission agents
Branch Offices: Ahmadi
Parent Company: Gharabally International Co

Principal Bankers: Commercial Bank of Kuwait

Principal Shareholders: Gharabally Int Co, Kuwait; Ishikawajima Harima Heavy Industries Co, Japan
Date of Establishment: October 1975
No of Employees: 200 permanent, 400 temporary

IBRAHIM A AL SALEM & CO

See AL SALEM, IBRAHIM A, & CO

INDEPENDENT PETROLEUM GROUP SAK

PO Box 24027 Safat, 13101 Kuwait
Tel: 5312840/7 (8 lines)
Cable: IPGROUP KUWAIT
Telex: 22766/46068 IPGROUP KT
Telefax: 5331472

Chairman: Khalaf Ahmed Al Khalaf
Directors: Abdulrazzak Khalid Zaid Al Khalid (Vice Chairman), Ali M Al-Radwan, Ghazi F Al Nafeesi, Mohamed M Al-Ghanim, Yusuf I Al Ghanim
Senior Executives: Waleed J Hadeed (Executive Managing Director), Jasem M Al Musallam (Managing Director, Marketing), Abdulla Mohammed Akil Zaman (Managing Director, Planning)

PRINCIPAL ACTIVITIES: Industrial, commercial, and consulting work in the oil and petrochemical industry
Branch Offices: London Office: Independent Petroleum Group of Kuwait Ltd, 112 Jermyn Street, London SW1Y 6LS, UK; Singapore Office: Independent Petroleum Group, 105 Cecil Street, The Octagon Mex 18-03/04, Singapore 0106
Principal Bankers: National Bank of Kuwait
Financial Information:

	1989 KD'000
Sales turnover	68,000
Profits	767
Authorised capital	5,000
Paid-up capital	5,000
Total assets	16,000

Principal Shareholders: Khalaf Al Khalaf, Waleed J Hadeed, Abdulla Akil Zaman, Jasem Al Musallem, Abdul Razak Al Khalid, Yusuf Al Ghanim, Ghazi Al Nafisi, Ali Al Radwan
Date of Establishment: 1976
No of Employees: 51

INDUSTRIAL BANK OF KUWAIT KSC

PO Box 3146 Safat, 13032 Kuwait
Tel: 2457661
Cable: BANKSENAEY, Kuwait
Telex: 22469, 22582 Senaey Kt

Directors: Abdul Salam A Al Awadi (Vice Chairman), Rabee Isa Al-Noumas, Mofarej I Al Mofarej, Saad M Al Azmee, Hussain A Al Khorafee, Nasser M Al Ajeel, Khaled A Al Sager, Mohammed A Al Saad, Atif H Al Zaabee
Senior Executives: Saleh Al Yousef (General Manager), Mohamad A Jamal (Deputy General Manager, Projects), Ali A Khaja (Deputy General Manager, Banking & Finance), Ibrahim Saad (Senior Legal Counsel), Dr Amr Mohie El-Din (Manager, Economics Department)

PRINCIPAL ACTIVITIES: Promoting and financing industrial projects in Kuwait, fixed income securities, direct investments
Financial Information:

	KD'000
Authorised capital	20,000
Paid-up capital	20,000

Principal Shareholders: The Government of Kuwait, Central Bank of Kuwait, The Public Institution for Social Security, plus 15 Kuwaiti shareholding companies
Date of Establishment: December 1973
No of Employees: 180

INDUSTRIAL BUILDING & CONSTRUCTIONS CO KSCC

PO Box 23891 Safat, 13099 Kuwait
Tel: 4674500, 4674602
Cable: Jahiz
Telex: 22145 IBC Kt
Telefax: 4675592

Chairman: Samer Al Omani
Directors: Suhair Khayat (AGMC), Adel Al Assoussi (AGMA), Khairy Yousef (AGMF)

PRINCIPAL ACTIVITIES: Precast construction, ready mix concrete and building materials
Principal Bankers: Industrial Bank of Kuwait, Al Ahli Bank of Kuwait, Gulf Bank of Kuwait

INDUSTRIAL INVESTMENT COMPANY

PO Box 26019 Safat, 13121 Kuwait
Tel: 2429073/5
Telex: 23132 Indvest
Telefax: 2448850

Chairman: Dr Taleb Ahmad Ali (also Managing Director)
Directors: Bader M Al Humaidhi

PRINCIPAL ACTIVITIES: Direct investments, financing, trading and management operations relating to assets of industrial projects
Subsidiary Companies: Kuwait Leather Industries Co, Electrical Boards Manufacturing Co, Kuwait & Gulf Carpets Manufacturing & Trading Co
Principal Bankers: Burgan Bank, Kuwait; United Bank of Kuwait, UK; National Bank of Kuwait, Kuwait
Financial Information:

	KD'000
Authorised capital	20,000
Paid-up capital	8,000

Principal Shareholders: Kuwait Investment Authority (31%), Kuwait Industrial Projects Co (21%), Public Institution for Social Security (10%), rest of shares owned by other Kuwaiti banks and companies
Date of Establishment: April 1983
No of Employees: 23

INDUSTRIAL SERVICES & SUPPLIES CO WLL

PO Box 5581 Safat, 13056 Kuwait
Tel: 4817877, 3911651
Cable: Inserply
Telex: 23884 Kt Isas
Telefax: 3921656

Chairman: Abdulla Ahmed Al-Eissa
Directors: Abdul Aziz Al Essa (Managing Director)
Senior Executives: Nabil Shtayyeh (General Manager)

PRINCIPAL ACTIVITIES: Importers, stockists and suppliers of industrial requirements especially for the oil and petrochemical industries; pipes, valves, tubes; brass and copper sheets; chemicals, safety equipment, scaffoldings
Principal Agencies: Hoke Intercontinental Ltd, USA; Yarwat Corp; John P Nissen Jr Co; Dow Corning Ltd; Takamisawa Koki Mfg Co Ltd; Carpenterie Fregerio, Italy; Okabe Co Ltd, Japan
Associated Companies: Arabi WLL, Kuwait; Abdul Aziz Yousuf Al Eissa & Co, Kuwait; Gulf Services & Industrial Supplies, Muscat; Furmanite Gulf, Kuwait
Principal Bankers: Gulf Bank

Date of Establishment: 1968
No of Employees: 50

INSTRUMENTS INSTALLATION & MAINTENANCE CO

PO Box 9309, Ahmadi, 61004 Kuwait
Tel: 3981661/2
Cable: IMCO Kuwait
Telex: 44270 IMCO KT
Telefax: 2451481

Chairman: Said Toufic Khoury
Directors: Abdul Karim Shawwa
Senior Executives: Omar A K Shawwa (Manager), Jawdat A Shawwa (Asst Managing Partner), Abdulla Batniji (Admin & Financial Manager), Samir Tibi (Manager Operations), Norman Allinson (Managing Engineer Technical Sales)

PRINCIPAL ACTIVITIES: Instruments and electrical construction and maintenance, motor rewinding, cathodic protection works, fire alarm systems, telecommunication installations, marketing of such products
Principal Bankers: National Bank of Kuwait, Ahmadi

Principal Shareholders: Sheikh Mishaal Al Ahmad Al Sabah, Abdul Karim Shawwa, Said Toufic Khoury
Date of Establishment: 1970
No of Employees: 450

INTER-ARAB INVESTMENT GUARANTEE CORPORATION

PO Box 23568 Safat, 13096 Kuwait
Tel: 2404740/6
Cable: Kafeel Kuwait
Telex: 22562 Kafeel KT, 46312 Kafeel KT
Telefax: 2405406

Directors: Mamoun Ibrahim Hassan (Director General), Guima Said Guima (Deputy Director General)
Senior Executives: Dr Al Fadel Nail Hassan (Director of Legal Dept), dr Abdel Rahman Taha (Director of Operations)

PRINCIPAL ACTIVITIES: Insurance coverage for Arab investors in the form of compensation for losses resulting from non-commercial risks; promotion of investment among member countries; insurance coverage for export credit against commercial and non commercial risks
Branch Offices: Riyadh, Saudi Arabia
Principal Bankers: National Bank of Kuwait; Gulf Bank; Al Ahli Bank of Kuwait; Commercial Bank of Kuwait; Bank of Kuwait and the Middle East
Financial Information:

	1988 KD'000	1989 KD'000
Net profit	2,200	3,026
Authorised capital	25,025	15,025
Paid-up capital	21,399	22,230
Total assets	46,610	50,970

Principal Shareholders: Algeria, Egypt, Iraq, Jordan, Kuwait, Lebanon, Libya, Mauritania, Morocco, Oman, Qatar, Saudi Arabia, Sudan, Syria, Tunisia, UAE, N Yemen and S Yemen, Somalia, Djibouti, Bahrain, Palestine
Date of Establishment: 1975
No of Employees: 52

INTER-CONSULT
Management & Computer Consultancy Co WLL

PO Box 23094 Safat, 13091 Kuwait
Tel: 2441317
Cable: Computer
Telex: 22069 Kt Yaas
Telefax: 2440325

Chairman: F S Al-Fozan

PRINCIPAL ACTIVITIES: Management and computer services consultancy in Kuwait and neighbouring Middle East countries
Principal Bankers: Commercial Bank of Kuwait

KUWAIT

Principal Shareholders: F S Al Fozan; S K Al Ghunaim; Jean A Marchand; Kutayba Y Alghanim; Bassam Y Alghanim; Ghassan Y Alghanim; Mubarak N Al Sayer

Date of Establishment: 1972

No of Employees: 30

INTERMARKETS KUWAIT

PO Box 20604 Safat, 13067 Kuwait
Tel: 4846540
Cable: Midmarket Kuwait
Telex: 22658 Intmar Kt
Telefax: 4846540

Directors: Bassam Soboh (General Manager)
Senior Executives: Mousa Qudaimat (Finance Manager)

PRINCIPAL ACTIVITIES: Advertising agency, sales promotions, public relations
Branch Offices: Bahrain; Dubai (UAE); Egypt; Saudi Arabia; Jordan; UK (London); Lebanon
Parent Company: Head Office in Lebanon

Date of Establishment: 1979
No of Employees: 22

INTERNATIONAL AUDIT BUREAU

PO Box 26154 Safat, 13122 Kuwait
Tel: 2452546/7/8
Telex: 46889 Kt
Telefax: 2452549

Chairman: Saad M Al Muhanna
Directors: Soliman H Maamoon (Managing Director)

PRINCIPAL ACTIVITIES: Chartered accountants and management consultants
Principal Bankers: Kuwait International Bank

Date of Establishment: 1978

INTERNATIONAL COMPUTERS LTD

PO Box 5234 Safat, 13053 Kuwait
Tel: 2401512/3, 2401534/6
Telex: 30523 ICLME KT

Senior Executives: R Gamage (General Manager), K Wilson (Oil Sector Manager), Omar Taha (Private & Government Sector Manager)

PRINCIPAL ACTIVITIES: Supply of data processing equipment and computers
Principal Agencies: ICL, UK

INTERNATIONAL CONTRACTING CO KSC

PO Box 23764 Safat, 13098 Kuwait
Tel: 2443820/21/22
Cable: Tameer Kuwait
Telex: 22559 Tameer Kt

Chairman: Abdulmohsen Yousef Al Hunaif
Directors: Abdul Rahman Moubark Al Kourod, Nasser Mohamed Abdulmohsen Al-Kharafi, Abdulmohsen Faisal Al-Thuwaini, Abdulmohsen H Al-Qattan, Abdulhadi A Al Dosari (Managing Director)

PRINCIPAL ACTIVITIES: Civil, electrical, mechanical and electronical contractors
Associated Companies: Kuwait Foreign trading, Contracting & Investment Co SAK; Mohamed Abdulmohsen Al-Kharafi; Ahmadiah Trading & Contracting Co; Lebanese Construction & Trading Co (SOLICO)
Principal Bankers: Commercial Bank of Kuwait; National Bank of Kuwait

Principal Shareholders: Associated companies as described
No of Employees: 400

INTERNATIONAL CONTRACTORS GROUP

PO Box 25068 Safat, 13111 Kuwait
Tel: 4736855
Cable: Takwa
Telex: 23040 Group KT, 44906 ICG KT
Telefax: 4747941

Chairman: Abdullah Saud Al Abdulrazzak
Directors: Abdul Aziz Abdul Rahman Al Zamel (Deputy Chairman), Khalil G Sarraf (Managing Director)
Senior Executives: Maher J Farah (General Manager), Mahrous Shaltout (Asst General Manager Construction), Ahmed Agha (External Affairs Manager), Abdullah Aboutaleb (Technical/Commercial/Purchasing Manager), A R Qishawi (Personnel & Admin Manager), Hamid Salha (Plant, Equipment & Vehicles Manager), Maajid Al Badri (Electrical Division Manager), Ibrahim Mohanna (Roads Manager), Tayseer Zidan (Iraq Office Manager), Mohammed Saeed (Egypt Office Manager)

PRINCIPAL ACTIVITIES: Building and civil contractors
Branch Offices: Riyadh, Saudi Arabia; Cairo, Egypt
Principal Bankers: Al Ahli Bank, Kuwait
Financial Information:

	US$'000
Sales turnover	50,000
Authorised capital	35,000
Paid-up capital	25,000

Principal Shareholders: Saud & Ibrahim Al Abdulrazzak Contracting Co; Al Mansour & Al Abdally Contracting Co; United Arab Contractors Co; Saud A Al Abdulrazzak; Abdullah S Al Abdulrazzak; Abdul Azeez A Al Zamel; Abdallah S Al Abdally; Khalil G Sarraf; Heir of Late Muram S Shammas
Date of Establishment: 1977
No of Employees: 1,700

INTERNATIONAL FINANCIAL ADVISERS KSC (C)

PO Box 4694 Safat, 13047 Kuwait
Tel: 2457842/3
Cable: IFA-Kuwait
Telex: 22385 IFA KT

Chairman: Saud K Al Azmi (Managing Director)
Directors: Abdul Wahab Al Bader (Vice Chairman), Jassim Al Daboos, Soheel Al Rasheed, Adel Al Nafisi

PRINCIPAL ACTIVITIES: Corporate finance, loan syndications, money and asset management, clearing and settlements, commodity and bullion dealings
Branch Offices: PO Box 2057, Dubai
Subsidiary Companies: IFA Banque SA Paris, 39 Av Pierre ler de Serbie, 73008 Paris, France
Principal Bankers: National Bank of Kuwait, Kuwait; National Westminister Bank, London; Citibank, New York; Dresdner Bank, Frankfurt
Financial Information:

	1990/91 KD'000
Authorised capital	23,300
Paid-up capital	23,300

Principal Shareholders: Kuwait Investment Authority
Date of Establishment: April 1974
No of Employees: 60

INTERNATIONAL MARINE CONSTRUCTION CO SAK

PO Box 24057 Safat, 13101 Kuwait
Tel: 2447061
Telex: 23187 KT Marinco
Telefax: 2447168

Chairman: Hisham Al Essa
Directors: Sulaiman Al Omani, Isamu Kita, Sulaiman Al Nasrallah, Tatsuo Nakatani, Hideki Shimozawa

PRINCIPAL ACTIVITIES: Marine construction and offshore services

Branch Offices: Khafji, Saudi Arabia

Parent Company: Contracting & Marine Services Co

Principal Bankers: Commercial Bank of Kuwait, Gulf Bank

Principal Shareholders: Contracting & Marine Services Co; Nippon Steel Corp; Mitsui & Co Ltd; Marubeni Corp; Nishio Iwai Corp; C Itoh & Co Ltd; Mitsubishi Corp; Toyo Menka Kaisha Ltd; Nittetsu Shoji Co Ltd

Date of Establishment: 1975

No of Employees: 100

INTERNATIONAL PAINT KUWAIT KSC

PO Box 42255, Shuwaikh Industrial Area, 70653 Kuwait

Tel: 4832471, 4832644, 4382698, 4832557

Telex: 23782 Inpakt KT

Telefax: 4843971

Chairman: Khalid Abdul Muhsin Al Bahtain

Directors: Saleh Abdul Muhsin Al Babtain, Barrak Abdul Muhsin Al Babtain, W G Hadman, Peter Rogers, David Brett

Senior Executives: Samir Sami Ghawi (General Manager)

PRINCIPAL ACTIVITIES: Manufacturing and trading in all kinds of paints including heavy duty marine and protective coatings, building paints etc; paint contracting

Principal Bankers: National Bank of Kuwait; Al Ahli Bank of Kuwait; Gulf Bank

Financial Information:

	1989 KD'000
Sales turnover	2,261
Profits	247
Authorised capital	720
Paid-up capital	720

Principal Shareholders: Al Babtain Group of Kuwait; International Paint Co, UK

Date of Establishment: 23/7/1978

No of Employees: 56

INTERNATIONAL SHIPPING AGENCY LTD

PO Box 20637 Safat, 13067 Kuwait

Tel: 2441860

Cable: Shipagent

Telex: 22208 Isaship; 22396 Isatug

Telefax: 2415732

Senior Executives: Hakan Granander (Managing Director)

PRINCIPAL ACTIVITIES: Shipping and forwarding agency, customs clearance, land transportation, air-freight, project cargo handling, warehousing, packing, removals

Principal Agencies: Niver Lines; Nippon Yusen Kaisha; Hinode Kisen Co Ltd; Hansa Projekt Transport; NOSAC; Fincarriers; Mammoet Shipping; Castle & Cooke; Beeco Shipping; Wallenius Lines, Lauritzen Reefers, Normudo Line, GCC Line

Parent Company: Group Administration: Gulf Agency Co Ltd, Administrative Office, Athens, PO Box 61087, GR-151 10 Amaroussiou, Greece

Associated Companies: Gulf Agency Company (GAC) Group

Principal Bankers: National Bank of Kuwait

Date of Establishment: 1956

No of Employees: 60

INTERNATIONAL SUPPLY CO LTD

PO Box 5514 Safat, 13056 Kuwait

Tel: 4814914, 4814389, 4830328

Cable: Iscol

Telex: 22449 Iscol KT

Chairman: Fahed Abdulrehman Al-Mojil

Directors: Mahmoud Hashim Borno

Senior Executives: S Lane (Commercial Manager)

PRINCIPAL ACTIVITIES: Stockist and suppliers of industrial, and oil-field equipment, pipes and fittings, valves, carbon steel and stainless electrodes, scaffoldings, pressure gauges, fire, oil steam and air hoses and fittings, wire ropes, forklifts, hoists, trucks, pumps, welding equipment, generators

Principal Agencies: Totectors Ltd, UK; Sumo Pumps Ltd, UK; Morganite Ceramic Fibres Ltd, UK Henry Wiggin & Co Ltd, UK; Copon International Wood Ltd, UK; Tom Shipman (Supplies) Ltd, UK

Branch Offices: International Supply Est, PO Box 34, Dammam, Saudi Arabia International Supply Co Ltd, PO Box 2360, Abu Dhabi

Principal Bankers: Commercial Bank of Kuwait

Principal Shareholders: Directors as described

Date of Establishment: 1972

No of Employees: 50

INTERNATIONAL TANK & PIPES CO

PO Box 9183, Ahmadi, 61002 Kuwait

Tel: 3982055, 2439596

Chairman: Abdulla Abdul Ghafar Ali Reda

PRINCIPAL ACTIVITIES: Metallurgical engineering, tank erection with Capper-Neill

Branch Offices: Kuwait; Fahed Salem St, PO Box 106, Tel 2439596

INTERNATIONAL TRAVEL CORPORATION

PO Box 24523 Safat, 13106 Kuwait

Tel: 2424962, 2424964, 2424969, 2424967, 2464396/8

Cable: Aldarmi

Telex: 23110 Aldarmi KT

Telefax: 2407842

President: Abdullah A Al Darmi

Directors: Sulaiman M K Malallah

Senior Executives: Emad M Sulaiman (Asst General Manager)

PRINCIPAL ACTIVITIES: Travel, tours and cargo agents

Branch Offices: Cargo Division: Al Sour Street, Kuwait; also Khaldiya Branch

Subsidiary Companies: Abdullah Al Darmi & Partners International Exchange & Precious Metals Co; Abdullah Ahmed Al Darmi Factory for Ready Made Garments

Principal Bankers: Gulf Bank, Commercial Bank of Kuwait

Principal Shareholders: Abdullah A Al Darmi

Date of Establishment: September 1977

No of Employees: 34

INTERNATIONAL TURNKEY SYSTEMS

PO Box 26729 Safat, 13128 Kuwait

Tel: 2409100

Telex: 23077 ITS

Telefax: 2408664

Chairman: Abdul Jalil Al Gharabally

Directors: Faisal Al Khatrash, Samir Al Nafisi, Mohammed Al Khudairi

Senior Executives: Saad Al Barrak (General Manager), Khalifa Al Soulah (Asst General Manager), Dr Costas Constantinidis (Manager Systems Dept)

PRINCIPAL ACTIVITIES: Marketing, support, installation and maintenance of tunrkey computer systems (hardware and software), computer consultancy services, etc

Principal Agencies: Tandem Computers, USA; Sequent Computer Systems, USA

Branch Offices: Bahrain (PO Box 1344), Dubai (PO Box 8687), Abu Dhabi (PO Box 3333), Saudi Arabia (Riyadh, Jeddah)

Parent Company: Kuwait Finance House

Principal Bankers: Kuwait Finance House, Kuwait; Dubai Islamic Bank, Dubai; Bahrain Islamic Bank, Bahrain

KUWAIT

Financial Information:

	1989
	KD'000
Sales turnover	2,500
Authorised capital	1,000
Paid-up capital	1,000

Principal Shareholders: Kuwait Sharing Closed Company (KSCC)
Date of Establishment: 1981
No of Employees: 60

ISOFOAM INSULATING MATERIALS PLANTS

PO Box 23053 Safat, 13091 Kuwait
Tel: 4812968, 4813671, 4844057
Cable: Isofoam
Telex: 23714 Isofoam Kt
Telefax: 4742689, 4844594

Chairman: Nasser Al-Kharafi
Directors: Mowafak El Chokhdar

PRINCIPAL ACTIVITIES: Manufacture of insulation and waterproofing materials
Branch Offices: Plants: UAE: PO Box 161, Ajman, Tel 422529, Telex 69564 Foam EM; Egypt: Cairo, Tel 724847, 720026 Telex 93433 Isfom Un; Morocco: PO Box 14294, Casablanca, Tel 251353, Telex 21761 UMI M
Parent Company: Mohamed Abdulmohsin Kharafi
Subsidiary Companies: Misrfoam Co; Isofoam Co; Misrpanel Co; United Moroccan Industries SA
Principal Bankers: National Bank of Kuwait
Financial Information:

	KD'000
Sales turnover	3,000
Authorised capital	1,000
Paid-up capital	1,000

Date of Establishment: 1973
No of Employees: 100

JAMAL, SALEH, & CO WLL

PO Box 179 Safat, 13002 Kuwait
Tel: 2445040 (60 lines)
Cable: Jamal
Telex: 22012 Almulla KT
Telefax: 2437285

Chairman: Najeeb Abdulla Al Mulla
Directors: Najeeb Abdulla Al Mulla, Anwar Abdulla Al Mulla, Nabil Abdulla Al Mulla, Lutfi Abdulla Al Mulla, Apkar Hovaguimian, D R Mirchandani, V Karamat, S Narenthiran, R K Sethi, H N Elowe, I Pacheco, Minoo Patel
Senior Executives: Anwar Abdulla Al Mulla (Deputy Chairman), Apkar Hovaguimian (Managing Director), D R Mirchandani (Deputy Managing Director), V Karamat (Financial Director), A S Narenthiran (Commercial Director)

PRINCIPAL ACTIVITIES: General agents, and manufacturers' representatives (electrical equipment, building materials, fire protection & security systems, telephone exchange & instruments, access control systems) and contractors; air passenger and cargo transportation services, chemicals & pharmaceuticals
Principal Agencies: GEC (Lamps & Lighting) Ltd, GEC (Street Lighting) Ltd, GEC Expelair and Telecommunications, Pirelli, MEA, Clyde Surveys Ltd, Pharmachemic, Woods of Colchester Ltd, Tann Synchronome Ltd, Carters of Burnley, UK Fire Int'l Ltd
Parent Company: Al Mulla Group
Associated Companies: Bader Al Mulla & Bros Co WLL; Maseelah Trading Co WLL; Al Mulla Rental & Leasing of Vehicles & Equipment Co; Al Mulla Security Services Co WLL; Al Mulla Environmental Systems Co WLL, Al Mulla International Trading & Contracting Co WLL, Al Mulla Travel Bureau, Al Mulla Cleaning & Maintenance Services Co WLL, Hiba Advertising Co WLL, Al Mulla Real Estate Co WLL, Al

Mulla Consultancy Co WLL, Gulf Trading Group WLL, Al Mulla Aviation Agencies
Principal Bankers: Bank of Kuwait & Middle East, Kuwait; National Bank of Kuwait; Commercial Bank of Kuwait
Financial Information:

	1988/98
	US$'000
Sales turnover	2,319
Authorised capital	2,097
Paid-up capital	2,097
Total reserves	826
Total assets	7,438

Principal Shareholders: Najeeb Abdulla Al Mulla; Anwar Abdulla Al Mulla; Nabil Abdulla Al Mulla; Lutfi Abdulla Al Mulla; Mrs Badriya Khalid Al Ghunaim; Abdulla Bader Al Mulla
Date of Establishment: 1938
No of Employees: 200

JASHANMAL & PARTNERS LTD

PO Box 5138 Safat, 13052 Kuwait
Tel: 2412797, 2420071/2, 2431457, 2432420
Cable: Jaypartner/Jashanmals
Telex: 22378 Kt

Chairman: Tony Jashanmal Jhangiani (also Managing Director)

PRINCIPAL ACTIVITIES: Department store, import and export of consumer goods
Principal Agencies: Hoover Limited, UK; Clarks Overseas Shoes Ltd, UK; Jaeger le Coultre, Switzerland; Max Factor & Co, UK; Yashica Co Ltd, Japan and Hong Kong; Parfum Christian Dior, France; Delsey, Paris; Thorn Emi Kenwood Small Appliances, UK; Etienne Agner Cosmetics, Germany; Nippon Sanso KK, Japan; Parfums Van Cleef & Arpels, France; Parfums Jean Louis Scherrer, France; Aladdin Industries Ltd, USA; Russell Hobbs products, UK; A T Cross, Ireland
Branch Offices: Location in Kuwait: Fahad Al Salem Street; also in Abu Dhabi; Al Ain; Bahrain; Das Island; Dubai; Ras Alkhaimah; Sharjah
Associated Companies: Rifai & Jashanmal Co WLL, PO Box 99, Kuwait; Jashanmal & Sons, PO Box 16, Bahrain; Jashanmal National Co, Dubai, PO Box 1545, UAE; Jashanmal National Co, Abu Dhabi, PO Box 316, UAE; Jashanmal Co for Printed Materials, PO Box 1545, Dubai, UAE
Principal Bankers: Bank of Kuwait and the Middle East; Alahli Bank of Kuwait; National Bank of Kuwait

JASSIM M A ALWAZZAN & MAHMOUD S ALI CO WLL

PO Box 3167 Safat, 13032 Kuwait
Tel: 2416092, 2429016
Cable: Mahnazco Kuwait
Telex: 23317 Mahnaz Kt

Directors: Jassim Al-Wazzan, Mahmoud Jeddi

PRINCIPAL ACTIVITIES: Import and wholesale of foodstuffs; distribution of batteries, tobacco, detergents, blankets, towels, tea, chocolates, biscuits, caramel, juices, nectars, sardines; industrial chemicals

JASSIM M AL BAHAR & PARTNERS WLL

See AL BAHAR, JASSIM M, & PARTNERS WLL

JULAIAH TRADING & CONTRACTING CO WLL

PO Box 26142 Safat, 13122 Kuwait
Tel: 4845171 (5 lines)
Cable: DIJLA KUWAIT
Telex: 22560 Dijla Kt
Telefax: 4841776

Chairman: Khalid A A Al Fahad
Directors: Jassim A A Al Fahad, Reyad Saleh Hijazi
Senior Executives: Reyad S Hijazi (Managing Partner/General Manager), Zeid H Nuwairan (Asst General Manager), Hamdi D

Ibrahim (Administration & Finance Manager), David A Kelso (General Sales Manager)

PRINCIPAL ACTIVITIES: Manufacturers'representatives and equipment & services suppliers to the oil, petrochemical and power generation industries; also marketing consultants

Principal Agencies: Arescon, John Crane Int, Lawrence Pumps, Dresser Randk Emco Wheaton, Parker Hannifin, Scama, Smith Meter, Vetco Gray, Veeder Root, Baker Hughes, Vetco Inspection & Vetco Pipeline Services, BTR Dunlop Industrial Hose, Dunlop Oil & Marine, David Brown, Ameron BV, Mandoval Coatings, Gordon Co, Lubriquip Inc

Principal Bankers: National Bank of Kuwait

Financial Information:

	1988/89 US$'000
Sales turnover	15,000
Authorised capital	500
Paid-up capital	500
Total assets	1,000

Principal Shareholders: Khalid A A Al Fahad; Jassim A A Al Fahad; Reyad S Hijazi
Date of Establishment: 1974
No of Employees: 35

K & M ALGHANIM CO

See ALGHANIM, K & M, CO

KADHMA CO FOR PUBLICATION, TRANSLATION & DISTRIBUTION

PO Box 24062 Safat, 13101 Kuwait
Tel: 2405845, 2405846

Chairman: N Al Awadi
Directors: N H Al-Saleh
Senior Executives: M M Barakat (General Manager), S Ali (Accountant), A Shareef (Secretary)

PRINCIPAL ACTIVITIES: Publication; translation; distribution
Principal Agencies: Agents for 25 publishers in the Arab World and World Book Encyclopedia Inc, USA
Principal Bankers: Gulf Bank

Principal Shareholders: Dar Al Watan; Massaleh Investment & Finance Co
Date of Establishment: November 1976
No of Employees: About 50

KAIS TRADING & CONTRACTING CO

PO Box 2028 Safat, 13021 Kuwait
Tel: 2457653, 2458404, 2458405, 2441609
Cable: Misharisons Kuwait
Telex: 44808 KAISALI KT

Chairman: Ali Hasssan Al Mishari
Directors: Mishari Sons

PRINCIPAL ACTIVITIES: Import, export, contracting; commission agents, caterers; dealing in cement, building materials, textiles, foodstuffs, soft drinks, machineries, carpets, toys, silverware
Branch Offices: Apollo Show Room, Sharq, Kuwait; Mishari International Jewellery; Jewellery Showroom, Kuwait; Foodstuff Store Mishari, Kais, Salmiah, Advertising Consultant Office
Associated Companies: Gulf Hotels Co KSC, Kuwait; Kuwait Toys Industries Co, Kuwait; Asia Kais Int'l Corp Osaka; Japan Kais Int'l Inv, Tokyo
Principal Bankers: National Bank of Kuwait

Principal Shareholders: Ali Hassan Al Mishari & Sons
Date of Establishment: 1942
No of Employees: 60

KARAM, MUSTAFA, TRADING & CONTG FIRM

PO Box 3128 Safat, 13031 Kuwait
Tel: 4744165, 4744169, 4744522 (Kuwait), 3981269, 3983880 (Ahmadi)
Cable: Karamco Kuwait
Telex: 23003 Karamco

Chairman: Mustafa Karam (Owner)
Senior Executives: Bader M Karam (General Manager, Trading Division), Saaid Shawa (General Manager, Contracting Division), Fawsi Karam (Deputy General Manager)

PRINCIPAL ACTIVITIES: Trading Division: distributors of motors cars, spare parts and accessories. Contracting Division: transport contractors to oil companies, private corporations and govt agencies for motor cars, coaches, trucks of all capacities, haulage trailers, cranes, forklifts, earthmoving machinery and oilfield equipments, car rental and lease
Principal Agencies: Leyland Trucks, Leyland Bus, Scammell Motors, Austin Rover, Dunlop Ltd, Automotive Products Group, Suzuki Motor Co Ltd
Principal Bankers: National Bank of Kuwait

KENOMAC
Kuwait Engineering, Operation & Management Co KSC

KFTCIC Bldg, Sharq, PO Box 22272 Safat, 13083 Kuwait
Tel: 2433352/3/4/7
Cable: Kenomac
Telex: 22217 Kt

Chairman: Dr Yousef K Shuhaibar (Managing Director)
Board Members: Salem Al Mussallam, Jassem Al Qattan, Abdul Aziz Shimali
Senior Executives: Mowaffaq Al-Fulaij (Project Coordinator), Dr Suliman Demir (Management Services Manager), Ramsis Boulis (Engineering Services Manager), Samir El Gohary (Project Director)

PRINCIPAL ACTIVITIES: Mechanical and industrial engineering consultants, operation and management of industrial installations; management services and corporate strategy
Branch Offices: Yemen: PO Box 884, Sanaa; Bahrain: PO Box 26901, Adliya
Subsidiary/Associated Companies: Unetec, United Engineering and Technical Consultants, Kuwait
Principal Bankers: National Bank of Kuwait; Gulf Bank of Kuwait

Principal Shareholders: Kuwait Metal Pipes Industries; Dr Yousef Shuhaibar; Salem Mussallam; Jassem Qattan
Date of Establishment: 1975
No of Employees: 172

KEO-KUWAITI ENGINEER'S OFFICE
Kuwaiti Engineer's Office

PO Box 3679 Safat, 13037 Kuwait
Tel: 2438011
Telex: 22522 LABBAD Kt
Telefax: 2443969

Owner: Dr Abdul Aziz Sultan (Managing Director)
Senior Executives: Paul Pawlowski (Design Director), Donna Sultan (Marketing Director), Abdul Hamid Darwish (Deputy Managing Director), David Todd (Director Infrastructure Engineering Services), Seif Kanaan (Director of Construction Management Services), David Raymond Jones (Director of Middle East Surveys), John Lesniewski (Chief Executive Officer for Sultan Systems)

PRINCIPAL ACTIVITIES: Architects, planners, engineers, interior & graphic designers, residential, educational, medical, municipal, and commercial developments, sanitary and water projects, roads design, environmental engineering, construction management and supervision, computer services and operation, maintenance consultancy

Branch Offices: Abu Dhabi: KEO International Consultants
Subsidiary Companies: CPM (Construction Management); Middle East Surveys (Soil Testing, Material Testing, Surveys); Sultan Systems (Computer Management Services)
Principal Bankers: Gulf Bank

Principal Shareholders: Dr Abdul Aziz Sultan
Date of Establishment: 1964
No of Employees: 350

KHALID ALI AL KHARAFI & BROS CO WLL (KHARAFI STEEL)

See AL KHARAFI, KHALID ALI, & BROS CO WLL (KHARAFI STEEL)

KHALIFA FULEIJ CONTRACTING & GENERAL TRADING EST

PO Box 9284, Ahmadi, 61003 Kuwait
Tel: 3982149, 3982148
Cable: Fadlalah
Telex: 44236 Fadelco Kt

President: Khalifa Al-Fulaij (also General Manager)
Senior Executives: Ahmad Farag (Technical Manager), Wadie G Ghali (Chief Electrical Engineer), Daoud Musallam (Office Manager)

PRINCIPAL ACTIVITIES: Civil, mechanical and electrical engineering and construction works including contracting and trading
Principal Agencies: E W Saybolt & Co SA, New York; Sembodja Holland NV Amsterdam, Holland; General Transportation Services, Beirut-Lebanon; IOMC Philippe Ports, Philippines; Int Medical Group Inc, Philippines; Claxy Catering, Philippines; CMP France; Korea Ship Bldg & Eng; Hans Leffer, West Germany
Principal Bankers: National Bank of Kuwait; Burgan Bank

No of Employees: 300

KHARAFI, MOHAMED ABDULMOHSIN, INDUSTRIES & ESTABLISHMENTS

PO Box 886 Safat, 13009 Kuwait
Tel: 813622/5
Cable: Alkharafi
Telex: 22071 Kharafi Kwt, 23569 Kharafi KWT

Chairman: Mohamed Abdulmohsin Al Kharafi
Directors: Nasser M Al Kharafi (President - Contracting Division), Fawzi Mohamed Al Kharafi (President - Factories Division)
Senior Executives: Mohsen Kamel Mustafa (Managing Director - Contracting Division), Omer D'Souki (Asst Director General - Finance & Administration), Khalifa Al Kharafi (Asst Director General - Public Relations), Ahmed Abdul Wahab (Manager - Business Development & Agencies Division)

PRINCIPAL ACTIVITIES: Civil engineering contractors, import-export, production of steel, aluminium, timber, terrazo tiles & steps, furniture, doors, windows, portable houses/offices, steel structures, drums, tanks, barrels, electrical, mechanical, plumbing, and HVAC Works, insulating materials and panels for roofing and cladding, piling, foundation, shoring, marine, supply of concrete readymix and aggregates, steel wire mesh, water wells drilling, agencies services, real estate, money exchange, hospitals' operation and maintenance, water treatment and chemicals, fast food restaurants and meat processing, etc
Principal Agencies: Compagnie D'Entreprises CFE, Belgium; IBIS Medical, UK; China State Construction Engineering, China; Institute for Computer Medicine, Austria; Hospilab, Switzerland; Errut, UK; Steinweg, West Germany; Hausermann, France; Paschal, West Germany; MacDonald, UK; Tremi, Sweden; Marmomacchine, Italy; Courmi, UK;

EMW, West Germany; Sulzer, West Germany; Chiyoda Shoji, Taiwan; Intergraph Al-Khaleej, Bahrain; Mediconsult, UK; AM Santos, Portugal; Bachert, West Germany; Amorin Trading, Portugal
Branch Offices: ADMAK General Contracting Co, PO Box 650, Abu Dhabi, UAE, Telex 22320 KHARAFI EM; Mohamed Abdulmohsin Kharafi Est, PO Box 423, Riyadh, Saudi Arabia, Telex 201206 KHARAFI SJ; Mohamed Abdulmohsin Kharafi, PO Box 2269, Sana'a, Yemen, Telex 2287 KHARAFI YE; MAK Contracting Co, PO Box 112, Giza, Cairo, Egypt, Telex 94112 MAK UN
Parent Company: Head Office in Kuwait
Subsidiary/Associated Companies: National Electro-Mechanical Co, Kuwait; National Piling Co, Kuwait; Kuwaiti British Readymix Co, Kuwait; Kuwait Steel Reinforcement Co, Kuwait; MAK Contracting Co, Egypt; Kuwait Aluminium Industries, Kuwait; Kuwait Terrazo Factory, Kuwait; Cassette Factory, Egypt; Yemen Hotels & Investment Co, Yemen; Drum Factory, Yemen; Tiles Factory, Yemen; Isofoam Insulating Materials Co, Kuwait/Egypt/UAE; Kuwait Food Co (Americana), Kuwait/UAE/Bahrain/Egypt/Saudi Arabia/Iraq; Al-Kharafi Drilling Co, Yemen; Sitar Co, Kuwait, etc
Principal Bankers: National Bank of Kuwait; Commercial Bank of Kuwait; Al Ahli Bank of Kuwait

Principal Shareholders: Mohamed Abdulmohsin Kharafi
Date of Establishment: 1930
No of Employees: 1,750 technical staff; 205 engineers; 3,200 labour

KIRBY BUILDING SYSTEMS-KUWAIT

PO Box 23933 Safat, 13100 Kuwait
Tel: 3262800
Cable: Kirbuilding
Telex: 44240 Kirbypt KT
Telefax: 3260323

Chairman: Kutayba Y Alghanim
President: Bassam Y Alghanim
Senior Executives: Marwan J Karadsheh (Vice President & General Manager), Mahmoud K Eid (Deputy General Manager), Alwin D'Souza (Engineering Manager), Taher Banker (Production & Quality Control Manager), Nabil F Sleiman (General Sales Manager)

PRINCIPAL ACTIVITIES: Manaufacture and supply of pre-engineered steel rigid frames, secondary members, prepainted claddings used in building factories, warehouses, offices, showrooms, camps, cold stores, industrial complexes, and residential units; also manufacture of a wide range of doors, windows, roofing, skylights, partitions, suspended ceilings, sandwich panels and other accessories
Branch Offices: Abu Dhabi Tel 332765, Bahrain Tel 276411, Cairo Tel 666866, Doha Tel 425267, Dubai Tel 373816, Jeddah Tel 6516844, Al Khobar Tel 8575967, Kuwait Tel 4842988, Muscat Tel 563749, Riyadh Tel 4648301, Sana'a Tel 207149
Parent Company: Alghanim Industries
Principal Bankers: Commercial Bank of Kuwait, Kuwait; Bank of Kuwait and the Middle East, Kuwait; Chase Manhattan Bank, Bahrain

Date of Establishment: 1976
No of Employees: 350

KITCHERAMA

PO Box 901 Safat, 13010 Kuwait
Tel: 814188 (12 lines)
Cable: Byblos Kuwait
Telex: 22509 Byblos

Directors: Omar Bakir (Managing Director)
Senior Executives: Ghassan Ali Hasan (General Manager), Hilary Barreto (Admin Manager), Sami Hindieh (Projects Engineer)

PRINCIPAL ACTIVITIES: Design, supply, installation and maintenance of heavy duty kitchen, food service, refrigeration and laundry equipment, catering, bakery and supermarket equipment

Principal Agencies: Zanussi Grandi Impianti Spa, Italy; Wodschow & Co; Dahlen Int; Jet Spray Int; Em D'hooge NV; Renzacci Spa; Santo Stefano Spa; Lan Elec Ltd; Manitowoc Equipment Works; Robot Coupe

Branch Offices: Showroom on Salem Al Mubarak Street, Salmiya

Parent Company: Supply & Building Company

Principal Bankers: Commercial Bank of Kuwait

Financial Information:

	KD'000
Sales turnover	15,000
Profits	1,500
Authorised capital	1,000
Paid-up capital	1,000

Principal Shareholders: Jassem M Al Bahar & Bros (51%); Omar M Bakir (49%)

Date of Establishment: 1975

No of Employees: 60

KUWAIT & GULF LINK TRANSPORT CO KSCC

PO Box 24565 Safat, 13106 Kuwait

Tel: 4815619, 4849355, 4845104, 4846507

Cable: Analez

Telex: 46263 Rabitku KT, 44519 Analeza KT

Telefax: 4845926

Chairman: Ismail Ali Dashti

Directors: Sa'ad Abdulaziz Al Rashid, Abdulla Yaqoub Al Wazzan, Ali Hussain Al Issa, Mahir Abdulla Marafi

Senior Executives: Saeed I Dashti (General Manager), Ahmed M Sadek (Asst General Manager)

PRINCIPAL ACTIVITIES: Inland and overland transporters; shipping agents; clearers & forwarders; container services & terminals; renting & leasing of trucks, trailers, forklifts, Ro-Ro, cranes, dumptrucks, tractors, equipment; garage services

Principal Agencies: Kalmar Forklift; Werklust Wheeloaders

Subsidiary Companies: Gulf Stevedor Contracting Co, PO Box 1153, Alkhobar 31952, Saudi Arabia

Principal Bankers: National Bank of Kuwait; Commercial Bank of Kuwait; Gulf Bank; Bank of Kuwait & the Middle East

Financial Information:

	KD'000
Authorised capital	20,000
Paid-up capital	11,000

Principal Shareholders: Chairman & directors as described

Date of Establishment: 1982

No of Employees: 1,800

KUWAIT AIRWAYS CORPORATION

Kuwait International Airport, PO Box 394 Safat, 13004 Kuwait

Tel: 4345555, 4346666, 4347777

Cable: Airkuwait

Telex: 23036

Telefax: 4714207, 4319204

Chairman: Ahmad Hamad Al Mishari (Managing Director)

Directors: Sheikh Jaber Al Mubarak Al Sabah, Ibrahim Al Shatti, Abdullah Khaled Al Samait, Mohammed Jassem Al Saqr, Habib Jawhar Hayat, Jamaan Salem Al Twaim, Abdel Aziz Al Roumi

Senior Executives: Ahmad Hamad Al Mishari (Chairman and Managing Director), Ahmad Faisal Al Zabin (Director General), Yousef Al Jassem (Dy Director General Financial & Admin), Abdul Karim Al Ibrahim (Dy Director General Engineering), Ghazi Al Mishaan (Dy Director General Commercial), Khalid Al Duwaisan (Dy Director General Flight Services), Capt Ali Al Dokhan (Dy Director General Operations)

PRINCIPAL ACTIVITIES: Air transport

Branch Offices: Temporary head office in Cairo, Egypt

Subsidiary Companies: Catering Supply & Aircraft Services Company; Air Taxi Service

Principal Bankers: All Kuwait banks

Financial Information:

	1988/89 KD'000
Sales turnover	127,439,556
Profits	3,333
Authorised capital	350,000
Paid-up capital	350,000
Total assets	453,116,690

Principal Shareholders: Government of Kuwait

Date of Establishment: 1954

No of Employees: 5,456

KUWAIT ALUMINIUM CO KSC

PO Box 5335 Safat, 13054 Kuwait

Tel: 4734600, 4710460, 4710475, 47344800

Cable: Kuwaital

Telex: 23025 Kuwaital Kt

Telefax: 965-4734419

Chairman: Nasser Naki

Directors: Mohammed Naki, Fawzan Al Fares

Senior Executives: Eng Ahmed Ibrahiem (R & D Manager), Omer Nemer (Production Manager), H W S Karunaratna (Technical Manager)

PRINCIPAL ACTIVITIES: Manufacture of aluminium products; aluminium doors, windows, curtain walls and cladding, partitions, facades, rolling shutters, handrails & balustrades, louvres, etc in non thermal and thermal break system and in anodised, powder coated and sandalor finishes

Subsidiary Companies: Arabian Light Metals KSC; United Glass Co WLL; Kuwaiti Sudanese Aluminium Co Ltd (Khartoum, Sudan)

Principal Bankers: Commercial Bank of Kuwait; Alahli Bank of Kuwait; Gulf Bamk

Financial Information:

	1989 KD'000
Sales turnover	1,319
Profits	82
Authorised capital	7,500
Paid-up capital	6,000
Total assets	6,263

Principal Shareholders: Arabian Light Metals Co KSC

Date of Establishment: 1968

No of Employees: 220

KUWAIT ALUMINIUM EXTRUSION CO KALEXCO

PO Box 24501 Safat, 13106 Kuwait

Tel: 4738509, 4745434, 4745745

Cable: Extrusion

Telex: 23068 Kalexco KT

Telefax: 4710694

Chairman: Husain Makki Al Juma

Senior Executives: Nazih Al Khudairy (Deputy General Manager), Nael Mousa (Sales & Marketing Manager), Altino F Coelho (Production Manager), Talib Omar (Personnel Manager)

PRINCIPAL ACTIVITIES: Extrusion and anodising plant, die making, cast house, electrostatic powder painting and fabrication of aluminium products

Principal Agencies: Syma System, Switzerland

Principal Bankers: Al Ahli Bank of Kuwait

KUWAIT

Financial Information:

	1989
	KD'000
Authorised capital	5,062
Paid-up capital	5,062

No of Employees: 200

KUWAIT ARC CO

PO Box 309 Safat, 13004 Kuwait
Tel: 812080, 834005
Cable: Arcweld
Telex: RH2437KT

Chairman: Abdullatif Yousuf Al-Oumi
Directors: Bader Al Bader, Taha A Aloumi

PRINCIPAL ACTIVITIES: Distributors for Hobert welding
 products, stainless, aluminium, brass sheets, decorative steel
 sheets, profiles pumps, wood working glue, aluminium cutting
 machines and industrial and hardware
Principal Agencies: Hobart Brothers Co, USA; Gisuke Konishi
 Japan
Branch Offices: Radiohouse Co, PO Box 1001 Safat, Kuwait
Subsidiary Companies: Supplying Stores WLL, PO Box 2154
 Safat, Kuwait
Principal Bankers: Alahli Bank of Kuwait; Bank of Kuwait and
 Middle East

Date of Establishment: 1954

KUWAIT ASBESTOS & PLASTIC INDUSTRIES

PO Box 3314 Safat, 13034 Kuwait
Tel: 4710700, 4710998, 3962979, 3962515
Cable: Asbestos
Telex: 23002, 44256

President: Mufarrej Ibrahim Al-Mufarrej (Chairman NIC)
Directors: Salah A Al Tarkait, S M Al-Sa'ad, A A Al-Obaidan, S
 K Al-Shallal, K F A Al-Fuleij, A I Al-Rabia, A A Al Shalfan, F M
 Al Kharafi
Senior Executives: Salah A Al Tarkait (General Manager)

PRINCIPAL ACTIVITIES: Production of asbestos pipes and
 sheets and PVC pipes and fittings
Parent Company: The National Industries Co SAK
Subsidiary/Associated Companies: Subsidiaries: Asbestos &
 PVC Factory; Lime Brick Factory & Quarry; Cement Products
 Plant; Detergent and Battery Plants. Associates (ownership
 of 5% up to 42%): Sand Lime Brick Factory; Kuwait Cement
 Co; Cement Factory; Cement Products Factory; Pre-fabricated
 Houses Factory; Metal Pipe Factory; Detergent Factory; Fiber
 Glass Pipes Factory; Car Battery Plant
Principal Bankers: National Bank of Kuwait; Gulf Bank;
 Commercial Bank of Kuwait; Bank of Kuwait and the Middle
 East
Financial Information:

	US$'000
Authorised capital	81,263
Paid-up capital	81,263

Principal Shareholders: Government of Kuwait 51%; private
 sector 49%
Date of Establishment: 1960
No of Employees: 2,500

KUWAIT ASPHALT EMULSION CO (ESHA)

PO Box 5989 Safat, 13060 Kuwait
Tel: 515175 (Office), 3981173 (Factory)
Cable: Emulsion
Telex: 23274 Sugar

Chairman: Hamoud Abdul Aziz Al Wazzan
Directors: Abdullah I Behbehani (Managing Director), Yousuf
 Abdul Aziz Al Wazzan; Ismail Ali Dashti

PRINCIPAL ACTIVITIES: Producing bituminous emulsions and
 asphaltic materials for roads

Branch Offices: Plant: East Ahmadi
Principal Bankers: Al-Ahli Bank of Kuwait

Principal Shareholders: Mohammad Al Wazzan, Yousuf Al
 Wazzan, Hamoud Al Wazzan, Ismail Ali Dashti
Date of Establishment: 1974

KUWAIT ASSOCIATED CONSULTANTS KASCON

PO Box 5443 Safat, 13055 Kuwait
Tel: 2429384, 2417744
Cable: Kascon Kuwait
Telex: 22116 Mazidi Kuwait

President: Feisal Mazidi

PRINCIPAL ACTIVITIES: Management, economic and technical
 consultancy
Principal Bankers: Commercial Bank of Kuwait

Principal Shareholders: President as described

KUWAIT AUTOMOBILE & TRADING CO WLL

PO Box 41 Safat, 13001 Kuwait
Tel: 4715314, 4741887, 4718960/1
Cable: Automobile
Telex: 23005 Mobile Kt, 44403 Zayani Kt
Telefax: 4744631

Directors: Qassim Abdul Rahman Al Zayani (Managing Director),
 Mohammad Qasim Abdul Rahman Al Zayani (Director)
Senior Executives: Nail Zayani (General Manager), Varughese
 Easaw (General Sales Manager), Mohammed Reedi (Finance
 Manager), Mohd Talat Othman (Legal Advisor), Michel Ayat
 (Commercial Vehicles Divn-Manager)

PRINCIPAL ACTIVITIES: Import and distribution of cars, trucks,
 buses, and related spare parts; garages
Principal Agencies: Rolls Royce; Jaguar; Land Rover; Range
 Rover; Rover; MAN (West Germany)
Branch Offices: Kuwait City, Shuaikh Al Rai Area
Associated Companies: Al Zayani Trading Company
Principal Bankers: Bank of Kuwait and the Middle East; National
 Bank of Kuwait; Commercial Bank of Kuwait; Bank of Bahrain
 & Kuwait; Alahli Bank; Gulf Bank

Principal Shareholders: Qassim Abdul Rahman Al Zayani;
 Mohamed Zayani
Date of Establishment: 1952
No of Employees: 375

KUWAIT AUTOMOTIVE IMPORTS CO WLL

PO Box 48 Safat, 13001 Kuwait
Tel: 2421276
Cable: Sayarat
Telex: 22430 Kt A/B SAYARAT
Telefax: 2401820

Chairman: Saleh Al Shaya
Senior Executives: Abdulla Al Shaya (General Manager)

PRINCIPAL ACTIVITIES: Automobiles, spare parts, lubricants,
 tyres
Principal Agencies: Peugeot Vehicles, Mazda Vehicles, Mobil
 Lubricants, Michelin Tyres & Car Rental
Branch Offices: Tyre & Oil Workshop, Canada Dry Street,
 Kuwait, Tel 4838028, 4849775
Parent Company: Mohammed Hamood Alshaya & Co; Abdullah
 Alhamed Alsager & Brothers
Principal Bankers: National Bank of Kuwait; Commercial Bank
 of Kuwait; Bank of Kuwait and the Middle East
Financial Information:

	1989
	KD'000
Sales turnover	10,000
Authorised capital	5,000
Paid-up capital	5,000

Principal Shareholders: Al Shaya and Al Sagar Families
Date of Establishment: 1928
No of Employees: 200

KUWAIT AVIATION FUELLING CO (KSC)

Kuwait International Airport, PO Box 1654 Safat, 13017 Kuwait
Tel: 4330483
Cable: Airfuel
Telex: 23056 Airfuel Kuwait
Telefax: 4330475

Chairman: Bader Hashim Al Refai
Directors: Abdulaziz Al-Bosiary, Abdulaziz F Al-Sirie, Yahya Moahmoud Al-Yahya
Senior Executives: Abdullaziz F Omar Al Sirie (Director & General Manager), Mustafa Bader Al Oun (General Services Manager), Ahmed Khalifa Al Shatti (Engineering Manager), John F Gardner (Accounts Manager), Adel Abdulwahab Al Roumi (Operations Manager), Awad Jawad Al Wadani (Safety & Inspection Manager)

PRINCIPAL ACTIVITIES: Aircraft refuelling and supply of aviation oil products
Parent Company: Kuwait Petroleum Corporation
Principal Bankers: Commercial Bank of Kuwait

Principal Shareholders: Wholly owned subsidiary of Kuwait Petroleum Corporation
Date of Establishment: July 1963
No of Employees: 80

KUWAIT BUILDING INDUSTRIES KSC
K.U.B.I.C.

PO Box 42318, Shuwaikh, 70654 Kuwait
Tel: 4845261, 4843716
Cable: FAWZI, KUWAIT
Telex: 23563 MSS Fact KT
Telefax: 4837987

Chairman: Yousif A Al Jassim
Senior Executives: Ataa Salah Shadi (Finance Manager), Zohair Ismail (Personnel Manager)

PRINCIPAL ACTIVITIES: Manufacture, supply and application/fitting of building materials: aluminium products, bituminous felt, vermiculite, building chemicals, ready mixed concrete, asphalt, reinforcing steel, equipment rental, scaffolding and formwork rental, waterproofing and insulation
Principal Agencies: Sika AG, Switzerland; Huld Troisorf (Dynamit Nobel), Germany; Promat, Germany; ChemBau, Italy
Branch Offices: Vermiculite & Roofing Felt Factory,Tel 3985664, 3982271; Aluminium Factory, Tel 3982271; Concrete & Asphalt Plant, Tel 4772833, 4774988
Parent Company: Musaad Al-Saleh Investment Group
Principal Bankers: Gulf Bank; Al-Ahli Bank of Kuwait; Burgan Bank; Commercial Bank of Kuwait; Kuwait Finance House
Financial Information:

	1988/89 KD'000
Sales turnover	5,500
Authorised capital	6,000
Paid-up capital	6,000

Principal Shareholders: Musaad Al Saleh Investment
Date of Establishment: 1964
No of Employees: 250

KUWAIT BUILDING MATERIALS MANUFACTURING CO (CKSC)

PO Box 24152 Safat, 13102 Kuwait
Tel: Admin Office: 4832554, 4834302, Factory & Accts Dept: 4674612, 4674622, Sales Dept: 4674260, 4674628
Cable: Manumatco
Telex: 23564 KBM KT

Chairman: Khalid A Rezooqi

Board Members: Sabar Al Jasar (Vice Chairman & Managing Director), Khalid A Razooqi, Abdullah Sarawi, Ali M Thunayan Alghanim, Hisham Abdulrazak S Aman, Salah Ghanum S Malallah, Omar Bader Al Kinaeye, Khalid Kalaf Al Salama
Senior Executives: Saud Mohammed Al-Rukhayes (General Manager)

PRINCIPAL ACTIVITIES: Manufacture all types of cement blocks, bricks, paving stones (interlockings), floor fillers etc. in various colours and designs
Branch Offices: Factory at Sulaibiyah and Administrative Office at Shuwaikh
Principal Bankers: Gulf Bank; Burgan Bank; Bank of Bahrain & Kuwait

Principal Shareholders: National Industries Co; Kuwait Cement Co; National Real Estate Co; Industrial Real Estate Co; Kuwait Real Estate Co; United Real Estate Co; Ali Mohammed Thunaiyan Alghanim Co
Date of Establishment: 27-11-1976
No of Employees: 90

KUWAIT CEMENT CO KSC

PO Box 20581 Safat, 13066 Kuwait
Tel: 2414033/039
Cable: Smeetco
Telex: 22205 Smeetco Kwt
Telefax: 2432956

Chairman: Abdulmohsin Abdul Aziz Al Rashed
Directors: Suleiman Khalid Al-Ghuneim (Vice Chairman), Khalid Abdulla M Al-Mishari, Abdulla Abdul Aziz Al-Obeidan, Mussaed Ahmed Al-Marzook, Saad Mohamed Al Saad, Adel Ahmad Al Wagyan, Abdul Aziz Suleiman Al Othman, Abdulla Mohamed Saud Al Baijan
Senior Executives: Khaled Abdulrazzak Rezooqi (General Manager), Abdulmutaleb Ismail Behbehani (Asst General Manager), Humoud Suleiman Khaled Al-Hamdan (Works Manager)

PRINCIPAL ACTIVITIES: Manufacturing and marketing of cement
Associated Companies: Saudi Kuwaiti Cement Manufacturing Co, Dammam, Saudi Arabia; Shuwaikh Cement Co, Kuwait
Principal Bankers: All banks operating in Kuwait
Financial Information:

	1988/89 KD'000
Sales turnover	14,258
Profits	75
Authorised capital	25,616
Paid-up capital	25,616
Total assets	43,904

Principal Shareholders: Government of Kuwait (28%); Al-Rashed Trading & Contracting Co Ltd, Kuwait (7.2%); Private shares (43.2%); National Industries Co SAK, Kuwait (21.6%)
Date of Establishment: 1968
No of Employees: 408

KUWAIT CHEMICAL MANUFACTURING CO KSC

PO Box 26011 Safat, 13121 Kuwait
Tel: 3262138, 3262143, 3262149, 3262151
Telex: 44925 RESINS
Telefax: 3261672

Chairman: Khalid Ibrahim Al Fassam
Senior Executives: T Y Durubi (Senior Manager), Adel Masoud (Finance Manager), John Hislop (Plant Manager), Barry T Scott (Sales Manager)

PRINCIPAL ACTIVITIES: Manufacturers of synthetic resins, alkyds, unsaturated polyesters, emulsions of polyvinyl acetate and styrene acrylics and also traders in chemicals
Principal Agencies: Exxon Chemicals; Akzo Chimie, Netherlands; Degussa AG, Germany; Kali Chemie, Germany

Branch Offices: Mina Abdulla Industrial Area, Kuwait
Subsidiary Companies: Middle East Chemical Manufacturing Co KSC
Principal Bankers: National Bank of Kuwait, Gulf Bank
Financial Information:

	1988/89 KD'000
Sales turnover	4,300
Authorised capital	2,500
Paid-up capital	2,268
Total assets	3,077

Principal Shareholders: Hempel Marine Paints; Abdul Aziz Al Muzaini
Date of Establishment: 1979; production started in July 1983
No of Employees: 90

KUWAIT COMMERCIAL AGENCY CO WLL

PO Box 20229 Safat, 13063 Kuwait
Tel: 2402011, 2402012
Cable: Comagency
Telex: 44217 Strolk Kt
Telefax: 2402013

Chairman: Najeeb Al Mulla
Directors: Anwar Abdulla Mulla
Senior Executives: Mustafa S Husseini (General Manager), V C James (Commercial Manager)

PRINCIPAL ACTIVITIES: Commission agents, distribution of oilfield equipment and supplies, and industrial machinery and equipment
Principal Agencies: Halliburton Services, USA; Raymond Int'l, UK; Hydril Co, USA; Maloney-Crawford Tank Corp, USA: Crouse Hinds Co, USA; Crouse Hinds of Europe, UK; Vinson Int, USA; Hawke Cable Glands, UK; Hockway, UK; Greywell Eng Services & Supply, UK; Gotco Int'l, USA; Cives Corp, USA; Oil Plus Ltd, UK; Maus Italia, Italy; Fugro Ltd, UK; Welex Division of Halliburton, USA; A.O.T. Division of Hydril Co, USA; Detektor, A Div of Semetex Corp, USA; Algoma Steel, Canada
Parent Company: Al Mulla Group of Companies
Principal Bankers: Bank of Kuwait and the Middle East, Kuwait
Financial Information:

	1989 US$'000
Sales turnover	850
Profits	420
Authorised capital	350
Paid-up capital	350
Total assets	450

Principal Shareholders: Abdullah Bader Al Mulla, Mrs Badriya Khaled Al Gunaim
Date of Establishment: 1958
No of Employees: 25

KUWAIT COMPUTER SERVICES

PO Box 5113 Safat, 13052 Kuwait
Tel: 2417965/7, 2417766/7, 2417966, 2458073, 2459018
Cable: Codiskap
Telex: 22790 Ksc Kt
Telefax: 2459019

Chairman: Anwar Essa Al Saleh
Directors: Marwan Salama (Vice Chairman), Saheb Behbehani, Ghazi B Al-Salem, Jamal Al Mutawa, Ghassan Fahad Al-Sultan (Managing Director)
Senior Executives: Taleb Nehmani (Marketing & Sales Manager), Ayman El Kaluobi, Boguslaw Zygalo (Service Manager)

PRINCIPAL ACTIVITIES: Computer supplies, turn-key systems, large computers, mini & micro computers, word processors, distributed DP networks, software support, service engineering, customer training

Principal Agencies: Wang Lab Inc; Acer Inc; TOM Software; SPI Software; Aztech; DEST Workless Workstation; Guttmann
Principal Bankers: National Bank of Kuwait; Gulf Bank; Burgan Bank
Financial Information:

	1989 KD'000
Sales turnover	1,000
Profits	150
Authorised capital	1,170
Paid-up capital	1,170
Total assets	1,300

Principal Shareholders: Closed shareholding company
Date of Establishment: 1976
No of Employees: 60

KUWAIT DAIRY CO SAK

PO Box 3240 Safat, 13033 Kuwait
Tel: 4670088, 4674632, 4671633, 4671617, 4671587, 4670205
Cable: KUDAIRCO
Telex: 23043 KUDAIRY KT
Telefax: 4676612

Chairman: Jassim Al Qatami
Senior Executives: Adel H Al Shaker (Deputy General Manager)

PRINCIPAL ACTIVITIES: Processing and distribution of fresh pasteurized milk, ice creams and fresh dairy products
Principal Bankers: Bank of Kuwait & the Middle East; Gulf Bank; Commercial Bank of Kuwait
Financial Information:

	1989 KD'000
Paid-up capital	3,000

Principal Shareholders: Jassim Al Qatami
Date of Establishment: 1978
No of Employees: 574

KUWAIT DANISH COMPUTER CO SAK

PO Box 25337 Safat, 13114 Kuwait
Tel: 830160/1, 2453830/1/2
Cable: KDCCOMP
Telex: 44074 KDC Comp KT

Chairman: Faisal Yousuf Al-Qatami
Directors: Khaled A Al Fares, Raeid Al Thuwaini, Sayed Ismail
Senior Executives: Sayed Ismail (General Manager), Dr Abdel Hamid Abed (Deputy General Manager)

PRINCIPAL ACTIVITIES: Computer systems (data processing, word processing and process control), supply, installation and maintenance of hardware and software; telecommunications systems ie telephone systems, EPABX's, key telephones, intercom systems and slow scan TV systems
Principal Agencies: Hoskyns Group Ltd; RC Computer; Arya Systems; C ITOH; Skan-A-Matic Ltd; ATEP; Data Link; CGCT; SLO; GNT Automatic; Colorado Video Inc; Digital Equipment Co; Matra Communication; Teleste Slocon
Branch Offices: Telephone & Tele-data Division; Computer Division
Subsidiary Companies: KDCC, 51 River St, Wellesley, Mass 02181 USA
Principal Bankers: National Bank of Kuwait; Commercial Bank of Kuwait
Financial Information:

	US$'000
Sales turnover	5,000
Authorised capital	2,500
Paid-up capital	2,200

Principal Shareholders: Ahmed Saleh Al-Shaya; Al Fares & Sons Co; Abdullah Al-Sharhan; Al Thuwaini Trading Co; Mohamed Sulaiman Sayed Ali; Mufarrej Al-Mufarrej; Nasser Al-Hajery;

Nasser Al Khorafi; Yousuf Al Nisf; Sultan Bin Essa & Sons
Co; Faisal Yousif Al Qatami

Date of Establishment: 1977

No of Employees: 50

KUWAIT DEVELOPMENT CO KSC

PO Box 2350 Safat, 13024 Kuwait

Tel: 2444780, 2444790, 2446682

Cable: Developko

Telex: 22683 Develop KT

Chairman: Ahmad Abdullah Al-Sharhan

Directors: Khalid Al-Babtein (Vice Chairman), Adnan A Al Sane
(Managing Director), Abdullah A Al-Sharhan (Director), Saleh
Salem Abdul Hadi (Member), Hamad Abdalla Al Hudib
(Member), Sou'd Abdul Aziz Al Gharabali (Member)

Senior Executives: S M Sejad (Commercial Manager), Wael B
Abdul Majeed (Adm & Financial Manager)

PRINCIPAL ACTIVITIES: Contracting and trading in building
materials, cement, steel bars & pipes etc

Principal Agencies: Nittetsu Cement Co Ltd, Japan; Clow Corp,
USA

Subsidiary Companies: Arab Contractors; Electrical Projects Co;
Gulf Paper Manufacturing Co

Principal Bankers: Commercial Bank of Kuwait

Financial Information:

	KD'000
Authorised capital	5,036
Paid-up capital	5,036

Principal Shareholders: Al-Sharhan Family; Al-Sane Family; Al-
Babtein Family

Date of Establishment: 1975

No of Employees: 30

KUWAIT DEVELOPMENTS & TRADING CO

PO Box 707 Safat, 13008 Kuwait

Tel: 4819144, 4815517, 4813421

Cable: Sultalim

Telex: 30207 Sultan B KT

Telefax: 4819059

Directors: Rashid Sultan Al Salim, Salim Al Salim, Yousuf Al
Salim, A Rahman Al Salim

Senior Executives: Abdul Rehman Sultan Al Salim (Managing
Director)

PRINCIPAL ACTIVITIES: Import and distribution of automobiles,
boats, marine engines, furniture, ceramics, lamps, gift articles,
playground equipment, children toys, inflatable and pedal
boats, marine sports wear

Principal Agencies: V/O Avtoexport, Moscow, USSR (cars);
Yamaha Motor Co, Japan (boats and marine engines);
Clabos, Italy; Pelican Inc, Canada; Woong Bee, Korea; Metal
Nova, Italy

Branch Offices: Automobile and Marine Workshop, Tel 4813421;
Furniture Division, Tel 4718820, 4834896, 4845931

Principal Bankers: Commercial Bank of Kuwait, Shuwaikh

Financial Information:

	1988/89 US$'000
Sales turnover	6,600
Profits	1,600
Authorised capital	1,500
Paid-up capital	600
Total assets	10,000

Principal Shareholders: Rashid Sultan Al Salim, Saleem Sultan
Al Salim, Yousaf Sultan Al Salim, Abdul Rehman Sultan Al
Salim

Date of Establishment: 1952

No of Employees: 100

KUWAIT DRILLING CO KSC

PO Box 9066, Ahmadi, 61001 Kuwait

Tel: 3981598

Cable: Kutdrill

Chairman: Hisham Al Otaibi

Directors: Ahmed Al Asfour, Hamad Al Hamad, Clyde F
Dawson, Charles L Barnhill, Larry D Swisher

PRINCIPAL ACTIVITIES: Drilling contractors; oilwell drilling and
workover

Associated Companies: Contracting & Marine Services Co SAK;
Santa Fe International Corporation

Principal Bankers: Commercial Bank of Kuwait; Industrial Bank
of Kuwait

Date of Establishment: 1962

No of Employees: 423

KUWAIT ENGINEERING BUREAU

PO Box 6567 Hawally, 32040 Kuwait

Tel: 2421550, 2423024, 2423025

Cable: Kuenbu

Telex: 23872 Delest KT

Telefax: 2424466

Chairman: Hisham H Al Issa

Directors: Adnan F Halawa (General Manager)

Senior Executives: M F Guncon, W A Khalaf (Office Manager)

PRINCIPAL ACTIVITIES: Consulting engineers, architects

Associated Companies: Architects Collaborative, USA; Rendel
Palmer & Tritton, UK; Colin Buchanan & Partners, UK

Principal Bankers: Burgan Bank, Kuwait; Al Ahli Bank, Kuwait

Principal Shareholders: Hisham H Al Issa, Adnan F Halawa

Date of Establishment: 1966

No of Employees: 45

KUWAIT ENGINEERING CENTRE

PO Box 11269 Dasma, 35153 Kuwait

Tel: 5316350, 5316353, 5316383

Telex: 22345 Balasem KT

Telefax: 5316299

Chairman: Ali Hassan Ibraheem (Partner & General Manager)

PRINCIPAL ACTIVITIES: Planners, architects and consulting
engineers

Principal Bankers: Burgan Bank

Principal Shareholders: Ali Hassan Ibraheem, Aziz Moharram
Fahim

Date of Establishment: 1976

No of Employees: 35

KUWAIT ENGINEERING GROUP

PO Box 960 Safat, 13010 Kuwait

Tel: 2435060

Cable: Majmuah Kuwait

Telex: 22806 Kengrup KT

PRINCIPAL ACTIVITIES: Consulting engineers, architects and
planners

KUWAIT FINANCE HOUSE

PO Box 24989 Safat, 13110 Kuwait

Tel: 2445050 (10 lines), 2445070 (10 lines)

Cable: BAITMAL

Telex: 23331 Baitmal KT

Chairman: Ahmad B Al Yassin

Directors: Faisal A Al-Khatrash (Vice Chairman), Bader A Al-
Mukhaziem (Managing Director), Abduljalil A Al-Gharabally,
Ali A Al-Fouzan, Mahammed A Al-Khodairy, Mohammed Y Al-
Roomi, Haza'a J Al-Hussain, Khaled A Al-Zeer, Samir Al-
Nafeesi

Senior Executives: Dr Khalid Boodai (Asst General Manager for
Financial & Administrative Sector), Adnan A Al-Musallem

(Asst. General Manager for Banking Sector), Faisal A Al-Zamel (Asst General Manager for Planning and Follow up), Waleed A Al-Rwaih (Asst General Manager for Trading Affairs), Solaiman A Al-Brikan (Asst General Manager for Real Estate Projects), Adnan A Al-Bahar (Asst General Manager for International Investment)

PRINCIPAL ACTIVITIES: A banking and investment institution conducting its business on an interest free basis according to Islamic economic principles
Branch Offices: 10 branches in Kuwait
Subsidiary Companies: Bahrain Islamic Investment Co; Islamic Banking Systems Luxembourg; International Turnkey Systems
Principal Bankers: Citibank (New York); United Bank of Kuwait (London); Banque Nationale de Paris (Paris); Dresdner Bank (Frankfurt); Bank of Tokyo (Tokyo)

Principal Shareholders: Ministry of Aqwaf and Islamic Affairs; Ministry of Justice; Ministry of Finance (49%); and Kuwaiti Nationals (51%)
Date of Establishment: 1977
No of Employees: 700

KUWAIT FINANCIAL CENTRE SAK

PO Box 23444 Safat, 13104 Kuwait
Tel: 2412131
Cable: Markazmal
Telex: 22477 Markaz Kt

Chairman: Diraar Yusuf Alghanim
Directors: Jassem Al-Mousa (Vice Chairman), Sheikh Bader Sabah Al-Salem Al-Sabah, Ibrahim Yusuf Al-Ragum, Ahdi Fahed Al-Marzouq, Abdulrahman Al-Mudahka, Faisal Al-Jallal, Ali Al-Bedah (Managing Director)

PRINCIPAL ACTIVITIES: Merchant banking and investment
Branch Offices: Al-Rehab Branch, Hawalli, Kuwait
Associated Companies: Korea Kuwait Banking Corp, Korea; Superior National Insurance Company, Los Angeles
Principal Bankers: First Chicago International, New York; J Henry Schroder Bank, New York; United Bank of Kuwait, London; Swiss Bank Corporation, Zurich; Deutsche Bank, Frankfurt; Swiss Kuwaiti Bank, Geneva; Kuwaiti French Bank, Paris; Swiss Bank Corporation, Tokyo
Financial Information:

	KD'000
Authorised capital	9,660
Paid-up capital	9,660

Principal Shareholders: Shareholding Company listed on Kuwait Stock Exchange
Date of Establishment: 22nd October 1974
No of Employees: 55

KUWAIT FLOUR MILLS & BAKERIES CO SAK

PO Box 681 Safat, 13007 Kuwait
Tel: 4841866
Cable: Matahen
Telex: 22209, 22263 Matahen Kt
Telefax: 4841866 ext 390

Chairman: Khalid A Al-Sagar
Directors: Bader A Al-Mousa (Managing Director)

PRINCIPAL ACTIVITIES: Manufacture of flour, wheat bread, marcaroni, biscuits, vegetable oils and fats (5 factories); and bakeries (8 bakeries)
Principal Bankers: All banks in Kuwait
Financial Information:

	1989 KD'000
Sales turnover	25,000
Authorised capital	30,000
Paid-up capital	30,000

Principal Shareholders: Government
Date of Establishment: 1961
No of Employees: over 2,000

KUWAIT FOOD CO SAK (AMERICANA)

PO Box 5087 Safat, 13051 Kuwait
Tel: 4815900,4815134, 4815362, 4815309, 4815323, 4815326
Cable: NUTRITION KWT
Telex: 22125 NUTRITION KWT, 22855 AMRCANA KWT
Telefax: 815914

Chairman: Nasser M Kharafi
Senior Executives: Moataz Al-Alfi (General Manager), Amgad El Mofti (Deputy General Manager Operations), Ismail El Sherbini (Deputy General Manager Finance & Admin), Mahmoud El Afifi (Regional Manager Kuwait), Sayed Deyab (Investment & Strategic Planning Manager)

PRINCIPAL ACTIVITIES: Fast food industry and consumer food industry
Principal Agencies: Wimpy; Kentucky Fried Chicken; Hardees; Pizza Hut; Sizzler Steak House; Chicken Tikka; Carvery
Branch Offices: Kuwait; Bahrain; UAE; Qatar; Saudi Arabia; Egypt; Morocco; Yemen; Jordan
Subsidiary Companies: Kuwait Food Co, UAE; Qatar Food Co, Doha/Qatar; Kuwait Food Co, Cairo/Egypt; Kuwait Food Co, Sanaa/N Yemen; National Meat Plant Co, Riyadh/Saudia Arabia; Al-Ahlia Restaurants Co, Riyadh/Saudia Arabia; Bahrain & Kuwait Restaurants Co, Manama/Bahrain; Sheba Poultry Co, Sanaa/N Yemen; Cairo Poultry Co, Cairo/Egypt; Tourism Projects Co, Cairo/Egypt; Gulfa Mineral Water, Ajman/UAE; Tourist Project & International Restaurants Co, Amman/Jordan; Americana International Co, Kuwait
Principal Bankers: National Bank of Kuwait SAK
Financial Information:

	KD'000
Authorised capital	11,288
Paid-up capital	11,288

Principal Shareholders: Public shareholding company
Date of Establishment: December 29th, 1963
No of Employees: 2,700

KUWAIT FOREIGN PETROLEUM EXPLORATION CO KSC

PO Box 26565 Safat, 13126 Kuwait
Tel: 455455
Cable: Petcorp
Telex: 44874/5/6/7/8 Petcorp KT

Chairman: Abdul Razak M Hussain (and Managing Director)
Directors: Faisal Al-Kazmawi, Khaled M Hussain, Nawal Al-Rushaid, Mahmoud Al Rahmani, Moustafa Al-Adasani, Abdulla Baroun
Senior Executives: Khaled M Hussain (Deputy Managing Director Finance & Administration), Youssef Al-Rushaid (Administration Manager), Arthur Menzies (Exploration Manager), Mahmoud Al Rahmani (Planning & Development Manager), John Small (Exploration Manager)

PRINCIPAL ACTIVITIES: Operations relating to the exploration and drilling for crude oil and natural gas; development and production of oil and gas fields
Branch Offices: Bahrain Office: PO Box 1808 - Manama; Tunisia Office: PO Box 65, 2080 - Ariana
Parent Company: Kuwait Petroleum Corporation
Subsidiary Companies: International Energy Development Corporation SA, Geneva; IEDC Exploration & Production Ltd, Bermuda; Kuwait Foreign Petroleum Exploration (Services) Co KSC; Santa Fe Minerals (Asia) Inc; Santa Fe Minerals (Ireland) Ltd; KUFPEC (Italy) Ltd; KUFPEC (Tunisia) Ltd; KUFPEC (Sudan) Ltd; KUFPEC (Sumatra) Ltd; KUFPEC (Indonesia) Ltd; KUFPEC (Congo) Ltd; KUFPEC (Egypt) Ltd; KUFPEC (Pakistan) Ltd; KUFPEC (Tanzania) Ltd; KUFPEC (Bahrain) Ltd; KUFPEC (Oman) Ltd; KUFPEC (Turkey) Ltd; KUFPEC (Alpha) Ltd; KUFPEC (Beta) Ltd; KUFPEC (Swiss Holdings) Ltd; KUFPEC (Operations) Ltd
Principal Bankers: Bank of Kuwait and the Middle East; United Bank of Kuwait, London

Financial Information:

	KD'000
Authorised capital	200,000
Paid-up capital	100,000

Principal Shareholders: Kuwait Petroleum Corporation
Date of Establishment: April 1981
No of Employees: 98

KUWAIT FOREIGN TRADING CONTRACTING & INVESTMENT CO SAK

K.F.T.C.I.C.

PO Box 5665 Safat, 13057 Kuwait
Tel: 2449031
Cable: Maaden Kuwait
Telex: 22021 Kt; 22053 Kt; 44655 Maaden Kt
Telefax: 2446173 CCITT G2 & G3

Chairman: Abdullah Ahmad Al Gabandi (also Managing Director)
Directors: Mohammed S Al Sabah (Deputy Chairman), Abdullah M Al Mansour, Adnan A Al Sultan, Ghassan A Al Subaih, Nassar A Al Nassar, Terki S Al Othman
Senior Executives: Abdullah Ahmed Al Gabandi (Chief Executive Officer), Youssef Essa A Hassawi (Senior Executive Vice President & General Manager), Abdulrahman A Al Dawood (SVP Follow Up/Direct Investments), Ahmad M Mohammed (SVP Credit Department), Anthony D Thornicroft (Treasurer), Fahad B Al Kuhailan (SVP Trading & New Issues), Khalid M Al Jeraiwi (SVP Real Estate Investments), Robert G Grimstead (SVP Operations), Subir K Ray (Financial Controller), Samir M A Seoud (Internal Auditor), Abdulaziz Al Jaser (VP Personnel & Administration), Abdulhadi H Al Gallaf (VP EDP Operations), Bader N AL Subaiee (VP Accounts), Ghazi Saqfuf Hait (VP Settlements/Operations), Maha K Al Ghunaim (VP Portfolio Management), Sulaiman N Al Qimlas (VP Local Investments)

PRINCIPAL ACTIVITIES: Private banking, direct investments and real estate. Banking: loan syndication, credit and guarantees, trade finance, primary issues, secondary market operations, portfolio management, also active treasury operations, currency hedging, forward and swap transactions. Direct Investments: equity participation, acquisitions and joint ventures. Real Estate: project & property management, trading, leasing, construction, development and maintenance
Subsidiary/Associated Companies: In Kuwait: Afro-Arab Co for Investment and International Trade (AFARCO), Al-Rawdatain Water Bottling Co, Al-Jahra Gate Real Estate Co, Fardous Al-Sharq Real Estate Co, Gulf Gravel Co, International Contracting Co, Kuwait Bakeries Co, Kuwait National Reinsurance Co, Kuwait Supply Co, Kuwait Insulating Materials Manufacturing Co, Kuwait Maritime Transport Co, Kuwait Markets Group Co, Kuwait Commercial Markets Complex Group, Kuwait Computer Trading & Services Co, Kuwait Clearing Co, Mubarakiah Poultry & Feed Co, National Real Estate Co, The Bank of Kuwait and the Middle East, The First National Investment Group, Technological Investment Co, The Industrial Real Estate Co, The Kuwait Desalination Plants Fabrication Co, Touristic Enterprises Co, Kuwait Real Estate Investment Consortium, Kuwait National Real Estate Management Co; Outside Kuwait: Bahrain: Bank of Bahrain & Kuwait, Arab Financial Services Co, National Hotels Co, Arab Iron & Steel Co; Brazil: Arab Brazilian Investment Co (ABICO); Cairo: Arab Petroleum Pipelines Co (SUMED), Kuwait Egyptian Investment Co; France: FRAB Bank International; Greece: Arab Hellenic Bank; Lebanon: Rif Bank; Luxembourg: FRAB Holding; Mauritania: Societe Arabe des Industries Metallurgiques (SAMIA); Morocco: Kuwait Moroccan Studies Co (SEKOM); Pakistan: Arabian Sea Enterprises (Sheraton Hotel - Karachi); Peru: Arab Latin American Bank (Arlabank); Senegal: Banque Senegalo Koweitienne; Spain: Banco Arabe Espanol (ARESBANK); Sudan: Sudanese-Kuwaiti Investment Co, Sudanese-Kuwaiti

Building & Construction Co, Sudanese-Kuwaiti Road Transport Co, Sudanese-Kuwaiti Animal Production Co; Switzerland: Credit des Bergues, Herlarb Management Co; Tunis: Compagnie Financiere Immobiliere et Touristique (COFIT); UK: United Bank of Kuwait; Vanatu: Asian Oceanic Holding Co; USA: PCA Crossroads Associate, L'Ermitage Palm Beach Project, Williston Basin Oil Exploration Project, Kansas Oil Resources Project
Financial Information:

	1988/89 KD'000
Authorised capital	54,000
Paid up capital	54,000
Deposits	485,787
Loans & advances	178,355
Reserves	3,797
Total assets	656,641

Principal Shareholders: 99.2% Government of Kuwait; 0.8% Shares held by Public
Date of Establishment: January 1965
No of Employees: 284

KUWAIT FOUNDRY CO SAK

PO Box 1393 Safat, 13014 Kuwait
Tel: 4712621, 4711641, 4717842
Cable: Foundry
Telex: 23032 Kt Foundry
Telefax: 4711641

Chairman: Abdulhamid Al-Fares
Senior Executives: Samy A Ibrahim (General Manager), Mohammed A Awad (Commercial Manager), Hussain Mustafa (Financial Manager)

PRINCIPAL ACTIVITIES: Manufacturers of all kinds of cast-iron products in accordance with British Standard specification and ISO, annual capacity 20,000 tons of cast iron comprising cast-iron pipes, pipe fittings of various shapes, manholes, sanitary fittings and ductile iron fittings
Branch Offices: Location in Kuwait: Shuwaikh Industrial Area
Parent Company: Al Reda Trading & Contracting Co, Saudi Arabia; Al Mureikhi Trading & Contracting Est, UAE
Principal Bankers: National Bank of Kuwait; Alahli Bank of Kuwait; Commerical Bank of Kuwait
Financial Information:

	KD'000
Authorised capital	3,000
Paid-up capital	3,000

Date of Establishment: 1962
No of Employees: 400

KUWAIT FRUIT & VEGETABLES SUPPLIERS LTD

PO Box 916 Safat, 13010 Kuwait
Tel: 2427181, 2427179
Cable: Conserve, Kuwait
Telex: 22093 Super Kuwait

Chairman: Albert P Abela
Senior Executives: Riad A Assafiri (Area Manager)

PRINCIPAL ACTIVITIES: General merchants, industrial catering and camp services, hotel management, tobacco distribution
Principal Agencies: Brown & Williamson (Europe) SA
Parent Company: Albert Abela International
Associated Companies: The New Supermarkets Ltd; Construction & Commercial Services Ltd: both companies are based at same address as above; representation of the Albert Abela Group of Companies
Principal Bankers: The Bank of Kuwait & The Middle East

Date of Establishment: 1956
No of Employees: 480

KUWAIT

KUWAIT FUND FOR ARAB ECONOMIC DEVELOPMENT
K.F.A.E.D.

PO Box 2921 Safat, 13030 Kuwait
Tel: 2468800 (40 lines)
Cable: ALSUNDUK, KUWAIT
Telex: 22025 Alsunduk, 22613 Kfaed KT, 22904 Kfaed KT, 46871 Kfinv KT
Telefax: 2419063 (Operations), 2436289 (Finance)

Chairman: Jassim Mohammad Al-Khorafi (Minister of Finance of the State of Kuwait)
Directors: Bader Al Humaidhi (Director General), Abdulwahab Al Bader (Deputy Director General Operations), Khaled Al-Shalfan (Deputy Director General Administration)
Senior Executives: Hisham Al Woqayan (Director of Operations), Fahed Al Dakheel (Director of Finance), Hamad Al Omer (Director of Administration)

PRINCIPAL ACTIVITIES: Provision of financial assistance to developing countries
Financial Information:

	1988/89 KD'million
Total income	73
Authorised capital	2,000
Paid-up capital	970
Total assets	1,896

Principal Shareholders: State-owned
Date of Establishment: December 1961
No of Employees: 250

KUWAIT GLASS FIBRE REINFORCED PLASTICS PRODUCTS CO SAK

PO Box 24947 Safat, 13110Kuwait
Tel: 4738781, 4743273
Cable: Kuglass
Telex: 23833 KRPCO KT

Chairman: Salem Al-Musallam
Directors: Abdul Malik R Al-Duaij (Managing Director)
Senior Executives: Saleh Abdul Mohsin Al-Musalem (Deputy General Manager)

PRINCIPAL ACTIVITIES: Manufacturers of GRP pipes and tanks
Principal Bankers: Commercial Bank of Kuwait; Al Ahli Bank of Kuwait; National Bank of Kuwait; Burgan Bank; Kuwait and the Middle East Bank; Gulf Bank

Principal Shareholders: Kuwait National Industries Co; Kuwait Sanitary Ware Industries Co; Kuwait Metal Pipes Industries Co; Kuwait International Investment Co
Date of Establishment: 1977
No of Employees: 60

KUWAIT GYPSUM MANUFACTURING & TRADING CO

PO Box 10013 Shuaiba, 65451 Kuwait
Tel: 3260421, 3260429, 3260438
Telex: 30131 GYPS KT

Chairman: Abdul-Mohsen Al-Asfour
Directors: Abdul Latif Hasan Al Sarraf (Vice Chairman)
Senior Executives: Taysir Husein Abdo (General Manager)

PRINCIPAL ACTIVITIES: Production of gypsum powder and gypsum boards
Principal Bankers: Al Ahli Bank of Kuwait; National Bank of Kuwait
Financial Information:

	1989 KD'000
Authorised capital	1,500
Paid-up capital	1,500

Principal Shareholders: Abed Ali Bahman; Ali Abdulrahman Al-Omar
Date of Establishment: March 1981; Production started on March 1984
No of Employees: 41

KUWAIT HILTON INTERNATIONAL

PO Box 5996 Safat, 13060 Kuwait
Tel: 2533000, 2530000
Cable: Hiltels Kt
Telex: 22039 Hiltels Kt

Chairman: Ali Ahmed Al-Ghanim Al-Jabr (Kuwait Hotels Co)

PRINCIPAL ACTIVITIES: Hotel management and operation
Parent Company: Hilton International
Principal Bankers: National Bank of Kuwait

Principal Shareholders: Kuwait Hotels Co
Date of Establishment: 1968
No of Employees: 340

KUWAIT HOTELS CO SAK

PO Box 833 Safat, 13009 Kuwait
Tel: 2520600, 2523197
Cable: Fanadiq
Telex: 22500 Kt KHC
Telefax: 2520276, 2550157

President: Ali Ahmed Al Ghanim Al Jabr
Directors: Abdul Latif Al Asfour (Vice-Chairman), Ahmed Behbehani, Faisal Al Houti, Hamed Al Rujaib, Abdulaziz Al Dhakheel, Yousef Al Jassim
Senior Executives: Faisal Yousef Al Mannaei (Vice President Finance & Administration), Mohamed A Najia (Vice President Operations)

PRINCIPAL ACTIVITIES: Hotel management company and catering services
Associated Companies: Kuwait International Hotel Kuwait; Messilah Beach Hotel, Kuwait; Airport Hotel, Kuwait; Khiran Resort, Kuwait; Bayan Palace, Kuwait; Dubaiya Resort, Kuwait; Safir Hotel, Cairo; Safir Zamelek Hotel, Cairo; Nile Cruiser "Safir Iman", Cairo
Principal Bankers: National Bank of Kuwait
Financial Information:

	1989 KD'000
Sales turnover	7,899
Profits	369
Authorised capital	5,000
Paid-up capital	5,000
Total assets	4,184

Principal Shareholders: 74% owned by the Govt of Kuwait, 26% owned by Kuwaiti shareholders
Date of Establishment: 1962
No of Employees: 1,700

KUWAIT INDUSTRIAL REFINERY MAINTENANCE & ENGINEERING CO
K.R.E.M.E.N.C.O.

PO Box 9021, Ahmadi, 61001 Kuwait
Tel: 3261366, 3262427, 3261367
Cable: Kremenco
Telex: 44218 Kt
Telefax: 3260533

Chairman: Eissa Ahmad Khafaf
Directors: Ghanim H Dabbous (Managing Director)
Senior Executives: John Carr (General Manager), Ghawi Shaker (Production & Engineering Manager), Shlemon Khamis (Field Maintenance Manager)

PRINCIPAL ACTIVITIES: Maintenance of oil refinery, heat exchangers and structural steel and piping manufacturing, oilfield engineering

Principal Bankers: National Bank of Kuwait; Kuwait Real Estate Bank; Commercial Bank of Kuwait

Financial Information:

	1988/89 US$'000
Sales turnover	25,687
Profits	32
Authorised capital	3,500
Paid-up capital	3,500
Total assets	6,611

Principal Shareholders: Khalifa Al-Fulaij; S T Khoury; The Industrial Investment Co; Ali & Fouad M T Al-Ghanim; Nayef Al-Dabbous; Al Mobader Co
Date of Establishment: 1969
No of Employees: 3,000

KUWAIT INSULATING MATERIAL MANUFACTURING CO SAK

PO Box 24609 Safat, 13107 Kuwait
Tel: 2452132, 2452131, 2415925
Cable: Thermo Glass
Telex: 44758 Kimmco Kt, 46016 Kimmco Kt

Chairman: Ahmad Mohammed Al-Najdi
Directors: Sulaiman Al-Brikan (Vice-Chairman), Bassam Al-Ghanim, Mahmood Al-Noori, Abdul Razzak Al-Nassar (Managing Director & General Manager)

PRINCIPAL ACTIVITIES: Manufacture and marketing of fibreglass (insulating materials)
Principal Agencies: Licence from Isover, Saint Gobain, France
Branch Offices: Saudi Arabia: M/S Abdul Hadi Est, PO Box 2845, Riyadh; PO Box 228 Thoqbah, Dammam/Al-Khobar; PO Box 1054, Jeddah; In Qatar: Laffan Trading & Contg Est, PO Box 6363, Doha
Principal Bankers: Bank of Kuwait and the Middle East

Principal Shareholders: Industrial Bank of Kuwait, Kuwait Foreign Trading Contracting & Investment Co, Refrigeration Industry & Cold Storage Co (KSC)
Date of Establishment: May 1977
No of Employees: 180

KUWAIT INSURANCE CO SAK

PO Box 769 Safat, 13008 Kuwait
Tel: 2420135, 2420139, 2420021 (8 lines)
Cable: Taminco
Telex: 22104 Taminco Kt; 44820
Telefax: 965-2428530

Chairman: Hamad Ahmad Al Bahar
Directors: Mustafa Jasim Boodai, Mohammad Saleh Yousuf Behbehani, Sulaiman Khaled Al Ghuneim, Abdul Rahman A Mughni, Faisal S Al Fozan, Ra'ed M A Al Hamad, Ali M Behbehani
Senior Executives: M S Ghunaim (Adviser to the Board of Directors), Rawhi M Terhi (General Manager), Aziz M Abdul Jawad (Deputy General Manager), George Nasr (Asst General Manager Marine Insurance), Subhi Al Asadi (Asst General Manager Non Marine Insurance)

PRINCIPAL ACTIVITIES: Life assurance and all classes of non-life insurance; marine and non marine insurance, investment
Associated Companies: Falcon Reinsurance Co, Switzerland; Middle Sea Insurance Co, Malta; Arab Reinsurance Co, Lebanon; Arab International Insurance Co, Egypt; Bahrain Kuwait Insurance Co, Bahrain; United Insurance Co, Ras Al Khaimah, UAE
Principal Bankers: Commercial Bank of Kuwait; Bank of Kuwait and the Middle East; National Bank of Kuwait

Financial Information:

	1988/89 KD'000
Sales turnover	17,587
Profits	5,450
Authorised capital	17,600
Paid-up capital	17,600
Total assets	79,130

Principal Shareholders: Owned by Kuwaiti individuals and firms
Date of Establishment: 1960
No of Employees: 275

KUWAIT INTERNATIONAL FAIR KSC

PO Box 656 Safat, 13007 Kuwait
Tel: 5387100
Cable: INTERFAIR
Telex: 23022, 30022 INFAIR KT

Chairman: Mohammad Al-Gharabally (Managing Director)
Senior Executives: Mohammad Saoud Al Dakheel (General Manager), Saleh Al-Harbi (Public Relations Manager), Riad Al-Dousari (Finance & Admim Manager), Mohammad Abdul Razzaq Razzooqi (Marketing Manager), Bader Al-Khalifa (Fairground Manager)

PRINCIPAL ACTIVITIES: International and Arabian fairs and local exhibitions
Subsidiary Companies: Union Exibition International, Paris, France
Principal Bankers: Gulf Bank, National Bank of Kuwait

Principal Shareholders: Government of Kuwait (49%); Kuwait Investment Co (51%)
Date of Establishment: 1971

KUWAIT INTERNATIONAL FINANCE CO SAK

PO Box 23792 Safat, 13098 Kuwait
Tel: 2448050/6, 2441578, 2444272, 2414618
Cable: Currency
Telex: 22569 Currency Kt; 23386 Alkifco Kt
Telefax: 2437792

Chairman: Faysal Saoud Al-Fulaij
Directors: N F Fulaij, Hussain Jawad Abdul Rasool, Mohammad Ataullah, Swaleh Naqvi, Saleem Siddiqi, Abdul Hafeez M Ahmad
Senior Executives: Ashraf Khan (Vice-Chairman & Managing Director)

PRINCIPAL ACTIVITIES: Project financing, underwriting Eurobond issues, syndicated multi-currency loans, investment advisory service, equity and real estate investments and portfolio management
Subsidiary Companies: Iz Company for Exchange, Kuwait
Principal Bankers: Commercial Bank of Kuwait, Kuwait; Bankamerica International, New York

Financial Information:

	1988/89 KD'000
Authorised capital	3,276
Paid-up capital	3,276
Total assets	77,148

Principal Shareholders: 51% Local interest, 49% BCCI
Date of Establishment: 1975
No of Employees: 30

KUWAIT INTERNATIONAL INVESTMENT CO SAK

PO Box 22792 Safat, 13088 Kuwait
Tel: 2438273/9, 2420762/3
Cable: Interinvest Kuwait
Telex: 22325 Intvest, 22997 Intvest
Telefax: (965) 2454931

Chairman: Jassim M Al Bahar (Managing Director)

Directors: Khalifa Y Al Roumy (Vice Chairman), Ahmed Y Behbehani, Mohamad A R Al Bisher, Abdulla R Al Hajeri, Salah F Al Marzouk, Eid A Al Rashidi, Wael J Al Sager

Senior Executives: Ibrahim S Al Therban (General Manager), Fuad S Al Shehab (Asst General Manager, Marketable Securities Div), Mohamad S Al Ghanim (Asst General Manager, Finance & Administration Div), Dr Imad Moosa (Asst General Manager, Research & Planning Div), Hussain Al Saeed (Asst General Manager, Banking Div), Mustafa Al Saleh (Asst General Manager Local & Direct Investments), Ahmed Al Mulla (Manager Trading), Muhammad Abu Fadaleh (Manager Finance), Husni Al Haroon (Manager EDP), Abeyya Al Qatami (Manager Marketing & Business Development), Saleh Al Selmi (Manager Local Shares), Khalid A Al Muraikhi (Manager Real Estate), Samih Al Daulah (Manager Real Estate Operations), Nabil Al Nassar (Manager New Issues), Mutasem Al Shihabi (Manager Direct Investments), Omar Saleh (Manager Internal Audit)

PRINCIPAL ACTIVITIES: Investment banking

Branch Offices: Kuwait Stock Exchange branch: Tel 2427641/3

Associated Companies: Al Salhia Real Estate Co SAK Kuwait (10.3%); Arab Brazilian Investment Co Brazil (12.5%); Arab International Finance SA Luxembourg (11.12%); International Transport Equipment Co KSC Kuwait (97.7%); Jordan Securities Corporation Jordan (5%); Kuwait Asia Bank EC Bahrain (9%); Kuwait Glass Fibre Reinforced Plastic Products Co SAK Kuwait (9.25%); Kuwait Real Estate Investment Consortium KSC Kuwait (0.13%); United Bank of Kuwait UK (6.41%); Pacific Centre Cayman Islands (41.25%); Saif Ltd Virgin Islands (15.4%); Kuwait Clearing Co SAK (7.69%); Overseas Princeton Placements NV Netherlands Antilles (5.7%); Bank of Bahrain & Kuwait EC Bahrain (2%); Kuwait Commercial Market Complex SAK Kuwait (2%); United Gulf Bank EC Bahrain (0.56%); Bahrain International Bank EC Bahrain (0.39%)

Principal Bankers: All local banks in Kuwait

Financial Information:

	1988/89 KD'000
Profits (loss)	(5,748)
Authorised capital	31,933
Paid-up capital	31,902
Total assets	146,905

Principal Shareholders: Private (69.9%); Government (30.1%)

Date of Establishment: September 1973

No of Employees: 175

KUWAIT INVESTMENT CO SAK (KIC)

PO Box 1005 Safat, 13011 Kuwait
Tel: 2438111
Cable: Estithmar
Telex: 22115 Estithmar
Telefax: 2444896

Chairman: Hamad Mohammad Al-Bahar (also Managing Director)

Directors: Abdullah Abdulatif Al-Shaya, Abdulaziz Abdulla Al-Shalfan, Abdulwahab Fahed Al Hamad Al Khalid (Deputy Chairman), Hamad Mishari Al Humaidhi, Ali Hussein Al Sayegh, Bader Abdullah Al Sumeit

Senior Executives: Hilal Mishari Al-Mutairi (General Manager), Mohammad Al Falah (Manager Banking Dept), Adel Al Mudaf (Manager Portfolio, Secondary Trading & New Issues Depts), Saleh Al Zouman (Manager Foreign Real Estate Dept), Issa Al Mishari (Manager Local Real Estate Dept)

PRINCIPAL ACTIVITIES: International and domestic money and capital markets, management and underwriting of new issues, secondary trading, portfolio management, local and foreign real estate development, direct investments

Subsidiary/Associated Companies: Arab Hellenic Bank SA, Greece; Arab Petroleum Pipelines Co, Egypt; Arab Turkish Bank, Turkey; Bank of Bahrain & Kuwait BSC, Bahrain;

Banque de Developpement Economique de Tunisis, Tunis; Banque Nationale pour le Developpement Economique, Morocco; Jordan National Bank SA, Jordan; Kuwait Catering Co KSC (C), Kuwait; Kuwait Clearing Co SAK (C), Kuwait; Kuwait Consulting & Investment Co KSC, Kuwait; Kuwait International Fair KSC (C), Kuwait; KIC Capital Corpoartion NV, Netherlands Antilles; Kuwait Pacific Finance Co Ltd, Hongkong; Kuwait Reinsurance Co KSC, Kuwait; Kuwait Supply Co SAK, Kuwait; Rifbank, SAL, Lebanon; SIFIDA Investment Co SA, Switzerland; Tourism Investment Co Ltd, Bahrain; Touristic Enterprises Co KSC, Kuwait; United Bank of Kuwait, UK; Yemeni Kuwaiti Real Estate Development Co, Yemen AR

Financial Information:

	1988/89 KD'000
Profits (loss)	(8,140)
Authorised capital	51,882
Paid-up capital	51,882
Total assets	312,715

Principal Shareholders: Government of Kuwait (50%), Kuwaiti nationals (50%)

Date of Establishment: 1961

No of Employees: 199

KUWAIT INVESTMENT GROUP

PO Box 25091 Safat, 13111 Kuwait
Tel: 2437595, 2434062, 2437754
Telex: 4475 KT KIGROUP

Chairman: Jassim Y Al-Marzook

Directors: Sabah Al-Rayyes, Hussain Makki Al-Jumma, Faisal Al-Khatrash, Jawad Bu Khamsin

PRINCIPAL ACTIVITIES: Investments in 'cash-flow' properties and real estate

Principal Bankers: Al-Ahli Bank of Kuwait, Commercial Bank of Kuwait, Gulf Bank

Principal Shareholders: Khalid Yousuf Al-Marzook, Jawad Ahmed Bu Khamsin, Shaikh Ali Abdulla Al-Salem Al-Sabah

Date of Establishment: 1977

KUWAIT LUBE OIL CO

PO Box 9748 Ahmadi, 61008 Ahmadi
Tel: 3261247/8/9
Telex: 31918 Kloc
Telefax: 3261240

Chairman: Salem K Al Marzouk

Directors: Yousef Al Omar, Abdulatif Al Manea, Bader Al Najjar

Senior Executives: Khalil Nafissah (Deputy General Manager), Khalid Salman (Local Sales Manager), Mohammed Yassin (Export Manager), Qassim Mustafa (Chief Accountant)

PRINCIPAL ACTIVITIES: Manufacture of lubricants and grease

Date of Establishment: 1981

No of Employees: 70

KUWAIT MARITIME & MERCANTILE CO KSC

PO Box 78 Safat, 13001 Kuwait
Tel: 2433755, 2418784, 2419126, 2434752, 2434181, 2442491, 2434993
Cable: Gray Kuwait
Telex: 22005 Gray Kt, 23371 KMMC Kt
Telefax: 2421396

Chairman: Ahmed Wahedi

Directors: Fahad Al Rashid, Abdulla Bassam, Khalid Al Mayoof, A A Macaskill, C Johnson, D Wakefield, (Representatives of Gray Mackenzie & Co Ltd)

Senior Executives: P A Whymant-Morris (General Manager), A J A Roff (Manager Transportation Div), Capt D Tomkiss (Manager Surveying Dept), C Howie (Travel Manager), J Cox (Trading Manager)

PRINCIPAL ACTIVITIES: Shipping & tanker agents, general trading, clearing & forwarding, travel agents, Lloyds agents and P+O representatives, industrial catering, general marine surveying, business & printing machines

Principal Agencies: P+O Containers Ltd; Cunard Ellerman; Avin Liners

Parent Company: Inchcape Plc, Gray Mackenzie & Co Ltd

Principal Bankers: The Bank of Kuwait & The Middle East KSC

Principal Shareholders: Fahad Al Rashid, Abdulla Bassam, Khalid Al Mayoof, Gray Mackenzie & Co Ltd

No of Employees: 60

KUWAIT MARRIOTT HOTEL & RESORT

PO Box 24285 Safat, 13103 Kuwait
Tel: 835344
Telex: 23596 Kt Mariota

Directors: A Al Mehri, M Muzaini, Yusuf Al Shimali, Abdulatiff Al Asfour, Abdulatif Al Wassan, Waleed Al Bajan

PRINCIPAL ACTIVITIES: Hotel and resort business

Parent Company: Kuwait National Hotels & Tourism Company

Subsidiary Companies: United International Hotels

Principal Bankers: Al Bank Al Tejari Kuwait

Date of Establishment: November 1979

KUWAIT MATTRESS CO LTD

PO Box 42305 Shuwaikh, 70654 Kuwait
Tel: 4819836, 4844258
Cable: Deepaj Kuwait
Telex: Kisco 22370 Kt
Telefax: (965) 4848310

Partners: Suleiman A Al Qudaibi, Ali Redha Kolaghassi (Managing Partner)

Senior Executives: Munir A Timani (Sales Manager)

PRINCIPAL ACTIVITIES: Manufacture of spring mattresses, quilts, bed spreads and pillows; manufacture of steel tube and office steel furniture, chairs, tables and beds; trading and contracting in office wooden and steel furniture

Principal Bankers: National Bank of Kuwait, Bank of Kuwait & the Middle East, Commercial Bank of Kuwait

Financial Information:

	1989
	KD'000
Sales turnover	700
Profits	30
Authorised capital	400
Paid-up capital	400
Total assets	1,500

Principal Shareholders: Partners as described

Date of Establishment: 1968

No of Employees: 30

KUWAIT METAL PIPE INDUSTRIES KSC

PO Box 3416 Safat, 13035 Kuwait
Tel: 4675622
Cable: Pipes Kuwait
Telex: 23064 Pipes Kt; 22182 Pipes Kt; 30065 Pipes Kt
Telefax: 4675897

Chairman: Khalid Fulaij Ali Al Fulaij

Directors: Dr Ahmad Yousif M Al Roudan (Vice Chairman & Managing Director)

Senior Executives: Emile Khair (Manager Marketing & Project Dept), Farouk Barsoum (Production Manager), Khalid Al Ali (Materials & Purchase Manager), Jasem Al Qattan (Personnel Manager), Mario A Padovani (Maintenance Manager)

PRINCIPAL ACTIVITIES: Manufacture of welded steel pipes from 1/2 to 180 inch dia., tanks, fittings with or without protective coating (zinc, coaltar epoxy, coaltar enamel) and lining (rubber, cement, steel)

Subsidiary/Associated Companies: Kuwait Engineering Operation & Management Co KSC

Principal Bankers: Gulf Bank of Kuwait; National Bank of Kuwait; Bank of Kuwait & the Middle East

Financial Information:

	1988/89
	KD'000
Sales turnover	4,697
Profits	1,641
Authorised capital	15,206
Paid-up capital	15,206
Total assets	31,989

Principal Shareholders: Kuwaiti shareholders (160)

Date of Establishment: 1966

No of Employees: 260

KUWAIT NATIONAL BOTTLING CO

PO Box 224 Safat, 13003 Kuwait
Tel: 4717155, 4717157
Cable: Kunabco, Kuwait
Telex: 23069 KT

Directors: Abdulaziz Hamad Sager

Senior Executives: Adnan H Dabbagh (General Manager)

PRINCIPAL ACTIVITIES: Manufacture of soft drinks (in bottles and cans)

Principal Agencies: Pepsi Cola and Mirinda

Branch Offices: Location in Kuwait: Sabhan Industrial Area

Principal Bankers: National Bank of Kuwait

Date of Establishment: 1954

No of Employees: 565

KUWAIT NATIONAL CINEMA CO

PO Box 502 Safat, 13006 Kuwait
Tel: 2611500
Cable: Cinkuwait
Telex: 22492 KT GRANADA
Telefax: (965) 2611590

President: Waleed Al Nisf

Directors: Ali Murad Behbehani (Vice Chairman), Adnan Y Al-Hunaif (Managing Director)

Senior Executives: Yousif Rashid Al-Shaheen (Board Member & General Manager)

PRINCIPAL ACTIVITIES: Import and distribution of video and cinima films, and cinema equipment for the Middle East, construction of cinema houses

Principal Bankers: National Bank of Kuwait

Financial Information:

	1989
	KD'000
Paid-up capital	7,000

Date of Establishment: October 1954

No of Employees: 280

KUWAIT NATIONAL FISHING CO KSC

PO Box 3389 Safat, 13034 Kuwait

Chairman: Sheikh Naser Sabah Al-Hamad Sabah

Directors: Hamed El Eissa

PRINCIPAL ACTIVITIES: Processing and export of frozen fish and shrimps

Parent Company: United Fisheries of Kuwait SAK

KUWAIT NATIONAL PETROLEUM CO KSC
K.N.P.C.

PO Box 70 Safat, 13001 Kuwait
Tel: 2420126
Cable: Kunpetco Kuwait
Telex: 22689, 22457, 22006 Kunpetco
Telefax: 2433839

Chairman: Ahmad Abdul Muhsin Al-Mutair (also Managing Director)

Directors: Abdul Aziz Al-Busairi (Deputy Chairman and Deputy Managing Director, Finance & Administration), Khaled Buhamra (Deputy Managing Director, Manufacturing), Mahmoud Al-Yahya (Deputy Managing Director, Planning), Bader Al-Refai (Director), Bader Hajji Yousef (Director), Mohammad Abbas (Director)

Senior Executives: Khaled Buhamra (Shuaiba Refinering Manager), Bader Hajji Yousef (Mena Abdullah Refinery Manager), Bader Al-Baijan (Major Projects Group General Manager), Mohammad Abbas (Coordinator Oil Refining & Gas Liquefaction Mina Al Ahmadi)

PRINCIPAL ACTIVITIES: Refining of crude oil and marketing of oil products and gas liquefaction

Branch Offices: Shuaiba Refinery: PO Box 9202, Ahmadi, Kuwait, Tel: 3262177/3260177; Mina Abdullah Ref.: PO Box 69, Safat, Kuwait, Tel: 3260233/3260461; Mina Al-Ahmadi Ref: PO Box 10252, Shuaiba, Kuwait, Tel: 3261888/3262888

Parent Company: Kuwait Petroleum Corporation
Subsidiary Companies: Kuwait Aviation Fuelling Company KSC
Financial Information:

	1988/89
	KD'000
Sales turnover	136,752
Profits	75,585
Authorised capital	260,000
Paid-up capital	260,000
Total assets	1,268,603

Principal Shareholders: Kuwaiti Government
Date of Establishment: October 1960
No of Employees: 6,428

KUWAIT OIL COMPANY KSC

PO Box 9758, Ahmadi, 61008 Ahmadi Kuwait
Tel: 3989111
Cable: Kuoco
Telex: 44211 Kwt
Telefax: 3983661

Chairman: Abdul Malik M Al Gharabally (Managing Director)
Directors: Khaled Y Al Fulaij (Dy Managing Director Operational Services), Yacoub Al Doub (Dy Managing Director Administration), Faisal Al Jassem (Dy Managing Director Operations)

PRINCIPAL ACTIVITIES: Exploration, drilling, production, and storage of oil and gas

Branch Offices: KOC, 54 St James's Street, 5th Floor, London SW1A 1GT, UK
Parent Company: Kuwait Petroleum Corporation
Financial Information:

	1988
	KD'000
Authorised capital	30,188
Paid-up capital	30,188
Total assets	453,564

Principal Shareholders: Kuwait Government
Date of Establishment: 1934
No of Employees: 5,106

KUWAIT OIL TANKER CO SAK

PO Box 810 Safat, 13009 Kuwait
Tel: 2455455
Cable: Tankerco
Telex: 22013 Kotc, 44755, 44766, 30850 KT
Telefax: 2445907, 2406605

Chairman: Abdul Fattah Sulaiman Al Bader (Managing Director)
Directors: Abdulla Al Roumi (Deputy Chairman)
Senior Executives: Hassan Ali Qabazard (Deputy Managing Director, Admin & Finance)

PRINCIPAL ACTIVITIES: Shipowners, sole agents for tankers calling at the ports of Mina al Ahmadi and Shuaiba and other ports in Kuwait, LP gas filling and distribution

Principal Agencies: Afran Transport Co; Aal Barwill; Agencies Maritime Pomme; Bahrain Maritime Mercantile; Ceylon Shipping Corp; Gleneagle Ship Management; Damanhour Shipping; Denholm Offshore; D A Knudsen & Co; Fin Services; Fekete & Co; Gesuri Lloyd; Gulf Agency Co (Dubai, Bahrain, Muscat); Hugo Trumpy; Intership Agency Abu Dhabi; Italnoli; Joroung Shipyard; Kirton; KNPC; KPC; Kee Yeh Maritime; Lamnalco Sharjah; Marine Agents & Brokers; Mackindon India; Merkezoiz Istanbul

Branch Offices: Agency Branch: PO Box 7055, Fahaheel, Kuwait, Tel 3911811, 3911758, Telex 44201: Minatank; Gas Branch: PO Box 810, Safat, Kuwait, Dry Cargo Group, Tel 3911811, Telex 46905 Mintak, PO Box 7055, Fahaheel, Kuwait

Parent Company: Kuwait Petroleum Corporation
Associated Companies: KOTC; KNPC; PIC; KOC; KUFPEC; SF; KPI
Principal Bankers: National Bank of Kuwait
Financial Information:

	1988	1989
	KD'000	KD'000
Net profit (loss)	(2,174)	12,127
Authorised capital	200,000	200,000
Paid-up capital	200,000	200,000
Total assets	218,440	234,913

Principal Shareholders: Kuwait Petroleum Corporation
Date of Establishment: 1957
No of Employees: 385

KUWAIT OXYGEN & ACETYLENE CO

PO Box 1462 Safat, 13015 Kuwait
Tel: 4810122, 4810132
Cable: Oxygen Kuwait
Telex: 22262 Oxygen Kt
Telefax: 4818902

President: Salim Said Huneidi
Senior Executives: Amer S Huneidi (General Manager), Ibrahim Y Hamadeh (Financial Manager), Omer Al Taher (Deputy General Manager)

PRINCIPAL ACTIVITIES: Producers of medical, industrial gases and gas mixtures; dealers in welding machines and equipment, medical equipment, safety equipment, chemicals and contractors

Principal Agencies: Union Carbide Corp, USA/Belgium; Miller Electric Mfg Co, USA; L'Air Liquide, France

Associated Companies: Kuwait Industrial Gases Corp, PO Box 23192, Kuwait; Salim Huneidi & Co, PO Box 102, Kuwait; Al Nasr Middle East, PO Box 23730 Safat, 13098 Kuwait

Principal Bankers: Bank of Kuwait and the Middle East; Commercial Bank of Kuwait; National Bank of Kuwait
Financial Information:

	1989
	KD'000
Authorised capital	500
Paid-up capital	500

Principal Shareholders: Salim S Huneidi, Khalad S Askar
Date of Establishment: 1956
No of Employees: 200

KUWAIT PAPER CO WLL

PO Box 23799 Safat, 13098 Kuwait
Tel: 2452638, 2455128
Telex: 44543 Rayesgrp Kt

PRINCIPAL ACTIVITIES: Manufacture of sensitised papers and polyester films. Supplies of office furniture and stationery

KUWAIT PETROLEUM CORPORATION

Salhiya Complex, PO Box 26565 Safat, 13126 Kuwait
Tel: 2455455
Cable: PETCORP
Telex: 44874, 44875, 44876, 44877, 44878 PETCORP KT
Telefax: 2423371, 2467159

Chairman: Shaikh Ali Al Khalifah Al Sabah (Minister of Oil)
Directors: Abdul Razzak Mohammad Mulla Hussain (Deputy Chairman & Managing Director Planning, Administration & Finance), Ahmad Abdul Muhsin Al Mutair (Managing Director Refining & LPG), Abdul Malik Mohammad Al Gharabally (Managing Director Exploration & Production), Al Jaber Al Ali Al Sabah (Managing Director Marketing), Abdul Baqi Abdullah Al Nouri (Managing Director Petrochemical Industries), Abdul Fattah Sulaiman Al Bader (Managing Director Transportation), Salim Abdullah Al Ahmad (Director), Ali Abdullah Saqer Al Benali (Director), Fuad Abdul Rahman Mulla Hussain (Director)
Senior Executives: Abdullatif Al Tourah (Exec Asst Managing Director Corporate Planning), Abbas Malik (Exec Asst Managing Director Administration), Abdul Hadi Al Awwad (Exec Asst Managing Director Finance), Abdullah H Al Roumi (Exec Asst Managing Director Sales Eastern Hemisphere), Nader H Sultan (Exec Asst Managing Director Sales Western Hemisphere), Hani A/Aziz Hussain (Exec Asst Managing Director Planning & Marketing), Mansour O Al Furaih (Exec Asst Managing Director Supply), Mahmoud Al Yahya (Exec Asst Managing Director Training)

PRINCIPAL ACTIVITIES: Coordination of petroleum activities: exploration and drilling for crude oil & natural gas in Kuwait and abroad; refining and processing of such substances; transport, distribution and marketing of crude oil, LPG & processed derivatives & products; engagement in petrochemical industry and marketing of its products; carrying out services connected with all the foregoing including designing, establishing and operating of plants and installations
Branch Offices: UK: 80 New Bond Street, London W1; USA: 45 Rockefeller Plaza, New York; Japan: 10th Floor South Wing, Tokyo 100; Singapore: 541 Orchard Road, Singapore
Subsidiary Companies: Kuwait Oil Company; Kuwait National Petroleum Company; Petrochemical Industries Company; Kuwait Oil Tanker Company; Kuwait Foreign Petroleum Exploration Co; Kuwait Santa Fe Braun for Engineering & Petroleum Enterprises; Kuwait Aviation Fuelling Company; KPC (US Holdings) Inc USA; KPC International NV; Petrochemical Industries Holding NV Europe
Financial Information:

	1988/89
	KD'million
Sales turnover	2,903
Net profit	121
Authorised capital	2,500
Paid-up capital	2,225
Total assets	5,512

Principal Shareholders: Government of Kuwait
Date of Establishment: 1980
No of Employees: KPC & Subsidiaries: 15,354

KUWAIT PHARMACEUTICALS CO SAK
Kuwait Pharmaceutical Industries Co SAK

PO Box 5846 Safat, 13059 Kuwait
Tel: 4748011
Telex: 23091 KOGCO KT
Telefax: 4714150

PRINCIPAL ACTIVITIES: Manufacturers of pharmaceuticals and pharmaceutical products

KUWAIT PLASTICS & MATS MANUFACTURING CO WLL

PO Box 42479 Shuwaikh, 70655 Kuwait
Tel: 4730286, 4730298
Cable: Bosabea Kuwait
Telex: 30007 Bosabea KT
Telefax: 4735580

Chairman: Suleiman A Al Qudaibi
Directors: Ali Redha Kolaghassi (Managing Partner), Yousuf M Al Sumait (Partner)
Senior Executives: Bashir Al Khateeb (General Manager)

PRINCIPAL ACTIVITIES: Manufacture of polythelene film, film roll for agriculture and construction, shopping bags, garbage and laundry bags, floor mats, twain and rope, hoses and tubes and fittings
Principal Bankers: Commercial Bank of Kuwait; Bank of Kuwait & the Middle East; National Bank of Kuwait
Financial Information:

	1989
	KD'000
Sales turnover	1,250
Profits	150
Authorised capital	600
Paid-up capital	600
Total assets	2,500

Principal Shareholders: Chairman and partners as described
No of Employees: 150

KUWAIT PORTLAND CEMENT CO

PO Box 42191, Shuwaikh, 70652 Kuwait
Tel: 844716, 835615-917, 818422
Cable: Porcem
Telex: 46553 PORCEM KT

Chairman: Naser Alquatami
Directors: Abed Ali Bahman
Senior Executives: Adel Al-Ghanim (General Manager), Mudaf Al-Mudaf (Asst. General Manager)

PRINCIPAL ACTIVITIES: Cement handling
Branch Offices: Factory at Shuwaikh, Tel 834129, 834108, Telex 23487 Porcem Kt
Principal Bankers: Gulf Bank of Kuwait; Industrial Bank of Kuwait
Financial Information:

	KD'000
Authorised capital	6,250
Paid-up capital	6,250

Date of Establishment: 1979
No of Employees: 200

KUWAIT PRECAST SYSTEM CO

PO Box 1800 Safat, 13018 Kuwait
Tel: 5728141, 5728393, 5729151, 5729030
Cable: Salwa Kuwait
Telex: 23172 Salwa KT

Chairman: Muhammed Ahmed Alghanim
Directors: Jasim Mohamed Alghanim, Hameed Mohamed Alghanim, Muayed Mohamed Alghanim
Senior Executives: Dr Qutaiba J Abdulwahab (General Manager)

PRINCIPAL ACTIVITIES: Precast building, ready mixed concrete, wire mesh, glass reinforced cement
Branch Offices: Factory: Tel 3262691/2, 3262815, Telex 30149 Kupresy KT
Principal Bankers: Burgan Bank, Kuwait; National Bank of Kuwait; Kuwait Real Estate Bank; Commercial Bank of Kuwait

Financial Information:

	KD'000
Sales turnover	9,000
Authorised capital	1,500

Date of Establishment: 1978
No of Employees: 400

KUWAIT PREFABRICATED BUILDING CO SAK

PO Box 5132 Safat, 13052 Kuwait
Tel: 4733055
Cable: Prefab, Kuwait
Telex: 23081, 23075 PREFAB KT

Chairman: Eng Abdulla Jassim Al-Rujaib

PRINCIPAL ACTIVITIES: Contractors for the construction of buildings using Precast Concrete System. Manufacturers of precast concrete elements, prestressed hollowcore slabs, claddings, beams, welded wire mesh, terrazzo tiles. Fabrication and erection of steel items and hot dip galvanization of steel sections
Principal Bankers: Commercial Bank of Kuwait; National Bank of Kuwait; Kuwait Real Estate Bank, Bank of Bahrain and Kuwait
Financial Information:

	KD'000
Authorised capital	6,500
Paid-up capital	6,500

Principal Shareholders: National Industries Company, Kuwait; National Bank of Kuwait; Kuwait Real Estate Bank; Commercial Bank of Kuwait; Gulf Bank; Industrial Bank of Kuwait
Date of Establishment: 1964
No of Employees: 1,446

KUWAIT PROJECTS CO FOR CONTRACTING & BUILDING SAK

PO Box 21281 Safat, 13073 Kuwait
Tel: 2445180
Telex: 22709 Murmur KT

President: Mohamad Ahmad Al Farhan

PRINCIPAL ACTIVITIES: Supply of building and construction equipment, plant hire

KUWAIT PROJECTS COMPANY SAK

PO Box 23982 Safat, 13100 Kuwait
Tel: 2444341
Cable: Cosha Kuwait
Telex: 22654 Kuproc Kt

Chairman: Mohammed Yousif Al Sumait
Directors: Anwar Abdul Aziz Al Osaimi, Bader Jassim Al Sumait, Issa Ibrahim Al Mishari, Dr Khalid Mohammad Bodai, Najib Mohammad Al Hamdan, Wael Jassim Al Saqer
Senior Executives: Abdulaziz Ali Al-Nahed (General Manager)

PRINCIPAL ACTIVITIES: Holding company for new and existing companies in real estate, financial and industrial fields
Associated Companies: Financial Group of Kuwait SAK; Kuwait Projects Company for Buildings and Real Estate SAK; Kuwait Investment Group
Principal Bankers: Real Estate Bank; National Bank of Kuwait; Al-Ahli Bank of Kuwait; Bank of Kuwait and the Middle East
Financial Information:

	KD'000
Authorised capital	8,500
Paid-up capital	8,500

Principal Shareholders: Government (51%), Kuwaiti individuals and institutions (49%)
Date of Establishment: August 2nd, 1975

KUWAIT PUBLIC TRANSPORT CO KSC

PO Box 375 Safat, 13004 Kuwait
Tel: 2469420, 2469485
Cable: Mowasalat
Telex: 22246 Ktc, 30629 Ktc
Telefax: 2401265

Chairman: Abdulwahab Rashid Al Haroon (Also Managing Director)
Directors: Abdul Aziz Hasan Al Jarallah (Vice Chairman), Ahmed Hamoud Al Khadda (Member), Sadeq Mohamed Al Aslawi (Member), Yousif Dekhail Al Dekhail (Member)
Senior Executives: Hilal Hamad Al Mutairi (Asst Managing Director for Admin & Services), Issam Mubarak Al Rifai (Asst Managing Director for Transport & Operations), Bader A Al Najjar (Asst Managing Director for Technical Affairs), Abdul Aziz M Al Shamroukh (Asst Managing Director for Finance & Stores)

PRINCIPAL ACTIVITIES: Public transportation
Principal Bankers: National Bank of Kuwait; Commercial Bank of Kuwait
Financial Information:

| | 1989 |
	KD'000
Authorised capital	40,000
Paid-up capital	40,000

Principal Shareholders: Government
Date of Establishment: December 1962
No of Employees: 6,343

KUWAIT REAL ESTATE BANK KSC

PO Box 22822 Safat, 13089 Kuwait
Tel: 2458177
Cable: Realbank
Telex: 22321 Akari, 46008 Rebank
Telefax: 2462516

Chairman: Saad Ali Al-Nahed (also Managing Director)
Directors: Khaled Yousuf Al-Marzouk (Deputy Chairman), Abdul Razzak Sultan Aman, Hamad Abdulla Al-Sager, Faisal Saoud Al Fulaij, Abdul Rahman Al Mohamed, Ahmad Abdulwahab Al Nakib, Yousif Ali Al Houfi
Senior Executives: Mohamed Al Farhan (General Manager), Wafa Al Qatami (Asst General Manager Investment), Fajhan Al Fahad (Asst General Manager Credit), Nasser Al Masaad (Operations Manager)

PRINCIPAL ACTIVITIES: Real estate and general commercial banking, foreign exchange trading
Branch Offices: Four Branches in Kuwait
Subsidiary/Associated Companies: Industrial Bank of Kuwait KSC; Kuwait Sanitaryware KSC; Bank of Kuwait & Lebanon KSC; Pearl Real Estate Co KSC; Kuwait Projects Co KSC; KPC for Real Estate & Reconstruction KSC; KPC for Building & Contracting KSC; Financial Group of Kuwait KSC; Misr America International Bank MSC; Jordan and Gulf Bank JSC; Pearl Investment Co BSC; Pearl Holding Co (Luxembourg); Bank of Kuwait & Asia EC (Bahrain)
Financial Information:

| | 1988/89 |
	KD'000
Profits	5,690
Authorised capital	25,742
Paid-up capital	25,742
Total assets	514,356

Principal Shareholders: 100% Kuwaiti public
Date of Establishment: May 1973
No of Employees: 320

KUWAIT REAL ESTATE CO

PO Box 1257 Safat, 13013 Kuwait
Tel: 2448330
Telex: 22644 Krec

Chairman: Khalid Yousuf Al Marzook
Directors: Abdel Razzak Sultan Aman (Vice Chairman), Abdul Aziz Abdul Muhsen Al-Rashed, Abdul Rahman Abdul Mughni Al-Moh'd, Faisal Saud Al-Felaij, Barrak Abdul Muhsen Al-Mutair, Sa'ad Ali Al-Nahedh, Yousef Moh'd Al-Nisf
Senior Executives: Faisal Yousuf Al Marzook (General Manager), Bader Jassim Al-Sumait (Deputy General Manager), Mehmood Taqui (Manager, Engineering Department), Saleh Qhanim Malallah (Manager, Real Estate Department)

PRINCIPAL ACTIVITIES: Real estate and property management
Financial Information:

	KD'000
Authorised capital	45,000
Paid-up capital	45,000

Date of Establishment: 16.5.1972

KUWAIT REAL ESTATE INVESTMENT CONSORTIUM KSC

PO Box 23411 Safat, 13095 Kuwait
Tel: 2448260 (10 lines)
Cable: Consortium
Telex: 22620 Consort Kt; 22849 Consort Kt
Telefax: 2434454, 2434440

Chairman: Rashid Abdulla Al Mijren Al Roumi
Directors: Shaker Jassim Al Sanea (Deputy Chairman), Husain Makki Al Juma, Abdulla Mohammed Al Sumait, Ali Abdul Rahman Al Hasawi, Majed Essa Al Ajeel, Bader Suleiman Al Othman
Senior Executives: Mishari Zaid Al Khaled (General Manager), Abdulla Ahmed Al Obaid (Real Estate & Investment Manager), Adel Adbulla Al Fowzan (Portfolio Manager), Sameer Abdul Aziz Al Loghani (Finance & Administration Manager), Hamed Mohammed Battash (Financial Advisor)

PRINCIPAL ACTIVITIES: All kinds of real estate investments; residential and low-income housing, hotels, commercial complexes worldwide; investments in various productive projects in Third World countries.
Branch Offices: Casablanca, Morocco; Tunis, Tunisia; Cairo, Egypt; Sanaa, Yemen; Dallas and New York, USA
Subsidiary/Associated Companies: Subsidiary Companies: (50-100%) KREIC (Singapore); KREIC Investment (Cayman Islands) Ltd; Al-Hubara Investments Antilles-NV; Loans & Investments Co (LINC); Societe Touristique Tunisie-Golfe; Arab Brick Co, Cairo; Saly Egypt Kuwait Woodworks Co; Associated Companies: (20-49%) Tourism & Conferences Co (Tunis); Arab Ceramic Co; Tawfiq Clinic, Tunis; Egyptian Gulf Bank; Saudi Hotel Services Co; Arab Multinational Finance Co (AMFCO); Moroccan Kuwaiti Development Consortium (CMKD); Yemeni Kuwaiti Real Estate Development Co; Banque Tuniso -International; Banque Tuniso - Koweitien de Developpement; United International Hotels Co (Sharjah); Saif Ltd (Lambert Brussels Corp); Kuwait Asia Bank, Bahrain; The United Bank of Kuwait, London; National Tourism & Development Bank
Principal Bankers: National Bank of Kuwait, Commercial Bank of Kuwait, Gulf Bank - Kuwait, Bank of Kuwait & The Middle East; Bahrain & Kuwait Bank
Financial Information:

	1989 KD'000
Authorised capital	40,000
Paid-up capital	36,800

Principal Shareholders: Kuwait Investment Authority, The Public Institution for Social Security, Kuwait Investment Co (KSC), Kuwait Foreign Trading Contracting & Investment Co (KSC), National Real Estate Co (KSC), Kuwait International Investment Co (KSC), Other Shareholders
Date of Establishment: October 1975
No of Employees: 74

KUWAIT REGENCY PALACE

PO Box 1139, Salmiyah, 22012 Kuwait
Tel: 5728000 (30 lines)
Telex: 46082 KREGPLH, 46863 KWREGPH
Telefax: 5723109

Chairman: Abdul Razzak Al Sane
Directors: Jameel Al Sane
Senior Executives: Ghassan Rahwangi (General Manager), Shatha Al Rihani (Director of Sales), Nigel Barlow (Financial Controller), Othman Al Ghanam (Director of Purchasing), Raja Khairallah (Director of Public Relations)

PRINCIPAL ACTIVITIES: Hotel business and conferences

Principal Shareholders: Privately owned

KUWAIT SHERATON HOTEL

PO Box 5902 Safat, 13060 Kuwait
Tel: 2422055, 2421005
Cable: Sheraton
Telex: 22434 Sheraton Kt; 22016 Sheraton Kwt
Telefax: 2448032

Chairman: Abdul Aziz Al Shaya (Oriental Hotels Co)
Directors: Hmoud Al Nusif, Khaled Al Shaya, Faisal Al Nusif

PRINCIPAL ACTIVITIES: Hotel management
Principal Agencies: Sheraton Corporation
Branch Offices: Location in Kuwait: Fahd Al Salem Street
Principal Bankers: National Bank of Kuwait

Date of Establishment: 1966
No of Employees: 498

KUWAIT SHIPBUILDING & REPAIRYARD CO SAK

PO Box 21998 Safat, 13080 Kuwait
Tel: 835488
Cable: Dockyard
Telex: 22438 Ksbryd Kt; 23745 Mishref Kt

Chairman: Hamad A Al-Sagar
Directors: Abdul Fatah Al-Bader (Deputy Chairman)
Senior Executives: Naif Al-Zufairy (General Manager), Dr Majid Al-Sani (Deputy General Manager), Robert Verburgt (Commercial Manager), Bassam Al Bassam (Purchasing & Marketing Manager)

PRINCIPAL ACTIVITIES: Ship repairing and building; steel construction, mechanical engineering; new shipbuilding; underwater cleaning services
Principal Agencies: Greece: Irmania Shipping & Trading Inc; UK
Subsidiary Companies: Gulf Dredging Co SAK; Kuwait Electrodes Co
Principal Bankers: Alahli Bank of Kuwait; Commercial Bank of Kuwait
Financial Information:

	KD'000
Authorised capital	30,000
Paid-up capital	30,000

Principal Shareholders: Ministry of Finance & Private Shareholders
Date of Establishment: 1974
No of Employees: 684

KUWAIT SHIPPING AGENCIES CO SAK

PO Box 20722 Safat, 13068 Kuwait
Tel: 832022, 831938
Cable: KuKeer
Telex: 22282, 23302

PRINCIPAL ACTIVITIES: Shipping agency
Branch Offices: Dubai
Parent Company: United Arab Shipping Co SAG

KUWAIT SILICONE PRODUCTS CO

PO Box 4281 Safat, 13043 Kuwait
Tel: 5721192, 5723979
Telex: 44080 SANEIUN KT

Chairman: Nasser Abdulmajeed Al-Sane
Directors: Mustafa Al Sane, Khalid Al Sane, Wayel Al Sane
Senior Executives: Momen Al Refai (Financial Controller)

PRINCIPAL ACTIVITIES: Manufacturing and sales of silicone
products such as: silicone sealants, greases, oils,
antifoamers, defoamers etc
Principal Agencies: CSL Silicones Ltd, Canada
Principal Bankers: Commercial Bank of Kuwait; National Bank
of Kuwait; Bank of Kuwait & The Middle East
Financial Information:

	KD'000
Authorised capital	2,000
Paid-up capital	2,000

Date of Establishment: March 1983
No of Employees: 18

KUWAIT SPANISH PETROLEUM CO KSC

PO Box 20467 Safat, 13065 Kuwait
Tel: 2435682
Cable: Kaspetco Kuwait
Telex: 22047 Kspc Kt

Chairman: Ahmed A Al-Mutair

PRINCIPAL ACTIVITIES: Oil exploration

Principal Shareholders: Kuwait Oil Co (KOC) and Hispanica de
Petroleos SA (Hispanoil)

KUWAIT SPONGE INDUSTRIES CO WLL

PO Box 3525 Safat, 13036 Kuwait
Tel: 4814755, 4814743
Cable: Esphingco
Telex: 22370 Kisco Kt
Telefax: 4848310

Chairman: Suleiman Ahmed Al Qudaibi
Directors: Ali Redha Kolaghassi (Managing Director & Partner)

PRINCIPAL ACTIVITIES: Manufacture of sponges, mattresses
and pillows; trading in oilfield and refinery supplies, pipes and
chemicals
Branch Offices: Polyglass Reinforced Plastics Factory, Kuwait;
Kuwait Mattress Co WLL, Kuwait
Principal Bankers: Commercial Bank of Kuwait; National Bank
of Kuwait; Bank of Kuwait & The Middle East
Financial Information:

	1989
	KD'000
Sales turnover	1,000
Profits	200
Authorised capital	500
Paid-up capital	500
Total assets	2,000

Principal Shareholders: S A Al Quadhaibi; A R Kolaghassi
Date of Establishment: 1968
No of Employees: 65

KUWAIT SUGAR COMPANY

PO Box 5989 Safat, 13060 Kuwait
Tel: 2414576

President: Yusuf Abdulaziz Al Wazzan

PRINCIPAL ACTIVITIES: Sugar production and processing

KUWAIT SUPPLY CO

PO Box 5932 Safat, 13060 Kuwait
Tel: 832562, 832411, 832845
Cable: Tamween
Telex: 22311 Kt

Directors: Tariq Al Barrak (Director General)

PRINCIPAL ACTIVITIES: Import of foodstuffs and general
trading

KUWAIT TRANSCONTINENTAL SHIPPING CO WLL

PO Box 25431 Safat, 13115 Kuwait
Tel: 2423753
Cable: Balship
Telex: 23275 Balship
Telefax: 2403823

Senior Executives: Bo Petterson (General Manager)

PRINCIPAL ACTIVITIES: Shipping and forwarding agency,
customs clearance, land transportation, air freight, project
cargo handling
Principal Agencies: American President Lines, Hyundai
Merchant Marine, Panalpina
Principal Bankers: Gulf Bank

Date of Establishment: 1977

KUWAIT TYRES COMPANY

PO Box 24338 Safat, 13104 Kuwait
Tel: 2410060
Cable: ETARCO
Telex: 22814 TYRES KT

Chairman: Eisa Abdullah Bahman

PRINCIPAL ACTIVITIES: Production and distribution of tyres
and rubber products
Principal Bankers: Gulf Bank of Kuwait; Commercial Bank of
Kuwait

Date of Establishment: November 1976

KUWAIT UNITED POULTRY KSC

K.U.P.C.O.

PO Box 1236 Safat, 13013 Kuwait
Tel: 2419901/2/3
Cable: Alkupco
Telex: 22573 Alkupco Kt
Telefax: 2436507

Chairman: Dr Yousef A Al Awadi
Senior Executives: Mahmood Nassar Al Nassar (Acting
Managing Director), Mohamed Al Thuwaini (Finance & Admin
Manager), Dr Bassam Nayfeh (Production Manager), Deia
Salama (Technical Manager)

PRINCIPAL ACTIVITIES: Poultry, meat, table-eggs and poultry
feed production. KUPCO has been formed to produce the
total requirements of poultry meat and eggs for Kuwait
Subsidiary Companies: Kuwait United Agricultural Production
Co KSC; Kuwait Catering Co
Principal Bankers: Alahli Bank; Commercial Bank of Kuwait;
Gulf Bank; Bank of Kuwait & the Middle East; Burgan Bank
Financial Information:

	1988/89
	US$'000
Sales turnover	20,139
Profits	6,597
Authorised capital	40,070
Paid-up capital	40,070
Total assets	56,027

Principal Shareholders: Government of the State of Kuwaiti; and
the public
Date of Establishment: 1974
No of Employees: 350

KUWAIT WOOD INDUSTRIES CO SAK

PO Box 25619 Safat, 13117 Kuwait
Tel: 4735420, 4745636
Telex: 30009 KWICO KT

Chairman: Khaled Al Fares
Senior Executives: Khaled Al Fares (General Manager)

PRINCIPAL ACTIVITIES: Manufacturers, importers and
exporters of internal/external/fire resistance doors, door
frames, kitchen cupboards, wardrobes etc
Branch Offices: Location in Kuwait: Sabhan Industrial Area
Principal Bankers: National Bank of Kuwait SAK; Kuwait
Finance House; Gulf Bank

Date of Establishment: 1978
No of Employees: 150

KUWAITI BRITISH READYMIX CO
PO Box 33273, Rawdah, 73453 Kuwait
Tel: 3710295, 3710297
Telex: 30121 RDYMIX KT
Telefax: 3710298

PRINCIPAL ACTIVITIES: Supply of readymix concrete
Parent Company: Redlands Ltd
Associated Companies: In Saudi Arabia; Abu Dhabi; Qatar

Principal Shareholders: Joint venture between Redlands
Readymix and M A Kharafi

LAMNALCO LTD
PO Box 11220, Dasmah, 35153 Kuwait
Tel: 831030, 840161
Cable: Lamnalco Kuwait
Telex: 22070 Rezayat Kt; 22962 Nalco Kt
Telefax: 831030

PRINCIPAL ACTIVITIES: Oil terminal operations, ship owners
and managers, pilotage, marine consultancy and trading, ship
repair and marine maintenance, maritime civil engineers -
submarine pipelines, hydrographic surveys
Parent Company: Royal Bos Kalis Westminster Group of
Holland and Abdulla Alireza Group of Kuwait
Principal Bankers: Bank of Kuwait & the Middle East; British
Bank of the Middle East

Date of Establishment: 1963
No of Employees: 250 (total Group)

LIVESTOCK TRANSPORT & TRADING CO KSC
PO Box 23727 Safat, 13098 Kuwait
Tel: 2434177, 2434187, 2434197
Cable: LIVETRADE KUWAIT
Telex: 22336 A/B LIVTRADE KT, 30324 A/B LIVTRDE KT

Chairman: Faisal Abdullah Al Khazam
Directors: Faisal Abdullah Al Khazam (Managing Director),
Ebrahim Abdullah Al Ghanim, Khalid Hamad Boodai, Abdullah
Dakheel Al Dakheel (Vice Chairman), Salah Yacoub Al
Homaizi, Mohammed Hamad Hassan Al Ebrahim
Senior Executives: Faisal Abdulla Al Khazam (Managing
Director), Dr Abdul Rahman Salman (Technical Consultant,
Chief of Studies & Research), Hamid Ahmed Al Homoud
(Finance & Administration Manager), Abdul Qader Nassir Al
Wohaib (Local Operations Manager), Jassim Abdul Hamid Al
Saquer (International Operations Manager), Captain Peter P C
Machado (Fleet Manager), Yousuf Dawood Makary (Financial
Controller), Mohammed Hassan Ebrahim Ahmed (Local
Operations Dept Manager), Zakariya Ibrahim Qasem (Meat
Preparation & Processing Manager), George Ariyanakum
(Farm Manager)

PRINCIPAL ACTIVITIES: Livestock trading and transportation,
fresh and frozen meat and meat products trading and
shipping
Subsidiary Companies: Rural Export & Trading (WA) Pty Ltd,
Perth, Western Australia; Emirates Livestock & Foodstuffs
Trading Co, Dubai, UAE
Principal Bankers: National Bank of Kuwait SAK

Principal Shareholders: Semi government
Date of Establishment: 1973
No of Employees: 1,200

MAHMOOD ALJASSIM & BROS
See ALJASSIM, MAHMOOD, & BROS

MAJIED, MUDHYAN & ABDUL, LTD
PO Box 4654 Safat, 13047 Kuwait
Tel: 2410095 (5 lines), 2411775
Cable: Lectrading
Telex: 22842 Majied
Telefax: 241894

Chairman: Hamood S Al-Mudhyan
Directors: A L Majied (Managing Director & General Manager)
Senior Executives: A Z Malik (Commercial Manager), J J
Hamdan (Admin Manager), Sameer Tahir (Finance Manager)

PRINCIPAL ACTIVITIES: Electrical trading and contracting
Principal Agencies: Dorman Smith Switchgears Ltd, Preston,
UK; Ta Tun Cable & Wires Co, Taiwan; Simplex Lighting Ltd,
UK; W J Parry, UK; JSB Electrical, UK
Principal Bankers: Alahli Bank of Kuwait; Bank of Kuwait & The
Middle East; National Bank of Kuwait

Date of Establishment: 1968
No of Employees: 650

MANAGEMENT CONSULTING CENTER
PO Box 25597 Safat, 13116 Kuwait
Tel: 2410216

Chairman: Ahmad El-Rashed
Directors: Shareef A H Massoud (Managing Director), Nair
Ewad, Abdula Al-Mulafi

PRINCIPAL ACTIVITIES: Management consulting, credit
reporting

Principal Shareholders: A division of Warba Auditing Office
Date of Establishment: 1977

MARAFI, MOHAMED SALEH, TRADING & CONTRACTING CO WLL
PO Box 26675 Safat, 13127 Kuwait
Tel: 4846884, 4840282
Cable: Ramases
Telex: 23568 Rameses KT
Telefax: 4849983

President: Mohamed Saleh Marafi
Directors: Hafez Amer Hafez (Managing Director & Partner)
Senior Executives: Walid Amer Hafez (Technical Manager),
Nimer Khalaf (Chief Engineer), Ashok Kumar
(Planning/Procurement & Cost Control Manager), Antwan
Ghanim (Financial Manager), Khalid Khuwaild (Marketing
Executive), Awad Mahmoud (Personnel Manager)

PRINCIPAL ACTIVITIES: Civil building construction, mechanical
contracting works, computer sales and services, electrical
material sales and general trading
Principal Agencies: Cables & Plastics Ltd, UK; Computers
Anyware Inc, USA
Branch Offices: Universe Computers Centre, Kuwait, Tel
2421812, Telefax 2421823; MSM Mechanical Division, Kuwait,
Tel 2421870, 2421861, Telex 44704 Rantis KT
Principal Bankers: Al Ahli Bank of Kuwait; National Bank of
Kuwait; Commercial Bank of Kuwait; Kuwait Real Estate Bank
Financial Information:

	1987/88 KD'000
Sales turnover	2,012
Profits	38
Authorised capital	400
Paid-up capital	400
Total assets	2,042

Principal Shareholders: Mohamed Saleh Marafi; Hafez Amer
  Hafez
Date of Establishment: November 1980
No of Employees: 968

MARAFIE, MOHD RAFIE HUSAIN, SONS CO

PO Box 122 Safat, 13002 Kuwait
Tel: 2449925
Cable: Rafie
Telex: 22661 Rafie KT
Telefax: 2444479

Chairman: Amir Marafie
Directors: Abdul Ilah Marafie, Abdul Fatah Marafie

PRINCIPAL ACTIVITIES: General trading and contracting; air
  handling; computers; domestic appliances; electronic and
  industrial equipment; power system; audio video;
  communications; elevators and swimming pools; medical
  supplies; cleaning equipment, construction, graphics,
  exhibition, stationery
Branch Offices: Sweden; USA
Parent Company: Wara Real Estate Co KSC
Subsidiary Companies: Al Moaeed Trading Co; Marafie Sons
  Co; Kuwait Clear Drains Co; Kuwait Danish Cleaning
  Equipment Co; Ducting & Servicing Co
Principal Bankers: Bank of Kuwait & Middle East; Al Ahli Bank
  of Kuwait

Principal Shareholders: Eleven brothers Marafie
Date of Establishment: 1919
No of Employees: 150

MASEELAH TRADING CO WLL

PO Box 2702 Safat, 13028 Kuwait
Tel: 2445040 (60 lines)
Cable: Matraco
Telex: 44853 Maseelh Kt
Telefax: 2437285, 2436079

Chairman: Najeeb A Al Mulla
Directors: Anwar A Al Mulla, Nabil A Al Mulla, Lutfi A Al Mulla,
  Apkar Hovaguimian, D R Mirchandani, Vaiz Karamat, R K
  Sethi, H N Elowe, Ivan Pacheco, A S Narenthiran, Minoo
  Patel
Senior Executives: Anwar A Al Mulla (Deputy Chairman), Apkar
  Havaguimian (Managing Director), D R Mirchandani (Deputy
  Managing Director), V Karamat (Financial Controller), A S
  Narenthiran (Commercial Director)

PRINCIPAL ACTIVITIES: General agents and merchants,
  manufacturers' representatives, industrial equipment and
  heavy machinery, passenger cars and commercial vehicles,
  parts and services, engineering products, domestic
  appliances, fire fighting and fire protection systems,
  foodstuffs, business machines, consumer products, etc
Principal Agencies: Distributorships: Chrysler Corp; Mitsubishi
  Heavy Industries; Mitsubishi Motors Corp; Kato Works Co;
  Industrie Zanussi; Nippon Yusoki Co; Luft; Maack & Co;
  Glyndova; Andrex Radiation Products; Radiographic
  Suppplies; Saval Kronenburg; Scientific Systems Corps, etc
Parent Company: Al Mulla Group
Associated Companies: Saleh Jamal & Co WLL; Al Mulla Rental
  & Leasing of Vehicles & Equipment Co WLL; Al Mulla Security
  Services Co WLL; Al Mulla Environmental Systems Co WLL;
  Al Mulla Consultancy Co WLL; Al Mulla Cleaning &
  Maintenance Co WLL; Bader Al Mulla & Bros Co WLL; Al
  Mulla International Trading & Contracting Co WLL; Gulf
  Trading Group WLL; Al Mulla Aviation Agencies; Al Mulla
  Travel Bureau; Hiba Advertising Co WLL; Al Mulla Real Estate
  Co WLL
Principal Bankers: Bank of Kuwait & the Middle East; National
  Bank of Kuwait; Commercial Bank of Kuwait; Gulf Bank

Financial Information:

	1988/89
	US$'000
Sales turnover	55,300
Authorised capital	3,356
Paid-up capital	3,356
Total reserves	7,912
Total assets	39,488

Principal Shareholders: Najeeb A Al Mulla, Anwar A Al Mulla
Date of Establishment: 1972
No of Employees: 300

MATROOK TRADING & CONTRACTING CO

Matrook Paint Factory

PO Box 320 Safat, 13004 Kuwait
Tel: Office: 2433448, 2432072, Factory: 832692, 810484
Cable: Alimatrook
Telex: 22607 Matrook Kt

Chairman: Ali Yousuf Al Matrook
Directors: Yousef Ali Al Matrook

PRINCIPAL ACTIVITIES: Manufacture of decorative, industrial,
  and marine paints and allied products
Principal Bankers: Al Ahli Bank of Kuwait; National Bank of
  Kuwait; Gulf Bank

Principal Shareholders: Fully owned by Ali Yousuf Al Matrook
Date of Establishment: 1966
No of Employees: 50

MAZIDI, ABDULHAMID MANSOOR,

PO Box 228 Safat, 13003 Kuwait
Tel: 442221
Cable: Mazidi
Telex: 22116 Mazidi Kt

Chairman: A H Mazidi (Proprietor)
Senior Executives: I M Mazidi (General Manager), Sulaiman
  Ibrahim (Head of Shares Department), Hussain Abdullah
  (Head of Real Estate Department)

PRINCIPAL ACTIVITIES: Trade, construction, investment, real
  estate
Subsidiary/Associated Companies: Mazidi Trading Co WLL,
  Kuwait & Dubai; Business Machines Co WLL, Kuwait & Dubai;
  Mazidi Contracting Co WLL, Kuwait; Euro-Kuwaiti Investment
  Co CSC, Kuwait; Euro Kuwaiti Trading Co Ltd, London

MAZIDI TRADING CO WLL

PO Box 228 Safat, 13003 Kuwait
Tel: 2467177
Cable: Mazidi
Telex: 22116 Mazidi KT
Telefax: 2468982

Chairman: A H Mazidi
Senior Executives: Mohammad Arqoob (General Manager)

PRINCIPAL ACTIVITIES: Import and distribution of various
  products and equipment, oilfield equipment, chemicals
Principal Agencies: Basf, Mapel, KDG-Mobrey, Nicola & Albia,
  Barton Hydraulic Eng Co, Golden Chemicals, Unichema,
  Sauer & Sohn, Maschinenbau, Actuated Controls
Principal Bankers: Al Ahli Bank of Kuwait
Financial Information:

	1988	1989
	KD'000	KD'000
Sales turnover	2,300	1,450
Profits	61	26
Authorised capital	500	100
Paid-up capital	500	100
Total assets	441	126

Principal Shareholders: Family owned
Date of Establishment: 1948 (reorganised in 1985)

MCDERMOTT KUWAIT

PO Box 8020, Salmiyah, 22052 Kuwait
Tel: 4715350
Telex: 22170 Jess KT

PRINCIPAL ACTIVITIES: Engineering and construction services
for the production and transportation of hydrocarbons in
offshore and onshore areas
Parent Company: McDermott International Inc

MIDDLE EAST DEVELOPMENT CO WLL
M.E.D.C.O.

PO Box 3340 Safat, 13034 Kuwait
Tel: 2425181, 2425182, 2425183
Cable: Mideastco Kuwait
Telex: 22499 Medco Kt
Telefax: 2409346

Chairman: Feisal Fuleij
Directors: M T El-Khalidi (Managing Director), Chafic Anis
Chehab (Finance Director)
Senior Executives: M Marsh (Chief Engineer)

PRINCIPAL ACTIVITIES: Contracting, trading, agencies
Principal Agencies: Arabian Drilling Co, PO Box 932, Riyadh,
Saudi Arabia
Principal Bankers: Gulf Bank; Commercial Bank of Kuwait
Financial Information:

	1988/89
	KD'000
Sales turnover	1,750
Authorised capital	112.5
Paid-up capital	112.5

Principal Shareholders: Feisal Fuleij; M T El-Khalidi; Chafic Anis
Chehab
Date of Establishment: 1958
No of Employees: 310

MIDDLE EAST GAS & PETROCHEMICAL CO

PO Box 89 Safat, 13001 Kuwait
Tel: 2438090
Telex: 22014 Bahar Kt

Chairman: Mishari Abdulrahman Al-Bahar

PRINCIPAL ACTIVITIES: LPG gas and petrochemicals
production, trading and transportation

MIDDLE EAST INTERNATIONAL CONTRACTING CO SAK

PO Box 1083 Safat, 13011 Kuwait
Tel: 2430725, 2439264/7
Telex: 22988 KT, 22142 Marata KT

President: Ali Mohamed Thunayan Al Ghanem

PRINCIPAL ACTIVITIES: General contracting, building and civil
engineering, mechanical engineering, pipeline contractors and
turnkey services

MIDDLE EAST OIL SERVICES CO WLL

PO Box 23960 Safat, 13099 Kuwait
Tel: 519450, 552180
Cable: Eastoil
Telex: 22617 Kt

Chairman: L Mutawa
Directors: K Mutawa
Senior Executives: M Mutawa (General Manager)

PRINCIPAL ACTIVITIES: Contractors and manufacturers'
agents for oil, gas and petrochemical industries
Principal Agencies: David Brown Vosper (Offshore) Ltd, UK; Joy
Mnfg Co, USA; Bautechnik AG, Germany; Petromat Products
Ltd, UK
Branch Offices: Middle East Oil Services Co, London, UK
Principal Bankers: Alahli Bank of Kuwait KSC

MODERN AIR CONDITIONING & REFRIGERATION CO

PO Box 4867 Safat, 13049 Kuwait
Tel: 2439471/2
Cable: Moryak
Telex: 23387
Telefax: 2411804

Chairman: Khaled Yusuf Al Mutawa
Directors: Abdul Muhsen Al Qattan (Managing Director), Khaled
Yousef Mutawa (President), Khaled Qattan (Director), Nihad
Haikal (General Manager)

PRINCIPAL ACTIVITIES: Import, distribution and installation of
air conditioning, water treatment, refrigerator and fire fighting
equipment
Branch Offices: Jordan: PO Box 2277, Amman
Principal Bankers: Ahli Bank of Kuwait; Gulf Bank of Kuwait;
Arab Bank, Amman

Principal Shareholders: Khaled Mutawa, A M Qattan, Khaled
Kattan
Date of Establishment: 1964
No of Employees: 210

MOHAMED ABDULMOHSIN KHARAFI INDUSTRIES & ESTABLISHMENTS

See KHARAFI, MOHAMED ABDULMOHSIN, INDUSTRIES &
ESTABLISHMENTS

MOHAMED ABDULRAHMAN AL-BAHAR

See AL-BAHAR, MOHAMED ABDULRAHMAN,

MOHAMED SALEH & REZA YOUSUF BEHBEHANI

See BEHBEHANI, MOHAMED SALEH & REZA YOUSUF,

MOHAMED SALEH MARAFI TRADING & CONTRACTING CO WLL

See MARAFI, MOHAMED SALEH, TRADING & CONTRACTING
CO WLL

MOHAMMED AL WAZZAN STORE CO WLL

See AL WAZZAN, MOHAMMED, STORE CO WLL

MOHAMMED HOMOOD ALSHAYA CO

See ALSHAYA, MOHAMMED HOMOOD, CO

MOHD NASER AL SAYER & SONS EST

See AL SAYER, MOHD NASER, & SONS EST

MOHD RAFIE HUSAIN MARAFIE SONS CO

See MARAFIE, MOHD RAFIE HUSAIN, SONS CO

MORAD YOUSUF BEHBEHANI

See BEHBEHANI, MORAD YOUSUF,

MOTOCAVE GENERAL CONTRACTING EST

PO Box 20465 Safat, 13065 Kuwait
Tel: 2453856, 2453857, 2431044
Telex: 22761 MOTOCAV KT
Telefax: 2431046

Chairman: Mushari M Al-Baddah
Directors: Salah Al-Baddah (Deputy Chairman)

PRINCIPAL ACTIVITIES: High tension and low tension electrical
contracts, air conditioning services, special air conditioning
units, raised floors and U.P.S. Systems for computers,
partitioning, plumbing and fire alarm and fire fighting
equipment, supply and installation of diesel generators,
transformers, also preparation of complete computer rooms
fitting contracting
Principal Agencies: E G & G Sealol, UK; I T E Gould World
Trade Corp., USA; Atwood & Morrill, USA; Milton Roy, USA;

Bestobell Mobrey Ltd, UK; Lanza, Italy; Ercolle Marelli, Italy; Pompe Gabionetta, Italy; Crane & Hoist Ltd, UK; Mark Control, UK; Hiross, Italy; Kane-May Ltd, UK
Subsidiary Companies: Sealol Kuwait KSC, PO Box 46833, Fahaheel, Kuwait; Al Baddah & Abdulla Co; Code Computer Co
Principal Bankers: Kuwait Finance House KSC; National Bank of Kuwait; Gulf Bank, Kuwait
Financial Information:

	KD'000
Sales turnover	3,000
Authorised capital	500
Paid-up capital	500

Principal Shareholders: Mushari M Al-Baddah
Date of Establishment: 1970
No of Employees: 200

MSS-MCKEE
Kuwait Co for Process Plant Construction & Contracting KSC
PO Box 1092 Safat, 13011 Kuwait
Tel: 315096, 314284
Telex: 44504 Hombre Kt

Chairman: Moayed H M Al Saleh
Directors: R K Young (Managing Director), Najeeb H M Al Saleh, Fawzi M Al Saleh, E W Sledjeski

PRINCIPAL ACTIVITIES: Engineering and construction of petroleum and petrochemical industries. Related projects and other industrial projects
Branch Offices: Main Office: Davy-McKee, London, UK; also Davy-McKee, Cleveland, Ohio, USA

Principal Shareholders: Musaad Al Saleh & Sons; McKee Overseas Corp
Date of Establishment: June 1979

MUBARAKIAH POULTRY & FEED CO
PO Box 24418 Safat, 13105 Kuwait
Tel: 4841786, 4841983, 4849085
Cable: Poultco
Telex: 44556 Poultco Kt
Telefax: (965) 4845634

Directors: Abdul Mohsin Farhan Al-Farhan (Managing Director)
Senior Executives: Tarek Abdul Baki (General Manager), Faisal Al-Wazzan (Sales Manager), Abdullah Mohd Al Sahli (Administration Manager)

PRINCIPAL ACTIVITIES: Poultry and feed production
Principal Bankers: Bank of Kuwait & Middle East; Commercial Bank of Kuwait
Financial Information:

	1989 KD'000
Sales turnover	5,000
Authorised capital	12,000

Principal Shareholders: Kuwait Foreign Trading & Investment Co; Kuwait United Fisheries
Date of Establishment: April, 1977
No of Employees: 428

MUDHYAN & ABDUL MAJIED LTD
See MAJIED, MUDHYAN & ABDUL, LTD

MUNAWER TRADING & CONTRACTING EST
PO Box 1090 Safat, 13011 Kuwait
Tel: 2425551
Cable: Montraco
Telex: 22286 Montrac KT

PRINCIPAL ACTIVITIES: Building, civil and general contracting

MUSAAD AL SALEH & SONS LTD
See AL SALEH, MUSAAD, & SONS LTD

MUSTAFA KARAM TRADING & CONTG FIRM
See KARAM, MUSTAFA, TRADING & CONTG FIRM

NADIA TRADING & CONTRACTING EST
PO Box 9072, Ahmadi, 61001 Kuwait
Tel: 985899
Cable: SALDWEEL
Telex: 44919 NAHILCO KT

Chairman: Miss Nadia Salem Abdul Jalil (General Manager)

PRINCIPAL ACTIVITIES: Trading and contracting, construction and maintenance works
Branch Offices: Ahmadi Printing Press; Ladies Tailoring branch
Principal Bankers: Burgan Bank, Commercial Bank of Kuwait

Date of Establishment: 22nd August, 1982
No of Employees: 250

NAFISI UNITED GROUP WLL
PO Box 23611 Safat, 13097 Kuwait
Tel: 2459595, 2460999
Cable: Nugpco Kuwait
Telex: 44620 NUGPCO KT
Telefax: 2402593

Chairman: Yacoub Y Al Nafisi
Directors: Rasheed Y Al Nafisi (Managing Director)

PRINCIPAL ACTIVITIES: Civil and mechanical engineering; petrochemical and chemical plants; pumping stations, sub-stations; oilfield plants; machines and equipment; also veterinary products and green houses
Principal Agencies: Medique, Italy; M S Nielsen, Denmark; Trendy; Closan; Belle Fleur; Carvena; Hyosung Corp, Korea
Subsidiary Companies: Nasifi Trading Co, PO Box 3333 Safat, Kuwait
Principal Bankers: Commercial Bank of Kuwait
Financial Information:

	1990 KD'000
Paid-up capital	1,000

NAIF H AL DABBOOS & SONS
See AL DABBOOS, NAIF H, & SONS

NASER SAYER & CO WLL
See SAYER, NASER, & CO WLL

NATIONAL & GERMAN ELECTRICAL & ELECTRONIC SERVICES CO
N.G.E.E.C.O.
PO Box 6612, Hawalli, 32041 Kuwait
Tel: 4831544, 4831887
Cable: Siemens KT
Telex: 22777 KT
Telefax: 4830156

President: Ali A Al Radwan
Senior Executives: F Hintermaier (General Manager), J Mohr (Commercial Manager)

PRINCIPAL ACTIVITIES: Supply of electrical and electronic equipment, cables and wires, computer systems, communication systems, pollution control equipment, power equipment, electrical engineering and services, power engineering and electrical installations
Principal Agencies: Siemens; Hell
Associates Companies: NGEECO is a joint venture with Siemens
Principal Bankers: National Bank of Kuwait; Gulf Bank

Financial Information:

	1988/89
	KD'000
Sales turnover	3,417
Profits	262
Authorised capital	200
Paid-up capital	200
Shareholders'funds	614
Total assets	818

Principal Shareholders: Siemens AG; Ali Radwan & Al Ghanim
    family
Date of Establishment: 29.4.79
No of Employees: 250

NATIONAL AUTOMOTIVE MANUFACTURING & TRADING CO KSC (NAMTCO)

PO Box 4555 Safat, 13046 Kuwait
Tel: 4747669, 4711966, 4713572, 4713922
Cable: Gulfcar
Telex: 30057 Gulfcar Kt
Telefax: 4735436 Namtco

Chairman: Masoud Jowhar Hayat
Directors: Issam Jassim Al Saqer (Vice Chairman), Abdul Aziz
    Mosa Abdul Razzaq, Ridwan Abdulla Jamal, Sulaiman Saud
    Al Zaid, Fahed Bader Al Kahailan, Ahmed Abdulla Al Kazmi
Senior Executives: Mahmoud Abu Hatab (General Manager), Ali
    Ghadhanfari (Asst General Manager for Marketing &
    Technical Affairs), Issam Al Quraini (Administrative Manager)

PRINCIPAL ACTIVITIES: Trading in automobiles, trucks, spare
    parts, repair and maintenance, assembly of trucks and
    industrial vehicle bodies, heavy equipment
Principal Agencies: Iveco Magirus, W Germany; KHD
    Agricultural Tractors, W Germany; PPM Mobile Cranes,
    France
Branch Offices: Show Room situated at Shuwaikh
Subsidiary Companies: Arabian Transport Vehicles Industrial Co
    (ATVICO); National Automotive & Special Machinery Co
    (NASMCO)
Principal Bankers: Alahli Bank of Kuwait; National Bank of
    Kuwait
Financial Information:

	1988/89
	KD'000
Sales turnover	2,337
Profits	103
Authorised capital	6,179.9
Paid-up capital	6,179.9
Total assets	9,187

Principal Shareholders: Government of Kuwait; Kuwait
    Investment Authority; Kuwait Foreign Trading & Contracting
    Co; Kuwait International Investment Co
Date of Establishment: 1973
No of Employees: 61

NATIONAL BANK OF KUWAIT SAK

Head Office, Abdullah Al Salem Street, PO Box 95 Safat, 13001
    Kuwait
Tel: 2422011 (20 lines)
Cable: National Kwt
Telex: 22043, 22451 Natbank KT
Telefax: 2466260, 2466261

Chairman: Mohamed Abdul Mohsin Al Kharafi
Directors: Mohamed Abdul Rahman Al Bahar (Deputy
    Chairman), Khaled Abdullatif Al-Hamad, Yousef Abdulaziz Al
    Fulaij, Yacoub Yousef Al-Hamad, Nasser Musaed Abdulla Al-
    Sayer, Hamad Abdul-Aziz Al Sager, Ghassan Ahmad Al
    Khaled
Senior Executives: Ibrahim S Dabdoub (Chief General Manager),
    Faisal M Al-Radwan (Deputy Chief General Manager), Yacoub
    Y Al-Fulaij (General Manager), Nemeh E Sabbagh (General
    Manager - International Banking Group), Roderic McKenzie

(General Manager - Treasury Group), Mohammed Tahboub
(General Manager - Domestic Credit & Marketing), Dr Ziad A
Taky (Asst General Manager, Chief Economist), Hussain
Abdel Khader Al Ali (Asst General Manager, Chief Auditor),
Ossama Al Naqib (Legal Advisor), Simon Clements (Executive
General Manager Operations Services), Ralph J Williams
(Executive Manager - Card Services), Antoine R Duwaida
(Executive Manager -Import Export & Guarantees), Mahmoud
Shehadeh (Executive Manager -International Marketing), M
Shunnar (Executive Manager - Domestic Branches),
Mohammed Farrag (Executive Manager - Human Resources)

PRINCIPAL ACTIVITIES: Commercial banking
Principal Agencies: Banking arrangements with 750
    correspondent banks all over the world
Branch Offices: 50 branches in Kuwait & 6 overseas (London
    (2), New York, Paris, Bahrain, Singapore)
Subsidiary/Associated Companies: Subsidiaries: NBK
    Investment Management Ltd, London, UK; NBK Finance SA,
    Geneva, Switzerland; Associated Banks: United Bank of
    Kuwait, 3 Lombard Street, London EC3V 9DT, UK; Rifbank
    SAL, PO Box 11-5727, Beirut, Lebanon; Bank of Bahrain &
    Kuwait (BSC), PO Box 597, Manama, Bahrain; Arab
    Reinsurance Co SAL, PO Box 11-9060, Beirut, Lebanon; in
    Kuwait: The Industrial Bank of Kuwait KSC, PO Box 3146
    Safat, 13032 Kuwait; Kuwait Reinsurance Co KSC, PO Box
    21929 Safat, 13080 Kuwait
Financial Information:

	1988	1989
	KD'000	KD'000
Profits	30,900	35,000
Loans & advances	1,554,100	1,673,500
Deposits	3,204,100	3,577,000
Authorised capital	77,300	87,400
Paid-up capital	77,300	87,400
Shareholders'funds	255,200	273,100
Total assets	3,476,200	3,867,600

Principal Shareholders: Kuwait Nationals - Private Sector
Date of Establishment: 1952
No of Employees: 1,700

NATIONAL COMMERCIAL ENTERPRISES

PO Box 8474, Salymiah, 22055 Kuwait
Tel: 735235, 2542314, 2522285, 2521285
Cable: Misstwenty KT
Telex: 22836 Oilland

Chairman: Abdullah Al Sumaie (Owner)
Directors: Mostafa Ahmad, Safwan Hadee
Senior Executives: J R Peter (Stock Controller), M D Lizzr
    (Purchasing Accountant), Mohamad Abdullah (Cargo
    Supervisor)

PRINCIPAL ACTIVITIES: Agents and general trading
Principal Agencies: Elegance; Renel; Rossitti, Ferragammo
Principal Bankers: Alahli Bank of Kuwait; National Bank of
    Kuwait

Date of Establishment: 1975
No of Employees: 50

NATIONAL COMPUTER SERVICES

PO Box 766 Safat, 13008 Kuwait
Tel: 4710576, 4731087, 4742274/5
Telex: 30166, 31930 Babtain KT
Telefax: 4713359

Chairman: Khalid Al Babtain
Senior Executives: Omer Taha (General Sales Manager)

PRINCIPAL ACTIVITIES: Installation and maintenance of
    computer systems
Principal Agencies: Digital; Timelink; Isoreg Corp; Infotron
    Systems; Compucorp; Denco; IES Data Systems; Paradyne;
    Black Box
Branch Offices: Bahrain: PO Box 26766, Manama

Parent Company: Al Babtain Group
Principal Bankers: Gulf Bank, Burgan Bank

Date of Establishment: 1978
No of Employees: 32

NATIONAL CONTRACTING CO LTD

Alireza Group of Companies

PO Box 60 Safat, 13001 Kuwait
Tel: 4843535, 4816836, 4840161, 4840163
Cable: Nalco Kuwait
Telex: 22070 Rezayat Kt, 22962 Nalco Kt
Telefax: 4831030

Chairman: Abdulla A Alireza
Directors: Teymour A Alireza (Deputy Chairman/President),
    Fahd A Alireza (Vice President)
Group Senior Executives: Noble Dreghorn (Group Finance
    Director), James H N Gibson (Group General Manager - Saudi
    Arabia), Ma'an Wafai (Group General Manager - Kuwait)

PRINCIPAL ACTIVITIES: Building and civil engineering
    contractors, importers/exporters, agents for foreign principals
Principal Agencies: G H Zeal; Armor Products, USA; Prakla
    Seismos, W Germany; Rezayat Brown & Root Ltd, Bahrain;
    BET Plant Services, UK
Branch Offices: National Contracting Co Ltd in Alkhobar, Riyadh
    and Jeddah Saudi Arabia
Associated Companies: Rezayat Trading Co, PO Box 106,
    Safat, Kuwait; Rezayat Europe Ltd, 52 Mount St, London
    W1Y 5RE, UK; Rezayat Co Ltd, PO Box 996, Riyadh, PO Box
    90, Alkhobar, and PO Box 6670 Jeddah, Saudi Arabia;
    Rezayat Europe Ltd, 34 Avenue George V, Paris-75008,
    France; Rezayat America Inc, 5177 Richmond Avenue, Suite
    780, Houston, Texas 77056, USA
Principal Bankers: Bank of Kuwait and the Middle East, Kuwait

Principal Shareholders: Abdulla Alireza and his Family Members
Date of Establishment: 1953
No of Employees: 2,650 (30 in Kuwait)

NATIONAL INDUSTRIES CO SAK

PO Box 417 Safat, 13005 Kuwait
Tel: 4849466, 4842863, 4844863, 4844739
Cable: Industrico Kuwait
Telex: 22165 Nic Kwt
Telefax: 4835982

Chairman: Mufarrej I Al Mufarrej (also Managing Director)
Directors: Saad M Al Saad (Vice Chairman), Musaed A Al
    Marzook (Head Office Director), Salah S Al Hussain (Director
    of Planning & Development)
Senior Executives: Salah A Al Tarkait (General Manager
    Marketing), Shallal K Al Shallal (General Manager Cement
    Products Unit), Sulaiman Al Zaid (General Manager Lime
    Asbestos & Plastic Unit)

PRINCIPAL ACTIVITIES: Manufacture of sand lime bricks,
    cement products, asbestos cement pipes and PVC pipes,
    batteries, detergents, and gas concrete blocks, quarrying and
    producing (lime) filler
Branch Offices: Lime Asbestos & Plastic Products Unit, Mena
    Abdulla, Tel 3262622, 3262677, Telex 44910; Cement
    Products Unit, Sulaibiyah, Tel 4674055, 4674127, Telex
    23024; Battery Plant, Al Rai, Tel 4731011; Detergent Plant, Al
    Rai, Tel 4731011
Associated Companies: Kuwait Metal Pipes Co; Kuwait Cement
    Co; Kuwait Pre-Fabricated Building Co; Kuwait Building
    Materials Manufacturing Co, Kuwait Glassfibre Reinforced
    Plastic Products Co; Industrial Bank of Kuwait
Principal Bankers: National Bank of Kuwait; Gulf Bank;
    Commercial Bank of Kuwait; Al Ahli Bank of Kuwait; Bank of
    Kuwait & the Middle East; Burgan Bank; Kuwait Finance
    House; Kuwait Real Estate Bank

Financial Information:

	1988/89
	KD'000
Profits	8,000
Authorised capital	26,727
Total assets	96,000

Principal Shareholders: Government of Kuwait (51%); Public
    (49%)
Date of Establishment: 1960
No of Employees: 1,700

NATIONAL MECHANICAL & ELECTRICAL WORKS CO

PO Box 24081 Safat, 13101 Kuwait
Tel: 4749655
Telex: 23809 Natcome
Telefax: 4730054

Directors: Ghalib Younis (Manging Director)
Senior Executives: Talal Qadan (Group Project Manager),
    Samer Younis (Group Project Manager), Shafqat Tariq
    (Tendering Manager), Mohammad Haggag (Financial & Admin
    Manager), Richard Rickards (Commercial Manager), Daoud
    Ershaid (Group Project Manager), Hassan Abu Madi (UAE
    Area Manager), Ghassan Younis (Yemen Area Manager)

PRINCIPAL ACTIVITIES: Contracting; oil and gas pipelines;
    mechanical and electrical works for hospitals, large
    commercial complexes, airports, highways; sewage treatment
    plants, building automation system and security systems
Principal Agencies: Johnson Controls, Kuwait
Branch Offices: Abu Dhabi: PO Box 1189 Al Ain, UAE, Tel
    3828937, Yemen: PO Box 2296, Sana'a, Tel 2234429;
    Representative Office in London: Unit 5, Yeoman Street,
    London SE8 5DU, Tel 071-232 2820, Fax 071-231 8305
Parent Company: M A Kharafi Group of Companies
Principal Bankers: Al Ahli Bank, Gulf Bank, Commercial Bank of
    Kuwait, National Bank of Kuwait
Financial Information:

	1990
	US$'000
Sales turnover	25,000
Authorised capital	2,900
Paid-up capital	2,900

Principal Shareholders: M A Kharafi, Ghalib Younis
Date of Establishment: 1974
No of Employees: 2,000

NATIONAL REAL ESTATE CO SAK

PO Box 22644 Safat, 13087 Kuwait
Tel: 2410190/8
Cable: Karra
Telex: 22681 Watnia Kt

Chairman: Mohammed Nasser Al Hamdhan
Directors: Yousef Ahmed Al Duaij (Deputy Chairman &
    Managing Director)

PRINCIPAL ACTIVITIES: Real estate investments
Principal Bankers: Gulf Bank of Kuwait; National Bank of
    Kuwait; Alahli Bank of Kuwait; Kuwait Foreign Trading
    Contracting and Investments Company; Burgan Bank;
    Commercial Bank of Kuwait
Financial Information:

	KD'000
Authorised capital	33,539
Paid-up capital	33,539

Principal Shareholders: Ministry of Finance, Ministry of Justice,
    Savings and Credit Bank, Kuwait Foreign Trading Contracting
    & Investment Co
Date of Establishment: July 1973
No of Employees: 100

NATIONAL TEXTILES CO SAK

PO Box 25186 Safat, 13112 Kuwait
Tel: 4736829, 4714347
Telex: 23810 Texmill Kt

President: Mustafa H Al Wazzan
Directors: Khalid Al Wazzan (Vice Chairman), Fadal M Abbas, Zaid Al Wazzan
Senior Executives: Michael Karunaharan (Mill Manager)

PRINCIPAL ACTIVITIES: Production and distribution of textiles
Principal Bankers: Burgan Bank; Gulf Bank

Date of Establishment: 1979
No of Employees: 50

NCR CORPORATION

PO Box 27380 Safat, 13134 Kuwait
Tel: 2413070/4
Cable: NACARECO, KUWAIT
Telex: 22059 NCR KT
Telefax: 2420930

Senior Executives: A Sawires (Resident Manager), S R H Krishnan (Manager Finance & Administration)

PRINCIPAL ACTIVITIES: Sale and distribution of business equipment, computers and terminals and electronic data processing equipment
Parent Company: NCR Corporation, Dayton, Ohio
Principal Bankers: Gulf Bank; National Bank of Kuwait

Date of Establishment: 1952
No of Employees: 55

NOURI INDUSTRIAL EST

PO Box 2829 Safat, 13029 Kuwait
Tel: 4814803, 4840219, 4840055
Cable: Nouriabd
Telex: 23887 Nouri Kt
Telefax: 4841055 G2/G3

Proprietor: Abdulkhaliq Al-Nouri
Directors: Nouri Al-Nouri (Managing Director)
Senior Executives: Dr Mitqhal Sartawi (Deputy Managing Director), Ibrahim Abdoh (Sales Engineer), Naser M Awad (Sales Engineer)

PRINCIPAL ACTIVITIES: Suppliers to oilfield and petrochemical industries, tendering, supply of building materials and industrial equipment
Principal Agencies: Hepworth Clay Products, Raychem, Marley Cooling Towers, Schlumberger Industries, Allen Bradley, Sundstrand Int'l, L & W Equipment, Nibco, Taco Inc, Pullen Pumps, Ameron, W H Pipe Int'l, Bilsom, Impalloy, Weksler Corp, Stanhope Seta, Wade Int'l, Trelleborg, Kurvers, R B Hilton, Space Decks, Sofrepost, Cleveland Bridge, Buck & Hickman, Struther Wells, Jeumont Schneider, GR Stein Refractories, Nuouo Pignone, Uniroyal, Grande Motori Trieste, GKN Bldg Services, Resinex, Cembre, John Zink
Branch Offices: N.I.E. International, Canada & Arabian Est for Technical Contracting, Bahrain
Principal Bankers: National Bank of Kuwait; Bank of Kuwait and the Middle East

Principal Shareholders: Private Company
Date of Establishment: 1958

OASIS TRADING CO LTD

PO Box 409 Safat, 13005 Kuwait
Tel: 2404001, 2426809, 2437231
Cable: Oasis Kuwait
Telex: 44035 Oasis KT
Telefax: 2413957

Chairman: Mohamed Abdulrahman Al Bahar

Directors: Jassim M Al Bahar (President), Issam M Al Bahar (Vice President)
Senior Executives: Walid Saleh (General Manager), Joseph Mathai (Sales Manager)

PRINCIPAL ACTIVITIES: General agents, distributors of office furniture, home furniture, false ceiling, venetian and vertical blinds, and other interior furnishing materials, weighing scales and weighbridges, storage systems and shelving, projectors and shredders, office equipment
Principal Agencies: Hunter Douglas, Holland; Avery, Warley, UK; TEC, Japan; Uniwell, Japan; Zambelli, Germany Geha, Germany
Parent Company: Mohamed A R Al Bahar
Associated Companies: Mohamed A R Al Bahar & Partners
Principal Bankers: National Bank of Kuwait; Bank of Kuwait & Middle East

Principal Shareholders: Mohamed Abdulrahman Al Bahar & Sons (Kuwait)
Date of Establishment: 1960
No of Employees: 55

ORGANISATION OF ARAB PETROLEUM EXPORTING COUNTRIES

O.A.P.E.C.

PO Box 20501 Safat, 13066 Kuwait
Tel: 2448200
Cable: Naftarab
Telex: 22166 Nafarab Kt
Telefax: 2426885

Chairman: Chairmanship of Ministerial Council and Executive Bureau on annual rotation basis
Directors: Members of the Ministerial Council which consists of the Oil Minister from each member country
Senior Executives: Members of the Executive Bureau which consists of a senior official from each member country. Also Members of the General Secretariat, Abdelaziz Alwattari (Acting Secretary General), Dr Usameh Jamali (Director, Information & Library Dept), Ismail Mahmoud Hussein (Director, Finance & Administrative Affairs Dept), Abdullatif Zarrug (Director, Technical Affairs Dept), Dr Jassim Al Gumer (Director, Economics Dept)

PRINCIPAL ACTIVITIES: Coordination and cooperation of the Member Countries in all activities and developments related to the oil industry
Principal Agencies: General Secretariat, Judicial Tribunal
Subsidiary Companies: Arab Maritime Petroleum Transport Company, Kuwait; Arab Shipbuilding & Repair Yard Company, Bahrain; Arab Petroleum Investments Corporation, Dammam, Saudi Arabia; Arab Petroleum Services Company, Tripoli, Libya; Arab Petroleum Training Institute, Baghdad, Iraq
Principal Bankers: National Bank of Kuwait
Financial Information:

	1990 KD'000
Budget for General Secretariat	1,316
Budget for Judicial Tribunal	164

Principal Shareholders: Member Countries: Eleven Arab oil producing countries: the Democratic and Popular Republic of Algeria, the State of Bahrain, the Arab Republic of Egypt, the Republic of Iraq, the State of Kuwait, the Socialist People's Libyan Arab Jamahiriya, the State of Qatar, the Kingdom of Saudi Arabia, the Syrian Arab Republic, the Republic of Tunisia (membership inactive since 1987), the United Arab Emirates
Date of Establishment: 1968
No of Employees: 63

KUWAIT

ORIENTAL IMPORT CO WLL

Jamal S Samerai

PO Box 21893 Safat, 13079 Kuwait
Tel: 2424930, 2410916
Cable: ERMAS KT
Telex: 22969 Orisam KT
Telefax: 2401519

Chairman: Jamal S Samerai
Directors: Jamal S Samerai, Ahmed Sayid Omar
Senior Executives: Sheikh Abd Al Vahed

PRINCIPAL ACTIVITIES: General contracting, dealing in capital
  goods and heavy machinery
Principal Agencies: Megator Pumps, UK; Vredstein, Holland;
  Cosmoter, Italy
Subsidiary Companies: J S Eastern Contracting Co Ltd; J S
  Eastern Finance Investment Co Ltd; J S Eastern
  Hydrocarbons Co Ltd; J Samerai Holding Co Ltd
Principal Bankers: National Bank of Kuwait; Alahli Bank;
  Commercial Bank of Kuwait
Financial Information:

	1989 KD'000
Sales turnover	36,492
Profits	1,960
Authorised capital	20
Paid-up capital	20
Total assets	34,290

Principal Shareholders: Jamal S Samerai
Date of Establishment: 1960
No of Employees: 30

OTIS ELEVATOR COMPANY

PO Box 11169, Dasma, 35152 Kuwait
Tel: 2445506
Cable: Lyndentree Kuwait
Telex: 22557 Otis Kt
Telefax: 2464862

Chairman: Sheikh Nasser Al Athbi Al Sabah
Directors: Sheikh Talal Nasser Al Athbi Al Sabah, Sheikh
  Abdullah Jaber Al Athbi Al Sabah, Mohamed Rasheed
  (Managing Director)

PRINCIPAL ACTIVITIES: Installation and maintenance of
  elevators and escalators, and travolators
Principal Agencies: Subsidiary of United Technologies
  Corporation
Parent Company: Otis Elevator Co, New Jersey, USA
Principal Bankers: Alahli Bank of Kuwait; Bank of Kuwait and
  the Middle East; Gulf Bank

Date of Establishment: March 1975
No of Employees: 98

OVERLAND TRANSPORT CO KSC

PO Box 24611 Safat, 13107 Kuwait
Tel: 4873994, 4873824, 4873752
Cable: Overland
Telex: 23817 Roads

Chairman: Abdullah Abdulaziz Al-Obaidan
Directors: Issam Mubarak Al-Refai (Vice Chairman), Salah
  Sulaiman Al Hassan (Managing Director), Saud Mohammad
  Al-Rkhais, Abdulrahman Fahed Buzaber, Abdulaziz Suad Al-
  Mutawa, Abdulaziz Mohammad Shuaib, Abdulaziz
  Mohammad Al-Shamroukh
Senior Executives: Fadl Saadeddin (Head of Sales Department),
  Saud Al Falah (Administration Manager), Kamal Hussein
  (Chief Accountant)

PRINCIPAL ACTIVITIES: Transportation of goods throughout
  the gulf area, specialising in transporting general construction
  materials and foodstuffs in bulk to Iraq; trading division for
  the sale of all truck related activities including tractors,
  trabosa trailers, tyres, batteries etc
Principal Agencies: Trabosa Trailers, Tip-Top Tyre Repairs,
  Bandag Tyre Re-Treading
Principal Bankers: Gulf Bank; Al Ahli Bank
Financial Information:

	KD'000
Authorised capital	10,000
Paid-up capital	9,985

Principal Shareholders: A publicly quoted company, the equity
  of which is currently distributed across 13,706 members
Date of Establishment: 1977
No of Employees: 324

PACC INTERNATIONAL

Pan Arab Computer Centre

PO Box 921 Safat, 13010 Kuwait
Tel: 848500
Cables: PACC Kuwait
Telex: 22901 PACC KT

Chairman: Abdul Rahman Al Shaya (Managing Director)
Directors: Ahmed Khalil (Executive Vice President)
Senior Executives: Rafi Razzak, Mourad Mankarios, Mokhtar
  Azmi, Sami Neseiri, Hassanein Tawfic, Omar Alami, Samir
  Debs

PRINCIPAL ACTIVITIES: Sale and service of computer and
  automated office equipment, advanced technology equipment
  - hotel systems etc
Principal Agencies: CII Honeywell Bull; Modular Computer
  Services Inc; Texas Instruments; Comterm Inc; Integro;
  Philips Data Systems; Datagraphix Inc; Benson; Cara Hotel
  Systems; Motorolla Inc
Branch Offices: Abu Dhabi, Dubai, Beirut, Bahrain, Jeddah, Al
  Khobar, Riyadh, Cairo, Amman
Parent Company: M H Al Shaya Co
Principal Bankers: Bank of Kuwait & the Middle East;
  Commercial Bank of Kuwait; National Bank of Kuwait; Bank
  of Bahrain & Kuwait

Date of Establishment: June 1976

PACKAGING & PLASTIC INDUSTRIES CO

PO Box 10044, Shuaiba, 65451 Kuwait
Tel: 3261322 (7 lines)
Cable: Package Kuwait
Telex: 44219 Package
Telefax: 3261762

Chairman: Dr Abdul Aziz Sultan Al Essa
Directors: Anwer Abdul Rehman Ateeqy (Vice-Chairman)
Senior Executives: Mazen A Khourshed (General Manager)

PRINCIPAL ACTIVITIES: Production of polypropylene sacks for
  the fertilizer industry; production of polyethylene sheeting for
  agricultural and construction industries; production of garbage
  bags, shopping bags, food storage bags, co-extruded flexible
  film packaging
Principal Bankers: Gulf Bank Kuwait; Commercial Bank of
  Kuwait

Principal Shareholders: Yousuf A A Al Mazini, Khaled Sultan,
  Saleh Sultan, Anwer Abdulrehman Ateeqy, Fawzi Musaad
  Saleh, Sheikh Nasser Sabah, Fahad Naif Daboos
Date of Establishment: 1974
No of Employees: 280

PALMS AGRO-PRODUCTION CO

PO Box 1976 Safat, 13020 Kuwait
Tel: 2438600
Cable: Kupalms
Telefax: (965) 2438940

Chairman: Faisal Ali Al Bahar

Directors: Hussain Ahmad Qabazard (Deputy Chairman &
Managing Director), Othman Al Bisher, Mohammed A Mohsen
Al Sayegh, Bader Al Salem, Anwar Sultan, Fahed Al Odeh
Senior Executives: Usama Al Azm (General Manager), Khalid
Baddad (Landscaping Section Head), Yousif Owais (Electro-
Mechanical Section Head), Mezian Barazi (Agricultural
Requisites Section Head), Rafi Ohanian (Gardening Requisites
Section Head)

PRINCIPAL ACTIVITIES: Landscaping; land reclamation and
improvement; design and execution of irrigation network
systems; design, supply and installation of greenhouses;
marketing of agricultural tools and equipment; supply of
seeds, soil, fertilisers, insecticides & pesticides; etc
Principal Agencies: Goldoni, Italy; Sierra Chemical Europe,
Netherlands; Plastika Kritis, Greece; Strella Group, UK;
Lowara, Italy; Douven, Netherland; Hasad, Jordan; Arab Drip,
Jordan
Subsidiary Companies: Jordanian Kuwait Agricultural Products
Co
Principal Bankers: National Bank of Kuwait, Kuwait, Al Hamra,
& New York; Gulf Bank, Kuwait
Financial Information:

	1988/89 KD'000
Sales turnover	5,000
Authorised capital	5,000
Paid-up capital	5,000
Total assets	6,520

Principal Shareholders: Public Investment Authority, Kuwait
Date of Establishment: May 1982
No of Employees: 450

PAN ARAB CONSULTING ENGINEERS P.A.C.E.

PO Box 1031 Safat, 13011 Kuwait
Tel: 2669600
Cable: Shaura
Telex: 22141 PACE KT
Telefax: (965) 2656830

Partners: Sabah Al-Rayes, Hamid A Shuaib
Senior Executives: Hakam Jarrar (Technical Manager), Geoff
Pollitt (General Manager Bahrain Office), Shawkat Odeh
(Financial & Admin Manager), Kais Dakkak (Head of
Supervision), Raad Al Shedidi (Manager for International
Projects), Gretchen Addi (Chief Interior Designer), Richard
Hattersley (Chief Quantity Surveyor), Michael Gebhart (Chief
Architect), Wid Al Amer (Act Chief Mechanical Engineer),
Mohammed Sabbagh (Chief Public Health Engineer), Hoda El
Sayyad (Chief Electrical Engineer), Michael Nason (Chief
Landscape Architect), Sunil Manchanda (Act Chief Structural
Engineer), Essam Al Khawam (Head of Computer Dept), Ali Al
Saleh (Personnel & Purchasing Manager), Hilda Jubran (Office
Executive Manager)

PRINCIPAL ACTIVITIES: Architects, engineers and planners
Branch Offices: Bahrain: PO Box 10207, Manama; and in UAE:
PO Box 315, Abu Dhabi
Subsidiary Companies: Pace UK Ltd, Grosvenor Gardens
House, 35/37 Grosvenor Gardens, London SW1W 0BS, Tel
071-834 7743, Fax 071 8285543
Principal Bankers: Gulf Bank of Kuwait; Commercial Bank of
Kuwait; Bank of Kuwait & the Middle East
Financial Information:

	1989/90 KD'000
Sales turnover	3,014
Profits	220
Authorised capital	600
Paid-up capital	600
Total assets	6,079

Principal Shareholders: Partners: Hamid A Shuaib, Sabah Al
Rayes
Date of Establishment: 1968
No of Employees: 255

PAN ARAB GROUP

PO Box 20230 Safat, 13063 Kuwait
Tel: 2416667, 2443559, 2443614
Telex: 23560, 22696 Panarab KT

PRINCIPAL ACTIVITIES: General contracting and representation
Principal Agencies: ITT; Grinnell Corp; Calorstat Pathway; Toyo
Menka Kaisha; Gardner Denver etc
Subsidiary Companies: Pan Arab UKCON; Pan Arab Tighe; Pan
Arab Ineco; Pan Arab Equipment & Gen Contracting Co WLL;
Pan Arab Flight Safety (Middle East); Pan Arab & Axe Design
& Consultancy Services

PAN ARAB MANAGEMENT KSC

PO Box 2081 Safat, 13021 Kuwait
Tel: 2416637, 2419762, 2419759, 542354
Cable: PANAFIN
Telex: 22425 KT PANAFIN, 22673 Mars Kt

President: Sulaiman A Al Mutawa

PRINCIPAL ACTIVITIES: Financial and management
consultants, money brokers

PARTS INTERNATIONAL CO WLL

PO Box 671 Safat, 13007 Kuwait
Tel: 835485
Cable: Partinco
Telex: 22768 Ikonkar

Directors: Mohammad H Qabazard, Mrs K K Bhasin
Senior Executives: B P S Bhasin (General Manager)

PRINCIPAL ACTIVITIES: Import-export of foodstuffs and
textiles, automotive spare parts and accessories, batteries,
oils and lubricants, and industrial products also commission
agents and manufacturers' representatives
Principal Bankers: Alahli Bank of Kuwait; Burgan Bank; Gulf
Bank of Kuwait

Principal Shareholders: M H Qabazard, Mrs K K Bhasin
Date of Establishment: 1965
No of Employees: 32

PETROCHEMICAL INDUSTRIES CO KSC

PO Box 1084 Safat, 13011 Kuwait
Tel: 2448280, 2422141
Cable: Petrokima
Telex: 22024 KCFC Kt
Telefax: 2447159

Chairman: Abdul Baqi Al-Nouri (also Managing Director)
Directors: Hussain Ibrahim Al-Jasim (Deputy Chairman), Tawfiq
Al Gharabally (Member/Dy Managing Director for Finance &
Administration), Adnan Yousef Al-Meer (Member/Dy Managing
Director for Manufacturing), Salman Mulla Hussain (Member),
Jamal Al Refai (Member)
Senior Executives: Nasser Al Tukhaim (Marketing General
Manager), Ahmed Al Duaij (Operations Manager), Hamad Al
Moshwet (Operations Manager), Suleiman AL Dosary
(Finance Manager), Waleed Al Sani (Materials Manager),
Fahad Al Khodar (Admin Manager), Waleed Al Nifesi
(Company Secretary)

PRINCIPAL ACTIVITIES: Manufacture of nitrogenous fertiliser
and salt and chlorine industry derivitives (ammonia, urea,
ammonium sulphate, sulphuric acid, salt, chlorine, caustic
soda, hydrochloric acid, sodium hypochlorite, compressed
hydrogen, distilled water)
Subsidiary/Associated Companies: Fertilizer Division: PO Box
9116 Ahmadi, 61002 Kuwait, Telex KUFERTCO 44212, CROP
44206 KT, Tel 3260622, 3261544; Salt & Chlorine Division: PO
Box 10277 Shuaiba, Kuwait 65453, Telex 46925 SCCOM Kt.

Associates: Gulf Petrochemical Industries Co (33.3%) Bahrain;
In Turkey: Mediterranean Fertiliser Industries (47.25%);
Turkish Arab Fertiliser Co (25%); In China: Sino Arab
Chemical Fertiliser Co Ltd (30%)
Principal Bankers: Kuwait National Bank; Bank of Kuwait and
the Middle East; Commercial Bank of Kuwait; Al Ahli Bank of
Kuwait; Burgan Bank; Gulf Bank
Financial Information:

	1988/89 KD'000
Sales turnover	29,730
Profits	303
Authorised capital	130,000
Paid-up capital	112,484
Total assets	137,978

Principal Shareholders: Kuwait Government 100%
Date of Establishment: July 1963
No of Employees: 1,608

PETROLEUM SERVICES CO WLL

PO Box 4098 Safat, 13041 Kuwait
Tel: 4732303, 4732304, 4732218, 4732318
Cable: Field
Telex: 46475 PETSERV KT, 46476 SBESCO KT
Telefax: 4732762

Chairman: Bader Sultan Al Essa
Directors: Abdullah Sultan Al Essa (Managing Director)
Senior Executives: Azzam Rafiq Al Masri (Finance & Admin
Director), Hatem Shaka'a (Sales Manager)

PRINCIPAL ACTIVITIES: Commision agents for manufacturers,
contractors for the supply of material and service for the oil,
power and the allied industries
Principal Agencies: Solar Turbine; Byron Jackson; Flexibox;
Turbodine, Dresser, etc
Parent Company: Sultan Ben Essa Sons Co Ltd
Principal Bankers: Gulf Bank of Kuwait

Principal Shareholders: Bader Sultan Al-Essa, Khaled Sultan Al
Essa, Anwar Sultan Al-Essa, Jameel Sultan Al-Essa,
Mohammad Sultan Al-Essa, Faisal Sultan Al-Essa, Abdullah
Sultan Al-Essa, Abdul Aziz Sultan Al-Essa
Date of Establishment: 1967
No of Employees: 38

PIRELLI CONSTRUCTION CO

PO Box 179 Safat, 13002 Kuwait
Tel: 5635512, 5632825, 5621718
Telex: 44794 PCCO KT

PRINCIPAL ACTIVITIES: Cable supply and installation services
Parent Company: Pirelli Construction, UK

POLYGLASS FACTORY

PO Box 3525 Safat, 13036 Kuwait
Tel: 4819834, 4835451
Telex: 22370 Kisco KT
Telefax: 4848310

Directors: Suleiman A Al Qudabi, Ali Redah Kolaghassi
Senior Executives: Eng Bassam Al Madani (Technical Manager)

PRINCIPAL ACTIVITIES: Manufacture of FRP water tanks,
boats, FRP furniture products, fiberglass panels, sun
breakers, foam coating and insulation work, etc
Principal Bankers: Commercial Bank of Kuwait, National Bank
of Kuwait, Bank of Kuwait & the Middle East
Financial Information:

	1989 KD'000
Sales turnover	1,000
Profits	100
Authorised capital	250
Paid-up capital	250
Total assets	2,500

Principal Shareholders: Directors as described
Date of Establishment: 1968
No of Employees: 80

PORTS PUBLIC AUTHORITY

PO Box 3874 Safat, Shuwaikh, 13039 Kuwait
Tel: 4812622
Telex: 22740 HMSHP KT
Telefax: 4830284, 4819714

Chairman: Issa Al Mazidi
Directors: Ibrahim Makki (Director General)
Senior Executives: Bader Al Rashud (Asst Director General-
Shuwaikh Port Affairs), A R Al Naibari (Asst Director General-
Shuaiba Port Affairs), Mohamed Ibrahim (Administration
Director), Eng Nouri A Al Saad (P & R Director), Tariq Al
Ziyab (Director of Computer Information Centre)

PRINCIPAL ACTIVITIES: Port authority and services
Principal Bankers: Central Bank of Kuwait

Date of Establishment: 1977
No of Employees: 2,975

PUBLIC WAREHOUSING CO

PO Box 25418 Safat, 13115 Kuwait
Tel: 2439783, 2425049 (5 lines)
Telex: 4119 Makhazan

Chairman: Abdul Aziz Al-Mutair
Senior Executives: Nasser Al-Rashed (Deputy General
Manager), Qais M Al-Nisf

PRINCIPAL ACTIVITIES: Building, renting and operating
warehouses
Subsidiary Companies: Link Transportation Co
Principal Bankers: Burgan Bank

Date of Establishment: 1979
No of Employees: 69

QABAZARD MARINE EQUIPMENT CO WLL

PO Box 1660 Safat, 13017 Kuwait
Tel: 4818817, 4849339, 5746579
Cable: Jasmin
Telex: 23624 Jasmin Kt
Telefax: 4837148, 5746578

Chairman: Jassim Qabazard
Directors: Abdul Majeed Qabazard

PRINCIPAL ACTIVITIES: Supply of marine and offshore
equipment, diving equipment, also scuba diving course
Principal Agencies: Technibub; Waterline; Simpson Lawrence;
Aifomotori FIAT; ITT Jabsco Pumps; GEC diesels; Kanab
Water Slides; Surf Partner; etc
Branch Offices: Showrooms: Shuwaikh, Tel 4849339; Salmiyah,
Tel 5746579
Parent Company: Mohammad Qabazard & Sons Co
Principal Bankers: Al Ahli Bank of Kuwait

Date of Establishment: 1955
No of Employees: 30

REAL ESTATE CONSTRUCTION & FABRICATION CO SAK (C)
R.E.C.A.F.C.O.

PO Box 24478 Safat, 13105 Kuwait
Tel: 3260054, 3262405, 3262582
Cable: Precast
Telex: 44248 Fabcret
Telefax: 3260067

Chairman: Abdul Aziz Al Abdulrazzak
Directors: Abdul Aziz Faisal Al Zaban (Deputy Chairman),
Abdullah Saud Al Abdulrazzak, Adel Yacoub Al Nafisi, Abdulla
Khalid Al Sumait, Abdul Majeed Mohamed Hussain Qabazard,
Saad Aref Al Suwaidi (Financial Counsellor)

Senior Executives: Muwafaq Elias (General Manager Technical
& Operations), Fazil K Al Abdul Razzak (General Manager
Admin & Finance), Natesan Chokkalingam (Factory Manager),
Khalid Ghali (Construction Manager), J L Khanna (Financial
Controller), Dhia Jaffer (Marketing Engineer)

PRINCIPAL ACTIVITIES: Precast concrete manufacture and
contracting
Principal Bankers: Commercial Bank of Kuwait, Al Ahli Bank of
Kuwait
Financial Information:

	1989
	KD'000
Authorised capital	2,000
Paid-up capital	1,900

Date of Establishment: 1977
No of Employees: 300

REFRIGERATION INDUSTRIES CO SAK
PO Box 22261 Safat, 13083 Kuwait
Tel: 4835804, 4835819, 4835779
Telex: 44809 Tabrid KT
Telefax: 4835809

Chairman: Mishari Abdulrahman Al-Bahar (also Managing
Director)
Directors: Yacoub Yousef Al-Juan (Vice-Chairman), Abdul Hadi
Al-Awadi, Faisal A Al-Kazemi, Bader Al-Farsi, Abdul Aziz
Yousef Al Flaij, Fawzi Abdul Rahman Al Joader, Mohamed
Ibrahim Al Rukayes
Senior Executives: Abdullah Al-Najadah (General Manager),
Mohammed Zeraie (Deputy General Manager), Qais Al Nisf
(Admin & Finance Manager), Qassim Abu Hijleh (Project
Manager), Adnan Awad (Marketing Manager), Adel Saad
(Sales Engineer), Mohammed Ramadan (Cold Stores Div
Manager), Tahir Khan (Maintenance Manager), R K Guha
(Acting Division Manager)

PRINCIPAL ACTIVITIES: Owners & operators of cold stores
with all other associated services, and manufacturing of
central air-conditioning equipment and mini split units
Principal Agencies: Manufacturing Central Air-conditioning
equipment under license from York, USA
Branch Offices: Shuwaikh Harbour cold store, Airconditioning
Factory at Sulabiyah
Subsidiary Companies: Kuwait Catering Co, United Gulf Bank,
Gulf Link Transportation Co, Industry Investment Co
Principal Bankers: All banks in Kuwait
Financial Information:

	1988/89
	KD'000
Sales turnover	5,217
Profits	1,801
Authorised capital	6,686
Paid-up capital	6,686
Total assets	19,231

Principal Shareholders: Public Shareholding Company
Date of Establishment: 1973
No of Employees: 555

REZAYAT TRADING COMPANY
Alireza Group of Companies
PO Box 106 Safat, 13002 Kuwait
Tel: 4816836, 4843535, 4840161, 4840163, 4842022
Cable: Rezayat
Telex: 22070 Rezayat Kt; 22962 Nalco Kt
Telefax: 4831030

Chairman: Abdulla Alireza
Directors: Teymour Abdulla Alireza (President), Fahd Abdulla
Alireza (Vice President)
Group Senior Executives: Noble Dreghorn (Group Finance
Director), James H N Gibson (Group General Manager - Saudi
Arabia), Ma'an Wafai (Group General Manager - Kuwait)

PRINCIPAL ACTIVITIES: Importers, exporters and
manufacturers' agents; the Alireza Group deals with trading,
industrial catering, hotels and motels, mechanical and
electrical engineering, trucking and plant hire, transport,
shipping and container services, pipe and structural steel
fabrication, building and construction, hospitals operation and
maintenance
Principal Agencies: BICC Ltd, UK; British Steel Corp, UK;
Northern Engineering Ind Ltd, UK; Badger Ltd, UK; Graham
Manufacturing Ltd, UK; Vokes Ltd, UK; GH Zeal Ltd, UK;
British Ropes Ltd, UK; Anderson-Greenwood, USA; Babcock
& Wilcox Co, USA; Alfa-Laval AB, Sweden; Hagen Int,
Denmark; RP Adam Chemical Products, UK; Stilwell Int Corp,
USA; Aqua-Chem Inc, USA; Du Pont, Switzerland; Union
Carbide, Dubai
Branch Offices: Alkhobar, Riyadh, Jeddah, London, Paris and
Houston
Subsidiary/Associated Companies: Rezayat Europe Ltd, 52
Mount St, London W1Y 5RE, UK; Rezayat Co Ltd, PO Box
90, Alkhobar, PO Box 996, Riyadh, and PO Box 6670,
Jeddah, Saudi Arabia; Rezayat Europe Ltd, 34 Avenue
George V, Paris 75008, France; National Contracting Co Ltd,
PO Box 60, Safat, Kuwait; Rezayat America Inc, Houston,
Texas 77056, USA
Principal Bankers: Bank of Kuwait and the Middle East, Kuwait;
British Bank of the Middle East, London; Saudi International
Bank, London; Manufacturers Hanover Trust Co, New York;
Union Bank of Switzerland, Switzerland

Principal Shareholders: Abdulla Alireza and his family members
Date of Establishment: 1948
No of Employees: 2,650 (30 in Kuwait)

ROLLS ROYCE INTERNATIONAL SA
PO Box 34073, 73251 Udailiyah, Kuwait
Tel: 5641972
Telex: 23889 Bestcar Kt

PRINCIPAL ACTIVITIES: Motor cars, service and parts
distribution, and promotion

SABA & CO
PO Box 1245 Safat, 13013 Kuwait
Tel: 438060
Cable: Sabaco Kuwait
Telex: 22111 Kwt

PRINCIPAL ACTIVITIES: Public accountants, management and
industrial property consultants
Branch Offices: Cyprus; Algeria; Bahrain; Egypt; Iraq; Jordan:
Kuwait; Libya; Morocco; Oman; Qatar; Saudi Arabia; Syria;
Yemen
Parent Company: Head office in Lebanon

SABAA CONTRACTING & CONSTRUCTION EST
PO Box 3939 Safat, 13040 Kuwait
Tel: 816330, 816770
Cable: Namashi
Telex: 22567 Namashi Kt

Chairman: Abdulwahab Saleh Al-Namash
Directors: Edmund John Rodrigues

PRINCIPAL ACTIVITIES: Trading agents, shuttering, falseworks,
concrete accessories; sub-contractors for concrete works
Principal Agencies: Construvit Ltd, Switzerland; Reuss GmbH,
West Germany; Euco Bauchemie, Switzerland
Branch Offices: Concrete Chemical Materials Co WLL
(Eucokwah)
Associated Companies: Al-Muhalab Trading & Contracting Co
Principal Bankers: Gulf Bank; Burgan Bank

Date of Establishment: 1974

SAFEWAY

PO Box 23828 Safat, 13099 Kuwait
Tel: 4811731, 48112731, 4811657
Cable: Safeway
Telex: 30546 Safway KT
Telefax: 4811643

Chairman: Khalifa Al Kharafi
Directors: Ossama Roshdy (General Manager)
Senior Executives: Moataz El Rafie (Finance Manager), Hatem Noweir (Sales Manager), William Tan (Operations Manager), Nasser Rahman (Purchasing Manager), Nagi Wali (Personnel Manager), Ali Nour El Din (EDP Manager)

PRINCIPAL ACTIVITIES: General trading, department store, supply of foodstuffs & dairy products, household goods & appliances, cosmetics & toiletries, garments, etc
Principal Agencies: Linde AG
Parent Company: Kuwait Food Company (Americana)
Principal Bankers: National Bank of Kuwait, Commercial Bank of Kuwait
Financial Information:

	1988/89
	US$'000
Authorised capital	35,700
Paid-up capital	14,280
Total assets	26,300

Date of Establishment: 1980
No of Employees: 340

SAFWAN TRADING & CONTRACTING ENTERPRISES

PO Box 20704 Safat, 13068 Kuwait
Tel: 8832017, 816488
Cable: Vibra Kuwait
Telex: 22112 Kt Cisco, 44569 Kt Sapharm

President: Hani Jamil Qaddumi
Senior Executives: Saad Qaddumi (Pharmaceutical Div), Usama A T Sharif (Pharmaceutical Div), Muzaffar Hasan (Commercial Div), Dr Nabil Qaddumi (Contracting Div)

PRINCIPAL ACTIVITIES: Wholesale and retail of pharmaceuticals and cosmetics, hospital and medical equipment; and supply to the oil refining industry of filtration and temperature sensing equipment, meteorological instruments, submergible pumps, civil and mechanical engineering contractors
Principal Agencies: May & Baker Ltd, UK; Warner-Lambert Group, USA; Pfizer Corp; Alcon Universal Group; Smith & Nephew Group; Hudson Products Corp, USA; Berol Kemi AB, Sweden; BYK Chemie GmBH, W Germany; TRW Reda Pump Co, USA; Degussa, W Germany; Parke Davis; Novo Industrie; American Optical Corp; Pall Trinity Micro Corp; Advanced Heat Technology Corp; Oil Skimmers; Montenay, France; Haver & Boecker, Germany; Van Swaay Int, Holland; PCI Polychemie, Germany; Alkor GmbH, Germany
Associated Companies: Chemical & Industrial Supplies Co, Kuwait and Sharjah (UAE); William Abou Kalil, Lebanon, Syria and Jordan
Principal Bankers: Commercial Bank of Kuwait; Bank of Kuwait and the Middle East

Principal Shareholders: Hani Qaddumi (Sole Owner)
Date of Establishment: 1963
No of Employees: 60

SALEH JAMAL & CO WLL

See JAMAL, SALEH, & CO WLL

SALEM AL MALIK'S SONS CO

See AL MALIK'S, SALEM, SONS CO

SALEM AL-MARZOUK & SABAH ABI-HANNA WLL

See AL-MARZOUK, SALEM, & SABAH ABI-HANNA WLL

SALHIA REAL ESTATE CO SAK

PO Box 23413 Safat, 13095 Kuwait
Tel: 2421260 (5 lines)
Cable: SAHREALTY
Telex: 22789 SAREC KT
Telefax: 2426606

Chairman: Ghazi Fahad Alnafisi (and Managing Director)
Directors: Salah F Almarzook (Vice Chairman), Hasan Abdulla Al-Mousa (Member) Abdul Aziz Sauod Al-Babtain (Member), Abdulrazak Yusuf Al-Khamees (Member), Anwar Abdul Aziz Al-Usaimi (Member), Faisal Abdul Rahman Al-Shayji (Member), Faisal Abdul Mohsen Al-Khatrash (Member), Abdullatif Abdul Kareem Al-Menies (Member)
Senior Executives: Ahmed M Boodai (Executive Manager), Jawad Mohammad Barakat (Deputy General Manager)

PRINCIPAL ACTIVITIES: Property and real estate investment and hotel owners
Subsidiary Companies: Meridien Kuwait Hotel
Principal Bankers: Commercial Bank of Kuwait; Burgan Bank; National Bank of Kuwait; Bank of Kuwait & Middle East; Gulf Bank
Financial Information:

	1989
	KD'000
Sales turnover	5,500
Authorised capital	19,200
Paid-up capital	19,200
Total assets	59,000

Principal Shareholders: Kuwait International Investment Co; Ghazi F Alnafisi, Marzouk Al Abdulwahab Al Marzouk, Faisal Saoud Al Zaben, Commercial Bank of Kuwait, Gulf Insurance Co
Date of Establishment: 16th September 1974
No of Employees: 500

SANITARY WARE CO SAK

PO Box 21999 Safat, 13080 Kuwait
Tel: 443088, 445080
Telex: 22721 Sanaware KT

Chairman: Faisal Saoud Al Fulaij

PRINCIPAL ACTIVITIES: Production and distribution of sanitary ware equipment

SAS KUWAIT HOTEL

PO Box 26199 Safat, 13122 Kuwait
Tel: 5657000
Cable: Sashotl
Telex: 44306 SASHOTL KT
Telefax: 5652999

Senior Executives: Werner Kuendig (General Manager), Steinar Bergvoll (Director of Sales), Jorgen Rathjen (Executive Asst Manager)

PRINCIPAL ACTIVITIES: Hotel business
Parent Company: SAS International Hotels

Principal Shareholders: The Marafie Group, Wara Real Estate Co Kuwait
Date of Establishment: 1980
No of Employees: 310

SAUD & IBRAHIM ABDULRAZAK TRADING & CONTRACTING CO

See ABDULRAZAK, SAUD & IBRAHIM, TRADING & CONTRACTING CO

SAUD AUJAN & BROS CO WLL
See AUJAN, SAUD, & BROS CO WLL

SAVINGS & CREDIT BANK
PO Box 1454 Safat, 13015 Kuwait
Tel: 2411301
Telex: 22211 Kt

Chairman: Abdul Razzaq Al-Askar
Directors: Yousef Ali Al-Houti, Ikab M Al-Khatib, Khaled Al Saleh, Ahmad Kh Al-Fouzan, Barrak A Al-Turki, Khalid S Al-Atiqui, Abdul Razak A Al-Asker, Abdul Latil Al Birjes, Ali Yousef Jamal, Abdul Rahman Al-Humeimidi
Senior Executives: Yousef Ali Al-Houti (General Manager)

PRINCIPAL ACTIVITIES: Real estate, agricultural and social credit, investments, savings
Branch Offices: Al-Ahmadi Branch

Principal Shareholders: Public institution
Date of Establishment: 1965
No of Employees: 400

SAYED ALI SAYED AWAZ
See AWAZ, SAYED ALI SAYED,

SAYER, NASER, & CO WLL
PO Box 186 Safat, 13002 Kuwait
Tel: 2421301, 2441031, 2441034
Cable: Nasersayer
Telex: 22392 Nesreen Kt

Chairman: Bader Abdulla Al Suhaim
Directors: Naser Mohd Naser Al Sayer, Abdul Rahman Abdul Mughni

PRINCIPAL ACTIVITIES: General trading and contracting, supply of building materials, hardware, sanitary ware, power equipment, household equipment, cables and wires, diesel engines
Principal Agencies: Josiah Parkes, UK; Makita Electric Works, Japan; Orient General Industries, India; Enfield India, India; Intersigma, Czechoslovakia; Serampore Industries, India; Osaka Seimitsu Electric, Japan
Branch Offices: PO Box 1825, Dubai, UAE, Telex 45825
Principal Bankers: Commercial Bank of Kuwait; National Bank of Kuwait

Principal Shareholders: Directors as described
Date of Establishment: 1954
No of Employees: 25

SAYID RAJAB AL RIFAI
See AL RIFAI, SAYID RAJAB,

SEALOL KUWAIT KSC
PO Box 46833, Fahaheel, 64019 Kuwait
Tel: 3984964, 3983457
Telex: 44287 Kt Sealol
Telefax: 3988517

Chairman: Mushari Al Baddah
Senior Executives: Abdul Ghafoor Munawar (General Manager)

PRINCIPAL ACTIVITIES: Manufacturers & reconditioners of mechanical seals, welded metal bellows devices, diaphragm couplings, bolt tensioning equipment & lapping machines
Principal Agencies: GKN Pilgrim Systems, UK, Lawrence Ind, UK
Branch Offices: Sealol, Jeddah, Saudi Arabia, Tel 6828206
Parent Company: EG&G Sealol Inc, USA
Associated Companies: Sealol Inc, USA; Sealol Europe SARL, France; Sealol GmbH, Germany; Sealol SpA, Italy; Eagle Industry Co Ltd, Tokyo; Sealol Ltd, UK
Principal Bankers: Gulf Bank, Kuwait; Kuwait Finance House; Commercial Bank of Kuwait

Financial Information:

	1989 US$'000
Sales turnover	1,200
Authorised capital	310
Paid-up capital	310
Total assets	1,110

Principal Shareholders: Kuwaiti Individuals (51%), EG&G Inc, USA (49%)
Date of Establishment: 1975
No of Employees: 20

SHAIKHAN AHMAD ALFARSI
See ALFARSI, SHAIKHAN AHMAD,

SHEZA TRADING CO LTD
PO Box 25155 Safat, 13112 Kuwait
Tel: 2422443, 2436959
Telex: 23732 Sheza Kt

Chairman: Asghar Ali Taj
Senior Executives: S Khalil (Manager)

PRINCIPAL ACTIVITIES: Import, export, wholesale and manufacturers' representation for leather products, gift articles, electronic watches, cameras, binoculars, perfumes
Principal Bankers: Gulf Bank KSC

SROUR TRADING CLEARING & FORWARDING CO WLL
PO Box 1468 Safat, 13015 Kuwait
Tel: 2433771, 2436211
Cable: Tarrad Co
Telex: 22490 Srour Kt

Directors: G N Tarrous Abu-Zoloff (Managing Director), Ahmad Y Nasrullah

PRINCIPAL ACTIVITIES: Trading, custom clearing, forwarding, transport
Principal Bankers: National Bank of Kuwait

SULTAN BIN ESSA SONS CO LTD
PO Box 4098 Safat, 13041 Kuwait
Tel: 4332555
Telex: 46476 SBESCO Kt
Telefax: 4332762, 4334217

Chairman: Bader Sultan Al Essa
Directors: Azzam Al Masri (Director Administration & Finance)
Senior Executives: Malek Mushtaq Ahmed (Manager Special Projects)

PRINCIPAL ACTIVITIES: Electronics, property, transport services
Subsidiary Companies: Bader Sultan & Bros Co; Petroleum Services Co; Sultan Center
Principal Bankers: Gulf Bank

Principal Shareholders: Bader Sultan, Faisal Sultan, Mohd Sultan, Khalid Sultan, Abdulaziz Sultan, Abdullah Sultan, Anwar Sultan, Jamil Sultan
Date of Establishment: 1974

SUPPLY & BUILDING COMPANY
PO Box 901 Safat, 13010 Kuwait
Tel: 814188 (12 lines)
Cable: Byblos Kuwait
Telex: 22509 Byblos
Telefax: (965) 4848772

Directors: Omar Bakir (Managing Director)
Senior Executives: Yehia Bakir (Chief Engineer Contracting Div), Jamal L Nahas (General Manager - Commercial Div), Sami Bakir (General Manager -Kitcherama Div), Rajeh Qunaibi (General Admin Manager), Ali Qatanani (Chief Accountant), Ali Saras (Financial Analyst)

PRINCIPAL ACTIVITIES: Civil and mechanical contractors, including offshore works; suppliers and erectors of commercial kitchen and laundry equipment; distributors of consumers' items (cosmetics, perfumes, cigarettes, confectionery, food items); retailers of clothing, footwear, gift items, leather goods

Principal Agencies: Centerline Co (for lining inner walls of pipes), Evergreen Helicopter Inc, Sumac Co (for offshore works); Zanussi Grandi Impianti, Ice-O-Matic, W M Cissel, Electro Dahlen, Wodschow, Jet spray, Frymaster, Traulsen; Estee Lauder, Unilever, Beecham, Trussardi, Lancetti, Ermenegildo Zeqna, Testoni, Christian Dior, Quintessence, Houbigant, Proteo, Christian Breton, Eagle Snacks, Hershey Int'l

Branch Offices: Retail Stores; Versailles, Salmiya; Byblos, 5 stores in Kuwait; Byblos House of Leather; Byblos Center; Kitcherama

Principal Bankers: Commercial Bank of Kuwait; Bank of Kuwait & the Middle East; Alahli Bank of Kuwait; National Bank of Kuwait

Financial Information:

	1989 US$'000
Paid-up capital & reserves	10,000

Principal Shareholders: Hissa Mohamad Al Marzook, Omar Bakir
Date of Establishment: 1956
No of Employees: 400

TALAL ABU GHAZALEH INTERNATIONAL

PO Box 4628 Safat, 13047 Kuwait
Tel: 2433004
Cable: Tagco
Telex: 30849 Tagco Kt
Telefax: 2440111

Chairman: Talal T Abu-Ghazaleh
Directors: Nazmi M Al Badawi (Vice Chairman), Dr Nabil S Faour, Munir H Al Borno, Tawfiq Ayoub, Monther Hammoudeh, Mahmoud Adileh, Mohammad Kalouti
Partners: Talal Abu-Ghazaleh, Nazmi M Al Badawi, Anwar Al Qatami, Akram Al Kadi, Dr Nabil S Faour, Munir H Al Borno, Tawfiq Ayoub, Akram El Husseini, Mahmoud Adileh, Amin Samara, Mohamed Al Kalouti, Nabil Suleiman, Fouad Khalil

PRINCIPAL ACTIVITIES: Audit, taxation and company formation; consultancy services: management, financial, industrial, business and economic; trade mark & patent registrations, project & patent registrations, project & investment bank advisory services, etc

Branch Offices: Regional Office in Amman, Chairman's Office in Kuwait and branches in Riyadh, Jeddah, Dammam, Jubail, Al-Ahssa, Doha, Manama, Abu-Dhabi, Dubai, Sharjah, Ras Al-Khaimah, Ajman, Muscat, Salalah, Sana'a, Hodeida, Taaz, Aden, Beirut, Cairo, Baghdad, Irbid, Algiers, Casablanca, Damascus, Nouakchott, Mogadishu, Tripoli, Tunis and Paris, New York, Switzerland, London and Luxembourg

Subsidiary/Associated Companies: Talal Abu Ghazaleh & Co (TAGCO); Talal Abu Ghazaleh Associates Ltd (TAGA); TMP Agents; Arab International Projects Co (AIPC); Abu Ghazaleh & Co Consulting (AGCOC); Al Dar Consulting Co (ADCO), First Project Management Co (FIPMAC); Saudi Arabia Projects Co (SAPCO); International Translation Center (ITC); Arab Bureau for Legal Services (ABLE)

Financial Information:

	1989 US$'000
Paid-up capital	10,000

Principal Shareholders: Chairman and directors as described
Date of Establishment: July 1972

TAREQ AL ESSA TRADING & CONTRACTING CO WLL

See AL ESSA, TAREQ, TRADING & CONTRACTING CO WLL

TECHNICAL APPLIANCES CO LTD

PO Box 5648 Safat, 13057 Kuwait
Tel: 2422259/60
Cable: Tart
Telex: 22241 Tac Kt

Chairman: Khalid Al Hassan
Directors: K I Shaheen (President)
Senior Executives: Farouk Al Hindi (Finance & Admin Manager), Nasser Al Hasan (Manager Office Automation Dept), Ibrahim Shaheen (Manager Consumer Products Dept)

PRINCIPAL ACTIVITIES: Dealing with all types of electrical, electronic, and telecommunication equipment
Principal Agencies: Sharp Corporation, Richard Hirschmann, Portacel Ltd, Sentinel Computers Inc, Aerotron Inc, Giesecke & Devrient, Iwatsu Electric Co, American District Telegraph
Subsidiary Companies: Technical Appliances International, Japan
Principal Bankers: Commercial Bank of Kuwait; National Bank of Kuwait
Financial Information:

	KD'000
Sales turnover	3,000
Authorised capital	1,000
Paid-up capital	1,000

Date of Establishment: 1968
No of Employees: 110

TECHNICAL STUDIES BUREAU

PO Box 2399 Safat, 13024 Kuwait
Tel: 2431754
Cable: Testbureau
Telex: 23784 Study KT

PRINCIPAL ACTIVITIES: Planners, architects and engineering consultants
Branch Offices: Saudi Arabia, Dubai, Oman

TECHNOLOGY AIDED SYSTEMS KUWAIT (TASK) WLL

PO Box 1367 Safat, 13014 Kuwait
Tel: 2421531, 2414740
Telex: 44770 COMTASK KT
Telefax: 2458742

Chairman: Faisal S Al Fozan (Managing Director)
Directors: Sabah Alghunaim
Senior Executives: Victor El Tawil (Operations Manager), John M John (Administration Manager), Brian E Ballagh (Marketing Manager)

PRINCIPAL ACTIVITIES: Data and wordprocessing, hardware maintenance and repair of all products, engineering services and training centre
Principal Agencies: Microdata UK Ltd; AES Data Ltd; Micom Borer; Micro Five; Telex Computer Products; Bankers Box; Actronics; Xios Europe; Memorex Telex

Date of Establishment: 1977

TEDKU LTD

PO Box 1405 Safat, 13015 Kuwait
Tel: 2434973, 2435346, 2433685
Cable: Tedku Kuwait

Chairman: H Abdullah Ben-Nekhi
Directors: Abdullah H Ben-Nekhi
Senior Executives: John Varghese (Import Manager), M Khalil (Sales Manager)

PRINCIPAL ACTIVITIES: Dealing in woollen goods, household furniture, carpets
Principal Agencies: Hield Brothers Ltd, Scabal, E Gomme Ltd
Principal Bankers: National Bank of Kuwait

Date of Establishment: 1958

TNT SKYPAK INTERNATIONAL (KUWAIT) WLL

PO Box 23959 Safat, 13100 Kuwait
Tel: 2454125, 2454126, 2463220, 2463221, 2465160
Cable: ALKATRAVEL
Telex: 44524 KT

Chairman: Diya Al Kazemi
Senior Executives: Tim Frank (General Manager)

PRINCIPAL ACTIVITIES: Worldwide courier service, collection, clearance and delivery of documents and commercial value items
Subsidiary/Associated Companies: TNT Skypak International operates in countries in Middle East and the rest of the world
Principal Shareholders: Al Kazemi Travel; TNT Skypak International
Date of Establishment: January 1981

TOURISTIC ENTERPRISES CO KSC (TEC)

PO Box 22310 Safat, 13084 Kuwait
Tel: 2412060
Cable: Tec
Telex: 22801 Trentco KT

Chairman: Abdulla Yousuf Abdul Aziz Al Qatami (also Managing Director); Deputy Chairman: Mohammed Saoud Al Dakheel (also General Manager)
Directors: Ahmad Hamza Mustafa, Abdul Wahab Rashid Al Haroon, Ali Abbas Al Abdullah, Abdul Rahman Yusif Al Mazrooei, Sami Fahid Al Ibrahim, Fisal Babir Al Tahous
Senior Executives: Ibrahim Al Samhan (Administration), Faisal Al Houti (Finance), Sulaiman Al Aoun (Training), Faisal Al Sharhan (Kuwait Towers), Khalid Al Mishri (Ice Skating Rink), Adel Al Fahed (Entertainment City), Abdul Hadi Yacoub (Sea Clubs), Sadiq Al Sargini (Failaka), Rashid Ibn Amara (Kheran Project), Abdul Wahab Taher (Marine), Mohamed Al Barges (Public Relations)

PRINCIPAL ACTIVITIES: To promote tourism and leisure projects in Kuwait

Principal Shareholders: 92% owned by Government of Kuwait; 8% owned by Kuwait Hotel Co, Kuwait Airways and Kuwait Real Estate Co
Date of Establishment: April 1976
No of Employees: 1387

TOWELL CONSTRUCTION CO LTD

PO Box 2560 Safat, 13026 Kuwait
Tel: 2436164, 2436169
Cable: Towell Kuwait
Telex: 23494 Towell Kt

Directors: Haji Ali Sultan, A H Forsyth, Maqbool Ali Sultan, R N Banerjee, S R Roessler

PRINCIPAL ACTIVITIES: Building and civil engineering contractors, construction of concrete domes for storage and handling of grains, maintenance and operation of completed facilities, utilities network
Branch Offices: PO Box 42612, Riyadh, Saudi Arabia, Tel 4657770, Telex 201989
Subsidiary Companies: Saudi Towell Construction Co Ltd, PO Box 42612, Riyadh, Saudi Arabia
Principal Bankers: Lloyd's Bank International, Bahrain; National Commercial Bank, Riyadh; Al Bahrain Arab African Bank, Bahrain; Alahli Bank, Kuwait; Rafidain Bank, Baghdad

Principal Shareholders: W J Towell & Co Agencies (Kuwait) WLL Kuwait; SEA Consultants 1973 Ltd, Hong Kong
Date of Establishment: January 1976
No of Employees: 700

TOWELL, W J, & CO AGENCIES (KUWAIT) WLL

PO Box 75 Safat, 13001 Kuwait
Tel: 4738732, 4738745, 4738311
Cable: Towell Kuwait
Telex: 23816 Towell Kt, 22096 Towell Kt
Telefax: 4739260

Chairman: Hussain Jawad Mohd Ali Abdul Rasosol
Directors: Tawfiq A Sultan (Managing Director), Murtadha A Sultan, Mohamed Ali A A Sultan, Mrs Sameera A A Sultan
Senior Executives: Jamil A Sultan, Mustafa A Sultan

PRINCIPAL ACTIVITIES: General trading and contracting, construction, telecommunication, computers, building materials, prefabricated housing, general merchandise (foodstuffs, clothing, toiletries and cigarettes)
Principal Agencies: R J Reynolds Tobacco; Hanes; Hochland; Bahlsen; Sultan Tea; Elizabeth Arden; Lagerfeld; Kohinoor Chemicals
Branch Offices: Oman, Dubai, Germany
Subsidiary Companies: Sultan Furnishing Co; Northern Gulf Trading Co; Gulf Transport; Middle East Telecommunications; Towell Construction; Gulf Cleaning & Contracting Co; Kuwait Snacks Production Co; Towell Tiles Co; Towell Computer Services
Principal Bankers: Burgan Bank; Commercial Bank of Kuwait; Gulf Bank; Bank of Kuwait and the Middle East
Financial Information:

	1989
	KD'000
Authorised capital	7,000
Paid-up capital	7,000

Principal Shareholders: Heirs of Qamar Sultan; Ali Sultan; Hussain Jawad; Heirs of Ahmed Sultan; Heirs of Abdul Amir Sultan
Date of Establishment: 1947
No of Employees: 350

TRADING & INDUSTRIAL EQUIPMENT CO (WLL)

PO Box 2159 Safat, 13022 Kuwait
Tel: 819179, 819188
Cable: Success
Telex: 22224 Kwt

Senior Executives: Yousef A Shurrab (Accountant), Faisal Al Kasadi (Sales Manager)

PRINCIPAL ACTIVITIES: Import and distribution of heavy machinery, construction equipment, earth-moving equipment, welding equipment, and agricultural machinery; well drilling equipment; etc
Principal Agencies: Lincoln (Australia); Pettibone; Ingersoll-Rand; American Hoist; Perkins; Cifa; Massey-Ferguson; Pingon
Branch Offices: Dubai (PO Box 5291, Deira)
Principal Bankers: National Bank of Kuwait

Principal Shareholders: Heirs of Mohd Yousuf Al Nisef; Heirs of Abdul Latif Al Nisef; Shukri Hanna Shammas
Date of Establishment: 1964
No of Employees: 95

UNION TRADING CO WLL

PO Box 28 Safat, 13001 Kuwait
Tel: 2423351, 2423360
Cable: Tradecoy Kuwait
Telex: 22202 Utc Kt
Telefax: 2410261

Chairman: Sayyid Abdur Razzaq Razzuqi
Senior Executives: Talal Razooqi (General Manager), Dimitri Anagnostaras (Deputy Manager)

PRINCIPAL ACTIVITIES: Import and distribution of consumers goods and electrical appliances; wholesale and department stores

Principal Agencies: General Corporation, Japan; General Foods International, USA/UK; Braun AG, W Germany; Gillette Industries, UK; Bourjois, France; Busterbrown Textiles; Yardley, UK; Cannon Mills, USA; BIC, France; Shulton, UK; Glem Gas, Italy; Lee, USA; Morphy Richards, UK; Prestige, UK; Sanford, USA; Stedman, USA; Jockey, USA; Tootal, UK; Vileda, W Germany

Principal Bankers: National Bank of Kuwait

Principal Shareholders: Sayid Abdul Razzaq Razzuqi, Daniel Bashir Hasso

Date of Establishment: 1949

No of Employees: 635

UNITED ARAB CONTRACTORS CO (UNARCO)

PO Box 2313 Safat, 13024 Kuwait
Tel: 4747712/3, 4747960/1/2
Cable: UNARCO KUWAIT
Telex: 22892 UNARCO KT

Directors: Khalil Ghattas Sarraf

Senior Executives: Bashir Owaijan (Financial & Administration Manager), Ibrahim Mohanna (Chief Engineer - Road Divn), Hani Farah (Area Manager -Bldg. Divn), Hamed Saleh (Manager - Equipment & Garage), Fairoz Miller (Technical Manager)

PRINCIPAL ACTIVITIES: Construction and maintenance of asphalt paved roads, RC bridges, box culverts, storm water drains, sanitary sewers, water distribution network, electrical and telephone, ducts crossing etc, construction and maintenance of multi-storey buildings

Principal Bankers: Alahlia Bank of Kuwait; Kuwait Real Estate Bank

Principal Shareholders: Abdulaziz Abdulrahman Al-Zamel; Khalil Ghattas Sarraf; Muram Shukri Shammas (Estate)

Date of Establishment: 1960

No of Employees: About 166

UNITED ARAB SHIPPING CO SAG

PO Box 3636 Safat, 13037 Kuwait
Tel: 4842160, 4843150
Cable: Uniship
Telex: 22018, 22176 Kunav Kt
Telefax: 965-4845388

Chairman: Abdul Aziz Hussain Salatt

Directors: Dr Yusuf Abdul Wahid Jasim, Eng Ahmed Al Turki, Abdulla Ahmed Lutah, Abdul Nabi Mansour, Mohammed Al-Daris (Vice Chairman), Abdulla Khalifa Huraiz, Abdul Rahman Jaber Muftah, Eng Khaled Saleh Ammar, Dr Ibrahim Makki (Vice Chairman), Eid Abdulla Yusuf, Shaker Jasem Al Sane

Senior Executives: Saud Al Zamil (Chief Executive), Faruk Mustafa Nafawa (Deputy Chief Exec-Fleet), Abdullah Madi Al Madi (Deputy Chief Exec-Personnel & Admin), Hamid Thulfikar Abdul-Rahman (Deputy Chief Exec-Liner)

PRINCIPAL ACTIVITIES: Ship owners, freight forwarders and liner service operators

Branch Offices: UAE (Abu Dhabi, Telex 23270; Dubai, Telex 45524); Bahrain (Manama Telex 9049); Saudi Arabia (Dammam, Telex 601331; Riyadh, Telex 202384; Jeddah, Telex 403254); Iraq (Baghdad, Telex 2696; Basrah, Telex 7070); Qatar (Doha Telex 4416); Jordan (Amman Telex 21353; Aqaba Telex 62232); Japan (Tokyo Telex 22970/22446); UK (London Telex 915184/5); USA (New York Telex 219162)

Subsidiary Companies: Kuwait Shipping Agencies, PO Box 20722, Safat, Kuwait, Telex 22282; Aratrans Kuwait, PO Box 20599, Telex 22659; United Arab Chartering Ltd (London), Telex 8811811

Principal Bankers: Gulf Bank; Commercial Bank; Burgan Bank; BKME, Kuwait; Chemical Bank & Bankers Trust Co, New York

Financial Information:

	1988/89 KD'000
Sales turnover	110,614
Profits	15,847
Authorised capital	500,000
Paid-up capital	280,000
Total fixed assets	146,496

Principal Shareholders: Governments of United Arab Emirates, Qatar, Iraq, Bahrain, Saudi Arabia, and Kuwait

Date of Establishment: 1976

No of Employees: Onshore: 838; Offshore: 2,077

UNITED BANK OF KUWAIT

PO Box 2616 Safat, 13027 Kuwait
Tel: 2527988
Telex: 30296 UBKCS KT
Telefax: 2520644

PRINCIPAL ACTIVITIES: Financial and banking services

Branch Offices: 3 in London; New York; Bahrain (representative office)

Parent Company: Head office in London, UK

Subsidiary Companies: UBK Customer Services Ltd, PO Box 2616, Safat, 13027 Kuwait; Venture Factors Plc, West Sussex, UK; UBK Asset Management (Guernsey) Ltd; UBK Leasing Finance Ltd; UBK Export Finance Ltd

UNITED BUILDING CO SAK

PO Box 22807 Safat, 13089 Kuwait
Tel: 2412160 (9 lines)
Cable: Unibuild
Telex: 44442 KT

Chairman: Bader Khalid Al Bader

Directors: Adnan Abdulla Al Asfour, Fahad Abdulla Al Hassawi, Omar Bader Al Qannai, Abdul Aziz Salem Al Abed Al Gaden

PRINCIPAL ACTIVITIES: All construction business, supply of related machinery and equipment, participation in other business as co-partners or agents

Principal Agencies: Thosti-Nurnburg, W Germany; Brochier-Nurnberg, W Germany

Branch Offices: Cairo, Egypt

Associated Companies: The United Prefab Building Co

Principal Bankers: Al Ahli Bank of Kuwait; Gulf Bank of Kuwait; National Bank of Kuwait; Commercial Bank of Kuwait

Financial Information:

	KD'000
Authorised capital	5,000
Paid-up capital	5,000

Principal Shareholders: United Realty Company SAK

Date of Establishment: 1973

UNITED CONTRACTING CO

PO Box 22350 Safat, 13084 Kuwait
Tel: 2435022, 2410945
Cable: Al-Kubra
Telex: 22581 Alkubra Kuwait

PRINCIPAL ACTIVITIES: Construction contracting

UNITED FISHERIES OF KUWAIT KSC

PO Box 22044 Safat, 13081 Kuwait
Tel: 2445020/27
Cable: SHEEM
Telex: 22285 KT, 22290 KT
Telefax: 2447970

Chairman: Abdullatif Al Asfoor (also Managing Director)

Directors: Ali Ahmed Al-Ghanim Al-Jaber (Vice Chairman), Dr Salem Yaseen Al Mahanne, Ghazi Khalid Al-Bader, Mohd

Hassan Al-Attar, Sheikh Nasser Sabah Al-Ahmed, Abdullatif Abdulwahab Al Zaidan

Senior Executives: Faisal M Al Shatti (Asst Managing Director), Abdulrazzaq K Al-Wazzan (Marketing Manager), Mahmoud Aweida (Manager, Fishing Operation)

PRINCIPAL ACTIVITIES: Fishing and fish industry, mainly prawns and shrimps, processing, packing and fast food restaurants
Principal Bankers: Bank of Kuwait & The Middle East; Bank of Bahrain & Kuwait; Al Ahli Bank of Kuwait; Burgan Bank
Financial Information:

	1987/88 KD'000
Sales turnover	5,260
Profits	825
Authorised capital	7,000
Paid-up capital	7,000
Total assets	10,208

Principal Shareholders: 48% Government; 52% Public
Date of Establishment: 16 May 1972
No of Employees: 650 (approx)

UNITED GLASS CO WLL

PO Box 24430 Safat, 13105 Kuwait
Tel: 3984705, 3985206
Cable: Uniglass
Telex: 23025 Kuwaital
Telefax: 3984925

Chairman: Mohammed A Naki
Directors: Anwar Naki, Nasser Naki
Senior Executives: Solaiman Ismail Solaiman, Hassan Mohie

PRINCIPAL ACTIVITIES: Import and export of all kinds of building and security glass, manufacture of insulating glass and tempered glass
Principal Bankers: Bank of Kuwait and The Middle East; Gulf Bank KSC; National Bank of Kuwait SAK

Principal Shareholders: Mohammed A Naki; Nasser A Naki
Date of Establishment: 1977
No of Employees: 40

UNITED GULF CONSTRUCTION CO WLL

PO Box 23495 Safat, 13095 Kuwait
Tel: 2415747, 2427899, 4747971/2/3
Cable: Jeeran
Telex: 23085, 44639 Jeeran KT
Telefax: 4718923

Chairman: Yousuf H Alomar
Partners: Yousuf H Alomar (Managing Director), Ali Yar Dehghani
Senior Executives: Abdel Rahman Al Hamamedi (Deputy General Manager), Mujahed H Taha (Chief Engineer), Abdel Rahim Tammam (Financial Manager)

PRINCIPAL ACTIVITIES: Construction: civil works, roads, infrastructure, buildings, housing projects, industrial buildings, warehouses; general trading: building materials & equipment
Principal Agencies: Hyundai Engineering & Construction, Korea; Aqua Engineering, Austria; United States Pipe & Foundry, USA; Terre Armee, France; Transroute, France
Principal Bankers: Commercial Bank of Kuwait, Gulf Bank
Financial Information:

	KD'000
Authorised capital	750
Paid-up capital	750

Principal Shareholders: Partners as mentioned
Date of Establishment: May 1975
No of Employees: 550

UNITED REAL ESTATE CO

PO Box 2232 Safat, 13023 Kuwait
Tel: 2412764, 2412760
Telex: 22383

Chairman: Shaikh Nasser Sabah Al Ahmad
Directors: Fawzi Mussad Al Saheh (Deputy Chairman)

PRINCIPAL ACTIVITIES: Real estate and construction operations in Kuwait and abroad
Associated Companies: Kuwait Real Estate Investment Consortium (10%)
Financial Information:

	KD'000
Capital	10,000

Date of Establishment: February 1973

UNITED TRADING GROUP

PO Box 1208 Safat, 13013 Kuwait
Tel: 2420115/6
Cable: Untroup
Telex: 22212 Untroupex Kt; 22160 Utg Kt; 22242 Utg Kt

Chairman: Shaikha Badria Saud Al Sabah
Directors: Shaikh Mubarak Fahd Al Salem Al Sabah (Executive Director)

PRINCIPAL ACTIVITIES: Foreign exchange
Principal Bankers: Al Ahli Bank of Kuwait, National Bank of Kuwait, Gulf Bank, Commercial Bank of Kuwait
Financial Information:

	1989 KD'000
Authorised capital	3,000
Paid-up capital	3,000

Date of Establishment: 1970

W J TOWELL & CO AGENCIES (KUWAIT) WLL

See TOWELL, W J, & CO AGENCIES (KUWAIT) WLL

W S ATKINS OVERSEAS LIMITED

See ATKINS, W S, OVERSEAS LIMITED

WAEL AL-NUSIF TRADING CO WLL

See AL-NUSIF, WAEL, TRADING CO WLL

WARBA INSURANCE CO SAK

PO Box 24282 Safat, 13103 Kuwait
Tel: 2445140, 2445147 (8 lines)
Cable: Warbinsco-KWT
Telex: 22779, 30230 WARINCO
Telefax: 2439629

Chairman: Abdullah Hassan Al Jarallah (Managing Director)
Directors: Abdul Ghani Khalid Al Ghunaim (Vice Chairman), Yacoub Yousuf Al Sager (Deputy Managing Director), Khalid Al Wogyan, Sabah Khalid Al Ghunaim, Faisal Al Hajiri, Khalifa Mousad Al Khorafi
Senior Executives: Ragheb Ishaq Abdo (General Manager), Talal Al Khuffash (Deputy General Manager), Tawfik Al-Bahar (Deputy General Manager)

PRINCIPAL ACTIVITIES: All types of insurance
Branch Offices: Ahmadi Branch; and Sabhan Branch
Principal Bankers: Gulf Bank; National Bank of Kuwait; Burgan Bank
Financial Information:

	1988 KD'000
Sales turnover	8,688
Profits	659
Authorised capital	5,753
Paid-up capital	5,753
Total assets	17,666

Principal Shareholders: State of Kuwait (51%)
Date of Establishment: 1976
No of Employees: 140

WARBA TRADING, CONSULTING & CONTRACTING CO WLL

PO Box 25104 Safat, 13112 Kuwait
Tel: 2424477, 2424488
Cable: Soquick
Telex: 44777 Soquick KT

PRINCIPAL ACTIVITIES: Mechanical and electrical contractors, building and construction, civil engineering, air conditioning, heavy engineering, commission agents etc

WATER ENGINEERING LTD

PO Box 24555 Safat, 13106 Kuwait
Tel: 3967446, 2457831, 2457833
Telex: 30237 Almidco KT
Telefax: 2457832

Senior Executives: William Carmichael (Project Manager)

PRINCIPAL ACTIVITIES: Water treatment

WORKS & BUILDING ESTABLISHMENT

PO Box 415 Safat, 13005 Kuwait
Tel: 814813, 816915
Cable: KATAMI
Telex: 22316 KATAMI, 44501 WOBUEST
Telefax: 4812763

Chairman: Yacoub Yousuf Al-Qatami
Directors: Faisal Yousuf Al-Qatami (General Manager), Waleed Yousuf Al-Qatami (Assistant Manager), Qatami Yousuf Al-Qatami (Admin Manager)

PRINCIPAL ACTIVITIES: Traders and agents, manufacturers of: prefab housing, industrial cold stores, insulating material styropor, street lighting poles and furniture
Principal Agencies: Hilti AG, Liechenstein; Hitachi Power Tools, Japan; Paul Hettich, West Germany
Branch Offices: Location in Kuwait: Shuwaikh Industrial Area, Plot No 102
Principal Bankers: Bank of Kuwait & The Middle East; National Bank of Kuwait
Financial Information:

	1989 US$'000
Authorised capital	10,000
Paid-up capital	10,000

Principal Shareholders: Yacoub Al-Qatami; Faisal Al-Qatami; Waleed Al-Qatami; Anwar Al-Qatami; Mohammed Al-Qatami; Qatami Al-Qatami; Maryam Al-Qatami; Sheikah Al-Qatami; Nassima Al-Qatami; Bassima Al-Qatami; Fedda Al-Qatami
Date of Establishment: 1952
No of Employees: 342

Y Y AL-DUAIJ TRADING & CONTRACTING

See AL-DUAIJ, Y Y, TRADING & CONTRACTING

YOUSEF ABDUL RAHMAN AL ROUMI

See AL ROUMI, YOUSEF ABDUL RAHMAN,

YOUSIF KHALID AL ADASANI ENT

See AL ADASANI, YOUSIF KHALID, ENT

YUSUF AHMAD ALGHANIM & SONS WLL

See ALGHANIM, YUSUF AHMAD, & SONS WLL

YUSUF IBRAHIM ALGHANIM & CO

See ALGHANIM, YUSUF IBRAHIM, & CO

ZAID AL KAZEMI SONS TRADING CO

See AL KAZEMI, ZAID, SONS TRADING CO

KUWAITI RELOCATED COMPANIES

The appendix lists Kuwaiti companies with their relocation addresses. This allows the reader to cross-refer the Kuwaiti company to its relocation entry in the relevant Arab country or to contact them direct if they have relocated in a non-Arab country.

At the time of going to press, some Kuwaiti companies and banks have returned to Kuwait. The reader is therefore also advised to consult the main Kuwaiti section when no relocation address is shown.

KUWAITI RELOCATED COMPANIES

ABDALLA CONTRACTING & TRADING
PO Box 6655, Dubai, United Arab Emirates
Tel: 971-4-295503

**AFRO ARAB CO FOR INVESTMENT &
INTERNATIONAL TRADE (AFARCO)**
PO Box 1929, Cairo, Egypt

AL AHLIA INSURANCE CO SAK
PO Box 3429, Dubai, United Arab Emirates
Tel: 971-4-222020

AL ALAHLI BANK OF KUWAIT KSC
PO Box 1719, Dubai, United Arab Emirates
Tel: 971-4-224175
Fax: 971-4-215527

ABDUL AZIZ S AL BABTAIN
C/o Abdul Lateef Al Babtain PO Box 2711, Riyadh, Saudi Arabia

**AL BAHAR & BARDAWIL SPECIALITIES CO
WLL**
PO Box 3880, Dubai, United Arab Emirates

MOHAMED ABDULRAHMAN AL BAHAR
PO Box 1170, Deira, Dubai, United Arab Emirates
Tel: 971-4-660255
Fax: 971-4-667342

AL DAR CONSULTING CO (ADCO)
PO Box 2195, Riyadh 11451, Saudi Arabia
Tel: 966-1-4630680
Fax: 966-1-4645939

ABDUL AZIZ YOUSUF AL ESSA & CO WLL
PO Box 290, Dubai, United Arab Emirates
Tel: 971-4-482915
Fax: 971-4-480584

**AL FAHED TRADING & CONTRACTING CO
WLL**
PO Box 2819, Dubai, United Arab Emirates

AL FARKAD TRADING ESTABLISHMENT
PO Box 55972, Dubai, United Arab Emirates
Tel: 971-4-226399
Fax: 971-4-285677

ADEL ALGHANIM ESTABLISHMENT
PO Box 55542, Dubai, United Arab Emirates
Tel: 971-4-625087
Fax: 971-4-625522

ALI & FOUAD ALGHANIM
PO Box 36, Dubai, United Arab Emirates
Tel: 971-4-260847

YUSUF AHMAD ALGHANIM & SONS WLL
PO Box 11288, Dubai, United Arab Emirates
Tel: 971-4-220278

AHMED SAYID HASHIM AL GHARABALLY
PO Box 1004, Dubai, United Arab Emirates
Tel: 971-4-223184

**AL GHAZAL CONSTRUCTION &
DEVELOPMENT CO KSCC**
PO Box 822, Manama, Bahrain
Tel: 973-245123
Telex: 9284 GIC BN

AL HADLAQ TRADING EST
PO Box 3731,Dubai
Tel: 971-4-625013
Fax: 971-4-622708

AL HAJERY COMMERCIAL BUREAU
PO Box 15749, Riyadh, Saudi Arabia

AL HAMRA GROUP OF COMPANIES
PO Box 769, Sharjah, United Arab Emirates
Tel: 971-6-591755

**ABBAS ALI AL HAZEEM & SONS TRADING
CO**
PO Box 10310, Dubai, United Arab Emirates

AL HOMAIZI FOODSTUFF CO WLL
PO Box 7372, Dubai, United Arab Emirates
Tel: 971-4-284196
Fax: 971-4-278907

ALINJAZ CONTRACTING CO SAK
C/o Abha Contracting Co, PO Box 4509, Al Medinah Al
Munawwara, Saudi Arabia

ALIREZA GROUP OF COMPANIES
C/o Rezayat Europe Ltd, 52 Mount Street, London W1Y 5RE,
UK
Tel: 44-71-499 6171
Fax: 44-71-499 2832

**AL MANSOUR & AL ABDALY TRADING &
CONTRACTING WLL**
PO Box 21, Riyadh 11411, Saudi Arabia
Tel: 966-1-4778745
Fax: 966-1-4769820

**MOHD ABDUL MOHSEN AL MERRI TRADING
EST**
PO Box 16443, Dubai, United Arab Emirates
Tel: 971-4-238746
Fax: 971-4-235819

**AL MUKABBER TRADING & CONTRACTING
CO WLL**
PO Box 3456, Amman, Jordan

ABDULAZIZ ALI AL MUTAWA
PO Box 1123, Riyadh 11431, Saudi Arabia

AL QABAS NEWSPAPER
Unit 4, Bramber Court, 2 Bramber Road, London W14 9PB, UK
Tel: 44-71-381 8011

ALI AL QURAISHI TRADING CO WLL
PO Box 339, Dammam 31411, Saudi Arabia
Tel: 966-3-8261596
Fax: 966-3-8271464

SAYID RAJAB AL RIFAI
PO Box 2000, Dubai, United Arab Emirates
Tel: 971-4-660755
Telex: 45439

A H AL SAGAR & BROS
PO Box 7080, Dubai, United Arab Emirates
Tel: 971-4-669595
Fax: 971-4-664680

AL SAHL TRADING CO
PO Box 15261, Al Ain, Abu Dhabi, United Arab Emirates

KUWAITI RELOCATED COMPANIES

MUSAAD AL SALEH & SONS LTD
PO Box 4093, Abu Dhabi, United Arab Emirates

SAUD AL SALEH GENERAL TRADING EST
PO Box 11057, Dubai, United Arab Emirates
Tel: 971-4-224502
Fax: 971-4-692923

AHMED AL SARRAF TRADING EST
PO Box 55972, Dubai, United Arab Emirates
Tel: 971-4-226399
Fax: 971-4-285677

ABBAS AHMAD AL SHAWAF & BROS CO WLL
PO Box 55608, Dubai, United Arab Emirates
Tel: 971-4-284565, 224834
Fax: 971-4-228255

MOHD NASER AL SAYER & SONS EST
PO Box 8765, Dubai, United Arab Emirates
Tel: 971-4-220682, 271520
Fax: 971-4-270253, 271884

NASSER AL SAYER & CO
PO Box 1825, Dubai, United Arab Emirates
Tel: 971-4-222471
Fax: 971-4-663972

MOHAMMED HOMOOD AL SHAYA CO
PO Box 1277, Dubai, United Arab Emirates
Tel: 971-4-664967
Fax: 971-4-692165

ADEL MOHD HAMAD AL SUMAIT (AL BOOM MARINE)
PO Box 5108, Dubai, United Arab Emirates
Tel: 971-4-690080
Fax: 971-4-661361

JASSIM MOHD ALI AL WAZZAN
PO Box 5344, Dubai, United Arab Emirates
Tel: 971-4-220941, 229396
Fax: 971-4-215248

AL YOUSIFI TRADING EST
PO Box 55673, Dubai, United Arab Emirates
Tel: 971-4-211754
Fax: 971-4-286136

ARAB BUILDING MATERIALS CO
PO Box 1596, Dubai, United Arab Emirates
Tel: 971-4-341330, 660454
Fax: 971-4-690138

ARAB COMMERCIAL ENTERPRISES (KUWAIT)
PO Box 667, Riyadh 11421, Saudi Arabia
Tel: 966-1-4774070
Fax: 966-1-4774081

ARAB PETROLEUM CONSULTANTS
C/o APC Services Inc, Dallas, Texas, USA

ARTHUR YOUNG BADER AL BAZIE & CO
PO Box 4235, Dubai, United Arab Emirates
Tel: 971-4-224147

W S ATKINS & PARTNERS OVERSEAS LTD
PO Box 5620, Dubai, United Arab Emirates
Tel: 971-4-522771
Fax: 971-4-523045

SAUD AUJAN & BROS CO WLL
PO Box 990, Dammam 31421, Saudi Arabia
Tel: 966-3-8570777
Fax: 966-3-8577923

ESSA & ABEDALI BAHMAN & CO
PO Box 1145, Dubai, United Arab Emirates

BANK OF BAHRAIN & KUWAIT
PO Box 597, Manama, Bahrain
Tel: 973-253388
Fax: 973-272785

BECH TEL LTD
PO Box 739, 245 Hammersmith Road, London W6 8DP
Tel: 44-81-846 5144
Fax: 44-81-846 6940

MOHAMED SALEH & REZA YOUSUF BEHBEHANI
C/o Behbehani Bros, PO Box 168, Manama, Bahrain
Tel: 973-253872, 255297, 252488

MORAD YOUSUF BEHBEHANI
C/o Behbehani Bros, PO Box 168, Manama, Bahrain
Tel: 973-253872, 255297, 252488

BOODAI TRADING CO LTD
PO Box 5108, Dubai, United Arab Emirates
Tel: 971-4-660080, 660975
Fax: 971-4-661361, 624027

BUILDING & ROADS CO (BARCO) WLL
C/o Contracting & Trading Co, PO Box 338, Alkhobar 31952
Tel: 966-3-8641455
Fax: 966-3-8950427

CHEMICALS & INDUSTRIAL SUPPLIES CO
C/o Industrial Chemicals Co PO Box 6349, Sharjah, United Arab Emirates

COAST INVESTMENT & DEVELOPMENT CO KSC
PO Box 5413, Ras Al Khaimah, United Arab Emirates
Tel: 971-77-26882
Fax: 971-77-99270

COMMERCIAL BANK OF KUWAIT SAK
49 Park Lane, London W1Y 4EQ, UK
Tel: 44-71-495 2096
Fax: 44-71-495 2094

COMMERCIAL FACILITIES CO SAK
C/o Financial & General Bank Plc 13 Lowndes Street, London SW1X 9EX, UK
Tel: 44-71-235 0036
Fax: 44-71-235 1488

CONSOLIDATED CONTRACTORS CO
Atrina Center, 32A Kifissias Avenue, PO Box 61092 Amoroussion, Athens, Greece
Tel: 30-1-219551

CONTRACTING & TRADING CO (CAT)
PO Box 338, Alkhobar 31952
Tel: 966-3-8951120
Fax: 966-3-8950427

EL HOSS ENGINEERING & TRADING CO
PO Box 113-5130, Beirut, Lebanon

FAJR DEVELOPMENT CO
PO Box 13691, Dubai, United Arab Emirates
Tel: 971-4-277767
Fax: 971-4-272525

FAWAZ GROUP INTERNATIONAL (FAWAZ REFRIGERATION & AIRCONDITIONING CO WLL)
PO Box 8037, Dubai, United Arab Emirates
Tel: 971-4-282733
Fax: 971-4-229418

GENERAL TRADING CO LTD
C/o Mahamy Trading (UK) Ltd 45 Cumberland Mansion,
   Seymour Place, London W1, UK
Tel: 44-71-723 6003

GENERAL TRANSPORTATION & EQUIPMENT CO
C/O General Transportation Enterprises PO Box 356 Alkhoban
   31952 Saudi Arabia
Tel: 966-3-8642377, 8643377

GULF BANK KSC
1 College Hill, London EC4R 2RA, UK
Tel: 44-71-248 2843
Fax: 44-71-489 0407

GULF INDUSTRIAL INVESTMENT CO
PO Box 50177, Irbid, Bahrain
Tel: 973-673311
Fax: 973-675258

GULF MARINE TRANSPORT CO KSC
C/o Gray MacKenzie & Co Ltd, PO Box 210, Manama, Bahrain
Tel: 973-712750
Fax: 973-712749

HALLIBURTON LTD
PO Box 515, Manama, Bahrain
Tel: 973-258866

ABBAS ALI HAZEEM & SONS CO
PO Box 10310, Dubai, United Arab Emirates
Tel: 971-4-857930
Fax: 971-4-850089

HEMPELS MARINE PAINTS (KUWAIT) WLL
PO Box 2000, Sharjah, United Arab Emirates
Tel: 971-6-356307
Fax: 971-6-546491

INDEPENDENT PETROLEUM GROUP SAK
112 Jermyn Street, London SW1Y 6LS, UK
Tel: 44-71-925 0505
Fax: 44-71-873 0923

INTER-ARAB INVESTMENT GUARANTEE CORPORATION
PO Box 56578, Riyadh 11564, Saudi Arabia
Tel: 966-1-4641400
Fax: 966-1-4649993

INTERNATIONAL CONTRACTORS GROUP
PO Box 21, Riyadh 11411, Saudi Arabia
Tel: 966-1-4778745
Fax: 966-1-4769820

INTERNATIONAL FINANCIAL ADVISERS KSC
PO Box 2057, Dubai, United Arab Emirates
Tel: 971-4-520638
Fax: 971-4-513687

INTERNATIONAL SHIPPING AGENCY LTD
C/O Gulf Agency Co Ltd, PO Box 61087, GR-151 10
   Amaroussiou, Greece

INTERNATIONAL SUPPLY CO LTD
PO Box 34, Damman 31411, Saudi Arabia
Tel: 966-3-8326261
Fax: 966-3-8346279

INTERNATIONAL TURNKEY SYSTEMS
PO Box 8687, Dubai, United Arab Emirates
Tel: 971-4-511022
Fax: 971-4-520419
also
PO Box 1344, Manama, Bahrain
Tel: 973-273280
Fax: 973-273281

ISOFOAM INSULATING MATERIALS
PO Box 161, Ajman, United Arab Emirates
Tel: 971-6-422529

KEO KUWAITI ENGINEERS' OFFICE
PO Box 27954, Abu Dhabi, United Arab Emirates
Tel: 971-2-788977
Fax: 971-2-786796

MOHAMED ABDULMOHSIN KHARAFI INDUSTRIES & ESTABLISHMENTS
PO Box 650, Abu Dhabi, United Arab Emirates
Tel: 971-2-322237
Fax: 971-2-322212
and
PO Box 11171, Dubai, United Arab Emirates
Tel: 971-4-377806

KIRBY BUILDING SYSTEMS KUWAIT
PO Box 9201, Dubai, United Arab Emirates
Tel: 971-4-373816
Fax: 971-4-374015

KUWAIT & GULF LINK TRANSPORT CO KSCC
C/o Gulf Stevedor Contracting Co PO Box 1153, Alkhobar
   31952, Saudi Arabia

KUWAIT AIRWAYS
4 Talat Harb Street, Cairo, Egypt
Tel: 20-2-747944
Fax: 20-2-747288

KUWAIT AUTOMOBILE & TRADING CO WLL
C/o A A Zayani & Sons, PO Box 932, Bahrain
Tel: 973-251411, 255921

KUWAIT AUTOMOTIVE IMPORTS CO WLL
C/o M H Al Shaya & Co, PO Box 1277, Dubai, United Arab
   Emirates
Tel: 971-4-664967
Fax: 971-4-692165

KUWAIT AVIATION FUELLING CO KSC
C/o KPC, 80 New Bond Street, London W1Y 9DA, UK
Tel: 44-71-491 4000
Fax: 44-71-493 7996

KUWAIT BUILDING INDUSTRIES KSC
C/o Musaad Al Saleh & Sons, PO Box 4093, Abu Dhabi, United
   Arab Emirates

KUWAITI RELOCATED COMPANIES

KUWAIT CEMENT CO KSC
PO Box 4536, Dammam 31412
Tel: 966-3-8273330
Fax: 966-3-8271923

KUWAIT DANISH COMPUTER CO SAK
51 River Street, Wellesley, Massachusset 02181, USA

KUWAIT DRILLING CO KSC
C/o Santa Fe International Parneli House 19/2 Wilton Road
London SW10 1LZ, UK
Tel: 44-71-828 7811
Fax: 44-71-828 0421

**KUWAIT ENGINEERING, OPERATION &
MANAGEMENT CO KSC (KENOMAC)**
PO Box 26901, Adliya, Bahrain

KUWAIT FOOD CO SAK
PO Box 3901, Dubai, United Arab Emirates
Tel: 971-4-224290
Fax: 971-4-259364

**KUWAIT FOREIGN PETROLEUM
EXPLORATION CO KSC**
C/o Santa Fe International Parneli House 19/2 Wilton Road
London SW10 1LZ
Tel: 44-71-828 7811
Fax: 44-71-828 0421
and
PO Box 1808, Dubai, United Arab Emirates

**KUWAIT INSULATING MATERIAL
MANUFACTURING CO SAK**
C/o Laffan Trading & Contracting Est PO Box 6363, Doha,
Qatar

KUWAIT INTERNATIONAL INVESTMENT CO
PO Box 1855, Dubai, United Arab Emirates
Tel: 971-4-230551
Fax: 971-4-273810

KUWAIT INVESTMENT OFFICE
St Vedast House, 150 Cheapside, London EC2V 6ET, UK
Tel: 44-71-606 8080
Fax: 44-71-606 1605

KUWAIT MARITIME & MERCANTILE CO KSC
C/o Gray MacKenzie & Co Ltd, PO Box 210, Manama, Bahrain
Tel: 973-712750
Fax: 973-712749

KUWAIT NATIONAL PETROLEUM CO KSC
C/o KPC, 80 New Bond Street, London W1Y 9DA, UK
Tel: 44-71-491 4000
Fax: 44-71-493 7996

KUWAIT OIL COMPANY KSC
26/28 Great portland Street, London W1N 5AD, UK
Tel: 44-71-436 1990
Fax: 44-71-436 4992
and
PO Box 20408, Sharjah, United Arab Emirates
Tel: 971-6-545361
Fax: 971-6-548931

KUWAIT OIL TANKER CO SAK
C/o KPC, 80 New Bond Street, London W1Y 9DA, UK
Tel: 44-71-491 4000
Fax: 44-71-493 7996

KUWAIT PETROLEUM CORPORATION
80 New Bond Street, London W1Y 9DA, UK
Tel: 44-71-491 4000
Fax: 44-71-493 7996

KUWAIT SHIPPING AGENCIES CO SAK
PO Box 3278, Dubai, United Arab Emirates
Tel: 971-4-210808
Fax: 971-4-272581

LAMNALCO LTD
PO Box 5687, Sharjah, United Arab Emirates
Tel: 971-6-359108
Fax: 971-6-547090
and
PO Box 61, Abu Dhabi, United Arab Emirates
Tel: 971-2-777772
Fax: 971-2-728158

**LIVESTOCK TRANSPORT & TRADING CO
KSC**
C/o Emirates Livestock & Trading Co PO Box 626, Dubai,
United Arab Emirates
Tel: 971-4-341072

**MASADER INTERNATIONAL GENERAL
TRADING CO**
PO Box 3449, Dubai, United Arab Emirates
Tel: 971-4-235754
Fax: 971-4-235753

MIDDLE EAST TRADING & INDUSTRIAL CO
PO Box 1767, Dubai, United Arab Emirates
Tel: 971-4-668461
Fax: 971-4-661573

**MODERN AIR CONDITIONING &
REFRIGERATION CO**
PO Box 2277, Amman, Jordan

NASER SAYER & CO WLL
PO Box 1825, Dubai, United Arab Emirates
Tel: 971-4-222471
Fax: 971-4-663972

NATIONAL BANK OF KUWAIT
9-13 George Street, London W1H 5PB, UK
Tel: 44-71-224 2277
Fax: 44-71-224 2101

NATIONAL COMPUTER SERVICES LTD
PO Box 26766, Manama, Bahrain
Tel: 973-261220

NATIONAL CONTRACTING CO LTD
C/o Rezayat Europe Ltd, 52 Mount Street, London W1Y 5RE,
UK
Tel: 44-71-499 6171
Fax: 44-71-499 2832

NATIONAL GLASS ESTABLISHMENT
PO Box 563, Dubai, United Arab Emirates
Tel: 971-4-221315
Fax: 971-4-275241

NATIONAL INVESTMENT CO
PO Box 1855, Dubai, United Arab Emirates
Tel: 971-4-286610

KUWAITI RELOCATED COMPANIES

NATIONAL MECHANICAL & ELECTRICAL WORKS CO

Unit 5, Yeoman Street, London SE8 5DU, UK
Tel: 44-71-232 2820
Fax: 44-71-231 8305
and
PO Box 1189, Al Ain, Abu Dhabi, United Arab Emirates
Tel: 971-3-828937
Fax: 971-3-828937

OASIS TRADING CO LTD

PO Box 1170, Deira, Dubai, United Arab Emirates
Tel: 971-4-660255
Fax: 971-4-667342

PACC INTERNATIONAL/PAN ARAB COMPUTER CENTRE

PO Box 1277, Dubai, United Arab Emirates
Tel: 971-4-664967
Fax: 971-4-692165

PAN ARAB CONSULTING ENGINEERS (PACE)

PO Box 10207, Manama, Bahrain
Tel: 973-533073
Fax: 973-533069

PETROCHEMICAL INDUSTRIES CO KSC

C/0 Gulf Petrochemical Industries Co BSC, PO Box 26730,
Manama, Bahrain
Tel: 973-731777
Fax: 973-731047

SECURITIES GROUP SAK

PO Box 55720, Dubai, United Arab Emirates
Tel: 971-4-217454
Fax: 971-4-270710

TALAL ABU GHAZALEH INTERNATIONAL

C/o Aldar Audit Bureau, PO Box 2195, Riyadh 11451, Saudi
Arabia
Tel: 966-1-4630680
Fax: 966-1-4645939

TOWELL CONSTRUCTION CO LTD

PO Box 42612, Riyadh, Saudi Arabia
Tel: 966-1-4657770

W J TOWELL & CO AGENCIES (KUWAIT) WLL

PO Box 4040, Ruwi, Sultanate of Oman
Tel: 968-708304
Fax: 968-793882

TRADING & INDUSTRIAL EQUIPMENT CO WLL

PO Box 5291, Deira, Dubai, United Arab Emirates
Tel: 971-4-246121
Fax: 971-4-246483

TRADING & MARKETING EST (DAKHIL A AL OSAIMI)

PO Box 36, Dubai, United Arab Emirates
Tel: 971-4-223651
Fax: 971-4-66-381

UNION CONSTRUCTION CO

PO Box 16638, Dubai, United Arab Emirates
Tel: 971-4-667870
Fax: 971-4-661790

UNITED ARAB SHIPPING CO SAG

PO Box 55586, Dubai, United Arab Emirates
Tel: 971-4-218222
Fax: 971-4-230652

UNITED BANK OF KUWAIT LTD (HEAD OFFICE)

3 Lombard Street, London EC3V 9DT, UK
Tel: 44-71-929 1000
Fax: 44-71-929 3966

KUWAITI RELOCATED COMPANIES

Major Companies of
LEBANON

A K NAAMANI & CO SARL

See NAAMANI, A K, & CO SARL

ABOU ADAL, ETS GEORGE, & CIE

PO Box 11-1332, Beirut
Tel: 334215
Telex: 20525 LE

PRINCIPAL ACTIVITIES: General trading and contracting, manufacturers' representation

ADCOM BANK

PO Box 11-2431, Beirut
Tel: 809100/2
Cable: Adcomco Beirut
Telex: 23200, 21397 Adcom LE

PRINCIPAL ACTIVITIES: Commercial banking

Date of Establishment: 1959

ALBERT ABELA SAL

PO Box 11-3203, Beirut
Tel: 343971, 353370
Cable: Alabela Beirut
Telex: 21187 EMC LE

Chairman: Albert Abela
Directors: Edwin G Abela, Joseph P Abela

PRINCIPAL ACTIVITIES: Industrial services; caterers and food suppliers, traders, and contrators, tobacco distribution, LPG distribution
Subsidiary Companies: Lebanese Air Transport (Charter) SAL

AL HAMRA ENGINEERING CO SAL

Al Hamra Group

PO Box 11-6040, Beirut
Tel: 340640/1/2, 483840, 483275
Cable: WAHACOM
Telex: 22211 Hameng, 44087 Hameng

Directors: Hanna Ayoub

PRINCIPAL ACTIVITIES: Industrial projects, airports, hospitals, sport field, housing schemes, water reservoir, drainage networks, power stations and other civil work. Import, distribution and supply of building materials - mainly waterproofing
Principal Agencies: Vandex, Denmark; Ruberoid, UK; Smid & Hollander, Holland; Swimquip, USA; Cementone, UK; Weka Sport, Holland; Rehau, Germany; Celotex, USA; CIB, France; Hamix, UK; Pyrok
Branch Offices: PO Box 2048 Safat, Kuwait; PO Box 769, Sharjah, United Arab Emirates; PO Box 926475, Amman, Jordan; PO Box 10223, Riyadh, Saudi Arabia; 77 Princedale Road, London, W11 4NS, UK
Parent Company: Al-Hamra Kuwait Co
Principal Bankers: Byblos Bank, Beirut; Allied Business Bank, Beirut

Date of Establishment: 1966

AL NISR INSURANCE CO SAL

PO Box 113-5113, Beirut
Tel: 350370
Cable: Nisrinsur
Telex: 20478 Nisr Le

PRINCIPAL ACTIVITIES: Insurance and reinsurance operations
Principal Agencies: Arab Commercial Enterprises, Saudi Arabia
Branch Offices: Tripoli, Jounieh, Sin El Fil, Saida, Lebanon; Muttrah, Sultanate of Oman
Parent Company: Saudi Arabian Insurance Company Ltd
Associated Companies: Arab Commercial Enteprises (ACE)

Principal Bankers: The First National Bank of Chicago, Beirut, Geneva; Arab Bank, Beirut

Date of Establishment: 1964

AMIN KAWAR & SONS

PO Box 11-4213, Beirut
Tel: 352525/6
Telex: 20865

Chairman: Tawfiq Amin Kawar

PRINCIPAL ACTIVITIES: Shipping and chartering agents, general traders, insurance and travel agents, land and property owners
Principal Bankers: Arab Bank Ltd; Grindlays Bank

ARAB ADVERTISING AGENCY

PO Box 11-2976, Beirut
Tel: 362540/1
Cable: Offarabe
Telex: 20443 Le Ofarab

PRINCIPAL ACTIVITIES: Advertising, marketing research and public relations
Associated Companies: Arab Advertising Agency, Kuwait

ARAB BANK PLC

PO Box 11-1015, Beirut
Tel: 250240/9, 251151/9
Cable: Bankarabi Beirut
Telex: 20704; 20789; 20964

PRINCIPAL ACTIVITIES: Commercial banking
Branch Offices: Bahrain, Cyprus, Egypt, France, Greece, Jordan, Lebanon, Oman, Qatar, Singapore, United Arab Emirates, United Kingdom, USA, Yemen
Parent Company: Head office in Amman, Jordan

ARAB COMMERCIAL ENTERPRISES SAL

PO Box 113-5112, Beirut
Tel: 340770
Cable: Comment Co
Telex: 21741 Ace Le

PRINCIPAL ACTIVITIES: Insurance and reinsurance agents and brokers
Branch Offices: Saudi Arabia; Kuwait; Bahrain; Qatar; Oman; Abu Dhabi; Al Ain; Dubai; Ras Al Khaimah; Yemen AR; Jordan
Parent Company: Head office in Greece
Associated Companies: Al Nisr Insurance Co SAL

ARAB DEVELOPMENT CO

PO Box 11-6106, Beirut
Tel: 804918, 804965
Cable: Ardevelop
Telex: 20481 Drilco Le

PRINCIPAL ACTIVITIES: Site investigations, land reclamation and development, civil and mechanical engineering, water well drilling
Branch Offices: Jordan, Syria, Saudi Arabia, Oman, Abu Dhabi, Ras Al Khaimah, London and the Liechtenstein
Principal Bankers: Arab Bank

Date of Establishment: 1971

ARAB FINANCE CORPORATION SAL

PO Box 113-5527, Beirut
Tel: 363020/4
Cable: Financorab
Telex: 21197 Le; 22098 Le

PRINCIPAL ACTIVITIES: Participation in the development of the national and Arab financial sectors, especially in capital markets. Mobilization of funds and their channelling into productive investments, whether directly for the account of the Corporation, or indirectly on behalf on owners of these funds

Parent Company: Al Saudi Bank Holding NV, Netherlands
Principal Bankers: Republic National Bank of New York, New York; Midland Bank Ltd, London; Deutsche Bank AG, Frankfurt; Al Saudi Banque, Paris, London & Bahrain

Date of Establishment: 1974

ARAB LIBYAN TUNISIAN BANK SAL

PO Box 11-9575, Beirut
Tel: 346320/2
Cable: Lituban
Telex: 20230 FETCO LE; 21582 LATBAN LE

PRINCIPAL ACTIVITIES: Commercial banking
Associated Companies: Libyan Arab Foreign Bank, Tripoli, Libya; Societe Tunisienne de Banque, Tunis, Tunisia

ARAB REINSURANCE COMPANY

PO Box 11-9060, Beirut
Tel: 814406, 814397
Cable: Arabre, Beirut
Telex: 20420 Arabre Le

PRINCIPAL ACTIVITIES: Reinsurance
Branch Offices: London Contact Office: 141/142 Fenchurch Street, 5th Floor, London EC3M 6BL, Tel 01-6267055/6, 01-6267712, Telex 8955104
Principal Bankers: UBAF Bank Ltd, Banque Libanaise Pour le Commerce; Gulf International Bank

Principal Shareholders: Arab insurance & reinsurance companies and institutions and Arab banks
Date of Establishment: 1972

ARABIA INSURANCE CO LTD SAL

Arabia House, Phoenicia St, PO Box 11-2172, Beirut
Tel: 363610 (10) Lines
Cable: Arabiaco
Telex: 21016 LE, 40060 LE, 43679 LE
Telefax: 9611-365139

Chairman: Badr Said Fahoum (General Manager)
Directors: Farouk Jabre (Deputy Chairman), W A Al Dajani, A Freij, M Al Masri, F M Assaid, N Baroudy, M Beydoun, C Nucho, H Sabbagh
Senior Executives: Francis Alonzo (Deputy General Manager)

PRINCIPAL ACTIVITIES: Fire, marine, burglary, motor, accident, life insurance and reinsurance
Branch Offices: Lebanon: Beirut, PO Box 11-3568, Tripoli, PO Box 224. Jordan: Amman, PO Box 543, Marka, PO Box 17085, Irbid, PO Box 1004, Zarqa. Akabah, PO Box 1165, Al Salt, PO Box 249, Al Karak, Ma'an, Jerash, PO Box 1004. Kuwait: PO Box 868 Safat. Bahrain: PO Box 745 Manama. Qatar: PO Box 771 Doha. Dubai: PO Box 1050. Sharjah: PO Box 6352. Abu Dhabi: PO Box 867. Al-Ain: PO Box 1216. Ras Al Khaimah: PO Box 1288. Muscat: PO Box 4905. Salalah: PO Box 18919. Saudi Arabia: Jeddah, PO Box 2114. Riyad, PO Box 4990. Dammam, PO Box 847. Mecca, PO Box 2997. Al-Khobar, PO Box 54. Al-Jubeil, PO Box 185. Al-Hofuf, PO Box 625. Al-Taef, PO Box 1575. Al Medina, PO Box 2963. Khamis Musheit, PO Box 1622
Associated Companies: GAT Tunisie; Ste Civile Immobiliere de Grand Large, Monaco
Principal Bankers: Arab Bank Ltd; Jordan National Bank; Bank of America, London
Financial Information:

	1988 LL'000
Sales turnover	9,848,364
Profits	612,000
Authorised capital	204,000
Paid-up capital	204,000
Total balance sheet	36,573,921

Principal Shareholders: Arab Bank Ltd; Al Mashreq Financial Investment Co; Badr S Fahoum; Fouad As-Said; Mohamed A R Al Bahar; Shaikh Abdul Aziz Suleiman; Suleiman Tannous & Sons
Date of Establishment: 1944
No of Employees: 324

ARABIAN CONSTRUCTION CO GROUP

PO Box 11-6876, Beirut
Tel: 362678, 362679
Cable: Matacont Beirut
Telex: 20385 ACC LE

PRINCIPAL ACTIVITIES: Multi-storey buildings and hotel, housing units, civil works, infrastructure projects, general contracting
Branch Offices: Abu-Dhabi, UAE, PO Box 2113, Telex 22333 Natasu Ah Sharjah, UAE, PO Box 609, Telex 68542 Accsh; Doha, Qatar, PO Box 1701, Telex 4540 Aramco Dh; Riyadh, Saudi Arabia, PO Box 5992, Telex 200245 SAACC Sj; Paris, France, 146 Ave des Champs Elysees, Telex 642757
Subsidiary/Associated Companies: Centronix, Gulf Timber; AMCC; MB Interdesign
Principal Bankers: Arab Bank; Citibank; National Bank of Abu-Dhabi; Bank of Credit and Commerce; Banque de la Mediterranee France; INVEST Bank; Societe Bancaire Arabe

ARABIAN TRANSPORT CO SARL

PO Box 11-3123, Beirut
Tel: 366694
Cable: Majory Beirut
Telex: 20981 Le; 20355

PRINCIPAL ACTIVITIES: Sea-air-land transport; forwarding clearing
Principal Agencies: Correspondents and agents all over the world
Principal Bankers: Banque Libano Francaise; Credit Commercial de France

ASSOCIATED CONSULTING ENGINEERS SAL A.C.E.

PO Box 11-3446, Beirut
Tel: 353430, 349151
Telex: 20412 ACE LE

PRINCIPAL ACTIVITIES: Civil engineering consultants

Date of Establishment: 1956

BANK OF BEIRUT SAL

PO Box 11-7354, Beirut
Tel: 360850, 360870
Cable: BANBETMAL
Telex: 23640 LE, 20439 LE

Chairman: HE William Kazan
Directors: Rida Abdujawdeh, Pierre Helou, Said Ayas, Cheikh Camille Geagea
Senior Executives: Rida Abdujawdeh (Managing Director), Elie Aboujawdeh (Asst General Manager), Mohammad Harb (Inspector), Hassan Maatouk (Manager Main Branch)

PRINCIPAL ACTIVITIES: Commercial banking
Branch Offices: Gefinor Branch; Jal El Dib Branch; Mar Elias Branch; Brumanna Branch; Hazmieh Branch
Principal Bankers: Banque de Paris Internationale, Paris; American Express Bank, USA/UK; Banca Commerciale Italiana, Italy
Financial Information:

	LL'000
Authorised capital	50,000
Paid-up capital	50,000

Principal Shareholders: HE William Kazan; Prince Mohamad Bin Fahd Bin Abdel Aziz Al Saoud; Said Ayas; Cheikh Camille Geagea; HE Pierre Helou; Rida Abujawdeh
Date of Establishment: 1970
No of Employees: 121

BANK OF CREDIT & COMMERCE INTERNATIONAL (LEBANON) SAL

PO Box 11-1889, Beirut
Tel: 353770/1, 354580/1
Cable: Charbank
Telex: 21676 Bocaci LE

PRINCIPAL ACTIVITIES: Commercial banking

Date of Establishment: 1974

BANK OF KUWAIT & THE ARAB WORLD SAL

PO Box 11-3846, Beirut
Tel: 297930/2, 341420
Cable: Bankut
Telex: 21524 Le, 43749 Le

PRINCIPAL ACTIVITIES: Commercial banking
Parent Company: Intra Investment Co
Principal Bankers: Chemical Bank, New York; Grindlays Bank Ltd, London; Dresdner Bank, Frankfurt; Societe Generale, Paris; American Express, Italy

Principal Shareholders: Intra Investment Co
Date of Establishment: 1966

BANK OF LEBANON & KUWAIT SAL

PO Box 11-5556, Beirut
Tel: 340270/2
Cable: Lebkubank
Telex: 23013, 20910 Kuleb Le

PRINCIPAL ACTIVITIES: Commercial banking
Branch Offices: Dora, Hamra, Tripoli, Saida
Principal Bankers: Irving Trust Co, New York, London, Tokyo; Midland Bank, London; Banque Libanaise Pour le Commerce, Paris; Deutsche Bank, Frankfurt

Principal Shareholders: Kuwaiti group (97%)
Date of Establishment: 1964

BANKERS ASSURANCE SAL

PO Box 11-4293, Beirut
Tel: 339538, 339448
Telex: 21672 Bassur Le

PRINCIPAL ACTIVITIES: All classes of insurance
Branch Offices: Tripoli; Saida; Jounieh
Associated Companies: Cedar Insurance & Reinsurance Co Ltd; Stewart Wrightson Ltd
Principal Bankers: Credit Libanais SAL

Date of Establishment: July 1972

BANQUE AUDI SAL

PO Box 11-2560, Beirut
Tel: 331600, 331299
Cable: BANAUDI
Telex: 21148, 20763, 43012/4 DIRODI LE
Telefax: 332293

Chairman: Georges W Audi
Directors: Raymond W Audi, Mrs Suad Hamad Al Homaizi, Sheikh Jazzaa Nasser Al Sabah, Mrs Arlette Jean Audi, Salim M Habis

PRINCIPAL ACTIVITIES: Commercial banking
Branch Offices: Beirut (5), Saida (2), Tripoli, Jounieh, Jal El Dib, Hazmieh, Chekka, Bhamdoun; Zouk; Hadeth; Jbeil
Associated Companies: Affiliated: Banque Audi (Suisse) SA, Geneva & Zurich; Banque Audi (France) SA, Paris; Bank Audi (USA), New York; INFIBANK - Investment & Finance Bank

SAL, Beirut; Associated: INVESTBANK -Investment Bank for Trade & Finance LLC, Sharjah, Abu Dhabi, Al Ain
Principal Bankers: Correspondents in New York, London, Paris and Switzerland
Financial Information:

	LL'000
Authorised capital	150,000
Paid-up capital	150,000

Date of Establishment: 1962
No of Employees: 531

BANQUE BEYROUTH POUR LE COMMERCE SAL

PO Box 11-0216, Beirut
Tel: 804525/6
Telex: 21457 BECOBA LE

PRINCIPAL ACTIVITIES: Commercial banking

Date of Establishment: 1961

BANQUE DE BEYROUTH ET DES PAYS ARABES SAL

Bank of Beirut & the Arab Countries SAL

PO Box 11-1536, Beirut
Tel: 366630, 360460
Cable: Arabcontribank
Telex: 40518 BBAC LE, 41698 BBAC LE
Telefax: 367877

Chairman: Toufic S Assaf
Directors: Nashat Sheikelard (Vice Chairman/General Manager), Ghassan Assaf (Joint General Manager), Fawzi Ghandour (Secretary), Mounir Abou Fadil, Edmond Gaspard, Dr Ali Al Khalil, Hassib Rassamny, Habib Maamari, Iyad Sheikelard, Abbas S El Halabi (Asst General Manager)

PRINCIPAL ACTIVITIES: Commercial banking
Branch Offices: Beirut & Suburbs (10), Outside Beirut (13), Overseas (1 OBU), Cyprus (1)
Subsidiary Companies: Informatic Co Sarl; Societe Libanaise de Services Sarl
Principal Bankers: Correspondents: Irving Trust Co; Manufacturers Hanover Trust Co; Midland Bank Plc; Deutsche Bank AG; Societe Generale; Banca Commerciale Italiana; Credito Italiano; UBAF; Union Bank of Switzerland
Financial Information:

	LL'000
Authorised capital	150,000
Paid-up capital	150,000

Date of Establishment: 1957
No of Employees: 435

BANQUE DE FINANCEMENT SAL

PO Box 11-5044, Beirut
Tel: 341420
Cable: TAMWILLBANK
Telex: 22334 FIBANK

PRINCIPAL ACTIVITIES: Banking (medium and long term credit)

Principal Shareholders: Intra Investment Company SAL
Date of Establishment: 1960

BANQUE DE LA MEDITERRANEE SAL

PO Box 11-348, Beirut
Tel: 335135, 337237
Cable: Combank
Telex: 20826 Le Cobank

PRINCIPAL ACTIVITIES: Commercial banking
Branch Offices: Achrafieh, Hamra, Raouche, Moussaitbeh, Furn el Chebbak, Choueifat, Zouk Mikayel, Jdeide, Mkalles, Chekka, Saida, Jbeil, Tripoli, Zahle
Parent Company: Banque de la Mediterranee France SA, Companie Financiere Mediterranee (Cofimed SA)

Principal Bankers: New York: Mantrust, Marine Midland, American Express, Chemical Bank; London: Midland Bank, Barclays Bank; Germany: Mantrust Frankfurt, Dresdner Bank, Deutsche Bank; France: Banque de la Mediterranee France SA; Switzerland: Compagnie Financiere Mediterranee COFIMED SA

Date of Establishment: 1956

BANQUE DE L'INDUSTRIE ET DU TRAVAIL SAL

PO Box 11-3948, Beirut
Tel: 364498, 368090
Cable: Bankasnaf
Telex: BANKAS 20698 LE, 41699 LE

PRINCIPAL ACTIVITIES: Commercial banking
Associated Companies: Saudi Lebanese Bank for the Middle East SA (Paris), 125 Ave des Champs Elysees, 75008 Paris; Tel 7202115, Telex A612777 F MIDBK; Affiliated Bank: Banque de l'Industrie et du Travail (Suisse) SA, 30 rue du Rhone, 1211 Geneva 3, Switzerland
Principal Bankers: London:- Manufacturers Hanover Trust Co, National Westminster Bank Ltd; New York:- Manufacturers Hanover Trust Co, Chemical Bank

Date of Establishment: 1960

BANQUE DU CREDIT POPULAIRE SAL

PO Box 11-5292, Beirut
Tel: 334102, 334944
Cable: Bancrepol
Telex: 22411, 40123 LE BANPOL

PRINCIPAL ACTIVITIES: Commercial banking
Parent Company: Kairouz Trust Co
Associated Companies: L'Union Nationale SAL (Insurance Company)

Date of Establishment: 1962

BANQUE DU LIBAN

PO Box 11-5544, Beirut
Tel: 341230/40
Cable: Loubnabank
Telex: 20744 LE; 21033 LE

PRINCIPAL ACTIVITIES: Central banking

Principal Shareholders: State-owned

BANQUE DU LIBAN ET D'OUTRE-MER SAL

PO Box 11-1912, Beirut
Tel: 346290/7
Telex: 20740, 21149, 21273, 42372 LE

Honorary Chairman: Mrs Boutros El Khoury
Directors: Dr Naaman Azhari (Chairman & General Manager), HE Philippe Takla, HE Sheikh Ghassan Shaker, Nicolas Saade, Mohamed Jaroudi, HE Fouad El Bizri, Jean Asfar, Sheikh Ghazi Shaker, Joseph Emile Kharrat, Sheikh Salim Boutros El Khoury

PRINCIPAL ACTIVITIES: Commercial banking
Branch Offices: UAE, Dubai, Sharjah; Oman, Muscat; UK, London
Associated Companies: Banque Indosuez, Paris
Financial Information:

	LL'000
Authorised capital	200,000
Paid-up capital	200,000

Date of Establishment: 1951

BANQUE G TRAD CREDIT LYONNAIS SAL

PO Box 11-113, Beirut
Tel: 417183, 336800
Cable: Tradionais
Telex: 20654 Trad Le; 20434

PRINCIPAL ACTIVITIES: Commercial banking
Branch Offices: Ras Beirut; Sin El Fil; Jounieh
Associated Companies: Banque Trad-Credit Lyonnais (France) SA, Paris; Credit Lyonnais, Paris, France

Date of Establishment: 1951

BANQUE LIBANAISE POUR LE COMMERCE SAL

PO Box 11-1126, Beirut
Tel: 240820
Cable: Bancoliba
Telex: 20703, 21565

PRINCIPAL ACTIVITIES: Commercial banking
Branch Offices: Beirut, Tripoli, Chekka, Kousba, Bechare, Batroun, Jbeil, Jounieh, Dammour, Saida, Tyr, Beit Chahab
Subsidiary Companies: Banque Libanaise Pour Le Commerce (France) SA, Paris, Abu Dhabi, Dubai, Ras Al Khaimah, Sharjah (UAE)

Principal Shareholders: Joint Stock Company
Date of Establishment: 1950

BANQUE LIBANO-FRANCAISE SAL

PO Box 11-808, Beirut
Tel: 328555
Cable: Libanofran
Telex: 21445 LIFRAC LE

PRINCIPAL ACTIVITIES: Commercial banking
Branch Offices: Beirut, Jounieh, Saida, Tyr, Tripoli, Batroun, Zahle, Bar Elias
Parent Company: Compagnie Financiere de Suez, Paris
Subsidiary Companies: Banque Libano-Francaise SA (France) in Paris, Nice & Monaco
Principal Bankers: N.Y.: Banque Indosuez, Bank of America (worldwide), Manufacturers Hanover Trust Co (worldwide) Chemical Bank, Irving Trust Co, French American Banking Corp, Deutsche Bank, Frankfurt; Banque Indosuez, London; Union Bank of Switzerland, Zurich & Geneve

Principal Shareholders: Compagnie Financiere de Suez
Date of Establishment: 1932 as Compagnie Algerienne, 1968 as present name

BANQUE NATIONALE DE PARIS (INTERCONTINENTALE)

PO Box 11-1608, Beirut
Tel: 336667, 337667, 216140
Cable: Nacinter Beirut
Telex: 20632 BNPI LE, 43016 LE, 20924 LE
Telefax: 337667

Chairman: Henry Tyan (General Manager of Lebanon Group)
Directors: Jean Paul Barrie
Senior Executives: Emile Rizk

PRINCIPAL ACTIVITIES: Commercial banking
Branch Offices: Hamra, Jounie, Dora, Saida
Parent Company: Head office in Paris, France
Subsidiary Companies: Societe Financiere de Beyrouth SAL
Principal Bankers: French American Banking Corp, New York; Banque Nationale de Paris, Paris/London/Frankfurt

Principal Shareholders: Banque Nationale de Paris, Paris
Date of Establishment: 1944
No of Employees: 209

BANQUE SARADAR SAL

PO Box 11-1121 & 11-3312, Beirut
Tel: 335067, 215492, 218430/4
Cable: Marsar Beirut
Telex: 21283, 23535 Marsar Le, 20343 Bansar Le
Telefax: 415472

Chairman: Joe Saradar (General Manager)
Directors: Mrs Henriette Saradar, Abdo Jeffi

PRINCIPAL ACTIVITIES: General banking business, foreign exchange, precious metals
Branch Offices: Hamra; Zouk; Broummana; Rabieh; Dora; Liaison Office: PO Box 4017, Nicosia, Cyprus
Financial Information:

	LL'000
Authorised capital	40,000
Paid-up capital	40,000

Principal Shareholders: Joe Saradar, Henriette Saradar, Lucienne Azar (born Saradar), Marianne Barakat (born Saradar)
Date of Establishment: 1948 as Banque Marius Saradar; 1956 as present name
No of Employees: 493

BARDAWIL & CIE
PO Box 110-967, Beirut
Tel: 894533, 891406
Cable: BARDAWILCO Beirut
Telex: 20822 LE, 41639 LE

PRINCIPAL ACTIVITIES: General trading and contracting, manufacturers' representation, construction engineering, industrial, agricultural equipment and special building materials
Principal Agencies: Benford Ltd (Mixers & Dumpers), Potain (Tower Cranes), Petbow Ltd (Generators), Putzmeister Werke (Concrete Pumps)
Principal Bankers: The British Bank of the Middle East

BEAUDART ISSA
PO Box 11-4950, Beirut
Tel: 447773, 447774
Cable: Trabossa Beirut
Telex: 44973 Limar LE

Chairman: Beaudart Issa
Directors: Dr Nicolas Abdouche, Joseph Gharios

PRINCIPAL ACTIVITIES: Counter trade; grains and fertilizers; contracting
Principal Agencies: Societe Soufflet & Co, France
Branch Offices: Paris, Tel 2561380/81, Telex 650187
Subsidiary/Associated Companies: Limar SARL: PO Box 6623, Beirut, Lebanon, Tel 446090/446091; Limar Shipping Ltd: 113/117 South Street, Romford, Essex RM1 1NX, UK; Limar: Paris; Cofinco SA: 16 Rue du Bourg, 1003 Lausanne, Switzerland
Principal Bankers: Credit Suisse SA, Paris; Credit Suisse, Beirut

Date of Establishment: 1962

BEIRUT EXPRESS (BEIRUT)
PO Box 11-3274, Beirut
Tel: 341400
Telex: 20880 BEXPR LE

PRINCIPAL ACTIVITIES: Packing, forwarding, storage, customs clearing, and travels
Principal Agencies: Home-Pack Transport, Inc New York; Endicott Oversea Express, Inc New Jersey, USA; Interdean Hellas Ltd, Greece; Airsea Freight Co Ltd London
Branch Offices: Beirut Express (Athens), 233 Syngrou Ave, Nea Smirney, Athens, Greece (Admn Office); Beirut Express (Bahrain), PO Box 113, Manama, Bahrain; Express Packing & Transport Co, PO Box 2657, Dammam, Saudi Arabia
Associated Companies: Oceanair International (Hellas) Ltd, Greece; Oceanair International (London) England; Oceanair International (Paris), France
Principal Bankers: Chase Manhattan Bank

BEIRUT RIYAD BANK SAL
PO Box 11-4668, Beirut
Tel: 240325, 240920
Cable: Banberi
Telex: 20610 Baberi LE

PRINCIPAL ACTIVITIES: Commercial banking and real estate management
Associated Companies: Arab Finance Corp SAL, Beirut

Date of Establishment: 1958

BRITISH BANK OF THE LEBANON SAL (THE)
PO Box 11-7048, Beirut
Tel: 340491, 250380/5
Cable: Bribanleb Beirut
Telex: 20598 Brileb Le

PRINCIPAL ACTIVITIES: Commercial banking
Branch Offices: Dora; Hamra; Jounieh
Associated Companies: British Bank of the Middle East (London)

Date of Establishment: 1971

BRITISH BANK OF THE MIDDLE EAST (THE)
PO Box 11-1380, Beirut
Tel: 340490, 340492
Cable: Bactria Beirut
Telex: 20762 BBMEBT LE

PRINCIPAL ACTIVITIES: Commercial banking
Branch Offices: Branches in Ras Beirut, Dora, Mazraa, Ashrafieh, Tripoli (Lebanon); and throughout the Middle East
Parent Company: The Hongkong and Shanghai Banking Corporation
Subsidiary Companies: Middle East Finance Co Ltd; BBME Nominees Ltd, London; Societe Immobiliere Atlas, Geneva; Dalbeattie Investments Ltd, Bahamas

Date of Establishment: 1946

BUILDING CHEMICALS CO SAL
PO Box 11-5712, Beirut
Tel: 420722
Telex: 21188 Le BCC

PRINCIPAL ACTIVITIES: Manufacture of expanded polystyrene sheets, packaging and food packaging; manufacture of emulsion and enamel paints, waterproofing and resins; expanded polyethylene pipe insulation
Subsidiary/Associated Companies: Building Chemicals Industries Co, Dammam, Saudi Arabia

BYBLOS BANK SAL
PO Box 11-5605, Beirut
Tel: 417830, 805325
Cable: Byblobank
Telex: BYBEX 20415 LE-BYBANK 41601-43364 LE

PRINCIPAL ACTIVITIES: Commercial banking
Branch Offices: London; Cyprus; In Lebanon: Dora, Jbeil, Verdun, Hamra, Tripoli, Ghobeiri-Okaybe; Sassine, Furn-El-Chebbak, Badaro, Bourj-Hammoud, Jiitawi, Antelias, Jounieh, Kosba, Chtaura, Aamchit, Saida, Batroun, Saifi
Parent Company: Byblos Invest Holding SA, Luxembourg
Subsidiary/Associated Companies: Adonis Insurance & Reinsurance; Societe d'Investissements Fonciers Byblos; Byblos Data Processing Center SARL; Societe Fonciere Generale SAL; Banque Byblos France; Byblos Arab Financing Holding (BARAF) SA; Byblos Bank Belgium
Principal Bankers: Irving Trust Co; Credit Suisse Zurich; Citibank NY; Manufacturers Hanover Trust Co; Chemical Bank; Saudi Cairo Bank, Jeddah; Byblos Bank Belgium; Banque Byblos France; Barclays Bank International, London; Banca Commerciale Italiana; Banque Nationale de Paris (Canada)

Date of Establishment: 1959

LEBANON

CAVES DE KSARA SAL

PO Box 16-6184, Beirut
Tel: 328417, 329800, 322169, 322170
Cable: Ksavinolib
Telex: 20257 Le Salber

President: Dr Albert Sara
Directors: J Pierre Sara (Vice President & Executive Director)

PRINCIPAL ACTIVITIES: Producer of wines and spirits (Ksarak)
Branch Offices: Cellars: Ksara (Lebanon) Tel 821662, 841544/8
Subsidiary Companies: Sodibal Sarl (Lebanon) to distribute the Ksara products on the Lebanese market; Sodicol SA (France) to produce and market Ksarak, the Arack of Ksara
Principal Bankers: Banque Libano-Francaise
Financial Information:

	LL'000
Authorised capital	20,000
Paid-up capital	20,000

Date of Establishment: Founded by Jesuits Fathers in 1857
No of Employees: 75

CHARLES E FROSST & CO (ME) SAL

See FROSST, CHARLES E, & CO (ME) SAL

CODIPHA

PO Box 11-3063, Beirut
Tel: 295716, 234655
Cable: Marleco Beirut

PRINCIPAL ACTIVITIES: Production and distribution of pharmaceutical and para-pharmaceutical products, manufacturers' representatives
Principal Agencies: Roussel Laboratories, UK; Laboratories Roussel, France; Ashe Laboratories Ltd, UK; Clin Midy International, France; Laboratories Beaufour, France; Laboratories Sarget-Ambrine SA, France; Brune Nadler & Cuffe, USA; Ets NV Lijempf, Holland; King Chemicals Co Ltd, Japan; Ravizza, Italy

COMATRA MIDDLE EAST SAL

PO Box 18-5012, Beirut
Tel: 300161, 303719
Telex: 21090 Comame LE

PRINCIPAL ACTIVITIES: Manufacturers' representation, import and distribution of construction equipment, heavy machinery and equipment, earthmoving equipment and construction plant, building contractors, plant hire

COMPAGNIE LIBANAISE DE TELEVISION

PO Box 11-4848, Beirut
Tel: 300360
Cable: Teve Liban
Telex: 20923 LE

PRINCIPAL ACTIVITIES: Television broadcasting
Principal Bankers: BNPI; Banque de la Mediterranee

Principal Shareholders: Sofirad, Intra

CONSOLIDATED CONTRACTORS CO SAL

PO Box 11-2254, Beirut
Tel: 352402
Cable: Concobeirut
Telex: 20515, 20905

PRINCIPAL ACTIVITIES: General construction and engineering contractors, pipeline contractors, marine, civil and mechanical works
Branch Offices: Managing Office: Consolidated Contractors International Co Ltd, Atrina Center, 32A Kifissias Ave, PO Box 61092, Amaroussion, Athens, Greece; Telex CCICL 219551-219734-219735 GR; Tel 6829200 (19 lines); also branches in Saudi Arabia (Riyadh and Dhahran); Abu Dhabi; Oman; Kuwait; Jordan, Iraq, Lebanon

Principal Bankers: Arab Bank, Bank of America

Date of Establishment: 1950
No of Employees: 10,000

CONSOLIDATED STEEL LEBANON SAL

PO Box 11-5198, Beirut
Tel: 227257, 297847
Cable: Steelian Beirut
Telex: 20543 Le Seel

PRINCIPAL ACTIVITIES: Hot rolling mill: reinforcing rounds small shapes; wire drawing plant: black annealed and galvanised wire
Principal Bankers: Litex Bank SAL

CONSTRUCTION MACHINERY TRADE SAL

PO Box 18-5012, Beirut
Tel: 303719, 300161
Cable: Comatramid
Telex: 21090 Comame Le

PRINCIPAL ACTIVITIES: Industrial marketing; trading and distribution of construction and earthmoving equipment and plants
Principal Agencies: FE Weatherill Ltd, Priestman Brothers Ltd, ACE Machinery Ltd, Edilmac SPA, Bukh AS, Phillips Drill Co
Branch Offices: Egypt: c/o Newtrend, G G Tarza, PO Box 10, Dokki, Giza, Cairo
Subsidiary/Associated Companies: Matra JCB Ltd, Cyprus; Comatra SA, Switzerland
Principal Bankers: British Bank of the Middle East; G Trad Credit Lyonnais SAL

Date of Establishment: 1973

CONTRACTING & TRADING CO (CAT)

PO Box 11-1036, Beirut
Tel: 221564/9, 252660/5
Cable: CAT Beirut
Telex: 20616 LE Cat

PRINCIPAL ACTIVITIES: Civil, mechanical and electrical engineering and pipeline and marine works contractors
Principal Agencies: Incotes Co Ltd, 1 Great Cumberland Place, London W1H 7AL
Branch Offices: Abu Dhabi, Bahrain, Dubai, Kuwait, Saudi Arabia, Sharjah, Ras Al Khaimah, Qatar, Sudan, Jordan
Subsidiary/Affiliated Companies: Mothercat Ltd (95%); Francat SA, Paris; Eurocat Sarl, Paris; Cycat Ltd, Limassol, Cyprus; Contracting & Trading (Iraq) Co Ltd; Dubai Hotels Ltd; Arab Contracting & Trading Co, Cairo; Arab Contracting & Trading Co Ltd, Amman; Building & Road Co(BARCO), Kuwait; Engineering Contractors Ltd, Lichtenstein
Principal Bankers: Hong Kong & Shanghai Banking Corp/British Bank of the Middle East; Grindlays Bank; Bank of America; Banque Indosuez, Banque Paribas

Date of Establishment: 1942

CREDIT COMMERCIAL DE FRANCE (MOYEN ORIENT) SAL

PO Box 11-8271, Beirut
Tel: 365100
Cable: Crefamo
Telex: 22224, 23266

PRINCIPAL ACTIVITIES: Commercial banking
Subsidiary Companies: Credit Commercial de France (Moyen Orient) SA, Paris, France

Principal Shareholders: Credit Commercial de France, Ets Georges Nicolas Shammas, Arab Investment Co SAL, Societe Financiere et Immobiliere de Beyrouth
Date of Establishment: 1964

CREDIT LIBANAIS SAL

PO Box 11-1458, Beirut
Tel: 582810/1, 582390, 809807/8
Cable: Creditlib
Telex: 42862, 43623, 41273, 43622
Telefax: 582390

PRINCIPAL ACTIVITIES: Commercial banking
Branch Offices: In Lebanon: Hamra, Ghobeiry, Mazraa, Ras
  Beirut, Verdun, Jisr, Bauchrieh, Bourj Hammoud, Rmeil, Zouk,
  Dora, Achrafieh, Furn El Chubbak, Sin El Fil, Broummana, Bar
  Elias, Chtaura, Jeb Jannine, Zahle, Machghara, Ferzol,
  Tripoli, Batroun, Saida; also in Cyprus: Credit Libanais SAL
  Offshore Banking Unit, Limassol, PO Box 3492, Telex 4702
  CRELIB CY, Tel (051) 35266, Fax 37032
Financial Information:

	LL'000
Authorised capital	60,000
Paid-up capital	60,000

Date of Establishment: 1961
No of Employees: 502

CREDIT SUISSE (MOYEN ORIENT) SAL

PO Box 11-9552, Beirut
Tel: 221720/1, 255321 (forex)
Cable: Suicredit
Telex: 21072 LE Cresui

Chairman: Dr Klaus Jenny (General Manager)
Directors: HE Me Fouad Boutros, Vahe Jazmadarian, Robert
  Matar

PRINCIPAL ACTIVITIES: Commercial banking
Branch Offices: In Lebanon: Dora, Hamra
Associated Companies: Credit Suisse, Zurich
Financial Information:

	LL'000
Authorised capital	15,000
Paid-up capital	15,000

Principal Shareholders: Credit Suisse Zurich (99.1%); Local
  shareholders (0.9%)
Date of Establishment: 1973

DAR AL-HANDASAH CONSULTANTS

Shair & Partners

PO Box 11-7159, Beirut
Tel: 319134, 300256
Cable: Darsah
Telex: 20697 Darsah; 22684

PRINCIPAL ACTIVITIES: Town planning and architecture, civil,
  structural, electrical, mechanical and industrial engineering,
  transportation, engineering consultants, advisory and
  management services
Branch Offices: Algeria; Bahrain; Egypt; Jordan; Kuwait;
  Morocco; Nigeria; Saudi Arabia; Sudan; Syria; Abu Dhabi;
  Dubai; Ras Al Khaimah; Yemen AR; Yemen PDR; France; UK
Subsidiary Companies: Research Associates for Technological
  Development
Principal Bankers: Arab Bank Ltd

Date of Establishment: 1956, 1970 (New Management)
No of Employees: 1,650

ELBA MIDDLE EAST

PO Box 11-6100, Beirut
Tel: 840800, 841106
Telex: 20152

PRINCIPAL ACTIVITIES: Manufacture of tipper bodies, trailers,
  semi trailers, tankers
Branch Offices: Plant at Chtaura (Bekaa plain)

Date of Establishment: 1968

ESCAT

Engineering Services Contracting & Trading

PO Box 11-3013, Beirut
Cable: Escat

PRINCIPAL ACTIVITIES: General contractors on turnkey jobs;
  importers of pre-engineered and pre-fabricated systems,
  reinforced concrete and masonry works
Branch Offices: Riyadh, Al-Kharj, Jubail
Principal Bankers: Al Bank Al Saudi Al Fransi, Saudi Arabia;
  Banque Paribas, Paris; British Bank of the Middle East, Beirut

Date of Establishment: 1960

ETS FOUAD SALIM SAAD SAL

See SAAD, ETS FOUAD SALIM, SAL

ETS GEORGE ABOU ADAL & CIE

See ABOU ADAL, ETS GEORGE, & CIE

EXERV CORPORATION SA

PO Box 11-7284, Beirut
Tel: 341198/9
Cable: Exervcorp
Telex: 21175 Exerv

PRINCIPAL ACTIVITIES: Holding company, marketing, financial,
  investment banking, international catering, manufacturers'
  representative. The corporation also has several joint
  ventures
Principal Agencies: Mosler (Div of American Standard). Hendrich
  Building Systems, Mieco, Aliand International, Jesup &
  Lamont Middle East, East; Polycast Technology
Branch Offices: Exerv Corp, PO Bo 6079, Sharjah, United Arab
  Emirates; Exerv Corp SA, PO Box 1704, Jeddah, Saudi
  Arabia; Exerv Corp, SA, 6 rue Bellot 1206 Geneva,
  Switzerland; 100 Park Ave, New York NY 1001; PO Box
  34605, 9490 Vaduz
Subsidiary/Associated Companies: ESI Management Corp;
  Hendrich Building Systems; Direct Design International; Jesup
  & Lamont Inc; Atco Sarl; Cincinatti Fan and Ventilator Co;
  Ariand International; PT Holding Co, Inc
Principal Bankers: Chase Manhattan Bank; British Bank of the
  Middle East; First National Bank of Chicago; Chemical Bank

Date of Establishment: 1968

F A KETTANEH SA

See KETTANEH, F A, SA

F TAMER & FILS SA

See TAMER, F, & FILS SA

FATTAL, KHALIL, & FILS

PO Box 11-0773, Beirut
Tel: 425450, 426120
Cable: Kafattal
Telex: 20747 KFF LE
Telefax: 494820 ext 431

Chairman: Georges Fattal
Directors: Khalil M Fattal, Bernard J Fattal

PRINCIPAL ACTIVITIES: General trading and contracting
Principal Agencies: Gillette; Unilever Export; Duracell; Xerox;
  John Dewar; Elizabeth Arden
Branch Offices: North Lebanon; Bekaa Valley; South Lebanon
Parent Company: Fattal Holdings
Subsidiary Companies: SNCI (Manufacture of toiletries);
  Midexport (representation in the Arab World); Assurex
  (Insurance Co)
Principal Bankers: BNPI; Banque Audi; Societe Generale
Financial Information:

	LL'000
Authorised capital	25,200
Paid-up capital	25,200

Principal Shareholders: Chairman and directors as described
Date of Establishment: 1897
No of Employees: 500

FEDERAL BANK OF LEBANON SAL

PO Box 11-2209, Beirut
Tel: 220733/5, 229918/9, 231837, 244946
Cable: FEDERALIBAN
Telex: 20267 Fedral LE, 22969 LE, 20267 LE

PRINCIPAL ACTIVITIES: Commercial banking
Branch Offices: Dora, Hamra, Jounieh, Jbeil, Aley, Damour, Bhamdoun; Representative Office: Nicosia, Cyprus
Subsidiary Companies: Federal Bank of the Middle East, Nicosia, Cyprus (offshore)
Principal Bankers: BNPI, Paris; Al Saudi Bank, Paris, National Westminster Bank Ltd, London; Chemical Bank, New York; Irving Trust Co, New York

Date of Establishment: 1952

FILATURE NATIONALE DE COTON SAL
ASSEILY & CIE

PO Box 11-4126, Beirut
Tel: 890610
Telex: 20018 LE

PRINCIPAL ACTIVITIES: Spinning and weaving, textiles

FONDERIES OHANNES H KASSARDJIAN SAL

PO Box 11-4150, Beirut
Tel: 462244
Cable: Okafond Beirut
Telex: 21117 Okafon LE

PRINCIPAL ACTIVITIES: Production of bronze, brass and chromium-plated sanitary fixtures; cast iron soil pipes and fittings, manhole covers and frames, gully gratings; manufacture of special high-pressure cast iron fittings for use with asbestos cement pipes, as well as cast iron sluice valves, check valves, air valves and fire hydrants, for water distribution and sewerage schemes

Date of Establishment: 1939

FRANSABANK SAL

BP 11-0393, Beirut
Tel: 340180/8, 860633, 860822, 861236
Cable: FRANSBANK
Telex: 20631, 23111, 40036

President: Adnan Kassar
Directors: Adel Kassar (Deputy Chairman), Habib Nauphal (General Manager), Mohammad Rabih Ammache, Rafic Charafeddine, Cheikh Abdul Rahman Mohd Mouminah, Me Raymond Rizk, Caisse Nationale de Credit Agricole (represented by Francois Jouven)

PRINCIPAL ACTIVITIES: Commercial banking
Branch Offices: In Lebanon: Beirut (13), Jbeil, Jounieh, Sarba, Tripoli, Chekka, Zahle (2), Baalbeck, Chtaura, Saida, Bint Jbeil, Jezzine, Marjayoun, Nabatieh, Tyr
Subsidiary/Associated Companies: Wholly owned subsidiaries: Societe Generale Fonciere SAL (SOGEFON), Societe de Participation et d'Entreprises pour le Moyen-Orient SAL (SOPEMO), Societe Generale d'Informatique SAL (SOGINFORM); Representative Offices: Budapest (Hungary); Long Kong; Subsidiary in Paris: Fransabank (France) SA; Affiliated Co in Geneva: Financiere Fransad SA
Principal Bankers: Manufacturers Hanover Trust Co, New York; Union des Banques Suisses, Zurich; Barclays Bank Plc, London

Financial Information:

	LL'000
Authorised capital	40,000
Paid-up capital	40,000

Date of Establishment: 1921
No of Employees: 486

FROSST, CHARLES E, & CO (ME) SAL

PO Box 11-962, Beirut
Tel: 930370
Cable: Frosst Beirut
Telex: 21615 LE

PRINCIPAL ACTIVITIES: Manufacture and sale of pharmaceuticals
Principal Bankers: Bank of America

GABRIEL ACAR & FILS

PO Box 80484, Dora
Tel: 582027, 494971, 493058
Cable: Acarfils Beirut
Telex: 21223 Acar LE

Chairman: Victor Acar
Directors: Gabriel Acar (Managing Director & Commercial Director)

PRINCIPAL ACTIVITIES: Contracting in hydro-electrical fields; import and distribution of mechanical and industrial products and equipment, fabricated steelwork, indusrial chemicals, water treatment and pumping plants, measuring instruments, rubber products; agents and general trading; agricultural equipment and services; telecommunications
Principal Agencies: Layne & Bowler Inc, Haenni SA, Amsler SA, Pilot Tools, Jung & Co, AEG-Telefunken AG, NKF, A Friedr Flender KG, Deer Island Ind (Japan), Guest & Chrimes Ltd, Rotork Controls Ltd, Skega AB, Mangels, Zacchi, Bristol Pneumatic Tools, Hoyt Metal, Itur, Chemetron, All State Weldng Alloys, Saunders Valve Co, Usocome Sew
Subsidiary/Associated Companies: Acar Concrete Blocks Factory (Lebanon); Victor & Charles Acar & Associes sarl; IVITA; Victor Acar Antiballe
Principal Bankers: Banque Trad - Credit Lyonnais SAL; Banque Saradar SAL; Ste Nlle Banque de Syrie & du Liban SAL

Date of Establishment: 1918

GANDOUR INDUSTRIAL CO SAL

PO Box 665, Tripoli
Tel: 630427/8

PRINCIPAL ACTIVITIES: Manufacture of vegetable oils and fats and its products, cold storage

GANDRA (MIDDLE EAST) SARL

PO Box 11-1652, Beirut
Tel: 221515/16
Cable: Gandra
Telex: 20247 LE

PRINCIPAL ACTIVITIES: Distribution of electrical, mechanical and agricultural equipment; hydro-electrical contractors
Principal Agencies: Bombas Ideal SA, Spain; Smith-Son, LA, USA; Johnson Gear; Clarke's Compressors Group; Girdlestone Pumps, UK; Gandra Intl Lubbock, Texas; Gandra Intl, NJ, USA
Principal Bankers: Almashrik Bank; Arab Bank Ltd

GARGOUR, T, & FILS

PO Box 11-371, Beirut

PRINCIPAL ACTIVITIES: Shipping agents and owners, importers and exporters specialising in automobiles and spare parts
Principal Agencies: Daimler-Benz
Branch Offices: PO Box 419, Amman, Jordan; 2 Albert Gate, London SW1X 7JX; 30 rue de Gramont, 75002, Paris, France

Subsidiary/Associated Companies: Lebanese Ceramic Factory (LECICO); Associated Levant Lines (ALL)

Principal Shareholders: Private company

GEMAYEL FRERES SAL

PO Box 11-3272, Beirut
Tel: 980122 (Plant), 260208/9 (Office)
Cable: Gemayelpack
Telex: 22713 LE Gempak

PRINCIPAL ACTIVITIES: Paperboard, corrugated, packaging
Branch Offices: Office in Dora, Lebanon, plant in Bikfaya, Lebanon
Principal Bankers: Banque Libanaise pour le Commerce SAL; Banque Libano-Francaise SAL; Byblos Bank SAL; Fransabank SAL

GHANDOUR, M O, & FILS

PO Box 494, Beirut
Tel: 431500, 431920
Telex: 20874 Choco LE

PRINCIPAL ACTIVITIES: Manufacturers, general traders and contractors

INDUSTRIAL DEVELOPMENT CO SARL

PO Box 11-2354, Beirut
Tel: 951445, 950856, 890680, 894339, 892347, 894322, 217530
Cable: STELHELM, BEIRUT/LEBANON
Telex: 22949 INDEV LE, 22336 PROFIN LE

PRINCIPAL ACTIVITIES: Promotion and execution of new projects and professional management; participation in industrial projects
Branch Offices: Washington, DC, USA; Riyadh, Saudi Arabia; Ajaltoun, Lebanon
Subsidiary Companies: Lebanon: Unipak, Masterpak, Sanita, Gespa, Mediapac, Agriroots, Hotel Du Roy, New Okal, Constrapak, Phoenicia Arab Hotel Management Pam Sarl, Tissue Mill Sarl, Saudi Arabia: NPPC, Carlton Al Moaibed Hotel, Safaripak, Badyapak, United Packaging; Dammam Farm; USA: Interstate Resources Inc; Merpas; Brazil: Plastpel Ltd, Cedarpak
Principal Bankers: Banque Libano Francaise, Lebanon; Chemical Bank, New York; Banque Indosuez, Lausanne

Date of Establishment: 1963 (Registration in 1972)

INTERCOOL LTD

PO Box 113-5372, Beirut
Tel: 364469, 364569
Cable: Johenriksen
Telex: 21112 Cool LE

PRINCIPAL ACTIVITIES: Designing, planning, supplying and erecting: ice cream plants, animal slaughter houses, dairy plants chicken slaughter houses, chicken farms equipment and hatcheries, cheese factories, freezing and cold stores
Principal Bankers: British Bank of the Middle East; Arab African Bank

INTERMARKETS SAL

PO Box 110-963, Beirut
Tel: 481475, 480477
Cable: Intermarkets Beirut
Telex: 40477 Market LE

PRINCIPAL ACTIVITIES: Advertising agency; production of films, handling of sales promotion schemes, and public relation programs
Branch Offices: Intermarkets Kuwait, PO Box 20604, Kuwait, Tel 414020, Telex 22658 Intmar KT. Intermarkets, Bahrain, PO Box 5047, Bahrain, Tel 250760, Telex 8400 Market GJ. Intermarkets, UAE, PO Box 7434, Deira, Dubai, Tel 665960, Telex 46361 Market db. Intermarkets, Egypt, 5 Dar el Shifa St, Garden City, Cairo, Tel 22978, Telex 7592 Integ Un.

Intermarkets, Saudi Arabia, PO Box 4635, Jeddah, Tel 6719929, Telex 400593 Inter SJ. Intermarkets, Jordan, PO Box 926976, Amman, Tel 63576, Telex 22167 Dajani JO Intermarkets, Europe, 29 Curzon Street, London W.I. Phone 6290898, Telex 296888 TWA.
Parent Company: Burson Marsteller/Intermarkets
Principal Bankers: Banque Audi Sal, American Express Banking Corp.

Date of Establishment: 1971

INTERNATIONAL COSMETIC MANUFACTURING CO SAL

PO Box 11-1332, Beirut
Tel: 280013, 288726
Cable: Geodal Beirut
Telex: 20525

PRINCIPAL ACTIVITIES: Manufacture and distribution of perfumes and cosmetic products
Principal Agencies: L'Oreal, Lancome, Guy Laroche, Bristol Myers, Vichy

JALLAD, M EZZAT, & FILS

PO Box 110208, Beirut
Tel: 932522
Cable: Jamla
Telex: 21614 Jamla LE

PRINCIPAL ACTIVITIES: Distribution of heavy equipment; industrial agricultural, marine and construction
Principal Agencies: Caterpillar Overseas SA, Geneva; Coles Cranes, UK; Consolidated Pneumatic Tool Co, UK; Hyster Europe, UK; FMC Peerless Pumps, USA
Branch Offices: M Ezzat Jallad & Fils pour le Commerce et la Representation (M Duried Jallad & Co), PO Box 23, Damascus, Syria Branches: Aleppo; Lattakia; Kamichlie Jordan Tractor & Equipment Co Ltd, PO Box 313, Amman, Jordan

JAMMAL TRUST BANK SAL

PO Box 11-5640, Beirut
Tel: 292340/47
Cable: Jamibk Beirut
Telex: 20854, 20939, 23192

PRINCIPAL ACTIVITIES: Commercial banking
Branch Offices: 3 Branches in Egypt
Subsidiary Companies: JTB Finance & Investment Trust Co Ltd; Malminster Ltd; Real Estate for Investment & Development Co SAL

Date of Establishment: 1963

KAMEL, PHILIPPE, SARL

PO Box 11-190, Beirut
Tel: 483940, 582842 (4 lines)
Cable: Philkamel Beirut
Telex: 21081 LE Philka, 43689 LE Filkad

President: Philippe Kamel
Directors: Samir Ph Kamel (General Manager)

PRINCIPAL ACTIVITIES: Marketing and distribution of generating sets, industrial machinery, construction equipment, marine equipment, heavy machinery and electrical equipment, data systems, computers, chemicals and paints
Principal Agencies: Dupont De Nemours, Ingersoll-Rand, ITT Data Systems, Mercury, Skil, Devilbiss, Sherwin Williams, John Deere Int, Rotary Lifts, Bennett Pumps, Graco France, STP Corp, F Parker Plc, CIFA SpA, AMF Mares Sub SpA, Multirep France Computers, Binks Int, ECO, Furnas, ABG GmbH, etc
Subsidiary Companies: Dubai (UAE) Equipment Int'l, PO Box 1871, Dubai, UAE
Principal Bankers: Banque de l'Industrie et du Travail SAL, Saifi Branch

LEBANON

Financial Information:

	US$'000
Authorised capital	1,000
Paid-up capital	1,000

Principal Shareholders: Samir Ph Kamel, Mrs Andree Tueni Kamel, Mrs Roula Kamel Jabbour
Date of Establishment: 1936
No of Employees: 50

KARAOGLAN NASCO & CO SARL
See NASCO, KARAOGLAN, & CO SARL

KAROUN DAIRIES SAL
PO Box 11-9150, Beirut
Tel: 269080, 264618
Cable: Laikaroun Beirut

PRINCIPAL ACTIVITIES: Production, distribution, wholesale and retail of milk and dairy products, import and export, representation of companies
Principal Bankers: Banque Nationale de Paris Intercontinentale; Banco di Roma

Date of Establishment: 1931

KETTANEH, F A, SA
Kettaneh Freres
PO Box 110-242, Beirut
Tel: 360757/8, 444560/4
Cable: Tanis Beirut
Telex: 20614 Tanis LE, 21772 Tanis LE

PRINCIPAL ACTIVITIES: General trading and contracting, import and distribution of passenger and commercial vehicles (Volkswagen & Audi), domestic appliances, air conditioners, drilling equipment and supplies, electrical, communication and industrial equipment, construction equipment, pharmaceuticals, cigarettes etc
Principal Agencies: VW Audi Group, GE Maid/GE Medical Systems, Atlas Copco, Siemens AG, Kohler, Buhler, FEB, Shering US; Philip Morris
Branch Offices: Tripoli, Zahle
Principal Bankers: British Bank of the Middle East; Societe Nouvelle de la Banque de Syrie et du Liban

Principal Shareholders: Kettaneh Family
Date of Establishment: 1952

KHALIL FATTAL & FILS
See FATTAL, KHALIL, & FILS

KHATIB AND ALAMI
Consolidated Engineering Co
PO Box 11-6203, Beirut
Tel: 300609
Cable: CONSING
Telex: 23523 CEC LE
Telefax: (9611) 862197

President: Prof Mounir El-Khatib
Director: Dr Zuheir Alami (Senior Partner)
Associates: Wail Sa'di (General Manager), Samir Abdulhadi (General Manager), Samir Moghrabi (Head of Transportation Dept), Dr Omar Omari (Head of Strutural Dept), Jacques S Ekmekji (Director of Special Assignments), Abdul Monem Ariss (Resident Manager Riyadh), Samir El Khatib (Resident Manager Jeddah), Othman Ayaso (Resident Manager Oman)

PRINCIPAL ACTIVITIES: Consulting engineers, architects, planners and designers
Branch Offices: Saudi Arabia: Riyadh, PO Box 3928, Tel 4766309, 4778384, Telex 401652, Fax 9661-4779793; Jeddah, PO Box 9330, Tel 6694541, Telex 602988, Fax 9662-6691340; AlKhobar, PO Box 1713, Tel 8946816, Telex 871441, Fax 9663-8942341; United Arab Emirates: Sharjah, PO Box 688, Tel 354144, Telex 68474, Fax 9716-354027; Abu Dhabi, PO Box 2732, Tel 662885, Telex 23790, Fax 9712-660289; Dubai, PO Box 5091, Tel 222203/4, Telex 45725, Fax 281014; Al Ain, PO Box 15860, Tel 55514; Bahrain: Manama, PO Box 5083, Tel 742131, Telex 8783, Fax 973-742120; Oman: Ruwi, PO Box 3238, Tel 702558, Telex 3452, Fax 705593; Jordan: Amman, PO Box 35256, Tel 822136, Telex 23012, Fax 822137
Parent Company: Head office in Beirut
Subsidiary Companies: Saudi CEC (Khatib & Alami); CEC Jordan (Alami & Abdulhadi)
Principal Bankers: Arab Bank Ltd
Financial Information:

	1988/89 US$'000
Sales turnover	15,000
Authorised capital	125
Paid-up capital	125

Date of Establishment: 1959
No of Employees: 410

LAHOUD ENGINEERING CO LTD
PO Box 11-4400, Beirut
Tel: 392922, 391403
Cable: Lencobey
Telex: 20203 Lencob LE

PRINCIPAL ACTIVITIES: Construction of industrial plants (cement plants, refineries, pipelines, desalination plants, power stations, etc)
Branch Offices: Al Owais Bldg, Bin Yas Street, Deira, PO Box 10111, Dubai, UAE; Tel 284131; Telex 47078 Lencd EM; Mohd Mansouri Bldg, Al Moushref Roundabout, Abu Dhabi, Tel 377282, Telex 23255
Associated Companies: Lahoud Engineering Co (UK) Ltd, 1 Hill St, Berkeley Square, London W1, UK

LE DAUPHIN - SKYPAK INTERNATIONAL
PO Box 116-2037, Beirut
Tel: 384156, 388870
Telex: 21218 SAGIT

PRINCIPAL ACTIVITIES: Worldwide courier service, collection, clearance and delivery of documents and commercial value items

LEBANESE AIR TRANSPORT (CHARTER) SAL
PO Box 11-1331, Beirut
Tel: 277570/2
Cable: Lebatra, Beirut
Telex: 20743 LE/Sita Beytolq

PRINCIPAL ACTIVITIES: Airport and in flight catering
Associated Companies: Albert Abela SAL
Principal Bankers: Audi Bank; Adcom Bank

Date of Establishment: 1958

LEBANESE ARAB BANK SAL (THE)
PO Box 16-5892
Tel: 297671/2
Cable: Larabank
Telex: 22060 LE

PRINCIPAL ACTIVITIES: Commercial banking
Branch Offices: Jal Al Dib, Beirut, Tripoli, Chekka, Jbeil
Subsidiary Companies: Lebanese Arab Bank (France) SA, Paris, France

Date of Establishment: 1973

LEBANESE CERAMIC INDUSTRIES SAL
PO Box 11-5147, Beirut
Tel: 431633/9, 432566
Cable: Khazaf
Telex: 20686 Khazaf LE; 20102

PRINCIPAL ACTIVITIES: Manufacture of sanitary ware, walls tiles and floor tiles
Subsidiary/Associated Companies: Lecico, Egypt, Alexandria, Egypt; Uniceramic, Zahle, Lebanon
Principal Bankers: British Bank of the Middle East; Bank of America; First Bank of Chicago; Bank Almashrek

Date of Establishment: 1959

LEBANON & GULF BANK SAL
PO Box 113-6404, Beirut
Tel: 340190, 370190, 813151, 371804
Cable: LEBGULF
Telex: 22097, 41693, 21074, 22538

PRINCIPAL ACTIVITIES: Commercial banking
Branch Offices: Mazrra; Dora; Zahle; Tripoli

Date of Establishment: 1963

LEBANON CHEMICAL CO SAL
PO Box 11-1113, Beirut
Tel: 421588
Telex: 20360 Elidou LE

PRINCIPAL ACTIVITIES: Chemicals production

LIBAN CABLES SAL
PO Box 11-6008, Beirut
Tel: 350040/6
Cable: Libcable Beirut
Telex: 21545 LE

PRINCIPAL ACTIVITIES: Production of all kinds of bare and insulated wire and cable, including overhead cables, building wire, flexible cords, power cables, telephone cables and special cables
Principal Bankers: Banque G Trad (Credit Lyonnais) SAL; Banque du Credit Populaire; Banque Libano-Francaise; Banque Libanaise pour le Commerce

Principal Shareholders: Cables de Lyon (France), Phelps Dodge (NY), Doumet Group (Lebanon), Jallad Group (Lebanon), Bechara Takla (Lebanon)

LIBANO INTERNATIONAL TRADING CORPORATION
PO Box 11-3604, Beirut
Tel: 230950, 300741
Cable: Lintro
Telex: 21637

PRINCIPAL ACTIVITIES: Tractors, pumps, hydraulic presses, and agricultural equipment, tyres etc; importers of fertilizers, paper, etc
Principal Agencies: Tractorexport, Moscow; Techmashexport, Moscow; Raznoimport, Moscow
Principal Bankers: Arab Bank

LIMITED TRADING CO OF LEBANON
PO Box 83, Beirut
Tel: 367136
Telex: 20980 LE

PRINCIPAL ACTIVITIES: Agricultural services
Branch Offices: Saida

M EZZAT JALLAD & FILS
See JALLAD, M EZZAT, & FILS

M O GHANDOUR & FILS
See GHANDOUR, M O, & FILS

MECHANICAL & CIVIL ENGINEERING CONTRACTORS LTD
M.A.C.E.
Maamari Street, Gardenia Building, Beirut
Tel: 343687
Telex: 22109

PRINCIPAL ACTIVITIES: Mechanical and civil Contracting
Branch Offices: Mechanical & Civil Engineering Contractors Ltd, PO Box 119, St Peter Port, Guernsey, CI; Mechanical & Civil Engineering Contractors Ltd, PO Box 12115, Tripoli, Libya; Mechanical & Civil Engineering Contractors (UK) Ltd, Brighton, UK; Mechanical & Civil Engineering Contractors (MACE) Ltd, PO Box 2307, Abu Dhabi, UAE; Al Mutlaq MACE Saudi Arabia Ltd, PO Box 429, Dhahran Airport, Saudi Arabia
Principal Bankers: British Bank of the Middle East

MECIS HOLDING
PO Box 50242, Beirut
Tel: 414830, 411887
Telex: 22011 Mecis LE, 23540 Mecis LE

PRINCIPAL ACTIVITIES: Finance and investment in touristic and industrial projects, construction, irrigation and agricultural projects, oil refineries
Branch Offices: Paris Office; Joannesburg Office
Subsidiary Companies: Mecis Middle East Commercial & Investment Services SAL; Medi Middle East Development & Investment SAL; Mecis Shipping Co SAL; TWT Trans World Tourism SAL; Mecis Insurance & Reinsurance Co SAL; Centre Anis et Hajj SAL
Principal Bankers: Foreign Trade Bank SAL

MEDITERRANEAN OIL SHIPPING & TRANSPORT CO SAL
M.E.D.C.O. SAL
PO Box 11-6274, Beirut
Tel: 260110, 265629, 264419
Cable: Geochammas Beirut
Telex: 22259 Menira; 20112 CTC TCO

PRINCIPAL ACTIVITIES: Marketing, transport and storage of refined petroleum products chemicals and petrochemicals

MEDITERRANEAN REFINING CO
PO Box 111925, Beirut

PRINCIPAL ACTIVITIES: Oil refining
Branch Offices: Refinery at Sidon

MERCURY SAL
PO Box 11-515, Beirut
Tel: 362354
Cable: Mercury
Telex: 20231 LE

PRINCIPAL ACTIVITIES: Distribution of pharmaceuticals, hospital products, veterinary products, poultry equipment, stationery, cosmetics, lighters and watches, towels and sheets
Principal Agencies: American Cyanamid, Kendall International, Laboratories Vifor, Terumo Corporation, Maruman, Yema, Fieldcrest, Carter-Wallace, Giordario Poultry Plast, Layla, Pierrel, Diversey Ltd, AR Wood
Principal Bankers: The First National Bank of Chicago; Banque Nationale de Paris Intercontinentale; Banque Libano-Francaise; Banque Francaise pour le Moyen-Orient

MERZARIO MIDDLE EAST
PO Box 11-1402, Beirut
Tel: 803814, 803782
Telex: 20069 MERZBE LE

PRINCIPAL ACTIVITIES: Shipping and forwarding

LEBANON

MIDDLE EAST AIRLINES AIR LIBAN SAL
M.E.A.
PO Box 206, Beirut
Tel: 272220, 316316
Cable: Cedarwings
Telex: 20820 LE Cedars

PRINCIPAL ACTIVITIES: Transportation of passenger and
cargo
Branch Offices: MEA London, 80 Piccadilly W1; MEA Dhahran,
Prince Nasser Street, Alkhobar; MEA Paris, 6 rue Scribe,
75009 Paris; MEA Cairo. 12 Kasr El Nile St
Associated Companies: Mideast Aircraft Service Co (MASCO);
Willis Faber (Middle East) SAL; Metra Insurance and
Reinsurance Co SAL
Principal Bankers: Chase Manhattan Bank

Principal Shareholders: Intra Investment Co; Air France
Date of Establishment: 1945

MIDDLE EAST BANKING CO SAL
MEBCO BANK
PO Box 11-3540, Beirut
Tel: 810600
Cable: Mebcobank
Telex: 20729 Mebcol LE

PRINCIPAL ACTIVITIES: Commercial banking
Subsidiary Companies: SOCOFI SA, Geneva; SCF Finance Co
Ltd, London; Petra Bank, Amman
Principal Bankers: Manufacturers Hanover Trust Co, New York;
Irving Trust Co, New York; Morgan Guaranty Trust Co,
London, New York; National Westminster Bank, London

Principal Shareholders: Merchants & businessmen from Arab
Countries
Date of Establishment: 1959

MIDDLE EAST CABLES SARL
PO Box 11-7769, Beirut
Tel: 251950, 320990
Cable: Midescab
Telex: 21066 Ceg LE

PRINCIPAL ACTIVITIES: Manufacture and distribution of
electrical cables and wires
Principal Bankers: Banque Nationale de Paris Intercontinentale;
Beirut Riyad Bank SAL

MIDDLE EAST PRESS
PO Box 90484, Jedeidet El-Matn
Tel: 260932
Cable: Mideast

PRINCIPAL ACTIVITIES: Printing and publishing
Principal Bankers: Byblos Bank, Beirut

Date of Establishment: 1947

MOTHERCAT LTD
PO Box 11-1036, Beirut
Tel: 252660/5
Cable: Mothercat Beirut
Telex: 20616 LE Cat

PRINCIPAL ACTIVITIES: Civil, mechanical and electrical
engineering, pipeline and marine works contractors
Principal Agencies: Incotes Co Ltd, 1 Great Cumberland Place,
London W1H7AL
Branch Offices: Bahrain; Dubai; Jordan; Oman; Abu Dhabi;
Qatar; Ras Al Khaimah; Sharjah; registered office: 175 West
George St, Glasgow, UK
Parent Company: Contracting & Trading Company (CAT), PO
Box 11-1036, Beirut, Lebanon
Subsidiary/Affiliated Companies: Mothercat Overseas Ltd;
Mothercat Overseas (Nigeria) Ltd; Mothercat Saudi Arabia

WLL; Dubai Hotels Ltd; Engineering Contractors Ltd; Refinery
Maintenance Services Ltd
Principal Bankers: Hong Kong and Shanghai Banking
Corp/British Bank of the Middle East; Grindlays Bank; Bank
of America; Banque Indosuez; Banque Paribas

Principal Shareholders: CAT (95%); Motherwell Bridge (Holding)
Ltd (5%)
Date of Establishment: 1951

NAAMANI, A K, & CO SARL
PO Box 11-347, Beirut
Tel: 297740
Cable: Kanaamani
Telex: 21167 LE Kamani

PRINCIPAL ACTIVITIES: Distribution of clothing; toiletries and
cosmetics; registration of trade marks and patents
Principal Bankers: Banque du Liban et d'Outre-Mer

NASCO, KARAOGLAN, & CO SARL
PO Box 11-4293, Beirut
Tel: 339538, 339448
Cable: Naskar Beirut
Telex: 21672 LE Bassur

PRINCIPAL ACTIVITIES: Insurance agents and brokers
Principal Agencies: La Fonciere, Paris; Bankers Assurance SAL
Associated Companies: Stewart Wrightson Ltd, London
Principal Bankers: Credit Libanais SAL

Principal Shareholders: Circocrest Investments Ltd (Stewart
Wrightson Ltd); Saba Nader; Maurice Karaoglan
Date of Establishment: 1969

NATIONAL BANK FOR INDUSTRIAL & TOURISTIC DEVELOPMENT
Banque Nationale pour le Developpement Industriel et Touristique
PO Box 11-8412, Beirut
Tel: 863834, 863645, 348319, 354751
Cable: Inmabank
Telex: 23086 LE

Chairman: Dr Talha Yaffi (General Manager)

PRINCIPAL ACTIVITIES: Medium and long term lending for the
development of industry and tourism
Branch Offices: Regional offices: Tripoli, Sidon, Zahle
Financial Information:

	LL'000
Authorised capital	66,000
Paid-up capital	66,000

Principal Shareholders: Lebanese Government (51%) and other
banks (49%)
Date of Establishment: March 1973
No of Employees: 65

NATIONAL CARPET MANUFACTURING CO SAL
PO Box 11-4126, Beirut
Tel: 264405, 264406
Cable: Carpetco

PRINCIPAL ACTIVITIES: Manufacture of tufted carpets and
wool and acrylic yarns

Date of Establishment: 1968

NATIONAL LIME CO SAL
SNACH
PO Box 11-4806, Beirut
Tel: 240160/61, 415163, 415214
Cable: Snach Beirut
Telex: 23538 LE Alita

PRINCIPAL ACTIVITIES: Production of quicklime, hydrated lime, limestone, whiting and related products
Branch Offices: Factory: Alita (Byblos), Tel 940266
Subsidiary Companies: Pan Arab Paints SAL, Lebanese Agencies & Trading Co. (Latco) SAL; Alita Industrial Group Ltd

NCR CORPORATION

PO Box 11-1185, Beirut
Tel: 365280
Cable: Nacareco
Telex: 20504 Ncrbey LE, 23545 LE NCR

PRINCIPAL ACTIVITIES: Marketing and maintaining electronic computers, cash registers, accounting machines and related supplies; manufacturers' representatives; printing
Parent Company: NCR Corp, Dayton, Ohio, USA
Principal Bankers: Citibank; The British Bank of the Middle East; Banque Trad (Credit Lyonnais)

Date of Establishment: 1949 (in Lebanon)

NEAR EAST COMMERCIAL BANK SAL

PO Box 11-4805, Beirut
Tel: 221077, 295452
Cable: BANKNEAST
Telex: 21432

PRINCIPAL ACTIVITIES: Commercial banking
Branch Offices: Representative office in Paris, France
Parent Company: Societe Nationale d'Assurances SAL

Date of Establishment: 1978

NEAR EAST RESOURCES

PO Box 11-966, Beirut
Tel: 341265, 245531
Telex: 20660 LE

PRINCIPAL ACTIVITIES: General trading and contracting, telecommunication and aviation equipment

PHILIPPE KAMEL SARL

See KAMEL, PHILIPPE, SARL

PHOENICIA CONTRACTING ENGINEERING & TRADING CO SAL

PO Box 11-4532, Beirut
Tel: 340615, 349130
Telex: 22056 LE

PRINCIPAL ACTIVITIES: Contracting; building materials; solar energy developers
Principal Agencies: Plextone Corp; Jadecor; Energy Systems Inc; ARCO Solar Inc
Principal Bankers: Royal Bank of Canada

Date of Establishment: 1965

PLASTEX SAL

PO Box 11-1778, Beirut
Tel: 430220, 431190
Cable: Plastex Beirut
Telex: 20481 Drilco LE

PRINCIPAL ACTIVITIES: Manufacture of polyethylene film/bag; printing: PE film, melamine tableware, melamine advertising ashtrays, industrial items
Principal Bankers: Arab Bank; Saudi National Commercial Bank; Societe Generale

Principal Shareholders: Munib R Masri; Tarif Ayoubi; Ahmad Stetie; Raif Kassem
Date of Establishment: 1958

PRODUITS ALIMENTAIRES LIBANAIS (PRALL)

PO Box 11-0122, Beirut
Tel: 221710, 236160
Cable: Experience
Telex: 20977 Sonat LE

PRINCIPAL ACTIVITIES: Production and processing of Lebanese food products (pickles, jams, fruits in syrup)
Branch Offices: Factory located in Chtaura Bekaa Valley, Lebanon

PROSPERITY BANK OF LEBANON SAL

PO Box 11-5625, Beirut
Tel: 894450, 890608, 894406
Cable: PROSPERBAN
Telex: 23426 Prosper LE

PRINCIPAL ACTIVITIES: Commercial banking

Date of Establishment: 1963

PUBLICO PUBLICITY COMPANY

PO Box 11-1675, Beirut
Tel: 242558, 296466
Cable: Publicoandrea
Telex: 22055 Publico LE

PRINCIPAL ACTIVITIES: Advertising, marketing, feasability studies, public relations, publishing, films production
Branch Offices: Dubai
Principal Bankers: Beirut Riyad Bank (Lebanon); First National Bank of Chicago (Dubai)

PURIPLAST-LIBAN SAL

PO Box 11-7814, Beirut
Tel: 931194, 933232, 331546
Cable: Lipuripla Beyrouth
Telex: 21560 Purpla LE

PRINCIPAL ACTIVITIES: Production of plastic laminated sheets
Branch Offices: Edde, Jbeil, Lebanon
Principal Bankers: The Bank of Nova Scotia, Fransabank, Banque Libanaise pour le Commerce

Date of Establishment: 1973

RAPHAEL & CO SAL

PO Box 11-7319, Beirut
Tel: 327900, 219670/1/2/3, 219859
Cable: Solfinka Beirut
Telex: 20524 Khdrco LE
Telefax: 403735

Chairman: Joe Raphael

PRINCIPAL ACTIVITIES: General trading; manufacturer's representative
Principal Agencies: Géha Werke GmbH, West Germany; Sun Oil Company, Belgium
Branch Offices: Sodeco, Beirut
Subsidiary Companies: Abdallah Al Ghoneim Trading Est, PO Box 3603, Jeddah, Saudi Arabia

RECHERCHES ET REALISATIONS INDUSTRIELLES

PO Box 16-6022, Beirut
Tel: 442174, 324280, 328757, 451216, 331582
Cable: SOTRELIB, BEYROUTH
Telex: 29125 LE, 29126 LE ATT RRI

Chairman: Naoum Homsy

PRINCIPAL ACTIVITIES: Development turnkey projects; electro-mechanical contractors; representation for industrial equipment; representation for medical equipment
Principal Agencies: Toshiba, Marconi, Lobry, Lequeux, Neu, IMS

LEBANON

Branch Offices: RRI, Damascus, PO Box 2932, Tel 228284, 222633, Damascus, Syria; RRI Baghdad, PO Box 542, Tel 7198584, Baghdad, Iraq
Parent Company: RRI Electro Mechanical Entreprises
Principal Bankers: Banque de l'Union Europeenne, Paris

Date of Establishment: 1960

RIF BANK SAL
PO Box 11-5727, Beirut
Tel: 362495/9; 368961/4
Telex: 20742 LE; 22083 LE; 23115 LE

PRINCIPAL ACTIVITIES: Commercial banking
Associated Companies: National Bank of Kuwait, Kuwait; Commerzbank, Germany; KFTCI, Kuwait; Commercial Bank of Kuwait SAK

Date of Establishment: 1965

SAAD & TRAD SAL
PO Box 11-1286, West Beirut, or, PO Box 16-6072, East Beirut
Tel: 366600, 366969, 364110/2 (West Beirut), 426793/4, 425940/2 (East Beirut)
Cable: Solibar Beirut
Telex: 42945 LE Satrad

Presidents: Ibrahim S Saad, Robert M Trad
Directors: Selim I Saad, Michel R Trad

PRINCIPAL ACTIVITIES: Agents and distributors of motor vehicles and components
Principal Agencies: Fiat, SPA, Torino; Jaguars Cars, UK; Rolls-Royce Motors International, Lausanne; Pol-Mot, Warszawa; Lancia, SpA, Torino
Branch Offices: Minet El Hosn Street, Ain Mreisseh, Beirut; Garage Fiat-Jaguar, rue Corniche du Fleuve, Beirut
Subsidiary Companies: Societe Intercontinentale d'Expansion Economique
Principal Bankers: Fransabank, Beirut; Banque de la Mediterranee-France, Paris
Financial Information:

	LL'000
Authorised capital	3,000
Paid-up capital	3,000

Principal Shareholders: Robert M Trad, Ibrahim S Saad, Selim I Saad, Michel R Trad
Date of Establishment: Saad & Trad: 1955; Saad & Trad SAL: 1972
No of Employees: 45

SAAD, ETS FOUAD SALIM, SAL
PO Box 11-3112, Beirut
Tel: 226201, 327249, 332887
Cable: FOSAAD
Telex: 20391 FOSAAD LE

PRINCIPAL ACTIVITIES: Importers and wholesalers of electrical home appliances and telecommunications equipment
Principal Agencies: Kelvinator, USA; Kelly (Italy); Safel, Spain
Subsidiary Companies: Systronics SAL, PO Box 11-3112, Beirut
Principal Bankers: British Bank of the Middle East, Banque Libano-Bresilienne, Saudi Lebanese Bank

Date of Establishment: 1959

SAUDI LEBANESE BANK
PO Box 11-6765, Beirut
Tel: 341010, 370173
Cable: Saulbank
Telex: 21469 LABANK LE

PRINCIPAL ACTIVITIES: Commercial banking
Branch Offices: Beirut, Saida
Subsidiary Companies: Saudi Lebanese Bank for the Middle East, Paris, France

Principal Shareholders: Sabbah Al Haj, Mohammad Halabi, Abdullah Bahamdan, Rafic Hariri, Mohammad Zatani, Yousef Bisat, Taha Mikati, and others

SOCIETE DYNAMIC SARL
PO Box 11-2421, Beirut
Tel: 262097, 264651
Telex: GERTEL 21319 LE

PRINCIPAL ACTIVITIES: Production of plastic advertising goods, bags, and silk screen printing and accessories
Principal Agencies: Sericol Group Ltd (UK)
Principal Bankers: Credit Libanais, Beirut

Date of Establishment: 1966

SOCIETE GENERALE DE PRESSE ET D'EDITION SAL
PO Box 11-2488, Beirut
Tel: 340560, 349010
Telex: 20817 Jaror LE

PRINCIPAL ACTIVITIES: Publication of L'Orient-Le Jour, a daily newspaper published in French and advertising

SOCIETE GENERALE DES PRODUITS ALIMENTAIRES ET DOMESTIQUES S.O.G.E.P.A. SAL
Sursock St, Sayegh Bldg, Beirut
Tel: 332570
Cable: Sogepa
Telex: 20525 Le (Geodal)

PRINCIPAL ACTIVITIES: Agents and distributors dealing with foodstuffs and alcoholic drinks
Principal Agencies: White Horse Distillers Ltd, UK; Panzani, France; Tattinger Champagne, France; Mercier Champagne, France; Simply & Wonderful, California; Olida, France
Associated Companies: Ets Georges Abou Adal & Cie SAL; Les Editions Orientales SAL; International Cosmetic Manufacturing Incoma SAL; Societe Libanaise de Developpement Agricole Solidar SARL; International Brands Inc SAL; Societe Libanaise Moderne de Bonneterie (Korrigan) SAL; Middle East Promotion SARL (Mepromo)

SOCIETE GENERALE LIBANO-EUROPEENNE DE BANQUE SAL
PO Box 11-2955, Beirut
Tel: 335200, 483001
Cable: SOGELIBAN
Telex: 40485 LE SOGELI, 42199 LE SOGELI

PRINCIPAL ACTIVITIES: Commercial banking
Branch Offices: Mazraa; Badaro; Bikfaya; Broummana; Antelias; Byblos; Tripoli
Associated Companies: Societe Generale, (France); Societe Generale de Banque, (Belgique)

Principal Shareholders: Sehnaoui family; Societe Generale, France; Societe Generale de Banque, Belgique
Date of Establishment: 1953

SOCIETE INDUSTRIELLE DES PRODUITS PIONEER-JABRE SAL
PO Box 11369, Beirut
Tel: 270650, 271590, 274170
Cable: Ednasco
Telex: 20988 LE

PRINCIPAL ACTIVITIES: Production of biscuits, wafers, chocolates, pasta confectionery corrugated cartons, tins, converting paper, halawa and tehineh and distribution of food products
Subsidiary/Associated Companies: Edward Nassar Group of Companies in England, Switzerland, Nigeria, Ghana and Liberia

Principal Bankers: Banque Libanaise Pour Le Commerce, Beirut; Banque de l'Industrie et du Travail, Beirut

Principal Shareholders: Edward Nassar
Date of Establishment: 1874

SOCIETE LIBANAISE DE CIMENTS BLANCS

Chekka
Tel: 645233, 645244, 645255
Cable: Cimenblanc - Chekka - Lebanon
Telex: 20405 LE Ciblan

PRINCIPAL ACTIVITIES: Production of white cement
Principal Bankers: Banque Nationale de Paris; Banque de Credit Populaire; Banque Libanaise pour le commerce

Principal Shareholders: Cimenterie Nationale, Chekka; Societe des Ciments Libanais, Chekka
Date of Establishment: 1962

SOCIETE LIBANO-EUROPEENNE POUR LA GESTION PRIVEE

Credit Lyonnais

PO Box 11-9472, Beirut
Tel: 258564, 334044
Cable: Sligest
Telex: 20342 LE Sligel

PRINCIPAL ACTIVITIES: Investment banking, general services, portfolio management
Subsidiary Companies: Sligest Establishment Vaduz
Principal Bankers: Credit Lyonnais Paris, New York, Geneva, Beirut; Berliner Handels Frankfurter, Frankfurt

Principal Shareholders: Credit Lyonnais, France (85%); Banco di Roma, Luxembourg (5%); Commerzbank, Germany (5%); Banque G Trad (CL), Lebanon (5%)

SOCIETE NATIONALE D'ASSURANCES SAL

PO Box 11-4805, Beirut
Tel: 250505/6/7/8/9
Cable: Natinsco
Telex: 20919 LE Sna

PRINCIPAL ACTIVITIES: All classes of insurance and reinsurance
Branch Offices: Zahle; Tripoli; Dbayeh
Subsidiary Companies: EIC, Hamra, Beirut, Lebanon

Principal Shareholders: SNA Holding (Bermuda) Ltd, Local Businessmen
Date of Establishment: 1963

SOCIETE NATIONALE D'ENTREPRISES

PO Box 11-7101, Beirut
Tel: 265560/3

PRINCIPAL ACTIVITIES: General and building contractors

SOCIETE NOUVELLE DE BANQUE DE SYRIE ET DU LIBAN SAL

PO Box 11-957, Beirut
Tel: 321833, 218733
Telex: 42282, 20735

PRINCIPAL ACTIVITIES: Commercial banking

Date of Establishment: 1963

SPINNEY'S LEBANON SAL

PO Box 11-746, Beirut
Tel: 315477/301206
Cable: Spinneys Beirut
Telex: 20766 Spinex LE

PRINCIPAL ACTIVITIES: Importers, retail and wholesale food distributors, agency representatives
Principal Agencies: Kraft, Rowntree McKintosh, Birds Eye, Walls, RHM, Burtons, Gordon Gin

Associated Companies: Spinney's (1948) Ltd, London, UK
Principal Bankers: British Bank of the Middle East - Mebco

Date of Establishment: 1981

STAL SAL

Steel & Aluminium Construction Co

PO Box 11-1962, Beirut
Tel: 400400, 409253, 400399, 400650/1, 409272, 400423
Cable: Kazanco Beirut
Telex: 20483 Stalco LE, 42269 STAL LE

President: Antoine Kazan
Directors: Maroun Kazan (Managing Director)
Senior Executives: Toufic Aris (Sales Director)

PRINCIPAL ACTIVITIES: Manufacture and supply of aluminium and steel products, doors, windows and building materials
Principal Agencies: Anaconda Aluminium Co, USA; Wespac Corp, USA; Overseas Operations Inc, USA; Avallon, W Germany; Masellis, Italy; Rehau Plastiks, W Germany
Principal Bankers: Banque de la Mediterranee; Banco di Roma; Bank Byblos; Banque Libano Francaise; Saudi Lebanese Bank for the Middle East
Financial Information:

	LL'000
Authorised capital	1,500
Paid-up capital	1,500

Principal Shareholders: Antoine Kazan, Maroun Kazan, Shukhri Shammas, Wolfgang Vogel, Dietrich Vogel
Date of Establishment: 1962
No of Employees: 50

STANDARD STATIONERY CO SAL

PO Box 11-1076, Beirut
Tel: 343819, 343820
Cable: Typroyal
Telex: 23398 SSCO LE

PRINCIPAL ACTIVITIES: Representation of manufacturers for office machines and equipment
Principal Agencies: A B Dick Co, Monroe International, General Binding Corporation, Okamura Corp, Hall-Welter Inc
Principal Bankers: Bank Almashrek SAL; Bank of Beirut & Arab Countries

Principal Shareholders: Dr Kamal E Khuri and others
Date of Establishment: 1956

SUPPLIES & CONTRACTS CO

PO Box 11-8914, Beirut
Tel: 345540, 347745/6
Cable: Sacleb
Telex: 20226 LE

PRINCIPAL ACTIVITIES: Mechanical, electrical, and civil engineering contractors. Services: hospitals, hotels, airports, etc; industrial: petrochemical plants. Value analysis, feasibility studies, project planning, design and engineering, process development and design, project management
Branch Offices: 3 Hans Crescent, London, SW1, UK; Saudi SAC Contracting Co Ltd, PO Box 9376, Riyadh, Saudi Arabia; PO Box 789, Manama, Bahrain; PO Box 748, Amman, Jordan
Principal Bankers: Arab Bank

Date of Establishment: 1966

SYRO LEBANESE COMMERCIAL BANK SAL

PO Box 11-8701, Beirut
Tel: 341261, 250975
Cable: SYRLICOM
Telex: 21720 SLCBNK

PRINCIPAL ACTIVITIES: Commercial banking

Date of Establishment: 1974

T GARGOUR & FILS

See GARGOUR, T, & FILS

TAMER, F, & FILS SA

PO Box 11-1139, Beirut
Tel: 270772
Cable: Atmer

PRINCIPAL ACTIVITIES: Manufacture of vegetable oils (milling and refining) and animal feeds; manufacture of paints and paint brushes

TAMER FRERES SAL

PO Box 84, Beirut
Tel: 282715/16
Cable: Tarem
Telex: 20609 LE Tamer

PRINCIPAL ACTIVITIES: General trading, distribution of building materials, petrochemicals, raw materials, hospital equipment, luxury products, dental goods, pharmaceuticals, foodstuffs, tobacco, cycles and motorcycles, security
Principal Agencies: BP Chemicals Ltd; BP Oil Ltd; S S White Dental; Dentsply; AD International Ltd; Castle and Cooke Foods Sales Corp; Lancaster Beauty Products; Alain Delon Perfumes; Loris Azzaro Perfumes; Maurer & Wirtz; Raleigh Cycles Co Ltd; Hauni Werke; Christian Dior lighters/pens
Branch Offices: Cyrus and Cairo
Parent Company: Slee-Eddco
Principal Bankers: Chase Manhattan, Geneva; Fransa Bank Beirut

Principal Shareholders: Jean Tamer; Gaby Tamer
Date of Establishment: 1917

TRANS-MEDITERRANEAN AIRWAYS SAL
T.M.A.

PO Box 11-3018, Beirut
Tel: 277510
Telex: 20736 TMA LE

PRINCIPAL ACTIVITIES: Air transportation of freight and passengers

TRANSMEDITERRANEAN SAL

PO Box 11913, Beirut
Tel: 803155
Telex: 20997 LE

PRINCIPAL ACTIVITIES: General trading and contracting, manufacturers' representation

TRANSORIENT BANK SAL

PO Box 11-6260, Beirut
Tel: 482983, 482984, 881197/8
Cable: Transorbank
Telex: 43685, 43701 LE
Telefax: 897705

Honorary Chairman: Hamed M Baki
Directors: Adib S Milad/Millet (Chairman), Wassef A Gandour (Vice Chairman), Farid S Milad/Millet, Ahmad Kabbarah, Gabriel Atallah, Chakib El Hayek, Rony Karam

PRINCIPAL ACTIVITIES: Commercial banking
Branch Offices: Bauchrieh; Bourj-Hammond; Ras Beirut; Sin El Fil; Ashrafieh; Tripoli; Chiah
Principal Bankers: Mantrust NY/Tokyo; Midland Bank, London; Deutsche Bank, Dusseldorf; BLPC, Paris; UBS, Zurich
Financial Information:

	LL'000
Authorised capital	22,500
Paid-up capital	22,500

Principal Shareholders: Adib S Milad (Millet), Wassef Gandour, Hikmat Tannous, Hamed Baki
Date of Establishment: 1966
No of Employees: 288

TRIAD CONDAS INTERNATIONAL SAL

PO Box 11-7063, Beirut
Tel: 345670, 345671
Cable: Condasint Beirut
Telex: 20849 LE

PRINCIPAL ACTIVITIES: Architecture and engineering, consultants; interior design and decoration; funiture manufacturing; interior turnkey projects and showroom retail sales
Branch Offices: Paris/France (Liaison Office): 16 avenue Hoche, 75008 Paris, Tel 9245186, 9245187, Telex 640180 F; Riyadh/Saudi Arabia: PO Box 5672, Telex 401112 Sj; Jeddah/Saudi Arabia: PO Box 6175, Telex 601208 Sj; Khobar/Saudi Arabia: PO Box 489, Telex 870024 Sj
Principal Bankers: Beirut-Riyad Bank, Beirut; Royal Bank of Canada, Beirut; First National City Bank, Riyadh; Credit Commercial de France, Geneva

Principal Shareholders: Triad Holding Corporation (Luxembourg)

UNITED BANK OF LEBANON & PAKISTAN SAL

PO Box 11-5600, Beirut
Tel: 813850, 812815
Telex: 20823, 22422

PRINCIPAL ACTIVITIES: Commercial banking
Branch Offices: Beirut, Tripoli
Associated Companies: Banque de Developpement Industriel et Touristique, Beirut

Principal Shareholders: Abdel Rahman Bin Hasan Sharabatly, Anis Yassine, Saleh Bourji, Edouard Karam, Salim Macksoud, Sardar Haq Nawaz, Tajammal Hussain, United Bank Limited
Date of Establishment: 1968

UNITED BANK OF SAUDIA & LEBANON SAL

PO Box 113-5072, Beirut
Tel: 350030, 350283
Telex: 21234 Salebk LE

PRINCIPAL ACTIVITIES: Commercial banking

Principal Shareholders: Shaikh Mahfouz Salim Bin Mahfouz and others
Date of Establishment: 1981

UNITED ELECTRIC OF LEBANON

PO Box 11-5710, Beirut
Tel: 237040, 294693
Cable: Unilec
Telex: 22297

PRINCIPAL ACTIVITIES: Distribution of electric and electronic equipment, and house appliances
Principal Agencies: Tokyo Shibaur Electric Co Ltd, Japan; O'Keefe & Merritt, A Division of Tappan Company, USA Krups, Germany
Principal Bankers: Credit Libanais SAL; Banque Libano-Francaise

VRESSO

A Saboundjian Mnfg Co

Jal-El-Dib, Beirut
Tel: 411300, 413445
Cable: Vresso, Jal el dib
Telex: 22719 Vresso LE

PRINCIPAL ACTIVITIES: Import, distribution and installation, food service equipment, refrigerators, laundry equipment; manufacture of food preparation equipment

Principal Agencies: USA: Jet Spray Int; Taylor Freezer;
Manitowoc; Blodgett; Vulcan Hart; France: Bonnet; Robot
Coupe; Rex; Bertrand; Italy: Cof; Carimali-Bergem; Sweden:
Electrolux CR; Belgium: IPSO
Branch Offices: Vresso International Corporation, 595 Broad
Avenue, Ridgefield NJ 07657, USA, Tel (201) 943-4577, Telex
421599 Vresso
Principal Bankers: Banque G Trad (Credit Lyonnais); Banque
Libano Francaise; Banque Audi

Principal Shareholders: Vrej Saboundjian, Anahid Saboundjian
Date of Establishment: 1942

WOODS CORP SAL (WOODCO)

PO Box 15-5010, Beirut
Tel: 244921, 225664
Cable: Timcobois
Telex: 21274 Timco LE

PRINCIPAL ACTIVITIES: Import and export of timber and
building materials; representation of European and Arab firms
Principal Agencies: Technoforest Export, Roumania; Degginger
and Hess, Austria; Franz Shweighover, Austria; Assi, Sweden;
Vapo, Finland
Subsidiary Companies: Timber Trading Corp TIMCO SAL; Ste
Internationale des Bois SARL; Sea and Land Transport Co
Marina SARL
Principal Bankers: Banque Libano Francaise, France; Ste Nlle
Banque Syrie et Liban; Bank El Mashrek

LEBANON

Major Companies of
LIBYA

ABDULRASUL RUHAYEM
See RUHAYEM, ABDULRASUL,

ADDALY SHIPPING & TRADING AGENCY
Shipping Department, PO Box 2310, Benghazi
Tel: 93964, 92111
Cable: Adsdalybenghazi

PRINCIPAL ACTIVITIES: Shipping agents, customs and clearing
agents, commercial representation, insurance brokers
Principal Agencies: Mediterranean Trading and Shipping Co,
Malta; Libyan Insurance Co, Castelletti Bologna; Rif
Navigation Co, Beirut; Lebmar Shipping Co, Beirut; Condos &
Son Co, Piraeus; Harisel Shipping Co, Piraeus; International
Chartering Co, Piraeus; M Fotopoulos, Piraeus
Branch Offices: Commercial Department, Hadada Sq, Benghazi;
and Tobruk, PO Box 34, Tel 2417, Cable Addalytobruck

AD-DAR AL JAMAHIRIYA FOR PUBLISHING DISTRIBUTION & ADVERTISING
PO Box 17459, Misurata
Tel: 21522, 29975, 28574, 17459
Telex: 30098 Matbuat LY
Telefax: 53-606086

Chairman: Salim A Al Shibani (Secretary of People's Committee)

PRINCIPAL ACTIVITIES: Printing, publishing, advertising
Branch Offices: Tripoli: PO Box 959, Tel 41418; Benghazi: PO
Box 321, Tel 97604, Telex 20222; Sebha: PO Box 20108;
Malta: PO Box 547, Vallitta; Morocco: PO Box 15977,
Casablanca
Principal Bankers: National Commercial Bank

Principal Shareholders: State-owned
Date of Establishment: 1974
No of Employees: 445

AFRICAN DRILLING COMPANY
PO Box 3245, Tripoli
Tel: 37223

PRINCIPAL ACTIVITIES: Oil production and drilling

AGHEILA, MOHAMMAD,
PO Box 603, Tripoli
Tel: 33025
Telex: 20060

PRINCIPAL ACTIVITIES: Public accountants and tax consultants
Branch Offices: Also office in Benghazi: PO Box 77, Benghazi,
Tel 93749

AHLYA BUILDING MATERIALS CO
PO Box 8545, Jumhouriya St, Tripoli
Tel: 36272, 36989, 38040
Telex: 20120

PRINCIPAL ACTIVITIES: Import and distribution of building
materials
Branch Offices: PO Box 1351, Benghazi, Tel 91808, Telex
40213

Principal Shareholders: State-owned company

AL AHLIYA CO FOR TRADING & MANUFACTURE OF CLOTHING
PO Box 4152, Benghazi
Tel: 91850
Telex: 40039, 40241

PRINCIPAL ACTIVITIES: Import, manufacture and trade of
textiles and clothing
Branch Offices: PO Box 15182, Tripoli, Tel 31899, Telex 20073
Financial Information: An amalgamation of the following
companies: Arab Co for Importation & Manufacture of
Clothing & Textiles; National Co for Trading & Manufacturing
of Clothing; The Modern Fashion Co for Trading and
Manufacturing of Clothing; Al Amal Co for Trading &
Manufacturing of Clothing

Principal Shareholders: State-owned
Date of Establishment: 1980

AL GAZEERA BENGHAZI
PO Box 2456, Benghazi
Tel: 93533
Telex: 40273 Gezclar

PRINCIPAL ACTIVITIES: Clearing and forwarding agency,
transport agency

Principal Shareholders: State-owned

AL MUKHTAR INSURANCE CO
230 Mohamed Lemgarief St, PO Box 2548, Tripoli
Tel: 44150/58
Cable: Mutamin
Telex: 20201 Mutamin

PRINCIPAL ACTIVITIES: Insurance business
Branch Offices: Benghazi: PO Box 557, Tel 94021, Telex 40074

AMAN CO FOR TYRES & BATTERIES
Tajura Km 19, PO Box 30737, Tripoli
Tel: (021) 690282/86
Cable: Aman Tajura
Telex: 20432, 20432 AMAN LY
Telefax: (021) 690283

Chairman: Ahmed Abdullatif
Senior Executives: Abduhafiz Sassi (Finance Manager),
Mohamed Marwan (Sales Manager), Abdurazag Zgouzi
(Personnel Manager), Ibraheem Al Shibani (R & D Manager),
Mohamed Abdulkader (Legal Manager), Ayad El Raai (Data
Processing Manager)

PRINCIPAL ACTIVITIES: Manufacture of tyres, auto batteries
Branch Offices: Benghazi Branch: PO Box 2394, Tel (061)
87569/70, Telex 40171; Tripoli Branch: Tel (021) 500060/61;
Misurata Branch: PO Box 17757, Tel (051) 24474; Sabha
Branch: Tel (071) 27054
Subsidiary/Associated Companies: Dry Battery Plant; Auto
Battery Plant; Tyre Plant; Tyres Retreading Centres
Principal Bankers: Umma Bank; National Commercial Bank
Financial Information:

	1990
	LD'000
Sales turnover	30,000
Profits	2,000
Authorised capital	4,000
Paid-up capital	5,400
Total assets	54,000

Principal Shareholders: State-owned
Date of Establishment: 1976
No of Employees: 1,600

ARAB BANKING CORPORATION
PO Box 3578, Tripoli
Tel: 33260, 42174
Telex: 20359 ABCG REP LY
Telefax: 32528

Senior Executives: Ali Dahmani (Chief Representative)

PRINCIPAL ACTIVITIES: Banking (Representative Office)
Parent Company: Head office in Bahrain

ARAB CO FOR GENERAL AGENCIES & TRADING
Suani Rd Km 3, Tripoli
Tel: 41354

LIBYA

PRINCIPAL ACTIVITIES: Import of earth-moving machines, road-equipment machines, Goodyear tyres, Lord batteries
Principal Agencies: Frisch, Germany; Marini, Italy; Benati, Italy; Goodyear, USA; Lord, Germany

ARAB CONTRACTING & CATERING CO LTD
PO Box 2078, Benghazi
Tel: 94804
Cable: Cacoil Benghazi

PRINCIPAL ACTIVITIES: Catering services and contractors

ARAB DRILLING & WORKOVER CO
PO Box 680, Tripoli
Tel: 801119, 800064/6
Telex: 20361 Adwoc LY
Telefax: 805945

Chairman: A El Badri
Directors: I Gritly, S El Nashmi, R A D Wright, F Al Rawi
Senior Executives: M A Attiga (General Manager), J G Harris (Chief Accountant), K Christensen (Operations Manager)

PRINCIPAL ACTIVITIES: Oil well drilling and workover contractors
Branch Offices: Syria: Ahmad Mrewed St, PO Box 5724, Damascus; Iraq: Al Mansour, PO Box 6490, Baghdad
Principal Bankers: Libyan Arab Foreign Bank
Financial Information:

	1989/90 US$'000	1989/90 LD'000
Sales turnover	37,690	-
Authorised capital	-	12,000
Paid-up capital	-	12,000
Total assets	80,641	-

Principal Shareholders: Arab Petroleum Services Co; Arab Petroleum Investments Corp; Santa Fe International Services Inc
Date of Establishment: February 1980
No of Employees: 693

ARAB PETROLEUM SERVICES CO
PO Box 12925, Tripoli
Tel: 45860, 45861, 45862
Cable: 719
Telex: 20405 ARPES LY

Chairman: Abdulla Salem Al Badri
Directors: Ismail Mohamed Gritly (Acting General Manager)
Senior Executives: Muftah M Buatig (Administration Manager), Abdulsalam K Musbah (Financial Manager)

PRINCIPAL ACTIVITIES: Petroleum services
Subsidiary Companies: Arab Drilling & Workover Co, Libya; Arab Well Logging Co, Iraq; Arab Geophysical Exploration Services Co, Libya
Principal Bankers: Libyan Arab Foreign Bank, National Commercial Bank
Financial Information:

	1988 LD'000
Authorised capital	100,000
Paid-up capital	14,625
Total assets	17,205

Principal Shareholders: OAPEC Member Countries
Date of Establishment: 1977

ARAB SHIPPING CO (LIBYA) LTD
PO Box 882, Tripoli
Tel: 39358, 40460
Cable: Araship

PRINCIPAL ACTIVITIES: Shipping agents
Principal Agencies: Det Forenede Dampskiba Selskab, NV Stoomvaart Maatschappij, Nederland; Royal Rotterdam Lloyd; United Levant Lines; Lebanese Shipping Co; Adriatic-Libya-Tunisia Line, Piraeus; Clausen Steamship Co, Copenhagen; Meandros Mediterranean Line, Buenos Aires
Branch Offices: PO Box 3036, Benghazi, Tel 93633

ARAB TRADING & CONTRACTING CO
PO Box 336, Ben Sassi Bldg, Omar Mukhtar St, Tripoli
Tel: 37600, 37701
Cable: Arabcat Tripoli
Telex: 20106

PRINCIPAL ACTIVITIES: Import, export, manufacturers' representatives, automobile dealers, electrical contractors, telecommunication engineering, services, sales, maintenance, civil contractors
Branch Offices: PO Box 431, 58 Abdel Nasser St, Benghazi, Tel 94891, 87848, Cable Arabcat Benghazi

ARAB UNION CONTRACTING CO
PO Box 3475, Tripoli
Tel: 48563
Telex: 20237

PRINCIPAL ACTIVITIES: Civil engineering contractors

Principal Shareholders: State-owned

ARABIAN GULF OIL CO
PO Box 263, Al Kish, Benghazi
Tel: 28931
Cable: Injaz Benghazi
Telex: 40033 Agoco

Chairman: Hamed A Layass (Secretary of Popular Committee)

PRINCIPAL ACTIVITIES: Exploration and production of crude oil and natural gas and carrying out refining, utilisation, storage, export, etc
Branch Offices: PO Box 325, Sharia Ben Ashour, Tripoli, Tel 35436, 32956, Telex 20209
Principal Bankers: Wahda Bank

Principal Shareholders: Member of the National Oil Corporation
Date of Establishment: 1971

ARKCO LIBYA MARITIME
230 Giaddat Istiklal, PO Box 401, Tripoli
Tel: 33567/8
Cable: Arkcomar

PRINCIPAL ACTIVITIES: Shipping agents
Branch Offices: Benghazi (PO Box 157, Tel 92236 Benghazi, Cable Arkcomar) and Tobruk (PO Box 16)

AZZAWIYA OIL REFINING CO
PO Box 6451, Tripoli
Tel: (021) 605389/93
Cable: ARC LY
Telex: 30423/4 ARC LY
Telefax: (021) 605948

Directors: Hammouda M El Aswad (Managing Director)
Senior Executives: Shaban A Ayad (Finance Manager), Taher O Mustafa (Purchasing Manager), Khaled A Baruni (Production Manager), Bedri T Ayad (Administration Manager), Mukhtar A Rabti (Technical Manager), Ramadan H Majdoub (Legal Manager), Mustafa El Amri (Engineering & Projects Manager), Abdallah J Salem (Loss Prevention Manager), Nuruddin Ashkundali (Services & Catering Manager), Frank R Tarry (Maintenance Manager), Bashir M Zreba (Training & Development Manager)

PRINCIPAL ACTIVITIES: Oil refining
Principal Agencies: Umm Al Jawaby Oil Services Co, London, UK; Mediterrranean Oil Services GmbH, Dussedorf, W Germany
Branch Offices: Benghazi Asphalt Plant Office, Benghazi
Parent Company: National Oil Corporation

Principal Bankers: National Commercial Bank; Central Bank of Libya

Financial Information:

	1989
	US$'000
Authorised capital	258,504
Paid-up capital	258,504

Principal Shareholders: National Oil Corporation
Date of Establishment: September 1974
No of Employees: 1,467

BEIDA CONSTRUCTION CO

PO Box 204, Benghazi

PRINCIPAL ACTIVITIES: Import and distribution of building materials, cement, iron and steel; also warehousing

BEN SASSI, MOHAMMED, ORGANISATION

Sharia Omar El Mukhtar, Tripoli
Tel: 41905

Chairman: Mohammed Ben Sassi
Directors: Khalif Ben Sassi

PRINCIPAL ACTIVITIES: Contractors and builders, general trading, major chain of hotels

BENGHAZI EST FOR BUILDING & CONSTRUCTION

PO Box 2118, Benghazi
Tel: 92639, 92392
Telex: 40158

PRINCIPAL ACTIVITIES: Building and construction works

Principal Shareholders: State-owned

BEY, IBRAHIM HUSNI,

138 Omar Moukhtar St, PO Box 198, Benghazi
Tel: 92487, 92762
Cable: Beyson
Telex: 40018 Beyson Ly

PRINCIPAL ACTIVITIES: Shipping agents, stevedores, forwarding and clearing, also packers. Import-export
Branch Offices: Head office in Benghazi, also banches in Tripoli; Mersa Brega; Tobruk; Derna; Ras Hilal; Ras Lanouf; Misurata; Zuara
Principal Bankers: National Commercial Bank

BREGA OIL MARKETING CO

PO Box 402, Sayedi St, Tripoli
Tel: 43041/47
Cable: Breganaft
Telex: 20090 Breganaft; 20203 Braganat; 20281 Breganaft; 20547 Bregan

Directors: Dr Al Dokali B Al Megharief (The Committe's Secretary), Eng Mohamed Al Wa'er (Member), Nasre El Din Tabak (Member), Mousa Abu Za'akouk (Member), Fathi Alqaramanli (Member)
PRINCIPAL ACTIVITIES: Marketing, distribution and transport of petroleum products and petrochemicals; international marketing of crude oil and refined products
Branch Offices: PO Box 1278, Benghazi, Tel 86366
Principal Bankers: Wahda Bank; Libyan Arab Foreign Bank

Principal Shareholders: National Oil Corporation
Date of Establishment: November 1971
No of Employees: 10,900

CENTRAL BANK OF LIBYA

PO Box 1103, Tripoli
Tel: 33951
Cable: Banklibya
Telex: 20196 Bank Ly

PRINCIPAL ACTIVITIES: Central banking

Principal Shareholders: State-owned

CHEMICAL & TECHNICAL SERVICES

PO Box 4285, Tripoli
Tel: 42460

PRINCIPAL ACTIVITIES: Oilfield contractors; import and distribution of equipment and bulk chemicals for the petroleum industry, industrial and municipal water treatment, chlorinators
Branch Offices: PO Box 1828, Benghazi

CIVIL & MILITARY CONSTRUCTION CO

PO Box 8185, Sharia el Nasr, Tripoli
Tel: 44756/7
Telex: 20287

PRINCIPAL ACTIVITIES: Building and civil engineering contract work for military constructions
Branch Offices: PO Box 412, Benghazi

Principal Shareholders: State-owned

CIVIL AVIATION AUTHORITY

Sharia El Saidi, Tripoli
Tel: 35109, 35101
Telex: 20353 CAA LY

PRINCIPAL ACTIVITIES: Civil aviation

Principal Shareholders: State-owned

CONSTRUCTION MATERIALS SUPPLY & SERVICES CO

PO Box 2426, Tripoli
Tel: 36083/4

PRINCIPAL ACTIVITIES: Window frame manufacturers, import of building materials, sanitary ware, air-conditioning equipment

CORE LABORATORIES LIBYA INC

PO Box 968, Tripoli
Tel: 38879, 608828
Cable: Corelab Tripoli

PRINCIPAL ACTIVITIES: Petroleum engineering

DERBI, MOHAMED AMIN,

PO Box 128, Benghazi
Tel: 2300

PRINCIPAL ACTIVITIES: Manufacture of explosive products, paints and chemicals

EL AYEB, HADI, & BROS

PO Box 923, Tripoli
Tel: 34544, 34712, 34752
Cable: Elayeb Tripolibya

PRINCIPAL ACTIVITIES: Import and distribution of earth-moving equipment, agricultural machinery, trailers and heavy machinery. Manufacture of paints for domestic and industrial purposes
Associated Companies: Gazella Plastic Paint Factory; National Sales Co

EL AZHAAR TRADING & CONTRACTING CO

1/3 Akaria Bldg, Sharia Gumhuria, PO Box 2806, Tripoli
Tel: 39028
Cable: Azhaar

LIBYA

PRINCIPAL ACTIVITIES: General trading and contracting, import and distribution of heating equipment, auto accessories and spare parts, pharmaceuticals, toiletries and consumer goods

EL BAIDA ROADS & UTILITIES CO

PO Box 232/561, El Baida
Tel: 2007/8
Telex: 50409

PRINCIPAL ACTIVITIES: Roads and public services

Principal Shareholders: State-owned

ELECTRICAL CONSTRUCTION CO

PO Box 5309, Tripoli
Tel: 48140
Telex: 20672

Chairman: Shaban Ramadan Kushad
Directors: A K Mitra (Managing Director)
Senior Executives: Ahmed El Sayah (Finance Director), Ahmed El Zaroog (Personnel Director), Mohamed El Mazogi (Technical Director), Siddiq El Khashek (Administration Director)

PRINCIPAL ACTIVITIES: Electrical works
Branch Offices: Tripoli (Head Office), Benghazi, Misurata, Sebha and Delhi (India)

Principal Shareholders: 51% Secretariat of Electricity, Libya; 49% Ministry of Industry, India
Date of Establishment: 1978
No of Employees: 450

EL FATAH AGENCY

PO Box 233, Tripoli
Tel: 31597, 36282
Telex: 20608

PRINCIPAL ACTIVITIES: Clearing and forwarding agency, transport agency

Principal Shareholders: State-owned

ELKHALEGE GENERAL CONSTRUCTION CO

PO Box 445, Agedabia
Tel: 22735, 22792, 22415
Cable: Khalegam Agedabia
Telex: 50602 Kalegam Ly

PRINCIPAL ACTIVITIES: General contracting, construction
Branch Offices: Sirti Office: PO Box 105, Tel 2396; Benghazi Office: Tel 96465, 96466
Principal Bankers: Jamahiriya Bank, Agedabia

Principal Shareholders: State-owned

EL MAMOURA FOOD COMPANY

PO Box 15058, Tripoli
Tel: (021) 34838, (021) 32329, (021) 28022/25
Cable: Mamoura Food Co
Telex: 20558 Mamfood LY
Telefax: 48977

Chairman: Mohammed Ali El Hemmali
Directors: Mohamed I El Mrabit (Technical Director), Mohammed Nass (Commercial Director), Salem Shanba (Financial Director), El Waier Bakeer (Administration Director)

PRINCIPAL ACTIVITIES: Production and processing of foodstuffs
Branch Offices: Tripoli & Benghazi
Parent Company: Responsible to the Secretariat of Light Industries
Principal Bankers: Jamahiriya Bank

Principal Shareholders: State-owned
Date of Establishment: 1979
No of Employees: 1,200

EMNUHOOD EST FOR CONTRACTS

PO Box 1380, Benghazi
Tel: 92786
Cable: Nakoo
Telex: 40226

PRINCIPAL ACTIVITIES: Contracting, building works

Principal Shareholders: State-owned

ENDER, HADI, ORGANISATION

30 Jakarta St, PO Box 3761, Tripoli
Tel: 30541
Cable: Enderco

PRINCIPAL ACTIVITIES: General trading, import and distribution of aluminium building products, suspended ceiling, venetian blinds, etc

GAMOENNS CONTRACTS & UTILITIES EST

PO Box 3038, Benghazi
Tel: 90160
Cable: Gamoenns
Telex: 40224

PRINCIPAL ACTIVITIES: Building and road contracting

Principal Shareholders: State owned

GAZAL & SONS

PO Box 204, Benghazi
Tel: 92643, 92225
Cable: Gazalship Benghazi

PRINCIPAL ACTIVITIES: General import/export, building materials, cement, iron and steel import, timber merchants, warehouse facilities, foodstuffs import, shipping agents, stevedores, shipbrokers
Principal Agencies: Kaha Products
Branch Offices: Branches in Tripoli (Al Debribi Bldg, Abu Hedra St, Tel 34644, Cable Gazalship, Tripoli); Derna; Tobruk; Marsa El Brega
Subsidiary Companies: Gazal Shipping (same address)

GENERAL CATERING CORPORATION

PO Box 491, Tripoli
Tel: 41809
Telex: 20604

PRINCIPAL ACTIVITIES: Catering services

Principal Shareholders: State-owned

GENERAL CLEANING COMPANY

PO Box 920, Tripoli
Tel: 32297, 32206

PRINCIPAL ACTIVITIES: General cleaning and garbage collection operations services

Principal Shareholders: State-owned

GENERAL CO FOR AGRICULTURAL MACHINERY & NECESSITIES

PO Box 324, Tripoli
Tel: 36288, 36746, 36130
Cable: Alziraia
Telex: 20022 Metrad Tp

PRINCIPAL ACTIVITIES: Import of all types of agricultural machinery and necessities required for the development of the agriculture sector
Branch Offices: Alziraia; Benghazi PO Box 2094, Tel 92329; Sebha; Zawia
Principal Bankers: Umma Bank, Tripoli; Sahara Bank, Tripoli

Principal Shareholders: State-owned

GENERAL CO FOR AGRICULTURAL PROJECTS

PO Box 2284, Tripoli
Tel: 600280, 607858
Cable: Mashruam
Telex: 20292 Gcap Ly

Chairman: Assaid A Dakhil
Directors: Ammar Abu Himida, Hadi M Deeb

PRINCIPAL ACTIVITIES: Construction of complete agricultural projects including farm buildings, roads, pipelines, installation of hydromechanical and electrical equipment as well as complete irrigation systems, Earthmoving
Branch Offices: PO Box 265, Gharian
Associated Companies: Agricultural Engineering Company
Principal Bankers: National Commercial Bank
Financial Information:

	1990
	LD'000
Authorised capital	3,000
Paid-up capital	2,750

Principal Shareholders: State-owned
Date of Establishment: November 1973
No of Employees: 300 approx

GENERAL CO FOR BUILDINGS

Omar El-Mukhtar St, PO Box 2916, Benghazi
Tel: 91639, 92687, 91867
Cable: Mabaniam Benghazi

PRINCIPAL ACTIVITIES: Promoting urbanisation in Libya through undertaking various building projects (schools, institutions, hospitals and general buildings for ordinary and industrial purposes)
Branch Offices: Tripoli Branch: PO Box 2885, 2 Somatra St, Tel 40427, 42193, Cable Mabaniam Tripoli

GENERAL CO FOR CERAMIC & GLASS PRODUCTS

Azizia, Amiri Bldg, Suani Ben Adam, PO Box 12581, Dhara-Tripoli
Tel: 22559

PRINCIPAL ACTIVITIES: Manufacture of all tyres of ceramic and glass products, sanitary equipment, etc
Subsidiary/Associated Companies: Azizia Bottle Plant, Tel 38462

Principal Shareholders: State-owned

GENERAL CO FOR CIVIL WORKS

PO Box 3306, Tripoli
Tel: 43647, 43975
Cable: Madaniaam
Telex: 20253

PRINCIPAL ACTIVITIES: Civil engineering works, building of factories, harbours, dams, bridges, water pipeline networks, sewage networks, etc
Branch Offices: PO Box 1299, Benghazi, Tel 91077

Principal Shareholders: State-owned

GENERAL CO FOR CONSTRUCTION & EDUCATIONAL BUILDINGS

PO Box 1186, Tripoli
Tel: 44116/7/8
Telex: 20390

PRINCIPAL ACTIVITIES: Construction of public services buildings (schools and educational buildings and other installations related to education purposes)
Branch Offices: PO Box 4087, Benghazi, Tel 90626, 90627

Principal Shareholders: State-owned

GENERAL CO FOR ELECTRIC WIRES & PRODUCTS

PO Box 1177, Benghazi
Tel: 20605, 90881
Cable: Silk Benghazi
Telex: 40121 Ly

PRINCIPAL ACTIVITIES: Manufacture of cables and wires, and electrical and electronic equipment
Branch Offices: PO Box 12629, Tripoli, Tel 43196
Subsidiary/Associated Companies: Electric Wires & Cables Plant

Principal Shareholders: State-owned

GENERAL CO FOR INDUSTRIAL & MEDICAL GASES (GECOMIG)

PO Box 15012, Bab Bangeshire, Tripoli
Tel: 602866, 600553
Telex: 20247 Libgas LY

PRINCIPAL ACTIVITIES: Import, manufacture and trade of industrial and medical gases, refrigerants and welding equipment
Branch Offices: PO Box 2219, Suani Road, Tripoli
Financial Information: Absorbed the National Sales Company in 1981

Date of Establishment: 1981

GENERAL CO FOR LAND RECLAMATION

PO Box 307, Souani Rd, Tripoli

PRINCIPAL ACTIVITIES: Land reclamation and agriculture

Principal Shareholders: State-owned

GENERAL CO FOR LEATHER PRODUCTS & MANUFACTURE

PO Box 2319, Tripoli
Tel: 690454/5
Telex: 20675 Leather

PRINCIPAL ACTIVITIES: Leather tanning and manufacture and distribution of shoes, suitcases and related products
Branch Offices: PO Box 152, Benghazi, Tel 96153, Telex 40071 Gldoura LY
Subsidiary Companies: Footwear Plant, Misurata; Tajoura Modern Tannery; Benghazi Tannery; Compressed Leather Board Fibre Plant, Tajoura; Okba Footwear Plant, Tajoura; Taharar Footwear Plant, Tripoli; 7th April Card Board Factory, Tajoura
Principal Bankers: Wahda Bank

Principal Shareholders: State-owned
Date of Establishment: 1976
No of Employees: 2,000

GENERAL CO FOR MARKETING & AGRICULTURAL PRODUCTION

PO Box 2897, Hadba Al Khadra, Tripoli
Tel: 43039, 43030
Telex: 20150

PRINCIPAL ACTIVITIES: Fruit and vegetable marketing; import of seeds and fertilizers
Branch Offices: PO Box 4251, Benghazi, Tel 97810

Principal Shareholders: State-owned

GENERAL CO FOR STATIONERY & OFFICE EQUIPMENT

PO Box 5314, Tripoli
Tel: 34081, 46097, 38718
Telex: 20395

PRINCIPAL ACTIVITIES: Import and distribution of office equipment and supplies, stationery and surveying equipment

Principal Shareholders: State-owned

GENERAL CO FOR TEXTILES
PO Box 1816, Benghazi
Tel: 97446/7
Telex: 40207 Miprint

PRINCIPAL ACTIVITIES: Production of textiles and cloth
Branch Offices: PO Box 3257, Tripoli, Tel 31936, Telex 20639

Principal Shareholders: State-owned

GENERAL CO FOR TOYS & SPORT EQUIPMENT
PO Box 3270, Tripoli
Tel: 31977, 35870
Telex: 20436, 20728

PRINCIPAL ACTIVITIES: Trading in toys, leisure goods, sport equipment, educational and training aids

Principal Shareholders: State-owned

GENERAL CONSTRUCTION COMPANY
PO Box 8636, Tripoli
Tel: 45158
Telex: 20198

PRINCIPAL ACTIVITIES: Civil engineering and construction
Branch Offices: Gharian: PO Box 178, Tel 497

Principal Shareholders: State owned

GENERAL CORPORATION FOR PUBLIC TRANSPORT
2175 Sharia Magaryef, Tatanaka Bldg, PO Box 4875, Tripoli
Tel: 30818, 30628
Telex: 20262

PRINCIPAL ACTIVITIES: Providing public transport throughout Libya
Branch Offices: PO Box 9528, Benghazi, Tel 95558

Principal Shareholders: State-owned

GENERAL DAIRIES & PRODUCTS CO
PO Box 5318, Tripoli
Tel: 800355, 800767, 800875, 801035
Cable: Aldalib
Telex: 20330 Gdp Ly

PRINCIPAL ACTIVITIES: Production and processing and import of milk and dairy products
Branch Offices: Benghazi Branch: PO Box 9118, Tel 91329, Telex 40136, also factories at Tripoli, Benghazi, Khoms and Jebel Akhdar
Principal Bankers: Sahara Bank, Tripoli
Financial Information:

	LD'000
Authorised capital	5,000

Principal Shareholders: State-owned

GENERAL ELECTRICITY CORPORATION
PO Box 3047, Benghazi
Tel: 93360, 21361
Cable: Kahraba
Telex: 50603, 50605

PRINCIPAL ACTIVITIES: Operation of power generating stations
Branch Offices: PO Box 668, Tripoli

Principal Shareholders: State-owned

GENERAL ELECTRONICS CO
PO Box 12580, Tripoli
Tel: 40435 (General), 38422, 34277 (Management)
Telex: 20397 ALECTRONAT LY

Secretary People's Committee: Mohamed Salehine Bsekri

PRINCIPAL ACTIVITIES: Import/distribution of all kinds of consumer electronic equipment
Principal Agencies: Distribution centres throughout Libya
Branch Offices: PO Box 2068, Benghazi, Tel 91772/93868, Telex 40239 GEEICO LY
Principal Bankers: Wahda Bank, Tripoli and Benghazi
Financial Information: Merged in late 1980 with General Electronic Equipments & Instruments Co (GEEICO), Benghazi, Libya

Principal Shareholders: State-owned
Date of Establishment: November 1976
No of Employees: 700

GENERAL EST FOR CIVIL WORKS
PO Box 85, Sebha
Tel: 30736
Cable: MADANIAN

PRINCIPAL ACTIVITIES: Civil engineering works

Principal Shareholders: State-owned

GENERAL FURNITURE CO
Suani Rd, Km 15, PO Box 12655, Tripoli
Tel: 31822
Cable: Furniture Libya

PRINCIPAL ACTIVITIES: Manufacture and distribution of furniture and timber and metal products
Subsidiary/Associated Companies: January Shuhada (Martyrs) Plant

Principal Shareholders: State-owned

GENERAL LIBYAN CO FOR ROAD CONSTRUCTION & MAINTENANCE
PO Box 2676, Swani Rd, Tripoli
Tel: 800454, 800455, 800456,
Cable: Torokam
Telex: 20249 Torokam

PRINCIPAL ACTIVITIES: Civil engineering contracts for road projects and supplementary activities and road maintenance as well as runways for airports and maintenance
Principal Bankers: Wahda Bank

Principal Shareholders: State-owned
Date of Establishment: 1973
No of Employees: 600

GENERAL NATIONAL CO FOR FLOUR MILLS & FODDER
Bab Bin Ghashir, PO Box 984, Tripoli
Tel: 600361, 600449
Cable: Tahlef
Telex: 20159

PRINCIPAL ACTIVITIES: Wheat milling, production of flour and fodder; import and marketing of premixed feed
Branch Offices: Benghazi: Gamel Abdumaser St, PO Box 209, Tel 96514
Subsidiary Companies: Tripoli Grain Mill; Zliten Grain Mill; Sebha Grain Mill; Garabulli Fodder Plant; Al Abiar Fodder Plant; Zliten Fodder Plant; Sorman Fodder Plant; Sebha Fodder Plant
Principal Bankers: Wahda Bank

Principal Shareholders: State-owned

GENERAL NATIONAL CO FOR INDUSTRIAL CONSTRUCTION

PO Box 953, Beida
Tel: 2672
Cable: Sanaam
Telex: 50410 Sinam

PRINCIPAL ACTIVITIES: Civil engineering and industrial
building, water supply and sewerage systems, prefabricated
buildings, electrical works
Branch Offices: Tripoli Branch: PO Box 295, Tel 54149;
Benghazi Branch: Gamal Abd El Naser St, PO Box 9502, Tel
24686, Telex 40203 Sinam
Principal Bankers: El Umma Bank, Tripoli, Benghazi; National
Commercial Bank, Beida, Shahat

Principal Shareholders: State-owned
Date of Establishment: 1974
No of Employees: 800

GENERAL NATIONAL MARITIME TRANSPORT CO (THE NATIONAL LINE OF LIBYA)

PO Box 80173, 2 Ahmed Sherif Street, Tripoli
Tel: 33155, 31818, 46046
Cable: NAKILBAHRI Tripoli Libya
Telex: 20208, 20239, 20627 Nakilbahri LY
Telefax: 34890

Chairman: Said Elahresh
Directors: Farid Geblawi (Vice Chairman)
Senior Executives: Mustafa Garadi (Finance & Administration
Director), Tahir Shtiwi (Manager Legal & Insurance Dept)

PRINCIPAL ACTIVITIES: Shipowners; maritime company,
commission agents, goods, packing, rescue and supplying all
kinds of ships, tankers, buoys, maritime transport supplies
Branch Offices: PO Box 2450, Benghazi, Tel 91705
Subsidiary Companies: Universal Shipping Agency, Tripoli,
Benghazi, Mersa El Brega, Zuetina, Misurata and all Libyan
ports
Principal Bankers: Central Bank of Libya; El Wahda Bank;
Umma Bank

Principal Shareholders: State-owned
Date of Establishment: 1971

GENERAL NATIONAL ORGANISATION FOR INDUSTRIALIZATION

Shaira Sana'a, PO Box 4388, Tripoli
Tel: 34995, 34559, 44680
Cable: Tasni Libya
Telex: 200990 Tr

PRINCIPAL ACTIVITIES: Promoting and developing all
industrialisation in Libya by the government
Branch Offices: Benghazi Branch: PO Box 2779, Tel 93318,
93036, Cable Tasnish Benghazi

Principal Shareholders: State-owned

GENERAL ORGANISATION FOR TOURISM & FAIRS

PO Box 891, Sharia Haiti, Tripoli
Tel: 32255, 40840, 41734

PRINCIPAL ACTIVITIES: All matters concerning tourism and
fairs in the Jamahiriya and the participation in the
international fairs abroad

Principal Shareholders: State-owned

GENERAL PAPER & PRINTING CO

PO Box 8096, Tripoli
Tel: 34955, 33194
Telex: 20594 Sherouq LY

PRINCIPAL ACTIVITIES: Import of printing equipment,
machines and supplies
Branch Offices: Benghazi, Sebha
Principal Bankers: Jamahiriya Bank

Principal Shareholders: State-owned
Date of Establishment: 1978

GENERAL POST & TELECOMMUNICATIONS CORP

Maidan al Jazair, Tripoli
Tel: 32586, 38587

PRINCIPAL ACTIVITIES: Providing services in the post and
telecommunications fields

Principal Shareholders: State-owned

GENERAL TOBACCO COMPANY

Sharia Maari, PO Box 696, Tripoli
Tel: 37766, 36184, 33828, 37628
Cable: Tritobac Tripoli
Telex: 20133

PRINCIPAL ACTIVITIES: Import and manufacture of cigarettes,
snuff and chewing tobacco and the growing of leaf tobacco

Principal Shareholders: State owned

GENERAL WATER AUTHORITY

Alfath Rd, PO Box 399, Tripoli

PRINCIPAL ACTIVITIES: Supply of water

Principal Shareholders: State-owned

GENERAL WATER WELL DRILLING CO

PO Box 2532, Sharia Omar Muktar, Mormesh Bldg, Tripoli
Tel: 36174

PRINCIPAL ACTIVITIES: Water well drilling, cleaning and
swabbing operations
Branch Offices: PO Box 2532, Benghazi, Tel 95969

Principal Shareholders: State-owned

GEOPHYSICAL SERVICE INT'L SA

Sharia El Gumhouria, Senussi, PO Box 592, Tripoli
Tel: 31819

PRINCIPAL ACTIVITIES: Geophysical services

GEZIRA HOTELS & TOURISM CO

PO Box 285, Benghazi
Tel: 96001/6
Telex: 40113

PRINCIPAL ACTIVITIES: Hotel business

HADI EL AYEB & BROS

See EL AYEB, HADI, & BROS

HADI ENDER ORGANISATION

See ENDER, HADI, ORGANISATION

LIBYA

HAFEZ, IBRAHIM, EST TRADING & CONTRACTING

5 Tozilli St, Garden City, PO Box 582, Tripoli
Tel: 30149, 34736, 41080
Cable: Hafez Tijara

PRINCIPAL ACTIVITIES: Production of building materials, general contracting and trading
Branch Offices: Benghazi: Gamal Abdel Nasser St, PO Box 439, Tel 6576

HOTEL UADDAN

Sharia Sidi Aissa, Tripoli
Tel: 30041, 39555
Cable: Uaddan Tripolibya

PRINCIPAL ACTIVITIES: Hotel business

HUSSEIN N SOUFRAKI

See SOUFRAKI, HUSSEIN N,

IBRAHIM HAFEZ EST TRADING & CONTRACTING

See HAFEZ, IBRAHIM, EST TRADING & CONTRACTING

IBRAHIM HUSNI BEY

See BEY, IBRAHIM HUSNI,

IRON & STEEL COMPLEX MISURATA

PO Box 17858, Misurata
Tel: (051) 24767, 23171, 23172
Cable: Solblibya
Telex: 30148, 30149, 30150 SOLB MS LY
Telefax: (051) 28332

Senior Executives: Shauki Belazi (Manager Industrial Engineering)

PRINCIPAL ACTIVITIES: Iron and steel plant
Branch Offices: Tripoli: PO Box 11108, Tel (021) 607151, 607152, 608690, 608691, Telex 20167

JAMAHIRIYA BANK (FORMERLY MASRAF AL-GUMHOURIA)

PO Box 3224, Tripoli
Tel: 33553
Cable: Jamaam
Telex: 20889, 10890 Lamaint LY
Telefax: 41587

Chairman: Mustafa S Gibril (General Manager)
Directors: Salem A Sheridi (Vice-Chairman & General Manager), Muhaddab Aljoumi, Mustafa A Albarsha, Emhemmed Eshtiwi
Senior Executives: Abulgassem A Bugsea (Asst General Manager), Abdulmajeed A Ghadamsi (Director of Foreign Relations), Mohamed Al Harati (Director of Administration & Staff Affairs), Mohamed Alwani (Director of Branches), Mohammad mansur (Director Advances Division), Suleiman Azzabi (Director of Accounts Division)

PRINCIPAL ACTIVITIES: Commercial Banking
Branch Offices: Libya (38 local branches; Benghazi, PO Box 1291, Telex 40008 Jamaghazi)
Financial Information:

	1988 LD'000
Capital	25,000
Legal Reserves	12,650
Unallocated reserves	25,200
Current accounts & deposits	589,126
Current a/c with foreign banks	46,459
Advances & loans	428,508
Bonds	286,400
Deposits with central Bank	105,871
Investments	2,629

Principal Shareholders: Wholly owned Government bank
Date of Establishment: 1969
No of Employees: 1,853

KCA DRILLING LTD (LIBYA)

PO Box 70050, Tripoli
Tel: 803334
Cable: Kaydrill Tripoli
Telex: 20296

PRINCIPAL ACTIVITIES: International onshore and offshore drilling and engineering contractors
Parent Company: KCA International PLC

Date of Establishment: 1957
No of Employees: 600

KELANY AGRICULTURAL CONSULTING ENGINEERS

PO Box 4285, Tripoli
Tel: 42460

PRINCIPAL ACTIVITIES: Agricultural consulting engineers, import and distribution of agricultural chemicals, insecticides, fertilizers, seeds etc
Branch Offices: PO Box 1828, Benghazi, Tel 93876

KHUELDI SHIPPING AGENCY

8/10/12 Mohamed El Magarief St, PO Box 2299, Tripoli
Tel: 30989
Cable: Shipagency

PRINCIPAL ACTIVITIES: Shipping agency

KUFRA AGRICULTURAL CO

PO Box 4239, Benghazi

PRINCIPAL ACTIVITIES: Agricultural development in the Kufra area
Branch Offices: Tripoli: PO Box 2306, Damascus St

Principal Shareholders: State-owned

KUFRA PRODUCTION PROJECT

PO Box 6324, Benghazi
Tel: 061-26268, 064-26352, 0652-2280
Cable: Kufrag
Telex: 40134 Kufrag, 50651 KPP KUF

PRINCIPAL ACTIVITIES: Responsible for the execution of the Kufra project in the south-eastern part of Libya (involving the exploitation of extensive underground water resources to grow wheat)
Branch Offices: PO Box 2306, Tripoli
Principal Bankers: Umma Bank

Principal Shareholders: State-owned
Date of Establishment: 1969
No of Employees: 500

LIBIMPORT

PO Box 496, Suani Rd Km 1.5, Tripoli
Tel: 30644
Cable: Libimport

PRINCIPAL ACTIVITIES: Trading in automobiles, generating sets and excavators

LIBYA PALACE

Sharia Sidi Issa, Tripoli
Tel: 31181
Telex: 20171

PRINCIPAL ACTIVITIES: Hotel business

LIBYAMAR LTD

PO Box 4452, Sharia Sidi Isa, Tripoli
Tel: 30062/63/67
Cable: Libyamar
Telex: 20130

PRINCIPAL ACTIVITIES: Shipping; insurance; claim adjusters; surveyors; customs clearing and forwarding agents
Branch Offices: Benghazi: PO Box 202; Tobruk: PO Box 3
Principal Bankers: Jamahirya Bank, Tripoli, Banghazi and Tobruk

LIBYAN AGRICULTURAL BANK

PO Box 1100, Tripoli
Tel: 38666, 33544
Cable: Agbank

PRINCIPAL ACTIVITIES: Banking

Principal Shareholders: State-owned

LIBYAN ARAB AIRLINES

Shahrah Haiti, PO Box 2555, Tripoli
Tel: 36021/29, 608860, 602090
Cable: Libair
Telex: 20333
Telefax: 218-22-30970

Chairman: Muflah S Eddlio
Directors: Aiad Al Abbar, Ahmed Zair, Abdulhamed Qadhi, Mahmoud Droug

PRINCIPAL ACTIVITIES: International airline, operating schedules services, transport of passengers, mail and cargo
Branch Offices: PO Box 360, Benghazi, Tel 94826; Bombay, India; London, UK
Principal Bankers: Libyan Foreign Bank
Financial Information:

	1990 LD'000
Profits	87,000
Authorised capital	25,000

Principal Shareholders: Understudy to be turned over to private owners
Date of Establishment: 1964
No of Employees: 6,671

LIBYAN ARAB CO FOR DOMESTIC ELECTRICAL MATERIALS

PO Box 12718, Tripoli
Tel: 37937
Telex: 20421

PRINCIPAL ACTIVITIES: Supply of electrical household appliances and equipment
Branch Offices: PO Box 453, Benghazi, Tel 90175, Telex 40223

Principal Shareholders: State-owned

LIBYAN ARAB FOREIGN BANK

PO Box 2542, 1st September St, Tripoli
Tel: 38107, 41428/9, 45610, 45611
Cable: Forebank
Telex: 20200 Adforbank; 20750/1 Forebank
Telefax: 42970

Chairman: Mohamed I Abduljawad (also General Manager)
Directors: Mohamed H Layas (Deputy Chairman), Salem A Zenaty (Member), Saddik M Hijjaji (Member), Ayad A Dheim (Member), Abdulmouneim H El Kaami (Secretary)

PRINCIPAL ACTIVITIES: Merchant banking (foreign exchange, money market transactions, finance investments and development projects)
Subsidiary/Associated Companies: Arab International Bank, Cairo; UBAF, London; Arab Libyan Tunisian Bank, Lebanon; Banco Arab-Espanol (Aresbank), Madrid; Arab Bank for Investment and Foreign Trade, Abu Dhabi; Libyan Arab Uganda Bank for Foreign Trade and Development; Banque Arabe Tchado-Libyenne pour le Commerce Exterieur et le Developpement; Banque Intercontinentale Arabe, Paris; Banque Arabe Libyenne Mauritanienne pour le Commerce exterieur et le Developpement; Arab Turkish Bank; Banque Arabe Libyenne Togolaise; UBAE, Rome; UBAAB, New York; UBAN, Hong Kong; Arab Jordanian Investment Bank; Banque de Development Economique de Tunisie; Banque Arabe Libyenne Malienne, Bamako; Banque Arabe Libyenne Nigerienne, Niamey; Arab Tunisian Libyan Bank for Developement and Foreign Trade, Tunis; Arab Hellenic Bank SA, Athens; Investment Finance Bank, Malta; Arlabank International, Bahrain; UBAC, Curacao; Arab Financial Services Co, Bahrain; AL UBAF Arab International Bank EC, Bahrain
Principal Bankers: London: UBAF Bank Ltd; New York: Bankers Trust Co; Paris: Banque Intercontinentale Arabe; Zurich: Union Bank of Switzerland; Tokyo: The Bank of Tokyo; Rome: Arab italian Bank (UBAE)
Financial Information:

	US$'000
Authorised capital	191,000
Paid-up capital	191,000

Principal Shareholders: Wholly owned by the Central Bank of Libya
Date of Establishment: 1972
No of Employees: 211

LIBYAN ARAB FOREIGN INVESTMENT CO

PO Box 4538, Maidan Masif El Baladi, Tripoli
Tel: 606570/71/72/73
Cable: ISTIHMARAT
Telex: 20598 LAFICO LY, 20911 NIC LY

Chairman: Mohamed Taher Hammuda Siala (General Manager)
Directors: Smeida El-Hosh El-Naili, Yousef Abd-El-Razegh Abdulmola, Mohamed Bubaker Al Dahmani, Mohamed Hussein Layas

PRINCIPAL ACTIVITIES: Investment and finance
Branch Offices: Malta Office, Rome Office and Athens Office
Principal Bankers: Libyan Arab Foreign Bank, Tripoli

Principal Shareholders: State-owned
Date of Establishment: 4th February 1981
No of Employees: 217

LIBYAN ARAB FURNITURE CO

PO Box 10557, Tripoli
Tel: 30643, 48355
Telex: 20506, 20285

PRINCIPAL ACTIVITIES: Import, distribution and manufacture of home and office furniture
Branch Offices: PO Box 9134, Benghazi, Tel 96638, Telex 40191

LIBYAN BRICK MANUFACTURING CO

PO Box 10700, Tripoli
Tel: 48781
Telex: 20274

PRINCIPAL ACTIVITIES: Manufacture of bricks and cement products
Branch Offices: PO Box 25, KM 17, Suani Rd, Suani

Principal Shareholders: State-owned

LIBYAN CEMENT CO

PO Box 2108, Benghazi
Tel: 21162, 21165, 94842, 87256
Cable: Cement Benghazi
Telex: 40133 Cement Ly; 40326

PRINCIPAL ACTIVITIES: Production of cement and hydrated lime; paper bags; hollow blocks, clay bricks, chalk

Subsidiary Companies: Benghazi Cement Plant; Benghazi Paper Bags Plant; Benghazi Lime Plant

Principal Shareholders: State-owned
No of Employees: 1,500

LIBYAN CINEMA CORPORATION

PO Box 878, Tripoli
Tel: 40661
Cable: Khayala Tripoli
Telex: 20308 Khalyala Ly

PRINCIPAL ACTIVITIES: Import and distribution of films; film production
Branch Offices: PO Box 2076, Benghazi, Tel 92259

Principal Shareholders: State-owned

LIBYAN CO FOR DEVELOPMENT & INVESTMENT

PO Box 2596, Imhamed Margeryef St, Tripoli
Tel: 40725, 37425

PRINCIPAL ACTIVITIES: General trade, contractors, export/import of electrical appliances, furniture, photographic equipment, etc

LIBYAN COMMERCE & INDUSTRY CO

8 Belkhair St, PO Box 20, Tripoli
Tel: 30441

PRINCIPAL ACTIVITIES: Construction, contracting and building materials imports

LIBYAN ELECTRONICS CO

Baghdad St, Andulos Bldg, PO Box 934, Tripoli
Tel: 36721

PRINCIPAL ACTIVITIES: Agriculture and industrial machinery, spare parts, tyres and tubes, batteries, electronics equipment, household appliances
Branch Offices: PO Box 318, Benghazi

LIBYAN ETERNIT COMPANY

PO Box 6103, Zanzour Km 17, Tripoli
Tel: 890106, 891381, 891020
Cable: Eternit Tripoli Libya
Telex: 20261

Chairman: Ali Suleiman

PRINCIPAL ACTIVITIES: Manufacture of asbestos, cement and PVC pipes
Principal Bankers: Wahda Bank, Tripoli; National Commercial Bank, Tripoli

Principal Shareholders: State-owned
Date of Establishment: 1967
No of Employees: 550

LIBYAN FISHING COMPANY

PO Box 3749, Tripoli
Tel: 41077

PRINCIPAL ACTIVITIES: Fishing, fish imports, fish processing and canning

Principal Shareholders: State-owned

LIBYAN HOTELS & TOURISM CO

PO Box 2977, Tripoli
Telex: 20242

PRINCIPAL ACTIVITIES: Hotels and tourism business

Principal Shareholders: State-owned

LIBYAN INSURANCE COMPANY

Ousama Bldg, 1st September St, PO Box 2438, Tripoli
Tel: 44150/8
Cable: Libinsure
Telex: 20071
Telefax: 44178

Secretary of People's Committee: K M Sherlala
Senior Executives: M Naas (Managing Director), M Salem (Finance Director), A Gheryani (Marketing Director), M El Ghoul (Personnel Director), S Al Arabi (Administration Director)

PRINCIPAL ACTIVITIES: Insurance and reinsurance
Branch Offices: Benghazi; Derna; Sebha; Gharian; Misurata; Zawiya; Homs
Subsidiary Companies: Libya Insurance Co (Cyprus Office) Ltd
Financial Information:

	1989 LD'000
Sales turnover	49,996
Profits	9,652
Authorised capital	30,000
Paid-up capital	30,000
Total assets	391,766

Principal Shareholders: 100% state owned
Date of Establishment: 1964
No of Employees: 970

LIBYAN METAL INDUSTRY

PO Box 809, Tripoli
Tel: 32004/5

PRINCIPAL ACTIVITIES: Iron and steel works, production of reinforcing bars

LIBYAN MILLS COMPANY

Sharia 1st September, PO Box 310, Tripoli
Tel: 36225, 31535

PRINCIPAL ACTIVITIES: Production of flour

Principal Shareholders: State-owned

LIBYAN NAVIGATION AGENCY

PO Box 1314, Benghazi
Tel: 94333, 94698
Cable: Navigation

PRINCIPAL ACTIVITIES: Shipping
Branch Offices: 21 Sharia Omar Ibn Abdelaziz, PO Box 3321, Tripoli, Tel 33459, 45104, Cable Libnan

LIBYAN SHIPPING & FISHING AGENCY

Sharia Sidi Dargout 47, PO Box 3909, Tripoli
Tel: 39086
Cable: Shallouf Tripoli

PRINCIPAL ACTIVITIES: Shipping agents, stevedores, forwarders, customs clearance, transport and chartering, door to door service, container services
Branch Offices: Benghazi: Omar Mukhtar St, PO Box 2976, Benghazi; also Agedabia; Zwara; and all Libyan ports)

LIBYAN TRACTOR ESTABLISHMENT

PO Box 12507, Dahra
Tel: 47562
Cable: Jarrar

PRINCIPAL ACTIVITIES: Trading of tractors

Principal Shareholders: State-owned

LIBYAN TRADE & INDUSTRIES CO

PO Box 578, Benghazi
Tel: 86395
Cable: Trustable

PRINCIPAL ACTIVITIES: Importers/commission agents for water/sewage pipes, valves, explosives, etc
Principal Bankers: Wahda bank

LIBYAN TRANSPORT COMPANY
PO Box 94, Sharia Omar El Mukhtar, Benghazi

PRINCIPAL ACTIVITIES: Transport

LINAIR
Libyan National Airways
18 Sharia Enasser, Tripoli
Tel: 33823/24

PRINCIPAL ACTIVITIES: Charter operations

MAGCOBAR (LIBYA) LTD
PO Box 867, Tripoli
Tel: 800327, 804748/9
Telex: 20050 MAGLIB LY

PRINCIPAL ACTIVITIES: Drilling muds, maintenance of Swaco machinery and oilfield equipment and Security Rock Bits
Branch Offices: Benghazi

Principal Shareholders: National Oil Company (51%); Dresser Industries (49%)

MEDICAL EQUIPMENT COMPANY
PO Box 12419, Tripoli
Tel: 41804, 39797
Telex: 20408

PRINCIPAL ACTIVITIES: Import and distribution of medical supplies and equipment, optical and scientific instruments
Branch Offices: PO Box 750, Benghazi, Telex 40167, Tel 95876; PO Box 464, Sebha, Telex 30631, Tel 23204

Principal Shareholders: State-owned

MERZARIO MIDDLE EAST
Badri Bldg, Baghdad Street, PO Box 985, Tripoli
Tel: 34316, 35308
Telex: 20028

PRINCIPAL ACTIVITIES: Shipping and forwarding

MIDDLE EAST OILFIELD SUPPLIES CO
PO Box 2465, Badri Bldg, Sharia Baghdad, Tripoli
Tel: 33422
Cable: Meos Tripoli

PRINCIPAL ACTIVITIES: Oilfield contractors, distribution of oilfield and allied equipment

MISURATA GENERAL ROADS CO
PO Box 200, Misurata
Tel: 21358, 20035, 20036, 20037
Cable: Misratork
Telex: 30260

PRINCIPAL ACTIVITIES: Building and civil engineering construction of roads and aircraft runways
Branch Offices: PO Box 958, Tripoli, Tel 45295
Principal Bankers: National Commercial Bank

Principal Shareholders: State-owned
No of Employees: 1,000

MOBIL OIL LIBYA
PO Box 690, Tripoli
Tel: 30081
Cable: Pegasus Libya
Telex: 20260 Mobpro Ly

PRINCIPAL ACTIVITIES: Oil and gas service and production
Principal Bankers: Sahara Bank; El Wahda Bank

Principal Shareholders: National Oil Corporation; Mobil Oil Corp; Gelsenberg AG
No of Employees: 766

MOHAMED AMIN DERBI
See DERBI, MOHAMED AMIN,

MOHAMMAD AGHEILA
See AGHEILA, MOHAMMAD,

MOHAMMED BEN SASSI ORGANISATION
See BEN SASSI, MOHAMMED, ORGANISATION

MOTHERCAT LTD
PO Box 2756, Tripoli

PRINCIPAL ACTIVITIES: Contractors for steel structures, pipelines, refinery installations and fertilizer complexes

MUDUROGLU LTD
PO Box 9314, Benghazi
Tel: 87816
Cable: Muduroglu

PRINCIPAL ACTIVITIES: Building and civil engineering contractors (rock blasting concreting and dredging operations)
Branch Offices: Cyprus (Head Office); Turkey

MUHARIKAAT GENERAL AUTOMOBILE CO
PO Box 259, Tripoli
Tel: 37090, 41671
Telex: 20079

PRINCIPAL ACTIVITIES: Trading in auto vehicles
Principal Agencies: Lada, Skoda, Seat, Zestawa, Pegaso
Branch Offices: PO Box 203, Benghazi, Tel 21982
Financial Information: An amalgamation of the following companies: Qafala General Automobile Co; General Rahila Automobile Co; Mahari General Automobile Co

Principal Shareholders: State-owned
Date of Establishment: 1980

NATIONAL AGRICULTURAL BANK OF LIBYA
PO Box 1100, Sharia Omar Mukthar, Tripoli
Tel: 33542
Cable: Agbank

PRINCIPAL ACTIVITIES: Loans to farmers

Principal Shareholders: State-owned

NATIONAL CEMENT & BUILDING MATERIALS EST
PO Box 628, Sharia Hayati 21, Tripoli
Tel: 2004, 39046
Cable: Cement Tripoli
Telex: 20137

PRINCIPAL ACTIVITIES: Production of cement, gypsum and other building materials. (Operation of cement factory at Homs producing 430,000 tons per year and a gypsum factory producing 5,000 tons per year)
Subsidiary Companies: Khoms, Cement Plant, Tel 2515, Khoms; Suani Gypsum Plant, Tel 38405; Tripoli Cement Silos, Tel 36417

Principal Shareholders: State-owned

NATIONAL CO FOR CHEMICAL PREPARATION & COSMETIC PRODUCTS
PO Box 2442, Tripoli
Tel: 39647, 39447
Telex: 20559

PRINCIPAL ACTIVITIES: Manufacture of chemical preparations and cosmetic products

Branch Offices: Benghazi, Tel 92182, Telex 40064
Financial Information: An amalgamation of the following
  companies: Al Jamal Trading Est (Benghazi) and Ahmad
  Qassem & Sons Co

Principal Shareholders: State-owned
Date of Establishment: 1980

NATIONAL CO FOR CONSTRUCTION & MAINTENANCE OF MUNICIPAL WORKS
PO Box 12908, Zavia Street, Tripoli
Tel: 41995, 47134
Telex: 20349, 20980

PRINCIPAL ACTIVITIES: Construction, maintenance of sewage
  and pumping station projects
Branch Offices: PO Box 441, Benghazi

Principal Shareholders: State-owned

NATIONAL CO FOR LIGHT EQUIPMENT
PO Box 8707, Tripoli
Tel: 30208
Telex: 20495

PRINCIPAL ACTIVITIES: Import of agricultural machinery and
  equipment, water pumps, and other light equipment
Branch Offices: PO Box 540, Benghazi, Tel 91210

Principal Shareholders: State-owned

NATIONAL CO FOR METAL WORKS
PO Box 2913, Tripoli
Tel: 32531, 35743
Cable: Mashgulat
Telex: 20264

PRINCIPAL ACTIVITIES: Steel structures and pipes,
  construction and metal works, structural design, storage
  tanks and doors, window shutters; sole importers and
  maintenance of lifts
Branch Offices: PO Box 4093, Benghazi, Tel 27733, Telex
  40196; Lift Department, PO Box 1000, Tripoli, Tel 39459,
  37449, 38813
Principal Bankers: Sahara Bank; Umma Bank

Principal Shareholders: State-owned
No of Employees: 300

NATIONAL CO FOR OILFIELD EQUIPMENT
PO Box 8707, Tripoli
Tel: 30208
Telex: 20495

PRINCIPAL ACTIVITIES: Supply of oilfield equipment

Principal Shareholders: State-owned

NATIONAL CO FOR ROAD EQUIPMENT
PO Box 12392, Tripoli
Tel: 37178, 48476, 41561
Cable: Tajhiz, Tripol
Telex: 20391 TJ LY

PRINCIPAL ACTIVITIES: Import of earthmoving, road building
  and construction equipment
Branch Offices: PO Box 700, Benghazi, Tel 98606, Telex 40169

Principal Shareholders: State-owned

NATIONL CO FOR ROADS & AIRPORTS
PO Box 4050, Benghazi
Tel: 21835, 24311
Cable: Mahabet
Telex: 40106 MAHABET LY

Chairman: Eng Mohamed N Salih

PRINCIPAL ACTIVITIES: Design and construction of roads and
  airports and maintenance

Branch Offices: PO Box 8634, Sharia Al Jaraba, Tripoli, Tel
  44975
Principal Bankers: Sahara Bank

Principal Shareholders: State-owned
Date of Establishment: 1972
No of Employees: 444

NATIONAL CO OF SOAP & CLEANING MATERIALS
PO Box 12025, Tripoli
Tel: 46566
Cable: Sabitri
Telex: 20288 Sabetry Ly

PRINCIPAL ACTIVITIES: Import and distribution of soap,
  detergents and chemical products
Branch Offices: PO Box 246, Benghazi; Cable Soapcler; Telex
  40127
Principal Bankers: Wahda Bank; Sahara Bank

Principal Shareholders: State-owned

NATIONAL COMMERCIAL BANK SAL
PO Box 4647, Shuhada Sq, Tripoli
Tel: 37191/6
Cable: Tijariwa Tani
Telex: 20169 Tijari

PRINCIPAL ACTIVITIES: All banking transactions
Branch Offices: PO Box 166, Benghazi, Tel 91140, Telex 40012
  Watani

Principal Shareholders: Central Bank of Libya
Date of Establishment: 1970

NATIONAL CONSTRUCTION & ENGINEERING CO
PO Box 1060, Sharia Sidi Issa, Tripoli
Tel: 35062, 33868

PRINCIPAL ACTIVITIES: Building and civil engineering
  contractors, sewerage, drainage work
Branch Offices: PO Box 259, Benghazi, Tel 94932

Principal Shareholders: State-owned

NATIONAL CONSULTING BUREAU
PO Box 12795, Tripoli
Tel: 48495, 48872
Telex: 20488

PRINCIPAL ACTIVITIES: Engineering consultants

Principal Shareholders: State-owned

NATIONAL CORPORATION FOR HOUSING
PO Box 4829, Sharia el Jumhuriya, Tripoli
Tel: 37104/5

PRINCIPAL ACTIVITIES: Construction and civil engineering,
  housing authority

Principal Shareholders: State-owned

NATIONAL DEPARTMENT STORES CO
PO Box 5327, Sharia El Jumhuriya, Tripoli
Tel: 40761
Telex: 20122; 20619 Aswaq

PRINCIPAL ACTIVITIES: Department stores

Principal Shareholders: State-owned

NATIONAL DEVELOPMENT COMPANY
PO Box 2285, Suani Rd, Km 2, Tripoli
Tel: 32993, 32108
Telex: 20221

PRINCIPAL ACTIVITIES: General trading and contracting operation for large mechanical and steel fabrication workshops, manufacture of trailers, air conditioning and prefabricated buildings

NATIONAL DRILLING COMPANY

PO Box 1454, Tripoli
Tel: 34995, 36034, 33738
Cable: Istmrar
Telex: 20332 ISTMRAR LY

PRINCIPAL ACTIVITIES: Oil drilling contractors and mining
Parent Company: National Oil Corporation, Libya

Date of Establishment: 1973
No of Employees: 430

NATIONAL FOODSTUFFS IMPORTS, EXPORTS & MANUFACTURING CO SAL

PO Box 11114, Tripoli
Tel: 48977
Telex: 20369

PRINCIPAL ACTIVITIES: Import and production of foodstuffs, dairy products, fish products and beverages
Branch Offices: PO Box 2439, Benghazi, Tel 96440, Telex 40126
Financial Information: Merged with Food Trading Company in Late 1980

Principal Shareholders: State-owned

NATIONAL GENERAL INDUSTRIAL CONTRACTING CO

Sharia al Jumhouria, PO Box 295, Tripoli
Tel: 45149

PRINCIPAL ACTIVITIES: Civil contracting works for factory buildings. Import of spare parts and raw materials for the establishment, operation and maintenance of factories

Principal Shareholders: State-owned

NATIONAL LIVESTOCK & MEAT CO

PO Box 389, Sharia Zawiet Dahmani, Tripoli
Tel: 45457
Telex: 20040

PRINCIPAL ACTIVITIES: Import of meat and livestock
Branch Offices: PO Box 4153, Sharia Jamal Abdulnasser, Telex 40020, Benghazi, Tel 91423

Principal Shareholders: State-owned
No of Employees: 150

NATIONAL NAVIGATION CO OF LIBYA

PO Box 2437, 67 Baghdad St, Tripoli

PRINCIPAL ACTIVITIES: Shipping and forwarding agency

NATIONAL OIL CORPORATION (NOC)

PO Box 2655, off Sharia Al Nasr, Tripoli
Tel: 46180, 46190
Cable: Linaft
Telex: 61508; 20270

PRINCIPAL ACTIVITIES: Development, management, marketing and exploitation of hydrocarbons, establishment of petroleum industries and distribution of locally manufactured and imported petroleum products
Branch Offices: PO Box 2978, Benghazi; Tel 86366; Telex 40032
Subsidiary Companies: Brega Petroleum Marketing; Arab Gulf Exploration Co; Umm Al-Jawaby Petroleum Co; Zawya Petroleum Co; National Methanol Co

Principal Shareholders: State-owned

NATIONAL OILFIELD SUPPLIES

Suani Rd, Km 3, PO Box 2745, Tripoli
Tel: 41354
Cable: Muttawe

PRINCIPAL ACTIVITIES: Oilfield supplies and tools, wire ropes, nylon ropes, manila ropes, all kinds of fittings and paints
Principal Bankers: National Commercial Bank, Tripoli; Jamahiriya Bank

NATIONAL PETROCHEMICALS CO (PREVIOUSLY NATIONAL METHANOL CO)

PO Box 5324, Garden City, Benghazi
Tel: (061) 21361, (021) 602105, 602106
Cable: Napetco
Telex: 50603, 50605

Chairman: A M Sahli

PRINCIPAL ACTIVITIES: Petrochemicals - methanol, ammonia, urea
Branch Offices: National Petrochemicals Company (Libyan), West Germany Tel (0211) 434956, Telex 8588234 NPCLD
Principal Bankers: Umma Bank, Benghazi

Principal Shareholders: 100% owned by Secretariat of Heavy Industry, Libya
Date of Establishment: December 1979
No of Employees: 1,500

NATIONAL PETROLEUM SERVICES CO

PO Box 2421, Tripoli
Tel: 42063, 33583
Telex: 20144 Ly

PRINCIPAL ACTIVITIES: Provide services to oil companies working in Libya. Engineering, consultant, maintenance and construction, workover and transport and other services required by oil companies only
Branch Offices: Benghazi, Tel 3822

NATIONAL PHARMACEUTICAL CO SAL

20 Jalal Bayer St, PO Box 2296, Tripoli
Tel: 32045
Cable: Aladwia
Telex: 20182 Aladwia

PRINCIPAL ACTIVITIES: Import, manufacture and distribution of pharmaceuticals, veterinary products, chemicals, and baby dietetics
Branch Offices: Tripoli Branch: Jamahiriya St, PO Box 10225, Tripoli, Cable Dwa Tripoli Benghazi branch: PO Box 2620, Benghazi, Telex 40044: Ben, Cable Dwa Benghazi
Principal Bankers: Umma Bank; Wahda Bank; Jamahiriya Bank

Principal Shareholders: State owned

NATIONAL SHIPPING & TRADING AGENCY

PO Box 610, Sharia Omar Mukhtar 132, Benghazi
Tel: 93709
Cable: Seatrade Benghazi

PRINCIPAL ACTIVITIES: Shipping agents, tourist agents, forwarding, stevedoring, packers, import, export, commission agents
Branch Offices: Branches in Tobruk and Derna

NATIONAL SOFT DRINKS EST

PO Box 559, Benghazi
Tel: 21690, 23728
Cable: SLIKO
Telex: 40157

Chairman: Abdulsallam I Haddad
Members of the General Committee: Abdulsallam I Haddad, Sailem F Hawat (Acting Chairman), Mahmud M Belgasim, Ali A Fazani, Farag A Fahazani

Senior Executives: Ismail M Ibrahim (Chairman's Office Manager)

PRINCIPAL ACTIVITIES: Production of soft drinks
Branch Offices: Litraco Impex Ltd, PO Box 5686, Benghazi, Fax 061-22836
Principal Bankers: Umma Bank of Libya
Financial Information:

	1990
	LD'000
Authorised capital	500
Paid-up capital	500
Total assets	12,000

Principal Shareholders: State-owned
Date of Establishment: 1979
No of Employees: 425

NATIONAL STORES & COLD STORES CO

PO Box 8454, Tripoli
Tel: 620439
Cable: Tabrid

Chairman: Salem Gamra (Chief of Popular Committee)

PRINCIPAL ACTIVITIES: Cold storage and warehousing
Branch Offices: Benghazi branch: PO Box 9250, tel: 97096, 98512, telex 40265

Principal Shareholders: National Investment Co; National Supply Corp; Port & Light Authority; General Co for Marketing & Agricultural Production

NATIONAL SUPPLIES CORPORATION (NASCO)

PO Box 3402, Sharia Omar Mukhtar, Tripoli
Tel: 43054/5/6, 37393, 36646
Telex: 20205

PRINCIPAL ACTIVITIES: Importer of bulk food items (salt, sugar, rice, coffee, olive oil, flour, grain, barley, rice)
Branch Offices: PO Box 2071, Benghazi, Tel 93614
Associated Companies: Consumer Products Corporation

Principal Shareholders: State-owned

NATIONAL TELECOMMUNICATIONS CO

PO Box 886, Shara Zawia, Tripoli
Tel: 605200, 605219
Cable: Silky
Telex: 20005 Ntc Ly

Chairman: Abdulla Kredly (Chairman of People's Committee)

PRINCIPAL ACTIVITIES: Undertaking the study, design, installation, trade, monopoly of import of electronics telecommunications systems, equipment and materials
Branch Offices: PO Box 4139, Benghazi, Telex 40116 Ntc Ly
Principal Bankers: Sahara Bank, Tripoli

Principal Shareholders: Wholly owned by the Government

NORTH AFRICA INDUSTRIAL TRADING & CONTRACTING CO

PO Box 245, Tripoli
Tel: 35052, 35767

PRINCIPAL ACTIVITIES: Trading and contracting in prefabricated buildings and office equipment

Principal Shareholders: State-owned

OASIS OIL CO OF LIBYA INC

PO Box 395, Tripoli
Tel: 31116
Cable: Oasisoil
Telex: 20158

PRINCIPAL ACTIVITIES: Crude oil and gas exploration and production
Principal Agencies: National Oil Corporation; Continental Oil Co; Marathon Petroleum, and Amerada Hess Corp

OEA DRINKS CO

PO Box 101, Ibn El Jarrah St, Tripoli
Tel: 36161, 36985
Cable: Oeadrinks Tripoli

Chairman: Mohamed Banoun

PRINCIPAL ACTIVITIES: Production of non-alcoholic beer and assorted soft drinks
Principal Bankers: Commercial Bank, Tripoli

Principal Shareholders: General National Organisation for Industrialisation

OILFIELD IMPORTS OF LIBYA LTD

PO Box 2421, Tripoli
Tel: 34822, 30602
Cable: Oil

PRINCIPAL ACTIVITIES: Industrial and oilfield sales; drilling and production rigs; plant hire; tug service
Subsidiary Companies: Sarco Ltd, Oil Service Department

POOL-INTAIRDRIL

PO Box 11828, Tripoli
Tel: 802385, 802246
Telex: 20852 POOLCO LY

PRINCIPAL ACTIVITIES: Oil drilling and workover contractors
Parent Company: Pool International

PRAKLALIBYA

PO Box 679, Tripoli
Tel: 42772
Telex: 20046

PRINCIPAL ACTIVITIES: Geophysical service company
Branch Offices: Libya and West Germany

PUBLIC COMPANY FOR GARMENTS

PO Box 4152, Benghazi
Tel: 91850
Telex: 40039, 40241

PRINCIPAL ACTIVITIES: Trading in clothing

Principal Shareholders: State-owned

PUBLIC ELECTRICAL WORKS CO

PO Box 8539, Sharia Halab, Tripoli
Tel: 35222, 35276, 47054
Telex: 20267, 20167

PRINCIPAL ACTIVITIES: Production of electrical power and distribution projects
Branch Offices: Benghazi, PO Box 32811, Tel 96667, Telex 40130

Principal Shareholders: State-owned

PUBLIC SAFETY COMMODITY IMPORTING CO (SILAMNIA)

PO Box 12942, Tripoli
Tel: 45341, 40226, 38528
Telex: 20426

PRINCIPAL ACTIVITIES: Import of ammunitions, weapons, explosives hunting and fishing equipment

Principal Shareholders: State-owned

RAED SHIPPING AGENCY

29 Mansur El Kikhya St, Benghazi
Tel: 92218, 93393
Cable: Raedship
Telex: 40023 Raemar

PRINCIPAL ACTIVITIES: Shipping agents, ships' brokers, transport of heavy lifts and operators of containers terminal
Branch Offices: PO Box 2902, Benghazi
Principal Bankers: Sahara Bank; Wahda Bank (Benghazi)

RAS HILAL MARITIME CO

PO Box 1496, Benghazi
Tel: 94471
Telex: 40019

PRINCIPAL ACTIVITIES: Shipping agency

Principal Shareholders: State-owned

RAS LANUF OIL & GAS PROCESSING CO

PO Box 75071, Tripoli
Tel: 601310

PRINCIPAL ACTIVITIES: Oil and gas processing
Branch Offices: Benghazi: PO Box 1971, Telex 40128; Ras Lanuf: Telex 50618

Principal Shareholders: State-owned

RUHAYEM, ABDULRASUL,

PO Box 3561, Tripoli
Tel: 41752

President: Abdulrasul Ruhayem
Directors: Mansour Ruhayem, Mohamed Ruhayem, Mahmoud Mohamed Mahmoud, Saleh Faraj

PRINCIPAL ACTIVITIES: Engineering and contracting, oilfield construction and maintenance
Branch Offices: PO Box 771, Benghazi, Tel 92503

SABRATA SHIPPING & STEVEDORING EST

Badri Bldg, PO Box 985, Tripoli
Tel: 34316, 35805, 42340, 39010, 43331, 35097
Cable: Sashipco
Telex: 20058 Libitra Ly, 20023 Sabgen, 20498

Chairman: Omar Burghiga (Head of People Committee)

PRINCIPAL ACTIVITIES: Shipping agents, shipbrokers, forwarders, stevedores, commerce, aviation, travel, tourism
Branch Offices: Misurata, Zuara, Pireaus
Principal Bankers: National Commercial Bank; Jamahiriya Bank; Wahda Bank

Date of Establishment: 1978
No of Employees: 328

SAHABI OIL FIELD PROJECT

PO Box 982, Tripoli
Tel: 34036/7/8/9, 34030
Cable: Linaft
Telex: 61508

PRINCIPAL ACTIVITIES: Oil and gas production

Principal Shareholders: State-owned

SAHARA BANK

PO Box 270, Sharia 1 September, Tripoli
Tel: 32771/3, 39804, 32129, 31229
Cable: Saharabank
Telex: 20009, 20545, 20678
Telefax: 37922

Chairman: Omar A Shabou (also Managing Director)
Directors: Abdel Majid Salem (Deputy Chairman), Tahier Nagah, Tahier El Haje, Ali G El Agely

Senior Executives: Mahmud Badi (Asst General Manager), Hassan T Elmadani (Asst General Manager), Mohamed M Swei (Managing Director Investment), Omar K Marsit (Managing Director Credit), Mohamed Lahresh (Managing Director Branches), Emhemed M Aboudib (Managing Director Inspection), Elhadi S Elsharef (Managing Director Personal), Abdel Hamid Almabruk (Managing Director Auditing)

PRINCIPAL ACTIVITIES: Commercial banking
Branch Offices: Benghazi, Tel 93138, Telex 40009; and 21 other branches in Libya
Financial Information:

	1990
	LD'000
Profits	6.968
Authorised capital	525
Paid-up capital	525
Total assets	658.109

Principal Shareholders: Central Bank of Libya (82%), Libyan Interests (18%)
Date of Establishment: 1964
No of Employees: 751

SAHARA DEVELOPMENT COMPANY

PO Box 4823, Tripoli
Tel: 39955, 47231
Cable: Ramy
Telex: 20114

PRINCIPAL ACTIVITIES: Hotel furnishings, hospital and medical equipment, general supplies for the army and government authorities
Branch Offices: Benghazi (PO Box 1283) and Sebha (PO Box 1919)

SAVING & REAL ESTATE INVESTMENT BANK

PO Box 2297, Tripoli
Tel: 49306/8
Cable: Sanabank
Telex: 20309 Sanabank
Telefax: 49309

Chairman: Ragiab Saad Madi
Directors: Eng Ramadan Milad Ragiab, Mohamed Bashir Al Bargati, Ayad Shtewe, Ahmed Saleh Balha
Senior Executives: Mohamed Bashir Al Bargati

PRINCIPAL ACTIVITIES: Finance for construction development and housing
Branch Offices: 24 branches in Libya
Financial Information:

	1988
	LD'000
Authorised capital	348,000
Paid-up capital	323,000
Total assets	423,000

Principal Shareholders: State-owned
Date of Establishment: 1965
No of Employees: 621

SAYED ABDALLA ABED SENUSSI CO (SAASCO)

PO Box 207, Benghazi

PRINCIPAL ACTIVITIES: Building and civil engineering contractors; import and distribution of building materials, agricultural machinery and equipment; export of esparto grass

SEBHA ROADS & CONSTRUCTION CO

PO Box 92, Sebha
Tel: 20622
Cable: Sebha General

PRINCIPAL ACTIVITIES: Building and civil engineering, construction of public buildings and public service buildings and maintenance of the necessary utilities required and other civil works
Branch Offices: Tripoli branch; PO Box 8264
Principal Bankers: National Commercial Bank; Umma Bank; Jamahiriya Bank

Principal Shareholders: State-owned
No of Employees: 1,000

SEZAI TURKES-FEYZI AKKAYA CONSTRUCTION CO

PO Box 3456, Tripoli
Tel: 218(21), 32142, 38060, 45462, 49148
Cable: Temel Tripoli
Telex: 20044 Temel Tp

PRINCIPAL ACTIVITIES: Heavy construction and civil engineering contracting
Branch Offices: Jeddah, Saudi Arabia; Tehran, Iran; Tunis, Tunisia; London, UK; Milan, Italy
Parent Company: Sezai Turkes Feyzi Akkaya Construction Co, Turkey

Principal Shareholders: Temel End Ins San ve Ticaret AS; Temel Insaat Taahhut Imalat San ve Ticaret AS; STFA Holding AS
Date of Establishment: 1938
No of Employees: 3,318

SHELL PETROLEUM DEVELOPMENT CO OF LIBYA

PO Box 1420, Benghazi
Tel: 99574
Telex: 40336 Shelben

PRINCIPAL ACTIVITIES: Petroleum services

Principal Shareholders: State-owned

SINTEC

International Engineering & Technical Services Co

PO Box 1309, 21 Sharia Omar Mikhtar, Benghazi
Tel: 94930, 94963, 93689
Cable: Sintec

Senior Executives: H M Zeidan, A H Zeidan

PRINCIPAL ACTIVITIES: Technical services, engineering maintenance, etc
Branch Offices: PO Box 2505, 16a Sharia 1st September, Tripoli, Tel 30101/2, 35690, Cable Sintec
Parent Company: Zeidan Group of Companies

SIRTE OIL CO FOR PRODUCTION MANUFACTURING OIL & GAS MARSA EL BREGA

PO Box 385, Tripoli
Tel: 30021
Telex: 20240
Telefax: 601487

Secretary People's Committee: M M Benniran
Members People's Committee: S M Ben Rahuma, K M Tabouli, A M Zregh, N N Khanfar

PRINCIPAL ACTIVITIES: Oil exploration, production of crude oil, gas and petrochemicals, liquefaction of natural gas
Principal Agencies: Umm Al Jawaby, London, UK; Medoil GmbH, Dusseldorf, Germany
Branch Offices: Benghazi, and Woking (UK)
Principal Bankers: UBAF Bank, London

Date of Establishment: 1955 as Esso Standard Libya, 1981 nationalised
No of Employees: 5,245

SOCIALIST EST FOR SPINNING & WEAVING

Zanzour Km 15, PO Box 30186, Tripoli
Tel: 73624, 73635
Cable: Nasij Zanzour
Telex: 20099

PRINCIPAL ACTIVITIES: Spinning and weaving, production of textiles, also dyeing, processing and sewing
Branch Offices: PO Box 852, Benghazi, Tel 91672
Subsidiary Companies: Weaving, Dyeing & Finishing Plant; Ready-Made Suits Plant, Derna; Wool Washing & Spinning Plant, Marj

Principal Shareholders: State-owned

SOUFRAKI, HUSSEIN N,

PO Box 3283, Sharia Haita, Ruhagiar Bldg, Tripoli
Tel: 35670
Cable: Soufracon

PRINCIPAL ACTIVITIES: Manufacturers' representative, import and distribution of earth-moving equipment and heavy machinery

SOUK EL KHAMIS GENERAL CEMENT & BUILDING MATERIALS CORP

Tarhuna, Sharia Bou Harida, PO Box 1084, Tripoli
Tel: 48243
Cable: Somes Tripoli

PRINCIPAL ACTIVITIES: Production of lime, cement and other building materials
Subsidiary Companies: Souk El Khamis Cement Co; Souk El Khamis Lime Factory

Principal Shareholders: State-owned

SOUSA SHIPPING & STEVEDORING EST

PO Box 2973, Benghazi
Tel: 92236, 93559, 92025, 94490
Cable: Senship
Telex: 40076, 40105

PRINCIPAL ACTIVITIES: Shipping agency
Principal Bankers: Wahda Bank

Principal Shareholders: State-owned and partnership
Date of Establishment: 27-8-78
No of Employees: 145

TARBAGHIA & SONS

PO Box 21, Benghazi
Tel: 94418, 96915
Cable: Tarbaghia
Telex: 40198
Telefax: 99616

Chairman: Mansour Tarbaghia
Directors: Eng Tarek Mansour Tarbaghia
Senior Executives: Eng Nabil Mansour Tarbaghia

PRINCIPAL ACTIVITIES: Shipping and forwarding agents
Branch Offices: Benghazi; Tripoli; Derna; Tobruk; Es Zuetina
Principal Bankers: Al Wahda Commercial Bank, Benghazi

Principal Shareholders: Mansour Tarbaghia
Date of Establishment: 1958

TATANAKI BROTHERS

PO Box 174, Tatanaki Bldg, Apt 10/3, Istiklal St, Tripoli
Tel: 34473, 43265
Cable: Tatanaki

Chairman: Salaheddin Tatanaki

PRINCIPAL ACTIVITIES: Civil engineering contractors, general dealers for OM trucks
Branch Offices: Branches in Benghazi and Tobruk

TECHNICAL CO FOR AGRICULTURAL PEST CONTROL
New Gourgy Rd, PO Box 6445, Tripoli
Tel: 71623
Cable: Pestco
Telex: 20487

PRINCIPAL ACTIVITIES: Import and marketing of chemical pesticides and spraying equipment
Branch Offices: Benghazi, Nacer St
Associated Companies: General Company for Agricultural Necessities; General Company for Marketing and Agricultural Production
Principal Bankers: Sahara Bank

Principal Shareholders: General Company for Agricultural Necessities (State-owned), General Company for Marketing and Agricultural Production (State-owned)

TIBESTI AUTOMOBILE GENERAL CO
PO Box 8456, Tripoli
Tel: 40990
Cable: Tibesti, Tripoli
Telex: 20438

Chairman: Abdalla T Abdulaziz

PRINCIPAL ACTIVITIES: Trading in automobiles, spare parts and accessories
Branch Offices: PO Box 5397, Benghazi, Tel 20528, Telex 40173; Derna, Misurata, Khums, Sebha, Gharian, Zawia and Tripoli.
Principal Bankers: Umma Bank, Tripoli

Principal Shareholders: State-owned
Date of Establishment: February 1972
No of Employees: 1,700

TOLMETHA SHIPPING ESTABLISHMENT
PO Box 208, Derna
Tel: 25256, 24123
Telex: 50002

PRINCIPAL ACTIVITIES: Shipping agency

Principal Shareholders: State-owned

UMM AL-JAWABY PETROLEUM CO SAL
PO Box 693, Tripoli
Tel: 37141
Cable: Pertel
Telex: 20202 Pertel

PRINCIPAL ACTIVITIES: Oil and gas exploration and production
Principal Bankers: Central Bank of Libya

Principal Shareholders: National Oil Corporation
No of Employees: 1,280

UMMA BANK SAL
PO Box 685, 1 Giaddet Omar Mukhtar, Tripoli
Tel: 21-34031 (5 lines), 31194/95, 32888, 40105, 41656
Telex: 20256 Umma Bank; 20748 Umma BK
Telefax: 30880, 41454, 32505, 42476

Chairman: Seddig Omar Elkaber
Directors: Hussein Abulaied Shairedi (Deputy Chairman & General Manager)
Senior Executives: Mahmoud M Zawia

PRINCIPAL ACTIVITIES: Commercial banking
Branch Offices: Benghazi, Tel 92048, Telex 40010, 40356 Umma Ly; and 32 branches throughout Libya

Financial Information:

	1989 LD'000
Profits	2,079
Authorised capital	23,000
Total assets	1,343,721

Principal Shareholders: 100% State-owned
Date of Establishment: 14th November 1969
No of Employees: 1,580

UNIVERSAL SHIPPING AGENCY
PO Box 3703, 69 Mhamed Mgarief St, Tripoli
Tel: 39361, 40566
Cable: Uniship Tripoli
Telex: 20263 Uniship

PRINCIPAL ACTIVITIES: Shipping, stevedoring, clearing, forwarding transport
Branch Offices: PO Box 2450, Benghazi, Cable Uniship Benghazi, Tel 91705, Telex 40101

VEBA OIL LIBYA GMBH - LIBYAN BRANCH
PO Box 2537, Tripoli
Tel: 38187, 42114
Telex: 20254

PRINCIPAL ACTIVITIES: Crude oil exploration and production in Libya
Parent Company: Veba Oel AG, Gelsenkirchen, West Germany
Principal Bankers: Libya Arab Foreign Bank, Tripoli; Sahara Bank, Tripoli

WAHDA BANK
Jamel Abdul Nasser St, PO Box 452, Benghazi
Tel: 91147/51
Cable: Wahdabank Headoffice
Telex: 40011; 40164

Chairman: Yousef A Hassadi (General Manager)

PRINCIPAL ACTIVITIES: Commercial banking
Branch Offices: PO Box 3427, Tripoli, Tel 34016, 41331, Telex 20011

Principal Shareholders: Central Bank of Libya
Date of Establishment: 1970

YASIN & COMPANY
PO Box 4285, Tripoli
Tel: 42460

PRINCIPAL ACTIVITIES: Construction and agricultural machinery and equipment, marine and diesel engines, pumps, and water and irrigation equipment, contractors' plant equipment
Branch Offices: PO Box 1828, Benghazi, Tel 93876
Subsidiary Companies: Chemical and Technical Services

ZEIDAN GROUP OF COMPANIES
PO Box 1309, Benghazi
Tel: 93689, 94930, 94963
Cable: Zeidanco

PRINCIPAL ACTIVITIES: Import/export, general agents, transport and general contractors, engineering and technical services, general suppliers (earth-moving equipment, agricultural equipment and machinery, irrigation pipes and pumps), deals promotors, computers
Branch Offices: PO Box 2505, Tripoli, Tel 30101, 30102, 35690, Cable Zeidanco
Subsidiary Companies: Zeidanco; Zeidsons and Sintec Companies

ZUETINA OIL COMPANY
PO Box 2134, Tripoli
Tel: 38011, 40956
Telex: 20289

Chairman: Dr N A Arifi (Chairman Management Committee)
Directors: A M Wazera (Member Management Committee)
Senior Executives: E Bergli (Manager Finance), M Oun
  (Manager Operations)

PRINCIPAL ACTIVITIES: Oil exploration and production
Parent Company: National Oil Corporation

Principal Shareholders: National Oil Corporation
Date of Establishment: 1986
No of Employees: 2,618

ZWAWA & CO

PO Box 2123, Benghazi
Tel: 93336, 93583, 94959
Cable: Zwawa
Telex: 40148 Zwawa

Chairman: Omar Zwawa
Directors: M Y Sedik
Senior Executives: Fawaz Khamash (Financial Director)

PRINCIPAL ACTIVITIES: Air conditioning and refrigeration
  appliances and equipment, supply of household goods,
  electronics, electrical and air conditioning contracting
Principal Agencies: GE of America, Danfoss, Grunding
Principal Bankers: Jamahiriya Bank, Benghazi

Date of Establishment: 1962

Major Companies of
MAURITANIA

AIR MAURITANIE

PO Box 41, Nouakchott

Chairman: Ahmed Ould Bah

PRINCIPAL ACTIVITIES: Airlines; domestic services from
Nouakchott and Nouadhibou and international services to
Dakar, Las Palmas and Casablanca

BANQUE ARABE AFRICAINE EN MAURITANIE

B.A.A.M.

Afarco Bldg, Rue Mamadou Konate, PO Box 622, Nouakchott
Tel: 52826
Cable: BAAM
Telex: 543

Chairman: Mohamed Seghir Mostafai
Directors: Sid Mohamed Abass (Deputy Chairman)
Senior Executives: Hussein Gamal El Din Gamgoum (General
Manager)

PRINCIPAL ACTIVITIES: Commercial banking
Branch Offices: Nouadhibou: rue Mediane, PO Box 324; Aioun;
Nema
Subsidiary/Associated Companies: Banque Centrale de
Mauritanie, Nouakchott; Banque Arabe Africaine
Internationale (Cairo)

Principal Shareholders: Banque Centrale de Mauritanie; Banque
Arabe Africaine Internationale (Cairo)
Date of Establishment: 1974

BANQUE ARABE LIBYENNE MAURITANIENNE POUR LE COMMERCE EXTERIEUR ET LE DEVELOPPEMENT

B.A.L.M.

PO Box 626, Ave Gamal Abdel Nasser, Nouakchott
Tel: 52142, 52827, 52370
Cable: Bankalm
Telex: 562 Bankalm Mtn

Chairman: Mohamed Salem Ould Mikhaitrat
Directors: Hadi M Fighi, Mohamed Yehdi Ould Moctar El
Hassan, Siddiq M Hijjaji, Ibrahim K Agha

PRINCIPAL ACTIVITIES: Foreign trade and development finance
Branch Offices: PO Box 239, Nouadhibou, Telex 2429;
Nouakchott
Principal Bankers: UBAF, Paris; UBAF Bank, London; UBAE,
Rome; Banco Hispano Americano, Madrid; Commerz Bank,
Frankfurt

Principal Shareholders: Libyan Foreign Arab Bank (51%), State
of Mauritania (Ministry of Finance) (49%)
Date of Establishment: 1972
No of Employees: 95

BANQUE CENTRALE DE MAURITANIE

B.C.M.

Avenue de l'Independence, PO Box 623, Nouakchott
Tel: 52206, 52888
Telex: 532 Rimbank; 572 Bcrim
Telefax: 52759

Chairman: Ahmed Ould Zein (Governor)
Directors: Cheikh Sidi El Moctar Ould Cheikh Abdallah (Deputy
Governor), Mohamdy Ould Memoune (Director Control of
Changes), Ahmed Ould Teyah (Director Foreign Banking
Services), Ahmed Ould Boucheiba (Director, Credit), Sidi
Mohamed Ould Nagi (Director, Economic Research)

PRINCIPAL ACTIVITIES: Central banking
Branch Offices: Nouadhibou; Rosso; Nema; Selibaby

Principal Shareholders: State-owned
Date of Establishment: 1973
No of Employees: 407

BANQUE INTERNATIONALE POUR LA MAURITANIE

B.I.M.A.

PO Box 210, Ave Gamal Abdel Nasser, Nouakchott
Tel: 52363
Cable: Bintmau Nouakchott
Telex: 574 Mtn

Chairman: Kane Hamedine
Directors: Mohamed Salem Ould Lekhal
Senior Executives: Thiam Mansour (Foreign Operations), Ahmed
Ould Abderrahmane (Inland Operations), Bertrand De Geloes
(Credit Department), James Sauret (Control General), Olivier
de Pouzilhac (Credit Department)

PRINCIPAL ACTIVITIES: Banking
Branch Offices: Nouadhibou; Zouerate; Rosso; Kiffa
Associated Companies: BIAO, 9 Ave de Messine, Paris

Date of Establishment: July 1974
No of Employees: 197

BANQUE MAURITANIENNE POUR LE DEVELOPPEMENT ET LE COMMERCE

B.M.D.C.

PO Box 219, Nouakchott
Tel: 52061, 51156
Telex: 564 Badec MNT

Chairman: Mohamed Ould Nany
Directors: Mohamed Abdallahi Ould Moctar Salem, Mohamed
Yeslem Ould El Vil, Y Alioune Bocar, Sidi Ould Bakha
Senior Executives: Ely Ould Selemetta, Mohamed Ould Sidi
Mohamed, Lemrabott Ould Oudeika, Sidi Mohamed Ould
Laghlal

PRINCIPAL ACTIVITIES: All banking transactions, finance to
agriculture and housing
Branch Offices: Kaedi, Nouadhibou

Principal Shareholders: State of Mauritania (76%), Societe
Tunisienne de Banque (20%), Banque Centrale de Mauritanie
(4%)
Date of Establishment: January 1961
No of Employees: 140

COMMERCIALE DE TRANSPORTS TRANSATLANTIQUES MAURITANIENNE

PO Box 41, Nouakchott

PRINCIPAL ACTIVITIES: General trading, and storage, cargo
handling and freight

COMPAGNIE TECHNIQUE MAURITANIENNE

C.O.T.E.M.A.

Route du Ksar, PO Box 313, Nouakchott
Tel: 51352
Telex: 588 Nt Tt

Chairman: Ba Bocar Alpha
Directors: Mohamed Salem Oul M'Kaitirat

PRINCIPAL ACTIVITIES: Import and distribution of trucks,
tractors and all automotive products
Principal Agencies: Rover, MAH Hyster, Perkins, Citroen
Poclain, Lister, Land Rover
Principal Bankers: Banque Arabe Africaine en Mauritanie
(BAAM); Banque Internationale pour la Mauritanie (BIMA);
Banque Arabe Libyenne Mauritanienne (BALM); Societe

Mauritanienne de Banque (SMB); Banque Mauritanienne pour le Developpement et le Commerce (BMDC)

Principal Shareholders: Ba Bocar Alpha, Dah Ould Minaha, Haba Ould Mohamed Fall, Abdella Ould Sidia

CONFEDERATION DES EMPLOYEURS ET ARTISANS DE MAURITANIE

PO Box 383, Nouakchott
Tel: 51990, 52160
Cable: Ceam

President: Cheikhna Ould Mohamed Laghdaf
Senior Executives: Ismail Ould Amar (Vice-President), Hadji Ould Sidina (Vice-President), Moktar Toure, Bamba Ould Sidi Badi, Abeidi Ould Gharraby, Boullaha Ould Moktar Lahi (Secretary General)

PRINCIPAL ACTIVITIES: Union of general merchants, contractors, manufacturers

ETS LACOMBE ET CIE SA

PO Box 204, Nouakchott

PRINCIPAL ACTIVITIES: General trading, distribution of general merchandise, trucking and road transport
Parent Company: Societe Commerciale de l'Ouest Africain, Paris, France

MAURITANIAN FISHERY CO SA

M.A.F.C.O. SA

BP 289, Nouadhibou

President: Kota Wada

PRINCIPAL ACTIVITIES: Fishing, export of fish, octopus

MINES DE FER DE MAURITANIE SA

PO Box 42, Nouadhibou

PRINCIPAL ACTIVITIES: Iron and copper ore mining

MOBIL OIL

PO Box 509, Nouakchott

PRINCIPAL ACTIVITIES: Oil and gas services and marketing

NOSOMACI/LIPAM

Ave Gamal-Abdel Nasser, PO Box 6242 & 600, Nouakchott
Tel: 51896, 52896, 52966
Telex: 565 Mtn Nosom

Chairman: M S Dahi (also Manager)
Directors: Mohamed Salem Badda

PRINCIPAL ACTIVITIES: Bookselling and stationery business, office supplies
Branch Offices: Registered offices Nouakchott; principal branch Ksar/Nouakchott
Principal Bankers: BIMA; BMDC; BAAM; SMB

Principal Shareholders: M S Dahi, D Ahmed, M Oufkih
Date of Establishment: 1973

SIRCOMA

PO Box 370, Nouakchott
Cable: Sircom
Telex: 576

Chairman: Mohamed Saleh o/Abdellahi
Directors: Mohamed Cheikh O/Dida

PRINCIPAL ACTIVITIES: Import and distribution of building materials, cement, wood, iron bars, sanitary ware, air-conditioning and welding equipment, water proofing materials, paints
Principal Agencies: Air conditioners Airwell; Ransome Concrete; Rene Dube Welding Equipment; Castolin
Associated Companies: Al Tawfik (Textiles)

Principal Bankers: SMB; BAAM

Principal Shareholders: Chairman and director as described
Date of Establishment: 1972

SOCIETE DE CONSTRUCTIONS METALLIQUES

S.O.C.O.M.E.T.A.L.

PO Box 174, Nouakchott
Tel: 51900, 52089
Cable: Soctal
Telex: 521 Mtn

Chairman: Sidi Mohamed O Abbas
Directors: Mohamed Salem (Marketing Director), Mohamed Yahya (Finance Director)

PRINCIPAL ACTIVITIES: Manufacture and distribution of cars and spare parts and metal products
Principal Agencies: Renault, Saviem, Dunlop, Philips, TRT
Branch Offices: PO Box 105, Nouadhibou, Tel 2038
Subsidiary Companies: STPM, SNIM-SEM
Principal Bankers: Societe Mauritienne de Banque; Banque Internationale pour la Mauritaine

Principal Shareholders: Sidi Abass; Hademine Abass
Date of Establishment: October 1971
No of Employees: 92

SOCIETE INDUSTRIELLE DE LA GRANDE PECHE

S.I.G.P.

PO Box 11, Nouadhibou

PRINCIPAL ACTIVITIES: Fishing, fish and lobster freezing and drying

SOCIETE MAURITANIENNE D'ALLUMETTES

S.O.M.A.U.R.A.L.

PO Box 44, Nouakchott
Tel: 52481
Telex: 539 Emanf

Chairman: Abdallahi Ould Noueigued
Directors: Mohamed Ould Saleck (Director General)

PRINCIPAL ACTIVITIES: Production of matches
Principal Bankers: SMB; BIMA; BAMIS; BMDC
Financial Information:

	UM'000
Authorised capital	18.000
Paid-up capital	20.000

Date of Establishment: 1971
No of Employees: 28

SOCIETE MAURITANIENNE DE BANQUE SA

S.M.B.

PO Box 614, Nouakchott
Tel: 2602
Cable: Mauritbank
Telex: 454 Mauritbank

President: Dion Boubacar
Directors: Mohamed Lemine Ould El Jailani (General Manager)

PRINCIPAL ACTIVITIES: Commercial banking

SOCIETE MAURITANIENNE DE BATIMENT ET REPRESENTATION

S.O.M.A.B.A.T.

PO Box 567, Nouakchott
Tel: 52367
Telex: 544 Mtn

Chairman: Ba Mamoudou Samba Bolly

Directors: Youssouph Arouna Ba (Director General), Kamara Abdoul Khoudous (Technical Director), Diakhite Sourouki (Architect)

PRINCIPAL ACTIVITIES: Building and civil engineering contractors, designing and architectural consultants
Principal Agencies: Schroder Planning KG, D 6100 Darmstadt
Associated Companies: Zouerat, Nouadhibou
Principal Bankers: BMDC

SOCIETE MAURITANIENNE DE CONSTRUCTION ET DE TRAVAUX PUBLICS
S.O.M.A.C.O. T.P.
PO Box 113, Nouakchott

Directors: B Ould Sidi Bady (General Manager)

PRINCIPAL ACTIVITIES: Civil engineering contractors, buildings, roads and public works

SOCIETE MAURITANIENNE DE GAZ INDUSTRIELS
S.M.G.I.
PO Box 39, Nouadhibou

Senior Executives: D Bender (Manager)

PRINCIPAL ACTIVITIES: Manufacture of industrial gas

SOCIETE MIXTE D'IMPORTATION ET D'EXPORTATION
S.O.N.I.M.E.X.
PO Box 290, Nouakchott

President: Hamoud Ould Ahmedou
Directors: Ahmed Ould Daddah (Director General)

PRINCIPAL ACTIVITIES: Monopoly of imports of consumer goods such as sugar, rice, tea, textiles, etc, and exports of gum-arabic

SOCIETE NATIONALE INDUSTRIELLE ET MINIERE
S.N.I.M./S.E.M.
PO Box 42, Nouadhibou
Tel: 41000, 41001, 41002
Cable: SNIM Fer Nouadhibou
Telex: 426 SNIM Fer MTN Nouadhibou

Chairman: Abdel Aziz Ould Ahmed
Directors: Mohamed Saleck Ould Heyine (General Manager)

PRINCIPAL ACTIVITIES: Mining and export of iron ore; reinforced concrete
Branch Offices: Nouakchott, BP 6259, tel 51254; SNIM-Paris: 5 Rue Scribes, Paris 75009, France; Las Palmas 1019 Paséo, 2 Shil
Associated Companies: SAMMA, Nouadhibou; SAFA, Nouadhibou
Principal Bankers: BNP, Paris; SMB; BIMA; UBS; BCM, Mauritania; Societe Generale, Paris; BIL, Luxembourg
Financial Information:

	UM'million
Authorised capital	9,059
Paid-up capital	9,059

Principal Shareholders: Islamic Republic of Mauritania; Kuwait Foreign Trading Contracting and Investment Co; Arab Mining Company; Iraqi Fund for External Development; Bureau de Recherches et de Participation Miniere (Maroc); Banque Islamique de Development
Date of Establishment: July 1972
No of Employees: Over 6,500

MAURITANIA

Major Companies of
MOROCCO

AETCO LEVER MAROC
Km 10 Route Cotiere, BP 519, Casablanca
Tel: 351097, 350692
Cable: Ethiope Casablanca
Telex: 21901

Senior Executives: M'Hamed Moumni (Manager)

PRINCIPAL ACTIVITIES: Manufacture and distribution of detergents, toilet preparations, exports
Principal Agencies: Unilever products
Associated Companies: Cofimar, Sofipar, Unilever
Principal Bankers: BMCE, BCM, BMCI, SMDC, CDM, ABN, FNCB

Principal Shareholders: Cofimar, Sofipar, Unilever
Date of Establishment: June 1959
No of Employees: 250

AFRETMA
Armement & Affretement au Maroc SA
242 Bis Blvd Mohamed 5, Casablanca
Tel: 304732, 307257
Cable: Afretma
Telex: 21869; 22827; 23015

Chairman: Hadj Taieb Sebti
Directors: Othman Sebti, Jaafar Sebti

PRINCIPAL ACTIVITIES: Ship agencies, custom brokers, chartering, stevedoring
Principal Agencies: Sub Agents in all Moroccan ports
Principal Bankers: SMDC; CMCB; BMCE;

AFRIC AUTO SA
147 rue Mostafa El Maani, Casablanca
Tel: 279294
Cable: Afrautofia
Telex: 21948

President: Aziz Alaoui (Director General)

PRINCIPAL ACTIVITIES: Import and distribution of cars, tractors, vans, and trucks
Principal Agencies: Fiat; Mazda; British Leyland
Principal Bankers: BMCE; CDM; BCM; BP

Date of Establishment: 1920

AFRICA PALACE MAROC
2 rue Abbou Abbas As Sebti, Casablanca
Tel: 256603
Telex: 21865

PRINCIPAL ACTIVITIES: Construction and management of hotels and tourist complexes (Almohades Hotel Agadir & Tangiers)
Principal Bankers: CMCB, BP

Date of Establishment: 1968
No of Employees: 450

AFRIQUIA
Rue Ibnou El Oinane, Ain Sebaa, BP 2545
Tel: 351735
Cable: Africa
Telex: 21049

PRINCIPAL ACTIVITIES: Wholesale of petroleum products and by-products
Branch Offices: Adagir; Marrakech; Meknes; Sidi Kacem; Sidi Ifni
Principal Bankers: BCM; BMCI; BMCE; CCDM

Date of Establishment: 1959

AGENCE GIBMAR SA
3 Rue Henri Regnault, Tangiers
Tel: 35875
Cable: Gibmar
Telex: 33091

Chairman: Jawad Ben Brahim
Directors: S Abecasis (General Manager), M Slaoui, D Tazi, S A Marbar

PRINCIPAL ACTIVITIES: Shipping and travel agents, stevedores, forwarding agents, customs brokers
Principal Agencies: P & O Passenger and Cargo Services, Mac Andrews & Co Ltd, American Export Lines, North America Line, Royal Viking Line
Branch Offices: Casablanca: 38 Rue Ibn Batouta
Associated Companies: Gibmar Travel SA
Principal Bankers: Credit du Maroc; Banque Commerciale du Maroc

Principal Shareholders: Marland Trading & Shipping Co Ltd, Marbar, SA

ALGEMENE BANK (MAROC) SA
Place du 16 Novembre, PO Box 13478, Casablanca
Tel: 221275, 221016, 221712
Cable: Marolanda
Telex: 21709

Chairman: Haj Mohamed Kassidi (General Manager)
Directors: Najem Abaakil (Vice Chairman), Messaud Agouzal, Habib Belkadi, Abdullah Ousalem, Willam J Slagter, J M H Van T Hoff

PRINCIPAL ACTIVITIES: All banking activities
Branch Offices: Casablanca; Tangiers; Rabat; Agadir

Principal Shareholders: Algemene Bank Nederland (50%), Moroccan Interests (50%)
Date of Establishment: 1948

AMERICAN PETROFINA EXPLORATION CO (APEX)
11 Zankat Gafsa, PO Box 433, Rabat
Tel: 32139, 26445
Telex: 31981 Fina Pex

PRINCIPAL ACTIVITIES: Petroleum exploration and production

ARAB BANK MAROC
Head Office & Main Branch, 174 Bld Mohamed V, Casablanca
Tel: 223152 (8 lines)
Cable: ARABMAROC
Telex: 22942, 23696
Telefax: (02) 200233

President: Abdellatif Laraki
Directors: Abdul Majeed Shoman (Vice-President), Abdelhak Abdi (Vice President), Salah Eddine Haroun (General Manager), Khalid Shoman, Faical Zemmama, Munib Rashid Masri, Nasr-Eddine Lahlou, Rachid Bennani Smires
Senior Executives: Rais Maati (Secretary General), Saher Abderrahim (Manager of Main Branch), Ahmed Assalhi (Manager of Rabat Branch), Abdelmounem Lahlou (Acting Manager of El Fida Agency), Azzedine Gassi (Head of Marketing & Studies Dept), Laanaya Omar (Head Loans Dept), Faouzi Zaid (Acting Manager of Tanger Branch), Rachid Chaouni (Acting Manager of Fes Branch), Mohammed Oueriagli Salim (Acting Manager of Marrakech Branch)

PRINCIPAL ACTIVITIES: Commercial banking
Branch Offices: Rabat Branch: PO Box 440, 2 Avenue Allal Ben Abdallah, Rabat, Tel 05-726314/19/27, Fax 05-738162, Telex 36032; El Fida Branch: 466 Bd El Fida, Casablanca, PO Box 4548, Tel 288457/96, 288501; Tanger Branch: 43 Bld Mohamed V, Tanger, Tel 940603/76, 940710/74, Fax 09-940774, Telex 33015; Fes Branch: 57 Bld Mohamed Slaoui, Po Box 2255, Fes, Tel 06-621803, 621808, Fax 06-621836,

MOROCCO

Telex 51784; Marrakech Branch: Bld Moulay El Hassan, Place Liberte, Tel 04-433105, 434400, Fax 431418, Telex 72775
Associated Companies: Arab Bank Ltd, Jordan; Banque Populaire, Morocco
Financial Information:

	1989/90 MDh'000
Deposits	419.280
Profits & reserves	24.952
Authorised capital	30.000
Paid-up capital	30.000
Total assets	609.271

Principal Shareholders: Arab Bank Plc, Amman (50%); Banque Centrale Populaire, Casablanca (50%)
Date of Establishment: July 1975
No of Employees: 230

ASAFIL
Safi Filature
7 Ave Hassan 11, Casablanca
Tel: 268395, 268296
Telex: 22733

PRINCIPAL ACTIVITIES: Weaving, bleaching and dyeing, textiles and man-made fibres
Branch Offices: Safi (factory); Casablanca (warehouse)
Principal Bankers: BMCE; UMB

Date of Establishment: 1971

ATLANTA
49 angle rues Lafuente/Longwy, Casablanca
Tel: 279325, 262971, 268931
Telex: 21644

Chairman: Abdelkader Ben Salah
Directors: Omar Bennani, Jean Chebaut, Mohamed Reyad

PRINCIPAL ACTIVITIES: Insurance and reinsurance
Branch Offices: Casablanca, Rabat, Meknes, Tanger
Parent Company: Preservatrice Fonciere, 18 rue de Londres, 75457 Paris Cedex 09
Principal Bankers: SMDC (Societe Marocaine de Depot et Credit)

Principal Shareholders: M Abdelkader Ben Salah; Holmarcom SA; Preservatrice Fonciere
Date of Establishment: 1947
No of Employees: 94

ATLAS COPCO MAROC
14 Rue Ibnou Adara, El Marrakouchi, La Jonquiere, Casablanca
Tel: 246685, 244850
Cable: Atlascopco
Telex: 25843

President: A El Glaoui
Directors: Max Brogli (Managing Director)

PRINCIPAL ACTIVITIES: Import and distribution of construction and mining machinery and equipment, trucks
Principal Agencies: Atlas Copco, Craelius, Sandvikens Jernverks, Alvenius, Dynapac, Sala, Galinet, Meynadier, Volvo
Parent Company: Atlas Copco AB Stockholm
Principal Bankers: SMDC; FNCB; BMCI; BCM; BPSBC; CMCB

Date of Establishment: 1948
No of Employees: 70

ATLAS SA
Societe Marocaine de Navigation
81 Ave Houmane Elfatouaki, Casablanca 01
Tel: 224190
Cable: Atlasnav
Telex: 23067

Chairman: Hassan Chami
Directors: Jawad Ben Brahim, Mohamed Lyoussi, Gilbert A Common, Abdellatif Ghazzali, Mohamed Slaoui, Common Brothers Ltd, Gomba Shipping Ltd, Marbar SA, Navex SA, John Malcon Fimister, N Speed

PRINCIPAL ACTIVITIES: Shipowners and charterers
Associated Companies: Common Brothers Ltd, Newcastle upon Tyne, UK; Gomba International, London, UK; Navex SA, Antwerp, Belgium
Principal Bankers: Credit du Maroc; Banque Commerciale du Maroc; Societe Marocaine de Depot et de Credit

Principal Shareholders: Mohamed Lyoussi, Mohamed Slaoui, Jawad Ben, Brahim, Abdellatif Ghazzali, Gilbert Common, Common Brothers Ltd, Gomba Shipping Ltd, Comaraf SA, Marbar SA, Navex SA
Date of Establishment: 1976

BAHIA PLASTIC
21 rue Termidi Maarif, Casablanca
Tel: 253313, 250138
Cable: Plastiba
Telex: 23711 M

President: Haj Ahmed Chraibi (Director General)
Directors: Said Allam

PRINCIPAL ACTIVITIES: Manufacture of plastic shoes and other plastic products
Branch Offices: Marrakech, Tel 31047 (Factory)
Principal Bankers: BMCI; BCM

Date of Establishment: 1960
No of Employees: 150

BANK AL MAGHRIB
PO Box 445, 227 Ave Mohammed V, Rabat
Tel: 763009
Cable: Marobank
Telex: 731006; 731909; 731612; 732759
Telefax: 761276

Chairman: Mohamed Seqat (Governor)
Directors: Abdellatif Laraqui, Mustapha Faris, Mohamed Brick, M'Fedel Lahlou, Rachid Haddaoui, Mohamed Dairi, Najib Benamour, Abdelhamid Bennani Smires, Mohamed Fettah, Saleh Hamzaoui, Mohamed Bijaad
Senior Executives: Mohamed Tazi (Central Manager Foreign Dept), Abelwahed Belhaj Soulami (Central Manager Credit Dept), Mohamed Benjelloun (Central Manager Professional Training Dept), Abdellatif Sekkat (Central Manager Budget/Control/Legal Studies Dept), Ahmed Bennani (Central Manager Research Dept), Mohamed Iraqui (Central Manager Dar As Sikah), Abdelhamid Benamour (Central Manage Inspection & Banks Control Dept), Abdelouahab Kissi (Central Manager Personal & Social Affairs Dept), Faddoul Rharnit (Central Manager Technical Dept)

PRINCIPAL ACTIVITIES: Central banking institution
Branch Offices: Rabat, Casablanca, Agadir, Al Hoceima, Nador, El Jadida, Fez, Kenitra, Al Ayoune, Larache, Marrakech, Meknes, Tangier, Oujda, Safi, Tetouan
Financial Information:

	1990 MDh'000
Profits	1.012.792
Authorised capital	30.000
Paid-up capital	30.000
Total assets	36.049.529

Principal Shareholders: 100% State-owned
Date of Establishment: 1959
No of Employees: 2,331

BANK OF CREDIT & COMMERCE INTERNATIONAL SA

5 rue Moulay Slimane, Rabat
Tel: 30806
Cable: BANCRECOM Kabat
Telex: 31829 M BCCI

PRINCIPAL ACTIVITIES: Banking (representative office)
Parent Company: Bank of Credit and Commerce International SA, Luxembourg

BANQUE CENTRALE POPULAIRE

B.C.P.

PO Box 10622, 101 Blvd Zerktouni, Casablanca
Tel: 270540, 272589, 220536
Cable: Bancepo
Telex: 21723, 22633

President: Abdellatif Laraki (Executive Officer)
Directors: Abdelhaq El Abdi (Deputy General Manager), Zemmama Faycal (Operations Manager), Msefer Mohamed (Production Manager), Lahlou Nasr Eddine (General Delegate External Relations), Bennani Smires Rachid (General Delegate International Developpement), Waazize Abdellah (Head of Foreign Trade)

PRINCIPAL ACTIVITIES: Commercial banking
Branch Offices: Paris, France; Brussels, Belgium; and 201 branches in Morocco; 2 Representative Offices in Belgium and Canada
Principal Bankers: UBAF, New York; Deutsche Bank; Barclays Bank, London; Caisse Centrale des Banques Populaires, Paris

Principal Shareholders: Government of Morocco, Banque du Maroc, Office Cherifien des Phosphates, Caisse de Depots et de Gestion, Societe Nationale d'Investissement, Caisse Nationale de Credit Agricole, Banque Nationale pour le Developpement Economique, Banque Marocaine du Commerce Exterieur, Credit Immobilier et Hotelier, Office National des Peches, Caisse Marocaine des Marches, Office National pour le Developpement Industriel
Date of Establishment: 1961
No of Employees: 4,127

BANQUE COMMERCIALE DU MAROC SA

B.C.M.

PO Box 141, 81 Ave de l'Armee Royale, Casablanca
Tel: 224169 (30 lines)
Telex: 22863, 21014

Chairman: Abdelaziz Alami (Director General)
Senior Executives: Fethallah Bennani (Deputy Director General), Mohamed Salmi (Credit Manager), Omar Benider (Branches Manager)

PRINCIPAL ACTIVITIES: Commercial Banking
Subsidiary/Associated Companies: Societe Immobiliere du Maghreb; COPROPAR; SOMGETI; Maghreb Bail; COFIMAR; etc

Principal Shareholders: Credit Industriel et Commercial, France; Deutsche Bank; and Moroccan Interests
Date of Establishment: 1911

BANQUE MAROCAINE DU COMMERCE EXTERIEUR

B.M.C.E.

140 Avenue Hassan II, PO Box 425, Casablanca
Tel: 272049, 273090
Cable: Crereb
Telex: 22804, 22950, 23053

Chairman: Abdellatif Jouahri (Director General)
Directors: Driss Gueddari (Managing Director), Mohamed Jouahri, Mohamed Ben Jilali Bennani, Louis Flaive, Carlo

---

Gragnani, Mohamed Karim Lamrani, Jose M Bravo, Abderrahman Slaoui, Lars Engstroem, Friedhelm Jost, Ali Kettani, Amaury Masquelier, S Zavatti

PRINCIPAL ACTIVITIES: Commercial Banking
Branch Offices: 114 (Morocco); Paris - 37, Rue Caumartin, Paris 9ème; Tanger Zone Franche, BP 513
Principal Bankers: BMCE Paris, Union de Banques Suisses, Zurich, BFCE, Paris

Principal Shareholders: Office Cherifien des Phosphates, Office de Commercialisation et d'Exportation, Office National Interprofessionnel des Cereales et Legumineuses, Office National du The et du Sucre, Banque Nationale de Developpement Economique, Caisse de Depots et de Gestion, Tresorerie Generale, Banque Francaise du Commerce Exterieur, Banco Exterior de Espana, Banca Commerciale Italiana, Societe Financiere du Credit du Maghreb, Commerzbank, Bank of America, Moulay Ali Kettani, Mohamed Karim Lamrani, Abderrahman Slaoui
Date of Establishment: September 1959
No of Employees: 2,203

BANQUE MAROCAINE POUR L'AFRIQUE ET L'ORIENT

B.M.A.O.

1 Place Bandoeng, Casablanca
Tel: 307070, 307955
Cable: Bamaocasablanca
Telex: 22039, 26720
Telefax: 301673

President: Mohamed Ait Menna
Directors: Ali Youssefi (Vice President), Abdelhamid Benani Dakhama (Deputy Director General)
Senior Executives: El Jai Mohamed (Marketing Dept), Rakib Miloud (Foreign Dept), Rouini Mohamed (Personnel Dept), Abdeljalil Rachad (Northern Branches Management), Belghali Benjelloun Mohamed (Casablanca Branch), Mrs Laghrani Saadia (Credit & Statistics Dept), Kharbachi Mustapha (Legal & Disputed Claims Dept), Bousfar Mohamed (Portfolio Dept), Smatou Benyacoub Miloud (Control & Inspection Dept), Chouitter Miloud (Processing Dept), Boulaajine Mohamed (Accounting Dept), Ouilali Abdellah (Research & Statistics Dept)

PRINCIPAL ACTIVITIES: Commercial banking
Branch Offices: in Casablanca: Bandoeng, Lalla Yacout, Anfa, 2 Mars, My Cherif, Goulmina, Tour Atlas, Oasis, Hay Hassani, Yacoub El Mansour, Route Mediouna, Haffari, Maarif; also in Rabat, Tanger, Meknes, Fes, Nador, Oujda, Tetouan, Agadir, Tiznit, Inezgane, Goulimine, Marrakech, Ait Melloul, Sale
Financial Information:

	1990 MDh'000
Authorised capital	100,000
Paid-up capital	100,000

Principal Shareholders: Mohamed Ait Menna, Ali Yousseif, Salah Kabboud, Gourvenec, Lyonnaise de Banque, Abdelaaziz El Manjra
Date of Establishment: 1961
No of Employees: 342

BANQUE MAROCAINE POUR LE COMMERCE ET L'INDUSTRIE SA

B.M.C.I.

PO Box 573, 26 Place Mohammed V, Casablanca
Tel: 224101, 223140
Cable: Marcomi Casa
Telex: 21092; 22092

President: Haj Ahmed Bargach
Directors: Mohamed Benkirane, Christian Weeger, Rene Thomas, Pierre Ledoux, Jean Gagne, Marcel Rinaudo, Larbi

Sekkat, Raissi Mohamed, Mohamed Lahbil Bekkai, Societe Nationale d'Investissement

PRINCIPAL ACTIVITIES: All banking transactions
Branch Offices: Paris, Frankfurt, Amsterdam
Associated Companies: Banque Nationale de Paris Intercontinentale

Date of Establishment: 1964

BANQUE NATIONALE POUR LE DEVELOPPEMENT ECONOMIQUE

B.N.D.E.

PO Box 407, Place des Alaouites, Rabat
Tel: 66040, 68844
Telex: Bademaroc 31942, 32758
Telefax: 63702

Chairman: Mustapha Faris (Chief Executive)
Senior Executives: Farid Dellero (Director & General Manager), Ahmed Rhoulami (Deputy General Manager), Mohamed Aissaoui (Deputy General Manager), A Berkia (Secretary General), R Frej (Finance Management), M Hafsi (Long & Medium Term Loans), A Bourassi (Shares Management), B Azzouzi (Long & Medium Sized Industries), A Chouikh (Specialised Credits & Promotion), F Jazouli (Economic Surveys & Documentation), M Amraoui (Technical & Project Study), M G Ameur (Follow-up), H Mikou (Outstanding Debts), S Ronda (Legal & Disputes), J Kadiri Hassani (Audit)

PRINCIPAL ACTIVITIES: Banking, promotion of agricultural and industrial development
Branch Offices: Casablanca: 46 avenue des Far, Tel 314453, 314488; Agadir: Avenue Hassan II, Batiment de la CCI, Tel 20235; Rabat: 13 rue Abou Inane
Subsidiary Companies: Somadet, Nouvelle Somatam, Caisse Marocaine des Marches, Sidet, Maroc Equipment, Maroc Leasing, SCH Sidi Harazem Limadet
Financial Information:

	1990 MDh'000
Authorised capital	210.000
Total assets	5.554.907

Principal Shareholders: The Moroccan Government (34.16%), Local Banks and financial Institutions, Moroccan private individuals (39.78%), Foreign financial institutions (26.06%)
Date of Establishment: 1959
No of Employees: 264

BATA SA MAROCAINE

228 bd Ibn Tachfine, Casablanca
Tel: 457-21
Telex: 25624

PRINCIPAL ACTIVITIES: Shoe business, manufacture of leather and plastic footwear and accessories
Principal Bankers: Credit du Maroc

No of Employees: 1,200

BERLIET MAROC

Km 10 Route de Rabat, BP 2624, Casablanca
Tel: 355650, 355666
Telex: 25960 Autoberl
Telefax: 355685

Chairman: Moulay Driss El Ouazzani
Directors: Omar Amraoui (Director General)
Senior Executives: Omar Bouzoubaa (Technical Director), Rene Petelat (Sales Director)

PRINCIPAL ACTIVITIES: Trucks and buses manufacturers
Principal Agencies: Berliet; British Leyland; Renault Vehicules Industriels
Parent Company: Renault Vehicules Industriels
Subsidiary Companies: Cimtex

Principal Bankers: Banque Marocaine du Commerce Exterieur; Credit du Maroc; Societe Generale Marocaine de Banque; Banque Commerciale du Maroc; Societe Marocaine de Credit et de Banque; Banque Marocaine pour le Commerce et l'Industrie
Financial Information:

	1989 MDh'000	1990 MDh'000
Sales turnover	377.814	473.280
Profits	6.938	17.610
Authorised capital	62.500	62.500
Paid-up capital	62.500	62.500
Total assets	218.502	268.800

Principal Shareholders: Renault Vehicules Industriels; Societe Nationale des Investissements; Banque Nationale pour Le Developpement Economique
Date of Establishment: 1958
No of Employees: 257

BRASSERIES DU MAROC

Avenue Pasteur, PO Box 15798, Casablanca
Tel: 245726, 240729, 241520
Cable: Brama Casablanca
Telex: 23931 M

Chairman: Bachir Benabbes Taarji
Directors: Hamid Benchekroun (Director General), Lahcen Bagoula (Managing Director), Mohammed Mellouk (Administrative Director), Gilles d'Agescy (Commercial Director), Abderrahman El Aoufi (Financial Director), Joseph Attias (Controle de Gestion & Informatique Director)

PRINCIPAL ACTIVITIES: Distillery, brewery and products of soft drinks
Branch Offices: Km3 700 route de Kenitra, Sale; Rue de l'Eglise, Oued-Zem; Avenue Sidi Mohamed Ben Abdellah, Safi; Avenue Ahmed Chawki, El Jadida; Quartier Anza, Agadir; Avenue de France, Marrakech
Subsidiary Companies: Societe des Brasseries du Nord Marocain, Fes; Societe de la Brasserie de Tanger, Tangiers, Societe du Thermalisme Marocain Sotherma, Sidi Harazem
Principal Bankers: Credit du Maroc; BMCI; BCM; CMCB; SGMB

Principal Shareholders: SNI, Rabat, Morocco; Enterprise Ouilmes, Luxembourg; Societe Europeenne et Africaine de Participations, 'Compeap', Djibouti; CIMR, Casablanca, Morocco; Al Amane, Casablanca, Morocco
Date of Establishment: 1919
No of Employees: 1,000

BRIMTEX SARL

96 rues des Oudayas, 21700 Casablanca
Tel: 241682, 241683
Cable: Brimtex
Telex: 25828, 22662
Telefax: 249175

Chairman: Aberrahman Chaoui

PRINCIPAL ACTIVITIES: Manufacture of textiles, spinning and weaving
Principal Bankers: BMCI; BMCE; BCM

Date of Establishment: 1962
No of Employees: 650

BUREAU DE RECHERCHES ET DE PARTICIPATIONS MINIERES

B.R.P.M.

5-7 Charia Moulay Hassan, BP 99, Rabat
Tel: 63035
Telex: 31066

Directors: Mohamed Chahid (General Manager), Assou Lhatoute (Assistant General Manager)

PRINCIPAL ACTIVITIES: State agency specialising in the exploration, development and marketing of Morocco's mineral resources

Subsidiary Companies: The Bureau is a state agency which participates either directly or indirectly in a majority of Moroccan mining enterprises

Date of Establishment: 1928
No of Employees: 750

CAISSE DE DEPOT ET DE GESTION
C.D.G.

BP 408, Sharia Moulay Hassan, Rabat
Tel: 65520
Telex: 31072 M
Telefax: 63849

President: Ahmed Bennani
Members: Hassan Lukasch, Mohamed Hassan, Mohamed Limamy, Abdelmajid Tazi
Senior Executives: M'Fadel Lahlou (Director General), Abdelhamid Dassouli (Secretary General)

PRINCIPAL ACTIVITIES: Financial institution

Subsidiary Companies: Societe Centrale de Reassurance (SCR); Compagnie Generale Immobiliere (CGI); Compagnie Nord-Africaine et Intercontinentale d'Assurances (CNIA); Compagnie Immobiliere et Fonciere Marocaine (CIFM); Societe Centrale pour l'Equipement du Territoire-Maroc (SCET-MAROC); Maroc-Tourist Societe Generale d'Amenagement Touristique (SOGATOUR), Societe de Financement d'Achats a Credit (SOFAC-CREDIT)

Principal Bankers: Bank of Morocco/Treasury
Financial Information:

	1988/89 MDh'000
Sales turnover	953.428
Profits	457.026
Total assets	14.189.104

Principal Shareholders: Public Institution
Date of Establishment: 1959
No of Employees: 434

CAISSE NATIONALE DE CREDIT AGRICOLE
C.N.C.A.

BP 49, 2 rue d'Alger, Rabat
Tel: 725920, 732555
Telex: CREDAGRI 36157 M; CNCA 32956 M
Telefax: 732580

Senior Executives: M Rachid Haddaoui (Directeur General)

PRINCIPAL ACTIVITIES: Agricultural investment fund, financing agriculture, agro-industry, rural housing, coastal fisheries, forestry, handicrafts, tourism, small and medium firms and banking services and advice

Branch Offices: 167 regional and local branches
Financial Information:

	1989/90 MDh'000
Total income	1.117.607
Profits	38.584
Authorised capital	1.487.654
Paid-up capital	1.487.654
Total assets	11.942.735

Principal Shareholders: State-owned
Date of Establishment: 1961
No of Employees: 2,935

CAOUTCHOUC ET PLASTIQUES DU MAGHREB (CAPLAM)

Km11-500 Autoroute de CasaRabat, Ain Sebaa
Tel: 351724
Cable: Caplam
Telex: 21950

PRINCIPAL ACTIVITIES: Manufacture of rubber and plastic products
Branch Offices: 168-170 Boulevard Emile Zola, Casablanca
Principal Bankers: BMCI

Principal Shareholders: Kleber-Colombes, Paris
Date of Establishment: 1943

CARGOS EUROAFRICAINS

17 Avenue de l'Armee Royale, PO Box 966, Casablanca
Tel: 266881/5
Cable: Transfrui
Telex: 21028

PRINCIPAL ACTIVITIES: Shipping agents, clearing and forwarding
Principal Agencies: Van Nievelt Goudriaan, Rotterdam; Compagnie Generale Transatlantique, Paris;Nedlloyd, Rotterdam
Branch Offices: Agadir; El Jadida; Essaioura; Kenitra; Safi; Tangiers

CARNAUD MAROC

83 Boulevard Hamad, Casablanca
Tel: 247445
Telex: 21821

PRINCIPAL ACTIVITIES: Manufacture of metal packaging materials
Branch Offices: Agadir; Safi
Principal Bankers: BMCI

Date of Establishment: 1938
No of Employees: 1,000

CARROSSERIE RAHALI SA
SOMAMI SA

Route Cotiere, 111 Km 11.200 Ain-Sebaa, Casablanca
Tel: 350438, 350400, 350915
Cable: Carrahali
Telex: 21970

President: Mohamed Rahali (Director General)

PRINCIPAL ACTIVITIES: Assembly of cars, trucks and buses, mechanical engineering, manufacturers' representatives
Principal Agencies: DAF, Holland
Associated Companies: DIFMA 166, Boulevard Moulay Ismail, Casablanca; (Agents for Jaguar, Triumph, Daihatsu)
Principal Bankers: Banque Marocaine du Commerce Exterieur; Societe Marocaine de Depot et de Credit

Principal Shareholders: Mohamed Rahali
No of Employees: 320

CASABLANCA TEXTILES
Blancatex

33 Allee des Troenes, BP 2514, Ain Sebaa
Tel: 350787/88, 351416
Cable: Blancatex
Telex: 26698 BLTEX

Chairman: Taki Laraki
Directors: Rachid Laraki
Senior Executives: Fouad Oudghiri (Sales Director)

PRINCIPAL ACTIVITIES: Spinning and weaving, production of textiles
Principal Bankers: Wafabank, BMCE, Arab Bank, BP

Financial Information:

	1988/89 MDh'000	1989/90 MDh'000
Sales turnover	45.000	46.000
Authorised capital	10.000	12.500

Date of Establishment: 1966
No of Employees: 300

CELLULOSE DU MAROC SA

16 rue Abou Inane, Immeuble Mamda, BP 429, Rabat
Tel: 68305
Cable: Celluma
Telex: 31086; 31825
Telefax: 67538

President: Abdeslam Berrada (President Delegue)
Directors: Ahmed Fizazi (Vice President), M'Hamed Mezzour (Director General)
Senior Executives: Amal Louraoui (Finance Director), Mohamed Benhamou (Sales Director), Abdelaziz Rmili (Production Director), Ahmed Hilmi (Mill Director), Mahjoub Hassouane (Maintenance Director)

PRINCIPAL ACTIVITIES: Manufacture of eucalyptus wood pulp
Principal Agencies: SCA Pulp Sales Int'l Ltd, UK; Nothern Pulp Shippers Ltd, UK
Principal Bankers: Wafabank, BCM, BMCE, BMCI, SGMB, CM, BCP
Financial Information:

	1988/89 MDh'million
Sales turnover	644
Profits	108
Authorised capital	123.5
Paid-up capital	123.5
Total assets	573

Principal Shareholders: TAIC; SNI; CDG; BNDE; Cellulose du Pin
Date of Establishment: 1953
No of Employees: 570

CEMENTOS MARROQUIES CMA

PO Box 174, Tetouan
Tel: 452245, 242900
Cable: Cementamuda
Telex: 33611 Cemenmar M

Chairman: Omar Qadiri
Directors: Mohamed Hassan El Amrani (Managing Director)

PRINCIPAL ACTIVITIES: Production and distribution of Portland cement
Branch Offices: Km 5,800, Route Torreta mers Tamuda, Tetouan
Principal Bankers: BCM; BMCI; BMCE; UNIBAN; BNDE

CEMENTOS TANGER SA

17 rue Rembrandt, Tangiers
Tel: 37748, 38538
Cable: Cementang
Telex: 33601

Senior Executives: S Said (General Manager)

PRINCIPAL ACTIVITIES: Production of cement
Principal Bankers: BMCE; BCM; CDM; Uniban

Date of Establishment: 1953

CENTRALE AUTOMOBILE CHERIFIENNE

84 Avenue Lalla Yacout, Casablanca
Tel: 278180
Cable: Centralgar
Telex: 21060 Gelco, 23676 CACVW

President: Victor Elbaz
Directors: Robert Marrache (Manager)

PRINCIPAL ACTIVITIES: Import and distribution of motor vehicles, manufacturers' representatives
Principal Agencies: Volkswagen, Audi, Porsche
Principal Bankers: BMCE; BCM; SMDC; CDM

No of Employees: 200

CENTRALE LAITIERE MAROC LAIT

83 rue Emir Abdelkader, Casablanca
Tel: 249796, 243000
Cable: Stassalait
Telex: 28939, 25764
Telefax: 249971

President: Fouad Filali
Directors: Mohamed Hamdouch (Managing Director), Driss Traki (Managing Director), Victor Cohen (Finance Director), Taieb Mestour (Director)

PRINCIPAL ACTIVITIES: Dairy products industry, production of pasteurised and sterilized milk (450,000/500,000 litres/day). Yoghourts (500,000 units/day), butter
Principal Agencies: BSN Gervais Danone, France
Parent Company: ONA
Principal Bankers: SGMB; BMCE; Credit du Maroc; BMCI; BCM; SBC
Financial Information:

	1989 MDh'000
Sales turnover	900.000
Net profit	30.000
Authorised capital	50.820
Paid-up capital	50.820

Principal Shareholders: Omnium Nord Africain
Date of Establishment: 1944
No of Employees: 1,600

CGE MAROC

Compagnie Generale d'Electricite

68 Bvd de la Resistance, PO Box 807, Casablanca
Tel: 277272
Telex: 21021 M

PRINCIPAL ACTIVITIES: Manufacture of electrical electronic equipment (wires and and cables transformers, batteries, accumulators)
Branch Offices: Mohammedia, Tel 2205
Principal Bankers: SGMB

CHARBONNAGES NORD AFRICAINS

BP 255, 27 Ave Moulay Hassan, Rabat
Tel: 24147, 21988
Cable: Charnor
Telex: 31923

PRINCIPAL ACTIVITIES: Coal mining

Date of Establishment: 1946
No of Employees: 5,000

CHERIFIENNE DE TRAVAUX AFRICAINS (CTRA)

1 Bvd du Fouarat, Casablanca
Tel: 242696, 243422
Telex: 21782

PRINCIPAL ACTIVITIES: Building and civil engineering contractors
Branch Offices: Safi, Oujda, Mohammedia
Subsidiary Companies: SCRC Societe Chimique et Routiere Cherifienne
Principal Bankers: BMCI; BCM; SMDC; SGMB; UMB; BMCE

Date of Establishment: 1960
No of Employees: 2,000

CHIMICOLOR SA

Sahat Dakar, Casablanca
Tel: 61751/3
Telex: 21748 M

Chairman: Jamil Bouhlal
Directors: Christian Abt (Director General), Jean-Louis Maldonado (Marketing Director)
Senior Executives: Frederic Fernandez (Secretary General), Etienne Hibon (Commercial Director), Jean Pierre Weber (Technical Director)

PRINCIPAL ACTIVITIES: Production of paints, putty, varnish and chemical products for domestic and industrial use
Principal Agencies: STE Lappartient, STE Carboline, STE Dresse, STE Matac Holfind, STE France Import
Principal Bankers: BCM; BMCI; Uniban; SMDC; SGMB; CMCB; BMCE

Principal Shareholders: Omnium Nord Africain

CIE AFRICAINE D'ASSURANCES

120 Avenue Hassan II, Casablanca
Tel: 224185
Cable: Comafassur
Telex: 21661
Telefax: 260150

Chairman: Fouad Filali
Directors: Elalamy My Hafid (Managing Director), Abakka Tahar (Director IARD)
Senior Executives: El Bouri Khalid (Finance/Accounts Manager), Wafaa Slaoui (Personnel Manager)

PRINCIPAL ACTIVITIES: Insurance and reinsurance
Principal Agencies: SAVA, Rabat
Branch Offices: Morocco, France
Parent Company: Assurances Generales de France, Omnium Nord Africain
Principal Bankers: SMDC; BCM; BMCE; CDM; SBC
Financial Information:

	1988/89 MDh'000
Sales turnover	172.041
Profits	5.352
Authorised capital	15.800
Paid-up capital	15.800
Total assets	667.296

Principal Shareholders: Assurances Generales de France, Omnium Nord Africain
Date of Establishment: 1950
No of Employees: 145

CIE AFRICAINE DE GEOPHYSIQUE (CAG)

BP 716, Rabat
Tel: 72359
Cable: Geomaroc Rabat

PRINCIPAL ACTIVITIES: Geophysic services

CIE CHERIFIENNE D'ARMEMENT

5 Bvd Abdellah Ben Yacine, Casablanca
Tel: 309455, 309032
Cable: Charmement
Telex: 27030, 27005
Telefax: 301890

President: Mohamed Bennani-Smires
Directors: Abdelwahab Laraki, Max Kadoch, Alain de Beauchamp
Senior Executives: Abdellaziz Mantrach

PRINCIPAL ACTIVITIES: Ship owners and brokers, ship and liners' agents, stevedores, forwarding agents
Principal Agencies: Odfjell, Oslo; Norwegian Caribbean Lines, Miami; Mafrebelines, Ermefer Geneve, Antwerp Maritiem Anvers, Armada Lines Kopenhaguen, Linea Transmare Genoa

Branch Offices: Bvd Imam Ali, Kenitra, Tel 4480-4253, Telex 91972
Parent Company: Transports Marocains S.A. Casablanca
Principal Bankers: BMCI; SGMB; BMCE

Date of Establishment: 1929
No of Employees: 90

CIE CHERIFIENNE D'ENTREPRISES ELECTRIQUES (CCEE)

PO Box 9607, Casa Bournazel, Bvd du Fouarat, Casablanca
Tel: 242746, 245410
Cable: Cherelec Casablanca
Telex: 22771 Cherelec

PRINCIPAL ACTIVITIES: Electrical equipment, central power plants, power generation, transmission, distribution, automation, controls, instrumentation, pumps stations, transformer stations
Principal Agencies: Entrelec, Villeurbanne (France); Rateau, La Courneuve (France)
Associated Companies: CGEE Alsthom, Levallois-Perret, France
Principal Bankers: Banque Marocaine du Commerce Exterieur; Societe Marocaine de Depot et Credit; Banque Commerciale du Maroc

CIE CHERIFIENNE DES TEXTILES

Route de Sidi Quassel, Safi
Tel: 2770, 3451
Telex: 71788
Telefax: (046) 3325

President: Abdelfattah Frej
Directors: Ahmed Bennani (Director General), Aziz Nadifi (Administrative Director)

PRINCIPAL ACTIVITIES: Production of jute products and man-made fibres and textiles
Branch Offices: Safi, Casablanca, Agadir

Date of Establishment: 1946
No of Employees: 700

CIE COMMERCIALE, CHARBONNIERE ET MARITIME

C.C.C.M.

24 Bvd Mohammed El Hansali, PO Box 704, Casablanca
Tel: 224131, 272256
Cable: Terem
Telex: 21074; 22836; 21778
Telefax: 222532

Directors: Gerard Klein
Senior Executives: Mohamed Barakat (Manager)

PRINCIPAL ACTIVITIES: Shipping lines and agents, stevedoring, clearing and forwarding
Branch Offices: Agadir, Tangier, Safi, Nador, Mohammedia, El Jadida
Parent Company: Mory & Cie Maroc
Subsidiary Companies: Comater
Principal Bankers: BMCE, SGMB, BCM, BMCI, CMCB

Date of Establishment: 1968
No of Employees: 60

CIE D'ASSURANCES SANAD

SANAD Societe Anonyme d'Assurances et de Reassurances

3 Bd Mohammed V, Casablanca 01
Tel: 260591/93, 270498, 270521
Cable: Sanadassur
Telex: 21927 Ellecram
Telefax: 293813

Chairman: Mohamed Aouad

MOROCCO

Directors: Andre Hernandez (Director General), Moulay Driss Alaoui, Abderrafih Menjour (SAMIR), Mehdi Joundy, Abdellatif Ghissassi

Senior Executives: Abdelatif Tahiri (Deputy Director General)

PRINCIPAL ACTIVITIES: Insurance and reinsurance
Principal Bankers: Societe Marocaine de Depot et Credit; BMCI; SBC
Financial Information:

	1988/89 MDh'000
Authorised capital	10.000
Total assets	253.395

Date of Establishment: 1946
No of Employees: 55

CIE DE TRANSPORT DU MAROC (LIGNES NATIONALES)

303 Bvd Brahim Roudani, BP 279, Casablanca
Tel: 252901
Cable: Transtour
Telex: 22943

President: S Abdelghani (Director General)

PRINCIPAL ACTIVITIES: Tourist agency and transport services

Date of Establishment: 1970

CIE ES SAADA

123 Avenue Hassan II, Casablanca
Tel: 62283, 62284, 24177
Cable: Groupassur
Telex: 22798

Chairman: Izarab Ouazzani
Directors: Mehdi Ouazzani, Hadi Arbyig, Musaed Saleh, Thami Ouazzani, Hamad Al Saleh, Armand E Araktingi, Said Ouazzani, Dr M'Hamed Sedrati

PRINCIPAL ACTIVITIES: All insurance and reinsurance activities
Associated Companies: Societe de Banque et de Credit; Assada Electronique; SEPO; SGCA
Principal Bankers: Banque Commerciale du Maroc; Societe de Banque et de Credit; Compagnie Marocaine de Credit et de Banques; Banque Marocaine pour le Commerce Exterieur; Credit du Maroc; Societe Marocaine de Depot et Credit; Arab Bank

Principal Shareholders: Musaed Al Saleh (Real Estate), Kuwait; Izarab, Ouazzani, Morocco; Marepar Co, Morocco

CIE FERMIERE DES SOURCES MINERALES (ETAT)

163 Bvd Yacoub El Mansour, Casablanca
Tel: 361940
Cable: OULMETAT
Telex: 23961 M

President: A Ben Salah
Directors: J P Sarrand, Zea Belmej Doub, (Managing Director)

PRINCIPAL ACTIVITIES: Production of mineral water
Principal Bankers: SMDC, BMCE, CDM, BCM, SGMB

Date of Establishment: 1933
No of Employees: 250

CIE GENERALE IMMOBILIERE

42 Sharia Al Alaouiynes, Rabat
Tel: 22571, 25434

Chairman: M'Fadel Lahlou
Directors: Abderrahmane Amrani (Director General), Abdelhafid Benjamaa (Secretary General)
Senior Executives: Mohamed Belgnaoui (Commercial Section), Omar Ouannane (Manager), Gerard Hoffman (Technical Section), Mohamed Mekkaoui (Financial Section), Mohamed Fellah (General Affairs Section)

PRINCIPAL ACTIVITIES: Real estate operations
Subsidiary Companies: Societe de Coordination et d'Ordonnancement Marocaine
Principal Bankers: Banque Commerciale du Maroc; Banque Marocaine pour le Commerce et l'Industrie

Principal Shareholders: Caisse de Depot et de Gestion and Morocain, Government

CIE INDUSTRIELLE DE TRAVAUX DU MAROC C.I.T.R.A.M.

BP 65, 55 Bvd des Almohades, Casablanca
Tel: 274442, 278820
Cable: Citravaux
Telex: 22709

Chairman: M Bargach
Directors: G Millet (Director General)

PRINCIPAL ACTIVITIES: Building and civil engineering contractors, production of cement and other building materials
Parent Company: Spie Batignolles
Subsidiary Companies: Elecam (Maroc)
Principal Bankers: CDM, BCM, BP, BMCE, BMCI, SMDC

Principal Shareholders: Spie Batignolles; SOMSI
Date of Establishment: 1974
No of Employees: 1,000

CIE MAROCAINE DE GESTION DES EXPLOITATIONS AGRICOLES COMAGRI

BP 297, 1 Ave John Kennedy, Rabat
Tel: 52806, 52808
Telex: 31633

PRINCIPAL ACTIVITIES: Agricultural services, production of cereal seeds, livestock rearing
Principal Bankers: BMCE, CNCA

Principal Shareholders: Ministere de l'Agriculture et de la Reforme, Agraire, CNCA, OCIC, ORMVA, Eaux et Forets
No of Employees: 2,300

CIE MAROCAINE DE METAUX ET D'ENTREPRISES COMAMETO

233-241 Bvd de la Liberte, Casablanca
Tel: 312040, 312082, 314950, 313197
Cable: Cuprifer
Telex: 21834, 26709

Chairman: Hadj Salah Kabboud
Directors: Ali Bourzigui

PRINCIPAL ACTIVITIES: Production of ferrous and non-ferrous building materials, and sanitaryware
Branch Offices: Agadir; Fes; Rabat; Oujda; Marrakech
Principal Bankers: SGMB; BCM; SMDC; CDM; Wafabank; BMCE
Financial Information:

	1988/89 MDh'000
Sales turnover	130.000
Profits	18%
Authorised capital	10.800
Paid-up capital	10.800
Total assets	55.000

Date of Establishment: 1948
No of Employees: 168

CIE MAROCAINE DE NAVIGATION
COMANAV
7 Bvd de la Resistance, BP 628, Casablanca 05
Tel: 303012, 302006 (25 lines)
Cable: Comanav
Telex: 26093, 26704 (7 lines)

Chairman: Abdellah Alaoui Kacimi
Senior Executives: Omar Bennani (Secretary General),
Abdelfattah Bouzoubaa (Advisor to the Chairman), Amaalaoui
Rezgui (Marine Director), Ali Bouassaba (Commercial
Director), Thami Boukentar (Superintendent & Supplies),
Abdelaziz Allouch (Director Passenger Div), Abdellah Imgli
(Financial Director), Fouad Azzabi (Director Legal Dept)

PRINCIPAL ACTIVITIES: Shipping transport, freight, clearing
and forwarding, handling, passenger transport and tourism
Branch Offices: France: 56 Rue de Londres, Paris 8; Germany:
KJ Kajen 10, Postfach 110.869 2 Hambourg 11
Subsidiary Companies: Acomar; Manuco; Comanav-Voyages;
Defmar
Principal Bankers: Banque Marocaine du Commerce Exterieur
and most other Moroccan banks
Financial Information:

	MDh'000
Authorised capital	224.500
Paid-up capital	224.500

Principal Shareholders: State-owned
Date of Establishment: 1946
No of Employees: 1,510

CIE MAROCAINE DES CARTONS ET
PAPIERS
Quartier Industriel, PO Box 94, Kenitra
Tel: 4644
Cable: Cartoma Kenitra
Telex: 91039

Chairman: Jim Verne
Directors: Abdelmajid Laroui (Director General)
Senior Executives: Louis-Pierre Perrazi (Secretary General),
Gabriel de Sagey (Commercial Director), Yves Monzies
(Marketing Director)

PRINCIPAL ACTIVITIES: Manufacture of pulp, paper,
cardboard, and packaging materials
Principal Bankers: SGMB; BMCI; BMCE; BCM; Credit du
Maroc; CMCB; SMDC

CIE MAROCAINE DES HYDROCARBURES
5 Bvd Abdellah Ben Yacine, PO Box 770, Casablanca
Tel: 42245/49
Telex: 47245; 47224

Directors: Hassan Agzenai (Director General)

PRINCIPAL ACTIVITIES: Marketing of oil and oil products

Principal Shareholders: Formerly Agip BP

CIE MAROCAINE INDUSTRIELLE ET
COMMERCIALE SA
C.M.I.C.
PO Box 236, 9 Bvd d'Oujda, Casablanca
Tel: 302211, 300318
Telex: 26872 M

Chairman: Mohamed Karim Lamrani
Senior Executives: Paul Vitalis (General Manager), Michel
Bouyssi (Manager), Abdelwahid Sekkat (Manager), Robert
Thomas (Manager)

PRINCIPAL ACTIVITIES: Production, import and distribution of
agricultural equipment and industrial and engineering
machinery
Principal Agencies: Massey Ferguson; Hanomag; Holman; PH
Harmischfeger

CIE MINIERE DE TOUISSIT
5 rue Ibnou Tofail, Casablanca
Tel: 251563
Cable: Royastur
Telex: 21713

PRINCIPAL ACTIVITIES: Mining of copper, lead, and silver ore
Principal Bankers: SGMB; BMCI; SMDC; CDM; BCM;

Date of Establishment: 1974
No of Employees: 700

CIE NORD AFRICAINE ET
INTERCONTINENTALE D'ASSURANCE
C.N.I.A.
157 Avenue Hassan II, Casablanca
Tel: 224118
Telex: 21096

PRINCIPAL ACTIVITIES: Insurance
Principal Bankers: BCM

Date of Establishment: 1949

CIE SUCRIERE MAROCAINE ET DE
RAFFINAGE SA
COSUMAR
PO Box 3098, 8 rue El Mouatamid Ibnou Abbad, Casablanca
(Roches-Noires)
Tel: 247345
Telex: 27656 Cosumar, .25032 Cosuc
Telefax: 241071

Chairman: Fouad Filali
Directors: Ahmed Tizniti (Director General)

PRINCIPAL ACTIVITIES: Sugar refining and trading
Subsidiary Companies: Societe Anonyme de la Sucrerie de
Doukkala, Societe Marocaine des Derives industriels du Mais,
Societe Anonyme de la Sucrerie des Zemamra
Principal Bankers: Credit du Maroc
Financial Information:

	1988/89 MDh'000	1989/90 MDh'000
Sales turnover	1.954.628	2.041.197
Profits	56.429	56.805
Authorised capital	60.000	60.000
Paid-up capital	20%	20%
Total assets	60.337	95.859

Principal Shareholders: Omnium Nord Africain; Societe
Nationale d'Investissements; CIMR
Date of Establishment: 1967
No of Employees: 2,757

CIMENTERIE DE L'ORIENTAL
2 rue Abi Chouaib Eddoukkali, Rabat
Tel: 68920
Telex: 31377 M

Chairman: Mohamed Belkhayat
Directors: Youssef Ennadifi (Director General)
Senior Executives: Louazani Mesrari (Factory Director), Nordine
El Ayoubi (Financial Director), Abdeljalil El Hassani
(Commercial Director), Lahcen Tamesna (Director of Centre of
Distribution at Fes)

PRINCIPAL ACTIVITIES: Production and marketing of cement
Branch Offices: Fes, Tel (06) 20715; Casablanca, Tel (02)
352640, Telex 25725; Factory at Oujda, Tel (069) 3240, Telex
61625

Subsidiary Companies: Briqueterie de Taza; Centre de Distribution - Fes; Centre de Distribution - Casablanca
Principal Bankers: BCM; BMCE; SGMB; CMCB
Financial Information:

	1988/89 MDh'000
Sales turnover	530.600
Profits	22.950
Authorised capital	245.000
Paid-up capital	245.000
Total assets	565.656

Principal Shareholders: Office Pour le Developpement Industriel; Banque Islamique de Developpement
Date of Establishment: 1976
No of Employees: 611

CITIBANK (MAGHREB)

52 Avenue Hassan II, PO Box 13362, Casablanca
Tel: 224168
Cable: Citibank
Telex: 21686

Chairman: Abdel-Latif Bennani Othmani
Directors: Othman Benjelloun, Sheldon E Boege, Christian J Bartholin, Mohamed Ambal, Thami Ammar, Abdelali Berrad, Abdel Rahim Cherkaoui, Abdel Kader Erzini, John C Botts, Timothy C Kelley, Thomas C Shortell, Jameleddine Touati

PRINCIPAL ACTIVITIES: Commercial banking
Branch Offices: Rabat Branch: 2 rue El Maousil Tel 24636, Cable Citibank Rabat; Beausejour Branch: 14 Residence El Mansour Casablanca, Tel 366245

Date of Establishment: 1967

COFITEX SA

Rue Gay Lussac, Quartier Dokkarat, BP 130, Fes
Tel: 23344, 23566
Telex: 23715

Senior Executives: B Hassan (General Manager), M Benchekroun (Administrator)

PRINCIPAL ACTIVITIES: Manufacture of cotton and synthetic fibres
Branch Offices: Casablanca: 53 rue Allal Ben Abdellah, Tel 276714
Principal Bankers: BMCE; BCM; BP; CMCB; CDM

Date of Establishment: 1961

COMADIT

72 Bvd Hassan Seghir, Casablanca
Tel: 270851

Directors: Rais Belaid (Managing Director)

PRINCIPAL ACTIVITIES: Import and distribution of foodstuffs and confectionery and household goods
Principal Agencies: Scripto Pens Ltd, Smedley-HP Foods Ltd, Shulton, Beecham Products Overseas, Laughton & Sons Ltd, Wilkinson Sword Ltd, Andre Philippe Ltd, Aladin Industries Ltd, Progress Shaving brush (Vulfix Ltd), General Foods Ltd, Newey Goodman Ltd, Johnson & Johnson, Mars Ltd Confectionery Division, Robertson Foods International Ltd, Bromley, Rowntree Mackintosh

COMAMUSSY SA

1 Place Mirabeau, Casablanca
Tel: 245562
Cable: Comamussy
Telex: 25673

Chairman: Michel Barrazza
Directors: Alain Perbet, Nustzpha El Kahlaoui

PRINCIPAL ACTIVITIES: Manufacture of wood products and packaging materials

Branch Offices: Ain Sebaa, Sidi Larbi, Berkane, Sidi Slimane
Principal Bankers: BMCE, BCM, SMDC

Principal Shareholders: Groupe Becob, Groupe Manorbois
Date of Establishment: 1960
No of Employees: 450

COMPANIA ELECTROQUIMICA MARROQUI, SA

COELMA SA

Route de Ouad-Laou Km 3, PO Box 194, Tetouan
Tel: 7005, 6954
Cable: Electroquimica
Telex: 43045 M

Chairman: Pedro Guitart Pujol
Directors: Abdelhaq Tazi, Enrique Jiminez Baez

PRINCIPAL ACTIVITIES: Production of hydrochloric acid, caustic soda, bleach, fertilisers, chemical products and animal feed
Principal Bankers: BMCE; Uniban; UMB; BCM;

Date of Establishment: 1948
No of Employees: 100

COMPLEXE CERAMIQUE DU MAROC

COCEMA

BP 179, Ain Kadous, Fes
Tel: 45125, 45126
Cable: Cocema
Telex: 51647

Chairman: El Hadi Tajmouati
Directors: Khalid Tajmouati, Abdellatif Tajmouati

PRINCIPAL ACTIVITIES: Manufacture of tiles and ceramics, and chinaware
Principal Bankers: BCM; SGMB
Financial Information:

	MDh'000
Authorised capital	55.000
Paid-up capital	55.000

Date of Establishment: 1966
No of Employees: 710

COMPLEXE TEXTILE DE FES

COTEF

PO Box 267, Route de Sefrou, Quartier Sidi Brahim, Fes
Tel: 22157, 23575, 23680
Telex: 51606; 22678

Chairman: A Ghissassi
Directors: M Mahrouch (General Manager)

PRINCIPAL ACTIVITIES: Spinning and weaving, production of textiles, threads reels
Branch Offices: Commercial Service for COTEF: 42 Avenue Hassan Seghir, Casablanca, Tel 223551

COMPTOIR DE L'AUTOMOBILE

Ets G Robin & Co

67 Avenue Lalla Yacout, Casablanca
Tel: 274765
Cable: Comptoirauto
Telex: 23052

Chairman: Mohamed Bennani Smires
Directors: Khadri Mohamed

PRINCIPAL ACTIVITIES: Import and wholesale of auto spare parts and accessories
Principal Bankers: BMCI; BMCI; SGMB

Principal Shareholders: Fismicom (Holding)
Date of Establishment: 1933
No of Employees: 28

COMPTOIR DES MINES ET DES GRANDS TRAVAUX DU MAROC

C.M.G.T.M.

BP 542, 4 rue Chevalier Bayard, Casablanca
Tel: 248954, 242377
Cable: Comines
Telex: 22737

Chairman: Mohamed Bensalah K Abboud
Directors: Farouk Benbrahim (Administrateur Directeur General)
Senior Executives: Mustapha Lakhdar, Abdelhaq Berrada, Ali Bourzigui

PRINCIPAL ACTIVITIES: Distribution of building materials, earthmoving heavy machinery, sanitaryware, metal products; construction timber
Principal Agencies: Grohe, Villeroy & Boch, Sarreguemines, John Deere, Pataud, Cadillon, Bohler, Outils Wolf, Silla, Moteurs Robin, STV
Branch Offices: Rabat, Kenitra, Meknes, Fes, Oujda, Marrakech, Agadir, Tangiers
Principal Bankers: CDM; BCM; BMCE; BMCI; CMBC; SGMB; BP; SMDC
Financial Information:

	MDh'000
Authorised capital	12.000
Paid-up capital	12.000

Date of Establishment: 1920
No of Employees: 200

COMPTOIR METALLURGIQUE MAROCAIN

80 Bvd de Paris, Casablanca
Tel: 224182
Cable: Cometal
Telex: 21979

President: Abdelkader Ben Salah
Directors: Louis Ravassod, Mylamine Alaoui, Meyer Benchimol

PRINCIPAL ACTIVITIES: Import, distribution and retailing of metallurgical products, hardware, tools, household equipment and electrical appliances
Principal Agencies: Sunbeam, Facom, Sauvageaux, Ingersoll Rand, Peugeot, General Electric, Hitachi, Allibert, AEG, Virax, Airco, Telitalia, Hampiaux, Latty Internl, Triplex, Stanley Works, Super Ego
Branch Offices: Branches at Rabat; Kenitra; Marrakech; Meknes; Fes; Oujda; Tangiers; Agadir
Parent Company: Descours & Cabaud, Lyon, France
Subsidiary Companies: Ollearis Maghreb SA
Principal Bankers: Societe Marocaine de Depot et Credit; Credit du Maroc; Banque Populaire; BCM; BMCI; BMCE; Societe Generale Marocaine de Banque; Wafabank
Financial Information:

	MDh'000
Sales turnover	200.000
Authorised capital	10.000
Paid-up capital	10.000

Principal Shareholders: Abdelkader Ben Salah Group, Descours et Cabaud, Comema
Date of Establishment: 1913; Marocanized in 1974
No of Employees: 265

CONSERVERIES CHERIFIENNES (LES)

Route du Djorf El Youdi, PO Box 96, Safi
Tel: 2500, 2502, 2513
Cable: Lescherif Safi
Telex: 71774, 71792 Lecherif Safi
Telefax: (212 46) 3226

Chairman: Hamou El Jamali
Directors: Mohamed El Jamali
Senior Executives: Abdelkarim El Jamali (Finance Director), Mohamed Kouy (Production Director), Abdeslam El Ouazzani (Technical Director)

PRINCIPAL ACTIVITIES: Fish and food processing and canning (fruits, vegetables)
Branch Offices: 59 Allee des Jardins, Ain Sebaa, Casablanca, Tel 356793, 356794, Telex 25700, 25768, Fax (212 35) 1447; and 4 factories in Safi
Subsidiary Companies: Societe MARIMPEX, 179 rue Paradis 13006, Marseille, France
Principal Bankers: Credit du Maroc; BMCI; BMCE
Financial Information:

	198990
	US$'000
Sales turnover	13,500
Authorised capital	2,000
Paid-up capital	2,000

Principal Shareholders: Group El Jamali (96.5%)
Date of Establishment: 1949
No of Employees: 2,500

CONSERVERIES LAHLOU

rue Moussa Ibn Noussair, BP 145, Agadir
Tel: 22343, 23543, 22625

PRINCIPAL ACTIVITIES: Fish processing and canning
Branch Offices: Essaouira; Casablanca
Principal Bankers: BMCI; BCM; Arab Bank; CMCB

CONTREPLAQUES & EMBALLAGES DU MAROC SA

C.E.M.A.

Sidi Maarouf, Route de Bouskoura, PO Box 203, Casablanca
Tel: 362742
Cable: Panocema
Telex: 22995 M

Chairman: Mohamed Karime Lamrani
Directors: Mohamed Bennis (Director General)

PRINCIPAL ACTIVITIES: Production of wood panels, plywood laths, and packaging materials
Associated Companies: Etablissements G Leroy, Lisieux, (France)
Principal Bankers: Societe Generale Marocaine de Banques; Credit du Maroc

Date of Establishment: 1948
No of Employees: 500

COOPER MAROC

Societe Marocaine de Cooperation Pharmaceutique

41 Rue Mohamed Diouri, Casablanca
Tel: 224116
Cable: Cooper Maroc
Telex: 21619

Chairman: Lahlou Jaouad Cheikh (Director General)
Directors: Bachir Benchekroun, Remi Cador, Cooperation Pharmaceutique Francaise, Mohamed Chraibi, Jean Deroux, Rene Lory, Mohamed Hadj Tazi, Claude Salmon

PRINCIPAL ACTIVITIES: Manufacture, import, distribution and wholesale of pharmaceutical products, toiletries, veterinary and chemical products
Principal Agencies: Andreu, Farmitalia, Faure, Hepatoum, Lafran, Leurquin, Martinet, Angellini, Nutricia, Oberval, Organon, Pfizer, Prodes, Robapharm, Carlo Erba, Roland Marie, Ucepha, Villette, Cooperation Pharmaceutique Francaise, Daniel Brunet, Dumex
Principal Bankers: BCM; BMCE; CMCB; SGMB

Principal Shareholders: Cooperation Pharmaceutique Francaise, Directors as described, also 75 chemists

MOROCCO

CORSIN, J J, SA
24 rue Saint-Savin, Casablanca
Tel: 244350, 241694
Cable: Corsinsa
Telex: 25967

President: Aziz Touzani
Directors: Mohammed Terrab (Director General)

PRINCIPAL ACTIVITIES: Import and distribution of motorcycles, industrial and agricultural equipment, auto spare parts

CREDIT DU MAROC SA
48-58 Bvd Mohamed V, PO Box 13.579, Casablanca
Tel: 212-2-224142
Cable: Crediroc
Telex: 21054; 22048; 22896 Crediroc
Telefax: 212-2-277127

Honorary Chairman: Mohamed Karim Lamrani
Chairman: Jawad Ben Brahim (Chairman and Managing Director)
Senior Executives: M'hamed Tazi Mezalek (Director - General Manager), Jean Pierre de Bellecombe (Director - Deputy General Manager)

PRINCIPAL ACTIVITIES: Banking
Branch Offices: 72 branches throughout Morocco: Casablanca (23), Rabat (6), Fes (5), Meknes (3), Marrakech (3), Agadir (2), Oujda (2), Tanger (2), Al Hoceima, Beni-Mellal, Berkane, Berrechid, El Jadida, Essaouira, Inezgane, Kenitra (2), Larache, Mohammedia (2), Nador (2), Ouarzazate, Safi, Sale (2), Settat, Sidi Slimane, Souk El Arbaa, Taza, Tetouan, Tiznit, Khouribga, Ain Taoujdate
Associated Companies: Credit Lyonnais, France
Financial Information:

	1988/89 MDh'000	1989/90 MDh'000
Total income	517.732	528.227
Profits	71.044	79.621
Authorised capital	124.080	124.080
Paid-up capital	124.080	124.080
Total assets	5.735.468	5.968.228

Principal Shareholders: Credit Lyonnais; Banque Marocaine du Commerce Exterieur; Societe Financiere et de Participations
Date of Establishment: 1963
No of Employees: 1,290

CREDIT IMMOBILIER ET HOTELIER
68 Rue de Reims, Casablanca
Tel: 273232
Telex: 22839 M Credotel

President: Othman Slimane (Director General)
Directors: Abdelhak Benkirane (Deputy Director General), Driss Aouachria (Secretary General), Abdellah Haimer (Central Senior)
Senior Executives: M Abdellatif Sadik (Sales Manager), Mustapha Amri (Credit Manager), Rkia Zarari (Financial Manager)

PRINCIPAL ACTIVITIES: Financing of investments to the building, hotels and tourist industry
Branch Offices: Casablanca; Rabat; Fes; Marrakech; Tangiers; Oujda; Agadir; Meknes
Subsidiary/Associated Companies: CMKD
Principal Bankers: BMCE; CMCB; SMDC

Principal Shareholders: Caisse de Depot et de Gestion; Banque du Maroc; Banque Marocaine du Commerce Exterieur
Date of Establishment: 1920
No of Employees: 389

CROWN CORK CO SA
Chemin des Glaieuls, BP 998, Ain Sebaa
Tel: 350954
Telex: 23881

PRINCIPAL ACTIVITIES: Manufacture of metal crowns, plastic caps, finishing of metals
Principal Bankers: SGMB; CDM; SMDC

Principal Shareholders: Crown Cork & Seal Co Inc, USA
Date of Establishment: 1951

DAVUM MAROC
8 Ave Khalid Bnou Loualid, PO Box 396, Casablanca
Tel: 248351/4
Cable: Salmofer

PRINCIPAL ACTIVITIES: Import and wholesale of metal products, machine tools, home electrical appliances, air-conditioning equipment

DELATTRE LEVIVIER MAROC
BP 2613, Km 9 Route de Rabat, Ain Sebaa, Casablanca 05
Tel: 350093, 352183
Telex: 25710 M

Chairman: Dr M Benhima
Directors: J C Bouveur

PRINCIPAL ACTIVITIES: Building and industrial steel structure; heavy and medium plate work, vessels and reservoirs piping, fabrication and erection
Parent Company: Delattre Levivier France
Principal Bankers: BMCI, BMCE, CDM, SGMB, BCM, SMDC

Principal Shareholders: Delattre Levivier (France)
Date of Establishment: 1949
No of Employees: 650

EBERTEC
12 rue Sad Ibnou Ouakkas, Casablanca
Tel: 242601, 243441, 244399
Cable: Ebertec

President: Abdelwahab Laraki

PRINCIPAL ACTIVITIES: Manufacture, import and distribution of drinks and foodstuffs
Principal Bankers: SGMB; BMCE; BCM; CDM;

Date of Establishment: 1929

E-H-M (MAROC) SA
32-34 rue de Barsac, Casablanca 03
Tel: 242997, 242023
Telex: 25675
Telefax: 243615

Chairman: Driss Lahlou
Directors: Guy Cosson (Managing Director)

PRINCIPAL ACTIVITIES: Distribution of heavy machinery, construction equipment, and earth-moving machinery, mechanical engineering, services and maintenance
Principal Agencies: Acrow; Aquatech; Benati; Douglas; Hyster; Morris; Nash; NEI; Parker; Perlini; Saxby; Simon; Storey; Windhoff

Date of Establishment: 1951

ELECTRA
BP 1015, Ain Sebaa, Casablanca (05)
Tel: 352411 (5 lines)
Cable: Elect-Casa
Telex: 25075

Chairman: Abdelfetah Frej
Directors: Abdelhamid Berrada (General Manager)

PRINCIPAL ACTIVITIES: Electrical and electronic equipment (radios, television, air-conditioning equipment, household electricals)
Principal Agencies: AEG Kelvinator; Chrysler; Airtemps; Fedders
Branch Offices: 45 branches in Morocco

Principal Bankers: Credit du Maroc; Banque Marocaine du Commerce Exterieur

Date of Establishment: 1932

ELECTRICITE ET CANALISATIONS DU MAROC
E.L.E.C.A.M.
BP 899, 8 rue Lapebie, Casablanca
Tel: 273243, 260781
Cable: Paralecop
Telex: 21029

PRINCIPAL ACTIVITIES: Electrical engineering, electrical and electronic equipment, civil engineering, water supply, irrigation services, electric power supply installations
Associated Companies: Spie Batignolles, France
Principal Bankers: CDM; SMDC; SGMB; BMCE; BMCI

Date of Establishment: 1975
No of Employees: 1,200

ENT. HADJ AOMAR SA
108 rue de Dinant, Casablanca
Tel: 242856, 247623, 245778

Chairman: Taissar Hadj Rachid
Directors: Albert Nahmani

PRINCIPAL ACTIVITIES: Public works enterprises, motorways, civil engineering, canals, agricultural works

ENT. TAISSIR CHAUFOUR DUMEZ
5 rue Yves Gay, Casablanca
Tel: 260711
Cable: Zemud maroc
Telex: 22949 Zemud Casa

Chairman: Ben Abdelkrim Hadj Omar
Directors: Mr Hadj Omar, Mme Hadj Omar, Melle Hadj Omar, Societe Marocaine des Entreprises Chaufour Dumez, Societe Dumez Afrique
Senior Executives: M Courjaret (General Manager), M Vovk (Technical Manager), M Fiard (Financial & Administrative Manager)

PRINCIPAL ACTIVITIES: Civil engineering and building contractors, public works, marine engineering
Principal Agencies: Societe Dumez Afrique, 325 Avenue Georges Clemenceau, 92000, Nanterre
Principal Bankers: Credit du Maroc; BCM; BMCE; SGMB; SBC

Principal Shareholders: Entreprise Hadj Omar (49.99%), Societe Marocaine des Entreprises Chaufour Dumez (47.76%), Societe Dumez, Afrique (2.24%)

ETS BOURCHANIN & CIE
72 Bvd Ibn Tachfine, Casablanca
Tel: 247534, 240631, 243836
Telex: 23725

Chairman: Omar Kabbaj
Directors: Mohamed Slaoui

PRINCIPAL ACTIVITIES: Manufacturers' representatives; import and distribution of wines, spirits, soft drinks and foodstuffs
Principal Agencies: Johnnie Walkers, Kronenbourg, Perriet & Jouet, Segrams, Produits Bardinet, Olida
Principal Bankers: Compagnie Marocaine de Credit et de Banque SA; Banque Marocaine du Commerce Exterieur; Banque Marocaine pour le Commerce et l'Industrie

ETS FRENDO
10, Rue Emile Brunet, Ain-Borja, Casablanca
Tel: 242239, 244068
Telex: 26617

President: Ahmed Benzakour Kabir

Directors: Andre Perez
Senior Executives: Yves Perez (Technical Manager)

PRINCIPAL ACTIVITIES: Manufacture, import and distribution of agricultural machinery and equipment
Principal Agencies: Smalley, Mahier, Allaeys, Comet, Zaga, Verbeke, Stafor, Cachapuz, Steyr, Fortschritt, Celli, Otma, Manza, Zetor, Mazotti, Didot
Subsidiary Companies: Somacom
Principal Bankers: BMCE, CMCB; BCM

FAMO SA
PO Box 2212, 12 bd Hassan El Alaoui, Casablanca
Tel: 246285, 240647
Telex: 25763

Chairman: Si Medersi Ben Larabi
Directors: A P Vignon
Senior Executives: Mohamed Khalil (Director)

PRINCIPAL ACTIVITIES: Food products (macaroni, couscous, biscuits)
Branch Offices: Rabat; Fes; Marrakech; Oujda; Agadir; Tetouan
Parent Company: Famo-Mauritanie; Nouakchott

Date of Establishment: 1949
No of Employees: 350

FILATURE NATIONALE DE LAINE
FILAINE SA
PO Box 2211, Casablanca
Tel: 241991/2/3

Chairman: G M Haggar
Directors: Ph M Haggar Khattabi Abdelmohsen, Haraba Marwan
Senior Executives: Ph M Haggar (Managing Director), Khattabi Abdelmohsen (Director)

PRINCIPAL ACTIVITIES: Spinners of polyester wool, polyester viscose, acrylics
Branch Offices: Sudan; London

FILROC
BP 39, rue de Casablanca, Rabat
Tel: 25576, 34431
Cable: Texafric

PRINCIPAL ACTIVITIES: Spinning and weaving, production of textiles, and knitted goods
Branch Offices: Casablanca, Sale
Principal Bankers: BMCI; CDM

Date of Establishment: 1952
No of Employees: 850

FRUITIERE MAROCAINE DE TRANSFORMATION
FRUMAT
BP 13155, 45 avenue des FAR, Casablanca
Tel: (212) 312840, 318434, 318462, 318465
Telex: 23872, 21707
Telefax: 314626, 310162

Chairman: M Guessouss
Directors: OCE, BNDE, Producteurs Agrumes, Orangina
Senior Executives: Abdelhamid Sedrati (Managing Director), Abdelmoula Sami (Finance Director), Tayeb Aboubakr (Purchasing & Personnel Director)

PRINCIPAL ACTIVITIES: Production of fruit juices, frozen and concentrate, essential oils
Branch Offices: Kenitre, Casablanca, Taroudant
Parent Company: Office de Commercialisation et d'Exportation (OCE)
Subsidiary Companies: Frusuma - Europe, Paris, France
Principal Bankers: BMCI; BMCE; SGMB; CDM

MOROCCO

Financial Information:

	1990
	MDh'000
Sales turnover	530.000
Authorised capital	80.000

Principal Shareholders: Producteurs d'Agrumes, OCE
Date of Establishment: 1976
No of Employees: 450

GENERAL TIRE & RUBBER CO OF MOROCCO

Km 10.600 Route No 111, PO Box 2608, Casablanca 05
Tel: 350094, 353342
Cable: Gentimaroc
Telex: 25009 Gentimar

Chairman: Gil Neal
Directors: Ramiro G de Moina (Managing Director), A Regragui (Asst General Manager), A Bennouna (Export Director), F Britel (Finance Director), D Drissi (Sales Director), A Abdelhak (Production Director)

PRINCIPAL ACTIVITIES: Production of tyres and inner tubes
Associated Companies: General Tire International Company, Akron, Ohio, USA
Principal Bankers: BMCE; CMCB; SMDC; SBC; CM; BMCI; BCM

Principal Shareholders: 42% Moroccan Government; 52% General Tire International Co; 6% various owners
Date of Establishment: 1958
No of Employees: 600

GOODYEAR MAROC SA

PO Box 2550, Ain Sebaa, Casablanca
Tel: 350831
Cable: Goodyear Casablanca
Telex: 22931

Chairman: Othman Benjelloun
Directors: M E Bryan (Managing Director)
Senior Executives: M Benabderrazak (Finance Director), A Muraglia (Production Director), A Abdessamad (Sales Director)

PRINCIPAL ACTIVITIES: Manufacture and distribution of tyres and tubes
Branch Offices: Km 13, Autoroute de Rabat, Casablanca
Parent Company: The Goodyear Tire & Rubber Co, Akron, Ohio, USA
Principal Bankers: Citibank, BMCE, CDM, BCM, SMDC, SBC, BMCI, Wafabank
Financial Information:

	MDh'000
Sales turnover	349.000
Authorised capital	17.500
Paid-up capital	17.500

Principal Shareholders: Goodyear Tire & Rubber Co; Othman Benjelloun
Date of Establishment: 1972
No of Employees: 650

GORDON WOODROFFE MOROCCO SA

Place Zallaqua, Imm Helvetia, Casablanca
Tel: 266531/32

Directors: A Boukantar (Administrative Director)

PRINCIPAL ACTIVITIES: Manufacture, import and distribution of heavy machinery and equipment, mining equipment, auto spare parts, trucks and heavy vehicles, agricultural machinery
Principal Agencies: Atco, Rolls-Royce, British Steel Corporation, Link 51

GRANDES MARQUES

37 rue des Aitbaamrane, Casablanca
Tel: 241985
Cable: Gramarq
Telex: 25081

PRINCIPAL ACTIVITIES: Production and export of fish products and canned fish
Branch Offices: Safi, Agadir
Principal Bankers: CDM; BCM; BMCE; CMCB

Date of Establishment: 1946
No of Employees: 1,500

GRAPHIC SYSTEM SA

25 rue de Provins, Casablanca
Tel: 301689
Telex: 25856

President: Samoudi Abdeddin
Directors: Pierre Finidori

PRINCIPAL ACTIVITIES: Distribution of printing machinery and equipment

HAMELLE MAROC

35 Bvd Hassan Seghir, BP 13682, Casablanca
Tel: 305115
Cable: Hamelaf
Telex: 27857

Chairman: Omar Benider
Directors: Abdelaziz Bencheqroun

PRINCIPAL ACTIVITIES: Distribution of industrial and agricultural equipment and machinery
Parent Company: SCOA, Paris
Principal Bankers: BCM; BMCE; BMCI; SMDC; BP
Financial Information:

	1989
	MDh'000
Paid-up capital	10.000

Principal Shareholders: Banque Commerciale du Maroc; Bencheqroun Brothers
Date of Establishment: 1956
No of Employees: 51

HILTON INTERNATIONAL RABAT

Aviation, PO Box 450, Rabat
Tel: 72151
Cable: Hiltels
Telex: 31913

PRINCIPAL ACTIVITIES: Hotel business
Branch Offices: Hilton hotels around the world
Principal Bankers: BMCE

Date of Establishment: 1967
No of Employees: 300

HOECHST MAROC SA

Route de Rabat-Ain Sebaa
Tel: 352167, 353395
Cable: Hostamar
Telex: 26623
Telefax: 350883

President: Bensalem Guessous
Directors: Edgar Winckler (Director General)
Senior Executives: Driss Tahiri (Sales Director), Eric Dupont (Financial Director), Mohamed Settaf (Production Director)

PRINCIPAL ACTIVITIES: Manufacture of chemicals
Parent Company: Hoechst AG, Frankfurt, W Germany
Subsidiary Companies: Laboratoires Polymedic SA

Financial Information:

	1988/89
	MDh'000
Sales turnover	364.000
Authorised capital	8.400

Principal Shareholders: Hoechst, Germany; Societe Matran; Societe Safari
Date of Establishment: 1954
No of Employees: 92

HOTEL LES ALMOHADES

Avenue des FAR, Tangiers
Tel: 940755, 940026
Cable: Mohadotel
Telex: 33075
Telefax: 946371

Chairman: A Ghissassi
Directors: F Chribi
Senior Executives: H Gmira

PRINCIPAL ACTIVITIES: Hotel business
Parent Company: Africa Palace SA and Palmariva Morocco
Principal Bankers: CMCB; BMCE
Financial Information:

	1990
	MDh'000
Sales turnover	20.000
Profits	8.000

Principal Shareholders: SOMED
Date of Establishment: 1970
No of Employees: 160

HOTEL MAMOUNIA

Ave Bab Jdid, Marrakech
Tel: 48981
Cable: Mamounia
Telex: 72018, 74036, 74037, 72041

Chairman: Moussa Moussaoui
Directors: Jacques Bouriot (General Manager)
Senior Executives: Mohammed Hammouti (Deputy General Manager)

PRINCIPAL ACTIVITIES: Hotel business
Branch Offices: Hotels Concorde
Principal Bankers: BMCE

Principal Shareholders: Societe La Mamounia
Date of Establishment: 1925, renovated in 1986
No of Employees: 600

HOTEL MARHABA

63 Ave de l'Armee Royale, Casablanca
Tel: 313199
Cable: Marhaba Casa
Telex: 21864

PRINCIPAL ACTIVITIES: Hotel business
Principal Bankers: BCM; CDM; SMDC; BMCI

Principal Shareholders: Chaine Hoteliere Marhaba Maroc
Date of Establishment: 1954

HOTEL MIRAMAR

BP 7, rue de Fes, Mohammedia
Tel: (32) 2021, 3271
Cable: Mirotel
Telex: 21964; 22692
Telefax: (32) 4613

Directors: Driss Ghazi (General Manager)

PRINCIPAL ACTIVITIES: Hotel business and leisure
Principal Bankers: BCM, SGMB, SBC, Credit du Maroc; BMCE

No of Employees: 125

HOTEL ROYAL MANSOUR

27 Avenue de l'Armee Royale, Casablanca 21000
Tel: 313011, 312112
Telex: 22912, 23005
Telefax: (212) 312583, 314818

Senior Executives: Guy Crawford (General Manager), Mrs Joan Gibbs (Director of Sales & Marketing)

PRINCIPAL ACTIVITIES: Hotel management and operation
Parent Company: Trusthouse Forte International Hotels

Date of Establishment: 1952, refurbished in April 1989

HOTEL TOUR HASSAN

BP 14, 26 Ave Abderrahmane Annegai, Rabat
Tel: 21401, 33814
Cable: Tourhassan
Telex: 31914

PRINCIPAL ACTIVITIES: Hotel business
Principal Bankers: BMCE; BP

Principal Shareholders: OMNT Maroc
Date of Establishment: 1965

HYATT REGENCY CASABLANCA

Place Mohammed V, Casablanca
Tel: 224167, 221332
Cable: HYATCASA
Telex: 22905, 22905
Telefax: 220180, 269645

Chairman: Dr Ghaith Rashad Pharaon
Senior Executives: Jacques L Morand (General Manager), Remi Cregut (Director of Sales), Keith Moorton (Financial Controller)

PRINCIPAL ACTIVITIES: Hotel management and operation
Parent Company: Hyatt International Corporation
Subsidiary Companies: 160 Hyatt Hotels Worldwide

Principal Shareholders: Moroccan Government
Date of Establishment: January 1984
No of Employees: 390

INDUSTRIE COTONNIERE DU MAROC
ICOMA

Boulevard Hassan II, BP 102, Mohammedia
Tel: 2123, 2125
Cable: Icoma
Telex: 21664

PRINCIPAL ACTIVITIES: Manufacture of textiles, and textiles processing
Principal Bankers: CDM; BCM; BMCI; BMCE; SMDC; SGMB; BP

Date of Establishment: 1946
No of Employees: 850

INDUSTRIE GENERALE DE FILATURE ET DE TISSAGE
NASCOTEX

BP 285, Km 7 route de Rabat, Tangiers
Tel: 419-88
Cable: NASCOTEX
Telex: 33669
Telefax: 425-65

Directors: Hadj Ahmed Nasreddin, Hassan Nasreddin
Senior Executives: Montasser Salhi (Administrative Manager)

PRINCIPAL ACTIVITIES: Spinning and weaving, printing on textiles, cotton and polyester
Branch Offices: Casablanca: 30 rue Mostafa El Maani
Parent Company: Nasco Milano (Italy); Raw-Mat - Chiasso (Switzerland)
Principal Bankers: BMCE; BCM

Financial Information:

	1989 MDh'000
Sales turnover	190.000
Authorised capital	25.000
Paid-up capital	25.000

Principal Shareholders: Hadj Ahmed Nasreddin
Date of Establishment: 1968
No of Employees: 800

INDUSTRIE MAROCAINE DES TEXTILES
IMATEX

47 Rue Emir Abdelkader, Casablanca
Tel: 241622, 246623
Cable: Lahloutex
Telex: 21887

Senior Executives: D Lahlou (General Manager)

PRINCIPAL ACTIVITIES: Manufacture of textiles and clothing
Principal Bankers: BMCI; BCM; Arab Bank; CMCB

No of Employees: 700

INTERCICAM SA
Ste Industrielle et Commerciale Anglo-Marocaine

88 Bvd Moulay Youssef, Casablanca
Tel: 222918
Telex: 23641

PRINCIPAL ACTIVITIES: General trading and distribution, promotion of foreign goods
Principal Agencies: Kwikform; Dexion; Thompson Cochran; Suffolk; Winger; Multibloc
Principal Bankers: BCM

Date of Establishment: 1974

INTERCONTINENTAL HOTEL

Blvd de Paris, Parc Brooks, Tangiers
Tel: 36053/9, 30150/8
Cable: Interotel Tangiers
Telex: 33067
Telefax: 37945

Chairman: A Bennani
Directors: J Bennani

PRINCIPAL ACTIVITIES: Hotel business
Subsidiary Companies: Part of Somatour
Principal Bankers: BPN; BMCE - UNIBAN

Date of Establishment: 1968
No of Employees: 110

ITT MAROC
International Telephone Telegraphe

BP 5306, 1 rue Soldat Louis Guillotte, Casablanca
Tel: 255294
Cable: Microphone
Telex: 21868

PRINCIPAL ACTIVITIES: Import, manufacture and distribution of electrical, electronic and telecommunication equipment
Branch Offices: Rabat, Marrakech, Fes, Agadir
Principal Bankers: SMDC; BMCI; FNCB

Date of Establishment: 1967

J J CORSIN SA

See CORSIN, J J, SA

LAFARGE MAROC

239 Bvd Moulay Ismail, Casablanca
Tel: 246733
Telex: 22986

PRINCIPAL ACTIVITIES: Manufacture of cement

Principal Shareholders: Lafarge-France
Date of Establishment: 1968
No of Employees: 500

L'ENTENTE

122 Avenue Hassan II, Casablanca
Tel: 267272, 267755
Cable: ENTENTAFRIC CASABLANCA
Telex: 27811 M
Telefax: 267023

President: Mohamed El Mehdi Boughaleb (Director General)
Directors: M'Hamed Bargach, Abdallah Belkeziz, Mohamed El Mehdi Boughaleb, Abderrahman Filali, Mohamed Cherkaoui, Jean-Marc Fiamma, Yvette Chassagne, Jacques-Henri Gougenheim, Farouk Bennis
Senior Executives: Mohamed El Mehdi Boughaleb (President Director General), Daniel Boulet (Director)

PRINCIPAL ACTIVITIES: Insurance and reinsurance
Associated Companies: UAP France
Principal Bankers: The majority of Moroccan Banks

Principal Shareholders: Compagnie d'Assurances Al Amane
Date of Establishment: 1950
No of Employees: 270

LESIEUR

BP 3095, 1 rue Caporal Corbi, Casablanca
Tel: 246636
Telex: 21674

PRINCIPAL ACTIVITIES: Production of vegetable oils, and soap products
Principal Bankers: SGMB; BCM; CDM; BMCE; BMCI

Date of Establishment: 1941

LIGNES MARITIMES DU DETROIT SA
Limadet-Ferry

3 rue Ibn Rochd, Tangiers
Tel: 933633, 933639, 933647
Cable: Limadet Tanger
Telex: 33013
Telefax: 937173

President: Faris Dellero
Directors: Rachid Benmansour (Director General)
Senior Executives: Vicente Ballarin (Commercial Manager), Mohamed Alioui (Purchasing Manager)

PRINCIPAL ACTIVITIES: Shipping agents; passenger ferry boat
Branch Offices: 13 Rue Prince Moulay Abdellah
Parent Company: Limadet-Ferry, Recinto del Puerto, Algeciras, Spain
Principal Bankers: BMCE, BNDE, BPT, BCM
Financial Information:

	1990 MDh'000
Authorised capital	58.880

Principal Shareholders: Banque Nationale pour le Developpement Economique, Rabat; Cia Trasmediterranea, Madrid
Date of Establishment: 1966
No of Employees: 140

LONGOMETAL AFRIQUE

178 Bvd Emile Zola, BP 587, Casablanca
Tel: 244233, 249515
Telex: 21064

PRINCIPAL ACTIVITIES: Manufacture of steel tubes, wire, plumbing and central heating equipment
Principal Agencies: Frigidaire; Bonnet; Usinor; Peugeot; Virax; etc

Branch Offices: Rabat; Tangiers; Agadir; Marrakech; Meknes; Oujda; Laayoun
Principal Bankers: SGMB

Date of Establishment: 1949

MAGHREB-ACCESSOIRES

37 rue Burger, PO Box 674, Casablanca
Tel: 270417
Cable: Maghauto
Telex: 23649

President: Mekhfi Ghaouti
Directors: Ahmed Benamar (Director General)

PRINCIPAL ACTIVITIES: Import and distribution of automobiles and spare parts, heavy machinery and garage equipment
Principal Agencies: SEV Marchal; FRAM; De Carbon; Sully; Flertex; DBA; Durol; DAV
Principal Bankers: SMCD; Credit Populaire Marocain, BCM

Principal Shareholders: A Benamar; M Bensalem Berrada; O Cherif; M Ghaouti

MANUDRA

51 rue Pelle, Casablanca
Tel: 306881, 309724, 309748
Cable: Manudra
Telex: 22989

Directors: A Ben Amour, L Ben Amour, Mohammed Ben Amour

PRINCIPAL ACTIVITIES: Manufacture of textiles and cloth
Principal Bankers: BMCE; BMCI; SBC; BPC

Principal Shareholders: Abdelouahed Ben Amour; Larbi Ben Amour
Date of Establishment: 1961
No of Employees: 500

MANUFACTURE MAROCAINE D'ALUMINIUM

Rue Fatima Zarah, Mohammedia
Tel: (032) 4406/4410
Cable: Manumarocal
Telex: 22975

President: Francois de Chassey (President Administrateur Delegue)
Directors: Paul Meley (Administrateur Delegue), Mohamed El Kabbaj (Directeur General)
Senior Executives: Mohamed El Kabbaj, Andre Body, Abdellah Benbouhou, Omar Taj, Toufik Bouzoubaa, Lahsen Aounsekt

PRINCIPAL ACTIVITIES: Manufacture of aluminium products, aluminium sheeting and household appliances, collapsible tubes, aluminium foil packaging
Branch Offices: Commercial Office: Immeuble Al Wifaq, Rue L, Route Cotiere Km 11.4, Ain Sebaa, Casablanca, Tel 352955, 352963
Parent Company: Pechiney, France
Subsidiary Companies: Mogalu, Mogalbat
Principal Bankers: BCM
Financial Information:

	MDh'000
Authorised capital	15.760
Paid-up capital	15.760

Principal Shareholders: Cebal, France (Groupe Pechiney)
Date of Establishment: 1948
No of Employees: 660

MANUFACTURE NATIONALE TEXTILE
MANATEX

164 Bvd de la Gironde, Casablanca
Tel: 246565
Cable: Manatextile
Telex: 26734

Chairman: Ali Kettani
Directors: Larbi Essakalli, Mohamed Lahlou, Mohamed Lazrak

PRINCIPAL ACTIVITIES: Manufacture of all kinds of textiles and furnishings
Principal Bankers: BMCE; CMCB; BCM; BMCI; BP

Date of Establishment: 1957
No of Employees: 1,250

MARBAR SA

81 Ave Houmane Eifetouaki, Casablanca
Tel: 224190
Cable: Barimer Casablanca
Telex: 21011, 21012, 22072, 24650

Chairman: Jawad Ben Brahim
Directors: Frank Barber (Vice-Chairman), Hassan Chami (Vice-Chairman), Mohamed Lyoussi, Mohamed Slaoui, Norman R P Speed

PRINCIPAL ACTIVITIES: Shipping and forwarding agents, claim settling agents, stevedores commercial agents
Principal Agencies: Lloyds; Imperial Chemical Industries
Branch Offices: 6 rue de la Poste, Safi; Immeuble Sibra, bd Mohammed V, Agadir; Immeuble Tijani, Nador; Vitadec 2 rue Ibn Albana
Associated Companies: UCAM SA, Casablanca; Gibmar Travel SA; Vitadec SA, Tangiers; 'Atlas' Societe Marocaine de Navigation, Casablanca; Tarik Navigation SA, Casablanca; Sodap Moroc
Principal Bankers: Credit du Maroc; SMDC; BMCE; SBC; Wafabank
Financial Information:

	MDh'000
Sales turnover	40.880
Authorised capital	6.000

Principal Shareholders: Barber Limited, Hassan Chami, Jawad Ben Brahim, Mohamed Lyoussi, Mohammed Slaoui
Date of Establishment: 1923 as L. Barber Ltd; 1968 as Marbar SA
No of Employees: 118

MAROC CHIMIE

BP 54, Route Djor El Youdi, Safi
Tel: 4-463089
Telex: 71707 MARPHORE, 71057 MARPHOR

Chairman: Mohammed Fettah (Director General)
Senior Executives: Mohamed Izelmaden (Director of Safi Industrial Facilities/DES Maroc-Chimie & Maroc Phosphore I & II)

PRINCIPAL ACTIVITIES: Production and sale of phosphoric acid and ammonium phosphate sulphate
Parent Company: Office Cherifien des Phoshates, Casablanca
Associated Companies: Exploitations Industrielles de Jorf Lasfar; Exploitations Industrielles de SAFI; Exploitations Minieres de Khouribga; Exploitations Minieres de PHOSBOUCRAA; Exploitations Minieres de Gantour; Societe Marocaine des Fertilisants (FERTIMA); MARPHOCEAN; Societe d'Etudes Speciales et Industrielles; Societe de Transports Regionaux (SOTREG)

Principal Shareholders: Office Cherifien des Phosphates, Casablanca; Moroccan State
Date of Establishment: 1965
No of Employees: 1,600

MAROC TOURIST

BP 408, 31 Charia Al Alaouyen, Rabat
Tel: 34471
Telex: 31072

PRINCIPAL ACTIVITIES: Exploitation and management of various hotels and tourist complexes

MOROCCO

Subsidiary/Associated Companies: Hotels: Boustane, Karabo, Mohammed V, Quemado, Tidighine, Parador de Chaouen, Rif Nador

Date of Establishment: 1962
No of Employees: 450

MAROPORT
6 rue Caporal Gastous, Casablanca
Tel: 269755, 221882

President: T Sebti (Director General)
Directors: J Sebti, T Taktak

PRINCIPAL ACTIVITIES: Import-export; manufacturers' representatives, distribution of raw materials and accessories for the textile industry

MILANO CRISTAL SA
37 rue Emile Brunet, Casablanca
Tel: 241654, 241656
Telex: MILCRIS 25950 M; PHILCO 28049 M

Chairman: Said Bounkit

PRINCIPAL ACTIVITIES: Manufacture of lighting equipment, low pressure regulator L.P.G., iron plates, gas cookers, chandeliers and others
Branch Offices: Angles rues Idriss Lahrizi et Peincarre, Casablanca
Principal Bankers: Societe Generale Marocaine de Banques, Casablanca
Financial Information:

	MDh'000
Authorised capital	10.000
Paid-up capital	10.000

Principal Shareholders: Moroccan (100%)
Date of Establishment: 1979
No of Employees: 220

MOBIL OIL MAROC
23 rue Allal Ben Abdallah, PO Box 485, Casablanca
Tel: 224173
Cable: Mobiloil Casablanca
Telex: 21961

President: Mohamed Sidiqui
Directors: A Alaoui (General Manager & Chief Executive)
Senior Executives: A Ghzali (Personnel Manager), M Temmar (Financial Manager), M Benkaddour (Sales Manager), E M Herradi (Operations Manager)

PRINCIPAL ACTIVITIES: Marketing of petroleum products
Principal Agencies: Casablanca, Rabat, Kenitra, Tanger, Marrakech, Agadir, Laayoum, Smara, Dakhla
Parent Company: Mobil Corporation and Societe Nationale des Produits Petroliers
Subsidiary Companies: Atlas Sahara, Petrocab, CEC
Principal Bankers: BMCE, BCM, Credit du Maroc, Wafabank
Financial Information:

	MDh'000
Authorised capital	33.000

Principal Shareholders: Mobil Oil, Corp, USA (50%), SNPP Casablanca (50%)
Date of Establishment: 1923
No of Employees: 202

MOROCCAN KUWAITI DEVELOPMENT CONSORTIUM
46 Ave de l'Armee Royale, Casablanca
Tel: 313185, 224185
Telex: 24627 CMKD
Telefax: (212) 311937

President: Zine El Abidine Alaoui
Directors: Rashed Al Mirjin, Ahmed Al Ibrahim, Ali Abdelrahman Al Hasawi, Hamad Mohamed Al Hajiri, Badr Al Roshood,

Moulay Ali El Kettani, Abdellatif Laraki, Othmane Slimani, Abdelhaq Benkirane, Mohamed Tazi
Senior Executives: Mondir H El Alami (Financial & Admin Director), Hassan Al Kacimi (Director of Real Estate Projects), Abdel Raoof Al Ahrash (Director of External Relations)

PRINCIPAL ACTIVITIES: Real estate development, investment and finance
Branch Offices: Safir, Farah Magreb, Deyar
Principal Bankers: Wafabank, BMCE, BMCI
Financial Information:

	1989/90 MDh'000
Profits	27.947
Authorised capital	315.000
Paid-up capital	315.000
Total assets	325.186

Principal Shareholders: Kuwait Real Estate Investment Co, Credit Immobilier et Hotelier, Banque Centrale Populaire, Cie Marocaine de Credit et de Banque, Banque Marocaine du Commerce Exterieur, Caisse de Depot et de Gestion, Banque Nationale pour le Developpement Economique, and other Moroccan interests
Date of Establishment: 1976
No of Employees: 25

MOROCCAN MODERN INDUSTRIES
Km 10/400 Ancien Route de Rabat, 2625 Ain Sebaa, Casablanca
Tel: 350759
Cable: Modinco
Telex: 21735

Chairman: M Marrakchi
Directors: M Bargach and representative of Procter & Gamble AG
Senior Executives: S A Sherif (General Manager)

PRINCIPAL ACTIVITIES: Manufacture and sale of synthetic detergents

NCR (MAROC)
12 rue Theophile Gauthier, PO Box 490, Casablanca
Tel: 278540, 274619
Cable: Nacareco
Telex: 22858

PRINCIPAL ACTIVITIES: Distribution of business equipment, computers and terminals electronic data processing equipment
Branch Offices: Morocco (1 Place Pietri, Rabat, Tel 26283) and in the Middle East; Bahrain; United Arab Emirates; Kuwait; Oman

OFFICE CHERIFIEN DES PHOSPHATES
Imm OCP, Angle Route d'El Jadida, et Bvd de la Grande Ceinture, Casablanca
Tel: 360025, 361025, 363025, 365025
Cable: Phosphat Casablanca
Telex: 21934, 24033, 24024

Directors: Mohammed Karim-Lamrani (Directeur General et Directeur Commercial), Abdallah Falaki (Directeur du Personnel et des Affaires Sociales), Abdelkrim Mikou (Directeur Charge de Mission), Mohammed El Arfaoui (Directeur Charge de Mission), Farouk Chaouni Benebdallah (Coordinateur a la Direction Commerciale), Abdelhadi Ninia (Directeur Financier), Sellam M'Hamedi (Directeur des Industries Chimiques), Abdelwahed Benchekroun (Directeur de la Planification), Yahia Saou di-Hassani (Directeur des Approvisionnements et Marches), Mohamed Molato (Directeur de la Production), Abdellatif Guerraoui (Chef du Secretariat du Directeur General), Abdelkrim Bekkali (Directeur de la SMESI), Abdeltif Belkouri (Directeur de la SOTREG), Mohammed Ksikes (Directeur de FERTIMA), Mostapha Jamaleddine (Directeur de PHOSBOUCRAA), Larbi El Omari (Directeur de

CERPHOS), Abdallah Falaki (Directeur d'IPSE), Taeb M'Rabet (Directeur de MAROTEC), M'hamed Benharouga (Directeur de MARPHOCEAN), Mohammed El Arfaoui (President-Directeur General de STAR), Mohamed Darkaoui (Directeur d'UIM)

PRINCIPAL ACTIVITIES: Production, processing and marketing of rock phosphate and derivatives, production of phosphoric acid and fertilisers

Branch Offices: Office in Paris

Subsidiaries Companies: CERPHOS (Centre d'etudes et de recherches des phosphates mineraux); FERTIMA (Societe Marocaine des Fertilisants); IPSE (Institut de Promotion socioeducative); MAROC-CHIMIE; MAROC-PHOSPHORE; MARPHOCEAN; PHOSBOUCRAA; (Phosphates de Boucraa SA); SOTREG; (Societe de Transports Regionaux); SMESI; (Societe Marocaine d'etudes speciales et industrielles); STAR; (Societe de Transports et d'Affretements reunis); U.I.M. (Union Industrielle et de montage); MAROTEC (Societe Marocaine de realisations techniques et d'ingenierie)

Principal Shareholders: State-owned
Date of Establishment: August 1920
No of Employees: 26,000 (OCP); 30,000 (OCP Group)

OFFICE DE COMMERCIALISATION ET D'EXPORTATION

45 Ave de l'Armee Royale, Casablanca
Tel: 314103
Cable: Ocexport
Telex: 21610

Senior Executives: Lahlou Abdallah (General Manager), Guessous Mohammed (Secretary General)

PRINCIPAL ACTIVITIES: Productivity planning, industrialisation and overseas trade-export fruits and vegetables, canned fish, fish oil and fish meal, wine and cotton

Branch Offices: Representations abroad: France (Paris, Marseille, Nantes, Bordeaux); Germany (Cologne, Hamburg); also in Brussels, Moscow, Montreal, London, Stockholm, Oslo

Subsidiary Companies: Soficom, Socamar, Serecaf, Sofruma, Sincomar, Panalfa, Ogden Maghreb, Imec, Socober, Slimaco, Frumat, Soplem, Ocas, Europe, Oca Scaninavia

Principal Bankers: BMCE and the other Moroccan banks

Principal Shareholders: Part of the Ministry of Commerce
Date of Establishment: July 1965
No of Employees: 2,060 (Subsidiaries not included)

OFFICE INDUSTRIEL ET AUTOMOBILE

M Bauchardon et Cie

218, Blvd Rahal El Meskini, Casablanca
Tel: 263041/42/82
Cable: Offindo
Telex: 212963 M Okab

Chairman: Abdellah Kadiri
Directors: Mohamed Ennail, Ernardo Roca, Albert Lo Bioudo

PRINCIPAL ACTIVITIES: Import and distribution of motor vehicles, heavy industrial machinery and equipment, electrical and power equipment

Subsidiary Companies: Seria, Casablanca; Semav, Casablanca; Ste Maghrebienne de Pneumatiques, Casablanca; Soprog, Casablanca; Metaluplast, Agadir; Technic Sauss, Agadir

Principal Bankers: BMCI; BMCE; BCM

OFFICE NATIONAL DE L'ELECTRICITE

65 rue Aspirant Lafuente, Casablanca
Tel: 224165, 223330
Cable: Ofelec
Telex: 22780 M, 22603 M
Telefax: 212-220038

Chairman: Ahmed Tazi (Director General)

Directors: Abdelhamid Mekki Berrada (Deputy Director General)
Senior Executives: Abdelkarim Berrada (Director Finance & Administration), Abd Er Rahmane Naji (Director of Distribution), Abd Er Rahmane Sekkaki (Director of Generation & Transmission), Mohamed Bekkali (Director of Equipment & Services), Abderrafii Berrada (Chief of Material Supply Dept)

PRINCIPAL ACTIVITIES: Generation, transmission and distribution of electricity
Principal Bankers: Banque du Maroc, Banque Nationale pour le Developpement Economique, Banque Marocaine du Commerce Exterieur, Banque Marocaine pour le Commerce et l'Industrie, Credit du Maroc, Banque Commerciale du Maroc, Societe Generale Marocaine de Banques, Banque Centrale Populaire
Financial Information:

	1989/90 MDh'000
Sales turnover	4.927.000
Profits	52.000
Authorised capital	879.000
Total assets	13.990.000

Principal Shareholders: Public company
Date of Establishment: 1963 (succeeded Energie Electrique du Maroc)
No of Employees: 9,328

OFFICE NATIONAL DES CHEMINS DE FER DU MAROC

O.N.C.F.M.

Rue Abderrahman El Ghafiki, Rabat Agdal
Tel: (212 7) 74747
Telex: 31907 M, 32711 M
Telefax: 74480

Director General: Moussa Moussaoui
Deputy Directors General: Abderrazak Benjelloun, Driss Kanouni, Abdellatif Benali, Zine El Abidine Achour, Mohamed El Aichaoui, Abraham Choukroun
Senior Executives: M'Hamed Naciri (Railways Director), Ahmed Tounsi (Buildings Director), Abdeslam El Ghissassi (Production Director), Abdallah Bouamri (Equipment Director), Ahmed Raissi (Purchasing Director), Mustapha Benmoussa (Data Processing Director)

PRINCIPAL ACTIVITIES: Railways (passenger and goods services) and hotel (chain of hotels ONCFM)

OFFICE NATIONAL DES PECHES

BP 21, 13 rue du Chevalier Bayard, Casablanca
Tel: 240551, 254964
Telex: 21708

PRINCIPAL ACTIVITIES: Fishing promotion and development
Branch Offices: El Ayoun, Agadir, Essaouir, Safi, Tangiers, Al Hoceima
Associated Companies: SOGEP, Agadir; Maropeche, Casablanca; PROMER, Casablanca; Promopeche, Casablanca; SOMAMER, Casablanca; Thonapeche; Casablanca; Codimer Asmak, Casablanca
Principal Bankers: BMCE; BCM; CDM; SGMB

Principal Shareholders: State-owned
Date of Establishment: 1969

OFFICE NATIONAL DES TRANSPORT

10 rue Annaba Chellah, Rabat
Tel: 31350, 31296
Cable: ONT
Telex: 31090

PRINCIPAL ACTIVITIES: National and International transportation, association for TIR, freight forwarding

Branch Offices: Casablanca: Ave Pasteur, Tel 249564, Telex 21691

Principal Shareholders: State-owned
No of Employees: 100

OFFICE NATIONAL DU THE ET DU SUCRE

BP 618, 137 Bd de la Gironde, Casablanca
Tel: 350873 Ain Sebaa
Telex: 21864 Ain sebaa

PRINCIPAL ACTIVITIES: Monopoly of tea import, and import of raw sugar for Moroccan refineries
Branch Offices: Ain Sebaa: Route de Tit Mellil; Casablanca; Fes
Principal Bankers: BMCE; CDM; BP

Principal Shareholders: State-owned
Date of Establishment: 1958

OFFICE NATIONAL MAROCAIN DU TOURISME (ONMT)

22 Avenue d'Alger, Rabat
Tel: 21252/3/4
Cable: TOURONMT
Telex: 31933, 32019

Chairman: Minister of Tourism
Senior Executives: El Manouar Mohamed (General Secretary)

PRINCIPAL ACTIVITIES: Promotion of tourism in Morocco
Branch Offices: Paris, Madrid, Dubai, Brussels, Dusseldorf, London, Milan, New York, Orlando, Los Angeles, Stockholm, Vienne, Lisbon, Torremolinos, Zurich, Tokyo, Sidney, Montreal, Jeddah, Las Palmas

Principal Shareholders: State-owned
Date of Establishment: 1918
No of Employees: 400

OFFICE POUR LE DEVELOPPEMENT INDUSTRIEL

Office for Industrial Development

10 Zankat Ghandi, BP 211, Rabat
Tel: 68460
Telex: 31053, 32078

Directors: Mohamed Belkhayat (Director General)
Senior Executives: Abdelhamid Belahcen (Secretary General)

PRINCIPAL ACTIVITIES: Promotion of industrial ventures
Branch Offices: Delegations in Paris, Brussels, Cologne, New York
Parent Company: Responsible to the Ministry of Commerce and Industry
Subsidiary/Associated Companies: SIMEF (Societe des Industries Mecaniques et Electriques de Fez); CIOR (Cimenterie de l'Oriental); SNEP (Societe Nationale d'Electrolyse et de Petrochimie); SONASID (Societe Nationale de Siderurgie); ICOZ (Industrie Cotonniere d'Oued Zem)
Principal Bankers: BMCE, Credit du Maroc, Tresorerie Generale

Principal Shareholders: State-owned
Date of Establishment: June 1973
No of Employees: 132

OMIUM TECHNIQUE

Ets J Barzach

32-40 Rue d'Anizy, PO Box 2197, Casablanca 05
Tel: 240183,245295
Cable: Omnitec
Telex: 25748 M

Chairman: M Benchehla
Directors: Y Hasnaoui
Senior Executives: M Maazouz

PRINCIPAL ACTIVITIES: Import and distribution of electrical and industrial machinery, hydraulic and power equipment

Principal Bankers: Compagnie Marocaine de Credit et de Banques SA; Banque Marocaine du Commerce Exterieur; BMCI

Principal Shareholders: M Benchehla; Y Hasnaoui
Date of Establishment: 1945

OMNIUM INDUSTRIEL DU MAGHREB

BP 343, 21 Rue de Sauternes, Casablanca
Tel: 245356,24836
Telex: 22691

PRINCIPAL ACTIVITIES: Sugar refinery
Branch Offices: Marrakech
Principal Bankers: BMCE; BMCI

Date of Establishment: 1915
No of Employees: 1,000

ORCOTEX

Organisme General de Controles Techniques et d'Expertises

1 rue de Toulon, Casablanca
Tel: 240530, 240205

Chairman: Mohamed Adnane

PRINCIPAL ACTIVITIES: General motor-component manufacturers, control equipment for cars, testing of lifting equipment, goods lifts, gas canisters, miscellaneous technical expertise
Branch Offices: 15 branches in Morocco
Principal Bankers: Banque Marocaine de Commerce et de l'Industrie, Casablanca

PARRENIN

145 Bvd de la Resistance, Casablanca
Tel: 40675
Cable: Paragricol
Telex: 21773

PRINCIPAL ACTIVITIES: Import and distribution of agricultural and industrial equipment and machinery
Principal Agencies: Caterpillar; Hyster; Blawknox; Bergeaud; Oshkosh
Branch Offices: Meknes; Sidi Silmane

Date of Establishment: 1932

PHOSBOUCRAA

Phosphates de Boucraa SA

Imm OCP, Angle Route d'El Jadida, et Bvd de la Grande Ceinture, Casablanca
Tel: 223628/30 Laayoune
Telex: 31727

President: Mohammed Karim Lamrani
Directors: Pardo de Santayana (Vice President), M'Hamed Nacer

PRINCIPAL ACTIVITIES: Production and processing of phosphate rock
Branch Offices: PO Box 76, Laayoune
Parent Company: OCP, Morocco; INI, Spain

Principal Shareholders: OCP, Morocco (65%); INI, Spain (35%)
Date of Establishment: 1962
No of Employees: 2,735

PIGNAL RADIO SA

29 bd Girardot, Casablanca
Tel: 304261
Cable: Piradio Casa
Telex: 21815

Chairman: E El Grichi
Directors: Jean Marie Gres (Director General), Ernest Naranjo (Commercial Director)

PRINCIPAL ACTIVITIES: Distribution and wholesale of electronic equipment and appliances, also air conditioning and household electrical equipment, hi-fi equipment and office equipment
Principal Agencies: Thomson, Sony, Pioneer, Bouyer, Centrad, Butterfly
Branch Offices: Tanger; Agadir
Principal Bankers: SMDC; Credit du Maroc; SGMB; UNIBAN; BMCE

Date of Establishment: 1947

PNEUMATIQUES RAOUL LECA SA

232 Bvd Emile Zola, Casablanca
Tel: 240644/45, 240533
Telex: 24059

President: Belemlih Abdellatif
Senior Executives: H Benmlih (Managing Director), A Hamzaoui (Sales and Administration Manager)

PRINCIPAL ACTIVITIES: Tyre retreading; sales of tyres and tubes all brands

Date of Establishment: 1945

PROMEGAL SA
Produits Metallurgiques Galvanises

Rue Abou Bakr Ibn Koutia, Oukacha, Casablanca
Tel: 240627, 245627
Telex: 22837 M

Chairman: Abid Abdelhak
Directors: Allalouche Mohamed, Mohamed Mennis, Kanematsu-Gosho Ltd, Kawasaki Steel Corp, Progress Investment SA

PRINCIPAL ACTIVITIES: Sales of galvanised iron sheets
Principal Bankers: FNCB; BCM; BMCE; BMCI

Date of Establishment: 1970

REGIE DES TABACS

51 Bvd Moulay Idriss Ier, Casablanca 03
Tel: 284109, 289714
Telex: 21090

Chairman: Abderrahim Salhi
Directors: Abderrahim Salhi (Directeur General), Mekki Bargach (Secretaire General), Ali Touima (Directeur du Personnel et des Affaires Sociales), Abdellatif Hatim (Directeur des Affaires Generales), Abdelhak Mikou (Directeur des Affaires Juridiques et du Contentieux), Driss Majdi (Inspecteur General)

PRINCIPAL ACTIVITIES: State Monopoly of tobacco, including tobacco farming and manufacture, import and export of tobacco products and ancillary industries
Branch Offices: 26 branches throughout Morocco
Principal Bankers: SMDC; BMCE; BMAO; BMCI; SGMB; Banque Populaire
Financial Information:

	1989/90 MDh'000
Sales turnover	4.066.000

Principal Shareholders: Moroccan state
Date of Establishment: 1967
No of Employees: 2,747

RENAULT MAROC

Place de Bauldoeng, BP 700 Casablanca
Tel: 270591, 224191
Telex: 21667

PRINCIPAL ACTIVITIES: Wholesale motor vehicles, auto spare parts for Renault agents
Principal Bankers: BCM; BMCI, CDM

Principal Shareholders: Regie Nationale des Usines Renault, France
No of Employees: 400

ROYAL AIR INTER
Compagnie Nationale des Lignes Interieures

Aeroport d'Anfa, Casablanca
Tel: 361251
Telex: 22058 Interair

Chairman: Mohamed Mekouar
Directors: Said Ben Ali Yaala (General Manager)
Senior Executives: Mostafa Melhaoui (Head of Financial Dept)

PRINCIPAL ACTIVITIES: Air transport, domestic flights
Associated Companies: Royal Air Maroc

Principal Shareholders: Royal Air Maroc (42.5%), Caisse de Depot et de Gestion, Office National Marocain du Tourisme, Office National des Chemins de Fer, Moroccan Government (50%)
Date of Establishment: April 1970

ROYAL AIR MAROC
Compagnie Nationales de Transports Aeriens

Aeroport d'Anfa, Casablanca
Tel: 364184
Telex: 21880 Marocair

Chairman: Mohamed Mekouar
Directors: Said Ben Ali Yaala (General Manager)
Senior Executives: Mostafa Mehlaoui (Head of Financial Dept)

PRINCIPAL ACTIVITIES: Air transport, international services
Branch Offices: Casablanca, Paris, New York, Montreal, Tunis, Tripoli, Cairo, Jeddah, Riyadh, Abu Dhabi, Kuwait, Rio de Janeiro, Abidjan, Geneva, Frankfurt, Brussels, London, Amsterdam, Rome, Madrid, Athens, etc
Subsidiary Companies: Royal Air Inter
Principal Bankers: Banque Marocaine du Commerce Exterieur; Banque Marocaine pour le Commerce et l'Industrie

Principal Shareholders: Moroccan Government
Date of Establishment: June 1957
No of Employees: 4,550

ROYALE MAROCAINE D'ASSURANCES

67/69 Ave de l'Armee Royale, Casablanca
Tel: 224163
Cable: Tamalino
Telex: 21818

PRINCIPAL ACTIVITIES: Insurance and reinsurance
Associated Companies: Societe Marocaine d'Assurances
Principal Bankers: All Moroccan banks

Date of Establishment: 1949

SABA & CO

Residence Zerktouni, 185 Bvd Zerktouni, BP 13921, Casablanca
Tel: 251530
Cable: Sabaco Casablanca
Telex: 21622 M
Telefax: 251603

Chairman: Suhail F Saba
Directors: Joseph Sanbar, George Ghali
Senior Executives: Joseph M Sanbar (Partner), Driss A El Hajjaji (Manager)

PRINCIPAL ACTIVITIES: Public accountants and management consultants, industrial property
Branch Offices: Lebanon; Cyprus; Bahrain; Egypt; Iraq; Jordan; Kuwait; Libya; Morocco; Oman; Qatar; Saudi Arabia; Syria; United Arab Emirates; Yemen
Parent Company: Saba & Co, Beirut
Associated Companies: Member firm in Touche Ross International

Principal Bankers: Arab Bank (Maroc); FNCB Maghreb; Banque Centrale Populaire

Date of Establishment: 1926; in Morocco 1962

SACEM
Ste Anonyme Cherifienne d'Etudes Minieres

BP 13241, 5 Ave de l'Armee Royale, Casablanca
Tel: 274411, 272471
Telex: 21740

Chairman: Jean Yves Eichenberger
Directors: Abdou El Kettani, Hassan Seqqat, Ahmed Louali, Ali Bennani, Othmane Khettouch, Moulay Hafid El Alaoui, Hadj Ahmed Bargach, Bureau de Recherches et de Participations Minieres, Comilog, Minemet Holding
Senior Executives: Abdou El Kettani (Director General)

PRINCIPAL ACTIVITIES: Mining and quarrying of manganese ore
Parent Company: Ste Imetal, Bureau de Recherches et de Participations Minieres; Comilog; Minemet Holding
Subsidiary Companies: Ste Nouvelle de Realisations Industrielles et Commerciales (SO.NO.RIC)
Principal Bankers: BMCI, Wafabank, BMCE, Credit du Maroc
Financial Information:

	1988/89 MDh'million
Sales turnover	68,5
Profits	2,7
Authorised capital	24
Paid-up capital	24
Total assets	84,5

Principal Shareholders: Bureau de Recherches et de Participations Minieres, Omnium Nord Africain, Comilog, Minemet Holding
Date of Establishment: 1929
No of Employees: 500

SAFIR
Ste Marocaine de Gestion Hoteliere

46 Av des FAR, Casablanca 01
Tel: 312211
Cable: SAFIR
Telex: 22892
Telefax: 311937

Chairman: Dr Zine Abidine Alaoui
Directors: Ahmad K Al Ibrahim (Vice President), Jaafar Alaoui (Finance Director, Abdessamad Masmoudi (Operations Director), Mehdi Ahmed (Personnel Director), Abdelghani Lahbari (Technical Director), Mohamed Zerouali (Sales & Marketing Director)

PRINCIPAL ACTIVITIES: Hotels management and travel business
Principal Agencies: Safir Voyages 39, rue de Foucauld, Casablanca
Branch Offices: Hotel Malabata, Tangiers; Hotel Siaha, Marrakech; Hotel Safir, Tetouan; Hotel Safir, Casablanca; Hotel Safir Kenitra; Hotel Safir Marrakech; Hotel Safir Khouribga; Hotel Safir Rabat; Hotel Safir Safi; Hotel Europa Safir Agadir; Hotel Safir Marrakech
Parent Company: KREIC (Kuwait)
Associated Companies: Moroccan Kuwaiti Development Consortium
Principal Bankers: BMCE; BMCI; CDM; Wafa Bank
Financial Information:

	1990 MDh'000
Paid-up capital	5.000

Principal Shareholders: Moroccan Kuwaiti Development Consortium (50%); Farah Maghreb (50%)
Date of Establishment: 1973
No of Employees: 2,000

SAIDA SA

269 Bvd Rahal El Meskini, Casablanca
Tel: 224161, 254428
Telex: 21850

Senior Executives: Omar Benjelloun (General Manager)

PRINCIPAL ACTIVITIES: Vehicle assembly, manufacture of trucks, motor vehicles and spare parts, aircraft parts; manufacturers' representative
Principal Agencies: Volvo, Mercedes, GM Trucks

Date of Establishment: 1960
No of Employees: 400

SAME

34 Bvd Mohammed V, BP 5156, Casablanca
Tel: 251771
Telex: 21684

PRINCIPAL ACTIVITIES: Import and distribution of heavy machinery and equipment

SAMINE
Ste Anonyme D'Entreprises Minieres

BP 657, 52 Ave Hassan 11, Casablanca
Tel: 224102
Cable: Omnafric
Telex: 21859

Chairman: Daniel Amar (ONA - AD)
Directors: Mourad Cherif
Senior Executives: Abdelaziz Abarro

PRINCIPAL ACTIVITIES: Mining of fluorine
Branch Offices: Mine at El Hammam
Principal Bankers: SMDC; BMCE; BP; SGMB; BCM; BMCI; CDM;
Financial Information:

	MDh'000
Authorised capital	26.000
Paid-up capital	26.000

Principal Shareholders: ONA; BRPM
Date of Establishment: 1961
No of Employees: 238

SAMIR

Route Cotiere de Casablance, BP 89, Mohammedia

PRINCIPAL ACTIVITIES: Oil refining

Principal Shareholders: State-owned

SAMPAC
Ste Anonyme Marocaine des Peintures Astral Celluco
Akzo Coatings SA

64 Bld Moulay Slimane, 21700 Casablanca
Tel: 354504
Telex: 28093 M
Telefax: 354443

Directors: Michel Laugier

PRINCIPAL ACTIVITIES: Manufacture of paints, varnish, and paint supplies
Branch Offices: Factory: 64 bd Moulay Slimane, Casablanca, Tel 354504, Telex 46191
Parent Company: Akzo Coatings SA, Saint-Denis, France
Principal Bankers: BMCE; SMDC; BCM; BMCI; SGMB; CDM; SBC

Financial Information:

	1988/89 MDh'000	1989/90 MDh'000
Sales turnover	290.000	310.000
Paid-up capital	46.502	46.502
Total assets	180.000	220.000

Principal Shareholders: Akzo Coatings SA (France) and Moroccan interests
Date of Establishment: 1922
No of Employees: 310

SAPRAF

Allee des Citronniers, Ain Sebaa, Casablanca
Tel: 350801, 351223

PRINCIPAL ACTIVITIES: Import and distribution of spirits and alcoholic drinks
Principal Agencies: Martini, St Raphael, Manor, Pastis Duval, champagne Laurent Perrier, champagne Ch de Cazanove, cognac Gaston de Lagange, cognac Hennessy, brandy Grand Trianon, gin Booth's, rhum Dakita, whisky William Lawson's, whisky White Label, whisky Ancestor, vodka Eristow, etc

SCTGF
Ste de Consignation Transports Generaux et Frigorifiques

238 Bvd Mohammed V, Casablanca
Tel: 300411/6
Cable: Gondrand Casa
Telex: 23973 M; 21034 M

President: Sebti Hadj Taieb
Directors: Sebti Othman (Managering Director), Sbihi Abdelghafour (General Manager), Knoerr Marcel (Administration Manager)

PRINCIPAL ACTIVITIES: Forwarders, international transporters (TIR), ship agencies all Moroccan ports, cargo supervisors, warehouses, custom brokers, road-air-sea transports
Principal Agencies: Gondrand, Griffith, Beckmann & Jorgensen, J H Wiggins, Knudsen Renou, Trans Bulk
Associated Companies: Etrama warehouses
Principal Bankers: BCM; BMCI; CMCB; BMCE

Principal Shareholders: Cotrafi, Mrs Sebti Hadj Taieb, Jaafar, Othman
Date of Establishment: 1940

SELS DE MOHAMMEDIA

30 rue Abou Faris, Al Morini, Rabat
Tel: (07) 66134, 66462
Telex: 23886
Telefax: 66462

Chairman: A Lhatoute
Directors: E Hilali (Managing Director)
Senior Executives: Omar Zaid (Finance Manager), Abdelwahab Tlemsani (Sales Manager), Tahar Saqalli (Production Manager)

PRINCIPAL ACTIVITIES: Salt mining
Parent Company: BRPM
Financial Information:

	1990 MDh'000
Sales turnover	13.229
Authorised capital	18.600
Net assets	45.300

Principal Shareholders: BRPM, Rabat
Date of Establishment: 1974
No of Employees: 60

SIMEF
Ste des Industries Mecaniques et Electriques de Fes

BP 41/A, Km 10 route d'aih Chkef, Fes
Tel: 41643, 41916
Cable: SIMEFES
Telex: 51962 M

Chairman: Minister of Industry
Directors: M Belkhayat, A Belahsen

PRINCIPAL ACTIVITIES: Mechanical and electrical engineering, production of heavy machinery and equipment and power equipment
Subsidiary Companies: SIMEF-LS
Principal Bankers: BMCE; BMCI; SBC; UMB; BP

Principal Shareholders: Office for Industrial Development, Rabat
Date of Establishment: 1974
No of Employees: 500

SOCIETE DE BANQUE ET DE CREDIT S.B.C.

26 Ave de l'Armee Royale, BP 13972, Casablanca
Tel: 310330, 314565, 263951/54
Cable: Sobac
Telex: 21848 Sobac

PRINCIPAL ACTIVITIES: Commercial banking
Branch Offices: Casablanca; Rabat; Meknes; Fes; Agadir; Marrakech; Beni Mellal

Principal Shareholders: Saada Insurance Co, Societe des Banques Suisses, Groupe Zellidja, Credit Commercial de France
Date of Establishment: 1951
No of Employees: 143

SOCOPIM

1 Rue d'Audenge, BP 47, Casablanca
Tel: 240894
Cable: Socopimar
Telex: 22978

PRINCIPAL ACTIVITIES: Import and distribution of agricultural, industrial, and construction machinery and equipment
Principal Bankers: CDM; CMCB

Date of Establishment: 1948

SOMADIR SA

Bvd Ouk'at Badi, Casablanca
Tel: 246897, 246479
Telex: 23651

PRINCIPAL ACTIVITIES: Manufacture and production of bread, yeast, polyurethane foam, glycerine
Principal Agencies: Germa; Moltopren
Principal Bankers: SGMB; CDM

Date of Establishment: 1938
No of Employees: 150

SOMAKOHOTEL
Moroccan Kuwaiti Hotels & Investment Co

187 Ave Lalla Yacout, Casablanca
Tel: 223350, 276139
Telex: 23695

PRINCIPAL ACTIVITIES: Promotion of tourist complexes, real estate investment, and hotels

Date of Establishment: 1973

STANDARD AUTO ACCESSOIRES

149 Rue Mohamed Smiha, Casablanca
Tel: 278623

Directors: M Hugues (Managing Director), M Boulet (Commercial Director)

PRINCIPAL ACTIVITIES: Import and distribution of auto spare parts and accessories
Principal Agencies: Lucas, Simms, CAV, Girling, Crosland

STE AFEMAR

Immeuble Helvetia, 1 Place Zallaga, Casablanca
Tel: 309906
Cable: Afemar Casablanca
Telex: 27818

Chairman: Jamil Bouhlal
Directors: J P Lechartier (Director General)

PRINCIPAL ACTIVITIES: Marine surveys, marine investments and consultants, underwater surveys - Harbour for Yacht consultant
Principal Agencies: American Bureau of Shipping; Det Norske Veritas; Nippon Kaiji Kyokai; United State Salvage Association
Principal Bankers: Societe Generale Marocaine de Banques

Principal Shareholders: J Bouhlal; J P Lechartier
Date of Establishment: 1974

STE AUTO-HALL

44/46 Ave Lalla Yacoute, Casablanca
Tel: 317044, 317052, 319056
Cable: Autohall
Telex: 21639
Telefax: 318915

President: Mohamed Karim Lamrani
Directors: Bouchaib Najioullah (Director General), Mohamed Larhouati (Commercial Director), Mohamed Karmaoui (Commercial Director), Brahim Ait Haddou (Technical Manager)

PRINCIPAL ACTIVITIES: Import and wholesale of agricultural, automobile and industrial equipment
Principal Agencies: Fiat; Ford; Ransomes; Champion; Ferodo; Cumins; Lorain; Richier; Winget; Sykes; Liebherr; Koehring; Steelfab; Welger; Ford New Holland; Gaspardo; Otma; Piva; Campeon; Itur; Pleuger; Allweiler; Mitsubishi; Dresser; Iseki; Fullspray; Maschio; Noder Gougis
Branch Offices: Rabat; Marrakech; Agadir; Kenitra; Meknes; Fes; Safi; El Jadida; Settat; Beni Mellal
Subsidiary Companies: Societe Nouvelle du Garage Universel, Tangiers
Principal Bankers: Credit du Maroc; SGMB; BMCI; BCM; CMCB; BMCE; SMDG

Date of Establishment: 1920
No of Employees: 537

STE CASABLANCAISE DE BOISSONS GAZEUSES
SOCABOGA

Routes des Oulad Ziane, angle rue d'Infi, Casablanca

PRINCIPAL ACTIVITIES: Production and distribution of soft beverages
Principal Bankers: BMCI

Date of Establishment: 1975
No of Employees: 400

STE CENTRALE DE REASSURANCE

Tour-Atlas, Place Zallaqa, PO Box 13.183, Casablanca
Tel: 308585, 309111, 304935
Cable: Centreas
Telex: 28084 Centreas
Telefax: 308672

Chairman: Farouk Bennis
Directors: Mohamed El Mehdi Boughaleb, Lahoucine El Bari, Ahmed Karim Bennani, Ahmed Es Saghir, Abdelaziz

Bensouda Korachi, Mohamed Sbiti, Ahmed Tazi, Abdelhamid Dassouli, Caisse de Depot et de Gestion Al Amane
Senior Executives: Yahia Filali (General Manager), Hassan Ouazzani Chahdi (Government Representative)

PRINCIPAL ACTIVITIES: All reinsurance transactions
Parent Company: Caisse de Depot & de Gestion Al Amane
Principal Bankers: BMCI, SGMB, Wafabank, BMAO, SMDC, BMCE, Midland Bank, Bank Al Maghrib, CCP, BMCE (Paris)
Financial Information:

	1989/90 MDh'000
Profits	861
Authorised capital	30.000
Paid-up capital	30.000
Total assets	1.945.739

Principal Shareholders: Caisse de Depot et de Gestion (Rabat) (94%); Mutuelle Electrique d'Assurances (Paris)
Date of Establishment: 1960
No of Employees: 193

STE CHERIFIENNE DE DISTRIBUTION ET DE PRESSE
SOCHEPRESS

Angle Rues Dinant/Saint Saens, Casablanca 05
Tel: 245745
Cable: Sochepress
Telex: 25786 Sochpres; 26660 Sochlivr; 25882 Sochedir; 25636 Sochpres

Chairman: Abdallah Lahrizi
Senior Executives: Mostafa Dnini (Press Manager), Mohamed Gounajjar (Books Manager), Miss Zhor Alaoui Belghiti (Financial Manager)

PRINCIPAL ACTIVITIES: Printing, publishing and distribution of books, post cards and newspapers throughout the country
Principal Agencies: Hachette, Delagrave (Paris), NMPP, MLP, etc
Branch Offices: Rabat: 8 Place Alaouite; Kenitra: Rue Moulay Abdallah; Meknes: 1 Avenue Ibnou Sina; Fes: 22 Avenue Hassan II No 9; Agadir: Imm Mauritania, Bd Mohammed V; Oujda: Rue Sijilmassa; Marrakech: Ave Med Zerktouni; Safi: 215 Route Sidi Ouassel; Casablanca A et B: 7 Rue Abou Ghaleb Achyani; Casablanca C: 16 Rue Saint Saëns
Subsidiary/Associated Companies: 'SOTADEC', 17-19 Rue Caid Riffi, Tangiers; Al Maghribiya Assaudia Littibaa, Casablanca; Radio Mediterranee Internationale, 3 Rue Emsallah, Tanger
Principal Bankers: SGMB; BMCE; Credit Du Maroc; SMDC; BMCI
Financial Information:

	MDh'000
Sales turnover	134.000
Authorised capital	4.800
Paid-up capital	4.800

Principal Shareholders: Government of Morocco; Nouvelles Messageries de la Presse Parisienne (France)
Date of Establishment: 1949
No of Employees: 325

STE CHERIFIENNE DE MATERIEL INDUSTRIEL ET FERROVIAIRE
S.C.I.F.

BP Box 2604, Allee des Cactus, Ain Sebaa, Casablanca
Tel: 353911, 351093, 353164
Telex: 26802

Chairman: Moussa Moussaoui
Directors: Mohammed Ouriaghli (Managing Director)
Senior Executives: M Arref (Finance), M Moucelin (Business), M Ghazani (Production)

PRINCIPAL ACTIVITIES: Production of industrial and
construction equipment and machinery, boiler works; gas
cylinders; waggons and railway cars
Principal Bankers: BMCI; BMCE; BCM; Credit du Maroc;
SGMB; SMDC
Financial Information:

	MDh'000
Sales turnover	95.500
Authorised capital	15.093
Paid-up capital	15.093

Principal Shareholders: Ets Fauvet Girel SA, Paris, France;
ONCF, Rabat, Morocco; BNDE, Rabat, Morocco; SCP, Rabat,
Morocco
Date of Establishment: 1946
No of Employees: 600

STE CHERIFIENNE DE PETROLES (SCP)

PO Box 79, 5-7 Charia Moulay Hassan, Rabat
Tel: 63075, 63128
Cable: Chetrol Rabat
Telex: 31084, 31946
Telefax: 63711

President: Larbi Chraibi
Directors: Mohamed Benabderrazik (Administrateur Delegue)
Senior Executives: S Alami (Technical Director), Anas Tazi
(Financial Director), Said Bouazzaoui (Social & Administrative
Director), Bachir Quemane (Budget Control), Abderrazak
Alami Souni (Director, Industrial Activities), Ahmed Mansouri
(Refining Director), Abdelali Lamhandez (Director Bottling
Plant)

PRINCIPAL ACTIVITIES: Refining of petrol and bottling of gas.
Production capacity: 1,200,000 tons per year
Principal Agencies: Office National de Recherches et
d'Exploitations Petrolieres (ONAREP); Societe Nationale Elf
Aquitaine (SNEA)
Branch Offices: Refinery at Sidi Kacem
Subsidiary Companies: Guigues Maroc; Somas; SCIF
Principal Bankers: BMCE; CDM; BCM; UMB; SBC; BCP;
SGMB; SMDC; BMCI; BMAO; Citibank; Arab Bank; Unibank;
Algemene Bank
Financial Information:

	1988/89 MDh'000
Sales turnover	3.433.300
Profits	27.442
Authorised capital	175.435
Paid-up capital	175.435

Principal Shareholders: ONAREP; SNEA
Date of Establishment: 1929
No of Employees: 895

STE CHERIFIENNE D'ENGRAIS ET DE PRODUITS CHIMIQUES

Km 6500 Route de Zenatas, BP 281, Casablanca
Tel: 246183, 243152
Cable: Engraimaroc
Telex: 25880

Directors: Driss Kandil (Commercial Director)

PRINCIPAL ACTIVITIES: Manufacture of chemical and fertilizer
products
Principal Agencies: Ugine Kuhlman; Francolor; CDF Chimie;
Vieille Montagne; Cabot; etc
Branch Offices: Sales Office: 204 Bd Emile Zola, Casablanca;
Kenitra; Fes; Berkane
Principal Bankers: CDM; SMDC; CMCB; BMCE; BMCI; BCM;
SBC

Date of Establishment: 1946

STE COMMERCIALE DE FRUITS ET LEGUMES DU MAROC

BP 2579, Ain Sebaa, Casablanca
Tel: 351611, 351772
Telex: 22883

PRINCIPAL ACTIVITIES: Cold storage and warehousing of fruit
and vegetables
Branch Offices: Agadir, Casablanca, Nouasseur
Principal Bankers: BMCE

Principal Shareholders: OCE (Maroc)
Date of Establishment: 1972
No of Employees: 200

STE DE FABRICATION RADIO-ELECTRONIQUES MAROCAINES

S.F.R.M.

59 Allee des Orangers, Ain Sebaa, Casablanca
Tel: 350833
Telex: 21924

Chairman: M de Riberolles
Directors: M Prince

PRINCIPAL ACTIVITIES: Manufacture of electrical and
electronic equipment
Principal Agencies: Thomson CSF
Associated Companies: Societe Commerciale Radio-Electrique
Marocaine (SCRM), 29 bd Girardot, Casablanca, Tel 276911,
Telex 21815 Piradi

Date of Establishment: 1952
No of Employees: 850

STE DE FINANCEMENT D'ACHATS-A-CREDIT

161 Avenue Hassan II, Casablanca
Tel: 277081
Telex: 22741, 21010

Directors: Ahmed Boufaim (Director General)
Senior Executives: Abdeljalil Agourram (Vice Director General)

PRINCIPAL ACTIVITIES: Consumer credit and financing
services
Branch Offices: Casablanca; Rabat; Marrakech; Fes; Agadir;
Meknes; Tangiers
Principal Bankers: All the Moroccan banks
Financial Information:

	1989/90 MDh'000
Sales turnover	334.000
Profits	37.000
Authorised capital	50.000
Paid-up capital	50.000
Total assets	399.000

Principal Shareholders: Caisse de Depot et de Gestion, Rabat,
Morocco
Date of Establishment: 1963
No of Employees: 110

STE DE PRODUCTION ET DE DISTRIBUTION DE MATERIEL ET D'EQUIPEMENT

SODIPI

242-246 Blvd Emile Zola, Casablanca
Tel: 243372/76
Cable: Sodipi Casa
Telex: 22614 M
Telefax: 243372

Chairman: Mohamed Marrakchi
Directors: Yves de Langre (General Manager)
Senior Executives: Mohamed Rachid Cadi (Finance Manager),
Claude Schageme (Commercial Manager), Ahmed Lahlou
(Commercial Manager), Hamed Zaki (Personnel Manager),
Mustapha Tala (Technical Manager)

PRINCIPAL ACTIVITIES: Manufacture of foam products, mattresses, furniture and products, also manufacture of gas ovens and appliances, butane, distributors of rubber for industries, tyres
Principal Agencies: Societe Application des Gas (Camping Gaz International), Pirelli
Principal Bankers: BMCE; BMCI; BCM; CMCB
Financial Information:

	1988/89 MDh'000	1989/90 MDh'000
Sales turnover	330.628	330.049
Profits	8.240	6.121
Authorised capital	25.000	25.000
Total assets	128.404	126.288

Date of Establishment: 1948
No of Employees: 498

STE DES CIMENTS ARTIFICIELS DE MEKNES SA

PO Box 33, Route de Fes Km 8, Meknes
Tel: 226-44
Telex: 41010, 41936

Senior Executives: Abbes Mandre (General Manager)

PRINCIPAL ACTIVITIES: Manufacture of cement
Principal Bankers: All Banks at Meknes

Principal Shareholders: Societe Nationale d'Investissements (SNI); Lafarge Coppe (France)
Date of Establishment: 1951
No of Employees: 309

STE DES CIMENTS D'AGADIR

BP 312, Km 7 Route d'Essaouira, Agadir
Tel: 22925, 23858, 21474
Cable: CIMAG
Telex: 81877, 82672
Telefax: (212-8) 23598

Chairman: Mustapha Faris
Directors: Philippe Ronsin, Mohamed Bargach, Bernard Laplace, Raymond M Doumenc, Dr Mohamed Benhima, BNDE, CNIA, Ciment Francais, SNI, CIMR
Senior Executives: Philippe Ronsin (Adminstrateur Delegue), Mohamed Chaibi (Managing Director)

PRINCIPAL ACTIVITIES: Production of cement (Sales: 560,000 tons of cement; production capacity: 1,000,000 tons of cement)
Branch Offices: Agadir
Parent Company: Ste des Ciments Francais
Subsidiary Companies: Ste des Ciments de Laayoune
Principal Bankers: SGMB, BMCI, SMDC, CDM, BMCE, Wafabank
Financial Information:

	MDh'000
Authorised capital	89.700
Paid-up capital	89.700

Principal Shareholders: Societe des Ciments Francais; CIMR; Banque Nationale pour le Developpement Economique; Compagnie Nord-Africaine et Intercontinentale d'Assurances; SNI
Date of Establishment: June 1951
No of Employees: 500

STE DES CIMENTS DE MARRAKECH

ASMAR

BP 550, Marrakech
Tel: 34263, 33311
Telex: 72078, 72025

Chairman: M Haj Omar Boucetta
Directors: M Allal Akouri

PRINCIPAL ACTIVITIES: Manufacture of cement
Principal Bankers: BMCE; BCM; BMCI; CMCB; SGMB; BP

Principal Shareholders: SNI, Abu Dhabi Fund, CIMR, SFI, Lafarge-Maroc, Cadem, BNDE
Date of Establishment: 1972
No of Employees: 275

STE D'EXPLOITATION DES BITUMES ET LUBRIFIANTS IRANO-MAROCAINE

SEBLIMA

PO Box 86, Mohammedia
Tel: 2892, 2893
Telex: 21882; 22998

President: Minister of Energy
Directors: Abdeslam Tajeddine (Director General), Benkirame Ghazi (Commercial Manager)

PRINCIPAL ACTIVITIES: Production of pure and oxidised bituminous products
Parent Company: Samir

Principal Shareholders: Samir (100%)
Date of Establishment: 1967
No of Employees: 83

STE D'EXPLOITATION DES MINES DU RIF

PO Box 14, Seferif, Nador
Tel: 4916, 4135
Telex: 61004

Chairman: M Chahid (Director General BRPM)
Directors: El Maghraoui Lahbib (Director General)

PRINCIPAL ACTIVITIES: Mining of iron ore and production of iron pellets, fines and lumps

Principal Shareholders: The mine was nationalised in 1967
No of Employees: 1,070

STE INDUSTRIELLE DE CONFECTION MAROCAINE

S.C.I.M.

122 Rue du Chevalier Bayard, Casablanca
Tel: 2469/33
Cable: Scimcasa
Telex: 22917

Chairman: Sekkat Larbi
Directors: Jacques Toledano, Pierre Lespagnol
Senior Executives: Habib Hazan (Commercial Director), Jean Robert Lamouliatte (Technical Director), Armand Cohen (Financial Director)

PRINCIPAL ACTIVITIES: Production of textiles, clothing and ready-made garments
Principal Bankers: SGMB; BCM; BMCE; BMCI

STE INDUSTRIELLE DE GRAINES OLEAGIEUSES DU GHARB

SIGO-GHARB

Quartier Industriel, PO Box 168, Kenitra
Tel: 2738, 5955, 5803
Cable: Sigrab
Telex: 91020

Chairman: Oulahna Idrissi Moulay Said
Directors: Naciri Bennani Abdelhaq (Director General)

PRINCIPAL ACTIVITIES: Production of vegetable oil and various agricultural produce
Subsidiary Companies: Societe Commerciale & Industrielle d'Aliment de betail; Societe Industrielle de Soubrerie de Ghout; Societe Kenitrienne de Trituration d'Olives; Entreprise

de Transport et de Manutention de Kenitra; Societe d'Industrie et de Commerce d'Outillage et de; Quincallerie
Principal Bankers: Banque Populaire; CMCB; BMCE

Principal Shareholders: Chairman as described

STE INDUSTRIELLE MAROCAINE (SIM)
BP 2070, 198 Bd Ibn Tachfine, Casablanca
Tel: 241915
Telex: 26967

Chairman: Abderrahman Bennani-Smires
Directors: Michel Macherey
Senior Executives: Moncef Djaidi (Financial Director)

PRINCIPAL ACTIVITIES: Production of soft beverages
Principal Agencies: Pepsi Cola; Seven Up; Orange Crush; Schweppes; Sim
Branch Offices: Fes; Marrakech
Subsidiary Companies: Seven Up Bottling Co, Tangiers
Principal Bankers: BMCE; BMCI; SGMB; BCM

Principal Shareholders: A Bennani-Smires
Date of Establishment: 1913
No of Employees: 700

STE INTER-AFRICAINE DE REPRESENTATIONS AUTOMOBILES
S.I.A.R.A.
133 Rue Mohamed Smiha, Casablanca
Tel: 272966, 261891/93, 302966, 301891/93

President: Hadj Beliout Bouchentouf
Directors: Filal Driss (Managing Director)

PRINCIPAL ACTIVITIES: Import and distribution of automobiles
Principal Agencies: Talbot

STE MAGHREBIENNE DE GENIE CIVIL
SOMAGEC
Angle Rues Corbi et Mesfioui, Casablanca 05
Tel: 248945, 246779, 246787, 246881
Telex: 25634, 25628
Telefax: 246881

Chairman: Rizkallah Riad Sahyoun
Directors: Roger Sahyoun, J F Catala

PRINCIPAL ACTIVITIES: Civil engineering contractors
Branch Offices: Marrakech
Parent Company: Cosima (Constructions Speciales pour l'Irrigation au Maroc)
Subsidiary Companies: SAERS (Societe des Anciens Ets Riad Sahyoun)
Principal Bankers: BCM; BMCE
Financial Information:

	MDh'000
Sales turnover	169.000
Authorised capital	15.750
Paid-up capital	15.750

Principal Shareholders: Riad Sahyoun, SAERS SA, Moulay Ismail Ben Hassan Alaoui
Date of Establishment: 1966
No of Employees: 2,050

STE MAGHREBINE DES BOIS DE L'ATLAS
300 route d'Agourai, Meknes
Tel: 30040
Cable: Boatlas
Telex: 41994

PRINCIPAL ACTIVITIES: Manufacture of timber and timber products
Principal Bankers: SGMB

Date of Establishment: 1972
No of Employees: 250

STE MAROCAINE AIGLEMER
38 Rue des Acacias, BP 5276, Casablanca
Tel: 258402/06
Cable: Aiglemer Casa
Telex: 22808 M
Telefax: 254291

Chairman: Abderrahim Zniber (President Delegue)
Directors: Mohamed Mellouki (Director General)

PRINCIPAL ACTIVITIES: Paper processing and production and wholesale of stationery and office supplies
Principal Agencies: Parker; Limpidol; Stypen; Caran d'Ache; Skreba; Mallat; Rapid; Pelikan; Arda; Reacto; Aussedat Rey; Finnpap; CTS
Parent Company: Buro Metal; Maroc Bureau
Principal Bankers: BMCE; SGMB; BCM; BCP; BMCI
Financial Information:

	1989 MDh'000
Authorised capital	10.000

Date of Establishment: 1966
No of Employees: 185

STE MAROCAINE DE CONSTRUCTIONS AUTOMOBILES
SOMACA
Km 12 Autoroute de Rabat, PO Box 2628, Casablanca
Tel: 353924, 350485
Cable: Somaca Casablanca
Telex: 21825 Ain Sebaa

President: Mehdi Benbouchta
Directors: Mohamed A Belarbi (Director General)
Senior Executives: Tahiri Driss (Administrative and Financial Director), Ajana Abdellatif (Technical Director)

PRINCIPAL ACTIVITIES: Assembly of motor vehicles
Principal Agencies: Fiat, Talbot, Simca
Subsidiary/Associated Companies: Maghreb Elastoplast; Siara; Sofac; Labefec; Locoto
Principal Bankers: BMCE; CMCB; SMDC; SGMB; CM; BMCI; BCM

Principal Shareholders: Government of Morocco, Fiat, Simca, SNI
Date of Establishment: July 1959
No of Employees: 1,175

STE MAROCAINE DE DEPOT ET CREDIT
S.M.D.C.
BP 13296, 79 Avenue Hassan II, Casablanca
Tel: 224114, 278059, 271041, 279090
Cable: Marodire
Telex: 21013, 24624
Telefax: 271590, 272815

Chairman: Abdel-Kader Ben Salah
Directors: Hubert de Saint Amand (Deputy Chairman), Jean Micheel Bloch Laine (Deputy Chairman), Thami Ammar, Mohamed Bargach, Moulay El Amine Al Alaoui, Ahmed Laski, Andre Azoulay, Mohamed Banhima, Loic de Fouchier, HE Moulay Cherif d'Ouezzane, Said Najim, Joel Retiere Lehideux, Omar Akalay, Marc Vuillermet, Michel Pariat
Senior Executives: Omar Akalay (General Manager), Robert Castel (Asst General Manager), Joseph Glaser (Asst General Manager), Brahim El Amiri (International Division Manager), Tahar Daoudi (Operations Manager)

PRINCIPAL ACTIVITIES: Commercial, merchant and investment banking
Branch Offices: Foreign Dept: 81 rue Colbert, Casablanca, Tel 224143, 220895, Telex 21800, Fax 267838; and 18 branches in Morocco, Rabat (2), Casablanca (9), Agadir, Bouznika, Nador, Fes, Sale, Rommani, Tanger; Representative Offive in Liechenstein

Principal Bankers: Banque Paribas, Banque Worms, Midland Bank, Philadelphia International Bank, Irving Trust Co

Principal Shareholders: Banque Paribas (26%), Banque Worms (24%), Moroccan Privates (50%)
Date of Establishment: June 1974
No of Employees: 420

STE MAROCAINE DE DEVELOPPEMENTS INDUSTRIELS & AGRICOLES

SMADIA

60 Bvd Yacoub El Mansour, Maarif, Casablanca
Tel: 251611, 251612, 251651
Telex: 22856 M

Directors: Omar Slaoui (Managing Director)
Senior Executives: Nadia Ibn Mansour (Administrative Director), Brahim Slaoui (Sales Manager), Omar Slaoui (Managing Director)

PRINCIPAL ACTIVITIES: Manufacture of diesel engines, Smadia pumps
Principal Agencies: R A Lister & Co Ltd; Lister Power Plant; Lister Marine; Bombas Ideal; Briggs-Stratton; International Pump Technology
Principal Bankers: BMCE; BCM
Financial Information:

	US$'000
Sales turnover	6,000
Authorised capital	1,000
Paid-up capital	1,000

Principal Shareholders: A Slaoui
Date of Establishment: 1930
No of Employees: 120

STE MAROCAINE DE L'INDUSTRIE DE RAFFINAGE SA

SAMIR

Route Cotiere, BP 89, Mohammedia
Tel: 4201, 2501, 7480, 7484
Cable: Samir Mohamedia
Telex: 22998, 21882, 23781
Telefax: 322954 (Commercial), 327489 (Secretariat), 327488 (General)

Chairman: Driss Alaoui M'Daghri (Ministry of Energy & Mines)
Directors: Abderrafie Menjour (General Manager), Abderrahman Benabderrazik (Secretary General)
Senior Executives: Rachid Bennouna (Financial Manager), Abdellatif Joudali (Industrial Manager), Driss Mansouri (Administrative Manager), Said Zebdi (Commercial Manager)

PRINCIPAL ACTIVITIES: Petroleum refinery; production of refined petroleum products, lubricating oils, bitumous products, paraffin wax
Subsidiary/Associated Companies: Societe Nationale de l'Electrolyse et de la Petrochimie (SNEP); Lubrifiant National (LUBNA); Societe Nationale d'Assurance (SANAD), Conseil de Placement d'Assurance (CPA), Hotel Samir
Principal Bankers: BMCE; BMCI; Citibank; Banque Populaire; Credit du Maroc; SGMB
Financial Information:

	1988/89 MDh'000	1989/90 MDh'000
Sales turnover	9.448.416	10.233.557
Profits	82.470	119.227
Authorised capital	563.000	563.000
Paid-up capital	413.000	563.000
Total assets	2.072.777	2.124.738

Principal Shareholders: Moroccan government
Date of Establishment: February 1959
No of Employees: 1,250

STE MAROCAINE DE NAVIGATION FRUITIERE

SOFRUMA

18 rue Colbert, 4eme Etage, Casablanca
Tel: 310003, 313500
Cable: Sofruma
Telex: 21890; 23097
Telefax: 310031

Chairman: Mohamed Guessous
Senior Executives: A Khammal (Director General)

PRINCIPAL ACTIVITIES: Shipping, freight transport; ship owners
Principal Bankers: BMCI; BCM; SGMB; BMCE
Financial Information:

	1988/89 MDh'000
Sales turnover	145.673
Profits	2.645
Authorised capital	9.000
Total assets	39.329

Principal Shareholders: OCE, Casablanca; REL New Jersey
Date of Establishment: 1962
No of Employees: 150

STE MAROCAINE DE TISSUS EPONGE

SPONTIS SA

28-32, Rue Termidi, Casablanca
Tel: 251665/66
Cable: Tisseponge
Telex: 22070
Telefax: 251668

Chairman: Tahar El Yacoubi
Directors: Saad El Yacoubi
Senior Executives: Badreddine Hachad (Commercial Director)

PRINCIPAL ACTIVITIES: Spinning and weaving, production of textiles and terry towels
Principal Bankers: BMCE; BCM; Banque Populaire
Financial Information:

	1990 MDh'000
Authorised capital	3.000

Date of Establishment: 1952
No of Employees: 250

STE MAROCAINE D'ENGRAIS ET PRODUITS CHIMIQUES AGRICOLES ET INDUSTRIELS

PROMAGRI SA

42 Ave Hassan Seghir, Casablanca
Tel: 277284
Telex: 21621 Omagri

Chairman: Abderrahmane Bouftas
Directors: Said Bouayad (Administrative and Financial Director), Mohamed Bouftas (Commercial Director), Houcine Bouftas (Secretary General)

PRINCIPAL ACTIVITIES: Production and marketing of fertilisers, import of chemicals and fertilisers, argicultural machinery and equipment and industrial materials for the tanning industry
Principal Agencies: Forestal Mimosa Ltd, Forestal Quebracho Ltd, Henkel, Stahl Iberica, Paule, Cofpa, Dicalite Espanola, Wilson & Sons
Branch Offices: 22 Avenue El Moukaouama, Agadir; 19 rue El Quassidia, Kenitra
Principal Bankers: BCM; BMCE; SGMB; BMAO

Principal Shareholders: Abderrahmane Bouftas, Said Tazit, Mohamed Bouftas

STE MAROCAINE DES DERIVES INDUSTRIELS DU MAIS

SOMADIM

Avenue D, Quartier Industriel Est, PO Box 2607, Ain Sebaa,
Casablanca 05
Tel: 353657, 350658, 352608

Chairman: M Abdelkebir El Fassi
Directors: Abdellatif Bennouna Louridi
Senior Executives: Abderhamane Badry (Commercial Manager),
Baghdad Chikhaoui (Administrative Manager)

PRINCIPAL ACTIVITIES: Manufacture of glucose, starch, corn
oil, industrial paste and gum and all derived products
Principal Bankers: SMDC, Credit du Maroc, BCM, BMCI,
BMCE, SBC

Principal Shareholders: Compagnie Sucriere Marocaine et de
Raffinage (Consumar), Banque Nationale pour le
Developpement Economique, Amylum GR (Belgium)
Date of Establishment: 1967
No of Employees: 100

STE MAROCAINE DES FERTILISANTS

FERTIMA

26 Bvd de la Resistance, Casablanca
Tel: 272231
Telex: 21846

PRINCIPAL ACTIVITIES: Import, manufacture and distribution of
fertilisers
Branch Offices: Berrechid, Safi, Agadir, Kenitra, Meknes
Principal Bankers: CDM

Date of Establishment: 1974
No of Employees: 200

STE MAROCAINE D'OXYGENE ET D'ACETYLENE

S.M.O.A.

80 Route des Oulad Ziane, Casablanca
Tel: 245076
Telex: 21775

PRINCIPAL ACTIVITIES: Manufacture and processing of gas,
oxygen, acetylene, ammonia
Branch Offices: Factories at Ain Sebaa; Meknes
Subsidiary Companies: Air Liquide, Paris, France
Principal Bankers: SMDC; CMCB; SGMB

Date of Establishment: 1956

STE MAROCAINE MARIX

18 rue d'Epernay, Casablanca
Tel: 245262, 240263

PRINCIPAL ACTIVITIES: Medical X-rays, monitoring, nuclear
medicine
Principal Agencies: Philips, Siemens

STE METALLURGIQUE AFRICAINE

SOMETAL

BP 2620, Chemin des Dahlias, Ain Sebaa, Casablanca
Tel: 350495, 350558, 350738
Cable: Sometal
Telex: 22039

President: Omar Benjelloun
Directors: H M Chraibi, M Chraibi (Commercial Director), M
Mokhtar (Planning Director), C H Hajj (General Manager)

PRINCIPAL ACTIVITIES: Manufacture of nuts, screws, bolts and
concrete reinforcing rods
Branch Offices: Morocco; Algeria; Tunisia; Mauritania; France

STE NATIONALE DE SIDERURGIE

SONASID

BP 485, Residence Kays, Immeuble E No 3, Rabat
Tel: 78348, 78350
Telex: 31721
Telefax: 78348

Directors: Abdallah Souibri (Director General)
Senior Executives: N Bouimadaghene (Rod Mill General
Superintendant at Nador), M Brraqui (Director), M Benamar
(Commercial Direcdtor), M Rabhi (Finance Director), M
Mouline (ADM Director)

PRINCIPAL ACTIVITIES: Iron and steel works and projects
Branch Offices: BP 151, Ave Youssef Ibn Tachfine, Nador, Tel
7070, 7028, 6054; Telex 65787, 65778 Nador; Fax 7086 Nador
Principal Bankers: Morgan Grenfell & Co Ltd; Lazard Bros;
BNP; Moroccan Treasury; BMCE
Financial Information:

	1990
	MDh'000
Authorised capital	500.000
Paid-up capital	390.000

Principal Shareholders: State of Morocco; ODI; BRPM;
SEFERIF
Date of Establishment: 1974
No of Employees: 650

STE NATIONALE DE TELECOMMUNICATIONS

Zankat Al Mansour Addahbi, BP 1067, Rabat 43
Tel: 21385, 21386
Telex: SONATEL 31789 M

Chairman: Minister of PTT
Directors: Mourad Akalay (General Manager)

PRINCIPAL ACTIVITIES: Telephone network, civil work,
engineering, radio transmission system
Branch Offices: Rabat; Casablanca; Marrakech; Tanger; Agadir;
Fes; Oujda; Meknes; Kenitra; Safi; Tetouan; Beni Mellal,
Ourzazate
Parent Company: Office National des Postes et
Telecommunications
Principal Bankers: BMCE; SGMB; SMDC; CM

Principal Shareholders: State-owned
Date of Establishment: 1964
No of Employees: 300 (permanent), 200 (temporary)

STE NATIONALE DE TEXTILE

SONATEX SA

73 Bvd Moulay Sliman, Casablanca
Tel: 242283
Cable: Sonatex

Senior Executives: Berrada El Ghali (General Manager)

PRINCIPAL ACTIVITIES: Manufacture of textiles, spinning and
weaving
Principal Bankers: BMCE; SMDC; Arab Bank

Date of Establishment: 1968

STE NATIONALE D'ELECTROLYSE ET DE PETROCHIMIE

S.N.E.P.

BP 94, route cotiere No 111, Mohammedia
Tel: 3520
Telex: 23702

Senior Executives: R Berrada (Administrative Director)

PRINCIPAL ACTIVITIES: Manufacture of petrochemicals
Principal Bankers: BMCE; BCM; CDM; CMCB

Principal Shareholders: State-owned
Date of Establishment: 1974
No of Employees: 500

STE NATIONALE DES PRODUITS PETROLIERS

S.N.P.A.

42 Avenue de l'Armee Royale, Casablanca

PRINCIPAL ACTIVITIES: Petroleum products
Subsidiary Companies: Compagnie Marocains des Hydrocarbures

Principal Shareholders: State-owned

STE NATIONALE D'INVESTISSEMENT

43 rue Aspirant Lafuente, Casablanca
Tel: 279269, 223081
Telex: 22736 M

Chairman: M'Hammed Bargach
Senior Executives: Abdallah Belkeziz (Director General), Abdelkrim Lahlou (Secretary General)

PRINCIPAL ACTIVITIES: Holding company
Subsidiary/Associated Companies: Lafarge Maroc, ASMAR, CADEM, SNCE, Longometal Afrique, Comameto, Cellulose du Maroc, Lesieur Afrique, Societe Cherifienne d'Engrais, General Tire & Rubber Co of Morocco, Brasseries du Maroc, Renault Maroc, etc
Principal Bankers: Banque Centrale Populaire; Societe Generale Marocaine de Banque; Banque Marocaine pour le Commerce et l'Industrie; Banque Marocaine pour le Commerce Exterieur

Principal Shareholders: Ministry of Finance; Banque du Maroc; Caisse de Depot et de Gestion; Banque Centrale Populaire; BNDE; etc
Date of Establishment: 1966
No of Employees: 40

STE NOUVELLE D'ASSURANCES

10 Rue Mohamed Diouri, PO Box 420, Casablanca
Tel: 300108
Cable: Nouvel
Telex: 21741

President: Ali Kettani
Directors: Abdelhak Bennani (Administrative Director)
Senior Executives: Jaouad Kettani (Director General), Felix Perez (Financial Director)

PRINCIPAL ACTIVITIES: Insurance and reinsurance
Branch Offices: 33 rue du Prince Moulay Abdallah, Tangiers
Principal Bankers: Compagnie Marocaine de Credit & de Banque; Societe Marocaine de Depot & Credit

Principal Shareholders: Societe Marocaine de Participation; Norwich Union Fire Insurance Co Ltd

STE NOUVELLE DES CHANTIERS NAVALS MAROCAINS SA

S.N.C.N.M.

Blvd des Almohades, Casablanca
Tel: 260161
Telex: 22664

President: Abderrazak El Bied
Directors: G Beal

PRINCIPAL ACTIVITIES: Ship building and repairing
Principal Bankers: SMDC; Credit du Maroc

Principal Shareholders: Beliard Murdoch, Antwerp, Belgium

STE NOUVELLE DES CONDUITES D'EAU

S.N.C.E.

Sahat Rabia El Adaouya, Residence Kays, Agdal, Rabat
Tel: 76714 (5 lines)
Telex: 31028 SNCE Rabat

Chairman: Omar Laraqui
Directors: Kamal Laraqui (Managing Director), Abdelhaq Laraichi
Senior Executives: Tayeb Abdallaoui (Development Manager), Ameur Chamich (Technical Manager), Abdessalem Zeghari (Administrative Manager)

PRINCIPAL ACTIVITIES: Manufacture of steel and cast-iron pipes and materials
Principal Agencies: Blaw Knox, Neyrpic, Stup, Precismeca, Socoman, Reel
Branch Offices: Sidi Aissa (Fquih Ben Salah); Ait Ourir, PO Box 744, Marrakech; Souk Jemma, PO Box 83, Sidi Slimane; PO Box 45, Berkane; PO Box 3, Sidi Bennour
Subsidiary Companies: SBBM, Casablanca; SEPROB, Casablanca; Asment; Rizq; Kays
Principal Bankers: BMCI; BMCE; Banque Populaire; BCM; SMDC; CMCB; SGMB

Principal Shareholders: Private and public interests
Date of Establishment: 1961
No of Employees: 2,500 to 3,000

STE NOUVELLE DES ETS ARVANITAKIS SA

42/50 Bld Lahcen ou Ider, Casablanca
Tel: 62401, 20017, 70664, 60802
Cable: Transip
Telex: 22074 M

PRINCIPAL ACTIVITIES: General trading, import and distribution of electrical and electronic equipment, air conditioners, refrigerators and electrical household appliances

STE NOUVELLE SOMATAM

Ste Marocaine de Tannerie et de Megisserie

11 Capitaine Thiriat St, Casablanca
Tel: 247687/56/89
Cable: Somatam Casa
Telex: 21814

Chairman: L Mounsif (Director General)
Senior Executives: E G Tarrusson (Technical Manager), A Sefraoui (Business Manager)

PRINCIPAL ACTIVITIES: Tannery and tawery, fancy-leather trade, manufacturing of leather clothes, shoes and boots
Principal Bankers: BPC; BMCI; BMCE

Principal Shareholders: Banque Nationale pour le Developpment Economique (BNDE), Docteur Hoffman (West Germany)

STE ORBONOR SA

20 rue Mustapha El Maani, Casablanca
Tel: 270701, 270947
Telex: 21078

Senior Executives: Abdelkader Ben Salah (General Manager)

PRINCIPAL ACTIVITIES: Processing wool and synthetic fibres; wholesale grain and dried vegetables
Principal Agencies: Tergal; Trevira; Chewitt; Crylor; Dolan
Principal Bankers: CDM

Date of Establishment: 1936
No of Employees: 700

STE SHELL DU MAROC

36 rue d'Azilal, Casablanca
Tel: 224162, 274130
Cable: Shell
Telex: 21055

PRINCIPAL ACTIVITIES: Wholesale petroleum products and by-products, chemical products

Date of Establishment: 1922

STE TISBROD

Tissage et Broderie Mecanique

56 rue d'Audenge, Casablanca 03
Tel: 304459
Cable: Tisbrod

Chairman: M Ali Kettani
Senior Executives: Drissi Mohamed (General Manager)

PRINCIPAL ACTIVITIES: Manufacture of textiles, knitted and embroidered goods
Principal Bankers: CMCB; CDM; BMCI; BMCE; BCM

Date of Establishment: 1959
No of Employees: 500

STOKVIS NORD AFRIQUE (SNA)

42 Bvd Emile Zola, Casablanca
Tel: 306475
Cable: Stokvisnoraf
Telex: 27059

Chairman: A Lyazidi
Directors: M Benchehla (Director General), J Duarte

PRINCIPAL ACTIVITIES: Distribution of moped bicycles, agricultural materials and accessories, climatisation boilers, cold air compressors, cold installations
Principal Agencies: Motobecane, Moulinex, Fiat, Claas, Ebra, York, Honeywell, Baltimore, Brunswerk, Wanson, Lindsay
Parent Company: Cie Optorg SA, Paris-Puteaux, France
Subsidiary Companies: Serit SA; Mobylette-Maroc
Principal Bankers: SGMB; BMCE; BP; Wafabank; Credit Du Maroc; BMCI

Principal Shareholders: Compagnie Optorg SA, France
Date of Establishment: 1950
No of Employees: 132

STRAFOR MAROC SA

Bvd Hassan II, Mohammedia
Tel: 2724, 2716
Telex: 22732
Telefax: 032 3233

President: Henri Lachmann
Directors: Raymond Delaviere (General Manager)

PRINCIPAL ACTIVITIES: Manufacture of metal furniture, household appliances and kitchen equipment
Branch Offices: Mohammedia; Ain Sebaa
Subsidiary Companies: CESAL
Principal Bankers: Credit du Maroc, BCM, BMCI, BMCE, BCP

Principal Shareholders: Forges de Strasbourg, France
Date of Establishment: 1948
No of Employees: 500

SUCRERIE DES DOUKKALA SA

SUDOUKA

Sidi Bennour, Province d'el Jadida
Tel: Sidi Bennour 3349031 (5 lines)
Cable: SUDOUKA
Telex: 78977 Sudouka
Telefax: 3349555

Chairman: Fouad Filali
Directors: Abdelmajid Bahbouhi (Director General)
Senior Executives: Ali Anba (Director of Agriculture & Human Relations Dept), Mohamed Eddahabi (Technical Director)

PRINCIPAL ACTIVITIES: Production of beet sugar
Parent Company: ONA
Associated Companies: Cosumar

Principal Bankers: Credit du Maroc; Banque Populaire; BMCI; SMDC; BCM; BMCE; Wafabank; Societe de Banque et de Credit
Financial Information:

	1990 MDh'000
Authorised capital	70.000
Paid-up capital	70.000

Principal Shareholders: Cosumar; CIMR; Eneifi; CMKD; ONA; SOMED; the Agricultural Farmers
Date of Establishment: 1968
No of Employees: 192

SUCRERIE NATIONALE DE BETTERAVES DE LOUKKOS

SUNABEL

18 rue de Taza, Rabat
Tel: 23637, 23647
Telex: 31812

PRINCIPAL ACTIVITIES: Production of white sugar
Branch Offices: Factory at Ksar El Kebir
Principal Bankers: BMCE; BCM

Date of Establishment: 1975
No of Employees: 400

SUCRERIE RAFFINERIE DE L'ORIENTAL

SUCRAFOR

30 rue Sidi Belyout, Casablanca
Tel: 313887
Telex: 22671 M

Chairman: The Minister of Commerce & Industry
Directors: Moulay Hassan El Alaoui (Director General)

PRINCIPAL ACTIVITIES: Sugar cane & sugar beet production and refinery
Branch Offices: Factory: BP 2 Zaio, Province de Nador; Tel 4155, 3327; Telex 65790
Principal Bankers: Credit du Maroc; BMCE; BCM; UNIBAN
Financial Information:

	MDh'000
Authorised capital	48.500

SUCRERIES NATIONALES DU GHARB

SUNAG

11 Ave Allal Ben Abdellah, Rabat

Senior Executives: Abdelhamid Senhaji (General Manager)

PRINCIPAL ACTIVITIES: Sugar refinery (beet sugar)

TECHNICAL EQUIPMENTS

121 Bd Emile Zola, Casablanca
Tel: 240621/22
Telex: 25860
Telefax: 248628

President: Mohamed Ghorfi
Senior Executives: Mohamed Laabi (Commercial Manager), Mohamed Chenni (Personnel Manager)

PRINCIPAL ACTIVITIES: Import and distribution of agricultural, industrial and mining equipment and machinery
Principal Agencies: Coles Cranes, Teddington, Petters, General Electric Co, Bryce Berger, Mirrlees, Blackstone, Aveling Barford, Duijeulaar, Europemill
Parent Company: SNI, Al Amane Group
Principal Bankers: Wafabank, SGMB, BCM, SMDC, BMCE, CDM, BMCI
Financial Information:

	1988/89 MDh'000
Sales turnover	21.500
Authorised capital	4.000

MOROCCO

Principal Shareholders: Societe Nationale d'Investissements
Date of Establishment: 1958
No of Employees: 63

TEXACO MAROC

rue Djillali Ghafiri, PO Box 2533, Ain Sabaa
Tel: 350301
Cable: Texaco Casablanca
Telex: 21047

PRINCIPAL ACTIVITIES: Marketing of petroleum products

Principal Shareholders: Texaco Inc, New York
Date of Establishment: 1937

TEXTILES DU NORD
TEXNORD

Angle Rues Bascunana & Lt Roze, Casablanca
Tel: 306453, 308703
Telex: 23818 Texnord

President: Ali Kettani
Directors: Abdellatif Drissi (General Manager), Ghali Squalli
(Commercial Manager)

PRINCIPAL ACTIVITIES: Weaving, dyeing, printing and finishing
of textiles and fabrics
Principal Bankers: Credit du Maroc; CMCB; BMCE; BCM;
Uniban

Principal Shareholders: Ste Sopar, Ste Amalfi
Date of Establishment: 1962
No of Employees: 700

TISMAR SA
Tissages Marocains Modernes

19 Ave Moulay Ismael, PO Box 159, Tangiers
Tel: 43553, 41123, 42033
Cable: Tismar Tanger
Telex: 33710

Chairman: Mohamed Tatari
Directors: Abdulaziz Tatari

PRINCIPAL ACTIVITIES: Textile industry
Branch Offices: 30 Rue Mostafa El Maani, Casablanca Tel:
312557, 310480, 313180, Telex 21645
Principal Bankers: Algemene Bank Marokko (A.B.M.) Tanger &
Casablanca

Principal Shareholders: A family company
Date of Establishment: 1963
No of Employees: 500

TOTAL-MAROC SA

146 Bvd Zerktouni, PO Box 638, Casablanca
Tel: 263401, 220471
Telex: 21817 Salpemo

PRINCIPAL ACTIVITIES: Marketing of oils and lubricants
Principal Bankers: SMDC; BMCE; BMCI; CMCB; BCM; Credit
du Maroc; UNIBAN; Banque Populaire

TUILERIES BRIQUETERIES DU MAROC

Bvd Hassan II, Mohammedia
Tel: 2013, 2778

Directors: Ali Youssefi

PRINCIPAL ACTIVITIES: Manufacture of tiles and concrete
products
Principal Bankers: Credit du Maroc; Banque Commerciale du
Maroc

Date of Establishment: 1914
No of Employees: 160

UNIGRAL CRISTAL

10-14 rue Mostafa El Maani, Casablanca
Tel: 311176
Cable: Unigral
Telex: 21063

Senior Executives: Mohamed Hamdouch (Manager)

PRINCIPAL ACTIVITIES: Production of vegetable oils, glycerine,
soaps and associated products
Branch Offices: Marrakech, Fes
Principal Bankers: CDM; BCM; SGMB; BMCE; BMCI; SMDC;
Uniban

Date of Establishment: 1974

UNIMAROC SA

59 rue des Quiconces, Casablanca
Tel: 240313
Telex: 23806

PRINCIPAL ACTIVITIES: Manufacture of metal products, cables
and accessories
Branch Offices: Oujda, 75 Bd Allah Ben Abdallah
Principal Bankers: CDM; SGMB; CMCB; SMDC

Date of Establishment: 1936

UNION BANCARIA HISPANO MARROQUI
UNIBAN

69 rue Prince Moulay Abdellah, Casablanca
Tel: 220230 (6 lines)
Cable: Uniban
Telex: 21678

President: Mohamed Jennane
Senior Executives: Pedro Landa Velon (General Manager),
Miguel Alvarez Rasero (Deputy Director General), Abdelkhalak
Mestassi (Deputy Director General), Jose Manuel Tejerina
(Controleur General)

PRINCIPAL ACTIVITIES: Commercial banking
Branch Offices: Casablanca; Tanger; Rabat; Marrakech
Subsidiary Companies: INFORBAN SA (Informatic Processing);
REMAR (Insurance Co); Cementos of Tetuan (Cement
Factory)

Principal Shareholders: Private Moroccan Shareholders; and
foreign shareholders: Banco Espanol de Credito, Spain;
Banco Central, Spain; Banco Hispano Americano, Spain;
Banco de Bilbao, Spain; Banco Exterior de Espana, Spain;
Banco Popular Espanol, Spain
Date of Establishment: 1958
No of Employees: 314

UNION MAROCAINE DE BANQUES

36 Rue Tahar Sebti, BP 611, Casablanca
Tel: 274961
Cable: Umarbank
Telex: 21926

Directors: Driss Alami (Directeur)

PRINCIPAL ACTIVITIES: Commercial banking
Branch Offices: Rabat, Tangiers, Nador, Tetouan, Al Hoceima

Date of Establishment: 1957

WAFABANK

163 Avenue Hassan II, BP 13057, Casablanca
Tel: 224105
Telex: 21051, 23771

President: Ali Kettani (Director General)
Directors: Abdelhak Bennani, Bernard Egloff, Abdullatif Drissi,
Izrab Kettani, Abdel Karim Lazrak, Georges Plescoff, Yves
Francois Martin

PRINCIPAL ACTIVITIES: Commercial banking

Financial Information:

	MD'000
Authorised capital	64.750
Paid-up capital	64.750

Principal Shareholders: SOPAR; Suez Group
Date of Establishment: 1964

ZELLIDJA SA

81 Avenue des FAR, Casablanca
Tel: 311194
Cable: Zellidja
Telex: 21804, 22891
Telefax: 311549

President: Abdellatif Ghissassi
Directors: Ahmed Chlyah (Administrative & Financial Director)
Senior Executives: Mohamed Hachimi (Asst Financial Director)

PRINCIPAL ACTIVITIES: Financial holding
Subsidiary Companies: Societe des Fonderies de Plomb de Zellidja (40%); Societe Fenie Brossette (50.71%); Societe de Banque et de Credit SBC (46.20%); Societe Nationale d'Electrolyse et de Petrochimie (4.69%); Societe Financiere d'Africa Palace (10%); Societe Protec (34%)
Principal Bankers: BCM; BMCE; CMC; SBC: SGMB; BMCI; Wafabank; SMDC
Financial Information:

	1990 MDh'000
Sales turnover	976.500
Profits	23.774
Authorised capital	57.283
Paid-up capital	57.283
Total assets	402.332

Principal Shareholders: SOMED; Societe d'Assurances Al Amane; REBAB; CDG
Date of Establishment: February 1929
No of Employees: 1,580

MOROCCO

Major Companies of OMAN

A&P (OMAN) LLC
PO Box 1102, Seeb Airport
Tel: 536066, 536206
Cable: Arpaco
Telex: 5486 ARPACO ON
Telefax: 535279

Directors: H H Sayed Faher Bin Taimur, G Paraskevaides
Senior Executives: P J Sotiriou (Manager)

PRINCIPAL ACTIVITIES: Electrical, mechanical, heating and
ventilating contractors
Branch Offices: PO Box 18207, Salalah, Oman
Associated Companies: A&P Paraskevaides (Overseas) Ltd,
Muscat & Saudi Arabia; A&P Electrical Agencies LLC, Muscat;
Ajman Polyesterene Factory, UAE; Conspel Construction
Specialists Ltd; North Yemen & Saudi Arabia; Arabian Gulf
Switchgear Co UAE; A&P Paraskevaides & Partners Limited,
UAE
Principal Bankers: Grindlays Bank plc

Principal Shareholders: A&P Paraskevaides (Overseas) Ltd; H H
Sayed Faher Bin Taimur
Date of Establishment: 1979
No of Employees: 850

ABDUL HUSAIN DAWOOD & SONS
See DAWOOD, ABDUL HUSAIN, & SONS

ABDULAZIZ & BROTHERS
PO Box 5, Muscat
Tel: 722399
Telex: 5373 Abdulaziz ON

Directors: Abdul Aziz Jaffer, Jaffer Abdulrahim

PRINCIPAL ACTIVITIES: Import and distribution of air
conditioners, electrical home appliances, foodstuffs and
beverages, hardware, tools and metal products and
pharmaceuticals

AHMED RAMADHAN JUMA & CO LLC
See JUMA, AHMED RAMADHAN, & CO LLC

AIRWORK LTD
PO Box 248, Muscat
Tel: 613061, 614523
Cable: Airwork
Telex: ON 5307
Telefax: 613084

Directors: J D Spottiswood (Managing Director), D Bolton
(Finance Director), R D Thurston, P N A Mosely (Commercial
Director & Secretary), S D Wharam (Non-Executive Director)
Senior Executives: A B Blackney (General Manager - Oman), A
D Whitfield (Admin Controller - Oman)

PRINCIPAL ACTIVITIES: Maintenance of aircraft, vehicles,
radar, communications, training of pilots and aeronautical
engineers, airports operation, air traffic control, aviation and
recruitment consultants, catering contractors, specialists in
medical recruitment, training and supplies
Branch Offices: Head Office: Bournemouth Int'l Airport
Christchurch, Dorset BH23 6EB, UK, Tel (0202) 572271, Fax
(0202) 573692, Telex 41282; Malawi, Zimbabwe, Oman
Parent Company: Rochfield Limited
Principal Bankers: Royal Bank of Scotland; Oman International
Bank
Financial Information:

	1989 St£'000
Sales turnover	65,000
Profits	5,975
Authorised capital	20
Paid-up capital	20
Total assets	25,924

Principal Shareholders: Rochfield Limited
Date of Establishment: 1928
No of Employees: 3,800

AL ADNAN TRADING & CONTRACTING EST
PO Box 5242, Ruwi
Tel: 702378, 702503, 701243
Cable: ADNAN MUSCAT
Telex: 3069 ADNAN ON
Telefax: 706147

Proprietor: Abdul Rasool Ali Mohd Al Raeesi
Senior Executives: Mahendra Kumar Sharma (General
Manager), B S Rana (Factory Manager)

PRINCIPAL ACTIVITIES: Aluminium allied products, building
materials supplies, building construction
Principal Agencies: Comalco; Phifer; Al Mog; Balterley; Heart
Kitchens; Porcher; Hellas Tiles; ARPA; Mandeli; E T Kitchens;
Regency; Bailey & Davison; Pla Products; Shaw Hereford
Tiles
Branch Offices: Al Adnan Building Materials (Showroom),
Khamis Al Shaqsi St, Ruwi, Tel 704140
Subsidiary Companies: Al Adnan Clinic (Hamria), PO Box 3327,
Ruwi, Tel 704940
Principal Bankers: Bank of Oman Bahrain & Kuwait, Wadi Kabir;
National Bank of Oman; Union Bank of Oman, Muttrah; Bank
of Muscat, Ruwi; Banque du Liban & d'Outre Mer, Ruwi;
Commercial Bank of Oman, Ruwi, Salalah

Principal Shareholders: Abdul Rasool Ali Mohd Al Raeesi
Date of Establishment: 18/1/1976
No of Employees: 71

AL AHLIA INSURANCE COMPANY SAO
PO Box 4463, Ruwi
Tel: 709441, 709442
Telex: 3518 Insure ON
Telefax: 797151

Chairman: Mohsin Haider Darwish
Directors: Mansor Talib Al Zakwani (Vice Chairman), Suleiman
Al Adawi, Essa Mohamed Al Essa, Suleiman Al Huqani, Salim
Ahmed Khalfan, Zakaria Mitry Meleka
Senior Executives: Michael A Burtonshaw (General Manager),
Anthony Caulfield (Asst General Manager)

PRINCIPAL ACTIVITIES: General and life insurance
Branch Offices: Salalah (PO Box 20299); Sohar; Seeb
Principal Bankers: Bank of Oman Bahrain & Kuwait
Financial Information:

	1989 RO'000
Sales turnover	3,270
Profits	293
Authorised capital	2,000
Paid-up capital	2,000
Total assets	2,511

Date of Establishment: July 1985
No of Employees: 43

AL AHRAM TRANSPORT COMPANY
PO Box 783, Muscat
Tel: 590368, 590725, 701392, 705028
Telex: 5146 Al Ahram ON, 3742 Aatsea ON
Telefax: 590542, 704858

Chairman: HE Saeed Bin Ahmed Al Shanfari
Directors: Abdul Aziz Ali Shanfari (Managing Director)
Senior Executives: Goerge Carr (General Manager)

PRINCIPAL ACTIVITIES: Transport, shipping, freight forwarding,
project cargo, heavy lift
Principal Agencies: Sea Land Service Inc; LEP Heavy Lift Int'l; F
H Bertling; Team Heavy Lift

Branch Offices: Al Ahram Shipping Agency, Marbat House, 2nd Floor, Qaboos Street; Shanfari Trading & Contracting, PO Box 18915, Salalah

Subsidiary Companies: OFSAT LLC, PO Box 1138, Seeb (rig moving company)

Principal Shareholders: Chairman and director as described
Date of Establishment: 1979
No of Employees: 210

AL ANSARI TRADING ENTERPRISE LLC

PO Box 4832, Ruwi
Tel: 703231 (5 lines)
Cable: Alansari Muscat
Telex: 3356 ANSARI ON
Telefax: 706829

Chairman: Mohd Ali Jumma
Directors: Kiran Asher (Managing Director)
Senior Executives: Yusuf Nalwala (Contracts Manager), Rajan Kanath (Contracts Manager), R O Pinto (Trading Manager), K Asokan (Irrigation Manager), B P Gandhi (Supermarket Manager), G J Cherian (Finance Manager)

PRINCIPAL ACTIVITIES: Trading, indenting, commission agents and manufacturers' representatives for building and construction materials, hardware, industrial goods, paints, carpets, sanitaryware, and safety equipment, commercial kitchen, laundry, bakery equipment, electro/mechanical contracting, painting and civil contracting, swimming pools, irrigation contracting, wholesale food distribution, supermarkets

Principal Agencies: Anandji V Kazi, India; Donald Macpherson & Co Ltd, UK; GEC Xpelair, UK; MSA Int, Pennsylvania, USA; Lupos Schuhfabrik, West Germany; A O Smith Corp, USA; Totectors Ltd, UK; Cepem Sauter Brand Waterheaters, France; Unibond Ltd, UK; Rainbird Int, USA; Sykes Pumps Ltd, UK; Jacuzzi Europa, Italy; Kingson, USA; Hobart, USA; Meridian Chemicals, USA; Crystal Tips, USA; JCD Bathroom, UK; King Gee, Australia; Glenco, USA; Esco, Holland; Moffat, USA; Acco, USA; Franklin Hodge, UK; Solar Industries, Australia; System Floors, UK; Certikin Ltd, UK; Wade Plumbing Products, UK

Branch Offices: Supermarket Division, Ruwi
Subsidiary Companies: Media Computer Supplies LLC; Al Manhal Sanitaryware & Kitchen Supplies
Principal Bankers: The British Bank of the Middle East, Bait Al Falaj, Bank of Muscat, Ruwi; Bank of Oman, Bahrain & Kuwait, Wadikabir; Bank Al Ahli

Financial Information:

	1989 RO'000	1990 RO'000
Sales turnover	3,200	3,750
Profits	140	140
Authorised capital	1,000	1,000
Paid-up capital	1,000	1,000
Total assets	2,000	2,000

Date of Establishment: 1975
No of Employees: 200

ALASFOOR FURNISHINGS LLC

PO Box 4812, Ruwi
Tel: 561400
Cable: Alasfoor
Telex: 5326 Alasfoor ON

Directors: Ali H Alasfoor, Monem H Alasfoor, Qais H Alasfoor
Senior Executives: E McDonagh (General Manager), P Baron (Sales and Contracts Manager)

PRINCIPAL ACTIVITIES: Retail and contract furnishing with interior design facilities
Principal Agencies: Velda; Van Pelt; Bevan Funnel; Derwent; Airsprung; Scanlife; Mobilar; Broyhill; Ferretti; Pierre Vandel; LDC; Brunati; Dyrlund; Tenani; Giaiotti; Antocks; Lairn; Vaghi; Okamura; Kokuyo; Westinghouse; Artifort; BCL; Burlington; Lano; Bremworth; Parkertex; Larsen; Tarian; Taunus; Pausa; Sekers; Creda; T I New Workd; Amana; Edesa; Decolite; Cresswell; Dauphin

Branch Offices: PO Box 490, Bahrain, Tel 254476
Principal Bankers: British Bank of the Middle East; Bank of Oman Bahrain & Kuwait

Principal Shareholders: Abdulla H Alasfoor, Hussain H Alasfoor
Date of Establishment: 1971
No of Employees: 150

AL BANK AL AHLI AL OMANI SAO

PO Box 3134, Ruwi, Muscat
Tel: 703044
Cable: BANKBO - MUSCAT
Telex: 3450
Telefax: 793536

Chairman: Sheikh Zaher Bin Hamad Al Harthy
Board of Directors: Sheikh Hamad Bin Eissa Al Taey, Sheikh Hashel Bin Mohd Al Mouselhy, Sheikh Hilal Bin Sultan Al Hosney
Senior Executives: Jean Maurice Beaux (General Manager), M Kamal Al-Zagha (Deputy General Manager), Muhammed Al Mahfudh (Senior Manager Administration), Daniel George Clement (Senior Manager Operations)

PRINCIPAL ACTIVITIES: Commercial bank activities, local and international
Branch Offices: Head Office: Greater Muttrah; and Branches - Medinat Qaboos, Fanja, Seeb, Rustaq, Salalah, Al Mudarib, Al Khuwair, Sultan Qaboos University, Firq (Nizwa), Al Wattayah (Al Harthy Complec)
Associate Companies: An affiliate of Societe Generale (France) who undertake the management of the Bank
Principal Correspondents: Societe Generale, France, London and New York; European-American Banking Corporation, USA; Manufacturers Hanover Trust Co, New York; American Express Int. Banking Corp, New York; National Westminster Bank, London; Bank of Baroda, Bombay; Habib Bank Ltd, Karachi

Financial Information:

	1989 RO'000
Profits after tax	380
Authorised capital	5,000
Paid-up capital + reserves	6,540
Total assets	85,460

Principal Shareholders: Societe Generale (20%); Omani Founders (80%)
Date of Establishment: November 1976
No of Employees: 162

AL BUSTAN PALACE HOTEL

PO Box 8998, Muttrah
Tel: 740200, 799666
Cable: Bustanhtl
Telex: 5477 Bushtl
Telefax: 799600

Senior Executives: Chris Cowdrey (General Manager), Mike Pilkington (Director of Sales), Issa Al Hajri (Executive Asst Manager), Woodrow Rebeira (Financial Controller)

PRINCIPAL ACTIVITIES: Hotel chain
Parent Company: Division of Intercontinental Hotels Group
Principal Bankers: Oman Arab Bank

Principal Shareholders: Fully owned by the Government of Oman
Date of Establishment: 1985
No of Employees: 410

AL DARWISH & AL MASHANI TRADING & CONTRACTING CO

PO Box 8289, Salalah, Dhofar
Tel: 461684
Cable: Musdar Salalah
Telex: 7673 Musdar ON

Chairman: Mohsin Haider Darwish (Proprietor)

PRINCIPAL ACTIVITIES: Distributors in Dhofar for motor vehicles and components, mechanical plant; building materials; construction plant; power equipment; household goods and hardware
Principal Agencies: British Leyland; Winget; Michelin; Ingersoll Rand; Pirelli; MK; Barford; Aveling Barford; Goodenough; Gum; Pioneer; Kismet; Crypton; Doulton; Erecto; Triumph Adler
Principal Bankers: British Bank of the Middle East; Bank of Oman Bahrain & Kuwait

ALDARWISH ENTERPRISES

PO Box 704, Muscat
Tel: 734624/25
Cable: Muwaffaq
Telex: 5357 Muwaffaq ON

Chairman: Hussain Haider Darwish (Proprietor)
Directors: Inder Lal (Group General Manager)

PRINCIPAL ACTIVITIES: Import and distribution of watches, motor cars, tyres, building materials, travel office
Principal Agencies: Rolls Royce Motors, Goodyear, TWA, TMA, PIA, Alitalia, Longines & Rotary, Sabena, Biman
Branch Offices: Aldarwish Tavels, PO Box 8767, Salalah Aldarwish Enterprises (Tyres), PO Box 8767, Salalah
Principal Bankers: Bank of Oman, Bahrain & Kuwait; Union Bank of Oman; National Bank of Oman; Arab Bank

Principal Shareholders: Hussain Haider Darwish
Date of Establishment: 1970
No of Employees: 150

AL ESSA TRADING & CONTRACTING EST (ESSACO)

PO Box 4826, Muscat
Tel: 705969/70, 795533/44
Cable: ESSACO
Telex: 3362 ESSACO ON
Telefax: 799153

President: Essa Mohd Essa Al Zedjali
Senior Executives: Aness Essa Mohd Al Zedjali (Vice President), Akbaraly Vahanvaty (Director Projects)

PRINCIPAL ACTIVITIES: General contracting and trading, building materials, engineering, metals, motorcycle dealers, spare parts, food products, security systems, livestock

ALFAIHA ENGINEERS ASSOCIATES

PO Box 4809, Ruwi
Tel: 701163
Cable: Assulaimy

Chairman: Shoeb Shipchandler
Directors: Mansoor Ali Assulaimy, N N Malbary (Senior Architect)

PRINCIPAL ACTIVITIES: Engineering consultants
Principal Bankers: Union Bank of Oman

ALFAIRUZ TRADING & CONTRACTING CO

PO Box 330, Muscat
Tel: 561399, 561626, 601183, 601568, 601838
Cable: Alfairuz
Telex: 5324 Alfairuz ON

Chairman: Haji Ali S Alfairuz

Directors: Salem S Alfairuz (President), Haji Mohammed Alfairuz, K A Menon (Managing Director Trading Division)
Senior Executives: Sumane K Iyer (General Manager - Automotive Division), Surinder Paul (Sales Manager), R G Shanker (Sales Manager -Construction Equipment)

PRINCIPAL ACTIVITIES: Import and distribution of automobiles, construction machinery, power equipment, outboard motors, agricultural machinery, desalination plants, pneumatic drilling tools, marine fenders & oil pollution control equipment, transit mixers and concrete pumps, vibratory compaction equipment, tower cranes, forklift trucks also construction works
Principal Agencies: Hino Motors, Japan; Furukawa, Japan; Hitachi Construction, Japan; Fuji Heavy Industries, Japan; Tohatsu, Japan; Dynapower, UK; F O'Brian & Co, UK; WECAM, West Germany; Bohler, Austria; Seaward Inc, USA, Yale, USA, IMT Agriculture Tractors, Yugoslavia; Schwing, West Germany; Cadillon, France; Aztec Inc USA
Branch Offices: Salalah (PO Box 8964, Telex 7637); Khaboura (PO Box 11511, Telex 8005); Buraimi (PO Box 16049); Al Bidaya (PO Box 11511); Sohar (PO Box 12835); Ibri, PO Box 16633
Subsidiary Companies: Packaging LLC, PO Box 5818, Ruwi, Oman; Vita Electrical & Mechanical LLC, PO Box 8195, Muttrah, Oman; Boats Manufacturing Co Ltd, Khabura, Oman
Principal Bankers: British Bank of the Middle East; National Bank of Oman; Bank of Credit & Commerce

Principal Shareholders: Haji Ali S Alfairuz; Salem S Alfairuz; Haji Mohamed Alfairuz
No of Employees: 600

AL FALAJ HOTEL SAO

PO Box 5031, Ruwi, Muscat
Tel: 702311
Cable: Falajotel
Telex: 3229 Hotel ON
Telefax: 795853

Chairman: HE Qais Abdul Munem Al Zawawi
Directors: Abdulla Moosa (Deputy Chairman), Warren M Woods (Managing Director), HE Mohamed Nasser Al Khaisibi, Eisa Bin Nasser Bin Abdullatif Al Serkal, HE Salem Bin Mohamed Bin Shaban, Mohsin Haider Darwish
Senior Executives: A C Papayannis (General Manager & Secretary to Board)

PRINCIPAL ACTIVITIES: Hotel catering, conferences, international seminars, sporting facilities
Branch Offices: Al Falaj Annexe
Parent Company: Oman Hotels Company Limited
Subsidiary Companies: Nizwa Motel, Nizwa; Arab Oryx Motels (Al Qabil, Al Ghaba, Al Ghaftain, Wadi Qitbit)
Principal Bankers: Bank of Oman; Bahrain & Kuwait; National Bank of Oman

Principal Shareholders: General public, Sultanate of Oman
Date of Establishment: November 1971
No of Employees: 250

ALHAMAD ENTERPRISES LLC

PO Box 5522, Ruwi, Muscat
Tel: 576002/4
Cable: AYMAN, MUSCAT
Telex: 5549 ALHAMAD ON

Directors: Indrajit C Shah (Managing Director)
Senior Executives: M Dasgupta (Chief Executive), Anup Shah (Manager), B S Srikanth (Chief Engineer)

PRINCIPAL ACTIVITIES: Contractors, designers, steel fabricators, interior decorators, traders, agricultural services
Principal Agencies: Zephyr Metal Craft, USA; True-Crete Ltd, UK; Hawker Siddely Water Engineering Ltd, UK
Group Companies: SABCO, SABCO LLC
Principal Bankers: Bank of Credit & Commerce International

Principal Shareholders: H H Sayed Badr Ahmad Bin Hamood, Sayed Nasr Badr Hamad Bin Hamood
Date of Establishment: 1976
No of Employees: 600

AL HAQ TRADING & CONTRACTING CO LLC

PO Box 18647, Salalah
Tel: 291044, 291278, 291428
Cable: AL HAQ
Telex: 7642 ALHAQCO ON
Telefax: 294535

President: HE Lt Col Said Bin Salem Al Wahaibi
Directors: Abdullah Bin Saleh Baabood (Managing Director), Abdul Aziz Bin Said Salem Al Wahaibi (Managing Director)
Senior Executives: Thomas Jacob (General Manager)

PRINCIPAL ACTIVITIES: General trading and contracting, modern furniture, supermarket and construction
Principal Agencies: Contract Interiors, UK; Annmed (Importers & Exporters), UK; Spearland, UK; FHH Koch & Co, West Germany; Charles Lawrence Scotland, UK
Subsidiary/Associated Companies: Saleh Bin Abdullah Baabood & Partners Co LLC, PO Box 18652, Salalah, Tel 292140, 290506, Telex 7666 BAABOOD ON, Cable BAABOOD; Baabood Travels, PO Box 18647, Salalah, Tel 292722, 290726, Telex 7642 ALHAQCO ON
Principal Bankers: National Bank of Oman Ltd, PO Box 18197, Salalah
Financial Information:

	US$'000
Sales turnover	30,000

Date of Establishment: 1976
No of Employees: 350

AL HARTHY CORPORATION

PO Box 4248, Ruwi
Tel: 702456, 702544, 703151, 701268
Cable: Harthcor
Telex: 5417 Harthcor ON

President: Sheikh Zaher Bin Hamad Al Harthy
Senior Executive: Ahmed Korayem

PRINCIPAL ACTIVITIES: Commercial, agriculture, industrial, construction, real estate, investments
Principal Agencies: Renault, Peugeot, Ital Dump Trucks, Haulamatic, Elf Lubricants, Fiat TTG, Bem Moller, Tecalemit, France
Associated Companies: Al Harthy Motors & Co; Poly Products LLC; Diners Club Oman; Modern Crusher Industries LLC; Al Harthy Building Materials LLC; Industrial Development Intl Agencies LLC
Principal Bankers: Al-Ahli Al-Oman Bank; Bank of Oman and the Gulf; Bank of Muscat; British Bank for the Middle East

Date of Establishment: 1974
No of Employees: 1,000

AL HASHAR GROUP OF COMPANIES

PO Box 7028, Mutrah
Tel: 702555, 706604
Cable: Motorco
Telex: 5245 Motorco ON, 3031 Motorco ON

Directors: Saeed Nasser Al Hashar, Nasser Saeed Al Hashar
Senior Executives: Musa Al Aruri (General Manager)

PRINCIPAL ACTIVITIES: Manufacturers' representatives; import, service and distribution of cars, trucks, commercial vehicles, trailers, and crane carriers, tyres and tubes, water-diesel tankers, batteries, cesspit emptiers, and supply of electronic equipment; household appliances; airconditioning equipment; office equipment and supplies; diesel generators and pump sets; LPG appliances; also tourism and travel; hotel

Principal Agencies: BMW, Nissan/Datsun cars, Nissan Diesel Heavy vehicles, Tata Buses, Firestone, Chloride Batteries, UK; Mikado Engineering, Japan; Berger Paints; Ariston; Rinnai; Primus; Frigor; Kardex; Sharp; Wisi; Mamiya Cameras; etc
Branch Offices: Salalah, Buraimi, Sohar, Nizwa, Ibri, Sur, Musanna, Qurum
Associated Companies: Al Hashar & Co, PO Box 7028, Muttrah; Saeed Bin Nasser Al-Hashar, PO Box 331, Muscat, Oman Modern Electronics Co, PO Box 7088, Mutrah; National Automobiles, PO Box 3818, Ruwi; National Hotels Co (Oman Sheraton Hotel); Al Hashar Tourism & Travel; Saeed Bin Nasser Al Hashar, PO BOx 1300, Deira, Dubai
Principal Bankers: Bank of Credit & Commerce International; Bank Dhofar Al Omani Al Fransi; Grindlays Bank; Arab Bank

Principal Shareholders: Directors as described
Date of Establishment: 1972
No of Employees: 400

AL HASSAN GROUP OF COMPANIES

PO Box 4948, Ruwi
Tel: (HO) 700575, (Showrooms) 703080, 707054, 708912, 700595/6, 713409
Cable: Ali Salman Muscat
Telex: 3589 AL HASSAN ON
Telefax: 704233

Directors: M A Salman (Managing Director)
Senior Executives: Z A Salam (General Manager), S M Rizvi (Manager -Electrical Division), N C Gupta (Manager - Building Materials Division), D Khotkar (Manager - Contracting Division), D M T Bandara (Manager - Finance & Admin), U Heble (Manager - Equipment Division)

PRINCIPAL ACTIVITIES: Dealers in electrical equipment, accessories & fittings, building materials, tools, hardware, sanitary ware, paint and coatings, safety products, decorative light fittings, office equipment also electrical, mechanical & plumbing contractors; instrumentation work; electro-mechanical projects
Principal Agencies: Ashley Accessories, UK; Dorman Smith Fuses, UK; Simplex GE, UK; Max Hellstern, West Germany; Geru Leuchten Fabrik, West Germany; Osaki Electric Co, Japan; TEC, Japan; Sigmaform, UK; IKO Kabels, Sweden; JOJO Cable Reels, Denmark; A N Wallis, UK; Berneray, UK; Dulmison, UK; Home Automation, UK; Natalarm Systems, UK; E H Jones, UK; Johnstone Safety, UK; Palace Chemicals, UK; NBS, UK; Hesse Andre, W Germany; Zippel, W Germany; Heim Electric, E Germany; Mitsubishi/CGE, Japan; Sanso Electric, Japan; Hitachi, Japan; Utax, Japan; Vega, Spain; Lorenzi Vasco, Italy; Solaic, France; etc
Subsidiary Companies: Al Hassan Building Materials Co (dealing in building materials, paints, kitchen units, sanitaryware, plumbing materials); Al Hassan Electricals (dealing in electrical equipment, accessories, decorative light fittings, transformers); Al Hassan Equipment Co (dealing in office equipment, telecommunication, office requisites, leisure equipment); Al Hassan Trading & Contracting Co (electromechanical projects, instrumentation projects)
Principal Bankers: Bank of Credit & Commerce International; Commercial Bank of Oman; Bank of Muscat; Bank of Oman Bahrain & Kuwait

Date of Establishment: 1975
No of Employees: 250

AL HAYTHEM TRADING & CONTRACTING CO LLC

PO Box 686, Muscat
Tel: 600412, 602471
Cable: ALHAYTHEM
Telex: 5640 HAYTHEM ON
Telefax: 601386

Chairman: Mahmood Macki (also Owner)

Directors: Hussain Al Rahma
Senior Executives: B D Amin (Marketing Manager)

PRINCIPAL ACTIVITIES: Sales and service of construction & mining machines, industrial and agricultural equipment, electro-mechanical services and equipment
Principal Agencies: Benford Ltd, UK; ACE Machineries, UK; Compair Construction & Mining, UK; Potain SA, France; Baranite, UK; Ransomes Sims & Jefferies Ltd, UK; Fyne Machinery & Engineering Ltd, UK; Demurger & Cie, France; SMG Machines & Abrasives, France; Finlay Screenig, UK; Hudig AG, W Germany
Branch Offices: Al Haythem Trading & Contr Co LLC, Sohar, Oman & Al Haythem & Partners, Salalah, Oman
Parent Company: Oman Technical Agencies, Muscat
Associated Companies: GETPCO Development General Trading Co, Dubai
Principal Bankers: British Bank of the Middle East; Union Bank of Oman; National Bank of Abu Dhabi; Bank of Oman Bahrain & Kuwait

Date of Establishment: 26th November 1974

AL IMAR ENTERPRISES
PO Box 4718, Ruwi
Tel: 705525, 701102, 659024
Cable: Entalamar
Telex: 5076 Alamar

Chairman: Abbas Jaffar Hussain
Directors: P S Dhingra (Managing Director)
Senior Executives: Mukesh K Babla (Senior Electrical Engineer), Darshan Singh Dhingra (Quantity Surveyor), Mobin Rizvi (Sales Manager), Mehmood Hudi (Public Relation Officer), S Sreekantan (Project Engineer), K Gopinathan Nair (Administrative Officer)

PRINCIPAL ACTIVITIES: Contracting and trading in electrical engineering field, electrical and instrumentation design consultancy
Principal Agencies: SIMPLEX GE, UK
Branch Offices: Al Amar Enterprises, PO Box 452, Muscat
Principal Bankers: British Bank of the Middle East, Muscat; Commercial Bank of Oman, Muscat

Principal Shareholders: Abbas Jaffar Hussain
Date of Establishment: 1970
No of Employees: 90

AL JAMALI EST
PO Box 4526, Ruwi
Tel: 706523
Telex: 3104 JEST CO ON, 3616 Mandlia ON

PRINCIPAL ACTIVITIES: Supply of building materials, furniture, carpets, flooring products, laboratory equipment, electrical materials, pollution control, chemicals, paints, coatings, water proofing materials
Principal Agencies: Foseco Minsep UAE, Dubai

AL JIZZI CO LLC
PO Box 4704, Ruwi, Muscat
Tel: 704795, 709618, 704903, 705153, 796628
Cable: ALJIZZI
Telex: 3058 REDHA ON
Telefax: 708334

Chairman: Hussain Saied Mohammed (also Managing Director)
Director: Abdul Amir Saied Mohammed
Senior Executives: K H Jeswani (Manager, Industrial & Engineering Div)

PRINCIPAL ACTIVITIES: Electrical, trading, industrial and engineering supplies/spares, various defence supplies; agents, general insurance
Principal Agencies: AB Chance Co USA; Black & Decker; Federal Mogul; National Seals

Subsidiary Companies: INDEC (interior decorators); Al Jizzi Electricals LLC
Principal Bankers: National Bank of Oman; Bank of Muscat

Principal Shareholders: Hussain Saied Mohammed & Brothers
Date of Establishment: 1978

ALKHALIJ ENTERPRISES
PO Box 3117, Ruwi, Muscat
Tel: 703506, 703385 (Darsait Main Showroom & Office)
Cable: Autoimpex
Telex: 3206 Autimp ON
Telefax: (968) 708211

Directors: Salim Essa Mansoor Assulaimi, Said Salim Assulaimi
Senior Executives: Ram Bhatia (General Manager), R S Manral (Sales Manager), G R Nath (Marketing Manager), G S Das (Chief Accountant)

PRINCIPAL ACTIVITIES: Retail and wholesale of bearings, filters, tools, pneumatic tools, garage equipment, welding equipment, nuts, bolts, spray paints, hoses, batteries, cork and rubber sheets, chemicals, pumps, batteries, compressors, welders, safety equipment, wire ropes, hoses, hydraulic jacks, etc
Principal Agencies: Fag Bearings, Germany; CRC Chemicals, Belgium; Vesta Batteries, Australia; Crosland Filters, UK; Stewart Warner, USA; Ajax, Australia; Creemers Air Compressors, Holland; Pioneer Weston, UK; R N Battery Chargers, USA; Sykes Pickavant Tools, UK; Champion Asbestos, India; Clayton, USA; Silver Beauty Charger, USA; Pedrollo, Italy; Black & Decker, UK; Imperial Eastman, USA; Dunlop, UK; General Motors, USA & Belgium; Carl Schlieper, Germany; Baudou, France; EPCO, UK; Automotive Products, UK; Finolex, India; Allanite Jointings, UK; Hempel Marine Paints
Associated Companies: Alkhalij Enterprises, PO Box 3320, Deira, Dubai, UAE; Alkhalij Enterprises, PO Box 4857, Abu Dhabi Assulaimi Trad. & Cont. Co, PO Box 321, Muscat, UAE; Bhatia & Co, PO Box 95, Bahrain
Principal Bankers: British Bank of the Middle East

Date of Establishment: 1975
No of Employees: 25

AL KHONJI, MOHAMED & AHMED,
PO Box 73, Muscat
Tel: 713188, showroom 704068, 704231
Cable: Khonji
Telex: 3525 Khonji ON

Chairman: Abdullah Mohamed Alkhonji (also Managing Director)
Senior Executives: Mahmood Alkhonji (General Manager), Najeeb Alkhonji (Sales Manager)

PRINCIPAL ACTIVITIES: Import, export and manufacturers' representation; building constructions; distribution of workshop equipment and implements, pumps, out-board motors, generators, car batteries, mechanical and electrical tools, agricultural material & equipment, fertilizers, pesticides, and services; fishing nets, nylon ropes, PVC hoses, G.I. pipes, all types of water pumps, generators and air compressors, wood working machines, hoists, mixers, impellents, block making machines, tile polishers, polythylene laminated sheets, wooden doors, tractors etc.
Principal Agencies: Robin Water Pumps & Generators; GFE Submersible Pumps; Arita Vertical Pumps; SCM Wood Working Machine; IHI-Shibaura Tractors; Davey Water Pumps, etc
Branch Offices: Main Showroom, Darsait, Muscat; Showroom, PO Box 7492, Muttrah, Muscat
Principal Bankers: Bank of Credit & Commerce International Ltd; Grindlays Bank plc; Arab Bank Ltd; British Bank of the Middle East

OMAN

Principal Shareholders: Mohamed Abdulla Alkhonji (100%)
Date of Establishment: 1895
No of Employees: 87

AL MACKI ESTABLISHMENT

PO Box 5088, Ruwi, Muscat
Tel: 705744, 702461, 793778
Cable: Macgroup
Telex: 3301 ON Macgroup
Telefax: (968) 703045

Chairman: Ahmed Abdul Rasool Macki (Proprietor & Managing Director)
Senior Executives: Robert J Stokes (General Manager), Francis Vieira (Trading Manager)

PRINCIPAL ACTIVITIES: General merchants and commission agents; import and distribution of vulcanising equipment, workshop and garage equipments, trailers and tippers, heavy steel structures, tyre retreading equipment; shipping services, clearing & forwarding, crane hire, transportation; safety and security systems; foodstuffs and pharmaceuticals
Principal Agencies: Tip Top Stahlgruber, W Germany; FMC Corp, USA; Kentredder, UK; Fram Filters, Holland; Water & Gas Industries, USA; CCL Systems, UK; Hella Products, West Falische Metals, W Germany; Scott & Huber, USA; Acco, USA; Martin Black, UK; Muller Water & Gas, UK; Bridport Gundry Cargo Nets, UK; Voest-Apline, Austria; American Science & Engineering, USA; Silvering Co Baby Products, Taiwan; Intercake, Butter Cookies, Denmark; STP - USA; Nordtend, Sweden; George Taylor, UK; Parsons Chains Kuplex, UK; John Shaw, UK; Citex, Holland; Airwert, UK
Branch Offices: PO Box 268, Muscat; PO Box 19343, Salalah; PO Box 5088, Ruwi; PO Box 5088, Gala
Subsidiary Companies: Al Macki Supermarket; Al Wadi Al Kabir Filling & Service Station; Al Macki Construction Company; Transport Services Oman; Riyam Development Company, Macktest
Principal Bankers: British Bank of the Middle East; Bank of Oman Bahrain & Kuwait SAO; Union Bank of Oman

Principal Shareholders: Sole proprietor
Date of Establishment: 1973
No of Employees: 105

AL MANARA TRADING CO

PO Box 3305, Ruwi, Muscat
Tel: 701920, 701860
Telex: 3207

PRINCIPAL ACTIVITIES: General trading; import and distribution of luxury goods and consumer goods
Principal Agencies: Asprey, Piaget, Luxor, Baume et Mercier, Patek Philippe, Jaeger Le Coultre, Audemas Piguet, Concord
Branch Offices: Ruwi and Muscat Intercontinental Hotel, Oman; Qatar; Abu Dhabi

AL MAZAARA ESTISHARIYA LLC (AME)

PO BOx 656, Muscat
Tel: 798373, 798376
Telex: 3323 MOM ON
Telefax: 793071

Chairman: HE Sheikh Mustahail Bin Ahmad Al Maashani
Directors: HE Salim Bin Mustahail Bin Ahmad Al Maashani
Senior Executives: Naeem Shakir (Group Chief Executive), V Seshadri (Group Financial Controller), Ahmad Hiraki (Manager Agriculture), Rajan Dewan (Manager Irrigation, Minoo Unwalla (Manager Landscaping), Mohd Aswad (Manager Farms)

PRINCIPAL ACTIVITIES: Engineering consultants, agro industries, irrigation and landscaping and water management
Principal Agencies: AS Bording, Denmark; BASF, W Germany; Ciba Geigy; Geder Holer, W Germany; Royal Sluis, Holland; Richard Sankey, UK; Kerry Pak, UK; Wolf Tools, UK; James Hardie Irrigation

Branch Offices: Barka, Tel 882960; Hail, Tel 536317; Salalah, Tel 210125, 210135
Parent Company: Qais Omani Establishment (Holding Company)
Principal Bankers: Bank of Oman Bahrain & Kuwait

Principal Shareholders: HE Sheikh Mustahail Bin Ahmad Al Maashani
Date of Establishment: 1975
No of Employees: 170

AL MUJTABA TRADING CORPORATION

PO Box 7344, Mutrah
Tel: 734663, 773103
Cable: Almujtaba Muscat
Telex: 5340 ON Mujtaba

Chairman: Ahmed Jaffer Suleiman (also Proprietor)

PRINCIPAL ACTIVITIES: Import and wholesale of foodstuffs, contract caterers to construction and other government organisations; also import and distribution of audio-video equipment, household appliances, air-conditioners and refrigerators
Principal Agencies: Imeko BV, Netherlands; Falcon, USA
Principal Bankers: Standard Chartered Bank (Muscat); British Bank of the Middle East (Mutrah)

AL NISR INSURANCE CO SAL (OMAN BRANCH)

Muttrah Business District, PO Box 4972, Ruwi
Tel: 798445, 798457, 798473
Cable: Comment Muscat
Telex: 3716 Comment ON
Telefax: 798456

Senior Executives: Ghassan Elias Ayoub (Branch Manager)

PRINCIPAL ACTIVITIES: Insurance agents and brokers
Branch Offices: Saudi Arabia; Lebanon; Kuwait; Bahrain; Qatar; United Arab Emirates; Oman; Yemen; Jordan
Parent Company: Head office in Greece

AL RASHDY, SAIF SAID, & SONS

PO Box 4746, Ruwi
Tel: 712958, 713450, 714654 (Office), 620878
Cable: AlRashdy MUSCAT
Telex: 5731 Alrashdy ON

Directors: Issa Saif Al-Rashdy (Managing Partner)

PRINCIPAL ACTIVITIES: General trading, import and supply of building materials, timber, paint, hardware, household appliances and bicycles and sewing machines
Principal Agencies: OLYMPIA Sewing Machines, Japan; Raleigh Bicycles, UK; Ultra Paints, UK
Principal Bankers: The British Bank of the Middle East; Grindlays Bank

Date of Establishment: 1960
No of Employees: 45

AL SERKAL, NASSER ABDULLATIF, EST

PO Box 3636, Ruwi
Tel: 703193, 703060
Cable: Nasser
Telex: 3375 ON
Telefax: 795118

Chairman: Nasser Abdullatif Al-Serkal
Directors: Eisa Bin Nasser Al-Serkal
Senior Executives: Nirantha de Silva (General Manager)

PRINCIPAL ACTIVITIES: Distribution of all types of centrifugal and turbine water pumps, diesel engines and spare parts, refrigerating, cooking and laundry equipment, storage and materials handling equipment, diesel generating sets, AC motors, marbles and tiles, carpentry machine, also water well drilling contractors

Principal Agencies: Petters, Electrolux, DPF, Peerless, Pleuger, Skjold, Newman, Hawker Siddeley Power Plant, Hydro Pumps, Treston, Electrolux Constructor (Germany), Gerni Cold/Hot Water High Pressure Cleaners
Branch Offices: Sohar, Oman (Head Office in Dubai: see separate entry)
Parent Company: Nasser Abdullatif Al Serkal & Son Establishment, PO Box 1219, Dubai, United Arab Emirates
Subsidiary Companies: Nal Parts Division Dubai; National Marble & Tiles Factory; Hydro Dynamic Industry Inc, Dubai
Principal Bankers: British of Bank of the Middle East; Al Bank Al Ahli Al Omani; Bank of Oman and the Gulf; Standard Chartered Bank

Principal Shareholders: Nasser Abdullatif; Eisa Bin Nasser Abdullatif
Date of Establishment: 1962
No of Employees: 30

AL SHIRAWI & COMPANY

PO Box 4511, Ruwi, Muscat
Tel: 705823, 702369
Cable: Al Shirawi
Telex: 3271 Shirawi ON
Telefax: 797762

Chairman: Abdulla Al Shirawi
Directors: M G Valrani (Senior Vice Chairman), Abdulla Al Khonji, Ebrahim Al Shirawi, G G Valrani
Senior Executives: G G Valrani (Managing Director)

PRINCIPAL ACTIVITIES: Dealing in all kinds of building and construction materials, hardware, tools, interior decoration materials
Principal Agencies: Bison, Holland; Sternson, Canada; Conybond, Japan; Union, UK; Marley, UK; Harris, UK
Branch Offices: Nizwa
Parent Company: Al-Shirawi Contracting & Trading Co, PO Box 93, Dubai (UAE)
Associated Companies: Asian Trading Co, PO Box 18692 Salalah, Tel 291578/291014, Fax 968-291014
Principal Bankers: National Bank of Oman Ltd, Ruwi, Muscat; Grindlays Bank plc, Ruwi, Muscat; Union Bank of Oman, Muttrah, Muscat; Bank of Muscat, Ruwi, Muscat
Financial Information:

	1989/90 RO'000
Sales turnover	3,500
Authorised capital	250
Paid-up capital	250

Principal Shareholders: Joint Stock Co (Al-Shirawi Contracting & Trading Co & Abdulla Al-Khonji)
Date of Establishment: 1972
No of Employees: 30

AL TAHER ENTERPRISES

PO Box 5670, Ruwi
Tel: 734602, 772227, 773493
Cable: Altaher
Telex: 5408 Altaher ON

Directors: Sheikh Saud Al Khalili

PRINCIPAL ACTIVITIES: Building and construction supplies; power generation; hardware, tools, metals
Principal Agencies: Velan; Crosby; Rosemont; Utica; Blackhawk

AL TURKI ENTERPRISES LLC

PO Box 5803, Ruwi
Tel: 590140
Cable: Al Turki
Telex: 5106 Al Turki

Chairman: H H Sayyed Turki Bin Mahmood Al Said
Directors: Gulabsi Ratansi Khimji, Chaitanya Gulabsi Khimji

Senior Executives: Pankaj Zaveri (Manager), Chandi Kumar (Contracts Manager)

PRINCIPAL ACTIVITIES: Construction, building materials, block manufacturing, crusher
Principal Agencies: Croda paints

AL YOUSEF INTERNATIONAL ENTERPRISES

PO Box 200, Muscat
Tel: 603936, 603937, 603955
Telex: 5247 AYIE ON

Chairman: H E Mohamed Bin Musa Al-Yousef
Directors: Yousuf Bin Salman Al Saleh (Vice Chairman)
Senior Executives: Mohsin Ghazi (Commercial Manager), N M Kasbekar (Manager Finance), P Prabhakaran (Investment Manager), A N Venugopal (Production Manager), Mustafa A Basset (Property Manager)

PRINCIPAL ACTIVITIES: Computers, telecommunications, oil field supplies; construction; power generation, water engineering; roofing; engineering consultancy, M & E Contracting, surveying; catering; finance; investment; insurance; loss adjusting; geotechnic engineering; petrochemical engineering; switchgear manufacturing; neon sign manufacturing
Principal Agencies: AT & T, Philips Telecommunications; TRT; NKF Cables; Airmech Eastern Engineering; Starr Roofing; Merrol Fire Protection; Halliburton; BKS Surveys; Soil Structures International; ABAY; Intergraph; Sumitomo Corporation; Toplis & Harding; Colcrete; IMES; W S Atkins Group; Kern; ACEC Gas Turbines; Protech International
Parent Company: Al Yousef Trading & Services Co LLC
Subsidiary Companies: Muscat Electronics Co (Sony); Oman Computer Services LLC (Wang); Voltamp Mfg Co LLC (Switchgear)
Principal Bankers: Oman International Bank; Commercial Bank of Oman

Principal Shareholders: H E Mohamed bin Musa Al-Yousef
Date of Establishment: 1977
No of Employees: (within group) 400

AMBOLA CONTRACTING & TRADING

PO Box 3158, Ruwi
Tel: 704367
Cable: Ambola
Telex: 3355 AMBOLA ON

Chairman: Qadar Bux Bin Charuk Ambola
Senior Executives: T K John (Trading Manager), Syed Imtiaz Ali (Office Manager)

PRINCIPAL ACTIVITIES: Building and civil engineering construction; shipowners; shipping agents and charterers, freight forwarding and clearing agents; building materials and paints distributors, lubricant oil and paints suppliers; plant hire
Principal Agencies: Smith & Walton Ltd, Mountain ROC Lubricants
Branch Offices: PO Box 18178, Salalah, Dhofar, Oman
Principal Bankers: British Bank of the Middle East (Muscat/Dubai)

No of Employees: 500

AMIANTIT OMAN SAO

C.P.O. Box 1417, Seeb
Tel: 626600, 626622, 626077
Cable: Amiantit Muscat
Telex: 5304 Amiantit ON
Telefax: 626611

Chairman: Suhail Bahwan
Directors: Saud Bahwan, Ismail Mansuri
Senior Executives: C N RaoRane (General Manager), Ranjith Cooray (Chief Accountant), Jack Hague (Technical Manager)

PRINCIPAL ACTIVITIES: Manufacture and distribution of asbestos cement, PVC/PE, GRP/FRP pipes for water, sewage, drainage and industrial piping applications; pipe fittings and other piping accessories; GRP/FRP tanks, tank lining, manholes and mouldings; GRP/GRC claddings, facias, facades and other architectural features; turnkey contracts for pipe-laying including irrigation; fishing boats; construction and maintenance of swimming pools

Principal Agencies: Formatura Inezione Polimeri, Italy; Maddalea, Italy; Sparling, UK; Yamaha Fishing Boats; Glasdon, UK; Pilkington, UK

Principal Bankers: Oman International Bank, Ruwi

Financial Information:

	1989/90 RO'000
Sales turnover	3,000
Authorised capital	2,100
Paid-up capital	2,100
Total assets	6,600

Principal Shareholders: Suhail & Saud Bahwan; Waleed Associates; Zawawi Trading

Date of Establishment: 1976

No of Employees: 200

ANZ GRINDLAYS BANK PLC

PO Box 3550, Ruwi

Tel: 702023, 7010102

Cable: Grindlays

Telex: 5393 Grindly ON

Telefax: 706911

Senior Executives: W S Harley (Chief General Manager), J T M McNie (General Manager)

PRINCIPAL ACTIVITIES: Commercial banking

Branch Offices: Bahrain; Oman; Qatar; United Arab Emirates (Abu Dhabi, Dubai, Sharjah, Ras Al Khaimah); Jordan; Pakistan and forty other countries

Parent Company: Head office: PO Box 280, 23 Fenchurch St, London EC3, UK

Principal Shareholders: ANZ Bank

Date of Establishment: 1969 in Oman

No of Employees: 62 in Oman

APOLLO TRADERS

PO Box 4639, Ruwi, Muscat

Tel: 734063

Telex: 5423 Opollo ON

Directors: Abdul Amir Abdul Husin Ebrahim (Partner), Hassan Abdullah Habib (Partner)

PRINCIPAL ACTIVITIES: Distribution of building materials and hardware, manufacturer's representatives, direct import of general goods

Principal Agencies: E I D Parry Ltd, Dalami, France

ARAB BUILDING MATERIALS CO LLC

PO Box 582, Muscat

Tel: 602420, 602422, 602460

Cable: Shiral

Telex: 5254 Shiral ON

Telefax: 602460

Chairman: Mohamed Ali Bdeir

Directors: Hassan Mango, Hussam Malas

Senior Executives: Tarek Hudhud (Executive Director)

PRINCIPAL ACTIVITIES: Supply of building materials, steel, timber, plywood, cement etc

Branch Offices: Jordan, Abu Dhabi, Dubai, Kuwait, Qatar, Bahrain, Saudi Arabia

Principal Bankers: Oman Arab Bank, Oman International Bank

Date of Establishment: 1972

No of Employees: 50

ARAB DEVELOPMENT CO LTD

PO Box 439, Muscat

Tel: 592159, 592101

Cable: Drilco Muscat

Telex: 3165 Drilco ON

Telefax: 592159

Directors: Munib R Masri, Tarif W Ayoubi

Senior Executives: Rashad R Masri (General Manager)

PRINCIPAL ACTIVITIES: Underground water exploration and water well drilling, geological and hydrological studies, geophysical surveys, well drilling and supply of pumps

Branch Offices: Salalah: PO Box 18201, Tel 211408, Fax 211408

Parent Company: Engineering and Development Group (EDGO), 186 Sloane Street, London SW1 X9QR, UK

Subsidiary Companies: Gulf Development Trading Enterprise

Principal Bankers: Oman Arab Bank SAO

Principal Shareholders: Munib R Masri and Tarif W Ayoubi

Date of Establishment: 1971

No of Employees: 170

ASHA ENTERPRISE

PO Box 6275, Ruwi

Tel: 734366

Cable: Ashaent Muscat

Telex: 5045 Asha ON

Senior Executives: S C Kandhari (Manager)

PRINCIPAL ACTIVITIES: General trading and contracting, furniture, fast food, consumer products

ASIAN TRADING COMPANY

PO Box 8692, Salalah, Dhofar

Tel: 461578, 461014

Cable: Asian

Telex: 7662 Asian ON

Senior Executives: Suresh D Choithramani (Sales Manager)

PRINCIPAL ACTIVITIES: Dealing in building and construction materials, hardware and tools

Subsidiary/Associated Companies: Al Shirawi & Co, Ruwi, Muscat

Principal Bankers: National Bank of Oman Ltd, Ruwi, Muscat; Grindlays Bank plc, Ruwi, Muscat

Date of Establishment: 1976

ASSARAIN ENTERPRISE

PO Box 4475, Ruwi

Tel: 564290 (6 lines)

Cable: ASSARAIN

Telex: 5293 ASSRAIN ON; 5338 ASSRAIN ON

Telefax: 564296

Chairman: HE Lt Col Said Bin Salem Al-Wahaibi

Directors: Abdulla Bin Saleh Baabood (Managing Director), Shiv Prakash Nanda (Finance Director), W I Mintowt - Czyz (Director/General Manager)

Senior Executives: Richard Siemicki (Asst General Manager Marketing), T D Samidon (Personnel & Adm Manager), D V Subbarao (Finance Manager)

PRINCIPAL ACTIVITIES: Furnishing and interior decorators, building products, construction, engineering, frozen foods, gardening and landscaping, irrigation, electronics and entertainment equipment, household appliances, airconditioning, specialised vehicles, telecommunications, travel, filling stations etc

Principal Agencies: EB Communication, Norway; Casa International, Denmark; Mobex Furniture, Italy; Index Furniture, Italy; Imex, USA; Johnston, UK; Troydence, UK; Lambown, UK; ASE, Belgium; Kone, Finland; ARMCO, UK; Taiyo, Japan; Automatic Lubrication System, Italy; Brooke Air Sales, UK; Burlington Slate, UK; Goodlass & Wall, UK; ITC,

Italy; A&T (Europe), Italy; Sports International, USA; Becker · Hellas, Greece; Marmaro, Greece; Bonsack Baths, UK; Emborg, Denmark; Hellaby, New Zealand; Watties, New Zealand; Jones, UK; Tweed Valley, UK; Englander, UK; Norman, UK; Sealy Sleep, UK; Sanderson, UK; Apexon, Italy; M Haupt, Austria; Hokyuo, Japan; Ital-line, Italy; Car Care, USA; Loewe, W Germany; Kable Metal Electro, W Germany; Krone, W Germany; Holden & Brooke, UK; DP Facilities, USA; Boring Irrigation, Denmark; Kirton Engg, UK; Albrecht Jung, W Germany; Norwood Partition, UK; Ancient Light, UK; Clearlight Roof Light, UK; Kalmar, Austria

Branch Offices: Assarain Building Products, Tel 603136; Assarain Construction, Tel 591255; Assarain Frozen Foods, Tel 603166, 698162; Assarain Furnishing, Tel 704464, 700368/9; Assarain Telecommunications, Tel 713295/6/7; Assarain Travels, Tel 795010/1/2/3; Wadi Adai Service Centre, Tel 561955; Assarain Service Centre, Tel 640213; Fibrous Plaster, Tel 603166; Assarain Enterprise (UK Office), Tel 01-930-1405

Subsidiary/Associated Companies: Drake & Scull Assarian LLC, PO Box 3116, Ruwi; Assarain International Construction Co LLC, PO Box 5910, Ruwi; Al Khuwair Gas Plant LLC, PO Box 4475, Ruwi; Assarian Garden Centre LLC, PO Box 4475, Ruwi; Al Haq General Trading & Contracting Co, PO Box 18647, Salalah; Assarain Concrete Products LLC, PO Box 7406, Ruwi; Hima Trdg & Cont Co, PO Box 3116, Ruwi; Oman International Trade and Exhibitions Co LLC, PO Box 4475, Ruwi

Principal Bankers: Bank of Baroda; National Bank of Oman; Al Bank Al Ahli Al Omani; Standard Chartered Bank

Principal Shareholders: Proprietorship
Date of Establishment: 1976
No of Employees: 1,300

ASSARAIN INTERNATIONAL CONSTRUCTION CO (LLC)

PO Box 5910, Ruwi
Tel: 704093, 794116, 794117, 794118
Cable: Asarain Co
Telex: 3453 AICC ON
Telefax: 3453 Cemint O ON

Chairman: H E Lt Col Said Salem Al Wahaibi
Senior Executives: Abdulla Saleh Baabood (Managing Director), Sudhir Keshavji (Managing Director), Salam Abdulla (Director), K R Lakdawala (Technical Director), H S C Swamy (Construction Manager), S P Nanda (Financial Director)

PRINCIPAL ACTIVITIES: Civil engineers and contractors
Principal Bankers: National Bank of Oman, Al Bank Al Ahli Al Omani

Date of Establishment: 1978
No of Employees: 1,400

ASSOCIATED ENTERPRISES

PO Box 5087, Ruwi
Tel: 704372, 707997
Cable: Assent
Telex: 3684 ON Elbualy
Telefax: 564784

Directors: Sheikh Majid Yahya Said Al Kindi (Proprietor)

PRINCIPAL ACTIVITIES: General traders, representatives for overseas companies, brokers and indentors, travel agents and estate agents, steel construction and fabrication, shipping agents and civil contractors, aviation services, textile merchants, building materials, auto paints and spare parts suppliers
Principal Agencies: Alomar Mechanical Engineering Co, Kuwait; CMC Surveys, UK; British Overseas & Export Trading Ltd, Diado Co, Japan; Meituko Busan, Japan; Cerberus, Switzerland; George Webb & Sons, UK; Sadolin Paints (Oman) Ltd

Branch Offices: Assent Super Market (Rumais) PO Box 10306, Barka; Assent Textiles Muttraah; Assent Paints & Auto Spare Parts Wadi Kabir (Ruwi)
Subsidiary/Associated Companies: National Travel & Tourism, Mutrah; Assent Distributors, Ruwi; Assent Estate Agents, Muscat; Assent Perfumeries, Muscat; Assent Surveys; Muscat; Yahya Al-Kindy Enterprises, Ruwi; Assent Shipping & Aviation Agency, Ruwi
Principal Bankers: British Bank of the Middle East; Union Bank of Oman

Date of Establishment: 1970

ATKINS, W S, INTERNATIONAL LTD

PO Box 5985, Ruwi
Tel: 702490, 798082
Telex: 3072 Atkins ON
Telefax: 708086

Senior Executives: B H Chapman (Resident Manager)

PRINCIPAL ACTIVITIES: Planning, engineering, management and agricultural consultants and architects
Branch Offices: In the Middle East: Bahrain, Kuwait, Dubai, Abu Dhabi, Saudi Arabia
Parent Company: W S Atkins Consultants, UK
Principal Bankers: British Bank of the Middle East

AZD HOCHTIEF CONSTRUCTION LLC

PO Box 338, Muscat
Tel: 621405, 605631
Telex: 3221 Hochtief ON
Telefax: 605632

Chairman: HH Kais Bin Tarik Bin Taimour Al Said
Directors: HH Haitham Bin Tarik Al Said (Director)
Senior Executives: Harold Wolf (General Manager), M K Naudakumar (Commercial Manager)

PRINCIPAL ACTIVITIES: Planning, design and construction; building and civil engineering contracting
Parent Company: Hochtief AG, West Germany
Principal Bankers: Oman International Bank

Principal Shareholders: AZD Enterprises; Hochtief AG
Date of Establishment: 1985

BAHWAN GROUP OF COMPANIES

PO Box 6168, Ruwi
Tel: 561256, 561377, 793741
Cable: Bahwan
Telex: 3724 Bahwan ON, 5501 BAHWAN ON
Telefax: 561631

Chairman: Suhail Bahwan
President: Saud Bahwan

PRINCIPAL ACTIVITIES: Import, distribution and after sales service of vehicles, construction and material handling equipment, watches, electronics and electrical appliances, building materials, steel, timber, plywood, pipes and fittings, sanitary-ware, refrigeration equipment, tyres and tubes; also building and civil engineering contract; travel; telecommunications and turnkey projects, cables, generators, elevators, mechanical and electrical projects, central air conditioning, cosmetics, pharmaceuticals, food products, supermarkets. Shipping and forwarding
Principal Agencies: Toyota, Komatsu, IBM, Seiko, Toshiba, Akai, Ford, Daewoo, Thermoking, Kato, Kubota, Bomag, MAN, Gloster Saro, Atlas, Yokohama, Kawasaki, Continental, Avialift, Manitou, Kuka, FB/GS Batteries, Simon Engineering, Carrier, Casio, Win, Ignis, Dunhill, Winston, Brown Boveri, Pye telecommunications, Bechtel, Dodsal, NEC Corp, Briathwaite, UTA, Jal, Thai Airways, Pan Am, Air France, etc
Branch Offices: Salalah, Buraimi, Sohar, Ibri, Nizwa, Barka, Sur, Al Kamil, Sinaw; Ibra; Khasab
Parent Company: Suhail & Saud Bahwan

OMAN

Associated Companies: Suhail & Saud Bahwan Building
   Materials LLC; Bahwan Contracting Co LLC; Bahwan
   Engineering Co LLC; Bahwan Travel Agency LLC; Bahwan
   Foods LLC; Edin Rushed Pharmacy LLC; Delta Limited; Rent-
   a-Car LLC; Arabian Engineering Services LLC; Al Mutawah
   Trading Co LLC; Arab Merchants Co LLC; Arabian Car
   Marketing Co LLC
Principal Bankers: Oman Arab Bank; Bank of Oman Bahrain &
   Kuwait; Citibank; Grindlays Bank; British Bank of the Middle
   East

Principal Shareholders: Suhail Bahwan, Saud Bahwan
Date of Establishment: 1967
No of Employees: over 4,000

BANK DHOFAR AL OMANI AL FRANSI SAOG

PO Box 4507, Ruwi
Tel: 798108, 798105, 798012/13
Telex: 3900 BDOF ON
Telefax: 798015

Chairman: HE Abdul Hafidh Bin Salim Bin Rajab Al Aujaili
Directors: Claude de Kemoularia, Francis Caze, Salim Oufaith,
   HE Yousuf Alawi, Ahmed Al Rawahi
Senior Executives: Noreddin Nahawi (General Manager)

PRINCIPAL ACTIVITIES: Commercial banking
Branch Offices: Salalah (Dhofar)
Parent Company: Head office: 3 rue d'Antin, 75002 Paris,
   France
Financial Information:

	1990 RO'000
Profits	250
Authorised capital	5,000
Paid-up capital	5,000
Total assets	35,524

Principal Shareholders: Private interest (40%); Banque Paribas
   (30%); Dhofar International Development & Investment
   Company (30%)
Date of Establishment: 1st January 1990?
No of Employees: 37

BANK MELLI IRAN

PO Box 410, Muscat
Tel: 722646, 722671
Cable: Mellibank
Telex: 5295 Bankml ON

PRINCIPAL ACTIVITIES: Commercial banking
Branch Offices: Salalah

BANK OF BARODA

PO Box 7231, Mutrah
Tel: 734556
Cable: Bank Baroda
Telex: 5470 ON

PRINCIPAL ACTIVITIES: Commercial banking

BANK OF CREDIT & COMMERCE INTERNATIONAL (OVERSEAS) LTD

PO Box 5230, Ruwi
Tel: 797240, 797247/9
Cable: Bancrecom
Telex: 3408 Bcci Mct ON

Senior Executives: Sajid Ali Abbasi (Manager)

PRINCIPAL ACTIVITIES: Commercial banking
Branch Offices: Branch in Salalah (Oman), PO Box 8550, Tel
   461631, Telex 7629; other branches in Oman: Seeb Airport;
   Greater Muttrah; Ruwi; Ibri; Nizwa; Rustaq; Sohar; Sook; Sur;

BANK OF MUSCAT SAOC (FORMERLY OMAN OVERSEAS TRUST BANK SAO)

PO Box 6326, Ruwi
Tel: 701769, 708490
Cable: Iddikhar
Telex: 3708 BK Muscat ON
Telefax: 707806

Chairman: HE Sheikh Hamood Bin Abdullah Al Harthy
Directors: HE Ali Bin Ahmed Al Ansari (Vice Chairman &
   Chairman Executive Committee), Ahmed Bin Saif Al Rawahy
   (Director), Major Waleed Bin Omar Bin Abdul Munem Al
   Zawawi (Director & Vice Chairman Executive Committee), HE
   Sheikh Salim Bin Mustahail Bin Ahmed Al Maashani
   (Director), Sayyid Badr Bin Hamad Bin Hamood Al Bu Said
   (Director & Member Executive Committee), Hussain Bin Saied
   Bin Mohamed (Director), Mohamed Jawad Bin Hassan
   (Director & Member Executive Committee)
Senior Executives: Yeshwant C Desai (General Manager), Abdul
   Razak Ali Issa (Deputy General Manager), J S George
   (Assistant General Manager Credit), A R I Parkar (Controller),
   Mohamed I Khan (Manager Computer Systems), Peter S
   Carvalho (Manager Correspondent Banking), Abbas Ghalib Al
   Kishri (Manager Personnel & Administration)

PRINCIPAL ACTIVITIES: Commercial banking
Branch Offices: 10 branches in Oman: Ruwi, Muscat, Hatat
   House, Jibroo, Salalah, Al Khuwair, Izki, Seeb, Samad e
   Shaan, Ghasab
Financial Information:

	1989 RO'000
Deposits	67,737
Profits	423
Authorised capital	5,500
Capital resources	6,127
Total assets	83,952

Principal Shareholders: Omani Interests
Date of Establishment: 1982 as Oman Overseas Trust Bank;
   1985 as present
No of Employees: 176

BANK OF OMAN, BAHRAIN & KUWAIT SAO

PO Box 4708, Ruwi
Tel: 700186/7/8, 701528, 701532, 701788, 705530
Cable: Bankom Muscat
Telex: 3290 OBK ON, 3674 OBK FX ON
Telefax: 705607

Chairman: Mohsin Haider Darwish
Directors: Ebrahim Eshaq Abdul Rahman (Joint Vice Chairman),
   Abdulla Moosa Abdul Rahman (Joint Vice Chairman),
   Mohamed Abdul Rasood Al Jamali (Managing Director), Hilal
   Mishari Hilal Al Mutairi (Deputy Managing Director), Suhail
   Salem Bahwan, Dr Yousef Abdulla Al Awadi, HE Ali Dawood
   Juma Al Raisi, Ibrahim Abdulla Al Hamer, Hassan Khalifa
   Mohd Al Jalahma, Mustafa Abdul Reda Sultan, Faisal Mohd
   Al Radwan

PRINCIPAL ACTIVITIES: Commercial banking
Branch Offices: Ruwi, Salalah, Muscat, Muttrah, Wadi Kabir, Al
   Falaj Hotel, Muscat Intercontinental Hotel, Wadi Hattat,
   Rusail, Birka, Bidaya, Suwaiq, Tharmad, Saham, Sohar,
   Mudha, Dibba Al Beya, Ghala, Gulf Hotel, Royal Hospital,
   Quriyat, Al Ashkara (Ja'alan), Bilal Bani Bu Hassan (Ja'alan),
   Baddia, Nizwa, Ibri, Al Khuwair, Al Hail and Hamriya
Financial Information:

	1988/89 RO'000
Profits	794
Authorised capital	15,000
Paid-up capital	8,250
Total assets	125,590

Principal Shareholders: Omani nationals (51%); Bank of Bahrain & Kuwait BSC (49%)
Date of Establishment: Incorporated in July 1973
No of Employees: 297

BANQUE SADERAT IRAN

PO Box 4269, Ruwi
Tel: 773474, 772844, 773478
Telex: 5191 Saderbnk ON

PRINCIPAL ACTIVITIES: Commercial banking

BEST ENTERPRISES

PO Box 3814, Greater Muttrah, Muscat
Tel: 703814, 704038, 703671
Cable: Bestelec
Telex: 3256 Best ON
Telefax: 798071

Proprietor: Moosa Baqer Suleiman (Chairman)
Senior Executives: V S Krishnamurthy (General Manager and Chief Engineer), M Jaiprakash (Administrative Manager)

PRINCIPAL ACTIVITIES: Dealers and contractors of electrical, electronic, mechanical and sanitary goods, central airconditioning and fire protection systems
Principal Agencies: Auto Diesels Braby Ltd, UK; Carters, UK; Braithwaite, India
Parent Company: Best Enterprises
Subsidiary Companies: Al Fakhr Establishment; Al Fakhr Pest Killer Fumigation Services
Principal Bankers: Bank of Credit & Commerce Int, Muscat; Bank of Muscat, Ruwi

Principal Shareholders: Sole proprietorship
Date of Establishment: 1978
No of Employees: Above 100

BHACKER HAJI ABDULLATIFF FAZUL

PO Box 4068, Ruwi
Tel: 714221/5 (5 lines)
Cable: Bhacker Muscat
Telex: 5220A Bhacker ON, 5220B Bhacker ON
Telefax: 711114

Chairman: Hassan Ali Abdullatiff
Directors: Ahmed Ali Abdullatiff (Managing Director), Hussain Ali Abdullatiff, Mahmoud Ali Abdullatiff, Mohamed Ali Abdullatiff

PRINCIPAL ACTIVITIES: Shipping agents, clearing, forwarding and transporting
Principal Agencies: Agents for Leading Shipping Companies
Branch Offices: PO Box 18389, Salalah (Dhofar), Tel 291013, Telex 7633
Subsidiary Companies: Abdullatiff Trading & Transport Co, PO Box 97, Muscat
Principal Bankers: British Bank of the Middle East; Union Bank of Oman

Principal Shareholders: (Partnership Firm) - Chairman & Directors mentioned above
Date of Establishment: 1895
No of Employees: 200 (approx)

BHATIA AND COMPANY

PO Box 78, Muscat
Tel: 722338
Cable: Bhatia

Directors: M I Bhatia, N I Bhatia

PRINCIPAL ACTIVITIES: Import and distribution of textiles, cosmetics and toilet preparations, toys, gift items, novelties, ready made gents, children and ladies garments (inner and outer), travelling clocks
Principal Agencies: Avon Cosmetics, UK, USA, France; Faberge Products, USA; Tip Top Hair Accessories USA; Lentheric Morny, UK; John Foster & Sons Ltd, UK

Associated Companies: Saar Corporation PO Box 1084, Salalah
Principal Bankers: The British Bank of the Middle East; Bank Melli Iran

BIN AMEIR ESTABLISHMENT

PO Box 100, Muscat
Tel: 701028, 773480
Cable: Al-Hinai
Telex: 5477 Al-Hinai ON; 3205 Binameir

Chairman: Nasser Mohamed Ameir Al Hinai
Directors: Saleh Mohamed Ameir Al Hinai

PRINCIPAL ACTIVITIES: Civil engineering and construction, import and distribution of tyres and air conditioners, refrigerators, ready-made garments; supermarket chain
Principal Agencies: Dunlop Tyres, UK; Linde Airconditioners & Refrigerators, Germany
Branch Offices: Falaj Supermarket: PO Box 3220, Ruwi
Associated Companies: Oman Engineering & Contracting; Al Bank Al Ahli Al Omani SAO; Al Jazira Establishment; Mohd Bin Ameir Al Hinai & Sons
Principal Bankers: Standard Chartered Bank (Muscat); Al-Bank Al-Ahli Al-Omani (Ruwi)

BIN SALIM ENTERPRISES

Al-Rawahy Building, Wattaya, Qaboos Street, PO Box 808, Muscat
Tel: 601708, 603078
Cable: Binsalim Muscat
Telex: 5430 Binsalim ON

Proprietor: Sheikh Hamed Salim Al-Rawahy, Chairman
Management Committee: Sheikh Aflah H S Al-Rawahy
Directors: Is-haq H S Al-Rawahy

PRINCIPAL ACTIVITIES: Import and distribution of drilling equipment, tools, home appliances and air-conditioning equipment, surface treatment equipment, pumps, and generating sets, concrete mixers, compactors and vibrators, dumpers, roof coating, fastening tools and accessories, brushes, welding sets, garage equipment
Principal Agencies: Atlas Copco, Hilti, Facom, Zoppas, Swan, Automan, Baromix, Errut, Mikasa, Johnson, Postgrand, Osborn, Telitalia, Tecalemit (Deutsche)
Parent Company: Al-Rawahy Limited
Subsidiary Companies: Bin Salim Enterprises - Ice Cream Division
Principal Bankers: Al Bank Al Ahli Al Omani SAO

Principal Shareholders: Sole proprietorship
Date of Establishment: 1975

BP MIDDLE EAST LIMITED

PO Box 51092, Mina Al Fahal
Tel: 561801 (10 lines)'
Cable: Beepee Muscat
Telex: 5419 Beepee ON
Telefax: 561283

Directors: P M Willis (Managing Director)
Senior Executives: A R Graham (General Manager Oman)

PRINCIPAL ACTIVITIES: Marketing of petroleum products
Branch Offices: BP Dhofar, PO Box 20309, Salalah
Parent Company: BP Middle East Ltd, PO Box 1699, Dubai
Associated Companies: Part of the British Petroleum Co plc, UK
Principal Bankers: Oman International Bank

Principal Shareholders: BP Co plc
Date of Establishment: 1957 (Oman)
No of Employees: 165

BRIAN COLQUHOUN & PARTNERS

See COLQUHOUN, BRIAN, & PARTNERS

OMAN

BRITISH BANK OF THE MIDDLE EAST (THE)

PO Box 3240, Ruwi
Tel: 799920/7
Cable: Bactria Muscat
Telex: 3110 BBME ME ON

Chairman: W Purves CBE DSO
Directors: J R H Bond, F J French, J M Gray, J A P Hill CBE, S Robertson, P J Wrangham
Senior Executives: R C Allenby (Manager Oman)

PRINCIPAL ACTIVITIES: All banking services
Branch Offices: Muscat, Muttrah, Bait Al Falaj (Main Office), Salalah
Parent Company: The Hongkong and Shanghai Banking Corporation
Principal Shareholders: The Hongkong and Shanghai Banking Corp Ltd
Date of Establishment: In Oman - 1948
No of Employees: In Oman - 249

BUILDING SUPPLIES & SERVICES CO LLC

PO Box 4006, Ruwi
Tel: (968) 714177
Cable: RASASI, MUSCAT
Telex: 5386 Rasasi ON
Telefax: (968) 711066

Directors: Iyad I Rasasi (Managing Director)
Senior Executives: C R Nair (Sales Executive)

PRINCIPAL ACTIVITIES: Supply of building materials and manufacturer's agents, specialists in waterproofing sewage treatment plant, installation and maintenance, swimming pool installation etc
Principal Agencies: Newman Tonks Worldtrade, UK; Buchtal GmbH, Germany; PCI Polychemie GmbH, Ausburg; Sigma Coatings, Holland; Maplex SA, Spain; Satec Ltd, UK; Chevron (CIM) USA; Krieg Et Zivy Industries, France; TRM, Austria; Niederberg, W Germany; Opiocolor, Hong Kong; Sealmaster, UK; J W Bollom & Co, UK; Nuway, UK; Wolliscroft, UK; Insuwrap, Saudi Arabia; Kassaab Steel Frames, Saudi Arabia; Isovolta, Austria; Corticeira Amorim, Portugal; Carl Freudenberg, Germany; Building Chemical Ind Co, Saudi Arabia; Robbins, USA; Sutcliffe Leisure, UK; Griffin Pipe Products, USA; Hydrex, France
Parent Company: Rasasi Commercial Enterprises
Principal Bankers: Union Bank of Oman, National Bank of Oman

BUSINESS INTERNATIONAL GROUP LLC

PO Box 499, Muscat
Tel: 600465 (8 lines), 603240
Cable: Fleet ON
Telex: 5502 Fleet ON
Telefax: 602406

Directors: Ziad Karim Al Haremi
Senior Executives: Salah Akhal (General Manager), Hemant Pajankar (Sales Manager), G Chandrasekar (Financial Controller), V S Mantha (Deputy Sales Manager)

PRINCIPAL ACTIVITIES: Vocational, technical and scientific equipment, laboratory equipment and furniture, testing and measuring instruments, language laboratories, storage shelving system, supermarket furnishing, fire fighting equipment, defence supplies, arts & crafts, sports and playground equipment, water testing equipment and treatment chemicals, material testing and workshop equipment, pipes and fittings, franchises, retail outlets
Principal Agencies: Philips Harris, UK; Reeves-Dryad, UK; Lloyd Instruments, UK; Boxford, UK; Shaw Scientific Instruments, Eire; Adam Rouily, UK; Palletower, UK; John Reid, UK; Potterycraft, UK; Armfield, UK; Feedback Instruments, UK; P A Hilton, UK; Greenings, UK; Tandberg Educational, Norway; Bork's Patentavler, Denmark; BTJ Products, Sweden; HKS, Germany; Eletrolux, Germany; Gametime, USA; GES Thomasson Darrouy, France; Dynamit Nobel, Germany; Joseph Gleave, UK; Pizza Inc, USA
Principal Bankers: Bank of Muscat, Ruwi; Bank of Oman Bahrain & Kuwait, Ruwi
Principal Shareholders: Ziad Karim Al Haremi, Osama Karim Al Haremi
Date of Establishment: 1990
No of Employees: 35

C JAYANT BROS (OMAN) LTD

See JAYANT, C, BROS (OMAN) LTD

CANSULT LIMITED

PO Box 443, Muscat
Tel: 601654, 601655
Cable: Cansult Muscat
Telex: 5382 Cansult ON

Chairman: J A Metcalfe
Senior Executives: H D Danesh (General Manager Oman)

PRINCIPAL ACTIVITIES: Consulting engineering, planning and architecture
Branch Offices: Saudi Arabia, United Arab Emirates
Parent Company: Cansult Group Ltd, Toronto, Canada
Principal Bankers: British Bank of the Middle East

CEMENT MARKETING CO LLC

PO Box 4890, Ruwi
Tel: 699171/4
Cable: Cementco Muscat
Telex: 5252 CMC ON
Telefax: 601487

Chairman: Abdullah Said Badr AlRawas
Directors: Ali Mohammad Akeel Ba-Omar (Managing Director), Salim Bin Abdullah Bin Said Al Rawas
Senior Executives: S Abdul Ghani El Sabir (General Manager), V Welihindha (Sales Manager), Hashim V Umar (Sales Manager)

PRINCIPAL ACTIVITIES: Trading and contracting, building products, timber, props, scaffolding, formwork, paints, hardware, ironmongery, GI pipes and fittings, PVC pipes and fittings, special coatings, sanitaryware, tiles, refrigerant gases, spray equipment, spare parts, electricals; supply and installation of waterproofing, kitchen units, steel ceilings, painting, electrical and civil works, GRP tanks, water treatment plants, reverse osmosis desalination, sewage treatment plants
Principal Agencies: Daiwa, Japan; Andamois IN, Spain; Noe Formwork, W Germany; Sadolin Paints, Oman, Rothenberger, W Germany; Modula, UK; GKN, UK; Liquid Plastics, UK; Lanstar, UK; Qualcast Grovewood Kitchens, UK; Qualcast Ceramics, UK; Supergress Tiles, Italy; Arcton ICI, UK; Wagner, W Germany; Varoline, W Germany; UTB, Switzerland; MMD, Switzerland; Watco, UK; Huntley & Sparks, UK; Burgess, UK; Contactum, UK; Elco, UK; Moka, USA
Branch Offices: Salalah: PO Box 18196, Dhofar, Salalah; Tel 290238, Telex 7670 CMC ON, Fax 293831
Subsidiary Companies: Ruwi Trading & Contracting Co
Principal Bankers: Bank of Credit & Commerce Int (Overseas) Ltd, National Bank of Oman Ltd, Union Bank of Oman Ltd
Principal Shareholders: Ali Mohammad Aqeel Baomar, Abdullah Bin Said Bin Badr Al Rawas
Date of Establishment: 1976
No of Employees: 50

CENTRAL BANK OF OMAN

PO Box 4161, Ruwi
Tel: 702222
Cable: Markazi ON
Telex: Administration Dept 3794 MARKZI ON, Accounts Dept
3070 MARKZI ON, International Relations Dept 3288
MRKZFX ON, 3493 MARKZI ON
Telefax: 702253

Deputy Chairman: HE Ahmed Abdul Nabi Macki
Board of Governors: Appointed by Royal Decree
Senior Executives: Dr Abdul Wahab Khayata (President),
Hamoud Sangour Hashim (Deputy Executive President),
Hassan Ali Salman (Senior Vice President), Dr Mohd
Abdulaziz Kalmoor (Vice President Research & Statistics),
Mohd Nasser Al Jahadhmy (Vice President Treasury
Investment & Settlement), Abdulla Daud Abdulla (Senior
Manager Research & Credit), Iqbal Ali Khamis (Senior
Manager Computer & Currency), Salim Mohamed Al Ghassani
(Senior Manager)

PRINCIPAL ACTIVITIES: Central banking, currency control and
regulation of local and foreign banks and money changers
Branch Offices: Salalah: PO Box 8356, Dhofar, Tel 461566,
Telex 7683 MARKAZI ON; Sohar: PO Box 12734, Sohar, Tel
842122, Telex 8040 MARKAZI ON
Financial Information:

	1990
	RO'000
Capital	100,000

Principal Shareholders: Government of Sultanate of Oman
Date of Establishment: December 1974; commenced business
April 1975
No of Employees: 295

CHAINLINK FENCING CO LLC

PO Box 42007, Rusayl Industrial Estate
Tel: 626024, 626211
Telex: 5222 Fences ON
Telefax: 968-626037

Chairman: Ali Mohammed Mirza Al Ajmi
Directors: Tariq Ali Mirza, Hani Ali Mirza
Senior Executives: G S Vasuki (General Manager), K S Kamath
(Finance Manager)

PRINCIPAL ACTIVITIES: Manufacture of chainlink fencing,
fencing systems, barbed wires, fabricated gates and
structures, gabion boxes, mattresses wire netting,
greenhouses, etc
Principal Bankers: National Bank of Oman
Financial Information:

	1990
	US$'000
Sales turnover	3,000
Authorised capital	1,000

Principal Shareholders: Chairman and directors as described
Date of Establishment: 1982
No of Employees: 50

CITIBANK NA

PO Box 8994, Ruwi
Tel: 795705, 795013, 700815
Telex: 3444 Citibk ON
Telefax: 795724

Senior Executives: Steven A Pinto (Country Corporate Officer &
Business Manager), M Zahran (Resident Vice President),
Muneer Khan (Operations Manager), Bassam Daoud (Credit
Manager), Anwer Iqbal (Treasurer & Financial Controller)

PRINCIPAL ACTIVITIES: Commercial banking
Parent Company: Head office in New York, USA

Date of Establishment: 1975

CIVIL CONTRACTING CO (OMAN) LLC

PO Box 4321, Ruwi
Tel: 590762/5
Cable: Civilco
Telex: 5083 Civilco ON
Telefax: 590541

Chairman: Ali Mohd Mirza
Directors: S M Rao
Senior Executives: B S Salehittal (General Manager)

PRINCIPAL ACTIVITIES: Electrical, plumbing, sanitation and air
conditioning contractors
Branch Offices: Buraimi, Salala
Subsidiary Companies: Masirah Electricals, Dubai
Principal Bankers: Oman International Bank
Financial Information:

	1989
	RO'000
Sales turnover	6,000
Authorised capital	150
Paid-up capital	150

Date of Establishment: 1974
No of Employees: 202

COLD STORAGE & TRADING CO LCC

PO Box 18055, Salalah
Tel: 290644, 460644
Cable: Spinsal Salalah
Telex: 7619 ON Spinsal

PRINCIPAL ACTIVITIES: Catering services, wholesale and retail
of foodstuffs and cold storage

COLQUHOUN, BRIAN, & PARTNERS

PO Box 402, Sultan Bldg, Ruwi, Muscat
Tel: 702909, 703539
Telex: 3129 Bricolp ON

PRINCIPAL ACTIVITIES: Consulting engineering service,
highways and bridges, airports, marine works, defence
installations, transportation planning, hotels and hospitals,
industrial, residential, commercial and institutional buildings,
electric power generation and distribution, water supply,
sewerage and sewage disposal
Parent Company: Head Office in UK, 22 Upper Grosvenor
Street, London W1X OAP

Date of Establishment: 1973

COMCENT INTERNATIONAL GROUP OF COMPANIES

PO Box 6558, Ruwi
Tel: 706752
Telex: 3499 Kharusi ON

Chairman: Muhammad Ali Said Al Kharusi
Senior Executives: Mohsen Fahmy (Group Public Relations
Manager), S George (Materials Controller)

PRINCIPAL ACTIVITIES: Office equipment, furniture, stationery,
supplies of hygiene and cleaning equipment, sewing
machines, photoproducts (professional and consumer),
phototypesetting printing equipment, electronics, telephone
systems/intercoms, security and communication equipment,
reprographic equipment
Branch Offices: Sohar: PO Box 12684; Salalah: PO Box 18679,
Tel 291154, Telex 7718 Khasala ON
Principal Divisions: Photocentre, PO Box 3115, Ruwi, Tel
706752, Telex 3499; Office Equipment Division, PO Box 3115,
Ruwi, Tel 706752, Telex 3499; Hygiene & Cleaning Division,
PO Box 3115, Ruwi, Tel 706752, Telex 3499;
Telecommunications Division, Colourlab LLC; Studios; Ijlaal
Trading, PO Box 3114, Ruwi; Almas Technical Services, PO
Box 3114, Ruwi; Comcent International LLC, PO Box 3115,
Ruwi, Tel 706752; Reprographic Division, Tel 706752;
Projects & Development Division

Principal Bankers: Grindlays Bank; Bank of Muscat; Bank of Oman & the Gulf

Date of Establishment: 1972

COMMERCIAL BANK OF OMAN LTD SAOG
PO Box 4696, Ruwi, Rami Plaza Muttrah Business District, Muscat
Tel: 793226/28, 793222/24
Cable: Combank Muscat
Telex: 3275 Combnkho ON
Telefax: 793229

Chairman: Maqbool Hameed
Directors: Maqbool A Soomro Mohammad Hassan Bin Ghulam Habib, Ahmed Bin Ali Bin Awadh Bin Rajab Alojaley, R T Gibson, Azizullah Menon, Hasan Yusuf
Senior Executives: Hasan Yusuf (Director & General Manager), Mohammad Afzal (Senior Manager Credit & Finance), Ali Hassan Suliman (Senior Manager Branches), M Riaz Ul Haq (Senior Manager Corporate Branch), Sadiq Mohammad Said (Senior Manager Personnel & Admin), Shaukat Mahmood Mir (Senior Manager Operations), M Luqman Khan (Senior Manager Data Processing), Ashfaq Ahmed Khan (Manager Operations), Tanweer A Sheikh (Manager Branches)

PRINCIPAL ACTIVITIES: Commercial banking
Branch Offices: Corporate Branch: PO Box 4696, Ruwi; Corniche Branch: PO Box 8265, Muttrah; Muttrah Branch: PO Box 7108, Muttrah, Ruwi Branch: PO Box 5330; Seeb Branch: PO Box 9647, Seeb; Nizwa Branch: PO Box 26592; Sohar Branch: PO Box 12579; Sur Branch: PO Box 30142; Salalah Branch: PO Box 18848; Adam Branch: PO Box 26974; Shinas: PO Box 13261; Al-Khuwair: PO Box 6486; Buraimi: PO Box 16227; Izki Branch: PO Box 26966; Greater Muttrah: PO Box 8218; Ibra: PO Box 32759; Liwa: PO Box 13729; Booth at Mina Qaboos; Al Suwaiq: PO Box 11311; Al Khaboura: PO Box 11923; Mahda: PO Box 15507; Taqa: PO Box 22007; Ibri: PO Box 17411, Ibri; Al Dareez: PO Box 17411, Ibri
Financial Information:

	1989 RO'000
Deposits	66,053
Advances	53,769
Share capital	5,000
Paid-up capital	5,000
Total assets	90,814

Principal Shareholders: Omani Nationals and United Bank Ltd, Karachi (Pakistan)
Date of Establishment: April 1976
No of Employees: 276

CONSOLIDATED CONTRACTORS COMPANY OMAN LLC
PO Box 614, Muscat
Tel: 700800 (10 lines)
Cable: Conco Muscat
Telex: 3420 Conco ON
Telefax: 708412

Chairman: HE Qais Abdul Munim Al Zawawi
Directors: HE Salem Bin Nasser Al Busaidi, HE Col Said Salem Al Wahaibi, HE Abdul Hafidh Salim Bin Rajab, Said T Khoury, Hassib J Sabbagh
Senior Executives: Youssef J Shammas (General Manager)

PRINCIPAL ACTIVITIES: General construction and engineering contractors, pipeline contractors, marine, civil and mechanical works
Branch Offices: Managing Office: Greece: PO Box 61092, Amaroussion, Athens, Tel 6829200, Telex 219551 CCIC GR, Fax 6841561
Parent Company: Consolidated Contractors Group (Holding) SAL

Principal Bankers: Oman Arab Bank SAO, Oman International Bank SAO
Financial Information:

	1990 RO'000
Sales turnover	7,300
Authorised capital	1,500
Paid-up capital	1,500
Total assets	5,000

Principal Shareholders: Consolidated Contractors Group (32.67%); Omani Businessmen (51%), Al Yusr Co for Contracting Trade & Industries WLL (16.33%)
Date of Establishment: Group: 1952; in Oman: 1971
No of Employees: 1,200

COOPERS & LYBRAND DELOITTE
PO Box 6075, Ruwi
Tel: 563717 (6 lines)
Cable: COLYBRAND
Telex: 5147 COLYBRND ON
Telefax: 564408

Partners: Safaa El Din Sadek (Managing Partner), Noel I Ferrand, Ian R Clay, Jeff Todd
Managers: Elena B Pattern (Senior Manager), David W Hannah (Senior Manager), R P Surana (Manager), Peter Clark (Manager), Ashok Rao (Manager)

PRINCIPAL ACTIVITIES: Public accountants and management consultants
Branch Offices: Salalah: PO Box 19386, Tel 290460

Date of Establishment: 1971
No of Employees: 45

CROWN DARWISH ENGINEERING OMAN LLC
PO Box 3729, Ruwi
Tel: 602104
Cable: Crowdar

Chairman: Mohsin Haider Darwish

PRINCIPAL ACTIVITIES: Electrical, mechanical and air conditioning engineering and contracting
Associated Companies: Mohsin Haider Darwish

D J SAMPAT & CO
See SAMPAT, D J, & CO

DARWISH, HAIDER,
PO Box 69, Muscat
Tel: 703377, 703677
Cable: Aldarwish
Telex: 3475 Haider ON

Chairman: Darwish Haider Darwish (also Proprietor)
Directors: Ahmed Darwish Haider (Managing Director)
Senior Executives: John C Sequeira (General Manager), Joseph Pinto (Chief Accountant)

PRINCIPAL ACTIVITIES: Importers, distributors and general merchants (cigarettes, tobacco and food-stuffs)
Principal Agencies: Rothmans of Pall Mall, London; Willem II Sigarenfabrieken, Holland; Consolidated Cigar; Douwe Egberts Tobacco Holland; International Cigarette Distributors, UK; Douwe Egbert Coffee & Tea, Holland
Branch Offices: PO Box 2706, Dubai, UAE
Subsidiary Companies: Ahmed and Fuad Darwish, PO Box 6069, Ruwi
Principal Bankers: British Bank of the Middle East (Bait Al-Falaj Branch)

Date of Establishment: 1921
No of Employees: 36

DARWISH, MOHSIN HAIDER, LLC

PO Box 3880, Ruwi
Tel: 703777
Cable: Areej Muscat
Telex: 3230 ON Lujaina
Telefax: 793256

Proprietor: Mohsin Haider Darwish
Directors: A Mehra (Director Finance)
Senior Executives: R N Spikins (General Manager Automotive),
P K Dutta (Manager Finance & Procurement), Ahmed E Qasim
(Manager Personnel & Admin), M V Ramaswamy (Manager
Internal Audit), M M Thomas (Vehicles Sales Manager), J
D'Souza (Manager Computer Services & Office Automation),
M P K Menon (Manager Retail Electrical & Projects), A C
Mogre (Manager Engineering Products), A K Paul (Manager
Gases Division), Bruno de Bonis (Manager Service Centre
Ruwi), Derek Brook (Manager Service Centre Azaiba), Robert
Pearce (General Manager UBM Division), S K Wig (Manager
Tyres & Batteries), S Ramaswamy (Manager Automotive
Parts)

PRINCIPAL ACTIVITIES: Importers, wholesalers, commission
agents for motor vehicles and spare parts, pumps, tyres and
tubes, electrical appliances and equipment, refrigeration,
airconditioning and kitchen equipment, building materials,
electronics, marine and sport equipment, household
appliances and lamps, computers and office automation,
telecommunications, gases and welding equipment, plant and
industrial products and equipment, safety and fire fighting
equipment, prefab, furnishings and contracting
Principal Agencies: British Leyland, Land Rover, Range Rover,
Jaguar, Austin Rover, UK; Aveling Barford, UK; Winget, UK;
Ingersoll Rand, Switzerland; Michelin, France; Chloride Int,
UK; Ferodo, UK; Sidchrome Pty, Australia; G & M Power
Plant, UK; Scottorn Trailers, UK; Pioneer Electronic Corp,
Japan; GEC, UK; Triumph Adler, Germany; British Oxygen,
UK; Cintec Ltd, UK; Ashok Leyland, India; Spencer Hydraulic,
UK; Metrix Engg, UK; Goodwin Barsby, UK; O & K Export,
Germany; Ransomes & Rapier, UK; Armitage Shanks, UK; H
D Sheldon & Co, USA; Hosoda Trading, Japan; Avon
Inflatables, UK; Foster Refrigerator, UK; Link 51, UK; MK
Electric, UK; Pirelli Cables, UK; Denby Tableware, UK; AEG
Telefunken, West Germany; Sunroc Corp, USA; Dunlop Ltd,
UK; Maskinfabrikken, Denmark; Minolta, Japan; Mitsubishi
Electric, Japan; Myson Copperad, UK; NCR, USA; Peabody
Barnes, USA; Pettibone, USA; Rediffusion, UK; Royal
Doulton, UK; Schrader, France; Unipart, UK; Yanmar Boats,
Japan; Draghwerk, Germany; Emip, France; Mcquay, Italy;
Casio Computer, Japan
Associated Companies: Al Darwish & Al Mashani Trading &
Contracting Co, Oman; Lujaini LLC, Oman; Special Oilfield
Services LLC, Oman; Areej Vegetable Oils & Derivatives SAO,
Oman; Darwish Ast Group of Companies, Oman; ADANCO
Trading, Dubai; ADANCO Technical Services, Dubai
Principal Bankers: Bank of Oman, Bahrain & Kuwait; National
Bank of Oman; Standard Chartered Bank; Union Bank of
Oman; British Bank of the Middle East

No of Employees: 600

DARWISH-AST GROUP OF COMPANIES LLC

PO Box 223, Muscat
Tel: 704177
Cable: Darast Muscat
Telex: 3238 DARAST ON

Chairman: Walter Strobl
Directors: Mohsin Haider Darwish, Dr Hans Seitz

PRINCIPAL ACTIVITIES: Civil engineering and contracting,
block and prefab factory
Branch Offices: Darwish-Ast & Partner Salalah LLC, PO Box
8289, Salalah, Oman; Darwish-Ast Construction Co, PO Box
223, Muscat; Darwish-Ast Block & Prefab Factory, PO Box
223, Muscat

Principal Bankers: British Bank of the Middle East; Standard
Chartered Bank; Bank of Oman, Bahrain & Kuwait
Principal Shareholders: Mohsin Haider Darwish, Overseas Ast A
G Fribourg, CH
Date of Establishment: 1964
No of Employees: 1,300

DAWOOD, ABDUL HUSAIN, & SONS

PO Box 7210, Muttrah
Tel: 773125

Chairman: Abdul Husain Dawood

PRINCIPAL ACTIVITIES: Supply of building materials and
sanitary-ware
Principal Agencies: Pillar Naco (UK) Ltd, Ogden (Otley) Ltd,
Ideal Standard (UK) Ltd

DESERT LINE PROJECTS LLC

PO Box 4880, Ruwi
Tel: 604153/4/5/6/7/8
Telex: 5169 Deed ON, 5128 Dlpgto ON
Telefax: 604159

Chairman: Ahmed Farid
Directors: Ayman Asfari (Managing Director)
Senior Executives: R J Brown (Contracts Manager), J A Fowler
(Commercial Manager), R L Inker (Project Manager), S Dodd
(Project Manager), J Hayhurst (Plant Manager), R Manon
(Head of Data Processing), N Khan (Stores Controller &
Purchasing Manager), P M Parakh (Management Accountant),
S N Garg (Finance Accountant)

PRINCIPAL ACTIVITIES: Civil engineering, mechanical, electrical
and instrumentation contractors; plant hire; construction
equipment and machinery; shipping and transport services
Branch Offices: Projects Office: Rusayl, Tel 510670
Associated/Subsidiary Companies: Desert Commercial
Enterprises LLC; Hazar International LLC, PO Box 4880,
Ruwi; Gulf Petrochemical Services LLC, PO Box 4880, Ruwi;
Desert Byrne Drilling Co, PO Box 1431, Ruwi; Modern Salt
Company LLC; Oman Industrial Safety LLC; Chemtech LLC;
Sharikat Al Marj LLC
Principal Bankers: Oman Arab Bank SAO, Ruwi

Principal Shareholders: Ahmed Farid, Saleh Ahmed Farid
Date of Establishment: 1977
No of Employees: 1,700

DHL INTERNATIONAL

PO Box 3833, Ruwi, Muscat
Tel: 708599
Telex: 5073 DHL MCT

PRINCIPAL ACTIVITIES: Worldwide courier service, air and sea
freight clearance and forwarding
Branch Offices: In the Middle East: Bahrain, Cyprus, Egypt
(Cairo, Alexandria), Iran, Jordan, Kuwait, Lebanon, Oman,
Qatar, Saudi Arabia (AlKhobar, Jeddah, Riyadh, Jubail, Tabuk,
Taif), Sudan, UAE (Abu Dhabi, Dubai, Sharjah)

DHOFAR CATTLE FEED CO SAOG

PO Box 19220, Salalah
Tel: 219228, 219071
Telex: 7738 DC Feed ON
Telefax: 219070

Chairman: Ahmed Taher Moqebal
Directors: Hafeez Taher Moqebal (Managing Director)
Senior Executives: Omar Alwi Mohamed Ibrahim (General
Manager)

PRINCIPAL ACTIVITIES: Production of cattle feed, milk, dairy
products
Subsidiary Companies: Dhofar Cattle Feed Co SAOG, Garzaiz
Farm, PO Box 18218, Salalah, Tel 225381, 225866, Fax
225482, Telex 7644 Garzaiz ON

Principal Bankers: Oman International Bank; National Bank of Oman

Financial Information:

	1990
	US$'000
Sales turnover	23,000
Profits	4,800
Authorised capital	11,759
Paid-up capital	11,759
Net asset	8,000

Date of Establishment: 1981
No of Employees: 300

DHOFAR TRANSPORT CO

PO Box 18316, Salalah
Tel: 460895
Telex: 7701 Deetesee ON

Senior Executives: Ibrahim K Eissa (Manager)

PRINCIPAL ACTIVITIES: Transportation contractors, supply of paints and building materials

DOUGLAS OHI LLC

PO Box 8639, Jibroo
Tel: 601402, 601422, 601562
Telex: 5104 DOUG OHI ON
Telefax: 601562

Chairman: Maqbool Hameed Mohamed Al Salah
Directors: J R T Douglas (Vice Chairman), M V Manzoni, R J Farndon, R Sengupta, D C Kelleher
Senior Executives: D C Kelleher (Director & General Manager), M R Cuttle (Chief Estimator), H G Joshi (Finance & Admin Manager)

PRINCIPAL ACTIVITIES: Civil, building and mechanical contractors
Branch Offices: PO Box 19886, Salalah
Parent Company: Oman Holdings International; R M Douglas Construction
Principal Bankers: Oman International Bank; British Bank of the Middle East
Financial Information:

	1988/89
	St£'000
Sales turnover	6,000
Authorised capital	375
Paid-up capital	375
Total assets	4,500

Principal Shareholders: R M Douglas Holdings PLC; Oman Holdings International LLC
Date of Establishment: September 1981
No of Employees: 1,300

ELECTROMAN LLC (OMAN)

PO Box 1082, Seeb Airport
Tel: 510315/6/7/8
Telex: 5015 Electrmn ON
Telefax: 510605

Senior Executives: L C Joachim (Managing Director), Peter Brunton (Sales Manager), A Philippides (General Manager), John Gerard (Area Manager Salalah)

PRINCIPAL ACTIVITIES: Communications and electronic systems contractors, representatives, service contracts, maintenance, after sales support, consultancy service
Principal Agencies: Thorn Security, Fire Alarm Systems; Arco Solar, Solar Energy Systems; Racal Electronics, Military Comms. Equip; G.E., Codan, Tait, Skanti, HF/VHF Radios; Arabrite, Epson, ICL, Computers; Pitney Bowes, Facsimile M/C; Magiboards, Office Equipment; De La Rue, Note Counting Machines; ARL, Laboratory Equipment; Multitone Electronics, Intercom & Paging; STC Telecommunications; Mitel Telecom Ltd; Dialatron; Hills Industries; Millbank

Branch Offices: PO Box 18743, Salalah, Tel 295104
Principal Bankers: The National Bank of Oman
Financial Information:

	1989
	RO'000
Sales turnover	10,000
Authorised capital	250
Paid-up capital	250

Date of Establishment: 1/7/1979
No of Employees: 160

ELF AQUITAINE OMAN

PO Box 3352, Ruwi
Tel: 704533, 704503, 704513
Cable: Elf Oman Muscat
Telex: 3314, 3559 Elf Oman ON

PRINCIPAL ACTIVITIES: Oil production
Branch Offices: Location: MCT Overseas Bldg, Qaboos Street, Ruwi
Parent Company: Head office in France

ERNST & WHINNEY

PO Box 4750, Ruwi
Tel: 703105, 702731, 702733/4
Cable: Ernstaudit Muscat
Telex: 3174 Ernst OM ON
Telefax: 702734

PRINCIPAL ACTIVITIES: Accountants and management consultants
Branch Offices: Algeria; Bahrain; Egypt; Iraq; Jordan; Kuwait; Lebanon; Libya; Morocco; Oman; Qatar; Saudi Arabia; United Arab Emirates; Yemen
Parent Company: Head office in the UK

EWBANK INTERNATIONAL CONSULTANTS (PVT) LTD

PO Box 6628, Ruwi
Tel: 600772, 600772
Telex: 5165 EWBANK ON

Chairman: R W H Reed
Directors: D A Lovie (Managing), R F Groom, T J Wiltshire, A R G Simmons, H S Willox, A Notman, M A Kitley

PRINCIPAL ACTIVITIES: Engineering consultants
Branch Offices: Dubai, Abu Dhabi, Doha
Parent Company: Ewbank - Preece
Principal Bankers: British Bank Middle East

Date of Establishment: June 1975
No of Employees: 35

FOUNDATION ENGINEERING LTD

PO Box 5282, Ruwi, Muscat
Tel: 591366
Cable: Cosdown Muscat
Telex: 5218 COSDON ON
Telefax: 591981

Senior Executives: J Mitchell (Contracts Manager)

PRINCIPAL ACTIVITIES: Site investigations, ground and materials testing, geotechnical consulting
Branch Offices: United Arab Emirates (Abu Dhabi and Dubai), Qatar, Saudi Arabia, Nigeria, Bahrain, Hong Kong, Singapore, Kuwait
Parent Company: Costain Group of Companies, UK

GALFAR ENGINEERING & CONTRACTING LLC

PO Box 533, Muscat
Tel: 591055/6/7
Cable: Alaremi Muscat
Telex: 5022 Galfar ON
Telefax: 591676

Chairman: Salim Saeed Hamed Al Araimi
Directors: P Mohamed Ali (Executive Director), Mohamed R Al Aremi (General Manager)

PRINCIPAL ACTIVITIES: Electrical, civil, building contractors, equipment and plant hire, manufacturers' representatives, supply of trucks, crushing and processing machinery, asphalt plants, tile and marble, all kinds of electrical fittings and fixtures, etc
Principal Agencies: Hillebrand; Ottermill Chilton Westinghouse; Legrand; Powerscreen; Arbau; Dieci; Loro & Parisini; Mondial MEC; Esto; Bamberger; Gent Ltd
Branch Offices: Electrical Division: Tel 703715; Trading Division: Tel 591708

GENERAL CONTRACTING & TRADING CO LLC

PO Box 3639, Ruwi, Muscat
Tel: 702006, 702025
Cable: Omandico
Telex: 5407 Omandico ON

Directors: Saeed Mohammed Rijab

PRINCIPAL ACTIVITIES: Import and sales of spare parts (automobile and fork-lifts, graders, wheel loaders, etc), furniture, batteries, acid, tyres; manufacture of cement blocks and supply of building materials and electrical equipment
Principal Agencies: Sumitomo Shoji Kaisha Ltd, Japan (Tyres); Chloride Batteries Australia Ltd (Batteries); Muhi Trading Corporation, Bombay (Acids); Dobson Bull Furnishing Co Ltd, London (Furniture); Yorkshore Switchgear Engineering Co (Electrical Equipment); Landis & Gyr, London (Electricity Meters)
Branch Offices: Mechanical engineering workshop; Supermarket
Subsidiary Companies: Oman Automotive Construction (heavy duty machine hire contracting work)
Principal Bankers: Grindlays Bank plc; National Bank of Oman; Arab Bank Ltd

Principal Shareholders: Saeed Mohammed Rijab, Abdul Khader Rijab, Mohammed Saeed Rijab, Jamal Saeed Rijab, Khalid Saeed Rijab

GENERAL DEVELOPMENT SERVICES LLC

CPO Box 2475, Seeb
Tel: 592816, 590866

Directors: Said M Sultan
Senior Executives: V M Hastak (Manager)

PRINCIPAL ACTIVITIES: General trading and contracting, manufacturers' representatives, agricultural services and consultancy, landscaping, construction
Principal Bankers: Bank of Oman & the Gulf SAO

Principal Shareholders: Said M Sultan
Date of Establishment: 1981
No of Employees: 159

GENERAL ELECTRIC & TRADING CO LLC
G.E.N.E.T.C.O.

PO Box 7006, Mutrah, Muscat
Tel: 704457, 704645
Cable: Genetco Muscat
Telex: 3332 Genetco ON
Telefax: 700032

Chairman: Sadiq Hassan Ali (also Managing Director)
Senior Executives: S Rajamani (General Manager), Mohamed Salahuddin (Financial Controller)

PRINCIPAL ACTIVITIES: Exporters, importers and distribution house dealing in electrical and electronic appliances and equipment, household goods, photographic and educational equipment
Principal Agencies: Sanyo Electric Trading Co, Japan; Siera Electronics BV, Holland; Grundig AG, W Germany; Aubry

Freres SA, Switzerland, Application des Gaz, France; Orient Watch Co, Japan; Northern Telecom, UK; Zanussi, Italy; Pfaff Gritzner Export GmbH, West Germany; Mitsubishi Electric Co, Japan; Admiral International Corp, USA; Canon Inc, Japan; Canon Europa NV, Netherlands; Yamaha Nippon Gakki Co, Japan
Branch Offices: PO Box 18215, Salalah, Dhofar, Oman
Subsidiary/Associated Companies: Oman Trading Contracting & Industries Ltd, PO Box 3826, Ruwi, Muscat; Fairtrade Ltd, PO Box 5636, Ruwi, Gulf Express Co, PO Box 5290, Ruwi
Principal Bankers: The British Bank of the Middle East, Muttrah; National Bank of Oman Ltd, Muttrah; Arab Bank Ltd, Muttrah; Bank of Credit & Commerce International SA, Ruwi; Bank of Oman Bahrain & Kuwait, Ruwi
Financial Information:

	US$'000
Authorised capital	1,450
Paid-up capital	1,450

Principal Shareholders: Sadiq Hassan Ali; W J Towell & Co LLC; Murtadha Hassan Ali
Date of Establishment: 1967
No of Employees: 200

GENERAL TELECOMMUNICATIONS ORGANISATION

PO Box 3789, Ruwi
Tel: 702568
Telex: 3400 Omantel ON

President: Nur Mohammad Nur
Senior Executives: Bakhit M Salim Al Qatan (General Manager Admin & Finance), Hamad Suleman Al Waihibi (General Manager General Services), Nasser Al Kindy (Manager Planning & Projects),

PRINCIPAL ACTIVITIES: Planning, execution and maintenance of the telecommunication system in Oman
Financial Information:

	RO'000
Revenues	40,000

GETCO GROUP OF COMPANIES
Getco Holdings & Investment LLC

PO Box 84, Muscat
Tel: 702133, 701454, 703121
Cable: Getco
Telex: 3278 ON
Telefax: 968-703826

Chairman: Kamal M Daud (Managing Director)
Directors: Ali K Daud
Senior Executives: Rafik El Toukhi (General Manager), Hameed Ibrahim (Finance Manager), A V S Hameed (Manager), Shafi U Wagle (Manager), A S Henderson (Manager)

PRINCIPAL ACTIVITIES: Manufacture of soft drinks, gases and architectural metal work, distribution of building materials and engineering products, telecommunications, and heavy machinery, civil construction, spare parts, industrial activities, investment and finance
Principal Agencies: AE Auto Parts, Access Equipment, Avalon Emergency Systems, Babcock Sweepers, BMA Italy, Briton Chadwick, Clarksteel, Coles Cranes, Coopers Payen, Co-Ro Foods Denmark; Crane Enfield, Crawley Refrigeration, Crittal Windows, Croda Hydrocarbons, Crown Decorative Products, Crush Procter & Gamble, Danish Telecom CGCT, Denso Imbema, De Jong Holland, Delbex, Dunbar Kapple, Durapipe, Elkosta, Essab Pipeline, Expandite, Firn Overseas, Fram Holland, Friedrich Grohe, Lincoln Electri, Ceramiche Gardenia, Hagenuk Telecom, Hanovia UK, Hargill Engg, Henderson Doors, Henkel Germany, Imporex, Interoll, Irish Telecom, ISS Electronics, Jakob Thaler, Joloda Loading Systems, Josiah Parkes, Keuco Germany, Key Terrain, King Trailers, Hermann Khoeler, Lake Electronics, Lancer Boss, Mafi Transport, Mapel, Marley Floors, Masafa Mineral Water, Metlex Ind,

Munsters Holland, Nibco ltd, Nicobond, Ofic, Petbow, Plan Transport, Planmarine, Polycell, Pullen Pumps, RC Cola, WF Rational Germany, Rehau Plastiks, Royal Doulton, Seven-up, Silver Paint, Southern Asbestos, Species Italy, Stanley Works, Stanton & Staveley, Stothert & Pitt, Techplastics, Thos Storey, Uponor, Valmet, Victaulic, Villeroy & Boch, Winn & Coales, Wash Perle, Wolseley Engg

Branch Offices: Nizwa, Sur, Salalah, Sohar

Parent Company: Getco Holdings & Investments LLC

Subsidiary/Associated Companies: In Oman:General Trading Co LLC; National Beverages Co Ltd SAOG; Getco Engineering Co LLC; Getco Aluminium Co LLC; Getco Gas Co LLC; Getco Construction Co LLC; In Dubai: Alrinasa Trading Est

Principal Bankers: National Bank of Oman SAO; Al Bank Al Ahli Al Omani SAO; Bank of Oman, Bahrain & Kuwait SAO

Date of Establishment: 1965

No of Employees: 600

GETCO PRESS INTERNATIONAL LLC

PO Box 3330, Ruwi
Tel: 702236
Telex: 5229 ON

PRINCIPAL ACTIVITIES: Petrochemical design and construction; mechanical and civil engineering

Principal Agencies: Wm Press International Ltd, Press Engineering & Management Services Ltd, Metal & Pipeline Endurance Ltd, Denco Holdings Ltd, Worley International Engineering Group Ltd; Pan Offshore Ltd

Principal Bankers: Grindlays Bank

Principal Shareholders: William Press International Ltd, Getco Group of Companies

GHAZALI GROUP OF COMPANIES

PO Box 4468, Ruwi
Tel: 575855 (10 lines)
Cable: Lavori
Telex: 5368 Ghazali ON, 5697 Lavori ON
Telefax: 575903

Chairman: HE Abdulla A Al Ghazali

Directors: Yusuf A Al Ghazali (Executive Director), Eng Hamid A Al Ghazali (Executive Director Technical)

PRINCIPAL ACTIVITIES: General trading and contracting, building and construction; manufacture of portacabins, rock blasting & drilling, electro-mechanical contracting, specialising in timber frame houses and offices

Principal Agencies: ENZED Hydraulic Hoses

Branch Offices: PO Box 19099, Salalah, Tel 211494, 210015, Fax 210771

Parent Company: ENZED, New Zealand

Associated Companies: GTC Enzed, Tel 591491; Lavori Oman LLC; Engineering Construction Co

Principal Shareholders: HE A A AlGhazali (sole owner)

Date of Establishment: 1978

No of Employees: Approx 200

GIBB, SIR ALEXANDER, & PARTNERS

PO Box 592, Muscat
Tel: 772147, 701811
Telex: 5335 Gibbosor ON

PRINCIPAL ACTIVITIES: Consulting engineers

Branch Offices: UK; Middle East

Associated Companies: Gibb, Peter Muller & Partners, PO Box 592, Muscat (Architects and Consulting Engineers)

GUARDIAN ROYAL EXCHANGE ASSURANCE PLC

PO Box 5899, Ruwi
Tel: 797536, 797537
Cable: Towell Muscat
Telex: 3214 Gremus ON
Telefax: 797539

Senior Executives: P K Mankad (General Manager), Ulhas Kajaria (Deputy Manager), K S Philip (Deputy Manager)

PRINCIPAL ACTIVITIES: Marine, motor, fire and general (non-life) insurance

Branch Offices: PO Box 19058, Salalah, Tel 292045, Fax 295610

Principal Bankers: National Bank of Oman Ltd

GULF AGENCY CO (OMAN) LLC

PO Box 3740, Ruwi
Tel: 707000 (5 lines)
Cable: Confidence Muscat
Telex: 3664 Gacship ON
Telefax: 703609

Chairman: Ahmed Ali Abdullatiff

Directors: Bjorn A Engblom, Hassan Ali Abdul Latiff

Senior Executives: Ehlert M Boberg (General Manager), E A Rebello (Shipping Manager), M A Fernandes (Operations Manager), Jan-Olof Andersson (Cargo Services Manager)

PRINCIPAL ACTIVITIES: Shipping, clearing, forwarding, packing and airfreighting agency

Principal Agencies: Nippon Yusen Kaisha, Tokyo; Finncarrier, Finland; Hinode Kisen Co, Tokyo; Lloyd Triestino, Italy; Polish Ocean Lines, Poland

Branch Offices: Salalah Branch: PO Box 19346, Tel 290405, 294662, Fax 294827, Telex 7647 Gacsal ON

Associated Companies: GAC Group of companies

Principal Bankers: British Bank of the Middle East

Date of Establishment: 1972

No of Employees: 55

GULF AIR

PO Box 4444, Ruwi
Tel: 703332, 703555, 703926, 703544
Telex: 3313 Gfcto ON
Telefax: 793381

Chairman: HE Yousuf Ahmed Shirawi

Directors: HE Salim Bin Ali Nasser Assiyabi (President & Chief Executive), Mohd Noor Sultan (Vice President Finance), Hamad Al Medfa (Vice President Marketing)

Senior Executives: Saleh Issa Al Kindy (Area Manager Oman)

PRINCIPAL ACTIVITIES: Airline transportation of passenger, cargo and mail

Branch Offices: Salalah, Tel 294145, 290527

Principal Bankers: National Bank of Oman, Greater Muttrah

Financial Information:

	1990 US$'000
Sales turnover	511,610
Profits	72,398
Share capital	169,761
Reserves	132,546
Total assets	654,880

Principal Shareholders: Jointly owned by the Governments of Bahrain, Qatar, Abu Dhabi and Oman

Date of Establishment: 1950

No of Employees: 116 in Oman

GULF DEVELOPMENT TRADING ENTERPRISE

PO Box 439, Muscat
Tel: 704687, 798216, Acctts: 592159
Cable: Gulfaprise Muscat
Telex: 3165 DRILCO ON
Telefax: 798449

Directors: Munib R Masri (Operating Director), Tarif W Ayoubi (Operating Director)
Senior Executives: Mohammed S Al Fahoum (General Manager)

PRINCIPAL ACTIVITIES: Agents, representatives, import and distribution of foodstuff, building materials, drilling equipments and materials; inspection, certification and third party engineering
Principal Agencies: Camco Reda Pump, USA; Reda Ras Al-Khaimah Ltd, UAE; F H Maloney Co, USA; Rohd & Schwartz, Germany; UGC Industries, USA; Groth Equipment Corp, USA; Electronic Systems, USA; Emerson Electric, USA; Dickirson Corp/Ackermann Int, USA; George E Failing, USA; TM Services Ltd, UK; Moody Tottrup Int, UK; Flexible Pipelines, UK; Hayward Tyler, UK; Bristol Babcock Ltd, UK; Moore Industries, UK; Williams & James Engg, UK; L G Mouchel & Partners, UK; EIC Industries, France; Robert Cort & Sons, UK; Dames & Moore, UK/USA; Rhone Poulenc, France; Atochem, France; Varel Manufacturing, USA; Germanischer Lloyd, Germany
Branch Offices: PO Box 18201, Salalah, Tel/Fax 211408
Principal Bankers: Oman Arab Bank SAO

Principal Shareholders: HE Qais Abdulmunim Al-Zawawi
Date of Establishment: 1979

GULF HOTELS (OMAN) CO SAOG

PO Box 4455, Ruwi, Muscat
Tel: 560100
Cable: Gulfotel Muscat
Telex: 5416 Gulfotel ON
Telefax: 560650

Chairman: HE Abdul Hafidh Salim Rajab
Directors: HE Salim Bin Nasser Al Busaidi, HE Salim Ahmed Khalfan, HE Sheikh Mustahail Al Maashani, Husain Haider Darwish, Hussain Bin Mohd Hassan Al Salih, HE Dr Al Yaqdhan Bin Talib Al Hinai, Sleyum Bin Said Sleyum Al Ma'ashary
Senior Executives: Mohsen Moursi (General Manager), Anil Abichandani (Chief Accountant), Peter J Lobo (Front Office Manager)

PRINCIPAL ACTIVITIES: Hotel and catering
Associated Companies: Gulf Air, Bahrain
Principal Bankers: Bank of Oman Bahrain & Kuwait; Bank Dhofar Al Omani Al Fransi
Financial Information:

	1989/90 RO'000
Sales turnover	1,370
Profits	294
Authorised capital	2,000
Paid-up capital	2,000
Total assets	5,287

Principal Shareholders: Government of Oman (32.1%), Gulf Air (25%), Omani and Gulf Nationals (42.9%)
Date of Establishment: 1975
No of Employees: 174

HABIB BANK LTD

PO Box 4326, Ruwi
Tel: 705272, 705276, 795282
Cable: Habibbank Muscat
Telex: 3283 ON
Telefax: 795283

Senior Executives: Syed Fazal Mabood (SEVP & General Manager)
PRINCIPAL ACTIVITIES: Commercial banking
Branch Offices: In Oman: Buraimi, Medinat Qaboos, Muttrah, Nizwa, Rusail, Ruwi, Ruwi Central, Salalah, Seeb, Sohar, Sur, Walja Area
Parent Company: Head office in Karachi, Pakistan

Date of Establishment: November 1972 in Oman

HAIDER DARWISH

See DARWISH, HAIDER,

HAMDAN GROUP OF COMPANIES

PO Box 18190, Salalah
Tel: 291984, 590549
Cable: Hamdan Salalah
Telex: 7667 Hamdan ON

Chairman: Sheikh Hamid Bin Hamood Al Ghafri (Owner)

PRINCIPAL ACTIVITIES: Heavy transport; shipping; construction; commercial importation; cold storage and trading; beverage bottling factory; tile factory; agriculture and fisheries; oilfield support services
Principal Agencies: Tube Investments Int, C Blumhardt GmbH, Dunlop Tyres, Racal Safety Equipment, Butler Building Systems
Branch Offices: PO Box 3608, Ruwi, Tel 590549, Telex 5548 Hamdan ON
Associated Companies: Perini Corporation, USA; Majestic Pipeline Co, Canada; Biwater Shellabear, UK; John Taylor & Sons, UK; Subtec France
Principal Bankers: British Bank of the Middle East; Arab Bank

Date of Establishment: January 1976
No of Employees: 1,000

HARIDAS LALJI TRADING LLC

PO Box 54, Muscat
Tel: 705485, 705486, 712716
Cable: Fullmoon
Telex: 3023 Fullmoon ON
Telefax: 705490

Chairman: Ajit Kumar Hamlai (Director)
Directors: Karsandas Haridas Hamlai (General Manager)

PRINCIPAL ACTIVITIES: Import and wholesale commission agents and general merchants, dealing in foodstuffs, animal feed and general beverages, textiles and defence supplies, manufacture and supply of perfumes
Branch Offices: PO Box 8962, Salalah, Oman
Subsidiary Companies: Farco Commercial Co, PO Box 4922, Ruwi; Ajay Enterprises, PO Box, 4922, Ruwi; Al Rashidi & Ajit Trading Co; PO Box 3933, Abu Dhabi, UAE; National Gift & Arab Perfume Center LLC, Ruwi; Al Khboorah Foodstuffs Packaging Co LLC, Ruwi; Oman Chemical Co LLC, Muscat
Principal Bankers: British Bank of the Middle East (Muscat); Standard Chartered Bank (Muscat); National Bank of Oman, (Muttrah)
Financial Information:

	1990 RO'000
Sales turnover	10,000

Principal Shareholders: Ajit Kumar Karsandas, Ajay Ajit Hamlai, Sujay Ajit Hamlai
Date of Establishment: 1947
No of Employees: 50

OMAN

HASHIMANI, MOHD HASSAN AL HAJ MOHSIN,

PO Box 130, Muscat
Tel: 702097, 708817, 700844
Cable: HASHIMANI
Telex: 3459 Hashmani ON
Telefax: 703006

Chairman: Mohamed Hassan Al Haj Mohsin Hashimani
Directors: Mehboob Mohammed Hassan Hashim

PRINCIPAL ACTIVITIES: Trading, furniture, carpets, household
and camping items
Branch Offices: Showrooms: Darsait and Wadi Kabir
Principal Bankers: National Bank of Oman; Bank of Oman,
Bahrain and Kuwait

Principal Shareholders: M H M Hashimani (Proprietor)
Date of Establishment: 1940
No of Employees: 55

HOLIDAY INN SALALAH

PO Box 8870, Salalah
Tel: 235333
Cable: Holisal
Telex: 7638 Holisal ON
Telefax: (968) 235137

Chairman: HE Mohamed Awfit Al Shanfary
Senior Executives: Hani Kafafi (General Manager), Naji Abi
Farah (Sales Manager), Rohith Fernando (Financial
Controller), Gamini Sooriyabandara (Chief Engineer)

PRINCIPAL ACTIVITIES: Hotel business
Parent Company: Holiday Corporation
Principal Bankers: Oman Arab Bank

Date of Establishment: October 1977
No of Employees: 120

HUCKLE AND PARTNERS (OMAN)

PO Box 4378, Ruwi
Tel: 601259, 601503, 601509
Telefax: 696066

Directors: T O R Nash (Resident Partner)
Senior Executives: K R Jarvis (Resident Associate)

PRINCIPAL ACTIVITIES: Architects and planners
Branch Offices: Medinat Qaboos
Parent Company: Huckle Tweddell Partnership
Principal Bankers: British Bank of the Middle East

Date of Establishment: 1975
No of Employees: 20

INMA OMAN LLC

PO Box 3760, Ruwi
Tel: 562100, 562092, 562096
Telex: 5196 Inma ON
Telefax: 562039

Chairman: Suhail Bahwan
Directors: Saud Bahwan, Samir Aweidah
Senior Executives: Job Raju (Commercial Manager), Harshad
Shah

PRINCIPAL ACTIVITIES: Import, sales and service of
construction plant and equipment
Principal Agencies: Power Curber, Gardner Denver, Hymac
Excavators, Linden Alimak Cranes & Hoists, Thwaites
Dumpers, Dynapac Rollers, Parker Crushers & Asphalt Plant,
Flygt Pumps, Stetter Concrete Plant, Hatz Engines
Branch Offices: Salalah
Principal Bankers: Oman Arab Bank SAO

Date of Establishment: 1974

INTERNATIONAL ELECTRIC CO (OMAN) LLC

PO Box 1364, CPO Seeb
Tel: 592351/2/3
Cable: ISCO MUSCAT
Telex: 5620 ISCO ON
Telefax: 590076

Chairman: Abdulla Mohamed Rabi
Directors: Mahmood Mohamed Rabi, Riadh Mohamed Abbas
Senior Executives: Sudhakaran Nair (General Manager), K U
Prem Kumar (Deputy General Manager)

PRINCIPAL ACTIVITIES: Electrical contractors, designing,
installations, testing, commissioning and maintenance of any
type of electrical installations and other systems
Subsidiary Companies: International Electric Co, PO Box 3223,
Dubai, UAE
Principal Bankers: National Bank of Oman Ltd; Grindlays Bank
plc; Bank of Muscat

Date of Establishment: 23-3-1977
No of Employees: 100

J & P (OMAN) LLC

PO Box 603, Muscat
Tel: 610200, 610323
Telex: 5242 Jaynpe ON

PRINCIPAL ACTIVITIES: Building and civil engineering
contractors (Seeb International Airport)
Branch Offices: Cyprus; Middle East; Oman; Dubai; Saudi
Arabia; Iraq; Libya; Abu Dhabi
Subsidiary Companies: J & P (Oman) LLC

JAFFER ENTERPRISES

PO Box 432, Muscat
Tel: 722854
Cable: Nida
Telex: 5371 ON

PRINCIPAL ACTIVITIES: General trading and contracting,
supply of building materials, furniture, electrical equipment,
and foodstuffs
Subsidiary/Associated Companies: Jaffer Contractors; Universal
Engineering Est (Electrical); Steel Fabricators (steel furnitue
and windows); Public Services Est (clearing and forwarding);
New Omar Khayam Restaurant
Principal Bankers: Grindlays Bank

JAMNADAS KHIMJI & CO

PO Box 251, Muscat
Tel: 704379, 700092, 751010
Cable: JKSONS Muscat
Telex: 3186 Jksons ON
Telefax: 700678

Partners: Pratapsinh Jamnadas, Madhursinh Jamnadas, Nitin
Jamnadas, Uday P Khimji, Pradeep M Khimji
Senior Executives: Uday P Khimji (Managing Partner), K R
Soman (Marketing Manager), Vinay Ashar (Admin Manager),
Harsh Sampat (Technical Manager)

PRINCIPAL ACTIVITIES: Building contractors and general
traders
Principal Agencies: Sika Chemicals; Gerland, France; Han
Sanitor, W Germany; Hillaldam Coburn, UK
Branch Offices: Salalah: PO Box 18018, Salalah, Tel 290459
Subsidiary Companies: Al Kahf Trading Co LLC
Principal Bankers: British Bank of the Middle East, Muscat;
National Bank of Oman, Ruwi

Date of Establishment: 1974
No of Employees: 400

JAPEX OMAN LTD

PO Box 3543, Ruwi
Tel: 602011, 602838
Telex: 5695 Japexom ON
Telefax: 602181

President: Hajime Fujita
Directors: Toshio Kushiro
Senior Executives: Toshihiro Ohara (General Manager)

PRINCIPAL ACTIVITIES: Oil exploration and production
Branch Offices: Location: Madinat Qabood Central Area,
Muscat
Parent Company: Japan Petroleum Exploration Co Ltd (Japex)

Principal Shareholders: Japan National Corporation
Date of Establishment: 1981
No of Employees: 32

JAYANT, C, BROS (OMAN) LTD

PO Box 50, Muscat
Tel: 773100
Cable: Kishor
Telex: 5526 Kishor ON

Directors: Champak V Pawani, Kishor V Pawani, Hemant V
Pawani
Senior Executives: Bharat V Pawani (Sales Executive), Subhash
V Pawani (Assistant Manager)

PRINCIPAL ACTIVITIES: General trading, import and distribution
of audio-video products, electrical and electronic home
appliances, building materials, photographical equipment
Principal Agencies: Asahi Pentax, Minolta, BASF (Tapes),
Lower-Opta, Korting (Germany), Henkel International GmbH,
Cabin (Projectors), Fuji (Films), Persil, Dixan, Patra, FA, ATA,
Pril, Phoenix USA
Branch Offices: PO Box 8814, Salalah
Principal Bankers: The British Bank of the Middle East;
Standard Chartered Bank; Grindlays Bank

Date of Establishment: 1920

JOHN R HARRIS PARTNERSHIP

PO Box 214, Muscat
Tel: 601922, 601925
Cable: Harrisplan Muscat
Telefax: 601923 G3

Partners: Alan Jones, John R Harris, Alfred Rigby
Senior Executives: Ian Buchanan (Resident Associate)

PRINCIPAL ACTIVITIES: Architecture and planning
Branch Offices: Salalah
Associated Companies: John R Harris Qatar Architects, Qatar;
John R Harris & Partners, Dubai and Hong Kong; John R
Harris Architects, London, UK; John R Harris Brunei
Architects, Brunei

Date of Establishment: 1971
No of Employees: 14

JUMA, AHMED RAMADHAN, & CO LLC

PO Box 6566, Ruwi, Muscat
Tel: 703170
Cable: Pumps
Telex: 3812 Arjuma ON
Telefax: 708305

Chairman: Ahmed Ramadhan Juma
Directors: Sheikh Salim Sulaiman Al Fairuz, Yasser Sulaiman Al
Fairuz
Senior Executives: R P Murthy (General Manager), V K Datta
(Sales Manager)

PRINCIPAL ACTIVITIES: Trading in agriculture equipment,
water pump sets
Principal Agencies: Lowara spa; Nemitsas Ltd; Rudolf Bauer
GmbH; Burnett & Co; etc

Subsidiary Companies: Ahmed Ramzan Juma Est, Dubai
Principal Bankers: Bank of Muscat, National Bank of Oman
Financial Information:

	1990 US$'000
Sales turnover	10,000

Date of Establishment: 1983

KAMEL ENTERPRISES

PO Box 765, Muscat
Tel: 704320, 700656
Cable: Kamel Muscat
Telex: 3586 Kamel ON
Telefax: 701988

President: Darwish Eidook Hassan
Directors: Shaokat Hussein (General Manager)

PRINCIPAL ACTIVITIES: Educational and hospital supplies,
leisure goods, laboratory equipment, dental equipment, X-ray
films and equipment, computer supplies, carpentry and
furniture, interior decoration, laundry, identification cards and
machines
Principal Agencies: Du Pont, W Germany; Broadhead-garrette,
USA; Scanzym, Denmark; HPS System, Technic, W Germany;
Toppan Moore Co Ltd, Japan; Leybold Heraus, West
Germany; Intradan Environmental Consultants, Denmark;
Cambridge Biomedical, Biotec Laboratories, UK; Impex,
France; SDI, Australia; Storz, W Germany
Subsidiary Companies: Majan General Contractors, PO Box
3500, Ruwi; Yacoob Mohammed Fakeer & Partner, PO Box
890, Muscat; Oman & Emirates Group Co Ltd, PO Box 765,
Muscat
Principal Bankers: National Bank of Oman; Bank of Oman
Bahrain & Kuwait; Oman International Bank, Ruwi

Principal Shareholders: Sole proprietor
Date of Establishment: 1970
No of Employees: 50

KANOO, YUSUF BIN AHMED, & CO

PO Box 7310, Mutrah, Muscat
Tel: 772252, 772253, 772254
Cable: Kanoo Muscat
Telex: 5352 ON KANOO

PRINCIPAL ACTIVITIES: Shipping agents, clearing and
forwarding agents, marine operators, warehousing, industrial
& domestic packers
Principal Agencies: Shipping: Blue Star Line, Norasia Line,
Mitsui Osk Line, Nosac, Hoegh-Ugland Auto Liners, Lloyd
Brasileiro, Gesuri Lloyd
Branch Offices: Saudi Arabia; United Arab Emirates; Oman;
representative offices in London and Houston, Texas (USA)
Parent Company: Head office in Bahrain
Principal Bankers: British Bank of the Middle East

Principal Shareholders: Yusuf Bin Ahmed Kanoo & Waleed
Associates
Date of Establishment: 1975

KHATIB & ALAMI
Consolidated Engineering Co

PO Box 3238, Muscat
Tel: 702558, 796402
Cable: CONSING
Telex: 3452 CEC ON
Telefax: 705593, 708412

President: Mounir El Khatib
Directors: Dr Zuheir Alami (Senior Partner)
Senior Executives: Faisal Alami (Resident Manager Oman)

PRINCIPAL ACTIVITIES: Consulting engineers, architects,
planners and designers

Branch Offices: Saudi Arabia, United Arab Emirates, Bahrain
Parent Company: Head office in Lebanon, Beirut
Principal Bankers: Arab Bank Ltd

KHIMJI RAMDAS

PO Box 19, Muscat
Tel: 795901 (8 lines)
Cable: Broker, Muscat
Telex: 3489 Broker ON
Telefax: 795988

Directors: Ajitsinh Gokaldas (Partner), Kanaksi Gokaldas
(Partner), Anil Mathradas (Partner), Ajay Mathradas (Partner)
Senior Executives: Pankaj Khimji, Umesh Khimji, Dharmesh
Khimji

PRINCIPAL ACTIVITIES: Import-export (foodstuffs, chemicals,
paints, toiletries, electrical and electronic equipment and
appliances, glass products, building materials, household
goods and photographical equipment); general merchants,
building contractors, commission agents; building materials
div, furniture div, air conditioning div, automotive div, electrical
div, foodstuff div, rolex div, construction div, duty free shop,
general stores, leisure division
Principal Agencies: Akzo Coatings, UK; Callard & Bowser, UK;
Formica Ltd, UK; Godrej, India; Cartier, France; Philip Morris
(Marlboro' Cigarettes), USA; Noritake, Japan; SGB (Export)
Ltd, UK; Magic Chef, USA; H & R Johnson Tiles, UK; Byford,
UK; Fitzgerald, UK; Bausch & Lomb, USA; Chanel, Caron,
Rochas, Rabanne, Ungaro, France; Servicised Ltd, UK;
Coleman, USA; General Corp, Japan; Hitachi Maxell, Japan;
Lacoste, France; Lindt, Switzerland; Rolex, Switzerland;
Moulinex, France; Nikon, Japan; Powersport Int'l, UK;
Karcher, W Germany; Swatch, Switzerland; Fissler, W
Germany; Rubberoid, UK; Samsonite, USA; Sheafer, USA;
Thomas Ness, UK; Whitmont, Australia; Zenith, Japan;
Snapon Tools, USA; Wicksteed Leisure Ltd, UK; Schelde
International, Belgium; Zephyr Flags & Banners, UK; Cross,
USA; Zojirushi, Japan; Delaneau, Switzerland; Procter &
Gamble, Switzerland; James Halstead, UK; Duracell, USA;
Oshkosh, USA; Arenson Int'l, UK
Branch Offices: Dubai, PO Box 3071 Tel 531484; also Salalah,
Tel 290736; Soor, Tel 440214; Sohar, Tel 840235 and Nizwa,
Tel 410145
Principal Bankers: British Bank of the Middle East; Bank of
Baroda; National Bank of Oman

Date of Establishment: 1870
No of Employees: 800

KOTHARY, RAMNIKLAL B, & CO LLC

PO Box 66, Muscat
Tel: 703863, 703086 (Head Office Ruwi)
Cable: Kothary Muscat
Telex: 3169 Kothary ON
Telefax: (968) 703110

Chairman: HE Ali Dawood
Directors: Madhukar R Kothary, Prabodh R Kothary

PRINCIPAL ACTIVITIES: General merchants and commission
agents, general consumer goods and foodstuffs
Principal Agencies: Beiersdorf, W Germany; M A Carven, UK;
Gillette, UK; Farley's Health Products, UK; Gist Brocades,
Holland; H J Heinz, Honig Foods, Holland; John Dickinson,
UK; Johnson & Johnson, John Palmer, UK; Kimberley-Clark,
Monarch Int, USA; Martin Brothers Tobacco, USA; P Sasso e
Figli, Italy; Reckitt & Colman, UK; Spillers French Milling, UK;
Shulton, UK; SEITA Usine des Tabacs de Dijon, France;
Standard Brands, USA; Robertson Foods, UK; Villiger Sohne,
Switzerland; Wrigley, USA; British Cod Liver Oils Ltd, UK
Branch Offices: Medinat Qaboss, Tel 602515; Salalah, Tel
290507; Sohar, Tel 842066
Principal Bankers: British Bank of the Middle East (Muscat)

Financial Information:

	1989/90 RO'000
Sales turnover	3,650
Authorised capital	350
Paid-up capital	350

Principal Shareholders: HE Ali Dawood, Madhukar R Kothary,
Prabodh R Kothary
Date of Establishment: 1935
No of Employees: 80

KPMG PEAT MARWICK MITCHELL & CO

PO Box 3641, Ruwi
Tel: 709181
Telex: 3651 PMM ON
Telefax: 700839

Senior Executives: Anwer Mateen (Partner), Khalid M Ansari
(Manager), Andrew Robinson (Manager)

PRINCIPAL ACTIVITIES: Auditing, accounting, taxation and
management consultancy
Branch Offices: KPMG offices in Dubai, Abu Dhabi, Sharjah,
Doha, Bahrain, Kuwait and Saudi Arabia

Date of Establishment: 1975

LAING OMAN LLC

PO Box 6006, Ruwi
Tel: 703757, 620661
Telex: 3243 LAING ON

PRINCIPAL ACTIVITIES: Building and civil engineering, design,
management and construction services
Parent Company: John Laing International Ltd, London, UK

LALBUKSH IRRIGATION & WELL DRILLING CO LLC

PO Box 6146, Ruwi, Muscat
Tel: 591721
Telex: 5613 LALVOL ON
Telefax: 592185

Chairman: Lalbuksh Essa Al Raise (also Director)
Directors: Ghazi Ahmed Razamiyan Shaikh
Senior Executives: N Visvanathan (Manager-Incharge), H P
Mishra (Drilling Engineer), V V Medhekar (Commercial
Manager)

PRINCIPAL ACTIVITIES: Water well drilling contractors,
irrigation, trading, drilling-irrigation and agricultural inputs,
also sewage/water treatment plants
Principal Agencies: Boode PVC Casings, Holland; Voltas Int'l,
India; Wade Rain Inc, USA
Parent Company: Lalbuksh Contracting & Trading Est, Voltas
International Ltd
Principal Bankers: Bank of Oman Bahrain & Kuwait (SAO)

Principal Shareholders: Lalbuksh Contracting & Trading Est,
Muscat; Voltas International Ltd, Bombay
Date of Establishment: April 1982
No of Employees: 100

LASHKO, NASSER, GROUP OF COMPANIES

PO Box 7839, Muttrah
Tel: 702873
Cable: Lashko, Muscat
Telex: 3286 Lashko ON

Chairman: Nasser Abdullah Lashko
Senior Executives: Mohammad Arif (General Manager)

PRINCIPAL ACTIVITIES: Import and distribution of building
materials, construction machines, industrial gases, medical
gases, cutting and welding equipment, medical equipment,
pesticides, fungicides, fertilisers, paints, industrial chemicals,
agricultural equipment

Principal Agencies: Caprari Pumps, Italy; Lombardini Pumps, Italy; Volund, Denmark; MIG Group, UK; Welding Industries Ltd, UK; MC Bauchemie, West Germany; Mitsubishi Daiya, Japan; Outboard Engines, Italy; Armourlite, UK; Bertolini, Italy; Aqualine Aquascreen, DANDO, UK; Hayter, UK; Horie E Fans, ANIC, Italy, MARC Radio Cassette Recorder, Japan
Associated Companies: Nasser Lashko & Sons Contracting Co; Nasser Lashko Trading Co; Nasser Lashko Crushers; Nasser Lashko Farms; Nasser Lashko Drilling Co
Principal Bankers: National Bank of Oman
Financial Information:

	RO'000
Sales turnover	5,000
Profits	500
Authorised capital	3,000
Paid-up capital	3,000

Principal Shareholders: Nasser Abdulla Lashko and Sons
Date of Establishment: 1982
No of Employees: 500

LAVORI OMAN LLC

PO Box 4468, Ruwi
Tel: 575855
Telex: 5697 Lavori ON, 5368 Ghazali ON
Telefax: 575903

Chairman: Abdulla A Al Ghazali
Directors: Yusuf A Al Ghazali

PRINCIPAL ACTIVITIES: Civil engineering and construction, rock blasting, water well drilling, portacabin construction; specialising in timber frame houses and offices, prefab buildings
Branch Offices: PO Box 19099 Salalah, Tel 211494, 210015, Telex 7650 Lavori ON
Parent Company: Ghazali Group of Companies

Principal Shareholders: Ownership
Date of Establishment: 1975
No of Employees: 300

LAXMIDAS THARIA VED & CO

PO Box 4418, Ruwi, Muscat
Tel: 772562/772563
Cable: Lakhoo
Telex: 5259 Lakhoo ON

PRINCIPAL ACTIVITIES: Import and distribution of all kinds of textiles, sundry items, watches, glasses and perfumes, also foodstuffs
Principal Agencies: QBB Brand Ghee, Australia; Lipton Tea, Spanish Brand Saffron, Zenith Steel Pipes, India; Rayban Sunglasses, USA; Estee Lauder Perfumes and Brut/Kiku Products, USA; Parker Pen Agency, Schick Blades
Branch Offices: Oman and Dubai (United Arab Emirates)
Principal Bankers: British Bank of the Middle East; Grindlays Bank

MALALLAH HAJI HABIB MURAD

See MURAD, MALALLAH HAJI HABIB,

MATRAH COLD STORES LLC

PO Box 4158, Ruwi, Muscat
Tel: 704333, 704539
Cable: Reefer
Telex: 5268 Reefer ON
Telefax: 793055

Senior Executives: J M Curtis (General Manager), T A Harker (Finance & Admin Manager), R W Higgins (Retail Manager), J S Lowe (Catering Manager), I W R Breen (Marketing Manager), A B Sneddon (Warehouse & Distribution Manager)

PRINCIPAL ACTIVITIES: Retail and wholesale, food & tobacco distributors, supermarkets and cold store operators, agency representatives; industrial catering and camp site management
Principal Agencies: Nestle, Rowntree Mackintosh, Kraft, Wellcome Foundation, Colgate Palmolive, Libby's, Wander, Pedigree petfoods, Ross Foods
Branch Offices: Sohar, Nizwa, Sur
Parent Company: The Bricom Group Ltd/W J Towell & Co LLC
Subsidary/Associated Companies: Cold Storage & Trading Co LLC, PO Box 18055, Salalah (Oman), Tel 290644, Telex 7619, Fax 292289
Principal Bankers: National Bank of Oman, Oman International Bank, Standard Chartered Bank, Al Bank Al Ahli Al Omani, Bank Dhofar Al Omani Al Fransi

Principal Shareholders: W J Towell & Co LLC, Oman; The Bricom Group Ltd, Uk
Date of Establishment: 1967
No of Employees: 525

MAZOUN EST FOR TRADING & GENERAL CONTRACTING

PO Box 415, Muscat
Tel: 561804, 561251, 561417, 561977
Cable: MAZOUN MUSCAT
Telex: 5336 ON Mazoun
Telefax: 562469

Chairman: Sheikh Yacoub Al Harthy
Directors: Sheikh Yousuf Al Harthy (Managing Director)

PRINCIPAL ACTIVITIES: Import and distribution of domestic appliances, building materials, refrigerators and cookers, heavy equipment, office equipment, power generators, general contractors
Principal Agencies: Kelvinator, USA/Italy; Areilos, Italy; Idrobeton, Italy; OCE, Netherland
Branch Offices: Salalah; Ibra
Associated Companies: Al Hamra Mazoun Civil & Const. Building; Technical Electric Co; Al Harthy Travels & Cargo; Road Markings & Manufacturing of Signs; Road Furniture; Guard Rails
Principal Bankers: Al Bank Al Ahli Al Omani

Date of Establishment: 1972
No of Employees: 40

MIDDLE EAST TRADERS (OMAN) LLC

PO Box 7406, Mutrah
Tel: 590694/6
Cable: Consort Muscat
Telex: 5215 CONSORT ON
Telefax: 590496

Directors: Mohammed Ali Jawad, S M Rao, U M Kini
Senior Executives: B Vijay Mallya (General Manager)

PRINCIPAL ACTIVITIES: Import and trade in all kinds of construction materials and special building products; manufacturers' representation on agency contracts and supply, installation & maintenance of elevators; waterproofing contractors
Principal Agencies: Adrian Stokes, UK; BICC Britmac, UK; Building Chemical Research Co, UK; Casco Nobel, Denmark; DZ Licht, W Germany; DWI Dermabit Waterproofing Industries, Saudi Arabia; Dean Reels, UK; Fischer, Italy; Hoogovens Aluminium, W Germany; Imper, Italy; Legrand, France; Lift Munich, W Germany; Martin Roberts, UK; Meynadier, Switzerland; Nittan, UK; Norton Clipper, Holland; RAK White Cement Factory, UAE; Swordsman, Australia; Vallances, UK
Branch Offices: Barka, Oman, Tel 882049
Principal Bankers: Oman International Bank, Ruwi; Grindlays Bank plc, Ruwi; National Bank of Oman Ltd, Muttrah

Date of Establishment: 1974

OMAN

MOHAMED & AHMED AL KHONJI

See AL KHONJI, MOHAMED & AHMED,

MOHAMMED KHAMIS & BROTHERS

PO Box 7022, Muttrah
Tel: 772454
Cable: Brothers
Telex: 5654 Brothers ON

Directors: Musa Haji Khamis Ali
Senior Executives: Irshad Musa Khamis

PRINCIPAL ACTIVITIES: Import and distribution of agricultural
  equipment and machinery, fertilisers, insecticides, irrigation
  equipment, building construction
Principal Agencies: Kloritz, Japan; Nibbi-Bruno, Italy; Jiffy,
  Norway; Hardi, Denmark; Nordisk-Alkali-Biokemi, Denmark;
  Webb Lawnmowers, England; KFC, Kuwait
Subsidiary Companies: Musa Khamis Trading, Building
  Construction
Principal Bankers: National Bank of Oman; Bank of Oman,
  Bahrain & Kuwait

Principal Shareholders: Musa Khamis Ali; Haider Musa Khamis
Date of Establishment: 1920
No of Employees: 25

MOHD HASSAN AL HAJ MOHSIN HASHIMANI

See HASHIMANI, MOHD HASSAN AL HAJ MOHSIN,

MOHSIN HAIDER DARWISH LLC

See DARWISH, MOHSIN HAIDER, LLC

MOORE STEPHENS (OMAN BRANCH)

PO Box 3933, Ruwi
Tel: 702082
Telefax: 703309

Senior Executives: John Adcock (Resident Principal)

PRINCIPAL ACTIVITIES: Auditing, accounting, management
  consultancy, tax consultancy

MOOSA ABDUL RAHMAN HASSAN & CO LLC

PO Box 4, Muscat
Tel: 701566, 701486
Cable: Moosa
Telex: 5222 ON

Chairman: Moosa A R Hassan
Directors: Abdulla Moosa (Managing Director), Ali Moosa
Senior Executives: Mohamed Abdulla Moosa (General Manager)

PRINCIPAL ACTIVITIES: Import and distribution of motor
  vehicles (cars and trucks), diesel engines, electrical
  equipment, generating sets, crusher plants, pumps, shovels
Principal Agencies: General Motors, Pontiac, Vauxhall/Bedford
  Cars and Trucks, Lister Generators, Diesel Engines, York
  Trailers, Arabia Insurance Co, Kawasaki Heavy Industries,
  Mitsubish Construction Equipment (Mitsubishi Heavy
  Industries)
Branch Offices: Salalah
Associated Companies: Oman Marketing & Services; Oman
  Concrete Products; Iskan Contracting; Amcat (Abdulla Moosa
  Contracting); Lamda Trading & Services Establishment
Principal Bankers: Bank of Oman, Bahrain & Kuwait
Financial Information:

	1989/90 RO'000
Authorised capital	5,000
Paid-up capital	5,000

Principal Shareholders: Moosa A R Hassan
Date of Establishment: 1918
No of Employees: 268

MOTHERCAT (OMAN) LTD

PO Box 1594, CPO Seeb
Tel: 591430, 592231
Cable: Mothercat Muscat
Telex: 5032 M/CAT ON
Telefax: 592200

Directors: Shukri H Shammas (Managing Partner), Mrs L Emile
  Bustani (Partner), Mrs N Abdullah Khoury (Partner)
Senior Executives: Anis Abu Khalaf (Resident Engineer)

PRINCIPAL ACTIVITIES: Building, mechanical and civil
  engineering, process plant and pipeline contractors
Branch Offices: In Oman: Salalah PO Box 19285, Telex 7728;
  and throughout the Middle East
Parent Company: Head office in Lebanon
Principal Bankers: British Bank of the Middle East; Bank Dhofar
  Al Omani Al Fransi

MUAMIR DESIGN ENGINEERING CONSULTANCY

PO Box 6271, Ruwi
Tel: 707594, 799394

Chairman: Ali Salem Al Hosni
Senior Executives: Bharat Parikh (Resident Architect/Manager)

PRINCIPAL ACTIVITIES: Planners, architects and engineering
  consultants
Branch Offices: Nizwa, Sohar, Ibri
Principal Bankers: Bank of Muscat

Date of Establishment: 1980

MUNA NOOR INCORPORATED

PO Box 8598, Muttrah
Tel: 590483 (5 lines)
Cable: Munanoor
Telex: 5273 Munanoor ON
Telefax: 590486

Directors: Mrs Maryam A M Al Zawawi (General Partner)
Senior Executives: B W Ritchie (Chief Executive), D N Tripathi
  (General Manager)

PRINCIPAL ACTIVITIES: Manufacture of PVC pipes and fittings
  for water supply, drainage, irrigation and telecommunication
  purposes and pipe laying services; also pest control division;
  import and sale of scientific instruments and equipment for
  laboratories and hospitals, geotextiles and plastic grids,
  valves and fittings, wall and roof claddings, packaged sewage
  treatment plants, agricultural and public health chemicals,
  irrigation design and installation of automatic irrigation
  systems
Principal Agencies: Uponor Ltd, UK; ICI, Agrochemicals; Exxon
  Terram; IMI Santon Water heaters, IMI Mouldings; Guest &
  Chrimes Valves; Peglers; H H Robertson Metal Claddings;
  Lake Irrigation Int'l, USA; Clearwater, UK; European Vinyls
  Corp
Branch Offices: PO Box 19450, Salalah, Tel 293702
Associated Companies: Hajar Explosives Trading Co Ltd; Hajar
  Explosives Manufacturing Co Ltd; Manazel Construction Co
  LLC; Environmental Engineering Services LLC; Science &
  Technology Equipment (Oman) LLC
Principal Bankers: Oman International Bank, Alkhuwair; Bank
  Melli Iran; Bank of Oman
Financial Information:

	1989/90 RO'000
Sales turnover	3,011
Authorised capital	256
Paid-up capital	256
Total assets	965

Principal Shareholders: Mrs Maryam A M Al Zawawi
Date of Establishment: 1975
No of Employees: 104

MURAD, MALALLAH HAJI HABIB,

PO Box 48, Mutrah
Tel: 773181, 773104, 773451
Cable: Muradani
Telex: 5372 ON

Chairman: Amin Malallah Haji Habib Murad
Directors: Moosa Malallah, Murtaza Malallah

PRINCIPAL ACTIVITIES: Import and export of foodstuffs, sugar, coffee, wheat, rice and wheat flour, canned fruits, canned vegetables, textiles
Principal Bankers: Habib Bank A G; National Bank of Oman; British Bank of the Middle East

MUSCAT COMMERCIAL AGENCIES LLC

PO Box 4050, Ruwi
Tel: 590442, 590443, 707147
Cable: Tijarah Muscat
Telex: 3258 Zubair ON

Senior Executives: U K Nair (Manager)

PRINCIPAL ACTIVITIES: Agricultural services, supply of agricultural produce and dairy products; also marine services, leisure crafts, marine equipment & engines and offshore engineering supplies
Branch Offices: General Trading Division; Marine Division
Parent Company: Zubair Enterprises

MUSCAT INSURANCE SERVICES LLC

PO Box 5063, Ruwi
Tel: 601860
Telex: 5239 MIS ON
Telefax: 601860

PRINCIPAL ACTIVITIES: Insurance brokers

MUSCAT INTER-CONTINENTAL HOTEL

PO Box 7398, Muttrah
Tel: 600500
Cable: Inhotelcor
Telex: 5491 IHC MCT ON

PRINCIPAL ACTIVITIES: Hotel management and operation, catering services
Branch Offices: In the Middle East: Jordan, Amman, Tel 41361; UAE, Dubai, Tel 227171; Saudi Arabia, Riyadh, Tel 465-5000; Bahrain, Tel 231777; UAE, Abu Dhabi, Tel 363777

Principal Shareholders: Government of Oman, Ministry of Commerce & Industry
Date of Establishment: November 1977
No of Employees: 400

MUSCAT (OVERSEAS) LLC

PO Box 3488, Ruwi
Tel: 703844
Cable: Overseas
Telex: 3323 MOM ON
Telefax: 793071

Chairman: HE Sheikh Mustahail Bin Ahmad Al Maashani
Directors: HE Salim Bin Mustahail Bin Ahmad Al Maashani
Senior Executives: Naeem Shakir (Group Chief Executive), Vijaya Seshadri (Group Financial Controller), Vinay Awati (Accounts Manager), Aqeel Ahmad Burham Ba Omar (Personnel, Administration & Public Relations Manager), Ajaya Kapoor (Manager Automotive Division), S M Anis (Service Manager), Sasi Kumar (Parts Manager), Glenn De Silva (Manager Industrial & Marine Division), Raju Pawar (Manager Business Development/Used Car Dept), Dattatray R Velankar (Manager Real Estate & Contracting), Salim Al Jabri (Property Manager), Sabu Abraham (Salalah Branch Incharge), Mohd Al Qyumi (Sohar Branch Incharge)

PRINCIPAL ACTIVITIES: Import and distribution of automotive, industrial and agricultural machinery and equipment, paint, engines, generators, tyres, compressors, garden tools, tractors, chemicals, safety and fire equipment, general trading, fertilisers, shade netting, marine engines, communication equipment, specialist roofing, travel and insurance, real estate and contracting, etc
Principal Agencies: General Motors (Chevrolet, Buick, Cadillac, Oldsmobile), USA; Isuzu Motors, Japan; Hyundai Motor Co, Korea; JCB Excavators, UK; Volvo Penta, Sweden; Rolls Royce, UK; Faun Cranes, Germany; Twin Disc, Hungary; Nu Swift, UK; Intex, UK; Petromin Lubricating Oil Co; National American Products Co; AC Delco; Gorghi; Automotive Products; Chaslyn Co USA; Floor Life Andek, UK; Chaoui, Portugal; Industrial Foam System, UK; Saudi Urethane Chemicals, Saudi Arabia, etc
Branch Offices: Sohar; Salalah
Parent Company: Qais Omani Establishment (Holding Company)
Principal Bankers: Bank of Muscat; Bank of Oman Bahrain & Kuwait; Commercial Bank of Oman

Principal Shareholders: HE Sheikh Mustahail Bin Ahmad Al Maashani
Date of Establishment: 1975
No of Employees: 400

MUSTAFA & JAWAD TRADING CO

PO Box 4918, Ruwi
Tel: 709955
Cable: Noorulamal
Telex: 3731 Mujatra ON
Telefax: 797277

Partners: Mustafa Abdul Reza Sultan, Mohamed Jawad Abdul Reza Sultan
Senior Executives: Sunit Shah (General Manager)

PRINCIPAL ACTIVITIES: General trading, import and distribution of consumer goods, readymade garments, pens, lighters, office equipment, toiletries, electronics
Principal Agencies: Philips, Polaroid, Christian Dior, Jean Patou, Giorgio, Lanvin, Jovan, Christofle, St Dupont, Rosenthal, Daum Cristal, Bell & Howell, Olympia, Tootal, Delsey, Mita Copiers, Nitsuko Telephones, OKI Fax & Teleprinter
Branch Offices: Capital Stores, Philips Showroom, Taj Restaurant, Mina Hotel, Al Nasr Cinema, Mustafa & Jawad Travel Agency, Office Equipment Division
Principal Bankers: British Bank of the Middle East; National Bank of Oman; Bank of Oman Bahrain & Kuwait; Oman International Bank
Financial Information:

	1989 US$'000
Sales turnover	19,500
Profits	1,075
Authorised capital	735
Paid-up capital	735
Total assets	5,350

Principal Shareholders: Partners as described
Date of Establishment: 1972
No of Employees: 293

MUTRAH HOTEL

PO Box 4525, Ruwi, Muscat
Tel: 714401/2/3/4
Cable: Mutrotel
Telex: 5226 Mutrotel ON

Chairman: Haji Ali Sultan

PRINCIPAL ACTIVITIES: Hotel owners and operators
Parent Company: Mutrah Cold Stores (Joint Venture between Spinneys (1948) Ltd, London & W J Towell & Co, Oman)
Subsidiary Companies: Several throughout Oman (non hotel)
Principal Bankers: British Bank of Middle East

Principal Shareholders: As Parent Co above
No of Employees: 50

OMAN

NARANJEE HIRJEE & CO LLC

PO Box 9, Muscat
Tel: 714842, 712764, 712244, 712826
Cable: Latwalla
Telex: 5183 Latwalla ON
Telefax: 714727

Directors: Lt Col Said Salem Al Wahaibi, Sudhir K Sampat,
  Mahesh K Sampat, Narendra K Sampat
Senior Executives: H F Bilimoria (General Manager)

PRINCIPAL ACTIVITIES: Importers of foodstuffs, household
  electrical appliances, nylon fishing nets, twines and ropes,
  chemicals, consumer goods, cigarettes
Principal Agencies: New Zealand Dairy Board; Braun, Germany;
  Kenwood Domestic Appliances, UK; Malaysia Int Palm Oil;
  Holland Canned Milk Products; Virginia Industries, UAE;
  Emirates Refining Co, UAE
Principal Bankers: Bank of Baroda; Standard Chartered Bank;
  British Bank of the Middle East; Oman International Bank
Financial Information:

	1990
	RO'000
Sales turnover	7,250

Principal Shareholders: Directors as described
Date of Establishment: 1905
No of Employees: 48

NASSER ABDULLATIF AL SERKAL EST

See AL SERKAL, NASSER ABDULLATIF, EST

NASSER LASHKO GROUP OF COMPANIES

See LASHKO, NASSER, GROUP OF COMPANIES

NATIONAL AUTOMOBILES

PO Box 3818, Ruwi, Muscat
Tel: 698520
Cable: Automobiles Muscat
Telex: 5186 BMW Oman ON
Telefax: 698942

Chairman: Sheikh Saeed Bin Nasser Al Hashar
Senior Executives: Klaus Wollin (General Manager)

PRINCIPAL ACTIVITIES: Sole importers of BMW motor cars,
  motor cycles and spare parts
Principal Agencies: Bayerische Motoren Werke AG, Germany
Branch Offices: Buraimi: PO Box 16129; Salalah: PO Box 19577
Principal Bankers: Al Bank Al Ahli Al Omani SAO, Ruwi; Bank
  Dhofar Al Omani Al Fransi, Ruwi
Financial Information:

	1990
	RO'000
Sales turnover	6,000
Profits	500
Paid-up capital	300
Total assets	2,800

Date of Establishment: 1975
No of Employees: 116

NATIONAL BANK OF ABU DHABI

PO Box 5293, Ruwi
Tel: 798841/2
Cable: Almasraf
Telex: 3740 Almasraf ON
Telefax: 794386

PRINCIPAL ACTIVITIES: Commercial banking
Branch Offices: United Arab Emirates (Dubai; Ajman; Sharjah;
  Fujairah; Ras-Al-Khaimah); Bahrain; Egypt; Sudan; Oman;
  London UK; France
Parent Company: Head office: PO Box 4, Abu Dhabi

NATIONAL BANK OF OMAN LTD SAO

Box 3751, Ruwi, Muscat
Tel: 708894
Cable: Natbank Muscat
Telex: 3281 NBO ON
Telefax: 707781

Chairman: Ali Bin Sultan Bin Mohammed Fadel
Directors: HH Sayyid Shabib Bln Taimur, Kamal Bin Abdul
  Redha Bin Sultan, Tawfiq Bin Ahmed Bin Sultan, Saleem
  Siddiqi, S Qaiser Raza, Sajid Ali Abbasi
Senior Executives: S Qaiser Raza (Director & General
  Manager), Sajid Ali Abbasi (Director & Deputy General
  Manager), Mohammed Swaleh (Executive Credit Div), Hassan
  Dawood (Executive System & Operation Div), Baqar Taki
  Mohammed (Executive International Div), Abdul Hameed
  Shahid (Executive Central Accounts Div), Dr Ahsanul Hassan
  Khan (Executive Central Inspection Div), Salim K Banatwalla
  (Executive Marketing Div), Qamar Azim Shaikh (Executive
  Establishment Div), Mehboob Alam Khan (Executive
  Management Services Div)

PRINCIPAL ACTIVITIES: Commercial banking
Branch Offices: Capital City Area Branches: 17: CBD (Main)
  Branch; Al Azaiba Round About; Al-Ghoubrah Round About;
  Areej (Ministry of Interior); Corporate; Corniche; Ghoubrah
  (Ministry of Health); Govt. Secretariate; Greater Muttrah;
  Hamriya; Mina Al Fahal PDO; Muscat; Muttrah; Qurum; Ruwi;
  Seeb Int'l. Airport; Wattaya; Salalah (Dhofar) Area Branches:
  4: Main Branch: Port Raysut; Hafa; Mirbat. Interior Area
  Branches: 28: Al-Hamra; Al-Kamil; Al-Khaboura; Al Mudaibi;
  Bahla; Barka; Bidaya; Bilad Bani Bu Ali; Bukha; Buraimi;
  Dhank; Falaj Al-Qabail; Fanja; Ibra; Ibri; Jallan; Khasab;
  Ma'abilla; Magan; Masirah; Musna; Nizwa, Qurriyat; Saham;
  Shinas; Sohar; Sumail; Sur. Overseas Branches: 3: Abu
  Dhabi, UAE; Alexandria, Egypt; Cairo, Egypt

Principal Shareholders: Omani Share Holding (60%); BCCI
  Holdings Luxembourg SA (40%)
Date of Establishment: February 1973
No of Employees: 795

NATIONAL BISCUIT INDUSTRIES LTD SAOG

PO Box 6926, Ruwi
Tel: 626034/5/6
Telex: 5278 Nabil ON
Telefax: 626048

Directors: Redha Bhacker Suleiman Jaffer (Managing Director),
  Ravi Chopra (Executive Director/General Manager), Hassan
  Ali Jawad Salman, Mohammed Bhacker Suleman Jaffer, K P
  Karnik (Representing Ominvest)
Senior Executives: S A Bhat (Production Manager), S L Rao
  (Chief Engineer), G S R Aponso (Financial Controller),
  Surinder Pal (Marketing Manager)

PRINCIPAL ACTIVITIES: Manufacture of biscuits, wafers and
  snacks
Branch Offices: Sohar; Sur; Nizwa
Principal Bankers: National Bank of Oman, Muttrah; Al Bank Al
  Ahli Al Omani, Ruwi; Bank of Oman Bahrain & Kuwait
Financial Information:

	1990
	RO'000
Sales turnover	2,000

Date of Establishment: 1982
No of Employees: 150

NATIONAL DETERGENT CO SAOG

PO Box 6104, Ruwi
Tel: 603824
Telex: 5635 Munazzaf ON
Telefax: (968) 602145

Chairman: Abdul Hussain Bhacker
Directors: Kishore Asthana (Director & General Manager)

Senior Executives: M S Iyer (Works Manager)

PRINCIPAL ACTIVITIES: Manufacturing and marketing of the following: Handwash and machine wash detergent powders, liquid detergents, toilet soaps, special laundry chemicals, industrial detergents

Principal Bankers: Bank of Oman Bahrain & Kuwait; National Bank of Oman

Financial Information:

	1989 RO'000
Sales turnover	4,037
Profits	603
Authorised capital	900
Paid-up capital	900
Total assets	3,670

Principal Shareholders: Omani public
Date of Establishment: 1981
No of Employees: 120

NATIONAL ENGINEERING & CONTRACTING CO

PO Box 4102, Ruwi, Muscat
Tel: 705310, 707234
Telex: 5430

Senior Executives: Aflah H S Al Rawahy (Managing Director)

PRINCIPAL ACTIVITIES: Building construction

NATIONAL MINERAL WATER CO LTD SAOG

PO Box 5740, Ruwi
Tel: 705817
Telex: 3782 TANUF ON
Telefax: 704960

Chairman: Sayyid Badr Bin Hamad Bin Hamood Al Busaid
Directors: HE Salim Bin Ali Bin Nasir Al Siyyabi, HE Sheikh Mustahail Bin Ahmed Al Ma'ashani, Abdul Hafidh Bin Salim Bin Rajab, Sheikh Zaher Bin Hamad Al Harthy, Sheikh Aflah Bin Hamad Bin Salim Al Rawahy, Mahmoud Bin Nasir Al Mahrezy
Senior Executives: Naveen K Kshatriya (General Manager)

PRINCIPAL ACTIVITIES: Bottling mineral water from the springs of Jabal Akhdar
Branch Offices: PO Box 26802, Nizwa
Principal Bankers: Oman Arab Bank, Al Bank Al Ahli Al Omani
Financial Information:

	1989/90 RO'000
Sales turnover	833
Profits	27
Authorised capital	800
Paid-up capital	800
Total assets	1,192

Date of Establishment: 1979
No of Employees: 48

NCR CORPORATION

PO Box 4728, Ruwi, Muscat
Tel: 793611
Cable: Nacareco Muscat
Telex: 3604 NCRMCT ON

PRINCIPAL ACTIVITIES: Sale and distribution of business equipment, computers and terminals and electronic data processing equipment
Principal Agencies: NCR
Branch Offices: Bahrain, Kuwait, Dubai, Abu Dhabi, Qatar
Parent Company: NCR Corporation, Dayton, Ohio
Principal Bankers: National Bank of Oman (in Oman)

Date of Establishment: 1966

OASIS TRADING & EQUIPMENT CO LLC

PO Box 7002, Mutrah
Tel: 592272
Cable: Moatasim Muscat
Telex: 5074 Moatasim ON
Telefax: 591626

Directors: Mohamed Al-Bahar, Sheikh Saud Al-Khalili, Sheikh Hamad Al-Taie
Senior Executives: Nicolas E Maas (Manager), Bahjat Al-Khairy

PRINCIPAL ACTIVITIES: Import and distribution of earth moving equipment and heavy machinery, marine engines, electric generating sets, uniterrupted power supply, maintenance and reconditioning of heavy equipment
Principal Agencies: Caterpillar; Lorain; Barber Greene; Merlin Gerin; Volvo Cars & Trucks; Hiab; Crane Fruehauf; Telsmith
Branch Offices: Salalah
Associated Companies: Associates in Abu Dhabi; Dubai; Sharjah; Al-Ain; Bahrain; Qatar; Kuwait
Principal Bankers: Oman Arab Bank; Oman International Bank; Al Bank Al Ahli Al Omani

Principal Shareholders: Mohamed Al-Bahar; Sheikh Saud Al-Khalili; Sheikh Hamad Al-Taie
Date of Establishment: 1976
No of Employees: 160

OCCIDENTAL OF OMAN INC

PO Box 5271, Ruwi
Tel: 603386, 603387
Telex: 5258
Telefax: 603358

Chairman: John J Dorgan
Directors: Paul C Hebner
Senior Executives: G E Grogan (President & General Manager), J B Heck (VP Operations), MIke Hauley (Controller)

PRINCIPAL ACTIVITIES: Oil & gas production and exploration in Oman
Parent Company: Occidental Petroleum Corp
Principal Bankers: Oman Arab Bank

Principal Shareholders: Occidental Petroleum Corporation

OMAK TRAVO LLC

PO Box 995, Muscat
Tel: 601127, 601402, 601422
Cable: Travo-Oman
Telex: 5409 Travomak ON

Senior Executives: Mohammad Imam Eid (General Manager), Ahmed Ismail (Finance & Admin Controller)

PRINCIPAL ACTIVITIES: Construction of multi storey buildings, laying of water pipelines, construction of villas, industrial buildings, sewage treatment plant, etc

Date of Establishment: 1973
No of Employees: 600 to 700

OMAN ARAB BANK SAO

PO Box 5010, Ruwi
Tel: 706265, 706266, 706277
Cable: OMANALARABI
Telex: 3285 & 3691 Arombnk On, 3623 Forex
Telefax: 797736 (Ruwi), 295005 (Salalah)

Chairman: HE Ahmad Bin Swaidan Al Baluchi
Directors: Murtardha Hassan Ali, Ali Bin Hussain H Alasfoor, Zakaria Mitry Melaka, Rashad Bin Mohd Bin Al Zubair, Muneeb Rashid Al Masri, Khalid A H Shoman, Abdul Hamid Shoman, Abdul Kader Askalan
Senior Executives: Abdul Kader Askalan (General Manager and Managing Director)

PRINCIPAL ACTIVITIES: Commercial banking

Branch Offices: Muttrah; Muscat; Khuwair; Salalah; Ruwi Main Branch; Al Bustan Palace Hotel Branch; Sohar Branch

Parent Company: Oman International for Development & Investment Co

Principal Bankers: Arab Bank Limited

Financial Information:

	1988 RO'000	1989 RO'000
Profits	1,084	1,188
Authorised capital	10,000	10,000
Paid-up capital	6,000	6,000
Total assets	107,074	108,128

Principal Shareholders: Oman International Development & Investment Co; Arab Bank Ltd, Jordan; Oman National Insurance

Date of Establishment: 1 October 1984

No of Employees: 160

OMAN AVIATION SERVICES CO SAOG

PO Box 1058, Seeb Airport
Tel: 519237
Cable: Omanavn
Telex: 5424 OAS Seeb ON
Telefax: 510805

Chairman: H E Sheikh Hamoud Bin Abdulla Mohd Al Harthy

Directors: Government Representatives: HE Sheikh Hamoud Bin Abdulla Mohd Al Harthy (Chairman), HE Salim Bin Ali Bin Nassir Assiyabi (Deputy Chairman), Sleyum Bin Said Bin Sleyum Al Ma'ashary (Member), Ahmed Bin Saleh Bin Ahmed (Member), Darwish Bin Ismail Bin Ali Al Baloushi (Member) Private Sector Representatives: HE Sayyid Badr Bin Saud Bin Hareb (Member), HE Yousuf Bin Alawi Abdullah (Member), HE Sheikh Mustahail Bin Ahmed Al Mahshani (Member), Sheikh Zaher Bin Hamed Bin Suleiman Al Harthy (Member), HE Abdul Aziz Mohd Al Rawas (Member)

Senior Executives: Seif Bin Hamood Al Behlany (General Manager), Saud Bin Dawood Al Raisy (Deputy General Manager & Financial Controller), Hamoud Al Behlany (Asst General Manager Operational Services), Seif H Mrs Sumaya Al Busaidi (Catering Manager), Max H Paulin (Manager Flight Operations), Mohd Zakwany (Manager Ground Services), B E Green (Chief Engineer), D K Dhir (Manager Internal Audit), Habib Bin Backer Bin Habib Al Lawatiya (Acting Manager Information & Computing), Mohd Said Al Aufy (Manager Finance), Said Bin Hilal Al Shidany (District Manager Dhofar), R Ealson (Quality Assurance & Technical Services Manager)

PRINCIPAL ACTIVITIES: Domestic airline; air charter operation and ground handling services; passenger and cargo handling, line maintenance on wide and narrow-body jets, base maintenance on light aircraft and both in-flight and restaurant catering; flight inspection of ground navigational aids

Branch Offices: Salalah Airport, Dhofar; Sales office at Ruwi, and offices at Khasab and Masirah; Agents in Sur, Bayah and Buraimi

Principal Bankers: National Bank of Oman, Oman Arab Bank, Oman International Bank, Bank of Muscat

Financial Information:

	1990 RO'000
Operating revenue	17,357
Operating profit	1,880
Share capital	5,000
Total assets	11,685

Principal Shareholders: 35% Government, 65% Public

Date of Establishment: 24 May 1981

No of Employees: 1,600 Approx

OMAN BANK OF AGRICULTURE & FISHERIES (THE)

PO Box 6077, Ruwi
Tel: 701761/3
Telex: 3046 AGFIBANK ON
Telefax: 706473

Chairman: HE Sheikh Mohamed Bin Abdallah Bin Zaher Al Hinai

Directors: HE Eng Mussallem Bin Salem Bin Mahad Qatan (Vice Chairman), HE Sheikh Ahmed Bin Mohammed Al Nabhani, HE Sheikh Said Bin Ali Al Kalbani, Sheikh Saudi Bin Ali Al Khalili, Sheikh Hamaad Bin Mohammed Al Shara Al Ghassassi, Salim Bin Abdullah Al Rawas, Sheikh Salim Bin Said Al Areimi Al Fanah, Hussain Bin Mohammed Bin Hassan Al Saleh

Senior Executives: Abdelhak Abdesalam Benani (Board's Chairman Advisor), Tariq Abdulredha Mohammed Al Jamali (General Manager), Ahmed Mohammed Al Massan (Deputy General Manager), Suleiman Dawood Abdulla Al Raiesi (Manager General Services & Public Relations), Qusai Hassan Yousuf Macki (Acting Manager Personnel Affairs & Training), Abdulaziz Mohammed Zaher Al Hinai (Acting Credit Manager), Saeed Salim Saeed Al Mubarak (Manager Banking Operations), Zainah Bint Nasser Al Namani (Acting Computer Manager)

PRINCIPAL ACTIVITIES: Agricultural and fisheries related finance

Branch Offices: Salalah, Nizwa, Sohar, Barka, Al Kamil, Ibri, Ibra, Khasab, Rustaq, Buraimi, Sinaw, Masirah

Principal Bankers: Oman International Bank

Financial Information:

	1990 RO'000
Authorised capital	19,000
Paid-up capital	16,730

Principal Shareholders: State-owned Government of Oman, Oman Chamber of Commerce & Industry, Oman Development Bank

Date of Establishment: May 19 1981

No of Employees: 134

OMAN BANKING CORPORATION SAO

PO Box 4175, Ruwi
Tel: 702383, 702385
Cable: Bankhalij Muscat
Telex: 3153 OBC ON
Telefax: 702469

Chairman: HH Es'ad Bin Tarik Al Said

Directors: HE Salim Bin Hassan Macki (Deputy Chairman), HE Awadh Bin Salim Al Shanfari, Yousuf Salman Al Saleh, Riadh A S Al Busaidi, Sadiq Bin Hassan Ali, Jawad A Sultan, David J Wilson

Senior Executives: Pradeep Saxena (General Manager)

PRINCIPAL ACTIVITIES: Wholesale commercial banking

Branch Offices: 82 Al Burj Street, Greater Mutrah

Principal Shareholders: Wholly Omani interests

Date of Establishment: 1978

OMAN CATERING CO LLC

PO Box 654, Muscat
Tel: 701353, 703057, 704932, 704946, 701353
Cable: Alabela-Muscat
Telex: 3565 Alabela ON

PRINCIPAL ACTIVITIES: Industrial catering and camp services, hotel management, cleaning services, tobacco & cigarettes distribution, liquor distribution, battery & canned fruit juice, cold storage, supermakets

Associated Companies: Catering & Supplies Co LLC; Marketing & Services Enterprises (MASE); Trading & Catering Enterprises (TACE); representation of Albert Abela Group of Companies

OMAN CEMENT CO SAO

PO Box 3560, Ruwi, Muscat
Tel: 626626 (10 lines)
Cable: Sarooj
Telex: 5139 Omancmnt ON
Telefax: 968-626414

Chairman: HE Dr Alyaqdhan Bin Talib Al Hinai
Senior Executives: Alladi Subramanyam (Financial Controller), Frank Antoniou (Sales Manager), Najim M Al Timami (Administration Manager), Stanley Edward (Production Manager), Sherif Marzouk El Sabea (Works Manager)

PRINCIPAL ACTIVITIES: Cement production and sales
Branch Offices: Cement plant at Rusail, Muscat
Principal Bankers: Bank of Oman Bahrain & Kuwait SAO
Financial Information:

	1990 RO'000
Sales turnover	14,266
Authorised capital	41,429
Paid-up capital	41,429

Principal Shareholders: Government of the Sultanate of Oman
Date of Establishment: 1977
No of Employees: 300

OMAN COMMERCIAL AGENCIES

PO Box 462, Muscat
Tel: 773444
Telex: 5322 Noor ON

Directors: Abdulla Suleiman (Partner)

PRINCIPAL ACTIVITIES: Import and distribution of building materials, GI pipes, water heaters, furniture, boats, motorcycles, sanitary-ware, aluminium doors and windows, paints
Principal Agencies: Yamaha, Japan

OMAN COMPUTER SERVICES LLC

PO Box 7917, Muttrah
Tel: 698352
Telex: 5043 OMCOMP ON
Telefax: 698356

Chairman: Mustafa A Sultan
Vice-Chairman: Anwar Al Essa Al Saleh
Senior Executives: Amrit S Chopra (Managing Director)

PRINCIPAL ACTIVITIES: Computer systems, installation and maintenance, turnkey systems, software development, project consultancy, facilities management
Principal Agencies: Wang, Radio Shack, Tom Software, DTS terminals, Optical Character Readers, Plotters, Daewoo Personal Computers, Rodias Hospital Systems, Aptech Hotel Management, Imunelec Line Conditioners, Star printers, Altos, Leo Personal Computers, Tetra, SCO, Oracle, Lampertz
Branch Offices: PO Box 19838, Salalah
Principal Bankers: Bank of Muscat, Ruwi
Financial Information:

	1990 US$'000
Sales turnover	6,500

Principal Shareholders: Jointly owned by: Kuwait Computer Services (Kuwait); Al Yousef International; HE Mohd Zubair; Mustafa Sultan; Mohd Jawad Sultan
Date of Establishment: February 1981
No of Employees: 70

OMAN CONSTRUCTION CO LLC (TOCO) (THE)

PO Box 142, Muscat
Tel: 590355
Cable: Toco Muscat
Telex: 5387 ON TOCO
Telefax: 591813

Chairman: Juman Ahour Rajab
Senior Executives: Jack Felton Furrh (General Manager), Latif A Razek (Administration Manager)

PRINCIPAL ACTIVITIES: Pipelines and oil field construction, transportation and equipment rental
Associated Companies: Willbros Energy Services Co, Tulsa, Oklahoma, USA

Date of Establishment: 1974
No of Employees: 250

OMAN DEVELOPMENT BANK SAO

PO Box 309, Muscat
Tel: 738021
Telex: 5179 Odebe ON

Chairman: HE Mohamed Moosa Al Yousuf
Members: Sheikh Zaher Al Harthy, Dr Faysal Al Amir, Ahmed Baqer, Dr Hamed Abdallah Al Riyami, Hugh Williams, Waleed Al Qattan, Ahmed Salim Al Shanfari, Mohammed Sadiq Dar, Andre Hovaguimian
Senior Executives: Bechir Ben Othman (General Manager)

PRINCIPAL ACTIVITIES: Investment and funding of development projects in the Sultanate of Oman
Principal Bankers: National Bank of Oman

Principal Shareholders: (40%): Government of Oman; (40%): The Hongkong and Shanghai Banking Corp; Kuwait Foreign Trading Contracting and Investment Co; Abu Dhabi Fund for Arab Economic Development; Arab Bank Ltd; Standard Chartered Bank; Grindlays Bank Plc; DEG of West Germany; National Bank of Oman Ltd SAO; International Finance Corp; (20%): Omani Nationals and Body Corporates
Date of Establishment: 1979

OMAN ENTERPRISES CO

PO Box 510, Muscat
Tel: 734642, 773202
Cable: Salim Muscat
Telex: 5366 Salim ON

Chairman: Khamis Al Hashar
Directors: Faisal Al Hashar

PRINCIPAL ACTIVITIES: Building contractors and traders, import and distribution of building materials, cement, steel, wood, sanitary-ware, electrical appliances and equipment, insurance agents
Principal Agencies: New Zealand Insurance Co; M A M Al Kharafi
Principal Bankers: Union Bank of Oman; Bank of Oman, Bahrain & Kuwait

Date of Establishment: 1970

OMAN FISHERIES CO SAOG

PO Box 5900, Ruwi
Tel: 714129
Cable: Omanfish Muscat
Telex: 5092 Samak ON
Telefax: 714765

Chairman: Dr Ali Bin Mohammed Moosa
Directors: HE Mohammed Bin Hassan Abdawani (Deputy Chairman), HE Sheikh Mohammed Bin Abdulla Bin Zahir Al Hinai, HE Salim Bin Abdulla Al Ghazali, HE Sheikh Amir Bin Shuwain Al Hosani, HE Dr Al Yaqdhan Bin Talib Al Hinai, HE Sheikh Salim Bin Mustahil Al Ma'ashani, HE Sheikh Said Bin Salim Al Shaksy, Sheikh Salem Bin Hilal Al Khalili, Sheikh Mohammed Bin Nasser Al Fanna, Mohammed Mussallam Al Alawi (General Manager)
Senior Executives: N Seshan (Financial Controller), Denzil Menezes (Marketing Manager), Abdulla Awad El Karim (Administration Manager), Zakaria Osman (Technical Manager), Andrew Mills (Quality Controller)

PRINCIPAL ACTIVITIES: Fishing, seafood production and processing
Branch Offices: Location: Salalah; Buraimi; Masirah
Principal Bankers: Bank of Oman, Jibroo; Oman International Bank, Ruwi
Financial Information:

	1989/90 RO'000
Sales turnover	4,000
Authorised capital	12,500
Paid-up capital	12,500
Total assets	15,200

Principal Shareholders: Government (24%); Founders (8%); Public (68%)
Date of Establishment: April 1989
No of Employees: 180

OMAN FLOUR MILLS CO LTD (SAO)

PO Box 3566, Ruwi
Tel: 711155, 711156, 711157, 711158
Cable: Omanmills
Telex: 5422 OFM ON
Telefax: 714711

Chairman: HE Dr Al Yaqdhan Bin Talib Al Hinai
Directors: HE Dr Ali Mohamed Moosa (Vice Chairman), Abdullah Moosa Abdul Rahman, HE Abdulla Ali Bakatheer, Sultan Salim Rashid, Zaher Mubarak, Mohamed Ali Said, HE Mohamed Ali Nasser Al Alawy
Senior Executives: Mahmoud Mostafa Elshorbagi (General Manager), Mohamed Thabit Al Battashi (Marketing Manager), Randhir Vithaldas (Flour Mill Manager), Ian Fraser Watson (Feed Mill Manager), Donald A Macdonald (Finance Manager)

PRINCIPAL ACTIVITIES: Operation of a modern flour mill, capacity 300 tons/24 hrs; production of atta, roller flour, wholewheat flour, semolina, and speciality flours, trading in wheat, maize and barley; operation of an animal feed mill, capacity 10 tons/hour, production of feeds for poultry, cattle, camels, horses, sheep, etc
Principal Bankers: National Bank of Oman
Financial Information:

	US$'000
Sales turnover	40,000
Authorised capital	10,000
Paid-up capital	10,000

Principal Shareholders: Government of the Sultanate of Oman (60%); Omani Public (40%)
Date of Establishment: 1976
No of Employees: 114

OMAN HOLDINGS INTERNATIONAL LLC (OHI)

Ammar Centre, PO Box 889, Muscat
Tel: 702666
Cable: Ammar
Telex: 3398 Ammar ON
Telefax: 703862

Chairman: Maqbool Hameed Mohd Al Saleh
Senior Executives: Raban Sengupta (Group Financial Controller), Behram Divecha (Group Commercial Director)

PRINCIPAL ACTIVITIES: Diversified Group of Companies acting as property developers with associated consultancy, architects, engineering, contracting, mechanical and electrical, building materials supply, security systems, landscaping and agriculture. Trading in marine equipment, motor vehicles (including car wash/petrol stations), pharmaceuticals, educational supplies, electronics. Dealing in insurance, oilfield supplies, supply and installation of telecommunications equipment. Hoteliers, caterers, travel agents, advertising agents, manufacture and export of garments
Branch Offices: OHI Salalah Branch, PO Box 18502, Salalah, Sultanate of Oman; OHI (UK) Ltd, 52/54 High Holborn, London WC1V 65U; OHI France SARL, 39 Avenue Pierre ler De Serbie, 75008 Paris; OHI Investments (Hongkong) Ltd, Prince's Building, 6th floor, Chater Road, Hongkong
Subsidiary/Associated Companies: Eihab Travels LLC; Hydromatic Construction Co; Jibroo Filling Stations & Services; Phoenix-Oman LLC; Rami Transport & Leasing Co LLC; Oman United Exchange LLC; IBN Sina Pharmacy LLC; Ghadeer Brothers LLC; Douglas-Ohi LLC; Nizwa Tourist Co LLC; Oman Tourist Corporation; Osco Imports & Marketing LLC; Voltamp Electricals; Oman Deutag Drilling Co Ltd; OHI Garments Manufacturing Co LLC
Principal Bankers: National Bank of Oman; Commercial Bank of Oman; British Bank of the Middle East; Banque Paribas
Financial Information:

	1988/89 US$'000	1989/90 US$'000
Sales turnover	40,000	50,000
Profits	2,000	2,000
Authorised capital	2,500	2,500
Paid-up capital	2,500	2,500
Total assets	23,000	49,000

Principal Shareholders: Private limited company
Date of Establishment: 1973; corporate registration of the Group 1976
No of Employees: 2,450

OMAN HOTELS CO LTD SAO

PO Box 5031, Ruwi, Muscat
Tel: 702311
Cable: Falajotel
Telex: 3229 Hotel ON
Telefax: 795853

Chairman: HE Qais Abdul Munem Al Zawawi
Directors: Abdulla Moosa (Deputy Chairman), Warren M Woods (Managing Director), Mohamed Nasser Al Khasibi, Eisa Bin Nasser Bin Abdullatif Alserkal, Salem Bin Mohammed Bin Shaban, Mohsin Haider Darwish
Senior Executives: Ashok Sharma (Regional Director & Secretary to Board), Vijay Verma (General Manager)

PRINCIPAL ACTIVITIES: Hotels operation and management, catering services, sporting, entertainment and health services
Branch Offices: Al Falaj Hotel; Al Falaj Annexe (City Centre, Ruwi)
Subsidiary Companies: Nizwa Motel, Nizwa
Principal Bankers: Bank of Oman Bahrain & Kuwait, National Bank of Oman
Financial Information:

	1990 US$'000
Authorised capital	8,700
Paid-up capital	8,700

Principal Shareholders: Joint stock company
Date of Establishment: 1971
No of Employees: 280

OMAN HOUSING BANK SAOC

PO Box 5555, Ruwi
Tel: 704444 (10 lines)
Cable: Oman Housing Bank, Ruwi
Telex: 3077 Iskan ON
Telefax: 704071

Chairman: HE Malik Bin Suleiman Bin Said Al Ma'mari
Directors: Mustafa Jassem Al Shamali (Deputy Chairman), HE Juma Hamad Al Nasry, Yousuf Bin Mohd Bin Abdul Rehman, Abdul Rehman Bin Issa Noor, Ali Al Hamood Al Finaini
Senior Executives: Mahmoud Bin Mohd Bin Omar Bahram (Acting General Manager), Adnan Bin Haider Bin Darwish (Manager Main Branch), Mahmoud Bin Ismail Bin Yousuf (Head of Organisation & Internal Audit), P N Choudhary (Head of Central Accounts), Ibrahim Bin Hamad Al Saqry (Head of Computer), Ali Bin Qassim Bin Mohd (Acting Head of Banking

Affairs), Hamdan Bin Hamoud Bin Ahmed Al Mahrooqi (Acting Head of Administrative Affairs)

PRINCIPAL ACTIVITIES: Long term loans financing for residential property
Branch Offices: Sohar, Soor, Salalah, Nizwa, Buraimi, Khasab, Rustaq, Ibra
Principal Bankers: Commercial Bank of Oman; Al Bank Al Ahli Al Omani; Bank of Oman Bahrain & Kuwait
Financial Information:

	1989 RO'000	1990 RO'000
Total loans	96,977	101,971
Profits	3,054	3,461
Authorised capital	30,000	30,000
Paid-up capital	30,000	30,000
Total assets	100,718	105,891

Principal Shareholders: Oman Government (60.9%); Kuwait Government (Ministry of Finance) (39.0%); Oman Development Bank (0.1%)
Date of Establishment: 1977
No of Employees: 233

OMAN HOUSING INDUSTRIES LTD

Sheikh Ali Bin-Zaher, Bloc Mutrah, PO Box 844, Muscat
Tel: 703409, 702243
Telex: 5313 Inoman ON

Directors: Farid Andraos, Yasser Idlibi

PRINCIPAL ACTIVITIES: Import and production of industrialised building products and light prefabrications
Principal Agencies: Polyfab (Lebanon)

Principal Shareholders: Part of the Oman International Corporation

OMAN INDUSTRIAL GAS CO

PO Box 5039, Ruwi
Tel: 703012
Cable: Khalil
Telex: 3795 Khalil ON

Chairman: Ibrahim Abdulla Lashro
Directors: Khalil Ibrahim Lashro (Managing Director)
Senior Executives: K F John (General Manager)

PRINCIPAL ACTIVITIES: Manufacture and distribution of gas welding equipment, chemicals, refrigeration equipment etc
Principal Agencies: Harris Europa; Exact, Denmark; Rothenberger, Germany

No of Employees: 250

OMAN INTERNATIONAL BANK

PO Box 4216, Ruwi
Tel: 793450 (10 lines)
Cable: Omin Bank
Telex: 3364 OMINBNK ON
Telefax: 707328, 796400

Chairman: HE Dr Omar Bin Abdul Muniem Al Zawawi
Directors: HE Hamood Bin Ibrahim Bin Soomar, HH Seyyid Shihab Bin Tariq Al Said, HE Maqbool Bin Ali Sultan, HE Noor Bin Mohammed Bin Abdulrahman, HE Sheikh Ahmed Bin Sultan Bin Saif Al Hosny, Ali Bin Thabit Al Battashi, Sheikh Ebrahim Al Ebrahim, Christopher Reeves, Salem Bin Said Bin Salem Al Wahaibi, John R Wright
Senior Executives: John R Wright ((General Manager & Chief Executive Officer), Basem Najjar (Chief Advisor & Secretary to Board), Ali Hassan Ali (Asst General Manager Banking), Yahya Said Abdulla (Asst General Manager Central Banking Services), K N Gopal Kurup (Chief Manager International), Amir Afzal (Chief Manager Computer Services), Rashid Ahmed Nasser (Manager Personnel), Vasanth Shetty (Manager Treasury), R Ganesan (Chief Accountant)

PRINCIPAL ACTIVITIES: Commercial banking

Branch Offices: Ruwi; Muttrah; Sidab; Al Khuwair; Mina Al Fahal; Ruwi High Street; Qurum; Muaskar Al Murtafa'a; Nizwa; Bahla; Ibri; Yanqul; Fahud; Marmul; Sohar; Musana'a; Buraimi; Khasab; Wudam; Mahadah; Salalah; Thumrait; Hafa'a; Ibra; Sinaw; Maseirah; Al Ashkara; Bani Bu Ali; Al Aiga; GTO; Manah; Nizwa (Police Academy); Qurum (Royal Oman Police); Saham; Rustaq; Seeb; Dima Tayeen; Al Hijj; Bombay (India)
Principal Bankers: London: Midland Bank; Bank of Scotland; National Westminster Bank; New York; Bankers Trust; Manufacturers Hanover Trust
Financial Information:

	1988 RO'000	1989 RO'000
Profits	753	1,868
Authorised capital	10,000	10,000
Paid-up capital	10,000	10,000
Total assets	163,955	191,790

Principal Shareholders: HE Omar Zawawi; HE Qais Al Zawawi; Omar Zawawi Group of Companies; Waljat Int'l Projects LLC; ROP Pension Trust LLC
Date of Establishment: 1984 (formerly subsidiary of Arab African Int Bank)
No of Employees: 494

OMAN INTERNATIONAL CONSTRUCTION EST

PO Box 286, Muscat
Tel: 702615, 702777
Cable: Natasha
Telex: 3239 Nasib ON

Chairman: Yahya Mohammed Nasib
Senior Executives: E Prabhakaran (Chief Accountant)

PRINCIPAL ACTIVITIES: Building and civil engineering contractors
Principal Agencies: Smith Steelwork, Int, UK; Sansui Electric Co Japan; Vercon International Ltd, UK; Doorware International Ltd, UK; Brandhurst Co Ltd, UK; Miltrain Ltd, UK
Branch Offices: PO Box 4195, Darsait; PO Box 7916, Ruwi
Parent Company: Yahya Enterprises (Joint Venture: Yahya Costain LLC)
Subsidiary Companies: Snow White Laundry, Sansui Shop
Principal Bankers: National Bank of Oman, Muscat; Union Bank of Oman, Ruwi

Principal Shareholders: Sole Proprietorship
Date of Establishment: 1973
No of Employees: 150

OMAN INTERNATIONAL CORPORATION

PO Box 4769, Ruwi
Tel: 602581, 602583
Cable: Oictrade, Muscat
Telex: 5096 Oictrade ON

Senior Executives: Awad El Karim Mohd Osman (General Manager)

PRINCIPAL ACTIVITIES: Diversified holding and commercial company operating in the following fields; agricultural enterprises, building materials, construction and civil engineering (joint ventures); housing; oilfield supplies; shipping; travel and freight forwarding; technical services; commercial representatives
Principal Agencies: Wild Heerbrugg Ltd, International Hough Dresser, Automobile M Berliet, Creusot Loire, Sita, Wertheim Werke, Acrow, Champion Road Machinery, SOGREAH, Fruehauf France, McDermott, Nestle & Fisher (NIDO), RFD Inflatables, 600 Services, Reliance Insurance, Ernest Leitz Wetzlar Wetzlar, Grove Cranes, Walter Kidde, Lincoln Electric, Baranite, Kawasaki, Opel, Magirus Deutz, etc
Branch Offices: Showroom in Al Khuwair & Workshop at Ghobra

Associated Companies: Hameed Associated International, PO
Box 4055, Ruwi, Tel 712862, Telex 5607

Principal Bankers: Bank Dhofar Al Omani Al Fransi; Union Bank
of Oman

Principal Shareholders: Sole proprietorship
Date of Establishment: July 1974
No of Employees: 20

OMAN INTERNATIONAL DEVELOPMENT & INVESTMENT CO SAOG

O.M.I.N.V.E.S.T.

PO Box 6886, Ruwi
Tel: 707772
Telex: 3770 Omivest ON
Telefax: 707519

Chairman: H E Mohammad Al Zubair
Directors: H E Mohamed Bin Musa Al Yousef (Deputy
Chairman), H E Sheikh Hamoud Bin Abdulla Bin Mohamed Al
Harthy, H E Ahmed Abdul Nabi Macki, H E Salim Ahmed Bin
Khalfan Al Barami, Murtadha Hassan Ali, Dr Ali Moosa,
Mohamed Al Jamali, Maqbool Ali Sultan, Abdul Kader Askalan
Senior Executives: L Charles Llewellyn (Chief Executive Officer)

PRINCIPAL ACTIVITIES: Investment Company
Subsidiary/Associated Companies: Oman Arab Bank SAO, Al
Ahlia Insurance Co SAO
Principal Bankers: Oman Arab Bank
Financial Information:

	RO'000
Authorised capital	16,000
Paid-up capital	8,000

Principal Shareholders: Oman Arab Bank SAO, Oman
International Bank, Al Bank Al Ahli Al Omani, Bank of Oman
Bahrain & Kuwait, Union Bank of Oman, National Bank of
Oman, Oman National Insurance Co, Oman National Electric
Co, Port Services Corp, Oman Aviation Services, Omar
Zawawi Est, Oman Investment & Finance Co, Royal Oman
Police Pension Fund, Zubair Enterprises, Fairtrade, Al Yousef
Intl Enterprises, Assarain Co, Desert Line Project, W J Towell
and others
Date of Establishment: December 1983

OMAN INVESTMENT & FINANCE CO LTD SAOG

PO Box 5476, Ruwi
Tel: 793170/2, 793204/8
Cable: OIFCO
Telex: 3826 OIFC ON
Telefax: 793043

Chairman: Mustafa Bin Abdul Redha Bin Sultan
Directors: Yousef Bin Salman Al Saleh, Warren M Woods,
Ismail N Mansuri, V Venkatesh, Hamza Khogali, D V
Subharao, Saghir Husain
Senior Executives: Saghir Husain (Managing Director)

PRINCIPAL ACTIVITIES: Investment company
Branch Offices: Ruwi, Quriyat, Nizwa, Ibri, Sur, Suwaiq, Sohar,
Ak-Kamil Ibra, Buraimi, Mudhaibi, Sumail, Khaboura, Salalah,
Taqah, Mirbat, Shinas, Sadah
Principal Bankers: National Bank of Oman Ltd
Financial Information:

	1989 RO'000	1990 RO'000
Sales turnover	63,908	70,409
Profits	1,048	1,101
Authorised capital	2,500	2,500
Paid-up capital	2,500	2,500
Total assets	8,654	9,368

Principal Shareholders: Omani joint stock company
Date of Establishment: 1.4.1980
No of Employees: 569

OMAN MARKETING & SERVICES CO

PO Box 5734, Ruwi
Tel: 562677, 562760
Cable: Fateh
Telex: 5319 Fateh ON
Telefax: 560372

Directors: Arvind Narain
Senior Executives: R U Baqai (Divisional Manager), G Sankaran
(Finance Manager), R J Rebello (Personnel & Admin Manager)

PRINCIPAL ACTIVITIES: Distributors and agents, trading in
electronics and home appliances, lube oil, tyres, pumps,
desalination plants, watches, etc
Principal Agencies: Matsushita Electric, National, Panasonic,
Technics, Japan; Fisher; Abu Dhabi National Oil Co for
Distribution; Toyo tyre; DE Danske Sukkerfabrikker; CFG;
Raymond Weil; Hattori Seiko
Branch Offices: Salalah: PO Box 18900; Sohar: PO Box 12646;
Nizwa: PO Box 27121; Ibri: c/o PO Box 5734
Principal Bankers: Standard Chartered Bank; Oman Arab Bank;
National Bank of Oman

Date of Establishment: 1974
No of Employees: 200

OMAN MECHANICAL ENGINEERING CONTRACTING CO

PO Box 3586, Ruwi
Tel: 794957, 794967
Cable: OMECCO
Telex: 3273 Alhusain ON

Senior Executives: Diab K El Zubeir (General Manager)

PRINCIPAL ACTIVITIES: Earthmoving contractors, civil
engineering and road building contractors, plant hire
Principal Bankers: Bank of Muscat SAO

Date of Establishment: 1974
No of Employees: 85

OMAN MECHANICAL SERVICES CO LTD

PO Box 4199, Ruwi
Tel: 563898, 563853, 563866
Cable: Omechsco
Telex: 5150 Omec ON
Telefax: 562691

President: Dr Omar Zawawi
Directors: Qais Zawawi
Senior Executives: R C Bajpai (Vice President Marketing), S
Rajamani (General Manager), Bertram Pereira (Finance
Manager), S Ananthakrishnan (Sales Manager), Stanley Vaz
(Automotive Sales Manager), N V Gashvi (Spare Parts
Manager), Suresh Madhav (Sales Engineer), Anwar Al Baluchi
(Administration Manager)

PRINCIPAL ACTIVITIES: General trading, agents for
mechanical, electrical, electronic and industrial equipment,
motor vehicles, mechanical and electrical engineering services
Principal Agencies: Rolls Royce Diesel, Perkins Engines, Hyster
Europe Ltd, Suzuki Motor Co, Mobil Oil Co, Nellen
Kraanbouw, General Electric (USA), AEG-Telefunken (WC); F
G Wilson; Goldstar Cable; Vecom Marine Chemicals
Branch Offices: Salalah
Parent Company: Member of Omar Zawawi Group of
Companies
Principal Bankers: British Bank of the Middle East; Bank of
Oman Bahrain & Kuwait SAO; Oman International Bank; Al
Bank Al Ahli Al Omani SAO
Financial Information:

	1990 RO'000
Sales turnover	3,000
Authorised capital	300
Paid-up capital	300

Principal Shareholders: Dr Omar Zawawi, Qais Zawawi
Date of Establishment: 1972
No of Employees: 55

OMAN MINING COMPANY LLC

PO Box 758, Muscat
Tel: 603501
Telex: 5492 ON

Chairman: HE Salim Shaban
Directors: Mohammad H Kassim, Dr Sherief Lutfi, Khalifa M Al
Hinai, Malek Al Adawi, Hassan Juma'a, Mustafa Mugeiry, Ali
Tamimi

PRINCIPAL ACTIVITIES: Developing three underground copper
mines for a production rate of 3,500 tonnes/day. Design,
construction and production of a 3,000 tonne/day copper
concentrator, and a 20,000 tonnes/year electric smelter, also
a 36 megawatt gas turbine generating plant, a townsite and a
jetty

Principal Shareholders: Private sector interests purchased by
the Government of the Sultanate of Oman in early 1980, thus
increasing its ownership to 100%
Date of Establishment: Incorporated 1978
No of Employees: 505

OMAN NATIONAL ELECTRIC CO SAOG

PO Box 4393, Ruwi
Tel: 796353, 700369
Cable: Electrico Muscat
Telex: 3328 ONEC ON
Telefax: 797394

Chairman: Sheikh Saud Ali Al Khalili
Directors: HE Ali Dawood Al Raisi, Murtadha Hassan, HE
Mohammad Ali Al Alawi, Abdul Rahman, Ahmed Saeed Zaki,
Abdul Aziz Al Shanfari
Senior Executives: M Osman Baig (General Manager), P B
Vanchi (Technical Manager)

PRINCIPAL ACTIVITIES: Electricity, power generation,
distribution and transmission, operation and maintenance of
power stations and desalination plants; computer software
services
Branch Offices: Salalah, Raysut, Masirah, Khasab, Beya,
Kumzar, Alfayy, Shisha, Lima, Mudha, Qidah
Principal Bankers: Bank of Oman Bahrain & Kuwait
Financial Information:

| | 1989 |
	RO'000
Sales turnover	2,252
Profits	126
Authorised capital	1,000
Paid-up capital	1,000
Total assets	1,843

Principal Shareholders: Al Taher Enterprises, Zawawi Trading,
Zubair Enterprises
Date of Establishment: 1978
No of Employees: 305

OMAN NATIONAL INSURANCE CO SAOG

PO Box 5254, Ruwi
Tel: 702677, 705527, 795020/21/22/23
Cable: Omanat
Telex: 3111 ONIC ON
Telefax: 702569

Chairman: HE Mohammed Bin Musa Al-Yousuf
Directors: HE Sheikh Hamoud Bin Abdullah Al-Harthy (Deputy
Chairman), HE Dr Omar Bin Abdul Muniem Al Zawawi, HE Dr
Ali Bin Moosa, Yusuf Bin Abdul Bari Al Zawawi, HE Mohamed
Bin Nasser Al Khasibi, Saad Bin Suhail Bin Bahwan, Hilal Bin
Amer Al Kiyumi, Rashid Bin Salim Al Masroori
Senior Executives: Michael J Adams (General Manager),
Mohammed H G Habib (Financial Controller), Nicholas R

Lehmann (Asst General Manager Finance), M J Oates (Asst
General Manager Insurance), Michael Leith Smith (Life
Manager)

PRINCIPAL ACTIVITIES: Insurance (life and non life business)
Principal Agencies: Al Bethran; Al Asfoor; Safeway Co LLC;
Saleh Mohd Talib; Oman Commercial Services; Muscat
Commercial Services; Al Jizzi Co; Basil Enterprises; Al Arama
Agencies; Trade Links & Services; Industrial & Trading Co;
Reham Enterprises; Al Haq General Trading; Eint Trading &
Contg LLC; Blue Eagle Shipping Co; Oman United Agencies,
Al Ahmedy Trading; Khulood Clearing; National Estate
Bureau; El Sukry Est; Salem Nasser Al Mahrooqi; Abu Hani
Est; Teejan Trading; Abu Anwar Trading; Al Jadwal Trading;
Wadi Mugmalas Trading
Branch Offices: Salalah Tel 292513; Buraimi Tel 650404; Nizwa
Tel 410494; Sohar, Tel 840720; Seeb Tel 622130
Subsidiary Companies: Salvage LLC; Alarm Equipment Co LLC
Principal Bankers: Bank of Oman Bahrain & Kuwait SAOG;
National Bank of Oman SAO; Oman International Bank SAOG
Financial Information:

| | 1990 |
	RO'000
Sales turnover	12,882
Profits	2,043
Authorised capital	5,000
Paid-up capital	5,000
Fixed assets	21,140

Principal Shareholders: Government of Oman; Omani
Shareholders
Date of Establishment: March 1978
No of Employees: 136

OMAN NATIONAL TRANSPORT CO SAO

PO Box 620, Muscat
Tel: 590046, 590601/4
Cable: Transerv Muscat
Telex: 5018 Transerv ON
Telefax: 590152

Chairman: Salim Bin Ali Bin Nasser Assiyabi
Directors: Suleiman Bin Muhana Al Adawi (Managing Director)
Senior Executives: Graham Fletcher (General Manager), Majid A
Al Mandhry (Deputy General Manager), Anthony Tallant
(Traffic Manager), Ali Bin Suleiman Amour Al Behlani
(Administration Manager), Mubarak Bin Khamid Al Shikely
(Personnel & Training Manager), S Balachandran (Deputy
Chief Engineer), V N Krishnan (Internal Auditor)

PRINCIPAL ACTIVITIES: Passenger transportation, fleet of 300
buses and coaches
Branch Offices: Salalah
Parent Company: Ministry of Communications
Principal Bankers: Oman International Bank, Al Khuwair Br
Financial Information:

	RO'000
Authorised capital	6,000
Paid-up capital	4,838

Principal Shareholders: Government of the Sultanate of Oman
Date of Establishment: 1984
No of Employees: 576

OMAN OIL INDUSTRY SUPPLIES & SERVICES CO

PO Box 3510, Ruwi
Tel: 590061/63/66/67
Cable: Tijarah Muscat
Telex: 5161 OOISS ON
Telefax: 590130

Directors: Mohammad Al Zubair, Jassim Jaidah
Senior Executives: N J Coates (General Manager), S Ganguly
(Financial Controller), Jihad Abu Hussain (Sales Engineer)

OMAN

PRINCIPAL ACTIVITIES: Agents and distributors for safety and survival equipment, fire fighting equipment, instrumentation, oilfield equipment

Principal Agencies: Bacharach Inc, Buveco, Detection Instruments, McKowan Lowe, Red Wing, Siebe Gorman, Tecsol, Tuffking Safety, Wolf Safety Lamp, Ansul Fire Protection, National Foam, Perren Fire Protection, Wormald Fire Hoses, Cyanamid, Dearborn Chemicals, Digitran, Foxboro, Magnetol, Mokveld Valves, PIC Automation Serivces, Scama Panalarm, Serck Controls, Ariel, Completion Tool, Dyckerhoff, Exploration Data Consultants, Global Cathodic Protection, Global Corrosion Consultants, Hughes Tool, Lynn, Baroid Ltd, NL Baroid Logging Systems, NL Sperry Sun, Oil Tools Int, Pronal, Raysut Cement, Solus Ocean Systems, Weatherford Oil Tools, etc

Branch Offices: Salalah: PO Box 19479, Salalah, Dhofar, Tel/Fax 294035

Parent Company: A joint venture between Zubair Enterprises, Muscat, Oman and Jaidah Motors & Trading Co, Doha, Qatar

Principal Bankers: Bank Dhofar Al Omani Al Fransi; National Bank of Oman; Bank of Oman Bahrain & Kuwait

Financial Information:

	1990 US$'000
Sales turnover	18,000
Authorised capital	660
Paid-up capital	660
Total assets	2,200

Principal Shareholders: Mohammad Zubair, Jassim Jaidah
Date of Establishment: October 1975
No of Employees: 50

OMAN OILFIELD SUPPLY CENTER LLC

PO Box 4160, Ruwi
Tel: 602044 (6 lines)
Cable: Oilfield
Telex: 5484 ON
Telefax: 698414

PRINCIPAL ACTIVITIES: Supply of engineering equipment to the oil, gas and other industries, also general engineering services

OMAN REFINERY COMPANY LLC

PO Box 6568, Ruwi
Tel: 561200
Cable: OMREF
Telex: 5123, 5123 ORC ON

Chairman: HE Salem Bin Mohammed Bin Shaban
Directors: Ali Bin Thabit Al-Battashi, Ali Bin Abdalla Al-Tamimi, Khalifa Bin Mubarak A-Hinai, Rashid Bin Ali Al Khaify, Haytham Bin Ali Al Qadi
Senior Executives: Donald E Aukerman (Managing Director), Charles R Smith (General Manager Operations), Ahmed J Galaal (General Manager Administration), Ahmed Bin Saleh Al Marhoon (Controller & Treasurer)

PRINCIPAL ACTIVITIES: Refining crude oil for production of refined oil products
Principal Bankers: Oman International Bank; National Bank of Oman

Principal Shareholders: Ministry of Petroleum and Minerals (99%); Central Bank of Oman (1%)
Date of Establishment: February 6th, 1982
No of Employees: 235

OMAN SERVICES & SUPPLY ORGANIZATION

PO Box 437, Muscat
Tel: 795721, 795722, 795736
Cable: Ossoman
Telex: 3228 OSSO ON
Telefax: (968) 796732

Chairman: Dr Omar Zawawi

Senior Executives: A A Bokhari (General Manager)

PRINCIPAL ACTIVITIES: Trading and contracting of technical items; manufacturers' representatives
Principal Agencies: ASEA AB, Sweden; ASEA-STAL Sweden; Sirti International, Italy; Sade-Sadelmi, Italy; Fujikura, Japan; Kongsberg Gasturbines & Power Systems, Norway; Feedback, UK; Tolley Industries, New Zealand; Sa Sakura Eng Co Ltd, Japan
Parent Company: Omar Zawawi Establishment (OMZEST)
Associated Companies: Waleed Associates
Principal Bankers: Bank of Oman Bahrain & Kuwait; Oman International Bank; Bank of Muscat

Principal Shareholders: HE Dr Omar Zawawi, HE Qais Zawawi
Date of Establishment: 1977
No of Employees: 50

OMAN SHAPOORJI CONSTRUCTION CO LLC

PO Box 4347, Ruwi, Muscat
Tel: 590297, 590629, 592072
Cable: Oscco Muscat
Telex: 5137 OSCO ON
Telefax: 591421

Chairman: HE Mohamed R Moosa
Directors: HE Lt Col Said Salem Al-Wahaibi, HH Sayed Hamed Bin Hamood, Maqbool Hameed, Pallonji S Mistry, Cyrus P Mistry
Senior Executives: K Venkata Rao (General Manager)

PRINCIPAL ACTIVITIES: Building and civil engineering contractors (office and residential blocks; government buildings etc)
Principal Bankers: National Bank of Oman, Ruwi; Bank of Muscat, Ruwi

Principal Shareholders: HE Mohamed R Moosa; HE Lt Col Said Salem Al-Wahaibi; HH Sayed Hamed Bin Hamood; Maqbool Hameed; Pascal Enterprises
Date of Establishment: July 1975
No of Employees: 1,000

OMAN SHERATON HOTEL

PO Box 6260, Ruwi, Muscat
Tel: 799899
Telex: 3353, 3357, 3358 Sheraton ON
Telefax: 795791

Chairman: Sheikh Saeed Bin Nasser Al Hashar (Owner)
Directors: Dieter Janssen (Vice President Sheraton South Asia)
Senior Executives: T Voss (Executive Asst Manager)

PRINCIPAL ACTIVITIES: Hotel operations
Principal Agencies: Managed By Sheraton Middle East Management Corporation
Parent Company: International Telephone & Telegraph (ITT), Boston, USA
Associated Companies: A member of Al Hashar Group of Companies
Principal Bankers: Bank Dhofar Al Omani Al Fransi

Principal Shareholders: Owned by National Hotels Co Ltd SAO
Date of Establishment: October 1985
No of Employees: 250

OMAN STEEL COMPANY LLC

PO Box 217, Muscat
Tel: 703143, 703515 (office), 591953 (factory)
Cable: Assulaimy
Telefax: 968-700010

Chairman: Salem Essa Assulaimy
Senior Executives: Shoeb Shipchandler (General Manager)

PRINCIPAL ACTIVITIES: Structural designers, suppliers, fabricators and erectors of steel structures, steel tanks; fabricators of windows, doors, ladders, pipeline works, equipment erection and power house relocation, etc

Associated Companies: Sister company: Technical Trading Co, PO Box 4693, Ruwi
Principal Bankers: Bank of Muscat
Financial Information:

	1989/90 RO'000
Sales turnover	300
Profits	10
Authorised capital	800
Paid-up capital	800
Total assets	1,070

Principal Shareholders: Successors of Mansoorali Mansoor Assulaimy
Date of Establishment: 1973
No of Employees: 55

OMAN TECHNICAL AGENCIES LLC

PO Box 423, Muscat
Tel: 700624
Telex: 3234 OMTAG ON

Senior Executives: K P Ramachandran (General Manager)

PRINCIPAL ACTIVITIES: Supply of agricultural equipment and products, agro chemicals, fertilisers, irrigation equipment turnkey projects; also industrial products, educational and recreational supplies, electronic parts and components, auto spare parts, manufacturers' representatives
Principal Agencies: Richter Harvesting Machinery; Warn Industrial Winches & Hoists; Danarim Hedge Trimmers; Olympia Power Sprayers; Bigtoys Recreational Equipment

OMAN TRANSPORT & CONTRACTING CO

PO Box 564, Muscat
Tel: 701155, 704014
Cable: Otcco
Telex: 3251 Otcco ON
Telefax: 750055

Partners: Hareb Ibrahim (Managing Director), Abdullah A M Hussain, Salah Hareb, Ahmed Hareb
Senior Executives: Abdullah A M Hussain (Administration Manager), Kuldeep K Hajela (Financial Controller), J C Bolaki (Chief Quantity Surveyor)

PRINCIPAL ACTIVITIES: Civil contractors, carpentry, steel factory, transportation
Principal Bankers: National Bank of Oman Ltd

Principal Shareholders: Partners as described
Date of Establishment: 1971
No of Employees: 500

OMAN UNITED AGENCIES LLC

PO Box 3985, Ruwi, Muscat
Tel: 701291, 701319, 702823, 793109, 793395, 708635
Cable: Omanunited
Telex: 3215 OUA ON
Telefax: 793390

Directors: HE Mohammad Al Zubair, Mohammed A Al Jamali, Abdulla Moosa, Shawqi Sultan, A G Davies, M Smith, R R Owens, P Srinivasan
Senior Executives: P Srinivasan (Manager Finance), H Shahab (Consumer Manager), G de Albuquerque (Manager Shipping), S Spencer (Manager Retail), T P Casey (Manager Travel), I Giulianott (Manager Oilfield Sales & Service)

PRINCIPAL ACTIVITIES: Travel agents and general traders; freight forwarders, Lloyds agents, shipping agents; engineering sales and services, general traders
Principal Agencies: General sale agents for British Airways, Air India, Qantas, KLM, American Airlines. Sales agents for Gulf Air. Manufacturers representatives for many UK and Continental companies
Parent Company: Gray Mackenzie & Co Ltd

Associated Companies: United Engineering Services LLC, PO Box 5638, Ruwi; Oman United Agencies (Dhofar) LLC, PO Box 18179, Salalah, Tel 290012, Telex 7614 ON
Principal Bankers: Grindlays Bank; Standard Chartered Bank; British Bank of the Middle East; National Bank of Oman

Date of Establishment: January 1978
No of Employees: 247

OMAN UNITED INSURANCE CO SAOG

PO Box 4522, Ruwi
Tel: 703990/1/4/6
Cable: OUICO Oman
Telex: 3652 OUI ON
Telefax: 796327

Chairman: HE Salim Bin Nassir Al Busaidi
Directors: Sheikh Suhail Bin Salim Al Bahwan (Deputy Chairman), Salim Bin Said Bin Salim Al Wahaibi, Sheikh Awad Bin Salim Al Shanfari, Ali Bin Hussain Hamza Al Asfoor
Senior Executives: Khalid Mansour Hamed (General Manager)

PRINCIPAL ACTIVITIES: All classes of general insurance and life assurance business
Branch Offices: PO Box 18716, Salalah, Tel/Fax 295040; PO Box 13920, Sohar, Tel 841533
Principal Bankers: Al Bank Al Ahli Al Omani, Oman Arab Bank
Financial Information:

	1988/89 RO'000	1989/90 RO'000
Sales turnover	4,651	5,031
Profits	488	562
Authorised capital	2,000	2,000
Paid-up capital	2,000	2,000
Total assets	4,150	5,483

Principal Shareholders: 100% Omani interests
Date of Establishment: December 1985
No of Employees: 54

OMANI CO FOR AGRICULTURAL SERVICES & DEVELOPMENT LLC

PO Box 6353, Ruwi
Tel: 564941, 701800
Cable: Shibly Muscat
Telex: 5271 Shibly ON
Telefax: 564947

Chairman: Saif Salem Shibly (Managing Director)

PRINCIPAL ACTIVITIES: Trading in agricultural and horticultural products, landscaping contractors, dealing in birds and fish, aquarium items, supply of bee keeping materials, live animals, veterinary and surgical items, poultry etc
Principal Agencies: Victa, UK; Dr Stahl, W Germany; Bulrush Peat, UK; Ets Salvy, France; Laurus Peter, W Germany; Andreas Stihl, W Germany; Uniroyal, UK
Branch Offices: Salalah: PO Box 19582, Tel 294600
Subsidiary Companies: Beit Al Munazim, PO Box 6353, Ruwi
Principal Bankers: British Bank of the Middle East, Ruwi; Oman Arab Bank, Ruwi

Principal Shareholders: Saif Salem Shibly; Mohamed Saif Shibly
Date of Establishment: 1981
No of Employees: 80

OMANI EST FOR AGRICULTURAL DEVELOPMENT & CONTRACTS

PO Box 4924, Ruwi
Tel: 704791, 705384, 793855
Cable: Zahara Oman
Telex: 3167 Zahara ON
Telefax: 709426

Chairman: Mohammed Abdulla Hashil Al Jardani (Managing Director)
Senior Executives: Ramanathan Krishnan (General Manager), P Suryanarayanan (Financial Controller)

OMAN

PRINCIPAL ACTIVITIES: Dealing in agro chemicals, agricultural equipment, vegetable & flower seeds, tools & equipment, pesticides, insecticides & fungicides, pots & planters; also landscaping contractors and civil contractors

Principal Agencies: Fisons, UK; Yates Cooper, New Zealand; Ludolf Beye, Holland; Hayters, UK; Hatsutah, Japan; Indo American Hybrid Seeds; Royal Slius Seeds; Grosfillex, France; Wilkinson Sword, UK; Igeba Foggers, W Germany; etc

Branch Offices: Salalah: PO Box 18832, Tel 290319; Nizwa: PO Box 27045, Tel 410655; Seeb Nursery: PO Box 4924, Ruwi, Tel 536907

Subsidiary Companies: Farms and green nurseries at Barkha, Seeb and Sohar

Principal Bankers: British Bank of the Middle East, Ruwi

Date of Establishment: 1974
No of Employees: 207

OMAR ZAWAWI ESTABLISHMENT O.M.Z.E.S.T.

PO Box 879, Muscat
Tel: 736239 (6 lines)
Cable: OMZEST
Telex: 5542 OMZEST ON
Telefax: 740230

President: Dr Omar Zawawi

Directors: Ismail Mansuri (Vice President Finance), Refaat Ghazawy (Vice President Legal & Personnel), N S Narasimhan (Senior Vice President)

Senior Executives: V Venkataraman (Manager Audit & Methods), K S Rao (Project Manager), Umesh Asaikar (Project Manager), S Subramani (Project Manager), A S Subbaraman (Mangaer Marketing Services), Pradeep Mehra (Finance Manager), D H Tambekar (Finance Manager)

PRINCIPAL ACTIVITIES: Corporate headquarters of OMZEST group of companies. Companies in the group deal with all types of agencies, banking, services, trading, manufacturing and construction activities

Principal Bankers: Oman International Bank; Bank of Muscat; Bank of Oman Bahrain & Kuwait; Commercial Bank of Oman; Union Bank of Oman

Principal Shareholders: 100% owned by Dr Omar Zawawi
Date of Establishment: August 1978
No of Employees: Omzest: 55; Group: 1,200

ORIENTAL INTERNATIONAL CO

PO Box 3359, Ruwi
Tel: 626130, 626131
Cable: Alsharqia
Telex: 5095 Orintal ON
Telefax: 626286

Chairman: Ali Awadh Ali
Directors: Mohammad Awadh Ali, Ibrahim Awadh Ali
Senior Executives: Khaldoun Al Hussayni (General Manager)

PRINCIPAL ACTIVITIES: Trading, commercial agencies, import/export

Principal Agencies: Liebherr-Export AG, Switzerland; Liebherr Mischtechnik, Germany; Liebherr-Werk Ehingen, Germany; Azienda Reggiana Construcione Electropompe, Italy; Terada Pump, Japan; Krislar Diesel Engines, India; Vedbysonder Maskinfabrik, Germany; Karl Kassbohrer, Germany

Subsidiary Companies: Oriental Crusher LLC; Oriental Building Material Industries LLC

Principal Bankers: Bank Melli Iran; Bank of Muscat; Oman International Bank

Date of Establishment: 1974

PAULING (OMAN) LLC

PO Box 4127, Ruwi
Tel: 602138
Cable: PAULING
Telex: 5286 Pauling ON

Directors: P A B Prosser, W A Barrage, R H White, V Venkatesh

PRINCIPAL ACTIVITIES: Construction and civil engineering
Associated Companies: UK Associate: Pauling (Middle East) Plc, 12-18 Grosvenor Gardens, London SW1W 0DZ
Principal Bankers: British Bank of the Middle East

Principal Shareholders: H E Mohammad Al Zubair; Pauling (Middle East) Plc
Date of Establishment: 1981
No of Employees: 200

PETROLEUM DEVELOPMENT OMAN

PO Box 81, Muscat
Tel: 678111
Cable: Petro, Muscat
Telex: 5212 ON
Telefax: 677106

Chairman: Salem Bin Mohammed Bin Shaban (Undersecretary Ministry of Petroleum and Minerals)

Directors: Ali Bin Abdulla Al Tamimi (Director General of Administrative & Financial Affairs - Ministry of Petroleum & Minerals), Salim Bin Mohamed Al Shanfari (Acting Director General of Petroleum & Gas Affairs - Ministry of Petroleum & Minerals), Mrs Rajiha Bint Abdul Ameer (Undersecretary Development Council), P Kassler (Shell International Petroleum Co Ltd -London), R M Charlton (Shell Internationale Petroleum Maatschappij - The Hague), B Madinier (Total Compagnie Francaise des Petroles - Paris), R Gulbenkian (Partex (Oman) Corp - Lisbon)

Senior Executives: H A Merle (Managing Director), Said Bin Ali Al Kalbani (Deputy Managing Director), Abdulla Bin Mohammed Al Lamki (Technical Director), Suleiman Bin Mohammed Al Lamki (Administration Manager), A Goldsmith (Finance Manager), P A C de Ruiter (Exploration Manager), J P M Buyzen (Operations Manager), Mohammed Samir Bin Soud Al Kharusi (Petroleum Engineering Manager), M A Brinded (Engineering Manager), Nasser Bin Sultan Bin Mohammed Al Maskari (Chief Medical Officer)

PRINCIPAL ACTIVITIES: Exploration and production of crude oil and gas

Branch Offices: Salalah, PO Box 19626, Tel 462585, Telex 7724 Petrosal, ON

Principal Bankers: Oman International Bank; National Bank of Oman

Principal Shareholders: Omani Government (60%); Royal Dutch Shell (34%); Total CFP (4%); Partex (2%)
Date of Establishment: By Royal Decree on 1st January 1980
No of Employees: 4,200

PHOTOCENTRE

PO Box 3115, Ruwi
Tel: 706752
Cable: Photocentre Muscat
Telex: 3499 Kharusi ON
Telefax: 968 794121

Chairman: Muhammad Ali Said Al Kharusi (Managing Director)

Senior Executives: Muhallab A H Al Busaidy (GM of Projects & Development), J Ramanan (Manager Finance & Administration), Bushan Drona (Marketing Manager), S N Jabbar (Sales Manager), Stanley Fernandes (Service Manager), Deepak Bhalla (Manager Computer Div)

PRINCIPAL ACTIVITIES: Manufacturers' representation; import and distribution of photographic and communications equipment, electronic components and audio-visual equipment, computers and reprographic equipment, musical instruments, health equipment

Principal Agencies: Fuji Film; Hasselblad; Leica; Apple; Chinon; Elmo; Sun Pak; Durst; Paterson; Trio Kenwood; Nakamichi; Bang & Olufsen; SABA; Revox; Yaesu Musen; Tektronix, TOA; JBL Kathrein; Eye DEntify; Minox, Broncolor, Bronica, etc

Branch Offices: Wadi Kabir; Ruwi; Greater Muttrah; Salalah; Sohar; Medinat Qaboos; Al Khuwair; Darsait

Parent Company: Comcent International Group of Companies

Subsidiary Companies: Colorlab LLC, PO Box 3114, Ruwi; Almas Technical Services; Abu Ijlaal Trading PO Box 3115, Ruwi

Principal Bankers: Citibank; Bank of Muscat; Standard Chartered Bank

Principal Shareholders: Sole proprietorship
Date of Establishment: 1972
No of Employees: 150

PORT SERVICES CORP LTD SAOG

PO Box 133, Muscat
Tel: 714000-6
Cable: Mina Qaboos
Telex: 5233 Mina Qaboos ON, 5203 Opsco On, 5276 Mina Qaboos
Telefax: 714007

Chairman: HE Sheikh Hamoud Bin Abdulla Al Harthy (Minister of Communications)

Directors: HE Salim Bin Ali Bin Nasser Al Assiyabi, HE Dr Al Yaqdhan Bin Talib Al Hinai, HE Hareb Bin Hamed Bin Soud, Fareeq Awal Said Bin Rashid Al Kalbani, Darwish Bin Ismail Bin Ali, Sheikh Mohd Bin Hilal Al Khalili, HE Qais Bin Abdul Muneim Al Zawawi, HE Dr Omar Bin Abdul Muneim Al Zawawi, Sheikh Suhail Bin Salim Bahwan, HE Sheikh Mustahil Bin Ahmed Al Mashani, Rashad Bin Mohammed Bin Al Zubair, HE Awad Bin Salim Al Shanfari, Eng Salim Bin Humeid Al Ghassani

Senior Executives: Awad Salim Al Shanfari (President), M M Shipchandler (Financial Controller), Hamed Bin Abdul Rehman Al Qadhi (Chief Engineer), Saud Al Nihari (Operations Manager), Capt Ahmed Said (Harbour Master), Said Bin Salim Al Marie (Manager Planning & Projects)

PRINCIPAL ACTIVITIES: Sole operator of Port Qaboos Muscat
Principal Bankers: Oman Arab Bank Ltd
Financial Information:

	1988/89 RO'000	1989/90 RO'000
Sales turnover	8,445	6,147
Profits	1,701	811
Authorised capital	2,400	4,800
Paid-up capital	2,400	4,800
Total assets	8,461	8,043

Principal Shareholders: Government of the Sultanate of Oman; Suhail & Saud Bahwan; Waleed Associates; Zubair Enterprises; Zawawi Trading Co; Qais Omani Establishment; Royal Oman Police Pension Trust LLC
Date of Establishment: 1976
No of Employees: 970

PREMIX LLC

PO Box 4939, Ruwi
Tel: 620092, 601992, 600935
Telex: 5214 ON

PRINCIPAL ACTIVITIES: Supply of building materials and cement

PRINTERS TRADE CENTER CO

PO Box 7116, Muttrah
Tel: 702699, 703492
Cable: Press
Telex: 3830 PTCC ON

Chairman: Syied Ali Alhashmi
Directors: Hammad Mubarak Al Mashry
Senior Executives: Mohamed Zaheer (Manager)

PRINCIPAL ACTIVITIES: Import and distribution of printing and allied machinery, equipment, and stationery
Principal Agencies: Heidelberg, Polar Mohr, Klimsch & Co, Harris Intertype, Dr Hell Klischograph, Roto Duplicators, ADS Cash Register, Hans Sixts, Hostmann Steinberg, Freudorfer, Warner Polinski, ING, Franksche Eisenwerke, Leibinger
Branch Offices: Dubai; Abu Dhabi; Saudi Arabia; Yemen; Kuwait; Oman
Parent Company: Printers Trade Center, Dubai
Principal Bankers: Al Bank Al Ahli Al Omani

Principal Shareholders: Syied Ali Alhashmi & Hammad Mubarak Al Mashry

QAIS OMANI ESTABLISHMENT (HOLDING COMPANY)

PO Box 3488, Ruwi
Tel: 703844
Telex: 3323 MOM ON
Telefax: 793071

Chairman: HE Sheikh Mustahail Bin Ahmad Al Maashani
Directors: HE Sheikh Salim Bin Mustahail Bin Ahmad Al Maashani (Vice Chairman)
Senior Executives: Naeem Shakir (Group Chief Executive), Vijay Seshadri (Group Financial Controller), Vinay Awati (Accounts Manager), Aqeel Ahmad Burham Ba Omar (Personnel, Administration & Public Relations Manager)

PRINCIPAL ACTIVITIES: General trading; import, distribution and installation of electrical and engineering equipment, mining, safety & fire equipment, marine engines, communication equipment, airconditioning, elevators and escalators, petrochemical, hospital and laboratory equipment, desalination and process industries; sewerage and waste disposal projects; general contracting and commission agents; sponsors; business promoters, advisors and consultants; real estate; travel and insurance
Principal Agencies: See Muscat (Overseas) LLC
Branch Offices: Sohar; Salalah
Parent Company: Holding Company
Subsidiary Companies: Muscat (Overseas) LLC; Al Mazaara Estishariya LLC (AME); Majan International Agencies Travel & Tourism LLC; Majan Brokerage House
Principal Bankers: Bank of Muscat; Bank of Oman Bahrain & Kuwait; Commercial Bank of Oman

Principal Shareholders: HE Sheikh Mustahail Bin Ahmad Al Maashani
Date of Establishment: 1975
No of Employees: 400

QURUM CONTRACTORS LLC

PO Box 7003, Muttrah
Tel: 562922, 562821, 562720, 563437, 562763
Cable: Surfacing Oman
Telex: 5008 Qcoman ON
Telefax: 562330

Chairman: Dr Omar Zawawi
Directors: H E Qais Zawawi, Abdulla Moosa, Mohsin Haider Darwish, Suhail Bahwan
Senior Executives: S M Gulatee (General Manager), N S Subramaniam (Financial Controller)

PRINCIPAL ACTIVITIES: Road engineers, building and civil engineering contractors
Principal Bankers: British Bank of the Middle East; Bank of Oman, Bahrain and Kuwait; Oman International Bank; National Bank of Oman; Al Bank Al Ahli Al Omani; Bank of Muscat

Financial Information:

	1988/89 RO'000	1989/90 RO'000
Sales turnover	2,560	2,977
Authorised capital	980	980
Paid-up capital	980	980
Total assets	1,898	1,935

Principal Shareholders: Waleed Associates; Mohsin Haider Darwish; Suhail Bahwan; Moosa Abdul Rahman; Zawawi Trading Company
Date of Establishment: October 1972
No of Employees: 500

RAMNIKLAL B KOTHARY & CO LLC

See KOTHARY, RAMNIKLAL B, & CO LLC

RASASI COMMERCIAL ENTERPRISES

PO Box 4020, Ruwi
Tel: 699745
Cable: Rasasi, Muscat
Telex: 5386 Rasasi ON
Telefax: (968) 699748

Proprietor: Iyad I Rasasi (Managing Director)
Senior Executives: C R Nair (Sales Executive Building Supplies), Dawood Hajjar (General Manager Restaurant)

PRINCIPAL ACTIVITIES: Supply of building materials and services, waterproofing, installation and maintenance of sewage treatment plants and swimming pools; road marking contractors, supply and installation of road safety products; food suppliers and caterers; restaurant; garden centres, landscape design and maintenance; installation of irrigation equipment
Principal Agencies: Sigma Coatings, Holland; Maplex, Spain; Buchtal, W Germany; Krieg & Zivy Industries, France; Laidlaw Thomson, UK; Satec Ltd, UK; PCI Polychemie; Chevron, USA; TRM, Austria; Niederberg, W Germany; Dekur, W Germany; Corticeira Amorim, Portugal; Opiocolor, Hong Kong
Subsidiary Companies: Building Supplies & Services Co LLC, PO Box 4006, Ruwi, Tel 699730, Telex 5386; Road Services Co LLC, PO Box 4114, Ruwi, Tel 699745, Telex 5386; Rasasi Farms & Gardens, PO Box 3898, Ruwi, Tel 699745, Telex 5386; La Terrazza Restaurant, PO Box 4020, Ruwi, Tel 699745, Telex 5386
Principal Bankers: Union Bank of Oman; Oman International Bank; Al Bank Al Ahli Al Omani SAO; Bank of Muscat SAO; National Bank of Oman SAO

Date of Establishment: 1979

RENARDET SAUTI ICE

PO Box 579, Muscat
Tel: 702522
Telex: 5274 Bahwan ON

PRINCIPAL ACTIVITIES: Consulting engineering, hydraulics, roads and airports, housing schemes, industrial facilities
Branch Offices: UAE; Saudi Arabia; Oman
Parent Company: Head offices in France (5 rue Keppler, Paris 75116) and Italy (Via Mattucci 33, Roma 00199)

RUWI NOVOTEL HOTEL

PO Box 5195, Ruwi
Tel: 704244
Cable: Ruwiotel
Telex: 3456 Ruwiotel ON
Telefax: 704248

Partner: HE Sayyid Badr Bin Hamad Al Bu Said
Chairman: Maqbool Hameed
Senior Executives: Daniel Cousin (General Manager)

PRINCIPAL ACTIVITIES: Hotel business
Principal Agencies: Novotel chain worldwide
Parent Company: Oman Tourist Corporation

Subsidiary Companies: Management of Sohar Hotel
Principal Bankers: Commercial Bank of Oman

Principal Shareholders: Private Partnership
Date of Establishment: 1975
No of Employees: 100

S M GHARIB TRANSPORT, CONTRACTING & GENERAL MERCHANTS

PO Box 431, Muscat
Tel: 701539
Cable: Suly
Telex: 3182 SULY ON

Directors: Suleiman Mohd Gharib (Managing Director)

PRINCIPAL ACTIVITIES: Heavy vehicle transport, building construction, supermarkets, pharmacy, carpentry and joinery works, boutique, gift shop
Principal Agencies: Fabia Stone Paints, UK; ABH Industrieanlagen, Germany; MB Impex, Germany; Medilas 2, Yag Laser and Accessories, Ercelas CO2 Laser 80S, Ercelas CO2 Laser 40S, Corbin Emhart, Italy; L Bodin, France
Principal Bankers: National Bank of Oman, Qurum; Al Bank Al Ahli Al Omani, Medinet Qaboos; Bank of Oman Bahrain and Kuwait

Date of Establishment: 1969
No of Employees: 140

SAAD EST FOR GENERAL TRADING

PO Box 3840, Ruwi
Tel: 704636, 7046444
Telex: 3584 OTOP ON

PRINCIPAL ACTIVITIES: Commission agents, and general traders

SABA & CO

PO Box 3258, Ruwi
Tel: 799425, 799426
Cable: SABACONY
Telex: 3580 SABACO ON
Telefax: (968) 799423

Chairman: Suhail Saba
Senior Executives: Saleh Humran (Manager)

PRINCIPAL ACTIVITIES: Chartered accountants and management consultants
Branch Offices: Throughout the Middle East and North Africa
Parent Company: Saba & Co, Member of Firm Touche Ross International
Principal Bankers: Oman Arab Bank SAO

Date of Establishment: 1976
No of Employees: 15

SABCO LLC

PO Box 6779, Ruwi
Tel: 704186, 708267
Telex: 3729, 3380 Sabco ON
Telefax: 700857

Chairman: Sayyid Badr Bin Hamad Al Bu Said
Directors: Sayyid Khalid Bin Hamad Al BuSaid (Co-Chairman), Hassan El Misbah (Chairman Executive Board)
Senior Executives: Hikmat Dandan (Chief Executive), B Natraj (Group Controller Finance & Admin)

PRINCIPAL ACTIVITIES: Commercial agencies, desalination, power generation, and gas projects, civil engineering & contracting, roads and ports, hotels, travel & tourism, national industries, property development, audio & video production, catering, advertising, production of confectionery, poultry
Subsidiary Companies: Sabdutco LLC PO Box 8481, Muttrah, Tel 795764, 795765, Telex 3350; Sabco Plant LLC; Sabco Catering LLC; Sabco Art LLC; Sabco Technical Services LLC; Sabco Advertising; Sabco Real Estate; Oman Perfumery LLC

Principal Bankers: Oman Arab Bank; National Bank of Oman

Principal Shareholders: The family of HH Sayyid Hamad Bin Hamoud Al Bu Said

Date of Establishment: 1977

No of Employees: 1,000

SABRY TRADING & CONTRACTING AGENCY S.A.T.C.O.

PO Box 617, Muscat

Tel: 590526, 590594, 704507 (Ruwi), 704081 (Wadi Kabir), 610526 (Azaiba)

Cable: Satco

Telex: 5688 Saabry ON

Chairman: Yacoub Mohammed Gharib Al Offy

PRINCIPAL ACTIVITIES: Civil, mechanical, electrical, engineers and contractors

Principal Agencies: Geoservices, France; Petrofina, Belgium

Principal Bankers: Grindlays Bank plc, Muscat, Bank of Oman and the Gulf SAO, Ruwi

Date of Establishment: 1973

No of Employees: 600

SAFEWAY COMPANY LLC

PO Box 4519, Ruwi

Tel: 601413

Telex: 5050 Safeway ON

Senior Executives: Ashok Chinnappa (Manager)

PRINCIPAL ACTIVITIES: Department stores, household goods, clothing, foodstuffs

SAIF SAID AL RASHDY & SONS

See AL RASHDY, SAIF SAID, & SONS

SALALAH HOLIDAY INN

PO Box 18870, Salalah

Tel: 461777

Telex: 7638 Holisal ON

PRINCIPAL ACTIVITIES: Hotel operation

SALEM ABDUL AZIZ RAWAS EST

PO Box 5712, Ruwi, Muscat

Tel: 704472

Chairman: Salem Abdul Aziz Rawas

Directors: Syed Younus Hussain Hashmi

Senior Executives: Maqsood-Uz-Zaman, Mazhar-Ul-Haque (Office Secretary)

PRINCIPAL ACTIVITIES: Trading, consultants, construction, contractors

Branch Offices: Salalah branch: PO Box 8097, Dhofar, Salalah

Principal Bankers: Central Bank of Oman

Date of Establishment: 1973

SAMPAT, D J, & CO

PO Box 4113, Ruwi, Muscat

Tel: 712566, 714510

Cable: Jaihind

Telex: 5325 Jaihind ON

Telefax: (968) 713694

Directors: Gulab Sampat (Managing Partner), Chandan Sampat (Managing Partner)

PRINCIPAL ACTIVITIES: Manufacturer's representatives, importers, retailers, wholesalers and indentors (all kinds of goods, except machinery, construction and medicines)

Principal Agencies: Aladdin Exco, USA; Corning (Pyrex), UK; Cussons, UK; Dorko Dortein, Germany; Gustav Winkler, Germany; HE Daniel, UK; Heinzerling, Germany; Houdret & Co, UK; JN Nichols, UK; Verreries du Gier, France; Milton

Lloyd, UK; Quaker Oats, Holland; Kai Cutlery, Japan; Senn & Co, Switzerland; Schwan Pencil, Germany; Prestige Group, UK; Trebor, UK; Wilheim Duncher, Germany

Branch Offices: Ruwi

Parent Company: Muttrah

Principal Bankers: British Bank of the Middle East; Bank of Baroda; Grindlays Bank; Habib Bank of Zurich AG

Date of Establishment: 1918

No of Employees: 20

SATA LLC

PO Box 814, Muscat

Tel: 592544, 592814

Telex: 5172 SKTE ON

Telefax: 592268

Chairman: Abdul Rassol Kassim

Directors: Samir A R Qassim

Senior Executives: George Nicolas (General Manager), Peter Humpston (Commercial Manager), Andriotis Georghiou (Workshop Manager), Wasim A Khan (Parts Manager)

PRINCIPAL ACTIVITIES: Trading, transport, insurance

Principal Agencies: Scania, Porsche, Pirelli, KHD-Deutz, Volvo-BM, Elba, Bunge, BPW, Jost, Puma

Branch Offices: Pirelli Tyre Showrooms at Wadi Kabeer, Al Ghobra, Birkha and Nizwa

Subsidiary Companies: Samir Kassim Trading Est, Muscat

Principal Bankers: Oman International Bank; Oman Arab Bank; Al Bank Al Ahli Al Omani, Bank of Oman Bahrain & Kuwait

Financial Information:

	1989/90 RO'000
Sales turnover	1,516
Profits	68
Authorised capital	465
Paid-up capital	465
Total assets	1,346

Principal Shareholders: Abdul Rasool Kassim, Samir A R Qassim

No of Employees: 75

SEEB NOVOTEL MUSCAT

PO Box 1069, Seeb Airport, Muscat

Tel: 510300

Telex: 5199 Seebnovo ON

Telefax: 510055

Senior Executives: J J Deutsche (General Manager), Ahmed Said (Manager), S Sivapalan (Administration & Finance Manager), K Romdane (Food & Beverage Manager)

PRINCIPAL ACTIVITIES: Hotel operation

Parent Company: ACCOR

Associated Companies: Ruwi Novotel, Oman Exhibition Centre, Government Guest Houses, Al Inshirah Restaurant

Principal Bankers: Bank of Credit & Commerce International, Bank Dhofar Al Omani Al Fransi

Principal Shareholders: Omani government

Date of Establishment: March 1984

No of Employees: 135

SHANFARI & PARTNERS LLC

PO Box 18026, Salalah

Tel: 291351, 291805, 290662

Cable: Shanfari

Telex: 7617 Shanfari ON

PRINCIPAL ACTIVITIES: Road works, plant and transport, construction and property development, agency and general trading, supermarket and cold storage, filling & service stations, printing and office supplies, carpentry and assembly work, metal works, cinema

Branch Offices: PO BOx 6072, Ruwi, Tel 708042, Telex 3798 Salaseas; also Shanfari & Partners in Dubai, PO Box 4226, Deira, Tel 226671, Telex 45954

Associated Companies: Salalah Construction; Salalah Carpentry; Dhofar National Printing Press; Dhofar Metal Works; National Laundry

SHANFARI TRADING & CONTRACTING CO LLC

PO Box 783, Muscat
Tel: 602596, 602608, 602712
Cable: Shanfari - MUSCAT
Telex: 5321 Shanfari ON
Telefax: 602714

Chairman: HE Saeed Ahmed Saeed Al Shanfari
Directors: Abdul Aziz Ali Shanfari (Managing Partner), Adel Saeed Shanfari, Abdullah Saeed Shanfari
Senior Executives: Khalid Shanfari (Abaiza Division Manager), O Terry Heselius (Commercial Manager), Gabriel Fernandez (Group Financial Controller), Amer A Rawass (Service Manager)

PRINCIPAL ACTIVITIES: Import and distribution of consumer goods, engineering equipment, electrical appliances and electronic equipment, automobile dealers, civil contractors, fleet owners, manufacturers representatives, printers and publishers, manufacture of furniture, production of aluminium, shipping agents
Principal Agencies: British Aerospace PLC, UK; Lec Refrigeration PLC, UK; Crescent of Cambridge Spiral Stairways, UK; Fiat Auto, Italy; Fiat Iveco, Italy; Fiat Carrelli, Italy; Fiat Aifo, Italy; Fiat Allis, Italy; Ferrari, Italy; Paccar Int Inc, USA; Transquip Trailers, UK; Marcantonini, Italy; Saab Scania, Sweden; Stothert & Pitt, UK; Sealand Shipping, UK; MJN, UK; Monenco Associates Ltd, UK; Fichtner, W Germany; FACE, UK; Jeumont Schneider, France; Associated Perforators & Weavers, UK; Winner Airconditioning, Spain; L G Harris & Co, UK; Lamborghini, Italy; Bertone, Italy; TVR Engg Ltd, UK; Vantagefield Ltd, UK; PPM, France; Holt Lloyd, UK; Jowat, W Germany; Taj Commisionning, Bahrain; Otis Engineering, USA
Branch Offices: PO Box 18915, Salalah, Tel 210810, 212812, Telex 7639 Adel ON, Fax 291086
Associated Companies: Shanfari Automotive; Shanfari Aluminium; Shanfari Carpentry & Furnishing Co; International Printing Press; Gulf Services & Industrial Supplies Co; International Paints; Serck Services; Shanfari & Partners
Principal Bankers: National Bank of Oman; Oman International Bank; Bank of Muscat; The British Bank of the Middle East
Financial Information:

	1990 RO'000
Authorised capital	853
Paid-up capital	853

Principal Shareholders: H E Said Ahmed Said Al Shanfari
Date of Establishment: 1973
No of Employees: 1,800

SHARIKAT FANNIYA OMANIYA (MUSCAT) LLC

PO Box 4949, Ruwi, Muscat
Tel: 704400
Cable: Fanniya Muscat
Telex: 3227 FANNIYA ON
Telefax: 700934

Chairman: M M J Matwani
Directors: M H Soparkar, A Z Nakhoda, A M J Matwani, E M J Matwani
Senior Executives: M H Soparkar (General Manager), A Z Nakhoda (Commercial Manager), J Dempsey (Technical Manager), P O'Brien

PRINCIPAL ACTIVITIES: Distributors of office equipment, liquor, beverages, toiletries, foodstuffs; engineers specialising in air conditioning and refrigeration. Suppliers of water treatment and irrigation plants, building chemicals, architectural iron mongery
Principal Agencies: Birds Eye; Walls; Pears; 3M Harris; Keeprite; Patterson Candy; Belling; Algor; Roneo BEAM; Union Carbide; Qualitair; Trane; Prestcold Searle; Farrow; Cormix; Chubb
Parent Company: Unilever Plc
Associated Companies: UAC International, PO Box 1, London SE1, UK
Principal Bankers: Standard Chartered Bank, Ruwi; Oman International Bank, Ruwi; British Bank of the Middle East, Ruwi
Financial Information:

	1989/90 RO'000
Sales turnover	8,000
Authorised capital	100
Paid-up capital	100

Principal Shareholders: M M J Matwani (51%), African & Eastern (NE) Ltd (49%)
Date of Establishment: 1968
No of Employees: 200

SHARIKAT HANI LLC

PO Box 4618, Ruwi
Tel: 562477, 562479, 562053
Cable: Maalas
Telex: 5053 Shaksy ON
Telefax: 564703

Chairman: Said Salim Al Shaksy
Directors: Salaam Said Al Shaksy
Senior Executives: David A Fryer (Manager)

PRINCIPAL ACTIVITIES: Sponsorship, representation in the oil industry, defence, civil engineering, electro-mechanical, water treatment, healthcare and management sectors
Principal Agencies: Arrow Oiltools, Gearhart Middle East, Core Laboratories, Eastman Christensen, Archirodon, Sir Bruce White, Barry & Partners, Gaffney, Cline & Associates, National Oilwell, A-Z Int'l, Tam Int'l, Technology Export, Serco
Subsidiary Companies: Shaksy Enterprises (General trading and supplies)
Principal Bankers: Al Bank Al Ahli Al Omani SAO

Principal Shareholders: Chairman and director as described
Date of Establishment: 1976
No of Employees: 50

SICO SAFEWAY

PO BOx 508, Muscat
Tel: 701166, 562918 (Warehouse)
Telex: 3415 SICO ON

PRINCIPAL ACTIVITIES: Import and distribution of comsumable goods, foodstuffs, general trading

SIR ALEXANDER GIBB & PARTNERS

See GIBB, SIR ALEXANDER, & PARTNERS

SIR M MACDONALD & PARTNERS

PO Box 3587, Ruwi, Muscat
Tel: 696242
Telex: 5510 Oman ON

PRINCIPAL ACTIVITIES: Civil engineering, mechanical, electrical and structural consultants
Branch Offices: In the Middle East: Abu Dhabi, UAE; Mogadishu, Somalia; Khartoum, Sudan; Hodeidah and Hadhramaut Governorate, Yemen
Parent Company: Sir M MacDonald & Partners, Cambridge, UK
Principal Bankers: Barclays Bank Plc

SOGEX - OMAN

PO Box 4739, Ruwi, Muscat
Tel: 563055, 563358, 600747
Cable: SOGEX
Telex: 5282 SOGEX ON
Telefax: 564608

Chairman: Suhail Bahwan
Directors: Saud Bahwan
Senior Executives: A R Abu Dayyeh (General Manager)

PRINCIPAL ACTIVITIES: Turnkey contractors for power &
desalination station, mechanical, electrical and civil works.
Operations and maintenance of power and desalination
station
Parent Company: Suhail & Saud Bahwan
Principal Bankers: Oman Arab Bank Ltd
Financial Information:

	1988/89 RO'000
Sales turnover	5,844
Authorised capital	350
Paid-up capital	350

Principal Shareholders: Suhail & Saud Bahwan; Universal
Engineering Services
Date of Establishment: 1978
No of Employees: 800

STANDARD CHARTERED BANK

PO Box 5353, Ruwi
Tel: 703574, 703796, 703999
Telex: 5217 ON

PRINCIPAL ACTIVITIES: Commercial banking
Branch Offices: Offices in the Middle East: Bahrain, Beirut,
Doha, Abu Dhabi, Dubai, Sharjah, Muttrah, Ruwi, Salalah,
Birka, etc
Parent Company: Standard Chartered Bank PLC, UK

STRABAG BAU OMAN

PO Box 444, Muscat
Tel: 591500, 591501, 591503
Cable: Strabag Muscat
Telex: 5244 Strabag ON
Telefax: 591502

Senior Executives: Eng W Kilian (General Manager)

PRINCIPAL ACTIVITIES: Civil engineering and general
contracting, construction plant
Parent Company: Strabag Bau AG, Germany

TALAL ABU-GHAZALEH & CO

Talal Abu-Ghazaleh Ass Ltd

PO Box 5366, Muscat
Tel: 793331/2, 704959
Cable: Auditors
Telex: 3379 TAGI ON
Telefax: 793351

Chairman: Talal Abu-Ghazaleh
Directors: Dr Nabil Faour, Nazmi Al Badawi, Akram Al Kadi
Senior Executives: Akram Al Husaini, Munir Al Borno, Tawfiq
Ayyoub

PRINCIPAL ACTIVITIES: Public accountants and management
and industrial consultants
Branch Offices: Kuwait (Head Office); Riyadh; Dammam;
Jeddah; Doha; Bahrain; Abu Dhabi, Dubai; Sharjah; Ras Al
Khaimah; Ajman; Muscat; Salalah; Sana'a; Hodeidah; Ta'az;
Aden; Beirut; Amman; Damascus; Cairo; Paris; Zurich;
Washington
Parent Company: Talal Abu-Ghazaleh International, Kuwait
Principal Bankers: Bank Dhofar Al Omani Al Fransi

Date of Establishment: 1972

TARGET LLC

PO Box 3574, Ruwi
Tel: 560438, 560446, 564956
Cable: Target Muscat
Telex: 5343 Target ON
Telefax: 968-560371

Senior Executives: Hani Bin Juman Ashour Rajab (Manager
Admin & Finance), Nijad Abdul Hadi (Construction Manager)

PRINCIPAL ACTIVITIES: Construction, mechanical and building
contractors

TAWOOS LLC

PO Box 8676, Muttrah
Tel: 796636
Telex: 3741 Tawoos ON
Telefax: 796639

Chairman: HH Sayyid Shabib Bin Taimur Al Said
Directors: Samir J Fancy (Vice Chairman), Mukhtar M Hasan
(Director Finance)
Senior Executives: Nigel Harris (Head of Technical &
Marketing), Hilal Al Harthy (Personnel Manager)

PRINCIPAL ACTIVITIES: Agriculture and agricultural services,
construction, computer and medical equipment, defence
support, exhibitions, industrial services, media publications,
and distribution, petroleum industry, waterproofing etc
Principal Agencies: Interbeton BV, Hewlett Packard, Oracle,
Novell, Gulf Oil Trading Co, Oilfields Supply Centre Dubai,
Smith Int Gulf Services, Geophysical Services Int, Grandmet
Industrial Services Middle East Ltd, Ameron BV, Compressor
Services Int, Deutsche Schachtbaun Tiefbohrgessellschaft,
Phoceenne de Metalurgie, Icare, Batignolles Technologies
Thermiques, Delft Hydraulics, Worlwide Pictures, Mott
MacDonald, Scott Wilson Kirpatrick, Neste Oy, Gulf COmputer
Lease, Litton Computer Services, Gerber Alley, Autodesk,
Gandalf, Cognos, Microsoft, Quinton, Amsco, Amersham,
Everest & Jennings, Imed, Fisher & Paykel, PB Puritan
Bennett, Medtel International, RH Industries, Soira Industries,
Geophysical Services Inc, AVM Filtration, Oil & Gas Project
Consultants, Begemann Pompen BV, Malbranque, Nicol &
Andrew, NL Atlas Bradford, Smit International, USA Today
International Corp, The Economist, Time Life International,
Time Warner Inc Dow Jones Publishing Co, International
Herald Tribune, The Conde Nast Publications, Readers
Digest, National Magazine House, National Geographic
Society, Le Point, Unistage, Paris Match, Dar Al Sayyad
Branch Offices: Major Divisions: Defence Sales Div, Property
Div, Investment Div, Waste Management Div
Subsidiary Companies: Tawoos Beton LLC; Tawoos
Waterproofing & Insulation LLC; Imtac LLC; Tawoos Oilfields
Supply Co LLC; Tawoos Industrial Services Co LLC; Oman
Expo LLC; United Media Services; United Scrap Services
LLC; Tawoos Agricultural Systems LLC; National Training
Institute; United Drug Stores LLC; Parks & Leisure Co LLC;
Insurance Management Services LLC
Principal Bankers: National Bank of Oman SAO

Principal Shareholders: HH Sayyid Shabib Bin Taimur Al Said,
HH Sayyid Tarik Bin Shabib Al Said, Samir J Fancy
Date of Establishment: 1982
No of Employees: 2,000

TAYLOR WOODROW-TOWELL CO (LLC)

PO Box 5835, Ruwi, Muscat
Tel: 603966 (6 lines), 591400 (5 lines)
Cable: Tayrow Muscat
Telex: 5224 ON Tayrow
Telefax: 696753

PRINCIPAL ACTIVITIES: Building, civil and mechanical
engineering contractors and consultants
Parent Company: A member of Taylor Woodrow Group of
Companies

OMAN

Principal Shareholders: Joint venture between Taylor Woodrow International, UK and W J Towell & Co, Oman
Date of Establishment: 1974
No of Employees: Approx 2,000

TECHNICAL TRADING COMPANY LLC

PO Box 4693, Ruwi, Muscat
Tel: 703515
Cable: Technical
Telefax: 700010

Chairman: Salim Essa Mansoor Assulaimy (Managing Director)
Directors: Mohamed Saud Mansoor Assulaimy
Senior Executives: Firoz Jariwala (General Manager), Shekhar Iyer (Commercial Manager), Anthony D'Souza (Manager Dubai Office)

PRINCIPAL ACTIVITIES: Trading in fire protection equipment, fire alarm and detection systems, maintenance and repair products, welding/cutting equipment, consumables and safety products, garage and lubrication equipment, structural steel, tools and oilfield supplies
Principal Agencies: Chubb Fire Overseas, UK; Lincoln Electric, USA; Clemco Int, Germany; Rigid Tools, USA; Ajax Machine Tools, UK; WD40, USA; Alentec Orion, Sweden; FKI Crypton, UK; Eutectic & Castolin, Switzerland; Thordon, Canada
Branch Offices: Salalah; and Dubai
Associated Companies: Oman Steel Company; Omanian Traders
Principal Bankers: Commercial Bank of Oman; National Bank of Oman; Bank of Muscat
Financial Information:

	1990 RO'000
Sales turnover	2,200
Authorised capital	500
Paid-up capital	500
Total assets	1,700

Principal Shareholders: Successors of Mansoor Ali Assulaimy
Date of Establishment: 1971
No of Employees: Company and Associated Cos: 100

TECHNIQUE LLC

PO Box 1089, Seeb
Tel: 591528, 591244, 590055, 592244
Telex: 5497 TEQUE ON, 5468 TEQUE ON
Telefax: 591478

Chairman: HH Sayyid Faher Bin Taimur Al-Said
Directors: Lukis C Joachim (Group Managing Director)
Senior Executives: K G Holdcroft (General Manager), W Weston (Workshop Manager)

PRINCIPAL ACTIVITIES: Agents for commercial trucks, military trucks, cranes, trailers, auto-spare parts, car paints, diesel generating sets, GRP panel tanks and claddings, ductile pipes and fittings, slings and lashings; satellite imagery
Principal Agencies: DAF; Steyr - Daimler - Puch; Sikkens; Palfinger; Dale Electric; Dewey Waters; Halberg; Spanset; Ashtec; Geo Systems
Branch Offices: Main office: Technique Bldg, Qaboos Street, Ghubrah Roundabout
Subsidiary Companies: Electroman; Muscat International Investment Co; Oman Trading Industrial & Engineering Organisation LLC; Risail Travels; Risail International Construction Est
Principal Bankers: National Bank of Oman Ltd

Principal Shareholders: HH Sayyid Faher Bin Taimur Al-Said
Date of Establishment: 1976
No of Employees: 100

TECODEV
Technical & Commercial Development Corporation

PO Box 520, Muscat
Tel: 700964, 794932, 795726, 704387
Cable: Tecodev
Telex: 3022 Tecodev ON
Telefax: 706443

Chairman: Dr Hamed Al Riyami
Directors: T V Mohan (Director)
Senior Executives: Abaya Shankar (General Manager), Rajendran Nair (Marketing Manager), M M Durani (Finance Manager), V V Lagu (Production Manager), B M Paul (Sales Manager), R Alemao (Finance Manager), Saleh Bookwala (Finance)

PRINCIPAL ACTIVITIES: General trading, importers & distributors of various types of water pumps, refrigeration and air conditioning equipments, generators, licenced applicators for thermal insulation and waterproofing, music and recording licenseee and distributor, reverse osmosis and water treatment plants, etc
Principal Agencies: Miele, Germany; ABS Pumpen, Germany; OASE Fountain Pumps, W Germany; Grundfos Pumps, Denmark; Varisco Pumps, Italy; 3M Co, USA; Claas, Germany, Emerson Electric, USA; Capital Controls, UK, BMG, Germany (Music & Records), Emco, USA
Subsidiary Companies: Al Farabi Pharmacy; BMR Contracting; Modern Technology Est; Oman Water Pumps Manufacturing Co; Tecodev Music House; Riyamco Trading Est
Principal Bankers: Omani European Bank, Oman International Bank, Al Bank Al Ahli, Middle East Bank, Bank of Oman, British Bank of the Middle East
Financial Information:

	1989 RO'000	1990 RO'000
Sales turnover	2,000	25,000
Net profit	150	160
Authorised capital	101	101
Paid-up capital	101	101
Total assets	892	950

Principal Shareholders: Dr Hamed Al Riyami and associates
Date of Establishment: 1974
No of Employees: 150

TOWELL, W J, & CO LLC

PO Box 4040, Ruwi
Tel: 708304
Cable: Towell Muscat
Telex: 3214A Towel ON, 3214B Gremus ON
Telefax: 793882

Chairman: Haji Ali Sultan (also Managing Director)
Directors: Kamal Abdulredha Sultan (Deputy Managing Director), Anwar Ali Sultan, Maqbool Ali Sultan, Hassan Kamer Sultan, Mustaq Kamer Sultan
Senior Executives: Reza K Sultan (General Manager THD), Naeem K Sultan (General Manager BMD), M S Khambete (Financial Controller), Harry Moore (General Advisor)

PRINCIPAL ACTIVITIES: General trade; agents & representatives, military equipment and provision supplies, computer services; foodstuffs; sanitary ware, building materials; automobile distribution, passenger and commercial vehicles, motor cycles and automotive spare parts, hardware and tools; tyres and lubricants; perfumes and toiletries, real estate developers; shipping and freight agents; insurance agents
Principal Agencies: Lucas-CAV, UK; Unilever, UK; Castrol, UK; Twyfords, UK; Mazda, Japan; Sandtex, UK; Suzuki, Japan; Bridgestone Tyres, Japan; Dormer Tools, UK; Rawlplug, UK/W Germany; Wilkinson Sword, UK; GS Allgood,UK; Akzo, UK; Snowcem, UK; Modulex, Denmark; Nauhaus, France; Bolton Brady, UK; Langley, UK; Kango Wolf, UK; James Neill,

UK; Concurrent Computers, USA; Mars, UK; Del Monte, USA; Eleizabeth Arden, USA; Margaret Astor, USA; Guardian Royal, UK; Barber Blus Sea, Norway; Willine, Norway; Barwill, Norway; Peter Grant, UK; Poclain Excavators, France; Foden Trucks, UK; Despa, W Germany; Tilsley & Lovatt, UK
Branch Offices: Salalah: PO Box 18553, Tel 461296, 463396, Telex 7675; also Nizwa, Sohar, Buraimi, Ibri, Sur, Sinaw, Barka, Ibra, Bidaya
Subsidiary/Associated Companies: W J Towell & Co Ltd, PO Box 5628, Sharjah, UAE; Taylor Woodrow-Towell Co LLC, PO Box 5835, Ruwi; Matrah Cold Stores, PO Box 4158, Ruwi; Oman National Dairy Products Co, PO Box 3610, Ruwi; Mazoon Printing Press LLC, PO Box 7178, Muttrah; Brown & Root Mid East LLC, PO Box 9182, Mina Al Fahal; Premix LLC, PO Box 4939, Ruwi; Readymix Muscat LLC, PO BOx 6887, Ruwi; Jotun LLC, PO BOx 1672, Seeb; W J Towell (Kuwait) WLL, OPO Box 75 Safat, Kuwait; National Bank of Oman Ltd SAO, PO Box 3751, Ruwi; Oman United Agencies LLC, PO Box 3985, Ruwi; International Furnishing Co LLC, PO Box 3308, Ruwi; Technical Parts Co LLC, PO Box 164, Muscat; General Electric & Trading Co LLC, PO Box 7006, Muttrah; Advance Services, PO Box 7061, Muttrah; Eint Trading & Contracting Co, PO Box 25, Muscat
Principal Bankers: British Bank of the Middle East; Grindlays Bank; Standard Chartered Bank; National Bank of Oman Ltd SAO

Principal Shareholders: Wholly owned by the Sultan family
Date of Establishment: 1866
No of Employees: 700

TRANS GULF CO LLC

PO Box 6431, Ruwi, Muscat
Tel: 709551
Cable: Towell Muscat
Telex: 3214 Towell ON
Telefax: 709552

Directors: Hassan Qamer Sultan, Maqbool Ali Sultan, Anwar Ali Sultan
Senior Executives: Arvind Kumar (Manager)

PRINCIPAL ACTIVITIES: Insurance surveyors and loss adjusters
Principal Bankers: Standard Chartered Bank

Date of Establishment: 1986

TRANSPORT SERVICES OMAN

PO Box 268, Muscat
Tel: 705744, 702461, 793778
Cable: Macgroup
Telex: 3301 Macgroup ON
Telefax: 703045

Propietor: Ahmed Abdul Rasool Macki (Also Managing Director)
Senior Executives: R J Stokes (General Manager)

PRINCIPAL ACTIVITIES: Clearing and forwarding, transportation, crane and trailer hire and shipping agents
Branch Offices: PO Box 5088, Ruwi; PO Box 19343, Salalah; Ghalla
Parent Company: Ahmed A Rasool Macki Est Group
Principal Bankers: British Bank of the Middle East, Muscat, Bank of Oman Bahrain & Kuwait

Principal Shareholders: Sole Proprietor
Date of Establishment: 1970
No of Employees: 105

TRIAD OMAN

PO Box 4397, Ruwi
Tel: 795031, 795017
Cable: Triad Muscat
Telefax: 795018

Chairman: Ahmed Hassan Ali (Proprietor)

PRINCIPAL ACTIVITIES: Architects, engineers
Associated Companies: Triad London, Triad Alkhobar, Triad Nairobi
Principal Bankers: British Bank of the Middle East

Date of Establishment: October 1974

UNION BANK OF OMAN (OSC)

Bank Al-Ittihad Al Omani

PO Box 4565, Ruwi, Muscat
Tel: 797410 (25 lines)
Cable: Etihadbank
Telex: 3492 ETIHAD ON, 3495 UBOFX ON, 3506 UBOCH ON

Chairman: Shaikh Khamis Al Hashar
Directors: Dawood Musaad Al Saleh (Deputy Chairman), Suleiman Al Adawy, Yousef Abdulbari Al Zawawi, Abdulla Abdul Aziz Al Muzaini, Salim Bin Hilal Al Khalili, Abdul Rasool Y Abul Hassan, Mohd Bin Nasser Al Kusiabi, HH Sayyid Talal Bin Tariq Al Said, Raymond Bravard

PRINCIPAL ACTIVITIES: Commercial banking
Branch Offices: Greater Muttrah; Ruwi; Snaw; Sur, Ibra, Bilad Bani Bu Ali, Muaskar Al Murtafa'a; Mintrib; Nakhal
Financial Information:

	RO'000
Authorised capital	6,300
Share capital	4,725

Date of Establishment: August 1976
No of Employees: 107

UNITED ENGINEERING SERVICES LLC

PO Box 5638, Ruwi
Tel: 592320/1/2
Telex: 5064 UES Eng ON
Telefax: 793390

Chairman: Mohamed A Al Jamali
Directors: HE Mohammed Zubair, Haji Ali Sultan, Abdulla Moosa, R R Owens, D J Wakefield, A A Macaskill, B L Saward

PRINCIPAL ACTIVITIES: Engineering contractors
Principal Agencies: Daniel Industries, Dresser Security, Dresser Rand, Alkhaja Cooperheat, Neyrfor, Swaco Geolograph
Parent Company: Gray Mackenzie & Co Ltd
Principal Bankers: Standard Chartered Bank, Ruwi

Principal Shareholders: Mohammed A Al Jamali, Zubair Enterprises, Moosa Abdul Rahman Hassan, W J Towell & Co LLC, Gray Mackenzie International
Date of Establishment: 1979
No of Employees: 90

UNITED ENTERPRISES CO

PO Box 3588, Ruwi
Tel: 705453, 701472
Cable: UNTER Muscat
Telex: 3457 UNTER ON

Directors: Hussain H Al Darwish, Hassan M Al Jamali

PRINCIPAL ACTIVITIES: General and building contractors, waterproofing, supply of building materials, concrete, tiles, glass products, asphalt & bitumen, sanitary ware, swimming pools, paint, building chemicals, tools and kitchen equipment
Branch Offices: Location: Jalan Street, Wadi Kabir; branch in Humood bin Ahmed St, PO Box 5125, Ruwi

UNIVERSAL ENGINEERING SERVICES LLC

PO Box 5688, Ruwi
Tel: 712470
Telex: 5712 UNIENG ON

Senior Executives: B R Bharath (General Manager)

PRINCIPAL ACTIVITIES: General, electrical, mechanical engineering contractors, power equipment, generators, pumps, water heaters, supply and installation, steel fabrication

Branch Offices: Al Kamil; Barka, Tel 629150; Buraimi, Tel 650275; Ibra; Ibri; Nizwa, Tel 410379; Salalah, PO Box 18144, Tel 290612; Sinaw; Sohar, Tel 640251; Sur, Tel 440086

VALTOS OMAN

PO Box 3199, Ruwi
Tel: 702509, 708457
Telefax: 793540

Senior Executives: Philip W Draper (Managing Director Oman)

PRINCIPAL ACTIVITIES: Architects and engineering consultants

Date of Establishment: 1976
No of Employees: 70 (group)

VOLTAMP ELECTRICALS LTD

Ammar Centre, Nasser Bin Murshid Street, PO Box 4237, Ruwi
Tel: 703311, 703326, 706895
Cable: Voltamp
Telex: 3166 Voltamp ON

Chairman: Maqbool Hameed Mohammed Al Saleh
Directors: HE Lt-Col Said Salem Al Wahaibi, HE Mohamed Musa Al-Yousef, Mehdi Abdulla Habib
Senior Executives: S P Talwar (General Manager), R R Lulla (Financial Controller)

PRINCIPAL ACTIVITIES: Electrical-mechanical project engineers and contractors, manufacturing of neon-signs and electrical switchboards, marketing of electro-mechanical products, building services, transmission line
Principal Agencies: Schlubach & Co GmbH, West Germany; Simplex Exports Ltd, UK; J D Beardmore & Co Ltd, UK; Erskine Systems Ltd, UK; Cuttler-Hammer, UK; Merlin Gerin Alps, France; Furakawa Electric Co (Cables), Japan
Branch Offices: PO Box 19011, Salalah
Principal Bankers: Grindlays Bank plc; Bank of Oman & the Gulf; Bank of Oman, Bahrain & Kuwait; Commercial Bank of Oman Ltd,

Principal Shareholders: Maqbool Bin Hameed Mohammed Al Saleh; H E Mohammed Bin Musa Al Yousef; Lt Col Said Salem Al Wahaibi; Mehdi Abdullan Habib
Date of Establishment: 1976
No of Employees: 400

W J TOWELL & CO LLC

See TOWELL, W J, & CO LLC

W S ATKINS INTERNATIONAL LTD

See ATKINS, W S, INTERNATIONAL LTD

WALEED ASSOCIATES

PO Box 437, Muscat
Tel: 738101-105
Cable: WALEED
Telex: 5270 ON
Telefax: 739930

Chairman: Dr Omar Zawawi
Partners: Dr Omar Zawawi, HE Qais Zawawi
Senior Executives: W H S Wilbourne (General Manager)

PRINCIPAL ACTIVITIES: Projects and agencies, manufacturers' representatives, import and distribution of electrical equipment, diesel engines and spares, oil-field equipment and services, water and sewage treatment plant equipment, water treatment plant, telecommunication equipment
Principal Agencies: Siemens, Cheverton Workboats, GEC Diesels; Harco Corp, USA; Sperrymarine, Vosper Thornycroft, etc
Principal Bankers: Oman International Bank, Ruwi; Bank of Muscat, Ruwi; Bank of Oman Bahrain & Kuwait, Ruwi

Principal Shareholders: Partners as above
Date of Establishment: 1972
No of Employees: 54

WALEED COMMUNICATIONS CO LTD (WACOM)

PO Box 5805, Ruwi
Tel: 704191, 793305
Telefax: 704401

Senior Executives: Don MacGilp (Sales & Engineering Manager)

PRINCIPAL ACTIVITIES: Supply and services of telecommunication equipment and systems

WALEED TECHNICAL SERVICES

PO Box 437, Muscat
Tel: 745101, 745105
Telex: 3270 Waleed ON

PRINCIPAL ACTIVITIES: General contracting

WESCON (OMAN) LLC

PO Box 8513, Ruwi
Tel: 703484
Telex: 3176 Gsis ON

PRINCIPAL ACTIVITIES: Civil, mechanical and general engineering contractors

WIMPEY ALAWI LLC

PO Box 4436, Ruwi, Muscat
Tel: 590347
Telex: 5240 WIMMUS ON
Telefax: 590893

Chairman: Sir C J Chetwood
Directors: D J Bowers, W Hollands, H Hayden
Senior Executives: M J Davies (Managing Director)

PRINCIPAL ACTIVITIES: Building, civil, mechanical and electrical engineering contractors
Branch Offices: UK (Head Office: Hammersmith Grove, London W6)
Parent Company: George Wimpey Plc
Principal Bankers: Standard Chartered Bank

YAHYA COSTAIN LLC

PO Box 5282, Ruwi
Tel: 591366
Cable: Cosdown Muscat
Telex: 5218 ON Cosdon
Telefax: 591981

Directors: Yahya Mohammed Nasib (Oman), A J D Franklin (UK, Alternate - J H Werrett), J W H Lawson (UK, Alternate - G G Luckhurst), N F Sale
Senior Executives: N F Sale (General Manager), J H Werrett (Company Secretary)

PRINCIPAL ACTIVITIES: Contractors, building and civil engineering, process engineering; site investigations; thrustboring; funiture and joinery manufacture
Associated Companies: Yahya Costain Furniture & Joinery LLC; Yahya Costain Process; Yahya Costain Foundation Engineering
Principal Bankers: National Bank of Oman; Standard Chartered Bank; Al Bank Al Ahli Al Omani; Grindlays Bank

Principal Shareholders: Yahya Mohammed Nasib (Oman); Richard Costain (Holdings) Ltd (UK)
Date of Establishment: March 1977 (previously joint venture from 1973)
No of Employees: 1,200

YAHYA COSTAIN PROCESS

PO Box 5282, Ruwi
Tel: 591366
Cable: Cosdon Muscat
Telex: 5218 Cosdon ON

PRINCIPAL ACTIVITIES: Process engineering, pipelines, electrical, mechanical engineering, and instrumentation construction
Parent Company: Part of Yahya Costain LLC

Principal Shareholders: Costain Group, UK; Yahya Mohammed Nasib, Oman

YAHYA ENTERPRISES

PO Box 286, Muscat
Tel: 702615, 702777
Cable: Natasha
Telex: 3239 NASIB ON Muscat
Telefax: 795056

Chairman: Yahya Mohammed Nasib
Senior Executives: Colonel Anthony Walker (General Manager)

PRINCIPAL ACTIVITIES: Consultants to international companies, local interests are International Clothing Industries, Snowwhite Laundry, and Sansui Radio Shops
Principal Agencies: Over 50 international companies are represented
Branch Offices: Snow White Laundry, PO Box 7916, Ruwi, Tel 703462; Sansui Shop, PO Box 4195, Ruwi, Ruwi 703758; International Clothing Industries, PO Box 2538, CPO Seeb, Tel 591891, 591804
Parent Company: Yahya Enterprises
Subsidiary Companies: Oman International Construction Company; Sansui Shops; Snowwhite Laundry
Principal Bankers: British Bank of the Middle East; National Bank of Oman

Principal Shareholders: Yahya Mahammed Nasib
Date of Establishment: 1973
No of Employees: 400

YUSUF BIN AHMED KANOO & CO

See KANOO, YUSUF BIN AHMED, & CO

ZAWAWI POWER ENGINEERING LLC

PO Box 3981, Ruwi
Tel: 610327
Telex: 5094 HSPE MO ON

Chairman: Dr Omar Zawawi
Directors: Dr Omar Zawawi, H E Qais Zawawi, M B Page, R Thornton-Jones, I Mansuri

PRINCIPAL ACTIVITIES: Electrical engineering
Parent Company: Head Office: Burton on the Wolds, Loughborough, Leicestershire, UK
Principal Bankers: Bank of Muscat

Principal Shareholders: Dr Omar Zawawi, HE Qais Zawawi
Date of Establishment: June 1982
No of Employees: 172

ZAWAWI TRADING COMPANY

PO Box 58, Muscat
Tel: 562077 (Head Office), 562102 (Qurum Office/Parts/Workshop/Accounts)
Cable: Zawawi Muscat
Telex: 5232 ON ZAWAWI

Directors: HE Qais Munim Al Zawawi (Managing Partner), Dr Omar Zawawi (Managing Partner)
Senior Executives: Michael H Akeroyd (General Manager), Roger L Shafer (Executive Director)

PRINCIPAL ACTIVITIES: Import and distribution of cars, agricultural machinery and implements, transport equipment

and machinery, electrical equipment, office equipment, generating sets
Principal Agencies: Daimler-Benz, Plessey Co Ltd, Mirrlees Blackstone Ltd, Hawker Siddeley Ltd, Massey-Ferguson, Wright Rain Ltd; Raychem; Simplex; Yorkshire Electric; South Wales Switchgear; Brush Power; John Brown; Mitsui; Higgins & Cattle; Blequip
Branch Offices: Oman (PO Box 18735, Salalah, Tel 460159 and PO Box 16238 Burami Tel 650170)
Principal Bankers: British Bank of the Middle East, Bank Dhofar Al Omani Al Fransi

ZIADFLEET

PO Box 4855, Ruwi, Muscat
Tel: 603240, 698551
Cable: Fleet
Telex: 5502 Fleet ON
Telefax: 602406

Chairman: HE Karim Ahmed Al Haremi
Directors: Ziad Karim Al Haremi (Managing Director)

PRINCIPAL ACTIVITIES: Civil, mechanical, structural engineering and building contracting; crushing plants; dedusting control plants; block making plant; batching & mixing plant; cable trays; wire screen mesh; generating equipment; pre-fabricated buildings; road safety equipment; fire fighting equipment; agricultural & irrigation equipment; marine equipment and power boats; defence supplies
Principal Agencies: E J Arnold & Son, UK; Philip Harris Int, UK; Dryad, UK; N Greenings, UK; Apex Storage System, UK; Kleemann + Reiner, W Germany; FAVO, W Germany; Zenith, W Germany; Wadkin Public, UK; Larchmill, UK; Whittakker & Gibb, UK; Pel Int, UK; J J Lloyd Instruments, UK; Reska Inventar, Denmark; Tandberg, Norway; James Galt Toys, UK; Longman, UK; Philip & Tacey, UK; Darnay, France; A Aubecq, France; Borks Pattentavler, Denmark; Adam Rouilly, UK; Potterycraft UK; Balmforth Library Shelving, UK; Palletower, UK; Ceemex, UK; Waimer Reiner, W Germany; John Reid, UK; Khandelwal, India; Terco, Sweden; Virklund, Denmark
Principal Bankers: Bank of Oman & the Gulf, Bank of Muscat
Financial Information:

	1990 RO'000
Authorised capital	539
Paid-up capital	539

Date of Establishment: November 1978
No of Employees: 180

ZUBAIR ENTERPRISES LLC

PO Box 4127, Ruwi
Tel: 707147
Cable: Zubair Muscat
Telex: 3258 ZUBAIR ON
Telefax: 796921

Chairman: Mohammad Al Zubair
Senior Executives: R H White (Senior Vice President), V Venkatesh (Vice President Investment), R M Zubair (Vice President Administration), Said Zaki (Vice President Finance), G Vallancey (Vice President Commercial)

PRINCIPAL ACTIVITIES: Holding company, joint ventures, sponsors, manufacturers' agents; vehicles, furnishing and furniture, electrical and electromechanical, chemicals, oil industry services, marine, agriculture and fisheries, steel structure buildings, construction, industrial equipment, turbines and diesel generators, telecommunications, surveying, remote sensing, mapping and digitising, oil and gas drilling services, engineering services, travel & tourism
Principal Agencies: Midland Electrical Manufacturing, Aston Martin, Rolls Royce, Bentley, Chrysler, Mitsubishi Motors, AEI Cables, Cable & Wireless, Ulferts, Dearborn, Cyanamid, GEC, Alfa-Laval, Evinrude, Gulfcraft, L M Ericsson, GDC Inc, Nortech Surveys, Hatteras, Kier International, Electricity

Supply Board, Hanscomb Consultants, Engineering & Power Development Consultants, IGN France Int'l, Spring AG, Coode Blizard, Indumont Industrie-Montage GmbH

Branch Offices: Salalah and Sohar - representation of all divisions

Subsidiary/Associated Companies: Divisions: Zubair Automotive LLC; Muscat Marine LLC; Zubair Furnishing LLC; Zubair Electric LLC; Muscat Commercial Agencies LLC; Associates: Zubair Travel & Service Bureau; Oman Oil Industry Supplies & Services; Zubair Kilpatrick; Pauling Oman; Prudential Assurance; OARC; EPDC; Intairdril Oman, Building Supplies & Services Co

Principal Bankers: British Bank of the Middle East, Ruwi; Bank of Oman, Bahrain & Kuwait, Ruwi

Financial Information:

	1989/90 US$'000
Group turnover	125,000
Paid-up capital	8,000
Total assets	65,000

Principal Shareholders: Mohammad Al Zubair
Date of Establishment: 1967
No of Employees: 500

ZUBAIR KILPATRICK LLC

PO Box 4999, Ruwi
Tel: 590577
Cable: Jelectrick
Telex: 5143 Zutrick ON
Telefax: 590811

Chairman: HE Mohammed Zubair
Directors: William Grattan Flood
Senior Executives: Nelson M Gibb, George G Houston

PRINCIPAL ACTIVITIES: Electrical, mechanical and multi-service engineering contractors; electronic supplies and service
Branch Offices: PO Box 18018, Salalah, Tel 235770
Parent Company: Balfour Beatty Ltd
Associated Companies: Balfour Kilpatrick Ltd
Principal Bankers: Al Bank Al Ahli Al Omani; British Bank of the Middle East

Principal Shareholders: Zubair Enterprises LLC; Balfour Kilpatrick Ltd
Date of Establishment: July 1976
No of Employees: 500

Major Companies of QATAR

ABDUL AZIZ ABDUL RAHMAN AL DARWISH AL FAKHROO EST

PO Box 1285, Doha
Tel: 415855, 415856, 424415
Cable: Abdulrahman Doha
Telex: 4310 Ard DH

Chairman: Abdul Aziz Abdul Rahman Al Darwish Al Fakhroo

PRINCIPAL ACTIVITIES: General trading, contracting,
automobiles and heavy equipment, supermarkets and storage
Branch Offices: Umm Said; Dukhan
Associated Companies: Qatar Cold Stores, PO Box 1717, Doha,
Tel 422674, 418245, 411330, Telex 4309; Darwish
Automobiles & Trading Co, PO Box 40, Doha, Tel 328110,
423131/3, Telex 4310
Principal Bankers: Grindlays Bank, Doha; British Bank of the
Middle East, Doha; Qatar National Bank, Doha

ABDUL WAHAB & ALI AKBAR TRADING & CONTRACTING CO

PO Box 3280, Doha
Tel: 328300
Cable: Bonvoo
Telex: 4420 Bonvo DH

Directors: Abdul Wahab, Ali Akbar (Managing Director)

PRINCIPAL ACTIVITIES: Importers of steel office furniture,
carpets, sewing machines, calculators, typewriters, etc
Principal Agencies: Hermes Precisa International SA,
Switzerland; Mobilex AG, Switzerland; Husqvarna AB,
Sweden; Yamamoto & Co Ltd, Japan; Kokuyo Co Ltd, Japan;
Mohammed Ahmed Brother, Pakistan

Date of Establishment: 1974

ABDULGHANI, ABDULLAH, & BROS CO WLL

Abdullah, Abduljaleel, Abdulghani Al Abdulghani

PO Box 1321, Doha
Tel: 423710, 426775, 423714, 437000 (6 lines)
Cable: Raissemotors
Telex: 4941 DH; 4464 Raismo DH
Telefax: 419660

Chairman: Abdullah Abdulghani Nasser
Directors: Abdulghani Abdulghani Nasser (Managing Director),
Abduljaleel Abdulghani Nasser (Asst Managing Director)

PRINCIPAL ACTIVITIES: Import and distribution of automobiles,
auto spares, tyres, electrical goods, carpets, stationery, and
civil engineering contracting
Principal Agencies: Toyota, Sumitomo
Associated Companies: Qatar National Trading & Contracting
Est (see separate entry); Dar al Uloom Est, PO Box 1671
(Printing & Publishing); Ultra Electric Doha (see separate
entry)
Principal Bankers: Arab Bank Ltd; Qatar National Bank;
Standard Chartered Bank; Banque Paribas; Al Ahli Bank of
Qatar; Commercial Bank of Qatar; United Bank; Doha Bank
Ltd; Qatar Islamic Bank

Date of Establishment: 1957
No of Employees: 200

ABDULLAH ABDULGHANI & BROS CO WLL

See ABDULGHANI, ABDULLAH, & BROS CO WLL

ABDULREHMAN BIN ABDULLA ABIDAN FAKHROO & SONS

See FAKHROO, ABDULREHMAN BIN ABDULLA ABIDAN, &
SONS

AHMAD ALUTHMAN & BROS

See ALUTHMAN, AHMAD, & BROS

AHMED BIN SALEH AL KHULAIFI & SONS

See AL KHULAIFI, AHMED BIN SALEH, & SONS

AK GROUP

PO Box 1991, Doha
Tel: 321800, 433305
Telex: 4138 AK Grp DH
Telefax: 444594

Chairman: Sheikh Abdulaziz Bin Khalifa Bin Ali Althani
(Managing Director)
Senior Executives: Paul G Reynolds (General Manager AK
Trading), M Golding (General Manager AKC Contracting), W
Vickery (Business Development Manager)

PRINCIPAL ACTIVITIES: Civil and building construction;
industrial, mechanical and electrical engineering; specialist
services to petrochemical industry; trading; sponsorship;
consultancy services; operations and maintenance
Subsidiary Companies: AKC Contracting; AK Trading
Principal Bankers: Grindlays Bank, Banque Paribas
Financial Information:

	1989/90 QR'000
Sales turnover	80,000

Principal Shareholders: Sheikh Abdulaziz Bin Khalifa Bin Ali
Althani and family
Date of Establishment: 1975
No of Employees: 1,100

AL AHED CONTRACTING CO

PO Box 4166, Doha
Tel: 414233/4/5
Telex: 4198 Alahed DH
Telefax: 414021

Chairman: Mohd Abdul Ghani Al Mansouri
Directors: Jaber A Al Sulaiti
Senior Executives: Mike Blacker (Manager), Steve Hutchinson
(Contracts Manager), H L Gray (Quantity Surveyor)

PRINCIPAL ACTIVITIES: Civil and building works contractors
Parent Company: Al Ahed Trading & Contracting
Subsidiary Companies: Al Ahed Trading Co
Principal Bankers: British Bank of the Middle East

AL AHED TRADING & CONTRACTING CO

PO Box 3266, Doha
Tel: 414022/3/4
Cable: AWAFI Doha
Telex: 4427 Awafi Dh
Telefax: 414021

Chairman: Mohd Abdul Ghani Al Mansouri
Directors: Jaber A Al Sulaiti

PRINCIPAL ACTIVITIES: General trading and contracting,
supply of building materials, tools, oilfield equipment, welding
equipment, protective clothing, etc
Subsidiary/Associated Companies: Al Ahed Contracting; Doha
Petroleum Equipment Workshop Services
Principal Bankers: British Bank of the Middle East

AL AHLI BANK OF QATAR QSC

PO Box 248, Doha
Tel: 436633
Telex: 5126 Alahli Dh

Chairman: Sheikh Mohammad Bin Hamad Al Thani
Directors: Sheikh Hamad Bin Jassem Bin Hamad Al Thani
(Deputy Chairman)
Senior Executives: Mustafa Ahmed Bashir (General Manager)

PRINCIPAL ACTIVITIES: Commercial banking

Financial Information:

	QR'000
Authorised capital	60,000
Paid-up capital	30,000

Date of Establishment: 1984

AL ANSARI, SALEM HASSAN, & SONS

PO Box 4355, Doha
Tel: 414068, 413181, 414793
Telex: 4354 Salem DH

Chairman: Salem Bin Hassan Al Ansari
Senior Executives: Tareq Murad (General Manager), Mohd Salem Al Ansari (Manager), Hassan Fouda (Asst Manager)

PRINCIPAL ACTIVITIES: General engineering, contracting and general trading, prefabricated houses, timber, building materials, designing and engineering consultancy, carpentry and decoration, office furniture
Subsidiary Companies: Salem Furniture; Dar Al Thaqafa Printing Press; Al Thaqafa Library; Block Factory

AL ATIYAH, ALI BIN HAMAD, & CO
QAPREFAB

PO Box 349, Doha
Tel: 323594, 421058
Cable: Windsor, Doha
Telex: 4450 Winsor DH

Chairman: Fares Tabet (Managing Director)
Senior Executives: Dr Georges F Tabet (Asst Managing Director), Joseph F Tabet (Architect), Adel Tohme (General Controller), Dr Nassim Daher (Legal Advisor)

PRINCIPAL ACTIVITIES: Civil engineering contractors and prefabricated building suppliers

Principal Shareholders: Ali Ben Hamad Al Atiyah; Fares Tabet
Date of Establishment: 1959
No of Employees: 700

AL ATTIYA MOTORS & TRADING CO

PO Box 2754, Doha
Tel: 420 520
Cable: Berliet
Telex: 4365 Gulcen DH

Directors: F M Kalla (Managing Director), Abdul Aziz Mohd Al Attiya (Deputy Managing Director), Robin T Barrett
Senior Executives: M H Maali (Sales Manager)

PRINCIPAL ACTIVITIES: Commercial vehicles, automative products, manufacturers representatives, national development projects, internal decoration and furnishing, building contractors, industrial contractors, electrical and mechanical contractors, transport contractors and services
Principal Agencies: Renault Vehicles, France; Paccar Int Inc (Kenworth), USA; Kia Industrial Co, Korea; Frederick Parker, UK; Kabag, W Germany; Hanomag, W Germany; Camiva, France; Tecalemit, France; MAN, W Germany; Cockerill Sambre, Italy; Wormald Int, UK; Rossigruppi Electrogeni, Italy; Rolba, Switzerland; Maruma, Japan; Facom, France; Cofran Lubricants, France; Valvoline Oil, USA; Martin Roberts, UK; IAL, UK; NBM, Holland; Marconi, UK; CSEE, France; Holec, Holland; SNCMP, France; LGA Gastechnik, W Germany; UIE, France; Vaisala, Finland; Rhone Poulenc, France
Branch Offices: Saudi Arabia; London; New York
Associated Companies: Gulf Centre, PO Box 229, Doha, Qatar; Doha Centre, PO Box 229, Doha, Qatar; Voltage Engineering Ltd, PO Box 6743, Doha, Qatar; Indage Industrial Agencies Corporation (I) PVT Ltd, PO Box 8341, Doha, Qatar; Asma Construction Co, PO Box 4654, Doha, Qatar; Al-Attiya Transport & Services Est, PO Box 9003, Doha, Qatar
Principal Bankers: Banque Paribas; Qatar National Bank; Grindlays Bank

Financial Information:

	QR'000
Sales turnover	60,000
Authorised capital	28,000
Paid-up capital	28,000

Principal Shareholders: Privately owned group
Date of Establishment: 1962
No of Employees: 1,282

AL ATTIYAH CONTRACTING & TRADING CO

PO Box 2681, Doha
Tel: 321920, 329127
Telex: 4246 Alcat DH

Directors: Khalifa Al Attiyah (Proprietor)

PRINCIPAL ACTIVITIES: Building and civil engineering contractors, general trading, import and export, joint ventures and sponsorship
Branch Offices: Qatar, United Arab Emirates (PO Box 2273, Abu Dhabi, Tel 41704)
Associated Companies: Howard-Alattiyah joint venture

AL BAHAR, MOHAMED ABDULRAHMAN,

PO Box 2171, Doha
Tel: 810222
Cable: Moatasim Doha
Telex: 4255 Bahar DH

Chairman: Mohamed Abdul Rahman Al Bahar
Directors: Mohamed Issam Al Bahar

PRINCIPAL ACTIVITIES: General trading and contracting and shipping; heavy construction, trucks dealers
Principal Agencies: Caterpillar; Koehring (Bantam & Lorain); Munster; Raygo; Ingram; Volvo Trucks; Oshkosh; Crane Fruehauf; Telsmith; Hiab
Branch Offices: Abu Dhabi, Bahrain, Dubai, Sharjah, Muscat
Parent Company: Mohamed Abdulrahman Al Bahar, Kuwait
Principal Bankers: British Bank of the Middle East, Arab Bank

AL BAKER ESTABLISHMENT

PO Box 9, Doha
Tel: 415059, 415062
Cable: Ahmed Albaker
Telex: 4239 Albker DH

Directors: Ahmed Khalil Al Baker (Owner)
Senior Executives: Yousef Ahmed Al Baker (General Manager)

PRINCIPAL ACTIVITIES: General merchants, import and distribution of pharmaceutical products and medical supplies; building materials division; electrical division
Principal Agencies: Glaxo, UK; Boots, UK; Sterling Products, UK; Ciba Geigy, Switzerland; Pfizer; May & Baker, UK; Abbott Laboratories; Beecham; Charles E Frosst; Cyanamid; Evans Medicals; Organon; Odoide; Roussel Laboratories; Astra Pharmaceuticals
Branch Offices: PO Box 1169, Deira, Dubai, UAE; PO Box 134, Abu Dhabi, UAE
Subsidiary Companies: National Pharmaceutical House; Al Baker Pharmaceutical House; Al Baker Trading Co for Sanitaryware; Al Baker Trading Co for Electrical Equipment; Qatar National Library; Al Baker Printing Press
Principal Bankers: Banque Paribas; Citibank; Grindlays Bank; Arab Bank; British Bank of the Middle East, Doha, London; Standard Chartered Bank, Doha, Dubai, Abu Dhabi

Principal Shareholders: Proprietorship concern
No of Employees: 275

ALDAFA TRADING & CONTRACTING

PO Box 2800 and 417, Doha
Tel: 428031, 428032, 422760
Telex: 4366 DH

Chairman: Omar Ismail Aldafa

Directors: Nizam M Jahami, Nasser O Aldafa, Bader O Aldafa
Senior Executives: Khattab O Dafa (Advisor), Majed Omaro (Chief Accountant)

PRINCIPAL ACTIVITIES: General trading, contracting, tendering, distributing electrical materials, electrical elevator installation, service air, ship and road cargo, clearing inward and forward, owners of petrol stations
Principal Agencies: American Morts Co General Contracting, Schadler Wetheim Elevators, Airlink Inc Ltd (Division of the Harper Group USA)

ALI BIN ALI & PARTNERS
PO Box 1993, Doha
Tel: 423911, 426201
Cable: Alipart doha
Telex: 4234 Binali DH

PRINCIPAL ACTIVITIES: Importers, retail and wholesale, food distributors; cold store operators and agency representatives

ALI BIN ALI EST
PO Box 75, Doha
Tel: 426201/5
Cable: Binali Doha
Telex: 4234 DH
Telefax: 433778

President: Ali Bin Ali
Directors: Adel Ali Bin Ali (Vice President)
Senior Executives: T Ghazal (General Manager), Mohd Hafez (Finance & Admin Manager)

PRINCIPAL ACTIVITIES: Soft drinks bottling, Govt contract, printing, diving, aluminium fabrication, consumer goods and pharmaceuticals importing, film processing, travel agency, wholesaling and retailing of food products and watches, cement block manufacturing, electrical, mechanical and civil engineering, etc
Principal Agencies: Kodak, Rothmans of Pall Mall, Pepsi Cola, Omega, OCE, Ampex, Chubb & Son, Lock & Sage, NCR, IBM, ITT, Siemens (Medical), F L Douglas Heavy Vehicles, Wiggins Teape Paper Products, Kores Stationery, Hoechst, Colgate-Palmolive, Johnson & Johnson, Wellcome Foundation, Wyeth International, Nestles, Kraft, Air France, Sudan Air, Alitalia, Singapore Airlines, etc
Branch Offices: Gulf Travel Agency; Modern Bookshop; Printing Press; Akhbar Al Usbou Magazine; Doha Drugstore
Associated Companies: Spinneys (1948) Ltd (Ali Bin Ali & Partners, PO Box 1993); Reliant Co; Higgs & Hill (Overseas) Ltd; joint venture Binali Contracting
Principal Bankers: British Bank of the Middle East; Qatar National Bank; Commercial Bank of Qatar

Principal Shareholders: Sole Proprietorship
Date of Establishment: 1945
No of Employees: About 1,000

ALI BIN HAMAD AL ATIYAH & CO
See AL ATIYAH, ALI BIN HAMAD, & CO

AL JABER TRADING & CONTRACTING CO WLL
PO Box 1120, Doha
Tel: 323737, 434493
Cable: JTC Doha
Telex: 4570 RANA DH
Telefax: (0974) 438002

Chairman: Sultan Mohd Al Jaber
Directors: Jaber Sultan Al Jaber (Managing Director)
Senior Executives: Ziad Abu Ajina (General Manager)

PRINCIPAL ACTIVITIES: Trading and contracting; architects, engineers, maintenance engineers, civil contractors, supply of building materials, sanitary fittings, swimming pools &

accessories, hardware and paints, diesel generating sets and spares, and electrical distribution products
Principal Agencies: Ciba-Geigy Ltd, Switzerland; Esscofoam, Kuwait; Melac Ltd, Kuwait; Hey'di, W Germany; Sipap Pipe systems, France; Ceramica Floor Gres, Italy; Modern Plastic Industry, Dubai; Redland Roof Tiles, Bahrain, Macnaughton Brooks, Italy
Branch Offices: Gulf Street, Doha
Subsidiary Companies: Al Jaber Consultancy & Design Services
Principal Bankers: Doha Bank Ltd; Al Ahli Bank of Qatar QSC

Date of Establishment: 1976
No of Employees: 60

AL JABOR TRADING COMPANY
Al Jabor Group of Companies
PO Box 295, Doha
Tel: 328500, 423869, 328501
Cable: Aljabor Doha
Telex: 4264 Jabor DH

Chairman: HE Sheikh Jabor Bin Mohamed Al Thani (Owner)
Directors: HE Sheikh Khalifa Bin Jabor Al Thani (Managing Director)
Senior Executives: S Sowani (General Manager), Colin D Trickett (Deputy General Manager)

PRINCIPAL ACTIVITIES: General traders, manufacturers' representatives; import and distribution of building materials, pipes and fittings, sanitary ware, electrical household appliances, chemicals, electrical household appliances
Principal Agencies: Armitage Shanks, Carron, Chemical Building Products of Fosroc, Gibson, Hepworth Iron Co Ltd, LEC, Leyland Paints, Luxor, ITT Computer UAE, Homecharm UK, Clark Steel Ltd, LEC Refrigeration, Leyland Paint & Wallpaper, Lowara Pumps Italy, Marley Extrusion, Sykes Pumps, TRM Austria, Sumitomo Corp Japan, Voltas Int India, Milliken Carpet USA, Mickey Thompson Tyres USA, Thorn EMI UK, Chubb UK, etc
Branch Offices: Doha: Darul Kutub Roundabout; Doha: Shk Jabor Road
Parent Company: Doha: (C) Ring Road
Principal Bankers: Doha Bank Ltd, Grindlays Bank
Financial Information:

	1990
Paid-up capital	QR9,000,000

Principal Shareholders: HE Sheikh Jabor Bin Mohamed Al Thani & Sons
Date of Establishment: 1962
No of Employees: 37

AL JABRI TRADING ORGANISATION
PO Box 253, Doha
Tel: 424170, 421502
Cable: Salmin Jabri

Senior Executives: Salmin Al Jabri

PRINCIPAL ACTIVITIES: General merchants and commission agents, import and distribution of electrical appliances, textiles, bicycles, auto spare parts, etc, transport services

Date of Establishment: 1954

AL JAZEERA INVESTMENT COMPANY
PO Box 22310, Doha
Tel: 882855, 882956
Telex: 5154 Islamb DH
Telefax: 880058, 882310

Chairman: Ahmad Ebrahim Seddiqi Al Emadi
Directors: Nasser Mohammad El Hajri (Chief Executive)
Senior Executives: Mohammad Jabre Youssef (Commercial Manager)

PRINCIPAL ACTIVITIES: Trading and contracting, commercial division, car division

Branch Offices: Commercial Division: Tel 882855, 881592, Fax 880058; Car Division: Tel 882310, 881596, Fax 882310
Parent Company: Qatar Islamic Bank
Principal Bankers: Qatar Islamic Bank

Date of Establishment: 1989
No of Employees: 20

AL KAABI CONTRACTING & TRADING CO (KCC)

PO Box 550, Doha
Tel: 329441
Telex: 4063 Kaabi DH

Chairman: Mohd Nasser Al Kaabi
Directors: George Daniel (Managing Partner)

PRINCIPAL ACTIVITIES: Building and civil engineering contractors

AL KAWARI, MOHD YOUSUF, & SONS EST

PO Box 2668, Doha
Tel: 425360
Cable: Mykco
Telex: 4036 Mykco DH

Chairman: Mohd Y Al-Kawari
Directors: A Qudeimat
Senior Executives: G Kawari

PRINCIPAL ACTIVITIES: Contracting; trading: building materials, sanitary ware, furniture for office and home, carpets and wallpaper, water pumps, paints etc; commission agents
Branch Offices: Mykco Steel, Industrial Area, Doha, Tel: 810870, 810871
Principal Bankers: Qatar National Bank
Financial Information:

	US$'000
Sales turnover	16,000
Authorised capital	2,000
Paid-up capital	2,000

Date of Establishment: 1974
No of Employees: 207

ALKHALEEJ INSURANCE COMPANY

PO Box 4555, Grand Hamad Avenue, Doha
Tel: 414151 (8 lines)
Cable: QATARI DOHA
Telex: 4692 QATARI DH
Telefax: 430530

Chairman: Sheikh Abdulla Bin Mohammed Jabor Al-Thani
Directors: Ahmed Bin Abdulla Al Ahmed Al Thani (Deputy Chairman), Jassim Mohamed Al Gefeiri (Managing Director), Sheikh Jabor Bin Mohd Al Thani, Qatar Flour Mills Company, Ahmed Abdul Rahman Obeidan Fakhru, Ahmed Hussain Al Khalaf, Sheikh Ali Bin Jabor Al Thani, Khaled Abdullaziz Al Baker
Senior Executives: Samir Yacoub Sawalha (General Manager)

PRINCIPAL ACTIVITIES: Transacts all types of insurance and reinsurance
Branch Offices: Traffic Dept: Tel 875038; Airport: Tel 772631; Souk Al Jabor: Tel 414151 Ext 225
Principal Bankers: Doha Bank; Commercial Bank of Qatar; Qatar National Bank
Financial Information:

	1988 QR'000	1989 QR'000
Sales turnover	25,543	22,251
Profits	4,209	3,737
Authorised capital	9,000	9,000
Paid-up capital	9,000	9,000
Total assets	48,614	48,553

Principal Shareholders: A Qatari National Shareholders Company
Date of Establishment: Established in 1978 by Emiri Decree
No of Employees: 45

AL KHARJI TRADING CO

PO Box 428, Doha
Tel: 414666
Cable: ALKHARJI DOHA
Telefax: (974) 430362

Directors: Abdul Aziz Saad Alkharji (General Manager)

PRINCIPAL ACTIVITIES: General merchants, commission agents, indentors, distributors and importers of household goods, hardware and tools, office equipment and supplies, paper, paint, timber, clothing, shoes, toiletries, etc
Principal Agencies: Win Lighter, Japan; Pilot Pen, Japan; Vileda, W Germany; Kutsuwa Stationery, Japan; Arcancil, France; Venilia, France; Elbrina, Holland; Mon Amie, USA
Principal Bankers: British Bank of the Middle East; Commercial Bank of Qatar; Qatar National Bank
Financial Information:

	1988/89 QR'000
Sales turnover	4,300
Profits	400
Authorised capital	2,000
Paid-up capital	2,000
Total assets	4,000

Principal Shareholders: Ali Saad Alkharji & Bros
Date of Establishment: 1960
No of Employees: 30

AL KHOLAIFI TRADING CO

PO Box 301, Doha
Tel: 423000, 423630
Cable: Alkholaifi
Telex: 4591 Mamk DH

Chairman: Majid A Al Kholaifi
Directors: Mohammad A Al Kholaifi, Khamis A Al Kholaifi
Senior Executives: Younis A N Al Agha

PRINCIPAL ACTIVITIES: Import and supply of heavy machinery for agricultural, industrial and marine uses
Principal Agencies: Lister Engines & Generators; Alta Water Pumps; Blackstone Diesel Engines; Godwin Pumps; Lucas Bryce Fuel Injection Equipment; Kato Pumps; Robin Generators
Principal Bankers: Qatar National Bank; Grindlays Bank

Date of Establishment: 1951
No of Employees: 20

AL KHULAIFI, AHMED BIN SALEH, & SONS

Al-Ahmed Street, PO Box 3414, Doha
Tel: 413729, 423878
Cable: KHALIFI
Telex: 4775DH KALIFI

Directors: Mohamed Bin Ahmed Al-Khulaifi (Managing Director), Saleh Bin Ahmed Al-Khulaifi (Managing Director)

PRINCIPAL ACTIVITIES: Building materials and general trade
Principal Bankers: Bank of Oman Ltd, Doha; Qatar National Bank, Doha

Date of Establishment: 1928
No of Employees: 58

AL-KHULAIFI ESTABLISHMENT

PO Box 1982, Doha
Tel: 424086
Cable: Zamil

Chairman: Essa Al Khulaifi
Directors: Essa Zamil Al Khulaifi

PRINCIPAL ACTIVITIES: Construction general trading, consultants, commission agencies,

Principal Agencies: Wuong Poong Ind Co, Korea; Hiyashi Motors, Japan; Combi-Camp, Denmark; Gulf-Air, Doha

Principal Bankers: Qatar National Bank

Date of Establishment: 1975

ALMANA & PARTNERS

PO Box 49, Doha
Tel: 423499, 422221, 422690/1/2
Cable: Ethiope Doha
Telex: 4305 DH
Telefax: 439610

Chairman: H E Khalid Abdul Latif Almana (Minister of Public Health)

Directors: Mohamed Hasan Baluchi (Managing Director)

Senior Executives: C D Isaac (Commercial Manager)

PRINCIPAL ACTIVITIES: Marketing, wholesaling, importing and distribution of general merchandise including provisions, building materials, furniture, clothing, electrical appliances and equipment, air conditioning and refrigerators equipment, office and business equipment, foodstuffs etc

Principal Agencies: Philips Export BV; Airedale Air-Conditioning, UK; Keeprite, Canada; Qualitari, UK; C Itoh & Co, Japan; CAC, Bangkok; Danfoss, Denmark; Atlas Foster, UK; Muller Brass, USA; Tecumseh, USA; Prestcold, USA; Nutek, USA; Algor, Intredas, Italy; Belling & Co, UK; Frigidaire International; International Air Monitors; Heatrae Sadia, UK; Henry Simon, UK; GEC Henley, UK; GEC Fusegear, UK; GEC Measurements; Electric Distribution, UK; Paterson Candy, UK; Portacel, UK; Sound Diffusion, UK; Farrow Irrigation, UK; Zapag Apprate, West Germany; Sunbeam/Rima; Interplastic; Hermes Precisa, Switzerland; Roneo Vickers, UK; Monroe, USA; Fordigraph Overseas, UK; 3M Middle East, Belgium, Cyprus, Sharjah, Dubai, USA, Germany, France and UK; Aerni Leuch, Switzerland; Project Office Furniture, UK; Kardex, UK; Ibico, Switzerland; Lebank Office Equipment, UK; Arnos Melborbe; Illingworth Carpets, UK; Security Lock and Safe; Office Systems Ltd; Minolta Camera, Japan; Al Jeel Reprographics; L C Bullock; Papeteries de Coiron et Desgorues, France; Pledge Office Chairs; Sibast, Denmark; Formode Office Furniture, UK; Kalmazoo; Hokuyo Marketing, Japan; Frank Kuhlman, Germany; Mutoh, Japan; Unilever Export, UK; Union Carbide, Singapore, Hong Kong, Germany; Wilkinson Sword, UK; Swedish Match, Sweden; Johnson Wax, UK; Hindustan Lever, India; African and Eastern Trading Co, Holland; Ajinomoto, Japan; Ripensa, Denmark; Lion Singapore Ltd; Sibra Management, Switzerland; Toms Chocolate, Denmark; Barker & Dobson, UK; Royal Foods, Dubai; United Foods, UAE; Reckitt & Colman Industrial Division; Eveready, Hong Kong; Honig Foods, Holland; UAE Ice Cream, Unikai; Delmonte, UK; Coroli, Holland

Branch Offices: in Bahrain: MH Baluchi Trading & Contracting Est, PO Box 5840, Manama, Tel 714643, Telex 9308 Fax 714647; M H Baluchi Contracting, PO Box 5840, Manama, Tel 714643, Telex 9308; in Qatar: Almana Inscape, PO Box 3895, Doha, Tel 416852, Fax 439610, Telex 4305

Associated Companies: Technical & Trading Co, Dubai; Thani Murshid & African & Eastern, Abu Dhabi; Sharikat Fanniya Omaniya Muscat and Salalah, Oman

Principal Bankers: Standard Chartered Bank; British Bank of the Middle East; Grindlays Bank

Financial Information:

	US$'000
Authorised capital	848
Paid-up capital	848

Date of Establishment: 1954
No of Employees: 200

AL MANA ENGINEERING & CONTRACTING CO

PO Box 1909, Doha
Tel: 328390, 328376, 328377
Cable: Almana
Telefax: 427294

Chairman: Khaled Al Mana

Directors: Azmi Nuseibeh (General Manager), Said Malak

Senior Executives: Jihad Abu Sitta (Project Engineer Dukham Area), Majed Abu Sitta (Project Engineer Doha), Adel Nusaybah (Building Materials Manager), Majed Abu Sitta (Manager of Almana Commercial Agency)

PRINCIPAL ACTIVITIES: Building contracting, import and distribution of various building materials and machinery

Principal Agencies: Hatz Motor Fabrik, West Germany; Lescha Concrete Mixers; Rover; Effepi, Italy; Girardi, Italy; SK Iron, India; GDA, Italy; Maffner, Austria; Export Drvo, Yugoslavia; Ozgur Atermit, Turkey

Subsidiary Companies: Almana Aluminium; Almana Commercial Agencies; United Co Quarries and Stone Crushers

Principal Bankers: Standard Chartered Bank; Arab Bank Ltd; United Bank; Doha Bank Ltd

Financial Information:

	1988/89 US$'000	1989/90 US$'000
Sales turnover	3,000	3,250
Profits	400	400
Authorised capital	4,000	4,000
Paid-up capital	4,000	4,000

Principal Shareholders: M A Almana & Bros; Associated Engineers & Contractors Co
Date of Establishment: 1950
No of Employees: 200

ALMANA TRADING COMPANY

PO Box 491, Doha
Tel: 418333 (10 lines)
Cable: Almanco
Telex: 4221 DH Manco; 4328 DH Mana

Chairman: Omar Almana

Senior Executives: Ahmed Almana (President), Mohamed Ismail (Vice President Projects & Joint Ventures), Said Abdul Jawad (Vice President International Projects), Mohd Sallam (Vice President Finance), Sulieman Al Ghazaz (Director of Personnel), Anton Sayegh (Projects), Mirza Khalil (Manager Almana Motors), Habib Dfouni (Transport Manager)

PRINCIPAL ACTIVITIES: Import and distribution of cars, spare parts, tyres and tubes, building materials and electrical goods such as refrigerators and air conditioners. Contractors and manufacturing agents, transportation contractors and crane hire, computers, customs clearance and shipment, medical and health care, security systems, communications systems

Principal Agencies: Peugeot, Citroen, Mitsubishi, Chiyoda, Kobe Steel, C Itoh & Co, Radpath Dorman Long Ltd, UK; Oman, USA; Tokyo Boeki; Whittaker Corporation; Systems Technik; IBM; ITT; Babcock & Wilcox

Branch Offices: Branches in Abu Dhabi; Dubai; Saudi Arabia; London

Subsidiary Companies: Manco, PO Box 5102, Doha, Tel 325374, Telex 4531 Mancon; Almana Boulton & Paul, PO Box 4987, Doha, Tel 27670, Telex 4328 Mana; Almana Transport, PO Box 491, Doha, Tel 26296, Telex 4221 Manco, 4328 Mana; Almana Banking & Finance Co, PO Box 5600, Doha, Tel 322626, Telex 4685 Manbnk Almana Maples, PO Box 491, Tel 26296, Telex 4221; Skyline Travel, PO Box 991, Doha, Tel 321880, Telex 4364 Skyla; INECO In Engineering Co AG, PO Box 2614, Doha, Tel 27644, Telex 4173, INECO; Almana Ottermill (Westinghouse) PO Box 491, Doha, Tel 418333; Almana-Circle Freight, PO Box 9308, Doha, Qatar

Principal Bankers: Citibank; Arab Bank; Commercial Bank of Qatar; Banque Paribas; Standard Chartered Bank; Grindlays Bank; Qatar National Bank

Principal Shareholders: Omar Almana
Date of Establishment: 1965
No of Employees: 800

AL MIHWAR CONSTRUCTION & REAL ESTATE DEVELOPMENT WLL

PO Box 688, Doha
Tel: 425087, 425187
Cable: Mahainst
Telex: 4179 Tamam DH

Chairman: Khamis Mohd Khamis Al Sulaiti
Directors: Hamza M S Al Kuwari, Khalid M Al Obaidly, Ahmed J Al Fehani, Nasser A Al Nuaimi, Ali I Al Khalaf, Mohd R Al Khalifa
PRINCIPAL ACTIVITIES: Civil construction & real estate development
Subsidiary Companies: Qatar Automobile Association; Automobile Sales & Services
Principal Bankers: Doha Bank, British Bank of the Middle East

Date of Establishment: April 1975
No of Employees: 135

ALMISNAD CONTRACTING & TRADING CO

PO Box 139, Doha
Tel: 867501/2/3/4
Cable: Al Misnad
Telex: 4350 Misnad DH

Chairman: Nasser Abdulla Almisnad (Sole Proprietor)
Directors: Mohamed Nasser Almisnad
Senior Executives: Mohamed Salem (General Manager)

PRINCIPAL ACTIVITIES: Building, civil and mechanical engineering contractors, importers and general traders, plant hire, supply of construction equipment and heavy machinery, waterproofing contractors, flooring products
Principal Agencies: MC Bauchemie; Reich Concrete System; Conmix Concrete Products; Simair A/C; Italy; Findlay, Canada; Sundial A/C, USA; Marshall, USA; U-Proof, Taiwan; Magna Welding Alloys-Hong Kong
Principal Bankers: Commercial Bank of Qatar Ltd; Arab Bank Ltd; Qatar National Bank; Citibank

Date of Establishment: 1950
No of Employees: 400

AL MISNAD, MISNAD BIN SAAD, EST

PO Box 2909, Doha
Tel: 320057, 421794, 425334
Telex: 4516 SAAD DH

PRINCIPAL ACTIVITIES: Agents, stockists and contractors, water proofing and insulation materials, fire protection equipment, and safety equipment

AL MUFTAH & PARTNERS
Al Muftah Transport

PO Box 1316, Doha
Tel: 328100, 426649, 324552
Cable: Rentcar
Telex: 4056 Rntca DH

Directors: Abdul Rahaman Muftah Al Muftah Qatari
Senior Executive: K P Abdul Hameed (General Manager), A K Usman (General Manager)

PRINCIPAL ACTIVITIES: Transportation, hiring of vehicles, trading and contracting, textile dealers and tailoring

Subsidiary Companies: Rent-a-car; Solar Corporation; Fashion Fabrics & Sharp Tailors
Principal Bankers: Banque Paribas; Qatar National Bank; United Bank Ltd

AL MUFTAH TRADING & CONTRACTING CO

PO Box 875, Doha
Tel: 446868 (4 lines)
Cable: Almuftah
Telex: 4295 DH
Telefax: 441415

Directors: Abdul Rehaman Muftah Al Muftah (Managing Director)
Senior Executives: P A Abubakker (General Manager), Samir Akl (Finance Manager), John Mathews (General Manager Restaurant & Catering)

PRINCIPAL ACTIVITIES: General merchants, contractors and manufacturers representative; distributors of electrical and electronic home appliances; HiFis; TVs; videos; electrical components; tyres and industrial parts; manufacturers of fibreglass watertanks and boats; wooden furniture; car hire and transport; textiles; leather goods and footwear; catering; travel; finance & exchange
Principal Agencies: Toyo Tyres, Kelly Springfield, Sharp Corporation, Clarion, Hyosung Corporation, David Brown, Hitachi Maxell, Technical Appliances Int Japan, Claudius Peters, Nilos, Pigeon Japn, General Electric Corp (HotPoint) USA, American Tourister USA, ADNOC
Branch Offices: Al Muftah Jewellery, Dubai; Caravan Restaurant, Dubai
Subsidiary Companies: Tristar Travel; Qatar Finance & Exchange; Video Centre; Altadamon Motors
Principal Bankers: Grindlays Bank; Bank Al-Mashrek; Qatar National Bank; United Bank Ltd
Financial Information:

	1988/89 QR'000
Sales turnover	150,000
Paid-up capital	18,000
Total assets	60,000

Date of Establishment: 1965
No of Employees: 1,000

AL MUSHIRI STORES

PO Box 1620, Doha
Tel: 324511, 426900, 425786
Cable: Al Mushiri
Telex: 4352 Mushri DH

Chairman: Mohd Noor Al Mushiri
Senior Executives: Mohd Irfan Chaudry (General Manager)

PRINCIPAL ACTIVITIES: Department stores, general trading, distribution of electrical and electronic equipment and household appliances, photographic equipment, and leisure goods, motorcycles, etc
Principal Agencies: Citizen Watch; General TV; Olympus; Chinon Camera; Minolta; Elna Sewing Machines; Kenwood; Yamaha
Branch Offices: 7 branches in Doha

AL NAHDA CONTRACTING & TRADING CO A.L.C.O.

PO Box 565, Doha
Tel: 321895, 321903, 321904
Cable: Nahda
Telex: 4163 Jaeng Dh
Telefax: 449411

Chairman: Sheikh Jabor Bin Mohammad Al Thani
Directors: George Jabbour (General Manager)
Senior Executives: Gordon Marshall (Chief Quantity Surveyor), Ibrahim Kamel Al Jausy (Financial Controller), Peter Cherry (Projects Manager), Hosni Ibrahim (Chief Accountant)

PRINCIPAL ACTIVITIES: Construction (civil enginering works; pipe lines, sewage, multi-storey buildings and flats, docks)
Branch Offices: Sharjah Office: PO Box 1053, Sharjah, UAE, tel 23109, 371219, telex 68357 Alco EM Water proofing
Subsidiary Companies: Al Jabor Engineering & Construction Co
Principal Bankers: Grindlays Bank; Doha Bank
Financial Information:

	1989 QR'000
Turnover	30,000
Authorised capital	7,000
Paid-up capital	7,000

Principal Shareholders: Sheikh Jabor Bin Mohammad Al-Thani
Date of Establishment: 1970
No of Employees: 450

AL NASR ENGINEERING GROUP

PO Box 28, Doha
Tel: 852452
Telex: 4401
Telefax: 853064

Chairman: Sultan Saif Al Easa
Directors: Mohd Sultan Saif (Managing Director)
Senior Executives: Hanny M Koubayssi (General Manager), M Girijan Menon (Finance Manager)

PRINCIPAL ACTIVITIES: Civil, electrical, mechanical and general engineering contractors, plant hire, pools division, distributors of construction and industrial equipment and spare parts
Principal Agencies: Perkins, Rolls Royce, Lucas, JCB, BBC, KSB, Kent Meters, etc
Parent Company: Al Nasr Trading Organisation
Principal Bankers: Grindlays Bank plc
Financial Information:

	1989 QR'000	1990 QR'000
Sales turnover	23,000	18,700
Profits	2,000	1,420
Authorised capital	10,000	10,000
Paid-up capital	10,000	10,000
Total assets	53,000	54,120

Principal Shareholders: Proprietorship
Date of Establishment: 1952
No of Employees: 125

AL NASR TRADING ORGANISATION

PO Box 28, Doha
Tel: 422280, 417333
Cable: Alnasr Doha
Telex: 4242 Alnasr DH
Telefax: (974) 423971

Proprietor: Sultan Saif Al Easa
Senior Executives: Mohd Sultan Saif (Managing Director), S Ejaz H Zaidi (General Manager), Majid Sultan Saif Al Issa (Asst Managing Director)

PRINCIPAL ACTIVITIES: General trading and government order suppliers, carpentry, civil engineering, structural steel designing, contracting and manufacturers' representatives, earth moving equipment, heavy machinery, chemicals, electrical and electronic equipment, air conditioning and refrigeration equipment, telecommunication equipment and household goods
Principal Agencies: Rolls-Royce, Coles Crane, Brown Boveri, Dale Electric, Hyster Overseas, ICI, Firestone, George Kent, NEC, Delta Enfield Cables, Perkins Engines, Hollman Bros, Kent Meters, British Ropes, Fisons Lab, Bohler Vienna, Borsig Beline, Prestair, Siemens, Fides, Brandt
Subsidiary/Associated Companies: Al Nasr Trading Group (in Dubai, Abu Dhabi, Sharjah); Al Nasr Travel, Doha; Al Nasr Novelties Stores (Doha); Al Nasr Mercantile, Doha, Al Nasr Airconditioning & Refrigeration, Doha; Al Nasr Carpentry,

Doha; Al Nasr Plant Hire, Doha; Al Nasr Machinery Division; Al Nasr Civil Division; Al Nasr Mechanical & Electrical Doha; Al Nasr (McAlpine) Construction
Principal Bankers: Qatar National Bank; City Bank; Arab Bank Ltd; Grindlays Bank plc; United Bank Ltd

Date of Establishment: 1955
No of Employees: 300

AL OBAIDLY & GULF ETERNIT TRADING CO

PO Box 1965, Doha
Tel: 437111 (4 lines)
Cable: ASEM DH
Telex: 4764 OBETCO DH
Telefax: 437217

Chairman: Ahmed Al Obaidly
Senior Executives: Mohiedeen Hamzi (General Manager), V K Luthra (Sales & Marketing Manager)

PRINCIPAL ACTIVITIES: Trading in building materials
Principal Agencies: Gulf Eternit Industries; Thyssen; Biwater Valves Ltd; Waterfit Ltd; Steinzeug GmbH; Marley Floors International; Rigips; Protektor; Mondo-Rubber; Chemrex; Stanton Plc; Pilkington; Muraspec; Butterley; Feb Building Chemicals; Hoesch; Sadi; System Floors
Parent Company: The Gulf Electrical Materials Co
Subsidiary Companies: Al Obeidly Trading Technology; Al Obeidly Trading Romance
Principal Bankers: Banque Paribas; Al Ahli Bank of Qatar
Financial Information:

	1988/89 QR'000
Sales turnover	18,902
Profits	733
Authorised capital	1,000
Paid-up capital	1,000

Principal Shareholders: The Gulf Electrical Materials Co; Ahmed S Al Obaidly
Date of Establishment: 1978
No of Employees: 30

AL OBAIDLY GROUP OF COMPANIES

PO Box 157, Doha
Tel: 433268, 431490, 321431, 323809
Telex: 4273, 4659

Chairman: Ahmed Saleh Al Obaidly
Senior Executives: Samir Arafa (Commercial Manager)

PRINCIPAL ACTIVITIES: Civil, electrical & general contracting and trading, heavy machinery & equipment, pest control & chemicals, travel, electrical equipment, planning & architecture, petrol centre
Subsidiary/Associated Companies: Gulf Electrical Materials Co, PO Box 157, Doha, Tel 433268, Telex 4273; Atlas Arabian Architectural & Constructional Co, PO Box 2206, Doha, Tel 323605, Telex 4355; Al Obaidly & Gulf Eternit Trading Co; Cibuilco, PO Box 1237, Doha, Tel 433332, Telex 4573; Al Obaidly Travel Bureau; Al Obaidly Contracting Co; PO Box 9154, Doha; Al Obaidly Trading Technology, PO Box 5549, Doha, Tel 321431, Telex 4581; Thomassen Gemco Qatar Ltd, PO Box 157, Doha, Tel 433268, Telex 4273

AL OBEIDLY TRADING TECHNOLOGY

PO Box 5549, Doha
Tel: 437111 (5 lines)
Cable: Obetco Doha
Telex: 4764 Obetco DH
Telefax: 437217

Chairman: Ahmed Saleh Al Obeidly

PRINCIPAL ACTIVITIES: Electrical and mechanical contractors, airconditioning, fire protection, import and trading in household appliances, electrical and electronic equipment, household goods, hardware, medical and hospital equipment, scientific instruments, etc

Principal Agencies: Karl Kolb; Beckman; Fisher Scientific; Philip Harris

Parent Company: Gulf Electrical Materials Co

Principal Bankers: Qatar National Bank; Al Ahli Bank

AL QAMRA INTERNATIONAL TRADE

PO Box 6302, Doha

Tel: 410975, 434415

Telex: 4091 STLTBR DH

Telefax: (0974) 411283

Chairman: Saleh Mohd Al Qamra

Senior Executives: M Kanjani (Chief Executive), Ramesh M Kanjani (Business Executive), T C Tilokani (Sales Executive)

PRINCIPAL ACTIVITIES: Manufacturers' representatives and agents; import and distribution of merchant steel, timber, metal sheets and bars, building materials, foodstuffs, government tenderers

Principal Agencies: Ueno Corp, Japan; Mitsui, Japan; Shri Anbica Tubes, India; Assan Ent, India; Standard Wirs, India; North Pacific, USA; Norddeutsche, W Germany; Mariotti G, Italy; Ceramiche Saloni, Spain; Alpha Business, Singapore; Chin Ming Trading, Singapore; DABG, Austria; Asun, Chile; Minmetals, China

Principal Bankers: British Bank of the Middle East, Doha

Principal Shareholders: M Kanjani

Date of Establishment: 1986

AL RAYES TRADING GROUP

PO Box 3312, Doha

Tel: 851774

Cable: Nasco

Telex: 4492 Nawaf DH

Telefax: 974-420768

Chairman: Ahmed N Al Rayes

Senior Executives: A M Khan (Manager Sales), Faiz ALi Khan (Asst Manager)

PRINCIPAL ACTIVITIES: General trading, electrical and electronic appliances and equipment, wholesale of household items, general maintenance, gas cylinders cookers, gift and antiques, car hire, dry cleaning, laundry, chemicals, video shop, workshop, restaurants, textiles, ready made clothing, auto spare parts

Principal Agencies: Syla, France; Family Products, USA; Pioneer, Thailand; OKO, UK

Principal Bankers: Doha Bank; Al Ahli Bank

Principal Shareholders: Sole proprietorship

Date of Establishment: 1980

No of Employees: 86

AL REHAB CONTRACTING & TRADING CO

PO Box 7192, Al Sudd Street, Doha

Tel: 441731/4

Cable: Al Rehab Doha

Telex: 4900 Rehab Dh

Telefax: (0974) 414654

Chairman: M R Al Khater

Directors: S M Al Khulaifi (Managing Director)

Senior Executives: Nehad M Habbab (General Manager)

PRINCIPAL ACTIVITIES: Landscaping, irrigation, roads, pipe laying (water, sewerage), buildings

Principal Bankers: Arab Bank Ltd, Doha; Al Ahli Bank of Qatar, Doha

Financial Information:

	1989 US$'000
Sales turnover	12,000
Profits	8%
Authorised capital	1,000
Paid-up capital	1,000
Total assets	2,500

Date of Establishment: 1980

No of Employees: 400

AL SHAIBEH ESTABLISHMENT

Rayyan Rd, PO Box 3975, Doha

Tel: 322141

Cable: Hatco

Telex: 4240 DH

Chairman: Said Mohd Al Fuhaid

Senior Executives: K P Abdulkader (General Manager)

PRINCIPAL ACTIVITIES: Import and trading in building materials, electrical and mechanical equipment, asbestos, PVC pipes and fittings; also civil engineering works, excavation and pipe laying, water reservoirs, sewerage, contracting

Principal Agencies: Canron of Canada, James H Lamont, Dewey Waters, SBD of UK

Associated Companies: Inter Benco, Benco Beton Consortium, Switzerland

Principal Bankers: Banque Paribas; Commercial Bank of Qatar

AL SHAIBI TRADING & CONTRACTING CO

PO Box 316, Doha

Tel: 413737

Telex: 4225

Chairman: Ahmed Al Shaibi

PRINCIPAL ACTIVITIES: General trading and contracting

Principal Shareholders: Sole proprietorship

AL SHARIF TRADING & CONTRACTING CO S.H.A.R.I.F.C.O.

PO Box 2897, Doha

Tel: 324311, 424981

Cable: Sharifco

Telex: 4849 Sharif DH

Chairman: Ismail Mohamed Sharif (also General Manager)

Directors: Ahmed Shaaban Noura (Financial Manager)

PRINCIPAL ACTIVITIES: General trading and contracting

Principal Agencies: Zodiac Watches, Switzerland; Maxi Wall Clocks, Japan; Rhythm Clocks, Japan; Sony, Japan

Principal Bankers: Bank Al Mashrek, Doha; Banque Paribas, Doha

Date of Establishment: 1973

AL SHOALA TRADING CO

PO Box 4694, Doha

Tel: 445502/3, 671905

Telex: 4673

Chairman: Sheikh Jabor Bin Mohd Al Thani (Owner)

Directors: Sheikh Khalifa Bin Jabor Bin Mohd Al Thani (Managing Director)

Senior Executives: I K Veshne (Electrical Engineer)

PRINCIPAL ACTIVITIES: Trading and contracting, transport, cement production, general agencies, electrical and mechanical engineering

Subsidiary Companies: Al Shoala Agencies; Al Shoala Cement Co; Al Shoala Transport; Unigulf

Principal Shareholders: Sheikh Jabor Bin Mohd Al Thani

ALTADAMON GROUP OF COMPANIES

PO Box 634, Doha
Tel: 321575
Cable: Tdamon Doha
Telex: 4267 Tdamon DH

Chairman: Ahmed A Al Malki
Directors: Nasir A Al Malki, Salah A Al Malki

PRINCIPAL ACTIVITIES: Supply and installation of all types of
suspended ceilings, aluminium doors and windows, wall and
floor tiles, building products; supply of electrical and
mechanical equipment; civil engineering and construction
Principal Agencies: Hunter Douglas, Holland; AEG, Germany;
Dynamit Nobel, Germany; Solus Schall International, UK; NKF
Cables, Holland; Clarke Chapman, England; BTR, England;
Ostara Fleisen, Germany
Subsidiary Companies: Altadamon Trading and Consulting;
Altadamon Plant Hire; Altadamon Engineering & Contracting;
Altadamon Furniture; Altadamon Aluminium
Principal Bankers: Bank Saderat Iran; Qatar National Bank

Principal Shareholders: Ahmed A Al Malki, Nasir A Al Malki,
Salah A Al Malki

ALTHANI, FAHAD BIN ABDULLAH, & SONS TRADING & CONTRACTING CO

PO Box 5013, Suk Abdullah Bin Thani, Doha
Tel: 320954, 320955
Telex: 4513 Fahad DH

Proprietor: Sheik Fahad Bin Abdullah Bin Thani Althani

PRINCIPAL ACTIVITIES: General traders, contractors and
commission agents, civil, electrical and mechanical
engineering and industrial engineering projects, etc
Principal Bankers: Grindlays Bank

AL THANI, GHANEM, HOLDINGS WLL

PO Box 5319, Doha
Tel: 428201
Telex: 4448 GAHLDG DH

Chairman: HE Sheikh Ghanem Bin Ali Al-Thani
Senior Executives: I D Halliday, M Al-Massri

PRINCIPAL ACTIVITIES: Retailing (department stores; watches,
jewellery and fashion goods boutiques), motor engineering,
hotel operation, residential developments, construction and
building supplies (aggregate, readymix, blocks and tiles,
carpentry), printing and paper converting, travel agents
Principal Agencies: BMW, Flygt, Magirus, Deutz, Ergen,
Putzmeister, Riva, Ferrari, Bayliner Patek-Philippe, IWC, Ebel,
Etienne Aigner, Cartier, Schlegel & Plana Perrier, Barbican,
Sainsbury, Brooke-Bond-Oxo, Safeway, Atari, Titus, Grand
Moulins de Paris
Branch Offices: In Doha: The Centre, PO Box 5316, Telex 4620;
New Trade Engineering, PO Box 5509, Telex 4046; New
Trade Co, PO Box 5591, Telex 4103; Ramada Renaissance
Hotel, PO Box 1768, Telex 4664; Al-Arab Contracting Co, PO
Box 112, Telex 4448; New Printing Co, PO Box 3359, Telex
4667; Gulf Tourist and Travel Bureau, PO Box 1541, Telex
4455
Subsidiary/Associated Companies: Ghanem Bin Ali Al-Thani &
Sons Co WLL; Ghanem Real Estate Investment Co WLL
Principal Bankers: Grindlays Bank; Standard Chartered Bank;
Qatar National Bank; Commercial Bank of Qatar

Principal Shareholders: HE Sheikh Ghanem Bin Ali Al-Thani and
His Sons

ALUGLASS

PO Box 2354, Doha
Tel: 422194, 441324
Cable: Aluglass
Telefax: 437138

Directors: Antoine Papadopoulos (Managing Director)
PRINCIPAL ACTIVITIES: Production and supply of aluminium
and glass products and materials
Principal Bankers: Banque Paribas
Financial Information:

	1989
	QR'000
Sales turnover	2,473
Profits	515
Authorised capital	1,000
Paid-up capital	1,000
Total assets	4,550

Date of Establishment: 1975
No of Employees: 32

ALUTHMAN, AHMAD, & BROS

PO Box 218, Doha
Tel: 423507/8, 323573
Telex: 4440 DH

Chairman: Ahmad Al Uthman (also Managing Director)

PRINCIPAL ACTIVITIES: General trading and contracting
commission agents, import and distribution of general
merchandise, building materials, prefabricated houses,
electrical appliances and equipment, communications,
photographical, and office equipment
Principal Agencies: Handy Angle, G A Harvey & Co, UK, Sansui,
Akai, Link 51, Alan Cooper, Grosfillex, GEC, Pioneer,
Socotec, Touvay Cauvin, SHRM

AL WAHA CONTRACTING & TRADING

PO Box 1486, Doha
Tel: 423213, 416306
Cable: Alwaco
Telex: 4390 Alwaco DH

Chairman: Omar Abbas (Managing Director)
Senior Executives: Nasser Mansour (Deputy Managing
Director), Ronan L Gardner (Contracts Manager), John Philips
(Manager Electrical & Mechanical Services), Marwan Abbas
(Construction Manager)

PRINCIPAL ACTIVITIES: Civil engineering contracting and
building supplies; electrical and mechanical engineering
Principal Bankers: Arab Bank; Al Mashrek Bank; Banque
Paribas; Qatar National Bank
Financial Information:

	QR'000
Sales turnover	37,000
Authorised capital	6,000
Paid-up capital	6,000

Principal Shareholders: Omar Abbas; Ahmed Obeidan Fakhro
Date of Establishment: 1967
No of Employees: 500

AMPEX

Abdullah M Al Ibrahim Al Mannai Est

PO Box 3958, Doha
Tel: 422233, 429333
Telex: 4364
Telefax: 438471

Directors: Abdullah M Al Mannai
Senior Executives: Rafiq Hamadi (Sales & Projects Coordination
Manager), Omer Oueini (Manager Interior Decoration)

PRINCIPAL ACTIVITIES: Trding, sponsoring of international
contractors, manufacturers' representatives
Principal Agencies: Sagem Data Processing; Quality Drilling
Tools; Meinecke Water Meters; UCB Pharma Australia
Principal Bankers: British Bank of the Middle East; Commercial
Bank of Qatar; Qatar National Bank

QATAR

Financial Information:

	1989/90 QR'000
Sales turnover	12,000
Profits	1,130
Authorised capital	3,000
Paid-up capital	1,000
Total assets	250

Principal Shareholders: Aboullah Al Mannai
Date of Establishment: 1983

ANSAR ENGG TRADE & CONT EST
Ansar Engineering Trading & Contracting Est
PO Box 1250, Doha
Tel: 325718
Cable: Inshaat
Telex: 4445 DH

PRINCIPAL ACTIVITIES: Contracting and general trading, import and distribution of building materials, steel stockists, and importers, domestic appliances, air conditioning and refrigeration, heavy and light equipment
Principal Agencies: Wix Filters, USA; General Deluxe Air Conditioners; JMA Vibrators UK; Uniroof UK
Principal Bankers: Grindlays Bank plc; British Bank of the Middle East; United Bank Ltd

Principal Shareholders: Jasim Kh Slaity, M S Turk

ANZ GRINDLAYS BANK PLC
Rayyan Rd, PO Box 2001, Doha
Tel: 327711/20
Cable: Grindlay Doha
Telex: 4209 Grndly DH
Telefax: 428077

Senior Executives: F J Gamble (Manager Qatar), Jacob Thomas (Manager Operations), Mohd Al Okar (Senior Manager Private Banking)

PRINCIPAL ACTIVITIES: International banking service
Branch Offices: Bahrain; Oman; Qatar; United Arab Emirates; Jordan; Pakistan
Parent Company: Australia & New Zealand Banking Group

No of Employees: 60

ARAB BANK PLC
PO Box 172, Doha
Tel: 437979
Cable: Bankarabi
Telex: 4202, 4752 Arabnk DH
Telefax: 410774

Senior Executives: Farouk Abdel Majeed (Regional Manager), Saad El Din Elayan (Assistant Manager)

PRINCIPAL ACTIVITIES: Commercial banking
Branch Offices: In Qatar: Alkhaleej Street Branch, PO Nox 3058, Doha, Tel 321850, Telex 4480 Arabgs DH (Adel Shaqadan Assistant Manager)
Parent Company: Head Office: PO Box 950544, Shmeisani, Amman, Jordan

Date of Establishment: 1957

ARAB BUILDING MATERIALS CO (QATAR)
PO Box 3221, Doha
Tel: 851768, 851540/1
Cable: Shiral
Telex: 4338 Shiral DH
Telefax: 851768

Chairman: Mohd Rasheed Al-Khater
Directors: Mohd Nazih Hudhud (Managing Director)

PRINCIPAL ACTIVITIES: Import of building materials, plywood, hard-board, redtimber, timber, nuts and bolts, asbestos sheets, steels bars, steel sheets, merchant bars, wall ties
Principal Agencies: Formica Laminates, GKN Mills, GKN Gridweld, GKN; Helix Reinforcement
Branch Offices: Kuwait; Dubai; Abu Dhabi; Bahrain; Oman
Parent Company: Arab Building Materials Group of Companies
Principal Bankers: Arab Bank Ltd, Doha; Bank Almashrek, Doha
Financial Information:

	1990 QR'000
Sales turnover	38,000
Authorised capital	8,000
Paid-up capital	2,000

Principal Shareholders: M R Khater
Date of Establishment: 1974
No of Employees: 30

ARAB COMMERCIAL ENTERPRISES (QATAR) LTD
Al Jasra, Shara Al Souq, PO Box 607, Doha
Tel: 422151, 425069
Cable: Comment Doha
Telex: 4266 Ace DH
Telefax: (0974) 325646

Chairman: Prince Fahad Bin Khaled Bin Abdullah Al Saud
Directors: Aziz A Abussuud (President & CEO)
Senior Executives: Aziz A Abussuud (President & CEO), Youssef H Kassim (Manager), Khalil Abu Hoseh (Finance Manager)

PRINCIPAL ACTIVITIES: Insurance agents and brokers
Principal Agencies: Libano - Suisse Sal, Beirut, Lebanon
Branch Offices: Greece; Saudi Arabia (Head office: Riyadh); Lebanon; Kuwait; Bahrain; Qatar; United Arab Emirates; Oman; Yemen; UK; USA
Parent Company: Arab Commercial Enterprises Ltd, Riyadh, Saudi Arabia
Associated Companies: ACE (Qatar) Ltd, PO Box 2745, Doha, Tel 324661; (Surveyors and Claims Settling Agents, Lloyd's Agents)
Principal Bankers: Qatar National Bank; Standard Chartered Bank; Commercial Bank of Qatar; Qatar Islamic Bank; Bank Al Masrek

Date of Establishment: 1960

ARABIAN CONSTRUCTION ENGINEERING CO (ACEC)
PO Box 1277, Doha
Tel: 414862, 417521, 413547,
Cable: Shahma
Telex: 4247 Shahma DH, 4086 ACECIT DH
Telefax: (0974) 430112

Chairman: H E Sh Hamad Bin Jassim Bin Mohamed Al Thani
Directors: G W Shousha'a
Senior Executives: G W Shousha'a (Managing Director)

PRINCIPAL ACTIVITIES: Traders and dealers; tenderers, contractors, importers of turn key industrial and earth moving equipment and construction plant and materials; electrical materials, industrial project and utilities, onshore, offshore drilling rigs, oilfield supplies
Principal Agencies: Fiat Allis, UK, USA, Italy, Euraquipments, UK; Siemens, W Germany; Kraftwerk Union, Germany; Westinghouse Brake & Signal Co, UK; Naylor Bros, UK; Robert Watson & Co, UK; Fyne UK; Aifo, Fiat, Italy; Van Roll, Switzerland; Mulder, Holland; NEI International Combustion Ltd, UK; Cementone-Beaver Ltd, UK; Ricchetti, Italy; Euroquipment, UK
Associated Companies: Skypak; Petrogas Industrial Coating; Gulf Agency Company; Qatar - Acec; Lemminkainen
Principal Bankers: Arab Bank; Al Ahli Bank; Bank of Oman; Standard Chartered Bank

Financial Information:

	1989 QR'000
Sales turnover	50,000
Authorised capital	12,000
Paid-up capital	12,000
Total assets current	43,000

Principal Shareholders: Sole proprietorship: HE Sh Hamad Bin Jassim Bin Mohd Althani
Date of Establishment: 19th April 1971
No of Employees: 550

ARABIAN ESTABLISHMENT FOR COMMERCE

PO Box 52, Doha
Tel: 423278, 425588 (central), 440014 (accounts), 440013 (commercial)
Cable: Arabian and Sahafa
Telex: 4497 Sahafa DH
Telefax: 429424, 325874

Directors: Abdulla Hussain Naama (General Manager/Owner), Khalid Abdulla Naama (Deputy General Manager)

PRINCIPAL ACTIVITIES: Importers, exporters, stationers, steel furniture, fixtures, office equipment, printing press, bookshop
Principal Agencies: Gunther Wagner Pelikan, Germany; J S Staedtler, Germany; M Myers & Sons, UK; Rexel Ltd, UK; Danza, Denmark; Ta Triumph Adler, Germany; Elba Rado, Germany; Ideal Werke, Germany
Branch Offices: Four shops in Doha
Associated Companies: Arabian Trading Co; Al Orouba Press & Publishing House, PO Box 633, Doha; Arabian Decoration & Construction Co, PO Box 3505, Doha; Al Shark Publicity & Service Agency, PO Box 2499, Doha
Principal Bankers: United Bank Ltd; Bank Al-Mashrek; Arab Bank Ltd, Doha Bank Ltd

Principal Shareholders: Proprietorship
Date of Establishment: 1957
No of Employees: 200

ASK CONTRACTING & TRADING EST

PO Box 4364, Doha
Tel: 410761, 323625
Cable: Ask Doha
Telex: 4436 Ask DH

Chairman: Ahmed Shaheen Al Kuwari
Senior Executives: T K Aboobacker (Manager)

PRINCIPAL ACTIVITIES: Engineering, construction, maintenance, earthmoving works, etc
Subsidiary Companies: Ahmed Transport Co, PO Box 2376, Doha, Tel 428858, 428896 (Vehicle hire, plant hire, transport)
Principal Bankers: Qatar National Bank

Date of Establishment: February 1977
No of Employees: 95

ASWAN TRADING & CONTRACTING CO

PO Box 2603, Doha
Tel: 410798, 414481
Telex: 4187 DH Piling
Telefax: 414319

Chairman: Nasser Hamad Al-Nuaimi (Sole Proprietor)

PRINCIPAL ACTIVITIES: Supply of construction equipment and heavy machinery, plant hire, supply of aggregates (stone products)
Parent Company: Aswan Trading & Contracting Co
Subsidiary Companies: Qatar Piling & Foundation Co, Aswan Stone Products
Principal Bankers: Qatar National Bank (SAQ)

Financial Information:

	QR'000
Authorised capital	3,300
Paid-up capital	3,300

Date of Establishment: 1974
No of Employees: 125

ATLAS ARABIAN ARCHITECTURAL & CONSTRUCTIONAL CO

PO Box 2206, Doha
Tel: 323605
Telex: 4355

Chairman: Ahmed S Al Obaidly

PRINCIPAL ACTIVITIES: Planners, architects and engineering consultants
Parent Company: Al Obaidly Group of Companies

ATLAS ASSURANCE CO LTD

PO Box 441, Doha
Tel: 422554

PRINCIPAL ACTIVITIES: General insurance
Branch Offices: Bahrain, PO Box 49; Abu Dhabi, PO Box 865; Dubai, PO Box 4585; Oman Muscat, PO Box 4865

AZIZCO
Aziz Trading & Contracting Co

PO Box 2455, Doha
Tel: 427765, 328897
Cable: Aziz
Telex: 4502 DH

Chairman: Abdulrehman Al Khather
Directors: R J S Mason (Managing Director), Khalid Al Khather, Fahid Al Khater

PRINCIPAL ACTIVITIES: Civil, mechanical, structural, marine and refractory engineering
Principal Agencies: Stran Steel (UK) Ltd; Morgan Refractories Ltd; Marconi Systems Ltd; F M Carter & Associates, USA
Branch Offices: Qatar; Bahrain; Saudi Arabia; Dubai; Iran; India; Pakistan
Subsidiary Companies: Oryx Pools; Gunform Ltd
Principal Bankers: Commercial Bank of Qatar

BANK AL MASHREK SAL

PO Box 388, Doha
Tel: 423981/3,411820
Cable: Almashrek
Telex: 4257 DH

PRINCIPAL ACTIVITIES: Commercial banking
Branch Offices: Jordan; Qatar; Sultanate of Oman
Parent Company: Head office in Lebanon

BANK OF OMAN LTD

PO Box 173, Doha
Tel: 413213 (5 lines)
Cable: Banoman Doha
Telex: 4235 DH
Telefax: 413880

Chairman: Saif Ahmed Al Ghurair (Head Office, Dubai)
Directors: Mohd Ibrahim Obaidullah (Deputy Chairman)
Senior Executives: Khawaja Zafarullah (Manager)

PRINCIPAL ACTIVITIES: Commercial banking
Parent Company: Head office in Dubai, UAE
Subsidiary Companies: Oman Insurance Co Ltd, PO Box 5209, Dubai, UAE; Oman Finance Co Ltd, PO Box 12920, Dubai, UAE

Financial Information:

	UAE Dh'000
Authorised capital	600,000
Paid-up capital	338,135

Principal Shareholders: Al Ghurair Family
Date of Establishment: 1967

BANK SADERAT IRAN

Sheikh Abdullah Bin Thani St, PO Box 2256, Doha
Tel: 424440/7/8/79, 329202/3
Cable: Saderbank
Telex: 4225 DH

PRINCIPAL ACTIVITIES: Commercial banking
Branch Offices: Regional Office: Bank Saderat Iran Bldg, Al
Maktoum Street, Deira, Dubai, UAE; Tel 221161/7, Tlx 45456,
46470

Date of Establishment: 1952 (Iran)
No of Employees: in the Region: 225

BANQUE PARIBAS

PO Box 2636, Doha
Tel: 433844/7
Cable: Parisbas
Telex: 4268 Pariba DH
Telefax: 410861

PRINCIPAL ACTIVITIES: Commercial banking and investment
banking
Branch Offices: Gulf Branches: Qatar; Abu Dhabi; Dubai; Oman;
Bahrain
Parent Company: Head office in Paris, France
Financial Information:

	QR'000
Authorised capital	5,000
Paid-up capital	5,000

Date of Establishment: 1973
No of Employees: 50

BIN NAYFA AL SHAHWANI INTERNATIONAL WLL

PO Box 5653, Doha
Tel: 325257, 433511, 327143
Cable: BINNYFA DH
Telex: 4048 BINYFA DH
Telefax: 410941

Chairman: Abdul Hadi Trahib Bin Nayfa Al Shahwani
Directors: Hazza Abdul Hadi Al Shahwani

PRINCIPAL ACTIVITIES: Mechanical, electrical, instrumentation
engineers and contractors, onshore/offshore engineering and
industrial services, fire and safety engineers, design and
draughting systems
Principal Agencies: CE Natco; Rockwell Intl; ICI; Commonwealth
Gases; BICC Pyrotenax; Seaweld Ltd; Static Systems Group;
Lincoln Welding; Merryweather; Beldam Packings; Sabre
Safety
Branch Offices: Abu Dhabi: PO Box 3350, Telex 23408 EM, Tel
336720/336721; Sharjah: PO Box 5113, Tel 547823
Subsidiary Companies: Shahwani Trading & Contracting Est, PO
Box 1949, Doha, Tel 424964/325257/323208, Telex 4048
BINYFA DH
Principal Bankers: Commercial Bank of Qatar; Bank of Oman
Financial Information:
Paid-up capital   QR5,000,000

Principal Shareholders: Abdul Hadi Trahib Bin Nayfa Al
Shahwani, Hazza Abdul Hadi Bin Nayfa Al Shahwani, Trahib
Abdul Hadi Bin Nayfa Al Shahwani, Hamed Abdul Hadi Bin
Nayfa Al Shahwani
Date of Establishment: 1977
No of Employees: 175

BLACK CAT CONSTRUCTION WLL

PO Box 12714, Doha
Tel: 322124, 411184
Telex: 4185 Trelco DH
Telefax: 429899

Chairman: George Salman (General Manager)
Senior Executives: Hassan Kassab (Project Manager), Elias
Salman (Resident Manager), Timothy Veigas (Finance
Manager)

PRINCIPAL ACTIVITIES: Mechanical construction, piping
fabrication, industrial construction, pipeline, structural
engineering, electrical & instrumentation, plant maintenance,
shutdowns, fibreglass lining, industrial coating, radiography,
non destructive testing, stress relieving, irrigation and
associated civil works
Branch Offices: International Technical Construction Co, PO
Box 950279, Amman, Jordan, Tel 677069, Telex 24099 Ghadi,
Fax 677069
Subsidiary Companies: International Inspection Co, PO Box
950279, Amman, Jordan, Tel 677069, Telex 24099, Fax
677069
Principal Bankers: Commercial Bank of Qatar, Doha

Date of Establishment: 1981
No of Employees: 200

BOODAI TRADING COMPANY

PO Box 4569, Doha
Tel: 432876, 322982, 601304
Cable: BOODAI
Telex: 4074 Boodai DH
Telefax: 415754

Senior Executives: Suresh Jagtiani (Sales Manager)

PRINCIPAL ACTIVITIES: Engineering supplies, construction
equipment, steel and building materials
Principal Agencies: Mitsubishi, TCM, Zenith, P & H, Elba,
Nordberg, Airman, Hudig, Lescha
Branch Offices: Dubai, Abu Dhabi, Saudi Arabia (Damman),
Oman (Muscat)
Parent Company: Boodai Trading Co Ltd, Kuwait
Principal Bankers: Doha Bank, Doha
Financial Information:

	1989 QR'000
Sales turnover	5,750
Authorised capital	1,800
Paid-up capital	1,200
Total assets	8,000

Date of Establishment: 1977

BRITISH BANK OF THE MIDDLE EAST (THE)

PO Box 57, Doha
Tel: 423124/10
Cable: Bactria-Qatar
Telex: 4204 DH
Telefax: 416353

Chairman: W Purves CBE DSO
Directors: J R H Bond, F J French, J M Gray, J A P Hill CBE, S
Robertson, P J Wrangham

PRINCIPAL ACTIVITIES: All banking transactions
Branch Offices: Branches throughout the Middle East
Parent Company: A Member of the Hongkong and Shanghai
Banking Corp Ltd
Financial Information:

	1988 St£'000	1989 St£'000
Deposits	1,466,415	1,757,230
Paid-up capital	100,000	100,000
Total assets	1,690,107	2,012,996

Principal Shareholders: The Hongkong and Shanghai Banking Corp Ltd
Date of Establishment: In Qatar 1954

BROTHER GROUP LIMITED
PO Box 2525, Doha
Tel: 322851, 428920, 428043, 428273, 322850, 852903, 852933
Cable: Brother Doha
Telex: 4360 Brthr DH
Telefax: 851734

Chairman: Abdullah A Almeer
Directors: Miss Maryam A Almeer, Ahmed A Almeer, Yousef Abdulla Almeer, Saleh A Almeer
Senior Executives: R Bhaskaran (Admin & Accounts Manager/Brother Group), V Gopalan (Manager/Brother Travel Co), Eng Yahya Damerdash (Manager/Brother Construction Co), S L Hussain (Public Relations Officer/Brother Group), Ahamed Saleh (Site Engineer/Brother Construction Co), Rafiqal Islam (Technical Manager/Brother Trading Co), K B Sharma (Manager/Brother Cleaning Co), Vaman Maroly (Thyssen Lift Division)

PRINCIPAL ACTIVITIES: Import and distribution of construction equipment and earthmoving equipment, office equipment, lifts & escalators, building materials, jewellery and watches, gift items, readymade garments, furniture, stationery, films, cleaning & maintenance, travel agents, construction, travel cases etc
Principal Agencies: Baromix Cement Mixers; Canon Photocopier; Mita Photocopiers; Thyssen Lifts; Milus Watches; Chatelain Watch, Frere Paris, Echolac Travel Cases, Segaud SA, France; GSA for Korean Airlines, British Caledonian Airways & Yugoslov Airlines (JAT); Finair; etc
Subsidiary Companies: Brother Travel Co; Brother Construction Co; Brother Stationery Co; Brother Cleaning Co; Arabian World Travel; Pan Arabian Motion Pictures & TV Co; Brother Jewellery Co; Pan Arabian Research & Marketing; Brother Trading Company, Brother Publishing Co; Brother Advertising & Promotion; Brother Petroleum Co Ltd; Panarabian Oil Co Ltd; Brother University & Educational Services
Principal Bankers: Doha Bank Ltd; Al Ahli Bank Ltd; Qatar Islamic Bank
Financial Information:

	1989/90 QR'000
Paid-up capital	20,000

Principal Shareholders: Proprietorship
Date of Establishment: August 20th, 1974
No of Employees: 200

BUKSHAISHA TRADING & CONTRACTING EST
PO Box 3100, Doha
Tel: 434361
Telex: 4756 BUTCO DH

Directors: Ismail Daud Mohd Bukshaisha, Hammad Ismail Abu Shanab
Senior Executives: Mohammed A Ra'Ouf (Sales Manager)

PRINCIPAL ACTIVITIES: Building construction and import of building materials

Date of Establishment: 1972
No of Employees: Approx 200

BUSINESS COMMUNICATIONS QATAR
PO Box 3656, Doha
Tel: 325851
Cable: Bcq Doha
Telex: 4454 DH
Telefax: 443871

Chairman: Kassem Mohammed Jaidah

Senior Executives: Tewfiq L Nahhas (General Manager), Michael Perkins (Technical Manager)

PRINCIPAL ACTIVITIES: Supply, installation and maintenance of communications systems, electronic systems, instrumentation systems, computer systems, UPS systems
Principal Agencies: Farinon; General Electric Mobile Radio, Multitone; Marconi Instruments; Tektronix; Kaypro; Case Modems; Erskine; Emerson; Racal Communications; Racal Antennas; Citizen Printers; SR-Telecom; Javelin; Park Air Electronics; Kaypro Computers; Exicom; Sherry Computers; Austin Computers; Racal Chubb Security Systems
Parent Company: Jaidah Motors & Trading
Principal Bankers: Standard Chartered Bank, Doha

Date of Establishment: 1974
No of Employees: 40

BUZWAIR, MOHD, ENGINEERING & CONTRACTING CO
PO Box 319, Doha
Tel: 324787, 423541
Cable: Buzwair
Telex: 4387 Buzco DH

Chairman: Mohammed Fahd Buzwair
Directors: Munir Mousa Jarjour (Managing Director)
Senior Executives: Mohd Bardawil (Senior Accountant), Ya'coub Ghulam (Engineer), Ya'coub Batty (Engineer)

PRINCIPAL ACTIVITIES: Building and civil engineering contractors; industrial gas plant
Principal Agencies: Speedstar Drilling Rigs, USA; Ditta Boscalo, Italy; ETPM, France
Subsidiary/Associated Companies: Orient Aluminium; Fahd Engineering; Buzwair Drilling Co; Buzwair Transportation
Principal Bankers: Qatar National Bank, Doha; Bank Saderat Iran, Doha; Standard Chartered Bank, Doha; Al-Mashrek Bank, Doha

Principal Shareholders: Private company

CCM SERVICES
Construction Commissioning & Maintenance Services
PO Box 1738, Doha
Tel: 321440, 325996
Cable: Comlex
Telex: 4144 Ressan DH

Directors: Abdul Rahman-Almannai, Costa Nasser (Managing Director), Nabih Nasser (General Manager)

PRINCIPAL ACTIVITIES: Civil, electrical, mechanical, instrumentation contractors and consultants
Principal Agencies: Verger-Delporte, France; Haden-International, UK; Instrument Services, France; etc
Branch Offices: UK; 97 Park St, London W1; France: 143 Bis Rue Saussure, Paris; Sharjah, PO Box 289, UAE
Principal Bankers: Banque Paribas

Principal Shareholders: Abdul Rahman Mannai, Costa Nasser

CENTRE (THE)
PO Box 5316, Doha
Tel: 321790 (5 lines)
Telex: 4620

Chairman: Sheikh Ghanem Bin Ali Al Thani (Proprietor)

PRINCIPAL ACTIVITIES: Department store, retail of foodstuffs, clothing, footwear, toiletries & cosmetics, pharmaceuticals, bakery, plants & flowers, electrical & electronic appliances and equipment, sport goods, textiles, books and stationery, etc

QATAR

CICO CONSULTANT ARCHITECTS ENGINEERS

PO Box 152, Doha
Tel: 421518
Cable: Cico
Telex: 4347 Triaco DH
Telefax: (974) 421542

Chairman: Ahmad Ismail Cheikha
Directors: James E Pearson (Managing Director)
Senior Executives: Ibrahim Jayoussi (Finance Manager)

PRINCIPAL ACTIVITIES: Architecture, planning, engineering
  consultants
Branch Offices: Beirut, London
Associated Companies: Triad Architects Planners, London; SPN
  & Associates, London
Principal Bankers: Qatar National Bank, Qatar Islamic Bank

Principal Shareholders: Ahmed Ismail Cheikha
Date of Establishment: 1968
No of Employees: 20

CITIBANK NA

Salwa Rd, PO Box 2309, Doha
Tel: 326611 (15 lines)
Cable: Citibank Doha
Telex: 4224 Citifx, 4884 Citiop DH

PRINCIPAL ACTIVITIES: Commercial banking
Branch Offices: In the Middle East: United Arab Emirates; Saudi
  Arabia; Bahrain; Jordan; Lebanon; Egypt; Oman
Parent Company: Head office: 399 Park Ave, New York, NY
  10043, USA

Principal Shareholders: Citibank NA, New York
Date of Establishment: 1970
No of Employees: 20

COMMERCIAL BANK OF QATAR QSC

PO Box 3232, Doha
Tel: 431010/9
Cable: Banktejari
Telex: 4351 Tejari; 4291 CBQ FX DH
Telefax: 438182

Chairman: Sheikh Ali Bin Jabor Al-Thani
Directors: Abdulghani Abdul Ghani (Deputy Chairman), Nasser
  Bin Falah Al Thani, Jassim Bin Mohd Al Jaidah, Hussain
  Ibrahim Al Fardan (Managing Director), Jassim Mohd Al
  Mosallam, Abdulla Khalifa Al Attiya, Abdulla A R Al Mannai,
  Khalifa Al Sobai
Senior Executives: T P Nunan (General Manager), M I Mandani
  (Manager Operation & Administration)

PRINCIPAL ACTIVITIES: Commercial banking
Branch Offices: Souk Al Ahmad Branch, Tel 413133; Wakrah
  Branch, Tel 641825/9; Ladies Branch, Tel 428686; West Bay
  Branch, Tel 831575
Financial Information:

	1988/89
	QR'000
Total income	60,401
Profits	10,519
Reserves	72,046
Paid-up capital	56,250
Total assets	827,713

Principal Shareholders: 100% Qataris
Date of Establishment: April 1975
No of Employees: 127

COMMERCIAL INDUSTRIAL CO

PO Box 5000, Doha
Tel: 423227, 426527
Cable: Comico
Telex: 4278 DH

Chairman: Sheikh Muhd Hamad Al Thani
Senior Executives: Issa M Dauleh (General Manager)

PRINCIPAL ACTIVITIES: Importers of building materials and
  commission agents
Parent Company: Muhd Hamad Al Thani & Sons Est
Associated Companies: Contracting & Trading Est; Qatar
  Industries Co; Trans-Orient Air Services; Doha Travel Agency;
  Trans-Arabian Travel Agency
Principal Bankers: Grindlays Bank; United Bank Ltd; Bank of
  Oman Ltd

COMPUTER ARABIA

PO Box 2750, Doha
Tel: 428555
Cable: COMPARAB
Telex: 4806 CMPARB

Chairman: Abdul Rahman Eissa Al-Mannai
Directors: Adel A R Al-Mannai (Managing Director)

PRINCIPAL ACTIVITIES: Supply of computers, word
  processors, microfilm, microfiche and all associated
  equipment
Principal Agencies: Apple; AES; Canon; Calcomp; Epson;
  Hewlett-Packard; Prime; Radio Shack; Sinclair
Branch Offices: Computer Arabia, 2nd Floor, HBK Building, Nr.
  Toyota Roundabout, Grand Hamad Avenue, Doha, Qatar
Parent Companies: Teyseer Group of Companies
Principal Bankers: Doha Bank Limited; Qatar Islamic Bank

Principal Shareholders: Privately owned
Date of Establishment: November, 1979
No of Employees: 26

CONSTRUCTION ENTERPRISES CO

PO Box 2277, Doha
Tel: 323379
Cable: Enterco
Telex: 4289 Cec DH
Telefax: 426105

Chairman: Sh Ali Bin Saoud Bin Abdul Aziz Althani
Directors: Joseph Abou Slaiman (Managing Director)
Senior Executives: Samir Sahyoun (Asst Managing Director)

PRINCIPAL ACTIVITIES: General contracting; concrete precast
  factory
Branch Offices: Beirut
Parent Company: Doha
Subsidiary Companies: Marketing & Trading Centre, PO Box
  6664, Doha
Principal Bankers: Qatar National Bank, Doha Bank Ltd
Financial Information:

	1988/89	1989/90
	QR'000	QR'000
Sales turnover	18,125	17,190
Authorised capital	5,000	5,000
Paid-up capital	5,000	5,000

Principal Shareholders: Sh Ali Bin Saoud Bin Abdul Aziz; Sh
  Ahmed Bin Ali Bin Saoud
Date of Establishment: 1973
No of Employees: 500

CONTRACTING & TRADING EST

PO Box 2344, Doha
Tel: 424641
Cable: Cato
Telex: 4278 DH

Chairman: Sheikh Muhd Hamad Al Thani
Senior Executives: Issa M Dauleh (General Manager)

PRINCIPAL ACTIVITIES: General contracting and trading
Parent Company: Muhd Hamad Al Thani & Sons Est

Associated Companies: Commercial Industrial Co; Qatar Industries Co; Trans Orient Air Services; Doha Travel Agency; Trans-Arabian Travel Agency

Principal Bankers: Grindlays Bank plc; United Bank Ltd; Bank of Oman Ltd

DAR-AL-BINAA CONTRACTING & TRADING

PO Box 3008, Doha
Tel: 424746, 424231, 321560
Cable: Darbi
Telex: 4369 Darbi DH

Senior Executives: Rabie Amash (General Manager)

PRINCIPAL ACTIVITIES: General contracting and trading, construction and building supply

Associated Companies: Darbi-Koch joint-venture, PO Box 3696, Doha

DARWISH & CO LTD

PO Box 889, Doha
Tel: 414747/8, 414238/9
Cable: Darco
Telex: 4272 DH
Telefax: 974-438805

Chairman: Ahmed K Darwish
Directors: Mustafa A Sherif (Managing Director)
Senior Executives: Emad A Moniem (Finance Manager), Ariel L Arcangel (Technical Manager)

PRINCIPAL ACTIVITIES: General trading; engineering and contracting, corrosion engineering, soil investigation and mechanical engineering

Principal Agencies: Cementation Chemicals UK; Schindler Lifts; Skanska; Nuovo Pignone; Petitjean; SW Farmer & Son Ltd; Foundation Engineering Ltd; Universal Incineration; Murata Machinery Ltd, Japan

Subsidiary Companies: Arab Trade Centre, Gulf Design, Darwish Foundation Engineering

Principal Bankers: Standard Chartered Bank; British Bank of the Middle East

Date of Establishment: 1969
No of Employees: 40

DARWISH ENGINEERING

PO Box 183, Doha
Tel: 433230, 422691/2, 422259, 422688/9, 421375
Cable: Dareng
Telex: 4308 DH

Directors: Sheikh Najib Izzedin (Managing Partner)
Senior Executives: Nicola Ghanem (Chief Engineer), J Tilden (Quantity Surveyor), Ghazi Abdul Majeed (Office Manager)

PRINCIPAL ACTIVITIES: Building and civil engineering contractors

Parent Company: Kassem & Abdullah Sons of Darwish Fakhroo

No of Employees: 600

DARWISH TRADING

PO Box 92, Doha
Tel: 422781, 428164
Cable: Tradar Doha
Telex: 4298 Tradar DH
Telefax: 426378

Chairman: Kassem Darwish Fakhroo
Directors: Yousuf K Darwish (Vice Chairman), Hassan K Darwish (Managing Director), Ahmed Kassem Darwish, Mohamed Kassem Darwish, Darwish Kassem Darwish, Nasser Kassem Darwish, Salman Kassem Darwish, Abdalla K Darwish (Executive Director)
Senior Executives: Cherif Hassouna (Group General Manager)

PRINCIPAL ACTIVITIES: General trading; imports; wholesale and retail of office equipment, electrical and electronic equipment, building materials, paint, heavy equipment and air conditioning equipment, construction plant, domestic appliances, commercial kitchen and laundry installations, cables, switchgear, accessories and tools

Principal Agencies: Barduct, UK; Berger, Jenson & Nicholson, UK; Berger Traffic Marketing, UK; Chloride Int, UK; Consolidated Pneumatic Tool, UK; CPT (India), India; Crawley (Refrigeration), UK; Crittal Windows, UK; Dunlop-Belting, UK; Dunlop Ltd, UK; Eichhoff-Weke, Germany; Emide Metallindustrie, W Germany; Expanded Metal Co, UK; Expandite, UK; Facit, Sweden; Friedrich Airconditioning & Refrigeration, USA; GEC Medical Equipment, UK; GEC X'pellair, UK; Henke Maschinenfabrik, W Germany; Hoover, UK; IMI Santon, UK; Olivetti, Italy; Iwai Ceramics, Japan; James Halstead, UK; Josiah Parks, UK; Kingson, USA; Kohler, USA; Lansing, UK; Lindner, W Germany; LM Ericsson, Sweden; Lyte Industries, UK; Mirrlees Blackstone, UK; Mitsui, Japan; Morphy Richards, Singapore; NV Philips, Holland; Orient General Industries, India; Peris Andreu, Spain; Phillips Consultants, UK; Pirelli General Cable, UK; Ramset Fasteners, Australia; Remington, UK; Ruberoid, UK; Snef, France; Texas, France; Thorn, UK; Trane, USA; Virax, France; Yorkshire Imperial Metals, UK; La Germania, Italy; Xerox, USA; Crabtree, UK; Cuprinol, UK; Ecenomic Laboratories, USA; Canficorp, Canada; Dynapac, Sweden; Barton Engineering, UK; Mirless Blackstone, UK; Al Zamil, Saudi Arabia; Allgood, UK; Baranite, UK; Datamation, Dubai

Parent Company: Kassem Darwish Fakhroo & Sons

Subsidiary/Associated Companies: Mechanical Division, PO Box 3898, Doha, Tel 422781, 422810, Telex 4298 TRADAR DH; Electrical Division, PO Box 3898, Doha, Tel 422781, 432899, Telex 4298 TRADAR DH; OTIS Elevator Division, PO Box 4887, Doha, Tel 428186, 328261, Telex 4298 TRADAR DH; Transport & Services, PO Box 3511, Doha, Tel 422781, 428866, Telex 4298 TRADAR DH; Computer Centre (Agents - Texas Instruments), PO Box 350, Doha, Tel 426383, Telex 4298 TRADAR DH; Arabesque GRC (Qatar), PO Box 4800, Doha, Tel 810107, Telex 4697 AGRCTA DH; Gulf Timber & Joinery Co, PO Box 4800, Doha, Tel 810822-4, Telex 4587 TIMBER DH; Gulf Housing Co, PO Box 3886, Doha, Tel 320997, 810714, Telex 4154 GULHOS DH; Inter Rent (Qatar), PO Box 3899, Doha, Tel 429753, Telex 4142 GATCO DH; Qatar Communication Co, PO Box 2481, Doha, Tel 424347, Telex 4395 DARTRA DH; American Express, PO Box 2481, Doha, Tel 422411, Telex 4144 QATCOM DH; K D Property Co, PO Box 350, Doha, Tel 422781; Gulf Automobile & Trading Co; PO Box 3899, Doha, Tel 810655, 446270, Telex 4142 GATCO DH

Principal Bankers: Qatar National Bank

Date of Establishment: 1911
No of Employees: 200

DARWISH TRAVEL BUREAU

PO Box 737, Doha
Tel: 418666 (7 lines)
Cable: Darair
Telex: 4334 DTB DH
Telefax: (974) 427711

Chairman: Kassem Darwish Fakhroo
Directors: Darwish Abdulla Darwish, Mohamed Abdul Rahman Darwish, Mohamed Kassem Darwish
Senior Executives: Hassan M Akhal (Chief Accountant), Mohamed Ibrahim (Sales & Reservations Manager)

PRINCIPAL ACTIVITIES: Travel agency

Principal Agencies: Air India, Alia, British Airways, Cyrprus Airways, Iran National Airlines, KLM, Kuwait Airways, Lufthansa, MEA, Pakistan Airlines, Qantas, Scandinavian Airlines, Swissair, TMA, TWA, Thai Airways

Branch Offices: Qatar Tours, Qatar Travels
Subsidiary Companies: Qatar National Travel
Principal Bankers: Standard Chartered Bank

Financial Information:

	1990
	QR'000
Sales turnover approx	117,000

Principal Shareholders: Owned by Kassem and Abdullah Sons of Darwish Fakhroo Est
Date of Establishment: 1950
No of Employees: 102

DESERT CONTRACTING & TRADING CO
PO Box 3389, Doha
Tel: 325212
Cable: Desco Doha
Telex: 4430 Q PLAS DH

Chairman: Brig Mohammad Bin Abdullah Al-Attiya
Senior Executives: Tarek Husseini (General Manager)

PRINCIPAL ACTIVITIES: General contracting, civil engineering and construction
Principal Bankers: British Bank of the Middle East

Principal Shareholders: Brig Mohammad Bin Abdullah Al-Attiya & Sons
Date of Establishment: December 1975
No of Employees: 300

DHL QATAR LTD
PO Box 9520, Doha
Tel: 420721
Telex: 4739 DHL DH

Senior Executives: S K Harman (General Manager)

PRINCIPAL ACTIVITIES: Worldwide express courier service, air and sea freight, packing clearance and forwarding
Branch Offices: In the Middle East: Bahrain, Cyprus, Egypt (Cairo, Alexandria), Jordan, Kuwait, Lebanon, Oman, Qatar, Saudi Arabia (AlKhobar, Jeddah, Riyadh, Jubail, Tabuk, Taif), UAE (Abu Dhabi, Dubai, Sharjah); Iraq; Djibouti
Parent Company: DHL International

Date of Establishment: 1978

DOHA BANK LTD
PO Box 3818, Doha
Tel: 435444
Cable: DOHABANK
Telex: 4534 DOHBNK DH, 4882 DBLFEX DH, 5051 DBL GEN DH
Telefax: 0974 - 416631

Chairman: Jabor Bin Mohamad Al Thani
Directors: Nasser Bin Abdullah Al Ahmad Al Thani (Deputy Chairman), Ali Bin Saud Bin Abdel Aziz Al Thani, Ali Bin Nasser Al Attiyah, Abdullah Bin Mohammad Bin Jaber Al Thani, Abdul Rehman Bin Mohamed Bin Jabor Al Thani, Ahmad Abdel Rahman Obaidan
Senior Executives: Maqbool H Khalfan (General Manager)

PRINCIPAL ACTIVITIES: Commercial banking
Branch Offices: Qatar: Mushaireb Street Branch, PO Box 2822, Doha; Umm Said Branch, PO Box 50111, Umm Said; Salwa Road Branch, PO Box 2176, Doha; Dukhan Branch, PO Box 100188, Dukhan; West Bay Branch, PO Box 9818, Doha; also New York Branch, 127 John Street, New York, NY 10038, USA; Karachi Branch, PO Box 6876, Karachi, Pakistan
Principal Bankers: BCCI, London; Chemical Bank, New York; Bank of Tokyo, Tokyo; Union Bank of Switzerland, Zurich; Qatar National Bank, Paris; Banca Commerciale Italiana, Italy
Financial Information:

	1988/89
	QR'000
Profits	24,444
Authorised capital	52,500
Paid-up capital	52,500
Total assets	1,915,712

Principal Shareholders: Qatar Flour Mills Co, Qatar National Navigation & Transport Co Ltd, Qatar Insurance Co Ltd, Al Khalij Insurance Co Ltd and private interests
Date of Establishment: 1979
No of Employees: Over 205

DOHA INTERNATIONAL AIRPORT
PO Box 3848, Doha
Tel: 351550
Telex: 4678 DH
Telefax: 418944

Directors: Abdulaziz Al Naoimi
Senior Executives: Mohammed Ali Al Hassan Al Mohanadi (Airport Manager)

PRINCIPAL ACTIVITIES: Airport management
Parent Company: Civil Aviation Department, Ministry of Communications & Transport
Principal Bankers: Qatar National Bank

Principal Shareholders: Government of Qatar

DOHA MOTORS & TRADING CO
PO Box 145, Doha
Tel: 424040, 325664
Cable: Alansari Doha
Telex: 4302 Ansari DH

Chairman: Jassim H Abu Abbass
Directors: A H Al Ansari, Ahmed H A Abbass (Managing Director)

PRINCIPAL ACTIVITIES: Dealing in motor cars and vehicles, auto spare parts, garage and petrol centre, technical division
Principal Agencies: SAAB SCANIA, Sweden; Jaguar, Daimler, Austin Morris Range, UK
Branch Offices: Salwa Industrial Estate, Qatar
Subsidiary Companies: Al Ansari Establishment; Al Ansari Technicals; Gulf Optics; Doha Modern Printing Press; Doha Library; Doha Furniture Showroom and Doha Petrol Center;
Principal Bankers: The British Bank of the Middle East

Principal Shareholders: Jassim Abu Abbass; A H Al Ansari; Ahmed H A Abbass
Date of Establishment: 1970
No of Employees: 200

DOHA SHERATON HOTEL & CONFERENCE CENTRE
PO Box 6000, West Bay, Doha
Tel: 833833
Telex: 5000 DOSHER
Telefax: 832323

Senior Executives: Gerhard Foltin (General Manager), Andreas Searty (Executive Asst Manager), Mohamed Akkad (Financial Controller), Shadi Hanafi (Director of Sales)

PRINCIPAL ACTIVITIES: Hotel, conference business
Branch Offices: Regional Offices: Cairo, Bahrain
Parent Company: The Sheraton Corporation, Boston, USA
Principal Bankers: Qatar National Bank
Financial Information:

	1989/90
	QR'000
Sales turnover	25,000

Date of Establishment: 22nd February 1982
No of Employees: 461

EASTERN TECHNICAL SERVICES
PO Box 4747, Doha
Tel: 441412
Telex: 4156 Eastec DH

Directors: Abdul Hamid Al-Mudhaiki (Managing Director)

PRINCIPAL ACTIVITIES: Sales, installation and servicing of two-way radio, telephone, marine airport, underwater, intercom, closed circuits TV, central TV Aerial, computer, fire, security and other telecommunications systems, steel erection
Principal Agencies: Digital Telephone Systems, USA; Wilcox Electric, USA; Raytheon Marine, USA; Ocean Applied Research, USA; Antiference, UK; Sailor Marineradio, Denmark; AEG Telefunken, W Germany; Barkway Electronics, UK; Teldis, UK; TOA Electric, Japan; Francis & Lewis, UK; Hewlett-Packard electronic instruments, USA; Alexander Manufacturing, USA; Group 4 Securitas, UK; Ceemex, UK; General Datacom, Bodet, Microdata, UK
Principal Bankers: Grindlays Bank plc; Commercial Bank of Qatar, Qatar National Bank

Date of Establishment: June 1st 1977
No of Employees: 36

ERNST & WHINNEY
PO Box 164, Doha
Tel: 414599
Cable: Ernstaudit Dh
Telex: 4415 Ernst DH
Telefax: 414649

Senior Executives: Ian Robinson (Managing Partner), Akram Mekhael (Manager)

PRINCIPAL ACTIVITIES: Accountants and management consultants
Branch Offices: Offices throughout the Middle East

Date of Establishment: Doha office opened in 1950
No of Employees: 25

FAHAD BIN ABDULLAH ALTHANI & SONS TRADING & CONTRACTING CO
See ALTHANI, FAHAD BIN ABDULLAH, & SONS TRADING & CONTRACTING CO

FAKHROO, ABDULREHMAN BIN ABDULLA ABIDAN, & SONS
PO Box 254, Doha
Tel: 423402
Cable: Al-Abidan
Telex: 4479 Abidan DH
Telefax: (0974) 416652

Directors: Abdulla A Fakhroo (Managing Director), Ahmad A Fakhroo (Director)

PRINCIPAL ACTIVITIES: Concrete machinery, welding sets, generator sets, pneumatic vibrators, diesel engines, marine engines and all types of pumps
Principal Agencies: Benford, UK; P F La Roche, UK; Grundfos, Denmark
Branch Offices: Show-Room for Heavy Equipment, Tel: 416652
Principal Bankers: Standard Chartered Bank; British Bank of the Middle East; Qatar National Bank

GENERAL CONTRACTING & TRADING CO
GENCO
PO Box 4243, Doha
Tel: 424801, 422466
Cable: Genco Doha
Telex: 4121 Genco DH

Chairman: Sheikh Ali Bin Saud Al Thani
Directors: Ismail Deeb Elashkar (Partner and General Manager)

PRINCIPAL ACTIVITIES: Construction; civil works, industrial projects, general trading
Principal Agencies: Officine Piccini, Italy; Comedil, Italy; Halbergerhutte, W Germany; Glynwed Wask Engineering, UK; Showcase Carpet Mills, USA; Aldek, Denmark
Associated Companies: Fairclough Ltd, London UK; H Klammt, West Germany

Principal Bankers: Bank Al Mashrek SaL

Principal Shareholders: Owned by Sheikh Ali Bin Saud Althani, Sons and Partners
Date of Establishment: 1958
No of Employees: 300

GETTCO
General Transport & Travel Co
PO Box 919, Doha
Tel: 327151/6, 422726, 324540
Cable: Gettco Doha
Telex: 4232 DH

Chairman: Faisal Bin Jassem Al Thani (Proprietor)

PRINCIPAL ACTIVITIES: Packing, clearing and forwarding agents; insurance; air, sea, land freight, storage, carpentry services, furnished apartments; import and distribution of building materials, timber, plywood, foodstuffs (canned foods, chocolate & biscuits), supermarkets, pharmacy, tyre showroom, refrigeration division, warehouse
Principal Agencies: Air India, Alia, Alitalia, BA, Gulf-Air, KLM, Lufthansa, MEA, Pan Am, PIA, Qantas, Swissair, Syrian Arab Airlines, Iraqi Airways, Bridgestone Tyres, Farco Batteries, Delacre Biscuits; Lindt
Subsidiary Companies: Intercontinental Trading Establishment, PO Box 1151, Doha; Gettco Carpentry, Doha; City Supermarket, Doha; Gettco Refrigeration, Doha; Ibn Sina Pharmacy, Doha; Gulf Pharmacy, Doha
Principal Bankers: Arab Bank Ltd, Qatar National Bank, Banque Paribas
Financial Information:
Paid-up capital   QR6,500,000

Principal Shareholders: (single ownership)
Date of Establishment: 1967
No of Employees: 110

GHANEM AL THANI HOLDINGS WLL
See AL THANI, GHANEM, HOLDINGS WLL

GHANEM BIN ALI AL THANI HOLDINGS CO
PO Box 5319, Doha
Tel: 428201
Telex: 4448

Chairman: Sheikh Ghanem Bin Ali Al Thani

PRINCIPAL ACTIVITIES: General trading and contracting; department store, hotel and real estate; building materials supply; garden centre; air conditioning contracting etc
Subsidiary/Associated Companies: Ramada Renaissance Hotel; The Centre; New Trade Co; Ghanem Gardens; Ghanem Real Estate; New Press & Converting Co; Prestige; Al Arab Contracting

GULF AGENCY CO QATAR
PO Box 6534, Doha
Tel: 323954
Cable: CONFIDENCE
Telex: 4327 GAC DH
Telefax: 433057

Senior Executives: Paul Haegeman (General Manager)

PRINCIPAL ACTIVITIES: Shipping agency, clearing and forwarding, heavy lift and transportation contractors, international removals
Associated Companies: In Kuwait; Bahrain; Saudi Arabia; Abu Dhabi; Dubai; Sharjah; Ras Al Khaimah; Oman; Lebanon; Syria; Yemen; Jordan; Egypt; Cyprus; Turkey; Nigeria; UK; Sweden; Italy; Norway; USA; Hong Kong; Singapore; Greece; Germany; Iran; India; Pakistan; Poland; Indonesia; Japan; Korea; Switzerland; Philippines; Vietnam; China
Principal Bankers: British Bank of the Middle East, Doha

Financial Information:

	1990
	QR'000
Sales turnover	12,000

Date of Establishment: 1979
No of Employees: 25

GULF AIR

PO Box 3394, Doha
Tel: 455455 (Admin), 455444 (Reservations)
Telex: 5150 GLFAIR DH

Chairman: HE Abdulla Bin Saleh Al Mana
Directors: HE Ali Ibrahim Al Malki (President & Chief Executive)

PRINCIPAL ACTIVITIES: Airline transportation of passenger, cargo and mail
Financial Information:

	1989/90
	US$'000
Sales turnover	511,610
Profits	72,398
Share capital	169,761
Reserves	132,546
Total assets	654,880

Principal Shareholders: Jointly owned by the Governments of Bahrain, Qatar, Abu Dhabi and Oman
Date of Establishment: 1950

GULF CONTRACTING EST

PO Box 2421, Doha
Tel: 324729
Cable: Buti
Telex: 4254 Buti DH

Chairman: Butti Bin Salem Khalifa
Senior Executives: Suleiman S Suleiman (Chief Executive)

PRINCIPAL ACTIVITIES: Building and road construction
Branch Offices: Saudi Gulf Est, PO Box 2420, Riyadh, Sauid Arabia
Principal Bankers: Grindlays Bank; Bank Saderat Iran; Banque Paribas

Date of Establishment: 1971
No of Employees: 120

GULF DANISH DAIRY & WILLIAMS

PO Box 2239, Doha
Tel: 422980
Telex: 4158 Dairy DH

Senior Executives: Mohd Ahmed Radwan (General Manager)

PRINCIPAL ACTIVITIES: Dairy products, ice cream and fruit juice

No of Employees: 60

GULF ELECTRICAL MATERIALS CO G.E.M.C.O.

PO Box 157, Doha
Tel: 321680
Cable: Asem
Telex: 4273 Asem DH

Directors: Ahmed Saleh Obaidally (Managing Director)

PRINCIPAL ACTIVITIES: General trading, import and distribution of central air conditioning equipment, heavy plant and equipment, electrical and mechanical engineering
Principal Agencies: Singer, USA; Dunham Bush, USA; Marley, UK; Aluminium Wire & Cable; Thomassen, Holland; Coppee Rust, Belgium; Seba Dynatronic, W Germany; Celamerck, W Germany; Utema, Belgium
Subsidiary Companies: Atlas Contracting & Trading, PO Box 2206, Doha; Cibuilco Contracting & Trading Co, PO Box 1237, Doha; Al Obaidally & Gulf Eternit Trading Co, PO Box 1965, Doha
Principal Bankers: Banque Paribas; Qatar National Bank; Bank Al Mashrek

Date of Establishment: 1969
No of Employees: 350

GULF FINANCE & EXCHANGE CO

PO Box 4847, Doha
Tel: 428211/2, 428285, 414278, 421744, 431273
Cable: GFECO
Telex: 4582, 4657
Telefax: 424055

Chairman: Ali Jaffer Sulaiman (Managing Director)
Partners: Ali Jaffer Sulaiman, Abdul Aziz Abdulla Khoshabi
Senior Executives: Ramesh Badjate (General Manager), Mustafa Abdulla Abdul Aziz (Asst Managing Director), Sohail A Hussain (Operations Manager)

PRINCIPAL ACTIVITIES: Dealing in foreign exchange and precious metals
Branch Offices: Souk Ahmed Bin Ali, Doha
Subsidiary Companies: Reem Jewellers
Principal Bankers: Qatar National Bank, Doha; Doha Bank Ltd, Doha; Credit Suisse, Bahrain
Financial Information:

	1988/89	1989/90
	QR'000	QR'000
Profits	4,841	5,234
Authorised capital	10,000	10,000
Paid-up capital	10,000	10,000
Total assets	51,256	60,803

Principal Shareholders: Partnership
Date of Establishment: 1978
No of Employees: 35

GULF GROUP CONTRACTING & TRADING

PO Box 3359, Doha
Tel: 325932, 61460
Telex: 4455 GLF GRP DH

Chairman: Sheikh Ghanim Bin Ali Al Thani

PRINCIPAL ACTIVITIES: General contracting and trading, telecommunications, electrical supplies, architectural design, real estate, industrial and mechanical engineering
Branch Offices: Beirut, Geneva, Amman, Khartoum
Subsidiary Companies: Gulf Electronics & Communications Division

GULF HELICOPTERS LIMITED

PO Box 811, Doha
Tel: 433991/2
Cable: Helicopters Doha
Telex: 4353 Glfhel DH
Telefax: 411004

Chairman: Abdulla Bin Hamad Al Attiya
Directors: Ahmed Ismiel Al Abdul Ghani, Mohd Noor Sultan, Hamid Al Alawi, Mohammad Rashid Al Muhanadi
Senior Executives: M J Evans (Manager), Capt D Laird (Chief Pilot), P M Giles (Chief Engineer), N K Darwish (Deputy Manager)

PRINCIPAL ACTIVITIES: Offshore and charter helicopter operations
Branch Offices: Gulf Helicopters Limited, UK
Parent Company: Gulf Air Co GSC
Principal Bankers: Qatar National Bank
Financial Information:

	1989/90
	QR'000
Sales turnover	23,938
Total assets	58,318

Principal Shareholders: State of Bahrain; State of Qatar; United Arab Emirates; Sultanate of Oman
Date of Establishment: July 1970
No of Employees: 68

GULF HOTEL

PO Box 1911, Doha
Tel: 432432
Cable: GLFHTL DOHA
Telex: 4250 GLFHTL DH
Telefax: 418784

Chairman: Ahmad Al Uthman
Senior Executives: L P Belsito (General Manager)

PRINCIPAL ACTIVITIES: Hotel business and catering
Principal Bankers: Qatar National Bank

Principal Shareholders: Qatar National Hotels Co Ltd
Date of Establishment: 1973
No of Employees: 600

GULF HOUSING CO LTD

PO Box 3886, Doha
Tel: 320997/8
Telex: 4154 Gulhos DH
Telefax: 449059

Chairman: Kassem Darwish Fakhroo
Directors: Yousuf K Darwish (Acting Chairman), Patrick Hegarty
Senior Executives: John Kennedy (Acting Deputy General Manager), John Fowler (Contracts Manager), Peter Happenny (Quantity Surveyor), V Jeyaraman (Manager Finance & Administration), S Krishnan (Factory Manager)

PRINCIPAL ACTIVITIES: General construction; system built housing; portable accommodation units - spacemakers
Parent Company: Kassem Darwish Fakhroo & Sons
Principal Bankers: Qatar National Bank
Financial Information:

	1990/91 QR'000
Sales turnover	50,000
Working capital	18,000

Principal Shareholders: Kassem Darwish Fakhroo & Sons
Date of Establishment: January 1976
No of Employees: 450

GULF MARKETS

PO Box 405, Doha
Tel: 672424
Telex: 4787
Telefax: 672574

Chairman: Yousef Kassem Darwish
Directors: Carlos G Saba (Managing Director), Dr M N Martini (Executive Director)

PRINCIPAL ACTIVITIES: General trading, supply of pharmaceuticals, foodstuffs; publishing and public relations agency; specialised oil services
Principal Agencies: Unigate, Australia; Evercrisp, Singapore; Hunter; Eli Lily; Boehringer Mannheim; Backer Production Services; Smit-Tak; Alite Foods
Subsidiary Companies: Oryx Publishing; Qatar Posters; Oasis Pharmacy; The Studio; Gulf Public Relations; Specialised Oil Services
Principal Bankers: Qatar National Bank, Al Ahli Bank, Standard Chartered Bank

Principal Shareholders: Yousuf K Darwish

GULF ORGANISATION FOR INDUSTRIAL CONSULTING

G.O.I.C.

PO Box 5114, Doha
Tel: 831234 (10 lines)
Cable: GOIC
Telex: 4619 DH
Telefax: 831465

Directors: Dr Naji Atallah (Projects Dept), Dr Badr Ul Islam Hashemy (Industrial Studies Dept), Dr Mohamed Hisham Khawajkiah (Industrial Informati on & Coordination Dept), Dr Ihsan Bu Hulaiga (Industrial Data Bank Dept), Mohamed Saleh Al Kuwari (Administration & Finance Dept)
Senior Executives: Dr Abdul Rahman A Al Jafary (Secretary General), Abdulla Ali Al Abdulla (Asst Secretary General)

PRINCIPAL ACTIVITIES: Collection & publication of information about industrial development projects and policies. Proposing the establishment of common industrial projects in the member states. Recommending ways and means of coordination among the industrial projects. Coordination and development of technical and economic cooperation among existing or planned industrial companies. Supplying of technical assistance to prepare and evaluate industrial projects. Preparation of information and studies concerning industry
Principal Bankers: Qatar National Bank

Principal Shareholders: (Member States) - Bahrain, Kuwait, Oman, Qatar, Saudi Arabia, United Arab Emirates
Date of Establishment: 1976
No of Employees: 85

GULF TIMBER & JOINERY CO WLL

PO Box 4800, Doha
Tel: 810822/3/4
Telex: 4298 Tradar
Telefax: (0974) 601282

Chairman: Amam Jassim Darwish
Directors: Hassan K Darwish (Managing Director)
Senior Executives: Jack Marsh (Manager), M Krishnaraj (Accountant)

PRINCIPAL ACTIVITIES: Manufacture of purpose made joinery, doors, windows, kitchen units, wardrobes, furniture items; also specialising in hand carving; manufacture and supply of playground equipment for parks, schools and zoo gardens
Principal Agencies: Hicksons Timber Products Ltd, UK

Date of Establishment: 1979
No of Employees: 80

HAMAD BIN KHALED CONTRACTING CO

H.B.K. Group

PO Box 1362, Doha
Tel: 433644
Cable: HAMENG
Telex: 4070 HBK DH

Chairman: Sh Hamad Bin Khaled Al Thani
Directors: Abraham G Dedeyan

PRINCIPAL ACTIVITIES: General contractors, air conditioning and electrical installations, ready mix concrete, grit blasting and painting, instrumentation, mechanical services, power cleaning
Subsidiary/Associated Companies: HBK Power Cleaning, Tel 887174, Telex 4539; J & H Readymix Concrete Co, Tel 883261; HBK Engineering Services, Tel 887611; Instrumentation & Mechanical Services, Tel 887612, Telex 41281
Principal Bankers: The British Bank of the Middle East; Grindlays Bank plc; Commercial Bank of Qatar Ltd

Financial Information:

	QR'000
Sales turnover	105,000
Authorised capital	18,000
Paid-up capital	18,000

Principal Shareholders: Sh Hamad Bin Khaled Al-Thani & Sons
Date of Establishment: 1/4/1971
No of Employees: 1,120

HAMAD BIN KHALED TRADING CO
H.B.K. Group
PO Box 1806, Doha
Tel: 425022, 416276
Cable: Hamadalthani
Telex: 4318 Hamad DH
Telefax: 438729

Chairman: Sh Hamad Bin Khaled Al Thani
Senior Executives: Abraham Dedeyan (General Manager), Maroun Namroud (Manager)

PRINCIPAL ACTIVITIES: Manufacturers' representation, import and distribution of fixing and fastening equipment, safety equipment, and genral merchandise
Principal Agencies: Hilti AG, Switzerland; Braithwaite Engineers Ltd, UK; Marubeni (Nippon Kukan Steel Casings), Japan; Construction Marine, UK; Cedar Link Int'l, UK; Engg & Metal Corrosion, UK; Tuffking Safety Ltd, UK; McKowan Lowe & Co Ltd, Hong Kong; Centurion, UK
Parent Company: Hamad Bin Khaled Contracting Co
Associate Companies: HBK Power Cleaning; HBK Engineering Services; HBK Instrumentation & Mechanical Services; HBK Drilling Co; J & H Readymix Concrete Co
Principal Bankers: British Bank of the Middle East (Doha)

Principal Shareholders: Hamad Bin Khaled Al Thani
Date of Establishment: 1985

HAMMAN TRADING & CONTRACTING CO
PO Box 672, Doha
Tel: 320236, 320066
Cable: Hammam
Telex: 4213 DH

Senior Executives: Osman Maniera (Manager)

PRINCIPAL ACTIVITIES: General trading and building contracting, Import and distribution of building materials, cement, iron, tiles, sanitary ware, electrical appliances, and spare parts for German cars

HASSAN ALI BIN ALI EST
PO Box 2863, Doha
Tel: 328526, 418181
Cable: Haba Doha
Telex: 4385 Haba DH

Chairman: Hassan Ali Bin Ali
Directors: Nouri Abed Al-Bahrani (General Manager), David Pearson (Manager/Road Construction Division), Tom Coyne (Director Agencies)
Senior Executives: Roger Gibson (Manager, Lighting Showroom), A Said (Manager Ready Mix), B Awad (Manager Electronic Division), A S Jamaludeen (Toys From Hamleys), A Ghafoor (Technical Marketing Centre), K Agar (Manager, Haba Controls)

PRINCIPAL ACTIVITIES: General trading, concrete mixing - patching plant, import and distribution of electrical household appliances and accessories, civil and electrical contracting, road construction division, toys showrooms
Principal Agencies: AEG, West Germany; Square D, UK; Afa Minerva, UK; Le Grand, France; Targatti, Italy; Hyundia; J-Harris; J A Crocker; Cementation; Scientific Design/USA; Bechtel, USA

Branch Offices: Lighting and Electrical Accessories Showroom (PO Box 1335, Doha); Ready Mix - Patching Plant Division (PO Box 2863, Doha); Electronic Division (PO Box 2863, Doha); Road Construction Division (PO Box 1343, Doha); Toys From Hamleys (PO Box 1355) Doha; Technical Marketing Centre (PO Box 2560, Doha); Habai Controls (PO Box 2863)
Principal Bankers: Qatar National Bank; Doha Bank
Financial Information:

	1989 US$'000
Authorised capital	2,500
Paid-up capital	2,500

Principal Shareholders: Private ownership
Date of Establishment: 1972
No of Employees: 406

HASSAN TRADING & CONTRACTING CO
PO Box 1509, Doha
Tel: 425998
Cable: Hastrad
Telex: 4418 Htc DH

Chairman: Sheikh Abdulrehman Bin Hassan Al Abdulla Al Thani
Directors: Sheikh Hassan Bin Abdulrehman Bin Hassan Al Abdulla Al Thani

PRINCIPAL ACTIVITIES: Manufacturers and suppliers of ceramic and marble tiling, building materials and sanitary ware, fire fighting equipment, manufacturers' representatives
Parent Company: Black Cat Construction
Subsidiary Companies: Mechanical Division
Principal Bankers: Grindlays Bank, Qatar National Bank

No of Employees: 300

HEMPEL PAINTS (QATAR) WLL
PO Box 3484, Doha
Tel: 810881/4 (main office & factory)
Cable: Hempaturi
Telex: 4864 Hempel DH
Telefax: 810901

Chairman: Mohamed Mubarak Al Khulaifi
Directors: Abdulaziz Yousef AlKhulaifi, Sheikh Hamad Sabah Al-Ahmed Al-Sabah, Saud Abdulaziz Al-Rashed, Saad Abdulaziz Al-Rashed, John Schwartzbach, Jorn H Lillelund
Senior Executives: Wilfred Thomas (General Manager)

PRINCIPAL ACTIVITIES: Manufacturers of paint and coatings for the marine, industrial, offshore, yacht and building sector uses; materials and tools for surface preparation and application of such coatings, inc provision of advisory services
Principal Agencies: ELCOMETER Instruments Ltd, UK; GRACO France SA; POLYCELL Products Ltd, UK; Clemco, Germany
Branch Offices: Doha Dept, Tel 413755
Principal Bankers: Banque Paribas, Doha; Grindlays Bank, Doha
Financial Information:

	1989 QR'000
Paid-up capital	3,600

Principal Shareholders: Chairman and directors as described
Date of Establishment: 1981
No of Employees: 40

HOTEL SOFITEL DOHA PALACE
PO Box 7566, Musheirib Street, Doha
Tel: 435-222
Cable: Sofitel Doha
Telex: 5151 Softel DH

PRINCIPAL ACTIVITIES: Hotel business
Parent Company: Sofitel/Novotel Sieh Groupe

IBRAHIM MOHAMED QASSEM FAKHROO TRADING EST

PO Box 77, Doha
Tel: 424268, 423542, 428231
Cable: Ibrahim Fakhroo
Telex: 4110 Imfakh DH

Chairman: Ibrahim Mohamed Qassem Fakhroo
Directors: Ahmed Fakroo (Civil Engineer), Abdul Rahman
Fakhroo (Commercial Manager)
Senior Executives: Ahmed Fakhroo (Contracting Manager),
Abdul Rahman Fakhroo (Commercial Manager)

PRINCIPAL ACTIVITIES: Commission agents, contractors and
traders, building materials, tools, heavy equipment
Principal Agencies: Stanley Tools Ltd, UK; Gebr Grundmann,
Austria; Enitor BV, Holland; Hansa Ueberseehandel, W
Germany; Crane Enfield, Australia; Briton Chadwick, UK;
Poral Cyclon, Australia; Moonsignal, Taiwan
Branch Offices: Qatar; Dubai; Bahrain
Principal Bankers: Grindlays Bank; Citibank; Banque Paribas;
Qatar National Bank

Date of Establishment: 1963

INTERBETON QATAR LTD (WLL)

PO Box 3810, Doha
Tel: 870130, 870131
Telex: 4133 inbet DH
Telefax: 865688

Owners: Abdul Aziz Alattiya, Hisham N Al Mannai
Directors: J L C M Poort (General Manager)
Senior Executives: T A Joyce (Factory Manager)

PRINCIPAL ACTIVITIES: General, civil, marine contractors and
precast/GRC manufacturers
Associated Companies: In technical collaboration with
Interbeton BV, subsidiary of Hollandes Beton Group (HBG),
Netherlands
Principal Bankers: Standard Chartered Bank, Doha; Grindlays
Bank, Doha

Date of Establishment: 1987
No of Employees: 250

ISHAQ BIN HUSSAIN MAHMOUD & SONS CO

PO Box 654, Doha
Tel: 422668, 328139
Cable: Ishaq Doha
Telex: 4432 DH

Chairman: Ishaq Bin Hussain Mahmoud
Directors: Ibrahim Ishaq (General Manager), Ali Ishaq (Managing
Director), Abdul Rehman Kosar (Commercial Manager)

PRINCIPAL ACTIVITIES: Commercial traders, building
contractors, supply and hiring of heavy transport.
Manufacture of aluminium, steelwork blocks and tiles,
carpentry, supply of building materials and sanitaryware
Principal Agencies: Interpoly, UK; Ceramica Venus, Italy
Principal Bankers: Qatar National Bank; Grindlays Bank; Bank
Saderat Iran

Date of Establishment: 1940
No of Employees: 320

JAIDAH MOTORS & TRADING CO

PO Box 150, Doha
Tel: 426161
Cable: Aljaidah
Telex: 4219 DH Jaidah
Telefax: 414100

Chairman: Jassem M Jaidah (also Managing Director)
Senior Executives: Tewfiq L Nahhas (General Manager), Carlos
G Saba (Asst General Manager)

PRINCIPAL ACTIVITIES: Import and distribution of automobiles,
plant, furniture, oilfield supplies and services, spare parts,
tools, earthmoving equipment, welding machines, forklift
trucks and generally all heavy duty equipment, safety
equipment, instrumentation, lubricants, business
communication, computers, telecommunication equipment
Principal Agencies: Shell, Baroid International, Redwing,
Dyckerhoff Oilwell Cement, Weatherford Lamb, Hydril,
Ingersoll-Rand, Drilco, Halliburton, Nissan Diesel, Chevrolet,
Oldsmobile, Buick, Isuzu, Komatsu, Foxboro, Farinon,
General Electric Mobile Radio, Multitone, Marconi
Instruments, Tektronix, Stentor, Kaypro, Case Modems,
Emerson, Racal Communications, Racal Antennas, Andrew
Antennas, Citizen Printers, SR-Telecom, Javelin, Kaypro
Computers, Racal Chubb Security Systems, Sherry
Computers, Austin Computers, Exicom
Branch Offices: Dubai
Subsidiary Companies: Oman Oil Industry Supplies and
Services
Principal Bankers: Qatar National Bank; British Bank of the
Middle East; Banque Paribas; Qatar Commercial Bank;
Standard Chartered Bank; ANZ Grindlays Bank

Principal Shareholders: Family owned
Date of Establishment: 1960
No of Employees: 400

JASSIM BIN KHALID (JBK)

PO Box 2202, Doha
Tel: 883203, 421924
Telex: 4817

Chairman: Sheikh Jassim Bi Khalid Al Thani
Senior Executives: Mahmoud Abu Rubb (General Manager JBK
Construction)

PRINCIPAL ACTIVITIES: Trading, construction, power
construction, supply of electrical and heavy equipment, real
estate and hotels
Principal Agencies: BICC Plc; Woden Transformers Ltd; GEC
Measurements Ltd; GEC Meters; Dearborn Chemicals Ltd
Subsidiary/Associated Companies: JBK BICC; Qatar Power
Construction Est; Qatar Decoration; Doha Palace Hotel;
Sofitel Hotel

JASSIM BIN MOHD BIN JASSIM AL THANI & SONS EST

PO Box 236, Doha
Tel: 425138/9
Cable: Jassim Al Thani
Telex: 4259 DH

Chairman: Sheikh Jassim Bin Mohd Bin Jassim Al Thani
(Owner)

PRINCIPAL ACTIVITIES: Building contractors and contractors'
plant importers, general merchants and manufacturers'
representatives. Import and distribution of building materials,
sanitary ware, pipes and fittings, steel and aluminium
products, air conditioning equipment, earth moving equipment
and heavy machinery, all types of motor vehicles and spare
parts, agricultural machinery, furniture, electrical appliances
for domestic and office use, household goods
Principal Bankers: Arab Bank; United Bank

JOHN R HARRIS QATAR ARCHITECTS

PO Box 8332, Doha
Tel: 441406
Telex: 4329 JRHQA DH
Telefax: 447197

Resident Partner: J N Hastings
Partners: John R Harris, A Rigby, J N Hastings
Senior Executives: Collin Somes (Senior Architect)

PRINCIPAL ACTIVITIES: Architecture and planning

Associated Companies: John R Harris Architects, London; John R Harris Brunei Architects, Brunei; John R Harris and Partners, Dubai and Hong Kong; John R Harris Associates, Muscat

KAMAL TRADING & CONTRACTING CO

PO Box 171, Doha
Tel: 421000
Cable: Kamalco
Telex: 4405 DH

PRINCIPAL ACTIVITIES: Import and distribution of electrical and electronic appliances and equipment, spare parts
Principal Agencies: Schaub, Lorenz, Belair

KASSEM & ABDULLAH SONS OF DARWISH FAKHROO

PO Box 71, Doha
Tel: 422781/9
Cable: Darwish
Telex: 4211 Darwish DH

Chairman: Kassem Darwish Fakhroo
Directors: Abdullah Darwish Fakhroo, Abdul Rahman Darwish Fakhroo (Partners)
Senior Executives: Abdul Aziz El Toukhi (General Manager), Dr Mohamed Magdi El Sherbini (Chief Accountant), Mohamed Abaza (Manager Oasis Hotel), Riad E Kuburcy (Manager QNT Airport), Riad Ofeish (Manager Qatar Tours), S G Welham (Manager Darwish Travel Bureau), Sheikh Najib Izzeddin (Manager Darwish Engineering)

PRINCIPAL ACTIVITIES: Travel, hotels, catering, motor vehicles, contracting, transport, import of industrial machinery, heavy equipment, air conditioners, household appliances
Branch Offices: Qatar; United Arab Emirates; Saudi Arabia (PO Box 153, Jeddah)
Subsidiary Companies: Darwish Travel Bureau, PO Box 737, Doha; Oasis Hotel; People's Car Company (Volkswagen); Darwish Engineering, PO Box 183, Doha; Qatar National Travel
Principal Bankers: Qatar National Bank; British Bank of the Middle East; Standard Chartered Bank; Grindlays Bank; Citibank; Arab Bank

No of Employees: 450

KASSEM DARWISH FAKHROO & SONS (KDF)

PO Box 350, Doha
Tel: 422781 (16 lines)
Cable: Tradar Doha
Telex: 4298 DH Tradar
Telefax: 426378

Chairman: Kassem Darwish Fakhroo
Directors: Yousuf K Darwish (Vice Chairman), Hassan K Darwish (Managing Director), Ahmed K Darwish, Mohammed K Darwish, Darwish K Darwish, Nasser K Darwish, Salman K Darwish
Senior Executives: Hassan K Darwish (Managing Director Contracting Divisions /Mechanical/Electrical/Otis and Managing Director Projects Dept), Salman K Darwish (Manager - Gulf Automobiles & Trading Co), Nasser K Darwish (Manager Qatar Communications Co & American Express Representative Office), Abdalla K Darwish (Executive Director Darwish Trading Doha), T V Balu (Manager Darwish Trading Dubai), Jack Marsh (Manager Gulf Timber & Joinery), John Kennedy (Acting General Manager Gulf Housing), David L Falconer (Manager Arabesque GRC), Ram Mohan (Manager Datamation Systems)

PRINCIPAL ACTIVITIES: General trading and contracting, building and electrical materials, automobiles; electrical, mechanical and civil contractors; timber and joinery; general construction; system built housing; transport; equipment for parks and playgrounds; tyres and batteries sales; CCTV, security and paging systems; glass reinforced concrete products; American Express service; car rentals; interior decoration and furnishing; hi-technology maintenance; sales and maintenance of computers and word processors
Principal Agencies: American Express; Asbestos Cement; Audi; Al Zamil (Saudi); Arrow Construction Equipment; Band-It Int, USA; Baranite Barduct Ltd; Berger Jenson & Nicholson UK; Benson Plotters; BKW Middle East; BRC Weldmesh (Gulf); British Sissal Kraft; Bruel & Kjaer; Buiscar BVC; Barton Conduits; Cannon; Casa Int; Chloride Int, UK; Cose Made in Italy, Italy; Crawley (Refrigeration); Crittal Construction; Crittal Windows; CMP Glands; Crabtree; Cuprinol; Canfi Corp; Decca Marine Radar; Delta Index UK; Diebold USA; Dunlop UK; Dynapac Eichoff Werke; Evode; Egatube; Expanded Metal UK; Expandite UK; Knoll Int; Kohler; Ericsson Telematerial; Lyte Ind; Mirrless Blackstone; Mitsui, Porsche; Putzmeister; Racal Milgo; Tokyu Cranes; Virax; Xerox; Lanmar; Facit AB, Sweden; Frederick Parker UK; Friedrich Airconditioning and Refrigeration USA; GEC Medical Equipment UK; Hoover UK; IMI Santon UK; Iris Ceramics, Italy; Isofoam, Kuwait; Iwai Ceramics, Japan; NEI Clarke-Chapman Cranes, UK; Olivetti, Italy; Otis Elevators, France; Philips Holland; Peonix Engin UK; Pirelli General Cable Works, UK; Qualcast Fleetway, UK; Ramset Fasteners, Australia; Remington Consumer Products, UK; Ruberoid Building Products, UK; Texas Instruments, France; Thorn Domestic Appliances, UK; Trane Airconditioning, USA; Yorkshire Imperial Metals, UK; Xerox
Branch Offices: United Arab Emirates (Abu Dhabi, Dubai)
Parent Company: Kassem Darwish Fakhroo & Sons
Subsidiary Companies: Darwish Trading, PO Box 92, Doha, Tel 422781, Telex 4298; Gulf Housing Co PO Box 3886, Doha, Tel 320997, Telex 4154; Gulf Automobile & Trading Co, PO Box 3899, Doha, Tel 446270, Telex 4142; Gulf Timber & Joinery Co Ltd, PO Box 4800, Tel 810822, Telex 4587; Arabesque GRC (Qatar), PO Box 4800, Doha Tel 810107, Telex 4697; InterRent (Qatar), PO Box 3899, Doha, Tel 429753, Telex 4142; Qatar Communication Co Ltd, PO Box 2481, Doha, Tel 424347, Telex 4414; American Express PO Box 2481, Tel 422411, Telex 4414
Principal Bankers: Standard Chartered Bank; Qatar National Bank
Financial Information:

	1990
	QR'000
Paid-up capital	45,000

Principal Shareholders: Owned by Kassem Darwish Fakhroo
Date of Establishment: Subsidiary Divisions: 1911; Corporate Group: 1972
No of Employees: Approx 1,000

KEMCO GROUP
Khalid Electrical & Mechanical Est

PO Box 2642, Doha
Tel: 321910/11/12/13
Cable: Kemco, Doha
Telex: 4773 Kemco DH
Telefax: 432506

Proprietor: Mohamed Bin Hammam (Managing Director)
Senior Executives: M I Farid (Manager - Accounts & Maintenance), P S Pai (Manager - Cable Laying Division), Jabor Abdul Latif (Manager Transport), Dileep R Sardesai (Contracts Manager)

PRINCIPAL ACTIVITIES: Electrical, airconditioning, plumbing, maintenance, mechanical (offshore and onshore) contractors
Principal Agencies: York, May & Christe
Subsidiary Companies: Hammam Trading & Contracting Co
Principal Bankers: Qatar National Bank; Grindlays Bank

Principal Shareholders: Proprietor: Mohamed Bin Hammam
Date of Establishment: 1st April 1975
No of Employees: Over 300

LOTUS CONTRACTING & TRADING CO

PO Box 3256, Doha
Tel: 434915/6/7/8
Telex: 4376 Lotus DH
Telefax: (974) 420310

Directors: Ali Hassan Dalaq (Managing Director)
Senior Executives: Magdy A Daoud (Finance & Admin Manager), George A Jabbour (Projects Manager), Waleed Nasrawi (Project Engineer), Imad Saliba (Project Engineer), S N Amin (Project Engineer), K K Sudha (Quantity Surveyor)

PRINCIPAL ACTIVITIES: General trading and contracting, civil, electrical and mechanical engineering
Subsidiary Companies: Lotus Carpentry; Lotus Garage; Lotus Import & Export (Egypt); Lotus Import & Export (Jordan); Lotus Maintenance Division; Mahames Shaheen Nuts & Candy
Principal Bankers: Doha Bank Ltd; Arab Bank Ltd; Qatar Islamic Bank
Financial Information:

	1990 QR'000
Sales turnover	37,000
Authorised capital	2,550
Paid-up capital	2,400
Total assets	4,400

Date of Establishment: 1973
No of Employees: 500

MANNAI CORPORATION LTD

Rayyan Road, PO Box 76, Doha
Tel: 412555 (10 lines), 412800
Cable: Mannai
Telex: 4208 Mannai DH
Telefax: 411982

Chairman: Ahmed Mannai (Managing Director)
Senior Executives: Peter V Quick (Chief Operating Officer), T A Hassiba (Corporate Manager), Anil Seth (Corporate Manager), Oscar A D'Souza (Consultant)

PRINCIPAL ACTIVITIES: Manufacturers' representation, general trading, marketing and servicing of automobiles & industrial vehicles, construction equipment, consumer products incl sound and video equipment & domestic appliances, office educational hospital and laboratoty equipment and supplies, computer software & hardware, telecommunications, engineering goods, landscaping and nursery products, oilfield products and services, air travel; contracting in the civil, mechanical, electrical and offshore construction fields
Principal Agencies: ASEA, Sweden; British Steel Corp, UK; Daewoo Motors, Korea; Detroit Diesel Allison, USA; Facit AB, Sweden; General Motors Overseas Distribution, USA; Grove Int Corp, USA; K Hattori & Co Ltd, Japan; Massey Ferguson, UK; McQuay Perfex, USA; Moulinex, France; Nashua Int Sales, Channel Islands; Ruston Gas Turbines Ltd, UK; Toshiba Corp, Japan; Weir Pump Ltd, UK; White-Westinghouse Int Ltd, USA; Atlas Maschinenexport, W Germany; Compair Construction & Mining, UK; GEC Power Transformers, UK; GEC Diesel, UK; GEC Machines, UK; GEC Switchgear, UK; GEC Turbine Generators, UK; GEC Distribution Switchgear, UK; John Deere Inter-Continental, Belgium; Dresser Europe SA, Belgium; Northern Telecom Int, UK; Shiroyama Industry Co, Japan; Schindler Management, Switzerland; Digital Equipment, UK; Ericsson Information Systems, Sweden; Franco Tosi Industrial, Italy; Grove Coles, UK; etc
Branch Offices: Salwa Industrial Complex, Salwa Road, Doha, Tel 810111, Telex 4765, Fax 601780; office in Riyadh, Saudi Arabia, PO Box 8451, Tel 4776474, 4774655, Telex 204214 MANNAI SJ; office in Dubai, UAE, PO Box 9204, Tel 373712, 440165, Telex 48244, Fax 373493

Parent Company: Mannai Corporation Ltd
Subsidiary/Associated Companies: Mannai Trading Co Ltd, PO Box 76, Doha (Marketing and trading); Mideast Constructors (MECON), PO Box 3325, Doha (Mechanical, electrical, air conditioning, civil and maintenance service); Technical Services Co Ltd (TECHSERV) PO Box 3325, Doha (Products and technical services, project management, consultancy, design work related to the petroleum industry); Manweir Ltd, PO Box 4038, Doha (Rotary and oilfield engineers and contractors, mechanical and electrical); Mannai Marine Co Ltd, PO Box 8776, Doha (Offshore engineering, manufacturing, construction, fabricating and offshore services); Mansal Offshore Ltd, PO Box 1310, Doha (Shipping, offshore supply services); and Nowsco Middle East
Principal Bankers: British Bank of the Middle East; Standard Chartered Bank
Financial Information:

	1990 QR'000
Authorised capital	210,000
Paid-up capital	210,000

Principal Shareholders: Ahmed Mannai (50%), HE Khalid Al Attiya (50%)
Date of Establishment: 1951
No of Employees: 1,300

MANSAL OFFSHORE LTD

PO Box 1310, Rayyan Rd, Doha
Tel: 425755, 421202
Cable: Mansal
Telex: 4279 Mansal DH
Telefax: 433626

Chairman: Ahmed Mannai
Senior Executives: A A Schmetz (General Manager)

PRINCIPAL ACTIVITIES: Marine contracting, offshore, maintenance, marine supplies, ship owners, offshore accomodation
Parent Company: Mannai Corporation
Principal Bankers: Qatar National Bank; British Bank of the Middle East; Banque Paribas

Principal Shareholders: Mannai Corporation, Qatar
Date of Establishment: 1974
No of Employees: 400

MANWEIR ENGINEERING SERVICES

PO Box 4038, Doha
Tel: 810220, 810099, 810111 Ext 290-295
Cable: MANWEIR
Telex: 4765 MANNAI DH
Telefax: 0974-601883

Owner: Mannai Corporation
Chairman: Ahmed Mannai
Senior Executives: Brian Grimley (Manager)

PRINCIPAL ACTIVITIES: Marine industrial and oilfield engineering; supply of oilfield products and services
Principal Agencies: Alfa Laval; British Steel Corp; Dresser Security; Eastman Christensen; Texas Iron Works; Union Pump; TI Flexible Tubes; Det Norske Veritas, Enterra Oil Field Services; PA International (Baker Tubular Services), SPS Technologies; King Wilkinson; Bowen Tools, Etc
Parent Company: Mannai Corporation
Sister Companies: Mannai Trading Co; Mideast Constructors; Mansal Offshore; Mannai Marine; Technical Services Co
Principal Bankers: Standard Chartered Bank, Doha

Principal Shareholders: Mannai Corporation
Date of Establishment: 1976
No of Employees: 65

MARCO TRADING & CONTRACTING CO

PO Box 2139, Doha
Tel: 327725, 320328, 325221
Telex: 4533 Marco DH

Chairman: Mohamed Rashid Al Kaabi
Senior Executives: Marwan Arekat (Personnel Manager), Saad G Ragheb (Marketing Manager), Rasmi Al Momani (Finance Manager), Sami Abd El Tawab (Legal Advisor)

PRINCIPAL ACTIVITIES: Civil engineering; building and electrical contracting; road maintenance; plant hire; plant servicing; readymix concrete; concrete pumps; asphalt supply
Subsidiary Companies: Readymix Plant; Road Division; University Service Est; Asphalt & Crusher Plants
Principal Bankers: Al Ahli Bank of Qatar; Banque Paribas

Principal Shareholders: Mohamed Rashid Al Kaabi, Mansoor Khalaf Al Kaabi
Date of Establishment: 1976
No of Employees: 350

MARS TRADING & CONTRACTING CO

PO Box 148, Doha
Tel: 447747 (5 lines), 423268
Cable: Mars Doha
Telex: 4375 Mars DH
Telefax: 427530

Chairman: Shaikh Jassem Bin Ahmed Al-Thani (also Proprietor)
Directors: Shaikh Fahad Bin Ahmed Al-Thani (General Manager)
Senior Executives: T S B Basha (Commercial Manager), P N Bhat (Electrical Engineer), T S Aman (Mechanical Engineer)

PRINCIPAL ACTIVITIES: Industrial supplies distribution to the oil, gas, cement, fertiliser, electricity and water industries, supplies to civil, mechanical, and electrical contractors, manufacture of oxygen, nitrogen, and acetylene gases
Principal Agencies: Angus Fire Armour, HCB Angus, NEI Reyrolle, NEI Peebles, NEI Electronics, Chloride Standby Systems, Chloride Int Marketing, Braham Millars, Wolf Electric Tools, Neil Tools, Rawl Plug, SKF & Dormer, Kango Tools, F.O. Brian Co, Colchester Lathes, AEG Elect Tools, FAG, Champion Spark Plug, Gates Europe, Enerpac, Dow Corning, General Descaling, Newman Hattersley, J Blakeborough, Worthington Simpson, Thor Tools, Loctite, Leslie Hartridge, Access Equipment, Spirax Sarco, Hawker Siddeley Brackett, Control Asco, Edward Wille, Reed Tools, Rabon Chesterman, Wagner Electric, Philips Drill, Dresser Products, Taprogge Pipe Cleaning; Parker Hannifin, Carborundum, Edward Barber & Co, F D Sims, Newman Electric Motors, Sparling Envirotech, Wemco, Copes Vulcan, Richard Klinger, Salter Industrial Measurement, Devilbliss, Dando Drilling Systems, Jacobs Young & Westbery, Sykes Pickavant, H F Epco, Norgren Martonaire, Neill Tools, Gloor Bros
Branch Offices: Mars & Company, PO Box 1180, Dubai
Principal Bankers: Qatar National Bank; Doha Bank; Standard Chartered Bank
Financial Information:

	1990 QR'000
Sales turnover	32,000
Total reserves	30,000
Paid-up capital	2,500
Total assets	38,000

Principal Shareholders: Proprietorship
Date of Establishment: 1958
No of Employees: 67

MAYSALOON TRADING & CONTRACTING CO

PO Box 3366, Doha
Tel: 446363, 446262
Cable: Maysaloon
Telex: 4137 GG DH
Telefax: 441102

Chairman: Abdulla Salem Al Sulaiteen (General Manager)
Senior Executives: Yacoub Yousuf Al Kawari (Deputy General Manager), Mahmoud Saoub (Head of Finance)

PRINCIPAL ACTIVITIES: Contracting and trading, real estate, furniture, computers, electrical and telecommunication equipment
Subsidiary Companies: Maysaloon Furniture; Telco; Qatar Computer Service
Principal Bankers: Qatar National Bank; Al Ahli Bank of Qatar
Financial Information:

	1989/90 QR'000
Authorised capital	3,633
Paid-up capital	3,633

Date of Establishment: 1975
No of Employees: 125

MECENG
Mechanical Engineering Workshop

PO Box 1223, Doha
Tel: 421116, 325480
Cable: Mecheng
Telex: 4382 Meceng
Telefax: 434117

Chairman: Yacoub Bulbul
Directors: Eng Mohamed Bulbul (Managing Director)

PRINCIPAL ACTIVITIES: Mechanical engineering, import and distribution of tools and equipment, constructional steel, stainless steel pipes and plates, steel pipes and plates, corrugated sheets, chain fencing, barbed wires, machinery, wire ropes, hand tools, mechanical tools, steel, brass, copper fittings, all kinds of valves, bolts, roller chains, block cranes, etc
Principal Bankers: Qatar National Bank
Financial Information:

	1990 SR'000
Sales turnover	20,000
Total assets	12,000

Date of Establishment: 1965
No of Employees: 70

MEDGULF CONSTRUCTION EST

PO Box 3603, Doha
Tel: 431516/7/8
Telex: 4472 MEDGLF DH
Telefax: 433586

Chairman: J M Jaidah
Directors: Zuhair Z Boulos (Managing Director)
Senior Executives: N Sarsar (Finance Manager), Ismail Al-Asaad (Project Manager), S Sahsuvaroglu (Project Manager)

PRINCIPAL ACTIVITIES: Contracting, pipelines, civil and construction, structural steel work
Branch Offices: Medgulf Construction Est, PO Box 495, Jubail, Saudi Arabia
Subsidiary/Associated Companies: Trags Electrical and Airconditioning Co, PO Box 470, Doha; Specialised Technical Services, PO Box 2763, Doha
Principal Bankers: Banque Paribas; Standard Chartered Bank; Commercial Bank of Qatar
Financial Information:

	1990 QR'000
Sales turnover	60,000
Authorised capital	10,000
Paid-up capital	10,000

Principal Shareholders: Private Company
Date of Establishment: 1975
No of Employees: 600

MIDDLE EAST BUSINESS SERVICES (MEBS)

PO Box 5414, Doha, Qatar
Tel: 873460
Telex: 4609 Audio DH att MEBS
Telefax: 424761 Att MEBS

Chairman: H E Shaikh Khalid Bin Ali Bin Abdulla Al Thani
Directors: Dr Roger Coleman (Managing Director), Mrs G
Coleman

PRINCIPAL ACTIVITIES: International recruitment, business
services, international trading, business promotion,
management consultancy, trade agents, advertising agents,
public relations and marketing services
Principal Agencies: Cashcount, Frequent Business Travellers
Club (FBTC)
Principal Bankers: Al Ahli Bank of Qatar

Principal Shareholders: H E Shaikh Khalid Bin Ali Bin Abdulla Al
Thani and Directors as mentioned
Date of Establishment: 1980

MIDDLE EAST TRADERS

PO Box 273, Doha
Tel: 325367, 423486, 320252, 428111/4
Telex: 4311 DH Wafa

Senior Executives: Mohammed H Bayyari (General Manager)

PRINCIPAL ACTIVITIES: Import and distribution of automobiles
and spares, air conditioning and refrigerating equipment
Principal Agencies: Rolls-Royce, Rover, Chrysler Intl, British
Leyland, Kelvinator, Winget, Rotary, ECO, Hockman Lewis,
Tecalemit, Mitsubishi Fuso, MAN Diesel

MIDEAST CONSTRUCTORS LTD

PO Box 3325, Doha
Tel: 415025 (10 lines)
Cable: Mecon
Telex: 4293 DH Mecon
Telefax: 415174

Directors: Ahmed Mannai (Managing Director)
Senior Executives: Ian K Matheson, (General Manager), Gordon
J Franklin (Deputy General Manager), P P Parasuraman
(Administration Manager), Bassam Abu Hijleh (Business
Development Manager), D Y Gurjar (Procurement Manager), K
A Chugani (Project Manager), A N Nair (Manager Operations),
F E Stacey (Sr Quantity Surveyor & Contracts Administrator),
R S Rathaur (Chief Engineer), G Stuart McKay (Manager
Quality Assurance)

PRINCIPAL ACTIVITIES: Civil engineering, supply and
installation of mechanical/electrical equipment; air
conditioning and ventilation equipment; fabrication of
structures/piping; supply, installation and servicing of
instrumentation/controls for industrial plants
Branch Offices: Mannai Trading Co Ltd, PO Box 7240,
Dammam 31462, Saudi Arabia
Parent Company: Mannai Corporation Limited, PO Box 76,
Doha, Qatar
Associated Companies: Manweir Limited; Mansal Offshore Ltd;
Mannai Marine Co Ltd; Mannai Engineering Co Ltd; Mannai
Trading Co Ltd; Technical Services Co
Principal Bankers: Banque Paribas (Doha); Commercial Bank of
Qatar (Doha)
Financial Information:

	1988/89 QR'000	1989/90 QR'000
Sales turnover	75,000	120,000
Authorised capital	20,000	20,000
Paid-up capital	20,000	20,000
Total assets	5,300	100,000

Principal Shareholders: A wholly owned subsidiary of Mannai
Corporation Limited
Date of Establishment: 1975
No of Employees: 900

MIDMAC CONTRACTING

PO Box 1758, Doha
Tel: 425125
Telex: 4240
Telefax: 440864

Chairman: Sheikh Ahmed Bin Khalifa Al Thani
Directors: Khalid Racy (Director)
Senior Executives: Abdallah Khabbaz (Area Manager), Majid
Bahouth (Financial & Commercial Manager)

PRINCIPAL ACTIVITIES: Civil, electrical and mechanical
engineering contractors
Principal Bankers: Commercial Bank of Qatar, Banque Paribas

Date of Establishment: March 1975
No of Employees: 300

MISNAD BIN SAAD AL MISNAD EST

See AL MISNAD, MISNAD BIN SAAD, EST

MODERN CONSTRUCTION CO

PO Box 3401, Doha
Tel: 851628, 851814
Cable: Mesco
Telex: 4031 Mesco DH

Chairman: Ibrahim Abdul Aziz Al Qatari
Directors: Nasrullah Lutfullah, Ali Iskender Al Hamad Al Karani,
Abdul Razak Qanbar, Abdul Aziz Bin Abbas
Senior Executives: Ismail Ali (Managing Director)

PRINCIPAL ACTIVITIES: Trading and contracting, dealing in
building materials, ceramics and sanitary ware, construction
plant; building contracting; plant hire; electrical and
mechanical engineering
Branch Offices: Modern Block Factory; Modern Aluminium
Factory, PO Box 4621, Doha, Qatar; Mercury Enterprise,
Mechanical & Electrical Division, PO Box 7480, Doha, Qatar
Principal Bankers: The Commercial Bank of Qatar; Grindlays
Bank

Date of Establishment: 1976
No of Employees: 400

MODERN HOME

PO Box 615, Al-Kahraba St, Doha
Tel: 422815, 422816, 422430
Cable: Al Hadith DH
Telex: 4342 Hadith DH
Telefax: 437002

Chairman: Bader Abdullah Darwish Fakhroo
Directors: Dr Majdi El Sherbini
Senior Executives: Hassan Ahmed Mahmoud Soliman
(Commercial Manager), Rahmat Ali Rahmat (Admin Manager)

PRINCIPAL ACTIVITIES: Department store supplying furniture,
carpets, clothing, shoes, luggage, perfumes, cosmetics,
cameras, radios, TV, tobacco products
Principal Agencies: Christofle, Samsonite Luggage, British
Luggage, Craven 'A' and Dunhill Cigarettes, Gillette Group,
Ronson, Dunhill, Sony, Yashica, Yardley, Shulton, Christian
Dior Perfumes and Clothings, Rochas, Guy Laroche, Lancome
Group, Chanel, Rolex and Piagett watches, Givenchy, Orlane,
Jean de D'Albret, Thermos, Dunlopillo & Dunlop Footwear,
John Tann Security Equipment, Clarks
Branch Offices: The Modern Home, Souk Ahmed Ali, Doha; The
Modern Home, Sh Abdul Aziz Bin Ahmed Street, Doha;
Dunhill Showroom, Souk Waqif, Doha; Shop at Oasis Hotel,
Doha
Parent Company: Abdulla Darwish Fakhroo Est
Principal Bankers: Standard Chartered Bank, Doha

Principal Shareholders: Heirs of Haj Abdulla Darwish Fakhroo
Date of Establishment: 1950
No of Employees: 130

MOHAMED ABDULRAHMAN AL BAHAR

See AL BAHAR, MOHAMED ABDULRAHMAN,

MOHD BUZWAIR ENGINEERING & CONTRACTING CO

See BUZWAIR, MOHD, ENGINEERING & CONTRACTING CO

MOHD YOUSUF AL KAWARI & SONS EST

See AL KAWARI, MOHD YOUSUF, & SONS EST

MOUCHEL MIDDLE EAST LTD

PO Box 7139, Doha
Tel: 420353
Telex: 4439 Nassa DH
Telefax: 420354

Directors: Peter R M Sproston (Resident Director)
Senior Executives: Keith Cogan (Resident Engineer)

PRINCIPAL ACTIVITIES: Civil and structural engineering
consultants, land surveyors
Parent Company: LG Mouchel & Partners, UK
Associated Companies: Mouchel Middle East Ltd, PO Box
26835 Safat, 13129 Kuwait, Tel 0965 5314620, Fax 0965
5339364

NAAMA CONTRACTING & TRADING CO

PO Box 23, Doha
Tel: 422124, 424405
Cable: Naama
Telex: 4269 Naama DH
Telefax: 427828

Chairman: Abdullah Ahmad Naama (also Managing Director)
Senior Executives: A Rahim Khan (Engineer in Charge of
Contracting Div), M A Sattar (Manager of Trading Div)

PRINCIPAL ACTIVITIES: Importers and commission agents,
contractors, sponsors, steel furniture, office furniture, safes,
drainage rods and plugs, etc
Principal Bankers: British Bank of the Middle East; Qatar
National Bank; Doha Bank Ltd

Principal Shareholders: Abdullah Ahmad Naama & Sons
Date of Establishment: January, 1952
No of Employees: 150

NASIR BIN ABDULLAH & MOHD SIDDIQ TRADING CO

N.A.M.S.

PO Box 329, Doha
Tel: 424249, 321486
Cable: UNICO-Doha
Telex: 4262 Unico Doha

Partners: Mian M Siddiq (Managing Partner), Sheikh Nasir Bin
Abdullah Al Ahmad Al Thani (Partner)
Senior Executives: Malik M Riaz (Manager), Syed Naseem
Ahmad (Group General Manager)

PRINCIPAL ACTIVITIES: Import and distribution of all types of
electrical and electronic appliances for domestic and
commercial use, cars, spare parts, and earthmoving
equipment, household items, kitchenware, crockery and
garments
Principal Agencies: National Home Appliances, JVC Electronics,
Fedders Central AC Units, Fides, Lombarde
(refrigerators/deep freezers, etc), Rimmel Cosmetics, Mazda
Pony, Chrysler, British Leyland, Kato, Kobelco, Telefunken
Colour TV, Zenith, Buster Brown, Janome, Brother, Ricoh,
Alba Watches
Branch Offices: Dubai (PO Box 2080); Abu Dhabi (PO Box
3672); Sharjah; and Sultanate of Oman
Subsidiary Companies: National Car Company; National
Engineering & Contracting Co; Nasir Siddiq Automobiles;
Nasir Siddiq Travels; National Electric & Decoration Co

Principal Bankers: United Bank Ltd; Doha Bank Ltd; Citibank;
Standard Chartered Bank; Banque Paribas, Doha

Date of Establishment: 1962
No of Employees: 1000 Approx.

NASIR BIN KHALID & SONS (NBK)

PO Box 82, Doha
Tel: 328211, 417388, 320037
Telex: 4203 Dh

Senior Executives: Munif Barghouthy (General Manager)

PRINCIPAL ACTIVITIES: Importers and dealers and contractors,
tenders & projects, transport, service station, tyres, spare
parts, lubricants, automobile agencies, carpentry and tiles
factory, heavy equipment, household appliances, engineering
Principal Agencies: Renault, Mercedes
Subsidiary/Associated Companies: Qatar Automobile; Doha
Petrol Station; Carpentry & Tiles Factory; Transport & Stores

NASSER TRADING & CONTRACTING CO

PO Box 1563, Doha
Tel: 422170, 423539
Cable: Nasser
Telex: 4439 Nasser DH
Telefax: 416980

Chairman: Sheikh Nasser Bin Ahmad Al Thani (also Proprietor)
Senior Executives: Joseph Ghanim (Manager Medical Section),
Salah Shaheen (Manager Contrating Section)

PRINCIPAL ACTIVITIES: General trading and contracting,
building and civil engineering; supply of medical equipment
and foodstuffs
Subsidiary Companies: Contractors International
Principal Bankers: Doha Bank, Doha

Date of Establishment: 1974
No of Employees: 108

NATIONAL CONTRACTING & TRADING CO

PO Box 637, Doha
Tel: 324092, 325873
Cable: ALAHMAD
Telex: 4099 NCT DH

Senior Executives: Mahdi El-Saheb (General Manager)

PRINCIPAL ACTIVITIES: Construction of office and residential
buildings; erection of steelwork, cladding; industrial turnkey
projects
Subsidiary/Associated Companies: Trade Promotion Centre
(Overseas) Ltd; Los Angeles, London & Cyprus
Principal Bankers: Qatar National Bank; Standard Chartered
Bank; Bank Almashrek; Doha Bank

Date of Establishment: 1960
No of Employees: Approx 350

NATIONAL INDUSTRIAL COMPANY

PO Box 235, Doha
Tel: 324531
Cable: Wibeco
Telex: 4203 NBKS DH
Telefax: 433652

Senior Executives: Fathi Al Asadi (Manager), Yahya Al Mahdy
(Agricultural Engineer)

PRINCIPAL ACTIVITIES: Agricultural materials, chemicals and
machinery also industrial chemicals
Principal Agencies: Ciba-Geigy, Switzerland; Union Carbide,
USA; Ferry Morse Seed Co, USA; Rohm and Hass, Italy;
Holder, West Germany; Ele International, UK; Soiltest Inc,
USA
Branch Offices: Dubai, Abu Dhabi
Principal Bankers: Banque Paribas

Date of Establishment: 1964

NATIONAL INDUSTRIAL CONTRACTING CO (NICC)

PO Box 3713, Doha
Tel: 883985/6/7, 883361, 887422
Cable: NICC
Telex: 4170 Nicc DH
Telefax: (974) 887511

Chairman: Sheikh Nasir Bin Khalid Althani (also Owner)
Directors: Hisham Dajani (Manager)
Senior Executives: Omer Mohsen (Chief Engineer), Dawoud S Tawil (Finance Manager), A Barghouthi (Project Engineer), Owni Kamel (Quantity Surveyor)

PRINCIPAL ACTIVITIES: Civil engineering contractors, water and sewerage networks
Parent Company: Nasir Bin Khalid & Sons
Principal Bankers: Arab Bank; Alahli Bank of Qatar; Qatar Islamic Bank
Financial Information:

	1989/90 QR'000
Sales turnover	33,688
Profits	1,866
Authorised capital	2,000
Paid-up capital	2,000
Total assets	30,996

Date of Establishment: 1972
No of Employees: 450

NATIONAL INDUSTRIAL GAS PLANTS

PO Box 1391, Doha
Tel: 324869, 433009, 422116, 428844, 411351, 427871, 432980, 810043
Cable: Oxygen
Telex: 4408 DH
Telefax: 974 435030

President: M H Almana
Vice President: Hamad Mohd Almana
Senior Executives: H M Khudair, A D K B Charles, Y Marei

PRINCIPAL ACTIVITIES: Production of industrial gas (oxygen, carbon dioxide, nitrogen, acetylene etc), medical gases (nitrous oxide and medical oxygen), liquid oxygen, liquid nitrogen and liquid argon; supply of other industrial gases (hydrogen, helium, chlorine and amonia), refrigeration gases and special high purity and ultra pure gases; stockists welding equipment, electrodes, welding rods, safety equipment, safety shoes, workwear, cutting & grinding discs, chemicals and rubber products
Principal Agencies: Murex (BOC) Welding Products, UK; Hancock Cutting Machines Ltd, UK; Alexandra Workwear Ltd, UK; Betts & Broughton, UK; Air Products Ltd, UK; Hoechst, Germany; Kestra, Germany; Hongkong European Mercantile Ltd, Hongkong; Trelleborg AB, Sweden; Faithful, UK; Rhone Poulenc Chemicals ISC Div, UK; Solvay Fluor & Derivate GmbH, Germany
Branch Offices: Dubai Oxygen Company, PO Box 11318, Dubai; Industrial Gas Company, PO Box 4279, Abu Dhabi, Riyadh Oxygen Company, PO Box 374, Riyadh, Saudi Arabia
Associated Companies: Gulf Gas Co; Almana Petrol Station, Qatar; Almana Lathe Work Shop, Qatar; International Gulf Trading Co, Qatar; National Tools & Trading Co, Qatar; Chubb Fire, Qatar; Gulf Lubricants, Qatar; Arabia Mechanical Engineering Workshop, Qatar; Electrical Engineering Centre, Qatar; Al Jazeerah Petrol Station, Qatar; K&H Readymix, Qatar; Concorde Trading Co, Abu Dhabi; Corodex Trading Co, Abu Dhabi
Principal Bankers: Grindlays Bank PLC, Doha
Financial Information:

	1990 US$'000
Sales turnover	30,000

Principal Shareholders: Sole Owner, M H Almana
Date of Establishment: 1954
No of Employees: 125

NATIONAL INSURANCE CO OF EGYPT

PO Box 207, Doha
Tel: 423424, 423422, 320872
Cable: Alinsure Doha
Telex: 4367 INSURE DH

Chairman: Dr Ahmed Fouad El Ansary
Directors: Ezzat Abd El Azim, Abd El Halim Mousa, Ahmed Talaat

PRINCIPAL ACTIVITIES: Insurance
Branch Offices: Head Offices in Egypt 41 Kasr El Nil St, Cairo, Telex 92372 INSUR and PO Box 446, Alexandria, Telex 54212 NICE, also branches in Kuwait, PO Box 2409 and UAE, PO Box 2558, Abu Dhabi
Parent Company: National Insurance Co of Egypt, Egypt
Principal Bankers: Arab Bank Ltd, Doha Bank Ltd, Bank of Oman Ltd, Citibank NA, Bank Al Mashrek

NATIONAL OIL DISTRIBUTION CO N.O.D.C.O.

PO Box 2244, Doha
Tel: 776555 (10 lines)
Cable: Nodco
Telex: 4324 Nodco DH
Telefax: 772880

Chairman: Abdullah Hussain Salat
Directors: M H El Hefnawi, M K Turki Al Sobai, Midhat Abdul Latif, Ali G Al Hagri, Hamed Al Bin Ali
Senior Executives: Dr Mahmood Hamid El Hefnawi (General Manager), Mohamed K T Al Sobai (Deputy General Manager), Ibrahim Bin Salem (Administration Manager), Abdul Hamid Abu El Saoud (Finance Manager)

PRINCIPAL ACTIVITIES: Refining and distribution of petroleum products
Branch Offices: Refinery at Umm Said (PO Box 50033), Tel 770651
Parent Company: Qatar General Petroleum Corporation
Principal Bankers: Qatar National Bank, Doha
Financial Information:

	1990 QR'000
Authorised capital	660,000
Paid-up capital	660,000

Principal Shareholders: 100% owned by Qatar General Petroleum Corporation
Date of Establishment: 1968
No of Employees: 600

NCR CORPORATION

PO Box 867, Doha
Tel: 671122/3/4
Cable: Nacareco Doha
Telex: 4841 NCR CO DH
Telefax: 671125

PRINCIPAL ACTIVITIES: Supplying, installing and maintaining of NCR computers and electronic data processing equipment
Branch Offices: Cyprus, Bahrain, Kuwait, Dubai, Abu Dhabi, Oman
Parent Company: NCR Corporation, Dayton, Ohio, USA
Principal Bankers: Standard Chartered Bank

NEW DOHA PALACE HOTEL

PO Box 710, Doha
Tel: 426131/2/3/4
Cable: Dohahotel
Telex: 4263 Newdph DH

Chairman: Sh Jassim Bin Khalid Al Thani

QATAR

Senior Executives: Fathi Q Samara (Managing Director)

PRINCIPAL ACTIVITIES: Hotel business
Principal Bankers: Al Ahli Bank of Qatar

NEW TRADE ENGINEERING CO
PO Box 5509, Doha
Tel: 444622
Telex: 4046 Neweng DH
Telefax: (974) 433141

Chairman: Sheikh Ghanem Bin Ali Al-Thani (Proprietor)
Directors: Aref M Akhal (General Manager)
Senior Executives: Marwan Barghouthi (Sales Manager), Rub
Nawaz Khan (Chief Accountant), Hany El Bendary (Service
Manager)

PRINCIPAL ACTIVITIES: Import and supply of heavy equipment,
cars, boats/marine equipment and air conditioners, stocking
of spare parts; fully supported by an experienced team of
engineers and comprehensive stock of spare parts
Principal Agencies: BMW, Magirus Deutz trucks, Flygt pumps,
Riva, Bayliner & Plancraft boats, Mariner outboard engines
Parent Company: Ghanem Al-Thani Holdings, PO Box 5319,
Doha, Qatar
Principal Bankers: Grindlays Bank; Standard Chartered Bank;
Qatar National Bank
Financial Information:

	1990 QR'000
Sales turnover	32,000
Profits	1,200
Authorised capital	30,000
Paid-up capital	30,000
Total assets	40,000

Date of Establishment: March 1978
No of Employees: Approx 100

OASIS HOTEL
PO Box 717, Doha
Tel: 424424
Telex: 4214 Oasis DH

PRINCIPAL ACTIVITIES: Hotel operation

ORIENT ARAB TRADING & CONTRACTING CO
PO Box 1632, Doha
Tel: 424035, 423405
Cable: Sharq Arabi
Telex: 4358 Oatco DH

Chairman: Mohd Bin Rashid Al-Khater
Senior Executives: Zeid Al-Zugheibi (General Manager)

PRINCIPAL ACTIVITIES: Garage equipment, tools and
accessories, welding and cutting equipment and accessories,
refrigeration and air conditioning products, hardware
Principal Bankers: Arab Bank Ltd

Date of Establishment: 1970
No of Employees: 25

ORIENTAL TRADING CO
PO Box 96, Rayyan Road, Doha
Tel: 423750, 423429
Cable: Oriental Doha
Telex: 4286 Orbet DH
Telefax: 418249

Chairman: Sh Jassim Bin Mohd Bin Jassim Althani
Directors: Sh Khalid Bin Jassim Althani, Sh Salman Bin Jassim
Althani, Sh Sultan Bin Jassim Althani
Senior Executives: Frank Ward (General Manager), Tony
McConnell (Technical Sales Manager), V S Narayanan
(Assistant Manager), V M Mathew (Accountant)

PRINCIPAL ACTIVITIES: Turnkey contractors, general
merchants, importers and distributors of heavy machinery;
pumps and air compressors, drilling equipment, diesel
engines, bearings and spare parts, generators, dumpers,
water desalination plant, electronics
Principal Agencies: Atlas Copco; SKF; Twaites Ltd; Lister-
Petter; Sidem; Pascon; Hawker Siddeley Power Plant
Parent Company: Petroserv Ltd, PO Box 7098, Doha, Qatar
Subsidiary Companies: National Pest Control Co
Principal Bankers: Banque Paribas; The British Bank of the
Middle East

Principal Shareholders: Sh Khalid Bin Jassim Althani, Sh
Salman Bin Jassim Althani, Sh Sultan Bin Jassim Althani
Date of Establishment: 1957
No of Employees: 40

ORYX FOR TRADING-INDUSTRY & CONTRACTING
PO Box 443, Doha
Tel: 426964
Cable: Abu Al Soud
Telex: 4166 Oryx DH

Chairman: A Aziz Fahed Bu Zwer
Directors: Riad Batarni (Manager)

PRINCIPAL ACTIVITIES: Import of aluminium frames, glass,
hardware, building materials, chemical materials and
prefabricated houses
Branch Offices: Orient Aluminium
Principal Bankers: Grindlays Bank

PENINSULAR PETROTECH ENGINEERING WLL
PO Box 4533, Doha
Tel: 432044/8
Telex: 5137 PETEC DH

PRINCIPAL ACTIVITIES: Fabrication and installation of
structural steel work, piping systems and pipelines,
installation of process equipment, and services to the
petroleum, petrochemical and fertiliser industry

PRICE WATERHOUSE
PO Box 6689, BBME Building, Doha
Tel: 415700
Telex: 4940 PW DH
Telefax: 416040

Senior Executives: D S Dunckley (Partner), D V Hurst (Partner),
C V Brown (Senior Manager)

PRINCIPAL ACTIVITIES: Public accountants and management
consultants

QATAR AUTOMOBILES CO
PO Box 1290, Doha
Tel: 426907, 323290
Cable: Automobiles
Telex: 4203 NBKS DH

Chairman: Nasser Bin Khalid

PRINCIPAL ACTIVITIES: Motor vehicle importers and
distributors
Principal Agencies: Chrysler; Mitsubishi
Parent Company: Nasser Bin Khalid Al Thani & Sons

QATAR BUILDING COMPANY
PO Box 1985, Doha
Tel: 426428, 426420
Cable: Tayebco Dh
Telex: 4381 Taybco DH
Telefax: 448376

Chairman: M T Mustafawi

Senior Executives: M B Browne (General Manager & Chief Engineer)

PRINCIPAL ACTIVITIES: Building, civil engineering
Subsidiary Companies: QBC Readymix; QBC Road Construction Division; QBC Precast

Principal Shareholders: Partnership
Date of Establishment: 1971
No of Employees: 500

QATAR CINEMA & FILM DISTRIBUTION CO SAQ

PO Box 1970, Doha
Tel: 671620, 671625
Cable: Cineqatar
Telex: 4037 Cinema DH

Chairman: SH Jassim Bin Khaled Al Thani
Directors: Yacoub Y Al Muharraqi

PRINCIPAL ACTIVITIES: Film supply and distribution
Principal Bankers: Qatar National Bank, Qatar Commercial Bank, Doha Bank
Financial Information:

	QR'000
Authorised capital	10,362
Paid-up capital	10,362

Date of Establishment: 1970
No of Employees: 57

QATAR COLD STORES

PO Box 1717, Doha
Tel: 422674, 418245, 419098
Cable: COLDSTORES
Telex: 4309 QCS DH

Chairman: Abdul Aziz Al Rehman Al-Darwish Al-Fakhroo
Senior Executives: Dr Magdi El Sherbini (Manager), Kamal El Assal (Commercial Manager)

PRINCIPAL ACTIVITIES: Wholesale and retail of foostuffs
Principal Agencies: Unilever Export, UK; Kimberley Clark, UK; Hochland Reich & Summer, West Germany; General Foods Corp, USA; Gerber Baby Foods, USA; Nestle; Libby's, Switzerland; Suchard Tobler, Switzerland; Strong & Co, Japan; Campbell Soup Co, USA
Branch Offices: Wakrah & Dukhan
Parent Company: Abdul Aziz Al Rehman Al-Darwish Al-Fakhroo Trading Est
Associated Companies: Darwish Motors & Trading Co
Principal Bankers: Qatar National Bank, Al Ahli Bank of Qatar

Principal Shareholders: Sole owner
Date of Establishment: 1960
No of Employees: 100

QATAR COMMUNICATIONS LTD

PO Box 2481, Doha
Tel: 424347, 424348
Telex: 4395 Dartra DH
Telefax: 426378

Directors: Hassan K Darwish (Managing Director), Nasser K Darwish (Executive Director)

PRINCIPAL ACTIVITIES: Electrical engineering and supplies, safety and security equipment, communication systems, computers; marine safety and navigational aids; operation and maintenance of Doha Maritime Coastal Radio Station; maintenance of all traffic signals in Qatar
Principal Agencies: LM Ericsson Telematerial AB; Farnell International; Racal Milgo; Koning en Hartman; Skanti; Racal Navigation; Racal Radar; RFD Limited; Millbank Electronics; Feedbank Instruments, Racal Instruments; Racal Recording; Racal Communications, Benson SA, Sogedex SA
Parent Company: Kassem Darwish Fakhroo and Sons

Principal Bankers: Standard Chartered Bank

Principal Shareholders: Solely owned by Kassem Darwish Fakhroo
Date of Establishment: 1972
No of Employees: 45

QATAR COMPUTER SERVICES WLL

PO Box 5711, Doha
Tel: 441101, 441212
Cable: COMPUTER
Telex: 4137 GG DH
Telefax: 441102

Chairman: Abdulla Salem Al Sulaiteen
Senior Executives: S M R Sarma (Executive Manager), A R Khan (Service Manager)

PRINCIPAL ACTIVITIES: Sale of computer and software systems; software support
Principal Agencies: WANG Lab Inc, Lans, Acer Computers; OKI Printers, Ashtontate, Accodata
Financial Information:

	1990 QR'000
Sales turnover	7,000
Profits	30%
Authorised capital	2,000

Date of Establishment: March 1978
No of Employees: 18

QATAR CONSTRUCTION & DEV CO

Qatar Construction & Development Co

PO Box 1421, Doha
Tel: 329885, 329293, 432545
Cable: SALMIN
Telex: 4294 Gcdc DH
Telefax: 432543

Chairman: Salmin Bin Khalid Al Sowaidi
Directors: Sameer M Fahmi (Managing Director)

PRINCIPAL ACTIVITIES: Civil engineering, road construction, readymixed concrete and precast concrete suppliers, asphalt and aggregate manufacturers
Subsidiary Companies: Salmeen Bin Khalid Trading & Contracting Est
Principal Bankers: Doha Bank
Financial Information:

	1989/90 QR'000
Sales turnover	19,688
Profits	2,172
Authorised capital	18,377
Paid-up capital	5,000
Total assets	22,600

Date of Establishment: 1955
No of Employees: 300

QATAR DAIRY COMPANY

PO Box 4770, Doha
Tel: 803814, 806165
Cable: QADARICO
Telex: 4430 QPLAS DH
Telefax: 802002

Chairman: Brig Mohammad Bin Abdullah Al Attiya
Directors: Abdullah Mohammad Al Attiya (General Manager), Abdulaziz Mohammad Al Attiya (Asst General Manager), Khalid Mohammad Al Attiya (Asst General Manager)
Senior Executives: Fred Draper (Dairy Technologist), Ian A Cheyne (Chief Veterinarian)

PRINCIPAL ACTIVITIES: Production of fresh homogenized, pasteurised milk, yoghurt, laban, labneh, cheese

Principal Bankers: Qatar National Bank; Arab Bank

Date of Establishment: 1973
No of Employees: 50

QATAR DANISH DAIRY COMPANY

PO Box 9310, Doha
Tel: 601107
Cable: QADDCO
Telex: 4972 QADDCO DH

Chairman: Omar Almana
Senior Executives: Salah Osman (Manager Finance & Administration)

PRINCIPAL ACTIVITIES: Production of fruit juices, ice creams and all dairy products
Parent Company: Almana Group, Qatar
Principal Bankers: Al Ahli Bank, Doha

Principal Shareholders: Sheikh Ahmed Bin Seif Al Thani, Mr Omar Almana
Date of Establishment: 1981
No of Employees: 65

QATAR ENTERPRISES & TRADING CO

PO Box 6671, Doha
Tel: 441295
Telex: 4179

Chairman: Nasser Abdullah Al Nuaimi
Directors: Mohd Bin Hamad Al Khalifa (Vice Chairman)
Senior Executives: G S Mohan (Deputy General Manager)

PRINCIPAL ACTIVITIES: Trading and contracting, catering services, gas supply, etc
Subsidiary Companies: Al Mehwar; Gulf Gas Supply; Qatar Catering Services

QATAR FERTILISER CO SAQ
Q.A.F.C.O.

PO Box 50001, Umm Said
Tel: 770252
Cable: Qafco
Telex: 4215 Qafco DH
Telefax: (974) 770347

Directors: Fouad Al Mahmoud (Executive Deputy Chairman), Sh Abdul Rahman Bin Jabor AlThani, Abdul Aziz Hamad Al Dulaimi, Ibrahim Nooh Al Mutawa, Sultan Al Kuwari, Abdel Rab El Malki, J B Holte
Senior Executives: Arnt Almendingen (Managing Director), Benjamin Brubakken (Financial Manager), Leif Fykerud (Personnel & Organisation Manager), Abdul Redha Abdul Rahman Ali (Deputy General Manager & Production Manager), Hakon Gran (Maintenance Manager)

PRINCIPAL ACTIVITIES: Production of liquid ammonia and urea fertilizers (46% nitrogen)
Principal Agencies: Worldwide Marketing: Norsk Hydro a.s, Oslo, Norway
Principal Bankers: Qatar National Bank SAQ, Doha; Hambros Bank Ltd, London
Financial Information:

	1990 QR'000
Authorised capital	100,000
Paid-up capital	100,000

Principal Shareholders: Qatar General Petroleum Corporation (75%), Norsk Hydro AS (25%)
Date of Establishment: 1969
No of Employees: 800

QATAR FLOUR MILLS CO (SAQ)

PO Box 1444, Doha
Tel: 770452, 671816, 671571, 671235
Telex: 4285 Flour DH
Telefax: 671611

Chairman: Sh Ahmed Bin Abdullah Al Thani
Directors: Sh Jabor Bin Mohammed Al Thani (Deputy Chairman), Sh Abdulla Bln Mohammed Al Thani, Sh Abdul Aziz Bin Mohammed Al Thani, Omer Al Mana, Abdulla Ali Al Nasari, Abdul Hadi Haider, Hussain Ali Kamal, Ibrahim Darhalli, Abdulla Ali Akber Al Ansari
Senior Executives: Ghazi Abdul Halim El Salimi (General Manager)

PRINCIPAL ACTIVITIES: Wheat, flour milling, bakery
Principal Bankers: Doha Bank
Financial Information:

	1990 QR'000
Authorised capital	12,564
Paid-up capital	12,564

Date of Establishment: 1969
No of Employees: 89

QATAR GAS COMPANY

PO Box 2954, Doha
Tel: 86252
Telex: 4500 DH

Senior Executives: Mohamed Al Amin Ali Orabi

PRINCIPAL ACTIVITIES: Utilisation and extraction of propane, butane and fuel from associated gas in the producing oilfields of Shell Co

Principal Shareholders: Qatar General Petroleum Corp (70%), Shell International (30%)

QATAR GAS IMPORT & DISTRIBUTION CO

PO Box 1140, Doha
Tel: 421892, 423262, 426020
Cable: Algas

PRINCIPAL ACTIVITIES: Import marketing and distribution of gascookers, water heaters
Principal Agencies: Ariston; Primus Sievert; Arj; Vaillant

QATAR GENERAL INSURANCE & REINSURANCE CO SAQ

PO Box 4500, Ras Abu Aboud Street, Doha
Tel: 417800, 425450
Cable: Genins Doha
Telex: 4742 Genins Dh, 4877 Genins Dh
Telefax: 437302

Chairman: Sheikh Ali Bin Saoud Al Thani
Senior Executives: Ghazi Abu Nahel (General Manager), Adham N Idrissi (Executive General Manager)

PRINCIPAL ACTIVITIES: All classes of insurance and reinsurance
Branch Offices: Jasra Branch, Tel 326314, Alkhor Branch, Tel 720974; Al Musherib Sofitel Branch, Tel 436620; Industrial Salwa Branch; in UAE: Dubai Branch, Tel 212500 & 212508, Telex 48878 GEINCO EM
Principal Bankers: Qatar National Bank; Bank Al Mashrek; Arab Bank; Al Ahli Bank of Qatar
Financial Information:

	QR'000
Authorised capital	15,000
Paid-up capital	15,000

Principal Shareholders: Sh Ali Bin Soud Bin Thani Al Thani; Sh Jasim Bin Mohd Bin Jasim Althani; Rashid Faisal Al Naimi and Messrs Pertroserv
Date of Establishment: 1979
No of Employees: 90

QATAR GENERAL PETROLEUM CORPORATION

PO Box 3212, Doha
Tel: 491491 (15 lines)
Cable: Petrol, Doha
Telex: 4343 Petcor DH
Telefax: 831125

Chairman: HE Sheikh Abdul Aziz Bin Khalifa Al-Thani
Members of Board: HE Dr Hassan Kamel (Vice Chairman), HE Issa Al Kuwari, Dr Jaber A Al Marri (Managing Director), Abdulla Salatt, Sheikh Abdulrahman Bin Mohammed Bin Jabr Al Thani, Fu'ad Al-Mahamoud
Senior Executives: Dr Jaber A Al Marri (Managing Director/Acting General Manager North Field Project), Mohammed Saud Al Dulaimi (Deputy Executive Manager Onshore Operations), Ajlan Al Kawari (Deputy Executive Manager Offshore Operations), Faisal Al Suwaidi (Administration Manager), Jum'a Al Boainain (Manager Personnel Dept), Farouk Abdullah Na'ma (Planning Manager), Abdulaziz Al Dulaimi (Exploration & Production Manager), Dr Hamad Khalifa Al Binali (Manufacturing & Investments Manager), Dr Khaled Al Shawi (Legal Dept Manager), Ibrahim Al Mutawa (Marketing & Transport Manager), Nassir M Al Nuaimi (Manager Services Dept), Isam Al Din Saed (Finance Manager), Abdulla Zaid Al Taleb (Information & Computer Services Manager), Ahmed Ali Al Boainain (A/Manager Public Relations Dept), Jassim Ibrahim Al Siddiqi (A/Manager Training Dept)

PRINCIPAL ACTIVITIES: Exploration, drilling, production, refining, transport and storage of oil, natural gas and other hydrocarbons and hydrocarbon derivatives and by-products. Trading, distribution, sale and export of hydrocarbon compounds
Branch Offices: Offshore Division, Onshore Division
Subsidiary/Associated Companies: National Oil Distribution Co (NODCO) (100%); Qatar Fertilizer Co Ltd (QAFCO) (75%); Qatar Petrochemical Co Ltd (QAPCO) (84%); Qatar Liquified Gas Co Ltd (QATARGAS) (77.5%); Norselore Company, France (7%); Arab Maritime Petroleum Transport Co, Kuwait (13.6%); Arab Shipbuilding and Repair Yard Co (ASRY); Bahrain (18.8%); Arab Petroleum Pipeline Co (SUMED), Egypt (5%); Arab Petroleum Investments Corp, Saudi Arabia (10%); Arab Petroleum Services Co, Libya (10%)
Principal Bankers: Qatar National Bank
Financial Information:

	1990 QR'million
Authorised capital	5,000

Principal Shareholders: State-owned corporation
Date of Establishment: August 1974
No of Employees: 5,550

QATAR GENERAL PETROLEUM CORPORATION (OFFSHORE OPERATIONS)

PO Box 47, Doha
Tel: 422514, 402437
Telex: 4201 QATOFF DH
Telefax: 402509, 402752

Senior Executives: Ajlan Al Kuwari (Deputy Executive Manager)

PRINCIPAL ACTIVITIES: Exploration and production of petroleum from the offshore oil and gas fields
Parent Company: Qatar General Petroleum Corporation

QATAR GENERAL PETROLEUM CORPORATION (ONSHORE OPERATIONS)

PO Box 70, Doha
Tel: 343287
Telex: 4253 QPADOH DH
Telefax: 444554

Directors: Sheikh Rashid O Al Thani (Managing Director), A K Howard (Executive Manager)

PRINCIPAL ACTIVITIES: Drilling, extraction, production, operations and export of crude oil and natural gas liquids
Parent Company: Qatar General Petroleum Corporation

No of Employees: 1,500

QATAR INDUSTRIES CO

PO Box 2345, Doha
Tel: 425669
Cable: Comico
Telex: 4278 DH

Chairman: Sheikh Muhd Hamad Al Thani
Senior Executives: Issa M Dauleh (General Manager)

PRINCIPAL ACTIVITIES: Stone crushing plants, quarries, transport, carpentry, mechanical engineering, steel erections
Parent Company: Muhd Al Thani & Sons Est
Associated Companies: Contracting & Trading Est; Commercial Industrial Co; Trans-Orient Air Services; Doha Travel Agency; Trans-Arabian Travel Agency
Principal Bankers: Grindlays Bank; United Bank Ltd; Bank of Oman Ltd

QATAR INSURANCE CO SAQ

Po Box 666, Doha
Tel: 831555 (10 lines)
Cable: Tamin Dh
Telex: 4216 Tamin DH

Chairman: Abdulla Hussain Naama
Directors: Ahmed Mannai (Deputy Chairman), State of Qatar, Ahmed Al Sowaidi, Abdul Ghani Abdul Ghani, Kassem and Abdullah Sons of Darwish Fakhroo, Jaidah Motors & Trading Co, Qatar National Navigation & Transport Co Ltd
Senior Executives: Fathi Ibrahim Gabr (General Manager), Mahmood Mufti (Deputy General Manager), Abdulla Marie (Financial & Administrative Manager)

PRINCIPAL ACTIVITIES: Insurance (all classes except life)
Branch Offices: Branches in Qatar: Souq Wakif, Doha, Tel 423052, 433822; Traffic Area, Doha, Tel 866371; Regional Branches: Riyadh, Saudi Arabia, PO Box 16729, Tel 4050169, 4056610, Telex 203479 QICRBR SJ; Deira, Dubai, UAE, PO Box 4066, Tel 224045, 223819, Telex 48067 TAMIN EM
Principal Bankers: Qatar National Bank; Commercial Bank of Qatar; Doha Bank Ltd
Financial Information:

	QR'000
Authorised capital	24,000
Paid-up capital	24,000

Principal Shareholders: Government of Qatar
Date of Establishment: 1964
No of Employees: 125

QATAR INTERNATIONAL COMMERCIAL CO

PO Box 2544, Doha
Tel: 321888, 421860, 426780, 426947, 872476
Cable: Qatarna
Telex: 4303 Qatrna DH; 4803 Ctlyts DH

Directors: Shaikh Ali Bin Ahmed Althani (Managing Director)
Senior Executives: Abboud A Mahfooz (General Manager), M Hameed Mohammed (Sales Manager)

PRINCIPAL ACTIVITIES: Electrical engineering, import and distribution of electrical appliances and equipment, building materials and machinery, lighting equipment
Principal Agencies: Dawson Keith Electric Ltd, UK; GEC Ltd, UK; American Standard, USA; Ideal Standard, West Germany
Subsidiary Companies: Qatar International Contracting Co
Principal Bankers: Grindlays Bank; Citibank

Date of Establishment: 1973

QATAR

QATAR INTERNATIONAL TRADING & INDUSTRIAL CO

Q.I.T.I.C.O.

PO Box 3211, Doha
Tel: 671443, 671393
Cable: Qitico Doha
Telex: 4449 TATCO DH

Chairman: Hamad Abu Salaa
Directors: Abdulla Abu Salaa, Fahed S Kawari, Farid Nakhla
(Managing Director)

PRINCIPAL ACTIVITIES: Trading; electrical, mechanical, civil
contracting; communication equipment, industrial catering
Principal Agencies: Harris Corp, USA; ABELA, Monaco;
Horwood, UK; Enka, Turkey; Snamprogetti, Italy; Complete
Pool Chemicals, UK
Parent Company: Qitico Head Office
Subsidiary Companies: Qitico - Industrial Projects Division;
Qatar International Communications; Catering Division;
Mechanical Services Division
Principal Bankers: Commercial Bank of Qatar Ltd, Doha

Date of Establishment: 1975

QATAR ISLAMIC BANK

PO Box 559, Grand Hamad Avenue, Doha
Tel: 409409 (20 lines)
Telex: 5177 Islamb Dh
Telefax: 412700

Chairman: Sheikh Abdul Rahman Bin Abdullah Al Mahmood
Directors: Abdul Rahman Essa Al Mannai (Vice Chairman),
Khalid Bin Ahmed Al Sowidi (Managing Director), Abdullah
Mohammed Al Dabbagh, Mohammed Hamad Al Manna, Abdul
Aziz Bin Saad Al Saad, Ahmed Ebrahim Seddiqi Al Emadi,
Hamad Bin Nasser Bin Jassem Al Thani, Nasser Bin
Mohammed Al Fehaid Al Hajiri, Saad Bin Fahad Al Mobarak,
Abdul Hadi Trahib Bin Nayfa Al Shahwani
Senior Executives: Ahmed Ebrahim Seddiqi Al Emadi (General
Manager), Bakr M Al Raihan (Asst General Manager Planning,
Research & Information), Rashid Saleem (Asst General
Manager International), Maher M Duweik (Executive Manager
Banking Operations), Walid Khalid (Manager Investment),
Ismail Khafagi (Manager Corporate Finance), Mohd Jassim
(Manager Public Relations), Nabil Osman (Manager Domestic
Banking), Abdul Rahman Khan (Manager EDP), Syed Khizer
Ahmed (Controller Treasury Dept), Taher Ahmad Bafagih
(Controller Foreign Exchange Dealing)

PRINCIPAL ACTIVITIES: Islamic banking
Branch Offices: Gharafa Br, Tel 866656, Fax 866056, Telex
5178; Salwa Road Br, Tel 881667, Fax 880123, Telex 5154;
Alkhor Br, Tel 721666, Fax 721888, Telex 4149
Subsidiary Companies: Al Jazeera Investment Co, PO Box
22310, Doha, Tel 882855, Fax 880058
Financial Information:

	1990
	QR'000
Deposits	1,793
Net profit	56
Authorised capital	200
Paid-up capital	100
Reserves	94
Total assets	2,046

Date of Establishment: 1983
No of Employees: 165

QATAR MONETARY AGENCY

PO Box 1234, Doha
Tel: 325987
Telex: 4335 DH

PRINCIPAL ACTIVITIES: Central banking

Principal Shareholders: State-owned

QATAR NATIONAL BANK SAQ

PO Box 1002, Doha
Tel: 413511 (20 lines)
Cable: Qatarbank
Telex: 4212; 4357; 4064; 4635 Qatbank DH
Telefax: 413753

Chairman: HE Sheikh Abdul Aziz Bin Khalifa Althani
Directors: HE Saleh Abo Dawood Al Muhanadi (Vice Chairman),
Dr Jaber Al Marri, Yousef Kamal, Sheikh Hamad Bin Faisal Al
Thani, Yousef Qassem Darwish, Ahmed Al Mannai, Mohamed
Marzouq Al Shamlan, Abdul Aziz Salat, Haider Suleiman
Haider
Senior Executives: Hany Osman Al Dana (General Manager),
Saeed Al Misnad (Deputy General Manager)

PRINCIPAL ACTIVITIES: Commercial banking
Branch Offices: 16 branches and offices in Qatar, 2 branches in
UK, 1 branch in Paris, 1 branch in the Cayman Islands
Financial Information:

	1988/89	1989/90
	QR'000	QR'000
Total deposits	7,796,040	7,526,907
Profits	201,147	207,021
Authorised capital	126,000	189,000
Paid-up capital	126,000	189,000
Total assets	10,809,071	11,095,080

Principal Shareholders: Government of Qatar (50%), Qatari
shareholders (50%)
Date of Establishment: 1965
No of Employees: 402

QATAR NATIONAL CEMENT CO SAQ

PO Box 1333, Doha
Tel: 412691, 423098, 421688 (office), 711811 (factory)
Cable: Qatarcement
Telex: 4337 Cement DH
Telefax: 974-417846

Chairman: Abdullah Hussain Salatt
Directors: Abdul Aziz Yousuf Al Kholefi, Mohamed Bargash Al
Noaimi, Salem Bati Al Noaimi, Khalil Redwani, Mohamed Al
Shamlan, AHmed Al Asiri, Khalid Ahmed Al Suwaidi
Senior Executives: Eng Saeed Mubarak Al Kuwari (General
Manager)

PRINCIPAL ACTIVITIES: Manufacture of cement, Portland
cement and sulphate-resistant cement, calcined lime and
hydrated lime
Branch Offices: Factory at Umm Bab
Principal Bankers: Al Ahli Bank of Qatar, Commercial Bank of
Qatar, Qatar National Bank
Financial Information:

	1990
	QR'000
Sales turnover	57,270
Profits	21,070
Authorised capital	65,007
Paid-up capital	65,007
Total assets	310,729

Principal Shareholders: Private interests (57%), Government
(43%)
Date of Establishment: 1965
No of Employees: 430

QATAR NATIONAL IMPORT & EXPORT CO

PO Box 490, Doha
Tel: 422577, 851154
Cable: Khiyamco
Telex: 4396 DH

Chairman: Ihsan Khiyami
Directors: Waleed Khiyami, Mohammed Khiyami

PRINCIPAL ACTIVITIES: Import of foodstuffs, especially frozen
  foods; chicken & meat; manufacture of ice cream, yoghurt,
  fruit juices and milk, also import of canned food and dairy
  products
Subsidiary Companies: Qatar Super Dairies Co; Umara Ltd;
  Doha
Principal Bankers: Qatar National Bank, United Bank, Citibank,
  Commercial Bank of Qatar

Date of Establishment: 1957
No of Employees: 80

QATAR NATIONAL NAVIGATION & TRANSPORT CO LTD

PO Box 153, Doha
Tel: (974) 321175, 422245, 434911
Cable: Navigation Doha
Telex: 4206 Melaha DH
Telefax: (974) 320921

Chairman: Ali Bin Khalifa Al Hitmi
Senior Executives: Abdulaziz H Salatt (Chief Executive)

PRINCIPAL ACTIVITIES: Sole shipping agents for all cargo
  vessels and passenger liners; shipowners; chartering agents;
  stevedores; clearance and forwarding agents; lighterage
  contractors; offshore services; gulf feedering and coastal
  transport; shiprepairs and fabrication yard; international land
  transport; trading agencies; claims and P & I representatives,
  travel agency; dredging, bunkering services, offshore
  construction and maintenance; sub sea services;
  anticorrosion contractors
Principal Agencies: Agents for Hino, Japan; KHD-Deutz, W
  Germany; Griesheim, W Germany; Hoogerwerff Staalkabel,
  Holland; Dong Yang Rope, Korea; Astran, etc
Branch Offices: Dubai, UAE and Abu Dhabi, UAE
Principal Bankers: Qatar National Bank; British Bank of the
  Middle East; Standard Chartered Bank; Bank of Oman
Financial Information:

	1988/89 QR'000	1989/90 QR'000
Sales turnover	369,676	396,243
Profits	51,357	71,023
Authorised capital	54,212	62,348
Paid-up capital	54,212	62,348
Total assets	780,636	826,172

Principal Shareholders: Qataris
Date of Establishment: 1958
No of Employees: 1,097

QATAR NATIONAL PLASTIC FACTORY

PO Box 5615, Doha
Tel: 803198 (3 lines)
Telex: 4430 QPLAS DH
Telefax: 802002

Chairman: HE Mohd Bin Abdullah Al-Attiya
Directors: Abdullah bin Mohd Al-Attiya (General Manager),
  Abdulaziz Mohammad Al Attiya (Asst General Manager)
Senior Executives: Abdullateef Abdulhalim (Production
  Manager), Paul Varghese (Sales Manager)

PRINCIPAL ACTIVITIES: Manufacturers of PVC pipes and
  fittings; low density polyethylene pipe, sheet, sleeving and
  bags (printed and plain); high density polyethylene bags

Principal Bankers: Qatar National Bank, Arab Bank Ltd
Date of Establishment: 1977
No of Employees: 80

QATAR NATIONAL TRADING & CONTRACTING

PO Box 1774, Doha
Tel: 325180
Telex: 4506

Senior Executives: Youssef Abu Ghaidah (General Manager)

PRINCIPAL ACTIVITIES: Civil engineering, contracting and
  general trading
Associated Companies: Abdullah Abdulghani & Bros

QATAR PETROCHEMICAL COMPANY Q.A.P.C.O.

PO Box 756, Doha
Tel: Doha: 321105, 323805, Umm Said: 770111
Cable: Qapco Doha
Telex: 4361 QAPCO DH, 4871 QAPS DH

Directors: Sheikh Rashed Awaida Al Thani(Vice-Chairman)
Senior Executives: Michel Fenain (General Manager)

PRINCIPAL ACTIVITIES: Operation of a petrochemical plant
  with an annual a capacity of 170,000 tons of LDPE, 50,000
  tons of solid sulphur and 280,000 tons of ethylene
Parent Company: Qatar General Petroleum Corporation (Qatar);
  CdF Chimie SA (France)
Principal Bankers: Qatar National Bank, Banque Paribas, Bank
  Al Mashrek
Financial Information:

	QR'000
Authorised capital	436,000
Paid-up capital	436,000

Principal Shareholders: 84% owned by Qatar General Petroleum
  Corporation, 16% foreign company (CDF-Chimie France)
Date of Establishment: 1974
No of Employees: 627

QATAR POWER CONSTRUCTION EST

PO Box 1297, Doha
Tel: 421922, 427614, 884922, 884010
Telex: 4442 Balkil DH

PRINCIPAL ACTIVITIES: Electrical, mechanical and multi-service
  engineering contractors
Parent Company: Jassim Bin Khalid JBK
Associated Companies: Balfour Kilpatrick International Ltd (UK)

QATAR STEEL COMPANY LTD Q.A.S.C.O.

PO Box 50090, Umm·Said
Tel: 770011
Cable: Qasco Doha
Telex: 4606 Qasco DH

Chairman: Mohd Said Al Mis'hal
Directors: Ahmed Mohamed Ali Al Subaie (Vice Chairman),
  Ibrahim Hamad Al Badr, Yousuf Hussain Kamal, S Yoshimura,
  Hiroshi Hasegawa (General Manager), Hye Baiesha

PRINCIPAL ACTIVITIES: Production of steel bars (Deformed
  and plain with diameters from 10mm to 32mm)
Branch Offices: PO Box 689, Doha, Qatar
Principal Bankers: Qatar National Bank, Bank Almashrek, Doha
  Bank Ltd

Principal Shareholders: The Qatari government (70%) and two
  Japanese companies Kobe Steel (20%) and Tokyo Boeki
  (10%)
Date of Establishment: October 1974
No of Employees: 1,200

QATAR TRACTOR & EQUIPMENT CO

PO Box 5257, Doha
Tel: 428709, 419021
Cable: Al Khouri
Telex: 4580 VICTOR DH

PRINCIPAL ACTIVITIES: Dealing in heavy machinery and spare parts, compressors and jack hammers, concrete vibrators, compactors, tyres and water pumps
Principal Agencies: Babcock-Allatt Finishers; Gilson Concrete Mixers; Clark Swimming Pools; Jonlaw Generators, CCL Plant; Vibromax Rollers; Conmech; IPD Spares
Principal Bankers: British Bank of the Middle East; Doha Bank

Date of Establishment: 1977

QATAR TRADING CO

PO Box 51, Doha
Tel: 323773, 431166, 432004, 432007
Telex: 4045 Qatco DH

Chairman: Mohammed M Al Shamlan (also Managing Partner)

PRINCIPAL ACTIVITIES: General trading, import and distribution of auto spare parts, heavy machinery, electrical and electronic equipment, tools and equipment, garage equipment, precision measuring instruments
Principal Agencies: Goodyear Tire, Arcos, Varta Batteries (Germany), Alemite Lubrication Equipment, Hazet Tools, Bosch Power Tools, Snap-On tools; Bem Muller garage equipment; Ti Crypton garage equipment; Fill-Rite fluid handling and dispensing equipment; PCL tyre inflation equipment; Merkel packings and seals; Forney arc welders; Silver Beauty battery chargers; Elektra wood working machines; Card Schlieper (Germany) hand tools; Goodyear industrial rubber products
Branch Offices: Goodyear Division, Musherib Street, PO Box 51, Doha, Tel 423418, Telex 4045 Qatco DH; Tools and Equipment Division, Sharin Al-Asmakh, PO Box 51, Doha, Tel 323773, 431166, 432004
Parent Company: Qatar Trading Co, Marzooq Shamlan and Sons, PO Box 51
Principal Bankers: Qatar National Bank; Commercial Bank of Qatar
Financial Information:

	QR'000
Sales turnover	12,000
Paid-up capital	3,000

Date of Establishment: 1954

RABBAN CONTRACTING & TRADING CO

PO Box 885, Doha
Tel: 423296, 422723
Telex: 4236 DH

Directors: Khalid Mohammed Al Rabban (General Manager)
Senior Executives: Issam Abdul Baki

PRINCIPAL ACTIVITIES: General trading and engineering contracting, import and distribution of timber, paints, building materials, production of tiles

RAFCO

PO Box 831, Doha
Tel: 328397, 423678
Cable: Rafco
Telex: 4270 Rafco DH

Chairman & Managing Director: Abdul Rahman Khalid Al-Khater

PRINCIPAL ACTIVITIES: Import and distribution of decorative building materials (interior furnishings), lighting equipment, survey equipment, precision instruments, boats, yachts and other marine equipment
Principal Agencies: Wild Heerbrugg, Switzerland; Bega, W Germany; Salubra, Switzerland; Dryad Metal Works, UK; AMF, USA; Heuga Overseas, UK; Int Accoustic, Belgium;

Orac Decor, Belgium; Ernst Leitz, W Germany; Outboard Marine, Belgium; Erco, W Germany; Zumtobel, Austria
Principal Bankers: British Bank of the Middle East, Doha; Qatar National Bank, Doha; Bank of Oman Ltd, Doha

Principal Shareholders: A K Al-Khater
Date of Establishment: 1968
No of Employees: 54

RAKO THE ENGINEERING CONTRACTING & GENERAL TRADING CO

PO Box 1139, Doha
Tel: 422015, 418768, 440234
Cable: Rako
Telex: 4640 Rako DH

Chairman: Issa Lahdan Al Mohanadi
Directors: Mohammad Issa Al Mohanadi
Senior Executives: Eng Mostafa Mashhour (Asst General Manager)

PRINCIPAL ACTIVITIES: General contracting and trading
Subsidiary Companies: RAKO Road Construction; RAKO Elec; RAKO Aluminium; RAKO Carpentry & Joinery
Principal Bankers: British Bank of the Middle East, Doha; Qatar National Bank SAQ, Doha; Grindlays Bank, Doha
Financial Information:

	QR'000
Authorised capital	3,000
Paid-up capital	3,000

No of Employees: 300

RAMADA RENAISSANCE HOTEL DOHA

PO Box 1768, Doha
Tel: 321321
Cable: Ramada
Telex: 4664 Ramada DH

Directors: Jose Von Gross

PRINCIPAL ACTIVITIES: Hotel
Branch Offices: Atlanta, Boston, Chicago, Dallas, Detroit, Houston, Los Angeles, Miami, New York, St. Louis, Washington, Toronto, Mexico, Tokyo, Osaka, Sydney, Frankfurt, London, Paris, Jonkoping, Brussels, Dusseldorf
Principal Bankers: Commercial Bank of Qatar

Principal Shareholders: Owned by Ghanem Al-Thani Holdings, WLL; Managed by Ramada Hotels International
Date of Establishment: 1979
No of Employees: 300

RAZAK TRADING & CONTRACTING CO

PO Box 1820, Doha
Tel: 421887, 422190
Cable: Alrazak Doha
Telex: 4104 Razak DH

Chairman: Abdul Razak Abdulla (Proprietor)
Senior Executives: R Desmonde (Managing Director), George Verghese (Engineer), M A Quddoos (Manager, Trading), George Cameron (Chief Quantity Surveyor)

PRINCIPAL ACTIVITIES: Civil contracting, trading in building materials, paints and electrical goods, commission agency
Principal Agencies: Bartoline Ltd, UK; Glolite Electricals, Bombay; Flex, W Germany
Principal Bankers: Grindlays Bank, Doha

No of Employees: 150

READYMIX (QATAR) WLL

PO Box 5007, Doha
Tel: 853070/1/2
Telex: 4668 RMQ DH
Telefax: 851534

Senior Executives: W D Forde (General Manager)

PRINCIPAL ACTIVITIES: Readymix concrete and quarry products

REDCO GROUP WLL

PO Box 2195, Doha
Tel: 328645/46, 439162
Telex: 4728 REDCO DH
Telefax: 436339

Chairman: Sheikh Abdul Rahman Bin Nasir Al Thani
Directors: Saif Ur Rehman Khan (Managing Director), Mujib Ur Rehman Khan (Deputy managing Director), Amanullah Khan (Director)
Senior Executives: John Vernon Hughes (Projects Manager), Asad Khan (Sales Manager)

PRINCIPAL ACTIVITIES: Trading, construction and manufacturing, oil field services, paints, kitchens, transport, precast manufacturing of construction units, waterproofing and heat insulation and mineral water bottling plant
Principal Agencies: ABT and QNCC for Cement; Silkbourne Exports, UK; Uniplast, Italy; Mineralite, UK; Dow Chemicals, ICI
Branch Offices: Redco Saudi Arabia, Riyadh
Parent Company: Redco Group WLL
Subsidiary Companies: Redco Pak(Pvt) Ltd, Pakistan
Principal Bankers: Bank of Oman, Doha; United Bank Ltd, Doha; Qatar National Bank, Doha

Principal Shareholders: Sh Abdul Rehman Bin Nasir Al Thani; Saif Ur Rehman Khan
Date of Establishment: 1981
No of Employees: 450

RELIANT CO

PO Box 2089, Doha
Tel: 321579, 418181
Cable: Reliant
Telex: 4207 DH

Chairman: Ali Bin Ali
Directors: Hassan Ali Bin Ali (General Manager - Qatar), Nouri Al-Bahrani (Assistant General Manager)

PRINCIPAL ACTIVITIES: Mechanical and electrical contractors
Principal Bankers: Grindlays Bank; Qatar National Bank; Doha Bank
Financial Information:

	QR'000
Authorised capital	4,000
Paid-up capital	4,000

Principal Shareholders: Owned by Ali Bin Ali
Date of Establishment: 1965
No of Employees: 800

RELIANT TRADING ALI BIN ALI EST

PO Box 75, Doha
Tel: 441621
Cable: Binali Doha
Telex: 4234 Binali DH
Telefax: 433778

President: Adel Ali Bin Ali
Directors: Nabil Ali Bin Ali (Vice President)
Senior Executives: T Ghazal (General Manager), Mohd Hafez (Finance & Admin Manager), Saleh Taweel (Manager of Reliant Trading Div)

PRINCIPAL ACTIVITIES: Trading in household and consumer goods, pharmaceutical & cosmetic products, electrical appliances
Principal Agencies: Gist Brocades, Holland; Impex, France; ROC, France; Wella, W Germany; Knoll, W Germany; Hoechst, W Germany; Health Care Int'l, USA; Johnson & Johnson, UK; Reckitt & Colman, UK; Wyeth, UK; Wellcome

Foundation, UK; Procter & Gamble, Switzerland; Rotary Watch, Switzerland Omega, Switzerland; Chubb, UK; Rothmans of Pall Mall, UK; Garrards, UK; IBM, France; Dupont, France; Eastman Kodak, USA; etc
Principal Bankers: British Bank of the Middle East; Qatar National Bank; Commercial Bank of Qatar

Principal Shareholders: Adel Ali Bin Ali son of late Ali Bin Ali
Date of Establishment: 1965
No of Employees: 96

ROOTS CONTRACTING & TRADING CO WLL

PO Box 6565, Doha
Tel: 411922, 320835/6/7
Cable: Roots
Telex: 4848 ROOTS DH
Telefax: (0947) 426040

Chairman: Abdullah Hamad Al-Attiya
Directors: Robert J Harmoush (Managing Director), Mohamed J Darwish (Director)
Senior Executives: Robert J Harmoush (Chief Engineer), Ian R Stapely (Project Manager), Farid N Aoude (Project Manager), Elie N Touma (Operations Manager), Martin J O'Hara (Contracts Co-ordinator), Tony Nasser (Project Engineer), Jacob George (Senior Projects Quantity Surveyor)

PRINCIPAL ACTIVITIES: Building and construction
Principal Bankers: Qatar National Bank; Paribas
Financial Information:

	1990 QR'000
Sales turnover	21,000
Authorised capital	2,700
Paid-up capital	1,000
Total assets	6,200

Principal Shareholders: Abdullah Hamad Al-Attiya; Mohamed J Darwish; Robert J Harmoush
Date of Establishment: 1979
No of Employees: 360

SABA & CO

PO Box 431, Doha
Tel: 422168, 425392
Cable: Sabaco Doha
Telex: 4182 Sabaco DH

PRINCIPAL ACTIVITIES: Public accountants and management consultants
Branch Offices: Cyprus; Algeria; Bahrain; Egypt; Iraq; Jodan; Kuwait; Libya; Morocco; Oman; Qatar; Saudi Arabia; Syria; United Arab Emirates; Yemen
Parent Company: Head office in Lebanon

SALEM HASSAN AL ANSARI & SONS

See AL ANSARI, SALEM HASSAN, & SONS

SALWA MECHANICAL & ELECTRICAL CONTRACTING CO

PO Box 2133, Doha
Tel: 810190, 810192
Telex: 4775 Salmec DH

PRINCIPAL ACTIVITIES: Mechanical and electrical engineering; pipeline installation; welding services; production of galvanised steel; aluminium stainless steel, PVC coated etc

SANTA FE INTERNATIONAL SERVICES INC

PO Box 4396, Doha
Tel: 342268
Telex: 4475 Sanafe DH

PRINCIPAL ACTIVITIES: Oil and gas well drilling

Date of Establishment: Qatar: 1976
No of Employees: 200

SHAHWANI CONTRACTING & TRADING EST

PO Box 1949, Doha
Tel: 424964, 323208, 325257
Telex: 4048 BINYFA DH

Chairman: Abdul Hadi Trahib Bin Nayfa Al Shahwani (Owner)
Directors: Syed Naseem Ahmad (Executive Director)

PRINCIPAL ACTIVITIES: Manufacturers' agents and importers, complete range of fire fighting equipment, installation of fire alarm security system, welding and cutting equipment, industrial packings and joints, chemicals etc
Principal Agencies: Siebe Gorman; National Foam; UK Fire Int'l Static Systems Group; Beldam Packing & Rubber Co Ltd, UK; Socado, Marseille; Newton Chambers Engineering Ltd, UK; Graviner Ltd, UK; Champion Chemicals; Flow Control Division, UK etc
Branch Offices: Abu Dhabi: PO Box 3350, Telex 23408 ALSHAH EM, Tel 336720/336721; Sharjah: PO Box 5113, Tel 547823
Principal Bankers: Qatar National Bank; British Bank of the Middle East

Principal Shareholders: Sole Proprietorship
Date of Establishment: 1969
No of Employees: 36

SHAMS MOHD ABDUL QADER

PO Box 898, Doha
Tel: 423339, 324353
Telex: 4093 Shams DH

Directors: Shams Mohd Abdul Qader (Owner)
Senior Executives: Saifuddin Pancha

PRINCIPAL ACTIVITIES: General merchants and building contractors
Principal Agencies: Crown Paints, UK; Ariston Water Heater, Italy; 7 Star Water Filter, India; Blue Circle
Principal Bankers: Qatar National Bank; Grindlays Bank; Standard Chartered Bank; Arab Bank; Doha Bank

Date of Establishment: 1964

SHELL MARKETS (MIDDLE EAST) LTD

PO Box 776, Doha
Tel: 426504
Telex: 4504 Aubit DH

PRINCIPAL ACTIVITIES: Supplies of petroleum products
Branch Offices: Oman
Parent Company: Head office in Dubai

STANDARD CHARTERED BANK

Government House Road, PO Box 29, Doha
Tel: 414252
Cable: Stanchart
Telex: 4217 DH

PRINCIPAL ACTIVITIES: Commercial banking
Branch Offices: Bahrain; Oman; Qatar; United Arab Emirates (Dubai, Abu Dhabi, Sharjah; Ras Al Khaimah)
Parent Company: Head office: 10 Clements Lane, London EC4, UK

TALAL ABU-GHAZALEH & CO
Talal Abu-Ghazaleh Ass Ltd

PO Box 2620, Doha
Tel: 424024, 425687
Cable: Auditors
Telex: 4368 DH

PRINCIPAL ACTIVITIES: Public accountants and management consultants
Branch Offices: Abu Dhabi; Dubai; Sharjah; Ras Al Khaimah; Bahrain; Qatar; Saudi Arabia; Lebanon; Jordan; Egypt; Libya; Tunisia; Yemen AR; Yemen PDR
Parent Company: Head office in Kuwait

TAWFEEQ TRADING & CONTRACTING CO

PO Box 187, Doha
Tel: 410644, 423173, 325638
Telex: 4220 Tawfeq DH

Senior Executives: Abdul Razak Mustafawi (General Manager)

PRINCIPAL ACTIVITIES: General engineering and contracting, general trading, import and distribution of electrical and electronic equipment, air conditioning and refrigeration equipment
Principal Agencies: Hitachi

TEYSEER GROUP OF COMPANIES

PO Box 1556, Doha
Tel: 321883
Cable: Yousr Doha
Telex: 4292 DH

Chairman: Abdul Rahman Issa Mannai (Group Managing Director

PRINCIPAL ACTIVITIES: Trading and commercial; construction and manufacturing and other services; stone crushing; cement and transport; aluminium products; airconditioning and refrigeration; mechanical and electrical engineering; computer services; fibreglass products; plant hire; auto and equipment centre; marine services
Principal Agencies: B F Goodrich; Suzuki; Mobiloil; Scania; Esab; Leonard; Lincoln; Dowidat; Metabo; Apple; Ardrox; Mitsubishi; Leigheit; Durametallic; Falcon Chemicals; Emelcold; Aeroquip; NGK; Tallatte
Subsidiary Companies: Teyseer Trading & Contracting; Teyseer Airconditioning & Refrigeration Co; Teyseer Cement Co; Teyseer Service Centre; Teyseer Stone Crushing Co; Teyseer Contracting Co; Teyseer CCM Services; Teysser Mechanical & Engineering Co; Gulf Inco; Ideal Home; Gulf Glass Fibre; AluArabia Aluminium & Glass; Qatar Plant Hire; Gulf Auto & Equipment Service Centre; Computerarabia
Principal Bankers: Grindlays Bank; United Bank; Standard Chartered Bank; Arab Bank

TRADING & AGENCY SERVICES WLL

PO Box 1884, Doha
Tel: 421101 (Sales Dept), 421100 (Showroom), 432212, 432213, 328550 (Head Office)
Cable: Trags
Telex: 4325 Trags Dh (Head Office)
Telefax: 422255

Chairman: Hussein Al Fardan
Directors: Jassim Jaidah
Senior Executives: Munir Issa (General Manager)

PRINCIPAL ACTIVITIES: Civil and electrical contracting, industrial and domestic maintenance, contracting and trading in pipes, pumps, industrial and commercial equipment, refrigeration and cold storage, catering equipment, building materials, swimming pools, water treatment, water and air pollution control and filtration, electrical and telephone cables, underwater pipe inspection and surveying, road marking etc
Principal Agencies: Avery Hardoll, UK; AAF, Netherlands; Bran & Luebbe, Germany; Fiat TTG, Italy; GEC Mechanical, UK; Mannesmann Demag, Germany; Mero, Germany; PAM, France; Penguin Pools, UK; Pilkingtons, UK; Stanley, UK; Geodetic, UK; Highway Safety, Australia; Hasler, Switzerland; CIT Alcatel, France; Marconi, UK; Rockwell Collins, USA; Telephone Cables, UK; Boulton & Paul, UK; Crypto Peerless, UK; Foster, UK; Stott Benham, UK; Werner & Pfleiderer, Germany; Ameron Fibreglass, Netherlands; Byron Jackson Pump & Seal, Netherlands; Blacksmith Chemical Services, UK; Existalite, UK; Gail, Germany; GEC, UK; Gripper, USA; Eala Audio, Netherlands; Howmaar, UK; Harry Stanger, UK; IGW Survey, UAE; IVO Int, Finland; Lyrec, Denmark; Marconi Radar Projects, UK; Otari, Japan; PAM, France; PLT Offshore, UK; Steelcase Straffor, France; Shell Trading (Middle East), Dubai; SHI Samsum Shipbuilding, Saudi Arabia;

Stewart & Hasting, UK; STC Telecom, UK; Saudi Vitrified Clay
Pipe, Saudi Arabia; Saudi Amiantit Co, Saudi Arabia;
Unipipeline System, Canada; Vallourec, France; Zaganite,
Australia
Branch Offices: Showroom in Ras Abu Aboud
Principal Bankers: Banque Paribas, Doha, Commercial Bank of
Qatar
Financial Information:

	1989 QR'000
Authorised capital	1,200
Paid-up capital	1,200
Total assets	17,699
Sales turnover	25,702
Profits	1,723

Principal Shareholders: Chairman and directors as described
Date of Establishment: 1972
No of Employees: 186

TRAGS ELECTRICAL ENGINEERING & AIRCONDITIONING CO

PO Box 470, Doha
Tel: 414211/12/2/4
Cable: Treecal-Doha
Telex: 4332 Trecal DH

Directors: Jassem Jaidah, Hussein Al Fardan
Senior Executives: Zuhair Z Bulos (General Manager), Elias A
Zakhem (Deputy General Manager)

PRINCIPAL ACTIVITIES: Electrical and mechanical engineering,
supply and installation of electrical, airconditioning, lifts,
escalators, plumbing and drainage systems, commercial
representation
Principal Agencies: Carrier International Corp, Siemens AG,
KHD Engineering GmbH, Kone Marryat & Scott International,
Hallam Group of Nottingham
Principal Bankers: Commercial Bank of Qatar; Banque Paribas;
Grindlays Bank; Qatar National Bank

Date of Establishment: June 1974
No of Employees: 250

TRAMARCO
Trading-Marketing Contracting Co WLL

PO Box 5803, Doha
Tel: 328881, 320853/4/5/7/8
Cable: Tramarco
Telex: 4359 TRMCCO DH
Telefax: 0974 - 425257

Chairman: Ali Hassan Khalaf
Senior Executives: H K A Bedrossian (Managing Director)

PRINCIPAL ACTIVITIES: Trading in building materials, paints,
sanitary ware; industrial equipment and machinery, power
equipment; civil engineering, mechanical engineering
contracting
Principal Agencies: George Fischer, Henkel, Int Adh, Walker
Crosweller, Caradon Terrain, Cuno Filters, Fratelli Pettinaroli,
Formatura Iniezione Polimeri, Lorenzi Vasco, Pedrollo,
Flamco, Winn & Coales, Rothenberger, Ripolin, Elcrom, Peta
Branch Offices: Main Showroom: B Ring Road, Doha
Principal Bankers: Commercial Bank of Qatar; Banque Paribas;
Grindlays Bank; Qatar Islamic Bank; Al Ahli Bank of Qatar;
Bank of Oman; Doha Bank
Financial Information:

	QR'000
Sales turnover	18,400
Paid-up capital	1,020

Date of Establishment: 1975
No of Employees: 80

TRANSORIENT ESTABLISHMENT

PO Box 363, Doha
Tel: 321237/9, 323963
Cable: Comico
Telex: 4278 Comico DH

Chairman: HE Sheikh Muhamad Bin Hamad Al Thani (Owner)
Directors: Mohd Ahmed Bashir (General Manager, Commercial,
Contracting & Travel Manager), Siddig Ali Eltayeb
(Administrative & Financial Manager)

PRINCIPAL ACTIVITIES: Agents and general trading
companies; civil engineering and construction; construction
plant; engineering consultants; travel and tourism and freight
forwarding; electronics; catering; livestock trading, petrol
service centre
Principal Agencies: Samsung Electronics
Branch Offices: Trans Orient Air Services, PO Box 93, Doha,
Doha Travel Agency, PO Box 1359, Doha, Trans Arabian
Travel Agency, PO Box 363, Doha, Express Travel, PO Box
2345, Doha, Tran West Travel, PO Box 363, Doha
Subsidiary Companies: Gulf Industrial Energy Services; Qatar
Livestock Trading & Transport Co
Principal Bankers: United Bank Limited

Date of Establishment: 1962
No of Employees: 200

ULTRA ELECTRIC

PO Box 856, Doha
Tel: 424669, 425933
Cable: Ultra Doha
Telex: 4288 DH

PRINCIPAL ACTIVITIES: Electrical engineering; import and
distribution of electrical equipment and appliances, wiring
accessories, fittings and lighting equipment
Principal Agencies: Klippon, Aerialite Cables and Wires, Nettle
Accessories Ltd, Ottermill Group, GEC Walshall Ltd, Relite
Electric Ltd
Associated Companies: Abdullah Abdulghani & Bros

UNION AUTOMOBILES CO

PO Box 82 and PO Box 3338, Doha
Tel: 328211, 423914, 323881
Telex: 4203 Wibeco DH

PRINCIPAL ACTIVITIES: Import and distribution of cars and
auto spare parts
Principal Agencies: Alfa Romeo; Renault; York
Branch Offices: Alfa Romeo Agency, PO Box 82, Doha, Tel
328211, Renault Agency, PO Box 3338, Doha, Tel 423914,
York Mobiles Showroom, PO Box 1991, Doha, Tel 323881

UNITED BANK LTD

PO Box 329, Doha
Tel: 321420
Cable: United Bank
Telex: 4222 DH

PRINCIPAL ACTIVITIES: Commercial banking
Branch Offices: In the Middle East: Abu Dhabi; Dubai; Sharjah;
Ras Al Khaimah; Umm Al Qaiwan; Ajman; Qatar; Saudi
Arabia; Yemen; Bahrain
Parent Company: Head office in Karachi, Pakistan

VENTURE GULF GROUP

PO Box 2515, Doha
Tel: 321367/9, 441367/8
Telex: 4892 Engulf DH

Directors: Said Bin Abdulaziz Al Nasr

PRINCIPAL ACTIVITIES: Metal recycling plant, construction and
trading, transport and plant hire, fibre glass products and
chemicals, supply of tanks, swimming pools contracting, car

hire and commercial vehicle hiring services, manufacturers' representation
Branch Offices: Bahrain, Dubai

WILSON MASON & PARTNERS - MIDDLE EAST

PO Box 7350, Doha
Tel: 440832
Telefax: 432451

Senior Partner: Duncan Mitchell
Partners: John Fenton, Bruce Aitken, William Thain
Senior Executives: Derek Southworth (Associate Partner)

PRINCIPAL ACTIVITIES: Architects, planners, engineers, landscape architects
Parent Company: Head office: 3 Chandoss Street, London W1M 0JU, UK
Principal Bankers: British Bank of the Middle East

Date of Establishment: 1974

Major Companies of
SAUDI ARABIA

A A MOFARRIJ
See MOFARRIJ, A A,

A BAHLAS CORPORATION FOR TRADE (BUILDMORE DIVISION)
See BAHLAS, A, CORPORATION FOR TRADE (BUILDMORE DIVISION)

A I AL KHORAYEF SONS CO
See AL KHORAYEF, A I, SONS CO

A K SAID FURNITURE
The Homemakers
PO Box 40656, Riyadh 11511
Tel: 4654847
Telex: 401843 AKSAID SJ
Telefax: 4645938

Chairman: Abdel Kader Said
Directors: Tarek A K Said (Managing Director)
Senior Executives: Salah A K Said (Sales Director), Ibrahim Said (Financial Manager), Salim Allawi (Admin & Personnel Manager), Nick M Broad (Project Manager -Furniture Div)

PRINCIPAL ACTIVITIES: Retail sales and turnkey projects, supply of furniture, lamps and accessories
Branch Offices: PO Box 14897, Jeddah 21434, Tel 6710131, Telex 401843 AKSAID SJ, Fax 6710131 (Branch Manager: Pierre Salhab); PO Box 40656, Riyadh 11511, Tel 4657911, Fax 4649266 (Branch Manager: Salah A K Said)
Parent Company: AK Said Trading & Contracting Est, PO Box 40656, Riyadh 11511
Principal Bankers: Riyad Bank, Riyadh
Financial Information:

	1989 US$'000
Sales turnover	15,000
Profits	4,000
Authorised capital	1,000
Paid-up capital	1,000
Total assets	5,000

Principal Shareholders: A K Said
Date of Establishment: 1976
No of Employees: 70

A R NAMLAH FACTORIES
See NAMLAH, A R, FACTORIES

A S BUGSHAN & BROS (KOMATSU DIVISION)
See BUGSHAN, A S, & BROS (KOMATSU DIVISION)

A W AUJAN & BROS
See AUJAN, A W, & BROS

ABAALKHAIL, SALAH, CONSULTING ENGINEERS
SACE
PO Box 4296, Riyadh 11491
Tel: 4766500 (5 lines)
Telex: 400376 Sace Sj
Telefax: 4768041

President: Salah Ali Abaalkhail
Senior Executives: Abdul Aziz Al Yousef (Vice President), Abdulkarim Jumma (Administration Manager)

PRINCIPAL ACTIVITIES: Consulting services; planning, investigation, design, project and construction management, safety studies and computer application and design for areas
Branch Offices: Jubail
Principal Bankers: Riyad Bank; Al-Bank Al-Saudi Al-Tejari Al-Mutahed; Albank Alsaudi Alhollandi

Principal Shareholders: Salah Ali Abaalkhail
Date of Establishment: 1978
No of Employees: 110

ABAHSAIN, SALEH & ABDULAZIZ, CO LTD
Head Office, PO Box 209, Alkhobar 31952
Tel: 8642025, 8642026
Cable: Bahsain Alkhobar
Telex: 871046 Abasen SJ, 870026 Basain SJ
Telefax: 8951542

President: Abdulaziz Ibrahim Abahsain
Senior Executives: Shaukat Sheikh (General Manager Commercial Div), Syed Khawaja Maqsood (General Manager Chemical Div), Zafar Naim (General Manager Heavy Equipment Div), Mohd Jaroudi (General Manager Foodstuff Div), Naeem Ansari (General Manager Automobile Div), Nael Marrar (General Manager Omega Pole Factory), Sh Ibrahim Saleh Abahsain (General Manager Road Construction)

PRINCIPAL ACTIVITIES: Trading in heavy machinery, construction machinery, generators, machinery for the oil and related industry, air compressors, welding equipment and supplies, pumps, mechanical seals, waterproofing materials, process industry machinery, solar turbines and logistic management; distribution and wholesale of foodstuff and industrial gases; manufacture of cable tray and electrical support systems and fixtures; civil and road construction, electrical and general engineering and fabrication; distribution of Saab cars in the Eastern and Central Provinces; service and repair of motors, pumps and mechanical seals
Principal Agencies: Alcoa Int Inc; Hudson Products USA; Tadano Cranes; Mitsubishi Heavy Industries; Solar Turbines; Byron Jackson Pumps; Hudson Italiana; Nippon Steel Corp; Mitsubishi Electric; Forney Engineering; Arrow Engineering; Lincoln Welders; SAAB Cars; NGK; IHI; Borg Warner Industrial Products; JCB UK; Yale Forklifts, Joy Manufacturing; Atochem; CECA
Branch Offices: PO Box 42127, Riyadh 11541, Tel 4951076/4950580, Fax 4954900, Telex 404689 Saherd Sj; PO Box 1300, Jeddah 21431, Tel 6829044, 6820935, Fax 6833124
Subsidiary Companies: Crown Furniture; Abahsain Cope SA Ltd; Abahsain Flame Controls; Abahsain Secem Ltd for electrical installations and HVAC services; Omega Poles Factory
Principal Bankers: Arab National Bank Ltd (Alkhobar, Riyadh); Al Bank Al Saudi Al Hollandi (Alkhobar, Riyadh, Jeddah)
Financial Information:

	1988/89 SR'000	1989/90 SR'000
Sales turnover	225,175	263,000
Authorised capital	50,000	50,000
Paid-up capital	50,000	50,000
Total assets	169,053	251,000

Principal Shareholders: Abdulaziz Abahsain & Sons; Saleh Abahsain & Sons
Date of Establishment: 1945
No of Employees: 1,400

ABBAR-MAHMOOD SALEH ABBAR CO
PO Box 461, Jeddah 21411
Tel: 6512764, 6512768, 6512940
Cable: Abbar
Telex: 601790 Abarjd Sj
Telefax: 6514032

Chairman: Ahmed Mahmood Abbar
Directors: Abdullah M Abbar (Vice Chairman), Rida M Abbar (Vice Chairman & Partner in Charge), Khalid A Abbar (President), Saleh M Balahwal (Vice President)
Senior Executives: Dr Abdul Aziz Abbar (Vice President, Medical Supply Div), Yehia A Abbar (Managing Director, Refrigeration Div), Mohammed A Abbar (Managing Director, Dammam Branch), Munir Y Chamas (General Manager, Central Air

Conditioning Div), Malek H Rayess (General Manager, Refrigeration Div), Samir Jum'a (General Manager, Riyadh Branch), Tariq Mahmoud (Financial Controller)

PRINCIPAL ACTIVITIES: Importers, wholesalers, retailers, distributors of household appliances and laundry equipment and of domestic and commercial air-conditioning and refrigeration equipment, contractors for the installation of central air-conditioning and commercial cold stores; distributors of electronic products including watches, calculators, musical instruments, and computers; also medical and surgical supplies, refrigerant gases. Joint venture to manufacture and assemble domestic air conditioners

Principal Agencies: White Westinghouse, McQuay-Perfex, Westinghouse Electric Corp, Wearever-Proctor Silex, H D Sheldon & Co, Thermo King, Master-Bilt, Global Systems Inc, all USA; Mitsubishi Heavy Industries, Casio, Toshiba Batteries all Japan; SMEG, Delchi, Isosirz, Frigas, Aspera, all Italy; Robot Coupe, France; Koxka, Spain; Gold Star, Korea; Electrolux-Wascator, Sweden; Wetrok, Switzerland; Caravell, Denmark

Branch Offices: Branches in Riyadh (PO Box 42739, Tel 4012735, 400615, Telex 400615); Makkah (PO Box 294, Tel 5429740, Telex 540072); Dammam (PO Box 5716, Tel 8267252, Telex 802374); Madinah (PO Box 462, Tel 8221453, Telex 570268); Yanbu (PO Box 475, Tel 3223640,Telex 661083)

Subsidiary Companies: Joint Venture with Mitsubishi Heavy Industries: Saudi Arabia Factory for Electrical Appliances Co Ltd

Principal Bankers: Al Bank Al Saudi Al Fransi; National Commercial Bank; Bank Al Jazira; Riyad Bank

Financial Information:

	1989 SR'000
Sales turnover	350,000

Principal Shareholders: Chairman and the two Vice Chairmen
Date of Establishment: 1953
No of Employees: 480

ABDALLA AL FARIS HEAVY INDUSTRIES
See AL FARIS, ABDALLA, HEAVY INDUSTRIES

ABDEL HADI ABDALLAH AL QAHTANI & SONS
See AL QAHTANI, ABDEL HADI ABDALLAH, & SONS

ABDUL AZIZ ABDULLAH AL SULEIMAN INSURANCE AGENTS
PO Box 1120, Dammam 31431
Tel: 8574385, 8572110
Cable: Naskaras Dammam
Telex: 801800 Rolaco SJ
Telefax: 8572321

Chairman: Sheikh Abdul Aziz Abdullah Al-Suleiman
Senior Executives: George Fouad Asmar (Branch Manager)

PRINCIPAL ACTIVITIES: All branches in insurance and reinsurance
Branch Offices: Location in Dammam: Rolaco Bldg, Airport Street; also branches in Lebanon: PO Box 4293, Beirut; and France: 6 rue de Berri, Paris 75008
Associated Companies: Stewart Wrightson Ltd

ABDUL GHANI EL-AJOU CORPORATION
See EL-AJOU, ABDUL GHANI, CORPORATION

ABDUL KADIR AL MUHAIDIB & SONS
See AL MUHAIDIB, ABDUL KADIR, & SONS

ABDUL LATIF A ALFOZAN & BROS
See ALFOZAN, ABDUL LATIF A, & BROS

ABDUL LATIF JAMEEL CO LTD
See JAMEEL, ABDUL LATIF, CO LTD

ABDUL LATIF SAUD AL BABTAIN & BROS
See AL BABTAIN, ABDUL LATIF SAUD, & BROS

ABDUL MAJEED MOHANDIS & CO
See MOHANDIS, ABDUL MAJEED, & CO

ABDUL MOHSEN AL TAMIMI EST
See AL TAMIMI, ABDUL MOHSEN, EST

ABDUL RAHMAN A A ALOTHMAN
See ALOTHMAN, ABDUL RAHMAN A A,

ABDUL RAHMAN DAWOOD AL GILANI
See AL GILANI, ABDUL RAHMAN DAWOOD,

ABDULAZIZ & MOHAMMED A ALJOMAIH CO
See ALJOMAIH, ABDULAZIZ & MOHAMMED A, CO

ABDULAZIZ & SAAD AL MOAJIL
See AL MOAJIL, ABDULAZIZ & SAAD,

ABDULAZIZ AL RASHED AL HUMAID CO
See AL HUMAID, ABDULAZIZ AL RASHED, CO

ABDULLA ABDULAZIZ ALRAJHI
See ALRAJHI, ABDULLA ABDULAZIZ,

ABDULLA AHMED QURAISHI & SONS
See QURAISHI, ABDULLA AHMED, & SONS

ABDULLA ALHOGAIL EST
See ALHOGAIL, ABDULLA, EST

ABDULLA B AL KHALIFA & SONS CO
See AL KHALIFA, ABDULLA B, & SONS CO

ABDULLA BUSBATE & PARTNERS CO LTD
PO Box 1683, Dammam 31441
Tel: 8574477
Telex: 801489 Busbat Sj
Telefax: (03) 8579257

Chairman: Abdulla Saleh Busbate
Senior Executives: Taher M S Taher (General Manager)

PRINCIPAL ACTIVITIES: Manufacture of polyethylene and UPVC pipes and UPVC, PE, PP, CI fittings, for water sewerage, drainage, irrigation and electrical installations, also manufacture of safety helmets and Petri dishes
Branch Offices: Riyadh, Jeddah, Al Qaseem, Al Hassa, Madina
Principal Bankers: Albank Alsaudi Alhollandi
Financial Information:

	1990 SR'000
Sales turnover	33,100
Authorised capital	22,985
Paid-up capital	22,985

Principal Shareholders: Abdulla S Busbate
Date of Establishment: 1975
No of Employees: 124

ABDULLA FOUAD & SONS CO
See FOUAD, ABDULLA, & SONS CO

ABDULLA HAMED AL ZAMIL GROUP OF COMPANIES
See AL ZAMIL, ABDULLA HAMED, GROUP OF COMPANIES

ABDULLA RASHID DOSSARY & PARTNER CO
See DOSSARY, ABDULLA RASHID, & PARTNER CO

ABDULLAH & SAID M OBINZAGRCO
See BINZAGR, ABDULLAH & SAID M O, CO

ABDULLAH A M AL-KHODARI EST
See AL-KHODARI, ABDULLAH A M, EST

ABDULLAH ABBAR & AHMED ZAINY
Administrative Office, PO Box 5700, Jeddah 21432
Tel: 6514104/8, 6514352/6
Cable: Moatasim Jeddah
Telex: 601062 Sj Motsim, 603256 Abazco Sj

Partners: Abdullah M Abbar, Ahmed A Zainy
Directors: Ghazi A Abbar, Adnan A Zainy, Gazi A Zainy, Osama
    A Zainy, Khalid H Zainy

PRINCIPAL ACTIVITIES: Import, wholesaling and retailing of
    foostuffs, cold storage facilities and ship chandlers, catering,
    meat processing, aviation and ship bunkering, distribution of
    deck and engine equipment, and home appliances, electrical,
    mechanical and agricultural equipment; computers,
    transportation and engineering contracting; tourism and travel
    services
Branch Offices: Branches in Riyadh (PO Box 393, Tel 4011392,
    Telex 401128); Dammam (PO Box 567, Tel 8261956, Telex
    801056); Mecca; Medina; Dhahran; Al Kharj; Qatif; Buraidah;
    Hofuf; Jizan; Jubail; Tabuk; Taif; Yanbu; Hasa; London (UK)
Subsidiary/Associated Companies: The United Arab Agencies
    (PO Box 1045, Jeddah); Petro-star Company; National Tahina
    and Tin Factory; Industry Services of Saudi Arabia (ISCOSA)
    (in partnership with Westinghouse Electric Corp); Ice Cream
    and Dairy Products Co; (CORTINA) (in partnership with Gelati
    Cortina Co, Beirut); Star Navigation Co Ltd; Chiyoda
    Petrostar; Saudi Meat factory; A & Z Boatel; A & Sodexho
    Catering; Saudi Multina Gas & Transportation Co; Ogem
    Saudi Arabia Construction; Saudi Aviation Services Co;
    Navigas International; Saudi Security & Technical Services
    Co; A & Z Mak Maschinenbau; A & Z Computers; A & Z Cold
    Stores, AZCO Travel; A & Z Clearing Agency; A & Z Electrical
    Appliances Div; A & Z Equipment Div; A & Z Food Div; A & Z
    French Bakery Systems; A & Z Pipes & Maintenance Div; A &
    Z Ship Chandling; A & Z US Beef; Al Aziziah Dairy Ltd; Bahra
    Hydroponic Farm; Ecology & Environment of Saudi Arabia Co
    Ltd; International Technology (Saudi Arabia) Ltd; Petro Trade
    Co Ltd; Wadi Fatima Poultry Farm etc
Principal Bankers: Al Bank Al Saudi Al Fransi, Riyad Bank,
    National Commercial Bank, Saudi American Bank, Al Bank Al
    Saudi Al Hollandi

Principal Shareholders: Partners as described
Date of Establishment: 1942
No of Employees: 3,000

ABDULLAH AL-HAMOUD AL SHUWAYER
See AL SHUWAYER, ABDULLAH AL-HAMOUD,

ABDULLAH EST FOR TRADING & INDUSTRY
PO Box 7778, Jeddah 21472
Tel: 6424879, 6426998/9
Cable: FAISALNA
Telex: 600688 JOHARA SJ, 601504 FISLNA SJ
Telefax: 6432645

Chairman: HRH Prince Abdullah Alfaisal Alsaud
Directors: Yousuf Abdul Shakour (Managing Director
Senior Executives: Shaikh M Tahir (Executive Manager)

PRINCIPAL ACTIVITIES: Shipping agency, stevedoring, general
    contracting
Principal Agencies: Ignazio Messina, Italy; Char Hsing Marine,
    Taiwan; Gesuri Lloyd, Indonesia
Principal Bankers: Albank Alsaudi Alfransi

Principal Shareholders: Sole proprietorship
Date of Establishment: February 1978
No of Employees: 20

ABDULLAH HASHIM CO LTD
See HASHIM, ABDULLAH, CO LTD

ABDULLAH MOHAMED BAROOM
See BAROOM, ABDULLAH MOHAMED,

ABDULLATIF A AL ISMAIL EST
See AL ISMAIL, ABDULLATIF A, EST

ABDULLATIF AL ISSA EST
See AL ISSA, ABDULLATIF, EST

ABDULREHMAN ALGOSAIBI GENERAL TRADING BUREAU
See ALGOSAIBI, ABDULREHMAN, GENERAL TRADING
BUREAU

ABHA INTERCONTINENTAL HOTEL
PO Box 1447, Abha
Tel: 2247777

PRINCIPAL ACTIVITIES: Hotel operation

ABUDAWOOD TRADING CO
PO Box 6060, Jeddah 21442
Tel: 6656364, 6673622, 6673670, 6657472
Telex: 600715 Sj
Telefax: 6652267

PRINCIPAL ACTIVITIES: Production of cleaning chemicals
Principal Agencies: Clorox, USA; Hail Cleaning Products; Arpal
Branch Offices: PO Box 20303, Riyadh, Tel 4910459, 4918927,
    Fax 4918927; PO Box 5993, Dammam, Tel 8574948, 8572291,
    Fax 8579419
Principal Bankers: Saudi American Bank; Riyad Bank

Principal Shareholders: Hussein Dawood

ABUKHADRA, SAAD H, & CO
PO Box 1340, Jeddah 21431
Tel: 6917700
Telex: 601794 GENCO SJ
Telefax: 6917479

Chairman: Saad H Abu Khadra
Senior Executives: Hal Warren (General Manager)

PRINCIPAL ACTIVITIES: Supply of construction materials and
    equipment
Principal Agencies: Hilti Fastening Systems
Branch Offices: Riyadh; Alkhobar; Yanbu; Medina; Jubail;
    Makkah; Khamis Mushait; Jeddah
Financial Information:

	1989/90 US$'000
Sales turnover	25,000

Principal Shareholders: Saad H Abu Khadra; Khalid Abu Khadra
Date of Establishment: 1965
No of Employees: Over 150

ABUNAYYAN, IBRAHIM, SONS CO
Head Office, PO Box 71, Riyadh 11411
Tel: 4593686, 4576054, 4576370
Cable: Drilimco
Telex: 401132 Drilab Sj, 404132 Sawco Sj
Telefax: 4583017

Owner: Sheikh Mohammed I Abunayyan (General Manager)
Directors: Fahad I Abunayyan (Deputy General Manager),
    Khaled I Abunayyan (Deputy General Manager)
Senior Executives: Sami Beyhum (Commercial Development
    Manager), Riaz AHmed (Contracts Manager), Nabil Hammoud
    (Asst General Manager), Awni Rifai (Drilling Manager),
    Mohammed Al Khateeb (Sales Manager)

PRINCIPAL ACTIVITIES: Deep water well drilling and
    maintenance, pumps supplies, installation and maintenance,

agricultural equipment, supply and installation of pipelines, manufacture of water meters, agricultural projects operations and maintenance, turnkey agriprojects, greenhouses, turf grass division
Branch Offices: PO Box 424, Alkhobar 31952, Tel 8574115, 8574525, Telex 871341 Drilog Sj, Fax 8578581; PO Box 8522, Jeddah 21492, Tel 6821544, Fax 6911544; PO Box 738, Jubail, Tel 3410594, Telex 632090 TCPIPE SJ, Fax 3410598
Subsidiary Companies: Abunayyan Hughes Tool Saudi Arabia Ltd Co; Saudi Meter Company (Joint venture with Schlumberger)
Principal Bankers: Al Bank Al Saudi Al Fransi
Financial Information:

	1990 SR'000
Sales turnover	300,000

Principal Shareholders: Mohammed Ibrahim Abunayyan, Fahd Ibrahim Abunayyan, Khaled Ibrahim Abunayyan
Date of Establishment: 1958
No of Employees: 1,300

ACEM-ASEA CONTRACTING CO LTD

PO Box 4441, Riyadh 11491
Tel: 01-4762644
Telefax: 01/476 7252
Telex: 404571 Aseard Sj
Telefax: 1-4769622

Chairman: Abdullah Al Hobayb
Directors: Lave Lindberg (Managing Director)

PRINCIPAL ACTIVITIES: Electrical contracting in power generation, transmission and distribution. Electrical and mechanical contracting for water and sewage plants. Turnkey deliveries of gas turbine power plants, transmission and distribution substations
Principal Agencies: The Abb, ASEA Brown Boveri Group
Branch Offices: PO Box 2873, Al Khobar 31952; PO Box 7937, Jeddah 21472
Parent Company: ASEA AB, Sweden
Principal Bankers: Saudi British Bank, Riyadh; Saudi American Bank, Riyadh

Principal Shareholders: Arabian Company for Electrical & Mechanical Works (ACEM), Riyadh; ABB Asea Brown Boveri Ltd, Zurich
Date of Establishment: February 1980 (1400H)
No of Employees: 100

ACMECON

Associated Civil & Mechanical Engineering Contractors

PO Box 990, Jeddah 21421
Tel: 6311214, 6310957
Cable: Acmecon Jeddah
Telex: 601533 Acmeco Sj

Chairman: Tosson Ahmad Al Barrawi
Directors: Berj B Kalaidjian, A S Gedeon
Senior Executives: Vahe Kabakian (Area Manager, Jeddah), Suheil Kafena (Area Manager, Riyadh), Fahd Sarkis (Area Manager, Damman)

PRINCIPAL ACTIVITIES: Civil, mechanical and electrical engineering contractors; building and steel erection contractors
Principal Agencies: Thyssen, Germany
Branch Offices: PO Box 283, Riyadh; PO Box 1033, Dammam
Principal Bankers: Banque Indosuez, Paris; Al Bank Al Saudi Al Fransi, Jeddah

Principal Shareholders: T A Al Barrawi; B B Kalaidjian; A S Gedeon
Date of Establishment: 1970
No of Employees: 500

ADRIAAN VOLKER SAUDI ARABIA LTD

PO Box 389, Dhahran Airport 31932
Tel: 03-3611905, 03-3613568
Fax: 03-3612800
Telex: 831195 ADVO SJ

Chairman: HRH Prince Khaled Ben Fahd Ben Abdulaziz
Directors: Sheikh Salah Hejailan, J B Cosijn, A Van Baardewijk, A Hoekstra

PRINCIPAL ACTIVITIES: Harbour works, pipeline works, sewerage & water networks, dredging and reclamation works including silt and mud removal
Branch Offices: PO Box 9501, Riyadh; PO Box 234, Jubail (Jubail 31951, Al Ventura Camp); PO Box 389, Dhahran Airport 31932
Parent Company: Royal Volker Stevin
Principal Bankers: Albank Alsaudi Alhollandi, Jubail

Principal Shareholders: Al Bilad Establishment for Trading and Economy (20%); Sheikh Salah Hejailan (10%); Adriaan Volker Dredging NV (70%)
Date of Establishment: 1978 (1398)
No of Employees: 350

ADWAN TRADING & CONTRACTING CO

PO Box 4913, Riyadh 11412
Tel: 4026011, 4026061
Telex: 401475 ADWAN SJ

President: Abdelaziz Bin Adwan
Directors: Mohamed Bin Adwan (Vice President)

PRINCIPAL ACTIVITIES: Retail and wholesale of electrical materials; turnkey construction power lines, power plants, sub-stations; sales and service of construction equipment, pole digging equipment, trencher and truck mounted cranes
Principal Agencies: AB Chance, USA; Wajax, Canada; Pesci, Italy; Hallmark, US/UK; Vermeer, Holland
Branch Offices: Construction Division, PO Box 17447, Riyadh, Tel 4055242, 4056804, Telex 403422 ADWANC
Subsidiary/Associated Companies: Power Services Co Ltd (Operation & Maint-electro mech); Al Mawrid Stationery Center (Office supplies, equipment)
Principal Bankers: National Commercial Bank; Riyad Bank; Arab National Bank

Principal Shareholders: Abdelaziz Bin Adwan (50%); Mohamed Bin Adwan (50%)
Date of Establishment: 05/02/1398H
No of Employees: 450

AGAP ARABIA LIMITED

PO Box 84, Dhahran Airport 31932
Tel: 8947665/7669/6248
Telex: 870398 Agap Sj
Telefax: (03) 8947893

Chairman: Khalid Ali AlTurki
Directors: Saleh Ali AlTurki, Peter M L Smith, Luis I Villanueva, Edgardo A Grau, R C Lombos
Senior Executives: James L Dunlap (General Manager), Renato S Umali (Engineering & Business Development Manager), Antonio A Atienza (Finance Manager), Hollis Fitch (Construction Manager), Manuel C de Vera (Administration Manager)

PRINCIPAL ACTIVITIES: General contractors for civil, structural, mechanical, piping, electrical, instrumentation and operation and maintenance of industrial plants and buildings
Parent Company: Atlantic, Gulf and Pacific Co of Manila, Inc (AG&P), Philippines; Trading & Development Co (TRADCO) of Alkhobar, Saudi Arabia
Principal Bankers: National Commmercial Bank, Damman; Al Bank Al Saudi Al Fransi, Al-Khobar

Financial Information:

	1989	1990
	SR'000	SR'000
Sales turnover	78,598	68,741
Profits	4,876	3,188
Authorised capital	5,000	5,000
Paid-up capital	5,000	5,000
Total assets	38,808	44,137

Principal Shareholders: Trading & Development Co (51%); Atlantic Gulf & Pacific Co of Manila Inc (49%)
Date of Establishment: December 16, 1978
No of Employees: 2,000

AGGAD INVESTMENT CO

PO Box 2256, Riyadh 11451
Tel: 4767911
Cable: Aggad
Telex: 400276 AGGAD
Telefax: (01) 4767895

Chairman: Omar A Aggad
Directors: Talal O Aggad
Senior Executives: Khalil Darawish (Chief Financial Officer)

PRINCIPAL ACTIVITIES: Establishing, managing and investing in industrial and other business enterprises
Subsidiary/Associated Companies: Saudi Plastic Products Co Ltd (SAPPCO), PO Box 2828, Riyadh (also Dammam); Arabian Plastic Manufacturing Co Ltd (APLACO), PO Box 6193, Riyadh 11442; Arabian Technical Contracting Co (ARTEC), PO Box 2987, Riyadh 11461; Aluminium Products Co Ltd (ALUPCO), PO Box 2080, Dammam 31451; Steel Products Co Ltd (STEPCO), PO Box 4930, Riyadh 11412; Manufacturing & Building Co (MABCO), PO Box 1549, Riyadh 11441; Health Water Bottling Co Ltd (NISSAH), PO Box 2948, Riyadh 11461; Hygienic Paper Co Ltd, PO Box 8160, Riyadh 21482; Saudi International Petroleum Carriers Ltd (SIPCA), PO Box 5572 Riyadh 11432; SAPPCO-Texaco Insulation Products Co (SAPTEX), PO Box 40042, Riyadh 11499; Aluminium Manufacturing Co (ALUMACO), PO Box 7661, Jeddah 21472; Mechanical Contracting Est (MCE), PO Box 5319, Riyadh 11422; Modern Medical Equipment Est (MEDISERV), PO Box 17550, Riyadh 11494; Arab Solar Energy Co ltd (SHAMSCO), PO BOX 52742, Riyadh 11573; Saudi Continental Insurance Co, PO Box 2940, Riyadh 11461; National Industrial Services Co Ltd (NISCO), PO Box 2821, Riyadh 11461; National Packing Products Co Ltd (WATANPAC), PO Box 25817, Riyadh 11476; Al Mira & Aggad Kone Elevators Ltd, PO Box 10142, Riyadh 11433; Arabian Confectionery Products Co Ltd (ACP), PO Box 25356, Riyadh 11466, GRC (Saudi Arabia) Ltd, PO Box 52743, Riyadh 11573; Saudi Finnish Contracting Co Ltd (SAFINCO), PO Box 2809, Riyadh 11461; Arab Technical Contracting Co Ltd (ARTEC), PO Box 55993, Riyadh 11544; National Advanced Systems Co Ltd (NASCO), PO Boc 50009, Riyadh 11523; Refreshment Manufacturing Co Ltd (REMACO), PO Boc 727, Jeddah 21421; National Marketing Co Ltd (NMC), PO Box 1848, Riyadh 11441
Principal Bankers: Gulf International Bank; Societe Generale; National Commercial Bank; Arab National Bank; Citibank; Bankers Trust Company; Manufacturers Hanover Trust Company; Brown Brothers Harriman & Co; Bahrain International Bank; Saudi American Bank; Banque Echanges Internationaux
Financial Information:

	1989
	SR'000
Sales turnover	462,000
Authorised capital	300,000
Paid-up capital	300,000
Total assets	648,000

Principal Shareholders: Omar A Aggad
Date of Establishment: 1975
No of Employees: 20 (Holding company only)

AGRI BULK TRADE LTD

PO Box 2194, Al Khobar 31952
Tel: (03) 894 4880, (03) 864 5351
Telex: 870354 SABUT SJ, 871096 ARBUT SJ
Telefax: 8640461

Chairman: Hisham A Alireza
Directors: Per Berg (President), Egil Sjulsen (Executive Vice President)
Senior Executives: Ali M Bamardouf (Vice President)

PRINCIPAL ACTIVITIES: Trading and marketing bulk agricultural commodities, feed grains, fertilizers, petro-chemical by-products
Principal Agencies: Norsk Hydro
Branch Offices: Jeddah: PO Box 16698, Tel (02) 6372024, Telex 605518 ABTTRA SJ; Buraydah: Tel (06) 3240381, Riyadh: Tel (01) 4789323, Telex 403106 BNEXRD SJ
Parent Company: Arabian Bulk Trade Ltd
Principal Bankers: Gulf International Bank; Saudi American Bank
Financial Information:

	1989/90
	SR'000
Sales turnover	125,000
Authorised capital	4,000
Paid-up capital	4,000

Principal Shareholders: A member of the Xenel Group of companies
Date of Establishment: 1983
No of Employees: 40

AGRICULTURAL DEVELOPMENT CORP

PO Box 1039, Jeddah 21431
Tel: 6428277, 6421879, 6422844
Cable: Nami
Telex: 601103 Dabagh Sj

Directors: Sheikh Abdalla Dabbagh (Managing Director)

PRINCIPAL ACTIVITIES: Promotion of agricultural projects, poultry industry, import and distribution of agricultural equipment and materials, feeds and veterinery supplies
Branch Offices: Riyadh: PO Box 437, Tel 4763965, 4771096; Dammam: PO Box 586, Tel 8321319; Taif and Medina

Date of Establishment: 1963

AGRICULTURAL EXPANSION EST

PO Box 456, Riyadh 11411
Tel: 4027845, 4055928
Cable: Al Tansheet
Telex: 405298 Tnshet Sj
Telefax: 4042502

Senior Executives: Adib H Mahmoud (General Manager), Mousa Al Issa (Accounting Manager), Tayseer Abdallah (Technical & Marketing Manager)

PRINCIPAL ACTIVITIES: Supply of fertilisers, seeds, agrochemicals, agricultural and horticultural equipment
Principal Agencies: Tezier, France; Harris Moran (Niagara), USA; Cequisa, Spain; Biesterfield, Germany; Kobe Industries, Japan; Cervic Plus, France
Branch Offices: Al Kharj
Principal Bankers: Riyad Bank; Arab National Bank; Al Bank Al Saudi Al Fransi

Date of Establishment: 1960
No of Employees: 30

AGRONOMICS ARABIA

PO Box 2615, Jeddah 21461
Tel: 6604539, 6673729
Telex: 600956 AGROS SJ

Chairman: Zuhair Omar Duhaiby

Senior Executives: Mohammad A Majeed (Asst General Manager), Kaleem A Sheik (Finance Manager), Ahmed Fiddah (Operations Manager), Mohammad Tawfiq (Admin Manager)

PRINCIPAL ACTIVITIES: Contractors, landscape and irrigation, nursery and management operators
Branch Offices: PO Box 58749, Riyadh 11515, Tel 4776164, 4776174
Parent Company: Afnan Business & Trading Co Ltd
Principal Bankers: National Commercial Bank

Principal Shareholders: Duhaiby family
Date of Establishment: 1976
No of Employees: 150

AHLIA REAL ESTATE EST
PO Box 3245, Riyadh 11471
Tel: 4113936
Telex: 400094 DOCON SJ (Attn: Moh Algossayyar)

Chairman: Mohammed Al-Gossayyar

PRINCIPAL ACTIVITIES: Manufacture and supply of cement blocks, tiles and other building materials, property development and construction
Parent Company: National House of Trade & Commission Corporation
Subsidiary Companies: Hajur Contracting Co Ltd
Principal Bankers: Riyad Bank

Date of Establishment: 1971

AHMAD HAMAD ALGOSAIBI & BROS
See ALGOSAIBI, AHMAD HAMAD, & BROS

AHMAD MOHAMED SALEH BAESHEN & CO
See BAESHEN, AHMAD MOHAMED SALEH, & CO

AHMED & MOHAMMAD SALEH KAKI (GROUP OF COMPANIES)
See KAKI, AHMED & MOHAMMAD SALEH, (GROUP OF COMPANIES)

AHMED & YOUSUF MOHAMED NAGHI
See NAGHI, AHMED & YOUSUF MOHAMED,

AHMED ALI BADOGHAISH
See BADOGHAISH, AHMED ALI,

AHMED ALI TURKI EST (AATE)
PO Box 1215, Jeddah 21431
Tel: 6674181, 6674185
Cable: International
Telex: 601240 Natali Sj
Telefax: 6601302

Owner: Ahmad Ali Turki
Directors: Hani A Turki (Managing Director)
Senior Executives: Basheer Al Abtah (Sales Manager), Ibrahim Omar (Marketing Manager), Iftikhar Ahmed (Technical Manager)

PRINCIPAL ACTIVITIES: Import of telecommunication and electrical equipment, office equipment contracting, manufacturers' representatives; footwear, toys, rubber products, aviation products, stationery, driers, project furniture, protective sprays/chemicals; supply, installation and maintenance of central airconditioning equipment, food packaging
Principal Agencies: International Aeradio Ltd, UK; Efficienta, Holland, Boyden, UK; Baby Deer Ltd, UK; Phillips Rubber Ltd, UK; Sutherland Ltd, UK; Anda Ltd, UK; Coba Int Ltd, UK; LPS Ltd, UK; Steweon, Holland
Principal Bankers: Arab National Bank, Jeddah

Financial Information:

	1989 SR'000
Sales turnover	5,000
Profits	1,250
Authorised capital	1,000
Paid-up capital	1,000
Total assets	1,800

Date of Establishment: 1980

AL ABBAD TRADING & CONTRACTING CO LTD
PO Box 5949, Riyadh 11432
Tel: 4763606, 4763608
Cable: Al Abbadiya
Telex: 401482 Alabad Sj

President: Abdullah S Al-Abbad
Directors: Ibrahim S Al-Abbad (Vice President)
Senior Executives: Khalid S Al-Abbad (Sales Manager)

PRINCIPAL ACTIVITIES: General trading, import and distribution of consumer goods, household appliances, furniture, agricultural machinery; paints, stucco for wood and walls, soft drinks, canned foodstuff, etc
Principal Agencies: Plextone Paints
Branch Offices: Branch in Jeddah
Principal Bankers: National Commercial Bank, Riyadh

Principal Shareholders: Al-Abbad Brothers
Date of Establishment: 1975

ALAFAK ALSAUDIA EST
PO Box 2195, Jeddah 21451
Tel: 6675992, 6675821, 6609687
Cable: Horizon Jeddah
Telex: 600137 Alafak Sj
Telefax: 6675821

President: Ramzi J Saab
Directors: Monir Salim Shamoon (Vice President), Mohammad Aslam Siddiqui (Managing Director)
Senior Executives: M D Ehteshamuddin (Personnel Manager), Abdullah Abdul Jabbar (Marketing Manager), Zafar Iqbal Butt (Sales & Purchasing Manager), Mahmood Said Babbour (Technical Manager)

PRINCIPAL ACTIVITIES: Civil engineering contracting and land development; leisure and amusement centres; general trading; building and maintenance of swimming pools; water treatment; fitness centers, tennis courts, landscaping; mobile cleaning and restoration
Subsidiary Companies: Alafak Bouhayrat; Alafak Yats; Lunapark; Sparkle Wash
Principal Bankers: Indosuez Bank (Nice, France); Al Bank Saudi Al Fransi, Jeddah, Saudi Arabia

Principal Shareholders: Ramzi J Saab
Date of Establishment: 1976
No of Employees: 150

AL AHGAAF CONTRACTING AGENCIES
PO Box 5273, Jeddah 21422
Tel: 6317573
Cable: Ahgaf, Jeddah
Telex: 600487 Ahgaf SJ, 601280 Hotman SJ

Chairman: Abubakr Bamatraf
Directors: Mohamed S Bathawab (Joint Managing Director), A M Bamatraf (Joint Managing Director)

PRINCIPAL ACTIVITIES: Civil engineering and construction, supply of steel buildings for turnkey projects, portable accommodation units and concrete finishing equipment
Principal Agencies: Errut Products Ltd, UK; SNOEI BV, Holland
Branch Offices: PO Box 7698, Riyadh Telex 400281 Ahgaaf SJ; Tel 4055984

Principal Bankers: Saudi British Bank; National Commercial Bank

Principal Shareholders: Abubakr Bamatraf
Date of Establishment: September 1976
No of Employees: 40

AL AIDAROUS TRADING CORP

PO Box 2238, Jeddah 21451
Tel: 6423029, 6424151, 6431278
Cable: JACOP JEDDAH
Telex: 600312 Jacop Sj

Chairman: Yousuf Ahmed Al Aidaroos
Directors: Yousuf Ahmed Al Aidarous, Yahya Ahmed Al Aidarous

PRINCIPAL ACTIVITIES: Generating, drilling, welding, safety equipment, tools and hardware, complete range of auto service equipment, material handling equipment, pipe tools, climbing equipment, packing equipment, measuring and precision measuring tools, turning tools, other machine shop hardware requirements, traffic hazard warning equipment, compressors, airconditioning servicing equipment
Principal Agencies: Hazet, Germany; Sykes Pickavant, UK; Ingersoll-Rand, Switzerland/USA; Peugeot, Electric Tools Div. France; Kango Wolf Power Tools, UK; Gloor Bors, Switzerland; Sandvik AB, Sweden; Mitutoyo, Japan; Protector Int'l Ltd, Australia/USA; SA GYS, France; Panther Equipment Ltd, UK
Branch Offices: Riyadh, Yanbu, Dammam
Principal Bankers: National Commercial Bank; Riyadh Bank

Principal Shareholders: Individual Ownership
Date of Establishment: 1962

ALAJAJI & ALZAYANI TRADING CO LTD

PO Box 828, Alkhobar 31952
Tel: 8952736
Telex: 871045 ZTT SJ

Chairman: Ghassan H Alajaji
Directors: Hamid R Alzayani
Senior Executives: Farooq A Chiragh (General Manager), Essa Alzayani (Commercial Manager)

PRINCIPAL ACTIVITIES: Electronics and home appliances
Principal Agencies: Samsung Electronics, Korea; Hightone, Japan; Beamscope, Japan
Principal Bankers: National Commercial Bank

Principal Shareholders: Hamad H Alajaji & Brothers, Alzayani Investments
Date of Establishment: June 1981

AL AJDA AUTOMOTIVE

PO Box 10974, Riyadh 11443
Tel: 4654950
Telex: 400534 HOUSE Sj

PRINCIPAL ACTIVITIES: Car agents and distributors, mechanical, electrical and body work
Principal Agencies: Ferrari; Lamborghini; Alfa Romeo; Riva; Rolls Royce; Bentley
Branch Offices: Jeddah: PO Box 9169, Jeddah 21643, Tel 6716183

AL AJINAH, ALI M, INC

PO Box 344, Alkhobar 31952
Tel: 8642641
Telex: 870086 Ajinah SJ

President: Ali Mohammed Al Ajinah (Owner)
Directors: Mohd A Al Ajinah, Fawaz A Al Ajinah

PRINCIPAL ACTIVITIES: General contracting, site preparation, road construction, airports, bridges, side development, utilities, highways, sewer and water systems, electromechanical and maintenance

AL ALAMIYA INSURANCE CO LTD

PO Box 2374, Jeddah 21451
Tel: (02) 6718851
Telex: 600941 ALINS SJ, 606456 ALAMIA SJ
Telefax: 6711377

Chairman: Sheikh Wahib S Binzagr
Directors: Sheikh Mohamed A Al-Fraih, Riyad Bank Ltd (represented by Mohammed Ammari), R A G Neville, D C Hulme (General Manager), Dr Mahsoun B Jalal
Senior Executives: D C Hulme (General Manager), C B Sequeira (Technical Manager), G Sridhar (Financial Manager), R P Gallagher (Branch Manager Jeddah), P Fernandes (Branch Manager Riyadh), A G Robertson (Branch Manager Alkhobar)

PRINCIPAL ACTIVITIES: Insurance
Branch Offices: Registered Office: 1 Bartholomew Lane, London EC2N 2AB; location in Jeddah: Al Rajhi Bldg, Palestine Street; Alkhobar: PO Box 1276, Alkhobar 31952, Tel 8983802, 8980745, Telex 870420 Alam Sj, Fax 8954051; Riyadh: PO Box 6393, Riyadh 11442, Tel 4651520, Telex 404409 ALINS SJ, Fax 4645457; Buraydah: PO Box 1214, Tel 3231724, Telex 801084 Alamia Sj
Associated Companies: Sun Alliance & London Insurance Group
Principal Bankers: Riyad Bank Ltd

Principal Shareholders: Sheikh Mohd Al Abdulrahman Al Fraih, National Industrialisation Co, Sheikh Abdulatif Al Ali Al-Issa, Ali Zaid Al Quraishi & Bros, Abdullah & Said M O Binzagr, Heirs of Sheikh Hamza Mohd Bogary, Riyad Bank Ltd, Sun Alliance & London Insurance Group
Date of Establishment: 1976
No of Employees: 70

ALAMDAR & CO LTD

PO Box 120, Dhahran Airport 31932
Tel: 03-8331116
Cable: ALAMDAR/DAMMAM
Telex: 802266 Alamco Sj
Telefax: 03-8339439

Chairman: Shaikh Omar Khaled Alamdar
Directors: Khaled Omar Alamdar (Managing Director)
Senior Executives: Moritz Kerler (General Manager), Khaled Omar Alamdar (Asst General Manager), Nabil A Z Thabit (Finance Manager), Abdul Rahman Kishk (Accounts Manager), Mansour Alamdar (Public Relations Officer), Tahseen Alkheder (Purchasing Manager), Mohammed Amin Higazy (Construction Manager), Hisham Shaikh Al Ard (Sales Manager), Fazlulla Khan (Company Secretary)

PRINCIPAL ACTIVITIES: Ready mix concrete, building materials and equipment, prefab and precast building, blocks, curbs, general construction, commerce, manufacturers, contracting, maintenance, operations, agencies, air and sea safety equipment, safety training, dewatering systems, heavy equipment, agricultural projects, machinery and equipment, green houses, meat, livestock, laundry services, transport, medical supplies and services, land development
Principal Agencies: Geho Dewatering Systems, Netherlands; Atlas Weyhausen, W Germany; Beaufort Air & Sea Equipment, UK; Krupp, W Germany etc
Branch Offices: Dammam; Dhahran; Jubail; Riyadh; Qassem; Jeddah; Abha; Tabouk; also overseas: Holland; West Germany; Canada; France
Principal Bankers: Saudi American Bank, Dammam; Riyad Bank, Damman; Saudi Cairo Bank, Dammam; Saudi British Bank, Dammam
Financial Information:

	1989 SR'000
Sales turnover	200,000
Profits	20,000
Authorised capital	10,200
Paid-up capital	10,200
Total assets	137,551

Principal Shareholders: Omar Khaled Alamdar, Khaled Omar
Alamdar, Ammar Omar Alamdar, Mrs Mona Omar Alamdar,
Mrs Ghada Omar Alamdar
Date of Establishment: November, 1975
No of Employees: 400

ALAMDAR VAPOTHERM CO LTD
PO Box 1428, Riyadh 11431
Tel: 4792964, 4770205
Cable: Alamdarco
Telex: 405581 Altaif Sj
Telefax: 4770987

Chairman: Sheikh Ahmed Jawad Alamdar
Directors: Sh A J Alamdar (General Manager), Dr Issam
Alamdar (Deputy General Manager)
Senior Executives: Eng Mohammed Othman (Technical Sales
Manager)

PRINCIPAL ACTIVITIES: Manufacturing rigid polyurethane
boards and pipe insulation sections for thermal insulation
Principal Bankers: National Commercial Bank
Financial Information:

	1990
	SR'000
Authorised capital	10,000
Paid-up capital	4,000

Principal Shareholders: Sh A J Alamdar (50%); Alamdar Co Ltd
For Trading, Industry & Contracting (50%)
Date of Establishment: 11/9/1396 H
No of Employees: 43

AL AMOUDI BROS CO
PO Box 8128, Jeddah 21482
Tel: 6721538, 6721750, 6714710, 6714550
Telex: 604970 Ambros SJ
Telefax: 6718628

Chairman: Sheikh Ahmed Abdullah Al Amoudi
Directors: Sh Ahmed A Al Amoudi, Sh Mohammed A Al Amoudi,
Sh Abdullatif A Al Amoudi, Sh Khalid A Al Amoudi

PRINCIPAL ACTIVITIES: Construction div, agricultural
machinery, pesticides, chemicals, agriculture, steel div,
foodstuff div, marine div, car div, computer div, commercial
div, transport div, hotel
Principal Agencies: Saab Scania, Sweden; Storebro Bruks AB,
Sweden
Subsidiary Companies: Saudi Red Bricks Co; Ahmed Abdullah
Al Amoudi Est, Printemps (department store), Prisunic
(supermarket), Asia Hotel, Middle Shopping Center
Principal Bankers: National Commercial Bank; Riyad Bank
Financial Information:

	1990
	US$'000
Sales turnover	100,000
Profits	20,000
Authorised capital	60,000
Paid-up capital	60,000
Total assets	200,000

Principal Shareholders: Sheikh Ahmed A Al Amoudi, Sheikh
Mohammed A Al Amoudi, Sheikh Abdullatif A Al Amoudi,
Sheikh Khalid A Al Amoudi
Date of Establishment: 1979
No of Employees: 1,500

AL AOUN CORPORATION
PO Box 4029, Jeddah 21491
Tel: 6721010, 6720123, 6717410
Cable: Alaoun
Telex: 601536 SAG Sj
Telefax: 6720059

Chairman: Suleiman Al Saiari
Directors: Saleh Al Saiari, Khalid Al Saiari

Senior Executives: Hamad Abu Idrees

PRINCIPAL ACTIVITIES: Industrial printing, graphic and screen
printing, equipment and inks, self adhesive labels printing
factory
Branch Offices: Riyadh, Dammam
Subsidiary Companies: Al Aoun Factory for Commercial Labels
Principal Bankers: National Commercial Bank, Jeddah

AL ARABI EST FOR TRADING & GENERAL CONTRACTING
PO Box 2435, Riyadh 11451
Tel: 4353834
Telex: 401531 Arbest Aj

President: Muslih A Harbi

PRINCIPAL ACTIVITIES: General trading and contracting,
construction and building contractors
Branch Offices: Jeddah, Tel 6653372

No of Employees: 230

ALARIFI TRADING & CONTRACTING CORPORATION
PO Box 345, Dammam 31411
Tel: 8322636, 8335825, 8337153, 8337154
Cable: PLANET
Telex: 802056 FARIFI SJ, 802619 SARIFI SJ
Telefax: 8341080

President: Sheikh Mohammad Abdullah Alarifi
Vice Presidents: Sheikh Abdullah Mohammad Alarifi (VP &
General Manager), Sheikh Abdulaziz Mohammad Alarifi (VP &
Promotions, Sales & Government Relations Director)
Senior Executives: Suhail M Pharaon (Commercial & Marketing
Manager), Roy Chadwick (Water Well Drilling & Pump
supplies Manager), Joseph Farah (Money Exchange &
Investment Manager), Ghattas Matar (Sales & Projects
Manager), Osama Khair (Supervision Investment &
Development Manager), Mohammad Abu Alwafa (Financial
Controller)

PRINCIPAL ACTIVITIES: General building contractors, water
well drilling contractors, real estate dealers and developers,
currency-banking transaction-precious metals dealers,
importers, stockists and suppliers of all kinds of building
materials, electrical goods, engineering & drafting materials,
all kinds of tools, valve pumps, pipes and fittings, steel
products, office products, furniture etc
Principal Agencies: SM Int'l, USA; Kelley Pumps; Veva Laterizi,
Italy; Pica Roof Tiles, Italy; Dennis & Robinson, UK;
Manhattan Kitchens; Daminco Marbles, Portugal
Branch Offices: Jeddah; Riyadh; Alkhobar; Dammam and Jubail
Subsidiary Companies: Alarifi Hotel; Alarifi Gulf Motel; Alarifi
Exchange Co
Principal Bankers: National Commercial Bank; Saudi American
Bank, Dammam
Financial Information:

	1990
	SR'000
Authorised capital	2,000
Paid-up capital	2,000
Total assets	300,000

Principal Shareholders: Sheikh Mohammed Abdullah Alarifi;
Sheikh Abdullah Mohammad Alarifi; Sheikh Abdel Aziz
Mohammad Alarifi
Date of Establishment: 14.3.1391 H (1971)
No of Employees: 250

ALATAS, S H, & CO LTD
Alatas Agencies
PO Box 1106, Dammam 31431
Tel: 8329379, 8329242
Cable: ALSHIP DAMMAM
Telex: 801591 Ship Sj

Chairman: M H Alatas
Directors: A H Alatas

PRINCIPAL ACTIVITIES: Shipping, customs clearing and forwarding services, transportation and crane rentals
Principal Agencies: Dock Express Shipping, Holland; Portakabin, UK; Hudsons International Freight Forwarding Services, UK & USA; Doornbos Tech, Holland
Branch Offices: Alatas Agencies (HO), PO Box 4, Jeddah; Alatas Agencies, PO Box 681, Jubail; Alatas Agencies, PO Box 270, Yanbu
Subsidiary Companies: Alatas Big Lift Co Ltd, HO Jeddah, Branches in Jubail, Yanbu; Alatas Transport Co Ltd, Jeddah; Alatas Nedlloyd Company Ltd, Jeddah
Principal Bankers: Albank Alsaudi Alhollandi - Dammam, Jubail, Jeddah

Principal Shareholders: 100% owned by S H Alatas Family
Date of Establishment: 1389H
No of Employees: 87

AL ATTAS, HUSSEIN BIN HASHIM,

PO Box 1299, Jeddah 21431
Tel: 6420400, 6420211, 6420418
Telex: 601158 Atasel Sj

Directors: Hussein Bin Hashim Al Attas (Managing Director)

PRINCIPAL ACTIVITIES: Hotel management and operation, general trading and contracting, travel agency, manufacture of furniture; import and distribution of building and decorative materials
Subsidiary Companies: Al Attas Hotels; Al Attas Holiday Beach Hotel, Al Haramain Hotel; Al Attas Oasis Decoration Centre; Al Attas Trading & Contracting; Montana Pastry & Bakery Shop; Al Attas Travel Agency; Al Attas Bamboo & Furniture Work Shop; Al-Attas Commercial Centre; Hussein Hashim Al Attas Est; Al Attas Trading Est

AL AZHAR TRADING DEVELOPMENT & CONTRACTING EST

Shobra for Trade & Hotels Services Co Ltd

PO Box 4521, Jeddah 21412
Tel: 5361661/62 (Makkah)
Cable: Sabagheen
Telex: 540113 Makkah Sj
Telefax: 5361108 (Makkah)

President: Sheikh Abdulghani Mahmoud Sabbagh (Owner)

PRINCIPAL ACTIVITIES: General trading and contracting, supply of building materials, ceramics, sanitaryware, carpets, furniture, construction equipment, hotel business
Branch Offices: Location in Jeddah: Madina Road, Al Faiha Bldg, 4th Floor; also branch in Mecca Mukarrama, Saudi Arabia
Subsidiary/Associated Companies: Shobra for Trade & Hotels Services Co Ltd; Oun Alqra Hotel Medana and Shobra Hotel Mecca, Saudi Arabia
Principal Bankers: Alrajhi Bank, Makkah
Financial Information:

	1988 SR'000
Paid-up capital	2,400
Total assets	80,000

Date of Establishment: 1975
No of Employees: 500

AL AZIZIA MARKETS CO

PO Box 752, Riyadh 11421
Tel: 4658103, 4633682
Telex: 403226 TARFA SJ

PRINCIPAL ACTIVITIES: Food processing and supply
Associated Companies: Great Atlantic and Pacific Tea Co, USA

AL AZIZIAH AGRICULTURAL PRODUCTS CO LTD

PO Box 54246, Riyadh 11514
Tel: 01-4630531, 01-4794525
Telex: 405352 Azizia Sj
Telefax: 01-4631802

Chairman: Sheikh Ahmed Zainy
Directors: Sheikh Fahad Al Athel (Executive Board Member)
Senior Executives: Mohammed Anwar Jan (Director General)

PRINCIPAL ACTIVITIES: Dairy farming, dairy processing and distribution
Branch Offices: Jeddah, Tel 02-6836820
Principal Bankers: Riyad Bank
Financial Information:

	1990 SR'000
Authorised capital	72,720
Paid-up capital	72,720

Date of Establishment: 1983
No of Employees: 163

AL BABTAIN, ABDUL LATIF SAUD, & BROS

PO Box 494, Alkhobar 31952
Tel: 8647420, 8643075
Cable: SHUROOK
Telex: 870178 Shrouk SJ
Telefax: 8983432

Chairman: Abdul Latif S Al Babtain

PRINCIPAL ACTIVITIES: General trading (Foodstuffs, tobacco, electrical & household equipment); real estate management; manufacture of polyurethane chemicals, insulators, furniture, plastic barrels
Branch Offices: Location in Alkhobar: Al Babtain Bldg, King Abdulaziz Street, also Riyadh, Jeddah, Hail, Najran, Arar, Dammam, Gassim, Medina, Khamis Mushait
Subsidiary Companies: AlBabtain Project Investment Company, Agri, Polyvest, Al Babtain Polyurethane Co Ltd, Al Babtain Plastic Barrel Co Ltd
Principal Bankers: Saudi American Bank, Riyadh

AL BABTAIN TRADING, INDUSTRY & CONTRACTING CO

PO Box 181, Riyadh 11411
Tel: 4028012, 4028023, 4025028, 2411222 (8 lines)
Telex: 401174 Babtan Sj
Telefax: 2410228

Chairman: Mohammed Al Babtain
Directors: Abdul Aziz Al Babtain, Abdul Aziz Al Wuhaibi, Wissa H Michael, Abdul Aziz Al Homaid
Senior Executives: Shaukat Naeem (Sales Manager Household Appliances Division), Mohkam Uddin (Sales Manager Electrical Division)

PRINCIPAL ACTIVITIES: Electrical, power, and air-conditioning equipment and contracting
Principal Agencies: Speed Queen Co, USA; Caloric, USA; Admiral, USA; Sigmaform, UK; Brush Fusegear, UK; Taichi Co, Japan; Catu, France; Legrand, France; Ilsa, Italy; Terim, Italy; El Cold, Denmark
Branch Offices: Alkhobar: PO Box 404; Jeddah: PO Box 4849; Khamis Mushait: PO Box 901; Buraydah: PO Box 3051; Riyadh: PO Box 181, Al Khazzan Street
Parent Company: Al Babtain Group of Companies
Subsidiary Companies: Al Babtain Trading Co; Al Babtain Contracting Co; Al Babtain Industries (Al Babtain Lighting Co; Al Babtain Washing Machine Factory; Al Babtain Panel Board Factory; Al Babtain Boiler Factory)
Principal Bankers: Riyad Bank; Al Bank Al Saudi Al Fransi; Albank Alsaudi Alhollandi

Financial Information:

	24/3/91
	SR'000
Sales turnover	60,000
Profits	6,000
Authorised capital	9,900
Paid-up capital	9,900
Total assets	16,000

Principal Shareholders: Hamad Al Babtain (Late), Ibrahim Al Babtain (Late), Mohammed Al Babtain
Date of Establishment: 1958
No of Employees: 140

AL BADER AMMACHE CONTRACTING CO LTD

PO Box 754, Jeddah 21421
Tel: 6514055, 6519687
Cable: BADER AFGO
Telex: 600319 Rabam Sj

Chairman: Rabih Ammache

PRINCIPAL ACTIVITIES: General contractors specialised in the building sector, feasibility studies, architectural designs, program scheduling, cost control, construction of building (hotels, residential, commercial), structural works, finishing works, exterior works, landscaping, furnishing, turn key basis
Principal Bankers: Banque Libano Francaise; National Commercial Bank

Principal Shareholders: Sheikh Wahbe Sansui Tahalwi; Rabih Ammache (the company was formed by incorporating Al Bader Contracting and Rabih Ammache Engineering General Cont Est of Lebanon)
Date of Establishment: 1980
No of Employees: work force 580

ALBADIA SAUDI TRADING CORPORATION

PO Box 7531, Jeddah 21472
Tel: 6475124
Telex: 602008 Badia Sj

Chairman: Saleh Ahmed El-Bayed
Directors: Zuhdi Mohamed Jibril (Managing Director)

PRINCIPAL ACTIVITIES: Importers/wholesalers/distributors for perfumes, cosmetics, consumer goods, health and beauty care items, commission agents, clearing and forwarding, transportation
Principal Agencies: Plough Int'l, USA; Bonne Bell, USA; Margaret Astor, W Germany
Branch Offices: Albadia Trading Corp, PO Box 5229, Dammam
Principal Bankers: Riyadh Bank

Principal Shareholders: Saleh A Elbayed; Saud A Elbayed; Zuhdi M Jibril
Date of Establishment: 1973
No of Employees: 35

AL BADR JEDDAH SHERATON HOTEL

PO Box 6719, Jeddah 21452
Tel: 6310000
Telex: 601512 SHER Sj

PRINCIPAL ACTIVITIES: Hotel operation

AL BAJJASH, HAMAD,

PO Box 862, Alkhobar 31952
Tel: 8647731, 8952740
Cable: Bajjash
Telex: 870197 BAJASH SJ

Proprietor: Hamad Al-Bajjash
Senior Executives: M Nasarullah Niazi

PRINCIPAL ACTIVITIES: General, civil and building contractors; electrical and food supplies; general services; land surveying; equipment rental and maintenance

Branch Offices: Hamad Al-Bajjash Overseas Inc, USA
Principal Bankers: Saudi British Bank, AlKhobar; National Commercial Bank, AlKhobar

Principal Shareholders: Hamad Al Bajjash
Date of Establishment: 1970
No of Employees: 360

AL BANK AL SAUDI AL FRANSI
Saudi French Bank

PO Box 56006, Riyadh 11554
Tel: 4042222 (50 lines)
Telex: 407666 SFGM SJ
Telefax: 4042311

Chairman: Sheikh Omran Mohamed Al Omran

Directors: Ibrahim A Al Touq (Vice Chairman), Antoine Jeancourt-Galignani, Abdulaziz R Al Rashed, Pierre Strub, Ibrahim A Alissa, Ibrahim M Al Issa, Abdullah Abu A Al Samh, Gerard Delaforge (Managing Director), Essam Al Sanie (Secretary General)

Senior Executives: Peter Willis (Investment Banking Manager), Alain Massiera (Credit Division Manager), Jean Pierre Jaffeux (System Operations Support Manager), Alain Mera (Corplan & Control Division Manager), Ibrahim A Shanak (Retail Banking Division Manager), C Marfaing (Internal Auditor)

PRINCIPAL ACTIVITIES: Commercial banking

Branch Offices: 58 branches in Saudi Arabia; Western Region Management Jeddah: PO Box 7888, Jeddah 21472, Tower Building, Al Madinah Road, Tel 6515151, Telex 601168, Fax 6533449; and 9 branches in Jeddah; Madina Main Branch: PO Box 462, Tel 8236618, Telex 570197 Fax 8256327; and 2 branches in Madina; Taif Branch: PO Box 1387; Makkah Main Branch: PO Box 3302; and 3 branches in Makkah; Abha Branch: PO Box 759; Yanbu Main Branch: PO Box 501; and 2 branches in Yanbu; Tabuk Branch: PO Box 675; Jizan Branch: PO Box 241; Najran Branch: PO Box 1020; Al-Jouf Branch: PO Box 332; Hail Branch: PO Box 1654; Arar Branch: PO Box 670; Baljurashy Branch: PO Box 99; Bisha Branch: PO Box 283; Al-Neemas Branch: PO Box 115, Baha Branch: PO Box 300; Khamis-Mushait Branch: PO Box 1180, Rabigh Branch: Main Road, Rabigh; Buraidah Branch: PO Box 1394; Regional Management Central Province: PO Box 1290, Riyadh 11431, Airport Road, Tel 4782066, Telex 401428, Fax 4770854; and 10 branches in Riyadh; Regional Management Eastern Province: PO Box 754, Dhahran International Airport, King Abdul Aziz Street, Al-Khobar Tel 8985760, Telex 871196, Fax 8945688 and 2 branches in Al Khobar; Dammam Main Branch: PO Box 2792; and 1 branch in Damman; Thugbah Branch: PO Box 122; Hofuf Main Branch: PO Box 779; and 1 branch in Hofuf; Mubarraz Branch: PO Box 330; Jubail Branch: PO Box 108; and 1 branch in Jubail; Qatif Branch, PO Box 427

Associated/Subsidiary Companies: Banco Saudi Espanol; Saudi Share Transfer Co; Saudi Travellers Cheque Co; Compagnie Financiere de Suez; Basic Chemical Industries

Financial Information:

	1988/89	1989/90
	SR'million	SR'million
Loans & advances	5,166	5,174
Deposits	12,386	13,170
Net income	86	103
Authorised capital	400	400
Paid-up capital	400	400
Total assets	29,086	27,823

Principal Shareholders: Saudi Nationals (60%); Banque Indosuez - Paris (40%)
Date of Establishment: December 1977
No of Employees: 1,316

ALBANK ALSAUDI ALHOLLANDI

Head Office, PO Box 1467, Riyadh 11431
Tel: 01-4067888
Cable: Saudilandahed
Telex: 405959 BSHRHO SJ
Telefax: 01-4067888 ext 523

Chairman: Sheikh Mohamed Abdulrahman Al-Fraih
Directors: HRH Prince Khalid Bin Fahd Bin Abdulaziz, Sheikh
  Ahmed Abdullah Al Juffali, Sheikh Ali Abdullah Al Tamimi,
  Sayed Mohamed Hussein Alatas, Dr Ibrahim Ali Al Khodair,
  Th J Bark, P J Kalff, JJ Oyevaar, E Merbis
Senior Executives: Th J Bark (Managing Director)

PRINCIPAL ACTIVITIES: Commercial banking
Branch Offices: Branches in Jeddah (5), Riyadh (5), Dammam
  (2), Makkah, Buraidah, Hofuf, Jubail (2), Alkhobar (3), Abha,
  Qatif, Yanbu, Tabuk, Taif, Madinah and Hail
Principal Bankers: Algemene Bank Nederland NV

Principal Shareholders: Algemene Bank Nederland NV (40%),
  Saudi Co-founders & Public (60%)
Date of Establishment: 1977
No of Employees: 760

AL BATEL EST FOR TRADING & SUPPLIES

PO Box 4211, Riyadh 11491
Tel: 4773788
Telefax: 4779124

Chairman: Suliman H Al Batel
Senior Executives: Syed Ibrahim (Finance Manager), Mahmood
  Al Hawt (Administration Manager), Jamal Abdel Basit
  (Marketing Manager)

PRINCIPAL ACTIVITIES: Import, export, trading, commission,
  tenders, advertising, publicity, companies' agents
Branch Offices: Zulfi, Medina, Jeddah
Principal Bankers: Saudi British Bank; Saudi Hollandi Bank,
  Saudi Cairo Bank

Date of Establishment: 1978

ALBAWARDI, MOH'D & A, CO

PO Box 217, Riyadh 11411
Tel: 4775301, 4775783, 4784550
Cable: AlBawardi
Telex: 406782 Bwardi SJ
Telefax: 4791342

President: Mohamed Saad AlBawardi
Directors: K M AlBawardi (Vice President)
Senior Executives: Fouad M Shaar (Commmercial Manager), D
  G Lee (Sales Manager)

PRINCIPAL ACTIVITIES: Import of all kinds of building
  materials, steel, cement, lumber, pipes, plywood, wire mesh,
  all kinds of tools, barley for animal feed; marine and motor
  surveyors, cargo superintendents, fire & machinery loss
  adjusters, valuation consultants
Branch Offices: Damman: PO Box 112, Tel 8324065, 8325346,
  8266105, Telex 801318 Bwardi SJ, Telefax 8334122;
  AlKhobar: Tel 8642473; Hasa: Tel 5821527, 5821018
Principal Bankers: National Commercial Bank; Saudi Cairo
  Bank; Riyadh Bank

Principal Shareholders: Mohamed and Abdul Rahman AlBawardi
Date of Establishment: 1956
No of Employees: 210

AL BAWARDY CONSULTING ENGINEERS

PO Box 8080, Riyadh 11482
Tel: 4782261, 4782355
Telex: 400448 Bawardy Sj
Telefax: 4767998

Chairman: Mohamed Al Bawardy

Directors: Dr Abdul Karim Shams Hamad (Director of Projects)
Senior Executives: Dr Najat Muhialdin

PRINCIPAL ACTIVITIES: Consulting engineering; power and
  water engineering
Branch Offices: Al Bawardy Consulting Engineers, PO Box
  28542, Riffa, Bahrain, Tel 233753, 233582, Telex 7420 SWCC
  BN
Principal Bankers: Saudi American Bank; National Commercial
  Bank

Date of Establishment: 1398H
No of Employees: 120

AL BAYDA TRADING CO

PO Box 7356, Jeddah 21462
Tel: 6713008, 6710644, 6718033
Cable: Center
Telex: 600430 Albyda Sj
Telefax: 6710644 Ext 415

Chairman: Sheikh Youssef Elakeel
President: Abdulaziz H Abulfaraj (Managing Director)
Senior Executives: Ralph M O'Dell (Vice President Marketing &
  Corporate Development), Essam Abdulmatloob (Finance
  Director), Saleh Bin Aquil (Purchasing Director), Osama
  Daoud (Personnel Director), Faysal I Al Aquil (Technical
  Director)

PRINCIPAL ACTIVITIES: Purchasing, construction, operation
  and maintenance, sales, procurement and logistics support,
  recruitment contractor, security systems
Principal Agencies: Superior Products Co, USA; Guerdon
  Industries Inc, USA; Hanjin Group, Korea; Shinwa Eng &
  Construction, Korea
Branch Offices: Riyadh, Yanbu, Dammam
Principal Bankers: National Commercial Bank; Saudi American
  Bank; Saudi British Bank; Saudi Cairo Bank
Financial Information:

	SR'000
Authorised capital	16,000
Paid-up capital	16,000

Principal Shareholders: Sheikh Youssef I Elakeel (50%);
  Abdulaziz H Abulfaraj; Essam Abdulmatloob; Saleh Bin Aquil;
  Faysal I Al Aquil; Osama Daoud
Date of Establishment: January 1978
No of Employees: 2,500

AL BILAD BCI TELECOMMUNICATIONS LTD

PO Box 6887, Riyadh 11452
Tel: 4657711
Telex: 402144 Belcor SJ

PRINCIPAL ACTIVITIES: Telecommunications consulting,
  engineering and operations and maintenance of
  telecommunication systems, training
Associated Companies: Bell Canada International, 1 Nicholas
  St, Ottawa Ont KIG 3J4, Canada
Principal Bankers: Albank Alsaudi Alhollandi

Principal Shareholders: Al Bilad Est for Trading & Economy;
  Bell Canada International
Date of Establishment: February 1980
No of Employees: 500

AL BINALI DRAKE & SCULL

PO Box 2, Dammam 31411
Tel: 8322285, 8322284
Telex: 801329 Sj

PRINCIPAL ACTIVITIES: Electrical, mechanical, general and
  building contractors

No of Employees: 300

AL BURAIDI EST FOR TRADING & GENERAL CONTRACTING

PO Box 6412, Riyadh 11442
Tel: 479-1870, 478-4867, 478-4866, 478-9872
Cable: Jareeco Braidi
Telex: 402037 Buraid Sj
Telefax: 4791496

Chairman: Mohammed J Al Buraidi
Directors: Abdullah J Al Buraidi (General Manager), Bandar J Al Buraidi (Civil Engineer - International Trading), Abdulrahman J Al Buraidi (Personnel & Transport Manager), Ali A Al Buraidi (Assistant Manager), Nayef A Atari (Financial Manager), John H Bond (Planning & Projects Controller)
Senior Executives: Mohammed Al Shamlan (Manager - Dammam), Ali Al Maiman (Manager - Hafr Al Batin), Ali Al Amro (Manager - Hail), Bandar A Al Buraidi (Manager - Gassim), Ismail Hussain (Manager - Jeddah), Abdulla Al Muneef (Manager- Abha)

PRINCIPAL ACTIVITIES: Building, construction
Branch Offices: PO Box 158, Hafr Al Batin, Tel (03) 722-3707; PO Box 429, Arar, Tel (04) 622-1158; PO Box 9042, Jeddah, Tel (02) 683-2713; PO Box 404, Buraidah, Tel (06) 323-4816; PO Box 7120, Dammam, Tel (03) 827-0954; PO Box 1287, Abha, Tel (07) 224-3744
Principal Bankers: Arab National Bank; Saudi American Bank; Riyad Bank; Al Bank Al Saudi Al Fransi
Financial Information:

	SR'000
Sales turnover	105,000
Authorised capital	40,000
Paid-up capital	40,000

Principal Shareholders: Privately owned by Mohammed J Al Buraidi
Date of Establishment: 1972
No of Employees: 1,750

AL DABAL CO

PO Box 1102, Dammam 31431
Tel: 8260578, 8266011
Cable: Dabal
Telex: 801124 Dabal Sj
Telefax: 8271580

Chairman: Abdullah K Al Dabal
Directors: Abdulrahman K Al Dabal

PRINCIPAL ACTIVITIES: Property and real estate, accommodation and office rentals, manufacturers' agents, paints, scaffolding & formwork, travel agency, insurance & reinsurance, manpower, advertising
Subsidiary Companies: Al Dabal Woodworks; Al Dabal Travel; SGB Dabal; First Travel Agency; Arabconsult; Alkairouan Manpower
Principal Bankers: Al Bank Al Saudi Al Hollandi; Al Bank Al Saudi Al Fransi; Riyad Bank
Financial Information:

| | 1989/90 |
	SR'000
Total assets	104,629

Date of Establishment: 1397H
No of Employees: 125

AL DAHLAWI, M JAMIL, CO

PO Box 1522, Jeddah 21441
Tel: 6470000
Cable: Al Dahlawi Jeddah
Telex: 601023 Dehlwi Sj
Telefax: 6474549

Chairman: M Amin Jamil Al Dahlawi
Directors: Hassan Jamil Al Dahlawi (Senior Vice President), Osman Al Dahlawi (Vice President), Ibrahim M H Al Dahlawi (Vice President), Abdullah M Amin Al Dahlawi (Vice President)

Senior Executives: Samir Al Karaki (General Manager), Abdus Salam (Banking Manager), Zahir Abdul Sattar Mobayed (Sales Manager Electronic), Anwar Khan Deshmukh (Sales Manager Home Appliances), M Anwar Ullah Khan (Import & Export Manager), S B Qadri (Manager Special Products System Dept), Essam El Sayed (Personnel Manager)

PRINCIPAL ACTIVITIES: Import and distribution of electrical and electronic equipment, fire and burglar alarm systems, low voltage engineering, studio and communication systems, home security, conference and language laboratory systems, office automation, sewing machines, foodstuffs, computers, sunrock water coolers, videa wall image expander & controller
Principal Agencies: Agents and sole distributors for Technics, National, National Panasonic
Branch Offices: Makkah: PO Box 28, Tel 5747272, Telex 540079, Fax 5745794; Taif: PO Box 15, Tel 7321425, Fax 7365771; Madina: PO Box 145, Tel 8366740, Fax 8363581; Riyadh: PO Box 738, Tel 4026707, Telex 405018, Fax 4026708; Dammam: PO Box 725, Tel 8326087, Alkhobar: PO Box 1092, Tel 8647840, Telex 871306, Fax 8950111; Khamis Mushait: PO Box 502, Tel 2223212, Fax 2223432; Al Hasa: PO Box 2107, Tel 5872208, Fax 5863578; Al Qasim: PO Box 620, Tel 3241233, Fax 3249165; Jizan: PO Box 574, Tel/Fax 3171328; Tabuk: PO Box 33, Tel/Fax 4220764
Subsidiary Companies: Dahlawi Nevada, Los Angeles; Convention Centre & Resort Hotel, Miami; Mecca International, Portland, USA
Principal Bankers: Arab National Bank, Makkah, Jeddah; Al Bank Al Saudi Al Fransi, Jeddah; Saudi American Bank, Jeddah; National Commercial Bank, Jeddah; Societe Generale, Bahrain; Arab Saudi Bank, Bahrain
Financial Information:

| | 1989/90 |
	SR'000
Sales turnover	520,000
Paid-up capital	75,000
Total assets	125,000

Principal Shareholders: Unlimited Liability Partnership
Date of Establishment: 1900
No of Employees: 650

AL DAKHEEL CORPORATION

PO Box 3625, Jeddah 21481
Tel: 6886167, 6886119
Telex: 600492 Dakhel Sj

PRINCIPAL ACTIVITIES: Civil engineering contractors, building and road works, electrical contractors
Branch Offices: Riyadh: PO Box 2088, Tel 4761968; Medina: PO Box 1279, Tel 8234940, Telex 570012

Principal Shareholders: Abdul Rahman Al Namelah, the Dakheel family

ALDAR AUDIT BUREAU
Talal Abu-Ghazaleh - Al Basri & Co
Grant Thornton International Group, a member firm of

PO Box 2195, Riyadh 11451
Tel: 4630680 (5 lines)
Cable: Tagauditors Riyadh
Telex: 401629 Tagco SJ
Telefax: (966-1) 4645939

Chairman: Talal Abu-Ghazaleh

Partners: Mahmoud M Adileh (Managing Partner), Abdullah Al Basri (Partner In Charge), Amin Samara, Mohammad Al Zaro, Bader Oudeh, Mohammad AL Kalouti, Akram Al Hussaini, Munir Al Borno, Mohammad Al Kadi

Managers: Mohammad Islam, Naim Dahbour, Khader Madhoon, Mahmoud Srour, Mahmoud Shaban, Najeh A Jawad, Mohammad N Sherif, Fayez Merebi, Waheeb Yousef, Salem Abu-Mahfooz, Khalil Okasha, Mahmoud Al Ansari, Tala'at Al Ali, Samir AL Sharqawi, Hani Al Abbasi, Jamil Salamah, Hatem Ghanem

PRINCIPAL ACTIVITIES: Accountants, auditing, tax consultants, management consultants, companies liquidators and financial services

Branch Offices: Saudi Arabia (PO Box 20135, Jeddah 21455, Tel 6716915, Fax 6711190; PO Box 3187, Alkhobar 31952, Tel 8986348; PO Box 2447 Al Qassim, Tel 3249693; Al Hofuf, Tel 5923255; Jubail, Tel 3611656); and Lebanon; Egypt; Bahrain; Jordan; Qatar; Oman; Tunisia; United Arab Emirates; Yemen

Parent Company: Head office in Kuwait

Subsidiary Companies: Talal Abu-Ghazaleh & Co (TAGCO), Talal Abu-Ghazaleh Associates Ltd (TAGA); Saudi Arab Projects Co Ltd (SAPCO), Saudi Arabia; International Translation Centre (ITC); Arab Bureau for Legal Services (ABLE); TMP Agents

ALDAR CONSULTING CO (ADCO)

PO Box 2195, Riyadh 11451
Tel: 4630680, 4630608, 4652673, 4656154
Cable: TAGAUDITORS
Telex: 401629 TAGCO SJ
Telefax: 4645939

PRINCIPAL ACTIVITIES: Project study and preparation, systems and organisation, financial analysis, technical and engineering studise, personnel, business consultancy services

Branch Offices: Jeddah: PO Box 2415, Jeddah 21451, Tel 6711190, Telex 601768, Fax 6711190; Alkhobar: PO Box 3187, Alkhobar 31952, Tel 8986348, Telex 872129, Fax 8986860; Jubail: Tel 3611656; Al Ahsa: Tel 5860101

Parent Company: Talal Abu Ghazaleh International
Associated Companies: Saudi Arab Projects Co (SAPCO)

AL DORAR TRADING & CONTRACTING CO LTD

PO Box 7257, Riyadh 11462
Tel: 4827767
Cable: Dorar
Telex: 400248 Dorar Sj
Telefax: 4827767

Chairman: Fahad Al-Anzan
Directors: Mansour Al Hamlan (Managing Director)

PRINCIPAL ACTIVITIES: Government contractors, civil engineering and building contractors, and general trading (building materials, electrical and safety equipment; toiletries, pharmaceutical and medical supplies), household ware distributors, cleaning and maintenance operation, commercial agencies and company's representative

Subsidiary Companies: Al-Dorar Pharmacy, Olaya, Riyadh
Principal Bankers: Saudi Investment Bank, Riyadh

Principal Shareholders: Mr Al-Anzan (50%); Mr Hamlan (50%)
Date of Establishment: 1976 as Al-Dorar Est, changed status in l985
No of Employees: 50

ALDOSSARY, YUSUF M, EST

PO Box 936, Dammam 31421
Tel: 8260925, 8271018, 8271038
Cable: Sonah
Telex: 801341 Ymde Sj
Telefax: 8266064

Chairman: Yusuf Mohamed Aldossary

Directors: Abdullah Ahmad Said Aldossary (General Manager)
Senior Executives: Makram Nassar (Technical Manager), Faoud Rashed Aldossary (Personnel Manager)

PRINCIPAL ACTIVITIES: General contracting and trading, water lines and sewage systems contract
Subsidiary Companies: Aldossary Block Factory; Aldossary Development & Contr Co; Dhahran National Crusher Co
Principal Bankers: Saudi British Bank, Alkhobar; Riyad Bank, Dammam

Date of Establishment: 1-12-1391 H
No of Employees: 300/540

ALDREES INTERNATIONAL CONTRACTORS SUPPLY CO

PO Box 369, Dammam 31411
Tel: 8576468
Telex: 802230 AICS SJ

PRINCIPAL ACTIVITIES: Construction contracting and management; supply and distribution of building materials
Branch Offices: PO Box 17236, Riyadh 11484, Tel: 4632421, 4630885, Telex: 404939 AICS SJ
Associated Companies: International Contractors Supply, USA

ALDREES, MOHAMMED ASSAD, & SONS CO

PO Box 609, Riyadh 11421
Tel: 4763875, 4763947, 4766319, 4762878, 4762879
Cable: IDREES
Telex: 405833 IDREES SJ
Telefax: 4763875

Chairman: Hamad Mohammed Aldrees
Directors: Eng Abdulmohsen Mohammed Aldrees (Managing Director), Eng Abdulilah Saad Aldrees (Finance Director), Saud Mohammed Aldrees (Administrative Director), Abdulaziz Assad Aldrees (Marketing Director), Fahd Assad Aldrees (Purchasing Director), Khaled Assad Aldrees (Production Director), Saad Hamad Aldrees (Technical Director)

PRINCIPAL ACTIVITIES: Mazda Division: Car, service and spare parts. Transport Division. Tools & Equipment Division: Supply of tools and spare parts, generators, air compressors, garage equipment, automatic car wash systems, paint systems etc. Irrigation Division: Supply, erection, maintenance of central pivot systems. Service Station Division:- Computerized and manuel fuel dispensing stations, lubrication and repair facilities, and accessories. Maintenance & Installation Division:- After sales service of all industrial equipment contract maintenance, installation, turn-key projects. Tender & Contracting Division: Management and operation of automatic slaughterhouses. Transport Division: Transport services throughout the Gulf. Scrap Division: Supply of scrap (metal, aluminium, copper)
Principal Agencies: USA: Alemite, Champion, Dresser Wayne, Kohler, Germany: Gedore; France: BEM-Muller; Japan: Hitachi, Daihatsu, Toyo, Yamaha, Solid Corp
Branch Offices: Riyadh, Dammam, Jeddah, Khamis Mushait, Bureidah, Hail, Wadi Dawasir
Subsidiary Companies: Saudi American Glass; Aldrees Modern Building Industries; Aldrees International Contractors Supply
Principal Bankers: National Commercial Bank, Riyadh
Financial Information:

	1989/90 US$'000
Sales turnover	70,000
Profits	5,000
Authorised capital	40,000
Paid-up capital	40,000
Total assets	109,000

Principal Shareholders: Aldrees Family
Date of Establishment: 1938
No of Employees: 1,000

AL EMAR GROUP ESTABLISHMENT

PO Box 22181, Riyadh 11495
Tel: 4632805
Telex: 404823 Alemar SJ
Telefax: (966 1) 4622452

Chairman: Abdul Latif Saleh Al Sheikh
Directors: Abdul Hafeez Khan (Vice Chairman), Abdul Aziz S Al Sheikh (Managing Director), Sultan Mohammad Al Dossary (Director Farming Division)
Senior Executives: Dr F M Chaudhry (Senior Manager & Chief Agronomist), Tariq R Sheikh (Financial Controller), Khalifa Imaduddin Ahmed (Manager Shipping & Overseas Procurement), Azmat Kamal (Office Manager)

PRINCIPAL ACTIVITIES: Farming (over 3000 hectares, grain, cereal, forage and vegetables), fresh water fish farming, trading in agro-chemicals, herbicides, insecticides, fungicides and micronutrients, veterinary, and laboratories for diagnosis and treatment of soil, water, crop and veterinary problems; shipping, real estate and trading in commodities
Principal Agencies: Bayer AG, Boral Cyclone, Conlee Int'l, Cresthale Seeds, Cyanamid, Fermenta, Fuller Seeds, HVH UK, Hoescht, Masstock, Melchemie, Petrisco, Pioneer Overseas, Portman, Rhone Poulenc, Unifert, Veterin SA, Wright Stephenson, Wuensche Handel, Willmot Industries, etc
Branch Offices: Buraidah, Al Kharj, Sajir, Wadi Dawasir, Hail in Saudi Arabia and in UK and in Pakistan
Principal Bankers: Saudi American Bank, Riyadh; Saudi British Bank, Riyadh; Trans Arabian Investment Bank, Bahrain
Financial Information:

	1990
	SR'000
Sales turnover	130,000
Authorised capital	53,074
Paid-up capital	53,074
Total assets	108,000

Principal Shareholders: Sole proprietorship
Date of Establishment: 1965
No of Employees: 200

AL ESAYI, OMAR K, & CO LTD

PO Box 8361, Jeddah 21482
Tel: 6440678, 6440224, 6445604
Cable: OKACO - Jeddah
Telex: 605677 OKECO SJ

Chairman: Omar K Al Esayi
Directors: Saleh A Al Esayi, Aidroos A Al Esayi, Said O Al Esayi, M O Al Esayi, A A K Al Esayi, A O Al Esayi
Senior Executives: Said O K Al Esayi (Manager), A A K Alesayi (Manager)

PRINCIPAL ACTIVITIES: Supply of building materials, cement, prefabricated buildings, heavy equipment, consumer products, computers, foodstuffs division, textile and clothing division, catering household goods, carpets and furnishing, office equipment, furnishing contractors safety & security equipment, safety contractors and consultants health and leisure equipment, graphic art, design and signmakers
Branch Offices: Riyadh: PO Box 6456, Tel 4773660, Telex 401163; Alqassim-Jizan, Dammam; Foodstuffs Division, PO Box 8680, Jeddah, Tel 6441580; Heavy Equipment Division, PO Box 8361, Jeddah, Tel 6879433; Carpets and Decoration Centre, PO Box 8361, Jeddah, Tel 6693169; Commercial Division & Contract Furniture Department, Jeddah, Tel 6440678, 6440224
Subsidiary/Associate Companies: Alesayi Travel Agency; Alesayi Saif Numan Douglas Co Ltd; Omar K Alesayi Office for Engineering & Arch Conts; Omar K Alesayi Trading & Contracting Corp (OMACO); Alesayi Trading Corp; Alesayi Alhoraibi Co
Principal Bankers: National Commercial Bank; Riyadh Bank; Saudi American Bank; Saudi French Bank

Principal Shareholders: Omar E Alesayi & Sons; Saleh A Alesayi; Aidroos H Alesayi
No of Employees: 260

AL ESAYI SAIF NOMAN DOUGLAS CO LTD

PO Box 2837, Jeddah 21461
Tel: 6712069, 6720854
Telex: 604407 RMDKSA

Chairman: Sheikh Saif Noman Said
Directors: Z A Golmohamed, M V Manzoni, C N Lambert, Saeed Ahmed Noman, J W Dalziel

PRINCIPAL ACTIVITIES: Building and civil engineering, construction
Branch Offices: Riyadh, PO Box 40843; Tel 4762525, 4792425; Telex 405156 SAIF SJ
Principal Bankers: Saudi British Bank
Financial Information:

	SR'000
Authorised capital	10,000
Paid-up capital	10,000

Principal Shareholders: Sheikh Omar K Al Esayi, Sheikh Saif Noman Said, R M Douglas Construction Ltd
Date of Establishment: June 1978
No of Employees: 375

ALESAYI TRADING CORPORATION

PO Box 1342, Jeddah 21431
Tel: 6208627, 6204676, 6210020
Cable: Alesayco
Telex: 601063 Esayico Sj, 604846 Atcorp Sj

Chairman: Sheikh Ali Abdullah Alesayi
Directors: Sheikh Omar Kassim Alesayi (Managing Director), Sheikh Khalid Ali Alesayi (Deputy Managing Director)

PRINCIPAL ACTIVITIES: Import and distribution of construction equipment, earthmoving and heavy machinery, trucks and motor vehicles, garbage collecting equipment and vehicles, incinerators
Principal Agencies: Chrysler Int SA, UK and USA; Mitsubishi Motors Corp, Japan; Neoplan, Germany; Faun Werke, Germany, Sulo - Garbage containers, Germany; Haller - Garbage containers, Germany; Atlas - Garbage collecting equipment, Germany; Shunt Italiana -Incinerators, Italy; VGT DK -Refractories, Germany
Branch Offices: Riyadh: PO Box 3983, Tel 4775817; Dammam: PO Box 2454, Tel 8572045; Abha, Tel 2230600; Buraidah, Tel 3230357; Abha, Tel 2230600
Principal Bankers: National Commercial Bank; Saudi American Bank; Beirut Riyadh Bank

Principal Shareholders: Sheikh Ali Abdullah Alesayi and Sheikh Omar Kassim Alesayi
Date of Establishment: 1960
No of Employees: 500

ALESSA, HAMAD ABDULLA, & SONS CO

PO Box 2091, Riyadh 11451
Tel: 4039295 (5 lines)
Cable: Alessa Riyadh
Telex: 401164 Alessa Sj
Telefax: 4035859

President: Abdulaziz Hamad Alessa
Senior Executives: Ali Adam Alsomali (Vice President Admin & Purchasing), Saud A Alessa (Vice President Finance),Ali A Alessa (Vice President Appliances Division), Ahmed Alessa (Vice President Cosmetics & Textiles Division), Fahad S Alessa (General Manager Manufacturing Division)

PRINCIPAL ACTIVITIES: Dealing in household appliances, audio-visual products, textiles, perfumeries. Manufacture of airconditioners through its subsidiary

Principal Agencies: Gibson, USA; Bauknecht, West Germany;
Win Lighter, Japan; Usha International, India; Hitachi, Japan;
Les Perfumes, France; Arvin, USA; Deltron, West Germany
Branch Offices: Location in Riyadh: Alessa Bldg, 8th Floor,
Airport Road; Dammam: PO Box 4965, Tel 8275181; Jeddah:
PO Box 2768, Sitteen St, Tel 6659226; Khamis Mushait:
Hitachi Centre, Main Street, Tel 2220924
Subsidiary Companies: National Factory for Air Conditioners,
6th Floor, Alessa Building, PO Box 12409, Riyadh, Tel
4027639, 4031719
Principal Bankers: Saudi American Bank; Saudi British Bank;
Saudi French Bank; United Saudi Commercial Bank
Financial Information:

	1989/90 SR'000
Turnover	460,000
Total assets	350,000

Principal Shareholders: Abdulaziz H Alessa, Saleh Hamad
Alessa
Date of Establishment: 1935
No of Employees: 420

AL FADHLI, FUAD, TRADING EST

PO Box 3506, Riyadh 11481
Tel: 4550807, 4566680, 4567760
Cable: Fadhliest
Telex: 400071 Fuad Sj
Telefax: 4543356

President: Fuad A J Al-Fadhli (Managing Director)
Senior Executives: Montasir Al-Shoaibi (General Manager),
Jawaid Qamar (Sales Manager)

PRINCIPAL ACTIVITIES: Dealing in medical, laboratory and
surgical equipment and suppliers, blood groups and
biochemical and diagnostic reagents
Principal Agencies: Hoechst Behring Int, West Germany;
Shandon Southern Products, UK; Oxoid Ltd, UK; Biomerieux,
France; Helena Laborories, USA; Carter-Wallace, USA;
Haemonetics, USA; Kawasumi, Japan; Bioself, Switzerland
Branch Offices: Jeddah, Dammam and Abha
Principal Bankers: Saudi Cairo Bank; Saudi French Bank

Date of Establishment: 1972
No of Employees: 30

ALFADL BIN LADEN & J&P CORPORATION LTD

PO Box 5028, Jeddah 21422
Tel: 6674551
Cable: Jayladco
Telex: 601417 Abjanp Sj

Chairman: Stelios Joannou
Directors: George Paraskevaides, Abdul Kader Alfadl, Salem
Bin Laden
Senior Executives: Marios Eleftheriades (Manager
Prefabrication), Constantine Shiacolas (Contracts Manager
Contracting)

PRINCIPAL ACTIVITIES: Manufacture and supply of
prefabricated building and building components, general
contracting, civil engineering and building
Principal Agencies: Joannou & Paraskevaides (Overseas) Ltd
Branch Offices: Riyadh Office: PO Box 5881, Tel 4040002/3/4;
Al Khobar Office: PO Box 720, Tel 8646107. Also Jubail,
Yanbu, Tabuk, Abha, Najran
Parent Company: Joannou & Paraskevaides (Overseas) Ltd, PO
Box 10064, Dubai, Tel 221283, Telex 46477 Jpgho Db
Principal Bankers: Saudi British Bank, Jeddah and Alkhobar;
Saudi American Bank, Riyadh
Financial Information:

	SR'000
Authorised capital	15,000
Paid-up capital	15,000

Principal Shareholders: Joannou & Paraskevaides (Overseas)
Ltd, Abdul Kader Mohd Alfadl, Bin Laden Brothers, Abdulaziz
Mohd Alfadl
Date of Establishment: 1971
No of Employees: 5,000

AL FADL GROUP

PO Box 15, Jeddah 21411
Tel: 6672653, 6603996
Cable: ALFADL
Telex: 601650 Alfadl Sj
Telefax: 6603682

Chairman: Abdulkader M Alfadl
Directors: Abdulaziz Alfadl (President), Mohamed A Alfadl
(Executive Vice President)
Senior Executives: Walid M Kastali (Finance Manager), Dr Faisal
M Nsouli (Marketing Manager), Hassan A Alfadl (Technical
Manager), Edgar O Cruz (Production Manager), Celso I
Isorena (Administration Manager), Mohammad Saleem
(Purchasing Manager), Abdallay Alqanzal (Sales Manager)

PRINCIPAL ACTIVITIES: Building and civil engineering
contractors, operation and maintenance contractors,
prefabricated houses and steel mesh manufacturers,
agricultural and industrial machinery distributors, electrical,
mechanical and electronic equipment suppliers, shipping
agents, fast food restaurants and general services
Branch Offices: Riyadh, Tel 4761603, Fax 4761633
Subsidiary Companies: Contracting: Sahara Building Contractor
Ltd; Rabya Landscaping Ltd; Services: Alpha Trading &
Shipping Ltd; Autoram Transport; Trans Arabia Ltd; Trading:
Economic Development Enterprises; Arabian Trading &
Industrial Services Ltd; Industry: Alfadl Bin Laden J & P Ltd;
B R C Alfadl Ltd; Aldewan Fast Food Co, Ltd
Principal Bankers: Riyad Bank; Al Jazirah Bank; Saudi
American Bank

Principal Shareholders: Sheikh Abdulqadir Alfadl, Sheikh
Abdulaziz Alfadl, Sheikh Mohamed A Alfadl
Date of Establishment: 1945
No of Employees: 3,000

AL FAHAD INTERNATIONAL EST

PO Box 3467, Jeddah 21471
Tel: 6691124
Telex: 606638 Sattar Sj

President: Abdul Aziz Nackshabandi
Senior Executives: Mrs Jamila Al-Shaer, Fahad Al Bitar

PRINCIPAL ACTIVITIES: Contracting; trading; operation and
maintenance of hospitals; supply of hospital equipment and
furniture; landscaping and supply of plants, PVC floors,
building materials & paints, koolshade screens, cladding, fire
protection sheets, surgical equipment, all kinds of pumps and
general spare parts
Principal Agencies: Eternit, Belgium; Koolshade, UK; Promat,
Germany; Fincraft, Kenya; FSBC, Switzerland; United
Aviation, USA; ECE European Export, France
Subsidiary Companies: Saudi Automation, Jeddah; Saudi
Automation, Republic of Djibouti; Bella Trading Establishment,
Jeddah; Al-Fahad International Establishment, Al-Khobar
Principal Bankers: Arab National Bank, Bank Al Jazira, Saudi
Cairo Bank

Principal Shareholders: 100% Saudi Company
Date of Establishment: 1976
No of Employees: 202

AL FAISALIYYAH AGRICULTURE & DAIRY EST (AL SAFI)

PO Box 10525, Riyadh 11443
Tel: 4951400 (6 lines)
Cable: Al safi
Telex: 402356 Dairy Sj
Telefax: 4954927

Chairman: HRH Prince Abdullah Al Faisal Al Saud

Directors: Eng Abdullah Abdullatif Al Saif (Director General)

Senior Executives: Ghazi H Gelidan (Commercial Manager), Khalid Al Qusair (Dairy Plant Manager), Ismaiel N Owaidah (Personnel Manager), Dr Robert Osland (Farm Operation Superintendent), Muhieddin Al Farra (Public Relations Officer)

PRINCIPAL ACTIVITIES: Production of fresh dairy products under Al-Safi brand name

Branch Offices: Location: Farm at Al Kharj, also branches in Riyadh, Jeddah, Dammam, Khamis Mushayt, Buraydah, Taif, Al Baha, Al Madinah

Principal Bankers: Arab National Bank; Saudi Cairo Bank; Riyad Bank

Financial Information:

	1990 SR'000
Authorised capital	100,000
Paid-up capital	100,000

Date of Establishment: 1979

No of Employees: 1,266

AL FALAK ELECTRONIC EQUIPMENT & SUPPLIES CO WLL

PO Box 1963, AlKhobar 31952

Tel: (966-3) 8946560, 8946568

Telex: 870841 KHALIJ SJ

Telefax: (966-3) 8946032

President: Ahmed Ali Ashadawi

Directors: Ahmed Mohammed Al Sari, Abdulaziz Al Sagr, Abdulaziz Al Bulaihid, Abdulaziz Al Rashed

Senior Executives: Tanweer Abbas (Product Manager SAS Software), Majeed Sharafudeen (Manager - Administration), Yousuf Abu Idris (Finance Manager), David Taylor (Manager Software Product Div), Maurice Tull (Manager Storage Tek Division)

PRINCIPAL ACTIVITIES: Mainframe and mini computre financial system and data centre management, software sales and support, IBM compatible computer peripherals, facsimile communication machines, computer supplies and accessories, projects, office stationery products, etc

Principal Agencies: Candle Corp; Systems Center; Storage Technology Corp; SAS Institute Inc; McCormack & Dodge; OKI Electric (OKIFAX); Progressive Ribbons Inc; Westra Office Equipment; Legent; Goldstar Telecom; 3M Magnetic Media Products

Branch Offices: Riyadh: PO Box 16091, Tel (966-1) 4656572, 4632143, Fax (966- 1) 4633230; Jeddah: PO Box 13401, Tel (966-2) 6676244/6253, Fax (966-2) 6676244

Principal Bankers: Arab National Bank, Alkhobar

Financial Information:

	1990 SR'000
Sales turnover	36,000
Authorised capital	2,300
Paid-up capital	1,000
Total assets	13,000

Principal Shareholders: Five Saudi shareholders

Date of Establishment: 1981

No of Employees: 150

AL FARIS, ABDALLA, HEAVY INDUSTRIES

PO Box 5987, Dammam 31432

Tel: (03) 8109897

Telex: 870135 Afaris Sj

President: Abdallo O Al Faris

Senior Executives: Hermann A Beimrohr (Vice President), Mohammed A Al-Quwaie (Assistant Vice President)

PRINCIPAL ACTIVITIES: Designers and builders of vehicles, semi-trailers, axles and hydraulic systems

Principal Agencies: Matzen & Timm, Hamburg, West Germany

Branch Offices: Location in Dammam: Abu Hadriyah Highway, Dammam

Subsidiary Companies: Abdalla Al Faris Universal Technical Works

Principal Bankers: Al Bank Al Saudi Al Fransi, Al Khobar

Financial Information:

	SR'000
Authorised capital	21,200
Paid-up capital	21,200

Principal Shareholders: Wholly owned by Abdalla O Al Faris

Date of Establishment: 1 July 1982

No of Employees: 200

AL FAYHAA TRADING EST

PO Box 224, Riyadh 11411

Tel: 4026237/8

Cable: Theqaa

Telex: 401398 Kassem Sj

Telfax: 4051818

Chairman: Sheikh Ibrahim M Al Kassem

Directors: Sheikh Khaled Al Kassem, Ibrahim Al Khlaif, Mansour Al Kassem

Senior Executives: Mosleh Sinjab (Technical Manager), Zuhair Jazairi (Sales Manager), Walid Al Far (Financial Manager), Walid Sinjab (Factory Manager), Yahya Mahdi (Jeddah Branch Manager), Hisham Oujal (Jeddah Sales Manager)

PRINCIPAL ACTIVITIES: Trading in natural stone, marble, granite; sanitary ware & fittings; ceramic tiles & porcelain tiles; tile adhesive cements & grouts

Principal Agencies: Armitage Shanks Bathrooms, UK; Nicobond Tile Adhesives, UK

Branch Offices: Jeddah Branch: Maakaroneh St, Opp Riyad Bank, Tel 6721791, 6728341, Telex 606802, Fax 6721791

Principal Bankers: National Commercial Bank, Riyadh; Saudi French Bank, Riyadh; Al Rajhi Exchange Co, Riyadh

Principal Shareholders: Ownership

Date of Establishment: 1953

No of Employees: 165

ALFOZAN, ABDUL LATIF A, & BROS

PO Box 38, Alkhobar 31952

Tel: 8642467, 8644014, 8984840

Cable: Alfozan Alkhobar

Telex: 870032 FOZAN SJ; 870412 FOZAN SJ

President: Abdullatif A Alfozan

Directors: Mohammad A Alfozan (Managing Director) , Abdul Aziz A Alfozan

Senior Executives: Khaled A Alfozan (Finance Director)

PRINCIPAL ACTIVITIES: Import and distribution of all types of building materials, cement, timber, plywood, steel products, pumps, electrical items, decorative items

Branch Offices: PO Box 8151, Riyadh, Tel 4485247; PO Box 1024, Dammam, Tel 8326604; PO Box 317, Jubail, Tel 3611165

Principal Bankers: Arab National Bank, Alkhobar; Saudi British Bank, Alkhobar

Financial Information:

	1989 SR'000
Sales turnover	449,600
Authorised capital	3,000
Paid-up capital	216,332

Date of Establishment: 19.11.1390 H

No of Employees: 150

AL GAHTANI, HASSAN ABDUL KARIM, SONS CO

PO Box 195, Alkhobar 31952
Tel: 8574102, 8576617
Cable: Abdul Karim
Telex: 870031 Hakm Sj
Telefax: (3) 8572504

Chairman: Khalid Hassan Algahtani
Directors: Mohsin H Algahtani, Paul S Booth
Senior Executives: Isaac B Nassereddin (Purchasing Manager), Aftab S Mohammed (Technical Manager), Abdul Gafoor (Secretary/Commercial/Admin Manager), Hussein Ismail (Marketing Manager), George Shannon (Production Manager), Ahmed Mansour (Personnel Manager)

PRINCIPAL ACTIVITIES: Heavy haulage and transportation, offshore drilling, construction, manufacture of dairy and bakery products, distributors for automobiles, and heavy construction machinery, equipment and cranes, printing and design work, computer supplies, technical management services, heavy electrical and mechanical work contracts, frozen meat and canned foodstuffs, air travel services and general suppliers
Branch Offices: PO Box 195, Alkhobar: AICO (Arabian Ind & Cont Co); Fadeco (Arabian Food & Dairy Products); Sahara Travel; Al-Eman Printing Press; HAK Algahtani DAF Trucks; HAK Computer Supplies; HAK Manpower & Rec. Div; Algatani International Maritime Agency; HAK Trading Div
Subsidiary Companies: GH Transport Ltd; Algahtani Clough Cont Ltd; Arabian Elmec Ltd; Arabian Offshore Int'l Ltd

Date of Establishment: 1967
No of Employees: 1,400

AL GHAITH CO LTD

PO Box 2721, Jeddah 21461
Tel: 6673569, 6657390
Cable: MUFTIPAK
Telex: 601425 MUFTI SJ

Chairman: Alsharief Jeraidi Bin Feten
Directors: Shakir S Mufti, Ahmed M Simbawa

PRINCIPAL ACTIVITIES: Trucking, agencies, supply of electrical materials and power equipment
Principal Agencies: Kienzle Apparate, Germany; Gustav Hensel, Germany; Mitsubishi, Japan
Branch Offices: Location in Jeddah: Prince Fahad Street, Jeddah
Principal Bankers: National Commercial Bank

Principal Shareholders: Chairman and directors as described
Date of Establishment: 1977
No of Employees: 200

AL GILANI, ABDUL RAHMAN DAWOOD,

PO Box 661, Jeddah 21421
Tel: 6870644
Cable: Al Gilani
Telex: 604498 AALLA SJ

Chairman: Abdul Rahman Dawood Al Gilani
Directors: Ali Ahmed Al Gilani (General Manager)
Senior Executives: Omer Al-Qaity (Sales Manager), Mohammed Sakkary (Riyadh Branch Manager)

PRINCIPAL ACTIVITIES: Import and distribution of heavy machinery, mechanical equipment, industrial machinery and electrical equipment
Principal Agencies: Acker Drill, USA; Conrad Stork, Holland; Schlosser, W Germany; Rieckerman, W Germany; Passavant, W Germany
Branch Offices: PO Box 1159, Damman, Tel 8330523; PO Box 3834, Riyadh, Tel 4024802

Principal Bankers: Saudi British Bank

Date of Establishment: 1956
No of Employees: 75

ALGOSAIBI, ABDULREHMAN, GENERAL TRADING BUREAU

PO Box 215, Riyadh 11411
Tel: 4793000 (10 lines)
Cable: FAHAD
Telex: 401125 Fahad Sj, 404877 Fahad Sj
Telefax: 4771374

Chairman: Fahad Abdulrehman Algosaibi
Directors: Fayez Fahad Algosaibi (President), Fawaz Fahad Algosaibi (Vice President)
Senior Executives: Dawood Abu Jobarah (General Manager)

PRINCIPAL ACTIVITIES: General trading, tender business, governmental supplies, real estate, import and distribution of electrical household appliances, medical and surgical equipment, and pharmaceuticals laboratory and scientific instruments; photographic materials etc
Principal Agencies: Many agencies from UK, West Germany, France, Italy, Belgium, Switzerland, Austria, USA, Denmark, Sweden, Japan, Spain, Pakistan, Jordan
Branch Offices: Location in Riyadh: Algosaibi Bldg, Airport Road; also branches in Jeddah: PO Box 1391; Alkhobar: PO Box 215; Mecca c/o Jeddah Branch; Dammam c/o Alkhobar Office; Medina: PO Box 4359; Al Qasim Buraidah: PO Box 892
Principal Bankers: National Commercial Bank; Saudi Cairo Bank, Riyadh
Financial Information:

	1989/90 SR'000
Sales turnover	335,000

Principal Shareholders: Sole ownership
Date of Establishment: 1942
No of Employees: 510

ALGOSAIBI, AHMAD HAMAD, & BROS

PO Box 106, Alkhobar 31952
Tel: 8642666
Cable: Ahmad Algosaibi
Telex: 870123 Algoso Sj
Telefax: 8949054

Chairman: Sh Ahmad Hamad Algosaibi
Directors: Sh Abdulaziz Hamad Algosaibi (President), Sh Sulaiman Hamad Algosaibi (Vice President), Sh Yousuf Ahmad Algosaibi (Vice President), Mohammad S Hindi (Vice President)

PRINCIPAL ACTIVITIES: Group of companies involved in shipping, insurance, hotels, trading, travel & tourism, airline agencies, ship owning/operation, stevedores, forwarding, transport & road haulage, can manufacturing, bottling, contracting, real estate, gas and water treatment, manufacturing of cement, oilfield chemicals, steel pipes, vegetable oils and ghee
Principal Agencies: Sumitomo, Japan (Steel Products, tyre, tubes & cables); Mirrlees Blackstone, UK (Diesel Engines & Generators); Fiat, Italy (Gas Turbines); Born Heater, UK; Damen Shipyards, Holland (Tug Boats); Borsig, W Germany (Valves, Compressors & Heat Exchangers); Fairmont Railway Motor, USA (Locomotives)
Branch Offices: Riyadh, Jeddah, Ras Tanura, Ras Al Khafji, Al Hassa
Subsidiary/Associated Companies: Algosaibi Trading Co; Algosaibi Real Estate; Algosaibi Service Station; National Bottling Co; Saudi Cement Co; Dhahran Electric Supply Co; El Khat Co Printing; Oilfield Chemical Co; Saudi Glass Manufacturing Co; Continental Can of Saudi Arabia Ltd; Saudi Vegetable Oil Co; Saudi National Pipe Co; Saudi Crowncaps Manufacturing Co; Algosaibi Hotel; Saudi Hotel Services Co

Ltd; Egyptian Saudi Hotel Co; Saudi Korean Stevedoring Co; Algosaibi Shipping Co; Gulf Agency Co; Algosaibi Marine Services Co; International Offshore Services Corp; Gulf Ro Ro Services; International Associated Cargo Carriers; International Air Cargo Corp; International Trucking Express Co; Yousuf Algosaibi Travel Agency; Gulf Marine Transport Co KSC (Kuwait); Al Jazira Contracting Co (Bahrain); Saudi United Insurance Co Ltd; Tecmo; Nafcel; JBCMC; SHI Arabia Ltd

Principal Bankers: Arab National Bank Ltd; Saudi British Bank; Riyad Bank; Saudi American Bank

Principal Shareholders: Sh Ahmad Hamad Algosaibi, Sh Abdul Aziz Hamad Algosaibi, Sh Sulaiman Algosaibi
Date of Establishment: 1946
No of Employees: 2,500

ALGOSAIBI DIVING & MARINE SERVICES

PO Box 133, Dhahran Airport 31932
Tel: 8570000
Telex: 870137 Dska Sj
Telefax: 8577315

Chairman: Muhammad Khalifa Algosaibi
Senior Executives: David Atkin (General Manager), J O'Callaghan (Finance Manager), John Mooney (Operations Manager)

PRINCIPAL ACTIVITIES: Provision of diving services; provision of vessels, bareboat or charter; ARAMCO contractor since 1964
Branch Offices: PO Box 5526, Manama, Bahrain
Parent Company: Khalifa Algosaibi & Sons
Principal Bankers: Albank Alsaudi Alhollandi, Alkhobar

Date of Establishment: 1964
No of Employees: 350

ALGOSAIBI ENGINEERING CONTRACTING CORP

PO Box 235, Riyadh 11411
Tel: 4762553, 4777727, 4778816
Cable: Algocorp Riyadh
Telex: 401123 Goseng Sj
Telefax: 4783946

Chairman: Adil A Algosaibi
Directors: Mohammed Wahbi (Director General), Hani Sinno (Director, Electrical Division)
Senior Executives: Badawy El Sayed Badawy (Chief Accountant), Mohammed Saleh Ballouli (Manager Marketing), Saleh Al Burqan (Manager Administration & Personnel), Omar Magdi (Projects Manager)

PRINCIPAL ACTIVITIES: Complete installation and maintenance of medical equipment for hospitals, hospital laundries, central air-conditioning, electrical engineering, import and distribution of household appliances and electrical goods, turnkey electrical distribution projects, operation and management of radio stations, hospitals, universities
Principal Agencies: Hospitalia Int GmbH, W Germany
Branch Offices: PO Box 606, Dammam 31421; PO Box 9477, Jeddah
Principal Bankers: Al Bank Al Saudi Al Fransi, Riyadh; Albank Alsaudi Alhollandi, Riyadh
Financial Information:

	1989/90 SR'000
Sales turnover	27,000
Profits	750
Authorised capital	4,000
Paid-up capital	4,000
Total assets	90,000

Principal Shareholders: Wholly owned by Sheikh Adil A Algosaibi
Date of Establishment: 1958
No of Employees: 1,200

AL GOSAIBI HOTEL

PO Box 51, Dhahran Airport 31932
Tel: 8942466, 8946466
Cable: Gosaibi Hotel
Telex: 870008 SJ GSTL SJ
Telefax: 8947533

Chairman: Sheikh Abdul Aziz Algosaibi
Directors: Mohamed S Hindi (Managing Director)
Senior Executives: Osama Dabbas (General Manager)

PRINCIPAL ACTIVITIES: Hotel business
Principal Agencies: Utell International
Parent Company: Ahmad Hamad Algosaibi & Bros
Associated Companies: Riyadh Palace Hotel

Principal Shareholders: Ahmad Hamad Algosaibi & Bros
Date of Establishment: 1973
No of Employees: 350

ALGOSAIBI, KHALIFA A, (GROUP OF COMPANIES)

PO Box 222, Dammam 31411
Tel: 8570000
Cable: Contracts Dammam
Telex: 801035 Gosaibi Sj
Telefax: 8577315

Chairman: Sheikh Khalifa A Algosaibi
Directors: Mohammed K Algosaibi (Executive Vice-Chairman and Managing Director), Saad K Algosaibi, Bader K Algosaibi, Sami K Algosaibi, Salah K Algosaibi
Senior Executives: Thayir K Al Aujan (Finance Manager), David A Cantrell (Marketing Manager), Mustafa N Nasr (Admin Manager)

PRINCIPAL ACTIVITIES: Import and distribution of frozen and dry food, shrimp fishing, general contracting and agency representation, catering and camp maintenance, diving and underwater maintenance, salvage services; production of calcium silicate bricks and blocks, manufacture of admixtures for concrete & roofing membranes, manufacture of fireproof caotings and artificial fertilisers, industrial and marine paints, thermoplastic road marking paints, road studs, agencies for pumps and industrial equipment, pipeline construction and internal cleaning in situ, tank manufacture and construction and additional services as required
Principal Agencies: Mitsui Group, Japan; CMC Manufacturing, USA; GEO Pipelines, USA; Motherwell Bridge, UK
Branch Offices: Saudi Arabia and neighbouring Gulf Area (branch offices in Riyadh, PO Box 701, and Jeddah, PO Box 408)
Subsidiary Companies: Khalifa Algosaibi Cold Stores, (frozen goods import/wholesaling); Khalifa Algosaibi Fisheries (shrimp fishing/processing), Khalifa Algosaibi Contracting (general contracting & property leasing), Algosaibi Services Co (catering & camp maintenance), Algosaibi Diving & Marine Services (diving & marine services), Construction Materials Co (bricks & blocks), Construction Materials Chemical Industries (admixtures & membranes), Arabian Vermiculite Industries (fireproof coatings), Sigma Paints (Saudi Arabia) Ltd (industrial & marine paints), Saudi Road Marking Co (thermoplastic paints), National Road Studs Company (road studs), Saudi Toyo Engineering Co (construction & maintenance)
Principal Bankers: Al Jazira Bank; Albank Alsaudi Alhollandi; Arab National Bank; National Commercial Bank; Saudi International Bank, London

Financial Information:

	1990
	US$'000
Sales turnover	150,000
Profits	12,000
Paid-up capital	15,000
Total assets	100,000

No of Employees: 2,500

ALGOSAIBI SERVICES CO LTD

PO Box 4131, Dammam Road, Dammam 31491
Tel: 8574555
Telex: 801471 AGML Sj
Telefax: 8573755

Chairman: Sheikh Khalifa Abdulrehman Algosaibi
Directors: Mohammed Khalifa Algosaibi, Sami Khalifa Algosaibi, Salah Khalifa Abdulrehman Algosaibi, R M Ross
Senior Executives: Hamad Mehmud (General Manager)

PRINCIPAL ACTIVITIES: All types of site catering and support services, operation and maintenance services, healthcare support services
Branch Offices: Riyadh: PO Box 41451, Riyadh 11461; Jeddah: PO Box 9328, Jeddah 21411
Principal Bankers: Al Bank Al Saudi Al Hollandi
Financial Information:

	1990
	SR'000
Sales turnover	73,409
Profits	8,025
Authorised capital	5,000
Paid-up capital	5,000
Total assets	30,626

Principal Shareholders: Sheikh Khalifa Abdulrehman Algosaibi, Mohammed Khalifa Algosaibi
Date of Establishment: 1976
No of Employees: 1,000

AL GOSAIBI TRADING & CONTRACTING CO

PO Box 2784, Dammam 31461
Tel: 8327221
Cable: Hiaco
Telex: 801382 Gtcc Sj

Chairman: Rashid Khalifa Al Gosaibi
Directors: Ghazi M M Al Gosaibi, Adel M M Al Gosaibi (Managing Director)
Senior Executives: Nabeel Al Gosaibi

PRINCIPAL ACTIVITIES: Import and distribution of foodstuffs, drinks, household goods, textiles, clothing, toiletries, tobacco, also catering services
Principal Agencies: ICC, Korea; Shinbeung Floor Mills Co Ltd, Korea; Pacific Int Mills Co, USA
Branch Offices: Riyadh Branch: Tel 4769849, 4766284; Al Hasa Branch
Principal Bankers: Saudi British Bank; Bank Al Jazira; National Commercial Bank

Principal Shareholders: Rashid Al Gosaibi; Adel Al Gosaibi; Ghazi Al Gosaibi
Date of Establishment: 1970
No of Employees: 100

AL HADA SHERATON HOTEL

PO Box 999, Taif
Tel: (02) 754 1400
Cable: Sheraton
Telex: 751092 sherhd sj
Telefax: 7544831

Senior Executives: Reda Darwish (General Manager)

PRINCIPAL ACTIVITIES: Hotel business
Branch Offices: Medina Sheraton Hotel, PO Box 1735, Medina; Tel (04) 823 0240, Telex 570076
Parent Company: Sheraton Hotels Inns & Resorts
Subsidiary Companies: ITT
Principal Bankers: Al-Saudi Al Fransi Bank, Taif

Principal Shareholders: The Ministry of Finance & National Economy (in Saudi Arabia)
Date of Establishment: 1978
No of Employees: 120

AL HAJRY COMPANY

PO Box 500, Dammam 31411
Tel: 8275909, 8275568, 8275590, 8269205
Cable: Alhajry Tarrak
Telex: 801024 Hajri Sj
Telefax: 8275846

Chairman: Saad Bati Al Hajry (General Manager)
Senior Executives: Khalid Saad Al Hajry (Commercial Manager)

PRINCIPAL ACTIVITIES: Trade, marine works, contracts, commission agents, shipchandlers, owners of water plants, polystyrene plant, tugs and barges, catering and ice plants
Principal Agencies: Wadsworth & Sons Ltd, UK; LM Liftmaterial, Germany
Branch Offices: Ras Tanura, Ras Al Khafji, Jubail, Seihat, Dammam
Subsidiary Companies: Saudi Arabian Catering Ent (SACE); Al Hajry Insulation Industries
Principal Bankers: National Commercial Bank

Principal Shareholders: Rashid B Al Hajry and Saad B Al Hajry
Date of Establishment: 1967 (2.1.1387H)
No of Employees: 102

AL HAMIDI CONTRACTING EST

PO Box 130, Riyadh 11411
Tel: 4774858
Cable: Al Hamidi
Telex: 401041 Hamidi Sj

Owner: Mohamed Abdul Aziz Al Hamidi
Directors: Samir M Al Hamidi (Director General), Khalid Al Hamidi (Technical Manager)
Senior Executives: Abdul Aziz Al Hamidi (Sales Manager), Riad Halabi (Finance Manager), Ahmed Awad (Marketing Manager), Hariss A Ahmed (Purchasing Manager), Kamal M Ibrahim (Personnel Manager), Faisal Al Attrash (Head of Data Processing)

PRINCIPAL ACTIVITIES: Roads and civil engineering construction; supply of building materials, fire fighting & safety equipment and systems
Principal Agencies: Total Walther
Branch Offices: PO Box 4142, Jeddah, Tel 6672585
Parent Company: Al Hamidi Trading Est
Subsidiary Companies: Saudi Sicli Co; Jeddah Industrial Materials Co; Saudi Co for Hardware
Principal Bankers: National Commercial Bank; Saudi Hollandi Bank; Al Bank Al Saudi Al Fransi
Financial Information:

	1989
	SR'000
Sales turnover	40,000
Profits	2,800
Authorised capital	21,000
Paid-up capital	21,000
Total assets	150,000

Date of Establishment: 1967
No of Employees: 220

ALHAMRA NOVA PARK HOTEL

PO Box 3757, Jeddah 21481
Tel: 6676132
Telex: 600749

PRINCIPAL ACTIVITIES: Hotel business
Branch Offices: Location in Jeddah: Palestine Road

ALHAMRANI & ALSULAIMAN UNITED CO

PO Box 6543, Medina Rd, Jeddah 21452
Tel: 6650745, 6600808, 6600816
Cable: Datsun Jeddah
Telex: 601556 Afaf Sj, 602931 Nisn Sj
Telefax: 6674394, 6600927

Chairman: Sheikh Mohamed Ali Alhamrani
Senior Executives: Essam A Banaja (General Manager
  Commercial Affairs)

PRINCIPAL ACTIVITIES: General trading and contracting,
  import, agencies
Principal Agencies: Nissan Motor Co Ltd, Japan; Gulf Oil Co,
  USA; Nissan Super Gold Motor Oil, Japan; Idemitsu Kosan
  Co, Japan
Branch Offices: Jeddah: Al Jama'a Br, PO Box 9354, Tel
  6884360; Jeddah: Al Mahjar Br, Tel 6366656; Makkah: Al
  Mansour Br, Tel 5365522, Al Rosayfa Br, Tel 5365959, Al
  Taysir Br, Tel 5424737; Khamis Mushayt, Tel 2220144; Al
  Baha, Tel 7253336; Al Namas, Tel 2820742; ArRass, Tel
  3335914; Abha, Tel 2241938; Tabuk, Tel 4234908; Medina Al
  Munwarra, Tel 8262826; Qaseem, Tel 3643559; Hail, Tel
  5332640
Principal Agencies: Main Dealers: Hamrani Trading & Imports
  Co, PO Box 2745, Riyadh, Tel 4766969; Al Jabre Trading Co,
  PO Box 600, Damman, Tel 8324300
Principal Bankers: National Commercial Bank; Al Bank Al Saudi
  Al Fransi, Jeddah; Saudi American Bank, Jeddah
Financial Information:

| | 1989 |
	SR'000
Sales turnover	1,200,000
Total assets	650,000

Principal Shareholders: Sheikh Abdul Aziz A Alsulaiman; Sheikh
  Mohamed A Alhamrani
Date of Establishment: 1952
No of Employees: 800

ALHAMRANI GROUP OF COMPANIES
(HOLDING COMPANY)

PO Box 1229, Jeddah 21431
Tel: 6827777
Cable: Alhamrani Jeddah
Telex: 601230 Danya Sj
Telefax: 6836085

Chairman: Sheikh Mohamed A Alhamrani
Directors: Sheikh Abdullah A Alhamrani (Vice Chairman &
  Executive President), Sheikh Siraj A Alhamrani (Senior
  Executive Vice President), Sheikh Khalid A Alhamrani
  (President Alhamrani Trading & Import Co), Sheikh Abdulaziz
  A Alhamrani (President Alhamrani Industrial Group)
Senior Executives: Sheikh Saeed H Jamaan (Vice President
  Alhamrani Trading & Import Co), Dr Salah Shehata (Vice
  President Finance), Mohamed El Shaer (Vice President
  Planning & Development), Isam Basrawi (President Alhamrani
  Universal Co Ltd)

PRINCIPAL ACTIVITIES: Sales and distribution of Nissan cars
  and spare parts, production and distribution of red bricks and
  steel drums, aviation and airport services, agents and
  contractors, automatic banking systems equipment,
  production of lubricants, grease, speciality products, brake
  fluid, and antifreeze

Principal Agencies: Nissan Motor Co, Japan; Krupp Stahlexport,
  Germany; Gebruder Uhl Corp, Germany; Chevron Chemical
  Co, USA; Air Seychelles; Gulf Oil; Neste Oy, Finland; Fuchs
  Petrolub, Switzerland
Branch Offices: PO Box 2745, Riyadh 11461, Tel 4766969,
  Telex 401246, Fax 4765276
Subsidiary Companies: Alhamrani Trade & Import Co Ltd,
  Riyadh; Alhamrani Fuchs Petroleum Productions Ltd, Jeddah;
  Alhamrani Co for Industry (Red Brick Factory), Jeddah;
  Alhamrani Trading Industry & Import Co (drum Factory),
  Jeddah; Mohammed A Alhamrani & Bros Co, (Drum Factory),
  Riyadh; Alhamrani Universal Co Ltd, Jeddah; International
  Airports Services Co Ltd, Jeddah
Principal Bankers: National Commercial Bank, Jeddah
Financial Information:

| | 1989/90 |
	SR'000
Sales turnover	490,000
Authorised capital	28,000
Paid-up capital	28,000
Total assets	501,000

Principal Shareholders: Family owned company
Date of Establishment: 15-11-1385 Hijra (1965)
No of Employees: 2,000

AL HARAMAIN COMPANY

PO Box 2233, Jeddah 21451
Tel: 6608301, 6608305, 6608309
Cable: Al Zarwa
Telex: 601404 Zarwah Sj

Chairman: Abdul Rehman Mohammed Al Howaish
Senior Executives: Mohamed A Al Howaish (General Manager),
  Othman Al Howaish (Manager), Abdul Wahab Al Howaish
  (Road Services Manager)

PRINCIPAL ACTIVITIES: General and building contractors,
  roads, tunnels, stadiums and housing compounds, real estate
  agents, road services, thermoplastic paints, roads markings,
  studs, (supply and installation)
Branch Offices: PO Box 940, Taif, Tel 7325610; PO Box 3459,
  Riyadh, Tel 4774781
Subsidiary Companies: Insulation Factory, Metal Work Factory,
  Saudi Metal; Al Howaish Trading Center, Jeddah
Principal Bankers: National Commercial Bank; Bank Al Jazira

Date of Establishment: 1969
No of Employees: 1,200 (Road, Building and Road Services
  Division)

AL HARBI, MISFER SULIMAN, EST

PO Box 1487, Jeddah 21431
Tel: 6878279, 6885386, 6883840, 6883688
Cable: Misfer Jeddah
Telex: 601326 Misfer Sj

President: Misfer Suliman Al-Harbi
Directors: Hamid Suliman Al-Harbi (Vice-President)
Senior Executives: Mohd Elyan (General Manager), A A Faruqi
  (Importers Executive), Ahmad Amin (Chief Accountant)

PRINCIPAL ACTIVITIES: Construction of buildings, roads,
  dams; import of decoration pieces, household electrical
  appliances, and construction machinery, crushing plants, etc
Principal Agencies: IBAG-Vertrieb GmbH; West Germany
Branch Offices: Alkhobar; Madina; Dammam; Makkah
Subsidiary/Associated Companies: Arabian Euroasia Corp
Principal Bankers: National Commercial Bank; Saudi Cairo
  Bank; Bank Aljazira

Principal Shareholders: Sole proprietorship
Date of Establishment: 1959

AL HARBI TRADING & CONTRACTING CO LTD

PO Box 5750, Riyadh 11432
Tel: 4775252
Cable: Alsaaedy
Telex: 401439 Heip Sj, 400629 Heip Sj
Telefax: 4775350

Chairman: Abdullah Olaitha Al-Harbi (also Managing Director)
Senior Executives: Abdullah Eid Al-Harbi (VP Finance & Admin), Eng Mustafa A El Hajjar (Technical Director)

PRINCIPAL ACTIVITIES: Civil engineering contractors (roads, bridges, airports etc); dealing in building materials and equipment
Branch Offices: Jeddah; Alkhobar; Jubail; Taif; Tabarjal; Al Jamum
Subsidiary Companies: Hadissah Electro-Mechanical Co, Al Bayan Advertising & Information Services, Heip for Educational & Informational Projects
Principal Bankers: Bank Al Jazirah, Bank Al Saudi Al Fransi, Riyadh Bank, National Commercial Bank

Principal Shareholders: Abdullah O Alharbi; Eid A Alharbi; Hamed A Alharbi
Date of Establishment: 1963
No of Employees: 2,500

AL HARITHY GENERAL CONTRACTING

PO Box 6249, Jeddah 21442
Tel: 6658195, 6658194
Cable: Colharithy
Telex: 601428 Reem Sj

Directors: Muwaffak Al Harithy (General Manager)

PRINCIPAL ACTIVITIES: Civil construction, electro-mechanical engineering, general maintenance; trade and representations; services and exhibitions; construction and paint division
Principal Agencies: Tropic Holz, Germany; Space Structures, USA; Keum Kang Construction, Korea; Fairs & Exhibits, UK; Memri, Saudi Arabia
Branch Offices: Riyadh, PO Box 7729, Tel 4766652
Subsidiary Companies: In Jeddah; Civil Construction Division; Mechanical Division; Electrical Division; Fibertex Division; In Riyadh: Maintenance Division; Finishing Division

AL HARITHY HOTEL

PO Box 7584, Jeddah 21472
Tel: 6670520, 6670540
Telex: 600687 Dalia Sj
Telefax: 6670540 ext 77

Chairman: Shareef Adel Mashur Al Harithy
Directors: Adel Mashur Al Harithy (Managing Director)
Senior Executives: Mohamed Jibreel Garcia (General Manager), Zubair Arooz Mohamed (Sales Manager)

PRINCIPAL ACTIVITIES: Hotel operation and catering
Parent Company: Al Harithy United Company
Associated Companies: Al Harithy Engineering, Al Harithy Exhibitions
Principal Bankers: Saudi American Bank
Financial Information:

	1989 SR'000
Sales turnover	8,000
Profits	2,000
Paid-up capital	2,500
Total assets	40,000

Principal Shareholders: Al Harithy family
Date of Establishment: 1980
No of Employees: 130

AL HATLANI, HAMAD AL NASER, & BROS

PO Box 751, Jeddah 21421
Tel: 6870103, 6871365, 6871756
Cable: Alhatlani
Telex: 601306 Htlani SJ

PRINCIPAL ACTIVITIES: Agents and dealers for cars and trucks; heavy transportation; construction, contracting, general trade, development projects
Principal Agencies: Berliet, Saviem, Daihatsu
Branch Offices: Riyadh: PO Box 560, Tel 4768924, Telex 401486; Dammam: PO Box 4209, Tel 8331154, Telex 801571

Date of Establishment: 1948
No of Employees: 395

ALHAYA MEDICAL COMPANY

PO Box 442, Riyadh 11411
Tel: 4414047, 4414056
Cable: Haya
Telex: 401499 Haya SJ, 405585 Haya SJ
Telefax: 4415368

Directors: Walid Amin Kayyali (Managing Director)
Senior Executives: Khalid Kayyali (Finance Director)

PRINCIPAL ACTIVITIES: Import and distribution of pharmaceuticals and medical supplies
Principal Agencies: Antigen, Beecham, Farmitalia, OM, Smith & Nephew, Asik, Antiseptica, Janssen, Norgine, Stiefel, Schwab, Clinipad, UCB, Duphar
Branch Offices: Jeddah, Alkhobar and Abha
Principal Bankers: Arab National Bank; Albank Alsaudi Alhollandi; Saudi American Bank; National Commercial Bank
Financial Information:

	1990 SR'000
Authorised capital	5,000
Paid-up capital	5,000

Principal Shareholders: Walid Amin Kayyali and family
Date of Establishment: 1967
No of Employees: 320

AL HILAL TRADING & CONTRACTING CO LTD

PO Box 8054, Jeddah 21482
Tel: 6510364, 6517316, 6517320
Telex: 600739

Directors: Gassan Ahmed Abdullah Al Sulaiman, Khaled Abdul Hadi Taher
Senior Executives: Haytham H El Abed

PRINCIPAL ACTIVITIES: Supply and installation of equipment, machinery, spare parts and maintenance, chemical products to the process industry; services: cathodic protection, surface preparation sand anticorrosion painting and coating
Principal Agencies: A W Chesterton; Teddington Bellows; Nikko Consulting Engineering; Thermon Manufacturing Company; Pfizer Chemicals
Branch Offices: Al-Khobar, Riyadh, Yanbu and Al-Jubail
Principal Bankers: Al Jazira Bank, Saudi-Cairo Bank

Principal Shareholders: Ghassan Ahmed A Al Sulaiman, Khalid Abdulhadi Taher
Date of Establishment: 1981
No of Employees: 37

ALHODA AHMED A ALHASHIM & SONS CO

PO Box 22, Dhahran Airport 31932
Tel: 8644873, 8642766
Cable: Alhoda
Telex: 870172 Alhoda Sj

Chairman: Ahmed A Alhashim (Managing Director)
Directors: Hesham A Alhashim, Fekri A Alhashim (General Manager)

PRINCIPAL ACTIVITIES: Suppliers of imported CPVC and PVC pipes, fittings and cement and manufacturers of flexible aluminium airducts for air-conditioning and plumbing contractor

Principal Agencies: Formatura Iniezioner Polimeri, Italy; Rehau Plastiks, W Germany; Osterreichesche Salen, Austria

Principal Bankers: Albank Alsaudi Alhollandi, Saudi British Bank, Riyad Bank Ltd

Principal Shareholders: Chairman and directors as described
Date of Establishment: 1973
No of Employees: 54

ALHOGAIL, ABDULLA, EST

PO Box 116, Alkhobar 31952
Tel: 8647408, 8953020
Telex: 871358 JHC Sj

President: Abdulla Ibrahim Al Hogail

PRINCIPAL ACTIVITIES: Dealers in underground construction, agricultural equipment, liquid displacement pumps; also accomodation rental and food catering

Principal Agencies: Ditch Witch Int, USA; Pengo-Jetco Equipment, USA; TCI Power Products, USA; Houdaille Industries, Viking Pump Div, USA; Tatra National Corp, Czechoslovakia

Branch Offices: PO Box 378, Jubail 31951, Tel 3611956, 3612484, Telex 831060 Golden Sj

Principal Bankers: Riyad Bank

Date of Establishment: 1963

AL HOTY-STANGER LTD

PO Box 1122, Alkhobar 31952
Tel: 03 8642539
Telex: 870778 Hodi SJ
Telefax: 03 8981466

Chairman: Abdulaziz Saleh Al Hoty
Directors: David H Stanger (Managing Director), Wendell R Cutting, Robert Barnes
Senior Executives: Dr Syed A Haider (General Manager), Richard Scales (Deputy General Manager), Thomas Sherriff (Senior Technical Consultant), Walter Pollock (Technical Consultant), Dr Sami Fahmy (Manager Chemical Dept), Bayani M Caparros (Finance Manager), Ibrahim A Wassif (Administration Manager)

PRINCIPAL ACTIVITIES: Chemicals and oil analysis (silicate, cement, concrete and raw materials services, analysis water, corrosion, agriculture and soil); inspection and non destructive services; geotechnical and site investigation, foundation evaluation services; concrete and soil analysis services (aggregate, concrete, mortar, bricks, soils, cement etc)

Branch Offices: Jeddah: PO Box 8129; Riyadh: PO Box 7359; Jubail: PO Box 467; Dubai (UAE): PO Box 16756

Associated Companies: Al Hoty Est, PO Box 175, Dhahran Airport 31932; Al Hoty Technical Services, PO Box 1122, Alkhobar 31952; Stanger Consultants Ltd, Fortune Lane, Elstree, Herts WD6 3HQ

Principal Bankers: Saudi British Bank, Dhahran Airport; National Commercial Bank, Alkhobar

Financial Information:

	1989/90 SR'000
Sales turnover	12,025
Profits	633
Authorised capital	6,689
Paid-up capital	6,689
Total assets	13,645

Principal Shareholders: Abdulaziz Saleh Al Hoty (75%); David Harry Stanger (25%)
Date of Establishment: 1976
No of Employees: 125

ALHOWAISH ELWIN G SMITH CO LTD (HESCO)

PO Box 11181, Jeddah 21453
Tel: 02-6378000
Cable: Al Howaish
Telex: 604230 Hesco Sj
Telefax: 6364566

Chairman: Abdulrahman Saad Alhowaish (Managing Director)
Directors: Abdulla Said Alhowaish
Senior Executives: Ahmad Gouda (Finance Manager), Nabil Jaber (Sales Manager), K T Ameen (Purchasing Manager), Osama Hijazi (Production Manager)

PRINCIPAL ACTIVITIES: Manufacture of insulated roof and wall cladding "Varifoam", cold store wall and ceiling panels, Variquiet accoustical, Varistyle liner and ceiling panels, etc

Principal Agencies: H H Robertson, UK; End Fasteners, Germany; Dryvit Systems, USA; Markus Doors, Netherlands

Branch Offices: Riyadh: PO Box 7714, Riyadh 11472, Tel 4775378, 4781997, Fax 4770116; Alkhobar: PO Box 1578, Alkhobar 31952, Tel 8953039, 8992417

Subsidiary Companies: Alhowaish Trading Est; Saudi Water Coolers & Frreezers Mnfg Co Ltd; Amana Refrigeration International, USA

Principal Bankers: Saudi British Bank, Riyad Bank

Financial Information:

	1990 SR'000
Authorised capital	4,000
Paid-up capital	4,000

Date of Establishment: 1971
No of Employees: 60

AL HOZAIMI EST FOR TRADING & AGENCIES

PO Box 7621, Riyadh 11472
Tel: 4768275, 4769041
Telex: 405751

Senior Executives: Mostafa Rhashab (Sales Manager)

PRINCIPAL ACTIVITIES: Supply of pharmaceuticals and medical and surgical equipment. Import of all types of stationery materials

Associated Companies: Development Group for Trading and Industrial Investment Ltd, PO Box 26764, Riyadh, Tel 47648275

Principal Bankers: Saudi American Bank

Principal Shareholders: Dr Khaled Al Hozaim

AL HUDA COMPANY

PO Box 733, Riyadh 11421
Tel: 4777079, 4771502, 4770917
Cable: ALHUDA
Telex: 402559 ALHUDA Sj, 400778 AKEEL Sj

Chairman: Sheikh Abdel Moneim Akeel
Directors: Sheikh Saud A Akeel (President), Sheikh Sami A Akeel (Executive Vice President)

PRINCIPAL ACTIVITIES: Supply and installation of all types of cold storage and refrigeration equipment, general contracting on turnkey basis; supply and installation of photographic and audio visual equipment

Principal Agencies: Electrolux, Sweden; Kuba, W Germany; Kipanel, Sweden; Bock GmbH, W Germany; Bell and Howell, UK; Hope, USA; Ilford, UK; Durst, UK

Branch Offices: Jeddah, Al Hamra Area, Telex 400917 Hudaco SJ, Tel 6673890, 6691067 and Damman

Principal Bankers: Saudi British Bank; Arab National Bank

Date of Establishment: 1966
No of Employees: 100

AL HUDAITHI EST FOR TRADING & CONTRACTING

PO Box 1254, Riyadh 11431
Tel: 4786315, 4789854
Cable: HUDAITHI
Telex: 400181 Hdathi Sj

President: Rashed Ibrahim Al-Hudaithi
Directors: Saleh Abdulrahman Al Ammar
Senior Executives: Eng Fayiz Swedian (Technical Manager), Eng Adil Mutava (Technical Manager), Eng Badvi Arnous (Technical Manager), Jamil Din (Legal Adviser)

PRINCIPAL ACTIVITIES: Building construction and road construction, trading in swimming pool equipment, water treatment, electrical and audio home appliances
Principal Agencies: Midas, W Germany; Astral and Espa, Spain; USA; Osmonics, USA; Gold Star Brand, Korea
Branch Offices: Dammam: PO Box 2044; and Abha: PO Box 74
Subsidiary Companies: Al-Zahria Est for Trading and Contracting & Road Construction
Principal Bankers: Bank Saudi Al-Hollandi; Bank Saudi Al-Fransi; Saudi British Bank; Riyadh Bank

Date of Establishment: 1969
No of Employees: 550

AL HUMAID, ABDULAZIZ AL RASHED, CO

PO Box 15586, Riyadh 11454
Tel: 4024243, 4020515, 4024484
Telex: 401938 RASHED SJ
Telefax: 4050555

Directors: Rashed Abdulaziz Al-Rashed (Managing Director)

PRINCIPAL ACTIVITIES: General, electrical, building and civil contracting; well drilling; building materials, construction equipment, suppliers, agriculture, investment
Branch Offices: Agricultural Division, Bureidah, Saudi Arabia

Date of Establishment: 13/10/1402

AL HUMEIDAN, IBRAHIM A, & BROS CO

PO Box 288, Riyadh 11411
Tel: 4025071, 4041902 (office)
Cable: ALHUMEIDAN
Telex: 401576 KWATER SJ

Chairman: Saleh A Al-Humeidan
Senior Executives: Hamad Al-Humeidan (Manager, Electrical Appliances Department), Sulaiman Al-Humeidan (Manager, Radios, Recorders Department), Saleh S Al-Humeidan (Manager, Jeddah Branch)

PRINCIPAL ACTIVITIES: Import and distribution of electrical appliances, wires and cables; power transformers; lighting fixtures, radio, recorders, etc
Branch Offices: Branch in Jeddah
Principal Bankers: National Commercial Bank

ALHUSEINI CORPORATION

PO Box 851, Jeddah 21421
Tel: 6310771/2
Cable: Alhuseini
Telex: 601163 Huseni Sj, 602160 Ahcorp Sj

Chairman: A Aziz M Alhuseini (Managing Director)
Directors: Fadl M Alhuseini (Assistant Managing Director)

PRINCIPAL ACTIVITIES: Manufacturers' representations; industrial projects and general contractors; importers of foodstuffs, grains, building materials; transport contractors, shipping and travel agents
Principal Agencies: BMW
Branch Offices: Riyadh: PO Box 10271, Tel 4647638, Telex 404775 AHCRUH SJ; Madinah: PO Box 1804, Tel 8244964, 8244724, Telex 570141 HUSEINI SJ; Dammam/Al-Khobar: PO Box 431, Thuqba, Tel 8572633, 8572637, Telex 802657 AHCKOB SJ

Subsidiary Companies: National Construction (Saudi Arabia) Co Ltd; Alhuseini-Ada (Saudi Arabia) Ltd
Principal Bankers: Saudi Cairo Bank; Bank Al Jazira

ALI AL THINAYYAN EST FOR TRADING & CONTRACTING

See AL THINAYYAN, ALI, EST FOR TRADING & CONTRACTING

ALI ASSAGGAFF EST FOR TRADING & CONTRACTING

PO Box 4144, Jeddah 21491
Tel: 6426670, 6444167
Cable: Dearjia Jeddah
Telex: 601657 Asagaf Sj

Chairman: Ali Assaggaff (Proprietor)

PRINCIPAL ACTIVITIES: Import, export, manufacturers' representatives, contracting, prefabricated buildings, steel and aluminium constructions, pharmaceuticals and cosmetics, photo colour finishing laboratory
Principal Agencies: Saira SPA, Italy; Proma, West Germany; Technica, West Germany; Encyclopaedia Britannica, USA; Montecoop, italy; Graziadio, Italy
Branch Offices: Riyadh
Principal Bankers: Albank Alsaudi Alhollandi; Saudi Cairo Bank

ALI HAMAD AL SHEBA EST

See AL SHEBA, ALI HAMAD, EST

ALI M AL AJINAH INC

See AL AJINAH, ALI M, INC

ALI ZAID AL QURAISHI & BROS

See AL QURAISHI, ALI ZAID, & BROS

ALIA TRADING CORPORATION

PO Box 551, Riyadh 11421
Tel: 4020483
Cable: Hebah
Telex: 402380 ALIA Sj

Chairman: Munir M Shanawani

PRINCIPAL ACTIVITIES: Distribution of electrical goods and domestic appliances
Principal Agencies: AEG Telefunken, Germany
Branch Offices: Riyadh and Jeddah
Principal Bankers: Saudi American Bank, Riyadh

AL IQBAL TRADING CO

PO Box 271, Alkhobar 31952
Tel: 8644235
Telex: 870143 Iqtrad Sj

Proprietor: Mohammed O Bamardouf

PRINCIPAL ACTIVITIES: Real estate agents, supply of electrical equipment, oilfield machinery, generators and pumps, hardware, steel products, general contracting
Branch Offices: Alkhobar, Dammam

No of Employees: 50

ALIREZA, HAJI ABDULLAH, & CO LTD

PO Box 8, Jeddah 21411
Tel: 647 2233 (11 lines)
Cable: Zainalreza
Telex: 601037 Reza Sj
Telefax: 648 4644

President: Ahmed Y Z Alireza
Directors: Mohamed Yousuf Alireza (Vice-President), Mahmoud Y Z Alireza (Director & Chairman of Supervisory Board), Abdullah Mohamed Alireza (Deputy Chairman of Supervisory Board), Zainal E Alireza (Member & Secretary of Supervisory Board), Tarik A Alireza (Member of Supervisory Board)

Senior Executives: Yahia Tewfeeq Hassan (General Manager, Personnel & Public Relations), M Q Zaman (General Manager, Projects & Commercial Affairs), Eugene Trioli (General Manager, General Technical Division GENTEC), Roger A Schami (General Manager, Accounts), B S Fadel (General Manager, Shipping), A K Ziriat (General Manager, Travel & Tourism), Yahia Zakaria (Internal Auditor), D H Williams (Legal Adviser)

PRINCIPAL ACTIVITIES: Telecommunication and security systems equipment suppliers and contractors; shipping lines and tankers agents; IATA agents; international insurance companies agents; representatives of international companies in different fields; dealing in watches and jewellery

Principal Agencies: Telecommunication: GEC Plessey Telecommunications; Shipping: Hapag Lloyd AG; Nippon Yusen Kaisha; China National Chartering Corp; Shipping Corp of India; Mobil Shipping & Transport Co; Compania Espanolia de Petroles SA CESPA. IATA agents, Insurance: Provincial Insurance PLC; Royal Insurance (Int) Ltd. Watches: Jaeger-Le Coultre, Juvenia and Vacheron & Constantin; Jewellery: Harry Winston

Branch Offices: Saudi Arabia (Riyadh: PO Box 361, Tel 4656428, 4645773, Fax 4650782, Telex 401080 Zenrza Sj; Dammam: PO Box 8, Tel 8337602, Fax 8337575, Telex 801008 Zainal Sj

Subsidiary/Associated Companies: Arabian Petroleum Supply Co SA (Marketing of lubricating oils, aircraft refueling and ships bunkering); Saudi Maritime Co Ltd (Transport of Petroleum by tankers); Alireza Delta Transport Co Ltd (Port terminal and transport operations); International Mechanical & Electrical Contracting Co Ltd

Principal Bankers: The Saudi British Bank; Union Bank of Switzerland and National Westminster Bank

Financial Information:

	1988/89 SR'000	1989/90 SR'000
Sales turnover	940,000	997,000
Paid-up capital	80,000	80,000
Total assets	-	504,000

Principal Shareholders: Ahmed Y Z Alireza; Mohamed Yousuf Alireza, Mahmoud Y Z Alireza, Abdullah Mohamed Alireza and Alireza family
Date of Establishment: 1845
No of Employees: 500 in parent company and 1,500 in related companies

ALIREZA, HAJI HUSEIN, & CO LTD

PO Box 40, Jeddah 21411
Tel: 6423509, 6423802
Cable: Huseinreza
Telex: 601221 Husreza
Telefax: 6426435

Chairman: Sheikh Husein A Alireza (also Chief Executive)
Directors: Sheikh Amin Abulhassan (Jeddah Head Office), Sheikh Hassan Abdulhassan (Al Khobar Branch)
Senior Executives: Alec Davis (General Manager), Mike Van Ooyen (Marketing Manager), Ali Alireza (Administration Manager), Martin Watson (Purchasing Manager), Mohammad Abdi (Personnel Manager), Donald Sharples (Accounting Manager), John Cook (Maintenance Manager)

PRINCIPAL ACTIVITIES: Manufacturers' representation, technical servicing specialists, import and distribution of power generating and diesel engines, agricultural equipment, motor vehicles, spare parts, tractors, tobacco and cigars, foodstuffs, tyres, batteries, electrical contracting
Principal Agencies: Mazda Cars, Nardi Agricultural Eqpt, Leibherr Construction Eqpt, NGK Spark Plugs, John Rusling Ltd Light Alloy Scaffolding, Havana Cigars, Mazda Commercial Vehicles; Industrial & Agricultural Diesel Engines; Ballotti Straddle & Container Cranes, Ford Mercury Cars; Kia Cars, Motorcraft Auto Accessories

Branch Offices: PO Box 269, Alkhobar, Tel 8642005; Riyadh, Tel 2323444
Principal Bankers: Al Bank Al Saudi Al Hollandi, Jeddah; National Commercial Bank, Jeddah
Financial Information:

	1990
Sales turnover	US$150,000,000
Paid-up capital	SR20,000,000
Total assets	SR300,000,000

Date of Establishment: 1906
No of Employees: 500

ALIREZA-DELTA TRANSPORT CO LTD

PO Box 8, Dhahran Airport 31932
Tel: 8320886/8
Telex: 801889 ADDCTW Sj
Telefax: 8576791

Chairman: Sheikh Zainal E Y Z Alireza
Directors: G Vissering, C P Kulenkampff Boedecker, B S Fadel
Senior Executives: J K V van den Brink (General Manager), C Meredith (Terminal Manager Port Operations)

PRINCIPAL ACTIVITIES: Port operations, road transport and terminal operations
Principal Agencies: Hapag Lloyd, Hamburg; Nippon Yusen Kaisha, Tokyo; Shipping Corp of India, Bombay; Hoegh Lines, Oslo; Jugo Linja, Yugoslavia, Lloyd Brasileiro, Brazil
Branch Offices: Yanbu PO Box 3; and Jeddah PO Box 8
Principal Bankers: Albank Alsaudi Alhollandi
Financial Information:

	1990 SR'000
Authorised capital	6,000
Paid-up capital	6,000

Principal Shareholders: Haji Abdullah Alireza & Co Ltd, Jeddah; Delta-Franke BV, Rotterdam
Date of Establishment: 1978
No of Employees: 700

AL ISMAIL, ABDULLATIF A, EST

PO Box 1308, Dammam 31431
Tel: 8348575, 8348627, 8348557
Cable: Ismailco
Telex: 801754 Aai Sj

Chairman: Abdullatif A Al-Ismail
Senior Executives: Saad Abdullah Abudeli (General Manager)

PRINCIPAL ACTIVITIES: General contracting (civil, mechanical and electrical construction/installation, repair and maintenance) and import
Principal Bankers: Saudi British Bank

Date of Establishment: 1974
No of Employees: 175

AL ISSA, ABDULLATIF, EST

PO Box 91, Riyadh 11411
Tel: 4037045, 4038038
Cable: Lateef Riyadh
Telex: 400305 Lateef SJ
Telefax: 4052218

Chairman: Abdullatif Ali Alissa
Directors: Saad A Alissa (President), Abdulmohsen A Alissa (Vice President)
Senior Executives: Najeeb A Alissa, Ziyad A Alissa

PRINCIPAL ACTIVITIES: Import and distribution of cars, and electrical appliances, real estate, supermarket
Principal Agencies: General Motors (Chevrolet/Oldsmobile), Isuzu Motors; AC-Delco, USA; Lucas, Bryce, UK
Branch Offices: Alkhobar: PO Box 192, Alkhobar 31952, Telex 870022, Jeddah: PO Box 5127, Jeddah 21422, Telex 603825 Lucas SJ

Subsidiary Companies: Clayco (Clay Pipes), Siporex (light
weight and insulation construction panel/block systems)
Principal Bankers: Saudi Hollandi Bank; Arab Bank; Saudi
Faransi Bank; National Commercial Bank
Financial Information:

	1989
	SR'000
Sales turnover	200,000
Authorised capital	3,000
Paid-up capital	3,000

Date of Establishment: 1950
No of Employees: 400

AL JABEEN EST FOR TRADING & CONTRACTING

PO Box 1167, Riyadh 11431
Tel: 4032449
Cable: Jabincotrade

Chairman: HE Prince Bandar Bin Musaed Bin Abdul Aziz

PRINCIPAL ACTIVITIES: General Building and civil engineering,
mechanical contractors, import of scientific and electronic
equipment and spare parts

No of Employees: 150

ALJABR TRADING CO

PO Box 600, Dammam 31421
Tel: 8324300, 8320891
Cable: ALJABR
Telex: 801140 ALJABR SJ

Chairman: Abdulatif H Aljabr
Directors: Abdulaziz H Aljabr (President), Mohammed H Aljabr
(Vice President)
Senior Executives: Maher A Aljabr (General Manager Autos &
Showrooms), Ibrahim M Aljabr (General Manager Africola
Beverage Dept), Abdulmohsin A Aljabr (General Manager
Laundry & Dry CLeaning Dept), Omar Aljabr (General
Manager Workshops), Abdullah Aljabr (General Manager
Spare Parts Dept), Said A Al Hurani (Company Secretary)

PRINCIPAL ACTIVITIES: Dealers of Nissan Motor Co; sole
agents GRE (Insurance); laundry and dry cleaning; Franchise
for bottling and canning of Afri Cola, Bluna Koln; investment
Principal Agencies: Nissan Motor Co; GRE (Insurance)
Branch Offices: Al-Khobar, Al-Hassa and Hafr Al-Baten
Subsidiary Companies: Atared Co, Al-Hassa
Principal Bankers: Arab National Bank, Dammam, Riyad Bank,
Dammam

Date of Establishment: 1952
No of Employees: 500

AL JALAHIMA & AL AMOUDI CO

PO Box 2173, Dammam 31451
Tel: 8336610
Telex: 801327 Jatco SJ
Telefax: 8320590

Chairman: A A Amoudi
Senior Executives: I Scott Hunter (General Manager), Colin
Clarke (Survey Manager)

PRINCIPAL ACTIVITIES: Surveying and mapping
Principal Agencies: Geotronics, Sweden; Ground Modelling
Systems, UK; Earth Anchors, UK
Branch Offices: Riyadh: PO Box 53133, Riyadh 11583; Jeddah:
PO Box 19208, Jeddah 21435
Associated Companies: Survey and Development Services Ltd,
Scotland, UK
Principal Bankers: Saudi British Bank, Dammam; Saudi
American Bank, Alkhobar

Financial Information:

	1989
	SR'000
Sales turnover	11,500
Profits	5,000
Authorised capital	1,000
Paid-up capital	1,000

Principal Shareholders: A A Amoudi (100%)
Date of Establishment: 1974
No of Employees: 120

AL JASSIM, EBRAHIM BIN JASSIM,

PO Box 102, Dammam 31411
Tel: (03) 8332109
Cable: Al Jassim Dammam
Telex: 801490 BNJASM SJ
Telefax: (03) 8330451

President: Ebrahim Bin Jassim Al Jassim
Directors: Mohammed Ebrahim Al Jassim (Managing Director),
Jamal Ebrahim Al Jassim (Technical Director - Electronics)
Senior Executives: K V Ravi (Manager)

PRINCIPAL ACTIVITIES: Supply of airconditioning and
refrigeration spares, electronics, domestic appliances,
industrial test instruments, computers and peripherals
Principal Agencies: ISC Chemicals, UK; G E Motors, USA;
Ranco Controls, USA/UK; Sun Oil, Belgium; Simpson Electric;
Haws Drinking Fountains, USA; Copeland, Germany; TVM
monitors, Taiwan; Ricoh, Japan; NEC, Japan; Graphtec
Plotters, Japan; Datex, Taiwan; Keydex, Taiwan; Baldor
Elelctric Co, USA; Airguard Industries, USA
Branch Offices: Alkhobar; Riyadh; Jeddah
Subsidiary Companies: Mohammed Al Jassim Trading Est,
Alkhobar; Gulf Refrigeration Est, Riyadh; Jamal Al Jassim
Electronics Est, Alkhobar/Riyadh/Jeddah
Principal Bankers: Albank Alsaudi Alhollandi; United Saudi
Commercial Bank
Financial Information:

	1990
	SR'000
Sales turnover	18,500

Date of Establishment: 1956
No of Employees: 115

AL JAWHRA EST SOIL FOUNDATIONS & MATERIALS ENGINEERS

PO Box 11074, Jeddah 21453
Tel: (2) 6878790
Telex: 604626 Jawhra Sj

Chairman: HRH Princess Jawhra Bint Mohammad Bin Abdulaziz
(Owner)
Senior Executives: Sartaj H Siddiqui (General Manager)

PRINCIPAL ACTIVITIES: Soil, foundations and materials
engineers; land, ocean and aerial surveyors, well drilling
Branch Offices: PO Box 8405, Riyadh; and PO Box 38, Madinah
Al Monawarah
Associated Companies: Terracon Consultants, Inc, Iowa 52406,
USA
Principal Bankers: National Commercial Bank

Date of Establishment: November 1982

AL JAZIRAH AL ARABIAH EST FOR TRADE & CONTRACTING

PO Box 357, Jeddah 21411
Tel: 6401655, 6604890
Cable: Aljazirah
Telex: 601409 Jazco

Owner: Sheikh Abdul Rahman Momenah
Directors: Mohamed Abbas

PRINCIPAL ACTIVITIES: Civil building and road construction contractors; cleaning and maintenance; telecommunication; air-conditioning; catering contractors
Branch Offices: PO Box 2529, Riyadh, Tel 4762374
Principal Bankers: Saudi Cairo Bank; National Commercial Bank

Date of Establishment: 18-5-85 Hijra
No of Employees: 479

AL JOHAR GROUP
Al Johar Trading & Import
PO Box 2518, Riyadh 11461
Tel: 4414481, 4949692
Telex: 400611 Johar Sj

PRINCIPAL ACTIVITIES: Supermarket claim dealing in foodstuffs and consumer products; fast food outlets
Principal Agencies: Kippling Cakes; Adam Food
Associated Companies: Al Johar Commercial Markets, PO Box 40611, Riyadh, Telex 402434 Khaled Sj
Principal Bankers: Saudi American Bank
Financial Information:

	SR'000
Sales turnover	120,000

No of Employees: 200

ALJOMAIH, ABDULAZIZ & MOHAMMED A, CO
PO Box 132, Riyadh 11411
Tel: 4788811 (10 lines), 4771443
Cable: Aljomaih
Telex: 401023 Jomh Sj, 400143 Jomaih Sj (Arabic)
Telefax: 4774038

Chairman: Mohammed Abdullah Aljomaih (and President)
Partners: Mohammed Abdulaziz Aljomaih (Vice Chairman & Vice President), Abdulrahman Abdulaziz Aljomaih (Vice President & Member of Board), Hamad Abdulaziz Aljomaih (Vice President & Member of Board)

PRINCIPAL ACTIVITIES: General importers and manufacturers'representatives, import of distribution of automobiles, spare parts, tyres and tubes, oils and lubricating oils, earthmoving and construction equipment, agricultural equipment, foodstuffs, owners of Pepsi Cola bottling plant; bus assembly plant; lubricating oil and blending plant
Principal Agencies: General Motors (Cadillac, Buick, Pontiac, Chevrolet, Oldsmobile, Opel, GMC), Agricultural equipment (Fiat Trattori, Claas, Ransomes), Fiat Allis (Excavators, Loaders, Graders), MTU AIFO (Generating Sets), ABG Road rollers & Asphalt Pavers, Leroi Air Compressors, Lurgi Desalination Plants, Shell OIl, Yokohama Tyres, Perkins Engines, Tumac Irrigation Systems, MAN Power Station, Cranes & Lifts
Branch Offices: Location of Head Office in Riyadh: Aljomaih Bldg, Airport Street, Riyadh; also branches in Jeddah: PO Box 467, Jeddah 21411, Tel 6605111, Telex 601147 Jomaih Sj; Dammam: PO Box 224, Dammam 31411, Tel 8337777, Telex 801054 Jomaih Sj; Buraydah, PO Box 2451, Tel 3243962, Telex 301238; Shaqra, PO Box 214, Tel 6223023
Principal Bankers: Arab National Bank; Saudi American Bank; National Commercial Bank; Riyad Bank
Financial Information:

	1990
	SR'000
Authorised capital	110,500

Principal Shareholders: Partners as described
Date of Establishment: 1936
No of Employees: 3,000

AL JOMAN EST
PO Box 6556, Riyadh 11452
Tel: 4044032, 4039492
Telex: 402871 Joman Sj
Telefax: 4043248

Chairman: M Kh Ghalayini (Managing Director)
Directors: Abdulrahman Al Ajouz (Admin & Financial Director), M Hassan Ghalayini (Technical Manager), Hussain Ghalayini (Jeddah Branch Manager), Nabil Jamal El Din (Marketing Manager)

PRINCIPAL ACTIVITIES: Mechanical and electrical equipment for fountains, waterfalls and swimming pools, design and implementation, garden lights and furniture, garden furniture, wood decoration products, general trading and government contractors
Branch Offices: Ghalayini Fountains, Riyadh & Jeddah
Subsidiary Companies: Al Joman Contracting; Al Joman Agriculture; Rawaj For Furniture & Decoration
Principal Bankers: National Commercial Bank

Date of Establishment: 1978
No of Employees: 90

AL JUBAIL INTERNATIONAL HOTEL
PO Box 215, Jubail 31951
Tel: 3610645, 3610167
Telex: 831027 Jubint SJ

PRINCIPAL ACTIVITIES: Hotel business
Branch Offices: (Sister-Hotels) Hotel Al Khozama, Riyadh; Red Sea Palace Hotel, Jeddah
Parent Company: Gustar AG, Zurich
Principal Bankers: Albank Alsaudi Alfransi

No of Employees: 110

AL JUBAIL PETROCHEMICAL CO (KEMYA)
PO Box 10084, Jubail Insdustrial City 31961
Tel: 3576000
Telex: 832058 Kemya SJ
Telefax: (03) 3587858

President: Khalil I Al Gannas
Directors: Clarence I Lewis Jr (Executive Vice President), Esam F Hamdi (Manufacturing Director), Stanley J Vanderleeuw (Technical Director), Mohammed A Dukhaikh (Finance Director), Ahmed A Al Mulla (Acting General Administration Director)

PRINCIPAL ACTIVITIES: Manufacturing various grades of linear low density polyethylene (LLDPE), high density polyethylene (HDPE) and higher alpha olefin polyethylene (HAO) with an annual capacity of 330,000 metric tons
Parent Company: Saudi Basic Industries Corporation (SABIC); Exxon Chemical Arabia Inc
Principal Bankers: Saudi British Bank; Albank Alsaudi Alhollandi
Financial Information:

	1990
	SR'000
Sales turnover	1,072,000
Authorised capital	1,099,200
Paid-up capital	1,099,200
Total assets	3,888,000

Principal Shareholders: A 50-50 joint venture between Saudi Basic Industries Corporation (SABIC) and Exxon Arabia Inc
Date of Establishment: April 1980
No of Employees: 430

AL KABLI CORPORATION
PO Box 3311, Jeddah 21471
Tel: 6513065, 6511796
Cable: Wafkobrothers
Telex: 607086 Wafco Sj
Telefax: 6516903

Chairman: Wasif A F Kabli (Owner)
Directors: Nehad Al Sheikh Hassan (Managing Director)
Senior Executives: Ibrahim Mahjoub (Sales Manager), Abdul Qader Al Haddad (Sales Manager)

PRINCIPAL ACTIVITIES: Dealing in foodstuffs, toiletries and toys
Branch Offices: Riyadh, Tel 4761350, Fax 4761350; Makkah, Tel 5449714; Taif, Tel 7320389, Fax 7381164
Principal Bankers: Bank Al-Rajhi, National Commercial Bank, Riyad Bank, Al Saudi American Bank, Al Saudi French Bank
Financial Information:

	1990
	SR'000
Sales turnover	13,587
Profits	765
Authorised capital	4,680
Paid-up capital	5,000
Total assets	9,680

Date of Establishment: 1968
No of Employees: 50

AL KAWTHER INDUSTRIES LTD

PO Box 7771, Jeddah 21472
Tel: 6360644
Cable: Kawther Water
Telex: 602907 Kawthr Sj
Telefax: 6374337

Chairman: HH Prince Fahad Bin Khaled Bin Abdullah Bin Abdul Rahman Al Saud
President: Eng Daud S Khumayyis
Senior Executives: Safwan Kabbara (Vice President Marketing & Projects, Production, Operations & Maintenance), Husni Sadaqa (Vice President Finance & Administration)

PRINCIPAL ACTIVITIES: Manufacturers of reverse osmosis water desalination equipment; design and construction of turn-key water desalination and treatment plants; manufacturers of sewage treatment plants and swimming pool equipment; operation and maintenance services
Principal Agencies: Licensee of DuPont PERMASEP permeators, USA; Pfizer Chemicals, USA; Klargester, UK; Trailigaz, France; Drew Chemicals, UK; Berson, Holland; Pura, USA
Branch Offices: PO Box 2220, Riyadh, Tel 4766716, Telex 404955, Fax 4787652; PO Box 20362, Al Khobar 31952, Tel 8953577, Telex 872078, Fax 8953085; Jeddah Sales Office: PO Box 7771, Jeddah 21472, Tel 6514730, 6511653, Fax 6514730, Telex 602907
Principal Bankers: Saudi British Bank, Jeddah; Riyad Bank, Jeddah
Financial Information:

	1989/90
	SR'000
Sales turnover	56,482
Net Profit	219
Authorised capital	21,000
Paid-up capital	21,000
Total assets	64,221

Principal Shareholders: Al Mawarid Investment, Saudi Center for Trading & Contracting, Mansour Al Badr Est
Date of Establishment: 1979
No of Employees: 170

AL KHALEEJ COMPUTERS & ELECTRONIC SYSTEMS

PO Box 16091, Riyadh 11464, Saudi Arabia
Tel: 4632143, 4656572, 4632368, 4656610
Telex: 870841 Khalij SJ
Telefax: 4633230

Chairman: Abdulaziz Hammad Al Bulaihed

Directors: Ahmed Ali Ashadawi, Abdelaziz Rashed Al Rashed, Dr Abdulaziz N Al Sagr, Ahmed M Al Sari, Abdulaziz H Al Bulaihed
Senior Executives: Salah Rady (VP Personnel & HRD), Nash Mikhail (VP Marketing), Hamza Al Sari (Administration Manager)

PRINCIPAL ACTIVITIES: Computer consultancy and software development, systems support services & systems integration and hardware maintenance
Principal Agencies: Information Associates, USA; Mini Computer Business Application Inc; Microlog Corp, USA
Branch Offices: Alkhobar: PO Box 2062, Alkhobar 31952, Tel 8649987, 8946564, Fax 8946032; Jeddah: PO Box 13401, Jeddah 21493, Tel 6676244, 6676253, Fax 6676244
Subsidiary Companies: Steria Al Khaleej; United Computer Services Co
Principal Bankers: Riyad Bank; Arab National Bank; National Commercial Bank
Financial Information:

	1989	1990
	SR'000	SR'000
Sales turnover	49,900	92,000
Profits	7,500	8,000
Authorised capital	1,500	2,000
Paid-up capital	1,500	2,000
Total assets	33,000	40,000

Principal Shareholders: Partnership
Date of Establishment: March 1979
No of Employees: 300

AL KHALIFA, ABDULLA B, & SONS CO

PO Box 1991, Dammam 31441
Tel: 8272332, 8267531, 8271277, 8268615
Telex: 801285 Akests Sj

Chairman: Abdulla B Al Khalifa
Senior Executives: Walter J Walmsley (Vice President)

PRINCIPAL ACTIVITIES: Construction, trading import sales of janitorial equipment, technical services, support services, computer services, agricultural services, medical services, fabrication services, applications division
Principal Agencies: Dubois International, Cincinnati, Ohio; Fabric Technic, Hong Kong
Branch Offices: Location in Damman: Dhahran Street, Damman; also PO Box 10251, Riyadh, Tel 4654581/4644985, Telex 403829 AKCOMP SJ; PO Box 9006, Jeddah, Tel 6823518/6826209, Telex 604556 AKSONS SJ
Associate Companies: International Belgium Services (ILPA), Brussels, Belgium; SK Business International, Bangkok, Thailand; Dubois Chemicals, Cincinnatti, Ohio, USA; Arable Aids Overseas Ltd, UK; Mirahdi Services Contractors, Manilla, Philippines
Principal Bankers: Saudi British Bank

Principal Shareholders: Abdulla B Al Khalifa
Date of Establishment: 1975
No of Employees: 1,200

ALKHODAIR TRADING & CONTRACTING EST

PO Box 3398, Riyadh 11471
Tel: 4781135, 4781136, 4781261
Cable: Mhasnpros Riyadh
Telefax: 4786761

Chairman: Mohammed Al Abdul Rahman Alkhodair (Managing Director)
Senior Executives: Eng Ehab Ahmed Essa (Executive Manager), Mohamed Abdul Fattah (Finance Manager), Abdullah Alhasson (Sales Manager), Mahdy Abdul Kader (Administration Manager)

PRINCIPAL ACTIVITIES: Building and civil engineering contractors
Branch Offices: Dhahran: Tel 2550918; Besha: Tel 6226019

Principal Bankers: Saudi Cairo Bank; Saudi British Bank
Financial Information:

	1990 SR'000
Sales turnover	140,000
Authorised capital	90,000
Paid-up capital	90,000
Total assets	120,000

Date of Establishment: 1389H
No of Employees: 415

AL-KHODARI, ABDULLAH A M, EST

PO Box 832, Dammam 31421
Tel: 8264549, 8263213, 8266761
Cable: Al-Khodari Dammam
Telex: 801087 Sj Kodari, 802782 Khodri Sj
Telefax: 8272902

Chairman: Abdullah Abdul Mohsin Al Khodari (Chief Executive
Officer)
Senior Executives: Shaban Abdullah Al Shaban (Finance &
Administration Manager), Maher Jamil Hammad (Chief of
Secretariat & Translation Dept), Basil Sudki (Purchasing
Manager), Ali Salamin (Personnel Manager), Eng Mohd Abu
Touk (Technical Manager), Misfer Harby Al Ghamdi (Public
Relations Manager)

PRINCIPAL ACTIVITIES: General contractors, road construction
and maintenance, general city cleaning, building, electrical
and mechanical works, water and sewerage works
Branch Offices: PO Box 3894, Riyadh 11142, Tel 4760117, Fax
4761351; PO Box 20520, Alkhobar 31952, Tel 8952840,
8952348 Fax 8986856; PO Box 2689, Al Ahsaa 31982, Tel
5822284; PO Box 789, Al Qatif 31911, Tel 8551657
Subsidiary Companies: Al Khodari & Sons Co, PO Box 6775,
Dammam 31452, Tel 8950048, Fax 8942427, Telex 870861
Khodari Sj

Principal Shareholders: Abdullah A M Al-Khodari (100%)
Date of Establishment: 1965
No of Employees: 7,439

AL KHORAYEF, A I, SONS CO

PO Box 305, Riyadh 11411
Tel: 4351479, 4351480, 4955452
Cable: Alkhorayef
Telex: 401388 Khoryf Sj, 404814 Kharif Sj
Telefax: 4358852, 4950261

President: Abdulrahman Alkhorayef
Directors: Hamad Alkhorayef (General Manager), Saad
Alkhorayef (Commercial Manager)
Senior Executives: Saeed Howail (Sales Manager), David
Henderson (Marketing Manager), Ahmed Hussain (Purchasing
Manager), Mohammed S Al Zaid (Personnel Manager),
Suleiman Abdulqadir (Acting Financial Controller & Chief
Accountant)

PRINCIPAL ACTIVITIES: Distribution of agricultural machinery
and equipment, motors, pumps; agricultural contracting;
marine services
Principal Agencies: John Deere; Layne; TRW Reda Pumps;
Volvo Penta; Ritz Pumps; US Motors; Valmont; Western;
Fletcher; Technisub; Bayliner; Phoenix; Zodia; Reflex Skis;
Italrope
Branch Offices: AlKhobar: PO Box 1383, Tel 8570324, Telex
802170 KHORAYF Sj; Jeddah: PO Box 7236, Tel 6911393,
Telex 603356 KHORYF SJ; Buraidah: PO Box 1078, Tel
3232064, Telex 301216 AIAAGD SJ
Subsidiary Companies: Alkhorayef Western Layne Pump Co
(AWL); Alkhorayef Irrigation Systems Co (AISCO)
Principal Bankers: Saudi American Bank, Riyadh; National
Commercial Bank, Riyadh

Financial Information:

	1989/90 SR'000
Sales turnover	450,000
Authorised capital	100,000
Paid-up capital	50,000
Total assets	300,000

Principal Shareholders: Abdulrahman, Hamad, Saad,
Mohammed, Bandar Alkhorayef
Date of Establishment: 1957
No of Employees: 826

AL KUHAIMI METAL INDUSTRIES LTD

PO Box 545, Dammam 31421
Tel: 3-8572777
Telex: 802174 Steel SJ
Telefax: 3-8572591

Chairman: Mohammad A Al Kuhaimi
Directors: Mahmoud A Al Kuhaimi

PRINCIPAL ACTIVITIES: Manufacture of fire rated hollow metal
doors, commercial and residential roll up doors, overhead
garage doors, sliding gates, light metal fabrication
Principal Agencies: Overhead Door Corp, USA; Dryad Simplan,
UK
Branch Offices: Riyadh: PO Box 17544, Riyadh 11494, Tel
4640677, Telex 406837; Jeddah: Tel 6671750
Subsidiary Companies: Sariya Co Ltd, PO Box 17544, Riyadh
11494
Principal Bankers: Riyad Bank, Alkhobar; National Commercial
Bank, Dammam; Arab National Bank, Dammam
Financial Information:

	1990 SR'000
Paid-up capital	9,750

Principal Shareholders: Chairman and director as described
(50/50)
Date of Establishment: 1975
No of Employees: 130

AL KURDI, M N, TRADING EST

PO Box 43379, Riyadh 11561
Tel: 01 4761918
Telex: 406134 Mkurdi SJ
Telefax: 01 4763810

Chairman: Ma'an Nizar Al Kurdi
Directors: Eng Ahmad A Issa (General Manager), Eng Nejm M
Tebshrani (Deputy General Manager)
Senior Executives: Eng George Daher (Jeddah Manager), Eng
Hassan Alkhatib (Alkhobar Manager), Eng Ahmad Machlab
(Mechanical Dept Manager), Eng George Sikali (Power Dept
Manager), Douglas Boyd (Fire & Security Dept Manager)

PRINCIPAL ACTIVITIES: Computer site preparation, electro-
mechanical works, electronics
Principal Agencies: Emerson Computer Power, UK & USA; Sola
Banner, UK & USA; Airedale A/C, UK; Thorn Security, UK;
Alcad Batteries, UK; Tungstone Batteries, UK; Belden Wire &
Cable, USA; USG Floor & Ceiling, USA
Branch Offices: Jeddah: PO Box 6256, Jeddah 21442, Tel 02
6726693, Telex 604246, Fax 02 6719860; Alkhobar: PO Box
3089, Alkhobar 31952, Tel 03 8954996, Telex 872119, Fax 03
8984557
Associated Companies: Al Muhandis Nizar Kurdi Consulting
Engineers, PO Box 2962 Riyadh, Tel 01 4765558, Telex
400743, Fax 01 4784186; Digital-Natcom, PO Box 7902,
Riyadh 11472, Tel 01 4793916, Telex 404807, Fax 01
4776355
Principal Bankers: Arab National Bank, Riyadh

Financial Information:

	1989/90 SR'000
Sales turnover	36,000
Profits	3,000
Authorised capital	500
Paid-up capital	500

Date of Establishment: 1980
No of Employees: 120

ALLIED ACCOUNTANTS
Mohandis, Abdul Majeed, & Co
PO Box 12187, Jeddah 21473
Tel: 6513816
Telex: 605179 Artand Sj
Telefax: 6531629

Directors: Abdul Majeed Mohandis (Managing Partner)
Senior Executives: Sami E Farah (Accounting & Audit), Abdul Hameid Musa (Tax), Abdul Hamid Bushnaq (Administration & Personnel), Rohit A Patel (Training) Rohit A Patel

PRINCIPAL ACTIVITIES: Accountants and auditors
Principal Agencies: A member of Arthur Andersen & Co
Branch Offices: Riyadh: PO Box 18366, Riyadh 11415, Tel 4787801, Fax 4773836, Telex 403631; Alkhobar: PO Box 20168, Alkhobar 31952, Tel 8954524, Fax 8954524, Telex 872143
Principal Bankers: Riyad Bank, National Commercial Bank, Saudi British Bank, Saudi Hollandi Bank

No of Employees: 35

ALMABANI GENERAL CONTRACTORS
PO Box 2781, Jeddah 21461
Tel: 6516532, 6516536, 6516772, 6516776
Cable: Almacont
Telex: 604326 Mabani Sj
Telefax: 6519184

President: Nehme Y Tohme (General Manager)
Senior Executives: Jihad Mikati (Asst General Manager), Alfred Hakim (Finance Manager), Souheil Haddad (Legal Advisor)

PRINCIPAL ACTIVITIES: General contractors, road works, and bridges, airports, dams, buildings, water networks, sewage, irrigation and drainage, electrical, electro mechanical, heavy pre-cast and pre-stressed elements, TV networks and all support industries
Branch Offices: Riyadh: PO Box 4339, Tel 4033701, Telex 401514 Mabani Sj; London: Almabani House, 147A Cromwell Road, SW5 0QD, Tel 071-3700522, Fax 071 3707716, Telex 23113 Mabani G; Beirut: PO Box 11-9385, Tel 216101, Telex 44116 Mabani Le; Paris: 77 rue la Boetie, 75008, Tel 42256946, Fax 42256930, Telex 642982 Cicfr F
Subsidiary/Associated Companies: Saudi Commercial & Industrial Co (SCIC); FREYSSINET Saudi Arabia; Saudia Electro Mechanical Co (SAEMCO); International Engineering & Contracting Co (INECC)
Principal Bankers: Al Bank Al Saudi Al Fransi, Jeddah; Saudi American Bank; Jeddah; Banque Indosuez, Bahrain
Financial Information:

	1989/90 SR'000
Sales turnover	656,301
Profits	13,956
Authorised capital	30,000
Paid-up capital	30,000
Total assets	273,154

Date of Establishment: 1972
No of Employees: 4,000 (Almabani G C and sister companies)

AL MADDAH CORPORATION
Al Khaleejia for Export Promotion & Marketing Co
PO Box 1892, Jeddah 21441
Tel: 62727746, 67190830
Telex: 605785 SJ
Telefax: 6719083

President: Adel S Almaddah (Owner)

PRINCIPAL ACTIVITIES: Agricultural services, general trading and contracting, general maintenance, advertisement, export promotion and marketing
Branch Offices: Riyadh, Al Khobar, Taif, Medina
Principal Bankers: Saudi Cairo Bank, National Commercial Bank, Saudi French Bank

Date of Establishment: 1977
No of Employees: 1,000

AL MAHA'AN TRADING & CONTRACTING CO
PO Box 295, Dhahran Airport 31932
Tel: 8575687, 8575685
Cable: AMTAC
Telex: 870071 Amtac Sj
Telefax: (966-3) 8571194

Chairman: Majed I Al Kahmous (also Managing Director)
Senior Executives: A G Farah (General Manager)

PRINCIPAL ACTIVITIES: Trading in auto spare parts, batteries, tyres, equipment, accessories, welding rods, water treatment equipment, filters; civil construction, fuel supplies, water supplies, road transportation, trailers and automotive workshop
Principal Agencies: Judo Water Treatment Equipment, W Germany
Principal Bankers: Saudi British Bank, Alkhobar
Financial Information:

	1989 SR'000
Sales turnover	21,100
Profits	3,990
Authorised capital	600
Paid-up capital	600

Principal Shareholders: Majed I Al Kahmous, Mufida Hamud Al Mubarak
Date of Establishment: 1978
No of Employees: 78

AL MAKTABA STORES
PO Box 1231, Jeddah 21431
Tel: 6601643
Cable: ALMAKTABA
Telex: 601749 Maktba Sj
Telefax: 6675905

President: Said I Boksmati
Senior Executives: Samih Boksmati (General Manager), Samir Boksmati (Commercial Manager), Mohamed Saif (Chief Accountant)

PRINCIPAL ACTIVITIES: Sales of stationery, office products/equipment, surveying/engineering equipment, office furniture, gift and novelty items through outlets and wholesale departments
Principal Agencies: Wilson Jones, USA; Swinglines, USA; Mead Products, USA; Eldon Office, USA; AW Faber Castell, Germany; Rotring, Germany; Staedtler, Germany; Schwan Stabilo, Germany; Leitz, Germany; Kalle, Germany; Neolt, Italy; Canson, France; Winsor & Newton, UK; Brother Industries, Japan
Branch Offices: Jeddah (3 branches); Jubail; Al Khobar; Dammam; Riyadh (3 branches); Tabuk; Gassim; Medina; Khamis Mushayt; Hail; Taif; Yanbu; Al Jauf; Hafraf Batin; Al Hassa

Associated Companies: Ambest Manufacturers NV, Los Angeles, USA
Principal Bankers: Saudi British Bank; Saudi Cairo Bank; Saudi American Bank; Saudi French Bank
Financial Information:

	1990 SR'000
Sales turnover	120,000
Authorised capital	5,000

Principal Shareholders: Sole proprietorship
Date of Establishment: 1958
No of Employees: 700

ALMANA, EBRAHIM MOHAMMAD, & BROTHERS CO

Almana, Mohammad Abdullah,

PO Box 3568, Alkhobar 31952
Tel: 8949400, 8949404
Cable: Mana
Telex: 870357 Najeeb Sj
Telefax: 8643603

Chairman: Ebrahim Mohammad Almana
Directors: Najeeb Mohammad Almana (Managing Director)
Senior Executives: Hasan Bilgrami (Marketing & Sales Manager, Medical Div), Ibrahim Taskin (Marketing & Sales Manager, Dental Div)

PRINCIPAL ACTIVITIES: Hospital supplies and medical equipment, health care project management, operation of a private general hospital
Principal Agencies: B Braun Melsungen, W Germany; Waterloo, USA: Bourmed, Bahrain; Forma Scientific, USA; Labline Instruments, USA; LIP, UK; 3M, USA; Anago Inc, USA; Flow Lab, UK; T F Herceg, USA; Bunny Line, USA; Medela, Switzerland; Denticator, USA; SDI, Australia; Beavers, Canada; Flow X Ray, USA; Komet, W Germany; Vivadent, Switzerland; Ceka, Belgium; Neoloy, USA; Harald Nordin, Switzerland; Ivoclar, Switzerland; Leleux, W Germany
Branch Offices: PO Box 56980, Olaiya, Riyadh 11564, Tel 4632834; PO Box 11447, Jeddah, Tel 6657469, Fax 6673805; PO Box 1707, Abha, Tel 2243984, Fax 2243984
Subsidiary Companies: Almana General Hospital; Almana Medical Services
Principal Bankers: Albank Alsaudi Alhollandi, Alkhobar; National Commercial Bank, Alkhobar
Financial Information:

	1990 US$'000
Paid-up capital	5,500
Total assets	100,000

Date of Establishment: 1980
No of Employees: 40

ALMANAR TRADING EST

PO Box 4940, Riyadh 11412
Tel: 4760548
Cable: Reslan
Telex: 402032 Almnar Sj

Owner: Ahmed S Najeeb

PRINCIPAL ACTIVITIES: Hospital supplies and equipment, turnkey projects, maintenance, stockists of pharmaceuticals and cosmetics
Principal Agencies: Dentex Inc, Switzerland; Davis & Geck; National Catheters; Davol; UMI; Stella, Belgium; Rougeri, Canada; Baxter, UK; Cent Ind Corp, Taiwan
Branch Offices: 2161 One World Trade Centre, New York NY 10048, USA. Tel (212) 432-0550, Telex 60518 JithCony; Further Branches in Saudi Arabia; Jeddah, Khamis Mushayt, Madina, Taif, Gizan
Subsidiary Companies: Najeeb Establishment; Najeeb Automatic Bakery, Riyadh; Najeeb Industrial United

Principal Bankers: Arab National Bank Ltd; Bank Al Cairo Al Saudia; Marine Midland Bank, New York, USA

Date of Establishment: 1966
No of Employees: 1,215

ALMANSOOR & ALABDALY TRADING & CONTRACTING CO

PO Box 21, Riyadh 11411
Tel: 4778745
Cable: Alabdaly
Telex: 401356 Mac Sj
Telefax: 4769820

Chairman: Abdulrahman Alzamil
Directors: Mansour A Alzamil (General Manager)
Senior Executives: M A Mansour (Financial Manager), F Musaid (Administrative Manager)

PRINCIPAL ACTIVITIES: General trading and civil engineering contracting (building materials, electrical equipment, industrial machinery); food processing and agricultural produce; plastics and hygienic towels industry
Branch Offices: PO Box 604, Dammam 31421
Subsidiary Companies: AIM Industries, PO Box 4667, Riyadh 11412
Principal Bankers: National Commercial Bank; Riyad Bank; Saudi Cairo Bank; Al Jazirah Bank

Principal Shareholders: Abdul Rahman Alzamil, Saleh Alabdaly
Date of Establishment: 1959
No of Employees: 150

AL MANSOUR AKRAM OJJEH EST

Airport St, PO Box 2814, Riyadh 11461
Tel: 4764030, 4762574
Cable: Akiojjeh
Telex: 401235 Akojjeh

Owner: Akram Ojjeh

PRINCIPAL ACTIVITIES: Manufacturers' representation, construction, water desalination, trading
Branch Offices: Jeddah; Tabuk; Khamis Myshait; Alkhobar
Subsidiary/Associated Companies: Diners Club of Saudi Arabia ltd; TAG Enterprises for Contracting & Trading Ltd; Al Mansour Trading; TAG Water Treatment; Trans Arabian Industrial Co Ltd
Principal Bankers: National Commercial Bank, Riyadh; Credit Commercial de France, Geneva

Principal Shareholders: Akram Ojjeh
No of Employees: 700

AL MANSOUR EASTERN DEVELOPMENT EST (AMEDE)

PO Box 655, Alkhobar 31952
Tel: 8645844
Cable: AMEDE
Telex: 870079 AMEDE SJ

Directors: Aref I Chafei (Managing Director)
Senior Executives: Bassem A Chafei (Asst Managing Director)

PRINCIPAL ACTIVITIES: General trading, construction machinery, trucks and tractors, generators, electrical equipment, freight transportation, engineering contracting, architectural and surveying services; gift items and paintings
Principal Bankers: National Commercial Bank, Alkhobar

Date of Establishment: 1975

ALMANSOUR INDUSTRIES

PO Box 8413, Jeddah 21471
Tel: 6917376, 6914400, 6915132
Telex: 604575 BPF SJ
Telefax: 6917224

Chairman: HRH Prince Talal Mansour Bin Abdulaziz Al Saud (Proprietor)
Directors: Mohamed Salem Bakheet (Chief Executive/Director), Ahmed Mohamed Nuraddin (General Manager/Director)
Senior Executives: Mohamed Aslam Anjum (Finance & Accounts Manager), Alan E Byrne (Sales & Marketing Manager)

PRINCIPAL ACTIVITIES: Manufacturers of concrete building materials, hollow blocks, pipes, tiles, paving tiles; also vehicle repair services; importers, wholesalers and retailers of toys and bicycles; advertising and production of video films, real estate
Branch Offices: BPF Division (concrete hollow block, pipes factory), Jeddah; Tiles Factory, Shumaysi; Al Mansour Auto Services Division, Jeddah; Al Mansour Toys Centre, Jeddah; Publicity Division, Jeddah
Subsidiary Companies: Al Manal Agencies
Principal Bankers: Arab National Bank, Jeddah

Principal Shareholders: Sole proprietorship
Date of Establishment: 1978
No of Employees: 110

ALMASHRIK CONTRACTING CO

PO Box 6108, Riyadh 11442
Tel: 4780330, 4775355, 4774561
Cable: Almashrik
Telex: 403232 Mashrk SJ
Telefax: 01-4776906

Chairman: HH Prince Sultan Bin Mohammad Bin Saud Alkabir
Directors: Abdalla Ibrahim Al-Tuwaijri (Managing Director and General Manager), Harb Salih Al Zuhair, Rashid Al Mubarak

PRINCIPAL ACTIVITIES: Construction, general contracting, civil works, landscaping and buildings; highway construction
Branch Offices: Dammam Branch: PO Box 1452, Tel 8325272, Fax 03-8983081; Buraidah Branch: PO Box 1794, Tel 06-3231996
Principal Bankers: Arab National Bank; Saudi American Bank; Saudi Investment Banking Corporation; National Commercial Bank; Union Bank of Switzerland; Societe Bancaire Arabe
Financial Information:

	SR'000
Sales turnover	160,000
Authorised capital	6,000
Paid-up capital	6,000

Principal Shareholders: Partners are the Directors
Date of Establishment: 1975
No of Employees: 1,650

AL-MATH'HAR GROUP OF COMPANIES (MTC)

PO Box 21636, Riyadh 11485
Tel: 4767145, 4765853
Cable: SELTELCOR
Telex: 402923 Ametac SJ
Telefax: 4765215

President: Homoud A Al Barrak
Director: Abdulaziz A Al Barrak (Deputy General Manager)

PRINCIPAL ACTIVITIES: Trading, contracting, maintenance and operations, advertising and publishing, representation and consultant for foreign companies
Principal Agencies: Metera Feuerschutztechnolgie; SAS R&D Services
Branch Offices: UK: 71 Flat K Park St, London W1
Principal Bankers: Saudi British Bank, Riyadh; Riyad Bank, Buraydah; Al Bank Al Saudi Al Fransi; Albank Alsaudi Alhollandi

Principal Shareholders: Homoud A Al-Barrak (sole owner)
Date of Establishment: 1980

AL MOAIBED CRESCENT HAMCO LTD

PO Box 2431, Dammam 31451
Tel: 8269860, 8349877
Telex: 802179 MOCHAM SJ

Chairman: Abdul Aziz Mohanna Al-Moaibed
Directors: Abdullah Al-Moaibed, Ibrahim Malouf, Elton D Arment, Terry J Hill (Managing Director)

PRINCIPAL ACTIVITIES: Construction contracting; electrical and mechanical contracting, HVAC and sheet metal work; vehicle maintenance
Subsidiary Companies: Hamco Ltd; Global Packaging Inc, Monroe, Ohio 45050, USA
Principal Bankers: Saudi French Bank, Dammam; Saudi British Bank, Al-Khobar

Principal Shareholders: Abdul Aziz and Abdullah Al-Moaibed; Hamco Ltd; Ibrahim Malouf
Date of Establishment: 1980
No of Employees: 392

AL MOAJIL, ABDULAZIZ & SAAD,

PO Box 207, Riyadh 11411
Tel: 4027357, 4028053
Cable: Moajilco
Telex: 401203 Moajil Sj

President: Abdulaziz Bin Muhammad Al Moajil, Saad Bin Muhammad Al Moajil
Directors: Abdulaziz Al Moajil (Riyadh), Saad Al Moajil (Dammam)

PRINCIPAL ACTIVITIES: General traders and contractors dealing in furniture, office equipment, electrical equipment and appliances, import of rice and sugar; building materials, industrial equipment, hardware
Principal Agencies: ACEC, Belgium; Crowse Hinds, USA; Rheem Manufacturing Co, USA; Mitsubishi, Japan; Yale Locks
Branch Offices: PO Box 53, Dammam, Tel 8321254, 8322756, Telex 801055
Principal Bankers: Saudi British Bank; Albank Alsaudi Alhollandi

AL MOAMMAR, M, & CO LTD

PO Box 907, Al-Khobar 31421
Tel: 8955020, 8647700, 8647438
Telex: 870320 PRIME SJ

Senior Executives: Mohammed Hijazi (Managing Director), Abdel Ghani Khatib (Director of Marketing)

PRINCIPAL ACTIVITIES: Sales and support of computer, hardware and software
Branch Offices: PO Box 16116, Riyadh 11464
Associated Companies: Prime Computer Inc, USA

AL MOBTY EST FOR TRADING & CONTRACTING

PO Box 325, Khamis Mushait
Tel: 2238015, 2230656
Cable: Al Mobty
Telex: 906622 Mobty Sj
Telefax: 07-2230648

President: Eng Abdullah Said Al-Mobty
Directors: Eng Saad Said Al Mobty (Managing Director), Dr Mohammad Siddique Jami, A H Al Zahrani, Fawzy Makki (Finance Director), Eng Adolf Brunner (R & D Director), Dr Abdul Wahb Al Husary

PRINCIPAL ACTIVITIES: Trading and contracting, construction
Branch Offices: Riyadh: PO Box 7705, Tel 4778686, 4778119; Jeddah: Tel 6715345; Al Baha: Tel 7502011
Subsidiary Companies: Saudi International Engineering Co (SIEC); Constructors & Architects (CONAR)
Principal Bankers: Arab National Bank; Saudi Cairo Bank

Financial Information:

	1989/90 SR'000
Sales turnover	65,181
Profits	6,318
Authorised capital	300,000
Paid-up capital	300,000
Total assets	308,870

Principal Shareholders: Sheikh Said Mohammad Al Mobty
Date of Establishment: 1390H
No of Employees: 700

ALMOHDAR TRADING CORPORATION

PO Box 3082, Jeddah 21471
Tel: 6606592, 6606596
Cable: Mohdarment
Telefax: 6607013

Chairman: Hassan M Almohdar (Owner & Managing Director)
Senior Executives: Farooq H Abdullah (Admin & Sales Officer)

PRINCIPAL ACTIVITIES: Importers, distributors of office
stationery and supplies
Principal Agencies: Hunt Int Co, USA; The Bates Mfg Co, USA;
Sanford Corp, USA; Datacom Inc, USA; Twink Int'l, New
Zealand; Bantex A/S, Denmark
Branch Offices: Dammam; Riyadh
Principal Bankers: Saudi British Bank; Albank Alsaudi Alhollandi

Date of Establishment: 1967
No of Employees: 30

ALMOUHAWIS EST

PO Box 142, Al-Khobar 31952
Tel: 8572944, 8573224, 8572672
Cable: Almouhawis
Telex: 802278 Muhwis Sj

Chairman: Abdullah A Almouhawis
Directors: Leo Loveniers (ADT), G Baradhie (Trading), Samir
Tawil (Aircond)

PRINCIPAL ACTIVITIES: Security systems, general trading,
cooling systems
Principal Agencies: ADT; Serex; Carrier
Principal Bankers: Saudi Cairo Bank; Saudi British Bank

Principal Shareholders: Abdullah Almouhawis
Date of Establishment: 1963
No of Employees: 65

AL MOUWASAT MEDICAL SERVICES

PO Box 1254, Dammam 31431
Tel: (966-3) 8263662, 8414444, 8410800
Telex: (0495) 801287 Mowasa Sj
Telefax: (966-3) 8263688, 8413436

Chairman: Mohammed Sultan Al Subaie
Directors: Nasser Sultan Al Subaie (General Manager)
Senior Executives: Mahmoud Solaiman Sharrab (Finance
Director), Marwan Khatib (Operations Director), Gerard J Kelly
(Marketing Director), Vincent E Conroy (Human Resources
Director), Dr Hussein Jabr (Medical Director), Mrs Mary
Follows (Nursing Director)

PRINCIPAL ACTIVITIES: Owners and operators of primary and
secondary health care facilities; contractors; operators of
retail pharmacies, suppliers of medical and dental equipment
& consumables; building and general contractors
Branch Offices: Al Mouwasat Hospital, PO Box 282, Dammam,
Tel 8410800, Fax 8263688, Telex 801287; Al Mouwasat
Medical Services, PO Box 10028, Madinat Al Jubail Al
Sinaiyah, Tel 3460862, Fax 3460861, Telex 832131; Al
Mouxasat Dispensary, PO Box 1254, Dammam, Tel 8260800,
Fax 8263688, Telex 801287

Date of Establishment: 1974
No of Employees: 650

AL MUHAIDIB, ABDUL KADIR, & SONS

PO Box 30, Dammam 31411
Tel: 8329014, 8327127
Cable: Musaab Dammam
Telex: 801106 Musaab Sj, 801487 Mhdbco Sj
Telefax: 8336082

Chairman: Abdul Kader Al Muhaidib
Directors: Sulaiman A Al Muhaidib, Emad A Al Muhaidib, Essam
A Al Muhaidib

PRINCIPAL ACTIVITIES: Supply of all building materials,
hardware, sanitary ware; also civil, electrical and mechanical
contracting; import of foodstuffs (sugar, barley, rice)
Branch Offices: Riyadh, PO Box 2063; and Jeddah, PO Box
16197
Principal Bankers: Al Bank Al Saudi Al Fransi; Al Bank Al Saudi
Al Hollandi; Saudi British Bank; Riyad Bank

No of Employees: 500

AL MURAIBIDH, SAOUD, EST FOR TRADE & GENERAL CONTRACTING

PO Box 3509, Riyadh 11481
Tel: 4774177 (10 lines), 4659779
Cable: ALMIRAIBID, RIYADH
Telex: 400531, 401370 MURABD SJ

Chairman: Shaikh Saoud Bin Birjis Al Muraibidh
Directors: Shaikh Sultan Al Muraibidh (Executive Director),
Shaikh Faisal Al Muraibidh (Executive Director)
Senior Executives: Dr Ismail M Fakhry (Executive Manager),
Eng Joseph Kuoyumjian (Technical Manager), Mohd Ahmad
Al Attar (Head of Accounting)

PRINCIPAL ACTIVITIES: General trade; road and building
construction; food products; telecommunications equipment;
commission agents; concrete works; ready mixed-concrete;
precast concrete for buildings; bridges and culverts; block
making factory; asphalt factory
Branch Offices: PO Box 3038, Jeddah, Telex 602361; PO Box
56, Al Khamis Mushayt, Abha, Telex 901091
Subsidiary/Associated Companies: Almuraibidh Est for
Telecommunication Projects, Saudi Industrial Centre,
Almurabibidh Real Estate Est; Muraibidh Constructions Est;
Manayer Trading Est
Principal Bankers: Saudi Cairo Bank, National Commercial
Bank, Saudi American Bank, Saudi British Bank

Principal Shareholders: Single Proprietorship
Date of Establishment: 1964
No of Employees: 400

ALMUSHAIKIH TRADING EST

PO Box 5820, Jeddah 21432
Tel: 6434838
Cable: Almushaikih

Chairman: Abdurahman Al Abdulaziz Almushaikih
Directors: Ibrahim A Almushaikih, Abdulmuhsin A Almushaikih
Senior Executives: Ahmed Hadad Karama (Acting Manager,
Riyadh), Abdulkarim A A Almushaikih (Clearing Manager,
Jeddah), Abdulaziz A A Almushaikih (Sales Manager, Jeddah)

PRINCIPAL ACTIVITIES: Datsun car sales; cement; building
materials; farming equipment
Principal Agencies: Sub-agent for Datsun cars
Branch Offices: Bureda; Riyadh; Yanbu; Afif; Dewadib; Uneza;
Hamil
Principal Bankers: National Commercial Bank; Saudi Cairo Bank
Financial Information:

	US$'000
Sales turnover	170,000

Principal Shareholders: Abdurahman, Abdulmuhsin and Ibrahim
Almushaikih

AL MUSSALLAM & AL SAYED MOTORS CO LTD

PO box 1850, Riyadh 11441
Tel: 4769689, 4769690
Telex: 401345 Saidco Sj

Directors: Ali Hussain Ibn Musallam (Partner), Saeed Abdullah Al Sayed (Partner)

PRINCIPAL ACTIVITIES: Sell, rent and lease of motor vehicles, trucks and cranes; import of motor vehicles, furniture, office equipment, household appliances, manufacturers' representation

Principal Shareholders: Partners are described

ALMUTLAQ BROTHERS CO (HOLDING COMPANY)

Almutlaq Centre, PO Box 153, Alkhobar 31952
Tel: 8644360, 8644253
Cable: Bader
Telex: 870015 Mutlaq Sj

Chairman: Abdulmuhsin A Almutlaq
Directors: Mutlaq A Almutlaq (President), Mohamed A Almutlaq (Vice President)
Senior Executives: Lutfi M Jalbout (Group General Manager)

PRINCIPAL ACTIVITIES: Almutlaq Brothers is a holding Co., operating through its subsidiaries/affiliates dealing in: production of upholstered and wooden furniture, spring mattresses and polyurathane foam, import and distribution of furniture, contract furnishing, general contractors, engineering, and supply of power stations; oilfield machinery, pumps and equipment, erection of steel structure supply and installation of cranes, instrumentation services and representation of foreign firms, supply and installation of central air conditioning system; building and environmental services, mechanical and electrical services-design, planning, procurement construction, operation and maintenance, servicing re-manufacture of radiators, oil coolers, fuel tanks, dealers in chinaware, silverware, gift, promotional articles and real estate development
Principal Agencies: Rochester Instruments, UK, USA; Serck GmbH, Germany; Sterling Foundry Specialists, UK; Serck Controls, Taylor Instruments UK; Tokyo Keiso Co, Japan; Svere Munck, Norway; Solidstate Controls, USA; Ludlam Sysco, UK; Hitachi, Japan; Singer, USA; Burlington, USA; Ebara, Japan; Flexibox, UK; Adrian Stokes, UK; AOT Flowmeters, UK; Nortech, USA; Plidco, USA; Summit Tools, Italy; Sella, Italy; Koyawood, Singapore; Wiggin Alloys, UK; Fuji Electric, Japan; Japan Steel Towers, Japan; Nichimen, Japan; Rockbestos, USA; Permali Glouster, UK; McGraw Edison, Greece; Valmont, USA; GF Business Equipment, USA; BTR Silvertown, UK; Richard Klinger, UK; Delens, France; Joslyn, USA; Sembawang, Singapore; Sterling Scaffolding, UK; Colt, UK; Lamons Metal Gasket, USA; Sorinc, USA
Branch Offices: Branches in Jeddah, PO Box 4645, Tel 682536, Telex 602082; Riyadh, PO Box 1321, Tel 4788040, Telex 401179; Dammam, PO Box 710, Tel 8322393; also branches and showrooms at Abha, Alkhobar, Dammam, Jubail, Khafji, Jeddah, Medina, Makkah, Qatif and Riyadh
Subsidiary Companies: Almutlaq Bossert Construction Co; Almutlaq Contracting and Trading Co (ACT), Almutlaq Furniture; Almutlaq Furnishing Co; Almutlaq Furniture Manufacturing Co; Almutlaq Mace Saudi Arabia Ltd; Almutlaq Mattress Manufacturing Co; Almutlaq Serck Services Ltd; Almutlaq Trading and Agencies (ATA); Saudi Industrial and Technical Services Co (SISCO); Haden International (Saudi Arabia) Ltd
Principal Bankers: Riyad Bank; Arab National Bank; Saudi British Bank; Al Saudi Al Hollandi Al Bank, Albank Alsaudi Alfransi

Principal Shareholders: Chairman and directors as described
Date of Establishment: 1952
No of Employees: over 1,800

AL MUTLAQ MACE SAUDI ARABIA LTD

PO Box 429, Dhahran Airport 31932
Tel: (03) 894-8887, (03) 898-2584
Telex: 870851 MACE SJ

Directors: W A T Haddad, B J Murr, A M A Al Mutlaq, M A Al Mutlaq

PRINCIPAL ACTIVITIES: Mechanical and civil contracting
Branch Offices: Riyadh: PO Box 20613, Tel (01)479-2100 Ext 172, (01)478-2516, Telex 400689 Mutlaq SJ; PO Box 117742, Beirut, Lebanon; PO Box 2307, Abu Dhabi, UAE; and Brighton, UK
Parent Company: MACE, PO Box 119, Commerce House, StPeters Port, Guernsey, Channel Islands
Principal Bankers: Saudi British Bank, Al Saudi Alhollandi Bank, National Commercial Bank, Lloyds Bank International

Principal Shareholders: Al Mutlaq Brothers, AlKhobar; Mechanical & Civil Eng Contractors, UK
Date of Establishment: 18th October, 1979
No of Employees: 398

AL MUTLAQ NOVOTEL

PO Box 3525, Riyadh 11481
Tel: 4763483
Telex: 405266 HOMTQ Sj
Telefax: 4780696

Chairman: Abdullah Al Mutlaq
Directors: Chaieb Kemel (General Manager)

PRINCIPAL ACTIVITIES: Hotel operation
Parent Company: Accor Groupe, Paris
Principal Bankers: Saudi American Bank
Financial Information:

	1990 SR'000
Sales turnover	16,000
Profits	45%
Total assets	57,000

Principal Shareholders: Abdullah Al Mutlaq
No of Employees: 95

ALMUTLAQ SERCK SERVICES

PO Box 1742, Alkhobar 31952
Tel: (03) 8575591, 8575587, 8575859, 8575867
Cable: ALMASEK
Telex: 870298 SERCK SJ
Telefax: 8574342

Chairman: Abdulmuhsin Al Mutlaq
Directors: P Wragg, A L G McKee, Mutlaq Al Mutlaq, K G Ansell
Senior Executives: K G Ansell (General Manager), J Skaria (Finance Manager), R Massey (Operations Manager), I Siyam (Sales & Purchasing Manager)

PRINCIPAL ACTIVITIES: Truck, plant, marine and automobile radiator and oil cooler repair and re-manufacture, also clutches and brake friction
Branch Offices: PO Box 13705, Jeddah; PO Box 1321, Riyadh; PO Box 325, Abha; Jubail; Yanbu & Buraidah
Subsidiary Companies: Almutlaq Serck Manufacturing Co
Principal Bankers: Albank Alsaudi Alhollandi; Grindlays - Bahrain

Principal Shareholders: Almutlaq Bros; Serck AG
Date of Establishment: 1978
No of Employees: 150

AL NAJIM SAUDI INTERNATIONAL CO LTD

PO Box 1017, Dammam 31431
Tel: 8572288
Cable: Firas
Telex: 801079 Nasico Sj
Telefax: 8578951

President: Abdul Rehman Eid Al Rakayan
Directors: Eid A R Al Rakayan (Executive Vice President),
Hisham A R Al Rakayan (Director)
Senior Executives: R Bhandari (Operations Manager), Tariq
Haider (Commercial Manager)

PRINCIPAL ACTIVITIES: Trading and contracting, catering;
electrical & mechanical engineering
Principal Agencies: GEC Alsthom Large Machines Ltd, UK; GEC
Henly Ltd, UK; Wavin Kls BV, Holland; Polyken, USA; Dymac,
USA; Larsen Toubro, India; Neles, Holland; ACEC Centrifugal
Pumps, Belgium; Dowding & Mills, UK; Pretrovalves, Italy;
Gemmo Impianti, Italy; Gulde, Germany
Subsidiary Companies: Al Najim Contracting & Trading Co;
Poong Lim Saudi Arabia Construction Co Ltd
Principal Bankers: Albank Alsaudi Alhollandi; Al Bank Al Saudi
Al Fransi; Riyad Bank; Saudi Investment Bank

Principal Shareholders: A R Al Rakayan and family
Date of Establishment: May 1979
No of Employees: 900

AL NAMLAH COMPANY

PO Box 1841, Riyadh 11441
Tel: 4767827, 4955050
Cable: Alkim
Telex: 401612 Alkim Sj, 400866 Bkeria Sj
Telefax: (966-1) 4913167

Chairman: Shaikh Ali A Al Namlah (General Manager)
Directors: Shaikh Abdullah A Al Namlah (Deputy General
Manager), Shaikh Abdul Aziz A Al Namlah (Deputy General
Manager)
Senior Executives: Abdullah Al Khutair (Manager)

PRINCIPAL ACTIVITIES: Trading and contracting
Principal Agencies: Plumeet Cable Laying Equipment,
Switzerland
Subsidiary/Associated Companies: Al Bekeria Trading Est; Al
Wajih Co
Principal Bankers: National Commercial Bank; Saudi American
Bank
Financial Information:

	SR'000
Sales turnover	67,977
Authorised capital	15,000
Paid-up capital	15,000

Principal Shareholders: Mohammad Shaikh, Shaikh Ali, Shaikh
Abdullah, Shaikh Abdul Aziz
No of Employees: 500

AL NASER, NASER, GROUP OF COMPANIES

PO Box 2942, Alkhobar 31952
Tel: 8950616, 8980226
Telex: 871048 Siamco Sj

Chairman: Naser B Al Naser
Directors: Abbas B Al Naser (Managing Director)
Senior Executives: Joe C Laxamana Jr (Technical & Personnel
Manager)

PRINCIPAL ACTIVITIES: Agents and general trading, transport,
freight forwarding, printing, plastic products, foodstuffs,
operation maintenance, janitorial services, landscaping and
pest control services, travel and advertising
Branch Offices: Dammam: 18th Street
Principal Bankers: Al Bank Al Saudi Al Fransi

Principal Shareholders: Naser B Al Naser
Date of Establishment: 1976

AL NASSAR, FOZAN MOHAMMAD, EST

PO Box 2254, Riyadh 11451
Tel: 4033124
Cable: Nassarco Riyad
Telex: 401435 Nassarco

Chairman: Fozan Mohammad Al Nassar

PRINCIPAL ACTIVITIES: Trading, contracting, agents; import of
building materials, agricultural equipment and tools
Principal Agencies: Japanese and Korean Firms
Principal Bankers: Riyad Bank, Riyadh

AL NIMRAN EST FOR ENGINEERING TRADING & CONTRACTING

PO Box 340, Alkhobar 31952
Tel: 8644867
Telex: 870669 Nimoff Sj
Telefax: 8649189

Chairman: Fahed Al-Nimran
Directors: Saud Al Dawood (Managing Director)

PRINCIPAL ACTIVITIES: Building contractors, architecture and
structural designs, engineering consultants, hotels, bakeries,
production of packaging materials

Date of Establishment: 1973
No of Employees: 180

ALOTHMAN, ABDUL RAHMAN A A,

PO Box 169, Dammam 31411
Tel: 8321161, 8326725
Cable: Alothman

Chairman: Abdul Rahman A A Alothman (Owner)

PRINCIPAL ACTIVITIES: General representatives and stockists,
construction contractors, specialised in arc/oxygen, tools,
welding equipment and industrial gases
Principal Agencies: Airco Welding products, USA
Principal Bankers: Albank Alsaudi Alhollandi; Arab National
Bank; Riyad Bank

AL OTHMAN, MOHAMMAD ABDULLAH, EST

PO Box 402, Alkhobar 31952
Tel: 8942113, 8640125, 8942208, 8942212
Cable: Al Othman
Telex: 871230 Mao SJ, 870812 Othman SJ

Chairman: Mohammad Abdullah Al-Othman
Senior Executives: Izzat Yousef (Administration Manager), E
Kharbat (Eng & Const Manager), T R Kumar (Sales
Representative)

PRINCIPAL ACTIVITIES: General contracting and trading
Principal Agencies: KVT-OTTO, Germany; Cable Laying
Equipment, Distributors: Raychem, ITT Blackburn, USA
Branch Offices: Location in Alkhobar: M A Alothman Bldg, Opp
Airline Centre, Al Bandariya, North Khobar
Subsidiary Companies: Technical Services Ltd, Alkhobar;
Marble Factory, Al Kalah Corp, Alkhobar
Principal Bankers: Albank Alsaudi Alhollandi

Date of Establishment: 1966
No of Employees: 800

AL OWAIDAH GROUP

PO Box 41880, Riyadh 11531
Tel: 4793700, 4774208
Telex: 400858 Owadco SJ, 403156 Kenrod SJ
Telefax: 4790437

Chairman: Sheikh Fahad Al Owaidah
Senior Executives: Sheikh Abdul Aziz Al Owaidah (Executive
Director), Ibrahim Al Juwini (Finance Director), Dr Abdul
Salam Babiker (Marketing Director), Salih Al Rubaish
(Purchasing Director), Mohammad Al Rusais (Production
Director), Ali Fahad Al Owaidah (Admin & Personnel Director),

Abdul Wahid Al Abdul Wahid (Technical Director), Kamal Fathi Hawana (Company Secretary), Ahmed Fahad Al Owaidah (Director of Al Owaidah Agricultural Co), Dr Mohammad S Al Rubaish (Head of Legal Dept), Eng Hisham Hamid Badawi (Head of Data Processing)

PRINCIPAL ACTIVITIES: Investments, real estate, agriculture, highway construction, civil works, earth moving equipment, travel & tourism, woodwork and furniture, steel works, manufacturing, trading and contracting

Subsidiary Companies: Contracting: Al Owaidah Contracting Co Ltd, Al Owaidah Est for Contracting, Al Owaidah Trading industries & Contracting; Agricultural: Al Owaidah Farm, Al Owaidah Agricultural Co; Real Estate: Khaldia Real Estate Office, Al Owaidah for Real Estate; Manufacturing: Al Owaidah Co for Industries, Al Owaidah Wood Works Co; Saudi Factory; Commercial: Al Owaidah Hexaco; Al Owaidah Trio Peninsula Co; Al Owaidah Development Co; Al Owaidah for Tourism & Aviation

Principal Bankers: Saudi French Bank; Arab National Bank; Al Rajhi Bank

Date of Establishment: 1938
No of Employees: 6,500

AL OWAIMER, MOHAMMAD, CONTRACTING & TRADING EST

OCEETEE

PO Box 338, Riyadh 11411
Tel: 4769846, 4782409
Cable: Oceetee
Telex: 401278 Ocetee Sj
Telefax: 4782281, 4765843

Chairman: Sheikh Mohammad J Al-Owaimer Aldossari (also Managing Director)
Senior Executives: Ibrahim Hamdan (Financial Manager), Yousef Abu Jarad (Commercial Manager), Salah Mijfer (Personnel Manager)

PRINCIPAL ACTIVITIES: Contracting; road construction, street lighting, power plants; importers and distributors of electrical materials, sanitary materials, pharmaceuticals and chemicals, building materials, cement, steel and timber
Principal Agencies: Holophane-Sabir, France; Jakob Thaler, Germany; Mitsui & Co, Japan; Breckwoldt & Co, Germany; Cigrange Freres, Belgium; Merten, Germany
Branch Offices: Jubail
Financial Information:

	1990 SR'000
Sales turnover	40,000
Authorised capital	750
Paid-up capital	44,000
Total assets	45,000

Date of Establishment: 1963
No of Employees: 370

AL QAHTANI, ABDEL HADI ABDALLAH, & SONS

PO Box 20, Dammam 31411
Tel: 8261477, 8261635, 8261831
Cable: Qahtani Dammam
Telex: 801017 Qahtani Sj
Telefax: 03-8269894

Chairman: Sheikh Abdul Hadi A Al Qahtani
Directors: Sheikh Abdul Aziz A Al Qahtani (Vice Chairman), Sheikh Khalid Al Qahtani (President), Sheikh Mohamed Al Qahtani, Faqir M Chaudhry (Executive Vice President)
Senior Executives: Salahuddin Ahmed (Manager, Commercial Affairs), Abdul Rahman Al Hamawi (General Manager, Finance), Saeed Shahrani (Personnel Manager)

PRINCIPAL ACTIVITIES: General trading and contracting; import and distribution of building materials, steel pipes, petrochemicals, industrial equipment, pumps, compressors, valves, batteries, instrumentation, electrical components, water treatment chemicals, canned food, etc
Principal Agencies: Fiberglass Resources Corp, USA; Elliott Turbomachinery, UK; Thomasen Service, Holland; Valtek Eng Corp, UK, USA; Powell Electric Mfg, USA; Daniel Ind, USA; Mitsui, Japan; Du Pont, USA; Texaco, USA; Calgon, USA; Conline Int, Holland; Milton Roy, USA; Sulta Mfg, USA; Brownal, UK; Vellaurec, France; Phoecenne, France; Bran & Lubbe, UK
Branch Offices: Riyadh, Jeddah and Abha
Subsidiary/Associated Companies: Alqahtani Marine & Oilfield Services Co, PO Box 2224, Dammam 31451, Tel 8576883, (machinery importers, industrial hoses, Conveyer belts, Good Year tyres); Al Qahtani Pipe Coating Terminal, PO Box 20, Dammam, Tel 8574150 (pipe coating contractors); Al Qahtani Travel Bureau, PO Box 20, Dammam 31411, Tel 82621741, 8262074 (travel and touring agency); The Arabian Commercial Services Est (ARCO); Al Maha Trading & Contracting Est (Airport operations and management services); Al Jazira (Supply of water treatment chemicals); Al Qahtani Pepsi Cola Factory, Abha; Al Qahtani Nail Factory, Jeddah; Al Qahtani Fisk (Electrical contractors)
Principal Bankers: Albank Alsaudi Alhollandi, Dammam; Al Bank Al Saudi Al Fransi, Alkhobar; Saudi American Bank, Dammam
Financial Information:

	1988/89 SR'000	1989/90 SR'000
Sales turnover	93,000	328,000
Profits	4,000	-
Authorised capital	3,000	3,000
Paid-up capital	3,000	3,000
Total assets	60,000	168,000

Date of Establishment: 1963
No of Employees: over 500

AL QAHTANI-FISK ELECTRICAL & TEL CO

PO Box 2221, Dammam 31451
Tel: 8570158, 8572858
Telex: 871491 QFETCO SJ
Telefax: 8576460

Chairman: Sheikh Abdulhadi Abdullah Al Qahtani
Directors: Sheikh Abdulaziz Abdulhadi Al Qahtani, M Haroon Satti
Senior Executives: Mohammad M A Masri Meery (Company Manager), Bernado Sj Sta Ana (Office Manager), Abdulah Mansoor Al Namshan (Governmemt Relations Manager)

PRINCIPAL ACTIVITIES: Communications, electrical equipment and services; power transmission lines, electrical installations, telephone installations and support operations, installation, testing, commissioning and repairs of all electronic and special systems
Parent Company: Al Qahtani Maritime, PO Box 2224, Dammam
Associated Companies: Abdulhadi Abdullah Al Qahtani & Sons Co, PO Box 20, Damman
Principal Bankers: Al Bank Al Saudi Al Fransi, Dammam
Financial Information:

	1989 SR'000	1990 SR'000
Sales turnover	3,850	5,178
Profits	747	809
Authorised capital	2,000	2,000
Paid-up capital	2,000	2,000
Total assets	9,632	9,636

Principal Shareholders: Al Qahtani Maritime (80%), Abdul Hadi Abdullah Al Qahtani (20%)
Date of Establishment: 1977
No of Employees: 53

AL QURAISHI, ALI ZAID, & BROS

PO Box 339, Dammam 31411
Tel: 8261596
Cable: Kreshan
Telex: 801058 Azaqco Sj, 603401 Azaqco Sj
Telefax: 8271464 (Dammam), 6653741 (Jeddah), 4786947 (Riyadh)

Chairman: Sheikh Ali Zaid Al-Quraishi
Directors: Sheikh Abdul Aziz Al Quraishi (Managing Director)
Senior Executives: Rashid Al Dahhan (Group General Manager), R A Hitchcock (Marketing Manager Household Products), C Walker (Marketing Manager Cigarettes), R Payne (Marketing Manager Leisure Products), Dr T Yamada (General Manager Al Sabah Trading Watches), J L Peeples (General Manager AQ Electrical), R Benson (General Manager Wescosa), D Morton (General Manager Teamwork), Y Al Qasaby (General Manager NMC)

PRINCIPAL ACTIVITIES: Trading and contracting, import and distribution of luggage, photographic equipment, tobacco, household goods, luxury goods, electrical and office equipment, furniture, foodstuffs, sport goods, toys, pharmaceuticals, watches and consumer goods, motor vehicles, construction, manufacturing
Principal Agencies: Samsonite, Canon, Sheaffer, AMF Bowling, Westinghouse, Taylor Woodrow, Reckitt and Colman, Tobacco Exporters Int, Citizen, Swatch, Favre-Leuba, Bic, Fisher Price, Mattel, Lego, Daewoo Motors Corp
Branch Offices: Location in Dammam: Al Quraishi Bldg, King Khalid Street; also in Riyadh; Jeddah; Gizzan; Khamis Mushayt; Taif; Medina; Mecca; Gassim; Tabuk; Jubail; Hofuf; Yanbu; Arar
Associated Companies: Al Quraishi Distribution Services; Al Quraishi Leisure Services; Al Quraishi Furniture; Al Sabah Trading; WESCOSA; Teamwork Saudi Arabia; AQ Electical Services; AQ Investments; AQ Real Estate; National Marketing Co Ltd; United Arab Motors; Gulf Glass Co Ltd
Principal Bankers: Saudi British Bank; Albank Alsaudi Alhollandi; Saudi American Bank; Riyad Bank
Financial Information:

	1989/90
	SR'000
Sales turnover	420,000
Authorised capital	10,000
Paid-up capital	10,000
Total assets	250,000

Principal Shareholders: Ali Zaid Al Quraishi; Abdul Aziz Zaid Al Quraishi; Khalid Zaid Al Quraishi; Saleh Zaid Al Quraishi; Abdul Razak Zaid Al Quraishi
Date of Establishment: 1957
No of Employees: 500

ALQURAISHI, SALEH ZAID, EST FOR TRADING & CONTRACTING

PO Box 688, Dhahran Airport 31932
Tel: 8646085 (Office), 8942408 (Showroom)
Telex: 871049 Alqu Sj
Telefax: 8953656

Chairman: Saleh Zaid AlQuraishi
Senior Executives: Khalid S Al Dakheel (General Manager), Sadik Mosawy (Technical Director), M K Raghavan (Stores Manager)

PRINCIPAL ACTIVITIES: Stockists of pipe hangers, crane valves and various piping accessories, exhaust fans, boilers, also contractors of heating, ventilation and airconditioning
Principal Agencies: Crane Valves & Fittings, UK; Flamco BV, Netherlands; Tozen, Japan; ILG Industries Inc, USA; York Shipley Inc, USA
Branch Offices: PO Box 25495, Riyadh 11466, Tel 4777346, Telex 206195 ALQU SJ
Principal Bankers: Saudi British Bank Ltd, Dhahran Airport

Financial Information:

	1990
	SR'000
Sales turnover	10,000
Profits	2,500
Paid-up capital	2,500
Total assets	6,000

Principal Shareholders: Sole Trader
Date of Establishment: July, 1981
No of Employees: 30

ALRAJA EST FOR COMMERCE

PO Box 121, Riyadh 11411
Tel: 4057511 (Office), 4028860/4540580 (Showroom)
Cable: Alraja Riyadh
Telex: 401124 Alraja Sj
Telefax: 4012516

President: Saied Mohamed Basmaih
Senior Executives: Ahmed Basmaih (Manager Jeddah Branch), Salim Basmaih (Manager Alkhobar Branch), Ali Basmaih (Manager Dammam Branch), Tariq M Butt (Commercial Manager), Higazi A Razig (Administrative Manager)

PRINCIPAL ACTIVITIES: Import and distribution of office furniture and equipment, household and school furniture, telecommunication equipment, test sets, cables and other telephone network materials, storage systems
Principal Agencies: Cazzaro, Italy; Mobilex, Italy; Project Office Furniture, UK; Leabank Office Equipment, UK; Puregas, USA; Stewing, W Germany
Branch Offices: Jeddah: PO Box 1667, Tel 6826086, 6826087, Telex 601654, Fax 6824000; Alkhobar: PO Box 1380, Tel 8950818, 8942285, 8644236, Fax 8954721
Principal Bankers: National Commercial Bank; Saudi American Bank

Date of Establishment: 1964
No of Employees: 160

AL-RAJEHI CONSULTING ENGINEERS

PO Box 7669, Riyadh 11472
Tel: 4644252, 4649629, 4644494, 4651345
Cable: Rajconsult
Telex: 402715 Rajcon Sj
Telefax: 4651527

President: Hamad N Al-Rajehi
Directors: Ahmed Al Rajehi (Vice President)
Senior Executives: Ayman Al Rajehi (Managing Director)

PRINCIPAL ACTIVITIES: Design, planning, construction supervision, architecture, engineering, soil investigation and material testing
Branch Offices: Athens, Greece
Subsidiary/Associated Companies: Al-Rajehi Law Engineering, Inc (Subs); Watson-Hawksley (Assoc); Reynolds Smith & Hills Inc (Assoc); A B Engineering (Assoc)
Principal Bankers: National Commercial Bank
Financial Information:

	1990
	US$'000
Sales turnover	8,783

Principal Shareholders: Hamad N Al-Rajehi
Date of Establishment: February 1976
No of Employees: 178

AL RAJEHI LAW ENGINEERING LTD

PO Box 51179, Riyadh 11543
Tel: 4640960, 4633153
Telex: 400842 LESAR SJ
Telefax: 4632306

Chairman: Hamad Nassar Al Rajehi
Directors: R K Sehgal, Mike Montgomery

Senior Executives: Craig R Clark (General Manager), Roger Hazell (Yanbu Branch Manager)

PRINCIPAL ACTIVITIES: Geotechnical engineering, testing of steel, masonry, soil, water, cement, asphalt, pipe and other construction materials, non destructive testing incl radiography, independent testing laboratory, failure analysis, inspection services

Branch Offices: PO Box 30034, Yanbu Al Sinaiyah, Tel 3962173, Telex 662310 PBTX SJ, Fax 3210963

Subsidiary Companies: Law International Inc, USA

Principal Bankers: National Commercial Bank

Financial Information:

	1989
	SR'000
Sales turnover	6,700
Authorised capital	1,500
Paid-up capital	1,500
Total assets	1,500

Principal Shareholders: H N Al Rajehi; Law International Inc
Date of Establishment: February 1978
No of Employees: 62

AL RAJHI & AL SEDAIS CO

PO Box 10554, Riyadh 11443
Tel: 4900168
Telex: 406748 Wtania SJ
Telefax: 4900520

Chairman: Soliman Abdul Aziz Al Rajhi
Senior Executives: Mohamad Soliman Al Rajhi

PRINCIPAL ACTIVITIES: Poultry farming, agricultural services, cold stores, manufacturer of plastics and bricks; jewellery
Branch Offices: Riyadh; Jeddah; Dammam; Buraidah; Abha; Tabuk; Jizan
Subsidiary Companies: Al Watania Poultry; Al Watania Plastics; Al Watania Bricks; Al Watania Jewellery
Principal Bankers: Saudi Cairo Bank; Arab National Bank; Alrajhi Banking & Investment Corporation
Financial Information:

	1989
	SR'000
Authorised capital	100,000
Paid-up capital	100,000
Total assets	1,069,736

Principal Shareholders: Chairman and director as described
Date of Establishment: 1979
No of Employees: 3,000

ALRAJHI, ABDULLA ABDULAZIZ,

PO Box 242, Riyadh 11411
Tel: 4023028, 4028684, 4485633
Cable: Alabdulaziz
Telex: 401312 Abdulla

Chairman: Abdulla Abdulaziz Alrajehi

PRINCIPAL ACTIVITIES: General agencies; distribution of building materials and equipment and cement, timber, paints, tiles, marble, ceramics, chemicals, portable generators
Principal Agencies: Kawasaki, Japan
Branch Offices: PO Box 1087, Jeddah, Tel 6432149, 6433615, Telex 601373; also branches in Dammam (PO Box 176); Abha; Gizan; Khamis Mushait (PO Box 438)
Principal Bankers: Saudi American Bank, Riyadh; Riyad Bank, Riyadh; Saudi Cairo Bank, Riyadh; Al Rajhi Establishment for Exchange

AL RAJHI BANKING & INVESTMENT CORP (ARABIC)

PO Box 28, Riyadh 11411
Tel: 4054244, 4013153, 4035588, 4034995
Cable: Alrajhi Riyadh
Telex: 401073, 401596, 401604, 401630
Telefax: 4032969, 4032169, 4036606, 4041594

Chairman: Saleh Ibn Abdul Aziz Alrajhi
Directors: Sulaiman Ibn Abdul Aziz Al Rajhi (General Manager & Managing Director), Abdullah Ibn Abdul Aziz Al Rajhi, Ismail Ali Sulaiman Abu Da'wd, Abdul Wahab Mohamed Saleh Sheikh, Sulaiman Al Mohamed Al Rasheed, Dr Abdullah Bin Naser Bin Mohamed Al Wehaibi, Eng Salah Ali Abdullah Aba Al Khail, Mohamed Bin Abdul Aziz Al Rajhi, Ali Bin Mohamed Bin Abdullah Al Rajhi, Abdul Rahman Bin Abdullah Bin Ogail, Mohamed Bin Abdullah Bin Abdul Aziz Al Rajhi, Saleh Bin Sulaiman Bin Abdul Aziz Al Rajhi, Sulaiman Bin Saleh Bin Abdul Aziz Al Rajhi, Mohamed Bin Osman Bin Ahmed Al Bishr, Naser Bin Mohamed Al Subai'y
Senior Executives: Saleh Sulaiman Al Rajhi (Deputy General Manager), Sulaiman Saleh Al Rajhi (Deputy General Manager), Abdullah Sulaiman Al Rajhi (Deputy General Manager)

PRINCIPAL ACTIVITIES: All types of commercial banking activities, including foreign exchange, international investments, etc
Principal Agencies: Representative office at Cairo, Egypt
Branch Offices: Saudi Arabia: 249 branches
Subsidiary Companies: Al Rajhi Company for Islamic Investments, 2 Copthall Avenue, London EC2R 7JQ, UK
Principal Bankers: Chemical Bank, New York; Deutsche Bank, Frankfurt; National Westminster Bank, London; Standard Chartered Bank, Singapore
Financial Information:

	1989
	SR'000
Total income	851,304
Net income	588,262
Share capital	750,000
Total assets	15,045,992

Date of Establishment: 19/3/1988 succeding Al Rajhi Currency Exchange
No of Employees: 4,000

AL RAJHI CHEMICAL INDUSTRIES

PO Box 7799, Riyadh 11472
Tel: 4983443, 4983179
Telex: 400967 Marco SJ
Telefax: 4981063

Chairman: Mohammed Abdullah Al Rajhi
Senior Executives: Fayek Hassan (Production Manager), Shihan Al Err (Sales Manager), Fathi Abdul Rahman (Accounts Manager)

PRINCIPAL ACTIVITIES: Manufacture of detergents, disinfectants, antiseptics, shampoos, creams, perfumes, cosmetics, distilled water, fertilisers and pesticides
Branch Offices: Jeddah, Madinah, Dammam, Khamis Mushayt, Arar, Hafar Al Baten
Principal Bankers: Al Rajhi Banking & Investment Corp, Riyadh; Arab National Bank, Riyadh

Principal Shareholders: Sole proprietorship
Date of Establishment: 1980
No of Employees: 82

AL RAJHI DEVELOPMENT CO LTD

PO Box 4301, Riyadh 11491
Tel: 4761581, 4769102, 4777576
Cable: Rajconsult
Telex: 401249 Nasser Sj
Telefax: 4769775

Chairman: A M Shawaf

Senior Executives: Mazin Al Rajhi (General Manager), Mahmoud Saud Koujan (General Manager), Yahya Al Shawaf (Financial Manager), Hazem A Shawaf (Production Manager), Ahmed Al Rajhi (Personnel Manager), Amer Shawaf (Technical Manager)

PRINCIPAL ACTIVITIES: Civil engineering and construction, supply of building materials and cement, transportation contractors, agencies, supply of pharmaceutical products
Principal Agencies: Transintra, Belgium; Jalite, UK; Power Curber Int, USA; Topos, Cyprus; Ferrosan Fine Chemicals, Denmark
Branch Offices: Amstelveen, Holland
Subsidiary Companies: Al Rajhi Hydrosoil; Al Nahdi & Al Rajhi & Partners Co; Brance for Trading & Construction Co; Al Shawaf Trading Est; Rajhi Topos; Al Rajhi & Shawaf Co; INMACO
Principal Bankers: National Commercial Bank; Al Saudi Al Fransi Bank; Arab National Bank; Albank Alsaudi Alhollandi

Principal Shareholders: Hamed N Al Rajhi & Brothers
Date of Establishment: 1975
No of Employees: 1,110

ALRAJHI, MOHAMMED A, CORP

PO Box 2632, Jeddah 21461
Tel: 6431298, 6447741, 6314577, 6314977
Cable: Marjcop
Telex: 601740 Wahest Sj, 602546 Marjco Sj

Senior Executives: Mohd Abdullah Al Rajhi (General Manager)

PRINCIPAL ACTIVITIES: Dealing in building materials, equipment and general agency
Branch Offices: PO Box 171, Khamis Mushait; Riyadh; Dammam

Date of Establishment: 1970

AL RASHED & AL OMRAN CO

PO Box 1238, Dammam 31431
Tel: 8338338, 8338211, 8335379
Cable: Romanco
Telex: 801427 Romnco Sj
Telefax: 03 8332986

Chairman: Rashed Abdulrahman Al Rashed
Directors: Omran M Al Omran (Managing Director), Abdulaziz Al Omran (Director & General Manager)
Senior Executives: Zaki A Alkhonaizy (Deputy General Manager, Dammam)

PRINCIPAL ACTIVITIES: Civil, mechanical and electrical engineering contractors, roads/highways and bridges, multi-storey buildings, site developments, off-shore and on-shore, industrial complex, etc
Branch Offices: PO Box 2743, Riyadh, Tel 01-4773500, Telex 402255 Omran Sj; PO Box 99, Al Hassa, Tel 5861566, 5864566, Telex 861023 Romnco Sj
Principal Bankers: Arab National Bank, Alkhobar, Riyadh; Al Bank Al Saudi Al Fransi, Riyadh; National Commercial Bank, Riyadh
Financial Information:

	SR'000
Authorised capital	50,000
Paid-up capital	50,000

Principal Shareholders: Omran Brothers, Rashed Alrashed & Sons
Date of Establishment: 1972
No of Employees: 1,580

AL RASHED, RASHED ABDULRAHMAN, & SONS

PO Box 99, Alkhobar 31592
Tel: 8642109, 8642150
Cable: Al Abdulrahman
Telex: 870040 Rshdco, 870324 Artico SJ
Telefax: 8649029

Chairman: Sheikh Rashed A Alrashed
Directors: Abdulaziz R Alrashed, Salah R Alrashed, Abdulmohsen R Alrashed
Senior Executives: Ahed S Shihadeh

PRINCIPAL ACTIVITIES: Import and sale of building materials, cement, steel, timber and allied products. Trading in real estate and leasing of transportation fleet
Branch Offices: PO Box 391, Dammam 31411, Tel 8323539, 8322443; PO Box 35, Alhassa, Tel 5865776, 5821863; PO Box 550, Riyadh 11421, Tel 4482222, Telex 403523 Rarruh SJ; PO Box 4311, Jeddah 21491, Tel 6724302, Telex 605540 RARUNO; Jubail, Tel 8100819
Subsidiary Companies: Alrashed Trading and Contracting Co, Alrashed & Alomran Co, Alrashed & Aljindan Co, Civil Works Co, National Factory
Principal Bankers: Arab National Bank, Saudi French Bank, Saudi American Bank; National Commercial Bank
Financial Information:

	SR'000
Authorised capital	25,000
Paid-up capital	25,000

Principal Shareholders: Sheikh Rashed A Alrashed; Abdulaziz Alrashed; Salah Alrashed; Abdul Mohsen Alrashed
Date of Establishment: 1950
No of Employees: 1,000

ALRASHID ABETONG CO LTD

PO Box 6058, Riyadh 11442
Tel: 2410507, 2412154
Telex: 403757 Araco Sj
Telefax: 2413419

Chairman: Abdulla S Al-Rashid
Senior Executives: Hisham Sheikh Khaled (General Manager), Ingemar Andersson (Executive General Manager), Mahmoud Judeh (Finance & Admin Manager)

PRINCIPAL ACTIVITIES: Manufacturers of precasts concrete products including planning, design, production, transportation and erection; ready-mixed concrete suppliers, buildings contractors
Branch Offices: Makka Site Factory
Parent Company: RTCC, Riyadh and Abetong-Sabema, Sweden
Principal Bankers: Saudi-American Bank, Riyadh; National Commercial Bank, Riyadh; Arab National Bank, Riyadh
Financial Information:

	1988/89 SR'000
Sales turnover	64,764
Authorised capital	10,600
Paid-up capital	10,600
Total assets	15,639

Principal Shareholders: Alrashid Trading & Contracting Co (RTCC, Saudi Arabia) (55%); Abetong Sabema AB (EUROC, Sweden) (45%)
Date of Establishment: 1977
No of Employees: 600

AL RASHID TRADING & CONTRACTING CO

PO Box 307, Riyadh 11411
Tel: 401-2550 (8 lines)
Cable: Shoraco
Telex: 401215 Shorac Sj
Telefax: 4012550 ext 480

Chairman: Abdullah S Al-Rashid
Directors: Rashid Abdul Rahman Al-Rashid, Abdul Rahman S Al-Rashid, Rashid S Al-Rashid
Senior Executives: Mutadel T Barghouty (Comptroller), Zuhair Ja'alouk (Assistant General Manager Contracting), Mamoun Diab (Manager Engineering Studies), Abdul Latif Shakaki (Manager Dammam Branch), Mouin I Bitar (Assistant Comptroller), Fawaz Tarazi (Technical Manager), Dr Hakim A

Jaradat (Real Estate Manager), Ossama Na'asan (Equipment Division Manager)

PRINCIPAL ACTIVITIES: General contractors
Branch Offices: Dammam: PO Box 1548, Telex 801334, Tel 8325174
Subsidiary/Associated Companies: Saudi Japan Construction Co Ltd (joint venture with Ohbayashi Gumi Ltd, Japan); Saudi Services for Electro-Mechanic Works Co Ltd; Al Rashid A Betong Co Ltd (joint venture with A Betong, Sweden); Consolidated Food Co (Subsidiary); Arak Operation & Maintenance Co Ltd
Principal Bankers: Arab National Bank; Riyadh Bank; Saudi American Bank; Al Bank Al Saudi Al Faransi; National Commercial Bank; Saudi Investment Bank

Date of Establishment: 1957
No of Employees: 3,000

AL RAYYAN EST FOR TRADING & CONTRACTING

PO Box 1517, Riyadh 11441
Tel: 4022894, 4020203, 4764406
Cable: Rawi
Telex: 401671 Rayyan Sj

Chairman: Rasheed M Al Rayyan (General Manager)

PRINCIPAL ACTIVITIES: Distribution of construction machinery and equipment, generating sets and steel frame building, spare parts and motor oils, electro mechanical works
Financial Information:

	SR'000
Turnover	50,000

No of Employees: 100

AL RUBAIYAT CO FOR INDUSTRY & TRADE LTD

PO Box 209, Jeddah 21411
Tel: 6476146, 6481286, 6478373, 6478038
Cable: BINZAGR JEDDAH
Telex: 600795 Asmob SJ, 601131 Iskal SJ
Telefax: 6476146

Chairman: Faisal S Binzagr (Chief Executive)
Directors: Wahib S Binzagr, Faisal S Binzagr, Mohamed O S Binzagr, Abdullah S Binzagr (President)
Senior Executives: R C Lester (Vice President Operations), E M Saleh (Vice President Finance)

PRINCIPAL ACTIVITIES: Import and distribution of household goods, perfumes and clothing; retail of ladies, mens and children clothing, fabrics, operation of Wimpy fast food restaurants and martinising dry-cleaning outlets
Principal Agencies: Kanebo Perfumes, Cutex, Healthtex, Wrangler, Lee Spatz, DIM, Playtex, Lanvin, Armani, Zegna, Valentino, Ferre
Branch Offices: Jeddah: Tel 6481286, 6484373; Alkhobar: Tel 8641430/1; Riyadh: Tel 4950076, 4951360
Parent Company: Beit Binzagr
Associated Companies: Binzagr Company; Abdullah & Said M.O. Binzagr Co; Wahib S Binzagr & Bros; International Agencies Ltd; Binzagr International Trading Co. Ltd (BITCO)
Principal Bankers: Riyad Bank, Jeddah; National Commercial Bank, Jeddah; Saudi British Bank, Jeddah; Arab National Bank, Riyadh
Financial Information:

	1990 SR'000
Paid-up capital	10,000

Principal Shareholders: Binzagr Family
Date of Establishment: January 1981
No of Employees: 122

AL RUSHAID INVESTMENT CO

PO Box 539, Dhahran Airport 31932
Tel: 8980028
Telex: 871314 Rushid Sj
Telefax: 03-8647320

Chairman: Sheikh Abdullah Rushaid Al Rushaid
Directors: Abdulrahman M Al Ibrahim (Senior Vice President)
Senior Executives: Vipen Kapur (VP & General Manager)

PRINCIPAL ACTIVITIES: Real estate operations, manufacturing and supplies of oilfield equipment and services, aviation and construction, hotel operation
Principal Agencies: Dresser Industries; Baker Hughes; FMC Corp; Cameron Iron Works; Dresser-Rand; Aerospatiale; Diamant Boart; IBC Containers
Associated Companies: Al Rushaid Trading Co; Western Atlas Arabia Ltd; Weatherford Saudi Arabia Ltd; Weatherford Al Rushaid Ltd; Saudi Shoe Co Ltd; Al Jubail Holiday Inn; Arabian Rockbits & Drilling Tools Ltd; Arabian Helicopters Ltd; Arabian Minerals Corporation Ltd; Noble Drilling Arabia Ltd
Principal Bankers: Saudi French Bank; Saudi American Bank
Financial Information:

	1990 SR'000
Sales turnover	1,340,000
Total assets	600,000

Principal Shareholders: Sheikh Abdullah Rushaid Al Rushaid and family
Date of Establishment: 1978
No of Employees: 1,900

AL RUSHAID TRADING CO

PO Box 540, Dhahran Airport 31932
Tel: 8980028
Cable: Interdevelop
Telex: 871314 Rushid SJ
Telefax: 03-8647320

Chairman: Sheikh Abdullah Rushaid Al-Rushaid
Senior Executives: Abdulrahman M Al Ibrahim (Senior Vice President), S D Shetty (Financial Controller), Daniel J Thompson (Manager Oilfield Products Div)

PRINCIPAL ACTIVITIES: Oilfield equipment division: manufacturers' representation; and water products division; water treatment, engineering services, water filtering products; safety shoes; helicopter sales and service, test, measurement and calibration equipment sales and service; computer software; computer graphics; aircraft service; personnel support services
Principal Agencies: Camco; Cameron Iron Works; Dresser Security Drill, Eastman Whipstock; Baker Oil Tools; Weatherford Lamb; Dresser Rand Compressors; Dresser Pacific Pumps; IBC Transport Containers Ltd; FMC Fluid Control; Dresser Rootes; Dresser Services; Baker CAC, Tristate Oil Tools, Diamant Boart; Aerospatiale Helicopter Division, Tektronix
Branch Offices: Main Office: Al Rushaid Building, Prince Hamood Street, AlKhobar; branch office: Riyadh, Suite 4302, New Akaria Bldg, Sitten Street, PO Box 58791, Riyadh 11515, Tel 01-4785328, Telex 406434 RUSHID SJ, Fax 01-4785327
Subsidiary Companies: Maintenance & Industrial Service Corp (MISCO)
Principal Bankers: Al Bank Al Saudi Al Fransi
Financial Information:

	1989 SR'000
Sales turnover	28,000
Authorised capital	2,000
Paid-up capital	2,000

Principal Shareholders: Chairman as described
Date of Establishment: 1976
No of Employees: 4,500

AL SAADA TRADING & CONTRACTING CO LTD

PO Box 5854, Jeddah 21432
Tel: 6435935, 6435426
Cable: Happyco
Telex: 601229 Al Saada Sj, 601634 Al Saada Sj

Chairman: HRH Prince Mishari Bin Abdul Aziz Al Saud
Directors: Sheikh Yousef Al Tawil (President), Sheikh Sami Ali Al Tawil (Managing Director)

PRINCIPAL ACTIVITIES: Transportation contractors, trucking, cargo handling, bunkering, clearing and forwarding, also building and civil contractors
Branch Offices: Dammam: PO Box 1778, Tel 8327860, Telex 801125; Riyadh: PO Box 1576, Telex 401299
Subsidiary Company: Al Saada Shipping Agencies, PO Box 5854, Jeddah

Date of Establishment: 1963

AL SAEED EST

PO Box 54092, Riyadh 11514
Tel: 4644368
Telex: 407425
Telefax: 4655447

Chairman: Mohammed Al Saeed
Directors: Dr S Amroussy, Adel M Al Saeed
Senior Executives: Talat Mahmoud (Refrigeration Sales Manager), Depak Paradan (Plastic Factory Manager)

PRINCIPAL ACTIVITIES: Airconditioning and refrigeration spare parts, building chemicals, waterproofing products, plastic factory, injection moulding and PVC products
Principal Agencies: Matsushita Compressors, CPC Construction Chemicals, Quaker Coatings for Waterproofing
Branch Offices: Sharjah: Tel 339965
Principal Bankers: National Commercial Bank; Saudi American Bank; Saudi British Bank
Financial Information:

	1990 SR'000
Sales turnover	25,000
Profits	6,000
Authorised capital	20,000
Paid-up capital	12,000
Total assets	17,000

Principal Shareholders: Sole proprietorship
Date of Establishment: 1972
No of Employees: 65

AL SAGHYIR TRADING & CONTRACTING CO LTD

PO Box 2792, Riyadh 11461
Tel: 4769475 (7 lines)
Cable: Ramada
Telex: 404655 Al-Sag SJ
Telefax: 4765405

Chairman: Hamad Saleh Al Saghyir
Directors: Abdul Aziz Al Goblan (President)
Senior Executives: Fahmy Sakoury (Sales Manager), Abdulaziz Sakoury, Jamal Khatab (Finance Manager), Mana Alsadoun (Marketing Manager), Abdul Hady Suliman (Purchasing Manager), Khalid Al Haidary (Production Manager), Mohamed Badawy (Personnel Manager), Bakry Hussain (Technical Manager)

PRINCIPAL ACTIVITIES: Engineering consultancy, building construction, trading import of furniture and laundry equipment; manufacture of aluminium windows and doors, and kitchen cabinets
Principal Agencies: Polymark, Spencer, Automations Int Ltd, Donini, Silc, Nybrorg, Ipso, Hawd, Lamborghini, ACS, Tac-o-Matic, Huebsch

Branch Offices: Jeddah, Dammam, Oniyzah, Khamis Mushait, Tabuk, Hail Buraidah
Subsidiary Companies: Al Saghyir Contracting Co; Al Motawasit Co; National Kitchens Factory; National Aluminium Factory; Al Saghyir Boiler Factory Co
Principal Bankers: Riyad Bank; Albank Alsaudi Alhollandi; Saudi American Bank
Financial Information:

	1990 SR'000
Authorised capital	12,000
Paid-up capital	12,000
Total assets	215,000

Date of Establishment: 1970
No of Employees: 500

AL SAGRI TRADING & CONTRACTING EST

PO Box 4302, Riyadh 11491
Tel: 4763631, 4766306, 4777931
Cable: Al-Sagri
Telex: 401852 Sagri Sj
Telefax: 4781658

President: Sheikh Saud Ali Al-Sagri (Owner)
Senior Executives: Abdulaziz Al Huwairini (Director General), Eng Hussain Fahmy (Manager Planning & Studies), Mohd S Bafail (Asst General Manager for Trading Division), Kamal Sabil (Asst General Manager for Aviation Centre)

PRINCIPAL ACTIVITIES: Import and export, general trade, contracting, operation and maintenance, chalk factories and aviation
Branch Offices: Dammam: PO Box 2720, Tel 8579314; Jeddah PO Box 7041, Tel 6484385
Subsidiary Companies: Al Sagri Trading Division, PO Box 86715, Riyadh 11632, Tel 2322295, Telex 406795, Fax 2318616; Canary Travel & Tourism, PO Box 58444, Riyadh 11594, Tel 4763535, Telex 406557, Fax 4761043
Principal Bankers: Al Bank Al Saudi Al Fransi, Riyadh; Saudi British Bank, Riyadh
Financial Information:

	1990 SR'000
Sales turnover	195,000
Authorised capital	4,000
Paid-up capital	4,000

Date of Establishment: 1395H
No of Employees: 2,000

AL SALAMAH ARABIAN AGENCIES CO LTD

PO Box 2041, Riyadh 11451
Tel: 4772317
Telex: 401766 UCARYD SJ
Telefax: 4784304

Senior Executives: Robert M Makhoul (Senior Vice President), Brian Richmond (Managing Vice President Dammam), Andrew Bentley (Managing Vice President Jeddah)

PRINCIPAL ACTIVITIES: Insurance broking and agency
Branch Offices: PO Box 3763, Dammam 31481, Tel 8948035, Telex 870740, Fax 8984582; PO Box 5019, Jeddah 21422, Tel 6440748, Telex 605864, Fax 6434248
Parent Company: Alexander Stenhouse (UK) Ltd

AL SALAMAH ARABIAN AGENCIES CO LTD

PO Box 2041, Riyadh 11451
Tel: 4772317
Telex: 401766 Ucaryd Sj
Telefax: 4784304

Senior Executives: Brian Richmond (Senior Vice President), Craig W Tauzin (Vice President)

PRINCIPAL ACTIVITIES: Consultants, risk managers, insurance and reinsurance brokers

Branch Offices: Alkhobar Tel 8649513, Fax 8984582; Jeddah
  Tel 6446252, Fax 6434258
Financial Information:

	1988/89 SR'000
Sales turnover	10,000
Authorised capital	1,000
Paid-up capital	1,000

Principal Shareholders: 100% Saudi owned
Date of Establishment: 1983
No of Employees: 45

AL SAMIYA CORPORATION

PO Box 6677, Riyadh 11452
Tel: 4659900, 4658077
Cable: SAFADCO
Telex: 402014 SAMIYA

Directors: Mustafa H Samy (Managing Director)

PRINCIPAL ACTIVITIES: Trading division: floor covering
  materials, marble, automatic vehicle washing machines;
  contracting division: thermal and water insulation works,
  elector-mechanical, marine construction and general
  construction; Services division: catering, general maintenance
  and camp management
Subsidiary/Associated Companies: Sitaf Saudia - Joint-Venture
Principal Bankers: Arab National Bank

Date of Establishment: 1977

AL SANIE CORP FOR AGRO INVESTMENT CO LTD

PO Box 4186, Riyadh 11491
Tel: 01-4983900, 4983688
Telex: 403675 Farms SJ
Telefax: 01-4986123

Chairman: Dr Abdullah Mohamed Ali Alsanie
Directors: Eng Nasir Mohamed Ali Alsanie (Manager of Yamama
  Agri Co), Eng Rashed M Al Debas (Manager of the
  Investment Dept)
Senior Executives: Abdul Rahman Alsanie (Sales Dept
  Manager), Abdul Aziz Alsanie (Manager of Alwadi Poultry
  Farms), Mohamed Salih Alsanie (Admin Dept Manager),
  Ibrahim Mohamed Alsanie (I Sanie Drilling Manager)

PRINCIPAL ACTIVITIES: Management of several agricultural
  projects including: Yamama Agricultural Co, Alwadi Poultry
  Farms, I Sanie Drilling Corp, Alyamama House for Agricultural
  Studies, Yamama Egg Tray Plant, Alwadi Poultry Farms Abha
Principal Agencies: Danish Nordsten Seeders; Vicon Equipment,
  Holland; Berkeley Pumps, USA; Hinomoto Tractors, Japan;
  Fendt Tractors, Germany; MWM Engines, Germany
Branch Offices: Algassim , Tel 06-3237035; Tabuk, Tel 04-
  4220540; Hail, Tel 06-5329662; Abha, Tel 07-2271495; Albaha,
  Tel 07-7251300; Najran, Tel 07-5222852
Subsidiary Companies: Alwadi Poultry Farms; Yamama Egg
  Tray Plant; Alyamama House for Agricultural Studies; Ibrahim
  Alsanie Drilling Corp; Yamama Agricultural Co
Principal Bankers: Saudi Cairo Bank; Albank Alsaudi Alhollandi;
  Riyad Bank
Financial Information:

	1989/90 SR'000
Sales turnover	66,000
Authorised capital	66,000
Paid-up capital	66,000
Total assets	76,000

Principal Shareholders: Ibrahim Mohamed Alsanie, Abdullah
  Mohamed Alsanie, Nasir Mohamed Alsanie, Abdul Rahman
  Mohamed Alsanie, Abdul Aziz Mohamed Alsanie
Date of Establishment: 1970
No of Employees: 450

AL SELOULY AGRICULTURAL EST

PO Box 826, Riyadh 11421
Tel: 4777425, 4773879, 4036630
Cable: Braslouly Riyadh
Telex: 401134 Slouly Sj
Telefax: 4773879

Chairman: Ibrahim A Al-Selouly
Directors: Saleh Al-Selouly (General Manager), Abdel Aziz Al-
  Selouly

PRINCIPAL ACTIVITIES: Agricultural machineries/equipments,
  all kinds of chemicals; insecticide, herbicide, pesticide,
  fertilizers, vegetables, flowers, seeds, plant/trees nurseries;
  veterinary products
Principal Agencies: Ciba-Geigy, Switzerland; American
  Cyanamide, USA; Rohm & Haas, Italy; Sharpstow Chemical
  Co, UK; Ferry Morse Seed Co, California, USA; Gebr Holder
  GmbH & Co, West Germany; Curtis Dyna Products Corp, USA
Branch Offices: Jeddah, Buryadah, AlKhraj, Dammam
Principal Bankers: National Commercial Bank, Riyadh
Financial Information:

	1990 SR'000
Sales turnover	21,000
Authorised capital	12,000
Paid-up capital	100,000

Date of Establishment: 1961
No of Employees: 164

AL SHAFAI CONSTRUCTORS

PO Box 1105, Dammam 31431
Tel: 5661317, 5661318, 5661530
Cable: Alshafai
Telex: 884010 Shafai Sj

President: Saud Abdul Aziz Al-Shafai
Directors: Abdul Munem Saud Al Shafai (Vice President)
Senior Executives: Mohammad Saud Al Shafai (General
  Manager), Sameer Saud Shafai (Manager)

PRINCIPAL ACTIVITIES: Major contractors to Arabian American
  Oil Company for construction of petro-chemical and gas
  industries
Principal Agencies: Eastern Trading Establishment represents
  several manufacturers of equipment, tools and parts in the
  United States and Europe
Branch Offices: Saudi Arabia; United Arab Emirates
Associated Companies: Eastern Trading Establishment (100%);
  Al-Shafai/Niklas, Jt Venture (37.5%)
Principal Bankers: Riyad Bank; Arab National Bank; National
  Commercial Bank, Abqaiq

Date of Establishment: 1960
No of Employees: 250

AL SHARQI CO (STACO)

PO Box 2870, Riyadh 11461
Tel: 4647129, 4788518, 4782205
Cable: Staco
Telex: 401228 Staco Sj

Senior Executives: Mohammed A Al-Sharqi (Chief Executive)

PRINCIPAL ACTIVITIES: Civil and building construction; general
  contracting, real estate; import; prefabricated houses;
  construction machinery etc
Branch Offices: Jeddah, Dammam, Sharjah (UAE)

No of Employees: 720

AL SHEBA, ALI HAMAD, EST

PO Box 1766, Dammam 31441
Tel: 8327323, 8329967
Telex: 801530 Jishah Sj

Chairman: Ali Hamad Al-Shehab

Directors: Fahad A Al-Shehab (Director and Vice-President), Yousif H Al-Shehab

PRINCIPAL ACTIVITIES: Trading, contracting and companies' representatives

Branch Offices: Ibgaig; Alhufoof; Alkhobar

Subsidiary/Associated Companies: General TC, Kuwait; IWKA, West Germany, IHTC, Bombay, India

Principal Bankers: Riyadh Bank; Al Bank Al Saudi Al Fransi; Saudi British Bank

Principal Shareholders: Ali Hamad

ALSHIFA MEDICAL SYRINGES MNFG CO LTD

PO Box 7917, Dammam 31472
Tel: 8574284, 8573617
Telex: 802826 RAMY SJ
Telefax: 8574033

Chairman: Sheikh Salim Abduljawad

Directors: Adel S Ashi (General Manager)

Senior Executives: Jihad A Hadi (Asst General Manager), Khalid A H Badi (Chief Financial Accountant)

PRINCIPAL ACTIVITIES: Manufacture of plastic medical disposable syringes and other hospital items

Principal Bankers: Riyad Bank; National Commercial Bank; Arab National Bank

Financial Information:

| | 1990 |
	SR'000
Sales turnover	24,000
Authorised capital	6,000
Paid-up capital	20,000
Total assets	26,000

Principal Shareholders: Ahmed Awad Saban; Fahmi Yousaf Basrawi; Ahdulaziz Rashed Al Rashed; Mubarak Omer Badgaish, Omer Khaled Alamdar, Azmi A Abdul Hadi

Date of Establishment: 1979

No of Employees: 45

AL SHIHA GROUP

PO Box 277, Dammam 31411
Tel: 8269081, 8265198
Cable: Alshiha
Telex: 801449 Shiotl Sj
Telefax: 8333444, ext 5

Chairman: Abdul Aziz Ebrahim Al Shiha

Directors: Khalid Ebrahim Al Shiha (Managing Director), Eng Aly Allam Mohamed Allam (Technical Director)

Senior Executives: Herbert Wey (Hotel Manager), Naji Abdul Aziz Al Shiha (Catering Manager), Anwar Sati Ahmed Lamy (Manager Carpentry & Decor), Ebrahim Abdul Aziz Al Shiha (Sales Manager), Ahamed Mohamoud Shilbayh (Finance Manager), Adil Allam Mohamed Allam (Purchasing Manager), Sultan Ahamed (Personnel Manager)

PRINCIPAL ACTIVITIES: Construction, building and civil contracting; hotel, outside catering services; carpentry and decoration, pickle factory, paper factory (in partnership)

Branch Offices: Al Hamra Hotel, PO Box 1411, Dammam

Parent Company: Al Shiha Contracting & Maintenance Corp, Dammam

Subsidiary Companies: Al Hamra Hotel, Dammam; Al Shiha Catering & Daily Services, Dammam; Al Shiha Carpentry & Decor, Dammam; Fine Paper Factory, Jeddah & Riyadh; Al Shiha Pickle & Marmalades Factories, Dammam

Principal Bankers: Riyad Bank, Dammam

Financial Information:

| | 1989/90 |
	SR'000
Sales turnover	2,250
Profits	450
Authorised capital	400
Total assets	2,200

Principal Shareholders: Chairman as described

Date of Establishment: 2/8/1381H

No of Employees: 300

AL SHUWAYER, ABDULLAH AL-HAMOUD,

PO Box 322, Dammam 31411
Tel: 8642821, 8642921
Cable: SHUAYER
Telex: 870042 Ashu Sj

Owner: Abdullah Al-Hamoud Al-Shuwayer

Senior Executives: Mohammad Al'Kaabi (Vice Chairman)

PRINCIPAL ACTIVITIES: Civil, mechanical, foundation and piling contractors; production and supply of building materials; machine shop services, testing and balancing HVAC systems

Principal Agencies: Moretrench (DeWatering Div), USA; Nissho Iwai Corp, Japan; Manitowoc Engineering Co, USA

Branch Offices: Jubail, Saudi Arabia

Parent Company: Abdullah Al-Hamoud Al-Shuwayer Trading & Contracting Est

Subsidiary Companies: Joint ventures with Santa Fe (USA); DeMauro Construction Corp (USA); Manitowoc Engineering Co (USA); A Long Int'l (Bahrain); Kong Yung Const Co (Korea); NDT & Corrosion Control Services (India); Middle East Const Co (Japan); Thuwainy Trading Co (Kuwait); Kolon Const Co (Korea); Fujikura Ltd (Japan)

Principal Bankers: Saudi British Bank

Principal Shareholders: Abdullah Al-Hamoud Al-Shuwayer (Sole Proprietor)

Date of Establishment: 1948

No of Employees: 2,287

AL SUBEAEI, MOHAMMED & ABDULLAH IBRAHIM,

PO Box 749, Jeddah 21421
Tel: 6722288 (5 lines)
Cable: Al Subeaei
Telex: 601120 Subeai Sj; 602112 Alsuba Sj
Telefax: 6725924

Chairman: Abdulla Ibrahim Al Subeaei

Directors: Ibrahim Abdulla Al Subeaei (Managing Director)

Senior Executives: Saleh Abdulla Al Subeaei (Sales Director)

PRINCIPAL ACTIVITIES: General trading and contracting; import and distribution of foostuffs, and agricultural products, textiles, furniture, hardware and gold; money exchange

Branch Offices: Riyadh: PO Box 467, Tel 4030289, Telex 401006 Subeaei Sj; Medina: PO Box 217, Tel 8234550, Telex 570005 Subeaei Sj; Mecca: PO Box 843, Al Godred St, Tel 5745006, Telex 751012 Subeaei Sj Dammam: PO Box 793, Tel 8323477, Telex 801573 Subeaei Sj

Parent Company: Mohamed & Abdulla Alsubeaei

Principal Bankers: Bank Al Jazira, Jeddah; Citibank, New York

Date of Establishment: 1934

No of Employees: 200

ALSUHAIMI CO (LTD PARTNERSHIP)

PO Box 161, Dammam 31411
Tel: 8264237 (4 lines)
Cable: Alsuhaimi
Telex: 801145 Suhimi Sj
Telefax: 8269595

Founders: Abdul Rahman Saleh Alsuhaimi, Mohammed Saleh Alsuhaimi

Directors: Abdul Aziz A R Alsuhaimi (President), Khalid A R Alsuhaimi (Vice President), Sulaiman A R Alsuhaimi (Vice President), Ahmad M Alsuhaimi (Vice President), Aziz M Alsuhaimi (Vice President), Khalid M Alsuhaimi (Vice President)

Senior Executives: Adel A Alsuhaimi (Manager)

PRINCIPAL ACTIVITIES: Oilfield supplies, water well drilling, architectural services, marble & terrazzo production, real estate and property, paint manufacture, metal cans manufacture, sandblasting, paint application & road marking, soil investigation & geotech activities, general trade and distribution of paints, construction and electrical materials, foodstuffs, manufacture of various chemicals, travel and tourism, air cargo handling, horticulturists, landscaping

Principal Agencies: Hans Leffer, Germany; Davidson Pipe Supply Co Ltd, USA; Hempel's Marine Paints (SA) Ltd, Saudi Arabia (Dammam & Riyadh areas); Branton Insulations Int'l, USA

Branch Offices: Alsuhaimi Trading & Contracting Est, 10th St, Dammam; Alsuhaimi Trading & Contracting Est, PO Box 1560, Hofuf 31982; Riyadh Office, PO Box 3494 Riyadh 11471; Alsuhaimi Tile & Marble Factory, PO Box 161, Dammam; Alsuhaimi Liaison Office, Al Sulaimaniah, Riyadh; Alsuhaimi Architectural Office, PO Box 161, Dammam; Alsuhaimi Travel & Tourism Agency, PO Box 161, Dammam 31411, Alsuhaimi Hortiplan, PO Box 161, Dammam 31411

Subsidiary/Associated Companies: Hempel's Marine Paints (SA) Ltd, Dammam; Saudi Arabian Packaging Industry, Dammam; Global Suhaimi Contracting, Dammam; McClelland Suhaimi Ltd, Dammam; Polybest Ltd, Dammam; New Projects: Alsuhaimi Albash Paints & Chemicals; Alsuhaimi Centre for Auto & Spare Parts; Annajma Opthalmic Centre; Gulf Environmental Services

Principal Bankers: Bank Al Jazira, Dammam, Albank Alsaudi Alhollandi, Dammam

Principal Shareholders: Heirs of late Abdul Rahman Saleh Alsuhaimi, heirs of late Mohammad Saleh Alsuhaimi

Date of Establishment: 1921

No of Employees: 600

AL SULAIMAN, GHASSAN AHMAD ABDULLAH, EST

PO Box 8054, Jeddah 21482
Tel: 6401661 (20 lines)
Telex: 606028 Wafaco Sj
Telefax: 966-2-6401924, 6400260

Chairman: Ghassan Ahmad Abdullah Al Sulaiman

Directors: Amin Mansour Jamal (Deputy Managing Director)

Senior Executives: Roy William Lee (Jeddah Store Manager), Jerry Best (Furniture Manager), Walid Al Sulaiman (Market Hall Manager), Bjarne Elmskov (Operations Manager), Shakeel Ansari (Purchasing Manager), Faek Mounla (Decoration Manager), Mustafa Awad (Contracts Manager), Tonny Svensson (Customers Service Manager), Usman A Ismail (Chief Accountant), Rasheed-Ur-Rehman (Warehouse Manager)

PRINCIPAL ACTIVITIES: Marketing a wide range of furnishing items

Principal Agencies: IKEA, Sweden

Branch Offices: Riyadh

Associated Companies: Al Sulaiman Intermarket Co Ltd, Jeddah; Horizon Development Co, Jeddah; Sawary Trading &

Contracting Est, Jeddah; Altajheezat General Trading & Marketing Co Ltd, Jeddah

Principal Bankers: Albank Alsaudi Alhollandi, Jeddah; Riyad Bank, Jeddah; Saudi Investment Bank, Jeddah

Principal Shareholders: Ghassan Ahmad Abdullah Al Sulaiman
Date of Establishment: 1979
No of Employees: 155

AL SULAIMAN INTERMARKET CO LTD

PO Box 8054, Jeddah 21482
Tel: 6401066 (20 lines)
Telex: 606028 Wafaco SJ
Telefax: 966-2-6400260, 6401924

Chairman: Ghassan Ahmad Abdullah Al Sulaiman
Senior Executives: Amin Mansour Jamal (General Manager), Hamid Rehman (Food Service Manager)

PRINCIPAL ACTIVITIES: Marketing of ice cream, frozen yorghurt, backed products and other foodstuffs

Principal Agencies: Honey Hill Farms, USA
Branch Offices: Six outlets in the Western Province
Principal Bankers: Albank Alsaudi Alhollandi, Jeddah; Riyad Bank, Jeddah; Saudi Investment Bank, Jeddah

Principal Shareholders: Ghassan Ahmad Abdullah Al Sulaiman
Date of Establishment: 1966
No of Employees: 30

ALSUWAIKET TRADING & CONTRACTING CO

PO Box 321, Alkhobar 31952
Tel: 8641436, 8646167, 8646717, 8980176
Cable: Alsuwaiket
Telex: 870193 Aziz Sj; 871223 Turki Sj; 871336 Stagro Sj

Chairman: Abdullah M Alsuwaiket
Directors: Fahad Alsuwaiket (Managing Director), Rashed Alsuwaiket (Deputy Managing Director)

PRINCIPAL ACTIVITIES: Trading, contracting, airport construction, electrical and mechanical engineering; travel agency; telecommunications, heavy duty equipments and plant hire

Branch Offices: Location in Alkhobar: King Khalid Street

Associated Companies: Alsuwaiket Miryung; Alsuwaiket Western; Azevedo Campos Suwaiket Co; Alsuwaiket Pentas; Arabian International Telecommunication; Alsuwaiket Catering; Saudi Arabian Condotte; Wasatch Saudi Arabia; Saudi Jurong Engineering Co; Stagro Suwaiket; Alsuwaiket Shipping & Oil Transport; Alsuwaiket Cold Storage; Alsuwaiket Industrial Project; Alsuwaiket Farm & Real Estate; Alsuwaiket Safety Support; Alsuwaiket Computer Services

Principal Bankers: Riyadh Bank Alkhobar; Bank Al Saudi Al Fransi; Saudi Cairo Bank; Saudi British Bank

Financial Information:

	1989
	SR'000
Sales turnover	1,300,000
Total assets	14,000,000

Principal Shareholders: Abdullah M Alsuwaiket
Date of Establishment: 1947
No of Employees: 1,700

ALTAJHEEEZAT GENERAL TRADING & MARKETING CO LTD

PO Box 8054, Jeddah 21482
Tel: 966-2-6608844, 6609959
Telex: 606028 Wafaco SJ
Telefax: 966-2-6605424

Chairman: Ghassan Ahmad Abdullah Al Sulaiman (Managing Director)
Senior Executives: Amin J Jamal (General Manager), Raef Fakhoury

PRINCIPAL ACTIVITIES: Supply distribution, marketing and servicing of household electrical appliances
Principal Agencies: Sears, Kenmore, Mr Coffee, Duracraft, Roebuck & Co
Branch Offices: Riyadh
Principal Bankers: Albank Alsaudi Alhollandi, Jeddah; Saudi Investment Bank, Jeddah
Financial Information:

	1990/91 SR'000
Paid-up capital	6,000

Principal Shareholders: Al Sulaiman Intermarket Co Ltd, Fahad Zahid
Date of Establishment: 1990

AL TAMIMI, ABDUL MOHSEN, EST

PO Box 12, Dhahran Airport 31932
Tel: 8641972, 8647774, 8948576, 8983956
Cable: Tamish
Telex: 870186 HUREST SJ, 870450 HUREST SJ
Telefax: 8949564

Chairman: Abdul Mohsen A H Al Tamimi
Directors: Dr Bassam Mitri (Managing Director), Najdat Jarrah (Legal Advisor)
Senior Executives: Dr A Homsi (Export Sales Director), Mohamed Attia Mohamed (Finance Director)

PRINCIPAL ACTIVITIES: Contracting, general trading, agriculture, distribution of consumer goods, glassware etc
Principal Agencies: Bohemia Crystals, Czechoslavakia; Semperit Tyres, Austria; Sanitaryware Lecico, Lebanon
Branch Offices: Showrooms in Alkhobar, Riyadh and Thoqbah
Principal Bankers: Arab National Bank; National Commercial Bank; Al Bank Al Saudi Al Fransi
Financial Information:

	SR'000
Authorised capital	30,000
Paid-up capital	30,000

Date of Establishment: 1970
No of Employees: 800

ALTAWIL TRADING ENTERPRISES

PO Box 377, Jeddah 21411
Tel: 6601887, 6659835
Cable: Altawil
Telex: 601795 Tawil Sj

President: Sheikh Yusuf M Altawil
Directors: Gerard Sikias (Vice President)
Senior Executives: Abdulaziz Raqtan, Husayn Altawil

PRINCIPAL ACTIVITIES: General merchants, contractors, commission agents, holdings and consultations, catering, hospital management and operation, stevedoring, shipping agents
Branch Offices: Riyadh: PO Box 5932, Tel 4766850, 4766190, Telex 401703 TAWIL SJ; Alkhobar: PO Box 1088, Tel 8645318, 8645028, Telex 870166 TAWIL SJ; Geneva: Rue du Rhone 23, Telex 428829; London: PO Box 139, 80 Cannon St, EC4P 4AE, Telex 886631; Washington DC: 1825 K St NW, 11th Floor, DC 20006, Telex 7108220065
Subsidiary Companies: Altawil Food Services, PO Box 40205, Riyadh, Tel 4782405, 4774758, Telex 202771 Foods SJ; Barge Company Arabia, PO Box 5932, Riyadh; Sperry Arabia Ltd, PO Box 5932, Riyadh; Altawil Medical Services, PO Box 844, Jeddah; Altawil Maintenance and Operations, PO Box 1088, Al Khobar
Principal Bankers: Saudi European Bank, Bahrain; Royal Bank of Canada, Bahrain; Saudi British Bank, Riyadh; Saudi American Bank, Riyadh
Financial Information:

	SR'000
Sales turnover	350,000

Date of Establishment: 1954
No of Employees: 2,500

AL THENAIAN CO

PO Box 2007, Jeddah 21451
Tel: 6880509, 6880868
Cable: Althenaian
Telex: 601311 Thenco Sj

Directors: Sheikh Abdul Aziz Elsedais
Senior Executives: Mohammad Tom (General Manager & Technical Consultant)

PRINCIPAL ACTIVITIES: Building construction, road construction, concrete and asphalt mixers, crushers, building materials
Branch Offices: Riyadh, Buraidah
Subsidiary Companies: Arabic Commercial House (Arco), PO Box 5193, Jeddah (trading in building materials)
Principal Bankers: Saudi Cairo Bank; Saudi American Bank

Date of Establishment: 1972
No of Employees: 380

AL THINAYYAN, ALI, EST FOR TRADING & CONTRACTING

PO Box 4928, Jeddah 21412
Tel: 6675967, 6691554
Telex: 603831

PRINCIPAL ACTIVITIES: Building contractors, supply of building materials, aggregates, crushing plant, plant hire, and car rentals, construction equipment

Date of Establishment: 1976

ALTOBAISHI, FAHD, & CO

PO Box 104, Riyadh 11411
Tel: 4772556, 4776588, 4770420
Cable: Fadco Riyadh
Telex: 402724 Fadco Sj

Chairman: HE Sheikh Fahd Abdul Rahman Altobaishi
Directors: Faisal F Altobaishi (President & Managing Director), Adel Ben Afeef (Executive Vice President - Jeddah), Maurice S Khoury (Executive Vice President Alkhobar), Elias Pendias (Executive Vice President Riyadh)

PRINCIPAL ACTIVITIES: Manufacturers' representatives; supply of drilling and completion equipment, marine equipment, water desalination and sewerage, oil, petrochemical and process industry equipment GRP pipes, control valves, process pumps, ball and gate valves, instrumentation, manufacturing of fibreglass (GRP div), industrial maintenance and cleaning (MSS div)
Principal Agencies: Cameron Iron Works Inc, USA; UK and France; Fisher Controls, USA, UK, Japan; Plenty Group, UK, USA; Labour, UK, USA; APG Hewitt Hoses, USA, UK; General Descaling, UK; Samson Ocean Systems, USA;

Mather & Platt; Orion, Italy; Frinlgiulia Mangiarotti, Italy; Imodco, USA; GRC Pilkington, UK; Flexintallic, UK; Sundstrand, UK; Ames Crosta Babcock, UK; CYEMS, Nicosia
Branch Offices: Jeddah, PO Box 1255, Tel 6655744, Telex 601233; Alkhobar, PO Box 304, Tel 8641069, 8646927, Telex 870029 Fadco Sj; London
Subsidiary/Associated Companies: Joint Ventures: Petrolite Saudi Arabia Ltd; Cameron Saudia; Cyems Saudi Arabia; Crane Saudi Arabia; Subsidiaries: Saudi Financial Services Co; GRP (Fibreglass); MSS (Industrial cleaning)
Principal Bankers: Saudi British Bank; Saudi American Bank; Alsaudi Alhollandi Bank; Al Saudi Banque, Bahrain; Saudi International Bank, London

Principal Shareholders: H E Shaikh Fahd A Altobaishi
Date of Establishment: 1961
No of Employees: 320

AL TORKI ORGANISATION

PO Box 69, Jeddah 21411
Tel: 6432618, 6435088
Cable: Bintorki
Telex: 601577 Altrki Sj, 600455

Directors: Ahmed Mohamed Al Sulaiman Torki

PRINCIPAL ACTIVITIES: General and building contractors, civil and electrical engineering
Branch Offices: Madinah, Tel 8234847; Riyadh; London

No of Employees: 140

AL TOUKHI EST FOR INDUSTRY & TRADING

PO Box 497, Riyadh 11411
Tel: 4633660 (4 lines)
Cable: Al-Toukhi
Telex: 401426 Toukhi SJ
Telefax: 4631150

Chairman: Eng Mohammad M Al-Toukhi
Senior Executives: Eng Abdulkarim Al-Toukhi (General Manager), Gazi Al-Toukhi (Finance & Accounts Manager), Eng Abdul Raheem Shehada (Tendering & Procurement Manager), Eng Omar Al Adel Abu Zlam (Marketing Manager), Eng Imad Abdul Karim Al Magrabi (Sales Manager), Serhal Hassan Darwish (Personnel Manager), Eng Issa Al A'bed (Deputy General Manager), Mohammed Al Digs (Office Manager)

PRINCIPAL ACTIVITIES: Electrical engineering and contracting, dealing in power equipment, transformers, electrical and mechanical equipment and network materials for electrical projects; construction of substations, transmission & distribution system of 33KV & 132KV
Branch Offices: Hail Office
Principal Bankers: National Commercial Bank; Saudi American Bank; Saudi French Bank
Financial Information:

	1990 SR'000
Sales turnover	45,900
Profits	3,071
Authorised capital	1,000
Paid-up capital	1,000
Total assets	62,513

Date of Establishment: 1972
No of Employees: 145

AL TUWAIJRI, M A, STORES

PO Box 111 Riyadh 11411
Tel: 4038974, 4039428
Telex: 403576
Telefax: 4024388

Chairman: Mohamed Abdullah Al Tuwaijri
Directors: Abdulaziz Hamad

PRINCIPAL ACTIVITIES: Supply of industrial equipment and tools
Principal Agencies: Finico, Berco, etc
Branch Offices: Jeddah, Tel 6872275
Principal Bankers: Arab National Bank; National Commercial Bank; Riyad Bank

Date of Establishment: 1977
No of Employees: 30

AL TWAIJRI, SAAD A, OFFICE

PO Box 968, Riyadh 11421
Tel: 4054015, 4069200
Telex: 401498 Saado Sj
Telefax: 4054015, 4069200 ext 218

President: Sheikh Saad Abdullah Al Twaijri
Senior Executives: Fahd Al Twaijri (General Manager Saad Construction Est), Salah Al Twaijri (Manager Procurement)

PRINCIPAL ACTIVITIES: Agency representation, industrial equipment, readymix cement, transformer manufacturing
Principal Agencies: AB Siwertell
Branch Offices: Dammam
Subsidiary Companies: As Safina; National Cement Products Co; Saudi Transformer Co
Principal Bankers: Saudi Cairo Bank; Saudi American Bank

Principal Shareholders: Saad Abdullah Al Twaijri
Date of Establishment: 1958
No of Employees: 1,500

ALUMINIUM ENTERPRISES EST (ALEESCO)

PO Box 2175, Riyadh 11451
Tel: 4951988, 4033173
Cable: Aleesco
Telex: 401069 Saudinn Sj
Telefax: 4955204

Chairman: Dr Mustafa H Badah
Directors: Bader Abu Hayah (Managing Director)
Senior Executives: M Wakeel (Personnel Manager), Jawad Fares (Finance Manager), Hasan Badah (Production Manager), Adly Abu Hayah (Purchasing Manager), Eng E Makage (Technical Manager), M Jaroudy (Sales Manager)

PRINCIPAL ACTIVITIES: Supply of prefabricated buildings, furniture and fittings, building materials
Principal Agencies: TUMAC
Associated Companies: Terrapin International Service, Milton Keynes, UK
Principal Bankers: Arab National Bank
Financial Information:

	1989 SR'000
Sales turnover	10,000
Profits	1,400
Authorised capital	26,000
Paid-up capital	6,000
Total assets	30,000

Principal Shareholders: Dr Mustafa H Badah
Date of Establishment: 1971
No of Employees: 75

ALUMINIUM MANUFACTURING CO LTD (ALUMACO)

PO Box 7661, Jeddah 21472
Tel: 6915666
Cable: Alumacool
Telex: 603327 Alumco Sj
Telefax: 6915722

President: Omar A Aggad
Senior Executives: Amir Shammaa (General Manager), Raif Kattar (Finance Manager), Ali Aboulhassan (Sales Manager), A P Sivasankaran (Production Manager), C P Hari (Purchasing Manager)

PRINCIPAL ACTIVITIES: High performance architectural aluminium systems, security windows/doors systems, curtain walls, skylights, retractable and rolling shutters
Principal Agencies: Schuco Int'l, W Germany
Branch Offices: PO Box 10644, Riyadh 11443
Principal Bankers: Al Bank Al Saudi Al Fransi; Arab National Bank; Riyad Bank
Financial Information:

	1989 SR'000	1990 SR'000
Sales turnover	23,000	29,000
Profits	2,000	3,200
Authorised capital	16,000	16,000
Paid-up capital	16,000	16,000
Total assets	38,000	21,000

Principal Shareholders: Trading & Industrial Group (TIG); Aggad Investment Co (AICO); Olayan Financing Co (OFC); Sheikh Mohammad I Al Issa; Commercial & Industrial Investment Co
Date of Establishment: 1979
No of Employees: 160

ALUMINIUM PRODUCTS CO LTD (ALUPCO)
PO Box 2080, Dammam 31451
Tel: 8570184 (6 lines)
Cable: Alupco
Telex: 801148 Alupco Sj, 801271 Alprod Sj

President: Omar A Aggad
Directors: Hashim S Hashim (Chairman), Omar A Aggad (President), Mohammed Imran (Member of Board), Saad F Arjani (Member of Board)
Senior Executives: Abdallah Y Al Mouallini (General Manager)

PRINCIPAL ACTIVITIES: Extrusion and anodising of aluminium profiles fabrication of aluminium windows, doors and other building products
Principal Agencies: Licensees of Swiss Aluminium Ltd for manufacturing windows and doors. Licensees of Industria Semilavorati Alluminio, Italy, for manufacturing windows
Branch Offices: PO Box 8717, Jeddah, Tel 6370027; PO Box 2249, Riyadh, Tel 4051735, 4051540
Subsidiary Companies: Alumaco, PO Box 1761, Jeddah
Principal Bankers: Arab National Bank Ltd, Dammam; Riyad Bank, Dammam; Al Bank Al Saudi Al Fransi
Financial Information:

	US$'000
Authorised capital	30,000
Paid-up capital	30,000

Principal Shareholders: Trading & Industrial Group (34%), Aggad Investment Co (28%), Olayan Finance Co Ltd (28%), Industrial & Commercial Investment Co (10%)
Date of Establishment: October 1975
No of Employees: 800

AL WALID CO LTD
PO Box 5957, Jeddah 21432
Tel: 6515152
Telex: 600097 Tareq Sj

Chairman: Khaled A Al Sulaiman

PRINCIPAL ACTIVITIES: Civil, mechanical, electrical projects on a turnkey basis, supply and installation of steel buildings, construction of cold stores

Date of Establishment: 1976

AL YAHYA INDUSTRIAL EST
PO Box 41051, Riyadh 11521
Tel: 4951052, 4953958
Telex: 402585 Al Yahya Sj

Chairman: Mohammad S Al Yahya
Senior Executives: Abdullah Al Yahya (Manager)

PRINCIPAL ACTIVITIES: Manufacture of cement products; crusher production and heavy equipment for hire; distribution of heavy equipment

AL YAMAMA HOTEL
PO Box 1210, Riyadh 11431
Tel: 4774035
Cable: Yamama Hotel
Telex: 401056 YAMTEL SJ

Chairman: Joseph Yazbeck
Directors: Joseph Otayek

PRINCIPAL ACTIVITIES: Hotel business
Branch Offices: Location in Riyadh: Airport Road

No of Employees: 200

AL ZAMIL, ABDULLA HAMED, GROUP OF COMPANIES
PO Box 9, Alkhobar 31952
Tel: 8642567, 8951240, 8950980, 8641299, 8647794
Cable: Alzamil Alkhobar
Telex: 870132 Zamil Sj, 870695 Zamil Sj
Telefax: 03-8949336

President: Mohamed A Al Zamil
Directors: Hamed A Al Zamil, Zamil A Al Zamil, Khaled A Al Zamil, Ahmed A Al Zamil, Suleiman A Al Zamil, Adib A Al Zamil, Fahad A Al Zamil

PRINCIPAL ACTIVITIES: Real estate, land development, property leasing; marketing and distribution of all products that the Group manufactures or represents
Principal Agencies: Allis Chalmers; Siemens Allis Inc; English Rose Kitchens; Carl Freudenberg & Co; Bayne Adjasters, Betz International; Bukeau Veritas; Mitsui/Toshiba; Hyundai; Hyosung; Emerson Motors; Cathodic Protection; Corelabs Export; DMT Corporation; GNB Batteries; Grove Italia; Truplo. Ceast; Getin Industries; Al Ahlia Insurance
Branch Offices: Location in Alkhobar: Al Zamil Bldg, Talal Street; also PO Box 251, Riyadh; Jubail PO Box 8076, Jeddah, Saudi Arabia; 194-27 Insadong, Seoul, Korea; 25 Chesham St, London SW1, UK; 1220 August Drive, Suite 402, Texas, USA
Subsidiary/Associated Companies: Zamil Refrigeration Industries, PO Box 294, Dhahran Airport; Zamil Aluminium Factory, PO Box 1633, Dammam; Zamil Steel Building Co Ltd, PO Box 270, Dhahran Airport; Yamama Factories for Red Brick and Clay Products, PO Box 4572, Riyadh; Zamil Food Industries Ltd, PO Box 9, Alkhobar; Arabian Gulf Construction Co Ltd, PO Box 1633, Dammam; Zamil Marine Services Co Ltd, PO Box 1922, Alkhobar; Zamil Corelab, PO Box 9, Alkhobar; Zamil Furniture, PO Box 9, AlKhobar; Zamil Travel Bureau, PO Box 9, Alkhobar; Bahrain Marble Factory, PO Box 285, Bahrain; Gulf Aluminium Factory, PO Box 285, Bahrain; Al Zamil Nails, Screws Factory, PO Box 285, Bahrain; Zamil Plastics Factory, PO Box 1748, Alkhobar
Principal Bankers: Saudi British Bank, Alkhobar; Al Bank Al Saudi Al Fransi, Alkhobar; Al Bank Al Saudi Al Alami Ltd, London
Financial Information:

	SR'000
Sales turnover	650,000

Date of Establishment: 1930
No of Employees: 7,500

AL ZAMIL REFRIGERATION INDUSTRIES
PO Box 294, Dhahran Airport 31932
Tel: 8571464
Cable: TABRIDCO
Telex: 801115 ARI Sj

Chairman: Ahmed Al Zamil
Directors: Adib Al Zamil

PRINCIPAL ACTIVITIES: Manufacture of airconditioning and refrigeration equipment
Branch Offices: Jeddah, Tel 6700020; Riyadh, Tel 4768177; Ras Tanura, Tel 6670679; Jubail, Tel 3416666; Al Hassa, Tel 5867700; Yanbu, Tel 3212151; Tabuk, Tel 4239548; Dammam, Tel 8571464; Onaiza, Tel 063649489; Buraidah, Tel 063245523; Madina, Tel 048366876; Gizan, Tel 073170489
Parent Company: Hamad Abdulla Al Zamil & Bros
Principal Bankers: Al Bank Alsaudi Alfransi, Dammam

Principal Shareholders: Al Zamil Group of Companies
Date of Establishment: 1974
No of Employees: 1,500

AMALCOM TRADING & CONTRACTING EST

PO Box 9438, Riyadh 11413
Tel: 4761412, 4768350
Cable: Amaltracont - Riyadh
Telex: 401350 Shams Sj

Chairman: Sheikh Mohammad M Shams
Directors: Ahmed Z Baradan (Manager)

PRINCIPAL ACTIVITIES: Direct import, distribution and packing of durable foodstuffs
Principal Agencies: Maktas, Turkey; Montesinos, Spain; International Food Corp, USA
Principal Bankers: National Commercial Bank, Riyadh

Principal Shareholders: Owner Sheikh Mohammad M Shams
Date of Establishment: 1975

AMERON SAUDI ARABIA LTD

PO Box 589, Dammam 31421
Tel: 8570092, 8571160
Telex: 802958 CCPDAM Sj
Telefax: 8570364

Chairman: HRH Prince Khaled Bin Abdullah Bin Abdul Rahman
Directors: Dr Abdulaziz S Al Jarbou (President)
Senior Executives: Theodore F Bevec (General Manager)

PRINCIPAL ACTIVITIES: Manufacturing and marketing of high pressure concrete cylinder pipes and fittings. Also mortar lining of steel pipes
Branch Offices: Cement Mortar Lining Plant, PO Box 589, Dammam 31421, Tel 8100829, Telex 802958 Ccpdam Sj, Fax 8570364; Prestressed Concrete Cylinder Pipe Plant, PO Box 10039, Madinat Al Jubail Al Sinaiyah 31961, Tel 3417360, Telex 832042 Ameron Sj, Fax 3417432; Concrete Cylinder Pipe Plant, PO Box 589, Dammam 31421, Tel 8571160, 8570092, Telex 802958 Ccpdam SJ; Concrete Cylinder Pipe Plant, PO Box 16450, Jeddah 21464, Tel 6101287, Telex 604678 Ameron SJ, Fax 6374551
Associated Companies: Saudi Arabia Concrete Products (SACOP) Ltd, PO Box 7727, Jeddah 21472, Tel 6374406, Telex 602305 Sacop Sj, Fax 6374551
Principal Bankers: Saudi International Bank, London; Al Bank Al Saudi Al Fransi, Dammam
Financial Information:

	1990 SR'000
Authorised capital	76,500
Paid-up capital	76,500

Principal Shareholders: Saudi Arabian Amiantit Co Ltd; Ameron Inc USA
Date of Establishment: 1978
No of Employees: 300

AMI SAUDI ARABIA LTD

Xenel Bldg, PO Box 2824, Jeddah 21461
Tel: 6448480, 6431134
Telex: 603843 AMISAL SJ
Telefax: 6431158

Chairman: Mohamed Ahmed Yousef Zainal Alireza

Directors: Khalid Ahmed Yousef Zainal Alireza (Vice Chairman), Ahmed Yehia (Director)
Senior Executives: Denis Ryan (President), Abdullah M Khadim (Senior Vice President), Nasser Al Zahim (Senior Vice President), Abdul Ilah Batterjee (Senior Vice President)

PRINCIPAL ACTIVITIES: Operation, management and maintenance of hospitals
Branch Offices: PO Box 2886, Riyadh 11481
Principal Bankers: Saudi French Bank; Riyad Bank
Financial Information:

	1989/90 SR'000
Authorised capital	16,000
Paid-up capital	16,000

Principal Shareholders: Xenel Industries Ltd, Jeddah
Date of Establishment: January 1981
No of Employees: 5,000

AMIANTIT FIBERGLASS INDUSTRIES LTD

PO Box 589, Dammam 31421
Tel: 03-8571160
Cable: Amiantit Dammam
Telex: 801825 Saac Sj
Telefax: 03-8579039

Chairman: HRH Prince Khaled Bin Abdullah Bin Abdul Rahman
President: Dr Abdul Aziz Al Jarbou
Senior Executives: Fareed Y Al Khalawi (Vice President), Toufic A Abahussain (General Manager), Saleh Al Hewaish (Administration Manager), Fadel H Jarjoura (Finance Manager)

PRINCIPAL ACTIVITIES: Manufacturing and marketing of (FRP) fiberglass reinforced pipes, fittings and tanks and manholes
Branch Offices: PO Box 2140, Jeddah, Tel 6534704,6515676, Telex 601431 Amijed SJ; PO Box 1029, Riyadh, Tel 4658409, 4658153, Telex 401008 Amiria Sj
Parent Company: The Saudi Arabian Amiantit Co Ltd
Subsidiary Companies: Owens Corning Fiberglass Corp, USA
Principal Bankers: Al Bank Al Saudi Al Fransi, Dammam
Financial Information:

	1990 SR'000
Sales turnover	77,000
Profits	14,600
Authorised capital	32,000
Paid-up capital	32,000
Total assets	61,776

Principal Shareholders: The Saudi Arabian Amiantit Co Ltd; Owens Corning Fiberglass
Date of Establishment: 1978
No of Employees: 264

AMIANTIT RUBBER INDUSTRIES LTD

PO Box 589, Dammam 31421
Tel: 8571164
Cable: Amiantit Dammam
Telex: 803298 Rubber Sj
Telefax: 8573200

Chairman: HH Prince Khaled Bin Abdullah Bin Abdul Rahman
President: Dr Abdulaziz S Al Jarbou
Senior Executives: Dr Abdulaziz S Al Jarbou (President), Fareed Al Khalawi (VP Operations), Kamal Pachisia (Manager)

PRINCIPAL ACTIVITIES: Manufacturing and marketing of rubber gaskets and rubber products
Principal Bankers: Al Bank Al Saudi Al Fransi, Dammam

Principal Shareholders: Saudi Arabian Amiantit Co Ltd, Dammam; Deccan Enterprises Private Ltd, India
Date of Establishment: 1977
No of Employees: 100

AMOUMI DEVELOPMENT CO LTD

PO Box 4445, Jeddah 21491

Tel: 6877326, 6873403

Cable: Almahmoudiah

Telex: 602139 Amoumi Sj

Directors: Alawi H Al Mihdar, Abdullah H Al Mihdar, Ali H Al Mihdar, Hamza H Al Mihdar

PRINCIPAL ACTIVITIES: Industrial, building and construction contractors manufacturers' representation, and commission agents, transportation contractors

Branch Offices: PO Box 6233, Riyadh, Tel 4037676

Associated Companies: Scan Arabia Division, PO Box 4445, Jeddah, Tel 6657581, Telex 603417

Date of Establishment: 1978

ANJALI TRADING ESTABLISHMENT

PO Box 2958, Riyadh 11461

Tel: 01 4771640

Cable: Redhead

Telex: 403487 Anjali Sj

Telefax: 01 4784058

Chairman: Mohammad Ahmed Salem Alay

Senior Executives: Hassan A Alay (Executive Sales Manager Jeddah), Qazi Munazzir (Executive Sales Manager Khamis Mushayt), Faheen Asif Jaswal (Executive Sales Manager Riyadh), S Saadat Ali (Executive Sales Manager Medical Division), Akmal Hanuk (Divisional Manager Industrial Maintenance), Imtiaz Ahmed (Divisional Manager), Michael William (Divisional Manager), Azhar Shafi (Divisional Manager)

PRINCIPAL ACTIVITIES: Supply of materials and equipment for the construction industry; scaffolding; building chemicals; prefabricated buildings; welding machines and electrodes, power tools, hand tools, hardware items, commercial kitchen equipment, plastering accessories, waterproofing materials; medical supplies etc

Principal Agencies: Alifabs, UK; Chesterton, USA; Esab, Sweden; Facom, France; Hako, W Germany; Harris, Italy; James Gibbons Format, UK; Link-51, W Germany; Zetweld, Italy; Steriseal, UK; Beaver, USA; Jedmed, USA; Ophtec, Netherlands; Autosyring, USA; Wisap, W Germany; Digilab, USA; Barnshind, W Germany; Clement Clark, UK

Branch Offices: Jeddah: PO Box 8308, Tel 6514549, 6513712, 6513292, Fax 6514670, Telex 603143; Dammam; PO Box 1643, Tel 8573147, 8573046, 8573050, Telex 803059, 802043; Khamis Mushait: PO Box 894, Tel 2237890, 2500537, Telex 906126; Riyadh: PO Box 42168

Subsidiary Companies: Sika Saudia Co Ltd; Sherwin Williams Saudi Arabia Ltd; Oras Trading & Contracting Est

Principal Bankers: Arab National Bank

Financial Information:

	1989 SR'000
Sales turnover	60,000
Profits	9,000
Authorised capital	55,000
Paid-up capital	55,000
Total assets	18,000

Date of Establishment: 1970

No of Employees: 150

AOUEINI, HUSSEIN, & CO LTD

PO Box 25, Jeddah 21411

Tel: 6431862, 6444899, 6445144

Cable: Aoueini

Telex: 602446 HAID SJ, 604034 HAIDHO SJ

Telefax: 6449761

Chairman: Sheikh Ghassan Ibrahim Shaker

Senior Executives: Toshihiko Kitayama (General Manager), Abdul Rafique Haroon Jeddavi (Company Secretary)

PRINCIPAL ACTIVITIES: Underwriting agents for The Tokio Marine & Fire Insurance Co Ltd, Japan and The Arab-Eastern Insurance Co Ltd EC, Bahrain; Insurance brokers & risk managemant consultants, surveyors & loss adjusters

Principal Agencies: Tokio Marine & Fire Insurance, Japan; Arab Eastern Insurance Co, Bahrain

Branch Offices: Riyadh 11421: PO Box 643; Alkhobar 31952: PO Box 290

Principal Bankers: Riyad Bank; Saudi American Bank

Financial Information:

	1990 SR'000
Sales turnover	50,000
Authorised capital	1,000
Paid-up capital	1,000

Principal Shareholders: Sheikh Ghassan Shaker & Sons Ltd

Date of Establishment: 1948

No of Employees: 50

AQUARIUS (SAUDI ARABIA) LTD

PO Box 9150, Riyadh 11413

Tel: 4784020 (5 lines)

Cable: AQUARIUS (RIYADH)

Telex: 400479 AQUASA SJ

Chairman: Sheikh Ibrahim Al Kassem

Directors: Salim Makhoul (General Manager), Amine Badro (Deputy General Manager)

Senior Executives: Bassem Makhoul (Riyadh Area Manager), Marwan Daher (Jeddah Area Manager)

PRINCIPAL ACTIVITIES: Water treatment plants (desalination plant, sewage water treatment plant, swimming pools)

Principal Agencies: Culligan International; Soaf, France

Branch Offices: Jeddah Branch, PO Box 8093, Jeddah 21482, Tel: 6822444

Associate Companies: Aquarius - Liban SAI, Beirut, PO Box 350, Lebanon

Principal Bankers: Saudi French Bank

Principal Shareholders: Sheikh Ibrahim Al Kaseem (75%); Khalid Ibrahim Al Kassem (25%)

Date of Establishment: January 1979

ARAB BUREAU OF EDUCATION FOR THE GULF STATES (ABEGS)

PO Box 3908, Riyadh 11481

Tel: 4789889, 4774644

Cable: Tarbia Riyadh

Telex: 401441 Tarbia Sj

Telefax: 4783165

Director General: Dr Ali M Towaigri

Directors: Hamed Al Fajeh, Abdul Rahman Al Sadhan, Dr Daham Alani, Mohammed S Al Hawas

PRINCIPAL ACTIVITIES: Coordination, cooperation and integration among Arab Gulf States in the fields of education, culture and science; aims to create an educational system for all the member Arab states

Associated Organs: The Arab Centre for Educational Research, PO Box 25566 Safat, Kuwait, Tel 830571, 831607, 830685, Telex 44118; Arabian Gulf University, PO Box 26809, Manama, Bahrain, Tel 262771/3, Telex 8674

Principal Shareholders: Member States: Bahrain, Iraq, Kuwait, Oman, Qatar, Saudi Arabia, United Arab Emirates

Date of Establishment: 1975

No of Employees: 108

ARAB COMMERCIAL ENTERPRISES LTD GROUP OF COMPANIES (ACE)

PO Box 667, Riyadh 11421
Tel: 4774070 (12 lines)
Cable: Comment Riyadh
Telex: 401091 Aceryd Sj, 407017 Saico Sj
Telefax: 4774081

Chairman: HRH Prince Fahd Bin Khalid Bin Abdullah Bin Abdul Rahman Al Saud
Directors: Prince Salman Bin Khalid Bin Abdulrahman Al Saud, Adrian Platt, Dr Ibrahim A Al Moneef, George S Medawar, Richard J W Titley, Abdulaziz A Abussuud
Senior Executives: Abdulaziz A Abussuud (President & Chief Executive Officer), Peter C Gibbs (Vice President International), Omar S Al Hoshan (Vice President Personnel & Admin), Amin M Lutfi (Regiional Vice President Central Region), Guy V Alfa (Regional Vice President Eastern Region), Albert G Akiki (Regional Vice President Western Region), Ahmad Abussuud (Asst Vice President), Suhail Abla (Manager ACE Lebanon), Subhi El Husseini (General Manager Al Nisr Lebanon), Khalil Abu Hoseh (Treasury), Abdul Samad Abdul Razzak (Financial Controller)

PRINCIPAL ACTIVITIES: Insurance and reinsurance agents and brokers, surveyors and claims settling agents
Principal Agencies: Saudi Arabian Insurance Co; Al Nisr Insurance Co; Arab Japanese Insurance Co; Mitsui Marine & Fire Insurance Co
Branch Offices: Insurance: Riyadh (PO Box 667); Jeddah (PO Box 1084); Al Khobar (PO Box 358,); Dammam (PO Box 401); Makkah (PO Box 586); Jubail (PO Box 726); Yanbu (PO Box 30036)
Parent Company: Mawarid Group
Subsidiary/Associated Companies: Qatar: PO Box 607, Doha; Kuwait: PO Box 2474 Safat; Bahrain: PO Box 781, Manama; Dubai: PO Box 1100, Deira; Abu Dhabi: PO Box 585; Oman: PO Box 4972, Ruwi; Lebanon: PO Box 113-5112, Beirut; Greece: PO Box 750594, Kallithea; USA: 505 Park Ave, New York NY 10022
Principal Bankers: Saudi American Bank; Saudi Hollandi Bank; Saudi British Bank; Citibank; Bankers Trust

Date of Establishment: 1952
No of Employees: 321

ARAB DEVELOPMENT CORPORATION

PO Box 88, Riyadh 11411
Tel: 4763776
Cable: Alsharif-Riyadh
Telex: 401285 Ads Aj

Chairman: Mrs Luftiah Rda Bizri (also Owner)
Directors: Shafic M Alsharif (Managing Director), Fayez S Bizri (Deputy Managing Director)

PRINCIPAL ACTIVITIES: General import, specialising in building, electrical and mechanical equipment and materials
Principal Agencies: Westinghouse Electric Corporation, USA; Sierra Industries, USA; Commercial Grorba, Spain; Chandris Cables, Greece; Technology Applications Corp, USA; Integrated Circuits Packaging, USA; Visual Effects Inc, USA; Italcavit Cables, Italy
Branch Offices: PO Box 2497, Jeddah, Tel 6604978; PO Box 16, Dammam, Tel 8343595
Principal Bankers: Saudi American Bank, Riyadh; Creditcorp, New York; Export Credit Corp, New York

Date of Establishment: 1975

ARAB EAST INDUSTRIAL CO LTD

PO Box 6938, Jeddah 21452
Tel: 6370125, 6379669
Telex: 604844 AEICO SJ

Directors: Shaik Mohamed Abdulla Al-Sulaiman, Majed Al-Sulaiman, Salah Al-Sulaiman

Senior Executives: Yousuf Mohamed Farah, Mohamed Ummer, Tony Balang
PRINCIPAL ACTIVITIES: Production of spare parts for heavy equipment, production of hydraulic and industrial hoses and fittings
Principal Bankers: National Commercial Bank

Principal Shareholders: Shaik Abdulla Al-Sulaiman; Majed Alsulaiman; Salah Al-Sulaiman
Date of Establishment: 28.7.1398 H
No of Employees: 35

ARAB EQUIPMENT EST

PO Box 1660, Dammam 31441
Tel: 8574988, 8573559, 8573571, 8570475
Telex: 870155 Eqpall Sj
Telefax: 8570463

Directors: Rushedan A R Al Rushedan
Senior Executives: Wasi Mirza (General Manager), Masleh Ud Din (Jeddah-Sales Manager), Mansoor A Khawaja (Dammam-Sales Manager), Masood Jahangir Durrani (Manager Accounts)

PRINCIPAL ACTIVITIES: Agents and distributors of construction equipment, building materials, industrial and workshop tools and machinery, manufacturers' representatives
Principal Agencies: Ridge Tool Co, USA; Warren Rupp Co, USA; Crosby International, USA; ELBA-WERK, W Germany; HUDIG, W Germany; Stanley Proto Tools, USA; Airman, Japan; Meiwa, Japan; Lescha, W Germany; Atika, W Germany; MGF, W Germany; Grindex, Sweden; TCM, Japan; SEAM, Italy; Furukawa, Japan; Ashurst Equipment, UK; Dreyco Inc, USA; Bruntons, UK; Dalex Werke, W Germany; Mogurt, Hungary; Enerpac Tools, Switzerland; Osborn, W Germany; Black & Decker, UK; CRC Crose Int, USA
Branch Offices: Dammam, Tel 8429066, 8429427; Jubail, PO Box 709, Tel 3611309; Riyadh PO Box 17139, Tel 2312841; Jeddah, PO Box 9741, Tel 6831560, 6835731, Telex 605843 EQPALL SJ
Principal Bankers: Saudi American Bank; United Saudi Commercial Bank, Dammam
Financial Information:

	1989 SR'000
Sales turnover	45,000
Authorised capital	120,000
Paid-up capital	85,000
Total assets	104,000

Date of Establishment: 1974
No of Employees: 65

ARAB INVESTMENT CO SAA (THE)

PO Box 4009, Umm Al Hamam, Riyadh 11491
Tel: 4823444
Cable: Amwal Riyadh
Telex: 401011 Arbvst Sj; 401236 Taic Sj
Telefax: 4823169

Chairman: HE Dr Ahmed Abdullah Al Malik
Board Members: Fahd Rashed Al-Ebrahim (Vice Chairman), Kamal Al-Shafai, Ali Al Sugair, Saqr Taher Al-Mureikhi, Ahmed Al-Badi, Walid Al Hindi, Hazim Hadi Al Said, Rashid Al-Meer, Mohammed Al Dahmani, Mohammed Al Morshed, Mohammed Dairi, Khalifa Bin Heweleel, Mohammed Al-Zaghal
Senior Executives: Dr Saleh Al Humaidan (Director General), Faisal M Al Alwan (Deputy General Manager OBU), Abdulwahid S Mearza (Finance Director), Ahmad Suweiti (Director Services Projects), Musa M Babiker (Director Industrial Projects), Kamel Al Ani (Director Agricultural Projects), Ali A Al Shiddi (Director of Administration), Waseem Y Abun Naja (Director Planning & Development), Mirghani A Malik (Legal Advisor), Salih I Al Kholaifi (Internal Auditor)

PRINCIPAL ACTIVITIES: Project Activities: Participation in and the establishment of major industrial, agricultural and service projects in the Arab World (this includes identification, evaluation, promotion and equity investment); Banking Activities: loans and facilities, trade financing, security trading and treasury operations

Branch Offices: Bahrain Branch (Offshore Banking Unit), PO Box 5559, Chartered Bank Bldg, Government Avenue, Manama, Tel 271126, Telex 8334 Taic, 7055 Taicfx, Fax 231034; Representative Offices: Khartoum, PO Box 2242 (Sudan), Tel 75571, Telex 22624 Taic; Amman, PO Box 950422 (Jordan), Tel 815491, Fax 815492, Telex 23072 Taic; Cairo, PO Box 139, Ghouria (Egypt), Tel 729585, Telex 92303; Tunis (Tunisia) PO Box 2080 Ariana Tunis, Immeuble Saadi (B-2), Tel 718539, Telex 13835, Fax 717906

Subsidiary Companies: Various equity participation in 27 companies in the Arab World

Principal Bankers: Morgan Guaranty Trust, Chase Manhattan, New York; Barclays Bank International, London

Financial Information:

	1988/89 US$'000	1989/90 US$'000
Total footing	856,940	747,867
Operating Profits	13,752	17,363
Authorised capital	300,000	300,000
Paid-up capital	290,500	290,500
Total assets	684,969	616,754

Principal Shareholders: The Governments of Saudi Arabia, Kuwait, Sudan, Egypt, Qatar, UAE (Abu Dhabi), Bahrain, Syria, Iraq, Jordan, Tunisia, Morocco, Libya, Yemen AR and Oman

Date of Establishment: July 1974

No of Employees: 113

ARAB NATIONAL BANK

PO Box 41090, Riyadh 11521
Tel: 4029000
Cable: Arabiwatani
Telex: 402660 Arna Sj

Chairman: HE Dr Abdallah M Al Omran

Directors: Dr Haidar Darwish (Managing Director), Sheikh Rashed Al-Rashed, Sheikh Abdullatif H Jaber, Abdullah I Al-Hudaithi, Fahed M Assaja, Mohammad S Abduljawad, Abdelmajeed A Shoman, Khalid A Shoman, Abdulhamid Attari

Senior Executives: Dr Haidar Darwish (Managing Director), Mohammed S Abdulkader (Asst Managing Director Credit Facilities & Administration)

PRINCIPAL ACTIVITIES: Commercial banking

Branch Offices: Offices in Jeddah: PO Box 344; Alkhobar: PO Box 15; Dammam: PO Box 18; Mecca

Financial Information:

	SR'000
Authorised capital	150,000
Paid-up capital	150,000

Principal Shareholders: Saudi Arabian Interests (60%); Arab Bank Ltd (40%)

Date of Establishment: 1980

No of Employees: 2,644

ARAB PETROLEUM INVESTMENTS CORPORATION
A.P.I.C.O.R.P.

PO Box 448, Dhahran Airport 31932
Tel: (03) 8647400, 8647164, 8640193, 8640196
Cable: Apicorp Dhahran Airport
Telex: 870068 Apic Sj
Telefax: (03) 8945076

Chairman: Abdullah A Al Zaid (Saudi Arabia)

Directors: Salem Farkash (Deputy Chairman - Libya), Ammari Abdul Aziz (Algeria), Ahmad Mohamed Al Kamdah (UAE), Abdul Hameed Al Aradi (Bahrain), Dr Nader Nabulsi (Syria),

Mohammed Ridha Al Shididi (Iraq), Sheikh Hassan Bin Sultan Al Thani (Qatar), Saleh A Al Haddad (Kuwait), Dr Hamdi Ali Al Banbi (Egypt)

Senior Executives: Dr Nureddin Farrag (Chief Executive and General Manager), Dr Hisham Elass (Deputy General Manager), Farouk Al-Rawi (Manager, Projects Dept), Kamal Shoukry (Manager Financial Control Dept), Michael Hamilton (Manager Project & Trade Finance), Dino Moretto (Head of Treasury & Capital Markets), Wim Schweer (Manager Money Markets), William O'Brien (Manager Capital Markets), El Tayeb El Gaily (General Legal Counsel), Maher El Bouhi (Manager Administration & Personnel Dept)

PRINCIPAL ACTIVITIES: Specialised in providing equity and loan financing for petroleum and petroleum related projects and industries, as well as other complementary activities in the Arab World and Third World countries with priority being given to Arab joint ventures which help build a regionally integrated Arab petroleum sector

Subsidiary Companies: The Corporation holds equity in: Jordan Phosphate Mining Co (JPMC) (1.7%); BAII Holdings, Paris, (6.8%); Bahrain National Gas Co -BANAGAS - (12.5%); Arab Drilling & Workover Co - ADWOC - based in the Libyan Jamahiriah (20%); Arab Detergent Chemicals Co - ARADET - based in Iraq (32%); Arab Engineered Systems & Controls Co -ARECSON based in Bahrain (30%); Saudi European Petrochemical Co - IBN ZAHR - based in Saudi Arabia (10%); Arab Geophysical Exploration Co - AGESCO - based in the Libyan Jamahiriah (10%); Paktank Mediterranee - PAKMED - based in Tunisia (20%)

Principal Bankers: National Commercial Bank, Jeddah; Swiss Bank Corporation, London and New York

Financial Information:

	1988/89 US$'000	1989/90 US$'000
Total shareholders funds	603,311	607,424
Net profit	16,342	24,113
Authorised capital	1,200	1,200
Share capital	400	400
Total assets	910,088	944,959

Principal Shareholders: Governments of the Member States of the Organisation of Arab Petroleum Exporting Countries (OAPEC), namely: Algeria (5%), Bahrain (3%), Egypt (3%), Iraq (10%), Libyan Jamahiriah (15%), Kuwait (17%), Qatar (10%), Saudi Arabia (17%), Syria (3%), UAE (17%)

Date of Establishment: 23rd November, 1975

No of Employees: 103

ARAB SATELLITE COMMUNICATION ORGANISATION
A.R.A.B.S.A.T.

PO Box 1038, Riyadh 11431
Tel: 4646666
Telex: 401300 Arbsat Sj
Telefax: 4643924

Directors: Ali Al Mashat, Abdulkader Bairi, Awad Al Karem Wada, Ahmed Al Amin, Said Abdullah Al Qahtani, Mohammed Othman Abdulghaffar

PRINCIPAL ACTIVITIES: Satellite communications

Branch Offices: Tunis, Tunisia

Principal Shareholders: Member States of the Arab League

ARAB SUPPLY & TRADING CORP

PO Box 3863, Riyadh 11481
Tel: 4771488
Cable: Esquire
Telex: 401707 Astra Sj
Telefax: 4780679

Chairman: Sabih Taher Masri

Directors: Zahi Nashat Masri (Managing Director)

Senior Executives: Salah Noubani (Sales & Marketing Manager), Bahjat Salloum (Purchasing Manager), Ali A Ghayyada (Production Manager), Iyad D Hajji (Personnel & Admin Manager), Sadiq A Arafat (Technical Manager), Salah Saleh (Financial Manager)

PRINCIPAL ACTIVITIES: Farming, production of vegetables, fruit, flowers and plants; sheep breeding and fattening projects; quail farms; catering and wholesale for foodstuffs, supermarkets & bakery; import and supply of military garments and accessories, menswear, bathroom accessories and pillow manufacturing; import and supply of fertilisers, seeds and agricultural materials; drip irrigation systems; construction; manufacturing of prefab housing, storage tanks, walk-in and mobile coldstores

Branch Offices: Tabuk, Jeddah, Dammam, Medina

Subsidiary Companies: Esquire Stores; Al-Masri & Al-Khalaf Trading Co; Astra Agricultural Co; National Metal Industries Co; Saudi Mais Equipment & Irrigation Systems Co; Nour Trading Co

Principal Bankers: Arab National Bank, Riyadh

Financial Information:

| | 1989 |
	SR'000
Sales turnover	457,909
Profits	4,777
Authorised capital	200,000
Paid-up capital	200,000
Total assets	375,359

Principal Shareholders: Wholly owned by Sabih T Masri
Date of Establishment: 1968
No of Employees: 2,500

ARABCO

PO Box 578, Riyadh 11421
Tel: 4771820, 4763292
Cable: ARABCO
Telex: 401605 ARABCO SJ
Telefax: 4763292

Chairman: Abdulrahman Bin Dannan
Directors: Hussein A Bastawici (General Manager)
Senior Executives: Eng Mohammad Afifi Mostafah, Eng Khalid M Al Ramahi

PRINCIPAL ACTIVITIES: Building and civil engineering contractors
Branch Offices: Dhahran, Cairo
Principal Bankers: Saudi Cairo Bank

Date of Establishment: 1960
No of Employees: 750

ARABIA ELECTRIC LTD

PO Box 4621, Jeddah 21412
Tel: 6605089, 6693516, 6693496, 6693412
Cable: Jufalisiemens
Telex: 601864 AELJED SJ

Chairman: A Juffali
Directors: J Askari, I Touq, D Ansar, W Seelig, H Franz, Dr B Mueller

PRINCIPAL ACTIVITIES: Electrical engineering, contracting and supply of electrical and telecommunication equipment
Principal Agencies: Siemens AG, Germany
Branch Offices: Riyadh, Dammam
Principal Bankers: Albank Alsaudi Alhollandi

Principal Shareholders: E A Juffali & Bros, Saudi Arabia (70%); Siemens AG, Germany (30%)
Date of Establishment: July 1976
No of Employees: 190

ARABIAN AEROSURVEY CO LTD

PO Box 6079, Riyadh 11442
Tel: 4542731
Telex: 405053 AERSUR SJ

Chairman: Sheikh Salim Binladen
Directors: Sheikh Omar Binladen, Sheikh Hassan Binladen, D A Francis, A D Bancroft (Managing)

PRINCIPAL ACTIVITIES: Aerial survey, photography and mapping, land survey and hydrography
Parent Company: Binladen Brothers; Hunting Surveys Ltd
Principal Bankers: Saudi-British Bank

Principal Shareholders: Binladen Bros for Contracting & Industry, Saudi Arabia; Hunting Surveys Ltd, UK
Date of Establishment: 1980

ARABIAN AUTO AGENCY

PO Box 2223, Jeddah 21451
Tel: 6695595
Telex: 601106 Sudair Sj

President: Zeid M Sudairi (also Managing Director)
Directors: Sheikh Abdulaziz Bin Hassan (Executive Vice President), Mohammad Zaki Siddiqui (Commercial Director)

PRINCIPAL ACTIVITIES: Distributors of heavy equipment, construction, earth moving, mining, material handling, truck and transportation, agriculture and well drilling equipment
Principal Agencies: Construction Equipment Division: Poclain Excavators, PPM/Poclain Cranes, France; Kawasaki Shovels and Rollers, Japan; American Hoist-Lattice Boom Cranes, USA; Gardner Denver- Mining Equipment Ent, USA; Potain Tower Cranes, France; Universal Crushers, USA; CCB-Batching Plants and Concrete Mixers, USA; Lancer Boss-Container Handlers and Lift Trucks, UK; NPK Hydraulic Hammers, Japan; Vibromax Losenhausen Vibrating Rollers and Compactors, West Germany; Energy Systems Generators, USA; Nisha Generators, Japan; Automotive/Truck Division: International Harvester Trucks, USA; Thomas Built Buses, USA; Elgin Sweepers, USA; Leach Refuse Trucks, USA; Unic Truck Mounted Cranes, Japan; Aztec Trailers, USA; Mol Bulk Carriers; Agriculture Division: Sperry New Holland Combines and Balers, Belgium; Lockwood Center Pivots and Irridelco Irrigation System, USA; White Farm Tractors, USA; Gardner - Denver Water Well Rigs, USA
Branch Offices: Riyadh 11481: PO Box 3691, Tel 4953330, Telex 401138 SUDARI SJ; Dammam 31451: PO Box 2111, Tel 8576024, Telex 871422 Sudari SJ; Buraidah: PO Box 7, Tel 3242141, Telex 801040 Sudari SJ; Jubail 31951: PO Box 399, Tel 3416800, Telex 632039 Sudari SJ; Khamis Mushait: PO Box 406, Tel 2223176
Principal Bankers: Saudi British Bank

Principal Shareholders: Emir Zeid M Sudairi
Date of Establishment: 1964
No of Employees: 1,050

ARABIAN AUTOMOTIVE COMPANY

PO Box 21767, Riyadh 11421
Tel: 4746644
Cable: OLAYANCO
Telex: 404786 Olayan Sj
Telefax: 4766644

Chairman: Sheikh Khalid S Olayan
Chief Executive: Imtiaz H Hydari (Vice President)
Senior Executives: Zaid Omar Al Dossary

PRINCIPAL ACTIVITIES: Sales and service of cars and their parts
Principal Agencies: Jaguar Cars Ltd, UK; Austin Rover Group, UK; Land Rover Ltd, UK; Unipart Ltd, UK
Branch Offices: PO Box 318, Al Thugba 31411, Tel 8642733, Telex 870019 Olayan SJ; PO Box 1227, Jeddah

Subsidiary Companies: General Contracting Company; General Trading Company; Saudi General Transportation Company; Project & Development Company
Principal Bankers: Saudi American Bank; National Commercial Bank; Riyadh Bank; Saudi British Bank
Financial Information:

	SR'000
Sales turnover	160,000
Authorised capital	2,000
Paid-up capital	2,000

Principal Shareholders: Sheikh Suliman S Olayan; Sheikh Khalid S Olayan
No of Employees: 300

ARABIAN BECHTEL CO LTD

PO Box 3477, Dammam 31471
Tel: 8540144
Cable: Wateka
Telex: 895011 KFIA Sj

PRINCIPAL ACTIVITIES: Engineering consultants
Parent Company: Bechtel Group of Companies
Subsidiary Companies: Saudi Arabian Bechtel Co; Bechtel Arabian Services Co; Saudi Arabian Bechtel Equipment Co
Principal Bankers: Saudi American Bank

No of Employees: 17,000

ARABIAN BULK TRADE LTD

PO Box 2194, Al Khobar 31952
Tel: (03) 8944880
Telex: 870354 SABUT SJ, 871096 ARBUT SJ
Telefax: (03) 8640461

Chairman: Hisham A Alireza
Directors: Per Berg (President)
Senior Executives: Egil Sjulsen (Executive Vice President)

PRINCIPAL ACTIVITIES: Trading in bulk commodities, cement
Branch Offices: Riyadh: PO Box 16896, Tel (01) 4789323, Telex 403106; Jubail: PO Box 151, Tel (03) 3612641; Jeddah: PO Box 16698, Tel (02) 6890568, Telex 605518 Abttra SJ
Parent Company: Xenel Industries
Associated Companies: Binex (Marketing Building Materials); Agri Bulk Trade Ltd (Trading and Marketing bulk agricultural commodities, feed grains, fertilizers, petro-chemical by-products); Saudi Scaffolding Factory (SSF) (Manufacture & Marketing tubular metal scaffold, access frames & towers, scaffolding & formwork components)
Principal Bankers: Gulf International Bank, Bahrain; Saudi American Bank, Alkhobar; Citibank, Bahrain

Principal Shareholders: Xenel Industries Ltd
Date of Establishment: 1977
No of Employees: 310

ARABIAN CEMENT CO LTD

PO Box 275, Jeddah 21411
Tel: 6828253, 6828270
Cable: Cementco
Telex: 600718 Arceco Sj
Telefax: (02) 6829989

Chairman: HRH Prince Turkey Bin Abdulaziz
Directors: HE Sheikh Abdul Aziz Al Abdalla Al Suleiman (Vice-Chairman), Eng Mohammed Najib Kheder (Director General)

PRINCIPAL ACTIVITIES: Production of ordinary grey portland and sulphate resisting cement (4,000 tons capacity daily)
Subsidiary Companies: Cement Product Industry Co Ltd, PO Box 3386, Jeddah; Technical Operation Maintenance & Services Co, Rabigh Cement Plant Management, PO Box 124, Rabigh, Tel 4222728, Telex 612021 Arceco Sj
Principal Bankers: National Commercial Bank; Riyad Bank; Bank Al Jazira; Saudi American Bank

Financial Information:

	1988/89 SR'000	1989/90 SR'000
Sales turnover	301,500	286,764
Profits	111,000	105,138
Authorised capital	600,000	600,000
Paid-up capital	600,000	600,000
Total assets	1,039,376	990,231

Principal Shareholders: Al Suliman; AlRajhi; National Commercial Bank; Riyad Bank and Binladin
Date of Establishment: 1954 (1374H)
No of Employees: 127

ARABIAN CHEMICAL CO (POLYSTYRENE)

PO Box 1049, Jeddah 21431
Tel: 6674640, 6673871, 6674818, 6607764
Cable: JUFFALICENT
Telex: 600991 Dochem Sj
Telefax: 6607268

Directors: Dr Souhail T Farouki
Senior Executives: L Wallin (Plant Manager), Hilal Kabbani (Regional Marketing Manager), Mansoor Munir (Financial Manager)

PRINCIPAL ACTIVITIES: Production of extruded polystyrene insulation boards (Styrofoam/Roofmate)
Principal Agencies: Dow Chemical Co

Principal Shareholders: E A Juffali & Bros; The Dow Chemical Co
Date of Establishment: 1982
No of Employees: 35

ARABIAN CHEVRON INC

PO Box 5536, Riyadh 11432
Tel: 4649053, 4640892
Telex: 401728 CHVRON SJ

Chairman: D Bonny
Directors: E R Lowry

PRINCIPAL ACTIVITIES: Technical service/support for Chevron's petroleum, petrochemical activities
Parent Company: Chevron Corporation, San Francisco, USA
Principal Bankers: Saudi American Bank, Riyadh

Date of Establishment: 1975

ARABIAN CLEANING ENTERPRISE LTD

PO Box 5736, Riyadh 11432
Tel: 4772237
Telex: 400893 WMSPFS SJ

PRINCIPAL ACTIVITIES: Maintenance services, municipal cleaning contractors and disposal of wastes
Branch Offices: PO Box 9366, Jeddah 21413, Tel 6600331, Telex 601972 ACEOFF SJ
Associated Companies: Waste Management Int Inc, USA

ARABIAN CO FOR ELECTRICAL & MECHANICAL WORKS (ACEM)

PO Box 556, Riyadh 11421
Tel: 4790100
Cable: Asemo
Telex: 401907 Acem SJ
Telefax: 4790171

Chairman: Abdullah Al-Hobayb
Directors: Sulaiman Al-Hamad (Managing Director)

PRINCIPAL ACTIVITIES: Electrical and mechanical contracting, civil works, sale of electrical materials
Principal Agencies: Asea, Sweden; NGK, Japan
Branch Offices: Location in Riyadh: Al Owaidah Bldg, Sitteen Street
Subsidiary Companies: Electrical Materials Centre (ELEMAC), Riyadh; ACEM-ASEA, Riyadh; Saudi Lighting Co, Riyadh;

Arabian Lighting Company, Riyadh (ALC); Arabian Electrical Industries Ltd, Riyadh

Principal Bankers: Arab National Bank, Riyadh; National Commercial Bank, Riyadh; Albank Alsaudi Al Fransi Bank, Riyadh; Albank Alsaudi Alhollandi, Riyadh; Saudi International Bank Ltd, London

Principal Shareholders: Abdullah Al-Hobayb
Date of Establishment: 1975
No of Employees: 80

ARABIAN COMPUTER MAINTENANCE & MARKETING CO

PO Box 53462, Riyadh 11583
Tel: 4761048, 4761578
Telex: 405139 Arbcom Sj

Chairman: Adel A Batterjee
Senior Executives: Dr Samir El Dardiry (Asst General Manager)

PRINCIPAL ACTIVITIES: Computer maintenance and installation; telex and telephone equipment

ARABIAN CONTRACTING & RESOURCES CO LTD

PO Box 435, Jeddah 21411
Tel: 6434054, 6471911
Telex: 601694

Chairman: Said Ahmad El Ajou
Directors: Ghassan Said Ahmad El Ajou

PRINCIPAL ACTIVITIES: Civil, building and general engineering contractors, supply of electrical and mechanical machinery and equipment; manufacturers' representatives

Principal Shareholders: Said El Ajou Trading Corp

ARABIAN DRILLING COMPANY

PO Box 932, Riyadh 11421
Tel: 4763571
Cable: Arabdrill Riyadh
Telex: 401058 Petromin Sj

Chairman: Saleh Alfadl
Directors: Djamal Jawa, Bernard Alpaerts, Andre Miens, Abdellaziz Zamzani

PRINCIPAL ACTIVITIES: Oil drilling onshore and offshore, mining core drilling
Branch Offices: Saudi Arabia (PO Box 1500, Jeddah, Tel 6432460, and PO Box 708, Dammam, Tel 8323222); and Kuwait

Principal Shareholders: Joint Venture between Petromin and Forex, France

ARABIAN ELECTRICAL INDUSTRIES LTD

PO Box 8796, Riyadh 11492
Tel: 4980088 (9 lines)
Telex: 404571 ABBRYD SJ
Telefax: 4985487, 4981939

Chairman: Abdullah Al Hobayb
President: Lave Lindberg
Senior Executives: Olof Westman (Executive Vice President)

PRINCIPAL ACTIVITIES: Manufacture of relay and control equipment, low and medium voltage switchgear, compact secondary substations
Branch Offices: Alkhobar: PO Box 2873, Alkhobar 31952, Tel 8985234, Fax 8946970, Telex 870254; Jeddah: PO Box 7937, Jeddah 21472, Tel 6654332, Fax 6694310, Telex 600627; Buraydah: PO Box 2669, Buraydah, Tel 3249590, Fax 3249582; Abha: PO Box 892, Abha, Tel 2270352, Fax 2270596, Telex 905002; Tabuk: PO Box 66, Tabuk, Tel 4230773, Fax 4230972, Telex 681051
Principal Bankers: Albank Alsaudi Alhollandi

Financial Information:

	1989 SR'000	1990 SR'000
Sales turnover	75,000	120,000
Authorised capital	15,000	15,000
Paid-up capital	15,000	15,000

Principal Shareholders: Abdullah Al Hobayb; ASEA Brown Boveri
Date of Establishment: 1406H
No of Employees: 250

ARABIAN ESTABLISHMENT FOR TRADE & SHIPPING LTD

PO Box 832, Jeddah 21421
Tel: 6422808, 6422852
Cable: Meyasser Jeddah
Telex: 601138, 602878 Aet Sj
Telefax: 6440285

Directors: HRH Prince Saud Al Abdullah Al Faisal (Managing Director)
Senior Executives: HRH Prince Sultan (Deputy Managing Director), Salah A Satti (General Manager Shipping), Brian R Johns (Deputy General Manager Shipping), Shafi Ahmed (General Manager Trading), Bora Altunsecen (AET Diving Division), Michael Knott (Finance Manager), Ahmed Eid S Al Harbi (Personnel & Admin Manager)

PRINCIPAL ACTIVITIES: Shipping agents, container base operation, clearing and forwarding, general trading; import and distribution of foodstuffs, storage (refrigerated and dry); inspection and survey of ships, cargo and materials; diving services, underwater maintenance, hull cleaning, salvage, stevedoring services, contractors to ports and public services
Principal Agencies: Numerous shipowners, incl Mitsui, Merzario, Cunard, Ellerman, Sudan Shipping Line, Black Sea Shipping, Baltic Shipping, Hual/Leif Hoech & Co, ACT, BLC; also Kraft Inc, Beatrice Foods, Lloyds, Salvage Association, class societies, The Institute of London Underwriters; Wijsmuller, Scruttons, Mersey Dock and Harbor Bond, Lloyds Register
Branch Offices: Dammam: PO Box 299, Dammam 31411, Tel 8322837, Telex 801051; Yanbu: PO Box 174, Tel 3222109, Telex 661030; Riyadh: PO Box 4767, Riyadh 11412, Tel 4773158, Telex 404957; Gizan: PO Box 145, Tel 3171824, Telex 911082; Rabigh: PO Box 218, Rabigh 21911, Tel 4222072, Telex 612035; London: 36 St James's Street, London SW1A 1JD, Tel 4912907, Telex 22610, Fax 4991250
Principal Bankers: Saudi British Bank
Financial Information:

	1990 SR'000
Authorised capital	60,000
Paid-up capital	60,000

Principal Shareholders: HRH Prince Abdullah Al Faisal and his sons and daughter
Date of Establishment: 1963
No of Employees: 250

ARABIAN FIBERGLASS INSULATION CO LTD

PO Box 1289, Dammam 31431
Tel: 8571519, 8572301
Telex: 801420 FGF SJ
Telefax: 8573605

President: Dr Abdulaziz S Al Jarbou
Directors: Eng Farid Y Al Khalawi (VP Operations)

Senior Executives: C Stokes Ritchie (General Manager), Antoine R Abou Mansour (Manager Marketing & Sales), Gerry F F Muhle (Production Manager), Asfand Iqbal (Financial Manager)

PRINCIPAL ACTIVITIES: Manufacture of thermal and accoustical fiberglass insulation products
Branch Offices: Riyadh: PO Box 1029, Riyadh 11431, Tel 4658665, Telex 401008, Fax 4633464; Jeddah: PO Box 2140, Jeddah 21451, Tel 6534704, Telex 601431, Fax 6516149
Parent Company: Amiantit Group of Companies; Owens-Corning Fiberglass Corp
Principal Bankers: Al Bank Al Saudi Al Fransi, Alkhobar

Principal Shareholders: Saudi Arabian Amiantit Co; Owens-Corning Fiberglass Corp, USA
Date of Establishment: 1980
No of Employees: 130

ARABIAN FOOD SUPPLIES

PO Box 1400, Jeddah 21431
Tel: 6514284, 6517229, 6512309
Cable: Catering Jeddah
Telex: 600602 AFSJED SJ
Telefax: 6512856

President: Yasser Y Naghi
Directors: Magdi N Yacoub (Vice President)
Senior Executives: T M Whitaker (Divisional Manager Support Services), S J Everest (Divisional Manager Retail), P R W Hole (Divisional Manager Effemex), J N Micallef (Divisional Manager Distribution), F S Mirza (Divisional Manager Finance & Administration), Ziyad Da'as (Sales Manager Consumer Products), Joseph N Hamouche (Marketing Manager Consumer Products)

PRINCIPAL ACTIVITIES: Full support services including compound management, catering, retailing stores, maintenance, laundry, housekepping, import and distribution of fast moving consumer goods
Principal Agencies: Mars, Hero, First Brands, Wrigleys, Ross, Pedigree Petfoods, Tate & Lyle, Loctite, Cooper, Normeat, Swan, Grosjean, Kodak, Lotus Paper Products, Carilla
Branch Offices: PO Box 2791, Riyadh 11461, Tel 4626842, Telex 404862, Fax 4632226; PO Box 341, Al Khobar 31952, Tel 8946126, 8946162, 8945726, Telex 871125, Fax 8945750
Parent Company: The House of Naghi, PO Box 704, Jeddah 21421
Principal Bankers: Saudi British Bank; Saudi American Bank
Financial Information:

	1990 SR'000
Sales turnover	302,000
Profits	12,500
Authorised capital	24,000
Paid-up capital	24,000
Total assets	141,000

Principal Shareholders: Yousef Mohamed Naghi, Mohamed Yousef Naghi, Yasser Yousef Naghi
Date of Establishment: 1967
No of Employees: 800

ARABIAN FREIGHT AGENCIES

PO Box 8352, Jeddah 21482
Tel: 6672818, 6695764
Telex: 602444 SAROUK SJ, 603304 AFAJED SJ
Telefax: 6692801

Senior Executives: H Al Amoudi (General Manager), S Taifur (Riyadh Branch Manager), M Varghese (Damman Branch Manager)

PRINCIPAL ACTIVITIES: International and local transportation, sea, land, air, international freight forwarding, delivery, storage, custom clearance, personal luggage service transportation

Branch Offices: PO Box 6360, Riyadh 11442, Tel 4768189, 4768195, Fax 4784638, Telex 406624 AFARUH SJ; PO Box 4825, Dammam 31412, Tel 8348842, fax 8349354, Telex 803223 AFADAM SJ
Associated Companies: Danzas Ltd, Switzerland

Date of Establishment: 1979
No of Employees: 60

ARABIAN GEOPHYSICAL & SURVEYING CO (ARGAS)

PO Box 2109, Jeddah 21451
Tel: 6710087, 6710183
Cable: Geosurvey Jeddah
Telex: 601786 Argas Sj
Telefax: (02) 6726352

Chairman: Jamal Hassan Jawa
Directors: Fadlullah Farouq (Managing Director), Yves Serres (Technical Managing Director)
Senior Executives: Abdul Wahab Hafez (Asst Managing Director), Mohammed Aslam (Chief Accountant)

PRINCIPAL ACTIVITIES: Geophysical exploration for oil, minerals and ground water as well as all types of land, airborne and marine surveys
Branch Offices: PO Box 2717, Riyadh, Tel 4650821; PO Box 535, Alkhobar, Tel 8943138, 8573138
Parent Company: Petromin, Saudi Arabia & CGG France
Principal Bankers: Al Bank Al Saudi Al Fransi, Jeddah; Saudi American Bank, Jeddah; National Commercial Bank, Jeddah; Al Bank Al Saudi Al Hollandi, Jeddah

Principal Shareholders: General Petroleum & Mineral Organisation (Petromin), Saudi Arabia; Compagnie Generale de Geophysique (CGG), France
Date of Establishment: 1966
No of Employees: 135

ARABIAN GULF CONSTRUCTION CO LTD

PO Box 1633, Dammam 31441
Tel: 8325347, 8320985
Telex: 801461 Zalalu Sj

President: Ahmed A Al-Zamil

PRINCIPAL ACTIVITIES: General and building contractors

No of Employees: 300

ARABIAN GULF ESTABLISHMENT

PO Box 162, Dammam 31411
Tel: 8331876, 8330352, 8332093, 8332111
Cable: Services
Telex: 802175 AGE SJ
Telefax: 8349664

Chairman: Hassan Abdullah Mira
Directors: Ghayoor H Siddiqui (Managing Director)
Senior Executives: Misbah H Siddiqui (General Manager), M A Hameed Javeed (Manager Finance)

PRINCIPAL ACTIVITIES: Importers, stockists and suppliers for all kind of building materials
Branch Offices: Riyadh: PO Box 17523, Tel 4954503, Fax 4954224, Telex 404732 AGE SJ
Principal Bankers: Bank Al-Jazira; Saudi British Bank; Saudi American Bank
Financial Information:

	1988/89 SR'000	1989/90 SR'000
Sales turnover	26,750	24,956
Paid-up capital	4,000	4,000
Total assets	3,750	3,000

Principal Shareholders: Proprietorship
Date of Establishment: 1976
No of Employees: 43

ARABIAN HALA CO LTD

PO Box 6164, Riyadh 11442
Tel: 01-4764875
Telex: 401969 Hala Sj
Telefax: 4764909

Chairman: Sheikh Suleiman Al Saleh
Directors: Aref El-Yafi (Managing Director)
Senior Executives: B Qaddoura, O Abou Gharbieh, Izzat
Nusaibah (Financial Controller), Suhail Harb

PRINCIPAL ACTIVITIES: Vehicle rental and leasing services,
limousine services, car maintenance services, gasoline sale,
mail orders
Principal Agencies: Al Ansa International Rent-A-Car, Freemans
Int'l of London, Franklin Mint Ltd
Branch Offices: Jeddah: PO Box 8410, Tel 02-6517643, Telex
604039; Al-Khobar: PO Box 1663, Tel 03-8954702, Telex
870590, Jubail: PO Box 898, Tel 03-3466777, Telex 632128;
Yanbu: PO Box 1171, Tel 04-3227588, Fax 04-3910822
Subsidiary Companies: Arabian Hala Co For Services
Principal Bankers: Riyad Bank; Al Bank Al Saudi Al Fransi; Arab
National Bank; Saudi American Bank, Saudi British Bank
Financial Information:

	1990 SR'000
Authorised capital	5,000
Paid up capital	5,000

Principal Shareholders: Suleiman Al Saleh, Hani Al Saleh,
Hussam Al Saleh
Date of Establishment: 1977
No of Employees: 600

ARABIAN HOMES CO LTD

PO Box 4553, Jeddah 21412
Tel: 6822201
Telex: 603229 Arahom SJ
Telefax: 6834560

Chairman: Ghassan N Pharaon
Directors: Hamad A Linjawi, Usman Mahmood
Senior Executives: Roger B Marshall (General Manager), John
Alexander (Deputy General Manager Operations), Sean Hunt
(Deputy General Manager Finance)

PRINCIPAL ACTIVITIES: Property developers, residential
housing contractors and managing agents, specialising in
luxury expatriate housing
Branch Offices: Riyadh: Tel (01) 4541888, Telex 404508
ARHOME SJ, Fax 4546420; Yanbu: Tel (04) 3225007, Telex
661184 ARHOMY SJ, Fax 3221055
Principal Bankers: National Commercial Bank
Financial Information:

	1989/90 SR'000
Sales turnover	100,000
Paid-up capital	41,500
Total assets	700,000

Principal Shareholders: Dr G N Pharaon, Talal Y Zahid, Osman
A Linjawi
Date of Establishment: 1976
No of Employees: 400

ARABIAN INDUSTRIES CO

PO Box 8069, Riyadh 11482
Tel: 4101790, 4773500
Telex: 402255 OMRAN SJ

Directors: Omran Al-Omran (Managing Director)

PRINCIPAL ACTIVITIES: Manufacturing building materials,
quicklime, hydrated lime, sand lime bricks and blocks
Principal Bankers: National Commercial Bank; Al Bank Al Saudi
Al Fransi

Financial Information:

	SR'000
Sales turnover	25,000

No of Employees: 220

ARABIAN INSPECTION & SURVEY CO LTD

PO Box 9963, Jeddah 21423
Tel: 6442635, 6435289
Telex: 600583 AIS SJ
Telefax: 6446296

Chairman: HRH Prince Saud Abdullah Al Faisal
Directors: HRH Prince Sultan Bin Abdullah Al Faisal
Senior Executives: Nizam Siddiqui (Manager), M Nazir Malik
(Senior Surveyor Cargo), A R M Jamal Mohiedeen (Maraine
Engineer Surveyor), John Carley (Marine Engineer Surveyor)

PRINCIPAL ACTIVITIES: Marine, cargo and industrial surveyors,
loss adjusters, surveyors to classification societies,
consultants
Principal Agencies: Managers AET Lloyd's agents, surveying
agents for several leading insurance companies
Branch Offices: Riyadh: PO Box 4767, Riyadh 11412, Telex
400580, Fax 4794498; Dammam: PO Box 6850, Dammam
31452, Telex 801750, Fax 8331052
Parent Company: SIGMA (Saudi Investment Group & Marketing,
PO Box 7972, Jeddah
Principal Bankers: Saudi British Bank, Jeddah

Date of Establishment: 1979

ARABIAN INVESTMENTS CO LTD

PO Box 6471, Jeddah 21442
Tel: 6692203/6
Cable: Jedbunkersco
Telex: 600043

Directors: Mazen Rashad Pharaon (Partner), Hattan Rashad
Pharaon (Partner)

PRINCIPAL ACTIVITIES: Import of industrial machinery and
equipment; textiles, clothing; building materials; sanitaryware,
chemicals, household and electrical appliances

Principal Shareholders: Partners as described
Date of Establishment: 1978

ARABIAN MECHANICAL & ELECTRICAL CONTRACTING CO (AMECCO)

PO Box 3488, Riyadh 11471
Tel: 4770080/4
Cable: Amelux Riyadh
Telex: 401233 Amecco SJ

Directors: Hamad Al Alaiwi (General Manager), Dr Roger
Chemali (Assistant General Manager)

PRINCIPAL ACTIVITIES: Electro-mechanical contractors
Branch Offices: Jeddah (PO Box 6935); Dammam; Taif
Principal Bankers: AlBank AlSaudi AlFransi; National
Commercial Bank

Principal Shareholders: Hamad Al Alaiwi (Debbas & Sons);
Abdul Khaliq Buksh (Rajab & Silsilah)
Date of Establishment: 1974
No of Employees: 600

ARABIAN MECHANICAL ENGINEERING CO LTD (AMEC)

PO Box 354, Dhahran Airport 31932
Tel: 8948029, 8948032, 8944068, 8952196
Cable: AMEC-DHAHRAN
Telex: 870235 AMEC SJ

Chairman: Teymour Abdulla Alireza
Directors: N Urmossy (Managing Director), A Weijburg, W A
Simpson (Chief Executive), H Norris, A A Alireza, J H N
Gibson

SAUDI ARABIA

PRINCIPAL ACTIVITIES: General Contracting, including, civil and building constrution work; also mechanical and electrical construction and maintenance work associated with the oil and petrochemical industry; desalination and water treatment plants, power generation; construction of portable office and accommodation units
Branch Offices: Jeddah, PO Box 8628, Tel 6690414, 6690109, 6691205
Associated Companies: Wimpey Arabian Services Co Ltd, PO Box 367, Dhahran Airport 31932, Tel 8757985, 8757978
Principal Bankers: Saudi British Bank, Saudi American Bank, Al Bank Al Saudi Al Fransi

Principal Shareholders: National Contracting Co Ltd, Saudi Arabi (51%), George Wimpey M E & Co (Overseas) Ltd, UK (49%)
Date of Establishment: 1973
No of Employees: 1,875

ARABIAN METAL INDUSTRIES LTD
PO Box 5937, Jeddah 21432
Tel: 6821410, 6821418, 6825033
Cable: Jarmet Jeddah, SA
Telex: 600075 Amind Sj

Chairman: Sheikh Ahmed Juffali
Directors: Jafar Askari, Nabeel Abillama, Samir Abillama
Senior Executives: Christoph Oertel (General Manager)

PRINCIPAL ACTIVITIES: Manufacture of tipper bodies, trailers, tankers and semi trailers
Branch Offices: Riyadh Branch; Tel (01) 4022222
Associated Companies: E A Juffali & Bros, PO Box 1049, Jeddah; Carrosserie Abillama, Beirut, PO Box 4482, Lebanon
Principal Bankers: Saudi American Bank; Arab National Bank
Financial Information:

	SR'000
Authorised capital	32,000
Paid-up capital	32,000

Principal Shareholders: E A Juffali & Bros; Carrosserie Abillama
Date of Establishment: 1976
No of Employees: 150 Approx

ARABIAN METALS CO LTD
PO Box 66, Dhahran Airport 31932
Tel: 3-8425639, 8429588
Telex: 871119 AMCO Sj
Telefax: 3-8422249

Chairman: Khalid Sulaiman Olayan
Directors: Saad F Al Arjani (Vice Chairman)
Senior Executives: C J Cooke (General Manager), Jassem M Al Gattry (Deputy General Manager), Graham Raeper (Sales Manager), Stephen Woods (Operations Manager), Mohammed Iqbal (Executive Secretary)

PRINCIPAL ACTIVITIES: Manufacture of steel pipes & joints and oil & petrochemical spare parts
Principal Agencies: Hydril; Atlas Bradford; Vallourec; Vetco Offshore
Parent Company: Olayan Financing Company
Principal Bankers: Riyad Bank, Alkhobar
Financial Information:

	1990 SR'000
Paid-up capital	7,100

Principal Shareholders: Olayan Financing Co; Sulaiman Saleh Olayyan
Date of Establishment: 1977
No of Employees: 55

ARABIAN MINERALS & CHEMICALS CO LTD
PO Box 2231, Dammam 31451
Tel: 8579285
Cable: AMC
Telex: 801608 AMC Sj
Telefax: 8573472

Senior Executives: E C Haynes Jr (Manager), Udhay Sharma (Financial Controller)

PRINCIPAL ACTIVITIES: Manufacturing and marketing oil well and water well drilling fluids
Principal Agencies: Dresser Industries Inc, Texas, USA
Principal Bankers: Al Bank Al Saudi Al Fransi
Financial Information:

	1990 SR'000
Authorised capital	5,000
Paid-up capital	5,000
Total assets	13,147

Principal Shareholders: Sheikh Abdel Hadi A Al Qahtani; Sheikh Abdullah Rushaid Al Rushaid; Al Bilad Establishment; Dresser Industries Inc
Date of Establishment: 1977
No of Employees: 20

ARABIAN MOTORS & ENGINEERING CO LTD
PO Box 166, Dammam 31411
Tel: 8262411, 8273363, 8273508
Cable: Ameco/Zahid
Telex: 801033 Amaeco Sj
Telefax: 8273491

President: Abdul Majid Zahid
Directors: Amr Zahid (Executive Vice President)
Senior Executives: Mohamed Hassan Abu Eideh (Vice President), Mustafa Bassuni (Vice President Finance), Sami Mansoor (Sales Manager), Christopher Burnell (Operations Manager), Yousuf Sultan (Personnel Manager), Joseph Lisko (Parts Director)

PRINCIPAL ACTIVITIES: GM dealer in Eastern Province for Chevrolet, Buick, Pontiac, Cadillac and GMC commercial pickups and trucks; sales, parts and service; vehicle leasing/rental contractors, lease purchase plan incl maintenance; heavy transport/cargo haulage, travel agency, specialised mechanical engineering, generator sets, fork lifts etc
Principal Agencies: GM; AC Delco; TWA; Saudia; Do-All (Tools); Isuzu Diesel; PAI; AE; Garrett; Eaton Fuller; KC Cummins; IPD; Diesel Kiki; Korody Colyer
Branch Offices: Al-Khobar, Ras Tanura, Jubail, Hofuf, Jeddah, Yanbu
Subsidiary Companies: Ameco Travel Agencies; Trans-Arabain Technical Services Co; Ameco Industrial Supply
Principal Bankers: Albank Alsaudi Alhollandi, Dammam; Riyad Bank, Dammam; Saudi Cairo Bank, AlKhobar; Saudi American Bank, AlKhobar
Financial Information:

	1990 SR'000
Sales turnover	242,658
Authorised capital	30,000
Paid-up capital	30,000
Total assets	229,615

Principal Shareholders: Shaikh Abdul Majid Zahid; Amr A Zahid; Mahmoud A Zahid; Amira A Zahid; Hoda A Zahid
Date of Establishment: 1948
No of Employees: 573

ARABIAN OIL COMPANY LTD
PO Box 256, Al-Khafji 31971, Divided Zone
Tel: (03) 7660555
Telex: 841011 SJ
Telefax: 7662001

President: H Eguchi

Directors: K Konaga, K Tono, K Yamauchi, Y Takeda, Y Ojimi, S Tsuge, T Kataoka, H Makie, M Onon, K Yamaura, K Okabe, Abdul Rahman Abdul Karim, Ahmad A Al Zamel, Jawad Omar Al Sakka, Abdul Razzak Mulla Hussain, Sulaiman Nisf Jasem Al Omani, Siham Abdul Razzak Rezouki

Senior Executives: Kiichi Konaga (Vice President), Ko Tono (Sr Managing Director / Resident Director Field Office), Kenjiro Yamauchi (Sr Managing Director / In charge of President's Office, Coordination and Finance & Accounting Dept), Soichi Tsuge (Managing Director / Field Chief Executive, Field Office), Takashi Kataoka (Managing Director / In charge of Planning Dept & Engineering Dept), Haruo Makie (Managing Director / In charge of Coordination Dept 2 & Terminal & Marketing Dept), Minora Ono (Director / In charge of Coordination Dept 1), Kiyu Yamaura (Director / In charge of Planning Dept & Engineering Dept), Katsura Okabe (Director / In charge of Finance & Accounting Dept)

PRINCIPAL ACTIVITIES: Exploration, development, production, refining, smelting and processing of oil and natural gas, halite, uranium and other mineral resources

Branch Offices: Dammam, Riyadh, Kuwait, London, New York; Field Office; Al Khafji, Divided Zone, Saudi Arabia.

Subsidiary Companies: AOC Energy Development Co Ltd

Principal Bankers: Industrial Bank of Japan

Principal Shareholders: Government of Saudi Arabia; Kuwait Oil Corporation; Tokyo Electric Co; Kansai Electric Co; Nippon Steel Co

Date of Establishment: 1958

No of Employees: 1,925

ARABIAN PETROLEUM CO LTD

PO Box 6471, Jeddah 21442
Tel: 6692203/6
Telex: 600042 Alda Sj, 600043 Hofna Sj

Directors: Mazen Rashad Pharaon (Partner), Hattan Rashad Pharaon (Partner)

PRINCIPAL ACTIVITIES: Drilling and prospecting for oil and minerals

Principal Shareholders: Partners as described

Date of Establishment: 1980

ARABIAN PETROLEUM MARINE CONSTRUCTION CO M.A.R.I.N.C.O.

PO Box 50, Dhahran Airport 31932
Tel: 8643411 ext 133
Cable: Marinco
Telex: 870047 Marico Sj

Chairman: Ali I Rubaishi

Directors: W L Higgins, A H Al-Shalian, R Howson, M Rahaimi

Senior Executives: W L Higgins (Technical Director), A H Al-Shalian (Administrative Director)

PRINCIPAL ACTIVITIES: Offshore, pipeline and oilfield construction

Branch Offices: Headquarters: Petromin Riyadh; Operations Offices: Dhahran and Alkhobar

Associated Companies: McDermott Saudi Arabia; McDermott Dubai

Principal Bankers: Citibank of New York; National Commercial Bank, Alkhobar

Principal Shareholders: Petromin Riyadh (51%), Jay Ray McDermott (49%)

Date of Establishment: January 1971

ARABIAN PETROLEUM SUPPLY CO SA

PO Box 1408, Jeddah 21431
Tel: 6366842, 6367164, 6367291, 6371120
Cable: Apsco
Telex: 602613 APSCO SJ
Telefax: 6377120, 6367164 Ext 275

Chairman: Sheikh Ahmed Y Z Alireza
Directors: Sheikh Ahmed Y Z Alireza (Managing Director)
Senior Executives: V C Caminiti (General Manager), M M Chebaclou (Accounting & Finance Manager)

PRINCIPAL ACTIVITIES: Lubricants and fuel sales, bunkering and refueling aircrafts
Principal Agencies: Mobil Oil
Branch Offices: Saudi Arabia: Yanbu; Jubail; Riyadh; Dammam
Parent Company: Haji Abdullah Alireza & Co Ltd; Mobil Marine Transportation Ltd
Subsidiary Companies: Saudi Can Company
Principal Bankers: Saudi British Bank; Saudi American Bank

Principal Shareholders: Alireza Group of Saudi Arabia; Mobil Oil Corp
Date of Establishment: 1961
No of Employees: 354

ARABIAN POWER CONSTRUCTION CO LTD

PO Box 381, Dammam 31411
Tel: 8322935
Telex: 871245 Sigma Sj

PRINCIPAL ACTIVITIES: Electrical power distribution and transmission network

Principal Shareholders: Bilal Co Ltd, Saudi Arabia; Power Constructions Co, USA

ARABIAN PUBLIC RELATIONS AGENCY

PO Box 5379, Riyadh 11422
Tel: 4654068, 4040542
Cable: Apraj
Telex: 401870 Apraj Sj

Chairman: Mahmoud Mashhady (also Proprietor)
Senior Executives: Farmanullah Khan

PRINCIPAL ACTIVITIES: Public relations consultants, advertising
Subsidiary Companies: International Trading Bureau, Riyadh; Overseas Catering Est, Riyadh
Principal Bankers: Saudi American Bank

ARABIAN SOLETANCHE SOIL CONTRACTORS

PO Box 2824, Jeddah 21461
Tel: 6602229, 6601757
Cable: Arsocontra
Telex: 600832 SJ Asolco

Chairman: Sheikh Mohammed Ahmed Youssef Zeinal Alireza
Directors: Rolland Venot, Walid Abboud
Senior Executives: Ibrahim Tawil (Managing Director)

PRINCIPAL ACTIVITIES: Soil and deep foundation specialist, testing and contracting
Branch Offices: Location in Jeddah: Anakesh, Mohammad Abdo Bldg
Parent Company: Soletanche, France; Soltravo, Lebanon
Principal Bankers: Al Bank Al Saudi Al Faransi
Financial Information:

	SR'000
Authorised capital	4,000
Paid-up capital	4,000

Principal Shareholders: Xenel Industries 25.5% (Saudi Arabia); Soletanche Ent. 50% (France); Soltravo 24.5% (Lebanon)
Date of Establishment: As J.V. in 1975 became A.S.S.C. in 1981
No of Employees: 60

ARABIAN SPRING MATTRESS FACTORY

PO Box 5635, Jeddah 21432
Tel: 6362855 (6 lines)
Cable: Sleep High
Telex: 600597 High Sj
Telefax: 6377015, 6374961

Chairman: Abbas Abdul Jawwad (also Owner)
Directors: Abdul Kader S Amudi, Abdul Latif Al-Azhary
Senior Executives: Mahmood Habashi (Financial Advisor)

PRINCIPAL ACTIVITIES: Production of spring mattresses and
raw materials for spring mattresses, production of foam
mattresses, polyester and foam pillows, box springs, mattress
pads & other bedding products
Principal Agencies: Merracare, UK; Tinsley Wire, UK; John
Cotton, UK; Beakert Mattress, Belgium; Fabric Factory Inc,
USA
Branch Offices: Riyadh, PO Box 3436; Dammam, PO Box 1314
Parent Company: Johaina Trading Establishment, PO Box 2037,
Jeddah 21451
Principal Bankers: Arab National Bank; Riyad Bank; National
Commercial Bank

Date of Establishment: 1963
No of Employees: 150

ARABIAN TECHNICAL CONTRACTING CO (ARTEC)

PO Box 1387, Jeddah 21431
Tel: 6711161, 6713485
Telex: 602876 Artec Sj
Telefax: 6725470

Chairman: Sheikh Omar Abdulfattah Al Aggad
Senior Executives: Mohammad Fawzi A Al Aggad (General
Manager), Dr Jamil A Al Azzeh (Deputy General Manager),
Eng Walid Al Aggad (Project Engineer)

PRINCIPAL ACTIVITIES: Road construction civil engineering
contracting, construction of roads, highways, bridges,
flyovers, tunnels and allied work
Branch Offices: PO Box 2987, Riyadh 11461, Tel 4650573,
Telex 401372
Principal Bankers: Arab National Bank; Saudi American Bank;
Riyad Bank
Financial Information:

	1990 SR'000
Sales turnover	58,000
Profits	2,000
Authorised capital	15,000
Paid-up capital	15,000
Total assets	31,000

Principal Shareholders: Sheikh Omar Aggad & Co
Date of Establishment: 1973
No of Employees: 800

ARABIAN TRADING CO FOR COLD STORAGE

PO Box 1393, Jeddah 21431
Tel: 6371239, 6364262
Cable: Naklyat Jeddah
Telex: 601065 Rijjal Sj
Telefax: 6363687

Chairman: Abdullah Mohammed Al Harbi
Directors: Qasim Jamil Al Rijjal (Managing Director)
Senior Executives: Mohammed Nazir Al Rijjal (Admin Manager),
Abdul Aal A Awad (Commercial Manager)

PRINCIPAL ACTIVITIES: Cold storage, import and distribution
of foodstuffs
Branch Offices: Saudi Arabia; United Arab Emirates
Associated Companies: Orient for Refrigeration & Foodstuffs
Co, Saudi Arabia; Shehab Cold Stores, Saudi Arabia; Jamil

Lines for Shipping & Trade, Lebanon; Fresh Fruits Co Ltd,
Sharjah & Kuwait
Principal Bankers: Riyad Bank, Saudi Cairo Bank, National
Commercial Bank
Financial Information:

	1989/90 SR'000
Sales turnover	250,000
Authorised capital	19,738
Paid-up capital	10,000
Total assets	80,000

Principal Shareholders: Abdullah Mohammed Al Harbi, Qasim
Jamil Al Rijjal
Date of Establishment: 1964
No of Employees: 45

ARABIAN WATERPROOFING INDUSTRIES CO (AWAZEL)

PO Box 2955, Riyadh 11461
Tel: 01-4981596, 4981604
Cable: AWAZEL
Telex: 400716 AWAZEL SJ
Telefax: 01-4981707, 4781078

Chairman: Khalid Ali Al Turki
Directors: Ali Ibrahim Al Sugair (Managing Director)
Senior Executives: Ibrahim A Yousef (Finance Manager), Firas I
Al Sugair (Research & Development Manager), Omar A Aziz
Al Madhi (Sales & Marketing Manager)

PRINCIPAL ACTIVITIES: Manufacture and sale of bituminous
roofing and waterproofing materials, bonding adhesives,
bitumous, paints and compounds
Branch Offices: Jeddah Manufacturing Plant, Tel 02-6601740;
Sales & Marketing Office: Riyadh, Tel 01-4782876; Dammam
Sales Office: Tel 03-8341853
Principal Bankers: United Saudi Commercial Bank
Financial Information:

	1989 SR'000	1990 SR'000
Sales turnover	46,000	50,000
Profits	2,700	3,500
Authorised capital	14,000	14,000
Paid-up capital	14,000	14,000
Total assets	42,000	50,000

Principal Shareholders: Khalid A Al Turki; Ali I Al Sugair; Nasser
A Al Salama; Marcel Steiger
Date of Establishment: 8.7.1401H
No of Employees: 180

ARABIAN WOODWORK CO LTD

PO Box 7177, Jeddah 21462
Tel: 6421549, 6210103
Cable: Alakhshab
Telex: 603224 Arwood SJ

Chairman: Sheikh Ahmed Abdullah Al-Sulaiman
Directors: Sheikh Gassan Ahmed Abdallah Al-Sulaiman
Senior Executives: Mohd Said Ali Bey (General Manager)

PRINCIPAL ACTIVITIES: Manufacture of all types of wooden
doors, furniture and other wooden products
Principal Bankers: Bank Al-Jazira; Saudi American Bank
Financial Information:

	SR'000
Sales turnover	22,000
Authorised capital	5,820
Paid-up capital	5,820

Principal Shareholders: 100% Saudi Owners
Date of Establishment: 1976
No of Employees: 45

ARCAN
Arabian Contracting Association
PO Box 252, Riyadh 11411
Tel: 4761090, 4761033, 4761086, 4766320, 4760135
Cable: Arco
Telex: 401279 Arcan Sj

President: Raja S Saab

PRINCIPAL ACTIVITIES: General contracting and trading
electrical and civil engineering
Principal Agencies: Saab, Sweden
Branch Offices: Jeddah Office; Al Johara Bldg, PO Box 1528,
Jeddah, Tel 6424325, Telex 601201
Associated Companies: Al Mabani Co Ltd

ARCHIRODON CONSTRUCTION (OVERSEAS) CO SA
PO Box 11948, Jeddah 21463
Tel: 6830253, 6831704, 6831790
Cable: Archirodon
Telex: 604358 Arcsmo Sj

PRINCIPAL ACTIVITIES: Construction and engineering, marine
works (Ports of Jeddah, Dammam, Yanbu, Jubail, Jizan
(Saudi Arabia); Sharjah (UAE); railroads, road and bridges;
dams and irrigation; airports; electrical/mechanical works;
industrial facilities; buildings; dredging; geotechnical
engineering
Parent Company: 20 rue Adrien Lachenal 20, 11207 Geneva,
Switzerland
Principal Bankers: Bank of America; Citibank: Arab Bank

Date of Establishment: 1967

ARDOGHAN TRADING & CONTRACTING
PO Box 1990, Jeddah 21441
Tel: 6691801
Cable: Doghaner
Telex: 401723 Ardog
Telefax: 6671788

Chairman: Ardoghan Jafar Asaad
Directors: Fuad Asaad, Kemal Asaad

PRINCIPAL ACTIVITIES: Trading and contracting, construction
plant, furniture, paints, electrical engineering, fishing, shipping
Branch Offices: Medina Muhawara: PO Box 2320, Medina
Principal Bankers: Saudi American Bank
Financial Information:

	1989 SR'000
Sales turnover	3,000
Profits	300
Authorised capital	1,000
Total assets	1,500

Date of Establishment: 1962
No of Employees: 20

ARIEB GROUP OF COMPANIES
PO Box 3790, Riyadh 11481
Tel: 4545912
Cable: Asseel Riyadh
Telex: 401171 Arieb Sj

President: Faisal Abdulrahman Al-Sudairy (Proprietor)

PRINCIPAL ACTIVITIES: Construction: roads, bridges, building
and other civil works; Trading: import and supply of industrial
and construction materials, electrical, plumbing, hardware and
tools; playground equipment; household goods and
appliances, furniture, kitchen and bathrooms; auto tyres,
batteries and accessories; clothing, shoes, toys and furniture;
Agriculture: agricultural and irrigation equipment sales and
services; farm management; Manufacturing: pre-cast concrete
slabs and panels, hollow blocks, curbstones, asphalt mix and

sand aggregates; reinforcement bars and steel supports;
doors, windows and other woodworks; Services: maintenance
services and manpower subcontracting; auto maintenance
Branch Offices: Saudi Arabia: Al-Ghat, Jubail, Al-Kharj,
Buraydah, Sajir, Al-Jouf
Parent Company: The Arieb Group of companies comprises:
ARIEB Development Co Ltd, ARIEB Enterprises, ARIEB
Marketing, ARIEB Services, ARIEB Agriculture
Subsidiary/Associated Companies: Arieb Marketing International
GmbH, Frankfurt, West Germany; Exporters Inc, Des Moines,
USA; Philsa Construction & Trading Co Ltd, Manila,
Philippines
Principal Bankers: In Riyadh: Saudi American Bank, Riyadh
Bank Ltd, Saudi Investment Bank, National Commercial Bank;
Northwest Bank, Minneapolis, USA; First Bank of
Minneapolis, USA; Citibank, Bahrain
Financial Information:

	SR'000
Authorised capital	43,750
Paid-up capital	43,750

Principal Shareholders: Faisal Abdulrahman Al Sudairy
Date of Establishment: 1974
No of Employees: 2,220

ARTHUR D LITTLE INTERNATIONAL INC
See LITTLE, ARTHUR D, INTERNATIONAL INC

AS SAWAFI AL THAHABIYAH ENTERPRISE
Golden Dunes
PO Box 6611, Jeddah 21452
Tel: 6601667, 6691369
Telex: 600086 Golhil SJ

Owner: I M Husseini (Manager)

PRINCIPAL ACTIVITIES: Specialising in maintenance materials;
safety clothing; light industry
Principal Agencies: Loctite Adhesives, Molykote Speciality
Lubricants, Cortec Volatitee Corrosion Inhibitors, Dow-
Corning Silastic RTV Silicones, Metal Filled Epoxies,
Fibreglass Resin Kits
Branch Offices: PO Box 2147, Dammam 31451, Tel 8910346;
Yanbu, Tel 3225774
Principal Bankers: Arab National Bank Ltd, Jeddah

Principal Shareholders: I M Husseini and family
Date of Establishment: July 1977

ASH-SHARQIYAH AGRICULTURAL DEVELOPMENT CO
PO Box 7118, Dammam 31462
Tel: 8429119
Cable: Shadco
Telex: 803030 SJ
Telefax: 8427573

Chairman: Rashid Abdulrahman Al Rashid
Directors: Muhammad Abdullah Abu Butain, Abdul Latif Hamad
Al Jabr, Nasser Abdul Rahman Al Muammar, Mahdi Al
Muhana, Mahdi Yasein Al Ramadan, Zaki Al Khoneizi
Senior Executives: Hassan Ali Al Sultan (Director General),
Yousef Qadan (Finance Manager), Ryong Byo Hong
(Workshop Manager), Zamil Al Mansour (Asst Director
General Administration), Abdullah Al Siddieg (Project
Manager), Ayyash Al Himsh (Asst Project Manager
Production), Maged Al Harazien (Technical Support Services
Coordinator), Abdullah Algam (Marketing Coordinator)

PRINCIPAL ACTIVITIES: Agricultural production
Branch Offices: Agricultural project at Alfadhili, 150 km North-
West of Dammam
Principal Bankers: Arab National Bank, Dammam; Albank
Alsaudi Alhollandi, Dammam

Financial Information:

	1990
	SR'000
Sales turnover	25,000
Profits	1,836
Authorised capital	356,687
Paid-up capital	89,172
Total assets	99,794

Principal Shareholders: Joint-stock company
Date of Establishment: 1984
No of Employees: 102

ASIA AL QURAISHI ELECTRO MECHANICAL CO LTD

PO Box 688, Dhahran Airport 31932
Tel: 8949067, 8646085
Telex: 871049 Alqu Sj
Telefax: 8953656

Chairman: Saleh Zaid Alquraishi
Directors: Mikhael Shaheen (Managing Partner), Riad Hussein (Managing Partner)
Senior Executives: Khalid S Aldakheel (General Manager), Sadik J Mosawy (Area Manager)

PRINCIPAL ACTIVITIES: Heating, ventilation and air conditioning contractors
Associated Companies: Asia Electro Mechanical Co Ltd, PO Box 24354, Safat, Kuwait, Tel 2516415, Telex: 23335 ASIAMEC KT
Principal Bankers: Saudi British Bank

Date of Establishment: 1980
No of Employees: 20

ASSAID STORES
Said Ahmad Badrig & Bros Co Ltd

PO Box 538, Jeddah 21421
Tel: 6422928, 6434136, 6423743
Telex: 601149 Assaid Sj

Chairman: Said Ahmad Badrig
Directors: Salem Ahmad Badrig (General Manager), Hassan Ahmad Badrig (Assistant General Manager)

PRINCIPAL ACTIVITIES: Import and distribution of household electrical appliances, kitchen utensils, glass wares, aluminium wares, crystal wares, stainless-steel wares, furniture, plastic wares, etc
Principal Agencies: Moulinex Electro-Menager, Sovirel (French Pyrex), Gunter Leifhett, Pento-Nett (Italy and Greece), Cosmopla SA, Biberon Remond, Rigolleau, etc
Branch Offices: Location in Jeddah: King Abdul Aziz Street, Prince Abdullah Al Faisal Bldg; also branches in Riyadh; Makkah; Medina; Dammam

AS'SAKKAF EST FOR ENGINEERING, TRADING & CONTRACTING

PO Box 232, Medina
Tel: 8363668, 8363672
Cable: Assakkaf
Telex: 570019 Sakkaf Sj, 570189 Sakkaf Sj

Chairman: Sheikh Alawi Abbas As'Sakkaf
Directors: Sheikh Ibrahim As'Sakkaf (Vice President)
Senior Executives: Eng Kamal Toukan (Jeddah Office), K Kassem (Medina Office)

PRINCIPAL ACTIVITIES: Civil construction, roads, trade import and distribution of office machinery, and computers
Principal Agencies: Hartford Fire Insurance Co
Branch Offices: Jeddah: PO Box 2240, Tel 6424211, Telex 601213
Subsidiary Companies: Al Akeek V Int'l Trading Co (Department Store)
Principal Bankers: Bank Al Jazeera, Medina

Principal Shareholders: Sole Proprietorship
Date of Establishment: 1959
No of Employees: Over 1,200

ASSOCIATED AGENCIES LTD

PO Box 419, Jeddah 21411
Tel: 6431820, 6447027, 6422429, 6422496
Cable: Loucas Jeddah
Telex: 601025 Sj

Directors: Abdul Raouf Abuzinadah (Managing Director)

PRINCIPAL ACTIVITIES: Shipping agents and general merchants, insurance agents, import and distribution of foodstuffs, travel agents, hospital
Principal Agencies: Comet Rice; Wessanen Flour Mills; General Mills of USA; AlSagr Insurance Co; Arab Belgian Insurance & Reinsurance Co
Branch Offices: Riyadh: PO Box 8707, Telex 400704, Tel 4010472, 4010376; Dammam: PO Box 6325, Telex 802273, Tel 8334551, 8334939
Associated Companies: Al Sagr Insurance Co, PO Box 419, Jeddah; Arabian Est for Food Products, PO Box 1450, Jeddah; Hatim Travel Agency, PO Box 419, Jeddah; Jeddah Medical Centre, PO Box 419, Jeddah
Principal Bankers: Saudi American Bank; National Commercial Bank; Al Jazirah Bank; Riyad Bank

Date of Establishment: 1960
No of Employees: About 40

AT&T INTERNATIONAL (SAUDI ARABIA)

PO Box 4945, Riyadh 11412
Tel: (01) 2411055
Telex: 401522 Atti Sj
Telefax: 2411055 ext 4148, 4104

President: John A Hinds
Senior Executives: Arthur J Davie (President - Europe, Middle East & Africa), Michael Parker (General Manager Saudi Arabia)

PRINCIPAL ACTIVITIES: Telecommunications and computer equipment and software, engineering, design, turnkey project implementation, consulting services, directory and videotex services, operations and maintenance and training
Principal Agencies: AT&T Technologies
Parent Company: American Telephone & Telegraph (AT&T)
Associated/Subsidiary Companies: Western Electric Saudi Arabia (WESA); AT&T International, Egypt; Ireland; Greece; UK; AT&T Network Systems; AS Bugshan Telecommunications; Modern Electronics Services Co Services Inc
Principal Bankers: Chase (Saudi Investment Banking Corporation); Citibank (Saudi American Bank)

Principal Shareholders: American Telephone & Telegraph Co (AT&T)
Date of Establishment: June 6, 1977
No of Employees: AT&T International (Saudi Arabia) 10; WESA 107

ATCO
A A Turki Corporation

PO Box 718, Dammam 31421
Tel: 8332339, 8335588
Cable: Atco Dammam
Telex: 801067 Turki Sj
Telefax: 8339881

President: Abdul Rahman Al Turki (also Managing Director)
Senior Executives: Fuad Tannous (Corporate Controller), Fritz Mair (Senior Manager), John Thorne (General Manager Commercial Division)

PRINCIPAL ACTIVITIES: Import and distribution of air-conditioning and refrigeration equipment, building materials,

electrical and electronic equipment, furniture, office equipment, paints, oil and gas equipment; general engineering, freight forwarding and customs agents; warehousing; municipal cleaning; catering; construction; printing; manufacturing electrical panels; manufacturing cement additives; maintenance
Principal Agencies: S&C Electric Co, USA; Pullen Pumps, UK; Honeywell Int'l Inc, USA; Kabel Metal, W Germany; Rosenthal, W Germany
Branch Offices: Riyadh; Jeddah; London (UK); Houston (USA)
Associated Companies: East & West Establishment, Alkhobar; East & West Express Ltd; Redland Industrial Service Ltd; Marine & Transportation Services (MATSS); Honeywell Turki Arabia Ltd; Saudi Danish Construction Corp; Al Turki BCR
Principal Bankers: Al Bank Al Saudi Al Hollandi, Dammam

Date of Establishment: 1976
No of Employees: 2,000

ATCO GENERAL SERVICES

PO Box 718, Dammam 31421
Tel: 8332339
Cable: ATCO Dammam
Telex: 801067 Turki Sj

President: Sh Abdul Rahman Ali Al-Turki
Senior Executives: Fritz Mair (Senior Manager)

PRINCIPAL ACTIVITIES: Hospital/camp catering, janitorial, maintenance, municipal cleaning and life support management
Branch Offices: Riyadh: PO Box 8077, Tel 4488845; Jeddah: PO Box 8694, Tel 6912419; Yanbu: PO Box 1086, Tel 3226784; Hofuf: PO BOx 3439, Tel 5801696
Parent Company: A A Turki Corporation (Saudi Arabia)
Principal Bankers: Albank Alsaudi Alhollandi, Dammam

Principal Shareholders: Sheikh Abdul Rahman Ali Al Turki
Date of Establishment: 1986
No of Employees: 500

ATCO PORT MANAGEMENT & MARINE SERVICES

PO Box 718, Dammam 31421
Tel: 03-8332460 (6 lines)
Cable: Fastmatss, Dammam
Telex: 801556 MATSSD SJ
Telefax: 03-8347331

Chairman: Sheikh Abdul Rahman Ali Al Turki
Directors: F E Tannous
Senior Executives: Saud Al Hafez (Contracts & Public Relations Manager), C R O'Kirwan (Marine Manager)

PRINCIPAL ACTIVITIES: The undertaking of contracts relating to the management and operation of ports, marine craft, and provision of cargo handling and technical services in such areas
Branch Offices: PO Box 5809, Jeddah, Tel 02-6918972, Telex 602954 GRAY Sj
Parent Company: A A Turki Corporation, Dammam
Principal Bankers: Albank Alsaudi Alhollandi, Saudi British Bank
Financial Information:

	1990
	SR'000
Authorised capital	2,000
Paid-up capital	2,000

Principal Shareholders: Sheikh Abdul Rahman Al Al Turki (Saudi Arabia)
Date of Establishment: May 1976, reorganised October 1988
No of Employees: 396

ATKINS, W S, AND ASSOCIATES

PO Box 22536, Riyadh 11416
Tel: 4651491, 4651495
Telex: 405317 Larco Sj
Telefax: 4650644

Senior Executives: B Davison (Resident Manager)

PRINCIPAL ACTIVITIES: Planning, engineering, management and agricultural consultants and architects
Branch Offices: In the Middle East: Bahrain, Kuwait, Oman, United Arab Emirates
Parent Company: W S Atkins Ltd, Woodcote Grove, Ashley Road, Epsom, Surrey KT18 5BW, UK
Financial Information:

	1990
	St£'000
Sales turnover	99,500

ATTAR, M SIRAJ, & BROS

PO Box 1765, Jeddah 21441
Tel: 6426241
Cable: Sirajbros
Telex: 601032 Attars SJ

Chairman: Shaikh Mohammed Siraj Attar
Directors: Shaikh Hesham Attar
Senior Executives: Omer M Baghazal (Manager)

PRINCIPAL ACTIVITIES: General trade, indenting, contracting, building and road construction etc.
Principal Bankers: National Commercial Bank

Principal Shareholders: Joint family organisation
Date of Establishment: 1935

ATTAR, SADDIK & MOHAMED,

PO Box 439, Jeddah 21411
Tel: 6447229, 6423437, 6423244
Cable: Attarco
Telex: 601075 Attarng

Chairman: Omar Saddik Attar
Directors: Sami M Attar
Senior Executives: Saddik O Attar (Manager, Commercial Department), Said S Attar (Regional Manager), Hassan Omar Attar (Manager, Shipping Department)

PRINCIPAL ACTIVITIES: Shipping, airlines agency, commerce (consumer goods) and transport services
Principal Agencies: British Airways, SAS, Swissair, Kuwait Airways, Diamond Reo Truck Inc, Hudson, Polish Ocean Lines, Yugoslav Shipping Cos, Montres Rolex SA, Muhammedi Steamship Co Ltd, Ashworth Ross & Co
Branch Offices: Riyadh (PO Box 364, Tel 4023047); Dammam (PO Box 142); Makkah (PO Box 22); Taif (Tel 7380709); Yanbu; Tabuk; Khamis Mushayt (Tel 2235288)
Principal Bankers: Al Bank Al Saudi Al Fransi

Date of Establishment: 1951

AUJAN, A W, & BROS

PO Box 990, Dammam 31421
Tel: 8570777
Cable: Aujan Dammam
Telex: 801300 AUJAN SJ
Telefax: 8577923

Chairman: Abdulwahab Al Aujan
Directors: Adel Abdul Rahman Al Aujan (Group Managing Director), Adnan Abdul Rahman Al Aujan (Managing Director), Faried Saud Aujan (Managing Director Kuwait)
Senior Executives: Abdul Aziz Al Obaid (Group Commercial Manager), Lloyd Glyn Partridge (Director of Sales & Marketing), Carl Richey (General Manager, Aujan Soft Drink Industries), Abdullah Al Shaigy (Finance & Admin Manager Aujan Soft Drink Industries), Tawfiq K Al Qadeeb (Director, Aujan Industrial Supplies AIS), Martin Howe (Act General Manager, Aujan Industrial Supplies AIS), Tariq Al Khalawi (Managing Director, Aujan Crestwood Co Ltd), Cedric Hackett (General Manager, Aujan Crestwood)

PRINCIPAL ACTIVITIES: Beverage and foodstuffs distributors; soft drink canners and bottlers; manufacturers of kitchen cabinets; distributors of industrial safety equipment

Principal Agencies: Rani Int Inc (Rani Drinks - Aujan own Brand); Mitsubishi Corporation; J N Nichols (VIMTO); Bass Exports; Crestwood Kitchens; Angus Fire Armour; Plus 50; Intersafe Int BV; Mine Safety Appliances; Cadbury Int'l; Stroh Int'l; Amerex; EAR Cabot Safety; RDI Safety Spectacles; Turner Entertainment; Ehime-ken Fruit Growers, Boeki Kaisha Ltd

Branch Offices: Jeddah: PO Box 6332, Jeddah 21442; Riyadh: PO Box 16458, Riyadh 16458; Hofuf: PO Box 639, Hofuf11461; Dammam: PO Box 990, Dammam 31421; Buraidah: PO Box 2887, Buraidah Qassim; Khamis Mushait: PO Box 147; Jizan: PO Box 107; Bahrain: PO Box 59, Manama; Hongkong Liaison Office

Associated Companies: Saud Aujan & Bros Co WLL, PO Box 29, Safat, Kuwait; Abdul Rahman Aujan & Sons, PO Box 59, Bahrain; Aujan Crestwood Co Ltd, PO Box 2232, Al-Khobar 31952; Aujan Industrial Supplies, Co, PO Box 2297, Al-Khobar 31952; Aujan Soft Drink Industries, PO Box 990, Dammam 31421; Rani Internation Ltd, Seaton House, 17 Seaton Place, St Helier, Jersey, Channel Islands

Principal Bankers: Saudi British Bank; Albank Alsaudi Alfransi; National Commercial Bank

Principal Shareholders: Members of the Aujan Family
Date of Establishment: 1905
No of Employees: 676

AZIZIYA MARKETS CO LTD

PO Box 1454, Riyadh 11431
Telex: 401109 Hejlan Sj

PRINCIPAL ACTIVITIES: Commercial markets, supermarkets, department stores
Financial Information:

	SR'000
Authorised capital	42,500

Principal Shareholders: Prince Talal Bin Abdul Aziz Al Saud; Taher Ahmad Ubaid

AZMI CORPORATION FOR TRADING & CONTRACTING

PO Box 5869, Jeddah 21432
Tel: 6650664, 6674875, 6650484
Telex: 600579 Azmico Sj

Chairman: Omar Azmi Abu El Said (Managing Director)

PRINCIPAL ACTIVITIES: Manufacturers' representation, distribution of building materials, sanitaryware and pipes; general and building contracting, consultants, management, manpower
Branch Offices: Alkhobar

Date of Establishment: 1975

BADOGHAISH, AHMED ALI,

King Khalid Street, PO Box 65, Alkhobar 31952
Tel: 8646786, 8641115

Chairman: Ahmed Ali Badoghaish

PRINCIPAL ACTIVITIES: Dealing in electronic equipment, and supplies
Principal Agencies: Pioneer; Sansui
Branch Offices: PO Box 815, Jeddah, Tel 6475813, 6832903; PO Box 1135, Riyadh, Tel 4765124; Khamis Mushayt, Tel 72232929; Dammam, Tel 8333542

Date of Establishment: 1961

BADRAH SAUDI FACTORIES CO LTD

PO Box 1678, Jeddah 21441
Tel: 6430255 (4 lines)
Cable: ALINTAJ Jeddah
Telex: 600178 Rashed; 601024 Badrah; 602114 Baker
Telefax: 6442645

Chairman: Abdul Rasheed Badrah
Directors: Aboulkhair Allaf (Deputy General Manager)
Senior Executives: Adan Badrah

PRINCIPAL ACTIVITIES: Manufacture of biscuits and sweets; import and trade of foodstuffs
Branch Offices: Makkah; Madina; Tabouk; Taif; Buraidah; Arar; Dammam; Riyadh; Jizan; Khamis Mushayt; Hail; Najran
Principal Bankers: Saudi American Bank; Albank Alsaudi Alfransi; Albank Alsaudi Alhollandi; Saudi Cairo Bank; Bank Al-Jazira
Financial Information:

	SR'000
Authorised capital	18,000
Paid-up capital	18,000

Date of Establishment: 1968
No of Employees: 700

BAESHEN & BANAGA

Head Office, PO Box 15611, Riyadh 11454
Tel: 405-9535
Telex: 403594 BBAYR SJ
Telefax: 403-5137

Managing Partners: Abdullah A Baeshen, Abdelgadir Banaga
Partners: J S G Bartlett (Partner Tax), Tim Downey (Partner Audit), Kevin O'Brien (Partner Audit)

PRINCIPAL ACTIVITIES: Auditors and certified accountants, tax translation and management consultants
Branch Offices: Jeddah: PO Box 6659, Jeddah 21452; Al Khobar: PO Box 619, Al Khobar 31952
Associated Companies: Arthur Young International, 277 Park Avenue, New York 10172
Principal Bankers: Arab National Bank; National Commercial Bank

Principal Shareholders: Partners Abdullah A Baeshen; Abdelgadir Banaga
Date of Establishment: 1978
No of Employees: 110

BAESHEN, AHMAD MOHAMED SALEH, & CO

PO Box 18, Jeddah 21411
Tel: 6431471, 6432964
Cable: Ameen
Telex: 601664 Friend Sj

Chairman: Ahmad Mohamed Saleh Baeshen
Directors: Ahmad Abubak Baeshen, Mrs Suad A S Baeshen
Senior Executives: Saed Ba-Amer (Chief-Personnel), Omar Baeshen (Senior Staff)

PRINCIPAL ACTIVITIES: Wholesale and import of foodstuffs, tea, jurak, rice, sugar, oils (edible), coffee beans, powdered whole milk, soap, fruit nectars, softdrinks, spices
Principal Agencies: MS Hebtulabhoy, Ceylon; La Societe du Sucre, Belgium; Lijempf, Holland; Foodmarketing, USA
Principal Bankers: Al Bank Al Saudi Al Fransi; National Commercial Bank
Financial Information:

	SR'000
Authorised capital	25,000
Paid-up capital	25,000

Principal Shareholders: Ahmad Abu Bakr Baeshen (Partner); Suad S Baeshen (Partner) and other shareholder of Baeshen Family
Date of Establishment: 1887

BAHARETH ORGANIZATION

PO Box 404, Jeddah 21411
Tel: 6423666, 6423734, 6445101
Cable: Arabintra
Telex: 601022 Hareth Sj

Chairman: Mohamed S Bahareth
Directors: Mazin M Bahareth
Senior Executives: Eng Fouad Chamoun, Eng Hassan Maleh, Eng Mohamed Younes

PRINCIPAL ACTIVITIES: Foodstuffs, construction materials and equipment; real estate, industrial development; building and construction, hospitals, clinics management, company representation, joint-ventures, foreign investments
Branch Offices: PO Box 2989, Riyadh, Tel 8332847, Telex 401491; PO Box 1190, Dammam, Tel 8323454, Telex 801268
Subsidiary Companies: Bahareth Contracting; Hotel & Catering Division; Sanitaryware Division; Specialities Division

Date of Establishment: 1958
No of Employees: 800

BAHLAS, A, CORPORATION FOR TRADE (BUILDMORE DIVISION)

PO Box 2564, Jeddah 21461
Tel: 6600796, 6602566
Telex: 601338 BLDMOR SJ

Chairman: Ahmed Abdullah Bahlas

PRINCIPAL ACTIVITIES: Importers and stockists of building materials, sanitaryware, tiles, pipes and fittings, furniture; sub-contractors
Principal Agencies: James Halstead, UK; Heuga Overseas, UK; Pilkington's Tiles, UK; Chloride Shires, UK; Annawerk, W Germany; Marley Extrusions, UK; Unibond, UK
Branch Offices: PO Box 4117, Riyadh, Tel 4633733, 4633554, Telex 401883 BAHLAS SJ

Date of Establishment: 1976

BAHRAWI TRADING COMPANY

PO Box 48, Jeddah 21411
Tel: 6652441, 6516676, 6376363
Cable: Bahrco Jeddah
Telex: 601699 Bahrco Sj
Telefax: 6652464

Chairman: Ibrahim A Bahrawi
Directors: Abdulmajeed A Bahrawi (Deputy Chairman), Fouad A Bahrawi
Senior Executives: Richard Thorne (General Manager Sales & Marketing), Dr Rafat Abdul Aziz (General Manager Pharmaceuticals), Yousri M Aly (Finance Manager), Maurice Collier (Project Dept), Robin Betser (Marketing Manager), Edmond Chedid (Food Division), David Simpson (Catering Equipment Division)

PRINCIPAL ACTIVITIES: Agents, manufacturers' representatives, distribution and marketing of foodstuffs, pharmaceuticals and cosmetics, detergents, food packing materials/equipment and industrial adhesives and chemicals, catering equipment, cold storage rooms, commercial floor maintenance equipment, ice and ice-cream making machines and cabinets, steel fabrications, modular shelving, coffee machines, commercial laundry equipment, kitchen utensils, crockery, water coolers etc, market research/study
Principal Agencies: Robertsons Jams, Palsgaard Bakeriy Products, Bohara Spices, Trebor Sweets, Danish Fancy Food Corp, Henkel, Continental Candy, BSN Groupe (Panzani, Evian, Vandamme, Pie Qui Chante, Amora, Maille), Dandy Chewing Gum, HP Bulmer, Lea & Perrins, Rayner, John Burgess, Joseph Wolf; Scandinavian Tobacco, Hillsdown, Smith Kendon, Lindt Chocolate, Witco Foods, LeoPharmaceuticales, Nougeaim Grace Italiana, Bras, Carpigiani Bruto, Hobart, ISA Inc, La Cimbali, Miele & Cie, Nilfisk, Scotsman, Vollrath, Steelite, etc

Branch Offices: Riyadh: PO Box 937, Tel 4023596, 4031706, Telex 402321, Fax 4027629; Dammam: PO Box 769, Tel 8323233, 8329147, 8333358 (Show Room), Telex 801385, Fax 8336507; Khamis Mushayt: PO Box 1049, Tel 2238168, Fax 2237828
Parent Company: Abdel Wahab Mohamed Aly Bahrawi Company
Associated Companies: Bahrawi Trading Company; Bahrawi Drug Stores; Ibrahim Abdel Wahab Bahrawi & Bros; Bahrawi International Company; Industrial Catering Eqpt Ltd
Principal Bankers: Saudi American Bank, Jeddah; National Commercial Bank, Jeddah; Saudi French Bank, Jeddah; Saudi British Bank, Jeddah

Date of Establishment: 1921

BAKER TRADING & CONTRACTING

PO Box 2985, Riyadh 11461
Tel: 4790052, 4766650
Cable: BAKER
Telex: 401242 BAKER SJ
Telefax: 4777190

President: Malih Baker
Directors: Sami Baker (Vice President), Mohamed Khawi, Suleiman Zarouby
Senior Executives: Elias Zoghbi (Deputy Manager, Construction Central & Western Province), Antoine Kordahi (Projects Manager)

PRINCIPAL ACTIVITIES: Trading, construction
Principal Agencies: Peugeot; Camping Gas; Nitrolac Paints; Duroplastiques
Branch Offices: Location in Riyadh: Sitteen Street; also branches in Alkhobar: PO Box 2082, Tel 8649695
Subsidiary/Associated Companies: Saudi Chamebel (Aluminium Curtain Walls); Center of Electrical Goods; Abeille Paix (Insurance Company); Pechiney; Saudi Mecam (Electro-mechanical Maintenance)
Principal Bankers: Saudi Hollandi Bank; Saudi American Bank; National Commercial Bank
Financial Information:

	SR'000
Sales turnover	35,000
Authorised capital	3,000

Principal Shareholders: Malih Baker, Sami Baker
Date of Establishment: 1970
No of Employees: 500

BAKHASHAB HEAVY EQUIPMENT EST

PO Box 1189, Jeddah 21431
Tel: 6873031, 6872295
Cable: Bahes Trade
Telex: 601015 Bakship Sj

Owner: M A Bakhashab Pasha

PRINCIPAL ACTIVITIES: Manufacturers' representation; import and supply of construction equipment, plant hire, trucking and transportation contractors
Principal Agencies: Mitsubishi, Hitachi, Denyo, Kawasaki
Principal Bankers: Arab National Bank

Date of Establishment: 1956

BAKHASHAB, MOHAMED ABUBAKR, CO

PO Box 66, Jeddah 21411
Tel: 6423051/4, 6423066
Cable: Bakhashab
Telex: 601015 Sj

Directors: Mohamed Abubakr Bakhashab

PRINCIPAL ACTIVITIES: General trading and contracting, transportation, import and distribution of trucks, buses and automobiles
Principal Agencies: Isuku Motor Co, Japan; Holden Co

SAUDI ARABIA

Subsidiary Companies: Saudi National Lines (Marine fleet);
Bakhashab Engineering & Electrical Services

Date of Establishment: 1956

BAKHASHWAIN, SALIM MOHAMMED,

PO Box 743, Jeddah 21421
Tel: 6431794, 6439987
Cable: Baekifah Jeddah
Telex: 601617 Bakifa Sj

Chairman: Salim M Bakhashwain

PRINCIPAL ACTIVITIES: Importers, distributors and commission
agents (household goods, hardware, electrical appliances,
glassware and carpets)
Principal Agencies: Anchor Hocking Corp; Cannon Mills; Aladdin
Exco Inc, USA; SEB; Tefal; Equipinox; J G Durand & Cie;
Massily; Aubecq Auxi, France; Braun; Turbo; Firehand; Jager,
Germany; Optimus, Sweden; Brabantia, Holland; Alessi
Fratelli, Italy; Prestige Group Ltd; E Wedgwood; Grindley Hot
Ware Co, UK
Branch Offices: Riyadh Branch: King Faisal St, Tel 4035140;
Taif Branch: Aladdas St, Tel 26751; Jeddah Showrooms:
Gabel St, Tel 6422251; King Faisal St, Tel 46713; Airport Rd,
Tel 6421009
Associated Companies: Commission & Trading Agency, Jeddah;
TETRACO, Jeddah; SMB Refrigeration Industry, Khamis
Mushayt; S M World Trade Corp, Beirut, Lebanon
Principal Bankers: National Commercial Bank; Al Bank Al Saudi
Al Hollandi

BAKHEET CO FOR MACHINERY LTD

PO Box 6101, Jeddah 21442
Tel: 6910550 (5 lines)
Cable: Bakheet Jeddah
Telex: 601807 Bakhet SJ
Telefax: 02-6910288

Chairman: Sheikh Abdullah Bakheet
Directors: Fuad M Bakheet, Ihsan Al Rifai
Senior Executives: Yasin A Bakheet, Adel A Aziz

PRINCIPAL ACTIVITIES: Supply and service of heavy
machinery, construction equipment, power equipment, garage
equipment, automobile repair equipment, medical disposable
items
Principal Agencies: Kobelco Excavators & Wheel Loaders;
Arbau Batching Plants; De Jong Concrete Mixers & Mobile
Hoists; Schwing Truck-Mounted Concrete Pumps; Munster
Tower Cranes; Fuchs Exavators on Wheels; Valmet
Excaloaders; Thomas Skid-Loaders; Alfelder Asphalt Plants;
DMT Generators; Finlay Hydra Screen; Commeto Transit
Mixers; Stetter Transit Mixer; Beissbarth Computerised Whell
Alignment; Blackhawk Chasis Denting & Painting Equipment;
Stahlwille Hand Tools; Faip Tyre Changer Equipment; Frank
Steam Washers; Abac Air Compressors; etc
Branch Offices: Riyadh: Tel 4912451; Damman: Tel 8572538;
Medina: Tel 8365548; Abha: Tel 2236532; Taif: Tel 7424166;
Tabuk: Tel 4227565; Gassim: Tel 3815214
Principal Bankers: Saudi British Bank
Financial Information:

	1990
	SR'000
Paid-up capital	6,000

Principal Shareholders: A Bakheet; F Bakheet; I Al Rifai
Date of Establishment: 1975
No of Employees: 250

BAKUR INT'L CORPORATION

PO Box 5610, Jeddah 21432
Tel: 6436511, 6429750
Cable: UNICOMMERCE
Telex: 600135 Binco Sj

Chairman: Abdullah Abubaker Malabari

Directors: Ahmed Abubaker Malabari
Senior Executives: Syed Abdullah Irshad (Import Manager)

PRINCIPAL ACTIVITIES: Commission agents; building, electrical
and mechanical contractors, agricultural equipment, fire
fighting equipment, industrial machinery, foodstuffs,
generators etc
Branch Offices: Riyadh, Telex 400482 Batco Sj; Dammam;
Makkah
Subsidiary/Associated Companies: Bakur Travel Agency; Bakur
Int Agencies Corp
Principal Bankers: Bank Melli Iran, Bank Al-Jazira, National
Commercial Bank

Principal Shareholders: Sole Proprietorship
Date of Establishment: 1975
No of Employees: 45

BALKHAIR TRADING ESTABLISHMENT

PO Box 11508, Jeddah 21463
Tel: 6445874, 6440442
Telex: 603588 Khair SJ
Telefax: (02) 6435219

President: Hassan Mohamed Balkhair
Directors: Omar Mohamed Balkhair, Hussein Mohamed Balkhair
Senior Executives: Omar Mohamed Balkhair (General Manager),
Mahmud Mohammed Osman (Sales Manager), Ali Arab
Zanhoor (Sales Representative)

PRINCIPAL ACTIVITIES: Commission agents dealing in building
materials, furniture, furniture fittings and accessories, paints,
glues, electric appliances, and components, foodstuffs,
toiletries; import of agriculture and garden tools and
equipment
Principal Agencies: Claber, Italy; Wolf Tools, UK; Solo
Kleinmotoren, W Germany; Colorificio, Italy; Klebertek, Italy;
Erba Luigi, Italy; ICSA Brabbrica Serrature, Italy; RDS La
Guarnimec, Italy; Galenco, Belgium, etc
Principal Bankers: National Commercial Bank, Jeddah; Alrajhi
Banking & Investment Corp, Jeddah

Date of Establishment: 1978

BALLAST ORIENT CONTRACTING CO

PO Box 185, Dhahran Airport 31932
Tel: 8644020, 8643228
Telex: 871213 Balor Sj

PRINCIPAL ACTIVITIES: Building and civil engineering
contractors, for building, factories, bridges, dams, harbours,
jetties dredging, earthwork, heavy construction, housing etc
Branch Offices: Location in Alkhobar: Al Mishari Road
Parent Company: Ballast Nedam Groep NV
Principal Bankers: Albank Alsaudi Alhollandi

Principal Shareholders: Abdulmajid Rabat; Ballast - Saudi
Arabia BV
Date of Establishment: 1974
No of Employees: 300

BALUBAID, OMAR ABUBAKER, EST

PO Box 213, Jeddah 21411
Tel: 6404444, 6405624
Cable: Omar
Telex: 601552 Omar SJ
Telefax: 6401093

President: Shaikh Omar Abubaker Balubaid
Directors: Khalid Omar Balubaid (Vice President), Ahmed Omar
Balubaid (Vice President)
Senior Executives: Salah A Said (General Manager), Khalid
Khan (Manager Sales & Marketing), Ali A Balubaid, Mustafa
Al Assad (Manager Finance), Khalid Al Amri (Personnel
Manager), Saeed A Saeed (Administration Manager), Omar
Bazaraa (Computer Manager)

PRINCIPAL ACTIVITIES: Automobile and spare parts dealers

Principal Agencies: Pontiac; GMC; Buick; Subaru; Opel
Branch Offices: Riyadh; Makkah; Madinah; Alkhobar; Khamis Mushait
Subsidiary Companies: Balubaid Motors Est, Madinah; Balubaid Service Equipment Est; Balubaid Decor; Oasis Insurance
Principal Bankers: Arab National Bank; Riyad Bank; Bank Al-Jazira

Principal Shareholders: Sole proprietorship
Date of Establishment: 1953

BANAWI INDUSTRIAL GROUP

PO Box 8281, Jeddah 21482
Tel: 6674057, 6674074
Cable: Alwataniya
Telex: 601670 Bangro Sj, 602670 BIG SJ

Chairman: Sheikh Ali Mohamed Banawi
President: Sheikh Hussein A Al-Banawi (Chief Executive Officer)
Senior Executives: Nabih G Nabti (Senior Vice President, Finance & Administration), George D Nakhle (Consumer Packaging & Building Products Division), Emile Y Chamoun (Corrugated Pkg & Plastics Div), Marwan Abdul-Malak (Director of Purchasing)

PRINCIPAL ACTIVITIES: Manufacturing of consumer & corrugated packaging, building products and plastics
Branch Offices: Dammam
Associated Companies: Overseas Industrial Trading GmbH, Dusseldorf, West Germany
Principal Bankers: Riyad Bank; National Commercial Bank; Saudi Cairo Bank; Bank Al Saudi Al Fransi
Financial Information:

	SR'000
Authorised capital	18,000
Paid-up capital	18,000

Principal Shareholders: Members of the Banawi Family
No of Employees: 1,000

BANDAR TRADING & CONTRACTING CO

PO Box 5174, Jeddah 21422
Tel: 6657317, 6431533
Cable: Bandarco
Telex: 601244 Bantac

Chairman: Prince Bandar Ahmed Sudeiry
Senior Executives: Fayez Abouchahine (Manager)

PRINCIPAL ACTIVITIES: Trading, contracting; manufacturers' representation; agents

Date of Establishment: 1974

BANK AL-JAZIRA

PO Box 6277, Jeddah 21442
Tel: 6670230
Cable: Raeesy
Telex: 601574 Hjaz Jeddah
Telefax: 6670230 ext 100

Chairman: Sheikh Mohammad Bin Saleh Bin Sultan
Directors: S Nasim Ahmed (Vice Chairman), Abdul Kader Mohammad Al Fadl, Abdul Raouf Mohammed Saleh Abu Zinada, Ibrahim Abdullah Al Subeaei, Ibrahim Mohammad Al Malik, Rashed M J Thahen, Hamad Saad Al Sulaiman
Senior Executives: R A Kaleemi (Actg General Manager), Mozaffar Iqbal (Manager Finance & International), Salah Ali Noori (Asst GM Int'l Div), Nosair Mohammad Nosair (Manager Management Support Dept), Abu Baker M I Khan (Secretary to the Board)

PRINCIPAL ACTIVITIES: Commercial banking
Branch Offices: Jeddah (6), Riyadh (3), Dammam, Makkah, Madina, Alkhobar, Abha, Taif, Jubail, Yanbu, Unaizah, Hafr Al Baten, Jizan, Najran, Al Hofuf, Tabuk, Buraidah, Khamis Mushait

Associated Companies: Arab African International Bank, Cairo, Egypt; Banco Saudi Espanol SA (Saudes Bank), Spain; Saudi Investment Bank, Riyadh; Al-Bahrain Arab African Bank, Manama, Bahrain
Financial Information:

	1989/90 SR'000
Deposits	4,540,307
Loans & advances	1,833,440
Authorised capital	100,000
Paid-up capital	100,000
Total assets	4,845,432

Principal Shareholders: Saudi Nationals (65%); National Bank of Pakistan (35%)
Date of Establishment: June 1975
No of Employees: 743

BARAKAH CORPORATION

PO Box 8734, Riyadh 11492
Tel: 4774118, 4760053 (showroom), 4760062, 4760063 (office)
Cable: BARACORP
Telex: 400201 BARAKA SJ
Telefax: 4760046

President: Usama I Al-Khudairy
Senior Executives: Ghassan Al-Khudairy (Trading Division Manager)

PRINCIPAL ACTIVITIES: General building and civil contractors; agents and distributors for commercial kitchen, refrigeration and laundry equipment, fire extinguishers, sprinkler systems, fire alarm systems, commercial water heaters; supply and installation of kitchen equipment and general maintenance
Principal Agencies: G S Blodgett, USA; Pitman, USA; Dorian, USA; EPC Elaine Products, USA; Fabrica-De-Cultaries, Brazil; Kalglas, USA; EDA Int'l, USA; Metro Int'l, USA; Gico, Italy
Principal Bankers: Saudi American Bank; National Commercial Bank
Financial Information:

	1989/90 SR'000
Sales turnover	3,000
Authorised capital	1,250
Paid-up capital	1,250
Total assets	5,000

Principal Shareholders: Proprietorship Usama I Al-Khudairy
Date of Establishment: 12/5/1975
No of Employees: 149

BAROOM, ABDULLAH MOHAMED,

PO Box 1346, Jeddah 21431
Tel: 6512222 (10 lines)
Cable: Portland
Telex: 601165 Brom Sj
Telefax: 6519181

Chairman: Sheikh Abdallah Mohamed Baroom (also Managing Director)
Directors: Ahmed Mohamed Baroom (General Manager)

PRINCIPAL ACTIVITIES: Civil engineering and contracting, architects and consultants, supply of diesel engines, power plant equipment and construction, equipment; import of contractors' plant and building materials, cement, iron, timber, steel bars, paints and varnish, also shipowners' and shipping agents; electronics showroom and servicing division
Principal Agencies: SGB Export Scaffoldings
Subsidiary Companies: Builmat Saudi Arabia; Barcom; Saudi Steel Reinforcement Ltd
Principal Bankers: Riyad Bank

Date of Establishment: 1956

BASAMH TRADING CO

PO Box 427, Jeddah 21411
Tel: 6606668
Cable: Basamh
Telex: 601017 Basamah SJ
Telefax: 6601544

Directors: Ali Saied Basamh (Chief Executive Officer), Salem
Ahmed Basamh (General Manager)
Senior Executives: Mohammed Ahmed Basamh (Deputy General
Manager)

PRINCIPAL ACTIVITIES: Import and distribution of foodstuffs,
grocery goods, maintenance and personal care products
Principal Agencies: Nestle; Findus; Buitoni; L'Oreal; Maggi;
Cross & Blackwell; Johnson Wax; General Mills; Brooke Bond
India; Perrier; Libbys; Ova; Ballantyne
Branch Offices: Riyadh: Tel 4779449; Damman: Tel 8330424;
Taif: Tel 4324181; Khamis Mushait: Tel 2232129; Hofuf: Tel
5821641
Subsidiary Companies: Saudi Modern Foods, Jeddah; Saudi
Food Industries, Jeddah
Principal Bankers: Saudi American Bank, National Commercial
Bank, Riyad Bank

Principal Shareholders: Heirs of Ahmed S Basamh and Ali
Saied Basamh
Date of Establishment: 1927
No of Employees: 500

BASIC CHEMICAL INDUSTRIES LTD

PO Box 1053, Dammam 31431
Tel: 8572466 (6 lines)
Cable: Chemicals
Telex: 801468 Bci SJ
Telefax: 8572648

Chairman: Abdulla Al Moaibed
Directors: Tarik Tamimi, M S Layous
Senior Executives: M S Layous (Group Managing Director),
Ashok Nanavati (Financial Controller), Dr James Ogg (National
Sales Manager), Ahmed Abu Aysha (Asst General Manager)

PRINCIPAL ACTIVITIES: Manufacture of chlorine, caustic soda,
hydrochloric acid, sodium hypochlorite; import and distribution
of chemicals concrete admixtures, industrial gas, and
industrial gas cylinders
Principal Agencies: Imperial Chemical Industries, Ellis &
Everard, Joseph Crossfield, Atlas Chemicals, Olin Chemical
Group, Chance & Hunt, Houseman Chemcials Tioxide Intl,
Columbiana Boiler, Peroxid Chemie, Blue Circle Textured
Coatings, Allied Colloids, John E Sturge, Kali Chemie,
National Adhesives & Resins, Rohm & Haas, Scottish
Agricultural Ind, Wackerchemie, William Blyth & Co, Air
Products, British Petroleum
Branch Offices: PO Box 41153, Riyadh, Tel 4769614, Fax
4762566, Telex 402823 BCIRYD; PO Box 11208, Jeddah, Tel
6821437, Fax 6833774, Telex 603780 BCIJED SJ; PO Box
2415, Buraidah, Tel 3239914
Subsidiary Companies: Arabian Polyol Company Ltd
(Polyurethane Chemicals); National Fruit Juice Company;
Saudi Water Treatment Company (Manufacture of water
treatment chemicals)
Principal Bankers: Riyad Bank, Dammam; Al Bank Al Saudi Al
Fransi
Financial Information:

	1990 SR'000
Sales turnover	140,000
Authorised capital	37,000
Paid-up capital	37,000

Principal Shareholders: Al Moaibed Family and Ali Tamimi
Date of Establishment: 1975
No of Employees: 275

BASSAM TRADING EST

PO Box 4611, Riyadh 11412
Tel: 4633059
Telex: 401589 Ribhi Sj
Telefax: 4641353

Directors: Dr Ribhi Ahmed Hamadeh (Managing Director)
Senior Executives: Basam Hamadeh (General Manager)

PRINCIPAL ACTIVITIES: Supply of pharmaceuticals and medical
disposables and instruments; security systems
Principal Agencies: B Braun; Porges; Beiersdorf; Weck; GMS;
Hoskins; 3M; Harris Lanier; Haagstaat Heine; Jalil; LRC;
Sempirit; Tawizara; SMAD; Unoplast; Wardray; Ferrosan;
Hardwood; Hollister; Invacare; DAYS; OMS; Trevilliton; TSI;
Vorling
Parent Company: Hamadeh Drugstore
Principal Bankers: Arab National Bank

Date of Establishment: 1967
No of Employees: 30

BATTERJEE INTERNATIONAL EST

PO Box 5853, Jeddah 21432
Tel: 6360166, 6364306
Cable: Batterjeeinter
Telex: 600172 Batrje SJ

Chairman: Abduraouf Ibrahim Batterjee
Directors: Abdulaziz A Batterjee (Managing Director), Shahir A
Batterjee (Finance), Tariq A Batterjee (Technical), Adnan A
Batterjee (Technical), Fahd A Batterjee (Architecture), Sayed
M Hassan (Management & Accounting)

PRINCIPAL ACTIVITIES: Manufacture of construction blocks,
plastic bags; supply of aluminium, windows and doors,
building materials, cosmetics, foodstuffs, stationery
Principal Agencies: Chevallier, France; Ital Genetrade, Italy; Ital
Chemi, Italy
Branch Offices: Concrete Block Factory; Plastic Factory;
Aluminium Window & Door Factory; Pastry Factory; Building
Materials Factory; Concrete Block Factory (Yanbu); Five
Pharmacies in the Kingdom
Principal Bankers: National Commercial Bank; Al Bank Al Saudi
Al Hollandi; Riyad Bank; Al Rajhi Banking & Investment Corp
Financial Information:

	1990 SR'000
Sales turnover	20,000
Profits	15%
Authorised capital	56,000
Paid-up capital	40,000
Total assets	35,000

Principal Shareholders: Abdulaziz Abduraouf Batterjee, Shahir
Abduraouf Batterjee, Tariq Abduraouf Batterjee
Date of Establishment: 1975
No of Employees: 150

BAWARETH ENTERPRISES FOR TRADE & CONTRACTING

PO Box 4721, Jeddah 21412
Tel: 6474044 (10 lines)
Cable: Bawareth
Telex: 601673 Wareth Sj
Telefax: (02) 6484115

Chairman: Eng Ali A Bawareth (General Manager)
Directors: Abdul Rahman A Bawareth (Assistant General
Manager)
Senior Executives: Mohammad A Bawareth (Manager Marketing
& Planning)

PRINCIPAL ACTIVITIES: Import and sales of electronic and
electrical material, telecommunication equipment, CCTV,
personnel and business computers, educational computer-
machines, answering devices, intercommunication, sound
equipment, video/audio entry systems, home computers

Principal Agencies: Cordata Computers, USA; Comelit Int, Italy; Electrodomesticos Eibar, Spain; Siemens Info Systems, USA; Jung Ang Electronics, Korea; Inkel Corp, Korea; Goldstar Telecom Co, Korea; Daewoo Corp, Korea; Otron Corp, Korea; Cherish Ent, Taiwan, Age Technology, Taiwan

Branch Offices: Showrooms in Jeddah: Southern Shopping Market; Bamehriz Center; Bin Zagr Street; and Showrooms in Riyadh: Al-Hijaz Road; Olia Riyadh; in Madina: Siteen Street; in Makkah: Siteen Street; in Khamis Mushayt: Al Am Street; in Dammam: King Saud Street

Subsidiary Companies: Bawareth for Construction, Bawareth for Advertising, Bawareth Engineering Office, Jeddah

Principal Bankers: Arab National Bank, Jeddah; Bank Al-Jazira, Jeddah; Al Rajhi Banking & Investment Corp, Jeddah; Saudi British Bank, Jeddah; Albank Alsaudi Alhollandi, Jeddah; Saudi American Bank, Jeddah

Financial Information:

	1990 SR'000
Sales turnover	28,000
Profits	2,200
Authorised capital	14,000
Paid-up capital	14,000
Total assets	30,000

Principal Shareholders: Chairman and director as described
Date of Establishment: 1966
No of Employees: 100

BECHTEL GROUP OF COMPANIES

PO Box 10488, Riyadh 11433
Tel: 01-4829051
Telex: 400698 Wateke Sj

Chairman: S D Bechtel Jr

PRINCIPAL ACTIVITIES: Engineering, construction, project & construction management, operations and maintenance, construction equipment leasing

Branch Offices: Dhahran: PO Box 88 Dhahran, Tel 03-894-8011, Telex 870028 WATEKA SJ; London: PO Box 739, 245 Hammersmith Road, London W6 8DP

Parent Company: Head Office: PO Box 3965, San Francisco, CA, USA 94110

Subsidiary Companies: Arabian Bechtel Company Ltd - Construction & Project Management; Saudi Arabian Bechtel Company - Engineering; Bechtel Arabian Services Company - Operations & Maintenance; Saudi Arabian Bechtel Equipment Company - Construction Equipment Leasing

Principal Shareholders: Privately held
Date of Establishment: Bechtel Group 1898; Arabian Subsidiaries 1940
No of Employees: Bechtel Group 25,000; Arabian Subsidiaries 3,000

BEIT BINZAGR

PO Box 209, Jeddah 21411
Tel: 6478502
Cable: BINZAGR JEDDAH
Telex: 600795 ASMOB SJ
Telefax: 6471131

Directors: Wahib Said Binzagr, Faisal Said Binzagr, Mohamed Obaid Said Binzagr, Abdullah Said Binzagr

PRINCIPAL ACTIVITIES: Commerce, distribution services, construction, manufacture, property, domestic and international investments, joint ventures through legal entities specifically established for selected activities

Branch Offices: London, Houston

Subsidiary/Associated Companies: Said M O Binzagr & Partners Co (Binzagr Co); Abdullah & Said M O Binzagr Co; Wahib S Binzagr & Bros; Al-Rubaiyat Co fpr Industry & Trade Ltd

Principal Bankers: Saudi French Bank, Saudi British Bank, National Commercial Bank, Riyad Bank, Saudi International Bank, London

Principal Shareholders: Binzagr Family Members
Date of Establishment: 1925
No of Employees: 2,000

BEST TRADING COMPANY

PO Box 1271, Jeddah 21431
Tel: 6692562, 6693441
Cable: Bestgroup
Telex: 601384 Best SJ
Telefax: 6693441

Chairman: Sheikh Abdul Mohsen Al-Sulaiman
Directors: Sheikh Fahd Al Sulaiman (Vice Chairman), Sheikh Ghassan A Al Sulaiman (President)

PRINCIPAL ACTIVITIES: Civil and marine engineering contracting, car hire services; general trading and representations, dealing in children' furniture, medical supply and contracting services and maintenance services

Principal Agencies: Avis Licensee

Branch Offices: Jeddah, Riyadh, Al-Khobar, Dhahran, Yanbu, Medina

Principal Bankers: Saudi British Bank; Saudi American Bank; Bank Al-Jazira; Al Bank Al Saudi Al Fransi

Principal Shareholders: Directors as described
Date of Establishment: 1973
No of Employees: 197

BICC MIDDLE EAST LTD

PO Box 11296, Jeddah 21453
Tel: 6671108, 6693131
Telex: 600835 BICC Sj

PRINCIPAL ACTIVITIES: Supply of electrical and electronic products

Branch Offices: PO Box 86, Riyadh 11411, Tel 4068479, Telex 404152; PO Box 24, Dammam 31411, Tel 8336116, Telex 802612

Parent Company: BICC Plc, London, UK
Principal Bankers: Al Bank Al Saudi Al Hollandi

No of Employees: 48

BIN THABIT TRADING & CONTRACTING

PO Box 11104, Jeddah 21453
Tel: 6691466, 6611548
Telefax: 6658852
Telex: 603996 ACTCO

Senior Executives: A M El Shafie (Managing Director)

PRINCIPAL ACTIVITIES: General trading and contracting, machinery, equipment, tools
Principal Bankers: National Commercial Bank
Financial Information:

	SR'000
Sales turnover	20,000

BINAYTI DEVELOPMENT CO

PO Box 3305, Jeddah 21471
Tel: 6654240, 6674406
Cable: Binayti
Telex: 600412 Binayti Sj

Chairman: Sheikh Umr M S Nassif
Directors: Sheikh Ali M S Nassif, Sheikh Othman M S Nassif, Sheikh Ibrahim M S Nassif, Sheikh Nabil A Nassif, Sheikh Ossama A Nassif, Dr Bakhashwin

PRINCIPAL ACTIVITIES: Building and construction contracting; manufacture and supply of building materials and pre cast concrete

Subsidiary/Associated Companies: Joint Venture: Saudi Italian Pre-Cast Co, Yanbu
Principal Bankers: Riyad Bank

Date of Establishment: 1975

BINEX, INTERNATIONAL CO FOR BUILDING MATERIALS LTD

PO Box 2194, AlKhobar 31952
Tel: 8944880, 8645351
Telex: 802388 BINEX SJ
Telefax: 8640461

Chairman: Hisham A Alireza
Directors: Per Berg (President), Egil Sjulsen (Executive Vice President), Abood M Bamardouf (Vice President Sales & Marketing)

PRINCIPAL ACTIVITIES: Supply of building materials
Principal Agencies: Blakeborough; Brickhouse Broads; Heatrae Sadia; Yorkshire Imperial, Ardex; Mueller Brass Co; Uponor Ltd; Schlegel (UK) Engineering Ltd; National Gypsum Co; Dupont; Typar; Spit; Binachem; Catric; Saudi Suspended Ceiling Co; Saudi Factory for Profile; Arabian Fibre Glass
Branch Offices: Jeddah - PO Box 8776, Jeddah, Tel (02) 6519524, 6519762, Tlx 602393 BINEX SJ; Riyadh - PO Box 16896, Riyadh, Tel (01) 4412115, 4413883, Tlx 403106 BNEXRD SJ
Parent Company: Arabian Bulk Trade Ltd (ABT)
Principal Bankers: Gulf International Bank, Saudi American Bank

Principal Shareholders: A member of the Xenel Group of companies
Date of Establishment: 1978
No of Employees: 40

BINLADEN BROS FOR CONTRACTING & INDUSTRY

PO Box 2734, Jeddah 21461
Tel: 6604778, 6604834, 6658633
Cable: Ladenco
Telex: 601071 Binbrs Sj; 601044 Binladn Sj

Chairman: Sheikh Salem Mohamed Binladen
Directors: Eng Haidar Abu Jaber (General Manager)
Senior Executives: Eng Yousif A Badra (Technical Manager), Ghassan El-Hussami (Administrative Manager), Kamil Makarem (Joint Ventures Dept Manager), Samir R Saady (Chief Accountant)

PRINCIPAL ACTIVITIES: Building and civil engineering contractors (roads and bridges)
Branch Offices: Saudi Arabia (Riyadh, PO Box 105, Telex 401104; Dammam PO Box 5803; United Arab Emirates (Dubai, PO Box 1555, Telex 45591 Binladen Db); Jordan (Amman, PO Box 5181, Telex 21207, 21267); UK (140 Park Lane, London W1); USA (Suite 1109, Fannin Bank Bldg, Houston, Texas)
Subsidiary/Associated Companies: Readymix Saudi, joint venture between Binladen Bros and Redland Readymix UK; Binladen Kaiser; Binladen Telecommunication; Binladen Emco; Saudi Aircraft Services; Al Fadl Binladen J & P; Binladen Electro Mechanical; Arabian Aerosurvey Co; Saudi International Properties
Principal Bankers: National Commercial Bank; Al Bank Al Saudi Al Hollandi; Saudi British Bank; Saudi Cairo Bank

Principal Shareholders: Sheikh Salem M Binladen; Sheikh Hassan M Binladen; Sheikh Bakr Binladen; Sheikh Ghaleb Binladen; Sheikh Thabet Binladen; Sheikh Omar Binladen; Sheikh Mahruus Binladen
Date of Establishment: 1972
No of Employees: 470

BINLADEN TELECOMMUNICATIONS CO LTD

PO Box 6045, Jeddah 21442
Tel: 6918787
Telex: 602109 Bintel Sj
Telefax: 6918525

Chairman: Sheikh Bakr Binladen
Directors: Sheikh Saleh Bin Mahfooz, Sheikh Galeb Binladen, Tahir M Bawazir, Alawi Baroum
Senior Executives: Tahir M Bawazir (Chairman Executive Committee), Alawi Baroum (Executive Director), Amer M Kabbara (Senior Manager Sales & Marketing and Acting General Manager), Mohd A Bajersh (Senior Manager Finance/Administration/Personnel and Corporate Secretary), Joseph Deckard (Senior Manager Data Products), J Gil Dickson (Senior Manager Central Region), Yvon Lafrance (Senior Manager Eastern Province)

PRINCIPAL ACTIVITIES: Import, marketing, installation, maintenance of all forms of communications equipment
Principal Agencies: Northern Telecom; North Supply; Multitone, Systems Reliability; Marconi Marine; Tellabs; Banyan Vines; Nokia Turrett Equipment; Digital Microwave
Branch Offices: Riyadh: PO Box 1223, Tel (01) 4650604; Alkhobar: PO Box 1674, Tel (03) 8646652
Principal Bankers: National Commercial Bank

Principal Shareholders: Binladen Bros; SEDCO
Date of Establishment: 1975
No of Employees: 125

BINLADEN-BEMCO ELECTRICAL & MECHANICAL CONTRACTING CO LTD

PO Box 3143, Jeddah 21471
Tel: 6695851, 6695857, 6692362, 6692380, 6692048, 6691840
Telex: 605630 Bemco SJ
Telefax: 6609432

Chairman: Sheikh Bakr Mohammed Binladen
Directors: Souren M Sarkissian (Managing Director), Henry M Sarkissian (Dy Managing Director)
Senior Executives: Henry Cabrera (Operations Manager), Raymond Kanan (Finance Manager), Raji Abou Haidar (Construction Manager), Yousuf Al Daajani (Personnel Manager), Shahe Kaloustian (Technical Manager), Sam Malouf (Administration Manager), Bassem Haddad (Supplies Dept Manager)

PRINCIPAL ACTIVITIES: Electrical and mechanical contractors of: HVAC and refrigeration; sanitary works, plumbing, piping and pipe fitting; pumping stations and distribution; sewage treatment, water and wastewater treatment systems; fire fighting and fire protection systems; instrumentation; power generation, transformation, substations and underground or overhead power distribution systems, street lighting; telephone, public address and audio visual systems as well as maintenance
Branch Offices: Riyadh; project offices: Taif; Makkah; Medinah
Subsidiary Companies: In Barcelona; Houston; Toronto; New Jersey
Principal Bankers: Al-Bank Al-Saudi Al-Fransi, Al-Bank Al-Saudi Al-Hollandi

Principal Shareholders: Binladen Bros for Contracting and Industry; The Saxsons Company (Lebanon)
Date of Establishment: 1975
No of Employees: 1,700

BINLADIN ORGANIZATION

PO Box 958, Jeddah 21421
Tel: 6879222, 6879850
Telex: 601258 Binorg Sj

Chairman: Sheikh Salem M Binladin
Directors: Sheikh Saleh Gazaz, Sheikh Mohamed Bahareth, Sheikh Abdullah Bin Said, Sheikh Mohamed Nur Rahimi,

Sheikh Bakr M Binladin, Sheikh Tarek M Binladin, Sheikh Omar M Binladin, Sheikh Yeslam M Binladin

Senior Executives: Bakr M Binladin (Authorised Board Member), Omar M Binladin (President Contracting), Yeslam M Binladin (President Administration)

PRINCIPAL ACTIVITIES: Civil construction and engineering
Branch Offices: Location in Jeddah: Mecca Road, Kilo 7; also branches in Riyadh, Mecca, Medina, Dammam
Subsidiary/Associated Companies: Binladin BAM Limited; Saudi Sweden Construction Co; Binladin Losinger Limited
Principal Bankers: Saudi American Bank, Jeddah; Al Bank Al Saudi Al Hollandi, Jeddah; Lloyds Bank, Bahrain; Bank of America NT & SA, Bahrain; National Commercial Bank, Jeddah; Saudi British Bank, Jeddah

Principal Shareholders: Members of the Binladin family
Date of Establishment: 1935
No of Employees: 5,000

BINZAGR, ABDULLAH & SAID M O, CO

PO Box 209, Jeddah 21411
Tel: 6478502
Cable: BINZAGR JEDDAH
Telex: 600795 Asmob SJ
Telefax: 6471131

Directors: Wahib S Binzagr, Faisal S Binzagr, Mohamed O S Binzagr, Abdullah S Binzagr
Senior Executives: Faisal S Binzagr (Chief Executive)

PRINCIPAL ACTIVITIES: Joint ventures in manufacturing, heavy transport, shipping, cleaning services, trading agencies, construction (civil, mechanical and electrical) and investment
Principal Agencies: Avon Products Inc, USA; Advance Linen Services, UK
Branch Offices: Alkhobar: PO Box 96, Tel 8641430, Telex 870021 Ikbal SJ; Riyadh: PO Box 392, Tel 4950076, 4951360, Telex 401702 Ikbal SJ
Associated Companies: Binzagr Lever Ltd; Binzagr Co-Ro Ltd; Binzagr Saudi Shipping Co Ltd; Binzagr Match Factory; Trans Arabia; Industrial Cleaning Services; Binzagr Co; Wahib S Binzagr & Bros; Al-Rubaiyat Co; Dywidag (Saudi Arabia) Ltd; Al-Alamiya for Commerce & Services; Binzagr Avon; Binzagr Lipton Ltd; Best Foods Saudi Arabia Ltd
Principal Bankers: Al Bank Al Saudi Al Fransi, Jeddah; Saudi British Bank, Jeddah; Saudi International Bank, London; United Overseas Bank, Switzerland

Principal Shareholders: Binzagr Family Members
Date of Establishment: 1967

BINZAGR COMPANY

Said M O Binzagr & Partners Co

PO Box 54, Jeddah 21411
Tel: 6474388
Cable: Ikbal - Jeddah
Telex: 601131 Ikbl SJ, 601830 Zgrbro SJ
Telefax: 6475856

Chairman: Mohamed O S Binzagr
Directors: Wahib Said Binzagr, Faisal Said Binzagr, Mohamed O S Binzagr, Abdullah Said Binzagr
Senior Executives: Mohamed O S Binzagr (Chairman), Abdullah Said Binzagr (President), Patrick C Arnold (Senior Vice President, Company Operations), Abbas A Morjan (Senior Vice President Finance)

PRINCIPAL ACTIVITIES: Import and distribution branded consumer goods such as food, drinks, frozen foods, chilled foods, tobacco, tyres, household products toiletries and catering supplies
Principal Agencies: Unilever Export, British American Tobacco (UK and Export), Brown & Williamson Int Tobacco, BAT (Deutschland) Export, Henri Wintermans Sigarenfabrieken BV, Lipton Export, H J Heinz, CPC Int Trading Corp, Kelloggs, UB (Biscuits), Uncle Bens, Royal Foods, Chupa Chups, Toshoku,

Hershey Int, Co-Ro Food A/S, Sibra Management, Dr Pepper Co, Wilkinson Sword, Tambrands, Duni Bila AG, Dunlop, General Tire
Branch Offices: Alkhobar: PO Box 96, Tel 8641430, Telex 870021; Riyadh: PO Box 392, Tel 4954029, Telex 401702 Also branches in Dammam, Khamis Mushayat, Hofuf, Medina, Taif, Makkah, Gassim, Jizan, Tabuk, Jubail, Yanbu, Najran, Al Baha, Al Kharj
Associated Companies: Abdullah & Said M O Binzagr Co, Wahib S Binzagr & Bros, Al Rubaiyat Company, Arabian Stores Co, Binzagr International Trading Co
Principal Bankers: Albank Alsaudi Alfransi, Albank Alsaudi Alhollandi, Saudi British Bank, National Commercial Bank, Riyad Bank, Saudi American Bank, Saudi Investment Banking Corporation, Saudi International Bank, London

Date of Establishment: 1922
No of Employees: Approx 500

BITUMAT COMPANY LTD

Bituminous Materials Factory

PO Box 7487, Dammam 31462
Tel: (03) 8424842, 8423688
Telex: 803165 BTUMAT SJ
Telefax: 8425717

Chairman: Mohammad A Bawazir
Directors: Hussain T Naqvi (Managing Director)
Senior Executives: J P Nair (General Manager), Amin Abdel Latif (Sales Manager)

PRINCIPAL ACTIVITIES: Manufacture of modified bitumen self adhesive and torchable membranes (polyester & glassfibre reinforced) for roofing, waterproofing, damproofing, on both new buildings and maintenance work; also traditional felts and coatings for built-up systems
Branch Offices: Corporate Head Office: PO Box 58698, Riyadh 11515, Tel (01) 4770443, 4762318, Fax 4762318, Telex 803165 Btumat Sj; also branch in Jeddah: PO Box 5044, Jeddah 21422, Tel (02) 6724816
Subsidiary Companies: Taroot Chemicals Factory
Principal Bankers: National Commercial Bank, Riyadh; Saudi British Bank, Dammam
Financial Information:

	1989 SR'000
Sales turnover	45,900
Profits	4,050
Authorised capital	15,200
Paid-up capital	9,000
Total assets	13,500

Date of Establishment: 11/9/1401 Hijra
No of Employees: 101

BMC ELECTRONICS SYSTEMS

PO Box 5641, Riyadh 11432
Tel: 4764934
Telex: 403272 SNARCR SJ
Telefax: 4760846

PRINCIPAL ACTIVITIES: Security equipment and services, electronic engineering

BODAL COMMERCIAL CORPORATION

PO Box 8167, Jeddah 21482
Tel: 6518140/8, 6517832
Telex: 602630 Bodal Sj

Chairman: Habib Mohammed Bodal

PRINCIPAL ACTIVITIES: Civil, drilling, communication contractors; metal works, plant hire, water treatment, transportation contractors; computer and business systems
Branch Offices: Taif; Medina; Muhawara

Date of Establishment: 1950

BOEING MIDDLE EAST LTD

Headquarters: PO Box 85319, Riyadh 11691
Tel: 4766700
Telex: 405039 BOEMEL Sj
Telefax: 4590226

Chairman: F A Shrontz
Directors: R R Albrecht, D P Beighle, B D Pinick
Senior Executives: Theodore H Bell (President), Stephen K
 Creighton (VP Business Management), Glenn E Lamb (VP
 Industrial Relations), J Edwards Parazinski (VP Aerospace &
 Electronics), Dwight Ayling (VP Commercial Airplanes)

PRINCIPAL ACTIVITIES: Operations and maintenance support
 and training services connected with aircraft; development of
 defense systems; computer services and training; engineering
 design and management
Parent Company: The Boeing Company
Principal Bankers: Saudi American Bank, Riyadh

Principal Shareholders: The Boeing Company
Date of Establishment: March 22, 1983
No of Employees: 200

BONDSTRAND LTD

PO Box 589, Dammam 31421
Tel: 8579836
Telex: 802958 CCPDAM SJ
Telefax: 8570364

Chairman: HRH Prince Khaled Bin Abdullah Bin Abdul Rahman
Directors: Dr Abdulaziz S Al Jarbou (President)
Senior Executives: Theodore F Bevec (General Manager), Isam
 Makansi (Product Manager), Fawzi M Ghanem (Finance
 Manager)

PRINCIPAL ACTIVITIES: Manufacture and marketing of
 reinforced thermosetting resin pipes and fittings;
 prefabricated reinforced thermosetting resin spools
Principal Bankers: Al Bank Al Saudi Al Fransi
Financial Information:

	1990
	SR'000
Authorised capital	20,000
Paid-up capital	20,000

Principal Shareholders: Saudi Arabian Amiantit Co Ltd, Saudi
 Arabia; Ameron Inc, USA
Date of Establishment: 1982
No of Employees: 96

BOUGARY TRADING & CONTRACTING EST

PO Box 1733, Jeddah 21441
Tel: 6821049, 6820802
Cable: LOEI JEDDAH
Telex: 601217 Logi Sj, 602610 Rizk Sj

Chairman: Abdul Razzak S Bougary
Senior Executives: Faisal M S Yamani, Nabil S Hallal

PRINCIPAL ACTIVITIES: Supply of construction machinery,
 earthmoving equipment, generating sets, plant hire
Principal Agencies: JCB; Fiori; Obim; Lambordini, Mikasa
Branch Offices: Riyadh; Makkah
Principal Bankers: Saudi Cairo Bank, National Commercial
 Bank, Riyad Bank

Date of Establishment: 1970
No of Employees: 100

BRC ALFADL (SAUDIA) LTD

PO Box 5489, Jeddah 21422
Tel: 6364724, 6379507, 6375285, 6374589
Cable: Brenforce Jeddah
Telex: 601888 Brc Sj
Telefax: 6375474

Directors: J Hall, R N C Hall, Sheikh Abdul Kader M Alfadl,
 Sheikh Abdul Aziz M Alfadl, Sheikh Mohammed Alfadl, Pavlos
 G Doukanaris
Senior Executives: P G Doukanaris (Managing Director), Nasser
 M Burji (Product Manager), Assaad Mawad (Product
 Manager), Shahid Mirza (Financial Controller)

PRINCIPAL ACTIVITIES: Manufacture, sales and distribution of
 welded wire mesh for use in reinforced concrete structures
 and roads, galvanised and PVC coated chainlink and
 weldmesh, barbed wire and ancillary wire and fencing
 products, rebars, blockmesh
Principal Agencies: Hall AG, Switzerland
Branch Offices: Sales Offices: Riyadh, Tel 4653698, Fax
 4630880; AlKhobar, Tel 8649972, Fax (03) 8649972
Principal Bankers: Saudi British Bank; Riyad Bank
Financial Information:

	1990
	SR'000
Sales turnover	68,000
Profits	1,200
Authorised capital	8,000
Paid-up capital	8,000

Principal Shareholders: Hall AG, Switzerland; Sheikh A K Alfadl
 and Sheikh A A Alfadl
Date of Establishment: 1974
No of Employees: 90

B.R.G.M.
Bureau de Recherches Geologiques et Minieres

PO Box 1492, Jeddah 21431
Tel: 6651104, 6604883
Telex: 601674 BRGM SJ
Telefax: 6651859

Senior Executives: J Caia (Managing Director), G Ozoux
 (Finance & Admin Director),

PRINCIPAL ACTIVITIES: Engineering consultants, geological
 and mining engineering

BRITISH AEROSPACE (MILITARY AIRCRAFT) LTD

PO Box 1732, Riyadh 11441
Tel: 4646600
Telex: 406935 BAE HQ SJ
Telefax: 4630738

Directors: D McClen (Chief Executive Saudi Arabia), D H Moss,
 F A Rutter, J A Allman, D A Griffiths, R L Reid
Senior Executives: J Arnold (Manager Riyadh Branch), P H
 Champniss (Manager Dhahran Branch), P J Hirst (Manager
 Tabuk Branch), R Blackburn (Manager Taif Branch), A J
 Stagg (Manager Khamis Mushayt Branch)

PRINCIPAL ACTIVITIES: Military aircraft, military training
Branch Offices: PO Box 3843, Riyadh 11481, Tel 4766566 Ext
 4350; PO Box 98, Dhahran Airport 31932, Tel 8917674; PO
 Box 2, Tabuk, Tel 4225064, PO Box 174, Taif Tel 7460166;
 PO Box 34, Khamis Mushayt, Tel 2233310
Parent Company: British Aerospace (Military Aircraft) Ltd,
 Warton Aerodrome, Preston, Lancashire PR4 1AX
Principal Bankers: Saudi British Bank

BROTHERS COMMERCIAL CO

PO Box 5604, Jeddah 21432
Tel: 6606802, 6606917
Telex: 605020 SJ
Telefax: 6606925

PRINCIPAL ACTIVITIES: Amusement park management,
 aviation services
Branch Offices: Dhahran, Dammam, Riyadh, Yanbu, Jubail
Principal Bankers: National Commercial Bank

BROWN & ROOT SAUDI LTD CO

PO Box 52926, Riyadh 11573
Tel: 4768700
Telex: 406204 BRSLTD SJ

Chairman: HRH Khalid Bin Fahad Bin Abdul Aziz
Directors: Dr Fahad Somait, Abdurrahman A Al Khamis, D K
  Dodson, S F Harris
Senior Executives: Dr Fahad Somait, Abdurrahman A Al Khamis
  (Managing Director)

PRINCIPAL ACTIVITIES: Engineering, construction, construction
  management
Parent Company: Brown & Root Inc
Principal Bankers: Saudi American Bank; National Commercial
  Bank

Principal Shareholders: Albilad Est For Trading & Contracting
  (51%); Brown & Root Inc (49%)
Date of Establishment: 1976
No of Employees: 200

BROWN BOVERI SAUDI ARABIA LTD

PO Box 4441, Riyadh 11491
Tel: 4762644
Cable: BROWNBOVER RIYADH
Telex: 401471 BBC SAR Sj
Telefax: 4767252

Chairman: Dr P Felix
Directors: Sheikh Ghassan Shaker, M D Ansar, Dr B Hess, P
  Klink

PRINCIPAL ACTIVITIES: Engineering and erection of turnkey
  power plants and supply of electrical components and
  systems
Branch Offices: PO Box 8900, Jeddah, Tel 6653151, Telex
  602889; PO Box 290, AlKhobar, Tel 8643058, Telex 871239
Parent Company: ABB Asea Brown Boveri Ltd, Switzerland
Principal Bankers: Saudi American Bank; Albank Alsaudi
  Alhollandi
Financial Information:

	SR'000
Authorised capital	4,000
Paid-up capital	4,000

Principal Shareholders: ABB Asea Brown Boveri, Sheikh Khalid
  Balghumaim, Sheikh Ghassan Shaker
Date of Establishment: 1979
No of Employees: 75

BTI OVERSEAS

PO Box 15357, Riyadh 11444
Tel: 4778577, 4777633
Telex: 402746 BTIAL SJ
Telefax: 4762808

PRINCIPAL ACTIVITIES: Telecommunications, computers and
  datacommunications

BUGSHAN, A S, & BROS (KOMATSU DIVISION)

PO Box 3329, Jeddah 21471
Tel: 6874793, 6875253, 6896028, 6870141
Cable: Komatsu Jeddah
Telex: 601336 Bugkom Sj
Telefax: 6804284 (Jeddah), 8575475 (Dammam), 4768530
  (Riyadh)

Senior Executives: S Mohammad Iqbal (Sales Manager Jeddah),
  Moe Fattah (Sales Manager Dammam)

PRINCIPAL ACTIVITIES: Distribution of earth-moving
  machinery, generators and forklift trucks
Principal Agencies: Komatsu
Branch Offices: Riyadh (PO Box 3586, Tel 4774004, 4768530,
  4760105, Telex 402337) and Dammam (PO Box 2277, Tel
  8946871, 8946186, 8948895, Telex 871389)

BUTLER INTERNATIONAL COMPANY

PO Box 8648, Jeddah 21492
Tel: 6370036 (8 lines), 6372423
Telex: 603449 SBSMFG SJ
Telefax: 6373152

Chairman: Robert West
Directors: Bill Chapman
Senior Executives: Moufid A Alossi (General Manager - Jeddah),
  Jawad Y Hallaq (Manufacturing Manager), Samir V Acra
  (Engineering Manager), Hassan Bahsoun (Marketing
  Manager), Desmond Hudson (Finance Manager), Hassan
  Bahsoun (District Manager - Jeddah), Nabil Azmeh (District
  Manager -Riyadh), Kheirallah Karam (District Manager -
  Dammam)

PRINCIPAL ACTIVITIES: Pre-engineered steel buildings (design,
  fabrication, supply and erection of pre-engineered steel
  buildings)
Branch Offices: PO Box 4980, Jeddah 21412, Tel 6370036 (8
  lines), Telex 602261 Sabsys Sj; PO Box 8823, Riyadh 11492,
  Tel 4647695, 4659212, Telex 403258 Sabsys Sj; PO Box
  4992, Dammam 31412, Tel 8275306, 8275324, Telex 870418
  Sabsys Sj
Parent Company: Butler Manufacturing Company, USA
Subsidiary Companies: Saudi Building Systems

No of Employees: 3,809

CABLE & WIRELESS SAUDI ARABIA LTD

PO Box 6196, Riyadh 11442
Tel: 4657092
Telex: 401691 CBLWIR SJ
Telefax: 4656426

Senior Executives: M J F Hayes (General Manager), T Graham
  (Engineering Manager), B Littlefair (Marketing Manager), M
  Gliddon (Manager Jeddah)

PRINCIPAL ACTIVITIES: Provision of datacommunication
  services and equipment, consultancy, facilities management,
  O & M contracts
Principal Agencies: Dynatech, Case/Dowty, Syntellect, Coherent
Branch Offices: Jeddah: PO Box 15056, Jeddah 21444, Tel
  6672967, Telex 606814 CABWIR SJ; Alkhobar: PO Box 1618,
  Alkhobar 31952, Tel 8983504, Telex 870825 CAWDAM SJ
Parent Company: Cable & Wireless Plc, Mercury House,
  Theobalds Road, London WC1, UK
Principal Bankers: Saudi British Bank

CALTEX (OVERSEAS) LIMITED SA

PO Box 8939, Jeddah 21492
Tel: 6823638, 6826293
Cable: CALTEX JEDDAH
Telex: 605440 CLTX SJ

Senior Executives: J P Taimni (Manager)

PRINCIPAL ACTIVITIES: Management services
Parent Company: Caltex Overseas Limited, Dallas, USA
Principal Bankers: Saudi American Bank

Principal Shareholders: Caltex Petroleum Corporation
Date of Establishment: July 1, 1982

CAMERON IRON WORKS

PO Box 304, Alkhobar 31952
Tel: 8646927, 8954468
Telex: 870029 FADCO SJ

PRINCIPAL ACTIVITIES: Oilfield equipment: tools, wellheads,
  valves
Subsidiary Companies: Cameron Iron Works, USA

CANAR TRADING ESTABLISHMENT

PO Box 2319, Alkhobar 31952
Tel: 8642568
Cable: CANAR
Telex: 870729 Camar Sj

Chairman: Saud Mohammed Al Gosaibi
Directors: Khalid Mohammed Al Gosaibi

PRINCIPAL ACTIVITIES: Sales and service of all office
equipment, calculators, cash registers, photocopiers,
computers, microfilm equipment, word processors, etc
Principal Agencies: C Itoh, Japan; Omron, Japan; Nashua, USA;
Qume, USA; Datagraphix, USA; Terminal Data, USA; Micron,
USA; New Burry Data, UK; Exxon Office Systems, USA
Branch Offices: Jeddah: PO Box 1723, Tel 6534003; Riyadh: PO
Box 9115, Tel 4054288
Principal Bankers: Saudi American Bank; Al Bank Al Saudi Al
Hollandi; National Commercial Bank

Principal Shareholders: Saud M Al Gosaibi
Date of Establishment: 1975
No of Employees: 200

CANSULT LIMITED

PO Box 324, Riyadh 11411
Tel: 4778700
Telex: 401327 CANRIY SJ
Telefax: 4779471

Senior Executives: Hesham M Sabra (General Manager)

PRINCIPAL ACTIVITIES: Design and supervision of construction
of housing developments, highways, bridges, sewerage
systems, hospitals, airports and water distribution systems,
electrical and mechanical engineering, etc
Branch Offices: PO Box 365, Medina, Tel 8232874; PO Box
7289, Dammam, Tel 8100783, 8323955; PO Box 8209,
Jeddah, Tel 6433181
Parent Company: Cansult Group Ltd, 30 Centurian Drive, Suite
206, Markham, Ontario, Canada (Head Office)
Principal Bankers: Saudi American Bank, Riyadh; National
Commercial Bank, Riyadh; Riyad Bank, Medina

Date of Establishment: 1961
No of Employees: 75 in Saudi Arabia

CARLSON AL-SAUDIA LTD

PO Box 6422, Riyadh 11442
Tel: 4657004, 4656972
Telex: 400968 Carlsn SJ

President: Frank A Pesa (Managing Director)
Directors: John I Carlson Jr, Robert Carlson, Bishr Haffar
Senior Executives: Atef B Souki (Vice President/Controller)

PRINCIPAL ACTIVITIES: Building and general construction
Branch Offices: Jeddah
Principal Bankers: National Commercial Bank; Bank Al-Jazira;
BCCI London
Financial Information:

	SR'000
Turnover approx	350,000
Authorised capital	5,000
Paid-up capital	5,000

Principal Shareholders: Carlson Group Ltd, Bermuda; HRH
Prince Abdul Aziz Bin Fahd Al-Faisal; Bishr Lutfi Al-Haffar;
Mohammad Daweesh; Said Ayas
Date of Establishment: 1976
No of Employees: 1,500

CARLTON AL MOAIBED HOTEL

PO Box 1235, Alkhobar 31952
Tel: 8575455, 8575214, 8575429
Cable: Carlton Alkhobar
Telex: 870064 CARLTN SJ
Telefax: 8575443

Directors: Sheikh Abdel Rahman Al Moaibed, Georges Frem
Senior Executives: Tony Ghosn (General Manager), Simon
Toubia (Sales & Marketing Executive)

PRINCIPAL ACTIVITIES: Hotel business
Principal Agencies: Best Western Worldwide Hotels; Golden
Tulip Worldwide Hotels; Supereps International
Parent Company: P A M, Beirut, Lebanon
Subsidiary Companies: Indevco Group of Companies
Principal Bankers: Al-Bank Al-Saudi Al-Faransi, Dammam
Financial Information:

	1990
	SR'000
Sales turnover	24,000
Authorised capital	30,000
Paid-up capital	30,000
Total assets	120,000

Principal Shareholders: Sheikh Abdul Rahman Al Moaibed,
George Frem
Date of Establishment: 1977
No of Employees: 200

CARRIER SAUDI SERVICE CO

PO Box 9784, Riyadh 11423
Tel: 4911333
Cable: Bared
Telex: 402596 Aacriy Sj

Directors: George Burk, Sheikh Kamal Adham, Sheikh Ghassan
Shaker, Philip Castelino, Wolf Laitner
Senior Executives: George Burk (Managing Director)

PRINCIPAL ACTIVITIES: Service, start up and commissioning,
maintenance of all types of airconditioning and electro-
mechanical equipment
Principal Agencies: A subsidiary of Carrier International Corp,
Syracuse, NY, USA
Branch Offices: Jeddah: PO Box 11728, Tel 6826453; Telex
603078 Aacjed Sj; Dammam: PO Box 690, Dhahran Airport,
Tel 8579320, Telex 801667 Swiarb Sj
Associated Companies: Carrier Arabian Air Conditioning
Company Ltd
Principal Bankers: Al Bank Al Saudi Al Fransi, Riyadh, Jeddah,
Al Khobar
Financial Information:

	SR'000
Authorised capital	3,000
Paid-up capital	3,000

Principal Shareholders: Carrier Service Company of USA (51%),
Sheikh Kamal Adham (45%), Sheikh Ghassan Shaker (4%)
Date of Establishment: September 1978
No of Employees: 210

CEMENTATION SAUDI ARABIA LTD

PO Box 3935, Riyadh 11481
Tel: 4784888, 4785851
Cable: Ghassan Shaker
Telex: 401561 Cemsau Sj

Chairman: Ghassan Shaker
Directors: C L E Edwards, Farouk Jabr

PRINCIPAL ACTIVITIES: Building and civil engineering,
contracting, specialist contracting, fabrication and erection
structural steelwork
Branch Offices: UK (London); Saudi Arabia (PO Box 4004,
Dammam)
Principal Bankers: Arab National Bank Limited
Financial Information:

	SR'000
Authorised capital	13,600
Paid-up capital	13,600

Principal Shareholders: Ghassan Shaker, Trollope Colls
Cementation Subsidiaries Limited, UK
Date of Establishment: November 1975
No of Employees: 270

CHBIB TRADING ESTABLISHMENT

PO Box 242, Dammam 31411
Tel: 8561962, 8561971, 8561950, 8560877
Cable: CHBIB DAMMAM
Telex: 801132 chbib Sj, 897020 CTEIND

Chairman: Marwan Chbib
Senior Executives: Abdul Latif Salem (General Manager), Khalid
Javaid (Senior Executive), Hamdy Fayed (Senior Executive),
Khalid Aziz (Senior Executive)

PRINCIPAL ACTIVITIES: Pre-cast concrete housing, fibreglass
manufacture, steel fabrication; pre-fab mini steel buildings,
prefab wooden portable bldgs, dry wall steel studs and
tracks, wooden doors and frames, wood work, general
construction and contracting
Principal Agencies: Plad Equipment, Canada; Inryco Inland
Steel, USA; Drake America, USA, Archidorme Steel Hangers,
Canada
Subsidiary Companies: Saudi Prefab Houses; Quick Concrete
Buildings; United Ships & Marine Service; United Electrical &
Refrigeration; Fiberglass Products Factory; Steel Fabrics;
United Catering & Motels; Saudi Products & Marketing Centre
Principal Bankers: Saudi American Bank, Dammam; Albank
Alhollandi AlSaudi, Dammam
Financial Information:

	SR'000
Authorised capital	100,000
Paid-up capital	50,000

Principal Shareholders: (Proprietor) Prince Bandar Bin
Mohammed Bin Abdul Rahman
Date of Establishment: 25/01/1388 Hijri
No of Employees: 300

CHEM TEC INDUSTRY & CONTRACTING

PO Box 4376, Jeddah 21491
Tel: 6711156, 6711283, 6714962
Telex: 601812 Kemtec Sj

PRINCIPAL ACTIVITIES: Building and civil engineering
contractors

Date of Establishment: 1976
No of Employees: 500

CHEMACO TRADING & CONTRACTING LTD

PO Box 10730, Riyadh 11443
Tel: (01) 4066060
Cable: Hisham
Telex: 402603 Chemco
Telefax: 4026807

Chairman: Ibrahim A Alissa
Directors: Abdulrahman A A Alissa (President & Managing
Director)
Senior Executives: Bashir Nawfal (General Manager), Samir
Haddad (Vice President)

PRINCIPAL ACTIVITIES: Specialist in joint sealing, roofing,
water proofing, reservoir lining, coating, concrete injection
Principal Agencies: Huls Troisdorf, W Germany; Hertel,
Netherland
Branch Offices: Jeddah 21431: PO Box 1270, Tel 6442467;
Alkhobar 31952: PO Box 1559, Tel 8578260, 8578512, Telex
802711 Alissa Sj
Parent Company: Alissa Trading & Contracting Co Ltd
Principal Bankers: Albank Alsaudi Alhollandi, Riyadh; Riyad
Bank, Riyadh

Financial Information:

	1990 SR'000
Sales turnover	40,000
Authorised capital	2,500
Paid-up capital	2,500
Total assets	3,500

Principal Shareholders: Ibrahim A Alissa, Abdulrahman A A
Alissa
Date of Establishment: July 1981
No of Employees: 165

CHIYODA PETROSTAR LTD

PO Box 6188, Jeddah 21442
Tel: 6470558, 6470646, 6476241, 6476424
Cable: Motasim
Telex: 602398 Chiyoj Sj
Telefax: 6471908

Chairman: Sheikh Ahmed Abbas Zainy
Directors: Osama A Zainy (Vice Chairman), Masataka
Shimoyama (President & Chief Executive Officer), Adnan A
Zainy (Director), Kazutoshi Sunohara (Director)

PRINCIPAL ACTIVITIES: Engineering, procurement and
construction of petroleum refinery and petrochemical plant,
electric power generation and desalination plant, maintenance
of mechanical plant and utilities
Branch Offices: PO Box 393, Riyadh 11411, Tel 4032700, Fax
4031721, Telex 401128 Motsim Sj; PO Box 602, Dhahran
Airport 31932, Tel 8558182, Fax 8553502, Telex 895015
Cpldia SJ
Principal Bankers: National Commercial Bank; Riyad Bank;
Saudi American Bank; Al Bank Al Saudi Al Fransi; Saudi
Investment Banking Corporation
Financial Information:

	1990 SR'000
Authorised capital	7,000
Paid-up capital	7,000

Principal Shareholders: Chiyoda Corporation, Japan; Petrostar
Company Ltd, Saudi Arabia
Date of Establishment: 1975
No of Employees: 47

COLLINS SYSTEMS INTERNATIONAL INC

PO Box 2375, Riyadh 11451
Tel: 4655549
Telex: 401276 RCKWELL SJ
Telefax: 4656563

Senior Executives: Tariq Aziz (General Manager)

PRINCIPAL ACTIVITIES: Supply, installation, maintenance of
telecommunications equipment in the military and defence
areas
Parent Company: Rockwell International, USA
Principal Bankers: Saudi American Bank, Riyadh

Date of Establishment: 1981

COMMERCIAL BUSINESS EST (CBE)

PO Box 2262, Jeddah 21451
Tel: 6604753, 6604750, 6653388
Cable: Shipjamal Jeddah
Telex: 601238 Jamal Sj

PRINCIPAL ACTIVITIES: Transport contractors, shipping,
packing, clearing, warehousing; dealing in agricultural
equipment, motor engines, generators etc
Branch Offices: PO Box 2803, Riyadh, Tel 45765012; PO Box
336, Dammam, Tel 8323885; Jubail; Yanbu; Taif; and London;
Houston

Principal Shareholders: Abdul Salam M Tayeb & Sons
Date of Establishment: 1962
No of Employees: 200

CONAM SERVICES SA LTD

PO Box 283, Jeddah 21411
Tel: 6828077, 6828284, 6828429, 6828574, 6828634, 6828735
Telex: 600072 CONAM SJ

PRINCIPAL ACTIVITIES: Technical consultants, O&M specialists
for water treatment, desalination and power plants, also
suppliers of chemicals, stainless steel, cutting tools, and
bitumen additives for roads, also operation of a laboratory
analysing service for water, sewerage, oil and soil samples,
flow meters, electrical motors and control gear, turbo
chargers, industrial/domestic/urban lighting, gas turbines
Principal Agencies: Pfizer; Schott; Champion Chem; Garrett;
Alenco; Sandvik; Diaprosim; Laurence Scott; Sparling;
Kenograro Smythe-Morris; Gulf Lighting
Branch Offices: Yanbu & Jubail
Parent Company: Olayan Financing Company - AlKhobar
Principal Bankers: Saudi-American Bank

Principal Shareholders: OFC; SK Sulieman S Olayan
Date of Establishment: 1976
No of Employees: 650

CONCRETE COMPANY LLP, THE

PO Box 5703, Jeddah 21432
Tel: 6820465, 6820305
Telex: 603023 Conelm Sj
Telefax: 6831973

Chairman: Sh Saleh Abdullah Kamel
Directors: Sh Abdul Aziz Abdullah Kamel (Vice President)
Senior Executives: Eng Yousef Nasif (General Manager), Eng
Talal Y Ashgan (Operations Manager)

PRINCIPAL ACTIVITIES: Manufacture and erectors of precast
and prestressed concrete and GRC products
Parent Company: Dallah Group
Principal Bankers: Saudi Cairo Bank, Jeddah
Financial Information:

	SR'000
Authorised capital	60,000
Paid-up capital	60,000

Principal Shareholders: Sheikh Saleh Abdullah Kamel
Date of Establishment: 1st January 1977
No of Employees: 200

CONSOLIDATED CONTRACTORS CO WLL
C.C.C. WLL

PO Box 234, Riyadh 11411
Tel: (01) 4650311
Cable: CONCO RIYADH
Telex: 401096 Conco Sj
Telefax: (01) 4645963

Chairman: HRH Prince Talal Ibn Abdul Aziz Al-Saud
Directors: Mohamad Z Seoudi (General Manager)
Senior Executives: Mustafa S Adawiyah (Asst General
Manager), Mohd Hussein Awaidah (Head of Accounts &
Administration), Omar A Abdelqader (Business Development
Representative)

PRINCIPAL ACTIVITIES: General construction and engineering
contractors: heavy civil, buildings, roads, bridges, industrial
plants, heavy mechanical, pipelines, and marine works
Branch Offices: AlKhobar; Jeddah; Medinah; Jubail
Parent Company: Consolidated Contractors Group, PO Box
61092, Amaroussion, Athens, Telex 219551, 219734, 219735
GR, Tel 6829200, Fax 6841561
Associated Companies: Consolidated Contractors Int'l Co;
National Petroleum Construction Co; Consolidated
Contractors Co SAL; CCC Oman; CCC Jordan; CCC Kuwait;

CCC Bahrain; CCC Yemen Arab Rep; CCC Egypt; CCC UAE;
CCC Morocco
Principal Bankers: Arab National Bank; Saudi American Bank
Financial Information:

	1989
	SR'000
Sales turnover	150,000

Principal Shareholders: Prince Talal Ibn Abdul Aziz Al-Saud;
Prince Waleed Ibn Talal Ibn Abdul Aziz. Full Management:
Consolidated Contractors Int'l Co Ltd (CCC)
Date of Establishment: 1965
No of Employees: 1,350

CONSTRUCTION & INDUSTRIAL
ENTERPRISES CO LTD

PO Box 1723, Riyadh 11441
Tel: 4022655, 4025552
Telex: 401281 Khoja Sj

Chairman: Abdul Maqsoud Muhammed Saeed Khoja

PRINCIPAL ACTIVITIES: Import of agricultural, electrical and
industrial machinery and equipment power, building, and civil
engineering contractors, sewage and water networks,
production of prestressed concrete slabs
Branch Offices: Jeddah, PO Box 97, Tel 6421900, Telex 600203

CONTRACTING & TRADING CO (CAT)

PO Box 338, Alkhobar 31952
Tel: 8641455, 8951120, 8984297
Cable: Catcompany
Telex: 870080 Cat Sj
Telefax: 8950427

Directors: Shukri H Shammas (Managing Partner), Mrs L Emile
Bustani (Partner), Mrs N Abdullah Khoury (Partner)
Senior Executives: K Noubani (Chief Executive Pipeline &
Mechanical), Z Shammas (Chief Executive Civil Engineering),
E Salem (Area Manager), M Matar (Project Manager), S
Ghattas (Resident Engineer)

PRINCIPAL ACTIVITIES: Civil engineering and building
contractors, pipelines, mechanical and electrical contractors
Branch Offices: PO Box 2994, Riyadh 11461, Tel 4793205,
4788909, Fax 4766607, Telex 401218; PO Box 1629, Jeddah
21441, Tel 6672080, 6672092, Fax 6691039; also branches in
Abu Dhabi, Sharjah, Oman, Kuwait
Parent Company: Contracting and Trading Co (CAT), PO Box
11-1036, Beirut, Lebanon
Subsidiary Companies: Mothercat Saudi Arabia WLL
Principal Bankers: Saudi British Bank; Al Bank Al Saudi Al
Fransi; Riyad Bank
Financial Information:

	SR'000
Authorised capital	10,000
Paid-up capital	10,000

Date of Establishment: June 1944
No of Employees: 2,000

CONTRACTOR CO LTD

PO Box 6372, Riyadh 11442
Tel: 4762149
Telex: 401505 Select Sj

Chairman: HRH Prince Saud Bin Naif Bin Abdul Aziz
Directors: Eng A M Abdel Moety (Vice President)

PRINCIPAL ACTIVITIES: General engineering, architectural,
mechanical and electrical contracting, power stations, sewage
and water networks
Branch Offices: Dammam
Principal Bankers: National Commercial Bank

Principal Shareholders: Prince Saud Ibn Naif Ibn Abdul Aziz;
Prince Abdul Aziz Ibn Salman Ibn Abdul Aziz; Ali Hamad Al

Mihdar, Muhammad Salahuddin Hussein Oman; Ahmad
Muhammad Mahmoud Ahmad
Date of Establishment: 1979
No of Employees: 50

CONTREX GROUP OF COMPANIES

PO Box 75, Jeddah 21411
Tel: 6659870, 6655234
Cable: Licontrex
Telex: 600077 Contrx Sj

Chairman: Sheikh Talal Khalid Idriss
Directors: Zaki A Beydoun, Richard C Alpha, Steven Beharrell,
Hans Gerlach

PRINCIPAL ACTIVITIES: Electrical and general contracting, soil
and foundation engineering and contracting, trading in
building materials hospital construction and management,
import of foodstuffs, steel materials, electrical and mechanical
equipment and transport
Principal Agencies: General Electric: Lowara; Pirelli; Monarch
Industries; T & R Generators; LST Manufacturing Co;
Legrand; Square D; Lithonia Lighting
Branch Offices: Branches in Jeddah, Riyadh, Dammam, Jubail,
Yanbu, Beirut, London, Chicago, Nigeria
Subsidiary Companies: Contrex Int, Jeddah; Consolidated
Engineering Co Ltd, London; MIDCO Jeddah; Idriss Trading &
Contracting Co, Jeddah; Contrex Research & Development
Co, Channel Islands; Contrex Transport, Jeddah; Electric
House, Jeddah; Contrex Trading, Jeddah; Saudi Hospitals Co,
Jeddah; Contrex Research & Development Co, London; Al
Amane Co, Beirut; Hospital & Supply International, Illinois;
Saudi Hospital Management Co, Jeddah; United Transport
Co, Jeddah; National Steel Trading Est, Jeddah; Electrical &
Mechanical Works Est
Principal Bankers: Saudi American Bank, Jeddah; National
Commercial Bank; Jeddah; Societe Bancaire Barclays,
Geneva; Saudi International Bank, London; BCCI, London

Principal Shareholders: Dr Khalid M Idriss, Sheikh Talal Khalid
Idriss

COOPERS & LYBRAND

C/o Fauzi F Saba CPA, PO Box 2672, Riyadh 11461
Tel: 4779532
Cable: COLYBRAND
Telex: 871486 C&L SJ
Telefax: 4779532

Chairman: Dr Fauzi F Saba
Senior Executives: A R Hepbrun (Resident Partner Al-Khobar),
S Y Sindaha (Resident Partner Jeddah), G A Karaman
(Resident Partner Riyadh)

PRINCIPAL ACTIVITIES: Auditors, accountants and tax advisors
Branch Offices: PO Box 6511, Jeddah 21452, Tel 6655343,
Telex 871486; PO Box 1131, Alkhobar 31952, Tel 8574041,
8570595, Telex 871486
Affiliated Companies: Coopers & Lybrand Deloitte, UK; Coopers
& Lybrand, USA

No of Employees: 30

COSTAIN INTERNATIONAL LTD

PO Box 6967, Jeddah 21452
Tel: 6722460
Telex: 602558 Nesma SJ
Telefax: 6713410

Chairman: A J D Franklin
Directors: J W H Lawson, P F Woods
Senior Executives: J V Hockin (General Manager Saudi Arabia)

PRINCIPAL ACTIVITIES: General contractors, building, civil
engineering, process petrochemical, dredging, mining and
geotechnical investigation

Branch Offices: Saudi Arabia (Riyadh); United Arab Emirates;
Oman; Bahrain; Nigeria; Australia; USA; Hong Kong
Parent Company: Costain Group, UK
Principal Bankers: Saudi American Bank, Jeddah; Lloyds Bank
PLC, London

Principal Shareholders: Costain Group Plc
No of Employees: 100

CRESCENT TRANSPORTATION CO LTD

PO Box 1232, Alkhobar 31952
Tel: 8339566, 8345915
Cable: Crescent
Telex: 802208 Crest Sj

Senior Executives: Israr Siddiqui (Chief Accountant)

PRINCIPAL ACTIVITIES: Transportation of containers and
general haulage work; terminal operations kingdomwide
Principal Agencies: Sea-Land Services Inc, CTI (Gelco),
Merzario
Branch Offices: PO Box 996, Riyadh, Tel 2312715, 2312181,
Telex 404533 CTCRIY SJ; PO Box 6670, Jeddah, Tel
6835442, 6830025, 6827353, Telex 604819 CRESNT SJ; PO
Box 216, Jubail, Tel 3415145, 3418845 Telex 632104
CTCJUB SJ; Yanbu, Tel 3225948, 3227464, Telex 661221
CTCYAN
Associated Companies: Rezayat Trading Company Ltd
Principal Bankers: Al Bank Al Saudi Al Fransi

Principal Shareholders: Rezayat Trading Co; National
Contracting Co
Date of Establishment: 1976
No of Employees: 300

DALLAH GROUP

PO Box 1438, Riyadh 11431
Tel: 4544455
Cable: Dallah Riyadh
Telex: 401036 Dallah Sj

President: Sheikh Saleh A Kamel
Directors: Sheikh Omer Abdallah Kamel (Vice President
Planning & Organisation)
Senior Executives: Ibrahim Mohamed Ali Mattar (Dir General Al
Baraka Al Saudia for Export Promotion), Ali Mohamed Ali
Hindi (Dir General Saudi Arabian Trading & Logistics Co), Eng
Gamal Hasan Hafifi (Dir General Industrial Sector), Khalid
Mohamed Al Nahdi (Dir General Real Estate Development
Sector), Ahmed Ghulam Haidar (Finance Director), Khalil
Ahmed Osman (Marketing Director), George T Berasley
(Technical Director), Farouk Ahmed Rashed Muhtasib
(Personnel Director), Ziada Abdallah Ziada (Secretary Board
of Advisors)

PRINCIPAL ACTIVITIES: Trading and manufacturers'
representation, contracting, servicing and maintenance;
import of electro-medical and radiological instruments and
equipment, drainage systems equipment and machinery,
furniture and heavy machinery
Principal Agencies: Trane, Kongsberg, Plessey, Bosch
Branch Offices: Saudi Arabia, PO Box 2618, Jeddah, Tel
6710000, Telex 600080 Dallah; and branches in Mecca,
Medina, Taif, Tabuk, Khamis Mushait, Shururah, Al Khobar
Subsidiary Companies: Dallah Est; Dallah Avco Trans Arabia Co
Ltd; Saudi Precast & Prefab Housing Co Ltd (SAPRECO);
Concrete Works Co; Dallah Industries Co Ltd; Arab Media Co
(ARAMED); Saudi Air Conditioning Co; Dallah Lilmabani;
Dallah Agriculture; Dallah Industries Co Ltd; Dallah Transport;
Food Service Group Co; Amertec; Al Baraka Al Saudia For
Export Promotion; Saidu Arabian Trading & Logistics Co; etc
Principal Bankers: Saudi American Bank; Saudi Cairo Bank;
National Commercial Bank; Al Bank Al Saudi Al Fransi

Financial Information:

	1990 SR'000
Sales turnover	426,000
Profits	53,000
Authorised capital	910,000
Paid-up capital	910,000
Total assets	1,942,000

Date of Establishment: 1969
No of Employees: 12,000

DALLAH-AVCO TRANS-ARABIA CO LTD

PO Box 430, Jeddah 21411
Tel: 6692628
Telex: 601482 AVCO SJ

Senior Executives: Dr A F Nazer (Director General Jeddah)

PRINCIPAL ACTIVITIES: Communications, heavy equipment and parts; full communications maintenance and installation, heavy equipment rental and log support
Branch Offices: PO Box 2304, Riyadh 11451, Tel 4544455, Telex 401036 DALLAH SJ
Subsidiary Companies: AVCO Corporation, USA

DANIEL INTERNATIONAL (SAUDI ARABIA) LTD

PO Box 8120, Jeddah 21482
Tel: 6532550, 6533554
Telex: 600188 DISA SJ
Telefax: 6519076

Chairman: Reda Nazer
President: Steven M MacLeod

PRINCIPAL ACTIVITIES: Project management; construction management; design management; architecture and engineering; maintenance and training
Parent Company: Daniel International Corporation, USA

Principal Shareholders: Reda Nazer; Daniel International
Date of Establishment: 1976
No of Employees: 210

DANISH SAUDI DAIRY CO LTD

PO Box 5043, Jeddah 21422
Tel: 6361440
Cable: Lawabin Jeddah
Telex: 601538 Albano SJ
Telefax: 6368727

Chairman: HE Shaikh Hamad Sabah Al Ahmed Al Sabah
Directors: Shaikh Hamdan A A Al Nassar (Deputy Chairman), Faisal Hamad Al Ayyar (Managing Director), Shaikh Abdulla A Ba-Quabas (Board Member), Faek Al Mutair (Board Member)
Senior Executives: Dr Abdul Aziz Hamdi (Deputy Managing Director), Ahmed Marzouki (General Manager Administration & Finance), Ben Ruscoe (General Manager Manufacturing), Bill Pace (General Manager Commercial)

PRINCIPAL ACTIVITIES: Dairy products and ice cream manufacturing and distribution (milk, cheese, yoghurt, juices, ice cream, tomato paste manufacturing and distribution)
Branch Offices: Riyadh; Makkah Al Mukarramah; Taif; Jizan; Khamis Mushait; Gassim; Abha; Al Baha; Najran; Dammam
Principal Bankers: National Commercial Bank, Saudi British Bank
Financial Information:

	1990 SR'000
Sales turnover	374,000
Authorised capital	60,600
Paid-up capital	60,600

Principal Shareholders: Saudi owned (22%); Kuwaiti owned (78%)
Date of Establishment: 1977
No of Employees: 1030

DAR AL AJYAAL PRINTING LTD
Dar Al Ajyaal for Printing Publishing & Distribution Ltd

PO Box 5750, Riyadh 11432
Tel: 6424333
Telex: 601023 Dehlawi Sj

PRINCIPAL ACTIVITIES: Printing, import and distribution of printing machinery and equipment

Principal Shareholders: Prince Faisal Ibn Fahed Ibn Abdul Aziz; Dr Abdul Aziz Al Fadda; Abdullah Ibn Ulaitha Al Harbi; Dr Abdullah Nafe Al Share; Dr Ahmad Muhammad Al Dubaib; Sheikh Mousa Abdullah Ismael

DAR AL RIYADH

PO Box 5364, Riyadh 11422
Tel: 4641611
Cable: Darconsult
Telex: 401405 Darcon Sj
Telefax: 4648853

President: Prince Turki Bin Abdullah Bin Abdulrahman
Directors: Dr Ayed Al Osaimi, Ahmad N Al Shalali (Director of Administration)
Senior Executives: Jesus J Flor (Director of Supervision & Chief Engineer)

PRINCIPAL ACTIVITIES: Consulting engineering, town planning and building, roads, airports, housing
Branch Offices: Jeddah, Dammam; and UK
Principal Bankers: National Commercial Bank

Date of Establishment: 1975

DAR ENGINEERING WORKS & CONTRACTING INTERNATIONAL CO LTD

PO Box 3648, Riyadh 11481
Tel: 4761144, 4785977
Cable: Darecol
Telex: 401424 Dar
Telefax: 4769068

Chairman: Sh Abdul Hameed Ghandourah
Directors: Yousef A As'ad, Sh Abdul Aziz Ghandourah
Senior Executives: Omar Issa (Financial Manager), M Zahid Anwar (Computer Dept Manager), Faisal S Nimer (Secretarial Manager)

PRINCIPAL ACTIVITIES: Building contractors specialising in computer buildings and highly technical specialised buildings
Branch Offices: Location in Riyadh: Farazdak Street, Malaz
Subsidiary Companies: Dar Aluminium Products Ltd (DALPCO), Dar Form Products Co (DFP); Dar Travel Agency, Dar Carpentry Plant
Principal Bankers: Arab National Bank Ltd, Riyadh
Financial Information:

	1989/90 SR'000
Sales turnover	5,621
Profits	1,685
Authorised capital	2,000
Paid-up capital	2,000
Total assets	16,239

Principal Shareholders: Sh Abdul Hameed Ghandourah, Yousef A As'ad
Date of Establishment: 1973
No of Employees: 250

DARWISH A DARWISH AGGREGATES

PO Box 427, Dammam 31411
Tel: 8325204, 8323352
Telex: 870039 Abtrac Sj

PRINCIPAL ACTIVITIES: Production of aggregates

Principal Shareholders: Yusuf Al Gosaibi; Yeoman International; Darwish A Darwish (DADCO) (PO Box 454, Dammam)

DE MAURO SHUWAYER CONSTRUCTION CO LTD

PO Box 5115, Dammam 31422
Tel: 8261654, 8250869
Cable: DeMauro-Shuwyaer
Telex: 801510 DSCO SJ

Chairman: Abdullah Al-Hamoud Al-Shuwayer
Directors: Michael DeMauro (Vice Chairman), Ernesto N Gnilo (General Manager)
Senior Executives: David N DeMauro (Deputy General Manager), Ahmed H Al-Shuwayer (Manager for Gov't & Business Dev'pt Affairs)

PRINCIPAL ACTIVITIES: General, building and civil engineering contractors; plant hire, supply of construction equiment and machinery
Principal Bankers: Saudi British Bank, Saudi American Bank

Date of Establishment: October 1977
No of Employees: 2,500

DELTA GROUP LIMITED

PO Box 11232, Jeddah 21453
Tel: 6440141, 6444046, 6445677, 6447254
Cable: Linjasco
Telex: 601516 Amal Sj
Telefax: 6444046

Chairman: Osman Abdullah Linjawi
Directors: Osman Abdullah Linjawi, Karim Osman Linjawi, Sultan Osman Linjawi

PRINCIPAL ACTIVITIES: Sponsorship and business support for Saudi based foreign companies, development of local assembly/manufacturing facilities, contracting, sales and services divisions, real estate divisions, auto design, painting and mechanical work
Principal Agencies: Hepworth Plastics, UK
Branch Offices: Location in Jeddah: Linjawi Bldg; also Riyadh: PO Box 61315, Tel 4646266, 4646822, Telex 403555 FLUIDS SJ
Associated Companies: Industrial Services Co; Unit Construction Co Ltd
Principal Bankers: Saudi British Bank

Principal Shareholders: Directors described above
Date of Establishment: January 1st, 1983
No of Employees: 550

DEVELOPMENT INT'L TRADE CO LTD

Development International Trade Co Ltd (DITCO)

PO Box 9057, Jeddah 21413
Tel: 6607000
Cable: Raad Jeddah
Telex: 601112 Ditco Sj

Chairman: Sheikh Raad El Khereiji
Vice Chairman: Sheikh Faisal El Khereiji
Senior Executives: John Philopoulos (General Manager)

PRINCIPAL ACTIVITIES: Civil contractors, buildings, housing, roads and bridges, steel fabrication, manufacturers, precast concrete, red bricks, mining and quarrying
Principal Agencies: Imeg; Imetal; Airtrust; BFI Arabia
Branch Offices: Riyadh; Yanbu

Associated Companies: ICG Ltd; Crown House Int; Bovay/Burns McDonnel; Saudi Pacific; AGA PVC Factory; Westinghouse; Archirodon
Principal Bankers: Saudi American Bank; Saudi Cairo Bank
Financial Information:

	1990
	SR'000
Sales turnover	185,000
Profits	10-15%
Authorised capital	29,000
Paid-up capital	29,000

Principal Shareholders: Sheikh Youssef Abdullah El Khereiji and Sons
Date of Establishment: 1968
No of Employees: 2,350

DHAHRAN INTERNATIONAL HOTEL

PO Box 428, Dhahran Airport 31932
Tel: 8918555
Telex: 801272 DIAH SJ
Telefax: 8918559

PRINCIPAL ACTIVITIES: Hotel business

DHAHRAN PALACE HOTEL RAMADA

PO Box 381, Dhahran Airport 31932
Tel: 8915444
Cable: Ramada, Dhahran
Telex: 801227 Ramada SJ
Telefax: 966-3 8915333

Chairman: Sheikh Said Ali Ghodran (owner)
Senior Executives: Mohammed Ismail Ibrahim (Personnel Manager), Mohamed Haladeen Lye (Chief Accountant)

PRINCIPAL ACTIVITIES: Hotel business
Branch Offices: Beljurashi Resort Hotel, Taif, Saudi Arabia
Parent Company: Said Ali Ghodran Trading Est
Associated Companies: Oilfields Supplies & Services, Ghodran Food Factory, Pan Arab Travel Agency, National Est for Agriculture & Industrial Sulphur, Ghodran Crusher Plant
Principal Bankers: Saudi Cairo Bank, Alkhobar; Riyad Bank, Dammam; National Commercial Bank, Dammam

Principal Shareholders: H E Said Ali Ghodran (Sole Owner)
Date of Establishment: June 1978
No of Employees: 83

DIHAN TRADING & CONTRACTING CO

PO Box 914, Al Khobar 31952
Tel: 8945069, 8947864
Telex: 871218 Diham Sj

Chairman: Qassim Dihan Al-Ameery
Directors: Ahmed Qassim Al-Ameery (Vice Chairman)
Senior Executives: Dihan Qassim Dihan (President), R D Secrist (General Manager), R J Capone (Business Development Manager)

PRINCIPAL ACTIVITIES: Transportation, fluid sealing, packing, roofing, trading, contracting, construction
Principal Agencies: A H I Roofing System
Branch Offices: Shedgum; Khafji; Jubail
Principal Bankers: Saudi British Bank, AlKhobar; Saudi American Bank, AlKhobar

Date of Establishment: 1972
No of Employees: 237

DONGKUK CONSTRUCTION CO LTD

PO Box 43109, Riyadh 11561
Tel: 4787023, 4787024
Telex: 400674 DKCONR Sj

Directors: Chough Byung Se (Head of Middle-East Division), Kim Thomas Man (Director of Technical Department)

PRINCIPAL ACTIVITIES: Building construction, civil works, plant construction, plant engineering, electrical and mechanical works, special construction works including dredging, dams, harbour and waterways, sewage and water supply system, oil tank farm

Branch Offices: PO Box 3321, Jeddah, Tel 6822179, Telex 603346 DKCONJ SJ

Parent Company: Dongkuk Steel Mill, CPO Box 4316, Seoul, Korea

Principal Bankers: National Commercial Bank; Riyad Bank

Financial Information:

	SR'000
Authorised capital	51,000
Paid-up capital	25,500

Principal Shareholders: Central Investment & Finance Co, Dongkuk Steel Mill

Date of Establishment: 1977

No of Employees: 1,000

DOSSARY, ABDULLA RASHID, & PARTNER CO

PO Box 139, Alkhobar 31952

Tel: 8645913, 8647459

Cable: Abdulla Dossary

Telex: 870129 ARD SJ

Senior Executives: H E Albinali (General Manager)

PRINCIPAL ACTIVITIES: Building contractors, electrical works, water and sewerage systems, road construction

No of Employees: 200

DOW CHEMICAL MID-EAST/AFRICA SA

PO Box 1049, Jeddah 21431

Tel: 6674818, 6673871

Cable: Jufalicent

Telex: 600991 DOCHEM SJ

Telefax: 6609028

Senior Executives: Dr Souhail El-Farouki (General Manager), Hilal Kabbani (Regional Manager), A Al Rawi (Senior Sales Jeddah)

PRINCIPAL ACTIVITIES: Manufacturing, marketing and distribution of chemical products

Branch Offices: Dammam: PO Box 24, Dammam 31411, Tel 8271652, Fax 8273623, Telex 801720 JUCHEM SJ; Riyadh: PO Box 86, Riyadh 11411, Tel 4655272, Fax 4655274, Telex 405028 ARCHEM SJ

Associated Companies: Dow Chemical Company, USA

DRILLING EQUIPMENT & CHEMICAL CO

PO Box 132, Dammam 31411

Tel: (966-3) 8325113, 8325115

Cable: Drecco

Telex: 801063 Drecco Sj

Telefax: (966-3) 8323619

Directors: Saleh Alfadl (General Manager), Suleiman Olayan

Senior Executives: Husam A Qanadilo (Manager)

PRINCIPAL ACTIVITIES: Oilfield equipment and materials, stocking and supplies

Principal Agencies: Adachi Paste Co, Japan; Atlas Powder Co, USA; Alsthom-Savoisienne, France; Belleli R, Italy; Bingham-Willamette Co, USA; Bowen Div, USA; Carbonisation et Charbons Actifs, France and Holland; Chicago Bridge, USA and UK; Compagnie des Ciments Belges, Belgium; Caproco Corrosion Prevention, Canada; David Brown Gear Industries, UK; Drilling Specialities Co, USA; Drilco, USA; Farbwerke Hoechst AG, West Germany; Grant Oil Tool Co, USA; Gray Tool Int, USA and UK; Goulds Pumps Inc, USA; Halliburton Services, USA; Hughes Tools Co, USA and UK; Hycalog Inc, USA; Hydril Co, USA; IMCO Services, USA; Importubi, SRL, Italy; Kawasaki Steel Corp, Japan; Le Grand, Canada; Magna Corp, USA; N Galperti & Figlio, Italy; Nakagawa corrosion

Protecting Co, Japan; National Supply Co (Armco), USA; Plicoflex, Inc, USA; SAPAG, France; SICES, Italy; Terry Steam Turbine Co, USA; Walworth Aloyco & Grove Int, Italy and UK; WABCO-Fluid Power Div, USA

Principal Bankers: Al Bank Al Saudi Al Fransi

Date of Establishment: 1958

DYNARABIA COMPANY LTD

PO Box 1491, Dammam 31431

Tel: 8331881, 8342593

Telex: 803062 Dyncom SJ

Directors: D E Shumate (President)

PRINCIPAL ACTIVITIES: Facilities operations and maintenance of telecommunications systems, industrial and vocational training, graphics, video production to include commercials for broadcast

Branch Offices: PO Box 40372, Riyadh, Tel 4915776, 4915736, Telex 405510 Dynrab SJ

Principal Bankers: National Commercial Bank, Dammam and Riyadh

Financial Information:

	SR'000
Paid-up capital	20,000

E A JUFFALI & BROS

See JUFFALI, E A, & BROS

EAST & WEST EXPRESS

PO Box 718, Dammam 31421

Tel: 8335588 (7 lines)

Cable: Atco Dammam

Telex: 801067 Turki Sj

Telefax: 8339881

Chairman: Sheikh Abdul Rahman Al Turki

Senior Executives: Ousama E Jureidini (Regional Manager), Fuad Tannous (Corporate Controller), Ikram Qureshi (Area Manager Riyadh), Salim Najjar (Area Manager Jeddah), Bassam Al Khatib (Customs Clearance Manager), Abdul Raouf A Latif (Marketing Manager), Kamal Y Sidawi (Area Manager Jubail), A A Baig (Operations Manager), Said Al Omeri (Personnel Manager)

PRINCIPAL ACTIVITIES: Packing specialists and internal removal contractors, air and sea freight, forwarding agents, storage, customs, clearing and general transportation

Branch Offices: Branch at Jeddah (PO Box 1298), Riyadh (PO Box 8077), Yanbu (PO Box 263) and Jubail (PO Box 686)

Parent Company: A A Turki Corporation

Subsidiary Companies: East & West Express Travel

Principal Bankers: Al Bank Al Saudi Al Hollandi

Principal Shareholders: Wholly owned by Sheikh Abdul Rahman Al Turki

Date of Establishment: 1964

No of Employees: 500

EASTERN CORPORATION

PO Box 792, Riyadh 11421

Tel: 4010051, 4032570

Cable: Etcorpe Riyadh

Telex: 404257 EASTRA SJ

Chairman: Mohamed Al Dughaither Al Hassan

Directors: Mohamed A Alfraih (Managing Director)

Senior Executives: Mohamed Ali Ibrahim (General Manager)

PRINCIPAL ACTIVITIES: Civil engineering contracting, trading, agencies (electrical, electronic and power equipment and appliances household and hospital linens and uniforms); travel agency

Principal Agencies: Hawker Siddeley Electric Export, UK; Crow Hamilton, UK; Cremar Marbles, Italy; Fielding and Platt, UK; Boomer Industries, UK

Branch Offices: Dammam: PO Box 375, Telex 801565; Jeddah; PO Box 1800, Telex 601080
Subsidiary Companies: General Building Co, PO Box 792, Riyadh, Tel 4023473, Telex 401089
Principal Bankers: Riyad Bank, Riyadh; Saudi Cairo Bank, Riyadh; National Commercial Bank, Riyadh; Saudi International Bank, London
Financial Information:

	SR'000
Sales turnover	115,000
Authorised capital	2,000
Paid-up capital	2,000

Principal Shareholders: Sheikh Mohamed Al-Dughaither Al Hassan; Sheikh Mohamed Alfraih
Date of Establishment: 1965
No of Employees: 420

EASTERN PETROCHEMICAL COMPANY (SHARQ)

PO Box 10035, Jubail Industrial City 31961
Tel: 3575000
Telex: 832037, 832064 Shafco
Telefax: (03) 3580383

Chairman: HE Mubarak Al Khafra
Directors: Ahmed Al Nekhilan (President), Nasser Al Sayari, Abdullah Al Humaidan, Kazuo Kume, Shigeki Itagaki, Hobuhiko Ozaki, Mustafa Al Sahan, Eiji Murata
Senior Executives: Nobuatsu Sanada (Executive Vice President)

PRINCIPAL ACTIVITIES: Manufacture of petrochemicals (Mono Ethylene Glycol, Tri Ethylene Ghycol, Linear Low Density Polyethylene)
Principal Bankers: Al Bank Al Saudi Al Fransi, Saudi American Bank
Financial Information:

	1990 SR'000
Authorised capital	1,140,000
Paid-up capital	1,140,000
Total assets	3,924,218

Principal Shareholders: Saudi Basic Industries Corporation (SABIC) and SPDC
Date of Establishment: 1981
No of Employees: 498

EBRAHIM BIN JASSIM AL JASSIM

See AL JASSIM, EBRAHIM BIN JASSIM,

EBRAHIM MOHAMMAD ALMANA & BROTHERS CO

See ALMANA, EBRAHIM MOHAMMAD, & BROTHERS CO

ECOLOGY & ENVIRONMENT CO OF SAUDI ARABIA LTD (EESAL)

PO Box 3793, Jeddah 21481
Tel: 6473121, 6473318
Telex: 602043 Starnv SJ

Senior Executives: R J King (Project Manager Al-Sanayiah), Khaled Zainy (General Manager Jeddah)

PRINCIPAL ACTIVITIES: Geotechnical research; ecological and environmental science
Branch Offices: Km 19, Yanbu Al Sanayiah, Tel 3211921, Telex 630310 Yicuts Sj
Subsidiary Companies: Ecology & Environment Inc, USA

ECONOMIC DEVELOPMENT ENTERPRISES

PO Box 82, Jeddah 21411
Tel: 6610865, 6675280
Cable: Amal Jeddah
Telex: 603112 Tede SJ
Telefax: 6603488

Chairman: Abdul Kader M Alfadl
Directors: Elias S Mazzawi (Managing Director)
Senior Executives: Abdul Aziz M Alfadl

PRINCIPAL ACTIVITIES: Agents, importers, distributors for government suppliers and contractors, broadcast and telecommunication equipment, electronic and electrical equipment, office equipment, cranes, generators, facsimile machines - tape recorders (professional and military), towers masts and aerials, CCTV, mechanical optical and electronic surveying and drawing instruments
Branch Offices: Riyadh (PO Box 764, Tel 4761603, 4761633) and Dammam
Parent Company: Al Fadl Group
Subsidiary Companies: Electronic Maintenance Services Ltd
Principal Bankers: Riyad Bank, Jeddah
Financial Information:

	23/3/91 SR'000
Sales turnover	3,000
Profits	400
Authorised capital	1,500
Paid-up capital	1,500

Date of Establishment: 1962
No of Employees: 35

EL-AJOU, ABDUL GHANI, CORPORATION

PO Box 78, Riyadh 11411
Tel: 4041717, 4056555
Cable: El-Ajou Trade
Telex: 401088 Elajou Sj, 400931/2 Elajou Sj, 401903 Al Hadi Sj
Telefax: 4041717, ext 158, 4066966 (direct line)

Chairman: Abdul Ghani El-Ajou
Directors: Marwan El-Ajou (Vice President & General Manager, Medical), Maher El-Ajou (Vice President & General Manager, Commercial & Marketing)
Senior Executives: Ahmed El Khayat (Area Manager Central Province), Sami Ghazal (Financial Consultant), Mohamed Rifa'at (Administration Manager), Mohamed El Zein (Area Manager Western Province), Salah Abu Al Adel (Deputy General Manager Medical), Dr Maher Idilbi (Western Province Area Manager Medical), Dr Ashraf Sobhi (Eastern Province Area Manager Medical), Dr Redouane Hamza (General Manager Ardico)

PRINCIPAL ACTIVITIES: Office machines, photographic equipment, scientific equipment, educational aids, computers, microfilming, stationery, medical supplies and office equipment
Principal Agencies: Canon; Triumph - Adler; Bieffe; Roth & Weber; Elite; Polaroid; Eiki; VGC; Bolex; Cinema Products; Fotomec, Kardex; Bell & Howell; Pitney Bowes; DelaRue; Hedman; Coulter; Otsuka; Heraeus; Stryker; Trophy; USA Air Shields (Healthdyne); Milton Roy; Orion; Imed; Kavo; Ticomed; Shirah: Merck; Ortho; Nikon; Assut; Cordis; CD Medical; Organon; Richards
Branch Offices: Riyadh Tel 01-4633635; Buraidah Tel 06-3235136; Haeil Tel 06-5330595; Jeddah Tel 02-6517240: Telex 600306 El-Jeel SJ; Makkah Tel 02-5452614; Yanbu Tel 04-3225434; Tabouk 04-4233509; Khamis Mishait Tel 07-2220200; Madina Tel 04-8269663; Al Khobar 03-8944744, Telex 870281 Ghani SJ; Dammam Tel 03-8347653; Jubail Tel 03-3610840; Hofuf Tel 03-5871660; Dhahran Tel 03-8792251; also in Syria; Jordan; Lebanon; Kuwait; Egypt; UK
Parent Company: El Ajou Group of Companies
Subsidiaries Companies: El-Ajou Trading Agencies, El-Ajou Trading Est, Al-Hady Saudi Est, Al-Jeel Medical & Trading Co Ltd, National Glass & Mirrors Factory, Arab Digital Computer Co Ltd, Shirah Trading Est
Principal Bankers: Saudi French Bank; Saudi Cairo Bank; Arab National Bank; Saudi American Bank

Financial Information:

	SR'000
Sales turnover	300,000
Authorised capital	12,000
Paid-up capital	12,000

Principal Shareholders: Sole Proprietorship
Date of Establishment: 1956
No of Employees: 510

EL AJOU, SAID, TRADING CORPORATION

PO Box 435, Jeddah 21411
Tel: 6471911, 6475412
Cable: Ajouco
Telex: 601694 S Ajou Sj

Chairman: Said Ahmad El Ajou (Owner)

PRINCIPAL ACTIVITIES: General trading, dealing in electrical
and electronic equipment, also import and distribution of
window glass and glass sheets
Principal Agencies: Celotex, USA; JVC, Japan; Graetz, Germany
Branch Offices: Alkhobar: PO Box 1589, Tel 8641237, 8641384;
Riyadh; PO Box 2213, Tel 4039853, 4014585; Dammam;
Yanbu; Makkah
Subsidiary Companies: Glass & Mirror Factories, Jeddah;
Modern Trading Agencies, Jeddah; Saudi Arabian Trading &
Resources, Jeddah; Nibal Trading Corp, Riyadh
Principal Bankers: Saudi Cairo Bank; Arab National Bank; Riyad
Bank; Saudi American Bank

Date of Establishment: 1975

EL AYOUTY, ISSA, & CO (IAC)

PO Box 489, Riyadh 11411
Tel: 4761696
Cable: Ayoutcom
Telex: 401964 Ayouty SJ
Telefax: 4766559

Chairman: Issa El-Ayouty
Partners: Sayed El-Ayouty, Salah El-Ayouty

PRINCIPAL ACTIVITIES: Auditors, accountants, financial
consultants and tax advisors
Branch Offices: Egypt, Cairo 17 Kasr El Nile St, (Head Office);
Saudi Arabia, Jeddah: PO Box 780, Tel 02-6693478, Fax
6602432, Telex 600032; Al-Khobar: Telex 870790, PO Box
200, Tel 03-8646361, 8642671, Fax 03-8943963; Makkah; Al-
Hasa; Khamis Mushait; Al Madeina Al Munawarah; Kuwait;
Dubai
Principal Bankers: National Commercial Bank; Bank Al Jazirah

Date of Establishment: 1938
No of Employees: 300

EL BADR TRADING & CONTRACTING

PO Box 9099, Jeddah 21413
Tel: 6433358
Telex: 600926 ISD SJ
Telefax: 6433120

Directors: Mazen Sabbah (General Manager), Abdul Rahman
Knio (Director)
Senior Executives: Khanjar Issa Musa (Sales Manager),
Shehzad A Qayyum (Purchasing Manager), Sayed A H
Hammoudah (Financial Manager)

PRINCIPAL ACTIVITIES: Stockist of pipes, fittings, valves,
controls, stainless steel and aluminium
Principal Agencies: Crane, UK; Hitachi, Japan; Sumitomo,
Japan; Benkan, Japan; Rubatex, USA; Nibco, USA; Honeywell
Braukmann, Germany; Jako, Austria
Principal Bankers: Al Bank Al Saudi Al Fransi, Jeddah; National
Commercial Bank, Jeddah

Financial Information:

	1990 SR'000
Sales turnover	25,000
Authorised capital	5,000
Paid-up capital	5,000
Total assets	8,000

Principal Shareholders: Single ownership
Date of Establishment: 1977

ELECTRICAL & ELECTRONIC CONTRACTING CO

Head Office, PO Box 4602, Jeddah 21412
Tel: 6690221
Cable: MOHANDISZAIDAN
Telex: 602044 Eecc Sj
Telefax: 6690225

Chairman: Sheikh Ahmed Mohammed Zaidan
Directors: Eng Mohammed Ahmed Zaidan (General Manager)
Senior Executives: Hisham Ahmed Attar (Deputy General
Manager), Muhsen Alshafi (Finance Manager), Eng Khalil
Alsalhi (Sales Manager), Emad Mohamed Fodah (Purchasing
& Marketing Manager), Eng Osman Alethy (Technical
Manager), Hadi Almoula (Personnel Manager)

PRINCIPAL ACTIVITIES: Electrical and electronic contracting,
telecommunications, import and supply of computers,
teleprinters, fascimile equipment, telex and electronic
equipment, office automation, communication security
systems
Principal Agencies: Italcable, Italy; Datotek, USA; Shinwa,
Japan; AEL, UK; Olivetti, Italy; BISCOM, USA; Stentofon,
Norway; Hills, Australia; IREM, Italy; Panasonic Office
Automation, Japan; Muirhead, UK; Ven-Tel, USA
Branch Offices: PO Box 7143, Riyadh 11462, Tel 4770406, Fax
4776866, Telex 403219 EECCRD SJ; PO Box 3005, Alkhobar
31471, Tel 8649534, Fax 8640553
Subsidiary Companies: EECC International, 178-202 Great
Portland Street, London W1N 5TB, UK, Tel 01-323 2731/6,
Telex: 894393 IDEAUK G
Principal Bankers: Al-Jazirah Bank, National Commercial Bank,
Saudi Cairo Bank, Jeddah; Barclays Bank Int'l, Bahrain; Royal
Bank of Canada, Bahrain
Financial Information:

	SR'000
Authorised capital	10,000
Paid-up capital	10,000

Principal Shareholders: Sheikh Ahmad Mohammad Zaidan;
Sheikh Mohammad Ahmad Zaidan
Date of Establishment: 1978
No of Employees: 140

ELECTRICAL WORK & MAINTENANCE

PO Box 3511, Riyadh 11481
Tel: 4761713, 4760372
Cable: Shabakgi
Telex: 401314 Ewm Sj
Telefax: 4776930

Chairman: Sheikh Ali Hussein Shobokshi
Directors: Sheikh Fahd Hussein Shobokshi (Managing Director)
Senior Executives: Asaad H Bakdash (Contracts Manager),
Walid Droubi (Marketing Manager), K Subramanian
(Commercial Manager)

PRINCIPAL ACTIVITIES: Electrical and mechanical installations,
maintenance contractors in power generation, transmission,
distribution telecommunication, water and sewerage, street
lighting and traffic control
Principal Agencies: Klein, Schanzlin & Becker AG, W Germany;
Moterenfabrik Hatz KG, W Germany; Klaus Dieterich
Shaltanlagenbau, W Germany; Auto Diesels Braby, UK;
Varisco Pompe, Italy

Branch Offices: PO Box 7240, Jeddah; PO Box 1058, Alkhobar; PO Box 4907, Medinah; PO Box 1569, Buraidah
Principal Bankers: Riyad Bank, National Commercial Bank, Saudi British Bank
Financial Information:

	1988/89 SR'000	1989/90 SR'000
Sales turnover	30,542	36,717
Profits	610	1,051
Authorised capital	15,000	3,000
Paid-up capital	15,000	3,000
Total assets	139,359	17,379

Principal Shareholders: Owner: Sheikh Ali Hussein Shobokshi
Date of Establishment: 1971
No of Employees: 146

ELECTRO-MECHANICAL CONSTRUCTION CO

PO Box 8997, Riyadh 11492
Tel: 4761000, 4785467
Cable: Conservice Riyadh
Telex: 400364 Elemco Sj

Chairman: Prince Khaled Bin Turki Al Sudairy
Senior Executives: Nadim Abou Samra (General Manager)

PRINCIPAL ACTIVITIES: Electrical and mechanical contracting
Branch Offices: Beirut; London
Associated Companies: Sister company: Saudi Catering & Contracting Co
Principal Bankers: Al Bank Al Saudi Al Fransi

Principal Shareholders: Prince Khaled Bin Turki Al Sudairy
Date of Establishment: 1969
No of Employees: 300

ELECTRONIC EQUIPMENT MARKETING CO

PO Box 3750, Riyadh 11481
Tel: 4771650, 4783662
Cable: Martel Riyadh
Telex: 401120 Zuhair Sj
Telefax: 4785140

Chairman: Harb Saleh Al-Zuhair (Owner)
Directors: Talal Harb Al Zuhair (Vice Chairman), Ghazi Ahmed Rashid Al Khayyat (Denior Vice President Finance), Abdullah Ibrahim Al Zuhair (Authorized Manager), Abdel Ghani Khatib (General Manager)
Senior Executives: Tarek Stouhy (Asst General Manager), Tariq M Raja (Manager Instrumentation Division), Dr Loui Ali Hassan Fakhri (Manager ISD)

PRINCIPAL ACTIVITIES: Marketing, supply, installation, maintenance, repairing and calibration of radio, satellite, microwave and security communications, test equipment and electro-mechanical works
Principal Agencies: Harris/RF Communications Group; Harris/Farinon; Mobile Telesystems Inc MII; TCC; Magnavox; Loral Terracom; Watkins Johnson; Canadian Marconi Co CMC; Hekimian Lab; Wiltron & Wavetek; Marconi Instruments; Lloyds Instruments; Carl Schenck; Thrane & Thrane; Thorn EMI; Bird Narda
Principal Bankers: Riyad Bank; Saudi French Bank; Saudi Cairo Bank; Societe Bancaire Arabe
Financial Information:

	1989 SR'000	1990 SR'000
Sales turnover	53,304	55,143
Profits	4,462	4,928
Authorised capital	4,000	4,000
Paid-up capital	4,000	4,000
Total assets	29,370	29,284

Principal Shareholders: Harb Saleh Al Zuhair; Talal Harb Al Zuhair
Date of Establishment: 1967
No of Employees: 81

EL KHEREIJI CORPORATION

PO Box 3971, Riyadh 11481
Tel: 4780925, 4784201
Cable: Khereiji
Telex: 401747 Kherji Sj
Telefax: 4772774

Chairman: Abdullah Abdulaziz Alkhereiji (Proprietor)
Directors: Ali Abdulaziz Elkhereiji (General Manager)
Senior Executives: Ahmed Safadi (Asst General Manager), Fahd Al Elkhereiji (Asst General Manager), Khalil Sarraf (Marketing Manager)

PRINCIPAL ACTIVITIES: General trading and contracting, real estate, supply of electrical and electronic equipment, household goods, insurance agents, commerce; airport services, maintenance, canned food supplies, motor oil, representation, laundry, hotel and catering, printing
Branch Offices: Jeddah, Dhahran, Medina, Qassim, Al Baha
Subsidiary/Associated Companies: El Khereiji Hotel; Nada Laundry; Lana Printing Press; Lana Furniture & Decoration Est
Principal Bankers: Riyad Bank; Arab National Bank; National Commercial Bank

Principal Shareholders: Sole proprietorship
Date of Establishment: 1970
No of Employees: 3,000

EL KHEREIJI TRADING & ELECTRONICS

PO Box 25, Dammam 31411
Tel: 8322985, 8322555
Cable: ELKHEREIJI DAMMAM
Telex: 801022 A/B KHREJI SJ

Chairman: Sheikh Abdulkarim Bin Abdulaziz El Khereiji
Senior Executives: Taysir Zeitoun (General Manager)

PRINCIPAL ACTIVITIES: General trading and contracting, insurance agents, real estate, electrical engineering, foodstuffs, data communications networks
Principal Agencies: General Electric, Hotpoint, Recal-Milgo, Leeds & Northrup, Kent Control Valves, Exide Electronics and Int'l Data Sciences
Branch Offices: Jeddah, Tel 6518197; Riyadh, Tel 4785518
Associated Companies: El Khereiji Corporation, El Khereiji Cold Stores, El Khereiji Machinery Division
Principal Bankers: Arab National Bank; National Commercial Bank, Saudi American Bank

Principal Shareholders: Sole ownership
Date of Establishment: 1962
No of Employees: 115

EL REDWAN TRADING & CONSTRUCTION CORP

Al Redwan General Co

PO Box 4061, Jeddah 21491
Tel: 6602070, 6692830, 6600505, 6602166
Cable: Rotacons
Telex: 601679 Redwan Sj

Chairman: Sheikh Abdullah Bakr Redwan
Directors: Eng Mokhtar Abdel Haleem Mamoun, Sameh Ibrahim El Sheikh, Nabil Ahmed Fahmee, Eng Mohammed Wageh Al Darwish, A Fattah Redwan, Kenneth Johnson

PRINCIPAL ACTIVITIES: Building and infrastructure construction; landscaping, trading, medical supply
Principal Agencies: Agra Ind Ltd, Becton Dickinson & Co, USA; Sherwood Medical, UK, USA; Johnson & Johnson, UK, USA
Branch Offices: Riyadh; Mecca; Abha; Al Baha
Associated Companies: El Bougary Trading & Contracting Est Jeddah; Agra Industries Ltd, Canada
Principal Bankers: Riyad Bank; National Commercial Bank; Al Bank Al Saudi Al Fransi

Principal Shareholders: Abdalla Bakr Redwan; Abdel Razag
   Saleh El Bougary
No of Employees: 678

EL SEIF DEVELOPMENT

PO Box 15665, Riyadh 11454
Tel: 4545996, 4546033
Cable: Elseif Co
Telex: 401872 Seifdv Sj
Telefax: 4540863

President: Mohamed Ben Musaed El Seif
Directors: Ali Otaki (Vice President)

PRINCIPAL ACTIVITIES: Operation & maintenance of hospitals;
   supply of medical equipment and consumables; turnkey
   projects, hospital equipping
Principal Agencies: General Electric Medical Systems, USA;
   Beckman Instruments, USA; Becton Dickinson, USA;
   Geometric Data, USA; Ortho Diagnostics, USA; Kendall, USA;
   etc
Branch Offices: Jeddah: PO Box 11284, Jeddah 21453, Tel
   6830978, 6833770, Telex 604164, Telefax 6821058; Dammam:
   PO Box 3775, Dammam 31481, Tel 8270970, Telex 802902,
   Telefax 8271720
Associated Companies: Arabian Medicare Co Ltd; Saudi
   Medicare Co Ltd; El Seif Engineering & Contracting; Saudi
   Lab Instruments
Principal Bankers: Saudi British Bank, Riyadh; Saudi American
   Bank, Riyadh

Date of Establishment: 1951
No of Employees: 200

EL SEIF, MUSAED, & SONS CO LTD

PO Box 2774, Riyadh 11461
Tel: 4542759, 4542763, 4549191
Cable: Alseifco
Telex: 401146 Elseif Sj
Telefax: 4540863

Chairman: Sheikh Musaed Ben Seif El Seif
Directors: Khaled Ben Musaed El Seif, Sami Ben Musaed El
   Seif, Mohammed Ben Musaed El Seif
Senior Executives: Fahed A Musharef (Vice-President),
   Abdulaziz Al Khamis (Vice-President), Wissam Shakkur (Vice-
   President), Ali Otaki (Vice-President), Roger Halvorson (Vice-
   President), Dawood Taylor (Vice-President)

PRINCIPAL ACTIVITIES: Holding company dealing in operation
   & maintenance, engineering, contracting & construction,
   consulting, sales & service of medical laboratory equipment,
   diagnostic imaging equipment, industrial & bio-research
   equipment, operation and management of hospitals, sales of
   pharmaceutical products, medical supplies & disposables,
   laboratory instruments & electro-mechanical supplies sales,
   transportation
Principal Agencies: General Electric; Beckman Instruments;
   Becton Dickinson; Ortho Diagnostics; Kendall
Branch Offices: Saudi Arabia: Tabuk, Turaif, Jeddah, Dammam,
   Khamis Mushayt, Taif; also in Beirut, Abu Dhabi and London
Subsidiary/Associated Companies: Intertransport Co Ltd; Elseif
   Engineering & Contracting Est; Elseif Est for Industry; Al Bilad
   Consultants; El Seif Development Est; Saudi Medicare Co Ltd;
   Arabian Medicare Co Ltd; Saudi Lab Est
Principal Bankers: National Commercial Bank; Saudi British
   Bank

Principal Shareholders: Sheikh Musaed Ben Seif El Seif, Khaled
   Ben Musaed El Seif, Sami Ben Musaed El Seif, Mohammed
   Ben Musaed El Seif
Date of Establishment: 1975
No of Employees: 3,420

ENDECO

PO Box 1097, Jeddah 21431
Tel: (02) 6659292, (02) 6659792
Cable: ENDECO, Jeddah
Telex: 602116 Endeco SJ
Telefax: (02) 6603515

Chairman: Shafic Ibrahim Hamza
Directors: Ibrahim Shafic Hamza
Senior Executives: Issam Adel Maher (Technical Director), Atif
   Souki (Finance Director), Adel Al Andari (Marketing Director),
   Fadi Milhim Al Awar (Production Director), Sayed Kamal
   Yakub (Purchasing Director)

PRINCIPAL ACTIVITIES: General contractors, construction of
   civil and architectural works incl site preparation, public
   utilities, roads, industrial buildings, residential and commercial
   buildings, earthworks, asphalt works, rock excavation,
   bridges, sewage system, dams, stomwater drainage,
   agriculture and irrigation, landscaping etc
Branch Offices: PO Box 8603, Riyadh, Tel (01) 4779049, (01)
   4764440; Telex 401596 ENDECO SJ, Fax (01) 4784996
Subsidiary Companies: Endeco Agriculture & Irrigation (The
   Landscaping Co), PO Box 8603, Riyadh 11492, Tel (01)
   4779049; Telex 405762; and Endeco Agricultural Projects
   (same address Riyadh)
Principal Bankers: National Commercial Bank, Jeddah; Saudi
   Cairo Bank, Jeddah
Financial Information:

	SR'000
Authorised capital	5,000
Paid-up capital	5,000

Principal Shareholders: Sheikh Shafic I Hamza, Sheikh Ibrahim
   S Hamza
Date of Establishment: 1969
No of Employees: 1,910

ESCAT
Engineering Services Contracting & Trading

PO Box 388, Alkhobar 31952
Tel: 8642619, 8645159
Cable: Escat
Telex: 871400 Escat Sj

Directors: Hamad I Al Saneh

PRINCIPAL ACTIVITIES: General construction contracting;
   specialised in industrial and residential buildings, reinforced
   concrete on preengineered, prefabricated structures; general
   utilities; irrigation and landscaping
Branch Offices: Riyadh, Jubail, Al Kharj
Principal Bankers: Al Bank Al Saudi Al Fransi
Financial Information:

	SR'000
Authorised capital	4,000
Working capital	10,000

Principal Shareholders: Saleh I Al Saneh & Bros, Escat, Beirut
   (Lebanon)
Date of Establishment: 1960
No of Employees: 290

EST FOR TECHNICAL ENTERPRISES & CONTRACTING (ETEC)

PO Box 5996, Riyadh 11432
Tel: 4039751,4043510
Cable: Etec
Telex: 401729 Etec Sj

Chairman: Prince Sultan Bin Mohamed Bin Saud Al Kabir (also
   Proprietor)
Senior Executives: Mohammed Alsultan (General Manager)

PRINCIPAL ACTIVITIES: Trading and contracting in electro-
   mechanical products, air-conditioning, steel construction;
   general agency

Parent Company: Al Nikhla Est, Riyadh
Principal Bankers: Arab National Bank; Saudi French Bank

Principal Shareholders: Prince Sultan Bin Mohammad Bin Saud Al Kabir
Date of Establishment: 1976
No of Employees: 120

EURABIA ENGINEERING & CONSTRUCTION CO

PO Box 431, Dhahran Airport 31932
Tel: 8980927, 8984560
Telex: 872086 Eurab SJ
Telefax: 8955027

Chairman: Khalid Abdul Hadi Taher
Directors: Tarek Taher, John F Franklin, Barry I Drinkel, David H Baty
Senior Executives: D Robinson (General Manager), John Franklin (Finance Director), G L Jones (Contracts Manager), C Ross

PRINCIPAL ACTIVITIES: Onshore and offshore (petroleum, gas, petrochemicals), instruments and electrical operations and maintenance, cathodic portection
Branch Offices: Jeddah: PO Box 1178, Jeddah 21431; Yanbu: PO BOx 30176, Yanbu Al Sinaiyah; Jubail: PO Box 10537, Madinat Al Jubail Al Sinaiyah
Parent Company: Roxby Engineering International Ltd, Sidcup, Kent, UK
Principal Bankers: Al Bank Al Saudi Al Fransi, Alkhobar; National Westminster Bank, Jersey
Financial Information:

	1990
	SR'000
Authorised capital	6,000
Paid-up capital	6,000

Principal Shareholders: Saudi Marketing & General Trading Corporation, Jeddah; Roxby Engineering International Ltd, UK
Date of Establishment: 1977
No of Employees: 150

EXPRESS CONTRACTING & TRADING

PO Box 2951, Jeddah 21461
Tel: 6829454, 6654203, 6651844
Cable: Development
Telex: 602640 ECTJED SJ, 601082 SINDIC SJ
Telefax: 6604324

Chairman: Ali Sindi
Directors: Kamel Sindi, Khalid Sindi
Senior Executives: Khalid Sindi (President), Mahmoud Kreidieh (Director)

PRINCIPAL ACTIVITIES: Import and distribution of construction equipment (cranes, air compressors, excavators, asphalt pavers, stone crushing plant, etc)
Principal Agencies: Frederick Parker Ltd, Hyster Europe Ltd, Coles Cranes, John Deere, BPR, Lambert, Putzmeister, Hoes
Branch Offices: Branches in Riyadh, Tel 2313375; Al Khobar, Tel 8645109; London
Subsidiary Companies: Express Gas Stations; Express Water Treatment Systems; Express Light Equipment Division
Principal Bankers: Riyad Bank; Al Bank Al Saudi Al Fransi; National Commercial Bank

Principal Shareholders: Ali Sindi, Kamel Sindi
Date of Establishment: 1965
No of Employees: 200

EXPRESS PACKING & TRANSPORT CO LTD (EPT)

Head Office, PO Box 14447, Jeddah 21424
Tel: 6911835, 6911753, 6914921
Telex: 605497 EPTOCE Sj
Telefax: 6916474

Chairman: Abdulrahman Al Rukkayan
Directors: Mounib J Seikaly (Managing Director), Richard Seikalay, Fred Seikaly, Jack Seikaly
Senior Executives: Talaat Mizari (Admin Manager), N Anwar Sandhu (Operations Manager), Issam Mizari (Operations Manager), Anwar Ghulam (Operations Manager), Malik Mikdad (Admin Assistant)

PRINCIPAL ACTIVITIES: Customs handling, linehaul trucking, packing and storage, household removal, freight forwarding, turnkey project logistics
Branch Offices: EPT-Dammam: PO Box 2657, Dammam 31461, Fax 8346992; EPT Riyadh: PO Box 59535, Riyadh 11535, Tel 4646784, 4655915, Telex 406436, Fax 4655915; also branches in Athens; Bahrain; Beirut; Khartoum; London; Paris; New York; Washington
Parent Company: Express Group
Principal Bankers: Saudi British Bank
Financial Information:

	1990/91
	SR'000
Paid-up capital	5,000

Date of Establishment: 1978
No of Employees: 103

EXXON SAUDI ARABIA INC

PO Box 4584, Riyadh 11412
Tel: 4769966, 4770920, 4778969
Cable: EXXONIND RIYADH
Telex: 401816 EXXON SJ
Telefax: (1) 4788878

President: Frank M Hardy

PRINCIPAL ACTIVITIES: Business services; development and implementation of Exxon investment projects
Parent Company: Exxon Corporation, USA
Principal Bankers: Saudi American Bank

FAHD ALTOBAISHI & CO

See ALTOBAISHI, FAHD, & CO

FAKHRY, MOHAMED SAID,

PO Box 88, Jeddah 21411
Tel: 6479507, 6477810
Cable: Nayem Jeddah
Telex: 601593 Fakhry SJ, 602704 Ezyrik SJ
Telefax: 6475089

Chairman: Sheikh Mohamed Said Fakhry
Directors: Sheikh Mahmoud Said Fakhry (Managing Director)
Senior Executives: M A Kfouri, Nayeem Fakhry

PRINCIPAL ACTIVITIES: Import and distribution of cigarettes, confectionery, foodstuffs, and industrial workclothing; manufacture of building materials; tiles, blocks, marbles etc
Principal Agencies: Philip Morris International, USA; Imperial Tobacco International Ltd, UK
Branch Offices: Medina, Tel 8221413; Taif, Tel 7328181; Khamis Mushait, Tel 2230848; Tabuk, Tel 4220035; Jizan, Tel 3221179
Subsidiary Companies: Industrial & Commercial Relations Co, PO Box 88, Jeddah 21411
Principal Bankers: Saudi American Bank; Saudi British Bank; National Commercial Bank

Principal Shareholders: Sheikh Mohamed Said Fakhry; Sheikh Mahmoud Said Fakhry
Date of Establishment: 1947
No of Employees: 160

FARHAN COMMERCIAL CO LTD

PO Box 5887, Riyadh 11432
Tel: 4828811 (4 lines)
Cable: Farhanco Riyadh
Telex: 401619 Afaisl SJ

President: Sheikh Ahmed N Al-Faisal
Directors: Eng Farhan N Al-Faisal (Vice President)

PRINCIPAL ACTIVITIES: Engineering and contractors, trading and consulting, electronic equipment, telecommunications, pharmaceutical supplies
Principal Agencies: GTC Gas Turbine Ltd, UK; TRT Co; Sopelem; Phillips; ITALCABLE, Italy
Branch Offices: Jeddah, Dammam and London
Subsidiary Companies: High Capabilities Operation & Maintenance Company Ltd (HICAP)
Principal Bankers: Saudi Cairo Bank; Saudi French Bank; Banque Indosuez Geneva, Switzerland

Principal Shareholders: Sheikh Ahmed N Al-Faisal, Sheikh Hamad Abdul-Aziz Al-Wanis
Date of Establishment: 1975
No of Employees: 185

FLUOR ARABIA LIMITED

PO Box 360, Dhahran Airport 31932
Tel: 8578577
Cable: FLUORAB KHOBAR
Telex: 871451 Falkho SJ
Telefax: 8576487

Chairman: Sheikh Ahmed A Juffali
Directors: H K Coble, J T Askari, C R Cox, K A Juffali, R W Dean, J P Powell (President & Managing Director), P E Lewis (Vice President, Sales), I Toup
Senior Executives: R A Pratt (VP Program Director), M J Abrey (Finance Manager), P M Olstad (Project Manager Offshore), G L Staggs (Project Manager Onshore), K S Spahr (Administration Manager), R L Reed (Construction Manager), L G Menegay (Material/Procurement Manager), S A Al Bakr (Manager Government Affairs)

PRINCIPAL ACTIVITIES: Feasibility studies, master planning, design and engineering, procurement, construction management for chemical, petrochemical, offshore facilities, telecommunications systems, industrial and commercial projects
Branch Offices: Saudi Arabia (Jeddah, Riyadh); USA; UK; Australia; Canada; West Germany; Netherland; Japan; Chile
Parent Company: Fluor Daniel Inc
Principal Bankers: Saudi American Bank, Alkhobar
Financial Information:

	1990 SR'000
Sales turnover	25,947
Profits	155
Authorised capital	4,000
Paid-up capital	4,000
Total assets	88,051

Principal Shareholders: E A Juffali & Bros, Jeddah; Fluor Daniel Inc, USA;
Date of Establishment: 1975
No of Employees: 249

FMC SAUDI ARABIA LTD

PO Box 1520, AlKhobar 31952
Tel: 8943377
Telex: 871204 Oshcok Sj

President: Kent Marshall
Directors: Robert Goodhouse (Vice President)

PRINCIPAL ACTIVITIES: Agricultural services and equipment; farm management; frozen food/beverage/lube oil processing plants, industrial chemicals; mining equipment; water treatment equipment and safety equipment
Branch Offices: Riyadh: PO Box 967, Tel 4659163, Telex 400405 Thelsa Sj

FOSAM COMPANY LTD

PO Box 11081, Jeddah 21453
Tel: 02 6602132
Telex: 603707 Fosam SJ
Telefax: 02 6601996

Chairman: Sheikh Mohammad Ashmawi
Directors: Hilmi Omari, Syed Al Jawhary, Ahmad Jad, Adel Sedki (Managing Director), A G T Chub, J Whitehead, G R M Purchase, Adnan Bokhary (Company Secretary)
Senior Executives: M Shahim (General Sales Manager), P T Walton (Production Manager), M A Zahoor (Technical Manager), A Lewis (Specification Manager), R Mohan (Financial Controller), M Rashid (Central Province Manager), M El Khub (Eastern Province Manager)

PRINCIPAL ACTIVITIES: Manufacture of construction chemicals and PVC water stops
Branch Offices: Riyadh: PO Box 50391; Dammam: PO Box 7807; Makkah: Anwar Shopping Centre; Jeddah: PO Box 11081; Yanbu: PO Box 1043; Khamis Mushayt: PO Box 1214
Principal Bankers: Saudi British Bank, Saudi French Bank, Lloyds Bank, Gulf Riyad Bank
Financial Information:

	1990 SR'000
Authorised capital	3,000
Paid-up capital	3,000

Principal Shareholders: Saudi Arabian Markets Co Ltd, HE Sheikh Kamal Adham, Fosroc AG
Date of Establishment: 1981
No of Employees: 110

FOSTER WHEELER SAUDI ARABIA CO LTD

PO Box 601, Dhahran Airport 31932
Tel: (03) 8954444
Cable: Foster Wheeler Alkhobar
Telex: 871088 Rewop SJ
Telefax: (03) 8945877

Chairman: HRH Prince Fahd Ibn Khalid Ibn Abdullah Ibn Abdulrahman Al Saud
Directors: Sheikh Abdulla Ali Kanoo, Dr William Jones, Neil William Atwater, Dennis Clement Smith
Senior Executives: Dennis C Smith (Managing Director), Roy Lewis Davies (Manager Finance & Administration)

PRINCIPAL ACTIVITIES: Civil, mechanical and electrical works for the construction of major plants and facilities
Principal Bankers: Albank Alsaudi Alhollandi, Alkhobar

Date of Establishment: 1396H (1976)

FOUAD, ABDULLA, & SONS CO

PO Box 257, Dammam 31411
Tel: 8324400, 8332600
Cable: Fouad Dammam
Telex: 801027 Fouad Sj; 801524 Fafco Sj
Telefax: 8345722

Chairman: Sheikh Abdulla Fouad
President: Fouad Abdulla Fouad
Senior Executives: Sardar M Ghalib (Vice President Commercial Affairs), Issac N Al Sharief (Vice President Administration), Peter Hesp (Vice President Finance), Yousef A Seyadi (Exec Vice President Health Care & Management), Samir K Samra (Vice President Planning & Development)

PRINCIPAL ACTIVITIES: Agency representation, distributors, stockist, manufacturers, contractors, importers, joint ventures, construction, travel agents, computer sales, educational aids sales, general services, real estate, health care and hospitals management
Principal Agencies: Kaiser Aluminium & Chemical, USA; L A Water Treatment, USA; Ecodyne Cooling Tower, USA; Cray Research Inc, USA; Datapoint, USA; Nelson Electric, USA; Computervision, USA; Bobrick International, USA; Ceilcote,

USA; Cyberex, USA; Bobcock & Wilcox SA, Spain; BKL Fittings Ltd, UK; Applied Equipment Corp USA; Japan Steel Works, Japan; Toshiba Corp, Japan; Takamisawa Koki Valves, Japan; Mitsubishi Kakoki Kaisha, Japan; Mitsui Engineering & Shipbuilding, Japan; A S E Europe (Technical Division); Treg SPA, Italy; IHC/TBM Controls BV, Holland; Servicised Ltd, UK; Controlec Ltd, UK; Impalloy Ltd, UK; Tubexport, Spain; Voest-Alpine AG, Australia

Branch Offices: Riyadh; Jeddah; also branches in Tokyo, Japan; Houston, Texas USA; London, UK

Associated Companies: Saudi Electro Mechanical Construction Co, PO Box 1664, Dammam; Basic Chemical Industries, PO Box 257, Dammam; Abdulla Fouad & Busbaite Co (FABCO), PO Box 1683, Dammam; Abdulla Fouad Impalloy Ltd, PO Box 257, Dammam; Fouad Travel Agency, PO Box 257, Dammam

Principal Bankers: Al Bank Al Saudi Al Fransi, Dammam; Al Bank Al Saudi Al Hollandi, Dammam; Banque Indochine, Paris

Financial Information:

	SR'000
Authorised capital	7,500

Principal Shareholders: Sheikh Abdulla Fouad; Fouad Abdulla Fouad

Date of Establishment: 1947

No of Employees: 2,500

FOUNDATION ENGINEERING LTD

PO Box 1020, Jeddah 21431

Tel: 6830016

Telex: 603422 Cosgrp Sj

PRINCIPAL ACTIVITIES: Site investigations, ground and materials testing, geotechnical consulting

Branch Offices: In the Middle East; Abu Dhabi, Dubai, Qatar, Oman, Saudi Arabia, Kuwait, Iraq; also in Nigeria, Singapore, Hong Kong, Kuala Lumpur

Parent Company: Head Office: 109 Blackfriars Rd, London SE1 8HW, UK

Principal Bankers: Saudi British Bank

Principal Shareholders: A member of the Costain Group of Companies

Date of Establishment: 1977 (Saudi Arabia)

No of Employees: 45 (Saudi Arabia)

FOUZ CHEMICAL COMPANY

PO Box 974, Dammam 31421

Tel: 3-8424738, 8427567

Cable: Fouz

Telex: 801778 Fouz SJ

Telefax: 3-8425284

President: Mohammad Ahmad Al Shubaili

Senior Executives: Mustafa H Hassan (General Manager), Ahmed H Brajinah (Finance & Administration Manager), Mohd Anwar Jalil (Dammam Branch Manager), Ali Safadi (Riyadh Branch Manager), Ghazi Howarri (Jeddah Branch Manager), Nizar Ayyad (O&M Dept Head), Hardeep Singh (Rubber Lining & Corrosion Control Div Manager)

PRINCIPAL ACTIVITIES: Import and trade in chemicals, transportation, O & M of chemical installations and allied functions; also rubber lining and corrosion control division; agrochemical division

Principal Agencies: Norit; Denad; Petrochemical Industries Co; SNF Floerger

Branch Offices: Dammam: PO Box 974, Dammam 31421; Riyadh: PO Box 57127, Riyadh; Jeddah: PO Box 21423, Jeddah 9823

Principal Bankers: National Commercial Bank; Arab National Bank

Financial Information:

	1990
	SR'000
Sales turnover	21,660
Authorised capital	1,000
Paid-up capital	1,000
Total assets	12,800

Principal Shareholders: Mohammed Ahmed Al Shubaili, Ahmed Mohammed Al Shubaili

Date of Establishment: 1979

No of Employees: 75

FOZAN MOHAMMAD AL NASSAR EST

See AL NASSAR, FOZAN MOHAMMAD, EST

FUAD AL FADHLI TRADING EST

See AL FADHLI, FUAD, TRADING EST

GADA MARKETING & TRADING

PO Box 6804, Jeddah 21452

Tel: 6657880, 6714416

Telex: 601275 Gmtco Sj

Chairman: HRH Prince Humoud Bin Abdul Aziz Al Saud

Directors: Sheikh Zuhdi Bushnak (Vice-Chairman), Imad Hakki (President)

Senior Executives: Hasan Kabir (Vice-President)

PRINCIPAL ACTIVITIES: General trading, construction and civil contracting

Principal Agencies: Hospitex, France; Marmac Systems Eng, USA; J G Mackin & Ass, USA

Branch Offices: PO Box 42442 Riyadh; Dammam; and Houston, Texas, USA

Subsidiary Companies: Gada Navigation Co Ltd, PO Box 6804, Jeddah (Saudi US joint venture)

Principal Bankers: Al Bank Al Saudi Al Fransi; Saudi American Bank

Principal Shareholders: HRH Prince Humoud Bin Abdul Aziz Al Saud; Sheikh Zuhdi Ahmed Bushnak

Date of Establishment: 1978

GENERAL AGENCIES & CONTRACTING CONSTRUCTION CO (GACCO)

PO Box 5371, Jeddah 21422

Tel: 6650410, 6604943, 6603391

Cable: Namcomes

Telex: 601485 Alheid Sj

Chairman: Mohamed Ibrahim Alheid

Directors: Nabil Abdul-Messie (Director General)

Senior Executives: Mohamed Maan Zahrawi (Executive Director)

PRINCIPAL ACTIVITIES: Construction, contracting

Principal Bankers: National Commercial Bank

Principal Shareholders: Chairman and director as described

Date of Establishment: 1972

No of Employees: 200

GENERAL AGENCIES CORPORATION (GAC)

PO Box 1988, Jeddah 21441

Tel: 6658208, 6658209, 6601659

Telex: 601008 Gac Sj

PRINCIPAL ACTIVITIES: General, building and civil engineering contractors; roads and bridges; water treatment and distribution; production of aggregate, ready-mix concrete and other building materials

Branch Offices: Riyadh, Dammam

Date of Establishment: 1963

SAUDI ARABIA

GENERAL ARABIAN MEDICAL & ALLIED SERVICES LTD
G.A.M.A.
PO Box 41726, Riyadh 11531
Tel: 4641361
Cable: Gama Riyadh
Telex: 400805 Gama SJ

PRINCIPAL ACTIVITIES: Hospital management and medical services

GENERAL ELECTRICITY CORPORATION (ELECTRICO)
PO Box 1185, Riyadh 11431
Tel: 4772722 (10 lines)
Telex: 401393 Electrc SJ

Chairman: Mahmoud Abdullah Taiba
Directors: Fahed Al Shareef, Atiyyah Al Zahrani

PRINCIPAL ACTIVITIES: Supervision of major power projects

Principal Shareholders: Public organisation

GENERAL MACHINERY AGENCIES
PO Box 139, Jeddah 21411
Tel: 6429501, 6429502, 6423791
Cable: Trust Jeddah
Telex: 601178 Saladin Sj
Telefax: 6659478

Chairman: Sheikh Salahuddin Abduljawad
Directors: Ghassan S Abduljawad, Mohammad S Abduljawad, Ziyad S Abduljawad, Raad S Abduljawad
Senior Executives: Mohammad S Abduljawad (General Manager), Salim Abduljawad (General Manager Eastern Province), Wahib F Nashashibi (Riyadh Branch)

PRINCIPAL ACTIVITIES: Import and distribution of motor vehicles, trucks, heavy machinery, building and road construction equipment, agricultural equipment, prefabricated houses
Principal Agencies: General Motor Corporation, Detroit Diesel Allison, Wacker Werke KG, Winget, Babbitless, P & H Harnischfeger, Braud & Faucheux, Moniton, ACE Machinery, Citroen Cars, Montabert, Arcair, Hap Lorry, Continental Diversified Industries, A C Material Handling Corp, Deutz Allis, Mannesmann Demag, Renault Vehicle Industries
Branch Offices: Location in Jeddah: Palestine Street; also branches in Riyadh, PO Box 793, Tel 4762320; Alkhobar, PO Box 287, Tel 8644184, Telex 870115 GMA Sj, Fax 8982484
Principal Bankers: Arab National Bank Ltd
Financial Information:

	1990 SR'000
Authorised capital	5,016
Paid-up capital	5,016

Principal Shareholders: Sheikh Salahuddin Abduljawad
Date of Establishment: 1957
No of Employees: 250

GENERAL MOTORS OVERSEAS DISTRIBUTION CORP
PO Box 5784, Jeddah 21432
Tel: 6530893, 6530902
Cable: JEMOTRJEN
Telex: 601748 GMOT SJ
Telefax: 6530897

Senior Executives: Thomas P Sorensen (Managing Director)

PRINCIPAL ACTIVITIES: Technical and scientific assistance to GMODC dealers and users of GM products
Principal Agencies: Al-Jomaih Co, Jeddah; GMA, Jeddah; Balubaid Est, Jeddah; Al-Nasar, Jeddah; Abdulaziz & MA Al-Jomaih, Riyadh; Abdul Latif Ali Issa, Riyadh; Sibie Est, Jeddah; Abdulaziz & MA Al-Jomaih, Dammam; GMA Al Khobar; Arabian Motors & Engineering Co Ltd, Dammam; Al-Hussaini Corp, Medina; Jubail Motors, Jubail
Parent Company: General Motors Corporation, USA
Principal Bankers: Saudi American Bank

Date of Establishment: 1397H

GENERAL ORGANISATION FOR SOCIAL INSURANCE
Headquarters, PO Box 2963, Riyadh 11461
Tel: 4777735
Cable: Taminat Riyadh
Telex: 400157 Tamin Sj
Telefax: 4779958

Governor: Musaad M Al Senany
Directors: Suliman S Al Humayyd (Deputy Governor)
Senior Executives: Mohamed A Al Fayez

PRINCIPAL ACTIVITIES: Government social insurance scheme
Branch Offices: Regional Offices: Central: PO Box 2952, Riyadh 11461; Western: PO BOx 4082, Jeddah 21491; Eastern: PO BOx 1203, Dammam 31431; and PO Box 877, Abha; Local Offices: Al Ahssa, Hail, Jizan, Jubail, Makkah, Medina, Najran, Qassim, Tabuk, Taif, Yanbu

Principal Shareholders: State owned

GENERAL TRADING COMPANY (GTC)
PO Box 319, Alkhobar 31952
Tel: 8575622
Cable: GENTRACOM
Telex: 871419 Gentra Sj
Telefax: 8575139, 8575834

Chairman: Khalid S Olayan
Directors: Suleiman S Olayan, Khaled S Olayan, Fahad A Olayan
Senior Executives: Ibrahim K Houri (General Manager), Khaled Salman Khan (Finance Manager), Mohib Khan (Product Group Manager), Serge Pensa (Marketing Manager), M Riaz Qureshi (Purchasing & Traffic Manager), Samir Bouari (Regional Manager Eastern Province - Based in Alkhobar), Vacant (Regional Manager Western Province - Based in Jeddah), Ghazi S Ismail (Regional Manager Central Province - Based in Riyadh)

PRINCIPAL ACTIVITIES: Import, distribution and marketing of food/non-food dry, frozen, confectionery, cosmetics, toiletries and tobacco product. Also manufacturers of paper cups, plates, tissue papers, sanitary napkins, toilet papers, kitchen towels and diapers
Principal Agencies: General Foods; Kimberly-Clark; Rowntree Mackintosh; Chesebrough Ponds; Emborg; Unigate; Duracell Batteries; Juvena; R T French; Martin Bros; Tulip; Tuborg; Borden; Britannia Int'l (Nabisco); Juice Bowl; Campbells; Pillsbury; Milkana Cheese; Beechnut; Warner Lambert; Societe Des Eaux Minerales (Sohat Water); Colgate Palmolive; Al Zamil Food Industries Ltd; Shulton; Carlton & United Breweries; Imperial Tobacco; Reemtsma Int'l (Davidoff Cigarettes), Polaroid Sunglasses & Photographic equipment
Branch Offices: Riyadh (PO Box 593) and Jeddah (PO Box 1085)
Parent Company: Olayan Saudi Holding Company (OSHCO)
Associated Companies: Arabian Health Care Supply Company (AHCSC); Industrial Converting Co (ICC); Arabian Paper Products Co (APPCO)
Principal Bankers: Saudi British Bank; Saudi American Bank; National Commercial Bank; Saudi Cairo Bank; American Express; Midland Bank
Financial Information:

	1990 US$'000	1990 SR'000
Sales turnover approx	150,000	-
Authorised capital	-	4,000
Paid-up capital	-	4,000

Principal Shareholders: Member of the Olayan Group of
   Companies
Date of Establishment: 1947
No of Employees: 500

GENERAL TRANSPORTATION ENTERPRISES (GTE)

PO Box 356, Alkhobar 31952
Tel: 8642377, 8643377
Cable: Olayanco
Telex: 870019 Olayam Sj; 871204 Oshcok Sj

Chairman: Suleiman Olayan

PRINCIPAL ACTIVITIES: Transport contractors (off-on highway
   heavy haulage)
Branch Offices: Saudi Arabia; Kuwait
Associated Companies: General Contracting Co, Alkhobar;
   General Trading Co, Alkhobar (see separate entries); Saudi
   General Transportation Co, Dammam
Principal Bankers: Bank of Kuwait and the Middle East; National
   Bank of Kuwait

Principal Shareholders: S S Olayan; A S Al Ageel
Date of Establishment: 1947

GEOREDA SAUDI INTERNATIONAL

PO Box 7952, Jeddah 21472
Tel: 02-6718721, 6710695
Telex: 603485 GEORED SJ
Telefax: 6710695

Chairman: Ali Murad Reda
Directors: Mrs Zain Ali Sifrah, Louay Ali Reda, Noumay Ali Reda
Senior Executives: Ihab Al Said Hassen (Finance Manager), Dr
   Ahmed Aissaoui (Production Manager), Eng Jamal Calouty
   (Technical Manager), Ziad Aref Ahmed (Admin Manager)

PRINCIPAL ACTIVITIES: Geotechnical investigation, mineral
   exploration, hydrographic surveys, GPS satelite surveys,
   geodetic services and related engineering
Branch Offices: Yanbu, Tel 04/3212815
Associated Companies: Geo/Hydro Inc, USA; Geo-Asa,
   Malaysia
Principal Bankers: National Commercial Bank, Jeddah; Saudi
   British Bank, Jeddah; Arab National Bank, Jeddah
Financial Information:

	1990
	SR'000
Profits	2,102
Authorised capital	500
Paid-up capital	500
Fixed assets	747

Principal Shareholders: Sheikh Ali Murad Reda (100%)
Date of Establishment: 1979
No of Employees: 70

GH TRANSPORT LTD

PO Box 269, Dhahran Airport 31932
Tel: 8560004
Telex: 897014 GHREEM SJ
Telefax: 8562003

Chairman: Khaled Hassan Al Gahtani
Senior Executives: P C Grainger (General Manager), M Ul-
   Hassan (Marketing Manager), P A Johnson (Controller), T
   Hollett (Maintenance Manager), J Holiday (Transport
   Manager), A Mansour (Personnel Manager)

PRINCIPAL ACTIVITIES: Customs clearance, transportation,
   warehousing, stevedoring and erection services services
Principal Agencies: Tyrfil, Oliver Retread Systems
Branch Offices: Jeddah; Riyadh; Jubail; Yanbu
Parent Company: HAK Algahtani Sons Co
Principal Bankers: Al Bank Al Saudi Al Fransi

Financial Information:

	1990
	SR'000
Authorised capital	10,590
Paid-up capital	10,590
Total assets	62,000

Principal Shareholders: Saudi owned 100%
Date of Establishment: 1976
No of Employees: 475

GHASSAN AHMAD ABDULLAH AL SULAIMAN EST

See AL SULAIMAN, GHASSAN AHMAD ABDULLAH, EST

GHASSAN AHMAD ABDULLAH AL SULAIMAN EST

See AL SULAIMAN, GHASSAN AHMAD ABDULLAH, EST

GKN KELLER ARABIA LTD

PO Box 718, Dammam 31421
Tel: 8333997, 8335325
Cable: Atco
Telex: 801067 TURKI SJ
Telefax: 8335325

Chairman: Sheikh Abdulrehman Ali Alturki
Directors: Dr J M West, N Boss, K Kirsch
Senior Executives: Ahmad Ali Mir (Resident Manager)

PRINCIPAL ACTIVITIES: Ground engineering contractors,
   vibrocompaction, piling, drilling, dewatering and grouting
Branch Offices: Jeddah: Tel 6912204, Telex 601759 ATURKI SJ
Parent Company: Keller Grundbau GmbH, Offenbach, Germany,
   Telex 4152745, 4152616, Fax 069-8051244
Associated Companies: Bahrain, UAE, Pakistan, Iraq, Qatar,
   Singapore, USA, UK, Austria, Portugal, Malaysia, Australia,
   Canada
Principal Bankers: Albank Alsaudi Alhollandi
Financial Information:

	1989	1990
	SR'000	SR'000
Sales turnover	9,600	7,200
Profits	137	283
Authorised capital	2,000	2,000
Paid-up capital	2,000	2,000
Total assets	5,300	3,500

Principal Shareholders: A A Turki and Keller Grundbau GmbH
Date of Establishment: 22 April 1978
No of Employees: 36

GLOBAL ARABIAN CO FOR ENGINEERING & CONSTRUCTION PROJECTS LTD

PO Box 4, Dhahran Airport 31932
Tel: 8640431, 8640531, 8640031, 8640631
Telefax: 8986496

Chairman: Ahmed Abdullah H Al-Shuwayer
Directors: Robert N Collins (Vice Chairman), Mohammad
   Al'Kaabi (Director), Leonard G Harris (Director)
Senior Executives: James G Kromas (General Manager), R D
   Santos (Finance Manager)

PRINCIPAL ACTIVITIES: Design, manage the construction of
   and construct onshore and offshore industrial and petroleum
   projects, port facilities, roads and housing projects, perform
   technical underwater support services (diving)
Associated Companies: Global Drilling Services, Alhambra,
   Calif, USA; Abdullah H Al-Shuwayer Trading & Contg Co (Ltd
   Partnership) PO Box 322, Dammam 31411, Saudi Arabia
Principal Bankers: Al Bank Al Saudi Al Fransi, Manufacturers
   Hanover Bank

Financial Information:

	1989/90 SR'000
Sales turnover	1,716
Authorised capital	5,000
Paid-up capital	5,000
Total assets	8,028

Principal Shareholders: Global Drilling Services Inc, Abdullah H
Al Shuwayer Trading & Contracting Co Ltd
Date of Establishment: 1983
No of Employees: 50/100

GLOBAL-SUHAIMI CONTRACTING (ARABIA) WLL

PO Box 2162, Dammam 31451
Tel: 03-8571937, 8571886, 8572776
Cable: Global
Telex: 802550 Glosuh Sj
Telefax: 8571953

Chairman: Khalid A R Al-Suhaimi
Directors: G H Smit, L J Leer, K M Alsuhaimi

PRINCIPAL ACTIVITIES: Abrasive blast cleaning, airless
application of protective materials, industrial coating of tanks,
vessels, pipes; concrete blasting and repair works, industrial
high pressure cleaning; roadmarking incl thermoplastic, road
studs accessories
Branch Offices: Riyadh, Tel 4641056; Jeddah, Tel 6657746;
Jubail, Tel 3611968
Associated Companies: Global Contracting (Qatar), PO Box 132,
Doha, Tel 22597, 327626, Telex 4536 SLEHCO DH; Global
Contracting (Abu Dhabi), PO Box 3629, Abu Dhabi, Tel 54980,
Telex 23057 GCAD EM; Global Al Darab Contracting LLC
(Oman), PO Box 1896, Tel 602128, Telex 5046 GCOM ON;
Global Gulf (Bahrain) WLL, PO Box 2897, Manama, Tel
702701, Telex 7317 Global BN; also P T Global UTama,
Jakarta; and GLobal Cor SA, Lausanne, Switzerland
Principal Bankers: Albank Alsaudi Alhollandi

Principal Shareholders: A R & M Saleh Al-Suhaimi; Saudi Arabia
(51%); Hemutech SA, Switzerland (49%)
Date of Establishment: 26th December 1976
No of Employees: 269

GOLDEN GRASS INC

PO Box 21570, Riyadh 11485
Tel: 01-4783024
Telex: 403717 GGI SJ
Telefax: 01-4784630

President: Turki Faisal Al Rasheed
Senior Executives: Rakesh Jain (Executive Vice President), John
Lawton (VP Farming), James Brown (VP Agro Chemicals),
Gary Campbell (VP Golden Grass USA), Salman Al Shabib
(Administration Manager), Nestor de Castro (Project
Coordinator Construction & Maintenance), Ray D Reyes (EDP
Manager), Manny Lorenzo (Chief Accountant), Faharan Al
Sadeed (Manager Hail), Taha Ibrahim (Manager Central),
Osman Fadlseed (Manager Gassim), Tayeb Abdullah
(Manager Sajir), Dr Salah Ghafoor (Manager Western Region),
Ghassan Masud (Manager Eastern Region), Mohammed Zaki
(Manager Wadi Dawasir), Amjad Sabri (Manager Tabuk), Dr
Hashim Taha (Manager Hail), Emad Al Bzour (Manager AL
Jouf), Ibrahim Khanji (Manager Durma), Naim Abu Thuraya
(Pesticides Advisor)

PRINCIPAL ACTIVITIES: Farming, farm management,
agriculture turnkey projects, plant protection, agrochemicals,
crop nutrition, animal health, public health, commercial and
residential maintenance and renovation, manpower supply
Principal Agencies: Hoechst; W R Grace Ltd; Coopers Animal
Health Ltd, UK; Rhone Poulenc; Ciba Geigy; Wellcome;
Fermenta; Monsantra

Branch Offices: Gassim Area Office: PO Box 1664, Buraidah,
Tel 3243100, Fax 3241191; Hail Area Office: PO Box 2174,
Hail, Tel 5321818, 5324769, Fax 5333010; Al Kharj Area
Office: PO Box 21570, Riyadh 11485, Tel 5501393; Sajir Area
Office: PO Box 204, Sajir, Tel 01 6321584; Jeddah Area
Office: PO Box 18467, Jeddah 21415, Tel 02 6440554; Wadi
Dawasir Area Office: PO Box 130, Wadi Dawasir, Tel 01
7861117; Tabuk Area Office: PO Box 93, Tabuk, Tel 04
4232678; Riyadh Showroom: PO Box 21570, Riyadh 11485,
Tel 4033096, Fax 4059125
Principal Bankers: Arab National Bank; Saudi Hollandi Bank;
Saudi British Bank; Saudi American Bank; National
Commercial Bank; Trans Arabian Investment Bank, Bahrain
Financial Information:

	1990 SR'000
Sales turnover	82,620
Profits	12,503
Authorised capital	1,000
Paid-up capital	1,000
Total assets	33,435

Principal Shareholders: Turki Faisal Al Rasheed (97%); other
members of his family (3%)
Date of Establishment: 1982
No of Employees: 500

GRAIN SILOS & FLOUR MILLS ORGANISATION

PO Box 3402, Olaya Street, Riyadh 11471
Tel: 4643500, 4649864, 4648585
Telex: 401052 Samawi Sj, 402580 Samawi Sj
Telefax: 4631943

Chairman: Dr Abdul Rahman Al Sheikh (Minister of Agriculture
& Water)
Directors: HE Saleh Bin Mohammad Al Sulaiman (Managing
Director)
Senior Executives: Dr Mohammad Al Al Bishr (Deputy Managing
Director), Abdul Aziz Al Bassam (Finance Director), Abdul
Rahman Ruwaita (Projects Execution Director), Hamad N Al
Toaimi (Purchasing Director), Abdullah Al Wahby (Personnel
Director), Mohammad Al Hassoun (Director Planning &
Budget), Saad Abu Nayan (Marketing Director)

PRINCIPAL ACTIVITIES: Storage of grain and manufacture of
flour and byproducts and animal feeds
Branch Offices: Plants at Riyadh, Dammam, Jeddah, Qassim,
Khamis Mushayt, Hail, Wadi Dawasir, Al Jouf, Tabouk, Al
Kharj
Parent Company: Responsible to the Ministry of Agriculture and
Water

Date of Establishment: 1972
No of Employees: 1,830

GRANADA TRADING & CONTRACTING

PO Box 1781, Jeddah 21441
Tel: 6425252, 6421422 (Office), 6430046 (Showroom)
Cable: Granadoffice
Telex: 604322 GRANAD SJ
Telefax: 6437367

Chairman: M H Yaghmour
Senior Executives: H Y Yaghmour (General Manager)

PRINCIPAL ACTIVITIES: Import of building materials and
foodstuffs
Principal Agencies: Annakeramik Architectural Ceramics, W
Germany
Branch Offices: Riyadh; Makkah; Medinah; Cairo (Egypt)
Principal Bankers: Saudi Cairo Bank

Date of Establishment: 1967
No of Employees: 37

GREYHOUND SERVICES SAUDI ARABIA LTD

PO Box 1892, Al Khobar 31952
Tel: 8640270, 8640281, 8949985, 8949986
Fax: 8949985
Telex: 871310 ALT SJ

Chairman: Abdulla Kanoo

Directors: Edward H Williams (Vice Chairman), Abdul Aziz Kanoo, John W Teets, Charles H Carpenter, Munib R Masri

PRINCIPAL ACTIVITIES: Complete camp catering, housekeeping, laundry, recreation, security, fire prevention, medical, maintenance, and related support services
Branch Offices: Al Khobar; Riyadh; Jeddah; Jubail-Ras Tanura
Associated Companies: Greyhound Support Services, Inc, Greyhound Tower, Phoenix Arizona 85077, USA, Telex 0668349, Tel (602) 248-6052
Principal Bankers: Saudi American Bank, Riyadh, Jeddah, Al Khobar

No of Employees: 1,600

GUARDIAN FENCING SYSTEMS LTD

PO Box 6765, Dammam 31452
Tel: 8571692
Telex: 802524 Fence Sj

Chairman: Sheikh Mohammed Al Ankary

Directors: Fahad Saja (Managing Director), A J Taylor

PRINCIPAL ACTIVITIES: Manufacture of chain link fencing systems and gates
Principal Agencies: Alan Kennedy grating glassfibre products; Barol Cyclone ringlok fencing
Branch Offices: Riyadh, Tel 4522545
Parent Company: Saudi Metal Industries Ltd
Principal Bankers: National Commercial Bank, Dammam
Financial Information:

	SR'000
Authorised capital	6,000
Paid-up capital	6,000

Principal Shareholders: Saudi Metal Industries Ltd (100%)
Date of Establishment: October 1984

GULF AGENCY COMPANY SAUDI ARABIA

Head Office, PO Box 72, Rahima 31941
Tel: 6670632, 6670636, 6673180
Cable: Confidence Ras Tanura
Telex: 851059 Gac Rt Sj, 851011 Gac Rt Sj

Chairman: Sheikh Ahmad Hamad Algosaibi

Directors: Sheikh Abdulaziz Algosaibi (Managing Director), Sulaiman Algosaibi, Yousef Algosaibi

PRINCIPAL ACTIVITIES: Shipping agents, bunker sales, ship supply services, underwater hull cleaning, Suez Canal transit service
Branch Offices: Throughout the Middle East; Saudi Arabia: Dammam: PO Box 86, Dhahran 31932, Tel 8323425/7, 8328762/4, Telex 801069, Fax 8323035, (General Manager: Amir Dhamee); Jeddah: PO Box 2038, Jeddah 21451, Tel 6531964, 6535060, Telex 601047, Fax 6510860, (General Manager: Jaafer A Maisari); Jubail: PO Box 12, Jubail 31951, Tel 3611064, Telex 831030; Riyadh: PO Box 74, Riyadh 11411, Tel 4632981, Telex 404922; Yanbu: PO Box 473, Yanbu, Tel 3223992, Telex 661084, Fax 3221231
Principal Bankers: Morgan Guaranty Trust, New York; Arab Bank (Overseas) Zurich

Principal Shareholders: Algosaibi Family
Date of Establishment: 1958
No of Employees: 150

GULF DANISH DAIRY CO LTD

PO Box 5360, Dammam 31422
Tel: 8426033
Cable: Haleib
Telex: 871022
Telefax: 8423128

Chairman: HE Sheikh Hamad Sabah Al Ahmed Al Jaber Al Sabah
Directors: Sheikh Faick Al Mutair, K E Knudsen, A M Strover, Sheikh Hamdan Abdalla Al Nassar
Senior Executives: Bill Pace (General Manager), Robert Pannewitz (Sales Manager), Mustafa Awad Al Seed (Finance Manager), David Lloyd-Williams (Production Manager), Tage L Jensen (Chief Engineer), Hassan K Al Arnaout (PR & Personnel Manager), Carl Xenophontos (Marketing Manager)

PRINCIPAL ACTIVITIES: Dairy products and juice drinks
Branch Offices: Riyadh; Hofuf; Gasim; Al Batin; Al Jouf
Principal Bankers: National Commercial Bank, Dammam; Ahmed Al Gosaibi Exchange Co, Dammam
Financial Information:

	1988/89 SR'000
Sales turnover	73,858
Profits	6,331
Authorised capital	13,215
Paid-up capital	13,215
Total assets	57,361

Principal Shareholders: Al Futtooh Investment Co WLL, Kuwait; Sheikh Abdul Aziz Mubarak A Hasawi, AlKhobar; Sheikh Hamdan Abdalla Al Nassar, Riyadh; Danish Turnkey Dairies Ltd, Denmark
Date of Establishment: 1980
No of Employees: 200

GULF MERIDIEN HOTEL

PO Box 1266, Alkhobar 31952
Tel: (966-3) 8646000
Cable: HOMER SJ
Telex: 870505 Homer Sj, 870524 Merhot Sj
Telefax: (966-3) 8981651

Chairman: Rodolphe Frantz (President Meridien SA)
Directors: Hussein Ghaleb (General Manager - AlKhobar)
Senior Executives: Georges Rispal (Executive Assistant Manager), Abdel Kader Muhtadie (Director of Sales & Marketing)

PRINCIPAL ACTIVITIES: Hotel business
Principal Agencies: Meridien Sales Offices, Air France Sales Offices
Branch Offices: Location in Alkhobar: Corniche Blvd, 28th Street
Parent Company: Air France
Principal Bankers: Arab National Bank

Date of Establishment: May 1981
No of Employees: 317

GULF STARS COMPUTER SYSTEMS

PO Box 52908, Riyadh 11573
Tel: 4643577
Telex: 407602 GSCS SJ
Telefax: (01) 4653146

Chairman: Sheikh Abdullah Rumaizan
Senior Executives: Rowland Griffiths (General Manager)

PRINCIPAL ACTIVITIES: Networking and computer systems
Principal Agencies: Novell, Micro Focus, Codenoll, Emerald, Storage Dimension, Micros, Hewlett Packard
Branch Offices: PO Box 16712, Jeddah; PO Box 3791, Alkhobar
Subsidiary Companies: Gulf Star Systems, PO Box 27050 Safat, 13131 Kuwait; Gulf Star Systems West, Florida, USA
Principal Bankers: Saudi Cairo Bank

Financial Information:

	1988/89 SR'000	1989/90 SR'000
Sales turnover	8,800	15,400

Date of Establishment: 1984 (as Sperry Arabia); 1988 (as GSCS)
No of Employees: 50

GULF UNION INSURANCE CO SAUDI ARABIA

PO Box 5719, Dammam 31432
Tel: 8333802, 8333646, 8333544, 8334556
Telex: 802458 Guincod Sj
Telefax: 8333517

Chairman: Sa'ad Mohammad Al Moajil
Directors: Dr Fouad Abdulsamad Al Falah (Vice Chairman), Abdul Aziz Ali Al Turki (Managing Director), Abdul Aziz Kanoo, Abdul Qader Al Mohaideb, Abdul Wahhab Al Babtain, Abdul Ghani El Ajou, Ali Yousif Fakhro, Percy Albert Sequeira
Senior Executives: Percy A Sequeira (Director & General Manager), Abdul Razak Al Khatab (Deputy General Manager), Muneeb Nazeer Mahmoud (Deputy General Manager)

PRINCIPAL ACTIVITIES: Insurance
Branch Offices: Riyadh: PO Box 8539, Tel 4656784, Telex 400686 Juma Sj, Fax 4656801; Jeddah: PO Box 17282, Tel 6518948, Fax 6518948; Kuwait: Gulf Insurance Brokers Office, PO Box 26330 Safat, Tel 435014/5/6/7/8, Telex 44548 Kuinb Kt
Principal Bankers: Saudi British Bank
Financial Information:

	US$'000
Authorised capital	20,000
Paid-up capital	20,000

Principal Shareholders: 22 Shareholders
Date of Establishment: 1982 in Bahrain
No of Employees: 36

HADI GENERAL SERVICES CO

PO Box 122, Dammam 31411
Tel: 8327301, 8323846, 8333138
Cable: Hadico
Telex: 801009 Hadico Sj
Telefax: 03-8333369

Directors: Mohammed Ahmed Hadi, Amin Ahmed Hadi

PRINCIPAL ACTIVITIES: Importers; distributors; clearing & forwarding agents; transporters
Principal Agencies: South East Food Co, Hong Kong; Milton Lloyd Associates, UK; Evercrisp Snacks, Singapore; Cheong Chan, Malaysia; Ushodaya Ent, India; American Dry Fruit, India
Branch Offices: PO Box 5169, Riyadh, Tel 01-4050917, 01-4058409, Fax 01-4011870; PO Box 16056, Jeddah, Tel 02-6519255, 02-6534401, Fax 02-6534179
Principal Bankers: Saudi British Bank, Dammam; Saudi Cairo Bank, Dammam

Date of Establishment: 1970
No of Employees: 70

HAJI ABDULLAH ALIREZA & CO LTD

See ALIREZA, HAJI ABDULLAH, & CO LTD

HAJI HUSEIN ALIREZA & CO LTD

See ALIREZA, HAJI HUSEIN, & CO LTD

HALWANI BROTHERS

PO Box 690, Jeddah 21421
Tel: 6366487, 6366496, 6369810
Cable: Al Nakhla
Telex: 601118 HALAWA, 600176 FAWAZ SJ

Chairman: Mohamed Munir Halwani
Directors: Mohammed A Halwani, Hicham A Halwani
Senior Executives: Nader A Houri (Executive Manager)

PRINCIPAL ACTIVITIES: Manufacture of dairy products, ice cream, processed meat, sesame extracts and oriental pastries, can, tins and plastic containers. Distribution of canned foods and foodstuffs; cold storage; general trading and contracting; catering, restaurants, supermarkets, readymade clothes, glassware; transportation, construction, travel agencies
Subsidiary Companies: Halwani Contracting Co; Halwani Cold Industries; Arabian Int'l Tourism Corp; M A M Co; Straco; Saudi Climate Control Est; Red Sea Establishment; Halwani Exchange; Halwani Cold Stores
Principal Bankers: National Commercial Bank
Financial Information:

	SR'000
Authorised capital	40,000
Paid-up capital	40,000

Principal Shareholders: M Munir Halwani; Mohammed A Halwani; Hisham A Halwani
Date of Establishment: 1952
No of Employees: 850

HAMAD ABDULLA ALESSA & SONS CO

See ALESSA, HAMAD ABDULLA, & SONS CO

HAMAD AL NASER AL HATLANI & BROS

See AL HATLANI, HAMAD AL NASER, & BROS

HAMAD AL BAJJASH

See AL BAJJASH, HAMAD,

HANAFI CONTRACTS & TRADING CORPORATION

PO Box 5995, Jeddah 21432
Tel: 6608411
Cable: Rowina
Telex: 601246 Hanafi Sj
Telefax: 6611755

Directors: Eng Abdulaziz A Hanafi (Managing Director)
Senior Executives: Rabie Ali Kabout (Technical Manager), K Viyajan Menon (Administration Manager)

PRINCIPAL ACTIVITIES: Building and civil engineering contractors, supply of building materials
Principal Bankers: National Commercial Bank, Jeddah

Date of Establishment: 1975
No of Employees: 50

HASHIM, ABDULLAH, CO LTD

PO Box 44, Jeddah 21411
Tel: 6470531, 6475222, 6472305, 6472200
Cable: Hashim
Telex: 601152 Hashim Sj
Telefax: 02-6481976

Chairman: Sheikh Abdullah Hashim
Directors: Mohammad A Hashim (Managing Director)
Senior Executives: Akram Kurabi (General Manager Finance), Saeed Ahmad (General Manager Machinery Division), Shakib Haider (General Manager Honda Division), Aladdin Mabofan (General Manager Administration), Hashim A Hashim (General Manager Western Region), Faisal El Miheina (General Manager Central Region), Badie S Al Kassir (General Manager Eastern Region)

PRINCIPAL ACTIVITIES: Import and distribution of automobiles, motocycles, generators, water pumps, lawn mowers, lawn tractors, agricultural equipment, marine engines, welding equipment, fire extinguishers, concrete mixers, industrial and medical gases, manufacture of industrial and medical gases, tin cans
Principal Agencies: Honda Motor Co Ltd, Japan; Honda Trading Corp, Japan; Honda Motor Co, USA; Yanmar Diesel Engine Co Ltd, Japan; WD-40 Co Ltd, UK; Marine Int'l Co, USA;

Deep Pumps, Holland; KYC Machine Industry, USA; FRP
Service, Japan

Branch Offices: Dammam: PO Box 307, Dammam 31411, Tel
03-8579877, Fax 03-8576311, Telex 801103; Riyaadh: PO Box
314, Riyadh 11411, Tel 01-4460637, Fax 01-4469740, Telex
401529; Madina: PO Box 3611, Madina, Tel 04-8224002, Fax
04-8222651; Makkah: PO Box 5841, Makkah, Tel 02-5425603,
Fax 02-5448358; Buraidah: PO Box 633, Buraidah, Tel 06-
3816751, Fax 06-3816153; Ras El Khafji: PO Box 59, Ras El
Khafji, Tel 03-7662584

Subsidiary Companies: Freon Products Saudi Arabia Ltd

Principal Bankers: Riyad Bank; National Commercial Bank;
Saudi American Bank

Financial Information:

	1990
	SR'000
Authorised capital	400,000
Paid-up capital	400,000

Principal Shareholders: Sheikh Abdullah Hashim (sole owner)
Date of Establishment: 1931
No of Employees: 600

HASSAN ABDUL KARIM AL GAHTANI SONS CO

See AL GAHTANI, HASSAN ABDUL KARIM, SONS CO

HASSAN ENTERPRISES

PO Box 4573, Riyadh 11412
Tel: 4212494, 4212506, 4212510
Telex: 402561 Hasan Sj

President: Hassan Saleh Al Sheikh
Directors: Abdul Latif Saleh Al Sheikh (Vice President)

PRINCIPAL ACTIVITIES: General contractors; manufacture and
supply of cement and marble tiles, and all building materials
Subsidiary Companies: Al-Emar Establishment: Agricultural &
Drilling (Tel 463-2702/463-2005)
Principal Bankers: Saudi American Bank; Arab National Bank;
National Commercial Bank

Date of Establishment: 1967
No of Employees: 150

HATHAL A OTAIBI EST

See OTAIBI, HATHAL A, EST

HAWA TRADING & CONTRACTING

PO Box 398, Alkhobar 31952
Tel: 8641464, 8641827, 8642295
Telex: 870052 Hawa Sj

Chairman: Younis M Hawa (Managing Director)

PRINCIPAL ACTIVITIES: Electrical engineering contractors,
distribution of electrical, air-conditioning and refrigerating
equipment and accessories
Branch Offices: Jeddah: PO Box 2879, Tel 6442125, Telex
600667; Riyadh: PO Box 2406

Date of Establishment: 1959

HAZAR GROUP OF COMPANIES

PO Box 41699, Riyadh 11531
Tel: (01) 464-2068, 465-5378
Telex: 400263 Hazar Sj, 403254 Sogrep Sj
Telefax: (966-1) 4644190

Chairman: Salman Bin Mohammad Bin Khalid Bin Hethlain
(Chief Executive Officer)
Senior Executives: Khalid A Al-Sadhan (Senior Vice President),
A B Kassir (Executive Vice President), Thomas E Thompson
(Vice President & General Manager)

PRINCIPAL ACTIVITIES: Agency representations, joint ventures
and wholly owned subsidiaries in aerospace and electronics
products, operations and maintenance, and agri-business

Principal Agencies: Plessey plc; Hydraulic Research Textron;
Bell Helicopter Textron Inc; Optic Electronics; Houchin Ltd;
Heckler & Koch; Chadwick-Helmut; CONAX; Systems &
Simulations Inc; Temet Oy
Branch Offices: Saudi Eastern Province: PO Box 490, Dhahran
31932, Telex 801962 Sogrep Sj, Tel 8910338; also
Switzerland: 145 Rue de Lausanne, 1202 Geneva, Telex
22939 HAZAR CH
Subsidiary Companies: Group companies: Hazar Est for
Trading; Bell Helicopter Arabia Ltd (JV with Bell Helicopter
Textron Inc); SOGEREP Ltd (Represents Bell Helicopter
Textron, Inc sales in KSA); HANI Animal Nutrition Industries
(Production, sales of animal food supplements); HIDIMCO
(Hazar Industrial Development & International Marketing Co)
Principal Bankers: Saudi American Bank; Saudi French Bank

Principal Shareholders: 100% Saudi - Salman Bin Mohammed
Bin Khalid Bin Hethlain
Date of Establishment: 1978
No of Employees: 186

HAZZA, NASSIR, & BROTHERS

PO Box 12, Alkhobar 31952
Tel: 8575588, 8573359
Cable: Alhazza
Telex: 870011 Sj
Telefax: 8576279

Chairman: Nassir Hazza
Directors: Salem Hazza, Fahad Hazza, Mohammed Nassir
Hazza (Managing Director), Hazza Nassir Hazza
Senior Executives: Hamdi Shabaan (Technical Manager),
Mohammed Eid Barakat (Administration Manager),
Mohammed Al Fateh

PRINCIPAL ACTIVITIES: Civil and mechanical engineering, road
building, plant hire
Branch Offices: Jubail, Riyadh, Bahrain, Abu Dhabi
Associated Companies: Procon Int Inc, Illinois, USA
Principal Bankers: Albank Alsaudi Alhollandi; Al Bank Al Saudi
Al Fransi; Saudi American Bank; United Saudi Commercial
Bank
Financial Information:

	1989
	SR'000
Turnover	183,329
Profits	4,832
Authorised capital	10,145
Paid-up capital	10,145
Total assets	569,092

Principal Shareholders: Chairman and directors as described
Date of Establishment: 1953
No of Employees: 1,000

HEALTH WATER BOTTLING CO LTD (NISSAH)

PO Box 2948, Riyadh 11461
Tel: 4033300, 4900244, 4900346, 4900172
Cable: Healthwater
Telex: 401102 Nissah SJ

Chairman: Sheikh A Al-Murshed
Directors: O A Aggad (Managing Director)
Senior Executives: S Weheibi (General Manager), M Husseini
(Assistant General Manager)

PRINCIPAL ACTIVITIES: Health water bottling and distribution
Branch Offices: Dammam and Jeddah
Principal Bankers: National Arab Bank, Riyadh
Financial Information:

	SR'000
Sales turnover	45,000
Authorised capital	20,150
Paid-up capital	20,000

Principal Shareholders: Aggad Investment Co; Olayan Financing Co; Sheikh Abdulrahman Al-Murshed
Date of Establishment: 1974
No of Employees: 200

HEMPEL PAINTS (SAUDI ARABIA) WLL

PO Box 1077, Dammam 31431
Tel: (03) 8576677 (7 lines)
Cable: Hempaturi
Telex: 801038 Hempel Sj
Telefax: (03) 8576643

Chairman: Khalid A R Al-Suhaimi
Directors: H E Sheikh Nasser Sabah Al-Ahmed Al-Sabah, Saud Abdulaziz Al-Rashed, Jorn H Lillelund, John W Schwartzbach
Senior Executives: Ebbe Finderup (General Manager), Yusuf Ahmed Al Sayed (Deputy General Manager), Mangesh S Mavinkurve (Financial Controller), David Thomas (Marketing Manager)

PRINCIPAL ACTIVITIES: Manufacturing and marketing of paint and coatings for marine, industrial, offshore, container, yacht and building sector uses; materials and tools for/and quality control of surface preparation and application of such coatings, including technical of advisory services
Principal Agencies: Graco, Airblast, Clemco, Elcometer, Hemco, Woma, Yamada, M G Duff, Eurogrit
Branch Offices: Jeddah, Riyadh, Yanbu, Jubail
Parent Company: J C Hempel Holding A/S - Denmark
Principal Bankers: Albank Asaudi Alhollandi, National Commercial Bank
Financial Information:

	1989
	SR'000
Sales turnover	95,000
Authorised capital	30,000
Paid-up capital	12,000
Total assets	69,000

Principal Shareholders: Al Suhaimi Company; Hempel Kuwait; Hempel Denmark
Date of Establishment: September 1972
No of Employees: 190

HESCO ALHOWAISH ELWIN G SMITH CO LTD

PO Box 11181, Jeddah 21453
Tel: 02 6378000
Cable: Alhowaish
Telex: 604230 HESCO
Telefax: 02 6364566

Chairman: Sheikh Abdul Rahman Saad Alhowaish (Managing Director)
Directors: Sh Abdullah S Alhowaish (Vice Chairman), Sh Khalid A Alhowaish (Director Nominated)
Senior Executives: Nabil Jaber (Sales Manager), Ahmed Gouda (Finance Manager), Massad Zamlot (Legal Adviser), K T Ameen (Procurement Manager), Ramon Rayco (Head Engineering Dept), Osama Hijazi (Operations Manager), A V Nair (Head Contracts Dept)

PRINCIPAL ACTIVITIES: Manufacture of varifoam insulated wall and roof cladding system, varifoam cold store panels, variquiet acoustic panel, varipanel single skin roof and cladding, varistyle ceiling and wall liner
Principal Agencies: Dryvit Systems, USA; End Fasteners, Germany
Branch Offices: Riyadh: PO Box 7714, Riyadh 11472, Tel 01 4775378, Fax 01 4770116; Alkhobar: PO Box 1578, Alkhobar 31952, Rel 03 8992417, Fax 03 8953039
Subsidiary Companies: Saudi Water Cooler & Freezers Manufacturing Co Ltd; Alhowaish Trading Est
Principal Bankers: Saudi British Bank, Riyad Bank

Financial Information:

	1990
	SR'000
Sales turnover	30,000
Profits	5,000
Authorised capital	8,540
Paid-up capital	8,540
Total assets	12,000

Principal Shareholders: Chairman and directors as mentioned
Date of Establishment: 1402H/1982
No of Employees: 70

HOLZMAN, PHILIPP, AG

PO Box 2996, Riyadh 11461
Tel: 4044166, 4025399, 4767599

PRINCIPAL ACTIVITIES: Building and civil engineering contractors; supply of building materials and aggregates
Branch Offices: Dhahran Airport: PO Box 407, Telex 801013 Holzman Sj; Jeddah: PO Box 6097, Tel 6652227; Alkhobar: Tel 8324536; Hofuf; Tayif and Medina
Associated Companies: Saudi Armoured Concrete Co
Principal Bankers: Riyad Bank

HONEYWELL TURKI ARABIA LTD

PO Box 718, Dammam 31421
Tel: 8342442, 8341919, 8342733, 8342147, 8347225, 8331645, 8331784
Telex: 803307 HTALDM SJ
Telefax: 8342828

Chairman: Sheikh Abdul Rahman Al Turki
Executive Directors: Fuad Tannous, Giannantonio Ferrari
Senior Executives: George T Chikhani (General Manager), Mehmoud Soliman (Area Manager), George E Azzam (Finance Manager), Kamal Habre (Commercial Sales Manager), Graham Gill (Industrial Sales Manager), M I Khan (Personnel Supervisor), John Clarke (Service Manager), Pierre Hourani (Customer Service Manager)

PRINCIPAL ACTIVITIES: Engineering, installaltion and commissions of building automation system and industrial process control system, training programme, service and maintenance of Honeywell and other products
Branch Offices: PO Box 8077, Riyadh 11482, Tel 4780252, 4793836, Telex 403849 HTALRD SJ; PO Box 10312, Jubail 31421, Tel 3419986, 3419987, Telx 832156 HTALJB SJ
Parent Company: Honeywell Inc USA; A A Turki Corporation KSA
Principal Bankers: Albank Alsaudi Alhollandi
Financial Information:

	1988/89	1989/90
	SR'000	SR'000
Sales turnover	35,600	34,878
Profits	1,426	1,847
Authorised capital	1,000	1,000
Paid-up capital	1,000	1,000
Total assets	31,465	22,673

Principal Shareholders: Sheikh Abdul Rahman Al Turki; Honeywell Inc USA
Date of Establishment: December 1979
No of Employees: 89

HOSHANCO

PO Box 25888, Riyadh 11476
Tel: 4761322, 4774290
Cable: Hoshan
Telex: 401436 Hoshan Sj
Telefax: 4775977

Chairman: Ahmed Hamad El Hoshan
Directors: Amir Hamad El Hoshan (Vice-President)
Senior Executives: Abdel Munhem Fakhoury (Director), Antoine Garabedian (Financial Manager), Vahe Yazedjian (General Manager Graphic Arts), Nabil Saab (General Manager

Stationery), Anas Yafi (General Manager Office Equipment), Hassan Hussni Omar (General Manager Medical Supply), Ahmed Al Harafi (General Manager Construction), Peter Sassoun (General Manager Insurance), Nadim Abou Nehme (General Manager Agriculture)

PRINCIPAL ACTIVITIES: Construction/commercial est. Sales and services of graphic arts equipment and business products, contracting, office furniture, catering, maintenance, farming/landscaping, medical/laboratory products, communications, military supply, insurance

Principal Agencies: Minolta; Sharp; 3M; Dr Hell; Pentel; Herman Miller; Hitachi; Oki; Liquid Paper; Wiggins Teape; Cartiere Baglini; Am Bruning; Kroy; Norfin; Jomac; Hohner; Nuarc; Challenge; Argon; Extec; Imtec; Plan Hold; K & E; Facit; Huyosung; Aurora; Secap; Glunz & Jensen; Gordon Russel; Compugraphic; Letrasetth

Branch Offices: PO Box 6389, Jeddah; PO Box 1856, Al-Khobar; Jubail; Dammam; Yanbu; Medina; Khamis Mushayt; Tabouk; Gassim

Associated Companies: Arab Supply Est, Riyadh; Pan Gulf Marketing Co; Gulf Telecommunications; Onama Catering; Amerco Inc, USA; Systems Srl, Lebanon; Peninsula Insurance Co; Arabian Agriculture & Livestock Investment Co

Principal Bankers: Saudi Cairo Bank; National Commercial Bank

Financial Information:

	1990 SR'000
Authorised capital	175,000
Total assets	250,000

Principal Shareholders: Ahmed Hamad El-Hoshan
Date of Establishment: 1965
No of Employees: 2,200

HOTEL AL HAMRA SOFITEL

PO Box 7375, Jeddah 21462
Tel: 6602000
Telex: 600749 Sofi Sj
Telefax: 6604145

Senior Executives: Habib Baccouche (General Manager), C Ranjith Manatunga (Financial Controller), Kingsley Ratnam (Sales & Marketing Manager)

PRINCIPAL ACTIVITIES: Hotel operation
Parent Company: ACCOR
Associated Companies: Novotel, Mercure, Ibis, Urbis, Formule No1

Principal Shareholders: Bougary & Sabban Tourism Company
Date of Establishment: 1980
No of Employees: 214

HOTEL AL KHOZAMA

Al Khozama Center

PO Box 4148, Riyadh 11491
Tel: 4654650
Cable: KHOZAMHOT
Telex: 400100 Khozam SJ
Telefax: 4648576

Senior Executives: Thomas Nikielewski (General Manager)

PRINCIPAL ACTIVITIES: Hotel business and property rentals
Branch Offices: Location in Riyadh: Olaya Street
Parent Company: King Faisal Foundation (as owner); Moevenpick Hotels International, Zurich, Switzerland (as managing company)
Principal Bankers: Saudi British Bank

Principal Shareholders: King Faisal Foundation
Date of Establishment: 1978
No of Employees: 420

HOTEL ALSALAM RAMADA JEDDAH

PO Box 6582, Jeddah 21452
Tel: 6314000
Cable: Hotaf Jeddah
Telex: 601276 Mersal Sj; 601327 Homer Sj

PRINCIPAL ACTIVITIES: Hotel, outside catering, banquets and conventions
Subsidiary Companies: Ramada Hotels International
Principal Bankers: Bank Al Saudi Al Hollandi

Principal Shareholders: Saudi Arabian Hotels Corporation
Date of Establishment: 1978
No of Employees: 300

HOTEL DAMMAM OBEROI

PO Box 5397, Dammam 31422
Tel: 8345555
Cable: Obhotel Dammam
Telex: 802071 OBHT Sj
Telefax: 8349872

Directors: Ratan Tata (Managing Director)
Senior Executives: Anil Kaul (Resident Manager), Shashi Khanna (Director of Sales & Marketing)

PRINCIPAL ACTIVITIES: Hotel business
Principal Agencies: Managing company: Oberoi Hotels International
Principal Bankers: Arab National Bank

Principal Shareholders: Sheikhs Abdullah Foud; Ali Tamimi; Rashed Al Rashed; Omran Al Omran; Abdul Aziz Al Omran
Date of Establishment: May 1981
No of Employees: 350

HOTEL MAKKAH INTERCONTINENTAL

PO Box 1496, Jeddah Road, Makkah
Tel: 6431580
Cable: INHOTELCOR MAKKAH
Telex: 440006 QCA IHC SJ

Senior Executives: Sameer Ayouby (General Manager)

PRINCIPAL ACTIVITIES: Hotel business

HOTEL MINHAL SOFITEL RIYADH

Airport Road, PO Box 17058, Riyadh 11484
Tel: 4782500
Cable: MINHAL
Telex: 403088 MNAL SJ
Telefax: 4772819

Directors: Georges Patenotte (General Manager)
Senior Executives: Mounir L Georges (Sales & Marketing Manager), M R Ashraf (Director of Finance)

PRINCIPAL ACTIVITIES: Hotel business
Branch Offices: Paris, New York, Abu Dhabi
Parent Company: Accor Group, Paris (France)
Financial Information:

	1990 US$'000
Sales turnover	6,000

Principal Shareholders: Prince Faisal Bin Khalid Bin A Aziz; PIA Investment
Date of Establishment: 1981
No of Employees: 200

HOUSSAM TRADING & CONTRACTING CO

PO Box 1826, Riyadh 11441
Tel: 4632833 (5 lines)
Cable: Houssamtrad
Telex: 401358 Houssam Sj
Telefax: 4649597

Chairman: Sheikh Ahmed A Al Saleh (Chief Executive)
Senior Executives: Abdulaziz A Al Saleh (General Manager)

PRINCIPAL ACTIVITIES: Supply, whole and retail sales of telecommunication materials and equipment, power cables, generating sets, PVC pipes, heat shrinkable products, agricultural equipment, drilling and excavation machinery and tools, compressors, airconditioning units, spare parts. Civil works contractors, telephone and water outside plants networks

Principal Agencies: Krone, W Germany; Taihan, S Korea; AEG Kabel, W Germany; Peter Lancier, W Germany; SEO Bong, S Korea; Donghak Corp, S Korea; Schiederwerk, W Germany; Yeonhab Electric Cable, S Korea; Kabelmetal Electro, W Germany; Ammann Duomat, W Germany; Philips, W Germany; Trane, USA; Arabian Gulf Mfg Co, Saudi Arabia; Raychem Ltd, Saudi Arabia

Branch Offices: Alkhobar: PO Box 20265, Alkhobar 31952, Tel 03-8941256, Fax 03-8941260

Principal Bankers: National Commercial Bank; Saudi American Bank; Saudi Cairo Bank

Financial Information:

	1989/90 SR'000
Sales turnover	32,829
Profits	6,245
Authorised capital	5,000
Paid-up capital	5,000
Total assets	35,420

Principal Shareholders: Sheikh Ahmed A Al Saleh, Abdulaziz Al Saleh, Mohammad Al Saleh, Khalid Al Saleh, Basil Al Saleh, Houssam Al Saleh, Abdullah Al Saleh

Date of Establishment: 1974

No of Employees: 1,000

HUSSEIN AOUEINI & CO LTD

See AOUEINI, HUSSEIN, & CO LTD

HUSSEIN BIN HASHIM AL ATTAS

See AL ATTAS, HUSSEIN BIN HASHIM,

HYATT REGENCY JEDDAH

PO Box 8483, Jeddah 21482
Tel: 6519800
Cable: HYATT
Telex: 602688 HYAT SJ
Telefax: (02) 6516260

Directors: Kamel Zayati (General Manager), Adnan Al Hadi (Regional Director of Sales), Rene Sommer (Financial Controller), Fouad Melhem (Director of Food & Beverage)

PRINCIPAL ACTIVITIES: Hotel services
Branch Offices: Location in Jeddah: Medina Road
Parent Company: Hyatt International Corporation
Principal Bankers: Saudi British Bank, Saudi French Bank, Saudi American Bank
Financial Information:

	1990 SR'000
Sales turnover	36,000
Profits	5,000

Principal Shareholders: Jeddah Hotels Co Ltd
Date of Establishment: October 1980
No of Employees: 280

HYATT REGENCY RIYADH

PO Box 18006, Riyadh 11415
Tel: 4791234
Telex: 402963 Hyatt Sj
Telefax: 4775373

Senior Executives: Abdullah Melhem (General Manager), Nadem Ikram (Director of Finance), Hamza Selim (Director of Sales)

PRINCIPAL ACTIVITIES: Hotel business
Branch Offices: Location in Riyadh: Airport Road, facing Ministry of Defense

Parent Company: Hyatt International Corporation
Principal Shareholders: REDEC
No of Employees: 310

HYATT YANBU

PO Box 300, Yanbu
Tel: 3223888
Cable: HyattYanbu
Telex: 661053

PRINCIPAL ACTIVITIES: Hotel business
Parent Company: Hyatt International Corporation

HYUNDAI ENGINEERING & CONSTRUCTION CO LTD

PO Box 2761, Riyadh 11461
Tel: 4919100, 4919070
Telex: 400197 HYDRYD SJ
Telefax: 4919161

Chairman: Myung-Bak Lee
Senior Executives: Hook-Mok Chung (President & Chief Executive Officer), Han Ho Yang (Executive Managing Director/General Manager Saudi Arabian Projects Operation Centre), Nae-Heun Lee (Senior Executive Vice President Domestic Business Development), Dae-Yoon Kim (Senior Vice President Overseas Contracting & Marketing), Eun-Bang Lee (Director Finance & Accounting)

PRINCIPAL ACTIVITIES: General engineering and contracts
Branch Offices: Jeddah, PO BOx 5678, Tel 6694404, Telex 600040, Fax 6830231; Dammam, PO Box 5090, Tel 8263835, Telex 801862, Fax 8267538; also in the Middle East: Abu Dhabi; Dubai; Oman; Kuwait; Yemen AR; Bahrain; Qatar; Iraq; Jordan; Turkey
Parent Company: Head Office: Korea
Subsidiary Companies: 24 subsidiary companies under Hyundai Group
Principal Bankers: Korea Exchange Bank; National Commercial Bank
Financial Information:

	1990 US$'000
Sales turnover	2,140,726
Profits	28,398
Authorised capital	588,236
Paid-up capital	294,118
Total assets	3,218,373

Principal Shareholders: The Asan Foundation
Date of Establishment: 1947
No of Employees: 5,200 (group)

IBRAHIM A AL HUMEIDAN & BROS CO

See AL HUMEIDAN, IBRAHIM A, & BROS CO

IBRAHIM ABUNAYYAN SONS CO

See ABUNAYYAN, IBRAHIM, SONS CO

I-MAN COMPANY

PO Box 3030, Riyadh 11471
Tel: 01-492003, 4920612, 4921402, 4931287, 4931543
Cable: Aimanamir
Telex: 401376 I-MAN SJ
Telefax: 01-4910703

Chairman: Ibrahim Mohamed Amer (also Director General)
Directors: Ayman Ibrahim Amer (General Manager)

Senior Executives: Rafe A Assad, Mohamed Majdi Toufiq (Finance Manager), Hussain Ali (Purchasing Manager), Eng Naji Al Wasseif (Technical Manager PTT), Eng Ali Mussallami (Technical Manager Hospitals), Eng Saad El Din Ahmed (Technical Manager Street Lighting), Eng Mahmoud Sulaiman (Technical Manager Power Stations), Eng Ahmed Fouad (R & D Manager)

PRINCIPAL ACTIVITIES: Agencies, commerce and contracting, operation and maintenance of biomedical projects, electromechanical engineering works, operation and management of hospitals, power station turnkey projects, etc
Principal Agencies: Schlichting Werft, W Germany; Copeland Boats, UK
Branch Offices: Jeddah, Tel 6915313, 6820900; Dammam, Tel 8981628
Subsidiary Companies: Nama International Enterprises
Principal Bankers: National Commercial Bank; Saudi Cairo Bank; Al-Jazira Bank

Principal Shareholders: Ibrahim M Amer, Ayman I Amer, Ms Najma I Amer and family
Date of Establishment: 1974
No of Employees: 1,613

INDUSTRIAL CO FOR CASTING & SANITARY FITTINGS

PO Box 3505, Riyadh 11481
Tel: 4480107, 4480130
Cable: Saudicast Riyadh
Telex: 400437 Sebaka Sj
Telefax: 4487814

Chairman: HH Prince Khalid Ibn Abdalla Ibn Mohamed
Directors: Abdalla Farid Khalifeh (Managing Director), Harb Saleh El-Zuhair
Senior Executives: Farid Khalifeh (Deputy Managing Director), Sami Elian (Financial Manager)

PRINCIPAL ACTIVITIES: Manufacture and distribution of cast-iron manhole covers and frames for sewage and storm water projects and other requirements in cast-iron
Branch Offices: PO Box 13453, Jeddah; PO Box 5230, Dammam
Principal Bankers: Riyad Bank; National Commercial Bank

Principal Shareholders: HH Prince Khalid bin Abdalla; Eng A F Khalifeh; Eng Harb S Zuhair
Date of Establishment: 1973
No of Employees: 140

INDUSTRIAL CONTRACTORS (INCO)

PO Box 437, Alkhobar 31952
Tel: 8570458, 8576330
Cable: INCO
Telex: 870103 INCO SJ
Telefax: 8570170

Proprietor: Mohammed Omar Babtain
Senior Executives: Tariq M Babtain (General Manager), Adil M Babtain (Admin Manager), Vahe H Ashjian (Technical Manager), Khalil A Khan (Construction Manager) (Technical Manager)

PRINCIPAL ACTIVITIES: General, mechanical and electrical engineering contracting; prefabricated houses; steel and sheet metal fabrication; aluminium joinery, wooden joinery and carpentry; precast concrete manufacturing and erecting
Principal Bankers: Riyad Bank, Alkhobar; Saudi French Bank, Alkhobar
Financial Information:

	SR'000
Authorised capital	10,000

Date of Establishment: 1966
No of Employees: 169

INDUSTRIAL MATERIALS ORGANISATION

PO Box 623, Riyadh 11421
Tel: 4028010, 4027504, 4028884
Cable: Industry
Telex: 400572 Alkaff Sj
Telefax: 4037970

Chairman: Ahmed Abu Bakr Alkaff (Owner)
Directors: Mohamed Ahmed Alkaff (Vice Chairman), Hamdi M Nour (Managing Director)
Senior Executives: Mohmood Syed Ahmed Shalaby (Chief Accountant), Mohd Ahmed Bashir (Executive Secretary), Mohd Y Amin (Sales Supervisor), Varghese Abraham (Manager), Sultan Mohmoud (Manager), Abdul Rehman Alkaff (Manager), Sultan Mahmoud (Marketing Supervisor)

PRINCIPAL ACTIVITIES: Import and distribution of machine tools, hardware, safety and security equipment, power equipment and mechanical machinery
Principal Agencies: Ridgid; Norton; Enerpac; Skil; Heyco; Sykes Pickavant; Proto; Black & Decker; Ingersoll Rand; Sidchrome
Branch Offices: Dammam: PO Box 1889, Dammam 31441, Tel 8336263, Telex 801853, Fax 8334452; Jeddah: PO Box 12285, Jeddah 21473, Tel 6324579, Telex 604734, Fax 6319740
Parent Company: Al Kaff Trading & Contracting Co, Po Box 3058, Riyadh 11471
Associated Companies: Addereyah Printing Press, Riyadh; Zekra Est Stationery Materials, Riyadh; Goba Est, Dammam
Principal Bankers: National Commercial Bank; Saudi American Bank, Riyadh; Saudi British Bank, Riyadh; Albank Alsaudi Alhollandi
Financial Information:

	1989/90 SR'000
Sales turnover	26,000
Total assets	25,992

Principal Shareholders: Sole proprietorship
Date of Establishment: 1965
No of Employees: 92

INDUSTRIALIZED BUILDING SAUDI FACTORIES (IBSF)

PO Box 7665, Jeddah 21472
Tel: 6203669, 6518883
Cable: Masanie IBSF
Telex: 601643 Kabli Sj, 606464 IBSF Sj
Telefax: 6533879

Chairman: Abdulaziz Kabli (General Manager)
Directors: Majdaldeen A Al Basher (Financial & Admin Director), Mohammed A Kabli (Production Division Director), Eng Maher Madkour (Contracting Manager)
Senior Executives: Eng Mohammed A Taki (Technical Manager), Eng Sayed Kamel (Sales Manager)

PRINCIPAL ACTIVITIES: Prefab building contractors, building systems, prefabricated buildings, portacabins, mobile cabins, cold stores, refrigerated trucks, manufacture of polystareen, insulation products, sandwich panels
Parent Company: Al Kabli Corporation, Jeddah
Principal Bankers: Riyad Bank
Financial Information:

	1989 SR'000
Sales turnover	24,000
Authorised capital	62,000
Paid-up capital	18,000
Total assets	42,000

Date of Establishment: 1976
No of Employees: 114

SAUDI ARABIA

INMA CONSTRUCTION MATERIALS CO LTD

PO Box 10016, Jubail Industrial City, Jubail 31961
Tel: (03) 3417377, 3411678
Telex: 832095 Savl Sj
Telefax: 3419564

President: Khalid Ali Al Turki (Owner)
Directors: Z M Khawaja (General Manager)
Senior Executives: W T de Lara (Manager Finance &
Administration)

PRINCIPAL ACTIVITIES: Suppliers of ready mixed concrete,
asphalt concrete, masonry block and miscellaneous precast
products throughout the Jubail Industrial City with ready mix
satellite operations at Khafji, Nuariyah, Dammam, Hofuf and
Dwadmi
Parent Company: Trading & Development Company (TRADCO)
Principal Bankers: Albank Alsaudi Alhollandi; Saudi British
Bank; Al Bank Al Saudi Al Fransi; National Commercial Bank;
all at Jubail Industrial City
Financial Information:

	1990 SR'000
Sales turnover	31,671
Profits	3,286
Authorised capital	17,033
Paid-up capital	17,033
Total assets	33,786

Principal Shareholders: Trading & Development Company
Date of Establishment: 19 February, 1980
No of Employees: 140

INTERBETON SAUDI ARABIA

PO Box 1227, Jeddah 21431
Tel: 02-6653555
Telex: 601424 OSHCOJ SJ

Chairman: A J L Nightingale
Directors: S Masri, A V Leeuwen, R S Sabban

PRINCIPAL ACTIVITIES: Contracting, engineering
Branch Offices: PO Box 1520, Alkhobar, Telex 871204
OSCHOK SJ; PO Box 6461, Riyadh, Telex 400405 THELSA
SJ
Parent Company: Hollandsche Beton Group Rijswijk Holland;
Olayan Saudi Holding Co
Principal Bankers: Saudi American Bank
Financial Information:

	SR'000
Authorised capital	10,000
Paid-up capital	10,000

Principal Shareholders: Olayan Saudi Holdings Co; Interbeton
BV
Date of Establishment: 1979

INTER-CONTINENTAL HOTEL

PO Box 3636, Riyadh 11481
Tel: 4655000
Cable: Inhotelcor
Telex: 401076 Ihc Hot Sj
Telefax: 4657833

Directors: Tom J Krooswijk (Regional Vice-President and
General Manager Riyadh Intercontinental), Pierre Boissel
(Manager), Maurice Batarseh (Regional Controller)

PRINCIPAL ACTIVITIES: Hotel business
Branch Offices: Location in Riyadh: Maazar Street; also Mecca
Intercontinental Hotel, PO Box 1496, Mecca; Massarrah
Intercontinental Hotel, PO Box 827, Taif; Abha
Intercontinental Hotel PO Box 1447, Abha, Saudi Arabia
Parent Company: Intercontinental Hotels Corp (Grand
Metropolitan)

Principal Shareholders: Ministry of Finance & National
Economy, Saudi Arabia
No of Employees: 1,400

INTEREDEC ASWAD CONTRACTING & ENGINEERING CO LTD (INASCO)

PO Box 2457, Dammam 31451
Tel: 8325240, 8325032, 8333720, 8335013
Cable: Inasco
Telex: 802016 INASCO SJ
Telefax: 8346495

Chairman: Dr Ghaith R Pharaon
Directors: Hazem F Aswad (Managing Director)
Senior Executives: Eng Edward A Blyth (Manager, Construction
& Engineering), Adel O Barkawi (Finance Manager)

PRINCIPAL ACTIVITIES: General civil engineering, electrical and
mechanical contracting, dealing in building materials,
sanitaryware, electrical appliances
Principal Agencies: Draka Cable, Holland; B V Industria,
Holland; Holec Transformer Group, Holland, Roland Kuhne
Eng, W Germany
Branch Offices: PO Box 1935, Jeddah, Tel 6652940, Telex
601122 Redec
Subsidiary Companies: INASCO Electrical Division, Dammam;
INASCO Jubail Division, Jubail
Principal Bankers: Albank Alsaudi Alfransi, Dammam; National
Commercial Bank, Dammam; Alsaudi Banque, Bahrain, Bank
Al-Jazira, Dammam

Principal Shareholders: International Research & Development
Co Ltd; Eng Hazem Fayez Al Aswad
Date of Establishment: June 1977
No of Employees: 236

INTERNATIONAL CENTRE FOR COMMERCE & CONTRACTING

PO Box 2388, Jeddah 21451
Tel: 6825961, 6825832, 6829487
Cable: Alamco
Telex: 600534 Incent Sj

Chairman: Sheikh Yousuf Elkhereiji
Directors: Sheikh Ibrahim Elkhereiji, Sheikh Abdulghani
Elkhereiji, Sheikh Solaiman Elkhereiji, Sheikh Mohamed
Elkhereiji
Senior Executives: Saad El-Shashtawi (Finance Manager),
Nadeem Naushad (Assistant Manager), Ahmed Shuja
(Marketing Manager), Ussamah Salaam (Project Manager)

PRINCIPAL ACTIVITIES: Contracting, mainly building
construction, commerce, representation and imports
Principal Agencies: American Desk Int Corp, USA; McDonough
Favorite & Co, USA; KLN Steel Products Co, USA
Branch Offices: Albuag Bldg, Riyadh
Subsidiary Companies: Solaiman Abdullah Elkhereiji
(Architecture Firm), Jeddah, Riyadh; Mohammed Abdullah
Elkhereiji (Law Firm), Jeddah, Riyadh
Principal Bankers: National Commercial Bank; Al Bank Al Saudi
Al Fransi

Date of Establishment: May 1977
No of Employees: 300

INTERNATIONAL MECHANICAL & ELECTRICAL CONTRACTING CO LTD
I.M.E.C.C.O.

PO Box 7155, Jeddah 21462
Tel: 6655688, 6651388
Telex: 604720 IMECCO SJ
Telefax: 6651291

Chairman: Ahmed Y Z Alireza
Directors: Mohamed Yousef Alireza, Mahmoud Y Z Alireza,
Glen T Conley, James J Walker, Greg B Noble

570

Senior Executives: Greg B Noble (Managing Director), Omar J Jama

PRINCIPAL ACTIVITIES: Electrical, mechanical, airconditioning, water and sewage contractors
Branch Offices: PO Box 831, Tabouk, Saudi Arabia
Parent Company: Haji Abdullah Alireza & Co Ltd (51%); Fischbach and Moore International Corp (49%)
Principal Bankers: Saudi British Bank, Jeddah; Republic Bank, Dallas, Texas, USA
Financial Information:

	SR'000
Authorised capital	5,000
Paid-up capital	5,000

Principal Shareholders: Haji Abdullah Alireza & Co (51%); Fischbach & Moore Int Corp (49%)
Date of Establishment: 1979
No of Employees: 210

INTERNATIONAL PRODUCTS EST

PO Box 17, Riyadh 11411
Tel: 4028730
Cable: Kaki, Riyadh

Partner: Sadaga Said Kaki

PRINCIPAL ACTIVITIES: General trading and contracting, import and distribution of air-conditioning and refrigerating equipment; also spare parts and accessories, household appliances, manufacture of ice
Principal Agencies: Prestone, Airwell
Branch Offices: PO Box 1159, Jeddah; PO Box 43, Dammam, Tel 8322864; PO Box 58, Alkhobar, Tel 8641734

INTERNATIONAL SUPPLY EST

PO Box 34, Dammam 31411
Tel: 8326261, 8347414
Cable: Iscol
Telex: 801699 Iscol Sj
Telefax: 8346279

Chairman: Abdulkarim Almojil
Directors: Ahmad H Almojil
Senior Executives: Sakhawat Parkar (Sales Manager), Mubarak Abdullah Al Arji (Public Relations)

PRINCIPAL ACTIVITIES: Supply of petrochemical/oilfield material and industrial equipment
Principal Agencies: Oster Teledyne, USA; Magnaflux, UK; GRI Sapag, France; Keystone Valves, USA
Principal Bankers: Arab National Bank Ltd

Date of Establishment: 1977

INTERNATIONAL TRADING BUREAU

PO Box 1249, Riyadh 11431
Tel: 4031245, 4659932
Cable: Intrab Riyadh
Telex: 401208 Intrab Sj

Chairman: Mahmoud Mashhady (also Proprietor)
Senior Executives: Farmanullah Khan

PRINCIPAL ACTIVITIES: General agents in construction, engineering, electronics, heavy machinery, industrial plants
Subsidiary Companies: Arabian Public Relations Agency, Riyadh; Overseas Catering Est, Riyadh
Principal Bankers: Riyad Bank

Date of Establishment: 1974

INTERSPAN CONSTRUCTION LIMITED

PO Box 999, Alkhobar 31952
Telex: 870098 Mepad Sj

Chairman: John Harris (Managing Director)
Directors: Michael McElligott, D Issac

PRINCIPAL ACTIVITIES: Supply and erection of steel framed buildings, steelwork for multi-storeys
Principal Agencies: Sanders & Forster Ltd; Ash Industries; Direct Fixings Ltd
Branch Offices: PO Box 2486, Jeddah, Telex 600470 Mafco Sj
Associated Companies: Mafco Structural, Jeddah, Saudi Arabia
Principal Bankers: Albank Alsaudi Alhollandi

Date of Establishment: September 1978

ISLAMIC DEVELOPMENT BANK

PO Box 5925, Jeddah 21432
Tel: 6361400 (10 lines)
Cable: Bankislami
Telex: 601137 ISDB Sj; 601407 ISDB Sj
Telefax: 6366871

Chairman: Dr Ahmad Mohamed Ali
Executive Directors: Aboajileh Al Rashid (Libya), Balghoula Bouasria (Algeria), Mamour Malick Jagne (Gambia), Ahmed Hamad Al Nuaimi (Qatar), Dr Zafir Al Omrana (Bahrain), Prof Korkut Ozal (Turkey), Kernaen A Perwataatmadja (Malaysia), Omar Abdullah Sejeini (Saudi Arabia), Yousuf Abdul Latif Al Sirkal (United Arab Emirates), Dr Syed Ali Ahmad Zaki (Sudan), Faisal Abdul Aziz Al Zamil (Kuwait)
Senior Executives: Dr Ahmed Mohamed Ali (President), Ousmane Seck (Vice-President Operation & Projects), Sidharta S P Soerjadi (Vice-President Administration), Fuad Abdullah Al Omar (Vice-President Finance), Abdul Rahman Nour Hersi (Bank Adviser)

PRINCIPAL ACTIVITIES: Financing of development activities in member countries and in Muslim communities in non-member countries in accordance with the principles of the Shariah of the Shariah
Principal Bankers: Saudi International Bank, London; Arab Banking Corporation, Bahrain; Gulf International Bank, London; UBAF, Paris
Financial Information: ID stands for Islamic Dinars; one ID is equivalent to one SDR of the International Monetary Fund

	1990/1410H ID'million
Authorised capital	2,000
Subscribed capital	1,958
Paid-up capital	1,624

Principal Shareholders: Member Countries: Afghanistan; Algeria; Bahrain; Bangladesh; Benin; Bourkina Fasso; Brunei Darussalam; Cameron; Chad; Comoro Is; Djibouti; Egypt; Gabon; Gambia; Guinea; Guinea Bissau; Indonesia; Iraq; Jordan; Kuwait; Lebanon; Libya; Malaysia; Maldives; Mali; Mauritania; Morocco; Niger; Oman; Pakistan; Palestine; Qatar; Saudi Arabia; Senegal; Sierra Leone; Somalia; Sudan; Syria; Tunisia; Turkey; Uganda; United Arab Emirates; Yemen AR; Yemen PDR
Date of Establishment: 1975 (1395 H)
No of Employees: 554

ISSA EL AYOUTY & CO (IAC)

See EL AYOUTY, ISSA, & CO (IAC)

ISSAM KABBANI & PARTNERS

See KABBANI, ISSAM, & PARTNERS

ITT AFRICA/MIDDLE EAST

ITT Africa - Middle East & Saudi Arabia

PO Box 8344, Jeddah 21482
Tel: 6601669
Telex: 603488 SEAL SJ

PRINCIPAL ACTIVITIES: Telecommunications, electronics, hotels, consumer products etc
Branch Offices: PO Box 20924, Riyadh 11465, Tel 4783826, Telex 404752 ITT RUH SJ

J N VALVIS

See VALVIS, J N,

JAHR COMPANY

PO Box 2527, Jeddah 21461
Tel: 6873267, 6875927
Cable: VERY JAHR
Telex: 600848 JAHR SJ

Owner: Sheikh Mohamed Hamed Al Ahmadi

PRINCIPAL ACTIVITIES: Road and bridges construction
Principal Agencies: Contracts from the Ministry of
Communications
Principal Bankers: Riyad Bank, Bank Al-Jazira

Date of Establishment: 1970

JAMEEL, ABDUL LATIF, CO LTD

PO Box 248, Jeddah 21411
Tel: 6604488
Cable: USEF
Telex: 601453 USEF SJ

Chairman: Abdul Latif Jameel
Directors: Yousef Jameel, Mohammed Jameel

PRINCIPAL ACTIVITIES: Import and distribution of vehicles,
trucks, and forklifts; vehicles leasing division
Principal Agencies: Toyota, Kubota, MAN Trucks
Branch Offices: Branches in Riyadh, Dammam, Al Khobar,
Makkah, Taif, Hofuf, Jubail
Principal Bankers: Saudi American Bank, Saudi British Bank;
Gulf International Bank

Principal Shareholders: Sheikh Abdul Latif Jameel and members
of his immediate family
Date of Establishment: 1955
No of Employees: 1,600

JAMJOOM GROUP OF INDUSTRIES

PO Box 59, Jeddah 21411
Tel: 6432578
Cable: Jamjoom
Telex: 601169 Jamjoom Sj

President: Sheikh Abdulgafar Mohammed Jameel Jamjoom
Directors: Mohammed Saleh Jamjoom, Isam Jamjoom, Abdullah
Jamjoom, Mohammed Jameel Jamjoom

PRINCIPAL ACTIVITIES: Import and distribution of air-
conditioning, heating, refrigeration, generating plants, also
water desalination, shipping/navigation, environmental
pollution control and pre-fabricated houses
Principal Agencies: Riley-Beaird Inc, USA; Pinckney Industries
Inc, USA; Southwest Manfg Co of 'Heatwave', USA; McQuay-
Perfex Inc, USA; Overseas Equipment Corporation, USA; Ets
Doisy-Houdart, France; Wescon International BV, Holland;
Hydro Construction Corp, Philippines
Associated Companies: The Jamjoom Group of Industries
comprises the following companies: Jamjoom Corporation for
Commerce & Industry, Jeddah (an electrical and mechanical
engineering concern); Chem Tec Industries, Jeddah
(environmental pollution control and pre-fabricated houses);
Wescon-Jamjoom Saudi Arabia Limited, Jeddah (dealing in
instrumentation work with modern workshop); Jamjoom-Hydro
Limited, Jeddah (all types of contracting business including
civil work); Joint Venture with an American Concern (a panel
board factory for local requirement); Joint Venture with Italian
concern (proposed field for shipping/navigation); Joint
Venture with Korean Concern (agreed business for fishing
and packing industries)
Principal Bankers: Riyad Bank

JAMJOOM VEHICLES & EQUIPMENT

PO Box 1247, Jeddah 21431
Tel: 6871708, 6872702, 6871876, 6872710, 6877096
Cable: Jamvehicle
Telex: 601324 Salah Sj
Telefax: 6879652, 6877525

Chairman: Ahmed Mohammad Salah Jamjoom
Directors: Dr Abdullatif Mohd Salah Jamjoom (Managing
Director), Hamza Salah Jamjoom, Yousuf Salah Jamjoom
Senior Executives: Marwan A Jamjoom (Deputy General
Manager), Waleed Y Jamjoom (Marketing Director), Faisal A
Jamjoom (Production Director), Abdul Ilah (Personnel
Manager), Mumtaz Husain (Company Secretary), Abdul
Rahman Abdullah (Sales Manager)

PRINCIPAL ACTIVITIES: Import and sales of vehicles, heavy
machinery and their spare parts
Principal Agencies: Hino Motors Ltd, Japan; Sakai Heavy
Industries, Japan; Benati Spa, Italy; Elba, Middle East; Cofian
Oil, France; Sun Oil, USA
Branch Offices: Riyadh (PO Box 8570, Tel 2310323), Dammam
(PO Box 2599, Tel 8573868)
Parent Company: Abdullatif Mohd Salah Jamjoom & Bros
Subsidiary Companies: Jamjoom General Agencies; Jamjoom
Drugstore; Middle East Medicine Store
Principal Bankers: Saudi American Bank; Riyad Bank; Saudi
British Bank; National Commercial Bank; Albank Alsaudi
Alhollandi; Saudi Cairo Bank

Date of Establishment: 1959
No of Employees: 208

JAMJOON CONSULT

PO Box 6285, Jeddah 21442
Tel: 6874288, 6877097, 6877098
Cable: Jam Consult
Telex: 600183 Gmcnsl Sj
Telefax: 6808464

Directors: Sh Osman Salah Jamjoom (Director General)
Senior Executives: Sh Jafar Salah Jamjoom (Deputy Director)

PRINCIPAL ACTIVITIES: Design and supervision of medium and
large size projects
Branch Offices: PO Box 10603, Riyadh; PO Box 2539, Medina
Munawarah
Associated Companies: Alex Gorden & Partners, UK; Mott, Hay
and Anderson Int, UK; Robert Matthew, Johnson-Marshall
and Partners, UK
Principal Bankers: Saudi British Bank

Date of Establishment: 1963
No of Employees: 90

JAWATHA EST FOR CIVIL WORKS & TRADING

PO Box 1832, Dammam 31441
Tel: 8335962, 8339716, 8325245, 8422242, 8100211
Telex: 801610 Ameer Sj

Chairman: Mubarak Am Al-Ameer
Senior Executives: Mohid Kobani (Branch Manager), Mussalem
Hurani (Branch Manager)

PRINCIPAL ACTIVITIES: Civil construction, maintenance
building materials, real estate development and general
trading
Branch Offices: National Timber & Building Materials Co, 23rd
St, Dammam; Jawatha Est for Maintenance, Khodharia,
Dammam
Principal Bankers: Riyad Bank, Dammam; Al-Jazira Bank,
Dammam

Principal Shareholders: Sole ownership
Date of Establishment: 1973
No of Employees: 200

JEDDAH CEMENT CO LTD

PO Box 1346, Jeddah 21431
Tel: 6422366, 6422377
Telex: 601165 Sj

Directors: Dr Ghaith Pharaon, Sayed Abdullah Muhammad Baroum, Salah Bin Salem Bin Mahfouz

PRINCIPAL ACTIVITIES: Import, storage and sale of bulk cement
Branch Offices: Yanbu, Tel 4288471

Principal Shareholders: Redec Intertrade; S A M Baroom; Saudi Economic & Development Co

JEDDAH INDUSTRIAL MATERIAL CO (JIMCO)

PO Box 6153, Jeddah 21442
Tel: 6672585, 6672629
Telex: 602616 Jimco Sj

Chairman: Mohamed Al Hamidi
Senior Executives: Abdelkader Djellouli (General Manager)

PRINCIPAL ACTIVITIES: Production and supply of building materials, aggregate, sand, concrete, road materials, asphalt etc
Associated Companies: Al Hamidi Contracting Est, PO Box 130, Riyadh; Cochery, 11 rue de Laborde, 75008 Paris
Principal Bankers: Al Bank Al Saudi Al Fransi, Jeddah; Albank Alsaudi Alhollandi, Jeddah
Financial Information:

	SR'000
Paid-up capital	8,700

Principal Shareholders: Al Hamidi Contracting Est, Saudi Arabia; Cochery, France
Date of Establishment: 1975
No of Employees: 140

JEDDAH MARRIOTT HOTEL

PO Box 6448, Jeddah 21442
Tel: 6714000
Telex: 605135 Mariot Sj
Telefax: 6715990

Directors: Anil V Sampat (General Manager)
Senior Executives: Ahmed Salama (Controller), John Louie (Director of Food & Beverages), Mohamad Dkeidek (Director of Sales)

PRINCIPAL ACTIVITIES: Hotel operation
Parent Company: Marriott Corporation, Washington DC 20058, USA
Principal Bankers: National Commercial Bank, Jeddah
Financial Information:

	1990 SR'000
Sales turnover	44,000
Profits	15,000
Authorised capital	150,000
Paid-up capital	150,000
Total assets	140,000

Date of Establishment: 1983
No of Employees: 260

JEDDAH OIL REFINERY CO

PO Box 1604, Jeddah 21441
Tel: 6426311, 6425495
Cable: Almisfat
Telex: 601150 Sj

Chairman: Dr A H Taher
Directors: M A Ajaj (Managing Director & Executive Asst to the Chairman)
Senior Executives: M A Sehaimi (Managing Director & Asst to the Chairman for Production), K H El Ghamri (General Manager, Finance), M O Sayes (General Manager Marine), Y A Al Zaid (General Manager Production), M S Nasief (General Manager Maintenance & Power), A S Gashlan (General Manager Administration), A O Attas (General Manager Marketing), A Hameed A Kayal (Asst General Manager Administration)

PRINCIPAL ACTIVITIES: Oil refining and distribution
Principal Bankers: Riyad Bank; National Commercial Bank
Financial Information:

	SR'000
Authorised capital	150,000
Issued capital	70,000

Principal Shareholders: Sarco (25%), Petromin (75%)

JERAISY COMPUTER SERVICES

PO Box 317, Riyadh 11411
Tel: 4620101
Telex: 401113 Jrairsy SJ
Telefax: 4625191

Chairman: Abdul Rahman Ali Al Jeraisy
President: Ali Abdul Rahman Al Jeraisy
Senior Executives: Khalaf Al Saad (Vice President Finance), Mohtashim Naveed (Operations Manager), Fouad Hamdan (General Manager Eastern Region), Sanjiv Krishen (General Manager Western Region)

PRINCIPAL ACTIVITIES: Computer services and supply, hardware and software
Principal Agencies: National Advanced Systems; Wang Lab Inc; Mitel Corp; JS Telecom; Iwatsu Systems; Victor Corp; Marvel; Mobel; Micro; BASF; AT&T Paradyne; Multitech Systems; Rittal Werk; ADC Telecommunications; OKI Data Printers; Acco Data; Lamperts; Modular Technology; Everex; Ocean Office Automation (Octek); Viewperfect
Branch Offices: Jeddah: PO Box 2830, Jeddah 21461; Dammam: PO Box 1244, Dammam 31431
Subsidiary Companies: Riyadh House Est; Jeraisytech Est; Jeraisy Computer Paper Products Co; Jeraisy Furniture Factory
Principal Bankers: Saudi American Bank; Saudi British Bank; National Commercial Bank

Principal Shareholders: Sole Proprietorship
Date of Establishment: 1978
No of Employees: 400

JOREPHANCO TRADING & CONTRACTING CO

PO Box 1046, Al Khobar 31952
Tel: (03) 8984028, 8947651, 8982366
Cable: Jorephanco Al Khobar
Telex: 870882 Jorphn Sj
Telefax: 8949554

President: Tawfiek Hassan Jorephani
Directors: Fawzi Hassan Jorephani (Vice President & Managing Director)

PRINCIPAL ACTIVITIES: Foodstuffs importers, traders and contractors
Principal Agencies: Stothert & Pitt Plc, UK; Yasar Holding Co, Turkey; Menghini Gomme, Italy
Branch Offices: Jeddah, Tel 6693914, Fax 6693914; Riyadh, Tel 4782017; Alkhobar, Tel 8955069
Parent Company: Jorephanco Trading & Contracting Co, AlKhobar
Subsidiary Companies: Jorephani Exports, Bath, UK; Citi Print, Bath, UK; Jorephani Productions, Weybridge, UK
Principal Bankers: Al Bank Al Saudi Al Fransi
Financial Information:

	1989 SR'000
Sales turnover	38,000
Profits	3,480
Authorised capital	400.
Paid-up capital	400

Principal Shareholders: T H Jorephani, F H Jorephani
Date of Establishment: 1976
No of Employees: 75

JUFFALI, E A, & BROS

PO Box 1049, Juffali Bldg, Jeddah 21431
Tel: 6672222
Cable: Juffalicent
Telex: 601130 EAJB SJ
Telefax: 6694010

Chairman: Sheikh Ali Juffali
Directors: Sheikh Ahmed Juffali (Managing Director), Sheikh Walid Juffali (Executive Director)
Senior Executives: Jafar Askari (Finance Director), Farouk Ostowani (General Manager Jeddah), Ibrahim Touq (General Manager Riyadh), Khaled Juffali (General Manager Dammam)

PRINCIPAL ACTIVITIES: Trading; civil construction, electro-mechanical, air-conditioning and telecommunications contracting, cement production, vehicle assembly, and body manufacture, super structure, fabrication, supply of heavy equipment, household appliances, prefab buildings, automobiles, refrigeration equipment, oilwell workover services, real estate and insurance
Principal Agencies: Barber Greene, Daimler-Benz, IBM, Kelvinator, Massey-Ferguson, Michelin, Klimich, Siemens, Sulzer, York, Compair, BICC, Demag, Worthington, FMC, Bosch, Heidelberger etc
Branch Offices: Branches in Riyadh (PO Box 86, Telex 401049); Dammam (PO Box 24, Telex 801025); also Beirut, PO Box 155327, Lebanon; Liaison Offices in Zurich, Switzerland; in London, England and in New York, USA
Subsidiary/Associated Companies: The Juffali Group's joint ventures and associated companies include: BICC Saudi Arabia; National Electric & Products Co (NEPCO); National Insurance Co; Arabian Metal Industries; National Automobile Industry; Pool-Arabia; Petro Chemical Engineering; Raychem; Saudi Cement Co; Saudi Bahraini Cement Co; Arabian Petroleum Services Co; Fluor Arabia; Saudi Building Systems (with Butler); Saudi Refrigerator Manufacturing Co; Saudi Tractor Manufacturing Co; Saudi Ericsson Communications; Arabia Electric; Marco; Saudi Air Conditioning Manufacturing Co; Saudi Business Machines (with IBM); Orient Transport Co; Arabian Chemical Co Ltd
Principal Bankers: Al Bank Al Saudi Al Hollandi

Date of Establishment: 1946
No of Employees: 5,000

KABBANI, ISSAM, & PARTNERS
Waterproofing Materials Co (BMC)
Prefabricated Buildings & Commerce Co Ltd (UNITECH)

PO Box 5338, Jeddah 21422
Tel: 6673180
Telex: 604406 UBM SJ
Telefax: 6658079

Chairman: Sheikh Issam Khairy Kabbani
Directors: Abdo A Sweidan (General Manager)
Senior Executives: Imad Mansour (Marketing & Sales Manager), Samir Yassine (Purchasing Manager), Hani Darwishe (Accounts & Administration Manager), Salim Takkoush (Western Region Area Manager), Fouad Khani (Central Region Area Manager), Ahmad Dawood (Eastern Region Area Manager)

PRINCIPAL ACTIVITIES: Roofing Contractors; water proofing membranes; concrete repairs, concrete resin coating and injection; trading, wholesale and retail of building materials, electrical components, tools, ironmongery, insulation products, hardware, bitumous products, sealants, marble fixing mechanical systems, expanded metal, geotextiles

Principal Agencies: Carlisle Syntec Systems, USA/Belgium; Derbit, Italy; AEG, W Germany; Colas Products/Shell, USA; Fischer Italia, Italy; GE Silicones, USA/France; Hawera, W Germany; Italex, Italy; Tremco, USA/UK; Wallmaster, USA; Weiser, UK; Kalis Expanded Metal, Jordan; DWI Dermabit, Saudi Arabia; Fibertex, Denmark
Branch Offices: Riyadh: PO Box 58951, Riyadh 11515, Tel 4651030, Telex 405057, Fax 4658648; Dammam: PO Box 6897, Damman 31452, Tel 8570034, Telex 803392, Fax 8578177
Parent Company: Isam Kabbani & Partners
Principal Bankers: Albank Alsaudi Alhollandi; Saudi American Bank
Financial Information:

	BMC 1991	UNITECH 1991
	SR'000	SR'000
Sales turnover	62,000	77,500
Profits	6,100	3,300
Authorised capital	1,300	20,000
Paid-up capital	1,250	750
Total assets	26,000	30,000

Principal Shareholders: Isam Kabbani, Rima Kabbani
Date of Establishment: 1980/81
No of Employees: 700 (BMC); 115 (UNITECH)

KAKI, AHMED & MOHAMMAD SALEH, (GROUP OF COMPANIES)

PO Box 1224, Jeddah 21431
Tel: 6602160
Cable: Watani Jeddah
Telex: 601503 Amskjd Sj; 600674 Gtrade Sj
Telefax: 6691968

Joint Presidents: Ahmed Saleh Kaki, Mohammad Saleh Kaki
Vice-Presidents: Mohammed Ahmed Kaki, Abdul Ellah Mohammed Kaki, Hisham Ahmed Kaki, Abdulwahab Ahmed Kaki, Ghaith Mohammed kaki
Senior Executives: Dr Maher Wasfi (Group & Technical Div Manager), Alaa El Din Ali (Contract Furnishing Div Manager), Salah A Haza (General Manager Scientific & Medical Division), Hardy Gabathuler (Technical Divi Manager Riyadh), Mahmood Al Dewal (Office Manager Riyadh), Chris Lockie (Marketing Manager Riyadh), Mohammed Bafadel (Finance Manager), Mohammed Ali Mahmood (Office Manager Dammam), Michael Holub (Manager Banking & Security Equip Div), Raymond Doumet (Resident Manager Kaki Hotel)

PRINCIPAL ACTIVITIES: Banking and investment; real estate; industrial development, joint ventures, hotels and commercial centres, civil, structural, electrical, mechanical and telecommunication contracting, aircraft sales, maintenance and training; supply of building materials and equipment; computer systems; contract furnishing, surveying, technical, medical, scientific and bank security equipment supply
Principal Agencies: Wild Heerbrugg; Ernst Leitz Wetzlar; Albert Nestler; Varian; Mettler; Technical Supply Co; Sheer Pride; Umberto Mascagni; Mobilest; Leyform; Alan Cooper; Daiichi Koguo Co; Kotobuki Tenani; Tec Equipment; 3M (Various); Magnavox; Planhold; LogEtronic; Fisher; MIE; Del Mar Avionics; Cape; Diasonics; Foss Electric; Balzars; Finnigan; LeFebure; Fieldcrest Mills; Karastan; Hille International; Captive Seas; Pace Collection; Skema; GIA; Mascagni; Mewaf; Dyrlund; De Havilland; Piper; Pilaetus; Kawasaki; Feal; ISOSIRZ; Monthern; Petrolutubin; Delfino; Technica; Petrolvalves; Metalfar; National Airoil Burners; Martex Spa; Medlux; Estel; Luparense; Kern; Hellige; Oxford Sonicaid; Haake; Ehret
Branch Offices: Location in Jeddah: PO Box 1224, Kaki Centre, Medina Road; also PO Box 208, Riyadh, Tel 4037455, Telex 401313; PO Box 263, Dammam, Tel 8271604, Telex 801506; PO Box 58, Medina, Tel 8224448; PO Box 49, Taif, Tel 7321665 and PO Box 234, Mecca, Tel 5421678

Subsidiary Companies: National Printing Press, Mecca; Jeddah
Kaki Hotel, Jeddah; National Workshop, Jeddah; Kaki Tent
Factory, Jeddah; Kaki Factory for Furniture, Jeddah; Kaki
Aluminium Factory, Jeddah
Principal Bankers: National Commercial Bank; Riyad Bank; Al
Bank Al Saudi Al Fransi
Financial Information:

	1990 SR'000
Sales turnover	160,000
Authorised capital	200,000
Paid-up capital	200,000
Total assets	250,000

Principal Shareholders: Ahmed Saleh Kaki and Mohammed
Saleh Kaki
Date of Establishment: 1915
No of Employees: 1,500

KANDARA PALACE HOTEL

PO Box 473, Jeddah 21411
Tel: 6312833, 6312944, 6312177
Cable: Kandara Palace
Telex: 601095 Kandar Sj

PRINCIPAL ACTIVITIES: Hotel business
Branch Offices: Location in Jeddah: Old Airport Road

Date of Establishment: 1953

KANOO, YUSUF BIN AHMED,
Kanoo Group

PO Box 37, Dammam 31411
Tel: 8323011, 8348880
Cable: Kanoo Dammam
Telex: 801011 YAKD SJ
Telefax: 8345639

Chairman: Abdulla Ali Kanoo
Directors: Abdul Aziz Qassim Kanoo (Deputy Chairman)
Senior Executives: Khalid Mohd Kanoo (Managing Director), Ali
Abdulaziz Kanoo (Deputy Managing Director), Akber Sa'ati
(Group General Manager)

PRINCIPAL ACTIVITIES: Manufacturers' representatives
(construction equipment and oilfield supplies), shipping
agents, travel agents, air cargo, communications, aircraft
handling, clearing and forwarding, insurance, computer and
business services; agricultural and horticultural consultancy,
livestock; consulting, contracting and management; various
service and manufacturing joint ventures
Principal Agencies: Priestman; Grove; Benford; Hyster; Lincoln;
BASF; Bridgestone; Exxon; Rocol; CPT; Hiab; Tremix;
Perkins, and many major shipping lines and international
airlines
Branch Offices: Jeddah: PO Box 812, Tel 6823759, Telex
601039; Riyadh: PO Box 753, Tel 4789578, Telex 401038;
Jubail: PO Box 122, Tel 033611860, Telex 631051; Al Khobar:
Tel 8642020, Telex 871298 KANOO SJ; Al Khalidia: Tel
8571502, Telex 602054 KANOO SJ; Ras Al Khafji/Ras Al
Mishab: PO Box 4, Tel 03766-0555, extn 2908, Telex 631051
KANOO SJ; Ras Tanura/Ju'Aymah Aramco: PO Box 711, Tel
6737147, Telex 651012 KANOO SJ; Yanbu: PO Box 88, Tel
22011, Telex 661027 KANOO SJ
Associated Companies: Associates in Bahrain; Abu Dhabi;
Dubai; Oman; UK; USA
Principal Bankers: Saudi British Bank; Al Bank Al Saudi Al
Hollandi; National Commercial Bank; Saudi American Bank;
Albank Alsaudi Alfransi; Riyad Bank; Arab Commercial Bank
Principal Shareholders: Collective name partnership
Date of Establishment: 1953
No of Employees: 2,000 in Saudi Arabia

KARA EST

PO Box 533, Jeddah 21421
Tel: 6516280, 6516284, 6516016, 6516020
Cable: Karatab
Telex: 601212 Kara Sj
Telefax: 6519084

Chairman: HE Sheikh Abdullah Al Kasabi (also Managing
Director)
Directors: Dr Majid Al Kasabi, Osama Al Kasabi
Senior Executives: Amin M Simbaw (Deputy General Manager),
Eng S Amin (Technical Director)

PRINCIPAL ACTIVITIES: Building and civil engineering
contractors (roads, bridges, tunnels), production of asphalt
and supply of building materials; sewerage and water
networks and town cleaning
Branch Offices: Riyadh; Makkah

Date of Establishment: 1966

KAYMART COMPANY LTD

PO Box 526, Jeddah 21421
Tel: 6712211, 6713311, 6716343
Telex: 601370, 600404 KAYNOR

Directors: Fouad Abdel Rahman Kayal, Rashad Abdullah Kayyal,
Abdul Majeed Abdullah Kayyal
Senior Executives: Salih Elamin, Zahid Ali Khan

PRINCIPAL ACTIVITIES: Shipping agencies, bunkering,
contractors, importers
Principal Bankers: Arab Bank, Geneva; Al Jazira Bank, Jeddah

Principal Shareholders: Directors as described
Date of Establishment: 1979

KHALDA CORP FOR COMMERCE
CONTRACTING AGENCIES & INDUSTRY

PO Box 99, Riyadh 11411
Tel: 4761175
Telex: 401186 Khalda Sj

Chairman: Sheikh Ali Mohammad Al-Awaji (Managing Director)

PRINCIPAL ACTIVITIES: General building contractors; import
and distribution of ready made garments, wood and metal
furniture, office equipment, dealing in trucks and parts

KHALIFA A ALGOSAIBI (GROUP OF
COMPANIES)

See ALGOSAIBI, KHALIFA A, (GROUP OF COMPANIES)

KHARAFI, M A, EST

PO Box 423, Riyadh 11411
Tel: 4764344, 4785866
Telex: 401206 Kharafi Sj

Senior Executives: Zakaria Zaidan (Saudi Arabia Area Manager)

PRINCIPAL ACTIVITIES: Civil and construction and
prefabricated buildings
Branch Offices: In Saudi Arabia: PO Box 43, Dhahran Airport,
Tel 8647618, Telex 870195; Jeddah, Tel 6604677, Telex
600674; in Abu Dhabi: PO Box 650; in North Yemen: PO Box
2296, Sanaa
Parent Company: Head Office in Kuwait
Principal Bankers: Arab National Bank

Principal Shareholders: Mohammed Abdul Al Kharafi (Kuwait)

KHUSHEIM COMPANY

PO Box 119, Dammam 31411
Tel: 8321010, 8325451, 8321083, 8333574
Cable: Khusheim
Telex: 801172 Khushim Sj
Telefax: 03-8325451

Chairman: Dr Reda Hassan Khusheim

SAUDI ARABIA

Directors: Khalifa Hamdan Al Argobi (Managing Director)
Senior Executives: Saeed Ahmed Bakhtir (Sales Manager)

PRINCIPAL ACTIVITIES: Industrial equipment, welding
equipment, water pumps, generators, air compressors,
hydraulic presses, drilling and milling machines, steel bars,
concrete mixers, elevators, cables, concrete cutting machines,
wood-working machines; forklifts; transformers, repair and
rewinding of motors, generators, transformers and other
electrical items
Principal Agencies: Makita Power Tools
Branch Offices: Al-Khobar, Tel 8641246; Riyadh, Tel 4489333;
Hofuf, Tel 5821220; Khamis Mushait, Tel 07-2230060; Jeddah,
Tel 02-6895835
Principal Bankers: The Saudi British Bank; United Saudi
Commercial Bank
Financial Information:

	1990 SR'000
Sales turnover	25,000

Principal Shareholders: Dr Reda H Khusheim
Date of Establishment: 1950
No of Employees: 60

KING-WILKINSON (SAUDI ARABIA) LTD

PO Box 1110, Alkhobar 31952
Tel: 8950536, 8951771
Telex: 871304 KWSA SJ
Telefax: 8649795

PRINCIPAL ACTIVITIES: Consulting engineers
Parent Company: King-Wilkinson Ltd, Middlesborough, UK

KITE ARABIA LTD

PO Box 2978, Riyadh 11461
Tel: 4641994, 4658141
Telex: 402748 GHAITH SJ

President: C Kenneth Kite

PRINCIPAL ACTIVITIES: General building construction; interior
and exterior finishes including special coatings, dry-wall,
tiling, flooring, partition and painting; operation and
maintenance of facilities
Branch Offices: PO Box 30118, Yanbu, Tel: 3968959
Associated Companies: Kite International Inc, USA

KUTBI FOR PETROLEUM & INDUSTRIAL EQUIPMENT

PO Box 3489, Jeddah 21471
Tel: 6835891, 6420450, 6429056
Cable: Batooltradeco
Telex: 607047 Batool SJ
Telefax: 6429054, 6533261

Chairman: Hasan Mohd Kutbi
Directors: Naji Hasan Kutbi (Managing Director)
Senior Executives: Faisal Hassan Kutbi

PRINCIPAL ACTIVITIES: Service station equipment, hand and
air tools, gasoline pumps, fire extinguishers, gasoline engine,
car washing equipment, vehicle lifts, air compressors
lubrication and greasing equipment, garage equipment,
battery chargers, computer wheel balancers, electric motors
and steam cleaners, tyre changers
Principal Agencies: Snap-on Tools Int, Bennett Pump Corp,
Smith Meter, Briggs & Stratton Corp, Walter Kidde, Fimec
Motori, Rotary Lift Corp, Kellogg American Compressors,
Black & Decker, Aro Corp, Graco Lubrication, Fog
Lubrication, Christe, Homestead, Diamonds Tools, Bennett,
Forney, Wheel Weights (Hodge), ARO
Branch Offices: Riyadh, Dammam, Taif, Medina, Khamis
Mushayat, Tabuk, Burayadah, Jeddah
Associated Companies: Kutbi for International Business
(automobiles and components)
Principal Bankers: National Commercial Bank, Jeddah

Financial Information:

	1990 SR'000
Authorised capital	25,000
Paid-up capital	15,000

Date of Establishment: 1949
No of Employees: 55

LAING WIMPEY ALIREZA LTD

PO Box 2797, Riyadh 11461
Tel: 4765995, 4764308
Cable: Airconsa Riyadh
Telex: 401404 Lawial Sj

Chairman: Sheikh Ahmed Y Z Alireza
Directors: Sheikh Ahmed Y Z Alireza, Sheikh Mahmoud Y Z
Alireza, Sheikh Mohamad Y Z Alireza, K S Bowden, R J
Astley, A D McDowall, J M K Laing, G O Whitehead, J A
Armitt, D C Evans

PRINCIPAL ACTIVITIES: Building and civil engineering
contracting
Branch Offices: PO Box 2059, Jeddah, Tel 6695935, Telex
600091
Principal Bankers: Saudi British Bank; Clydesdale Bank,
London; National Westminster Bank, London
Financial Information:

	SR'000
Authorised capital	6,000
Paid-up capital	6,000

Principal Shareholders: John Laing & Son BV; W G H
Investments Ltd; Haji Abdullah Alireza & Co
Date of Establishment: 1966 as JV, 1975 as Saudi Limited
Liability Company
No of Employees: 500

LAMA CO FOR DEVELOPMENT & CONTRACTING

PO Box 5305, Jeddah 21422
Tel: 6658339, 6675619
Cable: Tawsilatco
Telex: 600433 Lama Sj

President: Talib A Hafiz
Directors: Mohammad Talib, Hani Talib
Senior Executives: Talib A Hafiz (President & Managing
Director)

PRINCIPAL ACTIVITIES: General, civil, electrical, mechanical
contracting, buildings, roads, hospitals, community centres,
rough grading, landscape, sewerage and water pipelines
Branch Offices: Jubail: PO Box 446, Jubail 31951
Principal Bankers: Saudi American Bank, Albank Al-Saudi Al-
Hollandi, Bank Al-Jazira
Financial Information:

	SR'000
Authorised capital	5,000
Paid-up capital	5,000

Principal Shareholders: Talib A Hafiz, Mohammad Talib A Hafiz,
Hani Talib A Hafiz
Date of Establishment: July 1977
No of Employees: 290

LAMNALCO (SAUDI ARABIA) LTD

PO Box 90, Alkhobar 31952
Tel: 8640435, 8640835
Cable: Rezayat
Telex: 870502 Lam Kho Sj

President: Teymour Abdulla A A Alireza
Directors: J H N Gibson, A Weijburg, A Joustra

PRINCIPAL ACTIVITIES: Marine and offshore services and
consultancy; port and terminal operations and maintenance;
boat chartering; hydrographic surveys; offshore platform

maintenance and services; underwater pipeline inspections repair and installations; marine pilotage, oil pollution control/recovery services; marine training
Branch Offices: PO Box 203, Yanbu; PO Box 6670, Jeddah; PO Box 61, Abu Dhabi; PO Box 5687, Sharjah; PO Box 10316, Khorfakkan, UAE
Parent Company: Group Head Office: Sharjah
Associated Companies: A member of the Alireza Group of Companies
Principal Bankers: Saudi British Bank

Principal Shareholders: National Contracting Company, Saudi Arabia (75%); Bos Kalis Westminister Group (25%)
Date of Establishment: 1976 (Saudi Arabia); Lamnalco Group 1963
No of Employees: Saudi 755

LANA TRADING & CONTRACTING
PO Box 7604, Jeddah 21472
Tel: 6531672, 6534600
Cable: Afrodet
Telex: 602391 Lana Sj

Directors: Taha A Kumosani
Senior Executives: Samer A Kumosani (Manager)

PRINCIPAL ACTIVITIES: General trading and contracting; consultants; building materials; cleaning contractors
Principal Agencies: OTR, Milan; ITA, Milan; How Chi Enterprise, Tapei

Date of Establishment: April 1979
No of Employees: 50

LAND SEA TRANSPORT CO LTD
PO Box 5791, Jeddah 21432
Tel: 6658396
Cable: Lstco
Telex: 601260 Center Sj

Directors: Sheikh Faisal A Bushnak, Sheikh Zuhdi Ahmed Bushnak, Sheikh Baha Al Din Kashoej, Knut Kloster
Senior Executives: F A Bushnak (Managing Director)

PRINCIPAL ACTIVITIES: Stevedoring; navigation; port management; transportation
Principal Bankers: Riyadh Bank
Financial Information:

	SR'000
Authorised capital	10,000
Paid-up capital	10,000

LAW OFFICES OF M M J NADER
PO Box 3595, Jeddah 21481
Tel: 6652067
Cable: Saudicomp
Telex: 603285 Jaber SJ
Telefax: (02) 6608709

Directors: Mohamed M J Nader (Principal)
Senior Executives: R K Shah (Legal Consultant), M A Mallasi (Legal Consultant), Siddig M Ali (Legal Consultant), Dr Arnd Bernaerts (Legal Consultant), S M Kahtani (Legal Consultant), S A Pawlowski (Legal Consultant), Hussain M Al Sowyyed (Advocate), Akram M Nader (Debt Collector), K M Owaidah (Legal Consultant), Yousuf Badr (Legal Consultant)

PRINCIPAL ACTIVITIES: Legal consultancy, debt collection and translation
Principal Agencies: Member of the American Bar Association, International Bar Association, Arab British Chamber of Commerce, Institute of Chartered Arbitrators, Euro Arab Arbitration Systems
Branch Offices: Riyadh: PO Box 89704, Riyadh 11692, Tel 01-4793733, Fax 01-4792311
Principal Bankers: Saudi Cairo Bank, Jeddah; Al Bank Al Saudi Al Fransi, Jeddah; Riyad Bank, Riyadh

Principal Shareholders: Sole proprietorship
Date of Establishment: 1977
No of Employees: 28

LIGHTWEIGHT CONSTRUCTION CO (SIPOREX)
PO Box 6230, Riyadh 11442
Tel: 1-4981800
Telex: 402124 LCCSIP SJ
Telefax: 1-4982072

Chairman: Eng Abdullah Al Tharwa

PRINCIPAL ACTIVITIES: Manufacture of precast, lightweight, thermally insulating blocks and reinforced panels (wall panels, roof slabs, lintels)
Financial Information:

	1990 SR'000
Sales turnover	22,000
Profits	4,000
Authorised capital	30,000
Paid-up capital	30,000
Total assets	52,000

Date of Establishment: 1978
No of Employees: 130

LITTLE, ARTHUR D, INTERNATIONAL INC
PO Box 3266, Riyadh 11471
Tel: 4770153, 4770227
Telex: 400188 LITTLE SJ
Telefax: 4770134

Chairman: Harland A Riker
Directors: L Ray Kelly (Vice President Asia)
Senior Executives: Ghassan Barrage (VP & Managing Director Middle East), Martin Mankowski (Riyadh), Michael Sausman (Jeddah), William O'Neil (Financial Manager)

PRINCIPAL ACTIVITIES: Business management and technical consultants
Branch Offices: Jeddah
Parent Company: Arthur D Little Inc
Associated Companies: Saudi Consulting House - Arthur D Little Association, Riyadh
Principal Bankers: National Commercial Bank

Principal Shareholders: Employees Pension Fund

LOCKHEED ARABIA
PO Box 2811, Riyadh 11461
Tel: 4421133, 4417294
Telex: 400208 LOGGEP SJ
Telefax: (01) 4420484

Directors: Mansour Ibrahim Al-Tassan (Executive Director), C Stephen Jungers (General Manager)

PRINCIPAL ACTIVITIES: The design, installation, maintenance and operation of aerospace, communications and electrical systems and equipments relating to marine, environmental security, vocation and medical projects. Aircraft and helicopter maintenance, training and operational support
Branch Offices: PO Box 1963, Jeddah 21441, Tel: 6963694
Associated Companies: Lockheed Corporation, USA

Principal Shareholders: 803
Date of Establishment: 1982

M A AL TUWAIJRI STORES
See AL TUWAIJRI, M A, STORES

M A KHARAFI EST
See KHARAFI, M A, EST

M AL MOAMMAR & CO LTD
See AL MOAMMAR, M, & CO LTD

M JAMIL AL DAHLAWI CO

See AL DAHLAWI, M JAMIL, CO

M N AL KURDI TRADING EST

See AL KURDI, M N, TRADING EST

M SIRAJ ATTAR & BROS

See ATTAR, M SIRAJ, & BROS

MADINA ESTABLISHMENT

PO Box 198, Alkhobar 31952
Tel: 8642995
Telex: 870138 Madany Sj

President: Mansour Ahmed Madany (also Proprietor)

PRINCIPAL ACTIVITIES: Contracting, construction,
   maintenance, trading, industrial machineries, industrial
   projects (steel pipe mills, pre-cast units), trading in foodstuffs,
   light machineries and appliances and furniture
Principal Agencies: Custom Hydraulics Corp, USA
Branch Offices: Eastern and Central Saudi Arabia
Principal Bankers: Riyad Bank; Albank Alsaudi Alhollandi

MAGHRABI, MOHAMED ALI, & SONS

Trading Division, PO Box 61, Jeddah 21411
Tel: 6478322, 6471956, 6473570
Cable: Maghrabi
Telex: 601076 Mamtex
Telefax: 6474403

President: Mohamed Ali Maghrabi
Directors: Aaly Maghrabi (General Manager), Abdul Elah
   Maghrabi, Alaa Maghrabi
Senior Executives: M M A Gilmore (Commercial Manager),
   Iftekar Hassan (Finance Manager), Brian Reilly (General Parts
   & Service Manager), Ibrahim Moussa (General Sales
   Manager)

PRINCIPAL ACTIVITIES: Import and marketing of construction
   equipment, generating sets, commercial vehicles, paper
   products
Principal Agencies: Dresser; Atalanta; Thwaites; Irmer and Elze;
   J I Case; Baromix; Bomag GmbH; F Dieci; Pegaso; Kato
Branch Offices: Riyadh: PO Box 100, Tel 4769949, 4769115,
   Telex 400065; Alkhobar: PO Box 323, Tel 8641908, 8576664,
   Telex 870096; Buraidah; Abha; Madinah
Subsidiary Companies: Maghrabi Transport Co; Maghrabi
   Commercial Co
Principal Bankers: Riyad Bank
Financial Information:

	1990 SR'000
Sales turnover	120,000
Total assets	250,000

Principal Shareholders: Maghrabi family
Date of Establishment: 1940
No of Employees: 100

MAHMOOD SAEED COLLECTIVE CO

PO Box 1794, Jeddah 21441
Tel: 6474610, 6480084, 6436980, 6423566
Cable: Kudwah Jeddah
Telex: 601559 Saeed Sj

Chairman: Mahmood Saeed
President: Abdul Khaliq Saeed
Senior Executives: H Kamal, Taiseer Tamlieh, Abdul Hamid, A K
   Nagi, Souhail Bergawi

PRINCIPAL ACTIVITIES: Manufacture of foam mattresses and
   production of cans and canning of soft drinks (Pepsicola,
   Sunkist); import of textiles, cosmetics and toiletries, also
   manufacture of perfume and cosmetics items

Principal Agencies: J Casanova, France; General Cosmetics,
   Holland; Pacoma, France; Balestra, Italy; Intercosmo, Italy;
   Conair Hair, USA
Branch Offices: Riyadh: Tel 4020313; Medina: Tel 8229190;
   Dammam: Tel 8269311; Gaseem: Tel 3246294; Gizan: Tel
   3170935
Subsidiary Companies: Saudi Fruit Juice & Beverages Industry,
   Jeddah, Tel 6364153, Telex 603669; Saudi Perfume &
   Cosmetics Industry, Jeddah, Tel 6360020, Telex 603519;
   Jeddah Foam Laminates Factory, Tel 6377092, Telex 603671;
   Mahmood Saeed Est for Textile, Tel 6444247, Telex 601559;
   Jeddah Beverage Can Making Co Ltd, Tel 6363307, Telex
   605937
Principal Bankers: SIBC, Jeddah; Bank Al Jazira, Jeddah; Saudi
   Cairo Bank, Jeddah

Principal Shareholders: Sheikh Mahmood Saeed
Date of Establishment: 1952
No of Employees: 800

MANSOUR B JUMAH TRADING & CONTRACTING EST

PO Box 1179, Alkhobar 31952
Tel: 8645013, 8645517
Telex: 870198 Mansour SJ

Senior Executives: Nassir Al Sharif (General Manager)

PRINCIPAL ACTIVITIES: General contracting, mechanical and
   electrical works, travel agency, hotel services, agencies,
   automatic car wash
Branch Offices: PO Box 8539, Riyadh, Tel 4649237, Telex
   400686

No of Employees: 1,000

MANSOUR GROUP OF COMPANIES

PO Box 3362, Riyadh 11471
Tel: 4643975, 4643989
Telex: 401390 Mansur Sj

PRINCIPAL ACTIVITIES: Contractors and representatives,
   construction, electronic and defense systems, furniture,
   transportation
Branch Offices: Jeddah: PO Box 6231, Jeddah 21442, Tel
   6449997

MANSUR ATTAR FAKHRI CO
M.A.F.C.O.

PO Box 2486, Jeddah 21451
Tel: 6445512, 6429708
Cable: Commercial
Telex: 600470 Mafco Sj

Chairman: HRH Talal Bin Mansur Bin Abdulaziz Al Saud
Directors: Said Fakhri, Sami M Attar, Abdulrahim M Attar,
   Muhammad M Attar

PRINCIPAL ACTIVITIES: General trading & contracting, dealing
   in cement, wood, clearing and forwarding agents;
   warehousing; transportation; aircraft services; supply of
   building materials; furnishings; interior designers; office and
   domestic equipment
Subsidiary Companies: MAFCO Gulf United Freight Systems;
   MAFCO Medfurn; Mafco Structural
Principal Bankers: National Commercial Bank

Date of Establishment: 1978

MANUFACTURING & BUILDING CO LTD
M.A.B.C.O.

PO Box 1549, Riyadh 11441
Tel: 4778421
Cable: Precast
Telex: 401364 Mabco Sj
Telefax: 4790976

Chairman: HE Hassan Mishari Al Hussein

Directors: Omar Aggad (President), Yousif H Al Hamdan (Executive Vice President), Abdullah Al Hudaithi (Vice President), Nadim El Said (Vice President)

Senior Executives: Rifat Lubani (Manager Construction Div), Jawad Adra (Manager Manufacturing Div), Fida Jdeed (Marketing Manager), Fawaz Abbasi (Deputy Manager Finance & Admin), Ghassan Adra (Procurement Manager), Nassif Rizkallah (Manager Technical Support)

PRINCIPAL ACTIVITIES: Manufacturers of precast components for building construction including extruded prestressed hollow core slabs, external wall, internal walls and partitions, stairs, sunshades, parapets, fencing. Also general contractors undertaking turnkey construction projects

Branch Offices: Riyadh Factory: PO Box 52743, Riyadh 11573, Tel 4981222, Telex 404677 Mabco Sj; Dammam: PO Box 5374, Damman 31422, Tel 8430513, Telex 802082 Mabco SJ; Jeddah: PO Box 5406, Jeddah 21422, Tel 6533585, Telex 606428 Mabco Sj, Fax 6533585

Associated Companies: GRC (SA) Ltd, PO Box 52743, Riyadh 11573 Tel 4981222, Saudi Vetonit Co Ltd, PO Box 52235 Riyadh 11563, Tel 4650046; Saudi Finnish Contracting Co (SAFINNCO), PO Box 2809 Riyadh 11461, Tel 4773518; Arabian Parc Ltd, PO Box 1549, Riyadh 11441, Tel 4778421

Principal Bankers: Riyad Bank; Arab National Bank; Saudi American Bank; The Saudi Investment Bank

Financial Information:

	1989
	SR'000
Sales turnover	634,504
Authorised capital	100,000
Paid-up capital	100,000
Total assets	266,011

Principal Shareholders: A group of prominent Saudi businessmen

Date of Establishment: 1977

No of Employees: 3,590

MAPHAR COMPANY LTD

PO Box 1301, Jeddah 21431
Tel: 6653158, 6653141
Cable: MAPHAR - JEDDAH
Telex: 601055 Maphar Sj
Telefax: 6654742

Directors: Eng Khaled F Aswad (Managing Director)

Senior Executives: Eng Nazmi Khayat (Contracts & Technical Manager), Ahmed Rami Al Zetawi (Financial Manager), Mahmood Khaled Daas (Purchasing Manager), Saeed Abdallah Al Ghamdi (Personnel Manager)

PRINCIPAL ACTIVITIES: General contractors

Principal Bankers: Saudi American Bank; Al Bank Al Saudi Al Fransi

Financial Information:

	1990
	SR'000
Sales turnover	13,892
Profits	1,530
Authorised capital	5,000
Paid-up capital	5,000
Total assets	19,105

Principal Shareholders: Eng Khaled Fayez Al Aswad, Mrs Baria Shawki Keilani

Date of Establishment: 1970 as Maphar Est; 1978 as Maphar Co

No of Employees: 420

MARINE TRANSPORT INTERNATIONAL CO LTD

PO Box 4811, Jeddah 21412
Tel: 6514532, 6514772, 6512061
Cable: Martrans
Telex: 601777 Alreza Sj

Chairman: Sheikh Yousef Alireza
Directors: Sheikh Fahd M Alireza, Sheikh Tarik A Alireza

PRINCIPAL ACTIVITIES: Container terminal management at Jeddah
Branch Offices: 185/187 Brompton Road, London SW1 1NE, UK

Principal Shareholders: Alireza Organisation, Jeddah
Date of Establishment: 1976
No of Employees: 1,200

MARWAN TRADING & CONSTRUCTION EST

PO Box 1440, Jeddah 21431
Tel: 6518201, 6518205, 6518209
Cable: Marwanco
Telex: 605363 Mutcen Sj
Telefax: 6519159

President: Abdul Qadir Hassan Mutawalli
Senior Executives: Joseph Tawil (Manager)

PRINCIPAL ACTIVITIES: Supply of building materials; wooden doors; and all decorative materials; paints, granulite, van-tile, coral, etc
Branch Offices: Makkah: Tel 5432078, 5733749; Riyadh: Tel 4789192, Taif: Tel 7320049
Subsidiary Companies: Al Mutwalli Department Store, Jeddah
Principal Bankers: Riyad Bank, Jeddah

Principal Shareholders: Abdul Qadir H Mutawalli (Sole Proprietor)
Date of Establishment: 1972
No of Employees: 93

MASOOD CORPORATION FOR TRADING, INDUSTRY & CONTRACTING

PO Box 3900, Jeddah 21481
Tel: 6658352, 6427200
Telex: 601876 Masjed Sj

Chairman: Ahmed Omar Masood (Managing Director)

PRINCIPAL ACTIVITIES: General building contractors
Branch Offices: Makkah; Medina; Taif; Khamis Mushait

Date of Establishment: 1971

MASOOD TRADING & CONTRACTING EST

PO Box 324, Jeddah 21411
Tel: 6443842
Cable: Perdesi
Telex: 601798 Ilyas SJ

Chairman: Ghulam Masood (Owner)

PRINCIPAL ACTIVITIES: Importers, wholesalers and agents, tools, locks, canned goods
Principal Agencies: SICEM, Italy; Bleu d'Outremer et Couleurs; Gedore Tools (India) Ltd; Warren Tea Ltd, India
Branch Offices: Riyadh & Alkhobar
Subsidiary Companies: Masood Saree Centre, Jeddah
Principal Bankers: Bank Al-Jazira

Principal Shareholders: Sole Proprietor
Date of Establishment: 1954

MASSARAH INTERCONTINENTAL HOTEL

PO Box 827, Taif
Tel: 7328333
Cable: INHOTELCOR
Telex: 750055
Telefax: (2) 7361844

Senior Executives: Noel Massoud (General Manager), Mamoun Malhas (Sales Manager)

PRINCIPAL ACTIVITIES: Hotel business
Parent Company: Intercontinental Hotels Corporation

Date of Establishment: 1977
No of Employees: 197

MASSTOCK SAUDIA LTD

PO Box 8524, Riyadh 11492
Tel: 4776442, 4788400
Telex: 402328 Massdi Sj

Chairman: H H Prince Sultan Bin Mohameed Bin Saud Al Kabir
Directors: Alaistair K McGuckian, Patrick D McGuckian

PRINCIPAL ACTIVITIES: Turnkey contracting, extensive dairy and arable farms, land preparation, water well drilling, farm planning and construction, agricultural services, farm management, dairying, vegetables
Parent Company: Masstock International Ltd
Associated Companies: Almarai Ltd; Al Nakhlah Est For Trade & Industry; Richland Supplies Ltd

Principal Shareholders: Joint venture between Masstock Int (N Ireland) and Prince Sultan Ibn Mohammed Ibn Saud Al Kabir
No of Employees: over 1,000

MCCLELLAND-SUHAIMI LTD

PO Box 2165, Dammam 31451
Tel: 8577491, 8574200, 8572163
Telex: 801477 MEASL SJ
Telefax: (03) 8572035

Directors: G J Kramer, K J Koch, Khalid A R Alsuhaimi, Khalid M Alsuhaimi
Senior Executives: Niaz Ahmad (General Manager)

PRINCIPAL ACTIVITIES: Geotechnical and construction materials engineering and consultation; on-site quality control, testing of soil, concrete, asphalt, steel, chemical analyses; geotechnical and geophysical site investigations onshore/offshore
Branch Offices: Jubail, Riyadh and Jeddah
Parent Company: Fugro-McClelland BV; Alsuhaimi Company
Principal Bankers: Saudi American Bank, Dammam; Albank Alsaudi Alhollandi, Dammam
Financial Information:

	1988/89 SR'000
Sales turnover	15,401
Profits	975
Authorised capital	2,000
Paid-up capital	2,000
Total assets	7,649

Principal Shareholders: Fugro-McClelland BV; Alsuhaimi Company
Date of Establishment: August 1975
No of Employees: 74

MECHANICAL SYSTEMS CO LTD

PO Box 20935, Riyadh 11465
Tel: 4542560, 4540220
Telex: 403624 MSI SJ

Chairman: C Mel Smith
Directors: Khaled Ben Musaed El Seif

PRINCIPAL ACTIVITIES: Mechanical engineering contractors; supply of mechanical equipment and machinery; prefabricated buildings; waste treatment plants and incinerators
Principal Agencies: Mitchell Engineering Co; Clow Corp; Consumat Systems Inc; Johnson-Penn Controls; Marley Cooling Towers
Parent Company: Mechanical Systems, Inc, USA
Principal Bankers: National Commercial Bank, Saudi British Bank

Financial Information:

	SR'000
Authorised capital	4,000
Paid-up capital	4,000

Date of Establishment: September 1976
No of Employees: 75

MEDCO
Middle East Development Co

PO Box 1140, Alkhobar 31952
Tel: 8578804, 8578918
Cable: Mideastco
Telex: 871401/2 Medc Sj
Telefax: (3) 8579714

President: Sheikh Saleh A Alfadl (Senior Partner)
Directors: Ibrahim A Alfadl, Leif Johansson (General Manager)
Senior Executives: Yousef H Haddad (Finance Manager)

PRINCIPAL ACTIVITIES: Importers of heavy construction and earthmoving equipment, agricultural equipment, crushing and asphalt plants, road transport
Principal Agencies: Sweden: Volvo BM, Dynapac Heavy & Dynapac Light, Alimiak AB, Svedala-Arbra, Flygt; West Germany: Deutz Fahr, Stoll, Flygt Pumpen; Denmark: H A Agro Service Aps, Hartvig Jensen; USA: Sullair Corp, OMC, EDCO
Branch Offices: Riyadh: PO Box 19, Tel 4950828, Telex 403859, Fax (1) 4950832; Jeddah: PO Box 2680, Tel 6821333, Telex 602329, Fax (2) 6835496
Associated Companies: Medscan Terminal, Dammam
Principal Bankers: Al Bank Al Saudi Al Fransi; Albank Alsaudi Alhollandi; Banque Indosuez, Bahrain & Luxembourg
Financial Information:

	1988/89 SR'000	1989/90 SR'000
Sales turnover	27,000	37,000
Profits	2,000	4,000
Authorised capital	1,000	1,000
Paid-up capital	1,000	1,000
Total assets	85,000	89,000

Principal Shareholders: Saleh A Alfadl, Ibrahim A Alfadl
Date of Establishment: 1397H
No of Employees: 74

MEDINA ELECTRIC COMPANY

PO Box 5920, Jeddah 21432
Tel: 6650654, 6675818
Cable: Medinaelectric
Telex: 600870 MECJ SJ

Chairman: Sheikh Ahmed Juffali (Managing Director)

PRINCIPAL ACTIVITIES: Electrical power generation, transmission and distribution
Branch Offices: Medina: PO Box 128

Date of Establishment: 1957
No of Employees: 700

MEDINA SHERATON HOTEL

PO Box 1735, Medina
Tel: 8230240
Cable: Sherat
Telex: 570076 Medshr SJ
Telefax: 8251628

Senior Executives: Reda Darwish (General Manager), Mohamed Fahmy (Executive Assistant Manager), Nasser Abdine (Sales & Marketing Manager), Aftab Ansari (Financial Manager)

PRINCIPAL ACTIVITIES: Hotel business
Parent Company: ITT Corporation, New York
Principal Bankers: Bank Al Saudi Al Fransi, Medina

Financial Information:

	1989
	SR'000
Sales turnover	15,000
Profits	2,700
Authorised capital	2,000
Total assets	2,000

Principal Shareholders: Ministry of Finance & National Economy, Saudi Arabia
Date of Establishment: 1,979
No of Employees: 140

MERZARIO MIDDLE EAST

PO Box 832, Jeddah 21421
Tel: 6423799
Telex: 602217 MESAU SJ
Telefax: 6423799 ext 118

Senior Executives: F Poggi (General Manager), D Bianchi (Marketing Manager), Adel Ezzat (Branch Manager, Dammam), T Kayali (Branch Manager, Riyadh)

PRINCIPAL ACTIVITIES: Shipping and forwarding
Branch Offices: PO Box 299, Dammam 31411, Tel 8334943, Telex 803208, Fax 8334943; PO Box 4767 Riyadh 11412, Tel 4632946, Telex 406449, Fax 4644831
Parent Company: Andrea Merzario SpA Via Cavriana, 14 Milano
Principal Bankers: Bank Al Saudi Al Fransi; Saudi American Bank

METITO ARABIA INDUSTRIES LTD

PO Box 6133, Riyadh 11442
Tel: 4787001
Cable: METITO
Telex: 401878 METITO
Telefax: 4794250

Senior Executives: K Mazloum (President), J Wheatley (Vice President), M Fathallah (Vice President)

PRINCIPAL ACTIVITIES: Manufacturers, contractors and engineers in water treatment, water desalination, sewage treatment, chlorination, chemical treatment, maintenance and chemical cleaning, water supply
Branch Offices: Dammam: Tel 8576081, Telex 801852, Fax 8578208; Jeddah: Tel 6718757, Telex 603360, Fax 6710917; Factory Tel 8420607 (Dammam)
Parent Company: Metito (Overseas) Ltd
Principal Bankers: Saudi British Bank; Byblos Bank SAL
Financial Information:

	1989
	SR'000
Sales turnover	60,000
Authorised capital	9,010
Paid-up capital	2,252

Principal Shareholders: Al Ghanadi Ltd; Metito (Overseas) Ltd
Date of Establishment: 1982 (1402 H)
No of Employees: 165

MIDDLE EAST ENGINEERING & DEVELOPMENT CO LTD

PO Box 5090, Dammam 31422
Tel: 8263835, 8268378, 8265485, 8265468
Telex: 801862 MEEDCO SJ
Telefax: 8267538

Chairman: Abdullah M Al-Otaishan
Directors: Han Ho Yang, Saud Abdulla Al-Otaishan
Senior Executives: Abdul Rahman A Al Abdan (Vice President)

PRINCIPAL ACTIVITIES: Contracting, marine works, roads, dams, water and sewage works, industrial works, building, mechanical and electrical works, sanitary works and water well digging
Branch Offices: Riyadh, Jeddah
Parent Company: Hyundai Engineering & Construction Co Ltd

Principal Bankers: National Commercial Bank; Al-Bank Al-Saudi Al-Fransi
Financial Information:

	1988/89
	SR'000
Sales turnover	455,877
Profits	548
Authorised capital	10,000
Paid-up capital	10,000
Total assets	430,161

Principal Shareholders: Abdullah Muhammad Al Utaishan, Dammam; Hyundai Constructions, Co, Dhahran
Date of Establishment: Dec 1978
No of Employees: 1,559

MIDDLE EAST ENGINEERING LTD SAUDI ARABIA (MEELSA)

PO Box 2321, Dammam 31451
Tel: 8570032 (8 lines)
Telex: 801582 MEELSA SJ
Telefax: 8579469

Chairman: H A Downs
Directors: M C Hendry, M Sabir, Sheikh Ali Tamimi, V A Blando, C A Breese
Senior Executives: M C Hendry (Managing Director), G Goodall (Financial Manager), T Muallen (Manager Repair Facilities), M Madigan (Manager Engineering Services), H Ali (Manager Western Sales), N Shaffique (Manager Eastern Sales), D Drayton (Manager Admin/Materials), N Habayeb (Manager Southern Sales)

PRINCIPAL ACTIVITIES: Repair and engineering services of electrical and mechanical equipment, switchgear, pumps, compressors, gas and steam turbines, re-manufacture/overhaul & relocation of gas turbines
Branch Offices: PO Box 50, Jeddah 21411, Tel 6445043, Telex 602439 GEJED SJ; PO Box 10211, Riyadh 11433, Tel 4067622, Telex 400167 GETSCO SJ; PO Box 11549, Dubai, Tel 237755, Telex 46739
Associated Companies: General Electric Company, USA; Ali A Tamimi, Saudi Arabia
Principal Bankers: Saudi American Bank, Alkhobar
Financial Information:

	1989
	SR'000
Sales turnover	49,000
Authorised capital	19,800

Principal Shareholders: General Electric (USA), Sheikh Ali Tamimi
Date of Establishment: 1976
No of Employees: 235

MIDEAST TRADING AGENCIES CO (MTA)

PO Box 2106, Jeddah 21451
Tel: 6514132, 6514636, 6514384
Cable: Mideastrading
Telex: 600532 Mtaho
Telefax: 6510859

Chairman: Sheikh Abdulaziz Al Obeid
Directors: Sheikh Abdulaziz Al Obeid (Managing Director)
Senior Executives: Bassam Ahmad (Legal/Personnel/Transport Manager), Mohamed Zaman Khan (Regional Manager Shipping)

PRINCIPAL ACTIVITIES: Shipping agencies, stevedoring, forwarding, transportation and merchandise inspection, preshipment on discharge
Principal Agencies: CMA Marseille Container Line
Branch Offices: Riyadh: PO Box 3240, Tel 4028787; Dammam: PO Box 2105, Tel 8234903; and Yemen AR: PO Box 3225, Hodeidah
Principal Bankers: Bank Al Jazirah, Jeddah; National Commercial Bank, Jeddah

Principal Shareholders: Sheikh Abdulaziz Al Obeid
Date of Establishment: 1970
No of Employees: 103

MISFER SULIMAN AL HARBI EST

See AL HARBI, MISFER SULIMAN, EST

MISHA'AL ADHAM CORPORATION LTD

PO Box 7669, Jeddah 21472
Tel: 6652287, 6672392, 6672128, 6608412, 6609950
Telex: 603632 MATEST SJ

Chairman: Sheikh Mishaal Kamal Adham
Directors: H E Sheikh Kamal Adham, Sheikh Mishaal Kamal
Adham, Sheikh Sultan Kamal Adham

PRINCIPAL ACTIVITIES: Outdoor advertising, full-service
advertising agency; management and technical training;
computer services, data processing, systems programming;
military supplies; Government tenders, engineering and
construction (civil and military), procurement of equipment
and services; special projects; custom automobiles; general
maintenance, etc.
Branch Offices: Beverley Hills, CA, USA; Houston, Texas, USA;
Paris, France
Subsidiary Companies: Saudi Arabian Maintenance Company;
Saudi Arabian Data Services Ltd
Principal Bankers: Saudi Cairo Bank, Arab National Bank,
Chase Manhattan Bank
Financial Information:

	SR'000
Sales turnover	50,000
Paid-up capital	7,000

Principal Shareholders: Sheikh Mishaal Kamal Adham and
Family
Date of Establishment: 1978
No of Employees: 120

MISHARI ESTABLISHMENT

PO Box 1503, Alkhobar 31952
Tel: 8644349, 8644350, 8944302, 8984975
Telefax: 8984991

Senior Executives: Ahmed S Al Mishari (General Manager)

PRINCIPAL ACTIVITIES: Electronics Division: computers and
accessories, electronics, educational, telecommunications;
trading division: office supply and stationery, medical
supplies; construction division
Principal Agencies: Texas Instruments
Branch Offices: Riyadh: PO Box 59868, Riyadh 11535; Jeddah:
PO Box 14088, Jeddah 21424

MOBIL SAUDI ARABIA INC

PO Box 5335, Jeddah 21422
Tel: 6520000
Cable: Mobiloil Jeddah
Telex: 601877 Mobsaj SJ
Telefax: 6518021, 6517504, 6517761

Chairman: C W Brand
Senior Executives: W Wiggans (VP PEMREF/LUBEREF/ S&D
Coordination), S B Finch (VP Legal), J R Law (VP Marketing),
W H Ritchie (VP Relations, Industrial Projects & SVCS), C K
Hanna (VP Chemicals)

PRINCIPAL ACTIVITIES: Oil and gas services through
participation in Arab Petroleum Supply (APSCO) and joint
projects
Branch Offices: Riyadh: PO Box 40228, Riyadh 11499, Tel
4777341, Telex 402344 Mobsar SJ
Parent Company: Mobil Oil Corporation

Principal Bankers: Albank Alsaudi Alhollandi; National
Commercial Bank; Saudi International Bank; Riyad Bank;
Saudi French Bank; Saudi British Bank; Saudi American Bank

Date of Establishment: 1974
No of Employees: 400

MODERN ARAB CONSTRUCTION CO (MAC)

PO Box 855, Alkhobar 31952
Tel: 8572233
Cable: MAC Saudi Arabia
Telex: 871118 Mac Sj
Telefax: 8573554

Chairman: Harb Al Zuhair
Directors: Khaled El Seif, Fouad Malouf, Fahd Al Musharraf
Senior Executives: Naddem T Zakharia (General Manager),
Mouhannad Sadi (Engineering Manager), Samir Abu Saada
(Construction Manager), Mohammad Deeb (Finance
Manager), Mahmoud Bidawi (Marketing Manager), Farid Abu
Ghosh (Purchasing Manager), George Touma (Personnel &
Administration Manager)

PRINCIPAL ACTIVITIES: General contractors; engineering
consultants
Branch Offices: Riyadh; Paris; London; Belleville (NJ)
Principal Bankers: Saudi French Bank, Alkhobar; Banker Trust,
Zurich
Financial Information:

| | 1990/91 |
	SR'000
Sales turnover	80,000
Authorised capital	15,000
Paid-up capital	15,000
Total assets	19,000

Principal Shareholders: Modern Arab COntracting & Trading Co;
Khaled El Seif; Marketing & Construction Co
Date of Establishment: 1969
No of Employees: 685

MODERN ELECTRONICS EST

PO Box 1228, Jeddah 21431
Tel: 6436026
Cable: Electa
Telex: 601035 Modern Sj, 604221 Mdernj Sj
Telefax: 6441833

President: Mohammad Al-Areefy
Senior Executives: Rif Abou Richeh (General Manager),
Mohammad Al Segaih (General Manager Projects Division),
Sultan Al Otaibi (General Manager H.P. Division), Masaki
Terada (Marketing Manager), Ziad Sammour (Financial
Controller), Ousama Nasir (Admin & Personnel Manager)

PRINCIPAL ACTIVITIES: Sale, installation and maintenance of
electrical and electronic equipment, and computers
Principal Agencies: Sony Corporation, Hewlett Packard, Sony
Broadcast & Communications, UK
Branch Offices: Jeddah: PO Box 1228, Telex 604221 601035;
Riyadh: PO Box 2728, Telex 400756, 404782 & 402049;
Alkhobar: PO Box 193, Telex 870584 & 870136; Khamis
Mushait: PO Box 1161 Telex 906002; Madinah: PO Box 4051,
Telex 570327; Qassim: PO Box 2104, Telex 301309; Arar,
Telex 812071
Principal Bankers: Saudi Cairo Bank; Al Bank Al Saudi Al
Fransi; BAII - Bahrain
Financial Information:

| | 1989/90 |
	SR'000
Sales turnover	725,400
Authorised capital	95,000
Paid-up capital	95,000

Principal Shareholders: HRH Prince Abdullah Al Faisal Al Saoud
Date of Establishment: 1970
No of Employees: 430

MODERN FURNITURE FACTORY

PO Box 1919, Riyadh 11441
Tel: 4489170
Cable: Al Assree
Telex: 406857 Assree SJ
Telefax: 4462753

Chairman: Mohd Saddodin Aqqad
Directors: Omar Aqqad

PRINCIPAL ACTIVITIES: Manufacture of steel and wooden
   furniture
Branch Offices: PO Box 139, Buraidah, Qasem
Principal Bankers: Arab National Bank
Financial Information:

| | 1990 |
	SR'000
Sales turnover	10,000
Profits	1,500
Authorised capital	3,800
Paid-up capital	3,800
Total assets	7,000

Principal Shareholders: Limited liability
No of Employees: 90

MODERN INDUSTRIES COMPANY

PO Box 1435, Jeddah 21431
Tel: 6877266, 6877454, 6872463
Cable: Sinaat Jeddah
Telex: 601050 Micplt Sj
Telefax: 6875320

Chairman: Sheikh Ismail Abudawood
Senior Executives: Franz X Kundig (General Manager), Kamal S
   Dabbagh (Plant Manager)

PRINCIPAL ACTIVITIES: Manufacture and sale of synthetic
   detergents and soap
Branch Offices: Location in Jeddah: Kilo 5, Mecca Road
Associated Companies: Procter & Gamble AG, Geneva,
   Switzerland
Principal Bankers: Riyad Bank; Saudi American Bank
Financial Information:

| | 1990 |
	SR'000
Paid-up capital	26,000

Principal Shareholders: Sheikh I A Abudawood; Prince Badr Bin
   Saud; Sheikh A Al Nafeesi; Detergent Products AG
Date of Establishment: June 1964
No of Employees: 275

MODERN SCIENTIFIC & ELECTRONIC CORP

PO Box 1938, Riyadh 11441
Tel: 4765117
Cable: Moseco
Telex: 400434 Moseco Sj

President: Zuhair F Awartani

PRINCIPAL ACTIVITIES: General trade and agents, dealing in
   telecommunications, electronics, educational equipment,
   scientific and labs equipment, safety and security equipment,
   medical equipment, electrical equipment, and sports
   equipment
Principal Agencies: E-Systems, USA; ESA, UK; Magnavox, USA;
   GTE Sylvania, USA; Canberra, USA; Eberline, USA; Grunzig,
   West Germany; T-Cars, USA; Smith & Wesson, USA
Principal Bankers: Arab National Bank Ltd; Saudi Cairo Bank

Date of Establishment: 1974

MODERN TANNING INDUSTRIES

PO Box 1630, Jeddah 21441
Tel: 6364979, 6360551
Cable: Tanners
Telex: 601368 Taners Sj

Chairman: A R Bassam
Directors: Fawzi Bassam
Senior Executives: Ahmad Indil (Manager)

PRINCIPAL ACTIVITIES: Tanning sheep and goat skins; also
   camel and cow hides
Principal Bankers: Saudi British Bank, Jeddah; Riyad Bank,
   Jeddah

Date of Establishment: 1976

MODERN TECHNICAL SUPPLY CO (MTSCO)

PO Box 4951, Riyadh 11412
Tel: 4768246
Cable: Basalt
Telex: 401483 Mtsco Sj
Telefax: 4764509

Chairman: Bander Al Turki
Directors: Dr Khalid Al Turki
Senior Executives: M Arshad (Sales Manager), Mohamad Alagib
   (Administration Manager)

PRINCIPAL ACTIVITIES: Medical and dental equipment,
   supplies and instruments, laboratory and autopsy equipment
Principal Agencies: Jewett; Ritter GmbH; Baisch; Kerr;
   Cincinnati Sub-Zero; EMS; Girardelli; Jota; Ormeo; Planmeca;
   Roeko; W & H; Hawe-Neos; Revco
Branch Offices: Jeddah; AlKhobar
Principal Bankers: National Commercial Bank; Arab National
   Bank
Financial Information:

| | 1990 |
	SR'000
Sales turnover	11,000
Profits	2,000
Authorised capital	5,000
Paid-up capital	2,000

Date of Establishment: 1974

MOFARRIJ, A A,

PO Box 1337, Jeddah 21431
Tel: 6433115
Cable: Mofarri
Telex: 601423 Mofrij Sj

Chairman: Abdulrahim Abdullah Mofarrij (owner)

PRINCIPAL ACTIVITIES: General trading, import and distribution
   of foodstuffs and building materials, poultry farming
Branch Offices: Jizan

Date of Establishment: 1946

MOHAMED ABUBAKR BAKHASHAB CO
See BAKHASHAB, MOHAMED ABUBAKR, CO

MOHAMED ALI MAGHRABI & SONS
See MAGHRABI, MOHAMED ALI, & SONS

MOHAMED MOUDAYFER & BROS CO
See MOUDAYFER, MOHAMED, & BROS CO

MOHAMED SAID FAKHRY
See FAKHRY, MOHAMED SAID,

MOHAMMAD ABDULLAH ALMANA
See ALMANA, MOHAMMAD ABDULLAH,

MOHAMMAD ABDULLAH AL OTHMAN EST
See AL OTHMAN, MOHAMMAD ABDULLAH, EST

MOHAMMAD AL OWAIMER CONTRACTING & TRADING EST
See AL OWAIMER, MOHAMMAD, CONTRACTING & TRADING
EST

SAUDI ARABIA

MOHAMMED & ABDULLAH IBRAHIM AL SUBEAEI

See AL SUBEAEI, MOHAMMED & ABDULLAH IBRAHIM,

MOHAMMED A ALRAJHI CORP

See ALRAJHI, MOHAMMED A, CORP

MOHAMMED ASSAD ALDREES & SONS CO

See ALDREES, MOHAMMED ASSAD, & SONS CO

MOH'D & A ALBAWARDI CO

See ALBAWARDI, MOH'D & A, CO

MOHTASEB ESTABLISHMENT

PO Box 368, Riyadh 11411
Tel: 4020102, 4764069
Telex: 401608 Mohseb Sj

Chairman: A J Mohtaseb
Directors: M Akam Yaghmour (General Manager), Fawzi Mahmoud Kanana (Accountant), Abdul Rahman Rashid Araffah (Sales Manager)

PRINCIPAL ACTIVITIES: Import and distribution of electrical appliances and equipment and refrigeration; installation of heavy duty kitchens and catering equipment; general maintenance
Principal Agencies: FOEM Italy; Garland, Canada; Mafic Chef, USA; Junkers, Germany

MOSHEN STORES

PO Box 3498, Jeddah 21471
Tel: 6695887, 6693517
Cable: Mohsen Jeddah
Telex: 601513 Mohsen Sj
Telefax: 6693037

Owner: Mohsen Ali Mohsen

PRINCIPAL ACTIVITIES: Import of ready-made garments, giftware, jewellery, cosmetics, leather goods and shoes
Branch Offices: Riyadh: Tel 4655896, 4022827; Alkhobar: Tel 8980644, 8946959; Medina: Tel 8232149; Makkah: 5749583
Principal Bankers: Saudi American Bank

Principal Shareholders: Mohsen Ali Mohsen
Date of Establishment: 1950
No of Employees: 100

MOUDAYFER, MOHAMED, & BROS CO

PO Box 1378, Riyadh 11431
Tel: 4053311 (7 lines)
Cable: Moudayferco
Telex: 401423 Modfer Sj
Telefax: 4058478

Chairman: Mohamed Moudayfer
Directors: Aamer Mustafa Sehli (General Manager)
Senior Executives: A A Medawar (Jeddah Branch Manager), Abbas Hachem (Dammam Branch Manager), Mohamed Saleh Moudayfer (Al Hadissa Branch Manager), Saad Saleh Moudayfer (Buraidah Branch Manager)

PRINCIPAL ACTIVITIES: Customs clearance and forwarding agents, commerce
Branch Offices: Lebanon: PO Box 7569, Beirut; Saudi Arabia: PO Box 678, Dammam; Al Jubail; PO Box 1801, Jeddah; PO Box 95, Al Hadissa; PO Box 1546 Buraidah
Subsidiary Companies: Middle East Trading and Transport; Construction Material Co; Arabian Danish Paint Co; Saudi Lighting Co; Arab Lighting Co
Principal Bankers: National Commercial Bank, Riyad Bank, Saudi Cairo Bank

Financial Information:

	1989/90 SR'000
Sales turnover	10,216
Authorised capital	3,000
Paid-up capital	3,000
Total assets	4,753

Principal Shareholders: Mohamed Moudayfer & Bros
No of Employees: 120

MUNASSER ESTABLISHMENT

PO Box 804, Jeddah 21421
Tel: 6675896
Telex: 604041 Intag SJ
Telefax: 6608425

Chairman: Hussein Munasser
Senior Executives: Marwan Farra (Manager)

PRINCIPAL ACTIVITIES: Timber Division, timber trade, hardwoods, softwoods and panels
Principal Agencies: Baillie, Stora, EAC, Rilico, Balkanexport
Principal Bankers: Saudi American Bank

Date of Establishment: 1990

MUSAED EL SEIF & SONS CO LTD

See EL SEIF, MUSAED, & SONS CO LTD

NADCO

Hussein Al Harthy & Co

PO Box 789, Riyadh 11421
Tel: 4783336
Cable: Nadco
Telex: 401118 Nadco Sj

Chairman: Hussein Mohsen Alharthy
Directors: Sami H Fayez (Deputy General Manager)
Senior Executives: Abdul Hakim Gamil (Director Administration), Mohammed Fathy Hafez (Director Finance)

PRINCIPAL ACTIVITIES: Construction and civil engineering; electrical and mechanical contracting; supply of building materials; maintenance and operation of airports (civil, electrical and mechanical)
Branch Offices: Jeddah: PO Box 2424, Tel 6713313; Dhahran: PO Box 428, Tel 8948555; Taif: PO Box 400, Tel 7253368; Tabuk: PO Box 440, Tel 4228271
Subsidiary Companies: Saudi Arabian Gas Engineering Co Ltd (SAGE), PO Box 789, Riyadh; Saudi Arabian Mechanical & Engineering Co Ltd (SAMEC), PO Box 1001, Riyadh; National Quarries Co, PO Box 5953, Jeddah, Tel 6828509
Principal Bankers: Saudi Cairo Bank, Riyadh; National Commercial Bank, Riyadh; Saudi American Bank, Riyadh; American Express; Midland Bank

Principal Shareholders: Hussein M Alharthy
Date of Establishment: 3,100

NAGHI, AHMED & YOUSUF MOHAMED,

PO Box 273, Jeddah 21411
Tel: 6472225, 6470884
Cable: Alnaghi
Telex: 601107 Naghi Sj, 602349 Nabro Sj

Chairman: Ahmed Mohamed Naghi
Directors: Yousuf Mohamed Naghi, Mohamed Yousuf Naghi

PRINCIPAL ACTIVITIES: Import and distribution of consumer goods, pharmaceutical products, wholesalers
Principal Agencies: Rothmans of Pall Mall, Parke Davis Int, William R Warner, Boots Co Ltd, Charles E Frosst, Gillette Industries, Nicholas Laboratories, Sanitas Group Sales, Twinings Tea, Laurens Int, Turmac Tobacco Co, London Cigarettes Co, International Export Service, Bristol Myers Int, Mead Johnson, Berec Batteries Int, Carnation Int, Honig Foods, Allied Breweries, Bentley's Tea, Loctite Int, Kreuzer,

Dennison, Carand'ache, Matchbox Toys, R F Development, Marwolf, Sto-Rose
Branch Offices: Riyadh, Dammam, Mecca, Medina, Taif, Tabuk, Gizan, Khamis Mushayt
Subsidiary Companies: Naghi Bros, Naghi International, Abdul Wahab Naghi
Principal Bankers: Saudi British Bank, Saudi American Bank, Saudi Cairo Bank
Financial Information:

	SR'000
Sales turnover	500,000

Principal Shareholders: Ahmed & Yousuf Mohammed Naghi
Date of Establishment: 1911
No of Employees: 500

NAHDA CONTRACTING & ENGINEERING EST
PO Box 121, Dammam 31411
Tel: 8326008, 8322669
Cable: Nahda Dammam
Telex: 801110 Nahda Sj; 801709 Mostfa Sj

Chairman: Fouad Mohammed Darweesh Mostafa (Proprietor)
Senior Executives: Dr Khamis A Ashour (General Manager), Adib Jalajel (Commercial Manager)

PRINCIPAL ACTIVITIES: Import and supply of hardware, hand tools and electric power tools; civil, electrical and mechanical engineering and general contracting; manufacture of radiators, sale and maintenance of heavy duty vehicles
Principal Agencies: Uniweld Corp, USA; Remier Berlic, UK; Otto Suhner, Switzerland; Matador Tools, Germany; Taichung Machinery, Taiwan
Branch Offices: PO Box 7473, Jeddah; PO Box 3914, Riyadh
Principal Bankers: Riyad Bank, Dammam; Arab National Bank, Damman
Financial Information:

	SR'000
Sales turnover	50,000
Authorised capital	7,000
Paid-up capital	7,000

Date of Establishment: 1958
No of Employees: 530

NAJD EST FOR AGRICULTURE & TRADE
PO Box 3960, Riyadh 11481
Tel: 4351801, 4025033
Telex: 401698 Najd SJ

PRINCIPAL ACTIVITIES: Supply of agricultural chemicals, fertilisers and agricultural services

NAJEEB EST FOR GENERAL TRADING & CONTRACTING
PO Box 466, Jeddah 21411
Tel: 6422591, 6421595
Cable: Reslan
Telex: 601683 Najeeb Sj

PRINCIPAL ACTIVITIES: Import and distribution of heavy machinery, tractors, cranes, tyres, wire ropes, generators and spare parts for machinery, high pressure, water-jetting machines; general contracting, roads, bridges, etc
Principal Agencies: Hydrocon Crane Manufacturers, Caterpillar Tractors and Spare Parts, Semperit Tyres, British Made Ropes, Babcock Kina Jetting Machines; Remington Tyres; Electraplant Generators; Max Arc Welding Equip

Date of Establishment: 1964
No of Employees: 200

NAMLAH, A R, FACTORIES
PO Box 6989, Jeddah 21452
Tel: 6100172, 6719287, 6719364
Cable: Arefoun
Telex: 601396 Namlco Sj
Telefax: 6729253

Chairman: Solaiman Ibrahim Al Namlah
Directors: Farouk M Qiblawi (Financial & Admin Manager)
Senior Executives: Hilal M Qiblawi (Production & Admin Manager)

PRINCIPAL ACTIVITIES: Production and trade of concrete blocks, concrete tiles, kerbstones, aggregates and prefabricated concrete building materials
Branch Offices: Yanbu branch: PO Box 30231, Tel 3070027
Principal Bankers: Saudi American Bank, National Commercial Bank, Al Rajhi Bank, Arab National Bank, Riyad Bank
Financial Information:

	SR'000
Authorised capital	22,400
Paid-up capital	22,400

Date of Establishment: 1978
No of Employees: 118

NASER AL NASER GROUP OF COMPANIES
See AL NASER, NASER, GROUP OF COMPANIES

NASHAR TRADING COMPANY
PO Box 6697, Jeddah 21452
Tel: 02-6692878 (4 lines)
Cable: Nashar
Telex: 601156 Nashar SJ
Telefax: 02-6608011

President: Mahmoud M Nashar
Directors: W J Main
Senior Executives: W J Main (Finance Director), J P Ireland (Sales & Marketing Director Food Division), A W Sanders (General Manager Nashar Fresh Meat Co)

PRINCIPAL ACTIVITIES: Importers of dairy and other food products; owners/operators meat processing plant, meat retailers
Principal Agencies: United Dairymen, Holland; Campina Melkunie, Holland; New Zealand Dairy Board; Premier Brands, UK; Baxters, UK; Pillsbury, USA
Branch Offices: Jeddah; Riyadh; Dammam; Khamis Mushayt; Buraidah; Medina
Subsidiary Companies: Nashar Food Division; Nashar Saudi Lines; Nashar Fresh Meat Company
Principal Bankers: Riyad Bank, Bank Al Jazira; Saudi British Bank; Saudi Hollandi Bank; Saudi International Bank (London)
Financial Information:

	1990 SR'000
Sales turnover	178,000
Authorised capital	10,000
Paid-up capital	10,000
Total assets	126,000

Principal Shareholders: Family owned
Date of Establishment: 1942
No of Employees: 200

NASSIR HAZZA & BROTHERS
See HAZZA, NASSIR, & BROTHERS

NATIONAL AGRICULTURAL DEVELOPMENT CO (NADEC)
PO Box 2557, Riyadh 11461
Tel: 4783488, 4784011
Telex: 403681 Nadec Sj
Telefax: 4784127

Chairman: Dr Abdul-Rahman Abdul-Aziz Al-Esheikh (Minister of Agriculture & Water)

Directors: Sheikh Abdullatif Bin Saleh Al-Esheikh, Sheikh Abdulla Alhokail, Sheikh Abdulla S Alrashed, Sheikh Abdul-Rahman Alkhorayef, Sheikh Abdulmohsen Bin Saleh Al Rajhi, Sheikh Abdul Rahman Alfakih, Sheikh Fahd Abdul Rahman Althonayan, Mohammed Mohammed Alrashed

Senior Executives: Mohammed A Abu-Butain (Director General), Abdul-Rahman Alohali (Deputy Director General for Tech Affairs), Abdullah A Alkanhal (Deputy Director General for Financial & Admin Affairs), Ahmed Alhenti (Deputy Director General for Commercial Affairs), Hamood O Shammary (Public Relations Manager), Abdul Aziz A Albawardi (Marketing Director), Sulaiman I Alohaly (Purchasing Director), Abdul Aziz Saleh Alowain (Animal Welfare & Industry Director), Mansoor A Alsughayer (Personnel Director)

PRINCIPAL ACTIVITIES: Crop and vegetable production, animal production, land reclamation, food processing, dates, dairy farm and plant

Branch Offices: Haradh Project - Haradh; Hail Project - PO Box 1559, Hail; Wadi Dawser Project - PO Box 48, Sulayel; Wadi Al Sarhan Project -Nadec Dates Factory -Hofuf

Subsidiary Companies: The Eastern Agricultural Co, PO Box 7118, Dammam; Al-Quseem Agricultural Co, PO Box 1606, Buraida, Alquseem; Saudi Refrigerated Transportation Co

Principal Bankers: Riyadh Bank; Arab National Bank; Saudi British Bank

Financial Information:

	1989	1990
	SR'000	SR'000
Sales turnover	370,000	270,000
Profits	77,000	25,000
Authorised capital	400,000	400,000
Paid-up capital	400,000	400,000
Total net assets	663,000	835,000

Principal Shareholders: (10%) principal shareholders; The Government (20%); Plus 127,000 shareholders

Date of Establishment: June 1, 1981

No of Employees: 1,350

NATIONAL AUTO COMPANY

PO Box 999, Riyadh 11421

Tel: 4766555, 4766537

Cable: Autocar

Telex: 401232 AUTOS SJ

Chairman: Saud Awsaf Koraitem

Managers: Mohammad Samir Ibrahim (Finance Manager)

Senior Executives: Ghassan A Koraitem

PRINCIPAL ACTIVITIES: Import and distribution of Dodge cars, trucks, and auto spare parts

Principal Agencies: Chrysler, Dodge

Branch Offices: PO Box 2139, Jeddah

Principal Bankers: National Commercial Bank; Saudi American Bank; Saudi Cairo Bank

Principal Shareholders: Thabit Trading Est, Riyadh; Awsaf Trading Est, Riyadh

Date of Establishment: January 1979

No of Employees: 100

NATIONAL AUTOMOBILE INDUSTRY CO LTD

PO Box 5938, Jeddah 21432

Tel: 6822000

Telex: 600099 Naicar Sj

Chairman: Sheikh Ahmed Juffali

Directors: Dr Gernot Woerner (General Manager), Tahir Khan, G Kirchner, M Rawashdeh (Maintenance), M Ozdemir (Production), M Fouad (Personnel), H El Gamali (Material)

PRINCIPAL ACTIVITIES: Assembly of Mercedes Benz Trucks for Saudi Arabia

Parent Company: E A Juffali & Bros, Jeddah

Principal Bankers: Riyad Bank; Al Bank Al Saudi Al Hollandi

Financial Information:

	SR'000
Authorised capital	70,000
Paid-up capital	70,000

Principal Shareholders: Juffali (74%), Daimler Benz (26%)

Date of Establishment: 25.2.1395 Hijria

No of Employees: 270

NATIONAL BUNKERING CO LTD

PO Box 6471, Jeddah 21442

Tel: 6692203, 6692206, 6691707, 6691699

Cable: Jedbunkersco

Telex: 600042 ALDA; 600043 HOFNA SJ; 606870 SJ; 602080 AICO SJ

Telefax: 6691699

Chairman: Sheikh Mazen R Pharaon (Managing Director)

Directors: Capt A Kotsifis (General Manager)

Senior Executives: A Ghamdi (Shipping Manager)

PRINCIPAL ACTIVITIES: Shipowners, bunkers suppliers, shipping agents, chartering and brokers

Principal Agencies: National Shipping Agencies Co Ltd

Principal Bankers: Saudi American Bank; National Commercial Bank; Riyad Bank

Principal Shareholders: Sheikh Mazen R Pharaon

Date of Establishment: 1977

No of Employees: 35

NATIONAL CHEMICAL INDUSTRIES LTD

PO Box 1312, Jeddah 21422

Tel: 6512680, 6518796

Cable: Fiberchem

Telex: 601235 Nci J SJ

Chairman: Sheikh Mohammed Y Al Bedrawi

Directors: Adnan Kronfol (Vice President)

PRINCIPAL ACTIVITIES: Manufacturing reinforced plastic and chemicals, glass polyester, for pre-fabricated houses and buildings, sewage and water systems; also construction activities

Branch Offices: Riyadh: PO Box 7633, Tel 4642818; AlKhobar: Tel 8640270; London, UK

Subsidiary/Associated Companies: Bison Group, UK; Beyer Peacock Group, UK; Saudi Industrial Resins Ltd, Saudi Arabia; National Investments Co Ltd, Saudi Arabia

Principal Bankers: Saudi British Bank; Morgan Grenfell, UK

Financial Information:

	SR'000
Authorised capital	40,000
Paid-up capital	40,000

Date of Establishment: 1972

No of Employees: 2,500

NATIONAL COMMERCIAL BANK

PO Box 3555, Jeddah 21481

Tel: 6446644

Cable: Banksaudi

Telex: 605571 NCBH Sj, 605573 NCBH Sj, 605578 NCBK Sj, 601086 NCBG Sj

Telefax: (966-2) 6446644

Founders: Saleh and Abdullah Mousa Kaaki, Abdul Aziz Mohammed Kaaki, Salim Ahmed Bin Mahfouz

Management: Mohammed Bin Salim Bin Mahfouz (Deputy General Manager and Chairman of the Management Committee), Khalid Bin Salim Bin Mahfouz (Deputy General Manager International Relations & Investments), Abdullah Ahmed Bagabas (Deputy General Manager Inspection & Collection), Abdul Elah Bin Salim Bin Mahfouz (Deputy General Manager and Manager Central Region Riyadh), Mahfouz Salim Bin Mahfouz (Deputy General Manager and Manager Western Region Jeddah), Omar Abdul Qader

Bajamal (Deputy General Manager Planning, Business Development), Mohammed Salim Al Batati (Deputy General Manager Administration & Personnel), Abdullah Salim Bahamdan (Deputy General Manager Central Region Riyadh)

PRINCIPAL ACTIVITIES: All banking activities
Branch Offices: Over 190 branches throughout Saudi Arabia: General Management: PO Box 3555, Jeddah 21481; Western Region Management: PO Box 5171, Jeddah 21422, Tel 6446644, Telex 603548, Fax 6446644 ext 2745; Central Region Management: PO Box 22216, Riyadh 11495, Tel 4787877, telex 404231, Fax 4787877 ext 222 & 731; Eastern Region Management: PO Box 5558, Dammam 31432, Tel 8340088, Telex 803142, Fax 8346953; Southern Region Management: PO Box 605, Abha, Tel 2241408, Telex 901165, Fax 2244148; also branches in Lebanon; Bahrain; New York (USA); London (UK); and representative offices in Frankfurt (W Germany), Seoul (Korea); Singapore; Tokyo (Japan)
Financial Information:

	1988/89
	SR'million
Capital & reserves	3,200
Total deposits	73,447
Total loans & advances	31,832
Total assets less contra a/cs	79,117
Contra accounts	81,257

Date of Establishment: 1951
No of Employees: 6,200

NATIONAL COMPUTER SYSTEMS CO

PO Box 7902, Riyadh 11472
Tel: 4793916
Telex: 404807 Natcom Sj

PRINCIPAL ACTIVITIES: Installation and maintenance of computer systems
Principal Agencies: Digital; ARC CAD Systems; Benson; Santec; C Itoh
Branch Offices: Jeddah: PO Box 6256, Jeddah 21442, Tel 6726693, Telex 604246; Dammam: PO Box 3803, Dammam, Tel 8263671, Telex 802900

NATIONAL CONSTRUCTION CO

PO Box 1595, Riyadh 11441
Tel: 4773818, 4788162
Telex: 406267 KULIBI

President: Saub Al Kulaibi
Directors: A Al Mormer, K Peak, N W Kim

PRINCIPAL ACTIVITIES: Construction contracting, farm projects, project development
Branch Offices: Jeddah, Al Khobar, Jubail, Qassim, London, New York
Associated Companies: Hawaiian Agronomics, 745 Forst St, Honolulu, HA 96813, USA; Mechanical (SEMEC); Saudi Supply & Commerce, Saudi Electro
Principal Bankers: National Commercial Bank

Principal Shareholders: Privately held
Date of Establishment: 1979
No of Employees: 450

NATIONAL ENGINEERING SERVICES & MARKETING CO LTD

N.E.S.M.A.

PO Box 7195, Jeddah 21462
Tel: 6727970, 6717491, 6729577, 6722460
Cable: Nesmat
Telex: 602558 Nesma Sj, 604744 Namma Sj
Telefax: (02) 6713410

Chairman: Abdulaziz Ali Al Turki
President: Saleh Ali Al Turki
Senior Executives: Abdullah S Al Ghunaim (Vice President Administration), Saad Rashid Al Khamis (Director), Dr Marwan

Gholmieh (Director), Mohamed Wassef Hammad (Director), William R Evans (General Manager Operations), Mohamed W Hammad (General Manager Finance & Administration), Ted Millspaugh (Operations Manager)

PRINCIPAL ACTIVITIES: Marine services, offshore construction, petrochemical engineering and construction, operation and maintenance, training, electrical and mechanical installation, recreational services, general construction, overhead transmission lines, water and wastewater treatment, port management, freight forwarding, commercial trading, etc
Branch Offices: Riyadh: PO Box 9260, Riyadh 11413, Tel 4654200, 4654885; Yanbu: PO Box 30260, Yanbu, Tel 3960014; Al Khobar: PO Box 1498 Al Khobar 31952, Tel 8954580; Jubail: PO Box 10096, Jubail, Tel 3415838
Associated Companies: Pan Nesma Co Ltd, Nesma/Costain Process Co Ltd, Nesma & Alfadl Contracting Co Ltd, National Port Services, Arabian Trading & Industrial Services, National Maintenance & Marine Services Co Ltd, Namma Cargo Services Co Ltd, Telecom Australia Saudi Ltd, Lear Siegler Arabia Ltd, National Telecommunications Co Ltd, National Maintenance & Marine Services Co Ltd, Al Nawa Technical Services
Principal Bankers: National Commercial Bank, Bank Al Saudi Al Hollandi, Bank Al Jazira

Principal Shareholders: Abdulaziz Ali Al Turki, Saleh Ali Al Turki
Date of Establishment: 1979
No of Employees: 3,500

NATIONAL FACTORY FOR FASTERNERS & ENGINEERING FABRICATION SERVICES

PO Box 185, Alkhobar 31952
Tel: 8572008
Telex: 870149 Rarnat Sj
Telefax: 8576164

President: Rashed A Al Rashed (Proprietor)
Senior Executives: S A Malik (General Manager), Klaus Januche (Director Engineering), M H Chowdhry (Finance & Admin Manager), Nadeem H Malik (Sales Manager), Kamal Abul Ela (Materials Manager), Norbert R Harms (Manager Engineering Fabrication Services), K N Chishty (Manager Quality Assurance & Control), George Philips (Manager Data Processing)

PRINCIPAL ACTIVITIES: Manufacture of fasteners, galvanising division, heat treatment division, engineering fabrication services division, etc
Branch Offices: Riyadh: PO Box 21870, Riyadh 11485, Tel 4784833, Fax 4793454, Telex 407420 Rarico SJ; Jeddah: PO Box 10167, Jeddah 21433, Tel 67210247, Fax 6725979
Parent Company: Rashed A Al Rashed Group of Companies
Principal Bankers: Saudi American Bank, Alkhobar; Saudi Fransi Bank, Alkhobar
Financial Information:

	1990/91
	SR'000
Total assets	45,000

Principal Shareholders: Sole proprietorship
Date of Establishment: 1967, and ownership transferred in 1989
No of Employees: 150

NATIONAL FACTORY FOR PLASTIC INDUSTRY

National Co for Plastic Industry Ltd

PO Box 3449, Jeddah 21471
Tel: 6373058, 6372519
Telex: 604250 Masura Sj
Telefax: 6373764

Chairman: Abdullah Nassir Al Rashid (Managing Director)
Directors: Omer Abdullah Bin Madi (Sales Director)

PRINCIPAL ACTIVITIES: Manufacturing capacity of 13,000 tons per year of PVC pipes and fittings and capacity of 34,380 tons pf PVC compounds
Principal Bankers: Riyad Bank, National Commercial Bank, Saudi British Bank

Date of Establishment: 1402H

NATIONAL GAS INDUSTRIALISATION CO

PO Box 564, Riyadh 11421
Tel: 4024268, 4024271
Telex: 401274 Gasco Sj

Directors: Dr Ibrahim A Al Khudair

PRINCIPAL ACTIVITIES: Supply, transport, filling of LPG, and bulk LPG

NATIONAL GYPSUM COMPANY

PO Box 5229, Jeddah 21422
Tel: 6515452, 6515696
Cable: GYPSUM
Telex: 600123 Gypsco Sj

PRINCIPAL ACTIVITIES: Production of gypsum, juss and rough cast powder; manufacture of gypsum ceiling and wall panels, cornices, mouldlings trellis and rosettes, cement floor tiles
Principal Agencies: Sadi, Italy; Gartenman, Switzerland; Eurobrevets, Belgium
Branch Offices: Riyadh: PO Box 187; and Yanbu

Principal Shareholders: Limited company is which Triad is the single largest shareholder

NATIONAL INDUSTRIES COMPANY

PO Box 1085, Dammam 31431
Tel: 8323136
Cable: Malbusat
Telex: 801726 Dossary SJ
Telefax: 8349802

Chairman: Abdulla M Al Naimi
Senior Executives: Khalid Masood

PRINCIPAL ACTIVITIES: Manufacture of all kinds of ready-made garments
Subsidiary Companies: Jubail Shopping Centre
Principal Bankers: Al Bank Al Saudi Al Fransi
Financial Information:

	1989/90 SR'000
Sales turnover	2,000
Profits	500
Authorised capital	1,000
Paid-up capital	1,000
Total assets	1,600

Principal Shareholders: Abdulla M Al-Naimi
Date of Establishment: 1973
No of Employees: 28

NATIONAL INSURANCE CO SA

PO Box 5832, Jeddah 21432
Tel: 6606200
Telex: 601791 Nicom SJ

Chairman: Sheikh Ahmed Juffali
Directors: Ralph Roth (Vice Chairman), J Askari, Jean Choueiri, Mian Daud Ansar, Georges Kioes
Senior Executives: Samir T Jabbour (General Manager), Rashad A Harris (Assistant General Manager)

PRINCIPAL ACTIVITIES: Insurance
Branch Offices: PO Box 86, Riyadh 11411; PO Box 1933, Al Khobar 31952
Principal Bankers: Albank Alsaudi Alhollandi

Principal Shareholders: E A Juffali & Bros, Munich Reinsurance Co & Zurich Insurance Co
Date of Establishment: 1974 in Luxembourg
No of Employees: 65

NATIONAL MARKETING GROUP

PO Box 16375, Jeddah 21464
Tel: (02) 6475010, 6473714, 6479285
Cable: Conmark
Telex: 601668 Namat Sj, 604519 NATMAR SJ
Telefax: (02) 6474503

Chairman: Issam Kabbani
Directors: Samir J Kadi

PRINCIPAL ACTIVITIES: Trade, production and distribution of PVC & DCI pressure pipes and fittings and all construction materials (blocks, tiles, crushed aggregate, foam concrete); building contracting
Principal Agencies: Chemco, USA; Bayard, France; Von Roll, Switzerland
Branch Offices: Riyadh, PO Box 2729, Tel 4646669, 4657398, Telex 401321
Associated Companies: New Products Industries (NEPRO)
Principal Bankers: Albank Alsaudi Alfransi

Date of Establishment: 1965

NATIONAL METHANOL CO LTD (IBN SINA)

PO Box 10003, Jubail 31961
Tel: (03) 3405500
Telex: 832033 BNSINA SJ
Telefax: (03) 3405604

Chairman: Nasser A Sayyari
President: Khalid S Rawaf
Senior Executives: L N Anthony (Vice President), L G Ogden (Operations General Manager), A A Bu-Ali (Financial Manager), F A Suwaigh (Govt & Public Affairs Manager), M B Sadoon (Industrial Security Manager), A N Jaber (Industrial Relations Superintendent)

PRINCIPAL ACTIVITIES: Manufacture of petrochemicals including methanol and MTBE
Principal Bankers: Saudi International Bank; Al Bank Al Saudi Al Fransi
Financial Information:

	1990/91 SR'000
Authorised capital	516,000
Paid-up capital	393,000

Principal Shareholders: Saudi Basic Industries Corporation, Hoechst Celanese Corporation, Panhandle Eastern Corporation
Date of Establishment: 1981
No of Employees: 220

NATIONAL PAPER PRODUCTS CO

PO Box 538, Dammam 31421
Tel: 8571222
Cable: Napco
Telex: 801049 Napco Sj
Telefax: 8571918

Chairman: George Frem
Directors: Fawzi Saif (Chief Operating Officer)
Senior Executives: Khalil Khadij (Finance Manager), Jean Saad (General Manager Plastic), Bassem El Hibri (General Manager Tissue & Consumer Goods), Emile Chamoun (General Manager Paper Products), Mohamad Soudairy (Personnel Manager), Khalil Bounader (Manager Sales), George Kerbage (Manager Export Sales), Michel Shimlati (Marketing Manager), M I Simon (Purchasing Manager), Hikmat Saif (Technical Manager, Jean Badr (Administration Manager), George Karout (R & D Manager)

PRINCIPAL ACTIVITIES: Manufacture and export of flexible
packaging products (polyethelane, cling film, bags and rolls;
paper bags and rolls); tissue products; aluminium foil;
feminine pads, baby diapers, paper towels, napkins, facial
tissue

Branch Offices: Riyadh, PO Box 827, Tel 4791086; Jeddah, Tel
6370757; Hassa, Tel 5879768

Financial Information:

| | 1990 |
	SR'000
Sales turnover	170,000
Authorised capital	20,000
Paid-up capital	20,000
Total assets	160,000

Principal Shareholders: Sheikh Abed Al Rahman Abed Al Aziz
Al Moaibed, George Frem
Date of Establishment: 1956
No of Employees: 600

NATIONAL PIPE CO LTD

PO Box 1099, Alkhobar 31952
Tel: 8985263, 8985271, 8984873
Telex: 870966 PIPECO SJ

Chairman: Prince Saud Bin Naif Bin Abdul Aziz
Directors: Noboru Inui (Vice Chairman), Sheikh Teymour Abdulla
Abdul Ghaffar Alireza (Executive Director), Abdul Majeed
Mahmoud Zahid, Abdulla Taha Bakhs, Jun Suzuki (General
Manager), Masahiko Iwano

PRINCIPAL ACTIVITIES: Manufacturing and marketing of spiral
welded steel pipes used in oil, gas and water transmission;
structure usage: such as: piles, casing, dredging and sleeves
Parent Company: Sumitomo Metals Industries Ltd
Principal Bankers: Saudi British Bank; Saudi International Bank;
Saudi American Bank
Financial Information:

	SR'000
Authorised capital	50,000
Paid-up capital	50,000

Principal Shareholders: Prince Saud Bin Naif Bin Abdul Aziz;
Sheikh Teymour Abdulla Abdul Ghaffar Alireza; Sheikh
Ahmad Hamad Al Gosaibi & Bros; Sheikh Abdul Aziz & Saad
Mohammad Al Mojil; Sheikh Hashim Saeed Hashim; Sheikh
Jamal Hassan Jawa; Sheikh Abdulla Taha Bakhsh; Sheikh
Abdulla Abdul Aziz Al Seidairy; Sheikh Jamil Ibrahim Al
Hejailan; Sheikh Abdul Majeed Mahmoud Zahid; Sumitomo
Metal Industries Ltd, Japan; Sumitomo Corporation, Japan
Date of Establishment: August, 1978
No of Employees: 400

NATIONAL PORTS SERVICES CO

PO Box 7195, Jeddah 21462
Tel: 6727970, 6727971, 6717491
Telex: 602558 NESMA SJ

Senior Executives: R Evans (Manager Jeddah), Dr Marwan
Gholmieh (Manager Alkhobar)

PRINCIPAL ACTIVITIES: Port management and services
Branch Offices: PO Box 1498, Alkhobar, Tel 8954580, 8954942,
8954584, Telex 870603

NATIONAL QUARRIES COMPANY

PO Box 5953, Jeddah 21432
Tel: 6828526, 6828509
Cable: Granitekan
Telex: 600153 Nqc Sj

President: Hussain Al Harthy
Directors: Eng Mohammed Al-Durbi (General Manager)

PRINCIPAL ACTIVITIES: Production and supply of building
materials, (marble, granite, limestone quarries)
Branch Offices: Quarries: Yanbu; Riyadh; Tayif; Najran; Wady
Al-Jummom

Financial Information:

	SR'000
Authorised capital	25,000
Paid-up capital	25,000

Principal Shareholders: National Development Co; Hussain Al
Harthy; Saleh Kamel; Mohammed Fayez
Date of Establishment: 1975
No of Employees: 280

NATIONAL SHIPPING COMPANY OF SAUDI ARABIA (THE)

PO Box 8931, Riyadh 11492
Tel: 4785454
Cable: Melaha
Telex: 495-405624/6 Melaha SJ
Telefax: (966-1) 4778036, 4777478

Chairman: Dr Mohammad A Al Tawail
Directors: Eng Ahmad Y AL Turki, Dr Abdul Rahan A Al Zamil,
Ziad F Al Dghaither, Mohamed A Baker, Abdullah M Al Eissa,
Abdul Rahman M Abdou, Abdullah S Al Rajhi, Fahd S Al
Moajel
Senior Executives: Mohamed S Al Jarbou (Chief Executive),
Hazza B Al Qahtani (Vice Chief Executive, Admin & Finance),
Eng Mohamed A Al Ahmed (Vice Chief Executive, Lines)

PRINCIPAL ACTIVITIES: Ship owners; International liner
services operating US/Middle East, Europe/Middle East and
Far East/Middle East
Principal Agencies: Gastaldi, Italy; US Navigation, USA; Red
Burn, Canada; Transmeridian Navigation, Japan; Asia
Shipping, Korea; Maritime Transportation, Taiwan; HongKong
Maritime, Hongkong; NGOW Hock, Thailand; C F Sharf,
Philippines; Kim Shipping & Trading, Singapore; Segani
Agencies, Malaysia
Branch Offices: Jeddah; Dammam; Jubail; Yanbu (Saudi Arabia);
Dubai (UAE); Tokyo (Japan); New York (USA) and Antwerp
(Belgium)
Subsidiary/associated Companies: Saudi Livestock
Transportation & Trading Co, Riyadh (16%); Arabian Chemical
Carriers, Riyadh (50%); National Chemical Carriers, Riyadh
(80%)
Principal Bankers: Saudi American Bank; Riyad Bank; Saudi
International Bank; Citibank
Financial Information:

| | 1989/90 |
	SR'000
Sales turnover	535,944
Net income	68,810
Authorised capital	2,000,000
Paid-up capital	1,250,000
Total assets	1,344,606

Principal Shareholders: Saudi Government (29%); major
businessmen of Saudi Arabia; and about 42,000 public
shareholders
Date of Establishment: October 1979
No of Employees: 232

NATIONAL STRUCTURAL STEEL & CONTRACTING (THE)

PO Box 3971, Jeddah 21481
Tel: 6693822
Telex: 603648 WASAM Sj

Directors: Mohammed Salem Al Ghamdi, Essam A Banaja

PRINCIPAL ACTIVITIES: Civil engineering, structural steelwork,
fire protection
Branch Offices: Stalum Holloware Factory, Riyadh
Associated Companies: Mohammed Salem Est, PO Box 472,
Khamis Mushayt
Principal Bankers: Saudi American Bank

Date of Establishment: May 1980
No of Employees: 60-80

NATIONAL TRADING ESTABLISHMENT FOR CONTRACTING

Head Office, PO Box 2759, Riyadh 11461
Tel: 4771303, 4771311
Cable: Manima
Telex: 401317 Manima Sj
Telefax: 4765686

Chairman: Mohammad A Bawazir
Directors: Zahid Mahmoud
Senior Executives: S M Agha (Sales Manager Western Region), Magdi Wiliam (Sales Manager Central Region), Nabil Jomaa (Sales Manager Eastern Region)

PRINCIPAL ACTIVITIES: Suppliers and contractors for water-proofing, roofing, insulation, flooring and cladding
Principal Agencies: The Mearl Corporation, USA; Fiberlon, USA; Bitumat, Saudi Arabia; ORV, Italy
Branch Offices: Jeddah Branch: PO Box 5044, Jeddah 21422, Tel 6723308, Fax 6719910; Dammam Branch: PO Box 4899, Dammam 31412, Tel 8424305, Fax 8429464
Principal Bankers: National Commercial Bank, Riyadh

Date of Establishment: 1965
No of Employees: Over 100

NATIONAL UNITED SUPERMARKETS LTD

PO Box 60931, Riyadh 11655
Tel: 4916964, 4933294
Telex: 406083 Mokbil Sj
Telefax: 4920315

President: Ibrahim Mushareef
Directors: Hamood Ibrahim, Abdulrahman Jarboa, Abdulrahman Al Ajlan, Ibrahim Al Namla
Senior Executives: Ayad Al Aujan (General Manager)

PRINCIPAL ACTIVITIES: Import and distribution of foodstuffs and general consumer products to outlets throughout Saudi Arabia
Branch Offices: Ollayah Cash & Carry Centre, Riyadh and Dammam Branch
Associated Companies: Panda United Co; Al Amro Co for Trading; Abdullah Munajim & Sons Co; Al Jazeera Superstore; Hammad Shebl Est; Abdulrahman Al Ajlan Est, Al Shadaif Trading Est; Arabian Marketing Co; etc
Principal Bankers: Arab National Bank, Saudi United Commercial Bank, Albank Alsaudi Alhollandi
Financial Information:

	1990 US$'000
Authorised capital	3,866
Paid-up capital	3,866

Principal Shareholders: Panda United Corp, Abdul Rahman Al Ajlan Est, Abdullah Al Munajem & Sons Co, Al Jazeerah Superstore, Al Amro Trading Co
Date of Establishment: 1985
No of Employees: 56

NAWAL EST FOR TRADING & CONTRACTING

PO Box 1080, Alkhobar 31952
Tel: 8648884
Telex: 870145 Nawal Sj

PRINCIPAL ACTIVITIES: Civil contracting and general trading, supply to the oil and petrochemical industry; fasteners, tools and hardware
Principal Agencies: Bowman, USA; TNC, USA
Principal Bankers: Saudi American Bank; Saudi Fransi Bank; Saudi British Bank; Riyad Bank

NCR DIVISION SAUDI ARABIA

Zahid Industries & Investment Co

PO Box 13964, Jeddah 21414
Tel: 6512727
Cable: Nakareco Jeddah
Telex: 600020 NCR Jed SJ
Telefax: 6518804

Senior Executives: Mounib Mounir (General Manager), P K Choudhuri (Manager Systems Services/Education), John Rosser (Manager Field Engineering), Mehmoud Samara (Manager Finance & Administration)

PRINCIPAL ACTIVITIES: Marketing, installation, support and services for complete business systems, (computers, electronic business machines, data communication networks, software, etc) also field engineering, software support, educational programs etc
Branch Offices: Riyadh: PO Box 807, Riyadh 11421, Tel 4654156, Telex 402332, Fax 4654156; Dammam: PO Box 684, Dammam 31421, Tel 8333095, 8333860, Fax 8333877, Telex 803253; also in 17 countries in the Middle East
Parent Company: NCR Corporation, Latin America/Middle East/Africa Regional Headquarters, Dayton, Ohio, USA

Principal Shareholders: General Agents: Zahid Industries & Investment Co

NESMA-COSTAIN PROCESS CO LTD

PO Box 6967, Jeddah 21452
Tel: 6722460
Cable: Costain, Jeddah
Telex: 602558 Nesma Sj
Telefax: 6713410

Chairman: Sheikh Abdul Aziz Al-Turki
Directors: Sheikh Saleh Ali Al-Turki, Sheikh Abdullah S Al Ghunaim, Mohammed W Hammed, J W H Lawson, P F Woods
Senior Executives: J V Hockin (General Manager)

PRINCIPAL ACTIVITIES: Process engineering, mechanical engineering, and construction in the oil, gas and petrochemical industries
Branch Offices: Saudi Arabia (Dhahran: PO Box 607, Tel 8953504, 8954942, Telex 870603 NBSMA SJ). Head Office: Costain House, West Street, Woking, Surrey GU21 1EA
Parent Company: Costain Process Construction Ltd and National Engineering Services & Marketing Co Ltd
Principal Bankers: Albank Alsaudi Alhollandi, Jeddah

Principal Shareholders: Costain Process Construction Ltd (50%); National Engineering Services & Marketing Co Ltd (50%)
Date of Establishment: 1983
No of Employees: 200

NORTHROP CORPORATION REGIONAL OFFICE

PO Box 57270, Riyadh 11574
Tel: 4631120
Telex: 401258

PRINCIPAL ACTIVITIES: Defence contracting: aerospace equipment and services, fighter aircraft; operations, maintenance and training
Parent Company: Northrop Corporation, Los Angeles, CA, USA
Subsidiary Companies: Northrop Aircraft Division; Wilcox Electric; Ventura Division; Northrop Aircraft Services Division

No of Employees: In Saudi Arabia: 2,500

OASIS TRADING ESTABLISHMENT

PO Box 479, Alkhobar 31952
Tel: 8943684, 8943690, 8642336
Cable: Otesta Alkhobar
Telex: 870044 Otesta Sj

Chairman: Amir Abdul Aziz Bin Madhi

Directors: Bashar Khayat

PRINCIPAL ACTIVITIES: Manufacture of paints, import and distribution of hydraulic and electrical equipment, generators and flood lights, tools and pumps; manufacturers' representation, design, fabrication and erection of towers and masts

Principal Agencies: F E Myers, USA; R A Lister & Co, UK; Brown Boweri, West Germany; Speed Fasteners, USA; Verlinde, France; Creemers, Holland; Thompson Winch, UK; J S Production, Denmark

Branch Offices: Oasis Trading & Contracting Est, Al Ahsa St, Riyadh

Associated Companies: Oasis Sykes Pumps Ltd (Manufacture, sale, hire of pumps); Oasis-Ameron Ltd (Manufacture & supply of corrosion resistant protective coatings and industrial paints)

Principal Bankers: Saudi British Bank, Alkhobar

Date of Establishment: 1964

OBAID & ALMULLA CONSTRUCTION CO LTD (OBALCO)

PO Box 15467, Riyadh 11444
Tel: 4646784, 4655915
Cable: OBALCO
Telex: 400974 Obalco Sj

President: Essam Ahmed Obaid

Directors: Taher Ahmed Obaid (Chairman), Khalil Awad (Managing Director), Saeed Almulla (Director)

Senior Executives: Eng Mourad K Seliet (Assistant General Manager)

PRINCIPAL ACTIVITIES: Contractors for construction of: commercial buildings, highrise buildings, airports, residential buildings, roads, bridges, civil and earth works and maintenance of building complexes, etc

Parent Company: Almulla Construction Co Pvt Ltd, PO Box 59, Dubai, UAE

Principal Bankers: Bank Al Jazira, Riyadh; Al Saudi Banque, Bahrain

Financial Information:

	SR'000
Authorised capital	15,000
Paid-up capital	15,000

Principal Shareholders: Almulla Construction Co (Pvt) Ltd; Essam A Obaid; Taher A Obaid

Date of Establishment: 13/11/1399 H

No of Employees: 491

OGEM SAUDI ARABIA CONTRACTING CO LTD

PO Box 9310, Riyadh 11423
Tel: 4640388, 4645145
Telex: 402169 Ogemsa Sj

Directors: Abdulla Abbar, Ahmed Zainy, F C A A van Berkel, G G Kerkum (Managing Director)

PRINCIPAL ACTIVITIES: Engineering and contracting: civil works, industrial plants, housing, office buildings, treatment plants for water and sewage

Branch Offices: Jeddah: PO Box 7964, Tel 6826842, Telex 602210 Ogem Sj; Dammam: PO Box 2623, Tel 8268672, Telex 801450 Ogemby Sj

Principal Bankers: Albank Alsaudi Alhollandi; Algemene Bank Nederland; Amro Bank, Rotterdam

Principal Shareholders: Ogem Holding NV, Netherlands

Date of Establishment: 1975 (Jeddah)

No of Employees: 1,150

OILFIELD SUPPLIES & SERVICES

Said Ghodran

PO Box 131, Dammam 31411
Tel: 8323571, 8324089, 8322371
Telex: 801030 Sj

Chairman: Said Ali Ghodran

PRINCIPAL ACTIVITIES: Mechanical and electrical engineering equipment, particularly for oilfield use; importers of foodstuffs, rice, wheat, flour, building materials and motor oil, electrical household appliances

Subsidiary Companies: Saudi Gas Company

OKAZ ORGANIZATION FOR PRESS & PUBLICATION

PO Box 1508, Jeddah 21441
Tel: 6722630
Cable: OKAZ Jeddah
Telex: 601360 Okaz Sj
Telefax: 6724277

Chairman: Iyad Amin Madani (Director General)

Directors: Mohamed Al Hassoun (Deputy Director General)

Senior Executives: Dr Hashim Abdu Hashim (Editor-in-Chief, Okaz Daily Newspaper), Ridah Mohamed Larry (Editor-in-Chief, Saudi Gazette Daily Newspaper)

PRINCIPAL ACTIVITIES: Press and publication, Daily Newspaper - OKAZ (Arabic), Saudi Gazette (English) and Camera-3 (Video Sports Magazine)

Branch Offices: Major cities in Saudi Arabia, Washington DC, Paris, Tunis, Cairo, Athens, Sana'a

Principal Bankers: National Commercial Bank; Riyad Bank

Financial Information:

	1989 SR'000
Sales turnover	38,000
Authorised capital	13,921
Paid-up capital	13,921
Total assets	49,330

Principal Shareholders: 56 shareholders

Date of Establishment: 1960

No of Employees: 500

OLAYAN EQUIPMENT & AUTOMOTIVE GROUP (OEAG)

PO Box 5111, Dammam 31422
Tel: 8421216
Cable: OLAYANCO Dammam
Telex: 802024 GCCDAM SJ
Telefax: 8421708, 8431622

Chairman: Khaled S Olayan

Senior Executives: Imtiaz H Hydari (Vice President/General Manager), Abdul Mohsin Al-Ajaji (Assistant General Manager - Operations), Khalid S Khan (Assistant General Manager - Finance & Admin & Distribution)

PRINCIPAL ACTIVITIES: Major suppliers of equipment and machinery for construction, power generation, compressed air, agriculture and transportation. Extensive sales, parts and service facilities throughout Saudi Arabia. Part of the OLAYAN Group

Principal Agencies: Cummins, Paccar, Altas Copco, Scania, Warner & Swasey, Pierce, Fleetguard, Craelius, Fatih, AG-Chem, J I Case, Saudi Pump, Connor Shea, Koehring, Jaguar, Land/Range Rover

Branch Offices: Riyadh: PO Box 967, Tel 2333111, Fax 8421708, Telex 401365 Oshcor Sj; Jeddah: PO Box 1277, Tel 6653555, Telex 601424 Oshcoj Sj; Abha: PO Box 535, Tel 2235092, Fax 2235092, Telex 906055 Olayan Sj; Qassim: PO Box 147, Tel 3233464, Fax 3233464, Telex 301041 OLAYAN SJ. Kuwait: PO Box 1096 Safat, Tel 4833380, Fax 4833380, Telex 22279 GTE KT

Parent Company: Olayan Saudi Holding Company
Subsidiary Companies: General Contracting Company, Arabian
Automotive Company, Atlas Industrial & Equipment Company
Principal Bankers: Saudi British Bank, Saudi American Bank
Financial Information:

	1989 US$'000
Sales turnover	100,000
Total assets	60,000

Principal Shareholders: Suleiman S Olayan; Khaled S Olayan
Date of Establishment: 1947
No of Employees: 475

OLAYAN FINANCING COMPANY

PO Box 745, Alkhobar 31952
Tel: 8948011
Telex: 871450 Finsco Sj

Chairman: Suliman S Olayan
Directors: Khaled S Olayan (Vice Chairman)
Senior Executives: Saad F Al-Arjani (President)

PRINCIPAL ACTIVITIES: Equity investments in a wide range of
Saudi Companies and active management participation in a
variety of joint ventures, particularly in agriculture, basic
industrial development, and specialised technology
Branch Offices: Riyadh, Tel 4778740 & Jeddah, Tel 6829155
Subsidiaries/Associated Companies: Arabian Bechtel Co Ltd; Al
Bustan Co Ltd (subidiary); Aluminium Manufacturing Co;
Aluminium Products Co Ltd; Arabian Metals Co Ltd
(subsidiary); Bechtel Arabian Services Co; Carton Products
Co; Conam (Saudi Arabia) Ltd (subsidiary); Dammam Real
Estate Co Ltd; Drilling Equipment & Chemical Co; DST Saudi
Arabia; Saudi Automated Systems Co (subsidiary); Saudi
Graphco (subsidiary); Intermarine-Comex Saudi Arabia Ltd;
Intermarine Saudi Arabia Ltd (subsidiary); Investment &
Trading Co; Kashaaf Development Co (subsidiary); Olayan
Saudi Investment Co Ltd (subsidiary); PDM Saudi Arabia;
Mining Services Co; Near East Equipment Sales Co; Health
Water Bottling Co; Saudi Arabian Bechtel Co; Saudi Arabian
Bechtel Equipment Co; Saudi Agricultural Development Co;
Saudi Plastic Products Co Ltd; Saudi Poultry Co; Saudi
Chemical Co; Spanarabia Ltd; Steel Products Co Ltd; Saudi
Tugs Services; Thermo Electron Saudi Arabia; (OTIS) Elevator
SA; Vetco Saudi Arabia; Christensen Saudi Arabia;
Manufacturing & Prefabricated Building Co Ltd; Technical
Studies Bureau Saudi Arabia; Saudi Arabian Construction and
Repair Services Co Ltd; Hospital Management & Medical
Facilities Co Ltd (subsidiary);Arabian Plastic Manufacturing
Co; Sappco Texaco Insulation Products; Saudi Plastic
Products Co Ltd
Principal Bankers: Arab National Bank; Al-Bank Al-Saudi Al-
Fransi; Al-Bank Al-Saudi Al-Hollandi; National Commercial
Bank; Riyad Bank; Saudi American Bank; Saudi British Bank;
Banque Paribas; Credit Suisse; Chase Manhattan Bank NA;
Gulf International Bank BSC; Morgan Guarantee Trust Co;
First National Bank of Chicago; Manufacturers Hanover Trust
Co; Chemical Bank; Midland Bank

Principal Shareholders: Member of the Olayan Group of
Companies
Date of Establishment: 1969

OLAYAN SAUDI HOLDING COMPANY

PO Box 1520, Alkhobar 31952
Tel: 8943377
Cable: Olayanco
Telex: 871204 Oshcok Sj

Chairman: Khaled S Olayan (also Chief Executive Officer)

PRINCIPAL ACTIVITIES: Holding company and central services
for its subsidiaries
Branch Offices: Riyadh, PO Box 967 and Jeddah, PO Box 1227
Subsidiary Companies: General Contracting Co; General
Trading Co; Saudi General Transportation Co; Arabian

Automotive Co; Projects & Development Co; Arabian Health
Care Supply Co; Arabian Business Machines; Atlas Industrial
Equipment Co; Saudi Maritime Co; Saudi Forwarding &
Transportation Co; Arabian Telecommunications & Electronics
Co; Saudi Xerox Ltd; Saudi Box Co
Principal Bankers: Saudi American Bank, Riyad Bank, Al Bank
Al Saudi Al Fransi, National Commercial Bank

Principal Shareholders: Member of Olayan Group of Companies
Date of Establishment: Holding Co: l975 (Oldest company in
Group: l947)
No of Employees: 1,524

OMAR ABUBAKER BALUBAID EST

See BALUBAID, OMAR ABUBAKER, EST

OMAR K AL ESAYI & CO LTD

See AL ESAYI, OMAR K, & CO LTD

OMARIYA ORGANIZATION

PO Box 891, Riyadh 11421
Tel: 4780015, 4782567, 4052400
Cable: AL OMARIYA
Telex: 400357

Sole Proprietor: Abdulgader Omar Bagader
Senior Executives: M A Mills (General Manager)

PRINCIPAL ACTIVITIES: Importers and agents of European
construction machinery and equipment; office space rentals,
bookshops, stationery retailers and wholesalers, interior
decorators and warehousing facilities
Principal Agencies: De Jong, Holland; Rilco, West Germany;
Reita & Crippa, Italy; Petters, UK
Branch Offices: Jeddah: Telex 601048
Subsidiary Companies: Mod Decoration Est; Omariya Office
Building

No of Employees: 100

OMRAN & OMRAN & BROS

PO Box 550, Riyadh 11421
Tel: 4030059, 4022758
Cable: Vensco
Telex: 401935 Sascom Sj

Chairman: Sheikh Omran Bin Muhammad
Directors: Abdulaziz Bin Muhammad, Abdulrahman Bin
Muhammad

PRINCIPAL ACTIVITIES: Holding company; production of
building materials, cement, building contractors
Subsidiary/Associated Companies: Rashid & Al Umran Co, PO
Box 550, Riyadh; Arabian Industries Co, PO Box 550, Riyadh;
Civil Works Company, PO Box 550, Riyadh; Al Umran & Al
Toug Co, PO Box 2743, Riyadh, Tel 8337356; SABICO, PO
Box 987, Riyadh
Principal Bankers: Al Bank Al Saudi Al Fransi; National
Commercial Bank; American Express Bahrain

OMRAN BROS

PO Box 2743, Riyadh 11461
Tel: 4031440
Telex: 401082 Romanco

Directors: Omran Al Omran, Abdul Aziz Al Omran, Abdul
Rahman Al Omran

PRINCIPAL ACTIVITIES: Import export, construction,
contracting, trading agencies, commission agents, industrial
projects and maintenance operations
Financial Information:

	SR'000
Capital	9,000

Principal Shareholders: Directors as described

ORAIF FOR CONSTRUCTION & PROJECTS

PO Box 7517, Jeddah 21472
Tel: 6695438, 6675408
Cable: Apsanetraco
Telex: 600861 Apsa Sj
Telefax: 6691683

Chairman: Jamal M A Oraif
Senior Executives: Labeeb R Saba (Executive Manager)

PRINCIPAL ACTIVITIES: Building contractors, roads and
bridges engineering, cleaning, maintenance and operation,
commercial agencies and companies representatives
Branch Offices: Yanbu: PO Box 459, Tel 3968918
Principal Bankers: Saudi Cairo Bank, Jeddah; Saudi Bank Al
Fransi, Jeddah; Saudi American Bank, Jeddah

Date of Establishment: 1978
No of Employees: 250

ORIENT EST FOR REFRIGERATION & FOODSTUFFS

PO Box 2881, Riyadh 11461
Tel: 4026206
Cable: Naklyat Riyadh

Chairman: Nasouh Jameel Al-Rijjal
Directors: Abdulla Al-Harbi, Nazeer Al-Rijjal

PRINCIPAL ACTIVITIES: Import and distribution of foodstuffs,
such as frozen meat and chickens, fish, fruit
Branch Offices: Saudi Arabia and the Gulf States
Associated Companies: Arabian Trading for Cold Storage
(Saudi Arabia); Shehab Cold Stores (Saudi Arabia); Alharbi
Trading Foodstuffs Refrigeration and Industrial Co, Dubai
(UAE); Jamil Lines for Shipping and Trade, Lebanon

ORIENT MARKETING & TRADING CO (OMATRA)

PO Box 5039, Jeddah 21422
Tel: 6533683, 6511672
Telex: 601809 Omatra Sj

Directors: Ali H Shobokshi, Fahd H Shobokshi

PRINCIPAL ACTIVITIES: Import and distribution of industrial
equipment and heavy machinery, construction plant,
mechanical plant, heavy duty machinery etc
Principal Agencies: MAN; Magirus; Liebherr; Elba; Thyssen;
Deutz; Steeter; Clark; etc
Branch Offices: Riyadh: PO Box 17972, Tel 4770679, Telex
403048; Alkhobar: PO Box 2256, Tel 8649835, Telex 870576;
Yanbu: PO Box 19, Tel 22616, Telex 661021; Jubail: PO Box
209, Tel 3611900

Principal Shareholders: Ali & Fahd Shobokshi Group

ORIENT TRANSPORT CO LTD

PO Box 6983, Jeddah 21452
Tel: 6517248, 6511752
Cable: CONOTCOTRANS
Telex: 601832 Otc Sj
Telefax: 6533453

Chairman: Sheikh Ahmed Juffali
Directors: J Askari, H Puenjer
Senior Executives: H R Hartmann (General Manager)

PRINCIPAL ACTIVITIES: Freight forwarding, shipping and
transportation services
Branch Offices: Riyadh 11454: PO Box 15986, Tel 4776622,
Telex 403042
Parent Company: Kuehne & Nagel Int'l Switzerland; E A Juffali
& Bros, Jeddah
Principal Bankers: Al Bank Al Saudi Al Hollandi, Jeddah,
Dammam, Riyadh

Financial Information:

	1990
	SR'000
Sales turnover	48,000
Authorised capital	1,000
Paid-up capital	1,000

Principal Shareholders: Joint Venture between EA Juffali & Bros
and Kuehne & Nagel International
Date of Establishment: 1977

ORIENTAL COMMERCIAL & SHIPPING CO LTD

PO Box 160, Jeddah, 21411
Tel: 6481584
Cable: Overseas
Telex: 601203 Bokari Sj, 604737 Arbnav Sj, 602206 Arbshp Sj
Telefax: 6476775

President: Abdul Hameed M Zakir Bokhari (also Managing
Director)
Directors: Sami Ahmed Baghdadi (General Manager),
Mohammad Ahmad Naseem (Asst General Manager), Asif Ali
(Financial Manager)

PRINCIPAL ACTIVITIES: Ship owners, shipping agents, bunker
suppliers; ship chandlers, marine engineers, P & I
correspondents, insurance agents, containers storage and
haulage, clearing and forwarding, importers, exporters,
contractors, travel agents, stockists of BP Luboil and Drew
Ameroid chemicals and general agents
Branch Offices: PO Box 1060, Dammam 31431, Tel (03)
8348657, 8330176, 8331591, Telex 801253 Bokari Sj, 802259
Marine Sj, Fax 8331591; PO Box 324, Jubail, Tel (03)
3612778, Telex 831053 Bokari Sj; PO Box 239, Rahima, Ras
Tanura, Tel (03) 6673225, 6674077, Telex 851112 Bokari Sj;
PO Box 182, Gizan, Tel (07) 3221807, 3220620, Telex 911075
Bokari Sj; PO Box 388, Yanbu, Tel (04) 3223011, 3224486,
Telex 661057 Bokari Sj; PO Box 20638, Riyadh 11465, Tel
(01) 4768108, 4760987, Telex 404461 Bokari Sj, Fax 4760987;
also in Greece; Hong Kong and UK
Subsidiary Companies: Saudi Arabian Maritime Agencies,
Jeddah; Marine Services Co Ltd, Jeddah
Principal Bankers: Bank Al Jazira; Saudi American Bank
Financial Information:

	SR'000
Sales turnover	75,000
Authorised capital	1,500

Principal Shareholders: Sheikh Abdul Hameed Mohammed Zakir
Bokhari, Mrs Zainab Abdul Rahman Bokhari, Mrs Hind Abdul
Hameed Mohammed Zakir Bokhari, Mrs Abla Abdul Hameed
Mohammed Zakir Bokhari, Miss Nada Abdul Hameed
Mohammed Zakir Bokhari, Mohammed Abdul Hameed Zakir
Bokhari
Date of Establishment: 1956
No of Employees: 198

ORRI NAVIGATION LINES

PO Box 737, Jeddah 21421
Tel: 6476002, 6476181
Cable: Orrilines
Telex: 600133 Orri Sj

Chairman: Mohamed A R Orri
Directors: Ibrahim M Orri (Vice-President), Adel M Orri (Vice
President)
Senior Executives: Munir Ahmed Gondal (General Manager),
Zahid Rashid Khwaja (Shipping Manager)

PRINCIPAL ACTIVITIES: Shipowners, shipping agents,
stevedores; barge owners and commercial representatives,
local correspondents of various P&I clubs and also agents for
Bureau Veritas
Branch Offices: Dammam: PO Box 1504, Tel 8348469, 8349809,
Telex 801052 Orri Sj; Yanbu: PO Box 667, Tel 3225980, Telex

661155 Orri Sj; Jubail: PO Box 660, Tel 3611281; Ras Tanura:
Contact Dammam Office; Gizan: Contact Jeddah Office
Subsidiary/Associated Companies: Middle East Shipping
Agencies; PO Box 2313, Jeddah; Orri Traders, PO Box 737,
Jeddah; Oceantrade Agencies (Saudi Arabia), PO Box 2654,
Jeddah
Principal Bankers: Saudi British Bank

OTAIBI, HATHAL A, EST

PO Box 155, Dhahran International Airport, Dhahran 31932
Tel: 8641074, 8644127, 8982164, 8944533
Cable: Alotaibi Alkhobar
Telex: 870084 Otaibi Sj
Telefax: 8982808

President: Hathal Abdul Otaibi
Directors: Khalid A Al Otaibi (Vice President Operations), Fahad
H Al Otaibi (Vice President Operations), Ghazi A Al Otaibi
(Vice President & General Manager)
Senior Executives: Hamed M Al-Otaibi (General Manager
Relations), Norman G Rozario (Commercial Manager), Sudeer
Chandran (Marketing Executive),

PRINCIPAL ACTIVITIES: General trading, contracting,
manufacturers' representatives, import earth-moving,
transportation equipment, oilfield supplies, construction and
maintenance work
Branch Offices: Location in Alkhobar: Binthani Bldg, Prince
Nassir Street, also branch in Jubail, Tel 3417883, Telex
632014
Subsidiary Companies: H Otaibi & Sons Electric Co; Otaibi Tate
Ltd
Principal Bankers: Al Bank Al Saudi Al Fransi, Alkhobar
Financial Information:

	1990/91 SR'000
Sales turnover	60,000

Date of Establishment: 1952
No of Employees: 150

OVERSEAS CATERING EST

PO Box 6232, Riyadh 11442
Tel: 4649010, 4037049
Cable: OSCAT RIYADH
Telex: 400108 OSCAT SJ

Chairman: Mohamoud Mashhady (also Proprietor)

PRINCIPAL ACTIVITIES: General contractors and agents for
catering and general foods supply and agricultural equipment
Associated Companies: International Trading Bureau; Arabian
Public Relations Agency
Principal Bankers: Riyad Bank

OWAIDAH DEVELOPMENT COMPANY

PO Box 59369, Riyadh 11535
Tel: 4765242, 4768930, 4779275
Cable: Owaida
Telex: 401086 Owaida Sj
Telefax: 4771662

Chairman: Fahd Abdullah Al Owaidah
Directors: Saleh M Al Tayyar (General Manager)
Senior Executives: Saleem Abdul Aziz (Technical Manager)

PRINCIPAL ACTIVITIES: Import and distribution of construction
and earthmoving equipment; agricultural equipment and heavy
machinery
Principal Agencies: Watanabe; Frisch Grader; Furukawa; IMT
Yugoslavian Tractor; Thomas Edison Airconditioning; CMI
International
Branch Offices: Buraidah, Khamis Mushayt
Parent Company: Owaidah Group
Principal Bankers: Arab National Bank; Saudi American Bank

Date of Establishment: 1959
No of Employees: 150

P.A.M.A.S.
Prince Abdul Rahman Bin Mohamad Bin Abdul Aziz Al Saud Est

PO Box 8515, Jeddah 21492
Tel: 6600180, 6672813
Telex: 602603 ALBA SJ
Telefax: 6656453

Owner: HRH Prince Abdul Rahman Bin Mohamad Bin Abdul
Aziz Al Saud
Senior Executives: Jacob L Nishan (General Manager), Badih H
Salloum (Sales Manager), Ali El Hefni (Project Engineer), M M
Kassim (Office & Administration Manager), Joseph G Cavali
(General Manager Riyadh)

PRINCIPAL ACTIVITIES: Supply and installation of all types of
building materials and finishing products, demountable
partitions and screens, toilet cubicles, vinyl & rubber flooring,
carpets, wallcovering, false ceilings, swimming pool & roofing
tiles, ceramic, mosaic and terrazzo tiles, steel doors,
revolving doors, sun breakers, skylights, domes etc
Principal Agencies: Marley Floors, UK; Muraspec, UK; Dennis
Ruabon, UK; Esco, Holland; Intalite, Holland; HB Fuller,
Holland; Maplex, Spain; Heraklith, Austria; Gebr Knauf, W
Germany; Robbins, USA; W P Kickman, USA; Schiavello
Commercial Interiors, Australia; Gail, W Germany
Branch Offices: PO Box 17397, Riyadh 11484, Tel 4653349,
4653350, 4653440, Fax 4653445, Telex 404122 PAMASB SJ

PAN ARABIAN TRADING ENGINEERING & CONTRACTING
P.A.T.E.C.

PO Box 1137, Jeddah 21431
Tel: 6426983, 6432077
Cable: Patec Jeddah
Telex: 601522 Patec Sj

Chairman: Abdulla Siddik Sindi

PRINCIPAL ACTIVITIES: Engineering, contracting, imports (all
kinds of equipment, building materials, textiles, furniture)
factories and agencies
Principal Agencies: Marley Floors Ltd, UK; Crossley Carpets,
UK; Comag Carpets, Belgium; Mosvold Furnitures, Norway;
Anderson Roofs Materials, UK; Heraklith for roofs materials,
Austria

Date of Establishment: 1959

PENINSULAR AVIATION SERVICES CO LTD

PO Box 6369, Jeddah 21442
Tel: 6822564, 6823579, 6823596
Cable: PASCOTEX
Telex: 602372 PASCO SJ
Telefax: 6822580

Chairman: Sheikh Mohamed A Ashmawi
Senior Executives: O T Levent (General Manager), M J Ten
Brink (Finance Manager), M C Ling (Operations Manager)

PRINCIPAL ACTIVITIES: Refuelling of aircraft, and supply of
aviation lubricants and special products
Branch Offices: Operates at: Jeddah Airport (KAIA), and
Medina, Tabuk, Hail, Gizan, Qassim, Najran Airports
Principal Bankers: Saudi British Bank; Saudi French Bank
Principal Shareholders: Shell Petroleum Co Ltd; British
Petroleum Co Plc; Saudi Arabian Markets; Sheikh Kamal I
Adham
Date of Establishment: 1977
No of Employees: 130

SAUDI ARABIA

PETROLEUM SERVICES & CONTRACTING EST

PO Box 1040, Dammam 31431
Tel: 8577740, 8572348
Cable: Petroserv
Telex: 801242 Petser Sj

Chairman: Sheikh Abdulaziz Almouabed (Sole Owner)
Senior Executives: Khalid Rehmatulla (General Manager)

PRINCIPAL ACTIVITIES: Manufacturers' representation, general contracting and supply
Principal Agencies: Orbit Valves Co, Mead Corporation, Kaiser Chemicals, Cooper Energy Services, Ce-Natco (Div of Combustion Engineering)
Branch Offices: Offices in Riyadh, Jeddah
Subsidiary Companies: Ewan Constructions
Principal Bankers: Riyad Bank; Arab National Bank

Principal Shareholders: Sole ownership
Date of Establishment: 1973
No of Employees: 40

PETROMIN

General Petroleum & Mineral Organisation

PO Box 757, Riyadh 11189
Tel: 4781328, 4781332, 4774910, 4774947, 4781293
Cable: Petromin
Telex: 401490, 401615, 401058, 402802 (arabic)

Chairman: Hisham Nazer (HE Minister of Petroleum & Mineral Resources)
Directors: Abdel Hadi Taher (Governor), Abdullaziz Zamzami (Vice Governor)
Senior Executives: Jamal Jawad (Deputy Governor Operations)

PRINCIPAL ACTIVITIES: Refining, distribution, marketing and transportation of oil and other various operations related to oil performed through the following group of companies including joint ventures with national and foreign participants
Branch Offices: Jeddah: PO Box 1467, Jeddah 21189, Tel 6367411, 6367811, Telex 601150 Petromin Sj
Subsidiary/Associated Companies: ARGAS (Arabian Geophysical Surveying Co); Arabian Drilling Company; PETROLUBE (Petromin Lubricating Oil Co); LUBREF I Jeddah (Mobil); LUBREF II Yanbu (Mobil); LUBREF III Jubail (Shell); PETROMIN JET; Petromin Rabigh Infrastructure Project; Jeddah Oil Refinery Co; Riyadh Refinery Co; SAFCO (Saudi Arabian Fertilizers Co); PETROSHIP (Petromin Tankers and Mineral Shipping Co); PETROMARK (Petromin Marketing); MARINCO (Saudi Marine Petroleum Construction Co); PETROCID (Petromin Sulphuric Acid Plant); SULB (Steel Rolling Mill); PETROSERVE (Petromin Services); PETROMAR (Petromin Steel Project); Yanbu Oil Refinery; Petromin Mobil Yanbu Refinery (Export); Jubail Export Refinery (Petromin-Shell); Petromin Petrola Rabigh Oil Refinery Co; Jubail Iron & Steel Plant; Jubail Lube Oil Refinery (Petromin-Texaco-Chevron); PETROLINE (Crude Oil Pipeline); Saudi Sulphur Company

Principal Shareholders: Owned by the Saudi Arabian Government
Date of Establishment: 1962

PETROMIN LUBRICATING OIL CO

PETROLUBE

PO Box 1432, Jeddah 21431
Tel: 6510909
Cable: Petrolube
Telex: 601675 Petlub Sj
Telefax: 6512500, 6513117

Chairman: HE Ahmed Mohamed Al Khereiji
Directors: Rashad A Kayal, Dr Khalid Mansoor Al Aqeel, Curtis W Brand, Peter j J Ciapparelli

Senior Executives: HE Ahmed Mohamed Al Khereiji (President & CEO), Rashad A Kayal (Asst to the President), Abdullah S Owaida (Asst to the President Technical Affairs), Saud Bin Khalid Bin Turki (VP Marketing), Ali A Barasheed (VP Production), Baddah S Al Sabei (VP Industrial Relations), Abdul Rahman M Al Gabbani (General Manager Administration), Salvatore A Fontama (General Manager Finance & Planning)

PRINCIPAL ACTIVITIES: Manufacture and marketing of lubricating oils and greases
Branch Offices: Western Region Sales Office: PO Box 1432, Jeddah 21431, Tel 6474476; Central Region Sales Office: PO Box 3799, Riyadh 11481, Tel 4650987; Eastern Region Sales Office: PO Box 7720, Dammam 31472, Tel 8339613; Southern Region Sales Office: PO Box 1178, Abha, Tel 2270332
Parent Company: General Petroleum & Mineral Organisation (Petromin)
Principal Bankers: Riyad Bank, Saudi American Bank

Principal Shareholders: Petromin (71%); Mobil (29%)
Date of Establishment: April 1969
No of Employees: 576

PETROMIN MARKETING

PETROMARK

PO Box 50, Dhahran Airport 31932
Tel: 8643411, 8643883
Cable: Petmark
Telex: 870009 Petmark Sj

Senior Executives: S S Abu Al Jadayil (Executive Managing Director Marketing Affairs), A R Sabban (Managing Director, Finance & Administration)

PRINCIPAL ACTIVITIES: Responsible for operating petroleum products distribution and marketing
Branch Offices: PO Box 2396, Riyadh, Tel 4489625, Telex 402386
Principal Bankers: National Commercial Bank

Principal Shareholders: A subsidiary of the General Petroleum and Mineral Organisation (PETROMIN)
Date of Establishment: July 1967
No of Employees: 3,600

PETROMIN SHELL REFINERY

PO Box 10088, Jubail 31961
Tel: 3416889, 3410073, 3572040, 3572041
Telex: 632060 PSRC Sj

President: H Foxton
Directors: Alastair MacLachlan (Vice President Refinery)

PRINCIPAL ACTIVITIES: Oil refinery (capacity: 250,000 b/d)

PHILIPP HOLZMAN AG

See HOLZMAN, PHILIPP, AG

PROJECTS & DEVELOPMENT CO

PO Box 1520, Alkhobar 31952
Tel: 8573377
Telex: 871204 Oshcok Sj

Chairman: Khaled S Olayan

PRINCIPAL ACTIVITIES: Active joint venture participation with international partners in construction and allied projects; maintenance services & training, agricultural projects; and electrical and mechanical contracting
Branch Offices: Riyadh, Jubail, Jeddah
Associated Companies: Principal Joint Ventures; FMC Saudi Arabia; Interbeton Saudi Arabia; Olayan Held & Francke; Owens Corning Saudi Contracting Services; Protection Saudi Arabia; RSV Saudi Construction; Saudi Lord; Saudi Stylist; Technical Trading Corporation; Mitsubishi Olayan Machinery Industry Saudi Arabia; OSHCO-PAE Ltd; Northrop Saudi Services; Arabian Professional Training Co; SGV Arabia

595

Associated Companies: Olayan Saudi Holding Company; General Contracting Company; General Trading Company; Saudi General Transportation Company; Saudi Container Services; Saudi Maritime Company; Saudi Logistics Company

Principal Shareholders: Member of the Olayan Group of Companies

PROJECTS & TRADING CO

PO Box 412, Jeddah 21411
Tel: 6675237
Cable: Al-Mashroat, Jeddah
Telex: 601144 Ankary Sj
Telefax: 6650354

Chairman: Sheikh Abdulla Abdulaziz Al Ankary (also Managing Director)
Directors: Mohammad Abdulla Al Ankary (Managing Director), Mohammed Othman Al Ankary (Deputy Director General)
Senior Executives: Eng Fahad A Al Ankary (Technical Director), Turky Al Ankary (Manager Riyadh)

PRINCIPAL ACTIVITIES: Building and civil engineering contractors (roads and housing); trade; water and sewerage contractors, airports
Branch Offices: Riyadh: PO Box 297, Tel 4027421, Makkah: PO Box 638; Taif: PO Box 278
Principal Bankers: National Commercial Bank; Saudi Cairo Bank, Jeddah; Saudi American Bank, Riyadh
Financial Information:

	1990 SR'000
Sales turnover	250,000
Paid-up capital	15,000
Total assets	50,000

Principal Shareholders: Sheikh Abdulla A Al Ankary; Mohammed Othman Al Ankary; Khalid A Al Ankary
Date of Establishment: 1956
No of Employees: 500

PROTECTION SAUDI ARABIA LTD

PO Box 1520, Alkhobar 31952
Tel: 8643377, 8645601, 6848152, 8645884
Telex: 871204 Oshcok Sj

President: Dr J L Florakis

PRINCIPAL ACTIVITIES: Specialists in protection coatings for industry and marine
Subsidiary/Associated Companies: Protection Limited, UAE

Principal Shareholders: Protection Ltd; The Olayan Group
No of Employees: 1,100

QASSIM CEMENT COMPANY

PO Box 345, Buraydah, Al Qassim
Tel: 3236811, 3236495, 3236719
Telex: 801201 QACMNT Sj

Honorary Chairman: Prince Abdullah Al Faisal Al Saud
Chairman: Prince Sultan Al Abdullah Al Faisal Al Saud

PRINCIPAL ACTIVITIES: Production of cement
Branch Offices: Riyadh: PO Box 4089, Riyadh 11491, Tel 4762724
Financial Information:

	SR'000
Authorised capital	300,000

QURAISHI, ABDULLA AHMED, & SONS

PO Box 220, Dammam 31411
Tel: 8322242
Cable: Quraishi Dammam
Telex: 801036 Quraish Sj

Proprietor: Abdulla Ahmed Quraishi

PRINCIPAL ACTIVITIES: General contractors; plant hire; transportation contractors and customs agents; water well drilling; commission agents, property and real estate

RABIHA & NASSAR CO

PO Box 2889, Riyadh 11461
Tel: 4762519, 4767130
Telex: 401248 Ranco Sj

Directors: Khaled Al Rabiha, Tohme Al Nassar, Youssef Al Nassar

PRINCIPAL ACTIVITIES: Civil engineering, construction of roads and buildings; manufacturers' representation, supply of construction equipment, and power equipment, generators
Principal Agencies: Caterpillars, Allis Chalmers, Italdumper, Fracasso
Branch Offices: PO Box 216, Alkhobar

Principal Shareholders: Directors as described above

RADWA FOOD PRODUCTION CO LTD

PO Box 1178, Jeddah 21431
Tel: 6109196, 6532160, 6531940
Cable: Radomir
Telex: 601580 Towers Sj
Telefax: 6531912

Chairman: Dr Abdulhadi Taher
Directors: Khalid A Taher (President), Tarek A Taher
Senior Executives: A J Franklin (General Manager), J W H Graham (General Manager Finance)

PRINCIPAL ACTIVITIES: Poultry farm and feed mill, production and marketing of frozen chicken and a range of processed meats
Parent Company: Taher Group
Principal Bankers: Saudi American Bank

No of Employees: 250

RAJAB & SILSILAH (COMMERCIAL DIVISION)

Head Office, PO Box 203, Jeddah 21411
Tel: 6610006
Cable: Arandas Jeddah
Telex: 601180 Arndas Sj, 606393 Arasco Sj
Telefax: 6610164

Partners: Abdul Aziz Rajab (President), Abdullah Silsilah (Vice President)
Senior Executives: Osama Silsilah (Asst General Manager), Ali Omar Alkaff (Asst Executive General Manager), Mohamed Abu Saifan (Finance Manager), Abdul Kader Saad (Technical Manager)

PRINCIPAL ACTIVITIES: Importation, installation and maintenance of electrical, mechanical products and equipment, electronic supplies/systems, professional equipment, industrial supplies, consumer goods etc
Principal Agencies: Philips, Netherlands; Leonard, USA; Eveready, USA; Yamaha Musical Instruments, Japan; Benckiser Detergents, Germany
Branch Offices: Riyadh, Makkah, Taif, Dammam, Abha
Subsidiary Companies: Rajab & Tayeb; Saudi Minerva; Abdullah Silsilah & Co
Principal Bankers: National Commercial Bank; Riyad Bank; Albank Alsaudi Alhollandi
Financial Information:

	1990 SR'000
Sales turnover	339,000
Profits	7,000
Authorised capital	10,000
Paid-up capital	10,000
Total assets	509,000

Date of Establishment: 1937
No of Employees: 795

RAJAB & SILSILAH (PROJECTS DIVISION)

Head Office: PO Box 2815, Riyadh 11461
Tel: 4761092, 4781320, 4788070
Cable: Arandasco Riyadh
Telex: 401331 Arandas Sj
Telefax: 4774626

President: Abdul Aziz Rajab
Directors: Abdullah Silsilah (Vice President)
Senior Executives: Ahmed Taher Al Tayeb (General Manager)

PRINCIPAL ACTIVITIES: Design, supply, installation, operation
and maintenance of electrical/electronic and mechanical
engineering goods, X-ray baggage screening & passenger
scanning equipment, metal & explosives detection systems,
bomb disposal systems, etc
Principal Agencies: Philips, Holland & USA; Pye Unicam, UK;
Motoren Werke Mannheim, W Germany; ICL, UK; AGF Inc,
USA; Intex Inc, USA; Graseby Dynamics, USA; Union
Carbide, USA; Leonard, USA; Yamaha, Japan; Benckiser, W
Germany; Rapistan Lande, Holland; McGraw Elison Battery,
USA; Nederlandse Kunststf Ind, Holland; XID, USA
Branch Offices: Makkah, Taif, Dammam, Abha, Jeddah
Subsidiary Companies: Rajab & Tayeb Est for Trading &
Industry, Riyadh; Traffic Signal Factory, Dammam
Principal Bankers: Saudi American Bank, Riyadh; National
Commercial Bank, Riyadh; Albank Alsaudi Alhollandi, Riyadh

Principal Shareholders: Abdul Aziz Rajab; Abdullah Silsilah
Date of Establishment: 1945
No of Employees: 996

RAMZI TRADING & CONTRACTING EST

PO Box 355, Alkhobar 31952
Tel: 8643388, 8644233
Cable: Ramzi
Telex: 870125 Ramzi Sj

Chairman: A Ramzi Abdulwahab

PRINCIPAL ACTIVITIES: Construction materials
Principal Agencies: General Insurance Co (Sudan) Ltd
Branch Offices: Riyadh: Siteen St, PO Box 5297, Tel 4765517
Subsidiary/Associated Companies: Set Aluminium, Dammam;
Falcon Block Factory, Damma, Ras Tanura Rd; Modern
Exhaust Pipe Factory, Dammam
Principal Bankers: Arab National Bank, Alkhobar; Al Bank Al
Saudi Al Holandi, Alkhobar; Al Bank Al Saudi Al Faransi,
Alkhobar

Date of Establishment: 1971

RASHED ABDULRAHMAN AL RASHED & SONS

See AL RASHED, RASHED ABDULRAHMAN, & SONS

RASHID ENGINEERING

PO Box 4354, Riyadh 11491
Tel: 4641188
Cable: Recats
Telex: 402461 RANA SJ

Chairman: Dr Nasser I Al-Rashid
Senior Executives: Dr Adnan Abou-Ayyash (General Manager)

PRINCIPAL ACTIVITIES: Consulting engineers
Branch Offices: Alkhobar, Tel 8645141
Associated Companies: CRS Group Inc, Houston, USA
Principal Bankers: Arab National Bank Ltd

Date of Establishment: 1973
No of Employees: 600

RAYDAN ESTABLISHMENT

PO Box 551, Jeddah 21421
Tel: (02) 6604515, (02) 6604763
Cable: Raydan
Telex: 601789 Raydan Sj

Chairman: Ezzat Ibrahim Raydan (also General Manager)
Senior Executives: Raydan E Raydan (Deputy General
Manager), Zouheir S Kaedbey (Technical & Managing
Director), Hafez Souki (Administrative Manager)

PRINCIPAL ACTIVITIES: Construction: roads, buildings, bridges,
street lighting, tunnels, causeways, harbors, airports, dams,
water and sewage networks, irrigation and drainage projects
Branch Offices: Riyadh; Yanbu; Medinah, Buraidah
Principal Bankers: National Commercial Bank; Saudi Cairo Bank

Principal Shareholders: 100% owned by Ezzat I Raydan
Date of Establishment: 1961
No of Employees: 800

RAYTHEON MIDDLE EAST SYSTEMS CO

PO Box 1348, Jeddah 21431
Tel: 6823880
Telex: 600071 Raymes Sj

PRINCIPAL ACTIVITIES: Defence contracting; supply of defence
equipment
Branch Offices: PO Box 340, Alkhobar, Tel 8641454; Riyadh,
Tel 4767116, 4764995

Principal Shareholders: Raytheon Corp (USA)

READYMIX SAUDI LTD

PO Box 5948, Jeddah 21432
Tel: 6825702, 6827861
Telex: 605759 ALADIN SJ

PRINCIPAL ACTIVITIES: Production and supply of ready-mixed
concrete in Jeddah

Principal Shareholders: Bin Ladin Bros (Saudi Arabia); Almihdar
(Saudi Arabia)

RED SEA INDUSTRIAL SUPPLY & CONTRACTING CO

PO Box 2761, Jeddah 21461
Tel: 6605796, 6652966, 6653215
Telex: 600068 Resco Sj
Telefax: 6606656

Chairman: Abdul Khaliq Bakhsh
Directors: Hassan M Mazhar (Managing Director)

PRINCIPAL ACTIVITIES: Import and distribution of industrial
materials for the petrochemical industries
Principal Agencies: Brooks Instrument, USA; Flexitallic Gaskets
Ltd, UK
Branch Offices: In Alkhobar: RESCO, PO Box 642, Dhahran, Tel
8951708; Telex 870547 Resco Sj
Subsidiary Companies: Panta Lesco Saudi Arabia Co Ltd
Principal Bankers: Saudi American Bank

Date of Establishment: 1975

RED SEA INSURANCE (SAUDI ARABIA) EC

Head Office, PO Box 5627, Jeddah 21432
Tel: 6603538 (6 lines)
Cable: DAMANSURE
Telex: 601228 RESN Sj
Telefax: 6655418

Chairman: Sheikh Omar A K Bajamal
Directors: Sheikh Saleh Salim Bin Mahfouz, Sheikh Mohamed
Salim Bin Mahfouz, Sheikh Khaldoun B Barakat (Managing
Director & General Manager), Sheikh Mubarak A Baaramah,
Sheikh Saeed Bin Salim Bin Mahfouz, Sheikh Amin Hasan
Jawa, David S A Anslow-Wilson, Michael C Allemang,
Kazuchika Tokuhiro
Senior Executives: Ahmed Hussain Abul Ela (Deputy General
Manager), Idris Yousaf Balbale (Asst General Manager)

PRINCIPAL ACTIVITIES: All classes of insurance (excl life)
Branch Offices: Location in Jeddah: Al Hamra District, Al Watan
Al Arabi Street, Red Sea Bldg; also branches in Riyadh: PO

Box 5908, Riyadh 11432, Tel 4036643, Fax 4031992, Telex 402165; Dammam: PO Box 1939, Dammam 31441, Tel 8324256, Fax 8332548, Telex 802781; Makkah: PO Box 2174, Tel 5733132, Fax 5733133
Parent Company: Red Sea Development Co Ltd
Principal Bankers: National Commercial Bank; Saudi Cairo Bank
Financial Information:

	1989 US$'000
Sales turnover	8,740
Authorised capital	3,000
Paid-up capital & reserves	4,174
Total assets	8,572

Principal Shareholders: Red Sea Development Co Ltd; National Commercial Bank; Anslow Wilson & Amery Ltd, Firemens Fund American Insurance Co; Dowa Fire & Marine Insurance Co; Saudi businessmen
Date of Establishment: 1974 and 1989 as present status (EC)
No of Employees: 83

RED SEA PAINT FACTORY
PO Box 1642, Jeddah 21441
Tel: 6361271, 6369824
Telex: 603755 Bouyat Sj

Senior Executives: Khalid Mahmood Qureshi (General Manager)

PRINCIPAL ACTIVITIES: Manufacture of decorative and industry finishes
Principal Agencies: Goodlass Wall Co, UK
Branch Offices: Riyadh; Yanbu
Principal Bankers: National Commercial Bank
Financial Information:

	SR'000
Authorised capital	22,000

RED SEA TRADING & SHIPPING EST
PO Box 648, Jeddah 21421
Tel: 6422183, 6426123, 6436517
Cable: Phrontis
Telex: 601057 Redsea Sj

Chairman: Sheikh Ahmad Muhammed Aldainy (General Manager)
Directors: Alawi Ahmed Barakat (Dy General Manager)
Senior Executives: Mohammad Saeed (Shipping Manager)

PRINCIPAL ACTIVITIES: Trading, shipping, clearing and forwarding
Principal Agencies: Minerva SA Spain; Hungarofruct; Tungsram; Hungary
Branch Offices: Location in Jeddah: King Abdul Aziz Street, Al Mufti Bldg
Associated Companies: Saudi Road Guardrails Est; Saudi Est for Safety Electronic System (SESES); Saudi Arab Advertising Agency; Saudi Trade Centre
Principal Bankers: National Commercial Bank Ltd, Al Bank Al Saudi Al Fransi

Date of Establishment: 1956

REDEC DAELIM SAUDI ARABIA CO LTD
PO Box 361, Dhahran Airport 31932
Tel: 8648212, 8647137, 8648221
Telex: 871318 Delimsa Sj

Chairman: Dr Ghaith R Pharaon

PRINCIPAL ACTIVITIES: General construction services, civil, architectural, mechanical, electrical and other types of works including construction of power plants, petroleum refineries, chemical and petrochemical plants, gas processing plants; other heavy industrial and construction facilities
Branch Offices: Jeddah: Tel 6602043, Telex 600267; Riyadh: Tel 4643751
Principal Bankers: Al Bank Al Saudi Al Fransi; National Commercial Bank

Principal Shareholders: Daelim Industrial Co Ltd, Korea; Saudi Research & Development Corporation (REDEC), Saudi Arabia
Date of Establishment: August 1976
No of Employees: 13,203

REDLAND INDUSTRIAL SERVICES (ARABIA) LTD
PO Box 718, Dammam 31421
Tel: 03 8343343, 8343113
Telex: 803309 Risal Sj
Telefax: 8342937

Chairman: Sheikh Abdul Rahman Ali Al-Turki
Directors: Sheikh Rashid Al-Sunaid, Fouad Tannous

PRINCIPAL ACTIVITIES: Industrial and marine maintenance, catalyst handling, chemical cleaning, HPWJ, specialist maintenance services, surface preparation and special coatings, waste management consultants and contractors, tank cleaning, tank farm refurbishment
Branch Offices: Jubail: PO Box 388, Tel 03-3612126, 3610098; Jeddah: PO Box 5809, Tel 02-6911156, 6914123; Riyadh: Tel 01-4821663; Yanbu: Tel 04-3226788
Parent Company: A A Turki Corp
Principal Bankers: Saudi British Bank
Financial Information:

	1989 SR'000
Sales turnover	20,000
Profits	1,000
Authorised capital	1,000
Paid-up capital	1,000

Principal Shareholders: A A Turki Corporation for Trading & Contracting (100%)
Date of Establishment: September 1976
No of Employees: 250

REEM CORPORATION
PO Box 225, Riyadh 11411
Tel: 4024670
Cable: Reem-Riyadh
Telex: 401114 Remcor Sj

President: Nazih Odeh Karram
Directors: M Nabil Dabbagh, Pierre F Assioun

PRINCIPAL ACTIVITIES: Building, civil engineering and public works, commercial imports, agency, consultants
Branch Offices: Jeddah: PO Box 2336, Tel 6434185, Telex 601103; and Paris Office

Date of Establishment: 1966
No of Employees: 100

REFA TRADING & INDUSTRIAL CO
PO Box 6806, Riyadh 11452
Tel: 4353801, 4358618
Telex: 400520 Amajed SJ

Chairman: Ibrahim M Sayyar
Directors: Abdulkarim A Sayyar, Ahmed A Sayyar

PRINCIPAL ACTIVITIES: Import of all kind of electrical materials, furniture, carpets and rugs
Principal Bankers: Al-Jazirah Bank, Riyadh

RESOURCE SCIENCES ARABIA LTD
PO Box 58729, Riyadh 11515
Tel: 4633392
Telex: 870531 RSAL Sj
Telefax: 4630324

Chairman: Abdulla A Alireza
Directors: Mohammed A Alireza, Adnan Maimani, Newman A Howard, Earl P Gilmore, Joseph A Incaudo
Senior Executives: James L Rhyner (Managing Director), Sadi A Awwad (Marketing Manager)

PRINCIPAL ACTIVITIES: Operation and maintenance, training, supplemental manpower, construction management

Branch Offices: Branch in Alkhobar: PO Box 1272, Alkhobar 31952, Tel 8982500, Fax 8985100; also branch in Yanbu: PO Box 30108, Madinat Yanbu Al-Sinaiyah, Tel 396-8689, 396-6020

Parent Company: Resource Sciences Corporation, Tulsa, Oklahoma, USA; Xenel Industries Ltd, Xenel Bldg, Babjadid St, Jeddah

Associated Companies: Holmes & Narver, Inc, Orange, Calif. USA

Principal Bankers: Saudi French Bank

Financial Information:

	1989/90 SR'000
Sales turnover	78,106
Authorised capital	1,000
Paid-up capital	1,000

Principal Shareholders: Xenel Industries Ltd; Resource Sciences Corporation

Date of Establishment: 1975

No of Employees: 1,075

RET-SER ENGINEERING AGENCY

Saudi Arabian Branch Office, PO Box 3984, Jeddah 21481

Tel: 6510979, 6530702, 6531646

Cable: RSEA CHINE JEDDAH

Telex: 601343 Retser SJ

Telefax: 6519660

President: Arthur Y Chen (President of Ret-Ser Engineering Agency)

Senior Executives: Y Y Tseng (Vice President & Director of Overseas Operation Division), W N Liu (General Manager of Saudi Branch), Y T Ni (General Manager of Jordan Branch), K C Fun (General Manager of Bahrain Branch), C S Hsiao (General Manager of Egypt Branch)

PRINCIPAL ACTIVITIES: Construction of highways, railroads, bridges, dams and reservoirs, airfields, buildings, harbours, dredging, reclamation, hydraulic structures, power plants, sanitary and sewerage systems, integral steel mill, industrial complex

Principal Agencies: Xenel Industries Ltd

Branch Offices: Egypt Office: 1st Floor, Bldg 9, Str 23 Maadi, Cairo, Telex 22352 RSEA UN; Jordan Office: PO Box 2896, Jebel Ammam, Telex 22362 RSEA JO; Bahrain Office: PO Box 2588, Manama, Telex 7394 TETSER BN

Parent Company: Ret-Ser Engineering Agency, Taipei, Taiwan, Republic of China

Principal Bankers: Saudi American Bank; Saudi International Bank; National Commercial Bank; Bank of Taiwan; The International Commercial Bank of China; Citibank; Chase Manhattan Bank; Bank of America; Taipei

Financial Information:

	SR'000
Authorised capital	400,000
Paid-up capital	400,000

Principal Shareholders: Vocational Assistance Commission for Retired Servicemen, ROC

REZATRADE MARKETING & DEVELOP

Rezatrade Marketing & Development

PO Box 1555, Jeddah 21441

Tel: 6442993/5

Telex: 601777 Alreza Sj

PRINCIPAL ACTIVITIES: General trading and contracting, consultants, marketing, management, sponsors

Branch Offices: Riyadh

REZAYAT COMPANY LTD

Alireza Group of Companies

PO Box 90, Alkhobar 31952

Tel: 8570234 (10 lines)

Cable: Rezayat Alkhobar

Telex: 870006 Rezt Sj; 871250 Nalco Sj

Telefax: 8575643, 8572846

Chairman: Abdulla Alireza

Directors: Teymour Alireza (President)

Senior Executives: Saud Al Hejailan (Vice President), J H N Gibson (Group General Manager), C M Varghese (Chief Accountant), A W Huidekoper (General Manager Marine Division), F Haque (General Manager Electrical Projects Division), Abdul Majeed Al Yahya (General Manager Business Development & Commercial Division), James Anderson (General Manager Catering & Support Services Division), Magdi Elbitar (General Manager Maintenance Division), Owain Raw-Rees (General Manager Insurance Division), Dr Samy Hanna (General Manager Medical Division)

PRINCIPAL ACTIVITIES: Systems housing, camp construction and leasing; motels and industrial catering; heavy lift, heavy and general transportation; port activities, clearing and forwarding and marine services; steel pipe manufacture and steel fabrication; power projects, mechanical & electrical installation; engineering, plant overhaul and workshop services; utility operation and maintenance services; petrochemical engineering & civil construction; offshore & pipeline construction; oilwell drilling; corrosion control; general trading and business development; general medical services; operation and maintenance, general trading in medical; loss adjusting; calibration

Branch Offices: Saudi Arabia: PO Box 996, Riyadh, Tel 4772630, 4770587, Telex 402790, 401297; PO Box 6670, Jeddah, Tel 6657863, 6611333, Telex 600272; Kuwait: PO Box 106, Safat, Kuwait, Telex 22070; UAE: PO Box 256, Abu Dhabi, Telex 22255; PO Box 2752, Dubai, Telex 46598; UK: London, Telex 25997; France: Paris, Telex 641542; USA: Houston, Telex 792016

Subsidiary/Associated Companies: National Contracting Co Ltd; International Electronics Co Ltd; Brown & Root Alireza WLL Ltd; Arabian Mechanical Engineering Co Ltd; Crescent Transportation Co Ltd; Lamnalco Saudi Arabia Ltd; National Pipe Co Ltd; Rezayat Sparrow Arabian Crane Hire Co Ltd; Saudi Arabian Engineering Co Ltd; Wimpey Arabian Services Co Ltd; Taisei Saudi Arabia Co Ltd; Nadrico Saudi Ltd; Guest Spencer; Graham Miller; Caleb Brett; Saudi Arabian Fabricated Metals Industry Ltd; Rezayat for Water & Electric Resources Co Ltd; Rezayat Deutsche Babcock; Alireza Lyonnaise Water Co Ltd; Rezayat Daewoo Petrochemical Installations Co Ltd

Principal Bankers: Saudi British Bank; Riyad Bank; Morgan Guaranty Trust Co; Al Bank Al Saudi Al Fransi

Date of Establishment: 1.9.1971

No of Employees: 3,000

REZAYAT SPARROW ARABIAN CRANE HIRE CO LTD

PO Box 90, Alkhobar 31952

Tel: 8574134, 8574190, 8575247, 8576430

Cable: Rezayat

Telex: 870793 RESPAR SJ

Telefax: (03) 8575251

President: Teymour Abdulla Alireza

Directors: J H N Gibson, K Barnes

Senior Executives: Arthur Watt (General Manager)

PRINCIPAL ACTIVITIES: Crane hire, rigging, heavy lift specialists

Branch Offices: Jubail

Parent Company: Rezayat Trading Est, Saudi Arabia; BET Plant Services Plc, UK

SAUDI ARABIA

Principal Bankers: Saudi British Bank

Date of Establishment: October 1978
No of Employees: 140

RIYAD BANK
PO Box 22622, Riyadh 11416
Tel: 4013030
Cable: Riyadbank
Telex: 407490 RDX SJ
Telefax: 4041255

Chairman: Sheikh Ismail Abou Dawood
Directors: Sheikh Ahmed Abdullatif (Managing Director), Sheikh Abdul Mohsen Al Suwailem, Sheikh Khaled Al Gosaibi, Sheikh Rashed Abdulaziz Al Rashed, Dr Khaled Mohammed Al Fayez, Sheikh Khaled Suleiman Al Olayan
Senior Executives: Ibrahim M S Shams (General Manager), Abdul Majeed A Saiedi (Asst General Manager Public Relations), Mohammed Al Ammari (Asst General Manager Domestic Banking), Saud Al Fayez (Asst General Manager Credit Control), Talal Al Qudaibi (Asst General Manager International Banking), Mubarak Al Qahtani (Asst General Manager Personnel), Yahya M Sagga (Asst General Manager Training & Management Development)

PRINCIPAL ACTIVITIES: Commercial banking
Branch Offices: Over 157 throughout Saudi Arabia: Jeddah Main, PO Box 370, Telex 601799, Tel 6474777; Makkah Main, PO Box 160, Telex 750008, Tel 5741378; Madinah Main, PO Box 27, Telex 570015, Tel 8250876; AlKhobar Main, PO Box 229, Telex 870005, Tel 8983152; Dammam Main, PO Box 274, Telex 801127, Tel 8321056; Riyadh Main, PO Box 229, Telex 400282, Tel 4042889; Buraydah Main, PO Box 28, Telex 301016, Tel 3231960; Khamis Mushait, PO Box 267, Telex 906633, Tel 2239528; Tabouk Main, PO Box 72, Telx 681323, Tel 4229244; two branches in London, Temple Court, 11 Queen Victoria Street, London EC4N 4XP, Telex 8955154; and 49 Park Lane, London W1Y 4BR, Telex 915484, Tel 01-491 7950
Associated Companies: Gulf Riyad Bank EC, Bahrain; Arla Bank International EC, Bahrain; UBAF Arab American Bank, New York; Saudi Spanish Bank, Madrid; Arab Latin American Bank, Lima, Peru; Al Alamiya Insurance Co, London; UBAC Curacao, Curacao; Saudi Swiss Bank, Geneva
Financial Information:

	1988/89
	SR'000
Net profit	264,488
Authorised capital	200,000
Paid-up capital	200,000
Deposits	32,327,714
Loans & advances	9,513,714
Total assets	69,293,565

Principal Shareholders: Saudi Arabian Monetary Agency and Saudi Citizens
Date of Establishment: 1957
No of Employees: 4,361

RIYADH FURNITURE INDUSTRIES LTD
PO Box 5038, Riyadh 11422
Tel: 4980808
Cable: Rimth
Telex: 404643 Furn SJ
Telefax: (01) 4981216

Chairman: Mohammed Alomair

Directors: Abdul Rehman Al Mahmoud, Mohammad Alomair (President), Eng Omair Abdulaziz Alomair (Managing Director & General Manager), Eng Abdulaziz Abdullah Alomair (Deputy General Manager)
Senior Executives: Tariq Alomair (Stores & Procurement Manager), Eng Mohammed Al Shuhayeb (Marketing Manager), Eng Faraj Ayoub (Production Manager), Eng Abdulla Alomair (Production Manager Sheet Metal), Eng Ali Shamsan (Asst Marketing Manager)

PRINCIPAL ACTIVITIES: Manufacture of wooden, steel and upholstered furniture, contract furnishing, interior decoration, supply of complete fitted furniture, fixtures and equipment
Branch Offices: Riyadh Industries Corp, 81 Montecito Dr, CDM, California, USA
Associated Companies: Seating & Office Systems Industries Ltd, Arabiah Furniture Manufacturing Co
Principal Bankers: Riyad Bank, Arab National Bank
Financial Information:

	1990
	SR'000
Sales turnover	80,000
Authorised capital	99,000
Paid-up capital	25,000
Total assets	100,000

Principal Shareholders: Directors as described
Date of Establishment: 1975
No of Employees: 582

RIYADH HOUSE ESTABLISHMENT
PO Box 317, Riyadh 11411
Tel: 4624000
Cable: Aljeraisy
Telex: 401113 Jeraisy Sj

President: Abdulrahman Al Al-Jeraisy
Senior Executives: Saleh Al Mozeil (Executive Vice-President), Khaled Al Jeraisy (Vice-President Materials & Foreign Relations), Ibrahim Al Ghannam (Vice-President Manufacturing & Projects)

PRINCIPAL ACTIVITIES: Import and distribution of office communication and photographic machines and equipment, computers
Principal Agencies: Victor Intercontinental, Belgium; Canon Microfilm Systems, Japan; A B Dick, USA; Danza, Denmark; Olympia, W Germany; Harper & Tunstall, UK; Milta Holland BV; Wang Europe, Belgium; Apple; Mita; Konica U-Bix; Ricoh; 3M; Datacard; Dictaphone; Shako; Neolt
Branch Offices: Jeddah (PO Box 2830); Dammam (PO Box 1244); Alkhobar (PO Box 1643); Jubail; Khamis Mushayt; Al Ahsa; Tabuk; Yanbu; Mubaraz; Qaseem
Parent Company: Jeraisy Group of Establishments
Subsidiary Companies: Jeraisy Computer Services; Jeraisytech; Fraiha Est; Jeraisy Furniture Factory; Jeraisy Computer Paper Factory
Principal Bankers: National Commercial Bank; Saudi American Bank; Riyad Bank Ltd; Saudi British Bank; Al Bank Al Saudi Al Hollandi
Financial Information:

	1990
	SR'000
Sales turnover	900,000
Total assets	1,200,000

Principal Shareholders: Abdulrahman Al Jeraisy
Date of Establishment: 1958
No of Employees: 2000

RIYADH MARRIOTT HOTEL
PO Box 16294, Riyadh 11464
Tel: 4779300
Telex: 400983 Marr SJ
Telefax: 4779089

Directors: Mounir S Ami (General Manager)

Senior Executives: J G Heesbeen (Director of Marketing)

PRINCIPAL ACTIVITIES: Hotel business
Parent Company: Marriott Corporation

Date of Establishment: December 1980
No of Employees: 378

RIYADH NEW ORGANIZATION

PO Box 167, Riyadh 11411
Tel: 4781440
Cable: Alidrissi
Telex: 400906 Edrisy

Chairman: Ibrahim A Alidrissi
Directors: Hashim M Alidrissi (Vice Chairman), Hassan A
Alidrissi (Vice Chairman)

PRINCIPAL ACTIVITIES: Contracting: civil, building, roads,
factories; industry: wood works, steel works, aluminium;
commerce: construction materials, equipment, foodstuff;
agencies: investment
Branch Offices: Jeddah: PO Box 5800, Tel 6428943; Dammam:
Tel 8321441; Taif: PO Box 633, Tel 7367439; Abha: Tel
2238283
Subsidiary Companies: Saudi Sudanese Dev Co, Sudan;
Mediterranean Contracting and Trading, Cairo; Construction
Supplies Co, Saudi Arabia
Principal Bankers: Saudi Cairo Bank, Riyadh; Bank Melli Iran,
Jeddah
Financial Information:

	SR'000
Authorised capital	5,500
Paid-up capital	5,500

Principal Shareholders: Wholly owned by Sheikh Ibrahim A
Alidrissi
Date of Establishment: 1953
No of Employees: 911

RIYADH OXYGEN PLANT

PO Box 374, Riyadh 11411
Tel: 4485070
Cable: Oxoriyadh
Telex: 400822 Oxygen SJ
Telefax: 4468319

Chairman: Abdullah A Al Kharashi
Directors: Abdul Aziz Al Kharashi
Senior Executives: Bassam A Al Kharashi (Administration
Manager), Zafar I Khokhar (Production Manager), Waqar
Haleem Raza (Sales Manager)

PRINCIPAL ACTIVITIES: Production and distribution of medical
and industrial gases, hospital central gas distribution system,
supply of cryogenic tanks, high pressure cylinders and
welding equipment
Principal Agencies: L'Air Liquide, France; Japan Engg
Consultants & Exports, Japan; Iwatani Int'l Corp, Japan;
North American Cylinders, USA
Branch Offices: Al Khraj
Principal Bankers: National Commercial Bank, Riyadh; Riyad
Bank, Riyadh; Al Rajhi Banking & Investment Corp, Riyadh

Date of Establishment: 1967
No of Employees: 100

RIYADH PALACE HOTEL

PO Box 2691, Riyadh 11461
Tel: 4054444
Telex: 400312 RPH Sj
Telefax: 4053725

Chairman: Sheikh Abdulaziz Al Gosaibi
Senior Executives: Ghazi El Khatib (General Manager), Ibrahim
Balaha (Sales & Marketing Director)

PRINCIPAL ACTIVITIES: Hotel business

Principal Agencies: Utell International, Horis (Swissair), Goldin
Tulip (KLM)
Branch Offices: Location in Riyadh: Off Prince Abdulrahman Bin
Abdulaziz Ministerial Quarter
Parent Company: Saudi Hotel Services Company

Principal Shareholders: Arab Investment Co; General
Organisation for Social Insurance (GOSI); Riyad Bank Ltd;
National Commercial Bank; Saudi Hotels and Resort Areas
Co (SHARACO); Kuwait Real Estate Company; Ahmad Hamad
Al Gosaibi Group of Companies; Abdulaziz Al Suleiman &
Bros
Date of Establishment: 1979
No of Employees: 250

RIYADH REFINERY CO

PO Box 3946, Riyadh 11481
Tel: 4485033, 4485065
Cable: Almisfa
Telex: 401015 Almisfa Riyadh

PRINCIPAL ACTIVITIES: Petroleum refinery in the central
province

Principal Shareholders: A subsidiary of the General Petroleum
and Mineral Organisation (Petromin)

RIYADH SHERATON HOTEL

PO Box 90807, Riyadh 11623
Tel: 4543300
Cable: Sheraton Riyadh
Telex: 401415 Sher Sj
Telefax: 4541889

Senior Executives: Bento P Marcopoli (General Manager), Rolf
D Schmelcher (Executivr Asst Manager), Mohammed Javed
(Financial Controller), Willie D'Cunha (Director of Sales &
Promotion), Abdulaziz Tellawi (Personnel Manager), Maged
Berri (Purchasing Manager)

PRINCIPAL ACTIVITIES: Hotel operation
Principal Bankers: Saudi American Bank, Riyadh

Principal Shareholders: Owners: Saudi Oger Ltd, Riyadh
Date of Establishment: 1984
No of Employees: 195

ROAD CONSTRUCTION EST

PO Box 523, Alkhobar 31952
Tel: 8642137, 8644690
Cable: Inshaco
Telex: 870072 Rce Sj
Telefax: 03-8983401

Chairman: Nasser Ali Al Suhibani (General Manager)
Directors: Ali Nasser Al Suhibani (Technical Manager)
Senior Executives: Khalid Nasser Al Suhibani (Planning
Manager), Waleed Nasser Al Suhibani (Personnel Manager),
Abdul Rehman Al Suhibani (Administration Manager),
Mohammed Rajab (Finance Manager)

PRINCIPAL ACTIVITIES: Road construction, site preparation,
pipe line works, asphalt paving, equipment rental
Branch Offices: PO Box 1536, Al Qassim, Saudi Arabia
Principal Bankers: Arab National Bank; Saudi Cairo Bank
Financial Information:

	1990 SR'000
Sales turnover	14,462
Profits	605
Authorised capital	22,608
Paid-up capital	1,000
Total assets	46,121

Principal Shareholders: Nasser Ali Al Suhibani, Ali Nasser Al
Suhibani, Khalid Nasser Al Suhibani, Waleed Nasser Al
Suhibani
No of Employees: 450

ROLACO TRADING & CONTRACTING

PO Box 222, Jeddah 21411
Tel: 6518028, 6528456
Cable: Rolaco
Telex: 601029 Rolaco Sj
Telefax: 6534280

Chairman: HE Sheikh Abdul Aziz A Al Sulaiman

PRINCIPAL ACTIVITIES: Supply of cement, steel bars, heavy
equipment, building materials, scaffolding, civil and structural
engineering and mechanical and electrical works, general
contracting, catering, shipping, housing, cables, surveying
instruments, medical equipment, land transportation
Principal Agencies: Nissan Diesel Trucks; Kato Works Co;
Nissan Forklifts; Briab Cement Silos; Les Cables de Lyon;
Topcon Survey Instruments; Marubeni Medical Equipment
Branch Offices: Dammam: PO Box 4493, Tel 8572078, Telex
801800; Riyadh: PO Box 740, Tel 4917239, Telex 401380;
Yanbu: PO Box 579, Tel 3226716
Subsidiary Companies: Rolaco Cement Distributing Co Ltd;
Dalia Shipping Co; Lama Shipping Co; Zahran Contracting;
Rolaco for Animal Feed Trading & Packing Co Ltd (Barley)
Principal Bankers: Saudi Al Fransi Bank; Saudi American Bank;
Bank Al-Jazira; Bank Al Saudi Al Hollandi
Financial Information:

	SR'000
Sales turnover	450,000
Authorised capital	66,000
Paid-up capital	66,000

Principal Shareholders: H E Sheikh Abdul Aziz Al-Abdullah Al-
Sulaiman; Sheikh Saud Abdul Aziz Al-Sulaiman
Date of Establishment: 1968
No of Employees: 300/400

ROLLS-ROYCE INTERNATIONAL TURBINES SAUDI ARABIA LTD (RRITSA)

PO Box 1469, Jeddah 21431
Tel: 6692994
Telex: 604180 Rritsa Sj
Telefax: 6673892

PRINCIPAL ACTIVITIES: Engines and turbines, aerospace
components
Branch Offices: Riyadh Regional Office: PO Box 88215, Riyadh
11662, Tel 4541888 ext 438, Telex 404508, Fax 4546160

RUBEAAN FACTORIES CO LTD

PO Box 1375, Riyadh 11431
Tel: 4465640, 4480171
Cable: Robeaanco
Telex: 401917 SJ
Telefax: 4465644

Chairman: Mohamed Ali Al Rubeaan
Directors: Hamoud Ali Al Rubeaan (Finance & Administration
Director), Yousif Ali Al Rubeaan

PRINCIPAL ACTIVITIES: Manufacturers (construction
equipment, tools and machinery)
Branch Offices: Jeddah: PO Box 9599, Jeddah 21423, Tel
6373270, Fax 6364055; Dammam: PO Box 7483, Dammam
31462, Tel 8434877, Fax 8425286
Financial Information:

	1990 SR'000
Paid-up capital	18,000

Principal Shareholders: The Rubeaan brothers
Date of Establishment: 1397H
No of Employees: 131

S H ALATAS & CO LTD

See ALATAS, S H, & CO LTD

SAAD A AL TWAIJRI OFFICE

See AL TWAIJRI, SAAD A, OFFICE

SAAD CONSTRUCTION EST

PO Box 968, Riyadh 11421
Tel: 4069200
Cable: Saadico
Telex: 404913 Twajri Sj, 401498 Saado Sj
Telefax: 4069200 ext 220

President: Saad Abdullah Al Twaijri
Directors: Fahad Abdullah Al Twaijri (General Manager)
Senior Executives: Salah Khalid Al Twaijri (Procurement
Manager)

PRINCIPAL ACTIVITIES: Construction, buildings, landscaping,
turnkey furnishings
Principal Agencies: Consilium AB (materials handling marine);
Siwertell Div (conveying systems & ship unloaders/loaders)
Subsidiary Companies: NCP National Cement Products, Riyadh;
Saudi Transformer Co, Dammam; AS Safina Co Shipping &
Forwarding
Principal Bankers: Saudi Cairo Bank
Financial Information:

	SR'000
Paid-up capital	7,000

Principal Shareholders: Saad A Al Twaijri
Date of Establishment: 1958
No of Employees: 1,500

SAAD CORPORATION

PO Box 1, Dhahran 31411
Tel: 8324552
Cable: Trasadco Dammam
Telex: 801135 Saad Sj

Chairman: Prince Saad Bin Mohammad Bin Abdul Aziz Al Saud
Senior Executives: A I Souleiman (Executive Manager)

PRINCIPAL ACTIVITIES: Manufacturers' representatives,
engineering contractors; supply of electrical and power
equipment
Branch Offices: Riyadh: PO Box 6389, Tel 4769271, Telex
400410 Saads Sj
Associated Companies: The Saad Japanese Electric
Development Co (SEDEC); Saad Electric Co
Principal Bankers: Al Bank Al Saudi Al Fransi
Financial Information:

	SR'000
Authorised capital	15,000
Paid-up capital	15,000

Principal Shareholders: Prince Saad Bin Mohammad Bin Abdul
Aziz Al Saud
Date of Establishment: March 1976
No of Employees: 510

SAAD H ABUKHADRA & CO

See ABUKHADRA, SAAD H, & CO

SABA ABULKHAIR & CO

PO Box 442, Jeddah 21411
Tel: 6829495, 6825891
Cable: Sabaco Jeddah
Telex: 601625 Sabaco Sj
Telefax: 6829495

Chairman: George B Ghali (Managing Partner)
Partners: Joseph Sanbar, Bakr Abulkhair
Senior Executives: Khalil H Kashef, Fathi H Abbas, Fauji J
Awad, Krikor Sadikian, Shahed Zahur

PRINCIPAL ACTIVITIES: Public accountants and tax
management consultants
Branch Offices: PO Box 213, Riyadh 11411, Tel 4630018, Telex
201985 SABACO SJ; PO Box 182, Dammam 31411, Tel
8321144, Telex 801352 SABACO SJ

Parent Company: Saba & Co - Cyprus
Subsidiary Companies: Touche Ross, Saba & Co

No of Employees: Over 500

SABBAN INVESTMENT CO LTD

PO Box 4504, Jeddah 21412
Tel: 6530956, 6514690
Cable: Adjsabban
Telex: 601398 Novcom Sj

Chairman: Abdulbary M S Alsabban
Senior Executives: H F Shamsi (Manager)

PRINCIPAL ACTIVITIES: Investment, company development,
general contracting, manufacturers representation
Subsidiary/Associated Companies: Trading & Contracting
Corporation, Jeddah
Principal Bankers: National Commercial Bank

Principal Shareholders: Abdulbary M S Al Sabban; Khalid A M S
Sabban
Date of Establishment: 1978

SADDIK & MOHAMED ATTAR

See ATTAR, SADDIK & MOHAMED,

SADIQ CONTRACTING EST

PO Box 690, Dammam 31421
Tel: 8427639, 8100203, 3610572
Telex: 803437 Sadiq Sj
Telefax: 03-8429300, 03-3613970

President: Ali Sadiq Madani (Owner)
Directors: Nadir Hussni Mandil (General Manager)

PRINCIPAL ACTIVITIES: Civil engineering, airport, roads,
concrete and asphalt works, slurry seal works, aggregate
supply
Branch Offices: PO Box 618, Jubail 31951, Tel 03-3610572,
8100223
Principal Bankers: Saudi American Bank; Saudi British Bank;
National Commercial Bank; Al Bank Al Saudi Al Fransi

Date of Establishment: 1977
No of Employees: 94

SAFA CONTRACTING CO

PO Box 304, Jeddah 21411
Tel: 6725391, 6723076
Cable: Safzam
Telex: 601129 Safazam Sj
Telefax: 6723076

Chairman: Sheikh Adel Azzam
Directors: Sheikh Ahmad Azmi Azzam (Vice Chairman)
Senior Executives: Eng Ahmad Akl Helmy (Projects Manager),
Eng Wail Akl Helmy (Factories Manager), Hussein Nabil
(Finance Manager), Abdel Mohsin Al Hilbawi (Personnel
Manager)

PRINCIPAL ACTIVITIES: General contracting and construction;
building materials
Branch Offices: PO Box 368, Medina, Tel 8360205, 8360241,
8360778, Telex 570065
Subsidiary Companies: Al Shark Factories, PO Box 304, Jeddah
21411; Taibah Plants, PO Box 368, Madina Munawwara; Al
Faiha Poultry Farm, PO Box 3811, Madina Munawwara
Principal Bankers: Saudi Cairo Bank

Principal Shareholders: Chairman and director as described
Date of Establishment: 1966
No of Employees: 350

SAFID SAUDI FINN DUCTING CO LTD

PO Box 15300, Riyadh 11444
Tel: (01) 4982984
Telex: 400907 SAFID SJ
Telefax: (01) 4982497

President: Sheikh Mohamed Rahbani
Senior Executives: Tapio Leino (Managing Director), Jamal
Jawhari (Marketing Manager)

PRINCIPAL ACTIVITIES: Manufacture of air distribution
equipment, sound controls, and ducts of all kind
Principal Agencies: DEC International, Holland; Sound
Attenuators, UK
Branch Offices: Kuwait: PO Box 66519, Bayan 43756, Kuwait,
Tel 5390901, Fax 5390901
Parent Company: Nokia, Finland
Principal Bankers: Lloyds Bank Plc, Dubai; National Commercial
Bank, Riyadh
Financial Information:

	1990
	SR'000
Sales turnover	30,000
Paid-up capital	3,500
Total assets	20,000

Principal Shareholders: Sheikh Halim Rahbani; Nokia
Corporation, Finland
Date of Establishment: 1979
No of Employees: 200

SAGER INTERNATIONAL CO

PO Box 1453, Jeddah 21431
Tel: 02-6530551, 6532258
Telex: 601720 OTRAMO SJ
Telefax: 02-6533888

Chairman: Sheikh Othman Abdul-Aziz Sager Alghamdi
Directors: Saeed O Sager (Managing Director)
Senior Executives: Nadir Rahimtulla (Asst Managing Director)

PRINCIPAL ACTIVITIES: Import of home appliances, heavy duty
kitchen equipment and food service equipment and supplies,
seating and decor package for restaurants, hotels and homes
Principal Agencies: USA: Maytag, Garland, Lincoln, Duke
Manufacturing, American Permanent Wares, Wyott, Ice-o-
matic, Legion, Alto Shaam, Champion, Advance Food Service
Equip, Tabco, Chesterfried, Southbend, Traulsen, etc; Italy:
Angelo, Silko, Sima, Sagi, Brasilia, etc; Germany: Blanco,
Ratiotherm
Branch Offices: Location in Jeddah: First Floor, Suite 101/103,
Al Othman Commercial Centre, King Fahd Street; also
branches in Riyadh: PO Box 8992, Tel 01-4012121, Fax 01-
4042211; Alkhobar: PO Box 3533, Alkhobar 31951, Tel 03-
8983331, Fax 03-8985504
Parent Company: Sager Group of Companies
Principal Bankers: Al Rahji Banking & Investment Corp
Financial Information:

	1990/91
	SR'000
Authorised capital	16,000
Paid-up capital	16,000

Principal Shareholders: Chairman and directors as described
Date of Establishment: 1973
No of Employees: 85

SAHARA BUILDING CONTRACTORS

PO Box 11852, Jeddah 21463
Tel: 6653685, 6607564, 6650687, 6602312
Telex: 603039 Sahara Sj
Telefax: 6650710

Chairman: Abdul Aziz Alfadl
Directors: Bilal Nabahani (General Manager)
Senior Executives: Mohamed Hikmat (Area Manager), Mahmud
Shakir Al Hashimi (Construction Manager Jeddah), Bashir
Hamed (Sales Manager Riyadh), Allam Naji (Acting Manager
Alkhobar)

PRINCIPAL ACTIVITIES: Turnkey contractors of pre-engineered
steel buildings, designer/builders in civil, structural, electrical
and air conditioning. Specialist in construction of warehouses,

supermarkets, factories, aircraft hangers, and low rise office buildings

Principal Agencies: Certified builders in Saudi Arabia of Butler Steel Buildings

Branch Offices: Riyadh: PO Box 51478, Riyadh 11543, Tel 4059068, 4058642, Telex 405115 SAHARA SJ, Fax 4024872; AlKhobar: PO Box 2710, Alkhobar 31952, Tel 8953280, 8951252, Telex 870702 SAHARA SJ, Fax 8943872

Parent Company: Al Fadl Group

Principal Bankers: Riyadh Bank; Arab National Bank; Al Bank Al Saudi Al Fransi; Al Bank Al Saudi Al Hollandi

Financial Information:

	1990
	SR'000
Sales turnover	102,000
Authorised capital	3,000
Paid-up capital	3,000
Total assets	16,000

Principal Shareholders: Sheikh Abdul Aziz Al Fadl; Sheikh Abdul Kader Al Fadl

Date of Establishment: 1/11/1980

No of Employees: 650

SAID EL AJOU TRADING CORPORATION

See EL AJOU, SAID, TRADING CORPORATION

SAIF NOMAN SAID & PARTNERS CO

PO Box 4544, Jeddah 21412

Tel: 6884121, 6807176, 6806156

Cable: CIFKADORLI

Telex: 604524 SNSEST SJ

Chairman: Saif Noman Said

Directors: Omar El Esayi, Saif Noman Said, Khalid Salem Bin Mahfooz, Mohammed Salem Bin Mahfooz

PRINCIPAL ACTIVITIES: Manufacture of prestressed precast hollow core concrete roof/floor slabs, glassfibre reinforced (GRC) and prestressed concrete (railways sleepers)

Branch Offices: Riyadh: PO Box 40843, Tel 4762525, 4792425; Telex 405156 SAIF SJ; and London

Principal Bankers: National Commercial Bank, Main Branch, Jeddah

Financial Information:

	SR'000
Authorised capital	13,000
Paid-up capital	13,000

Principal Shareholders: Saif Noman Said

Date of Establishment: 1975

No of Employees: 500

SAIHATI WEIR ENGINEERING SERVICES CO LTD

PO Box 5172, Dammam 31422

Tel: 8560541, 8560386, 8500581

Telex: 897033 Swesco SJ

Telefax: 966-3-8501991

Chairman: Ibrahim Ali Bin Saihati

Directors: Ali Ali Bin Saihati

Senior Executives: K K N Nair (General Manager)

PRINCIPAL ACTIVITIES: Workshop machines, pump test, overhaul and repair, valve testing, mechanical seal lapping, dynamic balancing, industrial hard chrome plating, white metalling, welding, metal spray, heat treatment, etc

Principal Agencies: Weir Pumps Ltd, UK

Associated Companies: Weir Pumps Ltd, Glasgow, UK

Principal Bankers: Albank Alsaudi Alhollandi

Financial Information:

	1989/90
	SR'000
Sales turnover	6,000
Profits	10%
Authorised capital	6,400
Paid-up capital	2,000

Principal Shareholders: Chairman and directors as described

Date of Establishment: 1970

No of Employees: 32

SAKHRA CO FOR COMMERCE INDUSTRY & CONTRACTING

PO Box 5827, Riyadh 11432

Tel: 4645941, 4657327

Cable: Jahloof

Telex: 400033 SJ Sakhra

Telefax: 4645941

Directors: Mohammed Al-Ghamidi, Moshaal Al Ghamidi

Senior Executives: Salem Othman Neiroukh (Technical Manager)

PRINCIPAL ACTIVITIES: Contracting, commercial and industry; building construction, factory construction, civil works, surveying (land marking)

Branch Offices: Nimas

Principal Bankers: Arab National Bank, Riyadh; Riyad Bank, Riyadh

Financial Information:

	SR'000
Authorised capital	5,000
Paid-up capital	5,000

Date of Establishment: Oct 1976

No of Employees: 183

SALAH ABAALKHAIL CONSULTING ENGINEERS

See ABAALKHAIL, SALAH, CONSULTING ENGINEERS

SALEH & ABDULAZIZ ABAHSAIN CO LTD

See ABAHSAIN, SALEH & ABDULAZIZ, CO LTD

SALEH ZAID ALQURAISHI EST FOR TRADING & CONTRACTING

See ALQURAISHI, SALEH ZAID, EST FOR TRADING & CONTRACTING

SALEHIYA ESTABLISHMENT

PO Box 991, Riyadh 11421

Tel: 4351621, 4351684

Cable: Salehco

Telex: 401119 Saleco Sj

Senior Executives: Bassam B Barhoumy (Managing Director)

PRINCIPAL ACTIVITIES: Medical and hospital supplies and general contractors and builders

Branch Offices: Jeddah, Dammam

No of Employees: 250

SALIM MOHAMMED BAKHASHWAIN

See BAKHASHWAIN, SALIM MOHAMMED,

SALINE WATER CONVERSION CORP (SWCC)

PO Box 5968, Riyadh 11432

Tel: 4630501/3, 4780847, 4780942, 4780975, 4631780, 4631111

Telex: 400097, 400401 Tahlea Sj

Telefax: 4650852, 4631952

Governor: Abdullah M Al Gholaikah

Deputy Governors: Abdulrahman Al Khamis, Abdullah Abanmy, Abdulah Al Hossin

Senior Executives: Suliman Al Natheer (Planning & Follow up Director), Hamad Al Doaige (Housing Purchasing & Tenders Director), Abdulkareem Al Sadone (Construction Director), Saleh Butesh (Projects Director), Khalid Al Saawe (Training Director), Abdullah Al Azzaz (Research Director), Abdulatef Al Suliman (Public Relations Director), Abdulaziz Al Habdan (Personnel Director), Mohammad Al Kholify (Computers Director), Abdulrahman Al Issa (Information Centre Director), Ibrahim Al Habdan (Finance Director), Mosa Al Robian (Purchasing Director)

PRINCIPAL ACTIVITIES: Construction of desalination and power plants to produce fresh water from sea water
Branch Offices: SWCC Western Region: PO Box 7624, Jeddah, Tel 6821386, Telex 601473; SWCC Eastern Region: PO Box 752, Alkhobar, Tel 8646011, Telex 870093

Principal Shareholders: Government of Saudi Arabia
Date of Establishment: 1975
No of Employees: 5,000

SAMAMA COMPANY
PO Box 2781, Riyadh 11461
Tel: 4634005
Telex: 402430 Samama Sj
Telefax: 4631651

President: Eng Nasser Al Mutawa (Managing Director)
Directors: Eng Fahad Al Mutawa (Deputy Managing Director & Catering Director), Ali Al Mutawa (General Manager of Medina Projects), Ebrahim Shamsuldien Meisha (Deputy General Manager Medical Division)
Senior Executives: Abdul Malek A Omran (Finance & Accounts Manager), Ahmed Daoud Ayash (Sales Manager), Ibrahim Shaker (Personnel Manager), Eng Mahmoud Ziadeh (Operation Manager)

PRINCIPAL ACTIVITIES: Waste management, facility cleaning, M & E operation and maintenance, hospital management, catering, security services, landscaping, trading in cleaning chemicals, materials and equipment, and computer services
Branch Offices: Medina: PO Box 2781, Tel 8260679, Telefax 8260679; Makkah: PO Box 2264, Tel 5583730, Telefax 5589517; Buraidah: PO Box 2615, Tel 3245000, 3242075, Telefax 3247495; Al Kharj: King Khaled Hospital, Tel 5444444, 5443476, 5444015, Fax 5482665; Abha: PO Box 1110, Tel 2241703, 2246517; Al Ola: Prince Abdul Mohsen Hospital, Tel 8841524
Subsidiary Companies: Samama Linc Services
Principal Bankers: Arab National Bank; Al Bank Al Saudi Al Fransi
Financial Information:

	1989 SR'000	1990 SR'000
Sales turnover	54,508	100,721
Profits	2,771	9,686
Authorised capital	2,138	25,000
Paid-up capital	2,138	25,000
Total assets	59,954	68,057

Principal Shareholders: Prince Sultan Bin Mohd Bin Saud Al Kabir, Eng Nasser M Al Mutawa
Date of Establishment: 1980
No of Employees: 6,000

SAMMAN TRADING & IMPORT CO
PO Box 4180, Jeddah 21491
Tel: 6515251, 6515392
Cable: Nesyan
Telex: 601907 Samman Sj

Chairman: Sheikh Adnan Taha Samman
Partners: Sheikh Tawfiq Taha Samman, Sheikh Mohammad Taha Samman (Director General)
Senior Executives: Mohd Saeed Siddiqui (Financial Advisor/Chief Accountant)

PRINCIPAL ACTIVITIES: Import and distribution of building materials, furniture, carpets, wall coverings, etc
Principal Agencies: Dan River, USA; Sommer, France; Roisselier Durif; Laque d'Argent Marlin
Branch Offices: Riyadh: PO Box 4650, Tel 4774005/6, Telex 403844 Samdan Sj
Subsidiary/Associated Companies: Saudi Arabian Electronic Equipment Co, PO Box 1874, Jeddah; Tel 6603278, Telex 600167; Samman Trading & Industrial Investments Corp; Samman Construction & Contracting Corp, PO Box 5268, Jeddah, Tel 6655029
Principal Bankers: Saudi British Bank; Saudi Cairo Bank, Banque Libano Francaise (France)

Principal Shareholders: Chairman and partners as described
Date of Establishment: 1976

SAMODAH EST
PO Box 4537, Riyadh 21412
Tel: 4658740
Telefax: 4779149

Chairman: Abdullah S Al Shamsan
Directors: Mohammad A Al Shamsan

PRINCIPAL ACTIVITIES: Building, construction, trading in building materials, trading wholesale in foodstuffs
Principal Bankers: National Commercial Bank; Albank Alsaudi Alhollandi

No of Employees: 150

SAMWHAN CORPORATION
PO Box 4934, Jeddah 21412
Tel: 6713181, 6712957, 6710953, 6716986
Cable: SAMWANLIT JEDDAH
Telex: 602411 Swcjed Sj

PRINCIPAL ACTIVITIES: General contracting, engineering and developing
Branch Offices: Riyadh: PO Box 5743, Tel 4767014, 4762337, Telex 401414 Samwan Sj; Damman: Tel 8327540
Parent Company: SamWhan Corporation, Korea
Principal Bankers: National Commercial Bank, Jeddah; Korea Exchange Bank, Korea

No of Employees: 6,000 (in Saudi Arabia)

SAOUD AL MURAIBIDH EST FOR TRADE & GENERAL CONTRACTING
See AL MURAIBIDH, SAOUD, EST FOR TRADE & GENERAL CONTRACTING

SAPPCO-TEXACO INSULATION PRODUCTS CO LTD
PO Box 40042, Riyadh 11499
Tel: 4984676 4984676
Cable: SAPTEX
Telex: 403827 Saptex Sj
Telefax: 4980443

Chairman: Omar A Aggad
Directors: Abbas A Aggad, D E Six, M J Hurt, Rashed M J Thahen
Senior Executives: Alan J Pratt (President), Mohammed Jezry Sheriffdeen (Area Sales Representative Dammam), Emad Abdel Azim (Representative Jeddah), Atif Shareef (Asst Marketing Manager), Walid M Jamil (Production Manager), Liaqat Hussain (Administration Manager), Issam S Ghazal (Computer Manager), Mohammad Yahya (Laboratory Technician)

PRINCIPAL ACTIVITIES: Manufacturing and marketing of insulation materials for roof, wall, floor, pipe and duct
Branch Offices: PO Box 4916, Dammam 31412, Tel 8575784, Telex 801855, Telefax 8571969; and PO Box 5448, Jeddah 21422, Tel 6719285, Telefax 6719285; Dubai: PO Box 12927, Dubai, Tel 620555, 668997, Fax 694424

Parent Company: Saudi Plastics Products Co Ltd (SAPPCO)
Principal Bankers: Arab National Bank
Financial Information:

	1990
	SR'000
Authorised capital	105,000
Paid-up capital	30,000

Principal Shareholders: Saudi Plastic Products Co Ltd, Saudi Arabia; Texaco Saudi Investments, USA
Date of Establishment: 1980
No of Employees: 54

SAUDCONSULT
Saudi Consulting Services

PO Box 2341, Riyadh 11451
Tel: (01) 4659975
Cable: Saudconsult
Telex: 401231 Shawaf Sj
Telefax: (01) 4647540

Chairman: Tarek M A Shawaf (Chairman of the Board & President)
Directors: Ibrahim S Turkmani (Senior Executive Vice President), Fahad Al Tamimi (Executive Vice President), Syed Khedr (Excutive Vice President)
Senior Executives: Anas Shawaf (VP Architecture, Planning & Construction Management), Tarek Masri (VP & General Manager Western Region), Dr Adnan Kassab (VP Engineering & Computer Services), Sami Abdulghani (VP Electrical Engineering), Dr Murtada Kawakibi (Director of Mechanical Engineering), Khurram Karamat (Director of Site Development & Infrastructure Engineering), Osama Dahman (Director of Transportation & Roads), M Said Bairakdar (Chief Engieer, Construction Management), Ahmed Bilal Mehboob (Director, Coordination & Technical Resources), Fayek Khatib (Director of Structures), Bashar Yahya (Director of Computer Services)

PRINCIPAL ACTIVITIES: Studies, design, tender documentation, tenders evaluation, construction supervision, management in the fields of buildings, roads, recreational facilities, irrigation, water supply, desalination, wastewater disposal and treatment, storm water drainage, dams and flood control, transportation, marine planning and engineering, industrial engineering, electrical engineering & telecommunication
Branch Offices: Eastern Region: PO Box 1293, Dammam 31413, Tel 8571227, Telex 871496 Tarek Sj, Fax (3) 8570586; Western Region: PO Box 7352, Jeddah 21462, Tel 6445104, 6445191, Telex 607087 TSJED Sj, Fax (2) 6445826
Subsidiary Companies: Saudconsult International, UK
Principal Bankers: Riyad Bank, Riyadh
Financial Information:

	1990
	SR'000
Sales turnover	84,565
Profits	14,370
Authorised capital	5,000
Paid-up capital	5,000
Total assets	79,129

Principal Shareholders: Tarek M A Shawaf (Owner 100%)
Date of Establishment: 1965
No of Employees: 650

SAUDI ACCOUNTING BUREAU
K Y Fatani & A M Daghistani

PO Box 376, Riyadh 11411
Tel: 4775155, 4775078
Cable: Moragiun
Telex: 400175 Fatani Sj
Telefax: 4775121

Chairman: A M Daghistani
Executive Chairman: K Y Fatani
Senior Executives: Abdulatif Othman (General Manager)

PRINCIPAL ACTIVITIES: Account and audit office, financial consultation
Branch Offices: PO Box 445, Jeddah 21411, Tel 6322612, Fax 6320471; PO Box 1122, Dammam 31431, Tel 8330947, Fax 8330947
Principal Bankers: Riyad Bank

Date of Establishment: 1967
No of Employees: 55

SAUDI AGRICULTURAL BANK (SAAB)

PO Box 1811, Riyadh 11126
Tel: 4023934, 4023911, 4039303

Directors: Abdulaziz Muhammad Al Manqour (Director General)
Senior Executives: Husseini Abu Bakr Al-Kadi (General Manager)

PRINCIPAL ACTIVITIES: Provision of loans and credit facilities required for the development and promotion of agriculture and related activities
Branch Offices: Location in Riyadh: Omar Bin Al Khattab Street; also Jeddah: Tel 6690417; Al Kharj: Tel 5448527; Abha: Tel 2246175; Qassim: Tel 3231904; Qatif: Tel 8551984; Buraidah; Hail; Hofuf; Gizan; Jouf; Medina; Tabul; Taif

Principal Shareholders: Saudi Arabian Government
Date of Establishment: 1964
No of Employees: 1,900

SAUDI AGRICULTURAL DEVELOPMENT CO LTD (SADCO)

PO Box 5147, Riyadh 11422
Tel: 4955436, 4955440, 4955196
Cable: Saudi Tanmia
Telex: 402939 Sadcol Sj
Telefax: 4956068

Chairman: Prince Salman Bin Khalid Bin Abdullah Bin Abdul Rahman Al Saud
Directors: Elias G Rizkallah (Managing Director)
Senior Executives: Hafemi B Agra (Farm Manager), Jamil Zaroob (Marketing Manager), Masood Quraishi (Accounts Manager), Mohammed Abdullah Ash Shaya (Asst General Manager)

PRINCIPAL ACTIVITIES: Agricultural development, chickens eggs poultry feed production, carton products, poultry services
Branch Offices: , Hofuf, Jeddah, Gassim, Dammam
Subsidiary Companies: Saudi Poultry Co Ltd; SADCO Poultry Services; Carton Products Ltd
Principal Bankers: Saudi American Bank; Al Bank Al Saudi Al Faransi; Albank Alsaudi Alhollandi, National Commercial Bank; United Saudi Commercial Bank
Financial Information:

	1988/89
	SR'000
Sales turnover	72,844
Profits	5,632
Authorised capital	22,000
Paid-up capital	22,000
Total assets	82,242

Principal Shareholders: Mawarid Investment Co
Date of Establishment: 1975
No of Employees: 380

SAUDI AIRCONDITIONING MANUFACTURING CO LTD

PO Box 8755, Jeddah 21492
Tel: 6373202, 6380260, 6373092, 6372469
Cable: SRMCO Jeddah
Telex: 604256 AIRCON SJ
Telefax: 6363731

Chairman: Sheikh Ahmed Juffali

Directors: Sheikh Walid Juffali (Managing Director), H Shahine, M Casiraghi, J Walsh, M Macerollo
Senior Executives: M Wayne Climer (Executive Vice-President, Operations), S M Ali (Financial Controller), Abdullah Younis (Marketing Manager, Riyadh), Achilles Stragalis (Marketing Manager, Jeddah), Habib Khoury (Marketing Manager, Dammam)

PRINCIPAL ACTIVITIES: Manufacturing of room and central airconditioning units
Branch Offices: PO Box 86, Riyadh, Tel 4022222, Fax 4022122, Telex 401049; PO Box 24, Dammam, Tel 8323333, Fax 8325779, Telex 801025; PO Box 297, Jeddah, Tel 6601530, Fax 6607268, Telex 601530
Parent Company: E A Juffali & Bros, PO Box 1049, Jeddah 21431, Tel 6672222, Fax 6694010, Telex 601130
Affiliated Companies: Carrier Corporation, USA
Principal Bankers: Riyad Bank, Jeddah; Arab National Bank, Jeddah
Financial Information:

	1988/89 SR'000	1989/90 SR'000
Sales turnover	180,000	172,000
Authorised capital	13,000	13,000
Paid-up capital	13,000	13,000
Total assets	25,224	23,000

Principal Shareholders: E A Juffali & Bros (51.005%), Carrier Corporation (48.995%)
Date of Establishment: 4.8.1400H (1980)

SAUDI AMERICAN BANK
PO Box 833, Riyadh 11421
Tel: 4774770
Telex: 400195 Samba Sj

Chairman: Abdul Aziz Bin Hamad Al Gosaibi
Directors: Mohamed Hamoud Al Ohali, Husein Alireza, Dr Khalil Abdul Fattah Kordi, Khalid Al-Zamil, Rashed Mohamed Al Romaizan, Robert Botjer, John Beeman, Richard Lehman, Usama Mikdashi

PRINCIPAL ACTIVITIES: Commercial banking
Branch Offices: Regional Offices: Jeddah: PO Box 490, Jeddah 21411, Tel 6444111, 6442180, Telex 601968; Alkhobar: PO Box 842, Alkhobar 31421, Tel 8945630, Telex 870411; 29 Branches in Riyadh, Jeddah, Al-Khobar, Dammam, Hofuf, Jubail, Yanbu, Tabuk, Oneizah, Bureida, Al-Kharj, Al Madina, Abha, Khamis Mushayt, Taif, Hail, Marat; Turkey Branch: Istanbul; Representative Office: Buckingham House, 62/63 Queen Street, London EC4R 1AD; Geneva Office: Samba Finance SA, Geneva, Switzerland
Financial Information:

	1988/89 SR'000
Net income	235,225
Loans & advances	6,002,015
Cash & due from banks	11,937,197
Customer deposits	17,781,395
Total shareholders funds	1,634,055
Total assets	24,053,626

Principal Shareholders: Saudi Arabian interests (60%); Citibank NA (40%)
Date of Establishment: July 12th, 1980
No of Employees: 1,434

SAUDI AMERICAN CO LTD
PO Box 2450, Riyadh 11451
Tel: 4649313
Telex: 402276 Sacltd Sj

Directors: Helal Ex Swedy, Mamdouh Abdallah, Ray Stevens
Senior Executives: Dr M M Shamma (General Manager)

PRINCIPAL ACTIVITIES: Manufacturing of concrete masonry units according to ASTM and BS standards

Branch Offices: Jeddah: PO Box 900, Tel 6373158, Telex 603614 SAUAM SJ
Principal Bankers: Saudi Cairo Bank
Financial Information:

	SR'000
Authorised capital	17,000
Paid-up capital	4,372

Principal Shareholders: Helal El Swedy (40%); C - Block (30%); American Industrial International Inc (30%)
Date of Establishment: 1978
No of Employees: 30

SAUDI AMERICAN GENERAL ELECTRIC CO
PO Box 10211, Riyadh 11433
Tel: 4067622
Telex: 400167 Getsco Sj
Telefax: 4041561

Chairman: Sheikh Ali Tamimi
Directors: Alistair C Stewart (Managing Director), Shafiq Othman
Senior Executives: David R Dennemann (Finance Manager), Paul G Stokes (Manager Business Development), Peter M Robinson (Human Resources Manager), William T McCollum (Legal Counsel), Tarek Ragheb (Sales Manager), Said M Moraished (Administration Manager)

PRINCIPAL ACTIVITIES: Industrial equipment, power equipment, aircraft engines, communications, information systems and services, engineered materials, medical equipment and services, aerospace, construction engineering, transportation systems, power generation equipment and services, electrical and mechanical equipment and servicing and installation
Branch Offices: Jeddah, PO Box 50, Tel 6445043, Telex 602439
Parent Company: General Electric Co, Fairfield, Connecticut, USA
Associated Companies: General Electric Technical Services Co Inc
Principal Bankers: Saudi American Bank
Financial Information:

	1988/89 SR'000
Sales turnover	23,553
Profits	974
Authorised capital	5,000
Paid-up capital	5,000
Total assets	29,226

Principal Shareholders: Sheikh Ali Tamimi, Sheikh Salem Bin Laden, Shafiq Othman, General Electric Technical Services Co Inc
Date of Establishment: October 1980
No of Employees: 68

SAUDI AMERICAN GLASS CO LTD
PO Box 8418, Riyadh 11482
Tel: 4981212
Telex: 402733 Saglass SJ
Telefax: 4984007

Chairman: Abdulmohsen M Aldress
Directors: Abdullah S Aldress, Nikola M Antakali
Senior Executives: Abdulilah S Aldrees (President), Maurice L Chebli (Vice President), Khalid S Aldress (Asst Vice President), Jean Lelievre (Technical Manager), Fayyaz Ahmed (Financial Controller)

PRINCIPAL ACTIVITIES: Double glass unit, bullet proof glass, glass tempering, glass laminating, glass cutting, edging, polishing, bevelling, painting, etc; supply of all glass requirements on project basis including technical assistance
Branch Offices: Jeddah: Tel 6873664, Fax 6872053, Telex 601816 Dress Sj; Dammam: Tel 8576468, 8570844, Fax 8570356, Telex 802230 AICS Sj
Associated Companies: M A Aldrees & Sons, PO Box 609, Riyadh, Tel 4763875

SAUDI ARABIA

Principal Bankers: National Commercial Bank, Riyadh; Saudi British Bank, Riyadh

Financial Information:

	1990 SR'000
Sales turnover	27,700
Profits	4,050
Authorised capital	9,500
Paid-up capital	9,500
Total assets	21,000

Principal Shareholders: M A Aldrees & Sons, Riyadh (85%); Nikola M Antakali, USA (15%)

Date of Establishment: 1978

No of Employees: 91

SAUDI AMERICAN MACHINERY MAINTENANCE CO (SAMMCO)

PO Box 8136, Jeddah 21482

Tel: 6879222, 6886141

Telex: 602762 Sammco Sj

PRINCIPAL ACTIVITIES: Metal works, mechanical contractors, machinery maintenance, motors and generators diesel and marine engines, welding services, steel fabrications

Principal Shareholders: M Binladin Organisation, Jeddah; General Motors Corp, USA

Date of Establishment: 1980

SAUDI AMIAL EST

PO Box 5535, Jeddah 21432

Tel: 6656717, 6604465, 6656736

Cable: Fomkat

Telex: 600095 Amial Sj

Telefax: 6656717

Chairman: Mahmoud Medhat Fathi El Rayes

PRINCIPAL ACTIVITIES: Household electrical appliances, fitted kitchens, CTV's, HIFI, video and cassettes recorders

Principal Agencies: Robert Bosch Hausgerate, W Germany; Alno Mobelwerke, W Germany; ITT Schaub-Lorenz, W Germany

Branch Offices: Riyadh: PO Box 6307, Tel 4657887; Abha: PO Box 1443, Tel 2233391; Madina El Munawara: PO Box 3084, Tel 8224002/244

Principal Bankers: Saudi Cairo Bank, Jeddah

Principal Shareholders: Solely owned by Princess Fowzia, wife of HRH Prince Fawaz Bin Abdul Aziz

Date of Establishment: August 1974

No of Employees: 224

SAUDI AMOUDI GROUP

PO Box 2779, Jeddah 21461

Tel: 6830822, 6828640, 6830711

Telex: 601435 Ehsane Sj

Telefax: 6828402

Proprietor: Mohammed O A Al-Amoudi

Directors: Sheikh Ibrahim Al-Afandi

PRINCIPAL ACTIVITIES: Construction, trade, industry and contracting, pre-cast construction, airport maintenance, military projects, mining

Associated Companies: Saudi Letco Co Ltd, Al Afandi Est, ARINCO, Jeddah Geo-Research, Mohammed O A Al Amoudi, Letlock Saudi Arabia Ltd

Principal Bankers: National Commercial Bank

Financial Information:

	SR'000
Authorised capital	120,000
Paid-up capital	120,000

No of Employees: 217

SAUDI ARABIAN AIRLINES
SAUDIA

PO Box 620, Jeddah 21231

Tel: 6842000, 6860000 (Airport Headquarters), 6842334, 6842331 (Passenger Relations)

Cable: Saudair

Telex: 601007 1 COMM Sj, 600150 SDIPUR SJ

Chairman: HRH Prince Sultan Bin Abdulaziz

Directors: HH Prince Fahad Bin Abdullah Bin Mohammed Bin Saud Al Saud, HE Captain Ahmed Mattar, HE Sa'eed Yousef Ameen, HE Sulayman Al Mandeel, HE Ahmed Yoused Al Turki, HE Mohamed Mohamed Mufti, HE Hamad Abdullah Al Zamel, HE Abdullah Al Saad Al Rashid, HE Ibrahim Shams

Senior Executives: Capt Ahmed Khalifa Mattar (Director General), Ahmed I Boubshait (Exec VP Finance & Administration), Ibrahim Al Degaither (Exec VP Marketing), Rida T Hakeem (Exec VP Arab & International Affairs), Adnan A Dabbagh (Exec VP Operations)

PRINCIPAL ACTIVITIES: International air carrier

Branch Offices: Location in Jeddah: Airport Street, Saudia Bldg; branches throught Europe; Middle East; Africa; Asia; Far East and the United States

Principal Bankers: Riyad Bank

Principal Shareholders: Government owned

Date of Establishment: 1945

No of Employees: 24,064

SAUDI ARABIAN AMIANTIT CO LTD

PO Box 589, Dammam 31421

Tel: 8572160, 8571160

Cable: Amiantit Dammam

Telex: 801084 Amidam Sj

Telefax: 8579771

Chairman: HH Prince Khaled Ben Abdallah Ben Abdul Rahman

President: Dr Abdulaziz S Al Jarbou (Group President)

Senior Executives: Wehbe Rafih (Group Treasurer & Controller), Farid Al Khalawi (VP Operations)

PRINCIPAL ACTIVITIES: Production and marketing of fiber cement pipes, sheets and fittings, fiberglass reinforced plastic pipes, storage tanks, manholes, concrete cylinder pipes, prestressed concrete pipes, rubber products, reinforced thermosetting resin pipes, ductile iron pipes and fiberglass insulation products

Principal Agencies: FRE conduits, FRE Composite, Canada; VAG Valves, W Germany

Branch Offices: Saudi Arabia Sales Office: PO Box 1029, Riyadh, Tel 4658665, Telex 401008 Amiria Sj; Branch Office: PO Box 2140, Jeddah, Tel 6516920, 6534704, Telex 601431 Amijed Sj

Associated Companies: Amiantit Fibreglass Industries Ltd; Amiantit Rubber Industries Ltd; Ameron Saudi Arabia Ltd; Saudi Arabian Concrete Products Ltd; Bondstrand Ltd; Saudi Arabian Ductile Iron Pipe; Arabian Fiberglass Insulation

Principal Bankers: Al Bank Al Saudi Al Fransi, Damman; Saudi American Bank, AlKhobar, Banque Indosuez, Bahrain; Chase Manhattan Bank, Bahrain

Financial Information:

	1988/89 SR'000
Sales turnover	179,844
Authorised capital	160,000
Paid-up capital	160,000
Total assets	755,154

Date of Establishment: 1968

No of Employees: 1,400

SAUDI ARABIAN ANIMAL FEED CO

PO Box 173, Dammam 31411
Tel: 8570545, 8574920, 8579619, 8579687
Cable: PROVIMI DAMMAM
Telex: 801282 Ziyad Sj

Directors: Saleh A Sowayigh (Managing Director and Chairman)
Senior Executives: Hassan K Zameli

PRINCIPAL ACTIVITIES: Production and distribution of animal
feeds
Branch Offices: Riyadh, Al-Hasa, Hofuf
Principal Bankers: Albank Alsaudi Alhollandi, Arab National
Bank, Dammam, Saudi Arabia
Financial Information:

	SR'000
Authorised capital	10,000
Paid-up capital	10,000

Principal Shareholders: Sheikh Saleh A Sowayigh, Sheikh Abdul
Aziz Abahussain, Sheikh Yacob Alhumezi, Sheikh Ali Ahmed
Alsahati, Messrs Promico Holdings Limited
Date of Establishment: Registration: May 1965, Production:
December 1966
No of Employees: 62

SAUDI ARABIAN BANDAG LTD

PO Box 6478, Jeddah 21442
Tel: 6364391, 6364374
Cable: Bandagltd Jeddah
Telex: 600516 Tyreco Sj

Chairman: Abdul Aziz Abdullah Al Suleiman
Directors: Ahmad Abdullah Al Suleiman, Khalid Abdullah Al
Suleiman, Fahad Al Suleiman, Moosa Judatal Helaby
Senior Executives: Mirza Ishaq Beg (General Manager)

PRINCIPAL ACTIVITIES: Purchasing and marketing of tyres,
tubes and other accessories; repairing and retreading of tyres
Parent Company: Sawary Trading & Contracting
Subsidiary Companies: Saudi Tyre Est
Principal Bankers: Bank Al-Jazira; Massraf Faysal Al Islami

Principal Shareholders: Abdul Aziz Abdallah Al Suleiman;
Ahmed Abdallah Al Suleiman
Date of Establishment: 1978

SAUDI ARABIAN BECHTEL CORPORATION

PO Box 88, Dhahran Airport 31932
Tel: 4648011
Telex: 870028 Wateka Sj

PRINCIPAL ACTIVITIES: Chemical and petrochemical
engineering contractors, power plant, pipelines, underwater
and nuclear plant contractors
Branch Offices: Riyadh, PO Box 4103, Tel 4763036, Telex
401028; Jeddah: PO Box 5963, Tel 6653464, Telex 601158;
also branches in UK, Japan, Indonesia, Lebanon, Brazil, Peru,
Argentina, France, West Germany, Australia, Canada
Parent Company: Head Office: San Francisco, USA

Principal Shareholders: Bechtel Corp, USA; Sulaiman Olayyan

SAUDI ARABIAN BUNKERING SERVICES

PO Box 37, Dammam 31411
Tel: 8336617, 8336681
Cable: Kanoo
Telex: 802058 SABS SJ
Telefax: 8336778 SABS Damman

Chairman: Abdulla Ali Kanoo
Directors: Abdul Aziz Jassim Kanoo

PRINCIPAL ACTIVITIES: Bunkering services, supplying
intermediate fuel oil, marine gas oil
Parent Company: Y B A Kanoo, PO Box 37 Dammam, Saudi
Arabia

Principal Bankers: Saudi International Bank, London

Principal Shareholders: Chairman and director as described
Date of Establishment: 1975

SAUDI ARABIAN CARPETS FACTORY LTD

PO Box 2371, Jeddah 21451
Tel: 6363271, 6363254
Cable: Sudjadhome
Telex: 600503 Sujad Sj

Chairman: Mustafa Abdul Rahman Bin Sumait
Directors: Ali Abdulla Bugshan, Ali Abdulla Al-Esai, Ali Siraj
Bogari

PRINCIPAL ACTIVITIES: Manufacture of viscose/rayon carpets
and velvet, various kinds of velvet carpets
Principal Bankers: National Commercial Bank, Jeddah; Al Bank
Al Saudi Al Fransi
Financial Information:

	SR'000
Authorised capital	13,000

Principal Shareholders: Ali Abdulla Bugshan, Salim Ahmed
Bugshan, Ali Abdulla Al-Esai, Omer Kasim Ali-Esai, Siraj
Omer Bogari
Date of Establishment: 1970
No of Employees: 75

SAUDI ARABIAN CONSTRUCTION CONTRACTORS LTD

Saurabia Contractors

PO Box 6248, Jeddah 21442
Tel: 6515716, 6515968
Cable: Lawarsaud
Telex: 600612 Saurab Sj
Telefax: 6515968

Chairman: Sheikh Hussein Abdullah Siraj
Directors: Arif M Al-Awar (General Manager)
Senior Executives: Zouhair Sabra Al Awar (Chief Engineer),
Nadim A Al Awar (Administrative Manager)

PRINCIPAL ACTIVITIES: Contracting (roads, bridges, airports,
harbours, water supplies and buildings, electrical, mechanical,
pipeline, sewage)
Branch Offices: Saurabia: PO Box 3348, Riyadh, Tel 4642636;
Makkah
Associated Companies: Al-Awar & Co SAL, PO Box 1128,
Beirut, Lebanon,
Principal Bankers: National Commercial Bank, Jeddah; Saudi
Cairo Bank, Jeddah; Al Jazira Bank, Jeddah
Financial Information:

	1989 SR'000
Sales turnover	11,000
Profits	4,460
Authorised capital	5,000
Paid-up capital	5,000
Total assets	17,200

Principal Shareholders: Hussein Siraj, Al-Awar & Co SAL,
Lebanon
Date of Establishment: 1976
No of Employees: 300

SAUDI ARABIAN DAMES & MOORE

PO Box 2384, Riyadh 11451
Tel: 4650195, 4650831
Telex: 401864 Sadm Sj
Telefax: 4649764

Chairman: Farouk A Ahmed
Directors: Sheikh Fahd Muhammad Alireza, Sheikh Hamad
Abdullah Linjawi, Howard A Schirmer Jr, Usama B Jayyusi
Senior Executives: Farouk A Ahmed (Managing Director), Gavin
Hamilton (Managing Principal)

PRINCIPAL ACTIVITIES: Geotechnical, hydrological, environmental and planning engineering, quality control services

Parent Company: Dames & Moore International (USA)

Principal Bankers: National Commercial Bank, Riyadh

Financial Information:

	SR'000
Authorised capital	1,600
Paid-up capital	1,600

Principal Shareholders: Reza Investment Co (25%); Industrial Services (25%); Dames & Moore USA (50%)

Date of Establishment: 1977 in Riyadh

No of Employees: 45

SAUDI ARABIAN DEVELOPMENT CO LTD (SADC)

PO Box 7648, Riyadh 11472

Tel: 4781459, 4779464, 4775853

Cable: SARDECOM

Telex: 402389 SADCOL SJ, 403426 SSADCO SJ

Chairman: Mohammed Ahmed Al-Ibrahim

Directors: Munib R Masri, Tarif W Ayoubi

Senior Executives: Raja R Barbir (Vice President - Marketing), Nasuh A Muwafi (Senior Projects Coordinator)

PRINCIPAL ACTIVITIES: Oil, gas, chemical, petrochemical, civil and building contracting; management and engineering services; operation and maintenance services; education and training services; life support systems operation; sponsorship/agent

Principal Agencies: BS&B, UK; Moody Tottrop, UK; PLT Engineering, UK; Blohm & Voss, W Germany; Kamani Eng, India; Jaiprakash, India; G R Stein Refractories, UK; Kaldair, UK; Horwood Catering, UK; Ioncontract, Germany; Officine San Marco, Italy; Southern Petrochemical Industries, India

Branch Offices: AlKhobar: PO Box 1058, and Jeddah: PO Box 5470, also in London, UK

Associated Companies: Technip Saudi Arabia Ltd (TPSA); National Contracting & Development Co Ltd (NCDC); Shobokshi/Saudi Arabian Development Co Ltd (S/SADC)

Principal Bankers: Arab National Bank

Principal Shareholders: Mohammad Ahmed Al-Ibrahim; Ma'an M Al-Ibrahim

Date of Establishment: November 1977

No of Employees: 1,425

SAUDI ARABIAN DRUGSTORES CO LTD

PO Box 463, Jeddah 21411

Tel: 6422775, 6432838, 6422704

Cable: Pharma

Telex: 600031 Pharma Sj

Chairman: Gassan Massoud

PRINCIPAL ACTIVITIES: Agents and distributors of pharmaceuticals, cosmetics, hospital equipment, insecticides and toiletries

Principal Agencies: Wyeth Int USA, Ireland, Germany; C H Boehringer Sohn Ingelheim/Rh, Germany; Istituto de Angeli SpA, Italy; Whitehall Int Inc, USA; International Chemical Co, UK; Zyma SA, Switzerland; Takeda Chemical Industries, Japan; Apolab Ag, Norway; Nordmark-West GmbH, W Germany; Biobasal SA, Switzerland; Swiss Brush Mfg Co Ltd, Switzerland; Murray-Clarke & Jones Ltd, Sanitary Paper Co (Gyno), Lebanon, Princes Food Ltd, UK

Branch Offices: Riyadh: PO Box 661; and Alkhobar: PO Box 541

Subsidiary Companies: Gassan Massoud; Sadaga Sheikh; Mohd Ali Marzoogi; Fuoad Marzoogi; Abdullah Bagabas; Mohd Saleh Sheikh

Principal Bankers: Al Bank Al Saudi Al Fransi; National Commercial Bank

Date of Establishment: 1945

SAUDI ARABIAN ENGINEERING CO LTD (SAECO)

PO Box 384, Dhahran Airport 31932

Tel: 8570291, 8579519

Cable: SAECO

Telex: 870006Rezt SJ for SAECO

Telefax: 8579865

President: Teymour Abdulla Alireza

Directors: J H N Gibson

Senior Executives: Robert Taylor (General Manager), Miraj Uddin (Financial Controller), Keith Dempsey (Workshop Manager), Imtiaz Ahmad Sheikh (Marketing Manager)

PRINCIPAL ACTIVITIES: Repair, overhaul and test facilities for valves, diesel engines and components, heavy construction equipment; gas turbine components, instrument calibration, welding, fabrication, machining, sandblasting, painting; service back up for John Deere dealership

Principal Agencies: Detroit Diesel, Roosamaster, Regulateurs Europa, Barber Colman, Nippon Denso, John Deere Construction Equipment, Sapag, Borsig, Napier Turbochargers, John Brown Engg

Parent Company: Rezayat Group of Companies

Principal Bankers: Albank Alsaudi Alhollandi, Alkhobar

Financial Information:

	1990 SR'000
Sales turnover	7,230
Profits	560
Authorised capital	3,000
Paid-up capital	3,000
Total assets	4,837

Principal Shareholders: Rezayat Co Ltd; National Contracting Co Ltd

Date of Establishment: 1972

No of Employees: 55

SAUDI ARABIAN FABRICATED METALS INDUSTRY LTD
S.A.F.A.M.I.

PO Box 328, Dhahran Airport 31932

Tel: 8579086, 8579861, 8570234

Cable: Safami Alkhobar

Telex: 870006 Sj for Safami

Telefax: 8570246

President: Teymour Alireza

Directors: J H N Gibson

Senior Executives: Ian S Semple (General Manager)

PRINCIPAL ACTIVITIES: Fabricated pipe and structural steel, steel constructions for the oil and petrochemical industries; water/oil tanks, vessels

Associated Companies: Rezayat Group of Companies

Principal Bankers: Saudi British Bank, Alkhobar; Al-Bank Al Saudi Al Fransi, Dammam

Financial Information:

	1990 SR'000
Sales turnover	10,318
Profits	1,257
Authorised capital	15,280
Paid-up capital	3,820
Total assets	6,305

Principal Shareholders: Safami is a 100% Saudi owned company

Date of Establishment: 1974

No of Employees: 54

SAUDI ARABIA

SAUDI ARABIAN FERTILISER CO (SAFCO)

PO Box 553, Dammam 31421
Tel: (03) 8575011, (03) 8575208
Cable: Safco
Telex: 870117; 871356 Safco Sj

Chairman: Mahmood A Taiba (also Managing Director)
Directors: Ibrahim Bin Salamah, Ahmad S Al Tiweijri, Ali Abdulrahman Al Khalaf, Anwar Khair Badr, Muhammad Sulaiman Abanami, Jamal Joher Al Saud
Senior Executives: Hussein Eid Al-Jubeihi (General Manager), Saleh I Quraidis (Asst General Manager), Saeed A Khayat (Corporate Affairs Manager), Abdulaziz Al Muqaytib (Works Manager), Adel H Al Amad (Marketing Manager)

PRINCIPAL ACTIVITIES: Production and processing of chemical fertilizers using natural gas; also marketing and trading; production and marketing of sulfuric acid as an industrial chemical
Principal Agencies: Agents in different countries
Subsidiary Companies: SABIC, Riyadh - Ministry of Industry & Electricity
Principal Bankers: National Commercial Bank; Riyad Bank; Saudi American Bank; Bank Al-Saudi Al-Hollandi, Dammam
Financial Information:

	SR'000
Authorised capital	200,000
Paid up capital	200,000

Principal Shareholders: 41% owned by SABIC, 49% private Saudi sector and 10% by SAFCO Employees
Date of Establishment: 1965
No of Employees: 564

SAUDI ARABIAN GAS ENGINEERING CO LTD

NADCO-BOC, PO Box 789, Riyadh 11421
Tel: 4650535
Cable: Nadco
Telex: 401118 Nadco Sj

Directors: Dr G Winfield, K W Morley, H M Alharthy, S H Fayez

PRINCIPAL ACTIVITIES: Engineering in industrial and medical gases, fuel gases and associated processes, design, supply, installation, operation and maintenance of gas producing plants, and storage and distribution of heavy equipment for oxygen nitrogen, nitrous oxide, hydrogen, acetylene, argon, carbon dioxide, propane, butane and natural gas

Principal Shareholders: BOC International Ltd, UK; NADCO, Saudi Arabia

SAUDI ARABIAN INDUSTRIAL & TRADING EST (SAITE)

PO Box 2097, Dammam 31451
Tel: 8331696, 8345804, 8329102, 8344122
Cable: Saite
Telex: 801367 Saite Sj, 802305 Stasco Sj
Telefax: 8332783, 8349661

Chairman: Abdul Aziz Kanoo
Directors: Ali Sallam (Managing Director), Abdul Bari Saif (General Manager), Khalid Sallam (Asst General Manager)
Senior Executives: M J P Mitchell (Shipping Manager), Joseph Bothello (Manager, Petrochemical Services Division), N Vijaya Kumar (Accountant), A J Saldanha (Manager Jeddah Branch)

PRINCIPAL ACTIVITIES: Shipping, petrochemical services and general trading; industrial chemicals; oilfield supplies; electricals; instrumentation
Principal Agencies: American President Lines; West Asia Kontena Line; Cormorant Bulk Carriers
Branch Offices: Jubail; Ras Tanura; Riyadh; Jeddah
Parent Company: Y.B.A. Kanoo, PO Box 37, Dammam, Saudi Arabia

Principal Bankers: Saudi British Bank, Dammam; Albank Alsaudi Alhollandi, Dammam; Saudi American Bank, Dammam

Date of Establishment: June 1975
No of Employees: 75

SAUDI ARABIAN INVESTMENT CO

PO Box 2096, Jeddah 21451
Tel: 6433689, 6656193, 6673908
Telex: 601211 Saico Sj

Directors: HH Prince Mohamed Bin Fahed Bin Abdulaziz, HH Prince Abdullah Bin Musaid Bin Abdulrahman, Sheikh Mohamed Al Bedrawi, Sheikh Ahmed El-Maghraby

PRINCIPAL ACTIVITIES: Investment banking and financial advice, real estate development, joint ventures
Branch Offices: Location in Jeddah: Queens Bldg, King Abdul Aziz Street
Subsidiary Companies: Perini (Saudi Arabia); British Arabian Advisory Co Ltd, London; Saudi Arabian Investment Co (Overseas), Panama, USA

SAUDI ARABIAN MARKETING & REFINING CO

SAMAREC

PO Box 1600, Jeddah 21441
Tel: 6477200, 6477335, 6474819
Cable: Samarec
Telex: 607016 SMFO SJ
Telefax: 6473762

Senior Executives: Eng Ibrahim A Kurdi (Vice President Marine), Eng Hassan I Azzouz (Director Fleet Services), Eng Ali S Al Ghamdi (Manager Fleet Suppport), Eng Robert M Burrows (Engineer Superintendent)

PRINCIPAL ACTIVITIES: Operation and chartering of sea-going vessels for the transportation of oil
Principal Bankers: Riyad Bank, Jeddah; Saudi International Bank, London

Principal Shareholders: General Petroleum and Mineral Organisation (Petromin)
No of Employees: 200

SAUDI ARABIAN MARKETS LTD

PO Box 65, Jeddah 21411
Tel: 6883548, 6883448
Cable: Markets
Telex: 604331 Motors SJ
Telefax: 6515535

Chairman: Sheikh Mohamed Ahmed Ashmawi
Directors: Sheikh Issam Ahmed Ashmawi
Senior Executives: John Game (General Manager), Mohamed Thabit (Deputy General Manager), John Palmer (Trading Manager)

PRINCIPAL ACTIVITIES: Importers and distributors; import of cars, lubricants, gas turbine generators, construction chemicals, storage and handling equipment, forklift trucks; business systems, floor covering, manufacturers' representatives, ceramic tiles, carpets, synthetic grass
Principal Agencies: Rolls-Royce, Aston Martin, Dexion, Lansing Linde Forklifts; Forbo Flooring; Desso Syntigrass; Gail Ceramic Tiles; Heuga Carpet Tiles; H & R Johnson Ceramic Tiles; Lista; Chloride Batteries; Interface Carpet Tiles
Branch Offices: Riyadh: PO Box 246, Tel 4644909, 4646432, Telex 401271; and Alkhobar: PO Box 48, Tel 8571757, Telex 870065; Jeddah: PO Box 65, Tel 6518786, Telex 605343
Subsidiary/Associated Companies: Peninsular Aviation Services Co; Taylorplan Saudi Arabian Markets Catering; Shell Lubricants; Fosroc Construction Chemicals
Principal Bankers: Saudi British Bank; Al Bank Al Saudi Al Fransi; Riyad Bank

Financial Information:

	1990
	SR'000
Turnover	70,000
Profits	14,000
Authorised capital	9,000
Paid-up capital	9,000

Principal Shareholders: Sheikh Mohamed Ahmed Ashmawi; Sheikh Issam Ashmawi; Mrs Sabah Abdullah
Date of Establishment: 1947
No of Employees: 170

SAUDI ARABIAN MECHANICAL & ELECTRICAL CO LTD (SAMEC)

PO Box 789, Riyadh 11421
Tel: 4783336
Telex: 401118 Nadco Sj

Chairman: Hussein Al Harthy
Directors: Sami Fayez

PRINCIPAL ACTIVITIES: Mechanical and electrical contractors
Branch Offices: PO Box 428, Dhahran Aiport
Financial Information:

	SR'000
Turnover	55,000
Paid-up capital	1,000

Principal Shareholders: Totally owned subsidiary of NADCO, Saudi Arabia

SAUDI ARABIAN MONETARY AGENCY (SAMA)

PO Box 2992, Riyadh 11169
Tel: 4633000
Cable: Markazi Riyadh
Telex: 404390 MRKAZI SJ, 400353 SAMA SJ

PRINCIPAL ACTIVITIES: Central banking institution
Branch Offices: Jeddah: PO Box 392, Tel 6431122, Telex 601011 SAMAJD SJ; Dammam; Medina; Mecca; Taif; Jizan; Tabuk; Buraidah; Abha

SAUDI ARABIAN NATIONAL CENTRE FOR SCIENCE & TECHNOLOGY (SANCST)

PO Box 6086, Riyadh 11442
Tel: 4059696, 4788000
Cable: Mawsoah
Telex: 401590 Sancst Sj

Chairman: Dr Saleh Al Athel
Directors: Dr Abdullah Al Qadhi, Dr Suleiman Aqeely

PRINCIPAL ACTIVITIES: Promotion and coordination of scientific research

Principal Shareholders: Public organisation

SAUDI ARABIAN NATIONAL DEVELOPMENT CO (SAND)

Saudi German Hospital

PO Box 2550, Jeddah 21461
Tel: 6829000 (45 lines)
Cable: Sand Jeddah
Telex: 607062 SGHJED SJ
Telefax: 6835874

Chairman: Sheikh Abdul Jalil Batterjee
Directors: Sheikh Sobhi A Batterjee
Senior Executives: Dr Khalid Batterjee (General Manager), Mohammad Gulzar (Finance Manager), Yahia Bahrawy (Sales Manager)

PRINCIPAL ACTIVITIES: Civil, electrical and mechanical engineering contractors; real estate and property development; manufacturers' representatives, computer analysts and programmers, computer turn key installations, supply of furniture, office equipment and computers also electronic equipment and foostuffs, supermarkets, also hospitalisation and health care services through the Saudi German Hospital of Jeddah
Branch Offices: PO Box 3966, Riyadh
Subsidiary Companies: Computer Analysts & Programmers (CAP Saudi Arabia), PO Box 3966, Riyadh
Principal Bankers: Al Bank Al Saudi Al Fransi, Gulf International Bank (Bahrain), Al Bank Al Arabi; Saudi Investment Bank
Financial Information:

	1990
	SR'000
Turnover	860,000
Authorised capital	2,500
Paid-up capital	2,500

Principal Shareholders: Abdul Jalil Batterjee & Sons
Date of Establishment: 1975
No of Employees: 750

SAUDI ARABIAN OIL COMPANY

Saudi ARAMCO

PO Box 5000, Dhahran 31311
Tel: 8756110
Cable: Aramco Dhahran
Telex: 801220 ASAO Sj
Telefax: 8738190

President: Ali I Naimi (Chief Executive Officer)
Senior Executives: N M Ajmi (Executive Vice President), S A Al Ashgar (Sr Vice President - Operations Services), N I Al Bassam (Sr Vice President -Finance), A G Al Ghanim (Sr Vice President - Engineering & Project Management), A M Al Hokail (Sr Vice President - Manufacturing, Supply & Transportation), S I Husseini (Sr Vice President - Exploration & Producing), A S Jum'ah (Sr Vice President - Industrial Relations)

PRINCIPAL ACTIVITIES: Oil industry, exploration and petroleum engineering, drilling and pipelines, field operations, refining and NGL, terminal operations, support services

Principal Shareholders: Saudi Arabian Government
Date of Establishment: 1933
No of Employees: 43,500

SAUDI ARABIAN PACKAGING INDUSTRY WLL (SAPIN)

PO Box 1966, Dammam 31441
Tel: 8577300, 8577400
Telex: 801593 Sapin Sj
Telefax: 8574120

Chairman: Khalid A R Al-Suhaimi
Directors: HE Sheikh Nasser Sabah Al-Ahmed Al-Sabah, Saud Abdul Aziz Al-Rashed, Leif Nielsen, J Lillelund, Khalid M Al Suhaimi, Aziz Al Suhaimi
Senior Executives: Frede Kjaer (General Manager)

PRINCIPAL ACTIVITIES: Manufacture of tin plate metal containers for the packaging of industrial products and aerosols
Parent Company: PLM Haustrup International, Denmark
Principal Bankers: Albank Alsaudi Alhollandi, Dammam
Financial Information:

	1990
	SR'000
Paid-up capital	7,000

Principal Shareholders: A R Saleh Al-Suhaimi (Saudi Arabia), PLM Haustrup International (Denmark); Hempel Marine Paint (Kuwait)
Date of Establishment: 1976
No of Employees: 140

SAUDI ARABIAN PARSONS LTD

PO Box 611, Riyadh 11421
Tel: 478-4012
Telex: c/o 40133 Redec SJ

Chairman: Dr Ghaith R Pharaon
Senior Executives: Jaafar S Al-Hillawi (Business Development
Manager)

PRINCIPAL ACTIVITIES: Process, civil and mechanical
engineering and design; project and construction
management
Principal Bankers: Saudi American Bank, Jeddah
Financial Information:

	SR'000
Sales turnover	200,000
Authorised capital	15,000

Principal Shareholders: Parsons Middle East Corporation (USA);
Redec (Saudi Arabia)
Date of Establishment: 1976
No of Employees: 500

SAUDI ARABIAN PRINTING CO LTD

PO Box 6463, Riyadh 11442
Tel: 4633452 (Office), 4658990 (Factory)
Cable: SAPRINT
Telex: 402117 SAPRINT SJ

Directors: Abdullah H Al-Fohaid (General Manager)

PRINCIPAL ACTIVITIES: Printing of books, magazines,
stationery, etc

SAUDI ARABIAN PROJECTS DEVELOPMENT CO

PO Box 3330, Jeddah 21471
Tel: 6517460, 6517464, 6531538, 6531546
Cable: Projectsco Jeddah
Telex: 600258 Sapdco Sj; 600637 Predco Sj

Chairman: Sheikh Ali Abdullah Bugshan
Senior Executives: Ahmed Hassan Suleiman (President), Salem
Abdoulla Bugshan (Proprietor), Suleiman Hassan Suleiman
(Managing Director), Samir A Akkari (Manager Operations &
Administration)

PRINCIPAL ACTIVITIES: Contractors, joint ventures, electronics,
marine activities, machinery, civil works, telecommunications,
water and sewage treatment, agribusiness, agencies, etc
Principal Agencies: Smit Int, Holland; Bendix, USA; ECC, India;
E Systems Montek Div, USA; Strabag Bau AG, W Germany;
Walter Kiddie, USA; Schmidt & Clemens, W Germany; United
Paint Co, UK; Teledyne Hastings Raydist, USA
Branch Offices: Jeddah, Riyadh, Dammam
Associated Companies: Bugshan Group of Companies
Principal Bankers: Saudi American Bank

Date of Establishment: 1978

SAUDI ARABIAN SAIPEM LTD

PO Box 248, Dhahran Airport 31932
Tel: 8574282
Telex: 870160 SAS Sj
Telefax: 8573231

Chairman: Carlo Flore
Directors: Giuseppe Muratore
Senior Executives: Khaled Al Shoaibi (Commercial Manager)

PRINCIPAL ACTIVITIES: Pipeline and mechanical contracting
Parent Company: Saipem SpA, Milan, Italy
Principal Bankers: Saudi American Bank, Saudi Fransi Bank
Financial Information:

	1989 SR'000
Sales turnover	403,000
Paid-up capital	2,000

Principal Shareholders: Saipem (Italy); Qahtani Maritime (Saudi
Arabia); Al Bilad (Saudi Arabia)
Date of Establishment: 1976
No of Employees: 1,000

SAUDI ARABIAN STANDARDS ORGANIZATION

PO Box 3437, Riyadh 11471
Tel: 4793332, 4793062 (PR Office)
Cable: Giasy
Telex: 401610 Saso SJ
Telefax: 4793060

Chairman: HE Dr Saliman Al Solaim
Members: Dr Abdul Rahman Al Zamel, Dr Khaled Y Al Khalaf,
Dr Saleh Al Hazlol, Hamad Al Rushody, Eng Mubarak Al
Khafrah, Dr Galal Mohammad Ashi, Eng Saad Al Gohar,
Saliman Yousif Al Frihidi, Dr Habib Mostafa Zinul-Abidin,
Yousif Hamdan Al Hamdan, Saad Mohammad Al Maajal
Senior Executives: Dr Khaled Y Al Khalaf (Director General),
Nabil Amin Molla (Deputy Director General), Sirag Massode
(Director General Standards Dept), Fahad Bin Salamah
(Director General Laboratories General Dept), Abdullah A Al
Hamoudi (Director General Quality Control General Dept),
Ibrahim A Al Maayouf (Director General Administrative &
Financial Affairs General Dept), Abdul Mohsin Al Yousef
(Director Information Centre), Mohammed Al Subait (Director
General Services Dept), Yahya Sonbol (Makkah Zone Office),
Sami Al Mesfer (Eastern Zone Office), Dr Khaled Y Al Khalaf
(Secretary General Standardization & Metrology Organisation
for GCC Countries), Abdul Mohsin Al Yousef (Supervisor
Information Centre)

PRINCIPAL ACTIVITIES: Formulation and adoption of the texts
of national standards; issuance of certification of conformity;
setting rules for granting quality marks
Branch Offices: PO Box 9485, Jeddah-Al Hamra, Tel 6673652,
Telex 403553

Principal Shareholders: SASO is a governmental body. It is an
automomous and independent agency which operates under
the supervision of the board of Directors chaired by HE The
Minister of Commerce
Date of Establishment: 1972
No of Employees: 255

SAUDI ARABIAN TELECOMMUNICATIONS CO LTD
S.A.R.T.E.L.C.O.

PO Box 3515, Riyadh 11481
Tel: 4654551
Cable: Sirti Riyadh
Telex: 401014, 405314 SIRTI Sj

Chairman: Sheikh Fouad Abdul Wahab Bahrawi
Directors: Francesco Gelfi, Osamah O Fakieh, Giuliano
Invernizzi

PRINCIPAL ACTIVITIES: Execution of turnkey
telecommunications projects
Branch Offices: Jeddah, Dammam
Parent Company: Sirti International
Principal Bankers: Saudi American Bank, Riyadh; Saudi French
Bank, Riyadh; Riyad Bank, Riyadh, Yanbu; National
Commercial Bank, Riyadh
Financial Information:

	SR'000
Authorised capital	30,000
Paid-up capital	30,000

Principal Shareholders: Sirti International, Liechenstein; Heirs of
late Sheikh Hamza Mohamed Bogari; Sheikh Osamah Omar
Fakieh
Date of Establishment: May 1976 (27-5-1396 H)
No of Employees: 456

SAUDI ARABIA

SAUDI ARABIAN TRADING & CONSTRUCTION CO LTD (SATCO)

PO Box 346, Riyadh 11411
Tel: 4782655
Cable: Satco
Telex: 401484 Satco Sj
Telefax: 4760250

Chairman: Malek A Antabi
Directors: Jamal N Kanafani (Executive Vice-President), Chafic E Tabet (Vice President Legal & Int'l Affairs)
Senior Executives: Majed El Zein (Vice President Marketing)

PRINCIPAL ACTIVITIES: Trading, construction, contracting, manufacturers' representation, O&M, total life support services & catering, systems engineering, electro-mechanical construction, airport systems and equipment, training security systems, landscaping, fast food
Principal Agencies: Sietam, France; SCI Inc, USA; PA Int'l, UK
Branch Offices: Al Jubail: PO Box 157, Dhahran Airport, Tel (03) 8940864, 8645689, Telex 870867 SATKHO SJ; Jeddah: PO Box 9588, Jeddah; Tel (02) 6443175, 6448868, Telex 604279 SATCOJ SJ
Parent Company: Syantec; International Commercial Agencies
Subsidiary Companies: OMP Arabia Ltd; Arabian Catering & Maintenance Services Ltd; Al Jazira Food Services Ltd
Principal Bankers: Riyad Bank; Saudi American Bank

Principal Shareholders: Malek A Antabi; Bandar Antabi; Tarek Antabi
Date of Establishment: 1978
No of Employees: 1,185

SAUDI ARABIAN VIANINI

PO Box 4329, Jeddah 21491
Tel: 6654394
Telex: 601122 Redec Sj

PRINCIPAL ACTIVITIES: Civil engineering contracting
Branch Offices: PO Box 88, Gizan; PO Box 4654, Riyadh
Principal Bankers: Saudi American Bank, Jeddah; National Commercial Bank, Gizan

Principal Shareholders: Vianini SpA (Italy); Redec (Saudi Arabia)
Date of Establishment: June 1974
No of Employees: 311

SAUDI ASCON LTD

PO Box 2818, Medina
Tel: 8360318
Telex: 570021 ALRIDA SJ

Chairman: Shaikh Abdul Azeez Ahmed Saab
Directors: N D S Sathak Ansari
Senior Executives: S M Qudrathullah (General Manager), N Mohamed Ali (Project Engineer), Syed Hussain Shah (Project Engineer)

PRINCIPAL ACTIVITIES: Civil contractors and general builders
Branch Offices: PO Box 6591, Jeddah, Tel 6720186
Associated Companies: Saudi ETA Ltd, PO Box 1269, Medina
Principal Bankers: Bank of Oman Ltd, Dubai, UAE
Financial Information:

	SR'000
Authorised capital	10,000
Paid-up capital	7,000

Principal Shareholders: Shaikh Abdul Aziz Ahmed Saab (34%); Associated Constructions, Dubai (49%); Shaikh Honi Abdul Aziz Ahmed Saab (17%)
Date of Establishment: 30-11-1399H
No of Employees: 677

SAUDI BAHRAINI CEMENT CO

PO Box 2464, Dammam 31451
Tel: 8344500
Cable: Sabada, Dammam
Telex: 801359 Sbcdam Sj
Telefax: 8345460

Chairman: Sulaiman M Balghunaim
Directors: Muhammad A Zamil, Saleh Al-Rajhi, Abdulaziz Al-Gosaibi, Abdul-Rehman M Al-Abdul Karim, Sulaiman Al-Rajhi, Ahmed A Juffali, Abdul Rahman M Jamsheer
Senior Executives: Ahmed A Juffali (Managing Director), A Showail (General Manager), Yusuf A Ahmad (Senior Manager Administration), Ibrahim Anshassi (Senior Manager Marketing), Suresh B Gokhale (Senior Manager Operations), Fahd A Hawas (Senior Manager Relations)

PRINCIPAL ACTIVITIES: Manufacture, process and marketing of ordinary portland and sulphate resistant cement
Branch Offices: Location in Dammam: Saudi Cement Bldg, King Saud Street; also Riyadh Office: PO Box 87164, Riyadh 11642, Tel 4773021; Ain Dar Office (Plant): 20 Kms West of Abqaiq, Tel 5660600, Telex 884011 Sbcain Sj, Fax 5661992
Principal Bankers: National Commercial Bank; Riyad Bank; Al Bank Al Saudi Al Hollandi; Saudi American Bank
Financial Information:

	1990 SR'000
Sales turnover	246,858
Profits	72,488
Authorised capital	1,200,000
Paid-up capital	900,000
Total assets	1,592,260

Principal Shareholders: Shares are subscribed by Saudi Shareholders and by Bahraini Shareholders
Date of Establishment: April 1981
No of Employees: 850

SAUDI BASIC INDUSTRIES CORPORATION (SABIC)

PO Box 5101, Riyadh 11422
Tel: 4012033
Cable: Sabic
Telex: 401177 Sabic Sj, 400293 Sabic Sj
Telefax: 4012045

Chairman: Abdulaziz A Al-Zamil
Directors: Ibrahim A Bin Salamah, HRH Prince Faisal Ibn Sultan Ibn Abdulaziz Al Saud, Dr Saleh Al-Omair, Mubarak Al-Kafra, Mohammed Al Issa, Mohammed S Abanumy
Senior Executives: Ibrahim A Bin Salamah (Vice Chairman & Managing Director), Mohammed Al Mady (Director General Projects), Abdullah Nojaidi (President SABIC Marketing Ltd), Ghazi Al Hajjar (President SABIC Marketing Services Ltd), Saad N Salamah (Director General Administration & Organisation), Naser Al-Sayyari (Director General Planning & Studies), Moayyed Al Qurtas (Director General Research & Development), Yousuf Al Braik (Director General Finance & Investment)

PRINCIPAL ACTIVITIES: Implementation of basic industries in Saudi Arabia and manufacture and marketing of chemicals, petrochemicals, fertilisers, and metals
Branch Offices: Dammam: PO Box 2629, Telex 801661 Sabic Sj; Al Jubail: PO Box 10040, Telex 832165 Sabmrk SJ; London: Portland House, Stag Place, Telex 23411 SABMRK G; Hongkong: Unit 1204-8, 2 Pacific Place, 88 Queensway, Central Hong Kong, Telex 76973 SBMRK HX; USA: Metro Center, 1 Station Place, Stamford, Connecticut 06902, Telex 984950 SMAUS
Affiliated Companies: Saudi Iron & Steel Co (HADEED), Jubail; Steel Rolling Co (SULB), Jeddah; Saudi Methanol Co (AR RAZI), Jubail; National Methanol Co (IBN SINA), Jubail; Al Jubail Fertilizer Co (SAMAD), Jubail; Saudi Arabian Fertilizer Co (SAFCO), Dammam; Saudi Yanbu Petrochemical Co

(YANPET), Yanbu; Al Jubail Petrochemical Co (KEMYA), Jubail; Saudi Petrochemical Co (SADAF), Jubail; Arabian Petrochemical Co (PETROKEMYA), Jubail; Eastern Petrochemical Co (SHARQ), Jubail; National Plastic Co (IBN HAYYAN), Jubail; National Industrial Gases Co (GAS), Jubail; Saudi European Petrochemical Co (IBN ZAHR), Jubail; National Chemical Fertiliser Co (IBN AL BAYTAR), Jubail

Financial Information:

	1988/89 SR'000	1989/90 SR'000
Sales turnover	9,322,204	9,880,902
Profits	3,553,000	3,370,000
Authorised capital	10,000,000	10,000,000
Paid-up capital	5,000,000	7,500,000
Total assets	26,955,000	29,975,000

Principal Shareholders: Government (70%), citizens of Saudi Arabia and the neighbouring GCC states (30%)
Date of Establishment: 1976
No of Employees: 8,938

SAUDI BASIC TECHNOLOGIES LTD (SABAT)

PO Box 2548, Jeddah 21461
Tel: 6718050
Telex: 600480 KHALID SJ

Senior Executives: Ziad A Jamjoom (General Manager), Saleh Shata (General Manager - Al Khobar)

PRINCIPAL ACTIVITIES: Water desalination plant, water distribution
Branch Offices: PO Box 1220, Al Khobar 31431, Tel 8948835, Telex 870539 SBAT SJ
Associated Companies: Basic Technologies Inc, USA

SAUDI BAUER FOUNDATION CONTRACTORS LTD

PO Box 10740, Jeddah 21443
Tel: 6510281, 6513316
Telex: 603065 Bauers Sj
Telefax: 6510281

Chairman: Jafar S Jamjoom
Directors: Riaz H Malik (Managing Director)
Senior Executives: Muhammad Akram (Commercial Manager), K M Zimolong (Contracts Manager)

PRINCIPAL ACTIVITIES: Geotechnical contractors, foundation, ground improvement, ground water control, deep excavation
Parent Company: Bauer Spezialtiefbau, West Germany
Associated Companies: Bauer International, in Abu Dhabi, Egypt, Malaysia, USA, Austria, UK
Principal Bankers: Albank Alsaudi Alhollandi, Al Bank Al Saudi Al Fransi
Financial Information:

	1990 SR'000
Sales turnover	97,000
Authorised capital	1,000
Paid-up capital	1,000

Principal Shareholders: Bauer Spezialtiefbau, Jafar S Jamjoom, Osman S Jamjoom
Date of Establishment: 1979
No of Employees: 65

SAUDI BAZAAR

PO Box 11209, Jeddah 21453
Tel: 6534443, 6534060, 6534200
Cable: Soukshanco
Telex: 603645 Bazaar SJ
Telefax: 6510428

Chairman: Salem Ahmad Bugshan
Directors: Abdulmouin Auf (General Manager)

PRINCIPAL ACTIVITIES: Perfumes, cosmetics, toiletries, hardware and tools

Principal Agencies: Parfums Christian Dior, Giorgio, Clarins, Muko, Kent
Branch Offices: Riyadh: PO Box 16847, Tel 4043830; Dammam: PO Box 2913, Tel 8434308
Parent Company: Salem Ahmad Bugshan
Subsidiary Companies: Al Hamra Pharmacy; Al Hamra Gift Store; Bugshan Pharmacy; New Alhamra Pharmacy; Saudi Bazaar Tools Division
Principal Bankers: Al Bank Al Saudi Al Fransi, National Commercial Bank

Principal Shareholders: S A Bugshan (100%)
Date of Establishment: 1978
No of Employees: 50

SAUDI BIDDING & TRADING CO

PO Box 1187, Dammam 31431
Tel: 8325777, 8321278, 8320220
Telex: 801217 Albazi Sj

Senior Executives: Mohammed Al-Bazie (General Manager)

PRINCIPAL ACTIVITIES: Camp catering services; import and distribution of foodstuffs; cold storage plant installation; general contractors
Branch Offices: Jubail; Riyadh, Tel 4770806

SAUDI BRITISH BANK (THE)

Head Office, Dabaab St, PO Box 9084, Riyadh 11413
Tel: 4050677 (23 lines)
Cable: Sabrit Riyadh
Telex: 402349 Sabb Sj, 402351 Sabb Sj, 404081 Sabb Sj
Telefax: 4050660

Chairman: Sheikh Yousef Ebrahim Redwan
Board of Directors: Sheikh Abdullah Mohamed Al Hugail (Deputy Chairman), Aman Mehta (Manging Director), Andrew Dixon (Deputy Managing Director), Sheikh Sulaiman Saleh Olayan, Sheikh Omar Abdulfattah Aggad, Sheikh Khalifa Abdul Latif Al Mulhem, John A P Hill, Sir James Craig
Senior Executives: A Mehta (Managing Director), A Dixon (Deputy Managing Director), C A G Gibson (Senior Manager Finance), P Garstin (Senior Manager Treasury), Z J Cama (Senior Manager Corporate Banking), B J Howells (Senior Manager Retail Banking), F A Longi (Senior Manager Technical Services), S A Al Hamdan (Senior Manager Personnel)

PRINCIPAL ACTIVITIES: Commercial banking
Branch Offices: 45 Branches in Saudi Arabia: In Riyadh: Main Branch: PO Box 2907, Riyadh 11461, Tel 4794400 (14 lines), Telex 406303, 406383, 406191 SBBRYD Sj, 400149, 400426 SABB Sj; King Faisal Street Branch: PO Box 43069, Riyadh 11561; Olaya Branch: PO Box 10914, Riyadh 11443; Sharia Dabaab Branch: PO Box 17682, Riyadh 11494; Sanaiyah Branch: PO Box 2907, Riyadh 11461; In Alkhobar: Main Branch: PO Box 35, Dhahran Airport 31932, Tel 8642868, 8642869, Telex 870007 Sabb Sj; King Abdulaziz Bvd Branch; Thugbah Branch; In Dammam: Main Branch: PO Box 1618, Dammam 31441, Tel 8331553, 8331745, Telex 801314 Sabb Sj; Ibn Khildoun Branch Dammam; Hofuf Main Branch: PO Box 365, Tel 5820926, Telex 861172; Qatif Branch: PO Box 209, Qatif 31911, Tel 8552059, Telex 891020 Sabb Sj; Jubail Branch: PO Box 119, Tel 3610789, Telex 631029 Saab Sj; and Jubail Industrial City Branch, Tel 3419147, Telex 631029; In Jeddah: Main Branch: PO Box 109, Jeddah 21411, Tel 6512121 (12 lines), Telex 601051, 602048 Sabb Sj; King Abdulaziz St Branch: PO Box 7002, Jeddah 21462; Caravan Branch: PO Box 6885, Jeddah 21452; Caravan Ladies Branch: PO Box 6885, Jeddah 21452; Jeddah Int'l Markets Branch: PO Box 5383, Jeddah 21422; Makkah Road Branch: PO Box 11633, Jeddah 21463; Al Kharj Branch: PO Box 698, Al Kharj 11942; Buraidah Branch: PO Box 1829; Makkah Branch: PO Box 6052; Medinah Branch: PO Box 135; Abha Branch: PO Box 698; Taif Branch: PO Box 822; etc

SAUDI ARABIA

Financial Information:

	1989/90 SR'000
Profits	123,064
Authorised capital	400,000
Paid-up capital	400,000
Total assets	12,549,539

Principal Shareholders: Saudi Arabian Citizens (60%); The British Bank of the Middle East (40%)
Date of Establishment: 1 July 1978
No of Employees: 937

SAUDI BUILDING CO ABAHSAIN & PARTNERS LTD
S.A.U.L.E.X.

PO Box 676, Alkhobar 31952
Tel: 8645409
Cable: Saulex-Alkhobar
Telex: 871278 Saulex Sj

Chairman: Sheikh Abdulaziz Abahsain
Directors: Anas C Sinno (Managing Director)
Senior Executives: Vahan A Bezdikian (Project Director), William S Balesh (Business Manager), Nader Abu Ibrahim (Chief Administrator), Hassan A Dawi (Chief Accountant)

PRINCIPAL ACTIVITIES: General contractors
Principal Agencies: Armco Inc, USA USA
Branch Offices: Salman Al Farisi St, Riyadh
Subsidiary Companies: Saudi Tab-Faiyin Construction Co Ltd (Saudi-Tab); Saulex Confil Arabia Ltd
Principal Bankers: Arab National Bank; Al Bank Al Saudi Al Hollandi

Principal Shareholders: Saleh & Abdulaziz Abahsain Co Inc, Saudi Arabia; Ibrahim Al Mushari Al Hussain; Saudi Arabia; Mohamad Fahd Al Zahed; Saudi Arabia; Unibuild Limited, Jersey, Channel Islands
Date of Establishment: 1975
No of Employees: 750

SAUDI BUILDING MATERIALS EST

PO Box 3329, Riyadh 11471
Tel: 4484292, 4487441
Telex: 401112 Tricorp Sj

Chairman: Abdul Raouf Yusef Al Sharif

PRINCIPAL ACTIVITIES: Import and supply of building materials
Branch Offices: PO Box 5107, Jeddah, Tel 6433996; PO Box 2059, Dammam, Tel 8644490

SAUDI BUILDING SYSTEMS

PO Box 8648, Jeddah 21492
Tel: 6370036 (8 lines)
Telex: 603449 SBSMFG SJ

Chairman: Sheikh Ahmed Juffali
Directors: Jafar Askari, Robert West, Shaikh Walid Juffali, William D Chapman, Moufid Alossi
Senior Executives: Hassan Y Bahsoun (General Manager), Jawad Y Hallaq (Manufacturing Manager), Osama El Mabrook (Engineering Manager), Sharif Badawi (Export Manager), Zafarullah Qureshi (Finance Manager)

PRINCIPAL ACTIVITIES: Manufacture, supply, design, erection and construction of pre-engineered steel buildings for warehouses, offices, showrooms, shopping centres, aircraft hangars, school buildings, power plants and sub-stations
Branch Offices: Jeddah Office: PO Box 4980, Tel 6370036, Telex 602261; Riyadh Office: PO Box 8823, Tel 4647695, 4659212, Telex 403258; Alkhobar Office: PO Box 4992, Tel 8275306, 8275325, Telex 870418
Parent Company: E A Juffali & Bros; Butler International Co, USA

Principal Bankers: Saudi American Bank, Jeddah; Arab National Bank, Jeddah

Principal Shareholders: E A Juffali & Brothers, Butler International Co, Missouri, USA
Date of Establishment: 1976
No of Employees: 206

SAUDI BULK TRANSPORT LTD

PO Box 2194, Alkhobar 31952
Tel: 8944880
Telex: 870354 Sabut Sj
Telefax: 8640461

Chairman: Hisham A Alireza
Directors: Per Berg (President)

PRINCIPAL ACTIVITIES: Bulk transport contractors, handling and transportation of bulk cargo, including cement, aggregates, building materials, grain and fertiliser
Parent Company: Xenel Industries Ltd
Principal Bankers: Saudi British Bank; Gulf International Bank; Saudi American Bank

Principal Shareholders: A member of the Xenel Group of companies
Date of Establishment: 1977
No of Employees: 500

SAUDI BUSINESS MACHINES LTD

PO Box 5648, Jeddah 21432
Tel: 6651165, 6600007
Telex: 602428 IBM Sj
Telefax: 6651163

Chairman: Sheikh Ahmed Juffali
Senior Executives: Eric Arnaud (General Manager), Hasan Barraj (Asst General Manager)

PRINCIPAL ACTIVITIES: General marketing and services representative for IBM SEMEA SRL dealing in IBM data processing equipment, software, maintenance agreements and support services
Branch Offices: Riyadh: PO Box 818, Tel 4056910, Telex 401659; Al Khobar: PO Box 476, Tel 8571177, Telex 871440; Jubail: PO Box 150, Tel 3611438
Subsidiary Companies: Office Equipment Division: Saudi Business Machines, Information Products, PO Box 14730, Jeddah 21434, Tel 6671157, 6600812, Telex 606155 SBM IP SJ

Principal Shareholders: E A Juffali & Bros
Date of Establishment: 1981

SAUDI CABLE COMPANY

PO Box 4403, Jeddah 21491
Tel: 6694060 (10 lines)
Cable: Cablecom
Telex: 601751 Corp SJ
Telefax: 6693935

Chairman: Khalid Ahmad Yousuf Zainal Alireza
Directors: Abdallah Ahmad Yousuf Zainal Alireza, Abdul Karim Bakr Ahmad, Ibrahim Mohammad Said Shams, Abdallah Mohammad Taher Al Dabbagh, Omar Hashim Khalifati, Fawaz Al Alamy Al Hasani
Senior Executives: Hasmukh D Shah (Executive Vice President Planning & Business Development), Fawaz Al Alamy Al Hasani ((Executive Vice President Corporate Affairs and Company Secretary), Samir K Fayez (Senior Vice President Business Development), Jankut M Bilgen (Senior Vice President & Group Controller) Abdul Rahman Ali Al Hamdan (Vice President Company Affairs), Ala'a S Al Jabri (Vice President Finance), Mohammed Noor Joukhdar (Senior Vice President Saudi Operations)

PRINCIPAL ACTIVITIES: Manufacture of low and medium voltage wires and cables, insulated power cables, building wires and conductors for overhead lines of low, medium and high voltage for transmission and distribution, telecommunication cables, optical fibre cables, copper rods, PVC compounds, wooden reels and pallets; turnkey project services for electrical and telecommunication installations; marketing of electric/telecom cables, accessories and associated products

Branch Offices: Riyadh Branch: PO Box 6793, Riyadh 11452, Tel 4649080, Fax 4644148, Telex 406117; Alkhobar Branch: PO Box 2449, Alkhobar 31952, Tel 8981963, Fax 8982991, Telex 871027; Marketing & International Sales Branch: SCC Marketing, PO Box 9903, Jeddah 21423, Tel 6694147, Fax 6695581, Telex 607150

Associated Companies: Saudi Arabia: SCC Power Cables; SCC Marketing & Sales; SCC Materials; SCC Telecables; SCC Reel Plant; Bahrain: Midal Cables Ltd, PO Box 5939, Bahrain, Tel 662050, Fax 660259, Telex 9127; Turkey: Demirer Kablo Tesisleri Sanayi Ve Ticaret AS, Turkey; Kavel Kablo Ve Elektrik Malzemesi AS, Turkey

Principal Bankers: Saudi British Bank, Jeddah; Riyad Bank, Jeddah/Riyadh; Al Bank Al Saudi Al Fransi, Jeddah; Saudi International Bank, London; Gulf International Bank, Bahrain

Financial Information:

	1989/90 SR'000
Sales turnover	921,984
Profits	38,251
Authorised capital	270,000
Paid-up capital	270,000

Principal Shareholders: Xenel Industries Ltd (33.57%); HRH Princess Noha Bint Saud Bin Abdul Mohsen Bin Abdul Aziz (11.48%); Abdul Karim Bakr Ahmed (6.96%); and approz 990 other shareholders (48.0%)

Date of Establishment: September 1975
No of Employees: 1,590

SAUDI CAIRO BANK

PO Box 11222, Jeddah 21453
Tel: 6323044
Cable: SAUDICAIRBA JEDDAH
Telex: 600205, 602190 SCHO Sj; 602524 SCB Fx Sj

Chairman: Waheeb Bin Zagr

Directors: Waheeb Bin Zagr, Abdelaziz Nasrallah, Mansour Mayman, Taymour Abdullah Alireza, Dr Abdelaziz Al Jarbou, Mohamed Ebrahim Al Toaimi, Abdullah A Allohaidan, Fahad Sulaiman Al Misfer, Mahmoud Mohammed Youssef, Tawfeek Abdo Ismail

Senior Executives: Mohd F Daghistany (General Manager), Said Al Ghamdi (Asst General Manager Finance & EDP), Abdul Kader Bakkar (Asst General Manager Administration)

PRINCIPAL ACTIVITIES: Banking

Branch Offices: Over 46 branches in Saudi Arabia: Western Region Branches: Al-Faiha: PO Box 496, Jeddah; City: PO Box 472, Jeddah; Al Yamama: PO Box 17842, Jeddah; Al-Hamra: PO Box 8673, Jeddah: Bab-Makkah: PO Box 9053, Jeddah; King Abdul-Aziz University: PO Box 17843, Jeddah; Makkah Main: PO Box 2412; Ebn Khaldoon St: PO Box 3741, Makkah; Yanbu: PO Box 204; Medinah: PO Box 2457; Central Region Branches: Al-Sitteen: PO Box 42647, Riyadh; Al-Wazir St: PO Box 2848, Riyadh; Al-Malaz: PO Box 2804, Riyadh; Al-Batha: PO Box 4955, Riyadh; Eastern Region Branches: Al-Khobar: PO Box 43; Dammam: PO Box 1555; Jubail: PO Box 475; Southern Region Branches: Khamis Mushait: PO Box 711; Abha: PO Box 564; Jizan: PO Box 138, Hyatt Jizan Hotel; Northern Region: Tabuk: PO Box 720

Financial Information:

	SR'000
Authorised capital	300,000
Paid-up capital	300,000

Principal Shareholders: 30% Saudi Partners, 20% Banque du Caire SAE and 50% Public Investment Fund (Ministry of Finance)
Date of Establishment: October 1st, 1979
No of Employees: 1,301

SAUDI CATERING & CONTRACTING CO

Regional Head Office, PO Box 308, Riyadh 11411
Tel: 4773713 (5 lines)
Cable: Conservice
Telex: 401126 Caserv Sj, 400291 Kimma Sj
Telefax: 4780267

Owner: Prince Khalid Bin Turki Al Sudairi
Senior Executives: Ragi C Abouhaidar (Regional General Manager), Samir S Layous (Deputy Regional GM & Area Manager Central Zone), Jacques Daoud (Asst Area Manager Eastern Zone), Elie Ghorayeb (Asst Area Manager Western Zone)

PRINCIPAL ACTIVITIES: Catering and contracting, supply and erection of prefabricated buildings, design and construction of kitchens, electrical installation and maintenance, labour supply, transport, camp services, tobacco distribution
Principal Agencies: Kent products of Brown & Williamsons, USA; franchise of LeNotre, Paris
Branch Offices: Jeddah: PO Box 2266, Tel 6603708, 6603660 Telex 601220; Alkhobar: PO Box 258, Tel 8644220, 8644262, Telex 870038; Riyadh: PO Box 308, Tel 4773713 (5 lines), Telex 401126 Caserv Sj, 400291 Kimma Sj
Associated Companies: Electro Mechanical Construction Co, PO Box 8997, Riyadh, Tel 4761000, 4785467, Telex 400364 Elemco Sj; Saudi International Transport Co, PO Box 258, Alkhobar, Tel 8644262, 8954104, 8951200, Telex 870038 Caserv Sj
Principal Bankers: Saudi American Bank; Arab National Bank; Al Bank Al Saudi Al Fransi; Banque d'Indochine
Financial Information:

	US$'000
Annual turnover	200,000

Principal Shareholders: Saudi incorporated and owned
Date of Establishment: 1966
No of Employees: 6,500

SAUDI CEMENT COMPANY

PO Box 306, Dammam 31411
Tel: 8325177, 8322480
Cable: Cement Dammam
Telex: 801068 Cement sj
Telefax: 8325367

Chairman: Suleiman Balghoneim
Directors: Ahmed Juffali (Managing Director), Abdul Aziz Hamad Al Gosaibi, Saleh Al-Rajhi, Hamad Al Mubarak, Abdul Rehman Mohd Abdul Karim, Mohammad Al Faraj, Mohamad Al Saadi, Saleh S Al Rajhi
Senior Executives: Abdulaziz M Showail (General Manager), Mohammad Hossari (Works Manager)

PRINCIPAL ACTIVITIES: Manufacturing and marketing of sulphate resisting cement type V, high compressive strength cement type I, oil well cement and other special types of cement
Branch Offices: Riyadh: PO Box 973, Tel 4025290 and Al Hassa: PO Box 384, Tel 5821361
Principal Bankers: National Commercial Bank; Arab National Bank; Riyad Bank; Albank Alsaudi Alhollandi
Financial Information:

	1989/90 SR'000
Sales turnover	257,157
Profits	67,541
Capital	840,000
Paid-up capital	420,000
Total assets	666,967

Principal Shareholders: Chairman and directors as described
Date of Establishment: 1955
No of Employees: 949

SAUDI CERAMIC COMPANY

PO Box 3893, Riyadh 11481
Tel: 4770715
Cable: Ceramic
Telex: 401850 Cermco Sj
Telefax: 4792897

Chairman: Saleh A Aziz Al Rajhi
Senior Executives: M H Al Khuraisy (Administration & Personnel Manager), Salah Fayez Bader (Budgeting & Planning Manager), Abdul Aziz Suleiman (Showrooms & Branches Manager), Khalid Algadi (Wholesale Manager), Mohd Murad (Purchasing Manager), Salloum Aldabass (Project Sales & Export Manager), Richard Davies (Marketing Manager), M G Walton (Operations Manager)

PRINCIPAL ACTIVITIES: Manufacture and marketing of ceramic wall floor, and mosaic tiles, sanitaryware and accessories
Branch Offices: Jeddah, Dammam, Buraidah, Taif, Tabuk, and two showrooms in Riyadh
Principal Bankers: Riyad Bank; National Commercial Bank; Saudi American Bank; Saudi British Bank
Financial Information:

	1988/89 SR'000
Turnover	155,000
Profits	40,000
Authorised capital	150,000
Paid-up capital	150,000
Fixed assets	345,000

Principal Shareholders: Public and private sectors
Date of Establishment: 1976
No of Employees: 1,000

SAUDI CHEMICAL CO LTD

PO Box 2665, Riyadh 11461
Tel: 4767432 (8 lines)
Cable: Nitrosaud
Telex: 401031 Nitro Sj
Telefax: 4761275

Chairman: HH Amir Khaled Ibn Abdullah Ibn Abdulrahman
Directors: HH Amir Salman Bin Khaled Bin Abdullah, HH Amir Fahed Bin Khaled Bin Abdullah, Kjell Oyen (President)
Senior Executives: Mohamed Hamed Al Sogaih (Vice President), Arne Jansson (Business Dev & Marketing Manager), Roger Palmar (Finance Manager)

PRINCIPAL ACTIVITIES: Production and sale of explosives and accessories for civil use and blasting services
Branch Offices: Jeddah, PO Box 5765, and Alkhobar, PO Box 1117
Associated Companies: Nitro Nobel Ab Sweden
Principal Bankers: Albank Alsaudi Alhollandi, Alkhobar, Jeddah and Riyadh
Financial Information:

	1989 SR'000
Sales turnover	85,000
Profits	7,000
Authorised capital	70,000
Paid-up capital	70,000
Total assets	188,000

Principal Shareholders: Mawarid Holding Company
Date of Establishment: 1972
No of Employees: 160

SAUDI CHEMICAL INDUSTRIES CO LTD

PO Box 18417, Jeddah 21415
Tel: 6361815, 6380277, 6379074, 6374521
Telex: 605276 Saukem Sj
Telefax: 6374857

Owners: Sheikh Sulaiman Saleh Basahal, Sheikh Khalid Sulaiman Basahal
Senior Executives: M Anwarullah Khan (General Manager), F H Siddiqui (Technical Manager), M Azmatullah (Admin Manager)

PRINCIPAL ACTIVITIES: Manufacture of ICI decorative paints, Saudichem paints and textured coatings
Branch Offices: Jeddah (Factory): Tel 6361815, Telex 605276 SAUKEM SJ; Riyadh: Tel 01-4777341, Telex 402344 MOBSAR SJ
Parent Company: Sulaiman Saleh Basahal Establishment
Principal Bankers: Riyad Bank

Principal Shareholders: Sulaiman Saleh Basahal, Khalid Sulaiman Basahal
Date of Establishment: 1974
No of Employees: 56

SAUDI CHEMICAL INSECTICIDE & DISINFECTANT CO LTD (SCIDCO)

PO Box 3792, Industrial Area, Riyadh 11481
Tel: 4486792
Cable: Inscidco
Telex: 401566 Scidco Sj
Telefax: 4488079

Chairman: Prince Abdullah Bin Turki Al Saud
Directors: Prince Abdullah Al Fahd Al Faisal, Adel Yousef Khalil
Senior Executives: Dr Samy A S Mostafa (General & Research Manager)

PRINCIPAL ACTIVITIES: Manufacture of public health insecticides, industrial and domestic disinfectants, domestic chemical products and agricultural chemicals
Principal Bankers: Riyad Bank
Financial Information:

	1989/90 SR'000
Sales turnover	17,000
Authorised capital	34,240
Paid-up capital	8,560

Principal Shareholders: Directors as described above
Date of Establishment: November 1977

SAUDI COMMERCIAL & INDUSTRIAL CO (SCIC)

PO Box 349, Jeddah 21411
Tel: 6517200, 6517215
Telex: 603654 Scic Bp, 401182

Chairman: Nehme Tohme
Directors: Suham Maamari (Area Manager)

PRINCIPAL ACTIVITIES: Distribution and installation of air-conditioning equipment; construction materials; telephone equipment; gas turbine generators
Principal Agencies: Carrier, Ericsson, Rolls-Royce, OPTORG
Branch Offices: Jeddah: Tel 6530868, Telex 601182; Riyadh: Tel 4027287, Telex 404121; Dammam: Tel 8571827; Yanbu: Tel 3228472, Telex 661118
Subsidiary/Associated Companies: Almabani General Contractors
Principal Bankers: Saudi Cairo Bank; Al Bank Al Saudi Al Fransi

SAUDI COMPUTER SERVICES CO LTD

PO Box 1935, Jeddah 21441
Tel: 6448331, 6448880, 6449633
Telex: 601122 SRDC Sj
Telefax: 6448846

Chairman: Dr Ghaith Pharaon

Directors: M Saeed Alaya (General Manager)

Senior Executives: Wahaj Habib (Technical Manager), Sahel Masarani (Finance Manager)

PRINCIPAL ACTIVITIES: Computer distributors and service bureau

Principal Agencies: Texas Intruments, MEMOREX, Cincom, Systems, Retail Data Consultants

Branch Offices: Riyadh: PO Box 611, Tel 4766954, 4762657; Dhahran: PO Box 998, Tel 8311011, 8325421, 8325440

Parent Company: Saudi Research & Development Corporation

Principal Bankers: Saudi Investment Banking Corporation; National Commercial Bank; Saudi American Bank

Financial Information:

	1990
	SR'000
Sales turnover	19,000
Profits	7,600
Paid-up capital	5,000

Principal Shareholders: Dr Ghaith Pharaon; Saudi Research & Development Corporation (REDEC)

Date of Establishment: 1976

No of Employees: 60

SAUDI CONSOLIDATED ELECTRIC CO (CENTRAL REGION)

S.C.E.C.O. (Central)

PO Box 57, Riyadh 11411

Tel: 4031508, 4031557, 4032222

Cable: Riyadh Electric

Telex: 401016 Recs Sj; 402477 Rdel Sj

Telefax: 4051191, 4053063

Chairman: Eng Abdullah Abdulrahman Al Tassan

Directors: Eng Abdul Aziz Abdullah Al-Abdul Wahid (President), Eng Hamad Abdul Karim Al Hassoun (Vice President Engineering Affairs), Abdul Rahman M Al Medainy (Vice President Finance & Admin Affairs), Eng Ali Salih Al Barrak (Vice President Distribution & Customer Affairs), Dr Amir Mohamed Al Sawaha (Vice President Supporting Services)

Senior Executives: Mossad M Al Harbi (Director of Finance), Abdullah S Al Raees (Director of Materials), Saud A Al Rashid (Director of Technical Studies), Hussain Qutub (Director of Distribution Engineering), Abdul Rahman Al Bassam (Director of Transmission), Abdul Hameed Al Naeem (Director of Customer Affairs), Salim M Al Balawi (Director of Personnel)

PRINCIPAL ACTIVITIES: Generation, transmission, distribution and marketing of electric power

Branch Offices: Riyadh: PO Box 7604, Riyadh 11472 and all cities of the central region of Saudi Arabia

Principal Bankers: National Commercial Bank Ltd, Riyadh; Riyad Bank, Riyadh; Saudi American Bank, Riyadh; Arab National Bank, Riyadh

Financial Information:

	1409H/1989	1410H/1990
	SR'000	SR'000
Sales turnover	1,390,656	1,450,670
Profits	443,990	580,932
Authorised capital	8,000,000	8,000,000
Paid-up capital	8,000,000	8,000,000
Total assets	22,166,913	22,892,472

Principal Shareholders: Saudi Government; National and Government Companies; Citizens

Date of Establishment: 1979

No of Employees: 6,591

SAUDI CONSOLIDATED ELECTRIC CO (EASTERN REGION)

S.C.E.C.O. (Eastern)

PO Box 5190, Dammam 31422

Tel: 8572300

Cable: SCECO Dammam

Telex: 802030, 802720

Chairman: Fehied F Al Shareef

Directors: Sulaiman Al Alkadi (Managing Director), Sa'ad M Al Mojil, Mohammed H Al Bassam, Mahmud H Khalil

Senior Executives: H A Al Dulaijan (VP Finance & Industrial Relations), I A Al Bayat (VP Operations), A S Majhood (VP Engineering & Construction), M I Boubshait (VP Area Affairs), S I Al Bassam (VP Services)

PRINCIPAL ACTIVITIES: Generation, transmission, distribution and sale of electric power

Branch Offices: Throughout the Eastern Province of Saudi Arabia

Financial Information:

	1990
	SR'000
Authorised capital	5,000,000
Paid-up capital	4,100,000

Date of Establishment: 27 Sha'ban 1396 (23 August 1976)

No of Employees: 6,457

SAUDI CONSOLIDATED ELECTRIC CO (SOUTHERN REGION)

S.C.E.C.O. (Southern)

PO Box 616, Abha

Tel: 07-2271075

Telex: 905007, 905008

Telefax: 07-2271627

Chairman: Eng Abdulrahman A Al Tuwaijiri

Directors: Mohammad A Al Zarah (Director General)

Senior Executives: Mustafa A Bin Aziz (DDG for Financial Affairs), Abdul Rahman A Al Hasania (DDG for Services Affairs), Saad M Al Shahrani (DDG for Technical Affairs), Abdul Rahman A Al Hasania (DDG for Services Affairs), Safar M Shufaiyer (Generation Director)

PRINCIPAL ACTIVITIES: Generation, transmission and distribution of electricity in the southern region of Saudi Arabia

Branch Offices: Asir, Jizan, Najran, Al Baha, Bisha, Tihama

Principal Bankers: National Commercial Bank, Riyad Bank, Al Bank Al Saudi Al Fransi

Financial Information:

	1990
	SR'000
Sales turnover	257,339
Authorised capital	4,000,000
Paid-up capital	3,564,410
Total assets	5,583,187

Principal Shareholders: Government (98.1%), Nationals (1.3%)

Date of Establishment: 22.8.1399H

No of Employees: 3,354

SAUDI CONSOLIDATED ELECTRIC CO (WESTERN REGION)

S.C.E.C.O. (Western)

PO Box 9299, Jeddah 21413

Tel: 6511008

Cable: Kahrba Algharbia

Telex: 601970 Kahrba Sj, 604760 Electr Sj

Telefax: 6534139

Chairman: Eng Mahmoud A Taiba

Directors: Dr Bakr H Khoshaim (Director General)

Senior Executives: Anwar S Akbar (Asst Director General), Eng Yousef Balghunaim (DDG Operations), Eng Saleh M Abdoun (DDG Engineering & Projects), Dr Husein M Rida (ADG Manpower Development)

PRINCIPAL ACTIVITIES: Electric power generation, transmission and distribution

Branch Offices: All cities and villages in the western region of Saudi Arabia

Parent Company: Electricity Corporation, Riyadh

Principal Bankers: Riyad Bank, National Commercial Bank

Financial Information:

	1409H/1989 SR'000	1410H/1990 SR'000
Sales turnover	1,365,904	1,404,109
Authorised capital	8,000,000	8,000,000
Paid-up capital	7,272,697	7,328,312
Total assets	22,570,528	23,385,900

Principal Shareholders: Electricity Corporation; Shaikh Ali Juffali, Shaikh Ahmed Juffali, National Commercial Bank

Date of Establishment: 01.01.1402H

No of Employees: 7,581

SAUDI CONSOLIDATED ENGINEERING CO

Khatib and Alami

PO Box 3928, Riyadh 11481

Tel: 4778384, 4766309

Cable: CONSING

Telex: 401652 CEC SJ

Telefax: (966 1) 4779793

President: Prof Mounir El Khatib

Directors: Dr Zuheir Alami (Senior Partner)

Senior Executives: Abdul Monem Ariss (Resident Manager Riyadh), Samir El Khatib (Resident Manager Jeddah), Bassim Sayigh (Resident Manager Alkhobar)

PRINCIPAL ACTIVITIES: Engineering consultants and architects

Branch Offices: Saudi Arabia (Jeddah: PO Box 9330, Jeddah 21413, Tel 6694541, Fax 6691340, Telex 602988 CEC SJ; Alkhobar: PO Box 1713, Alkhobar 31952, Tel 8946816, Fax 8942341, Telex 871441 MECEC SJ), Abu Dhabi, Dubai, Sharjah, Bahrain, Oman

Parent Company: Khatib and Alami, Beirut, Lebanon

Subsidiary Companies: Alami & Abdulhadi, Amman, Jordan

Date of Establishment: 1961

No of Employees: 450

SAUDI CONSTRUCTION CO

PO Box 8073, Riyadh 11482

Tel: 4762835, 4785453

Cable: Osamcon

Telex: 400228 Ruhscc

Chairman: Architect Osama H Al-Sayed

Directors: Sheikh Abdullah Baroom (Partner), Mr Aiman Hamadallah (Partner)

Senior Executives: Omar El Shennawy (Chief Accountant), Abdel Salam El-Shafei (Commercial Manager)

PRINCIPAL ACTIVITIES: Building construction; civil engineering; reinforcement and cement supply; building materials supply; transport; trailers manufacture

Branch Offices: Medinah and Jeddah

Subsidiary Companies: Hana Establishment

Principal Bankers: National Commercial Bank; Saudi Cairo Bank; Saudi American Bank

Financial Information:

	SR'000
Sales turnover	81,000
Authorised capital	4,000
Paid-up capital	4,000

Principal Shareholders: Osama H Al-Sayed; Sheikh Abdullah Baroom; Aiman Hamadallah

Date of Establishment: November 1977

No of Employees: 450

SAUDI CONSULTING HOUSE (SCH)

PO Box 1267, Riyadh 11431

Tel: 4484688, 4484533, 4484588

Cable: Devind Riyadh

Telex: 401152, 404380

Telefax: 4484447

Chairman: HE Abdul Aziz Abdullah Al Zamil (Minister of Industry and Electricity)

Directors: Ahmed Saleh Al Twaijri (Vice Chairman and Managing Director), Prince Abdullah Bin Faisal Bin Turki, Mahmoud Abdullah Taiba, Mobarak Al Al Khafrah, Ibrahim A Bin Salamah, Reda M Abbar

Senior Executives: Dr Tajeddin Amin (Director General for Administration & Finance), Abulaziz A Al Khathlan (Director General for Economic & Management Consultancies), Abdul Hamid M Al Awadi (Director General for Engineering Consultancies), Siraj Qutah (Director SCH/Jeddah Branch), Salah Ahmad Al Obeidallah (Director Central Services), Mohammad Omar Ben Ateeq (Head of Information & Public Relations), Abdullah Al Salim (Director SCH/Dammam Branch)

PRINCIPAL ACTIVITIES: Technical, industrial, economic, management and engineering consultancy

Branch Offices: Jeddah: PO Box 1001, Jeddah 21431, Tel 6676388, Fax 6676392; Dammam: PO Box 1234, Dammam 31431, Tel 8576972, Fax 8571298

Principal Shareholders: Government owned

Date of Establishment: Formerly Industrial Studies & Development Centre

No of Employees: 263

SAUDI CONTRACTORS

Osman A Osman & Co

PO Box 5428, Riyadh 11422

Tel: 4262909

Telex: 401337 Osman Sj

PRINCIPAL ACTIVITIES: Building and civil engineering contractors; construction plant

Branch Offices: PO Box 1598, Makkah, Tel 5433658/9, Telex 750065; PO Box 624, Jeddah, Tel 6875621/3, 6872356, Telex 601314

Date of Establishment: 1975

SAUDI CREDIT BANK

PO Box 3401, Riyadh 11471

Tel: 4029128, 4029625

Cable: Taslif Riyadh

Chairman: Osama Jaafar Faqeeh

Directors: Abdullah M Al Dhabeib, Mohammad Al Dhabeib, Abdulrahman Eid Al Ami, Sulaiman Al Mandeel, Dr A Naiem, Abdulmuhsen Al Saleh, Abdulaziz Al Mehanna, Mohammed Al Hesani

PRINCIPAL ACTIVITIES: Providing interests free loans to Saudi lower income groups for specified purposes limited means

Branch Offices: Baha, Bishah, Buraydah, Dammam, Dawadmi, Hail, Hasa, Jizan, Jeddah, Jouf, Kharj, Khamis Mushayt, Majma, Makkah, Medina, Najran, Qunfutha, Riyadh, Tabuk, Taif, Wadi Al Dawasir, Namas, Qurayat

Date of Establishment: 1973

No of Employees: 350

SAUDI DANISH CONSTRUCTION CORPORATION LTD

PO Box 1296, Dammam 31431
Tel: 8571636, 8570372, 8578411
Telex: 801371 Sdcc Sj

Chairman: Sheikh Abdul Rahman A Al-Turki
Directors: Niels Uldall, Joern Rusz, Ziad Yamut, Robin Rathray

PRINCIPAL ACTIVITIES: Construction, civil, mechanical and electrical maintenance and operation. Turnkey industrial projects, specially in food-processing, vehicle and heavy equipment repair
Principal Bankers: Albank Alsaudi Alhollandi

Principal Shareholders: H Hoffmann and Sons, Copenhagen, Denmark; Sheikh Abdul Rahman Al Al-Turki, Dammam
Date of Establishment: 1975
No of Employees: 500

SAUDI DAVY CO LTD

PO Box 1006, Dammam 31431
Tel: 8344277, 8343781
Telex: 802615 Davydm Sj
Telefax: 8343057

Chairman: Sheikh Saleh Bin Salem Bin Mahfouz
Senior Executives: Edward Vasey (Managing Director), Martin J Parr (Finance Director), Daryl B Jones (Sales Manager), T Bawazir

PRINCIPAL ACTIVITIES: Engineering and contracting, services for process industries, oil and petrochemical, water treament, pollution control etc
Branch Offices: c/o Saudi Economic & Development Co, PO Box 7162, Riyadh, Tel 4763698, Fax 4765488, Telex 404603/4
Parent Company: Saudi Economic & Development Co, PO Box 4384, Jeddah; Davy McKee (London) Ltd, Davy House, 68 Hammersmith Road, London W14 8YW, UK
Affiliated Companies: Davy McKee Houston, 2925 Briarpark, Suite 700, Houston, Texas 77042
Principal Bankers: National Commercial Bank
Financial Information:

	1989 SR'000
Sales turnover	1,621
Profits	30
Authorised capital	11,000
Paid-up capital	11,000
Total assets	3,862

Principal Shareholders: Saudi Economic and Development Co; Davy McKee (London) Ltd
Date of Establishment: 1978

SAUDI DEVELOPMENT & TRADING CENTRE CO

PO Box 6554, Riyadh 11452
Tel: 4776981
Cable: Devcent Riyadh
Telex: 401886 Sdvtc Sj
Telefax: 4772447

Senior Executives: Abdul Kader M Hussein (General Manager), Osamah A M Hussein (Deputy General Manager)

PRINCIPAL ACTIVITIES: General trading, contracting and engineering; supply, installation of electrical, electronic and telecommunication equipment; construction
Parent Company: Beta Company/Abdul Aziz Zaidan & Partners
Principal Bankers: Arab National Bank, Riyadh

Principal Shareholders: Abdul Kader M Hussein, Osamah A M Hussein
Date of Establishment: 1978
No of Employees: 50

SAUDI DEVELOPMENT CORP

PO Box 4992, Jeddah 21412
Tel: 6658010
Telex: 601430 Focus Sj

PRINCIPAL ACTIVITIES: Insurance agents, brokers and services; scientific and optical instruments; safety and fire control equipment, electrical engineering and general contractors
Branch Offices: PO Box 542, Riyadh 11421, Tel 4766633, 4766635

Date of Establishment: 600

SAUDI DIESEL GENERATORS CO LTD

PO Box 87, Dhahran Airport 31932
Tel: 8576769, 8578028, 8578036, 8577816
Cable: Saudiesel
Telex: 802061 Saudsl SJ
Telefax: 8574681

Chairman: Mohammed S Abduljawad
Directors: Ghassan S Abduljawad, Ziyad S Abduljawad, Raad S Abduljawad
Senior Executives: Omar S Eanadeen (Managing Director), Rasheed Khan (Director of Finance), Javed Aslam (Director of Sales), Willie Neil (Director of Service & Manufacturing), Raad Abduljawad (Marketing Manager), David Field (Peace Shield Project Manager), Hank Thompson (Riyadh Branch Manager), Sikandar Bashir (Jeddah Branch Manager)

PRINCIPAL ACTIVITIES: Manufacturers of diesel generator sets from 30 KW to 2000 KW, plus rental units, spare parts and service
Principal Agencies: The sister co Saudi Diesel Marketing is the sole distributor for Detroit Diesel Corp; Allison Transmission Div of General Motors; Donaldson Co; Electro Motive Div of General Motors; Stewart & Stevenson Services Inc
Branch Offices: Riyadh: PO Box 17064, Riyadh 11484; Jeddah: PO Box 17001, Jeddah 21484
Associated Companies: Saudi Diesel Marketing, PO Box 87, Dhahran Airport 31932
Principal Bankers: Riyad Bank; National Commercial Bank
Financial Information:

	1989 SR'000	1990 SR'000
Sales turnover	85,000	67,000
Profits	10,500	6,700
Authorised capital	58,000	58,000
Paid-up capital	25,000	25,000
Total assets	61,000	62,000

Principal Shareholders: Abduljawad family (100%)
Date of Establishment: 1399H
No of Employees: 196

SAUDI ELECTRIC SUPPLY CO (SESCO)

PO Box 230, Al-Khobar 31952
Tel: (03) 8577738 (6 lines)
Telex: 871405 Sesco Sj
Telefax: 8573293

Chairman: Sheikh Ali A Tamimi
Directors: Jack E Denoe (Managing Director)

PRINCIPAL ACTIVITIES: Distributors of electrical supplies and equipment, also technical and commissioning services
Principal Agencies: USA: General Electric, Carol, Carlon, Wheatland, Crouse-Hinds, 0Z-Gedney, 3M, Lithonia, Steel City, Klein, Greenlee, Alpha Wire, Thomas & Betts, Chase-Shawmut, Prescolite, Ideal, Blackburn, Burndy, Asco, Hubbell, Powercon, Alflex, Precision Controls
Branch Offices: Riyadh: PO Box 7557, Riyadh 11472, Tel (01) 4983844, Fax 4985180, Telex 402842 SESCO SJ; Jeddah: PO Box 16704, Jeddah 21474, Tel (02) 6830416, 6820356, Fax 6820339, Telex 603287 SESCO SJ
Principal Bankers: Albank Alsaudi Alhollandi, Al-Khobar

Financial Information:

	SR'000
Sales turnover	123,000
Paid-up capital	3,500

Principal Shareholders: Sheikh Ali A Tamimi
Date of Establishment: 1976
No of Employees: 70

SAUDI ELECTRO MECHANICAL & AIR CONDITIONING CORP (SEMACOM)

PO Box 5411, Jeddah 21422
Tel: 6519021, 6518389, 6519536
Cable: Conditioning Jeddah
Telex: 600170 Smacom Sj
Telefax: 6519733

Directors: Eng Hazem Sammakieh (General Manager)
Senior Executives: Eng Amr Sammakieh (Deputy General Manager)

PRINCIPAL ACTIVITIES: Installation and erection of electrical projects and street lighting; supply and installation of power stations equipment. Distribution, installation and maintenance of air-conditioning equipment
Principal Agencies: Osram GEC, UK; Dorman Smith, UK; Thorn Lighting, UK; Rawlinson, UK; Concrete Utilities; Iwasaki Electric, Japan; Acec, Belgium; Philips, Netherlands; Adew/Isocel, France; Airwell, France; Cell Pack, Switzerland; Precision Multiple Control, USA; Kistenmacher, W Germany; Pissasco, Italy; Ghisalba, Italy; Borra, Italy; Comar Condensatori, Italy
Branch Offices: Location in Jeddah: Aljouhara Bldg, Baghdadia; also Riyadh: PO Box 192, Tel 4767690; Makkah; Medinah
Subsidiary/Associated Companies: Wooden Shutters Branch of Semocom Co; Sammakieh for Contracting & Central Agencies (ESTMAC); Sammakieh International Est
Principal Bankers: Saudi Cairo Bank, Jeddah; Saudi British Bank, Jeddah

Date of Establishment: 1967

SAUDI ELECTRONIC CIRCUITS LTD (FAAT)

PO Box 41811, Riyadh 11531
Tel: 4762184, 4777541, 4778837, 4778468, 4763941
Cable: FAAT, Riyadh
Telex: 401320 FAAT SJ
Telefax: 4769303

President: Fares M Attar
Senior Executives: Sami A Saeed (Managing Director), Rafik Taleb (Manager Finance & Administration)

PRINCIPAL ACTIVITIES: Electrical, mechanical and electronic works including erection, installation, and operation and maintenance of the same; turn-key projects; training courses
Branch Offices: Jeddah: PO Box 6359, Tel 6513352, Telex 601778 FAAT SJ
Subsidiary Companies: National System & Communication Co, PO Box 681, Riyadh 11421
Principal Bankers: National Commercial Bank, Nasseriya Branch, Riyadh; Societe Bancaire Arabe, Paris, France
Financial Information:

	SR'000
Sales turnover	40,000
Profits	3,000
Authorised capital	5,000
Paid-up capital	5,000

Principal Shareholders: L S Abou Zeid, W M Attar, S A Saeed
Date of Establishment: 1965
No of Employees: 175

SAUDI ELECTRONICS & TRADING CO LTD (SETCO)

PO Box 59993, Riyadh 11535
Tel: 01-4626276
Telefax: 01-4620235

Chairman: Ghassan Ahmed Abdallah Al Suleiman
Directors: Mohd Ali Alireza, Usama Kabbani
Senior Executives: Sufian M Azm (Managing Director)

PRINCIPAL ACTIVITIES: Electronic and telecommunication equipment, safety and security equipment, medical and scientific equipment etc, electronic engineering consultants, data processing and data communication, marine communication and navigation equipment, operation and maintenance
Principal Agencies: Rolm Corp, Taiko, Jutland, Schlage, Fujitsu, JRC
Branch Offices: Jeddah: PO Box 8122, Jeddah 21482, Tel 6431479
Parent Company: Alireza Group and Suleiman Group
Principal Bankers: Bank Al Jazira, Saudi American Bank, Albank Alsaudi Alhollandi

Date of Establishment: 1979
No of Employees: 40

SAUDI ELEVATOR & TRADE EST

PO Box 7517, Jeddah 21472
Tel: 6695438, 6675408
Cable: Apsanetraco
Telex: 600861 Apsa Sj
Telefax: 6691683

Chairman: Jamal M A Oraif
Senior Executives: Syed Munawar Hussain (Executive Manager)

PRINCIPAL ACTIVITIES: Import, sales and installation and servicing of elevators, electrical appliances, aluminium products, companies representation and general trade
Branch Offices: Yanbu, PO Box 459, Tel 3968918
Principal Bankers: Saudi Cairo Bank, Jeddah; Arab National Bank, Jeddah

Date of Establishment: 1977
No of Employees: 250

SAUDI ELEVATOR CO LTD (SCHINDLER)

Head Office, PO Box 1150, Jeddah 21431
Tel: 6515244 (6 lines)
Cable: Elevator
Telex: 601502 Liftco Sj
Telefax: 6512948

Chairman: Rizk Iskandar Rizk
Directors: Moh A Hafez El-Farra (General Manager), Selim A Dariane (Executive Manager)
Senior Executives: Ahmad Murad Harara (Finance Manager), Salah Abdullah Khamis (Sales Manager), Mohammad Aslam (Import Manager), Mohammad Fayyazuddin (Purchasing Manager), Mohammad Attieh (Technical Manager), Elie Abi-Aad (Erection Manager), Chafic Bechara (Maintenance Manager), Ahmad El Muzayyen (Personnel Manager), George Saad (Company Secretary)

PRINCIPAL ACTIVITIES: Supply, installation and servicing of elevators, escalators and belt-conveyers equipment
Principal Agencies: Schindler, Rapistan
Branch Offices: Regional Branches: Riyadh: PO Box 192, Riyadh 11411, Tel 4767690, Telex 402035, Fax 4765782; Al-Khobar; PO Box 505, Alkhobar 31952, Tel 8644194, Telex 870594, Fax 8946693; Makkah: PO Box 2921, Tel 5450526, Fax 5459822; Madinah: PO Box 402, Tel 8253954, Fax 8267663; Taif: PO Box 580, Tel 7328638; Tabouk: PO Box 172, Tel 4229220; Khamis Mushait: PO Box 748, Tel 7328638; Yanbu: PO Box 437, Tel 3223224; Buraidah: PO Box 936, Tel 3242473; Al-Ahsa: PO Box 1592, Tel 5875490; Jubail: PO Box 625, Tel 3613687

Principal Bankers: Saudi Cairo Bank, Jeddah; National Commercial Bank, Jeddah; Al-Bank Al-Saudi Al-Fransi, Jeddah; Banque Libano-Francaise, Paris

Financial Information:

	1989 SR'000
Sales turnover	47,000
Profits	5,427
Authorised capital	30,000
Paid-up capital	30,000
Total assets & investments	53,000

Principal Shareholders: Sheikh Kamal Adham; Sheikh Faisal K Adham
Date of Establishment: 1957
No of Employees: 500

SAUDI ENGINEERING & CONSTRUCTION CO LTD

PO Box 8747, Jeddah 21492
Tel: 6534456, 6531908
Telex: 601580 Towers Sj

President: Khalid A Taher

PRINCIPAL ACTIVITIES: Building, electrical and mechanical engineering, drilling and pipeline contractors, oil services, communications equipment
Branch Offices: Dhahran; Riyadh

Date of Establishment: 1979

SAUDI ENGINEERING CONSULTANTS BUREAU
S.E.C.O.N.

PO Box 7597, Riyadh 11472
Tel: (01) 4654836, 4656331
Cable: CONENSAB
Telex: 400168 Secon Sj
Telefax: 4631033

President: Kamal Akif Kazim
Senior Executives: Mohammad Qamaruddin (Vice President), Ahmed Bassiouny (Vice President)

PRINCIPAL ACTIVITIES: Consultants (engineering), architects/urban planners, electrical engineering, land survey
Branch Offices: Scet-Secon-Kattan Joint Venture, Makkah Housing Project, Po Box 6232, Makkah, Tel 5367070, 5364141, Telex 540529 SSK JV Sj, Fax 5363232
Associated Companies: Scet International, France
Principal Bankers: National Commercial BAnk, Riyadh

Principal Shareholders: 100% Saudi firm
Date of Establishment: 1975
No of Employees: 70

SAUDI ENGINEERING GROUP

PO Box 1835, AlKhobar 31952
Tel: 8644558, 8941064
Cable: ENGINEERCO
Telex: 870315 Segco Sj

President: Ghazi A Al-Shahwan
Directors: Thomas O'Hare (Managing Director)
Senior Executives: A H Al Dughaither (Deputy Managing Director Administration)

PRINCIPAL ACTIVITIES: Architects, planners, engineers
Subsidiary Companies: Lemco Engineers Inc, USA; Haiste & Partners, UK; Triad Architects, UK
Principal Bankers: Saudi British Bank; Saudi Al-Fransi Bank

Financial Information:

	1989 SR'000
Sales turnover	25,000
Profits	2,950
Authorised capital	1,000
Paid-up capital	1,000
Total assets	1,059

Principal Shareholders: Ghazi A Al-Shahwan, Ralf Young, G H Mathew
Date of Establishment: 1978
No of Employees: 95

SAUDI ENTERPRISES CO LTD
S.A.E.C.O.

PO Box 9233, Jeddah 21413
Tel: 6670084, 6670088
Cable: SAECO
Telex: 603261 Saesaj SJ
Telefax: 6672831

Senior Executives: Eng Gian Francesco Imperiali (General Manager)

PRINCIPAL ACTIVITIES: High & medium voltage power transmission lines, electrical substations, microwave telecommunication system, and radio antennae, railway electrification

SAUDI ERICSSON COMMUNICATIONS CO LTD

PO Box 9903, Riyadh 11423
Tel: 4785800
Cable: SAUDERIC
Telex: 400875 Saric Sj
Telefax: 4793622

Chairman: Sheikh Ahmed Al Juffali
Senior Executives: Abdullah S AL Banyan (General Manager), Ramzi Louza (Deputy General Manager), Robert L Merrill (Marketing Manager), Joseph Saqr (Economy Manager), Joseph Al Haddad (Riyadh Branch Manager), Wael Rawazik (Jeddah Branch Manager), Riad Hamdan (Dammam Branch Manager), David Jackson (Chief Accountant)

PRINCIPAL ACTIVITIES: Sales, installation and maintenance of telecommunication and datacommunications systems including telephone systems, security, hospital system, land mobile radio, paging, intercom, closed circuit TV, clock system, data products, facsimile, telephone cables and network material; turnkey projects and networks in telecommunications and datacommunications
Principal Agencies: Ericsson Group, Sweden; GNT, Denmark; Case Communications, UK; Benner Nawman, USA
Branch Offices: Jeddah: PO Box 8838, Jeddah 21492, Tel 667600; Dammam: PO Box 450, Dammam 31411, Tel 8262222
Parent Company: E A Juffali & Bros Group of Companies
Principal Bankers: Riyad Bank, Riyadh; Arab National Bank, Riyadh

Financial Information:

	1989 SR'000
Sales turnover	140,000
Authorised capital	10,000
Paid-up capital	10,000

Principal Shareholders: E A Juffali & Bros, Saudi Arabia
Date of Establishment: 1st July, 1980
No of Employees: 220

SAUDI EST FOR SAFETY EQUIPMENT

PO Box 17772, Riyadh 11494
Tel: 4760965, 4783511, 4783835
Telex: 400474 SESE SJ
Telefax: 4767670

PRINCIPAL ACTIVITIES: Manufacture and supply of fire fighting
and safety equipment
Branch Offices: Jeddah: PO Box 8605, Jeddah 21492, Tel
6673813, Telex 602820, Fax 6651258

SAUDI ETA LTD

PO Box 6591, Jeddah 21452
Tel: 6720186
Telex: 603083 Etajed Sj
Telefax: 6726753

Chairman: Abdul Aziz Ahmed Saab
Directors: N D S Sathak Ansari (Managing Director), Hani
Abdulaziz Saab (Administrative Director)

PRINCIPAL ACTIVITIES: Electromechanical services
Branch Offices: PO Box 20510, Riyadh; PO Box 1269, Medina;
PO Box 911, Dhahran
Subsidiary Companies: Emirates Trading Agency, PO Box 5239,
Dubai, UAE; Associated Constructions, PO Box 5238, Dubai,
UAE; Saudi Ascon Ltd, PO Box 12695, Jeddah, Saudi Arabia;
East Coast Construction & Industries, India
Principal Bankers: Bank of Oman Ltd; National Commercial
Bank; Bank Al-Jazira; Saudi Cairo Bank
Financial Information:

	SR'000
Authorised capital	10,000
Paid-up capital	6,000

Principal Shareholders: Abdul Aziz Ahmed Saab; Hani Abdulaziz
Saab; Emirates Trading Agency, Dubai
Date of Establishment: 23rd June 1979
No of Employees: 800

SAUDI EXPRESS COMPANY

PO Box 559, Alkhobar 31952
Tel: 8644260, 8945880
Telex: 870070 Riri Sj, 871416 Sekici Sj

Directors: Zuhair Amin Ghazzawi (Managing Director)

PRINCIPAL ACTIVITIES: General contracting and maintenance,
supply of tiles and building materials, motor scooters;
cleaning contractors
Branch Offices: Riyadh: PO Box 3362, Tel 4640866; Jeddah: PO
Box 12527, Tel 6832872
Principal Bankers: Riyad Bank

No of Employees: 200

SAUDI FIBREGLASS FACTORIES

PO Box 5645, Jeddah 21432
Tel: 6824337, 6824338
Telex: 600617 Dugeil SJ, 605469 DOKEL SJ

Chairman: Mohammed Salim Al-Dugeil
Senior Executives: Mohammed Saeed Bahakim (General
Manager)

PRINCIPAL ACTIVITIES: Manufacture of glass reinforced plastic
products; grp. water tanks, sanitary fittings, boats, etc
Branch Offices: Head office in Prince Fahad Road opposite
Medina Al Hujaj (Sherifia)
Principal Bankers: Arab National Bank

Date of Establishment: 1979
No of Employees: 60

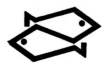

SAUDI FISHERIES COMPANY

PO Box 6535, Dammam 31452
Tel: 8573979
Cable: SAFISH
Telex: 802020 SAFISH SJ
Telefax: 8572493

Chairman: HE Dr Abdul Rahman Bin Abdul Aziz Al Sheikh
Directors: HRH Prince Mote'b Bin Abdul Aziz, Sheikh Ali Al
Tamimi, Sheikh Mohammad Abdul Aziz Al Nimr, Sheikh
Mohammad Khalifa Al Gosaibi, Dr Abdul Mohsen Al
Rowaished, Ibraheim Saudi Al Khoziem, Abdul Rahman Abdul
Aziz Al Hakbani
Senior Executives: Dr Nasser Othman Al-Saleh (General
Manager), Suleiman S Al-Sarraf (Dy General Manager
Operations), Musaid A Al Faiz (Dy General Manager
Marketing), Ahmed Al Amoudi (Manager Retail Operations),
Kamil Saadah (Manager Import-Export), Essam El Sharqawi
(Manager Finance), Mohammad Al Dossary (Wholesale
Manager), Nasser Al Jameel (Manager Riyadh Branch), Sa'd
Al Ghamdi (Manager Jeddah Branch), Riyadh Al Sarraf
(Manager Jizan Operations), Fahd Al Sunaid (Manager Dubai
Branch)

PRINCIPAL ACTIVITIES: Fishing, processing and marketing
Branch Offices: Dammam Operations Centre: Tel 8573479;
Riyadh: Tel 4051166, Fax 4056298; Jizan: Tel 3220633, Fax
3171096; Jeddah: Tel 6202246, Fax 6205061
Principal Bankers: National Commercial Bank, Dammam
Financial Information:

	1988/89 SR'000	1989/90 SR'000
Sales turnover	192,420	220,787
Profits	29,159	32,384
Authorised capital	100,000	100,000
Paid-up capital	100,000	100,000
Total assets	266,782	282,937

Principal Shareholders: 40% owned by the Government and
60% Saudi Citizens
Date of Establishment: 29.3.1401H (4/2/1981)
No of Employees: 863

SAUDI FOOD SUPPLIES & SUPERMARKETS CORP LTD

PO Box 1935, Jeddah 21441
Tel: 6448383
Telex: 600709 SAFA SJ

Chairman: Dr Gaith Rashad Pharaon
Directors: Wabel Rashad Pharaon
Senior Executives: Zuhair Hatahet (Executive Vice President)

PRINCIPAL ACTIVITIES: Import and distribution of fresh and
frozen foods, meat, poultry, fish, vegetables and fruits
Branch Offices: Riyadh; Dammam; Taif; Jizan; Nejran; Abha;
Medina
Subsidiary/Associated Companies: Saudi Research &
Development Corporation Ltd
Principal Bankers: National Commercial Bank, Jeddah
Financial Information:

	SR'000
Authorised capital	100,000
Paid-up capital	100,000

Principal Shareholders: Dr Gaith R Pharaon; Saudi Research &
Development Corporation Ltd
Date of Establishment: 1978
No of Employees: 250

SAUDI FRUIT JUICE & BEVERAGES INDUSTRY

PO Box 16302, Jeddah 21464
Tel: 6364153, 6377075
Cable: Kudwah
Telex: 603669 SFJI SJ
Telefax: 6375189

Chairman: Mahmood Mohamed Saeed
President: Abdul Khaliq Mohamed Saeed
Senior Executives: Taisir Tmelieh (General Manager)

PRINCIPAL ACTIVITIES: Production of fruit juices and soft drinks
Principal Agencies: Pepsi, Lazezah Juice
Branch Offices: Dammam, Tel 8422242; Medina, Tel 8371436; Agents: Riyadh, Tel 4985367; Yanbu, Tel 8234025; Makkah, Tel 5446003
Parent Company: Mahmood Saeed Establishment for Trade & Industry
Principal Bankers: Saudi Cairo Bank; National Commercial Bank; Bank Al Jazirah
Financial Information:

	1990 SR'000
Sales turnover	159,000
Authorised capital	30,000
Paid-up capital	30,000

Principal Shareholders: Mahmood Mohamed Saeed; Abdul Khaliq Mohamed Saeed
Date of Establishment: 1978
No of Employees: 300

SAUDI FUND FOR DEVELOPMENT

PO Box 50483, Riyadh 11523
Tel: 4640292 (5 lines)
Telex: 401145 Sunduq Sj; 401744
Telefax: 4647450

Chairman: HE Mohammad Ali Abalkhail (Minister of Finance & National Economy)
Directors: HE Mohammad A Al Sugair (Vice Chairman & Managing Director), Dr Abdulaziz Al Turki (Deputy Managing Director), Dr Saleh Al Humeidan (Deputy Managing Director Technical Affairs), Saleh Al Mos'ad (Deputy Managing Director International Relations), Saleh A Al Hegelan (Director General Loan Admin), Abdrahman Sehaibani (Director General Research & Economic Studies), Jameel Ameen (Director General Intenational Relations), Mohmmmad Al Kharashi (Director General Capital Admin), Abdullah Al Othaim (Director General Internal Audit), Abdullah Al Assaf (Director General General Admin), Yahya Kazim Baradah (Director Computer Dept), A Rahman Al Duwaihi (Director Public Relations), Othamn Abdul Karim (Director Vice Chairman's Office)

PRINCIPAL ACTIVITIES: Development fund, financing projects in developing countries in Africa and Asia
Financial Information:

	SR'000
Authorised capital	25,000,000

Date of Establishment: 1974
No of Employees: Approx 200

SAUDI GENERAL INSURANCE CO LTD

PO Box 1866, Jeddah 21441
Tel: 6516610, 6519442
Cable: Naskar
Telex: 602515 SAUGEN Sj
Telefax: 6511720

Chairman: Sheikh Abdul-Aziz Al-Abdullah Al-Suleiman
Directors: Maurice Karaoglan
Senior Executives: Pierre Chidiac (Managing Director), Eugene S Nader General Manager), Michel J Abu Jamra (Deputy General Manager), George T Asmar (Finance Manager)

PRINCIPAL ACTIVITIES: All classes of insurance and reinsurance
Branch Offices: PO Box 1866, Jeddah 21441; PO Box 1129, Dammam 31431; PO Box 5516, Riyadh 11432; PO Box 447, Tabuk
Parent Company: Saudi General Insurance Co Ltd, Bermuda
Financial Information:

	1989/90 US$'000
Sales turnover	10,883
Profits	224
Authorised capital	4,000
Paid-up capital	1,000
Total assets	6,576

Principal Shareholders: Sheikh Abdul-Aziz Al-Abdullah Al-Suleiman; Cedar Insurance & Reinsurance Co Ltd
Date of Establishment: May 1976
No of Employees: 80

SAUDI GOLD CO LTD

PO Box 8020, Riyadh 11482
Tel: 4980416, 4980128
Cable: Goldco
Telex: 400558 GOLDCO SJ
Telefax: 4981272

Directors: Nizar Abdul Aziz Al Raee (Managing Director)
Senior Executives: Aijaz Abdul Aziz Al Raee (General Manager)

PRINCIPAL ACTIVITIES: Gold refinery, all kinds of jewellery (gold 21K & 18K), coins and ingotes
Branch Offices: Saudi Gold & Jewellery Marketing Co Ltd, PO Box 4130, Jeddah 21491
Subsidiary Companies: Al Raee Group Ltd, PO Box 1513, Madina Munawara; Saudi Spinning & Weaving Industries Ltd, PO Box 4132, Jeddah
Principal Bankers: Saudi British Bank; Saudi American Bank
Financial Information:

	1989 SR'000	1990 SR'000
Sales turnover	383,900	-
Profits (loss)	4,287	(932)
Authorised capital	72,900	72,900
Paid-up capital	18,225	18,225
Total assets	38,184	23,000

Principal Shareholders: Sheikh Ibrahim Mohammad Al Fadel; Nizar Abdul Aziz Al Raee
Date of Establishment: 1398H
No of Employees: 165

SAUDI GULF CORPORATION

PO Box 3452, Jeddah 21471
Tel: 6422328, 6423040, 6432472
Telex: 601219 Somcol Sj

Directors: Abdullah A Kadi (Managing Director)

PRINCIPAL ACTIVITIES: General, building and civil contractors; import and distribution of motor vehicles, trucks and heavy equipment; plant hire; air services, etc

Date of Establishment: 1964

SAUDI HOSPITALS CO LTD

PO Box 75, Jeddah 21411
Tel: 6607172
Cable: Licontrex
Telex: 600077 Contrx Sj

Chairman: Sheikh Talal Khalid Idriss
Senior Executives: Bassam A Kawwass (Vice-President)

PRINCIPAL ACTIVITIES: Owns and operates private hospitals; management and operators, services to other private and government hospitals; pre-paid health insurance

Branch Offices: Location in Jeddah: Idriss Bldg, Off Medina Road; also branches in London, Chicago, Beirut
Parent Company: Idriss Group
Principal Bankers: Saudi American Bank; Saudi French Bank
Financial Information:

	SR'000
Authorised capital	6,300
Paid-up capital	6,300

Principal Shareholders: Dr Khalid Idriss Sons Company; Sheikh Abdulaziz Abdullah Al-Suleiman
Date of Establishment: 1980

SAUDI HOTELS & RESORT AREAS CO

PO Box 5500, Riyadh 11422
Tel: 4657177
Cable: FANADEK
Telex: 400366 SHRACO SJ
Telefax: 4657172

Chairman: Dr Faisal S Al Bashir
Members: Soliman S Al Humayyed (Vice Chairman), Soliman Al Mandeel, Eng Abdulla M Al Issa, Mohamed A Al Ankary, Eng Abdulaziz A Kamel, Mohamed H Al Ohali, Nasser M Al Subeiei, Abdulla I Al Hudaithi, Abdulmunem Rashed Al Rashed, Abdulaziz Al Jasser
Senior Executives: Eng Abdul Aziz S Al Ambar (Director General), Osama A Kamakhi (Deputy Director General), Abdulrahman Al Dohaim (Finance Director), Ghaleb Al Muqait (Central Purchasing Manager), Abdalla Al Shamsan (Director Projects Dept), Nabil Shono (Director Administration Dept), Saad Alkanhal (Director Recreation & Catering Dept), Hamdi Farag (Director Regional Operations), Abdulwahab Al Bakhett (Internal Auditor)

PRINCIPAL ACTIVITIES: Hotels and tourism (hotels, resorts and amusement parks)
Subsidiary Companies: Makkah Hotels Co; Tabuk Hotels Co; Al Madina Hotels Co; Daresco; Gulf Resort Areas Co; National Co for Development & Tourism Investment
Principal Bankers: Saudi French Bank; Riyad Bank; National Commercial Bank
Financial Information:

	1989/90 SR'000
Total revenue	110,811
Net income	48,013
Authorised capital	500,000
Paid-up capital	500,000
Total assets	773,947

Principal Shareholders: Saudi Government Agencies and Saudi Citizens
Date of Establishment: 1976
No of Employees: 1,300

SAUDI IMPORT CO

PO Box 42, Jeddah 21411
Tel: 6518084, 6518900, 6532536, 6517348
Cable: Central
Telex: 601507 Banaja Sj
Telefax: 6516237

Chairman: Abdellatif S Banaja
Directors: Abdel Salam S Banaja (Partner), Abdel Majid Banaja (Partner)
Senior Executives: Hassan Bashammakh (General Manager), Ghassan Husami (Deputy General Manager)

PRINCIPAL ACTIVITIES: Import and distribution of pharmaceuticals and toilet goods
Principal Agencies: F Hoffman La Roche & Co, Basle; Lederle Int (Cyanamid), New York; Vick International, New York; Glaxo Group, London; Sterling Winthrop, USA; Davis & Jeck, NY, USA; Allen and Hanburg; Elder Pharmaceuticals, Ohio; Geistlitch, Switzerland; British Cod Liver Oil, UK
Branch Offices: Riyadh; Dammam

Subsidiary Companies: Banaja Medical Agencies, Riyadh and Dammam
Principal Bankers: National Commercial Bank, Jeddah

Date of Establishment: 1934
No of Employees: 150

SAUDI INDUSTRIAL CONTRACTING CO LTD
S.I.C.C. Limited

PO Box 6148, Riyadh 11442
Tel: 4040328 (6 lines)
Cable: Selectric
Telex: 405707 SICC SJ
Telefax: 4040436

Chairman: Sheikh Abdul Aziz Al Sabhan
Directors: Nelson M Gibb, R K Elston
Senior Executives: G I Edisbury (General Manager),

PRINCIPAL ACTIVITIES: Electrical, mechanical and multi-service engineering contractors
Branch Offices: PO Box 19449, Jeddah, Tel 6712510, Telex 600228 SICC SJ
Parent Company: BICC - UK
Associated Companies: Balfour Kilpatrick International (BICC/Balfour Beatty Group)
Principal Bankers: Saudi British Bank

Principal Shareholders: Balfour Kilpatrick Ltd, UK (50%); A A Al-Sabhan (50%)
Date of Establishment: December 1975
No of Employees: 150

SAUDI INDUSTRIAL DEVELOPMENT FUND (SIDF)

PO Box 4143, King Abdulaziz Road, Riyadh 11149
Tel: 4774002
Cable: Banksinaie Riyadh
Telex: 401065; 402583 Sidfnd SJ
Telefax: 01-4790165

Chairman: Dr Saleh Al Omair
Senior Executives: Saleh A Al-Naim (Director General), Husni H Nahhas (Manager Projects Dept), Abdulmajeed Al Wohabe (Manager Operations & Admin), Dr Othman Al Houkail (Manager Legal Dept), Saleh Al Athel (Manager Human Resources), Ghassan Al Butairi (Controller)

PRINCIPAL ACTIVITIES: Supports local industrial development sponsored by the private sector, by providing long-term interest-free loans to industry. Offers marketing, technical financial and administrative advice. Manages lending programs for cold stores and dates packaging
Financial Information:

	1990 SR'000
Authorised capital	8,000,000
Paid-up capital	7,000,000

Principal Shareholders: Government of Saudi Arabia
Date of Establishment: March 1974
No of Employees: 350

SAUDI INDUSTRIAL GAS CO

PO Box 291, Alkhobar 31952
Tel: 8641190, 8641184/5, 8641396
Cable: Oxygen
Telex: 870012 Oxygen Sj

Directors: Othman Abdullah Alothman, Monther Mohd Almutlaq, Sami Mubarak Ba'armeh, Mohd A Aziz Almuammar, Khalid A Ullah Almuammar
Senior Executives: Monther Mohd Almutlaq (Executive Manager), Dr Eng Mahmoud Abdulfattah Al Sharif (Deputy Executive Manager)

PRINCIPAL ACTIVITIES: Production of gas for domestic and industrial purposes (liquid oxygen and nitrogen, argon,

acetylene, carbon dioxide and dry ice hydrogen plants, ammonia, chlorine, helium and other gases), welding and safety equipment, fire extinguishers
Branch Offices: Dammam, Tel 8321512; Riyadh, Tel 4024114; Jeddah, Tel 6319809; Khafji; Jubail
Principal Bankers: Arab National Bank; Riyad Bank; Al Bank Al Saudi Al Hollandi
Financial Information:

	1990
	SR'000
Paid up capital	80,000

Date of Establishment: 1955

SAUDI INDUSTRIAL SERVICES CO (SISCO)

PO Box 319, Dhahran Airport 31932
Tel: 8644252, 8955032
Cable: Sisco
Telex: 871311 SIS SJ

Chairman: Shaikh Abdulmuhsin Almutlaq
Directors: Abdulmuhsin A Almutlaq, Mutlaq A Almutlaq
Senior Executives: Samy Nihad (General Manager)

PRINCIPAL ACTIVITIES: Commercial Division: Provides materials and services to the oil, power and related industries. Contracting Division: Suppliers and erectors of structural steel buildings, ventilators systems, industrial cranes, industrial painting, roofing and insulation, sectional steel tanks and other related services
Principal Agencies: Taylor Instruments, Flexi Box, Colt Int'l, BTR, Fuji Electric, Ebara Corp, Wiggin Alloys, G F Business Equipment, Braithwaite, Summit Tools, Rockbestos, Permali Gloucester, McGraw Edison, Sembawang Engg, Bado Equipment, Burndy, etc
Branch Offices: PO Box 10508, Jeddah, Tel 6824530; PO Box 1321, Riyadh, Tel 4792100
Parent Company: Abdulmuhsin and Mutlaq A Almutlaq
Principal Bankers: Al Bank Al Saudi Al Fransi, Alkhobar; National Commercial Bank, Alkhobar

Principal Shareholders: Abdulmuhsin & Mutlaq A Almutlaq, Alkhobar, Saudi Arabia
Date of Establishment: 1394H
No of Employees: 150

SAUDI INTERNATIONAL AERADIO LTD

PO Box 15357, Riyadh 11444
Tel: 4767764, 4777633, 4778577
Telex: 402746 SIAL SJ
Telefax: 4762808

Chairman: Ali A R Sindi
Directors: Ahmed A Turki, G P Uttorson, E C Carpenter

PRINCIPAL ACTIVITIES: Aviation, training and computer services, equipment supply and installation of turnkey telecommunication projects, medical services and hospital maintenance
Principal Agencies: International Aeradio Ltd Divisions
Branch Offices: Jeddah: PO Box 1694, Jeddah 21441, Tel 6654010, Fax 6600453
Principal Bankers: Saudi British Bank, Riyadh

Principal Shareholders: International Aeradio Ltd, UK; two prominent Saudi partners
Date of Establishment: January 1980
No of Employees: 57

SAUDI INTERNATIONAL BUSINESS CENTRE

PO Box 10925, Riyadh 11443
Tel: 4646148, 4658417
Telex: 403146
Telefax: 4630740

Chairman: Prince Abdulaziz Bin Ahmed Bin Turkey Al Sudairy
Directors: Ibrahim Al Rediny(Deputy General Manager), Mohammed Hussein Al Shamy (Asst General Manager

Finance), Claudio Sandoval (Asst General Manager Planning & Project)

PRINCIPAL ACTIVITIES: Technical services and training, agricultural produce farms, agricultural equipment sales and maintenance services, poultry farm, deep water well drilling, irrigation equipment sales, plant seeds, chemicals and equipment, electronic safety and testing equipment, limousine operators, agents and general traders, TV promotion and advertising
Principal Agencies: Bender, Germany; Industrial Parts Depot, USA; Biccotest, UK; Metrix, France; Electro Location, UK; Fuji Sangyo, Japan; Faz Trading, Cyprus
Branch Offices: PO Box 21444, Jeddah; PO Box 6553, Dammam; Buraidah (Maintenance Equipment Sales & Services Centre)
Subsidiary Companies: SIBC Technical Services Inc, USA, PO Box 2023, Casselberry, Florida, 32707, USA
Principal Bankers: United Saudi Commercial Bank; Saudi Cairo Bank; Saudi French Bank
Financial Information:

	1990
	SR'000
Paid-up capital	10,000
Total assets	40,000

Principal Shareholders: Abdulaziz Bin Ahmed Bin Turkey Al Sudairy
Date of Establishment: 1970
No of Employees: 110

SAUDI INTERNATIONAL CORPORATION (SIACO)

PO Box 4571, Jeddah 21412
Tel: 6719185, 6432088
Cable: Kazadyou
Telex: 601501 Stitifo Sj; 601806 Tranco Sj; 601096 Genery Sj

Directors: Sheikh Adnan Abdulrahman Abdulmajeed (Partner), Sheikh Muhammad Ibrahim Al Hied (Partner)

PRINCIPAL ACTIVITIES: Marketing and manufacturers' representation; supply of medical equipment and services; agricultural services; transportation
Subsidiary Companies: Saudi Medical Services Co Ltd (SAMESCO); Saudi International Transportation Co Ltd (SIATRACO); Saudi American Modern Agricultural Co Ltd; Italian Saudi Co Ltd (ITASCO)

SAUDI INTERNATIONAL GROUP LTD

PO Box 6891, Jeddah 21452
Tel: 6670654, 6671041
Cable: SINGLIMITED
Telex: 600237 GROUP SJ

Chairman: Abdullah Khayat
Directors: Thaher A Amr (Director General)

PRINCIPAL ACTIVITIES: General trading and contracting, maintenance, operations, companies, representation, manufacturing, and aviation division. Construction, technology systems and computer services, cleaning operations, supply of prefab houses, furniture etc
Principal Agencies: Joint ventures with: Initial Services Ltd, of UK (for cleaning); and with Teledyne SA, Geneva, Switzerland (for engineering, avionics, electronics etc); Management Agreement with Technology Systems Inc of USA (for providing computerized information, computer software, services and equipment, computer hardware etc)
Branch Offices: Tabuk; Medina, Riyadh, Alkhobar
Principal Bankers: National Commercial Bank

Principal Shareholders: Abdullah Khayat, Mahfooz Salim bin Mahfouz
Date of Establishment: May 1978
No of Employees: 100

SAUDI ARABIA

SAUDI INTERNATIONAL INVESTMENT CO

PO Box 1716, Jeddah 21441
Tel: 6532511 (5 lines)
Cable: MYHOME
Telex: 601214 EMAN SJ

President: Hani S Emam
Senior Executives: S A Muneer Ahmad (Group Manager,
   Administration & Commercial), M Mohsin Ghayur (Finance
   Manager)

PRINCIPAL ACTIVITIES: Financial consulting and development
   of projects in Saudi Arabia, advisory services, investment
   services
Branch Offices: Location in Jeddah: Emam Centre, Madina
   Road
Principal Bankers: Bank Al Jazirah; Saudi British Bank

Principal Shareholders: Hussain Abdul Latif, Abdullah Mehdi,
   Jamal Hasan Jawa, Ali Abdullah Tamimi, Hani S Emam
Date of Establishment: 1978
No of Employees: 100

SAUDI INTERNATIONAL PROPERTIES

PO Box 2734, Jeddah 21461
Tel: (02) 6672098/99
Telex: 600577 Siprop Sj

Chairman: Sheikh Salem M Bin Laden
Directors: Christopher F Vock (Managing Director), Rupert
   Armitage, Douglas McLeod

PRINCIPAL ACTIVITIES: Property and real estate management
   and consultancy
Principal Bankers: Saudi Cairo Bank

Principal Shareholders: Sheikh Salem M Binladen
Date of Establishment: 1979

SAUDI INTERNATIONAL TRANSPORT & CONTRACTING CO LTD

PO Box 7006, Jeddah 21462
Tel: 6710951, 6712385
Cable: Siacoport
Telex: 601096 GENRAY SJ
Telefax: 6713571

Chairman: Sheikh Mohammed I El Heid
Directors: Adnan S Malas (Managing Director)

PRINCIPAL ACTIVITIES: International and local transportation,
   customs clearance and forwarding
Principal Agencies: Iveco Trucks
Branch Offices: Riyadh, Amman, Athens, Germany
Parent Company: General Agencies & Contracting Co PO Box
   1693, Jeddah
Subsidiary/Associated Companies: Saudi International
   Corporation (SIACO), PO Box 4571, Jeddah
Principal Bankers: National Commercial Bank; Arab Bank

Principal Shareholders: Sheikh Mohammed I El Heid, Adnan S
   Malas
Date of Establishment: 1977
No of Employees: 300

SAUDI INVESTMENT & DEVELOPMENT CENTRE

PO Box 5791, Jeddah 21432
Tel: 6658396, 6657880, 6600928
Telex: 601275 Gmtco, 601260 Center Sj

President: Sheikh Zuhdi Bushnak
Directors: HRH Prince Abdul Aziz Bin Turki, Faisal Bushnak,
   Eng Salah Abdul Fattah, Dr Adil Bushnak

PRINCIPAL ACTIVITIES: Investment, marketing, contracting,
   civil engineering, computer services, water desalination
Branch Offices: Head Office: PO Box 2220, Riyadh, Telex
   401413 Center Sj; also branch in AlKhobar

Subsidiary/Associated Companies: Land Sea Transport Co (PO
   Box 5791, Jeddah); Gada Marketing & Trading; Saudi
   International Center (PO Box 3396, Jeddah); Saudi Trading &
   Contracting Center (PO Box 3396, Jeddah); Al Kawther Water
   Treatment Ltd; Al Thara Co Ltd, Saudi Arabia
Principal Bankers: Riyadh Bank; Saudi Cairo Bank
Financial Information:

	SR'000
Turnover	200,000
Capital	60,000
Paid-up capital	18,000

Date of Establishment: 1976
No of Employees: 300

SAUDI INVESTMENT BANK (THE)

PO Box 3533, Riyadh 11481
Tel: (01) 4778433
Cable: Sibcorp Riyadh
Telex: 401170 SAIBRH SJ
Telefax: 4776781

Chairman: Dr Abdulaziz O'Hali
Directors: Khaled S Al-Olayan, Omar Abdul Qadir Bajamal,
   Rashid Al-Mubarek Al-Muraishid, Soliman S Al-Humayyd, Dr
   Khaled Nahas, Salman Abbasi, Mitsuo Seta
Senior Executives: Mohamed F Daghistany (General Manager),
   Morshed M Al-Zughaibi (AGM, Administration & Financial
   Planning & Controls), Jack J Knippenberg (AGM, Treasury
   Institutional Personal & Retail Banking), Ali Ayanlar (AGM,
   Credit Policy & Planning), Hans Schlee (AGM Corporate
   Banking), Michael H Grimsdell (General Auditor)

PRINCIPAL ACTIVITIES: All banking activities incl current &
   saving accounts, treasury services, remittances, cash
   management, letters of credit, guarantees, personal banking,
   short and medium term lending, local share dealing, and trade
   financing, fiduciary placements
Branch Offices: Jeddah: PO Box 5577, Jeddah 21432, Tel (02)
   6609585, Telex 601413 SAIBJD SJ; Alkhobar: PO Box 1581,
   Alkhobar 31952, Tel (03) 8944777, Telex 871333 SAIBAK SJ;
   Riyadh: PO Box 3533, Riyadh 11481 (Sulemaniyah Branch),
   Tel (01) 4632929, Telex 401170 SAIBRH SJ; Riyadh: PO Box
   3533, Riyadh 11481 (Takhassussi St Branch), Tel (01)
   4828340, Telex 401170 SAIBRH SJ
Financial Information:

	1990 SR'000
Deposits	4,310,870
Retained earnings	398
Authorised capital	90,000
Paid-up capital	90,000
Net income	13,357
Total assets	4,601,248

Principal Shareholders: Saudi Public (36%), National
   Industrialisation Co NIC (10%), General Organisation for
   Social Insurance Riyadh (8%), National Commercial Bank
   Jeddah (8%), Riyad Bank Jeddah (8%), Al Jazirah Bank
   Jeddah (8%), Chase Manhattan Bank USA (15%), J Henry
   Schrodder Wagg UK (5%), Industrial Bank of Japan (5%)
Date of Establishment: June 1976
No of Employees: 184

SAUDI INVESTMENT GROUP & MARKETING CO LTD

S.I.G.M.A.

PO Box 4767, Riyadh 11412
Tel: 4760491/3
Cable: Sigma Riyadh
Telex: 401399 SJ

PRINCIPAL ACTIVITIES: Diversified industrial and commercial
   activities
Branch Offices: PO Box 7972, Jeddah 21472, Tel 6440400,
   Telex 600584 SJ

Subsidiary/Associated Companies: Arabian Est for Trade, PO
Box 832, Jeddah 21421; Saudi Tourist & Travel Bureau Co
Ltd, PO Box 863, Jeddah 21421; Arabian Inspection & Survey
Co Ltd, PO Box 9963, Jeddah 21423; Saudi Aircrafts &
Equipment Maintenance Co Ltd, PO Box 863, Jeddah 21421;
Saudi Travel Co Ltd, PO Box 10028, Jeddah 21433; Saudi
Port Operations & Maintenance Co Ltd, PO Box 26460
Riyadh 11468

Principal Shareholders: Sons and daughter of HRH Prince
Abdullah Al Faisal founder of the company

SAUDI JAPAN CONSTRUCTION CO LTD
PO Box 10630, Riyadh 11443
Tel: 4763413, 4764981
Telex: 401215 SHORAL Sj

Directors: Rashid Saad Al-Rashid (General Manager)

PRINCIPAL ACTIVITIES: General building and civil contractors

SAUDI KUWAITI CEMENT MANUFACTURING CO
PO Box 4536, Damman 31412
Tel: 03-8273330
Cable: Saudi Kuwaiti Cement
Telex: 802495 SKC SJ, 832166 SKC KHP SJ
Telefax: 03-8271923

Chairman: Dr Abdullah Ibrahim Al Kuwaiz
Directors: Eng Humoud Sulaiman Al Hamdan (Managing
Director), Abdul Aziz Mohd AL Jamal (General Manager),
Khalid Abdul Razaq Rezooki, Saad Ibrahim AL Mo'ajil, Khalid
Abdullah Al Mishary, Abdullah Muhammed Noor Rehaimi,
Musaad Ahmed Al Marzook
Senior Executives: Othman Al Jindan (Administration Manager),
Ibrahim El Garawani (Finance Manager), Khalid Al Babtain
(Marketing Manager), Abdul Nasir Al Zain (Personnel
Manager), Mohammed Al Thonayan (Regional Manager),
Tafeeq Al Ohaideb (Deputy Purchasing Manager)

PRINCIPAL ACTIVITIES: Manufacturing and marketing of clinker
and cement (Sulphate Resistance Type V and Ordinary
Portland Cement Type 1)
Principal Bankers: National Commercial Bank; Al Bank Al Saudi
Al Fransi; Arab National Bank; Riyad Bank
Financial Information:

	1989 SR'000	1990 SR'000
Sales turnover	242,000	295,000
Profits	26,000	64,000
Authorised capital	967,500	967,500
Paid-up capital	645,000	645,000
Total assets	1,283,000	1,283,000

Principal Shareholders: Kuwait Cement Co KCC (45%); General
Organisation for Social Insurance (GOSI) (10%); Public
Pension Fund (PPF) (10%); Public Investment Fund (10%)
Date of Establishment: 1983
No of Employees: 623

SAUDI LIVESTOCK TRANSPORT & TRADING CO
PO Box 17363, Riyadh 11484
Tel: 4773474
Cable: MAWASHI
Telex: 403292 MSHI SJ
Telefax: 4788211

Chairman: Abdullah Al Ali Abalkhail
Directors: Maan Abdulwahed Al Sanaa, Dr Ibrahim Omar Nazer,
Fahad Saad Al Moajil, Mohammed Abdullah Al-Rajhi, Khalid
Solaiman Al Olian, Abdullah Ali Kanoo, Sulaiman Al-Suhaimi,
Ibrahim Mohammed Al-Jomaih, Saddik Omar Attar, Dr Abdul
Aziz Mohammed Al Turky
Senior Executives: Abdullah Ghazi Al Sherbi (Managing
Director), Mohammed A Al Hadithi (Finance Manager), Eid

Abdulaal (Australian Branch Manager), Adnan Al Mugreibi
(Marketing & Sales Manager), Mohammed Saleh AL Mahana
(Purchase Manager), Saleh Mohd Al Obeidi (Financial
Controller), Khalid Mansour Al Turki (P R Manager), Eng
Ahmed Faiz Al Aridh (Marine Operations Manager), Ali
Abdulaziz Al Hamidi (Land Transport Manager), Saleh Bin
Abdulaziz Al Mukhailed (Admin Manager), Abdullah Al Babtain
(Manager Meat Division)

PRINCIPAL ACTIVITIES: Transport and trading of livestock and
meat; trading in animal feed, skins; production of meat;
abattoir management; marine and land transport
Branch Offices: Australia (Adelaide, Perth), Saudi Arabia
(Jeddah, Riyadh and Dammam)
Principal Bankers: Saudi American Bank
Financial Information:

	SR'000
Authorised capital	500,000
Paid-up capital	309,222

Principal Shareholders: There are 24 principal shareholders, the
largest shareholders being the National Shipping company of
Saudi Arabia
Date of Establishment: December 1980
No of Employees: 345

SAUDI MAINTENANCE CORPORATION (SIYANCO)
Head Office, PO Box 2731, Riyadh 11461
Tel: 478-5410
Cable: SIYANCO RIYADH
Telex: 4205729 SYANCO SJ

Owner: Prince Abdul-Rahman Bin Abdulaziz
Senior Executives: Dr Abdullah M Al Shuaiby

PRINCIPAL ACTIVITIES: Life support activities, utilities &
facilities, hotel & catering services, municipal water supply
distribution, health care services, project management, design
& engineering, pharmaceutical & medical supplies, training,
port operations, stevedoring & cargo handling, airports
operations & maintenance, computer systems operations &
maintenance
Branch Offices: Jeddah, Al Kharj, Khamis Mushayt, Taif,
Dhahran, Alkhobar, Dammam, Tabuk, Hafar Al Batin, Jubail,
Al Khafj, Buraydah, Jizan; Overseas offices in Washington,
and New York
Parent Company: 100% Saudi-Owned
Principal Bankers: Saudi American Bank; Maryland Bank Int'l,
Virginia, USA
Financial Information:

	SR'000
Authorised capital	5,000
Paid-up capital	5,000

Date of Establishment: 1968
No of Employees: 4,833

SAUDI MAJOR CONSTRUCTION PROJECT
Saudi Major Construction Project Co
PO Box 2064, Jeddah 21451
Tel: 6431073
Telex: 601035 Modern Sj

Senior Executives: Hassan Abdul Fotouh (General Manager)

PRINCIPAL ACTIVITIES: General building and civil contractors
Branch Offices: Riyadh, Taif

SAUDI MAMMOTH CO LTD
PO Box 1040, Dammam 31431
Tel: 8326856
Telex: 801049 Napco Sj

PRINCIPAL ACTIVITIES: Heavy and light transportation inside
and outside of Saudi Arabia

Financial Information:

	SR'000
Capital	4,000

Principal Shareholders: Mammoth Transport BV, Netherlands (49%); Abdul Aziz Abdul Rahman Al Muaibed (23%); Muhammad Abdullah Ibrahim Al Muammar (23%); Fouad Abdul Rahman Al Suwaigh (5%)

SAUDI MARBLE CO

PO Box 1187, Jeddah 21431
Tel: 6713126, 6713348
Telex: 600147 Anab Sj
Telefax: 6712964

Chairman: Abbas Nour
Directors: Dr Kassem Nour
Senior Executives: Aziz Nour (Manager)

PRINCIPAL ACTIVITIES: Manaufacture of marbles and granites; import and distribution of building materials, tiles, marble, granite, insulation materials, steel doors, decorative materials, kitchen furniture, and decorative items
Parent Company: Abbas Nour & Bros
Subsidiary Companies: Istanbul Furniture Center
Principal Bankers: Al Bank Al Saudi Al Fransi, Riyad Bank
Financial Information:

	1989/90 SR'000
Sales turnover	500,000
Profits	60,000
Authorised capital	40,000
Paid-up capital	40,000

Principal Shareholders: Abbas Nour; Abdul Ghaffar Nour; Dr Kassem Nour; Aziz Nour
Date of Establishment: 1972
No of Employees: 500

SAUDI MARITIME COMPANY

PO Box 2384, Dammam 31451
Tel: 8339245, 8334726
Cable: Samar Dammam
Telex: 803224 SMC DMMSJ
Telefax: 8324793

Chairman: Khaled S Olayan
Senior Executives: Syed Mahmood Quadri (Marketing Executive)

PRINCIPAL ACTIVITIES: Shipping agents and operators, clearing, forwarding and chartering
Principal Agencies: Senator Linie
Branch Offices: Jeddah; Riyadh; Jubail
Parent Company: Olayan Saudi Holding Co
Associated Companies: General Contracting Co; General Trading Co; Olayan Industrial Group; Arabian Business Machines Co; Saudi Forwarding & Transportation Co
Principal Bankers: Saudi British Bank

Principal Shareholders: Member of the Olayan Group of Companies
Date of Establishment: 1973
No of Employees: 30

SAUDI MARITIME TRANSPORT CO LTD

PO Box 5977, Jeddah 21432
Tel: 6475661, 6482069
Cable: Saudiferry
Telex: 606016 SMOON SJ

Chairman: Dr Ghaith Rashad Pharaon
Senior Executives: Jamal Zein Tahir

PRINCIPAL ACTIVITIES: Shipping agents and transport contractors
Branch Offices: Saudi Maritime Transport Co Ltd, Cairo, Egypt
Associated Companies: Redec Group of companies
Principal Bankers: National Commercial Bank; Bank Al Jazirah; Saudi American Bank
Financial Information:

	SR'000
Authorised capital	10,500
Paid-up capital	10,500

Principal Shareholders: Redec, Jeddah
Date of Establishment: 1976
No of Employees: 29

SAUDI METAL EST FOR ALUMINIUM & BLACKSMITH EQUIPMENT

PO Box 5517, Riyadh 11432
Tel: 4482183, 4482173
Cable: Moftahco
Telex: 401881 Moftah Sj

Chairman: Yousef El Yamani Moftah
Directors: Rebhi El Yamani Moftah, Abdel Hamid Abou Selim

PRINCIPAL ACTIVITIES: Trade and enterprise, import and export, metal processing and fabrication, aluminium, blacksmith, hardware, wiring, glass
Branch Offices: Location in Riyadh: Industrial Area, Al Amir Sulman Street; also branches in Jeddah and Dammam
Principal Bankers: Al Jazira Bank; Arab National Bank Ltd; National Commercial Bank
Financial Information:

	SR'000
Authorised capital	6,000
Paid-up capital	6,000

Principal Shareholders: Yousef El Yamani Muftah

SAUDI METAL INDUSTRIES LTD

PO Box 6765, Dammam 31452
Tel: 8572190, 8575432
Cable: Smile
Telex: 801526 Smile Sj, 802524 Fence Sj
Telefax: 8572810

Chairman: Khalid M Kanoo
Directors: Khaled A Zamil (Deputy Chairman), Ali A Kanoo, Sulaiman Al Zamil, Fahad M Saja
Senior Executives: B G Sendall (Financial Controller), A B Thornhill (General Sales Manager), I J Fielder (Commercial Manager)

PRINCIPAL ACTIVITIES: Production of steel reinforcing fabric for concrete and production of all types of fence systems and related security systems
Principal Agencies: Shuwaikh Trading Co, Kuwait; Haji Hassan Group, Bahrain; YBA Kanoo
Branch Offices: Riyadh, Telex 400100 KHOZ SJ
Parent Company: Joint venture between YBA Kanoo and Al Zamil Group
Subsidiary Companies: Guardian Fencing Systems Ltd
Principal Bankers: National Commercial Bank
Financial Information:

	SR'000
Sales turnover	29,000
Authorised capital	10,500
Paid-up capital	10,500

Principal Shareholders: YBA Kanoo, Hamad Abdullah A Zamil & Brothers Co, Fahad Saja
Date of Establishment: 1978
No of Employees: 54

SAUDI METIN LTD

PO Box 6137, Jeddah 21442
Tel: 6650084
Telex: 600104 Metin Sj
Telefax: 6601598

Chairman: Sheikh Youssef El Khereiji
Directors: Sheikh Ibrahim El Khereiji (Executive Director)
Senior Executives: Abdul Rahman El Khereiji (General Manager)

PRINCIPAL ACTIVITIES: Steel manufacturing and structural
  engineering
Parent Company: Development International Trade Co (DITCO)
Principal Bankers: Arab National Bank; Al Bank Al Saudi Al
  Fransi
Financial Information:

| | 1989 |
	SR'000
Paid-up capital	6,000

Principal Shareholders: Sheikh Youssef El Khereiji
Date of Establishment: 1976
No of Employees: 70

SAUDI MINERVA CO LTD

PO Box 203, Jeddah 21411
Tel: 6610006 (10 lines), 6610225
Telex: 601180 Arndas Sj, 606393 Arasco Sj
Telefax: 6610558

Chairman: Sheikh Abdul Aziz Rajab
Directors: Sheikh Abdullah Silsilah, Sheikh Khalid A Rajab
Senior Executives: Sheikh Khalid A Rajab (General Manager),
  Zafar Ahmed (Marketing Manager), M El Sakran (Technical
  Manager), Abdul Rashid (Administration Manager)

PRINCIPAL ACTIVITIES: Fire protection and security systems
Principal Agencies: Thorn Security Ltd; Fire Control Instruments
  FCI
Parent Company: Rajab & Silsilah (Philips' dealers)
Principal Bankers: Saudi British Bank
Financial Information:

| | 1990 |
	SR'000
Authorised capital	2,200
Paid-up capital	2,200

Principal Shareholders: Sheikh Abdul Aziz Rajab; Sheikh
  Abdullah Silsilah; Sheikh Abdullah Silsilah and Company
Date of Establishment: 1980

SAUDI MODERN FACTORY

PO Box 894, Riyadh 11421
Tel: 4480483, 4480140, 4480072, 4480152
Cable: Ashi Riyadh
Telex: 401117 Ouimer Sj

Chairman: Haidar S A Al Ashi (General Manager)
Senior Executives: Nimer El Ashi (Deputy General Manager),
  Mamdouh Tolba (Production Manager)

PRINCIPAL ACTIVITIES: Manufacture of steel and wooden
  furniture and installation of air-conditioning equipment
Branch Offices: Dammam, PO Box 209
Principal Bankers: Saudi American Bank; Arab National Bank

Principal Shareholders: Haider El Ashi; Nimer El Ashi; Khalil
  Ouimer; Abdul Aziz Masoud Al Minyawi
Date of Establishment: 1965
No of Employees: 350

SAUDI NATIONAL LINES

PO Box 4181, Jeddah 21491
Tel: 6439216, 6423052
Cable: Dremship Jeddah
Telex: 601880 Snship Sj

Chairman: Sheikh Abubaker Mohammed Bakhashab

Directors: Dr Nicola Costa, Sheikh Mohammed Noor Rahimi, Dr
  Emanuele Costa

PRINCIPAL ACTIVITIES: Regular cargo services, shipping
  agents, transport
Principal Agencies: Costa Armatori SpA, Genoa, Italy; Costa
  Lines Cargo Services, New York, USA
Branch Offices: Location in Jeddah: Bakhashab Bldg
Principal Bankers: National Commercial Bank, Jeddah

Principal Shareholders: Sheikh Abubaker Mohammed
  Bakhashab Pasha, Costa Armatoria SpA
Date of Establishment: 1975

SAUDI OPERATION & MAINTENANCE CO (SOMC)

PO Box 8460, Riyadh 11482
Tel: 4645061
Telex: 400255 Manair Sj
Telefax: (966-1) 4644551

Chairman: Prince Khalid Bin Fahad Al Faisal
Directors: Abdul Rahman Al Rouji (Vice President and General
  Manager)
Senior Executives: Al Faleh Ahmed (Coordinating Supervisor for
  Tech & Admin), Eng Saad Al Kahki (Manager Project
  Operations), Eng Mohammad Adel El Shahat (Asst GM
  Technical Affairs), Abdulrahman Al Dubaeyan (Manager
  Personnel & Admin), Omar Abu Talib (Manager Purchase &
  Procurement), Wafiq Rahmah (Finance Manager), Eng
  Mithqual Abu Nasser (Project SS), Rusty Sharp (Facility &
  Transport Manager), Sharaf Ba Baker (Executive Secretary)

PRINCIPAL ACTIVITIES: Operation and maintenance of major
  hospitals in the Kingdom under the Ministry of Health, military
  facilities including base maintenance and expertise in O&M of
  telecommunication, electrical, mechanical, electronic, security
  services, catering, and landscaping services
Branch Offices: Washington DC; London; Athens
Principal Bankers: Saudi American Bank; National Commercial
  Bank
Financial Information:

| | 1989 | 1990 |
	SR'000	SR'000
Sales turnover	94,461	163,935
Profits	9,500	24,152
Authorised capital	6,000	6,000
Paid-up capital	6,000	6,000
Total assets	40,000	10,687

Principal Shareholders: Prince Khalid Bin Fahad Al Faisal,
  Prince Faisal Farhan Al Faisal, Princess Amal Farhan Al
  Faisal
Date of Establishment: 1400H
No of Employees: 6,500

SAUDI ORIENT MARITIME CO LTD

PO Box 5806, Jeddah 21432
Tel: 6422328, 6423040
Cable: Somcol
Telex: 601219 Somcol Sj

Chairman: HRH Prince Mishaal Bin Abdulaziz
Directors: Sheikh Abdulla A Kadi (General Manager), N
  Bellstedt, Hans J Tschudi

PRINCIPAL ACTIVITIES: Ship owners, operators, brokers and
  charters
Branch Offices: Location in Jeddah: Attar Bldg, 6th Floor, King
  Abdulaziz Street
Principal Bankers: Saudi British Bank, Jeddah

Principal Shareholders: HRH Prince Mishaal Bin Abdulaziz and
  Sheikh Abdulla A Kadi (55%); Deutsche Afrika Linien,
  Hamburg (West Germany) and A/S Consensio, Oslo (Norway)
  (45%)

SAUDI (OVERSEAS) MARKETING & TRADING CO (SOMATCO)

PO Box 1951, Riyadh 11441
Tel: 4025727, 4053845
Cable: Somatc
Telex: 401477 Somatc Sj
Telefax: 4055248

Chairman: Ibrahim Mohamed Almousa
Directors: M A Hammad, Omer Abdullah Kamel

PRINCIPAL ACTIVITIES: Supply of medical, educational, laboratory, hospital equipment
Principal Agencies: Takei & Co; Harshaw/Filtrol; Thomas Sceintific; Keithley Instruments; Biotronik; Leader Electronics; WTR Binder; Tennelec Inc; Nucleus Inc; Janke & Kundel; Kyowa Optical; Engelhard; Bicron; Adolf Thies; Camag; Andreas Hettichj
Branch Offices: King Abdulaziz St, Alkhobar (Tel 8986375); University Street, Jeddah (Tel 6872644)
Principal Bankers: Saudi Cairo Bank, Riyadh
Financial Information:

	1989 SR'000
Sales turnover	30,000

Date of Establishment: 1968
No of Employees: 47

SAUDI PAN GULF - UBM

PO Box 9313, Riyadh
Tel: 4633409, 4646039, 4646169, 4641750
Telex: 405698 SPGUBM SJ
Telefax: 4632230

Chairman: Fahad Saja
Senior Executives: Paul Gent (General Manager), Peter Cook (Manager Jeddah), Paul Lee (Manager Alkhobar), Abdul Rahim (Sales Manager Riyadh)

PRINCIPAL ACTIVITIES: Supply of building materials
Principal Agencies: Nibco, USA; Zurn, USA; Halstead, USA; Watts Regulator, USA; IMI Rycroft, UK; Griffin, USA; F C Frost, UK; Hamada, Japan; Cape Building Product, UK; Cape Durasteel, UK
Branch Offices: Jeddah: PO Box 18596, Jeddah 21425, Tel 6835840, 6831077, Telex 606213, Fax 6835840; Alkhobar: PO Box 2473, Alkhobar 31952, Tel 8579366, 8572025, Telex 871197, Fax 8575067

No of Employees: 30

SAUDI PHARMACEUTICAL DISTRIBUTION CO LTD (SAPHAD)

PO Box 16032, Riyadh 11464
Tel: 4658882
Cable: saphad sj
Telex: 404273 Saphad SJ
Telefax: 4630601

Senior Executives: Fahad Tamimi (General Manager), Ernest A Britton (Chief Executive), Reinhard Schellner (Sales & Distribution Manager), Keki Olia (Finance Manager), Ramzi Bou Serhal (Personnel & Administration Manager)

PRINCIPAL ACTIVITIES: Import and distribution of pharmaceuticals and health care products
Principal Agencies: Ciba-Geigy; Reckitt & Colman; Titmus; Ergon Sutramed; Belart; Servipharm; Ciba Vision; Watraco
Branch Offices: Jeddah: PO Box 8640, Tel 6695666, Fax 6695327, Telex 603121; Dammam: PO Box 6503, Tel 8343174, Fax 8344200
Principal Bankers: Albank Alsaudi Alhollandi; National Commercial Bank; Saudi British Bank

Financial Information:

	1987/88 SR'000	1988/89 SR'000
Sales turnover	120,326	131,946
Profits (loss)	107	(710)
Paid-up capital	4,000	4,000
Total assets	91,387	105,495

Principal Shareholders: Dr Saud Shawwaf
Date of Establishment: 1980
No of Employees: 100

SAUDI PLASTIC PRODUCTS CO LTD (SAPPCO)

PO Box 2828, Riyadh 11461
Tel: 4480448
Cable: Sappco Riyadh
Telex: 401025 Sappco Sj
Telefax: 4461392

Chairman: HRH Prince Abdullah Alfaisal
Directors: Omar A Aggad (Managing Director), Nasser M Al Saleh (Director), Rashed Zahan (Director)
Senior Executives: Abbas A Aggad (General Manager), Mohammad Al Qahtani (Deputy General Manager)

PRINCIPAL ACTIVITIES: Manufacture and supply of UPVC & PE pipe system and fittings, polystyrene & polyurethane insulation materials
Subsidiaries/Associated Companies: Arabian Plastic Manufacturing Co Ltd (Aplaco), PO Box 6193, Riyadh 11442, Tel 4480250, Telex 401745 Aplaco Sj, Fax 4480543; Saudi Plastic Products Co Ltd (Sappco/Dammam), PO Box 4916, Dammam 31412, Tel 8575784, Telefax 8571969, Telex 801855 Sapd Sj; Sappco-Texaco Insulation Products Co Ltd (Saptex), PO Box 40042, Riyadh 11499, Tel 4984676, Telex 403827 Saptex Sj, Telefax 4980443
Principal Bankers: Arab National Bank; Albank Alsaudi Alhollandi; Al Bank Al Saudi Al Fransi
Financial Information:

	1990 SR'000
Authorised capital	50,000
Paid-up capital	50,000

Principal Shareholders: HRH Prince Abdulla Alfaisal; Aggad Investment Co; Olayan Financing Co
Date of Establishment: 1969
No of Employees: 136

SAUDI POULTRY CO LTD

PO Box 4840, Riyadh 11412
Tel: 4781610, 4760724
Cable: Saudi Poultry
Telex: 402053 Poltry Sj
Telefax: 4785787

Chairman: Prince Salman Bin Khalid Bin Abdullah Bin Abed El Rehman Al Saud
Directors: Musa Suleiman Freiji (Managing Director), Dr Jamil Jaroudi
Senior Executives: Edgardo B Rerrer (Finance Manager), Ibrahim Suliman (Marketing Manager), George Abu Assali (Purchasing Manager), Khalil Arar (Production Manager), Mohamad S Al Saykhan (Personnel Manager), Abdul Wasay Khan (Administration Manager)

PRINCIPAL ACTIVITIES: Production of day-old chick for layers and broilers
Principal Agencies: Lohmann Tierzucht, W Germany
Branch Offices: Jeddah, PO Box 10634, Tel 6600320; Al Hassah, PO Box 1586, Tel 5823919 & 5867456; Gassim, PO Box 1854, Tel 3247645
Principal Bankers: Al Bank Al Saudi Al Holland; National Commercial Bank; Saudi American Bank, Al Bank Al Saudi Al Fransi

Financial Information:

	1989
	SR'000
Authorised capital	2,000
Paid-up capital	2,000

Principal Shareholders: Sadco Saudi Agricultural Development Co Ltd; Musa Suleiman Freiji
Date of Establishment: Feb 1976
No of Employees: 87

SAUDI PRECAST & PREFAB HOUSING CO LTD

PO Box 20580, Riyadh 11465
Tel: 4982275
Telex: 402246 Sapo Sj

PRINCIPAL ACTIVITIES: Contracting and trading, manufacture of precast concrete products, building systems, waste disposal systems
Principal Agencies: Glasdon Plastics, UK; GRP, UK; Buckingham Vehicles, UK
Parent Company: Dallah Corporation
Principal Bankers: Saudi American Bank; Saudi Cairo Bank

SAUDI PUBLIC TRANSPORT CO (SAPTCO)

PO Box 10667, Riyadh 11443
Tel: 4545000
Telex: 400987, 402414 Saptco Sj
Telefax: 4542100

Chairman: Eng Ahmed Yousuf Al Turky (Deputy Minister of Communications)
Directors: Dr Abdul Rahman Abdullah Al Zamil (Deputy Minister of Commerce), Mohammad Abdullah Al Shareef (Deputy Minister of Finance, for Financial & Accounting Affairs), Major Gen Abdul Gadir Abdul Hai Kamal (General Manager for traffic), Dr Abdul Fattah Muhieddeen Nazir, Ali Abdullah Al Tamimi, Ibrahim Mohammed Al Jomaih, Abdul Aziz Qasim Kanoo, Abdullah Abdulrahman Al Sinaidi
Senior Executives: Dr Saad A Al Ghamdi (Director General), Eng Abdullah A Al Sheraim (Deputy Director General Operations), Eng Yousuf Mohammed Bakhsh (Deputy Dirctor General for Finance & Administration), Eng Mohammad Muthana Abutaleb (Director of Maintenance), Eng Saad Ali Al Jumaah (Manager Administration & Support Services), Majed Attalla Al Shamrokh (Director of Finance & Accounting), Abdulaziz Saud Al Romaih (Director of Computer Dept), Mansur Al Baibi (Internal Auditor), Ali Ornasir (Budget Controller)

PRINCIPAL ACTIVITIES: Public transportation services in and between Riyadh, Jeddah, Dammam, Makkah, Madina, Taif, Gassim and Abha; contract and charter services
Branch Offices: Riyadh: PO Box 10667, Telex 402220, Tel 4545000; Jeddah: PO Box 7830, Telex 602220, Tel 6910019; Makkah: PO Box 1765, Telex 750232, Tel 5204949; Madina: PO Box 2231, Telex 570220, Tel 8244500; Dammam: PO Box 5034, Telex 851831, Tel 8434380; Taif: P Box 562, Telex 750157, Tel 7369646; Gassim: PO Box 956, Telex 801055, Tel 3234518; Abha
Principal Bankers: Riyad Bank
Financial Information:

	1989/90
	SR'000
Sales turnover	199,406
Profits	70,000
Authorised capital	1,000,000
Paid-up capital	1,000,000
Total assets	383,113

Principal Shareholders: General Investment Fund and General Organisation for Social Insurance (Founders) (30%); Public Shareholders (70%)
Date of Establishment: 1399H (1979)
No of Employees: 2,762

SAUDI RAILWAYS ORGANISATION

PO Box 36, Dammam 31241
Tel: 8322042, 8713001
Cable: Saudirail Dammam
Telex: 801050 Sarail Sj
Telefax: 8336337

President: Faysal M Alshehail
Vice President: A M Bashawri
Vice President Operations: Fahad Zamil Al Hazmi

PRINCIPAL ACTIVITIES: Railways operation
Branch Offices: Riyadh
Principal Bankers: SAMA Riyad; Riyad Bank, Dammam; National Commercial Bank, Dammam
Financial Information:

	1988/89
	SR'000
Total assets	11,582,295

Principal Shareholders: Government owned
Date of Establishment: 1951
No of Employees: 1,855

SAUDI REFRIGERATORS MANUFACTURING CO LTD

PO Box 3315, Jeddah 21471
Tel: 6373202, 6380260, 6373092, 6372469
Cable: SRMCO Jeddah
Telex: 604272 Srmco Sj
Telefax: 6363731

Chairman: Sheikh Ahmed Juffali
Directors: Sheikh Walid Juffali, Hassan Shahine, J Standeven
Senior Executives: M Wayne Climer (Executive Vice President, Operations), S M Ali (Financial Controller), Abdullah Younis (Marketing Manager Riyadh), Achilles Stragalis (Marketing Manager Jeddah), Habib Khoury (Marketing Manager Dammam)

PRINCIPAL ACTIVITIES: Manufacture of domestic and commercial refrigerators
Branch Offices: PO Box 86, Riyadh, Tel 4022222, Fax 4022122, Telex 401049; PO Box 24, Dammam, Tel 8323333, Fax 8325779, Telex 801025; PO Box 297, Jeddah, Tel 6672220, Fax 6607268, Telex 601530
Parent Company: E A Juffali & Bros, PO Box 1049, Jeddah 21431, Tel 6672222, Fax 6694010, Telex 601130
Affiliated Companies: Kelvinator International Company, USA
Principal Bankers: Riyad Bank, Jeddah; Arab National Bank, Jeddah
Financial Information:

	1988/89	1989/90
	SR'000	SR'000
Sales turnover	63,000	65,000
Authorised capital	7,000	7,000
Paid-up capital	7,000	7,000
Total assets	16,000	15,000

Principal Shareholders: E A Juffali & Bros (75%); Kelvinator International Co (25%)
Date of Establishment: 10-6-1399H (1979)
No of Employees: 120

SAUDI RESEARCH & DEVELOPMENT CORPORATION LTD
R.E.D.E.C.

PO Box 1935, Jeddah 21441
Tel: 6448880
Cable: Redec
Telex: 601122 SRDC Sj

Chairman: Dr Ghaith R Pharaon
Directors: Sheikh Wabel R Pharaon (Managing Director)
Senior Executives: Zuhair Hatahet (Executive Vice President), Ziyad Murad (Senior Vice President), Mohammed Al-Ali

(Senior Vice President), Jean Louis Eisenchteter (Senior Vice President), Mohammed Memmi (Senior Vice President), Daoud Yassin (Senior Vice President)

PRINCIPAL ACTIVITIES: Investment; contracting mainly in construction and civil works, industrial research and development engineering, electrical and mechanical engineering, shipping, catering, insurance, hotels, travel, general trading, cement

Branch Offices: Branches in Riyadh; Dammam; Beirut; Representative Offices: USA (Savannah), Canada, France, England, Hong Kong

Associated Companies: REDEC Intertrade, Jeddah; REDEC Daelim Co Ltd, Dammam; ARINCO; Interstal; Incas Bona; Intermec; Saudi Arabian Parsons Ltd; Saudi Arabian Vianini; Saudi Food Supplies & Supermarkets; Al-Sabah Maritime Services Co, Jeddah; Saudi Computer Services Co, Jeddah

Principal Bankers: National Commercial Bank, Jeddah; Saudi American Bank, Jeddah; National Bank of Georgia, USA

Principal Shareholders: Pharaon family
Date of Establishment: January 1966
No of Employees: 16,000

SAUDI SAC CONTRACTING CO LTD

PO Box 9376, Riyadh 11413
Tel: 4767545
Cable: Saudisac
Telex: 402393 Sudsac Sj

Chairman: O Aggad
Directors: G S Awad, N Saleh
Senior Executives: A Muhtaseb (General Manager)

PRINCIPAL ACTIVITIES: Mechanical, electrical and civil engineering contractors, industrial projects, design engineering management, electro-mechanical maintenance contractors

Parent Company: Libinvest Holdings Ltd
Principal Bankers: Arab National Bank Ltd

Principal Shareholders: Supplies & Contracts Holdings; Aggad Investment Co; N Saleh
Date of Establishment: 15.3.79
No of Employees: 350

SAUDI SAND LIME BRICKS & BUILDING MATERIALS CO

PO Box 3130, Riyadh 11471
Tel: 4981824, 4981816, 4983191, 4829097, 4826648
Cable: Toobramly
Telex: 402021 Bricks Sj, 407191 Blocks Sj
Telefax: 4981175, 4829528

Chairman: Mohammad A Aljomaih
Senior Executives: Abdul Mohsin A Al Reshaid (General Manager), Mohamed Abdul Aziz Al Zahim (Finance & Administration Manager), Nafi Masod (Sales & Marketing Manager)

PRINCIPAL ACTIVITIES: Manufacturers of lime and sand lime bricks and blocks

Branch Offices: Jeddah: PO Box 6724, Tel 6373365, Fax 6361138, Telex 601913 TOOBCO Sj

Principal Bankers: Arab National Bank; National Commercial Bank; Riyad Bank

Financial Information:

	1990 SR'000
Sales turnover	20,000
Authorised capital	194,000
Paid-up capital	126,000
Total assets	110,000

Date of Establishment: 1977
No of Employees: 144

SAUDI SCALES & EQUIPMENT

PO Box 3252, Jeddah 21471
Tel: 6675514, 6675515, 6657534
Telex: 602137 Sasa Sj
Telefax: 6601508

Chairman: Thabit Mansur Refae
Directors: Badr Mansur Refae (Managing Director), Harbi M Yousef (Deputy Managing Director)

PRINCIPAL ACTIVITIES: Weighing machine systems; mechanical and electronic equipment, material testing laboratory equipment, ground handling for airports. Banking and security systems, CCTV, access control, fire detection, physical security, currency counting & sorting machines; Turnkey projects

Branch Offices: Dammam: Tel 8331953, Telex 801833 Refae Sj; Riyadh: Tel 4025291, Telex 400213 Refae Sj; Yanbu, Tel 04/3227758, Fax 3224055; Abha Tel 07/2223442, Fax 07/2223442

Date of Establishment: 1966
No of Employees: 100

SAUDI SECURITY & TECHNICAL SERVICES CO LTD

PO Box 7187, Jeddah 21462
Tel: 6471565
Telex: 601062 Motsim SJ

Chairman: Sheikh Ahmed Zainy
Directors: Sheikh Abdul Raouf Khalil, Hani S Emam, Sheikh Adnan Zainy
Senior Executives: Johan Sanden (General Manager)

PRINCIPAL ACTIVITIES: International insurance brokers
Principal Agencies: Essar International Insurance Brokers A/S Ltd of Oslo, Norway manages the company
Branch Offices: PO Box 50427, Riyadh, Tel 4659546, 4659482, Telex 404728 SSTS SJ; PO Box 731 Dhahran Airport, AlKhobar, Tel 8983720, Telex 870791 SSTJ SJ
Principal Bankers: Saudi American Bank

Principal Shareholders: Abbar & Zainy Co; Abdul Raouf Khalil; Al-Arin; Hani Emam
Date of Establishment: 23.3.1978
No of Employees: 20

SAUDI SERVICES FOR ELECTRO-MECHANICAL WORKS CO LTD

PO Box 6341, Riyadh 11442
Tel: 4026809, 4026834, 4028215
Cable: SHORACO
Telex: 400235 SSEM SJ
Telefax: 4028213

Chairman: Sheikh Abdullah S Al Rashid
Directors: Abdul Rahman S Al Rashid, Rashid S Al Rashid
Senior Executives: Omar A Hamzeh (General Manager), Emad Haj Ibrahim (Head Mechanical Dept), Bashar Shaikhouni (Construction Manager), Mohd Nabil Mahgoub (Finance Manager), Hasan Al Eter (Purchasing & Services Manager), Hasan Fadel Bahjat (Personnel & Admin Manager)

PRINCIPAL ACTIVITIES: Electro mechanical contracting and maintenance; supply of equipment; power generation, overhead line and underground transmission and distribution network

Branch Offices: PO Box 12276, Jeddah, Tel 6727334; Abha, Tel 2233550; Jouf, Tel 6222662
Parent Company: Al Rashid Trading & Contracting Co
Subsidiary Companies: Al Rashid Abetong Co; Saudi Japan Constructions Co
Principal Bankers: Arab National Bank; Saudi American Bank; Al Bank Al Saudi Al Fransi; Albank Alsaudi Alhollandi

Financial Information:

	1989
	SR'000
Sales turnover	27,300
Profits	10,500
Authorised capital	5,000
Paid-up capital	5,000
Total assets	111,500

Principal Shareholders: Rashid Abdul Rahman; Abdullah S Al Rashid; Abdul Rahman S Al Rashid; Rashid S Al Rashid
Date of Establishment: 1976
No of Employees: 400

SAUDI STEEL (HADEED SAUDIA) REINFORCEMENTS LTD

PO Box 1296, Jeddah 21431
Tel: 6364775, 6377348, 6361462
Telefax: 6374991

Chairman: Ahmed Mohamed Baroom
Directors: Mohamed Baroom, Hassan Baroom
Senior Executives: Lucas Hesser (General Manager)

PRINCIPAL ACTIVITIES: Supply of reinforcing steel to the construction industry, cutting, bending and fixing of reinforcing steel; supply of epoxy coated reinforcing steel bars, structural steel, scrap collection
Principal Agencies: Saudi Manufactured Steel (Hadeed, Sulb)
Parent Company: Modern Trade & Development, Jeddah
Principal Bankers: Albank Alsaudi Alhollandi, Jeddah
Financial Information:

	1988/89	1989/90
	SR'000	SR'000
Sales turnover	57,000	60,000
Authorised capital	3,000	3,000
Paid-up capital	3,000	3,000
Total assets	17,965	14,000

Principal Shareholders: Modern Trade & Development, Jeddah
Date of Establishment: September 1976
No of Employees: 60

SAUDI STEEL PIPE CO LTD

PO Box 546, Dhahran, 31932
Tel: 3-8421563
Telex: 870512 SSPIPE SJ
Telefax: 966-3-8430582

Chairman: Khalid A Al Rabiah
Directors: Fahd Saja, Tami Nassar, Abdulrahman Khorayef, S J Yun, S H Kim
Senior Executives: Riyadh Al Rabiah (General Manager), K H Kim (Factory Manager)

PRINCIPAL ACTIVITIES: Manufacture of galvanised and black steel pipes and angular tubes
Branch Offices: Riyadh: Tel 4786648; Jeddah: Tel 6605607; Qassim: Tel 3235185
Parent Company: Korea Steel Pipe Co Ltd, Seoul; Rabiah & Nassar Co, Jeddah
Principal Bankers: Saudi American Bank; Saudi Investment Bank; Saudi United Commercial Bank
Financial Information:

	1990
	SR'000
Sales turnover	215,000
Authorised capital	150,000
Paid-up capital	80,000
Total assets	170,000

Principal Shareholders: Rabiah & Nassar Co; Korea Steel Pipe Co; Fahd Saja; Al Khorayef Co

SAUDI STEEL PRODUCT FACTORY (STEPRO)

PO Box 2532, Dammam 31461
Tel: 966-3-8572219
Telex: 801792 Stepro SJ
Telefax: 966-3-8574849

Chairman: Hassan Abdullah Mira
Senior Executives: Abdul Haq (General Manager)

PRINCIPAL ACTIVITIES: Manufacturing/fabrication of pressure vessels to ASME code, storage & atmospheric tanks, piping, structurals, machining, stress relieving
Principal Bankers: Albank Alsaudi Alhollandi

Date of Establishment: 1977
No of Employees: 100

SAUDI SUDANESE RED SEA JOINT COMMISSION

PO Box 5886, Jeddah 21432
Tel: 6610560, 6610564
Telex: 600221 RESEC SJ
Telefax: 6672265

Chairman: Dr Zohair Nawab (Acting Secretary General)
Directors: Sadik Illyass (Technical Director), Sami Fathi (Administration Director), Izzeldin Mahjoob (Purchasing Director)

PRINCIPAL ACTIVITIES: Exploitation of the Red Sea mineral resources
Branch Offices: Khartoum
Principal Bankers: Riyad Bank, Jeddah

Principal Shareholders: Governments of Saudi Arabia and Sudan
Date of Establishment: 1974
No of Employees: 47

SAUDI SUPPLY & COMMERCE CO

PO Box 1595, Riyadh 11441
Tel: 4773818
Telex: 406267 KULIBI SJ

President: Saud A Al Kulaibi
Senior Executives: Young Soo Park (Vice President), A A Almoamer (Vice President)

PRINCIPAL ACTIVITIES: Construction, trading, catering, maintenance, representing international firms
Branch Offices: Dammam; Jubail; London; Houston
Subsidiary Companies: AG Saudia; Semec; Sasuco Intl; Saudi Control System; WRH/Sasuco Joint venture; National Construction Co; International Travel Service
Principal Bankers: Saudi American Bank; Saudi British Bank; National Commercial Bank; Riyad Bank

Principal Shareholders: Private company
Date of Establishment: March 1978
No of Employees: 2,570 (inc subsidiaries)

SAUDI TARMAC CO LTD

PO Box 2644, Jeddah 21461
Tel: 6827644, 6832001
Telex: 601702 TRMC Sj
Telefax: 6827805

Chairman: Sheikh Saleh Bin Salem Bin Mahfouz
Directors: Sheikh Khaled Bin Salem Bin Mahfouz, Abdul Rahman Bin Mallouh, Tahir M Bawazir, B J Woodman, J A Sneden, Fazl Ameer, A R Chesters
Senior Executives: J A Sneden (Director and General Manager), Ian W Stirling (Administration Manager), Abubakr Buraei (Finance Manager)

PRINCIPAL ACTIVITIES: Civil engineering; building; turnkey projects
Principal Bankers: National Commercial Bank, Jeddah

Financial Information:

	SR'000
Authorised capital	85,000
Paid-up capital	85,000

Principal Shareholders: Al Ahlia Development Co (51%); Bin Mallouh Trading Establishment (5%); Tarmac (Jersey) Ltd (44%)
Date of Establishment: 1977

SAUDI TECHNICAL SERVICES & TRADING (STST)

PO Box 1716, Jeddah 21441
Tel: 6532511 (5 lines)
Cable: Myhome
Telex: 601214 Emam Sj

President: Hani S Emam
Directors: Qosay S Emam (Vice-President)
Senior Executives: S A Muneer Ahmad (Manager, Administration & Commercial, Public Relations & Services), M Mohsin Ghayur (Manager, Finance)

PRINCIPAL ACTIVITIES: Holding and trading company; import and trading of trucks, buses, trailers, furniture; operating fast food restaurants; holding/managing companies engaged in shipping, real estate, air-conditioning, chemicals, engineering, general insurance, supermarkets, production of precast roofing system and clay bricks
Principal Agencies: Mack Trucks Inc, USA; Tata Exports Ltd, India; Interdesign, Lebanon; Drexel Furnishing, USA; Hercules Trailers, USA
Branch Offices: Riyadh: PO Box 5669, Tel 4040445, Telex 404415 STST; Alkhobar: PO Box 1430, Tel 8947458, Telex 871474 EMAM SJ
Subsidiary/Associated Companies: Saudi Marine Transportation Co Ltd; Saudi Concrete Prefab Industries Ltd; Saudi Ensas Ltd; Saudi International Investment Co Ltd; Saudi Arabian Falcon Shipping & Transportation Co Ltd; Saudi Braun Ltd; Saudi Realestate Development Co; Saudi Security & Technical Services Ltd; National Realestate Development & Management; Arabian TR Oil Services Co Ltd; Saudi Vincotte Co Ltd; Tamimi Fouad & Al-Emam Food Co Ltd; National Clay Brick & Building Materials Industry Co Ltd
Principal Bankers: Bank Al-Jazira; Bank Al Saudi Al Fransi; Bank Al Saudi Al Hollandi; Saudi American Bank; Riyad Bank

Date of Establishment: 1971
No of Employees: 100

SAUDI TECHNOLOGISTS CONSULTING ENGINEERS

S.A.T.E.C.H.

PO Box 429, Dhahran Airport 31932
Tel: 8943025, 8951048
Telex: 871265 Satech Sj

PRINCIPAL ACTIVITIES: General engineers and architects
Branch Offices: Riyadh: PO Box 3455, Riyadh 11471, Tel 4767358, Telex 403119; also in Kuwait and England

SAUDI TEXTILE CO LTD

PO Box 3549, Jeddah 21481
Tel: 6363058, 6364277
Cable: Textfactory
Telex: 601291 Textco Sj

Chairman: Wasfi Hussain Ezzi
Directors: Fakhry Hussain Ezzi

PRINCIPAL ACTIVITIES: Production of yashmagh head covers, white voil head covers, face, bath and pilgrims towels and textiles
Branch Offices: Jeddah; Riyadh; Dammam; Khamis Mushayt; Tabuk
Subsidiary Companies: Ezzi Trading Establishment, PO Box 3824, Jeddah

Principal Bankers: Riyad Bank, Jeddah; National Commercial Bank, Jeddah
Financial Information:

	SR'000
Authorised capital	16,000
Paid-up capital	31,205

Principal Shareholders: Wasfi Hussain Ezzi, Ibraheem Shekh Ali, Fakhry Hussain Ezzi, Mohammed Ali Al-Syiari and brothers, Hamad Mohammed Alsaidan
No of Employees: 175

SAUDI TRADING & CONTRACTING CENTRE

PO Box 2220, Riyadh 11451
Tel: 4766715
Telex: 601260 Center Sj

Directors: H H Prince Abdul Aziz Al Turki (Partner), Zuhdi Ahmed Bushnak (Partner)

PRINCIPAL ACTIVITIES: General contractors
Branch Offices: Alkhobar; Madina; Jeddah, Tel 6658395, 6650929

SAUDI TRAFFIC SAFETY CO LTD

PO Box 4445, Jeddah 21491
Tel: 6874791, 6873403
Cable: Almahmoudiah
Telex: 601328 Mihdar Sj
Telefax: 6879668

Chairman: Salem Mohammed Bin Ladin
Directors: Abdallah Al-Mihdar (Managing Director), Alawi Al-Mihdar, Sheikh Bakr M Binladen, Sheikh Salem M Binladen
Senior Executives: M Sufian Abbasi (General Manager), Munir Ahmad (Operations Manager)

PRINCIPAL ACTIVITIES: Sprayplastic roadmarking and airfield marking contractors, slurry seal resurfacing contractors for roads and airfields, supply and fix of road studs and industrial maintenance chemicals. Manufacture of allied road safety products
Principal Agencies: Prismo (UK) Ltd; Syprop Ltd, W Germany; Corium Chemicals; Emcol
Branch Offices: PO Box 6233, Riyadh
Parent Company: Al Mihdar Development Company Ltd
Principal Bankers: Al Bank Al Saudi Al Fransi; National Commercial Bank
Financial Information:

	1989/90 SR'000
Sales turnover	8,000
Authorised capital	3,000
Paid-up capital	3,000
Total assets	6,500

Principal Shareholders: Binladen Bros; Abdallah Al-Mihdar
Date of Establishment: 1977. Converted to 100% Saudi Company in 1985
No of Employees: 45

SAUDI TRANSPORT SERVICES CO LTD (STRACO)

PO Box 2085, Jeddah 21451
Tel: 6446658, 6442032
Cable: Elnakla
Telex: 602323 STRUCK SJ
Telefax: 6446658

Chairman: Mohammed Mounir Halwani
Directors: Mossin S Chavdarian (Managing Director)
Senior Executives: Araya Kidani (Client Co-ordinator), Samir Saleh (Traffic Manager), Mohammed Fares (Personnel Manager), Mahmoud Joummieh (Finance Manager), Anthony Hoe (Workshop Manager)

PRINCIPAL ACTIVITIES: Long distance haulage of containerised and general cargo, cranage and forklifting

service, storage of full and empty containers, warehousing and storage, clearing and forwarding
Branch Offices: Dammam
Parent Company: Halwani Bros
Principal Bankers: Saudi Cairo Bank; Saudi American Bank
Financial Information:

	1990
	SR'000
Authorised capital	4,000
Paid-up capital	4,000

Principal Shareholders: Mounir Halwani; Mohammed Halwani; Halwani Bros
Date of Establishment: 1976
No of Employees: 128

SAUDI TRAVELLERS CHEQUE CO

PO Box 7915, Riyadh 11472
Tel: 4789311, 4789046
Telex: 405419, 405421 STCC Sj

Chairman: Ibrahim M S Shams
Directors: Abdullah I Samoum, Stanley Robertson, Abdullah Abu Al Khalil, Abdullah Abu Al Samh, Abdul R Al Medaini, Abdel Aziz Al Ajroush, Hamid Henaidy
Senior Executives: Mohammed S Ghaleb (General Manager)

PRINCIPAL ACTIVITIES: Issuing and marketing of Saudi Riyals travellers cheques
Financial Information:

	SR'000
Authorised capital	25,000
Paid-up capital	25,000

Principal Shareholders: National Commercial Bank, Riyad Bank, Saudi British Bank, Al Bank Al Saudi Al Hollandi, Al Bank Al Saudi Al Fransi, Arab National Bank, Saudi Cairo Bank, Bank Al Jazira
Date of Establishment: 1983

SAUDI UNITED FERTILISERS CO

PO Box 4811, Riyadh 11412
Tel: 4781304, 4781287, 4765341
Cable: Asmida
Telex: 401865
Telefax: (966-1) 4789581

Directors: Samer Ali Kabbani (Managing Director)
Senior Executives: Saifeldine Hamzah (Finance Manager), Redah Oweis (Technical Manager), Ibrahim Al Johar (Sales Manager)

PRINCIPAL ACTIVITIES: Importing & dealing in agricultural chemicals, fertilisers, seeds and insecticides, field sprayers
Principal Agencies: Hoechst, W Germany; Rhone Poulenc, France; Agrimont, Italy; Uniroyal, USA; Petoseed, USA; Protex, Belgium; Unifert, Belgium
Branch Offices: Qassim; Jeddah
Principal Bankers: Al Bank Al Saudi Al Fransi, Riyadh; Riyad Bank, Riyadh; National Commercial Bank, Riyadh
Financial Information:

	1989/90
	SR'000
Sales turnover	32,000
Paid-up capital	150

Principal Shareholders: T A Murad, S A Kabbani, A T Murad
Date of Establishment: 1975

SAUDI UNITED INSURANCE CO LTD EC

PO Box 933, Alkhobar 31952
Tel: 8642863, 8644898, 8949090
Cable: AMAN
Telex: 871335 Suico Sj
Telefax: 8949428

Chairman: Sh Ahmad Hamad Algosaibi

Directors: Sh Abdelaziz Hamad Algosaibi (Managing Director), Dr Walter Diehl (Vice Chairman), Sulaiman H Algosaibi, Yussif A Algosaibi, Luzius Gloor, James S Rattray
Senior Executives: A M Sabbagh (General Manager & Board Director), Roger A Bevan (Deputy General Manager), Abdul Mohsin A Algosaibi (Asst General Manager Administration), Abdul Rehman Qassas (Technical Manager)

PRINCIPAL ACTIVITIES: All classes of insurance except life
Branch Offices: Alkhobar: PO Box 2612, Tel 8952710, 8952737, Fax 8952748, Telex 872148; Riyadh: PO Box 74, Tel 4659270, Fax 4654895, Telex 401309; Jeddah: PO Box 6971, Tel 6534272, Telex 602258; Dammam: PO Box 5887, Tel 8332736, Fax 8340675, Telex 802408; Makkah: PO Box 1634, Tel 5455218, Telex 540332; Hofuf: PO Box 2204, Tel 5871712, Fax 5862696; Yanbu: PO Box 473, Tel 3223992, 3228765, Telex 661084
Parent Company: Ahmad Hamad Algosaibi & Bros, Alkhobar
Principal Bankers: Arab National Bank, Alkhobar; Ahmad Hamad Algosaibi & Bros Money Exchange Comm & Investment, Alkhobar; Saudi British Bank, Alkhobar
Financial Information:

	1989
	SR'000
Sales turnover	40,000
Authorised capital	17,800
Paid-up capital	17,800
Total assets	45,439

Principal Shareholders: Ahmad Hamad Algosaibi & Bros; Swiss Reinsurance Company; Commercial Union Assurance Co PLC; Baloise Insurance Co Ltd
Date of Establishment: 1st July 1976
No of Employees: 84

SAUDI VITRIFIED CLAY PIPE CO LTD

PO Box 6415, Riyadh 11442
Tel: 4769192, 4769162 (Office), 4980772, 4980768 (Factory)
Telex: 400019 Clayco
Telefax: 4782458

Chairman: H H Prince Faisal Bin Abdul Aziz Bin Faisal
Directors: Dr J Hartmann, H Wolf, A Koetter, Dr Saad Al Sayari, A Alissa
Senior Executives: Dr Saad Al-Sayari (General Manager), Mohan Murari (Finance Manager), Mahmoud Abu Jebara (Sales Manager), Muslim Al Ajmi (Technical Manager), Abdul Munim Attia (Production Manager)

PRINCIPAL ACTIVITIES: Production and sale of glazed vitrified clay pipes for sewage and drainage
Principal Agencies: Steinzeug Export Co, West Germany; Keramo, Belgium
Principal Bankers: Al Bank Al Saudi Al Hollandi, Riyadh; SIBC, Riyadh
Financial Information:

	1990
	SR'000
Capital	100,000
Paid-up capital	36,000

Principal Shareholders: HH Prince Faisal Bin Abdul Aziz Bin Faisal Al Saud (13.34%); Abdullatif Ali Al Issa (19.28%); National Industrialisation Company (21.81%); Heinrich Wolf Germany (5%); Cremer & Breuer Germany (5%); Keramo Belgium (0.67%); D E G, Germany (15%); Dr Saad Al-Sayari (7.86%), Abdullah Al Dabaan (5%), Abdullah Al Hugail (1%), Adnan H Bogari (4.03%), Amal H Bogari (2.01%)
Date of Establishment: 1979
No of Employees: 160

SAUDI WATER TECHNOLOGY CO LTD

PO Box 326, Dammam 31411
Tel: 8425546, 8420811
Telex: 803148 SWT Sj
Telefax: (03) 8425546

Chairman: Salah Mohammad Al Bassam
Directors: Hassan Ali Al Hudaib (General Manager)
Senior Executives: Munir Daoud Sulieman (Managing Director)

PRINCIPAL ACTIVITIES: Design, manufacture and installation of waste water treatment plants and related systems
Branch Offices: PO Box 61295, Riyadh 11565, Tel 4647185, 4633949, Fax 4634112, Telex 406674 IDG Sj
Principal Bankers: Saudi Fransi Bank; Riyad Bank; Arab National Bank
Financial Information:

	SR'000
Authorised capital	4,900
Paid-up capital	4,900

Principal Shareholders: Abdulla A Al Hudaib, Salah M Al Bassam, Abdul Aziz A Al Hudaib
Date of Establishment: 1984
No of Employees: 72

SAUDICORP
Abdulaziz A Al Sulaiman

PO Box 222, Jeddah 21411
Tel: 6514712, 6514716, 6510320
Telex: 600609 Scorp Sj

Chairman: Abdulaziz A Al Sulaiman
Directors: Amr Fouad (Managing Director)

PRINCIPAL ACTIVITIES: Projects development and promotion electrical engineering contracting; aluminium products; prefab housing; electrical products and pipe systems
Principal Agencies: GBA Geigy; Brown Boveri Electric; Alcan; G&W Electric; Cables of Lyon
Branch Offices: Riyadh; Al Khubar
Subsidiary Companies: Saudicorp Nordline Dean, PO Box 7763, Jeddah
Principal Bankers: Bank Al-Jazira, Al Bank Al Saudi Al-Faransi

Principal Shareholders: Abdulaziz A M Sulaiman
Date of Establishment: 1975
No of Employees: 200

SAUDIPHIL CONSTRUCTION CO LTD

PO Box 3362, Riyadh 11471
Tel: 4768282, 4768108
Telex: 401390 Mansur Sj

President: Sheikh Mansour I Badr

PRINCIPAL ACTIVITIES: General building and civil contractors; steel structural fabrication and erection; storage tanks, power equipment

SAWARY TRADING & CONTRACTING

PO Box 3420, Jeddah 21471
Tel: 6421549
Cable: Sawaryco
Telex: 601285 Sawary Sj
Telefax: 6425011

Chairman: Sheikh Ahmad Abdallah Sulaiman
President: Sheikh Ghassan A Al Sulaiman
Senior Executives: Arfan A Awwa (General Manager), Mohammad Safadi (Technical & Parts Director), Farouk Nabulsi (Sales & Marketing Manager)

PRINCIPAL ACTIVITIES: Supply, installation and maintenance of electrical power, generating and distribution systems, parts for diesel engines
Principal Agencies: Allis Chalmers, USA; Fram Filters, USA; Kubota Generators & Welders, Japan; Kohler Generator Sets, USA
Branch Offices: Riyadh, PO Box 6092, Tel 4764620, Telex 400864; Buraidah, PO Box 512, Tel 3234780; Dammam, PO Box 5278, Tel 8576440, Telex 802147; and New York (USA)
Principal Bankers: Saudi Cairo Bank, Jeddah; Al Bank Al Saudi Al Fransi, Jeddah

Financial Information:

	1989/90 SR'000
Sales turnover	50,000
Profits	1,600
Authorised capital	25,000
Paid-up capital	25,000
Total assets	9,500

Principal Shareholders: Sheikh Ahmad Abdallah Sulaiman
Date of Establishment: 1976
No of Employees: 80

SCAN ROAD MIDDLE EAST (BCI)

Head Office; PO Box 1053, Dammam 31431
Tel: 8573176
Telex: 802365 Malaco Sj

PRINCIPAL ACTIVITIES: Manufacture and supply of road chemicals, such as anti stripping agents, bitumen emulsifiers and bitumen emulsion plants
Branch Offices: Riyadh: PO Box 41153, Riyadh 11521, Tel 4766759, Telex 402823; Jeddah: PO Box 11208, Jeddah 21453, Tel 6821437, Telex 603780

Principal Shareholders: Kema Nobel, Sweden

SEATING & OFFICE SYSTEMS INDUSTRIES LTD

PO Box 56129, Riyadh 11554
Tel: 4984700
Telex: 407261 Karasi SJ
Telefax: 966-1 4982735

Chairman: Eng Omair Abdulaziz Alomair (Managing Director & General Manager)
Directors: Abdul Rehman Al Mahmoud, Mohammad Alomair, Eng Omair Abdulaziz Alomair, Eng Abdulaziz Abdullah Alomair
Senior Executives: Eng Mohammed I Al Shabnan (Factory Manager), Tariq M Alomair (Admin & Finance Manager)

PRINCIPAL ACTIVITIES: Manufacture of wooden and upholstered furniture, contract furnishing, interior decoration
Branch Offices: Riyadh Industries Corp, 81 Montecito Dr, GDM, California, USA
Associated Companies: Riyadh Furniture Inds Ltd, Arabiah Furniture Mfg Co
Principal Bankers: Riyad Bank, Riyadh; Arab National Bank, Riyadh
Financial Information:

	1990 SR'000
Sales turnover	20,000
Authorised capital	33,000
Paid-up capital	8,250
Total assets	35,000

Principal Shareholders: Directors/partners
Date of Establishment: 1982
No of Employees: 342

SEIARY, M O, EST

PO Box 40899, Riyadh 11511
Tel: 4770474, 4765240
Telex: 404492 Seiary Sj
Telefax: 4776935

Chairman: Mohammed Onn Eiary

Senior Executives: Rasheed K Ajjaj (General Manager), Philip George (Sales Manager)

PRINCIPAL ACTIVITIES: Suppliers of air conditioning and refrigeration equipment and spare parts
Principal Agencies: Flamco (Pipe support systems), Compac, Duro Dyne (Duct Work Accessories), Foster Adhsives, EFC Fliters, Afico Insulation Products
Branch Offices: Alkhobar
Principal Bankers: Arab National Bank, Riyadh
Financial Information:

	1989
	SR'000
Sales turnover	20,000
Total assets	15,000

Principal Shareholders: Sole proprietorship
Date of Establishment: 1982

SEMCO ARABIA LTD
PO Box 8898, Riyadh 11492
Tel: 4762645, 4771364, 4777771
Telex: 402054 SEMCO SJ

Chairman: Abdul Khaliq Bakhsh
Directors: Niels Schmidt

PRINCIPAL ACTIVITIES: Mechanical and electrical engineering contracting; power supply; electrical equipment, air-conditioning etc
Branch Offices: Dhahran Airport, Al Khobar, PO Box 478, Tel 8647615, Telex 871248 SEMCO SJ; Jeddah: PO Box 6752, Tel 6823954
Parent Company: Semco A/S, Park Alle 373, 2600 Glostrup, Denmark
Principal Bankers: Saudi American Bank, Riyadh

Date of Establishment: May 1976

SERVICE EQUIPMENT EST
PO Box 213, Jeddah 21411
Tel: 6803000, 6804212
Telex: 603541 SEEE Sj

President: Omar Abu-Baker Balubaid
Senior Executives: Ahmed O Balubaid (General Manager)

PRINCIPAL ACTIVITIES: Supplier/distributor of the following equipment and tools: car wash and cleaning system, injection pump and nozzle testing, garage body and workshops, petroleum and fuel stations
Principal Agencies: FMC Corporation, USA; Hanna Carwash Int'l, USA; Leslie Hartridge Ltd, UK; Gilbarco Inc, USA & Brazil; Ceccato, Italy; Sicam, Italy; Stenhoj, Denmark
Branch Offices: Riyadh: PO Box 20476; Dammam: PO Box 3515; Khamis Mushayt: PO Box 1215
Associated Companies: Omar A Balubaid Est
Principal Bankers: Arab National Bank

No of Employees: 82

SGB DABAL LTD
PO Box 1102, Dammam 31431
Tel: 8579572, 8571884
Cable: Dabal
Telex: 801124 Dabal SJ
Telefax: 8578707

Chairman: Abdullah K Al-Dabal
Directors: A R Al-Dabal, G Bayles, R Brigeman (Managing Director)
Senior Executives: David Webb (General Manager), Adel Al Dabal (Manager Dammam), Philip Munro (Manager Riyadh), Jon Shaw (Manager Jubail)

PRINCIPAL ACTIVITIES: Scaffolding and formwork equipment
Branch Offices: Riyadh: PO Box 58756, Riyadh 11515, Tel 4764036, Fax 4760258; Jubail: PO Box 667, Jubail 31951, Tel 3412130, Fax 3412165

Parent Company: SGB Int'l, Willow Lane, Mitcham, Surrey, UK
Principal Bankers: Albank Alsaudi Alhollandi, Dammam
Financial Information:

	1990
	SR'000
Sales turnover	11,532
Issued share capital	2,000
Paid-up capital	2,000
Total assets	4,239

Principal Shareholders: Al Dabal Co, Saudi Arabia; SGB Overseas Ltd, UK
Date of Establishment: 1977
No of Employees: 96

SHAHRAN TRADING EST
PO Box 8096, Riyadh 11482
Tel: 4034600, 4036900
Cable: Shatcorp
Telex: 401571 Rajest Sj

Chairman: Dirham M Shahrani
Directors: Fawzi A Tuffaha (General Manager)
Senior Executives: Tawfiq Tuffaha (Commercial Manager), Ahmed Attar (Sales Manager)

PRINCIPAL ACTIVITIES: Trading, contracting, agents and representatives for international companies, importers, custom brokers and packing
Subisiary/Assoicated Companies: Shahran Associates Inc, PO Box 2, Chelsea, Mass 02150
Principal Bankers: Bank Al-Jazira

Date of Establishment: April 1966

SHAKER, IBRAHIM, CO LTD
PO Box 15, Riyadh 11411
Tel: 4036763, 4024199, 4025431, 4020570
Cable: Atcom
Telex: 401087 Ghassan Sj, 401292 Shaker Sj
Telefax: 4025217

Chairman: Ghassan Shaker
President: Hussein Shaker
Managing Director: Hassan Shaker

PRINCIPAL ACTIVITIES: Import and distribution of air-conditioners, refrigerators and household electrical appliances
Principal Agencies: Electrolux; Norge; Trane Split A/C Units; Black & Decker
Branch Offices: Jeddah, Riyadh, Dammam, Alkhobar
Parent Company: Shaker Trading Co Ltd
Principal Bankers: Arab Bank Ltd
Financial Information:

	1990
	SR'000
Sales turnover	50,000
Profits	10%
Authorised capital	10,000

Principal Shareholders: Shaker Family
Date of Establishment: 1945
No of Employees: 100

SHAMEL EST
PO Box 22491, Riyadh 11495
Tel: 4631291, 4630975
Telex: 404779 Shamel Sj

PRINCIPAL ACTIVITIES: Manufacturers representatives. Medical division for medical and laboratory supplies
Principal Bankers: Saudi American Bank; Saudi British Bank

Principal Shareholders: Prince Nawwaf Bin Mohammed Bin Abdul Rahman Al Saud

SHARBATLY EST FOR TRADE & DEVELOPMENT

PO Box 293, Jeddah 21411
Tel: 6470149, 6470054, 6471844
Telex: 601226 Kamal Sj

Proprietor: Kamal Abdulla Sharbatly

PRINCIPAL ACTIVITIES: Import and distribution of furniture, foodstuffs, pre-fabricated buildings and building materials
Branch Offices: Riyadh, Dammam

Date of Establishment: 1971

SHEHAB COLD STORES

PO Box 104, Dammam 31411
Tel: 8323315, 8322153, 8322853
Cable: Shehab Dammam

PRINCIPAL ACTIVITIES: Import, storage and distribution of foodstuffs, cold storage
Associated Companies: Arabian Trading Co for Cold Storage, Saudi Arabia; Orient Est for Refrigeration & Foodstuffs, Saudi Arabia; Alharbi Trading Foodstuffs Refrigeration & Industrial Co, Dubai (UAE); Jamil Lines for Shipping & Trade, Lebanon

SHIPPING CORPORATION OF SAUDI ARABIA LTD (THE)

PO Box 1691, Jeddah 21441
Tel: 6471137, 6475650, 6472356
Cable: Albawakher
Telex: 601078 Arab, 602593 Scosa
Telefax: 6478222

Chairman: Abdulaziz Ahmed Arab
Senior Executives: Wajdi Aziz Arab (General Manager), Syed Azhar Hussain (Deputy General Manager), Mohd Sabir Khan (Deputy General Manager), Saleh Al Saggaf (Finance Manager), M Y Farooqui (Engineer Superintendent)

PRINCIPAL ACTIVITIES: Ship owners, shipping agents
Branch Offices: Head Office in Jeddah: National Marketing Bldg, 2nd Floor, Malik Khalid Street, also branch in Dammam: Arab Bldg, Amir Sultan Street, Haye Aladama, PO Box 302, Dammam, Tel 8264945, 8265271, Telex 801057 Arab, Fax 8264593 (Manager: Capt M Mohsin)
Principal Bankers: Bank Al Jazira; Saudi British Bank; National Commercial Bank

Date of Establishment: 1966

SHOBOKSHI, ALI & FAHD, GROUP

PO Box 5470, Jeddah 21422
Tel: 6658208, 6658209
Cable: GAC
Telex: 601008 Gac Sj

Directors: Sheikh Ali Shobokshi, Sheikh Fahd Shobokshi

PRINCIPAL ACTIVITIES: General, electrical, mechanical and civil engineering contractors, production of building materials, aggregate, asphalt, concrete products, hollow blocks, decorative products; commercial and industrial representations, power generation and distribution, water and sewage treatment, communication systems, transportation, clearing and forwarding, shipping services, motor vehicles and trucks distribution, manufacture, import and distribution of furniture; catering services, management services; advertising, market research, public relations; and aircraft operations; trading in foodstuffs, paper, clothing, electrical, and household appliances
Principal Agencies: Thorn Lighting, UK; Klein, Germany; Schanzin & Becker, Germany; Motoren Fabrik Hatz, Germany; Philips BV, Netherlands
Branch Offices: Riyadh: PO Box 3511, Tel 4761713, 4760372, Telex 401314 EWM; Dammam: PO Box 1058, Dhahran Airport, Tel 8331184, Telex 870074; Yanbu and Gizan

Subsidiary/Associated Companies: Electrical Work & Maintenance (EWM), PO Box 3511, Riyadh; Al Arousa Furniture Factory, PO Box 4515, Jeddah; Orient International Agencies (carpets, furnishings), PO Box 292, Jeddah; Saudi International Consulting Centre, PO Box 5470, Jeddah; Orient Co for Trading & Marketing, PO Box 5039, Jeddah; Shobokshi Maritime, PO Box 5470, Jeddah; Shobest Automotive Trading, PO Box 5470, Jeddah; Shobak Catering Group, PO Box 5470, Jeddah; Tihama for Advertising, Public Relations & Marketing, PO Box 5455, Jeddah; Shobokshi Commercial Enterprises, 173 Syngrou Ave, Athens, Greece

SIGMA PAINTS SAUDI ARABIA LTD

PO Box 7509, Dammam 31472
Tel: 8573436, 8573800, 8573996
Telex: 802341 Sigma Sj
Telefax: 8571734

Chairman: Sami K Algosaibi
Senior Executives: Jo Paffen (General Manager), Hennie Ansems (Area Manager), Mohammed Arif (Finance Manager), James Whalley (Production Manager), P H Isselmann (Technical Services Manager)

PRINCIPAL ACTIVITIES: Manufacture of paints, coatings and sealants
Branch Offices: Jeddah: PO Box 2285, Jeddah 21451, Tel 6911288, Telex 604162, Fax 6914648; Riyadh: PO Box 59738, Riyadh 11535, Tel 4654932, 4654943, Telex 406682, Fax 4654811
Principal Bankers: Albank Alsaudi Alhollandi, Dammam
Financial Information:

	1989/90 SR'000
Sales turnover	77,000
Authorised capital	8,175
Paid-up capital	8,175

Principal Shareholders: Khalifa Abdulrahman Algosaibi, Khaled Al Zamil, Mansour Al Zamil, Suleiman H Al Obeidallah, Sigma Coatings BV
Date of Establishment: 1981
No of Employees: 120

SNAS WORLDWIDE COURIER (IN ASSOCIATION WITH DHL)

PO Box 5641, Riyadh 11432
Tel: 4779653 (10 lines)
Telex: 403272 SNASCR Sj
Telefax: 4789846

PRINCIPAL ACTIVITIES: Worldwide courier service
Branch Offices: In Saudi Arabia: Dhahran, PO Box 756, Tel 8573333, Telex 870494; Jeddah, PO Box 7977, Tel 6693300, Telex 602559; Sub-Stations: Abha, Al Jouf, Arar, Baha, Buraidah, Gizan, Hafar Al Batin, Hail, Hofuf, Jubail, Khafji, Makkah, Medina, Nejran, Tabuk, Taif, Yanbu; In the Middle East: Bahrain, Cyprus, Egypt (Cairo, Alexandria), Iran, Jordan, Kuwait, Lebanon, Oman, Qatar, Sudan, UAE (Abu Dhabi, Dubai, Sharjah), Yemen

SOGEX ARABIA

PO Box 6929, Jeddah 21452
Tel: 6820120, 6820124
Telex: 602454 SOGEX SJ

Senior Executives: Mustapha Dernaika (Manager)

PRINCIPAL ACTIVITIES: Contractors, desalination and power plants; building, electrical, mechanical, general and precast building systems
Branch Offices: Riyadh & Dammam
Subsidiary Companies: Sogex International Ltd, USA

SOLTRAVO CONTRACTING CO

PO Box 2824, Jeddah 21461
Tel: 6656844
Cable: Arsocontra
Telex: 600832 Asolco Sj

Chairman: Sheikh Mohammad Ahmad Zainal Alireza
Directors: Said F Karam (General Manager)

PRINCIPAL ACTIVITIES: Civil works and construction, general
contractors
Principal Bankers: Al Bank Al Saudi Al Fransi, Jeddah

Principal Shareholders: Xenel Industries, Soltravo Lebanon
Date of Establishment: 1976
No of Employees: 300

SOUKS CO LTD (THE)

PO Box 200, Dhahran Airport 31932
Tel: 8579942
Cable: SOUKS
Telex: 870091 SOUKS SJ

Chairman: S A Alissa

PRINCIPAL ACTIVITIES: Supermarket operators in Eastern
Saudi Arabia, importers of chilled meats, dairy products and
fresh vegetables, cold store and warehouse operators
Branch Offices: Jubail; Qatif; Dammam; Dhahran; Al Khobar
Principal Bankers: Albank Alsaudi Alhollandi; Al Bank Al Saudi
Al Fransi

Date of Establishment: 1978
No of Employees: 200

SOUTHERN PROVINCE CEMENT CO

Head Office at Abha, PO Box 548, Abha
Tel: 2271500 (5 lines)
Cable: Southern Cement
Telex: 905010 SPCC Sj
Telefax: 2271407

Chairman: Prince Khalid Bin Turky Al Turky
Directors: Prince Abdullah Bin Musaed Bin Abdulrahman, Prince
Khalid Bin Fahd Bin Abdulaziz, Sheikh Saleh A Al Rajhi,
Sheikh Nasser M Bin Nabet, Sheikh Abdullah S Abu Melha,
Eng Amer Saeed Bargan, Sheikh Ahmed Abdullah Al Aqeel,
Sheikh Faleh Al Arjani
Senior Executives: Abdullah Bin Musaed (Vice Chairman), Amer
Saeed Bargan (Director/General Manager), Rida A Al
Ghazouli (Finance Manager), Mazhar Hussain (Marketing &
Purchasing Manager), Mohammad Saeed Awadh
(Administration Manager)

PRINCIPAL ACTIVITIES: Production and marketing of cement
Branch Offices: Jeddah: PO Box 7097, Jeddah 21462, Tel
6720822, 6727138, Fax 6716992, Telex 602381 SPCC Sj;
Factory: Gizan PO Box 119, Tel 3190755, Fax 3190544
Principal Bankers: Saudi American Bank, Saudi Cairo Bank,
Riyad Bank
Financial Information:

	1989/90 SR'000
Sales turnover	96,200
Authorised capital	700,000
Paid-up capital	700,000
Total assets	975,414

Principal Shareholders: Saudi Shareholders
Date of Establishment: 05.05.1394H (1974)
No of Employees: 793

SPECIALIZED ENTERPRISES CO (SPENCO)

PO Box 1731, Al-Khobar 31952
Tel: 8647431
Telex: 870245 Isaac Sj

President: I A Husseini (also General Manager)

PRINCIPAL ACTIVITIES: Engineering and architectural design,
construction of airport, harbours, desalination plant, water
treatment plants

No of Employees: 105

SPINNEY'S (SAUDI ARABIA) LTD

PO Box 2791, Riyadh 11461
Tel: 4784547 (4 lines)
Telex: 404862 Afscat Sj
Telefax: 4632226

PRINCIPAL ACTIVITIES: Catering and food supply

STEEL PRODUCTS CO LTD (STEPCO)

PO Box 4930, Riyadh 11412
Tel: Head Office & Factory: 4981888, Sales Office: 4053128,
4059546
Cable: STEPCO
Telex: 402285 STEPCO SJ
Telefax: 4982600 (HO & Factory), 4028022 (Sales Office)

Chairman: Ahmed A Juffali
Directors: Omar A Aggad (Managing Director), Rashed M
Thahen, Ibrahim A Touq, Peter H Koch
Senior Executives: Nabil M Atari (General Manager), Mohamed
A Afifi (Administration Manager), Ibrahim F Naddeh (Factory
Manager), Jamil Kamil (Financial Manager), Husam F Atari
(Asst Sales Manager)

PRINCIPAL ACTIVITIES: Manufacturing of deformed high
tensile wiremesh, lattice ribs, steel spacers, drawn wires in
coils & cut to length, block mesh galvanised or ungalvanised
Principal Agencies: Official distributors of Hadeed reinforcing
bars according to ASTM A615
Branch Offices: Jeddah: Tel 6726468, Fax 6726468
Principal Bankers: Arab National Bank; Albank Alsaudi
Alhollandi
Financial Information:

	1989 SR'000	1990 SR'000
Sales turnover	120,000	108,000
Authorised capital	16,400	16,400
Paid-up capital	16,400	16,400
Total assets	33,000	47,000

Principal Shareholders: E A Juffali & Bros; Aggad Investment
Co, Olayan Financing Company, Ibrahim Touq, Korf Transport
GmbH
Date of Establishment: 15th December 1976
No of Employees: 75

STEEL ROLLING MILL

PO Box 1826, Jeddah 21441
Tel: 6367462, 6367206, 6368706
Cable: Petsteel
Telex: 602127 Solb Sj

Chairman: Sheikh Youssef M Alireza
Directors: Eng Ali Al Ayed, Eng Ahmead Bakr Al Hibshi,
Abdullah Al Sulaim, Eng Abdulmohsin Al Otaibi
Senior Executives: Khalid A Al Sulaimani (Act General
Manager), Sameer A Al Dooseri (Asst Finance Manager),
Mohammad A Al Salim (Administration Manager), Mohamad
Al Mohdar (Commercial Manager), Mohammad H Al Oraini
(Production Manager), Adel A Al Qadi (Act Sales Manager)

PRINCIPAL ACTIVITIES: Producing reinforcing bars for building
and construction purposes
Parent Company: Saudi Iron & Steel Co (Hadeed)
Principal Bankers: Riyad Bank, Jeddah; Al Bank Al Saudi Al
Franci
Financial Information:

	1989/90 SR'000
Authorised capital	62,400
Paid-up capital	62,400

Principal Shareholders: Saudi Basic Industries Corp (SABIC);
Saudi Iron & Steel Co (Hadeed)
No of Employees: 230

STEVIN BAHARETH ENGINEERING & CONTRACTING CO LTD

PO Box 443, Jubail 31951
Tel: 3610556, 3611905
Telex: 831195 ADVO SJ
Telefax: 3612800

Owners: Shaikh Mohammed Saleh Bahareth, Hareth
Mohammed Bahareth

PRINCIPAL ACTIVITIES: Execution of all kinds of civil
construction projects, buildings, airports, roads, bridges,
dams, harbours, heavy foundations, piling/drilling, marine
dredging and reclamation works, soil investigations and
concrete repairs
Branch Offices: PO Box 404, Jeddah 21411, Tel 6440566,
6420234, 6423734, Telex 601022 Hareth Sj, Fax 6431747
Principal Bankers: Albank Alsaudi Alhollandi, Jubail
Financial Information:

	SR'000
Authorised capital	10,000
Paid-up capital	10,000

Principal Shareholders: Sheikh Mohammed Saleh Bahareth
(98%); Hareth Mohammed Bahareth (2%)
Date of Establishment: 1978
No of Employees: 80

SULTAN FOR GENERAL CONSTRUCTION & DEVELOPMENT

PO Box 6378, Jeddah 21442
Tel: 6655906, 6655907
Cable: SOLTAJED
Telex: 600155 SGC SJ

Directors: Mahmoud F El Kady (Managing Director)

PRINCIPAL ACTIVITIES: Construction, housing, commercial,
schools; factories for wood: doors, windows, furniture and
steel: fencing, tanks, also aluminium: windows, doors; quarry:
aggregates for concrete and asphalt. Import, wholesale, retail
of sanitaryware, tiles, kitchen equipment
Principal Agencies: Parodi Sanitaryware
Branch Offices: London, UK; Limassol, Cyprus
Principal Bankers: National Commercial Bank, Jeddah

Date of Establishment: 1977
No of Employees: 600

TAG SYSTEMS SAUDI ARABIA LTD

PO Box 2814, Riyadh 11461
Tel: 4022850

PRINCIPAL ACTIVITIES: Import and distribution of electrical
and sanitaryware, foodstuffs, heavy equipment, pipes,
chemicals, also public facilities, catering services and general
contracting

Principal Shareholders: Akram Subhi Al Ojjeh; Mansour Akram
Al Ojjeh; Osama Ali Al Qabbani

TAHER GROUP OF COMPANIES

PO Box 1178, Jeddah 21431
Tel: 02 6533668
Cable: Radomir
Telex: 601580 Towers SJ
Telefax: 02 6531912

Chairman: Khalid Abdulhady Taher
Directors: Tariq Taher, Nashwa Taher, Khadija Sidki
Senior Executives: John Francis Franklin (Executive Vice
President)

PRINCIPAL ACTIVITIES: Construction, hotels, trading, industry,
insurance, food, operation and maintenance

Principal Agencies: Du Pont, USA; Lubrizol, USA; Lafarge,
France
Branch Offices: Riyadh, Yanbu, Dammam, New York, Geneva
Principal Bankers: Saudi American Bank
Financial Information:

	1990 SR'000
Sales turnover	350,000
Authorised capital	40,000

Date of Establishment: 1977
No of Employees: 1,000

TAJ CO LTD

PO Box 4814, Jeddah 21412
Tel: 6313203, 6313204, 6313075
Cable: Al Taj Company Jeddah
Telex: 601637 Tajco Sj

Senior Executives: Waddah Al Dabbagh (Chief Executive)

PRINCIPAL ACTIVITIES: Boilers and process plant, process
engineering contractors, refrigeration and airconditioning
machinery, construction
Branch Offices: Riyadh, Damman, Yanbu

No of Employees: 200

TAJ PALACE HOTEL

PO Box 7727, Jeddah 21472
Tel: 6421288, 6439865
Telex: 601637 Tajco SJ

PRINCIPAL ACTIVITIES: Hotel business
Branch Offices: Location in Jeddah: Airport Road, Sharafia

TAMER, FAROUK, MAAMOUN, & CO

PO Box 180, Jeddah 21411
Tel: 6435600
Cable: Tamer Jeddah
Telex: 601215 Tamer Sj
Telefax: 6439834

Chairman: Farouk M S Tamer
Directors: Maanoun M S Tamer (Deputy Chairman), Ayman M M
S Tamer (Member of Board), Saeed M M S Tamer (Member
of Board), Talal F M S Tamer (Member of Board)
Senior Executives: Dr Subhi Alghanamah (General Manager)

PRINCIPAL ACTIVITIES: Import and distribution of
pharmaceutical products, medical equipment and hospital
supplies and consumer goods (toiletries, cosmetics,
foodstuffs, detergents & writing instruments)
Principal Agencies: Lab Anphar Rolland, France; Biochemie,
Austria; Boehringer Mannheim, W Germany; Lab Delagrange,
France; Lab Fumouze, France; Heinrich Mack, W Germany;
Kali Chemie, W Germany; Lab Latema, France; Gruppo
Lepetit, Italy; Luitpold, W Germany; Merrell Dow, France;
Norwich Eaton Hellas, Greece; Pharmax, UK; Sandoz
Wander, Switzerland; Schering Corp, USA; Searle, UK;
Specia, France; Rhone Poulenc, France; Swiss Serum &
Vaccine, Switzerland; Theraplix, France; Biolife, Italy;
Boehringer Mannheim Diagnostics, W Germany; Surgikos, UK
& USA; Bard, UK & USA; Steripak, UK; Spectramed Viggo,
UK; Boehringer Biochemia Robin, Italy; Hospal, Switzerland;
Johnson & Johnson, USA, Dubai, UK; Oticon, Denmark;
Quinton, USA; Sabre, UK; Seton, UK; S & S, Sweden; Bristol
Myers, Belgium; Mennen, USA; Shulton, UK; Maurer & Wirtz,
W Germany; Clairol, UK; Slendertone, Eire; Parfums Gucci,
France; A T Cross Export, USA; Borden, USA & UK;
Eurocoss, W Germany; AR Cross, Eire; Bristol Myers, USA,
UK & Sweden; Calirol Appliances, UK & Denmark; Dr Payot,
France; Ellenbetrix, W Germany; Leonard, France; Eurocos,
W Germany; Oral-B, UK & Eire; Lion Corp, Japan; Bonlac,
Australia; Nutricia, Holland; Bordan, USA; Roger Bellon,
France; Dansac, Denmark

Branch Offices: Riyadh: PO Box 388, Riyadh 11411; Alkhobar:
PO Box 352, Khobar 31411; Abha: PO Box 1141, Abha;
Buraidah, PO Box 740, Buraidah
Principal Bankers: Saudi American Bank, Albank Alsaudi
Alhollandi; Al Bank Al Saudi Al Fransi
Financial Information:

	1990
	SR'000
Annual turnover	300,000

Principal Shareholders: Farouk M S Tamer, Maamoun M S
Tamer
Date of Establishment: 1922
No of Employees: Approx 500

TAMIMI & FOUAD
PO Box 172, Dammam 31411
Tel: 8574050, 8574122, 8574130
Cable: Fouad Dammam
Telex: 801561 Tafco Sj

Chairman: Abdulla Fouad
Directors: Ali A Tamimi
Senior Executives: Tariq A Tamimi (President), Akram Arafeh
(Managing Director)

PRINCIPAL ACTIVITIES: Pipeline construction; mechanical and
civil construction; industrial catering, supermarkets, wholesale
and retail
Associated Companies: Arab American Constructors; T&F
Niigata; Tamimi & Fouad Global; Basic Chemical Industries
Ltd; Otis Engineering Saudi Arabia; T&F Reading & Bates;
Civil Works Co; Dammam Oberoi Hotel; National Shipping Co;
Tragex Insurance Co
Principal Bankers: Al Bank Al Saudi Al Fransi, Alkhobar
Financial Information:

	SR'000
Authorised capital	16,500
Paid-up capital	16,500

Principal Shareholders: Ali A Tamimi, Abdulla Fouad
Date of Establishment: 1963

TAMIMI COMPANY
Tamimi, Ali A,
PO Box 172, Dammam 3141152
Tel: 03-8574050, 8951128
Cable: Tamimi Alkhobar
Telex: 801561 Tafco SJ
Telefax: 03-8571592

Chairman: Ali A Tamimi (Owner)
Directors: Talal A Tamimi, Tariq A Tamimi
Senior Executives: Hisham Tamimi (General Manager Food
Div/Tamimi Safeway), Ahmad Tamimi (Asst General Manager
TAFGA O & M and Catering), H K Dossary (General Manager
Commercial Div), Mohammed Sabir (Finance Manager), Faez
AlBani (General Manager Real Estate Div), Stanley Doe
(General Manager Mechanical Div), John A McStay (General
Manager Construction Div), Adel A Azim (Purchasing
Manager), Samir N Beshara (Personnel Manager),
Mohammad Nada (Accounts Manager), Ahmed Al Arja
(Company Secretary)

PRINCIPAL ACTIVITIES: Contracting & trading. Contracting:
Tamimi Construction Division (general contractors of
buildings, roads & pipelines), Tamimi O & M and Catering
Division (operation & maintenance and catering contractors),
Tamimi Mechanical Division (mechanical & electrical
specialised contractors). Trading: Tamimi Food Division
(Supermarket chain), Tamimi Commercial Division (agents for
international firms), Tamimi Real Estate Division (development
and maintenance of group properties, compounds, buildings
and camps)
Principal Agencies: Cie Francaise de Produits Industriels;
General Electric; Manville; Pittsburg Corning; Red Wing;

Sterling Cable Co; Firestone Tires; Harris Control; Otis
Engineering; McProducts, Ireland; Stibbe BV Holland; Porta-
Test, Canada; Olympic, USA; Rockwool Lapinus, Holland;
Hamon Sobelco, Belgium; Dell, USA; Microsoft, USA
Branch Offices: Riyadh, Jubail, Dammam, Alkhobar, Dhahran,
Unaizah, Tabuk, Yanbu
Subsidiary Companies: Arabian T R Oil Services; Saudi Electric
Supply Co; Tamimi Technical Services & Trading; Middle East
Engineering Co (MEELSA); Taseco & Taseco T M S
(Transportation); Basic Chemical Industries (BCI)
Principal Bankers: Albank Alsaudi Alfransi; Albank Alsaudi
Alhollandi
Financial Information:

	1989	1990
	SR'000	SR'000
Sales turnover	700,000	720,000
Authorised capital	7,000	7,000
Paid-up capital	7,000	7,000
Total assets	1,100,000	1,200,000

Principal Shareholders: Ali A Tamimi, Mohammed A Tamimi
Date of Establishment: 1956
No of Employees: 2,800

TAYLORPLAN-SAUDI ARABIAN MARKETS LTD
PO Box 16446, Jeddah 21464
Tel: 6694151, 6694152, 6694274
Telex: 605051 TAYSAM SJ
Telefax: 6694274

Chairman: Sheikh Mohammad Ashmawi
Directors: Hilmi Omari, H N A Goodman, P A Hooper (Finance
Director), Sheikh Issam Ashmawi, Shabbir Ali (Managing
Director)
Senior Executives: Tim Abson (Commercial Manager), Ian
Wilkinson (Operations Manager)

PRINCIPAL ACTIVITIES: Contract catering, construction camp
management, all support services, for hotels, motels, schools,
hospitals, etc
Parent Company: Taylors International Services Limited, 5/7 St
Anne's House, Victoria Street, Alderney, Channel Islands
Principal Bankers: Saudi British Bank, Riyad Bank
Financial Information:

	1990
	SR'000
Authorised capital	1,000
Paid-up capital	1,000

Principal Shareholders: Saudi Arabian Markets Ltd, Jeddah,
Saudi Arabia (50%); Taylors International Services Ltd (50%)
Date of Establishment: 1976: In Saudi Arabia
No of Employees: 350

TEAMWORK SAUDI ARABIA LTD
PO Box 10747, Riyadh 11443
Tel: 4771519, 4783071
Telex: 400889 TAYCOM SJ
Telefax: 4785634

Chairman: Ali Zaid Al Quraishi
Directors: Khalid Zaid Al Quraishi, Bernard Moseley, Walter
Hogbin, Rashid Al Dahhan, Antony Jarvis, Geoffrey Hopkins,
Abdul Aziz Al Quraishi

PRINCIPAL ACTIVITIES: Building, civil and mechanical
engineering contractors
Branch Offices: Dammam; Jeddah
Principal Bankers: Saudi British Bank
Financial Information:

	1989
	SR'000
Turnover	7,000
Authorised capital	4,000
Paid-up capital	4,000

Principal Shareholders: Owned 50-50 by International Teamwork (a subsidiary of the Taylor Woodrow Group) and Ali Zaid Al Quraishi & Brothers
Date of Establishment: 1975
No of Employees: 190

TECHNICAL CONSTRUCTION CO
Abdulla Bin Moslem & Partners
PO Box 227, Dammam 31411
Tel: 8322276
Telex: 801096 Al Fanyah Sj

PRINCIPAL ACTIVITIES: General trading and contracting, real property; general building and civil contractors

TECHNICAL PROJECTS & CONTRACTING CO
PO Box 5467, Jeddah 21422
Tel: 6655458, 6650741, 6673064
Telex: 601112 Ditco Sj

Senior Executives: Sheikh Ibrahim Elkhereiji (Managing Director)

PRINCIPAL ACTIVITIES: Building and civil engineering contractors, building systems and materials
Branch Offices: Yanbu, Tel 3221144

Date of Establishment: 1975

TECHNICAL TRADING & CONTRACTING EST
PO Box 2302, Riyadh 11451
Tel: 4779395, 4778351
Cable: Modahi
Telex: 402911 Modahi Sj

Owner: Ali Abdulah Al-Qahtani
Directors: Bassam Fanush (Director of Marketing Department)

PRINCIPAL ACTIVITIES: General building and civil contractors, roads, bridges; import of building materials and, foreign firm's agents and representatives, marketing consultants
Principal Bankers: National Commercial Bank

Date of Establishment: 1974
No of Employees: 221

TECHNICAL WORKS CO
Technico
PO Box 2734, Riyadh 11461
Tel: 4021765, 4021768, 4027637
Cable: Izdhar
Telex: 401048 Algazal Sj

Directors: Abdel Aziz Albathi, Faisal Bin Turki Al Abdallah Al Saud, Mohamed Jawad Jaafar

PRINCIPAL ACTIVITIES: Building and civil engineering contractors (road building and bridge construction); production of asphalt

TECHNIP SAUDI ARABIA LTD
PO Box 7648, Riyadh 11472
Tel: 4781459, 4779464, 4773916
Cable: Sardecom Riyadh
Telex: 402389 Sadcol Sj

PRINCIPAL ACTIVITIES: Refineries, chemical/petrochemical, power utilities and desalination plants, contracting and construction

No of Employees: 1,200

TEXACO SAUDIA INC
PO Box 5572, Riyadh 11432
Tel: 4659077
Telex: 401709 TEXACO SJ
Telefax: 4641992

President: Richard G Grimler

PRINCIPAL ACTIVITIES: Local representation and coordination of business activities

THOMPSON COLE AZZAM
PO Box 12803, Jeddah 21483
Tel: 02 6718235
Telefax: 02 6722960

Directors: Clive Thompson, John Cole, Nabih Azzam, Gordon Hallewell, Gary Swinfield

PRINCIPAL ACTIVITIES: Quantity surveyors, cost consultants to the construction industry, project managers
Branch Offices: PO Box 3935, Riyadh 11481, Saudi Arabia; PO Box 5333, Amman, Jordan
Principal Bankers: Saudi American Bank

Date of Establishment: 1982
No of Employees: 30

TIHAMA FOR ADVERTISING, PUBLIC RELATIONS & MARKETING
PO Box 5455, Jeddah 21422
Tel: 644-4444 (30 lines)
Cable: Tihamco Jeddah
Telex: 601205 Tiha SJ
Telefax: 6512228

Chairman: Sheikh Saleh Abdullah Kamel
Directors: Mohammad Said Tayyeb (Delegated Member of the Board)
Senior Executives: Ghazi Abdul Aziz Jameel (General Manager), Adnan Kamel Slah (Dy General Manager for Media), Fahad Mohammad Bakhaidar (Dy General Manager for Planning & Control), Tareq Hassan Shata (Asst General Manager for Bookstores), Mansour Naser Lenjawi (Asst General Manager for Public Relations), Hussain Abdul Rahman Ramadan (Financial & Administration Manager)

PRINCIPAL ACTIVITIES: Advertising, media, public relations, market research, outdoor media, exhibition organisation, publishing, printing, distribution, bookstores, training and promotion
Branch Offices: Riyadh 11412: PO Box 4681; Makkah: PO Box 1074; Dammam 31461: PO Box 2666; Taif: PO Box 1245; Qasseem: Buraidah PO Box 232; Abha: PO Box 522; Yanbu: Tel 3223666; Hail: PO Box 1332; UK: International Press Centre, 76 Shoe Lane, London EC4A 3JB; France: 116 ave des Champs Elysees, 75008 Paris
Subsidiary Companies: Intermarkets; Saudi Expo; United Advertising Co (Shahba); Saudi Advertising Co; Tihama Al Mona International (TMI); Tihama Distribution & Bookstores; Interscope SA; Ad Art Al Medayan Co
Principal Bankers: National Commercial Bank; Saudi Cairo Bank; Riyad Bank; Jazirah Bank; Saudi American Bank; Saudi Hollandi Bank; French Saudi Bank
Financial Information:

	1989/90
	SR'000
Sales turnover	478,800
Profits	11,000
Authorised capital	120,000
Paid-up capital	120,000
Total assets	132,000

Principal Shareholders: HRH Saud Bin Naif Bin Abdul Aziz; Ali Hussein Shobokshi; Mohammad Said A Tayyeb; Ahmad Abdullah Sulaiman; Khalid Salem Bin Mahfooz; Abdul Aziz A Al-Rifai; Abdullah A Z Abu Al Samh; Dr Abdullah Sulaiman Man'aa; Hisham Ali Hafiz; Hamad A Al-Zamil; M Abdul Latif Jameel; Ibrahim M I Al-Esa; Saleh A Kamel; Dr Abdul Fattah Nazer
Date of Establishment: 1974
No of Employees: 425

TOONSI DEVELOPMENT & CONTRACTING CO

PO Box 262, Jeddah
Tel: 6872320/19, 6871957/58
Cable: Potatchips Jeddah
Telex: 600328 Toonsi Sj

Chairman: Abdullah B Toonsi
Directors: Faisal B Toonsi
Senior Executives: Yousef B Toonsi

PRINCIPAL ACTIVITIES: Furniture, jewellery, contracting, interior decoration
Branch Offices: Makkah: PO Box 91, Tel 5743981, 5745394
Parent Company: Bakr Toonsi Holding Co
Subsidiary Companies: Toonsi Investments Co; Toonsi-Bramm Co Ltd
Principal Bankers: Riyad Bank, Makkah

Principal Shareholders: Toonsi family
Date of Establishment: 1945
No of Employees: 224

TRADCO-VULCAN CO LTD (TVCL)

PO Box 10016, Jubail Industrial City, Jubail 31961
Tel: (03) 3417377
Telex: 832095 SAVL Sj
Telefax: 3419564

President: Nelson M Magee (Chief Executive Officer)
Directors: Khalid Ali Alturki (Trading & Development Co - Alkhobar), William J Grayson Jr (Vulcan Materials Co - USA), Kenneth E Boring (Dalton Rock Products Co - USA), W Clyde Shepherd Jr (Shepherd Construction Co Inc - USA)
Senior Executives: R Alan Hall (Manager Finance & Administration)

PRINCIPAL ACTIVITIES: Contractor/sub-contractor in paving and maintenance of roads, highways, airports, industrial sites, access facilities and other projects of similar nature
Principal Bankers: Al-Bank Al-Saudi Al-Fransi (Jubail Ind City Branch); Saudi American Bank (Jubail Ind City Branch)

Principal Shareholders: Trading & Development Co; Vulcan Materials Co; Dalton Rock Products Co; Shepherd Construction Co Inc
Date of Establishment: 1977

TRADING & CONTRACTING CORPORATION

PO Box 4504, Jeddah 21412
Tel: 6530956
Cable: Adjsabban
Telex: 601398 Novcom Sj

Chairman: Abdulbary M S Sabban (Owner)
Senior Executives: H Feroz Shamsi (Business Manager)

PRINCIPAL ACTIVITIES: Investment, manufacturing, trading, dealing in automobiles and leisure boats, catering, consumer goods
Branch Offices: Location in Jeddah: Medina Road
Parent Company: Sabban Investment Co Ltd
Principal Bankers: National Commercial Bank, Jeddah

Principal Shareholders: Abdulbary M S Sabban
Date of Establishment: 1973
No of Employees: 43

TRADING & DEVELOPMENT CO (TRADCO)

PO Box 84, Dhahran Airport, 31932
Tel: (03) 8644994, 8645381
Telex: 870151 PETSER SJ, 870176 TRADCO SJ
Telefax: 8952608

Chairman: Khalid Ali Alturki
Directors: Abdul Aziz Ali Alturki, Saleh Ali Alturki
Senior Executives: Peter M L Smith (Vice President Operations), Teck Boo Chow (Vice President), Dr Faisal Al Roumayyan (Vice President), Martin Mellish (Comptroller)

PRINCIPAL ACTIVITIES: Engineering; construction management; construction; general trading in industrial, agricultural and automotive products; steel fabrication; manufacture and sale of construction materials; lumber stocking and sales; training; instrumentation and electronic installation, repair and maintenance; operation and maintenance of industrial plants; telecommunications engineering, electrical engineering, supply and installation of roofing systems and insulation
Branch Offices: Alkhobar Office: PO Box 84, Dhahran Airport; Riyadh Office: PO Box 8082, Riyadh; Yanbu Office: PO Box 816, Madinat Yanbu Alsinaiyah
Subsidiary Companies: Agap Arabia Ltd; Roofing & Insulation Co Ltd (TASGEEF); Cegelec Contracting Co Ltd; Ebasco Arabia Ltd; Nedco Arabia Ltd; NKK Arabia Ltd; NKK Saudi Construction Co Ltd; Saudi Arabian Vulcan Ltd; TMSI Arabia Ltd; Tradco-Vulcan Co Ltd; Inma Lumber; Inma Electronics; Mannesmann Anlagenbau Arabia Ltd
Principal Bankers: National Commercial Bank; Albank Alsaudi Alfransi; Gulf International Bank

Principal Shareholders: Khalid Ali Alturki
Date of Establishment: 1973
No of Employees: 3,000

TRADING & INDUSTRIAL GROUP (HOLDING) LTD (TIG)

PO Box 2500, Jeddah 21451
Tel: 6531680 (5 lines)
Telex: 601110 Tig Sj, 603320 Hsh Sj
Telefax: 6519168

Chairman: Hashim Said Hashim
Directors: Said Hashim (Managing Director)
Senior Executives: Amr Hashim, Ali Saleem, Tawfic Al Gailani, Ali Salah (Finance Manager)

PRINCIPAL ACTIVITIES: Industrial engineering, construction, electrical and mechanical engineering, process control systems, data processing, precast concrete production, aluminium fabrication and extrusion, styropore and electro-mechanical engineering
Principal Agencies: Foxboro, Masoneilan, LWP Consortium
Branch Offices: Riyadh 11471, PO Box 3445, Tel 4786321, Telex 401656; Dammam 31421, PO Box 647, Tel 8338600, Telex 801073
Subsidiary/Associated Companies: TIG-Tesco Int'l Ltd, TIG-Foxboro Arabia Ltd, Arabian Contracting Company Ltd (ACC), ACC's Styropore Factory, ACC's Prefabricated Bathroom Factory, Aluminium Products Co Ltd (ALUPCO), Alumaco, Betonbau Koch Arabia Ltd, TIG-Galler-Informica, ACC-Ozok
Principal Bankers: National Arab Bank, Saudi European Bank, Saudi Investment Bank
Financial Information:

	1989 SR'000
Sales turnover	450,000
Authorised capital	10,000
Paid-up capital	10,000
Total assets	500,000

Principal Shareholders: Hashim S Hashim, Said H Hashim, Haifa H Hashim Amr H Hashim, Basma H Hasim
Date of Establishment: 1972
No of Employees: 1,500

TRANS-ARABIAN TECHNICAL SERVICES CO LTD (TATS)

PO Box 30, Dhahran Airport 31932
Tel: 8570095
Telex: 870259 TATS Sj
Telefax: 8577658

Chairman: Shaikh Abdul Majid Zahid
Directors: Amr A M Zahid (Managing Director)

SAUDI ARABIA

Senior Executives: Ayman Hussain (Director Finance & Administration), John G Salter Jr (Operations Manager), Georges Bizri (Parts Director)

PRINCIPAL ACTIVITIES: Rebuild/repair of diesel engine, construction/industrial equipment; fleet maintenance; facilities and installed equipment operation and maintenance
Principal Agencies: Korody-Colyer, Diesel Parts; PAI Diesel Parts; Industrial Parts Depot; Payen Gaskets; AE, Diesel Parts; United Technologies Diesel Systems; Garrett Aireisearch Turbochargers; DoAll Machine Tools & Supplies; Eaton Fuller Transmission & Axles, Zexel Corporation FIE Diesel Parts, Japan
Branch Offices: PO Box 16383, Jeddah 21464
Subsidiary Companies: Ameco Industrial Supply
Principal Bankers: Saudi Cairo Bank; Saudi Hollandi Bank; Saudi French Bank
Financial Information:

	1990
	SR'000
Sales turnover	10,000
Profits	200
Authorised capital	2,000
Paid-up capital	2,000
Total assets	8,500

Principal Shareholders: Shaikh Abdul Majid Zahid
Date of Establishment: 3-6-1393 (H) 1972
No of Employees: 150

TRIAD HOLDING CORPORATION LLC
PO Box 6, Riyadh 11411
Tel: 4027888, 4022305
Cable: Tricorp
Telefax: 4028577

Chairman: Adnan M Khashoggi
Directors: Adnan Khashoggi, Hussein Khashoggi
Senior Executives: Soufian A F Yassine (Vice President), Ibrahim Abdul Latif (Finance Director), Elias Farhat (Personnel Director)

PRINCIPAL ACTIVITIES: Industrial groups and promotion; economic, marketing and industrial consultants, investments, real estate, banking
Principal Agencies: Kenworth Trucks; MCI Construction Systems
Branch Offices: Jeddah
Subsidiary Companies: Triad Condas International; National Housing Co; System International; Triad International Markets; Al Nasr Co for Trade & Industry
Principal Bankers: Citibank; National Commercial Bank; Saudi American Bank
Financial Information:

	1990
	SR'000
Sales turnover	350,000
Authorised capital	10,000
Paid-up capital	10,000

Principal Shareholders: Adnan Khashoggi & Hussein Khashoggi
Date of Establishment: 1954
No of Employees: 200

TRUST INVESTMENT & DEVELOPMENT EST
PO Box 3750, Riyadh 21481
Tel: 4771650
Cable: Martel Riyadh
Telex: 401120 Zuhair Sj, 402211 Samark Sj

Chairman: Harb Al-Zuhair

PRINCIPAL ACTIVITIES: Civil and electro-mechanical contracting, electronics, manufacturing industry, trade, services and investment
Branch Offices: Riyadh, Al-Khobar, Dammam

No of Employees: 250

TUHAMAH CONTRACTING CO
PO Box 4730, Riyadh 11412
Tel: 4480330
Cable: Ormay
Telex: 401598 Tuhama Sj

Chairman: Abdullah Ibrahim Al Tuwaijri (also General Manager)
Directors: Abdul Mohsin Abdullah Al Tuwaijri, Abdul Mohsin Abdul Aziz Al Tuwaijri
Senior Executives: Kayid Omary (Technical Director), Saeed Sultan (Project Engineer), Jalal Malhas (Electrical Engineer)

PRINCIPAL ACTIVITIES: Civil engineering and construction (mainly buildings and roads construction)
Principal Bankers: Arab National Bank; Saudi Investment Banking Corp; Saudi American Bank
Financial Information:

	SR'000
Capital	15,000

Principal Shareholders: Chairman and directors as described above
No of Employees: 130

UNETCO
PO Box 1830, Dammam 31441
Tel: 8338021, 8337876
Telex: 802214 Unetco Sj

PRINCIPAL ACTIVITIES: Supplies of cement, white cement, steel bars, structural steel, transporters, contractors, and construction consultants
Branch Offices: Jeddah: PO Box 9096, Tel 6693409, Telex 602821; Riyadh: PO Box 6916, Tel 4772145, Telex 404528; Gizan; Khamis Mushait; Yanbu; Saihat

UNITED BROTHERS COMPANY
PO Box 6093, Jeddah 21442
Tel: 6441128, 6423859
Telex: 601177 Ubc Sj

Directors: Sheikh Sulaiman Bin Abdulaziz El Khereiji, Sheikh Abdulqader Bin Sulaiman El Khereiji, Sheikh Muhamad Bin Sulaiman El Khereiji, Sheikh Abdulaziz Bin Sulaiman El Khereiji

PRINCIPAL ACTIVITIES: Trading and dealing in automobiles and auto spare parts and accessories; import of medical equipment and supplies; engineering consultants
Principal Agencies: Renault; Ledcot; Creusot Loire; Elf Lubricants
Branch Offices: Riyadh; Yanbu
Principal Bankers: National Commercial Bank; Al Bank Al Saudi Al Fransi

Date of Establishment: 1976

UNITED COMMERCIAL AGENCIES LTD SA
PO Box 5019, Jeddah 21422
Tel: 6530068-72-76
Telex: 601906 Uca Sj
Telefax: 6511936

Chairman: Ghaith Pharaon
Directors: A Kanoo, S El Attas, Bakr Bin Laden
Senior Executives: Jacques G Sacy (Executive Vice President), Antoine H Ghattas (Senior Vice President), Machaal A Karam (Senior Vice President), Arziv Avakian (Branch Manager Jeddah), Daron Simonian (Branch Manager Riyadh), Robert Ayoub (Branch Manager Dammam)

PRINCIPAL ACTIVITIES: Insurance and reinsurance
Principal Agencies: Eastern Ins & Reins Co, Al Saudia Life Ins Co
Branch Offices: Dammam: PO Box 948; Riyadh: PO Box 2041; also UK: 16 Lovat Lane, London EC3R 8DT
Principal Bankers: Al Bank Al Saudi Al Fransi, Jeddah

Financial Information:

	1990
	SR'000
Sales turnover	56,000
Authorised capital	15,000
Paid-up capital	15,000

Principal Shareholders: Ghaith Pharaon, Heirs of Salem Binladen
Date of Establishment: 1974
No of Employees: 104

UNITED ENTERPRISES

PO Box 443, Port Rd, Dammam 31411
Tel: 8275440, 8276137, 8263044
Cable: Unenco
Telex: 801064 Sj Unenco
Telefax: 8275346

President: Sheikh Salim M Abduljawad
Directors: Sheikh Farid M Abduljawad, M I Siddiqui
Senior Executives: M J Siddiqui (General Manager), A I Qureshi (Shipping Manager), J A Khan (Transport & Container Manager)

PRINCIPAL ACTIVITIES: Shipping, stevedoring, freight brokers, imports, marketing, container handling and storage; transportation contractors
Principal Agencies: Toko, Fujiwara, Hkis, Sidermar Lines
Branch Offices: Jubail, Riyadh
Associated Companies: Globe Marine Services, Dammam; UNENCO (UK) Ltd, London; UNENCO (Pakistan) Ltd, Karachi; Associated Lubricants Co, Dammam
Principal Bankers: National Commercial Bank; Al Bank Al Saudi Al Fransi, Alkhobar

Principal Shareholders: Ownership Company
Date of Establishment: 1964
No of Employees: 1,050

UNITED HOTELS & SHOPPING CENTRES CO

PO Box 1178, Jeddah 21431
Tel: 6532515, 6533779
Cable: Radomir
Telex: 601580 Towerssj

Chairman: Khalid Abdulhadi Taher
Senior Executives: Jan Hilhorst (General Manager), John F Franklin (Executive Vice President)

PRINCIPAL ACTIVITIES: Ownership and operation of the Holiday Inn Hotel, Yanbu
Principal Bankers: Saudi American Bank

Principal Shareholders: Taher Group of Companies
No of Employees: 105

UNITED SAUDI COMMERCIAL BANK

PO Box 25895, Riyadh 11476
Tel: 4784200
Cable: Saucom Bank
Telex: 405461 Saucom SJ
Telefax: 4783197

Chairman: HRH Prince Al Waleed Bin Talal Bin Abdulaziz Al Saud
Directors: Saleh Ali Al Rashid, Hussain Alawi Al Bar, Hassan Ali Al Sairafi, Mustafa Ibrahim Al Hejailan, Esmat Mohiddine Nazer, Sulaiman A Al Saleh, Peter J de Roos, Maqbool Ahmed Soomro, Faridoun Towhidi Moqhddam
Senior Executives: Gerald Henry Kangas (General Manager & Chief Executive), M M Bailur (Senior Advisor), Abdulaziz Y Al Oraifi (Head of Operations & Bank Administration), Maher G Al Aujan (Head of Corporate Banking), Hussain M Al Fakhri (Head of Retail Banking)

PRINCIPAL ACTIVITIES: Commercial banking and investment

Branch Offices: Riyadh Sitteen St Br: PO Box 3335, Riyadh 11471, Telex 405815, Fax 4784200 ext 116; and 3 other branches in Riyadh; Jeddah Balad St Br: PO Box 482, Jeddah 21411, Telex 601068, Fax 6479971; and 1 other branch in Jeddah; Al Khobar Br: PO Box 1617, Al Khobar 31952, Telex 870967 Fax 8985964; Dammam Br: PO Box 619, Dammam 31421, Telex 803029, Fax 8330863; Makkah Br: PO Box 9080, Makkah, Telex 540525, Fax 5444500; Al Madinah Al Muawarah Br: PO Box 4126, Telex 570336, Fax 8365992; Hofuf Br: PO Box 2793 Hofuf 31982, Tel 5870456, Telex 861373, Fax 5878792
Financial Information:

	1990
	SR'000
Net income	125,300
Interest income	478,950
Authorised capital	250,000
Paid-up capital	250,000
Share capital & reserves	445,190
Deposits	5,612,971
Loans & advances	1,246,487
Total assets	6,237,092

Principal Shareholders: Saudi Nationals (70%); Saudi International Bank London (10%); Bank Melli Iran (10%); United Bank Limted Pakistan (10%)
Date of Establishment: October 1983
No of Employees: 262

UNITED TECHNOLOGY PRODUCTS CO LTD

PO Box 7997, Jeddah 21472
Tel: 6604488, 6656657
Telex: 601453 USEF Sj
Telefax: 6722753, 6719874

Chairman: Abdul Latif Jameel
Directors: Mohammed Jameel
Senior Executives: John Chan, Michel Elias (General Manager), Ahmed Iqbal Bangee (Financial Controller), Isam Nazmedin (Marketing Manager), Mohammed Hasim Kadi (Group Personnel Manager), Sahel Bushnaq (Technical Manager)

PRINCIPAL ACTIVITIES: Supply of household appliances and electronic equipment
Principal Agencies: Toshiba, Japan
Branch Offices: Riyadh, Tel 4652970; Dammam Tel 8263251, Jeddah Tel 6714488
Parent Company: Abdul Latif Jameel Co Ltd
Principal Bankers: Saudi British Bank
Financial Information:

	1990
	SR'000
Authorised capital	50,000
Paid-up capital	50,000

Date of Establishment: 1981
No of Employees: 167

UNITED TRANSPORT & HEAVY EQUIPMENT CORP (UTECORP)

PO Box 1768, AlKhobar 31952
Tel: 8642552
Cable: Mufreh
Telex: 871227 Mufreh Sj

President: Ali M Al-Ajinah

PRINCIPAL ACTIVITIES: General, civil, electrical and mechanical contractors, water distribution, drainage, landscaping, operation and maintenance of camps, buldings, transportation, vehicles and heavy equipment hire

URBAN & RURAL DEVELOPMENT CO

PO Box 3770, Riyadh 11481
Tel: 4024885
Cable: Urdco
Telex: 401927 Urdco Sj

Chairman: H R H Prince Khalid Bin Abdullah Bin Abdulrahman Al Saud

Directors: HE Suliman Olayan, HE Hassan Mishari, Conrad C Stucky

PRINCIPAL ACTIVITIES: Landscape design and implementation; irrigation systems, design and installation, soil stabilization, recreation and sport grounds

Principal Agencies: Rain Bird, California, USA; International Bitumen Emulsions (Chevron), California, USA

Branch Offices: PO Box 1468, Alkhobar, Tel 8644208; PO Box 6481, Jeddah, Tel 6514315; Jubail, Tel 8333000; Yanbu, Tel 3223124

Subsidiary Companies: Planning Development Services inc

Principal Bankers: Albank Alsaudi Alhollandi, Riyadh; Riyad Bank, Riyadh; First National Bank, Minnesota, USA

Financial Information:

	SR'000
Authorised capital	27,000

Principal Shareholders: HRH Prince Khalid Bin Abdullah Bin Abdulrahman Al Saud; Olayan Financing Company

Date of Establishment: June 16, 1976

No of Employees: 110

VETCO SAUDI ARABIA

PO Box 245, Dhahran Airport 31932
Tel: 8575883, 8576091
Cable: Vetco Dhahran
Telex: 870045 Vetco Sj
Telefax: 8579595

Senior Executives: Ian H Smith (General Manager), E G Navarro (Finance & Admin Manager), Stewart Smith (Sales & Marketing Manager), M Smith (Operations Supervisor), D Amos (Supervisor Technical Services)

PRINCIPAL ACTIVITIES: Service company specialising in quality control, industrial and oilfield inspection, destructive and non-destructive testing, welder qualification testing, site supervision, on stream inspection, commissioning, O & M, instrument calibration & manpower service

Branch Offices: Al Khobar Test Centre, Tel 857-9796; Yanbu, Tel 322-4128; Jubail, Tel 361-0331

Parent Company: Vetco Inspection Gmbh

Principal Bankers: Al Bank Al Saudi Al Fransi

Financial Information:

	1989 SR'000	1990 SR'000
Sales turnover	34,000	29,000
Authorised capital	4,000	4,000
Paid-up capital	4,000	4,000
Total assets	15,000	15,600

Principal Shareholders: Partners: Vetco Enterprises AG, Olayan Financing Company

Date of Establishment: March 1972

No of Employees: 250

W S ATKINS AND ASSOCIATES

See ATKINS, W S, AND ASSOCIATES

WAFRA UNITED

PO Box 756, Riyadh 11421
Tel: 4011486
Cable: Wafra Riyadh
Telex: 401775 Wafra Sj

Directors: Zouheir Sultani

Senior Executives: Wisam Sulayman (General Manager)

PRINCIPAL ACTIVITIES: Contracting and construction (civil, electrical and mechanical)

Principal Agencies: H H Robertson (UK) Ltd

Date of Establishment: 1962

WAHAH ELECTRIC SUPPLY CO OF SAUDI ARABIA

W.E.S.C.O.S.A.

PO Box 2389, Dammam 31451
Tel: 8572460, 8576457, 8577587
Telex: 801174 WESCOS SJ
Telefax: 8571684

Chairman: Ali Zaid Al Quraishi

Directors: Richard U Benson, Khaled Ben Ali

Senior Executives: Richard U Benson (General Manager), Khaled Bin Ali (Director of Marketing & Sales)

PRINCIPAL ACTIVITIES: Manufacture of transformers, panel-boards, switchboards, cable tray, electrical equipment

Parent Company: Ali Zaid Al Quraishi & Bros

Associated Companies: Westinghouse Electric Supply Co, USA; M P Husky, USA

Principal Bankers: Saudi British Bank, Dammam

Financial Information:

	1990 SR'000
Sales turnover	30,000
Paid-up capital	4,247.5
Total assets	14,000

Principal Shareholders: Ali Zaid Al Quraishi Brothers Co; Abdul Aziz Al Quraishi

Date of Establishment: 1976

No of Employees: 80

WASSIM TRADING ESTABLISHMENT

PO Box 409, Riyadh 11411
Tel: 4765000, 4762582
Cable: Wassim
Telex: 401617 Wassim Sj
Telefax: 4765000

Owner: Ibrahim Hassan Khashoggi

PRINCIPAL ACTIVITIES: Import and distribution of laboratory furniture, equipment, apparatus, supplies and chemicals

Principal Agencies: Kewaunee Scientific Equipment Corp, USA; Fluka, Switzerland; J Bibby, UK; GCA Precision Scientific Group, USA

Branch Offices: PO Box 18522, Jeddah 21142, Tel 6518785, Fax 6530676

Principal Bankers: Arab National Bank, Riyadh

Date of Establishment: 1976

WATSON (SAUDI ARABIA)

PO Box 2023, Jeddah 21451
Tel: 6655468, 6607949
Cable: Culvert - Jeddah
Telex: 601064 Culvet Sj
Telefax: 6607949

Resident Partner: Charles M Cullen

PRINCIPAL ACTIVITIES: Consulting engineers in the fields of water and public health engineering

Associated Companies: Watson Hawksley, High Wycombe, UK

Principal Shareholders: Partners

Date of Establishment: 1968

No of Employees: 50

WESTERN ELECTRIC INTERNATIONAL

PO Box 4945, Riyadh 11412
Tel: 4917700
Telex: 401522 WECORY SJ

Senior Executives: A D Wood (Vice President), J R Peddy (Manager -Jeddah), A Abdel Malek (Manager - Dammam)

PRINCIPAL ACTIVITIES: Telecommunications

Branch Offices: PO Box 6948, Jeddah 21452, Tel 6691698, 6657003, Telex 601179 Bugshan SJ; PO Box 4178, Dammam, Tel 8332188, 8339559, Telex 801065
Associated Companies: Western Electric Company, USA

WESTINGHOUSE ELECTRIC SA

PO Box 3779, Riyadh 11481
Tel: 4648000
Telex: 402209 WELSA SJ

PRINCIPAL ACTIVITIES: Power equipment supply and electrical contracting
Branch Offices: PO Box 620, Alkhobar, Tel 8949264; PO Box 461, Jeddah, Tel 6670290
Parent Company: Westinghouse Electric Corporation
Subsidiary Companies: Westinghouse Electric Supply Co of Saudi Arabia (WESCOSA); Industry Services Company of Saudi Arabia (ISCOSA)

Principal Shareholders: Westinghouse Electric Corp (USA)

WHINNEY MURRAY & CO

PO Box 213, Dhahran Airport 31932
Tel: 8571055 (7 lines)
Cable: Ernstaudit Dhahran Airport
Telex: 870146 ERNST SJ
Telefax: 8579831

Directors: K Dabir Alai (Managing Partner - Alkhobar), S T Badawi (Managing Partner - Jeddah), D W Perkins (Managing Partner - Riyadh)

PRINCIPAL ACTIVITIES: Accountants tax and management advisors
Branch Offices: Saudi Arabia (PO Box 2732, Riyadh 11461, Tel 4776272; Telex 401348, Fax 4776352; PO Box 1994, Jeddah 21441, Tel 6671040 (5 lines), Telex 601787, Fax 6652076); Dubai (Middle East Office); Bahrain; Egypt; Jordan; Kuwait; Lebanon; Oman; Qatar; United Arab Emirates (Abu Dhabi, Dubai, Ras Al Khaimah, Sharjah); Yemen

Date of Establishment: 1960

WHITTAKER SAUDI ARABIA LTD

PO Box 4347, Riyadh 11491
Tel: 4778755
Telex: 401447 WSAL SJ
Telefax: 4783166

Chairman: HRH Prince Fahd Bin Khalid
Directors: HRH Prince Saud Bin Khalid (Vice Chairman), Mohamed O Al Sanousi (Managing Director)
Senior Executives: John K Stroud (Finance Director), Salih Bulkhi (Business Development Manager), David Morgan (Recruitement Manager), Mohamed Alamudine (Project Manager MODA Hafr Al Batin Project), Abdul Rahman Nasser (Project Director MODA Dhahran Project), Jamil Odeh (Project Director MOH Project), Adnan Mugrabe (Project Manager MODA Jeddah Project), Awni Abu Sbaa (Regional Manager Abha)

PRINCIPAL ACTIVITIES: Hospital management
Parent Company: Mawarid Ltd (via Mawarid Services Ltd)
Principal Bankers: Albank Alsaudi Alhollandi
Financial Information:

	1989 SR'000
Sales turnover	650,000
Authorised capital	8,300
Paid-up capital	8,300
Total assets	386,000

Principal Shareholders: Mawarid Services Ltd
No of Employees: 5,000

XENEL INDUSTRIES LTD

PO Box 2824, Jeddah 21461
Tel: 6437619
Cable: Zenogram
Telex: 601166 Xenel Sj
Telefax: 6436344

Chairman: Mohamed Ahmed Yousuf Zainal Alireza
Directors: Abdullah A Y Z Alireza, Hisham A Y Z Alireza, Khalid A Y Z Alireza
Senior Executives: James A S Chapman (General Manager, Business Development & Construction), Mohamed Ashraf Tumbi (General Manager, Finance), Saleh Al Eisa (General Manager, Project Evaluation & Support Services), Fouad Al Humoud (General Manager, Riyadh), John A Bannerman (General Manager Systems Division)

PRINCIPAL ACTIVITIES: Multi purpose organisation in the fields of construction, marketing, investment, operation & maintenance, systems, property, transportation, general trading and manufacturing
Branch Offices: PO Box 3886, Riyadh 11481, Tel 4630550, Telex 401175 Xenel Sj, Fax 4650943; Xenel International USA, 1377 Oak Grove Place, Westlake Village CA91362, USA, Tel 805 497-0511, Telex 182613 Xenel WKVG
Associated Companies: Saudi Cable Co (Manufacture of electrical wire and cables); Resources Sciences Arabia Ltd (Construction, O&M management services); Saudi Bulk Transport Ltd (Cement supply and transportation in bulk); International Co for Building Materials (BINEX); AMI Saudi Arabia Ltd; Litton Saudi Arabia Ltd; Arabian Bulk Trade Ltd; Ret-Ser Saudi Arabia Ltd; Wexico Systems & Services Ltd; NEC Saudi Arabia Ltd; Saudi Services & Operating Co Ltd; Brown Daltas & Associates Saudi Arabia Ltd; Xenel Contracting Ltd; Xenel Marketing Ltd; Xenel Maintenance Ltd; CTCI Arabia Ltd; Arabian Soletanche Ltd; Furukawa Saudi Arabia Ltd; Hidada Ltd; Saudi Arabian Morrison Ltd; Dar Al Amana Lts; Xenel International; Saudi Cable Marketing Co; Hanjin Saudi Arabia Ltd; Kasktas Arabia Ltd, Spie-Capag Arabia Ltd; Gulf Pearl Trade Ltd; Agri Bulk Trade Ltd, Saudi Exploration Ltd; Saudi Scaffolding Factory; Xenel Systems Ltd; Tri-Continent Services Co Ltd; Micro Computer Company; Alujain Corporation Saudi Arabia; The Arab Company for Organic Fertilisers
Principal Bankers: Saudi French Bank; Albank Alsaudi Alhollandi; Saudi British Bank
Financial Information:

	1990 SR'000
Paid-up capital	50,000

Principal Shareholders: Chairman and Directors as described
Date of Establishment: 1973, became a limited liability company in 1979
No of Employees: Over 20,000 (in group)

YAMAMA FACTORIES FOR RED BRICKS & CLAY PRODUCTS

PO Box 26156, Riyadh 11486
Tel: 4763830, 4780509, 4783647
Cable: Tobelyamama
Telex: 405415
Telefax: 4780448

Chairman: Ali A Al Zamil
Directors: Abdulla Z Al Zamil, Khalid A Al Zamil, Abdulla H Al Naim
Senior Executives: Abdulla Z Al Zamil (General Manager), Claus Eberst (Production Manager), Ayyash Al Shamali (Sales Manager), Fathi Tolba (Chief Accountant)

PRINCIPAL ACTIVITIES: Manufacture of red clay bricks, ceiling bricks, paving bricks, and decorative bricks
Principal Bankers: Al Bank Al Saudi Al Fransi, Al Rajhi Co for Investment

Financial Information:

	1990
	SR'000
Sales turnover	18,600
Profits	3,600
Authorised capital	29,000
Paid-up capital	29,000
Total assets	65,000

Principal Shareholders: Hamad Ali Mubark, Fahad Al Deghaither, Abdulaziz A Al Zamil & Brothers, Abdulla Hamad Al Naim, Hamad Al Zamil & Bros, Abdulla Z Al Zamil
Date of Establishment: 1977
No of Employees: 120

YAMAMA SAUDI CEMENT CO LTD

PO Box 293, Riyadh 11411
Tel: 4058288
Cable: Yamama Cement
Telex: 401024 Yamama Sj
Telefax: 4033292

President: HH Prince Mohammed Bin Saud Alkabeer
Directors: HH Prince Mohammad Bin Abdul Aziz Bin Turky, HH Prince Sultan Bin Mohammad Bin Saud Alkabeer, HH Turky Bin Mohammad Bin Abdulaziz Bin Turky Al Saud, HE Sheikh Abdulla Bin Adwan, HE Sheikh Saleh Al Abdulaziz Al Rajhi, HE SHeikh Suliman Al Abdulaziz Al Mureishad, National Commercial Bank, Riyad Bank
Senior Executives: HH Prince Sultan Bin Mohammad Bin Saud Alkabeer (Managing Director), Malallah Hamid Al Tuhafi (General Manager)

PRINCIPAL ACTIVITIES: Manufacture and marketing of Portland cement capacity 350,000,000 tons/year; production of relevent paper bags
Branch Offices: Location in Riyadh: Batha Street, Yamama Cement Building
Principal Bankers: Saudi American Bank; National Commercial Bank; Saudi Cairo Bank
Financial Information:

	1990
	SR'000
Profits	100,000
Authorised capital	900,000
Paid-up capital	900,000
Total assets	1,000,000

Principal Shareholders: Saudi Nationals
No of Employees: over 1,000

YUSUF BIN AHMED KANOO

See KANOO, YUSUF BIN AHMED,

YUSUF M ALDOSSARY EST

See ALDOSSARY, YUSUF M, EST

ZAGZOOG & MATBOULI COMPANY

PO Box 556, Jeddah 21421
Tel: 6512111
Cable: ZAGZOOG
Telex: 601114 Zama Sj

Chairman: Sulaiman S Zagzoog
Directors: Suleiman Saeed Zagzoog (Partner), Mahmood Mohammad Ali Matbouli (Partner)
Senior Executives: Mohammad S Zagzoog

PRINCIPAL ACTIVITIES: Import and distribution of household appliances, electrical and electronic appliances and equipment
Principal Agencies: Samsung, Korea; Sampo, Shinho, Taiwan; Calor SA, France; Glem-Gas SPA, Italy; Toaco, Japan
Branch Offices: Jeddah, Tel 6422848 Mecca, Tel 5581094; Medina, Tel 8221031; Taif, Tel 6422456; Dammam, Tel 8334078; Riyadh, Tel 4121308

Principal Bankers: Albank Alsaudi Alhollandi, Saudi Cairo Bank, Jeddah; Massraf Faisal Al Islami, Bahrain
Financial Information:

	SR'000
Authorised capital	60,000
Paid-up capital	60,000

Principal Shareholders: Partnership
Date of Establishment: 1953
No of Employees: 150

ZAHA TRADING EST

PO Box 8018, Riyadh 11482
Tel: 4044523, 4043630
Cable: Akico
Telex: 400356

Chairman: Fahd Abdel Aziz Al-Akeel (also Owner and General Manager)

PRINCIPAL ACTIVITIES: Trading and import, export of all kinds of furniture and building materials. Also hotel owners and managers
Principal Agencies: Texas Instruments Inc, Texas, USA
Branch Offices: Hail, Saudi Arabia
Principal Bankers: National Commercial Bank; Riyadh Bank

ZAHID TRACTOR & HEAVY MACHINERY CO LTD

PO Box 8928, Jeddah 21492
Tel: 6671156
Cable: Zahidtractor
Telex: 602851 Zahtrac Sj, 602852 Zahgrp Sj
Telefax: 02-6690727

Chairman: Sheikh Talal Y Zahid
Directors: Sheikh Waleed Y Zahid (President), Sheikh Fahad Y Zahid (Executive Vice President), Sheikh Mohammad Y Zahid (Vice President)
Senior Executives: Edmond R Saoud (Director Finance & Accounting), Wafaa H Zawawi (Director Truck & Vehicle Division), Safwan H Zawawi (Director Personnel Development & Administration), Al Sharif Hazim Al Ghalib (Director Automotive Products Div), Roland Pflaumer (Director Construction & Machinery Div)

PRINCIPAL ACTIVITIES: Import/export and related services, dealing in earthmoving equipment, power generation, materials handling, mining, agricultural, automotive & rubber products, transport, travel services, real estate development, retailing, distribution, wholesale, maintenance and operation services, equipment rental
Principal Agencies: Caterpillar Tractor, Koehring International, Ingersoll-Rand Intl, Peerless Pumps, DJB, Volvo Cars & Trucks, Lorain, Ameise, JLG Lifts, Rome, Mannesmann DEMAG, Pirelli Tyres, Renault Cars, GEHL GmbH, Rammer Hammer
Branch Offices: Jeddah: PO Box 1588, Tel 6876366, Telex 601042 ZTRJ SJ; Riyadh: PO Box 814, Telex 401129 ZATRAC SJ, Tel 4319984; Damman: PO Box 579, Tel 8572595, Telex 801080 ZDRD SJ; Jubail: PO Box 10019, Tel 3416720, Telex 832047 ZATRAC SJ; Abha/Khamees: PO Box 598, Tel 2239875, Telex 906666 ZATRAC SJ; Gassim: PO Box 987, Buraidah, Tel 3234343/3246253, Telex 301254 ZATRAC SJ; Tabuk: PO Box 461, Tel 4239616/4428604, Telex 681085 ZHDTBK SJ; Madinah: PO Box 2861, Tel 8225483, Telex 570362 ZATRAC SJ; Yanbu: PO Box 30006, Yanbu Al-Sinaiyah, Tel 3960862, Telex 662350 ZATRAC SJ; Hail: PO Box 1510, Tel 5327467; Al Hofuf: PO Box 2834, Tel 5927889, Telex 801080 ZTRD SJ
Associated Companies: Zahid Industries & Investment Co Ltd, PO Box 8928, Jeddah; Zahid-Heanor Heavy Transport Co Ltd, PO Box 8923, Jeddah; Universal Car Rental Co Ltd (Budget Rent A Car), PO Box 18106, Jeddah; Zahid Travel Agencies Co Ltd, PO Box 4754, Jeddah; Zahid Industries Co Ltd, PO Box 30006, Yanbu Al Sinaiyah

Financial Information:

	1990
	SR'000
Authorised capital	50,000
Paid-up capital	50,000

Date of Establishment: 1967
No of Employees: 1,500

ZAHRAN CONTRACTING COMPANY

PO Box 1130, Jeddah 21431
Tel: 6518028, 6510320
Cable: Zahranco
Telex: 601029 Rolaco Sj
Telefax: 6534280

Chairman: Sheikh Abdul Aziz Al Sulaiman
Directors: Sheikh Saud Al Sulaiman (Director General)
Senior Executives: Pierre Kilzi (Deputy Director General Finance & Admin)

PRINCIPAL ACTIVITIES: General contractors, civil works, road, fly overs, water dams, buildings, harbours and airfields
Branch Offices: Taif Tel 7467343, 7467907; Riyadh Tel 4912220, Makka Tel 5563286
Parent Company: Rolaco Trading & Contracting; and Abdulaziz Al Abdullah Al Sulaiman Co Ltd
Subsidiary Companies: Zahran-KCL
Principal Bankers: Al Jazirah Bank, Saudi Cairo Bank, Saudi American Bank, Riyad Bank
Financial Information:

	1990
	SR'000
Authorised capital	10,000
Invested capital	26,941

Principal Shareholders: Sheikh Abdulaziz Al Sulaiman; Rolaco Trading & Contracting
Date of Establishment: 1961
No of Employees: 150

ZAIDAN, ABDUL AZIZ, & PARTNERS

Beta Company

PO Box 2824, Riyadh 11461
Tel: 4774040
Cable: Betangcom
Telex: 401044 BETACO SJ; 400621 BETAPR SJ
Telefax: 4772447

Chairman: Abdul Aziz Zaidan
Directors: Abdul Aziz Zaidan (Managing Director), Abdul Kader M Hussein (General Manager), Nabil Akbar Alireza (General Manager)
Senior Executives: Mohammed Sadik Khayat (Technical Director), Mohammed H E Shiry (Head of Legal Dept), Saleem Mahmood Janjua (Finance Manager), Abdul Kader Mohammad Hussein (Marketing Manager), Mohammad Sharaf Eldin (Purchasing Manager), Mohsen Monir (Personnel Manager)

PRINCIPAL ACTIVITIES: General trading and contracting, construction, supply of building materials, prefabricated houses, electrical and electronic equipment, computers, telecommunications equipment, power equipment, heavy machinery, scientific, educational and laboratory equipment and materials, contracting
Principal Agencies: E Co S Didattica Co, Italy; STI, Italy
Branch Offices: Beta Jeddah, PO Box 2011, Jeddah 21451; Beta Machinery, PO Box 2011, Jeddah 21451; Beta Investment, PO Box 2824, Riyadh 11461
Associated Companies: Al Yamamah Insurance Co, Riyadh; Turath Services, UK; EPC Ltd, Riyadh
Principal Bankers: Saudi American Bank, Riyadh; National Commercial Bank, Riyadh and Jeddah; Saudi Cairo Bank, Jeddah and Riyadh, Saudi French Bank, Riyadh

Financial Information:

	1988/89
	SR'000
Sales turnover	32,387
Profits (loss)	(95)
Authorised capital	100,000
Paid-up capital	100,000
Total assets	144,484

Principal Shareholders: Abdul Aziz Zaidan; Abdul Kader M Hussein; Nabil A Alireza; A S Bugshan & Bros Co
Date of Establishment: 1968
No of Employees: 986

ZAMIL ALUMINIUM FACTORY

PO Box 1633, Industrial Estate, Dammam 31441
Tel: 8570985
Cable: Aluminium
Telex: 801461 Zalalu SJ
Telefax: 8572193

Directors: Sulaiman A Al-Zamil (President, Saudi Arabia), Waleed A Al-Zamil (President, Bahrain)
Senior Executives: Imad Hassanin (Marketing Manager), Yousef Al-Rooq (Divison Manager of Al Zamil ICT), Omer Kannan (Automatic Door Manager), Khaled Al Rooq (Manager Zamil Glass), Ajlan Ajlan (Manager Zamil Ladders), Mazel Al Hamoudi (Manager Zamil Partitions)

PRINCIPAL ACTIVITIES: Fabrication of architectural aluminium products; distributors and agents for curtain walls, skylights, domes, doors and windows, space frames, hand rails, shop fronts, and all products made of aluminium; manufacture of aluminium ladders, double glazing, tempered glass, automatic entrances, wall and free standing office partition, distributors and agents for various aluminium machineries and accessories
Principal Agencies: B W N Industries, Australia; Phifer International Sales, USA; Kaltenbach Maschinenfabrik, Germany; Consturction Specialities, USA
Branch Offices: PO Box 285, Manama, Bahrain, Tel 727048, Telex 8381; and PO Box 251, Riyadh; PO Box 7504, Jeddah
Parent Company: A H Zamil Group of Companies
Associated Companies: Zamil Aluminium; Zamil Steel; Zamil Foods; Zamil Refrigeration; Zamil Marine; Zamil Nails & Screws; Zamil Ladder; Zamil Automatic Doors; Zamil Glass; Zamil Partitions
Principal Bankers: National Commercial Bank, Dammam; Al Bank Al Saudi Al Fransi, Dammam; Riyadh Bank Ltd, Al Khobar; Bank of Bahrain & Kuwait, Bahrain
Financial Information:

	1990
	SR'000
Authorised capital	7,700
Paid-up capital	7,700

Principal Shareholders: A H Al-Zamil & Sons
Date of Establishment: 1973
No of Employees: 450

ZAMIL STEEL BUILDINGS CO LTD

PO Box 270, Dhahran Airport 31932
Tel: (03) 8571840, 8571844
Telefax: 8571291
Telex: 801414 ZSBLDG SJ

President: Khalid Al-Zamil
Directors: Hamad Al Zamil, Khalid Al Zamil, Ahmad Al Zamil
Senior Executives: Alex Karakas (Vice President), James C Townsend (General Sales Manager), Mohd E Nabag (Finance Manager), Brian Malia (Operation Manager), Karim Itum (Engineering Manager), Ahmed Al Karawi (Administration & Purchasing Manager)

PRINCIPAL ACTIVITIES: Manufacture, design, consultantion, supply, testing, and erection of a variety of steel fabricated products including, pre-engineered buildings, structural steel,

steel lattice towers, B & D doors, Harley space frames, studs and runners, commercial steel panels, commercial galvanised sheets; design consulting service, steel erection service; galvanizing service

Branch Offices: Riyadh: PO Box 251, Tel 01-4768177, Fax 01-4766729, Telex 400439; Jeddah: PO Box 8076, Tel 02-6600012, Fax 02-6609707, Telex 600626; Bahrain: PO Box 285, Manama, Tel 23-1090, Fax 23-1803, Telex 8381; London, UK; Houston, USA

Parent Company: H A Al Zamil & Brothers Co

Principal Bankers: Al Bank Al Saudi Al Fransi, Dammam; National Commercial Bank, Dammam

Financial Information:

	1989/90 SR'000
Sales turnover	200,695
Authorised capital	14,000
Paid-up capital	14,000
Total assets	164,379

Principal Shareholders: H A Al Zamil & Brothers Co
Date of Establishment: 4th August 1976
No of Employees: 632

Major Companies of SOMALIA

A BESSE & CO (SOMALIA) LTD
See BESSE, A, & CO (SOMALIA) LTD

ABDULLAHI OMAAR
See OMAAR, ABDULLAHI,

ABUSITA, MOHAMED HAJ ABDULLAH,
PO Box 346, Hargeisa
Tel: 2444, 2585
Cable: Abusita Hargeisa

Proprietor: Mohamed H A Abusita
Directors: M H A Abusita (Managing Director), M H Mahmoud

PRINCIPAL ACTIVITIES: Import and distribution of building materials, auto spare parts and accessories
Principal Agencies: GMODC, Japan; Isuzu Trucks & Cars
Branch Offices: PO Box 810, Mogadishu, Somalia; PO Box 138, Berbera, Somalia
Principal Bankers: Commercial and Savings Bank of Somalia

AFRICAN MOTORS & ENGINEERING CO LTD (AMECO)
PO Box 427, Mogadishu
Tel: 3707, 3457
Cable: Ameco

President: Yusuf N Hassan

PRINCIPAL ACTIVITIES: Automobiles and commercial vehicles distributors; importers of diesel engines and equipment; electrical appliances; electrical and electronic equipment; heavy machinery, building materials and pumps
Principal Agencies: UK: British Leyland Ltd, R A Lister & Co Ltd, Lister-Blackstone Marine Ltd, H A Reikl Ltd, Europarts Ltd, Black & Decker Ltd.USA: F M C Walkerneer Co, Symington Wayne Pumps, Johnson Well Screen Ltd, General Electric, George E Failing. Italy: E Marelli & Co, Cablexport, Rejna, Rheem-Safim, Fauso Carello & Co Altissimo Aimone, Stab Bender & Martiny, Gilardoni, Utensileria. Germany: Volkswagen, Bosch

AL AHRAM TRADING CO SRL
PO Box 1885, Mogadishu
Tel: 33549
Telex: 3039 Almhara

Directors: Mohamud Abdullahi Hassan

PRINCIPAL ACTIVITIES: Commission agents, import of spare parts for cars, foodstuffs, building materials, general merchandise, export of livestock, marine produce, fossils

ASPIMA
PO Box 387, Mogadishu
Cable: Aspima

PRINCIPAL ACTIVITIES: Import of medicines and pharmaceutical products

BESSE, A, & CO (SOMALIA) LTD
PO Box 33, Mogadishu

Chairman: A Besse

PRINCIPAL ACTIVITIES: Shipping and forwarding agents, importers of electrical and electronic equipment, photographic equipment, office equipment, paint and varnish, foodstuffs, general merchandise
Principal Agencies: Phillips
Branch Offices: PO Box 121, Berbera; PO Box 23, Hargeisa

CENTRAL BANK OF SOMALIA
PO Box 11, Waddada Soomaaliya, 55, Mogadishu
Tel: 3111/15, 4121/25
Cable: Somalbanca
Telex: 900604 Somalbanca

Directors: Omar Ahmed Omar (Governor), Said Mohamed Ali (Director General)

PRINCIPAL ACTIVITIES: Regulates currency and credit; acts as banker to Government and public bodies; functions as bankers' bank; exercises supervision over commercial banks; manages external reserves of the country; operates exchange control and conducts economic and statistical research

COMMERCIAL & SAVINGS BANK OF SOMALIA
PO Box 203, Mogadishu
Tel: 2641/3
Telex: 609; 602

PRINCIPAL ACTIVITIES: Commercial banking
Branch Offices: International Division: PO Box 26, Mogadishu

Principal Shareholders: State owned
Date of Establishment: Formerly National Commercial Bank

COMMERCIAL AGENCY FOR VEHICLES & SPARE PARTS
PO Box 390, Mogadishu
Tel: 3135, 2785
Telex: 607

PRINCIPAL ACTIVITIES: Supply of all types of heavy vehicles and motor vehicles and their spare parts
Branch Offices: Hargeisa and Kismayo (Somalia)

Principal Shareholders: State-owned

FRATELLI LOCHE SPA
Via Scek Sakaoddin 39, PO Box 359, Mogadishu
Tel: 2662

PRINCIPAL ACTIVITIES: Agents and distributors of Castrol lubricants, import and distribution of chemicals, ready-made clothing, heavy machinery and equipment, toiletries and pharmaceuticals

HABO & CANDALA FISH FACTORY
PO Box 375, Mogadishu

PRINCIPAL ACTIVITIES: Canned fish manufacturers and exporters

HAJI ABDULLA SCIRUA
See SCIRUA, HAJI ABDULLA,

HANTIWARE TRADING CO
PO Box 69, Hargeisa, Eastern

Chairman: Ali Mohamed Gulaid (also Proprietor)

PRINCIPAL ACTIVITIES: Import and distribution of building materials, hardware and auto parts; export of hides and skins

INDUSTRIE CHIMICHE SOMALE (ICS)
PO Box 479, Mogadishu
Tel: 8426, 8557
Cable: Ics Industrie

Directors: Hirei Gassem (Managing Director)

PRINCIPAL ACTIVITIES: Production of detergents and toiletry goods

INTERNATIONAL BANK FOR RECONSTRUCTION & DEVELOPMENT
World Bank
PO Box 1825, Mogasishu
Telex: 767

PRINCIPAL ACTIVITIES: Banking (representative office)
Parent Company: Head office in Washington DC, USA

K PITAMBER & CO
See PITAMBER, K, & CO

LIVESTOCK DEVELOPMENT AGENCY
PO Box 929, Mogadishu
Tel: 21067
Cable: Stockagency
Telex: 742

Chairman: Dr Hassan Sheik Hussein (also General Manager)
Directors: Mahamud Ahmed Ali (Director of Development and
 Planning), Ahmed Dahir Hassan (Director of Marketing),
 Mohamed Mahamud Addawa (Director of Finance), Dr Abshir
 Ahmed Fareh (Project Director of Trans Juda)
Senior Executives: Mohamed Shabeel Awaleh (Marketing
 Officer), Abdillahi Mohamed Mahamud (Marketing Officer), Dr
 Mohamed Ghouse (Marketing Officer)

PRINCIPAL ACTIVITIES: Promotion, marketing and export of
 livestock and its related products, including live cattle, sheep,
 goats and camels; tinned beef, and frozen beef and mutton,
 animal feed, etc
Branch Offices: Branch in Hargiesa, and PO Box 60, Kismayu
Principal Bankers: Somali Saving and Commercial Bank

Date of Establishment: 1966
No of Employees: 730

M MOHAMEDALI M ABDULALI & BROS
PO Box 129, Mogadishu
Tel: 20368
Cable: Sodawala
Telex: 745 CROCEDSUD MOG ATT BROS

Chairman: Fakhruddin E M Mohamedali (Managing Director)
Directors: Ayub E M Mohamedali
Senior Executives: Hussain Fakhruddin (Manager)

PRINCIPAL ACTIVITIES: General trading; import and distribution
 of groceries, dairy products and household goods;
 manufacture of perfumes, cosmetics, toiletries, aerated
 waters and syrups
Principal Agencies: Kraft Foods, Australia, West Germany, UK;
 Quaker Oats, UK, Holland; United Biscuits, UK; Wilkinson
 Sword, UK; General Foods, France; also licencee
 manufacturers for Wella, West Germany; Paglieri, Italy; Avidal,
 Italy; Beecham Caze, France; Europarco, France
Principal Bankers: Commercial and Savings Bank of Somalia
Financial Information:

	Sh So'000
Sales turnover	12,500

Principal Shareholders: Directors as described
Date of Establishment: 1898

MOHAMED HAJ ABDULLAH ABUSITA
See ABUSITA, MOHAMED HAJ ABDULLAH,

NATIONAL AGENCY FOR TRADE
Ente Nazionale Commercio
PO Box 602, Mogadishu
Tel: 2487
Cable: Enc
Telex: 612 Enc

PRINCIPAL ACTIVITIES: Import and distribution of foodstuffs
 such as rice, vegetable oils and fats, tea, sugar, coffee,
 pasta, flour, and also detergents, rubber and plastic products,
 batteries, soaps, cement, cloths, etc; export of incense,
 myrrh, arabic gum and other gums
Branch Offices: Somalia (4 branches throughout the Somali
 Democratic Republic)

NATIONAL BANANA BOARD
PO Box 576, Mogadishu
Tel: 3652
Cable: Enb
Telex: 603

Chairman: M Yusuf Muro

PRINCIPAL ACTIVITIES: Production and export of bananas,
 import of fertilisers and agricultural equipment

NATIONAL BOTTLING CO
PO Box 939, Mogadishu
Tel: 8538/9

PRINCIPAL ACTIVITIES: Manufacture and distribution of soft
 drinks
Principal Agencies: Coca Cola, Sprite, Fanta, Nadifa table Water

NATIONAL ENGINEERING & CONSTRUCTION CO (NATCO)
PO Box 900, Mogadishu
Tel: 80886, 80887
Cable: Natco

Chairman: Mohmoud Abdi Arraleh (also Managing Director)
Directors: Haji Yusuf Egal, Nasir Nahar Hassan
Senior Executives: Abdulsalam Sahardeed Ismail (Assistant
 Managing Director and Chief Engineer), Ismail Abdi Aden
 (Finance Manager), Hassan Mahmoud Ali (Stores Manager),
 Ismail Haji-Jama (Mechanical Engineer)

PRINCIPAL ACTIVITIES: General construction contracting, civil,
 mechanical, water, agricultural and other allied works
Principal Agencies: Newton Chambers Engineering Ltd, UK;
 Warman Int Ltd, Australia
Branch Offices: Hargeisa; Kismayo
Principal Bankers: Somali Commercial & Savings Bank

Principal Shareholders: Chairman and directors as described

NATIONAL PETROLEUM AGENCY
Ente Nazionale Petroli
PO Box 573, Mogadishu
Cable: NPA Mogadishu

PRINCIPAL ACTIVITIES: Import and distribution of tyres of all
 kind, tubes, batteries, fuels, lubricants, bitumen, accumulators

OMAAR, ABDULLAHI,
PO Box 138, Berbera, Western

PRINCIPAL ACTIVITIES: General trading, import and distribution
 of communications and electronic equipment, electrical
 appliances, automobiles and commercial vehicles, cigarettes
 and tobacco, petroleum products, tyres and tubes
Principal Agencies: Marconi, English Electric Co, Agip, Dunlop

PACKING CLEARING & FORWARDING AGENCY
Furniture Express Co
PO Box 1189, Mogadishu
Tel: 25096
Cable: Hirabe Mugdisho

Chairman: Osman Ossoble Hirabe

PRINCIPAL ACTIVITIES: Packing, clearing and forwarding
 agency; manufacture of household and office furniture and
 general construction materials
Principal Agencies: Ingeco International SA (Refinery Project);
 Ipreso Besina (Road Project); Fra Murr (Road Project)
Principal Bankers: Savings & Commercial Bank of Somalia

PITAMBER, K, & CO
PO Box 33, Hargeisa (Eastern)
Cable: Kar Sandas

Chairman: Shah Prabhudas K (Partner)

PRINCIPAL ACTIVITIES: Manufacture of motor parts, distribution of hardware, cutlery, textiles and canned foodstuffs

SAIEMA SA
PO Box 32, Mogadishu

PRINCIPAL ACTIVITIES: General trading, manufacturers' representation, import and distribution of automobiles, motorcycles, tyres and tubes, diesel engines, electrical and electronic equipment and appliances, hardware and tools, office equipment and supplies, toiletries
Principal Agencies: Renault, Vespa, K H Deutz, Hanomag, Firestone

SCIRUA, HAJI ABDULLA,
PO Box 195, Mogadishu

Chairman: Haji Abdulla Scirua (also Proprietor)

PRINCIPAL ACTIVITIES: Import and distribution of building and construction equipment

SNAI
Wakaaladda Sonkorta Ee Jowhar
PO Box 25, 48 Corso Somalia, Mogadishu
Tel: 34064
Cable: Snai
Telex: 644

Chairman: Mohamed Hersi Bahal (General Manager)
Directors: Ahmed Ibrahim Hussein (Agriculture), Abdi Farah Isse (Industry); Abdul Karim Ali Mohamed (Accountancy), Jama Anshur (Commerce), Yacoub Sidow (Personnel), Ibrahim Hashi Fidow (BIASA)

PRINCIPAL ACTIVITIES: Manufacture, import and distribution of toiletries and cosmetics, rubber shoes and sandals; alcoholic beverages, and spirits, export of agricultural produce (grapefruit, sugar)
Subsidiary Companies: BIASA

Principal Shareholders: State-owned
Date of Establishment: SNAI: 1926; BIASA: 1971
No of Employees: 2,200 Permanent; 3,500-4,000 Seasonal

SOCIETA COMMERCIALE ITALO SOMALA
PO Box 113, Mogadishu
Tel: 20700,20290,21553, 20506
Cable: Scisomala Mogadishu
Telex: 3623 SCIS SM

Chairman: Dr Ahmed Scek Ibrahim
Directors: Avv Cenci Gianfranca (Managing Director), Rag Mohamed Mohamud Mursal (Finance Director)
Senior Executives: Hassan Aden Hassan (Export Sales Manager), Mohamed Abdulcadir Scek Ibrahim (Sales Manager), Hassan Abdulla Haile (Marketing Manager), Ahmad Haji Abdullahi (Purchasing Manager), Dr Hassan Abucar Izgow (Personnel Manager), Ibrahim Hussen Hassan (Technical Manager), Issak Hussen Hassan (Admin Manager)

PRINCIPAL ACTIVITIES: General trading, import and distribution of cars, medical supplies, foodstuffs, and electrical appliances, manufacturers' representation, shipping and insurance, commission agents
Branch Offices: Branches in Chrisimaio, Merca and Hargeisa
Parent Company: La FA.DE.CE. Trezzano Sul Naviglio, Milan, Italy
Principal Bankers: Commercial & Saving Bank of Somalia
Financial Information:

	US$'000
Authorised capital	5,000
Paid-up capital	5,000
Total assets	10,000

SOMALI AIRLINES
PO Box 726, Ex-Parliament Sq, Mogadishu
Tel: 2883/4/5, 2274
Cable: Somalair
Telex: 619

President: Hussein Mohamoud Mohamed

PRINCIPAL ACTIVITIES: Scheduled flights within Somalia and to Kenya, Saudi Arabia, United Arab Emirates, Oman, Egypt, Italy, Yemen Arab Republic. Charter and air taxi flights; general agents for airlines

SOMALI COMMERCIAL CO
PO Box 177, Hargeisa

PRINCIPAL ACTIVITIES: Automobile distribution and import
Principal Agencies: Toyota

SOMALI DEVELOPMENT BANK
PO Box 1079, Mogadishu
Tel: 21800, 22001/2
Cable: Bank Horumar
Telex: 635 Sdbmgdsr

President: Mohamud Mohamed Noor
Directors: Abbas Yussuf Ahmed, Mohamud Mohamed Noor, Ali Mohamed Ibrahim, Sherif Abubakar Mohamed, Jeelani Nur Mohamud, Hussein Hassan Farah
Senior Executives: Dr Osman Yussuf Farah (General-Manager), Issa Haagi Mussa (Deputy Director of Operations), Mohamed Sheck Elmi (Deputy General Director of Administration), Ali Hassan Farah (Central Director & Advisor), Hassan Noor Osman (Director of Resettlement & Rehabilitation Projects), Abdulcadir Adan Mohamud (Director of Agricultural Credit), Suleyman Omar Jama (Director of Projects), Mohamud Hagi Gele (Director of Administration), Hassan Ahmed Farah (Manager Hargeisa Branch), Libaan Khalif Hassan (Manager Kismayo Branch)

PRINCIPAL ACTIVITIES: Investment in agriculture, livestock, industry, mining and tourism, short and long term loans, financial assistance to foreign investors in joint-ventures
Branch Offices: Hargeisa, Kismayo
Subsidiary Companies: Pasta & Flour Industry
Principal Bankers: Central Bank of Somalia; Commercial and Saving Bank of Somalia
Financial Information:

	ShSo'000
Authorised capital	600,000
Paid-up capital	500,000

Principal Shareholders: Somali Government (55%); Central Bank of Somalia (27%); Commercial Bank of Somalia (9%); National Insurance Company (9%)
Date of Establishment: April 1970
No of Employees: 200

SOMALI EXPRESS FORWARDING AGENCY
PO Box 82, Mogadishu
Tel: 3218

PRINCIPAL ACTIVITIES: Shipping, clearing and forwarding agency

SOMALI LEATHER AGENCY
PO Box 1181, Mogadishu
Tel: 80026, 81007
Cable: Hasa
Telex: 634 Hasa Mog

Directors: Issa Ugas Abdulle (General Manager), Mohamed Suleiman Kahin, Mohamed Siyaad Naleye, Mukhtar Abukar, Abdi Adan Belel, Abdi Mohamed Warsame
Senior Executives: Abdirazak (Chief Accountant), Hassan Mohamed Nuur (Deputy Marketing Director)

PRINCIPAL ACTIVITIES: Sheep and goat skins, cattle and camel hides; leathers, raw, semi tanned and finished; manufacture of footwear and shoes and other leather goods
Branch Offices: Hargeisa, Kismaio, Garbaharey, Dhusamareb, Hudur, Burao, Baki, Erigavo & Buaale
Subsidiary Companies: Four tanneries in Mogadishu, Kismaio, Hargeisa, and Burao
Principal Bankers: Commercial and Savings Bank, Mogadishu
Financial Information:

	Sh So'000
Sales turnover	250,000
Profits	50,000
Authorised capital	90,000

Principal Shareholders: Somali Government (100%)
Date of Establishment: May 1973
No of Employees: 680

SOMALI PETROLEUM AGENCY

PO Box 920, Mogadishu
Cable: Comet Mog

PRINCIPAL ACTIVITIES: Import and distribution of fuels and lubricants, bitumen products for roads and airports

SOMALI SHIPPING AGENCY & LINE

PO Box 35, Mogadishu
Tel: 20231, 20312, 21948, 20054, 22209
Cable: Somship
Telex: 611 SSA Mog

Senior Executives: Dr Ahmed Issak Bihi (General Manager), Osman Dhel Abdulle (Deputy General Manager), Saeed Bihi Aded (Finance & Personnel Manager), Mohamud Mohamed Karshe (Commercial & Chartering Manager), Issa Ali Dhere (Operation Manager), Ahmed Mohamed Tarah (Economic Advisor), Ali Ahmed Amman (Planning & Insurance Manager), Eng Abdi Jama Aden (Technical Manager), Ahmed Nur Mohamed (Legal Advisor)

PRINCIPAL ACTIVITIES: Shipping agency, shipowners, brokers clearing and forwarding agents
Branch Offices: PO Box 124, Berbera; PO Box 42, Kismayo
Principal Bankers: Somali Commercial and Savings Bank

Principal Shareholders: Government Corporation
Date of Establishment: 1974
No of Employees: 260

SOMALTEX SPA

PO Box 28, Mogadishu
Tel: 22769
Cable: Somaltex
Telex: 3729 Somaltex Sm

Directors: Abdulcadir Mohamed Mohamud (Director General), Ismail Warsame Hagar (Commercial Director), Ahmed Suleiman Yusuf (Technical Director), Abdishakur Mohamed Adan (Personnel Director), Mohamed Abdi Abdulle (Financial Manager), Ismail Warsame Hagar (Purchasing Director), Hassan Olad Aden (Production & Mill Director)

PRINCIPAL ACTIVITIES: Spinning, weaving and printing of textiles, production of clothing goods and ready-made garments
Branch Offices: Kismayo and Jamaame
Principal Bankers: Somali Commercial & Savings Bank
Financial Information:

	SO Shs'000
Authorised capital	400.000
Paid-up capital	326.331

Principal Shareholders: Ministry of Finance; Somali Development Bank
Date of Establishment: 1974
No of Employees: 1,000

STATE INSURANCE CO OF SOMALIA SICOS

PO Box 992, Mogadishu
Tel: 32051/52, 32070
Cable: Sicos
Telex: 710 Sicos

Chairman: Said Mohamed Ali (General Manager)
Directors: Sherali Nassar Pira (Assistant General Manager)

PRINCIPAL ACTIVITIES: Monopoly of insurance and reinsurance business in Somali Democratic Republic
Branch Offices: Hargeysa; Berbera; Kismayo; Burao; Merca; Djibouti
Principal Bankers: Somali Central Bank; Somali Commercial Bank; National Westminister Bank, London

Principal Shareholders: Somali Government
Date of Establishment: 1972
No of Employees: 200

STATE MONOPOLY AGENCY

PO Box 12, Mogadishu

PRINCIPAL ACTIVITIES: Import and distribution of cigarettes, tobacco and matches

TRADING AGENCY FOR CONSTRUCTION MATERIALS

PO Box 1180, Mogadishu
Cable: Wagadh
Telex: 630

Senior Executives: Ahmed Haji Hashi (Acting Foreign Trade Department Director)

PRINCIPAL ACTIVITIES: Import and distribution of building materials

Principal Shareholders: State-owned

TUBEX

PO Box 347, Mogadishu

PRINCIPAL ACTIVITIES: Manufacture of plastic tubes and mouldings. Import and distribution of electrical equipment, radios and appliances

Major Companies of
SUDAN

ABA ELMUTASIM ENTERPRISES LTD

PO Box 228, Khartoum
Tel: 72084, 70505
Telex: 22288

Directors: Osman Elsheikh Mustafa, Nasr E Mustafa, Bashier E Mustafa, Elamin E Mustafa, Elsheikh Mustafa

PRINCIPAL ACTIVITIES: Manufacturers and exporters of oil seed products and general trade
Branch Offices: Port Sudan, New Halfa, Medani
Subsidiary Companies: Elsheikh Mustafa Elamin & Sons Co, Elsheikh Shipping Co, Elsheikh Oil Mills, Elsheikh Petroleum & Investment Group Ltd
Principal Bankers: Unity Bank, National Bank of Abu Dhabi, Citibank, National Bank of Sudan
Financial Information:

	S£'000
Authorised capital	15,000
Paid-up capital	15,000

Principal Shareholders: Family of Elsheikh Mustafa El Amin

ABDEL MONEIM INDUSTRIAL & ENGINEERING CO LTD

PO Box 2413, Khartoum
Tel: 70526, 77624
Cable: Makan
Telex: 22422 WAX

Directors: Dr Abdel Salem Abdel Moneim (Managing Director)
Senior Executives: Gamal Shawgi (Engineer in Charge)

PRINCIPAL ACTIVITIES: Import and distribution of industrial machinery, laboratory equipment and chemicals; manufacture of string, shoe laces, and wax candles
Principal Bankers: Sudan Commercial Bank

Date of Establishment: 1961
No of Employees: 73

ABOULELA CONTRACTING & MANUFACTURING CO

PO Box 541, Khartoum
Tel: 32903, 78970
Telex: 22903 DELTA KM

Chairman: Hamza Karim
Directors: Abbas Karim, Abdel Monem Karim
Senior Executives: Hanafi Karim, Abdel Rahim Karim

PRINCIPAL ACTIVITIES: Building contractors, manufacturers of building materials, (cement tiles, blocks, bricks, wood, steel) crushing, slabs granite, furniture, paint and steel products
Branch Offices: Abu Dhabi (PO Box 909)
Subsidiary Companies: Building & Construction Co Ltd; Seliet Quarrying Co Ltd; Aula Trading & Agencies Co Ltd
Principal Bankers: Sudan Commercial Bank, Abu Dhabi National Bank; Bank of Credit & Commerce; National Bank of Khartoum

Principal Shareholders: Members of the Aboulela family
Date of Establishment: 1930
No of Employees: 400

ABOULELA ENGINEERING CO LTD

Aboulela Bldg, Ghumhoria St, PO Box 1341, Khartoum
Tel: 73500, 77257, 77258, 75670
Cable: Handasiya
Telex: 22421 ABLE SD

Chairman: Saad Aboulela
Directors: Mustafa Aboulela, Hisham Aboulela
Senior Executives: Mohamed Abadi Ahmed, Mohamed Osman Eheymer, Abdullahi E El-Amin

PRINCIPAL ACTIVITIES: Manufacturers' agents, contractors and general merchants

Principal Agencies: Daimler-Benz AG, W Germany; Hawker Siddeley Group; Perkins Engines, UK; Biamax SA, Greece; Dresser Europe SA, UK; James Neill (Sheffield), UK; and others
Branch Offices: Port Sudan
Parent Company: Aboulela Group of Companies
Associated Companies: Aboulela Trading Co Ltd; Aboulela Plantation Co Ltd; Aboulela Estates Co Ltd; Aboulela Ginning Co Ltd; Massara Plantation Co Ltd
Principal Bankers: Bank of Khartoum; Unity Bank; Sudan Commercial Bank; Bank of Credit & Commerce Int; National Bank of Abu Dhabi; Habib Bank

Principal Shareholders: Members of the Aboulela family
Date of Establishment: 1958
No of Employees: 180

ABOULELA TRADING CO LTD

Aboulela Bldg, Abbas Sq, PO Box 121, Khartoum
Tel: 70020, 71173, 42968
Cable: Aboulela

PRINCIPAL ACTIVITIES: Export of cotton seeds, saesame seeds, oilcakes, groundnuts, domnuts, haricot beans, horse beans, chick peas, hides, skins and all other Sudanese produce; import of textiles, flour, rice, lentils, coffee, tea, soap, spices, general merchandise, owners of agricultural schemes, oil press mills, flour mills, glass manufacture, warehousing; general insurance agents
Branch Offices: Branches in Port Sudan; Omdurman; Wad Medani; Egypt (branch in Cairo, PO Box 1058, Tel 44045/6)
Associated Companies: Aboulela Plantation Co Ltd (PO Box 21, Khartoum); Aboulela Engineering Co Ltd; Aboulela Estates Co Ltd; Aboulela Ginning Co Ltd; Plantations Co Ltd

Principal Shareholders: Member of the Aboulela Group of Companies

ABUELIZZ CONTRACTING CO

PO Box 706, Khartoum
Tel: 73590, 73494
Cable: Gabriz
Telex: 22667 Gabriz Km

Chairman: Magdi Gabir Abdelhameed Abuelizz
Directors: Abil Gabir A Abuelizz
Senior Executives: A Abdalla (Commercial Manager)

PRINCIPAL ACTIVITIES: Investment, general trading, general contracting, supply of tiles and cement, steel works, and carpentry
Principal Agencies: Hunter Douglas, Holland; Bruno P Hartkopf, West Germany
Branch Offices: Buildmore Construction Co, PO Box 2808, Abu Dhabi, Telex 2610
Subsidiary Companies: Abuelizz Factories; The Industrial Safety Protectives Co Ld
Principal Bankers: El Nilein Bank; Sudan Commercial Bank; El Nilein Bank; National Bank of Abu Dhabi

Date of Establishment: 1956

AGRICULTURAL BANK OF SUDAN

PO Box 1363, Khartoum
Tel: 77466, 77432, 77424
Cable: Masraf
Telex: 22610

Chairman: Sid Ahmed Osman (also Managing Director)
Directors: Khider Ahmed Abdel Halim, Hassan Addar, Yousri Mohamed Gabr, Hassan Abdel Wahab, Omer Ali Omer, Tawfig Hashim, Dr Abdel Mohsin Hassan El Nadi, Dr Bashir Omer Fadlalla, Hassan Mutwakil, Ahmed El Gaily Abdel Mahmoud
Senior Executives: El Sheikh M El Hassan, Khidir Ahmed Abdel Halim, Khalid Mohamed Ibrahim, Ismail Mohamed Amara,

Babikir Osman, Salih Mahgoub Salih, Mohamed Salih Fadl, Ali
A El Nush

PRINCIPAL ACTIVITIES: Promotion and development of
agricultural projects
Branch Offices: Sennar; Kosti; Dongala; El Dilling; Port Sudan;
Shendi; Gedaref; Khartoum; Medani; New Halfa; Atbara;
Renk; Nyala; Zalingi; Kasala; El Obeid; Damazin; El Dabba;
Juba; Waw; Umm Ruaba; El Kamlin, El Nihud, Abu Gebaha, El
Leat
Financial Information:

	1990 S£'000
Authorised capital	50,000
Paid-up capital	50,000

Principal Shareholders: Bank of Sudan
Date of Establishment: 1957
No of Employees: 684

ALAKTAN TRADING CO

PO Box 2067, Khartoum
Tel: 81588, 76075
Telex: 22272 Confidence

PRINCIPAL ACTIVITIES: Cotton exporters

Principal Shareholders: Cotton Public Corporation

AL BARAKA BANK SUDAN

PO Box 3583, Hashim Hago Bldg, Khartoum
Tel: 73056, 73043, 76621, 80688
Telex: 22555, 22479 Braka

Chairman: Mohamed J Hassouba
Directors: Fathel Rahman El Bashier, Osman Ahmed Suliman,
Abbas A/Magid, Hashim Hagou, Mohd El Tayeb El Tounisi,
Suad M El Berier
Senior Executives: Muwia A/Wahab Taha (General Manager),
A/Magid El Amin Ali (Finance Director), A/Rahman Ali
A/Rahman (Internal Auditor), Hashim Mohamed Hamad
(Foreign Relations Director), A/Moneim Nagm El Din
(Personnel Director), Ibn Elhag M Salih (Admin Director),
Kamal A/Gadir Saied (Research & Statistics Director)

PRINCIPAL ACTIVITIES: Islamic banking and investment
services
Branch Offices: Khartoum, Omdurman, Gedarif, Sennar, Port
Sudan
Associated Companies: Al Baraka Agricultural Investment Co; Al
Baraka Export Promotion Co; Al Baraka Insurance Co
Principal Bankers: Al Baraka International Bank, London; UBAF,
France, Irving Trust Co, USA
Financial Information:

	1989 US$'000
Authorised capital	200,000
Paid-up capital	50,000

Principal Shareholders: 80% Saudi Citizens; 20% Sudanese
Citizens
Date of Establishment: March 1984
No of Employees: 211

ALBERERO TRADING & ENGINEERING CO

PO Box 78, Khartoum
Tel: 71721, 70893
Cable: Elhaga
Telex: 22112 Haga Sd

Chairman: Moutwakil Elberier (also Managing Director)

PRINCIPAL ACTIVITIES: Exporters, importers, manufacturers of
plastic products, textile and spare parts
Branch Offices: Omdurman, Industrial Area, Sudan
Principal Bankers: Unity Bank, National Bank of Sudan

Principal Shareholders: Moutwakil Elberier
Date of Establishment: 1979
No of Employees: 92

ALMAGBOUL BROS CORPORATION LTD

PO Box 1593, Khartoum
Tel: 76425, 72583, 80564
Cable: ALZAFER, KHARTOUM
Telex: 22039 Zeco Sd, 22377 Mgbc Sd

Chairman: Zoheir Ibrahim Almagboul (Managing Director)
Directors: Nagmeldin Almagboul (Marketing Director), Mohieldin
Almagboul

PRINCIPAL ACTIVITIES: Representation and general trade
Principal Agencies: P J Parmiter & Sons, Allman & Co,
Chubbfire International, American Motors Corp, Total Fire
Export; Independent Petroleum Group; Petrochemical
Industries of Kuwait
Branch Offices: Safarian Building, Abdal Moniem Street,
Khartoum
Subsidiary Companies: Fire Protection Services Ltd; Zoheir
Enterprise Company Ltd
Principal Bankers: Nilein Bank, Citibank, Khartoum; Bank of
Credit & Commerce International

Principal Shareholders: Z I Almagboul Family
Date of Establishment: 1948
No of Employees: 20

ANCHOR TRADING CO

PO Box 924, Khartoum
Tel: 81051, 79319
Cable: Anchor Km

Directors: Costas George Macris (Managing Director)

PRINCIPAL ACTIVITIES: Bottling, packing, foodstuff and
general trade
Principal Agencies: Pauls & White Ltd
Principal Bankers: Unity Bank, Bank of Khartoum

Principal Shareholders: C G Macris
Date of Establishment: 1954
No of Employees: 150

ARAB AFRICAN INTERNATIONAL BANK

PO Box 2721, Khartoum
Tel: 75573
Telex: 22624 TAIC

PRINCIPAL ACTIVITIES: Representative office
Parent Company: Head office in Cairo, Egypt

ARAB BANK FOR ECONOMIC DEVELOPMENT IN AFRICA

B.A.D.E.A.

Abdel Rahman El Mahdi Ave, PO Box 2640, Khartoum
Tel: 73646, 73709
Cable: Badea Khartoum
Telex: 22248 BADEA SD, 22739 BADEA SD

Chairman: Ahmed El Abdallah El Akil (Saudi Arabia)
Directors: Ahmed Harti El Wardi (Morocco/Director General),
Abdel Wahab El Badr (Kuwait), Youssef Abdellatif El Sirkal
(UAE), Dr Nour Abdel Salam Baryoun (Libya), Hameed J Al
Samir (Iraq), Khalifa Yassir El Musalam (Qatar), Mohammed
Terbeche (Algeria), Rifaat Sidki El Nimir (Palestine), Musa
Ibrahim Mohamed (Sudan), Mohamed Taha Baly (Syria),
Mansour Hanna Haddadin (Jordan)
Senior Executives: Ahmed Harti El Wardi (Director General),
Medhat S Lotfi (Director General Office), Dr Yahia Mohamed
Mahmoud (Director of Finance), Kamal Gaafar (Acting Director
of Projects Programmes & Legal Affairs), Ali Ahmed Kurdi
(Coordinator of Administration)

PRINCIPAL ACTIVITIES: BADEA is an international institution
enjoying full international legal status and complete autonomy

in administrative and financial matters. The objective of the Bank is to foster economic, financial and technical cooperation between the African states and Arab nations: BADEA assists in financing economic development projects in African countries (all OAU member countries, non-members of the Arab League); stimulates the contribution of Arab capital to African development; and helps to provide the technical assistance required for Africa's development

Financial Information:

	US$'000
Authorised capital	1,048,250
Paid-up capital	1,045,484

Principal Shareholders: Algeria, Bahrain, Egypt, Iraq, Jordan, Kuwait, Lebanon, Libya, Mauritania, Morocco, Oman, Palestine, Qatar, Saudi Arabia, Sudan, Syria, Tunisia and United Arab Emirates
Date of Establishment: 26th November 1973
No of Employees: 170

ARAB ORGANISATION FOR AGRICULTURAL DEVELOPMENT

PO Box 474, Khartoum
Tel: 78761/4
Cable: Motazeen
Telex: 22554 AOAD SD

Directors: Dr Hassan Fahmi Jumah (Director General), Dr Mohamed Osman M Salih (Deputy Director General)
Senior Executives: Dr Ibrahim Hag Musa (Legal Advisor)

PRINCIPAL ACTIVITIES: Studies for agricultural and fisheries projects within Arab League member states
Branch Offices: Syria, Jordan, Iraq, Yemen, Morocco, Libya, Mauritania, Algeria
Parent Company: The Arab League

ASSOCIATED CONSULTANTS & PARTNERS

PO Box 2960, Khartoum
Tel: 41808
Cable: Teckno Khartoum
Telex: 24204

Senior Executives: Y A Mageed (Manager)

PRINCIPAL ACTIVITIES: Civil engineering, mechanical, electrical and structural consultants
Branch Offices: In the Middle East: Abu Dhabi; Oman; Somalia; Yemen
Parent Company: Sir M MacDonald & Partners, Cambridge, UK
Principal Bankers: Barclays Bank Plc

ATBARA CEMENT COMPANY LTD

PO Box 96, Atbara
Tel: 2351, 2352
Telex: 22079 CEMS SD

Chairman: Dr Sabir Mohamed Salih
Directors: Brigadier Babiker Ahmed El Tigani (General Manager)
Senior Executives: Abas Khalid Idress (Financial Manager), Sameer Zakhir Shahata (Sales Manager), Ahmed Omer Agabaien (Stores & Purchasing Manager), Eng Babiker Osman Hamad (Engineering Manager)

PRINCIPAL ACTIVITIES: Cement manufacture
Branch Offices: PO Box 1498, Khartoum, Tel 80047, 73319, 34773, Telex 22079 CEMS SD
Principal Bankers: Bank of Khartoum

Principal Shareholders: Ministry of Finance & National Economy; Bank of Khartoum
Date of Establishment: 1947
No of Employees: 920

ATLAS TRADING CO LTD

PO Box 1024, Barlaman Ave, Khartoum
Tel: 73034, 77655, 77645
Cable: Success
Telex: 22289 Atlas-Km

Directors: John Sitinas, Roni Sikh

PRINCIPAL ACTIVITIES: The company comprises two divisions: Pharmaceutical Division: import and distribution of pharmaceutical preparations and chemical products; veterinary products and agricultural insecticides and Trading Division: manufacturers' representatives and contractors for construction or supply of diverse items, from rolling stock and accessories to complete industrial projects
Principal Agencies: Dumex, Merz & Co, Boats, Russel Laboratories
Branch Offices: Pharmaceutical Division, Trading Division
Principal Bankers: Citibank Khartoum & Elnilein Bank

Date of Establishment: 1963

AXIS TRADING CO LTD

PO Box 1574, Khartoum
Tel: 75521/6, 75875, 76981
Cable: Mihwar
Telex: 22294 HAMS SD

Chairman: Dr Hassan A M Suliman (General Manager)
Directors: M Hayat Hussein Sid A El Mufti

PRINCIPAL ACTIVITIES: Import and distribution of general merchandise, foodstuffs, sugar, milk powder, export of minerals (chrome ore, magnesite, iron scrap) and agricultural produce (wheat bran, oil cakes, sorghum, beans, durra)
Branch Offices: Branches in Port Sudan and Atbara
Subsidiary Companies: Tatco Trading Co Ltd; Tatco Transport Co Ltd; Swallow Shipping Co Inc
Principal Bankers: El Nilein Bank, Khartoum; Khartoum Bank, Khartoum; BCCI, Khartoum
Financial Information:

	S£'000
Authorised capital	4,000
Paid-up capital	2,500
Total assets	30,000

Principal Shareholders: H A M Suliman, M Hayat El Mufti
Date of Establishment: 1967
No of Employees: 72

B E BAMBOULIS & SONS LTD

See BAMBOULIS, B E, & SONS LTD

BAMBOULIS, B E, & SONS LTD

PO Box 1008, Khartoum

Directors: Basil E Bamboulis (Owner)

PRINCIPAL ACTIVITIES: Import and distribution of ironmongery; building materials, hardware and tools

BANK OF CREDIT & COMMERCE INTERNATIONAL OVERSEAS LTD

PO Box 5, Ahmed & Abdullah Awad El Saeed Bldg, Babikur Badur St, Khartoum
Tel: 73936/8
Cable: Bancrecom
Telex: 22662 BCCI SD

PRINCIPAL ACTIVITIES: Commercial banking
Branch Offices: Port Sudan and Omdurman

BANK OF KHARTOUM

PO Box 1008, Khartoum
Tel: 80137, 70198, 72880, 81071
Cable: Foreign Khartoum
Telex: 22181 BKHOF SD

Chairman: Abdel Rahman Ahmed Mahdi (General Manager)

Directors: Abdel Gadir Abdel Moneim, Salah El Dein El Zubair, Dr Ahmed Hassan El Jack, Mohamed Twfiek Ahmed

PRINCIPAL ACTIVITIES: Commercial banking
Branch Offices: Sh El Gamhoria, PO Box 312, Khartoum; Sh El Gama'a, PO Box 880, Khartoum; Omdurman Central, PO Box 67, Omdurman; Wad Medani, PO Box 131, Wad Medani; Port Sudan, PO Box 241, Port Sudan; El Obeid, PO Box 220, El Obeid; Atbara, El Damazeen, El Gedaref, El Hassa Heissa, Kassala, Kosti, Nyala, Sennar, El Dilling, Shendi, Singa, El Suki, El Managil, Um Ruwaba, El Fashir, El Dain, Berber, El Rahad, Halfa El Gadida, El Dinder, Rufa'a, etc
Financial Information:

	S£'000
Authorised capital	12,300
Paid-up capital	8,300

Principal Shareholders: Bank of Sudan, Ministry of Finance and Economic Planning
Date of Establishment: 1913
No of Employees: 2,310

BANK OF OMAN LTD

Regional Office, Baladia Street, PO Box 371, Khartoum
Tel: 72881, 72750, 72743, 72840, 72969
Cable: Banoman Khartoum
Telex: 22124 BOL SD, 22663 OMNFX SD

Senior Executives: Saiyed Arif Husain (Regional Chief Manager), Mahjoub Mohammad El Awad (Branch Manager), Zakaria Mohammed Abdo (Commercial Manager), Osman Awad El Karim (Accounts Manager), Mrs Margaret Kamel Bogtor (Advances Manager), Mohammed Khadir El Araki (Forex Manager)

PRINCIPAL ACTIVITIES: Commercial banking
Parent Company: Head office in Dubai, UAE
Principal Bankers: US Correspondents: Bank of Oman Overseas (USA) Inc, New York; Manufacturers Hanover Trust Co, New York

Date of Establishment: 1980
No of Employees: 40

BANK OF SUDAN

PO Box 313, Khartoum
Tel: 78064, 70206, 70765
Cable: El Bank Khartoum
Telex: 22352, 22559 El Bank

Governor: Ismail El Misbah Mekki
Directors: Mahdi El Faki, Mohamed El Makawi Mustafa, Dr Ali Mohamed El Hassan
Senior Executives: Awad El Karim Osman (General Manager)

PRINCIPAL ACTIVITIES: Central banking institution and note-issuing authority
Branch Offices: Port Sudan, Atbara, Wad Medani, El Gedaref, Kosti, Al Obeid, Ngala, Juba
Subsidiary Companies: Agricultural Bank, Khartoum; Sudanese Estates Bank, Khartoum; Industrial Bank, Khartoum

Principal Shareholders: 100% state owned
Date of Establishment: 1960
No of Employees: 1,353

BATA (SUDAN) LTD

PO Box 88, Khartoum
Tel: 32240
Cable: Batashoe
Telex: 22327, 26006

Chairman: Awad A Rahman Soghair, Syd. Awad El Karim Idreis
Directors: Amjad A Ali

PRINCIPAL ACTIVITIES: Footwear manufacturing and distribution
Parent Company: A member of the Leather Industries Corporation

Principal Bankers: Unity Bank; El Nilein Bank

Principal Shareholders: Sudan Government (45%), Bata Shoe Organization (51%)
No of Employees: 1,065

BITTAR ENGINEERING LTD

PO Box 1011, Khartoum
Tel: 70952, 71245
Cable: Engbox Khartoum
Telex: 22285 Bittar Sd

PRINCIPAL ACTIVITIES: Mechanical and electrical engineering; import of electrical, agricultural and cotton machinery; and spare parts
Principal Agencies: Campbell Oil Engine Co Ltd, W H Dorman & Co Ltd, Sigmund Pumps Ltd, Mono Pumps Ltd, Oliver Corporation, Paterson Engineering Co Ltd, Dale Electric Ltd

Principal Shareholders: A member of the Bittar Group of Companies

BITTAR GROUP OF COMPANIES

PO Box 1, Khartoum
Tel: 75400
Cable: Boxarabi
Telex: 22485 Bittar Km

Chairman: Gabriel M Bittar
Directors: S N Canaan, M Shehata, G M Brahamsha, George M Bittar, Michel G Bittar, Guy G Bittar

PRINCIPAL ACTIVITIES: Importers of steel products and wire mesh, cement, sanitaryware, asbestos sheets and pipes, plywood, butagas appliances, door locks, hardware, weighing machines, radios and fans, floor coverings, PVC plastic sheets, louvre windows, foodstuffs and flour, insecticides, fertilizers; industrial manufacturers; warehousing
Branch Offices: PO Box 1, Port Sudan
Subsidiary Companies: Bittar Engineering Ltd; Office Equipment Co; Building Materials Ltd; Soap & Allied Industries (Sudan) Ltd; Bittar & Co Ltd; Bittar Tyre Retreading Factory; BML Tiles Factory; Bittar Tins Factor
Principal Bankers: Nilein Bank; Bank of Khartoum; Unity Bank; Sudan CommercialBank; Citibank

Principal Shareholders: Bittar Family Members
Date of Establishment: 1924
No of Employees: 1,000

BLUE NILE BANK

PO Box 984, Khartoum
Tel: 78920, 78925, 79686
Telex: 22905 BNBAK SD

Chairman: C S Lee
Directors: Ibrahim Moneim Mansour, Hassan Abdel Salam Kambal, El Rashed A/Alla El Nour (Secretary of the Board)
Senior Executives: Elrasheed A/Alia Elnour (Acting General Manager), A/Rahman Ahmed Ibrahim (Deputy General Manager for Foreign Relations)

PRINCIPAL ACTIVITIES: Commercial banking
Branch Offices: Baladia branch, Khartoum
Parent Company: Daewoo Corporation
Financial Information:

	1990 US$'000
Profits	818
Authorised capital	20,000
Paid-up capital	17,000
Total assets	29,500

Principal Shareholders: Sudanese and Korean interests
Date of Establishment: October 1983
No of Employees: 80

BLUE NILE INTERNATIONAL

PO Box 1634, Khartoum
Tel: 73389, 79989, 77780
Telex: 22119 Suma Sd

Chairman: S M A Salah
Senior Executives: A Ismail (General Manager)

PRINCIPAL ACTIVITIES: General trade, import-export, livestock
and meats, commission agents
Principal Agencies: Philip Morris
Principal Bankers: Bank of Khartoum, Sudanese Commercial
Bank

Principal Shareholders: S M A Salah
Date of Establishment: 1981

BLUE NILE PACKING CORPORATION

PO Box 385, Khartoum
Tel: 80535
Cable: Cartonpaks

PRINCIPAL ACTIVITIES: Manufacture of packaging materials,
composite and folding boxes, corrugated board, polythene
bags, etc
Principal Bankers: Bank of Khartoum

Principal Shareholders: State owned

BODOURIAN, K A, & CO LTD

PO Box 21, Aboulela Bldg, Baladia Ave, Khartoum
Tel: 74222 (3 lines)
Cable: Bodourco
Telex: 22417 Khartoum Sudan

Chairman: Krikor Aram Bodourian
Directors: Jack K Bodourian, John A Bodourian, A K Bodourian

PRINCIPAL ACTIVITIES: Commission agents, manufacturers'
agents, importers and distributors of toiletries, pharmaceutical
products, radios, television sets and household appliances
Principal Agencies: National, Matsushita Trading, Smith &
Nephew, Nicholas Laboratories, Smith Kline & French
Laboratories, Union Carbide Sudan, Burroughs Wellcome,
Warner Lambert

BUILDING MATERIALS & REFRACTORIES CORP

PO Box 2241, Khartoum
Tel: 81128, 73831, 74245

Directors: Hassan Mohammed Ali (General Manager), Mohi el
Din Mousa (Deputy General Manager), Osman Mohed Hassan
(Deputy General Manager), Kamal Ahmed el Zubeir (General
Deputy Manager)

PRINCIPAL ACTIVITIES: Production of cement, paints, bricks
and building materials
Parent Company: Industrial Production Corporation
Subsidiary Companies: Maspio Cement Corporation, PO Box
96, Atbara; Nile Cement Factory, Rabak, PO Box 1502,
Khartoum; Arab Cement Co, Durdeib, PO Box 6180,
Khartoum; Rainbow Factories, PO Box 1768, Khartoum

BUILDING MATERIALS LTD

PO Box 645, Khartoum
Cable: Lilbinaa

PRINCIPAL ACTIVITIES: Import and production of building
materials; sanitary ware, hardware, plywood, steel products
and wire mesh, cement, asbestos sheets and pipes, PVC
plastic sheets, radios and fans
Principal Agencies: Blundell Permoglaze Ltd, Naco Louvred
Windows, Citroen, O M Trucks, CEAT Tyres, Mitsubishi
Radios, S A Eternit, Evode Ltd, Formica Ltd, Arthur Martin,
Junkers & Co, Ideal Standard, Coseley Steel Structure

Principal Shareholders: A member of the Bittar Group of
Companies

CARGO AIR SERVICES INTERNATIONAL

PO Box 8291, Khartoum
Tel: 40041, 40711
Telex: 24181 Casi Sd

Chairman: Mohamed Abass Osman
Directors: Musa Osman Musa
Senior Executives: Abraham Yayeh (Financial Officer)

PRINCIPAL ACTIVITIES: Courier services, clearing and
forwarding agents; agents for air traffic control; cargo
handlers
Principal Agencies: Tradewinds Express, UK; Overseas Courier
Services, Cairo, Egypt; Zahran Air Cargo, Jeddah; Riyadh,
Saudi Arabia; Abdul Wahab Mohamed Al Sani, Saudi Arabia
Branch Offices: Khartoum Airport Office: PO Box 8291, Tel
70988, 78259
Principal Bankers: Sudan Commercial Bank, Faisal Islamic Bank

Principal Shareholders: Mohamed Abass Osman, Musa Osman
Musa
Date of Establishment: 1981
No of Employees: 60

CENTRAL CO-OPERATIVE UNION

PO Box 2492, Khartoum
Tel: 80624

PRINCIPAL ACTIVITIES: Import and distribution of agricultural
machinery, grinding and flour mills, electrical equipment, etc

CENTRAL ELECTRICITY & WATER CORPORATION

PO Box 1380, Khartoum

PRINCIPAL ACTIVITIES: Government purchasing office,
generation of electric power and water supply

CHASE MANHATTAN BANK NA

PO Box 2679, Khartoum
Tel: 78703, 78740
Cable: CHAMANBANK KHARTOUM
Telex: 22618 Chase KM

PRINCIPAL ACTIVITIES: Commercial banking
Parent Company: Head office in New York, USA

CHEMICAL & PLASTICS CO (SUDAN) LTD

Elsheikh Mustafa Elamin Building, PO Box 1905, Khartoum
Tel: 78044, 78045, 75674, 79491
Cable: Chemiplast
Telex: 22205 Chem Sd
Telefax: 249-11-75674

Chairman: Farouk Diab (also Managing Director)
Directors: Abdel Aziz Safwat (Admin & Legal Director), Mrs F
Mousaad (Personnel Director), Dr Atif Anwar (Marketing
Director), Tag El Sir Mahgoub (Sales Director)

PRINCIPAL ACTIVITIES: Trading, industrial chemicals, plastics,
dyestuffs
Principal Agencies: Dow Chemical, USA; Industick, West
Germany; British Chrome, UK
Principal Bankers: Elnilein Bank, Khartoum; Tadamon Islamic
Bank, Khartoum

Principal Shareholders: Farouk Diab & Family
Date of Establishment: 1975

CITIBANK NA

PO Box 2743, Khartoum
Tel: 76654
Telex: 22454 Citibank

PRINCIPAL ACTIVITIES: Commercial banking
Parent Company: Head office in New York, USA

COLDAIR ENGINEERING CO LTD

PO Box 804, Khartoum
Tel: 72201, 71829
Cable: Koldair Khartoum
Telex: 22912 KOLDR SD

Chairman: V Christoforou (Managing Director)
Directors: J Christoforou, M H A Bashendi
Senior Executives: M H A Bashendi (Administration Director), P G Gounaris (Administration Assistant), L Abdel Sayed (Personnel Manager), Yahia El Fadil Eissa (Public Relations Officer)

PRINCIPAL ACTIVITIES: Manufacture of refrigerating and airconditioning equipment, air and water coolers, cold stores
Branch Offices: Showroom: 4 Zubeir Pasha Ave, Khartoum, Tel 71829 Factory: Plot 14, Block 5 east, Heavy Industrial Area, Khartoum North, Tel 31382, 33975, 31267
Principal Bankers: El Nilein Bank, Khartoum

Principal Shareholders: V Christoforou, J Christoforou
Date of Establishment: 1935
No of Employees: 105

CONTOMICHALOS SONS & CO LTD

PO Box 326, Khartoum
Tel: 74040/3, 72262
Cable: Controlos
Telex: 22284; 22414

PRINCIPAL ACTIVITIES: Shipping, clearing and forwarding agents, stevedoring, chartering, manufacturers' representatives, commission agents
Branch Offices: Port Sudan, PO Box 191, Tel 4908, 3705

COPTRADE CO LTD

PO Box 2893, Khartoum
Tel: 76225, 79154, 79243, 74220
Cable: Coptrade Kht
Telex: 22319 Copt A/B, 22172 Hisea A/B

Senior Executives: Assad Ismail Sheiboun (General Manager)

PRINCIPAL ACTIVITIES: Import, export, shipping and transportation, pharmaceuticals and chemicals, thread and cloth
Branch Offices: Thread Division: PO Box 148, Omdurman, Tel 54124, 51840, Telex 22319; Pharmaceutical & Chemical Division: PO Box 246, Khartoum, Tel 72412, 74501, Telex 22172; Port Sudan Branch: PO Box 74, Port Sudan, Tel 3179, 5802, 3200, Telex 70004
Financial Information:

	S£'000
Authorised capital	7,500

Principal Shareholders: Formed through the amalgamation of the Cooperative Trading Corporation and its subsidiaries: Commercial & Shipping Co, United African Drug Co, National Drug Co, Thread Import & Distribution Co
Date of Establishment: 24.1.1982

COPTRADE CO LTD (PHARMACEUTICAL & CHEMICAL DIVISION)

PO Box 246, Khartoum
Tel: 79151, 79152, 72456, 79154
Cable: COPTRADE KHTM.
Telex: 22319 COPT SD

Chairman: Sayed Mohmed Khogali El Sheikh
Directors: Assad Ismail Sheiboun

PRINCIPAL ACTIVITIES: Import and distribution of drugs, food stuffs, agricultural machinery, electric generators, shipping, insurance, clearing forwarding, inland transportation
Principal Agencies: Habag Lloyd and may other shipping lines M&B
Branch Offices: Port Sudan Branch

Principal Bankers: Bank of Khartoum, Bank of Abu Dhabi, Habib Bank, El Nilein Bank

Principal Shareholders: 90% owned by Government, 10% owned by employees
Date of Establishment: Formerly the National Drug Co
No of Employees: 350

DIGNA PETROLEUM CO LTD

PO Box 1235, Khartoum
Tel: 45171
Cable: Dignapeto
Telex: 22308 Khalignash/Dignapetco

PRINCIPAL ACTIVITIES: Distribution of petroleum and lubricating oil

Principal Shareholders: A member of the Gulf International (Sudan) Group

DUTY FREE SHOPS CORPORATION

PO Box 1789, Khartoum
Tel: 81461, 81435
Cable: Freeshop
Telex: 22487 Freeshop

Chairman: Sir Hassan Bashir
Senior Executives: Osman Said Yagoub (General Manager) Mohamed Elamin Abdel Magid (Commercial Manager), Hashim Radi (Financial Manager)

PRINCIPAL ACTIVITIES: Import and sale of duty free items, super markets operation
Branch Offices: Port Sudan Duty Free Shop, Juba Duty Free Shop, Wad Madani Duty Free Shop
Principal Bankers: Sudan Commercial Bank, Sudanese International Bank
Financial Information:

	1988/89 US$'000
Turnover	26,000
Profits	4,000
Authorised capital	2,500
Paid-up capital	2,500
Total assets	3,500

Principal Shareholders: Sudan Goverment
Date of Establishment: 1973
No of Employees: 450

EAGLE CO LTD

PO Box 2352, Khartoum
Tel: 42129, 42318
Cable: Omas
Telex: 22636 SAVP SD

Chairman: Dr Mohamed Osman Abdel Nabi (General Manager)
Directors: Dr Osman Abdel Nabi, Dr Osman Abdala, Elsayed Mohd Osman Elmirgani, Salah Sadik

PRINCIPAL ACTIVITIES: Importers and distributors of pharmaceuticals and medical equipment
Principal Agencies: Cimex AG, Switzerland; Promedica Labs, France; Cusson, UK; Artsana, Italy; Diaform, Switzerland; Zambeletti, Italy
Principal Bankers: Elnilein Bank, Sudan Commercial Bank, Sudanese Islamic Bank

Principal Shareholders: Chairman and directors as mentioned
Date of Establishment: 1971
No of Employees: 25

ELASHI, YOUSIF MOHAMED, & SONS CO LTD

PO Box 2189, Khartoum
Tel: 45598, 46514, 46511
Cable: Elrida Ktm & P/Sudan
Telex: 24100, 23026 Ashi Sd

Chairman: Yousif Mohamed Elashi

Directors: Hassan Yousif Elashi (Managing Director), Mohamed Yousif Elashi (Director), Mahmoud Yousif Elashi (Director)

Senior Executives: Adel Yousif Elashi (Manager), Baha Yousif Elashi (Manager)

PRINCIPAL ACTIVITIES: Import of all building materials, timber, steel, cement, boards, sanitary ware; transportation, handling, forwarding, warehousing, clearing, commission agents

Principal Agencies: Bayerische Motoren Werke (BMW); Mitsubishi Heavy Industries Fork Lifts; Yanmar Diesel Engines, Agricultural Tractors & Implements; Kawasaki Motor Cycles; Distributers for Mercedez Benz, Commercial Vehicles, Heavy Truck & Lorries

Branch Offices: Port Sudan Branch: PO Box 712, Tel 3453, 4291

Subsidiary Companies: Elashi Transport & Handling Services, Elashi Warehouses, Sudanese Steel Products Ltd, General Insurance, The Plastic Sacks Co

Principal Bankers: Unity Bank, National Bank of Sudan, Bank of Khartoum, BCCI Port Sudan

Financial Information:

	1988/89
	S£'000
Sales turnover	41,000
Authorised capital	1,000
Paid-up capital	1,000

Principal Shareholders: Yousif Mohamed Elashi Family

Date of Establishment: 1,907

No of Employees: 350

EL BARBARY, HAFEZ EL SAYED,

Head Office, PO Box 760, Khartoum

Tel: 41691, 42533, 76454

Cable: Ekhlas

Telex: 22469 Hafaz, 22932 NSAK

Telefax: 44894

Chairman: Kamil Mohamed H El Barbary

Directors: Hafez Ahmed Hafez El Barbary

Senior Executives: Lami Sidra Manious (Finance Manager), Magdi Mohamed H Elbarbary (Marketing Manager), Hassan Dahab (Personnel Manager), Mohamed Alamin Sadalla (Technical Manager), Yousif El Jack Taha (Administration Manager), Abdalla Alhasan (Company Lawyer)

PRINCIPAL ACTIVITIES: Building and engineering contractors, import and distribution of building materials, trucks and motorcars

Principal Agencies: Hino Motors Ltd, Japan; Honda Motors Ltd, Japan; Hankook Tire Mfg Co, S Korea

Branch Offices: PO Box 37, Port Sudan

Subsidiary Companies: National Shipping Agency; Transsudan Transportation Enterprise

Principal Bankers: Unity Bank, Khartoum

Financial Information:

	1989	1990
	S£'000	S£'000
Sales turnover	37,000	40,000
Profits	1,200	1,800
Authorised capital	8,000	8,000
Paid-up capital	3,000	3,000
Total assets	35,000	46,000

Principal Shareholders: Sons of late Mohamed H El Barbary, sons of late Ahmed E El Barbary

Date of Establishment: 1906

No of Employees: 750

ELBEREIR, MAMOUN, GROUP OF COMPANIES

Sheikh Mustafa Alamin Bldg, Ghumhoria Avenue, PO Box 2157, Khartoum

Tel: 74239, 78081

Cable: Vona

Telex: 22351 Rhino Sd

Chairman: Mamoun Elbereir

Directors: Saud Mamoun Elbereir, Idris El Haj, Ghazi Mamoun Elbereir, Murtada Elbereir

Senior Executives: Ahmed El Samani (Omdurman Soap & Chemical Factory Manager), Osman El Sheikh (Food Processing Factory Manager), Kamal Kambalawi (Financial Manager), Bakri Madani (Chief Accountant), Hafiz M A/Halim (Public Relations Manager)

PRINCIPAL ACTIVITIES: General trading, freight forwarding and clearing, dealing in agricultural produce, chemicals, electrical equipment, foodstuffs, plastic products and toiletries

Principal Agencies: Sekobe, Greece; Vimto, UK; Khalid Al-Hafi & Sons, Turkey

Branch Offices: Omdurman Soap & Chemicals Co, Mamoun Elbereir Food Processing Co, Mamoun Elbereir Plastic & Electrical Equipment Co, Mamoun Elbereir Agricultural Co

Subsidiary Companies: Stars International Co

Principal Bankers: BCCI, Khartoum; BCCI, Omdurman; Faisal Islamic Bank, Khartoum; Tadamon Islamic Bank, Middle East Bank

Principal Shareholders: Mamoun Elbereir, Saud Mamoun Elbereir, Ghazi Mamoun, Tilal Mamoun, Mohamed Mamoun

Date of Establishment: 1955

No of Employees: 400

EL DELTA INDUSTRIAL & TRADING CO LTD

PO Box 1998, Khartoum

Tel: 72076, 72966

Cable: Deltaco

Telex: 23053 AMIN SD

Chairman: Ali Awad El Kurdi

Directors: Mohd Ali El Kurdi, Bani Ali El Kurdi

PRINCIPAL ACTIVITIES: Distribution and sale of electrical equipment and agricultural machinery

Principal Agencies: GEC of England, Midland Electric Manu, Hawker Siddeley, Morrison Plant, Pirelli, Woods of Colchester

Principal Bankers: Unity Bank; Oman Bank; National Bank; Saudi Sudanese Bank

Principal Shareholders: A A El Kurdi, M A El Kurdi, B A El Kurdi

Date of Establishment: 1953

EL GEZIRA AUTOMOBILE CO

PO Box 232, Khartoum

Tel: 81215, 78555, 71094

Cable: Gezcar

Telex: 22455

PRINCIPAL ACTIVITIES: Automobile industry

Principal Agencies: Leyland

Principal Shareholders: Subsidiary of Automobile Corporation

EL NILEIN BANK

PO Box 466, Khartoum

Tel: 73939, 72740, 77686

Cable: Nilein Bank

Telex: 22243; 22220

Chairman: Mirghani Mohd Ahmed

Directors: Osman Ahmed Suleiman (Deputy Chairman & Managing Director)

PRINCIPAL ACTIVITIES: Commercial banking

Branch Offices: Branch in Abu Dhabi (UAE) and in Sudan: Khartoum, Port Sudan, Al Dueim, Wad Medani, Al Obeid,

Kadugli, El Gedaref, Karima, Kosti, Dongola, Kenana, El Nuhud, etc

Principal Shareholders: State-owned
Date of Establishment: 1964

EL NILEIN BUILDING MATERIALS CO

PO Box 588, Khartoum
Tel: 42370, 42011
Cable: Timber
Telex: 22616 Km

PRINCIPAL ACTIVITIES: Ironwork importers, distribution of boards, insulating and hard timber, building materials, timber, cement, methylated spirit, roofing felt, sanitary ware, and steel for construction
Associated Companies: El Nilein Industries

EL NILEIN INDUSTRIES

PO Box 701, Khartoum
Tel: 45884
Cable: Timber

PRINCIPAL ACTIVITIES: Manufacture of binding wire and wire nails, distribution of timber
Associated Companies: El Nilein Building Materials Co

EL ROUBI, TAHA EL SAYED, & CO

PO Box 467, Khartoum
Cable: Telroubi

PRINCIPAL ACTIVITIES: Mechanical engineers, commission and manufacturers' agents, importing and trading in electrical accessories, agricultural machinery, electric motors, engineering materials, fans, fire extinguishers, insecticides and fungicides, machine tools, radio, typewriters and wires and cables, exporting Sudanese produce

EL SHUHADA TRADING CORPORATION

PO Box 112, Khartoum
Cable: El Shuhada

PRINCIPAL ACTIVITIES: Export of groundnuts, cottonseed and oilcakes

EL TAKA AUTOMOBILE CO

PO Box 221, Khartoum
Tel: 75689, 72602
Cable: Sayarat
Telex: 22311

PRINCIPAL ACTIVITIES: Automobile industry

Principal Shareholders: Subsidiary of Automobile Corporation

EL TAYIB AHMED OSMAN (EL NUS)

PO Box 4089, Khartoum
Tel: 77771, 77520, 73841
Telex: 22047 Elnus Sd

Chairman: Eltayib Ahmed Osman

PRINCIPAL ACTIVITIES: Import, export, commission agents
Principal Agencies: Motor Iberia, Gulf East International
Principal Bankers: Faisal Islamic Bank
Financial Information:

	S£'000
Sales turnover	50,000

Principal Shareholders: Eltaib Ahmed Osman
Date of Establishment: 1977

EMIRATES & SUDAN INVESTMENT CO LTD

PO Box 7036, Khartoum
Tel: 79687, 73335
Cable: EMSU
Telex: 22524 Emsu

Chairman: Mohammad Khalifah Al Yousef

Directors: Abdalla Abdel Wahab (Managing Director), Abdullah Bin Ali, Mekki Hasan Abu Gawan Salim, Abdel Ali Mohammed

PRINCIPAL ACTIVITIES: Investment banking
Branch Offices: Khartoum, Port Sudan
Subsidiary Companies: Emirates & Red Sea Investment Co Ltd, Port Sudan; Emirates & Khartoum Investment Co Ltd, Khartoum; Emirates & Gezira Investment Co, Khartoum; Emirates & White Nile Investment Co, Khartoum
Financial Information:

	US$'000
Authorised capital	50,000
Paid-up capital	20,000

Principal Shareholders: Government of Sudan (50%), Government of UAE (50%)
Date of Establishment: 1977

ENGINEERING EQUIPMENT CORPORATION

PO Box 97, Khartoum
Tel: 73731, 76001
Cable: State Coe
Telex: 22274; 22331

PRINCIPAL ACTIVITIES: Import and distribution of agricultural machinery and implements, air compressors and exhausters, belting, diesel engines, earth-moving equipment, electrical appliances, electric motors, engineering materials, excavators, fans, lawn mowers, machine tools, marine engines, cars, motor cycles, tyres, oil engines, diesel engines, pumps, refrigerator machinery, ropes, steel furniture, steel office equipment, telecommunication and telephone equipment, tractors, weighing machines, welding plant and electrodes, wires and cables
Principal Agencies: Lewis & Tyler Ltd, Ford, Dunlop, Mather & Platt, Standard Telephones Ltd, Allis Chalmers, Ruston Bucyrus, Champion Spark Plug Co, British Oxygen Co, Electrolux, ITT Standard
Parent Company: State Trading Corporation
Subsidiary Companies: May Engineering Co; Refrigeration & Engineering Imports Co; Accounts & Electronics Equipments; Engineering Equipment Co; Khor Omer Engineering Co

EVEREADY (SUDAN) LTD

PO Box 974, Khartoum
Tel: 611884, 612534
Cable: Eveready Khartoum
Telex: 26021 Evrdy SD, 24006 Evbco SD

Chairman: N J Moden
Directors: D S Radley (Managing Director)
Senior Executives: P K Narayanan (Treasurer), F A Quashie (Plant Manager), F Y Maghoub (Marketing Manager)

PRINCIPAL ACTIVITIES: Manufacture and marketing of 'Eveready' dry cell batteries
Parent Company: Eveready Battery Co Inc, St Louis, Missouri, USA
Principal Bankers: Bank of Khartoum; Unity Bank, Citibank

Principal Shareholders: Ralston Purina Co (51%), Sudan Development Corporation (33%)
Date of Establishment: 1973
No of Employees: 385

FAHHAM TRADING AGENCIES

PO Box 720, Abouela Old Building, Khartoum
Tel: 81400, 79384, 71872
Telex: 22536 Faham Sd

Directors: Joseph M Faham, Edward M Faham, Shakir M Faham

PRINCIPAL ACTIVITIES: Importers and local industries distributors and commission agents
Principal Agencies: Societe Industrielle Lessafre, France; Esperia Machine Ind, Italy; Kaso Plastic Factory, Sudan

Principal Bankers: Elnilein Bank

Principal Shareholders: Family of Faham
Date of Establishment: 1960

FAISAL ISLAMIC BANK (SUDAN)
PO Box 10143, Khartoum
Tel: 81848, 81857
Cable: BANKISLAMI
Telex: 22163 FIBS SD, 22519 FIBS SD

Chairman: HRH Prince Mohammad Al Faisal Al Saud
Directors: Dar Al Mal Al Islami, Dafae Allah Al Haj Yousif, Yassin Omer Al Imam, Faisal Islamic Bank of Egypt, Dr Salah Ahmed Omer Kambal, Sheikh Ahmed Salah Jamjoom, Eng Beshir Hassan Bashir Osman, Ibrahim Al Tayeb Al Rayah, Dr Abdel Aziz El Fadda, Dr Ahmed Abdel Aziz Al Naggar, Sheikh Mohammed Salih Bahareth, Sheikh Saeed Ahmed Luttah, Sheikh Abdel Hamid Abdel Razig Al Obeid, Mohammed Abdo Rabu Mohammed
Senior Executives: Albagir Yousif Mudawi (General Manager)

PRINCIPAL ACTIVITIES: Islamic Banking
Branch Offices: Khartoum, Port Sudan, Omdurman, Gadarif, Kosti, El Obeid, Atbara, Kassala, Elfasher, Dongla, Eldmazin, Juba
Subsidiary Companies: Islamic Trading & Services Co, Real Estate Development Co
Financial Information:

	S£'000
Authorised capital	100,000
Paid-up capital	58,400

Principal Shareholders: 40% Sudanese interests, 60% Non-Sudanese interests
Date of Establishment: 1977
No of Employees: 826

FODIKWAN COMPANY LTD
PO Box 527, Port Sudan

Chairman: A A Basher

PRINCIPAL ACTIVITIES: The production and export of ferrous and non-ferrous ores

FOOD INDUSTRIES CORPORATION
PO Box 2341, Khartoum
Tel: 75463

Chairman: Mohamed el Ghali Suleiman (General Manager)
Directors: Babikir Mirghani Hassan (Deputy Managing Director), Khidir Osman Bashir (Chief Engineer)

PRINCIPAL ACTIVITIES: Production of foodstuffs, canned fruit, vegetables, dehydrated onions, packed dates, dried vegetables
Subsidiary Companies: Karima Fruit & Vegetable Canning Factory, PO Box 54, Karima; Wau Fruit & Vegetable Canning Factory, PO Box 110, Wau; Babanousa Milk Products Factory, PO Box 16, Babanousa; Kassala Onion Dehydration Factory, PO Box 22, Kassala; Rea Sweet Factory, PO Box 1027, Khartoum; Krikah Industries Group, PO Box 755, Khartoum North; Karima Date Factory, PO Box 31, Karima; Blue Nile Packing Corp, PO Box 385, Khartoum; Bahri Flour Mill, PO Box 1265, Khartoum North
Principal Bankers: Bank of Sudan; Bank of Khartoum

Principal Shareholders: Part of the Industrial Production Corporation

FRIENDSHIP PALACE HOTEL
PO Box 148, Khartoum North, Khartoum
Tel: 78204
Telex: 22470

PRINCIPAL ACTIVITIES: Hotel business

GAMAHIER TRADING CO
PO Box 4151, Khartoum Central
Tel: 76144, 81344
Cable: Gamahierco
Telex: 22626 Gamahierco SD

Directors: H H Hassanein (General Manager)

PRINCIPAL ACTIVITIES: Import of electric motors, water pumps, flour mills, diesel engines and spare parts
Principal Agencies: Electrimpex, Refimex, Futaba Electrading (Japan), Patel Engineering
Principal Bankers: Bank of Credit & Commerce Int, Sudan Commercial Bank, Faisal Islamic Bank

Principal Shareholders: H H Hassanein
Date of Establishment: 1967

GENERAL ADMINISTRATION FOR OIL TRANSPORTATION
New Mustafa El Amin Bldg, PO Box 1704, Khartoum
Tel: 78290, 79006, 78281
Cable: Pipes
Telex: 22649

Senior Executives: Mohammed Elmurtada Ibrahiem (Acting Managing Director), Ezzildin Mustafa (Financial Manager), Ali Awad Ali (Operations Manager), Mohamed Elamin Ahmed (Engineering Manager), Yousif Salih Ahmed (Maintenance Manager), Hussien Hakim Sharief (Purchasing & Stores Manager), Abubaker Mansour Suliman (Services & Admin Manager), Sid Ahmed Osman Khalifa (Personnel Manager)

PRINCIPAL ACTIVITIES: Petroleum products transportation via pipelines
Parent Company: General Petroleum Corporation

Principal Shareholders: Dept of the General Petroleum Corporation
Date of Establishment: 1977
No of Employees: 620

GENERAL INDUSTRIAL PRODUCTION CORPORATION
PO Box 1034, El Gamaa St, Khartoum
Tel: 74550, 75397, 71278
Cable: Sadak Khartoum
Telex: 22236

PRINCIPAL ACTIVITIES: Production of sugar, foodstuffs, and manufacture of leather and plastic products

GENERAL INSURANCE CO (SUDAN) LTD
Sharia El Gamhouria, PO Box 1555, Khartoum
Tel: 80616/7, 76820
Cable: Aman
Telex: 22303

Chairman: Dr Ibrahim M Al Moghrabi
Directors: Mohamed Tewfik Ahmed, Mahgoub Mohamed Ahmed, Zaki Ibrahim, Mohamed Salih Gereis, Mohamed Hassan Elsulimani

PRINCIPAL ACTIVITIES: Insurance and reinsurance
Subsidiary Companies: Branches at Port Sudan (PO Box 584) and Wad Medani (PO Box 194) (Sudan); Alkhobar (PO Box 355) (Saudi Arabia); Riyadh (PO Box 1220) (Saudi Arabia)
Principal Bankers: El Nilein Bank; Bank of Khartoum; Unity Bank; Sudan Commercial Bank; National Bank of Abu Dhabi; Bank of Credit & Commerce; Citibank

Date of Establishment: 1961
No of Employees: 125

SUDAN

GEZIRA TRADE & SERVICES CO LTD

Gamaa Avenue, PO Box 215, Khartoum
Tel: 81691, 70202, 84630, 84640
Cable: GZRA
Telex: 22302, 22315 GZRA SD

Directors: Dr Mohammed Osman Ibrahim (Managing Director),
Rahamtalla Ahmed Mohamed (Deputy Managing Director)
Senior Executives: Mohammed Salim Baasher (Asst Managing
Director Planning & Follow up), Mubarak Mahmoud (Asst
Managing Director Engineering), Omer A Basit (Asst
Managing Director Port Sudan Unit), Ibrahim M Ali (Asst
Managing Director Trading Unit), Rodulf George (Asst
Managing Director Automobile Unit)

PRINCIPAL ACTIVITIES: Export, import, agent of general
merchandise, shipping agents, and related services
Principal Agencies: Leyland Vehicles; Massey Ferguson
Tractors and Agricultural Implement; Lucas World Services;
SGS - Lloyds; Toplis & Hardings; Hoover; Gestetner; Facit
AB; Edible Products Ltd
Branch Offices: Port Sudan; Medani; Gedaref; Sennar; Kosti; El
Obied
Subsidiary Companies: El Wadi Export Enterprises
Principal Bankers: Unity Bank; El Nilein Bank; Citibank; Bank of
Khartoum; National Bank for Development
Financial Information:

	1990
	S£'000
Sales turnover	100,000
Profits	40,000
Authorised capital	5,200
Paid-up capital	5,200

Principal Shareholders: Ministry of Finance; Unity Bank
Date of Establishment: April 1980
No of Employees: 565

GOLDEN ARROW CO LTD

PO Box 465, Khartoum
Tel: 77178/9, 81857/9, 81985
Cable: Alsahm
Telex: 22399 Khartoum

Chairman: Awad Abdelmutaal
Directors: Mamoun Abdelmutaal (Managing Director)

PRINCIPAL ACTIVITIES: Distribution of cars, earthmoving
equipment, diesel engines, water engines, water pumps, tyres
and tubes
Principal Agencies: Toyota, Daihatsu, Komatsu, Rolls Royce,
Ebara, Ohtsu
Principal Bankers: Elnilein Bank, Bank of Credit & Commerce,
Middle East Bank

No of Employees: 175

GRAND HOTEL KHARTOUM

PO Box 316, Khartoum
Tel: 72782, 77758
Telex: 22436

PRINCIPAL ACTIVITIES: Hotel business

GROUPED INDUSTRIES CORPORATION

PO Box 2241, Khartoum
Tel: 81128, 73831, 74245

Chairman: Elshazali Mostafa A-Alla
Directors: Eng Omer Mohd Mohd Nour (General Manager), Abd
El Hafiez Abd El Kariem (Finance Director), Mohd Ali Abd El
Haliem (Sales Director), Eng Hamza Abd El Moniem
(Production Director)
Senior Executives: Eng Hag Bashier Ibrahiem (Plant Manager),
Eng Atif Mohd Abd El Gadir (Maintenance Manager)

PRINCIPAL ACTIVITIES: Holding company; manufacturing and
marketing of cement, perfumes, packing materials, spare
parts, laundry, minerals, iron, chromite and magnesite
Subsidiary Companies: Blue Nile Packing; Ingassana Mines Hills
Corp; El Taheer Perfumery Corp, Khartoum; El Tahreer
Perfumery Corp, Omdurmaon; The Modern Laundry Blue
Factory; Khartoum Central Foundry
Financial Information:

	1990
	S£'000
Sales turnover	60,569
Profits	18,383
Authorised capital	1,200
Paid-up capital	1,200
Total assets	90,178

Principal Shareholders: State-owned corporation
Date of Establishment: 1947
No of Employees: 1,222

GULF INTERNATIONAL (SUDAN)

PO Box 2316 and 1377, Khartoum
Tel: 34166, 32159, 32307, 76049, 71502
Cable: Khalignash
Telex: 22267 Theotext Khartoum; 22308 Khalignash Khartoum

Chairman: Dr Khalil Osman Mahmoud
Directors: Dafalla El Hag Yousif Medani, Osman Ahmed Kheir,
Mohmoud Sid Ahmed Swar El Dahab, Mahmoud Ahmed
Abdella

PRINCIPAL ACTIVITIES: Manufacture of textiles, matches,
chemicals, glass, packaging materials, cotton wool, medicines
and drugs, garments, particle board, operator of publicity,
hotels, aerial spraying, air taxi services
Principal Agencies: CIBA, North American Rockwell
Branch Offices: Kuwait; Nigeria; Egypt; Senegal; Lebanon;
Saudi Arabia; Austria; UK; France
Subsidiary Companies: Sudan Textile Industry Ltd, Modern
Match Producing & Distributing Co Ltd; Sudanese Chemical
Industries Ltd; Medical & Sanitary Products Ltd; Sudanese
Glass Co Ltd; Sudan Allwear Industry; Sudanese Kuwaiti
Packaging Co Ltd; National Agriculture Organization Ltd;
Tourism & Air Taxi Services; Particle Board Industries Ltd;
Khartoum Publicity Co Ltd; Meridien Hotel; Africa Plantation;
Digna Petroleum Co Ltd; Tagoog Mining Co Ltd; Gulf
International Training Centre

GUM ARABIC CO LTD

PO Box 857, Khartoum
Tel: 77288, 77707, 74028, 81646, 79714, 76338, 79713
Cable: Gumarab
Telex: 22314

Chairman: Fouad Mustafa Abu El Elia
Directors: Mubarak Mirghami, Dr M Hag Ali, Makawi S Akrat,
Mubarak M Logman, Mahmoud A Hafiz, Mustafa Daoud,
Salih M Salih, Mohamed El Hassan Abdallah, Osman M El
Hassan
Senior Executives: O M El Hassan (General Manager)

PRINCIPAL ACTIVITIES: Production, marketing and export of
gum arabic
Branch Offices: PO Box 378, Port Sudan
Principal Bankers: Bank of Khartoum; El Nilein Bank; Sudan
Commercial Bank; Bank of Abu Dhabi; Unity Bank; Islamic
Bank of Faisal

Principal Shareholders: Government (30%); Private (70%)
Date of Establishment: 1969
No of Employees: 120

HAFEZ EL SAYED EL BARBARY

See EL BARBARY, HAFEZ EL SAYED,

HASSOUNA AUTOWORK SHOPS & STORES CO LTD

PO Box 5032, Khartoum
Tel: 42729, 41842, 45206, 47482
Cable: Hassouna
Telex: 22382
Telefax: 47482

Chairman: Abdelmoniem M Hassouna
Directors: Mohamed A M Hassouna, Ahmed A M Hassouna
Senior Executives: Murtada A M Hassouna

PRINCIPAL ACTIVITIES: Dealers of motorcars, engines and spare parts
Principal Agencies: Nissan Diesels, Suzuki, Nissan Motor, Yokahama Tyres, Tadano
Branch Offices: Sales Office & Showroom: Khartoum 2, Tel 42729, 47482
Principal Bankers: Sudan Commercial Bank, Khartoum
Financial Information:

	1990 S£'000
Sales turnover	16,088
Profits	3,218
Paid-up capital	1,000
Total assets	38,350

Principal Shareholders: Abdelmoneim Hassouna & Family
Date of Establishment: 1963
No of Employees: 180

HILTON INTERNATIONAL KHARTOUM

PO Box 1910, Morgran, Khartoum
Tel: 74100, 78930
Cable: Hiltels-Khartoum
Telex: SD 22250

PRINCIPAL ACTIVITIES: Hotel and catering
Parent Company: Hilton International
Principal Bankers: Bank of Credit & Commerce

Principal Shareholders: Sudan/Kuwait Hotels Corporation
Date of Establishment: 1st March 1977
No of Employees: 400

IBRAHIM EL TAYEB A/SALAM & SONS

PO Box 1282, Khartoum
Tel: 78660, 76780
Cable: Ieas
Telex: 22081 Sudi SD

Chairman: Dr El-Tayeb Ibrahim
Directors: Abdel Gadir Suliman, Dr Gamal Mohamed Ahmed, Abdel Raouf Mustafa, Idris Bukhari Ali
Senior Executives: Abu Baker Ibrahim El Tayeb

PRINCIPAL ACTIVITIES: Raw skin dealers, export-import agents
Branch Offices: PO Box 626, Port Sudam, Tel 4858, Cable Tanneryco
Subsidiary Companies: Red Sea Tannery Co Ltd, PO Box 626, Port Sudan; Sudimpex International Consulting
Principal Bankers: Sudanese Investment Bank; El Nilein Bank
Financial Information: Member of the Iron and Steel Union

Principal Shareholders: Ibrahim El-Tayeb & Sons
Date of Establishment: 1930
No of Employees: 60

INDUSTRIAL & COMMERCIAL CONSULTANCY HOUSE

PO Box 2467, Khartoum
Tel: 71251, 71239
Cable: Yahanady
Telex: 22108 TACI, 22443 SEMAC

Chairman: Mohamed Malik Osman (General Manager)

PRINCIPAL ACTIVITIES: Import-export, agents, consultants, feasibility studies, information office, publishers
Subsidiary Companies: Sudan Industrial & Commercial Directory
Principal Bankers: Sudan Commercial Bank; El Nilein Bank; Bank Faisal

Principal Shareholders: Sole owner
Date of Establishment: June 1976
No of Employees: 20

INDUSTRIAL BANK OF SUDAN

United Nations Sq, PO Box 1722, Khartoum
Tel: 71223, 71208
Cable: Sinaie
Telex: 22456 Sinaire Km

Directors: The board of Directors is composed of 8 members, 5 of whom represent the public sector and the Bank senior management, and 3 represent the private sector

PRINCIPAL ACTIVITIES: Providing financial and technical assistance to industrial enterprises in Sudan

Principal Shareholders: State owned
Date of Establishment: 1961

INDUSTRIAL PRODUCTION CORPORATION

PO Box 1034, Khartoum
Tel: 71278, 75397, 74550/1, 72990
Cable: Sidce
Telex: 22236; 22298

Chairman: Omer Taha Abu Samra (also Director General)
Directors: Abdel Latif Widatalla (Deputy Chairman and Deputy Director General), Murtag Ahmed Gasim (Manager Industrial Relations & Training)

PRINCIPAL ACTIVITIES: Industrial development and holding company for the following organisations: Food Industries Corp, Sugar & Distilling Corp, Leather Industries Corp, Mining Corp, Building Materials & Refractories Corp, Oil Corp, Spinning & Weaving Corp, Public Corp for Oil Products & Pipelines, Petroleum General Administration

INDUSTRIAL RESEARCH & CONSULTANCY INSTITUTE

Po Box 268, Khartoum
Tel: 613225/28
Cable: Iris
Telex: 26008 IRCI SD

Chairman: Abdella A Wahab
Directors: Eng Zakria Abdel Nabi (Managing Director)
Senior Executives: Dr M O Arabi, M Majra, Dr Elhag Ahmed Elhag (Director of Industrial Information)

PRINCIPAL ACTIVITIES: Research, business and engineering consultants
Principal Bankers: Industrial Bank; Sudan Central Bank

Principal Shareholders: State-owned
Date of Establishment: 1965
No of Employees: 233

IZMIRLIAN SARKIS CORPORATION LTD
See SARKIS, IZMIRLIAN, CORPORATION LTD

J N VALVIS
See VALVIS, J N,

K A BODOURIAN & CO LTD
See BODOURIAN, K A, & CO LTD

KENANA SUGAR COMPANY

PO Box 2632, Khartoum

Chairman: Mohammad Al Bashir Al Wagie
Directors: Osman Abdalla Al Nazir (Managing Director), Faisal Al Kazemi (Deputy Chairman)

SUDAN

PRINCIPAL ACTIVITIES: Sugar refining and production
Financial Information:

	US$'000
Authorised capital	310,000

Principal Shareholders: Kuwait Foreign Trading, Contracting & Investment Co (KFTCIC), Kuwaiti Government, Sudanese Government, Sudan Development Corporation, Arab Investment Company, Saudi Arabian Government, Gulf Fisheries of Kuwait, Arab Authority in Agricultural Investment & Development, El Nilein Bank, etc

KHARTOUM COMMERCIAL & SHIPPING CO LTD

Head Office: Kasr Avenue, PO Box 221, Khartoum
Tel: 78555 (8 lines)
Cable: SAYARAT
Telex: 22311 SYRT; 22297 NTKM; 22306 SHIP SD

Directors: H M Ali (Acting Managing Director)

PRINCIPAL ACTIVITIES: Import, export, and manufacturers
Branch Offices: Port Sudan; Elobeid; Cairo
Associated Companies: Kordofan Co; African Drilling Co; Modern Electronic Co; El Amin El Gezai Co; Modern Plastic & Ceramics Industries Co; Wafra Chemicals & techno-medical Services Ltd

Principal Shareholders: Military Commercial Corporation
Date of Establishment: April 1982
No of Employees: 455

KHARTOUM COMMERCIAL AGENCY

PO Box 646, Khartoum
Tel: 80197, 70847, 72072, 76379
Cable: Tawkilat
Telex: 22626 FOM, 22183 DAIF

Chairman: Sami J Kronfli (Sole Proprietor & Director)
Senior Executives: Mrs Samira A Mortada (Administration & Finance Manager)

PRINCIPAL ACTIVITIES: Import and distribution of pharmaceuticals
Principal Agencies: Ciba, Switzerland; Merck Sharp & Dohme, USA, UK, Holland, Lebanon; Bristor Labs, USA, Italy; Syntex Pharmaceuticals, UK; London Rubber Co, UK; Stiefel Labs, UK; Emile Charpentier, France; Aron, France; Theramex Labs, France
Principal Bankers: Bank of Khartoum; Sudan Commercial Bank; Faisal Islamic Bank
Financial Information:

	1988/89 S£'000
Sales turnover	6,147
Profits	511
Authorised capital	655
Paid-up capital	163
Total assets	3,178

Principal Shareholders: Sami J Kronfli
Date of Establishment: 1949
No of Employees: 20

KHARTOUM MOTOR MART CO LTD

Al Khalifa Ave, PO Box 398, Khartoum
Tel: 70478, 73295, 76394
Cable: Motormart Khartoum

Chairman: Ali Abdalla Ali
Directors: Gamal Ali Abdalla (General Manager), Kamal Ali Abdalla (Sub Manager), El Rayeh Siddig Ali (Sales Manager)

PRINCIPAL ACTIVITIES: Import of spare parts
Principal Agencies: Taiyo, Japan; Helafrica, Greece; Omac, Italy; Mexim, England; Marmex, Holland

Principal Bankers: Unity Bank, El Nilein Bank

Principal Shareholders: Ali Abdalla Ali and Sons
Date of Establishment: 1942

KHARTOUM PUBLICITY CO LTD

PO Box 905, Khartoum
Tel: 70153, 70584, 70436
Cable: Kapservice
Telex: 22308 Khalignash/Kapservice

PRINCIPAL ACTIVITIES: Printing, publishing and advertising

Principal Shareholders: A member of the Gulf International (Sudan) Group

KHARTOUM SPINNING & WEAVING CO LTD

PO Box 193, Khartoum North
Tel: 32394, 34358
Cable: Naseeg Khartoum
Telex: 22277 Km

Chairman: Victor Kattan
Directors: Abdalla Siddik Gandour, George Hanna Kattan, Mohed Ahmed Abbas, Abdel Salam Aboulela (Managing Director), Mr Ichi, Mekkawi Mustafa (General Manager)

PRINCIPAL ACTIVITIES: Spinning and weaving
Principal Bankers: Sudan Commercial Bank

Principal Shareholders: International Finance Corporation, Kanematsu Gosho, Geretco, Kuwait Investment Co, Kattan Trading Co, Aboulela Co

KHARTOUM TANNNERY

PO Box 134, Khartoum South
Tel: 43752, 43904, 43170
Cable: Gotan
Telex: 22298 Sidg Kh Khartoum

Directors: El-Sheikh Mohamed Ahmed Tambal (Tannery General Manager)
Senior Executives: Abdalla A Gouda (Tannery Technical Manager)

PRINCIPAL ACTIVITIES: Conversion of raw cow hides and sheep and goat skins into finished and semi-finished leather of different varieties, marketing of leather products
Principal Agencies: Allison Marketing Inc, UK
Parent Company: Leather Industries Tanneries, Ministry of Industry
Principal Bankers: Bank of Khartoum; Commercial Bank of Sudan

Principal Shareholders: Sudan Government (public corporation)
Date of Establishment: 1962
No of Employees: 480

KHOR OMER ENGINEERING CO

Kordofan Trading & Engineering Co Ltd

PO Box 305, Khartoum
Tel: 72681, 79271
Cable: Khor Omer

PRINCIPAL ACTIVITIES: Engineering industry, supply of office equipment and engineering equipment
Principal Agencies: Olivetti; Rex Rottary typing machines; Daimler Benz; American Motors Corp; Thorn Consumer Electronics; Cinemeccanica SpA
Principal Bankers: El Nilein Bank; Sudan Commercial Bank; Faisal Islamic Bank

Principal Shareholders: State-owned

KORDOFAN AUTOMOBILE CO

PO Box 97, Khartoum
Tel: 80636
Cable: Stateco
Telex: 22331

PRINCIPAL ACTIVITIES: Automobile industry
Principal Agencies: Ford

Principal Shareholders: Subsidiary of Automobile Corporation

KOUTSOUDIS & CONTANINOU CO
PO Box 632, Khartoum

Chairman: George Koutsoudis

PRINCIPAL ACTIVITIES: Manufacturers' agents, distribution of
chemicals, bicycles and accessories, motor cars, perfumery
and toiletries and groceries

LABIB DEMIAN
PO Box 171, Khartoum

PRINCIPAL ACTIVITIES: General trading, import and distribution
of auto spare parts, batteries, tyres and tubes, rubber
products
Principal Agencies: Oldham Batteries, John Rubber Company

LEATHER INDUSTRIES CORPORATION
PO Box 1639, Khartoum
Tel: 78264, 79260
Cable: Glostic Khartoum
Telex: 22298

PRINCIPAL ACTIVITIES: Production of leather and shoes
Subsidiary Companies: Bata Nationalised Corporation, PO Box
88, Khartoum; Khartoum Tannery, PO Box 134, Khartoum
South; New Khartoum Tannery, PO Box 715, Khartoum;
White Nile Tannery, PO Box 4078, Khartoum Central; Gezira
Tannery; Omdurman Shoe Factory

Principal Shareholders: Part of the Industrial Production
Corporation

LIVESTOCK & MEAT MARKETING CORP (LMMC)
PO Box 1499, Khartoum
Tel: 45864, 42367, 46389
Cable: Limaco
Telex: 22342

Chairman: Osman A/Allah Bashari (Director General)
Directors: Dr Mohamed El Bagir Osman (Dept of Finance &
Administration), Dr Abu El Gasim Ahmed Shumu (Dept of
Regional Affairs), Dr Ismail Fakiri (Dept of Planning & Follow
Up), Hassan Mohd Ali (Dept of External Marketing), Dr Omer
Hassan El Dirani (Dept of Research & Information)

PRINCIPAL ACTIVITIES: Services and facilities required in
livestock and meat production & trade, purchase, sales,
distribution, shipment and delivery
Branch Offices: Omdurman, Wad Medeni, El Obied, Nyala, El
Fashir, Kosti, Portsudan, Mellit, El Da'an, Sinnar, Rabak,
Kadogli, Dilling
Parent Company: LMMC
Subsidiary Companies: Livestock Route Company
Principal Bankers: Bank of Sudan

Principal Shareholders: Sudanese Government (45.4%), IDA
(43.2%), Saudi Fund for Development (6.0%), ODA (5.4%)
Date of Establishment: October 1976
No of Employees: 364

M A MAHGOUB & CO LTD
See MAHGOUB, M A, & CO LTD

MAHGOUB, M A, & CO LTD
PO Box 577, Khartoum
Telex: 22602

Chairman: Mohamed Ahmed Mahgoub

PRINCIPAL ACTIVITIES: Import and distribution auto spare
parts
Associated Companies: Clark International Marketing, USA

MALIK INDUSTRIAL CO LTD
PO Box 1602, Khartoum
Tel: 31419, 33623, 77242
Cable: Ibrahim Malik Khartoum

Directors: Ahmed Ibrahim Malik

PRINCIPAL ACTIVITIES: Manufacture of edible oil and soap,
import and distribution of general merchandise

MAMOUN ELBEREIR GROUP OF COMPANIES
See ELBEREIR, MAMOUN, GROUP OF COMPANIES

MAY TRADING & SERVICES CO
PO Box 215, Khartoum
Tel: 77632, 79060, 81690
Cable: Mayo Khartoum
Telex: 22302 Mayo

PRINCIPAL ACTIVITIES: Insurance agents; shipping clearing
and forwarding agents; general trading; import and production
of cement, chemicals, building materials, hardboards, cotton
goods, flour, paints and oils, office equipment, sanitaryware,
steel, tarpaulins and timber; export of agricultural produce
Principal Agencies: General Insurance Co (Sudan) Ltd, Lloyds of
London, Facit Typewriters, Gestetner duplicators, Odhner
calculators, Universal Frankers, Steel Construction Ltd,
Gourok Ropework Co Ltd
Branch Offices: PO Box 17, Port Sudan, Tel 2437, 2029, Cable
Mayo Port Sudan; Wad Medani; El Obeid; Juba
Subsidiary Companies: Sudan Soap Factory; Sudan Cold
Stores; Red Sea Stevedoring; Sudan Warehousing Co
Principal Bankers: Bank of Khartoum; Nilein Bank; Unity Bank;
Commercial Bank of Sudan

MEDICAL & SANITARY PRODUCTS CO LTD
PO Box 2178, Khartoum
Tel: 611907, 611328, 611137
Cable: Shash
Telex: 26009 Km

Chairman: Joseph Makeen Iskander
Directors: Ishag Fagiri Mohammed
Senior Executives: El Sadik Abdullahi Elmahdi (General
Manager)

PRINCIPAL ACTIVITIES: Production of absorbent cotton wool,
sanitary towels, bandages and gauze
Principal Bankers: Unity Bank, Bank of Khartoum, Faisal Islamic
Bank
Financial Information:

	1988/89 S£'000	1989/90 S£'000
Sales turnover	6,103	12,327
Profits	1,296	3,460
Authorised capital	1,209	6,300
Paid-up capital	1,209	6,300
Total assets	6,300	18,500

Principal Shareholders: Joseph M Iskander, Ishag Fagiri
Mohammed, Dr M H Salih, Dr A A El Humidi, HE Sheikh Al
Sabah Al Ahmed
Date of Establishment: 1974
No of Employees: 210

MERIDIEN HOTEL
PO Box 1716, Khartoum
Tel: 75970/7
Telex: 22499

PRINCIPAL ACTIVITIES: Hotel business

MIDDLE EAST INTERNATIONAL FINANCE & DEVELOPMENT CO LTD
PO Box 2779, Khartoum
Tel: 75222

Chairman: Ahmed Ibrahim Draige

Directors: Ali Ahmed Draige

Senior Executives: Abdelrahman Ahmed Ibrahim (Commercial & Financial Manager)

PRINCIPAL ACTIVITIES: Imports, exports, tenders, commission agents, financial agents, engineering and management consultants, construction, transport and drilling

Principal Agencies: Renault, France; Stromberg, Finland

Subsidiary Companies: Elkhidir & Draiges Construction Co, Jabal Marah Drugs & Chemicals Co, Jabal Marah Water Drilling Co, Azoum Transport Co

Principal Bankers: Elnilein Bank, Sudanese International Bank, Unity Bank

Principal Shareholders: Family of Ahmed Ibrahim Draige

Date of Establishment: 1978

MILITARY COMMERCIAL CORPORATION

PO Box 221, Khartoum
Tel: 78555, 72659
Cable: Sayarat
Telex: 22297 NTKM; 22311 SYRT; 22306 SHIP SD

Chairman: E R M Tom
Directors: M O A Halim (Managing Director)

PRINCIPAL ACTIVITIES: Import of air compressors and exhausters, air conditioning, bearings, ball and roller, coal, coke and patent fuel, engineering materials, motor cars, trucks, cycles and parts, tyres, paints and oils. Owns the assembly plants in Port Sudan

Principal Agencies: Bedford CKD Trucks, British Leyland Trucks

Branch Offices: PO Box 242, Port Sudan

Parent Company: State Trading Corporation

Associated Companies: Khartoum Commercial & Shipping Co Ltd; Kordofan Trading & Engineering Co Ltd; Coptrade Trade & Shipping Co Ltd; El Amn El Gezaei Co Ltd; Wafra Chemicals & Techno - Medical Services Ltd

Principal Shareholders: Ministry of Finance & Bank of Khartoum

Date of Establishment: 1982

MINERAL WATER BOTTLING CO (SUDAN) LTD

PO Box 881, Khartoum

Chairman: Abdel Hafiz Abdel Moneim

PRINCIPAL ACTIVITIES: Manufacture of soft drinks and mineral waters

Principal Agencies: Al Cola

MOBIL OIL SUDAN LTD

PO Box 283, Khartoum
Tel: 77773
Cable: Mobiloil
Telex: 22269

Senior Executives: Mohd S Nagi (Operations Manager), Abbas Abdel Hafiz (Relations Manager), Abdel Moheim Abdallah (Sales Manager)

PRINCIPAL ACTIVITIES: Distribution and marketing of petroleum products

Branch Offices: PO Box 183, Port Sudan, Sudan

Principal Bankers: Bank of Khartoum; Bank of Credit & Commerce International, Citibank

Principal Shareholders: Mobil Petroleum Co

Date of Establishment: 1953

No of Employees: 250

MODAWI, MOHAMED AHMED,

PO Box 5136, Khartoum South
Tel: 42983, 44708, 45934, 42387
Cable: Modawi
Telex: 24068 Dawi SD, 22119 Afnan SD

Chairman: Mohamed Ahmed Modawi
Directors: Omer Modawi (Managing Director)
Senior Executives: Mohammed Adam Fadul (Finance Manager), Mahmoud A Alrahim (Admin Manager)

PRINCIPAL ACTIVITIES: Import of autospare parts, agricultural machinery, trucks, lubricating oil, glassware, tanneries and general trade

Principal Agencies: Burmah Castrol Oil, UK; Unimpex Ltd, Yasuda Trading; Technoimportexport, Roumania

Branch Offices: Port Sudan, Gedaref

Subsidiary Companies: Afnan Agricultural Co Ltd, Afnan International Co Ltd, Leena Agricultural Co Ltd

Principal Bankers: Habib Bank, Bank of Khartoum, Islamic Cooperative Development Bank, Tadamon Islamic Bank

Financial Information:

	1990 S£'000
Sales turnover	15,000
Profits	4,000
Authorised capital	5,000
Paid-up capital	2,000
Total assets	2,000

Principal Shareholders: Mohamed Ahmed Modawi
Date of Establishment: 1966
No of Employees: 100

MODERN MATCH PRODUCING & DISTRIBUTING CO LTD

PO Box 2316, Khartoum
Tel: 31442, 31909, 81117
Cable: Tumsah
Telex: 22326 Tumsah

Chairman: Khalil Osman Mahmoud

PRINCIPAL ACTIVITIES: Manufacture of safety matches

Parent Company: A member of the Gulf International (Sudan) Group

MODERN SUPPLIES AGENCY

PO Box 1805, Khartoum
Tel: 77192, 77244
Cable: Bamihemied
Telex: 22435 Osas Km

Chairman: El Fatih Ahmed El Sheikh
Directors: Y El Sheikh

PRINCIPAL ACTIVITIES: Import of industrial machinery, equipment and raw materials; manufacturers' representation

Principal Agencies: Soiltest Inc, Evanston; Gram A/S, Denmark

Principal Bankers: El Nilein Bank; People's Co-operative Bank

MOHAMED AHMED ABDEL LATIF & CO LTD

PO Box 241, Khartoum
Cable: Tantalus

Chairman: Mohamed A A Latif

PRINCIPAL ACTIVITIES: Commission agents, manufacturers' agents, sale of chick peas, insecticides and fungicides and motor tyres and import of flour

MOHAMED AHMED MODAWI

See MODAWI, MOHAMED AHMED,

NATIONAL AGRICULTURE ORGANISATION LTD

PO Box 1484, Khartoum
Tel: 75446, 75428
Cable: Agrinol
Telex: 22276 Theotext

PRINCIPAL ACTIVITIES: Agricultural development schemes, contractors, crop spraying and distribution of agricultural equipment

Parent Company: A member of the Gulf International (Sudan) Group

NATIONAL BANK OF ABU DHABI

PO Box 2465, Khartoum
Tel: 74892/5
Cable: Almasref Khartoum
Telex: 22249 Bankozabi

PRINCIPAL ACTIVITIES: Commercial banking
Branch Offices: Port Sudan: PO Box 596
Parent Company: Head office: PO Box 4, Abu Dhabi, UAE

NATIONAL CIGARETTES CO LTD

PO Box 2083, Khartoum
Tel: 74435/6/7/8
Cable: Watania-Tobac
Telex: 22330 Tobac

Chairman: Saad Aboulela
Directors: Charles A Kfouri, Hassan M Gangari, Beshir M Saeed, Abdalla El Hassan, Mohamed Khogali, Babiker El Khawad, Mohamed D El Khalifa
Senior Executives: Tawfig E Abugroon (General Manager)

PRINCIPAL ACTIVITIES: Production, import and distribution of cigarettes and tobacco products
Principal Agencies: British American Tobacco Co Ltd; Philip Morris Inc; Henri Winterman's; Willem II; Widmer & Cie; Villiger Sohne
Branch Offices: Wad Medani; Port Sudan; Atbara; El Obeid; Juba; Nyala; Kassala; Kosti
Parent Company: Sudanese Tobacco Corporation
Subsidiary Companies: Blue Nile Cigarette Co Ltd
Principal Bankers: Bank of Khartoum; El Nilein Bank; Abu Dhabi National Bank; Citibank
Financial Information:

	S£'000
Sales turnover	130,000
Authorised capital	2,000
Paid-up capital	1,000

Principal Shareholders: Public-owned
Date of Establishment: 1965
No of Employees: 120

NATIONAL COTTON & TRADE CO

PO Box 1552, Khartoum
Tel: 80040, 77084
Cable: Natcot
Telex: 22267 Natco

Chairman: Abdel Aati A Mekki
Directors: Abdel Rahman A/Moniem (Managing Director), Sayed Mohd Adam (Branch Manager), Salah Mohd Kheir (Deputy Manager), Tahir Mohd Kheir (Head of Shipping Dept), El Safi Suliman (Head of Port Sudan Office), El Amin Bannaga Mohd (Head of Finance Dept), Kamal Ali A/Hamid (Controller of Shipping Operations Port Sudan), Abdel Gadir Mohd Omer (Head of Technical Dept Port Sudan)

PRINCIPAL ACTIVITIES: Export of raw cotton
Branch Offices: Port Sudan: PO Box 549
Parent Company: Sudan Cotton Co Ltd
Principal Bankers: Bank of Khartoum; El Nilein Bank

Principal Shareholders: State-owned
Date of Establishment: 1970
No of Employees: 75

NATIONAL DEVELOPMENT BANK

PO Box 655, Khartoum
Tel: 79496, 79259, 81854
Cable: Rakha
Telex: 22835 Rakha Sd

Chairman: Sheikh Hussan Bileil
Directors: Abdel Rahim Mahmoud, Abdalla Imam, Dr Abdel Wahab Osman, Bashir Khamis, Elfatih Yousif, Mohd Ahmed Eljak, Mustafa Faiz Ahmed Hablas, Mohed Dawood Elkhalifa, Engineer Osman Ahmed Osman, Sid Ahmed Osman, Salih Mohamed Ali Sakran, Salah Eldin Ahmed Mohamed, Sayed Osman Elamin
Senior Executives: Kamal M A Elshaigi (General Manager), Hasan Bashir (General Manager)

PRINCIPAL ACTIVITIES: Banking
Branch Offices: Wad Medani, Port Sudan (Under establishment)
Associated Companies: Promoters & Shareholders in the following companies:- Iseilat Co for P D; Pop Dev Co for Drugs & Chemicals; Cold Storage Dev Co; Pop Co for Poultry; The Agricultural Services Co; Nimeri Youth Project
Principal Bankers: UBAF Bank Ltd, London

Principal Shareholders: Sudanese and Egyptian Banks and a Saudi Investment Company and Sudanese businessmen
Date of Establishment: 1982
No of Employees: 60

NATIONAL ENGINEERING CO LTD

PO Box 208, Khartoum
Tel: 46521, 42665, 41653
Cable: Natenco Khartoum
Telex: 22593 Toro SD, 24318 Vasko SD
Telefax: 46547

Chairman: Dikran N Partziguian
Directors: Edward Fahim Mansour
Senior Executives: Samir L Abdalla (Service Manager), Amr Al Jundi (Marketing Manager), Mohammed A Salih (Marketing Logistics)

PRINCIPAL ACTIVITIES: Import and distribution of construction and transport equipment
Principal Agencies: Brel, Scania, CPCS, Timken, Dynapac, ABB British Wheelsets, British Steel Corp, Benati
Associated Companies: Associated offices in Port Sudan and Atbara
Principal Bankers: Unity Bank, Khartoum
Financial Information:

	1989 US$'000
Sales turnover	5,000

Principal Shareholders: D N Partziguian
Date of Establishment: October 1957
No of Employees: 27

NATIONAL PRODUCTS CO (1956) LTD
ABC Trading Co (1966)

PO Box 315, Port Sudan
Tel: 3250, 3666, 2012, 5618
Cable: Napco
Telex: 70032 Zada SD, 22410 Napco, 70038, 22178 Derma SD
Telefax: 249-31-3491

President: Abbas El-Dawi A Galil (also Proprietor)
Directors: Issam Abbas El-Dawi, Salah El Dein Abbas El-Dawi, Tawfig A El Dawi

PRINCIPAL ACTIVITIES: Importers and commission agents, confirming houses agents, general and building materials, electric equipment and appliances, hardware, machinery and tools; exporters. Sudan produce raw hides and skins; owners of cold stores and ice factories; also lime and gypsum quarrying

SUDAN

Branch Offices: PO Box 1101, Khartown, tel 75485, 76118, 46583
Principal Bankers: Unity Bank; Sudanese International Bank; National Bank of Abu Dhabi, London
Financial Information:

	1990 US$'000
Sales turnover	1,000
Authorised capital	2,000
Total assets	6,000

Principal Shareholders: Family owned
Date of Establishment: 1956
No of Employees: 43

NATIONAL REINSURANCE CO (SUDAN) LTD

PO Box 443, Khartoum
Tel: 79118, 77325, 78416, 80464, 74174
Cable: Nationale
Telex: 22424 NATRE
Telefax: 75927

Chairman: Abdullahi Ahmed Abdullahi (Managing Director)
Directors: Mohamed El Amin Mirghani, Hashim Mohamed Ahmed El Bereir, Dr Ali Dafaalla Shibeika, Awad El Karim Osman Mustafa, Abdel Fattah Mohamed Siyam, Dr Sabir Mohamed Hassan, Jada Lorere
Senior Executives: Dr Mohamed Yousif Ali (Deputy General Manager), Mustafa Mohamedain Ismail (Asst General Manager Administration), Omer Mohamed Ahmed Tikail (Asst General Manager Finance)

PRINCIPAL ACTIVITIES: Reinsurance
Principal Bankers: Bank of Khartoum; Sudanese International Bank; El Nilein Bank; UBAF Ltd (London)
Financial Information:

	1989 S£'000
Gross premium	73,073
Profits	1,714
Authorised capital	5,000
Paid-up capital	2,300
Total assets	2,486

Principal Shareholders: Government of the Sudan (52.8%); Insurance Companies (25.23%); Commercial Banks (9.42%); Public (12.55%)
Date of Establishment: November 1973
No of Employees: 42

NATIONAL TEXTILE INDUSTRIES LTD

PO Box 810, Khartoum
Tel: 33630
Cable: Interlock

PRINCIPAL ACTIVITIES: Manufacture of textiles and clothing (underwear, sports-wear, socks)
Principal Agencies: Eagle Brand

NCR CORPORATION

PO Box 501, Khartoum
Tel: 70598
Cable: Satronico Ncr
Telex: 22655

PRINCIPAL ACTIVITIES: Import, distribution and service of data processing equipment, computers and supplies
Parent Company: NCR (Corporation, Dayton, Ohio, USA)
Principal Bankers: Unity Bank; Citibank; National Bank of Abu Dhabi

Date of Establishment: 1948, nationalised 1970 and denationalised 1980

NILE ARMOR CO LTD

PO Box 2648, Murad Bldg, Parliman Avenue, Khartoum
Tel: 77831, 76183
Telex: 22542

Directors: Yousif Badr (Managing Director), Amin Eltayeb

PRINCIPAL ACTIVITIES: Import of ice machines, motorcycles, safe deposit boxes and manufacturers agents
Principal Agencies: Scotsmanice Co, Fichbau, Trico Ltd
Principal Bankers: Sudanese International Bank, Sudan Commercial Bank

Principal Shareholders: Yousif Badr, Amin Eltayeb
Date of Establishment: June 1976

NILE CEMENT CO LTD

Po Box 1502, Khartoum
Tel: 40823
Cable: Asmant
Telex: 24196 Cemra SD, 22298 Sidc SD

Chairman: Hassan Ahmed Makki
Directors: Tag El Sir M Khogali, A Sharif, O Eltai, Dr Magrabi, E Elnour, Mustafa Arbab
Senior Executives: Tag El Sir Mohammed Kheir Khogali (Managing Director), Taha Mohamed Sourig (Deputy General Manager)

PRINCIPAL ACTIVITIES: Production of cement and cement products
Branch Offices: Sudan, factories at Rabak, Khartoum Extension St. 45-47
Principal Bankers: Unity Bank, Kosti; Sudan Commercial Bank, Khartoum

Principal Shareholders: 57% state-owned
Date of Establishment: 1960
No of Employees: 450

NILE EXPORT & IMPORT CO LTD

PO Box 292, Khartoum
Cable: Nileco

PRINCIPAL ACTIVITIES: Commission agents, manufacturers' agents, import of coffee, bedsteads, radios, tyres and tubes

NILE TRADING & ENGINEERING CO LTD

PO Box 226, Abouelella New Building, Gamhouria Avenue, Khartoum
Tel: 81136, 81484
Telex: 22287 Nitra

Chairman: Amin Eltayeb (Managing Director)
Directors: Hesham Omer Mohamed, Mohamed Abdelhalim

PRINCIPAL ACTIVITIES: Import of office equipment, computers, stationery and general trading
Principal Agencies: Rotaprint, Olivetti, Adler Triumph
Principal Bankers: Faisal Islamic Bank, Sudanese International Bank, Bank of Oman

Principal Shareholders: Amin Eltayeb, Hesham Omer Mohamed
Date of Establishment: 1979

OCTOBER NATIONAL TRADING CORP

PO Box 198, Khartoum
Cable: Octomat

PRINCIPAL ACTIVITIES: Commission agents, shipping agents, export of cotton seed, groundnuts, oils, oil cakes, import of flour, trading of building materials, cement, and pharmaceutical products, warehousing at Port Sudan
Subsidiary Companies: Sudan Oil Mill

OFFICE EQUIPMENT COMPANY

PO Box 1, Khartoum
Tel: 77381

PRINCIPAL ACTIVITIES: Import of office equipment and manufacture of office, kitchen and domestic steel furniture
Principal Agencies: Roneo Ltd, Olympia Werke GmbH

Principal Shareholders: A member of the Bittar Group of Companies

OIL CORPORATION
PO Box 64, Khartoum North
Tel: 32044, 34413/6
Cable: Oilsoap
Telex: 22198

Directors: Mohi el Din Yassin

PRINCIPAL ACTIVITIES: Production of vegetable and edible oils and by-products
Subsidiary Companies: Rabak Oil Mill, PO Box 2105, Khartoum; Sudan Oil Corp, PO Box 2, Khartoum North; Sudan Soap Corp, PO Box 23, Khartoum North; African Oil Corp, PO Box 1, Khartoum North; Port Sudan Edible Oils Storage Corp, PO Box 429, Port Sudan

Principal Shareholders: Part of the Industrial Production Corporation

PARTICLE BOARD INDUSTRIES CO LTD
PO Box 2593, Khartoum North
Tel: 34267
Cable: Sodaboard

Directors: Kamal Eltahir Abu Hawa (General Manager)
Senior Executives: Osman Ahmed Kheir

PRINCIPAL ACTIVITIES: Production of particle boards
Principal Bankers: Sudan Commercial Bank

Principal Shareholders: Dr Khalil Osman, El Sayed Ibrahim El Tayeb, El Sayed OsmanEl Tayeb

PETROLEUM GENERAL ADMINISTRATION
PO Box 2649, Khartoum

Chairman: Under-Secretary of the Ministry of Industry
Directors: Dr Omer el Sheikh Omer (Managing Director), Governor of the Bank of Sudan, Under-Secretary of the Attorney General's Office, Under-Secretary of the Ministry of Finance & National Economy, Director of Geology Dept, Director of Petroleum Administration (Ministry of Industry)

PRINCIPAL ACTIVITIES: Petroleum exploration and production

Principal Shareholders: Part of the Industrial Production Corporation

PORT SUDAN COTTON & TRADE CO
PO Box 590, Khartoum
Cable: Portcotco
Telex: 22270

PRINCIPAL ACTIVITIES: Cotton exporters
Branch Offices: PO Box 261, Port Sudan, Tel 5269, Telex 513
Parent Company: Sudan Cotton Co Ltd

PORT SUDAN REFINERY LTD
PO Box 354, Port Sudan
Tel: 3991/5
Cable: Refco
Telex: 70001 Refco P.Sudan

Chairman: Dr A/Rahman Osman A/Rahman
Directors: Hassan El Zubeir El Tahir
Senior Executives: H M Ali (Engineering Manager), Dawi Galal (Administration Manager), M Tambal (Operations Manager), B C A M Van Berden (Technology Manager)

PRINCIPAL ACTIVITIES: Oil refining
Principal Bankers: Unity Bank

Principal Shareholders: Sudan Government (50%); Shell International Petroleum Co (50%)
Date of Establishment: 1964
No of Employees: 181

PUBLIC CORPORATION FOR BUILDING & CONSTRUCTION
Po Box 2110, Khartoum
Tel: 74544

PRINCIPAL ACTIVITIES: Building and civil engineering

Principal Shareholders: State-owned

PUBLIC CORPORATION FOR IRRIGATION & EXCAVATION
Po Box 619, Khartoum
Tel: 80167, 33986, 32126, 32429

PRINCIPAL ACTIVITIES: Irrigation and excavation works
Branch Offices: PO Box 123, Wad Medani, Tel 2056, 400

Principal Shareholders: State-owned

PUBLIC ELECTRICITY & WATER CORPORATION
PO Box 1380, Khartoum
Tel: 81021, 80506, 76008, 76573

PRINCIPAL ACTIVITIES: Utilities and public services, electricity generation and distribution and water supply

Principal Shareholders: State-owned

RAINBOW FACTORIES LTD
PO Box 1768, Khartoum
Tel: 33669, 32406
Cable: Rainbow Khartoum

Chairman: Dr Yousif Daffalla Shebeika
Directors: Dr Ali D Shebeika, C A Kfouri, Magzoub Ibrahim Shoush, Armia Y Magar, Gaber A H Abuelizz, Ritchard Kahwati, Mohd Talaat Farid, Omer Abdel Ati

PRINCIPAL ACTIVITIES: Manufacture of paints and varnishes
Parent Company: Building Materials & Refractories Corp
Principal Bankers: Nilein Bank; Bank of Sudan; Sudan Commercial Bank

Principal Shareholders: Aziz Kfouri Sons Ltd; Shebeika Bros; Gaber & Mustafa Abuelizz

RED SEA IMPORTS & EXPORTS CO LTD
PO Box 420, Omdurman
Tel: 54325, 55367
Cable: Redsico
Telex: 28041 Start SD

Directors: B D Shah, D Dansukhlal Shah
Senior Executives: Yashor K Shah (Manager)

PRINCIPAL ACTIVITIES: Import of rice, tea, textiles, electronics and sundry goods, export of gum arabic
Principal Agencies: Japman Co, Kosmos Export & Import; China National Light Industry Production
Subsidiary Companies: Allied Traders Co Ltd; Star Agencies & Trading Co Ltd
Principal Bankers: Bank of Credit & Commerce International, Habib Bank, Unity Bank, Faisal Islamic Bank, Al Baraka Bank, Sudanese Islamic Bank

Principal Shareholders: DH J Shah, R A Bouqtour
Date of Establishment: 1980

REFRIGERATION & ENGINEERING IMPORT CO
PO Box 1092, Khartoum
Tel: 74414
Cable: Refengco

PRINCIPAL ACTIVITIES: Refrigeration and engineering equipment
Parent Company: Engineering Equipment Corporation

REYNOLDS ALUMINIUM ROLLING & SPINNING MILLS (SUDAN) LTD

PO Box 5031, Khartoum South
Tel: 79337/9
Cable: Patwee

Senior Executives: M S Patel (General Manager), M M A'Yazid (Financial Controller), Hassan Gibril (Production Manager)

PRINCIPAL ACTIVITIES: Manufacture of aluminium, brass, zinc, tin, iron and steel goods
Principal Bankers: Sudan Commercial Bank

ROADS & BRIDGES PUBLIC CORPORATION

PO Box 756, Khartoum
Tel: 70794, 71337

Chairman: Abdel Rahman Haboud
Directors: Abdu Mohammed Abdu (Director General)

PRINCIPAL ACTIVITIES: Civil engineering, infrastructure developments

Principal Shareholders: State-owned

SACKS FACTORY

PO Box 2328, Khartoum

PRINCIPAL ACTIVITIES: Production of sacks and containers

Principal Shareholders: 50% state owned

SARAGAS & COMPANY

PO Box 264, Khartoum
Cable: Saragas

PRINCIPAL ACTIVITIES: Commission and manufacturers' agents, distribution of cement, insulating and hardboards, dyestuffs, glass panes and plate-glass, brushes, building materials, ironmongery, ironwork, locks and padlocks, machine tools, methylated spirit, mirrors, paints and oils, radio, roofing, roofing felt, timber, tools

SARKIS, IZMIRLIAN, CORPORATION LTD

PO Box 112, Khartoum
Tel: 70981, 70951, 80160
Cable: Izmirco
Telex: 22305 Kooler; 22353

Chairman: A Izmirlian

PRINCIPAL ACTIVITIES: Import and distribution of agricultural and industrial machinery and equipment; construction and earthmoving equipment
Principal Agencies: Sulzer, Gardner, Denver, John Deere, J F Fabriken
Subsidiary Companies: Sheet Metal Industries Ltd; Sarkis Izmirlian Oil Mills Ltd

SAYED & COLLEY LTD

PO Box 807, Khartoum
Cable: Turbine

PRINCIPAL ACTIVITIES: Engineering contractors, import of aircraft, air compressors, ball and roller bearings, belting, engineering materials, fire extinguishers, fire protection, hoses, ropes, water control equipment, steam plant, steel piling, tools and welding plant and electrodes
Principal Agencies: Bristol Aeroplane Co, Reavell & Co Ltd, Mather & Platt, Babcock & Wilcox Ltd, Dewrance Ltd, Laidlew Drew Ltd, British Seagull Ltd; Bruntons Ltd; Hydraulic Engineering Co Ltd
Branch Offices: Wad Medani (PO Box 301)
Associated Companies: Sudanese Tractor Corporation

Principal Bankers: Unity Bank, Khartoum

Principal Shareholders: Sayed Daoud Abdel Latif and family
Date of Establishment: 1952
No of Employees: 40

SEFERIAN & CO LTD

PO Box 190, Khartoum
Tel: 70307, 81608, 81609
Cable: Seferco
Telex: 22620 A/B SEFCO SD

Chairman: A Seferian
Directors: Missak Padazian, Hratch Mardikian, Edward Seferian, Mrs Nelly Mardikian Boulos
Senior Executives: H Mardikian (Managing Director)

PRINCIPAL ACTIVITIES: Manufacturers agents, automobile dealers, spare parts, electrical equipment and agricultural equipment
Principal Agencies: Volkswagen, W Germany; Yanmar Diesel Engines, Japan
Principal Bankers: National Bank of Sudan; Bank of Khartoum

Principal Shareholders: Mardikian Family
Date of Establishment: 1928
No of Employees: 53

SHAM TRADING CO

PO Box 403, Khartoum
Tel: 31136, 72915, 78398
Telex: 22199 Sham Sd

Chairman: Abdalla Mohamed Hussein
Directors: Abdelmoniem Abdalla Mohamed (Managing Director)

PRINCIPAL ACTIVITIES: Import of foodstuffs, stationery, clothing, motor cars, electrical equipment and export of vegetables, fruits, cotton and Sudanese produce
Principal Agencies: Ganz Mavag, Licenena, Nikex
Branch Offices: Kosti: PO Box 148; Port Sudan: PO Box 126; Juba: PO Box 130
Subsidiary Companies: Sham Insoplastica Factory, Elniel Sham Trading Co, Sudanese Spanish Transportation Co Ltd, Sham Printing & Publicity Co, Sudanese International Agencies
Principal Bankers: Citibank, Khartoum; Bank of Khartoum; Islamic Development Bank

Principal Shareholders: Family of Abdalla Mohamed Hussein
Date of Establishment: 1963
No of Employees: 75

SHARAF INTERNATIONAL LTD

PO Box 1701, Khartoum
Tel: 75143, 73664, 78668, 78911, 75190, 73664
Cable: Alintisar
Telex: 22280 Sharaf Sd

Chairman: Fatah Elrahman Elbashier (Managing Director)
Directors: Ahmed Elbashier
Senior Executives: Ibrahim Yassin, Yousif Zaki

PRINCIPAL ACTIVITIES: Manufacturers of textiles, chemicals, cotton wool, metal products, transport, engineering, mining and commission agents, agriculture; farming-wheat flour mills, toothpaste manufacturing, export of cattle and sheep
Principal Agencies: Farmos Group, Sigma Tau, Wallace, Roter, Unigreg Ltd, Founier, Phillip Harris, Buckman Lab, C E C Diesel Ltd, Babcock & Wilcox, Kalser Spain, Hoover Marine, Daewoo, GEC-UK
Branch Offices: Sudan, Egypt, UK
Subsidiary Companies: Sharaf Metal Products Ltd, Sharaf Trading, Sharaf Chemical Industry Ltd, Sharaf Pharmaceutical & Chemical Ltd, Sharaf Transport Ltd, Blue Nile Spinning & Weaving Ltd, Red Sea Spinning Ltd, Wad Medani Textile Ltd, Gezeira Flour Mills Ltd, Sharaf Engineering Ltd, Modern Brushes Factory

Financial Information:

	S£'000
Authorised capital	10,000
Paid-up capital	10,000

Principal Shareholders: Fatah Elrahman Elbashier
Date of Establishment: 1964

SHEET METAL INDUSTRIES LTD
PO Box 112, Khartoum
Cable: Cooler
Telex: 22282, 22305

Chairman: A Izmirlian

PRINCIPAL ACTIVITIES: Import of air-conditioning and refrigeration machinery, manufacture of water cooling plants
Principal Agencies: Essick Manufacturing Co, Admiral International Corporation, Chrysler
Parent Company: Sarkis Izmirlian Corporation Ltd

SHELL CO OF SUDAN LTD
PO Box 320, Khartoum
Tel: 71143, 72787
Cable: Shell Khartoum
Telex: 22264; 22265

PRINCIPAL ACTIVITIES: Production of gas oils, lubricating oils and oil products

SILOS & STORAGE CORP
PO Box 1183, Khartoum
Cable: Takhzeen

PRINCIPAL ACTIVITIES: Owners of warehouses and silos throughout Sudan, storage and handling of all agricultural products
Parent Company: State Trading Corporation

Principal Shareholders: State owned

SOAP & ALLIED INDUSTRIES (SUDAN) LTD
PO Box 1, Khartoum
Tel: 75764
Telex: 22285 Bittar Km

PRINCIPAL ACTIVITIES: Manufacture of laundry and toilet soap, detergent, oils, plastic bottles and tins, glycerine, sulphuric acid

Principal Shareholders: A member of the Bittar Group of Companies

SPINNING & WEAVING CORP
PO Box 795, Khartoum
Tel: 76167, 78167, 76340, 74550
Cable: Textcorp

PRINCIPAL ACTIVITIES: Production of textiles and clothing
Subsidiary Companies: Kenaf Socks Factory, Abu Naama; Plastic Sacks Factory, PO Box 2328, Khartoum; Port Sudan Spinning Factory, Port Sudan; Friendship Spinning Factory, Hassaheisa

Principal Shareholders: Part of the Industrial Production Corporation

STATE CORPORATION FOR CINEMA
PO Box 6028, Khartoum
Tel: 43782, 43789, 43651, 43650

PRINCIPAL ACTIVITIES: Import and distribution of films and photographic equipment

Principal Shareholders: State-owned

STATE TRADING CORPORATION
PO Box 211, Khartoum
Tel: 78555, 78264, 79305
Cable: Doltigala
Telex: 22355; 22311

PRINCIPAL ACTIVITIES: The State Trading Corporation promotes Sudanese trade and controls the production of its branch corporations
Subsidiary Companies: Automobile Corporation; Engineering Equipment Corporation; Silos and Storage Corporation

Principal Shareholders: State owned

SUDAN AIRWAYS
PO Box 253, Khartoum
Tel: 70325

PRINCIPAL ACTIVITIES: Air transport
Branch Offices: Egypt, Saudi Arabia, Ethiopia, Kuwait, UAE, Nigeria, Kenya, Uganda, Chad, Greece, Italy, Germany, UK, Bahrain

Date of Establishment: 1947

SUDAN ALL-WEAR INDUSTRY LTD
PO Box 2384, Khartoum North
Tel: 33515, 80615, 31862
Cable: Malbisco
Telex: 22276 Theotext

PRINCIPAL ACTIVITIES: Manufacture of textiles, clothing and knitwear

Principal Shareholders: A member of the Gulf International (Sudan) Group

SUDAN COMMERCIAL BANK
PO Box 1116, Kasr Avenue, Khartoum
Tel: 71468, 76344
Cable: Elwatany
Telex: 22242 Watan SD

Chairman: Hussein A/Gader (and General Manager)
Directors: Babiker A/Allah El Banna (Vice Chairman & Deputy General Manager), Hassan Mohamed Adar (Member), El Misbah El Sadik (Member), Mohamed A/Karim Abbas (Member)
Senior Executives: Mohamed A/Rahman Ishag (Asst General Manager Foreign Dept), Abu Bakr Mohamed El Amin (Asst General Manager Audit & Accounts), A/Galil Hussein Nour (Asst General Manager Loans & Advances), Mahmoud Gamal Mohamed (Asst General Manager Training & Relations), Mostafa A/Rahman Sultan (Asst General Manager Personnel)

PRINCIPAL ACTIVITIES: Commercial banking
Branch Offices: Gamhoria Avenue, Kasr Avenue, Omdurman, Al Suk Al Afrangi, Port Sudan, El Obeid, El Gadaref, New Halfa, Industrial Area, El Nuhud, Khartoum North Market, El Mughtaribeen, El Damazin, El Fau. Sub-branches: New extension, El Hawata, Hillat Kuko, El Zubeir Basha. Agencies: Sudan Hotel Agency, Khartoum Airport Agency
Associated Companies: Shareholdings: Sudan Rural Development, Kenana Sugar Company, Sudanese Arab Starch & Glucose Co, Sudanese Arab Fruits & Vegetables, Sudanese International Bank, National Reinsurance Co
Financial Information:

	1990 S£'000
Authorised capital	15,000
Paid-up capital	10,000

Principal Shareholders: Bank of Sudan; Ministry of Finance and Economy
Date of Establishment: 1960
No of Employees: 555

SUDAN

SUDAN COTTON CO LTD

PO Box 1672, Khartoum
Tel: 75755, 71567, 79573, 71673
Cable: Publicot KHM
Telex: 22245 PCOT SD
Telefax: 70703

Chairman: Abdel Ati Abdella El Meki
Directors: Abdel Rahman Abdel Moneim (Managing Director)
Senior Executives: Sam Ibrahim El Khateem, Eltag Sir El Khatim Osman, Mohamed El Hassan Osman (Director of Marketing & Sales Dept), Mohamed Awad Ali Nagdi (Managing Director Port Sudan Cotton Co), Sayed Mohamed Adam (Managing Director National Cotton & Trade Co), Hunna Fouad Mahrous (Managing Director Alaktan Trading Co), Gabir Mahgoub (Acting Managing Director Sudan Cotton Co), Abd El Rahman Abd Ella (Director of Research & Statistics Dept), Abu Obaida Ali Osman (Finance Director), Yousif Mohd Salih (Sales Manager), El Gaili Hassan Gorashi (Regional Manager Port Sudan)

PRINCIPAL ACTIVITIES: Supervision of all cotton marketing in Sudan; exports and internal sales
Branch Offices: Office in Geneva (Switzertland)
Subsidiary Companies: National Cotton & Trade Co; Alaktan Cotton Trading Co; Port Sudan Cotton & Trade Co; Sudan Cotton Co
Principal Bankers: Bank of Sudan
Financial Information:

	1989/90 S£'000
Sales turnover	38,717
Profits	26,200
Authorised capital	110,000
Paid-up capital	82,500
Total assets	2,400

Principal Shareholders: Bank of Sudan, Ministry of Finance
Date of Establishment: June 1970
No of Employees: 568

SUDAN DEVELOPMENT CORPORATION

PO Box 710, Street No 21 Amarat, Khartoum
Tel: 47425/34 (10 lines)
Cable: DECORP, KHARTOUM SUDAN
Telex: 24078 SDC - SD
Telefax: 249-11-40473

Chairman: Abdalla Ahmed El Ramadi (and Managing Director)
Directors: Mubarak Abdel Azim (Deputy Chairman & Deputy Managing Director), Abdel Atti Abdalla El Makki, Khalil Ibrahim Hamid, Mohamed Khogali El Sheikh, Sid Ahmed Osman
Senior Executives: Izz El Dln Jubal (Director Finance & Administration Dept), Awad Abdalla Higazi (Director Project Dept), Salih Awad Salih (Legal Advisor)

PRINCIPAL ACTIVITIES: To identify, evaluate and implement technically feasible, economically sound and commercially viable joint venture projects between Sudanese and foreign technical and financial parties with emphasis on sound development projects in the agricultural, agri-business and industrial sectors
Principal Agencies: Chase Manhattan Bank, New York and London; Kleinwort Benson, London
Financial Information:

	1990 US$'000
Authorised capital	500,000
Paid-up capital	200,000

Principal Shareholders: Wholly owned by the Sudan Government
Date of Establishment: 1974
No of Employees: 70

SUDAN EXHIBITION & FAIRS CORPORATION

PO Box 2366, Khartoum
Tel: 79410, 77702
Cable: Sudanexpo
Telex: 22407

PRINCIPAL ACTIVITIES: Production of Sudanese trade and exports, representation abroad, and trade fairs

Principal Shareholders: State-owned
Date of Establishment: 1976
No of Employees: 120

SUDAN GEZIRA BOARD

Barakat, Gezira Province
Tel: 2412-464
Cable: Gezboard
Telex: 50001 Gezboard Barakat

Directors: Ezz El Deen Omer El Mekki (Managing Director)
Senior Executives: Adam Abdalla Daffalla (Deputy Managing Director)

PRINCIPAL ACTIVITIES: A co-operative organisation in the main cotton-producing area; production of cotton, wheat, vegetables, groundnuts, rice, sorghum and fodder
Branch Offices: PO Box 884, Khartoum; PO Box 185, Port Sudan; UK: 5 Cleveland Row, London SW1
Principal Bankers: Bank of Sudan

Principal Shareholders: The scheme is a partnership between the government, the Board and the tenants
Date of Establishment: 1910
No of Employees: Tenant farmers: 106,000; officials: 2,331; permanent labourers: 8,764

SUDAN OIL MILLS

PO Box 198, Khartoum
Cable: Sudoil

PRINCIPAL ACTIVITIES: Export of oil and production of soap

Principal Shareholders: Part of the October National Trading Corporation

SUDAN OIL SEEDS CO LTD

PO Box 167, Khartoum
Tel: 79614, 75294
Cable: Oil Seed Khartoum
Telex: 22312; 22613 SOSCO

Chairman: Salih Mohamed Salih (also General Manager)
Directors: Gindeel Ibrahim Gindeel, Mohamed Kailani Himat

PRINCIPAL ACTIVITIES: Export of oil seeds (groundnuts, sesame seeds and castor seeds)
Branch Offices: Branch at Port Sudan, Obied, Nyala, Tandalty
Parent Company: Sudanese Oilseed Processing Company
Principal Bankers: El Nilein Bank; Sudan Commercial Bank; Unity Bank

Principal Shareholders: The Government (the public sector) 58%
Date of Establishment: August 1974
No of Employees: 500 permanent staff, 10,000 seasonal labourers

SUDAN RAILWAYS CORPORATION (SRC)

PO Box 43, Atbara
Tel: 2000
Cable: Hadid
Telex: 22294

PRINCIPAL ACTIVITIES: Sudan Railways is the main mode of transport in the country
Branch Offices: Atbara, Port Sudan, Khartoum, Kosti, Babanousa
Principal Bankers: Bank of Sudan

Principal Shareholders: SRC is a public corporation under the sponsorship of the Ministry of Transport
Date of Establishment: 1897
No of Employees: 35,110

SUDAN SHIPPING LINE LTD

PO Box 426, Port Sudan
Tel: 2655, 4692, 4957/59
Cable: Ostool Port Sudan
Telex: 70025 Stolp SD, 70008 Stolp SD

Chairman: Ahmed Khalid Sharfi
Senior Executives: Capt Kamal Hassan (General Manager), Capt Abdu Mohd Osman (Deputy General Manager)

PRINCIPAL ACTIVITIES: Shipping, clearing and forwarding agents, chartering agents, stevedoring, warehousing, ship owners
Branch Offices: Branch and Chartering Office; PO Box 1731, Khartoum, Tel 70058, 75530, 80017, 75208; Telex 22301, 22332
Subsidiary Companies: Transline Company (inland road transport, door to door service), Head Office Khartoum, PO Box 1040, Tel: 78996, 70216, Telex 332, 301

Date of Establishment: 1962
No of Employees: 1,000

SUDAN TEA CO LTD

PO Box 1219
Tel: 81261/3

PRINCIPAL ACTIVITIES: Production and export of tea

SUDAN TEXTILE INDUSTRY LTD

PO Box 1377, Khartoum
Tel: 34166, 32611, 70584, 32674/6
Cable: Theotext
Telex: 22276

PRINCIPAL ACTIVITIES: Spinning, weaving, printing, bleaching, dyeing, embroidery end finishing of textiles

Principal Shareholders: A member of the Gulf International (Sudan) Group

SUDANESE CHEMICAL INDUSTRIES LTD

PO Box 40, Khartoum North
Tel: 31103, 31936
Cable: Farmaco
Telex: 26009 SCICO

Chairman: Dr Khalil Osman Mohamad
Senior Executives: Sadik Abdullahi El Mahdi

PRINCIPAL ACTIVITIES: Manufacture of chemicals, pharmaceuticals and cosmetics
Principal Bankers: Unity Bank

Principal Shareholders: A member of the Gulf International (Sudan) Group
Date of Establishment: 1973

SUDANESE ENGINEERING & DEVELOPMENT CO

PO Box 1214, Khartoum

PRINCIPAL ACTIVITIES: Import and distribution of agricultural machinery and equipment
Principal Agencies: International Harvester

SUDANESE ESTATES BANK

PO Box 309, Khartoum
Tel: 77017, 79465, 81061, 78061
Cable: Akri
Telex: 22439

Chairman: Mohammed Mekki Kanani

Directors: Salih El Ebeid, Mohd El Sayed Salam, El Fatim El Nur, Awad El Karim Mohd, Mohamed Abdulla El Kurdi, Abdel Aziz Mohamed Sadig, Osman El Shiekh
Senior Executives: Suliman Ibrahim Mohd, Hassan El Shiekh Mohd, Ahmed Mahmoud Khalifa, Ahmed Youssif Babiker

PRINCIPAL ACTIVITIES: Banking; investment for housing and building projects
Branch Offices: Obaid; Atbara; Khartoum
Subsidiary Companies: Sudanese Estates Insurance Co; Sudan Building Materials Co
Principal Bankers: Bank of Sudan; Bank of Khartoum; Unity Bank

Principal Shareholders: Government owned
Date of Establishment: 1967
No of Employees: 150

SUDANESE GLASS CO LTD

PO Box 286, Khartoum North
Tel: 33081/2, 32820
Cable: Zugag
Telex: 22438 Zugag

PRINCIPAL ACTIVITIES: Manufacture of glass and glass products
Parent Company: Gulf International (Sudan) Group
Subsidiary Companies: Sudan Textile Industry; Sudanese Kuwait Packing Co; Match Producing & Distributing Co; Air Taxi Co
Principal Bankers: Unity Bank

Principal Shareholders: Dr Khalil Osman (50%); El Shiekh Sabah El Ahmed El Gabir El Sabah (50%)
Date of Establishment: 1968
No of Employees: 400

SUDANESE INSURANCE & REINSURANCE CO LTD

PO Box 2332, Makkawi Bldg, Gamhoria Avenue, Nasir Square, Khartoum
Tel: 70812, 77797, 76381, 70026
Cable: SIRCO
Telex: 22292

Chairman: Izzeldein El Sayed
Directors: Widda Osman (Managing Director), Hassan El Sayed (General Manager)
Senior Executives: Ahmed Mohamed Fadul (Director of Finance), Makram Habib (Production & Marketing Manager), Tewfiq Yousif (Personnel Manager), Ahmed Sinada (Admin & PR Manager)

PRINCIPAL ACTIVITIES: Insurance and reinsurance agents
Branch Offices: Port Sudan, Wad Medani, Juba
Subsidiary Companies: Unity Insurance Company, Dubai
Principal Bankers: Elnilein Bank, Bank of Khartoum, Unity Bank, Commercial Bank of Sudan.

Principal Shareholders: Board of Directors
Date of Establishment: 1967
No of Employees: 115

SUDANESE INTERNATIONAL BANK

PO Box 2775, Khartoum
Tel: 71831, 71723, 76542, 71730
Cable: SIBANK KHARTOUM
Telex: 22204 SIBANK KM

Chairman: Khalid Farah
Directors: Alexis Saint Guily, Abdel Rahman Farah, Babika Al Bana, Dirdiri M Ahmad, Al Tayeb Mirghani Shakak, Ibrahim Elias, Makawi Sulaiman, Mahmoun Beheri, Mohammad Ali Husni, Salih Farah, Jean Anderelli, L Contomichalos, Al Amin Al Shaikh Mustafa, Ibrahim Ahmad, Antoine Larue de Charlus, Mehdi Sherif, Mirghani Mahgoub, Mubarak Mirghani

PRINCIPAL ACTIVITIES: Investment and finance

Branch Offices: Port Sudan

Principal Shareholders: Sudanese Public (50%), Societe Generale, Maninco SA, Bank of Sudan, Sudan Commercial Bank, Khalid Farah, Alimenta SA, local shareholders
Date of Establishment: 1978

SUDANESE KUWAITI ANIMAL PRODUCTION CO

51st, 23 Al-Khartoum, PO Box 2526, Khartoum 2
Tel: 79098
Telex: 22656 Skapco Km

PRINCIPAL ACTIVITIES: Joint venture company producing animal feed

Principal Shareholders: Sudanese Kuwaiti Investment Co Ltd

SUDANESE KUWAITI BUILDING & CONSTRUCTION CO

PO Box 1745, Khartoum
Tel: 79718
Telex: 22603 Inmmaa Km

PRINCIPAL ACTIVITIES: Joint venture company for building and civil engineering

Principal Shareholders: Sudanese Kuwaiti Investment Co Ltd

SUDANESE KUWAITI INVESTMENT CO LTD

PO Box 1745, Khartoum
Tel: 79520, 78470
Cable: Inmaa
Telex: 22603 Inmaa

Chairman: Osman Hashim Abdel Salam
Directors: Ahmed Abdulla Al-Nouri (Managing Director), Sid Ahmed Al-Sayed, Hayder Shihabi, Abdel Rahman Al-Gaoud, Dr Abdel Wahab Osman

PRINCIPAL ACTIVITIES: Identification and implementation of investment projects in different sectors of the economy
Subsidiary Companies: Sudanese Kuwaiti Animal Production Co; Sudanese Kuwaiti Road Transport Co; Sudanese Kuwaiti Building & Construction Co Ltd
Principal Bankers: El Nilein Bank; Khartoum Bank; Peoples' Co-operative Bank; Gulf Bank

Principal Shareholders: Government of Sudan; Kuwait Foreign Trading Contracting and Investment Co

SUDANESE KUWAITI PACKAGING CO

PO Box 727, Khartoum
Tel: 33068
Cable: Sudanpac
Telex: 26004 SKPC SD

Chairman: Abdalla Shulgami
Directors: M A Shulgami, K A Shulgami

PRINCIPAL ACTIVITIES: Manufacture of packaging materials
Branch Offices: UK: 21 Porchester Gardens, London W2 4DB
Parent Company: Khartoum Packaging Co Ltd
Principal Bankers: Al Baraka Bank, Sudan

Principal Shareholders: Khalid Shulgami, Mohamed Shulgami
Date of Establishment: 1972
No of Employees: 300

SUDANESE KUWAITI ROAD TRANSPORT CO LTD

PO Box 1156, Khartoum
Tel: 79721, 74244, 74261, 78030
Cable: Shahinat Khartoum
Telex: 22603 Inmaa Khartoum

Chairman: Dr Abdel Wahab Osman

Directors: Adel Al Atigi, Dr Yousif Atabani, Ahmed Mohed El Amin, Mohamed Al Hossayan, Suliman Al Braikan, Badr Al Rashoud
PRINCIPAL ACTIVITIES: Goods transport, warehousing clearance, vehicle agencies, local and long distance bus services
Branch Offices: Port Sudan; Kassala; Gedarif; Kenana
Associated Companies: Sudanese Kuwaiti Investment Co Ltd; Sudanese Kuwaiti Building & Construction Co Ltd; Sudanese Kuwaiti Animal Resources Co Ltd; Kuwait Investment & Contracting Co Ltd
Principal Bankers: El Nilein Bank; People's Co-operative Bank; Khartoum Bank; Bank of Kuwait; London; International Credit Bank

Principal Shareholders: Kuwaiti Government, Sudanese Government, Kuwaiti public sector, Sudanese public sector

SUDANESE LIQUID AIR CO LTD

PO Box 507, Khartoum

PRINCIPAL ACTIVITIES: Welding plant and electrodes, compressed gases and welding apparatus

SUDANESE MINING CORPORATION

PO Box 1034, Khartoum
Tel: 70840
Cable: Somincorr
Telex: 22298 Sidc Khartoum

Chairman: Dr Ibrahim Mudawi Babiker (Director General)
Directors: Mohamed Akasha (Technical Manager), Mahgoub Karoudi (Manager Ingessana Hill Mines Corp), Mohamed El Hassan Abdel Hafiz (Manager Shereik Mica Project)
Senior Executives: Ahmed Hamid Enani (Marketing Manager)

PRINCIPAL ACTIVITIES: Mining and mineral extraction (chronite-mica-gypsum)
Subsidiary Companies: Ingessana Hills Mines Corporation, PO Box 1108, Khartoum; Red Sea Hils Minerals Co; Shereik Mica Mines Co
Principal Bankers: Nilein Bank; Bank of Sudan

Principal Shareholders: Government of Sudan
Date of Establishment: 1975
No of Employees: 500

SUDANESE STEEL PRODUCTS LTD

PO Box 490, Khartoum
Tel: 32966, 32940, 31957
Cable: Fulaz
Telex: 22273

PRINCIPAL ACTIVITIES: Production of round steel bars, galvanised sheets and flat plates
Principal Bankers: El Nilein Bank; Unity Bank

Principal Shareholders: Hafez El Sayed El Barbary; Mitsubishi Corp; Nippon Steel Corp; Kyoei Steel Ltd
No of Employees: 300

SUDANESE TOBACCO CORPORATION

PO Box 2083, Khartoum
Tel: 74435
Cable: Watania

PRINCIPAL ACTIVITIES: Manufacture of cigarettes, cigars and tobacco
Subsidiary Companies: National Cigarettes Co Ltd

SUDANESE TRACTOR CORPORATION SUTRAC

PO Box 1840, Khartoum
Tel: 72828, 78888
Cable: Tractors
Telex: 22511 Trac SD
Telefax: 011 765774

Chairman: Daoud Abdel Latif
Directors: Osama Daoud Abdel Latif (Managing Director)
Senior Executives: G J Wooding (General Manager),
Abdelmoneim El Shaar (General Sales Manager), W J Bayer
(Product Support Manager), Abdelghani Ghandour
(Administration Manager), Ahmed Osman Daoud (Accounts
Manager)

PRINCIPAL ACTIVITIES: Manufacture and import of earth-
moving equipment, electric generating sets, agricultural
machinery, caterpillar tractors and allied equipment, marine
engines, tools and tractors
Principal Agencies: Caterpillar Overseas SA
Branch Offices: Branch in Wad Medani, PO Box 301, Tel
639/2416, Telex 50002 DEPO SD
Associated Companies: DAL Engineering Co Ltd, PO Box 807,
Khartoum
Principal Bankers: Sudanese International Bank

Principal Shareholders: Family of Daoud Abdel Latif
Date of Establishment: 1955
No of Employees: 470

SUGAR & DISTILLING CORP

New Mustafa el Amin Bldg, Barlaman Avenue, PO Box 511,
Khartoum
Tel: 78417, 75022, 78600/1, 74924, 74240, 70624
Cable: Sukrobat

PRINCIPAL ACTIVITIES: Production of sugar and distillery
operation
Subsidiary Companies: Gineid Sugar Factory, PO Box 1, Gineid;
New Halfa Sugar Factory, Khashm el Girba; Sugar Factory,
NW Sennar; Sugar Factory, Haggar Assalaya; Sugar Factory,
Malut; Sugar Factory, Mangala; Blue Nile Brewery, PO Box
1408, Khartoum; White Nile Brewery, PO Box 1378,
Khartoum; Aybee National Corporation, PO Box 159,
Khartoum; Watania Distillery Corporation, PO Box 1409,
Khartoum; El Tahair Perfume Corporation, PO Box 11,
Khartoum North

Principal Shareholders: Part of the Industrial Production
Corporation

TABALDI ENGINEERING CO

PO Box 463, Tabaldi Bldg, Baladiya Ave, Khartoum
Tel: 76018
Cable: Demco
Telex: 22337 Tabaldi Km

Chairman: Gaafar S A Goreish
Directors: Dimitri Zorzopoulos (Managing Director)
Senior Executives: Mohd S A Goreish, Mohamed El Hadi

PRINCIPAL ACTIVITIES: Manufacture of vehicle batteries, air
conditioners/refrigerators, estate owners, importers of motor
cars, trucks, auto-tyres, household appliances, electrical
equipment and accessories
Principal Agencies: Bridgestone Tires Co Ltd, Tokyo; White-
Westinghouse International Corporation, Pittsburg, USA
Subsidiary Companies: Tabaldi Battery Factory, Khartoum;
National Refrigeration Co, Khartoum
Principal Bankers: Bank of Khartoum; National Bank of Abu
Dhabi

Principal Shareholders: G A Goreish and Dimitri Zorzopoulos

TADAMON ISLAMIC BANK OF SUDAN

PO Box 3154, Parliament Avenue, Khartoum
Tel: 70417, 74432, 1877, 731145/6
Cable: Bankdaman
Telex: 22158, 22687/8 Daman SD
Telefax: 249 11 73840

Chairman: Khadir Hassan Kambal
Directors: Abdul Rahim Makkawi, Tigani Hassan Hilal, Abdulla
Ibrahim Subiea, Ahmed A Mohamed, Said Omer Kambal,

Ibrahim H Abdul Salam, Abdul Basit Ali, Osman Abdul Galil
Abazied, Hasim I Bashir, Abdul Gadir H Gaffar, Fathi Khalil,
Aljalsi Trading Marketing & Contracting, Kuwait Finance
House, Dr Ibrahim Obiedullah El Hussein, Mohamed Elkhair
Abdulgadir
Senior Executives: Salah Ali Abu El Naja (General Manager), Al
Rashid Saad El Sofi (Asst General Manager), Dr Ahmed Ali
Abdullah (Asst General Manager), Mohamed Shikh Mohamed
(Asst General Manager), Mostafa Omer Alawad (Asst General
Manager)

PRINCIPAL ACTIVITIES: Islamic banking
Branch Offices: Khartoum, Omdurman, Saggana, Port Sudan,
Nyala, Managil, Gedarif, Sinnar, Karima, Alobied, Aldalang,
Alrahad, Aldien, Saadgisha, Soque Alarabi, Kosti
Subsidiary Companies: Tadamon Isamic Co for Services Ltd;
Tadamon Islamic Co for Trade & Investment; Tadamon
Islamic Co for Agricultural Development; Tadamon Islamic Co
for Insurance; Tadamon Islamic Co for Real Estate
Development

Principal Shareholders: Faisal Islamic Bank (Sudan), Dubai
Islamic Bank, Kuwait Finance House, Abdullah Elsobie,
Aljalasi Trading CO, Bahrain Islamic Bank, Shikh Salih Al
Kamel
Date of Establishment: 1981

TAHA EL SAYED EL ROUBI & CO

See EL ROUBI, TAHA EL SAYED, & CO

TEA PACKETING & TRADING CO

PO Box 369, Khartoum
Tel: 54022

PRINCIPAL ACTIVITIES: Marketing of tea

Principal Shareholders: 505 state owned

TOURISM & AIR TAXI SERVICE LTD

PO Box 1484, Khartoum
Tel: 73307, 73482, 75451, 75207
Cable: Agrinol
Telex: 22383 Tasa SD

PRINCIPAL ACTIVITIES: Travel agency, air charterers, and
transport services

Principal Shareholders: A member of the Gulf International
(Sudan) Group

TOURISM & HOTELS CORPORATION

PO Box 7104, Khartoum
Tel: 74667, 74053, 74192
Cable: Karnaval
Telex: 22203 SIAHA

Chairman: Alam El Huda Mohed Sharief
Senior Executives: Alam El Huda Mohed Sharief (Director
General), Mustafa H Zarroug (Deputy Director General),
Anwar S El Kablli (General Manager Grand Hotel), Abdel
Gadir A/Wahab (Director of Tourism Administration),
Mahmoud Karamalla (Director of Catering & Supplies
Administration), Mohed Hassan Khalil (Director Hotels
Supervision & Control Administration)

PRINCIPAL ACTIVITIES: Hotel management and operation
Branch Offices: Port Sudan, Ed Damer, El Fasher, Khartoum
Airport
Subsidiary Companies: Sudanese International Tourism Co

Principal Shareholders: Sudanese Government
Date of Establishment: 1977
No of Employees: 433 (classified), 829 (unclassified)

TRADING & CONTRACTING CO LTD

PO Box 1233, Khartoum
Tel: 72123, 81730, 43270

SUDAN

PRINCIPAL ACTIVITIES: General merchants and commission agents, import and distribution of iron and steel, piping, fittings and valves

TRANS ARABIAN TRADING CO LTD

PO Box 1461, Khartoum
Tel: 80904, 81339
Telex: 22360 Supermax

Chairman: Hassan Gangari (also Managing Director)
Directors: Abbas Gangari (Export Manager), Hamza Gangari (Sales Manager), Yusri Gangari

PRINCIPAL ACTIVITIES: Export of meat and animal feed; import of general goods
Branch Offices: Sudan; Libya; Egypt; Saudi Arabia
Subsidiary Companies: Maxim Company Ltd

TRIAD NATURAL RESOURCES (SUDAN) LTD

PO Box 1069, Khartoum
Tel: 75069, 75070
Cable: Triad Khartoum
Telex: 22416, 22443 Triad Khartoum

PRINCIPAL ACTIVITIES: Business and planning consultants and financial management, agriculture, agribusiness, construction and industry

Date of Establishment: 1974

UNION TRADING CO LTD

PO Box 685, Khartoum
Tel: 76328, 71833, 76891
Cable: UNICO Khartoum
Telex: 22548 Unico

Directors: Robert B Boulos (Managing Director), Peter B Boulos (Finance Director), Paul B Boulos

PRINCIPAL ACTIVITIES: Import of chemicals, foodstuffs and auto spare parts, building materials, steel & timber, paper & engineering goods. Export of agricultural products
Principal Agencies: Mitsubishi, mitsui, Bethlehem Steel (USA), etc
Branch Offices: Port Sudan
Subsidiary Companies: Systel Khartoum
Principal Bankers: El Nilein Bank, Khartoum

Principal Shareholders: Robert B Boulos, Peter B Boulos, Paul B Boulos, Evelyn B Haggar
Date of Establishment: 1962

UNITED AFRICAN TRADING CORPORATION

PO Box 339, Khartoum
Tel: 71994, 70237, 76385, 80654
Cable: Aftraco
Telex: 22250

PRINCIPAL ACTIVITIES: Manufacturers' representation, insurance, forwarding and commission agents, shipping agents, stevedores, charterers, import and distribution of pharmaceuticals, and flour; manufacture and export of cereals, animal feed, soap, confectionery and sweets
Branch Offices: Port Sudan: PO Box 429, Tel 3058

UNITED CONSTRUCTION & TRADING (SUDAN) LTD

PO Box 8, Khartoum
Tel: 72447, 79790, 71542, 70021
Cable: Petrico
Telex: 22159 PETR SD

Chairman: E P Petrides
Directors: J E Petrides, H E Hassan, D E Petrides
Senior Executives: M A Adam

PRINCIPAL ACTIVITIES: Manufacture of brushes and abrasives, architects and engineering consultants, quantity surveyors,

building and industrial representatives and general contractors, property developers
Branch Offices: Port Sudan, Wad Medani, Juba
Associated Companies: Petrico Construction Ltd, Petrofin Int'l Ltd, Nubian Chemical Ind Ltd, Hermes Service & Maintenance Ltd, Petrozein Import & Export Ltd
Principal Bankers: Sudan International Bank, BCCI
Financial Information:

	1989 S£'000
Sales turnover	25,000
Profits	4,000
Authorised capital	8,000
Paid-up capital	8,000

Principal Shareholders: E P Petrides, B E Petrides
Date of Establishment: 1958
No of Employees: 800

UNITY BANK (FORMERLY JUBA OMDURMAN BANK)

PO Box 408, Khartoum
Tel: 74200/6
Cable: Unity Bank
Telex: 22231, 22238, 22239 UNIBK SD

Chairman: Makki El Manna
Directors: Abdalla El Mardi Karim Eldin, Ahmed Mohamed Nour
Senior Executives: Abdalla El Mardi Karim El Din (General Manager), Ahmed Mohamed Nour (Deputy General Manager), Ali Mohamed Salih (Assistant General Manager), Abdel Rahman Ali Barri (Assistant General Manager), Ali Mohmoud Obeid (Assistant General Manager), Abeeb Fouad Saeed (Assistant General Manager)

PRINCIPAL ACTIVITIES: Banking services
Branch Offices: Khartoum, Bralaman Avenue; Khartoum; El Tayer Murad; Khartoum North; Omdurman; Port Sudan; Juba; Kosti; Wad Medani

Principal Shareholders: Bank of Sudan; Ministry of Finance & National Planning
Date of Establishment: 1970
No of Employees: 900

VALVIS, J N,

PO Box 247, Khartoum
Cable: Glass

PRINCIPAL ACTIVITIES: Distribution of diesel engines, belting, glassware, hoses, tools, pumps, ironmongery, paints and oils
Principal Agencies: Bamford & Horizontal Blackstone Diesel Engines, Mulcott Belting (Cam)

WATER DRILLING & ENGINEERING CO LTD

Kassabian Bldg, Sharia El Gamhoria, Khartoum
Tel: 73591/3
Telex: 22392 Hafreyat Km

PRINCIPAL ACTIVITIES: General trading and contracting, import and supply of power equipment, steel and building materials and equipment, concrete mixers, diesel engines, also civil engineering, drilling and irrigation works
Principal Agencies: Hatz diesel engine; Loewe; Pleuger
Branch Offices: Factory in Khartoum North Industrial Area, Tel 31552, 31946

WHITE NILE IMPORT & EXPORT CO LTD

PO Box 7090, Khartoum
Tel: 74903, 76779
Telex: 22821 Sutra Sd

Chairman: Magdi F Girgis
Directors: Midhat F Girgis, Michael F Girgis

PRINCIPAL ACTIVITIES: Manufacturers, importers, exporters and general trading

Principal Agencies: Hyde Park Inter Trade, UK; National Foods, Holland
Branch Offices: PO Box 291, Omdurman
Subsidiary Companies: Sudanese Dyeing Finishing & Trading Co
Principal Bankers: Bank of Khartoum

Principal Shareholders: Magdi, Midhat & Michael F Girgis
Date of Establishment: 1980

YOUSIF MOHAMED ELASHI & SONS CO LTD
See ELASHI, YOUSIF MOHAMED, & SONS CO LTD

SUDAN

Major Companies of SYRIA

A S DERWICHE AHMAD

See DERWICHE, A S, AHMAD

ABDELNOUR FRERES

PO Box 300, Aleppo
Tel: 11176, 17071
Cable: Abdelnour Freres
Telex: 331028 Nourab SY

Chairman: Francois G Abdelnour
Directors: Edmond Lahlouh
Senior Executives: Francois Abdelnour (General Manager),
   Antoine Abdelnour (Vice-President)

PRINCIPAL ACTIVITIES: Import and distribution of cars, trucks,
   automotive spare parts and business machines
Principal Agencies: General Motors Overseas Distribution Corp;
   GM Parts; Vandervell Products Ltd; Wellworthy Products;
   Eaton-Nova Spa; Fiamm Spa
Branch Offices: Al Rashid St, Aleppo
Parent Company: United Machinery Co (UMC), Damascus
Subsidiary Companies: Ramac; Aleppo
Principal Bankers: Commercial Bank of Syria

Date of Establishment: Aleppo: 1940; Damascus (UMC): 1978

ADRA SUGAR COMPANY

PO Box 833, Abu Remmaneh
Tel: 332004, 334714
Cable: Sucraf

PRINCIPAL ACTIVITIES: Sugar processing and refining
Parent Company: Responsible to the General Organisation for
   Sugar

Principal Shareholders: State-owned company

AFFAKI FRERES

PO Box 139, Algezaer Street, Lattakia
Tel: 30181, 26303
Cable: Affaki
Telex: 51026 Affaki Sy

PRINCIPAL ACTIVITIES: Shipping agents, clearing and
   forwarding agents
Principal Agencies: Marseille Fret, Marseille; Carline, Paris;
   Gazocean, Paris; Dabinovic, Geneva; Koctug Line, Istanbul;
   Greek Maritime Exploitation, Piraeus; Ocean Gaz, Milano
Branch Offices: Tartous (PO Box 19); Banias (PO Box 12);
   Aleppo (PO Box 769); Damascus (PO Box 912)

AGRICULTURAL COOPERATIVE BANK

Euphrates Street, PO Box 5325, Damascus
Tel: 113461, 116461, 221393
Cable: Zeraisir
Telex: 98044

Chairman: Dr Naeim Jomaa
Senior Executives: Ayman Hamzawy (General Manager),
   Nasouh Bitar (Finance & Administration Manager), Kasem
   Bahbouh (Marketing & Purchasing Manager), Nizar Nashawy
   (Personnel Manager)

PRINCIPAL ACTIVITIES: Finance for the agricultural sector
Branch Offices: 67 branches in Syria
Parent Company: Responsible to the Ministry of Economy &
   Foreign Trade
Financial Information:

	1988 SP'000
Authorised capital	1,000,000
Paid-up capital	600,000
Total assets	300,000

Principal Shareholders: State-owned
Date of Establishment: 1888
No of Employees: 1,485

AGRICULTURAL MACHINERY DISTRIBUTION CO

Selim Jambart St, PO Box 1367, Aleppo
Tel: 36300/1
Cable: SYRTRAC
Telex: 331014 Tratco Sy

PRINCIPAL ACTIVITIES: Distribution of agricultural machinery
   and equipment, and tractors
Parent Company: Responsible to the Ministry of Industry
Subsidiary/Associated Companies: Al-Furat Tractors Co, PO
   Box 1802, Aleppo; Electric Motors Manufacturing Co, PO Box
   190, Lattakia

Principal Shareholders: State-owned company

AHLIEH SPINNING & WEAVING CO

Bolliarment, PO Box 230, Aleppo
Tel: 14557, 20610, 11213
Cable: Al-Ahlieh

PRINCIPAL ACTIVITIES: Spinning and weaving, cotton and
   woollen yarns and polyester fabrics
Parent Company: Responsible to the General Organisation of
   Textile Industries

Principal Shareholders: State-owned company

AL CHARK FOOD PRODUCTS CO

Ain-El-Tall, Moussallamiyah, PO Box 217, Aleppo
Tel: 447501, 447500
Cable: SYRBEER
Telex: 331267

Chairman: Mohammad Al-Mousa
Directors: A Jammal, Leila Shamoun, Musaleh Al-Shark, Bader
   Kezzeh, Anwar Jokhai

PRINCIPAL ACTIVITIES: Manufacture of food products, beer,
   biscuits, chocolates, dairy products
Parent Company: General Organization for Food Industries
Principal Bankers: Commercial Bank of Syria

Principal Shareholders: State-owned company
Date of Establishment: 1965

ALEPPO SILK WEAVING CORP (SATEX)

PO Box 462, Aleppo
Tel: 15179, 34374, 41225
Cable: Satex

PRINCIPAL ACTIVITIES: Manufacture of silk fabrics, brocades
   and silk rugs
Branch Offices: Salhieh, PO Box 1118, Damascus
Parent Company: Responsible to the General Organisation of
   Textile Industries
Associated Companies: Damascus Silk Cloth Corporation (PO
   Box 1230, Damascus, Tel 116420, Cable Harrieh)

Principal Shareholders: State-owned company

AL FRAT COMPANY

PO Box 1802, Aleppo
Tel: 336305, 333691
Cable: FRATCO
Telex: 331014

Chairman: Mahmoud Kaddour

PRINCIPAL ACTIVITIES: Production of agricultural tractors and
   equipment
Principal Bankers: Commercial Bank of Syria

Principal Shareholders: Syrian Government; Motor Iberica Co,
   Spain
Date of Establishment: 1974
No of Employees: 1070

SYRIA

AL RASTAN CEMENT & BUILDING MATERIALS CO

PO Box 336, Homs
Tel: 12844, 26100

PRINCIPAL ACTIVITIES: Production of cement and building
  materials
Parent Company: Responsible to the General Organisation for
  Cement

Principal Shareholders: State-owned company

AL-SHAHBA CEMENT & BUILDING MATERIALS CO

Mutanabbi St, PO Box 470, Aleppo
Tel: 11108, 15803, 13033

PRINCIPAL ACTIVITIES: Cement manufacture, and building
  materials, kraft paper bags
Parent Company: Responsible to the General Organisation for
  Cement

Principal Shareholders: State-owned company

AL-SHAHBA SPINNING & WEAVING CORP

Ain Al Tilal Rd, PO Box 514, Aleppo
Tel: 10257
Cable: Shams

PRINCIPAL ACTIVITIES: Manufacture of cotton yarns and all
  kind of grey textiles
Parent Company: Responsible to the General Organisation of
  Textile Industries

Principal Shareholders: State-owned company

ALTOUN CONTRACTING & TRADING CO

Port Said St, Houriah Bldg, PO Box 94, Lattakia
Tel: 12810, 13419
Cable: Altoun

Chairman: S G Altoun
Directors: Y G Altoun (Commercial Manager)

PRINCIPAL ACTIVITIES: Building contractors, manufacturers'
  representatives; supply of building materials and ceramics
Principal Agencies: Priestman Brothers Ltd, UK; Acrow
  Engineers (Export) Ltd, UK; F E Weatherill Ltd, UK; Sykes
  Pumps, UK; ACE Machinery Ltd, UK; Officine Riunite, Italy;
  Fiori Officine Meccaniche, Italy; Turbosol Al Spa, Italy;
  Edilmac Gru-Spa, Italy; Sacme SACME Spa, Italy
Branch Offices: PO Box 6299, Damascus, Telex 19135
  Altounco; Altoun Contracting & Trading Co, Rome, Italy,
  Europe Liaison Office Telex 68222 (Tibroma)
Principal Bankers: Commercial Bank of Syria

ALYAT AUTOMOTIVE ELECTRICAL & AGRICULTURAL IMPLEMENTS CORP

PO Box 2250, Al-Moutanabi St, Damascus

PRINCIPAL ACTIVITIES: General engineering, manufacture of
  mechanical, industrial and agricultural equipment,
  automobiles, etc

ANT MECATTAF & FILS

Ghassan St, Harika, PO Box 342, Damascus
Tel: 110136
Cable: Mectaf
Telex: 411243

Chairman: Pierre Mecattaf
Directors: Marcel Mecattaf, Ahmad Zarzour

PRINCIPAL ACTIVITIES: Import and export of electrical
  household goods, pharmaceuticals, toiletries, etc
Principal Agencies: Wilkinson Sword, UK; Hoover, UK; Albal,
  France; Venitex, France; Cussons, UK; Novacel, France;
  Yardley, UK

Branch Offices: PO Box 5833, Beirut, Lebanon
Associated Companies: Mecattaf Pharmaceutical Co SAL, PO
  Box 16-5366, Beirut/Lebanon
Principal Bankers: Commercial Bank of Syria

ARAB ADVERTISING ORGANIZATION

28 Moutanabbi St, PO Box 2842 and 3034, Damascus
Tel: 225219/20/21
Cable: Golan
Telex: 411923 Golan

Chairman: Minister of Information
Directors: Mazen Sabbagh (Director General), Samir Srour
  (Financial Director)

PRINCIPAL ACTIVITIES: Control, supervision and execution of
  advertising and publicity in the Syrian Arab Republic
Branch Offices: Aleppo; Homs; Lattakia; Hama
Parent Company: Responsible to the Ministry of Information,
  Damascus, Tel 660412, 669600, 667325
Principal Bankers: Central Bank of Syria; Commercial Bank of
  Syria

Principal Shareholders: State-owned organisation
Date of Establishment: 1963
No of Employees: 170

ARAB CEMENT & BUILDING MATERIALS CO

PO Box 5140, Aleppo
Tel: 38400, 38401
Cable: Arabcement
Telex: 331240 AC BMC SY

Directors: M S Owera (Managing Director)

PRINCIPAL ACTIVITIES: Production of cement
Parent Company: Responsible to the General Organisation for
  Cement
Principal Bankers: Commercial Bank of Syria

Principal Shareholders: State-owned company
Date of Establishment: 23-6-1977
No of Employees: 1,100

ARAB CO FOR LIVESTOCK DEVELOPMENT (ACOLID)

PO Box 5305, Damascus
Tel: 666039, 666037, 665687, 665688
Cable: ACOLID
Telex: 411376 Sy Acolid

Chairman: Eng Ahmed Al-Mana
Directors: Dr Abdullah Thenayan (Director General)

PRINCIPAL ACTIVITIES: All agricultural, industrial, commercial
  and all other technical works connected with the production,
  processing, transport of animal products and fodders;
  agribusiness feasibility studies, consultancy. The current
  projects are: Project for fattening lambs & calves, and
  breeding of sheep, Syria; project for the production and
  processing of green fodder, Saudi Arabia; the feedmill,
  Sudan; project for broiler chicken, Jordan; poultry project,
  Sudan
Branch Offices: Kamishly-Syria; Amman-Jordan; Quassim-Saudi
  Arabia; Kartoum-Sudan; Riyadh Regional Office-Riyadh Saudi
  Arabia: PO Box 18389, Telex 404355, Tel 4649255, 4651497,
  Fax (01) 4051497
Subsidiary Companies: Arab Qatar Co for Poultry Production,
  Qatar; Arab Co for Animal Production, United Arab Emirates;
  Arab Co for Poultry Production, United Arab Emirates; Arab
  Saudi Co for Poultry Production, Saudi Arabia; Arab Iraqi Co
  for Livestock Development, Iraq; Qatari Co for Dairy
  Production, Qatar
Principal Bankers: Al-Ahli Bank of Kuwait, Kuwait; Commercial
  Bank of Syria, Damascus; Al-Bank Al Saudi Al Hollandi,
  Riyadh

Financial Information:

	1988/89 KD'000
Authorised capital	60,000
Paid-up capital	56,025
Total assets	93,268

Principal Shareholders: Arab Governments and Organisations (the Governments of Syria; Jordan; Saudi Arabia; United Arab Emirates; Sudan; Iraq; Somalia; Egypt; North Yemen; Qatar; and the Arab Investment Company; Kuwait Real Estate Investment Group

Date of Establishment: Established in 1975 by the Arab League

ARAB DEVELOPMENT CO

Smadi Bldg, Malki St, PO Box 2390, Damascus
Tel: 33733, 33216
Cable: Philtay Damascus
Telex: 411292 Alicat

Directors: Munib R Masri, Tarif W Ayoubi

PRINCIPAL ACTIVITIES: Site investigations, land reclamation and development, civil and mechanical engineering, water well drilling
Branch Offices: Offices in Jordan, Lebanon, Saudi Arabia, Oman, Abu Dhabi, Ras Al Khaimah, London and the Liechtenstein
Principal Bankers: Arab Bank Ltd

Date of Establishment: 1971

ARAB INDUSTRIAL OIL & SOAP CO

PO Box 2489, Jaramana Rd, Damascus
Tel: 119393, 118618
Cable: Alteseir

PRINCIPAL ACTIVITIES: Producers and exporters of cake and linter cotton a variety of soaps; importers of oil for soap, palm and coconut oil, together with other chemicals and raw materials necessary for the soap and vegetable oil production
Parent Company: Responsible to the General Establishment for Chemical Industries

Principal Shareholders: State-owned company

ARAB MARITIME AGENCIES

PO Box 145, Lattakia
Tel: 2926
Cable: Tamar

PRINCIPAL ACTIVITIES: Shipping agents
Principal Agencies: Deutsche Orient Linie GmbH, Argo Nahost Linie GmbH
Branch Offices: Tartous; Banias; Damascus

ARAB MEDICAL COMPANY
THAMECO

Al Jessr-Afif St, PO Box 976, Damascus
Tel: 435515, 338965
Cable: Thameco
Telex: 411926 Tameco Sy

Chairman: Majed Koudsi
Directors: Dr Bassam Kabbani (Research Manager)

PRINCIPAL ACTIVITIES: Manufacture of pharmaceuticals and baby food, imports raw materials and packaging materials
Principal Agencies: Manufacture under Licence for Archifar Lepetit, Italy; Bayer, Germany; Germed, Germany; Beecham, UK, Schering Corporation, Eli Lilly USA
Parent Company: Responsible to the General Establishment of Chemical Industries
Principal Bankers: Commercial Bank of Syria

Principal Shareholders: State-owned company
Date of Establishment: 1963
No of Employees: 900

ARAB ORGANIZATION FOR AGRICULTURAL DEVELOPMENT

Mazza, Western Villas, PO Box 5450, Damascus
Tel: 662941
Cable: Agrarab
Telex: 411385 Agong Sy

PRINCIPAL ACTIVITIES: The Organization undertakes all sorts of investments pertaining to agriculture in order to realize agricultural development within the republics of the Union so as to secure self sufficiency and economic integration
Principal Bankers: Syrian Commercial Bank

Principal Shareholders: Syria, Egypt, and Libya

ARAB RUBBER PLASTIC & LEATHER PRODUCTS CO

Mutanabbi St, PO Box 369, Aleppo
Tel: 12965, 37405
Cable: NATACO

PRINCIPAL ACTIVITIES: Manufacture of rubber, plastic and leather products
Parent Company: General Establishment of Chemical Industries

Principal Shareholders: State-owned company

ARAB UNDERWEAR CO

PO Box 436, Rue El-Goumrok, Aleppo
Tel: 10458
Cable: Alarabiya

PRINCIPAL ACTIVITIES: Production of cotton and woollen underwear, pyjamas, towels, knitted goods, mercerised products, and ready made dresses for ladies
Parent Company: Responsible to the General Organisation of Textile Industries

Principal Shareholders: State-owned company

ARAB UNION REINSURANCE CO

New Damascus, Fayez Mansour Street, PO Box 5178, Damascus
Tel: 215600
Cable: ARABUNRE
Telex: 411387 Sy

Chairman: Dr Aziz Sakr
Members: Taha Kataf, Amin Abdullah, Suleiman Omar Ahtash, Abdel Hamid Al-Zaklaai, Abdul Salam Al-Ghomati, Sameer Al-Daoudi
Senior Executives: Mohamed Abugrain (General Manager)

PRINCIPAL ACTIVITIES: Reinsurance
Branch Offices: London Contact Office; Tripoli Branch, Libya
Principal Bankers: Commercial Bank of Syria
Financial Information:

	SP'000
Authorised capital	22,170
Paid-up capital	22,170

Principal Shareholders: Governments of Syria, Egypt and Libya
Date of Establishment: 11th June 1975
No of Employees: 60

ARAB WOOD INDUSTRY CO

PO Box 130, Bassa Mafrak El-Heffe, Lattakia
Tel: 22515
Cable: Ahshab
Telex: 451054 SY

Chairman: Eng Usama Ghannam
Directors: Najwan Akfali (Commercial Director), Edmond Jabbour (Financial Director), Abdulmajid Ghazi (Technical Director), Eng A Janzir (Production Director), Anis Baddour (Administration Director)

PRINCIPAL ACTIVITIES: Wood industry, manufacture of plywood, compressed wood, walnut veneer, prefabricated wooden houses
Parent Company: Responsible to the General Establishment for Engineering Industries
Principal Bankers: Commercial Bank of Syria, Lattakia
Financial Information:

	1989 SP'000
Sales turnover	30,000
Profits	10,000
Authorised capital	200,000
Paid-up capital	100,000
Total assets	500,000

Principal Shareholders: State-owned company
Date of Establishment: 1956
No of Employees: 675

AUTOMOTIVE & INDUSTRIAL EQUIPMENT CO

rue Sultan Selim, PO Box 789, Damascus

PRINCIPAL ACTIVITIES: Wholesale and retail of automobiles, and spare parts, tyres and tubes, mineral oils and electrical equipment

AZM, SUFIAN M,

55 Port Said St, PO Box 4184, Damascus
Tel: 211811
Telex: 419144

President: Sufian Azm

PRINCIPAL ACTIVITIES: Commercial advisors, manufacturers' representatives, and contractors in electronics; telecommunications, military electronics
Parent Company: SETCO, PO Box 8122, Jeddah, Saudi Arabia

Date of Establishment: 1975

BARADA METALLIC INDUSTRIES CO

Hosh Place, PO Box 2477, Damascus
Tel: 880520, 663200, 883200
Cable: Fricagable
Telex: 411207 Barada SY

PRINCIPAL ACTIVITIES: Production of household items, stoves, refrigerators, cables. Import of raw materials
Parent Company: Responsible to the General Establishment for Engineering Industries

Principal Shareholders: State-owned company

CENTRAL BANK OF SYRIA

Banque Centrale de Syrie

29 Ayar Sq, PO Box 2254, Damascus
Tel: 224800, 222471
Cable: Markazisyr
Telex: 411007 Marsyr

PRINCIPAL ACTIVITIES: Central banking institution
Subsidiary Companies: Industrial Bank, Damascus; Real Estate Bank, Damascus

Principal Shareholders: State owned
Date of Establishment: 1956

CHAM CO FOR HOTELS & TOURISM

Mayssaloun Street, Cham Palace Hotel, PO Box 7593, Damascus
Tel: 232300, 232320
Cable: CHAMHOTELS
Telex: SYRTEL 411966 SY

Chairman: Dr Osmane Aidi
Directors: Fouad Hammami, Imad Sabri, Ahmad Samir Al Daoudi, Eng Nizar Al Ass'Ad

PRINCIPAL ACTIVITIES: Hotel and tourism
Principal Agencies: Utell, Steingenberger
Branch Offices: Paris, Monte Carlo
Parent Company: Societe Arabe Syrienne des Etablissements Touristiques
Principal Bankers: Commercial Bank of Syria, Damascus; Banque Paribas, Paris; Societe Bancaire Arabe, Paris
Financial Information:

	SP'000
Authorised capital	15,000
Paid-up capital	15,000

Principal Shareholders: 40% the City of Damascus; 60% Syrian Arab Co for Touristic Establishments
Date of Establishment: 1979
No of Employees: 580

COMMERCIAL BANK OF SYRIA

Youssef Azmeh Square, Salhieh, PO Box 933, Damascus
Tel: 218890, 218891
Cable: Dircomersyr (Head Office), Comersyr & No (Branches)
Telex: 411002, 411205 Sy (General Management); 411025 Sy (Exchange)

Chairman: Riad Hakim (also General Manager)
Directors: Ibrahim Hajjar (Deputy Chairman), Rezkallah Nazha (Planning & Statistics Manager), Md Masri Zada (Internal Control Manager), Yasser Mourtada (Loans & Credit Manager), Adnan Kashalo (Accountancy Dept Manager), Shaher Shamout (Admin & Legal Dept Manager), Tarek Sarrag (Financial Dept Manager), Mustafa Issa Darwish (Secretarial Dept Manager), Najati S Shehabi (Technical Dept Manager)

PRINCIPAL ACTIVITIES: Commercial banking, banking services for domestic and foreign trade, foreign exchange transactions, and safe deposit
Principal Agencies: 31 Foreign Exchange Agencies
Branch Offices: 34 Branches throughout Syria
Associated Companies: Syro-Lebanese Commercial Bank, Beirut, Lebanon; Union des Banques Arabes & Francaises, Paris; UBAF Arab-American Bank, New York; UBAC Curacoa; Arab Bank
Principal Bankers: National Westminster Bank, Lloyds Bank, London; Citibank, UBAF Arab-American Bank, New York
Financial Information:

	1988 SP'000
Profits	94,237
Authorised capital	181,800
Paid-up capital	181,800
Total assets	61,375,700

Principal Shareholders: State-owned
Date of Establishment: 1st January 1967
No of Employees: 3,114

COMMERCIAL INDUSTRIAL & TECHNICAL ASSOCIATION

C.I.T.A.

PO Box 3220, Damascus
Tel: 330098
Cable: Tradly
Telex: 411951 Obeid Sy

PRINCIPAL ACTIVITIES: Engineering and contracting; turnkey projects; public works
Principal Agencies: Wavin Overseas, Massey Ferguson
Branch Offices: Aleppo: PO Box 530, Tel 12225
Subsidiary/Associated Companies: Syrian Engineering & Technical Association (SETA); APAD
Principal Bankers: Commercial Bank of Syria

Principal Shareholders: Association of Engineers, Contractors, Businessmen and Developers

CONVERTING INDUSTRIES CORPORATION
Kissweh Rd, PO Box 2803, Damascus
Tel: 110410
Cable: Hitex

PRINCIPAL ACTIVITIES: Production and export of tissues, paper handkerchiefs, medical products and toiletries. Import of hardrolls, wood pulp, chemicals and other raw and semi finished materials for use in its manufacturing operations
Parent Company: Responsible to the General Organisation of Mechanical Industries

Principal Shareholders: State-owned company

COTTON MARKETING ORGANISATION
Bab el Faraj St, PO Box 729, Aleppo
Tel: 238486, 239495
Cable: Cottonexport
Telex: 331227, 331210 COTSYR SY

Chairman: Rateb Jaber (also Director General)
Senior Executives: Ahmad Rajab (Finance Director), Abdul Sattar Osman (Marketing Director), Hasan Al Jasem (Production Director), Khaldoun El Sayed (Personnel Director), Walid Shoughouri (Technical Director), Nouri Dalati (Admin Director)

PRINCIPAL ACTIVITIES: Ginning and marketing of raw cotton (it is the sole government body authorised to purchase seed-cotton directly from producers)
Branch Offices: Lattakia, Hama, Deir-Zor (Syria)
Parent Company: Responsible to the Ministry of Economy & Foreign Trade
Principal Bankers: Commercial Bank of Syria, Aleppo; Central Bank, Damascus; Central Bank, Aleppo
Financial Information:

	1989/90 US$'000
Sales turnover	395,000
Authorised capital	51,282

Principal Shareholders: State-owned Organisation
Date of Establishment: 1965
No of Employees: Over 1,150 permanent staff

DAMASCUS FOOD PRODUCTS CO CAMELIA
Yarmouk, PO Box 1137, Damascus
Tel: 119406

PRINCIPAL ACTIVITIES: Manufacture and processing of food products
Parent Company: Responsible to the General Organisation of Food Industries

Principal Shareholders: State-owned company

DAMASCUS INTERNATIONAL HOTEL
Bahsa St, Damascus
Tel: 113400, 112400
Cable: Interhotel
Telex: 411062 Intrho

PRINCIPAL ACTIVITIES: Hotel business and catering

DAMASCUS SHERATON HOTEL
Omayyed Square, PO Box 4795, Damascus
Tel: 229300, 716664
Cable: Sherat Hotel
Telex: 411378, 411403, 411404 Sherat SY

Senior Executives: Said Abu Izzedin (General Manager), Hans Resl (Controller), Fahed Abu Sha'ar (Resident Manager), Nassouh Mounayyer (Director of Sales), Ahmed Awwad (Director of Purchasing), Khaldoun Kanaan (Director of Personnel), Walid Al Saadi (Director of Engineering & Maintenance)

PRINCIPAL ACTIVITIES: Hotel management and operation
Branch Offices: Sheraton Hotels Inns & Resorts Worldwide
Parent Company: International Telephone & Telegraph

Principal Shareholders: Hotel owned by the Ministry of Tourism, Syria
Date of Establishment: 1978
No of Employees: 520

DEHYDRATED ONIONS & VEGETABLES CO
Hama Rd, Salamieh
Tel: 64/1

PRINCIPAL ACTIVITIES: Production, processing and marketing of vegetables and dehydrated onions
Parent Company: Responsible to the General Organisation for Food Industries

Principal Shareholders: State-owned company

DERWICHE, A S, AHMAD
PO Box 192, Lattakia
Tel: (41) 34585, 34330, 33542
Cable: Derwiche
Telex: 451051 Derwic, 451105 Derwic
Telefax: (41) 33671

Chairman: A S Derwiche Ahmad
Directors: M Derwiche Ahmad, W Yazigi
Senior Executives: N Bitar (Shipping)

PRINCIPAL ACTIVITIES: Shipping agents; import-export; forwarders
Principal Agencies: Constellation Lines, Piraeus, Lignes de l'Etoile Blanche, Marseille, Neptune Orient Lines, Singapore
Branch Offices: Banias; Tartous
Parent Company: Papadopoulos & A S Derwiche Ahmad
Principal Bankers: Commercial Bank of Syria, Lattakia; Algemene Bank Nederland, Piraeus; Citibank, NY USA
Financial Information:

	1990 US$'000
Sales turnover	2,140
Profits	342
Authorised capital	500
Paid-up capital	500
Total assets	1,120

Principal Shareholders: A S Derwiche Ahmad
Date of Establishment: 1955

DIRECTORATE GENERAL OF CIVIL AVIATION
Nejmeh Sq, Damascus
Tel: 331306, 338720
Telex: 411928 Civair Sy

PRINCIPAL ACTIVITIES: Authority for civil aviation in Syria
Parent Company: Responsible to the Ministry of Transport, Damascus

Principal Shareholders: State-owned company

DIRECTORATE OF AGRICULTURE & AGRARIAN REFORM
Hedjaz Sq, Damascus
Tel: 227600

PRINCIPAL ACTIVITIES: Authority for agriculture and agrarian reform
Parent Company: Responsible to the Ministry of Agriculture & Agrarian Reform, Damascus

Principal Shareholders: State-owned company

DIRECTORATE OF ALEPPO CABLES PLANT
PO Box 1671, Aleppo

PRINCIPAL ACTIVITIES: Production of cables and wires

SYRIA

Parent Company: Responsible to the General Organisation of Mechanical Industries

Principal Shareholders: State-owned company

DIRECTORATE OF PRIVATE INDUSTRIAL & HANDICRAFTS SECTOR

Ministry of Industry Bldg, Damascus
Tel: 222680

PRINCIPAL ACTIVITIES: Authority for the production and control of the private industrial and handicrafts sector
Parent Company: Responsible to the Ministry of Industry, Damascus

Principal Shareholders: State-owned company

ELECTRIC MOTORS MANUFACTURING CO

PO Box 190, Lattakia
Tel: 21850, 21533
Cable: Motors

PRINCIPAL ACTIVITIES: Manufacture of electric motors and transformers

Date of Establishment: 1975
No of Employees: 453

ESTEFANE AND CO

PO Box 415, Damascus
Tel: 114665, 113421
Cable: Estefane Damascus

Chairman: Georges Estefane

PRINCIPAL ACTIVITIES: Import of electric and electronic equipment and home appliances
Principal Agencies: Sierra Electronics, Hitashi Ltd, KDK Fans, Casio Watches, Gibson Air conditioning
Associated Companies: Ets Estefane pour le Commerce, Beirut; Estefane Sargi and Co
Principal Bankers: Commercial Bank of Syria

ETICO

Hajjar Bros Co

Hajjar Bldg, Sabe Bahrat Square, PO Box 2425, Damascus
Telex: 411226 Etico Sy

Senior Executives: M S Hajjar (General Manager)

PRINCIPAL ACTIVITIES: Manufacture of mechanical and industrial equipment, general engineering and contracting

EZZAT M JALLAD & FILS

See JALLAD, EZZAT M, & FILS

FOREIGN TRADE ORGANISATION FOR MACHINERY & EQUIPMENT

SARAYAT

Maisaloun St, PO Box 3130, Damascus
Tel: 118480, 118156, 111870
Cable: Aftomachine
Telex: 411036 Aliyat Sy

Directors: Salim Dallal (Director General)

PRINCIPAL ACTIVITIES: Import of tyres, vehicles, spare parts, chassis, trucks, motorcyles
Principal Agencies: Scania, Volvo, Peugeot, Land-Rover, Fiat, Balkan, Mazda, Nissan, Mitsubishi, Hino, Toyota, Mogort
Branch Offices: Homs, Hama, Aleppo, Tantous, Latakia, Dir Al Zomr, Al Ruqa, Al Haska, Dara, Al Suwaida
Parent Company: Responsible to the Ministry of Economy & Foreign Trade
Principal Bankers: Commercial Bank of Syria

Principal Shareholders: State-owned
Date of Establishment: Formerly Aftomachine
No of Employees: 1,300

FOREIGN TRADE ORGANISATION FOR METALS & BUILDING MATERIALS

MAADEN

Huteen Square, (Al Maisat), PO Box 3136, Damascus
Tel: 420945, 420941
Cable: Maaden
Telex: 411459, 411005 Maaden Sy

Chairman: Muhammad Al Mahameed

PRINCIPAL ACTIVITIES: Import of steel, tin, portland white cement, timber products and building materials, export of portland grey cement, plain and stained glass, sanitaryware
Branch Offices: Lattakia, Tartous
Parent Company: Responsible to the Ministry of Economy & Foreign Trade
Principal Bankers: Commercial Bank of Syria, branch 5

Principal Shareholders: State-owned company
Date of Establishment: Formerly Aftometal
No of Employees: 760

FOREIGN TRADE ORGANISATION FOR PHARMACEUTICAL PRODUCTS

SAYDALAYA

PO Box 3052, Abou Firas Al-Hamadani St, Damascus
Tel: 110289
Cable: Saydalayah
Telex: 411001

PRINCIPAL ACTIVITIES: Monopoly of the import of all pharmaceutical products into Syria, including veterinary products
Parent Company: Responsible to the Ministry of Economy & Foreign Trade

Principal Shareholders: State-owned organisation
Date of Establishment: Formerly Pharmex

FOREIGN TRADE ORGANIZATION FOR CHEMICALS & FOODSTUFFS

GEZA

PO Box 893, Jamhouria St, Damascus
Tel: 228521, 218015, 225421, 218919
Cable: Geza Damascus
Telex: 411009; 411370

Chairman: Mohammed Sarakbi

PRINCIPAL ACTIVITIES: Import of foodstuffs (canned sardines, liquid glucose, butter ghee, vegetable oil, milk powder, sugar, rice, tea, coffee), pesticides, sodium , calcium, sukphur, printing inks, fertilizers, paper and board; export of cotton linters, ground nuts, dehydrated onion, molasses, fertilisers, mineral water, tomato juice, fruit jams, medical & industrial alcohol
Branch Offices: Branches in Lattakia, PO Box 87; and in Tartous
Parent Company: Public Consumption organisation and Agrobank
Principal Bankers: Commercial Bank of Syria
Financial Information:

	1990 SP'000
Paid-up capital	150,000

Principal Shareholders: State-owned organisation
Date of Establishment: 1969
No of Employees: 420

GARGOUR, SOUAYA, & CO

PO Box 5, Lattakia
Tel: 23602, 24614
Telex: 51025 Trust Sy

Chairman: Michel G Adbelnour (also Proprietor)

Directors: Michel Adbelnour, Nabil Abdelnour

PRINCIPAL ACTIVITIES: Shipping and commission agents
Principal Agencies: Associated Levant Lines, Beirut, Lebanon;
  Deutsche Levante Linie GmbH, Hamburg; Cory Brothers & Co
  Ltd, London; Mobil Shipping and Transportation, New York
Branch Offices: Syria and Lebanon
Subsidiary Companies: Banias and Tartous

GENERAL ASPHALT CO
Baghdad St, PO Box 6, Lattakia
Tel: 33121, 35674
Cable: Aspel
Telex: 451150 Aspel

Chairman: Nadim Al Skeif
Directors: Salim Darkoushi

PRINCIPAL ACTIVITIES: Production of asphalt, export of racks
  in blocks, crushing plant
Branch Offices: Kfarieh and Al Bishri
Parent Company: Responsible to the Ministry of Petroleum &
  Mineral Resources
Principal Bankers: Commercial Bank of Syria
Financial Information:

	1990 SP'000
Sales turnover	18,000
Authorised capital	12,000
Total assets	30,000

Principal Shareholders: State-owned company
Date of Establishment: 1927 then nationalised in 1968
No of Employees: 220

GENERAL CO FOR BUILDING
G.E.C.O.B.U.I.L.D.
Malki St, Abdul Mun'em Riad, PO Box 4574, Damascus
Tel: 332437, 661100, 228716
Cable: Bena
Telex: 411388 Gucobu

PRINCIPAL ACTIVITIES: Contractors specialising in
  prefabricated houses and buildings
Parent Company: Responsible to the Ministry of Public Works

Principal Shareholders: State-owned company

GENERAL CO FOR CABLE INDUSTRY
PO Box 827, Damas - Cadam - Hosh Blass
Tel: 883205
Telex: 11207

PRINCIPAL ACTIVITIES: Production of electrical cables and
  wires, bare conductors, telephone cables

Date of Establishment: 1978
No of Employees: 750

GENERAL CO FOR ENGINEERING & CONSULTING
Abassiyeen Sq, Koussour, PO Box 2350, Damascus
Tel: 453908, 453658
Telex: 411635 ENCO - SY

Chairman: Eng Ihsan Sham'a
Senior Executives: Hikmat Al Khudari (General Manager), Khalil
  Khouri (Finance Manager), Wajih Suliman (Purchasing
  Manager), Hikrat Al Khudari (Personnel & Admin Manager),
  Eng Farid Doumani (Technical Manager)

PRINCIPAL ACTIVITIES: Design, structural and civil engineering
  electrical, petroleum, chemical, petrochemical, mechanical,
  mining and civil feasibility studies
Branch Offices: Aleppo, Homs, Lattakia
Parent Company: Responsible to the Prime Minister Office
Principal Bankers: Syrian Central Bank

Financial Information:

	SP'000
Authorised capital	55,000
Paid-up capital	55,000

Principal Shareholders: State-owned organisation
Date of Establishment: 1981
No of Employees: 1,833

GENERAL CO FOR EXECUTING INDUSTRIAL PROJECTS
PO Box 2493, Damascus
Tel: 249601, 249602, 249603, 249604, 249605
Cable: Projects
Telex: 411734, 422483 INDPRO SY

Director General: Burhan Eldin Daghestain

PRINCIPAL ACTIVITIES: Execution of industrial projects
  (design, construction, erection) contracting
Branch Offices: 7 Branches throughout Syria
Parent Company: Responsible to the Ministry of Construction &
  Building
Principal Bankers: Industrial Bank of Syria; Commercial Bank of
  Syria

Principal Shareholders: State-owned company
Date of Establishment: 1957
No of Employees: 3,000

GENERAL CO FOR GLASS INDUSTRY & ELECTRIC LAMPS
V.E.R.A.L.E.P.
PO Box 1801, Aleppo
Tel: 464701-4
Cable: Veralep
Telex: 331207 SY

General Director: Chem Mohamad Anwar Mawaldi

PRINCIPAL ACTIVITIES: Production of flat glass, Pittsburgh
  method -various kinds of bottles, electric lamps - fluorescent
Principal Bankers: Industrial Bank; Commercial Bank of Syria
Financial Information:

	SP'000
Paid-up capital	250,000

Principal Shareholders: State-owned company
Date of Establishment: 1976

GENERAL CO FOR IRON & STEEL PRODUCTS
G.E.C.O.S.T.E.E.L.
PO Box 24, Al Assi Sq, Hama
Tel: 12224, 13304, 25304, 25308
Cable: Gecosteel
Telex: 331038 SY

PRINCIPAL ACTIVITIES: Production and distribution of all types
  of metal products; presently producing concrete
  reinforcement rods
Parent Company: Responsible to the General Establishment for
  Engineering Industries

Principal Shareholders: State-owned company

GENERAL CO FOR PHOSPHATE & MINES
G.E.C.O.P.H.A.M.
PO Box 288, Homs
Tel: 20405, 20505, 21536
Cable: Gecopham
Telex: 441000 Syrpho

PRINCIPAL ACTIVITIES: Production and export of phosphate
  rock
Branch Offices: PO Box 3160, Damascus, Syria

SYRIA

Parent Company: Responsible to the Ministry of Petroleum &
Mineral Resources

Principal Bankers: Commercial Bank of Syria; Central Bank of
Syria

Principal Shareholders: State-owned company

GENERAL CO FOR ROADS CONSTRUCTION
R.O.D.C.O.

PO Box 493, Homs
Tel: 20790, 20004
Cable: Rodco Homs
Telex: 441001 Rodco Sy

General Director: Eng Fares Samaan (Head of Management
Committee)

PRINCIPAL ACTIVITIES: Civil engineering and road construction
contractors
Branch Offices: Damascus; Aleppo; Lattakia; Deir Ezzor; Idlib;
Rakka; Jableh; Al-Kardaha; Al-Haffeh; Al-Hassakeh; Al-
Rmeilan; Al-Kamishly; Homs
Principal Bankers: Commercial Bank of Syria

Principal Shareholders: State-owned
Date of Establishment: September 1974
No of Employees: 5,000

GENERAL CO FOR STORAGE &
REFRIGERATION

Zablatani, the New Zuk Al Hall, PO Box 5603, Damascus
Tel: 411529, 419636
Cable: KHUDAR
Telex: 411914 GEF Sy

Chairman: Dr Eng Kassem AL Haj Ali

PRINCIPAL ACTIVITIES: Cold storage and refrigeration
contracting & transportation
Branch Offices: Refrigeraton Units
Parent Company: Responsible to the Ministry of Supply &
Internal Trade
Financial Information:

	SP'000
Authorised capital	310,000
Paid-up capital	102,190

Principal Shareholders: State-owned company
No of Employees: 700

GENERAL CO FOR THE MANUFACTURE OF
CHEMICAL DETERGENTS (EX SAR)
G.E.C.O.D.A.

PO Box 682, Damascus
Tel: 754875, 754876
Cable: Abyad Damascus
Telex: GECODA 412694 SY

Chairman: Wafik Makhloof (Director General)

PRINCIPAL ACTIVITIES: Producers and exporters of detergent,
cleansing and bleaching powders
Parent Company: Responsible to the General Establishment for
Chemical Industries
Principal Bankers: Commercial Bank of Syria, Damascus
Industrial Bank, Damascus
Financial Information:

	SP'000
Authorised capital	117,000
Paid-up capital	117,000

Principal Shareholders: State-owned company
Date of Establishment: June 1960
No of Employees: 480

GENERAL CO FOR VEGETABLES & FRUITS

PO Box 5603, Damascus
Tel: 419630, 419639, 419158
Cable: Kodaz
Telex: 411914

Chairman: Dr Chahim Nasser (Director General)

Directors: Ismail Monawer (General Relations Director)

PRINCIPAL ACTIVITIES: Trading in vegetables and fruits,
production and distribution
Branch Offices: 13 branches
Parent Company: Responsible to the Ministry of Supply &
Internal Trade
Principal Bankers: Commercial Bank of Syria

Principal Shareholders: State-owned company
Date of Establishment: 1977
No of Employees: 2,005

GENERAL DIRECTORATE OF THE
DAMASCUS INTERNATIONAL TRADE FAIR

Damascus International Trade Fair

Kouatly Street, Fair Grounds, Damascus
Tel: 229914, 117834, 117049
Cable: Marad
Telex: 411393 Marad Sy

PRINCIPAL ACTIVITIES: Organisation of the annual fair in
Damascus
Parent Company: Responsible to the Ministry of Ecomomy &
Foreign Trade

Principal Shareholders: State-owned organisation

GENERAL EST FOR CEREAL PROCESSING &
TRADE

Sahet Youssef Al-Azmeh, Hilal Al-Ahmar Bldg, Damascus
Tel: 111021, 113201, 113302
Cable: Hobbob Damascus
Telex: 411027 Sy Cereal, 411391

PRINCIPAL ACTIVITIES: Cereal processing, purchasing and
milling grain, import and export of grain (wheat, barley, lentil)
Parent Company: Responsible to the Ministry of Supplies &
Internal Trade
Associated Companies: General Milling Company; General
Bakeries Company

Principal Shareholders: State-owned

GENERAL EST OF CHEMICAL INDUSTRIES
G.E.C.I.

Unichem Bldg, Baramkeh St (opp free zone), PO Box 5447,
Damascus
Tel: 114650, 225214, 228216
Cable: Geci
Telex: 411035 Sy; 419145 Jissi

PRINCIPAL ACTIVITIES: Control and supervision of the works
of related chemical companies listed below:
Parent Company: Responsible to the Ministry of Industry
Subsidiary Companies: Paints & Chemical Products Co; Plastic
Products Co; General Detergents Co; National Co for Rubber
Products; Arab Rubber Plastic & Leather Products Co;
General Tanning Co; Syrian Glass & Porcelain Industries Co;
General Fertilizers Co; Arab Medical Co (Tameco); Arab Co
for Oil & Soap Industries; Shoe Manufacturing Co

Principal Shareholders: State-owned establishment

GENERAL EST OF GEOLOGICAL RESEARCHES & MINERAL RESOURCES

G.E.O.M.I.N.E.R.A.L.

Jade Al-Khatib, PO Box 7645, Damascus
Tel: 455426, 459518, 448501, 450507
Cable: Geomineral
Telex: 411528 GEO SY

Chairman: Dr Ahmad Khaled Al Maleh (Director General)
Directors: Dr Mohamad Mahfoud (Deputy Director General)
Senior Executives: Dr Talal Ballani (Director of Mining Projects), Dr Ghassan Abu Assaleh (Director of Prospecting), Dr Maziad Sharaf (Director of Surveying), Dr Rabah Hussein (Director of Planning), Mamoun Al Kurdi (Director of Finance)

PRINCIPAL ACTIVITIES: Geological research and mineral exploration
Branch Offices: Homs; Aleppo; Lattakia; Deir Azzour; Tartous; Idlib; Soveida; Hama
Parent Company: Responsible to the Ministry of Petroleum & Mineral Resources
Subsidiary Companies: General Co for Phosphates & Mining; General Asphalt Co; General Co for Marble & Gypsum
Principal Bankers: Commercial Bank of Syria

Principal Shareholders: State-owned company
Date of Establishment: 1977
No of Employees: 720

GENERAL FERTILIZERS CO

Kattineh, PO Box 280, Homs
Tel: 23332, 20515, 20535
Cable: Fertilizers Homs
Telex: 441005 Sy Fert

Chairman: Dr Eng Nazir Koussa
Directors: Dr Eng Ammar Makki (Director General)

PRINCIPAL ACTIVITIES: Production of chemicals and fertilisers
Parent Company: Responsible to the General Establishment of Chemical Industries
Principal Bankers: Industrial Bank
Financial Information:

	SP'000
Authorised capital	26,000

Principal Shareholders: State-owned company
Date of Establishment: 1967
No of Employees: 3,600

GENERAL ORGANISATION FOR CEMENT & BUILDING MATERIALS

PO Box 5265, Damascus
Tel: 661257, 666450, 666451
Cable: Milatt
Telex: GOC BM 411369 SY

Directors: Eng Ali-Trabulsi (General Director)

PRINCIPAL ACTIVITIES: Production of portland cement, asbestos pipes and sheets, wall tiles, sanitary ware; responsible for the supervision and operation of all cement factories in the country
Subsidiary/Associated Companies: Tartous Co for Cement & Building Materials; ADRA Co for Cement & Building Materials; The National Co for Cement & Building Materials; The Syrian Co for Cement & Building Materials; Al Rastan Co for Cement & Building Materials; Al Shahba Co for Cement & Building Materials; The Arabian Co for Cement & Building Materials; The Arabian Co for Porcelain & Sanitary Wares; Aleppo Co for Manufacturing Asbestos Cement Products
Principal Bankers: Syrian Industrial Bank

Principal Shareholders: State-owned organisation
Date of Establishment: 1975
No of Employees: 8,100 (incl affiliated companies in the organisation)

GENERAL ORGANISATION FOR FODDER

Port Said St, PO Box 4797, Damascus
Tel: 221689, 221893, 245347
Cable: Alaf
Telex: 411089 Alaf-Sy

Chairman: Eng Omar Kholani (General Director)
Directors: Dr Hasan Alio (Deputy General Director), Dr Mohamad Y Sbinati, Michel Barakat, Ismail Bakher, Kamal Shhaied, Mohsen El Daher, Ahmad Okar, Yousef Al Raies, Kamel Al Ahmed, Zouhair Al Emam

PRINCIPAL ACTIVITIES: Governmental body responsible for import, production, procurement and distribution of animal fodder in the private, public and co-operative sectors
Branch Offices: Throughout Syria
Parent Company: Responsible to the Ministry of Agriculture & Agrarian Reform
Principal Bankers: Commercial Bank of Syria, Branch 6
Financial Information:

	1990 SP'000
Sales turnover	3,196,131
Profits	500,000
Authorised capital	150,000
Paid-up capital	50,000
Total assets	278,596

Principal Shareholders: State-owned organisation
Date of Establishment: 1974

GENERAL ORGANISATION FOR FOOD INDUSTRIES

G.O.F.I.

Rue Fardoss, PO Box 105, Damascus
Tel: 225290/91, 222902, 116694
Cable: Gofi
Telex: 419154 Sy Gofood

PRINCIPAL ACTIVITIES: Production of cotton seed oil, linters, cotton seed cake, soap; also chocolate and biscuits; processing of peanuts, production of beer and alcoholic beverages; canning of fruits and vegetables, production of dehydrated vegetables, and noodles
Parent Company: Responsible to the Ministry of Industry
Subsidiary Companies: Syrian Industrial Co for Vegetable Oils; Hama Vegetable Oils Co; Arab Industrial Co for Soaps & Oils; Lattakia Vegetable Oil Co; Modern Conserves & Agricultural Products Co; Syrian Coastal Co for Conserves & Food Products; Syrian Arab Grape Processing Co; Homs Grape Processing Co; Al Shark Food Products Co; Damascus Food Products Co; Syrian Biscuits & Chocolate Manufacturing Co; Syrian Arab Dairy Products Co; Industrial Co for Dairy Products & Refrigeration; Dehydrated Onions & Vegetables Co; Syrian Arab Peanuts Processing & Marketing Co
Principal Bankers: Commercial of Syria

Principal Shareholders: State-owned organisation

GENERAL ORGANISATION FOR FREE-ZONES

Palestine Street, PO Box 2790, Damascus
Tel: 110951, 113834
Cable: Ozofranche

PRINCIPAL ACTIVITIES: Management and supervision on the industrial and commercial activities of the free zones in Syria: Damascus, Aleppo, Lattakia and Tartous ports, Damascus International Airport, and Adra
Branch Offices: Free Zones of Aleppo, Lattakia Port, Tartous Port, Adra, Damascus, Damascus International Airport
Principal Bankers: Syrian Commercial Bank

Principal Shareholders: State-owned
Date of Establishment: 1970

GENERAL ORGANISATION FOR HIJAZI RAILWAYS

Hedgaz St, PO Box 134, Damascus
Tel: 115815
Cable: Hedgazfer

PRINCIPAL ACTIVITIES: The administration is responsible for running the Syrian railway system. It is also in charge of the railways investment programme
Parent Company: Responsible to the Ministry of Transport

Principal Shareholders: State-owned company

GENERAL ORGANISATION FOR POULTRY

Victoria Bridge, PO Box 5597, Damascus
Tel: 111968, 112876, 117473
Cable: Gop

PRINCIPAL ACTIVITIES: Supervision of existing poultry institutions and execution of new poultry projects
Branch Offices: Branches, farms and connected organisations in Hama; Tartous; Aleppo; Homs; Lattakia; Al-Sweida; Moaret Al-Nooman; Hassake; Deraa; Raqqa and Deir Ez Zor
Parent Company: Responsible to the Ministry of Agriculture & Agrarian Reform
Associated Companies: Sednaya Poultry Establishment, PO Box 4355, Damascus
Principal Bankers: Commercial Bank of Syria; Central Bank of Syria

Principal Shareholders: State-owned organisation

GENERAL ORGANISATION FOR SUGAR

PO Box 429, Homs
Tel: 27600
Cable: Gofs
Telex: Gofs 441006 Sy

PRINCIPAL ACTIVITIES: Development of the sugar industry and derivatives; supervision of the following companies listed below:
Parent Company: Responsible to the Ministry of Industry
Subsidiary/Associated Companies: Homs Sugar Co, Ghab Sugar Co, Adra Sugar Co, National Yeast Co, Thawra Sugar Co, PO Box 45; Thawra Raqqa Sugar Co, Tal Salhab Sugar Co, Der-ez-Zore Sugar Co, Al-Fayhaa' Yeast Plant, Al Shahba Yeast Plant
Principal Bankers: Commercial Bank of Syria; Industrial Bank

Principal Shareholders: State-owned organisation
Date of Establishment: 1975

GENERAL ORGANISATION FOR SYRIAN RAILWAYS (CFS)

PO Box 182, Aleppo
Tel: 213900/2
Cable: Sikkethadid
Telex: 331009 CFS SY

Chairman: Eng Mohammed Ghassan El-Kaddour (Director General)
Directors: Abdel Gafour Khalousy (Director of Finance), Ahmad Mounir Battik (Director of Planning & Statistics), Zouhair Moomar (General Relations Director), Nizar Wafai (Technical Director), Zouhair Mousally (Administration Director), Ihsan Kalidy (Director of International Relations)

PRINCIPAL ACTIVITIES: Railway transport network in Syria
Branch Offices: Aleppo; Damascus; Homs; Hama; Lattakia; Tartous; Deirezzo; Rakka; Hassakeh
Parent Company: Responsible to the Ministry of Transport
Subsidiary Companies: General Company for Railways Construction, Aleppo
Principal Bankers: Commercial Bank of Syria; Central Bank of Syria

Principal Shareholders: State-owned company
Date of Establishment: 1897
No of Employees: 9,330

GENERAL ORGANISATION FOR TEXTILE INDUSTRIES

PO Box 620, Fardoss St, Damascus
Tel: 116200/1, 113802
Cable: Unitex
Telex: 411011

PRINCIPAL ACTIVITIES: Control and planning of the textile industry sector, supervision of textile manufacturing companies listed below:
Parent Company: Responsible to the Ministry of Industry
Subsidiary Companies: United Commercial Industrial Co; Modern Industries Corp; United Arab Industrial Co; Syrian Spinning & Weaving Co; Spinning and Weaving Co; Al-Ahlieh Spinning & Weaving Co; Al-Shahba Spinning & Weaving Co; Homs Spinning, Weaving & Dyeing Co; Aleppo Silk Weaving Co; Hama Spinning Corp; Synthetic Crimping & Socks Corp; Shark Underwear Corp; Arab Underwear Corp

Principal Shareholders: State-owned organisation

GENERAL ORGANISATION FOR THE EXECUTION OF TOURISTIC PROJECTS

Abbasieh Bldg, Damascus
Tel: 119685, 221176

PRINCIPAL ACTIVITIES: Promotion of the tourist industry in Syria
Branch Offices: Homs; Aleppo; Lattakia
Parent Company: Responsible to the Ministry of Tourism
Principal Bankers: Central Bank of Syria

Principal Shareholders: State-owned organisation

GENERAL ORGANISATION FOR THE GHAB EXPLOITATION

Al-Sakyabiyyeh, Hama

PRINCIPAL ACTIVITIES: Agricultural development in the Ghab area
Branch Offices: Damascus, tel 110802
Parent Company: Responsible to the Ministry of Agriculture & Agrarian Reform

Principal Shareholders: State-owned company

GENERAL ORGANISATION FOR TOBACCO

Salhieh St, PO Box 616, Damascus
Tel: 211282
Cable: MONOTAB
Telex: 411301 Sytomo

Chairman: Mohamed Ahmed Makhlouf

PRINCIPAL ACTIVITIES: Processing and export of the tobacco leaf and manufacture of cigarettes; import of virginian and burley tobacco and basic products related to cigarette manufacture
Parent Company: Responsible to the Ministry of Economy & Foreign Trade
Principal Bankers: Commercial Bank of Syria

Principal Shareholders: State-owned organisation
Date of Establishment: 1935
No of Employees: 9,264

GENERAL ORGANISATION FOR TRADE & DISTRIBUTION

PO Box 15, Damascus
Tel: 210396/7, 210949
Cable: Goutadim
Telex: 411355 Getra

Chairman: Mohamed Rateb Kweider

Directors: Noheil Khaldi (Manager of Duty Free Shops), Mohamed Younes (Asst General Manager/Admin & Legal Dept Manager)

PRINCIPAL ACTIVITIES: Imports: alcoholic drinks, cosmetics, general merchandise, domestic electrical appliances, office equipment, textiles, agricultural products, private arms and amunition, photographic equipment etc; exports: tobacco, crude oils, artisan products, dry batteries

Principal Agencies: Camus; Dewars; Capucci; Gillette; Olivetti; Hungarotex; Ferunion; Browning; Agfa Gevaert
Branch Offices: Aleppo; Lattakia
Parent Company: Responsible to the Ministry of Economy & Foreign Trade
Principal Bankers: Commercial Bank of Syria, Damascus
Financial Information:

	US$'000
Sales turnover	10/20,000
Profits	20%

Principal Shareholders: State-owned organisation
Date of Establishment: 1897 as Khalil Fattal & Fils, nationalised in 1963
No of Employees: 300

GENERAL PUBLIC CONSUMPTION ORGANISATION

Harika, PO Box 2552, Damascus
Tel: 226770, 216380
Cable: Maski
Telex: 419167 Maski SY

PRINCIPAL ACTIVITIES: Responsible for the wholesale and distribution of foodstuffs to local markets. Imports directly from abroad to meet consumption needs. In charge of meat trade, import and export of live sheep
Branch Offices: 12 branches in the main Syrian cities
Parent Company: Responsible to the Ministry of Supply & Internal Trade
Subsidiary Companies: Retail Co & General Co of Shoes & Leather Products
Principal Bankers: Commercial Bank of Syria

Principal Shareholders: State-owned
Date of Establishment: 1966
No of Employees: 180 in the Central Office & 1250 in the branches

GENERAL SHOES CO (EX-BATA)

Salhieh St, PO Box 496, Damascus
Tel: 452946, 450355, 452826

PRINCIPAL ACTIVITIES: Marketing and distribution of shoes
Parent Company: Responsible to the Ministry of Supply & Internal Trade

Principal Shareholders: State-owned company

GENERAL TANNING CO

Societe Generale de Tannage

Quartier Zablantani, PO Box 2019, Damascus
Tel: 458498, 457840, 458255
Cable: Satadas
Telex: 419145 Satadas SY

PRINCIPAL ACTIVITIES: Skin tanning and leather distribution
Parent Company: Responsible to the General Establishment of Chemical Industries

Principal Shareholders: State-owned company

GENERAL TARTOUS PORT CO

PO Box 86, Tartous
Tel: 20562, 20566
Cable: Tartous-Syria
Telex: 470004

Chairman: Ali Mahmoud Omran (Director General)

PRINCIPAL ACTIVITIES: Services in shipping, stevedoring, containers, ro-ro, warehousing of goods, import/export (ships are receive at draughts up to 39 feet)
Parent Company: Responsible to the Ministry of Transport
Principal Bankers: Syrian Commercial Bank

Principal Shareholders: State-owned company
Date of Establishment: 1969
No of Employees: 3,000

GHAB SUGAR COMPANY

PO Box 90, Jisr-El-Shoughour, Idleb
Tel: 11502
Cable: Suc Ghab

PRINCIPAL ACTIVITIES: Sugar processing and refining
Parent Company: Responsible to the General Organisation for Sugar

Principal Shareholders: State-owned company

HAMA SPINNING CORPORATION

Homs Rd, PO Box 11, Hama
Tel: 21744

PRINCIPAL ACTIVITIES: Spinning and weaving
Parent Company: Responsible to the General Organisation of Textile Industries

Principal Shareholders: State-owned company

HAMA VEGETABLE OILS CO

El-Mahatta Rd, PO Box 2702, Hama
Tel: 23492

PRINCIPAL ACTIVITIES: Production of vegetable oils
Parent Company: Responsible to the General Organisation of Food Industries

Principal Shareholders: State-owned company

HICHAM H JAFFAN

See JAFFAN, HICHAM H,

HOMS DAIRY PRODUCTS & REFRIGERATION CO

Hama Rd, PO Box 406, Homs
Tel: 12901, 25902
Cable: ALBAN Homs

PRINCIPAL ACTIVITIES: Production of dairy products and cold storage
Parent Company: Responsible to the General Organisation for Food Industries

Principal Shareholders: State-owned company

HOMS GRAPE PROCESSING CO

Zeidal, PO Box 294, Homs
Tel: 20970

PRINCIPAL ACTIVITIES: Processing of grapes
Parent Company: Responsible to the General Organisation for Food Industries

Principal Shareholders: State-owned company

HOMS PETROLEUM REFINERY CO

PO Box 352, Homs
Tel: 22771. 22767
Cable: Homs Refinery
Telex: 41004

Chairman: Eng A K Tarabishi
Directors: Eng T Zaina, Eng O Othman, Eng M Saadat, G Slaibi, A H Mohrat, R Salama, Eng T Quatrib, G Ubaid
Senior Executives: F Rostom, Eng K Shawysh, Eng W Sibaii, Eng A R Samman, W Hamoud, T Salama, A W Birini

PRINCIPAL ACTIVITIES: Petroleum refining

Parent Company: Syrian Petroleum Company
Principal Bankers: Commercial Bank of Syria, Homs

Principal Shareholders: State-owned company
Date of Establishment: 1959
No of Employees: 4,500

HOMS SPINNING WEAVING & DYEING CO

Mimas St, PO Box 365, Homs
Tel: 30701/3
Cable: Massabegh
Telex: 441002 SY

Chairman: Eng Salim Durbass
Directors: Eng R Haddad (Production Director), A R A Kareem
(Technical Director), A S Masud (Finance Director), K Ashee
(Commercial Director)

PRINCIPAL ACTIVITIES: Manufacture of cotton yarn and all
kinds of cotton fabrics
Parent Company: Responsible to the General Organisation of
Textile Industries
Principal Bankers: Commercial Bank of Syria, Homs
Financial Information:

	1990
	SP'000
Sales turnover	205,000
Profit	73,000
Authorised capital	43,500
Paid-up capital	33,000
Total assets	33,500

Principal Shareholders: State-owned company
Date of Establishment: 1946
No of Employees: 860

HOMS SUGAR COMPANY

PO Box 266, Homs
Tel: 21260, 21161
Cable: Sapic
Telex: 41006 Gofs Sapic

PRINCIPAL ACTIVITIES: Sugar processing and refining;
production of vegetable oils, yeast soaps
Parent Company: Responsible to the General Organisation for
Sugar
Principal Bankers: Industrial Bank of Syria

Principal Shareholders: State-owned company
No of Employees: 1,000

HOMSY, M Z, EST

PO Box 2476, Damascus
Tel: 235886
Cable: Seturep

Chairman: Mme Widad Homsy
Directors: M Z Homsy
Senior Executives: Dr M Radwan Homsy

PRINCIPAL ACTIVITIES: Manufacture of plastic products;
industrial studies, execution and representation
Associated Companies: Meico-Plastics, PO Box 75, Dokki,
Cairo, Egypt
Principal Bankers: Commercial Bank of Syria

Principal Shareholders: Mme Widad Homsy; Mohamad Zouheir
Homsy
Date of Establishment: 1965

HOTEL MERIDIEN DAMASCUS

Route de Beyrouth, PO Box 5531, Damascus
Tel: 223038, 718730
Cable: Homer Damas
Telex: 411379

PRINCIPAL ACTIVITIES: Hotel management and operation
Branch Offices: Hotels Meridien in Palmyra and Lattakia (Syria)
Parent Company: Part of Ste des Hotels Meridien (Air France)

INDUSTRIAL DEVELOPMENT BANK

29th May St, PO Box 2359, Damascus
Tel: 227100/2, 452500
Cable: Sinasory

PRINCIPAL ACTIVITIES: Finance for industry in the public
private sectors and general banking operations

Principal Shareholders: (100%) state-owned

INDUSTRIAL EST OF DEFENCE

PO Box 2330, Damascus
Tel: 225151, 225152, 119810, 228725, 451536
Cable: Etinde Damascus
Telex: 411029 Etinde Sy

PRINCIPAL ACTIVITIES: Import of detergents, chemical
products, industrial machinery, raw materials. Export and
production of water and electrical meters and gauges,
transformers, dry batteries, gas cylinders
Parent Company: Responsible to the Ministry of Defence

INDUSTRIAL TESTING & RESEARCH CENTER

PO Box 845, Damascus
Tel: 62438
Cable: Intest

Chairman: The Minister of Industry
Directors: Representatives from Ministry of Industry, Ministry of
Economy, Ministry of Planning, Chamber of Commerce,
Chambers of Industry, Damascus University

PRINCIPAL ACTIVITIES: Analysis and testing: standardisation;
documentation; and research
Parent Company: Responsible to the Ministry of Industry

Principal Shareholders: State-owned organisation

IRFAN JARJOUR

See JARJOUR, IRFAN,

JAFFAN, HICHAM H,

PO Box 618, Damascus
Tel: 210466, 226088
Cable: Jaffan
Telex: 411556 Jaffan

Chairman: Hicham Jaffan
Directors: Hayssam Jaffan, Tarif Jaffan

PRINCIPAL ACTIVITIES: Commission agents and
representatives dealing in all kinds of productive and packing
machines, raw and wrapping materials for the manufacturing
of chocolate, biscuit, wafers, sweets, chewing gum, soap
detergent, macaroni and snacks
Principal Agencies: Robert Bosch, W Germany; Cerestar Export,
Belgium; Loders Croklaan BV, Holland; Gerkens Cacao,
Holland; Acma, Italy; Cellografica Gerosa, Italy
Branch Offices: Beirut: PO Box 11-4625; Amman: PO Box 6065
Principal Bankers: Commercial Bank of Syria

Principal Shareholders: Hicham Jaffan; Hayssam Jaffan and
Tarif Jaffan
Date of Establishment: 1945

JALLAD, EZZAT M, & FILS

Aleppo St, Al Qaboun, PO Box 23, Damascus
Tel: 550321, 555012

PRINCIPAL ACTIVITIES: Import and distribution of earth moving
equipment, heavy machinery, and motor vehicles
Principal Agencies: Caterpillar, John Deere
Branch Offices: Jordan; Syria (branches in Lattakia, Aleppo)
Parent Company: Head office in Lebanon

JARJOUR, IRFAN,

PO Box 886, Damascus
Tel: 446453
Cable: Jarjouraf Damascus

Chairman: Eng Irfan Jarjour (also owner)

PRINCIPAL ACTIVITIES: Contracting and building; import of
building materials; inviting foreign suppliers to participate in
local tenders
Principal Agencies: Species, Marseille, Cedex 4, France;
Adshead Ratcliffe Int Ltd, Derby, UK
Principal Bankers: Commercial Bank of Syria

KARKOUR & KALLAS

PO Box 764, Immeuble Tibi, 2125 rue Bal Kis, Damascus

Chairman: Georges Karbour (also Partner)

PRINCIPAL ACTIVITIES: Manufacture of electrical, industrial,
agricultural equipment and machinery

KARNAK TOURIST & TRANSPORT CO

PO Box 5302, Damascus
Tel: 111755, 111756, 114116
Cable: Karnak
Telex: 411382 Sy

Chairman: Hasan Abdul Rahman

PRINCIPAL ACTIVITIES: Transport and tourism
Branch Offices: Homs: Walid St; Aleppo: Baron St; Lattakia:
Hurriya St; Head Office: 4 Bahsa, Damascus
Principal Bankers: Commercial Bank of Syria

Principal Shareholders: State-owned
Date of Establishment: 1952
No of Employees: 450

KRAYEM INDUSTRIAL TRADING EST

Bab Sharki, Ben Asaker St, PO Box 558, Damascus
Tel: 114634, 116021/714634
Cable: Freshup
Telex: 419150; 411921 KRAYEM IND SY

Chairman: Rateb Krayem (also Owner)
Directors: Zouheir Krayem

PRINCIPAL ACTIVITIES: Beverage bottling plants, plastic
production, mould-making
Branch Offices: Technical Bottling Factory, Amman/Jordan,
Mahatta St; Krayem Industrial Trading Est, Beirut/Lebanon,
PO Box 6947
Subsidiary Companies: Syrian Plastic Products Est, Damascus;
Automatic Bottling Est, Sweda; Modern Mechanic & Plastic
Factory, Damascus; ELAN Lebanese Shoes Production Co,
Mukalles, Beirut
Principal Bankers: Syrian Commercial Bank, Damascus;
Lebanese Credit-Bank, Beirut; Bank Handlowy for the Middle
East SAL

Date of Establishment: 1947
No of Employees: 268

LAHOUD ENGINEERING CO LTD

71 Ben Barka St, PO Box 3555, Damascus
Tel: 334300, 337075
Telex: 411087

PRINCIPAL ACTIVITIES: Building and civil engineering
contractors

LATTAKIA PORT COMPANY

PO Box 220, Lattakia
Tel: 11900
Cable: Latakiaport
Telex: 551008 St Lapoco

Chairman: Medhat Abu Al Shamlat
Directors: Nadim Mounzalji (Deputy General Manager)

PRINCIPAL ACTIVITIES: Port authority for Lattakia
Parent Company: Responsible to the Ministry of Transport
Principal Bankers: Commercial Bank of Syria; Central Bank of
Syria

Principal Shareholders: State-owned company
Date of Establishment: 1950
No of Employees: 3,000

M Z HOMSY EST

See HOMSY, M Z, EST

MECATTAF & CO

PO Box 531, Ghassan St, Harika, Damascus
Tel: 110136/7
Cable: Mecade
Telex: 411243 Sy

PRINCIPAL ACTIVITIES: Import and distribution of household
goods, electrical appliances, pharmaceuticals, cosmetics and
toiletries
Principal Agencies: Hoover Ltd, UK; Yardley Ltd, UK; Wilkinson
Sword Ltd, UK; Cussons Int'l Ltd, UK
Branch Offices: Branch in Aleppo, Tel 33970
Subsidiary/Associated Companies: Ant Mecattaf & Fils, PO Box
5833, Beirut, Lebanon; Ant Mecattaf & Fils, PO Box 342,
Damascus, Syria; Mecattaf Trading Co SAL, PO Box 648,
Beirut, Lebanon; Mecattaf Pharmaceutical Co, PO Box 648,
Beirut, Lebanon
Principal Bankers: Commercial Bank of Syria

MERIDIEN IBN HANI HOTEL

PO Box 473, Lattakia
Tel: 29000
Telex: 51064

PRINCIPAL ACTIVITIES: Hotel business

METALLIC CONSTRUCTION & MECHANICAL INDUSTRIES CO

PO Box 1149, Damascus
Tel: 113781, 113788
Cable: Metalco Damascus

PRINCIPAL ACTIVITIES: Production of steam boilers, fuel
tanks, hangars and sheds, trailers, dumpers, tanks and
cisterns for fuel transport, miscellaneous metal constructions
Branch Offices: Light Metals Factory, Qabun, Damascus, Tel
457191
Parent Company: Responsible to the General Establishment for
Engineering Industries

Principal Shareholders: State-owned company

MIDDLE EAST TRADE EST

PO Box 4316, Damascus
Tel: 452631, 446043, 236888
Cable: Sarawas
Telex: 419176 Sarwas SY

President: Said A K Rawas
Directors: Hasan Mardini (Managing Director)
Senior Executives: Abdul Karim Rawas (Finance Director), Wafa
Saadeh (Company Secretary)

PRINCIPAL ACTIVITIES: Agents and general trading, import of
medical equipment and hospital supplies, chemicals, fodder,
fertilisers, auto parts; export of phosphate, cotton towels, bed
covers, and clothing, and cereals ·
Principal Agencies: Heineken Brouwerijen BV; First
International Electronic Calculators, Japan; Fresenius AG,
Biotronik GmbH, Deknatel, W Germany; Tradingpor, Portugal;
Richco Grain, Switzerland; Isis, Italy; Silfe, Italy; Map, Italy;
Frabrica de Plasticos, Portugal
Branch Offices: Beirut; Amman; Riyadh; Cyprus
Principal Bankers: Commercial Bank of Syria, Syria Syrian
Lebanese Commercial Bank, Lebanon

Financial Information:

	1988/89 US$'000
Sales turnover	1,500

Principal Shareholders: Said A K Rawas
Date of Establishment: 1962 (Saudi Arabia); 1977 (Syria and Lebanon)
No of Employees: 38

MODERN CONSERVES & AGRICULTURAL INDUSTRIES CO

PO Box 345, Baghdad St, Damascus
Tel: 440384
Cable: Conserve

PRINCIPAL ACTIVITIES: Manufacture of foodstuffs, processing of fruits and vegetables
Parent Company: Responsible to the General Organisation for Food Industries

Principal Shareholders: State-owned company

MODERN INDUSTRIES CORP

Al-Ghouta Al-Sharkiyeh, PO Box 2701, Damascus
Tel: 225835, 222227, 113615
Cable: HADICE
Telex: 411127

Chairman: Dr Engineer Fawaz Al-Lahham (General Manager)

PRINCIPAL ACTIVITIES: Wool spinning and weaving, wollen, acrylic and blended yarns and fabrics manufacture, fabric dyeing
Parent Company: Responsible to the General Organisation of Textile Industries
Principal Bankers: Commercial Bank of Syria
Financial Information:

	SP'000
Sales turnover	100,000
Authorised capital	50,000

Principal Shareholders: State-owned company
No of Employees: 1,000

MODERN PLASTIC INDUSTRIES & PRINTING CO

Elbeik Co

PO Box 1642, Aleppo 6000
Tel: Office 241425, Factory 441525
Cable: Newplast ELBEIK
Telex: 331200 SYAHI SY

Chairman: Elbeik M Haitham

PRINCIPAL ACTIVITIES: Manufacture of polypropylene and polyethylene raw materials into flat and tubal sheets
Branch Offices: Abarah St Alepo
Subsidiary Companies: Brothers Massood, Zikak Al Mahkame, Damascus, Syria; Gazi Kawa, Jabel El Hossain, Amman, Jordan
Principal Bankers: Commercial Bank of Syria
Financial Information:

	US$'000
Profits	170
Authorised capital	800
Paid-up capital	600

Date of Establishment: 1972

MOUNIR HINEDI

PO Box 441, Aleppo
Tel: 13846, 23447
Cable: Motadi

Directors: Mounir Hinedi

PRINCIPAL ACTIVITIES: Marketing of oil and oil products

Principal Agencies: Ford Motor Co; Ransomes Sims & Jefferies, UK
Principal Bankers: Syrian Commercial Bank; Banque pour le Developpement des Echanges Internationaux

NABKI & CHARABATI

PO Box 122, Lattakia
Tel: 25025, 24474
Cable: Naze
Telex: 51014 Naze Sy

Chairman: David W Nabki
Directors: Joseph A Charabati

PRINCIPAL ACTIVITIES: Inland transportation, international transport, shipping agent, specialized in heavy lift transport
Principal Agencies: Jordan, Iraq, Saudi Arabia, all Arabian Gulf countries
Branch Offices: Tartous, Damascus, Aleppo
Principal Bankers: Commercial Bank of Syria; Fidelity Bank, London; Societe Bancaire Arabe, Paris

NASSARCO TRADE & AGENCIES

PO Box 2190, Damascus
Tel: 226433, 217899
Cable: Nassarco
Telex: 411419 RASHID SY

President: Atieh Nassar

PRINCIPAL ACTIVITIES: Import of cereals and grain, foodstuffs, animal feeds, chemicals and pharmaceuticals, agricultural machinery and implements
Branch Offices: Damascus; Homs; Aleppo

Date of Establishment: 1973

NATIONAL CEMENT & BUILDING MATERIALS CO

PO Box 309, Drummar, Damascus
Tel: 111820, 111586
Cable: Cimento

PRINCIPAL ACTIVITIES: Manufacture of cement, building materials (asbestos and cement), sheets and pipes, porcelain, sanitary ware, etc
Branch Offices: PO Box 733, Aleppo
Parent Company: Responsible to the General Organisation of Cement

Principal Shareholders: State-owned company

NATIONAL FILM ORGANIZATION

Rawda, Takriti St, Damascus
Tel: 334200
Cable: Filmor
Telex: 411944 Sy

PRINCIPAL ACTIVITIES: Production of feature films, documentary films, technical services in cinematic fields. Imports feature films, unexposed films, cine equipment, film industry accessories
Principal Bankers: Commercial Bank of Syria

Principal Shareholders: State owned organisation
Date of Establishment: 1963
No of Employees: 250

NATIONAL RUBBER PRODUCTS CO

PO Box 795, Tarek Bin Zayed St, Damascus
Tel: 11902, 222390
Cable: Alroco

PRINCIPAL ACTIVITIES: Production of rubber and plastic shoes, bicycle tyres, mattresses, neolite plates. Imports: natural rubber, synthetic rubber, plastic granules, chemicals

Parent Company: Responsible to the General Establishment of Chemical Inudstries

Principal Shareholders: State-owned company

OMAYAD HOTEL

4 Brazil St, Damascus
Tel: 217700/1/2, 235500/1/2/3
Cable: Omatel Damascus
Telex: 411206 Sy Omatel, 411600 Sy Omayad
Telefax: 217703

Chairman: H Salloum
Directors: N Kassouf, A Jabali

PRINCIPAL ACTIVITIES: Hotel business and catering
Parent Company: Riviera Hotel, Beirut
Principal Bankers: Commercial Bank of Syria
Financial Information:

	1990
	SP'000
Sales turnover	110,000
Profits	5,000
Authorised capital	10,000
Paid-up capital	10,000
Total assets	30,000

Principal Shareholders: H Salloum (100%)
Date of Establishment: 1953
No of Employees: 100

PETROLEUM RESEARCH CENTRE

Mutanabbi St, Damascus
Tel: 113613

PRINCIPAL ACTIVITIES: Petroleum research
Parent Company: Responsible to the Ministry of Petroleum & Mineral Resources

Principal Shareholders: State-owned company

PLASTIC PRODUCTS CO

Al Bounouk Street, PO Box 600 & PO Box 712, Aleppo
Tel: 38128/9, 33346 (Factory)
Cable: Plastics
Telex: 331207 Veralp SY

Chairman: Eng Mohamed Rashad Jatty (Director General)

PRINCIPAL ACTIVITIES: Manufacture of plastic products, household goods, office supplies, pipes, etc
Parent Company: Responsible to the General Establishment of Chemical Industries
Principal Bankers: Commercial Bank of Syria

Principal Shareholders: State-owned company
Date of Establishment: 1958
No of Employees: 300

POPULAR CREDIT BANK

Darwishieh, Fardoss Street, PO Box 2841, Damascus
Tel: 218376, 227604, 215752
Cable: Amchabi

Chairman: Hassan Al Houjayri
Directors: Hisham Al Awad (Deputy Chairman)

PRINCIPAL ACTIVITIES: Savings certificates, popular credit, savings, general banking operatins, public services
Branch Offices: 43 branches throughout Syria
Financial Information:

	1988
	SP'000
Authorised capital	25,000
Paid-up capital	25,000

Principal Shareholders: State-owned bank
Date of Establishment: 1967
No of Employees: 770

PUBLIC ELECTRICITY EST

Barada River Bank, PO Box 3386, Damascus
Tel: 223086, 227155
Cable: SYRLEC Damascus
Telex: 411056 SYRLEC SY

PRINCIPAL ACTIVITIES: Electricity generation and transmission
Parent Company: Responsible to the Ministry of Electricity
Subsidiary/Associated Companies: Directorate of Electricity Southern Area. Damascus; Directorate of Electricity Middle Area, Homs; Directorate of Electricity Northern Area, Aleppo; Directorate of Electricity, Lattakia

Principal Shareholders: State-owned company

PUBLIC POSTS EST

Saadallah Jabri St, Damascus
Tel: 112200
Cable: Gentel Damas
Telex: 411015 Gentel

PRINCIPAL ACTIVITIES: Supervision and operation of the communications and postal system
Parent Company: Responsible to the Ministry of Communications

Principal Shareholders: State-owned establishment

PUBLIC TELECOMMUNICATIONS EST

Saad'Alla Jabri St, Damascus
Tel: 112200, 119000
Cable: Gentel Damascus
Telex: 411015 Gentel Sy; 419174 Intrel Sy

Chairman: Eng Makram Obeid

PRINCIPAL ACTIVITIES: Providing local, regional and international telecommunications services and facilities
Branch Offices: Damascus; Aleppo; Homs; Hama; Lattakia; Tartous; Deraa; Sweda; Deir Ez-Zor; Rakka; Hassakeh; Idleb
Parent Company: Responsible to the Ministry of Communications
Principal Bankers: Central Bank of Syria; Commercial Bank of Syria
Financial Information:

	SP'000
Authorised capital	300,000
Paid-up capital	300,000

Principal Shareholders: State-owned organisation
Date of Establishment: July 10th, 1975
No of Employees: 11,653

PUBLIC TRANSPORT CO

PO Box 1219, Aleppo

PRINCIPAL ACTIVITIES: Passenger transport
Parent Company: Responsible to the Ministry of Transport

Principal Shareholders: State-owned company

QASSIOUN COMPANY

PO Box 5293, Damascus
Tel: 880056, 880039, 881256
Telex: 411217 Costra

Directors: Eng Mustafa Arratt (Director General)
Senior Executives: Eng Philip Abu Tara (Deputy Director General), Eng Farid Al Sabah (Deputy Director General), Abdulla Al Ahmar (Deputy Director General)

PRINCIPAL ACTIVITIES: Building and civil engineering contractors, highways, bridges, grain silo, specialised concrete work, concrete piles and foundations
Branch Offices: Lattakia; Homs; Dara; Aleppo
Parent Company: Responsible to the Ministry of Construction & Building

SYRIA

Financial Information:

	1990 US$'000
Sales turnover	35,000

Principal Shareholders: State-owned
Date of Establishment: 1987
No of Employees: 12,000

RAFIA PLAST

Omar Zouhair Hamo, PO Box 1663, Aleppo
Tel: 44309 (Office), 42105, 20728 (Factory)
Cable: Rafiaplast Aleppo

President: Omar Zouhair Hamo (also Director General)
Directors: Merwan Hamo

PRINCIPAL ACTIVITIES: Production of polythene film bags
Principal Bankers: Commercial Bank of Syria

No of Employees: 70

RAWAS & DABIAN CO

PO Box 693, Rue Rami, Damascus

Chairman: Mohamed Salim Rawas (also Partner)

PRINCIPAL ACTIVITIES: Manufacture of electrical household
  appliances and electric equipment

REAL ESTATE BANK

Al-Furat St, PO Box 2337, Damascus
Tel: 218602, 218603, 211186
Cable: Mudiritakari
Telex: 419171 Rebank Sy

Chairman: Mohammad Ahmed Makhlouf (General Manager)
Directors: Mohammed Majed Saadi (Vice Chairman & Deputy
  General Manager), Fayek Al-Noury, Isam Irabi, Hassan Safadi
  (Finance Director), Salim Akkad (Personnel Director), M Said
  Baghdadi, Tarek Kanawati

PRINCIPAL ACTIVITIES: Banking services; financing for
  construction projects, granting loans to cooperative housing
  associations, public & private sectors, and individuals for the
  building and of houses, hotels, hospitals, schools,
  restaurants, commercial and industrial premises
Branch Offices: Damascus (2 branches); Homs; Lattakia;
  Deirezzor; Aleppo; Hama; Tartous; Swaida; Deraa; Idleb;
  Hasakeh; Rakka
Financial Information:

	1989/90 SP'000
Profits	118,608
Authorised capital	515,000
Paid-up capital	515,000

Principal Shareholders: State-owned bank
Date of Establishment: 1966
No of Employees: 680

SABA & CO

Adib Khair Bldg, Fardos St, PO Box 460, Damascus
Tel: 215990, 226280
Cable: Sabaco
Telex: 419149

PRINCIPAL ACTIVITIES: Public accountants and tax
  consultants; industrial property registration
Parent Company: Saba & Co, PO Box 961, Beirut, Lebanon
Principal Bankers: Commercial Bank of Syria

Date of Establishment: 1926

SALAH BIZRI ENGINEERING CO
SABICO

PO Box 351, Damascus
Tel: 117043, 333877
Cable: Sabico Damas
Telex: 411095 Sumert SY

Chairman: Salah Bizri (also General Manager)
Directors: K S El-Bizri (Data Processing)
Senior Executives: Ali El Bizri

PRINCIPAL ACTIVITIES: Industrial supplies; contracting;
  electronic data processing; manufacturers' representatives
Branch Offices: Aleppo: PO Box 617, Syria, Lattakia: PO Box
  75, Syria
Principal Bankers: Syrian Commercial Bank

Principal Shareholders: Salah Bizri (50%), Dr K S El-Bizri (25%),
  Ali Bizri (25%)
Date of Establishment: 1954

SEA TRANSPORT AGENCY

PO Box 1153, Lattakia
Tel: 33964, 31929
Cable: Seatrans
Telex: 451044 Seatra

Directors: Saleem Jerjos Obeid

PRINCIPAL ACTIVITIES: Shipping brokerage, shipowners,
  clearing and forwarding
Principal Bankers: Commercial Bank of Syria

Principal Shareholders: John & Saleem Obeid
Date of Establishment: 1974

SHARK UNDERWEAR CORPORATION

Bab Sharky, Jaramana Rd, PO Box 1100, Damascus
Tel: 113763, 112448
Cable: Tricot

PRINCIPAL ACTIVITIES: Manufacture of clothing and
  underwear
Parent Company: Responsible to the General Organisation of
  Textile Industries

Principal Shareholders: State-owned company

SHIPPING AGENCIES CO
SHIPCO

PO Box 28, Lattakia
Tel: 1163, 2263
Cable: Shipco

PRINCIPAL ACTIVITIES: Shipping agents, clearing and
  forwarding
Principal Agencies: DSR Lines; United Arab Maritime Company,
  Alexandria; Baltic Steamship Co, Ismael, Black Sea
  Steamship Co, Odessa; Caspain Steamship Co; Manhart
  Hungarian Lines, Budapest
Branch Offices: PO Box 3, Tartous, Tel 21541, Cable Shipco

SOUAYA GARGOUR & CO

See GARGOUR, SOUAYA, & CO

SPINNING & WEAVING CO

PO Box 1167, Qabun, Damascus
Tel: 458501
Cable: Filages
Telex: 419129 Sparco

PRINCIPAL ACTIVITIES: Manufacturers of cotton yarn,
  synthetic yarn, and various cotton fabrics
Branch Offices: Sales branches in Aleppo (Tidal Rd) and
  Kamichli (Mouzha St)

Parent Company: Responsible to the General Organisation of Textile Industries

Principal Shareholders: State-owned company

SUFIAN M AZM
See AZM, SUFIAN M,

SYNTHETIC YARN CRIMPING & SOCKS CORP
SYCCONYL
Ghouta, PO Box 1275, Damascus
Tel: 225210
Cable: Sycconyl

PRINCIPAL ACTIVITIES: Manufacture of synthetic yarns and socks
Parent Company: Responsible to the General Organisation of Textile Industries

Principal Shareholders: State-owned company

SYRIAN ARAB AIRLINES
SYRIANAIR
PO Box 878, Damascus
Tel: 455600/1, 223434

PRINCIPAL ACTIVITIES: Passengers and cargo services
Branch Offices: 62 Piccadilly, London, W1, UK; 1 rue Auber Paris 9, France ; 2 Maximillianplatz 12A, 8 Munich, Germany; 13 Via Barberihi, Rome, Italy; United Arab Emirates; Egypt; Qatar; Iraq; Yemen; Iran; Kuwait; Eastern Europe; India

SYRIAN ARAB BUILDING CO
PO Box 797, Aleppo
Tel: 227267, 227268
Cable: Tamir
Telex: 331022 Tamir Sy

Director General: Eng Ahmed Haj Mousa
Directors: Kamel Shahid (Deputy Director)
Heads of Departments: Abdul Rasoul Nayef (Finance), Sate Barmada (Purchasing), Mustafa Al Shehne (Production), Eng Nabil Mansoury (Technical), Usama Labanieh (Administration)

PRINCIPAL ACTIVITIES: Construction and supply of building materials for hospitals, schools, universities, warehouses, residential and housing units
Branch Offices: Damascus; Tartous; Rakka; Idleb; Lattakia
Principal Bankers: Commercial Bank of Syria, Aleppo

Date of Establishment: 28-5-1967
No of Employees: 8,500

SYRIAN ARAB CO FOR ELECTRONIC INDUSTRIES
SYRONICS
Kaboun, PO Box 951, Damascus
Tel: 457404, 457309
Cable: Syronics, Damascus
Telex: 411052 Sacei Sy

Chairman: Eng Z Zabibi

PRINCIPAL ACTIVITIES: Production of CTV sets, LB & CB switch boards, printed circuits, telephone sets, Styropor packing material
Branch Offices: Aleppo
Parent Company: Responsible to the General Establishment for Engineering Industries
Principal Bankers: Commercial Bank of Syria

Principal Shareholders: State-owned organisation
Date of Establishment: 1960
No of Employees: 1,000 approx

SYRIAN ARAB CO FOR HOTELS & TOURISM
PO Box 5549, Damascus
Tel: 666286
Cable: SYRACOT
Telex: 412904 SYACOT SY

Directors: Mahmoud Dannoura (General Manager)

PRINCIPAL ACTIVITIES: Financing and management of hotels and tourist complexes
Branch Offices: Homs & Maalousa
Principal Bankers: Commercial Bank of Syria

Principal Shareholders: Ministry of Tourism, Syria; Arab Investment Co, Riyadh; Kuwait Real Estate Investment, Kuwait; Arab Libyan Co for Foreign Investments, Tripoli; Gefinor Investment SA, Genera
Date of Establishment: 1977

SYRIAN ARAB CO FOR IRRIGATION CONSTRUCTIONS
PO Box 9, Hama
Tel: 20975
Cable: SARICO
Telex: 31034 SY SARICO

Chairman: Abd El Razzak Naem (Director General)

PRINCIPAL ACTIVITIES: Civil engineering contractors for irrigation constructions
Parent Company: Responsible to the Ministry of Public Works & Water Resources

Principal Shareholders: State-owned company
Date of Establishment: 1967
No of Employees: Approx 3,000

SYRIAN ARAB CO FOR TOURISTIC ESTABLISHMENTS
Societe Arabe Syrienne des Etablissements Touristiques
Mayssaloun Street, Cham Place Hotel, PO Box 7265, Damascus
Tel: 232300, 232320
Cable: SYRITEL
Telex: Syrtel 411966 Sy

Chairman: Dr Osmane Aidi
Directors: Adel Al Saady, Youssif Kousseiri, Adam Moukhallalati, Fouad Hammami, Eng Mourhaf Sabouni, Eng Nizar Al Assad
Senior Executives: Dr Joseph Nseir (General Manager)

PRINCIPAL ACTIVITIES: Promotion and development of touristic projects in Syria
Subsidiary Companies: Al Cham Co for Hotels & Tourism; Lattakia Co for Hotels & Tourism; Homs Co for Hotels & Tourism
Principal Bankers: Commercial Bank of Syria; Banque Paribas; Banque de la Mediterrannee; Societe Bancaire

Principal Shareholders: 25% Ministry of Tourism; 75% private shareholders
Date of Establishment: 1977
No of Employees: 200

SYRIAN ARAB DAIRY PRODUCTS CO
PO Box 182, Bab Sharki St, Damascus
Tel: 435669, 435239
Cable: Alban, Damascus

PRINCIPAL ACTIVITIES: Producers of sterilised milk, cheese, butter, etc, importers of butter oil, powdered milk, milk bottles and machines
Parent Company: Responsible to the General Organisation of Food Industries

SYRIA

Principal Shareholders: State-owned company
Date of Establishment: 1968
No of Employees: 175

SYRIAN ARAB GRAPE PROCESSING CO

Kom El-Hessi, Suweida
Tel: 695

PRINCIPAL ACTIVITIES: Processing of grapes
Parent Company: Responsible to the General Organisation of
   Food Industries

Principal Shareholders: State-owned company

SYRIAN BATTERY & LIQUID GAS CO

PO Box 733, Mutanabi St, Aleppo
Tel: 337589

PRINCIPAL ACTIVITIES: Production of gas for domestic and
   industrial use, auto accumulators and batteries, liquid gases,
   oxygen and nitrogen
Parent Company: Responsible to the General Establishment for
   Engineering Industries

Principal Shareholders: State-owned company

SYRIAN BISCUIT & CHOCOLATE MANUFACTURING CO

Hosh Blass, PO Box 3006, Damascus
Tel: 226661, 880560

PRINCIPAL ACTIVITIES: Production of biscuits and chocolates
Parent Company: Responsible to the General Organisation of
   Food Industries

Principal Shareholders: State-owned company

SYRIAN CO FOR CEMENT & BUILDING MATERIALS

PO Box 8, Hama
Tel: 21400
Cable: Cement
Telex: 431035

Chairman: Osman Amir (General Director)

PRINCIPAL ACTIVITIES: Production of cement and building
   materials
Parent Company: Responsible to the General Organisation for
   Cement
Principal Bankers: Commercial Bank of Syria

Principal Shareholders: State-owned company
Date of Establishment: 1966
No of Employees: 966

SYRIAN CO FOR OIL TRANSPORT

PO Box 51, Homs
Tel: 23014, 12223
Telex: 41012

PRINCIPAL ACTIVITIES: Transport of Iraqi oil in pipelines
   through Syria to the Mediterranean and loading it on tankers
   at Banias Terminal
Branch Offices: PO Box 13, Banias (Tartous), Tel 26571, Cable
   Scot Banias, Telex 411031 Scot Sy, PO Box 310, Damascus,
   Tel 226571, 118469, Telex 411031 Scot
Parent Company: Responsible to the Ministry of Petroleum &
   Mineral Resources
Principal Bankers: Syrian Central Bank

Principal Shareholders: State-owned company

SYRIAN GENERAL AUTHORITY FOR MARITIME TRANSPORT

PO Box 730, 2 Argentina St, Damascus
Tel: 226350, 225710, 225592
Cable: Syriamar
Telex: 411012; 20012 Syrmar

PRINCIPAL ACTIVITIES: The Authority carries out maritime
   transport for import and export commodities on behalf of
   Government ministries and departments and also for the
   private sector
Branch Offices: Branch office in Lattakia (PO Box 225)
Parent Company: Responsible to the Ministry of Transport

Principal Shareholders: State-owned company

SYRIAN GLASS & PORCELAIN INDUSTRIES CO

Hosh Blass St, PO Box 439, Damascus
Tel: 110125, 225881
Cable: Glass Damascus

PRINCIPAL ACTIVITIES: Manufacture and export of window
   glass, household glass, bottles including candy jars,
   containers, milk bottles, etc, tumblers, dishes, bowls, drinking
   containers, porcelain dinner wares
Parent Company: Responsible to the General Establishment of
   Chemical Industries

Principal Shareholders: State-owned company

SYRIAN INDUSTRIAL CO FOR VEGETABLE OILS

Amawi St, Nached Bldg, PO Box 503, Aleppo
Tel: 334147
Cable: Aleppoils

PRINCIPAL ACTIVITIES: Production of refined vegetable oils
   and cotton seed cakes
Parent Company: Responsible to the General Organisation of
   Food Industries

Principal Shareholders: State-owned company

SYRIAN INSURANCE CO

Tajhiz St, PO Box 2279, Damascus
Tel: 118430, 111279, 222276
Cable: Syrassur Damascus
Telex: 411003

Chairman: Salem Haddad (General Manager)
Directors: Amin Abdullah, Adib Fakhri, Ghassan Baroudi, Mrs
   Walaa Muhanna, Abdul Majeed Khalouf, Ali Shafaamri, Mrs
   Najwa Essa, Miss Hayfa Joud, Issam Atrash, Akram Ayoubi,
   Ahmed Kiwan, Munthair Mahmoud

PRINCIPAL ACTIVITIES: All classes of insurance and
   reinsurance
Principal Bankers: Central Bank of Syria

Principal Shareholders: State-owned company
Date of Establishment: 1953
No of Employees: 530

SYRIAN MARITIME & TRANSPORT AGENCIES SAS

Baron St, PO Box 811, Aleppo
Tel: 211074, 221173, 219550
Cable: Maritime
Telex: 331003 Caton Sy

Chairman: Fouad Hilal
Directors: Fayez Hilal
Senior Executives: Antoine Boulos (Lattakia), George Kevork
   (Tartous), Sami Elias (Banias), Anis Jamal (Aleppo)

PRINCIPAL ACTIVITIES: Agencies, representation, shipping,
   transport, travel, forwarding, insurance
Principal Agencies: Lloyd's London; Lloyd's Register of
   Shipping London; KLM Airlines Holland
Branch Offices: Lattakia; PO Box 93, Tel 30210/1, Telex 451022
   Primar; Tartous: PO Box 17, Tel 21792, 21946; Banias: PO

Box 2, Tel 21246, 21446; Damascus: PO Box 700, Tel
219637, Telex 411198 Lloyd
Principal Bankers: Commercial Bank of Syria

Date of Establishment: 1953

SYRIAN PETROLEUM CO

Mountanabi St, PO Box 3378 & 2849, Damascus
Tel: 227007
Cable: Petsyria
Telex: 411031 Sypco

Chairman: Dr Eng Mohamad Khaddour (Director General)
Senior Executives: Eng Issam Jeiroudi (Deputy General
Manager), Dr Eng Youssef Houssamo (Deputy General
Manager), Dr Eng Zaki Haj Rashid (Chief Advisor), Eng Jamil
Rajah (Technical Director) Eng Bashir Kabbani (Hassake
Fields Director), Eng Adnan Al Jundi (Jbesse Fields Director),
Yassin Tutanji (Financial Director), Taj Din Kassaballi
(Commercial Director), Eng Wassif Al Youssef (Exploration
Director), Dr Eng Rizqallah Moussa (Petroleum Studies
Director), Eng Marwan Bashour (Planning Director), M Deeb
Qassem (Administration Director), Abdel Karim Moussa (Legal
Director), Eng Maher Jamal (Contract Service Director), Eng
Gassan Qaziha (Gas Development Director), Eng Mattar Karro
(Associated Gas Plant Director), Eng Mouhsin Wakkaf (Free
Gas plant Director)

PRINCIPAL ACTIVITIES: Exploration, production and marketing
of crude oil
Branch Offices: Hasake Oil Fields; Jibissa Oil Fields; Aleppo
Branch; Lattakia Branch; Tartous Branch
Parent Company: Responsible to the Ministry of Petroleum &
Mineral Resources
Subsidiary Companies: Homs Refinery: PO Box 352, Homs, Tel
22767, Telex 441004; Banias Refinery: Telex 441050
Principal Bankers: Commercial Bank of Syria; Central Bank of
Syria

Principal Shareholders: State-owned company
Date of Establishment: 1958
No of Employees: 11,468

SYRIAN SPINNING & WEAVING CO

PO Box 14, Ain El-Tall, Kastal El Hajjarin, Aleppo
Tel: 11903
Cable: Gaznas

PRINCIPAL ACTIVITIES: Manufacture of cotton yarns, fibranne
yarns, cotton and mixed fabrics
Parent Company: Responsible to the General Organisation of
Textile Industries

Principal Shareholders: State-owned company

SYRIAN TRANSPORT & TOURISM MARKETING CO SA

TRANSTOUR

PO Box 2319, Damascus
Tel: 667050, 669400, 664075
Cable: Transtour/Damascus
Telex: TRANST 411969 SY

Chairman: Saeb Nahas
Directors: Hussain Fadel (General Director)

PRINCIPAL ACTIVITIES: Transport, travel, tourism, tourism
marketing, conducted tours

SYRO-JORDANIAN SHIPPING CO

PO Box 148, Lattakia
Tel: 31635, 31636
Cable: SYJOMAR
Telex: 451002 SJOMAR

PRINCIPAL ACTIVITIES: Shipping (ownership and operation of
vessels)
Principal Bankers: Commercial Bank of Syria

Principal Shareholders: A joint stock company which is equally
owned by the governments of Syria and Jordan
Date of Establishment: November 1975

TASCO

Rue Chakib Arselan, PO Box 3585, Damascus
Tel: 334609, 114999
Cable: Tascodam Damas-Syrie
Telex: 411081 (Sy) Tasco

PRINCIPAL ACTIVITIES: Import-Export; manufacturers'
representation; distribution of building materials, sanitary
ware, hardware, ceramics, and heating equipment
Principal Agencies: Villeroy & Boch, Italy; ACIF, Italy; Ceramica
Olympia, Italy; Euroceramics, Spain Vitroceramics, Spain;
Compact, Italy
Principal Bankers: Commercial Bank of Syria

TEXTILES GENERAL FOREIGN TRADE ORGANISATION

NASIGE

PO Box 814, Jamhourieh St, Damascus
Tel: 228816, 228248, 211517
Cable: Nasige
Telex: 411008, 412036 Nasige SY

Chairman: Farhan Trabulsi
Senior Executives: Suheil Shaddad (Finance Dept), Ismail
Hammed (Import Dept), Nihad Abou Asaleh (Export Dept),
Tahsin Sattout (Personnel)

PRINCIPAL ACTIVITIES: Import of raw materials for the textile
industry (wool yarns, jute, nylon, viscose rayon, polyester,
blended yarns, acrylic yarns, spun rayons yarns, staple fibres,
staple viscose); export of machine made & hand made wool
carpets, cotton spun yarns, grey cloth and ready made
garments, cotton underwear, dralon pullovers, etc
Branch Offices: Aleppo Nasige, Latakia Nasige
Parent Company: Responsible to the Ministry of Economy
Principal Bankers: Central Commercial Bank of Syria; Syrian
Commercial Bank

Principal Shareholders: State-owned
Date of Establishment: 1969
No of Employees: 185

TRADE COORDINATION OFFICE

PO Box 242, Lattakia
Tel: 34184, 35434, 21329
Cable: Traco
Telex: 451019 Sy Naship, 451136 Sy Traco

Director: Ryad Azhari (Managing Director)
Senior Executives: Fouad Elias (Finance Director), Samir Hamod
(Marketing Director), Yasmina Azhari (Administration Director)

PRINCIPAL ACTIVITIES: Shipping consultancy and marketing
Principal Agencies: Nedlloyd Lines, Rotterdam; P & O, London;
Leif Hoegh & Co, Oslo; Scandutch I/S (Partnership),
Copenhagen
Branch Offices: Damascus: PO Box 3242, Tel 221646, Telex
412425 Sy Traco; Aleppo: PO Box 356, Tel 330331, Telex
331526 Sy Trado
Principal Bankers: Commercial Bank of Syria, Lattakia

Date of Establishment: 1962

UNITED ARAB INDUSTRIAL CO

Hosh Blass St, PO Box 895, Damascus
Tel: 221835/6
Cable: Debs Damascus

PRINCIPAL ACTIVITIES: Manufacture and export of textile
goods (spinning, weaving and dyeing); import of grey clothing
material, dyestuffs, chemicals, auxiliary products, textile
machinery, spare parts and accessories

Branch Offices: Sales offices in Damascus (29th Ayyar St) and
Hama (8th March Ave)
Parent Company: Responsible to the General Organisation of
Textile Industries

Principal Shareholders: State-owned company

UNITED ARAB MATCH & CHIPBOARD CO

Eastern Ghouta, PO Box 2672, Damascus
Tel: 435734, 229785
Cable: Kibrit

PRINCIPAL ACTIVITIES: Production of matches, chipboard, and
pencils; however, the marketing and distribution is delegated
to the Consumer Cooperative and Intrometal
Parent Company: Responsible to the General Establishment for
Engineering Industries
Principal Bankers: Commercial Bank of Syria

Principal Shareholders: State-owned company
Date of Establishment: 1961
No of Employees: 470

UNITED COMMERCIAL INDUSTRIAL CO (KHOMASSIEH)

Kabun Industrial Area, PO Box 546, Damascus

PRINCIPAL ACTIVITIES: Production and export of cotton wool,
and synthetic yarns, cotton goods, bleached and dyed
woollen carpets and medical bandages and sterilized cotton.
Import of rayon, tops, dyes, chemicals and auxiliary products
Branch Offices: Show Room and Sales: 29 Ayar St,
Khomassieh, Tel 554467, 554465, Cable Komassy Damascus
Parent Company: Responsible to the General Organisation of
Textile Industries

Principal Shareholders: State-owned company

Major Companies of TUNISIA

AFRICA HOTEL

50 Ave Habib Bourguiba, Tunis
Tel: 247477
Cable: Africa Tunis
Telex: 12536

PRINCIPAL ACTIVITIES: Hotel management and operation
Parent Company: Part of the Meridien Hotels Group

AGENCE DE PROMOTION DES INVESTISSEMENTS

A.P.I.

63 rue de Syrie, 1002 Tunis Belvedere
Tel: 287600
Cable: API/Tunis/Tunisie
Telex: 14166 Aprin

President: Ali El Hedda

PRINCIPAL ACTIVITIES: Assistance to industry with project planning and implementation, investment and promotion agency
Branch Offices: In Tunisia: 23; Abroad: 6 (France; Belgium; West Germany; Spain; Italy; Denmark)

AGIP SA

7 rue du Docteur Burnet, PO Box 473, Tunis
Tel: 288747, 288511
Cable: Mineragip Tunis
Telex: Agiptu 13649

Chairman: G Faverzani

PRINCIPAL ACTIVITIES: Oil exploration
Branch Offices: Sfax

AL MAADEN

14 rue 8611 La Charguia, BP 62, 1080 Tunis Cedex
Tel: 232514, 232400
Telex: 13687
Telefax: 792123

President: T Chaibi (PDG)
Senior Executives: H Chaabouni (Deputy Director General)

PRINCIPAL ACTIVITIES: Production of metal tubes
Principal Bankers: UIB, Arab Tunisian Bank, STB
Financial Information:

	1990 TD'000
Sales turnover	3.000
Profits	100
Authorised capital	600
Paid-up capital	600
Total assets	600

Date of Establishment: 1968
No of Employees: 120

ARAB BANKING CORPORATION

PO Box 57, 3 Avenue Jugurtha, Cite Mahragan, 1002 Tunis
Tel: 786752, 787638
Telefax: 788990

Senior Executives: Mohamed Ayoub (Chief Representative)

PRINCIPAL ACTIVITIES: Banking (Representative Office)
Parent Company: Head office in Bahrain

ARAB TUNISIAN BANK

BP 520, 9 rue de la Monnaie, Tunis
Tel: (216-1) 350147
Telex: 13065 ARTUBA TN, 14205 ARTUBA TN
Telefax: 247820, 349278, 348150

Chairman: Hatem Kchouk
Directors: Khalid Shoman (Vice Chairman), Abdelhamid Abdelmajid Shoman, Farouk K Jabr, Shoukri Bishara, Munib R Masri, Hasib J Sabbagh, Mohsen Trabelsi, Farid Abbes, Youssef Bayahi, Ridha Zerzeri, Chedly Ben Ammar
Senior Executives: Hamouda Belkhadja (General Manager)

PRINCIPAL ACTIVITIES: Commercial banking
Branch Offices: Tunis (4), Sousse, Sfax, Gabes, Bizerte, Nabeul, Hammamet, Djerba
Parent Company: Arab Bank Plc
Financial Information:

	TD'000
Authorised capital	10.000
Paid-up capital	10.000

Principal Shareholders: Arab Bank Ltd (62.4%), private Tunisian interests (37.6%)
Date of Establishment: 1982
No of Employees: 300

ASTRAL

Ste Tunisienne de Peintures

28 rue Ed Daghbagi, Tunis
Tel: 247365, 247266
Cable: Astralluco
Telex: 15089

Chairman: Saad Hadj Khelifa
Directors: Mustapha Ben Kheder
Senior Executives: M Kaffel (Technical Manager), M Bennour (Financial Manager), M Ben Kheder (Commercial Manager)

PRINCIPAL ACTIVITIES: Production of paints, varnish and colours
Branch Offices: Sfax, Route de Teniour Km 1,5
Parent Company: Akzo Coatings, France
Principal Bankers: Banque de Tunisie, Tunis

Date of Establishment: 1936
No of Employees: 146

ATELIERS MECANIQUES DU SAHEL

Route de Monastir, PO Box 63, Sousse
Tel: 0331111
Cable: Amesa
Telex: 30770 Ams Sousse

PRINCIPAL ACTIVITIES: Production, import and export of hardware, electrical and household equipment, cutlery, taps, locks bolts and screws
Principal Agencies: Sambonet Italy; Legrand, France; Vachette, France; Escurra, Spain; Iseo, Italy; GFD, France; Facom, France; Manoutil, France; Huot, France; Mamoli, Italy; Fontana, Italy
Subsidiary Companies: Sahelmob; STAEI
Principal Bankers: Societe Tunisienne de Banque; Union Tunisienne de Banques

Principal Shareholders: Societe Tunisienne de Banque; SGP; Sofiges
Date of Establishment: 1960
No of Employees: 820

BANKERS TRUST COMPANY

4 rue El Sahab Ben Abbad, Cite Jardins, Tunis
Tel: 280277, 281456, 284181
Telex: 13005 Bantru

PRINCIPAL ACTIVITIES: Representative office
Parent Company: Head office in New York, USA

BANQUE ARABE TUNISO LIBYENNE POUR LE DEVELOPPEMENT ET LE COMMERCE EXTERIEUR

B.A.T.L.D.C.E.

Arab Tunisian Libyan Bank for Development & Foreign Trade

BP 102 Le Belvedere, 25 Ave Khereddine Pacha, 1002 Tunis
Tel: 780335
Telex: 14938

Chairman: Hedi Touni

PRINCIPAL ACTIVITIES: Banking
Financial Information:

	TD'000
Authorised capital	100.000
Paid-up capital	25.000

Date of Establishment: 1984

BANQUE CENTRALE DE TUNISIE

B.C.T.

BP369, rue de la Monnaie, Tunis
Tel: 340588, 254000, 259977
Cable: Bancentun
Telex: 12375; 12320; 12138; 13308

Governor: Moncef Belkhodja
Directors: Tahar Sioud, Taoufik Karoui, Ezzedine Abbasi, Moncef Ben Abdallah, Mokhtar Bellagha, Ali Chaduachi, Abdel Majid Chedli, Salaheddine Ferchiou, Ahmed Smaoui, Mohamed Ali Souissi, Ahmed Triki

PRINCIPAL ACTIVITIES: Central banking, bank of issue
Branch Offices: Branches in Sousse; Sfax; Bizerte; Nabeul, Gabes

Principal Shareholders: State-owned (100%)
Date of Establishment: 1958

BANQUE DE COOPERATION DU MAGHREB ARABE

B.C.M.A.

BP 1012, 70 Ave de la Liberte, Le Belvedere, Tunis
Tel: 894311, 894526, 894738
Cable: BCMA Tunis
Telex: 13040 TN

Chairman: Mahfoud Zrouta
Directors: Nouri Zorgate (Vice Chairman)

PRINCIPAL ACTIVITIES: Finance for development projects
Financial Information:

	US$'000
Authorised capital	40,000
Paid-up capital	10,000

Principal Shareholders: Government of Algeria, Government of Tunisia
Date of Establishment: 1981

BANQUE DE DEVELOPPEMENT ECONOMIQUE DE TUNISIE

B.D.E.T.

34 rue 7050 El Menzah 1004, BP 48-1080 Tunis Cedex
Tel: 718000
Cable: BDETUN
Telex: 14382, 14133
Telefax: 713744

President: Tijani Chelli (PDG)
Directors: Ezzedine Souai (State), Mohamed Bouaoudja (BCT), Mohamed Bin Rashid Bin Obead El Khamyasi (Oman), Jean Pierre Gonon (CCCE), Omar Ali Shabbu (LAFB), Haus Joachim Blattner (DEG), Giovanni Vaccelli (DEG), Boubaker

Mabrouk (BT), Habib Nifar (BNA), Abdelssalem Ben Ayed (UBCI), Abdelmounem Souayah (STB), Mokhtar Fakhfakh (Adviser), Rachid Ben Yedder (Adviser), Chekib Nouira (Adviser)
Senior Executives: Brahim Riahi (Deputy Director General), Habib Ben Saad (Deputy Director General), Nejib Tnani (Inspector General)

PRINCIPAL ACTIVITIES: Development bank - loans and equity in the tourist and industrial sectors mainly, and also in other sectors (agriculture, services related to industry & tourism, transport, real estate)
Financial Information:

	1988/89 DT'000	1989/90 DT'000
Sales turnover	29.069	34.803
Profits	2.172	5.260
Authorised capital	30.000	30.000
Paid-up capital	30.000	30.000
Total assets	359.349	381.400

Principal Shareholders: Government of Tunisia, Banque Centrale de Tunisie, Tunisian banks and financial institutions, private Tunisian interests, Sultanate of Oman, Libyan Arab Foreign Bank, Kuwait Investment Co, International Finance Corp, Caisse Centrale de Cooperation Economique de France, Deutsche Gesellschaft fur Wirtschaftliche Zusammenarbeit
Date of Establishment: 1959
No of Employees: 237

BANQUE DE L'HABITAT

Housing Bank

4 rue Jean Jacques Rousseau, 1002 Tunis
Tel: 785277
Telex: 14349
Telefax: 784417

Chairman & General Manager: Slaheddine Mouelhi
Directors: Bechir Trabelsi (Deputy General Manager)
Senior Executives: Akrout Abderrazak (Loans & Credit Director), Raja Innoubli (Finance Director), Fadhel Ben Salah (Operations Director), Kamel Cherif (Inspection Director), Zine Bostangi (Personnel Director), Bahri Kouki (Dataa Processing Director)

PRINCIPAL ACTIVITIES: Housing finance
Branch Offices: 29 branches in Tunisia
Financial Information:

	1989/90 DT'000
Authorised capital	15.100
Paid-up capital	15.000
Total assets	594.053

Principal Shareholders: State-owned
Date of Establishment: 1989 (1973 as Caisse Nationale d'Epargne Logement)
No of Employees: 746

BANQUE DE TUNISIE

B.T.

BP 289, 3 Avenue de France, 1000 Tunis RP
Tel: 259999, 340544
Telex: 14070, 14170, 15387
Telefax: 350791 (Forex/Treasury), 352203 (Marketing), 352321 (General)

President: Boubaker Mabrouk (Director General)
Directors: Elyes Hayder, Mustapha Sellami, Mohamed ALi Souissi, Abderrahman Majoul, Jean Marie Weydert, Banque Transatlantique, Credit Suisse, Banca Nazionale del Lavoro, CIC
Senior Executives: Abdel Razzak Rassaa (Vice Chairman & General Manager)

PRINCIPAL ACTIVITIES: Commercial banking
Branch Offices: Tunis, Bizerte, Sousse, Sfax, Nabeul, El
  Menzah, Le Kram, Tunis Liberte, Tunis Mohamed V, Megrine
Financial Information:

	1990
	TD'000
Sales turnover	39.113
Profits	3.024
Authorised capital	10.000
Paid-up capital	10.000
Total assets	532.203

Principal Shareholders: Private Tunisian Interests, Credit
  Industriel et Commercial, Banque Transatlantique, Societe
  Generale, Credit Suisse, Banca Nazionale del Lavoro, etc
Date of Establishment: 1884

BANQUE DE TUNISIE ET DES EMIRATS D'INVESTISSEMENTS

B.T.E.I.

Tunisian & Emirates Investment Bank

5 bis bvd Philippe Thomas, Tunis
Tel: 282311, 282522, 282966
Telex: 13386 BTEI TN

Chairman: Moncef Kaouach
Directors: Abdullah Mazroui

PRINCIPAL ACTIVITIES: Investment banking
Financial Information:

	DT'000
Authorised capital	50.000
Paid-up capital	37.000

Principal Shareholders: Abu Dhabi Investment Authority (50%),
  Tunisian Ministry of Finance (35%), Banque Centrale de
  Tunisie (15%)
Date of Establishment: 1982

BANQUE DU SUD

B.S.

14 Avenue de Paris, Tunis
Tel: 256900
Cable: Bansud
Telex: 12351 Banksud

PRINCIPAL ACTIVITIES: Commercial banking, services to the
  industrial and agricultural sectors
Branch Offices: Sfax: Rue Aboul Kacem Chabbi Sousse: Ave H
  Bourguiba Bizerte: Rue Taieb El Mehiri Nabeul: Ave H
  Thameur Sid Bou Zid: Ave H Bourguiba Gabes: Ave H
  Bourguiba Medenine: Rue 18 Janvier
Subsidiary Companies: La Caisse Nationale de Securite Sociale;
  La Societe Nationale de Mise en Valeur de Sud; La
  Cooperative d'Assurances 'El Ittihad'; Groupement des
  transport petroliers; Societe Tunisienne d'Assurances et de
  Reassurances; Cie des phosphates Sfax-Gafsa; La Monte Dei
  Paschi Di Siena (Italie); L'Union de Banques a Paris (France)

Principal Shareholders: Government of Tunisia, private Tunisian
  interests, Monte Dei Paschi Di Siena, UBAF
Date of Establishment: 1968

BANQUE FRANCO-TUNISIENNE

B.F.T.

BP254, 13 rue d'Alger, Tunis
Tel: 242100, 242990, 240510
Cable: Banfrantu Tunis
Telex: 12092

PRINCIPAL ACTIVITIES: Commercial banking

Date of Establishment: 1887

BANQUE INTERNATIONALE ARABE DE TUNISIE

B.I.A.T.

70/72 Ave Habib Bourguiba, Tunis, BP 520, Tunis Cedex
Tel: 340733 (15 lines)
Cable: Biatun
Telex: 13090, 13091 Biatun, 15396, 14090, 14091
Telefax: 340680

Founder & Honorary Chairman: Mansour Moalla
President: Mokhtar Fakhfakh (PDG)
Directors: Habib Fourati (General Manager), Abdallah B Khaled
  Al Attia, Messaoud Jawhar Al Hayet, Abdul Razak Mohamed
  Abdul Kareem Al Khereiji, Hussain Ali Al Sayegh, Philippe
  Drillet, Gilles Leflambe, Jean-Paul Escande, Mario Angeli,
  Mohsen Hachicha, Mohamed Mohsen Ben Abdallah,
  Abdesselem Affes, Aziz Miled, Chekib Nouira, Rene Brousse,
  Mongi Ayoub

PRINCIPAL ACTIVITIES: All banking transactions
Branch Offices: Tunis (21); Sousse (2); Sfax (8); Nabeul;
  Hammamet; Mahdia; Gabes; Monastir; Bizerte; Jendouba;
  Kairouan; Tozeur; Mahres; Sakiet Ezzit; Al Alia; Mateur; Beja;
  M'Saken; Grombalia; El Hancha; Questatia; Kalaa Essaghira;
  Ksibet El Mediouni; Ksar Hellal; Djerba; Representative Office:
  97 Blvd Pereire, 75017 Paris, Tel 48888000, Fax 33-1-
  47665930, Telex 650282F
Subsidiary Companies: Groupe des Assurances de Tunisie
Financial Information:

	TD'000
Capital	10.000

Principal Shareholders: National Commercial Bank of Jeddah;
  Qatar National Bank; Investment Authority of Abu Dhabi;
  Bank of Kuwait and the Middle East; Al Ahli Bank of Kuwait;
  Banque de Neuflize Schlumberger Mallet, Paris; Caisse
  Centrale des Banques Populaires, Paris; Societe Marseillaise
  de Credit; Banque Paribas, Paris; Private Tunisian Companies
  and Individuals
Date of Establishment: April 1976
No of Employees: 1,230

BANQUE NATIONALE AGRICOLE

B.N.A.

19 avenue de Paris, Tunis
Tel: 258066
Swift: BNTETNTT
Telex: 15436 Banatu, 14130 Nabatu, 13220 Dirbnt
Telefax: 341929

Chairman: Habib El Hadj Said (Managing Director)
Directors: Mohamed Gharbi, Mohamed Amor, Mohamed Chatti,
  Zeine Mestiri, Office du Commerce de la Tunisie, Office des
  Cereales, Office National de l'Huile, CTAMA, Ali Chebbi
Senior Executives: Mohamed Ben Zoubir (Asst Managing
  Director), Mokhtar Atallah (Asst Managing Director), Mongi
  Ghariani (Director Internal Audit), Said Abassi (Director
  Branches Internal Audit), Mrs Hosn El Oujoud Maherzi
  (Budget Control Director), Mrs Fatma Dhrif (Personnel
  Director), Abdelwaheb Belaaj (Director Commercial &
  Industrial Loans), Mohsen Ben Yahia (Director Debt
  COllecting & Commercial & Industrial Loans Control), Fadhel
  Ben Othman (Director Treasury Dept), Laroussi Bouziri
  (Director Foreign Exchange Dealing), Mohamed Kharrat
  (Finance Director), Mohamed Meddeb (Director Trade
  Finance), M'Barek M'Barek (Director Resources Management,
  Studies & Development), Hassouna Namouchi (Director
  Project Evaluation & Subsidiary Companies) Babbou (Direct

PRINCIPAL ACTIVITIES: Commercial and agricultural banking
Branch Offices: 14 branches in Tunisia: Kheireddine Bacha,
  Tunisia International, Lafayette, Bizerte, Beja, Gabes,
  Kairouan, Nabeul, Sousse, Jendouba, Sfax, Monastir,
  Kasserine, Gafsa

TUNISIA

Subsidiary Companies: STIL, SIDPAD, SIMPAR, UTB, GIAB, SOCELTA, BTM, SODAD, Magasin General, Ets Louis Montenay, Ste d'Elevage Mateur Jalta, Ste de Dev Agricole Lakhmes - Siliana, Ste de Dev Agricole El Ghanima - Testour, Ste de Dev Agricole Sidi Saad - Sodass, Ste de Dev Agricole Zama Bouzid, Ste de Dev Agricole Baten El Ghazel, Ste les Fermes Laitieres de Medjez El Bab

Financial Information:

	DT'000
Authorised capital	33.000
Paid-up capital	33.000

Principal Shareholders: Government and governmental institutions (84.04%), other shareholders (15.96%)
Date of Establishment: 1959 (1989 as a merger between BNT and BNDA)
No of Employees: 2,367

BANQUE NATIONALE DU DEVELOPPEMENT TOURISTIQUE
B.N.D.T.
31 Ave de Paris, Tunis
Tel: 345200, 242690
Telex: 14265

PRINCIPAL ACTIVITIES: Finance to touristic projects

Principal Shareholders: Government of Tunisia, other Tunisian interests, foreign interests
Date of Establishment: 1969

BANQUE TUNISO KOWEITIENNE DE DEVELOPPEMENT
B.T.K.D.
3 avenue Jean Jaures, Tunis 1001
Tel: 340000
Telex: 13943, 14834
Telefax: 343106

Chairman: Abdul Rasoul Abulhasan
Directors: Hosni Toumi, Ali Debaya, Ahmed Al Ibrahim, Salah Mohamed Al Youssef, Abdellatif Saddam, Hesham Al Woqayan, Laroussi Bayoudh, Salah Al Qadhi, Rachid Kechiche
Senior Executives: Abdelghaffar Ezzedine (Director General), Mohamed Ali Hamdi (Director Development), Salah Souki (Director Studies & Control), Mohamed Khouja (Director Resources Management & Representation), Tawfik Ghrib (Director Budget Control)

PRINCIPAL ACTIVITIES: Development bank
Financial Information:

	DT'000
Capital	100.000

Principal Shareholders: Tunisian and Kuwaiti interests
Date of Establishment: 1981

BANQUE TUNISO QATARIENNE D'INVESTISSEMENT
B.T.Q.I.
Centre Urbain Nord BP 20, 1080 Tunis Cedex
Tel: 713555
Telex: 13601, 14754,14753
Telefax: 713111

Chairman: Taoufik Kalai (Managing Director)
Directors: Najmeddine Dajani (Vice Chairman), Mohamed Amor, Naceur El Hejri, Housni Toumi, Khalaf Mannai, Hassine Habboub
Senior Executives: Habiba Bouslama (Finance & Admin Director), J Touati (International Dept Director), Rachid Bouchaala (Project Development Director), Mohamed Chaker (Project Finance Director), Afif Chelbi (Project Evaluation Director)

PRINCIPAL ACTIVITIES: Medium & long term credit to local industrial, agricultural, and real estate projects; offshore banking
Principal Bankers: BAII, Paris; CFC, Paris; Dresdner Bank, Frankfurt; Bank of New York, New York; Barclays Bank, London
Financial Information:

	1989/90 TD'000
Sales turnover	7.992
Profits	5.687
Authorised capital	70.000
Paid-up capital	56.000
Total assets	115.248

Principal Shareholders: States of Tunisia (50%) and Qatar (50%)
Date of Establishment: 1982
No of Employees: 70

BATA TUNISIENNE SA
Route de Mornag Km 7, Ben Arous, Tunis
Tel: 295155, 295289, 295314
Cable: Bashoe
Telex: 12041

PRINCIPAL ACTIVITIES: Manufacture of shoes and sandals

CABLERIE CHAKIRA
40 rue du 18 Janvier, Tunis
Tel: 224000
Cable: Chakira Tunis
Telex: 14254 CHAKRA
Telefax: 511777

Chairman: Mohamed Taoufik Elloumi
Senior Executives: Hichem Elloumi (General Manager), Moncef Elloumi (Finance), Mounir Regaya (Sales), Sadok Bennour (Production), Charfeddine Ben Guiza (Personnel), A El Ghoul (Purchasing), A Smaoui (Technical)

PRINCIPAL ACTIVITIES: Production of cables and wires for electric energy and telephone, PVC compound, automotive harnesses
Branch Offices: Factory at Sedjoumi Tel 224000
Parent Company: Sotee, Ets M T Elloumi
Subsidiary Companies: Cofat International
Principal Bankers: STB; UBCI; BT; BEST; BTEI
Financial Information:

	US$'000
Sales turnover	17,000
Authorised capital	2,000

Principal Shareholders: Sotee; Elloumi Family; Private individuals
Date of Establishment: 1963
No of Employees: 350

CENTRE NATIONAL D'ETUDES INDUSTRIELLES
PO Box 5, Le Belvedere, Tunis
Tel: 286111
Cable: Cnei Bp No 5 Le Belvedere
Telex: 12171

Chairman: Moncef Belaid (Director General)

PRINCIPAL ACTIVITIES: General, mechanical and chemical engineering consultants
Branch Offices: Centre Regional D'Etudes Industrielles et de Productivite; Sfax
Principal Bankers: Societe Tunisienne de Banque; Banque de Sud; Union Internationale de Banque

Date of Establishment: 1968

CENTRE NATIONAL DU CUIR ET DE LA CHAUSSURE

6 Rue Djebel Mansour, 1002 Tunis
Tel: 287014, 287321, 287709
Telex: 14335

President: Habib Laroussi (Director General)

PRINCIPAL ACTIVITIES: Public establishment, providing technical assistance and consultancy, and quality control for the leather and shoe industry
Branch Offices: Sfax, Megrine

Principal Shareholders: State-owned

CERAMIQUE TUNISIENNE JENDOUBA

2 rue Joseph Giroud, Tunis
Tel: 243222
Cable: Tunisoise
Telex: 12181

Chairman: K Ben Ammar
Senior Executives: H Ktari (Commercial Manager)

PRINCIPAL ACTIVITIES: Production of ceramic tiles, bricks
Branch Offices: Jendouba, Tel 31338

Date of Establishment: 1967

CHIMIQUE DE TUNISIE

BP 52, Ben Arous
Tel: 384100, 384920
Cable: Cogepur Tunis
Telex: 14722 FEN

Chairman: F M'Zabi
Directors: L M'Zabi

PRINCIPAL ACTIVITIES: Manufacture of paints, varnish, pigments, resins, PVA and chemical products
Branch Offices: 51 Ave de Carthage, Tunis

CIE DES PHOSPHATES DE GAFSA

9 rue de l'Arabie Seoudite, Tunis
Tel: 283522
Cable: Gafsa
Telex: 14474, 14475 Gafs
Telefax: 288453

President: Nagib Ben Debba (Director General)
Senior Executives: Amor Chebbi (Commercial Director General)

PRINCIPAL ACTIVITIES: Production and marketing of phosphates
Parent Company: Head Office: Cite Bayache, Gafsa 2100

Principal Shareholders: 97% State owned; 3% private interests
Date of Establishment: 1897
No of Employees: 11,000

CIE EL ATHIR TUNISIENNE D'ELECTRONIQUE

27 ave Khereddine Pacha, Tunis
Tel: 283688
Telex: 12595

Chairman: Mohsen Allani

PRINCIPAL ACTIVITIES: Manufacture of TVs, transistor radios, car radios and electronic equipment

CIE FRANCO-TUNISIENNE DES PETROLES
C.F.T.P.

10 rue Jacques Cartier, Tunis
Tel: 287114, 289032, 280984
Cable: Petrocaise

Chairman: Karoui Khelifa
Directors: Jean Louis Corgnet (Director General), Zouheir Denguezli (Director Commercial)

PRINCIPAL ACTIVITIES: Petroleum exploration and production
Branch Offices: PO Box 387, Sfax
Subsidiary Companies: CODESK
Principal Bankers: Banque de Tunisie
Financial Information:

	TD'000
Sales turnover	10.000
Authorised capital	200
Paid-up capital	200

Principal Shareholders: TOTAL and Tunisian Government
Date of Establishment: 1969
No of Employees: 150

CIE GENERALE DES SALINES DE TUNISIE
C.O.T.U.S.A.L.

19 rue de Turquie, Tunis
Tel: 242245, 247043
Cable: Cotusal
Telex: 12354

Directors: Gerard Louis (Managing Director)
Senior Executives: Hedi Briki (Commercial Manager)

PRINCIPAL ACTIVITIES: Production of edible and industrial sea salt
Branch Offices: Branches in Megrine (Tel 259289); Sousse (Tel 65028); Sfax (Tel 20521)

CIE INDUSTRIELLE DE BONNETERIE (CIB)

2 quai des Voiliers, Tunis
Tel: 242951, 256663
Cable: Cibonnet
Telex: 12567

Senior Executives: Barim Mabrouk Bouzouita (General Manager), Mohamed Zarrad (Commercial Manager)

PRINCIPAL ACTIVITIES: Manufacture of hosiery articles and knitted goods
Branch Offices: Factory: 51 rue Abderazak Chraibi, Tunis

CIE INTERNATIONALE D'EQUIPEMENT DE MEUBLES ET D'EXPORTATION
C.I.E.M.E.X.

9 Avenue Khereddine Pacha, Tunis
Tel: 280759, 284048
Cable: Metagoz
Telex: 12023

Chairman: Naceur Makhlouf
Senior Executives: Claude Gozlan (Commercial Manager), Noureddine Kateb (Commercial Manager)

PRINCIPAL ACTIVITIES: Manufacture of metal furniture and wooden office furniture
Branch Offices: Branch in Menzel Bourguiba (Tel 60452)

CIE TUNISIENNE DE NAVIGATION
C.O.T.U.N.A.V.

5 Ave Dag Hammarskjoeld, Tunis
Tel: 242999, 341777
Cable: Cotunav/Tunis
Telex: 14202/3/4

President: Abdelhamid Douik

PRINCIPAL ACTIVITIES: Ship owners, regular liners, tramping, passenger transport, transport of oil products, chartering, ship agents
Principal Agencies: Somaskhir (Ste Maritime de Laskhirra), SNCM, Tirrenia, AEL, Sud Cargo, CNAN, Comanav, Seamalta, John Latsis, EVGE
Branch Offices: Tunis; Bizerta; Sousse; Sfax; Gabes; La Goulette
Subsidiary Companies: Navitour (Travel Agency); SOCOTU (Forwarding); TTT (Tunisian Transcontinental Transport)

Principal Bankers: STB; BNT; UBCI; Banque du Sud

Principal Shareholders: Tunisian State; BCT; STEG; STB; OPNT; Star; OCT
Date of Establishment: 1959
No of Employees: 1,614

CIMENT AMIANTE TUNISIE
CIAMIT

7 rue Saint Fulgence, Notre Dame, Tunis
Tel: 282873, 289554
Cable: Ciamit
Telex: 13149

Chairman: A Daldoul

PRINCIPAL ACTIVITIES: Production of asbestos
Branch Offices: Bizerte

Date of Establishment: 1976

CIMENTS ARTIFICIELS TUNISIENS

47 Avenue Farhat Hached, Tunis
Tel: 258477
Cable: Cimartificiel
Telex: 12735

Senior Executives: Lahbib Doghir (Commercial Manager)

PRINCIPAL ACTIVITIES: Manufacture of quicklime and cement
Branch Offices: Factory Djebel Djelloud, Tel 492321

Date of Establishment: 1932

CIMENTS DE BIZERTE

Baie De Sebra, Bizerte
Tel: 01.241960, 01.352409
Cable: Cimenport Bizerte
Telex: 21039 Cimenport; 12545 Cibcom
Telefax: 01.342194

Chairman: Charfeddine Guellouz
Senior Executives: Mahmoud Bettaieb (Secretary General), Badreddine Guerfali (Technical General Director), Tahar Dhaouadi (Financial Manager), M'Hamed Saidi (Commercial Manager)

PRINCIPAL ACTIVITIES: Manufacture of cement, limestone and distribution of construction materials
Branch Offices: Agence commerciale de Tunis, 61 Avenue Farhat Hached, Tunis; Jendouba; Sousse; Sfax; Gabes; Bizerte; Nabeul
Principal Bankers: STB; BNT; Banque Franco-Tunisienne; Banque du Sud

Principal Shareholders: Government of Tunisia (99%), private interests (1%)
Date of Establishment: 1951
No of Employees: 750

CIMENTS D'OUM EL KELIL (CIOK)
SICO

1 Cite Jardin, Le Kef
Tel: (08) 20884, 20936
Telex: 13902 Sicosa

Chairman: Salem Mansouri
Directors: Mohamed Kamel Bensouilah (Finance Director), Mohamed Larbi Hicheri (Purchasing Manager), Belgacem Jallali (Commercial Manager), Majid Khammassi (Technical General Director)

PRINCIPAL ACTIVITIES: Manufacture and distribution of cement and all other building materials
Branch Offices: Factories at Tajerouine and Djebel Oust
Principal Bankers: STB, BS, BNT

Financial Information:

	1989/90 TD'000
Authorised capital	28.000
Total assets	88.478

Principal Shareholders: Tunisian Government
Date of Establishment: June 1976
No of Employees: 608

CITIBANK NA

BP72, 3 Ave Jugurtha, Tunis
Tel: 890066, 890513
Telex: 15139 Citico

Senior Executives: Jaloul Ayed (General Manager)

PRINCIPAL ACTIVITIES: Offshore banking
Parent Company: Head office in New York, USA

COMPLEXE INDUSTRIEL DE ZERAMDINE (CIZ)

Route de la Corniche, Sousse
Tel: 21846, 21818, 21819

Chairman: Ali Mhenni
Directors: Mourad Mhenni

PRINCIPAL ACTIVITIES: Manufacture of bricks, prefabricated buildings, crockery, glasses and bottles, object d'art
Branch Offices: Factory: Route de Djemmal, Zeramdine, Tel 86113, 86213

Principal Shareholders: Member of Groupe Ali Mehni

COMPTOIR NATIONAL DU PLASTIQUE
C.N.P.

route de Tunis, Sousse
Tel: 21710, 21047
Cable: Plastic

Chairman: Mohamed Driss (General Manager)

PRINCIPAL ACTIVITIES: Manufacture of plastic products, pipes, sheets, household goods, bottles, etc
Branch Offices: Factory: Avenue Assad Ibn Fourat, Sousse
Sales Office: 48 rue Al-Djazira, Tunis, Tel 246835

COMPTOIR NATIONAL TUNISIEN
C.O.N.A.T.U.

15-17 Rue Garibaldi Tunis
Tel: 240789
Cable: Conatu
Telex: 12057

President: Dr Ahmed Akrout
Directors: Mustapha Sellami

PRINCIPAL ACTIVITIES: Production of building materials, all types of timber, sanitary ware, agricultural and industrial equipment
Branch Offices: Branch: rue de la Bienfaisance, Sfax

COMPTOIR SANITAIRE ET D'EQUIPEMENT MENAGER SARL
C.S.E.M.

3 Avenue de la Liberte, Tunis

Senior Executives: Hedi Driss (Manager)

PRINCIPAL ACTIVITIES: Import and distribution of electrical appliances, plumbing and heating equipment

COMPTOIR TEXTILE DU CENTRE (CTC)

Avenue Habib Bourguiba, Ksar Hellal
Tel: 0378375, 0375293
Cable: Cotec

President: Mohammed Dimassi (Director General)

PRINCIPAL ACTIVITIES: Manufacture of various kinds of textiles and fabrics; for household and commercial use
Branch Offices: Commercial Service: 20 Rue d'Espagne, Tunis, Tel 248094, 248095, Telex 12528: Tn Cotec

COMPTOIR TUNISIEN DES PAPIERS SA

PO Box 1147, rue Franklin, Tunis
Tel: 259282, 243094
Cable: Cotupapier

Chairman: Mahmoud Zerzeri (Director General)

PRINCIPAL ACTIVITIES: Paper processing production of stationery and office supplies

COPLACEL SARL

5 rue du Nil, Megrine, Tunis
Tel: 494200, 494318, 494754
Telex: 12288

Chairman: S Ben Sedrine

PRINCIPAL ACTIVITIES: Production of plastic products, household goods

Date of Establishment: 1963

COTAG SARL

10 rue de Hollande, Tunis
Tel: 256888
Cable: Cotag Tunis
Telex: 12450

Senior Executives: Mohamed Ben Khalifa (General Manager)

PRINCIPAL ACTIVITIES: Petroleum research and exploration

CREDIT FONCIER ET COMMERCIAL DE TUNISIE
C.F.C.T.

BP 52, 1080 Tunis Cedex, 13 Avenue de France, Tunis
Tel: 252133, 340511
Cable: Foncialbank
Telex: 14079 CFCT, 13930 CFCT
Telefax: 349909

Chairman: Rachid Ben Yedder (also Director General)
Directors: Mahmoud Babbou (Deputy Director General)
Senior Executives: Mohamed Methlouthi (Secretary General), Chedly Fayache (Corporate & Trade Finance Director)

PRINCIPAL ACTIVITIES: All banking transactions, service to the commercial and industrial sectors and property market
Branch Offices: 50 branches in Tunisia: Tunis; Nabeul; Sousse; Sfax; Jerba; Mareth; Gabes; Kelibia; Bizerte; etc
Financial Information:

	1990 DT'000
Authorised capital	20.000

Principal Shareholders: Tunis PGI (SA)
Date of Establishment: 1967
No of Employees: 695

EL ANABIB SA

route de Mornag, Ben Arous
Tel: 492233, 493968
Telex: 15090

Chairman: Arbi Soussi

PRINCIPAL ACTIVITIES: Manufacture of water and irrigation pipes and equipment
Principal Bankers: STB; UBCI

Date of Establishment: 1967

ELF AQUITAINE TUNISIE

116 Avenue de la Liberte, Tunis
Tel: 289600
Cable: ELFATU
Telex: 14995
Telefax: 783554

Chairman: Marc Cosse
Senior Executives: Roman Gozalo (General Manager), Jean Paul Blanc (Exploration Manager), Bernard Puthod (Operations Manager), Pierre-Louis de Cours Saint Gervasy (Finance & Administration Manager)

PRINCIPAL ACTIVITIES: Oil exploration and production
Parent Company: Societe Nationale Elf Aquitaine, France

ENGRAIS DE GABES

20 Rue d'Iraq, Tunis
Tel: 286488, 289088
Telex: 40935

Directors: M Sellami
Senior Executives: A Aloulou (Commercial Manager)

PRINCIPAL ACTIVITIES: Production of monoammonium phosphate
Branch Offices: Factory at Gabes, Tel 20899

Principal Shareholders: Central Resources Corpn (CRC) USA (70%), Societe Ind d'Acide Phosphorique et d'Engrais (SAIPE) (30%), Industries Chimiques Maghrebines, Banque de Developpement Economique de Tunisie
Date of Establishment: 1974
No of Employees: 100

ENT. ALI MHENI (EAM)

12 bis rue de Russie, Tunis
Tel: 252433
Cable: Entam
Telex: 12562

Chairman: Ali Mheni
Directors: Raouf Mheni, Bouraoui Mheni

PRINCIPAL ACTIVITIES: Construction and civil engineering. Public works, buildings, mechanical earthworks
Branch Offices: Sousse
Subsidiary Companies: Societe des Ateliers Metallurgiques; Tannerie Moderne de la Manouba; Briquetterie Ali Mheni; Prefrabique Ali Mheni; Societe Hoteliere et Touristique Mheni; Societe de la Marbrerie Centrale; Societe Nouvelle des Entreprises Jelloul et Ali Mheni; Societe Hotel Hadrumete
Principal Bankers: STB; UIB; Banque du Sud; BIAT

Principal Shareholders: Ali Mheni; Mme Ali Mheni; Raouf Mheni; Bouraoui Mheni; Mourad Mheni
Date of Establishment: 1934
No of Employees: 3,500

ENT. BOUZGUENDA MONCEF (EBM)

7 rue la Charguia, Tunis-Carthage
Tel: 283506, 283903
Telex: 12565

Chairman: Moncef Bouzguenda (Director General)

PRINCIPAL ACTIVITIES: Building and civil engineering contractors, public works
Subsidiary Companies: SFAX route de Tunis Km2, PO Box 326

ENT. GENERALES PETROLIERES
E.G.E.P.

BP 1069, 1045 Tunis
Tel: 287322
Cable: Egep Tunis

Senior Executives: P Marechal (General Manager)

TUNISIA

PRINCIPAL ACTIVITIES: Petroleum research and exploration
Branch Offices: 5 rue Michel-Ange, Paris 16e, France

Date of Establishment: 1956

ENT. TUNISIENNES D'ACTIVITES PETROLIERES

27 bis Avenue Khereddine Pacha, Tunis
Tel: 782288, 783233
Telex: 15128
Telefax: 784092

Chairman: Abdelwaheb Kesraoui
Directors: M Chine, M Amraoui, M Bouhamed, M Bin Ghorbel, M Saimanouli, M Akrout, M Metinet

PRINCIPAL ACTIVITIES: Oil exploration, prospection, drilling, production; engineering and professional formation
Principal Agencies: Total, Shell, AGIP, EAT, Fina, Svenska, Homt, Marathon, Amoco, Union Anadarco, Oxy, Petrex, Murphey, Canam, Kuppek, Enserch, Conoco, Natomas, Rutherfor
Subsidiary Companies: CTF; Sotrapil; Sotulub; Sodeps; Tofco; Sergaz; Sarost; Serept; Sotugat; Packmed; Teci; Sen; Bitumed; Stusid; ITF; Somatgaz
Principal Bankers: STB; BNT; BSud; BIAT; UIB

Principal Shareholders: Tunisian State
Date of Establishment: 1972
No of Employees: 300

ESSO STANDARD TUNISIE

12 avenue de Paris, Tunis
Tel: 245761/66, 341622
Cable: Esso Sales
Telex: 14392
Telefax: 341959

Chairman: Salim Taoufik Azzam (Director General)
Senior Executives: Ridha Mounir Goucha (Finance & Accounts Manager), Mahmoud Ben Ammar (Consumer Sales Manager), Mounir Irmani (Retail Sales Manager) , Noureddine Sakka (Operations Manager), Mohamed Mestiri (Human Relations Manager)

PRINCIPAL ACTIVITIES: Processing and production of oils, production of bitumen and asphalt, distribution of fuel
Branch Offices: Tunis; Sfax; Sousse
Parent Company: EXXON
Principal Bankers: Banque de Tunisie, UBCI

Principal Shareholders: Esso Europe-Africa Services Inc
Date of Establishment: 1904
No of Employees: 243

ETHA

Ste Tunisienne d'Hydraulique et d'Assainissement

6 rue du Niger, Tunis
Tel: 281217

Chairman: T Ben Ghanem

PRINCIPAL ACTIVITIES: Civil engineering, irrigation and water works

Date of Establishment: 1975

ETS SIALA FRERES

20-30 rue Bab Souika, Tunis
Tel: 260036, 510320, 510256
Telefax: (216-1) 223254

Chairman: Abdessalem Siala
Directors: Sadok Siala, Mondher Siala

PRINCIPAL ACTIVITIES: Production of tempered glass, glassware and mirrors
Branch Offices: Zone Industrielle, route de Bizerte Km 3, Cite Ibn Khaldoun, Tunis 2042
Subsidiary Companies: COGEM, 47 rue Bab Souika, Tunis 1006
Principal Bankers: STB; UIB

Date of Establishment: 1962
No of Employees: 58

EURAFRICAINE BREDERO

La Charguia, Tunis
Tel: 234955
Telex: 12559

Directors: Abdelaziz Ben Nasr (General Manager)

PRINCIPAL ACTIVITIES: Building and civil engineering contractors, distribution of building materials

FILTISS SA

Ste de Filature et de Tissage de Tunisie

21 rue de Blida, Jebel Jelloud, 1009 Tunis
Tel: 493022
Telex: 15423 Tn

President: M'hamed Ali Darghouth

PRINCIPAL ACTIVITIES: Spinning and weaving, printing, dyeing and finishing; production of luxury household linen
Principal Bankers: STB; BDET; Banque de Tunisie; Banque du Sud; CFCT

No of Employees: 480

FINA TUNISIENNE SA

26 ave Habib Bourguiba, Tunis
Tel: 245888
Cable: Fina-Tunis

Senior Executives: P Menant (General Manager)

PRINCIPAL ACTIVITIES: Import and marketing of petroleum products, lubricants and bitumen

FIRESTONE TUNISIE

PO Box 55, Ex-arsenal Manzel, Bourguiba
Tel: 60177, 60770, 60676, 60269

Directors: A M Pierrard

PRINCIPAL ACTIVITIES: Manufacture of tyres

Date of Establishment: 1966

FONDERIES REUNIES

Route de Sousse Km 5.500, Megrine
Tel: 295549, 295563, 295188
Telex: 12189 Fondex

Chairman: Tahar Ghenima (also Director General)
Directors: S Sassi (Technical Director), M Smaoui (Financial Director), N Guargouri (Administrative Director)

PRINCIPAL ACTIVITIES: Cast iron foundry, brass and aluminium alloys
Principal Agencies: Pont a Mousson (France), Compteur Schlumberger (France)
Subsidiary Companies: Maghreb Nautisme, Machine Maghreb a bois, Sotumeta, Ben Arous, Tunisia
Principal Bankers: Societe Tunisienne de Banque

Principal Shareholders: Ste Le Moteur, Ste La Sonede, and private interests
Date of Establishment: 1946
No of Employees: 449

GARGOUR, T, & FILS (TUNISIE) SARL

34 Rue de la Monnaie, PO Box 582, Tunis 1025 RP
Tel: 256232, 246558, 245236
Cable: Trust and Trstship
Telex: 15384 TRUST TN
Telefax: 354838

Directors: Rached Mouelhi (Managing Director), Abdulrahman
Majoul

PRINCIPAL ACTIVITIES: Shipping agency and brokers, freight
forwarding and clearing, general trading mainly in chemicals,
paper, and building materials, manufacturers' representatives
Principal Bankers: Banque Internationale Arabe de Tunisie

Date of Establishment: 1958

GRANDS ATELIERS DU NORD SA

GP1 Km 12, 2034 Ez Zahra
Tel: 292210, 291490
Cable: GAN Ezzahra
Telex: 13254, 15352
Telefax: 293748

President: Abdelwaheb Ben Ayed
Directors: Abdelaziz Guidara (General Manager)
Senior Executives: Moncef Daly (Finance Manager), Khaled
Karma (Sales & Marketing Manager), Habib Ben Amira
(Purchasing Manager), Badreddine Necib (Technical &
Production Manager), Mustapha Abdennadher (Personnel
Manager)

PRINCIPAL ACTIVITIES: Manufacture of agricultural and
building equipment, poultry equipment
Parent Company: POULINA
Subsidiary Companies: UNIT-PAF El Haykel
Principal Bankers: STB, UBCI, BIAT, BNT, BT

Date of Establishment: 1975
No of Employees: 1,000

GROUPE CHIMIQUE TUNISIEN

22 rue Pierre de Courbertin, Tunis
Tel: 249600
Cable: Chimag, Tunis
Telex: 12398 Chim

PRINCIPAL ACTIVITIES: Development and promotion of
chemical industries
Associated Companies: SIAPE (Societe Industrielle d'Acide
Phosphorique et d'Engrais; ICM (Industries Chimiques
Maghrebines); GCT (Gabes Chimie Transport); STEC (Societe
Tunisienne d'Engrais Chimiques)

GROUPE DES ASSURANCES DE TUNISIE

92 Avenue Hedi Chaker 1002, Tunis
Tel: 890800, 890900
Telex: 14941 TN

Chairman: Noureddine Skandrani
Directors: Habib Cheniti
Senior Executives: Habib Tounsi, Abdelmajid Ben Ahmed,
Adnane Kilani, Hichem Cherif

PRINCIPAL ACTIVITIES: Insurance and reinsurance
Branch Offices: Tunis; Beja; Bizerte; Sousse; Sfax; Gabes; Le
Kef; Mahdia; Zarzis; Gafsa; Sidi Bouzid; Nabeul; Kasserine;
Medenine; Kairouan; Jemmel; Jerba; Teboulba; Moknine;
Hammamet
Subsidiary Companies: Seca-Amina; Participation a la Carte,
Capi
Principal Bankers: BIAT; Banque du Sud

Principal Shareholders: GAN; BDET; BIAT; Secours; Banque du
Sud; Arabia Ins Co Ltd
Date of Establishment: 1976
No of Employees: 168

IMPRIMERIE OFFICIELLE DE LA REPUBLIQUE TUNISIENNE

Route de Rades, Km 2, Rades, Tunis
Tel: 299211, 299914

Chairman: Maamouri Taoufik (also General Manager)
Directors: Mohsen Abbes (Technical Director)

PRINCIPAL ACTIVITIES: Printing activities, offical gazette
(laws); official publications

Principal Shareholders: State-owned company

INDUSTRIE NOUVELLE DU PLASTIQUE I.N.O.P.L.A.S.T.

68 Ave Farhat Hached, Tunis
Tel: 240023
Cable: Inoplast
Telex: 12628

President: Mohsen Hachicha (also Director General)

PRINCIPAL ACTIVITIES: Plastic packaging, and plastic products
(bottles, boxes)
Branch Offices: Factory; Route de Mateur Km 7, Tunis, Tel
210143

INDUSTRIES CHIMIQUES DU FLUOR

47 rue Docteur Cotton, Tunis
Tel: 280733
Cable: Chimag
Telex: 12398

President: Redha Azzabi (Director General)

PRINCIPAL ACTIVITIES: Manufacture of chemicals and fluor

INDUSTRIES CHIMIQUES MAGHREBINES SA

20 Rue d'Iraq, Tunis
Tel: 286290, 286718, 289088
Cable: Chimag Tunis
Telex: 12398 Chim Tunis

President: Moncef Sellami (also Director General)
Directors: M Aloulou (Director General, Commercial)

PRINCIPAL ACTIVITIES: Manufacture of phosphoric and
sulphuric acid

Principal Shareholders: Tunisian banks and companies
(65.45%), ANIC (10.55%), SNPA (12.5%), Pierrefitte Auby
(6.5%), Windmill Holland (5.0%)
Date of Establishment: 1972

INDUSTRIES MAGHREBINES DE L'ALUMINIUM I.M.A.L.

12 rue de Quebec, Tunis
Tel: 249627, 342934
Cable: Imalum
Telex: Tubank 12376

Chairman: M Chekili
Directors: M M Ounais, M Nabli

PRINCIPAL ACTIVITIES: Manufacture and distribution of
aluminium products, doors and windows
Principal Bankers: STB, BFT

Principal Shareholders: STB
Date of Establishment: 1965
No of Employees: 50

LIPP

Laboratoire Industriel des Produits de Parfumerie

rue 8601 No 47, Zone Industrielle, La Charguia, Tunis
Tel: 233100
Cable: Liparfum
Telex: 12158

President: R Bismuth
Senior Executives: A Driaa (Commercial Manager)

PRINCIPAL ACTIVITIES: Production of toiletries, cosmetics, soaps, insecticides

Date of Establishment: 1964

MAGHREB NAUTISME SA

Zone Industrielle Ben Arous, Tunis
Tel: 298176, 298114
Telex: 13265

PRINCIPAL ACTIVITIES: Manufacture of fishing, service and pleasure boats; polyester sheets and furniture

Date of Establishment: 1977
No of Employees: 100

MANUFACTURE TUNISIENNE DE CERAMIQUE

Route de Tunis, Zarzouna, 7000 Bizerte
Tel: 31130, 31236
Cable: M.T.C.U.B.
Telex: 13572

President: Moncef Sifaoui (President Directeur General)
Directors: Chedi Ben Mustapha (Deputy Director General), Slaheddine Chaouch (Technical Director)

PRINCIPAL ACTIVITIES: Manufacture and distribution of sanitary ware and equipment
Principal Bankers: STB

Date of Establishment: 1966
No of Employees: 320

MANUFACTURE TUNISIENNE D'EXPLOITATION INDUSTRIELLE SA

M.T.E.I.

2 bis rue de Reservoir, Tunis
Tel: 260196
Cable: Ladjil
Telex: 12598

Chairman: Ali Djilani (also General Manager)

PRINCIPAL ACTIVITIES: Manufacture of textiles and woollen fabrics

MATERIEL FERROVIAIRE GANZ

PO Box 84, Gabes 6000
Tel: (05) 72200, (05) 72882, (05) 72337
Telex: 51976 METAGA
Telefax: (216 5) 71442

Chairman: Moncef Hachaichi
Directors: Andre Ladanyi (Director General), Bekri Med Charfi (Production)
Senior Executives: Lamine Abdeljelil (Financial Department), Karoui Abdelwaheb (Commercial Department), Zitouni Taieb (Development Dept)

PRINCIPAL ACTIVITIES: Railway material, general engineering, maintenance and erection of new plants, maintenance of petrol companies
Branch Offices: Tunis
Principal Bankers: STB, BETI, BIAT

Financial Information:

	1989/90 TD'000
Authorised capital	1.555
Paid-up capital	9.000

Date of Establishment: 1977
No of Employees: 700

MINOTERIE DES ABATTOIRS

Route de la Cagna, Tunis
Tel: 258984

President: T Zarrad
Senior Executives: Sadok Slamma (Commercial Manager)

PRINCIPAL ACTIVITIES: Production of flour
Principal Bankers: Banque Nationale de Tunisie

Principal Shareholders: Office National des Cereales

NORTH AFRICA INTERNATIONAL BANK

N.A.I.B.

BP 102, Le Belvedere, 1002 Tunis, 25 Ave Khereddine Pacha, Tunis
Tel: 785200
Cable: NAIBANK
Telex: 14940, 14959 NAIB TN

Chairman: Mohamed A Riany (General Manager)

PRINCIPAL ACTIVITIES: Offshore banking

OFFICE DE L'ELEVAGE ET DES PATURAGES

O.E.P.

30 Rue Alain Savary, Tunis
Tel: 289630, 289775, 284361
Cable: Ofelpat Tunis
Telex: 12185 Tn Ofelpa

President: Mohamed Habib Najar (Director General)

PRINCIPAL ACTIVITIES: Import and export monopoly for live animals, it also approves imports by other companies of livestock and poultry; production of animal feed and fertilisers
Parent Company: Responsible to the Ministry of Agriculture
Subsidiary Companies: SONAM; GRAFOU PAST
Principal Bankers: Banque de Tunisie; STB; UBCI; CFCT; BNT

Principal Shareholders: State-owned
Date of Establishment: 1967

OFFICE DES CEREALES

23 Bis Rue Al-Djazira, Tunis
Tel: 247/421/422
Cable: Ofible
Telex: 13449

Chairman: Tahar Zarrad (Director General)
Directors: Mohamed Lassaad Mouaffak

PRINCIPAL ACTIVITIES: Production of animal feeds and fertilisers, monopoly of trade for cereals, seeds, beans, rice, animal feeds, cotton seeds and condiments; Control of the cereal processing industry
Branch Offices: Rue Alain Savary, Tunis
Parent Company: Responsible to the Ministry of Agriculture
Subsidiary Companies: Societe Tunisienne de Levure; Societe Tunisienne des Industries Meunieres
Principal Bankers: All banks in Tunisia

Principal Shareholders: State-owned
Date of Establishment: 1962

OFFICE DES PORTS AERIENS

Aerodrome de Tunis, Carthage, PO Box 60, Tunis
Tel: 289000
Telex: 13809 Dttaye

Chairman: Mohamed El Hedi Merchaoui
Directors: Taoufik Regai (Administrative and Financial Director), Habib Kanoun (Maintenance Director), Mustafa Guiza (Administrative Director)
Senior Executives: Mohsen Menif (General Manager)

PRINCIPAL ACTIVITIES: Airport office and air traffic control
Principal Bankers: STB; BNT; BIAT; Banque du Sud; UBCI

Principal Shareholders: State-owned
No of Employees: 985

OFFICE DES PORTS NATIONAUX

Batiments Administratifs, Port de Goulette, La Goulette, Tunis
Tel: 275.300

PRINCIPAL ACTIVITIES: Maritime port administration
Parent Company: Office National de Peches (ONP)
Subsidiary/Associated Company: Direction Port Bizerte, tel 0233688; Direction Port Sousse, tel 0320401; Direction Port Sfax, tel 0420131; Direction Port Gabes, tel 0522922

Principal Shareholders: State-owned

OFFICE DES TERRES DOMANIALES (OTD)

43 rue d'Iran, Tunis
Tel: 280322, 280355
Telex: 13566 OTD TN

Directors: Bechir Ben Smail

PRINCIPAL ACTIVITIES: Agricultural production; management of state-owned lands
Subsidiary Companies: OTD Agro-Combinats

Principal Shareholders: State-owned
Date of Establishment: 1961
No of Employees: 10,000

OFFICE DU COMMERCE DE LA TUNISIE (OCT)

Avenue Mohammed V, Tunis
Tel: 247499
Cable: Oct Tunis
Telex: 12391

PRINCIPAL ACTIVITIES: Import monopoly for brown sugar, tea, coffee, spices; also supervision of foreign aid imports.
Parent Company: Responsible to the Ministry of Commerce

Principal Shareholders: State-owned
Date of Establishment: 1962

OFFICE DU VIN

44 Av Bourguiba, Tunis
Tel: 255052, 255173

Directors: H Sghaier (Director General)

PRINCIPAL ACTIVITIES: Wine Office, import and export

Principal Shareholders: State-owned

OFFICE NATIONAL DE L'ARTISANAT TUNISIEN (ONAT)

Den-Den, Tunis
Tel: 512400
Cable: Onart, Tunis
Telex: 15238

President: Hedi Chouchene
Senior Executives: Noureddine Gueddiche (Managing Director), Ali Tarchoun (Finance), Abdelaziz Berriri (Home Sales), Abdelfettah Khlif (Export Sales), Mustapha Abdelfettah (Purchasing), Noureddine Essaidi (Production), Lamine Mahdi (Administration)

PRINCIPAL ACTIVITIES: Production of ceramics, potteries, arts and crafts, carpets, etc

Branch Offices: Avenue Mohamed V, Tunis; and Avenue Habib Bourguiba, Tunis, Tel 259300; 197 factories throughout Tunisia
Subsidiary Companies: CECOTRAT, Paris, France
Principal Bankers: STB, UIB, BS
Financial Information:

	DT'000
Sales turnover	10.000
Authorised capital	3.000

Principal Shareholders: State-owned organisation
Date of Establishment: 1959
No of Employees: 8,000

OFFICE NATIONAL DE L'HUILE

10 avenue Mohamed V, 1001 Tunis
Tel: 258966, 258315
Cable: Zitfi Tunis
Telex: 14325, 15431
Telefax: 351883

Chairman: Abderrahman Tlili
Directors: Abdelhamid Reguigui (Managing Director), Abdelaziz Ben H'Riz (Finance Director), Fathi Mokthar (Commercial Director), Raouf Maoui (Production Director), Jabou Jalloul (Marketing Director)

PRINCIPAL ACTIVITIES: Import monopoly for vegetable and soap oils and export monopoly for olive oil. Responsible to the Ministry of Agriculture
Branch Offices: Branch in Marseille, 143 rue de Breteuil, France

Principal Shareholders: State-owned
Date of Establishment: 1930
No of Employees: 685

OFFICE NATIONAL DES MINES

26 rue d'Angleterre, Tunis
Tel: 253122, 258263, 258460
Telex: 12442, 12004

Directors: Mekki Zidi

PRINCIPAL ACTIVITIES: Mining of iron ores. Research and studies of mineral wealth. Import monopoly for marble which is sold locally by SOMACE
Subsidiary Companies: ONM Groupement des Exploitations Tamera, Douaria (22 rue Docteur Roux, Tunis, Tel 280030, Cable Sodjrissa)

Principal Shareholders: State-owned organisation

ORGANISME NATIONAL D'AVIATION AGRICOLE

Rue Taieb M'Hiri, Megrine-Riadh
Tel: 295469, 295696, 295544

President: Khaled Farhat (Director General)

PRINCIPAL ACTIVITIES: Agricultural services including crop spraying and pesticides

PENARROYA TUNISIE

47 rue Farhat Hached, Tunis
Tel: 258765, 258766
Cable: Pen Tunis
Telex: 12184

Directors: Sadok Borgi, A Benkhalifa, H Boussoffara, G Busquet, T Karoui, A Slama, P Peron, J Iche, J Napoly, P Waline, Ali Attya
Senior Executives: L Ben Fredj (Commercial Manager)

PRINCIPAL ACTIVITIES: Mining of lead, silver and zinc
Branch Offices: Factory at Meguine, Tunis, Tel 240539
Subsidiary Companies: Ste Miniere et Metallurgique de Penarroya

PHARMACIE CENTRALE DE TUNISIE

51 avenue Charles Nicolle, 1012, Tunis Belvedere
Tel: 283011, 283012
Cable: Phacet
Telex: 12424, 13824

Chairman: Dr Ali Stambouli
Senior Executives: Abdelkarim Ben Ezzedine (Commercial Manager)

PRINCIPAL ACTIVITIES: Manufacture of pharmaceutical products. Monopoly for import of pharmaceuticals and representations of pharmaceutical suppliers

Principal Shareholders: State-owned organisation

PLASTIC TUNISIE SA

Rue Laroussi Haddad, Megrine
Tel: 295719, 295255
Cable: Plastun
Telex: 12054

Senior Executives: Fathi Zendah (General Manager), Mohamed Salah-Jellouli, A H Okassi

PRINCIPAL ACTIVITIES: Plastic production household goods, shoes, packaging materials

Date of Establishment: 1958

RADIODIFFUSION TELEVISION TUNISIENNE
R.T.T.

71 Avenue de la Liberte, Tunis
Tel: 287300
Cable: RTT Tunis
Telex: 12356 Tn

Chairman: Slaheddine Maaoui (Director General)
Directors: Mokhtar Rassaa (TV Director), Ali Belarbi (Radio Director), Salah Chebil (Radio Monastir Director), Mohammed Abdelkefi (Radio Sfax Director), Abdelkader Marzouki (Director of International Affairs & Cooperation), Brahim Ghadab (Technical Director)

PRINCIPAL ACTIVITIES: Radiodiffusion and telecommunications
Branch Offices: Stations at Sfax and Monastir

No of Employees: 1,200

REGIE NATIONALE DES TABACS ET ALLUMETTES
R.N.T.A.

route de Zaghouan, Tunis Cedex 1008
Tel: 491432, 491155
Cable: Rnta Tunis
Telex: 12263

Directors: Ahmed Zorgati (Director General), Moncef El Kobbi (General Manager)

PRINCIPAL ACTIVITIES: Import monopoly for tobacco, cigarettes, matches and playing cards, manufacture of tobacco, cigarettes and matches
Parent Company: MTK
Principal Bankers: STB; BNA; UBCI
Financial Information:

	1989/90 TD'000
Sales turnover	61.770
Profits	7.040
Authorised capital	3,350

Principal Shareholders: State-owned
Date of Establishment: 1891
No of Employees: 1,902

SAIPEM SUCCURSALE DE TUNISIE

65 rue du ler Juin, Mutueville, Tunis
Tel: 287634, 288030

PRINCIPAL ACTIVITIES: Engineers, constructors, pipeline and sealine contractors, onshore/offshore drilling contractors
Branch Offices: Libya, Algeria, Tunisia, Iraq,
Parent Company: Head office in Italy

SIAPE
Ste Industrielle d'Acide Phosphorique et d'Engrais

5 rue de Khartoum, 1002 Tunis Belvedere
Tel: 784488, 783822
Cable: Trifos TN
Telex: 14705/6/7, 15003
Telefax: 783495

Chairman: Salah Jebali
Directors: Ennouri Ben Youssef, Hechemi Ayadi, Omar Elloumi

PRINCIPAL ACTIVITIES: Production of phosphoric acid and fertilisers
Subsidiary Companies: TECI (Consulting); Mezzouna (PLastic Bags); GCT (Shipping)
Principal Bankers: BIAT, STB, BT
Financial Information:

	1990 TD'000
Authorised capital	46.000

Principal Shareholders: Tunisian Government, Banque Centrale de Tunisie, Compagnie des Phosphates de Gafsa
Date of Establishment: 1952
No of Employees: 3,000

SICA
Ste Industrielle et Commerciale de la Chaussure

Route de Gabes Km 1.5, Sfax
Tel: 0422903
Cable: Sica Sfax
Telex: 40875 Chz Animex

Chairman: Taoufik Samet (also Director General)
Directors: Damak Mohamed El Hedi

PRINCIPAL ACTIVITIES: Manufacture and distribution of shoes
Branch Offices: Magasin SICA; Rue Yamel Abdennasser, Tunis
Principal Bankers: Societe Tunisienne de Banque; Banque de Tunisie; Banque de Sud

Principal Shareholders: Sorimex; Banque de Developpement Economique de Tunisie

SIP
Ste Industrielle de Peinture

Route de Gabes Km 3, BP 239, Sfax
Tel: 43116, 42503, 41767
Telex: 40860

Chairman: Abdellaziz Ben Abdallah
Senior Executives: Abdellaziz Henchiri (Manager)

PRINCIPAL ACTIVITIES: Production of paints
Parent Company: Sotim; Chaussures Aziz; EMS
Principal Bankers: BNT; STB; UBCI

Date of Establishment: 1971
No of Employees: 200

SKANES SA

35 avenue de Paris, Tunis
Tel: 255859

President: Ahmad Trimech (also Director General)
Senior Executives: Salem Harzallah (Commercial Manager)

PRINCIPAL ACTIVITIES: Manufacture of furniture and hotel equipment, toys, furnishings, interior decorators
Branch Offices: Gabes; Bizerte; Sousse; Sfax; Monastir; Jerba; Kairouam; Beja; Msaken; Tunis

SOCIETE TUNISIENNE DE BANQUE SA
S.T.B.
rue de la Monnaie, 1001 Tunis
Tel: 340477, 258000 (70 lines)
Cable: Sotubank
Telex: 14815, 15376, 15377, 14135, 14173, 14770
Telefax: 348400, 340009

Chairman: Abdelmoumem Souayah (General Manager)
Directors: Hedi Mamou, Anouar Azaiz Chibani, Abdesselem
Achour, Societe Tunisienne de L'Electricite et du Gaz, Taoufik
Ben Hamouda, Habib Ghenim, Naceur Makhlouf, Ezzedine
Souai, Mohamed Chaouech, Societe Tunisienne d'Assurances
et de Reassurances
Senior Executives: Ridha Besbes (Secretary General), Ali Majoul
(Deputy General Manager)

PRINCIPAL ACTIVITIES: Commercial, investment and
development banking
Branch Offices: 102 in Tunisia
Subsidiary Companies: Local: Banque Franco-Tunisienne; Union
Internationale de Banques; Banque du Sud; Banque de
Developpement Economique de Tunisie; Banque Nationale de
Developpement Agricole; Banque Nationale de
Developpement Touristique; International: Union Tunisienne
de Banques, France; Banque Senegalo-Tunisienne, Dakar;
UBAC, Curacao; Union des Banques de Developpement,
Mauritania; Banque Nigerienne de Developpement, Niger;
North Africa Commercial Bank, Lebanon
Financial Information:

	1988	1989
	TD'000	TD'000
Sales turnover	87.380	117.685
Profits	6.442	7.038
Authorised capital	30.000	30.000
Total assets	1.371.536	1.726.727

Principal Shareholders: Tunisian State (41.72%), public
companies (13.16%), private companies (6.50%), private
individuals (38.62%)
Date of Establishment: January 18th, 1957
No of Employees: 2,679

SOFACO
Ste de Fabrication et de Conditionnement
24 rue du Koweit, Tunis
Tel: 282877
Cable: Sofaco

President: B Bouslah

PRINCIPAL ACTIVITIES: Production of toiletries and cosmetics
Branch Offices: Rue No 13, Zone Industrielle, la Charguia, Tunis

Date of Establishment: 1975

SOGEMO SA
24 Rue de Bilda, Jebel-Jelloud
Tel: 492877
Telex: 12290

Chairman: Mohamed Mohsen Ben Abdallah

PRINCIPAL ACTIVITIES: Manufacture of textiles and clothing

Date of Establishment: 1966
No of Employees: 350

SOTACER SA
32 rue de Marseille, Tunis
Tel: 256748, 252213
Cable: Sotacer
Telex: 12595

Chairman: Mohsen Nouria
Senior Executives: Armand Nataf, Cherif Harzallah

PRINCIPAL ACTIVITIES: Manufacture of cooking, heating,
lighting equipment, and electrical household appliances
Branch Offices: Factory at Menzel Bourguiba, Tel 60139

SOTIM
route de Gabes Km 3, PO Box 5, Sfax
Tel: 21766
Cable: Sotim Sfax
Telex: 40860

President: Mohamed Ben Abdallah (Director General)
Directors: Abdelaziz Ben Abdallah (Manager)

PRINCIPAL ACTIVITIES: Production of polyurethane foam and
rubber and reclaimed leather Synderme

SOTUPLAST
Ste Tunisienne de Production d'Articles Plastiques SA
Route de Gabes Km 1, Sfax
Tel: 29307, 28441
Cable: Sotuplast
Telex: 40927 SOPLAS

President: Mohamed Fourati (Director General)

PRINCIPAL ACTIVITIES: Manufacture of plastic products
Associated Companies: Plasticom; Africa Plastic
Principal Bankers: CFCT, UIB, UBCI, Banque du Sud, STB,
BIAT

Principal Shareholders: Mohamed Fourati, Abdesselem Charfi,
Ali Abdermader, Rachid Mnif
Date of Establishment: 1970
No of Employees: 75

STE AFRICA
route de Monastir, Sousse
Tel: 20774, 21456
Cable: Africa Sousse

Senior Executives: Abdesselem Chaouch (General Manager),
Taieb Sridi (Commercial Manager)

PRINCIPAL ACTIVITIES: Production of soap, extraction of oil
from seeds and other sources

STE ANONYME TUNISIENNE DE PRODUCTION ET D'EXPANSION CINEMATOGRAPHIQUE
S.A.T.P.E.C.
20 rue Farhat Hached, Hauts de Gammarth, 2070 La Marsa
Tel: 740944
Cable: Satpecine
Telex: 15496 TN

President: Ali Zaiem (Director General)
Senior Executives: Mohsen Makni (Finance), Slah Dhaoui
(Marketing), Mustapha Ben Jemia (Production), Cherif
Bousnina (Technical)

PRINCIPAL ACTIVITIES: Production of films and
cinematographic equipment, laboratories
Principal Bankers: Union Internationale Des Banques (UIB)

Principal Shareholders: State (99.99%); State Companies and
Private interests (0.01%)
Date of Establishment: 1957
No of Employees: 128

STE ARABE DES ENGRAIS PHOSPHATES ET AZOTES
S.A.E.P.A.
5 rue de Khartoum, 1002 Tunis Belvedere
Tel: 784488, 783822
Telex: 14708 Tn Amofos
Telefax: 783495

Chairman: Moncef Sellami
Directors: Baouendi Houssine, Elloumi Risha

PRINCIPAL ACTIVITIES: Manufacture of phosphoric acid, DAP, ammonium nitrate
Principal Bankers: BT, STB, BIAT
Financial Information:

	1990
	DT'000
Authorised capital	42.000

Principal Shareholders: Government of Tunisia, Banque Centrale de Tunisie; Abu Dhabi Fund of Arab Economic Development; SIAPE, CPG
Date of Establishment: 1976
No of Employees: 900

STE COMMERCIALE TUNISIENNE SA
SOCOTU SA

59 rue du 18 Janvier, Tunis
Tel: 258100
Cable: Socotu Tunis
Telex: 14048, 13558

Chairman: Alouane Sfar
Senior Executives: M Ben Torkia (Marketing Manager)

PRINCIPAL ACTIVITIES: Shipping agents and trading, air and sea forwarding, P&I clubs representatives, surveyors
Principal Agencies: Lloyd's Register of Shipping
Branch Offices: at all Tunisian ports: Goulette, Bizerte, Sousse, Sfax, Gabes

No of Employees: 300

STE D'APPAREILLAGE MEDICAL ET
HOSPITALIER SA
S.A.M.O.S.

9 Ave Khereddine Pasha, Tunis
Tel: 285495, 284355

PRINCIPAL ACTIVITIES: Sale of medical and hospital material and equipment

STE DE CONSTRUCTIONS INDUSTRIELLES
ET NAVALES
S.C.I.N.

Avenue No 2 au port, Sfax
Tel: 20277
Cable: Sconina
Telex: 40818

President: W Tery
Directors: R Jallais (Technical Director), A Tumed (Commercial Director)

PRINCIPAL ACTIVITIES: Manufacture of metallic structures, boilers, oilfield equipment maintenance, ship repairing

STE DE FONDERIES ET DE MECANIQUE
S.O.F.O.M.E.C.A.

2014 Megrine Riadh, Route de Sousse Km 5, Tunis
Tel: 295088 (12 lines)
Cable: SFM Megrine
Telex: 14597, 14667 TN

Chairman: Mahmoud Sifaoui

PRINCIPAL ACTIVITIES: Iron and steel foundry, manufacture of metal products, mechanical equipment, machinery, diesel motors and spare parts for the agricultural, industrial, mining and transport sectors
Principal Bankers: Societe Tunisienne de Banque; Banque de Tunisie; Banque de Sud
Principal Shareholders: SNCFT (Ste Nationale du chemin de fer Tunisien), STEG (Ste Tunisienne d'Electricite et du Gaz), STB

(Ste Tunisienne de Banque), ONM (Office Nationale des Mines), ARMICO (Arab Mining Co), SAII (Ste Arabe d'Investissement Industriel), BID (Banque Islamique de Developpement), STUSID, BTKD, BEST, BTEI, BTQI
Date of Establishment: 1966
No of Employees: 620

STE DE MARBRE DE TUNISIE
S.O.M.A.T.U.

route de Sousse Km 6, Megrine
Tel: 295338, 295008
Cable: Somatu

Chairman: Ali Mhenni

PRINCIPAL ACTIVITIES: Exploitation of stone and marble quarries, manufacture of marble and building products, and objets d'arts, etc

Principal Shareholders: A member of the Groupe Ali Mheni

STE DE PROMOTION DES INDUSTRIES DE
CONFECTION
S.O.P.I.C.

Menzel Bourguiba
Tel: 60287, 60727
Telex: 12250

Directors: M Turki (Director General)

PRINCIPAL ACTIVITIES: Production of clothing

STE DE RECHERCHES ET D'EXPLOITATION
DES PETROLES EN TUNISIE
S.E.R.E.P.T.

6 rue du Venezuela, Tunis
Tel: 283288
Cable: Serept
Telex: 12393

PRINCIPAL ACTIVITIES: Exploration, development and production of crude oil and gas
Subsidiary Companies: Aquitaine Tunisie (PO Box 409, Tunis)

Principal Shareholders: ERAP, Tunisian Government, Cie Francaise des Petroles, CoFirep, Repfrance

STE DE TRANSPORT DE MARCHANDISES
S.T.M.

Km 5, Route de Mornag, PO Box 89, Tunis
Tel: 494766, 494089
Cable: TRAM Tunis
Telex: 12356 TN, 13356 TN

Chairman: Ahmed Ourir (Director General)

PRINCIPAL ACTIVITIES: All kinds of transportation by road (industrial and commercial freight)
Branch Offices: Port Goulette, Tunis; Sfax; Gabes; Bizerte
Principal Bankers: BIAT; BNT; UBCI; STB

Principal Shareholders: Tunisian State (66%); Private Interests (34%)
Date of Establishment: 1964
No of Employees: 1,700

STE D'ENGRAIS CHIMIQUES

6 rue de Bordeaux, Tunis
Tel: 252127
Cable: Grafos Tunis
Telex: 12584

Chairman: C Tnani

PRINCIPAL ACTIVITIES: Production of super phosphate
fertilisers, pesticides and agricultural chemicals
Branch Offices: El Afrane, Djebel Djelloud, Tunis, Tel 490050

Date of Establishment: 1968

STE DES CIMENTS DE GABES SA

58 Ave Farhat Hached, Tunis
Tel: 246509, 246314
Telex: 12400

Chairman: M Ben Othman

PRINCIPAL ACTIVITIES: Production of cement and lime
Branch Offices: Route d'El Hamma, Gabes, Tel 21722

Principal Shareholders: Tunisian Government
Date of Establishment: June 1977
No of Employees: 530

STE DES INDUSTRIES METALLURGIQUES
S.I.M.E.T.

route de Sousse Km 3, Jebel Jelloud, PO Box 311, Tunis
Tel: 255700
Cable: Sim et Tunis
Telex: 12248

President: Victor Berrebi (also Director General)
Senior Executives: Nourredine Ayed (Manager)

PRINCIPAL ACTIVITIES: Manufacture of galvanized pipes,
boilers, and metal products, iron foundry
Associated Companies: Societe Generale Industrielle

STE DES INDUSTRIES TEXTILES REUNIES
S.I.T.E.R.

Bir Kassaa, Par Ben Arous, Tunis
Tel: 297210, 297100
Telex: 12444

Directors: M Bouzgarrou (Director General)

PRINCIPAL ACTIVITIES: Production of man made fibres and
textiles
Branch Offices: Moknine, Tel 75093

STE DES MINES DE JEBEL JERISSA

6 rue Imam Rassaa, Tunis
Tel: 288676

Chairman: Habib Maamer
Directors: Rejeb Bel Gaida

PRINCIPAL ACTIVITIES: Mining of iron ore
Branch Offices: Factory at Jerissa
Principal Bankers: Banque du Sud
Financial Information:

	US$'000
Authorised capital	3,500

Date of Establishment: 1908
No of Employees: 750

STE DES PETROLES BP DE TUNISIE

2 rue Apollo XI, par l'av Charles Nicolle, Tunis
Tel: 283255
Cable: BEEPEE TN
Telex: 15368

Chairman: Ferid Abbas
Directors: Zohair Moalla (Marketing Director), Mortadha
Belkhodja (Operations Manager)

PRINCIPAL ACTIVITIES: Importers and distributors of
petroleum products in Tunisia
Principal Bankers: Arab Tunisian Bank; Union Bancaire pour le
Commerce et l'Industrie, Banque Internationale Arabe de
Tunisie

Principal Shareholders: BP Africa Ltd (51%), Group Abbas
(49%)
Date of Establishment: 1956
No of Employees: 100

STE DES PRODUITS CERAMIQUES
BERNARDAUD SA

Sotuver, Megrine
Tel: 29590

President: Sadock Lasram (also General Manager)
Directors: Michem Lasram (Manager)

PRINCIPAL ACTIVITIES: Manufacture and distribution of
ceramic and porcelain products
Associated Companies: Societe Tunisienne de Verrerie

STE DES PRODUITS CHIMIQUES
DETERGENTS SA

Voie 74, Megrine Er-Riadh
Tel: 295474
Cable: Chimoline Megrine
Telex: 12571

Senior Executives: Taoufik Elloumi (Director General)

PRINCIPAL ACTIVITIES: Production of chemicals and
detergents

STE D'IMPORTATION ET TRAVAUX
D'ELECTRICITE
S.I.T.E.L.E.C.

26 Avenue Farhat Hached, Tunis
Tel: 242860, 243003
Cable: Sitel
Telex: 12326

Senior Executives: Laroussi Mouelhi (Director General), Sauveur
Abita (Technical Director)

PRINCIPAL ACTIVITIES: Electrical engineering, import and
distribution of electrical and medical equipment
Principal Agencies: Siemens SA
Branch Offices: Imm Saadi, Tour C, l'Ariana, Tunis, Tel 231526

Date of Establishment: 1953

STE DU BOIS ET DERIVES (BOD)

Ave 2001, rue 2003, Port de Tunis, Tunis
Tel: 249563, 255720
Cable: BOD Tunis

President: Habib Bahri (also Director General)
Senior Executives: Bakar Snoussi (Technical Director)

PRINCIPAL ACTIVITIES: Industry of wood and ply wood
products, packaging materials; polystyrene
Principal Bankers: Societe Tunisienne de Banque

Principal Shareholders: Caisse Tunisienne d'Assurances
Mutuelles Agricoles (CTAMA); Héritiers Tahar Azaiez
Date of Establishment: 1960
No of Employees: 170

STE EAU ET ASSAINISSEMENT
S.O.C.E.A.

86 avenue Mohamed V, Tunis
Tel: 283267
Cable: Socea Y
Telex: 1925

PRINCIPAL ACTIVITIES: Supervision of public water supplies
and drainage

STE EL BOUNIANE

68 Avenue Farhat Hached, Tunis
Tel: 245966, 241110

PRINCIPAL ACTIVITIES: Cement production, building materials, industrial material, household, transport, sulphur, agricultural equipment, etc

Associated Companies: Cement: Ciments Artificiels Tunisiens (CAT), 47 Ave Farhat Hached, Tunis, Tel 258716 Building materials: Tunisoise Industrielle, 2 place Barcelone, Tunis, Tel 243222 Sulphur: Raffinerie Tunisienne de Soufre, 47 Ave Farhat Hatched, Tunis, Tel 258716 Agricultural equipment: Agricultor, 54 Rue de Turquie, Tunis, Tel 243200 Industrial material: Autotractor, 34 Rue Massicault, Tunis, Tel 245811 Industrial material: Mine-Usine, 11 Ave de Carthage, Tunis, Tel 243211 Household and sanitary goods: Batiment, 11 Ave de Cartha, Tunis, Tel 243211 Transport: Ennaki, Ave de Ghana, Tel 256411

STE ELLOUHOUM
Route de Zaghouan Km 3, Tunis
Tel: 256808
Telex: 12440

PRINCIPAL ACTIVITIES: Sole importer of meat

Principal Shareholders: State-owned
Date of Establishment: 1961

STE FRIGORIFIQUE ET BRASSERIE DE TUNIS
Route de l'Hopital Militaire, Bab Saadoun, Tunis
Tel: 260811
Cable: Frigobiere
Telex: 12059 Tunis

Chairman: Mohamed Bousbia

PRINCIPAL ACTIVITIES: Brewery, production of ice and soft drinks
Branch Offices: Sfax; Bizerte; Mahdia; Jerba
Principal Bankers: Banque Nationale de Tunisie; Banque de Tunisie; CFCT

STE GENERALE D'ENTREPRISES DE MATERIEL ET DE TRAVAUX
S.O.M.A.T.R.A.
8 Rue de Damas, Tunis
Tel: 781088 (7 lines)
Cable: Somatrapu Tunis
Telex: 14194 Matra

President: Houcine Daboussi (Director General)
Directors: Mohamed Kameleddine Gueddiche (Deputy Director General)

PRINCIPAL ACTIVITIES: Civil engineering contractors, construction of roads, buildings, irrigation works
Subsidiary Companies: SOMACAR Ste de Materiaux et de Carrieres, 8 rue Sanhaja, Mutuelleville, Tunis; SITEL Ste Industrielle Tunisienne d'Electricite, 37 Avenue Charles Nicolle, Tunis 1002
Principal Bankers: Union Internationale de Banque; Banque du Sud

STE GENERALE DES INDUSTRIES TEXTILES
S.O.G.I.T.E.X.
Bir Kassaa, Ben Arous, Tunis
Tel: 381133
Cable: Sogtex
Telex: 14444

Chairman: Habib Ben Cheikh
Directors: Moncef Bouzgarrou (Director SITER), Hedi Charfi (Director SOPIC), Abdellaziz Cheikhrouha (Director SOMOTEX), Abdellaziz Cheikhrouha (Director SITEX)

PRINCIPAL ACTIVITIES: Production of yarn, grey cloth, finished cloth, denim, ready-made clothing; import of threads and yarn
Subsidiary Companies: SITEX (Societe Industrielle des Textiles), Sousse; SITER (Societe Industrielle des Textiles Reuni), Bir

Kassaa, Ben Arous; SOMOTEX (Societe Monastirienne des Textiles), Monastir; SOPIC (Societe de Promotion des Industries de Confection), Menzel Bourguiba
Principal Bankers: All banks in Tunisia

Principal Shareholders: State banks
Date of Establishment: 1967
No of Employees: 4,500

STE GENERALE INDUSTRIELLE
route de Sousse Km 3, 2 Jebel Jelloud
Tel: 255700
Cable: Gindus Tunis
Telex: 12248

Chairman: Victor Berrebi
Directors: Joseph Maizil (General Manager)

PRINCIPAL ACTIVITIES: Copper and metal working; manufacture of gas bottles; construction of fully finished factories and mechanical structures, mechanical engineering
Associated Companies: Societe des Industries Metallurgiques

STE HOTELIERE ET TOURISTIQUE DE TUNISIE
Avenue Habib Bourguiba, Monastir
Tel: 61633, 61720
Cable: Soteltour
Telex: 30889

Chairman: Ahmed Freh
Senior Executives: Ahmed Slouma (Deputy Director General)

PRINCIPAL ACTIVITIES: Hotel owner and management, travel agency, and tourist transportation
Branch Offices: France (Paris)
Subsidiary Companies: Tourafric (Agency de Voyages), 52 Ave Habib Bourguiba, Tunis
Principal Bankers: STB; UIB; BS

Date of Establishment: June 1956
No of Employees: 1,800

STE HOTELIERE ET TOURISTIQUE MHENI
S.O.H.O.T.O.M.I.
Route de la Corniche, Sousse
Tel: 21846, 21818, 21819, 22900

PRINCIPAL ACTIVITIES: Hotel management and ownership

Principal Shareholders: Member of Groupe Ali Mheni

STE IMER
2 rue Flatters, Tunis
Tel: 240867, 243133

PRINCIPAL ACTIVITIES: Import of powdered sugar

Principal Shareholders: State-owned

STE IMMOBILIERE ET DE GESTION EL ISKAN SA
47 Avenue Habib Bourguiba, Tunis
Tel: 255200

Senior Executives: Abdel Motaleb Babai (General Manager)

PRINCIPAL ACTIVITIES: Construction and technical assistance, real estate management

STE INDUSTRIELLE D'ACIDE PHOSPHORIQUE ET D'ENGRAIS
S.I.A.P.E.
1 Rue El Arbi Zarrouk, BP'S' - 229 - 393, Sfax
Tel: 21866, 41866, 21000
Telex: 40844 TN, 40893 TN, 40838 TN

PRINCIPAL ACTIVITIES: Manufacture of fertilisers, fabricant and export of granular triple superphosphate gisp (fertiliser with 46% P205 APA)
Branch Offices: 7, Rue Royaume d'Arabie Seoudite, Tunis, Telex 12.347 Tel 289.088, cable ACIPHOS

STE INDUSTRIELLE DE CARROSSERIE AUTOMOBILE ET MATERIEL ELEVATEUR

S.I.C.A.M.E.

Rue No 14, Cherguia II, Tunis Carthage
Tel: 233300
Cable: Sicame Tunis
Telex: 12516

President: Abdelaziz Essassi (also Director General)
Directors: Tahar Kacem, Bechir Ladjimi

PRINCIPAL ACTIVITIES: Manufacture of trucks, earth-moving equipment, lorries, trailers
Branch Offices: Tunis, Sfax, Sousse, Gabes
Subsidiary Companies: Hydromeca (Hydraulic body, flow pumps); Reno Moteurs; Iso Frigo (commercial vehicle); Cotrel (the Tunisian Leaf Spring Company)
Principal Bankers: UTB; STB

Date of Establishment: 1970
No of Employees: 300

STE INDUSTRIELLE DE CONSTRUCTIONS METALLIQUES SARL

S.I.C.M.

Route de Mornag, Sida Fathallah
Tel: 256925, 248005
Cable: Sicmetal

Senior Executives: Habib Rias (General Manager), Hamadi Msakiri (Commercial Manager)

PRINCIPAL ACTIVITIES: Production of metal structures, boilers, frames, hardware, cisterns, semi-trailers and trailers for use in agriculture and public works and hydraulic installations
Branch Offices: Factory: 36 Avenue Sinan Pacha, Tunis

STE INDUSTRIELLE DE DISTRIBUTION DES PRODUITS ALIMENTAIRES ET DIETETIQUES

S.I.D.P.A.D.

PO Box 329, 27 rue Garibaldi, Tunis
Tel: 240444, 244106, 242460
Cable: Sidpad Tunis

Chairman: Moncef Belkhodja (also Director General)
Directors: Habib Gharbi (Commercial Manager)

PRINCIPAL ACTIVITIES: Manufacture of ice cream, children's food, and health foods

STE INDUSTRIELLE DE GRILLAGE

Route de Gabes Km 2, Sfax
Tel: 0442382, 0440085
Cable: Sigfil

President: Mahmoud Sellami (Director General)
Directors: Youssef Drira (Deputy Director General)

PRINCIPAL ACTIVITIES: Production of steel wires and cables and other metal products
Principal Bankers: STB; Banque de Tunisie; CFCT

STE INDUSTRIELLE DE LINGERIE (SIL)

Avenue Mohamed Hedi Khefacha, Sfax
Tel: 23736, 25935, 25647, 25552
Cable: Sil Sfax
Telex: 40887 SIL TN
Telefax: 25566

President: Habib Achich (Director General)

Directors: Mohamed Jamoussi (Deputy Director General), Abdessalem Fourati (Director)
Senior Executives: Rachida Jamoussi (Technical Director)

PRINCIPAL ACTIVITIES: Production of knitted goods, underwear and fine textiles
Branch Offices: 9 rue d'Annaba, Tunis
Subsidiary Companies: SILEX; Les Soutiens Gorges MANEL
Principal Bankers: UBCI; Banque du Sud; CFCT; STB
Financial Information:

	1988/89 DT'000	1989/90 DT'000
Sales turnover	3.970	3.400
Authorised capital	1.665	1.900
Paid-up capital	1.665	1.900

Date of Establishment: 1964
No of Employees: 500 (160 in SILEX)

STE INDUSTRIELLE DE PECHES ET DE CONSERVES ALIMENTAIRES SA

S.I.P.C.A.

Avenue Habib Bourguiba, Megrine-Riadh
Tel: 295500
Cable: Spica
Telex: 12240

Senior Executives: Ali Mabrouk (Director General), Mahmoud Gaddouna (Commercial Manager)

PRINCIPAL ACTIVITIES: Fish, fruit and vegetable processing and canning
Branch Offices: Route de Monastir, Sousse

STE INDUSTRIELLE DES TEXTILES

S.I.T.E.X.

Ave Habib Bouguiba, Ksar Hellal
Tel: 75267, 75133
Telex: 30708 TN, 30763 TN, 13736 TN
Telefax: 890685, 32306, 75262

President: Abdelaziz Cheikh Rouha (Director General)
Senior Executives: Mohamed Khaled (Technical Director), Mohamed Sayah (Production Director), Amor Ghodbane (Financial Director)

PRINCIPAL ACTIVITIES: Weaving and textiles, blue denim
Branch Offices: Sousse, Tel 31177, 31204, Telex 30763; Tunis, Tel 282054, 892734, Telex 13736
Subsidiary Companies: Ksar Hellal (Weaving Factory); Sousse (Spinning Factory); Tunis (Clothing Factory)
Principal Bankers: STB
Financial Information:

	1987/88 TD'000
Sales turnover	51.140
Profits	4.405
Authorised capital	17.741
Paid-up capital	17.741
Total assets	62.905

Principal Shareholders: SOGITEX Holding
Date of Establishment: January 1979
No of Employees: 1,750

STE INDUSTRIELLE D'OUVRAGES EN CAOUTCHOUC

S.I.O.C.

route de Gabes Km 3, PO Box 362, Sfax
Tel: 24072, 20333, 24022
Cable: Sotpri
Telex: 40836

Chairman: Rachid Mnif
Directors: Adebl Karray (Managing Director)

Senior Executives: Ahmed Mnif (Commercial Manager)

PRINCIPAL ACTIVITIES: Manufacture of rubber pipes and tubes and various rubber products

STE INDUSTRIELLE ET COMMERCIALE DE TEXTILES ET CONFECTION DE SFAX
S.I.N.T.E.X.

Ave 18 Janvier, PO Box 193, Sfax
Tel: 22107

President: A Sellami

PRINCIPAL ACTIVITIES: Textiles and clothing
Principal Bankers: Banque Nationale de Tunisie, Sfax

Date of Establishment: 1962
No of Employees: 38

STE ITALO TUNISIENNE D'EXPLOITATION PETROLIERE
S.I.T.E.P.

92/94 Rue de Palestine, Tunis
Tel: 289244
Cable: Sitep
Telex: 15439

President: Abdelmajid Slama (Director General)
Directors: Eduardo Rico (Asst Director General)
Senior Executives: Ridha Grira, Hassen Dachraoui, Sadok Rabah, Omrane Ellouze, Baoubaker Bachraoui, Gianfranco Borella, Gianfranco Digosciu, Lucio Cangi, Silvio Mercante, Francesco Salvo

PRINCIPAL ACTIVITIES: Petroleum exploration and development. Exploration of the Elborma field

Date of Establishment: 1960
No of Employees: 600

STE LE CONFORT SA

7 rue d'Annaba, Tunis
Tel: 243555
Cable: Confortu
Telex: 12426

President: Mahjoub Ben Ali (also Director General)

PRINCIPAL ACTIVITIES: General trading, distribution of electrical household appliances, hardware, air-conditioning and refrigerating equipment
Branch Offices: Sousse; Sfax; Jerba
Principal Bankers: STB; CFCT; BNT; BIAT

Principal Shareholders: State (25%); Societe Batiment (53.3%); Societe El Bouniane and others (21.7%)
No of Employees: 1,110

STE LE METAL SA

Zone Industriel de la Charguia, Tunis
Tel: 232452, 232715
Cable: Lemetal Tunis
Telex: 13287
Telefax: 780418

President: Lucien Ronco (Director General)
Senior Executives: Robert Vinci (General Manager), Sadreddine Lasram (Finance Manager)

PRINCIPAL ACTIVITIES: Production of metal furniture and kitchenware in aluminium
Subsidiary Companies: Ste Jardin et Maison
Principal Bankers: CFCT

Date of Establishment: 1971
No of Employees: 120

STE LE MOTEUR SA

54 avenue de Carthage, Tunis
Tel: 237002, 237711
Cable: Somoteur
Telex: 12040

Senior Executives: A Trabelsi (Financial Manager)

PRINCIPAL ACTIVITIES: Production and distribution of vehicles, and transport equipment, maintenance
Principal Agencies: Fiat, Mercedes, Land-Rover, British Leyland, David Brown, Claas, Ransomes, Allis Chelmer, Khoring, etc
Branch Offices: Factory Cherguia, Tunis, Tel 237711; Branch: Sfax, Tel 0420286

Date of Establishment: 1931
No of Employees: 470

STE NATIONALE DE CELLULOSE ET DE PAPIER ALFA
S.N.C.P.A.

6 Ave Bourguiba, Tunis
Tel: 243833
Cable: CPALFA Kasserine
Telex: 14430 Cellulex Cpalfa

Chairman: Belgacem Ouchtati (also General Manager)
Senior Executives: Mohamed Besbes (Director General)

PRINCIPAL ACTIVITIES: Production of Esparto pulp, and paper
Branch Offices: Headquarter and mill at Kasserine, Tel 0770811, 0770824, Telex 40881
Associated Companies: Societe de Commercialisation des Papiers, Tunis

Principal Shareholders: State-owned
Date of Establishment: 1980
No of Employees: 1,200

STE NATIONALE DES CHEMINS DE FER DE TUNISIE
S.N.C.F.T.

67 avenue Farhat Hached, Tunis
Tel: 249999
Cable: Sonafertu
Telex: 12019

Chairman: Noury Chaouch (Director General)
Directors: Kamel Ben Amor (Deputy Director General Management), Abdelmajid Bazarbacha (Deputy Director General Technical)

PRINCIPAL ACTIVITIES: Tunisian national railways
Branch Offices: Tunis; Sousse; Sfax; Gafsa; Gafour
Subsidiary Companies: SOTRAFER
Principal Bankers: STB; BNT; BFT; BIAT; UBCI
Financial Information:

	DT'000
Sales turnover	62.800
Total assets	72.500

Principal Shareholders: State-owned organisation
Date of Establishment: 1956
No of Employees: 9,200

STE NATIONALE DES TRANSPORTS
S.N.T.

1 Avenue Habib Bourguiba, BP 660, Tunis
Tel: 259422
Cable: Sonatra
Telex: 12196

President: Abdellatif Dahmani (Director General)
Directors: Abdelwaheb Ben Khlifa, Lamine Riahi, Slaheddine Bouguerra, Moncef Chebil, Fathi Kanoun, Lotfi Mami, Hedi Tlili, Salim Zlitni (Technical Director), Mohamed Soudani (Financial Director)

PRINCIPAL ACTIVITIES: Passenger transport within Tunis and suburbs

Subsidiary Companies: Transtours

Principal Bankers: STB; UBCI; Union Internationale des Banques; Banque de Tunisie; Banque de Sud; BNT

Principal Shareholders: State-owned

Date of Establishment: March 1963

No of Employees: 5,082

STE NATIONALE D'EXPLOITATION ET DE DISTRIBUTION DES EAUX

S.O.N.E.D.E.

23 rue Jawaher El Nehru, Montfleury, Tunis

Tel: 493700

Cable: Sonede

Telex: 14262

Telefax: 390561

Chairman: Tahar Delloua (PDG)

Directors: B Abid Abdeljelil (Admin & Financial Director), Frikha Ali (Director of Home Management), Marzouk Abdelaziz (Research Director), Chaabouni Abdelkerim (New Projects Director), Fekih Mohamed (Technical Cooperation & PR Director)

PRINCIPAL ACTIVITIES: Distribution of water for drinking and industrial use

Branch Offices: Tunis, Sousse, Sfax, 31 Districts

Parent Company: Responsible to the Ministry of Agriculture

Principal Bankers: STB; Banque du Sud; UBCI

Financial Information:

	1989/90 TD'000
Sales turnover	85.585
Profits	1.749
Authorised capital	15.929
Total assets	592.394

Principal Shareholders: State-owned organisation

Date of Establishment: 1968

No of Employees: 4,472

STE NATIONALE IMMOBILIERE DE TUNISIE

S.N.I.T.

Immeuble Intilak, Cite Mahrajane, El Menzah, Tunis

Tel: 286155

Telex: 12230

President: Hassouna M'Nara (Director General)

PRINCIPAL ACTIVITIES: Property and real estate promotion and investment, civil engineering

Subsidiary Companies: Omnium des Materiaux Prefabriques

Principal Bankers: STB; BNT; Banque de Tunisie; Banque du Sud; Banque Franco-Tunisienne; Union International de Banques

STE NOUVELLE DES ENTREPRISES JELLOUL ET ALI MHENI (JAM)

Ent Jelloul et Ali Mheni (JAM)

Route de Kalaa Sghira, PO Box 31, Sousse

Tel: 20958, 21669

President: Ali Mheni

Directors: Abdelkarim Mheni (General Manager)

PRINCIPAL ACTIVITIES: Brick manufacture, joinery, metalwork, public works

Principal Shareholders: A member of the Groupe Ali Mheni

STE REGIONALE D'IMPORTATION & EXPORTATION SA

S.O.R.I.M.E.X.

Rue Habib Maazone, PO Box 392, Sfax

Tel: 21617, 20080

Telex: 40875 Sfax Sorimex

PRINCIPAL ACTIVITIES: Import and distribution of general foodstuffs, building materials, household articles and electrical goods, motorcycles and bicycles, various other articles

Branch Offices: 72-74 Rue Pierre de Coubertin, Tunis, Tel 248026, 240578

STE ROUTIERE TUNISIENNE DE GRANDS TRAVAUX COLAS

S.R.T.G.T. Colas

Rue de la Gare, Megrine

Tel: 295933

Cable: Colas Megrine

Telex: 13377 Colas

Chairman: Mohsen Ghedira

Directors: Mehdi Ayed (Technical Director)

PRINCIPAL ACTIVITIES: Civil engineering works, buildings and roads, supply of building materials

Branch Offices: Sousse; Immeuble Allala Bchir; Sfax; Route de Gabes

Associated Companies: Societe Tunisienne de Grands Travaux (STGT); Societe des Marbres Agglomeres (SOMAG)

Principal Bankers: Banque Nationale de Tunisie, Tunis; Societe Tunisienne de Banques, Megrine

No of Employees: 525

STE SHELL DE TUNISIE

24-26 place d'Afrique, PO Box 269, Tunis

Tel: 24711

Cable: Shell Tunis

Telex: 12394

PRINCIPAL ACTIVITIES: Manufacture of insecticides, detergents and lube oil

Branch Offices: La Goulette

STE TUNISIENNE AUTOMOBILE FINANCIERE IMMOBILIERE & MARITIME

S.T.A.F.I.M.

85 avenue Louis Braille, 1003 Cite El Khadra Tunis

Tel: 785055

Cable: Peugeotunis

Telex: 14581

Telefax: 782467

Senior Executives: Herve Guillot-Tantay (General Manager) Kamel Ben Jemaa (Commercial Manager)

PRINCIPAL ACTIVITIES: Manufacture of automobiles, spare parts, engines, and mechanical machinery

Principal Agencies: Peugeot

Date of Establishment: 1932

STE TUNISIENNE D'ALUMINIUM SA

S.O.T.A.L.

Avenue No 6 au Port, Tunis

Tel: 242351, 242836

Cable: Sotalu

Telex: 12461

President: Youssef Bayahi

Senior Executives: Hassan Sassi (Vice-President), Farhat Azzabi (Commercial Manager)

PRINCIPAL ACTIVITIES: Manufacture of aluminium products, household goods, stoves, etc

TUNISIA

STE TUNISIENNE D'APPLICATIONS MECANIQUES
S.T.A.M.
6 Avenue au Port, Tunis
Tel: 258501/2, 246156
Cable: Stamec Tunis

Directors: Taieb Hachicha (Managing Director)

Senior Executives: Hedi Kamoun (Commercial Manager)

PRINCIPAL ACTIVITIES: Construction and civil engineering contractors; public works, building and mechanical earthworks

STE TUNISIENNE D'ASSURANCES ET DE REASSURANCES
S.T.A.R.
PO Box 420, Avenue de Paris, Tunis
Tel: 256800, 340866
Cable: Stareass
Telex: 13420
Telefax: 340835

Chairman: Mohmaed Salah Bouaziz

Directors: Mohamed Hedi Darghouth (Insurance General Director), Mustapha Mourali (Reinsurance General Director), Hedi Daaloul (Finance Director)

PRINCIPAL ACTIVITIES: Insurance and reinsurance
Branch Offices: Sfax; Sousse; Bizerte; Beja; Menzel Bourguiba; Gabes; Mahdia; Grombalia
Principal Bankers: Ste Tunisienne de Banque

Principal Shareholders: State-owned company
Date of Establishment: 1958
No of Employees: 800

STE TUNISIENNE DE BISCUITERIE
S.O.T.U.B.I.
Avenue Bourguiba, Megrine Riadh, Tunis
Tel: 295500, 295069

President: Ali Mabrouk (General Manager)

Senior Executives: M Gaddouna (Commercial Manager)

PRINCIPAL ACTIVITIES: Biscuits and cakes manufacturers

STE TUNISIENNE DE BOISSONS GAZEUSES SA
Megrine Riadh, Tunis
Tel: 295200
Cable: Boga Tunis
Telex: ST BOGA 14729

President: Faycal Ben M'Barek (General Manager)

Senior Executives: Tahar Zaouali

PRINCIPAL ACTIVITIES: Manufacture of carbonated beverages and soft drinks
Principal Agencies: Coca-Cola, Fanta, Boga, Apla, Schweppes
Associated Companies: Societe-Frigorifique et Brasserie de Tunis
Principal Bankers: Banque Nationale de Tunisie

Principal Shareholders: Societe Frigorifique et Brasserie de Tunis; Banque Nationale de Tunisie; Office du Commerce de Tunisie; Banque de Developpement Economique de Tunisie; Societe Tunisienne d'Assurances et de Reassurances
Date of Establishment: 1948
No of Employees: 450

STE TUNISIENNE DE CONSTRUCTIONS ET DE REPARATIONS MECANIQUES ET NAVALES
S.O.C.O.M.E.N.A.
Menzel Bourguiba, Bizerte
Tel: 0260155, 0260656
Cable: Socomena
Telex: 21016 Renav

President: Moncef Driss (Director General)
Senior Executives: Lamine Tekaya (Commercial Director), Abdallah Benaceur (Financial Director), Amor Jilani (Admin Director), Moncef Mellaiem (Purchasing Director), Cherif Jerbi (Technical Director)

PRINCIPAL ACTIVITIES: Metal and wooden naval and mechanical construction and repairs, dry dock
Branch Offices: PO Box 10, Menzel Bourguiba
Principal Bankers: Societe Tunisienne de Banque (STB)

Principal Shareholders: Tunisian State, Societe Tunisienne de Banque (STB), Societe El Bouniane, CTN
Date of Establishment: 1963
No of Employees: 1040

STE TUNISIENNE DE CONSTRUCTIONS METALLIQUES
S.T.U.C.O.M.
Megrine, Riadh, Tunis
Tel: 296325
Cable: Stucom
Telex: 13297

Chairman: M Fourati
Directors: A Boccara

PRINCIPAL ACTIVITIES: Manufacture of metal structures, boilers, tubes and pipes, foundry
Subsidiary Companies: CICEM (Constructions Industrielles Cles en Main); Ceramik-Zleiz (Usine de Carreaux de parement)
Principal Bankers: Banque de Tunisie; UBCI; Banque du Sud

Date of Establishment: 1946

STE TUNISIENNE DE DIFFUSION
5 avenue de Carthage, PO Box 440, Tunis
Tel: 255000
Cable: Studiffusion
Telex: 12521

Chairman: Moncef Laroussi
Senior Executives: Zein Bostangi (Secretary General)

PRINCIPAL ACTIVITIES: Production of books, papers, stationery, records, business machines printing and publishing
Principal Agencies: Maison Tunisienne de l'Edition; Maison Arabe du Livre; Ceres
Associated Companies: Centre Industriel du livre; Usine Ennagham
Principal Bankers: STB; UIB; BIAT; BT; Arab Bank; UBCI-CFCT

Principal Shareholders: State-owned
Date of Establishment: 1964

STE TUNISIENNE DE FABRICATION DE MOUSSE
S.O.T.U.M.O.U.S.
route de Sousse, Km 6, Megrine
Tel: 296348, 296181, 296348
Cable: Mzabi Tunis
Telex: 12583, 13684

President: Fetbi Mzabi (Director General)

PRINCIPAL ACTIVITIES: Manufacture of foam mattresses and foam and rubber products; PVC and polyethylene tubes
Principal Bankers: CFCT; Arab Bank; BFT

STE TUNISIENNE DE FILATURE ET DE TISSAGE

S.T.U.F.I.T.

Avenue Louis Braille, Tunis
Tel: 287899
Cable: Stufit
Telex: 12419

President: Mustapha Chenik (Director General)
Directors: Mansour Guerfali (Secretary General), Mohamed E Hedi Chenik (Commercial Director)

PRINCIPAL ACTIVITIES: Spinning and weaving, production of yarns, greycloth and fabrics
Principal Bankers: BDET; UBCI; STB; BS; BIAT;

No of Employees: 400

STE TUNISIENNE DE FRUITS ET LEGUMES

S.O.T.U.F.R.U.I.T.S.

24 rue Gamal Abdel Nasser, Tunis
Tel: 246286, 257605
Cable: Ethimar Pagna

Directors: Othman Makni

PRINCIPAL ACTIVITIES: Food processing, fruit and vegetables, cold storage

STE TUNISIENNE DE L'ACCUMULATEUR NOUR SA

Route de Sousse Km 6, Megrine, Tunis
Tel: 298833
Cable: Nourtunis
Telex: 12517

President: Habib Cheikh Rouhou (Director General)
Senior Executives: Abdesselem Hachicha (General Manager), Mondher Cheikh Rouhou (General Manager)

PRINCIPAL ACTIVITIES: Manufacture of auto and industrial batteries

STE TUNISIENNE DE L'ELECTRICITE ET DU GAZ

S.T.E.G.

BP 190, 1080 Tunis Cedex
Tel: 341311, 243522
Cable: Gazelec
Telex: 12020, 13060, 13061, 14744
Telefax: 349981

President: Tahar Hadj Ali
Senior Executives: Mohamed Elloumi (Deputy General Manager), Khereddine Guellouz (Development & Research Manager), Habib Amara (Administrative & Legal Affairs Manager), Khaled Hammou (Distribution Manager), Touhami Mankai (General Affairs Manager), Amor Mokhtar (Financial Affairs Manager), Amor Jebalia (Gas Branch Manager), Othman Arfa (Equipment Manager), Mahmoud Lakhoua (Exploitation Manager), Fadhel Baccouri (Head of Data Processing Dept), Hedi Turki (Head of Study & Planification Dept)

PRINCIPAL ACTIVITIES: STEG has the exclusive responsibility for producing, transporting, distribution and sale of electricity as well as natural and manufactured gas for all of Tunisia. Main installations are a gas plant at Tunis, a gas pipeline from El Borma to Gabes and four electric power stations and a dispatching centre
Branch Offices: 33 districts throughout Tunisia
Associated Companies: STE, SACEM, SIAME, SIALE, CELEC

Principal Shareholders: State-owned company
Date of Establishment: 1963
No of Employees: 8,000

STE TUNISIENNE DE L'INDUSTRIE DU BOIS

S.T.I.B.

17 Rue Garibaldi, Tunis
Tel: 255488, 255349, 245711
Cable: Stibois
Telex: 13893

Chairman: Mustapha Sellami (Director General)
Directors: Mohsen Sellami (Vice-President)

PRINCIPAL ACTIVITIES: Timber industry
Branch Offices: Factory; Bir Kassaa, Tunis, Tel 295280
Subsidiary Companies: Stramica, Tunis
Principal Bankers: UBCI; Banque du Sud; Banque de Tunisie; BDET

STE TUNISIENNE DE L'INDUSTRIE LAITIERE SA

S.T.I.L.

24 Avenue de France, Tunis
Tel: 253487, 253011
Cable: Stilait
Telex: 12378 Stil

Chairman: Ferid El Mokhtar

PRINCIPAL ACTIVITIES: Production of dairy products, cold stores, production and processing of dates, canning of fruit and vegetables. Owns State departmental store chain
Branch Offices: Chain of 26 stores

Date of Establishment: May 1961
No of Employees: 5,000

STE TUNISIENNE DE MATIERES PREMIERES TEXTILES

S.O.T.U.M.A.T.E.X.

88 Avenue Barthou, Tunis
Tel: 280947, 280188
Cable: Rags

President: Bechir Ben Nijima (Director General)

PRINCIPAL ACTIVITIES: Manufacture of yarns and textiles, dyeing and processing cotton, wollen, and acrylic fabrics

STE TUNISIENNE DE PRODUCTION INDUSTRIELLE

SOTUPRI

route de Gabes Km 1, Sfax
Tel: 20157, 20299
Cable: Sotuprisfax
Telex: 40836

Senior Executives: Rachid M'Nif (Director General), Abdelmajid Maazoun (Manager)

PRINCIPAL ACTIVITIES: Production of leather and cloth shoes and soles

STE TUNISIENNE DE SIDERURGIE

ELFOULADH

Route de Tunis KM3, BP 23 & 24, 7050 Menzel Bourguiba
Tel: 60522, 60385, 60698
Cable: Siderm
Telex: 21036, 21055, 21060
Telefax: (02) 61533

Chairman: Mohamed Fadhel Zerelli (PDG)
Directors: Mokhtar Robei (Deputy Director General), Houcine Kassassi (Sales & Purchasing Director)

PRINCIPAL ACTIVITIES: Production and marketing of iron and steel products, rolled bars, wires, drawn wires and metallic structures

Branch Offices: Head office and Factory at Menzel Bourguiba; Tunis: 122 rue de Yougoslavie, 1000 Tunis, Tel 244188, Telex 15427; Sales Office: Rolled Bars & Drawn Wires: Route de Tunis KM3, 7050 Menzel Bourguiba; Metallic Structures: 7 rue Mustapha Sfar, Tunis Belvedere, Tel 780036, Teled 15427

Financial Information:

	TD'000
Sales turnover	90.000
Authorised capital	5.910
Paid-up capital	5.910

Principal Shareholders: Government of Tunisia (87.43%), mixed sector (12.30%), private sector (0.27%)
Date of Establishment: 1963
No of Employees: 2,350

STE TUNISIENNE DE VERRERIE

S.O.T.U.V.E.R.

Rue Taieb Mehiri, Megrine, Riadh
Tel: 295900, 295117
Cable: Sotuver

Chairman: R Djait
Senior Executives: M Karghani (Commercial Manager)

PRINCIPAL ACTIVITIES: Manufacture of glass, bottles and glass products
Associated Companies: Societe des Produits Ceramiques Bernardaud

STE TUNISIENNE D'ENGRAIS CHIMIQUES

S.T.E.C.

6 rue de Bordeaux, Tunis
Tel: 252127
Cable: Grafos Tunis
Telex: 12584

President: C Trani

PRINCIPAL ACTIVITIES: Manufacture and export of chemical products, superphosphates, hyperphosphates, ammonia, fertilisers and pesticides
Branch Offices: Factory at Djebel Djelloud, Tel 490050
Subsidiary Companies: Granufos

Principal Shareholders: A member of The Groupe Chimique Tunisien
Date of Establishment: 1968

STE TUNISIENNE DES ATELIERS MHENNI

S.A.M.M.I.

route de Sousse Km 5m, Megrine, Tunis
Tel: 295556
Cable: Sammi Tunis

Chairman: Ali Mheni
Senior Executives: Hassen Driss (Commercial Manager)

PRINCIPAL ACTIVITIES: General metal working, joinery, aluminium, copper

Principal Shareholders: A member of the Groupe Ali Mheni
Date of Establishment: 1962

STE TUNISIENNE DES EMBALLAGES METALLIQUES

S.T.U.M.E.T.A.L.

24 Rue Belhassen Ben Chaabane, Tunis
Tel: 260877
Telex: 12437 Emetal

Chairman: Bechir Yaiche
Directors: Ahmed M'Halla (Secretary General)

PRINCIPAL ACTIVITIES: Manufacture of metal cases, boxes, cans, bottles and other packaging products
Principal Bankers: STB; Banque de Tunisie; Banque Franco-Tunisienne

Principal Shareholders: Societe Tunisienne de Banque (STB), Banque de Developpement Economique de Tunisie (BDET), Government of Tunisia, Carnaud SA, France
No of Employees: 542

STE TUNISIENNE DES ENTREPRISES CHAUFOUR-DUMEZ

Entreprises Chaufour-Dumez

25 avenue Farhat Hached, Tunis
Tel: 242117
Cable: Chaufour-Dumez Tunis
Telex: 15237 Zemud TN

Chairman: M Wuchner
Directors: M Leriche

PRINCIPAL ACTIVITIES: Civil engineering and construction, marine engineering, general contractors
Financial Information:

	DT'000
Sales turnover	11.300
Authorised capital	1.000

Principal Shareholders: Dumez International, France
Date of Establishment: 1935

STE TUNISIENNE DES ETS BROSSETTE

18 Ave de Madrid, Tunis
Tel: 243466
Telex: 12380

PRINCIPAL ACTIVITIES: Specialists in building services: tubes, pipes, sanitary installations, taps, laboratory installations, heating, warehousing, covers, pumps, non-ferrous metals, steel, and other industrial supplies

Principal Shareholders: Brossette SA, Lyon, France

STE TUNISIENNE DES INDUSTRIES DE RAFFINAGE

S.T.I.R.

PO Box 46, Zarzouna, Bizerte
Tel: 31744
Cable: Stiraf
Telex: 12445

President: Kamel Belkahia

PRINCIPAL ACTIVITIES: Oil refining

Date of Establishment: 1960

STE TUNISIENNE DES MATERIAUX DE CONSTRUCTION SA

S.O.T.I.M.A.C.O.

2 Place Barcelone, Tunis
Tel: 243222
Telex: 12181 Simaco

President: Khaled B Ammar

PRINCIPAL ACTIVITIES: Manufacture of building materials and construction equipment
Subsidiary Companies: Les Carrieres Tunisiennes; La Ceramique; Les Carrelages Tunisiens; Les Faienceries Tunisiennes; Les Refractaires de Tunisie; Les Platriers Tunisiens; Les Platres Tunisiens; Les Marbres et Granites Tunisiens; La Ceramique de l'Ouest

Principal Shareholders: State-owned
No of Employees: 2,200

STE TUNISIENNE DES MOTEURS
S.O.T.U.M.O.
2 rue Danton, Tunis 1002
Tel: 289355
Cable: Sotumo
Telex: 15126

President: Ridha Dhaoui (PDG)
Senior Executives: Bechir Rouatbi

PRINCIPAL ACTIVITIES: Production of diesel engines
(stationery and marine) for fishing industry and irrigation
Principal Agencies: Hatz, Bukh, British Seagull motors
Branch Offices: Factory: Menzel Bourguiba, Tel 0260471 Shop:
66 Ave de Carthage, Tunis, Tel 240321

Date of Establishment: 1964
No of Employees: 90

STE TUNISIENNE D'ETUDES TECHNIQUES ET ECONOMIQUES
S.O.T.U.E.T.E.C.
23 rue de Khartoum, Tunis
Tel: 287000
Telex: 14016 TN

Chairman: Moncef Thraya
Directors: Ahmed El Aouani (Director General)

PRINCIPAL ACTIVITIES: Consultancy, technical and economic
studies and data processing for building and public works
and transport
Associated Companies: Societe Tunisienne d'Informatique et
d'Organisation (SOTINFOR); Societe d'Etudes et de
Realisations Agricoles et Hydrauliques (SERAH)
Principal Bankers: BIAT

Date of Establishment: 1963
No of Employees: 185

STE TUNISIENNE D'IMPRIMERIE ET DE CARTONNAGE
S.T.I.C.
route de Rades, Foudouk Choucha, Tunis 2040
Tel: 299533, 297452
Cable: Stic Rades
Telex: 15418
Telefax: 297267

President: Chatti Rachid (Director General)
Directors: Layouni Samir (Managing Director)

PRINCIPAL ACTIVITIES: Paper industry, cardboard, packaging

Date of Establishment: 1960
No of Employees: 220

STE TUNISIENNE D'INDUSTRIE AUTOMOBILE
S.T.I.A.
19 rue de Turquie, Tunis
Tel: 256233
Cable: Stiauto
Telex: 12001

Chairman: Mokhtar Cheniti (Director General)
Directors: Bechir Ladjimi (Deputy Director General)

PRINCIPAL ACTIVITIES: Assembly of buses, cars, lorries,
trucks, estate cars and spare parts
Principal Agencies: Peugeot, Renault, Citroen, Berliet, Fiat,
Ford, Van Hool
Principal Bankers: STB; BNT; BDET;

Date of Establishment: 1961
No of Employees: 1,500

STE TUNISIENNE D'INDUSTRIE MEUNIERE
S.T.I.M.
53 rue Al Djazira, Tunis
Tel: 245366
Cable: STIM Tunis

Chairman: T Zarrad
Senior Executives: M Yahiaoui (Commercial Manager)

PRINCIPAL ACTIVITIES: Milling, production and sale of
semoulina, flour and pasta
Parent Company: Office des Cereales
Principal Bankers: BIAT
Financial Information:

	TD'000
Sales turnover	6.000
Authorised capital	951
Paid-up capital	951
Total assets	7.620

Principal Shareholders: State owned
Date of Establishment: 1952
No of Employees: 200

STE TUNISIENNE D'INFORMATIQUE ET D'ORGANISATION
S.O.T.I.N.F.O.R.
Ste d'Etudes et de Realisation Agricole et Hydraulique
S.E.R.A.H.
5 rue de Liberia, 1002 Tunis
Tel: (216-1) 287046, 781243, 781637
Telex: 14053 TN
Telefax: 783315

Chairman: Ahmed El Aouani
Directors: Mohsen Tounsi

PRINCIPAL ACTIVITIES: Management, economical studies,
feasibility studies, project management, data processing
computer service, urban hydraulics, sanitation, roads and
networks, urban and rural development, agriculture and
irrigation, public works, building
Associated Companies: L'Ordinateur SA
Principal Bankers: Banque Internationale Arabe de Tunisie

Date of Establishment: 1973
No of Employees: 45

STE TUNISIENNE DU SUCRE
70 Avenue de la Liberte, Tunis
Tel: 287422

Chairman: Morched Boubaker (Director General)

PRINCIPAL ACTIVITIES: Production of sugar and by-products
Branch Offices: Factory: Route de Tabarka, Beja, Tel 0851655
Subsidiary Companies: Societe d'Industrie Alimentaire et de
Conditionnement
Principal Bankers: STB; BNT; Banque de Sud

Principal Shareholders: Government of Tunisia; CNSS, and
Tunisian banks

STE TUNISIENNE LAFARGE SA
58 avenue Farhat Hached, Tunis
Tel: 345977
Telex: 14948

Chairman: Mohamed Salah Sanakli Turki
Senior Executives: M Cheriaa (Administration & Finance
Manager)

PRINCIPAL ACTIVITIES: Manufacture of cement, mosaic and
reconstituted marble tiles, building materials
Branch Offices: Factories: Zone Industrielle La Charguia, Tel
232579

Subsidiary Companies: Carrelages & Prefabrications du Sud a Gabes; Carrelages du Nord a Beja
Financial Information:

	1990
	TD'000
Authorised capital	1.700

Date of Establishment: 1984
No of Employees: 300

STRAMICA

17 rue Garibaldi, Tunis
Tel: 255488
Cable: Stramica
Telex: 12057 Tunis

Chairman: Mohsen Sellami
Directors: Mahmoud Sellami

PRINCIPAL ACTIVITIES: Wood industry, manufacture of plywood, formica, wood products, doors and windows
Branch Offices: Factory: 67 Avenue Louis Braille, Tunis
Associated Companies: STIB, Tunis
Principal Bankers: UBCI; BIAT; BDET

T GARGOUR & FILS (TUNISIE) SARL

See GARGOUR, T, & FILS (TUNISIE) SARL

TANNERIES MODERNES DE LA MANOUBA

Rue de la Tannerie, La Manouba
Tel: 220004, 222005
Cable: Moderntan La Manouba

President: Ali Mheni (also Director General)
Senior Executives: Mohamed Ghali (General Manager)

PRINCIPAL ACTIVITIES: Tannery, leather processing for shoes, bags, and similar articles
Principal Bankers: STB

Principal Shareholders: A member of the Groupe Ali Mheni
No of Employees: 200

TUNIS AIR

Societe Tunisienne de l'Air

113 Avenue de la Liberte, Tunis
Tel: 288100
Cable: Tunair
Telex: 15283 Tunair TN

PRINCIPAL ACTIVITIES: Air transport
Branch Offices: Algiers; Brussels; Cairo; Geneva; London; Munich; Paris; Rome; Marseille; Nice; Lyon; Toulouse; Strasbourg; Bordeaux; Milan; Frankfurt; Dusseldorf; Amsterdam; Luxembourg; Copenhague; Zurich; Casablanca; Dakar; Tripoli; Jeddah; Khartoum; Damascus; Kuwait; Abu-Dhabi; Athens; Dubai; Madrid; Barcelona; Istanbul, Vienna
Principal Bankers: STB

Principal Shareholders: State-owned
Date of Establishment: 1948
No of Employees: 4508

TUNIS HILTON HOTEL

Avenue Salammbo, PO Box 1160, Tunis 1045
Tel: 282000, 782800
Cable: Hiltel Tunis
Telex: 15372, 13306

PRINCIPAL ACTIVITIES: Hotel management and operation
Parent Company: Part of Hilton International Corp, 301 Park Av, New York, NY 10022, USA
Principal Bankers: Societe Tunisienne de Banques

Date of Establishment: 1965
No of Employees: 320

TUNIS INTERNATIONAL BANK

T.I.B.

18 Avenue des USA, BP 81, 1002 Tunis Belvedere
Tel: 782411 (7 lines)
Cable: TIB TN
Telex: 14049, 14051, 14052
Telefax: 782223

Chairman: Ebrahim Al Ebrahim
Senior Executives: John S Callaghan (Chief General Manager), Mohamed Fekih (General Manager), Syed Ali Abbas (Deputy General Manager), Yves Chaulet (Asst General Manager Credit), George Tabet (Asst General Manager Foreign Exchange), Paul Asmar (Asst General Manager Marketing), Abderrahman Ben Ghezala (Manager Correspondent Banking Dept)

PRINCIPAL ACTIVITIES: Offshore, commercial banking, trade finance, letters of credit, corporate finance, international bonds, private banking, portfolio management, savings accounts
Branch Offices: Sousse: 2 Avenue Taha Hussein, Khaezama, 4051 Sousse, Tel 3-43397/8, Fax 3-43399; Paris Representative Office: 26 rue de Bassano, 75016 Paris, Tel 47239069, Fax 40701383
Subsidiary Companies: Tunis Investment Holding (100%)
Financial Information:

	1989
	US$'000
Loans & discounts	259,337
Deposits	245,387
Authorised capital	70,000
Paid-up capital	55,000
Total assets	476,190

Principal Shareholders: Arab African International Bank, Egypt; Brent Walker Overseas, Netherlands; Comec Financial, UK; Yemen Bank for Reconstruction & Development, Yemen; First Gulf Bank, Ajman UAE; Oman International Bank, Sultanante of Oman
Date of Establishment: 1982

TUNISACIER SA

5 rue d'Angola, Tunis
Tel: 284267
Telex: 14113
Telefax: 784875

Chairman: V Berrebi
Directors: M Ksomtini (Commercial Director), M Cherif (Financial Director)

PRINCIPAL ACTIVITIES: Metal processing, galvanazing
Branch Offices: Bizerte
Parent Company: Ilva, Italy; SIMET, Tunisia, SGI, Tunisia
Principal Bankers: BIAT, BS, Citibank, STB, BNT, UIB, UBCI

Principal Shareholders: M Berrebi, Ilva, BDET, BS, SIMET, SGI
Date of Establishment: 1976
No of Employees: 170

TUNISIA OILFIELD CONTRACTORS

T.O.F.C.O.

14 rue Imam Mouslim, El Menzah, Tunis
Tel: 232643, 230241
Cable: Tofco Tunis
Telex: 13873

President: Tewfik Mazigh
Directors: Jacques Perrin (Deputy General Manager)
Senior Executives: Pierre Gomez (Technical Manager)

PRINCIPAL ACTIVITIES: Oil and industry, piping, structural fabrication and erection in oil business, including construction of offshore steel platforms.
Branch Offices: Factory: 2 rue 103, Sousse
Principal Bankers: UBCI; CFTP; STB

Principal Shareholders: AMREP, France (49%); Entreprise
Tunisienne d'Activites Petrolieres (ETAP) (17.5%); Societe
Tunisienne d'Electricite et de Gaz (STEG) (17.5%); Banque
Tuniso Koweitienne de Development (BTKD) (16%)
Date of Establishment: 1977
No of Employees: 250

TUNISIAN KUWAITI DEVELOPMENT BANK

3 Avenue Jean Jaures, Tunis
Tel: 340000
Telex: 13943

Chairman: Abdul Rasoul Abulhasan
Directors: Mohamed Ali Souissi (Vice Chairman), Abdulbaki Al
Nouri, Salah Muhammed Al Youssef, Ahmed Al Ibrahim, Salah
Al Kadhi, Khalifa Karoui, Noureddine Koubaa, Mohamed
Ghannouchi, Ali Rekik

PRINCIPAL ACTIVITIES: Development banking, financial
assistance to industry

TUNISIE CABLES SA

22 rue 8600, Zone Industrieele, La Charguia II, Tunis Cedex
1080
Tel: 286305, 289703, 782011
Telex: 13380
Telefax: 780464

Chairman: Moncef Sellami
Directors: Anouar Esseghir, Tahar Touil

PRINCIPAL ACTIVITIES: Manufacture of electrical and
telephone cables and wires
Branch Offices: Plant at Grombalia Industrial Area, Nabeul
Governorate
Principal Bankers: BIAT, BNT, UIB, BT, BS
Financial Information:

	1988/89 US$'000
Sales turnover	15,000
Profits	1,000

Date of Establishment: 1978
No of Employees: 180

TUNISIE LAIT SOCIETE INDUSTRIELLE SA

Tunisie Lait

42 avenue de la Republique, Sousse
Tel: (03)23174
Telex: 30775 Tulait

Chairman: Mustapha Chahed

PRINCIPAL ACTIVITIES: Production of milk and dairy products
Branch Offices: Centrale Laitiere de Sidi Bou Ali, Tel (03)68544,
68551
Principal Bankers: Banque Nationale de Tunisie, Tunis

TUNISIENNE DE CONSERVES ALIMENTAIRES

T.U.C.A.L.

15 rue Sidi Bou Mendil, Tunis
Tel: 241617, 241748
Cable: Tucal Tunis

President: Amor Ben Sedrine (Director General)

PRINCIPAL ACTIVITIES: Manufacture and distribution of
canned food products (fruits, fish and vegetables, etc)

TUNISIENNE DE MINOTERIE & DE SEMOULERIE

48 Avenue Habib Bourguiba, Tunis
Tel: 241308

Chairman: M'hamed Sfar (Director General)
Directors: Sadok Ben Yahmed, Roger Sfez

PRINCIPAL ACTIVITIES: Production of flour, semoules and by-
products
Branch Offices: Factory at Djebel Djelloud, Tunis
Principal Bankers: All Tunisian banks

UNION BANCAIRE POUR LE COMMERCE ET L'INDUSTRIE

U.B.C.I.

BP 829, 7-9 rue Gamal Abdel Nasser, Tunis
Tel: 245877
Cable: Unicomi
Telex: 14490

Chairman: Abdessalam Ben Ayed
Directors: Khaled Abdel Wahab, Jean Thamazeau, Tahar
Bouricha, Mustafa Chenik, Abdullah Lachhab, Marcel
Rinaudo, Henri Stalin, Rene Thomas

PRINCIPAL ACTIVITIES: All banking transaction
Branch Offices: Tunis, Sfax, Gafsa, Bizerte, Gabes, Sidi Bouzid,
Nabeul, Sousse, Hammamet, Kairouan, Menzel Bouzelfa, La
Manouba, Megrine, Mahares
Subsidiary/Associated Companies: Banque pour le Commerce
et l'Industrie de la Mer Rouge, Djibouti

Principal Shareholders: Banque Nationale de Paris
Intercontinentale, private Tunisian interests
Date of Establishment: 1951
No of Employees: 450

UNION GENERALE

5 rue de Hollande, Tunis
Tel: 242611, 242620, 242613

Chairman: Mustapha Kamel Bourguiba
Senior Executives: Mohamed Ben Yahia (Managing Director)

PRINCIPAL ACTIVITIES: Manufacture of concrete blocks,
bricks, and red pottery

UNION INTERNATIONALE DE BANQUES

U.I.B.

BP 224, 1080 Tunis Cedex, 65 avenue Habib Bourguiba, Tunis
Tel: 247000, 347000 (20 lines)
Cable: Unibank
Telex: 14397 TN Unib, 13700, 13701

President: Neji Skiri (Director General)
Directors: Tawfik Moalla (Deputy General Manager), Julien Paul
Koszul (Deputy General Manager)

PRINCIPAL ACTIVITIES: Banking and commercial operations
Branch Offices: 48 branches in Tunisia
Associated Companies: Credit Lyonnais
Financial Information:

	DT'000
Authorised capital	10.000
Paid-up capital	10.000

Principal Shareholders: Credit Lyonnais; Banca Commerciale
Italiana; Groupe Societe Tunisienne de Banques; Office
National de l'Huile, others
Date of Establishment: 1963
No of Employees: 1,221

UNION TUNISIENNE DE BANQUES

50 Ave Habib Bourguiba, Tunis
Tel: 341211, 340241
Telex: 13160 UTBANK

PRINCIPAL ACTIVITIES: Offshore banking
Parent Company: Head office in Paris, France

TUNISIA

Major Companies of the UNITED ARAB EMIRATES

Abu Dhabi

ABDUL JALIL & HENSON CO

Po Box 323, Abu Dhabi
Tel: 341731
Cable: Henson
Telex: 22280 EM

Directors: Abdul Jalil Al-Fahim, T D Henson (Joint Partners)

PRINCIPAL ACTIVITIES: Vertical transportation; mechanical,
electrical and air conditioning contractors
Principal Agencies: Marryatt and Scott (International) Ltd,
Simplex GE, Airtemp Corporation, Woods of Colchester
Associated Companies: Reliant Co, PO Box 2089, Doha, Qatar,
Reliant Co, Dubai, UAE
Principal Bankers: British Bank of the Middle East

ABDUL RAHMAN DARWISH TRADING & CONTRACTING CO

See DARWISH, ABDUL RAHMAN, TRADING & CONTRACTING
CO

ABDUL RAHMAN HAMAD AL HADLAQ CO & PARTNERS

See AL HADLAQ, ABDUL RAHMAN HAMAD, CO & PARTNERS

ABDULLA BIN AHMED ZAROUNI & BROS

See ZAROUNI, ABDULLA BIN AHMED, & BROS

ABDULLA NASSER & ASSOCIATES

Abdulla Nasser Bldg, Al-Salam St, PO Box 46611, Abu Dhabi
Tel: 773300
Telex: 23499 Abnaas EM
Telefax: 770003

President: Abdulla Nasser
Directors: Fadhel M Khan (Managing Director), M A Al-Muhairy
Senior Executives: Ganpat Singhvi (Group Finance Director),
Moezz Dhialdeen (Technical Manager)

PRINCIPAL ACTIVITIES: General trading, import and export
light industries, commercial representation and consultancy
Principal Agencies: Hawker Siddeley Power Engineering,
Chicago Bridge International, Foster Wheeler, Byron-Jackson,
Yorkshire Imperial Alloys
Branch Offices: Dubai, Al Ain
Subsidiary/Associated Companies: Amalgamated National
Diversified Offshore Co, PO Box 6611, Abu Dhabi; Al-Muhairy
Trading Co, PO Box 95, Abu Dhabi; Al-Mansoori Specialised
Engineering, PO Box 3374, Abu Dhabi; Awlad Nasser Corp;
Business Management Ent
Principal Bankers: British Bank of the Middle East

Principal Shareholders: Abdulla Nasser; S T Al-Nahayan; Matter
Al-Muhairy; Mubarak Al-Muhairy
Date of Establishment: 1977
No of Employees: 300

ABU DHABI AIRPORT SERVICES

PO Box 3668, Abu Dhabi
Tel: 757500
Cable: Abuaps
Telex: 23272 Abuaps EM
Telefax: 757157

Directors: Sa'ad Dajani (General Manager), Abdulla Abdulrazak
Ali (Deputy General Manager)
Senior Executives: Samir Farajallah (Customer Services
Manager), Hani Khorsheed (Freight & Mail Manager), K D
Wade (Personnel & Administration Manager), Samir Abou
Zahr (Ramp Operations Manager)

PRINCIPAL ACTIVITIES: Ground handling at Abu Dhabi
International Airport
Principal Bankers: Emirates Commercial Bank, Abu Dhabi

Principal Shareholders: ADAS is a government sponsored
organisation
Date of Establishment: June 1976
No of Employees: 1,180

ABU DHABI AVIATION

PO Box 2723, Abu Dhabi
Tel: 449100
Cable: Adavco
Telex: 22656 Adaco EM
Telefax: 449081

Chairman: HE Ali Bin Khalfan Al Dhahry
Directors: Salem Rashid Saeed Al Mohandy, Mohamed Ahmed
Saeed Al Qasimi, Abdulla Sultan Abdulla Al Shamsi, Hamed
Mohamed Abdulla Brook, Issa Mohamed Al Suwaidy, Khalifa
Al Kindi
Senior Executives: Ali Bin Saeed Al Shamsi (General Manager),
Ali Hassan Ali (Deputy General Manager), Yahya Murtadha Al
Qaimi (Finance & Admin Manager), George Tucker
(Operations Manager), Michael W Conomos (Chief Engineer),
Issa Abdulatif Saif (Deputy Computer Manager)

PRINCIPAL ACTIVITIES: Helicopter services
Principal Bankers: Abu Dhabi Commercial Bank; National Bank
of Abu Dhabi
Financial Information:

	1989 St£'000
Sales turnover	16,120
Profits	6,280
Authorised capital	34,188
Paid-up capital	15,385
Total assets	43,214

Principal Shareholders: (30%) Abdu Dhabi Government; (70%)
UAE Nationals
Date of Establishment: 1976
No of Employees: 317

ABU DHABI BAGS FACTORY

PO Box 6828, Abu Dhabi
Tel: 554100
Telex: 22580 Adbag EM
Telefax: 554404

PRINCIPAL ACTIVITIES: Production of paper and plastic bags
Parent Company: General Industry Corporation, Abu Dhabi

ABU DHABI BUILDING MATERIALS & CONTRACTING CO

PO Box 558, Abu Dhabi
Tel: 772713, 770431
Cable: Amalcom
Telex: 22387 Amalcom EM
Telefax: 782581

Chairman: Mukhtar Farra
Directors: Akram Farra (Managing Director)
Senior Executives: Maher Farra (Sales Manager), Sunil Bhatia
(Senior Salesman & Marketing)

PRINCIPAL ACTIVITIES: Import of building materials, mainly
ceramic floor and wall tiles; sanitary ware
Principal Agencies: Armitage Shanks Sanitaryware; Formica,
UK; Niclar Exports, Italy; Iris, Italy; Hoganas, Sweden;
Stalotan, Germany; KCH Extruded Pool Tiles; Cerabati,
France; Steinbok, Netherlands; Goldbach, Germany; Friedrich
Grohe, Germany
Associated Companies: Al Falah Building Materials & Trading
Co: PO Box 1864, Dubai, UAE
Principal Bankers: Banque Paribas; United Bank; Bank of Credit
& Commerce Intl; Banca Commerciale Italiana

UAE (Abu Dhabi)

Financial Information:

	1990
	Dh'000
Authorised capital	1,250
Paid-up capital	1,250

Date of Establishment: 1969

ABU DHABI CO FOR ONSHORE OIL OPERATIONS
A.D.C.O.

PO Box 270, Abu Dhabi
Tel: 666100
Cable: PETRUCIAL ABU DHABI
Telex: 22222 ADCO EM
Telefax: 720099, 664888

Chairman: HE Shaikh Tahnoun Bin Mohammed Al Nahayan

PRINCIPAL ACTIVITIES: Exploration, drilling, production and export of crude oil on behalf of national and foreign shareholders
Principal Bankers: Abu Dhabi National Bank

Principal Shareholders: ADNOC (60%); BP (9.5%); Shell (9.5%); CFP (9.5%); Exxon (4.75%); Mobil (4.75%); Partex (2%)
Date of Establishment: 1939
No of Employees: 1,450

ABU DHABI COMMERCIAL BANK

PO Box 939, Abu Dhabi
Tel: 02 720000
Telex: 22244 ADCBCR EM (General), 23229 ADCBTR EM (Forex)
Telefax: 02 776499

Chairman: HE Shaikh Suroor Bin Sultan Al Dhaheri
Directors: Fadhel Saeed Al Darmaki (Vice Chairman), Sultan Nasser Al Suwaidi (Managing Director & CEO), Mohamed Abdul Aziz Al Rubaiyea, Khalifa Mohammad Al Muhairy, Nasser Bin Muthker AL Shafi, Mohammed Abdulla Al Sayed, Rashid Humaid AL Mazroui, Mohammed H Bin Ali Al Dhaheri
Senior Executives: Sultan Nasser Al Suwaidi (Managing Director & CEO), Alexander Anderson (General Manager - UAE Branches), Ebrahim Abdul Rehman (Asst General Manager Corporate Banking Group), Mohamed A Ashraf (Senior Manager Treasury & Private Baking Div), Dr H K N Mishra (Senior Manager Head Credit Div), Arif Harianawalla (Senior Manager Head Operations Div), Dr Kamlesh N Agarwala (Senior Manager Corporate Accounts), Ziad Nsouli (Manager Corporate Accounts), Hemant J Jethwani (Manager Loan Syndications & Trade Financing), Sharat Anand (Manager Investments), Sasi Menon (Senior Dealer Money Market), Lancelot Sequeira (Asst Manager Setlement Dept), V G Nair (Asst Manager L/C & Financial Services Dept), F J Mathew (Head Correspondent Banking)

PRINCIPAL ACTIVITIES: Retail/wholesale commercial banking with some investment/merchant banking activities. Established in 1985 through a merger of Khalif Commercial Bank, Emirates Commercial Bank, and Federal Commercial Bank
Branch Offices: 25 branches and offices in UAE (7 in Abu Dhabi, 3 in Al Ain, 4 in Dubai, 11 in other areas) and 1 overseas in Bombay
Principal Bankers: Correspondents: New York: Manufacturers Hanover Trust Co, First Chicago International; London: Barclays Bank Plc; Frankfurt: Dredsner Bank AG; Tokyo: Bank of Tokyo Ltd; and correspondents worldwide
Financial Information:

	1989	1989
	Dh'000	US$'000
Total assets	9,710,052	2,642,181
Total deposits	6,903,592	1,878,529
Capital & reserves	1,402,052	381,239
Net income	102,588	27,915

Principal Shareholders: Abu Dhabi Investment Authority (state owned) (64%); United Arab Emirates Institutions and nationals (36%)
Date of Establishment: July 1st, 1985 (merger date)
No of Employees: 664

ABU DHABI COMMERCIAL CORP

PO Box 2214, Bani Yas St, Abu Dhabi
Tel: 336672, 336673
Cable: Artinovel
Telex: 22676 Al Namat EM

Chairman: Abdullah Namat Mohammed Khocry
Directors: Khalid Abdullah, Yusuf Abdullah
Senior Executives: Saif Ur Rahman (Manager)

PRINCIPAL ACTIVITIES: Tenderers, contractors and agents to foreign principals; import of all kinds of machinery; industrial and construction equipment, road construction equipment, electrical and electronic equipment, chemicals, building materials and sanitary ware
Principal Agencies: Fujikura Ltd, Japan; Inoue Machinery, Japan; Seba Dyntronic, West Germany; Universal Generators, UK; Madar Engineering, Italy; Megra Edison, USA; Critchley Brothers, UK; James Walls & Co, UK; GEC Henlay, UK; Rey Rolle Industries, UK; Legrand, France; Merlin Gerin, France; Telemecanique, France
Parent Company: Al Naim Transport & Contracting Est
Subsidiary Companies: Al Naim & Partners (Clearing & Forwarding Agent)
Principal Bankers: Bank of Credit & Commerce (Emirates), SA

Principal Shareholders: Abdullah Namat Mohammed Khoory and his sons
Date of Establishment: 1974

ABU DHABI DRILLING CHEMICALS & PRODUCTS LTD
A.D.D.C.A.P.

PO Box 46121, Abu Dhabi
Tel: 772400
Telex: 23267 EM
Telefax: 773725

PRINCIPAL ACTIVITIES: Manufacture and marketing of drilling mud and other products

Principal Shareholders: Abu Dhabi National Oil Co (ADNOC) (75%)

ABU DHABI ENGINEERING CO

PO Box 876, Abu Dhabi
Tel: 324247, 324248
Cable: Engcon

Chairman: Atteg Khalaf Al Mazroui
Directors: Hamid Shamkhi (Managing Director)

PRINCIPAL ACTIVITIES: Electrical, building and civil engineering contractors
Subsidiary/Associated Companies: AEC Roberts; AEC Kitchenmakers
Principal Bankers: National Bank of Abu Dhabi; Rafidain Bank

Principal Shareholders: Atteg Khalaf Al Mazroui; H Shamkhi
Date of Establishment: 1975
No of Employees: 320

ABU DHABI FLOUR & FEED FACTORY

PO Box 6622, Abu Dhabi
Tel: 722300
Telex: 23022 Ansom EM
Telefax: 724730

PRINCIPAL ACTIVITIES: Production of flour and animal feed
Parent Company: General Industry Corporation, Abu Dhabi

ABU DHABI FUND FOR ARAB ECONOMIC DEVELOPMENT
A.D.F.A.E.D.

PO Box 814, Abu Dhabi
Tel: 725800, 822865/6
Cable: Fund
Telex: 22287 Fund EM
Telefax: 728890

Chairman: HH Sheikh Khalifa Bin Zayed Al-Nahyan

Directors: HE Sheikh Sultan Bin Zayed Al Nahyan (Vice Chairman), HE Rashid Abdullah Al Nuaimi, HE Sheikh Hamdan Bin Zayed Al Nahyan, HE Sheikh Saeed Bin Zayed Al Nahyan, HE Nasser Mohammad Ali Al Nuwais (General Manager), HE Ju'an Salem Al Dhaheri, HE Hareb Massod Al Darmaki, HE Khalifa Mohammad Obeid Al Muhairi

Senior Executives: Nasser Al Nuwais (General Manager), Ahmed Hussein Baqer (Asst Director General), Miss Hamda Al Suweidi (Director Accounts Department) Miss Fawzia Al Mubarak (Director Investments Department), Abdullah Saleh (Director Projects Department), Dr Saeed M A El Mahdi (Legal Advisor), Hussein Al Medfa (Director Loans Department), Talib A Abdullatif (Director Administration)

PRINCIPAL ACTIVITIES: Provides development aids to Arab, African and Asian Countries
Financial Information:

	1990/91 Dh'000
Paid-up capital	2,132,023
Total assets	3,286,838

Principal Shareholders: Government Organisation
Date of Establishment: July 1971
No of Employees: 85

ABU DHABI GAS INDUSTRIES LTD
GASCO

PO Box 665, Abu Dhabi
Tel: 651100
Cable: Ongas Abu Dhabi
Telex: 22365 Cogas EM
Telefax: 6047414

Chairman: Suhail Fares Al Mazrui

Directors: S Al Mazrui, S Al Shamsi, K Al Otaiba, D G Turner, A Ait Said, R Gulbenkian

Senior Executives: Andrew B Pirrie (General Manager), Jean Philippe Hillaireaud (Operations Manager), Ali S Anoon (Personnel Manager), Jose Pereira (General Secretary), F Hanselman (Finance Manager), Pierre Chateau (Projects Manager)

PRINCIPAL ACTIVITIES: Recovery of condensate from the gas fields of Asab, Bab and Buhasa, and further separation into commercial products (Propane, Butane and Pentane Plus) at the fractionation plant in Ruwais
Principal Bankers: Abu Dhabi Investment Authority (ADIA); National Bank of Abu Dhabi
Financial Information:

	1989/90 US$'million
Authorised capital	425
Long term loan from ADIA	1,600

Principal Shareholders: Abu Dhabi National Oil Company (ADNOC) (68%), Compagnie Francaise des Petroles (CFP) (15%), Shell Gas BV (SHELL) (15%); Participations & Explorations Corporation (PARTEX) (2%)
Date of Establishment: Incorporated 1978, production 1981
No of Employees: 825

ABU DHABI GAS LIQUEFACTION CO LTD
A.D.G.A.S.

PO Box 3500, Abu Dhabi
Tel: 333888
Cable: Adgas Abu Dhabi
Telex: 22698 ADGAS EM

Directors: HH Dr M Saeed Otaiba, Sohail Al Mazrui, Khalaf Al Otaiba, Dr D A Claydon, C E Bonnet, T Takada, M Matsunaga
Senior Executives: R I Wiseman (General Manager), E S Haboosh (Deputy General Manager), C de Fraissinette (Plant Manager), K Bydford (Finance Manager), A Al Jafri (Commercial Manager), A Anoon (Personnel & Admin Manager),Dr H A Fattah (Engg & Technical Services Manager)

PRINCIPAL ACTIVITIES: Production and export of LNG and LPG from Das Island, Abu Dhabi
Branch Offices: Tokyo Liaison Office
Principal Bankers: National Bank of Abu Dhabi; Bank of Credit and Commerce Int SA

Principal Shareholders: Abu Dhabi National Oil Company, British Petroleum Company Ltd, Compagnie Francaise des Petroles, Mitsui & Co, Mitsui Liquefied Gas Co Ltd
Date of Establishment: 1973
No of Employees: 850

ABU DHABI GENERAL TRANSPORT CO

PO Box 493, Abu Dhabi
Tel: 822760
Cable: Brook
Telex: 22439 EM

Chairman: Saeed Khalfan Al Qumzi
Directors: Ahmed Saeed Khalfan
Senior Executives: Jirair Tozlikian (Deputy General Manager), Mohammad Hamdan (Finance Manager), Mujbil Yousef (Manager of Transp & Equip Dept)

PRINCIPAL ACTIVITIES: Transportation, road construction and civil engineering contractors
Branch Offices: Al Ain (UAE)
Parent Company: Saeed Khalfan & Sons Co
Associated Companies: Brook & Khalfan Contracting Co, PO Box 493, Abu Dhabi; Abu Dhabi Oasis Residence, Furnished Apartments, PO Box 6336, Abu Dhabi; Bin Eid Trading Est; Abdullah Khalfan Bunkering; Khalfan Transport & General Contracting Co; National Crushers (Saeed Bin Khalfan)
Principal Bankers: National Bank of Abu Dhabi; Banque du Caire; Bank of Oman Ltd; National Bank of Sharjah

Principal Shareholders: Equal partnership
Date of Establishment: 1965
No of Employees: 1,000

ABU DHABI GULF HOTEL

PO Box 3766, Abu Dhabi
Tel: 377260
Telex: 22904 Gulftl EM
Telefax: 376537

Chairman: H E Nasser Al Nowais
Directors: Selim El Zyr (General Manager)
Senior Executives: Adel Hallaba (Exec Asst Manager)

PRINCIPAL ACTIVITIES: Hotel business
Parent Company: Abu Dhabi National Hotel Company
Principal Bankers: National Bank of Abu Dhabi

Date of Establishment: March 1977
No of Employees: 230

ABU DHABI INTER-CONTINENTAL HOTEL

PO Box 4171, Abu Dhabi
Tel: 666888
Cable: IHCAD Abu Dhabi
Telex: 23160 Inhot EM
Telefax: (971 2) 669153

Senior Executives: Sameer Z Ayouby (General Manager), Michael Kappes (Director of Sales), Helma Eppstein (Regional Housekeeper), Goerge Samara (Finance Director), Abdul Aziz (Purchasing Manager), Atef Gabbani ()Personnel & Training Manager), Keith Tose (Chief Engineer)

PRINCIPAL ACTIVITIES: Hotel business
Principal Bankers: National Bank of Abu Dhabi
Financial Information:

	1990
	US$'000
Sales turnover	21,000

Principal Shareholders: Abu Dhabi Government
Date of Establishment: 1980
No of Employees: 450

ABU DHABI INVESTMENT CO (ADIC)

PO Box 46309, Abu Dhabi
Tel: 328200 (general), 328605, 331660 (loans & syndications), 324205, 329051 (treasury), 333026 (new issues), 331595/319452 (equities)
Cable: Adinvestco Abu Dhabi
Telex: 23824 ADICGN EM, 22968 ADICCR EM
Telefax: 212903

Chairman: Hareb Al-Darmaki
Directors: Hareb Al-Darmaki, Obeid Al Nassiri, Salem Al Muhannadi, Khalifa Mohammed Al Muhairi, Mohammed Ahmed Al Fahim, Khalifa Al Kindi, Mohammed Bin Hamoodah
Senior Executives: Khalifa Mohammed Al Muhairi (Director & Acting General Manager), Humaid Darwish (Asst General Manager), Fakhruddin Goga (Financial Controller)

PRINCIPAL ACTIVITIES: Merchant and investment banking activities in the UAE and overseas
Parent Company: Abu Dhabi Investment Authority (ADIA)
Subsidiary Companies: Plaza Residential Developments Ltd, ADIC Finance Co BV
Principal Bankers: National Bank of Abu Dhabi, Abu Dhabi; First Chicago Int'l Banking Corp, New York; Deutsche Bank, Frankfurt; Union Bank of Switzerland, Zurich; Mitsui Taiyo Kobe Bank, Tokyo; Lloyds Bank (Overseas) Plc, London; National Bank of Abu Dhabi, London
Financial Information:

	1989	1990
	Dh'000	Dh'000
Profits	26,435	25,030
Deposits	3,681,234	3,384,089
Loans & advances	599,767	563,362
Authorised capital	200,000	200,000
Paid-up capital	110,250	110,250
Total assets	4,296,000	4,019,600

Principal Shareholders: Abu Dhabi Investment Authority (90%), National Bank of Abu Dhabi (10%)
Date of Establishment: 24 February, 1977
No of Employees: 41 (including subsidiaries)

ABU DHABI MARINE OPERATING CO A.D.M.A.- O.P.C.O.

PO Box 303, Abu Dhabi
Tel: 776600
Cable: Admarine
Telex: 22284 Adma EM
Telefax: 669785, 776600 ext 4888

Board Chairman: HE Shaikh Tahnoun Bin Mohammad Al Nahyan
Board of Directors: S Al Mazroui (ADNOC), J C Davies (BP), B Madinier (TOTAL-CFP), Y Tamura (JODCO)
Senior Executives: A Durand de Bousingen (General Manager), D Woodward (Deputy General Manager - Operations), M N Shanti (Asst General Manager -Technical), Saif N Al Suweidi (Asst General Manager - Administration)

PRINCIPAL ACTIVITIES: Oil and gas exploration, production and export
Parent Company: ADNOC (Abu Dhabi) and Adma Ltd (London)
Principal Bankers: National Bank of Abu Dhabi

Principal Shareholders: Abu Dhabi National Oil Co (ADNOC) (60%), British Petroleum (BP) (14.67%), TOTAL-Compagnie Francaise des Petroles (TOTAL-CFP) (13.33%), Japan Oil Development Co (JODCO) (12%)
Date of Establishment: July 1977 (took over operations from ADMA)
No of Employees: Approx 1,650

ABU DHABI MARITIME & MERCANTILE INTERNATIONAL

PO Box 247, Abu Dhabi
Tel: 323131
Cable: ADMMI Abudhabi
Telex: 22245 EM
Telefax: 213661

Chairman: Rahma bin Mohammed Al Masaood
Directors: HE Shaikh Suroor bin Sultan Al Daheri, HE Shaikh Saeed bin Mohammed Al Nahyan; Butti bin Ahmed Al Otaiba, Ahmed Hamdan Bu Debs
Senior Executives: S D Blake (General Manager)

PRINCIPAL ACTIVITIES: Lloyds Agents, travel agents, marine operators, dry cargo ship and tanker agents, general merchants, import and distribution of oilfield related equipment and foodstuffs
Principal Agencies: OCL Hapag Lloyd; Yugolinija; Schenkers; Nalco Italiana; Nalfloc; W & J Leigh; Saunders Valves; Crosby Valves; Beechams; Yardley; United Biscuits
Branch Offices: Branches in Abu Dhabi; Al Ain; Jebel Dhanna/Ruwais
Parent Company: Inchcape Group Plc
Associated Companies: Gray Mackenzie & Co Limited, London SW1, UK
Principal Bankers: Standard Chartered Bank; National Bank of Abu Dhabi; British Bank of the Middle East; Grindlays Bank

Date of Establishment: August 1982
No of Employees: 95

ABU DHABI NATIONAL CO FOR BUILDING MATERIALS (BILDCO)

PO Box 2443, Abu Dhabi
Tel: 773834
Cable: Buildco
Telex: 22299 BILDCO EM
Telefax: (971 2) 771863

Chairman: Faraj Bin Ali Bin Hamoodah
Directors: Mohamed Abdulla Brook (Vice Chariman), Sultan Bin Rashid (Managing Director), Rashid Al Mansouri, Hamil Al Gaith, Mohamed Abdul Azeez Al Rubayeh, Matar Al Muheiri
Senior Executives: Ahmed Sami Aboul Ezz (General Manager), Ali Osman Ali (Financial Manager)

PRINCIPAL ACTIVITIES: Import and marketing of all kinds of building materials and supplies and services to oil operating companies and related industries
Principal Agencies: M C Bauchemie Mueller, Germany; Armitage Shanks, UK; Sangyong Corp, Korea; David Roberts (Bottle) Ltd, UK; Mitsubishi Corp, Japan; Klockner, Germany
Branch Offices: BILDCO Agencies, PO Box 2443, Abu Dhabi
Principal Bankers: National Bank of Abu Dhabi; United Bank Ltd; Abu Dhabi Commercial Bank; BCC (Emirates), ANZ Grindlays Bank
Financial Information:

	1989
	Dh'000
Sales turnover	25,000
Authorised capital	3,000
Paid-up capital	3,000
Total assets	25,000

Principal Shareholders: Chairman and directors as described
Date of Establishment: 1974
No of Employees: 21

ABU DHABI NATIONAL HOTELS CO

PO Box 46806, Abu Dhabi
Tel: 447228 (l2 lines)
Cable: HOTELCORP
Telex: 23183 Hotlco EM
Telefax: 448495

Chairman: Nasser Al Nowais
Directors: Sayed Abdullah Al-Mousawe (General Manager)
Senior Executives: Abdullah Ali Al-Saadi (Deputy General
 Manager), Ahmed Ender (Executive Manager - Catering
 Division), Nael Hashweh (Administration & Finance Manager),
 Sheikh Omar Mahjoub (Head of Technical Department)

PRINCIPAL ACTIVITIES: Hotel owners, developers, catering
 operations (food, maintenance and cleaning)
Principal Agencies: Hilton, Sheraton, Intercontinental, Meridien
Subsidiary Companies: AMAR Hotel Investment Corp NV;
 Nederland; Overseas Tourist Investment Co Ltd, Jersey; Al
 Ghazal Taxi Co, Abu Dhabi
Principal Bankers: National Bank of Abu Dhabi, Abu Dhabi;
 Arab Bank for Investment & Foreign Trade, Abu Dhabi;
 BCCE, Abu Dhabi
Financial Information:

	1988/89	1989/90
	Dh'000	Dh'000
Sales turnover	317,090	347,122
Profits	58,578	64,986
Authorised capital	121,000	121,000
Paid-up capital	121,000	121,000
Total assets	488,427	501,098

Principal Shareholders: Government of Abu Dhabi (35%); UAE
 Nationals (65%)
Date of Establishment: April 1978
No of Employees: 5,500

ABU DHABI NATIONAL INSURANCE CO

Sh Khalifa St, PO Box 839, Abu Dhabi
Tel: 343171
Cable: Adinsure
Telex: 22340 Adinc EM
Telefax: 02 211358

Chairman: HE Khalaf A Al Otaibah
Directors: Sheikh Ahmed Bin Saif Al Nahyan, Butti Bin Ahmed
 Al Otaibah, Ghanim Bin Ali Bin Hamoodah, Sultan Bin Rashid,
 Mohamad Abdul Aziz Al Rubaya, Matar Abdulla Al Muhairy,
 Abdullah Nasser, Ghanim Al-Mazrouie, Yousif Omair Al-Yousif
Senior Executives: HE Khalaf A Al Otaibah (General Manager),
 Wagdi Hamdi (Deputy General Manager Corporate Finance &
 Services), James W Stafford (Asst General Manager Marine &
 Aviation), Wael Khatib (Asst General Manager Non-Marine)

PRINCIPAL ACTIVITIES: All classes of insurance and
 reinsurance
Branch Offices: United Arab Emirates: Abu Dhabi, PO Box
 3275, Tel 325274; Al-Ain, PO Box 1407, Tel 641834; Dubai,
 PO Box 11236, Tel 222223, Telex 47076; Sharjah, PO Box
 3674, Tel 350743; Saudi Arabia: Riyadh, PO Box 42841, Tel
 4765451, Telex 404064; UK: Abu Dhabi National Insurance Co
 (Services) Ltd, 40 Lime St, London EC3M 5BY, Tel 01-929
 0268, Telex 8951284 ADNIC G, Fax 01-626 0884; France: Abu
 Dhabi National Insurance Co France (SARL), 2 rue de la Paix,
 75002 Paris, Tel 49270306, Telex 214371 ADNIC FR, Fax 01-
 49278325
Subsidiary Companies: Abu Dhabi National Insurance Co
 (Services) Ltd, London; Abu Dhabi National Insurance Co
 France (SARL)
Principal Bankers: National Bank of Abu Dhabi; Abu Dhabi
 Commercial Bank; Bank of Credit & Commerce International;
 Bank of Credit and Commerce (Emirates); United Bank Ltd

Financial Information:

	1988/89
	Dh'000
Sales turnover	351,197
Profits	100,176
Authorised capital	150,000
Paid-up capital	150,000
Total assets	787,657

Principal Shareholders: Government of Abu Dhabi and citizens
 of UAE
Date of Establishment: 1972
No of Employees: 223 (H O & Branches), 159 (H O)

ABU DHABI NATIONAL OIL CO
A.D.N.O.C.

PO Box 898, Abu Dhabi
Tel: 666000
Cable: Adnoc
Telex: 22215 Adnoc EM, 23688 Adnoc EM
Telefax: 6023389

Chairman of Supreme Petroleum Council: HH Sheikh Khalifa Bin
 Zayed Al-Nahyan
Members of Supreme Petroleum Council: HH Sheikh Tahnoun
 Bin Mohammed Al Nahyan, HH Sheikh Surour Bin
 Mohammed Al Nahyan, HH Sheikh Sultan Bin Zayed Al
 Nahyan, HH Sheikh Mohammed Bin Zayed Al Nahyan,
 Mohammed Khalifa Al Kindi, Dr Mana Saeed Al Otaiba,
 Mohammed Habroush Al Suweidi, Ali Bin Ahmed Al Dhahiri,
 Jau'an Salem Al Dhahiri, Mohammed Eid Al Mureikhi, HE
 Sohail F Al Mazrui
Senior Executives: Sohail F Al Mazrui (ADNOC General
 Manager & General Secretary of Petroleum Supreme
 Council), Mohammed S Al Hamli (Marketing Director), Khalaf
 Al Oteiba (Procesing Director), Rashid S Al Suweidi
 (Exploration & Production Director), Salah Salem Al Shamsi
 (Projects Director), Abdulla Nasir Al Suweidi (Planning &
 Coordination Director), Walid S Al Mehairi (Personnel
 Director), Ahmad Al Sayegh (Administration Director), Ali Al
 Yabhouni (DPS Director), Dr Atef Suleiman (Legal Advisor),
 Waleed Al Muhairi (GMO Manager)

PRINCIPAL ACTIVITIES: Deals in all phases of the oil industry
 such as: exploration, drilling, development, production,
 refining, gas processing, chemical, petrochemical industry,
 marine transportation, storage, distribution and marketing the
 Company's share of crude oil, liquefied gas and refined
 products
Branch Offices: Wholly Owned Plants by ADNOC: Umm Al-Nar
 Refinery (Capacity: 60,000 bpd); Ruwais Refinery (Capacity:
 120,000 bpd); Habshan Gas Treatment Plant; Salt & Chlorine
 Plant
Subsidiary/Associated Companies: Wholly Owned Subsidiaries:
 Abu Dhabi National Oil Co for Distribution (ADNOC FOD)
 (100%); National Drilling Co (NDC) (100%); Abu Dhabi National
 Tankers Co (ADNATCO) (100%); Oil Operating Companies:
 Abu Dhabi Marine Co (ADMA-OPCO) (60%); Abu Dhabi Co for
 Onshore Oil Operations (ADCO) (60%); Zakum Development
 Co (ZADCO) (50%); Other Companies: Abu Dhabi Gas
 Liquefaction Co (ADGAS) (51%); Abu Dhabi Gas Industries
 Ltd (GASCO) (68%); Abu Dhabi Drilling Chemicals & Products
 Co Ltd (ADDCAP) (75%); National Petroleum Construction Co
 (NPCC) (70%); Abu Dhabi Petroleum Ports Operating Co
 (ADPPOC) (60%); National Marine Services (NMS) (60%);
 Fertilizers Industries Ltd (FERTIL) (66.66%); The Liquefied
 Gas Shipping Co Ltd (LGSC) (51%); Overseas Affiliates: Arab
 Petroleum Pipeline Co (SUMED) (15%); Pak Arab Fertilizers
 Ltd (PAFCO) (48%); Pak Arab Refinery Ltd (PARCO) (40%)

Principal Shareholders: Abu Dhabi Government
Date of Establishment: 1971
No of Employees: ADNOC 3,350; ADNOC Group of Companies
 19,300

ABU DHABI NATIONAL PLASTIC PIPES CO

PO Box 2915, Abu Dhabi
Tel: 724400/1/2, 554400
Cable: Adpipe
Telex: 22627 Adpipe EM
Telefax: 782685, 554531

Chairman: Hasan Mousa Al Qumzi
Directors: Essa A Ateek (Director General)
Senior Executives: Eng Ezzat K Fahmy (General Manager),
John Hughes (Technical Manager)

PRINCIPAL ACTIVITIES: Production and marketing of PVC
pipes and fittings
Principal Bankers: National Bank of Abu Dhabi; Bank of Credit
& Commerce (Emirates)

Principal Shareholders: 100% Government
Date of Establishment: September 1974
No of Employees: 72

ABU DHABI NATIONAL TANKER CO
A.D.N.A.T.C.O.

PO Box 2977, Abu Dhabi
Tel: 331800
Cable: ADNTCO
Telex: 22747 ADNTCO EM
Telefax: 322940

Chairman: Khalaf R Al Oteiba
Senior Executives: Bader Al Sowaidi (General Manager), Moshin
Nassar (Finance & Admin Manager), Mohd Aziz Ansari
(Commercial Manager), Nohd Nooraldeen (Chartering
Manager), Sydney Ferguson (Fleet Manager), J J Bruegmann
(Marine Manager), Ismail Abu Salem (Personnel Manager)

PRINCIPAL ACTIVITIES: Holding company, transportation of
crude oil and petroleum products, chartering and shipbroking
Parent Company: Abu Dhabi National Oil Co (ADNOC)
Subsidiary Companies: Tanker Marine Services Company Ltd
(tanker operators); Tanker Marine Chartering Company Ltd
Principal Bankers: National Bank of Abu Dhabi

Principal Shareholders: 100% Abu Dhabi National Oil Company
Date of Establishment: April 1975
No of Employees: 45 (office staff)

ABU DHABI OIL CO (ADOC)

PO Box 630, Abu Dhabi
Tel: 661100
Cable: OILJAPAN ABU DHABI
Telex: 22260 Adoco EM
Telefax: 665956

President: Y Kasahara
Directors: M Dohi (Managing Director), Dr S Iwasa (Executive
Vice President)
Senior Executives: K Komai (Finance Manager), T Hirota
(Materials Supply Manager), K Kawamura (Production
Manager), H Noguchi (Development Manager), K Murakami
(Maintenance & Engineering Manager), A Tamiya (Marine &
Transport Manager)

PRINCIPAL ACTIVITIES: Operations of the Mubarraz offshore
field
Parent Company: Abu Dhabi Oil Co Ltd, 1-19 Akasaka, 8-
Chome, Minato-Ku, Tokyo, Japan
Principal Shareholders: Cosmo Oil (51.1%), Nippon Mining
(25.6%), Japan National Oil Corp (17.8%), other Japanese
companies (5.5%)
Date of Establishment: January 17, 1968
No of Employees: 183

ABU DHABI OILFIELD SERVICES EST

PO Box 4015, Abu Dhabi
Tel: 322768/9
Cable: Ados
Telex: 22312 Ados EM

Proprietor: Musallam Maktoom Rashed Al Mazroui
Directors: Musallam Maktoom Rashed Al Mazroui (Chairman),
M R Sturt (Managing Director), E E Lovett, D Salisbury-Jones

PRINCIPAL ACTIVITIES: Representation of major suppliers of
industrial equipment to the oilfield industry; supply, repair and
maintenance of offshore and onshore oilfield equipment
Principal Agencies: Burleigh Marine; B S & B Safety Systems,
UK; Cameron Iron Works, UK, USA, France; Coppus
Engineering, USA; Crane Packing, UK; Diamant Boart,
Belgium; Drilltec, W Germany, USA; Dow Corning, UK, USA;
Gilbarco, UK, USA; Hamworthy Engineering Ltd, UK; James
Howden, UK; IMODCO, USA; Industrial Control Services Ltd,
UK; Ocean Technical Systems; Oil Plus, UK; Oilfield
Inspection Services, UK; Plenty Group Ltd, UK; Pipeline Seal
& Insulator Co UK; NL Sperry-Sun, USA; Sundstrand USA;
TBV; Vallourec, France; Tideland Signal; Teledyne Farris Eng,
USA; Chemische Fabrick Servo, Holland; Brissonneau & Lote
Marine, France; Graham Manufacturing, USA; Kenmac Controls
Ltd, UK; Richard Klinger Ltd, UK; Pipeline Seal & Insulator
Co, Ltd; Sundstrand Fluid Handling; Hydrolex Inc, USA;
Kleber Industrie, France; PSI Telecommunications; Lapmaster
Int Ltd; Wilson Walton Int; Opsco Ind Ltd, Canada; Cormon
Ltd, UK; Neutra Rust Int'l Ltd, UK; KeyMed Ind Ltd, UK
Associated/Subsidiary Companies: ADOS Holdings Ltd, UK;
Subsidiary: Middle East Oilfield Supplies Est, Dubai; MEOS
Workshop, Jebel Ali
Principal Bankers: First National Bank of Chicago, Abu Dhabi;
Arab Bank for Investment & Foreign Trade, Abu Dhabi; British
Bank of the Middle East, Abu Dhabi

Principal Shareholders: Musallam Maktoom Rashed (Proprietor)
Date of Establishment: 1971
No of Employees: 220

ABU DHABI PETROLEUM CO LTD

PO Box 26696, Abu Dhabi
Tel: 328288
Telex: 24203 ADPC EM
Telefax: 211248

Senior Executives: D Heard (Representative)

PRINCIPAL ACTIVITIES: Representative company of the non-
ADNOC shareholders in ADCO
Associated Companies: Abu Dhabi Petroleum Co, 33 Cavendish
Square, London W1, UK

ABU DHABI PETROLEUM PORTS
OPERATING CO
A.D.P.P.O.C.

PO Box 61, Abu Dhabi
Tel: 336700
Cable: Adppoc Abu Dhabi
Telex: 22209 Adppoc EM
Telefax: 216002

Chairman: F S Al Mazrui (Adnoc)
Directors: T Alireza (Lamnalco), Y Al Nowais (Adnoc), R S Al
Suweidi (Adnoc), H Masri (Adnoc), I Zalatimo (Adnoc)
Senior Executives: Tony E Dennis (General Manager), Moeen Al
Sarraj (Company Secretary & Finance Manager), B Al Jarah
(Operations Manager), M Al Bahti (Technical Manager), Y Al
Hosani (Personnel & Administration Manager)

PRINCIPAL ACTIVITIES: The marine operations, maintenance of
offshore loading terminals and management of the
petrochemical ports of Jebel Dhanna Ruwais, Zirqu Island,
Umm Al Nar and Mubarras Island. To provide port traffic and
emergency control, pilotage, berthing and mooring, collection
of port dues, navigational aids and channel maintenance,

pollution control, shiphandling and firefighting tugs, mooring launches, diving, jetty and berth maintenance services, marine surveys and all port authority duties. All marine services are available to third parties both in UAE and Overseas

Branch Offices: ADPPOC Port Control: PO Box 61 Jebel Dhanna, Tel 052-72018, Telex 52207 APOCRUEM

Parent Company: Abu Dhabi National Oil Company (ADNOC)

Associated Companies: Alireza Group of Companies (Lamnalco Ltd)

Principal Bankers: Bank of Credit & Commerce (Emirates)

Financial Information:

	1989/90 Dh'000
Sales turnover	78,000
Profits	19,000
Authorised capital	100,000
Paid-up capital	25,000
Total assets	49,000

Principal Shareholders: Abu Dhabi National Oil Company (ADNOC) (60%); Lamnalco Limited (40%)

Date of Establishment: 1 February, 1979

No of Employees: 338

ABU DHABI SERVICES OFFICE
A.D.S.O.

PO Box 746, Abu Dhabi
Tel: 335567 (5 lines)
Cable: Adsoff
Telex: 22406 Adsoff EM
Telefax: 344886

Chairman: Philip F Khoury

Directors: Fayek El Khoury (Managing)

Senior Executives: Victor Thanikkal (Operations Manager), Elias Amoury (Chief Accountant), Abdullah Jarrar (Clearing Manager)

PRINCIPAL ACTIVITIES: Shipping, clearing and international forwarding

Principal Agencies: Astran; Whittle Int'l, UK; Amerford Int'l, USA; Transworld, Italy; General Transportation Services

Branch Offices: Abu Dhabi Services Office, PO Box 2300, Dubai, UAE; Abu Dhabi Services Office, Silaa Branch, Silaa, Abu Dhabi, UAE

Subsidiary Companies: Al Jahani Est, Saudi Arabia

Principal Bankers: Arab African International Bank

Financial Information:

	1989/90 Dh'000
Sales turnover	36,000
Profits	3,000
Authorised capital	10,000
Paid-up capital	10,000
Total assets	7,000

Principal Shareholders: Juma Bin Khadim Al Muhairy; Philip F Khoury

Date of Establishment: 1968

No of Employees: 100

ABU DHABI SHERATON HOTEL

PO Box 640, Abu Dhabi
Tel: 823333
Cable: Sheraton Abu Dhabi
Telex: 23453 Sherad EM

Chairman: Nasser Al Nowais

PRINCIPAL ACTIVITIES: Hotel operation

Principal Agencies: Managed by the Sheraton Middle East Management Corporation

Principal Bankers: National Bank of Abu Dhabi

Principal Shareholders: Owned by the Emiri Court, Government of Abu Dhabi

Date of Establishment: 24th August 1979

No of Employees: 370

ABU DHABI SHIPPING AGENCY

PO Box 46103, Abu Dhabi
Tel: 721228, 314100, 316644, 312626, 318877
Cable: Adgent
Telex: 22819 Adgent EM
Telefax: 311814

Proprietor: S Moherbie

Senior Executives: P M Reilly (Managing Director), G Yung (Manager), P Babu (Commercial Manager), J Thomas (Financial Controller), J Percy (Freight Services Manager), D Sequeira (Station Manager Airfreight)

PRINCIPAL ACTIVITIES: Shipping agents; freight forwarders; clearing and forwarding; container groupage; air freight agents; project contractors; international courier agents; international exhibitions; international removals; general insurance agents

Principal Agencies: Orient Overseas Container Line (OOCL); Norasia Shipping Line; MSAS Cargo Int'l, New India Assurance Co Ltd

Branch Offices: Al Ain: PO Box 80200, Al Ain, Tel 666100, Fax 666200

Principal Bankers: Commercial Bank of Dubai

Date of Establishment: April 1979

No of Employees: Abu Dhabi 50

ABU DHABI TRADING & CONTRACTING CO

Hamdan St, Rashid Aweidha Bldg, PO Box 266, Abu Dhabi
Tel: 330930
Cable: Alaweidha
Telex: 22563 Aweida EM

Chairman: Rashid Aweidha

PRINCIPAL ACTIVITIES: General trading and contracting, transportation, import and distribution of storage systems; domestic appliances; machinery; office machines; furniture; air conditioning

Principal Agencies: Dexion, Westinghouse, Simon, White Westinghouse

Parent Company: Aweidha Sons & Bin Sagar Group of Companies

Associated Companies: Baniyas Trading Co; Aljamal Stores; Abu Dhabi Gas Co; Abu Dhabi Hospital Supplies

Principal Bankers: National Bank of Abu Dhabi

ABU DHABI TRAVEL BUREAU
Travel-Cargo Packers & Forwarders

Sh Hamdan Bldg, Corniche Road, PO Box 278, Abu Dhabi
Tel: 338700
Cable: Al Falahi
Telex: 22427 ATB EM
Telefax: 346020

Chairman: Mohammed Bin Saqr Saadoun Al Falahi

Senior Executives: Mohammed Radhi Mohammed (General Manager), Georges Khoury (Financial Controller), Raymond Kourban (Sales Manager)

PRINCIPAL ACTIVITIES: Travel, freight forwarding and cargo handling

Principal Agencies: Air India, Kuwait Airways, Saudia, Yemenia, KLM, Korean Airlines, Somali Airlines, Garuda Indonesia, Iran Air, Iraqi Airways; Sub Agencies: Singapore Airlines, PIA, Royal Jordanian Airlines, Gulf Air, Sabena, Bangladesh Biman, Sudan Airways, Emirates Air, Cathay Pacific, Eastern Airlines, Swiss Air, GSA

Branch Offices: Two branches in Abu Dhabi, branch in Al Ain and branch in Abu Dhabi International Airport

Subsidiary Companies: Delma Travels

UAE (Abu Dhabi)

Principal Bankers: National Bank of Oman, Abu Dhabi
Financial Information:

	1990 Dh'000
Sales turnover	136,153
Profits	1,000
Authorised capital	350

Date of Establishment: 1966
No of Employees: 125

ABU DHABI WORKSHOP SERVICES CO

PO Box 4015, Abu Dhabi
Tel: 322768
Telex: 22312 ADOSEM

PRINCIPAL ACTIVITIES: Service and repair of oil field
  machinery
Principal Agencies: Hunting oilfield services
Branch Offices: Musafa, Tel 554106; Sadiyat, Tel 578393

ADMAK GENERAL CONTRACTING CO

PO Box 650, Abu Dhabi
Tel: 322237
Cable: ALKHARAFI ABU DHABI
Telex: 22320 Kharafi EM
Telefax: 322212

Chairman: Mohamed Abdulmohsin Kharafi
Directors: Mohsen Kamel (Managing Director), Mounir Mustafa
  (Executive Director)
Senior Executives: Omar Dessouki (Finance & Administration
  Director)

PRINCIPAL ACTIVITIES: General civil engineering contractors,
  such as building, roads, bridges, sewerage and water
  projects (lines, pumping stations & treatment plants)
Branch Offices: Al Ain (UAE): PO Box 1189, Tel 825700, Telex
  22320 Kharafi EM, Fax 828936
Parent Company: Mohamed Abdulmohsin Kharafi, PO Box 886,
  Safat, Kuwait
Principal Bankers: Grindlays Bank, Abu Dhabi; Arab Bank, Abu
  Dhabi; Arab African Intl Bank, Abu Dhabi

Principal Shareholders: Ahmed Bin Hadir Al Murekhi (UAE
  National) 51%; M A Kharafi (Kuwaiti) 49%
Date of Establishment: 1968 in Abu Dhabi; and under present
  status: 1980
No of Employees: Total in UAE: 500 - 700

AHMED KHALIL AL BAKER & SONS

See AL BAKER, AHMED KHALIL, & SONS

AL AHLIA OILFIELDS DEVELOPMENT CO

PO Box 4399, Abu Dhabi
Tel: Head Office: 338622, Operations Base: 553555
Cable: Aodco EM
Telex: (Head Office) 24322 Aodco EM, (Operations Base) 23927
  Opad EM

Chairman: Saeed Bin Sultan Al Darmaki
Directors: Samir Zaabri (Managing Director)
Senior Executives: Camille Atie (General Manager)

PRINCIPAL ACTIVITIES: Well testing, wire line and coil tubing
  services, well safety systems, and supply of associated
  equipment
Principal Agencies: Al Ahlia Otis; Al Ahlia Mather & Platt;
  Teledyne Geotech; Gray Oil Tool; Serck Baker; Mainworks;
  Procor; Industrial Security Supplies; Champion Chemicals;
  Prime Mover Maintenance; Cyanamid; Durometalic; Airflex
  Containers Ltd; Gilbert Gilkes Gordon; Epic Inc; Seismograph
  Service Ltd; Seatech; Burgess Manning; Raysut Cement;
  Wormald Engineering
Parent Company: Al Ahlia General Trading Company (Private)
  Ltd
Principal Bankers: Arab Bank for Investment and Foreign Trade

Financial Information:

	US$'000
Sales turnover	20,400
Paid-up capital	2,800

Principal Shareholders: H E Shaikh Tahnoun Bin Mohammad Al
  Nahyan, H E Shaikh Saif Bin Mohammad Al Nahyan, H E
  Shaikh Mohammad Bin Butti Al Ahmed, Sa'eed Bin Sultan Al
  Darmaki, Shabib Bin Mohammad Al Dhaheri, Hamad Bin
  Sultan Al Darmaki, Ali Bin Khalfan Al Dhaheri, Hilal Bin
  Sa'eed Mohammad Al Dhaheri, Ali Bin Ahmad Al Dhaheri,
  Rashid Bin Khalfan Al Dhaheri, Sa'eed Hilal Al Darmaki,
  Sa'eed Mohammad Al Kalili
Date of Establishment: 21st July 1982
No of Employees: 50

AL AHMADIAH CONTRACTING & TRADING

PO Box 2752, Abu Dhabi
Tel: 344895, 323811
Telex: 22877 Wafa EM

PRINCIPAL ACTIVITIES: Building and construction, supply of
  building materials
Principal Agencies: Unibond, UK; Cardisa, Italy

AL AIN AHLIA INSURANCE CO

PO Box 3077, Abu Dhabi
Tel: 323551 (9 lines)
Cable: Ahlin
Telex: 22352 Ahlin EM

Chairman: Hamil Al Gaith
Directors: Ahmed Ghanoum Al Hameli (Deputy Chairman),
  Rashid Bin Awaidha, Rahma Al Masaood, Ibrahim Al Mazroui,
  Mohamad Juan Al Badi, Mohmed Abdulla Bin Brook,
  Mohammed Al Fandi Al Mazroui, Obaid Ahmed Al Dahiri

PRINCIPAL ACTIVITIES: All classes of insurance and
  reinsurance
Subsidiary Companies: Branch Office: Al Ain, PO Box 1770, Tel
  642142, 656254, Telex 33569 HALA EM; Dubai, PO Box 3541,
  Tel 222240, 281829, Telex 47416 AL AIN EM
Principal Bankers: National Bank of Abu Dhabi; Arab African
  International Bank; Arab Bank for Investments & Foreign
  Trade; BCCI
Financial Information:

	Dh'000
Authorised capital	60,000
Paid-up capital	30,000

Principal Shareholders: Government and citizens of Abu Dhabi
Date of Establishment: 1975
No of Employees: 55

AL AIN CEMENT FACTORY

PO Box 1114, Al Ain, Abu Dhabi
Tel: 3-828600
Telex: 33527 Aincmt EM
Telefax: 3-828711

PRINCIPAL ACTIVITIES: Production of cement
Parent Company: General Industry Corporation, Abu Dhabi

AL AIN GENERAL CONTRACTING CO (ALGECO)

PO Box 6397, Al Ain, Abu Dhabi
Tel: (03)25606
Cable: Algeco
Telex: 33503 EM Algeco

Chairman: Amal I Hourani
Directors: Mohammed Salem
Senior Executives: Fouad Touma (Chief Engineer), Salim Isber
  (Administrator)

PRINCIPAL ACTIVITIES: Building and sewerage works
Branch Offices: Lebanon: PO Box 113-5585, Beirut

Principal Bankers: Grindlays Bank

Date of Establishment: 1969
No of Employees: 600

AL AIN INTER-CONTINENTAL HOTEL
PO Box 16031, Al Ain
Tel: 686686
Cable: INHOTELCOR
Telex: 34034 IHCAAN EM
Telefax: 686766, 686868

Senior Executives: Chawki H Ayoub (General Manager), Philip D'Cruze (Controller), Ahmed Kamel (Sales Manager), Herve Baguenard (Food & Beverage Manager), Simon Lorenzo (Executive Assistant Manager)

PRINCIPAL ACTIVITIES: Hotel business
Principal Agencies: Inter-Continental Hotels Corporation
Parent Company: Abu Dhabi National Hotels Company
Principal Bankers: National Bank of Abu Dhabi; Citibank
Financial Information:

	1990 Dh'000
Sales turnover	25,000
Profits	10,000

Principal Shareholders: Abu Dhabi National Hotels Company
Date of Establishment: May 1982
No of Employees: 195

AL AIN MINERAL WATER BOTTLING PLANT
PO Box 16020, Al Ain, Abu Dhabi
Tel: 3-686500
Telex: 34133 Ainwtr Em
Telefax: 3-686515

PRINCIPAL ACTIVITIES: Mineral water bottling plant
Parent Company: General Industry Corporation, Abu Dhabi

AL ATTIYAH CONTRACTING & TRADING CO
PO Box 2273, Abdul Jalil Bldg, Abu Dhabi
Tel: 341704, 344792
Telex: 22444 Attiyah EM

PRINCIPAL ACTIVITIES: Civil engineering contractors, supply of building materials and construction plant equipment

ALAWI TRADING CO
Sheikh Hamdan St, Al Mallah Bldg, PO Box 983, Abu Dhabi
Tel: 322485/6
Cable: Alnasr
Telex: 22207 Alwai EM

Chairman: Ghaffair Al Alawi (Owner)

PRINCIPAL ACTIVITIES: Import and distribution of heavy machinery, engines, pumps, welding machines, tools and machines, fork lifts and dumpers
Principal Agencies: Dale Electric Ltd, British Ropes, Blackhawk Hand Tools, Coles Cranes, Rolls-Royce Motors, Sigmund Pumps, Lincoln, Bonser Engineering
Parent Company: Al Nasr Trading Organisation
Principal Bankers: National Bank of Dubai, Abu Dhabi

AL BAHAR, MOHAMED ABDULRAHMAN,
PO Box 441, Abu Dhabi
Tel: 554200
Cable: Moatasim Abu Dhabi
Telex: 22988 BAHAR EM
Telefax: 553061

Chairman: Mohamed Abdulrahman Al-Bahar
Directors: Jassim Mohamed Al-Bahar (Vice President), Issam Mohamed Al-Bahar (Executive Vice President)
Senior Executives: Ashfaque Azad (Area Manager, UAE), Wassim Charara (Branch Manager Abu Dhabi)

PRINCIPAL ACTIVITIES: Distribution of earthmoving, material handling, compaction & asphalt equipment, generators and control systems
Principal Agencies: Caterpillar; Koehring (Bantam & Lorain); Barber Greene; Atlet; Ingram; Oshkosh; Telsmith; Hiab
Branch Offices: Arabian Gulf States
Parent Company: Head office in Kuwait
Principal Bankers: Arab Bank; National Bank of Abu Dhabi; Grindlays Bank, Abu Dhabi

Principal Shareholders: Mohamed Abdulrahman Al-Bahar
Date of Establishment: 1964
No of Employees: 100

AL BAKER, AHMED KHALIL, & SONS
PO Box 134, Abu Dhabi
Tel: 324241, 341357
Cable: Al-Baker Pharmacy
Telex: 33213 Albakr EM

PRINCIPAL ACTIVITIES: Import and distribution of pharmaceuticals, chemicals, cosmetics, perfumes, baby foods and supplies of hospital equipments, laboratory instruments
Principal Agencies: Glaxo Group Ltd, UK; Fisons, Armour, Roussel Labs, Boots Co, UK; G D Searle & Co, UK; Sterling Products (Winthrop), Evans Medical, Optrex Ltd, Ortho, UK and USA; Norwich-Eaton, USA; Allergan Intl, USA; Pfizer Corpn, Schering Corpn, USA; Cyanamid (Lederle), etc and ATC Group, West Germany
Branch Offices: PO Box 1169, Deira, Dubai (UAE)
Parent Company: Head office: PO Box 9, Doha, Qatar
Principal Bankers: Banque Paribas; British Bank of the Middle East; Standard Chartered Bank

AL BAWARDI GROUP
PO Box 4118, Abu Dhabi
Tel: 2-349999
Telex: 22433 ABHO EM
Telefax: 2-318181

Chairman: Juma Ahmed Al Bawardi
Directors: Hasan Ali Darwish (President)
Senior Executives: Imad Abolhosn (Manager Mechanical & Process Dept), Bashar Dajani (Manager Control & Instrumentation Dept), Naresh Goplani (Manager Electrical & Telecoms Dept), Mukul Sarin (Financial Controller)

PRINCIPAL ACTIVITIES: Trading, distribution, supply and services of products related to: exploration and products, mechanical & process, electrical & telecoms, control & instrumentation
Principal Agencies: Algoma Steel, Canada; Dril Quip, USA; Ingram Cactus, USA; Itag, Germany; Petrolite, UK; Site Oil Tools, Canada; TSK, Japan; TriMax, USA; Trico Submersible Systems, USA; Tam Int'l, USA; Tryad, USA; Tubular Fiberglass, USA; Agriandre, France; Begemann Pumps, Holland; Hydrotech System, USA; Master Flo, Canada; Prime Actuators, UK; Stockdale, UK; Tomoe Saunders, UK; Woma, Germany; Trico Industries, USA; Bruel & Kjaer, Denmark; Costain Telecom & Systems, UK; Gard Controls, Norway; GE Fanuc, USA; Norcontrol, Norway; Petrotech, USA; Silvertech, UK; Texas Instruments, USA; Vonk Systems, Holland; Hapam, Holland; Iskra, Yugoslovia; Phillips Cables, Canada; Sarrat Industries, France; Transpak Elektro, Pakistan; Alan Dick, UK; Atis Assmann, Germany; Attel, France; Dynacord, Germany; Hitachi, Japan; Matra Communication, France; Plantronics, USA; SAT, France; Standard Communications, USA
Branch Offices: Al Bawardi Dubai, PO Box 3711, Dubai; Al Bawardi Jebel Ali
Subsidiary Companies: Al Bawardi Computers; Al Bawardi Marine Services; Al Bawardi Alan Dick; Al Bawardi All Metal; Graphic International Est; Al Bawardi General Maintenance
Principal Bankers: Arab Bank for Investment & Foreign Trade; British Bank of the Middle East

UAE (Abu Dhabi)

Financial Information:

	1990 US$'000
Sales turnover	34,000
Profits	3,000
Authorised capital	3,000
Paid-up capital	3,000
Total assets	1,000

Principal Shareholders: Juma Ahmed Al Bawardi
Date of Establishment: 1979

ALBERT ABELA CO (ABU DHABI)

PO Box 143, Abu Dhabi
Tel: 661520
Cable: Alabela Abu Dhabi
Telex: 22264 Abelas EM
Telefax: 665448

Directors: A Nadar (Senior Vice President, Dubai)
Senior Executives: Hani Abdelnour (Area Manager, Abu Dhabi),
Fawaz Masri (Trading Manager, Abu Dhabi), Wael Kremid
(Area Accountant, Abu Dhabi)

PRINCIPAL ACTIVITIES: Caterers and food supplies for oil
companies; contractors; hotels; airport catering and
manufacturers' representation (foodstuffs); tobacco
distribution
Principal Agencies: Brown & Williamson (Kent Cigarettes), USA;
Ceylon Tea Delma, Sri Lanka; Sunbright Canned Fruit Juices,
USA; Akvina Portion Products, Netherlands; Lorado Dairy
Products, Germany
Branch Offices: Supermarkets in Abu Dhabi and Dubai
Parent Company: Albert Abela Corporation Inc, Monte Carlo,
Monaco
Associated Companies: The New Supermarket Ltd;
Representation of the Albert Abela Group of Companies
Principal Bankers: Banque Paribas, Abu Dhabi

Date of Establishment: 1960
No of Employees: 300

AL DHAFRA INSURANCE CO SA

PO Box 319, Al Dhafra Bldg, Zayed 2nd Street, Abu Dhabi
Tel: 721444
Cable: Frasure
Telex: 23040 FRA EM
Telefax: 729833

Chairman: Sh Suroor Bin Sultan Al Dhahiri
Directors: Al Shaibah Saeed Al Hamily (Deputy Chairman), HE
Faraj Bin Hamoodah, HE Sayeh Mohammed Mousa Al
Qubeisy, Saleh Rashid Al Dhahery, Abdullah Al Massoud, Saif
Mubarak Al Riamy, Dr Mohammed Bin Khamis Al Rumaithy,
Sultan Bin Nasser Al Suweidi, Hussein Bin Jasem Al Nowais,
Obaid Khalifa Al Jaber
Senior Executives: Waked Rushdi Al Jayyusi (General Manager),
Sharif M Osman (Finance Manager), Mohamad Y Othman
(Manager Fire & General Accident Dept), Nabil Al Hakkim
(Manager Marine & Reinsurance), Fawaz Moukayed
(Marketing Manager), Mohamad Al Masri (Motor Manager),
Khader Shahin (Claims Superintendent)

PRINCIPAL ACTIVITIES: Domestic and international insurance
Branch Offices: Al Ain Town and Al Ain Traffic Office, Bida
Zayed and Abu Dhabi Traffic Office
Principal Bankers: Abu Dhabi Commercial Bank
Financial Information:

	1988 Dh'000	1989 Dh'000
Sales turnover	47,106	48,900
Profits	6,511	6,647
Authorised capital	60,000	60,000
Paid-up capital	32,624	32,624
Total assets	72,019	75,647

Principal Shareholders: Citizens of Abu Dhabi
Date of Establishment: 1979
No of Employees: 51

AL DHAHERI GROUP

PO Box 6676, Abu Dhabi
Tel: 332377
Telex: 23347 DAHERY

Chairman: Sheikh Suroor Bin Sultan Al Dhaheri
Directors: Sheikh Mohammed Bin Sultan Al Dhaheri, Sheikh
Saeed Bin Sultan Al Dhaheri
Senior Executives: Ragheb M Kanaan (General Manager)

PRINCIPAL ACTIVITIES: General trading, contracting and
representation of international firms, business consultancy, oil
& gas fields (onshore/offshore) services
Principal Agencies: Fiat Engineering,Italy; Italimpianti, Italy;
Remtech, France; Mearsk Drilling, Denmark; Bertin & Cie,
France; Al Dhaheri Group, Abu Dhabi (joint venture); Nordic
Chemical Co, Norway; Kongsberg Datamation System,
Norway; Anchor Drilling Fluids, Norway; Quillery, France;
Diesel Energie, France; Sodeteg, France; Henrich Hirdes, W
Germany
Subsidiary Companies: Al Dhaheri Raidan Contracting; Abu
Dhabi Refreshments Co (Pepsi); Electrical & Mechanical
Const Co (EMCC); Al Dhaheri Drilling & Oil Services; Al
Dhaheri Air Services; Pollensky & Zoellner, Abu Dhabi; Al
Dhaheri Enterprises; Emirates Consultancy Services
Principal Bankers: Abu Dhabi Commercial Bank Ltd; Bank of
Oman Ltd
Financial Information:

	Dh'000
Authorised capital	10,000
Paid-up capital	3,000

Date of Establishment: May 1st 1981
No of Employees: 310

AL FAHAD GENERAL TRADING & CONTRACTING CO

PO Box 866, Abu Dhabi
Tel: 332386
Cable: Al Fahad
Telex: 22412 Al Fahad EM

Chairman: Hamed Saif Al Fahad (also Managing Director)
Senior Executives: T V Varughese (Manager)

PRINCIPAL ACTIVITIES: Building, roads, major projects
contracting; transportation contracting; supply of building
materials, heavy construction equipment, power equipment
and general trading
Principal Bankers: Bank of Credit and Commerce International
Inc; Bank of Baroda; United Bank Ltd; United Arab Bank

AL FAHIM GROUP

PO Box 279, Corniche Road, Abu Dhabi
Tel: 211500
Telex: 22301 Fahim EM
Telefax: 344366

Chairman: Abdul Jalil Al Fahim
Directors: Mohamed Abdul Jalil Al Fahim (Managing Director),
Abdulla Abdul Jalil Al Fahim, Abbas Abdul Jalil Al Fahim,
Taha Abdul Jalil Al Fahim, Ahmed Abdul Jalil Al Fahim (Asst
Managing Director)
Senior Executives: Majed Barakat (Group Financial Controller),
Mohd Ahmed Hasan Khoury (Group Personnel Manager)

PRINCIPAL ACTIVITIES: Importers, exporters, commission
agents, estate and travel agents, vehicles and tyre
distributors, heavy machinery, diesel engines, water pumps,
electrical goods, computers, oilfield services, manufacturers'
representation; business consultants

Principal Agencies: Agents: Daimler Benz, Michelin, Petters Ltd, Robert Bosch GmbH, Brown & Root, Camco Inc, American Jeep

Subsidiary Companies: Abdul Jalil Travel Agency, Al Jallaf Trading, Emirates Motor Co, Emirates Property Investment Co, Abdul Jalil Industrial Development Co; Marjan Oilfield Services, Al Jallaf Jeep, Holiday Inn Abu Dhabi, Corniche Residence Hotel Abu Dhabi, Dalma Centre Hotel Abu Dhabi

Principal Bankers: British Bank of the Middle East; First National Bank of Chicago

Financial Information:

	1989/90 Dh'000
Sales turnover	402,000
Profits	25,000
Authorised capital	50,000
Paid-up capital	50,000
Total assets	440,000

Principal Shareholders: Abdul Jalil Al Fahim & Family
Date of Establishment: 1961
No of Employees: 1,032

AL FUTTAIM TOWER SCAFFOLDING (PVT) LTD

PO Box 555, Abu Dhabi
Tel: 727510
Telex: 23957 Scafom EM
Telefax: 783357

Senior Executives: William H Ball (Divisional Manager)

PRINCIPAL ACTIVITIES: Scaffolding, sale, contract, hire
Parent Company: Tower Scaffolding UK, Bristol, UK

AL GAITH TRADING & CONTRACTING CO

PO Box 306, Abu Dhabi
Tel: 341513, 361073
Cable: Al Gaith
Telex: 22232 EM

Directors: Hamil Bin Khadim Al Ghaith

PRINCIPAL ACTIVITIES: General trading and contracting; manufacturers' representatives; distribution of heavy machinery, cranes, lifts, water pumps, building materials, electrical equipment, surgical instruments, foodstuffs, paints, generators, furniture, gas cookers, etc
Principal Agencies: Lancer Bos; Stothert & Pitt, UK; Pye Unicam, UK; Sumitomo Tyres; Marelli & Co; Thorn Appliances; Tuncova, Spain; Yintan Corp, Japan

ALGEEMI & PARTNERS CONTRACTING CO

PO Box 2877, Abu Dhabi
Tel: 328438, 335682
Cable: Algeemi
Telex: 23171 Geemi EM
Telefax: 338135

Chairman: Ghanim Bin Hamoodah
Directors: Munzer Farah (General Manager)
Senior Executives: Wafaie Kamel Yani (Project Manager), Omer Ibrahim Dahlan (Project Manager), Maged Ramzy (Project Manager), Wagih Zaki Soliman (Project Manager), Stephen Varghese (Senior Accountant), Nassif Habib Nassif (PMV Manager)

PRINCIPAL ACTIVITIES: Contracting
Branch Offices: PO Box 17281, Al Ain
Associated Companies: Bin Hamoodah Trading & General Service, PO Box 203, Abu Dhabi; Gasos of Bin Hamoodah, PO Box 203, Abu Dhabi; Gisco, PO Box 6625, Abu Dhabi
Principal Bankers: National Bank of Abu Dhabi; Abu Dhabi Commercial Bank Ltd

Financial Information:

	1988/89 US$'000	1989/90 US$'000
Sales turnover	11,229	15,370
Profits	630	2,2512
Authorised capital	5,400	5,400
Paid-up capital & reserves	8,152	8,152
Total assets	12,866	17,108

Principal Shareholders: Ghanim Bin Hamoodah, Faraj Bin Hamoodah, Munzer Farah
Date of Establishment: 1966
No of Employees: 750

ALGEMENE BANK NEDERLAND NV

Faraj Bin Hamoodah Bldg, Sheikh Hamdan St, PO Box 2720, Abu Dhabi
Tel: 335400 (4 lines), 327346/7/8 (forex)
Cable: Bancolanda
Telex: 22401 Abn EM

PRINCIPAL ACTIVITIES: Commercial banking
Branch Offices: PO Box 2567, Dubai; PO Box 1971, Sharjah; PO Box 350, Bahrain
Parent Company: Head office: PO Box 669, Amsterdam

ALHAMRA TRADERS

PO Box 556, Sh. Suroor Bldg, Hamdan Rd, Abu Dhabi
Tel: 823456 (6 lines)
Cable: Alhamra
Telex: 23920 Hamra EM

President: Shaikh Abdus Salam
Directors: Shaikh Mohd Abdullah, Shaikh Mohd Hanif, Shaikh Abdu Samad

PRINCIPAL ACTIVITIES: Textile, ready made garments, industrial garments, hotel and hospital supplies, tailoring contractors, etc
Principal Agencies: 'Ranger' Workwear
Branch Offices: Dubai Tel 214912 (6 lines), Sharjah, Alain
Parent Company: Alhamra Traders, Incorporated in Abu Dhabi
Subsidiary Companies: AlNafees Textiles & Tailoring, Abu Dhabi; Al Hamra Ice Creams & Snacks, Abu Dhabi; Al Hamra Garments, Sharjah; Green House Trading, Hong Kong
Principal Bankers: Bank of Credit & Commerce (Emirates)

Principal Shareholders: President and directors as described
Date of Establishment: 1967
No of Employees: 53

AL HARBI GENERAL TRADING & CONTRACTING EST

PO Box 3472, Abu Dhabi
Tel: 325493, 344599
Telex: 23779 Harbi EM

Chairman: Ali Sultan Al Harbi

PRINCIPAL ACTIVITIES: General trading and contracting, supply of furniture, office equipment, household goods, electrical and electronic goods

AL HEBAISHI, ALI & ABDULREHMAN,

PO Box 275, Abu Dhabi
Tel: 341291
Cable: Alhumaid

Directors: Ali Bin Abdulla Al Hebaishi, Abdulrehman Al Hebaishi, G I Motwani

PRINCIPAL ACTIVITIES: Import and distribution of building materials, timber, cement, steel, diesel machinery, floor covering, motorcycles, motor engines, spare parts, agricultural equipment, pumps
Principal Agencies: Kawasaki, Japan; Dunlop Semtex Ltd, UK; Crittall-Hope Ltd, UK; Kirloskar Oil Engines Ltd, India

UAE (Abu Dhabi)

ALI & ABDULREHMAN AL HEBAISHI
See AL HEBAISHI, ALI & ABDULREHMAN,

ALI & SONS COMPANY
P O Box 915, Abu Dhabi
Tel: 723900
Cable: ABKACORP
Telex: 23900 ABKA EM

Chairman: Ali Bin Khalfan Al Dhahry
Directors: Abdallah M Khabbaz (Managing Director)

PRINCIPAL ACTIVITIES: Business consultants, representation
of companies, general trading, oilfield supplies and services

AL JABER ESTABLISHMENT (GROUP)
PO Box 2175, Abu Dhabi
Tel: 554300, 553707
Cable: Al Jaber
Telex: 22379 EM Aljabr
Telefax: 553370

Chairman: Obeid Khalifa Al Jaber
Directors: Wahib Ghais (Managing Director), Ismail Fikri
(Finance Director), Alex Mullins (Marketing Director)
Senior Executives: Youssef Ghais (General Manager -
Commercial), Badri Ghais (General Manager - Technical),
Salman Ghais (General Manager -Construction), David Abdo
(Production Manager), Dr Faouzi Abou Reslan (Controller
General)

PRINCIPAL ACTIVITIES: Road and building construction and
civil engineering contractors, suppliers of building materials
(crushed stone aggregate, ready mix cement) and
construction plant, also transport contractors and plant hire.
Principal Agencies: Kenworth Trucks; Shell Lubricants
Branch Offices: London (Interlift UK Ltd)
Subsidiaries Companies: Al Jaber Transport & General
Contracting Est; Al Jaber Trading; Al Jaber Marine Services,
Al Jaber Heavy Lifting
Principal Bankers: National Bank of Abu Dhabi, Grindlays Bank
Financial Information:

	1989 Dh'000
Sales turnover	240,000
Paid-up capital	120,000
Total assets	375,000

Date of Establishment: 1973
No of Employees: 1,560

AL JALLAF TRADING
PO Box 46193, Abu Dhabi
Tel: 344300
Cable: Al Jallaf
Telex: 23220 Jallaf EM
Telefax: 344366

Chairman: Abdul Jalil Al Fahim
Directors: Mohammed A Al Fahim (Managing Director)
Senior Executives: Moutaz Al Kaissi (General Manager)

PRINCIPAL ACTIVITIES: Distribution of motor components,
electrical equipment, engines, tyres, specialised vehicles and
equipment
Principal Agencies: Michelin, Bosch, Jeep Vehicles, Petter,
Blaupunkt, Metrix Engineering, Peabody Myers, Mico, Diesel
Kiki, Schrader
Branch Offices: Al Ain, PO Box 1359; Dubai, PO Box 11393;
Sharjah, PO Box 1984; Fujeirah: PO Box 990, Fujeirah
Parent Company: Al Fahim Group
Principal Bankers: British Bank of the Middle East; Banque
Paribas

Principal Shareholders: Al Fahim Group
Date of Establishment: 1976
No of Employees: 180

AL JAMAL
Hamdan Street, Rashid Aweidha Bldg, PO Box 266, Abu Dhabi
Tel: 330930, 330630
Cable: Alaweidha
Telex: 22563 Aweida EM

Chairman: Rashid Aweidha (Owner)

PRINCIPAL ACTIVITIES: Import and distribution of watches,
silverware, porcelaine, cristal, lighters, pens and suitcases
Principal Agencies: Patek Philippe, Christofle, Bernardaud,
Baccarat, Daum, S T Dupont, Lanvin, Longines, Chopard,
Halliburton, Favo, Royal Worcester, Porcelaine de Paris
Parent Company: Aweidha Sons & Bin Sagar Group of
Companies
Principal Bankers: National Bank of Abu Dhabi

ALLIED ENGINEERING ENTERPRISES (ABU DHABI)
PO Box 2655, Abu Dhabi
Tel: 770075
Cable: Allied Abu Dhabi
Telex: 22625 Allied EM
Telefax: 770864

Chairman: Mohamad Abdul Jalil Al Fahim
Directors: Mansour Abu Jamra (Partner), Walid Boutros Samaha
(Partner), Sameer Nassib Hammam (Partner), Zikar George
Masruah (Partner)
Senior Executives: Samir N Hammam (Managing Director),
Mansour Abu Jamra (General Manager), Walid B Samaha
(Managing Director), Zikar George Masruah (Regional
Manager UAE)

PRINCIPAL ACTIVITIES: Contracting engineering dealing in
industrial works; building construction; and specialised civil
works
Branch Offices: Allied Engineering Enterprises, PO Box 8594,
Riyadh, Saudi Arabia, Tel 4765348, Telex 200462, Fax
4782725
Parent Company: Allied Engineering Enterprises (Lebanon)
Principal Bankers: Citibank; United Arab Bank; National Bank of
Abu Dhabi

Principal Shareholders: Mohamad Abdul Jalil Al Fahim; Mansour
Abu Jamra; Walid Boutros Samaha; Sameer Nassib
Hammam; Zikar George Masruah
Date of Establishment: 1973
No of Employees: 600

ALLIED MEDICAL GROUP LTD
PO Box 3788, Abu Dhabi
Tel: 724900
Telex: 23367 Deilla EM
Telefax: 720782

Senior Executives: R Cross (UAE Representative)

PRINCIPAL ACTIVITIES: Health care management and supply
of medical equipment
Parent Company: Evered Plc, Solihull, West Midlands, UK

ALLIED PROJECTS (OVERSEAS) LTD
PO Box 4543, Abu Dhabi
Tel: 351524
Telex: 23858 Alproj EM
Telefax: 352438

Senior Executives: A M Barakat (General Manager)

PRINCIPAL ACTIVITIES: Oilfield and technical supplies and
services, offshore and onshore engineering, security services,
general trading, chemicals, mechanical parts, industrial
equipment, insecticides and pesticides, timber, cement, oil
lubricants, additives and foodstuffs
Parent Company: Head office in Jersey

AL MAHMOOD BUILDERS (FORMERLY AL-FALAJ TRADING & CONTRACTING)

PO Box 4400, Abu Dhabi
Tel: 326027
Cable: Falaj
Telex: 33223 EM Haig

Chairman: Y Shahnazarian (also Managing Director)
Directors: Y Shahnazarian, Abdul Hameed Al Mahamood, Mrs Brigitte Shahnazarian

PRINCIPAL ACTIVITIES: Civil engineering and building construction contractors, mechanical engineering
Principal Bankers: Citibank

Principal Shareholders: Partnership firm

AL MARIAH UNITED COMPANY

PO Box 206, Abu Dhabi
Tel: 771741, 770553
Cable: Almariah Abu Dhabi
Telex: 22323 Mariah EM
Telefax: (971 2) 782628

Chairman: Saeed Khalaf Al Mazroui
Directors: Attiq Khalaf, John Doyle (General Manager)
Senior Executives: Anura Dissanayake (Engineering), Ahmed Fayez Kamal (Finance), Syed Abdul Qader (Commercial), M J R Anthony (Transport), Wipula Fernando (Telecommunication), Mohd Gamal (Public Relations/Admin)

PRINCIPAL ACTIVITIES: Import and distribution of air-conditioning plants, electrical appliances; household goods, spare parts; telecommunication, and data processing equipment, office furniture, commercial refrigeration, freezers, refrigerators, cookers, washing machines and other home appliances, household furniture, cathodic protection and corrosion control, industrial filters, transportation service, labour supply, transportation of passengers, catering and maintenance of residential camps, etc
Principal Agencies: Fedders, USA; Dollinger, USA (Filtration); BASCO, UK (Cathodic Protection & Corrosion Control); Trend Telecommunications, UK; Storno, Denmark; Winner, Switzerland; Century, Korea; Zodiac, Italy; Blick Paging System, UK; Uchida, Japan
Branch Offices: Dubai; AlAin; Residential Camps in Ruwais RLIP Area, Ruwais
Subsidiary Companies: Bin Khalaf Est, Abu Dhabi
Principal Bankers: Commercial Bank of Dubai Ltd; Standard Chartered Bank
Financial Information:

| | 1989/90 |
	US$'000
Sales turnover	2,980
Profits	690
Authorised capital	1,000
Paid-up capital	1,000
Total assets	3,000

Principal Shareholders: Saeed Khalaf, Attiq Khalaf
Date of Establishment: 1970
No of Employees: 296

AL MASAOOD ENGINEERING & CONTRACTING CO (METCO)

PO Box 102, Abu Dhabi
Tel: 822396, 822621
Cable: Metco
Telex: 23342 Metco EM

Chairman: Rahma Masaood
Directors: Abdullah Masaood
Senior Executives: Michel A Joukhadar (General Manager)

PRINCIPAL ACTIVITIES: Civil engineers and contractors
Parent Company: Mohammed Bin Masaood & Sons

Principal Bankers: Grindlays Bank; National Bank of Abu Dhabi; Abu Dhabi Commercial Bank; British Bank of the Middle East
Financial Information:

	Dh'000
Sales turnover	122,000
Authorised capital	10,000

Principal Shareholders: Chairman and Directors as described
Date of Establishment: 1967
No of Employees: 800

AL MASAOOD OIL INDUSTRY SUPPLIES & SERVICE CO

PO Box 4352, Abu Dhabi
Tel: 344900
Telex: 22825 Masoil EM
Telefax: 341423

Chairman: Rahma Al Masaood
Senior Executives: Ahmed Tamim (General Manager), Jeremy Weeks (Sales Manager)

PRINCIPAL ACTIVITIES: Oil service company and supply of oilfield equipment and machinery
Principal Agencies: NL Baroid, TIW, Tri-state Oil Tools, BJ Hughes, Redwing Int'l, Completion Tool Co, Rohrback Cosasco Systems, PA Int'l, Bran & Luebbe, Midland Pipe Co, Corroless, Drilex Systems, Omsco Industries, Wire Rope Industries, Thermon, Kalibur Engineering, Custom Safety, Furmanite Int'l, Tamsa, Travis
Branch Offices: Dubai, Sharjah, Ras Al Khaimah
Parent Company: Mohamed Bin Masaood
Subsidiary Companies: Al Masaood Casing Services
Principal Bankers: Arab Bank for Investment & Foreign Trade

Date of Establishment: 1974
No of Employees: 30

AL MAZROUI & PARTNERS

PO Box 2035, Abu Dhabi
Tel: 826138 (4lines)
Cable: Mapad
Telex: 22353 EM

Chairman: Rashid Al-Mazroui
Directors: Asem Bibi (Managing Partner)
Senior Executives: Roger D'Souza (Commercial Manager), Eid Abou Jerad (Sales Manager)

PRINCIPAL ACTIVITIES: Import and distribution of office equipment, photographic equipment and accessories; business and industrial promotions, computers, software, copy bureau, airport ground support equipment
Principal Agencies: Triumph-Adler AG; Alpia, Planhold, Harper & Tunstall, Solvit, Khalex, Kis France, Coated Specialities Ltd
Parent Company: Al Mazroui Trading & General Services
Subsidiary Companies: Mazroui Construction Technology (Civil Contractors); Mazroui Int Cargo Co, Mapco
Principal Bankers: Bank of Credit and Commerce International

Principal Shareholders: Chairman and director as described
Date of Establishment: 1974
No of Employees: 30

AL MOHERBIE THERMOPLAS

PO Box 46767, Abu Dhabi
Tel: 775936
Telex: 23294 TMPLAS
Telefax: 722714

Partners: S S Al Moherbie, Zaidy Family
Senior Executives: R M Bailey (General Manager), D Pryce (Export/Sales Manager)

PRINCIPAL ACTIVITIES: Manufacture of PVC, LDPE, HDPE pipes and irrigation fittings
Principal Agencies: FIP, Italy; Wingfield, Australia
Principal Bankers: Bank of Credit & Commerce (Emirates)

Principal Shareholders: S S Al Moherbie / Zaidy Family
Date of Establishment: 1976
No of Employees: 36

AL MUHAIRY GENERAL CONTRACTING CO

PO Box 1288, Al Ain
Tel: 41031, 25600
Cable: Al-Muhairy
Telex: 33538 EM

Chairman: Mubarak Bin Abdullah (also Managing Director)
Directors: Mattar Bin Abdullah, Hamad Bin Mubarak

PRINCIPAL ACTIVITIES: Agents and distributors of BP
products, building and general contractors, transportation
Principal Agencies: British Petroleum Co, UK
Branch Offices: PO Box 6687, Abu Dhabi, Tel 334100, Telex
23031
Subsidiary Companies: Contracting Company; Catering
Company; Transportation Company; Stone Crusher Company;
BP Products Company; Travel Agency
Principal Bankers: Bank of Credit and Commerce; National
Bank of Abu Dhabi; Bank of Oman

Principal Shareholders: Private company for the Al-Muhairy
directors

AL MULLA SERVICES EST

PO Box 2406, Abu Dhabi
Tel: 336627
Cable: thayeb
Telex: 22409 THAYEB EM

Chairman: A Q Al Mulla
Directors: Bassam N Saab

PRINCIPAL ACTIVITIES: Marketing logical business machines
Associated Companies: Al Mulla Construction; Al Rawdatain
Engineering; Al Mulla Ready Mix; Al Mulla Fiber Glass
Factory; Al Mulla Crushers
Principal Bankers: Bank Saderat Iran

Date of Establishment: 1960
No of Employees: 100

AL MUREIKHI CONTRACTING & TRADING EST

PO Box 211, Abu Dhabi
Tel: 770590
Cable: Almaco
Telex: 22652 Almaco EM
Telefax: 725475

Chairman: Eng Adel G Jabbour (Managing Partner)
Directors: Ahmed Bin Hader Al Mureikhi, Adel G Jabbour
Senior Executives: Eng Samir Nasser (Manager), Eng Pierre
Bassil (Factory Manager), Eng Pierre Bassil (Head of Design),
Eng Antoine Diab (Projects Manager), Sherif Lotfi (Head of
Accounts Dept), Eng Ezat Mahmoud (Sales Manager Precast)

PRINCIPAL ACTIVITIES: Building contractors; manufacturers of
precast building structures
Branch Offices: Al Ain
Principal Bankers: Invest Bank; United Bank; Banque Paribas

Principal Shareholders: Ahmed Bin Hader Al Mureikhi; Adel G
Jabbour
Date of Establishment: 1970
No of Employees: 750

AL NAHIYA GROUP

PO Box 3278, Abu Dhabi
Tel: 333201
Telex: 22874 CLBT EM, 23701 NIRMIL EM

PRINCIPAL ACTIVITIES: Petroleum and chemicals, inspection
services, laboratories and technical services

ALNASR TECHNICAL TRADING AGENCIES

PO Box 7355, Abu Dhabi
Tel: 332565
Cable: Alnasr Abu Dhabi
Telex: 22207 Attag Em
Telefax: 9712-332212

Chairman: Ebrahim Al Shaker (also Managing Director)

PRINCIPAL ACTIVITIES: Trading in oilfield and construction
supplies and equipment, hotel and catering supplies,
engineering repair services to the oilfield industry
Principal Agencies: British Ropes, UK; Spanset, UK; Castolin
Eutectic, Switzerland; George Taylor & Co; Lifting Gear
(Midlands) Ltd, UK; Avon Inflatables, UK; Bridon Fibres, UK
Branch Offices: Alnasr Engineering, Sadiyat Island
Associated Companies: Crescent Oilfield Supplies
Establishment
Principal Bankers: Naitonal Bank of Sharjah, Abu Dhabi

Principal Shareholders: Ebrahim Mohamed Jassim Al Shaker
(Sole Proprietor)
Date of Establishment: 1965
No of Employees: 40

AL OTAIBA ESTABLISHMENTS

PO Box 467, Abu Dhabi
Tel: 446100, 448818
Cable: Atabagroup
Telex: 22329 EM Kantot

Chairman: HE Dr Mana Saeed Al-Otaiba

PRINCIPAL ACTIVITIES: General trading, and distribution of
cars and spare parts; and tyres, electrical goods, air-
conditioners, civil construction, mechanical and electrical
engineering, safety and fire prevention, transportation
contracting
Principal Agencies: Chevrolet, Cadillac, Isuzu, Land Rover,
Range Rover, Jaguar, Austin Rover
Branch Offices: Al Ain

AL OTAIBA GROUP

PO Box 310, Abu Dhabi
Tel: 335700
Cable: Alotaiba
Telex: 22348 Otaiba EM
Telefax: 330167

Chairman: Hareb Mohammed Al Otaiba
Senior Executives: George A Topping (General Manager),
Digvijay Singh (Group Financial Controller), A S Rao
(Divisional Manager Food Service Equipment & Domestic
Appliances), Gopal Khrishnan (Divisional Manager Office
Systems), Ashraf Hamed (Divisional Manager Leisure & Sport
equipment)

PRINCIPAL ACTIVITIES: Import, distribution and retailing of
leisure and sport equipment; food service equipment,
domestic appliances, office equipment, commercial &
domestic kitchens, TV broadcasting equipment,
transportation; commercial agencies
Principal Agencies: Bosch Domestic Appliances, BTS TV
Sustems, Foster Walk-In Cold Stores, Scotsman Ice Makers,
Nashua Copiers, Xerox Products, Brunswick Bowling
Equipment, Sovereign Snooker Tables
Branch Offices: Dubai: PO Box 5009, Tel 691575, Telex 45594;
Al-Ain: PO Box 1358, Tel 641497
Parent Company: Mohd Hareb Al Otaiba
Subsidiary Companies: Avis Rent-a-Car (UAE); Al Otaiba
Ferretti; Zerox Emirates; Tidex International Abu Dhabi
Principal Bankers: British Bank of the Middle East; Commercial
Bank of Dubai; Abu Dhabi Commercial Bank

Principal Shareholders: Hareb Mohd Al Otaiba
Date of Establishment: 1949
No of Employees: 100 (excluding subsidiaries)

AL RASHID TRADING COMPANY

Al Rashid Group of Companies

PO Box 4172, Abu Dhabi
Tel: 344222. 343695
Cable: Rashidco
Telex: 22399 Rashidco EM

Directors: Hassan Ali Rashid, Buti Bin Beshr

PRINCIPAL ACTIVITIES: Manufacturers' representation, contracting, import, distribution and wholesale of motor vehicles, heavy machinery, electrical equipment, air-conditioning equipment, building materials, paints and household goods
Principal Agencies: Adolph Saurer Ltd, Switzerland; Karl Muller AG, Switzerland; SA Levis, NV, Belgium; Tokyo Car Corp, Japan; Sabro Kaltetechnic, Germany; CCS & Engineering Co, Hong Kong; Caravell, Denmark; Southwestern Petroleum Corporation, Texas, USA; Emil Huggler AG, Switzerland
Subsidiary Companies: Al Rashid Trading Co, PO Box 1954, Sharjah, UAE, Tel 25594; Khorfakkan Export & Import, PO Box 3080, Khorfakkan, UAE; Al Rashid Trading Co, PO Box 4777, Dubai, UAE, Tel 20445; Al Jasmy & Al Rashid Cont Co, PO Box 255, Fujairah, UAE, Tel 419; Al Hosany Trading Establishment, PO Box 1371, Muscat, Sultanate of Oman; Al Rashid General Contracting Co, PO Box 4172, Abu Dhabi, UAE, Tel 43695
Principal Bankers: Bank of Baroda, Abu Dhabi; Bank Saderat Iran, Sharjah; British Bank of the Middle East, Khorfakkan

Principal Shareholders: Directors as described

AL RUBAYA GROUP

PO Box 107, Abu Dhabi
Tel: 341356, 342356
Cable: Al Rubaya
Telex: 22278 Rubaya EM

Chairman: Mohamed Abdul Aziz Rubaya (also Managing Director)
Directors: Abdul Aziz Rubaya
Senior Executives: Das Kakodkar (General Manager)

PRINCIPAL ACTIVITIES: General trading and contracting; catering; engineering contracting and transport; sponsorships, tenders, agents
Principal Agencies: General Electric Co of America; Landis & Gyr, UK; W Lucy & Co, UK
Parent Company: Abdul Aziz Bin Rubaya & Son
Associated Companies: Abdul Aziz Bin Rubaya & Son; Al Rubaya Contracting Co; Electromechanical Co Ltd; Pecon; Al Rubaya Sodexho Catering Co; General Construction Co
Principal Bankers: British Bank of the Middle East; Abu Dhabi Commercial Bank, National Bank of Abu Dhabi

Principal Shareholders: Mohamed Abdul Aziz Rubaya
Date of Establishment: 1955
No of Employees: 280

AL RUMAITHY

Al Rumaithy Bldg, Nazda St, PO Box 4356, Abu Dhabi
Tel: 324910, 342050, 342190, 324502
Cable: Rumaithiship/Cos Mig
Telex: 22377 EM A/B Rumaithi

Chairman: Mohd Khamis Al Rumaithy
Directors: Thomas Abraham

PRINCIPAL ACTIVITIES: Shipping, travel, general transportation, general trading, and contracting, clearing, forwarding, distribution of electrical goods, household goods, chemicals, auto parts, building materials, and sanitary ware
Branch Offices: PO Box 2115, Dubai; PO Box 6045, Sharjah
Subsidiary Companies: Gulf Building Materials; Gulf International Marine Supplies, PO Box 4356, Abu Dhabi
Principal Bankers: Bank of Credit and Commerce International; Habib Bank

AL SAGAR ENGINEERING CO

PO Box 697, Abu Dhabi
Tel: 778700
Cable: Hamadsagar
Telex: 22315 Sytco EM
Telefax: (9712) 728980

Chairman: Hamad Abdul Aziz Al Sagar
Directors: Imad Jassim Hamad Al Sagar (Managing Director)
Senior Executives: Poul Bakmand (Commercial Manager), Parvez Masood (Accounts & Administration Manager)

PRINCIPAL ACTIVITIES: Electrical and mechanical engineering contractors, import and distribution of generators, electrical motors, pumps, RO desalination plants
Principal Agencies: Mitsubishi, Japan; SPP, UK; GEC Machines, UK; Sprecher & Schuh, Switzerland; Berkeley, USA; NKT, Denmark; Tsurumi, Japan, Duijvelaar Pompen, Holland; Osmotec, Germany; Applied Membranes Inc, USA; Desmi, Denmark; Gould Pumps Inc, USA
Branch Offices: Dubai; Musaffah; Al Ain; Ras Al Khaimah; Fujeirah
Parent Company: A H Al Sagar & Bros, Kuwait
Principal Bankers: Commercial Bank of Dubai; Abu Dhabi; National Bank of Ras Al Khaimah, Abu Dhabi

Principal Shareholders: A H Al Sagar & Bros, Kuwait; Sukri Saleh Zaki, Abu Dhabi
Date of Establishment: 1971
No of Employees: 75

AL SAGR INSURANCE (UAE) CO LTD

PO Box 4907, Abu Dhabi
Tel: 339705
Telex: 23537 ARIC EM
Telefax: 215046

Chairman: Abdulla Al Sari
Directors: Yusri Dweik (Managing Director)
Senior Executives: Abdul Hamid El Mahi (Manager Abu Dhabi Branch)

PRINCIPAL ACTIVITIES: All classes of insurance
Branch Offices: Sharjah, Alkhobar, Jeddah
Parent Company: Head office in Dubai

AL SAHEL CONTRACTING & TRADING CO

PO Box 915, Abu Dhabi
Tel: 323456
Telex: 23900 Abka

Chairman: H E Khalifa Jumaa Al Nabooda
Directors: HE Ali Bin Khalfan Al Dhahiri (Executive Director), Nicolas Habib Nasra (Managing Director)

PRINCIPAL ACTIVITIES: Building and construction, manufacture of building materials, sale of building materials and equipment
Branch Offices: PO Box 15473, Al Ain, Tel 54080
Principal Bankers: Emirates Commercial Bank

Principal Shareholders: Chairman and Directors as described
Date of Establishment: 1980
No of Employees: 400

AL SAHEL CONTRACTING CO

PO Box 2153, Abu Dhabi
Tel: 721932
Telex: 23903 ASAHEL EM

Chairman: H E Ali Bin Khalfan Al Dhahry
Directors: Joseph Yared

PRINCIPAL ACTIVITIES: Building and construction
Principal Bankers: Emirates Commercial Bank Ltd; Arab Bank for Investment & Foreign Trade

UAE (Abu Dhabi)

AL SAMAN, SALEM EBRAHIM,

Shaikh Hamdan Street, PO Box 271, Abu Dhabi
Tel: 319116, 319336
Cable: Al Saman
Telex: 22292 Manara EM
Telefax: 971-2- 330787

Chairman: Salem Ebrahim Al Saman
Senior Executives: Ebrahim Salem Al Saman (General
  Manager), P A M Ilias (Manager)

PRINCIPAL ACTIVITIES: General trade, office furniture, and
  equipment, electrical equipment and appliances; kitchen
  equipment, safes and vault doors
Principal Agencies: AEG Olympia, Memofax A/S, Sunroc
Subsidiary Companies: Al Manara Trading Est, Abu Dhabi;
  Salem Travel Agency, Abu Dhabi
Principal Bankers: Bank of Credit & Commerce (Emirates),
  Indosuez Bank

Principal Shareholders: Wholly owned by Salem E Al Saman
Date of Establishment: 1963

ALSHAGGA TRADING ESTABLISHMENT

PO Box 2050, Abu Dhabi
Tel: 344155, 323453, 344577
Cable: Alshagga
Telex: 22550 Shagaco EM

Chairman: Salem Abdulla Alshagga
Directors: Ali Abdulla Alshagga
Senior Executives: Ahmed Abdulla Alshagga (Manager)

PRINCIPAL ACTIVITIES: Importers, exporters, manufacturers,
  representatives, general merchants and contractors; suppliers
  of air-conditioning equipment, heavy machinery, electrical
  equipment and timber
Principal Agencies: Daf, Netherlands; Ariston, Italy; Argos,
  Poland; Kawasaki Heavy Industries; Mitsubishi Air Condition;
  Finlux, Finland; Tong Shin Tyres, Korea
Branch Offices: PO Box 5165, Dubai, UAE
Principal Bankers: Bank Saderat Iran; Standard Chartered
  Bank; Rafidain Bank

AL SHAHEEN GYPSUM PRODUCTS

PO Box 2618, Abu Dhabi
Tel: 361240, 54673
Cable: ELLAMA
Telex: 22926 ELLAMA EM

Directors: Obaid Al Mansouri, Francois Lama

PRINCIPAL ACTIVITIES: Fabrication of gypsum blocks for use
  in dry wall partitioning
Principal Agencies: In technical association with Lambert
  Freres, Paris
Principal Bankers: Citibank NA

Date of Establishment: 1978

AL SHIRAWI TRADING & CONTRACTING CO

PO Box 811, Abu Dhabi
Tel: 829400 (4 lines), 820104, 828492, 327076, 342602
Telex: 23469 Global EM

Chairman: Abdullah Al Shirawi

PRINCIPAL ACTIVITIES: Import and distribution and building
  materials, cement, textiles, air-conditioning equipment,
  manufacture of welded wire mesh, steel fabrication, also
  transportation, printing, construction
Branch Offices: Abu Dhabi; Al-Ain; Dubai; Sharjah; Khorfakkan;
  Ras Al Khaimah (UAE); Muscat and Salalah (Oman); Iraq

AL WAHA ENGINEERING CO

PO Box 2618, Abu Dhabi
Tel: 362856, 361240
Cable: Ellama
Telex: 22926 Ellama EM

Chairman: Francois Lama
Directors: Saif Al Mansouri

PRINCIPAL ACTIVITIES: Civil contracting; specialized in high
  quality concrete and prefabricated concrete
Principal Agencies: Al Shaheen Gypsum Products; Al Habara;
  Lambert Industries
Associated Companies: Alhabara (Imports and Maintenance)
Principal Bankers: Citibank, Abu Dhabi

Principal Shareholders: Francois Lama, Saif Al Mansouri
Date of Establishment: 1974
No of Employees: 280

AL WATHBA CONCRETE BLOCKS FACTORY

PO Box 4781, Abu Dhabi
Tel: 051-211158
Telex: 22938 Gicorp
Telefax: 051-325034

PRINCIPAL ACTIVITIES: Production of concrete blocks
Parent Company: General Industry Corporation, Abu Dhabi

AL WIMPEY ROADS & CONSTRUCTION (ABU DHABI) LTD

PO Box 46464, Abu Dhabi
Tel: 216234
Telex: 22919 Alwimp EM
Telefax: 335965

Directors: M R Kay (Managing Director Dubai)

PRINCIPAL ACTIVITIES: Building and civil engineering
  contractors
Branch Offices: Al Ain: PO Box 15075, Tel 825709, Telex
  34057; and Dubai
Parent Company: Wimpey Int, 27 Hammersmith Grove, London
  W6, UK

Date of Establishment: 1979
No of Employees: 500

AL YOUSUF, YOUSUF HABIB,

PO Box 2846, Abu Dhabi
Tel: 335816, 328259
Cable: Habibani
Telex: 45436 Habib EM
Telefax: 233268

Chairman: Ali Yousuf Habib Al Yousuf
Directors: K M Polad (Managing Director), Kassim M Al Hassan
Senior Executives: Yousuf Abdul Hussain (Branch Manager)

PRINCIPAL ACTIVITIES: Dealing in cars, motorcycles, outboard
  engines, boats, tyres, water pump, generators, batteries, auto
  paints and parts
Principal Agencies: Daihatsu; Yamaha; Suzuki; Nitto &
  Roadstone Tyres; Golden Battery, Nippon & Kansai Paints;
  Daewoo Cars/trucks; Chevrolet Passenger & Commercial
  Vehicles; Buick Passenger Cars
Parent Company: Yousuf Habib Al Yousuf, PO Box 25, Dubai
Subsidiary Companies: Al Yousuf Computers; Al Yousuf
  Electronics, Al Yousuf Commodities
Principal Bankers: Habib Bank AG Zurich; Citibank
Financial Information:

	1989 US$'000
Sales turnover	125,000

Date of Establishment: 1972 in Abu Dhabi; 1961 in UAE
No of Employees: 650

AMERADA HESS OIL CORPORATION

PO Box 2406, Abu Dhabi
Tel: 829500
Telex: 23275

PRINCIPAL ACTIVITIES: Operations of 10 production wells in 2
  reservoirs in the Arzana field

Principal Shareholders: Amerada Hess (41.25%), Pan Ocean Oil (31.5%), Bow Valley Industries (10%), Canada Superior (10%), Wington Industries (4.75%), Sunningdale Oil (2.5%)

ANZ GRINDLAYS BANK PLC

PO Box 241, Abu Dhabi
Tel: 330876
Cable: Grindlay
Telex: 22252 Grndly EM
Telefax: 331767, 330876

Senior Executives: D B Crane (General Manager)

PRINCIPAL ACTIVITIES: Commercial banking
Branch Offices: In the Middle East: Bahrain; Oman; Qatar; United Arab Emirates (Abu Dhabi, Al-Ain, Dubai, Sharjah, Ras Al Khaimah); Jordan; Pakistan
Parent Company: Head office: PO Box 7 Minerva House, Montague Close, London SE1 9DH, UK

ARAB AFRICAN INTERNATIONAL BANK

PO Box 928, Abu Dhabi
Tel: 323400
Cable: Arabafro Abu Dhabi
Telex: 22587 ARAFRO EM, 23498 AFRBNK EM, 23792 AAIBFX EM
Telefax: 216009

Chairman: Ali Abdul Rahman R AlBader
Directors: Mohamed I Farid (Managing Director & Deputy Chairman)
Senior Executives: Mohamed Aly Faramawi (Asst General Manager & Manager of Abu Dhabi Branch), Kamal Abdel Moneim Aly Amin (Asst Manager)

PRINCIPAL ACTIVITIES: Commercial banking
Branch Offices: Deira-Dubai; Beirut; Cairo; Alexandria; Heliopolis; New York; London
Parent Company: Arab African International Bank, 5 Midan El Saraya El Kobra, Garden City, Cairo, Egypt
Subsidiary/Associated Companies: Subsidiaries: Tunis Arab African Bank, Tunis; Egypt Arab African Bank, Cairo; Associates: UBAF, France; UBAF-Arab American Bank, USA; UBAF (Hongkong) Ltd, Hongkong; UBAF Group Holding (Panama), Panama; Banque Nationale de Developpement Touristique (BNDT), Tunisia; El Gezirah Hotels & Tourism Co, Cairo, Egypt

Principal Shareholders: Ministry of Finance, Kuwait; Central Bank of Egypt; Rafidain Bank, Baghdad; Central Bank of Algeria; Ministry of Finance, Jordan; Bank Al-Jazira, Jeddah; Ministry of Finance, Qatar; Individuals and Arab Institutions
Date of Establishment: May, 1976
No of Employees: 32

ARAB BANK FOR INVESTMENT & FOREIGN TRADE

Arbift Bldg, Hamdan St, PO Box 46733, Abu Dhabi
Tel: 721900 (20 Lines), 721600 (10 lines)
Cable: Arbift
Telex: 22455 (General) Arbift EM, 22833 (Forex) Arbift EM
Telefax: 777550

Chairman: Abdul Hafid M Zlitni
Directors: Ahmed H Al Tayer (Vice Chairman), Mohamed I Shtewi, Mohamed Ali Zayed, Ramadan M Omeish, Houcine Hannachi, Mabrouk Belgroun, Abdulla Khalifa Al Hariz
Senior Executives: Hadi M Giteli (General Manager), Mohamed Al Qassimi (Deputy General Manager), Yousuf Bapputty (Manager Foreign Exchange & Money Operations), Hassan Osman Abdel Karim (Manager Int'l Finance Dept), Osman H Suleiman (Manager Foreign Relations Dept), Saidi Zobair (Manager Banking Operations Dept), Hassan Said Kishko (Manager Administration & Financial Dept), Sadeq Khalifa Abu Hallalah (Manager Treasury Dept), Merghani A Ahmed (Manager Advances & Commercial Dept), Saidi Zouhair

(Manager Abu Dhabi), Mahmoud A Al Khalifa (Manager Dubai Branch), Yousuf Mahgoub Mohamed (Manager Al Ain Branch), Taha Abdul Qader Budair (Manager Souk Branch)
PRINCIPAL ACTIVITIES: Commercial, merchant and investment banking
Branch Offices: Abu Dhabi Branch: PO Box 2484, Tel 724049, Telex 22455; Al Ain Branch: PO Box 16003, Tel 665133, 656482, Telex 34022; Souk Branch: PO Box 7588, Abu Dhabi, Tel 213500, Telex 23116/7; and Dubai Branch: PO Box 5549, Dubai, Tel 220151, Telex 46243
Principal Bankers: Bankers Trust Co, New York; UBAF, London; Midland Bank, London; Manufacturers Hanover Trust, New York; Dresdner Bank, Frankfurt; European Arab Bank, Frankfurt; Banque Intercontinentale Arabe, Paris; Banque Nationale de Paris, Paris; Hypobank, Munich; UBAF, Tokyo; etc
Principal Shareholders: United Arab Emirates Government; Libyan Arab Foreign Bank; Banque Exterieure d'Algerie
Date of Establishment: 1976

ARAB BANK PLC

PO Box 875, Abu Dhabi
Tel: 334111
Cable: Bankarabi
Telex: 22257 Arabnk EM

Chairman: Abdul Majeed Shoman
Senior Executives: Fathi Shaik (Snior Manager Abu Dhabi Branch)

PRINCIPAL ACTIVITIES: Commercial banking
Branch Offices: Bahrain; Abu Dhabi; Dubai; Sharjah; Ras Al Khaimah; Ajman; Fujairah; Al Ain; Qatar; Oman; Lebanon; Yemen AR; Egypt; Cyprus; Greece; France; Singapore; UK; USA
Parent Company: Head Office: Shmeisani, Amman, Jordan

ARAB BUILDING MATERIALS CO LTD

PO Box 56, Abu Dhabi
Tel: 554052, 554053, 553989
Cable: Shiral Abu Dhabi
Telex: 22313 Shiral EM
Telefax: 554532

Chairman: Mohamed Ali Bdeir
Directors: Nadim Hudhud, Bassam Malas, A Idilbi
Senior Executives: Hassan Mango (Purchasing Director), Hussam Malas (Managing Partner), Mazen Malas

PRINCIPAL ACTIVITIES: Supply of building materials, steel, timber, plywood, cement etc
Branch Offices: Jordan, Dubai, Oman, Kuwait, Qatar, Bahrain
Parent Company: Jordan Construction Materials Company
Subsidiary Companies: Trizac
Principal Bankers: Arab Bank Limited; Banque de Paribas; Indosuez Bank

Date of Establishment: 1969
No of Employees: 193 in all branches

ARAB ENGINEERING CO (AREC)

PO Box 7658, Abu Dhabi
Tel: 339900
Cable: AREC
Telex: 24493

Chairman: Dr Mahmoud Hamra Krouha
Senior Executives: Aziz Amara Korba (General Manager)

PRINCIPAL ACTIVITIES: Involved in oil related projects, techno-economic studies, providing basic designs and detailed engineering of offshore refining, petrochemical, water treatment and water desalination plants
Branch Offices: London, Libya, Algeria, Tunisia

Financial Information:

	US$'000
Authorised capital	20,000
Paid-up capital	12,765

Principal Shareholders: UAE, Saudi Arabia, Kuwait, Qatar, Bahrain, Iraq, Syria, Algeria, Libya
Date of Establishment: June 1981
No of Employees: 255

ARAB GULF EQUIPMENT CO WLL

PO Box 936, Abu Dhabi
Tel: 461898
Cable: Equipment
Telefax: 9712-463151

Chairman: Ahmed A Al Katami
Directors: Mohammed A Al Khonaini
Senior Executives: Mohd Banat (Finance Manager)

PRINCIPAL ACTIVITIES: Supply of heavy machinery and industrial equipment; also supply of office equipment
Parent Company: Arab Gulf Equipment Co WLL, PO Box 1777, Dubai
Principal Bankers: Arab Bank; Alahli Bank
Financial Information:

	1990 Dh'000
Authorised capital	15,000
Paid-up capital	15,000

Principal Shareholders: Ahmed A Al Katami (50%), Mohd A Al Khonaini (50%)
No of Employees: 55

ARAB MONETARY FUND

PO Box 2818, Abu Dhabi
Tel: 215000
Cable: Arab Monetary Fund
Telex: 22989 AMF EM
Telefax: 971-2-326454

Chairman: Osama J Faquih (Director General)
Directors: Rasheed O Khalid (Advisor and Director of Economics & Technical Dept), Salaheddin Hassan (Direcctor of Legal Dept), Arfan El Azmeh (Director of Economic Policy Institute), Muhammad Said Shahin (Director of Investment Dept), Abdul Majid Qasim (Advisor and Director of Finance & Computer Dept), Shawket A H Aleyan (Director of Administration Dept), Mahmoud Al Shaibani (Director of Internal Audit Bureau)

PRINCIPAL ACTIVITIES: Arab Monetary Fund is an inter-governmental regional Arab financial organisation. Its main objectives are: to help correct disequilibria in the balance of payments of member countries; to promote the stability of exchange rates among Arab currencies; to promote the development of Arab financial markets; to coordinate the positions of member states in dealing with international monetary and economic problems and to settle current payments between member states in order to promote trade among them
Financial Information: Currency AAD (Arab Accounting Dinars equal to 3 SDR (Special Drawing Rights)

	1990 AAD'000
Total income	26,846
Net profit	22,983
Authorised capital	600,000
Paid-up capital	311,840
Reserves & liabilities	196,102
Total net assets	474,292

Principal Shareholders: Twenty, all members of the Arab League
Date of Establishment: 1976
No of Employees: 109

ARABCONSTRUCT INTERNATIONAL LTD

PO Box 238, Abu Dhabi
Tel: 322668
Cable: Conrab

Chairman: Adnan M Derbas (General Manager)
Directors: Ra'ouf Derbas (Asst General Manager)

PRINCIPAL ACTIVITIES: Building construction; engineers and contractors

Principal Shareholders: Adnan M Derbas
Date of Establishment: 1967
No of Employees: 1,500

ARABIAN CONSTRUCTION COMPANY

PO Box 2113, Abu Dhabi
Tel: 771225 (8 lines)
Cable: Natasu
Telex: 22333 Natasu EM; 22785 ACCG
Telefax: 770513

Honorary Chairman: Sheikh Ahmed Bin Hamdan Al Nahyan
Directors: Ghassan Merehbi (Chairman), Taha Mikati, Anas Mikati
Senior Executives: Abdul Ghani Mikati (Area Manager), Riad Mikati (Asst General Manager), Hamed Mikati (Chief Estimator), Omar R Mikati (Asst Finance Manager), Abdul Hamid Mikati (Plant Manager)

PRINCIPAL ACTIVITIES: Building and civil engineering contractors
Branch Offices: Lebanon: PO Box 6876, Beirut
Parent Company: Arabian Construction Company - Lebanon
Principal Bankers: National Bank of Abu Dhabi; Investbank
Financial Information:

	1989/90 Dh'000
Turnover	44,404
Equity	23,844
Paid-up capital	20,000
Total assets	88,533

Principal Shareholders: Directors as described and Sheikh Ahmed Bin Hamdan Al Nahyan (51%)
Date of Establishment: 1968
No of Employees: 907

ARABIAN TECHNICAL & TRADING CO LTD

PO Box 2610, Abu Dhabi
Tel: 322110
Cable: Autoimpex
Telex: 22436 EM

Directors: Sulaiman Ahmad Al Hoqani (Partner), Prem Chandra Bhatia (Partner), Nandu Bhatia (Manager)

PRINCIPAL ACTIVITIES: Dealers in industrial and engineering goods, machinery, spare parts, tyres and tubes, bearings, cables, marine equipment, pumps, batteries, etc
Principal Agencies: Lincoln Electric Co of Canada; Clayton Manufacturing Co, USA; Willex Batteries
Branch Offices: All over the UAE; Muscat; Bahrain
Subsidiary Companies: Bhatia & Co, Bahrain; Alkhalij Enterprises, Dubai; Alkhalij Enterprises, Muscat

ARABIAN TRADING & CONTRACTING EST

Musallam Maktoom Enterprises

PO Box 294, Abu Dhabi
Tel: 334455
Cable: MUSALLAM
Telex: 22296 Maktum EM

Chairman: Musallam Maktoom
Senior Executives: Shaker Saleh (General Manager)

PRINCIPAL ACTIVITIES: Import and distribution of cars and spare parts, pharmaceuticals, cigarettes; hospitals and oil companies suppliers

Principal Agencies: Peugeot, Citroen, Aston Martin, Onan Generators, Gillette Products, Johnson & Johnson Products

Branch Offices: Al Ain, UAE

Date of Establishment: 1965

ARABIAN TRADING & IMPORTING EST

PO Box 1846, Al Ain, Abu Dhabi
Tel: 643959
Cable: Al Darmaki
Telex: 34053 Sultn Em
Telefax: 645272

Chairman: H E Mohammed Sultan Al Darmaki (Owner)
Senior Executives: Hisham Hassan Sharkass (General Manager)

PRINCIPAL ACTIVITIES: Manufacturers' representatives, importers

Principal Agencies: Haller, W Germany; Teha, W Germany; Otto, W Germany; Optimal Vertrieb Opitz, W Germany; Vetter, W Germany; Voest Alpine, Austria; Chemie Linz, Austria; Ames Crosta Babcock, UK; Johnston Engineering, UK

Branch Offices: PO Box 6190, Abu Dhabi, Tel 781041
Principal Bankers: Arab Bank, Al Ain

Date of Establishment: 1978

ASCO

Arabian Consulting & Organising Co

PO Box 2204, Abu Dhabi
Tel: 727879
Cable: Abudasco
Telex: 22418 Ascoad EM

Chairman: F Mazzucchelli
Directors: Philid Bond, R G Mazzucchelli

PRINCIPAL ACTIVITIES: Architecture, civil engineering planning and engineering consultants

Branch Offices: Associated Offices: UK, Zambia, Qatar, Monaco, Nigeria

Parent Company: Interasco
Principal Bankers: Citibank, Abu Dhabi

Date of Establishment: 1969

ASEA BROWN BOVERI

PO Box 267, Abu Dhabi
Tel: 328328, 323018
Telex: 24467 ABBAD EM
Telefax: 338092

Senior Executives: Dr Michael Fiorentzis (General Manager)

PRINCIPAL ACTIVITIES: Electrical equipment for power, industry and transportation

Parent Company: ABB Asea Brown Boveri Ltd, PO Box 8131, Zurich, Switzerland

ASTRACO CONSTRUCTION

PO Box 46370, Abu Dhabi
Tel: 325227
Cable: Astraco
Telex: 22784 Astra EM
Telefax: 314361

Chairman: Sultan Bin Rashed Al-Dhahiri
Directors: Rafik Mansour (Director Administration), Sami Abu Rahmeh (Director Projects)
Senior Executives: Sami Afifi (Construction Manager)

PRINCIPAL ACTIVITIES: Water and sewage works, civil and mechanical engineering, and building construction

Subsidiary Companies: Matrix Services Ltd, 17a Connaught Street, London W2 2AY, UK

Principal Bankers: National Bank of Abu Dhabi

Date of Establishment: 1975

ATKINS, W S, & PARTNERS OVERSEAS

PO Box 7562, Abu Dhabi
Tel: 331326
Telex: 22574 Fandi EM
Telefax: 784823

Chairman: T Wyatt
Directors: P A Brown, M T Foley, R C French, D R S Harris, D O Hyett, F A Isola, M H S Muller, B J Patrick, D Slater, A V Stagnetto
Senior Executives: B Chapman (Resident Manager UAE)

PRINCIPAL ACTIVITIES: Planning, engineering, management and agricultural consultants and architects

Branch Offices: In the Middle East: Abu Dhabi, Dubai, Bahrain, Kuwait, Oman, Saudi Arabia

Parent Company: W S Atkins Group, Epsom, Surrey, UK
Principal Bankers: Standard Chartered Bank, Dubai

Date of Establishment: 1978 in Abu Dhabi
No of Employees: 35 in UAE

ATTO ENGINEERING & CONTRACTING

PO Box 66, Abu Dhabi
Tel: 322550, 322207
Cable: Makjara
Telex: 22451 Atto EM

Chairman: Victor N Hashem
Senior Executives: Eng Antoine Nassar (Jobs Coordinator), Eng Mohamed Samaha (Senior Engineer)

PRINCIPAL ACTIVITIES: Civil and mechanical engineering contractors

Branch Offices: PO Box 1029, Al Ain, Tel 25036, United Arab Emirates; PO Box 114642, Beirut, Tel 340310 Lebanon

Subsidiary Companies: GPC Pile Driving
Principal Bankers: Grindlays Bank Ltd, Abu Dhabi

Principal Shareholders: Privately owned by Victor N Hashem

AWEIDHA SONS & BIN SAGAR GROUP OF COMPANIES

Rashid Aweidha Bldg, Hamdan St, PO Box 266, Abu Dhabi
Tel: 330930
Cable: Alaweidha
Telex: 22563 Aweidha EM

Chairman: Rashid Bin Aweidha
Directors: Mohamed Bin Sagar (Vice Chairman)
Senior Executives: Samir Abu Dehays (General Manager), Fazle Hasan (Financial Controller)

PRINCIPAL ACTIVITIES: General trading and contracting, supply of building materials, office equipment, electrical equipment, furniture, heavy machinery, medical supplies, household goods and general consumer products, also travel agency, department stores and printing

Principal Agencies: Dexion; White Westinghouse, Hestair Dennis; Mobilest Furniture and various airlines

Subsidiary Companies: Abu Dhabi Trading & Contracting Co; Abu Dhabi Travel Bureau; Baniyas Trading Co; Al Jamal Stores

Principal Shareholders: Rashid Bin Aweidha, Mohamed Bin Sagar, Mohamad Aweidha

Date of Establishment: 1963
No of Employees: 250

BALFOUR CONSULTING ENGINEERS

Balfour International Services Co

PO Box 1419, Al Ain
Tel: 03-641929
Telex: 33510 Balfour EM
Telefax: 03-654727

Senior Executives: D C Craib (Resident Partner)

PRINCIPAL ACTIVITIES: Consulting engineering specialising in environmental and public health engineering
Parent Company: Balfour Maunsell, Yeoman House, 63 Croydon Road, London SE20 7TW, UK

BANCA COMMERCIALE ITALIANA SPA

PO Box 3839, Abu Dhabi
Tel: 324330, 326661/2/3
Cable: Comitbanca
Telex: 23299 COMIT EM
Telefax: 323709

Senior Executives: Paolo Tescari (Chief Manager)

PRINCIPAL ACTIVITIES: Wholesale commercial banking, treasury, bonds and securities, private banking
Parent Company: Head office in Milan, Italy

Date of Establishment: 1977 in UAE
No of Employees: 21

BANIYAS TRADING CO

Hamdan St, Rashid Aweidha Bldg, PO Box 266, Abu Dhabi
Tel: 330930
Cable: Alaweidha
Telex: 22563 Aweida EM

Chairman: Rashid Aweidha

PRINCIPAL ACTIVITIES: Import and distribution of construction machinery
Principal Agencies: Bonser, Millars, ICL (Sponsor)
Branch Offices: Abu Dhabi; Dubai
Parent Company: Aweidha Sons & Bin Sagar Group of Companies
Principal Bankers: National Bank of Abu Dhabi

BANK MELLI IRAN

PO Box 2656, 16 Sheikh Khalifa St, Abu Dhabi
Tel: 345802/3
Cable: Bankmelli
Telex: 22400 EM

PRINCIPAL ACTIVITIES: Commercial banking
Parent Company: Head office in Tehran, Iran

BANK OF BARODA

PO Box 2303, Abu Dhabi
Tel: 333266, 333253
Cable: Bankbaroda
Telex: 22391 Baroda EM, 23803 Zonbob EM
Telefax: 335293

Senior Executives: I C Shah (Senior Vice President UAE Branches)

PRINCIPAL ACTIVITIES: Commercial banking
Branch Offices: 6 branches in UAE; 3 branches in Sultanate of Oman; offshore unit in Bahrain
Parent Company: Central office in Bombay, and head office in Mandvi, Baroda, India
Subsidiary Companies: BOB Fiscal Services Ltd

Principal Shareholders: Owned by Government of India
Date of Establishment: 1974 in UAE
No of Employees: 160 in UAE and Oman

BANK OF CREDIT & COMMERCE (EMIRATES)

Head Office, Corniche Road, PO Box 3865, Abu Dhabi
Tel: 321600
Cable: BCCAMARAT
Telex: 23693 BCCAMA EM
Telefax: 331709

Chairman: HE Sh Nahyan Bin Muharak Al-Nahyan
Directors: Obaib Humaid Al-Tayer, Mohammed Juma Al-Naboodah, Eid Bakheet, Mosllam Bin Himila Al-Masroai, Ashraf Nawabi, Saleem Siddiqi, Zafar Iqbal
Senior Executives: Zafar Iqbal (Managing Director & Chief Executive), Bashir Tahir (General Manager), Mahmoud S Allarakhia (Accounting Control), Ghulam Hannani (Advances Control), Ajmal Sheikh (Area Manager Dubai), Hamid Ashraf (Legal Dept), Javed Ali Khan (Marketing Dept), Anwar Qayum Sher (Corporate Business & Investment Dept), Mohammed Ramzan (Chief Dealer), Fateh Mohammed (International Dept)

PRINCIPAL ACTIVITIES: Commercial banking
Branch Offices: City Centre, Hazzaa Airport, Najda Road, Sea View, Main Abu Dhabi, Al-Maktoum Street, Deira Dubai, Al Fahidi Street Branch, Rashidiya, Ras-al-Khaimah, Fujairah, Sharjah, Al Ain, Khalidiya, Baniyas, Sweihan
Parent Company: BCCI Holdings (Luxembourg) SA
Principal Bankers: Bank of Credit & Commerce Int'l SA, UK; First American Bank of New York, USA
Financial Information:

	US$'000
Authorised capital	108,962
Paid-up capital	79,256

Principal Shareholders: BCCI (Holdings) Luxembourg SA (40%); UAE Nationals (45%); Founders (15%)
Date of Establishment: January 1983

BANK OF CREDIT & COMMERCE INTERNATIONAL SA

PO Box 4021, Sh Sultan Al Nahyan Bldg, Corniche Tower, Abu Dhabi
Tel: 322255
Cable: Bancrecom
Telex: 22841 Bcci EM
Telefax: 9712 213630

President: Agha Hasan Abedi
Directors: Y C Lamarche, J D van Oenen, P C Twitchin, Ghanim Faris Al-Mazrui, Dr Alfred Hartmann, Swaleh Naqvi
Senior Executives: Ashraf Nawabi (General Manager - Middle East Region), Nasser Durrani (Manager)

PRINCIPAL ACTIVITIES: Commercial banking including investment and merchant banking
Branch Offices: UAE (Abu Dhabi, Al Ain, Dubai, Sharjah, Ajman); Oman; Jordan; Morocco; Lebanon; Yemen AR; Djibouti; France; United Kingdom; West Germany; Luxembourg; Australia; Bahrain; Cyprus; Hong Kong; Indonesia; Italy; Japan; Seychelles; Spain; USA; Venezuela; Isle of Man; Netherlands
Subsidiaries and Associated Companies: BCCI SA, Luxembourg; BCCI (Overseas) Ltd, Grand Cayman; BCCI (Lebanon) SAL, Beirut; BCCI (Swaziland) Ltd, Manzini; BCC Canada, Montreal; BCC (Zambia) Ltd, Lusaka; BCC (Botswana) Ltd, Gaborone; BCC Zimbabwe Ltd, Harare; BCC Cameroon SA, Yaounde; BCC Hong Kong Ltd; Hong Kong; BCCI Finance Int Ltd, Hong Kong; Credit and Finance Corp Ltd, Grand Cayman; BCCI Finance Int (Kenya) Ltd, Nairobi; Italfinance Int SpA, Rome; BCC Credit & Finance (Uruguay), Montevideo; BCCI SAE Madrid; Banco Mercantil, Bogota, Colombia; BCC (Emirates), Abu Dhabi; BCCI (Nigeria) Ltd, Lagos; BCC (Misr) SAE, Cairo, Egypt; National Bank of Oman Ltd, (SAO), Muscat; BCCI (Ghana) Ltd, Accra, Ghana; KIFCO-Kuwait International Finance Co, SAK, Kuwait; BCC Finance & Securities Ltd, Bangkok; BCCI Leasing (Malaysia) Sdn Bhd, Kuala Lumpur; Banque de Commerce et de Placements SA,

Geneva, Switzerland; BCCI Niger, Niamey; BCC SA
(Argentina); BCC Australia Ltd; Banco de Credito Y Comercio
de Investimento SA, Brazil
Financial Information: Consolidated

	US$'million
Pretax profits	115
Authorised capital	1,000
Paid-up capital	660

Date of Establishment: September 1972
No of Employees: 3,752

BANK OF OMAN LTD

PO Box 858, Abu Dhabi
Tel: 343693, 342287/8
Telex: 22251 OMANBK EM

PRINCIPAL ACTIVITIES: Commercial banking
Parent Company: Head office: PO BOx 1250, Deira, Dubai

BANK OF TOKYO LTD

PO Box 2174, Abu Dhabi
Tel: 339622, 339611
Cable: Tohbank Abu Dhabi
Telex: 23500 Tohbk EM
Telefax: 331410

Senior Executives: Kenichi Nakagawa (Chief Representative)

PRINCIPAL ACTIVITIES: Representative office
Parent Company: The Bank of Tokyo Ltd, Japan

BANK SADERAT IRAN

Sheikh Khalifa St, PO Box 700, Abu Dhabi
Tel: 335155
Cable: Saderbank
Telex: 22263 EM

PRINCIPAL ACTIVITIES: All banking transactions
Branch Offices: Lebanon; Abu Dhabi; Dubai; Sharjah; Al Ain;
Ras Al Khaimah; Fujairah; Umm Al Qaiwan; Bahrain; Qatar;
Sultanate of Oman
Parent Company: Head office in Tehran, Iran

BANQUE DU CAIRE SAE

Regional Management, PO Box 533, Abu Dhabi
Tel: 328700
Cable: Bancaire
Telex: 22304 EM
Telefax: 323881

Chairman: Mamdouh S El Nadoury

PRINCIPAL ACTIVITIES: Commercial banking
Branch Offices: Abu Dhabi; Dubai; Sharjah; Ras Al Khaimah;
and Bahrain
Parent Company: Head office: PO Box 1495, Cairo, Egypt
Financial Information:

	1989 Dh'000
Total income	16,000
Authorised capital	40,000
Paid-up capital	40,000
Total assets	168,000

Date of Establishment: 1952
No of Employees: 130 in Gulf branches

BANQUE INDOSUEZ

PO Box 6786, Abu Dhabi
Tel: 338400
Cable: Indosuez
Telex: 22464 Indosu EM

PRINCIPAL ACTIVITIES: Commercial banking
Branch Offices: Dubai
Parent Company: Head office in Paris, France

Date of Establishment: 1981

BANQUE LIBANAISE POUR LE COMMERCE (FRANCE)

PO Box 3771, Abu Dhabi
Tel: 320920
Telex: 22862 Balib EM

PRINCIPAL ACTIVITIES: Commercial banking
Branch Offices: Branches in UAE; Dubai, PO Box 4207;
Sharjah, PO Box 854; Ras Al Khaimah, PO Box 771

BANQUE NATIONALE DE PARIS

PO Box 930, Abu Dhabi
Tel: 332530
Cable: Natiopar
Telex: 23047
Telefax: 320634

Senior Executives: Gerard Bouley (Representative)

PRINCIPAL ACTIVITIES: Representative office
Parent Company: Head office in Paris, France

BANQUE PARIBAS

PO Box 2742, Abu Dhabi
Tel: 335560
Cable: Paribas
Telex: 22331 EM

Senior Executives: P Maveyraud (General Manager), G Achkar

PRINCIPAL ACTIVITIES: Commercial banking
Branch Offices: Gulf branches: Abu Dhabi; Dubai; Qatar; Oman;
Bahrain
Parent Company: Head office: 3 rue d'Antin, 75002 Paris,
France

BARCLAYS BANK PLC

PO Box 2734, Abu Dhabi
Tel: 345313
Telex: 22893 Barabu EM
Telefax: 345815

Senior Executives: I M Revolta (Manager)

PRINCIPAL ACTIVITIES: Commercial banking
Parent Company: Head Office: PO Box 544, 54 Lombard St,
London EC3V 9EX, UK

BICC AL JALLAF

PO Box 6707, Abu Dhabi
Tel: 779767/8/99769
Telex: 23413 BICC MEEM
Telefax: 720187

Senior Executives: K K Ramaseshan (Regional Manager)

PRINCIPAL ACTIVITIES: Supply of electrical and electronic
cables, fire survival cables (Pyrotenax), and associated
accessories
Parent Company: BICC Cables Ltd, PO Box 1, Prescot,
Merseyside L34 5SZ, UK

BIN HAMOODAH TRADING & GENERAL SERVICES CO

PO Box 203, Abu Dhabi
Tel: 211366
Cable: Alhamoodah
Telex: 22404 Hamcom EM

Chairman: Ghanim A Bin Hamoodah
Directors: Faraj A Bin Hamoodah (President)
Senior Executives: Khalil R Traboulsi (General Manager)

PRINCIPAL ACTIVITIES: General merchants and contractors;
import and distribution of motor vehicles; electrical equipment
and appliances; heavy machinery and equipment; building
materials; engineering contractors; oil and gas services;
telecommunications and transport contractors; catering;
insurance; sponsorships; agency; supply of laboratory

equipment, medical products, educational material and laboratory chemicals

Principal Agencies: General Motors (Oldsmobile, Pontiac, GMC, Opel, Holden)

Branch Offices: Sharjah; Dubai; Al Ain

Subsidiary/Associated Companies: (Gasos) Gulf Automation Services & Oilfield Supplies; National Food Products; Sahara Transport & Cont Co; Tareef Heavy Equipment & Trading Co Ltd; Howard Algeemi Construction Co

Principal Bankers: Abu Dhabi Commercial Bank; National Bank of Abu Dhabi; First Chicago Bank; Banque Paribas

No of Employees: 250

BIN MASAOOD, MOHAMMED, & SONS

PO Box 322, Abu Dhabi
Tel: 772000
Cable: Almasaood
Telex: 22249 Mastor EM
Telefax: 776689

Chairman: Rahma Masaood

Directors: Abdulla Masaood (Managing Director)

Senior Executives: Mike Dickens (Group General Manager), Stuart Griffiths (Group Commercial Manager), John Mahon (Group Financial Controller)

PRINCIPAL ACTIVITIES: Import and distribution of motor vehicles, generating sets, tyres, engines, pumping sets, oilfield equipment, telecommunication equipment, marine craft & equipment, aviation, travel agents, property development, stevedoring, electrical and mechanical engineering contractors

Principal Agencies: Nissan Motor Co Ltd, Japan; Nissan Diesel Motor Co Ltd, Japan; Bridgestone Tire Co Ltd, Japan; R A Lister & Co Ltd, UK; Mirrlees Blackstone Ltd, UK; John Brown Engineering Gas Turbines Ltd, Scotland; Weir Westgarth Ltd, Scotland; Pompes Guinard, France; Saab-Scania; Volvo-Penta; Alcatel; Standard Telephones & Cables; Fluor Daniels; Coutinho Caro & Co; Texas Iron Works; B J Hughes; Redpath Dorman Long; British Aerospace; De Havilland; Lufthansa Airways; Air France; Sabena Airways; UTA; Egypt Air; American Express

Branch Offices: Al-Ain: PO Box 1241; Abu Dhabi: PO Box 322; Dubai: PO Box 3954

Associated Companies: Al Masaood Engineering & Contracting Co; Masaood Marine Services; Emirates Air Services; Abu Dhabi Marina Club; Masaood Travel & Services; Masaood Jewellery; Masaood John Brown; Masaood Bergum

Principal Bankers: National Bank of Abu Dhabi; Arab Bank for Investment & Foreign Trade; Standard Chartered Bank

Principal Shareholders: Partnership concern

BOODAI TRADING COMPANY

PO Box 6027, Abu Dhabi
Tel: 320581
Cable: Boodai
Telex: 22983 Boodai EM

Chairman: Mustafa Jassim Boodai

Directors: Jassim Boodai, Idris Ismail

Senior Executives: Zubair Ahmed (Area Manager), Khalid Mahmoud (Branch Manager

PRINCIPAL ACTIVITIES: Importers, distributors and manufacturer's representatives for construction equipment, industrial and engineering products and oilfield supplies

Principal Agencies: P&H Cranes, Bros Road Rollers, Blaw Knox Pavers, Mitsubishi Excavators, Furukawa Loaders, TCM & Manitou Forklifts, Zenith Block Making Machines, Hudig Dewatering Pumps, Airman Compressors, Lesha Concrete Mizers, Westco Dumpers, Kubota Tractors, Grindex Dewatering Pumps, Lincoln Welding Machines, Seam Bar Bending & Cutting Machines, Sioux Steam Cleaners, Meiwa Compactors & Trowels, etc

Branch Offices: PO Box 5108, Dubai, UAE; PO Box 4569, Doha, Qatar; PO Box 1287 Safat, Kuwait; PO Box 5215, Ruwi, Muscat, Oman

Parent Company: Boodai Trading Co, PO Box 1287, Safat, Kuwait (Head Office)

Subsidiary Companies: Arab Equipment Est, PO Box 1660, Dammam, Saudi Arabia

Principal Bankers: Al Ahli Bank, Dubai; Bank of Credit & Commerce (E), Dubai

Principal Shareholders: Mustafa J Boodai, Jassim Boodai, Idris M Ismail

Date of Establishment: 1976

No of Employees: 32

BOSKALIS WESTMINSTER ME LTD

PO Box 4831, Abu Dhabi
Tel: 772306
Telex: 23068 BKWAD EM
Telefax: 728158

Senior Executives: H B Huisman (General Manager)

PRINCIPAL ACTIVITIES: Dredging and land reclamation, pipelines, offshore works, building and civil engineering, survey and site investigations, drilling and blasting

Parent Company: Westminster Dredging Co Ltd, Fareham, Hampshire, UK

BRENT EUROPE LTD (MIDDLE EAST)

PO Box 43539, Abu Dhabi
Tel: 333359
Telex: 23562 Brent EM
Telefax: 311816

Senior Executives: K G Sinclair (Technical Sales Manager)

PRINCIPAL ACTIVITIES: Specialised chemical systems for cleaning, non-destructive testing and related equipment; supplies to the oil industry, power generation and general engineering

Parent Company: Brent Europe Ltd, Iver, Buckinghamshire, UK

BRITISH AEROSPACE PLC

PO Box 4049, Abu Dhabi
Tel: 211780, 211797
Telex: 22450 Baeabu EM
Telefax: 211085

Senior Executives: Keith Monson (Regional Director), Andrew Scott (Regional Executive)

PRINCIPAL ACTIVITIES: Manufacture and sales of civil and military aircraft and defence systems, associated training and maintenance support, civil engineering

Parent Company: Head office: 11 Strand, London WC2, UK

BRITISH BANK OF THE MIDDLE EAST (THE)

PO Box 242, Dalma Centre, Sheikh Hamdan St, Abu Dhabi
Tel: 332200
Cable: Bactria Abu Dhabi
Telex: 22231 BBME EM
Telefax: 2-331564

Chairman: W Purves CBE DSO

Directors: J R H Bond, F J French, J M Gray, J A P Hill CBE, S Robertson, P J Wrangham

Senior Executives: J E Anderson (Manager, Abu Dhabi)

PRINCIPAL ACTIVITIES: Commercial banking

Branch Offices: In the Middle East & Africa: Bahrain, Jordan, Lebanon, Oman, Qatar, United Arab Emirates, Egypt, Cyprus, Zambia

Parent Company: The HongKong and Shanghai Banking Corporation

Associated Companies: Saudi British Bank; Middle East Finance Co Ltd

BROOK & KHALFAN CONTRACTING CO

PO Box 493, Abu Dhabi
Tel: 822760
Telex: 22439 EM

Chairman: Saeed Khalfan Al Qumzi
Directors: Ahmed Saeed Khalfan
Senior Executives: Jirair Tozlikian (Deputy General Manager),
Omar Akkad (Manager)

PRINCIPAL ACTIVITIES: Road and building construction
Parent Company: Saeed Khalfan & Sons Co
Associated Companies: Abu Dhabi General Transport Co, PO
Box 493, Abu Dhabi; Oasis Residence, PO Box 6336, Abu
Dhabi; Bin Eid Trading Est; Abdullah Khalfan Bunkering;
Khalfan Transport & General Contracting Co; National
Crushers (Saeed Bin Khalfan)
Principal Bankers: National Bank of Abu Dhabi; Banque du
Caire; Bank of Oman; National Bank of Sharjah

BUNDUQ OIL COMPANY

PO Box 46015, Abu Dhabi
Tel: 213380
Telex: 23692
Telefax: 321794

Chairman: H Iwasaki
Directors: Sohail F Al Mazrui, Abdulaziz Al Dulaimi, F Shiraishi,
K Ikeda, T Yamagata, W T J Digins, L J Brown, A A Said, J L
de Vaux, M Lefregvre
Senior Executives: T Negishi (General Manager), K Kanda
(Administration Manager), T Yamauchi (Finance Manager), M
Aoki (Development Manager), K Imanishi (Production
Manager), H Ikegami (Head of Material Supply)

PRINCIPAL ACTIVITIES: Oil exploration and production in the
Al Bunduq oil field
Branch Offices: PO Box 1183, Doha, Qatar
Principal Bankers: National Bank of Abu Dhabi

Principal Shareholders: United Petroleum Development Co,
Japan (33.1/3%), CFP (33.1/3%), BP (33.1/3%)
Date of Establishment: 1975
No of Employees: 167

BUSINESS COMMUNICATIONS UAE (PVT) LTD ABU DHABI

PO Box 2534, Abu Dhabi
Tel: 720646
Telex: 22457 EM

PRINCIPAL ACTIVITIES: System design, consultancy, supply,
installation, commissioning and subsequent maintenance of
radio systems, mini computers, hotel and hospital low voltage
systems, airport communications, security and surveillance
systems, marine communications
Principal Agencies: Marconi, Awa New Zealand, Stentor,
Electronic, Millbank
Branch Offices: PO Box 233, Dubai, UAE, tel 225135, telex
47631 DUTEN EM
Parent Company: Dubai Transport Company
Principal Bankers: National Bank of Dubai

CALEB BRETT ABU DHABI

PO Box 3278, Abu Dhabi
Tel: 666389
Telex: 22874 CLBT EM
Telefax: 667675

Senior Executives: G Boyazoglou (Area Manager)

PRINCIPAL ACTIVITIES: Petroleum and chemical inspection
services, cargo surveyors, industrial surveyors, laboratories
testing, tank calibrators and flow measurements
Parent Company: Caleb Brett & Son International, Chelmsford,
Essex, UK

CAMERON IRON WORKS

PO Box 4015, Abu Dhabi
Tel: 328596
Telex: 22312 ADOS EM
Telefax: 345952

Senior Executives: B H Gronski (District Manager)

PRINCIPAL ACTIVITIES: Oilfield supply and services, drilling
control systems, heavy equipment
Parent Company: Head office: 205 Holland Park Avenue,
London W11 4XB, UK

CANSULT LIMITED

PO Box 53, Abu Dhabi
Tel: 344615
Cable: Cansult Abu Dhabi
Telex: 22483 EM

PRINCIPAL ACTIVITIES: Consulting engineering, planning and
architecture (Abu Dhabi Airport terminal, Muqta's bridge,
dredging and reclamation in Abu Dhabi)
Branch Offices: Saudi Arabia; United Arab Emirates
Parent Company: Head office: 275 Duncan Mills Road, Don
Mills, Toronto, Canada
Principal Bankers: National Bank of Abu Dhabi, Abu Dhabi

CAPE CONTRACTS INTERNATIONAL LTD

PO Box 347, Abu Dhabi
Tel: 555199
Telex: 23242 Cape EM
Telefax: 553229

Senior Executives: R W McAndrew (General Manager)

PRINCIPAL ACTIVITIES: Supply of thermal insulation and fire
protection materials, sand blasting and anti corrosion
engineering
Parent Company: Head office in Watford, Herts, UK

CEGELEC DIVISION COMSIP

PO Box 47055, Abu Dhabi
Tel: 332680
Cable: Comsip
Telex: 22810 Comsip EM
Telefax: 326363

Senior Executives: Andre Termat (Resident Manager for UAE)

PRINCIPAL ACTIVITIES: Engineers & contractors, electrical &
instrumentation
Parent Company: CEGELEC, France
Associated/Subsidiary Companies: CACEM, Algeria; Comsip Al
A'Ali WLL, Bahrain; Comsip Automation Benelux, Belgium;
Entrelec do Brasil, Brazil; Orteng Ltd, Brazil; Cegelec
Entreprises Inc, Canada
Principal Bankers: National Bank of Abu Dhabi

Principal Shareholders: Compagnie Generale de Electricite
Date of Establishment: 1978 (Abu Dhabi)
No of Employees: 150 (Abu Dhabi)

CENTRAL BANK OF THE UAE

PO Box 854, Abu Dhabi
Tel: 652220
Telex: 22330, 24153, 22396, 23316 Markzi EM
Telefax: 668483

Chairman: HE Sheikh Suroor Bin Mohammed Al Nahyan
Directors: Mohammed Abdullah Al Kaz (Vice Chairman), Abdul
Malik Yousef Al Hamar (Governor), Juma Al Majid (Member),
Harib Masood Al Dharmaki (Member), Abdullah Mohammed Al
Mulla (Member)
Senior Executives: Abdul Malik Yousef Al Hamar (Governor),
Mohammed Bin Sultan Al Dhahri (Deputy Governor), Ahmed
M Shareef Folathi (Executive Director), Saeed Abdullah Al
Hamiz (Executive Director), Salim Ahmed Al Hammadi

(Executive Director), Salim Ibrahim Darwish (Executive Director), Saif Hadef Al Shamsi (Executive Director)

PRINCIPAL ACTIVITIES: Central Banking
Branch Offices: Dubai, Sharjah, Ras Al Khaimah, Fujairah, Al Ain
Financial Information:

	1990 Dh'000
Authorised capital	300,000
Paid-up capital	300,000
Total assets	17,415,000

Principal Shareholders: State-owned
Date of Establishment: 1980
No of Employees: 532

CIMEL CO UAE
PO Box 2889, Abu Dhabi
Tel: 773963
Telex: 23390 Cimel EM
Telefax: 722805

Directors: G Dierckx
Senior Executives: E Vanbelleghem

PRINCIPAL ACTIVITIES: Contractors, electrical, instrumentation, piping, mechanical, building, overhead line power station, drainage system, industrial field (chemical and petroleum)
Branch Offices: Cimel Ajman, PO Box 597, Tel 422631, Fax 422890
Parent Company: ABFIN SA, Leuvensesteenweg 540, 1930 Zaventen, Belgium
Principal Bankers: Banque Indosuez, Abu Dhabi
Financial Information:

	1990 Dh'000
Authorised capital	5,000
Paid-up capital	2,926

Principal Shareholders: ABFIN of Financial Groupe Empain Schneider Belgium
Date of Establishment: 1975
No of Employees: 80

CITIBANK NA
PO Box 999, Abu Dhabi
Tel: 341410
Cable: Citibank
Telex: 22243 Citibk EM
Telefax: 334524

Chairman: John S Reed
Senior Executives: Andre Sayegh (Vice President)

PRINCIPAL ACTIVITIES: Commercial & private banking
Branch Offices: Middle East Branches: Abu Dhabi; Dubai; Sharjah; Al Ain; Bahrain; Qatar; Jordan; Lebanon; Oman; Morocco; Egypt; Sudan; Tunisia
Parent Company: Head Office: 399 Park Ave, New York, NY 10022, USA
Associated Companies: Saudi American Bank, Saudi Arabia

Date of Establishment: 1964 in UAE

COMEX MIDDLE EAST
PO Box 46273, Abu Dhabi
Tel: 342367
Telefax: 347617

Senior Executives: Michel Bourhis (Area Manager), Wasfi Cheaitou (Administration Manager)

PRINCIPAL ACTIVITIES: Underwater services; diving contractors, marine support and services
Parent Company: Comex Services SA Ltd, France
Subsidiary Companies: Comex Saudi Arabia Ltd, Alkhobar, Saudi Arabia
Principal Bankers: Banque Paribas

Financial Information:

	1990 FF'million
Authorised capital	49.3
Paid-up capital	49.3

Principal Shareholders: H G Delauze
No of Employees: 1915

COMMERCIAL BANK OF DUBAI LTD
PO Box 2466, Abu Dhabi
Tel: 345700/1
Cable: Trubank Abu Dhabi
Telex: 22507 Trubak EM

PRINCIPAL ACTIVITIES: Commercial banking
Branch Offices: Abu Dhabi, Sharjah, Ras Al Khaimah
Parent Company: Head office in Dubai

Date of Establishment: 1969

COMMERCIAL SERVICES AGENCY
Airport Rd, PO Box 3629, Abu Dhabi
Tel: 324439
Cable: Comserva
Telex: 22430 Alsaman EM

Chairman: Salem Ebrahim Al Saman

PRINCIPAL ACTIVITIES: Import and distribution of building materials, construction equipment, agricultural machinery
Principal Agencies: Staub (Agricultural machinery)
Principal Bankers: Arab Bank for Investment and Foreign Trade

CONCORDE TRADING CO (CTC)
PO Box 2617, Abu Dhabi
Tel: 668770, 668771
Cable: Concorde
Telex: 22590 Concrd EM
Telefax: 667863

Chairman: Saeed Mohd Saeed Al Qubaisi
Directors: Mahmoud S Awad
Senior Executives: V J George, Fakhri Sammar, Nimer A Rahim

PRINCIPAL ACTIVITIES: Trade and import and stockist
Principal Agencies: Sides, France; Bristol Uniform, UK; Leyco, Belgium; Sabo, Italy; Ginge Kerr, Denmark; Sabre Safety, UK; Holmatro, Holland; Buveco, Holland; Houseman, UK; Vecom, Holland; Catu, France; Norit, Holland; Eversafe, Malaysia
Branch Offices: Dubai Branch, Tel 284313; Al Ain Branch, Tel 642267
Associated Companies: Industrial Gas Plant, Abu Dhabi
Principal Bankers: Bank of Credit and Commerce; United Bank Ltd
Financial Information:

	1990 Dh'000
Authorised capital	3,000
Paid-up capital	3,000

Principal Shareholders: Mahmoud S Awad, Mohammed Al Mana
Date of Establishment: 1975
No of Employees: 45

CONSOLIDATED CONTRACTORS CO (UNDERWATER ENGINEERING) SAL
PO Box 224, Abu Dhabi
Tel: 553656
Telex: 23441 CCCUWE EM
Telefax: 553641

Chairman: Fawzi Kawash
Senior Executives: R V Burns (General Manager), Victor A Jarrous (Manager Finance & Administration), Christopher H Tapley (Commercial Manager), Craig Whale (Operations Manager)

PRINCIPAL ACTIVITIES: Underwater engineering, marine engineering, offshore diving contractors
Branch Offices: CCC (UE) SAL, Dhahran, Saudi Arabia
Parent Company: Consolidated Contractors Group of Companies
Associated Companies: Consolidated Contractors International Co
Principal Bankers: Investment Bank of Trade & Finance

CONSOLIDATED CONTRACTORS INTERNATIONAL CO SAL

PO Box 224, Abu Dhabi
Tel: 333656 (10 lines)
Cable: Conco
Telex: 22256 Conco EM
Telefax: 337012

Chairman: Hasib J Sabbagh
Directors: Said T Khoury (President)
Senior Executives: Samih Zaben (Area General Manager)

PRINCIPAL ACTIVITIES: Contractors for all engineering works
Branch Offices: Bahrain, Egypt, Iraq, Jordan, Kuwait, Lebanon, Oman, Saudi Arabia, Qatar, Yemen, Tunisia, Mauritania, UK, USA
Parent Company: Managing Office: Atrina Center, 32A Kifissias Av, PO Box 61092, Amaroussion, Athens, Tel 682920, Telex 219551
Subsidiary Companies: CCC Underwater Engineering
Principal Bankers: Arab Bank Ltd, Abu Dhabi; Investbank, Abu Dhabi; Banque Paribas, Abu Dhabi, National Bank of Abu Dhabi
Financial Information: Consolidated

	1990 US$'000
Sales turnover	361,000
Retained earnings	84,655
Authorised capital	12,000
Paid-up capital	12,000
Total assets	265,000

Principal Shareholders: Hasib J Sabbagh, Said T Khoury
Date of Establishment: 1952
No of Employees: 1,900

CONSOLIDATED INVESTMENT & CONTRACTING CO
C.I.C.O.N.

PO Box 660, Abu Dhabi
Tel: 345811/4
Cable: Cicon
Telex: 22265 Cicon EM

Directors: Farouk Toukan

PRINCIPAL ACTIVITIES: Import and distribution of building materials, steel and timber, sanitary ware, foodstuffs and electrical goods
Branch Offices: Dubai

CONTRACTING & TRADING CO (CAT)

PO Box 250, Abu Dhabi
Tel: 721626, 727329
Telex: 22362 CAT EM
Telefax: 727329

Directors: Shukri H Shammas (Managing Partner), Mrs L Emile Bustani (Partner), Mrs N Abdullah Khoury (Partner)
Senior Executives: Abdallah Ghantous (Resident Engineer)

PRINCIPAL ACTIVITIES: Civil engineering and building contractors, pipelines, mechanical and electrical contractors
Branch Offices: Riyadh, Jeddah, Sharjah, Oman (Seeb), Kuwait
Parent Company: Contracting & Trading Co (CAT), PO Box 11-1-36, Beirut, Lebanon

COOPERS & LYBRAND DELOITTE

PO Box 46163, Blue Tower Bldg, Sh Khalifa Bin Zayed St, Abu Dhabi
Tel: 02 211123
Telex: 23973 DHS ABU EM
Telefax: 333193

Senior Executives: Malcolm Best (Partner)

PRINCIPAL ACTIVITIES: Chartered accountants, management consultants and computer services
Branch Offices: Offices in the Middle East: Abu Dhabi, Bahrain, Dubai, Oman, Sharjah, Saudi Arabia
Parent Company: Head offices in London and New York

COPRI CONSTRUCTION ENTERPRISES WLL

PO Box 4233, Abu Dhabi
Tel: 342544, 335145, 322270
Cable: Coprico
Telex: 22923 Copri EM

Chairman: H E Saeed Sultan Al Darmaki
Directors: Joseph Anton Khalifeh
Senior Executives: Khalil Anshasi (Area Manager), Yousef Humadi (Administrative & Financial Manager)

PRINCIPAL ACTIVITIES: Civil engineering and construction works
Branch Offices: PO Box 4720, Kuwait
Principal Bankers: Al Ahli Bank, Dubai; Bank of Credit & Commerce (Emirates), Abu Dhabi
Financial Information:

	US$'000
Authorised capital	7,000
Paid-up capital	7,000

Principal Shareholders: Joseph Anton Khalifeh, HE Saeed Al Darmaki
Date of Establishment: 1972
No of Employees: 350

CORDOBA DEVELOPMENT CO

Shk Khalifa St, Rashed Al Rashed Bldg, PO Box 2386, Abu Dhabi
Tel: 326717, 326718, 335118, 344119
Cable: Cordoba
Telex: 22482 EM

Chairman: Jaweed Al Ghussein
Directors: Garbis Kesheshian (General Manager), Nader Shraideh (Financial Manager), Fouad Aljamal (Cost and Planning Manager)

PRINCIPAL ACTIVITIES: General contracting
Branch Offices: Cordoba Development Co, PO Box 1928, Sharjah, UAE
Subsidiary/Associated Companies: Alsalmeen General Contracting Co; Alsalmeen Trading Co; DNCC-Cordoba J V, PO Box 9247, Dubai, UAE; Sharjah Automobile & Equipment Co, PO Box 3618, Sharjah, UAE
Principal Bankers: Arab Bank; Bank of Baroda; Bank of Credit and Commerce, International (Overseas) Ltd

Principal Shareholders: Jaweed Al Ghussein (Proprietor)
Date of Establishment: 1974
No of Employees: 800

COSTAIN ABU DHABI CO

PO Box 3069, Abu Dhabi
Tel: 553920
Cable: COSDOWN ABU DHABI
Telex: 24290 COSDEP EM
Telefax: 559598

Chairman: Abdulla Nasser Hawaileel
Senior Executives: J Booth (Manager)

PRINCIPAL ACTIVITIES: Building and civil engineering
contractors, mechanical engineering and construction,
geotechnical engineering, process engineering
Parent Company: Costain International Ltd, Woking, Surrey, UK
Associated Companies: Costain Dubai Co
Principal Bankers: The British Bank of the Middle East, Abu
Dhabi

Principal Shareholders: Joint venture company owned 51% by
Amlad Nasser Corporation and 49% by Costain International
Ltd
Date of Establishment: 1987
No of Employees: 275

CREDIT LYONNAIS
PO Box 4725, Abu Dhabi
Tel: 337493
Telex: 23727
Telefax: 344995

Senior Executives: Jean Paul Barge (General Representative)

PRINCIPAL ACTIVITIES: Representative office
Parent Company: Head office in Paris, France

Date of Establishment: 1977

CREDIT SUISSE
Representative Office, PO Box 47060, Abu Dhabi
Tel: 325048
Telex: 22975 Cresui EM
Telefax: 324109

Senior Executives: Eduard Schmid (Representative), Peter
Waldburger (Assistant Representative), Thomas Greter
(Assistant Representative)

PRINCIPAL ACTIVITIES: Representative Office
Parent Company: Head office in Zurich, Switzerland

Principal Shareholders: Public
Date of Establishment: 1978 Rep Office Abu Dhabi

CTMS (UAE) LTD
PO Box 46983, Abu Dhabi
Tel: 344726
Telex: 23099 HPCTMS EM
Telefax: 212056

Chairman: I W Reeves (High-Point Plc)
Directors: R V Wharton (Chief Executive High-Point Plc), A S
Toates (Director CTMS (UAE) Ltd), A K Zakaria (JV
Partner/Director CTMS (UAE) Ltd
Senior Executives: M S Robinson (Regional Manager)

PRINCIPAL ACTIVITIES: Construction, technology, commercial
and contractual management services
Parent Company: High-Point Plc, Birmingham, UK
Associated Companies: Rendel, Palmer & Tritton; High-Point
Schaer; BR Wood; Rendel Meckel; Transportation Planning
Associates; Economic Studies Group; London Scientific
Services-Environmental Consultants
Principal Bankers: British Bank of the Middle East, Abu Dhabi;
Barclays Bank, UK

Date of Establishment: 1981

DAFF TRADING & OIL SERVICES
Muroor Road, PO Box 7399, Abu Dhabi
Tel: 477218, 477219
Telex: 23890 DAFF EM

Chairman: Khalfan Khalifa Al Mazroui (Managing Director)
Senior Executives: M K Abdul Rahman (Office Executive), K K
Koshy (Sales Executive), Deepak Vaswani (Sales Executive)

PRINCIPAL ACTIVITIES: Import, wholesale and retail of oil-field
equipment, pumps, valves, pipes, fittings, lubricants,
chemicals etc, agency and sponsorship of foreign companies

Principal Agencies: Robert Cort & Son, UK; Copes-Valcan, UK;
John Zink, France, UK, Luxembourg; Balcke-Duerr, W
Germany; Goulds Inc, USA; Kubota Ltd, Japan; Magnetrol
Int'l NV, Belgium; Machinfabriek Mokveld BV, Holland; Nat,
France; Bowen, USA; Interweld (UK), UK; Best International,
USA; Van Leeuwen BV, Holland; C M Kemp Mfg, USA;
Simtran Corp, USA; Amco Naardan BV, Holland
Principal Bankers: Arab Bank for Investment & Foreign Trade

Date of Establishment: 1980

DALMA INTERNATIONAL CORP
PO Box 6550, Abu Dhabi
Tel: 363921, 724876
Cable: Mustjab
Telex: 23428 Mustja EM

Chairman: Mohd Saeed Salem Al Qubaisi
Directors: Saeed Akhtar (Managing Partner)

PRINCIPAL ACTIVITIES: Civil and building contractors, turnkey
services, sewage treatment plant, structural steelwork
Subsidiary Companies: Joint-ventures: Dalma Conforlar
(Portugal); Cora Eng Abu Dhabi (Switzerland); Bond Const Co
(Germany); Interag Co Ltd (Hungary); Meto Bau (Switzerland)
Principal Bankers: BCCI

Principal Shareholders: Partners as described
Date of Establishment: October 1980

DAMES & MOORE
PO Box 2621, Abu Dhabi
Tel: 335622
Telex: 22893 DMAD EM
Telefax: 727602

Senior Executives: R Beake (Manager)

PRINCIPAL ACTIVITIES: Geotechnical, environmental and water
resources consultants
Parent Company: Dames & Moore, Twickenham, UK

DANWAY ABU DHABI
PO Box 47142, Abu Dhabi
Tel: 725617
Telex: 22782 Danway EM
Telefax: 727373

PRINCIPAL ACTIVITIES: Trading and servicing, control and
components, high gland power supplies AC/DC, laboratory,
testing and weighing equipment, pumps, electric motors,
mechanical plant, instrumentation
Parent Company: Associated British Engineering Group,
Southall, Middlesex, UK

DAR AL BINAA CONTRACTING CO
PO Box 201, Abu Dhabi
Tel: 667024, 666371, 665695
Cable: Darbina
Telex: 23465 EM Darbna
Telefax: 669902

Chairman: Mohamad Khalid
Senior Executives: Nidal Mohammed (Project Manager &
Resident Engineer)

PRINCIPAL ACTIVITIES: Building contractors
Subsidiary Companies: National Cold Stores
Principal Bankers: National Bank of Abu Dhabi; United Bank
Ltd, Abu Dhabi, Invest Bank of Abu Dhabi
Financial Information:

	1990
	Dh'000
Authorised capital	5,000
Paid-up capital	5,000

Principal Shareholders: Mohamad Khalid
Date of Establishment: November 1973
No of Employees: 150

DARCO MACHINERY

PO Box 2263, Abu Dhabi
Tel: 562712
Cable: Darma EM
Telex: 22431
Telefax: 562810

Chairman: A Haidar
Senior Executives: Mohd Haidar (General Manager)

PRINCIPAL ACTIVITIES: Import and distribution of construction
equipment and heavy machinery
Principal Agencies: Cummins Engine, USA; Maschinenbau Ulm,
W Germany; Warner & Swasey, USA; Fleetguard Inc, USA
Branch Offices: Sharjah
Parent Company: Darco Road Construction
Principal Bankers: Dubai Islamic Bank, Abu Dhabi

Principal Shareholders: Saeed Bin Daen Al Mansouri; A Haidar
Date of Establishment: 1977

DARCO ROAD CONSTRUCTION

Airport Rd, PO Box 520, Abu Dhabi
Tel: 341708, 326833
Cable: Darco
Telex: 22614 EM

Chairman: Ali Haidar
Directors: Azmi Zorba (Chief Engineer)
Senior Executives: Hikmat Baya (Office Engineer), Samir Shini
(Chief Accountant)

PRINCIPAL ACTIVITIES: Road works construction; machinery
distributors
Branch Offices: Darco Machinery, PO Box 2263, Abu Dhabi
Principal Bankers: Arab Bank of Investment & Commerce; Al
Rafidain Bank

Principal Shareholders: Said Bin Daen Al Mansoori
No of Employees: 240

DARWISH, ABDUL RAHMAN, TRADING & CONTRACTING CO

PO Box 2434, Abu Dhabi
Tel: 822385, 822910, 820705
Cable: Darwishco
Telex: 22382 Darwis EM

Chairman: Ahmed Yusuf Ali
Senior Executives: Abdul Rahman Moughrabi (Manager)

PRINCIPAL ACTIVITIES: General trading, and contracting,
specialising in sport complexes
Principal Agencies: GES Thomasson, Paris; Bafferey
Hennebique, Paris; Eclatec Technic, Paris; S A Enregistreurs
Lambert, Paris
Branch Offices: PO Box 1285, Doha, Qatar
Subsidiary Companies: Darwish Engineering, PO Box 11175,
Dubai (UAE)
Principal Bankers: Grindlays Bank, Abu Dhabi

Date of Establishment: 1974

DARWISH TRADING EST

PO Box 222, Abu Dhabi
Tel: 827402, 827403
Telex: 22213 Trader EM

Chairman: Kassem Darwish Fakhroo
Directors: Hasan Darwish Fakhroo (Managing Director)
Senior Executives: Syed Faiyaz Husain (Manager)

PRINCIPAL ACTIVITIES: General trading and contracting,
distribution of cars
Principal Agencies: Audi; Volkswagen
Branch Offices: Dubai

Parent Company: Kassem Darwish Fakhroo & Sons, Doha -
Qatar
Principal Bankers: British Bank of the Middle East

No of Employees: 500 (Group)

DECCA NAVIGATOR OVERSEAS LTD

PO Box 251, Abu Dhabi
Tel: 667703, 345152
Telefax: 666506

Senior Executives: A Smith Taylor (Area Manager)

PRINCIPAL ACTIVITIES: Electronic navigation systems for
shipping, aircraft and survey
Parent Company: Racal Decca Navigator Co Ltd, New Malden,
Surrey, UK

DHAFIR & JALAL ENGINEERING EQUIPMENT CO

PO Box 6372, Abu Dhabi
Tel: 325336, 324161
Telex: 22987 DHAJAL EM

Directors: Jalal M Jalal, Sultan Bin Ghanoum Al Hamely
Senior Executives: K V Samuel (Manager)

PRINCIPAL ACTIVITIES: Supply, installation, maintenance of
lifts, cranes, construction equipment, excavators
Principal Agencies: Schindler Lifts; Mannesmann Demag
Baumaschinen; Mannesmann Demag Fordertechnik
Associated Companies: Mohammed Jalal and Sons, Bahrain,
Dubai, Sharjah; Dhafir Group of Companies, Abu Dhabi
Principal Bankers: National Bank of Abu Dhabi

Date of Establishment: August 1976
No of Employees: 145

DHAFIR GROUP OF COMPANIES

PO Box 4330, Dhafir Bldg, Banias St, Abu Dhabi
Tel: 774670, 774656
Cable: Dhafir
Telex: 22385 EM
Telefax: 776786

President: Sultan Ghanoum Al Hameli
Directors: Sherif El Kurdi (Managing Director)
Senior Executives: S A Mebarek (General Manager), K K Refai
(Commercial Manager), Ibrahim Mashal (Personnel & Admin
Manager), Asaad S Arar (Finance Manager)

PRINCIPAL ACTIVITIES: Manufacturers' representation,
distribution of electrical equipment and appliances, cables,
generators, motors, lighting equipment, household appliances,
marine equipment, construction equipment and machinery,
agricultural equipment, building materials, refrigeration
equipment, communication & office equipment, security
systems, testing & measuring systems, pharmaceuticals, also
printing press and stationery, travel agency and cargo
services, central air-conditioning projects and civil engineering
construction and services
Principal Agencies: Alfa Romeo, Italy; Aluminium Wire & Cable
Co, UK; Merlin Gerin, France; Yorkshire Switgear, UK;
Raychem, USA; Invest Import, Yugoslavia; Industrija Kablova,
Yugoslavia; France Transfo, France
Branch Offices: Dhafir Group, PO Box 9027, Dubai, Tel 227075,
Telex 48977, Fax 280822; Dhafir Group, PO Box 1439, Al Ain,
Tel 661661, Telex 34145, Fax 669895; Dhafir Group, PO Box
7604, Industrial Zone, Musafah, Tel 554151; Dhafir Group, PO
Box 11766, Ruwais, Tel 75115, Telex 22365
Subsidiary Companies: Dhafir Engineering Services; Oilfield &
Industrial Supplies; Dhafir Travel Services; Dhafir Printing
House; Dhafir General Contracting & Maintenance; Dhafir
Garage Alfa Romeo; Dhafir Educational Institutes; Dhafir
Development & Contracting; Bin Ghanoum Est; Gulf
Commercial
Principal Bankers: Bank of Credit & Commerce (Emirates); Bank
of Oman Ltd

UAE (Abu Dhabi)

Financial Information:

	1989/90 Dh'000
Sales turnover	180,000
Profits	12,000
Paid-up capital	15,000
Total assets	80,000

Principal Shareholders: Proprietorship
Date of Establishment: 1971
No of Employees: 300

DHL UAE

PO Box 7041, Abu Dhabi
Tel: 321860
Telex: 23821 DHL AUH EM

PRINCIPAL ACTIVITIES: Worldwide courier express service
Branch Offices: In the Middle East: Bahrain, Cyprus, Egypt
(Cairo, Alexandria), Iran, Jordan, Kuwait, Lebanon, Oman,
Qatar, Saudi Arabia (AlKhobar, Jeddah, Riyadh, Jubail, Tabuk,
Taif), Sudan, UAE (Abu Dhabi, Dubai, Sharjah)
Parent Company: DHL Middle East, Bahrain

DOWELL SCHLUMBERGER (WESTERN) SA

PO Box 4020, Abu Dhabi
Tel: 554600
Cable: Bigorange Abu Dhabi
Telex: 22537 EM
Telefax: 554200

PRINCIPAL ACTIVITIES: Oil service company
Branch Offices: Middle East Division Office Dubai: PO Box
2964, Tel 420299, Fax 434299
Parent Company: Dowell Schlumberger Corporation

DRAKE & SCULL ENGINEERING

PO Box 915, Abu Dhabi
Tel: 727664, 725938
Telex: 22493 Dasbmi EM

Senior Executives: C Harman (Area Manager Dubai)

PRINCIPAL ACTIVITIES: Mechanical, electrical and sanitation
contractors
Branch Offices: Dubai
Parent Company: Drake & Scull Engineering, London N19, UK

DUCTO TENNANT (ME) PVT LTD

PO Box 2534, Abu Dhabi
Tel: 701386, 720646
Telex: 22457 Dunn EM
Telefax: 782702

Senior Executives: I M Mack (General Manager Dubai)

PRINCIPAL ACTIVITIES: Agent representatives and trading
Branch Offices: Area Office in Dubai

EASTERN LIMITED

PO Box 6790, Abu Dhabi
Tel: 827869
Telex: 23466 Eastrn EM

Chairman: Abdulrahman M Bukhatir
Senior Executives: G Bhandari (General Manager), C J
Sabavala (Dy General Manager), R Ganapathy (Dy General
Manager)

PRINCIPAL ACTIVITIES: Engineers and contractors
Branch Offices: PO Box 15421, Al Ain, UAE, Tel 642976; PO
Box 5231, Dubai, UAE, Tel 236300; PO Box 5676, Baghdad,
Iraq, Tel 7182658; PO Box 5927, Ruwi, Oman, Tel 601010
Parent Company: Bukhatir Investment Ltd, Sharjah
Subsidiary Companies: Conforce (Gulf) Ltd; Bucomac Ltd;
Touchwood, Sharjah
Principal Bankers: National Bank of Abu Dhabi; Habib Bank AG
Zurich; National Bank of Sharjah

Financial Information:

	Dh'000
Authorised capital	50,000
Paid-up capital	20,000

Date of Establishment: 1974
No of Employees: 2,000

EASTMAN WHIPSTOCK INC

PO Box 4563, Abu Dhabi
Tel: 328543, 58065
Telex: 23682 Ewi EM

PRINCIPAL ACTIVITIES: Directional drilling and surveying
services and equipment
Branch Offices: UK; Norway; Denmark; Nigeria; Egypt; United
Arab Emirates; Saudi Arabia; Greece
Parent Company: Eastman Whipstock Inc, Houston, USA

EL NILEIN BANK

PO Box 6013, Abu Dhabi
Tel: 326451/3
Cable: Nileinbank
Telex: 22884 EM

PRINCIPAL ACTIVITIES: Commercial banking
Parent Company: Head office: PO Box 466, Khartoum, Sudan

ELENCO GENERAL TRADING & CONTRACTING CO

PO Box 103, Abu Dhabi
Tel: 828880
Cable: Elenco
Telex: 22295 Elenco EM

Chairman: Antoine Iskander Farah

PRINCIPAL ACTIVITIES: Electrical engineering contractors,
manufacturers representation, supply of electrical fittings and
equipment
Principal Agencies: J A Crabtree, UK; Kelvinator, USA; Pirelli
Cables, UK; Bamberger, W Germany; Ottermill, UK; BICC
Pyrothene, UK; Puma Generators, UK; Eclatic Paris, Univolt,
Austria; W J Furse & Co, UK; Condiesel Power, USA
Subsidiary Companies: Electrical Trading & Contracting Co, PO
Box 6012, Sharjah, Tel 356178; Lara Trading Est, PO Box
6012, Sharjah, Tel 222909; Technical Electric Co, PO Box
415, Muscat, Oman; Elenco Enterprise, PO Box 55100, Beirut,
Lebanon
Principal Bankers: National Bank of Abu Dhabi

Principal Shareholders: Said Hilal; Antoine Farah
Date of Establishment: 1968
No of Employees: 350

EMIRATES HOLDINGS

PO Box 984, Abu Dhabi
Tel: 823553
Cable: EMHOLD EM
Telex: 23011 Emhold EM

Directors: Hussein J Al Nowais (Managing Director)
Senior Executives: Michel Sawaya (General Manager), M
Narayan (Group Finance Manager), Saad Abdul Baky
(Manager Power & Water Div), Ashok Kumar (Engineer
Telecommunications Div - Emircom), Fred Schaefer (Manager
International Transport Div - OTC), Gordon Kirkman (Manager
Diving & Inspection - Solus), Roland Larsson (Manager
Cleaning & Maintenance -Electrolux/EMCS)

PRINCIPAL ACTIVITIES: Sponsorship/representation, business
development, international transport/clearing and forwarding,
health care, contracting, insurance,
investments,telecommunications, maintenance and services to
the oil and gas industry
Principal Agencies: Allied Medical; Nuovo Pignone; Conline Int'l;
Norton Chemical Process Products; Robertson Research;
Descon Engineering; Geophysical Services Inc; Maersk

Drilling; Degremont; Sigmund Pulsometer Pumps; Colcrete; Italtel; Mid East Data Systems
Branch Offices: Dubai and Egypt
Subsidiary Companies: Orient Transport Co, Abu Dhabi; Oceanroutes Emirates; Emirates General Energy Co; Global Gulf Emirates, Abu Dhabi; Solus Emirates; Motherwell Bridge Emirates; Consafe Emirates; Pharmatrade; Laing Abu Dhabi; Transelektro Emirates; Emirates Swire Pacific Offshore; Fire Protection Emirates; Teleco Drilltech Emirates; Nowsco Emirates; Emircom; Emirates Maintenance & Cleaning Services; Memo
Principal Bankers: Banque Paribas

Principal Shareholders: Hussain Al Nowais
Date of Establishment: 1979
No of Employees: Joint Ventures 500 (UAE); Total Group 2,000 (UAE)

EMIRATES HOSPITAL SUPPLIES LTD

PO Box 366, Abu Dhabi
Tel: 823311
Cable: Hosplies
Telex: 22622 HOSPLY EM

Directors: Rashid Aweidha, Rasul Al Jishi

PRINCIPAL ACTIVITIES: Import and distribution of pharmaceuticals; medical supplies lab and industrial chemicals, laboratory supplies
Principal Agencies: Hoffman La Roche & Co, 3M Riker Laboratories, Eisai Co Ltd, Chas F Thackray, Beckmann Instruments, Albright and Wilson, Aesculap, OEC, Vickers Medical, E Scheurich, Robert Bosch, Leo Pharmaceutical, Lohmann, Keeleroptics
Branch Offices: Hospital Supplies, PO Box 3321, Dubai
Principal Bankers: British Bank of the Middle East

Date of Establishment: 1967

EMIRATES INDUSTRIAL BANK

Head Office, PO Box 2722, Abu Dhabi
Tel: 339700
Telex: 23324 INDBNK EM
Telefax: 326397

Chairman: HE Ahmed Humaid Al Tayer
Directors: HE Sh Surour Bin Sultan Al Dhaheri (Vice Chairman), Jaffar Al Fardan, Mohamed K Kharbash, Ebrahim F Humaid, Anis Al Jallal, Juaan Salim Al Dhaheri, Jamal M Al Ghurair, Hussain Jassim Al Nowais, Mohamed Abdulla Al Ghurair
Senior Executives: Mohamed Abdulbaki (General Manager), Muzafar Al Haj Muzafar (Deputy General Manager), Ahmad Mohd Bakhit Khalfan (Dubai Branch Manager), Wisam M Shaheen (Manager Administration), Mohamed Munir Maklid (Manager Finance), Radwan Ghanimah (Manager Audit), Abdulrahim Kazim (Manager Loans), Mustafa K Khan (Manager Projects), Abdullah Omran (Manager Evaluation & Follow Up), Dr Mohamed Al Assoomi (Manager Economical Research)

PRINCIPAL ACTIVITIES: Banking
Branch Offices: Dubai
Financial Information:

	1989/90 Dh'000
Income	54,598
Profits	36,538
Authorised capital	500,000
Paid-up capital	200,000
Total assets	708,904

Principal Shareholders: 51% UAE Ministry of Finance & Industry; 49% UAE banks and insurance companies
Date of Establishment: 1982
No of Employees: 43

EMIRATES SAFETY SERVICES

PO Box 322, Abu Dhabi
Tel: 721155
Telex: 68697 Safety EM
Telefax: 774290

Directors: W Wigan (Director)

PRINCIPAL ACTIVITIES: Certification of lifting gear, advice on safety, fire and environmental matters
Parent Company: Eurmaco Engineering ltd, Meldreth, Cambridgeshire, UK

EMITAC LIMITED

PO Box 2711, Abu Dhabi
Tel: 770420
Cable: Emitad Ad
Telex: 48710 Emitac EM
Telefax: 723058

Chairman: Abdul Rahman Bukhatir
Directors: Ghobash Ahmed Saeed
Senior Executives: Viren Naroola (Chief Executive)

PRINCIPAL ACTIVITIES: Electronics and communication equipment, computers, calculators, medical equipment, test and measuring instruments, peripherals for computers, computer supplies, training
Principal Agencies: HP, B&K, Amersham, IMED, Gandalf, SPSS, Chemshare
Branch Offices: Dubai
Parent Company: Head Office in Sharjah
Principal Bankers: National Bank of Sharjah

Principal Shareholders: UAE Nationals own 100% of the Company
Date of Establishment: 1974
No of Employees: 140

ENGINEERING & TRADING CO

Nasser M Shaffi Bldg, Electra Rd, PO Box 4170, Abu Dhabi
Tel: 343158
Cable: Entraco
Telex: 22337 Entrac EM

Chairman: Abdullah Syed Hashim Al Gharabally
Directors: Muzher Abdulla Al Gharabally, K T B Menon, Ahmed Huma Al Dharif

PRINCIPAL ACTIVITIES: Contractors/manufacturers' representatives, trading in chemicals, building material, air-conditioning and refrigerating equipment and spare parts
Principal Agencies: Takenaka Kumagai, Japan; Sumitomo Construction Co, Japan; Korean Overseas Construction; Curtiss Wright Corn, New Jersey, USA; Bridge & Roof, India; Fibreglass Pilkington; Asian Paints; X-Ray Engineering Works; Enamelled wires, Singapore; Tropimere, UK
Subsidiary Companies: Marine Transport Services Co Ltd (Offshore Services)·
Principal Bankers: Bank of Commerce & Credit International Ltd

ERNST & YOUNG

PO Box 136, Abu Dhabi
Tel: 322224
Cable: Ernstaudit Abu Dhabi
Telex: 22672
Telefax: 342968

Partners: J I Channo, P D Sharp, N J Love
Senior Executives: S A H Ali, Adel Hussein, R F Akbar, B Hajj

PRINCIPAL ACTIVITIES: Accountants and management consultants
Branch Offices: In the Middle East; Bahrain; Egypt; Jordan; Kuwait; Lebanon; Oman; Qatar; Saudi Arabia; United Arab Emirates; Yemen

Date of Establishment: Middle East - 1923; Abu Dhabi - 1966
No of Employees: Middle East - 500; Abu Dhabi - 41

ETISALAT

PO Box 300, Abu Dhabi
Tel: 333111
Telex: 22144 EM

PRINCIPAL ACTIVITIES: Telecommunications, telephone and
telegraph systems
Branch Offices: Throughout the United Arab Emirates
Principal Bankers: National Bank of Abu Dhabi, National Bank
of Dubai

No of Employees: 4,350

EURO MECHANICAL & ELECTRICAL CONTRACTORS

PO Box 46153, Abu Dhabi
Tel: 781133
Telex: 23269 Euro EM
Telefax: 783419

Chairman: John Manna
Directors: Rashed Mohammed Hamad Al Hurr Al Suwaidi,
Hamad Mohammed Hamad Al Hurr Al Suwaidi
Senior Executives: Matthew Greenslade (General Manager),
Michael Farley (Manager Agencies), Larry Howie (Operations
Manager), Joseph Bernard (Company Accountant)

PRINCIPAL ACTIVITIES: Electrical and mechanical engineering
contractors, agents and manpower suppliers
Principal Agencies: ABB Kent Taylor, ABB Kent Introl, Neles
Jamesbury, Krautkramer, Enraf Nonius, Sydney Smith Dennis
Ltd, Delta Controls Ltd, McAlpine Kershaw Ltd, IRD
Mechanalysis, KDG Mobrey, Schroedahl, Tokheim Corp,
Measurement Inc, Highland Electronics Ltd, D W Munro
Ltd, Inpipe Products
Branch Offices: Das Island, Ruwais
Parent Company: United Trading Co
Principal Bankers: Abu Dhabi National Bank Ltd, Barclays Bank
Financial Information:

	1990
	Dh'000
Sales turnover	35,000
Profits	3,700
Authorised capital	750
Paid-up capital	750
Total assets	9,894

Principal Shareholders: 100% owned by Directors stated above
(UAE Nationals)
Date of Establishment: April 1976
No of Employees: 485

EUROPEAN EXHIBITION FOR MODERN FURNITURE

Al Hadlaq, Abdul Rahman Hamad, Co & Partners

PO Box 4127, Abu Dhabi
Tel: 822871, 821034, 822242
Cable: Dinar, Abu Dhabi
Telex: 22925 Dinar EM
Telefax: 729028

Partners: Musallam Bin Hum, Abdulrahman Hamad Al Hadlaq
Senior Executives: Mohammed Shaker (Manager)

PRINCIPAL ACTIVITIES: Import and distribution of furniture,
carpets and curtain materials and furnishing and decoration
consultants
Principal Bankers: Arab Bank of Investment and Foreign Trade,
Abu Dhabi

Date of Establishment: 1971
No of Employees: 45

EWBANK PREECE LTD

PO Box 4336, Abu Dhabi
Tel: 02-724603
Telex: 22871 RIDER EM
Telefax: 02-725477

Senior Executives: R F Groom (Resident Manager)

PRINCIPAL ACTIVITIES: Multi-discipline consulting engineers
and projects managers
Branch Offices: PO Box 15663, Al Ain, Tel 03-634621, 634246
Parent Company: Ewbank Preece Ltd, Brighton, UK, Tel 0273-
724533
Associated Companies: Ewbank International Consultants (Pvt)
Ltd, Dubai, Tel 04-228801
Principal Bankers: BBME, Abu Dhabi
Financial Information:

	1990/91
	Dh'000
Sales turnover	7,000

Date of Establishment: 1977
No of Employees: 50

EXXON (AL-KHALIJ) INC

PO Box 3500, Abu Dhabi
Tel: 336091, 213104
Telex: 24342 EXONAK EM
Telefax: 215178

President: John Ehardt

PRINCIPAL ACTIVITIES: Representation office
Parent Company: Exxon Corporation, New York, USA
Principal Bankers: Citibank

Date of Establishment: July 1984

FALAKNAZ HABITAT

PO Box 46613, Abu Dhabi
Tel: 318121
Telefax: 346848

Senior Executives: Lars Lund (Manager)

PRINCIPAL ACTIVITIES: Supply of furniture and furnishings
Parent Company: Habitat Design ltd, Wallingford, Oxfordshire,
UK

FEB MIDDLE EAST

PO Box 5280, Abu Dhabi
Tel: 726580
Telex: 22728 Rimal EM
Telefax: 776058

Senior Executives: J Day (Area Manager)

PRINCIPAL ACTIVITIES: Construction chemicals supplies
Parent Company: Feb (GB) Ltd, Swinton, UK

FIRST GULF BANK

PO Box 3820, Abu Dhabi
Tel: 341367, 328089
Telex: 22582 Ajbankem

PRINCIPAL ACTIVITIES: Commercial banking
Branch Offices: Sharjah
Parent Company: Head office in Ajman UAE

FIRST INTERSTATE BANK OF CALIFORNIA

PO Box 46643, Abu Dhabi
Tel: 321896/7
Cable: Ficalem
Telex: 23496 FICAL EM
Telefax: 330209

Senior Executives: Osman Morad (Vice President and Middle
East Representative)

PRINCIPAL ACTIVITIES: Commercial banking, representative office
Parent Company: First Interstate Bancorp, Los Angeles, California, USA

Date of Establishment: 1978

FLOPETROL TECHNICAL SERVICES INC
South Gulf District Office, PO Box 4362, Abu Dhabi
Tel: 321794
Telex: 22318 Flopret EM

PRINCIPAL ACTIVITIES: Oil field services; well testing; snubbing workover; sampling; PVT Laboratory; drill stem testing

FOSROC
PO Box 7268, Abu Dhabi
Tel: 721719
Telex: 22372 Algurg EM
Telefax: 782658

Senior Executives: A McKee (Regional Sales Manager)

PRINCIPAL ACTIVITIES: Supplies of construction chemicals
Associated Companies: Foseco Plc, Birmingham, UK

G & T CONSTRUCTION CO
PO Box 4072, Abu Dhabi
Tel: 343801, 343408, 345307
Telex: 22316 Tarmac EM

Chairman: Saif Al Ghurair

PRINCIPAL ACTIVITIES: Building construction, civil engineering, contracting, asphalt road paving, construction products and quarrying
Principal Agencies: G & T Construction is the Construction Division of Ghurair-Tarmac (Private) Limited and totally managed by Tarmac Group
Branch Offices: Dubai: PO Box 2285, Dubai Al Ain: PO Box 15569, Al Ain
Principal Bankers: Bank of Oman Ltd, Abu Dhabi; Commercial Bank of Dubai, Dubai

Principal Shareholders: Public
Date of Establishment: 1976
No of Employees: (1,500 Qualified Engineers)

G.A.S.O.S.
Gulf Automation Services & Oilfield Supplies
PO Box 203, Abu Dhabi
Tel: 211366
Telex: 22603 GASOS EM
Telefax: 972-336184

Chairman: HE Hamoodah Bin ALi
Directors: Faraj Ali Bin Hamoodah (President), Ghanem Ali Bin Hamoodah
Senior Executives: Samir Al Gharbi (General Manager), M Omar Yusuf (Financial Controller), S Nath (Sales Manager), A K Bazara (Marketing Manager), F Shaltony (Technical Manager)

PRINCIPAL ACTIVITIES: Mechanical contractors; oilfield supplies and services; water desalination units; safety equipment; power generation equipment etc
Branch Offices: GASOS Bin Hamoodah, PO Box 9082, Dubai
Parent Company: Bin Hamoodah Group
Subsidiary Companies: Bin Hamoodah Trading & General Services; Gisco; AlGeemi and Partners; Milco; Weatherford Bin Hamoodah; Wesco
Principal Bankers: National Bank of Abu Dhabi; Arab Bank Ltd

Principal Shareholders: Bin Hamoodah Company (100%)
Date of Establishment: 1972
No of Employees: 40

GEC PLESSEY TELECOMMUNICATIONS LTD
PO Box 2570, Abu Dhabi
Tel: 770302
Telefax: 777652

Senior Executives: D Harris (Resident Manager)

PRINCIPAL ACTIVITIES: Planning, installation, and maintenance of telecommunication systems, network and business systems
Parent Company: Head office in Coventry, UK

GENERAL INDUSTRY CORPORATION (GIC)
PO Box 4499, Abu Dhabi
Tel: 20214900
Cable: Gicorp
Telex: 22938 Gicorp EM
Telefax: 2-325034

Chairman: Hassan Moosa Al Kimji
Directors: Essa Abdul Rahman Al Atiq (Director General)
Senior Executives: Dr M A Zaher (Director of Planning & Operation), Sultan Mohd Jaassim Al Aali (Administration Director), Awn Al Sayegh (Finance Director), Dr Abdul Majeed Ginena (Economic Advisor), Salah Abduljaleel (Legal Advisor)

PRINCIPAL ACTIVITIES: Establishment and management of industries in Abu Dhabi; issuing of licenses for industry; promotion of industries in the private sector
Branch Offices: PO Box 1602, Al Ain
Subsidiary Companies: GIC is the head office in control of the following factories: Abu Dhabi Flour & Feed Factory, PO Box 6622, Abu Dhabi; National Plastics Pipe Factory, PO Box 2915, Abu Dhabi; Abu Dhabi Bags Factory, PO Box 6828, Abu Dhabi; Abu Dhabi Pipe Factory, PO Box 4526, Abu Dhabi; Al Ain Cement Factory, PO Box 1114, Al Ain; Al Wathba Concrete Blocks Factory, PO Box 4781, Abu Dhabi; Al Ain Mineral Water Bottling Plant, PO Box 16020, Al Ain
Principal Bankers: Bank of Credit & Commerce (Emirate), Abu Dhabi

Principal Shareholders: 100% owned by the Government of Abu Dhabi
Date of Establishment: 1979
No of Employees: 900

G.I.B.C.A.
General International Business Contracting Associates
Head Office, PO Box 2570, Abu Dhabi
Tel: 330866 (8 lines)
Cable: Gibca
Telex: 22384 Gibca EM
Telefax: 323445

Chairman: HE Sheikh Faisal Bin Sultan Al-Qassimi (Owner)
Directors: Sheikh Khalid Bin Saqr Al-Qassimi (Managing Director), Sheikh Sultan Bin Saqr Al-Qassimi, Colonel Eric Johnson (Finance Director)
Senior Executives: Bassam Helayl (Technical Manager), Rusi Sorabji (Manager GIBCA Petroleum Service), Anthony G White (Manager Emirates Arab Electronics), Shafiq Hussein (Manager Al Yoha International), Samir Dakik (Sales & Marketing Manager), Mohammad Farid (Manager Commercial), Norman Hamady (Manager A/C Division)

PRINCIPAL ACTIVITIES: Representation of companies, sponsors, consultants, marketing advisors, concentrating in electric power generation and transmission, oil and gas, central airconditioning supplies, electronics and telecommunications, defense
Principal Agencies: Representations: Plessey; Rolls Royce Aero & Industrial; Worthington Pump; Ruston; Teledyne; Cables de Lyon; Fiat TTG; Skoda Export; Instromet; Gorter; Phoceenne; Hitachi Central Air Conditioning
Branch Offices: Dubai

Associated Companies: Gibca Ltd, PO Box 289, Sharjah, UAE, Tel 591433, Telex 68082; Gibca Petroleum Services, Head Office Abu Dhabi; Al Yoha International, PO Box 2570, Abu Dhabi

Principal Bankers: United Arab Bank, UAE

Principal Shareholders: 100% Sheikh Faisal bin Sultan Al-Qassimi

Date of Establishment: 1974
No of Employees: 300 approx

GLOBAL CONTRACTING (ABU DHABI)

PO Box 3629, Abu Dhabi
Tel: 554890
Telex: 23057 gcad em
Telefax: 554386

Chairman: G Smit
Directors: J L Leer
Senior Executives: J N Roggeveen (General Manager UAE)

PRINCIPAL ACTIVITIES: Abrasive blasting protective coating, industrial cleaning, fire-proofing, internal lining of tanks and pipes, cathodic protection, roadmarking, concrete repairs
Branch Offices: Branches in Saudi Arabia, UAE, Qatar, Sultanate of Oman, Bahrain, Kuwait, Indonesia, Italy and North Africa
Parent Company: Vendex Int'l NV, De Klencke 6, 1083HH Amsterdam, The Netherlands
Principal Bankers: Algemene Bank Nederland

Principal Shareholders: Hemutech SA, Switzerland (Fully owned by Vendex Int'l)
Date of Establishment: Global - Abu Dhabi 1979
No of Employees: Abu Dhabi (120); Arabian Gulf (800)

GRAY MACKENZIE & PARTNERS (ABU DHABI) LTD

PO Box 247, Abu Dhabi
Tel: 323131
Cable: ADMMI Abudhabi
Telex: 22245 Gray EM
Telefax: 213661

Chairman: Rahma bin Mohammed Al Masaood
Directors: HE Shaikh Suroor bin Sultan Al Daheri, HE Shaikh Saeed bin Mohammed Al Nahyan, Butti bin Ahmed Al Otaiba, R R Owens, A A Macaskill, C Johnson
Senior Executives: S D Blake (Managing Director), P Srinivasan (Finance Director), C Boother (Marketing Director), J Fuller (Technical Director)

PRINCIPAL ACTIVITIES: Managers of: Lloyds Agents, travel agents, dry cargo ship and tanker agents, general merchants, import and distribution of oilfield related equipment, foodstuffs and beverages
Principal Agencies: Schenkers, Jugolinija, Beechams, Yardley, Wallace & Tiernan, OCL, Hapag-Lloyd, Ellerman City Line, Nalco, Nalfloc, W & J Leigh, Brickhouse Broads, Saunders Valves, Crosby & Co, United Biscuits
Branch Offices: Branches in Abu Dhabi; Al Ain; Jebel Dhanna; Ruwais
Parent Company: In association with the Gray Mackenzie Group of Companies
Associated Companies: Abu Dhabi Maritime & Mercantile International
Principal Bankers: Standard Chartered Bank, Abu Dhabi; National Bank of Abu Dhabi; Grindlays Bank

Principal Shareholders: Rahma bin Mohammed Al Masaood; HE Shaikh Suroor bin Sultan Al Daheri; HE Shaikh Saeed bin Mohammed Al Nahyan; Butti bin Ahmed Al Otaiba; Ahmed Hamdan Bu Debs; Gray Mackenzie & Co Ltd
Date of Establishment: 1981
No of Employees: 95

GULF AIR

PO Box 573, Abu Dhabi
Tel: 331700
Telex: 22305

Chairman: HE Abdulla Bin Saleh Al Mana
Directors: HE Ali Ibrahim Al Malki

PRINCIPAL ACTIVITIES: Airline transportation of passenger, cargo and mail
Financial Information:

	1989/90 US$'000
Sales turnover	511,610
Profits	72,398
Share capital	169,761
Reserves	132,546
Total assets	654,880

Principal Shareholders: Jointly owned by the governments of Bahrain, Qatar, Abu Dhabi and Oman
Date of Establishment: 1950
No of Employees: 4,200

GULF AIRCRAFT MAINTENANCE CO (GAMCO)

PO Box 46450, Abu Dhabi
Tel: 971-2 767504
Cable: Sita Auhgmgf
Telex: 23258 Gamcom EM
Telefax: 971-2 757263

Chairman: Ali Bin Khalfan Al Dhaheri
Directors: Sultan Ghanoom Al Hameli (Managing Director)
Senior Executives: Viet Nguyen (General Manager), Seif Al Mugheiry (Director Aircraft Maintenance), Alan Vandersluis (Director Customer Relations), Michael Windle (Director, Operations Planning & Support), Brian Wilkie (Director Data Services)

PRINCIPAL ACTIVITIES: Aircraft maintenance support
Principal Agencies: Service centre for Bendix/King Electronics Equipment
Principal Bankers: Abu Dhabi Commercial Bank, National Bank of Abu Dhabi

Principal Shareholders: UAE Government, Gulf Air
Date of Establishment: 1987
No of Employees: 1,220

GULF INDUSTRIAL SERVICES CO (GISCO)

PO Box 6625, Abu Dhabi
Tel: 334800
Telex: 23041 Esdgas EM
Telefax: 322871

Chairman: Faraj Bin Hamoodah
Directors: S M Khalifa (General Manager)
Senior Executives: T Primrose (Manager-Fire Engineering)

PRINCIPAL ACTIVITIES: Electrical, instrumentation, mechanical installations, fire protection, security, rotating equipment, supply of specialist staff, workshops, halon filling rig maintenance, instrument control systems, etc
Principal Agencies: Thorn Security, UK
Branch Offices: Dubai: 16th Floor Dubai Trade Centre
Parent Company: Bin Hamoodah Company
Principal Bankers: National Bank of Abu Dhabi

Principal Shareholders: Bin Hamoodah, Abu Dhabi Associates: ME&C, UK; GEC Gas Turbines Ltd, UK
Date of Establishment: July 1978
No of Employees: 120

GULF PILES (VIBRO) CO LTD

PO Box 2352, Abu Dhabi
Tel: 323062, 343769
Cable: Vibro Abudhabi
Telex: 22415 Gupco EM

Directors: Hazim Mohd Abdulla (Managing Director)
Senior Executives: Rauf Riad Michael (Senior Project Engineer)

PRINCIPAL ACTIVITIES: Building contractors specialising in
construction of pile foundations of buildings, bridges, tanks
Branch Offices: Mechanical Foundation Company (Vibro), PO
Box 1552, Deira, Dubai
Principal Bankers: Arab Bank Ltd, Abu Dhabi, Dubai; Bank of
Credit and Commerce International

Principal Shareholders: Hazim Mohd Abdulla, Shukri Saleh Zaki,
Kadhim Mustafa Hillawi, Thani Bin Murshid
No of Employees: 155

GULF PRINTING SYSTEMS

Hamdan Street, Rashid Bin Aweidha Bldg, PO Box 4475, Abu
Dhabi
Tel: 330930
Cable: Al Aweidha
Telex: 23853 JALDI EM

Chairman: Rashid Bin Aweidha (Owner)
Senior Executives: Salahuddin Khursheed

PRINCIPAL ACTIVITIES: Printing and graphic products
Principal Agencies: (Screen) Dainippon Screen, Manderr Kidd
(UK), Ryobi, Guilleminot Boespflug & Cie, Japo Co Ltd
Branch Offices: UAE (branch in Dubai, PO Box 3060); Oman
Parent Company: Bin Aweidha Group of Companies
Principal Bankers: National Bank of Abu Dhabi; First Gulf
Bank/Ajman

Principal Shareholders: Rashid Bin Aweidha
No of Employees: 200

HABIB BANK LTD

PO Box 897, Abu Dhabi
Tel: 325665, 330188
Cable: Habibank
Telex: 22332 Habib EM

President: Abdul Jabbar Khan
Senior Executives: Tajjamal Hussain, Kasim Parekh

PRINCIPAL ACTIVITIES: Commercial banking
Branch Offices: Bahrain; Abu Dhabi; Dubai; Sharjah; Ras Al
Khaimah; Al Ain; Ajman; Umm Al Qaiwan; Yemen; Lebanon
Parent Company: Head office in Karachi, Pakistan

HACCO ENGINEERING & CONSTRUCTION CO

PO Box 3524, Abu Dhabi
Tel: 329629
Cable: Hacco
Telex: 23360 HACCO EM
Telefax: 328143

Chairman: Sadru Damji (also Managing Director)
Directors: Jimmy Kheraj, Jameel Damji
Senior Executives: Mukesh Kiswani (Projects Manager), Abdul
Gafur (Administrator), Stiburt Pinto (Accounts Manager),
Narayanan Muralidharan (Personnel Manager), N Rajan (Head
of Data Processing)

PRINCIPAL ACTIVITIES: Building and civil engineering
contractors
Branch Offices: Al Ain
Subsidiary Companies: Hassan Ahmed General Trading Est
(HASTE), PO Box 3524, Abu Dhabi; Hassan Ahmed Al
Mazrooi Trading Est (HASTE), PO Box 13229, Dubai
Principal Bankers: Standard Chartered Bank, Abu Dhabi; ABN
Bank, Abu Dhabi

Financial Information:

	1990
	US$'000
Authorised capital	1,000
Paid-up capital	1,000

Principal Shareholders: Sadru Damji
Date of Establishment: 1976
No of Employees: 165

HALCROW INTERNATIONAL PARTNERSHIP

PO Box 46024, Abu Dhabi
Tel: 790804
Telex: 22465 Hipad Em
Telefax: 785422

Senior Executives: I McLennan (Resident Representative)

PRINCIPAL ACTIVITIES: Consulting engineers and architects
Parent Company: Sir William Halcrow & Partners, London W6,
UK

HALLIBURTON GEODATA SERVICES (OVERSEAS) LTD

PO Box 71399, Abu Dhabi
Tel: 725776
Telex: 22793 GOAD EM
Telefax: 781502

Senior Executives: M Redmond (Middle East Manager)

PRINCIPAL ACTIVITIES: Geological and engineering services
for the oil industry
Parent Company: Halliburton Geodata, Aberdeen, Scotland, UK

HASAN MANSOURI

See MANSOURI, HASAN,

HEMPEL'S MARINE PAINTS (ABU DHABI)

PO Box 377, Abu Dhabi
Tel: 327749
Cable: Hempaturi

PRINCIPAL ACTIVITIES: Sale of paints for marine, industrial
and domestic use
Principal Agencies: Graco paint spray equipment; Elcometer
instruments
Branch Offices: Sharjah and throughout the Middle East

HILTON INTERNATIONAL ABU DHABI

PO Box 877, Abu Dhabi
Tel: 661900
Cable: Hiltels Abu Dhabi
Telex: 22212 Hiltels EM
Telefax: 669696

Senior Executives: Imad Elias (General Manager), Fahim Khan
(Sales Director)

PRINCIPAL ACTIVITIES: Hotel management and operation
Parent Company: Hilton International Hotels
Principal Bankers: National Bank of Abu Dhabi

Principal Shareholders: Abu Dhabi National Hotels Co
Date of Establishment: 1973
No of Employees: 260

HILTON INTERNATIONAL AL AIN

PO Box 1333, Al-Ain
Tel: 641410
Cable: Hiltels Al Ain
Telex: 33505 HILTON EM
Telefax: 654958

Chairman: John Jarvis
Directors: John Wilson
Senior Executives: Norbert Spichtinger, Imad W Elias (General
Manager Abu Dhabi)

PRINCIPAL ACTIVITIES: Hotel management and operation
Parent Company: Hilton International Hotels, Ladbroke Plc
Principal Bankers: Arab Bank for Foreign Trade & Investment

Date of Establishment: 1971
No of Employees: 175

HOLIDAY INN HOTEL

PO Box 3541, Abu Dhabi
Tel: 335335
Telex: 23030 Hol Inn EM
Telefax: 335766

Directors: Samir A Ghanime (General Manager)
Senior Executives: R Kirupananthan (Financial Controller), G
Wichremasinghe (Executive Housekeeper), Michel Yazbeck
(Sales Director)

PRINCIPAL ACTIVITIES: Hotel accommodation and restauration
Branch Offices: Hotels in the M.E.: Bahrain, Kuwait, Oman
(Muscat, Salalah), Saudi Arabia (Yanbu, Jeddah, Jubail)
Parent Company: Holiday Inn Worldwide, Woluwe Office, Park
1, rue Neerveld 101, POBox 2, 1200 Brussels, Belgium
Principal Bankers: Banque Indosuez, Abu Dhabi

Principal Shareholders: Emirates Property Investment Co
Date of Establishment: May 1980
No of Employees: 240

HYUNDAI ENGINEERING & CONSTRUCTION CO LTD

PO Box 6101, Abu Dhabi
Tel: 829612, 829615
Telex: 233811 Hyndai EM

PRINCIPAL ACTIVITIES: Building and general contracting
Branch Offices: Saudi Arabia, Oman, Bahrain
Parent Company: Head office in Seoul, Korea

I.A.L.

International Aeradio Ltd

PO Box 3164, Abu Dhabi
Tel: 341666
Telex: 22820 Intaer EM
Telefax: 346199

Chairman: Ali Al Bwardi
Directors: A Ball, C Sansom, J Baker
Senior Executives: R Thompson (Manager)

PRINCIPAL ACTIVITIES: Radio and electronic equipment
consultancy, maintenance and installation services
Principal Agencies: G E Mobile Radio, Lear Siegler, Feedback
Instruments, Casella, IAL Security, Astrophysics, Budde Int
(USA), Mitel, Racal Mildo, Tait Mobile Radio, Mannesman
Tally, British Telecom, Howells Radio, Dancall
Parent Company: IAL, PO Box 9197, Dubai, UAE
Principal Bankers: BBME, Abu Dhabi

Date of Establishment: 1982
No of Employees: 50

IGW SURVEYS LTD

PO Box 6737, Abu Dhabi
Tel: 829222 (4 lines)
Telex: 23933 IGW UAE EM
Telefax: 727584

Chairman: R F Aird
Directors: K J Lake, D Taylor
Senior Executives: C A Mott (General Manager), R Neilson
(Operations Manager), E Guild (Technical Manager)

PRINCIPAL ACTIVITIES: Geophysical surveys, positioning and
related survey services
Branch Offices: Kuwait, Bahrain, Muscat, Doha, Dubai, Bombay,
Singapore, UK

Parent Company: Oceanics Plc, UK
Principal Bankers: Algemene Bank Nederland

Date of Establishment: 1980
No of Employees: 30

INDUSTRIAL ENGINEERING & CONTRACTING CO

I.N.D.E.C.O.

PO Box 656, Khalifa St, Rashed El Yateem Bldg, Abu Dhabi
Tel: 344039
Cable: Indeco Abu Dhabi
Telex: 22297 Indeco EM

Chairman: Konrad Hinricks
Directors: Walter Hoffman
Senior Executives: Omar Sharif (Area Manager)

PRINCIPAL ACTIVITIES: Contracting, civil engineering
Principal Bankers: Grindlays Bank plc

Principal Shareholders: Ed Zublin AG, Germany
Date of Establishment: 1970
No of Employees: 200

INDUSTRIAL GAS PLANTS

PO Box 4273, Abu Dhabi
Tel: 554040, 554190/1
Cable: Oxygen
Telex: 23699 IGC EM
Telefax: 555124

Chairman: M H Al Mana
Directors: Mahmoud Fayez Abdel Khalik (Managing Director)

PRINCIPAL ACTIVITIES: Manufacture of industrial and medical
gases, supply of chemicals, welding equipment and gases
Principal Agencies: AGA Welding Equipment
Parent Company: National Industrial Gas Plant, PO Box 1391,
Doha, Qatar
Principal Bankers: Arab Bank Ltd, Abu Dhabi

Date of Establishment: 1969
No of Employees: 40

INMA THE GULF DEVELOPMENT & CONSTRUCTION CO

PO Box 798, Abu Dhabi
Tel: 338787
Cable: INMA, Abu Dhabi
Telex: 23334 INMA EM
Telefax: 330320

Chairman: Juma Al Majid
Directors: Samir Aweidah (Managing Director), Rashid Al Majid,
Mohamed Al Makhawi
Senior Executives: Amin Dayani (Manager), Mohyiddin Sukaik
(Commercial Manager)

PRINCIPAL ACTIVITIES: Building and civil engineering; import
and distribution of equipment and machinery for the
construction industry
Principal Agencies: Atlas Copco; Dynapac, Flygt Pumps, Hatz
Diesel Engines, Hymac, Lancer Boss, Alimak, Frederik
Parker, Thwaites, Stetter, Mustang, Liebherr, Phoenix,
Wirtgen
Branch Offices: Al Ain: PO Box 15533, Tel 656356, Telex 34027
INMA EM
Parent Company: Head office in Dubai, PO Bpx 4560, Tel
226231, Telex 45632 INMA EM, Fax 236481
Principal Bankers: United Bank Ltd, Abu Dhabi

Principal Shareholders: Chairman and Directors as described
Date of Establishment: 1972

INTERNATIONAL BECHTEL INC

PO Box 2661, Abu Dhabi
Tel: 345509, 216066
Telex: 22463 Wateka EM
Telefax: 216010

Senior Executives: J Love (Resident Manager)

PRINCIPAL ACTIVITIES: Engineering and construction
Parent Company: Bechtel International Ltd, PO Box 7329, 245
  Hammersmith Road, London W8, UK

INTERNATIONAL COMPUTERS LTD

PO Box 7237, Abu Dhabi
Tel: 335200
Telex: 23970 ICL ABU EM
Telefax: 338724

Senior Executives: T J Finney (General Manager)

PRINCIPAL ACTIVITIES: Marketing and support of computer
  systems
Principal Agencies: Abu Dhabi Computer Centre
Parent Company: ICL, London SW13, UK

INTERNATIONAL DEVELOPMENT CO

PO Box 2621, Abu Dhabi
Tel: 774170
Telex: 22417 IDC EM
Telefax: 727602

Senior Executives: R Urfali (General Manager)

PRINCIPAL ACTIVITIES: Business promotion, manufacturers'
  representatives, and projects development in oil and gas
  industries and in water and electricity supplies, civil and
  mechanical engineering
Principal Agencies: TRW Reda Pump, Acrow Group, Brooks, F
  H Maloney, Breda Fucine, Brewporter, Confab Industrial SA
  Flimon Industrie, Fluid Data, Howden Oil Engineering, Kaldair,
  London Bridge Engineering, Ludlam Sysco, OMB, OGTS,
  Petrolvalves, Owatrol Rhone Poulenc, Sau du Tarn,
  Skeltonhall, SBPI Spiro Gills, Stockdale Engineering, Thyssen
  Rhurpumpen Transchem Valves, Wagi, Waugh Controls
Branch Offices: Offices in Jordan, Lebanon, Syria, Saudi Arabia,
  Qatar, Oman, Abu Dhabi, London and the Liechtenstein
Parent Company: Engineering & Development Group, London
  SW1, UK
Subsidiary Companies: Arab International Development
  Company (Water Well Drilling)
Principal Bankers: Arab Bank Ltd

Date of Establishment: 1978

INTERNATIONAL PAINT (GULF) LTD

PO Box 245, Abu Dhabi
Tel: 775890
Telex: 22282 Kanoo EM
Telefax: 782548

Senior Executives: David Woodward (Area Manager)

PRINCIPAL ACTIVITIES: Manufacture of paints
Parent Company: International Paint Plc, 18 Hanover Square,
  London W1, UK

INTERNATIONAL SUPPLY EST

PO Box 2360, Abu Dhabi
Tel: 331250
Cable: ISCOL
Telex: 22355 ISCOL EM

Chairman: Mohamed Amin Zainal Khoory
Directors: Leslie P Nassey (Managing Director)
Senior Executives: Peter L Nassey (Sales Manager)

PRINCIPAL ACTIVITIES: Trading and import of industrial
  chemicals, oil field equipment, engineering products and
  electronic testing equipment

Principal Agencies: Texaco, Dresser, TPS Technitube
Principal Bankers: Abu Dhabi Commercial Bank

Principal Shareholders: 100% Local National Ownership
Date of Establishment: 1974

INTERNATIONAL TURNKEY SYSTEMS

PO Box 3333, Abu Dhabi
Tel: 726111
Telex: 22918
Telefax: 772160

PRINCIPAL ACTIVITIES: Engaged in marketing, support and
  maintenance of turnkey computer solutions (hardware and
  software), computer consultancy services, etc
Branch Offices: Bahrain, Dubai, Saudi Arabia
Parent Company: Head office in Kuwait
Principal Bankers: Dubai Islamic Bank, Dubai

INVESTMENT BANK FOR TRADE AND FINANCE

INVESTBANK

PO Box 2875, Abu Dhabi
Tel: 02 324594, 324596
Cable: Investbank Abu Dhabi
Telex: 22665 EM
Telefax: 02 324592

Chairman: HH Sheikh Saqr Bin Mohammad Al Qassimi
Senior Executives: Afif N Shehadeh (Asst General Manager,
  Incharge of Abu Dhabi Branch)

PRINCIPAL ACTIVITIES: Commercial banking
Branch Offices: Al Ain: PO Box 1933, Tel 03-644446, Fax 03-
  645335, Telex 33587 EM
Parent Company: Head office in Sharjah

JANANA TRADING COMPANY

PO Box 2502, Abu Dhabi
Tel: 324999
Cable: JANANA
Telex: 22409 JANANA EM

Chairman: Mattar Abdulla Al Muhairy
Directors: Hamad Bin Tahnoon Al Nahyan, Mubarak Abdulla Al
  Muhairy, Hamad Mubarak Al Muhairy
Senior Executives: Saad Salem Tohme (Managing Director),
  Gleason Pinto (Finance Manager), Yousef Sabha (Sales
  Manager), Andreas Papaphilotheou (Commercial Manager)

PRINCIPAL ACTIVITIES: Companies representation and
  sponsorship; lubrication oils; drilling fluids; asphalt
Principal Agencies: British Petroleum BP
Branch Offices: Al Ain, Tel 825100
Parent Company: Al Muhairy Group
Subsidiary Companies: Al Muhairy General Contracting Co; Al
  Muhairy Trading Co; Abu Dhabi Maintenance & General
  Services Co (ADMASCO); Abu Dhabi Bitumen Co Ltd; Janana
  Technical Co Ltd
Principal Bankers: Bank of Credit & Commerce
Financial Information:

	Dh'000
Paid-up capital	15,000

Principal Shareholders: Directors as described above
Date of Establishment: 1972

JANATA BANK

PO Box 2630, Abu Dhabi
Tel: 344542/3, 331400
Cable: Janatabank
Telex: 22402 EM

Chairman: Dr Abdullah Farouk
Directors: A A Qureishi

PRINCIPAL ACTIVITIES: Commercial banking

Branch Offices: Abu Dhabi, Dubai, Sharjah, Al-Ain
Parent Company: Head office in Dhaka, Bangladesh

No of Employees: 100 in UAE

JASHANMAL NATIONAL CO (UAE)

PO Box 316, Abu Dhabi
Tel: 335569
Cable: Jashanmal Abu Dhabi
Telex: 22376 Jashan EM
Telefax: 338322

Chairman: Sheikh Suroor Bin Sultan Al Dhahiry
Directors: Abdulla Mohamed Al Mazroui, Abdul Rahim E
  Galadari, Gangu Batra, Tony Jashanmal
Senior Executives: Mohan Jashanmal (General Manager)

PRINCIPAL ACTIVITIES: Department store (retail and
  wholesale) supply of all kind of consumer commodities
Principal Agencies: Hoover Ltd, UK; Alladin Industries, USA; A T
  Cross, USA; Yashica Co Ltd, Japan; Clark Overseas Shoe
  Co, UK; Charles Lett, UK; Jacobs Suchard Export,
  Switzerland; T I Russell Hobbs, UK; Johnson International
  News, UK; Levnat Distributors, France; Parfums Christian
  Dior, Eleizabeth Arden; Lagerfield; Francesco Smalto;
  Davidoff International; Parfums Gucci; Jean Louis Scherrer;
  Giorgio Armani; Christine Darvin, etc
Branch Offices: Jashanmal National Co, Al Ain, Abu Dhabi; Das
  Island, Abu Dhabi; and Dubai
Associated Companies: Jashanmal and Partners Ltd, PO Box
  5138, Safat, Kuwait; Jashanmal and Sons, PO Box 16,
  Manama, Bahrain
Principal Bankers: National Bank of Abu Dhabi

Date of Establishment: 1982
No of Employees: 100

JIBARAH BIN HASSAN & THANI BIN MOHD

PO Box 99, Abu Dhabi
Tel: 342187, 343820
Cable: Jibarah
Telex: 23899 Jibara EM

Chairman: Jibarah Bin Hassan (Partner)
Directors: Thani Bin Mohd (Partner)

PRINCIPAL ACTIVITIES: Importers and dealers of petrol, diesel
  and electrical pumping sets, agricultural machinery and
  equipment, electrical generators and garage equipment
Principal Agencies: Yuasa Batteries (Japan), Tokai Pumps
  (Japan)
Branch Offices: Musafah (Industrial area) and Al Ain
Subsidiary Companies: Jibarah Contracting Co
Principal Bankers: Standard Chartered Bank; Abu Dhabi; United
  Bank; Abu Dhabi

Date of Establishment: 1964

JOANNOU & PARASKEVAIDES (OVERSEAS) LTD

PO Box 2536, Abu Dhabi
Tel: 463800
Cable: Jaynpee
Telex: 22462 EM

PRINCIPAL ACTIVITIES: Civil engineering contractors, (roads
  and buildings and airports)
Branch Offices: Cyprus; United Arab Emirates; Oman; Saudi
  Arabia; Iraq; Libya; Syria; Qatar; UK; Nigeria; Greece; Bahrain

JOINT ARAB INVESTMENT CORPORATION

PO Box 917, Abu Dhabi
Tel: 341883
Telex: 24167

PRINCIPAL ACTIVITIES: Merchant banking and investment
Parent Company: Head office in Cairo, Egypt

Date of Establishment: 1983

KANOO GROUP, THE

PO Box 245, Abu Dhabi
Tel: 774444824444
Cable: Kanoo Abu Dhabi
Telex: 22282 Kanoo EM
Telefax: 722505

Chairman: Hamed Ali Kanoo (Chairman UAE & Oman)
Directors: Yusuf Ahmed Kanoo (Managing Director UAE &
  Oman)
Senior Executives: A E H Johnson (Manager)

PRINCIPAL ACTIVITIES: Shipping agents, marine craft
  operators, clearing and forwarding, insurance agents,
  household and industrial packing and removals,
  manufacturers' agents and distributors of construction
  equipment and oilfield supplies, heavy equipment and
  machinery, tobacco, also business consultants
Principal Agencies: BASF; Bedford; Blakeborough; BTR TEK;
  CPT; Clark Bobcat; Grove; Hyster; Lincoln; Massey Ferguson;
  Renold; International Paints, Survival System; Cortest
  Instrument; Powerbank Marlow; Panametrics; Hamworthy;
  Perkins; Agema; Norton; Vicon; Crawford Fittings; Fawlett; A
  O Smith; L D Duiker; Betist Broughten; Cabot Safety;
  Chapman & Smith; Checkmate; Uvex
Branch Offices: Regional Office: PO Box 290, Dubai, PO Box
  153, Sharjah, UAE; PO Box 151, Ras Al Khaimah; PO box
  245, Jebel Dhanna, Abu Dhabi, UAE; PO Box 1779, Al Ain,
  UAE; PO box 1310, Muscat, Sultanate of Oman
Principal Bankers: British Bank of the Middle East, Abu Dhabi;
  Citibank, Abu Dhabi

Principal Shareholders: Members of the Kanoo family
Date of Establishment: 1890
No of Employees: 102

KENNEDY & DONKIN GROUP LTD

PO Box 3374, Abu Dhabi
Tel: 333052
Telex: 24183 MSE EM
Telefax: 720345

Senior Executives: B T Daniels (Marketing Consultant)

PRINCIPAL ACTIVITIES: Consulting engineers
Parent Company: Head office in Godalming, Surrey, UK

KEO INTERNATIONAL CONSULTANTS

PO Box 27594, Abu Dhabi
Tel: 788977
Telefax: 786796

Directors: Dr Abdul Aziz Sultan (Managing Director)

PRINCIPAL ACTIVITIES: Planning and design of residential,
  educational, medical, municipal and commercial
  developments, sanitary and water projects, roads design,
  environmental engineering, construction management,
  construction supervision, computer services and operations
  and maintenance consultancy
Parent Company: Head office in Kuwait
Principal Bankers: Gulf Bank

KHANSAHEB SYKES (ABU DHABI)

PO Box 4056, Abu Dhabi
Tel: 554131, 554126
Telex: 23972 Sykes EM
Telefax: 559875

Senior Executives: D Pudney (General Manager)

PRINCIPAL ACTIVITIES: Sale and hire of pumps, dewatering
  systems, and drill rigs, sale of marine propulsion units,
  sewage pumps, and complete sewage treatment works
Parent Company: Sykes Pumps Ltd, London SE7, UK

KHARAFI, MOHAMED ABDULMOHSIN, INDUSTRIES & ESTABLISHMENTS

UAE Area Main Office, PO Box 650, Abu Dhabi
Tel: 322237 (9 lines)
Cable: Alkharafi Abu Dhabi
Telex: 22320 Khrafi EM
Telefax: 322212

Chairman: Mohamed Abdulmohsin Al Kharafi
Directors: Mohsen Kamel (Managing Director)

PRINCIPAL ACTIVITIES: Civil engineering contractors, import-export, production of steel, aluminium, timber, terrazo tiles & steps, furniture, doors, windows, portable houses/offices, steel structures, drums, tanks, barrels, electrical, mechanical, plumbing and HVAC works, insulating materials and panels for roofing and cladding, piling, foundation, shoring, marine, supply of concrete readymix and aggregates, steel wire mesh, water wells drilling, agencies services, etc
Branch Offices: Saudi Arabia; Yemen; Egypt; Botswana
Parent Company: Head office in Kuwait
Principal Bankers: Grindlays Bank; Arab Bank plc; Arab African International Bank

KHATIB & ALAMI

Consolidated Engineering Co

PO Box 2732, Abu Dhabi
Tel: (9712) 662885
Cable: Consing
Telex: 23790 CEC EM
Telefax: (9712) 660289

President: Prof M Khatib
Directors: Dr Z Alami (Vice President), S Abdulhadi
Senior Executives: Saba Saba (Financial Manager), Adnan Zakoui (Personnel Manager), Mohamad Sadiyyah (Head of Design Dept), U Hassouneh (Resident Manager Abu Dhabi)

PRINCIPAL ACTIVITIES: Consulting engineers and architects
Branch Offices: Dubai, Sharjah, Al Ain and Fujairah (UAE); Riyadh, Jeddah and Al Khobar (Saudi Arabia); Manama (Bahrain); Muscat (Oman); Amman (Jordan)
Parent Company: Head office in Beirut, Lebanon
Subsidiary Companies: Alami & Abdulhadi, Jordan
Principal Bankers: Arab Bank Ltd

Principal Shareholders: Prof M Khatib, Dr Z Alami
Date of Establishment: 1963
No of Employees: Total: 540; Abu Dhabi: 28

KIER INTERNATIONAL LTD

PO Box 23622, Dubai
Tel: 4-453260, 774001
Telefax: 4-450780, 774108

Chairman: M B Jardine
Directors: D E Crouch (Managing Director)
Senior Executives: D S Hook (Area Manager)

PRINCIPAL ACTIVITIES: Building and civil engineering contractors
Branch Offices: Saudi Arabia; Riyadh, PO Box 7648, Tel 4781459, Telex 402389; Jordan, PO Box 6147, Amman, Tel 625261, Telex 21227
Parent Company: Kier International Ltd, Sandy, Bedfordshire, UK
Principal Bankers: Barclays Bank; Citibank; Grindlays Bank

KPMG PEAT MARWICK

PO Box 7613, 7th Floor, Bin Hamoudah Tower, Sh Khalifa St, Abu Dhabi
Tel: 343318, 323476
Telex: 23613 PMM AD EM
Telefax: 327612

Senior Executives: Michael G W Armstrong (Partner)

PRINCIPAL ACTIVITIES: Audit, accounting, corporate finance services, corporate recovery and management consultancy (including information technology, financial management and human resources)
Parent Company: Member firm of Klynveld Peat Marwick Goerdeler (KPMG)

Date of Establishment: 1973
No of Employees: 25

LAMNALCO LTD

PO Box 61, Abu Dhabi
Tel: 777772
Telex: 22631 LAMAH EM
Telefax: 728158

Directors: T A Alireza, R Van Gelder, A H Godri, J N H Gibson
Senior Executives: A C Wilkinson (Chief Executive Officer), M H Smyth (Finance & Administration Manager), Capt J R Murray (Shipping & Agency Manager), W S Trought (Marine & Engineering Manager), A Jackson (Sales & Marketing Manager)

PRINCIPAL ACTIVITIES: Marine and offshore services, oil terminal contractors; generators hire; maritime civil engineers; shipping and agency
Principal Agencies: Agents for Vikoma Int in the Middle East; Dunlop Oil & Marine; Bridon Fibres
Branch Offices: Kuwait; Abu Dhabi; Saudi Arabia (Alkhobar); Sharjah; Khorfakkan; Fujairah
Parent Company: Royal Bos Kalis Westminster; Alireza Group Kuwait
Subsidiary Companies: Abu Dhabi Petroleum Ports Operating Co (Joint venture between Abu Dhabi National Oil Co and Lamnalco); Lamnalco (Sharjah) Ltd; Lamnalco (Fujairah) Ltd; Lamnalco Saudi Arabia Ltd
Principal Bankers: The British Bank of the Middle East

Principal Shareholders: Alireza Group & RBKW Group
Date of Establishment: 1963
No of Employees: 52

LIQUEFIED GAS SHIPPING CO (LGSC)

PO Box 3500, Abu Dhabi
Tel: 333888
Telex: 22698

PRINCIPAL ACTIVITIES: Shipping liquefied gas products
Financial Information:

Authorised capital	US$1,000,000

Principal Shareholders: Adnoc (51%)

LIWA TRADING ENTERPRISES

PO Box 46611, Abu Dhabi
Tel: 211242, 662212
Telex: 23499 Abnaas EM
Telefax: 338773

Senior Executives: G Walters (Retail Store Manager)

PRINCIPAL ACTIVITIES: Department stores
Branch Offices: Main Store: Al Otaiba Tower, Hamdan Street, Abu Dhabi; Branch Store: Sh Zayed 11 Street, Khalidiya, Abu Dhabi
Associated Companies: BHS Plc, London NW1, UK

LOTUS CO

PO Box 41, Abu Dhabi
Tel: 324289
Cable: Lotus

Chairman: Adel Kamel Siddiq
Directors: M Mansour Kambal (Sales Manager), S Mohd Hassan

PRINCIPAL ACTIVITIES: Import and distribution of gas and electrical household appliances

Branch Offices: Kuwait; Egypt
Principal Bankers: Bank of Credit and Commerce International;
Banque du Caire

MAC CONTRACTING & ENGINEERING

PO Box 586, Abu Dhabi
Tel: 344606
Cable: Mac Co
Telex: 22292 Manara EM

Chairman: Salim Chamoun
Directors: Munir Chamoun, Mansour Chamoun

PRINCIPAL ACTIVITIES: Building and civil engineering
contractors
Subsidiary Companies: MAC Al-Ain (PO Box 1297, Tel 47222)
Principal Bankers: National Bank of Abu Dhabi; Bank of Oman

MAINTENANCE SERVICES GULF LTD (MSG)

PO Box 7604, Abu Dhabi
Tel: 739600, 824358
Telex: 23403 EM

PRINCIPAL ACTIVITIES: Installation, erection, maintenance of
mechanical rotating machines, instrumentation, diesel
engines, gas turbines, pumps
Parent Company: Rolls Royce Ltd, Industrial Marine Division,
Coventry, UK

MANSOOR COMMERCIAL GROUP OF COMPANIES

PO Box 2840, Abu Dhabi
Tel: 345351/3
Telex: 22492 EM

PRINCIPAL ACTIVITIES: General trading and contracting,
supply of building materials and construction equipment, civil
engineering works, sales and commission agency
Subsidiary Companies: Gulf Contractors Ltd, PO Box 2840, Abu
Dhabi

MANSOORI INDUSTRIAL SUPPLY

PO Box 287, Abu Dhabi
Tel: 779795/6
Cable: Almansoori
Telex: 22237 Motmec EM
Telefax: 782613

Chairman: Hilal Mubarak Al Mansoori
Directors: Nabil Al Alawi
Senior Executives: Khalid A Baobeid (General Manager)

PRINCIPAL ACTIVITIES: General trading and mechanical
engineering; import and distribution of oilfield equipment and
industrial equipment and machinery, spare parts and water
distilling plant
Principal Agencies: Abex Denison, France; BKL, UK; Newman
Hattersley, UK; Versa, USA; Prosper, UK; RGB, UK; Krupp,
WGermany; Parker, USA; Sykes Pickavant, UK; Laycock, UK;
Gachot, France; Molex, UK; Plidco, USA; Gloor, Switzerland;
Epco, UK; etc
Parent Company: Al Mansoori Specialised Engineering, Abu
Dhabi
Principal Bankers: National Bank of Abu Dhabi; Bank of Credit
& Commerce (Emirates)

Date of Establishment: 1965

MANSOURI, HASAN,

PO Box 2426, Abu Dhabi
Tel: 344151, 322344
Telex: 32584 Cranes EM

PRINCIPAL ACTIVITIES: Supply of building materials and
equipment, crane and plant hire
Parent Company: Head Office in Bahrain, PO Box 5185,
Manama, Tel 252214

MAPCO

PO Box 2035, Abu Dhabi
Tel: 770430
Cable: Mapad
Telex: 22353 Mapad EM
Telefax: (9712) 783640, 724452

Chairman: Rashid Al-Mazroui
Directors: Mohd S Al Hudhud (Managing Partner)
Senior Executives: Mansoor Ali (Chief Mechanical Engineer),
Maurice Al Abd (Chief Electrical Engineer)

PRINCIPAL ACTIVITIES: Electro-mechanical contracting,
industrial kitchen and laundry equipment, airconditioning,
plumbing and sanitary works
Branch Offices: Al Ain branch: PO Box 1682
Principal Bankers: National Bank of Abu Dhabi; Bank of Credit
& Commerce Intl; Bank of Credit & Commerce (Emirates)
Financial Information:

	1990
	US$'000
Sales turnover	11,800
Paid-up capital	2,000

Principal Shareholders: Chairman and director as described
Date of Establishment: 1974
No of Employees: 550

MARKETING & CONSTRUCTION CO (MAC)

PO Box 750, Abu Dhabi
Tel: 363834, 366443, 363243
Cable: Macad
Telex: 22895 Macad EM

Chairman: Fouad Malouf
Directors: Farouk W Agha (President), Wajih M Sleiman (Vice
President)
Senior Executives: D G Salameh (Engineering & Development
Manager), Marwan W Agha (Finance & Administration
Manager)

PRINCIPAL ACTIVITIES: Mechanical engineering, erectors of
industrial plants, power plants, water desalination plants,
cement plants, gas processing and petrochemical plants and
pipeline contractors
Principal Agencies: Babcock & Wilcox, USA; Control
Components Intl USA; Bailey Meter Co, USA
Branch Offices: Saudi Arabia: PO Box 855, Al-Khobar, Tel
8572233, 8574069, Telex 671118 Mac Sj; and PO Box 7819,
Riyadh, Tel 4780516, 4776772, Telex 200524 Maccon Sj
Parent Company: MAC, PO Box 4841, Beirut, Lebanon
Subsidiary Companies: Building Chemical Industries Co (BCIC),
Al Khobar, Saudi Arabia; Technical Trading Co (TTC), Al
Khobar, Saudi Arabia
Principal Bankers: National Bank of Abu Dhabi; First National
Bank of Chicago; The National Westminster Bank, London; Al
Bank Al Saudi Al Fransi, Saudi Arabia
Financial Information:

	Dh'000
Authorised capital	10,000
Paid-up capital	10,000

Principal Shareholders: F W Agha, F M Malouf
Date of Establishment: 1973 in Abu Dhabi
No of Employees: 1,629

MASAOOD JOHN BROWN LTD

PO Box 322, Abu Dhabi
Tel: 323570
Telex: 23681
Telefax: 331102

Chairman: Rahma Masaood
Directors: Chris J Packard (Technical Director), Norman
Simpson (Finance Director), Abdulla Masaood (Sales Director)
Senior Executives: Steve Winton (General Manager)

PRINCIPAL ACTIVITIES: Service centre for gas turbines and associated power plants; supply of spare pats; repair workshop, service and overhauls, emergency call-outs
Branch Offices: Dubai: PO Box 11931, Tel 452974, Telex 47436
Parent Company: John Brown Engineering Ltd, Scotland, UK
Principal Bankers: Standard Chartered Bank
Financial Information:

	1990 Dh'000
Sales turnover	28,000
Profits	2,500

Principal Shareholders: John Brown Engineering Ltd, Mohamed Bin Masaood & Sons
Date of Establishment: 1979

MAZROUI CONSTRUCTION TECHNOLOGY (MAZCOT)

PO Box 2035, Abu Dhabi
Tel: 825967/8
Cable: MAZCOT
Telex: 23844 Mazcot EM

Chairman: Rashid Al Mazroui
Directors: Sabah Rumani (Managing Partner), Mohammed Hudhud (Partner)
Senior Executives: N Abdullah (Senior Contracts Manager), A N Khan (Senior Accountant)

PRINCIPAL ACTIVITIES: General contracting; foundations; steel framed industrial buildings
Associated Companies: Mazroui and Partners
Principal Bankers: Arab Bank for Investment and Foreign Trade; Bank of Credit & Commerce (Emirates)

Principal Shareholders: Chairman and Partners
Date of Establishment: January 1976
No of Employees: 200

MAZROUI SUPPLIES, CONTRACTS & MAINTENANCE EST

PO Box 4265, Abu Dhabi
Tel: 723185
Cable: Sacad
Telex: 22397 EM
Telefax: 777075

Chairman: Ibrahim Mohd Abdulla Al-Mazroui
Senior Executives: A Rahman (Operations Manager)

PRINCIPAL ACTIVITIES: Design, installation and commissioning of mechanical and electrical services for hotels, hospitals, commercial buildings and airports and planned general building services maintenance
Principal Agencies: CEN Lifts, Italy
Subsidiary Companies: Union General Transport & Contracting Co
Principal Bankers: Barclays Bank, Abu Dhabi, National Bank of Bahrain, Abu Dhabi; Bank of Oman Ltd
Financial Information:

	1990 Dh'000
Sales turnover	5,760
Profits	1,098
Authorised capital	7,000
Paid-up capital	2,000
Total assets	4,114

Principal Shareholders: Ibrahim M A Al-Mazroui
Date of Establishment: 1982
No of Employees: 180

MAZROUI-SONAT DRILLING

PO Box 890, Abu Dhabi
Tel: 341384
Cable: OFDRIL Abu Dhabi
Telex: 22309 Ofdril EM
Telefax: 333475

PRINCIPAL ACTIVITIES: Offshore drilling contractors
Parent Company: M & Al-Mazroui Trading Est; Sonat Offshore Drilling Inc, Houston

MECHANICAL & CIVIL ENGINEERING CONTRACTORS LTD
M.A.C.E.

PO Box 2307, Abu Dhabi
Tel: 330144, 325889
Cable: Contractomace
Telex: 22816 MACE EM

Chairman: William A T Haddad (Managing Director)
Directors: Bishara J Murr
Senior Executives: Maurice I Abboud (Finance and Administration Manager), Muwaffaq E Matti (Operations Manager)

PRINCIPAL ACTIVITIES: Civil and mechanical contracting; construction and buildings and pipelines
Branch Offices: Mace-Libya; PO Box 2993, Benghazi, and PO box 12115, Tripoli, Libya; Al Mutlaq Mace SA: PO Box 429, Dhahram Airport, Saudi Arabia; Mace-Beirut: PO Box 117741, Beirut, Lebanon
Principal Bankers: British Bank of the Middle East; National Bank of Abu Dhabi; Bank of Credit and Commerce International; Investbank

Principal Shareholders: Directors as described
No of Employees: 2,000

MERIDIEN HOTEL ABU DHABI

PO Box 46066, Abu Dhabi
Tel: 776666
Cable: Homer
Telex: 23794, 22233 Homer EM
Telefax: 727221

Chairman: Rodolphe Frantz (President Societe des Hotels Meridien Chain)
Directors: Michel Noblet (General Manager - Abu Dhabi), Nohad Selman (Director of Sales & Marketing)
Senior Executives: D Sanousi (Financial Controller), Hafeel Sadardeen (Purchasing Manager), Hussam Abbas (Personnel Manager), Fouad Nohra (Technical Manager), Nada Andari (Executive Secretary)

PRINCIPAL ACTIVITIES: Hotel business
Parent Company: Air France

Date of Establishment: 1979

M-I OVERSEAS

PO Box 4076, Abu Dhabi
Tel: 729940
Telex: 24155 IMCO EM
Telefax: 723606

President: Jim Bryan
Directors: Bill Bishop (Vice President), Jim Emerick (Vice President Joint Ventures)
Senior Executives: Satish K Mahajan (District Manager)

PRINCIPAL ACTIVITIES: Supply of oilwell drilling fluids, products and services
Branch Offices: PO Box 515, Manama, Bahrain
Parent Company: M-I Drilling Fluids Co, Houston, Texas, USA
Principal Bankers: Citibank NA, Abu Dhabi

Principal Shareholders: Dresser and Halliburton Ltd through the parent company M-I Drilling Fluids Co
Date of Establishment: 1973

MIDDLE EAST BANK LTD

PO Box 6077, Abu Dhabi
Tel: 328400
Cable: Mebasnk
Telex: 22883 Mebank EM

PRINCIPAL ACTIVITIES: Commercial banking
Parent Company: Head office in Dubai, Tel 220121, Telex 46074 Mebnk EM

MIDDLE EAST OIL CO LTD

PO Box 672, Abu Dhabi
Tel: 322883/7 322154
Cable: Chutosekiyo Abu Dhabi
Telex: 22246 EM

PRINCIPAL ACTIVITIES: Supply of petroleum and mining equipment and transportation; the company holds concessions covering 15,000 Sq Kms

Principal Shareholders: Mitsubishi Group

MIDDLE EAST TRADING & CONTRACTING CO (METCO)

PO Box 851, Abu Dhabi
Tel: 341322, 322662
Cable: MIDCAT
Telex: 22389 MIDCAT EM
Telefax: 02 336068

Chairman: Abdul Rahman Abdulla Al Habaishi
Directors: Talib Mustafa Khan (Director General)
Senior Executives: Hamish Emmerson (Asst General Manager), Ramuel Garcia (Operations Manager), Mohd Ashraf (Accounts Manager)

PRINCIPAL ACTIVITIES: General trading and contracting; inspection and service of all type of pipelines
Principal Agencies: DuPont, USA; Steinzeug, W Germany; US Pipe & Foundry, USA; PDM, USA; Belgo Cables, Belgium; Alsthom Atlantique, France; Sprecher Energie, Switzerland; Caird Rayner Bravac, UK; Rausch TV, W Germany; Madison Chemical Industries, Canada; H & G Engineering, UK; Gasunie, Netherlands; Pipeline Equipment Benelux, Netherlands; Rosen Engineering, Germany; Tubacex, Spain
Associated Companies: A R A Al-Habaishi, General Contractors, PO Box 851, Abu Dhabi; Al-Habaishi Cont, PO Box 3068, Dubai
Principal Bankers: Bank of Credit & Commerce (Emirates), Abu Dhabi

Principal Shareholders: Directors as described
Date of Establishment: 1969

MODERN DEVELOPMENT CONTRACTING CO

PO Box 3742, Abu Dhabi
Tel: 333042
Cable: DEVELOP
Telex: 22927 DEVELP EM

Directors: HE Abdulla H Al Mazroie, Colonel Humaid Ali Saif
Senior Executives: C D Vaidya (Managing Director)

PRINCIPAL ACTIVITIES: Construction, general contractors
Branch Offices: PO Box 15376, Al Ain
Associated Companies: Modern Development Trading Co, PO Box 2344, Abu Dhabi

Date of Establishment: August 1977
No of Employees: 480

MODERN PRINTING PRESS & STATIONERY

PO Box 950, Abu Dhabi
Tel: 826076, 826077, 826543/5
Cable: Modernpress
Telex: 23452 Modern EM

Owner: Hassan Mohd Bin Al-Shaikh
Senior Executives: Mohd Saeed Al-Qassimi (General Manager)

PRINCIPAL ACTIVITIES: Printing, publishing, suppliers of office stationery and furniture
Branch Offices: PO Box 1042, Dubai; Sharjah, UAE; Al-Ain, UAE
Associated Companies: Hassan Bin Al-Shaikh Paper Converting Industries, Dubai
Principal Bankers: Bank of Oman Ltd, Abu Dhabi, Dubai; BBME, Abu Dhabi, Dubai

Date of Establishment: 1968
No of Employees: 250

MOHAMED ABDULMOHSIN KHARAFI INDUSTRIES & ESTABLISHMENTS

See KHARAFI, MOHAMED ABDULMOHSIN, INDUSTRIES & ESTABLISHMENTS

MOHAMED ABDULRAHMAN AL BAHAR

See AL BAHAR, MOHAMED ABDULRAHMAN,

MOHAMMED BIN MASAOOD & SONS

See BIN MASAOOD, MOHAMMED, & SONS

MOTHERWELL BRIDGE EMIRATES

PO Box 3343, Abu Dhabi
Tel: 823750
Telex: 22857 Mother EM

Chairman: H J Al Nowais

PRINCIPAL ACTIVITIES: Storage tanks and pipework, engineering contractors to the oil gas and petrochemical industries
Parent Company: Emirates Holdings; Motherwell Bridge Constructors Ltd

Principal Shareholders: Emirates Holdings, Motherwell Bridge Constructors Ltd
Date of Establishment: UK: 1898 / UAE: 1976
No of Employees: UK: 2,000 / UAE: 80

MUTAWA INTERNATIONAL CONSTRUCTION

PO Box 46100, Abu Dhabi
Tel: 324200, 826300
Telex: 23626 Mutawa EM
Telefax: 325710

Chairman: Abdulla M Al Mutawa
Senior Executives: S E Guy (General Manager)

PRINCIPAL ACTIVITIES: Supply of building partitions, and office furniture
Principal Agencies: Ergonom Int; Modulo 3
Associated Companies: Mutawa Lloyds British; Mutawa Montin

MUTAWA TECHNICAL TRADING EST

PO Box 46100, Abu Dhabi
Tel: 324200
Cable: Mutawa
Telex: 23626 Mutawa Em
Telefax: 325710

Chairman: A Al Mutawa
Senior Executives: Saad Bunni (Business Development Manager)

PRINCIPAL ACTIVITIES: Oil & gas engineering and supply services
Principal Agencies: Ferranti Int'l Engineering; GTC Gas Turbine; Iscosa (Westinghouse)
Subsidiary Companies: Mutawa Marine Est

Financial Information:

	1990 US$'000
Sales turnover	10,000
Authorised capital	2,000
Total assets	1,500

Principal Shareholders: Proprietorship
Date of Establishment: 1979

NATIONAL ABU DHABI OFFSHORE CONTRACTORS
N.A.D.O.C.
PO Box 6488, Abu Dhabi
Tel: 342194
Telex: 22505

PRINCIPAL ACTIVITIES: Engineering and offshore contractors

NATIONAL BANK OF ABU DHABI
Sheikh Khalifa Street, PO Box 4, Abu Dhabi
Tel: 335262
Cable: Almasraf
Telex: 22266/7 Masrip EM
Telefax: 336078

Chairman: HE Mohammed Habroush Al Suwaidi
Directors: Khalaf Bin Ahmed Al Otaiba (Deputy Chairman), Jouan Salem Al Dhaheri, Sheikh Saeed Bin Mohammed Bin Khalifa Al Nahayan, Hamil Bin Khadem Al Gaith, Rahma Al Masaood, Faraj Bin Ali Bin Hamoodah, Shabib Bin Mohammed Al Dhahiri, Mohammed Joaan Al Badi, Mohammed Bin Brook, Sultan Bin Rashid Al Dhahiri, Humaid Darwish Bin Karam, Obaid Saif Al Nasseri
Senior Executives: John S W Coombs (Chief Executive), Barry K Noden (General Manager Treasury), Mohammed Sharief Al Mutawa'a (Asst General Manager Services), Marshall W Lewis (Asst General Manager Domestic Banking), Paul Meek (Chief Advances Manager)

PRINCIPAL ACTIVITIES: Commercial banking
Branch Offices: 34 Branches throughout the United Arab Emirates (Abu Dhabi (24), Ajman, Dubai (2), Fujairah (2), Ras Al Khaimah (2), Sharjah (3); 14 Overseas Branches, offices and rep office: Bahrain (2); Cairo (2), Alexandria, Port Said (Egypt); Muttrah (Oman); Khartoum (Sudan); Washington DC (USA)(1 wholly owned subsidiary); London (3) (UK); Paris (France); Sydney Rep Office (Australia)
Subsidiary Companies: Abu Dhabi International Bank NV, Washington DC (Wholly owned subsidiary); National Bank of Abu Dhabi - Nominee Limited, London (wholly owned subsidiary)
Financial Information:

	1988 Dh'million	1989 Dh'million
Net profit	86	107
Loans & advances	7,013	6,820
Deposits & other Accts	16,610	12,988
Authorised capital	1,000	1,000
Paid-up capital	942	942
Reserves	789	801
Total assets	24,605	20,977

Principal Shareholders: Abu Dhabi Investment Authority and UAE nationals
Date of Establishment: 1968
No of Employees: 1,069

NATIONAL BANK OF BAHRAIN
PO Box 6080, Abu Dhabi
Tel: 335288, 335299
Telex: 24344 Natbah EM

PRINCIPAL ACTIVITIES: Commercial banking
Parent Company: Head office in Manama, Bahrain

NATIONAL BANK OF DUBAI LTD
PO Box 386, Abu Dhabi
Tel: 330611 (5 lines)
Cable: National Abu Dhabi

PRINCIPAL ACTIVITIES: Commercial banking
Parent Company: Head office in Dubai

NATIONAL BANK OF FUJAIRAH
PO Box 786, Abu Dhabi
Tel: 333300
Telex: 22666
Telefax: 211336

Chairman: Sheikh Saleh Bin Mohammed Al Sharqi
Directors: Easa Saleh Al Gurg, Khalaf Saeed Al Ghaith, Sheikh Saud Bin Khalid Al Qasimi, Khalifa Juma Al Naboodah, Sulaiman Mousa Al Jassim, Sayed Abdullah Al Mousawi, Eid Obeid Khalfan, Mohamed Ahmed Abdul Rahman, Dr Salem Abdo Khalil
Senior Executives: Asad A Ahmed (Senior Manager Abu Dhabi)

PRINCIPAL ACTIVITIES: Commercial banking
Branch Offices: Dubai, Fujairah, Dibba
Parent Company: Head office in Fujairah
Financial Information:

	1988 Dh'000	1989 Dh'000
Profits	9,234	13,965
Authorised capital	400,000	400,000
Paid-up capital	150,000	150,000
Total assets	387,986	426,202

NATIONAL BANK OF OMAN LTD SAO
PO Box 3822, Abu Dhabi
Tel: 325354, 325358
Telex: 22866 NBO EM

PRINCIPAL ACTIVITIES: Commercial banking
Parent Company: Head office in the Sultanate of Oman

NATIONAL BANK OF RAS AL KHAIMAH
PO Box 2289, Abu Dhabi
Tel: 722211/6
Telex: 24343 Nbrak Em

PRINCIPAL ACTIVITIES: Commercial banking
Branch Offices: Dubai
Parent Company: Head office in Ras Al Khaimah

NATIONAL BANK OF SHARJAH
PO Box 7650, Abu Dhabi
Tel: 337255, 337445
Cable: Banksha
Telex: 23907 BnkSha Em
Telefax: 320828

Chairman: HE Shaikh Ahmed Bin Sultan Al Qasimi

PRINCIPAL ACTIVITIES: Commercial banking
Parent Company: Head office in Sharjah

NATIONAL BANK OF UMM AL QAIWAIN
PO Box 3915, Abu Dhabi
Tel: 339100
Telex: 23114 Nbuaq EM

PRINCIPAL ACTIVITIES: Commercial banking
Parent Company: Head office in Umm Al Qaiwain

NATIONAL CATERING & SERVICES
PO Box 464, Abu Dhabi
Tel: 341088
Cable: Unitrace
Telex: 22228 Alhurr EM

Chairman: Ahmed Bin Jumma Al Suweidi
Directors: John Manna

PRINCIPAL ACTIVITIES: Catering services and contractors to the Abu Dhabi Government Hospital, Al Ain Government Hospital, Adnoc Refinery and for other major companies
Associated Companies: United Trading & Services Co
Principal Bankers: British Bank of the Middle East; United Bank Ltd

Principal Shareholders: Mohamed Alhurr, Ahmed Bin Jumma Al Suweidi

NATIONAL CHLORIDE INDUSTRIES (NCI)
PO Box 6557, Abu Dhabi
Tel: 52911
Telex: 24152

Senior Executives: Ghalan Al Azzawy (General Manager)

PRINCIPAL ACTIVITIES: Manufacture of chlorine, hydrochloric acid, caustic soda, industrial and table salt

Principal Shareholders: Adnoc (100%)

NATIONAL COMPUTER SERVICES LTD
PO Box 6386, Abu Dhabi
Tel: 725652/3
Telex: 24276 NCSAUH EM

Directors: A Quadri, J H Pugsley (General Manager)

PRINCIPAL ACTIVITIES: Installation and maintenance of computer systems
Principal Agencies: Digital Equipment Corp, Infotron
Branch Offices: Dubai; Bahrain; Kuwait
Principal Bankers: Abu Dhabi Commercial Bank

Date of Establishment: 1978

NATIONAL DRILLING CO (NDC)
PO Box 4017, Abu Dhabi
Tel: 316600, 770330
Cable: NATDRIL Abu Dhabi
Telex: 22553 Nadril EM
Telefax: 317045

Chairman: HE Mohamed Habroush
Directors: Rashid Saif Al Swedi, Suhail Faris Al-Mazroui (ADNOC)
Senior Executives: Ahmed Juma Al Dharif (General Manager), Mohd Omar Abdulla (Finance Manager), Najeeb Hassan Al Zaabi (Operations Manager), Robert Jon Taylor (Materials & Purchasing Manager), Musbah Timraz (Maintenance Manager)

PRINCIPAL ACTIVITIES: Drilling contractors, onshore and offshore drilling work (oil & gas), in addition to water well drilling
Parent Company: ADNOC
Principal Bankers: National Bank of Abu Dhabi
Financial Information:

	1990 Dh'000
Paid-up capital	105,000

Principal Shareholders: ADNOC (100%)
Date of Establishment: 1972
No of Employees: 1,144

NATIONAL INDUSTRIAL COMPANY
PO Box 706, Abu Dhabi
Tel: 721000
Cable: Wibeco
Telex: 22421 Wibeco EM
Telefax: 770011

Directors: Issa Rishmawi (Managing Director)

PRINCIPAL ACTIVITIES: Trading and import of agricultural equipment and services
Principal Agencies: Ferry Morse Seed Co, USA seeds; Holder, Germany spraying equipment; Ciba Geigy, Switzerland

chemicals, Fendt- Germany Tractors, American Cyanamid-Insecticides etc
Branch Offices: National Industrial Co, Al Ain, PO Box 1071, UAE; National Agricultural Equipment & Chemicals Co, PO Box 5127, Dubai, UAE
Subsidiary/Associated Companies: National Industrial Co, PO Box 235, Doha, Qatar
Principal Bankers: Banque Paribas, Abu Dhabi; United Arab Bank, Abu Dhabi

Principal Shareholders: Mohamad Al Mana, Issa Rishmawi, Zetoun Bin Mohamad Al Mansouri
Date of Establishment: 1968
No of Employees: 35

NATIONAL MARINE DREDGING CO
PO Box 3649, Abu Dhabi
Tel: 562800
Telex: 22750 NMDC EM
Telefax: 971-2-562027

Chairman: Humeid Rashid Al Hamly
Directors: Ghanim Mohamed Al Sowaidi, Ahmed Said Al Mureikhi, Abdulla Mohamed Al Mulla, Masha Allah Mohd Abas Khoory, Saif Said Mohd Al Dhahiri, Nasser Ben Mudker Al Shafi Al Hajri, Hamad Mohd Brook, Mohd Abdulla Saleh Al Sowaidi
Senior Executives: Donald Rae (General Manager), Shahir Mikhail (Deputy General Manager Plant & Operation), Ahmed Nagi Alawi (Asst General Manager Finance & Administration)

PRINCIPAL ACTIVITIES: Dredging and reclamation
Financial Information:

	1990 Dh'000
Sales turnover	350,000
Authorised capital	100,000
Paid-up capital	100,000

Principal Shareholders: Abu Dhabi Government (40%); UAE Nationals (60%)
Date of Establishment: 1976
No of Employees: 1,000

NATIONAL MARINE SERVICES (NMS)
PO Box 7202, Abu Dhabi
Tel: 339800
Cable: MARINCO
Telex: 22965 NMS EM

Chairman: S F Al Mazrui
Directors: K W Waldorf, Rashid Al Suwaidy, Yusuf Al Nowais, Gary Pope
Senior Executives: Capt H A Shareef (General Manager), H Klemp (Deputy General Manager), Y Mukadam (Finance & Admin Manager), J Brennan (Operations Manager)

PRINCIPAL ACTIVITIES: Operation, chartering and leasing of specialised offshore support vessels
Parent Company: Abu Dhabi National Oil Co (ADNOC); Zapata Gulf Marine Corporation
Principal Bankers: National Bank of Abu Dhabi
Financial Information:

	1989 Dh'000	1990 Dh'000
Sales turnover	34,633	42,142
Profits	8,992	10,948
Authorised capital	60,000	60,000
Paid-up capital	25,000	25,000
Total assets	130,233	122,892

Principal Shareholders: Abu Dhabi National Oil Co (ADNOC) (60%)
Date of Establishment: 8 October 1978
No of Employees: 270

NATIONAL MECHANICAL & ELECTRICAL WORKS CO

PO Box 1189, Al Ain, Abu Dhabi
Tel: 3-828937
Telex: 22320 Khrafi Em
Telefax: 3-828937

Directors: Ghalib Younis (Managing Director)
Senior Executives: Hassan Abu Madi (UAE Area Manager)

PRINCIPAL ACTIVITIES: Contracting, oil and gas pipelines, mechanical and electrical works for hospitals, large commercial complexes, airports, highways, sewage treatment plants, building automation systems and security systems
Branch Offices: Yemen: PO Box 2296, Sana'a; representative office in London, UK
Parent Company: Head office in Kuwait

Principal Shareholders: M A Kharafi, Ghalib Younis

NATIONAL PETROLEUM CONSTRUCTION CO (NPCC)

PO Box 2058, Abu Dhabi
Tel: 774100 (15 lines)
Cable: NAPECO
Telex: 22638 NPCC EM
Telefax: 727763

Chairman: HE Mohamed Khalifa Al Kindi
Directors: Juaan Salem Al-Dhahiri, Suhail F Al Mazroui, Abdullah Nasser Al Suweidi, Rashed Saif Al Suwaidi, Said Khoury, Fawzi Kawash, Munir E Khoury (Supervising Director), Bishara Zabaneh (Board Secretary)
Senior Executives: Najjad A Zeenni (General Manager), David F Winning (Asst General Manager Marketing & Business Development), Ralph E Conder (Special Advisor - Offshore), Ibrahim E Khoury (Manager Finance & Accounts), Michel E Lattouf (Manager Onshore Projects), Sa'ed F Shawwa (Manager Personnel & Administration), Toufiq Hamad (Plant Manager), Sami E Ghandour (Manager Offshore Operations), ANtoine Y Hayek (Contracts Manager), Bassem A Kardoush (Manager Maintenance), Sami A Kurban (Manager Marketing & Business Development), Ahmed Kharboush (Manager Yards)

PRINCIPAL ACTIVITIES: Turnkey construction and maintenance of offshore platforms, topsides, storage tanks and modules for the oil and gas industry, including submarine laying and coating of pipelines
Branch Offices: NPCC Alkhobar: PO Box 34, Dhahran Airport 31932, Saudi Arabia, Tel 8576801, Telex 871461 CONCO SJ, Fax 8576364; NPCC Dubai: PO Box 1741, Dubai, UAE Tel 377508, Telex 48971 CCICL EM; NPCC Sharjah: PO Box 11, Sharjah, UAE, Tel 522238, Telex 68032; NPCC Cairo: 12 Rashdan Street, Dokki, Cairo, Egypt Tel 3484743, 3484759, Telex 22825 CCIC UN; and NPCC Bombay, Fax 2872664, India; NPCC SDN BHD, Kuala Lumpur, Fax 4410880, Malaysia
Parent Company: Abu Dhabi National Oil Company; Consolidated Contractors Group SAL
Subsidiary Companies: NPCC Sdn Bhd, Malaysia; NPCC Singapore Pte Ltd; NPCC UK; Zamil-NPCC Saudi Arabia; Malmarine Sdn Bhd, Malaysia
Principal Bankers: Arab Bank Ltd; National Bank of Abu Dhabi; Abu Dhabi Commercial Bank Ltd
Financial Information:

	1988/89	1989/90
	Dh'000	Dh'000
Sales turnover	237,000	223,000
Authorised capital	100,000	100,000
Paid-up capital	100,000	100,000
Total assets	571,000	568,000

Principal Shareholders: Abu Dhabi National Oil Co (ADNOC) (70%); Consolidated Contractors Group SAL (Holding Company) (CCC) (30%)
Date of Establishment: 2nd April 1973
No of Employees: 1,571

NATIONAL PLASTICS PIPE FACTORY

PO Box 2915, Abu Dhabi
Tel: 724400 (office), 554400 (factory)
Telex: 22627 Adpipe EM
Telefax: 782658

PRINCIPAL ACTIVITIES: Manufacture of plastic pipes
Parent Company: General Industry Corporation, Abu Dhabi

NATIONAL SHIPPING GULF AGENCY CO (ABU DHABI) LTD

PO Box 377, Abu Dhabi
Tel: 334300 (10 lines)
Cable: Confidence Abu Dhabi
Telex: 22248 Gacauh EM
Telefax: 339350

Chairman: HE Mohd Khalifa Al Yusuf
Directors: Mohd Khakifa, Saed Al Otaiba, P Lindstrom, Faris Bin Faris
Senior Executives: Per Lindstrom (General Manager), J Ray (Operations Manager), Tulsi Bhatia (Forwarding Manager), T George (Finance Manager)

PRINCIPAL ACTIVITIES: Shipping, clearing and forwarding agents, marine contracting, warehousing and packing, tugs and barges
Branch Offices: Jebel Dhanna: PO Box 377, Jebel Dhanna, Tel 72214, Fax 72033
Associated Companies: In Dubai; Sharjah; Ras Al Khaimah; Kuwait; Bahrain; Qatar; Saudi Arabia; Oman; Lebanon; Cyprus; Syria; Turkey; Iran; Greece; Nigeria; UK; Sweden; Norway; USA; Hong Kong; Singapore
Principal Bankers: British Bank of the Middle East

Date of Establishment: 1967

NCR CORPORATION

PO Box 350, Abu Dhabi
Tel: 333700
Cable: Nacareco Abu Dhabi
Telex: 23657 NCR AUH EM

PRINCIPAL ACTIVITIES: Sale and distribution of business equipment, computers and terminals and electronic data processing equipment
Branch Offices: Bahrain, Kuwait, Dubai, Qatar, Oman

Date of Establishment: 1962
No of Employees: 45

NEWAGE COMPANY

PO Box 7645, Abu Dhabi
Tel: 774548
Cable: Newage Abu Dhabi
Telex: 47927 Newage EM Dubai
Telefax: 728880

Directors: Mohamed Omran Taryam, Rajni C Shah (Managing Director)
Senior Executives: Dinesh Singare (Sales Manager)

PRINCIPAL ACTIVITIES: Engineers, traders, manufacturers' representatives, importers, suppliers and distributors of technical building equipment, pumping equipment, fire detection and protection equipment, water coolers, fountains, and servicing
Principal Agencies: Jung Pumpen, W Germany; Pompes Salmson, France; Haws Drinking Faucets Co, USA; Dunlop, UK; Albin Sprenger; Gollmer & Hummel, W Germany; Crane, UK; Noha, Norway; H J Godwin Ltd, UK; Apollo Fire Detectors, UK; H Warner & Sons, UK; Bayham Ltd, UK

UAE (Abu Dhabi)

Branch Offices: Dubai, Sharjah
Parent Company: Omram Investment Ltd, PO Box 82, Sharjah
Subsidiary Companies: Newage Company, Dubai; Haws Middle
East, Dubai; Spot Int, Sharjah; Gulf Lebanese Ent, Sharjah
Principal Bankers: Bank of Baroda, Abu Dhabi; Bank of Oman,
Abu Dhabi
Financial Information:

	1990 Dh'000
Sales turnover	12,000
Authorised capital	1,000
Paid-up capital	1,000

Principal Shareholders: Directors as described
Date of Establishment: 1976

NITCO CONCRETE PRODUCTS

PO Box 654, Abu Dhabi
Tel: 341776, 344255, 554787, 554788
Cable: Sultan
Telex: 22360, 22407 Nitco EM; Zafira EM
Telefax: 310147

Chairman: Farah Abdel Rahman Hamed
Directors: Ibrahim Farah, Mahdi Farah, Yahya Farah
Senior Executives: Abdullahi Farah (Managing Director)

PRINCIPAL ACTIVITIES: Producers and suppliers of readymix
concrete, interlocking concrete paving stones, kerb stones
Branch Offices: Mussaffah, Abu Dhabi
Subsidiary Companies: Nitco National Industry, Trading &
Contracting Co; Nitco Printing Press,Arak General
Maintenance Est, Farah Public Relations Est
Principal Bankers: Arab Bank for Investment & Foreign Trade,
Abu Dhabi
Financial Information:

	1989/90 Dh'000
Sales turnover	4,000
Profits	800
Authorised capital	10,000
Paid-up capital	8,000
Total assets	7,600

Date of Establishment: 1980; commercial production March
1981
No of Employees: 60

NORWICH WINTERTHUR INSURANCE (GULF) LTD

PO Box 245, Abu Dhabi
Tel: 774444 ext 226/230/224/248
Telex: 22282 Kanoo EM
Telefax: 722505

Directors: K H Williams, G C Larn, H B Gilmore, G W H Jones,
E J Sainsbury, J D Campbell, Yusuf Ahmed Kanoo
Senior Executives: F O'Sullivan (Manager UAE)

PRINCIPAL ACTIVITIES: All classes of insurance and
reinsurance (except life)
Branch Offices: Bahrain, Abu Dhabi, Dubai, Sharjah, Oman
Parent Company: Norwich Union Insurance Group, Norwich, UK
Subsidiary Companies: Norwich Winterthur Insurance (Arabia)
Ltd, Jeddah; Riyadh; Al Khobar (Saudi Arabia)

Principal Shareholders: Norwich Union Fire Insurance Society
Ltd (45%); Winterthur Swiss Insurance Group of Switzerland
(45%); Chiyoda Fire and Life Insurance Companies of Japan
(10%)
Date of Establishment: 1979

OFFSHORE SUPPLY ASSOCIATION LTD

PO Box 465, Abu Dhabi
Tel: 332963
Cable: RAIS EM
Telex: 22477 EM

Chairman: Dr H Matthies
Directors: H Sikora (Deputy Chairman), W Plate (Managing
Director, Bremen), H D Ahlrichs, L Hoare, A M R Sylvester
(London)

PRINCIPAL ACTIVITIES: Operators of offshore supply ships
and diving support vessels for the international oil and
offshore construction industries
Branch Offices: Bremen, London, Houston, Paris, Rio de
Janeiro, Singapore, Port Gentil, Aberdeen, Port Harcourt, Abu
Dhabi, Dubai, Shekou (China)
Parent Company: VTG Vereinigte Tanklager und Transportmittel
GmbH, Hamburg

Date of Establishment: 1968
No of Employees: 40

OILFIELD INSPECTION SERVICES (ME)

PO Box 4074, Abu Dhabi
Tel: 333105
Telex: 22639 OIS EM
Telefax: 325972

Senior Executives: K McIntosh (Area Manager)

PRINCIPAL ACTIVITIES: Non destructive testing
Associated Companies: Inspectorate Oilfield, Aberdeen,
Scotland, UK

OMAN NATIONAL ELECTRONICS

PO Box 555, Abu Dhabi
Tel: 328180, 333432
Cable: Al-Futtaim
Telex: 23304 Futgrp EM

President: Majid Al-Futtaim
Directors: Abdullah Al-Futtaim (Vice President), Enver Masood
(Executive Vice Chairman), Z U Sabri (Managing Director)

PRINCIPAL ACTIVITIES: Trading in electrical and electronic
consumer products, home appliances, systems engineering in
communications, security surveillance CCTV, fire alarm and
music systems
Principal Agencies: Matsushita Electric Trading Co, Japan
Branch Offices: A branch of Dubai based Oman National
Electronics
Parent Company: Al Futtaim Group of Companies
Associated Companies: Al-Futtaim Motors Toyota, Abu Dhabi;
Al-Futtaim Electronics Auto & Machinery Co, Abu Dhabi; Al-
Futtaim Ltd, Abu Dhabi
Principal Bankers: Bank of Oman, Abu Dhabi

Principal Shareholders: Family Partnership
Date of Establishment: 1970
No of Employees: 150

OMEIR BIN YOUSEF & SONS
Omeir Travel Agency

PO Box 267, Abu Dhabi
Tel: 344477, 342737
Cable: Omeir
Telex: 22305 OMEIR EM
Telefax: 337310

Proprietor: Omeir Bin Youssef
Senior Executives: Fathi I Elwan (General Manager), Ghazi
Helaihil (Finance Manager), Mahmoud I Elwan (Sales Manager
Buick & Bedford), Mrs Zainab Habib (Sales Manager Travel
Agency), J J Benny (Service Manager Buick & Bedford), A
Salam (Personnel Manager), Munir K Said (Sales Engineer)

PRINCIPAL ACTIVITIES: Travel agents, clearing and forwarding
agents, real estate agents; dealers for cars and trucks and
spare parts, contrctors for turnkey electrical projects,
installation and commissioning of radio/TV stations,
desalination plants, power generation and distribution
systems, switch gears etc

Principal Agencies: AWD Bedford Commercial Vehicles; GM Buick Passenger Cars; Asea Brown Boveri Ltd
Branch Offices: Al Ain, Mussaffah
Parent Company: Omeir Travel Agency
Principal Bankers: British Bank of the Middle East, Abu Dhabi

Principal Shareholders: Local Owned Company 100%
Date of Establishment: 1959
No of Employees: 65 in Omer Bin Youssef & Sons and 409 in Travel Agency

OMEST TRADING & GENERAL AGENCIES
PO Box 4091, Abu Dhabi
Tel: 331641
Telex: 23680 OMEST EM

Chairman: Sheikh Omar Abdulla Al Qasimi
Senior Executives: Zahiruddin Khan (General Manager)

PRINCIPAL ACTIVITIES: Suppliers of gas turbines, electrical equipment, generators, cables, trading, local sponsoring
Principal Agencies: Hispano Suiza, France, Biwater Shellabear Int'l, UK; AVM Systems, USA; Oreco Switzerland
Branch Offices: PO Box 103, Ras Al Khaimah (Head Office)
Parent Company: Omest Group
Subsidiary Companies: Omest Investment, Omest Contracting
Principal Bankers: Bank of the Arab Coast; National Bank of Ras Al Khaimah

Date of Establishment: 1979

ORIENT CONTRACTING COMPANY
PO Box 348, Abu Dhabi
Tel: 322622
Cable: Orient
Telex: 22250 EM

Directors: Moufid F Dabaghi, Joseph Chamieh, Rafik Mansour

PRINCIPAL ACTIVITIES: Water and sewerage pipelines; submarine water pipelines; pumping stations; civil engineering contracting
Branch Offices: Orient Overseas Organisation Ltd, 192 Sloane St, London SW1, UK; Orient Contracting Co, PO Box 1171, Al Ain
Principal Bankers: Grindlays Bank plc

P&O CONTAINERS LTD
PO Box 247, Abu Dhabi
Tel: 323131
Telex: 22245 Gray Em
Telefax: 213661

Senior Executives: S D Blake (General Manager)

PRINCIPAL ACTIVITIES: Shipping and freight forwarding
Parent Company: OCL, London E1, UK

PAN ARABIA INTERNATIONAL
PO Box 600, Rashid Al Rashid Bldg, Sheikh Khalifa St, Abu Dhabi
Tel: 344244
Telex: 22443 Panar EM

Chairman: Colonel Mohamed Ismail Shadid
Directors: A Boulhabel, O Boulkadid

PRINCIPAL ACTIVITIES: Electromechanical installations, construction, industrial and gas and oil field projects
Principal Agencies: Hitachi Ltd, Japan; Robert Bosch, Spain; Goldbach GmbH, West Germany; Dai Vera, Italy; K Span, USA
Principal Bankers: National Bank of Abu Dhabi; Gulf Bank; United Arab Bank

Principal Shareholders: Colonel Mohamed Ismail Shadid; Dr A Boulhabel
Date of Establishment: 1972

PAULING (MIDDLE EAST) PLC
PO Box 282, Abu Dhabi
Tel: 464885, 463654
Cable: Pauling Abu Dhabi
Telex: 22433 EM
Telefax: 461545

Directors: W A Barrage, L Novelli, J R Coulson

PRINCIPAL ACTIVITIES: Building and civil engineering contractors
Branch Offices: Abu Dhabi; Dubai; Oman; Libya; Jeddah (Saudi Arabia)
Parent Company: Pauling Plc, London SW1, UK
Principal Bankers: British Bank of the Middle East

Principal Shareholders: Pauling Plc
Date of Establishment: 1964

PENCOL INTERNATIONAL LTD
PO Box 46562, Abu Dhabi
Tel: 661944
Telex: 23420 Pencol EM
Telefax: 665624

Directors: R S Bradley (Director)

PRINCIPAL ACTIVITIES: Civil engineering consultants, specialising in oil, gas, water and sewerage pipeline work
Parent Company: Pencol Engineeering Consultants, 20 Grosvenor Place, London SW1X 7HP, UK

PETROLEUM ENGINEERING & CONSTRUCTION EST (PECON)
PO Box 3262, Abu Dhabi
Tel: 553662
Cable: Pecon
Telex: 23230 Pecon EM

Chairman: Moh A A Rubaya
Directors: Wim L Buker (Managing), Basim A Azzam

PRINCIPAL ACTIVITIES: Mechanical and MV/HV electrical installations, instrumentation, telecomms, installation and maintenance, heavy transport (up to 1000 tons/unit) and rigging, company representation
Branch Offices: Pecon (Transport Division), Abu Dhabi
Parent Company: Rubaya Group of Companies
Subsidiary Companies: Pecon Technicare Joint Venture, Abu Dhabi
Principal Bankers: British Bank of the Middle East; Abu Dhabi

Principal Shareholders: Member of the Rubaya Group of Companies
Date of Establishment: January 2nd 1974
No of Employees: 80

PETROLEUM TECHNOLOGY ENTERPRISES
PO Box 25868, Abu Dhabi
Tel: 216099
Telex: 24246
Telefax: 217195

Senior Executives: T B Long (Managing Director)

PRINCIPAL ACTIVITIES: Onshore/offshore petrochemical and power generation projects
Parent Company: Head office in Glasgow, Scotland, UK

PIPELINE CONSTRUCTION CO P.I.L.C.O.
PO Box 2021, Abu Dhabi
Tel: 554500
Cable: Pilcoest
Telex: 23210 Pilco EM

Directors: E N Hawa (General Manager)

PRINCIPAL ACTIVITIES: Design, material procurement and fabrication of pressure vessels, air receivers, storage tanks, structural steelwork, pipe spools, lighting poles, gantries, isometrics, general fabrication, radiographic and NDT inspection
Principal Bankers: Grindlays Bank PLC

Date of Establishment: June 1968
No of Employees: 200

POWER TRANSMISSION (GULF) LTD

PO Box 376, Abu Dhabi
Tel: 771385
Telex: 22247 Powertran EM, 23413 BICC EM
Telefax: 720187

Senior Executives: N M Gibb (General Manager)

PRINCIPAL ACTIVITIES: Electrical, mechanical and multi-service engineering contractors
Branch Offices: Abu Dhabi; Dubai; Sharjah
Parent Company: Balfour Kilpatrick Int'l, Wallington, Surrey, UK
Associated Companies: Gulf Electrical Engineering SAK, Kuwait; Zubair Kilpatrick LLC, Oman; Qatar Power Construction Est, Qatar; Saudi Industrial Contracting Co Ltd, Jeddah; Interstal Saudi Arabia Ltd, Dhahran

PRICE WATERHOUSE

PO Box 3646, Abu Dhabi
Tel: 334138
Telex: 24178 PWCO EM
Telefax: 330672

Senior Executives: Simon J Chapman (Partner), Amrjit A Atkar (Partner)

PRINCIPAL ACTIVITIES: Chartered accountants and management consultants
Branch Offices: In the Middle East: Bahrain, Doha, Dubai, Cairo, Qatar, Oman, Riyadh
Parent Company: Price Waterhouse, 32 London Bridge Street, London SE1, UK

No of Employees: 20

PRISMO UNIVERSAL (GULF) CO LTD

PO Box 367, Abu Dhabi
Tel: 774450
Telex: 22350 Sbrad EM
Telefax: 725538

Senior Executives: M S Nasser (General Manager)

PRINCIPAL ACTIVITIES: Road and airport marking, anti skid surfacing, resurfacing, traffic safety products
Parent Company: Prismo Ltd, Crawley, West Sussex, UK

QUEBEISI SGB

PO Box 7574, Abu Dhabi
Tel: 661783
Telex: 24337 SGB AD EM
Telefax: 669740

Senior Executives: M Rafferty (Branch Manager)

PRINCIPAL ACTIVITIES: Scaffolding and formwork equipment
Principal Agencies: Youngman; Boulton; SGB
Branch Offices: Dubai and Sharjah
Parent Company: SGB International Ltd, Mitcham, UK
Principal Bankers: British Bank of the Middle East

RAFIDAIN BANK

PO Box 2727, Abu Dhabi
Cable: Rafdbank Abu Dhabi
Telex: 22522 EM

PRINCIPAL ACTIVITIES: Commercial banking
Parent Company: Head office in Baghdad, Iraq

RAIS HASSAN SAADI & CO

PO Box 465, Abu Dhabi
Tel: 322929
Cable: Raishassan
Telex: 22477 EM

President: A R S Rais

PRINCIPAL ACTIVITIES: Shipping and forwarding agents; barge owners; insurance and general trading
Parent Company: Head office in Dubai

RANA & SONS

Sh Hamdan St, PO Box 273, Abu Dhabi
Tel: 341577, 323029, 327486
Cable: Rana Abudhabi

Proprietor: Farzand Ali Rana
Directors: Farook Ahmed Rana (Manager)

PRINCIPAL ACTIVITIES: Importers and dealers of building materials, hardware, paint, plastic products, safety equipment, rubber goods, tools, generators, water pumps and chemicals
Principal Agencies: Stockists: Phillips Drill Co (UK) Ltd, UK; Wolf Electric Tools Ltd; Burnett Atlanta Int, Black & Decker, Starrett Tools, Presto Tools, Baranite Ltd
Principal Bankers: British Bank of the Middle East; Standard Chartered Bank

Date of Establishment: 1974

RANYA TRADING, CONTRACTING & INDUSTRIAL

PO Box 602, Abu Dhabi
Tel: 822416
Cable: Tabari
Telex: 22386 Rtcc EM

Chairman: Marwan R Tabari, Hisham R Tabari
Directors: Nayef Serhan

PRINCIPAL ACTIVITIES: Trading in electrical equipment, chemicals, pharmaceuticals, building materials, also contracting for electrical, mechanical and civil engineering, water treatment cooling, plumbing etc
Principal Agencies: Thorn; MK; Bowthorp; Acro Cool; Petit Jean, France; FPE, USA; Laur Knudsen, Denmark; Caloremag; Germany; Pauwels Traffu, Belgium; Beecham, UK; Bayer, Germany, Schering, Germany; Hoescht, Germany; GE, USA
Branch Offices: Dubai; Abu Dhabi; Sharjah; Ras Al Khaimah; Jordan

Principal Shareholders: M Tabari, H Tabari

RAPCO BUILDINGS

PO Box 692, Abu Dhabi
Tel: 775949
Telex: 23817 RBLDG EM
Telefax: 720252

Managing Partner: Abdallah D Sha'
Directors: Khalil Khalid Al Mureikhy (Owner), Ahmad Khalil Al Mureikhy (Holding General Power of Attorney)
Senior Executives: Mouine N El Saghir (Deputy General Manager), S H Nazumudin (Office Engineer), Joseph Saouma (Chief Accountant)

PRINCIPAL ACTIVITIES: General contracting for all types of civil works, sewerage works and electro-mechanical works
Principal Agencies: Joint venture with Asea Brown Boveri, Germany
Associated Companies: Rapco Roads, PO Box 2315, Abu Dhabi
Principal Bankers: Bank of Credit & Commerce (Emirates), Abu Dhabi; Bank of Credit & Commerce International, Abu Dhabi; Bank of Oman Ltd, Abu Dhabi

Financial Information:

	1989/90 US$'000
Current assets	9,805
Other assets	2,350
Equity	1,752

Principal Shareholders: 100% local company (owner Khalil Khalid Al Mureikhy)
Date of Establishment: 1976
No of Employees: 300

RAPCO TRADING ENTERPRISES

PO Box 2315, Abu Dhabi
Tel: 772204 (4 lines)
Cable: RAPCO-ABU DHABI
Telex: 23291 Rapco EM
Telefax: 725405

Chairman: Ahmad Khalil Al Mureikhi
Directors: N Moje (Manager)

PRINCIPAL ACTIVITIES: Importers, distributors and manufacturers representatives; chemicals, construction equipment, water pumps and desalination plants, oilfield equipment and sewerage equipment
Principal Agencies: Norclean, Norway; Cole Parmer, USA; Lamarche, USA; Gates Rubber Co, USA & Belgium; Vac/All by Leach, USA
Parent Company: Roads & General Contracting Projects (RAPCO)
Principal Bankers: National Bank of Abu Dhabi; Bank of Oman

Date of Establishment: 1981

READY MIX BETON

PO Box 3610, Abu Dhabi
Tel: 337580, 554062, 554924
Telex: 22916 Beton EM
Telefax: 333715

Chairman: Osman Ghandour
Directors: Khaled Gandour (Managing Director)
Senior Executives: Riad Al Sayegh (Engineer), Khaled Awad (Engineer), Mouhamad Awaida (Engineer)

PRINCIPAL ACTIVITIES: Supply of ready mix concrete
Branch Offices: Abu-Dhabi; Moussafah
Parent Company: Climatex, Tripoli, Lebanon
Subsidiary Companies: Ready Mix Beton, Cairo; Ready Mix Beton, Lebanon
Principal Bankers: Investbank

Principal Shareholders: Osman Ghandour; Omar Ghandour; Khaled Ghandour
Date of Establishment: 1976
No of Employees: 120

READYMIX ABU DHABI LTD

PO Box 7289, Abu Dhabi
Tel: 553425
Telex: 23619 RMAD EM
Telefax: 553512

PRINCIPAL ACTIVITIES: Supply of readymix concrete and pumping services
Branch Offices: Al Ain
Parent Company: Redland International, Reigate, UK

RELIANT CO

PO Box 323, Abu Dhabi
Tel: 326943
Cable: Relia
Telex: 22280 Relia EM

Directors: T D Henson, Ali Bin Ali

PRINCIPAL ACTIVITIES: Mechanical, air-conditioning and electrical services

Principal Agencies: Marryat & Scott (International) Ltd, Airtemp Corporation
Branch Offices: Reliant Co, Doha, Qatar; Reliant Co, Dubai, UAE; Reliant Co, Muscat, Oman
Associated Companies: Reliant Technical Services, UK; Intercommerce (UK) Ltd, UK
Principal Bankers: Grindlays Bank; British Bank of the Middle East

RENARDET SAUTI ICE

PO Box 625, Abu Dhabi
Tel: 341106
Telex: 22426 Ice EM

PRINCIPAL ACTIVITIES: Consulting engineering; hydraulics, roads and airports, housing schemes, industrial facilities
Branch Offices: UAE; Saudi Arabia; Oman
Parent Company: Head office in Paris, France

RENCO

PO Box 221, Abu Dhabi
Tel: 341624, 341097
Cable: Renco
Telex: 22766 Renco EM

Chairman: Baqer Nimat Khoory

PRINCIPAL ACTIVITIES: Import and distribution of air conditioners, refrigerators, washing machines, water heaters, electrical equipment, chemicals, also electrical engineering contractors

ROADS & GENERAL CONTRACTING PROJECTS (RAPCO)

PO Box 2315, Abu Dhabi
Tel: 772204
Cable: Rapco
Telex: 23291 Rapco Em
Telefax: 725405

Directors: Ahmad Khalil Al Meraikhy (Executive Director)
Senior Executives: Jane T Shaheen (General Manager), Eng Mohammad M Ali Al Hadidi (Technical Director), Sulayman Ali Sulayman (Administration Manager), Abas Khan (Finance Director), Eng Guma Hamdan Barhoom (Production Manager)

PRINCIPAL ACTIVITIES: Contracting for roads and bridges, surface drainage and sewerage systems
Branch Offices: Al Ain, Tel 637357
Principal Bankers: National Bank of Abu Dhabi
Financial Information:

	1990 Dh'000
Authorised capital	30,500
Paid-up capital	30,500

Principal Shareholders: Khalil Khalid Al Mureikhy
Date of Establishment: 1968
No of Employees: 1,800

RUWAIS FERTILISER INDUSTRIES (FERTIL)

PO Box 46159, Abu Dhabi
Tel: 727100
Cable: Fertil Abu Dhabi
Telex: 24205 Fertil Em
Telefax: 2-728084

Chairman: Salah Salem Al Shamsi
Senior Executives: Yousef Al Nowais (General Manager), Jean Roussennac (Deputy General Manager), Abdul Hakim Al Suwaidi (Marketing Manager), Mahmoud I Bhutta (Plant Manager), Francois Michel Fay (Administration & Finance Manager)

PRINCIPAL ACTIVITIES: Production of fertilisers; 1,000 tonnes/day ammonia; 1,500 tonnes/day urea
Parent Company: Abu Dhabi National Oil Co (ADNOC); Total-Compagnie Francaise des Petroles (TCFP)

Principal Shareholders: (66-2/3%) ADNOC; (33-1/3%) TCFP
Date of Establishment: 1980
No of Employees: 360

SABA & CO

PO Box 202, Abu Dhabi
Tel: 335658, 341659, 322282
Cable: Sabaco Abu Dhabi
Telex: 23645 Sabaco EM
Telefax: 343904

Chairman: Suhail Saba
Directors: Joseph Sanbar, George Ghali
Senior Executives: Joseph M Sanbar (Responsible Partner),
   Elias G Sanbar (Resident Partner), Eid A Awwad (Resident
   Manager)

PRINCIPAL ACTIVITIES: Public accountants and management
   consultants
Principal Agencies: Touche Ross & Co (DRT International)
Branch Offices: Lebanon; Algeria; Bahrain; Egypt; Iraq; Jordan;
   Kuwait; Libya; Morocco; Oman; Qatar; Saudi Arabia; Syria;
   United Arab Emirates; Yemen; London (UK)
Parent Company: Saba & Co, Beirut, Lebanon
Subsidiary Companies: Saba & Nagle International Ltd of
   London
Principal Bankers: Arab Bank Ltd

Principal Shareholders: Partnership
Date of Establishment: 1967
No of Employees: 25

SADIQ BROTHERS

Obaid Al Mazroui Building, Sh. Zayed 2nd Street, PO Box 169,
   Abu Dhabi
Tel: 344333, 341542
Cable: Sadiq Abu Dhabi
Telex: 22272 United EM
Telefax: 322691

Chairman: S M Sadiq
Directors: S Dilawar Ali (Partner), S A N Al-Sadiq (Partner)

PRINCIPAL ACTIVITIES: Manufacturers' representation;
   distribution of hardware, tools, building materials, electric
   equipment, garage and workshop equipment, electric and gas
   welding accessories, sanitary ware, pumps and hoses,
   transformers and electric/diesel generating sets, tents and
   tarpaulins
Principal Agencies: Hilti Fasting Tools; Presto Threading Tools
Principal Bankers: United Bank Limited; Middle East Bank Ltd

Date of Establishment: 1964

SAINRAPT CONTRACTING CO

PO Box 661, Abu Dhabi
Tel: 554545
Cable: Etabrisaint
Telex: 22423 Brisad EM
Telefax: 553758

Chairman: HE Sheikh Nahyan Bin Hamdan Al Nahyan
Directors: Abdulla Ali Al Hashli, P Laborie, J Treffandier
Senior Executives: Bernard Martin (Managing Director), Nigel C
   Greenhalgh (Contracts Manager), A Collin (Finance Manager),
   N H Pham (Project Manager), P Delaunay (Plant Manager),
   Mustafa Shabbir (Company Secretary)

PRINCIPAL ACTIVITIES: Civil engineering works, dredging &
   reclamation works
Parent Company: SOGEA France
Associated Companies: SGE SOGEA Group, France
Principal Bankers: Banque Indosuez, Abu Dhabi; Banque
   Paribas, Abu Dhabi; Bank of Credit & Commerce (Emirates),
   Abu Dhabi; National Bank of Abu Dhabi

Financial Information:

	1989/90
	Dh'000
Sales turnover	16,000
Authorised capital	20,000
Paid-up capital	20,000
Total assets	20,000

Principal Shareholders: HE Sheikh Nahyan Bin Hamdan Al
   Nahyan (51%); Sainrapt et Brice (SOGEA) (49%)
Date of Establishment: 1968

SALEM EBRAHIM AL SAMAN

See AL SAMAN, SALEM EBRAHIM,

SAMER GROUP

PO Box 2764, Abu Dhabi
Tel: 325740, 216753, 325744
Telex: 23268 Smrgp EM
Telefax: 312351, 333475

Directors: N Majdalini
Senior Executives: S Abou Chacra (Manager)

PRINCIPAL ACTIVITIES: Civil engineering, telecommunications,
   consultancy, design and architecture, construction
   management
Associated Companies: R H Sanbar Projects (UK) Ltd, London
   W1, UK

SANTA FE INTERNATIONAL SERVICES INC

PO Box 591, Abu Dhabi
Tel: 344191/2
Cable: Santa Fe Abudhabi
Telex: 22236 EM

PRINCIPAL ACTIVITIES: Drilling contractors
Parent Company: Santa Fe International Corp, California, USA

SCOTT W KIRKPATRICK & PARTNERS

PO Box 2768, Abu Dhabi
Tel: 776769
Telex: 23355 SWK EM
Telefax: 777334

Senior Executives: M J E Potter (Resident Project Manager)

PRINCIPAL ACTIVITIES: Civil engineering consultants,
   transportation planners
Branch Offices: Al Ain; Dubai; Sharjah
Parent Company: Scott Wilson Kirkpatrick & Partners,
   Basingstoke, Hants, UK

SEA & LAND DRILLING CONTRACTORS INC

PO Box 2155, Abu Dhabi
Tel: 343003, 820051
Telex: 22216 EM

PRINCIPAL ACTIVITIES: Offshore and onshore drilling
   contractors
Branch Offices: Office in Dubai

SHANKLAND COX LTD (UAE)

PO Box 1333, Al Ain
Tel: 03-687324
Telex: 33505
Telefax: 03-686962

Chairman: John McEwan
Directors: Iain Findlay (Managing Director), Ken Jones, Michael
   Wellbank
Senior Executives: Michael C Smith (UAE Manager)

PRINCIPAL ACTIVITIES: Consultants in town and regional
   planning, architectural design, project management and site
   supervision, landscape architecture, transportation planning,
   tourism planning, and design of tourism projects
Branch Offices: Hongkong

Parent Company: Shankland Cox is a member of the Robertson Group Plc, UK

Principal Bankers: British Bank of the Middle East, UAE; Lloyds Bank, UK

Financial Information:

	1990
	Dh'000
Sales turnover	3,000

Date of Establishment: 1962
No of Employees: 80

SHELL GAS ABU DHABI BV

PO Box 46807, Abu Dhabi
Tel: 321973
Telex: 23607 SGAD EM
Telefax: 334942

Senior Executives: T E Ridley (Managing Director & General Representative)

PRINCIPAL ACTIVITIES: Trade and export of shell/gasco products
Parent Company: Shell Gas BV
Principal Bankers: British Bank of the Middle East

Date of Establishment: 1981

SIEMENS PLESSEY ELECTRONIC SYSTEMS LTD

PO Box 2570, Abu Dhabi
Tel: 326366, 322874
Telex: 23922 Ples EM
Telefax: 211488

Senior Executives: J Gill (Resident Manager)

PRINCIPAL ACTIVITIES: Electronic and telecommunications engineering contractors
Parent Company: Siemens Plessey Systems ltd, Weybridge, Surrey, UK

SIR ALEXANDER GIBB & PARTNERS

PO Box 528, Abu Dhabi
Tel: 727214
Telex: 23301 GIBAL EM
Telefax: 728920

Senior Executives: J O Hall (Senior Representative)

PRINCIPAL ACTIVITIES: Architects and consulting engineers
Parent Company: Head office in Reading, UK
Principal Bankers: Barclays Bank; Grindlays Bank

SIR M MACDONALD & PARTNERS

PO Box 47094, Abu Dhabi
Tel: 725526
Telex: 22673
Telefax: 783195

Directors: G M Fenton, M E George
Senior Executives: J T Hancock (Resident Manager)

PRINCIPAL ACTIVITIES: Civil engineering, mechanical, electrical and structural consultants
Branch Offices: In the Middle East: Abu Dhabi, UAE; Muscat, Oman; Mogadishu, Somalia; Khartoum, Sudan; Hodeidah, and Hadhramaut Governorate, Yemen
Parent Company: Mott MacDonald International, Cambridge, UK
Subsidiary/Associated Companies: Groundwater Development Consultants Ltd; MacDonald Agricultural Services Ltd; Cambridge Education Consultants
Principal Bankers: Barclays Bank Plc

SIX CONSTRUCT LIMITED

PO Box 226, Abu Dhabi
Tel: 322579, 322228
Cable: Sixconstruct Abu Dhabi
Telex: 22339 Sixco EM
Telefax: 523453

Chairman: Roger Lemaire
Directors: John Beerlandt, B E Soussou, G Ejjeh
Senior Executives: B E Soussou (General Manager)

PRINCIPAL ACTIVITIES: Building and civil engineering contractors (Harbours, cement factories, power plants, roads, jetties, etc)
Branch Offices: Belgium (Head Office); Holland; France; Spain; Zaire; Sudan; Saudi Arabia; Oman; UAE (Abu Dhabi, Sharjah, Ras Al Khaimah, Ajman, Fujairah, Umm al Quwain)
Parent Company: Les Entreprises SBBM and Six Contruct SA, Brussels
Subsidiary Companies: Bel Hasa Six Construct Co (Pvt) Ltd
Principal Bankers: BCC(E), Banque Indosuez, Banque Paribas, ABN Bank
Financial Information:

	1989/90
	US$'000
Sales turnover	40,000
Authorised capital	10,000
Paid-up capital	10,000

Date of Establishment: 1964
No of Employees: 1,100

SKYPAK INTERNATIONAL

PO Box 7860, Abu Dhabi
Tel: 339449
Telex: 24471 SKYAUH EM
Telefax: 336351

Senior Executives: S Bradley (Country General Manager)

PRINCIPAL ACTIVITIES: Worldwide courier service, collection, clearance and delivery of documents and commercial value items.
Parent Company: Head office in Hounslow, Middlesex, UK
Principal Bankers: National Bank of Sharjah

Principal Shareholders: Skypak Int'l (Pty) Ltd
Date of Establishment: March 1980

SODETEG ENGINEERING

PO Box 2764, Abu Dhabi
Tel: 322454
Cable: Sodeteg
Telex: 22475 EM

PRINCIPAL ACTIVITIES: General engineering contractors and technical studies; desalination projects, transport
Parent Company: Head office in France

SOGEX SPECIALISED ENGINEERING

PO Box 948, Abu Dhabi
Tel: 343660
Telex: 22321 Sogex EM

PRINCIPAL ACTIVITIES: Turnkey contractors, desalination, power station, pipe lines, precast building, roads, and other heavy industrial and civil engineering projects
Branch Offices: UAE (Abu Dhabi, Dubai, Sharjah); Oman

SOLUS EMIRATES

PO Box 47044, Abu Dhabi
Tel: 725118
Telex: 23753 Solus EM
Telefax: 785261, 725565

Chairman: Hussain Al Nowais
Directors: D Derbyshire, J Walker

Senior Executives: G Kirkman (General Manager), N Harvey (Operations Manager)

PRINCIPAL ACTIVITIES: Engineering inspection and underwater services
Parent Company: Solus Schall, Aberdeen, UK
Principal Bankers: Standard Chartered Bank, Abu Dhabi

Date of Establishment: March 1983
No of Employees: 100

SPICER & PEGLER

PO Box 7649, Abu Dhabi
Tel: 772526
Telex: 47297 Mtgco EM
Telefax: 785545

Senior Executives: S S S Ahmed (Branch Manager)

PRINCIPAL ACTIVITIES: Chartered accountants, international taxation, joint venture management, financial consultants
Parent Company: Head office in London, UK

SPINNEY'S (ABU DHABI)

PO Box 243, Abu Dhabi
Tel: 770200
Cable: Spinneys Abu Dhabi
Telex: 22271 EM
Telefax: 720532

Chairman: Michael C E Hemery
Senior Executives: Rodney G James (General Manager), Samir E Suleiman (External Relations Manager), Ian Anderson (General Sales Manager)

PRINCIPAL ACTIVITIES: Catering services and contractors, cold store supermarkets, retail and wholesale food distribution and agency representatives
Parent Company: Bricom Plc, Dorking, Surrey, UK
Principal Bankers: British Bank of the Middle East; ANZ Grindlays; Standard Chartered
Financial Information:

	1990
	Dh'000
Sales turnover	250,000
Authorised capital	16,000
Paid-up capital	16,000

Principal Shareholders: Spinneys 1948 Ltd
Date of Establishment: 1962
No of Employees: 980

STALCO

PO Box 3768, Abu Dhabi
Tel: 323282
Cable: STALCO
Telex: 22561 STALCO EM
Telefax: 2-344660

Chairman: Mohammed Abdu Thabet
Directors: Mohammad Yassin A Ghafoor (Managing Director)
Senior Executives: Feizulla A Abdulali (Shipping Manager)

PRINCIPAL ACTIVITIES: Shipping agents, stevedores, clearing, forwarding, packing and transport contractors, airfreight agents
Branch Offices: Head Office in Dubai; branch offices in Abu Dhabi and Sharjah
Parent Company: STALCO - Dubai
Subsidiary Companies: STALCO - Sharjah & Khorfakhan
Principal Bankers: Abu Dhabi Commercial Bank

Principal Shareholders: STALCO - Dubai; Rashid Mohd Al Hurr; Ahmed Sultan Al Yousuf; Mohammed Abdul Aziz Al Rubaya
Date of Establishment: 1975

STANDARD CHARTERED BANK

PO Box 240, Abu Dhabi
Tel: 330077
Cable: Stanchart
Telex: 22274
Telefax: 341511

Senior Executives: D G D Mauritzen (Manager), P J Butler (Manager Operations)

PRINCIPAL ACTIVITIES: Commercial banking
Branch Offices: Al Ain
Parent Company: Head office: 38 Bishopsgate, London EC2, UK

STEEL CONSTRUCTION ENGINEERING CO

PO Box 3922, Abu Dhabi
Tel: 773117
Cable: SCECO
Telex: 22680 SCECO EM
Telefax: 782483

Chairman: Sayeed Mattar Sayeed Hamr'ain Al Mohairbi
Directors: Issa Sheikh Hassan
Senior Executives: Shafqat Zaheer Mohamed Zaheer (Chief Engineer)

PRINCIPAL ACTIVITIES: Mechanical engineering, fabricating and erection of storage tanks, filling stations, gas petrol pipelines etc, construction of warehouses
Principal Agencies: Dirickx Fencing System, France
Parent Company: Hamarain Group of Companies
Principal Bankers: Bank of Oman; BCCI; National Bank of Abu Dhabi; Rafidain Bank
Financial Information:

	1990
	Dh'000
Sales turnover	12.350
Profits	2,250
Authorised capital	3,500
Paid-up capital	2,000
Total assets	3,000

Principal Shareholders: Sayeed Mattar Sayeed Hamarain Al Mohrbi; Issa Sheikh Hassan
Date of Establishment: 1977
No of Employees: 150

STONE & WEBSTER ABU DHABI (UAE)

PO Box 4722, Abu Dhabi
Tel: 339578
Telex: 23480 SWMEIN EM
Telefax: 211033

Directors: K White (Vice President)
Senior Executives: M Imran Butt (General Manager), J F Waters (Senior Design Engineer), L I Smith (Principal Resident Engineer)

PRINCIPAL ACTIVITIES: Consulting engineers, project management and construction management to the oil, gas, petrochemical and power industries
Parent Company: Stone & Webster Engineering Corporation, Milton Keynes, UK
Subsidiary Companies: DSS Engineers Inc
Principal Bankers: Standard Chartered Bank; Midland Bank; Chase Manhattan Bank

SULTAN BIN RASHED & PARTNERS

Head Office, PO Box 965, Tourist Club Area, Abu Dhabi
Tel: 774450 (7 lines)
Cable: Sultaco
Telex: 22350 SBRAD EM
Telefax: 725538

Senior Executives: Sultan Rashed Saeed Al Dhahiri (General Manager), Nizam Abdul Baki (Deputy General Manager), Godfrey M D'Costa (Technical & Sales Manager), Nabil

Abulaban (Finance & Administration Manager), Julian Lewis (Manager Sharjah/Dubai), Mike O'Neill (Sales Manager Dubai/Sharjah), George Rejeilly (Sales Manager AL Ain)

PRINCIPAL ACTIVITIES: Dealers, import & export, and distributors of sanitaryware and fittings, tiles, (vinyl, ceramic, rubber, industrial), plumbing/drainage materials, sports flooring, paints, kitchen furniture, waterproofing membranes and coatings, anticorrosion pipe wrapping tapes, structural and bridge deck expansion joints and bearings, desalination chemicals, textured finishes and specialised building materials

Principal Agencies: Ideal Standard group of companies (USA, UK, Italy, France, Greece, W Germany); Marley Floors UK; Marley Extrusions UK; Bolidt BV, Holland; Mondo Rubber, Italy; Servicised, UK; Serviwrap, UK; Intervandex, Switzerland; Wash-Perle Intl, France; Cuprinol, UK; Ciba-Geigy (Desalination Chemicals), Switzerland; Maurer Sohne, W Germany; SK Bearings, UK; IMI Yorkshire Imperial Plastics, UK; Robert Bosch, W Germany; Pilkington's Tiles, UK; JCD Creations, UK; EMCO, W Germany; Solaria, Italy; Humes, Australia; Keramo, Belgium; Intraco, Belgium; Annawerk, W Germany; Jasba, W Germany; Awyco Sanitar, W Germany; Thermafex, Holland; IMI Rycroft, UK; Merati, Italy; Ceramiche, Italy; Sanitarprodukte, W Germany; Sitam, Italy; Evergreen, Cyprus; Vandex, Switzerland

Branch Offices: PO Box 3402, Bur-Dubai, Tel 377834/377631; also PO Box 5829, Sharjah, Tel 331844, Fax 330093, Telex 68183 SULTCO EM; and PO Box 15011, Al Ain, Tel 631609/631610, Fax 632003

Principal Bankers: National Bank of Abu Dhabi

Financial Information:

	1989/90 Dh'000	1990/91 Dh'000
Sales turnover	49,000	57,000
Paid-up capital	12,000	12,000

Principal Shareholders: Sultan Rashed Saeed Al Dhahiri (100%)
Date of Establishment: 1969
No of Employees: 140

SULTAN BIN YOUSUF & SONS

PO Box 698, Abu Dhabi
Tel: 326258, 327124
Telex: 22607 Harson EM
Telefax: 324312

Chairman: Harib Sultan Al Yousuf
Directors: M A Qureishi (Director Airline Admin, Finance & Planning)
Senior Executives: Khalid Aziz (General Manager)

PRINCIPAL ACTIVITIES: Travel agencies
Principal Agencies: PIA; Sudan Airways; Turkish Airlines; Austrian Airline; Olympic Airways; Air Malta; Eastern; Air Canada; ZAS Airline
Branch Offices: PO Box 16026, Al Ain
Parent Company: Harib Sultan Group of Companies
Principal Bankers: Bank of Credit & Commerce International; United Bank Limited

Date of Establishment: 1972

TALAL ABU-GHAZALEH & CO

PO Box 4295, Abu Dhabi
Tel: 343242
Cable: Auditors
Telex: 22437 EM

PRINCIPAL ACTIVITIES: Public accountants and management consultants
Branch Offices: United Arab Emirates (Abu Dhabi, Dubai, Sharjah, Ras Al Khaimah); Lebanon; Egypt; Bahrain, Jordan; Qatar; Oman; Libya; Tunisia; Saudi Arabia; Yemen
Parent Company: Head office in Kuwait

TAREQ TRADING ESTABLISHMENT

PO Box 2673, Abu Dhabi
Tel: 323345, 323479
Cable: Hudaco-Abu Dhabi
Telex: 22629 Ebtsam EM

President: Mohamed F Bindhafari
Directors: M F Obeid

PRINCIPAL ACTIVITIES: Supply of pharmaceuticals, electronic appliances, prefabricated houses, scientific equipment, educational materials, laboratory furniture and electrical goods
Branch Offices: Tareq Trading Est, Sharjah, UAE, Tel 354507 Bindhafari Gen Trading, Dubai, UAE, Tel 282996
Principal Bankers: BCCI SA; Bank of Oman Ltd

TEBODIN MIDDLE EAST LTD

PO Box 2652, Abu Dhabi
Tel: 828400
Telex: 22772 Tebo EM
Telefax: 727406

Directors: W Quaak (Managing Director)
Senior Executives: A S De Vries (Manager, Abu Dhabi), N Abdulla (Manager Dubai)

PRINCIPAL ACTIVITIES: Consulting engineers for water supply, hydrocarbon production and industrial projects
Branch Offices: Dubai; PO Box 8092, Tel 215839, Telex 48438 TEBOM
Parent Company: Tebodin BV, The Hague, Holland
Principal Bankers: Algemene Bank; Abu Dhabi & Dubai

Principal Shareholders: Tebodin BV; The Hague, Holland
Date of Establishment: 1973
No of Employees: 60

TECHNICAL PARTS CO

PO Box 337, Abu Dhabi
Tel: 771500 (5 lines)
Cable: Technical
Telex: 22346 Tecpts EM
Telefax: 9712-771958, 782462

Chairman: V B Bhatia
Directors: G B Whabi (General Manager)
Senior Executives: Deepak Chopra (Sales Manager), Vijay Ganju (Sales Executive)

PRINCIPAL ACTIVITIES: Import, stocking and distribution of oilfield supplies, petrochemical products, engineering goods, fire fighting equipment, safety products, pipes and fittings, valves, mechanical and fabrication contractors
Principal Agencies: Aeroquip, UK and USA; Crane, UK; Lincoln St, Louis; Stewart-Warner; Hoke; Jallatte, France; Kango Wolf, UK; etc
Branch Offices: Bhatia Bros, PO Box 275, Dubai; Technical Parts Co, PO Box 5071, Dubai; Oilfield Supply Centre, PO Box 5855, Ruwi, Oman; Technical Parts Co, PO Box 1369, Al Ain
Parent Company: Bhatia Bros
Subsidiary Companies: Technical Oilfield Supplies Centre, PO Box 2647, Abu Dhabi; Eastern Union Corp, PO Box 3489, Abu Dhabi
Principal Bankers: British Bank of the Middle East
Financial Information:

	1989/90 Dh'000
Sales turnover	32,000
Profits	2,500
Authorised capital	1,000
Paid-up capital	1,000
Total assets	43,000

Principal Shareholders: Private Company
Date of Establishment: 1965
No of Employees: 150

TECHNICAL SERVICES & SUPPLY CO

PO Box 277, Abu Dhabi
Tel: 824400
Cable: Techserve
Telex: 22643 U T S EM

Directors: Ziad J Al Askari (Owner)
Senior Executives: Omar Z Al Askari (Chief Executive)

PRINCIPAL ACTIVITIES: Mechanical and electrical engineering, trading and contracting, manufacturers' representation; mechanical, electrical and air-conditioning equipment
Principal Bankers: Algemene Bank Nederland N.V.

Principal Shareholders: Z Al Askari (Owner)
Date of Establishment: 1962

TECHNICAL SUPPLIES & SERVICES CO

PO Box 410, Abu Dhabi
Tel: 772912, 772325
Cable: Rima
Telex: 23624 Rima Em
Telefax: 726175

Chairman: Jamil G Nasr (Managing Director)

PRINCIPAL ACTIVITIES: Manufacture of insulated panels (polyurethance injected) and profiled insulated steel claddings for steel buildings
Branch Offices: Dubai
Parent Company: Head office & Factory in Sharjah
Principal Bankers: First Gulf Bank, Dubai; Bank of Credit & Commerce, Sharjah; National Bank of Abu Dhabi
Financial Information:

	1990 Dh'000
Paid-up capital	6,000
Total assets	3,000

Principal Shareholders: Sole proprietorship
Date of Establishment: 1962
No of Employees: 110

THANI MURSHID & AFRICAN & EASTERN LTD

PO Box 49, Abu Dhabi
Tel: 825600, 775600
Cable: Ethiope
Telex: 22276 EM
Telefax: 777780

Senior Executives: A N Wallace (District Manager), B E Fawcett (Technical Manager)

PRINCIPAL ACTIVITIES: Engineers specialising in air conditioning and refrigeration design, installation and servicing in the Arabian Gulf, also general trading, consumer products, soaps, detergents, toiletries and foodstuffs, office equipment and furniture, business equipment, beverages division
Principal Agencies: Unilever Products, C C Friesland, Carlton United Breweries
Branch Offices: Arabian Gulf countries (Abu Dhabi, Dubai, Qatar, Bahrain, Oman)
Associated Companies: Unilever Plc, Bristol, UK
Principal Bankers: British Bank of the Middle East, Standard Chartered Bank, Grindlays Bank

TOTAL ABU AL BUKHOOSH (ABU DHABI BRANCH)

PO Box 4058, Abu Dhabi
Tel: 335566
Telex: 22347 Totabk EM
Telefax: 322948

Chairman: Aziz Ait Said
Senior Executives: Michel Contie (General Manager), P Raab (Finance Manager), J M Salvadori (Operations Manager), Kamal Hassan (Human Resources & Administration Manager), H Nusseibeh (Planning & Development Manager), R Hadjimegrian (Technical Services Manager)

PRINCIPAL ACTIVITIES: Oil production

Principal Shareholders: Compagnie Francaise des Petroles (51%), Sunningdale Oil Ltd (12.25%), Nepco Exploration Corporation (24.5%) and Amerada Hess (12.25%)
Date of Establishment: 1973

TOUCHE ROSS SABA & CO

PO Box 202, Abu Dhabi
Tel: 335658, 322282, 341659
Telex: 23645 Sabaco EM
Telefax: 343904

Directors: E Sanbar (Partner)

PRINCIPAL ACTIVITIES: Audit and accountancy, management consultancy
Associated Companies: Touche Ross & Co, London EC4, UK

UMM AL DALKH DEVELOPMENT CO (UDECO)

PO Box 6866, Abu Dhabi
Tel: 722600
Cable: Udeco
Telex: 23686 EM

Chairman: Suhail AlMazrui (ADNOC)
Directors: Suhail AlMazrui (ADNOC), Khalaf R Al Otaiba (ADNOC), Dr H Hosoi (JODCO), H Fujita (JODCO), O Kanno (JODCO)

PRINCIPAL ACTIVITIES: Exploration, development and production of hydrocarbons in Umm Al Dalkh field or other field as may be agreed
Parent Company: Abu Dhabi National Oil Co (ADNOC); Japan Oil Development Co (JODCO)
Principal Bankers: National Bank of Abu Dhabi, Bank of Credit & Commerce Int'l

Principal Shareholders: Abu Dhabi National Oil Co, (Adnoc) 50%, Abu Dhabi; Japan Oil Development Co (JODCO) 50%, Abu Dhabi
Date of Establishment: 1978
No of Employees: 187

UNION TRANSPORT & CONTRACTING CO

PO Box 616, Abu Dhabi
Tel: 822592
Cable: Hilal
Telex: 22718 Khalil EM

Directors: Ibrahim Mohammed Al Mazroui (Chairman), Mohammed Tayser Khreis (General Manager)

PRINCIPAL ACTIVITIES: General trading and contracting, import and distribution of building materials, sanitary ware, and prefabricated buildings
Principal Agencies: Rilco Maschinenfabric, Germany; Blue Circle, Permoglaze Paints, CMC Ravenna, Steiner
Branch Offices: M A Al Mazroui & Sons, Abu Dhabi; IBM Al Mazroui & Partners, Al Ain
Principal Bankers: National Bank of Abu Dhabi

Principal Shareholders: Mohd Abdulla Al Mazroui
Date of Establishment: 1967
No of Employees: 150

UNITED ARAB BANK

PO Box 3562, Abu Dhabi
Tel: 325000
Cable: UABANK
Telex: 22759 Uabank EM
Telefax: 338361

Chairman: HE Sheikh Faisal Bin Sultan Al Qassimi

Directors: Martial Lesay, M du Halgouet, Sheikh Sultan Bin Saqr Al Qassimi, Sheikh Khalid Bin Saqr Al Qassimi, Ahmed Mohd Hamad Al Midfa, Mohammed Saleh Bin Badouh Al Darmaki, Hassan Mohd Abdul Rehman Khansaheb, Khalid Al Alami, Mohammed Saeed Al Qassimi, Saeed Ahmed Omran Al Mazroui, Abdullah Rashid Al Majid

Senior Executives: J Dubois (General Manager), Awni Alami (Deputy General Manager), J L Alvernhe (Manager Head Office), J C Robert (Manager Credit)

PRINCIPAL ACTIVITIES: Commercial banking
Branch Offices: Abu Dhabi; Sharjah; Dubai; (Deira - Dubai); Ras Al Khaimah; Al Ain; Jebel Ali; Ajman
Parent Company: Societe Generale (Paris)
Principal Correspondents: Societe Generale - Paris; New York; London; Zurich
Financial Information:

	1988 Dh'000	1989 Dh'000
Income	109,442	135,077
Profits	25,958	26,048
Authorised capital	150,000	150,000
Paid-up capital	90,000	90,000
Total assets	1,054,269	1,198,470

Principal Shareholders: Societe Generale (20%); Local Shareholders (80%)
Date of Establishment: August 1975
No of Employees: 221

UNITED BANK LTD

PO Box 237, Abu Dhabi
Tel: 345667, 326597, 338240, 338932
Cable: Unitedbank
Telex: 22272 United EM

PRINCIPAL ACTIVITIES: Commercial banking
Branch Offices: Abu Dhabi; Dubai; Sharjah; Qatar; Bahrain; Yemen; Representative Office: Cairo, Egypt
Parent Company: Pakistan Banking Council, Karachi-Pakistan
Subsidiary/Associated Companies: United Bank AG Zurich, Switzerland; United Bank of Lebanon & Pakistan, Lebanon; Commercial Bank of Oman, Muscat; United Saudi Commercial Bank SA

UNITED GENERAL AGENCIES EST

PO Box 6447, Abu Dhabi
Tel: 822212
Telex: 23362 MCGCO EM

Senior Executives: Sameh Masry (General Manager)

PRINCIPAL ACTIVITIES: General trading and commissions agents

Date of Establishment: 1977
No of Employees: 35

UNITED TECHNICAL SERVICES

PO Box 277, Abu Dhabi
Tel: 774400
Cable: Techserve
Telex: 22643 UTS EM
Telefax: 722012

President: Omar Z Al Askari
Senior Executives: S Ahmed (Commercial Manager), Varouj Arslanian (Division Manager), Mohan Kumar (Finance Manager)

PRINCIPAL ACTIVITIES: Mechanical and engineering products, oilfield supplies and services, company representations and joint-ventures
Principal Agencies: Bureau Veritas, France; Carrier Int, USA; J C Carter, USA; Hughes Tool Co, USA; King Wilkinson, UK; C E Lummus, USA; Meco, USA; C E Natco, USA; Petbow, UK; Perkins Engines, UK; Sumitomo Shoji Kaisha, Japan; Union Pump, USA; Western Oceanic, USA; Westinghouse Electric,

USA; Yokogawa Electric Corp, Japan; Dresser Magcobar, USA; M F Kent, Eire; AVA Int'l, USA; BJ Machinery, Netherlands; Ebara Corp, Japan; Jennis & Leblanc Communications, Australia; Ontario Hydro, Canada; Platypus, UK; Sentry Piping System, Canada; UTS Servicemaster Emirates, USA; Alfa Laval, Sweden
Subsidiary Companies: Abu Dhabi Magcobar, UTS Carrier
Principal Bankers: Arab Bank for Investment & Foreign Trade; Standard Chartered Bank

Principal Shareholders: Omar Z Al Askari; Abdulla Darwish Al-Katbi
Date of Establishment: 1980
No of Employees: 30

UNITED TRADING & SERVICES CO

PO Box 691, Abu Dhabi
Tel: 341463/4
Cable: Unitrace
Telex: 22228 EM

PRINCIPAL ACTIVITIES: Mechanical engineering contractors, import and distribution of electrical and mechanical equipment, generators, diesel engines, medical equipment
Principal Agencies: Riva Boats, GEC X-ray Equipment, Cox Safes, Braithwaite, Taiyo, etc

Principal Shareholders: Ahmed Bin Juma Al Suweidi, Mohammed Al Hurr Al Suweidi

UNIVERSAL TRADING CO

PO Box 4399, Universal Centre Bldg, Abu Dhabi
Tel: 335331, 344265
Cable: Al Dhaheri
Telex: 22343 Unisal EM

Chairman: Shabeeb Al Dhaheri
Directors: Hilal Al Dhaheri (Partner), Samir Zaabri (Managing Partner)

PRINCIPAL ACTIVITIES: Trading, engineering, sponsorships
Principal Agencies: AEG, Germany; Twinlock, UK; Lancing Henley Forklift Trucks, UK; Woden Distribution Transformers, UK; Sanderson Forklifts, UK; Klockner-Humboldt-Deutz AG, Germany; Lindenberg Aggregate, Germany; Fox Bompani, Italy; Universal Airconditioners, Japan
Branch Offices: PO Box 1594, Dubai; PO Box 5826 Sharjah; PO Box 15320, Al Ain
Subsidiary and Associated Companies: Subsidiaries: Universal-Continental Co (Office equipment); Universal Computers Co (with USA); Universal Voltas Co (Air condit) Universal Design Co (with Belgium); Universal Service Co (with Germany); Universal Rent-a-car Co (with France 'EuropCar'); Associated: Federal Motor Co (agents for Renault cars & MAN trucks); Target Engineering & Construction Co; Al Ahlia General Trading Co Ltd
Principal Bankers: National Bank of Abu Dhabi; Arab Bank for Investment & Foreign Trade

Date of Establishment: 1973
No of Employees: 700

W S ATKINS & PARTNERS OVERSEAS

See ATKINS, W S, & PARTNERS OVERSEAS

WEATHERFORD BIN HAMOODAH

PO Box 4503, Abu Dhabi
Tel: 825963/4
Telex: 22644

Chairman: Faraj Ali Bin Hamoodah
Directors: L C S Gambrill, K K Bushati, R A Heureithi

PRINCIPAL ACTIVITIES: Oilfield services
Principal Bankers: Algemene Bank Nederland

Date of Establishment: 1983
No of Employees: 69

WEIR ENGINEERING SERVICES
WESCO
PO Box 4752, Mussafah, Abu Dhabi
Tel: 554108, 554436
Telex: 23336 Wplauh EM
Telefax: 553688

Senior Executives: J O'Neill (Works Manager), B Chew (Sales Engineer)

PRINCIPAL ACTIVITIES: General mechanical and electrical engineering, pump installation and repair, metal spraying, diesel engines repair, steel fabrication and welding, electric motor rewinding, field services to the oil, marine, industrial and power generation industries, oilfield services
Principal Agencies: Weir Pumps, Mather & Platt, NEI Peebles, Rolls Royce Engines, Petbow Generators
Parent Company: Weir Pumps Ltd, Glasgow, Scotland, UK

YOUSUF HABIB AL YOUSUF
See AL YOUSUF, YOUSUF HABIB,

ZAKUM CONSTRUCTION
PO Box 3611, Abu Dhabi
Tel: 825094
Cable: Zakum
Telex: 23005 ZAKUM EM

Chairman: Awad Mohd Al Otaiba
Directors: Mohan Kulkarni (Financial Controller), Alapati Ranga Rao (General Manager)
Senior Executives: D N Sardesai (Engineering Manager)

PRINCIPAL ACTIVITIES: Civil and mechanical engineering contractors
Principal Bankers: Emirates Commercial Bank; Abu Dhabi Commercial Bank; National Bank of Abu Dhabi; Commercial Bank of Dubai
Financial Information:

	Dh'000
Sales turnover	85,000
Authorised capital	5,000
Paid-up capital	5,000

Principal Shareholders: 100% owned by Chairman
Date of Establishment: 1976
No of Employees: 500

ZAKUM DEVELOPMENT CO (ZADCO)
PO Box 46808, Abu Dhabi
Tel: 661700
Cable: Upper Zakum Abu Dhabi
Telex: 22948 ZDC AUH EM
Telefax: 669448

Chairman: HE Suhail F Al Mazroui
Senior Executives: Y Hirai (General Manager), T Inahara (Asst General Manager Admin), M Viallard (Asst General Manager Operations), R Al Jarwan (Asst General Manager Technical)

PRINCIPAL ACTIVITIES: Oil producing and exporting
Parent Company: Abu Dhabi National Oil Company (ADNOC)

Principal Shareholders: ADNOC
Date of Establishment: 1977
No of Employees: 1,200

ZAROUNI, ABDULLA BIN AHMED, & BROS
PO Box 283, Abu Dhabi
Tel: 341823
Cable: Zarouni
Telex: 22351 EM

Chairman: Abdulla Bin Ahmed Zarouni
Directors: Mahmoud Bin Ahmed Zarouni (Managing Director)

PRINCIPAL ACTIVITIES: Manufacturers' representation, import and distribution of road construction equipment, rotary and stationary compressors, generators, tyres and pumps; engineering contractors
Principal Agencies: Sakai, Airman, Iwata, Denyo, Goodyear, Matra
Branch Offices: PO Box 1020, Al-Ain; PO Box 184, Dubai
Principal Bankers: Grindlays Bank, Abu Dhabi

Ajman

AJMAN BEACH HOTEL

PO Box 874, Al Khaleej Street, Ajman
Tel: 423333
Telex: 69519 BEOTEL EM

Senior Executives: Wadi Khoury (General Manager), S Nabil (Asst Manager), S Guptia (Financial Controller), J Khan (Chief Accountant), A Sharma (Personnel & Room Division Manager), R Chawdry (Food & Beverage Manager)

PRINCIPAL ACTIVITIES: Hotel business
Parent Company: Bhatia Bros
Subsidiary Companies: Pearl Hotel, Umm Al Quwain; Ajman Marina, Ajman
Principal Bankers: Abu Dhabi National Bank; Bank of Credit & Commerce

Date of Establishment: 1977
No of Employees: 70

AJMAN CEMENT COMPANY

PO Box 940, Ajman
Tel: 971-6-544611
Telex: 69563 AJCEM EM
Telefax: 971-6-544610

Senior Executives: Mohammed Al Shather (General Manager), Mohd Shariff (Finance & Admin Manager), Abdulkarim H Abusittah (Marketing Manager), T K Sen (Maintenance Manager), Mohd Manna (Production Manager)

PRINCIPAL ACTIVITIES: Cement manufacturing, OP & SR cement in bulk and bags
Principal Bankers: Bank of Oman Ltd, First Gulf Bank

Date of Establishment: 1984
No of Employees: 60

AJMAN INDUSTRIAL GASES CO

PO Box 1034, Ajman
Tel: 422209

Chairman: Raghib El Saqqa

PRINCIPAL ACTIVITIES: Industrial gases

AJMAN NATIONAL TRAVEL AGENCY

PO Box 641, Ajman
Tel: 422300

Chairman: HH Sheikh Mohammed Bin Ali Al Nuaimi
Directors: Syed M Salahuddin (Managing Director), Khalid Al Ghurair
Senior Executives: B Ramesh Kumar (General Manager)

PRINCIPAL ACTIVITIES: Travel agency
Principal Agencies: Air France; Alia; Sabena; Kuwait Airways; Syrian Arab Airlines; Air Lanka; MEA; Iraqi Airways; Thai Airways; SAS
Principal Bankers: Bank of Oman, Ajman
Financial Information:

	Dh'000
Authorised capital	1,000
Paid-up capital	1,000

Principal Shareholders: HE Sheikh Ammar Bin Humaid Al Nuaimi, HE Sheikh Mohammad Bin Ali Al Nuaimi, Abdul Rahman Saif Al Ghurair, Khalid Abdullah Al Ghurair, ETA Electro Mechanical Co
Date of Establishment: October 1976
No of Employees: 20

AL FOORAH TRADING & CONTRACTING CO

PO Box 1171, Ajman
Tel: 422459, 422655

Chairman: Mohammed Bin Khalifa Al Foorah

PRINCIPAL ACTIVITIES: General trading and contracting

ANZ GRINDLAYS BANK PLC

PO Box 452, Ajman
Tel: 22007
Cable: Grindlay
Telex: 69537 EM

PRINCIPAL ACTIVITIES: Commercial banking
Branch Offices: In the Middle East; Bahrain, Jordan, Oman, Pakistan, Qatar, United Arab Emirates (Abu Dhabi, Ajman, Dubai, Fujeirah, Sharjah, Umm Al Qaiwan)
Parent Company: Head office in London, UK

ARAB BANK PLC

PO Box 17, Ajman
Tel: 422431, 423192
Cable: Bankarabi

PRINCIPAL ACTIVITIES: Commercial banking
Branch Offices: Bahrain; Abu Dhabi; Dubai; Sharjah; Ras Al Khaimah; Ajman; Qatar; Oman; Lebanon; Saudi Arabia; Yemen; Tunisia; Morocco
Parent Company: Head office in Amman, Jordan

ARAB HEAVY INDUSTRIES LTD SA

PO Box 529, Ajman
Tel: 06-422134
Telex: 69511 Ahil EM
Telefax: 06-422137

Chairman: Obeid Ali Al Muheiri
Directors: Ali Abdullah Al Hamarni (Deputy Chairman), Majid Bin Mohammed Al Futtaim, Abdulla Bin Hamad Al Futtaim, Nasser Al Shazar, Hameed Khan, Mounir Y Moustafa, Mohammed Nasser Al Owais, Tetsuo Takeuchi, Kiyoshi Harada
Senior Executives: Kiyoshi Harada (General Manager), Tetsuo Kawashima (Production Manager), Haruo Imai (Marketing Manager)

PRINCIPAL ACTIVITIES: Maintenance and repair work for tug boats, barges, rigs, supply boats and other oil related equipment, steel fabrication work
Branch Offices: Mohd Bin Masood Bldg, Hamdan Street, Abu Dhabi, UAE
Associated Companies: Modec Inc, Japan
Principal Bankers: British Bank of the Middle East, Sharjah; Commercial Bank of Dubai, Sharjah; Middle East Bank, Dubai; National Bank of Abu Dhabi, Sharjah; Bank of Tokyo, Bahrain; Mitsui Taiyo Bank, Tokyo
Financial Information:

	1989/90 Dh'000
Sales turnover	25,103
Profits	3,635
Authorised capital	52,000
Paid-up capital	48,000
Total assets	56,429

Principal Shareholders: Ajman Government; Modec Inc; UAE citizens
Date of Establishment: 30 June 1975
No of Employees: 190

BANK OF CREDIT AND COMMERCE INTERNATIONAL SA

PO Box 146, Ajman
Tel: 422313
Cable: Bancrecom
Telex: 68121, 69509 BCCI AJ EM

PRINCIPAL ACTIVITIES: Commercial banking

UAE (Ajman)

Branch Offices: UAE (Abu Dhabi, Dubai, Sharjah, Ajman); Oman; Jordan
Parent Company: BCCI (Holdings) Luxembourg SA

BANK OF OMAN LIMITED

PO Box 11, Ajman
Tel: 422440
Cable: Banoman Ajman
Telex: 69575 EM

PRINCIPAL ACTIVITIES: Commercial banking
Branch Offices: Abu Dhabi, Dubai, Fujairah, Ras Al Khaimah, Sharjah, Umm Al Quwain
Parent Company: Head office in Dubai

BANK SADERAT IRAN

PO Box 16, Ajman
Tel: 22232
Cable: Saderbank
Telex: 45456 Dubai EM

PRINCIPAL ACTIVITIES: All banking transactions
Branch Offices: Abu Dhabi, Dubai, Fujairah, Ras Al Khaimah
Parent Company: Head office in Tehran, Iran

EMIRATES COAST ELECTRICAL TRADING & CONTRACTING CO

PO Box 120, Ajman
Tel: 22258

PRINCIPAL ACTIVITIES: Electrical engineering contractors, import and distribution of electrical and electronic equipment

ETISALAT

PO Box 40, Ajman
Tel: 422659, 422359
Telex: 69500 EM

PRINCIPAL ACTIVITIES: Telecommunications, telephone and telegraph systems
Branch Offices: Throughout the United Arab Emirates

FIRST GULF BANK

PO Box 414, Ajman
Tel: 423450
Cable: Firstgulf
Telex: 69510, 69512, 69565 Figulf EM
Telefax: 446503

Chairman: Rashid Bin Owaidah
Directors: Jawad Ahmad Bu Khamseen (Deputy Chairman)
Senior Executives: Abdullah Showaiter (Manager Credit & Marketing)

PRINCIPAL ACTIVITIES: Commercial banking, local and international, merchant and investment banking
Principal Bankers: Citibank, New York; Deutsche Bank, Frankfurt; Credit Suisse, Zurich; Tokai Bank, Tokyo; Lloyds Bank, London
Financial Information:

	1989/90 Dh'000
Profits	8,653
Authorised capital	120,000
Paid-up capital	120,000
Total assets	456,426

Date of Establishment: October 1979
No of Employees: 73

GULF INVESTMENT & REAL ESTATE CO

PO Box 172, Sh Rashid Bldg, Al Khour Street, Ajman
Tel: 422980
Cable: GIRECO
Telex: 69522 Gireco EM

PRINCIPAL ACTIVITIES: Investment advisors, real estate

GULFA MINERAL WATER & PROCESSING INDUSTRIES CO LTD

PO Box 929, Ajman
Tel: 422981/2
Cable: Gulfa
Telex: 69542 Gulfa EM

Chairman: Naser Mohamed Al Kharafi
Directors: Jawad Bu Khamseen, Abdul Wahab Al Mutawa, Mahmoud Razouqi, Moataz El Alfi
Senior Executives: Mohamed Ragheb Shakankiri (General Manager), Mukhtar Abdul Latif (Finance Manager), Esam Bakr (Factory Manager)

PRINCIPAL ACTIVITIES: Processing of mineral water and distribution
Subsidiary/Associated Companies: Gulf Investment and Real Estate Co (GIRECO); Kuwait Food Company (Americana) (KFC)
Principal Bankers: National Bank of Abu Dhabi; First Gulf Bank
Financial Information:

	Dh'000
Sales turnover	22,000
Authorised capital	20,000

Principal Shareholders: Government of Ajman; Gulf Investment and Real Estate Co; Kuwait Food Company
Date of Establishment: 1975
No of Employees: 90

ISLAMIC INVESTMENT CO OF THE GULF

PO Box 1388, Ajman
Tel: 421306
Telex: 68596

PRINCIPAL ACTIVITIES: Islamic investment banking
Branch Offices: Abu Dhabi
Parent Company: Head office in Sharjah

Principal Shareholders: Dar Al Maal Al Islami Group

ISOFOAM INSULATING MATERIALS PLANTS

PO Box 161, Ajman
Tel: 422529
Telex: 69564 Foam EM

PRINCIPAL ACTIVITIES: Manufacture of insulation and waterproofing materials
Branch Offices: Egypt, Morocco
Parent Company: Head office in Kuwait

NATIONAL BANK OF ABU DHABI

PO Box 988, Ajman
Tel: 422996
Telex: 69595 EM

PRINCIPAL ACTIVITIES: Commercial banking
Branch Offices: Abu Dhabi, Dubai, Fujairah, Ras Al Khaimah, Sharjah
Parent Company: Head office in Abu Dhabi

Date of Establishment: 1978

NATIONAL CONTRACTING CO LTD

PO Box 824, Ajman
Tel: 423244
Cable: NALCO
Telex: 69559 Nalco EM

Chairman: Abdulla Alireza

PRINCIPAL ACTIVITIES: General engineering contractors, electro-mechanical, civil, building, oil and gas, transport, shipping and forwarding agents; plant hire
Branch Offices: Main Office in Kuwait, PO Box 106, Safat, Tel 816836/840163, Telex 22962 NALCO KT/22070 REZAYAT KT and branches in Al Khobar, Riyadh, Jeddah (Saudi Arabia), Oman, London, Paris, New York, Boston

Principal Bankers: British Bank of the Middle East; Bank of Kuwait & the Middle East; Riyadh Bank Ltd; Morgan Guaranty Trust Co, Credit Suisse

Date of Establishment: 1977
No of Employees: 60

NATIONAL STEEL FACTORY

PO Box 99, Ajman
Tel: 22311

PRINCIPAL ACTIVITIES: Metal processing

SALAMAH INTERNATIONAL GENERAL CONTRACTING CO

PO Box 1566, Ajman
Tel: 548477
Telex: 68012 Cartel EM

PRINCIPAL ACTIVITIES: General and building contractors

SILENTNIGHT (UAE) LTD

PO Box 973, Ajman
Tel: 06-424511
Telex: 69560

Senior Executives: S Noonan (Managing Director)

PRINCIPAL ACTIVITIES: Supply of beds and furnishings
Parent Company: Silentnight Export, Barnwick, UK
Principal Bankers: Barclays Bank plc

Date of Establishment: 1978

STYRIA ENGINEERING WORKS

PO Box 301, Ajman
Tel: 424502, 424933
Telex: 69524 Styria EM

President: Heinz Adam (also Managing Director)

PRINCIPAL ACTIVITIES: Machine-shop, fabrication, plant-hire and repair
Associated Companies: Hiebel and Co, PO Box 301, Ajman, UAE
Principal Bankers: BCCI, Ajman

Dubai

ABBAS AHMAD AL SHAWAF & BROS CO WLL
See AL SHAWAF, ABBAS AHMAD, & BROS CO WLL

ABBAS ALI AL HAZEEM & SONS TRADING CO
See AL HAZEEM, ABBAS ALI, & SONS TRADING CO

ABDALLA CONTRACTING & TRADING
PO Box 6655, Dubai
Tel: 295503

Chairman: Abdalla Saleh Al Bassam

PRINCIPAL ACTIVITIES: Trading in commodities, import of iron and steel, cement and other building materials, civil, mechanical and electrical contracting, fabrication of oil and chemical tanks, fire fighting systems, suppliers of industrial and protective footwear, telephone/power cables
Parent Company: Head office in Kuwait

ABDUL AZIZ YOUSUF AL ESSA & CO WLL
See AL ESSA, ABDUL AZIZ YOUSUF, & CO WLL

ABDULLA SULTAN ALSHARHAN
See ALSHARHAN, ABDULLA SULTAN,

ABELA & CO PVT LTD
PO Box 1556, Deira, Dubai
Tel: 225251
Cable: Alabela Dubai
Telex: 45477 Abela EM

Chairman: Albert Abela
Directors: Adeeb Nadar (Senior Vice President), Saleh Tassabehji (Area Manager), Hani Abdelnour (Asst Area Manager), Issam Zorob (Area Accountant)

PRINCIPAL ACTIVITIES: Caterers and food suppliers for oil companies, contractors, hotels, airports' catering and manufacturers' representations (foodstuffs)
Branch Offices: Abu Dhabi, Dubai, Sharjah, Ras Al Kahimah
Parent Company: Albert Abela Corporation
Principal Bankers: Commercial Bank of Dubai; Banque Paribas

No of Employees: 1800

ADEL ALGHANIM ESTABLISHMENT
See ALGHANIM, ADEL, ESTABLISHMENT

ADEL MOHD HAMAD AL SUMAIT
See AL SUMAIT, ADEL MOHD HAMAD,

AEROGULF SERVICES CO (PVT) LTD
PO Box 10566, Dubai
Tel: 245157
Telex: 46674 Aero EM
Telefax: 246035

Chairman: Abdulla Hassan Al Rostamani
Directors: Major Juma Saif Rashed Bin Bakhit (Executive Vice Chairman), Khalifa Juma Al Nabooda, Mohamed Mir Hashem Khoory
Senior Executives: U J Sobiecki (General Manager), P Mortimer (Chief Engineer)

PRINCIPAL ACTIVITIES: Operation of helicopter, offshore support operation, helicopter and aircraft maintenance facility

Principal Agencies: King Radio; Avco Lycoming Engines; MBB Service Station; Aeromaritime (Allison Engines); Chadwick - Helmuth
Principal Bankers: Emirates Bank International

Principal Shareholders: Chairman and directors as described
Date of Establishment: 1976
No of Employees: 70

AHMAD BAHMAN
See BAHMAN, AHMAD,

AHMED AL SARRAF TRADING EST
See AL SARRAF, AHMED, TRADING EST

AHMED SAYID HASHIM AL GHARABALLY
See AL GHARABALLY, AHMED SAYID HASHIM,

AIRDYNE SERVICES
PO Box 10620, Dubai
Tel: 258990
Telex: 46508 ELGLF EM

PRINCIPAL ACTIVITIES: Mechanical, electrical and plumbing system suppliers, and contractors
Parent Company: A Division of Ellis Gulf Ltd

AL ABBAS TRADING COMPANY
PO Box 327, Dubai
Tel: 521000, 377770, 222656
Cable: Burhan
Telex: 45654 Burhan EM
Telefax: 521200

Directors: Ebrahim Abdulnabi Al Abbas (President), Ismail Abdulnabi Al Abbas (Vice President)
Senior Executives: T E Fernandes (General Manager), V O Sebastian (Sales Manager)

PRINCIPAL ACTIVITIES: Import and distribution of office equipment, household appliances and office furniture, mini/micro computers, computer related products, word processors, medical equipment, technical parts, pharmaceutical products
Principal Agencies: IBM, Minolta, Adler, Postalia, Ideal, Steelcase, Korody-Colyer, 3M, Wabco, Zippel, Lanier, Creda, Fantoni, Dauphin, Lineager, Archiutti, Datacard, Fireking Int'l, Interfinish, Neusielder, Life Fitness, Woheico
Branch Offices: PO Box 3471, Abu Dhabi, UAE, Tel 463656; PO Box 5423, Sharjah, UAE, Tel 591744, PO Box 1484, Al Ain, UAE Tel 642534
Subsidiary Companies: International Office Supplies, PO Box 2994, Dubai; Publilink Advertising, Marketing, Public Relations, PO Box 6712, Dubai; Hadi Enterprises, PO Box 5833, Dubai; National Medical Supplies, PO Box 327, Dubai; Al Abbas Technical Supplies & Services, PO Box 10172, Dubai
Principal Bankers: Citibank, Dubai
Financial Information:

	1990 Dh'000
Sales turnover	76,000

Principal Shareholders: Directors as described
Date of Establishment: 1967
No of Employees: 300

AL ACCAD TRADING COMPANY
PO Box 4194, Dubai
Tel: 224777, 222970, 220111
Telex: 45604 Accad EM

PRINCIPAL ACTIVITIES: Scientific and medical equipment and supplies, motor spare parts, glassware, bakery and supermarket

Branch Offices: Scientific Dept, PO Box 5335, Dubai, Tel
281333, Telex 47420; Spare Parts Dept, PO Box 2166, Dubai,
Tel 660606
Subsidiary Companies: Modern Bakery & Supermarket, PO Box
5558, Dubai, Tel 471100, Telex 47112; Bohemian Crystal Co,
PO Box 3407, Dubai; Crystal Stores, PO Box 200, Dubai

AL AHLI BANK OF KUWAIT KSC

PO Box 1719, Dubai
Tel: 224175/9
Cable: Ahlibank
Telex: 45518 EM
Telefax: 215527

Chairman: Saoud Al Abdul Razzak
Directors: Suleiman Sukkar, Bernard Thiolon, Mohammad
Abdel-Aziz Al-Wazzan, Husain Makki Al-Juma, Abdel-Kader
Tash, Khalifa Youssef Al-Roumi, Bruno Davezac

PRINCIPAL ACTIVITIES: Commercial banking
Parent Company: Alahli Bank of Kuwait, Kuwait
Associated Companies: Al-Ahli Bank, Kuwait; Jordan National
Bank, Jordan; Credit Lyonnais, France; UBAF, France
Financial Information:

	Dh'000
Authorised capital	40,000
Paid-up capital	40,000

Principal Shareholders: Al-Ahli Bank of Kuwait (50%), Jordan
National Bank (25%), Credit Lyonnais (25%)
Date of Establishment: 1969
No of Employees: 30

AL AHLIA INSURANCE CO SAK

PO Box 3429, Dubai
Tel: 222020

Chairman: Yousef Ibrahim Alghanim
Directors: Yacoub Yousef Al Humaidi, Issa Ahmad Al Khalaf,
Hamad Abdullah Al Saqr, Fawzi Mohammed Al Kharafi, Isam
Mohammed Al Bahar, Osamah Mohammed Al Nisf, Abdul
Aziz Abdul Razzaq Al Jassar

PRINCIPAL ACTIVITIES: Insurance and reinsurance
Parent Company: Head office in Kuwait

AL AHMADIAH CONTRACTING & TRADING

PO Box 2596, Dubai
Tel: 450900 (10 lines)
Cable: Comatco
Telex: 45703 CNTRA EM
Telefax: 450327

President: HE Sheikh Hasher Maktoum Juma Al Maktoum
Directors: Ramesh Menda (Acting President), Mahesh Menda, S
K Joshi, Cyrus J Sabavala
Senior Executives: A K Vora (Executive Engineer), Shiv Datt
(Finance Manager)

PRINCIPAL ACTIVITIES: Building and civil engineering
contractors engaged in various major construction projects;
import and distribution of building materials
Branch Offices: PO Box 2752, Abu Dhabi, Tel 461434, Telex
22877; PO Box 1267, Al Ain
Parent Company: Al Fajer Enterprises (Holding Company), PO
Box 1600, Dubai
Associated Companies: Lunar Electro, Dubai; Al Fajer Est,
Dubai; Al Fajer Decoration Co, Dubai; Al Fajer Department
Stores, Dubai; Al Fajer Information & Services, Dubai; Al Fajer
Medical Supplies, Dubai; Al Fajer Fashions, Dubai; Al Fajer
Engineering Consultants, Dubai
Principal Bankers: British Bank of the Middle East, Dubai
Financial Information:

	1989/90 Dh'000
Sales turnover	100,000
Paid-up capital	25,000

Principal Shareholders: Fully owned by President
Date of Establishment: 1970
No of Employees: 1,500

AL AMAR ENGINEERING & CONTRACTING CO

PO Box 2449, Dubai
Tel: 257153, 257154
Cable: ALAMAR
Telex: 46229 Alamar EM

Senior Executives: Issa I Farah (General manager)

PRINCIPAL ACTIVITIES: Building and civil engineering,
contractors
Branch Offices: Sharjah; Ras Al Khaimah; Ajman; Umm Al
Qaiwan; Fujeirah, Abu Dhabi
Subsidiary Companies: Alamar Engineering & Contracting Co
(Abu Dhabi)
Principal Bankers: Arab African International Bank, Dubai; Arab
Bank plc, Dubai

Principal Shareholders: Proprietor: Issa I Farah
Date of Establishment: August, 1967
No of Employees: 289

AL ASHRAM CONTRACTING CO

PO Box 1290, Dubai
Tel: 257812/3
Telex: 46913 Nasag EM

Partner: Saif Al-Ashram
Directors: Nabil N Ghazal (Managing Partner)

PRINCIPAL ACTIVITIES: Building construction and civil work
Branch Offices: Al- Ashram Contracting Co, PO Box 15494, Al-
Ain, UAE
Subsidiary Companies: Al-Ashram Contracting Co, E.T.P.O. &
L.T.P.A., PO Box 1290, Dubai, UAE
Principal Bankers: Bank of Oman Ltd, Deira - Dubai; Banque de
l'Orient Arabe et d'Outre-Mer, Deira - Dubai

Principal Shareholders: Said Al-Ashram, Nabil N Ghazal
Date of Establishment: Mid June 1974
No of Employees: 850

AL BAHAR, MOHAMED ABDULRAHMAN,

PO Box 1170, Deira, Dubai
Tel: (04) 660255
Cable: Moatasim Dubai
Telex: 45445 Bahar EM
Telefax: (04) 667342

Chairman: Mohamed Abdulrahman Al-Bahar
Directors: Jassim Al-Bahar (President), Issam Al-Bahar
(Executive Vice President), Mohamed Numan (Deputy Group
General Manager)
Senior Executives: Ashfaque Azad (Area Manager - UAE),
Anton Hayek (General Parts & Service Manager), Walid
Shtayyeh (Central Personnel Manager)

PRINCIPAL ACTIVITIES: Distribution of earthmoving, material
handling, compaction and asphalt equipment, generators and
control systems
Principal Agencies: Caterpillar Overseas, Switzerland;
Caterpillar Tractor Co, USA; Koehring Int, USA; Oshkosh Int,
USA
Branch Offices: Arabian Gulf (Abu Dhabi, Sharjah, Doha,
Bahrain)
Parent Company: Head office in Kuwait
Associated Companies: Oasis Trading & Equipment Co, PO Box
7002, Muttrah, Oman
Principal Bankers: British Bank of the Middle East; Arab Bank

Principal Shareholders: Mohamed Abdulrahman Al-Bahar
Date of Establishment: 1964 in Dubai
No of Employees: 140

AL BAQER CORPORATION (PIMS DIVN)

PO Box 2551, Dubai
Tel: 434597, 436297
Telex: 46792 Pims EM

Directors: Adam Haggart (Managing Director)

PRINCIPAL ACTIVITIES: Manufacturers' representatives, supply
of air-conditioning equipment, and spares, flooring materials;
commission agents, environmental control for computer areas
Principal Agencies: Temperature Ltd, UK; Wacpac Ltd, UK;
Floating Floors Inc, USA; Environmental Span Floors Ltd, UK
Principal Bankers: National Bank of Dubai

Date of Establishment: 1977

AL BOGARI TRADING COMPANY

PO Box 4048, Dubai
Tel: 229645 (Sales), 224530 (Office)
Cable: Consotrade
Telex: 45896 Constd EM
Telefax: 228741

Directors: Farook Kassim (Managing Director)

PRINCIPAL ACTIVITIES: Trading, export, import and re-export
of general merchandise including chemicals, foodstuffs,
general trading activities, wholesale
Principal Bankers: Habib Bank AG, Zurich; Bank of Oman; Bank
of Credit and Commerce (Emirates)

AL BOOM MARINE

Al Sumait, Adel Mohd Hamad,

PO Box 5108, Dubai
Tel: 690080
Telex: 45597
Telefax: 661361

Chairman: Adel Mohd Hamad Al Sumait

PRINCIPAL ACTIVITIES: Boats, generators, pumps, marine
equipment, diving equipment, etc
Parent Company: Head office in Kuwait

ALBWARDY INTERNATIONAL AERADIO

PO Box 9197, Dubai
Tel: 523331
Cable: Intaerio
Telex: 46296 ABIAL EM
Telefax: 529128

Chairman: Ali Saeed Juma Albwardy
Directors: Colin J Sansom, A F P Ball, Mohd Beyatt
Senior Executives: A F P Ball (General Manager)

PRINCIPAL ACTIVITIES: Aviation and communication equipment
supply
Branch Offices: Abu Dhabi International Aeradio, PO Box 3164,
Abu Dhabi
Parent Company: Head office in Southall, Middlesex, UK
Principal Bankers: Lloyds Bank Plc, Dubai
Financial Information:

	1990
	Dh'000
Sales turnover	13,500
Authorised capital	1,000
Paid-up capital	1,000
Total assets	3,455

Principal Shareholders: A S Albwardy (51%), IAL (49%)
No of Employees: 65

ALBWARDY MARINE ENGINEERING

PO Box 6515, Dubai
Tel: 520014, 520319
Cable: Bwardy Dubai
Telex: 47263 Bwrdy EM
Telefax: 524909

Chairman: Ali Saeed AlBawardy
Directors: Mohammed Bayat, Renier Meuleman (Managing
Partner)
Senior Executives: R Bhesania (Shipyard Manager), Chen Yo
Sin (Ship's Manager), H Deweers (Operations Manager)

PRINCIPAL ACTIVITIES: Ship repairers, mechanical repairs on
engines, fabrication-steel repairs, electrical rewinding of
motors, generators, wet docking and hydro blasting, under
water cleaning, C.O.W. installation, AC repairs, fully equipped
machine shop, remetalling of bearings, owners of supply
boats, crewboats and tugboats
Principal Agencies: G.M. Detroit Diesel Engines; Deep Sea Seal;
Yamamizu -Crude Oil Washing Machines
Associated Companies: Spinney's, Marine Inspection Company,
Albwardy Shipping Agency; Deepsea Fisheries
Principal Bankers: ABN Bank, Dubai
Financial Information:

	1988/89	1989/90
	Dh'000	Dh'000
Sales turnover	30,000	34,000
Paid-up capital	4,500	5,500
Total assets	12,000	16,000

Principal Shareholders: Ali Saeed Albwardy; Mohammed Bayat;
Reinier Meuleman; Sembawang Maritime
Date of Establishment: 1st March 1979
No of Employees: 280

ALBWARDY-IAL

PO Box 10380, Dubai
Tel: 257111
Cable: Intaerio Dubai
Telex: 46296 ABIAL EM

Chairman: Ali Saeed Al Bwardy
Directors: Mahmoud Gassim, Colin Sansom, Alastair Ball
Senior Executives: A F P Ball (General Manager), R Thompson
(Marketing Manager), Oliver Moraes (Financial Controller), P
Ellis (Engineering Manager)

PRINCIPAL ACTIVITIES: Telecommunications, technical
services, marine navigation, fire-safety-security, hotel
management, electronics
Principal Agencies: Racal-Milgo Limited; Japan Radio Corpn;
General Electric Mobile Radio; Sperry Marine Systems; Aga
Navigation Aids; Kelvin Hughes; Calcomp; AWA; AEL;
Casella; Trioving,; Budde; Mannesmann Tally
Parent Company: British Telecom Plc UK / International Aeradio
Plc
Principal Bankers: Lloyds Bank International
Financial Information:

	1988/89	1989/90
	Dh'000	Dh'000
Sales turnover	11,255	12,845
Profits	809	721
Authorised capital	1,000	1,000
Paid-up capital	1,000	1,000
Total assets	2,992	2,671

Principal Shareholders: British Telecom Plc UK; Ali Saeed Al
Bwardy, Dubai, UAE
Date of Establishment: January 1980
No of Employees: 55

AL ESSA, ABDUL AZIZ YOUSUF, & CO WLL

PO Box 290, Dubai
Tel: 482915
Telefax: 480584

Chairman: Abdul Aziz Yousuf Al Essa

PRINCIPAL ACTIVITIES: Supplies of chemical products, welding
equipment and generators, engineering products, oilfield
equipment, safety equipment, hospital and laboratory supplies
and equipment
Parent Company: Head office in Kuwait

ALEXANDER STENHOUSE

PO Box 50832, Dubai
Tel: 345641
Telex: 45704 Alzsh EM
Telefax: (0971-4) 344348

Directors: Peter J Bleach (Managing Director)
Senior Executives: Nandu Babur (Manager)

PRINCIPAL ACTIVITIES: Risk management and insurance
broking
Parent Company: Alexander & Alexander International Inc, New
York, USA
Associated Companies: Al Salamah Arabian Agencies Ltd,
Saudi Arabia
Principal Bankers: Standard Chartered Bank

Date of Establishment: 1971

AL FAJER DEPARTMENT STORES

PO Box 1600, Umm Hurair Road, Dubai
Tel: 371600
Cable: Dawn
Telex: 47126 ALFJR EM
Telefax: (9714) 371611

President: H H Sheikh Hasher Maktoum Juma Al Maktoum
Senior Executives: Ahmed Mazhar (Sales Manager), S K Joshi
(Executive Vice President)

PRINCIPAL ACTIVITIES: Department stores in ladies', men's
and children's fashions, household goods and appliances,
furniture, home furnishing, supermarket, gifts, watches,
books, luggage, sports goods, pharmacy, perfumes and
cosmetics, electronics etc; also wholesalers of consumer
products and suppliers of printing machineries/accessories,
graphic equipment and news print paper throughout the UAE
Principal Agencies: K Shoes Makers, UK; Spring AG,
Switzerland, Rug Doctor, USA; J W Bonser, UK; Uves Winter
Optik, W Germany; Aqualona, UK; Garfield Glass, UK; Miller
Johannisberg Druckmashinen, W Germany; Hartmann, W
Germany; Polychrome, W Germany; Toyobo, Japan;
Mitsubishi, Japan; Kimoto, Switzerland; Konica, Japan;
Crosfield, UK; Eskofot, Denmark, Harris Graphics, France
Subsidiary/Associated Companies: Al Fajer Enterprises; Al
Ahmadiah Contg & Trading; Lunar Electro; Al Fajer
Information & Media Services; Al Fajer Decoration Co; Al
Fajer Display & Fittings; Al Fajer Fashions
Principal Bankers: United Arab Bank; Middle East Bank

Principal Shareholders: Proprietorship
Date of Establishment: 1978
No of Employees: 150

AL FALAH BUILDING MATERIALS & TRADING CO

PO Box 1864, Dubai
Tel: 661568, 667125, 663230
Cable: Farraco Dubai
Telex: 46369 Farra EM
Telefax: 691766

Chairman: Muktar Farra
Directors: Akram Farra
Managing Partner: Zeki Farra

PRINCIPAL ACTIVITIES: Import of building materials; ceramic
wall and floor tiles, and sanitary ware; formica; adhesives;
kitchen and wardrobe furniture
Principal Agencies: Iris Ceramic Tiles; Formica Brand Laminate;
Manhattan Furniture
Associated Companies: Abu Dhabi Building Materials & Cont Co
(Sister Co), PO Box 558, Abu Dhabi
Principal Bankers: Arab Bank Ltd; Banque de l'Orient Arab et
d'Outre Mer; Lloyds Bank Ltd

Principal Shareholders: Farra family
Date of Establishment: 1972

AL FARDAN EXCHANGE CO

PO Box 2095, Dubai
Tel: 226111/2, 224788
Telex: 46240 Farbk EM

PRINCIPAL ACTIVITIES: Money exchange
Branch Offices: Abu Dhabi, Sharjah
Parent Company: Head office in Qatar

AL FARKAD TRADING ESTABLISHMENT

PO Box 55972, Dubai
Tel: 226399
Telefax: 285677

PRINCIPAL ACTIVITIES: Supply of printing machines, computer
peripherals, industrial equipment, spare parts, electrical
cables, etc
Parent Company: Head office in Kuwait

ALFULAIJ & COMPANY

PO Box 1008, Dubai
Tel: 226411, 222037, 222461
Cable: Alfulaij Dubai
Telex: 45935 Alfco EM

Directors: M/S Fahad Abdulaziz Alfulaij & Bros, Mohammad
Abdullah Aljamea (Managing Partner)
Senior Executives: Imtiaz Uddin (Manager)

PRINCIPAL ACTIVITIES: Import and distribution of drilling
equipment, light machinery, welding equipment, garage
equipment and tools
Principal Agencies: Snap-on Tools, Ridgid Tools, Joy
Compressors, Hartridge Diesel Test Equipments, Lincoln
Welding Equipment, Osborn Brushes, Link 51 Storage and
Shelving Equipment, KPT Kawasaki Pneumatic Tools, Toshiba
Electric Tools
Branch Offices: Kuwait; Bahrain
Subsidiary Companies: Alfulaij & Co Trading Centre, PO Box
7664, Abu Dhabi, UAE
Principal Bankers: National Bank of Dubai Ltd

Principal Shareholders: Fahad Abdul Aziz Alfulaij Bros;
Mohammad Abdullah Aljamea
Date of Establishment: 1963
No of Employees: 40

AL FUTTAIM GROUP (HOLDING COMPANY)

PO Box 152, Dubai
Tel: 224101/9
Cable: Alfuttaim
Telex: 45462 EM

President: Majid Al Futtaim
Directors: Sheikh Hamad Al Futtaim, Abdulla Hamad Al Futtaim
(Vice President)

PRINCIPAL ACTIVITIES: Trading, industry, real estate,
construction, contracting, engineering, insurance & advertising
Principal Agencies: Toyota, Honda, Chrysler & Dodge, Volvo
BM, Hino Trucks, National Panasonic, Fisher, Sanyo,
Toshiba, Seiko Watches, Timex, Alba, Pentel, Caran D'Ache,
Toyo Tyres, Yanmar Marine Engines, G S Batteries, Rob Roy,
General Tire, Siera, Zoppas, Zettler, Wisi Product, Raymond
Weil, Volvo Trucks & Cars, Kolber
Branch Offices: UAE Branches: Abu Dhabi, Sharjah, Al Ain, Ras
Al Khaimah, Fujairah, Umm Al Qaiwain, Ajman, Dhaid, Khor
Fakkan; Overseas Operations: USA, Egypt, Qatar, Oman,
Singapore, Pakistan
Parent Company: Al Futtaim (Private) Limited
Subsidiaries/Associated Companies: Al Futtaim (Pvt) Ltd, PO
Box 152, Dubai, Tel 224101/9, Telex 45462 Futaim Em; Al
Futtaim Trading (Pvt) Ltd, PO Box 7880, Dubai, Tel 224101/9,
Telex 45462 Futaim Em; Al Futtaim Industries (Pvt) Ltd, PO
Box 152, Dubai, Tel 224101, Telex 47730 Indus Em; Al
Futtaim Real Estate (Pvt) Ltd, PO Box 152, Dubai, Tel
224101/9, Telex 45462 Futaim Em; Al Futtaim Wimpey (Pvt)

Ltd, PO Box 1811, Dubai, Tel 236200, Telex 47523 Alwim Em; Al Futtaim Willis Faber (Pvt) Ltd, PO Box 152, Dubai, Tel 236082, 236089, Telex 45665 Arion Em; Arab Orient Insurance Co (Pte) Ltd, PO Box 152, Dubai, Tel 236069, 236082, 213425, Telex 45665 AROIN

Principal Bankers: Middle East Bank; Bank of Oman; National Bank of Abu Dhabi; Amro Bank; Standard Chartered Bank; Royal Bank of Canada; Arab African Bank; Arab Bank Ltd; British Bank of the Middle East; United Bank

Principal Shareholders: Majid Al Futtaim, Abdulla Hamad Al Futtaim, Sheikh Hamad Al Futtaim
Date of Establishment: 1952, incorporated 1980
No of Employees: 3,500

AL FUTTAIM TOWER SCAFFOLDING (PVT) LTD

PO Box 5502, Dubai
Tel: 251368, 257726
Cable: AFTOWER
Telex: 46086 Scaff EM

Chairman: Peter Bonner
Directors: Michael C H Hemery, K C Mohan, Hasan Irshad

PRINCIPAL ACTIVITIES: Manufacture of scaffolding and steel products for sale, rental and contract; and general fabrication
Principal Agencies: Western Gear, Belgium; London & Midland Steel Scaffolding Co, UK; F Amadio Ind, Italy; Pressco, UK; Cradle Runways, UK
Branch Offices: PO Box 555, Abu Dhabi, Tel 727510, Telex 23957, Fax 783357
Parent Company: Al Futtaim Group, PO Box 152, Dubai
Principal Bankers: Grindlays Bank; Middle East Bank

Principal Shareholders: Majid Al-Futtaim, Abdullah Al-Futtaim
Date of Establishment: June 1975
No of Employees: 150

AL GARGAWI TRADING STORES

PO Box 558, Dubai
Tel: 221013, 283768, 223006, 227718, 258096
Cable: Gargawi Dubai
Telex: 45996 Grgawi EM

Chairman: Mohd Noor Gargawi
Directors: Ali Ebrahim Gargawi
Senior Executives: S G Pillai

PRINCIPAL ACTIVITIES: Importers, manufacturers' representatives, wholesalers commission agents
Principal Agencies: Dico, Holland; Meblo, Yugoslavia; Stkarasek, Austria; Cooperative Spazzolai, Italy; Chin Yang Chemicals, Korea; Lius Wheel Com Ltd, Taiwan; Eurofloor, Luxembourg; Goodwill Coir Manufacturing, India
Branch Offices: Al Gargawi Trading Organisation, PO Box 1258, Dubai, UAE; Al Gargawi Furniture Centre (Showroom), Dubai, UAE
Subsidiary Companies: Al Gargawi Furniture Centre; Al Gargawi Trading Est
Principal Bankers: British Bank of the Middle East, Dubai; National Bank of Dubai Ltd, Dubai; Bank of Oman Ltd, Dubai; Middle East Bank, Dubai

Principal Shareholders: Mohamed Noor Gargawi, Ali Ebrahim Gargawi
Date of Establishment: 1956

AL GARSH GROUP OF COMPANIES

PO Box 24925, Dubai
Tel: 480464 (4 lines), 480342, 480971, 341619, 341152
Cable: Al-Garsh
Telex: 46629 GARSH EM
Telefax: (971 4) 481530

Proprietor: Ahmed Obaid Al-Garsh
Directors: Radwan Wahba (Managing Director)

PRINCIPAL ACTIVITIES: Manufacture of mosaic tiles, paving and plain roof cement tiles, marble (all kinds of natural and granite marble) and aluminium products for the construction industry also general transport, contracting
Subsidiary Companies: Satwa Automatic Mosaic Tiles & Marble Factory PO Box 4925, Dubai; Al Farashah General Trading, PO Box 982, Dubai; Al Jarsh Transport & Contracting, PO Box 982, Dubai; Al Garsh Aluminium Factory, PO Box 982, Dubai
Principal Bankers: British Bank of the Middle East; Bank of Oman; Bank of Credit & Commerce International; Citibank NV, Dubai

Date of Establishment: 1969
No of Employees: 200

ALGEMENE BANK NEDERLAND NV

PO Box 2567, Dubai
Tel: 225156
Cable: Bancolanda
Telex: 45610 Abn EM

PRINCIPAL ACTIVITIES: Commercial banking
Branch Offices: Abu Dhabi, Sharjah
Parent Company: Head Office: Algemene Bank Nederland NV, Amsterdam, Netherlands

AL GHANDI, SAEED MOHAMED, & SONS

PO Box 1034, Dubai
Tel: 663500
Cable: FLASI
Telex: 45822 Flasi EM
Telefax: 664702

Chairman: Saeed Mohamed Al Ghandi
Directors: Matar Al Tayer (Managing Director)
Senior Executives: J Kurup (Manager Machinery Div), Harbi Sandouk (Manager Lube & Tyre Div), M John (Manager Al Ghandi Marketing)

PRINCIPAL ACTIVITIES: General trade, agents, dealing in construction and transportation equipment also bathroom and kitchen furniture and accessories through Al Ghandi Marketing; and electrical engineering and equipment through Al Ghandi General Trading Co; electronics equipment appliances and lighting systems of Philips products, through Al Ghandi Electronics
Principal Agencies: FMC, USA; Terberg, Holland; Furukawa Battery, Japan; Kumho, S Korea; Fina Chemicals, UK; Jacob delafon, France; Schock, Germany; Carron, UK; Isoklepa, Germany; Zucchetti, Italy; Brown Boveri; SACE, Italy; CEAG, Germany; BBC-CEM, France; Pogliano, Italy; Philips, Holland; Linkbelt, USA
Branch Offices: PO Box 365, Abu Dhabi, Tel 329292, Fax 314437
Subsidiary/Associated Companies: Al Ghandi Marketing, Tel 237595; Al Ghandi General Trading Co, PO Box 5991, Dubai, Tel 420550, Telex 47068; Al Ghandi Electronics, PO Box 9098, Dubai, Tel 376600
Principal Bankers: Bank of Oman

Date of Establishment: 1970
No of Employees: 150

ALGHANIM, ADEL, ESTABLISHMENT

PO Box 55542, Dubai
Tel: 625087
Telefax: 625522

Chairman: Adel Alghanim

PRINCIPAL ACTIVITIES: Civil contracting, oilfield services
Parent Company: Head office in Kuwait

ALGHANIM, ALI & FOUAD, EST

PO Box 36, Dubai
Tel: 260847

Directors: Ali Mohd Thunian Alghanim, Fouad Mohd Thunian Alghanim

PRINCIPAL ACTIVITIES: Manufacturers' representatives, civil, mechanical and electrical contractors, import and distribution of electrical equipment, building materials, heavy machinery and earthmoving equipment, transportation
Parent Company: Head office in Kuwait

ALGHANIM, YUSUF AHMAD, & SONS

PO Box 11288, Dubai
Tel: 220278

Chairman: Kutayba Yusuf Alghanim
President: Bassam Yusuf Alghanim

PRINCIPAL ACTIVITIES: Contracting, electronics and electrical engineering, general trading, import and distribution of cars and spare parts, domestic electrical appliances, industrial lubricants, communication equipment, mechanical and industrial equipment, also shipping and forwarding, car hire and travel agency, toys retailing, cameras, insulation materials, etc
Parent Company: Head office in Kuwait
Principal Bankers: Chase Manhattan Bank, Citibank, ABN, Lloyds Bank, Algemene Bank, Gulf International Bank, Credit Suisse, all Kuwaiti and Saudi banks

AL GHARABALLY, AHMED SAYID HASHIM,

PO Box 1004, Dubai
Tel: 536603, 223184/5/6
Cable: Gharabally
Telex: 55690 Gharab EM

Chairman: Ahmed Sayid Hashim Al Gharabally
Directors: Hameed Gharabally
Senior Executives: Ali Mohd Abdulla Al Sharhan (General Manager)

PRINCIPAL ACTIVITIES: General trading, manufacturer's representation, show rooms and service station
Principal Agencies: Fiat Gruppo Automobili, Italy; Seat, Spain; Bata; Royal Insurance Co Ltd, UK
Branch Offices: PO Box 191, Bahrain; PO Box 471, Muscat
Parent Company: Head Office: PO Box 98, Kuwait
Principal Bankers: British Bank of the Middle East, Dubai; Commercial Bank of Dubai; National Bank of Dubai; BCCI (Overseas) Ltd

Date of Establishment: 1965
No of Employees: 110

AL GHURAIR GROUP OF COMPANIES

PO Box 1, Dubai
Tel: (04) 693311 (15 lines)
Cable: GRAIR
Telex: 45438 GRAIR EM
Telefax: (04) 660850

Chairman: Saif Ahmed Majed Al-Ghurair
Directors: Abdulla Ahmed Majed Al-Ghurair (Vice Chairman), Abdulrahman Saif Al-Ghurair, Jamal Majed Al-Ghurair, Abdulaziz Abdulla Al-Ghurair
Senior Executives: Marwan Ahmed Al Ghurair (General Manager), Eissa Abdulla Al Ghurair (General Manager), Juma Ahmed Al Ghurair (General Manager), Abdulla Majed Al Ghurair (General Manager), Ahmed R Hatahet (General Manager Gulf Extrusions), Khaid Abdullah Al Ghurair (General Manager Property Services), Ahmed Adam Awad (General Manager Administration), Zeyad S Suhaimat (General Manager Union Mosaic & Marble Co), K Thomas (General Manager Gulf Utensils), Khalil Mattar (Manager Abu Dhabi Br), Mohamed H Al Kailani (Legal Advisor), Khawaja R Ahmed (Manager Accounts & Audit)

PRINCIPAL ACTIVITIES: General contracting, extrusion of aluminium sections, and manufacture and distribution of aluminium windows, doors, utensils, PVC pipes, tiles and marbles, cement, mineral waters. Also banking and exchange dealers, real estate, owners of flour mills, printing press, concrete mixers and packaging factory; importers and exporters
Branch Offices: Abu Dhabi, PO Box 727, Tel 820176; Sultanate of Oman and other neighbouring Arab Countries
Parent Company: Al Ghurair Holdings (Private) Ltd (Al Ghurair Industries (Private) Ltd)
Subsidiary Companies: Gulf Extrusions Ltd; Arabian Aluminium Co; Gulf Utensils; Gulf Import & Export Co; Arabian Mix; National Floor Mills Co Ltd; Al Ghurair Publishing & Printing House; Union Mosaic & Marble Co; Masafi Mineral Water Co; Al Ghurair Exchange; Al Ghurair Industries (Pvt) Ltd; Al-Ghurair Centre; Associated Companies: Ghurair Crown (Engineering) Ltd; Emirate Trading Agency; National Cement Co Ltd; National Concrete Products Ltd; Associated Constructions Ltd; Rawda Quarries Ltd; Arabian Packaging Company
Principal Bankers: Bank of Oman Ltd, Dubai
Financial Information:

	1989/90 Dh'000
Sales turnover	800,000
Authorised capital	1,300,000

Principal Shareholders: Saif Ahmed Majed Al Ghurair; Abdulla Ahmed Majed Al Ghurair
Date of Establishment: 1960/61
No of Employees: 3,000

AL GURG BUILDING SERVICES (PVT) LTD CO

PO Box 325, Dubai
Tel: 857770
Cable: GURG DUBAI
Telex: 46349 Fabrik EM

Chairman: Easa Saleh Al Gurg
Directors: Saleh Easa Al Gurg
Senior Executives: Martin J Pollock (Manager)

PRINCIPAL ACTIVITIES: Manufacturers & suppliers of steel mesh/fabric reinforcement for concrete (fusion bonded epoxy coated reinforcement mesh & rebar); building products and services
Branch Offices: Abu Dhabi Office: PO Box 7268, Abu Dhabi, Tel 777485, Telex 22372 AL GURG EM
Parent Company: Easa Saleh Al Gurg Group
Subsidiary Companies: 12 companies within the Group
Principal Bankers: Lloyds Bank, Dubai

Principal Shareholders: Easa Saleh Al Gurg
Date of Establishment: 1976
No of Employees: 60

AL GURG, EASA SALEH,

PO Box 325, Dubai
Tel: 522500
Cable: Gurg Dubai
Telex: 48170 Gurg EM
Telefax: 522518

Chairman: Easa Saleh Al Gurg
Directors: Saleh Easa Al Gurg
Senior Executives: Hamidduddin Ahmed, G S Nivas, S B Jeyaseelan, Talib Rubai, Abdulla Ali, J Gregory, P G Evans, Stephen Mather, Huw A Rees

PRINCIPAL ACTIVITIES: Import and distribution of furniture, cigarettes, building materials, stationery, radios, televisions, tyres, supply and installation of electrical and electronic goods, manufacture of building materials, construction chemicals, explosives, switchgears, etc
Principal Agencies: British American Tobacco, Grundig, Siemens, Weir Pumps, Albright & Wilson, Osram, United Technologies, Trafo-Union, Dunlop, Rest Assured, Gautier, Gefmo, G Plan, Schriber, Armitage Shanks, British Gypsum,

Dover Engineering, Hepworth, Catnic-Holston Ltd, Unilever Products, Stanton & Stavely, Yorkshire Copper Tubes, Benetton, etc
Branch Offices: Dubai, Abu Dhabi, Sharjah, Ras Al Khaimah, Ajman, Fujairah, Umm Al Quwain, Khorfakkan, Kalba
Parent Company: Easa Saleh Al Gurg Group
Associated Companies: Scientechnic; Interiors; Easa Saleh Al Gurg & Sons; Grundig Sales & Services; Al Gurg Building Services; Mac al Gurg; Target Auto Services; BAT Agencies; Al Gurg Stationery. Joint Ventures: Al Gurg Fosroc (Pvt) Ltd; Technical and Trading Co; Arabian Explosives (Pvt) Ltd
Principal Bankers: lloyds Bank, Dubai

Date of Establishment: 1962
No of Employees: 600

AL HABTOOR ENGINEERING ENTERPRISES CO (PVT) LTD

PO Box 320, Dubai
Tel: 257215, 257551 (7 lines)
Cable: Hee
Telex: 45603 Hee EM

Directors: Khalaf A Al Habtoor, Riad T Sadek

PRINCIPAL ACTIVITIES: Civil and building contracting, contractors for major building projects in UAE
Branch Offices: Dubai; Abu Dhabi (PO Box 4284, Tel 822420, Telex 24121 HEE AD); Jordan (PO Box 7401, Amman, Tel 32661, Telex 23325); UK (London, 16 Berkeley Street, London W1X 5AE)
Associated Companies: Construction Machinery Centre Co (Pvt) Ltd, PO Box 5261, Dubai, Telex 45956 HABTR EM; Al Habtoor for Marble Co (Pvt) Ltd, PO Box 320, Dubai, Telex 48223 HEEMD; Al Habtoor Holding Co (Pvt) Ltd, PO Box 320, Dubai, Telex 45603 HEE EM
Principal Bankers: Commercial Bank of Dubai Ltd; Bank of Credit & Commerce; Lloyds Bank; Citibank

Principal Shareholders: Directors as described
Date of Establishment: 1971
No of Employees: Approx 2,000

AL HADLAQ TRADING EST

PO Box 3731, Dubai
Tel: 625013
Telefax: 622708

Chairman: Abdul Rahman Hamad Al Hadlaq

PRINCIPAL ACTIVITIES: Supply of building and construction materials, cleaning materials
Parent Company: Head office in Kuwait

AL HAMRA ENGINEERING CO

PO Box 11801, Dubai
Tel: 521254
Telex: 68048

Directors: Ali Mohd Ahmed Al Shihhe, Yacoob Yousuf Al Hamad, Hanna Nicholas Ayoob, Joseph Bemans Iskandar

PRINCIPAL ACTIVITIES: Building contractors, multi storey buildings
Associated Companies: Al Hamra Group of Companies, Kuwait

Principal Shareholders: Directors as mentioned above

ALHARBI TRADING, FOODSTUFF REFRIGERATION & INDUSTRIAL CO

PO Box 4345, Dubai
Tel: 222042, 222046
Cable: Alharbi Dubai

PRINCIPAL ACTIVITIES: Cold storage, import and distribution of foodstuffs
Branch Offices: Saudi Arabia; United Arab Emirates

Associated Companies: Arabian Trading Co for Cold Storage, Saudi Arabia; Orient Est for Refrigeration & Foodstuffs, Saudi Arabia; Shebah Cold Stores, Saudi Arabia; Jamil Lines for Shipping & Trade, Lebanon

AL HAREB GROUP OF COMPANIES

PO Box 2357, Dubai
Tel: 283216, 481949, 480505, 480991
Telex: 45899 HARBCO EM

President: Abdulla Mohammed Hareb
Directors: Hareb Mohammed Hareb, Khalifa Mohammed Hareb
Senior Executives: Khalifa Mohammed Hareb (Group General Manager)

PRINCIPAL ACTIVITIES: General trading, sponsors, government tenders, importers and distributors of furniture and furnishings, production/manufacturing, retreaded tyres and rubber products, PVC stationery and welded products, carpentry and joinery division, steamer agents, clearing and forwarding agents, airline agents and tourism, air courier services, air cargo and freight
Branch Offices: Member Companies: Al Hareb Trading Co, Dubai; Al Hareb Trdg Est, Abu Dhabi; Queen's Palace Furniture, Dubai; Falcontyre & Rubber Co, Dubai; Dubai Creative Plastics;, Dubai; Al Wasl Carpentry, Dubai; United Tourist Services & Travel, Dubai/Abu Dhabi; Al Ain Travel & Tourism, Alain
Principal Bankers: Barclays Bank Intl, Dubai

Principal Shareholders: Sole Proprietorship - Abdulla Mohammed Hareb
Date of Establishment: 1977
No of Employees: Approx 200

AL HASHAR, SAEED BIN NASSER,

PO Box 1300, Dubai
Tel: 223881, 228388, 231118
Telex: 45738 EM
Telefax: (971-4) 622811

Chairman: Saeed Nasser Al Hashar
Directors: Musa Al Arudi (Group General Manager)
Senior Executives: Ravinder Kumar Bhatia (Sales Manager)

PRINCIPAL ACTIVITIES: General trading and contracting, import and distribution of LP Gas
Principal Agencies: Ariston Products; Rinnai & Primes Sievert Gas Appliances
Branch Offices: PO Box 4810, Abu Dhabi, Tel 775127/8
Parent Company: Al Hashar & Co, PO Box 7028, Muscat, Sultanate of Oman
Principal Bankers: Grindlays Bank; Bank of Oman

Date of Establishment: 1962
No of Employees: 45

AL HATHBOOR GROUP OF COMPANIES

PO Box 2246, Dubai
Tel: 246124
Telex: 46468 Becop Em
Telefax: (971-4) 245922

Proprietor: Saif Obaid Al Hathboor
Directors: Abdulla Saif Al Hathboor, Jamal Saif Al Hathboor
Senior Executives: Mohamad Y H El Hasan (Chief Executive), M Salahuddin (General Manager Electrical/Mechanical), R Sharma (General Manager Foods & Stationery), P Menon (General Manager Cosmetics), B S Sandhu (General Manager Supermarket Equipment)

PRINCIPAL ACTIVITIES: Trading: import, wholesale and retail of food items, mechanical and industrial supplies, electrical supplies, stationery and office supplies, cosmetics and beauty products, supermarket equipment and laundry supplies
Principal Agencies: WD-40 Co, UK; Crosby Europe, Belgium; International Distributor Centre (Loctite), UK; SKF Intertrade, Belgium; John Prior Inc, USA; Swedish Battery, Sweden;

Barton Engineering Ltd, UK; Hawke Cable Glands, UK; Legrand, France; Avon Products, UK; Omega, Italy; Shulton, USA; Arneg, Italy; Brodrene Gram, Denmark; General Refrigeration, Italy; Apostolou, Greece; Shriram Refrigeration, India; Burton Son & Sanders, UK; William Sinclair, UK; Ejidius Janssen, Holland; Galt, UK; Kopex, UK; Shairco, Saudi Arabia; T M Mullick, UK; Thermos, UK; Royal Sovereign, UK

Subsidiary Companies: Member companies of the Group: Gulf Mechanical Engineers & Suppliers, PO Box 2605, Dubai; Al Hathboor Electrical Est, PO Box 6069, Dubai; Consumer & Beauty Products Division, PO Box 6785, Dubai; Arabian Gulf Agencies, PO Box 1183, Dubai; Al Hathboor General Trading, PO Box 6972, Dubai; Al Hathboor Food Est, PO Box 5754, Dubai; Al Hathboor Martinizing, PO Box 2246, Dubai

Principal Bankers: Bank of Credit & Commerce International, Deira; Commercial Bank of Dubai, Dubai; Emirates Bank International, PO Box 2923, Dubai; Bank of Oman, Dubai

Principal Shareholders: Proprietorship
Date of Establishment: Group in 1982, flagship co in 1971
No of Employees: 200

AL HAZEEM, ABBAS ALI, & SONS TRADING CO

PO Box 10310, Dubai

Chairman: Abbas Ali Al Hazeem
Directors: Shaker Abbas A Al Hazeem, Fadhel Abbas A Al Hazeem, Saheb Abbas A Al Hazeem, Ali Abbas A Al Hazeem, Hassan Abbas A Al Hazeem

PRINCIPAL ACTIVITIES: Interior furnishings and building cleaning
Branch Offices: Abu Dhabi, Oman, Egypt, USA
Parent Company: Head office in Kuwait: PO Box 273, Safat 13003 Kuwait, Tel 4745200, 2448290, Fax 2419976

AL HINNA TRADING EST

PO Box 1113, Deira, Dubai
Tel: 226146, 229526
Cable: Insha
Telex: 45784 Hinna EM

Chairman: Shaikh Zafar Hussain
Directors: M Amin Agha

PRINCIPAL ACTIVITIES: Importers and stockists of building materials, electric cables, etc
Subsidiary/Associated Companies: Emirates Plastic Industry, Deira, Dubai; Dascopp, Deira, Dubai
Principal Bankers: Middle East Bank Ltd, Deira, Dubai; Habib Bank Ltd, Deira, Dubai

AL HOMAIZI FOODSTUFF CO WLL

PO Box 7372, Dubai
Tel: 284196
Telefax: 278907

Chairman: Yaqoob Yousuf Al Homaizi
Directors: Fadwa Yaqoob Y Al Homaizi, Saleh Yaqoob Y Al Homaizi

PRINCIPAL ACTIVITIES: Foodstuff trading
Parent Company: Head office in Kuwait

ALI & FOUAD ALGHANIM EST

See ALGHANIM, ALI & FOUAD, EST

ALI BIN ABDULLA AL OWAIS

See AL OWAIS, ALI BIN ABDULLA,

ALI HAJI ABDULLA AWAZI

See AWAZI, ALI HAJI ABDULLA,

ALI HAJI ABDULLA AWAZI - GARGASH

PO Box 1047, Deira, Dubai
Tel: 282151,214182,660154,662047,663898
Cable: Awazi
Telex: 46218 Awash EM, 24448 Gargash EM, 45673 Grgas EM

Directors: Abdul Ghafoor Awazi, Mohamed Abdul Khaliq Awazi, Abdulla Bin Ali Gargash
Senior Executives: S Gohari (Director), Abdul Jabbar Gargash (Managing Director)

PRINCIPAL ACTIVITIES: Distributors of vehicles and spares, electrical equipment and accessories, power cables, tyres; manufacturer's representation, power, telecommunication contractors, civil contractors
Principal Agencies: Bedford Motors; Pirelli General Cable Works; GEC Group; New Zealand Insurance Co Ltd; Petbow; Victor; Bowthorpe Hellermann; A P W Cable Trays; B&R Electricals
Branch Offices: Ali Haji Abdulla Awazi, PO Box 2296, Abu Dhabi and PO Box 5808, Sharjah
Subsidiary Companies: Al Sagr Insurance Co Ltd
Principal Bankers: British Bank of the Middle East; National Bank of Dubai

Principal Shareholders: Family concern
Date of Establishment: 1921
No of Employees: 500

AL JAMIL SUPPLY COMPANY

PO Box 1486, Deira, Dubai
Tel: 231502, 224312
Cable: Tanco
Telex: 45760 Tanco EM

Directors: Jamil N Haoula (Proprietor)

PRINCIPAL ACTIVITIES: Dealing in all kinds of foodstuffs
Principal Bankers: Arab African International Bank; Banque de l'Orient Arabe et d'Outre-Mer

Date of Establishment: April 1979

AL KAITOOB, MOHAMED & ABDULSAMAD,

PO Box 1052, Dubai
Tel: 221723, 224340, 221569
Cable: Alkaitoob

PRINCIPAL ACTIVITIES: Import and distribution of ball and roller bearings, diesel engines, marine engines, pumping sets
Principal Agencies: Ramsome Hoffman Pollard Ltd (UK); Farymann Diesel (Germany); Motorfabriken Bukh A/S (Germany), John Cherry & Sons Ltd (UK), Warwick Pump and Engineering Co Ltd (UK)

AL KAZIM TRADERS

PO Box 5013, Dubai
Tel: 225959, 221352
Cable: Aialkazim
Telex: 45663 Akt EM

Chairman: Abdul Razak Kazim
Directors: Ahmed Kazim, Ismail Kazim

PRINCIPAL ACTIVITIES: Agents, importers, wholesale dealers, indentors
Principal Agencies: W Thomas & Co (WA) Pty Ltd, Australia; Kajaria Exports Private Ltd Calcutta, India; Uni-Ol B V Holland,etc
Principal Bankers: Barclays Bank International; Habib Bank AG Zurich

ALKHALIJ ENTERPRISES

PO Box 3320, Deira, Dubai
Tel: 225208, 225209, 223838
Cable: Autoimpex
Telex: 45843 Autimp EM

Directors: P C Bhatia (Managing Director), C S Bhatia (Director)

Senior Executives: P S Advani (Sales Manager)

PRINCIPAL ACTIVITIES: Import and distribution of batteries, bearings, cables, marine equipment, lubrication systems, hoses, wire ropes, hand tools, welding equipment, angles and shelvings, compressors, generators

Principal Agencies: Kugelfisher George Schafer, Germany; Dunlop, UK; Clayton Co, USA; Alco Int, Japan; Pioneer Weson, UK; Vesta Batteries, Alenite, Singapore; Johnstone Safety International, UK

Subsidiary Companies: Alkhalij Enterprises, PO Box 3117, Muscat; Arabian Technical & Trading Co, PO Box 2610, Abu Dhabi; Alkhalij Enterprises, PO Box 4857, Abu Dhabi; Bearing Sales Co, PO Box 7149, Sharjah; Alkhalij Enterprises, PO Box 17136, Al Ain

Principal Bankers: Commercial Bank of Dubai; ABN Bank

Principal Shareholders: Partnership
Date of Establishment: 1970
No of Employees: 35

AL KHARJI

PO Box 4379, Dubai
Tel: 282863, 224649, 227705
Cable: Comisgent
Telex: 45933 Kharji EM

Directors: Abdulla Rashid Alkharji

PRINCIPAL ACTIVITIES: Indenting, importing, distributors and general trading (household goods, cosmetics, toiletries, stationery, garments and clothing)

Principal Agencies: Vileda GmbH, Germany; N Kioleides SA

Principal Bankers: Bank of Oman Ltd; National Bank of Dubai Ltd

Principal Shareholders: Sultan Rashid Alkharji; Omer Rashid Alkharji; Rasheed Rashid Alkharji
Date of Establishment: 1972
No of Employees: 25

ALLIED ENTERPRISES LTD

PO Box 1579, Dubai
Tel: 223265, 221538
Cable: Alent EM
Telex: 45475 EM
Telefax: 221609

Chairman: A Bukhatir
Directors: C D Motiwalla, R D Motiwalla, N D Motiwalla
Senior Executives: Rusi N Motiwalla (Sales & Marketing Manager), A A Sayed (Sales Manager Wholesale), K N Tarapore (Finance & Accounts Manager)

PRINCIPAL ACTIVITIES: Department stores; general trading; import and distribution of clothes, household appliances, giftware, silverware

Principal Agencies: L'Oreal; Christofle; Lladro; Christian Dior Clothing; Wedgwood; Cacharel; Swatch; S T Dupont; Paloma Picasso, Fissla

Branch Offices: Dubai; Abu Dhabi; Sharjah

Principal Bankers: Barclays Bank Plc, Emirates Bank International

Financial Information:

	1990 Dh'000
Sales turnover	43,000
Profits	2,000
Authorised capital	5,000
Paid-up capital	5,000
Total assets	28,000

Principal Shareholders: Pearl Investments Ltd; Bukhatir Investments Ltd
Date of Establishment: 1968
No of Employees: 151

AL MAJID, JUMA, GROUP

Al Majid, Juma, Est

PO Box 156, Dubai
Tel: 665210, 660655
Cable: Arab Dubai
Telex: 45440 Arab EM
Telefax: 695867

Chairman: Juma Al Majid
Executive Directors: Abdullah Rashid Al Majid, Tariq Rashid Al Majid, Khalid Al Majid, Mohd Rashid Daour (Managing Director), Ismail Nashash, Tetsuji Yamada, Walid Omer Yousuf

PRINCIPAL ACTIVITIES: General contractors; import and distribution of household appliances, carpets, curtains, watches, heavy machinery, refrigeration equipment, electronic and electrical equipment, office equipment, tyres, automobiles, concrete products plant, fire fighting equipment, air conditioning equipment, electro mechanical contractors, telecommunications, etc

Principal Agencies: General Electric Company; USA; Yokohama Rubber Tyre Co, Japan; Citizen Trading Co, Japan; Gibson, USA; Samsung Electronics, Korea; Hyundai Motor Co, Korea; Daikin Airconditioners, Japan; Westinghouse A.S.D., USA; Angus Fire Armour, UK; Trane Airconditioning, USA; General Foods, USA; Express Lift Co, UK; U-Bix Copiers, Japan; L M Ericsson, Sweden, Isuzu Motor Co Japan; S C Johnson, Wrigley; Lion Corp; Renault, France

Branch Offices: Abu Dhabi; Sharjah; Ras Al Khaimah; Al Ain; Ajman, Fujairah, Umm Al Quwain

Subsidiary/Associated Companies: Al Majid Electronics; Al Majid Contracting Co; Automatic Laundry Services; Dubai Automatic Bakery; Gulf Trading & Refrigerating Co; National Refreshments (7-Up); Al Jadeed Bakery; Al Aweer Construction Co; INMA Gulf Development & Construction Co; Arab Sea International Trading; General Navigation & Commerce Co (GENAVCO); Al Majid Express Lift Co; Al Majid Ellis Fire Protection; Al Majid Samsung Co; Al Majid Travel Agency; Freon Products Dubai; Gulf Testing Laboratory; Intermarkets; Barber Dubai Shipping Agencies; Al Hana Jewellery; Stalco Shipping; Best Food Co; Al Majid Motors

Principal Bankers: United Arab Bank; National Bank of Dubai; Bank of Oman

Financial Information:

	1990 US$'000
Sales turnover	300,000

Date of Establishment: 1950
No of Employees: 4,000 (Group)

AL MAKAWI, MOHAMED, EST

PO Box 1059, Dubai
Tel: 470793
Cable: AM RATCO DUBAI
Telex: 46890 Em
Telefax: 373194

Chairman: Mohamed Al Makawi
Senior Executives: Michael Sullivan (General Manager)

PRINCIPAL ACTIVITIES: Electrical installations telecommunications, power generating plant, building systems, airfreight clearing and forwarding, shopfitting, office furniture, stationery, supermarket equipment

Principal Agencies: AEG Telefunken, GKN Mills Building Services Ltd, Twinlock, Zaf, Norpe, Sima, Windsor & Newton

Branch Offices: PO Box 7516, Abu Dhabi, Tel 724141 Telex 24437 EM

Subsidiary Companies: Emirates Trading Co, Dubai; Pandair Freight, Dubai; Mohd Abdulaziz Almakhawi & Associates, Abu Dhabi; Mohd Almakhawi Est for Airfreight, Clearing & Forwarding, Abu Dhabi

Principal Bankers: Emirates Bank International, Commercial Bank of Dubai, Citibank, National Bank of Dubai

Principal Shareholders: Sole proprietorship
Date of Establishment: 1974
No of Employees: 100

AL MATROUSHI TRADING COMPANY

PO Box 11001, Dubai
Tel: 661588, 661589
Telex: 46996 Sport EM

Directors: Rashid Al Matroushi

PRINCIPAL ACTIVITIES: Supply of marine equipment
Principal Agencies: Glastron American Make Speed boats,
Evinrude motors, Abu Fishing Rods, Bombard inflatable
boats, Dacor diving equipment

AL MOOSA GROUP OF COMPANIES

PO Box 24775, Dubai
Tel: 371270 (8 lines)
Telex: 47304 Pcon EM; 46020 Pwata EM
Telefax: 379034

President: Salim Ahmed Abdullah Al Moosa
Directors: Imad Abdul Fattah (Vice President Engineering &
Contracting), Mohsen El Badramany (Vice President Business
& International Affairs), Kamal Abu Saqr (Director of Legal
Affairs)
Senior Executives: Khalil Roz (Manager Painting Div), S T
Ahmed (Manager Travel Agency), Tito Mathson (Trading
Division Manager), Nabil Kayali (Manager Transport & Plant
Hire)

PRINCIPAL ACTIVITIES: Civil engineers and contractors,
building services, fleet owners and general transport, painting
contractors, interior decorators, advertising and travel agents,
general trading, kitchen furniture, supplies and services to the
oil, gas and energy related industries
Principal Agencies: Colora Products; Xey Kitchen; Slovenijales
Kitchen, Allen & Bradley Control Equipment; Gorenje
Appliances, Amana Microwave Ovens, Nippon Antenna;
Mannesmann Demag Fordertechnik, Federal Express
Branch Offices: PO Box 3821, Abu Dhabi, Telex 23910 AMPCO
EM
Subsidiary/Associated Companies: Dubai International
Reinforced Plastics (Pvt) Ltd; Solar Gulf Bldg Services Pvt
Ltd; Osalco Construction Co; Arabian Gulf Petroleum
Construction Supplies & Services Est; National Wheel J&P;
Wheel International (UAE) Co
Principal Bankers: Arab African International Bank; British Bank
of the Middle East; National Bank of Dubai; Bank of Credit &
Commerce International

Principal Shareholders: Proprietory concern
Date of Establishment: 1974
No of Employees: 1,500

AL MUHAIDEB TRADING & CONTRACTING EST

PO Box 2147, Dubai
Tel: 370133, 471119, 470133, 470390
Cable: Al-Mohaideb Dubai
Telex: 46276 Mohdeb EM
Telefax: 667924

Chairman: Abdul Latif Khalid Al Muhaideb
Directors: Abdul Mohsen Hamood Al Mohaisen, Sahoo Ali
Hamood Al Sahoo

PRINCIPAL ACTIVITIES: Importers, distributors, manufacturer's
representatives and agents, building materials, sanitaryware,
paint and varnish
Principal Agencies: Societa Italiana Smeriglio (Tenax), Italy;
Merloni (Ariston); Lgienico Sanitari, SpA, Italy; Ceramiche
ALCo, Italy; Ceramica Floor Gres, Italy; Fas Glass, Italy;
Ceramiche Piemme, Italy; Ottone & Meloda, Italy
Principal Bankers: National Bank of Dubai Ltd, Dubai; Bank of
Oman Ltd, Dubai

Principal Shareholders: A Al-Muhaideb (50%), Sahoo Modern
Exhibition (50%)
No of Employees: 50

ALMULLA, MOHAMMED SAEED, & SONS (PVT) LTD

Almulla Group of Companies

PO Box 59, Dubai
Tel: 221241/2/3, 221539
Cable: Almulla
Telex: 45444 Mulla EM

Chairman: HE Mohamed Saeed Almulla
Directors: Saeed Mohamed Almulla
Senior Executives: Abdulla Mohamed Almulla (General
Manager)

PRINCIPAL ACTIVITIES: Holding company dealing in
construction contracting, mechanical and transport services,
building materials, hotels, jewellery, watches, home and office
furniture, electrical appliances
Branch Offices: PO Box 700, Riyadh, Saudi Arabia, Tel
4645872, Telex 200974 OBALCO Sj; PO Box 439, Mosul,
Iraq, Tel 73492, Telex 298041 Mulla IK; Singapore, Telex
39005 WISDEV RS
Subsidiary Companies: Almulla Mechanical & Transport
Services, PO Box 1983, Dubai, Tel 667100, Telex 45444 Mulla
EM; Almulla Jewellery Co (PVT) Ltd, PO Box 5111, Dubai, Tel
225970, Telex 45877 Jwelry EM; Almulla Enterprises (PVT)
Ltd, PO Box 59, Dubai, Tel 221241, Telex 45611 Mulla EM;
Almulla Trading Corporation (PVT) Ltd, PO Box 817, Dubai,
Tel 471132, Telex 46259 Bagara EM; Almulla Construction Co
(PVT) Ltd, PO Box 59, Dubai, Tel 221241, Telex 45444 Mulla
EM
Principal Bankers: National Bank of Dubai Ltd; Bank of Credit &
Commerce, Bahrain

Principal Shareholders: HE Mohamed Saeed Almulla and family
No of Employees: 850

AL MUTAIWIE AGRICULTURE MATERIAL EST

PO Box 9310, Dubai
Tel: 236769, 481308
Telex: 48094 Amam EM
Telefax: 04 279688

Chairman: Obaid Ghanem Al Mutaiwie
Directors: Dr Nabil Agha (Managing Director)
Senior Executives: Eng Saleh Attieh (Sales Manager)

PRINCIPAL ACTIVITIES: Agricultural machinery and equipment,
horticulture, crop cultivation, irrigation and water
Branch Offices: AFCO, PO Box 17109, Amman, Jordan; AFCO,
Ontario, Canada
Parent Company: Al Mutaiwie Group
Principal Bankers: Grindlays Bank, Dubai

Date of Establishment: 1988
No of Employees: 25

AL NABOODAH, SAEED & MOHAMED, GROUP

PO Box 1200, Dubai
Tel: 660601
Telex: 45651
Telefax: 667602

Chairman: Saeed Juma Al Naboodah
Directors: Mohamed Juma Al Naboodah, Abdulla Mohamed Al
Naboodah, Ahmed Saeed Al Naboodah, Juma Mohamed Al
Naboodah
Senior Executives: Dr Salwan Yousif (General
Manager/International Resources Overseas Co), Nabeel
Mahmood (General Manager/Real Estate Co), Mahmood
Gamal (Finance Manager), Abdul Aziz Shoukry (Manager Al

Naboodah Travel Agency), Mufid Abbas (Finance &
Commercial Manager/Swaidan Trading Co), Mahmood Ismail (
Administration Manager), Ibrahim Desmal (Manager Gulf
Technical Trading & Services Co)

PRINCIPAL ACTIVITIES: General trading and contracting,
construction, airconditioning, electrical services, travel agency
and tours, import & export
Principal Agencies: Goodyear Tyres, USA; Peugeot Cars,
France; BASF, Germany; Via Nova, Italy; Iveco, Italy; Ashok
Leyland, India; BMC, Turkey; Marve, Italy; Wolf Tools, UK;
Dresser, USA; Mikasa, Japan; Agroflor, Austria; Virax,
France; Auto Diesel, UK; Cathay Pacific; Air France; Air
Canada; Austrian Airline; Hungarian Airline; Turkish Airline
Branch Offices: PO Box 2239, Abu Dhabi; PO Box 371,
Fujairah; PO Box 1250, Al Ain
Subsidiary Companies: Swaidan Trading Co; Al Naboodah
Contracting Co; International Resources Overseas Co; Gulf
Technical Trading & Services Co; Al Naboodah Laing; Trans
Electrical Co; Al Naboodah Travel Agencies; Al Naboodah
Cargo Centre; Al Naboodah Real Estate Co
Principal Bankers: National Bank of Dubai, Dubai
Financial Information:

	1990 Dh'000
Sales turnover	520,000
Profits	84,000
Authorised capital	263,000
Paid-up capital	135,000
Total assets	207,000

Principal Shareholders: Saeed J Al Naboodah, Mohamed J Al
Naboodah
Date of Establishment: 1978
No of Employees: 1600

AL NASR GROUP

PO Box 1106, Deira, Dubai
Tel: 661625
Cable: Alnsr
Telex: 45638 Alnasr EM

Chairman: Abdul Rahman Abdul Ghaffar Al Alawi (Sole
Proprietor)

PRINCIPAL ACTIVITIES: General contractors and civil
engineering; import and distribution of heavy machinery,
agricultural equipment, mechanical and industrial equipment,
film distribution, cinema operation
Principal Agencies: Rolls Royce Diesels; British Ropes; Bosch
Tools; Chas Thacknay; Merryweather Fire Fighting
Equipment; Lincoln Electric; Crosby Group; Bahco Tools;
Horseley Bridge Steel Tanks; Avon Inflatables
Branch Offices: Alawi Trading Co, Abu Dhabi; Al Nasr Trading &
Contracting Co; Sharjah; Technical Supplies Co, Ras Al
Khaimah; Al Nasr Engineering, Abu Dhabi
Parent Company: Al Nasr Trading Organisation, Qatar
Subsidiary Companies: Crescent Industrial Supplies; Al Nasr
Novelty Stores; Trucial States Film Co, NOLTE; TRASHCO;
Plant & Equipment Ltd
Principal Bankers: Commercial Bank of Dubai; Royal Bank of
Canada

Date of Establishment: 1959
No of Employees: 900

AL OTAIBA GROUP OF COMPANIES

Mohamed Hareb Al Otaiba

PO Box 5009, Dubai
Tel: 691575/76/77
Cable: Alotaiba
Telex: 45594 Otaiba EM
Telefax: 694940

Chairman: Hareb Mohammed Al Otaiba

Directors: Martin A Hardcastle (Group General Manager),
Santosh Talathi (Group Finance Manager)
Senior Executives: M Gopalakrishnan (Divisional Manager Office
Systems), Oscar Netto (Sales Manager Food Service
Equipment), M Nandakumar (Manager Domestic Appliance),
Joseph Silveira (Sales Manager Leisure & Sports)

PRINCIPAL ACTIVITIES: Sales, installation and after-sales
service and maintenance of food service equipment, domestic
appliances, leisure and sports equipment and office systems
Principal Agencies: Robert Bosch Hausgerate GmbH, Germany;
Foster Refrigerator (UK) Ltd, UK; Steelite Int Plc, UK;
Rubbermaid, USA; Litton Microwave, USA; Blanco, Germany;
La Cimbali, Italy; Hobart Corp, USA; Renzacci, Italy; Aurea,
Italy; Mareno Industriale, Italy; Catering Specialities, Canada;
Frimont, Italy; Vestfrost, Denmark; Domicor, USA; Terim, Italy;
Brunswick, USA & Germany; Balsam, Germany; Nashua Int,
UK; Schneider, Switzerland
Branch Offices: Abu Dhabi: PO Box 310, Abu Dhabi, Tel 02-
335700; Al Ain: PO Box 1358, Al Ain, Tel 03-641497
Subsidiary Companies: Xerox Emirates; Avis; Al Otaiba Ferretti
Principal Bankers: Abu Dhabi Commercial Bank, Dubai

Principal Shareholders: Hareb Al Otaiba
Date of Establishment: 1946
No of Employees: 200

AL OWAIS, ALI BIN ABDULLA,

PO Box 4, Dubai
Tel: 223935/6
Cable: Aliowais
Telex: 45450 Alwais EM

PRINCIPAL ACTIVITIES: Import and distribution of cars and
spare parts, electrical household appliances, tyres and tubes,
batteries, office equipment
Principal Agencies: Automobiles; British Leyland International
Ltd, UK; Suzuki Motor Co, Japan; Household Appliances;
General Electric Co, USA; Hotpoint Brand; Office Equipment;
Facit AB, Sweden
Branch Offices: Head Office in Dubai; Offices in Abu Dhabi (PO
Box 205, Tel 41408) and Sharjah (PO Box 39)
Principal Bankers: National Bank of Dubai Ltd

AL RIFAI, SAYID RAJAB,

PO Box 2000, Dubai
Tel: 660755, 221155, 222481, 223245
Telex: 45439 EM

Chairman: Abdullah Sayid Rajab Al Rifai

PRINCIPAL ACTIVITIES: Electrical and civil engineering
contracting, general trading, import and distribution of cars
and spare parts, agricultural machinery, furniture and
electrical appliances
Principal Agencies: Castrol, JCB Scaffolding, Leyland, Jaguar,
General Motors Overseas, Rolls-Royce, IBM, Riva Boats,
International Harvester, Fuji Heavy Industries, Piaget Watches
Branch Offices: Abu Dhabi
Parent Company: Head office in Kuwait

AL RUMAITHI SHIPPING CO

Oceantrade

PO Box 6380, Dubai
Tel: 434318
Cable: Rumaithiship
Telex: 46066 EM

Chairman: Mohd Khamis Al Rumaithi
Directors: Thomas Abraham (Managing Director)

PRINCIPAL ACTIVITIES: Shipping agents, freight forwarders
and general traders
Branch Offices: PO Box 4356, Abu Dhabi and PO Box 6045,
Sharjah
Principal Bankers: Bank of Credit & Commerce International
(Overseas) Ltd; Abudhabi, Dubai, Sharjah

AL SAGAR ENGINEERING CO

PO Box 7080, Dubai
Tel: 669595
Telefax: 664680

Chairman: Shukri Saleh Zaki
Directors: Abdulla Al Hamad Al Sagar & Bros

PRINCIPAL ACTIVITIES: Supply of pumps, generators, spare
parts, machinery and industrial equipment, workshop
equipment
Parent Company: Head office in Kuwait

AL SAGR INSURANCE (UAE) CO LTD

PO Box 10276, Dubai
Tel: 666285
Cable: Interesco
Telex: 47213 ASIC EM
Telefax: 668957

Chairman: Abdulla Al Sari
Directors: Yusri Dweik (Managing Director), Saeed Ghoubash,
Taryam O Taryam, Abdulla O Taryam, Khalfan Al Roumi
Senior Executives: Rifat R Abdo (General Manager), Ahmed
Khater (Deputy General Manager), Mohamad A R Chahine
(Deputy General Manager Saudi Arabia), Salim M Said
(Finance & Administration Manager), Majid Shaheen (Claims
Manager & Legal Advisor)

PRINCIPAL ACTIVITIES: All classes of insurance
Branch Offices: Sharjah, PO Box 4412, Tel 374686; Abu Dhabi,
PO Box 4907, Tel 339705; Alkhobar, Tel 8648644; Jeddah Tel
6515219
Principal Bankers: Investbank, Bank of Sharjah
Financial Information:

| | 1990 |
	Dh'000
Sales turnover	25,500
Profits	2,100
Authorised capital	10,000
Paid-up capital	10,000
Total assets	28,730

Principal Shareholders: Abdulla Al Sari, Yusri Dweik, Saeed
Ghobash, Taryam O Taryam, Abdulla Omran Taryam, Khalfan
Al Roumi
Date of Establishment: 1979
No of Employees: 55

AL SAHEL CONTRACTING CO

PO Box 3815, Dubai
Tel: 857324/5
Telex: 47001 Sahel EM
Telefax: 371080

Chairman: HE Khalifa Juma Al Naboodah
Senior Executives: Obaid S Al Naboodah (Manager), Lachman
Parwani (Manager/Engineer)

PRINCIPAL ACTIVITIES: Building and construction
Parent Company: Khalifa Juma Al Naboodah Group
Principal Bankers: Banque Paribas

Principal Shareholders: HE Khalifa Juma Al Naboodah
Date of Establishment: 1973
No of Employees: 180

AL SALEH, SAUD, GENERAL TRADING

PO Box 11057, Dubai
Tel: 224502
Telefax: 692923

Chairman: Wael Saud Al Saleh

PRINCIPAL ACTIVITIES: Trading in foodstuffs, water pumps,
building materials, etc
Parent Company: Head office in Kuwait

AL SARRAF, AHMED, TRADING EST

PO Box 55972, Dubai
Tel: 226399
Telefax: 285677

Chairman: Ahmed Abdulla Jassim Al Sarraf

PRINCIPAL ACTIVITIES: Building materials, hardware, electrical
fittings
Parent Company: Head office in Kuwait

AL SAYER, MOHD NASER, & SONS

PO Box 8765, Dubai
Tel: 220682, 271520
Telex: 46271
Telefax: 270253, 271884

Chairman: Nasser Mohd Nasser Al Sayer
Directors: Faisal Bader Mohd Al Sayer, Musaed Bader Mohd Al
Sayer, Sayer Bader Mohd Nasser Al Sayer
Senior Executives: Ali Shawki (Manager)

PRINCIPAL ACTIVITIES: General trading, dealing in
automobiles, auto spare parts, forklifts, engineering goods,
generators, electrical goods, furniture, transportation, car
rental, manufacturers' representatives, electrical contractors,
etc
Principal Agencies: Toyota, Japan; Beecham, UK; Kawasaki,
Japan; Yokohama Rubber, Japan; Hitachi Excavators, Japan;
Lotus Cars, UK; Nippon Shario, Japan, etc
Parent Company: Head office in Kuwait

Principal Shareholders: Chairman and directors as described

AL SAYER, NASSER, & CO

PO Box 1825, Dubai
Tel: 222471
Telex: 45825
Telefax: 663972

Directors: Nasser Mohd Nasser Al Sayer, Abdul Rahman Abdul
Moghni, Bader Abdulla Al Suhaim

PRINCIPAL ACTIVITIES: General trading and contracting, metal
furniture, airconditioning and refrigeration equipment, cold
storage equipment, building materials, hardware, tools,
electrical goods, etc
Parent Company: Head office in Kuwait

ALSERKAL, NASSER ABDULLATIF, & SON EST

PO Box 1219, Dubai
Tel: 237145, 221374
Cable: Nasser Dubai
Telex: 45540 Naser Em

PRINCIPAL ACTIVITIES: General trading and contracting,
pumps, generators, construction plant, water treatment, heavy
machinery, tractors and agricultural equipment
Principal Agencies: Bridgestone, Japan; AEI Cables, UK; Petter,
UK; Electrolux, Sweden; Newman Motors, UK; Massey
Ferguson, USA; Kawasaki, Japan; Coutinho Caro, Germany;
Woden, UK; Peerless Pumps, USA; Simon Hartley, UK;
Kurogame, Japan
Subsidiary Companies: Oman Trading Company, PO Box 4062,
Dubai

ALSHARHAN, ABDULLA SULTAN,

PO Box 1675, Dubai
Tel: 660417, 661718
Cable: Pacific
Telex: 45883 Asas EM
Telefax: 695913

Chairman: Abdulla Sultan Alsharhan
Directors: Ghazi Swaidani (Managing Director)

PRINCIPAL ACTIVITIES: Importers, commission agents,
manufacturers' representatives and contractors

Principal Agencies: GEC, UK; Candy, Italy; Toyoset, Japan;
Foemm, Italy; Hotpoint, UK; Art Metal Furniture, UK; Admiral,
USA; MWM - Diesel Engines, W Germany; PKB Yuguslavia;
Dutch Bacock, W Germany; Cherry Tree, UK; BMM Weston,
UK; ENKA Construction Co, Turkey; Emco Engineering, USA;
Projektror I Glumslov AB, Sweden; Skopos Fabrics, UK;
Samick, Korea; Peavey, USA; Elettronica Montarbo, Italy
Branch Offices: Head Office and Main Showrooms: At Dubai
Sharjah Rd, Dubai Branches: Ras Al Khaimah (PO Box 179);
Sharjah (PO Box 5285)
Subsidiary Companies: Gulf Electrical Supply Agency, Dubai; A
S Alsharhan; Energy Projects, Sharjah Musical Gallery -Dubai
Principal Bankers: National Bank of Dubai, UAE; Commercial
Bank of Dubai, UAE; Bank of The Arab Coast, Dubai
Financial Information:

	1989 Dh'000
Sales turnover	35,000
Profits	800
Authorised capital	1,000

Date of Establishment: 1965
No of Employees: 100

AL SHAWAF, ABBAS AHMAD, & BROS CO WLL

Al Shawaf, Saleh, Trading Est

PO Box 55608, Dubai
Tel: 284565, 224834
Telex: 46561
Telefax: 228255

Chairman: Abbas Ahmad Al Shawaf
Directors: Saleh Ahmad Mohd Ali Al Shawaf

PRINCIPAL ACTIVITIES: Trading in medical and surgical
equipment and instruments, scientific and laboratory
equipment, foodstuffs, electrical goods, auto spares, etc
Parent Company: Head office in Kuwait

Principal Shareholders: Saleh Al Shawaf (100%)

ALSHAYA TRADING COMPANY

PO Box 1277, Deira, Dubai
Tel: 664967
Cable: Alshaya Dubai
Telex: 45865 Shaya EM
Telefax: 692165

Chairman: Abdul Azeez Alshaya
Directors: Hamad Alshaya (Group Managing Director), Ayman
Alshaya (Executive Director)
Senior Executives: K M Dharmaraj (Area Sales Manager),
Shabbir A Udaipurwala (Financial Controller)

PRINCIPAL ACTIVITIES: Stockists and dealers in various types
of sanitary ware, wall and floor tiles, pipes and bathroom
equipment, consturction materials and consumer products,
sponsorships
Principal Agencies: Allia (France); H&R Johnson Tiles Ltd;
Symphony Group, UK; Cesame, Italy
Branch Offices: Al Shaya Trading Agencies Est, PO Box 543,
Riyadh, Saudi Arabia
Parent Company: M H Alshaya Co, PO Box 181, Safat, 13002
Kuwait
Principal Bankers: Bank of Oman

Date of Establishment: November 1968
No of Employees: 60

AL SHIRAWI CONTRACTING & TRADING CO

PO Box 93, Dubai
Tel: 245251
Cable: Alshirawi
Telex: 45483 Shrwi EM; 46564 Actco EM
Telefax: 245534 (GIII)

Chairman: Abdulla Al Shirawi
Directors: Ibrahim Al Shirawi, Mohan G Valrani (Managing
Director)
Senior Executives: Mohamed Al Shirawi (Executive Director),
Hisham Al Shirawi (Executive Director), P R Patel (Finance
Director), D G Valrani (Executive Director), S B Jain
(Executive Director), Yasin Jumah (Personnel Director)

PRINCIPAL ACTIVITIES: Building and civil engineering
contractors. Supply of building materials, steel, wood and
cement. Printing, electronics, shipping, transport, air travel
and foodstuffs
Principal Agencies: Scania Trucks; Postman Cooking Oil, Rani
Orange Float, JVC, Castrol, Haushahn
Branch Offices: UAE: PO Box 542, Sharjah; PO Box 811, Abu
Dhabi; PO Box 93, Dubai; PO Box 10083, Khorfakkan;
Sultanate of Oman: PO Box 4511, Muscat
Parent Company: Veam Corporation, Dubai
Subsidiary/Associated Companies: Arabian Oasis Industries;
National Aluminium Co; Emirates Printing Press; Global
Shipping Co; Al Shirawi Airconditioning Co; Al Shirawi
Equipment Co; Al Ghazal Iron Works; Arabian Oasis Food Co;
Oasis Enterprises; Al Shirawi Air Travel & Tourism Agency; Al
Shirawi Enterprises; Aswan Engineering & Auto Works; Al
Ahram General Transport Co; Modern Plastic Industries
Principal Bankers: Commercial Bank of Dubai; Bank of Oman
Ltd
Financial Information:

	Dh'000
Authorised capital	70,000
Paid-up capital	70,000

Principal Shareholders: Chairman and directors as described,
and Pary Ltd, Guernsey, Channel Islands
Date of Establishment: 1971
No of Employees: 800

AL SHIRAWI EQUIPMENT CO

PO Box 10983, Dubai
Tel: 480606, 480977, 481769
Cable: ASECO
Telex: 49517 Crane EM
Telefax: 482157

Chairman: Abdulla Al Shirawi
Directors: Mohan G Valrani (Senior Vice Chairman), Ibrahim
Shirawi (Vice Chairman), S K Ramchandani (Executive
Director)

PRINCIPAL ACTIVITIES: Products Division: design and
fabrication of storage and transportation equipment, such as
tanks, silos, pressure vessels, trailers, tankers, tippers and
municipal vehicles, cesspit emptiers; Structural Division:
design, fabrication and installation of factory sheds,
warehouses, and other structural steel works; Aluminium
Division: aluminium joinery and glass fittings for building
complexes
Principal Agencies: Bergische Achsenfabrik (BPW), Germany;
Metalair, UK; Verlinde, France; Ramsay Winches, USA;
Nummi (Partek OY Group), Finland
Branch Offices: Sultanate of Oman; Iraq; Saudi Arabia
Subsidiary Companies: Veam Corporation Group Companies
Principal Bankers: Commercial Bank of Dubai; Bank of Oman,
Dubai
Financial Information:

	1989 Dh'000
Sales turnover	9,500
Authorised capital	1,000
Paid-up capital	1,000

Principal Shareholders: Veam Corporation
Date of Establishment: 1976
No of Employees: 110

AL TAYER, OBAID HUMAID,

PO Box 2623, Dubai
Tel: 282241, 212272
Telex: 46808 Ohatem, 46771 Ohted Em

PRINCIPAL ACTIVITIES: Medical and educational equipment division, engineering division
Principal Agencies: Brown Boveri & Co Ltd, Sulzer Bros Ltd, Hauserman Overseas Contracting, Gray Tool Co, James Clark and Eaton Ltd, Crescent of Cambridge Ltd
Branch Offices: Al Tayer Travel Agency

AL WASL MARINE LTD

PO Box 24981, Dubai
Tel: 084-56400
Telex: 45622 GFME EMEM
Telefax: 084-56428

Chairman: Ken Waldorf
Directors: H H Sheikh Hamdan Bin Rashid Al-Maktoum, Ahmed Lufti, H L Aycock, G D Pope

PRINCIPAL ACTIVITIES: Marine support services for all offshore drilling and oil exploration work
Principal Bankers: National Bank of Dubai

Principal Shareholders: Zapata Gulf Marine Corp, Texas, USA; His Highness Sheikh Hamdan Bin Rashid Al-Maktoum
Date of Establishment: 1974
No of Employees: 236

AL WAZZAN, JASSIM MOHD ALI,

PO Box 5344, Dubai
Tel: 229396, 220941
Telefax: 215248

Senior Executives: R Hampton (Manager)

PRINCIPAL ACTIVITIES: General trading, commission agents, foodstuffs, pharmaceuticals, consumer goods
Parent Company: Head office in Kuwait

Principal Shareholders: Heirs of Jassim Mohd Al Wazzan, Kuwait (100%)

AL YOUSIFI, ESSA HUSAIN, TRADING EST

PO Box 55673, Dubai
Tel: 211754
Telefax: 286136

Chairman: Essa Husain Al Yousifi

PRINCIPAL ACTIVITIES: Suppliers of electrical goods and lighting
Parent Company: Head office in Kuwait

AL YOUSUF, YOUSUF HABIB,

Head Office, PO Box 25, Dubai
Tel: 224261 (4 lines), 221640, 223976
Cable: Habibani Dubai
Telex: 45436 EM
Telefax: 233268

Chairman: Yousuf Habib Al Yousuf
Directors: Ali Yousuf Habib Al Yousuf (Vice Chairman), Eqbal Yousuf Habib Al Yousuf (Deputy Chairman), Ahmed Yousuf Habib Al Yousuf (Deputy Chairman), Kersie Merwan Polad (Managing Director, Auto Division) Hossein Asrar Haghighi (Director Finance), Kassim M Al Hassan (Director Auto Division)
Senior Executives: Arif Rashid (General Manager Vehicle), Prem Srivastava (General Manager Electronics), Ghulam Ali

(Manager Commodities), M Nayebi (Asst Director Finance), P Z Cherian (Chief Accountant)

PRINCIPAL ACTIVITIES: Real estate, construction, money exchange, shipping, advertising, general trading, import, export and distribution of: Automotives: motor-cycles, cars and spare parts, outboard engines, FRP boats, generators and parts, tyres and tubes, batteries, paints, agricultural tractors and allied products. Electronics: gas cookers, home appliances, HiFi systems, air conditioners, water coolers. Commodities: rice, sugar, oils, tomato paste, salt & coconut powder. Computers and peripherals
Principal Agencies: Automotives: Yamaha Motor, Japan; Suzuki Motor, Japan; General Motors Corp, USA/Japan; Cunrel Motors, Brazil; Isuzu Motors Overseas, Japan; Daewoo Motors, Japan; Daihatsu Motor, Japan; Toyo Tyre & Rubber, Japan; Woosung Industrial, Korea; Yuasa Battery, Japan; Uniroyal Goodrich Tire, USA; Nippon Paint, Japan; Toyota Tsusho, Japan; Iysaka, Japan; Daewoo, Korea; Kansai Paint, Japan; Electronics: Sharp, Japan; Gold Star, Korea; Yamaha, Japan; Yenmade (YHAY Brand); Glemgas, Italy; Tecnogas, Italy; Rowenta, W Germany; Maspro Denkoh, Japan; Sumida Fastener, Japan; Leonard Int'l, USA; Ocean, Italy; Computers: Casio, Japan; Alalamiah, Japan; Sord/Chatani, Japan; Arc Plus, Taiwan; Daewoo, Korea; Xerox Emirates, UAE; NEC, Japan; Samsung, Korea; Miniscribe Corp, USA
Branch Offices: United Arab Emirates (Abu Dhabi, Sharjah, Ras Al Khaimah, Fujairah, Al Ain) and Oman (Muscat, PO Box 462)
Parent Company: Yousuf Habib Al Yousuf (Sole trader)
Subsidiary/Associated Companies: Group holding divisions: Automotive; Electronic & Home Appliances; Commodities; Computers; Exchange; Real Estate & Property Development. Al Yousuf Int'l Construction; Al Sadique Islamic English School; Yasmeen Trading & Contracting Est, Oman; Gulf Shipping Co; Seagal Shippping; Chinese Joint Venture, Oman; Al Yousuf Exchange; Al Yousuf Jewellery; Al Yousuf Real Estate & Trading Agency; Afeeyat Corp; Habibani General Trading Est; Al Yousuf Universal Import & Export; Arab Commercial Enterprises
Principal Bankers: American Express Bank; Bank of Credit & Commerce Int'l; Bank of Credit & Commerce (Emirates); Banque Paribas; Citibank; Gulf Riyad Bank, Bahrain; Middle East Bank; National Bank of Sharjah; Standard Chartered Bank
Financial Information:

	1990 AED'million
Turnover trading	517
Owner's equity	242

Principal Shareholders: Sole proprietorship
Date of Establishment: 1952
No of Employees: 595 (UAE) 81 (Other countries)

AL ZOROONI AIR CONDITIONING CO

PO Box 3253, Dubai
Tel: 225161
Cable: Airco Dubai
Telex: 45601 EM

Chairman: Abdulrahim Mohamed Al-Zarooni
Directors: K K Tata
Senior Executives: Syed Iqbal Ahmad

PRINCIPAL ACTIVITIES: Manufacturers' representatives, design and installation of air-conditioning, import and distribution of air-conditioning and refrigerator equipment
Principal Agencies: Typhoon
Branch Offices: Al Ain, Abu Dhabi, Sharjah
Associated Companies: Asian Trading Co; Zarooni Electronic; Zarooni Trans Emirates Gen Cont Co; Trans Emirates Gen Cont Co; Trans Gulf Electronics
Principal Bankers: Bank of Credit & Commerce International; Union Bank of the Middle East

Principal Shareholders: Abdul Rahim Mohd Al Zarooni
Date of Establishment: 1970
No of Employees: 52

AMERICAN EASTERN (DUBAI) LTD
AMEASTER Dubai
PO Box 3827, Apt 304, Al Mulla Bldg, Bin Yas Street, Deira-Dubai
Tel: 223486 (5 lines)
Cable: Ameaster
Telex: 45676 Amster EM
Telefax: 225142

Chairman: Mohamed Abdul Rahim Al Ali
Directors: Brig Mohammed Abdul Rahim A Al Ali (Honorary Chairman), Robert M Wagner (President & CEO), Uschi Wagner, Sathish S Shenoy
Senior Executives: Robert M Wagner (Director & Chief Executive Officer), Sathish S Shenoy (General Manager & Treasurer), Uschi Wagner (Public Relations Director), David Fernandes (Deputy General Manager & Marketing Director)

PRINCIPAL ACTIVITIES: General trading, distribution and marketing services
Principal Agencies: Amity, American Tourister, Blow Past, Sainberg, BBSOL, Costa Del Mar, Doakkar Noir, Guy Laroche, K-One, Maseratti, Opti-Vision, Opti-Ray, Serengeti, Gorham & Co, Neely Manufacturing, Crayola, Landscape Structures, Ohio Arts, Priss Prints, Peri, Parker Pen Co, Collection 2000, Constance Carroll, Eyelure, Jolen Creme, Woods of Windsor, Faberge, DIM, Diamant, Hanes, L'Eggs, Nursemate, Rosy, Daylite, Revelations, Soft Spots, AKRO, GFI, Polyloom, World Carpets, Duro-Lite, EKCO, Fafco, Glad, Grosfillex
Branch Offices: Abu Dhabi, Oman, Kuwait
Parent Company: Ameaster International Inc, Geneva, Switzerland
Subsidiary Companies: Ameaster Shipping & Trading Co SRL, Port Said, Cairo, Alexandria (Egypt); Ameaster International Inc, Lausanne (Switzerland); American Eastern Ltd, Kuwait; Ameaster Oman
Principal Bankers: Commercial Bank of Dubai; Emirates Bank International

Date of Establishment: 1969
No of Employees: 100

AMERICAN EXPRESS BANK LTD
PO Box 3304, Dubai
Tel: 223236
Cable: AMEXBANK
Telex: 46245 Amexbk EM
Telefax: 213516

Senior Executives: Ian Longhurst (First Vice President), Ashok Bablani (Asst Treasurer)

PRINCIPAL ACTIVITIES: Bank representative office
Branch Offices: Bahrain; Cairo
Parent Company: Head office in New York, USA
Subsidiary Companies: Egyptian American Bank SAE, Cairo (49%); American Express Middle East Development Co SAL, Amman

AMRO BANK - DUBAI BRANCH
Amsterdam-Rotterdam Bank NV
PO Box 2941, Dubai
Tel: 373180 (General), 374142 (Investment), 374211 (Forex)
Cable: Amro Bank
Telex: 46778 Amro EM (General); 46777 Amros EM (Forex)
Telefax: 373799

PRINCIPAL ACTIVITIES: Corporate Banking, commercial banking, investment banking, foreign exchange and money market

Parent Company: Amro Bank NV, PO Box 1220, Amsterdam, Holland

Date of Establishment: May 1978 (Dubai Branch)
No of Employees: 27

ANTICORROSION PROTECTIVE SYSTEMS
PO Box 8091, Dubai
Tel: 372877 (8 lines)
Telex: 45952 WSC EM
Telefax: (971-4) 377389

Chairman: R A Walters
Directors: Graham R Young (Managing Director)
Senior Executives: S Williams (Contracts Manager), P Sayed (Accountant)

PRINCIPAL ACTIVITIES: Supply of anti corrosion coatings, cathodic protection, glassflake lining systems, GRP laminates, rubber lining, neoprene claddings for splashzone, cocoon mothballing systems, fireproofing, concrete repair systems and waterproofing
Principal Agencies: Harco Corp; Ceilcote; Webco; Pipeline Maintenance Services; Prodorite UK
Branch Offices: PO Box 4705, Abu Dhabi, Tel 327070
Parent Company: Belminster Holdings, Shepperton, Middlesex, UK
Principal Bankers: Grindlays Bank, Dubai
Financial Information:

	1990 Dh'000
Sales turnover	9,500
Profits	1,000
Authorised capital	1,000
Paid-up capital	1,000
Total assets	5,500

Principal Shareholders: Robert Walters
Date of Establishment: 1980
No of Employees: 40

ANZ GRINDLAYS BANK PLC
PO Box 4166, Deira, Dubai
Tel: 285663
Cable: Grindlay
Telex: 49265 Minerv EM

PRINCIPAL ACTIVITIES: Commercial banking
Branch Offices: In the Middle East: Bahrain, Iran, Jordan, Oman, Pakistan, Qatar
Parent Company: Australia & New Zealand Banking Group

ARAB AFRICAN INTERNATIONAL BANK
PO Box 1049, Deira-Dubai
Tel: 223131 (10 lines) (Forex 283824/5)
Cable: Arabafro
Telex: 45503 ARAFR EM (General), 47433 AABFX EM (Dealers)
Telefax: 222257

Chairman: Ali El Badr
Directors: Mohamed Shokair (Dubai Branch Manager and Asst General Manager)
Senior Executives: Abdel Latif Abou Oura

PRINCIPAL ACTIVITIES: Commercial banking
Branch Offices: Dubai, Abu Dhabi, London, New York, Tunis
Parent Company: Head Office: 5 Midan Al-Saray Al-Kobra, Garden City, Cairo, Egypt, Tel 3555448, Telex 22304 UN, 22306 UN
Subsidiary Companies: Egypt Arab African Bank

Principal Shareholders: Egypt Central Bank; Kuwait Investment Authority
Date of Establishment: 1964
No of Employees: 40 (Dubai)

ARAB BANK PLC

PO Box 11364, Dubai
Tel: 228845
Cable: BANKARABI
Telex: 46126 ARBNK EM
Telefax: 285974

Chairman: Abdulmajeed A H Shoman
Senior Executives: Fathi Shaik (Senior Manager), Jamil Nabih (Manager)

PRINCIPAL ACTIVITIES: Commercial banking
Branch Offices: Main Branches in the Arab Countries: King Faisal Str, Amman; Shmeisani, Amman; Riad Solh Str, Beirut; Tell St, Tripoli; Saida; Manama; Doha; Abu Dhabi; Al Maktoum, Dubai; Sana'a; Main Offshore Banking Units: Manama, Bahrain; Cairo, Eygpt; Singapore; Main Branches in Europe and USA: London, UK; Paris, France; Athens, Greece; New York, USA; Nicosia, Cyprus; Representative Office: Beijing (Peking), China
Parent Company: General Management: Amman, Jordan
Subsidiaries/Associates Companies: Sister Institution: Arab Bank (Switzerland) Ltd, Zurich & Geneva; Subsidiaries: Arab Bank Investment Co Ltd, London; Finance, Accountancy, Mohassaba SA, Geneva; Arab Tunisian Bank, Tunis; Associated Companies: Arab Bank Maroc, Casablanca; Oman Arab Bank, Ruwi (Oman); Arab National Bank, Riyadh, Saudi Arabia; Nigeria Arab Bank Ltd, Lagos; Ubae Arab German Bank, Luxembourg & Frankfurt; Arabia Insurance Co, Beirut

Date of Establishment: 1930

ARAB BUILDING MATERIALS CO

PO Box 1596, Dubai
Tel: 341330, 660454, 660485, 660469
Cable: Shiral
Telex: 45584 Shira EM
Telefax: 690138

Chairman: Hassan Hamdi Mango
Directors: Mohd Taher Mohd Al Houdhoud, Mohd Ahmed Malas, Mohd Ali Bdeir, Saeed Hamzeh Malas, Abdul Hussain Haji Mohd Bahman, Hussan Saeed Malas

PRINCIPAL ACTIVITIES: Trading of building materials, (steel, timber, plywood, cement etc)
Branch Offices: Jordan Construction Materials Co, PO Box 6125, Amman, Jordan, Telex 23033; Arab Building Materials Co Ltd, PO Box 56, Abu Dhabi (U.A.E.), Telex 22313 Shiral EM; Arab Building Materials Co WLL, PO Box 582 Muscat, Oman; Arab Building Materials Co WLL, PO Box 697, Kuwait, Telex 3117 Arma KT; Arab Building Materials Co, PO Box 3221, Doha, Qatar, Telex 4338 Shiral DH
Parent Company: Jordan Construction Materials Co, PO Box 6125, Amman, Jordan, Telex 23033 OMRAN Jo
Principal Bankers: Arab Bank Ltd; The First National Bank of Chicago; Banque Paribas; Bank of Oman Ltd; Commercial Bank of Dubai Ltd

Date of Establishment: 1968
No of Employees: 105

ARAB EMIRATES INVESTMENT BANK LTD

303 New Sheikh Rashid Bldg, PO Box 5503, Deira, Dubai
Tel: 222191
Cable: Aremin
Telex: 46080 Aremin EM
Telefax: 274351

Chairman: HE Mohammed Saeed Al-Mulla
Directors: Majid Mohamed Al-Futtaim, Sultan Ali Al-Owais, Abdulla Hamad Al Futtaim
Senior Executives: Sajjad Ahmad (General Manager & Chief Executive), Abdul Malik Ismail (Manager Finance & Administration), Imran Afzal Khan (Manager Investments & Securities), Khawaja Asadullah (Manager Banking), Umar Hayat (Manager Private Banking & Public Relations)

PRINCIPAL ACTIVITIES: Investment banking
Principal Bankers: United Bank Ltd, Dubai; Union Bank of Switzerland, New York
Financial Information:

	1989
	Dh'000
Authorised capital	80,000
Paid-up capital	40,852

Principal Shareholders: Mohammed & Obaid Al-Mulla (Pvt) Ltd; Majid Mohd Al-Futtaim, Sultan Ali Al-Owais
Date of Establishment: February 1976

ARAB GULF EQUIPMENT CO WLL

PO Box 1777, Dubai
Tel: 226276/9
Cable: Equipment Dubai
Telex: 45536 Eqpmt EM

Chairman: Ahmed Al Katami
Directors: Mohammed Al Khonaini
Senior Executives: Mohamed Banat (Financial Manager)

PRINCIPAL ACTIVITIES: Import and distribution of furniture and furnishings, heavy machinery and equipment
Principal Agencies: Benford, Hermanns, Eversafe, Sheer Pride, Lion, Tadano, ACE, Phoenix, Potain, Bomag, Mitsubishi, Kubota, ECE, Compair, Fyne, Steelcase USA, Liebherr, Swan, ACI Holland, etc
Branch Offices: PO Box 936, Abu Dhabi, UAE
Parent Company: Al Khonaini Al Katami Trading & Contracting Co, PO Box 593, Safat, Kuwait
Principal Bankers: Al Ahli Bank Ltd, Dubai; Arab Bank Ltd, Dubai
Financial Information:

	Dh'000
Authorised capital	15,000
Paid-up capital	15,000

Date of Establishment: 1966
No of Employees: 55

ARAB TECHNICAL CONSTRUCTION CO (ARABTEC)

PO Box 3399, Dubai
Tel: (9714) 223753, 282527
Cable: Arabtec
Telex: 46255 Arabtec EM
Telefax: (9716) 333957

Chairman: Riad Kamal
Senior Executives: Riad Kamal (Managing Director), Usama Abdulhadi (Deputy Manager), Thomas Barry (Deputy Manager), Ali M Zayed (Administrative Manager), Peter Bruce (Director)

PRINCIPAL ACTIVITIES: Building and civil engineering works including electrical contracts, lifts and escalators, partitions and interiors, ready mix concrete and precast concrete
Principal Agencies: Thyssen Aufzuge GmbH, W Germany; Consolidated Partition Industries Holdings Pty Ltd, Australia; G&H, W Germany; Knauf, W Germany; Hatema, Holland; DLW, W Germany
Branch Offices: PO Box 1358, Al Ain, Tel 661610; PO Box 5645, Sharjah, Tel 332300, Telex 68397; Abu Dhabi, Tel 779872
Principal Bankers: Banque Libanaise pour le Commerce SA, Dubai; Banque de l'Orient Arabe et d'Outre-Mer, Dubai
Financial Information:

	1989/90
	Dh'000
Sales turnover	48,000
Authorised capital	10,000
Paid-up capital	10,000

Date of Establishment: 1965
No of Employees: 550

ARABIA INSURANCE CO LTD SAL

PO Box 1050, Dubai
Tel: 236955
Cable: Arabiaco
Telex: 45901 Arabia EM
Telefax: 233790

Chairman: Badr Said Fahoum
Senior Executives: Ibrahim Hannoun (Area Manager Northern Emirates)

PRINCIPAL ACTIVITIES: All types of insurances
Branch Offices: Sharjah, Ras Al Khaimah, Abu Dhabi, Al Ain, Jordan, Bahrain, Kuwait, Lebanon, Qatar, Saudi Arabia, Oman
Principal Bankers: Arab Bank Plc; Banque de L'Orient Arabe et D'Outre Mer; Invest Bank

Principal Shareholders: Arab Bank Ltd
Date of Establishment: 1944
No of Employees: 1,250

ARABIAN AUTOMOBILES COMPANY

PO Box 2128, Dubai
Tel: 226222/6
Cable: AUTOMOTIVE
Telex: 45484 Marwan EM

Chairman: Abdulla Hasan Rostamani
Directors: Abdul Wahed Rostamani
Senior Executives: T M Nair

PRINCIPAL ACTIVITIES: Import and distribution of cars, trucks, buses, trailers, tyres and spare parts
Principal Agencies: Nissan, Datsun, United Diesel Japan, Hargil Trailers, Blue Star Water Coolers
Branch Offices: United Arab Emirates, Dubai, Sharjah, Ajman; Umm Al Quwain, Ras Al Khaimah, Fujairah
Parent Company: Arabian Automobiles Company
Subsidiary Companies: United Diesel; General Impex
Principal Bankers: The British Bank of The Middle East, Dubai; Lloyds Bank, Dubai

Date of Establishment: 1968
No of Employees: 326

ARABIAN GENERAL INVESTMENT CORPORATION (SHUAA)

A.G.I.C.O.

PO Box 3501, Dubai World Trade Centre, 17th Floor, Dubai
Tel: 373320
Cable: Shuaa
Telex: 47878 Shuaa EM, 48586 Agico EM (FX)
Telefax: 370371

Chairman: Abdul Aziz Hamad Al Sagar
Directors: Juma Al Majid (Vice Chairman), Adnan Kassar (Vice Chairman), Ismail Abu Dawood, Saeb Nahas, Walid Al Nusif, Yacoub Y Al Jouaan, Yousef Al Fulaij, Hilal M Al Mutairi, Ibrahim Y Al Ghanim, Abdul Salam A Al Awadi, Majed Jamaluddin (Advisor to the Board)
Senior Executives: Radwan M Termanini (General Manager), Adham K Haddad (Administration Manager), Daniel Greenwald (Corporate Finance Manager), Iyad Duwaji (Treasurer & Finance Manager), Paul Debenedictis (Marketing Manager), Jack Greenwald (General Counsel), John Poole (Corporate Banking Manager)

PRINCIPAL ACTIVITIES: Project promotion & consulting, money market operations, lease finance, trade finance, forex dealing, equity participation, direct investments
Associated Companies: Societe Delma d'Investissements Touristiques et Immobiliers, Tunis; Technopak, Egypt; Gefinor Finance SA, Luxembourg; Tagas, Turkey, Agrosyr, Syria; First Venture Investments Corp, Cayman Islands; Hosteleria Unida SA, Spain; Babcock & Prebon, UK; Amrit, Syria
Principal Bankers: American Express Bank Ltd, New York; Deutsche Bank, Frankfurt; Bank of Oman Ltd, Dubai; Lloyds

Bank, London; Banque Indosuez, Paris; Bank of Tokyo, Tokyo; Barclays Bank, Barcelona
Financial Information:

	1990 Dh'000
Total income	40,038
Net profit	23,622
Authorised capital	700,000
Paid-up capital	290,759
Shareholders' equity	356,352
Total assets	474,407

Principal Shareholders: Public shareholders company listed on Kuwait Stock Exchange
Date of Establishment: April 1979
No of Employees: 36

ARABIAN OASIS INDUSTRIES

PO Box 10983, Dubai
Tel: 480606, 480977, 481769
Cable: ASECO
Telex: 49517 CRANE EM
Telefax: 482157

Chairman: Abdulla Al-Shirawi
Directors: Moham G Valrani (Senior Vice Chairman), Ebrahim Al Shirawi (Vice Chairman), S K Ramchandani (Executive Director)

PRINCIPAL ACTIVITIES: Construction of steel-framed buildings on turnkey basis; fabrication and erection of steel structures; installation of pipelines & equipment; supply and fixing of cladding systems; manufacturers' representatives
Branch Offices: Abu Dhabi (UAE), PO Box 811, Tel 335509, Telex 23845 Aoi EM; Baghdad (Iraq), PO Box 18022, Palestine St, Tel 96225, Telex 213478 Oasis IK; Al-Khobar (Saudi Arabia), PO Box 1425, Tel 8640188, Telex 671378 Ghrare SJ; Riyadh (Saudi Arabia), PO Box 1230, Tel 4650984/8, Telex 203043 Jamsup SJ
Parent Company: Holding Company: Veam Corporation, PO Box 93, Dubai, Tel 245251, Telex 46564 Actco EM
Principal Bankers: Commercial Bank of Dubai, Bank of Oman, Dubai
Financial Information:

	1989/90 Dh'000
Authorised capital	3,500
Paid-up capital	3,500

Principal Shareholders: Abdulla Al Shirawi; Ebrahim Al Shirawi; Parv Ltd; M G Valrani
Date of Establishment: May 1976
No of Employees: 101

ARATRANS DUBAI SAK

PO Box 3278, Dubai
Tel: 210808
Telex: 45524
Telefax: 230650

Chairman: Saud Abdulaziz Al Zamel

PRINCIPAL ACTIVITIES: International forwarders by land, sea and air, cargo packing, forwarding and clearing services
Parent Company: Head office in Kuwait

ARENCO REAL ESTATE

Arenco A A Al Moosa & Associates

PO Box 2622, Dubai
Tel: 370550
Cable: Arenco
Telex: 45726 ARNCO EM
Telefax: 378349

Chairman: Abdullah A Almoosa

Senior Executives: A Majid (General Manager), D D Patkar (Chief Architect), A Bhardwaj (Financial Controller), D Cobban (Chief Architect), E G Daniel (Real Estate Marketing Manager)

PRINCIPAL ACTIVITIES: Accomodation leasing, architects and engineering consultants
Branch Offices: Liaison Offices: Abu Dhabi; Houston
Principal Bankers: British Bank of the Middle East, Citibank, Emirates Bank International; National Bank of Dubai

Date of Establishment: 1971
No of Employees: 150

ARTHUR YOUNG BADER AL BAZIE & CO

PO Box 4235, Dubai
Tel: 224147
Telex: 46034

Directors: Arthur Young & Company, Bader Bazie Al Yaseen, Shuaib Abdulla Mohd Shuaib

PRINCIPAL ACTIVITIES: Chartered accountants
Associated Companies: Bader Al Bazie & Co, Kuwait; Arthur Young & Co, USA

ASEA BROWN BOVERI REGIONAL OFFICE

PO Box 11070, Dubai
Tel: 521424
Telex: 45759 ABBDU EM
Telefax: 521988

Senior Executives: Svein Torgersbraten (General Manager), Simaan Boutros (Manager Distribution and Oil & Gas Dept), Jihad Badaro (Manager Power Project Equipment), Boerje W Lundavist (General Manager Gas Turbine Services), John Williams (General Manager Major Projects)

PRINCIPAL ACTIVITIES: Electrical equipment for power, industry and transportation
Parent Company: Head Office: ABB Asea Brown Boveri Ltd, PO Box 8131, Zurich, Switzerland

Date of Establishment: 1975

ASSOCIATED CONSTRUCTIONS & INVESTMENTS

PO Box 5238, Dubai
Tel: 666220
Cable: ASCON
Telex: 46162 ASCON EM
Telefax: 622761

Chairman: Saif Ahmed Al Ghurair
Directors: Abdullah Al Ghurair (Executive Vice Chairman), B S Abdul Rahman (Vice-Chairman), Syed Mohamed Salahuddin (Managing Director), Khalid Al Ghurair (Director), Juma Al Ghurair (Director), Abdul Rahman Al Ghurair (Director), Arif B Rahman (Director)
Senior Executives: V S Sanghvi (General Manager), P H M Syed Ismail (Technical Manager), M Shahul Hameed (Project Manager), P V Mathai (Project Manager), M Murugappan (Project Engineer)

PRINCIPAL ACTIVITIES: Builders and construction contractors
Branch Offices: Associated Constructions & Investments Ltd, PO Box 3532, Abu Dhabi, UAE; Associated Constructions, Syed Ahmed Bldg, Umm Traffa, Sharjah, UAE; Ascon Constructions, PO Box 778, Ras Al Khaimah, UAE; Saudi-Ascon, PO Box 1269, Medina; PO Box 6591, Jeddah; PO Box 17338, Riyadh, Saudi Arabia
Associated Companies: ETA-Melco Elevator Co Pvt Ltd, PO Box 5239, Dubai, UAE; ETA-Melco Elevator Co, Colombo, Sri Lanka; Emirates Trading Agency, PO Box 5239, Dubai, UAE; Emirates Trading Agency Ltd, PO Box 3532, Abu Dhabi, UAE; Emirates Trading Agency, PO Box 779, Ras-Al-Khaimah, UAE; Electromech Technical Associates, PO Box 6304, Abu Dhabi; also PO Box 119, Doha, Qatar; and Muscat, Oman; Al-

Bahar-ETA, PO Box 26672, Safat, Kuwait; Saudi-ETA Ltd, Jeddah, Medina & Riyadh, Saudi Arabia. Modern Building Maintenance, Dubai, Abu Dhabi, Sharjah & Ras-Al-Khaimah. Computerized Auto Repairs & Services (CARS), Dubai & Abu Dhabi. Engineering Maintenance Company (EMCO), Dubai, Sharjah & Abu Dhabi.
Principal Bankers: Bank of Oman Ltd; Deira Main, Dubai
Financial Information:

	1989	1990
	Dh'000	Dh'000
Sales turnover	63,781	95,680
Authorised capital	20,000	20,000
Paid-up capital	20,000	20,000

Principal Shareholders: Saif Ahmed Al Ghurair, Dubai, UAE; Abdullah Ahmed Al Ghurair, Dubai, UAE; Amana Investments Ltd, Hong Kong
Date of Establishment: May 1974
No of Employees: 1,560

ATKINS, W S, & PARTNERS (OVERSEAS)

PO Box 5620, Dubai
Tel: 522771
Telex: 46615 ATKINS EM
Telefax: (971-4) 523045

Chairman: T Wyatt
Directors: P A Brown, M T Foley, R C French, D R S Harris, D O Hyett, F A Isola, M H S Muller, B J Patrick, D Slater, A V Stagnetto
Senior Executives: B H Chapman (Resident Director)

PRINCIPAL ACTIVITIES: Planning, engineering, management and agricultural consultants and architects
Branch Offices: In the Middle East: Abu Dhabi, Dubai, Bahrain, Kuwait, Oman, Saudi Arabia
Parent Company: W S Atkins Ltd, UK
Principal Bankers: Standard Chartered Bank, Dubai

Date of Establishment: 1975 in Dubai
No of Employees: 365 in UAE

ATLAS ASSURANCE CO LTD

PO Box 5862, Dubai
Tel: 473842/3, 470335
Telex: 45764 UNANCE EM

PRINCIPAL ACTIVITIES: All types of insurance
Branch Offices: Branches in Abu Dhabi (PO Box 865); Ras Al Khaimah (PO Box 571); Bahrain (PO Box 49); Qatar (PO Box 441, Doha); Oman (PO Box 4865, Muscat)
Parent Company: Guardian Royal Exchange Assurance

ATLAS COPCO INTERNATIONAL

Gulf Office, PO Box 6795, Dubai
Tel: 377140, 377145
Telex: 46049 COPCO EM

PRINCIPAL ACTIVITIES: Drilling contractors, suppliers of pneumatic & hydraulic rock drills and breakers

ATTAR BROS COMPANY

PO Box 1592, Dubai
Tel: 221642
Cable: 45706 Atarco EM

Chairman: Abdul Kader Attar (General Manager)
Directors: Yousef Attar, Farid Attar

PRINCIPAL ACTIVITIES: General merchants, importers of foodstuffs, and cold storage
Principal Agencies: Knorr Soups & Bouillons, CPC Products (USA), Knorr Egg Ravioli, Adler Cheese, Oxenia Olives, Kaha Canned Foodstuffs, Frozen Vegetables, Dandy Chewing Gum, ICI, UK
Branch Offices: United Arab Emirates and Oman

UAE (Dubai)

AWAZI, ALI HAJI ABDULLA,

PO Box 1047, Deira, Dubai
Tel: 223121/2/3, 661617/8
Cable: Awazi
Telex: 46218 Awash EM

Chairman: Ali Haji Abdulla Awazi
Directors: Abdul Ghafoor Awazi, Mohamed Abdul Khaliq Awazi, Abdulla Bin Ali Awazi

PRINCIPAL ACTIVITIES: Distributors of vehicles and spares, electrical equipment and accessories, power cables, tyres; manufacturer's representation, power, telecommunication contractors
Principal Agencies: Vauxhall Motors Ltd, General Motors, Pirelli General Cable Works, GEC Group, New Zealand Insurance Co Ltd
Branch Offices: Ali Haji Abdulla Awazi, PO Box 2296, Abu Dhabi and PO Box 5808, Sharjah
Principal Bankers: British Bank of the Middle East; National Bank of Dubai; Chartered Bank; Citibank

Principal Shareholders: Family concern

BADRI GROUP OF COMPANIES

PO Box 4380, Dubai
Tel: 666216
Cable: Badribros
Telex: 45902 Badri EM
Telefax: 971-4-660745

President: Mohamed Badri
Directors: Yousuf Badri (Vice President & Managing Director), Mohd Ali Badri, Nasser Badri
Senior Executives: D J Babani (General Manager), Mohan Bhambani (Financial Controller)

PRINCIPAL ACTIVITIES: Import-export, general merchants, real estate, business investments, distribution of electronics and electrical home appliances, communication equipments, optical goods, auto spares, toys, games, gift articles, clocks; printing press and advertising agency, distibution of TV and video films, etc
Principal Agencies: Hitachi, Japan; Channel Master, USA; China National Products, China; Aiphone, Japan; Lenox, USA
Branch Offices: Abu Dhabi, Sharjah, Ras Al Khaimah, Fujairah
Subsidiary Companies: Eros Electricals, Dubai; International Trade Linkers, Dubai; Oriental Electronics, Dubai; Asian Printing Press, Dubai; Asian Advertising Agency, Dubai; Badri Electro Supply & Trading Co, Dubai; M Ali Badri Trading Est, Dubai; Badri General Trade Enterprises, Dubai; Oriental Enterprises, Dubai; Bestco Film Distributions, Dubai; B & F Food & Beverages Co, Dubai; Golden Electronics, Dubai; Auto World, Dubai
Principal Bankers: Emirates Bank International, Dubai; Citibank, Dubai; Lloyds Bank, Dubai; Algemene Bank Nederland, Dubai

Date of Establishment: 1967
No of Employees: 200

BAHMAN, AHMAD,

PO Box 1145, Deira, Dubai
Tel: 232682, 214210
Cable: Bahman Dubai
Telex: 45572 BAMAN EM
Telefax: 224730

Proprietor: Haji Ahmad Bahman
Directors: Mohammed A Bahman

PRINCIPAL ACTIVITIES: Manufacturers' representatives, indentors and general merchants; foodstuff, household goods, building materials, footwear, gift's toys, garments and blankets, curtains and carpets, gold, silver plated items and crystal ware
Branch Offices: PO Box 88, Safat, Kuwait
Subsidiary Companies: Kingsway, PO Box 437, Dubai; East Asia Trading Est, PO Box 437, Dubai; Zodiac Commercial

Enterprises, PO Box 1145, Dubai; Modern Kitchen Supplies, PO Box 1145, Dubai
Principal Bankers: National Bank of Dubai; the British Bank of the Middle East, Bank of Oman Ltd; Union Bank of the Middle East
Financial Information:

	1989
Sales turnover	$25,475,000
Paid-up capital	Dh1,500,000

Principal Shareholders: Ahmad Bahman
Date of Establishment: 1960
No of Employees: 85

BANK MELLI IRAN

PO Box 1894, Deira, Dubai
Tel: 282171, 221462
Cable: Regmelli Dubai
Telex: 46404 Rgbmi EM
Telefax: 278405

Senior Executives: Aziz Azimi Nobar (General Manager & Regional Director)

PRINCIPAL ACTIVITIES: Commercial banking
Branch Offices: Dubai, Abu Dhabi, Al Ain, Sharjah, Ras Al Khaiman, Fujairah, Bahrain, Muscat (Oman)
Parent Company: Head office in Tehran, Iran

Date of Establishment: UAE 1969; Iran 1928

BANK OF BARODA

PO Box 5107, Deira, Dubai
Tel: 227579
Telex: 46979 Bobde EM

PRINCIPAL ACTIVITIES: Commercial banking
Parent Company: Head office in Baroda, India

Principal Shareholders: Government of India Undertaking
Date of Establishment: 1908: in India

BANK OF CREDIT & COMMERCE INTERNATIONAL

Middle East Regional Office, PO Box 6925, BCC Bldg, Deira, Dubai
Tel: 285161
Cable: Bancrecom
Telex: 48870 BCCRO EM
Telefax: (971-4) 237732

President: Agha Hasan Abedi
Directors: Yves C Lamarche, J D Van Oenen, Ghanim Faris Al Mazrui, Dr Alfred Hartmann, P C Twitchin, Khalid Salim Bin Mahfouz, Swaleh Naqvi (Chief Executive Officer)

PRINCIPAL ACTIVITIES: Commercial banking
Branch Offices: In the Middle East: UAE (Abu Dhabi, Al Ain, Dubai, Dubai Main Branch; PO Box 5032, Deira, Dubai, Tel 227526, Telex 45778 BCCI EM, Sharjah, Ajman); Bahrain; Oman; Jordan; Egypt; Lebanon; Morocco; Sudan; Yemen
Parent Company: BCCI (Holdings) Luxembourg, 39 Boulevard Royal, 2449 Luxembourg

Date of Establishment: September 1972
No of Employees: 13,998

BANK OF CREDIT AND COMMERCE (EMIRATES)

HH Shaika Maryum Bldg, PO Box 6811, Bin Yas Street, Deira, Dubai
Tel: 227613
Cable: BANCRECOM
Telex: 48834 BCCI Em

Chairman: H E Sh Nahayan Bin Mubarak Al Nahayan
Directors: Obaid Humaid Al-Tayer, Ahmed Al Kamda, Eid-Bakheet Al Massroai, Ashraf Nawabi, Saleem Siddiqi

Senior Executives: Zafar Iqbal (Managing Director and Chief Executive), Bashir Tahir (General Manager), Fateh Mohammed (Manager International Dept), Mahmood S Allarakhia (Executive Accounting Control), Ghulam Hannani (Executive Advances Control), Hamid Ashraf (Manager Legal Dept)

PRINCIPAL ACTIVITIES: Commercial banking
Parent Company: BCCI Holdings (Luxembourg) SA
Principal Bankers: Bank of Credit & Commerce International SA, UK; First American Bank of New York, USA
Financial Information:

	1990 US$'000
Authorised capital	108,962
Paid-up capital	87,182

Principal Shareholders: BCCI Holdings (Luxembourg) SA (40%); UAE Nationals (45%); Founders (15%)
Date of Establishment: January 1983
No of Employees: 564

BANK OF NOVA SCOTIA
PO Box 3859, Deira, Dubai
Tel: 226257
Cable: Scotiabank
Telex: 46665 Scotia EM

PRINCIPAL ACTIVITIES: Commercial banking
Branch Offices: PO Box 5260, Manama, Bahrain; PO Box 656, Cairo, Egypt; PO Box 4446, Beirut, Lebanon

BANK OF OMAN LTD
Head office, PO Box 1250, Deira, Dubai
Tel: 229131 (30 lines)
Cable: Banoman
Telex: 45429 Oman EM; 45464 Omank EM; 45674 Omnfx EM
Telefax: 226061

Chairman: Saif Ahmed Al-Ghurair
Directors: Mohammad Ibrahim Obaidullah (Deputy Chairman), Ali Bin Khalifa Al-Hitmi, Abdullah Ahmed Al Ghurair, Jamal Majid Al Ghurair, Abdul Aziz Abdulla Al Ghurair, Mohammed Ali Al Gaizi
Senior Executives: Abdulla Ahmed Al Ghurair (General Manager & Managing Director), Abdul Aziz Abdulla Al Ghurair (Executive Director), Jamal Majid Al Ghurair (Executive Director), Sultan M Khan (Deputy General Manager), Usama Mohammed Khader (Board Secretary)

PRINCIPAL ACTIVITIES: Commercial banking
Branch Offices: Abu Dhabi (3 branches); Ajman; Dubai (9 branches); Fujairah (2 branches); Ras Al Khaimah (2 branches); Sharjah (4 branches); Umm Al Qaiwan; Egypt (Cairo, Alexandria); Qatar (Doha); Bahrain; UK (London / 2 branches); Pakistan (Karachi, Lahore, Peshawar); Sri Lanka (Colombo); Sudan (Khartoum); India (Bombay); Kenya (Nairobi); USA (New York)
Subsidiary Companies: Oman Insurance Co Ltd, Dubai (6 branches in UAE); Oman Finance Co Ltd, Dubai, (7 branches in UAE); Oman International Finance Ltd, Hong Kong (2 branches), Bank of Oman Overseas (USA) Inc
Financial Information:

	1990 Dh'000
Authorised capital	600,000
Paid-up capital	371,948

Principal Shareholders: Al Ghurair Family
Date of Establishment: 1967
No of Employees: 1,826

BANK OF THE ARAB COAST
PO Box 5536, Dubai
Tel: 223101/4
Cable: ARCOBA
Telex: 46177 Arcoba EM, 47096 BACFX EM

PRINCIPAL ACTIVITIES: Commercial banking
Branch Offices: General Management: Dubai. Registered Office: Ras Al Khaimah (PO Box 342)

Date of Establishment: 1975, reconstituted in November 1980

BANK SADERAT IRAN
Al Maktoum Street, PO Box 4182, Deira, Dubai
Tel: 221161-7
Cable: Saderbank
Telex: 45456 SADBK EM, 46470 SADRM EM

PRINCIPAL ACTIVITIES: Commercial banking
Branch Offices: UAE (8 branches), Dubai, Abu Dhabi, Al Ain, Sharjah, Ajman, Fujairah
Parent Company: Head Office: Tehran, Iran

Principal Shareholders: Nationalized Institution
Date of Establishment: In the UAE: 1968
No of Employees: 136

BANQUE BRUXELLES LAMBERT
PO Box 4296, Deira, Dubai
Tel: 226206
Telex: 46460 BBL EM
Telefax: 282836

Senior Executives: Michel Sterckmans (Gulf Regional Representative)

PRINCIPAL ACTIVITIES: Banking (representative office)
Parent Company: Head office in Brussels, Belgium

BANQUE DE L'ORIENT ARABE ET D'OUTRE MER
BANORABE
PO Box 4370, Dubai
Tel: 284655
Cable: BANO EM
Telex: 45801 Bano EM
Telefax: 236260

Chairman: Dr Naaman Azhari
Senior Executives: Bassem M El Ariss (Regional Manager), Samir El Kaissi (Inspector), Mrs Taghrid Al Rashdan (Supervisor Operations), Georges Yazbeck (Supervisor Credit)

PRINCIPAL ACTIVITIES: Commercial banking
Branch Offices: Paris, London, Muscat (Oman), Dubai and Sharjah (UAE)
Parent Company: Banque de l'Orient Arabe et d'Outre Mer, Paris, France
Subsidiary Companies: Banque du Liban et d'Outre Mer SAL (Beirut); Banorient (Geneva); Banafrique (Ivory Coast)
Principal Bankers: American Express, Manufacturers Hanover Trust Co

Date of Establishment: 1974
No of Employees: 56

BANQUE DU CAIRE
PO Box 1502, Dubai
Tel: 225175/6
Cable: Bancaire
Telex: 45780 EM

PRINCIPAL ACTIVITIES: Commercial banking
Parent Company: Head office: 22 Adly St, PO Box 1495, Cairo, Egypt

BANQUE INDOSUEZ
PO Box 9256, Dubai
Tel: 379211
Cable: Indosu Dubai
Telex: 45860 Indosu EM
Telefax: 379201

Senior Executives: A Monclar (Regional Manager), E Aubrun (Manager)

PRINCIPAL ACTIVITIES: Commercial banking
Branch Offices: In the Middle East: Bahrain (OBU), Abu Dhabi, Dubai, Yemen (Sana'a, Hodeidah, Taiz), Turkey
Parent Company: Head Office: 96 Blvd Haussman, 75008, Paris, France
Subsidiary Companies: Affiliated banks in Saudi Arabia and Sultanate of Oman

Principal Shareholders: Compagnie Financiere de Suez

BANQUE LIBANAISE POUR LE COMMERCE (FRANCE) SA

PO Box 4207, Dubai
Tel: 222291
Cable: Bancoliba
Telex: 45671 Balib EM

Chairman: Jean Aboujaoude (also General Manager)
Senior Executives: Jean Maher (Regional Manger UAE Branches)

PRINCIPAL ACTIVITIES: Commercial banking
Branch Offices: Abu Dhabi; Sharjah; Ras Al Khaimah
Parent Company: Head office in France: 7 rue Auber, 75009 Paris

BANQUE PARIBAS

PO Box 7233, Dubai
Tel: 532929
Cable: PARIBAS
Telex: 45755 PARIBAS EM

PRINCIPAL ACTIVITIES: Commercial banking
Branch Offices: Gulf Branches: Abu Dhabi; Dubai; Qatar; Oman; Bahrain
Parent Company: Head office in France: 3 rue d'Antin, 750002 Paris

Date of Establishment: 1974

BAQER MOHEBI EST

PO Box 267, Dubai
Tel: 859565
Cable: Mohebi Dubai
Telex: 45606 Mhebi Em
Telefax: 858274

President: Zainal Mohebi
Directors: S H Siadat (General Manager)

PRINCIPAL ACTIVITIES: Agents, importers, distributors of foodstuffs, tobacco, toiletries and household goods, disposable paperware, luggage products, department store owners
Principal Agencies: Honig Foods, Holland; Twining, UK; Volvic, France; American Tourister, USA; BT Export, Spain; Cross Paperware, UK; DCL Yeast, UK; Ducros, France; Hills Bros Coffee, USA; Needlers, UK; Puratos, Belgium; Pal Int'l, UK; Scott Paper, Belgium; Unibon/Hirtschler, Germany
Branch Offices: Abu Dhabi, Ras Al Khaimah, Al Ain
Associated Companies: Mohebi Centre Department Store; Mohebi Shipping & Intl Forwarding; MTE Middle East; Mohebi Marine Services; GSA & Air Cargo Service for Aeroflot
Principal Bankers: National Bank of Dubai, Deira

Date of Establishment: 1938
No of Employees: 100

BARCLAYS BANK PLC

PO Box 1891, Dubai Pearl Bldg, Bin Yas St, Deira, Dubai
Tel: 226158
Telex: 45820 EM

PRINCIPAL ACTIVITIES: Commercial banking

Branch Offices: Abu Dhabi: PO Box 2734, Tel 335313, Fax 345815
Parent Company: Head office: 54 Lombard St, London EC3V 9EX, UK

BASTI & MUKTHA ASSOCIATES

PO Box 2393, Dubai
Tel: 282111/4
Cable: Swamiji
Telex: 46041 Muktha EM

Chairman: S K Pathak (also Managing Director)
Directors: Lahej Bin Khalifa Al-Basti, J K Patel, C K Sibal
Senior Executives: Y N Khanna (General Manager Construction), Sharad Arora (Projects Manager), Ashok K Hazra (Projects Manager), N Purushothaman (Financial Controller)

PRINCIPAL ACTIVITIES: Civil engineering and contracting and general trading
Subsidiary Companies: Bilt Middle East Ltd, Dubai
Principal Bankers: Union Bank of the Middle East Ltd; Grindlays Bank Plc

Principal Shareholders: S K Pathak; J K Patel; Lahej Bin Khalifa Al Basti
Date of Establishment: 1974
No of Employees: 900

BICC MIDDLE EAST LTD

PO Box 683, Dubai
Tel: 432335
Telex: 46286
Telefax: 432202

Chairman: P Bibby
Directors: C J Paskins, J G Davis, H H Vasi (Company Secretary)

PRINCIPAL ACTIVITIES: Supply of electric cables, switchgear and accessories
Branch Offices: BICC Pyrotenax Ltd, PO Box 11292, Dubai; BICC (ME) Ltd, PO Box 5996, Sharjah, Tel 354497, Telex 68576
Parent Company: BICC Plc, London, UK

BILT MIDDLE EAST (PVT) LTD

PO Box 2393, Dubai
Tel: 282142
Cable: Swamiji
Telex: 46041 Muktha EM

Chairman: S K Pathak
Directors: L M Thapar, C K Sibal, Prem Patnaik
Senior Executives: Rakesh Talwar (General Manager), K B Mohan Chandran (Projects Manager), N Purushothama (Financial Controller)

PRINCIPAL ACTIVITIES: Electrical engineering, contracting and trading
Branch Offices: PO Box 306, Abu Dhabi
Parent Company: Al-Basti & Muktha Associates, Dubai
Principal Bankers: Grindlays Bank, Dubai; Union Bank of the Middle East, Dubai

Principal Shareholders: Al-Basti & Muktha Associates, Dubai; Ballarpur Industries Limited, India
Date of Establishment: 15th March, 1978
No of Employees: 100

BIN HAIDER, MOHAMMAD OMAR, EST

PO Box 3555, Dubai
Tel: 245191/4
Cable: Khair Dubai
Telex: 45487 KHAIR EM
Telefax: 246260

Chairman: Mohammad Omar Bin Haider

Senior Executives: R P Murgai (General Sales Manager), Yousuf Abed Raba (Accounts Manager), Saed Abu Sharben (Personnel Manager), K S Premkumar (Real Estate Manager)

PRINCIPAL ACTIVITIES: General trading and contracting. Manufacturers' representatives. Production, import and distribution of tools, machinery, welding equipment, aluminium products and industrial gases; automobiles and tyres, real estate, hotel, etc
Principal Agencies: Victor Equipment, USA; Ridge Tool, USA; CMC, Italy; Nippon Electrodes, Japan; Nitchi Chain Block, Japan, etc
Subsidiary Companies: Dubai Equipment Co, PO Box 3044, Dubai; Dubai Industrial Gas Plants, PO Box 1174, Dubai; Aluminium Factory, Dubai; Hotel Excelsior; Abu Dhabi Equipment Co, PO Box 4303, Abu Dhabi; SISCO Abu Dhabi

No of Employees: 200

BIN HAIDER, SALEH OMER,

PO Box 229, Dubai
Tel: 660291
Telex: 45680 EM

Chairman: Saleh Omer Bin Haider

PRINCIPAL ACTIVITIES: Electrical engineering, import and distribution of electrical equipment and appliances
Subsidiary Companies: Bin Haider Butane Gas Agency; Bin Haider Electrical Contractors; Bin Haider Commercial Agency

BIN HUSSAIN ALUMINIUM FACTORIES

PO Box 1535, Dubai
Tel: 660643, 661567
Cable: Binhussain Dubai
Telex: 45947 Husain EM

Chairman: Hussain Mohamed Bin Hussain

PRINCIPAL ACTIVITIES: Processing and fabrication of aluminium doors, windows, shop fronts, balustrade, rolling shutters, etc
Principal Agencies: International Aluminium Corporation, California, USA
Subsidiary Companies: Shanfari and Bin Hussain Aluminium Co, PO Box 3340, Ruwi, Sultanate of Oman

Principal Shareholders: Hussain Mohamed Bin Hussain

BIN LADIN CONTRACTING & TRADING CO

PO Box 1555, Dubai
Tel: 691500
Telex: 45991 Binldn EM
Telefax: 691350

Chairman: Sheikh Bakr M Bin Laden
Directors: Sheikh Ghaleb M Bin Laden, Abu Bakr Salim Al Hamid (Managing Director)
Senior Executives: Hashim Alawi Al Safi (Asst Managing Director), Michael F Deery (Financial Adviser), Wim Domisse (Technical Adviser), Ian Shanly (Construction Manager), Kais Al Dhandashi (Personnel Manager)

PRINCIPAL ACTIVITIES: Civil engineering, roadwords, piling, ground services, building, electrical contracting
Branch Offices: PO Box 2014, Sharjah, UAE; PO Box 539, Ras Al Khaimah, UAE; PO Box 762, Fujairah
Subsidiary Companies: Binladin Overseas Private Ltd
Principal Bankers: British Bank of the Middle East; Citibank; Lloyds Bank; Bank of Oman; Indosuez Bank

Principal Shareholders: Sheikh Bakr M Bin Laden
Date of Establishment: UAE 1967; Saudi Arabia 1935
No of Employees: 4,000

BIN MASOOD, MOHAMMED, & SONS

PO Box 3945, Dubai
Tel: 226151/4
Telex: 45556 Masood EM

Directors: Hamed Buti Al Masood

PRINCIPAL ACTIVITIES: Import and distribution of air-conditioning and refrigeration equipment, electrical equipment; and building materials
Branch Offices: Abu Dhabi

BINALI DIVING SERVICES

PO Box 2876, Dubai
Tel: 480481
Cable: Binalidiv
Telex: 45922 Teams EM

PRINCIPAL ACTIVITIES: Diving services (oilfield, shipping, civil engineering), marine craft
Branch Offices: PO Box 6985, Abu Dhabi
Parent Company: Head office in Qatar: PO BOx 3687, Doha

BIX (GULF) LTD

PO Box 2976, Dubai
Tel: 436625
Telex: 46044

Directors: L M Schmidt (Managing Director), M D McAllister

PRINCIPAL ACTIVITIES: Quality control, consultancy and inspection, non destructive testing, heat treatment etc
Branch Offices: Abu Dhabi, Qatar, Bahrain, Kuwait, Oman, Saudi Arabia
Parent Company: BIX Holdings Ltd
Principal Bankers: Barclays Bank plc

BOC HEALTHCARE

Ohmeda BOC Healthcare

PO Box 7021, Dubai
Tel: 665506
Telex: 46060

Senior Executives: G J Haslam (Business Manager)

PRINCIPAL ACTIVITIES: Healthcare products and services
Parent Company: BOC Ltd, London, UK

BOODAI TRADING COMPANY

PO Box 5108, Dubai
Tel: 690080, 660975
Cable: Boodai
Telex: 45597 Bodai EM
Telefax: 661361, 624027

Chairman: Mustafa Jassim Boodai
Directors: Jassim Marzouk Boodai (Deputy Chairman), Marwan M Boodai (Managing Director), Jassim Mustafa Boodai (Regional Director)
Senior Executives: Fawaz Ibrahim Al Qattan (Corporate Manager), Walid F Kaassamani (Corporate Treasurer), Aziz H Siddiqui (Corporate Financial Controller)

PRINCIPAL ACTIVITIES: Manufacturers' representaton, import and distribution, construction equipment, industrial & engineering products and equipment, oilfield supplies, home appliances and sewing machines
Principal Agencies: P&H Cranes, Blaw Knox Pavers, Furukawa Loaders, TCM & Manitou Forklifts, Zenith Block Making Machines, Hudig Dewatering Pumps, Airman Compressors, Lescha Concrete Mixers, Westco Dumpers, Kubota Tractors, Grindex Dewatering Pumps, Lincoln Welding Machines, Seam Bar Bending & Cutting Machines, Sioux Steam Cleaners, Meiwa Compactors & Trowels, Singer Sewing Machines & Home Appliances
Parent Company: Boodai Trading Co Ltd, PO Box Safat 1287, Kuwait
Subsidiary Companies: Arab Equipment Est, PO Box 1660, Dammam, Saudi Arabia; Boodai Trading Co, PO Box 4569, Doha, Qatar
Principal Bankers: Al Ahli Bank; Bank of Credit & Commerce (Emirates)

Principal Shareholders: Mustafa Jassim Boodai, Jassim Boodai, Marwan Boodai
Date of Establishment: 1975
No of Employees: 90

BRITISH ALCAN BUILDING PRODUCTS LTD

PO Box 5639, Dubai
Tel: 581035
Telex: 45936 TCTI EM
Telefax: 581140

Senior Executives: P Ellerby (General Manager)

PRINCIPAL ACTIVITIES: Manufacture of aluminium building products
Parent Company: Head office in Worcester, UK

BRITISH BANK OF THE MIDDLE EAST (THE)

UAE Management Office, Sheikh Rachid Bldg, Bur Dubai, PO Box 66, Dubai
Tel: 535000 (General)
Cable: Bactria Dubai
Telex: 45424 BBMED EM
Telefax: 531005

Chairman: W Purves CBE DSO
Directors: J R H Bond, F J French, J M Gray, A P Hill CBE, S Robertson, P J Wrangham
Senior Executives: D C Howells (Chief Executive Officer UAE), Abdul Jalil Yousuf (Deputy Chief Executive Officer UAE), W E Garbett (Manager Finance), T S T Major (Manager Services), C A Ewin (Manager Treasury & Foreign Exchange), Mohammed Noor Hussain Tahlak (Manager Private Banking), S R Bannister (Manager Dubai Branch)

PRINCIPAL ACTIVITIES: Commercial banking
Branch Offices: in the UAE: Al Ain, Deira, Dubai, Jebal Ali, Fujairah, Ras Al Khaimah, Sharjah; In the Middle East & Africa: Bahrain, Jordan, Lebanon, Oman, Qatar, United Arab Emirates, Egypt, Cyprus, Zambia
Parent Company: The Hongkong & Shanghai Banking Corporation Ltd, 1 Queen's Road Central, PO Box 64, Hong Kong, Tel 8221111, Fax 8101112
Associated/Subsidiary Companies: Saudi British Bank; Middle East Finance Co Ltd
Financial Information:

	1988 St£'000	1989 St£'000
Deposits	1,470,432	1,761,605
Advances	733,482	904,687
Net profit	17,403	22,560
Authorised capital	150,000	150,000
Share capital	100,000	100,000
Total assets	1,702,193	2,030,016

Principal Shareholders: The Hongkong and Shanghai Banking Corporation Limited
Date of Establishment: Inc by Royal Charter 1889, founded in UAE 1946
No of Employees: 821 in the UAE

BUILDERS MERCHANTS & GENERAL AGENCIES

PO Box 4112, Dubai
Tel: 665101/9
Cable: Bumga Dubai
Telex: 45501 Bumga EM

Sole Proprietor: G V Eswar

PRINCIPAL ACTIVITIES: Import, stocking and distribution of all kinds of building materials, structural steel, pipes, and oilfield supplies
Branch Offices: PO Box 6572, Abu Dhabi
Subsidiary Companies: Bumga Autoparts, PO Box 4112, Dubai; Bumga Enterprices, PO Box 6572, Abu Dhabi

Principal Bankers: National Bank of Dubai Ltd

Date of Establishment: 1968
No of Employees: 150

BUSINESS COMMUNICATIONS UAE (PVT) LTD (BCL)

PO Box 233, Dubai
Tel: 225135
Telex: 47631 DUTEN EM

Senior Executives: Ian M Mack (General Manager), Russell Jones, Ken Mason, Roy Davis, Shaun Kirk

PRINCIPAL ACTIVITIES: Fire protection systems, system design, consultancy, supply, installation, commissioning and subsequent maintenance of: radio and audio visual systems, mini-computers, hotel and hospital low voltage systems, airport communications, security and surveillance systems, marine communications, digitising and scanning services
Principal Agencies: Marconi, Awa New Zealand, Stentor, Electrosonic, Millbank, McDonnell Douglas Information Systems, August Systems, Coherent, Andrew, Chloride, Ascoa, Morris Merryweather
Branch Offices: PO Box 2534, Abu Dhabi, Tel 720646, Telex 22457 BCLAHEM
Parent Company: Dubai Transport Company (Dutco)
Subsidiary Companies: Dutco Tennant (ME) Pvt Ltd
Principal Bankers: National Bank of Dubai

Date of Establishment: 1976

C ITOH & CO LTD (DUBAI LIAISON OFFICE)

See ITOH, C, & CO LTD (DUBAI LIAISON OFFICE)

CALTEX AL KHALIJ

PO Box 2155, Dubai
Tel: 470332, 373220
Telex: 45544 Caltx EM

PRINCIPAL ACTIVITIES: Manufacture and supply of lube oils and greases
Branch Offices: Bahrain

CARLTON HOTELS COMPANY

Carlton Tower Hotel, PO Box 1955, Dubai
Tel: 227111
Cable: Carlton Dubai
Telex: 46410 Cartel; 46328 Cartow EM
Telefax: 228249, 273907

Chairman: Sheikh Abdul Aziz Al-Masaeed
Directors: Sheikh Hassan Harmouch, Sheikh Sami Assaf
Senior Executives: Mohammed Tufail (General Manager), Samir Chami (Asst General Manager)

PRINCIPAL ACTIVITIES: Hotel and catering management
Branch Offices: Carlton Hotel, Kuwait
Principal Bankers: Arab African Int'l Bank Dubai

Date of Establishment: 1976
No of Employees: 200

CENTRAL BANK OF THE UAE

PO Box 448, Dubai
Tel: 536655
Telex: 45645 Markzi EM
Telefax: 532955

Chairman: Sheikh Suroor Bin Mohammed Al Nahyan
Directors: Mohammed Abdullah Al Kaz (Vice-Chairman)
Senior Executives: Mohammed S Al Marri (Branch Manager)

PRINCIPAL ACTIVITIES: Central banking
Branch Offices: Ras Al Khaimah; Sharjah; Fujairah; Al Ain
Parent Company: Head office in Abu Dhabi

CGEE ALSTHOM

181 Deira Tower, PO Box 1178, Dubai
Tel: 239539
Telex: 48856 CGEAT Kt
Telefax: 239538

Directors: J Richer (Honorary Chairman), G Glasser (Honorary
Chairman), M H Marty (Honorary Chairman & Director), P
Boisseau (Chairman & Chief Executive Officer), M A Rivet
(President & Chief Operating Officer), D Leger (Vice President
& Secretary)
Senior Executives: Aejazuddin Shaikh (Regional Delegate)

PRINCIPAL ACTIVITIES: Electrical equipment and contracting,
instrumentation and control
Parent Company: CGEE Alsthom, Paris, France
Associated Companies: Cegelec Contracting Co, PO Box 84,
Dhahran Airport 31932, Saudi Arabia; Comsip Al A'Ali, PO
Box 26949, Manama, Bahrain; Division Comsip, PO Box
7055, Abu Dhabi, UAE
Principal Bankers: Societe Generale, Credit Lyonnais

Date of Establishment: 1971
No of Employees: 20,798 (Group)

CHEMICAL BANK

PO Box 4619, Deira, Dubai
Tel: 225279, 225270
Telex: 45885 CHEMBK EM

PRINCIPAL ACTIVITIES: Banking (representative office)
Parent Company: Chemical Bank, New York

Date of Establishment: 1975

CHOITHRAM, T, & SONS

PO Box 5249, Dubai
Tel: 666670
Cable: Choithson
Telex: 45812 Bytco EM
Telefax: 691137

Chairman: T C Pagarani
Directors: R D Rajwani, V L Pamnani (Managing Director), R P
Thanwani (Resident Director), L T Pagarani
Senior Executives: K C Rajwani (General Manager)

PRINCIPAL ACTIVITIES: Chain of supermarkets, retailers and
wholesalers of consumer goods, foodstuffs and novelties
Principal Agencies: Lipton; C C Friesland; Giant; Heinz; Natco;
El Almendro; Weetabix; Nalleys; Supercook; Schwartz; Rauch;
Fruitella; Smith Kendon; Callard & Bowser; Primo; Drackett;
Hochland; Dairy Crest; Plough; Britvic; SPC; Americana;
Ajinomoto; Kandos; 3M Scotch Brite; Terry's; Hipp; McCain;
Blue Diamond; Lensi; Albal (Dow); Lilypak; Kimball; Crystal;
etc
Branch Offices: PO Box 1142, Ras Al Khaimah, UAE; PO Box
5663, Sharjah, UAE; PO Box 470, Abu Dhabi, UAE; PO Box
15257, Al Ain, UAE
Subsidiary/Associated Companies: T Choithram & Sons
(London) Ltd, UK; T Choithram & Sons, Freetown; National
Confectionery Co Ltd, Freetown; T Choithram & Sons
(Canary) SA, Las Palmas; T Choithram & Sons (HK) Ltd, Hong
Kong; T Choithram & Sons Cameroun SARL; T Choithram &
Sons (USA) INc, New York; T Choithram E Hijos (Canarias)
SA, Spain; T Choithram & Sons (Japan) Ltd, Osaka; T
Choithram & Sons (HK) Ltd, Taiwan; Shiva Import & Export
(Thai) Ltd, Bangkok; Technical & Consumer Services Co Ltd,
Muscat; P T Choithram Sakti, Indonesia
Principal Bankers: Standard Chartered Bank; Grindlays Bank;
Barclays Bank; Banque Paribas
Financial Information:

	1990 US$'000
Sales turnover	86,000

Date of Establishment: 1975
No of Employees: 865

CITIBANK NA

PO Box 749, Dubai
Tel: 522100
Cable: Citibank
Telex: 45422 Citibk EM
Telefax: 9714-512239

Senior Executives: Ahmed Bin Breek (General Manager UAE),
Anjun Iqbal (International Banking & Finance Manager UAE)

PRINCIPAL ACTIVITIES: Commercial, retail and private banking
Branch Offices: In the UAE: Al Ain; Dubai; Deira; Sharjah; Abu
Dhabi
Parent Company: Citicorp
Subsidiary Companies: In the Middle East: Saudi American
Bank

CKK MIDDLE EAST (PVT) LTD

PO Box 6589, Dubai
Tel: 4-370923, 370525
Telex: 46325 Ckk EM
Telefax: 971-4-373189

Senior Executives: Nick Willemse (General Manager), Sipco de
Jonge (Technical Sales Manager), Zain Moh'd Ali (Chief
Accountant), Tim Hoefsloot (Contracts Coordinator)

PRINCIPAL ACTIVITIES: Roofing systems, steel & aluminium
cladding, suspended ceilings, insulation
Principal Agencies: Ruberoid Roofing Felt; SBS modified
Flexobit Waterproofing Membrance; EPDM; PVC Hypalon
Roofing Membrane; Extruded Polystyrene Insulation
Branch Offices: Abu Dhabi, Bahrain, Qatar, Oman
Parent Company: Key & Kramer NV
Principal Bankers: Algemene Bank Nederland NV; Amro Bank
Dubai; Banque Indosuez Dubai

Principal Shareholders: Key & Kramer Divisie Bouw BV,
Maassluis, Holland
Date of Establishment: 1975
No of Employees: 120

CLEVELAND BRIDGE & ENGINEERING MIDDLE EAST (PVT) LTD

PO Box 16765, Dubai
Tel: 35551 (Jebel Ali)
Telex: 47440 CBEJA EM
Telefax: (97184) 35416 (Jebel Ali)

Chairman: Annis Jallaf
Senior Executives: J J Beeton (Director & General Manager), M
A Khawar (Finance Manager), B Towlard (Works Manager), G
Broad (Marketing Manager), D H Shaw (Construction
Manager)

PRINCIPAL ACTIVITIES: Structural steel design, fabrication and
erection for buildings, bridges, pipeline supports, refineries,
power plants and off-shore structures
Branch Offices: Abu Dhabi: PO Box 6133, Tel 3232142/3;
Bahrain; PO Box 26137, Tel 728334/5; Oman: PO Box 169,
Tel 697068
Parent Company: Trafalgar House Plc, London, UK
Principal Bankers: British Bank of the Middle East; Barclays
Bank
Financial Information:

	1988/89 Dh'000	1989/90 Dh'000
Sales turnover	55,000	75,000
Profits	5,000	8,000
Authorised capital	20,000	20,000
Paid-up capital	8,500	8,500

Principal Shareholders: Government of Dubai; Trafalgar House
PLC, UK
Date of Establishment: 1977
No of Employees: 510

UAE (Dubai)

CLUTTONS CHARTERED SURVEYORS

PO Box 1446, Dubai
Tel: 282428
Telefax: 218337

Senior Executives: R C Hinchey (Resident Partner)

PRINCIPAL ACTIVITIES: Property valuations, property
management, residential and commercial letting, feasability
studies
Branch Offices: Bahrain, Sharjah, Muscat
Parent Company: Cluttons, 45 Berkeley Square, London W1,
UK

Principal Shareholders: A member of the Lincoln Property
Group of Companies
Date of Establishment: 1975

COASTAL TRADING & CONTRACTING CO

PO Box 2323, Dubai
Tel: 660648, 660848
Cable: Cotco EM
Telex: 45656 Cotco EM
Telefax: 664795

Directors: Yousuf M Najibi, Abdul Aziz Eshaq, Ebrahim Eshaq
Senior Executives: D K Sadekar (Chief Accountant)

PRINCIPAL ACTIVITIES: Dealers in imported furniture,
furnishings, buidling products such as kitchen units, built-in
wardrobes, ironmongery items
·*Principal Agencies:* Dunlopillo Ltd, UK; Adrian Stokes (O) Ltd,
UK; Northcol A/s, Denmark; Mobilia Italia, Italy; B & B Italia,
Italy; Interlubke, W Germany; Saporiti Italia, Italy; Crossley
Carpets, UK; Silent Gliss, UK; HK Furniture, UK; Leicht
Einbaukuchen, Germany; Doimo Salotti, Italy, etc
Associated Companies: Precast Concrete Products; Union
Industries
Principal Bankers: United Bank; Union Bank of the Middle East

Date of Establishment: 1967
No of Employees: Over 100

COMEX MIDDLE EAST

Dnata Bldg, PO Box 4596, Dubai
Tel: 224164, 224165
Cable: Comdive
Telex: 45546 Comdiv EM

PRINCIPAL ACTIVITIES: Underwater services; diving
contractors
Principal Bankers: Banque Paribas; United Arab Bank Ltd

COMMERCIAL BANK OF DUBAI LTD

PO Box 2668, Dubai
Tel: 523355 (20 lines)
Cable: Trubank Dubai
Telex: 49600 Trbnk EM, 45468 Trbnk EM, 46310 Trfox EM
Telefax: 520444, 524796

Chairman: Ahmed Humaid Al Tayer
Directors: Saeed Mohamed Al Ghandi (Deputy Chairman),
Saeed Ahmed Ghobash (Deputy Chairman), Ali Abdulla Al
Noman, Abdul Rehman Saif Al Ghurair, Abdul Wahed Hassan
Al Rostamani, Khalid Juma Al Majid, Saeed Mohammed Al
Mulla
Senior Executives: Omar Abdul Rahim Leyas (General
Manager), Shabib Khansaheb (Deputy General Manager
Admin & Finance), Yacoub Y Hassan (Deputy General
Manager Credit & International)

PRINCIPAL ACTIVITIES: Banking
Branch Offices: Dubai: PO Box 2668, Dubai; Deira: PO Box
1709, Dubai; Sharjah: PO Box 677, Sharjah; Al Maktoum: PO
Box 3393, Deira, Dubai; Jumairah: PO Box 2668, Dubai; Ras
Al Khaimah: PO Box 5849, Ras al Khaimah; Abu Dhabi: PO

Box 2466, Abu Dhabi; Jebel Ali: PO Box 2668, Jebel Ali
Village, Dubai; Central Military Command (Cash Office), PO
Box 2668, Dubai
Financial Information:

	1989 Dh'000	1990 Dh'000
Deposits	828,750	914,127
Loans & advances	778,623	808,127
Retained profit	35,568	40,120
Authorised capital	500,000	500,000
Paid-up capital	200,000	200,000
Shareholders'funds	284,378	297,998
Total assets	1,274,792	1,401,481

Principal Shareholders: Publicly held shares; The Government
of Dubai holding 20% of share capital
Date of Establishment: 1969
No of Employees: 282

CONSOLIDATED INVESTMENT & CONTRACTING CO (CICON)

PO Box 3311, Dubai
Tel: 664472/3/4
Cable: Cicon Dubai
Telex: 22265 Cicon EM

Senior Executives: Nasser Masri (Dubai Branch Manager)

PRINCIPAL ACTIVITIES: Import and distribution of building
materials, sanitary ware
Parent Company: Head Office: PO Box 660, Abu Dhabi, Telex
22265 Cicon EM
Subsidiary Companies: United Sanitary Co, Abu Dhabi; Civil
Construction Gulf, Abu Dhabi; Studio 2000, Abu Dhabi;
Consolidated Garment, Abu Dhabi
Principal Bankers: Arab Bank; Grindlays Bank; National Bank of
Abu Dhabi

Date of Establishment: Head Office Abu Dhabi: 1968, Dubai
Branch: 1971

CONSTRUCTION MACHINERY CENTER CO (PVT) LTD

PO Box 5261, Deira, Dubai
Tel: 258959
Cable: HEE DUBAI
Telex: 45956 HABTR EM

President: Khalaf Ahmed Al Habtoor
Senior Executives: Subhi M Duraidi (General Manager), Abdul
Hamid Duraidi (Administration & Sales Manager), Jihad
Bizzari (Branch Manager), S N Arshad (Chief Accountant)

PRINCIPAL ACTIVITIES: Marketing of construction machinery
and spare parts and after sales service
Principal Agencies: Friedrichn Wilh Schwing; Arbau
Baumaschinen; Eder Maschinenfabrik; Arrow Construction
Eqpt; Solid Corp; Silla Macchine Edili e Stradali; F LLI Dieci;
Wacker Werke; Welding Industries Ltd; Baranite Ltd; Liebherr-
Export; Karrena; L'Europea; Tokyo Car Corp; Mannesmann
Demag Pokorny; Hazemag Dr E Andreas; Daihatsu Diesel
Mfg; Toyo Kensetsu Kohki; Ohatsu; Nippon Sharyo Seizo
Kaisha; Kramer Werke
Branch Offices: Abu Dhabi; Al Ain
Associated Companies: Al Habtoor Eng. Ent. Co. (PVT) Ltd;
Dubai Metropolitan Hotel; Al Habtoor Motors; Al Habtoor
Marble Factory
Principal Bankers: Commercial Bank of Dubai Ltd; Bank of
Credit & Commerce Intl; Bank of Credit & Commerce
(Emirates)

Principal Shareholders: Khalaf Ahmed Al Habtoor; Riad T Sadik
Date of Establishment: 1977

COOPERS & LYBRAND DELOITTE

PO Box 11339, 7th Floor, Dubai Pearl Bldg, Deira, Dubai
Tel: 233400
Cable: Dehands
Telex: 46696 DHS DB EM
Telefax: 232863

Directors: D Brewer, Dr F Saba
Senior Executives: Tim Heaton, Malcolm Best, Andrew Evans,
Habib Nehme, Alfred Strolla, Camille Sifri

PRINCIPAL ACTIVITIES: Chartered accountants, management
consultants and computer services
Branch Offices: In the Middle East: Abu Dhabi, Bahrain, Dubai,
Oman, Sharjah, Saudi Arabia, Egypt and Lebanon
Parent Company: Head offices in London and New York

Date of Establishment: 1970
No of Employees: 55

COST PARTNERSHIP (GULF)

PO Box 12857, Dubai
Tel: 213609
Telefax: 212900

Partners: A P Davey, R J Thorpe (Consultant), R C Hawthorn

PRINCIPAL ACTIVITIES: Building consultants and quantity
surveyors
Branch Offices: PO Box 26122, Manama, Bahrain, Tel 256826,
Fax 256826
Parent Company: CP Group UK, London, UK
Principal Bankers: Barclays Bank International, Grindlays Bank

Date of Establishment: 1961
No of Employees: 30

COSTAIN INTERNATIONAL LTD

Area Office, PO Box 2526, Dubai
Tel: 450756/7/8/9
Telex: 45434 Cosdb EM

Chairman: J E Langford
Directors: L F C Tarrant (Managing Director)

PRINCIPAL ACTIVITIES: Building and civil engineering
contractors, property development, housing, dredging, mining,
mechanical engineering
Branch Offices: United Arab Emirates; Australia; Canada;
Nigeria; Hong Kong; Muscat (Oman)
Parent Company: Costain Group Plc, UK
Principal Bankers: Lloyds Bank Plc, UK

Principal Shareholders: 100% owned subsidiary of Costain
Group Plc, UK

D G JONES & PARTNERS LTD

See JONES, D G, & PARTNERS LTD

DANWAY

PO Box 1576, Dubai
Tel: 226121
Cable: Danlesco
Telex: 45547 Danco EM

Chairman: Michael Barry
Directors: Y Daneshvar, A Hawkins, A C Ridgway, P I
Jandraman
Senior Executives: J B Fernandes (Senior Manager), F R
Khaleel

PRINCIPAL ACTIVITIES: Electrical engineers; sale, hire and
service of motor controls, AC/DC power supplies, heat
shrinkable products, industrial batteries, U.P.S. systems
Principal Agencies: Dawson Keith; Havant; Hamps; Raychem
Inc; Cutler Hammer Inc; Harmer & Simmons; Klippon;
Waukesha Engines; Polar Engines; Widdop Engines
Parent Company: Associated British Engineering Group,
Southall, Middlesex, UK

Associated Companies: Abu Dhabi: PO Box 47142, Tel 725617,
Telex 22782, Fax 727375
Principal Bankers: Bank of Credit & Commerce, Dubai

Date of Establishment: 1976
No of Employees: 75

DARWISH ENGINEERING

Darwish Bldg, Ras Deira, PO Box 11175, Dubai
Tel: 222285
Cable: Dareng Dubai
Telex: 46146 Dareng EM
Telefax: 211330

Chairman: Kassem Darwish Fakhroo
Senior Executives: Bahas Nahawi (Area Manager UAE)

PRINCIPAL ACTIVITIES: Civil engineering, road and building
contracting
Branch Offices: PO Box 51, Abu Dhabi; PO Box 873, Ajman; PO
Box 183, Doha, Qatar
Parent Company: Kassem & Abdullah Sons of Darwish Fahkroo
Principal Bankers: Invest Bank, Dubai
Financial Information:

	1989
	Dh'000
Sales turnover	55,000
Profits	6,000
Authorised capital	25,000
Paid-up capital	25,000
Total assets	46,000

Principal Shareholders: Qassem & Abdullah Sons of Darwish
Fakhroo, Qatar
Date of Establishment: 1952
No of Employees: 700

DARWISH TRADING COMPANY

PO Box 380, Dubai
Tel: 221667, 212540, 221693
Cable: Tradar
Telex: 45576 Trada EM

Chairman: Haj Kassem Darwish Fakhroo
Directors: Hassan Kassem Darwish (Managing Director)
Senior Executives: Shareef Hassounah (General Manager), T V
Balasubramanian (Area Manager - UAE)

PRINCIPAL ACTIVITIES: Trading in air-conditioners, typewriters
& office equipments, fire proof safes, sanitaryware, building
materials, gift articles etc
Principal Agencies: Mobileast, Italy; Diebold Banking
Equipments; Olivetti Office Equipments; Friedrich Air
conditioners
Branch Offices: Darwish Trading Co, PO Box 222, Abu Dhabi,
UAE; Darwish Trading Co, PO Box 350, Doha, Qatar (Head
Office); Darwish Engineering, PO Box 380, Dubai, UAE
Subsidiary Companies: Kassem Darwish Fakhroo & Sons,
Doha, Qatar; Gulf Automobiles, Doha, Qatar; Orient
Automobiles, Dubai, UAE
Principal Bankers: Standard Chartered Bank; Bank of Credit &
Commerce Emirates

Principal Shareholders: Darwish & Sons
Date of Establishment: 1955
No of Employees: 450

DAWOOD TRADING COMPANY

PO Box 7513, Dubai
Tel: 225036, 281750
Cable: Henabi
Telex: 46092 Farzin EM

President: Arjan M Bhatia
Directors: Jairaj Arjan Bhatia, Vinod Arjan Bhatia
Senior Executives: Mohammed Khamass (Manager), Dawood
Abdul Rehman (Chief Accountant)

PRINCIPAL ACTIVITIES: Import, export, indentors,
manufacturers' representative, shipping agents
Principal Bankers: National Bank of Dubai; Bank of Oman; First
National City Bank of Chicago

Date of Establishment: 1969

DESERT ROOFING & FLOORING CO

PO Box 185, Dubai
Tel: 341003, 341009
Telefax: 341427

Chairman: M A Saleem (Managing Director)
Senior Executives: Kaleem Khan (General Manager), Akhtar
Razvi (Company Secretary)

PRINCIPAL ACTIVITIES: Sub-contracting sales of waterproofing
materials, concrete additives and admixtures, thermal
insulation, concrete repairs
Principal Agencies: Cement Marketing Co, UK; Ronacrete Ltd,
UK; Burt Boulton (Timber) Ltd, UK; Index-Italy; British Uralite,
UK; Plastic & Resins, UK; Interpur, Germany
Branch Offices: PO Box 6716, Abu Dhabi Tel 335349
Principal Bankers: United Bank Ltd, Dubai; Habib Bank AG
Zurich, Abu Dhabi; BCCI
Financial Information:

	1990 Dh'000
Authorised capital	2,000
Paid-up capital	2,000

Principal Shareholders: M A Saleem
Date of Establishment: January 1978
No of Employees: 60

DHL INTERNATIONAL (UAE) LTD

PO Box 6252, Dubai
Tel: 473500
Telex: 45799 DHL DXB EM

PRINCIPAL ACTIVITIES: Worldwide courier service, air and sea
freight clearance and forwarding, marketing of word
processors and related office equipment
Branch Offices: In the Middle East: Bahrain, Cyprus, Egypt
(Cairo, Alexandria), Iran, Jordan, Kuwait, Lebanon, Oman,
Qatar, Saudi Arabia (AlKhobar, Jeddah, Riyadh, Jubail, Tabuk,
Taif), Sudan, UAE (Abu Dhabi, Dubai, Sharjah)

DNATA & DNATA WORLD TRAVEL

Airline Centre, Flame Roundabout, PO Box 1515, Dubai
Tel: 222151 (10 lines)
Cable: Airtravel
Telex: 45728 Dnata EM
Telefax: 214560

Chairman: HH Shiekh Ahmed Bin Saeed Al Maktoum
Senior Executives: Maurice Flanagan (Group Managing
Director), Sultan Dhiyab Saqer (Group Deputy Managing
Director), Ismail Ali Albanna (Director), Gary Chapman
(General Manager Finance), Keith A Longstaff (Senior General
Manager DNATA Agencies), G G K Nair (Company Secretary)

PRINCIPAL ACTIVITIES: IATA approved passenger and cargo
sales agency; aircraft handling, general sales agents
Branch Offices: Sharjah, Fujairah and throughout Dubai
Principal Bankers: British Bank of the Middle East

Date of Establishment: 1959
No of Employees: 2,200

DOWELL SCHLUMBERGER (WESTERN) SA

PO Box 2964, Dubai
Tel: 371976
Cable: Bigorange, Dubai Arabian Gulf
Telex: 46302 DS MEO EM
Telefax: 344572

Senior Executives: Alberto Bertolin (Vice President/General
Manager), Fred Peters (Marketing Manager), Herve Prigent
(Technical Manager), Rod Ritchie (Safety/Environmental
Manager), Alistair Ferguson (Financial Controller), Mumtaz
Khan (Sales Manager), Ian Crane (Personnel Manager)

PRINCIPAL ACTIVITIES: Oil service company, specializing in
cementing, stimulation, enhanced oil recovery, pipeline and
industrial cleaning services
Branch Offices: Saudi Arabia, Abu Dhabi, Dubai, Kuwait, Oman,
Egypt, Pakistan, Syria
Parent Company: Joint venture between Dow Chemical and
Schlumberger Limited
Subsidiary Companies: Dowell Schlumberger Middle East;
Services Dowell Schlumberger; DS Technical Services Inc
Principal Bankers: Citibank, Dubai

Date of Establishment: 1960
No of Employees: 265

DUBAI ALUMINIUM CO LTD
DUBAL

PO Box 3627, Dubai
Tel: Jebel Ali 46666
Cable: Dubal Db
Telex: 47240 Dalja EM (General), 47463 Ingot EM (Sales)
Telefax: Jebel Ali 46646 (Sales), 46292 (General), 46919 (Public
Relations)

Chairman: HE Shaikh Hamdan Bin Rashid Al Maktoum
Senior Executives: I D Livingstone (Chief Executive), B A Mills
(General Manager), C R W Morley (Company Secretary)

PRINCIPAL ACTIVITIES: Primary aluminium smelter;
manufacture of desalinated water (1990: hot metal production:
171,299 tonnes; and water supplies to Dubai: 26.8 million
gallons/day)
Principal Bankers: Lloyds Bank Int, London and Dubai; Citicorp,
London and Dubai; National Bank of Dubai

Principal Shareholders: Government of Dubai
Date of Establishment: May, 1975
No of Employees: 1,300

DUBAI AUTOMATIC BAKERY

PO Box 1705, Riqa, Dubai
Tel: 666615
Cable: Autobakery
Telex: 46138 BAKRY

Chairman: Juma Al Majid
Directors: Mohamed Rashid Daur

PRINCIPAL ACTIVITIES: Production and distribution of bakery
products
Branch Offices: Dubai, Clock Tower, Sharjah; Ras Al Khaima,
Khorfakhan
Subsidiary Companies: Al Jadeed Bakery, Dubai
Principal Bankers: National Bank of Dubai Ltd, United Arab
Bank; Bank of Oman
Financial Information:

	Dh'000
Sales turnover	30,000
Authorised capital	12,000
Paid-up capital	12,000

Principal Shareholders: Juma Al Majid; Mohamed Al Makhawi;
Saif Al Hathboor; Rashid Al Majid
Date of Establishment: 1964
No of Employees: 400

DUBAI CABLE COMPANY (PRIVATE) LIMITED

PO Box 11529, Dubai
Tel: 084-35354 (Jebel Ali)
Telex: 47350 Ducab EM
Telefax: 084-35382

Chairman: HE Mohammed Mahdi Al Tajir
Directors: R W Evans (Managing Director)
Senior Executives: H H Vasi (General Manager Finance), W Bailey (General Manager Sales & Marketing), M M Roy (General Manager Technical), N H Blackwell (General Manager Manufacturing)

PRINCIPAL ACTIVITIES: Manufacture of power cables and building wires
Principal Agencies: BICC Plc, UK
Branch Offices: Northern Emirates Sales Office, Dubai; Oman Sales Office, Muscat; Bahrain Sales Office; Riyadh Sales Office
Parent Company: BICC Plc, UK
Subsidiary Companies: BICC Al Jallaf, Abu Dhabi
Principal Bankers: British Bank of the Middle East, Dubai; National Bank of Dubai, Dubai
Financial Information:

	1990
	Dh'000
Sales turnover	167,000

Principal Shareholders: Government of Dubai; BICC Plc of UK
Date of Establishment: 1979
No of Employees: 185

DUBAI CONTRACTING CO WLL

PO Box 232, Dubai
Tel: 222331/2, 221151
Cable: Dubaico
Telex: 45432 Dcc EM; 46938 Dccb EM

Chairman: Hasan A Yabroudi (also General Manager)

PRINCIPAL ACTIVITIES: Building and civil engineering contractors
Branch Offices: United Arab Emirates (Office in Abu Dhabi, PO Box 324, Tel 829300); Sultanate of Oman (Office in Mutrah, PO Box 1149, Tel 734647)
Associated Companies: Saudi Contracting Co; PO Box 195, Al Khobar, Saudi Arabia
Principal Bankers: National Bank of Abu Dhabi; Banque du Caire; Citibank; Banque Paribas

Date of Establishment: August 1961
No of Employees: 1,000

DUBAI DRYDOCKS

PO Box 8988, Dubai
Tel: 450626
Telefax: 450116
Telex: 48838 Docit Em

Directors: E S Ware (Chief Executive), I K Drever (Financial Director), U I Nielsen (Production Director), J W van der Veer (Commercial Director)

PRINCIPAL ACTIVITIES: Dry dock, complete tank cleaning, galvanising plant, cranage, transport sytems, maintenance and repair of ships of any size
Principal Agencies: Agencia Maritima Laurits Lachmann, Brazil; Eberhardt Agencies, Denmark; CET Werft Und-Handelsvertreturgen Grunewald, W Germany; Arrow Iberica SA, Spain; A & P Appledore Intl, UK; Euro Shipbuilders & Marine Agencies, Netherlands; Henning Astrup, Norway; Transma Ltd, Hong Kong; Henning Astrup, Norway; Nissho Iwai Corp, India
Principal Bankers: The British Bank of the Middle East

Principal Shareholders: 100% Dubai Government
Date of Establishment: Operations started May 1983
No of Employees: approx 700

DUBAI EASTERN GENERAL INSURANCE CO

PO Box 154, Dubai
Tel: 226486, 228685
Cable: Degins
Telex: 45441 Zrwani EM

PRINCIPAL ACTIVITIES: All classes of insurance
Branch Offices: Offices in Abu Dhabi and Sharjah, representatives in UK and Pakistan

DUBAI ELECTRICITY CO

PO Box 564, Dubai
Tel: (971-4) 222111, 226216, 237745
Cable: Kahraba
Telex: 45838 KAHRBA EM
Telefax: (971-4) 281930

Senior Executives: S P Kim (General Manager and Chief Engineer), P P Manghnani (Chief Transmission and Distribution Engineer), S H Lee (Station Manager), Syd Mohd Bin Ghanim (Executive Coordinator), M P Thomas (Financial Manager)

PRINCIPAL ACTIVITIES: Generation and supply of electricity to the Emirate of Dubai
Principal Bankers: Emirates Bank International Ltd
Financial Information:

	1989/90
	Dh'000
Sales turnover	376,904
Authorised capital	140,000
Paid-up capital	49,792
Total assets	2,678,469

Principal Shareholders: HH The Ruler of Dubai
Date of Establishment: 1959
No of Employees: 2,527

DUBAI EQUIPMENT COMPANY

PO Box 3044, Dubai
Tel: 228426, 228427 (Clocktower Division), 281925, 281186 (Al Nasr Square Division)
Cable: Alkhair
Telex: 45487 Khair EM
Telefax: 246260, 228253

Chairman: Mohammed Omer Bin Haider
Senior Executives: G Govind Rao (Senior Marketing Executive)

PRINCIPAL ACTIVITIES: Import and distribution of tools, machinery, welding equipment and industrial oxygen, oilfied supply and building materials, construction equipment
Principal Agencies: Rigid, Victor, OTC, CMC, Jamsdring, Johnshaw, Nippon, Kew
Branch Offices: Al Nasr Square, Dubai; and Abu Dhabi; and Mussaffa
Parent Company: Mohd Omer Bin Haider Est
Subsidiary Companies: Orient Food Factory
Principal Bankers: Dubai Commercial Bank

Principal Shareholders: Mohammed Omer Bin Haider
Date of Establishment: 1957
No of Employees: 140

DUBAI GENERAL TRADING CO (MARINA SHIPCHANDLERS)

PO Box 169, Dubai
Tel: 470755/54
Cable: Marina
Telex: 46039 Marina EM

Chairman: Hamed Butti Al Masood
Senior Executives: Shavak Homi Dubash (Manager)

PRINCIPAL ACTIVITIES: Ship chandling and allied services
Branch Offices: Fujairah and servicing at all major ports of UAE
Principal Bankers: Union Bank of the Middle East; Standard Chartered Bank; Bank of Baroda

DUBAI INSURANCE CO (SAD))

PO Box 3027, Dubai
Tel: 693030
Cable: Assurance
Telex: 45685 EM Dubins
Telefax: 693727

Chairman: Majid Al Futtaim
Directors: Abdulla Rostamani (Deputy Chairman)
Senior Executives: Farouk Huwaidi (General Manager), Elias
   Khoury (Asst General Manager), Mrs Rashida Abdullabhoy
   (Chief Accountant)

PRINCIPAL ACTIVITIES: Insurance and reinsurance
Principal Bankers: National Bank of Dubai Ltd
Financial Information:

	1990 Dh'000
Authorised capital	10,000
Paid-up capital	10,000

Date of Establishment: 1970
No of Employees: 24

DUBAI INTER-CONTINENTAL HOTEL

PO Box 476, Dubai
Tel: 227171
Cable: Inhotelcor
Telex: 45779 Ihchot EM

PRINCIPAL ACTIVITIES: Hotel and catering

Date of Establishment: March 1975
No of Employees: 560

DUBAI INTERNATIONAL HOTEL

PO Box 10001, Opp Dubai Int'l Airport, Dubai
Tel: 245111
Telex: 47333 DIHTL EM
Telefax: 246438

Senior Executives: Aldo Grosso (General Manager), Andrew
   Bushe (Director of Sales & Marketing), S Nadarajah (Financial
   Controller)

PRINCIPAL ACTIVITIES: Hotel business
Parent Company: Trusthouse Forte Hotels Limited

Date of Establishment: 27 September 1979
No of Employees: 337

DUBAI INTERNATIONAL REINFORCED PLASTICS LTD

PO Box 2202, Dubai
Tel: 858080
Cable: Dirpl
Telex: 46081 EM
Telefax: 850956

Chairman: Salim Al Moosa
Directors: A G Hopkins, P Lydiard, P C W Lunt
Senior Executives: P Lydiard (Managing Director), D R Lewis
   (Sales Manager), C Tometzki (Works Manager)

PRINCIPAL ACTIVITIES: Manufacture of glass-fibre reinforced
   plastics products (watertanks, building materials, moulds for
   concrete), decorative gypsum, gypsum tiles, GRC products,
   leisurecraft upto 30ft length and 10ft beam
Principal Agencies: BTR Hydroglas Tanks
Branch Offices: Oman, Saudi Arabia, Kuwait, Qatar, Bahrain
Principal Bankers: Standard Chartered Bank, Dubai
Financial Information:

	1990 Dh'000
Sales turnover	15,000

Date of Establishment: 1974
No of Employees: 130

DUBAI ISLAMIC BANK

PO Box 1080, Dubai
Tel: 214888
Cable: Islami Dubai
Telex: 45889 Islami EM
Telefax: 237243

Chairman: Saeed Ahmad Lootah (and Managing Director)
Directors: Sultan Ahmed Lootah, Merza Al Sayegh, Al Shaikh
   Khalid Al Nohyan, Yousuf Jassem Al Hajji, Nasser Ahmed
   Lootah, Mohd Saleh Al Rayees, Salem Al Mohanadi, Abdul
   Latif Janahi
Senior Executives: Mohamed Ayoub Mohamed (Asst Managing
   Director & General Manager), Ahmed Mohammed Al Shamsi
   (Planning & Follow Up Manager), Hussain Al Rifai (Head of
   General Accounts), Ahmed Nuseirat (Head of Administration),
   Sultan Majid Lootah (Head of Real Estate), Mahmoud Saif
   Uddin (Head of Legal Affairs), Zohair Saeed Al Rabii (Head of
   Computer)

PRINCIPAL ACTIVITIES: General banking following the rules of
   the Islamic religion; finance for major projects
Branch Offices: Abu Dhabi, Al Ain, Ras Al Khaimah, Fujairah,
   Sharjah, Murshid Bazar
Subsidiary Companies: Al Ahli Aluminium; Dubai Islamic Bank
   Printing Press
Financial Information:

	1990 Dh'000
Profits	180,000
Authorised capital	500,000
Paid-up capital	200,000
Total assets	3,261,000

Principal Shareholders: Government of Dubai (10%);
   Government of Kuwait (10%); private interests (80%)
Date of Establishment: 1975 (1395 H)
No of Employees: 430

DUBAI MARITIME TRANSPORT CO

PO Box 855, Dubai
Tel: 371341, 370751
Cable: Promar DUBAI
Telex: 45746 Promar EM
Telefax: 369599

Directors: Hussain M Sultan (Managing Director)
Senior Executives: Darayes F Patel (Administration Manager)

PRINCIPAL ACTIVITIES: Ship owners, operators, charterers,
   shipping agents and ship management
Associated Companies: Technical Engineering and Marine
   Services; Inspection Control (Overseas) Ltd
Principal Bankers: BCC Emirates (BCCE); BCC International

Principal Shareholders: Privately owned by HH The Ruler of
   Dubai
Date of Establishment: 1973

DUBAI METROPOLITAN HOTEL

PO Box 4988, Dubai
Tel: 440000
Cable: Methotel Dubai
Telex: 46999 MTHTL EM
Telefax: 441146

Chairman: Khalaf A Al-Habtoor

PRINCIPAL ACTIVITIES: Hotel business
Principal Agencies: The Representation Business Ltd, London,
   UK
Parent Company: Al-Habtoor Engineering Enterprises Co (Pvt)
   Ltd (Khalaf Al-Habtoor)
Principal Bankers: Bank of Credit & Commerce (Emirates)

Date of Establishment: February 1979
No of Employees: 195

DUBAI MINERAL WATER COMPANY

Zaabeel Road, Al Kola Roundabout, Dubai Side, Dubai
Tel: 371110
Cable: Monish Dubai
Telex: 46804 Kola Em
Telefax: 04 370296

Chairman: HH Sheikh Hamdan Bin Rasheed Al Maktoum
Directors: Mirza Hussain Al Sayegh
Senior Executives: Nazih Abu Kamel (Financial Manager), Hilmi
  Afif Abdulla (Chief Accountant)

PRINCIPAL ACTIVITIES: Bottling and distribution of soft drinks
Principal Agencies: Akras International, Austria
Subsidiary Companies: Dubai Ice Company

Principal Shareholders: HH Sheikh Hamdan Bin Rasheed Al
  Maktoum, Her Highness Maryam Bint Rasheed Al Maktoum,
  HE Mahdi Al Tajer
Date of Establishment: 1964
No of Employees: 50

DUBAI NATIONAL SHIPPING CORP

PO Box 154, Dubai
Tel: 222756, 223644
Cable: Dunasco
Telex: 45441 EM

Senior Executives: Ebrahim Zarwani (Managing Director),
  Mohamed Saleh Zarwani, Capt Rashid Hamlani

PRINCIPAL ACTIVITIES: Shipping lines and agents, steamship
  transportation

DUBAI NATURAL GAS CO (DUGAS)

PO Box 4311, Dubai
Tel: 56234 (Jebel Ali)
Cable: NATGAS
Telex: 45741 DUGAS EM
Telefax: 56118 (Jebal Ali)

Chairman: HH Sheikh Hamdan Bin Rashid Al Maktoum

PRINCIPAL ACTIVITIES: Production of propane, butane and
  heavier NGL

Principal Shareholders: 100% Dubai Government
Date of Establishment: April 1980

DUBAI OXYGEN COMPANY

PO Box 11318, Dubai
Tel: 660983
Cable: Acetylene Dubai
Telex: DOC EM 47963
Telefax: 690168

Chairman: Abdul Rehman Zayed
Senior Executives: Ralph S Moore (VP & General Manager
  Operations), James A Tilley (VP & General Manager
  Administration)

PRINCIPAL ACTIVITIES: Manufacture and distribution of
  industrial and medical gases and dealers in welding and
  safety equipment
Parent Company: National Industrial Gas Plant - Doha - Quatar
Subsidiary/Associated Companies: Industrial Gas Company, PO
  Box 4273, Abu Dhabi; National Industrial Gas Plant, PO Box
  1391, Doha
Principal Bankers: British Bank of the Middle East
Financial Information:

	1989/90 Dh'000
Sales turnover	6,800
Profits	800
Paid-up capital	3,000
Total assets	5,000

Principal Shareholders: Mohammed Hamed Al Mana
Date of Establishment: 1970

DUBAI PETROLEUM COMPANY

PO Box 2222, Dubai
Tel: 442990
Cable: Dupetco
Telex: 45423 Dupetco; 45557 EM
Telefax: 462200

President: J I Horning
Senior Executives: Daniel L McWilliams (Vice-President &
  General Manager of Operations), James A Tilley (Vice-
  President & General Manager of Administration), Allen R
  Thyssen (Manager Government & Partner Affairs)

PRINCIPAL ACTIVITIES: Crude oil exploration and production

Date of Establishment: 1963
No of Employees: 975

DUBAI RADIO & COLOUR TELEVISION

PO Box 1695, Dubai
Tel: 470255
Telex: 45605 Drctv EM

Chairman: Shaikh Hasher Maktoum (Director of Information
  Department)
Directors: Abdul Ghafoor Sayed Ibrahim (Director General)

PRINCIPAL ACTIVITIES: Broadcasting, production, distribution
Subsidiary/Associated Companies: Arabian Gulf Productions
  Corporation, TV Production Centre
Principal Bankers: British Bank of the Middle East

Date of Establishment: 1974 Television, 1971 Radio
No of Employees: 400

DUBAI RAMADA HOTEL

PO Box 7979, Dubai
Tel: 521010
Telex: 48333 Ram DB EM
Telefax: 521033

Senior Executives: Miranda Brabon (Executive Assistant
  Manager), Charles Barks (Financial Controller), Mohammed
  Farid (Director of Sales)

PRINCIPAL ACTIVITIES: Hotel business

No of Employees: 200

DUBAI REAL ESTATE CO

PO Box 1897, Dubai
Tel: 228680, 227335

Directors: Elias S Bahou (Partner), Saif Al Ashram

PRINCIPAL ACTIVITIES: Real estate agency and management
Principal Bankers: Bank of Oman

Principal Shareholders: Partnership

DUBAI TOBACCO COMPANY

PO Box 1001, Dubai
Tel: 225251
Cable: Alabela
Telex: 45477 Abela EM
Telefax: 06-333764

Chairman: Albert Abela
Directors: Ghazal Younis (Gulf Manager)
Senior Executives: Riyad Sartan (Area Sales Manager)

PRINCIPAL ACTIVITIES: Distribution of tobacco and products
Principal Agencies: Kent Cigarettes; Brown & Williamson Int
  (Oman)
Branch Offices: PO Box 2941, Abu Dhabi; PO Box 650, Muscat,
  Oman
Associated Companies: Albert Abela Dubai
Principal Bankers: National Bank of Abu Dhabi

Principal Shareholders: Mehdi Al Tajer, Nahyan Bin Hamdam Al Nahyan, Saif Al Zawawee
Date of Establishment: 1964
No of Employees: 23

DUBAI TRADE & TRUST CO (PVT) LTD

PO Box 9243, Dubai
Tel: 373030 (10 lines)
Cable: MOHAFA
Telex: 48626 MOHAFA EM
Telefax: 373367

Senior Executives: John C Hitchcock (General Manager)

PRINCIPAL ACTIVITIES: Shipping, clearing and forwarding agents, charterers
Principal Agencies: Orient Overseas Container Line; Lloyd Triestino; Contship Containerlines Lts; Danzas AG
Subsidiary Companies: Sotinmar Shipping Co; IML Air Couriers (UAE); Sotinmar Airfreight Services
Principal Bankers: Lloyds Bank

Principal Shareholders: Mohamed Al Fayed, Ali Al Fayed, Salah Al Fayed, Emad Al Fayed
Date of Establishment: 1976
No of Employees: 53

DUBAI TRADE CENTRE MANAGEMENT CO

Dubai World Trade Centre, PO Box 9292, Dubai
Tel: (971-4) 372200
Telex: 47474 DITC EM
Telefax: (971-4) 373493

Chairman: Sheikh Hamdan Bin Rashid Al Maktoum
Directors: Christoph Bettermann (Director), Adnan Abdul Karim (Director), Ahmed Lutfi (Director)
Senior Executives: Ian Luxton (General Manager), John Lake (Manager, Apartments), Simon Horgan (Sales & Marketing Manager), Abdullah Mohammed (Administration Manager), Clive Lowe (Property and Office Leasing Manager)

PRINCIPAL ACTIVITIES: Management, leasing and marketing of office, exhibition, conference and serviced apartments complex, management training centre
Branch Offices: International Office: UK: Trade Centre Management Company, 17 Waterloo Place, London SW1Y 4AR, Tel 01-930-3881, Telex 919916, Fax 071-976-1772
Principal Bankers: National Bank of Dubai

Principal Shareholders: HH Sheikh Rashid Bin Saeed Al Maktoum
Date of Establishment: 1978
No of Employees: 360

DUTCO BALFOUR BEATTY CO (PVT) LTD

PO Box 8944, Dubai
Tel: 858867
Telex: 47026 DBBRA EM
Telefax: 859087

PRINCIPAL ACTIVITIES: Civil and building engineering contractors
Parent Company: Balfour Beatty Construction Ltd, UK; DUTCO Group, Dubai

DUTCO GROUP

PO Box 233, Dubai
Tel: 660311
Cable: Dtco
Telex: 45491 Dtco EM
Telefax: 665157

Chairman: Ahmed Baker
Directors: Abdullah Saleh, Najeeb Baker
Senior Executives: James A Hancock (Group General Manager), Simon R Essex (Group Financial Controller), Paul Pieterse (Group Construction Manager)

PRINCIPAL ACTIVITIES: Roadworks, earthworks, construction, civil engineering, dredging, hotels, trading
Subsidiary/Associated Companies: Dutco Construction Co (Pvt) Ltd; Dutco Balfour Beatty (Pvt) Ltd; Dutco Commercial Enterprises; Dutco Pauling (Pvt) Ltd; Dutco Tennant (ME) Pvt Ltd; Dutco Hotels; Gulf Cobla (Pvt) Ltd; BK Gulf (Pvt) Ltd
Principal Bankers: National Bank of Dubai Ltd

Principal Shareholders: Ahmed Baker; Abdullah Saleh; Najeeb Baker
Date of Establishment: 1947
No of Employees: 5,000

DUTCO PAULING (PVT) LTD

PO Box 5240, Dubai
Tel: 857175
Telex: 46906 DPPCO EM
Telefax: 858925

Chairman: A Baker
Directors: Ahmed Baker, Abdullah Saleh, Najeeb Y Baker, Tariq A Baker
Senior Executives: P P Pieterse (Group Construction Manager), M J Copping (Company Secretary), M Cudby (Group Commercial Manager)

PRINCIPAL ACTIVITIES: Building and civil engineering contractors
Parent Company: DUTCO Group; Pauling Plc
Principal Bankers: National Bank of Dubai, British Bank of the Middle East

Principal Shareholders: Dutco Group
Date of Establishment: 1974
No of Employees: 500

DUTCO TENNANT (ME) PVT LTD

PO Box 233, Dubai
Tel: 220186/8
Telex: 47631 EM

Senior Executives: Ian M Mack (General Manager), Russell Jones, Ken Mason

PRINCIPAL ACTIVITIES: Manufacturers' representatives, distributors and services to the oil, gas and power industries; building, civil, mechanical and electrical contractors; specialist suppliers of valves, GRP pipes, measuring and indicating instruments, control systems and pumps
Principal Agencies: Alfa Laval, Lionweld Kennedy, Anderson, Braithwaite, BSP, Fibretex, GEC Ruston, Solarex, Valmet Sisu, Wailes Dove, Angus Wellmaster, Wemco, Dresser Rand Power
Branch Offices: PO Box 2534, Abu Dhabi, Tel 720646, Telex 22457 BCLAH EM
Parent Company: Dubai Transport Company (DUTCO)
Subsidiary Companies: Business Communication UAE (Pvt) Ltd
Principal Bankers: National Bank of Dubai

Date of Establishment: 1976

EASA SALEH AL GURG

See AL GURG, EASA SALEH,

EAST & WEST CORP

PO Box 121, Dubai
Tel: 431400
Cable: Chainani
Telex: 45482 CHNAN EM

Managing Director: V M Chainani

PRINCIPAL ACTIVITIES: Import of consumer goods, clothing and textiles and watches
Principal Agencies: Ricoh; Tressa; Nino watches; Voken; Longines
Principal Bankers: Grindlays Bank, Dubai; The British Bank of the Middle East, Dubai

Principal Shareholders: Mohd Saleh Zarawani; V M Chainani
Date of Establishment: 1958
No of Employees: 200

EASTERN COMMERCIAL AGENCIES

PO Box 45, Dubai
Tel: 222977
Cable: Comage
Telex: 45988 Comage EM
Telefax: 225762

Directors: R V Kore (Managing Director)
Senior Executives: J T Lilwa (Manager)

PRINCIPAL ACTIVITIES: Wholesalers, retailers, manufacturers'
representatives (electrical and electronic equipment, office
equipment, household goods)
Principal Agencies: Pioneer Electronics Corp, Japan; Canon Inc,
Japan; Crown Gas Lighter Co Ltd, Japan; Riccar, Japan;
Raaco, Denmark; Mikado, Germany; Taiyo Electric Ind, Japan;
BASF, Germany; Kyoritsu Electrical Instruments, Japan
Branch Offices: Bango Electronics, PO Box 3574, Abu Dhabi;
ECA Electronics, PO Box 6751, Sharjah
Principal Bankers: British Bank of the Middle East

Date of Establishment: 1971
No of Employees: 30

EASTERN LTD

PO Box 5231, Dubai
Tel: 236300, 232217

Chairman: Abdul Rahman M Bukhatir
Senior Executives: G Bhandari (General Manager), C J
Sabawala (Dy General Manager, Technical), R Ganapathy (Dy
General Manager, Technical), V Seshadri (Services Manager),
A B Pakvasa (Manager Development), D Dhingra
(Procurement Manager), N K Manihar (Chief Accountant)

PRINCIPAL ACTIVITIES: Building and civil contractors
Branch Offices: Sharjah, Abu Dhabi, Al Ain, Iraq and India
Parent Company: Bukhatir Investments Ltd, Sharjah
Associated Companies: Bucomac Ltd, Sharjah
Principal Bankers: National Bank of Abu Dhabi; Habib Bank AG
Zurich; National Bank of Sharjah

Date of Establishment: 1974
No of Employees: 2,000

EASTMAN CHRISTENSEN

PO Box 567, Dubai
Tel: 224806, 211749
Telex: 45841 Ewi EM
Telefax: 227930

Directors: Martin R Reid (Chief Executive Officer)

PRINCIPAL ACTIVITIES: Directional drilling and surveying
services and equipment, diamond bits, core bits
Branch Offices: UK; Norway; Denmark; Nigeria; Egypt; United
Arab Emirates; Saudi Arabia
Parent Company: Norton Christensen and Texas Eastern

No of Employees: 20 (UAE)

EID MOHAMMED & SONS

PO Box 1350, Deira, Dubai
Tel: 245026 (5 lines)
Cable: Almodein Dubai
Telex: 46140 Eidson EM
Telefax: (04) 245093

Proprietor: Eid Mohammed Medeya
Directors: Khalid Eid Medeya (Partner)
Senior Executives: M Dhanapalan (Manager), G Reghu (Sales
Manager), Abdul Sattar (Accountant)

PRINCIPAL ACTIVITIES: Manufacturers of chainlink fencing,
barbed wire, dealers in polythene pipes, PVC pipes; GI pipes

and sheets, MS plates and angles, aluminium sheets, beams,
tents, etc
Branch Offices: Abu Dhabi, Al Ain, Deira
Principal Bankers: The British Bank of the Middle East; Bank of
Oman Ltd; Grindlays Bank Plc; The National Bank of Dubai
Ltd

Date of Establishment: 1935
No of Employees: 53

ELCOME INTERNATIONAL

PO Box 1788, Dubai
Tel: 371335
Cable: Communic
Telex: 47116 Elcom EM
Telefax: 373426

Chairman: Saif Al Shaffar
Directors: W J Hardman (Managing Director), K S Grewal
(Deputy Managing Director)
Senior Executives: T R Bates (General Manager)

PRINCIPAL ACTIVITIES: Electronic and communications
engineers, specialists in the supply, installation and
maintenance of electronic, communications, radar, gyro,
navigational aids, instrumentation and marine safety
equipment
Branch Offices: Elcome Int, PO Box 306, Abu Dhabi; Colortel
Gulf Ltd, PO Box 1788, Dubai
Associated Companies: Elcome Marine Services Pvt Ltd, India
Principal Bankers: Chartered Bank Banque Paribas
Financial Information:

	1988/89 Dh'000	1989/90 Dh'000
Sales turnover	17,000	17,800
Authorised capital	8,000	8,000
Paid-up capital	8,000	8,000
Total assets	10,725	10,862

Principal Shareholders: Saif Al Shaafar; W J Hardman; K S
Grewal
Date of Establishment: 1969
No of Employees: about 50

EMIRATES DESIGN CONSORTIUM

PO Box 3662, Dubai
Tel: 520644
Cable: SABTCO
Telefax: 520889

Directors: Mohd Khamis Bin Sabt, Malik A Omer
Senior Executives: Malik A Omer (Resident Architect/Director)

PRINCIPAL ACTIVITIES: Consulting architects, engineers and
town-planners
Branch Offices: New Dehli and Calcutta, India
Associated Companies: C P Kukreja & Associates; K-13 Hauz
Khas Enclave, New Delhi 110016, India

Date of Establishment: 1976
No of Employees: 85

EMIRATES GENERAL PETROLEUM CORPORATION

PO Box 9400, Dubai
Tel: 373300
Cable: EMPET EM Dubai
Telex: 47980 EMPET EM
Telefax: 373200

Chairman: HE Dr Mana Saeed Al Otaiba
Directors: HE Ahmad Al Tayer, HE Sheikh Ahmed Sultan Al
Qassimi, HE Humaid Nasser Al Owais, HE Saif Al Jarwan, HE
Sheeba Al Hamily, HE Ahmed Atiq Al Jumairi, HE Nasser Al
Sharhan, HE Sheikh Mohamed Saqr Al Qassimi, HE Juma Al
Bawardi, HE Fadhel Khadem Al Muhairbi, HE Mohammed
Ghanem Al Falasi

Senior Executives: Ahmed Mohammed Al Kamdah (General Manager), Mohd Ghanem Al Falasi (Deputy General Manager), B M Lightfoot (Marketing Manager), P E Robinson (Finance & Accounts Manager), Abdul Aziz Al Nemer (Sales Manager), W V T F von Huth (Operations Manager), C G Coulter (Gas Operations Manager)

PRINCIPAL ACTIVITIES: Marketing and distribution of refined petroleum products and natural gas in the UAE
Principal Bankers: National Bank of Dubai

Date of Establishment: November 1980

EMIRATES INDUSTRIAL BANK

PO Box 5454, Dubai
Tel: 211300
Telex: 47691 Indbk EM
Telefax: 232320

Chairman: H E Ahmed Humaid Al Tayer
Directors: HE Shekih Surour Bin Sultan Al Dhaheri (Vice Chairman), Jaffar Al Fardan, Mohamed K Kharbash, Ebrahim F Humaid, Youssef A Al Serkal, Juaan Salim Al Dhaheri, Jamal M Al Ghurair, Hussain Jassim Al Nowais, Mohamed Abdulla Al Ghurair
Senior Executives: Ahmed Khilfan (Manager Dubai Branch)

PRINCIPAL ACTIVITIES: Banking
Parent Company: Head office in Abu Dhabi
Financial Information:

	1990
	Dh'000
Authorised capital	500,000
Paid-up capital	200,000

Principal Shareholders: 51% Government of United Arab Emirates, 49% UAE banks and insurance companies
Date of Establishment: 1982
No of Employees: 48

EMIRATES INDUSTRIAL GASES CO

PO Box 3763, Dubai
Tel: 660775, 660649
Cable: Cylinder
Telex: 47553 EM
Telefax: 664168

Chairman: Abdel Jawad Hassouneh
Directors: Saudi Faris Hassouneh (General Manager)
Senior Executives: Abdul Muttalib Zamer (Admininstration Services Manager)

PRINCIPAL ACTIVITIES: Production and marketing of industrial and medical gases
Principal Agencies: Ruwais Industrial Gases Co, Abu Dhabi
Branch Offices: Ajman
Parent Company: Refrigeration & Oxygen Co, Kuwait
Subsidiary Companies: Industrial Welding Materials & Equipment
Principal Bankers: Citibank N.A.
Financial Information:

	1989/90
	Dh'000
Sales turnover	20,000
Profits	3,000
Authorised capital	21,000
Paid-up capital	21,000
Total assets	42,000

Principal Shareholders: Mohammed Khalid Zayed Al Khalid, Abdulrazak Khalid Zayed Al Khalid, Abdul Jawad Abdul Qader Hassouneh
Date of Establishment: 1978
No of Employees: 130

EMIRATES LIVESTOCK & MEAT TRADING CO

PO Box 626, Dubai
Tel: 341072
Telex: 47001
Telefax: 371073

PRINCIPAL ACTIVITIES: Livestock trading, fresh and chilled meat trading, poultry and dairy products trading, fodder and animal feed trading
Associated Companies: Livestock Transport & Trading Co, Kuwait; Al Naboodah General Enterprises Est, Dubai

EMIRATES MCALPINE CONTRACTORS (PVT) LTD

PO Box 9273, Dubai
Tel: 663388520325
Telex: 48440 Jasap EM
Telefax: 661136

Senior Executives: Alan B Ashurst (General Manager)

PRINCIPAL ACTIVITIES: Building and civil engineering, road works, pipelines contracting, open cast mining
Parent Company: Alfred McAlpine International Ltd, UK

EMIRATES PRECAST CONSTRUCTION CO

PO Box 10062, Dubai
Tel: 257844
Cable: Precast-Dubai
Telex: 46863 Epcco EM

Owner: Mohd Juma'a Al Naboodah
Senior Executives: Faruk Sadik (General Manager)

PRINCIPAL ACTIVITIES: Production and erection of precast concrete elements
Principal Bankers: Union Bank of the Middle East Ltd

Date of Establishment: 1976
No of Employees: 150

EMIRATES SPECIALITIES CO

PO Box 3880, Dubai
Tel: 222181/2/3/4/5/6
Cable: Specialities
Telex: 46171 SPECIA EM
Telefax: (04) 235442

Chairman: Fouad Bardawil
Directors: Gibca Limited, M A Al Mazroui (General Trading Est), Yusuf Ibrahim Alghanim, Abdullah Yusuf Alghanim, Jassim Al Katami, Mohammad Saeed Al Ghaith
Senior Executives: Abdel Karim Karroum (General Manager), John P Kirby (General Sales Manager)

PRINCIPAL ACTIVITIES: Manufacturers' representation, import and distribution of building materials, jointing compounds, sealants, bitumen paint, concrete admixtures, adhesives, lightweight concrete, also wall coverings, decking & flooring systems, tiles, rubber flooring and doors, ironmongery, plastic moulds, sliding and folding doors and walls, also tools and industrial equipment, hardware, nails and accessories, steam cleaners, compressors, welding machines and alloys, fire extinguishers etc
Principal Agencies: Expandite, UK; BCR, UK; Deflex Bautentechnik, W Germany; Dow Corning, USA; Mandelli, France; Permanite, UK; Attema, Holland; Dennis Ruabon, UK; Harefield Rubber, UK; Aplix SA, France; NOE, Germany; The Rawlplug Co Ltd, UK; GEC Mechanical Handling Ltd, UK; Permaquik (Canada), Norton, Luxemburg; Swordsman, Australia; Jenny, USA; Turbine Supplies, USA; Reliance Mercury, UK; Expanded Metal Co Ltd, UK; DWI Dermabit Waterproofing Co, Saudi Arabia
Branch Offices: Emirates Specialities Co, PO Box 6564, Abu Dhabi, Tel 461780, 461581/2, Telex 23337 Specia EM, Fax (02) 463895; also PO Box 6156, Sharjah, UAE, Tel 592529

Associated Companies: Bardawil & Company, Beirut; Al Bahar & Bardawil Specialities Co WLL, Kuwait; Syria Equipment Co SA, Damascus; Bahareth Organisation (Specialities Div), Jeddah, Saudi Arabia; Saudi Co for Chemical Products (Al Turki-BCR), Dammam, Saudi Arabia

Principal Bankers: British Bank of the Middle East; Arab Bank Plc; Al Ahli Bank of Kuwait; United Arab Bank Ltd

Financial Information:

	1988/89 Dh'000	1989/90 Dh'000
Sales turnover	14,000	17,065
Authorised capital	8,000	8,000
Paid-up capital	4,000	4,000
Total assets	11,500	13,077

Principal Shareholders: Directors and Chairman as mentioned above

Date of Establishment: 1967

No of Employees: 37

EMIRATES TRADING AGENCY

PO Box 5239, Dubai

Tel: 666335

Cable: Emirates

Telex: 46716 Eta EM

Chairman: Saif Ahmed Al Ghurair

Directors: Abdullah Al Ghurair (Vice Chairman), B S Abdul Rahman (Executive Vice-Chairman), Syed Mohamed Salahuddin (Managing Director), P S M Seyed Abdul Khadir (Managing Director), N D S Sathak Ansari (Managing Director - ETA/ASCON Saudi)

PRINCIPAL ACTIVITIES: Engineering, and electromechanical contracting, shipping and trading

Principal Agencies: Mitsubishi Electric, Japan; Trane Co, USA; Ottermill Products of Westinghouse, UK; Dainichi-Nippon Cables, Japan; AEG, Germany; National Cement Co, Dubai

Branch Offices: Emirates Trading Agency, PO Box 6304, Abu Dhabi, UAE; Emirates Trading Agency, PO Box 119, Doha; Electromech Technical Associates, PO Box 3532, Abu Dhabi, UAE; Saudi-ETA, Medina Riyadh & Jeddah, Saudi Arabia

Subsidiary/Associated Companies: Associated Constructions, Dubai, UAE; Ras Al Khaimah, UAE; Al Ain, UAE; Abu Dhabi, UAE; Saudi-Ascon, Medina Riyadh & Jeddah, Saudi Arabia

Principal Bankers: Bank of Oman; Banque Indosuez

Date of Establishment: August 1975

No of Employees: 700

EMITAC LIMITED

Emirates International Trading & Contracting Co Ltd

PO Box 8391, Dubai

Tel: 377591

Cable: Emitac

Telex: 48710 Emitac Em

Telefax: 02-723058, 04-370899

Chairman: Abdul Rahman Bukhatir

Directors: Ghosbash Ahmed Saeed

Senior Executives: Viren Naroola (Chief Executive), Ashok Sharma (Marketing Support Manager), Atef Rafla (Marketing Manager), S Mani (Medical/Analytical Manager), Kapil Saigal (Instruments Manager), Jawed Alavi (Technical Services Manager), R Rajaram (Financial Controller)

PRINCIPAL ACTIVITIES: Computers, medical, analytical and test measurement equipment, airconditioning equipment, trading, manufacturing of polystyrenes, calculators, sicientific equipment

Principal Agencies: Hewlett Packard; Imed Intal, USA; Hill Rom Co, USA; Nicolet Instruments, USA; Bruel & Kjaer, Denmark; Hertel & Reuss, W Germany; Amersham Intal, UK; Industrie Guito Malvestio, Italy; Century Mnfg, USA; Consort, Belgium;

Amsco, USA/UK; A H Robins, USA/UK; Arredi, Italy; Baird Europe, USA/Holland; Biological Systems, UK; Dionex, USA; Electric Nucleanics, Holland; Fukuda Sanyo, Japan; Haake Mess Technic, W Germany; Ito Co, Japan; Lifecare, USA; Nippocolin, Japan; Parker Research, USA; PJP, UK; Promeda, Italy; Puritan Bennett, USA/UK; Reynolds Medical, UK; Shimatzu, Japan; Simon Keller, Switzerland; Spex Automatic, UK/USA; Ticombs, UK; Universal Hospital Supplies, UK; Kyoto Daiishi Kagagu, Japan; Raytest Isotopenmessgerate, W Germany

Branch Offices: PO Box 2711, Abu Dhabi, Tel 770420; PO Box 1641, Sharjah, Tel 331811

Subsidiary Companies: Plastifoam (UAE) Ltd, PO Box 1641, Sharjah; Technology Equipment Agencies, PO Box 8121, Dubai

Principal Bankers: AMRO Bank; National Bank of Shrjah; Bank of Sharjah

Principal Shareholders: Bukhatir Investments Ltd (50%); Ghobash Ahmed Saeed (50%)

Date of Establishment: October 1974

No of Employees: 130

ENGINEERING CONTRACTING CO

PO Box 1050, Dubai

Tel: 232161

Telex: 45976 ECC EM

Telefax: 04-236299, 06-332171

Chairman: Hatem Farah (also Managing Director)

Senior Executives: Ibrahim Hannoun (Partner Manager), Khador Mohd Al Doh (Contracting Manager)

PRINCIPAL ACTIVITIES: Building construction and civil works; manufacturing, interior designers, decorators, postforming fabricators, High-Tech woodworks

Branch Offices: Sharjah & Fujairah

Subsidiary Companies: ECC Furniture Industries

Principal Bankers: Banque de l'Orient Arabe et d'Outre Mer, Dubai

Financial Information:

	1990 US$'000
Sales turnover	15,000
Authorised capital	750
Paid-up capital	750
Total assets	5,000

Date of Establishment: 1975

No of Employees: 600

ERNST & WHINNEY

Middle East Office, PO Box 9267, Dubai

Tel: 375025

Cable: Ernstaudit Dubai

Telex: 45944

Telefax: 374999

Partners: Edward Quinlan (Managing Partner)

PRINCIPAL ACTIVITIES: Accountants and management consultants

Branch Offices: Dubai (Middle East Office); In the Middle East: Bahrain; Egypt; Jordan; Kuwait; Lebanon; Oman; Qatar; Saudi Arabia; United Arab Emirates; Yemen

ESSA HUSAIN AL YOUSIFI TRADING EST

See AL YOUSIFI, ESSA HUSAIN, TRADING EST

ETISALAT

PO Box 400, Dubai

Tel: 228111, 228121

Telex: 46010, 46012 EM

PRINCIPAL ACTIVITIES: Telecommunications, telephone and telegraph systems

Branch Offices: Throughout the United Arab Emirates
Parent Company: Head office in Abu Dhabi
Principal Bankers: National Bank of Abu Dhabi

EWBANK INTERNATIONAL CONSULTANTS (PVT) LTD

PO Box 11302, Dubai
Tel: 228801/2/3
Cable: Ewbanpart Dubai
Telefax: 231552

Chairman: R W H Reed
Directors: D A Lovie (Managing Director), R F Groom, T J Wiltshire H S Willox, V A Smith

PRINCIPAL ACTIVITIES: Consulting engineers and projects design contractors, power plant and process plant, civil, structural, mechanical and electrical plants for oil/petrochemical, utility and industry, building services
Branch Offices: PO Box 2692, Doha, Qatar; PO Box 6628, Muscat, Oman; PO Box 4336, Abu Dhabi, UAE
Parent Company: Ewbank Preece Ltd, Brighton, UK
Principal Bankers: British Bank of the Middle East, Dubai

Principal Shareholders: Ewbank Preece Ltd, Brighton, UK
Date of Establishment: 1975
No of Employees: 170

FAJR DEVELOPMENT CO

PO Box 13691, Dubai
Tel: 277767
Telefax: 272525

Senior Executives: M Kavalekar (Manager)

PRINCIPAL ACTIVITIES: Supply of telecommunication equipment, security and safety equipment
Parent Company: Head office in Kuwait

FARAIDOONI, MOHAMED ZAINAL,

PO Box 3, Dubai
Tel: 221373, 222946, 222947
Cable: Faraidooni
Telex: 45744 EM

Chairman: Mohamed Zainal Faraidooni

PRINCIPAL ACTIVITIES: Import and distribution of cement, building, materials, sanitary ware, chemical building products
Principal Agencies: The Cement Marketing Co, UK; Crittal Windows Ltd UK; Key Terrain Ltd, UK; Twyfords Ltd, UK; Sealocrete Exports Ltd, UK; James Halstead Ltd, UK

FARDAN STORES

PO Box 182, Dubai
Tel: 282256, 225447
Cable: Alfardan
Telex: 45963 Fardan EM
Telefax: (971-4) 282258

Partners: Fardan Bin Ali, Syed Adnan Syed Mohd
Senior Executives: Ahmed Adnan (Manager)

PRINCIPAL ACTIVITIES: Importers, re-exporters, wholesalers and retailers of perfumes, toiletries and cosmetics and leisure goods
Principal Agencies: Jovan, Inc.; Juvena; Renato Balestra, Italy; Gres; Shiseido Cosmetics; Loris Azzaro; etc
Branch Offices: 5 branches in Dubai, 1 branch in Abu Dhabi, Sharjah and Al Ain, 3 branches in Doha (Qatar)
Subsidiary Companies: Al Musawi Stores, Dubai; Vishal Stores, Dubai
Principal Bankers: Union Bank of the Middle East Ltd; Citibank N.A.

Date of Establishment: 1946
No of Employees: 50

FAROUK MOHAMED & CO

PO Box 1620, Dubai
Tel: 221314, 227785
Cable: Nyrmin
Telex: 45748 Nyrmin EM
Telefax: 226182

Senior Executives: Farouk Mohamed (Senior Partner), Allan Forster (Partner)

PRINCIPAL ACTIVITIES: Public accountants
Principal Agencies: Representing Grant Thornton International
Branch Offices: PO Box 1968, Sharjah, Tel 23196
Principal Bankers: British Bank of the Middle East

FAWAZ REFRIGERATION & AIRCONDITIONING CO WLL

PO Box 8037, Dubai
Tel: 282733
Telex: 49662 Fawaz EM
Telefax: 229418

Chairman: Mubarak Abdul Aziz Al Hassawi
Directors: Abdul Jaleel Mahmood Al Baqer, Osama Mohd Hussain Ali
Senior Executives: Basil Khartabil (Manager)

PRINCIPAL ACTIVITIES: General contracting, refrigeration and cold storage equipment, airconditioning, spare parts and equipment
Parent Company: Head office in Kuwait

FIBROPLAST INDUSTRIES CO (PVT) LTD

PO Box 10192, Dubai
Tel: 257575 (5 lines)
Cable: FIBROPLAST
Telex: 46912 FPI EM

Chairman: Butti Bin Bishr
Directors: G Buttiker, Louis Ruess, Edward Woods

PRINCIPAL ACTIVITIES: Manufacture of glassfibre reinforced polyester pipes, tanks and fittings
Principal Bankers: Commercial Bank of Dubai; Banque de l'Orient Arabe et d'Outre Mer; Banque Indosuez

Principal Shareholders: Gulf PICOM SA
Date of Establishment: February 1977
No of Employees: 187

FIRST NATIONAL BANK OF CHICAGO

PO Box 1655, Deira, Dubai
Tel: 226161
Telex: 45633 Frchgo EM

PRINCIPAL ACTIVITIES: Commercial banking
Parent Company: Head office in Chicago, USA

FLOPETROL TECHNICAL SERVICES INC

Middle East Region, DNATA Airline Centre, Level 4, PO Box 4959, Dubai
Tel: 211184
Cable: Flopet
Telex: 46950 FLOIN EM

PRINCIPAL ACTIVITIES: Services for the oil industry; well testing, wireline, sampling, early production facilities, snubbing workover, drill stem testing, well test interpretation, PVT laboratory
Branch Offices: South Gulf District: PO Box 4362, Abu Dhabi, UAE; Near East District: PO Box 35, Naadi, Cairo

FOSECO MINSEP UAE (PVT) LTD

PO Box 657, Dubai
Tel: 258606
Cable: Foseco
Telex: 45900 Foseco EM

Chairman: Dr D V Atterton

Directors: J S Newsome, Dr D S Belford, E S Gurg, S E Gurg, A G T Chubb, M R J MacDiarmid

PRINCIPAL ACTIVITIES: Manufacture and marketing of chemical products for the building and construction industry in Kuwait, Saudi, Bahrain, Qatar, UAE, Oman and Jordan
Branch Offices: FOSAM, Jeddah; FOSROC, Cairo
Parent Company: FOSROC International Limited, 285 Long Acre, Nechells, Birmingham B7 5JR, UK
Principal Bankers: British Bank of the Middle East, Dubai

Principal Shareholders: Foseco Minsep Group (UK), E S Al Gurg (Dubai)
Date of Establishment: 1975
No of Employees: 78

FUGRO MIDDLE EAST

PO Box 2863, Dubai
Tel: 442655
Telex: 46186 FUGRO EM

PRINCIPAL ACTIVITIES: Consulting geotechnical engineers and geologists; land, engineering and hydrographic surveyors
Branch Offices: PO Box 4447, Abu Dhabi, Tel 476487; Fugro Int BV, Oman; UK; USA; Hong Kong; Singapore
Parent Company: Fugro BV, Netherlands

Principal Shareholders: Calland Holding
No of Employees: 35

G & M INTERNATIONAL

PO Box 1229, Deira, Dubai
Tel: 669000
Cable: ETEQAD, DUBAI
Telex: 45505 Etqad Em
Telefax: 669216

Chairman: Taher T Muhieldeen
Directors: Mohiuddin T Muhieldeen
Senior Executives: Jalil Ahmed (General Manager)

PRINCIPAL ACTIVITIES: General trading, household goods, watches, electronics, HiFi systems
Principal Agencies: Bose Speaker, Barco Monitors, Delmon TV, Fuji Watches & Clocks, Kenwood, Maxell, Peter Clocks, Sangean Radio, Koss
Branch Offices: Abu Dhabi, Al Ain, Sharjah
Principal Bankers: Union Bank of the Middle East Ltd, Dubai; Habib Bank AG Zurich, Dubai
Financial Information:

	19898 US$'000
Sales turnover	8,400
Profits	400
Authorised capital	1,500
Paid-up capital	1,500
Total assets	6,500

Principal Shareholders: Taher T Muhieldeen; Mohiuddin T Muhieldeen
Date of Establishment: 1st April 1977
No of Employees: 62

GALADARI BROTHERS GROUP

PO Box 138, Dubai
Tel: 664000 (23 lines)
Cable: Galadari
Telex: 45443 Gabros EM

Chairman: Abdulrahim E Galadari (Partner), Abdul Latif E Galadari (Partner)

PRINCIPAL ACTIVITIES: General trading of consumer goods and foodstuffs, import and distribution of cars and spare parts, engines, generators, air-conditioning equipment, electrical appliances, heavy machinery, building materials. Car repairs and maintenance; building and civil engineering contracting, property development; travel agency,

manufacture of plastic products, ceramics, textiles, ice cream, tyre retreading, printing, insurance brokerage, barge operators, precast designing, manufacture and stone erection
Principal Agencies: Euclid Europe; Fedders, USA; Norge, USA; Marler Haley, UK; Gleenhill, UK; Butler Building Systems, USA; Mazda Auto
Branch Offices: Branch in Abu Dhabi, PO Box 4069, Tel 43314; London, UK; New York, USA
Subsidiary/Associated Companies: Galadari Automobiles (Pvt) Ltd; Business Services & Information Corp; Plaza Cinema; Jumeira Textile Mills (Dubai) Ltd; Allied Insurance Brokers; Dubai Bank Ltd; Guthrie Galadari; Interstate Shipping & Resources Corp; Al Quraish General Trading; Axis Construct; G & M International; Gulf Beton Ltd; Galadari Progressive Industries Co; Arab Plastic & Chemicals; Arab Emirates Bandag Ltd; Dubai Food Processing; Sun Engineering & Contracting Co; Arabian American Stone Builders Ltd; Galadari Truck & Heavy Equipment Ltd; Galadari Airconditioning & Refrigeration Co; Galadari Printing & Publishing Est; Galadari Ice Cream Co (Put) Ltd
Principal Bankers: Standard Chartered Bank; Citibank; Royal Bank of Canada

Principal Shareholders: Abdul Rahim E Galadari
Date of Establishment: 1930
No of Employees: 4,000

GALADARI ENGINEERING WORKS (PVT) LTD

PO Box 355, Dubai
Tel: 667318, 666408
Cable: Galenco
Telex: 48378 Galen EM

Chairmen: Abdul Rahim E Galadari, Abdul Latif E Galadari
Senior Executives: Arun Goudar (General Manager)

PRINCIPAL ACTIVITIES: Manufacture of various types of parts & accessories, repair and reconditioning of components for cars, heavy vehicles, earthmoving machinery, oil drilling equipment, fabrication of steel structures, erection of prefabricated steel buildings, ferrous & non ferrous castings, shiprepairs, and turnkey projects
Branch Offices: Branch in Abu Dhabi, PO Box 2797
Parent Company: A R E Galadari Brothers
Associated Companies: Galadari Automobiles (Pvt) Ltd; Galadari Truck & Heavy Equipment (Pvt) Ltd; Gulfbeton (Pvt) Ltd; Galadari Airconditioning & Refrigeration Co; Galadari Printing & Publishing Est (Khaleej Times); Galadari Ice Cream Co; Hotel Intercontinental Dubai; Khaleej Automobiles
Principal Bankers: Dubai Bank; Lloyds Bank Int Ltd; Bank of Credit & Commerce International
Financial Information:

	Dh'000
Sales turnover	20,000
Authorised capital	25,000
Paid-up capital	25,000

Principal Shareholders: Fully owned by Abdul Rahim E Galadari and Abdul Latif E Galadari
Date of Establishment: 1969
No of Employees: 140

GALADARI TRUCKS & HEAVY EQUIPMENT (PVT) LTD

Heavy Equipment Division, PO Box 11080, Dubai
Tel: 667443
Cable: GALENCO
Telex: 46887 GALEQ EM
Telefax: 690858

Chairmen: A R E Galadari, A L E Galadari
Directors: A R E Galadari, A L E Galadari
Senior Executives: Bijan Sheibani (Group General Manager), Parveez Namazie (Finance & Admin Manager), Eshanul Haq (Sales Manager), John F Coleshill (Plant Manager)

PRINCIPAL ACTIVITIES: Heavy engineering equipment, in the field of construction/earth moving and truck tractors

Principal Agencies: Komatsu Earthmoving Equipment; Japan; International Trucks & Commercial Vehicles, USA; JCB Earthmoving Equipment, UK; Kumatsu Forklifts Japan; Parker Plant Mixers, Dumpers, Conveyors, UK; Krupp Hydraulic Hammers, Germany

Branch Offices: PO Box 2797, Abu Dhabi, UAE; PO Box 15064, Al Ain, UAE

Parent Company: Galadari Brothers

Associated Companies: Galadari Automobiles (P) Ltd; Galadari Engineering

Principal Bankers: Bank of Credit & Commerce International

Financial Information:

	Dh'000
Authorised capital	100,000
Paid-up capital	10,000

Principal Shareholders: Galadari Brothers
Date of Establishment: 1974
No of Employees: 70

GAS & OIL SERVICES COMPANY GOSCO

Dubai International Trade Centre, PO Box 9240, Dubai
Tel: 373230
Telex: 48359 GOSCO EM

PRINCIPAL ACTIVITIES: International maintenance and operating services on all rotating, reciprocating and associated equipment in the oil and gas power generation industries

Principal Shareholders: Cooper Industries

GEEBEE TRADING COMPANY

PO Box 56, Dubai
Tel: 432555, 531873
Cable: Geebee
Telex: 45472 GBTCO EM
Telefax: 532555

President: Choithram V Jethwani
Directors: Girish Choithram Jethwani

PRINCIPAL ACTIVITIES: Indentors, suppliers and importers of building materials, machinery, textiles, cement, electronics and industrial equipment; jewellery showroom; and plastic manufacturers

Branch Offices: Singapore
Parent Company: Geebee Trading Company, Bombay, India
Subsidiary Companies: Eterna Manufacturing & Trading Company; Al Hana Jewellery
Principal Bankers: British Bank of the Middle East; Union Bank of the Middle East

Financial Information:

	1989 Dh'000
Authorised capital	50,000
Paid-up capital	24,000
Total assets	50,000

Date of Establishment: 1950
No of Employees: 54

GENERAL ACCIDENT FIRE & LIFE ASSURANCE CORP PLC

PO Box 7017, Dubai
Tel: 281819
Telex: 46614 Genac EM
Telefax: 225310

Senior Executives: A S Armstrong (Middle East Manager), Mustafa A Vazayil (Operations Manager)

PRINCIPAL ACTIVITIES: All classes of general insurance
Branch Offices: Bahrain: Abdulla Yusuf Fakhro Est, PO Box 39, Manama; Saudi Arabia: International Corp for Trade & Commerce Services, PO Box 276, Dammam 31411
Principal Bankers: Standard Chartered Bank, Dubai

GENERAL ELECTRIC TECHNICAL SERVICES CO

PO Box 11549, Dubai
Tel: 283138, 283139
Telex: 46739 GEINT EM

Senior Executives: Regional Manager-Consumer Products Middle East & North Africa

PRINCIPAL ACTIVITIES: Sales and marketing support operation for franchised distribution companies handling general electric room air conditioners, domestic appliances, and household goods

Principal Agencies: Hotpoint; General Electric

GENERAL ENTERPRISES CO (GECO)

PO Box 363, Dubai
Tel: 224131
Cable: Geco Dubai
Telex: 45528 Geco EM
Telefax: 281703

Chairman: Sheikh Ahmed Bin Mohammed Sultan Al Qasimi
Directors: Sheikh Salem Bin Mohammed Al Qasimi (Vice Chairman)
Senior Executives: D F Boyle (General Manager), M G Jacob (Finance & Administration Manager), Hakim K Sarpanch (Sales Manager)

PRINCIPAL ACTIVITIES: Trading and distribution of consumer electronics, domestic appliances and housewares, chinaware, airconditioning equipment, civil survey equipment, explosives

Principal Agencies: Akai Electric Co Ltd; Casio Computer Co, Japan; Hotpoint, USA; Texas Instruments; Indesit Spa; Servis Domestic Appliances Ltd; Noritake Co, Japan; Singer Sewing Machine Co, USA; Nordemende Vertriebes, Germany; Westpoint; Mellerware

Branch Offices: PO Box 289, Abu Dhabi; PO Box 28, Sharjah
Parent Company: Al Batha Trading & Industry Co, PO Box 1145, Sharjah
Associated Companies: GECO Mechanical & Electrical Co Ltd; GECO Marine Co Ltd; GECO Chemical Co Ltd
Principal Bankers: Arab Bank; Bank of Oman; Banque du Caire

Principal Shareholders: Wholly owned by Sheikh Ahmed Bin Mohammed Al Qasimi and brothers of the ruling family of Sharjah

Date of Establishment: 1959
No of Employees: 140

GENERAL FOODS EST

PO Box 1528, Dubai
Tel: 4-227715,6-331833
Cable: Genfoods
Telex: 46139 Genfod EM
Telefax: 971-6-337793

Chairman: Fares Naim Otaky (also General Manager)

PRINCIPAL ACTIVITIES: Indentors, representatives, importers and general traders for foodstuffs, paper products, consumer products and household equipments

Branch Offices: Sharjah: PO Box 1377, Tel 6-331833
Principal Bankers: Banque du Liban et d'Outre-Mer, Deira, Dubai; Banorabe

Financial Information:

	1990
	Dh'000
Sales turnover	5,000
Authorised capital	500
Paid-up capital	500

Date of Establishment: 1973
No of Employees: 23

GENERAL IMPEX COMPANY

PO Box 812, Dubai
Tel: 222301, 223564
Cable: Gimco Dubai
Telex: 45484 Marwan EM

President: Abdulla Hassain Rostamani
Directors: Abdul Wahed Rostamani (Managing Director), T M Nair (General Manager)

PRINCIPAL ACTIVITIES: Assembly and installation of aluminium ceilings, doors and windows; manufacturers' representations; supply of electrical equipment, refrigerators and cookers, household equipment
Principal Agencies: Firestone Tyre & Rubber Co (USA), Siltal SPA (Italy), Blue Star Limited (India), Hunter Douglas (Holland)
Branch Offices: General Impex Co, PO Box 2974, Abu Dhabi (UAE)
Associated Companies: Arabian Automobiles Co; United Diesel Co
Principal Bankers: Bank of the Middle East; British Bank of the Middle East; National Bank of Dubai Ltd

Principal Shareholders: President and Managing Director as described

GETPCO

Development General Trading Co

PO Box 3335, Dubai
Tel: 229818, 225296, 229723
Cable: Getpco/Dubai
Telex: 45702 Getpco EM

Chairman: Husain Al Rahmah
Directors: Khalil Al Nimer, Mohamood Macki

PRINCIPAL ACTIVITIES: Import and distribution of construction equipment (cranes, concrete vibrators, welding equipment, dumpers, generators, etc)
Principal Agencies: Ferro, Italy; ABG, Germany; Vibratechniques, France; Officine Piccini, Italy; Pumpex, Sweden; H Steinweg, Germany; Velox, Italy; Irmer & Elze, Germany; Piener, Germany
Branch Offices: Getpco-Development General Trading Co, PO Box 3559, Abu Dhabi, Tel 321648/9
Associated Companies: Al-Haythem Trading & Contracting Co, PO Box 686, Muscat, Oman, Tel 702349, Telex 3323; Gentraco-General Trading Enterprises Co, PO Box 4191, Ruwi, Muscat, Oman, Tel 600991
Principal Bankers: Bank of Oman; Citibank; American Express; British Bank of the Middle East; Union Bank of the Middle East

Principal Shareholders: H Al Rahmah, Khalil Al Nimer, Mahmood Macki
Date of Establishment: 1974

GIBCA

General International Business Contracting Associates

PO Box 1579, Dubai
Tel: 228480
Telex: 45693 Peace EM

Chairman: HH Sheikh Faisal Bin Sultan Al-Qassimi

PRINCIPAL ACTIVITIES: Manufacturers' representatives (building materials, air-conditioning equipment, electronic equipment, industrial and marine product); transport contractors
Principal Agencies: See GIBCA; Sharjah, UAE
Branch Offices: Abu Dhabi, Dubai, Ras Al Khaimah
Parent Company: Head office in Sharjah
Principal Bankers: National Bank of Abu Dhabi; United Arab Bank of Sharjah

GLOBAL SHIPPING CO (PVT) LTD

PO Box 2022, Dubai
Tel: 852666, 858568
Cable: Global
Telex: 46994 Global EM
Telefax: 859255

Chairman: Abdullah Al Shirawi
Directors: Ebrahim Al Shirawi, M G Valrani
Senior Executives: Capt S K Bhasin (General Manager)

PRINCIPAL ACTIVITIES: Charterers, operators and brokers, agency operators, inter gulf shipping specialists
Branch Offices: UAE ports and Oman ports
Parent Company: Al Shirawi Group of Companies
Associated Companies: Global Towage & Lighterage Co; Arabian Shipwares
Principal Bankers: Citibank; American Express; Commercial Bank of Dubai

Date of Establishment: August 1975

GREAT CIRCLE LINE

PO Box 2506, Dubai
Tel: 371216/18/19/20
Cable: Circle Dubai
Telex: 46958 CCL EM, 45631 Circl EM
Telefax: 370577

Directors: Remu Nagji (Managing Director)
Senior Executives: A Navaratnam (General Manager), K Nagarasa (Office Manager/Chief Accountant), S R Hassan (Sales Manager), M T M Mahir (Operations Superintendent), Stanley Suresh (Container Controller)

PRINCIPAL ACTIVITIES: Shipping agents, managers, charterers, tug & barge operators
Principal Agencies: Norasia Shipping Line, Hong Kong; Arabian Maritime Line, Sharjah; Central Gulf Line, New Orleans; Watermann Steamship Corp, New Orleans; Tsakos Shipping & Trading, Greece; Maritime Transport Ent, Antwerp

GREEN COAST ENTERPRISES

PO Box 552, Dubai
Tel: 660167, 661664
Telex: 46464 Green EM

Chairman: Abdul Ghaffar Hussain
Directors: Khalid Hussain

PRINCIPAL ACTIVITIES: General agents and traders (paint, printing inks, PVC pipes, plastics); also holding company involved in general and property investments
Principal Agencies: Owens Corning Fiberglas; Jotungruppen; Hepworth Plastics; Satchwell Control Systems; William Steward Group; James Budgett; Sharpstow Chemical Co; American Life Insurance Co; Taikisha; Hanway Trading
Subsidiary/Associated Companies: Jotun UAE Ltd; Kangaroo Plastics; Hepworth Plastics; Torda UAE
Principal Bankers: National Bank of Dubai

No of Employees: 30

GULF AGENCY CO (DUBAI) PVT LTD

PO Box 2404, Dubai
Tel: 457555
Cable: Confidence
Telex: 45448, 45809 GACDB EM
Telefax: 457202

Chairman: A R Saadi Rais
Directors: Salim S Rais, Saadi S Rais, Tor H Sandgren, Rolf Muchardt
Senior Executives: Rolf Muchardt (Managing Director), Lars Safverstrom (General Manager Shipping Services Div), Ingvar Svedberg (General Manager Forwarding Div), Christer Borjesson (General Manager Finance & Administration), William Hill (Forwarding Sales Manager), Michael Maloney (Shipping Manager)

PRINCIPAL ACTIVITIES: Shipping agents, clearing & forwarding; international transport, ships supply services, P&I correspondents, chartering
Branch Offices: Port Rashid; Port of Jebel Ali; Dubai International Airport
Associated Companies: In Abu Dhabi, Ras Al Khaimah, Fujairah, Sharjah, Qatar, Bahrain, Kuwait, Saudi Arabia, Jordan, Lebanon, Iran, India, Hongkong, Singapore, Sweden, Greece, Turkey, UK, Nigeria, Cyprus, Egypt (Suez Canal), Norway, Oman, Philippines, USA, Japan, Korea, Switzerland, Poland, Yemen, Pakistan, China, Indonesia, Vietnam
Principal Bankers: British Bank of the Middle East

Principal Shareholders: The Rais Hassan Family
Date of Establishment: 1967
No of Employees: 217

GULF COBLA (PVT) LTD

PO Box 5708, Dubai
Tel: 373260
Telex: 45676 GC Dub EM

PRINCIPAL ACTIVITIES: Dredging and reclamation work

GULF ETERNIT INDUSTRIES CO

PO Box 1371, Dubai
Tel: 857256
Cable: Eterind
Telex: 47040 Geind EM
Telefax: 851935

Chairman: Mohammed Bin Dhaher
Directors: Fouad Makhzoumi (Managing Director/President), Ahmad Saleh Al Obeifally (Member), Michel Klat (Member), Edward Elias (Member)
Senior Executives: Fady Klat (Controller/Treasurer), Saad E Khadem (VP Sales & Marketing), Antoine Habib (VP Export), Robert I Akl (VP Operations)

PRINCIPAL ACTIVITIES: Manufacture of asbestos cement, PVC, GRP and PE pipes and accessories; distribution of cast iron brass and PVC fittings
Branch Offices: Gulf Eternit Trading Co, PO Box 2140, Abu Dhabi; Gulf Eternit Trading Co, PO Box 9690, Dubai
Associated Companies: Al Obeidly & Gulf Eternit Trading Co WLL PO Box 1965, Doha, Qatar; Qasim Fakhro & Gulf Eternit, PO Box 2569, Manama, Bahrain
Principal Bankers: Bank Indosuez, Banque Paribas, Banque de l'Orient Arabe et d'Outre Mer, Standard Chartered Bank
Financial Information:

	1989 Dh'000	1990 Dh'000
Sales turnover	127,822	124,000
Profits	7,035	10,500
Authorised capital	20,000	20,000
Paid-up capital	20,000	20,000

Principal Shareholders: Eternit Investments Ltd, New Jersey, Channel Islands, UK; Mohammed Bin Dhaher; Ahmed Bin Mohammed Bin Dhaher
Date of Establishment: 1971
No of Employees: 474

GULF EXPLOSIVES CO LTD

PO Box 5596, Dubai
Tel: 420500
Telex: 47738 Explo EM

Directors: Ulf Mossberg, Anders Eklund, Lars Laven
Senior Executives: Lars Laven (Managing Director)

PRINCIPAL ACTIVITIES: Blasting contractors; manufacture, sales and distribution of explosives
Branch Offices: PO Box 5175, Doha, Qatar

Date of Establishment: 1976
No of Employees: 75

GULF FLEET MIDDLE EAST INC

PO Box 4981, Dubai
Tel: Jebel Ali 56400
Telex: 45622 GFME EM

PRINCIPAL ACTIVITIES: Marine transportation, supply boats, crew boats, tugs and materials barges
Associated Companies: Gulf Fleet Abu Dhabi, PO Box 4876, Abu Dhabi; Gulf Fleet Arabia Ltd, PO Box 154, Alkhobar, Saudi Arabia

Principal Shareholders: Gulf Fleet Marine Corporation
Date of Establishment: 1971
No of Employees: 250

GULF GENERAL TRADING EST

PO Box 1860, Dubai
Tel: 224321
Telex: 45486
Telefax: 215071

Chairman: Bader Hamoud Al Roudhan

PRINCIPAL ACTIVITIES: General trading
Parent Company: Head office in Kuwait

GULF INTERNATIONAL

PO Box 2870, Deira, Dubai
Tel: 374525
Cable: Gulfintel Dubai
Telex: 46487 Glfint EM
Telefax: 377090

Chairman: Sheikh Ahmed Bin Mohammed Al Qasimi
Senior Executives: David L Smith (General Manager)

PRINCIPAL ACTIVITIES: Distribution of consumer goods (grocery goods, toiletries, adhesives, consumer and industrial, etc)
Principal Agencies: Carnation, USA; Henkel, W Germany; Knorr Food Products, Switzerland; CPC International, USA; Kjeldsen, Denmark; Shell Markets, Dubai; H Bahlsens, W Germany; Lindt, Switzerland; Johnson & Johnson, UK; Wander, Switz; Crosse & Blackwell, UK; Findus, UK; Del Monte, UK; Shulton, UK; Gillette Ltd; Hero, Switzerland
Branch Offices: PO Box 7594, Abu Dhabi; PO Box 28, Sharjah
Parent Company: Al Batha Trading & Industry Co, PO Box 1145, Sharjah
Principal Bankers: British Bank of the Middle East; Standard Chartered Bank

Principal Shareholders: 100% owned by Sheikh Ahmed Al Qasimi
Date of Establishment: 1973
No of Employees: 100

GULF SHIPPING COMPANY

PO Box 2578, Dubai
Tel: 521451 (6 lines)
Cable: Seagull
Telex: 45520 EM
Telefax: 524024

Chairman: Yousuf Habib Al Yousuf
Directors: M Shamim Anwer (Managing Director)
Senior Executives: Syed Manzar Alam (Shipping Executive), A R M Farouk (Operations Manager), Ravinder Ghasin (Marketing Executive)

PRINCIPAL ACTIVITIES: Liner and trampship agents, charterers and ship brokers, freight forwarding and customs clearing, airfreight
Branch Offices: Sharjah, Fujairah, Khor Fakkan, Ras Al Khaimah and Abu Dhabi
Associated Companies: UAE Marine Consultants & Services, Dubai
Principal Bankers: Middle East Bank, Dubai

Date of Establishment: 1968
No of Employees: 40

GULF TRADING & REFRIGERATING (PVT) LTD
GULFCO

PO Box 1003, Dubai
Tel: 371400, 373185
Cable: Gulfco Dubai
Telex: 45523 Gulfo EM
Telefax: 372898

Chairman: Juma Al Majid
Directors: Mohamed Rashid Daour (Managing Director)
Senior Executives: Naser Ali Odeh (General Manager), Hashim S Hafeez (Accounts Manager), Mahmoud AL Bayari (Sales Manager/Frozen Division), Anand Kumar (Sales Manager/Dry Division), Hussain Abu Assaf (Wholesale Manager)

PRINCIPAL ACTIVITIES: Importers, wholesalers and retailers of all kinds of foodstuffs (canned and frozen) and allied products
Principal Agencies: General Foods, USA; Monarch Int'l, USA; Campbell's Soups Int'l, USA; Gerber Products, USA; Johnson & Son Inc, USA; The Wrigley Co USA; Campbell's Soups Ltd, UK; Johnson Wax Ltd, UK; General Foods Ltd, UK; Oemolk, Austria; S & W Fine Foods Inc, USA; General Mills Inc, USA; American Rice Inc, USA; Perrier Export, France; Cebag BV, Holland; Danpo Foods, Denmark; Lion Corp, Japan; Eastern Company SAE, Egypt; Nordex Food, Denmark; Eureka, Pakistan
Branch Offices: Gulfco Sales Offices in Abu Dhabi, Al Ain, Fujairah and Ras Al Khaimah
Parent Company: Al-Majid Group of Companies, PO Box 156, Dubai
Principal Bankers: Arab Bank Ltd, Dubai; Arab African Bank, Dubai; United Arab Bank, Dubai
Financial Information:

	1989 Dh'000	1990 Dh'000
Sales turnover	80,000	85,000
Authorised capital	15,000	15,000
Paid-up capital	15,000	15,000

Principal Shareholders: Juma Al-Majid (68%), Khalid Juma Al-Majid (16%), Miss Hana Juma Al-Majid (8%), Miss Lubna Al-Majid (8%) (All shareholders are UAE nationals)
Date of Establishment: 1962
No of Employees: 100

GULFBETON (PVT) LTD

PO Box 831, Dubai
Tel: 660734
Cable: Gulf beton Dubai
Telex: 45602 Beton EM

Chairman: Abdul Rahim E Galadari
Directors: A J M Boersma (Managing Director), A Mitchell (Marketing Director)

PRINCIPAL ACTIVITIES: Structural steel works, civil and marine construction; commercial and industrial buildings, general and public works contractors
Branch Offices: (Regional) Interbeton Abu Dhabi nv, PO Box 7100, Abu Dhabi UAE
Parent Company: Interbeton bv, PO Box 84, Rijswijk - Holland
Principal Bankers: Citibank; ABN Bank

Principal Shareholders: Joint venture between ARE Galadari & Bros, Dubai and Interbeton BV, Netherlands
Date of Establishment: 1976
No of Employees: 250

H & R JOHNSON TILES (UK) LTD

PO Box 1277, Dubai
Tel: 664967
Telex: 45865 Shaya EM
Telefax: 692165

Senior Executives: Alec Hedley (Regional Manager)

PRINCIPAL ACTIVITIES: Sales and marketing of ceramic wall and floor tiles, swimming pool tiles, industrial tiles, ceramic murals and giftware
Principal Agencies: Johnson Tiles, Cristal Tiles, Minton Hollins, Maw & Co, Building Adhesives Ltd

Date of Establishment: 1980 in Dubai

HABIB BANK LTD

PO Box 888, Dubai
Tel: 284631, 284447
Cable: Habibank
Telex: 46875 HBUAE EM
Telefax: 272712

President: Safdar Abbas Zaidi (Karachi)
Directors: Himayat Ali Khan, Masoof Akhtar
Senior Executives: Saghir M Siddiqui (Senior Vice President & General Manager)

PRINCIPAL ACTIVITIES: Commercial banking
Branch Offices: In the Middle East; Bahrain; Abu Dhabi; Dubai; Sharjah; Ras Al Khaimah; Al Ain; Oman; Lebanon etc
Parent Company: Head office in Karachi, Pakistan
Subsidiary/Associated Companies: Habib Finance International Limited, Hong Kong; Joint ventures: Perwira Habib Bank, Kuala Lumpur; Habib Nigeria Bank Ltd, Kaduna; Rep offices: Amman, Cairo, Jakarta, Tehran and Sydney; Managing agencies: Kuwait Bahrain International Exchange Co, Kuwait

HADI ENTERPRISES

PO Box 5833, Dubai
Tel: 369530, 274733, 850148
Cable: Hadiprise
Telex: 45654 Burhan EM
Telefax: 521200

Directors: Ebrahim Abdulnabi Al Abbas (President), Ismail Abdulnabi Al Abbas (Vice President)
Senior Executives: T E Fernandes (General Manager), C C Chandy

PRINCIPAL ACTIVITIES: Department stores, importers and retailers/wholesalers
Principal Agencies: Hoya, Luigi Bormioli, Superior, Impas, Anchor Hockings, VMC, AR Trading, Meyer Mfg Co, Ozecu, Chung's Corp, Newell Int'l, UTC, Harry Hyman, Paduana, Westpoint Pepperill, Pioneer, Bohemia Cristal, Crivisa, Car Bonboniere, Coloroll, Sobral Invicta, CALP Crystalware, Shin KWA Int'l Corp, Emsa Werke Wulf, Tajimi Pottery Ltd
Parent Company: Al Abbas Trading Company, PO Box 327, Dubai

Associated Companies: International Office Supplies, National Medical Supplies, Al Abbas Technical Supplies & Services, Publilink Advertising Marketing & Public Relations
Principal Bankers: Citibank, Dubai; British Bank of the Middle East, Dubai; Commercial Bank of Dubai, Dubai
Financial Information:

	1990 Dh'000
Sales turnover	75,980

Principal Shareholders: Ebrahim Al Abbas, Ismail Al Abbas
Date of Establishment: 1979
No of Employees: 300 (Group), 35 (Hadi)

HADISON TRADING AGENCY
PO Box 281, Dubai
Tel: 435789, 435790
Cable: Haidson Dubai
Telex: 46560 Hadis EM

Proprietor: Mohammed Sharif Al-Hadi

PRINCIPAL ACTIVITIES: Trading, import of textiles, clothing, foodstuffs (canned), toys, video cassettes
Branch Offices: Hadison Commercial Establishment; Hadison Clearing & Forwarding, Dubai; Hadison Audio & Video; Tom & Jerry
Principal Bankers: Union Bank of the Middle East

HALCROW INTERNATIONAL PARTNERSHIP
PO Box 360, Dubai
Tel: 370380
Telefax: 379239

Chairman: A R Kopec
Partners: A R Kopec, R W Rothwell, T D Casey, A C Cadwallader, M S Fletcher, D O Lloyd, V J W Hoad, D Buckley, H G Johnson, D J Pollock, R S Gray, D S Kennedy, C J Kirkland, M R Stewart, I C Millar
Senior Executives: M R Stewart (Resident Partner Middle East)

PRINCIPAL ACTIVITIES: Civil engineering consultants, design and project management of roadworks, marine structure, highway structures, airports, water supply projects, sewerage and sewage treatment works, town planning, environmental and public health projects
Branch Offices: Abu Dhabi: PO Box 46024, Tel 331998; Sharjah: PO Box 673, Tel 543133; Muscat: PO Box 220, Tel 699142
Principal Bankers: British Bank of the Middle East

Date of Establishment: 1959
No of Employees: 66

HASSANI TRADING COMPANY
PO Box 286, Dubai
Tel: 220166
Cable: Hasni EM
Telex: 45499 Hasni EM
Telefax: 285396

Chairman: Mohd H Hassani
Directors: Ahmed Hassani
Senior Executives: Mohan Nair (Commercial Manager)

PRINCIPAL ACTIVITIES: Distribution of foodstuffs, consumer items, table & household wares, supermarket chain, importers
Principal Agencies: H J Heinz, Kellogg (Deutchland), Premier Brands Food Exports, Corning Ltd
Principal Bankers: British Bank of the Middle East

Date of Establishment: 1930
No of Employees: 280

HEMPEL'S MARINE PAINTS (UAE) LTD
PO Box 696, Dubai
Tel: 459359
Cable: Hempaturi
Telex: 68197 HEMPEL EM

Chairman: Saud Abdulaziz Al Rashed
Directors: HE Sheikh Mohammad Bin Sultan Al Qasimi, HE Sheikh Nasser Al Ahmed Al Sabah, Saad Abdulaziz Al Rashed, J H Lillelund (Representative of J C Hempel Holding A/S)
Senior Executives: Allan Christensen (General Manager)

PRINCIPAL ACTIVITIES: Manufacture of paints and coatings for the marine, industrial, container, offshore yacht and building sectors; import and marketing of materials and tools for surface preparation and application of such coatings, incl provision for advisory services
Branch Offices: UAE Head Office: Sharjah
Parent Company: J C Hempel Holdings A/S, Denmark
Principal Bankers: National Bank of Dubai, Dubai; Banque Paribas, Dubai; National Bank of Abu Dhabi, Sharjah; British Bank of the Middle East, Sharjah

HEPWORTH PLASTICS GULF
PO Box 2345, Dubai
Tel: 370124
Cable: Corcon
Telex: 45965 Corcon EM
Telefax: 371298

Chairman: Abdul Ghaffar Hussain
Senior Executives: Robert Hughes (General Manager), Simon Murray (Sales Manager Middle East), Lester McIlwaine (Technical Marketing Manager), Sayeed Alavi (Sales Manager Dubai), Saleh Mahmoud Hussein (Sales Manager Abu Dhabi), Ajith Kumar (Sales Manager Sultanate of Oman), Gary Harris (Sales Manager Bahrain), Craig Tattersall (Sales Manager Saudi Arabia), David McDonald (Sales Manager Qatar), Ronald Hallett (Financial Controller), Varghese Thomas (Chief Accountant)

PRINCIPAL ACTIVITIES: Manufacture and supply of plastic and GRP pipes and fittings to the building industry incl valves and other pipeline accessories
Principal Agencies: Hepworth Building Products, George Fischer, Talbot, Guest, Chrimes, McAlpine
Branch Offices: PO Box 4894, Abu Dhabi, Tel 727585, Fax 783578
Parent Company: Hepworth Building Products Plc, Hazlehead, Stocksbridge, Sheffield S30 5HG, UK
Associated Comanies: Sultanate of Oman: Ajay Enterprises (Hepworth Plastics Gulf Division), PO Box 1667, Seeb, Tel 590911, 592128, Fax 592310; Saudi Arabia: Delta Group Ltd (Hepworth Plastics Gulf Division), PO Box 11232, Jeddah 21453, Tel 6942005, Fax 6990890; Bahrain: YKA Hepworth Gulf, PO Box 143, Manama, Tel 211518, Fax 211885; Qatar: Al Andalus Trading (Hepworth Plastics Gulf), PO Box 9475, Doha, Tel 432827
Principal Bankers: National Bank of Dubai Ltd
Financial Information:

	1990 Dh'000
Sales turnover	35,000

Principal Shareholders: Abdul Ghaffar Hussein
Date of Establishment: 1974
No of Employees: 70

HILTON INTERNATIONAL DUBAI
PO Box 927, Dubai
Tel: 370000
Cable: HILTELS Dubai
Telex: 46670 Hiltl EM
Telefax: (971-4) 371383

Chairman: Michael Hirst
Senior Executives: Walter Annen (Director UAE), Clive Ostler (Director of Sales), Sadiq Ibrahim (Business Development Manager)

PRINCIPAL ACTIVITIES: Hotel business

Parent Company: Hilton International
Principal Bankers: National Bank of Dubai

No of Employees: 372

HYATT REGENCY DUBAI & GALLERIA

PO Box 5588, Dubai
Tel: 221234
Cable: Hyatt Dubai
Telex: 47555 HYATT EM, 47403 HYSAL EM
Telefax: (971-4) 211868

Senior Executives: Uli Hoppe (General Manager), Edward
   Chaaya (Senior Food & Beverage Manager), Munir Ahmed
   (Director of Marketing), Tim Wise (Financial Controller), Nigel
   Cumber (Galleria Manager)

PRINCIPAL ACTIVITIES: Hotel business
Parent Company: Hyatt International Corporation
Principal Bankers: National Bank of Dubai Ltd

Date of Establishment: May 1980
No of Employees: 590

IBM WORLD TRADE

PO Box 9226, Dubai
Tel: 373155
Cable: Inbusmach
Telex: 45773 Ibmdxb Em

PRINCIPAL ACTIVITIES: Marketing (purchase, lease or rental)
   and maintenance of data processing equipment and services

IMCO SERVICES

Middle East Division, PO Box 11628, Jumeirah, Dubai, UAE
Tel: 375155
Telex: 46027 Imco EM

President: G L Jackson

PRINCIPAL ACTIVITIES: Supplier of oil well drilling fluids,
   products and services
Branch Offices: Bahrain: PO Box 515, Tel 728733, Telex 8372;
   Abu Dhabi: PO Box 4076, Tel 344216, Telex 24155; Oman:
   PO Box 5796, Ruwi, Tel 602533, Telex 5485
Parent Company: IMCO Services, A Division of Halliburton
   Company, Houston, Texas, USA
Principal Bankers: Interfirst Bank NA, Houston, Texas, USA;
   Citibank NA, Dubai

IMECO INTERNATIONAL MOTOR & EQUIPMENT CO LTD

PO Box 2229, Dubai
Tel: 471018
Telex: 46607 IMECO EM

Chairman: Yousuf Habib Al Yousuf

PRINCIPAL ACTIVITIES: Car and truck dealers
Principal Agencies: Berliet

IML AIR COURIERS (UAE)

PO Box 50875, Dubai, UAE
Tel: 344646, 344606
Cable: IML Dubai
Telex: 47340 IMLDB EM

Senior Executives: J C Hitchcock (General Manager)

PRINCIPAL ACTIVITIES: International courier operators,
   operators of skydata, skypacket and skycourier, clearing and
   forwarding, airfreight operators
Branch Offices: IML Air Couriers (UAE), PO Box 6103, Abu
   Dhabi Tel 821578
Parent Company: Dubai Trade & Trust Co (Private) Ltd
Subsidiary Companies: Sotinmar Shipping Co, Dubai; Sotinmar
   Airfreight Services, Dubai

Principal Bankers: Lloyds Bank

Date of Establishment: 1st April 1981
No of Employees: 17

INMA THE GULF DEVELOPMENT & CONSTRUCTION CO

PO Box 4560, Dubai
Tel: 226231 (5 lines)
Cable: Inma Dubai
Telex: 45632 Inma EM
Telefax: 236481

Chairman: Juma Al Majid
Directors: Samir Aweidah (Managing Director), Rashed Al Majid,
   Mohamed Al Makhawi
Senior Executives: M Sukaik (Commercial Manager)

PRINCIPAL ACTIVITIES: Import and distribution of plant and
   machinery for the construction industry; building and civil
   contracting
Principal Agencies: Atlas Copco; Dynapac; Flygt Pumps; Hatz
   Diesel Engines; Hymac; Lancer Boss; Linden Alimak; Fred
   Parker; Thwaites; Stetter; Mustang; Liebherr; Phoenix;
   Wirtgen
Branch Offices: Branches in Abu Dhabi (PO Box 798, Tel
   338787, Telex 23334, Fax 330320) and in Al Ain (PO Box
   15533, Tel 656356, Telex 34027)
Associated Companies: INMA-Oman, PO Box 3760, Ruwi,
   Oman, Tel 562092, 602100, Telex 5196 Inma ON and INMA-
   Oman, PO Box 18851, Salalah, Tel 212815, Telex 7709 Inma
   Sal ON
Principal Bankers: United Bank; Bank of Oman
Financial Information:

	1990 Dh'000
Authorised capital	15,000
Paid-up capital	15,000

Principal Shareholders: Chairman and directors as described
Date of Establishment: 1972
No of Employees: 85

INTERNATIONAL FINANCIAL ADVISERS KSC

PO Box 2057, Dubai
Tel: 520638, 515540
Telefax: 513687

Chairman: Saud K Al Azmi (Managing Director)
Directors: Abdul Wahab Al Bader (Vice Chairman), Jassim Al
   Daboos, Soheel Al Rasheed, Adel Al Nafisi

PRINCIPAL ACTIVITIES: Corporate finance, loan syndications,
   money and asset management, clearing and settlements,
   commodity and bullion dealing
Parent Company: Head office in Kuwait
Principal Bankers: National Bank of Kuwait, Kuwait; National
   Westminster Bank, London; Citibank, New York; Dresdner
   Bank, Frankfurt

Principal Shareholders: Kuwait Investment Authority

INTERNATIONAL FOAM & FURNISHING CO

PO Box 10310, Dubai
Tel: 857930
Telex: 48025
Telefax: 850089

Chairman: Salem Khamis Sabt
Directors: Abbas Ali Al Hazeem, W J Towell & Co

PRINCIPAL ACTIVITIES: Manufacture of artificial sponge,
   sponge mattresses and spring mattresses
Branch Offices: Kuwait; Sultanate of Oman

Principal Shareholders: Chairman and directors as mentioned
   above

INTERNATIONAL FURNISHING CO

PO Box 5077, Deira, Dubai
Tel: 246201, 246030
Cable: Furnishing (Dubai)
Telex: 49184 Nofal EM

Chairman: Mohamed Ahmed Al Shangiti (Owner)
Directors: Rashid Ahmed Al Shangiti (General Manager)
Senior Executives: Syed Atta Maamaun (Manager)

PRINCIPAL ACTIVITIES: Importers and distributors of carpets, furniture, curtain materials
Principal Bankers: Bank of Credit & Commerce International SA, Dubai

Date of Establishment: 1965
No of Employees: 50

INTERNATIONAL INSURANCE SERVICES GULF (PVT) LTD

Dubai World Trade Centre, Level 28, PO Box 9215, Dubai
Tel: 373150
Cable: Insco Dubai
Telex: 46264 Insco EM
Telefax: 375812

Chairman: Abdullah M Saleh
Directors: HE Ahmed Al Tayer, S J C Minoprio, D F McKenzie, Toufic H Barakeh (Managing Director), National Bank of Dubai Ltd, J G Hogg
Senior Executives: N R Thiruvengadam (Director Agency Operations), R T Jagtiani (Manager Dubai Branch), Miss E A Mascarenhas (Administration Officer)

PRINCIPAL ACTIVITIES: Insurance and reinsurance brokers, surveyors and consultants, managing agents
Principal Agencies: Prudential Assurance, UK; Insurance Co of North America, USA
Branch Offices: Deira: PO Box 1019, Dubai, Tel 238080; Abu Dhabi: PO BOx 46771, Abu Dhabi, Tel 351536
Principal Bankers: National Bank of Dubai
Financial Information:

	1990 Dh'000
Sales turnover	26,124
Profits	751
Authorised capital	1,500
Paid-up capital	1,500
Total assets	15,349

Principal Shareholders: Abdullah M Saleh, National Bank of Dubai Ltd, HE Ahmed Al Tayer, Hogg Robinson Gardner Mountain Ltd (UK), Toufic H Barakeh
Date of Establishment: 1976
No of Employees: 30

INTERNATIONAL MARINE SERVICES

PO Box 1882, Dubai
Tel: 521545, 522515
Telex: 47234 Imsar EM; 45750 Marser EM
Telefax: (971-4) 526771

PRINCIPAL ACTIVITIES: Provides tugs, supply vessels, barges and equipment serving the offshore industry, marine operations, fabrication, engineering, offshore maintenance, catering
Branch Offices: International Marine Services, PO Box 1246, Sharjah, UAE; Abu Dhabi Marine International Services, PO Box 7141, Abu Dhabi, UAE: International Marine Services Inc, PO Box 3199, Doha, Qatar; IMS, PO Box 38284, Safat, Kuwait
Subsidiary Companies: Timsah International Marine Services (TIMS) 5 Abdel Rahman el Rafei, Cairo, Egypt
Principal Bankers: Commercial Bank of Dubai, Grindlays Bank PLC, Dubai; Amrobank NV, Dubai

Date of Establishment: 1969
No of Employees: 600 approx

INTERNATIONAL PAINT (GULF) LTD

PO Box 290, Dubai
Tel: 480491
Cable: Kanoo Dubai
Telex: 48246 PAINT EM
Telefax: 481339

Chairman: Hamed Ali Kanoo
Directors: W H C Brien, J B Bradley, P Rogers, D L Brett, H Baltiner

PRINCIPAL ACTIVITIES: Manufacture and sale of a wide range of paints and protective coatings for the environment of the Gulf
Branch Offices: Abu Dhabi Office: C/o Kanoo, PO Box 245, Abu Dhabi, Tel 7758808; Bahrain Office: PO Box 45, Manama, Bahrain, Tel 727408, 727091; Oman Office: C/o Shanfari Trading & Contg Co, PO Box 783, Muscat, Tel 600794; Qatar Office: C/o Al Ghorairi & Partners, PO Box 3547, Doha, Tel 324959
Associated Companies: International Paint PLC; Kanoo Group
Principal Bankers: Royal Bank of Canada; British Bank of the Middle East

Principal Shareholders: International Paint Company Ltd; Kanoo Group
Date of Establishment: 1975
No of Employees: 60

INTERNATIONAL TRADERS (ME) LTD

PO Box 6, Dubai
Tel: (971-4) 521155
Cable: Distinct
Telex: 45452 ITLDB EM
Telefax: (971-4) 521294

Chairman: Gopaldas B Mahbubani
Directors: Murij J Manghnani (Managing Director), U D Chotirmall (Vice Chairman), Parmanand Balani, Ram J Buxani
Senior Executives: S D Thawrani (Deputy General Manager)

PRINCIPAL ACTIVITIES: Importers, exporters, commission agents, manufacturers' representatives, wholesalers and retailers (photographic goods, household goods, textiles and clothing, electrical and electronic equipment, etc)
Principal Agencies: Remington Shavers; Minolta Cameras; Sharp Products of Japan; Win Lighters; TDK Cassettes; Felca Swiss Watches; Europa German Clocks; Rhythm Japanese Clocks & Watches, etc
Branch Offices: Cosmos, PO Box 2134, Ab2 Dhabi, Tel 335556, 336583, Fax 212914; Cosmos, PO Box 2643, Sharjah, Tel 377961, Fax 545670; Cosmos, PO Box 607, Fujairah, Tel 22685 Fax 22685; Cosmos, PO BOx 1841, Ras AlKhaimah, Tel 24674, Fax 24674; Cosmos, PO BOx 15334, Al Ain, Tel 656878, Fax 656878; Universal Est, PO Box 2436, Dubai, Tel 534638, 535688, Fax 521294, Telex 45452; International Traders (Oman) LLC, PO Box 7515, Jibroo, Muttrah, Oman, Tel 714016, 712795, Telex 5363, Fax 713555
Subsidiary Companies: Ambassador Hotel, Dubai; Astoria Hotel, Dubai; Pure Ice Cream Co Ltd, Sharjah; Crescent Enterprises Ltd, Sharjah; Al Wafa Engineers Ltd, Sharjah; Al Razouki International Exchange Co, Dubai
Principal Bankers: British Bank of the Middle East, Bank of Oman Ltd, Standard Charterd Bank, ANZ Grindlays,Banque Paribas, Barclays Bank, Emirates International Bank, Bank of Baroda, National Bank of Fujairah, National Bank of Abu Dhabi, Middle East Bank, United Bank Ltd, Dubai; Bank of Credit & Commerce International

Principal Shareholders: Intra Group (Holdings) Co Inc, Panama
Date of Establishment: 1953
No of Employees: 205

INTERNATIONAL TURNKEY SYSTEMS

PO Box 8687, Deira, Dubai
Tel: 511022
Telex: 48599 ITS EM
Telefax: 520419

Chairman: Abdul Jalil Al Gharabally
Directors: Abdul Jalil Al Gharabally, Faisal Al Khatrash, Samir Al
  Nafisi, Mohammed Al Khudairi
Senior Executives: Saad Al Barrak (General Manager), Mustafa
  Shehata (UAE Country Manager), Ebrahim Ali (Bahrain
  Country Manager)

PRINCIPAL ACTIVITIES: Engaged in marketing, support,
  installation and maintenance of turnkey computer solutions
  (hardware and software), computer consultancy services, etc
Principal Agencies: Tandem Computers Inc; Sequent Computer
  Systems Inc; Alis Thechnologies
Branch Offices: Dubai, Abu Dhabi, Bahrain, Riyadh and Dhahran
Parent Company: Head office in Kuwait
Principal Bankers: Dubai Islamic Bank, Dubai; Bahrain Islamic
  Bank, Bahrain; Al Rajhi Banking & Investment Corp, Saudi
  Arabia

Principal Shareholders: Kuwait Finance House
Date of Establishment: 1981
No of Employees: 65

INVESTMENT BANK FOR TRADE & FINANCE LLC

INVESTBANK

PO Box 12955, Dubai
Tel: 04 285551
Telex: 49316 Invest EM
Telefax: 04 220818

Chairman: HE Sheikh Saqr Bin Mohammad Al Qassimi

PRINCIPAL ACTIVITIES: Commercial banking
Parent Company: Head office in Sharjah

ITOH, C, & CO LTD (DUBAI LIAISON OFFICE)

PO Box 3472, Dubai
Tel: 223348, 282231/6
Cable: Citoh-Dubai
Telex: 45734 Citoh EM

PRINCIPAL ACTIVITIES: General industries and trading,
  including textiles, plastics, chemicals, marine, aircrafts,
  telecommunications, iron and steel, foodstuffs, energy (oil,
  gas and nuclear), constructions, etc; project coordinating
Branch Offices: Worldwide: 20 Offices in the Middle East
Principal Bankers: Algemene Bank Nederland NV, Dubai, British
  Bank of the Middle East

JANATA BANK

PO Box 3342, Dubai
Tel: 223360, 281442, 282310
Telex: 46237 Janata EM

PRINCIPAL ACTIVITIES: Commercial banking
Branch Offices: Abu Dhabi, Al Ain, Sharjah
Parent Company: Head office in Bangladesh

JASHANMAL NATIONAL CO (UAE)

PO Box 1545, Dubai
Tel: 212579
Cable: Jashanmal Dubai
Telex: 45705 Jashan EM
Telefax: 212651

Chairman: Sheikh Suroor Bin Sultan Al Dhahiry
Directors: Abdullah Mohamed Al Mazroui, Abdul Rahim E
  Galadari, Gangu Batra, Tony Jashanmal, Mohan Jashanmal,
  Hiro Jashanmal
Senior Executives: Gangu Batra (Chief Executive Officer)

PRINCIPAL ACTIVITIES: Commission agents, general trading,
  importers, indentors, manufacturers' representatives; chain of
  department stores, distribution of consumer goods,
  newspapers and periodicals, pharmaceuticals
Principal Agencies: Nippon Sanso KK, Japan; Hoover Ltd, UK;
  Jacobs Suchard Tobler, Switzerland; Yashica Co Ltd, Japan;
  Hong Kong; Maurier & Writz, West Germany; Delsey, France;
  Clarks Shoes, UK; Parfums Christian Dior, France; Elizabeth
  Arden (Lagerfeld), Switzerland; Parfums Gucci, France;
  Georgio Armani, France; Imeko, Holland; Kenwood, UK;
  Times of India, India; MEED, Financial Times, The Economist,
  Newsweek, Letts Diary, UK
Branch Offices: Al Ain (Abu Dhabi); Das Island (Abu Dhabi)
Associated Companies: Jashanmal and Partners Ltd, PO Box
  5138 Safat, Kuwait; Jashanmal and Sons, PO Box 16,
  Manama, Bahrain
Principal Bankers: Banque Paribas; Middle East Bank Ltd
Financial Information:

	1990 Dh'000
Sales turnover	95,932
Profits	5,209
Authorised capital	10,000
Paid-up capital	10,000

Date of Establishment: 1956
No of Employees: 230

JASSIM MOHD ALI AL WAZZAN

See AL WAZZAN, JASSIM MOHD ALI,

JAWAD SAJWANI GROUP OF COMPANIES

See SAJWANI, JAWAD, GROUP OF COMPANIES

JEBEL ALI FREE ZONE AUTHORITY

PO Box 3258, Dubai
Tel: 56578
Cable: PAJADUB
Telex: 47398 Paja Em
Telefax: 56093

PRINCIPAL ACTIVITIES: Free zone authority allowing 100%
  foreign ownership; unlimited transfer of profit and capital; no
  import duties or export taxes; etc
Principal Agencies: Black & Decker, Caltex, McDermott,
  Mitsubishi Motors, Reebok Middle East, Shell, Sony, Toppan
  Moore, Toyo Warehouse, Union Carbide, York Airconditioners

JEEVAN TRADERS

PO Box 2775, Dubai
Tel: 431561, 431583, 431844
Cable: Jeevan Dubai
Telex: 46043 Jeevan EM

PRINCIPAL ACTIVITIES: General trading, electrical engineering
  goods and accessories, kitchen cabinets and appliances,
  textiles, retailers, wholesalers and indentors
Principal Agencies: Crompton Parkinson, UK; Gower Furniture
  Ltd, UK; Falcon Home Care, UK
Subsidiary/Associated Companies: Mayfair Stores, Dubai;
  Mayfair Textiles, Dubai; Union Plastics Industries, Dubai
Principal Bankers: Union Bank of the Middle East

Principal Shareholders: Partnership firm
Date of Establishment: 1968

JOANNOU & PARASKEVAIDES (OVERSEAS) LTD

PO Box 4624, Dubai
Tel: 212248, 246387
Cable: Jaynpee Dubai
Telex: 45537 Jaynp EM, 46477 Jpgho EM

Directors: St Chr Joannou (Joint Chairman), G E Paraskevaides
  (Joint Chairman), R H J Hoare, D V Willis, P A Hudson

PRINCIPAL ACTIVITIES: Building and civil engineering contractors; buildings, roads, bridges, airports, prefabricated dwellings, etc; also electrical and mechanical installations through associated companies

Branch Offices: Oman: PO Box 603, Muscat, Telex 5242 Jaynpe ON; Saudi Arabia: PO Box 5881, Riyadh, Telex 201384 Jaynpe SJ; Libya: PO Box 2055, Benghazi, Telex 40046 Jaynp LY; Iraq: PO Box 5422, Baghdad, Telex 212539 Jaynpee IK; Syria: PO Box 3257, Damascus, Telex 11337 Jasoum SY

Associated Companies: J & P (UK) Ltd, 7 Hanover Square, London; J & P (Cyprus) Ltd, PO Box 1178, Nicosia; Alfadl Bin Laden and J & P Corpn Ltd, PO Box 5028, Jeddah, Telex 401417 Abjanp SJ; A & P Paraskevaides & Partners Ltd, PO Box 10641, Dubai, Telex 45868 Elecap EM

Principal Bankers: Grindlays Bank, British Bank of the Middle East

Principal Shareholders: St Chr Joannou, G E Paraskevaides
Date of Establishment: 1961

JOHN R HARRIS & PARTNERS

PO Box 2825, Dubai
Tel: 372481/2
Cable: Harrisplan Dubai
Telex: 46070 Condtc EM
Telefax: 377057

PRINCIPAL ACTIVITIES: Architecture and planning, consulting engineering
Parent Company: John R Harris Partnership, London, UK
Associated Companies: John R Harris Associates, Muscat; John R Harris Brunei Architects, Brunei; John R Harris Qatar Architects, Qatar

Date of Establishment: 1974

JONES, D G, & PARTNERS LTD

PO Box 1801, Dubai
Tel: 226197/8
Telex: 45644 Surdub EM

Senior Executives: C E McGrory, P C Barker, R J Cook

PRINCIPAL ACTIVITIES: Construction consultancy services
Branch Offices: In the Middle East: Bahrain, Iraq, Jordan, Kuwait, Lebanon, Qatar, Oman, UAE (Abu Dhabi)

JOTUN UAE LTD

PO Box 3671, Airport Road, Rashidiya, Dubai
Tel: 851515 (10 lines)
Cable: Jotun Dubai
Telex: 45798 Jotun EM
Telefax: 859051

Chairman: Abdul Ghaffar Hussain
Directors: Knut Hanssen (Managing Director), Odd Gleditsch Jr, Anwar Sultan
Senior Executives: Arne Skjonberg (Technical Production Manager), Paul Richardson (Decorative Sales Manager), Z Hegazi (Sales Adviser), John C Swan (Heavy Duty Sales Manager), Bjorn Tveitan (Marine Sales Manager), Mohamed Hossam (Branch Manager Abu Dhabi)

PRINCIPAL ACTIVITIES: Production of paints for marine, decorative and industrial uses
Principal Agencies: Penguin Paints
Branch Offices: PO Box 3714, Abu Dhabi, Tel 771697, 724037, Telex 23448; PO Box 363, Manama, Bahrain, Tel 211155, Telex 8267; PO Box 76, Doha, Qatar, Tel 601291, Telex 4876, Fax 810325; PO Box 75 Safat, Kuwait 13001, Tel 4738732, Fax 4739260, Telex 23816
Parent Company: Jotun A/S, PO Box 400, 3201-Sandefjord, Norway
Principal Bankers: Bank of Credit & Commerce (Emirates)

Principal Shareholders: HH Sheikh Hamdan Bin Rashid Al Maktoum; Abdul Ghaffar Hussain; Jotun A/S
Date of Establishment: 1975
No of Employees: 140

JUMA AL MAJID EST
See AL MAJID, JUMA, EST

JUMA AL MAJID GROUP
See AL MAJID, JUMA, GROUP

JUMAIRAH MARINE & TRADING CO

PO Box 2370, Dubai
Tel: 432300
Cable: Jumairah
Telex: 45510 EM

Chairman: Khalil Ibrahim Al Saygh

PRINCIPAL ACTIVITIES: Shipping agents, trading and diving services
Principal Agencies: Tuboscope, Carboline Worldwide Corp, Rochem International, Dennis Motors, Owatonna Tool International Corp, Carlisle Europe SA
Associated Companies: Jumairah Marine Contracting Services; Oceaneering/JMI; Lamprell/Jumairah
Principal Bankers: First National City Bank

JUMBO ELECTRONICS CO LTD

PO Box 3426, Riga Dubai
Tel: 523555
Cable: Jecol Dubai
Telex: 45845 EM
Telefax: 523910

Chairman: M R Chhabria
Directors: Moosa Habib Al Yousuf, Abdul Karim Mohamed, Shorafa Mohamed Saleh, Siddique Mohamed Ebrahim
Senior Executives: M P Sharma (General Manager Marketing)

PRINCIPAL ACTIVITIES: Import and distribution of electrical and electronic equipment
Principal Agencies: Sony Corp, Japan; Asahi Corp, Japan; Casio Computer, Japan; Tanita Corp, Japan; Hermes Precisa Int, Switzerland; Thorn EMI Ferguson, UK; Morphy Richards, UK; Robert Krups, W Germany; Brother Ind, Japan; Telefunken, W Germany; Ricoh, Japan; Electrolux, Sweden; Pifco, UK; Delchi, Italy; Thomson, France
Branch Offices: Offices and Showrooms in: Dubai - PO Box 3426; Abu Dhabi -PO Box 3832; Sharjah - PO Box 5331; Ras Al Khaimah - PO Box 1054; Al Ain -PO Box 15444; Fujairah - PO Box 868
Principal Bankers: Grindlays Bank, Dubai; Banque Paribas, Dubai; Standard Chartered Bank, Dubai; National Bank of Abu Dhabi, Dubai

Date of Establishment: 1974
No of Employees: 300

K M BROTHERS

PO Box 2044, Dubai
Tel: 370110
Cable: Quality
Telex: 45598 Kmbro EM
Telefax: 378852

Directors: K M Bhatia (Managing Director), Kamlesh K Bhatia (Director)
Senior Executives: K T Bhatia (Import Manager)

PRINCIPAL ACTIVITIES: Supermarkets, shipchandling, wholesale and retail trade; supplies for hospitals, oil rigs, supply and work boats, and restaurants etc
Principal Agencies: John Burgess, UK; Barilla, Italy; Juice Bowl Products, USA; British Tissues, UK; Arnotts Mills & Ware, Australia; Haco, Switzerland; etc

Branch Offices: PO Box 1839, Sharjah; PO Box 3962, Abu Dhabi
Subsidiary/Associated Companies: Pure Ice Cream (UAE) Ltd, PO Box 6172, Sharjah; Golden Dragon Restaurant, PO Box 2044, Dubai; Emirates Ship Supply and Catering Co, PO Box 2044, Dubai; Dubai General Trading Co, PO Box 169, Dubai; K M International, PO Box 370, Ajman
Principal Bankers: British Bank of the Middle East; Middle East Bank
Financial Information:

	1989/90 Dh'000
Sales turnover	65,000
Authorised capital	20,000
Paid-up capital	18,500

Principal Shareholders: K M Bhatia, Kamla K Bhatia, Kamlesh K Bhatia
Date of Establishment: 1969
No of Employees: 275

KANOO GROUP, THE

PO Box 290, Dubai
Tel: 521525
Cable: Kanoo Dubai
Telex: 45451, Kanoo EM
Telefax: 524532, 522497

Chairman: Hamed A Kanoo
Directors: Yusuf Kanoo (Managing Director)
Senior Executives: A E H Johnson (Senior Executive Manager)

PRINCIPAL ACTIVITIES: Shipping agents; marine craft operators; clearing and forwarding; packing and removals; travel agents; courier and rapid transit; sales and service of heavy equipment and machinery construction plant, and mechanical engineering plant; insurance agents; project and management services; joint ventures; agents and distributors (chemicals, workshops, agricultural equipment, cranes, forklifts, construction equipment, oilfield supplies)
Principal Agencies: BASF, Bedford, Clark Bobcat, Grove Cranes, Massey Ferguson Equipment, Perkins Engines, CPT Compressors & Tools, Hyster Forklift Trucks, Lincoln, Tennant, Tremix, International Paints, etc
Branch Offices: UAE & Oman Offices: PO Box 245, Abu Dhabi, UAE; PO Box 151, Ras Al Khaimah, UAE; PO Box 771, Fujeirah, UAE; PO Box 10339, Khor Fakkan, UAE; PO Box 245, Jebel Dhanna, UAE; PO Box 1779, Al Ain, UAE; PO Box 7310, Muscat, Oman
Associated Companies: Yusuf Bin Ahmed Kanoo, Manama, Bahrain; Yusuf Bin Ahmed Kanoo, Dammam, Saudi Arabia; Kanoo Group Ltd, 1 Battersea Bridge Road, London SW11 3BG, UK
Principal Bankers: Citibank; British Bank of the Middle East; Royal Bank of Canada

Principal Shareholders: Members of the Kanoo family
Date of Establishment: Group 1890, UAE 1957
No of Employees: Group 3,200, UAE & Oman 500

KHANSAHEB CIVIL ENGINEERING CO

PO Box 2716, Dubai
Tel: 257251/4
Telex: 45471 Kansab EM

Chairman: Husain Abdul Bahman

PRINCIPAL ACTIVITIES: Civil engineering, building and contracting, oilfield contracting
Branch Offices: Branch Offices at Abu Dhabi and Sharjah
Associated Companies: R M Douglas Int'l, UK

KHARAFI, MOHAMED ABDULMOHSIN, EST

PO Box 11171, Dubai
Tel: 377806

Chairman: Mohamed Abdulmohsin Al Kharafi

Directors: Nasser M Al Kharafi, Fawzi Mohamed Al Kharafi

PRINCIPAL ACTIVITIES: Civil engineering contractors, import-export, production of steel, aluminium, timber, terrazzo tiles, building materials, insulating materials, readymix concrete, etc
Parent Company: Head office in Kuwait

KHATIB AND ALAMI

Consolidated Engineering Co

PO Box 5091, Dubai
Tel: 222203
Cable: Consing
Telex: 68474 CEC EM
Telefax: 281014

President: Prof Munir El Khatib
Directors: Dr Zuheir Alami (Senior Partner)
Senior Executives: Wail Sa'di (General Manager), Samir Abdulhadi (General Manager), Saba Saba (Admin & Financial Manager), Jacques S Ekmekji (Director Special Assignments)

PRINCIPAL ACTIVITIES: Engineering consultants and architects
Branch Offices: In UAE: Sharjah, PO Box 688; Abu Dhabi, PO Box 2732; also branches in Saudi Arabia, Bahrain and Oman
Parent Company: Head office in Beirut, Lebanon, Tel 300609, Telex 23523 CEC LE, Fax 862197
Subsidiary Companies: Alami & Abdulhadi (Consolidated Engineering Co), PO Box 35256, Amman, Jordan, Tel 822136, Telex 23012 CEC JO, Fax 822137
Principal Bankers: Arab Bank

Date of Establishment: 1961
No of Employees: 450

KHOORY, MOHAMED ABDULLAH HAJI YOUSUF, & CO

M A H Y Khoory & Co

PO Box 41, Dubai
Tel: 223271, 666300
Cable: Khoory Dubai
Telex: 45545 Khory EM
Telefax: 222651, 661642

Chairman: Mohamed Abdulla Khoory
Directors: Abdul Hamid Khoory, Salahuddin Sharafi

PRINCIPAL ACTIVITIES: Import and distribution of water pumps, desalination plants, diesel engines, marine engines, generating sets, electric motors and starters, gate valves, cold/hot/gas meters; manufacture of kraft liner and fluting medium (Union Paper Mills), and column and riser pipes (Al Khoory Engineering)
Principal Agencies: Grundfos Int'l, Denmark; DDS Filtration, Denmark; Lister Petter, UK; Hawker Siddeley Power Plant, UK; Hawker Siddeley Marine, UK; Mirrlees Blackstone Diesels, UK; Hawker Siddleley Electric Export, UK; Godwin Pumps, UK; Samson, Netherlands; GWF Gas & Water Meter Mnfg, Switzerland
Branch Offices: PO Box 3175, Abu Dhabi; PO Box 15005, Al Ain; PO Box 251, Ras Al-Khaimah; PO Box 12510, Dhaid
Subsidiary Companies: Al Khoory Engineering; Union Paper Mills
Principal Bankers: British Bank of the Middle East; Bank of Oman Ltd

Principal Shareholders: Directors as described
Date of Establishment: 1931
No of Employees: 600

KIRBY KUWAIT BUILDING SYSTEMS CO

PO Box 9201, Dubai
Tel: 373816
Telex: 47632
Telefax: 374015

Chairman: Kutayba Y Alghanim
President: Bassam Y Alghanim

PRINCIPAL ACTIVITIES: Supply of pre-engineered steel rigid frames used in building factories, warehouses, offices, showrooms, camps, etc, and doors, windows, roofing, skylights, partitions, suspended ceilings, panels etc
Parent Company: Head office in Kuwait

KPMG PEAT MARWICK

PO Box 3800, Chamber of Commerce Bldg, Dubai
Tel: 231447
Telex: 45878 PMNDB EM
Telefax: 214450

Chairman: M D U Rake (Senior Partner)
Partners: V N Malhotra, D M J Smith, A Mateen, M Dajani, M G W Armstrong

PRINCIPAL ACTIVITIES: Accountants and consultants
Branch Offices: Abu Dhabi, Sharjah, Jebel Ali, Fujairah, Oman, Qatar
Parent Company: Peat Marwich McLintock, London
Principal Bankers: Barclays Bank Plc

No of Employees: 95

KUWAIT FOOD CO (AMERICANA)

PO Box 3901, Dubai
Tel: 224290
Telex: 68349
Telefax: 59364

Chairman: Nasser M Kharafi

PRINCIPAL ACTIVITIES: Fast food industry and consumer food industry
Branch Offices: Jumairah Branch: PO Box 12054, Dubai, Tel 453933, Telex 47094, Fax 452738
Parent Company: Head office in Kuwait

KUWAIT INTERNATIONAL INVESTMENT CO

PO Box 1855, Dubai
Tel: 230551
Telex: 49558
Telefax: 273810

Chairman: Jassim M Al Bahar
Directors: Khalifa Y Al Roumy, Ahmed Y Behbehani, Mohamad A R Al Bisher, Abdulla R Al Hajeri, Salah F Al Marzouk, Eid A Al Rashidi, Wael J Al Sager

PRINCIPAL ACTIVITIES: Regional liaison office
Parent Company: Head office in Kuwait

KUWAIT SHIPPING AGENCIES CO SAK

PO Box 3278, Dubai
Tel: 210808
Telex: 45524
Telefax: 272581

PRINCIPAL ACTIVITIES: Freight agency, maritime transport, cargo
Parent Company: United Arab Shipping Co, Kuwait

LAING EMIRATES

PO Box 4588, Dubai
Tel: 667300
Telex: 46894 LAING EM
Telefax: 662180

Chairman: Obaid Humaid Al Tayer
Directors: B W Foot (Managing Director), W D Hewetson
Senior Executives: S Metcalfe (Financial Director), J E Alford (Commercial Director), J A Marks (Contracts Director)

PRINCIPAL ACTIVITIES: Building and civil engineering contractors

Subsidiary Companies: Laing Emirates Joinery
Principal Bankers: British Bank of Middle East

Principal Shareholders: Obaid Humaid Al Tayer; Laing Projects BV
Date of Establishment: January 1984
No of Employees: 600

LAMNALCO (DUBAI) CORP

PO Box 2752, Dubai
Tel: 431341
Cable: 45575 Helicon EM

PRINCIPAL ACTIVITIES: Marine and offshore services, oil terminal contractors
Branch Offices: Abu Dhabi; Jebel Dhanna; Saudi Arabia (Al Khobar)
Parent Company: Head office in Kuwait

LLOYDS BANK PLC

PO Box 3766, 29th Floor, Dubai International Trade Centre, Dubai
Tel: 375005
Cable: Interloyd Dubai
Telex: 46450 LBI EM
Telefax: 375026

PRINCIPAL ACTIVITIES: Commercial banking
Parent Company: Lloyds Bank Plc London

Date of Establishment: 1977
No of Employees: 42

LOOTAH, SAEED & SULTAN, CONTRACTING CO

PO Box 553, Dubai
Tel: 221682, 221813, 223314, 221682, 229948
Cable: Saeedlootah Dubai
Telex: 45923 Slotah EM, 45934 Slota EM
Telefax: 212648

Chairmen: Saeed Ahmed Lootah, Sultan Ahmed Lootah
Directors: Majid Rashid Lootah (Managing Director)
Senior Executives: Eng Mohammed Fathi Abdul Latif (General Manager), Atiq Ahmed Chishti (Commercial Executive)

PRINCIPAL ACTIVITIES: General contractors (civil construction, mechanical, electrical), merchants and manufacturer's agents. Supply of building materials, mechanical equipment and automotive equipment. Steel and carpentry works, tiles and block factory, gypsum factory, crusher plant, garage (maintenance of vehicles and heavy equipment)
Principal Agencies: Carborundum, UK; Suhner, Switzerland; Itakura Ceramic Tiles, Japan; Armitage Shanks, UK; Achilli Ercole, Italy; TA Rokal, W Germany; Polypipe, UK; Faris, Italy; Hunter Building Products, UK; Delta Crompton Cables, UK; Dubai Cables, Dubai
Branch Offices: Trading Division, Tel 668459, 668356; Steel Workshop, Tel 221880; Carpentry Workshop, Tel 225496; Garage, Tel 660319; Tiles Factory, Tel 223948; Crusher Plant & Block Factory, Tel 482313; Gypsum Factory (Jebel Ali), Tel 56197; New Showroom: Dubai/Shj Road, Tel 668356, 668459, Telex 45934 SLOTA EM, Fax 660703
Principal Bankers: Dubai Islamic Bank
Financial Information:

	1990
	Dh'000
Total assets	100,000

Principal Shareholders: Saeed Ahmed Lootah, Sultan Ahmed Lootah
Date of Establishment: 1964
No of Employees: 1,500

M R DEVELOPMENT & COMMERCIAL CO LTD

PO Box 5406, 3rd Floor, Al Shamsee Bldg, Dubai
Tel: 664041, 664280/81
Cable: Devco Dubai
Telex: 46321 Mrdevc EM
Telefax: 693910

Chairman: M M Rai

PRINCIPAL ACTIVITIES: Insurance and re-insurance agents; credit financing, industrial and business promotion; import and export of industrial machinery, motor vehicles and spares, tractors, diesel engines, pumps, and pipes
Principal Agencies: Assurances Generales de France, France; Swati Ent, India; Gadre Ind, India; Product Supply Co, USA
Branch Offices: Offices and agencies in Arab countries, Lebanon
Associated Companies: Intercontinental General and Life Assurance Co SAL; Federal Insurance Services & Consultancy Co
Principal Bankers: Banque Paribas, London, Dubai

MAAROUF ALUMINIUM

PO Box 5280, Dubai
Tel: 258003
Telex: 45854

Directors: Abdul Rahim Ibrahim Ismail Maroof, Mustafa Al Haj Mohd Abu Saleh, Nabil Saood Haroon

PRINCIPAL ACTIVITIES: Manufacture of doors, windows and other building aluminium products

MAC AL GURG (UAE)

PO Box 672, Dubai
Tel: 661291, 212481
Telex: 46040 Macag EM

Chairman: Easa Saleh Al Gurg
Directors: Saleh Easa Al Gurg, Nabil Easa Al Gurg

PRINCIPAL ACTIVITIES: Suppliers of complete range of building and construction materials, sewage systems, sanitary wares etc
Principal Agencies: Stockists: Hepworth Clay Pipe; Yorkshire Imperial Metals; Stanton & Staveley; Armitage Shanks; B Lilley & Sons; IMI Santon; British Gypsum; Catnic; Dover Engineering; Cape Boards; Schlegal Engineering; IMI Pacific; Lilley; Tuke & Bell; Mark Reiner
Branch Offices: Abu Dhabi
Parent Company: Easa Saleh Al Gurg Group
Principal Bankers: British Bank of the Middle East

Date of Establishment: 1975
No of Employees: 25

MARITIME & MERCANTILE INTERNATIONAL (PVT) LTD

PO Box 70, Dubai
Tel: 228181, 282161, 282221
Cable: Gray Dubai
Telex: 45425 Gray EM
Telefax: 228070

Chairman: S D Nasser Bin Abdulla Hussain Lootah
Directors: A G Davies, M Smith, R W T Tatham, Ahmed Al Mansouri, Mohammed Said Al Ghaith, Nasser Abdulrazak Al Said, Abdulrahman Midfa, Khalfan Kahrbash
Senior Executives: R W T Tatham (Area Director), G R Busby (Financial Controller), C A Boother (Manager Wines & Spirits), B I Gray (Manager Consumer), T G Lawrence (Manager Industrial), J C Baldwin (Manager Shipping), D F Profit (Manager Grayship), L E Fewtrell (Manager Travel), P R Bott (Manager On Trade Retail), R Karmall (Manager Freight Forwarding), K V Nainan (Manager Lloyds & Insurance), L Pinto (Manager Admin & Personnel)

PRINCIPAL ACTIVITIES: Shipping agents, travel agents, ship, and offshore supply vessels' operators; clearing and forwarding; general merchants; Lloyds agents
Principal Agencies: Beecham Overseas; Brickhouse Dudley Ltd; Delta Switchgear & Accessories; Yardley Int Ltd; P & OCL; BP Tankers; Shell Tankers; NCHP; Jugolinija; Hapag Lloyd; Esso Tankers; IATA; American Airlines; Finnair; Cunard Ellerman; Lloyds; Mobil Marine Lubricants; Nalfloc; Sea Containers; Scotpac; Texaco
Associated Companies: Abu Dhabi Maritime & Mercantile, PO Box 247; Ras Al Khaimah MMI, PO Box 140; Fujairah MMI, PO Box 259; also at Sharjah, Al Ain, Ummal Qawain, Ajman, Khorfakhan, Jebel Dhanna and Bahrain MMI; Oman United Agencies; United Engineering Services, Oman; KMMC Kuwait
Principal Bankers: British Bank of the Middle East; Standard Chartered Bank
Financial Information:

	1989/90 Dh'000
Sales turnover	250,000
Authorised capital	25,000
Paid-up capital	25,000

Principal Shareholders: Gray Mackenzie & Co Ltd (Member of the Inchcape Group)
Date of Establishment: Before 1860
No of Employees: 298

MASADER INTERNATIONAL GENERAL TRADING CO

PO Box 3449, Dubai
Tel: 235754
Telex: 48864
Telefax: 235753

Chairman: Sheikh Mana Rashid Mana Al Maktoum

PRINCIPAL ACTIVITIES: General trading and contracting
Branch Offices: Kuwait

Principal Shareholders: Sh Mana Rashid Mana Al Maktoum, UAE (51%), Masader General Trading Co, Kuwait (49%)

MATERIAL MARKETING COMPANY

PO Box 10886, Dubai
Tel: 227395
Telex: 46653 Matco EM

Senior Executives: David Walker (Area Manager)

PRINCIPAL ACTIVITIES: Supply of building materials
Principal Agencies: Expamet
Branch Offices: Abu Dhabi

MAZZAWI BROTHERS COMPANY

PO Box 1548, Dubai
Tel: 221208/9, 220575
Cable: Mazzawi-Dubai
Telex: 46143 Mazawi EM

Chairman: Gabi R Mazzawi
Directors: Fouad R Mazzawi

PRINCIPAL ACTIVITIES: Electrical engineers and contractors, import and export of electrical materials and luxury goods
Principal Agencies: British Lightning Preventor Ltd., UK; Westinghouse Electrical Co., USA; ITT, USA; La France, USA; Wells Fargo, USA; E.P.I. Gas, UK
Subsidiary Companies: Wakeling Instruments Ltd, UK
Principal Bankers: Citibank; Banque de l'Orient Arabe et d'Outre-Mer

Principal Shareholders: Partnership
Date of Establishment: 1967

UAE (Dubai)

MCDERMOTT INTERNATIONAL INC

PO Box 3098, Dubai
Tel: (971-4) 35100
Cable: Jaramac Dubai
Telex: 45437 Jarmc EM
Telefax: (971-4) 35527

Senior Executives: Mervyn W Raynor (General Manager Middle East Operations)

PRINCIPAL ACTIVITIES: Engineering and construction services for the production and transportation of hydrocarbons in offshore and onshore areas
Branch Offices: McDermott Arabia Co Ltd, PO Box 188, Dhahran Airport 31932, Saudi Arabia; McDermott International, Inc (ARE Branch), 15 Mohammed Hafez Street, Dokki, Cairo, Egypt
Parent Company: McDermott International, Inc
Subsidiary Companies: Babcock & Wilcox; Hudson Products; Hudson Engineering & Project Management Corp
Principal Bankers: Citibank, New York

Date of Establishment: 1946 in Delaware (ME operations began in 1968)
No of Employees: 39,000 worldwide (2,500 in Middle East)

MIDDLE EAST BANK LIMITED

Head Office, PO Box 5547, ARBIFT Tower, Deira, Dubai
Tel: 220121 (10 lines)
Cable: Memainbank
Telex: 46074 EM

Chairman: Majid Mohammad Al-Futtaim
Directors: Mohammad Uaman (Vice Chairman), Thomas Welsh, D W A Blye, Abdel Moneim Abdel Azim
Management: Majid Al Futtaim (Chief Executive)

PRINCIPAL ACTIVITIES: Commercial and investment banking
Branch Offices: Local branches: 9 (Abu Dhabi 2, Dubai 4, Ras-Al-Khaimah, Sharjah, Umm Al Quwain). Foreign branches: 8 (Karachi, Lahore; Islamabad, Pakistan; Cairo, Egypt; London, UK; New York, USA; Khartoum, Sudan; Colombo, Sri Lanka)
Subsidiary/Associated Companies: Middle East Bank Kenya Limited, Nairobi; Owena Bank (Nigeria) Limited, Akure; Banque de Djibouti et du Moyen Orient SA, Djibouti; Middle East Bank Int Ltd, Cayman Islands; Middle East Finance Int Ltd, Hong Kong
Financial Information: Capital was fully paid up on 30th April 1986

	Dh'000
Authorised capital	300,000
Paid up capital	200,000

Principal Shareholders: Majid Mohammad Al-Futtaim, Dubai (51%); Government of Dubai (21%); Muslim Commercial Bank Ltd, Karachi (10%); UAE Nationals (18%)
Date of Establishment: 1976

MIDDLE EAST EXCHANGE & TRADE

PO Box 1356, Dubai
Tel: 223286/9, 215934
Cable: Meet
Telex: 45558 Meet EM

Chairman: Hamdan Habib Sajwani
Directors: Hussain Hamdan Sajwani, Shawqi Hamdan Sajwani

PRINCIPAL ACTIVITIES: Import-export of foodstuffs, chemicals, electronics, travel agents and manufacture, canning and beverages filling industries (dixi cola); national plastics and building material industries
Principal Agencies: Aimor; Funai; Sampo; Corona
Branch Offices: Abu Dhabi; Sharjah; Tehran (Iran)
Subsidiary Companies: Canning and Beverage Filling Industries; Green Coast Electronics; Emirates Express Travel Agency; National Plastics and Building Material Industries; International Furnishing and Foam Factory; Sajwani Insurance Company

Principal Bankers: Union Bank of the Middle East Ltd; Bank of the Arab Coast; Al-Ahli Bank

Date of Establishment: 1969

MIDDLE EAST TRADING & INDUSTRIAL CO

PO Box 1767, Dubai
Tel: 668461
Telex: 45552
Telefax: 661573

Chairman: Mahmoud Mohd Abu Ghazalah
Directors: Ahmed Mohd Abu Ghazalah

PRINCIPAL ACTIVITIES: General trading, fooodstuffs, vegetables and fruit
Branch Offices: Jordan
Parent Company: Head office in Kuwait

MODERN FREIGHT COMPANY

PO Box 5727, Dubai
Tel: 521625
Cable: Modcom
Telex: 47977
Telefax: 520612

Senior Executives: T S B Challis (General Manager), C Steibelt (Deputy General Manager), M K Prakash (Administration Manager), A S Braganza (Operations Manager), S Jainudeen (Special Projects Manager), D Menon (Chief Acccountant), I Jodha (Marketing Manager)

PRINCIPAL ACTIVITIES: Shipping agency, liner and trampship agency, clearing and forwarding, shipchartering, brokerage, surveying, airfreight, sea air cargo, project forwarding, warehousing
Principal Agencies: American President Lines; Merzario; Normudu Lines, Panalpina, Air Sea Brokers Ltd, Hyundai Merchant Marine
Branch Offices: Sharjah, Khor Fakkan, Fujairah, Doha (Qatar)
Principal Bankers: Citibank, Dubai; National Bank of Dubai, Dubai

Date of Establishment: 1977
No of Employees: 68

MOHAMED & ABDULSAMAD AL KAITOOB

See AL KAITOOB, MOHAMED & ABDULSAMAD,

MOHAMED ABDULLAH HAJI YOUSUF KHOORY & CO

See KHOORY, MOHAMED ABDULLAH HAJI YOUSUF, & CO

MOHAMED ABDULMOHSIN KHARAFI EST

See KHARAFI, MOHAMED ABDULMOHSIN, EST

MOHAMED ABDULRAHMAN AL BAHAR

See AL BAHAR, MOHAMED ABDULRAHMAN,

MOHAMED AL MAKAWI EST

See AL MAKAWI, MOHAMED, EST

MOHAMED ZAINAL FARAIDOONI

See FARAIDOONI, MOHAMED ZAINAL,

MOHAMMAD OMAR BIN HAIDER EST

See BIN HAIDER, MOHAMMAD OMAR, EST

MOHAMMED ABDUL MOHSEN AL MERRI TRADING EST

PO Box 16443, Dubai
Tel: 238746
Telefax: 235819

Chairman: Mohammed Abdul Mohsen

PRINCIPAL ACTIVITIES: Supply of generators,
telecommunication equipment, household equipment,
electrical, electronic and medical equipment, etc
Parent Company: Head office in Kuwait

MOHAMMED BIN MASOOD & SONS
See BIN MASOOD, MOHAMMED, & SONS

MOHAMMED SAEED ALMULLA & SONS (PVT) LTD
See ALMULLA, MOHAMMED SAEED, & SONS (PVT) LTD

MOHAMMED TAYYEB KHOORY & SONS
PO Box 4664, Dubai
Tel: 229684, 223251 (8 lines)
Cable: Taykhoory
Telex: 45943 Tayyeb EM
Telefax: 212750

Chairman: Mohammed Tayyeb Khoory
Directors: Abdulqadir Sharafi (Director), Mohammed Mohd
Tayyeb Khoory (Director & Partner), Abdulla Mohd Tayyeb
Khoory (Director & Partner)

PRINCIPAL ACTIVITIES: Stockists and distributors of motor
vehicles (SUBARU), diesel engines, pumps, generators &
engines, construction machinery, sprayers, water well drilling
rigs, alternators, air compressors, fire fighting equipment,
ductile iron pipes and fittings, wire ropes, spare parts
(general)
Principal Agencies: Caprari Fabbrica Italiana Pompe, Italy;
Lombardini Fabbrica Italiana Motori, Italy; Stabilimenti
Meccanici VM, Italy; Jori, Italy; Fuji Heavy Industries, Japan;
D Nagata & Co, Japan; FF Luft, Denmark; De Smithske,
Denmark; Dando Drilling System, UK; Varisco, Italy; Cristanini,
Italy; Marcati, Italy; Bruntons, UK; Kubota, Japan; Ferrari,
Italy; Radaelli Sud, Italy; Benfra, Italy; Slanzi Motors, Italy;
Fondocianes Metalicas, Spain; MTK Automatic Fire Fighting
Unit
Branch Offices: PO Box 51812, Ras Al Khaimah; PO Box
15514, Al Ain; PO Box 6528, Sharjah; PO Box 12694, Al
Dhayd; PO Box 3869, Abu Dhabi; PO Box 1003, Fujairah
Principal Bankers: Bank of Credit & Commerce International,
Deira, Dubai; Emirates Bank International, Deira, Dubai;
Commercial Bank of Dubai, Deira, Dubai

Principal Shareholders: Proprietory concern
Date of Establishment: 1976
No of Employees: 109

MOHD NASEEM MOHD SALEEM
PO Box 2999, Dubai
Tel: 225436, 225656, 283391/2
Cable: SUPER - DUBAI
Telex: 46263 Super Em

Chairman: Naseem Farooque
Directors: Saleem Farooque, Naeem Farooque

PRINCIPAL ACTIVITIES: Dealers and stockists of auto spare
parts and all types of belts, noses and bearings, batteries, oil
seals and safety items
Principal Agencies: AC Delco, Land Rover, Range Rover,
Bedford
Branch Offices: Abu Dhabi, UK
Subsidiary Companies: J & N Export Co (Int) Ltd, Milton
Keynes, UK; Mohd Naseem Mohd Saleem (Pte) Ltd,
Singapore; International Auto Corporation, Abu Dhabi
Principal Bankers: Standard Chartered Bank; Union Bank of the
Middle East, Dubai

Date of Establishment: 1967

MOHD NASER AL SAYER & SONS
See AL SAYER, MOHD NASER, & SONS

MONA TRADING CO
PO Box 5012, Dubai
Tel: 245451/2, 245004, 245972, 245499
Cable: Monatco
Telex: 45727 MONCO EM
Telefax: 245944

Chairman: Abdul Rahman Al Jalaf
Directors: Suhail Awartani (Managing Director), Mohammed H
Mefrej (Finance Director), Abdul Razzaq (Technical Director),
Kaleed Mohamed

PRINCIPAL ACTIVITIES: Manufacturers' representation,
distribution of agricultural equipment, welding equipment,
mechanical engineering plant, heavy machinery, tools,
materials handling equipment, wood working machines, rock
breakers, Mercedes spare parts, all types of tools and garage
equipment
Principal Agencies: Miller, USA; Briggs & Stratton, USA; Nike,
Sweden; Montabert, France; Steton Wood Working Mach,
Italy; Beta Tools, Italy; CISE Air Compressors, Italy; Cormach
Workshop Equpt, Italy; International Hardware Grinding Disc,
UK; AC Workshop Crane, Denmark
Subsidiary Companies: Contractors Supply Co, PO Box 3379,
Abu Dhabi; Al Gondool Auto Parts, PO Box 7093, Sharjah
Principal Bankers: United Arab Bank; Commercial Bank of
Dubai Ltd

Date of Establishment: 1973

MONNRIS ENTERPRISES
PO Box 11398, Dubai
Tel: 282017, 232239
Cable: Monnris Dubai
Telex: 47250 Monrs EM
Telefax: 239354

Managing Partner: Kunhi Muhammed
Senior Executives: A Awan, P M Sebastian

PRINCIPAL ACTIVITIES: Import/export/stockists of chemicals
and acids for oil well drilling, petroleum production, water
treatment, water well drilling and other industrial purposes;
also stockists of lubricants, cleaning products and
maintenance products
Principal Bankers: Standard Chartered Bank, Dubai; Bank of
Baroda, Dubai

Principal Shareholders: Partnership Company
Date of Establishment: November 1978

MOSTAFA & NAJIBI SHIPPING & TRADING CO
PO Box 3197, Dubai
Tel: 431771, 431519, 431520
Cable: Manco Dubai
Telex: 45909 Manco EM

Directors: Nooruddin Mostafa (Managing Director), Yousouf
Najibi (Partner)
Senior Executives: D P Sukthankar (Executive Director)

PRINCIPAL ACTIVITIES: Shipping; Trading; Import; Export;
technical and management consultants; commodities, joint
venture sponsorship
Principal Bankers: Bank of Baroda, Dubai

Date of Establishment: 1967

MOSTAFA BIN ABDULLATIF
PO Box 44, Dubai
Tel: 534192, 536421
Cable: Mostafa
Telex: 46573 Mostaf EM
Telefax: 532174

Chairman: Abdul Rahman Arif
Directors: G V Mehta (Acting Chief Administrator)

PRINCIPAL ACTIVITIES: Importers, exporters, indentors and general merchants, distributors and agents

Principal Agencies: Rothmans of Pall Mall (O/S) Ltd, BICC Ltd, UK; Chubb & Sons Lock & Safe Co Ltd, UK; Braun AG, Kronberg, West Germany; Krimpen, Holland; NCR Corp, USA; Systema & Checker Co Ltd, Denmark; Vickers, UK; Alan Cooper, UK; General Binding Corporation, USA; Comforto Systemes, Switzerland; Efficienta BV, Holland; Modulex, Denmark

Branch Offices: Abu Dhabi, Sharjah, Fujairah, Kalba

Subsidiary Companies: Axon Business Systems, Dubai and Abu Dhabi; The New Store, Dubai, Abu Dhabi and Sharjah; BICC Mostafa Bin Abdullatif Dubai; Dubai Ice Plant & Cold Stores, Dubai

Principal Bankers: British Bank of the Middle East; National Bank of Dubai Ltd; Union Bank of the Middle East Ltd; Emirates International Ltd

Date of Establishment: 1930
No of Employees: 119

MOTHERCAT LTD

PO Box 1820, Dubai
Tel: 232538
Cable: Mothercat
Telex: 68014 Cat EM

Chairman: Mrs Loura El Bustani
Directors: Mrs Nadia El Khoury, Shukri H Shammas, Fuad El Khazen, Khalil Noubani, Andre Geha
Senior Executives: Ibrahim Khawaja (Area Manager, UAE)

PRINCIPAL ACTIVITIES: General contracting, building and civil engineering works, mechanical engineering and pipeline contractors, steel structure fixtures, fitting out and interior decorating works and manufacture and supply of prefabricated building & caravans

Branch Offices: Branches throughout the UAE, also in Lebanon, Saudi Arabia, Kuwait, Bahrain, Qatar, Oman, Libya, Pakistan, Nigeria, UK (London), France (Paris)

Parent Company: Contracting & Trading Co (C.A.T)

Principal Bankers: British Bank of the Middle East, Grindlays Bank, Arab Bank Ltd

Financial Information:

	1990 St£'000
Authorised capital	5,000

Principal Shareholders: Directors as described
Date of Establishment: 2nd January 1963
No of Employees: Over 2,000

NAAZ TRADING CORPORATION

PO Box 4378, Deira, Dubai
Tel: 223457, 281893
Cable: Naazco Dubai
Telex: 45839 Naazco EM

Chairman: Najmuddin E Ali
Directors: Abbas E Ali (Managing Director)
Senior Executives: Asgar Ali (General Manager)

PRINCIPAL ACTIVITIES: Manufacturers, importers and exporters; woodworking machines, building materials, including timber, plywood, hardware, auto spare parts and machine tools; manufacture of fibre glass products, steel fabrications, wooden and steel doors, windows and furniture, packaging materials etc

Subsidiary/Associated Companies: Naaz Steel Works; Naaz Industrial Tools Supplies Co; Naaz Industrial Enterprises, Naaz, Enterprises Associated companies in Bombay; Kuala-Lumpur; Hong Kong; Tokyo; Bangkok; Taipei; Cairo; Muscat; Amman; Jeddah

Principal Bankers: British Bank of the Middle East; Barclays Bank

Principal Shareholders: N E Ali, A E Ali, K Wassia and their families
Date of Establishment: 1968
No of Employees: 80

NASCO, KARAOGLAN & CO LTD

Clock Tower Area, Rostomani Bldg, PO Box 7108, Deira, Dubai
Tel: 282871
Telex: 46496 Naskar EM

PRINCIPAL ACTIVITIES: Insurance brokers and underwriting agents
Principal Agencies: CAMAT, Paris; Bankers Assurance SAL, Beirut
Branch Offices: Head Office in Paris
Principal Bankers: Banque Indosuez; Banque Paribas; First National Bank of Chicago

Principal Shareholders: Circocrest Investments Limited; Saba Nader; Maurice Karaoglan
Date of Establishment: 1976

NASER MOHD SAYER & CO

PO Box 1825, Deira, Dubai
Tel: 222471, 284314, 669280
Cable: Naser Sayer
Telex: 45825 Nesma EM
Telefax: 663972

Directors: Naser Mohd Nasser Sayer, Abdul Rehman Abdul Mughni, Bader Abdulla Al-Suhaim

PRINCIPAL ACTIVITIES: General trade; office furniture and equipment; tools; hardware; airconditioning and refrigeration equipment and parts, measuring and control systems, building materials, electrical fittings
Principal Agencies: Josiah Parkes & Sons Limited, UK; Alco International Ltd, Japan; Mita, Holland; Virginia Chemicals, USA; Mueller Brass, USA
Parent Company: Head Office: Naser Sayer & Co WLL, PO Box 186, Kuwait
Principal Bankers: Commercial Bank of Dubai Ltd

Principal Shareholders: Directors as described
Date of Establishment: 1965
No of Employees: 45

NASIR BIN ABDULLAH & MOHD SIDDIQ TRADING CO

PO Box 2080, Dubai
Tel: 471469, 470277
Cable: Elba
Telex: 45766 Elba EM

Chairman: Mian M Siddiq

PRINCIPAL ACTIVITIES: General trading and distribution of heavy machinery, air-conditioning equipment, electrical equipment
Principal Agencies: Hyundai, Kaelable, Kato, Singer, Frimont, Fjdes
Branch Offices: Nasir Bin Abdullah & Mohd Siddiq Trading Co, PO Box 329, Doha; Nasir Bin Abdullah & Mohd Siddiq Trading Co, PO Box 3672, Abu Dhabi
Principal Bankers: Banque Paribas; Commercial Bank of Dubai Ltd; Bank of Oman; Habib Bank Ltd

NASSER ABDULLATIF

PO Box 1219, Dubai
Tel: 221374, 222081
Cable: Nasser
Telex: 45540 Nasser EM

Directors: Nasser Abdullatif (Proprietor), Eisa Bin Nasser (Proprietor)

PRINCIPAL ACTIVITIES: Importers, stockists, general
merchants (mechanical and industrial equipment, motor
vehicles), water well drilling and contractors
Principal Agencies: AB Electrolux, Sweden; Bridgestone Tire Co
Ltd, Japan; F M C Corporation, USA; Hayward Tyler & Co
Ltd, UK; Hawker Siddeley International UK; Irrigation &
Industrial Development Corpn, USA; Mirrless Blackstone Ltd,
UK; Massey Ferguson, UK; Petters Ltd, UK; Newman Electric
Motors, UK; Outboard Marine NV, Belgium
Branch Offices: Branch in Abu Dhabi; Sultanate of Oman
(Muscat Branch, PO Box 36)
Associated Companies: Nasser Abdullatif & Co, PO Box 3636,
Ruwi, Muscat, Oman)
Principal Bankers: National Bank of Dubai, Dubai; Standard
Chartered Bank Ltd, Dubai; British Bank of the Middle East,
Dubai

NASSER ABDULLATIF ALSERKAL & SON EST

See ALSERKAL, NASSER ABDULLATIF, & SON EST

NASSER AL SAYER & CO

See AL SAYER, NASSER, & CO

NASSER RASHID LOOTAH & SONS

PO Box 1187, Deira, Dubai
Tel: 223218/19/10
Cable: Badiah, Dubai
Telex: 45831 Badie EM
Telefax: (971-4) 274631

President: Nasser Rashid Lootah (also Managing Director)
Directors: Khaled Nasser Lootah (Senior Vice President),
Ibrahim Nasser Lootah (Vice President)

PRINCIPAL ACTIVITIES: Dealers in building materials,
hardware, plastic products, concrete mixers; manufacturers of
ball pens, galvanizing wires; building and road construction;
travel agents; hotels; supply of lighting systems
Principal Agencies: Yale Security Products, Italy, UK, W
Germany, USA; Ifo Sanitar AB, Sweden; Armitage Shanks,
UK; Concrete Utilities, UK; F O'Brian, UK; China Airlines;
Ethiopian Airlines; Olympus Optical Co; PC Henderson, UK
Branch Offices: UAE: PO Box 4796, Abu Dhabi, Telex 22489
Lootah, Tel 334551; Hong Kong Office: PO Box 7136, Hong
Kong
Subsidiary Companies: Asian Air Travel & Tours Agency, Dubai;
NRL Factories for wire drawing, galvanising, ball pens, etc
Principal Bankers: Lloyds Bank, Dubai; Hang Seng Bank Ltd,
Hong Kong; United Bank Ltd, Dubai; Bank of Credit &
Commerce Intl, Dubai; The British Bank of the Middle East,
London; United Bank Ltd, London

Principal Shareholders: N R Lootah & Sons
Date of Establishment: 1966
No of Employees: 1,012

NATIONAL ALUMINIUM COMPANY

PO Box 5326, Dubai
Tel: 257851, 257376
Cable: Bronzal
Telex: 45660 ASECO EM

Chairman: Abdulla Al-Shirawi, Mohan G Valrani (Senior Vice
Chairman)
Directors: Arjun Bulchandani (Managing Director), Darshan G
Valrani (Executive Director)
Senior Executives: R M Ramchandani (General Manager)

PRINCIPAL ACTIVITIES: Architectural aluminium products:
fabricated doors and windows, aluminium staircases, curtain
wallings, aluminium balustrade; import and sale of glass, clear
sheet, clear float glass, double glazed panels and tempered
glass

Principal Agencies: Amarlite Anaconda Aluminium Co; Saint
Gobain (stockist), Pilkington-(stockist), Fla-chglass
Branch Offices: PO Box 18056, Baghdad, Iraq
Parent Company: Al-Sharawi Group of Companies, PO Box 93,
Dubai
Principal Bankers: Commercial Bank of Dubai Ltd

Principal Shareholders: Ajit India Pvt Ltd Bombay (India); Al
Shirawi Group of Industries (Dubai)
Date of Establishment: March 1975
No of Employees: 100

NATIONAL BANK OF ABU DHABI

PO Box 4436, Dubai
Tel: 226141
Cable: Almasraf Dubai
Telex: 45668 EM

PRINCIPAL ACTIVITIES: Commercial banking
Branch Offices: Abu Dhabi, Dubai, Fujairah, Ras Al Khaimah,
Sharjah
Parent Company: Head office in Abu Dhabi, UAE

Date of Establishment: 1974

NATIONAL BANK OF DUBAI LTD

PO Box 777, Dubai
Tel: 222241, 222255
Cable: National
Telex: 45421 Natnal EM
Telefax: 215939

Chairman: Sultan Ali Al-Owais
Directors: HE Mohamed Al Mulla (Deputy Chairman), Abdullah
Mohamed Saleh (Managing Director), Mir Hashim Khoory,
Yousuf Habib, HE Mohamed Mahdi Al Tajir, Saeed Juma Al
Naboodah
Senior Executives: D F McKenzie (General Manager)

PRINCIPAL ACTIVITIES: All banking services
Branch Offices: PO Box 386, Abu Dhabi; PO Box 22, Umm Al
Quwain; PO Box 16122, Al Ain; UK: 207 Sloane Street,
London SW1X 9QX
Financial Information:

	1988	1989
	Dh'000	Dh'000
Profits	396,217	437,946
Authorised capital	1,000,000	1,000,000
Paid-up capital	861,769	861,769
Total assets	22,120,820	23,087,016

Principal Shareholders: UAE Nationals
Date of Establishment: 1963
No of Employees: 787

NATIONAL BANK OF FUJAIRAH

PO Box 2979, Dubai
Tel: 511700
Telex: 47211
Telefax: 526001

Chairman: HH Sheikh Saleh Bin Mohammed Al Sharqi
Directors: Easa Saleh Al Gurg (Deputy Chairman), Khalaf Saeed
Al Ghaith, Sheikh Saud Bin Khalid Al Qasimi, Khalifa Juma Al
Naboodah, Sulaiman Mousa Al Jassim, Sayed Abdullah Al
Mousawi, Eid Obeid Khalfan, Mohamed Ahmed Abdul
Rahman, Dr Salem Abdo Khalil (Secretary to the Board)
Senior Executives: Michael J Connor (General Manager),
Alberto F T Martins (Senior Manager Operation & Admin),
George Cromar Collie (Senior Manager Dubai)

PRINCIPAL ACTIVITIES: Commercial banking
Branch Offices: Abu Dhabi, Dubai, Fujairah, Dibba
Parent Company: Head office: PO Box 887, Fujairah, UAE

Financial Information:

	1989	1990
	Dh'000	Dh'000
Profits	13,965	15,207
Authorised capital	400,000	400,000
Paid-up capital	150,000	150,000
Total assets	426,202	484,145

Principal Shareholders: Government of Fujairah (43%), Government of Dubai (19.6%)
Date of Establishment: September 1984
No of Employees: 96

NATIONAL BANK OF RAS AL KHAIMAH

PO Box 1531, Dubai
Tel: 226291/5
Telex: 46757 Nbrak EM

PRINCIPAL ACTIVITIES: Commercial banking
Branch Offices: Abu Dhabi, Ras Al Khaimah
Parent Company: Head office in Ras Al Khaimah

Date of Establishment: 1979

NATIONAL BANK OF UMM AL QAIWAIN

PO Box 8898, Dubai
Tel: 233314
Telex: 48818

PRINCIPAL ACTIVITIES: Commercial banking
Branch Offices: Abu Dhabi
Parent Company: Head office in Umm Al Qaiwain

Date of Establishment: 1983

NATIONAL CEMENT CO LTD

PO Box 4041, Dubai
Tel: 480671, 480950
Cable: Cement Dubai
Telex: 47202 NACEM EM

Chairman: Saif Ahmed Al Ghurair
Senior Executives: Eng Mohammed Nizar Sibai (General Manager), Mohammed A Al Ghurair (DY General Manager), Mohammed Ezzat Daaji (DY General Manager)

PRINCIPAL ACTIVITIES: Manufacture and sale of cement
Principal Bankers: Bank of Oman Ltd, Dubai

Principal Shareholders: Public Limited Company
Date of Establishment: 1968
No of Employees: 500

NATIONAL FLOOR MILLS CO

PO Box 780, Dubai
Tel: 534700
Cable: Nafmills
Telex: 48795 Nafco EM
Telefax: 533095

Chairman: Abdulla Al Ghurair
Directors: Saif Al Ghurair
Senior Executives: Essa Al Ghurair (General Manager), Juma Al Ghurair (Deputy General Manager), A J Shetty (Production Manager), Farook Assassa (Administration Manager), Rashid Mubarak (Sales Manager), Anwar Ali Khan (Chief Accountant)

PRINCIPAL ACTIVITIES: Milling of wheat flour and marketing of feed barley
Principal Bankers: Bank of Oman, Dubai
Financial Information:

	1990
	Dh'000
Sales turnover	131,172
Profits	9,580
Authorised capital	35,000
Paid-up capital	35,000
Total assets	83,053

Principal Shareholders: Saif Al Ghurair, Abdulla Al Ghurair
Date of Establishment: 1976
No of Employees: 90

NATIONAL GLASS ESTABLISHMENT

PO Box 563, Dubai
Tel: 221315
Telefax: 275241

Chairman: Nayrous Ali Hussain

PRINCIPAL ACTIVITIES: Glass for windows and doors, mirrors, non ferrous metal products, crude plastics and nylons, etc
Parent Company: Head office in Kuwait

NATIONAL PRINTING PRESS

PO Box 1120, Deira, Dubai
Tel: 660784, 660626, 664219, 214930, 214926
Cable: Press
Telex: 45679 Press EM

Chairman: Jafar Ali Bustani (also Managing Partner)
Directors: A Karim Ali Bustani (Manager, Abu Dhabi), Khalid Ali Bustani
Senior Executives: Mohamed Homs (Financial Controller)

PRINCIPAL ACTIVITIES: Printing; sale of stationery and office equipment; manufacture of boxes
Principal Agencies: Rexel Ltd, UK; J S Staedtler, Germany; G W Pelikan, Germany; M Mayers & Sons, UK
Branch Offices: PO Box 147, Abu Dhabi; PO Box 333, Sharjah

Principal Shareholders: Jafar Ali Bustani & Bros
Date of Establishment: 1961
No of Employees: 200

NATIONAL TRADING & DEVELOPING EST (SMOKERS CENTRE)

PO Box 3139, 1st Floor, Dubai Tower, Deira, Dubai
Tel: 220115 (6 lines), 225520
Cable: Intaj Dubai
Telex: 45867 Intaj EM
Telefax: 281372

Directors: Hassan Ahmadi (Proprietor)
Senior Executives: Hossein Ahmadi (General Manager)

PRINCIPAL ACTIVITIES: Exclusively dealing in tobacco goods and smokers' requisites, food products, confectionery items, consumer goods and household items
Principal Agencies: Cadbury International Ltd, UK; Gallaher International, UK; American Tobacco Co, USA; Martin Brothers Tobacco Co Inc, USA; Willem II Sigarenfabriekan BV, Holland; General Cigars, USA; T Neimeyer, Holland; GTC Industries, India; Imperial Tobacco, UK; Villiger Cigars, Switzerland; Swedish Tobacco, Sweden; Ritmeester, Holland, Reemtsma Int'l, W Germany; Alfred Dunhill, UK; Sarome, Japan; Rowenta, W Germany; Pokka Juice, Japan; Arrow Honey, Australia; Pezzullo Macaroni, Italy; Life Savers Chocolates, Australia; Dandy, Denmark; Red Tulip Chocolates, Australia; Blue Bird Confectionery, UK; Almond Roca, USA; Buitoni, Italy; Fuji Electrochemical, Japan; Keen, UK; DIM Soaps, W Germany; Eagle Flasks, India; Oster Int'l ,USA; Hawkins Cookers, India
Branch Offices: Abu Dhabi (6 branches); Al Ain; Sharjah; Ras Al Khaimah, Dubai (4 branches)
Principal Bankers: British Bank of the Middle East, Citibank, Standard Chartered Bank, ABN Bank, Bank of Oman, Middle East Bank, Bank Melli Iran

Date of Establishment: 1969
No of Employees: 180

NATIONAL TRADING COMPANY

PO Box 1316, Deira, Dubai
Tel: 695914
Cable: Motorist
Telefax: 691250

Directors: Bahrat A Bhatia (Partner)

PRINCIPAL ACTIVITIES: Wholesale, retail, export-import, hardware, hand tools, building materials, batteries, chemicals, rubber sheets, packaging, safety equipment, welding and garage equipment

Principal Agencies: Elora Tools, Germany; Weiding, Germany; Bosny Products, Thailand

Principal Bankers: Emirates Bank International, National Bank of Abu Dhabi

Financial Information:

	1990 Dh'000
Sales turnover	3,000
Authorised capital	1,000

Date of Establishment: 1965

NCR CORPORATION

PO Box 1185, Dubai
Tel: 231500
Cable: Nacareco Dubai
Telex: 45874 NCR EM

PRINCIPAL ACTIVITIES: Distribution of business equipment, computers, terminals, electronic data processing equipment

Branch Offices: United Arab Emirates; Kuwait; Bahrain; Oman; Qatar

Date of Establishment: 1962
No of Employees: 40

NEWAGE COMPANY

PO Box 4396, Deira, Dubai
Tel: 664000 (4 lines)
Cable: Newage
Telex: 47927 NEWAG EM
Telefax: 664044

Chairman: Mohmed Omran Taryam
Directors: Rajni C Shah
Senior Executives: R V Shah

PRINCIPAL ACTIVITIES: Engineers, traders and manufacturers representatives, importers, suppliers, distributors of technical building service equipment, fire detection and protection equipment, pumping equipment, hot water and steam boilers, water coolers and drinking fountains, playground equipment, washroom appliances, etc including service and repair

Principal Agencies: Jung Pumpen, W Germany; Crane Pumps, UK; Gollmer & Hummel, W Germany; Norsk Hammerverk AS, Norway; Bahyam Ltd, UK; Pompes Salmson, France; Haws Drinking Faucets, USA; Dunlop, UK; Albin Sprenger, W Germany; Eurocall Ltd, UK; J T Wade, UK; Apollo Fire Detectors, UK; Cefex International, UK

Branch Offices: PO Box 5001, Sharjah, UAE, Tel 338798, Telex 47927; PO Box 7645, Abu Dhabi, UAE, Tel 774548, Telex 47927, Fax 728880

Parent Company: Omran Investment Co, PO Box 82, Sharjah

Subsidiary Companies: Haws Middle East, Dubai

Principal Bankers: Bank of Oman, Deira, Dubai; Investmentbank for Trade & Finance LLC, Dubai

Financial Information:

	1990 Dh'000
Sales turnover	9,084
Profits	1,527
Authorised capital	650
Paid-up capital	650
Total assets	3,016

Principal Shareholders: Mohmed Omran Taryam, Rajni C Shah
Date of Establishment: June 1976

NICO INTERNATIONAL UAE

PO Box 12068, Dubai
Tel: 582135
Cable: Nicoship
Telex: 45961 Nico EM
Telefax: 581832

Chairman: Goran Wijkmark
Directors: Inge Wernersson (Managing Director)
Senior Executives: Henk Carstens (Manager Industrial Div), Charlie Zickerman, (Ship Repair Manager), Ragnar Andersson (Workshop Manager), Thomas Barth (Deputy General Manager), Satya N Bhutra (Accounts Manager)

PRINCIPAL ACTIVITIES: Marine services, ship repair and maintenance, diving services, anti corrosion services, offshore maintenance services, onshore industrial services, steel fabrication, electrical rewinding services

Principal Agencies: AB Hagglund & Soner; Asea AB; Goltens Atlantic Diesel; Lincoln Diesels; Twin Disc; Berl UK; Van Der Horst of England; Reintje Gears; Esab; Wartsila Diesel; Holset Dampers; Camesa Cable; B&W Man; Fincantieri Divisione Grandi Motori, Aalborg Boilers

Subsidiaries Companies: Nico International (Fujairah) Ltd, Fujairah; Nico International Abu Dhabi; Maintenance Services Gulf (Abu Dhabi), Gulf Rock Engineering Co Ltd (Ras Al Khaimah)

Principal Bankers: Grindlays Bank plc; Bank Indosuez

Financial Information:

	1989/90 Dh'000
Sales turnover	65,000
Authorised capital	1,300
Paid-up capital	1,300
Total assets	7,700

Principal Shareholders: Nordstjernan Group
Date of Establishment: April 1973
No of Employees: 430

NORWICH WINTERTHUR INSURANCE (GULF) LTD

PO Box 290, Dubai
Tel: 421525
Cable: Kanoo Dubai
Telex: 45451 Kanoo EM
Telefax: 524532

Chairman: Yusuf Ahmed Kanoo
Directors: I L Reid, H R Strickler, G W H Jones, E J Sainsbury, J D Campbell, G A Gilmour
Senior Executives: I L Reid (General Manager), H A Hussain (Non-Marine Underwriter), F D Evans (Marine Underwriter), J F O'Sullivan (Manager for UAE and Oman), Mohamed Makee (Chief Accountant & Manager)

PRINCIPAL ACTIVITIES: All classes of insurance and reinsurance (except life)

Branch Offices: Bahrain, Abu Dhabi, Dubai, Sharjah, Oman

Parent Company: Norwich Winterthur Holdings Ltd

Associated Companies: In the Middle East: Norwich Winterthur Insurance (Saudi Arabia) EC, Jeddah, Riyadh, Al Khobar

Principal Shareholders: Norwich Union Fire Insurance Society Ltd (46.5%); Winterthur Swiss Insurance Group of Switzerland (46.5%); Chiyoda Fire and Marine Insurance Company of Japan (7%)

Date of Establishment: 1979
No of Employees: 16 (Dubai)

OBAID HUMAID AL TAYER

See AL TAYER, OBAID HUMAID,

UAE (Dubai)

OILFIELDS SUPPLY CENTER LTD

PO Box 1518, Dubai
Tel: 226171/6
Cable: Servoil Dubai
Telex: 45454 OSC EM
Telefax: 279778

Chairman: HH Sheikh Hamdan Bin Rashid Al Maktoum
Directors: Mirza Al Sayegh, I M A Abedin, Byron Green
Senior Executives: A J Rogers (General Manager)

PRINCIPAL ACTIVITIES: Oil and gas industry, supply and
  services
Branch Offices: Sharjah Oilfields Supply Co
Subsidiary Companies: Joint Ventures: Smith Int Gulf Services;
  Cansult; Christensen Gulf Services; Dresco Pvt Ltd
  (Magcobar); Irongard Ltd
Principal Bankers: Commercial Bank of Dubai; National Bank of
  Dubai
Financial Information:

	1990 US$'000
Sales turnover	95,000
Authorised capital	3,000
Paid-up capital	3,000

Principal Shareholders: UAE Nationals
Date of Establishment: 1963
No of Employees: 360

OMAN FINANCE CO LTD

PO Box 12920, Deira, Dubai
Tel: 693331
Cable: Omanfinco
Telex: 49692 Ofco EM
Telefax: 695357

Chairman: Saif Al Ghurair
Directors: Abdullah Ahmad Al Ghurair

PRINCIPAL ACTIVITIES: Hire purchase financing, LBD financing
  and real estate
Branch Offices: Branch in Abu Dhabi, Al Ain, Karama, Sharjah,
  Ajman, Ras Al Khaimah, Fujeirah, Deira
Principal Bankers: Bank of Oman Ltd

Principal Shareholders: Bank of Oman Ltd

OMAN NATIONAL ELECTRONICS

PO Box 531, Dubai
Tel: 282201
Cable: Fateh
Telex: 45691 Fateh EM
Telefax: 213284

President: Majid Mohammed Al-Futtaim
Directors: Abdullah Al Futtaim (Vice-President), Philip Best
  (Group Managing Director)
Senior Executives: Z U Sabri (Managing Director), O Boers
  (Group Director Personnel & Administration), Abdel Moneim
  Abdel Azim (Group Legal Advisor & Director), Manager), K C
  Mohan (Managing Director Real Estate), A Kotwal (General
  Manager Management Service Division)

PRINCIPAL ACTIVITIES: Agents and distributors of electrical
  and electronic appliances, consumer goods, lighting products,
  system engineering and office automation
Principal Agencies: National; Panasonic; Technogas; Technics;
  Daewoo; Wisi; Rainbow; Audix; Schooner Dis
Branch Offices: PO Box 531, Dubai; PO Box 555, Abu Dhabi;
  PO Box 5471; Sharjah; PO Box 389, Ras Al Khaimah; PO
  Box 33561, Al Ain; PO Box 89053, Fujairah
Parent Company: Al Futtaim (Pte) Ltd
Principal Bankers: Bank of Oman; Arab Bank; Middle East
  Bank; Lloyds Bank

Date of Establishment: 1970/71
No of Employees: 350

OMAN TRANSPORT ESTABLISHMENT

PO Box 1034, Dubai
Tel: 663500, 341435
Cable: Flasi
Telex: 45822 EM

Chairman: Saeed Mohamed Al-Ghandi (Proprietor)
Directors: Matar Al Tayer (Managing Director)

PRINCIPAL ACTIVITIES: Land transportation, container
  haulage, crane and trucks rental, heavy lifts, rental of earth
  moving equipment, also quarry and aggregate production
Subsidiary Companies: Oman Transport Crusher Plant (Tel
  23242 Hatta)
Principal Bankers: Bank of Oman

Date of Establishment: 1962
No of Employees: 252

OMRAN INVESTMENT LTD

Al Maktoum Street, PO Box 4396, Deira, Dubai
Tel: 237748
Cable: NEWAGE
Telex: 47927 NEWAG EM

Chairman: Mohmed Omran Taryam; Abdullah M Taryam; Omran
  M Taryam
Senior Executives: Rajni C Shah (Manager)

PRINCIPAL ACTIVITIES: Real estate development, investment
  in industrial and housing projects
Parent Company: Head office in Sharjah, Telex 68222
Subsidiary Companies: New Age Industries, Abu Dhabi, Dubai,
  Sharjah and San Francisco, USA; Sport International, Abu
  Dhabi and Sharjah; Gulf Lebanese Enterprises, Sharjah; Haws
  Middle East, Dubai; Halwan Filling Station, Sharjah
Principal Bankers: Bank of Credit and Commerce

Date of Establishment: 1980

ORIENT AUTOMOBILE & TRADING CO PVT LTD

PO Box 10773, Dubai
Tel: 660748, 667312
Telex: 47544 Oatco Em

PRINCIPAL ACTIVITIES: Motor dealers
Principal Agencies: Audi, Porsche
Branch Offices: PO Box 859, Abu Dhabi, Tel 829190

ORIENT IRRIGATION SERVICES

PO Box 10581, Dubai
Tel: 691985
Telex: 48519 Orient EM
Telefax: 04-693655

Chairman: HE Sheikh Faisal Bin Khalid Bin Sultan Al Qasimi
Directors: Peter Harradine (Managing Director)
Senior Executives: Suheil Al Najjar (Finance Manager), Nick
  Lavender (Technical Manager), Dr Saaman Asmar (Marketing
  Manager), Nawaz Zaidi (Sales Manager)

PRINCIPAL ACTIVITIES: Irrigation and water treatment,
  agriculture, landscaping
Principal Agencies: Rain-Bird, FIP
Branch Offices: Sharjah: PO Box 1165, Tel 356446
Associated Companies: Harradine AG, Switzerland
Principal Bankers: AMRO, Dubai; Barclays Bank, Sharjah;
  BCCE, Sharjah
Financial Information:

	1990 Dh'000
Authorised capital	2,000
Paid-up capital	2,000

Principal Shareholders: Chairman and Director as described
Date of Establishment: 1976
No of Employees: 112

ORYX MERCHANT BANK LTD

PO Box 1855, Deira, Dubai
Tel: 221110, 221119
Cable: Oryx
Telex: 45795 Oryx

Chairman: Abdul Aziz Al Abdullah Al Sulaiman
Directors: Paul Jeanbert, D J Lenihan

PRINCIPAL ACTIVITIES: Merchant Banking

OTAC CONTRACTING LTD

PO Box 2925, Dubai
Tel: 660855/6/7, 660969
Cable: Baaklini
Telex: 45517 Otac EM

Chairman: Mursheed Baaklini (also General Manager)
Senior Executives: Hanna Hawa (Area Manager), Emile Jabbour
(Financial Controller)

PRINCIPAL ACTIVITIES: Contractors for sewerage and sewage
disposal works in the Gulf
Branch Offices: Throughout the Arab countries (with Dubai
being temporarily OTAC Head Office); UK
Principal Bankers: First National Bank of Chicago, Dubai

No of Employees: 2,000

OTIS ENGINEERING CORP

PO Box 2222, Dubai
Tel: 257865, 228374, 222265, 221106/7
Cable: Otis Dubai

PRINCIPAL ACTIVITIES: Engineering, well drilling and
completion, engineering equipment manufacturing and service
Branch Offices: Worldwide

OVERSEAS AST CO LTD

PO Box 350, Dubai
Tel: 221106
Cable: Akec Dxb
Telex: 45428 EM

PRINCIPAL ACTIVITIES: Civil engineering and construction
Branch Offices: Sharjah (PO Box 1179); Abu Dhabi (PO Box
2961)
Parent Company: Ed Ast & Co, GmbH, Graz, Austria
Subsidiary Companies: Darwish-Ast Co Ltd, Muscat (PO Box
223, Telex 3238 Mb)
Principal Bankers: Citibank; British Bank of the Middle East;
Standard Chartered Bank

Date of Establishment: 1959
No of Employees: 500

PAN GULF GROUP LTD

PO Box 5710, Dubai
Tel: 450823
Cable: Pangulf, Dubai
Telex: 46109 Pancn EM; 46635 Arti EM

Chairman: Ghazi Abdulaziz Alwan
Directors: P A L Vine, Pratap B Shirke, Christopher Chambers

PRINCIPAL ACTIVITIES: Construction of turnkey projects
involving, construction of buildings and houses, schools,
mosques, townships, industrial buildings etc, using pre-fab
building materials
Branch Offices: PO Box 2309, Sanaa, Yemen; PO Box 28024,
Dawoodi, Baghdad, Iraq
Subsidiary Companies: Gulf Contractors Ltd, PO Box 9313,
Riyadh, Saudi Arabia; Pan Gulf Developments (USA) Inc,
Atlanta, USA; Pan Gulf Constructions (UK) Ltd, UK
Principal Bankers: Standard Chartered Bank; American Express

Financial Information:

	US$'000
Authorised capital	2,300
Paid-up capital	2,300

Date of Establishment: March 1, 1975
No of Employees: 1,500

PIRELLI CABLES

PO Box 1047, Dubai
Tel: 211621, 282151
Telex: 46714 PGICO EM
Telefax: 235034

Senior Executives: G S Palmer (Sales Manager Arabian Gulf)

PRINCIPAL ACTIVITIES: Representative office of Pirelli Cable
Group of Companies; suppliers of cables, electrics and
telecommunications
Parent Company: Cablexport Spa, Viale Sarca 222, 20126
Milan, Italy
Principal Bankers: Standard Chartered Bank

PORT RASHID AUTHORITY

PO Box 2149, Dubai
Tel: 451545
Cable: Portrashid
Telex: 47530 PRA EM
Telefax: 552005

Chairman: Administered by the Government of Dubai
Directors: Khalid Khalifa Al Jallaf (Asst Director General, Dept of
Ports & Customs Port Rashid - Dubai)
Senior Executives: John Arundell (General Manager)

PRINCIPAL ACTIVITIES: Port operations
Principal Bankers: British Bank of the Middle East

Date of Establishment: 1970
No of Employees: 1,200

PRAKASH TRADING COMPANY

PO Box 778, Deira, Dubai
Tel: 222374, 236327
Cable: Peeteecee
Telex: 45927 Prktc EM
Telefax: 279609

Directors: M M Karani (Managing Director)
Senior Executives: W M Siddique (Manager), C Reddy (Finance
Manager)

PRINCIPAL ACTIVITIES: Importers and distributors of electrical
light fittings, wires and cables, switch boards and accessories
Principal Bankers: ANZ Grindlays Bank, Dubai
Financial Information:

	1990 Dh'000
Sales turnover	42,000

Principal Shareholders: M M Karani; P M Karani
Date of Establishment: 1963
No of Employees: 40

PRICE WATERHOUSE

PO Box 11987, 15th Floor, Dubai International Trade Centre,
Dubai
Tel: 377888
Telex: 47471 PWCO EM
Telefax: 378138

PRINCIPAL ACTIVITIES: Public accountants and consultants
Parent Company: Price Waterhouse, London, UK

PUBLICO

PO Box 4538, Dubai
Tel: 221887, 229024
Cable: Publico Dubai
Telex: 46282 PUBCO EM

UAE (Dubai)

President: Antoine Andrea (also Managing Director)
Directors: Antoine Rached, Elis Rached
Senior Executives: Babu Chacko

PRINCIPAL ACTIVITIES: Advertising, marketing, public
relations, promotions, print, photography and film production
Principal Agencies: Henkel, W Germany; Wander Ltd,
Switzerland; Akai Electric Co, Japan; Merloni Elettrodomestici,
Italy; Rinnai Corp, Japan; Karim Overseas, Australia; National
Foods Holland, Netherlands
Branch Offices: Dubai; Kuwait
Parent Company: Head Office in Beirut, Lebanon

Date of Establishment: 1959
No of Employees: 30

RAIS HASSAN SAADI & CO
PO Box 7, Dubai
Tel: 421515
Cable: Raishassan
Telex: 45522 Rais EM
Telefax: 436412

Chairman: A R S Rais
Directors: Saadi Rais, Salim Rais

PRINCIPAL ACTIVITIES: Shipping agents, tug boat and barge
owners; exporters and importers; insurance representatives;
ship-chandlers, manufacturers' agents, freight forwarders
Principal Agencies: DSR Lines, PNSC Lines, Cosco Lines,
Golden Lines, Pan Islamic Lines, Sinotrans Lines, New India
Assurance Co
Branch Offices: PO Box 465, Abu Dhabi, Tel 332963, 332319,
Telex 22477; PO Box 339, Fujairah, Tel 24327, Telex 89062,
Fax (070) 24329; PO Box 10078 Khor Fakkan, Tel 87207,
Telex 89045, Fax (070) 87208; PO Box 7294, Sharjah
Subsidiary/Associated Companies: United Bakery, Dubai;
Middle East Catering Co, Dubai; Rais Shipping Agency, Dubai
Principal Bankers: British Bank of the Middle East; Standard
Chartered Bank; Citibank; Union Bank of the Middle East;
Bank of Credit & Commerce Int'l

RANYA TRADING COMPANY
PO Box 5374, Dubai
Tel: 226395, 224278/9
Cable: Tabari
Telex: 68292, 46165 RTC EM

Chairman: Hisham R Tabari (also Managing Director)
Directors: Marwan R Tabari, Tareq Al Husseini (General
Manager)

PRINCIPAL ACTIVITIES: Trading and contracting (electrical and
civil); sale of pharmaceutical goods
Principal Agencies: Thorn Lighting, Permanite, FPE, Polybond
Ltd, Haden International, Flintkote, Contech, Petitjean S
Troye, CMP Glands, General Electric, Gold Star Cables, PDL
Accessories, Shin-Etsu Polymer Tiles, Lucky Ltd
Branch Offices: Ras Al Khaimah, Tel 21196; Sharjah, Tel
593784, 357950, 357459
Subsidiary Companies: Ranya Trading: Abu Dhabi, (PO Box
602, Tel 22416, Telex 2386); (Amman) Jordan; Union
Pharmacy; Abu Dhabi, Dubai, Sharjah
Principal Bankers: Banque Paribas; Arab Bank

Principal Shareholders: Marwan R Tabari, Hisham R Tabari
Date of Establishment: 1968
No of Employees: 100

ROBERTSON CONSTRUCTION SERVICES (UAE)
PO Box 9228, Dubai
Tel: 373682, 373687
Telex: 45777 RCS EM

PRINCIPAL ACTIVITIES: Sales and installation of protected
metal roofing, cladding, ventilators, flooring systems; curtain
walling systems; sales of vibration analysis and balancing
equipment; sales and erection of pre-engineered steel
buildings and industrial doors
Principal Agencies: H H Robertson Group; IRD Mechanalysis;
Freemans Chemical Co; Bostwick Doors (UK) Ltd

Date of Establishment: 1976
No of Employees: 80

ROSTAMANI GROUP OF COMPANIES
PO Box 261, Dubai
Tel: 226222
Cable: Automotive
Telex: 45484 Marwa EM

Chairman: Abdulla Hassan Rostamani
Directors: Abdul Wahed Rostamani

PRINCIPAL ACTIVITIES: Automobiles, construction, general
trading, agents, travel, foreign exchange, civil projects
Principal Agencies: Nissan, Datsun, Castrol, Firestone, Hunter
Douglas, Thomas Cooks, Hargill, Ralph M Parsons, Hyundai
International, Gifelec
Branch Offices: Throughout the UAE
Principal Bankers: British Bank of the Middle East; Union Bank
of the Middle East

Principal Shareholders: Family business
No of Employees: 600

ROYAL BANK OF CANADA
PO Box 3614, Deira, Dubai
Tel: 225226
Telex: 45926 Roybk EM
Telefax: 215687

Senior Executives: G S Klein (General Manager), R Watfa
(Senior Account Manager), R Harper (Marketing Manager), R
Almeida (Treasurer), B Drover (Operations Manager)

PRINCIPAL ACTIVITIES: Banking
Parent Company: Head Office: Montreal, Canada

SAEED & MOHAMED AL NABOODAH GROUP
See AL NABOODAH, SAEED & MOHAMED, GROUP

SAEED & SULTAN LOOTAH CONTRACTING CO
See LOOTAH, SAEED & SULTAN, CONTRACTING CO

SAEED BIN NASSER AL HASHAR
See AL HASHAR, SAEED BIN NASSER,

SAEED MOHAMED AL GHANDI & SONS
See AL GHANDI, SAEED MOHAMED, & SONS

SAJWANI, JAWAD, GROUP OF COMPANIES
Sajwani, Jawad Haji Abdulhussain & Co
PO Box 178, Dubai
Tel: 223099, 226365
Cable: Sajwani
Telex: 45583 Sajwan EM

Chairman: Fuad M Sajwani
Directors: Fuad M Sajwani, A Hussain Sajwani, Kamal M
Sajwani, Iqbal M Sajwani, Ali M Sajwani

PRINCIPAL ACTIVITIES: Import/export of commodities,
foodstuffs, dairy products
Branch Offices: Jawad Haji Abdulhussain Sajwani & Co, Sharjah
Subsidiary Companies: Sajwani Exchange Co, PO Box 178,
Dubai

Principal Shareholders: Directors as described above
Date of Establishment: 1865

SALEH AL SHAWAF TRADING EST
See AL SHAWAF, SALEH, TRADING EST

SALEH OMER BIN HAIDER
See BIN HAIDER, SALEH OMER,

SAUD AL SALEH GENERAL TRADING
See AL SALEH, SAUD, GENERAL TRADING

SAYID RAJAB AL RIFAI
See AL RIFAI, SAYID RAJAB,

SCIENTECHNIC
PO Box 325, Dubai
Tel: 666000
Cable: Scientecnic
Telex: 46072 SCITC EM
Telefax: 971-4 666176

Chairman: Easa Saleh Al Gurg
Directors: Saleh Easa Al Gurg
Senior Executives: Hamiduddin Ahmed (General Manager)

PRINCIPAL ACTIVITIES: Electrical, electronics & mechanical
engineering; trading and contracting; assembly of electrical
switchboards
Principal Agencies: Siemens AG; Siemens Electrogerate GmbH;
Osram GmbH; Transformatoren Union AG; Weir Pumps Ltd;
United Technologies (Power Systems Div); Sikorsky
Helicopters; Kaise Instruments; Hamilton Standard; Erco
Lighting; Peil & Putzler Lighting; Kaise Instruments; Witton
Chemicals; Maehler & Kaege
Branch Offices: Deira - Dubai, Sharjah & Ras Al Khaimah
Parent Company: Easa Saleh Al Gurg Group
Subsidiary Companies: Al Gurg Building Services, Electrical-
Mechanical Div, Abu Dhabi
Principal Bankers: Lloyds Bank, Dubai

Principal Shareholders: Fully owned by Easa Saleh Al Gurg
Date of Establishment: October 1972
No of Employees: 115

SEA-LAND SERVICE INC
PO Box 11328, Dubai
Tel: 523422
Telex: 47846 SLDXB EM
Telefax: 525615

Senior Executives: A H Gaskell (Marketing Manager)

PRINCIPAL ACTIVITIES: Container shipping line, regional office

SEDCO INTERNATIONAL SA
PO Box 702, Dubai
Tel: 224141/5
Cable: Sedco Dubai
Telex: 45469 Sedco EM

President: Carl F Thorne

PRINCIPAL ACTIVITIES: Drilling contractors, marine operations
Branch Offices: Sedco Int SA, Qatar and Oman

SHELL MARKETS (MIDDLE EAST) LTD
PO Box 307, Dubai
Tel: 533900
Cable: Shell Dubai
Telex: 45478 SMME EM
Telefax: 533861

Senior Executives: J J L R Schoonbrood (Chief Executive), A H
Pooley (General Manager Main Products), P B Merry (General
Manager Lubricants & Special Products)

PRINCIPAL ACTIVITIES: Marketing and distribution of
petroleum and petrochemical products
Associated Companies: Shell Markets (Middle East) Ltd, PO
Box 776, Doha, Qatar; Shell Markets (Middle East) Ltd, PO
Box 9038, Mina Al Fahal, Oman
Principal Bankers: British Bank of the Middle East

Principal Shareholders: Royal Dutch Shell Group

SHERATON DUBAI HOTEL
PO Box 4250, Dubai
Tel: 281111
Telex: 46710 EM
Telefax: 213468

Chairman: HE Mohd Said Al Mulla
Senior Executives: Richard Pfeifer (General Manager), Maan
Halabi (Director of Sales), Hugo Gerritsen (Financial
Controller)

PRINCIPAL ACTIVITIES: Hotel business
Parent Company: Sheraton Management Corporation
Principal Bankers: The National Bank of Dubai

Principal Shareholders: Al Mulla Enterprises (Pvt) Ltd
Date of Establishment: April 1978
No of Employees: 295

SHIPPING, TRADING & LIGHTERAGE CO LTD
S.T.A.L.C.O.
PO Box 464, Dubai
Tel: 367367
Cable: Stalco
Telex: 45495 Stalco EM
Telefax: 345105, 368226

Chairman: Rashid Al Majid
Directors: Rashed Almajid, Mohamed Yasin Abdul Ghafoor,
Abdul Gabbar Thabet (Managing Director)
Senior Executives: Mohamed Yasin Abdul Ghafoor (General
Manager), Vivian Mascarenhas (Senior Shipping Manager),
Capt Mansoor Yasin A Ghafoor (Shipping Manager),
Maqdoom Mohiuddin (Operations Manager), Shiv Prakash
Sadasivam (Marketing Manager), Barjoer Bajan (Chief
Accountant)

PRINCIPAL ACTIVITIES: Stevedores, shipping agents, clearing,
forwarding, packing and transport, air cargo agents, air/sea
freight, container sales, feedering
Principal Agencies: Ever Green Line, Uniglory Line, Lauritzen
Reefers, Messina Line, Pacific Int'l Lines, Irano Hind Shipping
Co, West Reefer Lines, Blue Star Line, Sea Containers Line,
General Accident, Fire & Life Assurance Corp of Perth, Pacific
International Line, Ignazio Messina, Evergreen, Lauritzen
Reefers, Sea Containers, General Accident Life Assurance of
Perth, Uniglory, Irano Hind
Branch Offices: Sharjah, Abu Dhabi & Khorfakkan
Subsidiary Companies: Stalco Air Cargo, Feltham Middlesex,
UK
Principal Bankers: Bank of Oman, Deira, Banque Indosuez,
Deira
Financial Information:

	1988/89 Dh'000	1989/90 Dh'000
Sales turnover	11,000	12,000
Profits	1,500	2,000
Authorised capital	600	600
Paid-up capital	600	600
Total assets	2,500	2,900

Principal Shareholders: Rashid Al Majid, Khaled Juma Al Majid,
Thabet Group of Companies
Date of Establishment: February 1974
No of Employees: 115 (including Sharjah and Abu Dhabi)

SIAMCO ENGINEERING CO
PO Box 2653, Dubai
Tel: 281432, 851553, 223082
Cable: SIAMCO DUBAI
Telex: 46387 Siamco EM
Telefax: (971-4) 851986

President: Mohammad Siddique Chaudry
Directors: Sarfraz Mohammad Siddique, Ijaz Mohammad
Siddique

UAE (Dubai)

Senior Executives: A G Khan (Manager Engineering), D B Chimulkar (Projects Engineer Civil)

PRINCIPAL ACTIVITIES: Mechanical and electrical engineering contractors, airconditioning and refrigeration servicing and repairs, anti corrosion services, marine engineering and ship repairs, suppliers of 60 Hz equipment and spares
Branch Offices: AC & Refrigeration Divn, Tel 851553; Electrical Divn, Tel 851553; Mechanical Divn, Tel 851553; Marine Divn, Tel 851553; Auto Machineshop Divn, Tel 226845; Construction Divn, Tel 851553; Trading Divn, Tel 223082
Subsidiary Companies: Night Prince Electric, Dubai
Principal Bankers: Emirates Bank International Ltd, Dubai; Abu Dhabi Commercial Bank Ltd, Dubai

Principal Shareholders: Proprietory
Date of Establishment: 1976
No of Employees: 150

SIGMA CHEMIE CO
PO Box 6148, Dubai
Tel: 446346, 443112
Telex: 47524 Mixic Em

Chairman: Ferozuddin Khan
Directors: Rashid N Hasan

PRINCIPAL ACTIVITIES: Suppliers and stockists of welding machinery electric and pneumatic tools, chemicals, generators
Principal Agencies: Blackgold, USA; Dearman, USA; Widder, USA
Parent Company: Tubular Products of America (TPA), USA
Principal Bankers: Bank of Oman, BCCI

Date of Establishment: 1978

SLS & SONS
PO Box 1769, Dubai
Tel: 489394
Cable: Ebasco
Telex: 45497 Ebasco EM
Telefax: 480859

Chairman: S L Sharma
Directors: Ashwani K Sharma (Managing Director), Arvind K Sharma, Miss Binu Sharma
Senior Executives: Y N Khanna (Vice President Asia), D B Kutubuddin (Chief Engineer), N Prithviraj (General Manager-Hotel), P Kumar (General Manager MEP Services), V N Bhattacharya (Vice President Trading Middle East)

PRINCIPAL ACTIVITIES: Civil engineering contractors, manufacturing and trading, hoteliers, resorts, leisure and amusement, MEP contractors, maintenance contractors
Subsidiary/Associated Companies: Al Rashid Construction Co, PO Box 1769, Dubai, Tel 440800, Telex 45497 EBasco EM; Dubai Plaza Hotel, PO Box 7646, Dubai, Tel 459000, Telex 47978 DUPLA EM; Ebasco Trading Corp, PO Box 1769, Dubai, Tel 346009, Fax 345982, Telex 46172 EM; Roxbury Enterprises, Hongkong
Principal Bankers: BCCI; Bank of Credit & Commerce (Emirates)
Financial Information:

	1990 US$'000
Sales turnover	12,000
Authorised capital	3,000
Paid-up capital	3,000

Principal Shareholders: Sohan Lal Sharma; Mrs Pushpa Lata Sharma; Ashwani Kumar Sharma; Arvind V Sharma
Date of Establishment: 1967
No of Employees: 800

SNOWDEN MCLEOD & ASSOCIATES
PO Box 9243, Dubai
Tel: 374845
Telex: 48626 Mohafa EM
Telefax: 373367

Senior Executives: R Taylor (Manager Middle East)

PRINCIPAL ACTIVITIES: Marine consultants and surveyors
Branch Offices: Pacmarine Services, Singapore

SOCOIN INTERNATIONAL
PO Box 3997, Deira, Dubai
Tel: 232208, 211405,341612
Cable: SOCOIN
Telex: 46330 SOCOIN EM
Telefax: 223014

Directors: Ibrahim Abdul Malik, N Jeewakhan
Senior Executives: N Jeewakhan (Managing Partner)

PRINCIPAL ACTIVITIES: Import and marketing of oilfield, mud and industrial chemicals
Principal Agencies: Threshvale Ltd; Guest Medical Ltd
Branch Offices: PO Box 27486, Abu Dhabi
Principal Bankers: Banque Indosuez; Habib Bank AG Zurich

Principal Shareholders: Directors as above
Date of Establishment: 1976

SOGEX DUBAI
PO Box 1589, Dubai
Tel: 257315, 257237
Telex: 45589 Sogex EM

PRINCIPAL ACTIVITIES: Turnkey contractors, desalination, power stations, pipe lines, precast buildings, roads, etc
Branch Offices: UAE (Abu Dhabi, Dubai, Sharjah); Oman; Iraq

SOTINMAR AIRFREIGHT SERVICES
Dubai International Airport, PO Box 33, Dubai
Tel: 245716/8
Cable: Soair Dubai
Telex: 47870 Soair EM
Telefax: 245718

Senior Executives: J C Hitchcock (General Manager)

PRINCIPAL ACTIVITIES: Airfreight Agents, clearing and forwarding, air chartering, breakbulk agents, sea/air agents
Principal Agencies: Danzas, IML Airfreight
Parent Company: Dubai Trade & Trust Co (Pvt) Ltd
Subsidiary Companies: Sotinmar Shipping Company
Principal Bankers: Lloyds Bank

Date of Establishment: 1976

SOTINMAR SHIPPING CO
19th Floor, Dubai Trade Centre, PO Box 33, Dubai
Tel: 373030 (10 lines)
Cable: MOHAFA
Telex: 48626 MOHAFA EM

Senior Executives: J C Hitchcock (General Manager)

PRINCIPAL ACTIVITIES: Steamship agents and operators, clearing, forwarding and chartering contractors, airfreight agents and charterers, container groupage consolidators
Parent Company: Dubai Trade & Trust Co (Pvt) Ltd
Subsidiary Companies: IML Air Couriers UAE; Sotinmar Airfreight Services
Principal Bankers: Lloyds Bank

Principal Shareholders: Al Fayed Brothers
Date of Establishment: 1976

SPINNEYS LTD
PO Box 677, Dubai
Tel: 374050, 370170
Cable: Spinneys Dubai
Telex: 45666 Spinn EM
Telefax: 371210

Chairman: Ali Albwardy
Directors: B P Skinner, M Bin Bayat, M C E Hemery

PRINCIPAL ACTIVITIES: Catering services and contractors, retail and wholesale, food distribution and agency representatives
Principal Agencies: Nestle, Rowntree Mackintosh, Kraft, Reckitt & Colman, Kimberley Clark, Colgate Palmolive
Parent Company: Spinneys 1948 Ltd
Principal Bankers: BBME, Standard Chartered Bank, Royal Bank of Canada
Financial Information:

	1990 Dh'000
Paid-up capital	36,000

Principal Shareholders: Associated with Spinneys (1948) Ltd, UK; British & Commonwealth Plc
Date of Establishment: 1973
No of Employees: 430

STANDARD CHARTERED BANK

PO Box 999, Dubai
Tel: 422455
Cable: STANCHART
Telex: 45431 SCBDUB EM

PRINCIPAL ACTIVITIES: Commercial banking
Branch Offices: In the Middle East: Bahrain; Abu Dhabi; Sharjah; Qatar; Oman; Lebanon
Parent Company: Standard Chartered PLC, UK

Date of Establishment: 1957/12/15
No of Employees: 261

STEEL CORPORATION OF DUBAI LTD

PO Box 4168, Plot No 19, Industrial Zone, Khawanij, Dubai
Tel: 257322
Telex: 45553 EM

Directors: M Issa (Sales and Purchase Management), Ahmad Chappra (Works and Technical Director), T Shaban (Financial Director)

PRINCIPAL ACTIVITIES: Production of mild-steel reinforcing bars, high-tensile deformed bars, and mild-steel flat bars

Principal Shareholders: Private limited company

SWAIDAN TRADING CO (PVT) LTD

PO Box 1200, Dubai
Tel: 660601 (20 lines)
Cable: Alnaboodah
Telex: 45511 SMA EM
Telefax: 660198

Chairman: Saeed Juma Al Naboodah
Directors: Mohamed Juma Al Naboodah (Vice Chairman), Ahmed Saeed Juma Al Naboodah (Managing Director), Abdullah Mohd Al Naboodah (General Manager), Adel Jasim Al Midfa (Deputy General Manager)
Senior Executives: Mufid Abbas (Finance & Commercial Manager), Mahmoud Ismail (Administration Manager), Ahmed Al Husseini (Manager Agrochemical Div), Thomas Koshy (Manager Heavy Equipment & Commercial Vehicles), Wagdy Helmy (Manager Goodyear Tyre Div), M Marchoud (Sales Manager Peugeot Automobile Div), R Kumar (Manager Industrial Rubber Products), Costas Hadjicosti (Manager Service Div), Shahab Uddin (Manager Auto Spare Parts), A A Shoukry (Manager Al Naboodah Travel Agencies), Safwat Munir (Manager Data Processing)

PRINCIPAL ACTIVITIES: General trading; import and distribution of light and heavy machinery and construction equipment, agricultural equipment, commercial vehicles, light and heavy duty trucks, tyres and industrial rubber products, agrochemicals, fertilizer, green house, seed, pharmaceutical products, electronics and household appliances; also fuel injection services workshop, auto electrical and turbocharger engineering; travel and cargo agencies

Principal Agencies: Auto Diesels, UK; Aveling Barford Int, UK; Ashok Leyland, India; Automobiles Peugeot, France; BASF, W Germany; BMC Sanayi, Turkey; De Jong, Holland; Dresser, USA; Gloria, W Germany; Leyland DAF, UK; Goodyear, USA; Iveco Aifo, Italy; Lombard, Italy; Marve, Italy; Mikasa, Japan; Olympia, Japan; etc and general sales agents for various airlines
Branch Offices: PO Box 2239, Abu Dhabi, Tel 725070; PO Box 1250, Al Ain, Tel 655818; PO Box 371, Fujeirah, Tel 22731
Parent Company: Saeed & Mohamed Al Naboodah Group
Subsidiary Companies: Al Naboodah Contracting Co; Al Naboodah Laing (Pvt) Ltd; Al Naboodah Real Estate; Al Naboodah Gypsum Products; Transgulf Electric Company; Gulf Technical Trading & Services Co; Al Naboodah Cargo Centre; International Resources (Overseas) Co Pvt Ltd
Principal Bankers: National Bank of Dubai; British Bank of the Middle East; Citibank; BCC (Emirates); BCCI

Principal Shareholders: Saeed Juma Al Naboodah, Mohamed Juma Al Naboodah, Ahmed Saeed Al Naboodah, Abdulla Mohd Al Naboodah
Date of Establishment: 1958
No of Employees: 3,000 (Group), 350 (Trading Division)

SYSTIME GULF LTD

PO Box 9246, Dubai
Tel: 533535
Telex: 47990
Telefax: 531662

Senior Executives: Aman Ullah Quadri (Managing Director), Rahmat Ullah Quadri (General Manager)

PRINCIPAL ACTIVITIES: Installation and maintenance of computer systems, supply of software
Branch Offices: Abu Dhabi: PO Box 4874, Tel 346200, Bahrain: PO Box 10664, Tel 213319, Telex 8212; Qatar: PO Box 4877, Doha, Tel 661430, Telex 5106; Oman: PO Box 4031, Muscat, Tel 601734, Telex 3149
Parent Company: Head office in Leeds, UK

T CHOITHRAM & SONS

See CHOITHRAM, T, & SONS

T I GULF (PVT) LTD

PO Box 8937, Dubai
Tel: 444695
Telex: 46686 Tigulf EM

PRINCIPAL ACTIVITIES: Supply of all building materials and equipment
Principal Agencies: Baco Building Structures; Baco Aluminium; Baco marine craft; Becker lifts; Creda catering equipment; Gibbons ironmongery; Metsec ceilings; Pel office furniture; John Tann safes; Tann Synchromone
Associated Companies: Tube Investments Group

TECHNICAL & TRADING CO

PO Box 49, Dubai
Tel: 370335
Cable: Ethiope Dubai
Telex: 45514 EM
Telefax: 378390

Chairman: Easa Saleh Al Gurg
Directors: P G Evans (General Manager)
Senior Executives: M C Sharples (Commercial Manager), J R Jones (Consumer Products Manager), P S Thompson (Manager Industrial Products), B E Fawcett (Technical Manager), R Dias (Office Furniture Manager), S Khoory (Head of Personnel & Admin)

PRINCIPAL ACTIVITIES: Import and distribution of refrigeration and air-conditioning equipment, office furniture, consumer products, industrial detergents, bakery products
Principal Agencies: Unilever Export Ltd, Keeprite, Qualitair, Prestcold, Hindustan Lever Ltd, C C Friesland, CORO, Project

Office Furniture, Dauphin, Wilkhahn, Heuga, Swedish Match, Wilkinson Sword, etc
Branch Offices: Throughout the Northern Emirates UAE
Principal Bankers: Standard Chartered Bank

Principal Shareholders: A partnership between Easa Saleh Al Gurg and African & Eastern (Near East) Ltd (a subsidiary of Unilever Plc)
Date of Establishment: As partnership 1/1/1986
No of Employees: 198

TECHNICAL PARTS COMPANY

PO Box 5071, Dubai
Tel: 225904, 284007
Cable: Teepeecee
Telex: 46343 Tepar EM

Chairman: B V Bhatia
Senior Executives: N G Menon (Manager)

PRINCIPAL ACTIVITIES: Manufacturers representatives and distributors for oil field, marine supplies and general engineering goods
Principal Agencies: Applied Power Int (Enerpac), Bourdon France; Crane Ltd, UK; Kango Electric Hammers Ltd, UK; Dow Corning, Belgium/USA; Mac Arc Ltd, UK; Stewart Warner Ltd, UK; Serck AG, UK; Tubela Engg Co Ltd, Kito Corp, Japan; Dixon Valve & Coupling Co, USA; The WM Powell Company, Ohio, USA; Jenkins Ltd, Canada; Smith ·Valve Int, USA; Winn & Coales, UK; Ajax Nettlefolds, Australia; Spirax Sarco, UK
Branch Offices: Technical Parts Co, PO Box 337, Abu Dhabi; Technical Parts Co, Sharjah
Principal Bankers: Union Bank of the Middle East Ltd

Date of Establishment: 1974

TECHNICAL SUPPLIES & SERVICES CO

Sales Office, PO Box 69, Dubai
Tel: 223211/2/3
Cable: Rima Dubai
Telex: 45751 Rima EM

Directors: Jamil G Nasr (Proprietor & Managing Director)
Senior Executives: R Hewlett, J Assal

PRINCIPAL ACTIVITIES: Manufacturers of polyurethane rigid foam products for the building and refrigeration industry; modular coldstores and refrigerated vehicles; sandwich elements for walls and roof cladding, insulated pre-fab buildings and portacabins; roofboard insulation and spraying; central air conditioning systems; profiled cladding for steel buildings
Branch Offices: Sales & Execution Office: Abu Dhabi, PO Box 410
Parent Company: Head Office & Factory: Sharjah, PO Box 1818
Principal Bankers: First Gulf Bank, Dubai; Bank of Credit & Commerce, Sharjah; National Bank of Abu Dhabi
Financial Information:

	1990 Dh'000
Sales turnover	15,000
Paid-up capital	6,000
Total assets	3,000

Principal Shareholders: Sole ownership
Date of Establishment: 1962
No of Employees: 110 (all branches)

THOMAS COOK AL ROSTAMANI (PVT) LTD

Thomas Cook Al Rostamani Exchange Co

PO Box 10072, Al Nasser Square, Al Maktoum St, Deira, Dubai
Tel: 236060, 223564
Cable: Cookrostam
Telex: 47482 T Cook Em

Chairman: Abdullah Hassan Al Rostamani
Directors: Abdul Wahed Hassan Al Rostamani, T M Nair, Abdul Jalil Yousuf Darwish, Farooq Huwaidi

PRINCIPAL ACTIVITIES: Travel agents, foreign exchange dealers
Principal Agencies: Cosmos Tours, Eurail Passes, Britrail, Thomas Cook Travellers Cheques, State Bank of India Travellers Cheques
Branch Offices: Abu Dhabi: PO Box 2974, Tel 727500, 727717, Telex 24134
Principal Bankers: British Bank of the Middle East; National Bank of Umm Al Qaiwain

Principal Shareholders: Abdullah Hassan Al Rostamani, Abdul Wahed Hassan Al Rostamani
Date of Establishment: 1979
No of Employees: 24

TIDEX INTERNATIONAL

PO Box 3640, Dubai
Tel: 660078, 660829, 661683
Telex: 45696 Tidex EM

PRINCIPAL ACTIVITIES: Marine support services to hydrocarbon industry
Parent Company: Tidewater Marine Service Inc, New Orleans, USA

TNT SKYPAK INTERNATIONAL UAE LTD

TNT Building, Al Mulla Plaza Roundabout, Dubai
Tel: 665050
Telex: 48816 Skydxb EM

Directors: J G Robertson (Regional Director Africa & Middle East), Sean Bradley (General Manager UAE), J Sancheti (Regional Financial Controller), David Stacey (Regional Sales & Marketing Manager), Anton Barneveld (Regional Operations Manager)
Senior Executives: Ashok Natarajan (Finance & Administration Manager), Antony Davison (Operations Manager), Nick Webb (Sales Manager), Julian Skyrme

PRINCIPAL ACTIVITIES: Worldwide courier service, collection, clearance and delivery of documents & commercial value items, domestic road couriers
Branch Offices: Sharjah, Jebel Ali, Abu Dhabi
Parent Company: TNT Limited
Principal Bankers: British Bank of the Middle East

TOUCHE ROSS SABA & CO

PO Box 1222, Dubai
Tel: 224297, 220518
Cable: SABACONY
Telex: 46036
Telefax: 213640

Senior Executives: Hani K Tarazi (General Partner)

PRINCIPAL ACTIVITIES: Accountants and management consultants
Branch Offices: PO Box 5470, Sharjah, Tel 351034; PO Box 462, Fujairah, Tel 22320; PO Box 435, Ras Al Khaimah, Tel 29360
Associated Companies: Saba & Co

TOWELL, W J, TRADING EST

PO Box 2581, Dubai
Tel: 221121
Telex: 46133
Telefax: 211492

Chairman: Hussain Jawad Mohd Ali Abdul Rasool

PRINCIPAL ACTIVITIES: General trading and contracting, construction, telecommunications, computers, building

materials, prefabricated housing, general merchandise (foodstuffs, clothing, toiletries, tobacco)
Branch Offices: Oman
Parent Company: Head office in Kuwait

TRADING & INDUSTRIAL EQUIPMENT CO WLL (TIECO)

PO Box 5291, Deira, Dubai
Tel: 246121, 226254
Cable: Tieco
Telex: 45595 Tieco EM
Telefax: 246483

PRINCIPAL ACTIVITIES: Import and distribution of heavy machinery, earth-moving equipment; generating sets; garage equipment and construction plant; well drilling equipment; and spare parts
Principal Agencies: Ingersoll Rand; Petibone; Wiwa; Clemco; Cifa; Band it; American Hoist; Dia Pumps; Fagersta Secoroc; Ferguson Compactors; IMI Norgren; Uryu Pneumatic Tools; BF Goodrich Air Hoses; Istobal Garage Eqpt
Parent Company: Trading & Industrial Equipment Co, Kuwait
Principal Bankers: National Bank of Dubai

Principal Shareholders: Heirs of Mohd Yousuf Al Nisef, Heirs of Abdul Latif Al Nisef, Shukri Hanna Shammas

UNION BANK OF THE MIDDLE EAST LTD

PO Box 2923, Dubai
Tel: 281181
Cable: Unionbank
Telex: 46425 Unidb EM

Chairman: H E Ahmed Humaid Al Tayer
Directors: Juma Al Majid (Vice-Chairman), Sheikh Mohammed bin Sultan Al Dahiri, Easa Saleh Al Gurg, Fardan Bin Ali Al Fardan, Khalifa bin Mohammed Al Shamsi

PRINCIPAL ACTIVITIES: All merchant and commercial banking facilities
Branch Offices: 5 in Dubai; 3 in Pakistan, 1 in Sri Lanka
Subsidiary Companies: 1 in Hong Kong
Financial Information:

	Dh'000
Authorised capital	1,000,000
Issued and paid-up capital	335,225

Principal Shareholders: Government of Dubai (73%)
Date of Establishment: March 1977
No of Employees: 305

UNION CONSTRUCTION CO

PO Box 16638, Dubai
Tel: 667870
Telex: 661790

Directors: Saif Rashid Saeed Hamarain, Ghanem Ibrahim Nasser Al Dheeb, Yousuf Rashid Boresly, Samir Fahmi Hakoura

PRINCIPAL ACTIVITIES: Building contractors, multi storey buildings
Branch Offices: Kuwait

Principal Shareholders: Directors as described above

UNITED ARAB AGENCIES

PO Box 410, Dubai
Tel: 224241/4
Telex: 45516 Naa EM

Chairman: Mohammed Abdullah Al Gaz (also Proprietor)
Senior Executives: Mohammed Abdullah Al Houl (General Manager), M M Balakrishna (Sales Manager)

PRINCIPAL ACTIVITIES: General trading and contracting. Import and distribution of building materials, automobiles and spare parts, air-conditioning and refrigerating equipment,

diesel engines, electrical and electronic equipment, paints and varnish, and foodstuffs (cold storage)
Principal Agencies: Opel, Frigidaire, MWM Engines, Philips, etc

UNITED ARAB ASIAN DEVELOPMENT CORPORATION

PO Box 3472, Dubai
Tel: 667399
Cable: Uaadco, Dubai
Telex: 45918 Uaadco EM

Directors: Moiz Jabir (Partner), Akbar Khan (Partner), Abdul Qadir Al Tawil (Partner)

PRINCIPAL ACTIVITIES: Importers/distributors of timber, timber products, plywood, steel, and all other building materials
Subsidiary/Associated Companies: Tropical Timber Industries Ltd, Singapore; Moiz Yoosuf & Co, Malaysia
Principal Bankers: Grindlays Bank; Banque Paribas; Middle East Bank

Date of Establishment: 1974

UNITED ARAB BANK

PO Box 4579, Dubai
Tel: 220181
Telex: 46356 UABANK EM

Chairman: HE Sh Feisal Bin Sultan Al Qassimi
Directors: Jean Marie Weydert (Vice Chairman), Sh Sultan Bin Saqr Al Qassimi, Sh Khalid Bin Saqr Al Qassimi, Ahmed Mohd Hamdad Al Midfa, Sayyah Mohd Moussa Al Qobaissi, Sayed Hasan Mohd Abdul Rehman, Khalid Alami, M Lesay, Abbas Abdul Jalil Al Fahim, Said Omram Al Mazroui

PRINCIPAL ACTIVITIES: Commercial banking
Branch Offices: Registered office: Sharjah, General Management: Abu Dhabi, Branches: Deira - Dubai, Ras Al Khaimah, Al Ain
Financial Information:

	Dh'000
Authorised capital	150,000
Paid-up capital	75,000

Principal Shareholders: Societe Generale (20%)
Date of Establishment: August, 1975
No of Employees: 157

UNITED ARAB SHIPPING CO SAG

PO Box 55586, Dubai
Tel: 218222
Telex: 49799
Telefax: 230652

PRINCIPAL ACTIVITIES: Freight agency, maritime transport, cargo, ship chartering, passenger yacht rental, barges and tugs chartering, ships and boats repairing
Parent Company: Head office in Kuwait

UNITED BANK LTD

PO Box 1000, Dubai
Tel: 222532, 223191/2/3, 285952/3
Cable: Unitedbank Dubai
Telex: 45433 EM, 47181 EM

President: Tajammal Hussain
Directors: S M Abdullah, K N Cheema, A Majid Khan, Muhammad Usman, M Saleem Malik, Muhammad Zaki
Senior Executives: S Mojib Raza (Secretary)

PRINCIPAL ACTIVITIES: Commercial banking
Branch Offices: Branches: 1,592
Parent Company: Head Office: 11 Chundrigar Rd, Karachi, Pakistan
Subsidiary Companies: Zurich: United Bank AG Zurich, PO Box 1176, 8022 Zurich, Switzerland; Beirut: United Bank of Lebanon & Pakistan, PO Box 5600, Beirut, Lebanon; Joint Venture: Commercial Bank of Oman Ltd, PO Box 4696 Ruwi,

Matrah/(Muscat), Sultanate of Oman; United Saudi
Commercial Bank, PO Box 3335, Riyadh, Saudi Arabia

Principal Shareholders: Fully owned by Government of Pakistan

UNITED FOODS LIMITED

PO Box 1416, Dubai
Tel: 223214/5/6
Cable: Vegoil
Telex: 46689 Vegoil EM

Chairman: Abdul Aziz Al-Owais
Directors: Saeed Mohammad Al-Mulla, Humaid Nasser Al-
Owais, Sajjad Ahmed

PRINCIPAL ACTIVITIES: Manufacturing and trading of
hydrogenated vegetable oil and cooking oil
Principal Bankers: Commercial Bank of Dubai Ltd

Principal Shareholders: Arab Emirates Investments Ltd, Dubai;
Sultan Ali Al-Owais; Mohd and Obeid Al-Mulla
Date of Establishment: 1976
No of Employees: 100

UNITED RICE (DUBAI) LTD

PO Box 2229, Dubai
Tel: 222072, 223601, 221737
Cable: Unirice
Telex: 45529 Uniric EM

Chairman: Yousaf Habib Al-Yousaf
Directors: Abdul Karim Ahmadi, Moosa Habib Al-Yousaf

PRINCIPAL ACTIVITIES: Trading in foodstuffs and food
commodities

UNIVERSAL CONCRETE PRODUCTS (PVT) LTD

PO Box 11091, Dubai
Tel: 370810 (4 lines)
Telex: 47245 UCP EM
Telefax: 372891

Chairman: Mohd Salem Bakhit
Directors: Khalid Mohd Bakhit (Managing Director)
Senior Executives: Omar Abu Shamla (Financial Controller),
Salah Hijazi (Sales Manager)

PRINCIPAL ACTIVITIES: Production of ready mixed concrete
Branch Offices: Jebel Ali, Fujeirah, Hatta
Principal Bankers: Arab Bank Plc

Principal Shareholders: Mohd Salem Bakhit
Date of Establishment: 1977
No of Employees: 60

VENTURE GULF GROUP

PO Box 1885, Dubai Pearl Bldg, Dubai
Tel: 281360, 281460
Telex: 41894 VGULF EM

PRINCIPAL ACTIVITIES: Metal recycling plant, manufacturers'
representation, supply of fibreglass products, chemicals,
tanks, swimming pools contracting, transport and commercial
vehicles hiring service, car hire, plant hire, supply of industrial
and construction equipment
Branch Offices: Bahrain, Qatar

VERSONS TRADING COMPANY

PO Box 3069, Dubai
Tel: 524115 (4 lines)
Cable: VERSONS
Telex: 46047 VERSON EM
Telefax: 524093

Parners: Bhagwan V Jethwani, Vijay V Jethwani

PRINCIPAL ACTIVITIES: Indentors and importers of textiles,
cement, building materials, foodstuffs and gold jewellery;
garments manufacturers

Branch Offices: Versons (Singapore) Pte Ltd, PO Box 364,
Singapore 9117
Subsidiary Companies: Vetco Int (Vetco Textiles), PO Box
11800, Jumeirah-Dubai; Vertex (Textile), PO Box 3069, Dubai;
Vetco Garments, PO Box 435, Ajman
Principal Bankers: British Bank of the Middle East; Bank of
Oman

Principal Shareholders: Bhagwan V Jethwani; Vijay V Jethwani
Date of Establishment: 1975
No of Employees: 200

W J TOWELL & COMPANY

PO Box 2581, Dubai
Tel: 450910, 450858
Cable: Towell-Dubai
Telex: 46133 Towell EM
Telefax: 6-339919

Chairman: Haji Ali Sultan
Directors: Murtadha A Sultan, Muqbool A Sultan, Hussein
Jawad, Anwar A Sultan, Mushtak Sultan
Senior Executives: S K Bhanji (General Manager), H Fayyad
(Operations Manager), J Toutikian (Manager - Royale Trading)

PRINCIPAL ACTIVITIES: General merchants, readymade
garments, linen, consumer products, government supplies
and contracts
Principal Agencies: Hanes, USA; Household Trading Corp, USA;
Intex, Brazil; Tilda Rice, India; Sultan Cereals, W Germany;
Feudor Lighters, France; Trussardi Cigarettes, Austria; DAC
Detergents, Saudi Arabia; Al Jameel Diapers, Oman
Branch Offices: W J Towell & Co Agencies WLL, PO Box 75,
Safat, Kuwait
Parent Company: W J Towell & Co, PO Box 4040, Ruwi,
Muscat, Oman
Subsidiary Companies: W J Towell & Co Limited, PO Box 2093,
Sharjah
Principal Bankers: Standard Chartered Bank, Dubai
Financial Information:

	1990
	Dh'000
Sales turnover	25,381
Profits	1,833
Authorised capital	2,250
Paid-up capital	2,250
Total assets	27,712

Principal Shareholders: Haji Qamer Sultan; Haji Ali Sultan;
Kamal Abdul Redha Sultan; Ahmed Sultan; Amir Sultan
Date of Establishment: 1866
No of Employees: 40

W J TOWELL TRADING EST

See TOWELL, W J, TRADING EST

W S ATKINS & PARTNERS (OVERSEAS)

See ATKINS, W S, & PARTNERS (OVERSEAS)

WARDLEY MIDDLE EAST LTD

PO Box 4604, 8th Floor/BBME Bldg, Nasser Square, Deira,
Dubai
Tel: 221126/7/8/9
Cable: Wardley Dubai
Telex: 45806 Wardub EM

PRINCIPAL ACTIVITIES: Merchant and investment banking
Branch Offices: Bahrain and Cyprus (representative offices)
Parent Company: Wardley Limited, Hong Kong
Principal Bankers: The Hongkong & Shanghai Banking Corp
Financial Information:

	Dh'000
Authorised capital	40,000
Paid-up capital	40,000

UAE (Dubai)

Principal Shareholders: A Member of the Hongkong Bank
    Group
Date of Establishment: April 1975
No of Employees: 35

WATSON HAWKSLEY

PO Box 3020, Dubai
Tel: 371355
Telex: 45538 Culvt EM
Telefax: 375789

PRINCIPAL ACTIVITIES: Consulting engineers for sewerage,
    sewage disposal and water supply
Branch Offices: Bahrain, Oman
Parent Company: Watson Hawksley, Terriers House, Amersham
    Road, High Wycombe, Bucks UK

No of Employees: 45

WEATHERFORD OIL TOOL MIDDLE EAST LTD

PO Box 4627, Dubai
Tel: 432550
Telex: 45613 EM

PRINCIPAL ACTIVITIES: Oilfield services, cementing
    engineering, oilfield equipment, water blasters, chemical
    injection pumps, rubber products for the oil industry, marine
    cranes

WEIR PUMPS LTD

PO Box 11419, Dubai
Tel: 480154/9
Telex: 48590 WPDXB
Telefax: 482317

PRINCIPAL ACTIVITIES: Suppliers of pumps and electric
    motors
Parent Company: Weir Pumps Ltd, Cathcart, Glasgow,
    Scotland, UK
Principal Bankers: BBME, Dubai

WESCON INTERNATIONAL BV

PO Box 4949, Dubai
Tel: 421746, 435784
Telex: 48159 WSCON EM

Directors: F H Saarberg

PRINCIPAL ACTIVITIES: Mechanical, electrical, instrumentation
    and maintenance contractors for public utilities, oil and
    petrochemical industries
Branch Offices: PO Box 636, Abu Dhabi UAE; PO Box 1553,
    Sharjah UAE; PO Box 8513, Mutrah, Sultanate of Oman
Parent Company: Wescon BV
Principal Bankers: Algemene Bank Nederland BV

Principal Shareholders: Verenigde Machinefabrieken- Stork NV;
    Amsterdam
Date of Establishment: 26th April, 1974
No of Employees: 450

WILLIAMS INTERNATIONAL GROUP

PO Box 290, Dubai
Tel: 435222/3
Cable: Willbro Dubai
Telex: 45743 EM

PRINCIPAL ACTIVITIES: Pipeline construction and construction
    of oil and gas related facilities
Branch Offices: Projects in Algeria, Iran, Oman, Saudi Arabia,
    Bolivia, Peru, Nigeria
Parent Company: Head office: Tulsa, Oklahoma, USA
Associated Companies: Saudi Arabian Fabricated Metals
    Industry; The Oman Construction Company; Rezayat and
    Williams Construction Company, Saudi Arabia
Principal Bankers: British Bank of the Middle East

YOUSUF HABIB AL YOUSUF

See AL YOUSUF, YOUSUF HABIB,

YUSUF AHMAD ALGHANIM & SONS

See ALGHANIM, YUSUF AHMAD, & SONS

ZENER ELECTRICAL & ELECTRONICS SERVICES

PO Box 389, Dubai
Tel: 522880
Cable: Zener
Telex: 46300 Timber EM
Telefax: 524410

Managing Partner: Muneer A Shk Mohd Sharif
Partners: Salim A Shk Mohd Sharif, Muneer A Shk Mohd Sharif,
    Ayaz Farooq, Robert Nairn, Abdul Ellah Saleh, Saqr Bin Majid
    Saqr
Senior Executives: Muneer A Shk Mohd Sharif (Managing
    Director)

PRINCIPAL ACTIVITIES: Electrical contracting; electronic
    systems for audio-visual; fire; security systems;
    telecommunications, radar electronics and marine services
Principal Agencies: Sola Electric Inc, USA; Photain Controls Ltd,
    UK; Aerotron Inc, USA; Multitone, UK; OAR Corp Inc, USA;
    Tandberg A/S, Norway, ITT MacKay, USA; Sperry Marine
    Systems, UK; Sperry International, USA; Regency Inc, USA;
    Repco Inc, USA; King Radio, USA; Teletec Corp, USA;
    Spectrum Communications & Electronics, USA; Quintron
    Corp, USA; REL, USA; Protect Ltd, UK; Malling Kontrol,
    Denmark; Amplidan, Denmark
Branch Offices: Abu Dhabi, PO Box 3905, Tel 668720
Associated Companies: Zener Colston Electrical Co; Electrical
    Engineers & Contractors
Principal Bankers: National Bank of Dubai Ltd, Dubai;
    Commercial Bank of Dubai Ltd, Dubai
Financial Information:

	1988/89 Dh'000	1889/90 Dh'000
Sales turnover	21,624	52,328
Profits	139	2,080
Authorised capital	6,000	6,000
Paid-up capital	6,000	6,000
Total net assets	6,621	8,104

Principal Shareholders: Partners as described
Date of Establishment: 1974
No of Employees: 85

UAE (Dubai)

THE RECONSTRUCTION AND RE-EQUIPMENT OF KUWAIT:

NEW BUSINESS OPPORTUNITIES

WRITTEN AND RESEARCHED BY ROBERT BAILEY AND JOHN WHELAN

In response to the urgent need for detailed information on the current situation, Graham & Trotman is delighted to announce the publication of *The Reconstruction and Re-Equipment of Kuwait: New Business Opportunities.* This is a major new series of quarterly Reports, which will identify the essential requirements and priorities as Kuwait seeks to reactivate its infrastructure, industry and commerce.

Each Report provides a detailed and systematic overview on a sectoral basis, advising subscribers on where to focus attention and conduct business and identifying the right channels through which to direct prequalification particulars, secure tender documents and enter contract negotiations. It also includes commentaries on legal and contractual matters affecting all aspects of the reconstruction of Kuwait.

This publication is produced on a quarterly basis to ensure that it remains completely up-to-date and flexible enough to adapt to the developing political, economic and commercial situation in Kuwait. Each quarterly Report is a self-contained working document - together the Reports will build into a complete overview of Kuwait's changing requirements as the reconstruction process develops, and will be an invaluable source of information and advice for all companies seeking to capitalise on the new business opportunities available.

Make sure your Company is not left behind in the race for business - enter your subscription without delay.

Contents

Introduction; After the Storm; Decision Makers; Tendering; Private Sector; Manpower; Trading Partners; GCC States; Financing Recovery; Government; Legal, Regulatory and Contractual Requirements; Appendices; Cumulative and Classified Index.

1991 Subscription (3 issues) -- £297.00/US$645.00
Issue No. 1 due: June 1991.

For further details please contact:
The Marketing Department, Graham & Trotman, Sterling House, 66 Wilton Road, London SW1V 1DE
Telephone 071-821 1123   Fax 071-630 5229

Major Companies Database

supplied as

Mailing Lists or Disks

for the following areas

- **Europe**
- **Arab World**
- **Far East**
- **Australasia**
- **Eastern Europe**

The European Database now has over 14,500 of the leading European companies. Selections are available by **Company Size, Business Activity** and/or **Country**. With up to 17 named individuals at board and senior management level.

As well as Europe the database covers the Far East and Australasia with 7,000 of the regions leading companies. In the Arab World, covering 19 countries, the database offers 6,000 companies. New for 1991 are the East European and Soviet business organisations with over 2,000 entry organisations.

This is a unique list that has been built up over 15 years by constant research for Graham & Trotman's publishing activities, therefore offering you a highly responsive international marketing vehicle.

Lists can be provided on disk, labels, or print-out including telephone, fax and telex numbers.

Contact: Pauline Isbel, List Manager
Graham & Trotman Ltd, Sterling House, 66 Wilton Road
London SW1V 1DE.
Tel: 071-821 1123, Fax: 071-630 5229

Graham & Trotman
A member of the Kluwer Academic Publishers Group

Fujairah

ABU DHABI COMMERCIAL BANK

PO Box 770, Abu Dhabi
Tel: 23052
Telex: 89015

PRINCIPAL ACTIVITIES: Commercial banking
Branch Offices: Al Ain, Dubai, Sharjah, Ras Al Khaimah
Parent Company: Head office in Abu Dhabi

Date of Establishment: 1985

AL JASSIM AUTOMATIC TILES & MARBLE INDUSTRY

PO Box 444, Fujairah
Tel: 971-9-228559, 228452
Telex: 89038 Jassim EM
Telefax: 971-9228225

Chairman: Dr Sulaiman M Al Jassim (Proprietor)
Directors: Mohammed Moosa Al Jassim
Senior Executives: Eyad Kayyem (General Manager)

PRINCIPAL ACTIVITIES: Manufacture and export of mosaic tiles and marble products
Subsidiary Companies: Al Jassim Trading Group; Al Jassim Contracting
Principal Bankers: National Bank of Fujairah; British Bank of the Middle East; Bank of Oman; National Bank of Abu Dhabi

Principal Shareholders: Proprietorship
Date of Establishment: 1978
No of Employees: 70

ARAB BANK PLC

PO Box 300, Fujairah
Tel: 22050, 22421
Telex: 89051

PRINCIPAL ACTIVITIES: Commercial banking
Branch Offices: Abu Dhabi, Dubai
Parent Company: Head office in Amman, Jordan

BANK MELLI IRAN

PO Box 248, Fujairah
Tel: 22551
Telex: 89014 Bk Meli EM

PRINCIPAL ACTIVITIES: Commercial banking
Branch Offices: Abu Dhabi, Dubai, Ras Al Khaimah, Sharjah
Parent Company: Head office in Tehran, Iran

BANK OF CREDIT & COMMERCE (EMIRATES)

PO Box 268, Fujairah
Tel: 22747
Cable: Bancrecom
Telex: 89068 BCC Fj EM

PRINCIPAL ACTIVITIES: Commercial banking
Branch Offices: Abu Dhabi, Al Ain, Dubai, Ras Al Khaimah, Sharjah
Parent Company: Head office in Abu Dhabi

Date of Establishment: 1976

BANK OF OMAN LTD

PO Box 270, Fujairah
Tel: 224493
Telex: 89078

PRINCIPAL ACTIVITIES: Commercial banking
Branch Offices: Abu Dhabi, Ajman, Dubai, Fujairah, Ras Al Khaimah, Sharjah, Umm Al Quwain
Parent Company: Head office in Dubai

BANK SADERAT IRAN

PO Box 55, Fujairah
Tel: 22241
Cable: Saderbank
Telex: 45456 Dubai EM

PRINCIPAL ACTIVITIES: All banking transactions
Branch Offices: Abu Dhabi, Dubai, Ajman, Sharjah
Parent Company: Head office in Tehran, Iran

BRITISH BANK OF THE MIDDLE EAST (THE)

PO Box 21, Hamed Bin Abdulla Street, Fujairah
Tel: 9-222221
Telex: 89011 BBMEFJ EM
Telefax: 9-227150

Chairman: W Purves CBE DSO
Directors: J R H Bond, F J French, J M Gray, J A P Hill CBE, S Robertson, P J Wrangham
Senior Executives: G Burr (Branch Manager)

PRINCIPAL ACTIVITIES: Commercial banking
Branch Offices: Throughout the Middle East
Parent Company: The Hongkong & Shanghai Banking Corp Ltd

CENTRAL BANK OF THE UAE

PO Box 768, Fujairah
Tel: 224040
Telex: 89065 Markzi Em
Telefax: 26805

Chairman: Sheikh Suroor Bin Mohammed Al Nahyan
Directors: Mohammed Abdullah Al Kaz (Vice Chairman)
Senior Executives: Ali Mubarak Saeed Abbad (Branch Manager)

PRINCIPAL ACTIVITIES: Central banking
Branch Offices: Al Ain, Dubai, Sharjah, Ras Al Khaimah
Parent Company: Head office in Abu Dhabi

ETISALAT

PO Box 14, Fujairah
Tel: 22201
Telex: 89090 EM

PRINCIPAL ACTIVITIES: Telecommunications, telephone and telegraph systems, electrical engineering
Branch Offices: Throughout the United Arab Emirates

FUJAIRAH ANDRITZ & INDUSTRIAL ENGINEERING CO

PO Box 111, Fujairah
Tel: 070 22594
Telex: 89031 FUJAN EM

PRINCIPAL ACTIVITIES: Steel buildings, erection

FUJAIRAH BEACH HOTEL

PO Box 283, Fujairah
Tel: 22001
Telex: 89013 Motel EM

PRINCIPAL ACTIVITIES: Hotel business

FUJAIRAH BUILDING INDUSTRIES

PO Box 383, Fujairah
Tel: 22051
Telex: 89060 EM

PRINCIPAL ACTIVITIES: Manufacturers of concrete blocks
Branch Offices: PO Box 15666, Dibba, Tel 44751

FUJAIRAH CEMENT INDUSTRIES

PO Box 600, Fujairah
Tel: 223110, 223111
Telex: 89020 FCIDIB EM
Telefax: 444016, 227718

Chairman: HH Shaikh Hamad Bin Saif Al Sharqui
Directors: HE Sayed Ragbani, Mohamed Madoh, A G Bahraoozian, M D Darwish Al Marri, Abdul Malik Duaij, Mohamed Saeed Al Dwisaw

PRINCIPAL ACTIVITIES: Cement manufacture and supply
Branch Offices: Factory: PO Box 11477, Dibba, Tel 444011
Principal Bankers: National Bank of Abu Dhabi
Financial Information:

	1990 Dh'000
Sales turnover	65,000
Authorised capital	555,000
Paid-up capital	275,816
Total assets	328,000

Principal Shareholders: Government of Fujairah
Date of Establishment: 1979
No of Employees: 200

FUJAIRAH MARITIME & MERCANTILE INTERNATIONAL

PO Box 259, Fujairah
Tel: 23238
Telex: 89017 Grayfuj EM
Telefax: 228070

PRINCIPAL ACTIVITIES: General trading and contracting, supply of building materials, chemicals, etc, shipping and engineering

FUJAIRAH NATIONAL GROUP

PO Box 802, Fujairah
Tel: 24448, 24151
Telex: 89001 Natgrp EM

PRINCIPAL ACTIVITIES: Transport contrators

FUJAIRAH NATIONAL INSURANCE CO

PO Box 277, Fujairah
Tel: 22526/7
Telex: 89012 Finsco EM

Senior Executives: Naim Abou Samah (Technical Manager)

PRINCIPAL ACTIVITIES: General insurance

FUJAIRAH NATIONAL SHIPPING AGENCY

PO Box 234, Fujairah
Tel: 24151
Cable: FENSA
Telex: 89081 FNSA EM
Telefax: 09-228640

Chairman: HH Shaikh Saleh Bin Mohd Al Sharqi
Directors: Mohammed Ahmed Natafji
Senior Executives: Capt S K Bhasin (General Manager)

PRINCIPAL ACTIVITIES: Shipping agency
Principal Agencies: American President Lines, Rachid Fares Enterprises, West Asia Kontena Line
Parent Company: Fujairah National Group

Principal Bankers: National Bank of Fujairah; Bank of Credit & Commerce (E); Arab Bank Ltd
Date of Establishment: 1982
No of Employees: 33

FUJAIRAH PHARMACY

PO Box 232, Fujairah
Tel: 222395, 222495
Telex: 89091 Faleh EM
Telefax: (971 9) 226782

Chairman: Dr Rawhi M Faleh
Directors: Dr Omar Taher Baba'a
Senior Executives: Dr Issam Mohammed (Pharmacist)

PRINCIPAL ACTIVITIES: Import, trading and wholesale and retail of pharmaceuticals, baby care items, cosmetics, toiletries, chain of pharmacies
Principal Agencies: Health Life (UK); Thornton & Ross Ltd (UK); Hobon, Spain
Branch Offices: Dibba Pharmacy; New Fujairah Pharmacy; Fujairah Tower Pharmacy; Middle East Pharmacy
Parent Company: Fujairah Pharmacy
Subsidiary Companies: Fujairah Trading Establishment
Principal Bankers: Arab Bank; Bank Melli Iran
Financial Information:

	1990 Dh'000
Sales turnover	12,000
Authorised capital	240
Paid-up capital	240

Principal Shareholders: Dr Rawhi M Faleh, Shaikh Hamad Bin Saief Hamad Bin Al Sharqi
Date of Establishment: 1977
No of Employees: 35

GHURAIR TARMAC (PVT) LTD

PO Box 402, Fujairah
Tel: 22043
Telex: 47015

PRINCIPAL ACTIVITIES: Building and civil engineering

GULF AGENCY CO (FUJAIRAH) PVT LTD

PO Box 590, Fujairah
Tel: 228300, 228301
Cable: Confidence, Fujairah
Telex: 89046 GACFUJ EM
Telefax: 09-228269

Senior Executives: Capt C R Smylie (General Manager)

PRINCIPAL ACTIVITIES: Shipping agents, ships supply service, clearing and forwarding, trading; oilfield support vessel owners tugs barges, sea/air cargo
Branch Offices: Dubai; Abu Dhabi; Qatar; Oman; Bahrain; Saudi Arabia; Kuwait; Egypt; Athens; Stockholm; London; New York
Parent Company: Gulf Agency Co Ltd
Principal Bankers: British Bank of the Middle East

Principal Shareholders: Gulf Agency: Sulimann Al Jassim, Fusairah
Date of Establishment: 1975
No of Employees: 220 Overall

HILTON INTERNATIONAL FUJAIRAH

PO Box 231, Fujairah
Tel: 222411
Cable: Hiltels Fujairah
Telex: 89018 Hilton EM
Telefax: 226541

President: M Hirst
Directors: W Annen
Senior Executives: Slaheddine Hefaf (General Manager)

PRINCIPAL ACTIVITIES: Hotel operation

Principal Shareholders: H H Sheikh Hamad, Ruler of Fujairah
Date of Establishment: April 1978
No of Employees: 107

KHATIB AND ALAMI
Consolidated Engineering Co
PO Box 699, Fujairah
Tel: (971700 23377
Telex: 68474 CEC EM

PRINCIPAL ACTIVITIES: Engineering consultants and architects
Branch Offices: In UAE: Abu Dhabi, Al Ain, Dubai, Sharjah
Parent Company: Head office in Beirut, Lebanon
Principal Bankers: Arab Bank

NATIONAL BANK OF ABU DHABI
PO Box 79, Fujairah
Tel: 22345
Telex: 89010 Masraf EM

PRINCIPAL ACTIVITIES: Commercial banking
Branch Offices: Abu Dhabi, Ajman, Dubai, Fujairah, Ras Al
  Khaimah, Sharjah
Parent Company: Head office in Abu Dhabi

Date of Establishment: 1974

NATIONAL BANK OF FUJAIRAH
PO Box 887, Hamad Bin Abdulla Street, Fujairah
Tel: (070) 24518
Telex: 89050 Bankfj EM
Telefax: 24516

Chairman: H H Sheikh Saleh Bin Mohammed Al Sharqi
Directors: Easa Saleh Ál Gurg (Deputy Chairman), Khalaf Saeed
  Al Gaith, Sheikh Saud Bin Khalid Al Qasimi, Khalifa Juma Al
  Naboodah, Sulaiman Mousa Al Jassim, Sayed Abdullah Al
  Mousawi, Eid Obeid Khalfan, Mohamed Ahmed Abdul
  Rahman, Dr Salem Abdo Khalil (Board Secretary)
Senior Executives: Michael J Connor (General Manager),
  Alberto F T Martins (Senior Manager Operations &
  Operations)

PRINCIPAL ACTIVITIES: Commercial banking
Branch Offices: Abu Dhabi: PO Box 786, Tel 333300, Fax
  211336, Telex 22666; Dubai: PO Box 2979, Dubai, Tel
  511700, Fax 526001, Telex 47211; Dibba, Fujairah: PO Box
  17000, Tel 43788, Fax 43785, Telex 89024
Financial Information:

	1988 Dh'000	1989 Dh'000
Profits	9,234	13,965
Authorised capital	400,000	400,000
Paid-up capital	150,000	150,000
Total assets	387,986	426,202

Principal Shareholders: Government of Fujairah (43%);
  Government of Dubai (19.6%)
Date of Establishment: September 1984 (Operations started)
No of Employees: 74

PORT OF FUJAIRAH
PO Box 787, Fujairah
Tel: 228800
Telex: 89085
Telefax: 228811

Chairman: Sheikh Saleh Bin Mohammad Al Sharqi
Directors: Mohammad Al Salami, Dr Salem Abdo Khalil, Ibrahim
  Saad, Capt R M Saunders
Senior Executives: Capt R M Saunders (General Manager),
  Alistair Arthur (Marketing Manager), Michael Middleton
  (Engineering Manager), Capt R Turnbull (Harbour Master)

PRINCIPAL ACTIVITIES: Port management

Date of Establishment: 1982

SAFI TRADING & REFRIGERATING CO
PO Box 140, Fujairah
Tel: 22560, 22470
Cable: Fadi Fujairah
Telex: 89022 Fadi Fujairah EM

Chairman: Rafic Saifi

PRINCIPAL ACTIVITIES: General trading in textiles; foodstuffs;
  spare parts, dairy products, also shipping agency, tourism
  and travel, petrol filling station
Branch Offices: Ras Al Khaimah; Sharjah; Ajman; Khofakkan
Principal Bankers: Grindlays Bank

Principal Shareholders: HH The Sheikh Hamad Bin Mohammad
  Al Sharqi (Ruler of Fujairah) and Rafic Saifi

Ras Al Khaimah

ABDULLA AHMED RASHID EST
See RASHID, ABDULLA AHMED, EST

ABU DHABI COMMERCIAL BANK
PO Box 1633, Ras Al Khaimah
Tel: 32200
Telex: 99224 ADCBRK EM

PRINCIPAL ACTIVITIES: Commercial banking
Parent Company: Head office in Abu Dhabi

Date of Establishment: 1985

AL AHLIA INSURANCE CO LTD
PO Box 128, Ras Al Khaimah
Tel: 21479
Cable: Insure

Chairman: HE Sheikh Omar Bin Abdullah Al Qassimi
Directors: Abdullah Yousuf Abdullah, Abdullah Sultan Al-Sharhan, Saif Rashid Hamrein

PRINCIPAL ACTIVITIES: General insurance and reinsurance
Branch Offices: Branch in Dubai, PO Box 6730, Tel: 233289, Telex: 47677 Ahlia EM
Principal Bankers: Bank of Oman Ltd; National Bank of Ras Al Khaimah; Bank of the Arab Coast

Principal Shareholders: Directors as described
Date of Establishment: 26th April, 1977

AL BADAWI ENGINEERING CONTRACTING & GENERAL TRADING CO
PO Box 562, Ras Al Khaimah
Tel: 29240

PRINCIPAL ACTIVITIES: Civil, mechanical engineering contractors, building materials suppliers

ALBERT ABELA RAS-AL-KHAIMAH
PO Box 56, Ras-Al-Khaimah
Tel: 29436
Cable: Alabela Rak
Telex: 99161 Abela EM

PRINCIPAL ACTIVITIES: Industrial catering and camp services, construction, hotel management, tobacco distribution
Associated Companies: Representing the Albert Abela Group of Companies

AL BURG ENTERPRISES CO
PO Box 121, Ras Al Khaimah
Tel: 29310
Telex: 99128 Flex EM

PRINCIPAL ACTIVITIES: General trading and building contracting

AL KHARAZ TRADING & CONTRACTING EST (RAZCO)
PO Box 75, Ras Al Khaimah
Tel: 29312
Cable: Razco

Chairman: Mohamed Jassim Al Kharaz

PRINCIPAL ACTIVITIES: Supply of building materials, carpentry work, block factory, transportation contractors

AL MOSSABAH TRANSPORT CO
PO Box 102, Ras Al Khaimah
Tel: 51486, 51476
Cable: Mossabah
Telex: 99140 EM Tegara

Chairman: Ali Abdulla Mussabeh
Senior Executives: Mohamed Hassanain (Manager)

PRINCIPAL ACTIVITIES: General trading and contracting, supply of heavy transportation and auto spare parts
Principal Bankers: The British Bank of Middle East
Financial Information:

	Dh'000
Authorised capital	2,913
Paid-up capital	2,913

No of Employees: 30

AL NAHDA FOR GENERAL CONSTRUCTION CO
PO Box 446, Ras Al Khaimah
Tel: 21715
Cable: Alnahda

Chairman: Mohd Saleh Quasim
Senior Executives: Mohd Khatib (General Manager)

PRINCIPAL ACTIVITIES: Supply of building materials, timber, pipes, sanitaryware, paints; building construction
Branch Offices: National Aluminium Factory; Nayagra & Nameco Electrical Contracting

Principal Shareholders: Mohd Saleh Quasim; Mohd Al Basti; Haji Anwer Hussain
Date of Establishment: 1973
No of Employees: 500

AL SALEM ENGINEERING & CONTRACTING CO
PO Box 566, Ras Al Khaimah
Tel: 21369
Telex: 99183 Sect EM

PRINCIPAL ACTIVITIES: General engineering contracting

ARAB BANK PLC
PO Box 4972, Al Nakheel, Ras Al Khaimah
Tel: 28437, 28438
Cable: Bankarabi
Telex: 99152 EM Arabnk

PRINCIPAL ACTIVITIES: Commercial banking
Branch Offices: Bahrain; Abu Dhabi; Dubai; Sharjah; Ras Al Khaimah; Ajman; Fujairah; Qatar; Oman; Lebanon; Saudi Arabia; Yemen; Tunisia; Morocco
Parent Company: Head office in Amman, Jordan

ARAB COMMERCIAL ENTERPRISES
PO Box 412, Ras Al Khaimah
Tel: 28188
Cable: Comment Ras Al Khaimah
Telex: 99185 EM

Senior Executives: Kundapur G Rao (Manager)

PRINCIPAL ACTIVITIES: Insurance brokers, surveyors and travel agents
Branch Offices: Branches throughout the Middle East

BANK MELLI IRAN
PO Box 5270, Ras Al Khaimah
Tel: 28797
Telex: 99212

PRINCIPAL ACTIVITIES: Commercial banking

Branch Offices: Abu Dhabi, Dubai, Fujairah, Sharjah
Parent Company: Head office in Iran

Date of Establishment: 1978

BANK OF BARODA
PO Box 295, Ras Al Khaimah
Tel: 29293
Telex: 99159 Baroda EM

PRINCIPAL ACTIVITIES: Commercial banking
Branch Offices: Abu Dhabi, Dubai, Fujairah, Sharjah, Umm Al Quwain
Parent Company: Head office in Baroda, India

BANK OF CREDIT & COMMERCE (EMIRATES)
PO Box 553, Ras Al Khaimah
Tel: 29424
Cable: Bankover
Telex: 99260 BCCI EM

Senior Executives: Zafar Iqbal (Managing Director & Chief Executive), Khawaja T Rasheed (Manager)

PRINCIPAL ACTIVITIES: Commercial banking
Branch Offices: Branches throughout the Middle East
Parent Company: Bank of Credit & Commerce (Luxembourg) Holding Company

BANK OF OMAN LTD
PO Box 700, Ras al-Khaimah
Tel: 29344, 21178
Telex: 99219 Oman EM

PRINCIPAL ACTIVITIES: Commercial banking
Branch Offices: In Ras Al Khaimah: Al Nakheel Branch, Tel 21621; Masafi Branch, Tel 64334
Parent Company: Head office in Dubai

BANK OF THE ARAB COAST
Al Nakheel, PO Box 342, Ras Al Khaimah
Tel: 29548, 21480
Cable: Arcoba
Telex: 99149 Arcoba EM

PRINCIPAL ACTIVITIES: Commercial banking
Branch Offices: Ras Al Khaimah, Dubai

Date of Establishment: 1975 reconstituted under new ownership in 1980

BANQUE LIBANAISE POUR LE COMMERCE
PO Box 771, Ras Al Khaimah
Tel: 29547
Telex: 99174 Balib EM

PRINCIPAL ACTIVITIES: Commercial banking
Branch Offices: Abu Dhabi, Dubai, Sharjah
Parent Company: Head office in Paris, France

BIN LADEN ORGANISATION
PO Box 539, Ras Al Khaimah
Tel: 21360, 21241

PRINCIPAL ACTIVITIES: Civil engineering contractors

BIN MASAOOD, MOHAMMAD, & SONS
PO Box 173, Ras Al Khaimah
Tel: 28465

PRINCIPAL ACTIVITIES: Import and distribution of building materials, tyres and tubes, household goods, electrical appliances, motor vehicles, etc
Principal Agencies: Dunlop, Electrolux, etc
Branch Offices: Branches throughout the United Arab Emirates
Parent Company: Head office in Abu Dhabi

BRITISH BANK OF THE MIDDLE EAST (THE)
PO Box 9, Sheikh Mohd Bin Salem Street, Ras Al Khaimah
Tel: 333544
Cable: Bactria
Telex: 99160 BBME EM
Telefax: 7-330200

Chairman: W Purves CBE DSO
Directors: J R H Bond, F J French, J M Gray, J A P Hill CBE, S Robertson, P J Wrangham
Senior Executives: C B Gregory (Manager Ras Al Khaimah)

PRINCIPAL ACTIVITIES: Commercial banking
Branch Offices: Throughout the Middle East
Subsidiary Companies: The Middle East Finance Co Ltd

Date of Establishment: In Ras Al Khaimah: January 1964

CENTRAL BANK OF THE UAE
PO Box 5000, Ras Al Khaimah
Tel: 23330
Telex: 99126 MARKZI EM
Telefax: 23009

Chairman: Sheikh Suroor Bin Mohammed Al Nahyan
Directors: Mohammed Abdullah Al Kaz (Vice Chairman)
Senior Executives: Salim J Al Baker (Branch Manager)

PRINCIPAL ACTIVITIES: Central banking
Branch Offices: Dubai; Sharjah; Fujairah; Al Ain
Parent Company: Head office in Abu Dhabi

Date of Establishment: 1973
No of Employees: 243

CITIBANK NA
PO Box 294, Oman St, Ras Al Khaimah
Tel: 29235
Cable: Citibank
Telex: 99119 EM

PRINCIPAL ACTIVITIES: Commercial banking
Parent Company: Head Office: New York, USA

COAST INVESTMENT & DEVELOPMENT CO
PO Box 5413, Ras Al Khaimah
Tel: 26882
Telex: 99270

Chairman: Sheikh Saud Bin Sagar Al Qassimi
Directors: Mohammad Jasim Al Sagar (Managing Director)

PRINCIPAL ACTIVITIES: Investment company
Parent Company: Head office in Kuwait
Financial Information:

	US$'000
Authorised capital	100,000
Paid-up capital	100,000

COMMERCIAL BANK OF DUBAI LTD
PO Box 454, Ras Al Khaimah
Tel: 28447
Telex: 99180 Trubnk EM

PRINCIPAL ACTIVITIES: Commercial banking
Branch Offices: Abu Dhabi, Dubai, Sharjah
Parent Company: Head office in Dubai

CONTRACTING & ENGINEERING ENTERPRISES LTD
PO Box 756, Ras Al Khaimah
Tel: 45886
Cable: CEENTREP
Telex: 99171 Center EM

Chairman: Dr Osmane Aidi
Directors: Dr Amine Mreiden

PRINCIPAL ACTIVITIES: Building and engineering contractors, suppliers of building materials, mechanical and electrical works
Branch Offices: PO Box 2226, Abu Dhabi, UAE, Tel 331095/96, Telex 24380 Ceeadh EM; Factory at Jazeerah Al Hamra, Tel 45886; 8, Avenue Hoche, 75008 Paris, France, Tel 5637172, Telex 640182 OSDI F

CONTRACTING & TRADING CO

Civil Division, PO Box 207, Ras Al Khaimah
Tel: 81168, 81325
Telex: 99199 EM

PRINCIPAL ACTIVITIES: Building materials; mechanical and civil engineering contractors

Principal Shareholders: Mothercat (Lebanon)

DAR AL HANDASAH

PO Box 361, Ras Al Khaimah
Tel: 21615
Telex: 991925 Darsah EM

PRINCIPAL ACTIVITIES: Architects and consulting engineers
Branch Offices: Throughout the Middle East

DEVELOPMENT TRADING & CONTRACTING CO WLL

PO Box 153, Ras al Khaimah
Tel: 28464
Cable: Development
Telex: 99186 Dtc EM

Chairman: HH Sheikh Abdul Malik Kayed Al-Qasimi (Partner)
Directors: Ali Abdullah Nussabeh (Partner), Sadiq Shallita Sadiq (Partner/General Manager), Yousif Roumanus Hanna (Partner/Executive Manager)

PRINCIPAL ACTIVITIES: Civil works (building and construction) contracting; trading; properties and real estate
Principal Bankers: National Bank of Abu Dhabi; Bank of Oman Ltd; Grindlays Bank plc; United Arab Bank

Principal Shareholders: Chairman and Directors as described above

DST RAS AL KHAIMAH

PO Box 374, Ras Al Khaimah
Tel: 21633
Telex: 99112 Dst EM

PRINCIPAL ACTIVITIES: Drilling contractors

EMIRATES TRADING CO

PO Box 309, Ras Al Khaimah
Tel: 21431, 28262
Cable: Etcom
Telex: 99118 Et Comp EM

PRINCIPAL ACTIVITIES: General trading, distribution of building materials, electrical appliances, household goods, toiletries and general consumer goods
Principal Agencies: Yaskwa generators

EMITAC LTD

PO Box 473, Ras Al Khaimah
Tel: 28133
Cable: Emitac RAK
Telex: 68136 Emitac EM

Chairman: Abdul Rahman Bukhatir

PRINCIPAL ACTIVITIES: Supply and maintenance of electronic equipment, mechanical engineering etc
Principal Agencies: Hewlett Packard; CPT; McQuay; IMED; Bruel & Kjaar
Branch Offices: Abu Dhabi, Dubai
Parent Company: Head office in Sharjah

Principal Bankers: National Bank of Sharjah

Date of Establishment: 1975
No of Employees: 350

ERNST & WHINNEY

PO Box 5579, Ras Al Khaimah
Tel: 21022
Telex: 99150

PRINCIPAL ACTIVITIES: Accountants and management consultants
Branch Offices: In the Middle East: Dubai, Bahrain, Egypt, Jordan, Kuwait, Lebanon, Oman, Qatar, Saudi Arabia, Abu Dhabi, Sharjah, Yemen AR
Parent Company: Middle East Regional Office: Dubai

ETISALAT

PO Box 245, Ras Al Khaimah
Tel: 21111, 28470
Telex: 99100 EM

PRINCIPAL ACTIVITIES: Telecommunications telephone and telegraph systems

GULF CEMENT COMPANY

PO Box 5295, Ras Al Khaimah
Tel: 668222
Telex: 99187 GCC EM
Telefax: 668038

Chairman: Saleh A Al Shalfan
Directors: Abdul Wahab Al Qallaf (Vice Chairman and Managing Director)

PRINCIPAL ACTIVITIES: Cement manufacturers and products suppliers
Principal Bankers: Al Ahli Bank of Kuwait, Kuwait
Financial Information:

	1990 Dh'000
Authorised capital	240,590
Paid-up capital	240,590

Principal Shareholders: Kuwait Real Estate Investment (19.5%), Government of Ras Al Khaimah (16.5%), Consortium KSC (Kuwaiti governmental company)
Date of Establishment: May 1977
No of Employees: 355

GULF CONTRACTING & ENTERPRISES CO

PO Box 159, Ras Al Khaimah
Tel: 21414

PRINCIPAL ACTIVITIES: General trading and contracting, import and distribution of building materials, etc

GULF EXPLOSIVES CO LTD

PO Box 731, Ras Al Khaimah
Tel: 21777
Telex: 99173 Explos EM

Directors: M Kjellquist, V Mossberg, A Ekluna, J Kallenback
Senior Executives: J Kallenback (Managing Director)

PRINCIPAL ACTIVITIES: Blasting contractors; manufacture, sales and distribution of explosives
Branch Offices: PO Box 5175, Doha, Qatar

Date of Establishment: 1976
No of Employees: 75

HABIB BANK LTD

Maftul Bldg, Sabah Rd, PO Box 205, Ras Al Khaimah
Tel: 21549
Cable: Habibank
Telex: 45430 via Dubai

PRINCIPAL ACTIVITIES: Commercial banking

Branch Offices: In the Middle East: Abu Dhabi; Dubai; Sharjah; Ras Al Khaimah; Al Ain; Ajman; Umm Al Qaiwan; Oman; Yemen AR; Lebanon
Parent Company: Head office in Karachi, Pakistan

HAMRAIN TRANSPORT CO

PO Box 166, Ras Al Khaimah
Tel: 24035
Telex: 99176 Seif EM

Directors: B Parseghian

PRINCIPAL ACTIVITIES: Transportation contractors, air charterers

JASSIM DARWISH TRADING EST

PO Box 104, Ras Al Khaimah
Tel: 21148
Cable: Al Darwish Est RAK
Telex: 99137 EGTA

Chairman: Jassim Mohamed Darwish

PRINCIPAL ACTIVITIES: Import and distribution of pharmaceuticals, toiletries and general commodities, printers and stationers
Branch Offices: Ras Al Khaimah and Dubai
Subsidiary Companies: Al Shifa Pharmacy, Nakheel, Dira Pharmacy, Dubai, Ras Al Khaimah Pharmacy, RAK (UAE)
Principal Bankers: Bank of the Arab Coast

Date of Establishment: 1965
No of Employees: 68

KARKABAH ELECTRICAL EST

PO Box 34, Oman St, Nakhill, Ras Al Khaimah
Tel: 21336, 21290, 28862, 28078
Cable: Karkabah

PRINCIPAL ACTIVITIES: General trading and electrical contracting. Import and distribution of electrical and electronic appliances, air-conditioning and heating equipment, etc

KIER INTERNATIONAL LTD

PO Box 729, Ras Al Khaimah
Tel: 29525
Telex: 99110 Kircat EM

PRINCIPAL ACTIVITIES: Civil engineering contractors
Branch Offices: Sharjah, PO Box 5173, Tel 355176, 357159, Telex 68396
Parent Company: Head office: Tempsford Hail, Sandy, Beds, UK

MIDDLE EAST BANK LTD

PO Box 302, Ras Al Khaimah
Tel: 21366
Telex: 46074 MEBNK EM

PRINCIPAL ACTIVITIES: Commercial banking
Branch Offices: Abu Dhabi, Dubai, Sharjah, Umm Al Quwain
Parent Company: Head office in Dubai

Date of Establishment: 1977

MOHAMMAD BIN MASAOOD & SONS

See BIN MASAOOD, MOHAMMAD, & SONS

NATIONAL BANK OF ABU DHABI

PO Box 5744, Ras Al Khaimah
Tel: 21753
Telex: 99194 Masraf EM

Chairman: HE Mohammed Habroush Al Suweidi
Directors: Khalaf Bin Ahmed Al Otaiba (Deputy Chairman)

PRINCIPAL ACTIVITIES: Commercial banking

Branch Offices: Abu Dhabi (24), Ajman, Dubai (2), Fujairah (2), Ras Al Khaimah (2), Sharjah (2)
Parent Company: Head office in Abu Dhabi

Date of Establishment: 1978

NATIONAL BANK OF RAS AL KHAIMAH

PO Box 5300, Ras Al Khaimah
Tel: 21127
Cable: Bankwatani
Telex: 99109 Nbrak EM

Chairman: HH Sheikh Khalid Bin Saqr Al-Qasimi
Directors: HE Sheikh Omar Bin Abdallah Al-Qasimi, Mohammed Khalifa Al Yousuf, Saeed Ibrahim Darwish, Faisal Yusuf Al-Qatami, Hamad Abdul-Aziz Al-Sagar

PRINCIPAL ACTIVITIES: Commercial banking
Branch Offices: Dubai, Abu Dhabi, Ras Al Khaimah
Principal Bankers: Hill Samuel & Co Limited, UK; Brown Brothers Harriman & Co, New York

Principal Shareholders: The Government of Ras Al Khaimah (30%), Citizens of the UAE (25%), Citizens of Kuwait (20%), Hill Samuel & Co Ltd (10%)
Date of Establishment: March 1978
No of Employees: 41

R A K GENERAL TRADING EST

PO Box 59, Ras Al Khaimah
Tel: 21512, 28631
Cable: Sahawat
Telex: 99618 Sahawat EM

Proprietor: Saleh Mohd Saleh

PRINCIPAL ACTIVITIES: Import and wholesale of all types of paints
Branch Offices: Sharjah
Principal Bankers: British Bank of the Middle East, Commercial Bank of Dubai

Date of Establishment: 1976

RAKNOR (PVT) LTD

PO Box 883, Ras Al Khaimah
Tel: 66351
Telex: 99251 Raknor EM
Telefax: 66910

Chairman: H H Sheikh Saud Bin Saqr Al Qassimi
Directors: Sami Rida Sami (General Manager)

PRINCIPAL ACTIVITIES: Concrete product manufacturers
Principal Bankers: National Bank of Ras Al Khaimah
Financial Information:

	Dh'000
Authorised capital	8,000

Principal Shareholders: HH Sheikh Saqr bin Mohammed Al Qasimi (Ruler of Ras Al Khaimah)
Date of Establishment: July 1976
No of Employees: 65

RAS AL KHAIMAH ASPHALT CO

PO Box 586, Ras Al Khaimah
Tel: 29535
Telex: 99169 Oudeh EM

PRINCIPAL ACTIVITIES: Production of building materials

RAS AL KHAIMAH HOTEL

PO Box 56, Ras Al Khaimah
Tel: 28251
Cable: Alabela Rasalkaima
Telex: 99113 EM

PRINCIPAL ACTIVITIES: Hotel management and operation

UAE (Ras Al Khaimah)

RAS AL KHAIMAH MARITIME & MERCANTILE INTERNATIONAL

PO Box 4888, Ras Al Khaimah
Tel: 21701, 21213, 28586, 23232
Cable: Gray
Telex: 99284 Grayrk EM
Telefax: 23646

Chairman: Sh Saqr Bin Khalid Al Qasimi
Directors: Sh Khalid Bin Humaid Al Qasimi, Sh Mohamed Bin Saqr Al Qasimi

PRINCIPAL ACTIVITIES: General trading and contracting, import and distribution of electrical equipment, foodstuffs, Lloyds agents, cargo ship and tanker agents, travel agents and general merchants
Principal Agencies: Shipping: OCL, Hapag-Lloyd, CMB, NCHP, Jugolinija, Showa, Avin Liners, Lloyds Agents; Trading: Beechams, Yardley, Berec, SSI, Fix, Planned Storage Systems; Tankers: BP, Shell, Texaco and Esso
Branch Offices: Associates throughout the United Arab Emirates and the Arabian Gulf
Parent Company: Associated with the Gray Mackenzie and Inchcape Groups
Principal Bankers: The National Bank of Ras Al Khaimah

Principal Shareholders: Sh Saqr Bin Khalid Al Qasimi; Gray Mackenzie International
Date of Establishment: June 1983
No of Employees: 20

RAS AL KHAIMAH NATIONAL INSURANCE CO

PO Box 506, Ras Al Khaimah
Tel: 07-228145
Cable: RASASSURE
Telex: 99116 Rasure EM
Telefax: 07-228500

Chairman: H H Sheikh Sultan Bin Saqr Al-Qasimi
Directors: Khaled Safarini, Saba Nader, Maurice Karaoglan, Nassib Boulos
Senior Executives: Antoine M Stephan (General Manager)

PRINCIPAL ACTIVITIES: All classes of insurance and reinsurance
Principal Agencies: Nasco Karaoglan, PO Box 7108, Dubai, UAE, Tel (04) 523133, Fax (04) 520544, Telex 46496 Naskr EM
Branch Offices: Traffic Police Premises, Tel (077) 351157, Ras Al Khaimah, UAE; Ras Al Khaimah National Insurance Co, PO Box 46440, Abu Dhabi, UAE, Tel (02) 344565/566, Telex 23913 RAKNIC EM, Fax (02) 344795
Parent Company: Management Company: Nasco Karaoglan, 171 rue de Buzenval, 92380 Garches, France
Associated Companies: Cedar Insurance & Reinsurance Co Ltd
Principal Bankers: National Bank of Ras Al Khaimah, The British Bank of the Middle East
Financial Information:

	1988	1989
	Dh'000	Dh'000
Sales turnover	14,843	31,054
Profits	2,101	2,102
Authorised capital	10,000	10,000
Paid-up capital	10,000	10,000
Total assets	22,791	25,895

Principal Shareholders: Government of Ras Al Khaimah; Nationals of the Emirates
Date of Establishment: December 1974
No of Employees: 19

RAS AL KHAIMAH OILFIELDS SUPPLY CENTRE LTD

PO Box 447, Ras Al Khaimah
Tel: 21630
Cable: RAKOSC
Telex: 99172 Rakosc EM

Chairman: Sheikh Khalid Bin Saqr Al Qassimi

PRINCIPAL ACTIVITIES: Supply of oilfield equipment, warehouse facilities and base services
Branch Offices: Mina Saqr, Ras Al Khaimah, UAE
Parent Company: Oilfields Supply Center Limited, Dubai, UAE
Principal Bankers: National Bank of Ras Al Khaimah

Principal Shareholders: Government of Ras Al Khaimah & Oilfields Supply Center Ltd, Dubai, UAE
Date of Establishment: 1st November 1976
No of Employees: 23

RAS AL KHAIMAH PLASTICS LTD

PO Box 838, Ras Al Khaimah
Tel: 45777
Telex: 99191 RAKP EM

PRINCIPAL ACTIVITIES: Manufacture of glass reinforced plastics

RAS AL KHAIMAH PORT SERVICES

PO Box 5130, Ras Al Khaimah
Tel: 66444
Cable: Minasaqr Ras al Khaimah
Telex: 99280 RAKPS EM

Chairman: Sheikh Mohammed Bin Saqr Al Qasimi
Senior Executives: Capt H R Assaad (Port Manager), J Duncan (Port Engineer), M Iqbal (Port Accountant)

PRINCIPAL ACTIVITIES: Port operators at Mina Saqr
Associated Companies: Inchcape Group, London
Principal Bankers: National Bank of Ras Al Khaimah

Principal Shareholders: Government of Ras Al Khaimah (majority); Inchcape Group (minority)
Date of Establishment: 1977
No of Employees: 53

RAS AL KHAIMAH POULTRY & FEEDING CO

PO Box 184, Ras Al Khaimah
Tel: 441477
Cable: Rapco
Telex: 99220 Rapco
Telefax: 442220

Chairman: Hamad Abdulla Al Mutawa
Directors: Dr Marzouq Al Ghunaim (Vice Chairman), Abdullah Khalfan Mohd (Managing Director), Mohamed Badr Al Katami (Asst Managing Director)
Senior Executives: Mohamed Ali Al Noosh (General Manager), Mohamed Siddiq Al Emam (Production Manager)

PRINCIPAL ACTIVITIES: Production and distribution of all poultry products
Branch Offices: Sales centres in Dubai, Sharjah and Ajman
Principal Bankers: Bank of Credit & Commerce; Abu Dhabi Commercial Bank
Financial Information:

	1990
	Dh'000
Sales turnover	35,000
Profits	6,400
Authorised capital	72,000
Paid-up capital	72,000
Total assets	100,000

Principal Shareholders: Government of Ras Al Khaimah (Majority shareholding); and shareholders from Kuwait and United Arab Emirates
Date of Establishment: 1977
No of Employees: 200

RAS AL KHAIMAH ROCK CO

PO Box 86, Ras Al Khaimah
Tel: 66251
Cable: Rakrock
Telex: 99235
Telefax: (971) 77 66994

Chairman: Shaikh Sultan Bin Saqr Al Qasimi
Directors: Shaikh Saud Bin Saqr Al Qasimi (Vice Chairman), Sami Rida Sami
Senior Executives: Sami Rida Sami (General Manager)

PRINCIPAL ACTIVITIES: Supply of limestone and gabbro aggregates and sand

Date of Establishment: 1972
No of Employees: 304

RAS AL KHAIMAH SPINNEY'S

PO Box 115, Ras Al Khaimah
Tel: 21317

PRINCIPAL ACTIVITIES: Catering contractors, wholesale and retail of foodstuffs
Branch Offices: Lebanon; Jordan; UAE; (Abu Dhabi, Dubai, Sharjah, Ras Al Khaimah); Kuwait; Bahrain; Qatar; Oman; Saudi Arabia; Iran; Libya; Cyprus; Indonesia

RASHID, ABDULLA AHMED, EST

PO Box 3, Ras Al Khaimah
Tel: 24875, 21221
Cable: Hisham
Telex: 99133 Aarest EM

PRINCIPAL ACTIVITIES: Building and transportation contractors

REDA RAS AL KHAIMAH LTD

PO Box 518, Ras Al Khaimah
Tel: 81154
Cable: Reda
Telex: 99138 Reda EM

Directors: Munib R Masri, Tarif W Ayoubi

PRINCIPAL ACTIVITIES: Site investigations, land reclamation and development, civil and mechanical engineering, water well drilling
Branch Offices: Offices in Jordan, Lebanon, Syria, Saudi Arabia, Oman, Abu Dhabi, London and the Liechtenstein
Principal Bankers: Arab Bank Ltd

SABA & CO

PO Box 435, Ras Al Khaimah
Tel: 29360
Cable: Sabaco Ras Al Khaimah

PRINCIPAL ACTIVITIES: Chartered accountants and management consultants

TALAL ABU-GHAZALEH & CO

PO Box 403, Ras Al Khaimah
Tel: 28427
Cable: Auditors
Telex: 99151 Audit EM

PRINCIPAL ACTIVITIES: Public accountants, management and industrial consultants
Branch Offices: Abu Dhabi; Dubai; Sharjah; Ras Al Khaimah; Lebanon; Egypt; Bahrain; Jordan; Qatar; Oman; Libya; Saudi Arabia; Tunisia; Yemen AR; Yemen PDR
Parent Company: Head office in Kuwait

UNION CEMENT CO

PO Box 170, Ras Al Khaimah
Tel: 66166
Cable: Cement
Telex: 99117 Unicem EM
Telefax: 66635

Chairman: HE Sheikh Saqr Bin Khalid Humaid Al Qasimi
Directors: Hammad Harazeen (Vice Chairman & Managing Director), Dr Ali Ismail Al Embaby (Member), Abdulla Ahmed Rashed (Member), HE Sheikh Taleb Bin Saqr Al Qasimi (Member), Jaber Saif Jaber (Member), Ahmed Hamdan Malek (Member)

PRINCIPAL ACTIVITIES: Production and sale of cement to BS and ASTM specifications, also producing oil well cement to API specifications
Subsidiary Companies: Union Cement Norcem Co Ltd, PO Box 170, Ras Al Khaimah
Principal Bankers: National Bank of Ras Al Khaimah, Ras Al Khaimah

Principal Shareholders: Government of Ras Al Khaimah
Date of Establishment: 25.6.1972
No of Employees: 323

UNION CONTRACTING CO (UNCO)

PO Box 162, Ras Al Khaimah
Tel: 07-445627
Cable: Unco
Telex: 99253 UNCO EM
Telefax: 07-445474

Directors: Mohammad Abu Dayah (General Manager)
Senior Executives: Zareh Hadajian, Haryr Soghomonian, Allam Shadid

PRINCIPAL ACTIVITIES: Plant hire; supply of construction equipment
Branch Offices: UNCO (PO Box 16638, Dubai); UNCO (PO Box 3896 Abu Dhabi); UNCO (PO Box 2033, Sharjah)
Principal Bankers: National Bank of Abu Dhabi; Bank of Credit & Commerce (E); United Arab Bank; Arab Bank Ltd
Financial Information:

	1990 Dh'000
Paid-up capital	10,125

Principal Shareholders: Saif Hamarain; Ghanem Al Deeb; Yousuf Boresly
Date of Establishment: 1972
No of Employees: 600

UNITED ARAB BANK

PO Box 615, Ras Al Khaimah
Tel: 29356
Telex: 99145 Uabank EM

PRINCIPAL ACTIVITIES: Commercial banking
Branch Offices: Abu Dhabi, Dubai, Sharjah
Parent Company: Registered Office: Sharjah; Head Office: Abu Dhabi

UNITED DEVELOPING ENTERPRISES CO

PO Box 309, Ras Al Khaimah
Tel: 223122, 223133, 223144
Telex: 99118 Yousef EM
Telefax: 07-226000

Chairman: Abdulla Yousef Abdulla
Partner: HE Sheikh Muntaseer Khalid
Senior Executives: Abdulla Yousef Abdulla (Managing Director), Arch Adnan Yousef Abdullah (Asst Managing Director & Technical Manager)

PRINCIPAL ACTIVITIES: Civil engineering & construction, and ship management
Associated Companies: AYA Group of Companies

Principal Bankers: National Bank of Ras Al Khaimah; Bank of
    Credit & Commerce International; Middle East Bank
Financial Information:

| | 1990 |
	Dh'000
Authorised capital	10,000
Paid-up capital	10,000
Total assets	36,000

Principal Shareholders: Abdulla Yousef Abdulla; HE Sheikh
    Muntaseer Khalid
Date of Establishment: 1971
No of Employees: 500

VITOL EXPLORATION BV
PO Box 374, Ras Al Khaimah
Tel: 21633, 28445
Telex: 99112 Vitex EM

PRINCIPAL ACTIVITIES: Petroleum exploration

Sharjah

ABDUL JALIL AL FAHIM
See AL FAHIM, ABDUL JALIL,

ADRECO
Arab Development Real Estate Co
PO Box 1887, Sharjah
Tel: 355485
Telex: 68031 Marblo EM

Chairman: Said Khoury

PRINCIPAL ACTIVITIES: Real estate development, studies,
construction, commercial enterprises

Principal Shareholders: Government of Sharjah, Renault Group
(France), Said Khoury, Marblo Group

AIR INTERGULF LTD
PO Box 289, Sharjah
Tel: 357549, 354301
Telex: 68249 Aigops EM

Chairman: HE Sheikh Faisal Bin Sultan Al-Qassimi
Directors: Zaki Shuwayhat (Managing Director), Abdul R
Bukhatir

PRINCIPAL ACTIVITIES: Cargo airlines, clearing and forwarding
Principal Agencies: Halbart Air Consolidator System,
Amsterdam; Cargoman, Muscat (Oman)
Subsidiary Companies: Pan Arabian Aircraft
Principal Bankers: Grindlays Bank, London; United Arab Bank,
Sharjah

Principal Shareholders: United Arab Aviation

AL ATTIYAH CONTRACTING & TRADING CO
PO Box 525, Sharjah
Tel: 23891, 22352, 23005
Cable: Alattiyah
Telex: 68042 Attiay EM

PRINCIPAL ACTIVITIES: General trading and civil engineering
contracting. Supply of building materials and construction
plant equipment

AL BADAWI ENGINEERING CONTRACTING & GENERAL TRADING CO
PO Box 1147, Sharjah
Tel: 23890, 23868
Telex: 68434 Batha EM

PRINCIPAL ACTIVITIES: General trading and civil engineering
contracting

AL BAHAR, MOHAMMED ABDULRAHMAN,
PO Box 6038, Sharjah
Tel: 331271
Cable: Moatasim
Telex: 68680 Bahar EM
Telefax: 06-335132

Chairman: Mohamed Abdulrahman Al-Bahar
Directors: Jassim Al-Bahar (President), Issam Al-Bahar
(Executive Vice President)
Senior Executives: Mohamed Numan (Deputy Group General
Manager), Anton Hayek (General Parts & Service Manager),
Walid Shtayyeh (Central Personnel Manager), Ashfaque Azad
(Area Manager, UAE)

PRINCIPAL ACTIVITIES: Distribution of earthmoving, material
handling, compaction and asphalt equipment; generators and
control systems
Principal Agencies: Caterpillar, Switzerland; Caterpillar Tractor
USA; Koehring, USA; Oshkosh, USA
Branch Offices: Abu Dhabi; Bahrain; Dubai; Qatar; Oman
Parent Company: Head office in Kuwait
Subsidiary Companies: Oasis Trading & Equipment Co, PO Box
7002, Muttrah, Muscat (Oman)
Principal Bankers: Arab Bank; British Bank of the Middle East

Principal Shareholders: Mohamed Abdulrahman Al-Bahar
Date of Establishment: 1964 in Dubai
No of Employees: 140

AL BORJ TRADING CO
PO Box 127, Sharjah
Tel: 353000
Telex: 68668 Alborj EM

Chairman: Shaikh Mohammed Bin Saud Al-Qasemi and Bros
Directors: Eng Arsalan Anwar A Murshed
Senior Executives: V C Unnikrishnan

PRINCIPAL ACTIVITIES: General trading, fertilisers, agricultural
services
Principal Agencies: Porcelli Pumps, Italy; Saer Pumps, Italy;
Nardi Francesco & Figli, Italy; Grinding Mills of R Frimodt
Pederson, Denmark
Principal Bankers: Invest Bank, Sharjah

Date of Establishment: 1967
No of Employees: 30

AL FAHIM, ABDUL JALIL,
PO Box 1445, Sharjah
Tel: 354169, 354573
Cable: Igmaco
Telex: 68065 EM

Chairman: Abdul Jalil Al Fahim

PRINCIPAL ACTIVITIES: Electrical engineering, import and
distribution of electrical equipment, cables and accessories;
mechanical equipment
Principal Agencies: BICC, Bosch
Branch Offices: Sharjah; Dubai; Abu Dhabi

AL FUTTAIM
PO Box 5471, Sharjah
Tel: 357648, 352017, 358240
Telex: 68528 Alfel EM; 68497 Futaim EM

PRINCIPAL ACTIVITIES: General trading and contracting,
distribution of motor vehicles, auto spare parts, electrical and
electronic equipment, diesel engines, generators, also building
contracting, supply of construction plant
Branch Offices: Branches throughout the United Arab Emirates
Parent Company: Head office in Dubai

ALGEMENE BANK NEDERLAND NV
Al Zahra Square, PO Box 1971, Sharjah
Tel: 355021
Cable: Bancolanda
Telex: 68467 Abnsh EM
Telefax: 546036

PRINCIPAL ACTIVITIES: Commercial banking
Branch Offices: In the Middle East: Bahrain; Saudi Arabia; Abu
Dhabi; Dubai; Sharjah; Lebanon; Morocco; Pakistan
Parent Company: Algemene Bank Nederland NV, Amsterdam

AL HAMRA ENGINEERING CO WLL
PO Box 769, Sharjah
Tel: 591755 (4 lines)
Cable: Al Hamra Sharjah
Telex: 68048 Hamra EM

Chairman: Yacoub Yousuf Al Hamad

Directors: Hanna Nicola Ayoub (President), Joseph Bermens Iskander (Managing Director)

PRINCIPAL ACTIVITIES: Construction division: general contracting and trading; mechanical section: plumbing and water supply services, fire fighting, drainage, swimming pool, airconditioning services etc; electrical section: power supply and distribution services, power generation etc; commercial division: sale and application of specialized materials for roofing and waterproofing and insulations, sports flooring

Principal Agencies: Vandex, Denmark; Ruberoid Building Products, UK; Isolite, Swimquip, USA; Fire Protection Equipments, CIB, France; Smid & Hollander ESHA, Netherlands; Inter Plastic (Austria); Weka Sports (Holland) etc

Branch Offices: In the UAE: PO Box 11801, Dubai; PO Box 6968/3835, Abu Dhabi; PO Box 15985 Al Ain

Parent Company: Hameng Holdings Ltd, PO Box 2048, Safat, Kuwait

Associated Companies: Al Hamra Eng Co SARL, PO Box 6040, Beirut, Lebanon; Al Hamra Kuwait Co WLL, PO Box 2048, Safat, Kuwait, Al Hamra Eng (London) Ltd, 77 Princedale Road, Holland Park, London W11 4NS (UK); Al Hamra Saudia Ltd, PO Box 10223, Riyadh, Saudi Arabia; Hameng Holdings Ltd, PO Box 2048, Safat, Kuwait; Hamra Mazoun Civil Const & Buildings LLC, PO Box 415, Muscat, Sultanate of Oman

Principal Bankers: Arab Bank Ltd, Sharjah; Commercial Bank of Dubai Ltd, Sharjah

Financial Information:

	Dh'000
Authorised capital	5,000
Paid-up capital	5,000

Principal Shareholders: Directors as described above
Date of Establishment: 1974 (Sharjah - UAE)
No of Employees: 275

ALJABOR SHIPPING & FORWARDING CO

PO Box 5906, Sharjah
Tel: 357450, 354553
Cable: ALJABOR
Telex: 68184 JABOR

Chairman: Sheikh Jabor Bin Mohamad Al Thani
Senior Executives: M Nazir Hossain (General Manager), S S A Meerza (Shipping Manager), S A Zafar

PRINCIPAL ACTIVITIES: Shipowners, agency, clearing and fowarding and intergulf road transportation
Branch Offices: Doha
Principal Bankers: United Bank Ltd; Middle East Bank Ltd

Date of Establishment: 1976

ALLIED ENGINEERING ENTERPRISES

PO Box 1876, Sharjah
Tel: 24573, 25667, 25668
Cable: Allied Sharjah
Telex: 68071 Allied EM

PRINCIPAL ACTIVITIES: Building and civil engineering contractors
Branch Offices: Abu Dhabi, Dubai, Ras Al Khaimah, Ajman

AL MANAR TRADING & CONTRACTING CO LTD

PO Box 621, Sharjah
Tel: 356284

Chairman: Salem Ali Al Mahmoodh (Owner)

PRINCIPAL ACTIVITIES: General trading and contracting, transportation
Subsidiary Companies: Al Manar Medco; Sharjah Express

AL MASHREK MARBLE CO (MARBLO)

PO Box 682, Sharjah
Tel: 333121, 332683
Cable: Al Marblo
Telex: 68031 Marblo EM
Telefax: 330126

Chairman: Said Khoury
Directors: Jamil Shammas (President), Antoine Daou (General Manager)
Senior Executives: Imad T Saad (Emirates Manager)

PRINCIPAL ACTIVITIES: Import, export of all kinds of marble and granite
Branch Offices: Arabian Gulf countries
Subsidiary Companies: Arab Marble Co, Beirut, Lebanon; Al Jazirah Marble Co, Riyadh; San Dikili Mermer Co, Turkey
Principal Bankers: Investbank, Sharjah
Financial Information:

	1988/89 Dh'000	1989/90 Dh'000
Sales turnover	3,500	3,000
Profits	350	310
Authorised capital	3,000	3,000
Paid-up capital	3,000	3,000
Total assets	8,200	4,800

AL NASR TRADING COMPANY

PO Box 204, Sharjah
Tel: 22657
Cable: Alnasr Sharjah

PRINCIPAL ACTIVITIES: General trading and contracting and civil engineering
Parent Company: Al Nasr Trading Organisation, Qatar
Associated Companies: Al Nasr Trading Co (Dubai, Abu Dhabi); Al-Alawi Factories (Bahrain)

AL OMRAN TRADING AGENCIES

PO Box 1694, Sharjah
Tel: 593597/8
Telex: 868414 Omran

PRINCIPAL ACTIVITIES: Electrical engineering, motors, pumps, sewage systems, hardware
Principal Agencies: Valley Pumps, USA; Fortunia, Italy; Holden & Brooke, UK; Crompton Greaves, India; Jones & Attwood Ltd, UK; Kodai Dorloc, Japan
Branch Offices: Mohamed Abdulla Al Omran Est, PO Box 804, Dubai, Tel 220916, Telex 46266; Al Omran Company, PO Box 501, Abu Dhabi, Tel 822263, Telex 23371

AL QASEMI TRADING & INDUSTRY CO

PO Box 3050, Sharjah
Tel: 545702, 353000
Telex: 68668 Alborj EM

Chairman: Sheikh Mohammed Bin Saoud Al Qasemi
Directors: Eng Arsalan Anwar A Murshed (Managing Director)

PRINCIPAL ACTIVITIES: Trading in furniture, carpets, furnishings and agricultural equipment
Principal Agencies: Jose Serret, Spain; Dita Dolfi; Nisshiki Trdg, & Industrial Co; Piltex; Aminco Orient, W Stallmann-Germany
Subsidiary Companies: Al Zahra Shopping Centre; Al Borj Trading Co
Principal Bankers: Investbank, Sharjah; National Bank of Sharjah, Sharjah
Financial Information:

	1989 Dh'000
Sales turnover	15,000
Profits	2,000
Authorised capital	1,000
Paid-up capital	1,000
Total assets	7,000

Principal Shareholders: Shaikha Naema Bint Mohd Al Qasemi;
Shaikh Saoud Bin Mohd Al Qasemi
Date of Establishment: 1967
No of Employees: 45

AL SAGR INSURANCE (UAE) CO LTD

PO Box 4412, Sharjah
Tel: 374686
Telex: 68125 ARIC EM
Telefax: 526771

Senior Executives: Cesar Geadah (Manager Sharjah Branch)

PRINCIPAL ACTIVITIES: All classes of insurance
Parent Company: Head office in Dubai

AL SAQA TRADING EST

PO Box 438, Sharjah
Tel: 354477, 23840, 22281
Cable: Al Saqa Sharjah
Telex: 68087 EM

PRINCIPAL ACTIVITIES: General trading, import and distribution
of building materials and foodstuffs

ALSHAMSI TRADING & CONTRACTING CO

PO Box 559, Sharjah
Tel: 354237
Cable: SHAMSICO
Telex: 68194 ALSHAM EM

Chairman: Abdullah Hamad Alshamsi
Senior Executives: Farooq Sultan (General Manager)

PRINCIPAL ACTIVITIES: Civil engineering contracting, block
factory, ready mix concrete, aluminium factory, joinery,
crushing plant, quarry, trading, building materials
Branch Offices: Abudhabi; Khorfakan, Zaid
Subsidiary Companies: Multi Link Enterprize; Sharjah Aluminium
Factory
Principal Bankers: Bank of Credit & Commerce Sharjah;
National Bank of Sharjah
Financial Information:

	Dh'000
Paid-up capital	28,000

Principal Shareholders: Sole Proprietorship
Date of Establishment: 1967
No of Employees: 500

AL SHIRAWI TRADING & CONTRACTING CO

PO Box 542, Sharjah
Tel: 22826

PRINCIPAL ACTIVITIES: General trading and contracting;
import and distribution of building materials, sanitary ware,
paints, etc

ANZ GRINDLAYS BANK PLC

PO Box 357, Al Bourj Ave, Sharjah
Tel: 359998
Cable: Grindlay
Telex: 68011 Grndly EM

PRINCIPAL ACTIVITIES: Commercial banking
Branch Offices: In the Middle East: Bahrain; Oman; Qatar; Abu
Dhabi; Al Ain; Dubai; Sharjah; Ras Al Khaimah; Jordan and
Pakistan

No of Employees: 24

ARAB BANK PLC

PO Box 130, Sharjah
Tel: 22333/4
Cable: Bankarabi
Telex: 68223 Arabnk EM

PRINCIPAL ACTIVITIES: Commercial banking

Branch Offices: Bahrain; Abu Dhabi; Dubai; Sharjah; Ras Al
Khaimah; Ajman; Qatar; Oman; Lebanon; Saudi Arabia;
Yemen; Tunisia; Morocco
Parent Company: Head office in Amman, Jordan

ARABCO ALUMINIUM

PO Box 638, Sharjah
Tel: 353185
Cable: Arabco
Telex: 68542 Zarab EM

PRINCIPAL ACTIVITIES: Dealers in all kinds of aluminium
joinery, windows, doors and all aluminium products

ARABIAN CONSTRUCTION CO SHARJAH LTD

PO Box 609, Sharjah
Tel: 354665 (3 lines)
Cable: ACC
Telex: 68542 ACCSH Em
Telefax: 549304

Chairman: Ghassan Merehbi
Directors: Riyad Mikati (General Manager)
Senior Executives: Abdul Hamid Mikati (Plant Manager), Hamed
Mikati (Chief Estimator), Omar Mikati (Asst. Finance Manager)

PRINCIPAL ACTIVITIES: Construction of buildings and civil
works
Branch Offices: PO Box 6876, Beirut, Lebanon; PO Box 2113,
Abu Dhabi, UAE; PO Box 5350, Doha Qatar; PO Box 17713,
Riyadh, Saudi Arabia
Parent Company: Arabian Construction Company Group SA,
Luxembourg
Principal Bankers: Investbank, Sharjah
Financial Information:

	1988/89 Dh'000
Sales turnover	78,321
Profits	3,559
Authorised capital	6,000
Paid-up capital	6,000
Total assets	218,633

Principal Shareholders: Ghassan Merehbi, Taha Mikati, Anas
Mikati
Date of Establishment: 1976
No of Employees: 1,070

ARABIAN GULF TRADING CO

PO Box 46, Sharjah
Tel: 971-6-330122 (4 lines), 330194
Cable: AGTCO
Telex: 68117 AGTCO EM
Telefax: 971-6-337244

Chairman: Mohammed Sherif Zaman
Directors: Mohammed Abdullah Khayal
Senior Executives: Othman Sherif Zaman (General Manager),
Yousuf Ali (Chief Accountant)

PRINCIPAL ACTIVITIES: Import and stockists of building
materials, steel, timber, plywood, cement
Principal Agencies: Qatar Steel Co, Doha
Principal Bankers: National Bank of Sharjah; Commercial Bank
of Dubai, Sharjah

Date of Establishment: 1969
No of Employees: 80

ARCHIDORON GULF CO LTD

PO Box 1930, Sharjah
Tel: 356672
Cable: Archidoron
Telex: 68111 Arcdon EM

PRINCIPAL ACTIVITIES: Building and general contractors

UAE (Sharjah)

ATLAS TRADING & CONTRACTING CO

PO Box 1240, Sharjah
Tel: 592329
Cable: Lakis
Telex: 22713 EM Hamcon

Senior Executives: Antoine Lakis (General Manager and Owner)

PRINCIPAL ACTIVITIES: General trading, building and civil
engineering contractors
Principal Bankers: Invest Bank; Commercial Bank of Dubai
Financial Information:

	Dh'000
Sales turnover	10,000
Authorised capital	2,000
Paid-up capital	2,000

Date of Establishment: 1973
No of Employees: 250

BANK MELLI IRAN

PO Box 459, Al Arooba St, Sharjah
Tel: 23710, 22510
Cable: Bankmelli
Telex: 68461 Bkmeli EM

PRINCIPAL ACTIVITIES: Commercial banking
Branch Offices: Regional Office: PO Box 1894, Deira, Dubai
Parent Company: Head office in Tehran, Iran

BANK OF BARODA

PO Box 1671, Sharjah
Tel: 358273
Telex: 68133 Baroda EM

PRINCIPAL ACTIVITIES: Commercial banking
Branch Offices: Abu Dhabi, Dubai, Fujairah, Ras Al Khaimah,
Umm Al Quwain
Parent Company: Head office in Baroda, India

BANK OF CREDIT & COMMERCE (EMIRATES)

PO Box 5106, Sharjah
Tel: 354151
Telex: 68241 BCC OS EM

PRINCIPAL ACTIVITIES: Commercial banking
Branch Offices: Abu Dhabi, Al Ain, Dubai, Fujairah, Ras Al
Khaimah
Parent Company: Head office in Abu Dhabi

Date of Establishment: 1982

BANK OF CREDIT & COMMERCE INTERNATIONAL SA

PO Box 713, Sharjah
Tel: 549935 (6 lines)
Cable: Bancrecom
Telex: 68121 Bcci EM

PRINCIPAL ACTIVITIES: Commercial banking
Branch Offices: Abu Dhabi, Dubai, Sharjah, Ajman

BANK OF OMAN LTD

PO Box 2082, Sharjah
Tel: 351366 (4 lines)
Cable: BANOMAN SHARJAH
Telex: 68628 OMNSHJ EM
Telefax: 372903

Senior Executives: Amjad Nawaz (Manager), S Shahnawaz
Bokhari (Operations Manager)

PRINCIPAL ACTIVITIES: Commercial banking
Branch Offices: Abu Dhabi, Dubai, Ajman, Fujairah, Ras Al
Khaimah, Sharjah, Umm Al Qaiwain
Parent Company: Head office in Dubai

BANK OF SHARJAH LTD

Al Bourj Avenue, PO Box 1394, Sharjah
Tel: 352111
Cable: Sharjabank
Telex: 68039 Bank EM, 68065 Bosfx EM
Telefax: 350323

Honorary Chairman: HH Dr Sheikh Sultan Bin Mohamed Al
Qassimi; Chairman: Mubarak Abdul Aziz Al-Hassawi
Directors: Salem Al-Mazroa (Vice President), HE Humeid Naser
Al Owais, Mohamed Hamad Al Shamsi, Ahmad Al Noman,
Abdul Aziz Al Midfa, Abdul Rahman Bukhater, Omran Al
Borno, Saud Al Besharah, Hubert de Saint Amand, HE Claude
de Kemoularia, Francis Caze
Senior Executives: Rachid Naceur B H (General Manager),
Varouj Nerguizian (Manager)

PRINCIPAL ACTIVITIES: Commercial banking
Branch Offices: Abu Dhabi Branch: PO Box 27391, Tel 213555,
215936, Telex 23104
Principal Bankers: Manufacturers Hanover Trust (New York);
Fidelity International Bank (New York); National Westminster
Bank (London); Banque Paribas (London); Banque Paribas
(Paris)
Financial Information:

	1990 Dh'000
Profits	12,035
Authorised capital	70,000
Paid-up capital	70,000
Total assets	811,417

Principal Shareholders: Government of Sharjah (9.64%); Banque
Paribas (France) (15%); Mubarak Abdul Aziz Al Hassawi
(Kuwait) (5%), public subscription (70.36%)
Date of Establishment: December 1973
No of Employees: 98

BANK SADERAT IRAN

Sheikh Saif Rd, PO Box 316, Sharjah
Tel: 355155
Cable: Saderbank
Telex: 8145

PRINCIPAL ACTIVITIES: Commercial banking
Branch Offices: Abu Dhabi; Dubai; Sharjah; Al Ain; Ras Al
Khaimah; Fujairah; Umm Al Qaiwan
Parent Company: Head office in Tehran, Iran

BANQUE DE L'ORIENT ARABE ET D'OUTRE MER

BANORABE

PO Box 5803, Sharjah
Tel: 06-593361
Telex: 68512 Bano EM
Telefax: 596413

PRINCIPAL ACTIVITIES: Commercial banking
Branch Offices: Dubai
Parent Company: Head office in Paris, France
Subsidiary Companies: Banque du Liban et d'Outre-Mer SAL

BANQUE DU CAIRE

PO Box 254, Sharjah
Tel: 22946
Cable: Bancaire
Telex: 66780 EM, 68228 EM

PRINCIPAL ACTIVITIES: Commercial banking
Branch Offices: Abu Dhabi, Dubai, Ras Al Khaimah
Parent Company: Head office in Cairo, Egypt

BANQUE INDOSUEZ

PO Box 2086, Sharjah
Tel: 356362, 354404
Cable: Indousuez
Telex: 68190 Indosu EM

PRINCIPAL ACTIVITIES: Commercial banking
Branch Offices: In the Middle East; Dubai; Bahrain; Yemen AR; Saudi Arabia; Lebanon
Associated Companies: Banque Libano Francaise, Beirut; Banque Sabbag et Francaise pour le Moyen Orient, Beirut

Principal Shareholders: Compagnie Financiere de Suez
Date of Establishment: 1850

BANQUE LIBANAISE POUR LE COMMERCE SA

PO Box 854, Sharjah
Tel: 355161
Telex: 68088 EM

PRINCIPAL ACTIVITIES: Commercial banking
Branch Offices: Abu Dhabi, Dubai, Ras Al Khaimah
Parent Company: Head office in Paris, France

BARCLAYS BANK PLC

PO Box 1953, G 2 Al Boorj Avenue, Sharjah
Tel: 355288 (5 lines)
Cable: Barint, Sharjah
Telex: 68100 BARSHA EM
Telefax: 543498

Chairman: Sir John Quinton
Senior Executives: G Abbas Khawaja (Branch Manager), S V Pai (Accountant)

PRINCIPAL ACTIVITIES: Commercial banking
Branch Offices: In UAE: PO Box 1891, Dubai and PO Box 2734, Abu Dhabi
Parent Company: Barclays Bank Plc, 54 Lombard Street, London, UK

Date of Establishment: In Sharjah: 1975
No of Employees: 22

BICC MIDDLE EAST LTD

PO Box 1445, Sharjah
Tel: 354497
Telex: 68147 Bicc EM

PRINCIPAL ACTIVITIES: General trading and contracting, supply of electrical equipment and fittings, generators, power and welding equipment
Branch Offices: Abu Dhabi; Dubai; Ras Al Khaimah

BIN MASOOD, MOHAMMED, & SONS

PO Box 390, Sharjah
Tel: 22737

PRINCIPAL ACTIVITIES: Import and distribution of tyres and spare parts, motor vehicles, electrical equipment, building materials, household goods, etc
Principal Agencies: Dunlop, Electrolux
Parent Company: Head office in Abu Dhabi

BLAKEDOWN GULF LTD

PO Box 88, Sharjah
Tel: 356682
Telex: 68608 BDOWN EM

Chairman: Les Bailey
Directors: John H May, Parvez Amin, Norman Turner

PRINCIPAL ACTIVITIES: Contractors in landscaping, irrigation and related agricultural and horticultural activities
Branch Offices: PO Box 3636, Doha, Qatar, Tel 831041 Telex 4645 Dico Dh; Blakedown Manterak Int, PO Box 7093, Jeddah, Saudi Arabia, Tel 665-7029, Telex 400120 Tamco SJ; Blakedown Gulf, Tel 3865 2226, Telex 336913 Blkdwn G

Principal Bankers: State Bank of India, OBU, Bahrain

Date of Establishment: 1977
No of Employees: 100

BRITISH BANK OF THE MIDDLE EAST (THE)

PO Box 25, Sh Faisal Bldg, Al Arooba St, Sharjah
Tel: 350055
Cable: Bactria
Telex: 68044 BBMESH EM
Telefax: 06-374440

Chairman: W Purves CBE DSO
Directors: J R H Bond, F J French, J M Gray, J A P Hill CBE, S Robertson, P J Wrangham
Senior Executives: A Gent (Manager Sharjah)

PRINCIPAL ACTIVITIES: Commercial banking
Branch Offices: Other branches in the UAE: Abu Dhabi, Jebel Ali (FTZ), Al Ain, Deira, Dubai, Fujairah, Ras Al Khaimah
Parent Company: The Hongkong & Shanghai Banking Corporation
Subsidiary Companies: Middle East Finance Co Ltd, Dubai

Principal Shareholders: The Hongkong and Shanghai Banking Corporation (100%)
Date of Establishment: Sharjah Office established in February 1953

BRITISH ELECTRICAL REPAIRS LTD (ME)

BERL Middle East

PO Box 6480, Sharjah
Tel: 545118
Cable: Berl Em
Telex: 68524 Berl Em

Chairman: The Hon G H Wilson
Directors: A G Adlington (Managing Director), John Broadbent, Paul Anslem, Sulieman Jassim

PRINCIPAL ACTIVITIES: Electrical motors and transformers repairing
Branch Offices: BERL Middle East, PO Box 247, Abu Dhabi
Principal Bankers: British Bank of the Middle East, Sharjah

Principal Shareholders: Delta Group PLC, Sulieman Jassim
Date of Establishment: 1977
No of Employees: 32 in the middle east

BUILDING MATERIALS IMPORT CO

PO Box 6098, Al Wahda St, Nasser Ibrahim El Dheeb Bldg, Sharjah
Tel: 592651
Telex: 68154 Bumat EM

Chairman: Berj K Bedrossian (General Manager)

PRINCIPAL ACTIVITIES: Import and trade of building materials, sanitary ware, ceramics, reconstituted marble and kitchen furniture
Principal Agencies: Pozzi-Ginori, Salvarani, Astra, Rover S.p.a.
Branch Offices: Dubai, Tel 660874; Ras Al Khaimah, Tel 28224
Principal Bankers: Banque Libanaise Pour Le Commerce
Financial Information:

	Dh'000
Paid-up capital	1,500

Principal Shareholders: B K Bedrossian; Youssef R Boresly; Ghaneh Ibrahim Al Dheeb, Seif R Hamarein
Date of Establishment: 1975
No of Employees: 28

BUKHATIR INVESTMENTS LTD

PO Box 88, Sharjah
Tel: 3524401/2/3
Cable: Salaah Sharjah
Telex: 68033 Burkat EM

Chairman: Abdulrahman Mohamed Bukhatir

UAE (Sharjah)

Directors: Abdulla Bukhatir

PRINCIPAL ACTIVITIES: Building and civil engineering contractors, real estate and land development, property management, hotel owners, trading and contracting, import and distribution of building materials, cement, electrical and electronic equipment, refrigeration and air-conditioning equipment, photographic equipment, sole agents for excavators and lorry-mounted hydro cranes, concrete pumps, manufacture of polystyrene and polyurethane products, aluminium doors and windows

Associated Companies: Eastern Contracting Co, National Hotels Ltd, Modern Hotels Ltd, Marbella Club, Conmix Ltd, Emitac Ltd, Alumtech (UAE) Ltd, Euro-Arab Investments Ltd, German Gulf Enterprises, Bucomac Ltd, Nitco-Miller Ltd, Plastifoam (UAE) Ltd, Flotilla Ltd, Sharjah Real Estate Co, Trade House Inc, Conforce (Gulf) Ltd, Architectural Consultants, Bukhatir Mackinnon

Principal Bankers: National Bank of Sharjah; Bank of Sharjah

BYRNE DRILLING CO

PO Box 5228, Sharjah
Tel: 332810, 338913
Telex: 68080 Bydrco EM
Telefax: 336097

Chairman: Francis James Byrne

PRINCIPAL ACTIVITIES: Drilling, oilfield services, plant hire
Associated Companies: Desert Byrne Drilling LLC, PO Box 1431, Seeb, Sultanate of Oman
Principal Bankers: Barclays Bank, Sharjah

Principal Shareholders: F J Byrne
Date of Establishment: 1977
No of Employees: 25

CARLTON SHARJAH HOTEL

PO Box 1198, Sharjah
Tel: 523711
Cable: Carlton Sharjah
Telex: 68012 Cartel EM
Telefax: 374962

Chairman: Mubarak Abdulaziz Al Hassawi
Directors: Jamal Al Alami (Managing Director)
Senior Executives: Rafic Habib (General Manager)

PRINCIPAL ACTIVITIES: Hotel operation
Parent Company: Kuwait Commercial Real Estate Co
Associated Companies: Continental Hotel, Sharjah; Chicago Beach Hotel, Dubai
Principal Bankers: United Arab Bank, Sharjah
Financial Information:

| | 1990 |
	Dh'000
Sales turnover	10,000
Profits	2,682
Authorised capital	3,325
Paid-up capital	3,325
Total assets	4,423

Date of Establishment: 1973
No of Employees: 118

CENTRAL BANK OF THE UAE

PO Box 645, Sharjah
Tel: 354515
Telex: 68078 Markzi EM
Telefax: 543967

Chairman: Sheikh Suroor Bin Mohammed Al Nahyan
Directors: Mohammed Abdullah Al Kaz (Vice Chairman)
Senior Executives: Mohammed S Al Musharikh (Branch Manager)

PRINCIPAL ACTIVITIES: Central banking

Branch Offices: Dubai; Ras Al Khaimah; Fujairah; Al Ain
Parent Company: Head office in Abu Dhabi

Date of Establishment: 1975

CITIBANK NA

PO Box 346, Shiekh Zamid Bldg, Al Arooba St, Sharjah
Tel: 22533
Cable: Citibank
Telex: 68075 EM Citbk

PRINCIPAL ACTIVITIES: Commercial banking
Branch Offices: Dubai; Deira; Abu Dhabi; Al Ain
Parent Company: Citicorp, New York, USA

CME CONTRACTING MARINE ENGINEERING

PO Box 1859, Sharjah
Tel: 354511
Cable: Figawly
Telex: 68069 Cme EM

Chairman: Dr F El-Gawly
Senior Executives: Eng S Tawfik (Mechanical Superintendent), Eng K Mehta (Civil Superintendent)

PRINCIPAL ACTIVITIES: Turnkey industrial projects, water and electricity plants, building construction, marine works
Branch Offices: Greece, Piraeus, 17 King Paul's Ave, Tlx 213365; Cairo, 21 Morad Street; Stuttgart, Olgastr 77, Tlx 723770; Ajman (UAE), PO Box 1513, Tel 421538, Telex 68069
Subsidiary Companies: CME (Buildings); CME (Real estate); Prince offshore Bunkering Co; Al Mazroei Trading and Contracting Co
Principal Bankers: Bank of Credit and Commerce International, Deira, Dubai; Investbank, Sharjah
Financial Information:

	Dh'000
Authorised capital	18,000

Principal Shareholders: Dr F El-Gawly; Klaus Stufft; Helma Greuel-Mainz
Date of Establishment: 1975
No of Employees: 180

COMMERCIAL BANK OF DUBAI

PO Box 677, Sharjah
Tel: 355201, 22520
Cable: Trubank
Telex: 68116 EM

PRINCIPAL ACTIVITIES: Commercial banking
Branch Offices: Abu Dhabi, Dubai, Ras Al Khaimah
Parent Company: Head office in Dubai

COOPERS & LYBRAND DELOITTE

PO Box 3615, Sharjah
Tel: 546499
Telex: 46696 DHS DB EM

Chairman: D Brewer, Dr F Saba
Partners: Tim J B Heaton, Malcolm Best, Andrew Evans, Habib Nehme, Alfred Strolla, Camille Sifri

PRINCIPAL ACTIVITIES: Chartered accountants, management consultants and computer services
Branch Offices: Offices in the Middle East: Abu Dhabi; Bahrain; Dubai; Oman; Sharjah; Saudi Arabia and Lebanon
Parent Company: Head offices in London and New York

COSMOPLAST INDUSTRIAL CO WLL

PO Box 6032, Sharjah
Tel: 6-331264
Cable: Coplast
Telex: 68578 Copol EM
Telefax: 6-331917

Chairman: Yousri Dweik

Directors: Harout Ohanesian, Amjad Dweik, Taryam Omran Taryam, Abdulla Omran Taryam

Senior Executives: Peter B Spencer (General Manager), Walid Najjar (Technical Manager), Ian Mitchell (Finance Manager), Munir Ahmed (Chief Accountant)

PRINCIPAL ACTIVITIES: Manufacture and distribution of uPVC and polyethelene pipes, injection and blow moulded household and refrigerating items, well casing, polythelene sheets, shopping bags, etc

Associated Companies: Interplast Co Ltd, PO Box 4679, Sharjah

Principal Bankers: Standard Chartered Bank, Sharjah

Financial Information:

	1990
	Dh'000
Paid-up capital	12,000

Principal Shareholders: Chairman and directors as above
Date of Establishment: 1977
No of Employees: 320

CRESCENT PETROLEUM COMPANY

PO Box 211, Sharjah
Tel: 543000
Cable: Crespt
Telex: 68015 Crespt EM
Telefax: 542000

Chairman: Hamid D Jafar (Chief Executive Officer)
Directors: Dr Hilmi Samara, John F Martin
Senior Executives: Hosam A Raouf (Deputy Chairman), Michael Woolgar (Director, Finance), Martin F Whitehead (VP Operations), Walter Sequiera (Chief Accountant), Dr Hilmi Samara (Senior Director, Technical), Mazher A Alvie (Petroleum Sales Coordinator), Kamal A Ataya (VP Commercial), Daniel Oscar Mascarenhas (Administration Manager), Sadiq Jafar (Legal Counsel)

PRINCIPAL ACTIVITIES: Petroleum exploration, production and marketing
Principal Bankers: Investment Bank for Trade & Finance, Sharjah

Date of Establishment: 1972
No of Employees: 200

DELMON OILFIELD SUPPLY CO

PO Box 1297, Sharjah
Tel: 354765, 356171
Telex: 68193 Delmon EM
Telefax: 354705

Chairman: Saeed Mohamed Ali Al Salman
Directors: Mohamad Shams
Senior Executives: Bob White (Operations & Sales Manager), K V Kumar (Accountant)

PRINCIPAL ACTIVITIES: Supply of oilfield equipment, tools and machinery, plant hire
Principal Agencies: Bowen; David Brown Vosper; Dunlop; FMC Weco Chiksan; Oteco; Polyken; Rapid Supply Co; Resinex; Rush Johnson, Uniroyal
Parent Company: Delmon Oilfield Supply Company, PO Box 880, Bahrain
Subsidiary Companies: Al Salman General Trading, Dubai
Principal Bankers: Union Bank of the Middle East Ltd, Dubai
Financial Information:

	1988/89
	Dh'000
Sales turnover	10,000
Profits	1,000
Authorised capital	1,000
Paid-up capital	1,000
Total assets	5,000

Principal Shareholders: Mohamed Shams, Saeed Mohamed Ali Al Salman
Date of Establishment: 1975

DEMAS & AL FARHAN ENGINEERING & CONTRACTING CO

PO Box 515, Sharjah
Tel: 593333, 592222
Cable: Dafco
Telex: 68106 EM
Telefax: 596531

Chairman: Rashid Ali Rashid Al Demas
Directors: Mahmood Abdul Wahid Al Farhan (Managing Director)
Senior Executives: Hamed Abdul Rahman (Property Director), Mohammadi Abu Zaid (Technical Director), Abdul Moiez Al Sabaee (Production Director), Akeel Hamoudi (Sales Director),Ahmed Mabrook (Finance Advisor), Mrs Sohaer Mohammed Ahmed (Personnel Manager)

PRINCIPAL ACTIVITIES: Contracting, ready mixed concrete, concrete products of hollow and solid blocks, paving slabs, kerbstones, interlocking blocks
Branch Offices: Dafco Block Factory, Dhaid, Sharjah, Dafco Kor Fakkan, Tel 86888
Associated Companies: Dafco Ready Mixed Concrete Plant Co WLL; Dafco Concrete Products Industries Co WLL
Principal Bankers: British Bank of the Middle East; Grindlays Bank; National Bank of Abu Dhabi; United Arab Bank
Financial Information:

	1990
	Dh'000
Authorised capital	4,000
Paid-up capital	4,000
Total assets	35,000

Principal Shareholders: Rashid Ali Demas, Mehmood Abdul Wahad Al Farhan
Date of Establishment: 1969
No of Employees: 200

DHL INTERNATIONAL (SHARJAH) LTD

Hassan Habid Bldg, King Faisal Street, PO Box 5771, Sharjah
Tel: 357462, 353568
Telex: 45799 DHL EM (DUBAI)

PRINCIPAL ACTIVITIES: Worldwide courier service for documents and small parcels; air and sea freight clearance and forwarding; marketing word processors and related office equipment

EASTERN (TRADING & MARKETING DIVISION)

PO Box 4621, Sharjah
Tel: 333233
Telex: 68074 EASTRN EM
Telefax: 332020

Chairman: Abdul Rahman Bukhatir
Directors: Obeid Rashid Shamsi
Senior Executives: Mario R Cordeiro (Manager), Deepak Dhingra (Manager International Division)

PRINCIPAL ACTIVITIES: Trading and marketing of electrical, mechanical, civil materials, sport equipment, exclusive agencies
Principal Agencies: Brush Switchgear Ltd, UK; Irish Cable & Wires Ltd, Ireland; Keyson Ltd, UK; Halfeneisen GmbH Co, Germany; Ott International, Germany; Industrie Face Standard (ITT), Italy; Filli Campion, Italy; Schroder & Henzelmann, Germany, Zephyr Flag Poles, UK; Brush Transformer, Italy; Sport Gerlach, Germany, NSF, Denmark
Branch Offices: PO Box 5231, Dubai; PO Box 6790, Abu Dhabi
Parent Company: Bukhatir Investments Ltd, PO Box 88, Sharjah
Subsidiary and Associate Companies: Eastern Trading Ltd, PO Box 6790, Abu Dhabi; Conforce/Eastern Trading, PO Box 5231, Dubai

Principal Bankers: National Bank of Sharjah; United Bank Ltd, Abu Dhabi
Financial Information:

	1989
	Dh'000
Sales turnover	12,000
Authorised capital	1,000
Paid-up capital	1,000

Principal Shareholders: Abdulrahman M Bukhatir, Obaid Rashid Al Shamsi
Date of Establishment: 1984
No of Employees: 20

ELECTRONIC & ENGINEERING INDUSTRIES

PO Box 5088, Sharjah
Tel: 592114, 592010
Telex: 68188 EEI

Chairman: George N Hawi

PRINCIPAL ACTIVITIES: Manufacture of insulation products, and insulated panels for building and coldstorage buildings and coldrooms
Branch Offices: Abu Dhabi, PO Box 3877, Tel 363481, Tlx 23155 JSEST
Principal Bankers: British Bank of the Middle East; Banque du Liban et d'Outre-Mer
Financial Information:

	Dh'000
Authorised capital	5,000
Paid-up capital	5,000

Principal Shareholders: George Hawi; Joan Salem Al Dahri; George Sarkis; Assaad Sarkis; Samir Khoury; Khalil Khoury
Date of Establishment: 1976
No of Employees: 30

EMELCO CONSTRUCTION & GENERAL TRADING

PO Box 1159, Sharjah
Tel: 23458/9

PRINCIPAL ACTIVITIES: Construction contractors; steel works; supply of electrical and air-conditioning equipment and maintenance

EMIRATES MARINE SERVICES EST

PO Box 5868, Sharjah
Tel: 357570, 351771
Telex: 68303 MASOOR

PRINCIPAL ACTIVITIES: Ship repair, electrical rewinds, steel fabrication, offshore maintenance
Subsidiary/Associated Companies: Kuwait Mechanical & Steel Fabrication Works
Principal Bankers: Barclays

Date of Establishment: 1977
No of Employees: 106

EMIRATES TECHNICAL SERVICES LTD

PO Box 2025, Sharjah
Tel: 334158
Telex: 680033 Burkat EM
Telefax: 971-6-336540

Chairman: Abdulrahman Bukhatir
Directors: A K Kamlani (Finance Director), Salah A Bukhatir (Marketing Director)
Senior Executives: Vikas B Mankar, Y Trinath (Group Manager)

PRINCIPAL ACTIVITIES: Contracting, fabrication, trading, interior, scaffolding hire, plant hire
Parent Company: Euro Arab Investments Ltd
Principal Bankers: Dubai Islamic Bank

Principal Shareholders: Abdulrahman Bukhatir
Date of Establishment: 1990
No of Employees: 100

EMITAC LIMITED

Emirates Technology Co Ltd

PO Box 1641, Sharjah
Tel: 591181
Cable: Emitac
Telex: 68136 Emitac EM

Chairman: Abdul Rahman Bukhatir
Directors: Brig Saqr Ghobash
Senior Executives: V Naroola (Chief Executive)

PRINCIPAL ACTIVITIES: Computers, medical, analytical and test instruments, air conditioners
Principal Agencies: Hewlett Packard; Imed International; Hill-Rom Company Inc, USA; Nicolet Instruments, UK; Bruel & Kjaer, Denmark; Exacon, Denmark; Amersham International PLC, UK; Industrie Guido Malvestio, Italy; Gandale Ltd, Canada, Hill Room, USA
Branch Offices: Emitac Limited, PO Box 2711, Abu Dhabi (UAE) Tel 820419; Emitac, PO Box 8040, Dubai (UAE) Tel 377591/373600
Subsidiary Companies: Datamation Systems, PO Box 8040, Dubai, (UAE); Technology Equipment Agencies, PO Box 8121, Dubai (UAE), Qatar Datamation Systems, Doha, Qatar
Principal Bankers: National Bank of Sharjah; Bank of Sharjah
Financial Information:

	1990
	Dh'000
Sales turnover	70,000
Authorised capital	10,000
Paid-up capital	6,000

Principal Shareholders: Bukhatir Investments Ltd (50%); legal heirs of Ghobash Ahmed Saeed (50%)
Date of Establishment: October 1974
No of Employees: 160

ERNST & WHINNEY

PO Box 1350, Sharjah
Tel: 23725, 352231
Telex: 68567
Telefax: 546751

PRINCIPAL ACTIVITIES: Accountants and management consultants
Branch Offices: In the Middle East; Bahrain; Jordan; Kuwait; Lebanon; Oman; Qatar; Saudi Arabia; Tunisia; United Arab Emirates (Abu Dhabi, Dubai, Sharjah), Yemen AR
Parent Company: Head office in the UK

Principal Shareholders: A member firm of Ernst & Whinney International

ETISALAT

PO Box 980, Sharjah
Tel: 355111
Telex: 68005 EM

PRINCIPAL ACTIVITIES: Telecommunications, telephone and telegraph systems
Branch Offices: Throughout the United Arab Emirates

E.T.P.M.

Entrepose G.T.M. pour les Travaux Petroliers Maritimes

Middle East Headquarters, PO Box 255, Sharjah
Tel: 355206 (18 lines)
Cable: Shentrapema
Telex: 68034 Etpm EM

Chairman & President: Andre Jarrosson

Directors: Gerard Fondimare (Executive Officer), Andre Lamarque (Executive Officer), Henri de Metz (Executive Officer), Jacques Touret (Vice-President Middle East)

PRINCIPAL ACTIVITIES: Design, engineering, fabrication and installation of: drilling platforms; production platforms; living quarters platforms; terminals, loading and unloading facilities for oil products; submarine pipelines, including trenching and burying operations; maintenance of offshore facilities; onshore pipe laying. Rental of derrick barges

Branch Offices: Head Office, Courcellor II, 33/35 rue d'Alsace, 92531 Levallois-Perret Cedex, France, Telex 612021 Etpm F; Middle East Branches: PO Box 6488, Abu Dhabi, UAE, Tel 342194, Telex 22505 Etpm; PO Box 998, Damman, Saudi Arabia, Tel 8263042, 8263187; Telex 601019 Redec; PO Box 1307, Tehran, Iran, Tel 656733

Parent Company: GTM-Entrepose

Financial Information: Consolidated

	US$'000
Authorised capital	14,500
Paid-up capital	14,500

No of Employees: 1,950

EURO ARAB INVESTMENTS LTD

PO Box 2025, Sharjah
Tel: 375062
Telex: 68033 Burkat EM

Chairman: Abdul Rahman Bukhatir
Directors: Q Noorani

PRINCIPAL ACTIVITIES: Real estate development and management
Parent Company: Bukhatir Investments Ltd
Principal Bankers: Barclays Bank Int Ltd

Principal Shareholders: Bukhatir Investments Ltd

EXPLORATION LOGGING ARABIAN GULF LTD

PO Box 5932, Sharjah
Tel: 592461, 592463
Telex: 68558 Beach EM

Chairman: HE Sheikh Sultan Bin Khalid Al-Qassimi
Senior Executives: Mohammed Saleem (Resident Engineer)

PRINCIPAL ACTIVITIES: Supply of mud logging services to the oil exploration industry, geological and petroleum engineering, wellsite consultants, geochemistry and other laboratory services, computerised instrumentation for oil rigs
Branch Offices: Abu Dhabi, PO Box 3374, Tel 722837, Telex 24183 Almans EM; Muscat, Sultanate of Oman, PO Box 919, Tel 602886, Telex 5113 SPONSOR ON

FAWAZ REFRIGERATION CO WLL

PO Box 1170, Sharjah
Tel: 594917, 591344
Cable: Fawazhawa
Telex: 68056 Fawaz EM
Telefax: 591342

Chairman: Mubarak Abdul Aziz Al Hasawi
Directors: Osama Hussain
Senior Executives: Bassam Saffarini (General Manager/Marketing & Sales), Helmi Badawieh, Basil Khartabil

PRINCIPAL ACTIVITIES: Refrigeration, central air conditioning and electromechanical services, trading, contracting and manufacturing
Branch Offices: Dubai, Abu Dhabi, Fujairah, Kuwait, Doha, Riyadh, Jeddah, Al Khobar, Baghdad, Amman, Aden
Principal Bankers: United Bank Ltd, Abu Dhabi Commercial Bank Ltd

No of Employees: 1100 (all branches)

FIRST GULF BANK

PO Box 3244, Sharjah
Tel: 357025
Telex: 68255

PRINCIPAL ACTIVITIES: Commercial banking
Branch Offices: Abu Dhabi
Parent Company: Head office in Ajman

Date of Establishment: 1979

FIRST NATIONAL BANK OF CHICAGO

PO Box 1278, Sharjah
Tel: 23532
Telex: 68073 Frchgo EM

PRINCIPAL ACTIVITIES: Commercial banking
Branch Offices: Abu Dhabi, Dubai
Parent Company: Head office in Chicago, USA

GAC TRADING (SHARJAH) LTD

PO Box 435, Sharjah
Tel: 22163

PRINCIPAL ACTIVITIES: General traders, suppliers and indentors; distribution of marine and industrial equipment, chemical plants, heavy electrical machinery, chemicals, foostuffs, pharmaceuticals, and medical supplies
Principal Agencies: Diversey, Asea, Gamlen

GECO MECHANICAL & ELECTRICAL LTD

PO Box 1150, Sharjah
Tel: 331727 (9 lines)
Cable: Geco Shj
Telex: 68020 Geco EM
Telefax: 336470

Chairman: Shaikh Ahmed Bin Mohammed Bin Sultan Al Qassimi
Vice Chairman: Shaikh Salem Bin Mohammed Bin Sultan Al Qassimi
Senior Executives: A A Mousoulides (Managing Director), S A S Rizvi (Contracts General Manager)

PRINCIPAL ACTIVITIES: Mechanical and electrical engineers and roofing contractors, i.e., airconditioning, refrigeration, cold storage, power generation and distribution, fire detection and protection, building services, electrical, plumbing, sanitary and maintenance, water distribution, water and effluent treatment and disposal, roof waterproofing
Principal Agencies: York International (Airconditioning Equipment), SWEPCO Water Proofing Products
Branch Offices: Abu Dhabi, PO Box 3298, Tel 339625, Fax 335610, Telex 24387 Geco EM; Dubai, PO Box 16297, Tel 667801, Telex 45528 Geco Em; Al Ain, Tel 666906; Fujairah PO Box 704, Tel 27116
Parent Company: Al Batha Trading & Industry Co
Associated Companies: Tecon Ltd; Gulf International; Al Oufouk; Arabian Gulf Mechanical Centre
Principal Bankers: Bank of Sharjah Ltd; National Bank of Sharjah
Financial Information:

	1988/89 Dh'000	1989/90 Dh'000
Sales turnover	25,000	30,000
Profits	1,250	1,750
Authorised capital	13,000	13,000
Paid-up capital	13,000	13,000
Total assets	21,000	22,000

Principal Shareholders: Chairman as described, Al Batha Trading & Industry Co, A A Mousoulides
Date of Establishment: 1957
No of Employees: 300

GENERAL MARINE SERVICES

PO Box 989, Sharjah
Tel: 23023, 23025, 355321, 355322
Telex: 68038 Genmar EM

PRINCIPAL ACTIVITIES: Shipping agents; supply of marine equipment and services; tug and barge owners and operators; offshore oilfield vessel brokers; bunkering and catering services

GERMAN GULF ENTERPRISES LTD

PO Box 5937, Sharjah
Tel: 591161, 591100
Telex: 68631 GGE EM
Telefax: 591128

Chairman: Abdul Rahman M Bukhatir
Directors: Rudolf Eller
Senior Executives: Siegfried Sammler (Administration Manager)

PRINCIPAL ACTIVITIES: General trading and contracting; import and distribution of earth moving equipment, construction equipment and heavy machinery, planning, construction and underwater grouting
Principal Agencies: Atlas Excavators and Cranes, Putzmeister Pumps, Mannesmann - Rexroth (HYDR Components), Griesheim Welding Equipment
Associated Companies: Bukhatir Investments Ltd; Conmix Ltd
Principal Bankers: National Bank of Sharjah, Commercial Bank of Dubai

Date of Establishment: 1974

GGP GROUP OF COMPANIES

PO Box 17, Sharjah
Tel: 22051, 351411
Telex: 68021 Khaldon EM

Chairman: HE Sheikh Abdul Aziz Bin Mohammed Al Qasimi (Owner)
Directors: V Damodar
Senior Executives: Peter O Walz, Walid Nounou, S N Mohsin, Hiralal Punjabi, N Shriram, S Rajan, Robi Chakravarti

PRINCIPAL ACTIVITIES: Trading, transport, joint-ventures, construction, real-estate, travel, vehicles, minerals, concrete, aluminium, glass, carpentry, lifts and electrical equipment, agriculture, fibre glass, advertising marketing, public relations consultancy, building systems
Principal Agencies: General Motors, USA; Lift Munich, Germany; Schoeller Hallen Bau, Austria; Mysore Plywood, India
Branch Offices: PO Box 4100, Abu Dhabi
Subsidiary/Associated Companies: GGP Construction Co, PO Box 17, Sharjah, Tel 22051, 351411 (Construction, Civil engineering); GGP Batching Plant, PO Box 17, Sharjah, Tel 355743, 351251 (Concrete); International Heated Forms Co Form Works, PO Box 17, Sharjah, Tel 22074, 354013; GGP Aluminium Co, PO Box 17, Sharjah, Tel 22168, (Aluminium/Glass/Carpentry) ABC Real Estate Co, PO Box 17, Sharjah, Tel 22051, 351411 (Real Estate); GGP Transport Co, PO Box 17, Sharjah, Tel 354167 (Transport); Sharjah National Travel Tourist Agency, PO Box 17. Sharjah, Tel 22051, 351411 (Travel, Freight and Aircraft Maintenance, Charters); Liberty Automobiles, PO Box 5506, Sharjah, Tel 23589, 23926 (Vehicles, Sales and Service); GGP Trading Co, PO Box 17, Sharjah, Tel 22051, 351411 (Trading/Joint Ventures); Agricultural Development Co, PO Box 17, Sharjah, Tel 354167, 82232 (Irrigation, Plantation); International Agency for Publishing Advertising & Marketing, PO Box 17, Sharjah, Tel 22051, 351411; Union Lift Co, PO Box 17, Sharjah, Tel 22151, 351411
Principal Bankers: United Arab Bank; Bank of Credit and Commerce International SA; Bank of Baroda; National Bank of Abu Dhabi; Investment Bank

Date of Establishment: 1975
No of Employees: 700

GIBCA

PO Box 289, Sharjah
Tel: 591433, 591444
Cable: Gibca Sharjah
Telex: 68082 Gibca EM

Chairman: HE Sheikh Faisal Bin Sultan Al-Qassimi
Directors: Sheikh Sultan Bin Saqr Al-Qassimi (Managing Director Sharjah), Sheikh Khalid Bin Saqr Al-Qassimi (Vice Chairman Abu Dhabi)

PRINCIPAL ACTIVITIES: Building and civil engineering contractors; manufacturers of aluminium windows, profiles, architectural castings; suppliers of crushed aggregates, readymixed concrete, cleaning materials; project developers and manufacturers' representatives
Principal Agencies: Plessey, Rolls Royce, Hitachi, Ruston Gas Turbines, Heras Fencing
Parent Company: Head office in Abu Dhabi
Associated Companies: Gibca Abu Dhabi; Gibca Crushing & Quarry Operations Co; Gibca Transport Corporation Ltd; Gibca Electro-mechanical Co (GEMCO); Readymix Gulf Ltd; Inter Emirates Trading & Contracting; Arabian Profile Ltd; Ema Lubricants Co; Alico Industries Co Ltd; Aluminium & Light Industries Co (ALICO); Continental Trading Est; Specialities
Principal Bankers: United Arab Bank Abu Dhabi, Sharjah; Grindlays Bank, Sharjah
Financial Information:

	Dh'000
Authorised capital	20,000
Paid-up capital	20,000

Principal Shareholders: HE Sheikh Faisal Bin Sultan Al-Qassimi
No of Employees: 800

GIBCA TRANSPORT CORP LTD

PO Box 289, Sharjah
Tel: 23163
Cable: Gibca
Telex: 68082 EM

PRINCIPAL ACTIVITIES: Transport contractors, supply of hydraulic excavators, air compressors, dumpers, also aggregate and sand

GULF AGENCY CO (SHARJAH) WLL

PO Box 435, Sharjah
Tel: 544446
Cable: Confidence
Telex: 68019 GAC SHJ EM
Telefax: 524091

Senior Executives: Joseph Chacko (General Manager)

PRINCIPAL ACTIVITIES: Shipping, ship supply services, clearing and forwarding, warehousing
Principal Agencies: NYK, Hinode, Sanko, CCWW, Yukiong Lines
Branch Offices: Operation Offices: Sweden; UK; Norway; Turkey; Lebanon; Saudi Arabia; Kuwait; Bahrain; Oman; United Arab Emirates; Qatar; Greece; Korea: Singapore; USA; Pakistan; Nigeria; India; Hong Kong
Parent Company: Gulf Agency Company
Principal Bankers: British Bank of the Middle East, National Bank of Sharjah

Date of Establishment: 1969

GULF AGRICULTURE DEVELOPMENT CO

PO Box 5686, Sharjah
Tel: 356711, 356714, 356715, 356712, 356713
Cable: GADCO
Telex: 68330 GADCO EM

Chairman: Fawzi Mousaed Al-Saleh
Senior Executives: Hamad Al-Salman (Deputy Chairman), Abdulwahab Ali Almutawa (Managing Director), Mansour

Bandar Husain (Deputy Managing Director & General Manager)

PRINCIPAL ACTIVITIES: Agriculture produce, agriculture equipment, fishing and fish processing, food processing, animal feeds, poultry raising

Branch Offices: Agriculture Investment Company, PO Box 25062, Safat, Kuwait, Tel 45775/4, Telex 44864 GADCO KT

Subsidiary Companies: Agriculture Trading and Development Company; International Plant; Ra'ad Food Stuff Co

Principal Bankers: Burgan Bank, Kuwait; First Gulf Bank, Ajman, UAE; Gulf Bank, Kuwait; Al-Ahli Bank, Kuwait

Financial Information:

	Dh'000
Authorised capital	200,000
Paid-up capital	200,000

Principal Shareholders: Abdulwahab Al-Ali-Al-Mutawa; Sharjah Group; Mansour Bandar Husain; Mousaed Al-Saleh Real Estate

Date of Establishment: 1977
No of Employees: 120

GULF BUILDING MATERIALS CO LTD

PO Box 1612, Sharjah
Tel: 354683
Telex: 68089 EM

PRINCIPAL ACTIVITIES: Production and supply of building materials. The company comprises a cement blocks plant, a woodwork plant, a tile and marble plant, an aluminium plant

Associated Companies: Engineering, Trading and Contracting Co Ltd, Sharjah

GULF CONVERTING INDUSTRIES CO

PO Box 1019, Sharjah
Tel: 592008, 592112
Cable: CONICO
Telex: 68184 JABOR
Telefax: 592956

Proprietor: HE Shaikh Jabor Bin Mohd Al Thani

Senior Executives: Malik M Riaz (General Manager), Maqbool Hussain (Production Engineer), Asif Ali Mirza (Sales Executive)

PRINCIPAL ACTIVITIES: Manufacture of consumer paper products, and distribution of allied paper and plastic products

Branch Offices: Doha (Qatar)

Associated Companies: Aljabor Shipping & Forwarding Co, Sharjah

Principal Bankers: Grindlays Bank; United Bank Ltd; Bank of Credit & Commerce International

Principal Shareholders: Proprietory Concern
Date of Establishment: 1974
No of Employees: 69

GULF FINANCIAL CENTRE

PO Box 5037, Sharjah
Tel: 358681/82
Cable: Almal
Telex: 68429 Almal EM

PRINCIPAL ACTIVITIES: Investment, financial services and real estate

Branch Offices: Kuwait

Date of Establishment: 1980

GULFTAINER CO LTD

PO Box 225, Sharjah
Tel: 354201/2
Telex: 68413 Tainer EM; 68207 Servic EM
Telefax: (971-6) 357711

Chairman: Hamid D Jafar

Directors: B R Coughlan (Managing Director)

Senior Executives: T Danesh (Finance Manager), A Gorton (Commercial Manager)

PRINCIPAL ACTIVITIES: Container terminal operators, shipping and forwarding agents; road haulage

Branch Offices: Khorfakkan Port

Associated Companies: Gulftainer Agencies; Sharjah Contaner Terminal; Trucktainer; Speedtrux Khorfakkan Container Terminal

Principal Bankers: Barclays Bank; Invest Bank

Date of Establishment: 1976
No of Employees: 300

HABIB BANK LIMITED

PO Box 300, Sharjah
Tel: 22441, 22173
Cable: Habibbank
Telex: 68061 EM

PRINCIPAL ACTIVITIES: Commercial banking

Branch Offices: Abu Dhabi, Dubai, Ras Al Khaimah, Sharjah

Parent Company: Head office in Karachi, Pakistan

Date of Establishment: 1967

HALCROW INTERNATIONAL PARTNERSHIP

PO Box 673, Sharjah
Tel: 357755
Telex: 68199 Propul EM

PRINCIPAL ACTIVITIES: Civil engineering consultants, construction, planning and architecture (Sharjah Deep Water Harbour, Sharjah International Airport, etc)

Branch Offices: UAE; Saudi Arabia; Oman; Ghana; Tanzania; Malaysia; Venezuela; Bahrain; Libya; Indonesia; Guyana, etc

Parent Company: Head office in London, UK

HEMPEL'S MARINE PAINTS (UAE) LTD

PO Box 2000, Sharjah
Tel: 356307 (6 lines)
Cable: Hempaturi Sharjah
Telex: 68197 Hempel EM
Telefax: 546491

Chairman: Saud Abdulaziz Al-Rashed

Directors: HE Sheikh Mohammad Bin Sultan Al-Qasimi, HE Sheikh Nasser Al-Ahmed Al-Sabah, Saad Abdulaziz Al Rashed, J H Lillelund, JC Hempel Holding A/S

Senior Executives: Allan Christensen (General Manager)

PRINCIPAL ACTIVITIES: Manufacture of paint and coatings for the marine, industrial, container, offshore, yacht and building sector uses; import and marketing of materials and tools for surface preparation and application of such coatings, including provision of advisory services

Branch Offices: PO Box 696, Dubai, Tel 459359; PO Box 47006, Abu Dhabi, Tel 721694

Associated Companies: J C Hempel Holding A/S Group

Principal Bankers: British Bank of the Middle East, Sharjah; National Bank of Abu Dhabi, Sharjah; Banque Paribas, Dubai; National Bank of Dubai, Dubai

Financial Information:

	1990 Dh'000
Authorised capital	2,500
Paid-up capital	2,500
Total assets	16,000

Principal Shareholders: Saud Abdulaziz Al Rashed, HE Sheikh Mohammad Bin Sultan Al Qassimi, HE Sheikh Nasser Al Ahmed Al Sabah, Saad Abdulaziz Al Rashed, and J C Hempel Holding A/S, Denmark

Date of Establishment: 1976
No of Employees: 49

UAE (Sharjah)

HOLIDAY INN SHARJAH

PO Box 5802, Sharjah
Tel: 357357
Cable: Holidayinn
Telex: 68305 Holinn EM

PRINCIPAL ACTIVITIES: Hotel operation
Principal Agencies: Holiday Inn International
Principal Bankers: National Bank of Sharjah

Date of Establishment: March 1st, 1978

HONEYWELL MIDDLE EAST LTD

PO Box 6034, Sharjah
Tel: 356143 (3 lines)
Cable: Honeywell Sharjah
Telex: 68211 Honwel EM
Telefax: 356165

Chairman: G A Ferrari
Directors: M F F Abdel Shafei (Managing Director)

PRINCIPAL ACTIVITIES: Supply of automatic control for oilfield
  equipment and mechanical engineerng plant, computers,
  precision and safety equipment
Principal Agencies: Branch of Honeywell
Parent Company: Honeywell Inc
Principal Bankers: Commercial Bank of Dubai, Sharjah; British
  Bank of the Middle East, Sharjah
Financial Information:

	1990
	Dh'000
Authorised capital	2,775
Paid-up capital	2,775

Principal Shareholders: Honeywel Middle East BV Amsterdam
Date of Establishment: November 1976

HOTEL NOVA SHARJAH BEACH

PO Box 6015, Sharjah
Tel: 356566
Telex: 68213 NOVTEL EM

Directors: Ahmed Al-Noman-Managing (Director), R N Rekhi
  (Group General Manager)

PRINCIPAL ACTIVITIES: Hotel business
Parent Company: Gulf International Tourism Company

Date of Establishment: 1977
No of Employees: 102

INCA TANVIR ADVERTISING

PO Box 5320, Sharjah
Tel: 06-593711
Telex: 68623 Inca EM
Telefax: 06-591226

Directors: Tanvir Kanji (Managing Director)
Senior Executives: Pinky Daniels (Deputy Managing Director),
  Sunil Anand (Finance Manager)

PRINCIPAL ACTIVITIES: Advertising agency, marketing
  consultancy, market research, clients throughout the Gulf
Principal Bankers: Union Bank of the Middle East, Dubai

Date of Establishment: April 1976
No of Employees: 31

INDUSTRY & BUSINESS DEVELOPMENT CONSORTIUM

PO Box 1247, Sharjah
Tel: 23535
Cable: Buscon
Telex: 68127 EM

PRINCIPAL ACTIVITIES: Import and export services, industrial
  group, business consultancy

Branch Offices: United Arab Emirates; Bahrain; Kuwait; Oman;
  Liechtenstein
Associated Companies: Sharjah Shipyard & Engineering Works
  Co Ltd

INTERGULF SHIPPING CO (SHARJAH)

PO Box 2066, Sharjah
Tel: 355091
Cable: Anchor
Telex: 68535 Anchor EM

PRINCIPAL ACTIVITIES: Shipping, clearing, forwarding and
  stevedoring agents

INTERNATIONAL TRADING & CONSTRUCTION CO LTD

PO Box 6284, Sharjah
Tel: 359311
Cable: Itcee
Telex: 68626 Itcee EM

Chairman: V K Khandelwal
Directors: Mrs Smith Khandelwal, Timothy Ridley

PRINCIPAL ACTIVITIES: Scaffolding systems, structural
  systems including accessories and household appliances
Principal Agencies: Stenson Ltd, Canada; Khandelwal
  Manufacturing, India; Conrad Kern, Switzerland; Fichtel &
  Sachs, W Germany; Kaiser Aluminium, W Germany; Mero
  Werke, W Germany; GEA Haffel Industrie Technik, W
  Germany
Subsidiary/Associated Companies: Arabian Est for Tech Cont,
  PO Box 143, Bahrain; Motocave, PO Box 20465, Kuwait; Al
  Shirawi & Co, PO Box 4511, Muscat, Oman; Qatar Int Com
  Co, PO Box 2544, Doha, Qatar; Works & Trade Co Ltd, PO
  Box 1199, Alkhobar, Saudi Arabia, Arabian Oasis Ind, PO Box
  811, Abu Dhabi, UAE; and PO Box 2032, Dubai, UAE; Ahmed
  Ibrahim Isaaq, PO Box 2, Sanaa, Yemen AR; Consolidated
  Ent, PO Box 79, Port Louis, Mauritius

Date of Establishment: April 1978
No of Employees: 100

INVESTMENT BANK FOR TRADE & FINANCE LLC
INVESTBANK

PO Box 1885, Sharjah
Tel: (06) 355391
Cable: Investbank Sharjah
Telex: 68083; 68218 Invest EM
Telefax: (03) 546683

Chairman: HE Sheikh Saqr Bin Mohammad Al Qassimi
Directors: Said T Khoury (Executive President), Samir N Hanna
  (Managing Director), HE Sheikh Abdullah Bin Mohammad Al
  Qassimi, HE Sheikh Saoud Bin Khalid Al Khalid Al Qassimi,
  HE Sheikh Faysal Bin Khalid Bin Sultan Al Qassimi, Taryam
  Omran Taryam, Abdallah Omran Taryam, Raymond O Audi,
  Mohammad Yusri Dweik, Obeid Bin Issa Ahmad, Mohammad
  Al Hosseini
Senior Executives: Paul M Choufani (General Manager), Afif N
  Chehadeh (Assistant General Manager, Incharge of Abu
  Dhabi Branch)

PRINCIPAL ACTIVITIES: Commercial banking
Branch Offices: Abu Dhabi (PO Box 2875, Tel 02-324594, Fax
  02-324592, Telex 22665); Al Ain (PO Box 1933, Tel 03-
  644446, Fax 03-645335, Telex 33587); Dubai (PO Box 12955,
  Tel 04-285551, Fax 04-220818, Telex 49316)
Financial Information:

	1989
	Dh'000
Profits	20,141
Authorised capital	121,000
Paid-up capital	121,000
Total assets	2,525,100

Principal Shareholders: Several prominent local businessmen and companies; Said T Khoury, Co-Owner of Consolidated Contractors International Co Ltd
Date of Establishment: 1975
No of Employees: 136

ISLAMIC INVESTMENT CO OF THE GULF

PO Box 6129, Sharjah
Tel: 597075
Telex: 68595 ASAS EM
Telefax: 548204

Chairman: HRH Prince Mohamed Al Faisal Al Saud
Directors: Khedher Mohamed Ali (Managing Director)
Senior Executives: Omar Abdi Ali (Chief Executive)

PRINCIPAL ACTIVITIES: Islamic investment banking
Branch Offices: Abu Dhabi, Ajman, Al Ain, Sharjah, Umm Al Quwain, Doha (Qatar), Saudi Arabia
Parent Company: Dar Al Maal Al Islami
Subsidiary Companies: Islamic Investment Co of the Gulf; Massraf Faisal Al Islami Bahrain; Massraf Faisal AL Islami Bahamas; Islamic Takafol Co
Principal Bankers: Dubai Islamic Bank, Dubai; Qatar Islamic Bank, Doha; National Commercial Bank, Saudi Arabia

Principal Shareholders: Dar Al Maal Al Islami

JALAL, MOHAMMED, GENERAL TRADING

ꞏPO Box 1041, Sharjah
Tel: 593903, 592190, 593901
Telex: 68380 Jalal EM

Chairman: Mohammed Yousuf Jalal

PRINCIPAL ACTIVITIES: General trading: construction machinery, lifts and escalators, overhead travelling cranes, stationery and office equipment
Principal Agencies: Mannesmann Demag, Schindler, J Arthur Dixon, Anton Piller, Ardrox Chemicals
Branch Offices: PO Box 1905, Dubai, Tel 222246, 237150
Parent Company: Mohd Jalal & Sons, PO Box 113, Bahrain
Principal Bankers: Standard Chartered Bank; Banque Paribas; Banque de Libanaise pour le Commerce; Arab Bank

Date of Establishment: 1968

JANATA BANK

PO Box 5303, Sharjah
Tel: 357031
Telex: 68316 Janata EM

PRINCIPAL ACTIVITIES: Commercial banking
Branch Offices: Abu Dhabi, Dubai, Al Ain
Parent Company: Head office in Dacca, Bangladesh

KANOO GROUP, THE

PO Box 153, Sharjah
Tel: 22436, 356058
Cable: Kanoo Sharjah
Telex: 68607 EM

Chairman: Hamed A Kanoo
Directors: Yusuf Kanoo (Managing Director)
Senior Executives: A E H Johnson (Senior Executive Manager)

PRINCIPAL ACTIVITIES: Shipping agents, tug and barge operators, packing & removals, courier, freight handling agents, manufacturers' agents and distributors, (chemicals, workshops, cranes, forklifts, agricultural equipment, construction equipment, oilfield supplies), travel agents, insurance
Parent Company: Yusuf Bin Ahmed Kanoo WLL, Bahrain
Associated Companies: Saudi Arabia; Bahrain; Abu Dhabi, Dubai, Fujairah, Ras Al Khaimah, Oman; Representative Office in London, UK

Principal Bankers: British Bank of the Middle East; Standard Chartered Bank; Royal Bank of Canada

No of Employees: 500

KHANSAHEB SYKES LTD

PO Box 1848, Sharjah
Tel: 330542, 330543
Telex: 68265 KSPUMP EM
Telefax: 06-334031

Directors: Hussain Abdul Rehman Khansaheb, S Ross
Senior Executives: Derek L Pudney (General Manager), Robert Van Dyke (Sales & Operations Manager)

PRINCIPAL ACTIVITIES: Hire, sale, installation and servicing of pumps and dewatering equipment
Principal Agencies: Bauer Quick Action Coupling, Austria; Wire Armoured Hose; Weda Electric Submersible Pumps; Sweden; EIM Sewage Pumps, Japan; Pilcon Drill Rigs; Sykes/Pumps & Dewatering Equipment
Branch Offices: PO Box 4056, Abu Dhabi, Tel 554126/554131, Telex 23972 Sykes EM, Fax 2-559875
Parent Company: Braithwaite PLC, UK
Principal Bankers: The British Bank of the Middle East, Sharjah

Date of Establishment: 1975

KHATIB & ALAMI
Consolidated Engineering Co

PO Box 688, Sharjah
Tel: 354144
Cable: Consing
Telex: 68474 EM
Telefax: 354027

President: Prof Munir El Khatib
Vice President: Dr Zuhair Alami
Senior Executives: Wail Sadi (General Manager), Samir Abdulhadi (General Manager), Saba Z Saba (Admin & Financial Manager), Jack S Ekmekji (Design & Development Manager), Faisal Alami (Business & Development Manager)

PRINCIPAL ACTIVITIES: Consulting engineers, architects, planners and designers
Branch Offices: Abu Dhabi, Dubai, Al Ain, Fujairah (UAE); Manama, Bahrain; Muscat, Oman; Riyadh, Jeddah, AlKhobar, Mekka, Madinah (Saudi Arabia), Amman, Jordan
Parent Company: Head office in Beirut, Lebanon, Tel 300609, 300613, Telex 21360, Fax 300384
Associated Companies: Alami & Abdulhadi (Consolidated Engineering Co), Jordan
Principal Bankers: Arab Bank Ltd

Principal Shareholders: Prof Mounir El Khatib, Dr Zuhair Alami, Wail Saidi, Samir Abdulhadi, Omar Omari, Samir Moghrabi, Joe Ounanian, A M Ariss, Jack S Ekmekji, Saba Z Saba, Samir El Khatib, Othman Ayano
Date of Establishment: 1961
No of Employees: 450

KUWAIT OIL COMPANY KSC

PO Box 20408, Sharjah
Tel: 6-545361
Telex: 66849 Kotcsh EM
Telefax: 6-548931

Chairman: Abdul Malik M Al Gharabally (Managing Director)
Directors: Faisal Al Jassem (Deputy Managing Director Operations)

PRINCIPAL ACTIVITIES: Exploration, drilling, production and storage of oil and gas (the company is planning the reconstruction of its oilfields in Kuuwait and is in immediate need of all types of oilfield equipment)
Parent Company: Head office in Kuwait

UAE (Sharjah)

LAMNALCO (SHARJAH) LIMITED

PO Box 5687, Sharjah
Tel: 359108
Cable: LAMNALCO SHARJAH
Telex: 68433 Lamshj EM
Telefax: (9716) 547090

Directors: Teymour Alireza, Salim Ali Al Mazroa, Mohammed Al Shamsi, Ahmed Abdulla Al Nooman, J H N Gibson, R V Gelder, A H Godri
Senior Executives: A C Wilkinson (Chief Executive Officer), M H Smyth (Finance & Administration Manager), Capt S W Trought (Marine & Engineering Manager), Capt J R Murray (Manager Shipping & Agency), A Jackson (Sales & Marketing Manager)

PRINCIPAL ACTIVITIES: Marine and offshore related services to the oil industry, oil terminals management and operations, ship management, marine oilfields, sypply bases, ship to ship transfer, deep sea services, agency, crew change and pilotage, marine consultancy and survey, marine safety products, navigational aids, rubber fenders, pollution control, liferafts recertification, plant hire, generators hire, etc
Branch Offices: Agency Crew change & Pilotage Division: PO Box 10316, KhorFakkan, UAE, Tel 85748, 85713, Fax 83032, Telex 89034 Pilot KF EM
Parent Company: Royal Bos Kalis Westminster Group and Alireza Group of Kuwait
Associated Companies: Lamnalco Group Ltd offices throughout Saudi Arabia, Kuwait, UAE
Principal Bankers: Bank of Kuwait & the Middle East, British Bank of the Middle East

Principal Shareholders: Alireza Group; Royal Boskalis Westminster
Date of Establishment: 1978
No of Employees: 241

MERCANTILE & MARINE (ME) LTD

PO Box 2066, Sharjah
Tel: 971-6-547353
Cable: Mermar Sharjah
Telex: 68387 Mermar EM
Telefax: 971-6-358994

Chairman: Capt S K A Mahmoodi (Managing Director)
Senior Executives: Hamid Baig (General Manager Operations), Capt Khalid Humail (Senior Manager Operations), A Razak A Hussain (Financial Controller), Fida Ali Mirza (Manager Finance)

PRINCIPAL ACTIVITIES: Chartering, freight brokers, tally and cargo supervision, ship's supply service, crew change, bunkering, fresh water supply, hull cleaning, dry docking, surveys, custom brokers, clearing and forwarding, warehousing, transhipment, air cargo, tugs and barges, road haulage
Principal Agencies: Atlas Ship Management, HongKong; Gulfeast Ship Management, HongKong; Middle East Tanker Transport, Liberia; Scirroco Shipping Inc, Liberia; Trident Shipping Co, Liberia; Waveney Marine Services, UK
Branch Offices: PO Box 10488, KhorFakkan, Tel 971-70-86605, Fax 971-70-87264
Principal Bankers: Royal Bank of Canada, Dubai; Bank of Credit & Commerce International, Sharjah

Date of Establishment: December 1981
No of Employees: 35

MIDDLE EAST BANK LTD

PO Box 5169, Sharjah
Tel: 356166
Telex: 68074 EM, 68814 EM

PRINCIPAL ACTIVITIES: Commercial banking

Branch Offices: In the UAE: Abu Dhabi, Ras Al Khaimah, Umm Al Quwain
Parent Company: Head office in Dubai

Date of Establishment: 1976

MOHAMMED ABDULRAHMAN AL BAHAR

See AL BAHAR, MOHAMMED ABDULRAHMAN,

MOHAMMED BIN JASEM GENERAL TRADING & CONTRACTING CO

PO Box 949, Sharjah
Tel: 354344

PRINCIPAL ACTIVITIES: Transportation contractors, supply of auto spare parts and components, chemicals, lubricants, etc

MOHAMMED BIN MASOOD & SONS

See BIN MASOOD, MOHAMMED, & SONS

MOHAMMED JALAL GENERAL TRADING

See JALAL, MOHAMMED, GENERAL TRADING

MOTHERCAT LIMITED

PO Box 121, Sharjah
Tel: 06-331233, 332152
Cable: Mothercat
Telex: 68014 Cat EM
Telefax: 06-331442

Chairman: Mrs Loura El Bustani
Directors: Mrs Nadia El Khoury, Shukri H Shammas (Managing Director), Fuad J El Khazen, Khalil Noubani (Technical Director), Andre Geha (Finance Director)
Senior Executives: Ibrahim Khawaja (Area Manager, UAE)

PRINCIPAL ACTIVITIES: General contractors; heavy civil engineering works, mechanical engineering works, pipeline and tankage; steel structure builders, etc
Branch Offices: Branches in all UAE states; also offices in: Lebanon, Saudi Arabia, Kuwait, Bahrain, Qatar, Sultanate of Oman, Libya, Pakistan, Nigeria, UK (London), France (Paris)
Parent Company: CAT Group of Companies
Associated Companies: Contracting and Trading Co (CAT); Nigercat Ltd
Principal Bankers: British Bank of the Middle East; Arab Bank; Grindlays Bank
Financial Information:

	1990 St£'000
Authorised capital	5,000
Paid-up capital	5,000

Principal Shareholders: Chairman and directors as described
Date of Establishment: 1963
No of Employees: approx 2,000

NATIONAL BANK OF ABU DHABI

PO Box 1109, Sharjah
Tel: 22601
Telex: 68179 Masraf EM

PRINCIPAL ACTIVITIES: Commercial banking
Branch Offices: Abu Dhabi, Ajman, Dubai, Fujairah, Ras Al Khaimah, Sharjah
Parent Company: Head office in Abu Dhabi

Date of Establishment: 1974

NATIONAL BANK OF SHARJAH

Al Boorj Avenue, PO Box 4, Sharjah
Tel: 547745 (16 lines)
Cable: Natbank Sharjah
Telex: 68085 Natbnk EM
Telefax: 543483

Chairman: HE Shaikh Ahmed Bin Sultan Al Qasimi

Directors: HE Sheikh Sultan Bin Khalid Al Qasimi (Executive Director), HE Khalfan Mohd Al Roomi (Vice Chairman), HE Sheikh Abdulla Bin Mohd Al Thani, Hussain Abdulrahman Khansaheb, Mohd Abdulla Al Khayal, Mohamed Sharif Al Zaman, Omran Salim Al Owais, Ismail Abdul Wahid Al Sayeedi, Eissa Ali Al Mazroo, Rolf G Dellborg

Senior Executives: Gordon D Abernethy (General Manager & Chief Executive), Mohd Ali Merchant (Manager Exchange & Money Market), J B Campbell (Asst General Manager Operations), Mohd Saeed Soruji (Asst General Manager Credit & Marketing), M Balaubramaniam (Manager Credit), Essa J Al Mutawa (Asst Manager Head Office), Sean Roche (Manager Data Processing), Hugh J Mullan (Manager Financial Control & Planning), Sami Mowaswes (Manager Main Branch)

PRINCIPAL ACTIVITIES: All banking transactions
Branch Offices: 34 branches in Sharjah; 1 branch in Abu Dhabi; 1 branch in Dubai; 1 branch in Dibba; 1 branch in Khorfakkan; 1 branch in Al Ain
Financial Information:

	1990 Dh'000
Authorised capital	500,000
Paid-up capital	260,000

Principal Shareholders: Government of Sharjah (26.35%), UAE Nationals (73.65%)
Date of Establishment: March 1976
No of Employees: 241

NATIONAL INVESTMENT CO (PVT) LTD

PO Box 17, Sharjah
Tel: 522959, 355121/2
Cable: Khaldon
Telex: 68021 SNTTA EM
Telefax: 971-6-374968

Chairman: HE Sheikh Abdul Aziz Bin Mohd Al Qasimi
Directors: HE Sheikh Khalid Bin Abdul Aziz Al Qasimi (Deputy Chairman), M Musharraf Hussain (Executive Director and Group Finance Director)
Senior Executives: Baher Nabulsi, Tareq Ali, J Gore

PRINCIPAL ACTIVITIES: Investment, financing, trading
Principal Agencies: General Motors, Lada, Lift Munich, Emirates Airlines, PIA, Panam, Swiss Air, Budget Rent-a-Car
Branch Offices: West Germany and UK under joint ventures
Subsidiary Companies: National Real Estate Co Pvt Ltd; Liberty Automobiles Co Pvt Ltd; Sharjah National Travel & Tourist Agency Pvt Ltd; Asia General Contracting Co Pvt Ltd; Unesia Building Materials Co; Express Spare Parts Service; Sharjah Aviation; Union Lift Co; Gulf Union Shipping & Trading Co
Principal Bankers: AMRO Bank, Bank of Baroda, Citibank, Bank of Sharjah
Financial Information:

	1990 Dh'000
Sales turnover	160,000
Profits	10,000
Authorised capital	100,000
Paid-up capital	75,000
Total assets	115,000

Principal Shareholders: Dependents of HE Sheikh Abdul Aziz Bin Mohd Al Qasimi
Date of Establishment: 1980
No of Employees: 350

NATIONAL PLASTIC & BUILDING MATERIAL INDUSTRIES

PO Box 1943, Sharjah
Tel: 331830, 331831
Cable: Plastpipe
Telex: 68529 Pipe EM
Telefax: 335629

Directors: Antoune N Kronfli (Managing Director), Dr M Shunnar,
Senior Executives: Philip Morcos (Manager), Yossri Abdallah (Assistant Manager), H Mohammed

PRINCIPAL ACTIVITIES: Manufacture of PVC pressure pipe, drain pipe, duct, conduit, LD & HD, polythene pipe; import of plastic building materials and pipe fittings and irrigation equipment; manufacture of adhesives and bonding agents for all applications, export of chemicals
Principal Agencies: Hardy Irrigation; Hunter Plastics; FIP; Spears; Weldon Adhesives, Fitco Netting
Branch Offices: Dubai
Subsidiary Companies: In UK; Canada; Jebel Ali
Principal Bankers: United Arab Bank, Sharjah; ABN Bank, Sharjah

Date of Establishment: 1975

NATIONAL TILES & MOSAIC EST

PO Box 1855, Sharjah
Tel: 22739
Cable: Ali
Telex: 68538 EM

Chairman: Ali Saeed Al Khayaili
Senior Executives: Mohammad Ahmad Shmandi (Accountant), Azizul Hasan Siddiqui (Sales and Marketing Manager), Mohammad Faiz (Foreman)

PRINCIPAL ACTIVITIES: Production of mosaic tiles, ceramics, cement and concrete blocks, wooden doors, windows, and building materials
Subsidiary/Associated Companies: Al Khayaili Trading Enterprises; Al Khayaili Contracting & Transport
Principal Bankers: Bank of Sharjah; National Bank of Abu Dhabi

NCR CORPORATION

Systemedia Plant

PO Box 6293, Sharjah
Tel: 549330
Cable: Nacareco Sharjah
Telex: 68051 NCRSH EM

PRINCIPAL ACTIVITIES: Manufacture of high quality business forms, continuous stationery, and other associated printed forms
Branch Offices: Bahrain, Kuwait, Dubai, Abu Dhabi, Qatar, Oman
Parent Company: NCR Corporation
Principal Bankers: Standard Chartered Bank

Date of Establishment: 1978
No of Employees: 30

NEWAGE INDUSTRIES

Industrial Area No 2, Off Green Belt Street, PO Box 5001, Sharjah
Tel: 353798
Cable: Newage
Telex: 68388 Oij EM

Chairman: Mohmed Omran Taryam
Directors: Rajni C Shah
Senior Executives: R V Shah

PRINCIPAL ACTIVITIES: Engineers, traders and manufacturers representatives, importers, suppliers, distributors of technical building service equipments including service and repair
Branch Offices: Dubai, Abu Dhabi and San Francisco (USA)

Parent Company: Omran Investment Ltd, PO Box 82, Sharjah
Subsidiary Companies: Haws Middle East, Dubai
Principal Bankers: Bank of Oman, Dubai; Investment Bank for Trade & Finance, Dubai

Principal Shareholders: Mohmed Omran Taryam, Rajni C Shah
Date of Establishment: May 1976

OCEANIC AT KHOR FAKKAN BEACH

PO Box 10444, Khor Fakkan, Sharjah
Tel: 85111
Telex: 89089 Batha EM
Telefax: 87716

Chairman: Sheikh Ahmed Bin Mohamed Al Qasimi
Vice Chairman: Sheikh Salem Bin Mohamed Al Qasimi
Senior Executives: Nawaz Qureshi (General Manager)

PRINCIPAL ACTIVITIES: Hotel operation and tourim
Parent Company: East Coast Hotels & Tourism Ltd, UAE
Subsidiary Companies: Affiliated unit: East Coast Diving Centre; Sea Sports Centre
Principal Bankers: National Bank of Sharjah

Date of Establishment: October 6, 1979
No of Employees: 80

OFFSHORE ELECTRONICS & SAFETY EQUIPMENT

PO Box 5272, Sharjah
Tel: 332930, 333591
Telex: 68636 OFFSHO EM
Telefax: 06-336860

Directors: Ali Abdul Jalil
Senior Executives: E M S Edirisinghe (General Manager), C A Ramadasan (Chief Engineer)

PRINCIPAL ACTIVITIES: Marine, industrial, educational, electronics and safety equipment, sales, service and installation
Principal Agencies: Dancom Communication Equip, Denmark; Comet Pyrotechniks, W Germany; DSB Life Rafts & Boats, W Germany; Northern Radio, USA; Skanti Radio, Denmark; Debeg, W Germany; Aero Marine Life Raft, India; Tokyokeiki, Japan; Hickok Teaching System, USA; Tanus Fire Extinguisher, W Germany; Rakon, Singapore; ITT, Denmark; Danish Marine Communication, Denmark; Jaybeam Antennas, UK; Gold Star Precision, Korea; B F Goodrich Inflatables, USA; Marineter Fishfindees, Australia
Branch Offices: PO Box 6644, Abu Dhabi, Tel 461273
Principal Bankers: Bank of Oman, Sharjah; National Bank of Sharjah
Financial Information:

	1988/89
	Dh'000
Sales turnover	5,500
Profits	650
Authorised capital	750
Paid-up capital	750

Date of Establishment: December 1976

OMRAN INVESTMENT CO

Head Office: Spinney's Bldg, King Faisal Street, PO Box 5001, Sharjah
Tel: 373737
Cable: NEWAGE
Telex: 68388 OIJ EM

Chairman: Mohmed Omran Taryam
Directors: Abdullah Mohamed Taryam, Omran Mohamed
Senior Executives: Rajni C Shah (Manager)

PRINCIPAL ACTIVITIES: Real estate development and investment

Branch Offices: Dubai
Subsidiary Companies: Newage Industries Dubai, Sharjah, Abu Dhabi; Gulf Lebanese Enterprises; Omran Italian Jewellery, Sharjah; Halwan Filling Station, Sharjah
Principal Bankers: Bank of Credit and Commerce Intl (Emirates) Sharjah; Investbank Sharjah; Bank of Baroda, Deira-Dubai

Principal Shareholders: Taryam family members
Date of Establishment: 1981

ORIENT IRRIGATION SERVICES

PO Box 1165, Sharjah
Tel: 691985
Cable: Orient
Telex: 48519 Orient EM
Telefax: 693655

Chairman: HE Sheikh Faisal Bin Khalid Bin Sultan Al Qasimi
Directors: Peter Harradine (Managing Director)

PRINCIPAL ACTIVITIES: Agriculture, landscaping and irrigation, and water treatment
Principal Agencies: Rain- Bird, Sisis, Ransomes
Branch Offices: Dubai
Principal Bankers: Amro, BCC(E), Barclays Bank

Date of Establishment: 1977
No of Employees: 107

ORIENT TRAVEL & TOURING AGENCY

PO Box 772, Sharjah
Tel: 357323
Cable: Orient Travel
Telex: 68268 Orient EM

Chairman: Sheikh Faisal bin Khalid Al Qasimi
Directors: Sheikh Sultan Bin Khalid Al Qasimi (Director), Sheikh Saud Bin Khalid Al Qasimi (Director)
Senior Executives: Godwin E Fernandez (General Manager), Asim Arshad (Assistant Sales Manager)

PRINCIPAL ACTIVITIES: Travel agency
Branch Offices: Orient Travel, PO Box 10408, Khor Fakkan, UAE
Principal Bankers: Invest Bank, Sharjah
Financial Information:

	Dh'000
Authorised capital	10,000
Paid-up capital	5,000

Date of Establishment: 1962
No of Employees: 50

PAUWELS MIDDLE EAST TRADING & CONTRACTING

PO Box 5730, Sharjah
Tel: 357078, 351492
Cable: Pauwme Sharjah
Telex: 68274 Pauwme EM
Telefax: 378077

Chairman: Victor Pauwels
Directors: Frans Michiels (Managing Director)
Senior Executives: M Sharif Ahmed (Resident Manager), S S Arfeen (Regional Manager)

PRINCIPAL ACTIVITIES: Trading and contracting (mainly electrical)
Principal Agencies: Pauwels Int, Belgium; Inimex, Belgium; Fulton Ent, Belgium; International Contracting, Belgium; Fulton Marine, Belgium
Parent Company: Pauwels International NV
Principal Bankers: Bank of Sharjah; Banque Paribas

Date of Establishment: May 1977

PETRA TRADING & CONTRACTING CO

PO Box 5189, Sharjah
Tel: 354811
Telex: 68354 Petra EM

PRINCIPAL ACTIVITIES: Building and civil engineering; supply
of building materials

PORT MANAGEMENT SERVICES LTD

Seatrain Gulf Services Ltd

PO Box 5509, Sharjah
Tel: 356793
Cable: Ctrain
Telex: 68250 Ctrain EM

PRINCIPAL ACTIVITIES: Port management and operation
management of Port Khalid, Sharjah
Subsidiary Companies: Seatrain Gulf Services Ltd, PO Box 356,
Damman

Principal Shareholders: Wholly owned subsidiary of Seatrain
Lines Inc, New York, USA

PROJECT DEVELOPMENT CO LTD SA

PO Box 2200, Sharjah
Tel: 354068
Telex: 68176 EM Prodco

PRINCIPAL ACTIVITIES: Holding company; promotions and
investment in development projects, Gulf wide, Europe, and
the USA
Principal Bankers: Investbank, Sharjah

QUEBEISI-SGB

PO Box 5682, Sharjah
Tel: 594839
Telex: 68430 SGB EM
Telefax: 591808

Chairman: M G Blair
Directors: B Al Quebeisi, H Lorimer
Senior Executives: David D Webb (General Manager UAE &
Gulf)

PRINCIPAL ACTIVITIES: Suppliers of formwork; scaffolding sub
contractors
Principal Agencies: SGB Export Ltd, UK; Youngmans Ltd, UK;
Ulma, Spain; Plasclip Spacers
Branch Offices: PO Box 7574, Abu Dhabi, UAE
Parent Company: SGB International
Principal Bankers: British Bank of the Middle East

Principal Shareholders: B Al Quebeisi, Abu Dhabi; SGB Group
Ltd, Jersey
Date of Establishment: 1976
No of Employees: 50

RANYA TRADING CO

PO Box 1433, Sharjah
Tel: 593784 (5 lines)
Cable: Tabari
Telex: 68292 RTC EM

Chairman: Hisham R Tabari (also Managing Director)
Directors: Marwan R Tabari, Tareq Al Husseini (General
Manager)

PRINCIPAL ACTIVITIES: Electrical, mechanical engineering
contractors; supply of building materials, electrical equipment
Principal Agencies: Thorn Lighting, Permanite, Federal Pacific
Electric, Polybond, Haden Int, Flintkote, Contech, Petitjean,
CMP Glands, General Electric, Gold Star Cable, PDL
Accessories, Shin-Etsu Polymer Tiles, Lucky
Branch Offices: Ras Al Khaimah - Tel 21196; Dubai - Tel
226395
Subsidiary Companies: Ranya Trading Co, PO Box 602, Abu
Dhabi - Tel 822416; Ranya Trading Co, PO Box 23113,
Amman, Jordan; Union Pharmacy -Dubai, Sharjah, Abu Dhabi

Principal Bankers: Banque Paribas, Arab Bank Ltd

Principal Shareholders: Marwan R Tabari & Hisham R Tabari
Date of Establishment: 1968
No of Employees: 100

RAPID METAL DEVELOPMENTS

PO Box 5801, Sharjah
Tel: 06-357289
Telex: 68376
Telefax: 06-377260

Chairman: Hussain Abdul Rahman Khansaheb
Senior Executives: Ken Ross (Manager), Colin Turner (Technical
Manager), Richard C Gain (Export Sales Manager)

PRINCIPAL ACTIVITIES: Formwork, scaffolding, support
systems, precast concrete formwork
Branch Offices: Abu Dhabi, Tel 722039
Parent Company: RMD Ltd, Aldridge, UK
Principal Bankers: British Bank of the Middle East, Sharjah

Date of Establishment: 1977

READYMIX GULF LTD

PO Box 289, Sharjah
Tel: 592614
Telex: 68082 GIBCA EM

PRINCIPAL ACTIVITIES: Supply of concrete readymix, and
pumping services
Branch Offices: Kuwait, Qatar
Parent Company: Redpath Readymix Ltd, UK; Gibca Ltd,
Sharjah

SABA & CO

PO Box 5470, Sharjah
Tel: 351034
Cable: Sabaco Sharjah
Telex: 46036 Sabaco EM
Telefax: 971-4-213640

Chairman: Suhail F Saba
Directors: George B Ghali, Joseph M Sanbar
Partners: Fathi H Abbas, Bakr A Abulkhair, Ibrahim A Al Tarazi,
Samir I Bawarshi, Haid H Chiad, Mazen K Dajani, Toufic A El
Khatib, George B Ghali, Khalil H Kashef, Joseph F Nakfour,
Suhail F Saba, Krikors Sadikian, Elias G Sanbar, Joseph M
Sanbar, Hani K Tarazi, Usama J Tuqan, Shahid Z Zahur

PRINCIPAL ACTIVITIES: Chartered accountants and
management consultants
Branch Offices: Throughout the Middle East
Parent Company: Saba & Co
Principal Bankers: Arab Bank, Alahli Bank of Kuwait

Date of Establishment: 1926
No of Employees: 300 (group)

SAFAA TRADING & REFRIGERATING CO

PO Box 1932, Sharjah
Tel: 355071
Cable: Fadi
Telex: 68353 Fadi Sharjah EM

Chairman: Rafic Saifi (Proprietor)
Directors: Salim Saifi (Manager), Yousuf Saifi (Production
Manager)

PRINCIPAL ACTIVITIES: General trading in textiles, foostuffs,
spare parts, furniture, dairy products, also shipping agency,
tourism and travel, and freight forwarding
Branch Offices: Fujairah; Khorfakkan; Ras Al Khaimah
Principal Bankers: Grindlays Bank

Date of Establishment: 1974
No of Employees: 253

SANA CONSTRUCTION LIMITED

PO Box 6018, Sharjah
Tel: 332145, 331210
Telex: 47798 Cone EM
Telefax: 04 581842

Chairman: Nakhleh Saqar
Directors: Saif Al Nouman, N Saqar
Senior Executives: Xavier Paravana (Chief Accountant), Basil
  Awad (Manager)

PRINCIPAL ACTIVITIES: Building construction and civil
  engineering
Parent Company: Constructive Enterprises Co (Consent), PO
  BOx 136, Dubai
Associated Companies: Consent Company, PO Box 6018,
  Sharjah and Consent Blocks, PO Box 136, Dubai, Tel 582759,
  Telex 47798, Fax 581842
Principal Bankers: National Bank of Abu Dhabi, Banque
  Libanaise pour le Commerce (France), Dubai

Principal Shareholders: Saif Al Nouman & N Saqar
Date of Establishment: 1980
No of Employees: 350

SAWWAN CONTRACTING & TRADING

PO Box 600, Sharjah
Tel: 22979
Cable: Sawwan
Telex: 68230 EM

PRINCIPAL ACTIVITIES: Building and civil engineering
  contractors, import and distribution of sanitary ware,
  galvanised iron piping and fittings

SEDANA TRADING CO

PO Box 1919, Sharjah
Tel: 334631, 330551
Telex: 68252 Sedana EM
Telefax: 337368

Senior Executives: Assad Semaan (General Manager), Ziad E
  Saoud (Managing Partner), Walid Daniel (Sales Manager)

PRINCIPAL ACTIVITIES: Stockists and distributors of tools and
  garage equipment, and car care products
Principal Agencies: Cem; Metabo; Karcher; Wagner;
  Markisches; Hofmann; Sice & Ammco; Stahlwille; Fasep;
  Ceccato; Celette; Fini; Omia
Branch Offices: Abu Dhabi, PO Box 6861, Tel 337112, Telex
  24224, Fax 337104; Dubai, Tel 665211, 665225

Date of Establishment: 1974
No of Employees: 25

SHARJAH AIRPORT AUTHORITY

PO Box 8, Sharjah
Tel: 581111
Cable: Civilair
Telex: 68185 Airpt EM
Telefax: 581167

Chairman: Sheikh Abdullah Bin Mohammad Al Thani (Chairman
  of Civil Aviation)
Directors: Sheikh Isam Bin Saqr Bin Humaid Al Qassimi (Deputy
  Chairman), Mohammad Saif Al Hajri (Director of Civil Aviation)
Senior Executives: Ghanem Al-Hajri (General Manager), Robert
  Tabet (Deputy General Manager), Egon Kumpa (Manager
  Administration) E G Avery (Manager Technical Services), B
  Marshall (Manager Engineering), J Klawiter (Manager Aircraft
  Maintenance)

PRINCIPAL ACTIVITIES: Airport operation and administration
Principal Bankers: National Bank of Sharjah

Principal Shareholders: Government of Sharjah
Date of Establishment: 1977
No of Employees: 682

SHARJAH CEMENT & INDUSTRIAL DEVELOPMENT CO LTD

PO Box 2083, Sharjah
Tel: 356102, 354681
Telex: 68152 Natico EM

Chairman: Sheikh Faisal Bin Sultan Bin Salim Al Qassimi
Directors: Ahmed Abdulaziz Al Jarallah (Vice Chairman),
  Abdulrahman Mohamed Bukhatir, Obaid Rashid Al Shamsi,
  Salim Bin Ali Al Mazrou, Abdulla Juma Al Sari, Fahad
  Abdulaziz Al Muzaini, Salah A Al Ayoub, Khalid Ajran Hussein
  Al Ajran, Adnan Mohamed Al Wazaan, Mohamed Al Roumi,
  Adnan Abdulaziz Al Fulaij (Managing Director)

PRINCIPAL ACTIVITIES: Industrial development
Branch Offices: PO Box 23679, Safat, Kuwait
Subsidiary Companies: Sharjah Cement Factory, PO Box 5419,
  Sharjah; Sharjah Paper Sacks Factory, PO Box 2083,
  Sharjah; Sharjah Rope Factory, PO Box 2083, Sharjah
Principal Bankers: National Bank of Sharjah; Bank of Credit &
  Commerce International (Overseas) Ltd; Standard Chartered
  Bank; United Arab Bank; Bank of Sharjah; Crocker National
  Bank, London

Principal Shareholders: Government of Sharjah
Date of Establishment: Re-established on 12th May 1979
No of Employees: 350

SHARJAH CONTAINER TERMINAL

PO Box 225, Sharjah
Tel: 354205/6
Telex: 68207 Servic EM; 68207 Servic EM
Telefax: (971-6) 354513

Chairman: H D Jafar
Directors: B R Coughlan (Managing Director)
Senior Executives: T Danesh (Finance Manager), A Gorton
  (Commercial Manager)

PRINCIPAL ACTIVITIES: Container handling, warehousing,
  immediate berthing and discharge of container vessels
Branch Offices: Khorfakkan Port
Parent Company: Gulftainer Company Limited
Principal Bankers: Invest Bank; Barclays Bank

Principal Shareholders: A subsidiary of Gulftainer Co Ltd
Date of Establishment: 1976
No of Employees: 100

SHARJAH CONTINENTAL HOTEL

PO Box 3527, Sharjah
Tel: 371111
Telex: 68123
Telefax: 524090

Directors: Jamal Al Alami (Managing Director)
Senior Executives: Timothy Craig (Deputy General Manager),
  Ghassan Ghobar (Sales Manager), Atef Salama (Front Office
  Manager)

PRINCIPAL ACTIVITIES: Hotel, catering, conferences
Branch Offices: Chicago Beach Hotel, PO Box 11416, Dubai;
  Sharjah Carlton Hotel, PO Box 1198, Sharjah

Date of Establishment: January 1982
No of Employees: 300

SHARJAH ELECTRODES

PO Box 2019, Sharjah
Tel: 593888, 591000
Cable: Agtco
Telex: 68117 Agtco EM

Directors: Mohd Shareef Zaman (Director), Mohd Abdulla Al-
  Khayyal (Managing Director)
Senior Executives: P K Varghese (Manager)

PRINCIPAL ACTIVITIES: Manufacture and distribution of arc
  welding electrodes and wire nails

Parent Company: Welding Industries Oerlikon Buehrle, Switzerland
Principal Bankers: National Bank of Sharjah

Principal Shareholders: Mohd Abdullah Al Khayal & Mohd Shariff Zaman
Date of Establishment: 1976
No of Employees: 37

SHARJAH GROUP COMPANY

PO Box 5440, Sharjah
Tel: 356465
Telex: 68134 Shargo EM

Chairman: Sheikh Nasser Sabah Al Ahmad Al Sabah
Directors: Fawzi Musaed Al Saleh, Sheikh Saud Bin Khalid Al Qasimi, Fayez Abdel Aziz Saleh Al Mutawa, Abdel Jalil Sayed Hassan behbehani, Nouri Abdel Salam Shuaib, Yousri Mahmoud Dweik, Bader Nasser Al Bisher, Samer Khanchet

PRINCIPAL ACTIVITIES: Investment services
Branch Offices: London, UK; Kuwait

Principal Shareholders: Gulf Nationals (100%)
Date of Establishment: 1976

SHARJAH INSURANCE & REINSURANCE CO

PO Box 792, Sharjah
Tel: 357768, 355090, 22516, 546551
Cable: Taminsure
Telex: 68060 Tamin EM
Telefax: 06-352545

Chairman: Mahmood Khairulla Al Haji
Directors: Abdulla Yacoub Al Wazzan (Vice Chairman), Mohamed Abdulla Al Khayal (Deputy Managing Director), Hussain Al Mazroui, Faisal Fahad Al Ma'jil, Saad Abdullatif Al Dousry
Senior Executives: Adeeb Abed (General Manager)

PRINCIPAL ACTIVITIES: Underwriting all classes of business (insurance and reinsurance)
Branch Offices: Offices in Abu Dhabi, Dubai, Khorfakhan, Al Ain
Principal Bankers: National Bank of Sharjah; Bank of Sharjah; United Arab Bank; Invest Bank
Financial Information:

	1989 Dh'000
Authorised capital	100,000
Paid-up capital	100,000

Principal Shareholders: UAE and Kuwaiti Nationals
Date of Establishment: 1970
No of Employees: 46

SHARJAH INVESTMENT GROUP

PO Box 5440, Sharjah
Tel: 356465, 351317
Telex: 68134 Shagro EM

Chairman: Sheikh Nasser Sabah Al-Ahmed Al-Sabah
Directors: Sheikh Saoud Bin Khalid Al-Khalid Al Qassimi (Vice Chairman), Fawzi Musaad Al-Saleh (Managing Director), Sheikh Hamad Sabah Al-Ahmed Al-Sabah, Abdul Jalil Sayyid Hassan Behbehani, Nouri Abdul Salam Shuaib, Yousri Mahmoud Dowaik

PRINCIPAL ACTIVITIES: Investment in Arab projects
Branch Offices: Sharjah

Principal Shareholders: Arab Nationals only
Date of Establishment: 1977

SHARJAH MARITIME & MERCANTILE INTERNATIONAL

PO Box 186, Sharjah
Tel: 357696
Cable: Gray
Telex: 68273 Gray EM

PRINCIPAL ACTIVITIES: General trading and contracting; import and distribution of electrical equipment, foodstuffs, Lloyds' agent, cargo ship and tanker agents, travel agents and general merchants
Branch Offices: Branches in the UAE; Abu Dhabi, PO Box 247; Dubai, PO Box 70; Khorfakkan; Ras Al Khaimah; Umm-Al-Qaiwan

SHARJAH MERIDIEN HOTEL

Sultan Al Awal Rd, PO Box 6059, Sharjah
Tel: 356557
Cable: Homer Shj
Telex: 68204 Homer EM

PRINCIPAL ACTIVITIES: Hotel operation

SHARJAH NATIONAL LUBE OIL CO LTD

PO Box 1575, Sharjah
Tel: 354435, 355354
Cable: Sharlu Sharjah
Telex: 68091 Sharlu EM
Telefax: 549366

Senior Executives: Shafquat Hussain (General Manager), Najm Ul Haque (Marketing & Operations Manager), Manzar Zuberi (Finance & Admin Manager)

PRINCIPAL ACTIVITIES: Blending and packaging of lubricants; technical consultancy on lubricants and lubrication with full laboratory back up service
Principal Agencies: Polyester Resins (Midex AB Sweden); Fiber Glass (Owens-Corning Fiber Glass)
Branch Offices: Dubai, Abu Dhabi, Al Ain, Ras Al Khaimah, Fujairah
Associated Companies: Falcon Oil Co Ltd, PO Box 3461, Sharjah; Sharlu Enterprises (Oman), PO Box 4504, Ruwi, Oman; Nufins Sharlu Ltd, PO Box 1575, Sharjah; Sharlu Group of Companies, PO Box 12877, Dubai
Principal Bankers: Banque Paribas, Dubai; Barclays Bank, Sharjah; Royal Bank of Canada, Dubai
Financial Information:

	1990 Dh'000
Authorised capital	12,000
Paid-up capital	10,500

Date of Establishment: 1975
No of Employees: 135

SHARJAH OXYGEN CO

PO Box 800, Sharjah
Tel: 336481
Cable: OXYGEN Sharjah
Telex: 68057 Oxygen EM
Telefax: 330942

Chairman: Anwer Asadi
Senior Executives: Assad Assadi (Marketing Manager), Irshad Ali Shah (Plants Engineer)

PRINCIPAL ACTIVITIES: Manufacture and supply of industrial and medical gases
Principal Agencies: Hoechst - Refrigerant (Frigen) for UAE
Branch Offices: Abu Dhabi Oxygen Co, PO Box 4512, Abu Dhabi, Tel 554351, Fax 553827; Abu Dhabi Oxygen Co, Al Ain, Tel 666014; Ras Al Khaimah Oxygen Co, PO Box 5136, Ras Al Khaimah, Tel 21029
Principal Bankers: Bank of Oman, Sharjah

Date of Establishment: 1972
No of Employees: 95

UAE (Sharjah)

SHARJAH PORTS & CUSTOMS AUTHORITY

PO Box 510, Sharjah
Tel: 541666
Cable: Seagul
Telex: 68138 EM
Telefax: 06-541425

Chairman Ports & Customs: Shaikh Saud Bin Khalid Al Qasimi
Directors: Abdul Aziz Suleiman Al Sarkal (Director General of
 Ports)
Senior Executives: Capt Mohamed Saleh (Operations Manager),
 Simon G Keen (Marketing Manager)

PRINCIPAL ACTIVITIES: Port authority offering specialised
 facilities for container traffic, Ro-Ro traffic, reefer cargo and
 project and general cargo

Principal Shareholders: Government Organisation
Date of Establishment: 1976
No of Employees: 670

SHARJAH SHIPPING CO LTD

PO Box 1477, Sharjah
Tel: 354411/3
Cable: Shipco Sharjah
Telex: 68024 EM

Chairman: Mohd Sherif A Zaman
Directors: Karim J Haider (Managing Director), Mohd A Khayal

PRINCIPAL ACTIVITIES: Shipowners, shipping agents, and
 charterers
Branch Offices: Offices in Dubai; Abu Dhabi; Ras Al Khaimah;
 UK (London); Singapore; Pakistan
Subsidiary Companies: Gulf Marine Services (Marine and civil
 engineering), PO Box 1477, Sharjah

SHARJAH SHIPYARD & ENGINEERING WORKS CO LTD

PO Box 6026, Sharjah
Tel: 357813
Telex: 68362 SSEW EM

Directors: P Bakker, T Alireza, A Weijburg, J Teensma, M
 Thomassen, O Al Shamsi

PRINCIPAL ACTIVITIES: Marine engineering and heavy
 equipment; fuel injection and dynanometer testing, retail
 earthmoving equipment and trucks
Principal Agencies: Damen Shipyards; Lohman and Stolterfoht;
 Stork Werkspoor; Faun; Holec; John Deere; Twin Disc;
 Roosanastor; DAF trucks
Subsidiary Companies: Geveke Holland; Geveke Intl, NY, USA;
 SAECO, Dhahran, Saudi Arabia; Mits, Curacao, STS Oman;
 STS Abu Dhabi; STS Jebel Dhanna
Principal Bankers: Algemene Bank; British Bank of the Middle
 East

Principal Shareholders: SHV (Holland); Damen Shipyards
 (Holland); International Business Development Corp (UAE); Al
 Shamsi Trading Co Ltd (UAE); National Contracting Company
 (Kuwait)
Date of Establishment: 1977
No of Employees: 240

SHARJAH SPECIALIZED INDUSTRIES

PO Box 1083, Sharjah
Tel: 523748, 354628
Telex: 68558 EM BEACH
Telefax: 350364 Abu Dhabi

Chairman: Ziad Matta (Managing Director)
Directors: Jack El Lati (Finance Manager), M Ramchandani
 (Production Manager), Rajesh C B (Sales Manager), Wassim
 Nsouli (Administration Manager)
Senior Executives: M Ramchandani (Production Engineer)

PRINCIPAL ACTIVITIES: Manufacture of polystyrene products,
 lightweight concrete panels and coated steel bars for
 reinforced concrete
Principal Agencies: Metprep Industrial Products, UK
Branch Offices: Abu Dhabi, Tel 780500, Fax 785151
Parent Company: SIFICO
Subsidiary Companies: Abu Dhabi Specialized Industries
Principal Bankers: United Bank Ltd, Sharjah; Banque Libanaise
 pour le Commerce, Abu Dhabi
Financial Information:

	1988/89 Dh'000	1989/90 Dh'000
Sales turnover	4,500	9,400
Profits	480	2,150
Authorised capital	5,000	5,000
Paid-up capital	5,000	5,000
Total assets	5,500	6,000

Principal Shareholders: A Matta, Z G Matta
Date of Establishment: 1976
No of Employees: 37

SHARJAH TRADING & MECHANICAL WORKS K.U.T.M.E.C.

PO Box 5830, Sharjah
Tel: 356363
Telex: 68389 Kutmec EM

PRINCIPAL ACTIVITIES: Mechanical engineering contractors,
 supply of building materials fittings, pipes and tubes, and
 steel products

SHARJAH TYRE & GENERAL TRADING CO

PO Box 14, Sharjah
Tel: 22126

Directors: Ibrahim Obaid Al-Shaer

PRINCIPAL ACTIVITIES: Import and distribution of electrical
 appliances and equipment, tyres and tubes, auto spare parts
 and gas cookers
Principal Agencies: Riken Tyres, Belanger Refrigerators, Boreal
 Gas Cookers
Branch Offices: Dubai

SHATTAF ANAND STEEL ROLLING MILLS CO PVT LTD

PO Box 574, Sharjah
Tel: 6-592740
Telex: 68354 Shataf EM
Telefax: 6-592760

Chairman: Mohd Humaid Mohd Shattaf
Directors: Dheerajmal Bastimal Siroya, Ashok Bastimal Siroya
Senior Executives: Manhar Sharda (Senior Sales Manager)

PRINCIPAL ACTIVITIES: Manufacture of steel bars
Subsidiary Companies: Shattaf Jewellers Ltd, PO Box 819,
 Dubai; Shattaf Trading Co, PO Box 574, Sharjah; Shattaf
 Construction, PO Box 574, Sharjah
Principal Bankers: Commercial Bank of Dubai, Sharjah; National
 Bank of Fujairah, Dubai; Bank of Oman, Dubai
Financial Information:

	1990 Dh'000
Sales turnover	20,000
Profits	3,000
Authorised capital	1,000
Paid-up capital	1,000
Total assets	3,000

Principal Shareholders: Mohd Humaid Mohd Shattaf,
 Dheerajmal Bastimal Siroya
Date of Establishment: 1982
No of Employees: 150

SIFICO GROUP

PO Box 1083, Sharjah
Tel: 06-523748
Telex: 68558 Beach EM
Telefax: 06-525422

Chairman: Dr Gabriel Matta
Directors: Albert Matta, Ziad Matta

PRINCIPAL ACTIVITIES: Construction, property, hotels and catering
Branch Offices: Abu Dhabi: PO Box 71453, Abu Dhabi, Tel 02-776000, Fax 02-785151; also branch in France
Parent Company: Head office in Lebanon: Old Damascus Road, Dr Matta Bldg, Hazmieh, Tel 450711, 450712, Telex 424477
Subsidiary Companies: Sharjah Specialised Industries; Abu Dhabi Specialised Industries; Gulf Swissotel; Sifico WLL; Summerland Real Estate; Patisserie Bourgeoise; Acapulco Laundries; Gulf Insecticides
Principal Bankers: United Bank Ltd, Sharjah; Banque Libanaise pour le Commerce, Abu Dhabi
Financial Information:

	1990 US$'000
Sales turnover	31,000
Profits	4,300

Principal Shareholders: Chairman and directors as described
Date of Establishment: 1958
No of Employees: 465

SIX CONSTRUCT LIMITED SA

PO Box 1472, Sharjah
Tel: 23453, 354136
Cable: Sixconstruct Sharjah
Telex: 68023 Sixco EM

PRINCIPAL ACTIVITIES: Civil engineering and construction (harbours, cement factories, power plants, roads, jetties, etc
Branch Offices: Belgium; Holland; France; Spain; Zaire; Sudan; Saudi Arabia; UAE (Abu Dhabi, Sharjah, Ras Al Khaimah, Ajman)

SOGEX SHARJAH

PO Box 598, Sharjah
Tel: 22045
Cable: Sogex

PRINCIPAL ACTIVITIES: Turnkey contractors, desalination, power stations, pipe lines, roads and other heavy industrial and civil engineering projects
Branch Offices: UAE (Abu Dhabi, Dubai, Sharjah); Oman; Germany

SOLO INDUSTRIES COMPANY

PO Box 6187, Sharjah
Tel: 06 330581
Cable: Solo Ind Sharjah
Telex: 68633 Solo EM
Telefax: 06 335617

President: M Patel
Senior Executives: P Thottan (General Manager)

PRINCIPAL ACTIVITIES: Non ferrous alloys smelter
Branch Offices: London, UK
Principal Bankers: ABN Bank, ANZ Grindlays Bank, Barclays Bank
Financial Information:

	1989 Dh'000	1990 Dh'000
Sales turnover	201,000	438,000
Profits	7,000	19,000
Paid-up capital	20,000	40,000
Total assets	72,000	142,000

Date of Establishment: 1980
No of Employees: 62

SPINNEYS (1948) LTD

PO Box 199, Sharjah
Tel: 357011, 357000

Directors: J B Hay, J M Lunn, R J Tatlow, R D Thurston

PRINCIPAL ACTIVITIES: Importers and supermarket operators
Principal Agencies: Nestle; Rowntree MacKintosh; Kraft; Coopers Wellcome
Branch Offices: Lebanon; Jordan; UAE (Abu Dhabi, Dubai, Sharjah, Ras Al Khaimah); Kuwait; Bahrain; Qatar; Oman; Saudi Arabia; Cyprus; Singapore; Indonesia
Parent Company: British & Commonwealth Holdings Plc

STANDARD CHARTERED BANK

PO Box 5, Sharjah
Tel: 357788
Cable: Stanchart
Telex: 68245 EM
Telefax: 546676

Senior Executives: A F King (Manager)

PRINCIPAL ACTIVITIES: Commercial banking
Branch Offices: In the Middle East: Bahrain; Oman; Qatar; Abu Dhabi; Dubai; Sharjah
Parent Company: Head office in London, UK

Date of Establishment: 1957
No of Employees: 45

SWISS ARAB INVESTMENT SERVICES (EX SOPADIF)

PO Box 3361, Sharjah
Tel: 375654, 355249, 23637
Telex: 68820 Swarab EM

President: Hamad Bin Saif Al Tounaiji
Directors: Vincent J Derudder (Vice President), Sheikh Omar El-Eid, Adnan Mehio

PRINCIPAL ACTIVITIES: Investment consultant and broker (precious metals, and precious stones, investment insurance plan, direct investment)
Principal Agencies: Legal and General; Royal Insurance; Swiss Arab Finance & Trade; Euro-Arab Commodities and Securities; Dunn & Hargitt
Branch Offices: Dubai, Abu Dhabi, Beirut, London, Geneva, Brussels
Parent Company: Swiss-Arab Bank & Trust; United Arab Leasing & Tourism
Associated Companies: Sopadif SA, Switzerland; International Investment & Sales, PO Box 14-5895, Beirut, Lebanon; United Arab Diamond PO Box 14, 5895 Beirut Lebanon; Kentucky Trading Ltd
Principal Bankers: Amro Bank (Dubai Branch); ABN (Sharjah); Swiss Arab Bank & Trust

Principal Shareholders: UALT
Date of Establishment: 1981

TALAL ABU-GHAZALEH & CO

Al Dar Audit Bureau

PO Box 952, Sharjah
Tel: 592484
Cable: Auditors
Telex: 68338 TAGI EM
Telefax: 596947

Chairman: Talal Abu Ghazaleh
Directors: Ali H Shalabi (Partner In-Charge)

PRINCIPAL ACTIVITIES: Public accountants, management and industrial consultants
Branch Offices: Kuwait (Head Office); Abu Dhabi; Dubai; Sharjah; Ras Al Khaimah; Lebanon; Egypt; Bahrain; Jordan;

Qatar; Oman; Libya; Saudi Arabia; Tunisia; Yemen AR; Yemen PDR
Parent Company: Talal Abu Ghazaleh International

Date of Establishment: 1972

TARMAC OVERSEAS LTD

PO Box 1499, Sharjah
Tel: 352338
Cable: Tarconst Sharjah
Telex: 68131 TARPNT EM

PRINCIPAL ACTIVITIES: Building and civil engineering constructions
Parent Company: Tarmac Plc

TECHNICAL & TRADING CO

PO Box 749, Sharjah
Tel: 23240

PRINCIPAL ACTIVITIES: General trading and contracting. Import and distribution of air-conditioning equipment, refrigerators, irrigation equipment and agricultural equipment
Principal Agencies: Tempair, Keeprite, Prestcold Int, English Electric, ICC, Exomet Plastics, Chloride Alcad Ltd, Du Pont, 3M, Sasco, Aglor, Belling, Fenner International, Copperweld
Branch Offices: Branches in Ras Al Khaimah and Dubai
Associated Companies: UNAMEC

TECHNICAL SUPPLIES & SERVICES CO

Head Office & Factory, PO Box 1818, Sharjah
Tel: 332344
Cable: Rima
Telex: 68221 Rima Em
Telefax: 331086

Chairman: Jamil G Nasr (Managing Director)

PRINCIPAL ACTIVITIES: Manufacture of insulated panels (polyurethane injected) and profiled insulated steel claddings for steel buildings
Branch Offices: Sales offices in Dubai and Abu Dhabi
Principal Bankers: First Gulf Bank, Dubai; Bank of Credit & Commerce, Sharjah; National Bank of Abu Dhabi
Financial Information:

	1990 Dh'000
Sales turnover	15,000
Paid-up capital	6,000
Total assets	3,000

Principal Shareholders: Sole proprietorship
Date of Establishment: 1962
No of Employees: 110

TERRAZZO INC

PO Box 5934, Sharjah
Tel: 333609 (5 lines)
Cable: Terazo
Telex: 68568 Terazo Em
Telefax: 333058

Chairman: Abdulrahman Bukhatir
Directors: Lovraj Talwar (Managing Director), Vijay Talwar (Director)
Senior Executives: Lave Malhotra (General Manager)

PRINCIPAL ACTIVITIES: Manufacturers of cement mosaic tiles and pre-cast mosaic elements, also cement roofing and paving tiles, manufacturers of fibreglass products, trading in granites and marble, etc
Branch Offices: Abu Dhabi: PO Box 6790, Tel 451829; Al Ain: PO Box 1932, Tel 657247; Bahrain: PO Box 5562, Manama, Tel 257078; Doha - Qatar: PO Box 5982, Tel 412659
Parent Company: Bukhatir Investments Ltd
Associated Companies: Trade House; German Gulf Ltd; Conmix; Emitac; Eastern; etc

Principal Bankers: Banque Indosuez; Banque Paribas; Commercial Bank of Dubai; BBME; Al Ahli Bank; First Gulf Bank
Financial Information:

	1990 US$'000
Sales turnover	7,000
Authorised capital	1,500
Paid-up capital	500
Total assets	3,000

Principal Shareholders: Bukhatir Investments Ltd
Date of Establishment: 1976
No of Employees: 250

TNT SKYPAK INTERNATIONAL UAE LTD

PO Box 3746, Skypak Bldg, 11 King Faisal Road, Sharjah
Tel: 373857 (4 lines)
Telex: 48816 Skydxb EM

Directors: J G Robertson (Regional Director), Sean Bradley (General Manager UAE)
Senior Executives: A Natarajan (Finance Manager UAE), A Davison (Operations Manager UAE)

PRINCIPAL ACTIVITIES: Worldwide courier service, collection, clearance and delivery of documents and commercial value items, also domestic road couriers, air freight, personal effects, household removals
Parent Company: TNT Limited
Principal Bankers: National Bank of Sharjah

Date of Establishment: March 1980

TRADE HOUSE INC

PO Box 1829, Al Wahda Street, Sharjah
Tel: 593745
Cable: Traho
Telex: 68539 Traho EM
Telefax: 06 596357

Chairman: Abdulrahman M Bukhatir
Directors: Lovraj Talwar (Managing Director)
Senior Executives: S R Munot (General Manager)

PRINCIPAL ACTIVITIES: Import and distribution of building materials, cement, sanitary ware, steel, tiles, timber
Principal Agencies: Settef Paints, Italy; Rock Tile, Japan; Heisterholz roof tiles, W Germany
Branch Offices: Abu Dhabi, Al Ain, Dubai
Parent Company: Bukhatir Investment Ltd
Associated Companies: Terrazzo Inc
Principal Bankers: Grindlays Bank, Banque Indosuez, Bank of Sharjah, National Bank of Sharjah, Banque Paribas, Al Ahli Bank of Dubai
Financial Information:

	1989 Dh'000
Sales turnover	30,000
Authorised capital	1,500
Paid-up capital	1,500

Principal Shareholders: Private Limited Company
Date of Establishment: 1975
No of Employees: 75

UNION BEVERAGES FACTORY

PO Box 5112, Sharjah
Tel: 331525
Cable: Omran Sharjah
Telex: 68148 Omran EM
Telefax: 330360

Chairman: Mohamed Abdulla Omran (Owner)
Senior Executives: George M Lazar (Deputy General Manager)

PRINCIPAL ACTIVITIES: Beverage bottling & mineral water production

Principal Agencies: Parle (Exports) Ltd, India; Royal Crown Cola
  Co, International, USA
Branch Offices: PO Box 501, Abu Dhabi, PO Box 541, Fujairah
Principal Bankers: Bank of Sharjah; Union Bank of the Middle
  East
Financial Information:

	1990 Dh'000
Sales turnover	25,000
Authorised capital	11,300
Paid-up capital	11,300

Principal Shareholders: Sole proprietorship
Date of Establishment: 1975
No of Employees: 180

UNION EST FOR ALUMINIUM & GLASS

PO Box 1770, Sharjah
Tel: 330368
Telex: 68259 Hetco Em
Telefax: (971-6) 330869

Chairman: Rashid Brously
Directors: Saif Rashid Saeed Hamarian, Ghanem Ibrahim Nasir
  Al Dheeb, Munir Abdul Qader Mansour
Senior Executives: Saleh Abdul Hameed (Technical Manager),
  Antoun Knayzeh (Project Manager), Mohd Abdul Wahid (Sales
  Manager), Mohd Khalique Akhtar (Accounts Manager)

PRINCIPAL ACTIVITIES: Manufacture of all types of aluminium
  and glass work for doors, windows, shopfronts, security
  grills, automatic door system with manual, electrical and
  remote control operations; import and export of glass,
  hardware and accessories
Subsidiary Companies: Al Rashid Glass Co, PO Box 6204,
  Sharjah; Khat Trading Est, PO Box 6990, Dubai
Principal Bankers: United Arab Bank, Sharjah; Abu Dhabi
  Commercial Bank, Sharjah
Financial Information:

	1989/90 US$'000
Sales turnover	6,500
Profits	550
Authorised capital	500
Paid-up capital	1,500

Date of Establishment: 1974
No of Employees: 115

UNITED ARAB BANK

PO Box 881, Sharjah
Tel: 354111/2/3
Cable: Uabank Sharjah
Telex: 68092 Uabank EM

Chairman: Sheikh Faisal Bin Sultan Al Qassimi
Directors: Martial Lesay (Vice Chairman), Melec du Halgouet,
  Sheikh Sultan Bin Saqr Al Qassimi, Sheikh Khalid Bin Saqr Al
  Qassimi, Ahmed Mohd Hamad Al Midfa, Mohammed Saleh
  Bin Badouh Al Darmaki, Hassan Mohd Abdul Rehman
  Khansaheb, Mohammed Saeed Al Qassimi, Saeed Ahmed
  Omran Al Marzroui, Abdullah Rashid Al Majid
Senior Executives: Jean Dubois (General Manager)

PRINCIPAL ACTIVITIES: Commercial banking
Branch Offices: PO Box 3562, Abu Dhabi; PO Box 4579, Deira,
  Dubai; PO Box 615, Ras Al Khaimah; PO Box 16077 Al Ain;
  PO Box 16823, Jebel Ali; PO Box 2700, Ajman
Parent Company: Societe Generale (France)
Financial Information:

	1989/90 Dh'000
Profits	26,048
Authorised capital	150,000
Paid-up capital	90,000
Total assets	1,198,470

Principal Shareholders: Societe Generale (20%), Local
  Shareholders (80%)
Date of Establishment: August 1975
No of Employees: 220

UNITED BANK LTD

PO Box 669, Sharjah
Tel: 22666
Cable: Sharjunited

PRINCIPAL ACTIVITIES: Commercial banking
Branch Offices: In the Middle East; Abu Dhabi, Dubai; Sharjah;
  Ras Al Khaimah; Umm Al Qaiwan; Qatar; Saudi Arabia;
  Bahrain; Yemen; Lebanon
Parent Company: Head office in Karachi, Pakistan

UNITED INDUSTRIAL & TRADING CO

PO Box 2057, Sharjah
Tel: 356408, 23010, 355060
Cable: Unitco Sharjah
Telex: 68101 Unitco EM

Chairman: Tarek A R Kaddouri (also Managing Director)
Directors: Shireen N M Kaddouri (Partner)

PRINCIPAL ACTIVITIES: Consultants (construction, engineering,
  industry) and general traders
Principal Agencies: Schaefer Systems International, Pepsi Cola,
  Vinora, Morris Ashby Ltd
Principal Bankers: Bank of Credit & Commerce International

Principal Shareholders: Tarek A R Kaddouri; Shireen N M
  Kaddouri

UNITED TRADING GROUP WLL

PO Box 1388, Sharjah
Tel: 332859
Cable: LUNA TRADE
Telex: 68356 Luna EM
Telefax: 332938

Senior Executives: Eng Ali Mahrous (Manager)

PRINCIPAL ACTIVITIES: Manufacture and supply of fibreglass
  products
Branch Offices: Arabian Gulf States
Parent Company: UTG Kuwait
Principal Bankers: United Bank Limited, Sharjah

Date of Establishment: 1974
No of Employees: 65

VINTO ENGINEERING GROUP

PO Box 5739, Sharjah
Tel: 357906/7
Telex: 68383 Candu EM

Chairman: Len Heerema (also Managing Director)
Directors: E Hedegaard, B Braithwaite

PRINCIPAL ACTIVITIES: Design and installation of electrical,
  plumbing and air-conditioning systems
Branch Offices: Vinto Engineering Ltd, Canada

Principal Shareholders: Vinto Engineering Ltd, L Heerema

WELLCOME ARABIAN GULF LTD

PO Box 5916, Sharjah
Tel: 356184, 545570
Telex: 68160 Wellco Em
Telefax: 523369

Senior Executives: N Kafisheh (Manager)

PRINCIPAL ACTIVITIES: Distribution of medical supplies and
  pharmaceuticals
Parent Company: The Wellcome Foundation Ltd, UK

Date of Establishment: 1977

ZAKHEM GULF LTD

PO Box 1510, Sharjah
Tel: 331752
Cable: Zakhemeng
Telefax: 335009

Chairman: A S Zakhem
Directors: George S Zakhem, Khalil H Zakhem (Managing
    Director), Abdalla S Zakhem

PRINCIPAL ACTIVITIES: General contracting
Parent Company: Zakhem International Construction Ltd, Jersey
Principal Bankers: Banque Libanaise pour le Commerce
    (France), Dubai
Financial Information:

	1990
	Dh'000
Authorised capital	2,400
Paid-up capital	2,400

Principal Shareholders: Zakhem International Construction Ltd,
    Jersey
Date of Establishment: 1974
No of Employees: 150

Umm Al Quwain

ABDUL RAHMAN ABUBAKKER
See ABUBAKKER, ABDUL RAHMAN,

ABUBAKKER, ABDUL RAHMAN,
PO Box 63, Umm Al Quwain
Tel: 666534

Chairman: Abdul Rahman Abubakker

PRINCIPAL ACTIVITIES: General trading and contracting

BANK OF OMAN
PO Box 127, Umm Al Quwain
Tel: 666448, 666948
Cable: BANOMAN

PRINCIPAL ACTIVITIES: Commercial banking
Branch Offices: In the UAE: Abu Dhabi, Ajman, Dubai, Fujairah, Ras Al Khaimah, Sharjah
Parent Company: Head office in Dubai

ETISALAT
PO Box 17, Umm Al Quwain
Tel: 666559
Telex: 69700 EM

PRINCIPAL ACTIVITIES: Telecommunications, telephone and telegraph systems
Branch Offices: Throughout the United Arab Emirates

MIDDLE EAST BANK LTD
PO Box 315, Umm Al Quwain
Tel: 666670, 666050
Cable: Mebank
Telex: 46074 EM

PRINCIPAL ACTIVITIES: Commercial banking
Branch Offices: Abu Dhabi, Dubai, Ras Al Khaimah, Sharjah
Parent Company: Head office in Dubai

Date of Establishment: 1979

NATIONAL BANK OF DUBAI
PO Box 22, Umm Al Quwain
Tel: 666151

PRINCIPAL ACTIVITIES: Commercial banking
Parent Company: Head office in Dubai

NATIONAL BANK OF UMM-AL-QAIWAIN LTD (THE)
PO Box 800, Umm-Al-Qaiwain
Tel: 665225, 665441/3
Cable: UMMBANK
Telex: 69733 NBUAQ EM
Telefax: 665440

Chairman: H H Shaikh Saud Bin Rashid Al-Moalla
Directors: Rashid Humaid Sultan (Deputy Chairman), Shaikh Nasser Bin Rashid Al-Moalla (Managing Director), Saeed Nasser Al-Talai, Abduljaleel Yousef Darwish, Abdullah Al Rustomani, Issa Abdulrahman Ateeq

PRINCIPAL ACTIVITIES: Commercial banking
Branch Offices: Umm Al-Qaiwain; Dubai; Abu Dhabi; Falaj Al-Moalla; Masfout
Principal Bankers: Chase Manhattan Bank NA, New York; First Interstate International of California, New York; Grindlays Bank PLC, London; Banco Di Roma, Milan; Fuji Bank Ltd, Tokyo; Sanwa Bank Ltd, Tokyo; Mitsubishi Bank Ltd, Tokyo;

Dresdner Bank AG, Frankfurt; Deutsche Bank AG, Frankfurt; Union Bank of Switzerland, Zurich
Financial Information:

	Dh'000
Authorised capital	500,000
Paid-up capital	250,000

Principal Shareholders: 100% UAE Nationals and Organisations
Date of Establishment: August 5, 1982
No of Employees: 85

NATIONAL ENGINEERING & CONTRACTING CO
PO Box 19, Umm Al Quwain
Tel: 666542
Cable: NOVAL-DUBAI
Telex: 46734 NOVAL EM

Chairman: Mohammed Abdullah Hussain
Directors: Jaffer Abdullah Hussain
Senior Executives: Sankara Narayanan (Manager)

PRINCIPAL ACTIVITIES: Civil contruction; importers and stockists of building materials and electrical materials; indentors and commission agents
Principal Agencies: Orient Wire, India; Laxmi Metal, India; China National Metals & Minerals, Shanghai; Kwok Hing Electrical, Hong Kong; Ferrosttal, Taiwan; Dawoo, Korea; Chronicle Trading, Hong Kong
Branch Offices: PO Box 5247, Dubai, Tel 282467
Associated Companies: Huda General Trading Est, PO Box 195, Umm Al Quwain; Noval General Trading Est, PO Box 5247, Dubai
Principal Bankers: Bank Credit & Commerce Int, Umm Al Quwain; Middle East Bank, Umm Al Quwain; Union Bank of the Middle East, Dubai

Date of Establishment: 1964
No of Employees: 750

UMM AL QUWAIN ASBESTOS CEMENT INDUSTRIES
PO Box 547, Umm Al Quwain
Tel: 666641/42
Cable: Arabit
Telex: 69711 Moalla EM

Chairman: Shaikh Saud Bin Rashid Al Moalla
Senior Executives: Abdul Aziz Salim Al Molahi (General Manager)

PRINCIPAL ACTIVITIES: Manufacture of asbestos cement pressure pipes, asbestos cement corrugated sheets, compressed flat sheets and coloured sheets
Principal Bankers: National Bank of Umm Al Quwain Ltd, Umm Al Quwain; Middle East Bank Ltd, Umm Al Quwain

Principal Shareholders: Government of Umm Al Quwain
Date of Establishment: 1979
No of Employees: 180

UMM AL QUWAIN MOTEL & RESTAURANT
PO Box 216, Umm Al Quwain
Tel: 666647
Telex: 47472 Rover EM

PRINCIPAL ACTIVITIES: Hotel business

UNION INSURANCE CO LTD
PO Box 460, Umm Al Quwain
Tel: 666223
Cable: Ticost
Telex: 45800 EM

Chairman: Sheikh Mohamed Bin Sultan Al-Moalla

PRINCIPAL ACTIVITIES: General insurance
Branch Offices: PO Box 4623, Riqa, Dubai; PO Box 3196, Abu Dhabi

UAE (Umm Al Quwain)

Principal Bankers: Grindlays Bank plc; Bank of Credit and
Commerce

Principal Shareholders: Prudential Assurance Co Ltd, London,
UK; Maynard, Reeve & Wallace Ltd, London, UK; Sudanese
Insurance & Reinsurance Co Ltd, Khartoum (Sudan)

Major Companies of YEMEN

ABDO MOHAMED SAEED ABOUDAHAB

See ABOUDAHAB, ABDO MOHAMED SAEED,

ABDUL KARIM A-R FARA AL-ASWADI

PO Box 3586, Hodeidah
Tel: 210923/28 (6lines)
Cable: Alfadhila
Telex: 5670, 5722 Fadhila YE
Telefax: (03) 211571

Chairman: Abdul Karim Abdu Rehman Fara Al-Aswadi
Senior Executives: Fadhle Hasson Yehia (Commercial Manager),
  Salah Abdul Sheikh (Director Chairman's Office)

PRINCIPAL ACTIVITIES: Import and supply of iron and steel,
  plywood, cement, galvanished steel pipes, timber
Branch Offices: Abdul Karim A R Fara Al-Aswadi, Sanaa
Subsidiary Companies: Abdul Rehman A K A Al Aswadi,
  Hodeidah; Mustafa A Hafeed Co, Hodeidah
Principal Bankers: Yemen Bank for Reconstruction &
  Development; Banque Indosuez; Arab Bank

Principal Shareholders: Chairman and director
Date of Establishment: 1968
No of Employees: 120

ABDUL KHALIL SULAIMAN

See SULAIMAN, ABDUL KHALIL,

ABDULLA M FAHEM & CO

See FAHEM, ABDULLA M, & CO

ABDULLAH HASSAN AL SONIDAR & SONS

See AL SONIDAR, ABDULLAH HASSAN, & SONS

ABDULLAH SALEH EL-AGHIL & SONS

See EL-AGHIL, ABDULLAH SALEH, & SONS

ABOUDAHAB, ABDO MOHAMED SAEED,

PO Box 5252, Taiz
Tel: 226325
Cable: Aboudahab Taiz
Telex: 8801 Abdhab YE
Telefax: 219623

President: Abdo Mohd Saeed Abu Dhahab
Directors: Waleed Abdo Mohamed Saeed (Managing Director)
Senior Executives: Jamal Abdo Mohamed Saeed (Manager)

PRINCIPAL ACTIVITIES: Agency trading in stationery, office
  equipment, furniture, glass, household goods, jewellery and
  leather products; general merchants and commission agents,
  sportswear
Branch Offices: Mokha
Principal Bankers: Yemen Bank for Reconstruction &
  Development, Taiz; Arab Bank, Taiz

Date of Establishment: 1948

ADEN BUS CO LTD

Adbusco Bldg, Ma'alla, PO Box 905, Aden

Chairman: Saeed Fara Salim (also Managing Director)

PRINCIPAL ACTIVITIES: Public transport

ADEN EMULSION & PAINT CO LTD

PO Box 5153, Ma'alla, Aden
Tel: 24292
Cable: Emulsion
Telex: 2500 AD

Chairman: Mohammed Ali Assakkaf
Directors: A M Khader, A O Assafi, A N Gaber, M A AlKirbi, F
  M Khalifa, A A Awad, F A Kassim, M A Bari
Senior Executives: M A Assakkaf (General Manager), A Aziz
  Mustafa (Technical Manager), Awad S Hassan (Production
  Manager), A K Farawi (Chief Accountant)

PRINCIPAL ACTIVITIES: Production of all types of marine
  paints and emulsions and gloss enamels
Principal Bankers: National Bank of Yemen

Principal Shareholders: Government (58%), private sector (42%)
Date of Establishment: 1966
No of Employees: 95

ADEN REFINERY COMPANY

PO Box 3003, Little Aden 110
Tel: 76234, 76258, 76244, 76251, 76214
Cable: Refineries Aden
Telex: 2213 YD RFINRY

Directors: Mohamed Hussein Al Haj (Executive Director)
Senior Executives: Ahmed Hasson Al Gifri (Refinery Manager),
  Jaffer Mohamed Al Sakkaf (Chief Engineer), Omer Awadh
  Bamatraf (Chief Accountant), Mostafa Othman Salem
  (Operations Superintendent), Yehia Murshed Ahmed
  (Production Coordinator), Eng Mohamed Ali Noor (Refinery
  Maintenance Engineer), Mohsen Ali Saeed (Refinery Stores
  Superintendent), Mahfoodh Mohd Saeed (Marine
  Superintendent), Abdulla Mohsen Saleh (Power Engineer)

PRINCIPAL ACTIVITIES: Refining crude petroleum on behalf of
  national oil companies and international oil groups. Total
  capacity 8,000,000 tons/annum. Production of vacuum gas oil
  and drummed asphalt; transportation of petroleum products
  by coastal tankers within the Red Sea and Gulf Areas
Subsidiary Companies: The Aden Bunkering Company
Principal Bankers: National Bank of Yemen
Financial Information: Assets insured to value of 450,000,000
  dollars

	1990 YD'000
Authorised capital	101,000
Paid-up capital	24,349

Principal Shareholders: Wholly owned subsidiary of Ministry of
  Oil & Mineral Resources
Date of Establishment: September 1952
No of Employees: 2,400

ADHBAN TRADING CORPORATION

PO Box 1105, Sana'a
Tel: 74501, 76540, 78111
Cable: Adhban Sanaa
Telex: 2260 Adhban YE, 2462, 2212

Chairman: Mohamed Mubarak Adhban
Directors: Hussain Mubarak Adhban
Senior Executives: Ahmed Sarhan, Abdullah Nadeesh, Mubarak
  Logman, Dr A M Al Husseini

PRINCIPAL ACTIVITIES: Manufacturers' representation, import
  and distribution of agricultural machinery and equipment;
  export of agricultural produce; transportation contractors
Principal Agencies: Nissan Diesel; Mitsubishi Motors; Mitsubishi
  Heavy Industries; Group Renault
Branch Offices: 14 branches in Yemen AR (Sana'a, Hodeidah,
  Taiz, etc); Saudi Arabia; Somalia; Yemen PDR; Tokyo;
  London; Paris
Subsidiary/Associated Companies: Al Halal Maritime Co;
  Adhban Trading Corp; Associates: Agricultural Cooperative
  Co; Adhban Co for Agriculture & Transportation; Adhban
  Corp for Trade & Industry; Adhban Brothers (Yemen) Ltd;
  Adhban Travel & Tourism; Adhban Industrial & Petroleum
  Services
Principal Bankers: Yemen Bank for Reconstruction &
  Development; Arab Bank Ltd; British Bank of the Middle East
Financial Information:

	US$'000
Sales turnover	100,000

Principal Shareholders: Chairman & directors as described
Date of Establishment: 1947
No of Employees: 600

YEMEN

AGRICULTURAL SOLIDARITY CO

PO Box 1105, Sana'a
Tel: 72780
Cable: Adhban

PRINCIPAL ACTIVITIES: Import and distribution of agricultural
equipment and machinery, pumps and grinding machines

AKLAN & MOHAMED SAEED GHANNAMI

See GHANNAMI, AKLAN & MOHAMED SAEED,

AL ABSI TRADING CORPORATION

Omer Mohamed Taleb Al Absi Stores

PO Box 3914, Hodeidah
Tel: 245400, 245617
Cable: Omabsi
Telex: 5678 Bureau YE

Proprietor: Omer Mohamde Taleb Al Absi

PRINCIPAL ACTIVITIES: General trading and contracting
dealing in foodstuffs, tea, building materials, sanitary ware,
paints, textiles, glassware, water pumps, tractors, auto spare
parts
Branch Offices: Sanaa, Tel 217025; Taiz, Tel 230028/9
Subsidiary/Associated Companies: Yemen United Beverages Co
(Canada Dry Hodeidah); Maeen Mineral Waters Co Ltd;
Yemen Co for Ghee & Soap Manufacture Ltd; Subsidairies:
Factory for Textiles; Factory for Sewing; Factory for Cotton
Towels; Factory for Bed Sheets; Factory for Canning Fruits;
Factory for Electric Wires; Factory for Galvanized Steel Pipes;
Factory for Packing Honey
Principal Bankers: Arab Bank Ltd; Habib Bank Ltd
Financial Information:

	YR'000
Sales turnover	70,000

Date of Establishment: 1962

AL ASNAG, SHAHER SAIF AHMED, & BROS

PO Box (4) 411, Taiz
Tel: 72355, 72021
Cable: Abdulsmad

Chairman: Shaher Saif Al Asnag (Partner)

PRINCIPAL ACTIVITIES: Import and distribution of foodstuffs,
building materials, cars and spare parts, commission agents
Principal Agencies: Lipton Ltd, UK; Sikkens Groep NV
Sassenheim, Holland; Auto Export, Moscow; Energymash
Exports, Moscow; Machine Export, Moscow; Techmash
Export, Moscow; Water Pumps; and Danish manufacturers for
biscuits, soaps and cooking oil
Branch Offices: Branches in Sana'a, PO Box 1486; and
Hodeidah

ALBUKARI, HUSSEIN SULEIMAN, & CO

Albukari Building, PO Box 3358 or 3607, Hodeidah
Tel: 245320, 245514, 72381
Cable: Al Bukari Hodeidah
Telex: 5548 Bukari YE

Directors: Hussein S Albukari (Managing Director), Faisal A
Albukari

PRINCIPAL ACTIVITIES: Import of foodstuffs (wheat, wheat
flour, sugar, rice) cement, multiwall paper sacks etc
Principal Agencies: Thomas Cook Bankers
Branch Offices: Sanaa, Tel 227373/75326
Subsidiary Companies: Albukari Shipping Co Ltd
Principal Bankers: Yemen Bank for Re-Construction &
Development, Hodeidah; Arab Bank, Hodeidah; Habib Bank
Ltd, London

Date of Establishment: 1912

ALBUKARI SHIPPING CO LTD

Albukari Building, PO Box 3358 or 3607, Hodeidah
Tel: 245320, 245514, 72381
Cable: Bukariship Hodeidah
Telex: 5548 Bukari Ye

Directors: Hussein S Albukari (Managing Director), Faisal A
Albukari (Director)

PRINCIPAL ACTIVITIES: Shipowners, managers, charterers,
liner and charterers agents, clearing and forwarding agents,
stevedores and lighterman many shipping lines/compaines
Associated Companies: Hussein Suleiman Albukari & Co
Principal Bankers: Yemen Bank for Re-Construction &
Development, Hodeidah; Arab Bank, Hodeidah; Habib Bank
Ltd, London

Date of Establishment: 1978
No of Employees: 100

ALGHALEBI SHIPPING CO (YEMEN) LTD

PO Box 3113, Sanaa Road, Hodeidah
Tel: 73806, 73807, 238396, 231424
Cable: Alghalebi
Telex: 5547 Chlabi YE

Directors: S S Alghalebi (Managing Director)
Senior Executives: A I Kadhi

PRINCIPAL ACTIVITIES: Insurance, surveyors, general trading,
shipping agency
Principal Bankers: Arab Bank Ltd

Date of Establishment: 1962

ALGUNDI PLASTIC FACTORY

PO Box 4206, Khormaksar, Gamal Camp, Crater, Aden
Tel: 53890
Cable: Algundi
Telex: 2273 Industry Aden

Chairman: Abdulla Humza Mohamood
Directors: Mrs Aida Salem Abood, Hasson Mahmoud Abdul
Rehman (Director General)

PRINCIPAL ACTIVITIES: Manufacture and marketing of plastic
household utensils; manufacture of polyethylene bags of
various sizes, and crates
Principal Bankers: The National Bank of Yemen

ALI OMAR AHMED BAZARA

See BAZARA, ALI OMAR AHMED,

ALMUTAHAR MOTOR & ENGINEERING CO

PO Box 522, Al Zubeiri Street, Sana'a
Tel: 207020, 207021, 207018
Cable: Almutahar
Telex: 2242 Ameco YE

Chairman: Abdussamad Mutahar Said
Directors: Abdul Wahed Mutahar Said

PRINCIPAL ACTIVITIES: Civil works and roads contractors;
general importers (electrical appliances and equipment,
tractors, tiles, building materials and equipments, spare parts
for trucks), also carpentry, vehicles assembly, tiles and
marble factory, manufacturers' representatives
Principal Agencies: Lancia, Fiat, Massey Ferguson, Landini,
Benati, Aifo
Branch Offices: Hodeidah Branch: PO Box 633, Hodeidah, Tel
224312; Telex 5535
Associated Companies: Joint Venture Almutahar/YCON; Joint
Venture Jean Lefebve/Almutahar
Principal Bankers: Yemen Bank for Reconstruction &
Development, Sana'a, Banque Indosuez, Hodeidah, Yemen

Bank for Trade & Investment, Sanaa; Bank of Credit of Commerce, Sanaa

Principal Shareholders: Abdussamad Mutahar Said, Abdul Wahed Mutahar Said

AL SONIDAR, ABDULLAH HASSAN, & SONS

PO Box 11, Sana'a
Tel: 224142, 224141
Telex: 2226 YE

Chairman: Ali Abdullah Al Sonidar
Directors: Mohamed Abdullah Al Sonidar (Managing Director), Hassan Abdullah Al Sonidar (Joint Managing Director)

PRINCIPAL ACTIVITIES: Import and distribution of diesel engines, and heavy machinery; agricultural equipment etc
Principal Agencies: Caprari Pumps, Tractors; Valpadana Tractors; Sicar Wood Working Machines; VM Diesel Engines; Blackstone Engines, Equipment for Agricultural Machinery and Heavy Machinery

AL SUFFARI, MOHAMED SAEED GHALEB,

PO Box 4309, Taiz

PRINCIPAL ACTIVITIES: Import and distribution of cars and spare parts, pharmaceuticals, household goods, foodstuffs and general merchandise
Branch Offices: Branches in Sana'a and Hodeidah (PO Box 593)

ALTHOR INDUSTRIAL & TRADING CO

PO Box 29, Sana'a
Tel: 72557, 72528
Cable: Althor Sanaa
Telex: 2258

President: Mohamed Althor
Directors: Ismail Althor (Director General)

PRINCIPAL ACTIVITIES: Manufacturers' representation, import and distribution of automobiles, and agricultural equipment, construction and building contractors
Principal Agencies: BMW, Pluger Pumps, Kolb Kelb, Striver (Abdullah Moh. Althor); Cellpack, Cablex (Switzerland), Walsall (UK), Coutinho (W Germany) (Althor Corporation); Harrath, G&M, Haywar Tailor & Associates (Althor Company)
Branch Offices: Branch in Hodeidah, PO Box 3155
Parent Company: Alhag Mohd Abdullah Althor & Sons Corp, Sana'a
Principal Bankers: Yemen Bank for Reconstruction & Development; Kuwait and Yemen Bank

Principal Shareholders: Mohd Mohd Abdullah Althor, Ismail Mohd Abdullah Althor, Ali Mohd Abdullah Althor, Abdullah Mohd Abdullah Althor
Date of Establishment: 1945

ALWATAARY GENERAL TRADING & AGRICULTURAL DEVELOPMENT CO

PO Box 61-2207, Sana'a
Tel: 71791, 71796, 73808
Cable: Wataary
Telex: 2268 Wataary YE, 2595 AITC YE

Chairman: Al-Haj Hussein Ali Alwataary
Directors: Al-Haj Mohamed Ali Alwataary, Ali Hussein Alwataary (General Manager), Abdulla Mohamed Alwataary (Deputy General Manager)

PRINCIPAL ACTIVITIES: Importers-exporters and general merchants; heavy and light equipment, etc, agricultural tractors, autos, tippers, commercial vehicles, drilling services, workshop facilities, manufacturing, mineral water plant
Principal Agencies: JCB Sales, UK; Ingersoll Rand, USA; Honda Motors, Japan; Detroit Diesel Allison, USA; X Fendt & Co, W Germany; Nardi, Italy; DAF Trucks, Holland
Subsidiary Companies: Azal Industrial Development Co

Principal Bankers: Yemen Bank for Reconstruction & Development; Bank of Credit & Commerce International

Principal Shareholders: Al-Haj Hussein Alwataary, Al Haj Mohamed Alwataary

ALYEMDA AIR YEMEN

PO Box 6006, Khormakser Aden
Tel: 31339, 33251, 31060, 31954
Cable: Alyemda
Telex: 2269
Telefax: 33287

Chairman: Abdalla A Abdalla (General Manager)
Directors: Saeed N Sinan (Deputy General Manager Technical), Ali A Althahs (Deputy General Manager Commercial Administration & Finance), S M Fulais (Technical Director), Salem M Saeed (Planning Director), Mohammed Saif (Finance Director), Fadle Kassim (Purchasing Director), Adel A Alawi (Commercial Director)
Senior Executives: Gamal A Hubaishi (Ground Handling Manager), Ali Muthana (Manager Chairman's Office), A M Remman (Manpower Manager)

PRINCIPAL ACTIVITIES: National airline
Principal Agencies: 35 international airlines
Branch Offices: Abu Dhabi; Addis Ababa; Bombay; Beirut; Cairo; Damascus; Doha; Dubai; Djibouti; Jeddah; Kuwait; Mogadishn; Sharjah; Ajman; Fujairah; Sanaa; Taiz; Sofia; Cairo; Budapest; Larnaca; Tripoli
Principal Bankers: National Bank of Yemen

Principal Shareholders: Wholly owned by the Government
Date of Establishment: March 1971
No of Employees: 1,180

ANAM & THABET CONSTRUCTION & DEVELOPMENT EST LTD

PO Box 32, Sana'a
Tel: 72272, 72606
Cable: Inshaat
Telex: 2221 Bilquis YE

PRINCIPAL ACTIVITIES: Contractors; tenderers for international projects in Yemen. Main projects: Sana'a Water Supply, Sana'a Industrial Estate, Military Police College, Meterological Station

ARAB BANK PLC

PO Box 1301 & 475, Zubairi Road, Sana'a
Tel: 240922, 240924, 240926, 240927
Cable: Bankarabi
Telex: 2239 Arbank YE, 2641

PRINCIPAL ACTIVITIES: Commercial banking
Branch Offices: Hodeidah; PO Box 3812, Hodeidah, Telex 5523; Taiz: PO Box 5234, Jamal Abdul Nasser Street, Taiz, Telex 8911 Arbank, Tel 231523, 213525
Parent Company: Head office in Amman, Jordan

Date of Establishment: 1972

ARAB COMMERCIAL ENTERPRISES LTD

PO Box 2073, Sana'a
Tel: 76677, 76678
Cable: Comment Sanaa
Telex: 2451 Acesan YE

Senior Executives: Said M Midani (Manager)

PRINCIPAL ACTIVITIES: Insurance and travel agents

ARAB GENERAL TRADING CO

PO Box 4195, Zafaran St, Crater 101, Aden
Tel: 52479, 53450, 82266
Cable: Amana Aden
Telex: 607

Chairman: Hassan Ali Bazara (Owner)

Directors: Omer Hassan Bazara (General Manager)

PRINCIPAL ACTIVITIES: Distribution and sale of marine diesel engines, agricultural tractors, industrial tractors, cranes, petrol pumps, electric generators, water vertical turbine pumps; contractors and engineers for oil companies, government and private companies, manufacturers representatives

Principal Agencies: Gardner Engines Ltd; David Brown Tractors Ltd

Branch Offices: Berbera; Mukalla; Hodeidah

Date of Establishment: 1873

ARABIAN MATCH CO

PO Box 4184, Crater, Aden
Tel: 43511/2
Cable: Kibrit
Telex: 2257 Kibrit YD

Chairman: Taha Mohammed Shaker
Directors: Salem Abdulrahman Al Ammari (General Manager)
Senior Executives: Ahmed Abdo Mohamed (Finance Manager), Saleh Abdul Rab (Commercial Manager), Mohamed Hanif Abdul Majid (Purchasing Manager), Hassan Ahmed Al Sakkaf (Production Manager)

PRINCIPAL ACTIVITIES: Manufacture of all kinds of matches
Principal Bankers: National Bank of Yemen

Principal Shareholders: Mixed sector company
Date of Establishment: 1973
No of Employees: 580

ARWA MINERAL WATER CO LTD

PO Box 1108, Sana'a
Tel: 272901
Telex: 2203

Chairman: Hayel Saeed Anam

PRINCIPAL ACTIVITIES: Production of mineral water at Shamlan near Sana'a

Principal Shareholders: Hayel Saeed Anam & Company
Date of Establishment: 1979

BADANI TRADING AGENCY

PO Box 1129, Sanaa
Tel: 72791
Cable: Badani

Chairman: Mansoor Nasher Albadani
Directors: Naser M Nasher Albadani
Senior Executives: Omer M Albadani (Ship Manager), Mohid M Albadani (Shop Manager, Branch), Saleh M Albadani (Shop Manager, Branch)

PRINCIPAL ACTIVITIES: Property owners, and real state developers; agents, import, export, distribution of shoes, ready-made garments, cosmetics & toiletries, electrical appliances, textiles, blankets, foodstuffs
Principal Agencies: Noel (shoes), Labelle (shoes), Tootal (exclusive), Marie-Claire (France), Arataki (New Zealand)
Branch Offices: Hodeidah: PO Box 3069; Aden: PO Box 659
Principal Bankers: Yemen Bank, Sana'a; Middle East Bank, Hodeidah; Arab Bank, Hodeidah

BANK OF CREDIT & COMMERCE INTERNATIONAL SA

PO Box 160, Al Qasr St, Sana'a
Tel: 73953/4
Cable: Bancrecom
Telex: 2267 Bcci YE

PRINCIPAL ACTIVITIES: Commercial banking
Branch Offices: Hodeidah: PO Box 3473, Tel 2127640, Telex 5575

Date of Establishment: 1975

BANQUE INDOSUEZ

PO Box 651, Al Kasr Al Gumhuria Street, Sana'a
Tel: 27801/3
Cable: Indosuez Yemen
Telex: 2412 Indobk YE

PRINCIPAL ACTIVITIES: Commercial banking
Branch Offices: Hodeidah, Taiz
Parent Company: Head office in Paris, France

BAZARA, ALI OMAR AHMED,

Sheikh Abdulla St, PO Box 899, Aden
Tel: 52625
Cable: Bawagih

Chairman: Abdulrehman Ali Omar Ahmed Bazara

PRINCIPAL ACTIVITIES: Export of gum myrrh, cow bladder stone, kid skins, civet and Persian carpets and marine products; import of machine and hand-made carpets, spices, French and Japanese second-hand motor cars and general merchandise
Principal Bankers: National Bank of Yemen

CENTRAL BANK OF YEMEN

PO Box 59, Ali Abdel Moghi Street, Sana'a
Tel: 79351-56
Cable: Markazi Sanaa
Telex: 2210 Markazi

PRINCIPAL ACTIVITIES: Central banking
Branch Offices: Aden (PO Box 452), Taiz, Hodeidah, Sana'a, Ibb, Dhamar, Hajjah, Beidha, Mareb, Mahweet

Principal Shareholders: State-owned
Date of Establishment: 1971

CITIBANK NA

PO Box 2133, Zubeoro Rd, Sana'a
Tel: 75796
Cable: Citibranch/Citibank
Telex: 2276 Citibk YE

PRINCIPAL ACTIVITIES: Commercial banking
Parent Company: Head office in New York, USA

COMMERCIAL CO-OPERATION CO

PO Box 5291, Taiz
Tel: 225838, 225837
Cable: Makhafy Taiz
Telex: 8835 Mak -cco YE
Telefax: 212369

Chairman: Yahya Ali Makhafy
Directors: Abdul Aziz Ali Makhafy (General Manager), Ahmed Ali Makhafy (Partner)

PRINCIPAL ACTIVITIES: Import of pharmaceuticals, baby food and articles, cosmetics and perfumes; building materials and general trade and domestic appliances
Principal Agencies: Boehringer Ingelheim, W Germany; Grunenthal, W Germany; Novo Industri, Denmark; H Lundbeck, Denmark; ABC Torino, Italy; Menarini, Italy; Plasmon Dietetici Alimentare, Italy
Branch Offices: Sana'a: PO Box 203, Tel 271964; Hodeidah: PO Box 3424, Tel 238418
Subsidiary Companies: The Central Pharmacy; International Drugstore
Principal Bankers: Yemen Bank for Reconstruction & Development

Financial Information:

	1989
	YR'000
Sales turnover	30,000
Authorised capital	1,000
Paid-up capital	1,000
Total assets	50,000

Principal Shareholders: Partners as described above
Date of Establishment: 1953

EL-AGHIL, ABDULLAH SALEH, & SONS

PO Box 72, Sana'a
Tel: 72573
Cable: Yemstore

Chairman: Abdullah Saleh El-Aghil (Proprietor)

PRINCIPAL ACTIVITIES: Import and distribution of building
materials, cement and tiles

EL AGHIL GROUP OF COMPANIES

PO Box 66, Sanaa
Tel: 78123, 77172
Cable: ELAGHIL SANAA YEMEN
Telex: 2373

Chairman: A A El Aghil
Directors: Ali Nasser El Aghil

PRINCIPAL ACTIVITIES: Supply of heavy duty equipment,
construction plant; electrical and electronic equipment and
appliances, motor engines, batteries, general trading; shipping
etc
Principal Agencies: Volvo; Westinghouse; Electrolux; Facit
Branch Offices: Hodeidah: PO Box 3686, Tel 72181, Telex 5667
Subsidiary Companies: El Aghil Trading Co; Yemen Garment
Co; Yemen Shipping Co; Yemen Cement Silos Co; Yemen Dry
Cell Battery Co
Principal Bankers: Yemen Bank for Reconstruction and
Development, Sana'a

Date of Establishment: 1932
No of Employees: 500

ELKIRSHI SHIPPING & STEVEDORING CO

PO Box 3813, Al Hanidi Street, Hodeidah
Tel: 224263, 224338
Cable: Kirship
Telex: 5569 Sultan YE

PRINCIPAL ACTIVITIES: Clearing, forwarding, shipping,
transportation
Branch Offices: Ports: Hodeidah; Mokha; Saleef

ELMOHDAR & AHMED ABDULLAH ZEID

PO Box 1473, Sana'a
Tel: 207433, 207434
Cable: Mohdar Sanaa
Telex: 2272 MOHDAR YE, 2300 KIRBEE YE

Chairman: Elmohd Ar Abdullah Zeid
Directors: Abdullah Ahmed Zeid (General Manager)

PRINCIPAL ACTIVITIES: Manufacturers' representation, import
and distribution of agricultural machinery and equipment,
construction heavy machinery, and heavy trucks
Principal Agencies: Fiat, Fiat-Allis Construction Machinery
Branch Offices: Branches in Hodeidah, PO Box 3074, and in
Taiz, PO Box 4304
Principal Bankers: Yemen Bank for Reconstruction and
Development

Principal Shareholders: Elmohdar A Zeid, Ahmed A Zeid
Date of Establishment: 1948

ERNST & WHINNEY

PO Box 137, 1st Floor, Al Matari Bldg, Zubeiry Street, Sana'a
Tel: 275068, 275042
Cable: TCC Sana'a
Telex: 2813
Telefax: 274106

PRINCIPAL ACTIVITIES: Accountants and management
consultants
Branch Offices: Offices throughout the Middle East

FAHEM, ABDULLA M, & CO

PO Box 3637, Hodeidah
Tel: 79062, 72518, 245387
Cable: Fahem
Telex: 5611 Fahem YE

Chairman: Abdulla Mohd Fahem
Directors: Mohed Fahem (Manager)
Senior Executives: Ahmed Haider Fahem

PRINCIPAL ACTIVITIES: Import and distribution of food
products, detergents, soap, building materials
Branch Offices: Sanaa Office

Principal Shareholders: Abdulla Mohd Fahem, Haider Mohd
Fahem
Date of Establishment: 1955
No of Employees: 50

GENERAL CORPORATION FOR FOREIGN
TRADE & GRAINS

PO Box 77, 163 Al Matar Street, Sana'a
Tel: 223858, 223860
Cable: Gftcorp
Telex: 2348, 2349, 2262 GCFTG YE

Chairman: Dr Ahmad Al Hamdani
Directors: Abdullah Al Aghbari (Managing Director)
Senior Executives: Qassim Al Sabri, Ahmad Al Arashi
(Commercial Manager), Yahia Zaffan (Financial Manager),
Ahmad Al Kadadi (Personnel Manager), Nasher Hashem
(Technical Manager)

PRINCIPAL ACTIVITIES: Import of building materials, heavy
equipment, furniture, foodstuffs
Branch Offices: Hodeidah, Taiz
Principal Bankers: Central Bank of Yemen; Yemen Bank for
Reconstruction & Development
Financial Information:

	YR'000
Sales turnover	2,000,000
Authorised capital	205,000
Paid-up capital	205,000

Principal Shareholders: State-owned
Date of Establishment: 1976
No of Employees: 950

GENERAL INDUSTRIES & PACKAGES

PO Box 5302, Taiz
Tel: 218027
Telex: 8946 Genpack YE
Telefax: 4-218024

Chairman: Ali Mohamed Saeed
Directors: Ahmed Hayel (Managing Director), Abdul Gabbar
Hayel Saeed
Senior Executives: Khaled Ahmed Hayel (General Manager),
Mahfouz Ali Mohamed Saeed

PRINCIPAL ACTIVITIES: Manufacture of cosmetics, disposable
diapers and sanitary towels, chocolate bars, snacks,
confectionery, pasta, etc
Branch Offices: Sana'a, Hodeidah
Parent Company: Hayel Saeed Anam & Co
Principal Bankers: Yemen Bank for Reconstruction &
Development; Indosuez Bank, Taiz; Arab Bank

YEMEN

Principal Shareholders: Hayel Saeed Anam & Co
Date of Establishment: October 1985
No of Employees: 605

GHAILANS CO FOR GENERAL TRADE & DISTRIBUTION
PO Box 4860, Taiz

Chairman: Ghailan Hassan

PRINCIPAL ACTIVITIES: Import and distribution of clothing, food products, household electrical appliances, water heaters, washing machines, radios, watches

GHANNAMI, AKLAN & MOHAMED SAEED,
PO Box 4812, Taiz
Tel: 2287
Cable: Ghannami Taiz
Telex: 8845 Ghannami YE, 5657 Canal YE

Chairman: Hag Mohamed Saeed Ghannami
Directors: Ali M Ghannami, Abdulla M Ghannami, Saeed M Ghannami

PRINCIPAL ACTIVITIES: Importers, distributors, wholesalers of automotive spare parts and accessories
Principal Agencies: Bridgestone Tire Co Ltd; ICI Paints Division, England; Lucas Group products; AP Group products, England; OHK Brand spring & leaves, Japan; NGK Brand sparkplugs, Japan; Vauxhall/Bedford cars and trucks; AC/General Motor spare parts
Branch Offices: Hodeidah: Main St, Tel 73637, 73246, Telex 5657
Principal Bankers: Yemen Bank for Reconstruction and Development, Taiz; British Bank of the Middle East, Taiz; Arab Bank, Hodeidah

Principal Shareholders: Aklan and Mohamed Saeed Ghannami
Date of Establishment: 1951
No of Employees: 80

HABIB BANK LTD
Al-Akhwa Bldg, Sana'a Rd, PO Box 3927, Hodeidah
Tel: 239205, 239208
Cable: Habibank
Telex: 5518 YE HABIB

PRINCIPAL ACTIVITIES: Commercial banking
Parent Company: Head office in Karachi, Pakistan

Date of Establishment: 1971

HALAL SHIPPING CO (YEMEN) LTD
PO Box 3147, Hodeidah
Tel: 231579, 231580, 224330
Cable: Halal
Telex: 5508 Halal YE, 5573 ADHBAN YE
Telefax: 211524

Chairman: Haj Mohammed Mubarak Adhban
Directors: Haj Mohd Adhban, Haj Hussein Adhban (Vice Chairman)
Senior Executives: Mubarak Abdo Rabo Adhban (General Manager)

PRINCIPAL ACTIVITIES: Shipping agents, stevedores, lighterage, warehousing, clearing and forwarding agents, insurance representatives and surveyors
Principal Agencies: NYK; CMA; Hoegh; Hual; CMB; Continental; CGM; Kaybee; Jugolinija; IAAC; DMC; Korea Tonghae; Afram; etc
Branch Offices: Branch offices in Mokha and Saleef; liaison offices in Sana'a and Taiz
Parent Company: Adhban Trading Corporation, Sana'a
Associated Companies: Adhban Brothers Co (Yemen) Ltd; Adhban Trading Corporation Agricultural Cooperative Co; Adhban Co for Trade and Industry; Adhban Co for Agriculture

& Transport; Adhban Travel & Tourism; Adhban Industrial & Petroleum Services Co Ltd; Adhban Trade & Marketing Co
Principal Bankers: Yemen Bank for Reconstruction and Development; Banque Indosuez

Principal Shareholders: Adhban Trading Corporation
Date of Establishment: 1969
No of Employees: 50

HAYEL SAEED ANAM GROUP OF COMPANIES
Hayel Saeed Anam & Company
PO Box 5302, Taiz
Tel: 215171/2
Cable: Hayelsaeed
Telex: 8804 HSAYE
Telefax: 212334

Chairman: Hayel Saeed Anam
Directors: Ali Mohamed Saeed (Vice-Chairman), Ahmed Hayel Saeed (Managing Director), Abdul Rahman Hayel Saeed (Deputy Managing Director), Abdul Wasa Hayel Saeed (Executive Director), Abdul Gabar Hayel Saeed (Executive Director), Abdulla Abdo Saeed (Finance Director), Mahfouz Ali Mohamed Saeed (Director Technical)
Senior Executives: Mohamed Abdo Saeed, Abdul Galil Gazem, Ahmed Gazem Saeed, Mahfouz Ali Mohamed Saeed, Kaid Gazem Saeed, Saeed Abdo Saeed, Dirham Abdo Saeed, Ibrahim Hayel Saeed

PRINCIPAL ACTIVITIES: Import, cold storage and distribution of a wide range of foodstuffs including, wheat, flour, sugar, spices, tea, milk & dairy products, rice, ghee, edible oil and canned foodstuffs, cigarettes, fertilizers, cement, metallurgical and other building materials, house appliances, electrical equipment, furniture, stationery, textiles, also shipping agents, insurance and travel agents, etc
Principal Agencies: Rothmans of Pall Mall (Overseas), UK; Unilever Export, UK; Standard Brands, USA; Wrigley Co Ltd; Bunge (Australia) Pty, Australia; Gillette Industries, UK; Aladdin; British Cellophane; BP Chemicals; Kraft; Shell; Borden Foods; Mitsubishi, UK; Heracles, Greece; Lipton Exports; Ciba Geigy; ICI; Shupbach; GIG Duisburg, W Germany; Conserven Hero; Beecham Products Overseas, UK; Beirsdorf AG, W Germany
Branch Offices: Branches in Sana'a (PO Box 1108, Tel 272901, Telex 2203); Hodeidah (PO Box 3376, Tel 217276, Telex 5600)
Subsidiaries/Associated Companies: Yemen Co for Industry & Commerce Ltd; National Co for Sponge & Plastic Industry Ltd; Yemen Co for Ghee & Soap Industry; Arwa Mineral Water Co Ltd; National Dairy & Food Co Ltd; General Industries & Packages Ltd; Yemen Co for Agriculture & Livestock Development; United Industries Co; Arabia Felix Industries Ltd; Middle East Trading Co; Middle East Shipping; United Insurance Co; Hayel Saeed Anam Trading Co Ltd; National Trading Co
Principal Bankers: Yemen Bank for Development and Reconstruction; Banque Indosuez; Arab Bank Ltd

Principal Shareholders: Hayel Saeed Anam Group
Date of Establishment: 1938
No of Employees: 66000

HODEIDAH SHIPPING & TRANSPORT CO LTD
PO Box 3337, Hodeidah
Tel: 238130/1, 238270
Cable: Hodship Hodeidah
Telex: 5510 Hdship YE
Telefax: 3-211533

Chairman: Mohamed Abdo Thabet
Directors: Abdul Gabbar Thabet, Ali Abdo Thabet, Abdul Wahab Thabet
Senior Executives: Abdul Gabbar Thabet (Chief Executive)

PRINCIPAL ACTIVITIES: Shipping agency, stevedoring, lighter operations, transport
Branch Offices: Sanaa; Taiz; Mocha

Principal Shareholders: Thabet Investment Co Ltd

HORTICULTURAL CO-OPERATIVE UNION LTD

Wholesale Market, Khormaksar, Aden
Tel: 24828/9, 24850, 22845
Cable: Cen Prod

PRINCIPAL ACTIVITIES: Representation of all producers of fresh fruits and vegetables, import and distribution of seeds, fertilizers, insecticides, sprayers, etc

HUSSEIN SULEIMAN ALBUKARI & CO

See ALBUKARI, HUSSEIN SULEIMAN, & CO

INDUSTRIAL BANK OF YEMEN

PO Box 323, Zubeiry Street, Sanaa
Tel: 207379, 207381, 207384, 206619, 206620
Cable: Banksinaie
Telex: 2580 Indbnk YE

Chairman: Abbas Abdo Mohammed Al Kirshy (also Managing Director)
Directors: Mohammed Abdulwahab Jubari, Lotf Hamoud Al Habori, Ali Hussein Al Huthi, Mohammed Ahmed Saleh, Abdullah Mohammed Beshr, Rashed Abdulhaq Beshr
Senior Executives: Abdulkarim Ismail Al-Arhabi (General Manager)

PRINCIPAL ACTIVITIES: Promoting industrial development and financing industrial projects (medium and long-term credit facilities)
Branch Offices: PO Box 6518, Taiz, Tel 230861
Financial Information:

	1988 YR'000
Portfolio investment	98,638
Authorised capital	100,000
Paid-up capital	95,094
Total shareholders equity	117,624
Total assets	262,897

Principal Shareholders: Government of Yemen Arab Republic (70%), Yemen Petroleum (0.5%), Yemen Co for Investment & Finance Ltd (5%), Deutsche Entwicklungsgesellschaft (5.75%), Shahir Company for Trade (5%), Others
Date of Establishment: 1976
No of Employees: 62

INTERNATIONAL BANK OF YEMEN

PO Box 2847, Zubeiry Street, Sanaa
Tel: 272920/5
Telex: 2523, 2540 Intbnk YE

Chairman: HE Ahmed Kaid Barakat
Directors: Ali Lutf Al Thor, Sheikh Khalid Bin Mahfouz, Sheikh Abdul Elah Bin Mahfouz, Abbas Al Kirshi, Abdul Wase Hayel Saeed, Nasser Ali Ziad, Zakir Mahmood, Mohammed Salim Al Batati, Shaher Abdul Haq
Senior Executives: Mohammadmian Soomro (General Manager), Khurshed M Tengra (Dy General Manager Head Operations), Fida M Malik (Dy General Manager Head Marketing)

PRINCIPAL ACTIVITIES: Commercial banking
Branch Offices: Sanaa, Hodeidah, Shahrahi Taiz
Principal Correspondents: Bank of America, New York, London; Dredsner Bank, Frankfurt; UBS, Zurich; BNP, Paris; NCB, Jeddah

Financial Information:

	1990 YR'000
Total deposits	1,741,389
Profits	24,518
Authorised capital	50,000
Paid-up capital	50,000
Total assets	2,389,360

Principal Shareholders: Khalid Bin Mahfouz (25%), Bank of America (20%), prominent Yemeni businessmen (55%)
Date of Establishment: 1979
No of Employees: 139

ISCANDER HUSSAIN ALI

PO Box 444, Sana'a
Tel: 75897
Cable: Gemsage
Telex: 2238 Gemage YE

President: Iscander Hussain Ali

PRINCIPAL ACTIVITIES: Dealing in electrical products
Principal Agencies: National Panasonic, Japan; Matsushita Electric Trading Co Ltd, Japan
Branch Offices: Taiz and Hodeidah
Principal Bankers: Banque Indosuez; United Bank Ltd

JUMAAN TRADING & INDUSTRIAL CORP (JUTICO)

PO Box 213, Sanaa
Tel: 272232/4, 272261
Cable: Jumaan
Telex: 2255, 2828 Jumaan YE
Telefax: 274185, 272232

Chairman: Mohamed Ahmed Jumaan (Managing Director)
Directors: Dr Bameshmesh (Treasurer & Auditor), Obad Ahmed Jumaan (General Manager for Branches & Domestic Services)

PRINCIPAL ACTIVITIES: Import and distribution of agricultural, industrial, road construction and heavy equipment
Principal Agencies: (Japan) Yanmar, Yamaha, Sakai, Ebara, Tokyo crane, MAN Commercial Vehicles; Nemitsas Water Pumps, Cyprus; Bertolla Water Pumps, Italy; Agricultural Implements, UK; Hosking Equipment, UK; Fermont, USA
Branch Offices: Taiz: Tel 210265, Telex 8914, Fax 211468; Hodeidah: Tel 231162, Telex 5707, Fax 211556
Associated Companies: Jahran Poultry Production Co, Zubeiry Street, Sanaa, Tel 207409, Telex 2676, Fax 209505; Yemen Aluminium & Accessories Co Ltd, PO Box 10349, Sanaa, Tel 224863, Telex 2665
Principal Bankers: Yemen Bank for Reconstruction and Development; Yemen Kuwait Bank for Trade & Investment

Principal Shareholders: Hussain Ahmed Jumaan; Obad Ahmed Jumaan; Mohamed Ahmed Jumaan
No of Employees: 220

KHARAFI, M A,

PO Box 2296, Sana'a
Tel: 73145, 73421
Telex: 2287 Karafi YE

Chairman: Mohamed Abdulmohsin Kharafi
Senior Executives: Samir Youssef (North Yemen Area Manager)

PRINCIPAL ACTIVITIES: General contractors for civil works, roads, buildings, agencies for building products and materials
Branch Offices: Abu Dhabi, Saudi Arabia, Egypt, Lebanon, Sharjah
Parent Company: Head office in Kuwait

KUWAITI YEMENI REAL ESTATE DEVELOPMENT CO

PO Box 888, Zubeiry Street, Sana'a
Tel: 215607
Telex: 2404 Ekarat YE

Chairman: Ahmad Ali Al Duaij

Directors: Abdel Wahhab Al Noman, Youssef Rifai, Abdullah Hashem Al Kabsi, Amin Al Shibani, Ahmad Abdel Razzaq Shihin

PRINCIPAL ACTIVITIES: Investment housing and building projects

Principal Shareholders: Yemen Arab Republic Government, Yemen Bank for Reconstruction & Development, Kuwait Real Estate Investment Consortium, Housing Credit Bank, Yemen Cement Corporation, Sharjah Group, Gulf Bank, Kuwait Investment Co, Social Insurance General Organisation of Kuwait

Date of Establishment: 1977

M A KHARAFI

See KHARAFI, M A,

MAIN TRADING CO (YEMEN) LTD

PO Box 676, Hodeidah

Directors: Radman Saeed Abdo

PRINCIPAL ACTIVITIES: Distribution of agricultural foodstuffs, textiles, building materials, lumber

Branch Offices: PO Box 4964, Taiz

MAREB TRADING & DEVELOPMENT CORPORATION

PO Box 189, Sana'a
Tel: 224145, 226044
Cable: Mareb
Telex: 2306 Bashar YE
Telefax: 226093

Directors: Abdulla Saleh Al Shaba

Senior Executives: Ahmed Saleh Al Shaba

PRINCIPAL ACTIVITIES: General agents and tenderers representing international companies in construction, communications, education and consultancy

Principal Agencies: LM Ericsson, Sweden; SR Telecom, Canada; GNB, USA; Kurogane Kosakuso Ltd, Japan

Principal Bankers: Yemen Bank for Reconstruction & Development, Sanaa

Date of Establishment: 1975

MAREB YEMEN INSURANCE CO (YSC)

AlZuberi St, PO Box 2284, Sanaa
Tel: 206111-116
Cable: Yemtamin
Telex: 2279 Yemtam YE, 2789

Chairman: Mohamed Abdulla Abdo

Directors: Akil A Alsakkaf (Managing Director), Abdulaziz Kumaim, Ali M AlHabouri, Ahmed Alwajeeh, Amin Hizam, Leslie Lainson, Ali AlDuais, Ahmed Murgham, Abdulwahab Sinan

PRINCIPAL ACTIVITIES: All kinds of insurance and reinsurance business

Branch Offices: Taiz Branch: PO Box 5077; Hodeida Branch: Mareb Ins Co Building, 26th Sept Street and EBB Agency

Principal Bankers: Yemen Bank for Reconstruction & Development

Principal Shareholders: Yemen Company Investment & Finance, Sana'a Kuwait Insurance Co SAK Kuwait; and J H Minet & Co Ltd London, General Corp for Foreign Trade

Date of Establishment: 1974

No of Employees: 95

MIDDLE EAST SHIPPING CO

PO Box 3700, Hodeidah
Tel: 217276, 217277,217418
Cable: Mideast Hodeidah
Telex: 5505 Midest YE; 5600 HSA YE
Telefax: 211529

Chairman: Abdulwasa H Saeed

Directors: Abdul Gabbar H Saeed, Abdulla Abdo Saeed, Abdul Galil Gazem Saeed, Ahmed Gazem Saeed, Abdulrahim A Ghafur, Matook A Bari

Senior Executives: Abdul Rehim A Ghafur (General Manager), Matook A Bari (Deputy General Manager)

PRINCIPAL ACTIVITIES: Shipping agents and stevedores, clearing and forwarding agents, crude oil export tanker agents, and P & I correspondents

Branch Offices: Offices in Sana'a, Taiz, Hodeidah, Mokha and Saleef

Parent Company: Hayel Saeed Anam & Co Ltd

Principal Bankers: Yemen Bank for Reconstruction and Development; Banque Indosuez, Arab Bank Ltd

Principal Shareholders: A member of the Hayel Saeed Anam & Co Group

Date of Establishment: October 1962

No of Employees: 142

MIDDLE EAST TRADING CO

PO Box 5927, Taiz
Tel: 215172
Cable: Metco Taiz
Telex: 8825 Metco Ye
Telefax: (967 4) 212334

Directors: Abdul Gabbar H Saeed (Managing Director), Abdul Rahman H Saeed, Abdul Wasa H Saeed, Abdulla Abdo Saeed, Mohamed Abdo Saeed, Abdul Galil G Saeed

Senior Executives: Mohd Suhaibi (General Manager)

PRINCIPAL ACTIVITIES: General trading, import and distribution of foodstuffs, toiletries, furniture, carpets, wall coverings, tobacco products, and general household goods; also import of raw materials for confectionery, margarine, plastic pipes, polyurethene, corrugated cartons, packaging, tannery, canning industry

Principal Agencies: Beecham Products Overseas UK; Fay International, UK; General Foods Ltd, Gillette, Parker Pen International Inc, Shulton (Gt Britian), UK; Reckitt & Coleman, UK; Beiersdor AG, W Germany; Camping Gaz, France; Faberge Inc, Willem II, Holland; HP Smedley Foods, UK; Slovenijales, Yugoslavia; K O Braun, W Germany; Jacques Bogart, France; CIE, France; Revillon, France; Coleman Co, USA; Shell Trading (ME) Ltd

Branch Offices: PO Box 1108, Sana'a, Tel 204227, Telex 2409; PO Box 3376, Hodeidah, Tel 245910, Telex 5505

Parent Company: Hayel Saeed Anam Group

Associate Companies: Yemen Co for Industry and Commerce Ltd; National Co for Sponge and Plastic Industry Ltd; Yemen Co for Ghee and Soap Industry Ltd; National Dairy and Food Co Ltd; General Industries and Packages Ltd; United Industries Co Ltd; Mass Advertising Agency Ltd; Arwa Mineral Water Co Ltd; Yemen Refreshment and Industry co; Saeed Kalpatarn Industries Ltd; Middle East Shipping Co Ltd; Prefabcon Ltd; Yemen Travel Agencies; Yemen Gulf Trading & Contracting Co; National Trading Company; Arabia Felix Industries Ltd; Pacific Inter-Link SDN BHD

Principal Bankers: Banque Indosuez; Yemen Bank for Reconstruction & Development

Date of Establishment: 1970

No of Employees: 6,000 (Total Group)

MOHAMED SAEED GHALEB AL SUFFARI

See AL SUFFARI, MOHAMED SAEED GHALEB,

MOHAMMED ISMAIL GHAMDAN ORGANISATION

PO Box 3106, Hodeidah
Tel: 79024, 75850
Cable: MIGO Hodeidah
Telex: 5524 MIGO YE

Senior Executives: Mushtaq S Jaffer (Director for Foreign Affairs)

PRINCIPAL ACTIVITIES: General trading and contracting

MOHDAR CORPORATION

PO Box 1082, Sanaa
Tel: 78121, 272215, 74431
Cable: Pharmahouse
Telex: 2377 Ossan YE

Chairman: Sayed Mohsen Aboobaker Almohdar
Directors: Sayed Mustafa Abdulla Almohdar (Managing Director)
Senior Executives: Dr Hashed Taleb (Technical Manager)

PRINCIPAL ACTIVITIES: Import and distribution of pharmaceuticals, chemical products and medical appliances
Principal Agencies: Glenmark; MSD; Wellcome; Astra, Sweden; Ayerst, Canada; Codal Synto, Cyprus; Berkeley Pharmaceuticals; Dar Al Dawa, Jordan; Nile Co, Egypt; JPM, Jordan; Eisai, Japan; Nippon Kayaku, Japan; Opal, Pakistan; Denis, France; Reckitt & Coleman, UK; Transbussan, Switzerland; International Genetics, UK
Branch Offices: Taiz, Hodeidah
Principal Bankers: International Bank of Yemen, Sana'a

Date of Establishment: 1970
No of Employees: 50

NATIONAL BANK OF YEMEN

Head Office, PO Box No 5, Crater, Aden
Tel: 52481/2
Cable: National ADEN
Telex: AD 2224, AD 2274, AD 2308 NATIONAL

Chairman: Salem Al-Ashwali
Directors: Mohamed A Muqbil Al-Amry (General Manager)

PRINCIPAL ACTIVITIES: Commercial banking
Branch Offices: Aidroos, Queen Arwa Road, Maalla, Khormaksar, Sheikh Othman, Steamer Point, Little Aden, Airport Branch (Aden International Airport), Seiyun, Mukalla, Shihr, Alqatan, Huraidah, Lahej, Dhala, Laboos, Shuaib, Tooralbaha, Zingibar, Zara (Lodar), Mukeiras, Moodia, Beihan, Attaq, Maifa'ah, Ghaida, Al Rusod, etc

Date of Establishment: April 1970
No of Employees: 657

NATIONAL BOTTLING ORGANIZATION

PO Box 352, Crater, Aden
Tel: 82237/8
Cable: Mogasbot

Chairman: Ahmed Omer Saleh (General Manager)

PRINCIPAL ACTIVITIES: Manufacture and distribution of soft drinks, ice, distilled water and carbon dioxide
Principal Agencies: Canada Dry W Wide
Principal Bankers: National Bank of Yemen

Principal Shareholders: State owned organisation
Date of Establishment: 1972
No of Employees: 360

NATIONAL DAIRY & FOOD CO LTD

PO Box 5302, Taiz
Tel: 215171
Telex: 8804

PRINCIPAL ACTIVITIES: Four manufacturing plants for the production of cans, evaporated milk, beans & peas, and milk & juices

Principal Shareholders: Hayel Saeed Anam & Co
Date of Establishment: 1985

NATIONAL DOCKYARDS CO

PO Box 1244, Aden
Tel: 23837, 24484
Cable: Dockyard Aden
Telex: 2268 AD

Chairman: Yousef Ali Bin Ali (also Managing Director)
Senior Executives: Dr Saleh Mehdi Al Muntaser (General Manager)

PRINCIPAL ACTIVITIES: Maintenance and repair of ships and vessels of various types; mechanical and marine engineering
Principal Bankers: National Bank of Yemen

Principal Shareholders: State owned
Date of Establishment: 1969
No of Employees: 420

NATIONAL DRUG COMPANY

PO Box 192, Crater Aden
Tel: 24912, 23928, 23271 (General Manager), 22971 (Import Manager)
Cable: Aqqar
Telex: 2293 Aqqar YD

Chairman: Dr Awadh Salem Issa Bamatraf (General Manager and Chairman of Board)

PRINCIPAL ACTIVITIES: Import of pharmaceutical products, cosmetics, chemicals, medical supplies, scientific instruments, and baby requirements, wholesales and retailers for all imports
Branch Offices: Mukalla: PO Box 8305
Principal Bankers: National Bank of Yemen

Principal Shareholders: State owned
Date of Establishment: 1972
No of Employees: 450

NATIONAL FOREIGN TRADE CO

PO Box 90, Crater, Aden
Tel: 51347/8, 51632/3
Cable: Foreigntrade
Telex: 2211 Foreigntrade Aden; 2266 Nattrade Aden

Senior Executives: Ahmed Mohamed Saleh (Deputy Director General), Khaled M Kalim (Import Manager)

PRINCIPAL ACTIVITIES: Import of all types of goods; foodstuffs, cigarettes, tyres, batteries, soap, electrical goods, refrigerators, radios, television sets, marine engines, diesel pumps, consumer goods, provisions, building materials, timber, heavy machinery, motor cars, spare parts, medical and hospital requirements; export of all national produce of the Republic, raw cotton, tobacco, coffee, hides and skins, fish
Principal Agencies: GMOC, Caterpillar, Massey Ferguson, Kelvinator, Philips, Toyota

Principal Shareholders: Public sector company
Date of Establishment: 1969
No of Employees: 130

NATIONAL HOME TRADE CO

PO Box 90, Crater, Aden
Tel: 51134
Cable: Home Trade Aden
Telex: 2211 Adn, 2266 Hometrade

Directors: Abdulrahman Al Sailani (Managing Director)

PRINCIPAL ACTIVITIES: Equipment sales, marketing of building materials, auto spares, photographic and electrical goods, consumer goods

NATIONAL SHIPPING COMPANY

PO Box 1228, Steamer Point, Aden
Tel: 24861/5
Cable: Natship
Telex: 2216; 2217 Natship Ad

Chairman: Minister for Communications
Directors: Mohamed Bin Mohamed Shaker (General Manager)
Senior Executives: Rashid Ali (Freight Manager), M Othman A Kader (Chief Accountant), Ahmed M Hadeira (Shippping Manager)

PRINCIPAL ACTIVITIES: Shipping, bunkering, passenger/freight booking agents and clearing and forwarding agents
Principal Agencies: Agents for all shipowners/charters/operators trading with Aden, Mukalla and Nishton ports
Branch Offices: PO Box 8089, Mukalla
Parent Company: Responsible to the Ministry of Communications
Associated Companies: Yemen Navigation Lines, Adentel 22849, cable Yemhavco, Telex 2295 AD
Principal Bankers: National Bank of Yemen, Aden

Principal Shareholders: State owned
Date of Establishment: Nationalised in 1970
No of Employees: 250

NATIONAL SPONGE & PLASTIC INDUSTRY CO LTD

PO Box 5302, Al-Houban Area, Taiz
Tel: 72941
Cable: Plasphing
Telex: 8804 HSA YE; 8825 Metco YE

PRINCIPAL ACTIVITIES: Manufacture of corrugated cartons and PVC plastic pipes; polyrethene foam mattress; foam furniture; tissue paper etc

NATIONAL TANNERY FACTORY

PO Box 4073, Crater Aden
Tel: 81449
Cable: TANNERY

Chairman: Mansoor A Mansoor (General Manager)

PRINCIPAL ACTIVITIES: Manufacture of leather goods; export of raw skins, cured sheep and goat skins
Principal Bankers: National Bank of Yemen, Crater, Aden

Principal Shareholders: State-owned company
Date of Establishment: 10 January 1972
No of Employees: 70

NATIONAL TOBACCO & MATCHES CO

PO Box 3571, Hodeidah
Tel: 72375, 72481, 72281
Telex: 5529 Attabgh YE

Chairman: Abdel Rahem Ali Nagi

PRINCIPAL ACTIVITIES: Manufacture 'Mareb' brand filter cigarettes; import of raw materials for manufacture of cigarettes; monopoly of import of safety matches

NATIONAL TRADING CO (NATCO)

PO Box 1108, Sana'a
Tel: 272986/7/8
Telex: 2203 HSA YE, 2409 Metco YE

Chairman: Ali Mohamed Saeed
Directors: Ahmed Hayel Saeed, Abdul Rahman Hayel Saeed, Abdul Gabbar Hayel Saeed

Senior Executives: Nabil Hayel Saeed (General Manager)

PRINCIPAL ACTIVITIES: Marketing and trading in consumer goods, electrical goods, educational and recreational goods, agricultural & farm machinery, irrigation equipment, toiletries & pharmaceuticals, medical equipment, etc
Principal Agencies: Cussons; Lotus; Schwarzkopf; SPC; Rain Bird; Irrifrance
Branch Offices: Taiz, Hodeidah
Parent Company: Hayel Saeed Anam & Co
Principal Bankers: Banque Indosuez; International Bank of Yemen
Financial Information:

	US$'000
Sales turnover	12,000

Date of Establishment: 1978
No of Employees: 48

PETROLEUM & MINERAL BOARD

PO Box 5780, Maalla, Aden
Tel: 424151, 41985
Cable: Ynoc
Telex: 2215 YNOC Aden

PRINCIPAL ACTIVITIES: Refining, marketing of petroleum products, exploring hydrocarbon alone or in joint venture, and exploring for minerals; supplying water and electricity
Subsidiary Companies: Aden Refinning Company; Yemen National Oil Company; Petroleum Exploration Dept; Geology and Minerals Exploration Department; Public Corporation for Electric Power; Public Water Corporation; Affiliate: Yemen Kuwait Terminal Company
Principal Bankers: National Bank of Yemen

Date of Establishment: 1969
No of Employees: 4,000

RAFIDAIN BANK

PO Box 1023, Sana'a
Tel: 77257
Telex: 2392 Rafdbk YE

PRINCIPAL ACTIVITIES: Commercial banking toiletries, cosmetics
Parent Company: Head office in Baghdad, Iraq

RAMADA HADDA HOTEL

Po Box 999, Sanaa
Tel: 215215, 215214, 215212
Cable: Ramada Hadda Sana'a
Telex: 2227 Ramada YE

Chairman: Nassr El Kharafi
Senior Executives: Abd Rabbo Mohamed (General Manager)

PRINCIPAL ACTIVITIES: Hotel business
Branch Offices: International Ramada Inns
Parent Company: Yemen Hotels & Investment Co
Principal Bankers: Yemen Kuwait Bank for Trade & Investment

Principal Shareholders: Kuwaiti Businessmen, Kharafi
Date of Establishment: 29th March 1979
No of Employees: 120

SABA & CO

Hadda Commercial Complex, Bldg 3/Floor 7, Hadda Road, PO Box 1493, Sana'a
Tel: 215676, 215716
Cable: Sabaco Sanaa
Telex: 2596 Sabaco YE

Directors: Hadi Chiad (Partner in Charge)

PRINCIPAL ACTIVITIES: Chartered accountants, management consultants and tax advisers

Branch Offices: Lebanon; Cyprus; Algeria; Bahrain; Egypt; Iraq; Jordan; Kuwait; Libya; Morocco; Oman; Qatar; Saudi Arabia; Syria; United Arab Emirates; Yemen
Principal Bankers: Arab Bank

No of Employees: 30

SAEED NOMAN AL HAJ & SONS

PO Box 4994, 26th September St, Taiz
Tel: 2706
Cable: Saeed Noman
Telex: 8856 Ksnomn

Directors: Khaled Saeed Noman (Director)

PRINCIPAL ACTIVITIES: Import and supply of building materials, galvanised pipes, and sheets, tiles, household furniture, and appliances, timber, metal bars and products
Branch Offices: PO Box 3441, Hodeidah, Tel 72441
Principal Bankers: Yemen Bank for Reconstruction & Development

SALEM MOHAMMED SHAMMAKH & CO

See SHAMMAKH, SALEM MOHAMMED, & CO

SANA'A SHERATON HOTEL

PO Box 2467, Sanaa
Tel: (02) 237500
Cable: Sheraton Sana'a
Telex: 2222 SHSAN YE

Vice Chairman: O Al Wasabi (Yemen Kuwait Real Estate)
Senior Executives: Adel Hafez (General Manager), Awad Saleh (Resident Manager)

PRINCIPAL ACTIVITIES: Hotel business and catering
Parent Company: The Sheraton Corporation
Associated Companies: Sheraton Middle East Management Co
Principal Bankers: BCCI, Yemen Kuwait Bank for Investment and Trade

Date of Establishment: November 1980

SAUDI BAHAMISH TRADING CO

PO Box 3553, Hodeidah
Tel: 72679, 75378
Cable: Zalri Hodeidah
Telex: 5549 Radman Ye attn Kumar

Chairman: Ahmed Mohamed Bahamish
Directors: Kumar J Shrimanker (Director and Executive), Mohamed Bahamish

PRINCIPAL ACTIVITIES: Import, commission and indenting agency; industrial construction and engineering, shipping agency and chartering, hotel management, insurance, consultants, import of foodstuffs and building materials
Principal Agencies: Comet Rice Mills Inc, USA; World Marine & General Insurance Co Ltd, UK; George Payne & Co Ceylon; Lipton Tea Co, UK
Branch Offices: PO Box 478, Sanaa
Associated Companies: Shrimanker Export Corporation, Bombay, India; Famy Enterprises, PO Box 2060, Dubai, Tel 231450, Telex 46807
Principal Bankers: Habib Bank Ltd; Yemen Bank for Reconstruction and Development

Date of Establishment: 1972

SHAHER SAIF AHMED AL ASNAG & BROS

See AL ASNAG, SHAHER SAIF AHMED, & BROS

SHAHER TRADING CO LTD

PO Box 28, Sana'a
Tel: 78110, 77330, 272968/9
Cable: Albashair Sana'a
Telex: 2205 Bashair YE
Telefax: 274112

Chairman: Shaher Abdul Hak
Directors: Rashid Abdul Hak (Vice Chairman), Hayel Abdul Hak (Executive Director), Abdul Galil Abdulhak (Director), Fareed Abdul Gabbar (Director)

PRINCIPAL ACTIVITIES: Import of foodstuffs such as sugar, wheat, flour, rice, tourism industry, agents, motor vehicles and spares, data processing equipment
Principal Agencies: Mercedes-Benz AG, Rank Xerox Corp, Thomas de la Rue
Branch Offices: Hodeidah; Cairo, Egypt; London, UK
Subsidiary Companies: Sabaa Hotels Co Ltd; Sanaa Beverages Co Ltd; United Investment & Trading Co Ltd; United Engineering & Automobile Co Ltd
Principal Bankers: United Bank Ltd; International Bank of Yemen

SHAMMAKH, SALEM MOHAMMED, & CO

PO Box 3372, Hodeidah
Tel: 217299, 217685, 217305
Cable: Shammakh
Telex: 5534 Shammakh YE; 2437 Shamak YE
Telefax: 217369

Chairman: Abubaker Salem Mohammed Shammakh
Directors: Ahmed S Shamnmakh (General Manager), Mahfoodh S Shammakh (Managing Director), Maroof S Shammakh (Sales & Marketing Director)
Senior Executives: Mohammad Bin Mubarak

PRINCIPAL ACTIVITIES: Importers of vehicles, household and commercial appliances, foodstuffs. Exporters: dry salted skins and hides and wet blue skins, buying and selling of lands, general tender contractors; leather tanning and industry
Principal Agencies: Daihatsu Motor Sales Co Ltd; Merloni Group, Italy; General Electric Co, USA; Rinnai Corporation, Japan; Thomson Brandt, France; Fisher, Japan; Mitsubishi Air Conditioners, Japan; Goldstar, South Korea
Branch Offices: Sanaa, Taiz
Subsidiary Companies: Modern House Exhibition, PO Box 2981, Sanaa, Tel 225803, 225805, Cable Shammakh Sanaa, Telex 2437 Shammakh YE; Shammakh Tanning & Leather Industries Ltd, PO Box 3372, Hodeidah, Telex 5534 SHAMAK YE
Principal Bankers: Banque IndoSuez; Bank of Credit & Commerce International, Hodeidah

Principal Shareholders: Abubaker, Mahfoodh, Ahmed & Maroof S Shammakh
Date of Establishment: 1955
No of Employees: 120

SHEIBANI GROUP OF COMPANIES

PO Box 5726, Taiz
Tel: 230402/5
Telex: 8843, 8847 Shbani YE

PRINCIPAL ACTIVITIES: Manufacture of paint, chemical, cosmetics, ice, carbon dioxide, perfume, beverages, aerosols etc, sale and distribution of consumer goods, engines and parts
Principal Agencies: Coca Cola, USA; ICI, UK; Vittel, France; Sunquick, Denmark; Berger Paints, Rolls Royce Engines; Dale Power Generators; Yorkshire Switchgear; HE Daniel; Ciba-Geigy Chemicals
Branch Offices: Sanaa, Tel 207415; Hodeidah, Tel 238512; UK (Bradford)
Associated Companies: Sheibani Manufacturing & Trading Co Ltd, UK; Overseas Contracting Co, UK

SHIHAB INSURANCE & TRADING AGENCIES (YEMEN) LTD

PO Box 3699, Hodeidah
Tel: 72631
Cable: Chihabion
Telex: 2247 Chisana

Chairman: S U A Shihab
Directors: Akil U A Shihab (Hodeidah Branch), Sakr U A Shihab (Sanaa Branch), Fahd U A Shihab (Taiz Branch)

PRINCIPAL ACTIVITIES: Aviation and tourist agents, commission agents, insurance brokers and underwriting agents, shipping and forwarding agents, stevedores, chartering, soft-drinks bottling plant, and general trading, import-export
Principal Agencies: Norwish Union Insurance Group, Colgate-Palmolive Ltd, Quaker Oats, Nestle, Libbys, Crosse and Blackwell, Findus, Keillers, Clarks Machinery (USA), Tyler Refrigeration (USA), Glaxo, Allenburys, Farleys (UK), Patterson Pharmaceuticals
Branch Offices: Taiz: PO Box 4251; Sana'a: PO Box 1241
Principal Bankers: Bank of Credit and Commerce International

SULAIMAN, ABDUL KHALIL,

PO Box 571, Hodeidah

Senior Executives: Abdul Khalil Sulaiman

PRINCIPAL ACTIVITIES: General trading and contracting
Principal Agencies: Massey Ferguson

TAJ SHEBA HOTEL

PO Box 773, Ali Abdolmoghni St, Sanaa
Tel: 272202-08, 272301-8, 272372
Cable: SABA HOTEL
Telex: 2551, 2561 SHEBA YE

Chairman: Shaher Abdul Hak
Directors: Abdul Galil Abdul Hak, Hayel Abdul Hak (Managing Director), B D Khole (General Manager)

PRINCIPAL ACTIVITIES: Hotel business
Principal Agencies: Yemen Travel and Tours
Parent Company: Sabaa Hotels Co Ltd
Principal Bankers: Yemen Bank for Reconstruction & Development

Principal Shareholders: Shaher Trading Company
Date of Establishment: July 15th, 1980
No of Employees: 200

THABET GROUP OF COMPANIES

PO Box 3337, Hodeidah
Tel: 238958, 238130/2
Telex: 5510 HDSHIP YE

Chairman: Mohamed Abdo Thabet
Directors: Abdul Gabbar Thabet, Ali Abdo Thabet, Abdul Wahab Thabet

PRINCIPAL ACTIVITIES: Heavy machinery and agricultural equipment, vehicles, building contracting, prefab houses; import and manufacture of foodstuffs and dairy products; insurance; office equipment etc
Principal Agencies: M F Tractors; Caterpillar; Peugeot; Nissan; Lloyds; Massey Ferguson; Dynafac; Perkins Engines; Olympia; DJB Engineering
Branch Offices: Sanaa: PO Box 73, Tel 208925, 208926, Telex 2218
Parent Company: Thabet Investments Ltd
Members of Group: Tihama Trading Co; Hodeidah Shipping & Transport Co; Red Sea Construction Co; Yemen Dairy & Juice Ind Co; Thabet Bros & Co Ltd; Yemen General Insurance Co; National Co for Vegetable Oil and Ghee Industries Ltd; Yemen Stores for Fruit and Meat Ltd; The Thabet Institute; Thabet International Ltd, London; Shipping Trading & Lighterage Co, Dubai (Associate); International Carton Manufacturing Co Ltd; Almaraee Yemen Co Ltd (Dairy Farm)

Principal Shareholders: Thabet Investments Ltd
Date of Establishment: 1976
No of Employees: 1,500

THABET SON CORPORATION

PO Box 2205, Sana'a
Tel: 272338
Cable: TSCORP Sana'a
Telex: 2607 TBT SNS YE
Telefax: 967-2-272310

Proprietor: Saif Thabet A Galil (Managing Director)
Senior Executives: Adel Saif Thabet (General Manager), Adnan Saif Thabet (Asst General Manager)

PRINCIPAL ACTIVITIES: Printers, stationers, office equipment furniture, drafting, printing machines/equipment and commission agents
Principal Agencies: John Dickinson & Co, UK; Mutoh Industries, Japan; Minolta Camera Co Ltd, Japan; Hermes Precia International, Switzerland; Rotring-Werke Riepe, W Germany; Asian Paints, India; Paul Ferd, W Germany; Precisa Ltd, Switzerland; Pelikan, W Germany; Este Kombi, W Germany; Kumahira, Japan; Rholac, France; KAS, UK; Memofax, Denmark; Laurel BM, Japan; Weka, Austria; KAS, UK
Branch Offices: Ali A Moghni St, PO Box 2205, Sana'a, Tel 73613 and Hadda Street, Sana'a; Tel 207691
Principal Bankers: Yemen Bank for Reconstruction & Development, Taiz
Financial Information:

	1989/90 YR'000
Sales turnover	10,000
Profits	1,600
Authorised capital	3,000
Paid-up capital	3,000
Total assets	10,000

Principal Shareholders: Proprietorship
Date of Establishment: 1957

TIHAMA TRACTORS & ENGINEERING CO LTD

PO Box 49, Sana'a
Tel: 967-2-76960, 273044, 273590
Cable: Tihama
Telex: 2217 Tihama YE
Telefax: 967-2-274119

Chairman: A Dirhem
Vice Chairman: M K Abdo
Directors: J L de Sa (Commercial Director), Y M Saleh (Technical Director)

PRINCIPAL ACTIVITIES: Electrical and mechanical engineering; turnkey projects in all fields; small and large scale projects; installation and maintenance work on electrical and mechanical plants. Import and distribution of heavy machinery, building materials and medical equipment
Principal Agencies: Siemens AG, W Germany; Kloeckner-Humboldt-Deutz AG, W Germany; Kloeckner Industrieanlagen AG, Humboldt, Wedag, W Germany; Atlas Copco AB, Sweden; Hospitalia Int'l GmbH, W Germany; Jos Hansen & Soehne, W Germany; Raychem NV, Belgium; Kent Meters Ltd, UK; Snap on Tools, USA; OSRAM, W Germany; Alfa Laval AB, Sweden; Nokia Engineering, Finland; Trafo Union AG, W Germany; Inak GmbH, W Germany; KSB Ag, W Germany, Beckman Instruments Int'l, Switzerland
Branch Offices: Branches in Taiz, PO Box 437, and Hodeidah, PO Box 3717
Subsidiary Companies: Tihama Travel Tours; GSA Lufthansa German Cargo Services; Yemen Air Conditioning & Refrigeration Co Ltd
Principal Bankers: Yemen Bank for Reconstruction and Development; Arab Bank Ltd

Date of Establishment: 1963
No of Employees: 52

UNITED BANK LTD

PO Box 1295, Sana'a
Tel: 75012/3/4, 71781
Telex: 2228

PRINCIPAL ACTIVITIES: Commercial banking
Parent Company: Head Office: PO Box 4306, Karachi, Pakistan

UNITED INDUSTRIES COMPANY

PO Box 5302, Taiz
Tel: 215171
Telex: 8804 HSAYE

PRINCIPAL ACTIVITIES: Manufacture of Rothmans King Size
cigarettes
Principal Agencies: Rothmans

Principal Shareholders: Hayel Saeed Anam & Co

WADI HADHRAMAUT AGRICULTURAL PROJECT

Seiyun, Hadhramaut Governorate, PO Box 9177
Cable: MacDonalds Seiyun
Telex: 2293

PRINCIPAL ACTIVITIES: Civil engineering, mechanical, electrical
and structural consultants
Branch Offices: PO Box 3258, Hodeidah, Tel 231212, Telex
5678; also in the Middle East: Abu Dhabi, Oman, Sudan,
Somalia
Parent Company: Sir M MacDonald & Partners, Cambridge, UK

YEMEN AIRWAYS CORPORATION YEMENIA

PO Box 1183, Sana'a
Tel: 232381/90
Cable: Yemenair
Telex: 2204 YE (Head Office), 2532 Yemair YE (Airport)

Chairman: Mohammad A Al Haimy
Directors: Rida Hakeem (Managing Director), Mohamed Al Anisi,
Capt Jazzaa Al Ghanem, Ahmed Hussein Basha, Adnan A
Dabag, Mohamed Al Haidary

PRINCIPAL ACTIVITIES: Airline offering internal and external
services
Branch Offices: London Office: 5 Cork Street, W1X 1PB
Financial Information:

	YR'000
Authorised capital	260,000
Paid-up capital	260,000

Principal Shareholders: Saudi Arabian Government (49%),
Yemeni Government (51%)
No of Employees: 1,891

YEMEN BANK FOR RECONSTRUCTION & DEVELOPMENT (THE)

PO Box 541, Sana'a
Tel: 271622, 271627, 271630, 73176
Cable: BANYEMEN
Telex: 2202, 2291, 2533

Chairman: Ahmed Abdul Rahman Al Samawi
Directors: Ahmed M Al Eryani, Mohammad Al Haimi, Ismail Al
Fadhli, Abduraboh Garadah, Kayed Al Hirwi, Al Haj Hussein
Ali Al Watari, Ali Mohd Said Anaam, Abdul Samad Mutahar,
Hussain Al Suffari, Mohamed Said Thabet
Senior Executives: Abdul Aziz Y Al Maktari (General Manager)

PRINCIPAL ACTIVITIES: Banking, investment in industrial and
development projects and commercial banking
Branch Offices: Over 40 throughout Yemen; UK: 2 Fore Street,
London EC2Y 5DA
Subsidiary Companies: Yemen Co for Investment & Finance, PO
Box 2789, Sana'a

Financial Information:

	YR'000
Share capital	100,000

Principal Shareholders: Government (51%), Private Sector (49%)
Date of Establishment: 1962

YEMEN CEMENT INDUSTRY CORPORATION

PO Box 3393, Hodeidah
Tel: 72952
Cable: Yemcement

Chairman: Amin Abdul-Wahid Ahmed
Directors: Ali Kaid Al-Adashi
Senior Executives: Wahib Mohamed Saleh (Secretary to the
Chairman), Ahmed Faki Mozare (Chief Accountant)

PRINCIPAL ACTIVITIES: Production of cement
Branch Offices: Sana'a Branch: Alkeada Street
Principal Bankers: Central Bank of Yemen; Yemen Bank for
Reconstruction and Development

YEMEN CO FOR GHEE & SOAP INDUSTRY

PO Box 5273, Taiz
Tel: 230665, 230664
Cable: El Zeyoot
Telex: 8804 HSA YE, 8928 YCGSI YE
Telefax: 212338, 212334

Chairman: Ali Mohamed Saeed Anam
Directors: Abdulla Abdo Saeed, Ahmed Abdulla Al Aquil, Abdul
Gabbar Hayel Saeed, Amin Hurab, Abdul Hamid Ali Noman,
Abdul Ghani Ali
Senior Executives: Abdulla El Kershi (General Manager),
Muneer Ahmed Hayel (Deputy General Manager), M S
Panchal (Technical Manager), K C Goyal (CHief Engineer),
Abdul Rahman Kassim (Sales Manager)

PRINCIPAL ACTIVITIES: Production of ghee (cooking fat),
margarine, soap, detergents and oxygen
Principal Agencies: Unilever Export Ltd, UK
Branch Offices: Sana'a, Hodeidah, Jeddah, Dubai, London
Principal Bankers: Yemen Bank for Reconstruction and
Development; Arab Bank Ltd; Banque Indosuez
Financial Information:

	1988/89 YR'000
Sales turnover	735,000
Dividend	25%
Authorised capital	150,000
Paid-up capital	150,000
Total assets	150,000

Principal Shareholders: Hayel Saeed Anam & Co Ltd
Date of Establishment: May 1975
No of Employees: 790

YEMEN CO FOR INDUSTRY & COMMERCE LTD

PO Box 5423, Taiz
Tel: 218058, 218055, 218059/60
Cable: Assinaah
Telex: 8942 YCIC YE
Telefax: 4-218054

Chairman: Ali Mohamed Saeed
Directors: Ahmed Hayel Saeed (Managing Director)
Senior Executives: Shawki Ahmed Hayel Saeed (General
Manager), Abdul Gani Abdul Rab (Finance Manager), Ali Al
Shebani (Marketing Manager), Abdulla Rashid Mukrid (Export
Manager), Wahib Abdul Razaq (Personnel Manager), Mohd
Akhter (Technical Adviser)

PRINCIPAL ACTIVITIES: Manufacture of biscuits, wafers and
confectionery
Parent Company: Hayel Saeed Anam & Co
Principal Bankers: Yemen Bank for Reconstruction &
Development, Taiz; Banque Indosuez, Taiz; Arab Bank, Taiz

Financial Information:

	1990
	YR'000
Authorised capital	150,000

Date of Establishment: 1971
No of Employees: 1,500

YEMEN CO FOR INVESTMENT & FINANCE (YCIF)

PO Box 2789, Sana'a
Tel: 72089, 71457
Cable: Invest Yemen
Telex: 2564 Invest YE

Chairman: Abdulla Mohd Ishaq
Senior Executives: Ahmed Mohd Saleh (Deputy General Manager)

PRINCIPAL ACTIVITIES: Investment and finance
Parent Company: Yemen Bank for Reconstruction & Development
Subsidiary Companies: National Co for Tobacco & Matches; Yemen Drug Co; Mareb (Yemen) Insurance Co
Financial Information:

	YR'000
Authorised capital	100,000
Paid-up capital	100,000

Principal Shareholders: Yemen Bank for Reconstruction and Development
Date of Establishment: 1981
No of Employees: 43

YEMEN CO FOR TANNERY & INDUSTRY LTD

PO Box 4302, Taiz
Tel: 2325, 3368
Cable: Alglood
Telex: 8804, 8852

PRINCIPAL ACTIVITIES: Processing of hides and skins and export to many overseas countries

YEMEN COMPUTER CO LTD

PO Box 340, Sanaa
Tel: 208811/2/3/4
Cable: Yemcom
Telex: 2406 Ycc YE
Telefax: 2-2-9523

Directors: Abdulmalik Zabarah (Managing Director), Abdulaziz Murshid (Sales Director), Mohammed A'Amer Ali A'Amer (Finance Director)

PRINCIPAL ACTIVITIES: Specialised sales and service for data processing equipment, computer and computer room hardware and supplies; business equipment and allied security fields
Principal Agencies: Wang Laboratories, Inc, USA; Hugin Sweda, UK, Sweden; Pitney Bowes, UK; Crotan, UK; Liebert, USA; BASF, W Germany; Otto Lampertz, W Germany
Branch Offices: Hodeidah, Taiz
Principal Bankers: Yemen Kuwait Bank for Trade & Investment YSC, Sana'a; International Bank of Yemen YSC, Sana'a

Date of Establishment: September 1977
No of Employees: 38

YEMEN DRUG CO FOR INDUSTRY & COMMERCE

PO Box 40, Sana'a

PRINCIPAL ACTIVITIES: Production, import and distribution of pharmaceuticals
Principal Agencies: Beecham; Bencard; Ciba Geigy; Farmitalia; Merck; Natterman; Organon; Pfizer; Rivopharm; Roche; Schering; Searle; Specia; Squibb; Wallace; Wander; Warner Lambert; Wyeth; Zyma

YEMEN ELECTRONICS CENTRE

PO Box 1489, 26th September St, Sana'a
Tel: 74656
Cable: Mastoor
Telex: 2311 Akabat YE

Chairman: Ali A Akabat
Directors: Abdallah Akabat (Assistant Local Manager)

PRINCIPAL ACTIVITIES: Electronics appliances, solar energy equipment, etc; plus tenders supervision, import
Principal Bankers: Bank of Credit and Commerce Int SA

Date of Establishment: 1975

YEMEN ENGINEERING CO LTD

PO Box 550, Sana'a
Tel: 72266
Cable: Engineering
Telex: 2231

PRINCIPAL ACTIVITIES: Importers and dealers in vehicles; car maintenance

YEMEN GENERAL INSURANCE CO SYC

PO Box 2709, Sana'a
Tel: 265191/2
Cable: Assurance Sana'a
Telex: 2451 Assure YE
Telefax: 2-263109

Chairman: Abdul Jabbar Abdo Thabet
Directors: Abdul Wahab Thabet, Abdul Wahed Saeed Al Mutahar
Senior Executives: Hosny El Zanfaly (General Manager), Saleh Bashanfer (Deputy General Manager), Abdul Aziz Saleh (Sana'a Branch Manager), Jaman Hamid (Hodeidah Branch Manager), Abdul Sallam Kassim (Taiz Branch Manager), Abdullah Tamimi (Reinsurance Manager)

PRINCIPAL ACTIVITIES: All classes of insurance and reinsurance
Branch Offices: PO Box 5844, Taiz, Tel 221561/2, Telex 8872; PO Box 3952, Hodeidah, Tel 239184/5, Telex 5563, 5720
Associated Companies: Thabet Bros Group; Saudi Arabian Insurance Co Ltd
Principal Bankers: Banque Indosuez; Arab Bank Ltd
Financial Information:

	1988	1989
	YR'000	YR'000
Sales turnover	41,667	40,025
Underwriting	4,618	6,912
Authorised capital	5,000	10,000
Paid-up capital	5,000	10,000
Total assets	38,707	46,451

Principal Shareholders: Thabet Investment Co Ltd; Saudi Arabian Insurance Co Ltd
Date of Establishment: 1977
No of Employees: 45

YEMEN INSURANCE & REINSURANCE CO

PO Box 456, Crater, Aden
Tel: 51464/8
Cable: Shameen - Aden
Telex: 2245 AD

Chairman: Farouq Nassir Ali
Managers: Ali Abdu Salam, Hussain Abdo Hamza, Salem Mohamed Wadi, Jaffer Mohamed Saleh, Ibrahim Ahmed Mockbel, Ali Nasser Mohamed, Mustafa Abdo Hussain, Ahmed Jaffer Al-Katheri, Gazi Saeed Abdulla, Abdu Mohamed Saad, Ahmad Mustafa Ghanim
Senior Executives: Farouq Nassir Ali (General Manager), Salem Mohamed Wadi (Financial Manager)

PRINCIPAL ACTIVITIES: Insurance and reinsurance

Branch Offices: Lahej; Abyan; Shabwa; Mukalla; Seyoun; Al Ghida
Principal Bankers: National Bank of Yemen, Aden

Principal Shareholders: State-owned
Date of Establishment: January 1970
No of Employees: 195

YEMEN INSURANCE AGENCIES LTD

PO Box 3876, Hodeidah
Tel: 72543, 72941, 75022, 74407, 74402
Cable: Yeminag Hodeidah
Telex: 5505 Midest YE

Chairman: Hayel Saeed Anam
Directors: Ahmed Hayel, Ali Moahmed Saeed, Abdul Rehman Hayel, Abdul Wasa Hayel, Abdul Gabbar Hayel (Managing Director)

PRINCIPAL ACTIVITIES: Underwriters' agents, marine claims survey and settling agents
Principal Agencies: American International Underwriters Med Inc, Institute of London Underwriters, People's Insurance Co of China, Nippon Fire and Marine Insurance Co
Associated Companies: Hayel Saeed Anam & Co
Principal Bankers: Yemen Bank for Reconstruction and Development; Banque Indosuez

YEMEN KUWAIT BANK FOR TRADE & INVESTMENT YSC

PO Box 987, Zubairi Street, Sanaa
Tel: 71757, 78047, 240783
Cable: YEMKUBANK
Telex: 2449, 2478 YKBANK

Chairman: Bader N Al Bisher (also Managing Director)
Directors: Hussein Mohd Al Maswari (Vice Chairman), Farooq Al Herwi, Marzooq Al Bahr, Hamed Ali Ahmed Al Salem, Ibrahim Al Manaee, Abdullah Al Ghabri, Mohammed Abdo Saeed, Abdulmoula Mohd Mokbel

PRINCIPAL ACTIVITIES: Commercial banking
Principal Bankers: Bank of Tokyo, London; Irving Trust Co, New York
Financial Information:

	YR'000
Authorised capital	100,000
Paid-up capital	50,000

Date of Establishment: 1977
No of Employees: 48

YEMEN NATIONAL OIL CO

PO Box 5050, Maalla, Aden
Tel: 24151
Cable: YNOC Aden
Telex: 2215 YNOC AD

Chairman: Ali Ahmed Hasson
Senior Executives: Ali Ahmed Hasson (General Manager), M A Hussein (Deputy General Manager), M A Awad (Financial Manager), A M S Bushadi (Technical Manager), M S Bashbail (Operation Manager), A M Noaman (Import Manager), S A Mohamed (Admin Manager)

PRINCIPAL ACTIVITIES: Marketing and distribution of petroleum products
Principal Agencies: Shell/BP/Caltex/Mobil lubricants; BP Aviation
Branch Offices: Mukalla-Hadramouth; Nishtun-Mahara
Parent Company: Petroleum & Mineral Board
Principal Bankers: National Bank of Yemen

Principal Shareholders: Government owned
Date of Establishment: 1969
No of Employees: 1,200

YEMEN OIL & MINERAL RESOURCES CORP (YOMINCO)

PO Box 81, Sana'a
Tel: 70432
Telex: 2257 Yomin Ye

PRINCIPAL ACTIVITIES: Petroleum products and oil services
Principal Agencies: Shell Lubricants

YEMEN PETROLEUM COMPANY

PO Box 187, Sanaa
Tel: 202321, 202318, 202320
Cable: YEM PET
Telex: 3106 YEM PET
Telefax: 209598

Chairman: Ahmed Ali Al Mohany (Minister of Oil & Mineral Resources)
Directors: Fathi Salem Ali (Director General Yemen Petroleum Co)
Senior Executives: Avdul Ghani Aqlan (Finance Manager), Abdul Latif Muthahr (Commercial Manager), Ahmed Hussain Alhalali (Personnel & Admin Manager), Kais Shaher (Technical Manager), Mohamed Al Baheri (Legal Advisor)

PRINCIPAL ACTIVITIES: Production and marketing of oil and oil products
Branch Offices: PO Box 3360, Hodeidah, Telex 5526

Date of Establishment: 1961
No of Employees: 1,200

YEMEN PRINTING & PUBLISHING CO

PO Box 1081, Sana'a

Chairman: Ahmad Muhammad Hadi

PRINCIPAL ACTIVITIES: Newspaper publication and commercial printing

YEMEN STEEL & ALUMINIUM MANUFCTURING CO LTD

PO Box 5286, Taiz
Tel: 72521
Cable: Mahyoub
Telex: 8865 Mahyoub YE

Chairman: Mohamed Mahyoub Abbas (General Manager)
Directors: Shawki Mahyoub (Managing Director), Saeed Mahyoub (Assistant Manager)

PRINCIPAL ACTIVITIES: Import of steel sheets, pipes, tubes and profiles, for the manufacture of home furniture, beds, office equipment and aluminium doors and windows
Principal Bankers: Banque Indosuez; Yemen Bank for Reconstruction and Development

Principal Shareholders: Mahyoub Family
Date of Establishment: January 1974

YEMEN TRADING & MARKETING CO LTD

PO Box 32, Sana'a
Tel: 241065, 241149, 241150
Cable: Yemtamarco
Telex: 2221 BILQIS YE
Telefax: 263037

Chairman: Mohamed Saif Thabet
Directors: Talal M S Thabet
Senior Executives: Tawfeek M S Thabet (General Manager), Abdulla S Ali (Finance Manager), Kaid A Mohamed (Sales Manager), Zainuddin Kaderally (Admin Manager)

PRINCIPAL ACTIVITIES: Agency distributing detergents, foodstuffs, confectionery, cigarettes, insecticides, and general merchandise
Principal Agencies: Brooke Bond; Clorox; H J Heinz; Kelloggs; Mars; Procter & Gamble; Philip Morris; Warner Lambert; Wellcome Foundation; Top Knott Int'l

Branch Offices: Branches at Hodeidah and Taiz
Principal Bankers: Yemen Bank for Reconstruction and
Development; International Bank of Yemen

Date of Establishment: 1972
No of Employees: 32

YEMEN TRAVEL AGENCIES

PO Box 4302, 26th September St, Taiz
Tel: 72804
Cable: Yemtravel
Telex: 8804

PRINCIPAL ACTIVITIES: Airlines and travel agents
Branch Offices: PO Box 1108, Ali A Mughni St, Sana'a, Tel
72096, Telex 2285, Cable Temtravel

ZUBIERI TRADING COMPANY

1 Zubieri Street, PO Box 535, Sana'a
Tel: 79149, 79336, 244400
Cable: Zubieri
Telex: 2285 Zubiri YE
Telefax: 2-245838

President: Mohamed Hassan Zubieri
Directors: A H Zubieri (Deputy General Manager)
Senior Executives: Ismail Sabry (Sana'a Branch Manager), Alwi
Abubaker (Commercial Manager)

PRINCIPAL ACTIVITIES: Import and distribution of tyres, trucks,
spare parts, electronlc products, office equipment and
cameras
Principal Agencies: Goodyear Tyres; Facit Addo Machines; FMC
Vehicle Sweepers; Ericsson Information Systems; Becker
Autoradios; AMA Universal Dryclening Machines; Perc
Solvent; Hofmann Roadmarking Equipment; Wylie Bldg &
Road equipment; Lake Electronics Telephone Switching
Systems; Cummins Diesel Engines
Branch Offices: Hodeidah
Subsidiary Companies: Zubieri Drilling Co, PO Box 2459,
Sana'a
Principal Bankers: Yemen & Kuwait Bank for Trade &
Investment

Principal Shareholders: Zubieri family
Date of Establishment: 1962

Alphabetical Index

Index by Country

BAHRAIN

IRAQ

JORDAN

KUWAIT

MOROCCO

SOMALIA

SUDAN

SYRIA

UAE — Abu Dhabi

INDEX: By Country

Index to Business Activities

INDEX: Business Activities Subdivided by Country

Architecture and town planning

Baking and flour milling

Banks, finance and investment

Cereal products

Commodity trading

Computer software and services

Confectionery

Electrical engineering

INDEX: Business Activities Subdivided by Country

Fish and fish processing

Fishing

Food and beverage plant

Food and drink retailing

Footwear

INDEX: Business Activities Subdivided by Country

Furniture and components

General chemicals

INDEX: Business Activities Subdivided by Country

General mechanical engineering

Generators

Hand tools

Health care

Heating, ventilation and refrigeration

Industrial ceramics

Iron and steel

Irrigation equipment

Machine tools

Management services and consultants

Mechanical engineering plant

Metal fabrication

Motor vehicles

Motorcycles and bicycles

Natural gas supply

Non-alcoholic beverages

Nuclear engineering

Office equipment

Oil and gas exploration and production

Oil refining

Paints, inks and dyestuffs

Photographic and copying equipment and services

Plastics and plastic products

Pollution control equipment

Postal services

Power equipment

Precious metals

Printing and binding

Public services

Publishing and information services

Pumps, valves and compressors

Scientific instruments

Security services

Ship and boat building and marine engineering

Snack products

Storage and warehousing

Telecommunications services

Toiletries and cosmetics

INDEX: Business Activities Subdivided by Country

Vegetable products

Watches and clocks

Water supply and treatment services

Woollen goods

Writing equipment